VOLUME I

Lewis's Medical-Surgical Nursing

Assessment and Management of Clinical Problems

Eleventh Edition

Mariann M. Harding, RN, PhD, FAADN, CNE
Professor of Nursing
Kent State University at Tuscarawas
New Philadelphia, Ohio

Section Editors

Jeffrey Kwong, RN, DNP, MPH, ANP-BC, FAAN, FAANP
Professor
Division of Advanced Nursing Practice
School of Nursing
Rutgers University
Newark, New Jersey

Dottie Roberts, RN, EdD, MSN, MACI, OCNS-C, CMSRN, CNE
Executive Director
Orthopaedic Nurses Certification Board
Chicago, Illinois

Debra Hagler, RN, PhD, ACNS-BC, CNE, CHSE, ANEF, FAAN
Clinical Professor
Edson College of Nursing and Health Innovation
Arizona State University
Phoenix, Arizona

Courtney Reinisch, RN, DNP, FNP-BC
Undergraduate Program Director
Associate Professor
School of Nursing
Montclair State University
Montclair, New Jersey

ELSEVIER

Elsevier
3251 Riverport Lane
St. Louis, Missouri 63043

LEWIS'S MEDICAL-SURGICAL NURSING, ELEVENTH EDITION
ISBN (two-volume set): 978-0-323-55200-4
Copyright © 2020 by Elsevier, Inc. All rights reserved.
ISBN (Volume 1): 978-0-323-55150-2

Notice

Practitioners and researchers must always rely on their own experience and knowledge in evaluating and using any information, methods, compounds or experiments described herein. Because of rapid advances in the medical sciences, in particular, independent verification of diagnoses and drug dosages should be made. To the fullest extent of the law, no responsibility is assumed by Elsevier, authors, editors or contributors for any injury and/or damage to persons or property as a matter of products liability, negligence or otherwise, or from any use or operation of any methods, products, instructions, or ideas contained in the material herein.

Previous editions copyrighted 2017, 2014, 2011, 2007, 2004, 2000, 1996, 1992, 1987, and 1983.

International Standard Book Number: 978-0-323-55149-6

Senior Content Strategist: Jamie Blum
Senior Content Development Specialist: Rebecca Leenhouts
Publishing Services Manager: Julie Eddy
Book Production Specialist: Clay S. Broeker
Design Direction: Amy Buxton

Printed in Canada

Last digit is the print number: 9 8 7 6 5 4 3 2

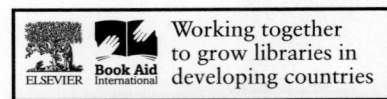

Working together
to grow libraries in
developing countries

www.elsevier.com • www.bookaid.org

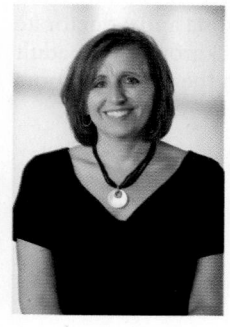

MARIANN M. HARDING, RN, PHD, FAADN, CNE

Mariann Harding is a Professor of Nursing at Kent State University Tuscarawas, New Philadelphia, Ohio, where she has been on the faculty since 2005. She received her diploma in nursing from Mt. Carmel School of Nursing in Columbus, Ohio; her Bachelor of Science in nursing from Ohio University in Athens, Ohio; her Master of Science in Nursing as an adult nurse practitioner from the Catholic University of America in Washington, DC; and her doctorate in nursing from West Virginia University in Morgantown, West Virginia. Her 29 years of nursing experience have primarily been in critical care nursing and teaching in licensed practical, associate, and baccalaureate nursing programs. She currently teaches medical-surgical nursing, health care policy, and evidence-based practice. Her research has focused on promoting student success and health promotion among individuals with gout and facing cancer.

JEFFREY KWONG, RN, DNP, MPH, ANP-BC, FAAN, FAANP

Jeffrey Kwong is a Professor at the School of Nursing at Rutgers, the State University of New Jersey. He has worked for over 20 years in the area of adult primary care with a special focus on HIV. He received his undergraduate degree from the University of California—Berkeley, his nurse practitioner degree from the University of California—San Francisco, and completed his doctoral training at the University of Colorado—Denver. He also has a Master of Science Degree in public health with a focus on health education and behavioral sciences from the University of California—Los Angeles, and he was appointed a Hartford Geriatric Interprofessional Scholar while completing his gerontology education at New York University. In addition to teaching, Dr. Kwong maintains a clinical practice at Gotham Medical Group in New York City. He is a Fellow in the American Association of Nurse Practitioners.

DOTTIE ROBERTS, RN, EdD, MSN, MACI, CMSRN, OCNS-C, CNE

Dottie Roberts received her Bachelor of Science in nursing from Beth-El College of Nursing, Colorado Springs, Colorado; her Master of Science in adult health nursing from Beth-El College of Nursing and Health Sciences; her Master of Arts in curriculum and instruction from Colorado Christian University, Colorado Springs, Colorado; and her EdD in healthcare education from Nova Southeastern University, Ft. Lauderdale, Florida. She has over 25 years of experience in medical-surgical and orthopaedic nursing and holds certifications in both specialties. She has also taught in two baccalaureate programs in the Southeast and is certified as a nurse educator. She currently serves as contributing faculty for the RN-BSN program at Walden University. For her dissertation, Dottie completed a phenomenological study on facilitation of critical-thinking skills by clinical faculty in a baccalaureate nursing program. She has been Executive Director of the Orthopaedic Nurses Certification Board since 2005 and editor of *MEDSURG Nursing*, official journal of the Academy of Medical-Surgical Nurses, since 2003. Her free time is spent traveling, reading, and cross-stitching.

DEBRA HAGLER, RN, PhD, ACNS-BC, CNE, CHSE, ANEF, FAAN

Debbie Hagler is a Clinical Professor in the Edson College of Nursing and Health Innovation at Arizona State University in Phoenix. She is Deputy Editor of *The Journal of Continuing Education in Nursing*. She received her Practical Certificate in Nursing, Associate Degree in Nursing, and Bachelor of Science in Nursing from New Mexico State University. She earned a Master of Science from the University of Arizona and a doctorate in Learning and Instructional Technology from Arizona State University. Her clinical background is in adult health and critical care nursing. Her current role focuses on supporting students through the Barrett Honors program and helping faculty members develop their scholarly writing for publication.

COURTNEY REINISCH, RN, DNP, FNP-BC

Courtney Reinisch is the Undergraduate Program Director and Associate Professor for the School of Nursing at Montclair State University. She earned her Bachelor of Arts in biology and psychology from Immaculata University. She received her Bachelor of Science in nursing and Masters of Science in family practice nurse practitioner degree from the University of Delaware. She completed her Doctor of Nursing Practice degree at Columbia University School of Nursing. Courtney's nursing career has focused on providing care for under-served populations in primary care and emergency settings. She has taught in undergraduate and graduate nursing programs in New York and New Jersey. Courtney enjoys playing tennis, snowboarding, reading, and spending time with her family and dogs. She is the biggest fan for her nieces and nephews at their soccer games, cross-country events, and track meets. She is an active volunteer in the Parents Association of her son's school and advocates for the needs of students with learning differences and the LGBTQ community.

Vera Barton-Maxwell, PhD, APRN, FNP-BC, CHFN
Assistant Professor
Advanced Nursing Practice, Family Nurse
    Practitioner Program
Georgetown University
Washington, District of Columbia
Nurse Practitioner
Center for Advanced Heart Failure
West Virginia University Heart and Vascular
    Institute
Morgantown, West Virginia

Cecilia Bidigare, MSN, RN
Professor
Nursing Department
Sinclair Community College
Dayton, Ohio

Megan Ann Brissie, DNP, RN, ACNP-BC, CEN
Acute Care Nurse Practitioner
Neurosurgery
Duke Health
Durham, North Carolina
Adjunct Instructor
College of Nursing
University of Cincinnati
Cincinnati, Ohio

Diana Taibi Buchanan, PhD, RN
Associate Professor
Biobehavioral Nursing and Health Systems
University of Washington
Seattle, Washington

Michelle Bussard, PhD, RN
RN to BSN Online eCampus Program Director
College of Health and Human Services
Bowling Green State University
Bowling Green, Ohio

Kim K. Choma, DNP, APRN, WHNP-BC
Women's Health Nurse Practitioner
Independent Consultant and Clinical
    Trainer
Kim Choma, DNP, LLC
Scotch Plains, New Jersey

Marisa Cortese, PhD, RN, FNP-BC
Research Nurse Practitioner
Hematology/Oncology
White Plains Hospital
White Plains, New York

Ann Crawford, RN, PhD, CNS, CEN
Professor
Department of Nursing
University of Mary Hardin-Baylor
Belton, Texas

Kimberly Day, DNP, RN
Clinical Assistant Professor
Edson College of Nursing and Health Innovation
Arizona State University
Phoenix, Arizona

Deena Damsky Dell, MSN, RN, APRN, AOCN(R), LNC
Oncology Advanced Practice Registered
    Nurse
Sarasota Memorial Hospital
Sarasota, Florida

Hazel Dennison, DNP, RN, APNc, CPHQ, CNE
Director of Continuing Nursing Education
College of Health Sciences, School of Nursing
Walden University
Minneapolis, Minnesota
Nurse Practitioner
Urgent Care
Virtua Health System
Medford, New Jersey

Jane K. Dickinson, PhD, RN, CDE
Program Director/Lecturer
Diabetes Education and Management
Teachers College Columbia University
New York, New York

Cathy Edson, MSN, RN
Nurse Practitioner
Emergency Department
Team Health—Virtua Memorial
Mt. Holly, New Jersey

Jonel L. Gomez, DNP, ARNP, CPCO, COE
Nurse Practitioner
Ophthalmic Facial Plastic Surgery
    Specialists
Stephen Laquis, MD
Fort Myers, Florida

Sherry A. Greenberg, PhD, RN, GNP-BC, FGSA
Courtesy-Appointed Associate Professor
Nursing
Rory Meyers College of Nursing
New York University
New York, New York

Diana Rabbani Hagler, MSN-Ed, RN, CCRN
Staff Nurse
Intensive Care Unit
Banner Health
Gilbert, Arizona

Julia A. Hitch, MS, APRN, FNPCDE
Nurse Practitioner
Internal Medicine—Endocrinology
Ohio State University Physicians
Columbus, Ohio

Haley Hoy, PhD, APRN
Associate Professor
College of Nursing
University of Alabama in Huntsville
Huntsville, Alabama
Nurse Practitioner
Vanderbilt Lung Transplantation
Vanderbilt Medical Center
Nashville, Tennessee

Melissa Hutchinson, MN, BA, RN
Clinical Nurse Specialist
MICU/CCU
VA Puget Sound Health Care System
Seattle, Washington

Mark Karasin, DNP, APRN, AGACNP-BC, CNOR
Advanced Practice Nurse
Cardiothoracic Surgery
Robert Wood Johnson University Hospital
New Brunswick, New Jersey
Adjunct Faculty
Center for Professional Development
School of Nursing
Rutgers University
Newark, New Jersey

Patricia Keegan, DNP, NP-C, AACC
Director Strategic and Programmatic
    Initiatives
Heart and Vascular Center
Emory University
Atlanta, Georgia

Kristen Keller, DNP, ACNP-BC, PMHNP-BC
Nurse Practitioner
Trauma and Acute Care Surgery
Banner Thunderbird Medical Center
Glendale, Arizona

Anthony Lutz, MSN, NP-C, CUNP
Nurse Practitioner
Department of Urology
Columbia University Irving Medical Center
New York, New York

Denise M. McEnroe-Petitte, PhD, RN
Associate Professor
Nursing Department
Kent State University Tuscarawas
New Philadelphia, Ohio

Amy Meredith, MSN, RN, EM Cert/ Residency
APN-C Lead and APN Emergency Department
Emergency Department
Southern Ocean Medical Center
Manahawkin, New Jersey

Helen Miley, RN, PhD, AG-ACNP
Specialty Director of Adult Gerontology
Acute Care Nurse Practitioner Program
School of Nursing
Rutgers University
Newark, New Jersey

Debra Miller-Saultz, DNP, FNP-BC
Assistant Professor of Nursing
School of Nursing
Columbia University
New York, New York

Eugene Mondor, MN, RN, CNCC(C)
Clinical Nurse Educator
Adult Critical Care
Royal Alexandra Hospital
Edmonton, Alberta
Canada

Brenda C. Morris, EdD, RN, CNE
Clinical Professor
Edson College of Nursing and Health Innovation
Arizona State University
Phoenix, Arizona

Janice A. Neil, PhD, RN, CNE
Associate Professor
College of Nursing, Department of Baccalaureate Education
East Carolina University
Greenville, North Carolina

Yeow Chye Ng, PhD, CRNP, CPC, AAHIVE
Associate Professor
College of Nursing
University of Alabama in Huntsville
Huntsville, Alabama

Mary C. Olson, DNP, APRN
Nurse Practitioner
Medicine, Division of Gastroenterology and Hepatology
New York University Langone Health
New York, New York

Madona D. Plueger, MSN, RN, ACNS-BC CNRN
Adult Health Clinical Nurse Specialist
Barrow Neurological Institute
Dignity Health
St. Joseph's Hospital and Medical Center
Phoenix, Arizona

Matthew C. Price, MS, CNP, ONP-C, RNFA
Orthopedic Nurse Practitioner
Orthopedic One
Columbus, Ohio
Director
Orthopedic Nurses Certification Board
Chicago, Illinois

Margaret R. Rateau, PhD, RN, CNE
Assistant Professor
School of Nursing, Education, and Human Studies
Robert Morris University
Moon Township, Pennsylvania

Catherine R. Ratliff, RN, PhD
Clinical Associate Professor and Nurse Practitioner
School of Nursing/Vascular Surgery
University of Virginia Health System
Charlottesville, Virginia

Sandra Irene Rome, MN, RN, AOCN
Clinical Nurse Specialist
Blood and Marrow Transplant Program
Cedars–Sinai Medical Center
Los Angeles, California
Assistant Clinical Professor
University of California Los Angeles School of Nursing
Los Angeles, California

Diane M. Rudolphi, MSN, RN
Senior Instructor of Nursing
College of Health Sciences
University of Delaware, Newark
Newark, Delaware

Diane Ryzner, MSN, APRN, CNS-BC, OCNS-C
Clinical Nursing Transformation Leader
Orthopedics
Northwest Community Healthcare
Arlington Heights, Illinois

Andrew Scanlon, DNP, RN
Associate Professor
School of Nursing
Montclair State University
Montclair, New Jersey

Rose Shaffer, MSN, RN, ACNP-BC, CCRN
Cardiology Nurse Practitioner
Thomas Jefferson University Hospital
Philadelphia, Pennsylvania

Tara Shaw, MSN, RN
Assistant Professor
Goldfarb School of Nursing
Barnes-Jewish College
St. Louis, Missouri

Cynthia Ann Smith, DNP, APRN, CNN-NP, FNP-BC
Nurse Practitioner
Renal Consultants, PLLC
South Charleston, West Virginia

Janice Smolowitz, PhD, DNP, EdD
Dean and Professor
School of Nursing
Montclair State University
Montclair, New Jersey

Cindy Sullivan, MN, ANP-C, CNRN
Nurse Practitioner
Department of Neurosurgery
Barrow Neurological Institute
Phoenix, Arizona

Teresa Turnbull, DNP, RN
Assistant Professor
School of Nursing
Oregon Health and Science University
Portland, Oregon

Kara Ann Ventura, DNP, PNP, FNP
Director
Liver Transplant Program
Yale New Haven
New Haven, Connecticut

Colleen Walsh, DNP, RN, ONC, ONP-C, CNS, ACNP-BC
Contract Assistant Professor of Nursing
College of Nursing and Health Professions
University of Southern Indiana
Evansville, Indiana

Pamela Wilkerson, MN, RN
Nurse Manager
Primary Care and Urgent Care
Department of Veterans Affairs
Veterans Administration, Puget Sound
Tacoma, Washington

Daniel P. Worrall, MSN, ANP-BC
Nurse Practitioner
Sexual Health Clinic
Nurse Practitioner
General and Gastrointestinal Surgery
Massachusetts General Hospital
Boston, Massachusetts
Clinical Operations Manager
The Ragon Institute of MGH, MIT, and Harvard
Cambridge, Massachusetts

TEST BANK

Debra Hagler, RN, PhD, ACNS-BC, CNE, CHSE, ANEF, FAAN
Clinical Professor
Edson College of Nursing and Health Innovation
Arizona State University
Phoenix, Arizona

CASE STUDIES
Interactive and Managing Care of Multiple Patients Case Studies

Mariann M. Harding, RN, PhD, FAADN, CNE
Professor of Nursing
Kent State University at Tuscarawas
New Philadelphia, Ohio

Brenda C. Morris, EdD, RN, CNE
Clinical Professor
Edson College of Nursing and Health Innovation
Arizona State University
Phoenix, Arizona

POWERPOINT PRESENTATIONS

Bonnie Heintzelman, RN, MS, CMSRN
Assistant Professor of Nursing
Pennsylvania College of Technology
Williamsport, Pennsylvania

Michelle A. Walczak, RN, MSN
Associate Professor of Nursing
Pennsylvania College of Technology
Williamsport, Pennsylvania

TEACH FOR NURSES

Margaret R. Rateau, RN, PhD, CNE
Assistant Professor
School of Nursing, Education, and Human Studies
Robert Morris University
Moon Township, Pennsylvania

Janice Sarasnick, RN, PhD, CHSE
Associate Professor of Nursing
Robert Morris University
Moon Township, Pennsylvania

NCLEX EXAMINATION REVIEW QUESTIONS

Mistey D. Bailey, RN, MSN
Lecturer, Nursing
Kent State University Tuscarawas
New Philadelphia, Ohio

Shelly Stefka, RN, MSN
Lecturer, Nursing
Kent State University Tuscarawas
New Philadelphia, Ohio

STUDY GUIDE

Collin Bowman-Woodall, RN, MS
Assistant Professor
Samuel Merritt University
San Francisco Peninsula Campus
San Mateo, California

CLINICAL COMPANION

Debra Hagler, RN, PhD, ACNS-BC, CNE, CHSE, ANEF, FAAN
Clinical Professor
Edson College of Nursing and Health Innovation
Arizona State University
Phoenix, Arizona

EVIDENCE-BASED PRACTICE BOXES

Linda Bucher, RN, PhD, CEN, CNE
Emerita Professor
University of Delaware
Newark, Delaware

NURSING CARE PLANS

Collin Bowman-Woodall, RN, MS
Assistant Professor
Samuel Merritt University
San Francisco Peninsula Campus
San Mateo, California

REVIEWERS

Kristen Ryan Barry-Rodgers, RN, BSN, CEN
Emergency Department Charge and Staff Nurse
Virtua Memorial Hospital
Mt. Holly, New Jersey

Michelle Bussard, PhD, RN
RN to BSN Online eCampus
    Program Director
College of Health and Human Services
Bowling Green State University
Bowling Green, Ohio

Margaret A. Chesnutt, MSN, FNP, BC, CORLN
Nurse Practitioner
Primary Care
Veterans Administration Medical Center
Decatur, Georgia

Ann Crawford, RN, PhD, CNS, CEN
Professor
Department of Nursing
University of Mary Hardin-Baylor
Belton, Texas

Jonel L. Gomez, DNP, ARNP, CPCO, COE
Nurse Practitioner
Ophthalmic Facial Plastic Surgery Specialists
Stephen Laquis, MD
Fort Myers, Florida

Jennifer Hebert, MSN, RN-BC, NE-BC
Manager, Patient Care Services
Nursing Administration
Sentara Princess Anne Hospital
Virginia Beach, Virginia

Haley Hoy, PhD, APRN
Associate Professor
College of Nursing
University of Alabama in Huntsville
Huntsville, Alabama
Nurse Practitioner
Vanderbilt Lung Transplantation
Vanderbilt Medical Center
Nashville, Tennessee

Coretta M. Jenerette, PhD, RN, CNE, AOCN
Associate Professor
School of Nursing
University of North Carolina at
    Chapel Hill
Chapel Hill, North Carolina

Beth Karasin, MSN, APN, AGACNP-BC, RNFA, CNOR
Advanced Practice Nurse
Neurosurgery
Atlantic Neurosurgical Specialists
Morristown, New Jersey

Mark Karasin, DNP, APRN, AGACNP-BC, CNOR
Advanced Practice Nurse
Cardiothoracic Surgery
Robert Wood Johnson University Hospital
New Brunswick, New Jersey
Adjunct Faculty
Center for Professional Development
School of Nursing
Rutgers University
Newark, New Jersey

Kristen Keller, DNP, ACNP-BC, PMHNP-BC
Nurse Practitioner
Trauma and Acute Care Surgery
Banner Thunderbird Medical Center
Glendale, Arizona

Suzanne M. Mahon, DNSc, RN, AOCN(R), AGN-BC
Professor
Division of Hematology/Oncology
Department of Internal Medicine
Adult Nursing, School of Nursing
Saint Louis University
St. Louis, Missouri

Helen Miley, RN, PhD, AG-ACNP
Specialty Director of Adult Gerontology
Acute Care Nurse Practitioner Program
School of Nursing
Rutgers University
Newark, New Jersey

Linda L. Morris, PhD, APN, CCNS, FCCM
Clinical Nurse Educator
Associate Professor of Physical Medicine and Rehabilitation
    and Anesthesiology
Academy Department
Shirley Ryan Ability Lab
Northwestern University Feinberg School of Medicine
Chicago, Illinois

Louise O'Keefe, PhD, CRNP
Assistant Professor and Director
Faculty and Staff Clinic
College of Nursing
University of Alabama in Huntsville
Huntsville, Alabama

Catherine R. Ratliff, RN, PhD
Clinical Associate Professor and Nurse Practitioner
School of Nursing/Vascular Surgery
University of Virginia Health System
Charlottesville, Virginia

Lori M. Rhudy, RN, PhD, CNRN, ACNS-BC
Clinical Associate Professor
School of Nursing
University of Minnesota
Minneapolis, Minnesota
Nurse Scientist
Division of Nursing Research
Mayo Clinic
Rochester, Minnesota

Cynthia Ann Smith, DNP, APRN, CNN-NP, FNP-BC
Nurse Practitioner
Renal Consultants, PLLC
South Charleston, West Virginia

Janice Smolowitz, PhD, DNP, EdD
Dean and Professor
School of Nursing
Montclair State University
Montclair, New Jersey

Charity L. Tan, MSN, ACNP-BC
Acute Care Nurse Practitioner
Neurological Surgery
University of California Davis Health
Sacramento, California

Kara Ann Ventura, DNP, PNP, FNP
Director
Liver Transplant Program
Yale New Haven
New Haven, Connecticut

Robert M. Welch, MSN, FNP, CRNO
Nurse Practitioner
Ophthalmology—Retina
Neveda Retina Associates
Reno, Nevada

Mary Zellinger, APRN-CCNS, MN, ANP-BC, CCRN-CSC, FCCM
Clinical Nurse Specialist
Cardiovascular Critical Care
Nursing Department
Emory University Hospital
Atlanta, Georgia

To the Profession of Nursing and to the Important People in Our Lives

Mariann

My husband Jeff, our daughters
Kate and Sarah,
and my parents, Mick and Mary.

Jeff

My parents, Raymond and Virginia,
thank you for believing in me and
providing me the opportunity to become a nurse.

Dottie

My husband Steve and my children Megan, E.J., Jessica, and Matthew, who have
supported me through four college degrees and countless writing projects; and to
my son-in-law Al, our grandsons Oscar and Stephen, and my new daughter-in-law
Melissa.

Debbie

My husband James, our children Matthew,
Andrew, Amanda, and Diana, and our granddaughter Emma.

Courtney

To future nurses and the advancement of health care globally.

The eleventh edition of *Lewis's Medical-Surgical Nursing: Assessment and Management of Clinical Problems* incorporates the most current medical-surgical nursing information in an easy-to-use format. This textbook is a comprehensive resource containing the essential information that students need to prepare for class, examinations, clinical assignments, and safe and comprehensive patient care. The text and accompanying resources include many features to help students learn key medical-surgical nursing content, including patient and caregiver teaching, gerontology, interprofessional care, cultural and ethnic considerations, patient safety, genetics, nutrition and drug therapy, evidence-based practice, and much more.

To address the rapidly changing practice environment, all efforts were directed toward building on the strengths of the previous editions while delivering this more effective new edition. To help students and faculty members focus on the most important concepts in patient care, most chapters open with a conceptual focus that introduces students to the common concepts shared by patients experiencing the main exemplars discussed in the chapter. This edition features more body maps and has many new illustrations. Lengthy diagnostic tables in the assessment chapters have been separated into specific categories, including radiologic studies and serology studies. The previously combined visual and auditory content is now in separate chapters focusing on the assessment and management of vision and hearing disorders. New Promoting Population Health boxes address strategies to improve health outcomes.

For a text to be effective, it must be understandable. In this edition, great effort has been put into improving the readability and lowering the reading level. Students will find more clear and easier-to-read language, with an engaging conversational style. The narrative addresses the reader, helping make the text more personal and an active learning tool. The language is more positive. For example, particular side effects and complications are referred to as *common,* as opposed to *not uncommon.*

International Classification for Nursing Practice (ICNP) nursing diagnoses, one of the terminologies recognized by the American Nurses Association, are used throughout the text and ancillary materials. The language is similar to that of NANDA-I. ICNP nursing diagnoses are used in many facilities worldwide to document nursing care in electronic health records. By introducing students to the ICNP nursing diagnoses, students will learn a more shared vocabulary. This should translate into the more accurate use of diagnostic language in clinical practice across healthcare settings.

Contributors were selected for their expertise in specific content areas; one or more specialists in a given subject area have thoroughly reviewed each chapter to increase accuracy. The editors have undertaken final rewriting and editing to achieve internal consistency. The comprehensive and timely content, special features, attractive layout, full-color illustrations, and student-friendly writing style combine to make this the textbook used in more nursing schools than any other medical-surgical nursing textbook.

ORGANIZATION

Content is organized into 2 major divisions. The first division, Sections 1 through 3 (Chapters 1 through 16), discusses general concepts related to the care of adult patients. The second division, Sections 4 through 13 (Chapters 17 through 68), presents nursing assessment and nursing management of medical-surgical problems. At the beginning of each chapter, the Conceptual Focus helps students focus on the key concepts and integrate concepts with exemplars affecting different body systems. Learning Outcomes and Key Terms assist students in identifying the key content for that chapter.

The various body systems are grouped to reflect their interrelated functions. Each section is organized around 2 central themes: assessment and management. Chapters dealing with assessment of a body system include a discussion of the following:

1. A brief review of anatomy and physiology, focusing on information that will promote understanding of nursing care
2. Health history and noninvasive physical assessment skills to expand the knowledge base on which treatment decisions are made
3. Common diagnostic studies, expected results, and related nursing responsibilities to provide easily accessible information

Management chapters focus on the pathophysiology, clinical manifestations, diagnostic studies, interprofessional care, and nursing management of various diseases and disorders. The nursing management sections are presented in a consistent format, organized into assessment, nursing diagnoses, planning, implementation, and evaluation. To emphasize the importance of patient care in and across various clinical settings, nursing implementation of all major health problems is organized by the following levels of care:

1. Health Promotion
2. Acute Care
3. Ambulatory Care

SPECIAL FEATURES

The 6 competencies for registered nursing practice identified by QSEN serve as the foundation of the text and are highlighted in the core content, case studies, and nursing care plans.

- *New!* **Nursing Management** tables and boxes focus on the actions nurses need to take to deliver safe, quality, effective patient care.
- *New!* **Diagnostic Studies** tables focus on the specific type of study, such as interventional, serologic, or radiologic, with more detailed information on interpreting results and associated nursing care.
- **Cultural and ethnic health disparities** content and boxes in the text highlight risk factors and important issues related to the nursing care of various ethnic groups. A special Culturally Competent Care heading denotes cultural and ethnic content related to diseases and disorders. Chapter 2 (Health Equity and Culturally Competent Care) discusses health status differences among groups of people related to access to care, economic aspects of health care, gender and cultural issues, and the nurse's role in promoting health equity.
- **Interprofessional care** is highlighted in special Interprofessional Care sections in all management chapters and Interprofessional Care tables throughout the text.

- **Focused Assessment boxes** in all assessment chapters provide brief checklists that help students do a more practical "assessment on the run" or bedside approach to assessment. They can be used to evaluate the status of previously identified health problems and monitor for signs of new problems.
- **Safety Alert boxes** highlight important patient safety issues and focus on the National Patient Safety Goals.
- **Pathophysiology Maps** outline complex concepts related to diseases in a flowchart format, making them easier to understand.
- **Patient and caregiver teaching** is an ongoing theme throughout the text. Chapter 4 (Patient and Caregiver Teaching) emphasizes the increasing importance and prevalence of patient management of chronic illnesses and conditions and the role of the caregiver in patient care.
- *New!* **Conceptual Focus** at the beginning of each chapter helps students focus on the key concepts and integrate concepts with exemplars affecting different body systems.
- **Gerontology and chronic illness** are discussed in Chapter 5 (Chronic Illness and Older Adults) and included throughout the text under Gerontologic Considerations headings and in Gerontologic Differences in Assessment tables.
- **Nutrition** is highlighted throughout the textbook. Nutritional Therapy tables summarize nutritional interventions and promote healthy lifestyles in patients with various health problems.
- *New!* **Promoting Population Health boxes** present health care goals and interventions as they relate to specific disorders, such as diabetes and cancer, and to health promotion, such as preserving hearing and maintaining a healthy weight.
- **Extensive drug therapy** content includes Drug Therapy tables and concise Drug Alerts highlighting important safety considerations for key drugs.
- **Genetics content** includes:
  - Genetics in Clinical Practice boxes that summarize the genetic basis, genetic testing, and clinical implications for genetic disorders that affect adults
  - A genetics chapter that focuses on practical application of nursing care as it relates to this important topic
  - Genetic Risk Alerts in the assessment chapters, which call attention to important genetic risks
  - Genetic Link headings in the management chapters, which highlight the specific genetic bases of many disorders
- **Gender Differences boxes** discuss how women and men are affected differently by conditions such as pain and hypertension.
- **Check Your Practice boxes** challenge students to think critically, analyze patient assessment data, and implement the appropriate intervention. Scenarios and discussion questions are provided to promote active learning.
- **Complementary & Alternative Therapies boxes** expand on this information and summarize what nurses need to know about therapies such as herbal remedies, acupuncture, and yoga.
- **Ethical/Legal Dilemmas boxes** promote critical thinking for timely and sensitive issues that nursing students may deal with in clinical practice—topics such as informed consent, advance directives, and confidentiality.
- **Emergency Management tables** outline the emergency treatment of health problems most likely to require emergency intervention.

- **Nursing care plans** on the Evolve website focus on common disorders or exemplars. These care plans incorporate ICNP nursing diagnoses, Nursing Interventions Classification (NIC), and Nursing Outcomes Classification (NOC) in a way that clearly shows the linkages among NIC, NOC, and nursing diagnoses and applies them to nursing practice.
- Coverage on delegation and prioritization includes:
  - Specific topics and skills related to delegation and the nurse's role in working with members of the interprofessional team, which are detailed in Nursing Management tables.
  - Delegation and prioritization questions in case studies and Bridge to NCLEX Examination Questions.
  - Nursing interventions throughout the text, listed in order of priority.
  - Nursing diagnoses in the nursing care plans, listed in order of priority.
- **Assessment Abnormalities tables** in assessment chapters alert the nurse to commonly encountered abnormalities and their possible etiologies.
- **Nursing Assessment tables** summarize the key subjective and objective data related to common diseases. Subjective data are organized by functional health patterns.
- **Health History tables** in assessment chapters present key questions to ask patients related to a specific disease or disorder.
- **Evidence-based practice** is covered in Applying the Evidence boxes and evidence-based practice-focused questions in the case studies. Applying the Evidence boxes use a case study approach to help students learn to use evidence in making patient care decisions.
- **Informatics boxes and content** in Chapter 4 (Patient and Caregiver Teaching) reflect the current use and importance of technology as it relates to patient self-management.
- **Bridge to NCLEX® Examination Questions** at the end of each chapter are matched to the Learning Outcomes and help students learn the important points in the chapter. Answers are provided just below the questions for immediate feedback, and rationales are provided on the Evolve website.
- **Case Studies** with photos bring patients to life. Management chapters have case studies at the end of the chapters. These cases help students learn how to prioritize care and manage patients in the clinical setting. Unfolding case studies are included in each assessment chapter, and case studies that focus on managing care of multiple patients are included at the end of each section. Discussion questions with a focus on prioritization, delegation, and evidence-based practice are included in all case studies. Answer guidelines are provided on the Evolve website.

LEARNING SUPPLEMENTS FOR STUDENTS

- The handy **Clinical Companion** presents approximately 200 common medical-surgical conditions and procedures in a concise, alphabetical format for quick clinical reference. Designed for portability, this popular reference includes the essential, need-to-know information for treatments and procedures in which nurses play a major role. An attractive and functional four-color design highlights key information for quick, easy reference.
- An exceptionally thorough **Study Guide** contains over 500 pages of review material that reflect the content found in

the textbook. It features a wide variety of clinically relevant exercises and activities, including NCLEX-format multiple choice and alternate format questions, case studies, anatomy review, critical thinking activities, and much more. It features an attractive four-color design and many alternate-item format questions to better prepare students for the NCLEX examination. An answer key is included to provide students with immediate feedback as they study.

- The **Evolve Student Resources** are available online at *http://evolve.elsevier.com/Lewis/medsurg* and include the following valuable learning aids organized by chapter:
  - Printable **Key Points** summaries for each chapter.
  - 1000 NCLEX examination **Review Questions.**
  - **Answer Guidelines** to the case studies in the textbook.
  - **Rationales for the Bridge to NCLEX® Examination Questions** in the textbook.
  - 55 **Interactive Case Studies** with state-of-the-art animations and a variety of learning activities, which provide students with immediate feedback. Ten of the case studies are enhanced with photos and narration of the clinical scenarios.
  - Customizable **Nursing Care Plans** for over 60 common disorder or exemplars.
  - **Conceptual Care Map Creator.**
  - **Audio glossary** of key terms, available as comprehensive alphabetical glossary and organized by chapter.
  - **Fluids and Electrolytes Tutorial.**
  - **Content Updates.**
- More than just words on a screen, **Elsevier eBooks** come with a wealth of built-in study tools and interactive functionality to help students better connect with the course material and their instructors. In addition, with the ability to fit an entire library on one portable device, students have the ability to study when, where, and how they want.

TEACHING SUPPLEMENTS FOR INSTRUCTORS

- The **Evolve Instructor Resources** (available online at *http://evolve.elsevier.com/Lewis/medsurg*) remain the most comprehensive set of instructor's materials available, containing the following:
  - **TEACH for Nurses Lesson Plans** with electronic resources organized by chapter to help instructors develop and manage the course curriculum. This exciting resource includes:
    - Objectives
    - Pre-class activities
    - Nursing curriculum standards
    - Student and instructor chapter resource listings
    - Teaching strategies, with learning activities and assessment methods tied to learning outcomes
    - **Case studies** with answer guidelines
  - The **Test Bank** features over 2000 NCLEX examination test questions with text page references and answers coded for NCLEX Client Needs category, nursing process, and cognitive level. The test bank includes hundreds

of prioritization, delegation, and multiple patient questions. All alternate-item format questions are included. The ExamView software allows instructors to create new tests; edit, add, and delete test questions; sort questions by NCLEX category, cognitive level, nursing process step, and question type; and administer and grade online tests.

- The **Image Collection** contains more than 800 full-color images from the text for use in lectures.
- An extensive collection of **PowerPoint Presentations** includes over 125 different presentations focused on the most common diseases and disorders. The presentations have been thoroughly revised to include helpful instructor notes/teaching tips, unfolding case studies, illustrations and photos not found in the book, new animations, and updated audience response questions for use with iClicker and other audience response systems.
- Course management system.
- Access to all student resources listed above.
- The **Simulation Learning System (SLS)** is an online toolkit that helps instructors and facilitators effectively incorporate medium- to high-fidelity simulation into their nursing curriculum. Detailed patient scenarios promote and enhance the clinical decision-making skills of students at all levels. The SLS provides detailed instructions for preparation and implementation of the simulation experience, debriefing questions that encourage critical thinking, and learning resources to reinforce student comprehension. Each scenario in the SLS complements the textbook content and helps bridge the gap between lecture and clinical. The SLS provides the perfect environment for students to practice what they are learning in the text for a true-to-life, hands-on learning experience.

ACKNOWLEDGMENTS

The editors are especially grateful to many people at Elsevier who assisted with this revision effort. In particular, we wish to thank the team of Jamie Blum, Rebecca Leenhouts, Denise Roslonski, Clay Broeker, and Julie Eddy. In addition, we want to thank Kristin Oyirifi in marketing. We also wish to thank our contributors and reviewers for their assistance with the revision process.

We are particularly indebted to the faculty, nurses, and student nurses who have put their faith in our textbook to assist them on their path to excellence. The increasing use of this book throughout the United States, Canada, Australia, and other parts of the world has been gratifying. We appreciate the many users who have shared their comments and suggestions on the previous editions.

We sincerely hope that this book will assist both students and clinicians in practicing truly professional nursing.

Mariann M. Harding
Jeffrey Kwong
Dottie Roberts
Debra Hagler
Courtney Reinisch

CONTENTS

SECTION THIRTEEN Care in Specialized Settings

APPENDIXES

CONCEPTS EXEMPLARS

Acid–Base Balance
Chronic Kidney Disease
Diarrhea
Metabolic Acidosis
Metabolic Alkalosis
Respiratory Acidosis
Respiratory Alkalosis

Cellular Regulation
Anemia
Breast Cancer
Cervical Cancer
Colon Cancer
Endometrial Cancer
Head and Neck Cancer
Leukemia
Lung Cancer
Lymphoma
Melanoma
Prostate Cancer

Clotting
Disseminated Intravascular
   Coagulopathy
Pulmonary Embolism
Thrombocytopenia
Venous Thromboembolism

Cognition
Alzheimer's Disease
Delirium

Elimination
Benign Prostatic Hypertrophy
Chronic Kidney Disease
Constipation
Diarrhea
Intestinal Obstruction
Pyelonephritis
Prostatitis
Renal Calculi

Fluids and Electrolytes
Burns
Hyperkalemia
Hypernatremia
Hypokalemia
Hyponatremia

Gas Exchange
Acute Respiratory Failure
Acute Respiratory Distress Syndrome
Asthma

Chronic Obstructive Pulmonary Disease
Cystic Fibrosis
Lung Cancer
Pulmonary Embolism

Glucose Regulation
Cushing's Syndrome
Diabetes Mellitus

Hormonal Regulation
Addison's Disease
Hyperthyroidism
Hypothyroidism

Immunity
Allergic Rhinitis
Anaphylaxis
HIV Infection
Organ Transplantation
Peptic Ulcer Disease

Infection
Antimicrobial Resistant Infections
Health Care–Associated Infections
Hepatitis
Pneumonia
Tuberculosis
Urinary Tract Infection

Inflammation
Appendicitis
Cholecystitis
Glomerulonephritis
Pancreatitis
Pelvic Inflammatory Disease
Peritonitis
Rheumatoid Arthritis

Intracranial Regulation
Brain Tumor
Head Injury
Meningitis
Seizure Disorder
Stroke

Mobility
Fractures
Low Back Pain
Multiple Sclerosis
Osteoarthritis
Parkinson's Disease
Spinal Cord Injury

Nutrition
Gastroesophageal Reflux Disease
Inflammatory Bowel Disease
Metabolic Syndrome
Malnutrition
Obesity

Perfusion
Acute Coronary Syndrome
Atrial Fibrillation
Cardiogenic Shock
Endocarditis
Heart Failure
Hyperlipidemia
Hypertension
Hypovolemic Shock
Mitral Valve Prolapse
Peripheral Artery Disease
Septic Shock
Sickle Cell Disease

Reproduction
Early Pregnancy Loss
Ectopic Pregnancy
Infertility

Sleep
Insomnia
Sleep Apnea

Sensory Perception
Cataracts
Glaucoma
Hearing Loss
Macular Degeneration
Otitis Media

Sexuality
Erectile Dysfunction
Leiomyomas
Menopause
Sexually Transmitted Infection

Thermoregulation
Frostbite
Heat Stroke
Hyperthyroidism

Tissue Integrity
Burns
Pressure Injuries
Wound Healing

SPECIAL FEATURES

DIAGNOSTIC STUDIES TABLES

DRUG THERAPY TABLES

NURSING ASSESSMENT TABLES

NURSING MANAGEMENT BOXES

NUTRITIONAL THERAPY TABLES

PATIENT & CAREGIVER TEACHING TABLES

PROMOTING HEALTH EQUITY

PROMOTING POPULATION HEALTH BOXES

Professional Nursing

Mariann M. Harding

Caring is the essence of nursing.

Jean Watson

http://evolve.elsevier.com/Lewis/medsurg/

CONCEPTUAL FOCUS

Care Competencies
Leadership

Professional Identity

LEARNING OUTCOMES

1. Describe professional nursing practice in terms of domain, definitions, and recipients of care.
2. Compare the different scopes of practice available to professional nurses.
3. Describe the role of critical thinking skills and using the nursing process to provide patient-centered care.
4. Apply the SBAR procedure and effective communication techniques in the clinical setting.

5. Explore the role of the professional nurse in delegating care to licensed practical/vocational nurses and unlicensed assistive personnel.
6. Discuss the role of integrating safety and quality improvement processes into nursing practice.
7. Evaluate the role of informatics and technology in nursing practice.
8. Apply concepts of evidence-based practice to nursing practice.

KEY TERMS

advanced practice registered nurse (APRN), p. 2
case management, p. 7
clinical pathways, p. 9
clinical reasoning, p. 8
critical thinking, p. 8

delegation, p. 9
electronic health records (EHRs), p. 13
evidence-based practice (EBP), p. 13
interprofessional team, p. 8
nursing, p. 2

nursing process, p. 4
SBAR (Situation-Background-Assessment-Recommendation), p. 9
serious reportable event (SRE), p. 10
telehealth, p. 8

This chapter presents an overview of professional nursing practice, discussing the wide variety of roles and responsibilities that nurses fulfill to meet society's health care needs. This overview includes several key concepts that are part of competent nursing practice. These include safety, quality, informatics, and collaboration.

PROFESSIONAL NURSING PRACTICE

Domain of Nursing Practice

Nursing practice today consists of a wide variety of roles and responsibilities necessary to meet society's health care needs. As a nurse, you are the frontline professional of health care (Fig. 1.1). You can practice in virtually all health care settings and communities. You have never been more important to health

care than you are today. As a nurse, you (1) offer skilled care to those recuperating from illness or injury, (2) advocate for patients' rights, (3) teach patients to manage their health, (4) support patients and their caregivers at critical times, and (5) help them navigate the complex health care system. Although many nurses work in acute care facilities, nurses also practice in long-term care, home care, community health, public health centers, schools, and ambulatory or outpatient clinics. Wherever you practice, recipients of your care include individuals, families, groups, or communities.

The American Nurses Association (ANA) states that the authority for nursing practice is based on a contract with society that acknowledges professional rights and responsibilities, as well as mechanisms for public accountability.[1] The knowledge and skills that make up nursing practice are based on

1

FIG. 1.1 Nurses are frontline professionals of health care. (© Michael Jung/iStock/Thinkstock.)

society's expectations and needs. Nursing practice continues to evolve according to society's health care needs and as knowledge and technology expand. This chapter introduces concepts and factors that affect professional nursing practice.

Definitions of Nursing

Well-known definitions of nursing show that the basic themes of health, illness, and caring have existed since Florence Nightingale described nursing. Following are 2 such examples:

- Nursing is putting the patient in the best condition for nature to act (Nightingale).[2]
- The nurse's unique function is to aid patients, sick or well, in performing those activities contributing to health or its recovery (or to peaceful death) that they would perform unaided if they had the necessary strength, will, or knowledge—and to do this in such a way as to help them gain independence as rapidly as possible (Henderson).[3]

In 1980 the ANA defined nursing as "the diagnosis and treatment of human responses to actual and potential health problems."[1] In this context, your care of a person with a fractured hip would focus on the patient's response to impaired mobility, pain, and loss of independence. The 2010 edition of the ANA's *Nursing: A Social Policy Statement* provided a new definition of nursing that reflects the continuing evolution of nursing practice:

Nursing is the protection, promotion, and optimization of health and abilities, prevention of illness and injury, alleviation of suffering through the diagnosis and treatment of human response, and advocacy in the care of individuals, families, communities, and populations.[1]

Nursing's View of Humanity

A person has physiologic (or biophysical), psychologic (or emotional), sociocultural (or interpersonal), spiritual, and environmental components or dimensions. In this book, we consider a person to be in constant interaction with a changing environment. A person is composed of interrelated dimensions and not separate entities. Thus a problem in 1 dimension may affect 1 or more of the other dimensions. A person's behavior is meaningful and oriented toward fulfilling needs, coping with stress, and developing one's self. However, at times a person needs help to meet these needs, cope successfully, or develop his or her unique potential.

Scope of Nursing Practice

The essential core of nursing practice is to deliver holistic, patient-centered care. It includes assessment and evaluation, giving a variety of interventions, patient and family teaching, and being a member of the interprofessional health care team.

The extent that nurses engage in their scope of practice depends on their educational preparation, experience, role, and state law. To enter practice, a nurse must complete an accredited program and pass an examination verifying that the nurse has the knowledge necessary to provide safe care. Entry-level nurses with associate or baccalaureate degrees are prepared to function as generalists. At this level, nurses provide direct health care and focus on ensuring coordinated and comprehensive care to patients in a variety of settings. Nurses work collaboratively with other health care providers to manage the needs of persons and groups.

With experience and continued study, nurses may specialize in a specific practice area. Certification is a formal way for nurses to obtain professional recognition for having expertise in a specialty area. A variety of nursing organizations offer certification in nursing specialties.[4] Certification usually requires a certain amount of clinical experience and successful completion of an examination. Recertification usually requires ongoing clinical experience and continuing education. Common nursing specialties include critical care, women's health, geriatric, medical-surgical, perinatal, emergency, psychiatric/mental health, and community health nursing.

Additional formal education and experience can prepare nurses for advanced practice. An advanced practice registered nurse (APRN) is a nurse educated at the master's or doctoral level, with advanced education in pathophysiology, pharmacology, and health assessment and expertise in a specialized area of practice. APRNs include clinical nurse specialists, nurse practitioners, nurse midwives, and nurse anesthetists. APRNs play a vital role in the health care delivery system. In addition to managing and delivering direct patient care, APRNs have roles in leadership, quality improvement, evidence-based practice, and informatics.

The doctor of nursing practice (DNP) degree is a practice-focused terminal nursing degree. With raising the educational preparation for APRNs to the doctoral level, nursing is at the same level as other health professions that offer practice doctorates (e.g., pharmacy [PharmD], physical therapy [DPT]). Nurses with a research-focused doctorate (PhD) typically are used in health care settings as nurse faculty, clinical experts, researchers, and health care system executives.

Standards of Professional Nursing Practice

To guide nurses in how to perform professionally, the ANA defined Standards of Professional Nursing Practice. There are 2 parts, Standards of Practice and Standards of Professional Performance.[5] The Standards of Practice describe a competent level of nursing care, based on the nursing process. The Standards of Professional Performance describe behavioral competencies expected of a nurse. You are following the performance standards when you practice ethically and use evidence-based practice. Communicating effectively and staying competent in practice are important. You must be able to work in collaboration with other interprofessional team members, patients, and caregivers.

INFLUENCES ON PROFESSIONAL NURSING PRACTICE

Expanding Knowledge and Technology

Ever-changing technology and rapidly expanding clinical knowledge add to the complexity of health care. The increased treatment, diagnostic, and care options available are changing care delivery and extending patients' lives. Discoveries in genetics are changing the way we think about diseases such as cancer and heart disease. For example, genetic information guides breast cancer screening. If a woman has cancer, this information allows for treatment and drug therapy based on her genetic makeup. Ethical dilemmas and controversies arise about the use of new scientific knowledge and the disparities that exist in patients' access to technologically advanced health care. Throughout this book, genetics, informatics, and ethical/legal boxes highlight expanding knowledge and technology's impact on nursing practice.

Diverse Populations

Patient populations are more diverse than ever. Americans are living longer, with the number of people with chronic illnesses and multiple co-morbidities increasing. Unlike those who receive acute, episodic care, patients with chronic illnesses have complex needs. They see different health care providers in various settings over an extended period. With care shifting from hospitals and nursing homes to managed care in the community, you need to be able to manage and coordinate care when patients are transitioning among different settings.

At the same time, you will be caring for a more culturally and ethnically diverse population. When delivering care, you must consider the patient's and caregiver's cultural beliefs and values. Immigrants, particularly undocumented immigrants, often lack the resources necessary to access health care. Inability to pay for health care is related to a tendency to delay seeking care, resulting in illnesses that are more serious at the time of diagnosis. Boxes throughout this book emphasize the influence of such factors as gender, culture, and ethnicity on nursing practice.

Consumerism

Health care is a consumer-focused business, and patients today are more involved in their health care. They want more control over their health care and expect high-quality, coordinated, and financially reasonable care. Health information is readily available. Many patients are very knowledgeable about their health and seek information about health problems and health care from media and Internet sources. They gather information so that they can have a voice in making decisions about their health care. As a nurse, you must be able to help patients access, interpret, and use safe health care information (Fig. 1.2).

Health Care Financing

High health care costs are a growing problem. There are many reasons for the continued increase in costs. These include the rising use of prescription medications, administrative costs, and new medical innovations and treatments.[6] Many changes in health care systems that influence nursing care delivery are

FIG. 1.2 The patient, family, and nurse collaborate as part of coordinating high-quality care. (© monkeybusinessimages/iStock/Thinkstock.)

started by the government, employers, insurance companies, and regulating agencies. They are usually in effort to contain spending and provide more cost-effective health care. Historically, the most notable event related to reimbursement was the establishment of prospective payment systems in the Medicare program. With this system, payment for hospital services for Medicare patients are based on flat fees determined by the diseases and problems treated during the admission. For example, if a patient had a total knee replacement, the hospital receives a set sum of money, such as $45,000, for the patient's care.

Other health care systems followed by introducing managed care systems that use prospective payment as a means of offering cost-effective health care delivery. In health maintenance organizations (HMOs) and preferred provider organizations (PPOs), charges are negotiated before the delivery of care using fixed reimbursement rates or capitation fees for medical care, hospitalization, and other health care services.

Now, quality and performance initiatives are driving further changes in health care financing. Value-based purchasing programs base reimbursement to health care providers on their performance on certain quality measures. These quality measures include clinical outcomes, patient safety, patient satisfaction, and the provider's adherence to evidence-based practice. Those who provide quality care at a lower cost may receive more payment.

As part of value-based purchasing, payment for care can be withheld if a patient experiences events such as developing a pressure injury during a hospital stay or having something happen that is considered preventable (e.g., a fall-related injury, having wrong-site surgery).[7] This type of event is considered a *serious reportable event (SRE)*. SREs are discussed later in this chapter on p. 10.

Health Policy

Legislation has serious implications for health care delivery and nursing practice. The 2010 Patient Protection and Affordable Care Act (ACA) was the most important health care legislation since the creation of Medicare in 1965. The ACA triggered changes throughout the health care system. The ACA's main goal was to increase access to health care. The ACA created new health care delivery and payment models that emphasized teamwork, care coordination, and quality care.

The ACA encourages the creation of accountable care organizations (ACOs). ACOs are groups of physicians, hospitals, and other health care providers who unite to coordinate care for Medicare patients. The goal of an ACO is to ensure that patients, especially the chronically ill, get the right care at the right time, while avoiding duplicate services and preventing errors. As a nurse, you must take a leadership role in creating health care systems that provide safe, quality, patient-centered care.

Professional Nursing Organizations

The ANA is the primary professional nursing organization. There are many professional specialty organizations, such as the American Association of Critical-Care Nurses (AACN), National Association of Orthopedic Nurses (NAON), and Oncology Nursing Society (ONS). Professional organizations play a role in promoting quality patient care and professional nursing practice. These roles include developing standards of practice and codes of ethics, supporting research, and lobbying for legislation and regulations. Major nursing organizations promote research into the causes of errors, develop strategies to prevent future errors, and address nursing issues that affect the nurse's ability to deliver patient care safely. Nurses join a professional organization to keep current in their practice and network with others who are interested in a specific practice area.

A program that supports nurses is the American Nurses Credentialing Center's Magnet Recognition Program. The Magnet program "recognizes health care organizations for quality patient care, nursing excellence and innovations in professional nursing practice."[8] Magnet designation shows a high quality of nursing care and achievement of a positive practice environment for nurses. Nurses who work in Magnet facilities have low turnover and burnout rates and more opportunities for professional and personal growth. This leads to better patient outcomes and greater career satisfaction.

Nursing Core Competencies

Several high-profile reports over the past 20 years have highlighted problems with the quality of health care. One of these reports, *The Future of Nursing: Leading Change, Advancing Health,* acknowledged the link between professional nursing practice and health care delivery. The report discussed how health care providers, including nurses, were not being adequately prepared to provide the highest quality care possible. It recommended making changes so that nurses will have the skills to advance health care and play leadership roles in the health care system[9] (Table 1.1).

To address nursing's role in solving these problems, the Robert Wood Johnson Foundation funded the *Quality and Safety Education*

for Nurses (QSEN) Institute. QSEN has made a major contribution to nursing by defining specific competencies that nurses need to have to practice safely and effectively in today's complex health care system. The rest of this chapter describes each of the 6 QSEN nursing core competencies and the knowledge, skills, and attitudes (KSAs) necessary in each area: (1) patient-centered care, (2) teamwork and collaboration, (3) safety, (4) quality improvement, (5) informatics, and (6) evidence-based practice[10] (Table 1.2). When you are licensed as a registered nurse, you accept responsibility to base your practice on these core competencies.

PATIENT-CENTERED CARE

Nurses have long shown that they deliver patient-centered care based on each patient's unique needs and understanding of the patient's preferences, values, and beliefs. Patient-centered care is interrelated with quality and safety. In a patient-centered care model, patients and caregivers seek and receive care from competent and knowledgeable health care professionals. In addition, patients and caregivers are involved in making decisions and coordinating care.

Nursing Process

Nurses provide patient-centered care using an organizing framework called the *nursing process*. The nursing process is a problem-solving approach to the identification and treatment of patient problems that is the foundation of nursing practice. The nursing process framework provides a structure for delivering nursing care and the knowledge, judgments, and actions that nurses use to achieve best patient outcomes. Once started, the nursing process is continuous and cyclic.

The nursing process consists of 5 phases: assessment, diagnosis, planning, implementation, and evaluation (Fig. 1.3). There is a basic order to the nursing process, beginning with assessment. *Assessment* is the collection of subjective and objective patient information on which you will base your plan of care. *Diagnosing* is the act of analyzing the assessment data and making a judgment about the nature of the data. It includes your identifying nursing diagnoses or problems and collaborative problems. During *planning,* you use nursing diagnoses and problems to develop patient outcomes or goals and identify nursing interventions to accomplish the outcomes. *Implementation* is the activation of the plan with the use of nursing interventions. *Evaluation* is a continual activity. During evaluation you decide whether the patient outcomes have been met because of the nursing interventions. If the outcomes were not met, a review of the steps of the process is necessary to figure out why not. You may need to revise the assessment (data collection), nursing diagnoses, planning (determining patient outcomes), or implementation (nursing interventions).

Standard Nursing Terminologies

The demands of the health care system challenge nursing to define its contribution to health care. The nursing profession can describe its unique role by answering questions such as: What do nurses do? How do they do it? How does it make a measurable difference in the health of those for whom they care? How are nursing's contributions different from those of medicine?

In response to these questions, nursing uses standard terminologies (also called *classification systems* or *taxonomies*) to define and evaluate nursing care. This promotes continuity of patient care and gives data showing nursing's impact on patient outcomes. Instead of using a variety of words to describe the

---

TABLE 1.1   Key Messages for the Future of Nursing

- Nurses should practice to the full extent of their education and training.
- Nurses should achieve high education and training through an improved education system that promotes seamless academic progression.
- Nurses should be full partners with physicians and other health professionals in redesigning health care.
- Effective workforce planning and policy making require better data collection and information infrastructure.

Source: IOM (now HMD) recommendations. Retrieved from *www.thefutureofnursing. org/recommendations.*

TABLE 1.2 QSEN Competencies

Competency	Knowledge, Skills, and Attitudes
Patient-Centered Care Recognize the patient and caregiver as full partners in providing compassionate and coordinated care based on respect for patient's preferences, values, and needs	• Provide care with sensitivity and respect, taking into consideration the patient's perspectives, beliefs, and cultural background • Assess level of comfort and treat appropriately • Engage the patient in an active partnership that promotes health, well-being, and self-care management • Facilitate patient's informed consent for care
Teamwork and Collaboration Function effectively within nursing and interprofessional teams	• Value the expertise of each interprofessional member • Initiate appropriate referrals • Follow communication practices that minimize risks associated with hand-offs and transitions in care • Take part in interprofessional rounds
Safety Minimize risk of harm to patients and providers	• Follow recommendations from national safety campaigns • Appropriately communicate concerns related to hazards and errors • Contribute to designing systems to improve safety
Quality Improvement Use data to monitor the outcomes of care and to improve the quality and safety of health care systems	• Use quality measures to understand performance • Identify gaps between local and best practices • Take part in investigating the circumstances surrounding a sentinel event (never event) or serious reportable event (SRE)
Informatics Use information and technology to communicate, manage knowledge, reduce errors, and support decision making	• Protect confidentiality of patient's protected health information • Document appropriately in electronic health records • Use communication technologies to coordinate patient care • Respond correctly to clinical decision-making alerts
Evidence-Based Practice Integrate best current evidence with clinical expertise and the patient/family preferences and values for delivery of optimal health care	• Read research, clinical practice guidelines, and evidence reports related to area of practice • Base patient care plan on patient's values, clinical expertise, and evidence • Continuously improve clinical practice based on new knowledge

Source: QSEN competencies. Retrieved from *www.qsen.org/competencies*.

FIG. 1.3 *Nursing process.*

same patient problems and nursing interventions, nurses use a common language to improve communication.

Standard languages are essential in exchanging information between different electronic records systems. The need for quality care makes it necessary to be able to share information in a meaningful way across care settings. Using the same language reduces ambiguity and confusion. For example, do the patient problems of pressure injury and skin breakdown mean the same thing? Does turning the patient every 2 hours mean the same thing as repositioning the patient every 2 hours? If you turn or reposition the patient every 2 hours, what is the result? Does placing the patient on a pressure-relieving mattress or a standard mattress change the results? When you use a standard language, each nurse reading and documenting in the electronic record understands the diagnosis, can provide the interventions, and can measure the outcome.

The ANA recognizes several nursing and multidisciplinary languages. Three nursing languages focus on specific phases of the nursing process: (1) NANDA International (NANDA-I): Nursing Diagnoses, Definitions, and Classification; (2) the Nursing Outcomes Classification (NOC); and (3) the Nursing Interventions Classification (NIC). Two other nursing languages, each with their own nursing diagnoses, outcomes, and interventions, include the International Classification of Nursing Practice (ICNP) and the Clinical Care Classification (CCC).

Nursing Diagnoses. The ANA defines a nursing diagnosis as the nurse's clinical judgment about the patient's response to actual or potential health conditions or needs.[11] You determine nursing diagnoses based on your analysis of the assessment data. Delivering care based on accurately identified nursing diagnoses results in more effective and safer patient care. They are the basis for selecting nursing interventions to achieve patient outcomes for which nursing is accountable. This book uses the ICNP nursing diagnosis terminology (see Appendix B).

Outcome Identification. The next step is to create the framework for delivering care by identifying outcomes and goal indicators. After choosing an outcome, you need to identify short- and/or long-term measurable goals and then list the behaviors or observations you will use to determine if the goal was attained. By identifying the right outcomes and goals, you can measure and evaluate the impact of the interventions you provide as part of your nursing practice. They also guide the interprofessional team so that we are all working to achieve the same outcomes. The outcomes achieved by patients are the most important indicator of quality in health care.[12]

Nursing Interventions. An intervention is "a single nursing action, treatment, procedure, activity, or service designed to achieve an outcome of a nursing or medical diagnosis for which the nurse is accountable."[13] This includes treatments that you perform in all settings and includes direct and indirect care. The ICNP includes more than 1100 interventions. That many interventions may seem overwhelming. You will discover the interventions you will use most often with your patient population. When planning care for a patient, choose specific interventions for the patient based on the nursing diagnosis and desired patient outcomes. You make the crucial decision of when and which interventions to use for a specific patient and situation based on your knowledge of the patient and the patient's condition.

Nursing Care Plans

In any clinical setting, you are responsible for providing a custom plan of care that includes nursing diagnoses, outcomes, and interventions. In clinical practice, electronic care plans often follow a standard format that has been adapted for that specific setting. These plans are guides for routine nursing care. You customize each to your patient's unique needs and problems.

In nursing education, the nursing process is often documented differently from clinical practice. The nursing process is often recorded in nursing care plans similar to those found on the website for this book (http://evolve.elsevier.com/Lewis/medsurg). These nursing care plans are teaching and learning tools. You practice and learn the nursing process by collecting assessment data, identifying nursing diagnoses, and selecting patient outcomes and nursing interventions. You usually should give rationales for the selected interventions.

⊚ NURSING CARE PLAN 1.1

*Patient With Heart Failure**

Nursing Diagnosis†*

Impaired Gas Exchange

Etiology: Increased preload, alveolar-capillary membrane changes
Supporting data: Abnormal O_2 saturation, hypoxemia, dyspnea, tachypnea, tachycardia, restlessness, patient's statement, "I am so short of breath"

Patient Goal

Maintains adequate O_2/CO_2 exchange at the alveolar-capillary membrane to meet O_2 needs of the body

Outcomes (NOC)	Interventions (NIC) and Rationales
Respiratory Status: Gas Exchange	**Respiratory Monitoring**
• O_2 saturation ___	• Monitor pulse oximetry, respiratory rate, rhythm, depth, and effort of respirations *to detect changes in respiratory status.*
• Arterial pH ___	• Auscultate breath sounds, noting areas of decreased or absent ventilation and presence of adventitious sounds *to detect presence of pulmonary edema.*
• PaO_2 ___	• Monitor for increased restlessness, anxiety, and work of breathing *to detect increasing hypoxemia.*
• $PaCO_2$ ___	**Oxygen Therapy**
• Chest x-ray findings ___	• Administer supplemental O_2 or other noninvasive ventilator support (e.g., bilevel positive airway pressure [BiPAP]) as needed *to maintain adequate O_2 levels.*
Measurement Scale	• Monitor the O_2 liter flow rate and placement of O_2 delivery device *to ensure O_2 is adequately delivered.*
1 = Severe deviation from normal range	• Change O_2 delivery device from mask to nasal prongs during meals as tolerated *to sustain O_2 levels while eating.*
2 = Substantial deviation from normal range	• Monitor the effectiveness of O_2 therapy *to identify hypoxemia and establish range of O_2 saturation.*
3 = Moderate deviation from normal range	**Positioning**
4 = Mild deviation from normal range	• Position patient to alleviate dyspnea (e.g., semi-Fowler's position), as appropriate, *to improve ventilation by decreasing venous return to the heart and increasing thoracic capacity.*
5 = No deviation from normal range	
• Dyspnea with exertion ___	
• Dyspnea at rest ___	
• Restlessness ___	
• Impaired cognition ___	
Measurement Scale	
1 = Severe	
2 = Substantial	
3 = Moderate	
4 = Mild	
5 = None	

*This example presents 1 nursing diagnosis for heart failure. The complete nursing care plan for heart failure is available on *http://evolve.elsevier.com/Lewis/medsurg.*
†Nursing diagnoses are listed in order of priority.

The nursing care plans associated with this book list nursing diagnoses, in order of priority, based on the ICNP, along with outcomes and interventions (NCP 1.1). When you use these care plans, you will need to customize the plan for your specific patient. You must use critical thinking to continually evaluate the situation and revise the nursing diagnoses, outcomes, and interventions to fit each patient's unique care needs.

Collaborative problems are certain physiologic complications that nurses must monitor to detect the onset of or changes in patient status.[14] Nurses manage collaborative problems using physician and nurse prescribed interventions to prevent morbidity and mortality. You identify these risks during the diagnosis phase of the nursing process. Identifying collaborative problems requires knowledge of pathophysiology and possible complications of medical treatment. Collaborative problem statements are usually written as "potential complication: _____" or "PC: _____" without a *related to* statement. An example is "PC: pulmonary embolism."

A *concept map* is another method of recording a nursing care plan. A concept map records the nursing process in a visual diagram. The map displays patient problems and interventions and shows relationships among clinical data. Nurse educators use concept mapping to teach nursing process and care planning. There are various formats for concept maps.

Conceptual care maps blend a concept map and a nursing care plan. On a conceptual care map, assessment data used to identify the patient's primary health concern are centrally positioned. Diagnostic test data, treatments, and medications surround the assessment data. Positioned below are nursing diagnoses or problems that represent the patient's responses to the health state. Listed with those are the supporting assessment data, outcomes, nursing interventions with rationales, and evaluation. After completing the map, you draw connections between identified relationships and concepts. A conceptual care map creator is available online on the website for this book. Concept maps for select case studies at the end of management chapters are available on the website at *http://evolve.elsevier. com/Lewis/medsurg.*

Continuum of Patient Care

Nursing is part of health care at all points along the patient care continuum. Depending on their health status, patients often move among a multitude of different health care settings. For example, a young man is in a trauma unit of an acute care hospital following a motor vehicle crash. After he is stable, he is transferred to a general medical-surgical unit and then to an acute rehabilitation facility. After rehabilitation is complete, he is discharged home to continue with outpatient rehabilitation, with follow-up by home health care nurses and care in an ambulatory clinic.

Decisions about the best setting for obtaining health care often depend on the cost of care and the patient's health care insurance plan and personal finances. Although the hospital is the mainstay for acute care interventions, community-based settings offer patients the opportunity to live or recover in settings that maximize their independence and preserve human dignity.

Community-based health care settings include ambulatory care, transitional care, and long-term care. *Transitional care* settings provide care in between the acute care and the home or long-term care setting. Patients may receive transitional care at an acute rehabilitation facility after head trauma or a spinal cord injury.

Long-term care refers to the care of patients for a period longer than 30 days. It may be needed for those who are severely developmentally disabled, who are mentally impaired, or who have physical deficits requiring continuous medical and nursing care (e.g., patients who are ventilator dependent or have Alzheimer's disease). Long-term care facilities include skilled nursing facilities, assisted living facilities, and residential care facilities.

There is a new emphasis on care coordination when patients transition between care settings. *Transitions of care* refer to patients moving among health care practitioners, settings, and home as their condition and care needs change.[15] As a nurse, you are an essential part of care coordination by stressing actions that meet patients' needs and facilitate safe, quality care. Collaborating with other members of the interprofessional team is critical. A lack of communication can result in an ineffective care transition, leading to drug errors and higher hospital readmission rates. For example, you are a nurse in acute care admitting a long-term care patient who has been receiving propranolol 20 mg/5 mL twice a day. The admitting orders read "propranolol 20 mg/mL, give 5 mL twice a day." You avert a potential drug error by using communication techniques to reconcile the difference.

Delivery of Nursing Care

Nurses deliver patient-centered care in collaboration with the interprofessional health care team and within the framework of a care delivery model. A care delivery model outlines how responsibilities and authority are structured to carry out patient care.[16] More positive care outcomes occur when the number and type of care providers match patient needs and there is a designated care coordinator.

In acute care settings, 2 basic models are used: team care and total patient care. *Team care* models involve a group of providers who work together to deliver care. A professional nurse is usually the team leader. As team leader, you manage and coordinate care with others, such as licensed practical/vocational nurses (LPN/VNs) and unlicensed assistive personnel (UAP). You have accountability for the quality of care delivered by team members during a work period. In total patient care models, you are responsible for planning and providing all care.

Other care models include case management and telehealth. Case management is "a collaborative process of assessment, planning, facilitation, care coordination, evaluation, and advocacy for options and services to meet an individual's and family's comprehensive health needs through communication and available resources to promote quality, cost-effective outcomes."[17] Although health care agencies implement case management in various ways, it involves managing the patient's care with other interprofessional team members across multiple care settings and levels of care.

A professional nurse often serves as the case manager. In this role, the nurse assesses the needs of patients and/or caregivers, coordinates services for them, makes appropriate referrals, and evaluates the progress toward meeting care goals. For example, a nurse case manager in an outpatient clinic has been working for 3 months with an older male patient who has multiple co-morbidities, including severe coronary artery disease, diabetes, and osteoarthritis. After he is scheduled for a coronary artery bypass, the nurse manager coordinates his care with other members of the interprofessional team. She arranges his preoperative appointments and informs the other team members so that all health care providers understand the patient's unique needs. After the patient has surgery, he develops a deep venous thrombosis in his leg. The case manager then works with the interprofessional team to evaluate the patient's discharge needs and decide whether rehabilitation or home health care is necessary for the patient. With the patient and caregiver, the team decides to discharge the patient to a rehabilitation facility. The case manager helps with the transition, again coordinating care so that the providers at the rehabilitation facility are aware of the patient's needs.

Telehealth nursing is the delivery of health care and information through telecommunication technologies, including high-speed Internet, wireless, satellite, and video communications.[18] Among the many uses of telehealth are triaging patients, monitoring patients with chronic or critical conditions, helping patients manage symptoms, providing patient and caregiver education and emotional support, and providing follow-up care. Telehealth can increase access to care. The nurse engaged in telehealth can assess the patient's health status, deliver interventions, and evaluate the outcomes of nursing care while separated geographically from the patient (Fig. 1.4).

Critical Thinking

Complex health care environments require that you use critical thinking and clinical reasoning skills to make decisions that

FIG. 1.4 An older adult performing remote blood pressure monitoring. (From Cooper K, Gosnell K: *Foundations of nursing,* St Louis, 2015, Elsevier.)

lead to the best patient outcomes. Critical thinking, your ability to focus your thinking to get the results you need in various situations, has been described as knowing how to learn, be creative, generate ideas, make decisions, and solve problems.[19]

Critical thinking is not memorizing a list of facts or the steps of a procedure. Instead, it is the ability to make judgments and solve problems by making sense of information. Learning and using critical thinking is a continual process that occurs inside and outside of the clinical setting.

Clinical reasoning is using critical thinking to examine and analyze patient care issues.[19] It involves understanding the medical and nursing implications of a patient's situation when making decisions about patient care. You use clinical reasoning when you identify a change in a patient's status, consider the context and concerns of the patient and caregiver, and decide what to do about it.

Given the complexity of patient care today, nurses need to learn and implement critical thinking and clinical reasoning skills before they gain those skills through experience in professional practice. Various experiences in nursing school offer opportunities for you to learn and make decisions about patient care. Various education activities, including interactive case studies and simulation exercises, promote practice in critical thinking and clinical reasoning. Throughout this book, select boxes, case studies, and review questions promote your use of critical thinking and clinical reasoning skills.

TEAMWORK AND COLLABORATION

Interprofessional Team

To deliver high-quality care, you need to have effective working relationships with members of the health care team. The interprofessional team is made up of providers from various disciplines, working together and sharing their expertise to provide customized care. It may consist of physicians, nurses, pharmacists, occupational and physical therapists, and others (Table 1.3). To be competent in interprofessional practice, you must collaborate in many ways by exchanging knowledge, sharing responsibility for problem solving, and making patient care decisions. You may be responsible for coordinating care among the team members, taking part in interprofessional

TABLE 1.3 Interprofessional Team Members

Team Member	Description of Services Provided
Dentist	Provides preventive and restorative treatments for problems affecting the teeth and mouth
Dietitian	Provides general nutrition services, including dietary consultation about health promotion or specialized diets
Occupational therapist (OT)	May help patient with fine motor coordination, performing activities of daily living, cognitive-perceptual skills, sensory testing, and the construction or use of assistive or adaptive equipment
Pastoral care	Offers spiritual support and guidance to patients and caregivers
Pharmacist	Prepares medications and infusion products
Physical therapist (PT)	Works with patients on improving strength and endurance, gait training, transfer training, and developing a patient education program
Physician (medical doctor [MD])	Practices medicine and treats illness and injury by prescribing medication, performing diagnostic tests and evaluations, performing surgery, and providing other medical services and advice
Physician assistant	Conducts physical exams, diagnoses and treats illnesses, and counsels on preventive health care in collaboration with a physician
Respiratory therapist	May provide oxygen therapy in the home, give specialized respiratory treatments, and teach the patient or caregiver about the proper use of respiratory equipment
Social worker	Assists patients with developing coping skills, meeting caregiver concerns, securing adequate financial resources or housing, or making referrals to social service or volunteer agencies
Speech pathologist	Focuses on treatment of speech defects and disorders, especially by using physical exercises to strengthen muscles used in speech, speech drills, and audiovisual aids that develop new speech habits

TABLE 1.4 Guidelines for Communicating Using SBAR

Purpose: SBAR is a model for effective transfer of information by providing a standard structure for concise factual communications from nurse-to-nurse, nurse-to-physician, or nurse-to–other health professionals.

Steps to Use: Before speaking with a physician or other health care professional about a patient problem, assess the patient yourself, read the most recent physician progress and nursing notes, and have the patient's chart available.

S **Situation**	• What is the situation you want to discuss? What is happening right now? • Identify self, unit. State: I am calling about: *patient, room number.* • Briefly state the problem: what it is, when it happened or started, and how severe it is. State: I have just assessed the patient and am concerned about: *describe why you are concerned.*
B **Background**	• What is the background or circumstances leading up to the situation? State pertinent background information related to the situation that may include: • Admitting diagnosis and date of admission • List of current medications, allergies, IV fluids • Most recent vital signs • Date and time of any laboratory testing and results of previous tests for comparison • Synopsis of treatment to date • Code status
A **Assessment**	• What do you think the problem is? What is your assessment of the situation? State what you think the problem is: • Changes from prior assessments • Patient condition unstable or worsening
R **Recommenda-** **tion/Request**	• What should we do to correct the problem? What is your recommendation or request? State your request. • Specific treatments • Tests needed • Patient needs to be seen now

Source: Institute for Health Care Improvement: SBAR technique for communication: A situational briefing model. Retrieved from *www.ihi.org/resources/Pages/Tools/SBAR-TechniqueforCommunicationASituationalBriefingModel.aspx.*

team meetings or rounds, and making referrals when you need expertise in specialized areas to help the patient. To do so, you must be aware of the knowledge and skills of other team members and be able to communicate effectively with them.

To help you develop the competencies necessary to practice within an interprofessional clinical environment, you may take part in education activities with students from other disciplines. Throughout this book, case studies and review questions discuss the roles others have in managing patient care.

Coordinating Care

Communication. Effective communication is key to fostering teamwork and coordinating care. To provide safe, effective care, everyone involved in a patient's care should understand the patient's condition and needs. Unfortunately, many issues result from a breakdown in communication. Miscommunication often occurs during transitions of care. One structured model used to improve communication is the SBAR (Situation-Background-Assessment-Recommendation) technique (Table 1.4). This technique offers a way to talk about a patient's condition among members of the health care team in a predictable, structured

manner. Other ways to enhance communication during transitions include using bedside rounds, having standard processes for patient hand-offs, and conducting interprofessional rounds to identify risks and develop a plan for delivering care.

Clinical Pathways. Clinical pathways, also known as care maps, are interprofessional care plans that outline the care and desired outcomes for a specific time period for patients with a specific diagnosis. Think of a clinical pathway as a road map the patient and health care team should follow. As the patient progresses along the road, the patient should receive specific care and accomplish specific goals. If a patient's progress differs from the planned path, a variance has occurred. A negative variance occurs when specific goals are not met. The nurse usually identifies when a negative variance is present and works with the interprofessional team to create a plan to address the issue.[16]

The exact content and format of clinical pathways vary among agencies and settings. Each agency usually develops its own pathways based on evidence-based practice guidelines. Common components include assessment guidelines, laboratory and diagnostic testing, medications, activity, diet, and teaching. In acute care, clinical pathways often describe which patient care components are needed at specific times (Fig. 1.5). The case types selected for this type of pathway are usually those that are high volume or high risk and predictable, such as myocardial infarction and surgical procedures (e.g., endoscopy, cholecystectomy, cataract surgery).

Delegation and Assignment. As a registered nurse (RN), you will delegate nursing care and supervise those who are qualified to deliver care. Delegation allows a care provider to perform a specific nursing activity, skill, or procedure that is beyond their usual role.[20] Delegating and assigning nursing activities is a process that, when used appropriately, results in safe, effective, and efficient patient care. Delegating can allow you more time to focus on complex patient care needs. Delegating care and supervising others will be one of your essential roles as a professional nurse.

Delegation usually involves tasks and procedures that licensed practical/vocational nurses (LPN/VNs) and unlicensed assistive personnel (UAP) perform. Nursing interventions that require independent nursing knowledge, skill, or judgment (e.g., initial assessment, patient teaching, evaluating care) are your responsibility and cannot be delegated. State nurse practice acts and agency policies identify activities that you can delegate to LPN/VNs and UAP. You will use professional judgment to select which activities to delegate. Your decision will be based on the patient's needs, the LPN/VN's and UAP's education and training, and the amount of supervision needed. The most common delegated nursing actions occur during the implementation phase of the nursing process. For example, you can delegate measuring oral intake and urine output to UAP, but you use your nursing judgment to decide if the intake and output are adequate.

The general guideline for LPN/VN practice is that they can function independently in a stable, routine situation. However, they must work under the direct supervision of a professional nurse in acute, unstable situations in which a patient's condition can rapidly change. In most states, LPN/VNs may give medications, perform sterile procedures, and perform a wide variety of interventions planned by the RN. The procedure itself is not the issue when an RN is determining what to delegate. Rather, the stability of the patient determines whether it is appropriate for an RN to delegate a procedure to an LPN/VN. For example, the LPN/VN can change a dressing on an abdominal surgical wound, but the RN should do the first dressing change and wound assessment.

Patient Name _____   Date _____

DRG# _____   Expected LOS _____<23 hours_____

	Preprocedure	Preoperative	Intraoperative	Postoperative Phase I PACU	Postoperative PHASE II PACU	Discharge	Postoperative PHASE II PACU
Medication	Review medical history	Start IV	Administer meperidine, propofol, midazolam	Administer naloxone, flumazenil pm	Pain med prn	Start on Rx omeprazole	Continue medications
Diagnostic tests	H-&-P chest x-ray, ECG, blood work	Review tests	Endoscopy procedure	None, unless complications	None	None	None
Diet	Regular	NPO	NPO	NPO	Clear liquids & progress	Regular	Regular
Activity	Not restricted	Ambulate	None	Turn, cough, and deep breathe	Increase activity to ambulation	Normal ambulation	Not restricted
Nursing action	Assessment	Vital signs	Vital signs, O_2 saturation	Vital signs, level of consciousness, O_2 saturation	Monitor as before	Prepare for discharge	Follow-up evaluation via phone
Teaching/ discharge planning	Phone call	Patient education about procedure	Transport to PACU	Discharge when Aldrete criteria I met	Discharge when Aldrete criteria II met	Instructions reviewed	Phone call for follow-up

FIG. 1.5 Clinical pathway for endoscopy. (From Arnold EC, Boggs KU: *Interpersonal relationships,* ed 6, St Louis, 2011, Mosby.)

UAP hold many titles, including nurse aides, certified medication aides, nursing assistants, patient care assistants, or technicians. The activities UAP perform typically include obtaining routine vital signs on stable patients, feeding and helping patients at mealtimes, ambulating stable patients, and helping patients with bathing and hygiene.

Delegation can occur among professional nurses. For example, if 1 RN has accountability for an outcome and asks another RN to perform a specific intervention related to that outcome, that is delegation. This type of delegation typically occurs when 1 RN leaves the unit/work area for a meal break.

Assignment is different from delegation. The term *assign* is used when you direct an LPN/VN or UAP to do an activity or procedure that is part of their everyday job.[20] An assignment must be within the authorized scope of practice of the LPN/VN or part of the routine function of the UAP. For example, you can assign an LPN/VN to give medications to a patient, because this is within the LPN/VN's scope of practice. You cannot assign an LPN/VN to a patient who needs an admission assessment because an RN must perform the initial patient assessment.

Whether you delegate or are working with staff to whom you assign tasks, you are responsible for the patient's total care during your work period. You need to decide what patient care tasks must be carried out during the given period, identify who will do them, and prioritize the order in which the tasks must be completed. You are responsible for supervising UAP or LPN/VNs. Clearly communicate the tasks that must be done and give

necessary guidance. Because you are accountable for ensuring that delegated tasks are completed in a competent manner, evaluate the care given, follow up as needed, and make sure no care was missed.

Delegation is a skill that is learned, and you must practice to be proficient in managing patient care. You need to use critical thinking and professional judgment to ensure that you follow the 5 Rights of Delegation (Table 1.5). To help you, information on delegation is presented in the nursing management tables and case study questions at the end of the management chapters.

SAFETY

It is estimated that about 250,000 patients each year die because of preventable medical errors.[21] Several groups are addressing this issue by outlining safety goals for health care organizations and identifying safety competencies for health professionals. By implementing various procedures and systems that improve patient safety, health care systems are working to attain a culture that minimizes the risk of harm to the patient. Because of your closeness to patients, you are in a unique position to promote patient safety.

Serious Reportable Events

The National Quality Forum (NQF) uses the term **serious reportable event (SRE)**, also called a *never event,* to describe

TABLE 1.5 5 Rights of Delegation

The 5 Rights of Delegation

The registered nurse uses critical thinking and professional judgment to be sure that the delegation or assignment is:

1. The right task
2. Under the right circumstances
3. To the right person
4. With the right directions and communication
5. Under the right supervision and evaluation

Rights of Delegation	Description	Questions to Ask
Right Task	One that can be delegated for a specific patient	Is it appropriate to delegate based on legal and agency factors? Has the person been trained and evaluated in performing the task? Is the person able and willing to do this specific task?
Right Circumstances	Appropriate patient setting, available resources, and considering relevant factors, including patient stability	What are the patient's needs right now? Is staffing such that the circumstances support delegation strategies?
Right Person	Right person is delegating the right task to the right person to be performed on the right person	Is the prospective delegatee a willing and able employee? Are the patient needs a "fit" with the delegatee?
Right Directions and Communication	Clear, concise description of task, including its objective, limits, and expectations	Have you given clear communication about the task? With directions, limits, and expected outcomes? Does the delegatee know what and when to report? Does the delegatee understand what needs to be done?
Right Supervision and Evaluation	Appropriate monitoring, evaluation, intervention, and feedback	Do you know how and when you will interact about patient care with the delegatee? How often do you need to directly observe? Will you be able to give feedback to the staff member if needed?

Source: National Guidelines for Nursing Delegation. Retrieved from *www.ncsbn.org/1625.htm.*

serious, largely preventable, and harmful clinical events.[22] The current list of SREs consists of 29 events. These events include such things as a patient acquiring a stage III or greater pressure injury while hospitalized and death or disability from a fall or hypoglycemia.

To reduce the occurrence of SREs, the NQF has a list of effective *Safe Practices* that health care settings should use to provide safe patient care *(www.qualityforum.org)*. You are implementing NQF practices when you perform a time-out before a surgical procedure, reconcile medication records, and implement interventions to prevent hospital-acquired infections, pressure injuries and falls.

National Patient Safety Goals

The Joint Commission (TJC), the accrediting agency for health care organizations, gathers and reports data on serious errors they call sentinel events. A *sentinel event* is a patient safety event not related to the patient's illness or underlying condition that reaches a patient and results in death, permanent harm, or severe temporary harm.[23] Events are "sentinel" because they signal the need for immediate investigation and response. Many sentinel events are also serious reportable events. If the patient undergoes a wrong-site or wrong-procedure surgery, experiences an assault in the health care setting, or receives an incompatible blood product, the occurrence is both a sentinel event, reportable to TJC, and a serious reportable event, reportable to NQF.

To address specific patient safety concerns, TJC issues National Patient Safety Goals (NPSGs).[24] NPSGs promote patient safety by offering evidence-based solutions to common safety problems. The 2017 NPSGs are listed in Table 1.6.

The latest safety goal, focusing on improving the safety of clinical alarm systems, greatly affects nursing. Patient monitoring systems provide vital information. Alarms that work well improve patient safety and care by telling you when a patient needs your attention. However, so many alarms can go off that *alarm fatigue* occurs, and nurses can become desensitized to the sounds. By better managing alarms, we reduce alarm fatigue and improve patient safety.

Because you have the greatest amount of interaction with patients, you play a key role in promoting safety. Many describe nurses as the patient's last line of defense. Every nurse has the responsibility to ensure the patient receives care in a manner that prevents errors and promotes patient safety. Throughout this book, safety alerts highlighting patient care issues and NPSGs will help you in learning to apply safety principles.

QUALITY IMPROVEMENT

Quality care and safety are related: the higher the culture of safety, the better the quality of care. Health care systems focused on quality outcomes use practice standards and protocols based on best evidence while considering the patient's unique preferences and needs. Your role is to coordinate the complex aspects of patient care, including the care delivered by others, and identify and correct issues associated with poor quality and unsafe care.

Quality improvement (QI) programs involve systematic actions that monitor, assess, and improve health care quality. QI is an interprofessional team effort that is required by accrediting agencies. As part of professional nursing practice, you need to be able to collect data using QI tools, implement interventions to improve quality of care, and monitor patient outcomes. Several public and private groups focusing on improving health care quality have developed standard QI measures. These performance measures assess how well the health care team cares

TABLE 1.6 National Patient Safety Goals

Safety Goal	Examples
Identify patients correctly	• Use at least 2 ways to identify patients (e.g., have them state full name and date of birth). • Give the correct patient the correct blood with every blood transfusion.
Improve communication among the health care team	• Get critical test results to the right person on time.
Use medicines safely	• Before a procedure, label all medicines. Discard any found unlabeled. • Use proper precautions with patients who take anticoagulants. • Find out what medicines each patient is taking. Make certain that it is safe for the patient to take any new medicines with his or her current ones. • Give a medication list to the patient and the caregiver before discharge. Explain the list.
Use alarm systems safely	• Respond to alarms promptly. • Do not turn alarms off.
Prevent health care–associated infections	• Use soap, water, and hand sanitizer before and after every patient contact. • Use evidence-based practices to prevent infections related to central lines, indwelling urinary catheters, and multidrug-resistant organisms
Identify patient safety risks	• Assess patients at risk for suicide. • Assess any risks, such as fires, for patients who are getting home oxygen therapy.
Prevent mistakes in surgery	• Conduct a time-out before the start of any surgery. • Confirm correct patient, procedure, and site.

Adapted from The Joint Commission (TJC): *2016 National patient safety goals*, Oakbrook Terrace, IL. Retrieved from *www.jointcommission.org/assets/1/6/2017_NPSG_HAP_ER.pdf.*

Aim
Improve care of patients with asthma by implementing evidence-based practices

Goals
• >90% of asthma patients will have an asthma action plan
• >90% of asthma patients will receive flu vaccine
• >90% of asthma patients will have an asthma flow sheet

Measures
• % of asthma patients with an asthma action plan
• % of asthma patients who receive the flu vaccine
• % of asthma patients with an asthma flow sheet

Data Collection Plan
Survey 25 charts every week for flu shots, action plans, and flow sheets

FIG. 1.6 Quality improvement system. (Adapted from Courtlandt CD, Noonan L, Leonard GF: Model for improvement—Part 1: A framework for health care quality, *Pediatr Clin North Am* 56:757, 2009.)

for a patient with a certain condition or receives a specific treatment. They describe what data the team must collect and monitor. Fig 1.6 shows an example of a QI system for adult patients with asthma. In this example, you would review patient medical records to decide if the rate of flu vaccine administration exceeds 90%. You would share the results with the team and, if the identified standard was not met, work as a team to implement measures to correct the deficiency.

National Database of Nursing Quality Indicators

The National Database of Nursing Quality Indicators (NDNQI) provides data on nursing-sensitive measures to evaluate the impact of nursing care on patient outcomes. Patient outcomes are nursing sensitive if they improve with a greater quantity or quality of nursing care. NDNQI outcomes are unique because they identify how nursing workforce factors, including nurse staffing and skill mix, directly influence patient outcomes. NDNQI data show the incidence of falls and health care–associated pressure injuries and infections decreases with adequate staffing and increased nurse education and satisfaction with the work environment. Table 1.7 lists the current NDNQI.

INFORMATICS

Nursing is an information-intense profession. Advances in informatics and technology have changed the way nurses plan, deliver, document, and evaluate care. All nurses, regardless of their setting or role, use informatics and technology every day in practice. Informatics has changed how you obtain and review diagnostic information, make clinical decisions, communicate with patients and health care team members, document, and provide care.

Technology advances have increased the efficiency of nursing care, improving the work environment and the care nurses provide. Computers and mobile devices allow you to document at the time you deliver care and give you quick and easy access to information, including clinical decision-making tools, patient education materials, and references. Texting, video chat, and e-mail enhance communication among health care team members and help you deliver the right message to the right person at the right time.

Technology plays a key role in providing safe, quality patient care. Medication administration applications improve patient

TABLE 1.7 National Database of Nursing Quality Indicators

• Structure indicators
  • RN turnover rate
  • Nursing hours per patient day
  • RN education and certification
  • Staff mix: RNs, LPN/VNs, UAP, agency staff
• Process and outcome indicators
  • Patient falls and falls with injury
  • Pressure injury rate
  • RN surveys on job satisfaction and practice environment scale
• Outcome indicators
  • Physical/sexual assault rate
  • Restraint use
  • Health care–associated infections (HAI) rate

Source: National Database of Nursing Quality Indicators. Retrieved from *www.nursingquality.org.*

safety by flagging potential errors, such as look-alike and sound-alike medications and adverse drug interactions, before they can occur. Computerized provider order entry (CPOE) systems can reduce errors caused by misreading or misinterpreting handwritten orders. Sensor technology can decrease the number of falls in high-risk patients. Care reminder systems give cues that decrease the amount of missed nursing care.

Being able to use technology skills to communicate and access information is now an essential part of your professional nursing practice. You must be able to use word processing software, communicate by e-mail and book messaging, access information, and follow security and confidentiality rules. You need to have the ability to safely use patient care technologies and navigate electronic documentation systems.

Protected health information (PHI) is highly sensitive. The *Health Insurance Portability and Accountability Act (HIPAA)* is part of federal legislation that addresses actions for how PHI is used and disclosed. With the increased use of informatics and

FIG. 1.7 Members of the interprofessional team review a patient's electronic health record. (From Arnold EC, Boggs KU: *Interpersonal relationships*, ed 6, St Louis, 2011, Mosby.)

ETHICAL/LEGAL DILEMMAS
Social Networking: HIPAA Violation

Situation
You log into a closed group on a social networking site and read a posting from a fellow nursing student. The posting describes in detail the complex care the student gave to an older patient in a local hospital the previous day. The student comments on how stressful the day was and asks for advice on how to deal with similar patients in the future.

Ethical/Legal Points for Consideration
- Protecting and maintaining patient privacy and confidentiality are basic obligations defined in the Code of Ethics for Nurses, which nurses and nursing students should uphold.[1]
- As outlined in the Health Insurance Portability and Accountability Act (HIPAA), a patient's private health information is any information that relates to the person's past, present, or future physical or mental health. This includes not only specific details such as a patient's name or picture but also information that gives enough details that someone may be able to identify that person.
- You may unintentionally breach privacy or confidentiality by posting patient information (diagnosis, condition, situation) on a social networking site. Using privacy settings or being in a closed group does not guarantee the secrecy of posted information. Others can copy and share any post without your knowledge.
- Potential consequences for improperly using social networking vary based on the situation. These may include (1) disciplinary action by the state board of nursing; (2) being disciplined, suspended, or fired by an employer; (3) dismissal from a nursing program; and (4) civil and/or criminal charges.
- A student nurse who experienced a stressful day and is looking for advice and support from peers (e.g., "Today my patient died. I wanted to cry.") could share the experience by clearly limiting the posts to the student's personal perspective and not sharing any identifying information. This is 1 area in which it is safest to err on the side of caution to avoid the appearance of impropriety.

Discussion Questions
1. How would you deal with the situation involving the fellow nursing student?
2. How would you handle a situation in which you saw a staff member who violated HIPAA?

Reference
1. Code of Ethics for Nurses. Retrieved from *www.nursingworld.org/DocumentVault/Ethics-1/Code-of-Ethics-for-Nurses.html.*

technology come new concerns on how to comply with HIPAA regulations and maintain a patient's privacy. Wireless technologies, increased use of e-mail and computer networking, and the ongoing threat of computer viruses increase the need for properly protecting a patient's privacy. We must assure patients of their privacy and that only those with a right to know are accessing protected information.

As a nurse, you have an obligation to ensure the privacy of your patient's health information. To do so, you need to understand your agency's policies about the use of technology. You need to know the rules about accessing patient records and releasing PHI, what to do if information is accidentally or intentionally released, and how to protect any passwords you use. If you are using social networking, you must be careful not to place any individually identifiable PHI online. Throughout this book, Informatics in Practice boxes offer suggestions on how to use informatics in your practice.

Electronic Health Records
The largest use of informatics is **electronic health records (EHRs)**, also called *electronic medical records*. An EHR is a computerized record of patient information. It is shared among all health care team members involved in a patient's care and moves with the patient—to other providers and across care settings. The ideal EHR provides a single place for team members to review and update a patient's health record, document care given, and enter patient care orders, including medications, procedures, diets, and diagnostic and laboratory tests (Fig. 1.7).

Several obstacles are still in the way of fully implementing EHRs. Systems are technologically complex, requiring many resources and training to implement and maintain. Communication is still lacking among computer systems and software applications. Finally, perceived challenges in the use of EHRs, including increased workload and the need for workarounds, affect implementation.

EVIDENCE-BASED PRACTICE

Evidence-based practice (EBP) is a problem-solving approach to clinical decision making. Using the best available evidence (e.g., research findings, QI data), combined with your expertise

TABLE 1.8 **Steps of Evidence-Based Practice (EBP) Process**
1. Ask the clinical question using the **PICOT** format: Patients/population Intervention Comparison or comparison group Outcome(s) Time (as applicable) 2. Search for the best evidence based on the clinical question. 3. Critically appraise and synthesize the evidence. 4. Implement the evidence in practice. 5. Evaluate the practice decision or change. 6. Share the outcomes of the decision or change.

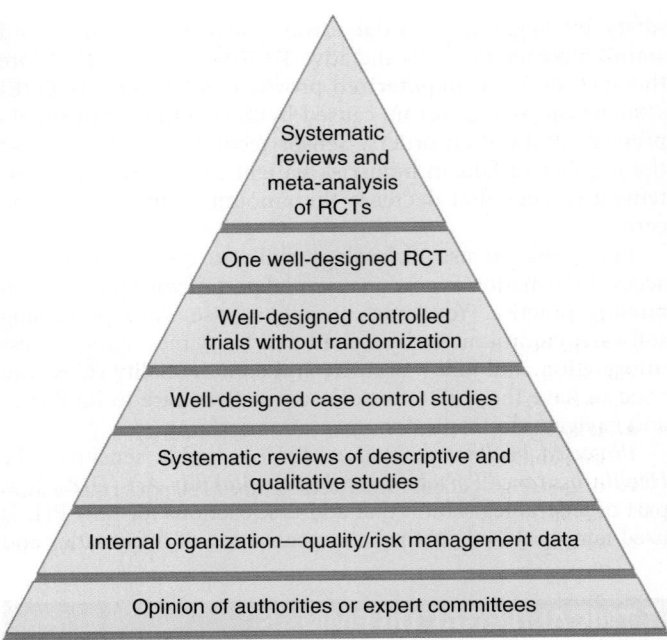

FIG. 1.8 Hierarchy of evidence. (Modified from Melnyk BM, Fineout-Overholt E: *Evidence-based practice in nursing and healthcare: A guide to best practice,* ed 3, Philadelphia, 2014, Lippincott Williams & Wilkins.)

and the patient's unique circumstances and preferences, leads to better clinical decisions and improved patient outcomes. EBP closes the gap between research and practice, providing more reliable and predictable care than that based on tradition, opinion, and trial and error.

EBP does not mean that you conduct a research study. Instead, EBP depends on you to take an active role in using the best available evidence when delivering care. You need to have an ongoing curiosity about what are the best nursing practices and routinely ask questions about your patient's care. Recognize when you need more information. When you base your practice on valid evidence, you are solving problems and supporting best patient outcomes.

Steps of EBP Process

The EBP process has 6 steps (Table 1.8).

Step 1. Step 1 is asking a clinical question in the PICOT format. Developing the clinical question is the key step in the EBP process.[25] A good clinical question sets the context for integrating evidence, clinical judgment, and patient preferences. In addition, the question guides the literature search for the best evidence to influence practice.

An example of a clinical question in PICOT format is, "In adult abdominal surgery patients (**P** = patients/population) is splinting with an elasticized abdominal binder (**I** = intervention) or a pillow (**C** = comparison) more effective in reducing pain associated with ambulation (**O** = outcome) on the first postoperative day (**T** = time period)?" A clinical question may not have all components of PICOT. Some only include 4 components. The (T) timing or (C) comparison components are not appropriate for every question. The (C) component of PICOT may include a comparison with a specific intervention, the usual standard of care, or no intervention at all.

Step 2. Step 2 is searching for the best evidence that applies to the clinical question. Technology provides you with ready access to data. You can easily search several online resources and collect large amounts of clinical information and evidence. It is important to evaluate all data sources for their credibility and reliability. Not all evidence is equal. Fig. 1.8 presents the hierarchy of evidence. As you go down the pyramid, the strength of the evidence becomes weaker. Systematic reviews and evidence-based clinical practice guidelines save time and effort in the EBP process. However, they are available for only a limited number of clinical topics and may not suit all types of clinical questions. When insufficient research exists to guide practice, recommendations from expert panels and authority figures may be the best evidence available.

Step 3. Step 3 is to critically appraise the evidence you found. A successful critical appraisal process focuses on 3 essential questions: (1) What are the results? (2) Are the results reliable and valid? and (3) Will the results help me in caring for my patients? You decide the strength of the evidence and synthesize the findings related to the clinical question to conclude what is the best practice. For example, you find strong evidence supporting effectiveness of elasticized binders and pillows in reducing pain associated with ambulation. However, the binder appears to be more effective if the patient is obese or has had prior abdominal surgery.

Step 4. Step 4 involves implementing the evidence in practice. The decision to implement change is made by combining the evidence, clinical judgment, and preferences and values of patients and caregivers. You may be part of an interprofessional team charged with implementing a practice change or applying evidence in a specific patient care situation. This may include developing clinical practice guidelines, policies and procedures, or new assessment, teaching, or documentation tools. For example, you may be part of a team implementing a new postoperative protocol focused on using elasticized abdominal binders with patients who are obese or had prior abdominal surgery.

Step 5. Step 5 is evaluating the outcome of the practice change. After implementing the change for a specific period, you should monitor outcomes to determine whether the change has improved patient outcomes. Accrediting bodies require documentation of outcome measures to show that the organization is using evidence to improve patient care.

Step 6. Step 6 is sharing the results of the EBP change. If you do not share the outcomes of EBP, then other health care providers and patients cannot benefit from what you learned from your experience. You can share information locally using unit- or hospital-based newsletters and posters and regionally and nationally through journal publications and presentations at conferences.

Implementing EBP

To implement EBP, you must develop the skills to be able to seek and incorporate into practice scientific evidence that supports best patient outcomes. Throughout this book, Evidence-Based Practice boxes provide an opportunity for you to practice your critical thinking skills in applying EBP to patient scenarios. To help you identify the use of evidence in this book, an asterisk (*) in the reference list at the end of each chapter indicates evidence-based information for clinical practice.

BRIDGE TO NCLEX EXAMINATION

The number of the question corresponds to the same-numbered outcome at the beginning of the chapter.

1. An example of a nursing activity that best reflects the American Nurses Association's definition of nursing is
   a. treating dysrhythmias that occur in a patient in the coronary care unit.
   b. diagnosing a patient with a feeding tube as being at risk for aspiration.
   c. setting up protocols for treating patients in the emergency department.
   d. offering antianxiety drugs to a patient with a disturbed sleep pattern.

2. A nurse working on the medical-surgical unit at an urban hospital would like to become certified in medical-surgical nursing. The nurse knows that this process would most likely require
   a. a bachelor's degree in nursing.
   b. formal education in advanced nursing practice.
   c. experience for a specific period in medical-surgical nursing.
   d. membership in a medical-surgical nursing specialty organization.

3. The nurse is assigned to care for a newly admitted patient. Number in order the steps for using the nursing process to prioritize care. (Number 1 is the first step, and number 5 is the last step.)
   ___ Evaluate whether the plan was effective.
   ___ Identify any health problems.
   ___ Collect patient information.
   ___ Carry out the plan.
   ___ Decide a plan of action.

4. Using the SBAR format, number in order the steps for how the nurse would communicate information with the provider. (Number 1 is the first step, and number 4 is the last step.)
   ___ "I would like you to order an IV medication and come evaluate the patient as soon as possible."
   ___ "This is Nurse M.H. I am calling from the unit because your patient, D.R., has a new onset of atrial fibrillation."
   ___ "The atrial fibrillation started about 10 minutes ago. The heart rate is 124; BP 90/60. The patient is experiencing dizziness."
   ___ "D.R., who is 2 days postoperative for a bowel resection for diverticulitis, has a history of mitral valve disease."

5. The nurse is caring for a diabetic patient in the ambulatory surgical unit who has undergone wound debridement. Which task is appropriate for the nurse to delegate to unlicensed assistive personnel (UAP)?
   a. Check the patient's vital signs.
   b. Assess the patient's pain level.
   c. Palpate the patient's pedal pulses.
   d. Monitor the patient's IV catheter site.

6. The nurse's role in addressing the National Patient Safety Goals established by The Joint Commission includes (select all that apply)
   a. answering all patient monitoring alarms promptly.
   b. memorizing all the rules published by The Joint Commission.
   c. obtaining a correct list of the patient's medications on admission.
   d. encouraging patients to be actively involved in their own health care.
   e. using side rails and alarm systems as necessary to prevent patient falls.

7. Advantages of using informatics in health care delivery are (select all that apply)
   a. reduced need for nurses in acute care.
   b. increased patient anonymity and confidentiality.
   c. the ability to achieve and maintain high standards of care.
   d. access to standard plans of care for many health problems.
   e. improved communication of the patient's health status to the health care team.

8. When using evidence-based practice, the nurse
   a. must use clinical practice guidelines developed by national health agencies.
   b. should use findings from randomized controlled trials to plan care for all patient problems.
   c. uses clinical decision making and judgment to decide what evidence is appropriate for a specific clinical situation.
   d. analyzes the relationship of nursing interventions to patient outcomes to discover evidence for patient interventions.

1. b, 2. c, 3. 5, 2, 1, 4, 3, 4. 4, 1, 3, 2, 5. a, 6. a, c, e, 7. c, d, e, 8. c.

For rationales to these answers and even more NCLEX review questions, visit http://evolve.elsevier.com/Lewis/medsurg.

EVOLVE WEBSITE/RESOURCES LIST

http://evolve.elsevier.com/Lewis/medsurg
Review Questions (Online Only)
Key Points
Answer Key for Questions
• Rationales for Bridge to NCLEX Examination Questions
Conceptual Care Map Creator
Audio Glossary
Content Updates

REFERENCES

1. American Nurses Association: *Nursing: A social policy statement*, 3rd ed, Washington, DC, 2010, The Association. (Classic)
2. Nightingale F: *Notes on nursing: What it is and what it is not* (facsimile edition), Philadelphia, 1946, Lippincott. (Classic)
3. Henderson V: *The nature of nursing*, New York, 1966, Macmillan. (Classic)
4. American Nurses Credentialing Center. Certification. Retrieved from *www.nursingworld.org/ancc/*.

5. American Nurses Association. *Nursing: Scope and standards of practice*, Washington, DC, 2010, The Association. (Classic)
6. Thorpe KE The rise in health care spending and what to do about it, *Health Affairs* 24:1436, 2017.
7. Robert Wood Johnson Foundation. Achieving the potential of health care performance measures. Retrieved from *www.rwjf.org*.
8. ANCC Magnet Recognition Program. Retrieved from *www.nursingworld. org/organizational-programs/magnet/*.
9. Committee on the Robert Wood Johnson Foundation Initiative on the Future of Nursing at the Institute of Medicine. *The future of nursing: Leading change, advancing health*, Washington, DC, 2011, National Academies Press. (Classic)
10. QSEN Institute. Retrieved from *http://qsen.org*.
11. American Nurses Association: The nursing process. Retrieved from *www. nursingworld.org/practice-policy/workforce/what-is-nursing/the-nursing-process/*.
12. Rabelo-Silva ER, Dantas Cavalcanti AC, Ramos MC, et al: Advanced nursing process quality: Comparing the ICNP with the NANDA-International and Nursing Interventions Classification, *J Clinical Nurs* 26:379, 2017.
13. Clinical Care Classification. Nursing interventions. Retrieved from *www. sabacare.com/framework/nursing-interventions/*.
14. Carpenito LJ: *Handbook of nursing diagnoses*. 17th ed, Philadelphia, 2017, Lippincott Williams & Wilkins.
15. The Joint Commission: Transitions of care portal. Retrieved from *www. jointcommission.org/toc.aspx*.
16. Motacki K, Burke K. *Nursing delegation and management of patient care*. 2nd ed, St Louis, 2016, Elsevier.
17. What is a case manager? Retrieved from *www.cmsa.org*.
18. Zerwekh J, Garneau AZ. *Nursing today: Transitions and trends*, 9th ed, St Louis, 2017, Elsevier.
19. Alfaro-LeFevre R. *Critical thinking, clinical reasoning, and clinical judgment*, 6th ed, St Louis, 2017, Saunders.
20. Delegation. Retrieved from *www.ncsbn.org/1625.htm*.
*21. Makary MA, Daniel M: Medical error—The third leading cause of death in the US, *BMJ* 3:353, 2016.
22. Safe practices for better healthcare. Retrieved from *www.qualityforum. org/Topics/Patient_Safety.aspx*.
23. Sentinel events policy and procedures. Retrieved from *www.jointcommission. org/sentinel_event_policy_and_procedures/*.
24. National patient safety goals. Retrieved from *www.jointcommission.org/ standards_information/npsgs.aspx*.
25. Melnyk BM, Gallagher-Ford L, Fineout-Overholt E: *Implementing the evidence-based practice competencies in healthcare: A practical guide for improving quality, safety, and outcomes*, Indianapolis, 2016, Sigma Theta Tau.

*Evidence-based information for clinical practice.

2

Health Equity and Culturally Competent Care

Andrew Scanlon

> *We may have different religions, different languages, different colored skin, but we all belong to one human race. We all share the same basic values.*
>
> ***Kofi Annan***

e http://evolve.elsevier.com/Lewis/medsurg/

CONCEPTUAL FOCUS

Culture

Health Disparities

LEARNING OUTCOMES

1. Identify the key determinants of health and equity.
2. Describe the factors that contribute to health disparities and health equity.
3. Define the terms *culture, values, acculturation, ethnicity, race, stereotyping, ethnocentrism, cultural imposition, cultural competency,* and *culture-bound syndrome.*
4. Explain how culture and ethnicity may affect a person's physical and psychologic health.

5. Apply strategies for incorporating cultural information in the nursing process with all patients.
6. Describe the role of nursing in promoting health equity.
7. Examine ways that your own cultural background may influence nursing care.
8. Describe strategies for successfully communicating with a person who speaks a language that you do not understand.

KEY TERMS

acculturation, p. 21
cultural competence, p. 22
culture, p. 20
culture-bound syndromes, p. 27
determinants of health, p. 17
ethnicity, p. 18
ethnocentrism, p. 21

folk healers, p. 23
health disparities, p. 18
health equity, p. 18
health status, p. 17
lesbian, gay, bisexual, transgender, and queer or
    questioning (LGBTQ), p. 20
place, p. 19

race, p. 18
sexuality, p. 20
stereotyping, p. 21
transcultural nursing, p. 22
values, p. 20

This chapter discusses health disparities and culture. Health is a cultural concept because culture frames and shapes our experiences. Cultural beliefs influence health promotion practices and attitudes about seeking health care. Cultural differences can lead to problems that decrease the chance of receiving equitable health care. Nurses play a key role in recognizing and reducing health disparities. Understanding the concept of culture is important in your ability to provide patient-centered care.

DETERMINANTS OF HEALTH

Why are there differences in people's health status? How do these differences occur? The determinants of health are factors that (1) influence the health of individuals and groups and (2) help explain why some people experience poorer health than others.[1] Where people are born, grow up, live, work, and age helps determine their health status, behaviors, and care.

Health status is a holistic concept that is more than the presence or absence of disease. It encompasses life expectancy as well as self-assessment of health. As such, many measures make up the concept of health status. For individuals, this means the sum of their current health problems plus their coping resources (e.g., family, financial resources). For a community, health status is the combination of health measures for all people living in the community. Community health measures include birth and death rates, life expectancy, access to care, and morbidity and mortality rates related to disease and injury.

Factors in a person's social and physical environment, including personal relationships, workplace, housing, transportation, and neighborhood violence, contribute to health status.[1] For example, the risk of youth homicide is much higher in neighborhoods with gang activity and high crime rates. The physical environment in which one lives, works, and plays may expose a person to such risks as environmental hazards (workplace injuries), toxic agents (chemical spills, industrial pollution), unsafe traffic patterns (lack of sidewalks), or absence of fresh and healthy food choices.

A person's behavior is influenced by his or her environment, education, and economic status. Behaviors such as tobacco and illicit drug use are strongly linked to many health conditions (e.g., lung cancer, liver disease). A person's biologic makeup, such as genetics and family history of disease (e.g., heart disease), can increase the risk for specific diseases.

The availability of health care also contributes to a person's health. Though government initiatives are striving to reduce the number of uninsured Americans, millions remain uninsured and have limited access to care. This affects both individual and community health.

HEALTH DISPARITIES AND HEALTH EQUITY

Health disparities are differences in the incidence, prevalence, mortality rate, and burden of diseases that exist among specific population groups. In the United States this is because of social, economic, or environmental disadvantages. Health disparities can affect population groups based on gender, age, ethnicity, socioeconomic status, education, location, sexual orientation, or disability status.[2] Health equity is achieved when every person has the opportunity to attain his or her health potential, and no one is disadvantaged.

ETHICAL/LEGAL DILEMMAS
Health Disparities

Situation

E.M., a 47-yr-old Mexican American woman living with type 2 diabetes mellitus, comes to the clinic to have her blood glucose measured. It has been 12 months since her last visit. At that time, the nurse asked that she bring along her glucometer and strips to show how she checks her blood glucose because her glucose values were high at her previous visits.

When you check E.M.'s equipment and glucose strips, you find that the strips are for a different machine and they expired more than 2 years ago. When you inquire about the situation, E.M. explains that she cannot afford to come to the clinic or to buy new equipment and supplies to check her blood glucose level. During the day, E.M. cares for her 3 grandchildren so her daughter can work. E.M. spends most of her income on food for her family, so she has little money left for her health care.

Ethical/Legal Points for Consideration

• Ethnic minorities and other vulnerable or disadvantaged groups experience certain chronic illnesses at higher rates. Limited access to high-quality, accessible, and affordable health care services is associated with an increased incidence of illness and complications, as well as a reduced life span.
• People with certain health problems such as diabetes may have difficulty obtaining health care insurance. Consider these issues in the broader context of social justice.
• In many states, the legal definition of the role of the professional nurse includes patient advocacy. Advocacy includes the obligation to provide adequate follow-up care for all patients, especially those who are experiencing health care disparities.
• A nurse who observes disparities must consider the possibility of discrimination and abuse. Professional nurses are legally and ethically responsible for patient advocacy. The nurse may incur legal liability if failure to fulfill this obligation results in patient harm.

Discussion Questions

1. How would you work with E.M. to help her obtain the necessary resources and knowledge to care for her diabetes?
2. What can you do to begin working on the problems of health disparities in your community?

Factors and Conditions Leading to Health Disparities

Many factors and conditions can lead to the development of health disparities (Table 2.1). Awareness of these factors will help you provide optimal care for your patients.

Ethnicity and Race. The terms ethnicity and race are subjective and based on self-report. These terms are used interchangeably in conversation and are not defined by genetic markers. Social context and lived experiences influence people's decision about the ethnic and race category to which they identify or are assigned. For example, ethnic and race categories may differ on a person's birth certificate and death certificate.

People often identify their own ethnicity and race for health data collection (e.g., health plans, birth certificates). Collection of health data based on self-reported ethnic and race categories is important for research, to inform policy, and to understand and eliminate disparities. People identify their race using 1 or more categories. Law requires federal agencies to list a minimum of 5 race categories: white, black, American Indian or Alaska Native, Asian, and Native Hawaiian or other Pacific Islander. Federal agencies must also list a minimum of 2 ethnicities for people who self-identify as either *Hispanic or Latino* and *Not Hispanic or Latino*. A Hispanic or Latino is typically a person of Cuban, Mexican, Puerto Rican, South or Central American, or other Spanish descent, regardless of race. In this book, we use the terms *ethnicity* and *race* interchangeably or together.

Although dramatic improvements in treatments have prolonged life and improved quality of life for many, racial and ethnic minorities have benefited far less from these advances. Disparities are generally determined by comparing population groups. In the United States, minority groups include Hispanics/Latinos (17.8% of the U.S. population), blacks (13.3%), Asian Americans (5.7%), Native Hawaiians and other Pacific Islanders (0.2%), Native Americans and Native Alaskans (1.3%), and 2 or more races (2.6%) population.[3] The number for most of these groups is expected to increase in the coming decades.

Obesity and chronic illness rates for diabetes, hypertension, chronic obstructive pulmonary diseases, cancer, and stroke are higher among minority people. Racial, ethnic, and cultural differences exist in health services, treatments provided, and access to health care providers (HCPs). Race and ethnicity also influence disease risk and outcomes. For example, after myocardial infarction, minority patients are at greater risk of rehospitalization and death but are less likely than nonminority patients to receive potentially beneficial treatments.[4] Native Americans have a higher incidence of several types of cancers and are often diagnosed at later stages of disease, resulting in a poorer prognosis.[5] Numerous strategies are being developed to promote health equity and reduce disparities.

TABLE 2.1 Factors and Conditions Leading to Health Disparities

• Age	• Income status
• Disability status	• Lack of health care services access
• Education	• Language barrier
• Ethnicity and race	• Occupation or unemployment
• Gender	• Place
• Health care provider attitudes/biases	• Sexual orientation
• Health literacy	

🌐 PROMOTING HEALTH EQUITY

Promoting Health Equity Boxes Throughout Book

Place. Place refers to the geographic and environmental location where a person is born, grows, lives, works, and ages. Place affects the use of health services, health status, and health behaviors.

About 20% of Americans live in nonurban or rural areas.[6] Differences in access to health care services between rural and urban settings can create geographic health disparities. For example, rural populations and Native Americans living on reservations may need to travel long distances to receive health care. This can result in inadequate or less-frequent access to health care services. Some parts of the rural United States are "medically underserved" because of decreased numbers of HCPs per population.

People living in rural areas have higher rates of cancer, heart disease, diabetes, depression, and injury-related deaths than people living in urban areas. For example, in rural Appalachia the rates of lung, colon, cervical, and colorectal cancer are higher than the national average. Rural populations tend to be older than urban populations. Many rural areas have higher rates of obesity and chronic disease. The impact of social and physical environment on health choices can be illustrated by the problem of intimate partner violence in rural communities.[7] The decision to seek help is affected by geographic isolation, traditional gender roles, patriarchal attitudes, fear of lack of confidentiality, and economic factors that exist in some small rural communities.

Living in urban centers may also predispose a person to health disparities. Concerns about personal safety (e.g., clinics located in high-crime neighborhoods) can make patients reluctant to visit HCPs. High rates of chronic health problems and premature deaths occur in neighborhoods with social inequalities, including high poverty rates and residential segregation.

Among the most obvious health behaviors affected by place are physical activity and nutrition. Safe, walkable neighborhoods with playgrounds and sources of healthy foods promote physical activity and healthy eating. Social support positively affects coping with illness. Social networks are more likely to be found in communities where neighbors interact and rely on one another.

Income, Education, and Occupation. People of lower income, education, or occupational status experience worse health. In addition, they die at a younger age than those who are more affluent. Adults without a high school diploma or equivalent are 3 times more likely to die before age 65 than those with a college degree. Health care costs are 1 of the key factors that contribute to health disparities. People who have no insurance, are underinsured, or lack financial resources to pay for treatment of diseases may forgo health care visits, screenings, and treatments. Patients who lack the knowledge and/or access to apply for government assistance programs (e.g., Medicaid) are also at risk. Hazardous work environments and high-risk occupations of laborers increase health risk and contribute to higher rates of illness, injury, and death.

Health Literacy. *Health literacy* is defined as the degree to which a person has the capacity to obtain, process, and understand basic health information and services needed to make appropriate health decisions. This includes the ability to (1) read, understand, and analyze information; (2) understand instructions; (3) weigh risks and benefits; and (4) make decisions and take action. Low health literacy is associated with more hospitalizations, greater use of emergency department care, decreased use of cancer screening and influenza vaccine, decreased ability to use medications correctly, and higher mortality rates among older adults.

On a daily basis, patients need to self-manage conditions such as diabetes and asthma. For example, patients with diabetes may not be able to maintain adequate blood glucose levels if they cannot read or understand the numbers on the home glucose monitoring system. The inability to read and understand medication labels can result in taking medications at the wrong time or in the wrong dose. See Chapter 4 for more about health literacy.

Gender. Health disparities exist between men and women. Adult women use health care services more than men. Women may not receive the same quality of care (Fig. 2.1). For example, women are less likely than men to receive procedures (e.g., coronary angiography) for cardiovascular disease.[8] When gender is combined with racial and ethnic differences, the disparities are

FIG. 2.1 Older Asian women are especially at risk for health disparities. (© szefei/iStock/Thinkstock.)

even greater. Gender Differences boxes throughout this book highlight gender differences in disease risk, manifestations, and treatment.

Age. Older adults are at risk for experiencing health disparities in the number of diagnostic tests done and aggressiveness of treatments used. Biases toward older adults that affect their care, or ageism, are discussed in Chapter 5. Older people of low socioeconomic status experience greater disability, more limitations in activities of daily living, and more frequent and rapid cognitive decline. Black and Latino older adults, in particular, are disproportionately affected by chronic illnesses, disability, depression, and substandard quality of life.[9]

Sexual Orientation. Sexuality is defined as a person's romantic, emotional, or sexual attraction to another person.

Lesbian, Gay, Bisexual, Transgender, and Queer or Questioning. Lesbian, gay, bisexual, transgender, and queer or questioning (LGBTQ) is a term that refers to the sexual orientation of these groups of people. LGBTQ persons encompass all races and ethnicities, religions, and social classes. Being LGBTQ places a person at risk for health disparities resulting from social, economic, or environmental disadvantages. Personal, family, and social acceptance of sexual orientation and gender identity affects the mental health and personal safety of LGBTQ persons. Discrimination against LGBTQ people has been associated with high rates of psychiatric disorders, substance abuse, and suicide.

LGBTQ people are more likely to be obese when compared with their heterosexual counterparts. Lesbian and bisexual women have higher rates of breast cancer and increased risk factors for cardiovascular disease. Gay and bisexual men have higher rates of human immunodeficiency virus and hepatitis infections than other groups.[10] Older LGBTQ persons may face added barriers to health because of isolation and a lack of social services and culturally competent providers.[9]

Understanding the cause of disparities among LGBTQ persons is essential to providing safe and high-quality care. One of the barriers to accessing high-quality health care by LGBTQ adults is the current lack of HCPs who are knowledgeable about their health needs. LGBTQ people may also experience fear of discrimination in health care settings.

Some health care settings are addressing the negative stereotypes that health care professionals may have, but of which they may not be aware. The Joint Commission (TJC) requires that patients be allowed the presence of a support person of their choice. In addition, hospitals must adopt policies that bar discrimination based on factors such as sexual orientation and gender identification and expression.

♥ PROMOTING POPULATION HEALTH

Improving the Health and Well-Being of LGBTQ Persons

- Provide supportive social services to reduce suicide among young LGBTQ persons.
- Inquire about and be supportive of a patient's sexual orientation to enhance the patient-provider interaction and patient's regular use of care.
- Implement antibullying policies in schools.
- Provide health care professionals with knowledge of the health needs of the LGBTQ community and training on LGBT mental health issues.
- Continue efforts to expand domestic partner health insurance coverage.
- Establish community advisory boards and LGBTQ health centers.
- Disseminate effective HIV and sexually transmitted infections interventions.

Health Care Provider Attitudes. Certain behaviors and biases of the HCP can contribute to health disparities. Factors such as bias and prejudice can affect health care-seeking behavior in minority populations. The health care system may also contribute to the problem of health disparities. For example, a clinic located in an area with a large population of Vietnamese immigrants that does not provide interpreters or educational materials and financial forms in Vietnamese may limit these families' ability to understand how to access health care.

Discrimination and *bias* based on a patient's race, ethnicity, gender, age, body size, sexual orientation, or ability to pay are likely to result in less aggressive or negative treatment practices. Discrimination can result in the delay of a proper diagnosis due to assumptions made about the patient. Sometimes discrimination is hard to recognize, especially when it occurs at the institutional level.

Because an HCP's overt discriminatory behavior may not be clear to the patient or yourself, it may be difficult to confront. Even well-intentioned providers who try to eliminate bias in their care can show their prior beliefs or prejudices through nonverbal communication. Many policies are in place to eliminate discrimination, but it still exists.

▌CULTURE

Culture is a way of life for a group of people. It includes the behaviors, beliefs, values, traditions, and symbols that the group accepts, generally without thinking about them. This way of life is passed along by communication and imitation from 1 generation to the next. You can also think of culture as cultivated behavior that one acquires through social learning. It is the totality of a person's learned, accumulated experience that is socially transmitted. The 4 classic characteristics of culture are described in Table 2.2.

Values are the sets of rules by which persons, families, groups, and communities live. They are the principles and standards that serve as the basis for beliefs, attitudes, and behaviors. Although all cultures have values, the types and expressions of those values differ from 1 culture to another. These cultural values develop over time, guide decision making and actions, and may affect a person's self-esteem. Cultural values often unconsciously develop early in life as a child learns about acceptable and unacceptable behaviors. The extent to which a person's cultural values are internalized influences that person's tendency toward judging other cultures, while usually using his or her own culture as the accepted standard. Table 2.3 provides some examples of cultural characteristics of different ethnic groups in the United States.

Although persons within a cultural group may have many similarities through their shared values, beliefs, and practices, there is also diversity within groups (Fig. 2.2). Each person is culturally unique. Such diversity may result from different perspectives and interpretations of situations. These differences may be based on age, gender, marital status, family structure, income, education level, religious views, and life experiences. Within any cultural group, there are smaller groups that may not hold all the values of the dominant culture. These smaller cultural groups have experiences that differ from those of the dominant group. These differences may be related to ethnic background, residence, religion, occupation, health, age, gender, education, or other factors that unite the group. Members

TABLE 2.2 Basic Characteristics of Culture

- *Dynamic* and ever-changing
- *Not always shared* by all members of a cultural group
- *Adapted* to specific conditions such as environmental factors
- *Learned* through oral and written histories, as well as socialization

TABLE 2.3 Cultural Characteristics of Different Ethnic Groups

Asian American
- Cultural foods
- Family loyalty
- Folk healing
- Harmonious relationships
- Harmony and balance within body vital for preservation of life energy
- Respect for elders
- Respect for one's parents and ancestors

Black
- Cultural foods
- Family networks
- Folk healing
- Importance of religion
- Interdependence within ethnic group
- Music and physical activities valued

European American
- Equal rights of genders
- Independence and freedom
- Individualistic and competitive
- Materialistic
- Self-reliance valued
- Youth and beauty valued

Hispanic/Latino
- Cultural foods
- Folk healing

- Extended family valued
- Interdependence and collectivism
- Involvement of family in social activities
- Religion and spirituality highly valued
- Respect for elders and authority

Native American
- Doing the honorable thing
- Folk healing
- Living in harmony with people and nature
- Respect for tribal elders and children
- Respect for all things living
- Return what is taken from nature
- Spiritual guidance

Pacific Islander American
- Collective concern and involvement
- Kinship alliance among nuclear and extended family
- Knowledge is collective; belongs to group, not a person
- Natural order and balanced relationships

Adapted from Andrews MM, Boyle JS: *Transcultural concepts in nursing care*, ed 7, Philadelphia, 2016, Lippincott Williams & Wilkins; and Giger JN, Davidhizar RE: *Transcultural nursing: Assessment and intervention*, ed 7, St Louis, 2016, Mosby.

of a subculture share certain aspects of culture that are different from those of the overall cultural group. For example, among Hispanics some seek professional health care right away when symptoms appear. Other Hispanics rely first on folk healers. Others first seek the opinion of family and friends before seeking formal health care.

Cultural beliefs about symptom tolerance and health care–seeking behavior can contribute to health disparities. Some cultures consider pain something to be endured or ignored, and as a result, the patient does not seek help. Some cultures may view diseases or problems fatalistically; that is, people see no reason to seek treatment because they believe it is unlikely to have any benefit. Some cultures view the signs and symptoms of an illness as "God's will" or as a punishment for some prior behavior. In some cultures, it may not be acceptable to see an HCP who is not of the same gender or ethnic group. Such beliefs can result in delays in seeking health care or inadequate treatment.

FIG. 2.2 Members of this family share a common heritage. (© Jack Hollingsworth/Photodisc/Thinkstock.)

Acculturation is the lifelong process of incorporating cultural aspects of the contexts in which a person grows, lives, works, and ages.[11] Acculturation is often bidirectional. In other words, the context changes as a person's culture influences it. Change may be in attitudes, behaviors, and values. For example, a sedentary person who loves to cook may change his or her attitude toward exercise when living with athletic roommates, who in turn also change as they begin to appreciate cooking. Behaviors change when an immigrant child learns the local language while influencing the conduct of classmates. A deeply held value such as self-sufficiency may change for a person exposed to a culture in which reliance on others dominates.

Newcomers may adopt both the strengths and limitations of the dominant culture. This is relevant when considering health behaviors and the quality of health care delivered by professionals. For example, an immigrant may be negatively influenced by a dominant cultural context in which unhealthy eating habits prevail.[12]

The result of acculturation may be new cultural variations in attitudes, behaviors, and values. All people take part in this process over their lives. People who move to a new cultural context are more aware of the acculturation experience than people who are not exposed to new experiences. Exposure to new cultural contexts increases a nurse's cultural competency.

Stereotyping refers to an overgeneralized viewpoint that members of a specific culture, race, or ethnic group are alike and share the same values and beliefs. This oversimplified approach does not consider the individual differences that exist within a culture. Being a member of a particular cultural, ethnic, or racial group does not make the person an expert on other members of that same group. Such stereotyping can lead to false assumptions and affect a patient's care. For example, it would be inappropriate for you to assume that just because a nurse is Mexican American, he would know how a Mexican American patient's beliefs may affect that patient's health care practices. As another example, a young Mexican American nurse born and raised in a large city has experienced a different culture than the older patient who was born and raised in a rural area of Mexico.

Ethnocentrism refers to the belief that one's own culture and worldview are superior to those of others from different cultural, ethnic, or racial backgrounds.[11] Comparing others' ways to your own can lead to seeing others as different or inferior. HCP's ethnocentrism can result in poor communication, patient alienation, and potentially inadequate treatment. To avoid ethnocentrism, you need to remain open to a variety of perspectives and maintain a nonjudgmental view of the values, beliefs, and practices of others. Failure to do this can result in ethnic stereotyping or cultural imposition.

Cultural imposition occurs when we impose our own cultural beliefs and practices on another person or group of people. In health care, it can result in disregarding or trivializing a patient's health care beliefs or practices. Cultural imposition may happen when an HCP is unaware of the patient's cultural beliefs and plans and implements care without taking them into account.

Cultural safety describes care and advocacy for a person of another culture determined by that person or family. Care that is culturally safe prevents cultural imposition. Culturally safe practice requires cultural competency and action to ensure that cultural histories, experiences, and traditions of patients, their families, and communities are valued and shape health care approaches and policies.[13]

Madeleine Leininger coined the term transcultural nursing in the 1950s. Transcultural nursing is a specialty that focuses on the comparative study and analysis of cultures and subcultures. The goal of transcultural nursing is the discovery of culturally relevant facts that can guide the nurse in providing culturally appropriate care.[11]

CULTURAL COMPETENCE

Cultural competence is the ability to understand, appreciate, and work with people from cultures other than your own. It involves an awareness and acceptance of cultural differences, self-awareness, knowledge of the patient's culture, and adaptation of skills to meet the patient's needs. The 4 components of cultural competence are (1) cultural awareness, (2) cultural knowledge, (3) cultural skill, and (4) cultural encounter (Table 2.4).

We present specific information throughout this book to help you develop an awareness of cultural differences and learning assessment skills for different cultural groups. Table 2.8 (later in this chapter) presents a cultural assessment guide. It may be helpful to review general cultural characteristics associated with a cultural group when preparing to interview a patient. However, recognize that the patient may not identify with the assumed cultural group and the provider's own biases and stereotypes may affect the patient and result in more patient-provider barriers.

Providing culturally competent care may increase patient satisfaction, promote health equity, increase patient safety, and prevent misunderstandings between you and your patients.[14] It also involves integrating cultural practices into Western medicine. For example, before some diagnostic procedures and interventions, it is typical to have patients remove personal objects they are wearing on the body. Ask patients whether they wear personal objects and the significance of their removal, since they may have cultural or spiritual significance. You should know whether wearing these objects will compromise patient safety, test results, or outcomes of the intervention.

CULTURAL DIVERSITY IN THE HEALTH CARE WORKPLACE

Poorer health outcomes for minorities are linked to the shortage of culturally and ethnically diverse HCPs, who have historically

TABLE 2.4 How to Develop Cultural Competence

Description	Role of Nurse
Cultural Awareness	
• Ability to understand patients' unique cultural needs	• Understand your own cultural background, values, and beliefs, especially as related to health and health care. • Examine your own cultural biases toward people whose cultures differ from your own culture.
Cultural Knowledge	
• Process of learning key aspects of a group's culture, especially as it relates to health and health care practices • Patients are best source of information about their culture	• Learn basic general information about predominant cultural groups in your geographic area. Cultural pocket guides can be a good resource. • Assess patients for presence or absence of cultural traits based on an understanding of generalizations about a cultural group. • Do not make assumptions based on cultural background because the degree of acculturation varies among persons. • Read research studies that describe cultural differences. • Read ethnic newspaper articles and books. • View documentaries about cultural groups.
Cultural Skill	
• Ability to collect relevant cultural data • Performance of a cultural assessment	• Be alert for unexpected responses with patients, especially as related to cultural issues. • Become aware of cultural differences in predominant ethnic groups. • Develop assessment skills to do a competent cultural assessment for any patient (see Table 2.8). • Learn assessment skills for different cultural groups, including cultural beliefs and practices.
Cultural Encounter	
• Direct cross-cultural interactions between people from culturally diverse backgrounds • Extended contact with a cultural group to enhance understanding of its values and beliefs	• Create opportunities to interact with predominant cultural groups. • Attend cultural events, such as religious ceremonies, significant life passage rituals, social events, and demonstrations of cultural practices. • Visit markets and restaurants in ethnic neighborhoods. • Explore ethnic neighborhoods, listen to different types of ethnic music, and learn games of various ethnic groups. • Visit or volunteer at health fairs in local ethnic neighborhoods. • Learn about prominent cultural beliefs and practices and incorporate this knowledge into planning nursing care.

been underrepresented in the health professions. A diversity gap exists between the ethnic composition of the interprofessional health care team and the overall population in the United States (Fig. 2.3). For example, the diversity of nurses in the United States is increasing but still lags that of the overall population. Blacks, Hispanic/Latino Americans, and Native Americans make up more than 35% of the population but only

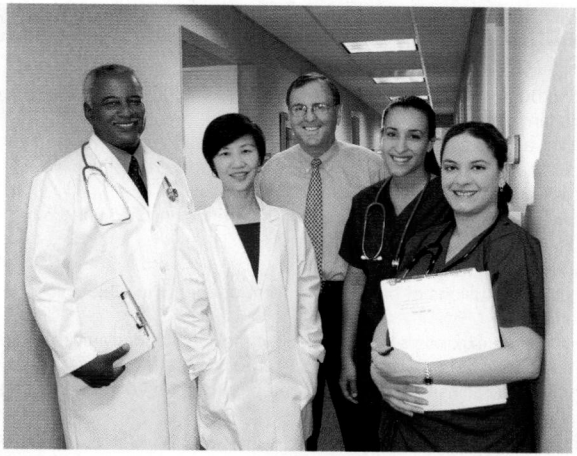

FIG. 2.3 Interprofessional team working together in a multicultural health care environment. (© Thinkstock/Stockbyte/Thinkstock.)

24% of the nation's nurses.[3,15] Biased behaviors against nurses of diverse cultural and ethnic backgrounds by patients and health care professionals may contribute to their underrepresentation.

Cultural differences exist in how well patients think they can communicate with their HCP. In the United States, minority patients are more likely to have difficulty communicating with their HCP.[16] Communication issues include not understanding the HCP, feeling that they are not listened to, and having questions but not asking them. As more internationally educated nurses join the workforce, sufficient training and transitional support must be in place to ensure communication and quality of care.

When HCPs from different cultures work together as members of the health care team, opportunities for miscommunication and conflict can occur. This is termed *cultural conflict*. The cultural origins of miscommunication and conflict in the workplace are often interconnected with cultural beliefs, values, and etiquette. Seeking clarification about misperceptions and misunderstandings is a communication strategy to foster effective teamwork among a multicultural health care team. To ensure the recruitment and retention of nurses from minority populations, all members of the health care team and leadership must create an environment that promotes effective cross-cultural communication and reduces bias and discrimination.

CULTURAL FACTORS AFFECTING HEALTH AND HEALTH CARE

Many cultural factors affect the patient's health and health care. Several potential factors are outlined in Table 2.5.

Folk Healers and Traditions

Many cultures have folk healers, who are also known as *traditional healers*. Most folk healers speak the person's native language and cost less than conventional HCPs. Among the many folk healers found worldwide, Hispanics, particularly from regions in Mexico and Central and South America, may choose to use a *curandero* (or *curandera*); blacks may visit a *hougan*; Native Americans may seek help from a medicine man or *shaman*; and Asian Americans may use folk healers such as a Chinese herbal therapist. In addition to folk healers, some cultures involve lay midwives (e.g., *parteras* for Hispanic women) in the care of pregnant women.

TABLE 2.5 Cultural Factors Affecting Health and Health Care

Beliefs and Practices
- Care provided in established health care programs may not be perceived as culturally relevant.
- Religious reasons, beliefs, or practices may affect a person's decision to seek (or not seek) health care.
- Patients may delay seeking health care because of fear or dependence on folk medicine and herbal remedies.
- Patients may stop treatment or visits for health care because the symptoms are no longer present and they think that further care is not needed.
- Some patients associate hospitals and extended care facilities with death.
- The patient may have had a previous negative experience with culturally incompetent HCPs or discriminatory practices.
- Some people mistrust the majority population and institutions dominated by them.
- Some patients may feel apprehensive about unfamiliar diagnostic procedures and treatment options.

Communication and Language
- Patients may not speak English and may not be able to communicate with the HCP.
- It may be hard to communicate, even with interpreters.

Economic Factors
- Patients may not get health care because they cannot pay for it or because of the costs associated with travel for health care.
- Refugee or undocumented immigrant status may deter some patients from using the health care system.
- Immigrant women who are heads of households or single mothers may not seek health care for themselves because of child care costs.
- Patients may lack health insurance.

Health Care System
- Patients may not make or keep appointments because of the time lag between the onset of an illness and an available appointment.
- Hours of operation of health care facilities may not accommodate patients' need to work or use public transportation.
- Requirements to access some types of care may discourage some patients from taking the steps to qualify for health care or health care payment assistance.
- Some patients have a general distrust of HCPs and health care systems.
- Lack of ethnic-specific health care programs may deter some people from seeking health care.
- Transportation may be a problem for patients who must travel long distances for health care.
- Adequate interpreter services may be unavailable.
- Patients may not have a primary HCP and may use emergency departments or urgent care centers for health care.
- Shortages of HCPs from specific ethnic groups may deter some people from seeking health care.
- Patients may lack knowledge about the availability of existing health care resources.
- Facility policies may not be culturally competent (e.g., hospital policy may limit the number of visitors, which is problematic for cultures that value having many family members present).

Time Orientation
- For some cultures, it is more important to attend to a social role than to arrive on time for an appointment with an HCP.
- Some cultures are future oriented; others are past or present oriented.

TABLE 2.6 Health-Related Beliefs and Practices of Selected Religious Groups

Amish
- Prohibit drinking alcoholic beverages
- Prohibit abortion, artificial insemination, and stem cell use
- Seldom buy commercial health insurance
- Prohibit drugs unless prescribed by HCPs

Buddhism
- Prohibit drinking alcoholic beverages and using illicit drugs
- Practice moderation in diet and avoidance of extremes
- Central tenets are maintaining right views, intentions, speech, actions, livelihood, effort, mindfulness, and concentration

Catholicism
- Fast and abstain from meat and meat products on Ash Wednesday and the Fridays of Lent
- Prohibit artificial contraception and direct abortion
- Indirect abortion (e.g., treatment of uterine cancer in a pregnant woman) may be morally justified
- Sacrament of the Sick includes anointing of sick with oil, blessing by a priest, and communion (unleavened wafer made of flour and water)

Church of Jesus Christ of Latter-Day Saints (Mormons)
- Strict dietary code called Word of Wisdom prohibits all alcoholic beverages, hot drinks (nonherbal teas and coffee), tobacco, and recreational drugs
- Fast for a 24-hour period each month on "Fast Sunday"
- During hospitalization or serious illness, an elder anoints the ill person with oil while a second elder seals the anointing with a prayer and blessing (laying on of hands)
- Prohibit abortion except when the mother's life is in danger

Hinduism
- Prohibit eating meat because it involves harming a living creature
- Cremation is the usual form of body disposal, but fetuses or newborns are sometimes buried

Islam
- Fasting during daytime hours occurs during a month-long period called Ramadan
- Perform a ritual cleansing with water before eating and before prayer
- Prohibit eating pork or taking medicines with pork derivatives
- Prohibit drinking alcoholic beverages
- Artificial insemination is permissible only if from the husband to his own wife

Jehovah's Witness
- Prohibit transfusions of blood in any form or agents in which blood is an ingredient
- Blood volume expanders are acceptable if they are not derivatives of blood
- Prohibit transplants that involve bodily mutilation
- Prohibit artificial insemination and therapeutic and on-demand abortions

Judaism
- Prohibit eating pork, shellfish, or predatory fowl or mixing milk dishes and meat dishes when preparing foods
- Certain foods and drinks are designated as kosher, which means "proper." All animals must be ritually slaughtered
- On the eighth day after birth, boys are circumcised in a ritual called Brit Milah. Girls are given a dedication ceremony involving prayers and blessings
- Prohibit abortion except when the mother's life is in danger
- Organized support system for the sick includes a visit from the rabbi. The rabbi may pray with the sick person alone or in a minyan, a group of 10 adults over age 13
- If an autopsy is done, all body parts must be returned for burial

Seventh-Day Adventism
- Encourage a vegetarian diet
- Nonvegetarian members do not eat foods derived from any animal having a cloven hoof that chews its cud (e.g., pigs, goats).
- Prohibit eating shellfish; eating fish with fins and scales is acceptable
- Prohibit drinking alcoholic beverages
- Healthy church members practice voluntary fasting

Data from Andrews MM, Boyle JS: *Transcultural concepts in nursing care,* ed 7, Philadelphia, 2016, Lippincott Williams & Wilkins.

Folk medicine and traditions are culturally based forms of prevention and treatment. They traditionally rely on oral transmission of healing techniques from 1 generation to the next. The patient may not use the term *folk medicine* but thinks of these as cultural home remedies or treatment practices. A patient can be practicing folk medicine at home without using a folk healer. It is important to assess whether the patient is practicing traditional or folk healing.

Some traditions that are practiced as a rite of passage in some cultures are considered harmful in the dominant culture in the United States. For example, female genital cutting is a tradition that is illegal in most countries yet still practiced in many countries in Africa and the Middle East. It results in physical and emotional trauma and may affect childbirth. Nurses can advocate for immigrant women who have experienced this trauma and to prevent return of young girls to their country of origin for the procedure.

Spirituality and Religion

Spirituality and religion are aspects of culture that may affect a person's beliefs about health, illness, and end-of-life care. They may also play a role in nutrition and decisions related to health, wellness, and how to respond to or treat an illness.

Spirituality refers to a person's effort to find purpose and meaning in life. It is influenced by a person's unique life experiences and reflects one's personal understanding of life's mysteries. Spirituality relates to the soul or spirit more than to the body, and it may provide hope and strength for a person during an illness.

Religion is a more formal and organized system of beliefs, including belief in or worship of God or gods. Religious beliefs include the cause, nature, and purpose of the universe and involve prayer and rituals. Religion is based on beliefs about life, death, good, and evil. You can use several interventions to meet a patient's religious and spiritual needs, including prayer, scripture reading, listening, and referral to a chaplain, rabbi, or priest.

Many patients find that rituals help them during times of illness. Rituals help a person make sense of life experiences and may take the form of prayer, meditation, or other rituals that the patient may create. You should include spiritual questions in your patient assessment and plan care accordingly. Table 9.5 has a spiritual assessment guide that may be used with patients. Table 2.6 summarizes health-related beliefs and practices of selected religious groups.

Cross-Cultural Communication

Communication refers to an organized, patterned system of behavior that may be verbal or nonverbal (Fig. 2.4). *Verbal communication* includes not only one's language or dialect, but also voice tone, volume, timing, and ability to share thoughts and feelings. More than 45 million people in the United States speak a language other than English in their home, with Spanish being

FIG. 2.4 Co-workers from different cultures communicate with verbal and nonverbal cues. (© BananaStock/Thinkstock.)

FIG. 2.5 Family roles and relationships differ from 1 culture to another. (© Jupiterimages/Photos.com/Thinkstock.)

the most common. Hispanic people who do not speak English at home are less likely to receive a variety of health care services even if they are comfortable speaking English.

Nonverbal communication may take the form of writing, gestures, body movements, posture, facial expressions, and personal dress in some cultures. It also includes eye contact, use of touch, body language, style of greeting, and spatial distancing. Eye contact varies greatly among cultural groups. Patients who are Asian, Arab, or Native American may avoid direct eye contact and consider it disrespectful or aggressive. Hispanic patients may expect you to look directly at them but may not return that direct gaze. Other variables to consider include the role of gender, age, acculturation, status, or appropriate eye contact. For example, Muslim-Arab women exhibit modesty when avoiding eye contact with men other than their husbands and when in public situations.

Silence has many meanings. It is important to understand the meaning of silence for different cultural groups. Some people are comfortable with silence. Others become uncomfortable and may speak to decrease the amount of silent time. It is important to clarify what silence means in an interaction with a patient. Patients sometimes nod their head or say "yes" as if agreeing with you or to show they understand. Actually, they may be doing this because it is a culturally acceptable manner of showing respect, not because they understand or agree.

Many Native Americans are comfortable with silence and interpret silence as essential for thinking and carefully considering a response. In these interactions, silence shows respect for the other person and shows the importance of the remarks. In traditional Japanese and Chinese cultures, the speaker may stop talking and leave a period of silence for the listener to think about what was said before continuing. Silence may show respect for the speaker's privacy. In some cultures (e.g., French, Spanish, and Russian) the person may interpret silence as meaning agreement. Asian Americans may use silence to show respect for elders. Blacks may use silence as a response to what they perceive to be an inappropriate question.

Racism and microaggression affect communication. *Racism* is a belief that differences among the various racial/ethnic groups determine cultural or individual achievement. It usually involves the idea that one's own race/ethnicity is superior and involves the idea that one's own race/ethnicity is superior and has the right to dominate others or that a particular racial/ethnic group is inferior to the others.

Microaggression is social exchanges in which a person says or does something that can either intentionally or unintentionally belittle or alienate a person, especially someone of a different racial/ethnic group. It is imperative that nurses seek to understand racism and microaggression through education, self-awareness, and open dialogue with peers.[17]

Family Roles and Relationships

Family roles differ from 1 culture to another (Fig. 2.5). It is important for you to determine who should be involved in communication and decision making related to health care. Some cultural groups emphasize interdependence rather than independence. In the United States, many in the mainstream culture have strong beliefs related to autonomy. We expect a patient to sign consent forms when receiving health care. In some cultural groups, the patient may expect a family member to make health care decisions. When you encounter a patient who values interdependence over independence, the health care system may have difficulty with how the patient makes decisions. We may have to delay treatment while the patient waits for family members to arrive before giving consent for a procedure or treatment. In other instances, the patient may make a decision that is best for the family despite adverse outcomes for the patient. Being aware of such values will better prepare you to advocate for the patient.

Some cultural differences relate to expectations of family members in providing care. In some cultures, family members expect to provide care for the patient even in the hospital. The patient may expect that the family, along with the HCPs, will provide all care. This view is the opposite of the predominant Western expectation that the patient will assume self-care as quickly as possible.

Ask about culturally relevant gender relationships. For example, in some cultures, such as many Arab groups, it is not appropriate for a man to be alone with a woman other than his wife. Nor is it appropriate for a woman other than a man's wife

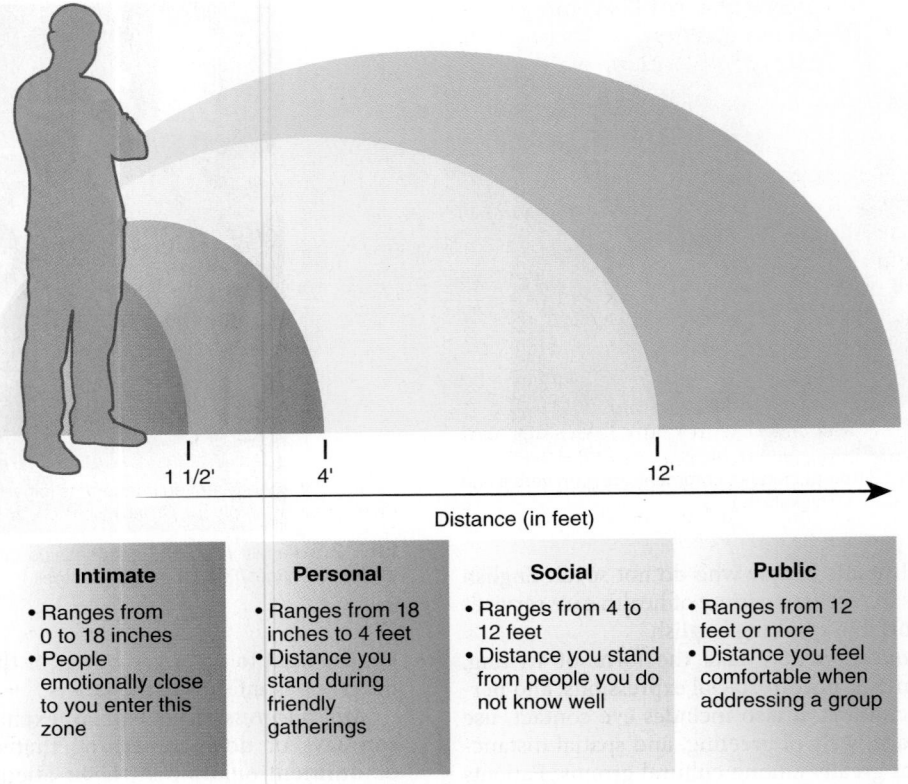

1 1/2'   4'   12'

Distance (in feet)

Intimate	**Personal**	**Social**	**Public**
• Ranges from 0 to 18 inches • People emotionally close to you enter this zone	• Ranges from 18 inches to 4 feet • Distance you stand during friendly gatherings	• Ranges from 4 to 12 feet • Distance you stand from people you do not know well	• Ranges from 12 feet or more • Distance you feel comfortable when addressing a group

FIG 2.6 Personal space zones.

to provide physical care for him. The clinical implication of this cultural belief is that for many patients from Arab cultures, nurses cannot provide direct physical care for patients of the opposite gender. In some instances, patients may only receive procedures or treatments from providers of the opposite gender if a third party is present.

Personal Space

Personal space zones are the variable and subjective distance at which 1 person feels comfortable talking to another. A representative example of personal space zones for European Americans is shown in Fig. 2.6. Personal space distances vary from culture to culture, as well as within a culture. As a nurse, you often interact with patients in the intimate or personal distance, which may be uncomfortable for the patient.

Cultural groups have wide variations in their perception of appropriate distances. An American nurse of European descent may be comfortable with a certain distance. A person from a Hispanic or Middle Eastern background may believe that the distance is too far and will move closer, perhaps causing you to feel uncomfortable. If you then move away to a more comfortable distance, this may cause the other person to think that you are unfriendly or the person may be offended.

Touch

Physical contact with patients conveys various meanings depending on the culture. Performing a comprehensive assessment requires touching a patient. Many people of Asian and Hispanic heritage believe that touching a person's head is a sign of disrespect because the head is the source of one's

strength and/or soul. Many people in the world believe in the evil eye, or *mal ojo*. In this culture-bound syndrome, the illness—usually in a child or a woman—resulted from excessive admiration by another person. In some cultures, the proper way to ward off the evil eye is to touch the area of admiration. For example, if the person admires the hair, the top of the head may be touched. It is important for you to ask permission before touching anyone, particularly if it is necessary to touch the person's head.

Nutrition

An important part of cultural practices is food, including both the foods that are eaten and rituals and practices associated with food. Muslims fast during the daytime during the Islamic month of Ramadan. Such practices may affect when and how patients take medications. Patients may need to make major changes in their diets because of health problems. A person may use food to cope with life changes such as homesickness. Specific foods may be considered essential to good health during pregnancy or other life stages. The HCP should consider food-related cultural beliefs, practices, and habits when discussing nutrition with patients and planning their diets.

When people immigrate to an area that is very different from their country of origin, they may experience unfamiliar foods, food-storage systems, and food-buying habits. They may come from countries that have limited food supplies because of poverty, wars, and poor sanitation. They may arrive with conditions such as malnutrition, diarrhea, and dental caries. Other problems may develop after the person arrives in the new country. For example, second-generation

Hispanic immigrants have a greater chance of becoming over-weight than their first-generation counterparts. The increase in weight is related to the degree of acculturation experienced by the immigrant.

Immigrants and Immigration

Several conditions drive migration, such as overcrowding, nat-ural disasters, geopolitical conflict, persecution, and economic forces. Because of these migrations, a rich diversity of cultures exists in many communities and countries today (Fig. 2.7).

Recent immigrants may be at risk for physical and mental health problems for many reasons. Conditions in their countries of origin (e.g., malnutrition, poor sanitation, civil war) may have resulted in chronic health problems. In addition, recent immi-grants are at increased risk for health problems after arriving in a new area. Relocation is associated with many losses and can cause economic hardship, physical stress, and mental distress.

As new immigrants go through the acculturation process, many have cultural stress as they adjust to their new environ-ment, especially if they have left relatives behind or are unable to return to their home country. Older immigrants are especially affected by changes in role and social position. This may result in depression. Immigrants who have survived wars and violence may have posttraumatic stress disorder. Immigrants may face barriers to social acceptance, such as prejudice or discrimina-tion, and experience a lack of ethnic and cultural resources. For some, it may mean loss of the social status that they experienced in their countries of origin.

Another potential problem is tuberculosis (TB). Two-thirds of the TB cases in the United States occur in people born out-side the country.[18] Those who have recently immigrated from areas that have a high endemic rate of TB are more likely to have TB. Foreign-born Hispanics and Asians combined account for 48% of the nation's TB cases. The top 5 countries of the ori-gin of foreign-born people with TB are Mexico, Philippines, Vietnam, India, and China. The *Refugee Health Guidelines* from the Centers for Disease Control and Prevention supports early identification and treatment.[19]

During the past 45 years, the migration pattern of North America has shifted. Once most immigrants came from Europe. Now, most originate from Asia, Latin America, and Africa. Additionally, an increased number of first- and second-gener-ation immigrants enter the United States after visiting friends and relatives. They have a higher risk for malaria, typhoid fever, cholera, and hepatitis A than people born in the United States. Many immigrants lack health insurance and may primarily obtain their health care in emergency departments and urgent care clinics. Therefore nurses in all settings need to be aware of refugee health screening, treatment recommendations, and resources for access to health care and social services.

Drugs

Genetic differences among people from diverse ethnic or racial groups may explain differences in drug choice, dosage, or administration. For example, some drugs are more effective in certain ethnic groups than others. Side effects may vary among persons from diverse backgrounds.

Genetic variations can affect how the body processes a drug and the overall effect of selected drugs on the body. Although race and ethnicity are imprecise indicators of genetic dif-ferences, they can be helpful in predicting variations in the

FIG. 2.7 Recently arrived immigrants join a neighbor for a barbecue, a com-mon American tradition. (© Jack Hollingsworth/Photodisc/Thinkstock.)

response to drugs. For example, European Americans respond better to angiotensin-converting enzyme (ACE) inhibitors and β-blockers than blacks. Genetics and drug metabolism are dis-cussed in Chapter 12.

Regardless of their cultural origins, many people use cul-tural remedies and prescription drugs to treat illness. Problems can result from interactions of these substances. For example, some Mexican Americans may treat gastrointestinal problems with preparations that contain lead. Some people may self-treat their depression with St. John's wort, which can result in adverse effects if taken with prescription antidepressants.

Patients may avoid standard Western medicine until herbs and other remedies become ineffective or the illness becomes acute. The challenge for you is to try to accommodate the patient's desire for traditional aspects of care while using evi-dence-based approaches that are appropriate and acceptable to the patient. Evaluate the safety and appropriateness of the patient's traditional cultural healing therapies.

Develop a collaborative, trusting relationship with patients and encourage them to discuss their traditional approaches to healing. Seek out information on potential drug and herbal product interaction from the pharmacist. Honor the patient's choices, if safe and effective, since this will enhance collabora-tion and may have a positive impact on health outcomes.

Psychologic Factors

Symptoms are interpreted through a person's cultural norms and may vary from the recognized interpretations of Western medicine. All symptoms have meaning, and the meanings may vary from 1 culture to another. For example, the degree of depression following a cardiac diagnosis is mediated by cultural views. It is important to ask patients what their illness means to them, what they believe is the cause, and what they think is the best treatment.

Culture-bound syndromes are illnesses or afflictions that are recognized only within a cultural group (Table 2.7). The symptoms, course of the illness, and people's reactions to the ill-ness are limited to specific cultures. Culture-bound syndromes are expressed through psychologic or physical symptoms.

TABLE 2.7 Culture-Bound Syndromes

Syndrome	Description
Blacks	
Brain Fag	Term describing brain "fatigue" caused by the challenges of school. Symptoms include difficulties concentrating, remembering, and thinking.
Thin Blood	Affects older adults, women, and children. Weakens a person and increases susceptibility to illness.
Cambodians	
Koucharang or Kit Chroeun	Translates as "thinking too much," brought about by having seen or experienced a horrific trauma. Characterized by physical and emotional exhaustion, immobilization, and constant preoccupation with past suffering and loss.
Caribbean and Southern United States	
Falling Out	Characterized by a sudden collapse, which may sometimes be preceded by dizziness or "swimming" in the head. The person can hear but is unable to move.
Chinese	
Shenjing Shuairuo	Characterized by physical and mental fatigue, headaches and other pains, dizziness, sleep disturbances, and concentration difficulties.
Hispanics/Latinos	
Bilis or Colera	Caused by strong anger or rage. Anger results in excess bile that gets into the systemic circulation. Symptoms include acute nervous tension, headache, trembling, stomach disturbances, and, in severe cases, loss of consciousness.
Ataque de Nervios	Brought on by a stressful family event (e.g., death, divorce). Symptoms may include uncontrollable shouting, crying, trembling, and verbal or physical aggression.
Empacho	The perception that an undigested food bolus is "stuck" somewhere in the gastrointestinal tract, causing nausea, pain, and diarrhea.
Susto	Sometimes referred to as "fright sickness" or "soul loss." A traumatic anxiety-depressive state that may result from a frightening experience, such as a loud sound or some threat. Can cause anxiety, insomnia, listlessness, loss of appetite, and social withdrawal. One treatment is to have the affected person lie on the floor. The healer then sweeps indigenous herbs over the person's body while praying to release the evil wind.
Koreans	
Hwa-Byung	Ailment characterized by resentment that is brought about by bitterness and discontent.
Native Americans	
Ghost Sickness	Condition sometimes associated with witchcraft and a preoccupation with death. Symptoms include general weakness, loss of appetite, a feeling of suffocation, recurring nightmares, and a pervasive feeling of terror

❖ NURSING MANAGEMENT: PROMOTING HEALTH EQUITY AND INCREASING CULTURAL COMPETENCY

Nurse's Self-Assessment

The first step in promoting health equity and providing culturally competent care is for you to assess your own cultural background, values, and beliefs, especially those that are related to health and health care. Many tools are available to help you with this process (*http://nccc.georgetown.edu*).

Table 2.4 suggests ways for you to improve your cultural competence. This information can help you better understand patients and provide culturally competent care. It is important to understand that cultures evolve and change over time. Culturally competent care requires continual learning and self-reflection. Many other important aspects of culture related to health care are included in the Culturally Competent Care sections throughout this book.

In today's increasingly multicultural environment, you will meet patients, families, significant others, and members of the health care team from many different cultures. You will find yourself in patient care situations that require an understanding of the patient's cultural beliefs and practices. Even when you provide care for patients from your own cultural background, you may be from a different subculture than the patient. For example, there are more than 550 federally recognized Native American tribes in the United States. It would be inappropriate for you to assume that a Native American nurse can give culturally appropriate care to a Native American patient when the nurse may be from a different tribe. A white nurse from an urban upbringing may find cultural differences with a white patient from a rural community. Cultural competence is a lifelong process that involves self-reflection and continual learning.[20]

Patient Assessment

HCPs play a key role in promoting health equity. However, the causes of health disparities are not always easy to identify. Assess patients for their risk for reduced health care services because of limited access, inadequate resources, age, or low health literacy.

A cultural assessment should be included in the nursing process.[21] Table 2.8 lists important components of the assessment. Determine the patient's (1) health beliefs and health care practices and (2) perspective of the meaning, cause, and preferred treatment of illness. Ask questions that you are comfortable with based on your own culture.

How can you be aware of the differences among ethnic groups? Using guides for cultural assessment will facilitate the nursing process when working with patients, families, or other groups who are from different cultures. Although guides can help in this process, you need to be careful not to stereotype or assume that common cultural characteristics pertain to each patient. Use guides to explore the degree to which patients share commonalities with the traits attributed to their cultural group. You need to know about traditional characteristics of cultural groups while recognizing that culture is constantly evolving and unique for each person.

Nursing Implementation

Although the issues associated with health disparities can seem overwhelming, several strategies are available to reduce and eliminate health disparities. Table 2.9 presents nursing interventions to promote health equity.

Advocacy. The solutions to reduce health disparities often rest with the policymakers. Economic issues often determine health care delivery. Access and public policy decisions determine who is eligible for federal and state health insurance coverage. You, along with the social worker, can help by identifying key resources in the community, including transportation services,

TABLE 2.8 Cultural Assessment

A cultural assessment should include the following:
- Brief history of the cultural group with which person identifies
- Communication
- Cultural sanctions and restrictions
- Educational background
- Health-related beliefs and practices
- Nutrition
- Organizations providing cultural support
- Religious affiliation
- Socioeconomic considerations
- Spiritual considerations
- Values orientation

Adapted from Jarvis C: *Physical examination and health assessment,* ed 7, Philadelphia, 2016, Saunders.

TABLE 2.9 Nursing Management

Interventions to Promote Health Equity
- Treat all patients equally.
- Be aware of your own biases or prejudices and work toward eliminating them.
- Learn about services and programs that focus on specific cultural/ethnic groups.
- Inform patients about health care services available for their specific cultural/ethnic group.
- Make sure the same standards of care are followed for all patients regardless of culture or ethnicity.
- Recognize health care practices and cultural practices that are important to cultural and ethnic identity.
- Take part in research focused on understanding and improving care to culturally and ethnically diverse populations.
- Identify stereotypic attitudes toward a culture/ethnic group that may interfere with getting appropriate health care.
- Support patients who are fearful about traveling outside the accepted neighborhood for health care services.
- Advocate for patients of specific cultural/ethnic groups to receive health care services that pay special attention to English-language limitations and cultural health practices.
- Learn advocacy and interpersonal strategies from leaders of specific cultural/ethnic groups. For example, blacks may respond to themes such as "do it for your loved ones." Asian Americans may respond to fear of dependency themes.
- Ensure availability of culturally appropriate patient educational resources.

FIG. 2.8 A Navajo nurse teaching a Navajo patient. (From Giger JN: *Transcultural nursing,* ed 7, St Louis, 2016, Mosby.)

The National Standards for Culturally and Linguistically Appropriate Services in Health Care (CLAS standards) are guidelines that improve the quality of health care.[22] The CLAS standards provide practical guidance for care of people with limited English proficiency and of diverse cultural backgrounds.

Communication. Improving interpersonal skills is an important first step in providing culturally competent care. To show respect for the patient, consider the patient's usual communication style. For instance, conduct a health history in an unhurried manner and in a way that is appropriate for the culture. In some cultures, it is best to start with general rather than direct questions. For some cultures, it is most effective to engage in "small talk," with the discussion including answers that may seem to be unrelated to the questions. If you appear to be "too busy," communication may be impaired.

When meeting patients or family members, introduce yourself and indicate how you would like them to address you—whether they should use first names; Mr., Ms., or Mrs.; or a title, such as Nurse. Ask the patient how he or she prefers to be addressed. This shows respect and will help you begin the relationship in a culturally appropriate manner.

If you need to gather personal information, it is important to understand the most effective approach to use. For instance, when talking with people from some cultural groups, it is imperative that you take time to establish trust and listen to the patient's responses to questions. There may be long silences as the person thinks about the question, showing respect by giving the question proper consideration before answering. Take time to listen and help establish trust.

Consider how the patient's age may affect his or her views and communication. For example, black older adults with mental health concerns may struggle with shame, uncertainty, and lack of trust in the system.

Do not try to serve as an interpreter if your patient does not understand English, because this could lead to misunderstandings. Get the help of a person who is qualified to do medical interpretation when you cannot speak the patient's primary language (Table 2.10). Interpreters are available by phone anywhere in the United States through a fee-based service. Use them rather than a family member. Table 2.11 offers guidelines for communicating when no interpreter is available.

reduced-fee screening programs, and appropriate federal and state offices for Medicaid and Medicare.

You can be an advocate in your health care setting by helping to create a community advisory group. Such a group can be very helpful when setting up health programs within a community. This can increase the distribution of culturally sensitive information. Another powerful strategy is to increase the number of underrepresented populations in the health care professions (Fig. 2.8).

Standardized Guidelines. The use of standardized, evidence-based care guidelines can reduce disparities in diagnosis and treatments. For example, the management of hypertension should be based on guidelines and the patient's BP, symptoms, history, and laboratory values rather than other characteristics such as gender, age, or culture. Following the guidelines reduces racial or cultural differences in outcomes. In addition, recommendations related to cultural competency will guide you in your learning and practice.

TABLE 2.10 Using a Medical Interpreter

Choosing an Interpreter
- Use an agency interpreter if possible.
- Use a trained medical interpreter who knows how to interpret, has a health care background, understands patients' rights, and can help with advice about the cultural relevance or appropriateness of the health care plan and instructions.
- Use a family member only if necessary. Be aware of limitations if the family member does not understand medical terms, is younger or a different gender from the patient, or is not aware of the health care procedures or medical ethics.
- Interpreter should be able to do the following:
  - Interpret the patient's nonverbal as well as verbal communication.
  - Translate the message into understandable terms.
  - Act as a patient advocate to represent the patient's needs to the health care team.
  - Be culturally competent and understand how to give teaching instructions.

Strategies for Working With an Interpreter
- If possible, have the interpreter meet with the patient ahead of time to establish rapport before the interpreting begins.
- Speak slowly.
- Maintain eye contact with the patient.
- Talk to the patient, not the interpreter.
- Use simple language with as few medical terms as possible.
- Speak 1 or 2 sentences at a time to allow for easier interpretation.
- Avoid raising your voice during the interaction.
- Obtain feedback to be certain the patient understands.
- Plan to take twice as long to complete the interaction.

INFORMATICS IN PRACTICE
Use of Translation Applications

- Communication barriers can negatively affect the type of care received by non–English-speaking patients.
- Use a language translation app to help you translate 1 language into another language.
- Some apps allow you to speak critical phrases and the translation is immediately spoken back to you or the patient in a natural human voice with the proper accent.
- Check the policy of the health care institution on the use of medical interpreters or translators, including the use of translation apps.

A dictionary that translates from both your language and the patient's language (e.g., Spanish-English/English-Spanish dictionary) is useful. Patients may find it helpful if you have a list of questions and potential answers in several languages prepared by using these types of dictionaries. Many websites and applications translate words and documents from 1 language into another (see Informatics in Practice box). It is helpful to have resources for persons from cultural groups who often use the health care facility. This is especially beneficial when a qualified medical interpreter is not readily available, and you need to learn important phrases in another language.

TABLE 2.11 Overcoming Language Barriers

1. Be polite and formal.
2. Pronounce name correctly. If unsure, ask about the correct pronunciation of the name. Use proper titles of respect, such as "Mr.," "Mrs.," "Ms.," "Dr." Greet the person using the last or complete name.
3. Gesture to yourself and say your name.
4. Offer a handshake or nod. Smile.
5. Proceed in an unhurried manner. Pay attention to any effort by the patient or family to communicate.
6. Speak in a low, moderate voice and avoid excess hand gestures. Remember that there is a tendency to raise the volume and pitch of your voice when the listener appears not to understand. The listener may perceive that you are shouting or angry.
7. Use any words that you might know in the person's language. This shows that you are aware of and respect his or her culture.
8. Use simple words such as "pain" instead of "discomfort." Avoid medical jargon, idioms, and slang. Avoid using contractions (e.g., don't, can't, won't). Use nouns repeatedly instead of pronouns. *Example:*
   Do not say: "He has been taking his medicine, hasn't he?"
   Do say: "Does Juan take medicine?"
9. Pantomime words and simple actions while you say them.
10. Give instructions in the proper sequence. *Example:*
    Do not say: "Before you rinse the bottle, sterilize it."
    Do say: "First, wash the bottle. Second, rinse the bottle."
11. Discuss 1 topic at a time. Avoid using conjunctions. *Example:*
    Do not say: "Are you cold and in pain?"
    Do say: "Are you cold [while pantomiming]? Are you in pain?"
12. Validate whether the person understands by having him or her repeat instructions, demonstrate the procedure, or act out the meaning.
13. Write out several short sentences in English and determine the person's ability to read them.
14. Try a third language. Many Indochinese people speak French. Europeans often know 2 or more languages. Try Latin words or phrases. Use English words that have Latin roots (e.g., use precipitation instead of rain).
15. Ask the person's family and friends who could serve as an interpreter.
16. Use websites that translate words from 1 language to another. Some of them also have audio to help you know how to say the word correctly.
17. Obtain phrase books from a library or bookstore, make or purchase flash cards, contact hospitals for a list of interpreters, and use both a formal and an informal network to find a suitable interpreter.

Source: Jarvis C: *Physical examination and health assessment,* ed 7, Philadelphia, 2016, Saunders.

CASE STUDY
Health Disparities

(© Luevanos/ iStock/ Thinkstock.)

Patient Profile

M.S. is an 81-yr-old woman who came to the United States from India 4 years ago with her son and daughter-in-law and their 4 children. She has several health problems, including coronary artery disease, hypertension, osteoarthritis in her right hip, and diabetes. Her daughter-in-law is the primary caregiver and often brings her to the urban community health clinic for a variety of health-related problems. Recently, M.S. has been having memory problems.

The entire family comes to the health clinic with M.S. Because English is a second language (Hindustani is their first language) for all the adult family members, the staff relies on the oldest granddaughter to interpret.

At this clinic visit, M.S. is presenting with shortness of breath. Through her granddaughter's interpretation, she tells the nurse that she is having trouble walking up the stairs in the apartment building. The nurse does the history and assessment, checks her blood glucose (which is within normal limits), and tells her that she should get more exercise. Given M.S.'s memory problems and limited English, the nurse does not complete a 24-hour dietary recall or teach her or the family about diabetes management. M.S. is scheduled for an appointment with the cardiologist for an evaluation of her hypertension and heart disease. Two weeks later, when she sees the cardiologist, her shortness of breath is much worse, and she is having chest pain. She is hospitalized immediately.

Meanwhile, the clinic supervisor is completing a chart audit for the clinic's quality review program. She is reviewing M.S.'s chart and notices that, although she has been a patient in the clinic for 3 years, she has never received instructions on blood glucose monitoring or general diabetes management. The clinic has a nurse diabetes educator who teaches individual patients and groups of patients with diabetes. The clinic manager reviews these findings with the nurse and asks why she has not recommended that M.S. see the diabetes educator. The nurse states that with M.S.'s memory problems and the language barrier, she assumed that M.S. and her family would not benefit from the consultation.

Discussion Questions

1. What type of health disparity has M.S. experienced?
2. What factors led to her not receiving the standard of care?
3. What other assessment should have been done at the initial visit?
4. ***Patient-Centered Care:*** What strategies may have worked to enhance patient education?
5. ***Patient-Centered Care:*** How would you assess M.S.'s religious and spiritual needs?
6. ***Quality Improvement:*** If you were the clinic manager, how would you recommend that the nurse improve her practice?

Answers available at *http://evolve.elsevier.com/Lewis/medsurg.*

BRIDGE TO NCLEX EXAMINATION

The number of the question corresponds to the same-numbered outcome at the beginning of the chapter.

1. What are the *leading* determinants of a patient's health *(select all that apply)*?
   a. Genetics
   b. Health behaviors
   c. Family history of disease
   d. Social and physical environment
   e. Type and quality of medical care received

2. In identifying patients at the *greatest* risk for health disparities, the nurse would note that
   a. patients who live in urban areas have readily available access to health care services.
   b. cultural differences exist in patients' ability to communicate with their health care provider.
   c. a patient receiving care from a health care provider of a different culture will have decreased quality of care.
   d. men are more likely than women to have their cardiovascular disease symptoms ignored by a health care provider.

3. Forcing one's own cultural beliefs and practices on another person is an example of
   a. stereotyping.
   b. ethnocentrism.
   c. cultural relativity.
   d. cultural imposition.

4. Which statement *most* accurately describes cultural factors that may affect health?
   a. Diabetes and cancer rates differ by cultural/ethnic groups.
   b. There are limited ethnic variations in physiologic responses to drugs.
   c. Most patients find that religious rituals help them during times of illness.
   d. Silence during a nurse-patient interaction means the patient understands the instructions.

5. As part of the nursing process, cultural assessment is *best* accomplished by
   a. judging the patient's cultural values based on observations.
   b. using a cultural assessment guide as part of the nursing process.
   c. seeking guidance from a nurse from the patient's cultural background.
   d. relying on the nurse's previous experience with patients from that cultural group.

6. Nurses play a key role in promoting health equity. An important mechanism to do this is to
   a. discourage use of evidence-based practice guidelines.
   b. insist that patients adhere to established clinical guidelines.
   c. teach patients to use the Internet to find resources related to their health.
   d. engage in active listening and establish relationships with patients and families.

7. What is the *first* step in developing cultural competence?
   a. Create opportunities to interact with a variety of cultural groups.
   b. Examine the nurse's own cultural background, values, and beliefs about health and health care.
   c. Learn about a multitude of folk medicines and herbal substances that different cultures use for self-care.
   d. Learn assessment skills for different cultural groups, including cultural beliefs and practices and physical assessments.

8. When communicating with a patient who speaks a language that the nurse does not understand, it is important to *first* attempt to
   a. have a family member interpret.
   b. use a trained medical interpreter.
   c. use specific medical terminology so there will be no mistakes.
   d. focus on the translation rather than nonverbal communication.

1. a, b, d, 2. b, 3. d, 4. a, 5. b, 6. d, 7. b, 8. b

For rationales to these answers and even more NCLEX review questions, visit *http://evolve.elsevier.com/Lewis/medsurg.*

EVOLVE WEBSITE/RESOURCES LIST

http://evolve.elsevier.com/Lewis/medsurg
Review Questions (Online Only)
Key Points
Answer Keys for Questions
- Rationales for Bridge to NCLEX Examination Questions
- Answer Guidelines for Case Study on p. 31

Conceptual Care Map Creator
Audio Glossary
Content Updates

REFERENCES

1. World Health Organization: Health impact assessment. Retrieved from *www.who.int.hia.en.*
2. Kaiser Family Foundation: Disparities in health and health care. Retrieved from *www.kff.org/disparities-policy/issue-brief/disparities-in-health-and-health-care-five-key-questions-and-answers/.*
3. U.S. Census Bureau : Population estimates. Retrieved from *www.census.gov/programs-surveys/popest.html.*
*4. Hess CN, Kaltenbach LA, Doll JA, et al Race and sex differences in post-myocardial infarction angina frequency and risk of 1-year unplanned rehospitalization, *Circulation* 135:532, 2017.
*5. Willman CL: Cancer health disparities in American Indian and Alaskan Native populations, *Cancer* 77:13, 2017.
6. U.S. Census Bureau: Measuring America, our changing landscape. Retrieved from *www.census.gov/library/visualizations/2016/comm/acs-rural-urban.html.*
*7. DeKeseredy WS, Hall-Sanchez A, Dragiewicz M, et al Intimate violence against women in rural communities. In Donnermeyer JF, editor: *The Routledge international handbook of rural criminology,* London, 2016, Routledge.
*8. Shaw LJ, Pepine CJ, Xie J, et al Quality and equitable health care gaps for women: Attributions to sex differences in cardiovascular medicine, *J Am Coll Cardiol* 70:373, 2017.
9. Correa-de-Araujo R: *Health disparities: Access and utilization,* New York, 2017, Springer.
10. Cigna: LGBT and health disparities. Retrieved from *www.cigna.com/healthwellness/lgbt/lgbt-disparities.*
11. Giger JN: *Transcultural nursing: Assessment and intervention,* ed 7, St Louis. 2016, Mosby.
12. Schwartz SJ, Unger J. *The Oxford handbook of acculturation and health,* New York, 2017, University Press.
*13. Darroch F, Giles A, Sanderson P, et al The United States does CAIR about cultural safety, *J Transcult Nurs* 28:269, 2017.
*14. Betancourt JR, Green AR, Carrillo JE, et al Defining cultural competence: A practical framework for addressing racial/ethnic disparities in health and health care, *Public Health Rep* 118:293, 2016.
15. Minority Nurse: *Nursing statistics.* Retrieved from *http://minoritynurse.com/nursing-statistics/.*
*16. Han W, Lee S: Racial/ethnic variation in health care satisfaction: The role of acculturation, *Soc Work Health Care* 55:694, 2016.
*17. Hall JM, Carlson K: Marginalization, *Adv Nurs Sci* 39:200, 2016.
*18. Schmit KM: Tuberculosis—United States 2016, *MMWR* 66:289, 2017.
19. Centers for Disease Control and Prevention: Refugee health guidelines. Retrieved from *www.cdc.gov/immigrantrefugeehealth/guidelines/refugee-guidelines.html.*
20. American Association of Colleges in Nursing: Cultural competency in baccalaureate nursing education. Retrieved from *www.aacnnursing.org/Education-Resources/Tool-Kits/Cultural-Competency-in-Nursing-Education.*
21. Jarvis C: *Physical examination and health assessment,* ed 7, Philadelphia, 2016, Saunders.
22. U.S. Department of Health and Human Services: Think cultural health. Retrieved from *www.ThinkCulturalHealth.hhs.gov.*

*Evidence-based information for clinical practice.

3

Health History and Physical Examination

Courtney Reinisch

We make a living by what we get, but we make a life by what we give.

Winston Churchill

http://evolve.elsevier.com/Lewis/medsurg/

CONCEPTUAL FOCUS

Clinical Judgment
Collaboration

Communication

LEARNING OUTCOMES

1. Explain the purpose, components, and techniques of a patient's health history and physical examination.
2. Obtain a nursing history using a functional health pattern format.

3. Select appropriate techniques of inspection, palpation, percussion, and auscultation for physical examination of a patient.
4. Distinguish among emergency, comprehensive, and focused types of assessment in terms of indications, purposes, and components.

KEY TERMS

auscultation, p. 38
database, p. 33
functional health patterns, p. 35

inspection, p. 38
nursing history, p. 34
objective data, p. 34

palpation, p. 38
percussion, p. 38
subjective data, p. 34

During the assessment phase of the nursing process, you will obtain a patient's health history and perform a physical examination. This serves as part of the interprofessional team evaluation. The interprofessional team, also known as an inter-disciplinary, transdisciplinary, or multidisciplinary team, is made up of a number of health care professionals who provide care to a patient. The findings of your nursing assessment (1) contribute to a database that identifies the patient's current and past health status and (2) provide a baseline against which future changes can be evaluated. The purpose of the nursing assessment is to enable you to make clinical judgments about your patient's health status.[1] Assessment is the first step of the nursing process. It is performed continually throughout the nursing process to validate nursing diagnoses, evaluate nursing interventions, and determine whether patient outcomes and goals have been met.

The language of assessment is complex, with many overlapping and confusing terms. In this text, *assessment* describes a hands-on data collection process and a *database* identifies a specific list of information (data) to collect.

DATA COLLECTION

The **database** is all the health information about a patient. It includes (1) nursing history and physical examination, (2) the medical history and physical examination, and (3) laboratory and diagnostic test results. A nurse and health care provider (HCP) perform a patient history and a physical examination using formats and data based on each discipline's focus.

Medical Focus

A *medical history* is designed to collect data to be used primarily by the HCP to determine risk for disease and diagnose medical conditions. The medical history is usually collected by a member of the health care team (e.g., physician, advanced practice nurse [APN], resident, physician's assistant, medical student). The HCP's physical examination and diagnostic tests aid in establishing medical diagnoses and implementing and monitoring the medical treatment plan. The information collected and reported by the HCP is used by nurses and other health care team members (e.g., pharmacist, physical therapist, dietitian, social worker) based on the focus of their care. For example, the abnormal results of a neurologic examination by an APN may aid in diagnosing a stroke. You may use the same results to identify a priority nursing diagnosis of fall risk. A physical therapist may use this information to plan therapy involving range-of-motion exercises.

Nursing Focus

The focus of nursing care is the diagnosis and treatment of human responses to actual or potential health problems or life processes. The information obtained from the nursing history and physical examination is used to determine the patient's strengths and responses to a health problem. For example, a patient with a diagnosis of diabetes may respond with anxiety or a lack of knowledge about self-managing the condition. This patient may experience the physical response of fluid volume deficit because of the abnormal fluid loss caused by hyperglycemia. These human responses to the condition of diabetes are diagnosed and treated by nurses. During the nursing history interview and physical examination, you will obtain and record the data to support the identification of nursing diagnoses (Fig. 3.1).

Types of Data

The database includes subjective and objective data. Subjective data, also known as *symptoms,* are collected by interviewing the patient and/or caregiver during the nursing history. This type of data includes information that can be described or verified only by the patient or caregiver. It is what the person tells you either spontaneously or in response to a direct question.

Objective data, also known as *signs,* are data that can be observed or measured. You obtain this type of data using inspection, palpation, percussion, and auscultation during the physical examination. Objective data are also acquired by diagnostic testing. Patients often provide subjective data while you are performing the physical examination. You will observe objective signs while interviewing the patient. All the findings related to a specific problem, whether subjective or objective, are known as *clinical manifestations* of that problem.

Interview Considerations

The purpose of the patient interview is to obtain a health history (i.e., subjective data) about the patient's past and present health state. Effective communication is needed in the interview process. Creating a climate of trust and respect is critical to establishing a therapeutic relationship.[2] You need to communicate acceptance of the patient as a person by using an open, responsive, nonjudgmental approach. You communicate through spoken language, as well as in your manner of dress, gestures, and body language. Culture influences the words, gestures, and postures one uses and the information that is shared with others (see Chapter 2).

In addition to understanding the principles of effective communication, you will develop a personal style of relating to patients. One style of communication does not fit all. The wording of questions can increase the likelihood of obtaining the needed information. The ease of asking questions, particularly those related to sensitive areas such as sexual functioning, comes with training and experience.

The amount of time you need to complete a nursing history varies with the format used and your experience. The nursing history may be completed in 1 or several sessions, depending on the setting and patient. For example, an older adult patient with a low energy level may need a few brief interviews to allow time for the patient to give the needed information. You must make a judgment about the amount of information to collect on initial contact with the patient. In interviews with patients with chronic disease, patients in pain, and patients in emergency situations, ask only those questions that are pertinent to a specific problem. You can complete the health history interview at a more appropriate time.

Judge the reliability of the patient as a historian. An older adult may give a false impression about his or her mental status because of a prolonged response time or visual and hearing impairments. The complexity and long duration of health problems may make it hard for an older adult or a chronically ill younger patient to be an accurate historian.

It is important for you to determine the patient's priority concerns and expectations, since your priorities may be different from the patient's. For example, your priority may be to complete the health history, while the patient is interested only in relief from symptoms. Until the patient's priority need is met, you will probably be unsuccessful in obtaining complete and accurate data.

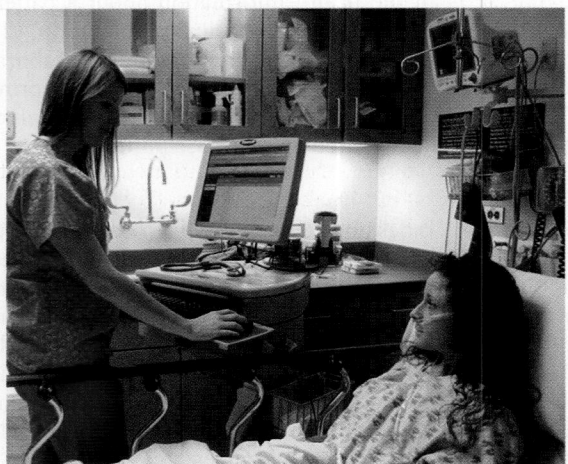

FIG. 3.1 Conducting a nursing focused interview. (Courtesy Linda Bucher, RN, PhD, CEN, CNE, Staff Nurse, Virtua Memorial Hospital, Mt. Holly, N.J.)

■■ NURSING MANAGEMENT
Assessment and Data Collection

In acute care, a registered nurse (RN) must complete the initial (admission) nursing assessment within the timeframe determined by the agency. Ongoing data collection is expected of all members of the health care team.

- On admission, complete a comprehensive assessment (Table 3.4).
- Obtain patient's health history by interviewing patient and/or caregiver.
- Perform physical examination using inspection, palpation, percussion, and auscultation as appropriate.
- Document findings from the health history and physical examination in the patient's record.
- Organize patient data into functional health patterns (Table 3.2).
- Develop and prioritize nursing and collaborative problems for the patient.
- Throughout hospitalization, perform focused assessments based on patient's history or clinical manifestations (Table 3.7).
- Oversee aspects of data collection by UAP.
  - Vital signs, including oxygen saturation
  - Height and weight, oral intake, and output
  - Per agency policy, point-of-care testing (e.g., glucose)

Symptom Investigation

At any time during the assessment the patient may report a symptom such as pain, fatigue, or weakness. Because we do not observe symptoms patients experience, the symptoms must be explored. Table 3.1 shows a mnemonic (PQRST) to help you remember the areas to explore when a symptom is reported. The information you receive may help determine the cause of the symptom. A common symptom that you will assess is pain (see Chapter 8). For example, if a patient states that he has "pain in his leg," you would assess and record the data using PQRST.

Has right midcalf pain that usually occurs at work when climbing stairs after lunch (P). Pain is alleviated by stopping and resting for 2 to 3 minutes. Patient states he has been "eating a banana every day for extra potassium" but "it hasn't helped" (P). Pain is described as "stabbing" and is non-radiating (Q, R). Pain is so severe (rating 9 on 0-10 scale) that patient cannot continue activity (S). Onset is abrupt, occurring once or twice daily. It last occurred yesterday while cutting the lawn (T).

Data Organization

You must systematically obtain and organize assessment data so you can readily analyze and make judgments about the patient's health status and any health problems. Some assessment forms are organized using body systems. Although helpful, these types of forms may be incomplete because they may omit areas such as health promotion behaviors, sleep, coping, and values.

Functional health patterns, developed by Gordon,[3] provide the framework used throughout this book for obtaining a nursing history. This format includes an initial collection of important health information followed by assessment of 11 areas of health status or function (Table 3.2). Data organized in this format allow for the identification of areas of wellness (or positive function) and health problems.[2]

Culturally Competent Care: Assessment

The process of obtaining a health history and performing a physical examination is an intimate experience for you and the patient. Culture influences patterns of communication and the information one shares with others. During the interview and physical examination, be sensitive to issues of eye contact, space, modesty, and touching, as discussed in Chapter 2. Knowing the cultural norms related to male-female relationships is especially important during the physical examination. To avoid violating any culturally based practices, ask the patient about cultural values. Determine if the patient would like to have someone present during the history or physical examination or someone of the same gender to perform the history and physical examination.[1]

NURSING HISTORY: SUBJECTIVE DATA

Important Health Information

Important health information offers an overview of past and present medical conditions and treatments. Past health history, medications, allergies, and surgery or other treatments are included in this part of the history.

Past Health History. The past health history provides information about the patient's prior state of health. Ask the patient about major childhood and adult illnesses, injuries, hospitalizations, and surgeries. Specific questions are more effective than simply asking whether the patient has had any illness or health problems in the past. For example, asking "Do you have a history of diabetes?" elicits better information than asking "Do you have any chronic health problems?"

Medications. Ask the patient for specific details related to past and current medications, including prescription and illicit drugs, over-the-counter (OTC) drugs, vitamins, herbs, and dietary supplements. Patients often do not consider herbs and dietary supplements as drugs. It is important to specifically ask about their use because they can interact adversely with existing or newly prescribed medications (see the Complementary & Alternative Therapies box).

COMPLEMENTARY & ALTERNATIVE THERAPIES

Assessment of Use of Herbs and Dietary Supplements

Why Assessment Is Important
- Herbs and dietary supplements may have side effects or may interact adversely with prescription or OTC drugs.
- Patients at high risk for drug-herb interactions include those taking anticoagulant, antihypertensive, antidepressant, or immune-regulating therapy and patients undergoing anesthesia. Most herbs must be stopped 2 to 3 weeks before surgery.
- Many patients do not tell HCPs that they are using herbs and dietary supplements. They may fear HCPs will disapprove of their use.
- Many herbal preparations have a variety of ingredients. Ask the patient or caregiver to bring labeled containers to the health care site to determine product composition.

Nurse's Role
- Patients typically share information about the use of herbs and dietary supplements with you if you ask them.
- Create an accepting and nonjudgmental attitude when assessing use or interest in herbs or dietary supplements.
- Use open-ended questions such as, "What types of herbs, vitamins, or supplements do you take?" and "What effects have you noticed from using them?"
- Document the use of any herb(s) or dietary supplements in the patient record, including the name, amount, frequency of use, and any side effects.
- Inform patients of the following:
  - Risks and benefits associated with herbal use, including drug-herb interactions
  - Health food store employees are not licensed HCPs
  - Importance of carefully reading the labels of herbal therapies and dietary supplements and taking only the recommended amount
  - Moisture, sunlight, and heat may change the components of herbs
  - Many herbal therapies have side effects. Report these to the HCP at once.

Question older adult and chronically ill patients about medication routines. Look for issues related to medication cost and polypharmacy. Changes in absorption, metabolism, and elimination of drugs can pose serious potential problems for these patients.[4]

Allergies. Explore the patient's history of allergies to drugs, latex, contrast media, food, and the environment (e.g., pollen). Include a detailed description of any allergic reaction(s) reported by the patient.

Surgery or Other Treatments. Record all surgeries, along with the date, reason for the surgery, and outcome. The outcome includes whether the problem was resolved or has residual effects. Ask about and record any blood products the patient has received.

TABLE 3.1 Investigation of Patient-Reported Symptom

	Factor	Questions for Patient and Caregiver	Record
P	Precipitating and Palliative	Were there any events that came before the symptom? What makes it better? Worse? What have you done for the symptom? Did this help?	Influence of physical and emotional activities. Patient's attempts to alleviate (or treat) the symptom
Q	Quality	Tell me what the symptom feels like (e.g., aching, dull, pressure, burning, stabbing).	Patient's own words (e.g., "Like a pinch or stabbing feeling")
R	Radiation	Where do you feel the symptom? Does it move to other areas?	Region of body. Local or radiating, superficial or deep
S	Severity	On a scale of 0–10, with 0 meaning no pain and 10 being the worst pain you could imagine, what number would you give your symptom?	Pain rating number (e.g., 5/10)
T	Timing	When did the symptom start? Was it sudden or gradual? Any particular time of day, week, month, or year? Has the symptom changed over time? Has the symptom happened before? What are you doing when the symptom occurs?	Time of onset, duration, periodicity, and frequency. Course of symptoms. Where patient is and what patient is doing when the symptom occurs

Functional Health Patterns

Assess the patient's functional health patterns to identify effective, dysfunctional, and potential dysfunctional health patterns. *Dysfunctional health patterns* occur with disease. *Potential dysfunctional patterns* identify risk conditions for problems. You may identify patients with effective health function who want a higher level of wellness. Table 3.2 gives examples of possible questions to ask the patient related to functional health patterns.

Health Perception–Health Management Pattern. This pattern focuses on the patient's perceived level of health and well-being and on personal practices for maintaining health. Ask the patient to describe his or her personal health and any concerns about it. Explore the patient's feelings of effectiveness at staying healthy by asking what helps and what hinders his or her well-being. Ask the patient to rate his or her health as excellent, good, fair, or poor. When possible, record this information in the patient's own words.

Next, ask about the type of HCP the patient uses. For example, if the patient is Native American, a medicine man may be considered the primary HCP. If the patient is of Hispanic origin, a *curandero*, a Hispanic healer who uses folk medicine and herbs to treat patients, may be the primary HCP (see Chapter 2).

Other questions seek to identify risk factors by obtaining a thorough family history (e.g., heart disease, cancer, genetic disorders), history of personal health habits (e.g., tobacco, alcohol, drug use), and history of exposure to environmental hazards (e.g., asbestos). If the patient is hospitalized, ask about the expectations for this experience. Have the patient describe his or her understanding of the current health problem, including its onset, course, and treatment. These questions obtain information about a patient's knowledge of the health problem and ability to use appropriate resources to manage the problem.

Nutritional-Metabolic Pattern. This pattern assesses the processes of ingestion, digestion, absorption, and metabolism. Obtain a 24-hour diet recall from the patient to evaluate the quantity and quality of foods and fluids consumed. If a problem is found, ask the patient to keep a 3-day food diary for a more careful analysis of dietary intake. Assess the impact of psychologic factors such as depression, anxiety, stress, and self-concept on nutrition. Evaluate socioeconomic and cultural factors such as food budget, who prepares the meals, and food preferences. Determine whether the patient's present condition has interfered with eating and appetite by exploring any symptoms of nausea, intestinal gas, or pain. Food allergies should be distinguished from food intolerances, such as lactose or gluten intolerance.

Elimination Pattern. This pattern involves bowel, bladder, and skin function. Ask the patient about the frequency of bowel and bladder activity. Ask about urgency, incontinence, and diuretic use. Inquire about stool consistency, color, and laxative use. Assess the skin in the elimination pattern in terms of its excretory function.

Activity-Exercise Pattern. Assessing this pattern looks at the patient's usual pattern of exercise, work activity, leisure, and recreation. Question the patient about his or her ability to perform activities of daily living (ADLs) and note any specific problems. Table 3.2 includes a scale for rating the functional levels of common activities.

Sleep-Rest Pattern. This pattern describes the patient's perception of his or her pattern of sleep, rest, and relaxation in a 24-hour period. Elicit this information by asking, "Do you feel rested when you wake up?"

Cognitive-Perceptual Pattern. Assessing this pattern involves a description of all the senses and cognitive functions. Assess pain as a sensory perception (see pain assessment in Chapter 8). Ask the patient about any sensory deficits that affect the ability to perform ADLs. Record ways in which the patient compensates for any sensory-perceptual problems. Ask the patient how he or she learns best and in what language. Ask what he or she understands about the illness and treatment plan. Plan patient teaching according to identified needs and preferences (see Chapter 4 for details on patient teaching).

Self-Perception–Self-Concept Pattern. This pattern describes the patient's self-concept, which is critical in determining the way the person interacts with others. Included are attitudes about self, perception of personal abilities, body image, and general sense of worth. Ask the patient for a self-description and about how his or her health condition affects self-concept. Patients' expressions of hopelessness or loss of control often reflect an inability to care for one's self.

TABLE 3.2 Health History

Functional Health Pattern Format

Demographic Data

Name, address, age, occupation, gender
Race, ethnicity, culture, spirituality

Important Health Information

Past health history
Medications, supplements
Allergies
Surgery or other treatments

Health Perception–Health Management Pattern

1. Reason for visit?
2. General state of health?
3. Most important things done to keep healthy? Testicular self-examination? Colorectal cancer, hypertension, and heart disease risk screening? Papanicolaou (Pap) test? Immunizations such as tetanus, pneumonia, hepatitis, and flu vaccines?
4. Who is your primary health care provider?
5. Health adherence problems?
6. Cause of illness? Action taken? Results?
7. Things important to you while here?
8. Family health history (e.g., cardiovascular disease, hypertension, cancer, diabetes, psychiatric illness, genetic disorders)?
9. Illness and injury risk factors (e.g., sexual abuse, intimate partner abuse, violence, use of tobacco or alcohol, substance abuse)?

Nutritional-Metabolic Pattern

1. Typical daily food intake (describe)? Supplements?
2. Typical daily fluid intake (describe)?
3. Weight loss or gain (amount, time span, intentional)?
4. Desired weight?
5. Appetite?
6. Food or eating: Discomfort? Diet restrictions?
7. Change in appetite with anxiety?
8. Heal well or poorly?
9. Skin problems: Lesions? Dryness?
10. Dentition: Dental problems? Well-fitting dentures?
11. Food preferences?
12. Food allergies?

Elimination Pattern

1. Bowel elimination pattern (describe): Frequency? Character? Discomfort? Laxatives? Enemas?
2. Urinary elimination pattern (describe): Frequency? Problem in control? Diuretics?
3. Any external devices?
4. Excess perspiration? Odor problems? Itching?

Activity-Exercise Pattern

1. Sufficient energy for desired or required activities?
2. Exercise pattern? Type? Regularity?
3. Spare time (leisure) activities?
4. Dyspnea? Chest pain? Palpitations? Stiffness? Aching? At rest? With activity?
5. Perceived ability for (rate Functional Level 0–III for each):
   Eating __ Cooking __ Grooming __
   Transfer (e.g., bed to chair) __ Toileting __
   Bathing __ Dressing __ Shopping __ General mobility __

   Functional Levels
   Level 0: Full self-care
   Level I: Requires use of equipment or device
   Level II: Needs help or supervision from another person
   Level III: Is dependent and does not participate

Sleep-Rest Pattern

1. Generally rested and ready for daily activities after sleep?
2. Sleep onset problems? Aids (e.g., drugs, CPAP)? Dreams (nightmares)? Early awakening?
3. Usual sleep rituals?
4. Usual sleep pattern?

Cognitive-Perceptual Pattern

1. Hearing impairment? Hearing aids?
2. Vision? Wear glasses? Wear contact lens? Last checked?
3. Any change in taste? Any change in smell?
4. Any recent change in memory?
5. Easiest way to learn things?
6. Any discomfort? Pain (rating on scale of 0–10)? How managed?
7. Ability to communicate (e.g., primary language)?
8. Understanding of illness?
9. Understanding of treatments?

Self-Perception–Self-Concept Pattern

1. Self-description? Self-perception?
2. Effect of illness on self-image?

Role-Relationship Pattern

1. Live alone? Family/caregiver? Family structure?
2. Family problems?
3. Family problem solving?
4. Family dependence on you for things? How managing?
5. Family's and others' feelings about illness or hospitalization?*
6. Problems with children? Hard to handle?*
7. Belong to social groups? Have close friends? Feel lonely (frequency)?
8. Work (school) satisfaction? Income sufficient for needs?*
9. Feel part of or isolated from neighborhood where living?

Sexuality-Reproductive Pattern

1. Any changes or problems in sexual relations?*
2. Effect of illness?
3. Use of contraceptives? Problems?
4. When menstruation started? Last menstrual period? Menstrual problems? Gravida? Para?†
5. Effect of present condition or treatment on sexuality?
6. Sexually transmitted infections?

Coping–Stress Tolerance Pattern

1. Tense a lot of the time? What helps? Use any drugs, alcohol?
2. Have someone to confide in? Available to you now?
3. Recent life changes?
4. Problem-solving techniques? Effective?

Value-Belief Pattern

1. Satisfied with life?
2. Religion important in your life?
3. Conflict between treatment and beliefs?

Modified from Gordon M: *Manual of nursing diagnosis,* ed 13, Boston, 2014, Jones & Bartlett.
CPAP, Continuous positive airway pressure.
*If appropriate.
†For women.

Role-Relationship Pattern. This pattern reveals the patient's roles and relationships, including major responsibilities. Ask the patient to describe family, social, and work roles and relationships and to rate his or her performance of the expected behaviors related to these. Determine whether patterns in these roles and relationships are satisfactory or whether strain is evident. Note the patient's feelings about how the present condition affects his or her roles and relationships.

Sexuality-Reproductive Pattern. This pattern describes satisfaction or dissatisfaction with personal sexuality and describes reproductive issues. Assessing this pattern is important because many illnesses, surgical procedures, and drugs affect sexual function. A patient's sexual and reproductive concerns may be expressed. Teaching needs may be identified through information obtained in this pattern.

You may feel uncomfortable obtaining information related to sexuality. However, it is important to take a health history and screen for sexual function and dysfunction in a nonjudgmental way. Provide appropriate information or refer the patient to a more experienced HCP.

Coping–Stress Tolerance Pattern. This pattern describes the patient's general coping and the effectiveness of the coping mechanisms. Assessing this pattern involves analyzing the specific stressors or problems that confront the patient, the patient's perception of the stressors, and the patient's response to the stressors. Document any major losses or stressors experienced by the patient in the previous year. Note strategies used by the patient to deal with stressors and relieve tension. Ask about persons and groups that make up the patient's social support networks.

Value-Belief Pattern. This pattern describes the values, goals, and beliefs (including spiritual) that guide health-related choices. Document the patient's ethnic background and effects of culture and beliefs on health practices. Note and respect the patient's wishes about continuation of religious or spiritual practices and the use of religious articles.

PHYSICAL EXAMINATION: OBJECTIVE DATA

General Survey

After the nursing history, make a *general survey statement*. This is your general impression of a patient, including behavioral observations. The initial survey begins with your first encounter with the patient and continues during the health history interview.

The major areas included in the general survey statement are (1) body features, (2) mental state, (3) speech, (4) body movements, (5) obvious physical signs, (6) nutritional status, and (7) behavior. Vital signs and body mass index (BMI) (calculated from height and weight [kg/m^2]) may be included. The following is a sample of a general survey statement:

A.H. is a 34-yr-old Hispanic woman, BP 130/84, P 88, R 18. No distinguishing body features. Alert but anxious. Speech rapid with trailing thoughts. Wringing hands and shuffling feet during interview. Skin flushed, hands clammy. Overweight relative to height (BMI = 28.3 kg/m^2). Sits with eyes downcast, shoulders slumped, and avoids eye contact.

Physical Examination

The *physical examination* is the systematic assessment of a patient's physical status. Explore any positive findings using the same criteria used when investigating a symptom in the nursing history (Table 3.1). A *positive finding* shows that the patient has or has had the particular problem or sign under discussion (e.g., if the patient with jaundice has an enlarged liver, it is a positive finding). Relevant information about this problem should then be gathered.

Negative findings may be significant. A pertinent *negative finding* is the absence of a sign or symptom usually associated with a problem. For example, peripheral edema is common with advanced liver disease. If edema is not present in a patient with advanced liver disease, specifically note this as "no peripheral edema."

Techniques. Four major techniques are used in performing the physical examination: inspection, palpation, percussion, and auscultation. The techniques are usually performed in this sequence: inspection, palpation, percussion, and auscultation. The abdominal examination is an exception. Inspection is first, followed by auscultation, percussion, and palpation. Performing percussion and palpation before auscultation can alter bowel sounds and produce false findings. Not every assessment area requires the use of all 4 assessment techniques (e.g., musculoskeletal system requires only inspection and palpation).

Inspection. Inspection is the visual examination of a part or region of the body to assess normal conditions or deviations. Inspection is more than just looking. This technique is deliberate, systematic, and focused. Compare what is seen with the known, generally visible characteristics of the body part that you are inspecting. For example, most 30-yr-old men have hair on their legs. Absence of hair may indicate a vascular problem and the need for further investigation, or it may be normal for a patient of a particular ethnicity (e.g., Filipino men have little body hair). Always compare 1 side of the patient's body to the other to assess bilaterally for any abnormal findings.

Palpation. Palpation is the examination of the body using touch. Using light and deep palpation can yield information related to masses, pulsations, organ enlargement, tenderness or pain, swelling, muscular spasm or rigidity, elasticity, vibration of voice sounds, crepitus, moisture, and texture. Different parts of the hand are more sensitive for specific assessments. For example, use the palmar surface (base of fingers) to feel vibrations, the dorsa (backs) of your hands and fingers to assess skin temperature, and tips of your fingers to palpate the abdomen[1] (Fig. 3.2).

Percussion. Percussion is a technique that produces a sound and vibration to obtain information about the underlying area (Fig. 3.3). The sounds and vibrations are relative to the underlying structures. A change from an expected sound may indicate a problem. For example, dullness in the right lower quadrant instead of the normal sound of tympany should be explored. Specific percussion sounds of various body parts and regions are discussed in the appropriate assessment chapters.

Auscultation. Auscultation involves listening to sounds produced by the body with a stethoscope to assess normal and abnormal conditions. This technique is useful in evaluating sounds from the heart, lungs, abdomen, and vascular system. The bell of the stethoscope is more sensitive to low-pitched sounds (e.g., heart murmurs). The diaphragm of the stethoscope is more sensitive to high-pitched sounds (e.g., bowel sounds). Some stethoscopes have only a diaphragm, designed to transmit low- and high-pitched sounds. To listen for low-pitched sounds, hold the diaphragm lightly on the skin. For high-pitched sounds, press the diaphragm firmly

FIG. 3.2 Palpation is the examination of the body using touch. (From Jarvis C: *Physical examination and health assessment,* ed 7, St Louis, 2015, Saunders.)

FIG. 3.4 Auscultation is listening to sounds produced by the body to assess normal conditions and deviations from normal. (Courtesy Linda Bucher, RN, PhD, CEN, CNE, Staff Nurse, Virtua Memorial Hospital, Mt. Holly, N.J.)

FIG. 3.3 Percussion is tapping of the patient's skin with the middle finger or striking finger of the dominant hand. Hyperextend the middle finger of the nondominant hand and place its distal joint and tip firmly on the patient's skin. Normal percussion sounds: *resonant*—lung tissue; *tympany*—air-filled viscus (e.g., intestines); *dull*—dense organs (e.g., liver); *flat*—no air present (e.g., bone, muscle). (Adapted from Jarvis C: *Physical examination and health assessment,* ed 7, St Louis, 2015, Saunders.)

TABLE 3.3 Common Physical Examination Equipment

- Alcohol swabs
- Blood pressure cuff
- Cotton balls
- Examining table or bed
- Eye chart (e.g., Snellen eye chart)
- Paper cup with water
- Patient gown
- Pocket flashlight
- Reflex hammer
- Stethoscope (with bell and diaphragm or a dual-purpose diaphragm; tubing 15–18 inches [38–46 cm])
- Tongue blades
- Watch (with second hand or digital)

on the skin (Fig. 3.4).[1] Specific sounds and auscultation techniques are discussed in the appropriate assessment chapters.

Equipment. Collect the equipment needed for the physical examination before you begin (Table 3.3). This saves time and energy for you and the patient. It promotes trust by showing a level of professionalism. The use of specific equipment is discussed in the appropriate assessment chapters.

Organization of Examination. Perform the physical examination systematically and efficiently. Give explanations to the patient as the examination proceeds and consider the patient's comfort, safety, and privacy. Follow the same sequence every time to avoid omitting a procedure, a step in the sequence, or a part of the body. Table 3.4 presents a comprehensive, organized physical examination outline.

Adapting the physical examination is often useful for the older adult patient, who may have age-related problems such as decreased mobility, limited energy, and perceptual changes.[5] An outline listing some useful adaptations is found in Table 3.5.

A nurse with appropriate education can perform advanced techniques. A retinal reflex examination would be done with an eye examination. Speculum and bimanual examination of women and the prostate gland examination of men would be performed after inspecting the genitalia.

Recording Physical Examination. At the end of the examination, record the normal and abnormal findings in the patient's health record. See Table 3.6 for an example of how to record findings of a normal physical examination of a healthy adult. See Table 5.5 to find age-related assessment findings in the book.

TYPES OF ASSESSMENT

Different types of assessment are used to obtain information about a patient. These approaches are divided into 3 types: emergency, comprehensive, and focused (Table 3.7). Decide what type of assessment to perform based on the clinical situation. Sometimes the health care agency provides guidelines, and other times it is a nursing judgment.

Emergency Assessment

An *emergency assessment* may be done in an emergency or life-threatening situation. This involves a rapid history and examination of a patient while supporting vital functions.

TABLE 3.4 Physical Examination Outline

1. General Survey
Observe general state of health (patient is seated).
- Body features
- Mental state and level of orientation
- Speech
- Body movements
- Physical appearance
- Nutritional status
- Behavior

2. Vital Signs
Record vital signs.
- Blood pressure—both arms for comparison
- Apical/radial pulse
- Respiration
- Temperature
- Oxygen saturation

Record height and weight; calculate body mass index (BMI).

3. Integument
Inspect and palpate skin for the following:
- Color
- Integrity (e.g., lacerations, lesions, breakdown)
- Scars, tattoos, piercings
- Bruises, rash
- Edema
- Moisture
- Texture
- Temperature
- Turgor
- Vascularity

Inspect and palpate nails for the following:
- Color
- Lesions
- Size
- Shape
- Angle
- Capillary refill time

4. Head and Neck
Inspect and palpate head for the following:
- Shape and symmetry of skull
- Masses
- Tenderness
- Condition of hair and scalp
- Temporal arteries
- Temporomandibular joint
- Sensory (CN V, light touch, pain)
- Motor (CN VII, shows teeth, purses lips, raises eyebrows)
- Looks up, wrinkles forehead (CN VII)
- Raises shoulders against resistance (CN XI)

Inspect and palpate (occasionally auscultate) neck for the following:
- Skin (vascularity and visible pulsations)
- Symmetry
- Range of motion
- Pulses and bruits (carotid)
- Midline structure (trachea, thyroid gland, cartilage)
- Lymph nodes (preauricular, postauricular, occipital, mandibular, tonsillar, submental, anterior and posterior cervical, infraclavicular, supraclavicular)

Test visual acuity.
Inspect and lightly palpate eyes/eyebrows for the following:
- Position and movement of eyelids (CN VII)
- Visual fields (CN II)
- Extraocular movements (CN III, IV, VI)
- Cornea, sclera, conjunctiva
- Pupillary response (CN III)
- Red reflex

Inspect and palpate nose and sinuses for the following:
- External nose: Shape, blockage
- Internal nose: Patency of nasal passages, shape, turbinates or polyps, discharge
- Frontal and maxillary sinuses

Inspect and palpate ears for the following:
- Placement
- Pinna
- Auditory acuity (whispered voice, ticking watch) (CN VIII)
- Mastoid process
- Auditory canal
- Tympanic membrane

Inspect and palpate mouth for the following:
- Lips (symmetry, lesions, color)
- Buccal mucosa (Stensen's and Wharton's ducts)
- Teeth (absence, state of repair, color)
- Gums (color, receding from teeth)
- Tongue for strength (asymmetry, ability to stick out tongue, side to side, fasciculations) (CN XII)
- Palates
- Tonsils and pillars
- Uvular elevation (CN IX)
- Posterior pharynx
- Gag reflex (CN IX and X)
- Jaw strength (CN V)
- Moisture
- Color
- Floor of mouth

5. Extremities
Observe size and shape, symmetry and deformity, involuntary movements. Inspect and palpate arms, fingers, wrists, elbows, shoulders for the following:
- Strength
- Range of motion
- Joint pain
- Swelling
- Pulses (radial, brachial)
- Sensation (light touch, pain, temperature)
- Test reflexes: Triceps, biceps, brachioradialis

Inspect and palpate legs for the following:
- Strength
- Range of motion
- Joint pain
- Swelling, edema
- Hair distribution
- Sensation (light touch, pain, temperature)
- Pulses (dorsalis pedis, posterior tibialis)
- Test reflexes: Patellar, Achilles, plantar

6. Posterior Thorax
Inspect for muscular development, scoliosis, respiratory movement, approximation of AP diameter.
- Palpate for symmetry of respiratory movement, tenderness of CVA, spinous processes, tumors or swelling, tactile fremitus
- Percuss for pulmonary resonance
- Auscultate for breath sounds
- Auscultate for egophony, bronchophony, whispered pectoriloquy

7. Anterior Thorax
- Assess breasts for configuration, symmetry, dimpling of skin
- Assess nipples for rash, direction, inversion, retraction
- Inspect for apical impulse, other precordial pulsations
- Palpate the apical impulse and the precordium for thrills, lifts, heaves, tenderness
- Inspect neck for venous distention, pulsations, waves
- Palpate lymph nodes in the subclavian, axillary, brachial areas
- Palpate breasts
- Auscultate for rate and rhythm; character of S_1 and S_2 in the aortic, pulmonic, Erb's point, tricuspid, mitral areas; bruits at carotid, epigastrium

TABLE 3.4 Physical Examination Outline—cont'd

8. Abdomen
- Inspect for scars, shape, symmetry, bulging, muscular position and condition of umbilicus, movements (respiratory, pulsations, presence of peristaltic waves)
- Auscultate for peristalsis (i.e., bowel sounds), bruits
- Percuss then palpate to confirm positive findings; check liver (size, tenderness), spleen, kidney (size, tenderness), urinary bladder (distention)
- Palpate femoral pulses, inguinofemoral nodes, abdominal aorta

9. Neurologic

Observe motor status:
- Gait
- Toe walk
- Heel walk
- Drift

Observe coordination:
- Finger to nose
- Romberg sign
- Heel to opposite shin

Observe the following:
- Proprioception (position sense of great toe)

10. Genitalia
Male External Genitalia
- Inspect penis, noting hair distribution, prepuce, glans, urethral meatus, scars, ulcers, eruptions, structural changes, discharge
- Inspect epidermis of perineum, rectum
- Inspect skin of scrotum; palpate for descended testes, masses, pain

Female External Genitalia
- Inspect hair distribution; mons pubis, labia (minora and majora); urethral meatus; Bartholin's, urethral, Skene's glands (may be palpated, if indicated); introitus; any discharge
- Assess for presence of cystocele, prolapse
- Inspect perineum, rectum

AP, Anteroposterior; *CN,* cranial nerve; *CVA,* costovertebral angle.

TABLE 3.5 Gerontologic Assessment Differences

Adaptations in Physical Assessment Techniques

General Approach
Keep patient warm and comfortable because loss of subcutaneous fat decreases ability to stay warm. Adapt positioning to physical limitations. Avoid unnecessary changes in position. Perform as many activities as possible in the position of comfort for the patient.

Skin
Handle with care because of fragility and loss of subcutaneous fat.

Head and Neck
Provide a quiet environment free from distraction because of possible sensory impairments (e.g., decreased vision, hearing).

Extremities
Use gentle movements and reinforcement techniques. Avoid having patient hop on 1 foot or perform deep knee bends if patient has limited range of motion of the extremities, decreased reflexes, or diminished sense of balance.

Thorax
Adapt examination for changes related to decreased force of expiration, weakened cough reflex, and shortness of breath.

Abdomen
Use caution in palpating patient's liver because it is readily accessible because of a thinner, softer abdominal wall. The older adult patient may have diminished pain perception in the abdominal wall.

Comprehensive Assessment

A *comprehensive assessment* includes a detailed health history and physical examination of all body systems. This is typically done on admission to the hospital or onset of care in a primary care setting.

Focused Assessment

A *focused assessment* is an abbreviated health history and examination. It is used to evaluate the status of previously identified problems and monitor for signs and symptoms of new problems. It can be done when a specific problem (e.g., pneumonia) is identified. The patient's clinical manifestations guide a focused assessment. For example, abdominal pain signals the need for a focused assessment of the abdomen. Some problems need a focused assessment of more than 1 body system. A patient with a headache may need musculoskeletal, neurologic, and head and neck examinations. Examples of focused assessments for the various body systems are found in each assessment chapter of this book.

Using Assessment Approaches

Assessment in an inpatient, acute care hospital setting is different from assessment in other settings. Focused assessment of the hospitalized patient is frequent and performed by many different HCPs. A team approach demands a high degree of consistency among HCPs from a variety of disciplines.

As you gain experience, you will be able to form a mental image of a patient's status from a few basic details, such as "85-yr-old Hispanic woman admitted for COPD exacerbation." Details from a complete verbal report, including length of stay, laboratory results, physical findings, and vital signs will help you make a clearer picture. Next, perform your own assessment using a focused approach. During your assessment, you will confirm or revise the findings that you read in the medical record and what you heard from other HCPs.

Remember, the process does not end once you have done your first assessment on a patient during rounds. Continue to gather information about all your patients throughout your shift. Everything you learned previously about each patient is considered in light of new information. For example, when you are doing a respiratory assessment on your patient with COPD, you hear crackles in her lungs. This finding should lead you to

TABLE 3.6 Findings From a Physical Examination of a Healthy Adult

Example

General Status

Well-nourished, well-hydrated, well-developed white (woman) or (man) in NAD, appears stated age, speech clear and evenly paced; is alert and oriented ×3; cooperative, calm; BMI 23.8

Skin

Clear s̄ lesions, warm and dry, trunk warmer than extremities, normal skin turgor, no ↑ vascularity, no varicose veins

Nails

Well-groomed, round 160-degree angle s̄ lesions, nail beds pink, capillary refill <2 sec

Hair

Thick, brown, shiny, normal (male, female) distribution

Head

Normocephalic, nontender

Eyes

Visual fields intact on gross confrontation

Visual acuity:	Right eye	20/20
	Left eye	20/20
	Both eyes	20/20
	s̄ glasses	

EOM: Intact on all gazes s̄ ptosis, nystagmus
Pupils: PERRLA, negative cover and uncover tests

Ears

Pinna intact, in proper alignment; external canal patent; small amount of cerumen present bilaterally; TMs intact; pearly gray LM, LR visible, not bulging; whisper heard at 3 ft bilaterally

Nose

Patent bilaterally; turbinates pink, no swelling
Sinuses nontender

Mouth

Moist and pink, soft and hard palates intact, uvula rises midline on "ahh," 24 teeth present and in good repair

Throat

Tonsils surgically removed, no redness

Tongue

Moist, pink, size appropriate for mouth, no lesions

Neck

Supple, s̄ masses, s̄ bruits, lymph nodes nonpalpable and nontender
Thyroid: Palpable, smooth, not enlarged
ROM: Full, intact strong
Trachea: Midline, nontender

Breasts

Soft, nonpendulous, s̄ venous pattern, s̄ dimpling, puckering
Nipples: s̄ inversion, point in same direction, areola dark and symmetric, no discharge, no masses, nontender

Axilla

Hair present, no lesions, no palpable lymph nodes

Thorax and Lungs

Respiratory rate 18, regular rhythm, oxygen saturation 98% on room air; AP < transverse diameter, no ↑ in tactile fremitus, no tenderness, lungs resonant throughout, diaphragmatic excursion 4 cm bilaterally, chest expansion symmetric, lung fields clear throughout

Heart

Rate 82, regular rate and rhythm; blood pressure: RA: 122/76, LA: 120/78; no lifts, heaves
Apical impulse: 5th ICS at MCL; no palpable thrills; S_1, S_2 louder, softer in appropriate locations; no S_3, S_4; no murmurs, rubs, clicks
Carotid, femoral, pedal, and radial pulses present; equal, 2+ bilaterally

Abdomen

No pulsations visible, rounded, positive bowel sounds in 4 quadrants, no bruits or CVA tenderness, no palpable masses

Liver

Lower border percussed at costal margin, smooth, nontender; approx. 9-cm span

Spleen

Nonpalpable, nontender

Neurologic System

Cranial nerves I–XII intact
Motor (drift, toe stand) intact
Coordination (FN, Romberg) intact
Reflexes: See diagram

Grading Scale

0 No response
1+ Diminished
2+ Normal
3+ Increased
4+ Hyperactive
Sensation (touch, vibration, proprioception) normal bilaterally, upper and lower extremities

Musculoskeletal System

Well developed, no muscle wasting; s̄ crepitus, nodules, swelling; no scoliosis
ROM: Full and equal bilaterally, upper and lower extremities
Strength: Equal, strong 5/5 bilaterally, upper and lower extremities
Gait: Walks erect 2-foot steps, arms swinging at side s̄ staggering

TABLE 3.6 Findings From a Physical Examination of a Healthy Adult—cont'd

Female Genitalia*	**Male Genitalia***
External genitalia: No swelling, redness, tenderness in BUS; normal hair distribution, no cysts	Normal male hair distribution, negative inguinal hernia
Vagina: No lesions, discharge; bulging, pink	Penis: Urethral opening patent; no redness, swelling, discharge; no lesions, structural changes
Cervix: Os closed; pink, no lesions, erosions, nontender	Scrotum: Testes descended; no redness, masses, tenderness
Uterus: Small, firm, nontender	Rectal: No lesions, redness; sphincter intact; prostate small, nontender
Adnexa: No enlargement; nontender	
Rectovaginal: Sphincter intact; confirms above findings	

AP, Anterior-posterior; *BMI*, body mass index; *BUS*, Bartholin's gland, urethral meatus, Skene's duct; *CVA*, costovertebral angle; *EOM*, extraocular movements; *FN*, finger to nose; *ICS*, intercostal space; *LA*, left arm; *LM*, landmarks; *LR*, light reflex; *MCL*, midclavicular line; *NAD*, no acute distress; *PERRLA*, pupils equal, round, reactive to light and accommodation; *RA*, right arm; *ROM*, range of motion; $\overline{s}$, without; S_1, S_2, S_3, and S_4, heart sounds; *TM*, tympanic membrane.

*Some data would be obtained only if the nurse has the appropriate education.

TABLE 3.7 Types of Assessment

The following describes types of assessment that you may use in various situations.

Description	When and Where Performed	Where to Find in Book
Emergency		
• Limited to assessing life-threatening conditions (e.g., inhalation injuries, anaphylaxis, myocardial infarction, shock, stroke) • Conducted to ensure survival. Focuses on elements in primary survey (e.g., airway, breathing, circulation, disability) • After life-saving interventions are started, perform brief systematic assessment to identify other injuries or problems	• Performed in any setting when signs or symptoms of a life-threatening condition appear (e.g., emergency department, critical care unit, surgical setting)	• Chapter 68, Table 68.3 and Table 68.5 • Emergency management tables throughout the book and listed in Table 68.1
Comprehensive		
• Detailed assessment of all body systems (head-to-toe assessment)	• Onset of care in primary or ambulatory care setting • On admission to hospital, rehabilitation, or long-term care setting • On initial home care visit	• Assessment chapters for each body system • Physical examination outline (Table 3.4) • Findings from physical examination of a healthy adult (Table 3.6)
Focused		
• Abbreviated assessment that focuses on 1 or more body systems that are the focus of care • Includes an assessment related to a specific problem (e.g., pneumonia, specific abnormal laboratory findings) • Monitors for signs and symptoms of new problems	• Throughout hospital admission—at beginning of a shift and as needed throughout shift • Revisit in ambulatory care setting or home care setting	• Focused assessment boxes in each assessment chapter • Tables on nursing assessment of specific diseases throughout book

do a cardiovascular assessment because heart problems (e.g., heart failure) can also cause crackles. As you gain experience, the importance of new findings will be more obvious to you. Assessment case studies integrated into all the assessment chapters will help you develop your assessment skills and knowledge.

Table 3.8 shows how you perform different types of assessments based on a patient's progress through a given hospitalization. When a patient arrives at the emergency department with a life-threatening condition, you will perform an emergency assessment based on the elements of a primary survey (e.g., airway, breathing, circulation, disability) (see Table 68.3).

Once the patient is stable, you can begin a focused assessment of related body systems. After the patient is admitted, a comprehensive assessment of all body systems is completed.

PROBLEM IDENTIFICATION

After completing the history and physical examination, analyze the data to develop a list of nursing and collaborative problems. See Chapter 1 for a description of the nursing process, including the identification of nursing and collaborative problems.

TABLE 3.8 Clinical Applications for Types of Assessment

The following is an example of how different types of assessment would be used as a patient progresses from the emergency department to a clinical unit of a hospital.

Timeline	Type of Assessment
Emergency Department Patient arrives in acute respiratory distress. Problem is found, and critical interventions are performed. Patient stabilizes.	• Perform emergency assessment (see Table 68.3). • Conduct a focused assessment of the respiratory and related body systems (e.g., cardiovascular). • May begin comprehensive assessment of all body systems.
Clinical Unit Patient is admitted to a monitored clinical unit. Beginning of each shift: Reassess per orders and more frequently as determined by the nurse.	• Complete comprehensive assessment of all body systems within proper timeframe. • Perform focused assessment of respiratory system and other related body systems per agency protocol. • Perform focused assessment of appropriate body system(s) if new symptoms are reported.

BRIDGE TO NCLEX EXAMINATION

The number of the question corresponds to the same-numbered outcome at the beginning of the chapter.

1. The patient health history and physical examination provide the nurse with information primarily to
   a. diagnose a medical problem.
   b. investigate a patient's signs and symptoms.
   c. classify subjective and objective patient data.
   d. identify nursing diagnoses and collaborative problems.

2. The nurse would place information about the patient's concern that his illness is threatening his job security in which functional health pattern?
   a. Role-relationship
   b. Cognitive-perceptual
   c. Coping–stress tolerance
   d. Health perception–health management

3. The nurse is preparing to examine a patient's abdomen. Place in order the proper steps for an abdominal assessment, using the numbers 1–4, with 1 = the first technique and 4 = the last technique:
   ___ Inspection
   ___ Palpation
   ___ Percussion
   ___ Auscultation

4. Which situation would require the nurse to obtain a focused assessment *(select all that apply)*?
   a. A patient denies a current health problem.
   b. A patient reports a new symptom during rounds.
   c. A previously identified problem needs reassessment.
   d. A baseline health maintenance examination is needed.
   e. A patient with an emergent problem needs immediate care.

1. d, 2. a, 3. 1, 4, 3, 2, 4. b, c.

For rationales to these answers and even more NCLEX review questions, visit *http://evolve.elsevier.com/Lewis/medsurg*.

EVOLVE WEBSITE/RESOURCES LIST

http://evolve.elsevier.com/Lewis/medsurg
Review Questions (Online Only)
Key Points
Answer Key for Questions
• Rationales for Bridge to NCLEX Examination Questions
Conceptual Care Map Creator
Audio Glossary
Content Updates

REFERENCES

1. Jarvis C: *Physical examination and health assessment*, ed 7, St Louis, 2015, Saunders.
2. Wilson S: Giddens J. *Health assessment for nursing practice*, ed 6, St Louis, 2016, Mosby.
3. Gordon M: *Manual of nursing diagnosis*, ed 13, Boston, 2014, Jones & Bartlett.
4. Lehne R: *Pharmacology for nursing care*, ed 9, St Louis, 2016, Saunders.
5. Touhy T, Jett J: *Ebersole and Hess' gerontological nursing and healthy aging*, ed 5, St Louis, 2017, Mosby.

Patient and Caregiver Teaching

Brenda C. Morris

True compassion lies in what you can do for someone else.

Billy Graham

http://evolve.elsevier.com/Lewis/medsurg/

CONCEPTUAL FOCUS

Adherence

Communication

Health Promotion

Patient Education

Self-Management

LEARNING OUTCOMES

1. Apply the teaching-learning process to diverse patient populations.
2. Apply strategies to support patient learning.
3. Evaluate the role of the caregiver in patient teaching.
4. Relate the physical, psychologic, and sociocultural characteristics of the patient and caregiver to the teaching-learning process.

5. Prioritize patient teaching goals for patients and caregivers.
6. Choose appropriate teaching strategies for patients and their caregivers.
7. Choose appropriate methods to evaluate patient and caregiver teaching.

KEY TERMS

caregivers, p. 48

health literacy, p. 50

learning, p. 46

learning needs, p. 51

motivational interviewing, p. 46

positive reinforcement, p. 51

self-efficacy, p. 47

teaching, p. 46

teaching plan, p. 45

teaching process, p. 49

This chapter describes the process of patient and caregiver teaching and strategies that contribute to successful teaching and learning experiences. The concept of patient and caregiver (family member or significant other) teaching is central to delivering quality patient care. It is a dynamic, interactive process that involves a change in a patient's knowledge, behavior, and/or attitude to maintain or improve health. You will find that teaching is 1 of your most challenging and rewarding roles. Teaching patients and caregivers is a key nursing intervention that makes a difference in their lives.

ROLE OF PATIENT AND CAREGIVER TEACHING

The general goals of patient teaching include health promotion, disease prevention, management of illness, and appropriate choice and use of treatment options. In patients with acute and chronic health problems, teaching can prevent complications and promote recovery, self-care, and independence. Chronic diseases are responsible for 7 of 10 deaths each year in the United States.[1] Whether patients adequately manage their health problems and maintain quality of life depends on what they learn about their conditions and what they do with this knowledge. Patients who have the knowledge, skills, and desire to take responsibility for managing their health are less likely to visit the emergency department or be readmitted.[2]

Teaching may occur wherever you work. Although agencies may employ advanced practice nurses and patient educators to establish and oversee patient teaching programs, you are always responsible for patient and caregiver teaching.[3] It is a responsibility that cannot be delegated to unlicensed assistive personnel (UAP).

Every interaction with a patient and a caregiver is a potential *teachable moment*. On any given day, more informal opportunities to teach occur than formal opportunities. Take advantage of and document all these moments. For example, when you teach a patient with asthma how to use a peak flow meter, you do not need a formal teaching plan. However, when your patient has a specific learning need about health promotion or management of a health problem, you should develop a teaching plan. A **teaching plan** includes (1) assessment of the patient's ability and readiness to learn, (2) identification of teaching needs, (3) development of learning goals with the patient, (4) implementation of the teaching, and (5) evaluation of the patient's learning.

TEACHING-LEARNING PROCESS

Teaching is "a complex process intended to facilitate learning" (p. 75).[4] When a nurse is teaching a patient about health, the nurse becomes the teacher and the patient becomes the learner. Nurses often teach patients using various methods such as direct instruction, coaching, counseling, and behavior modification. Teaching may be formal, such as giving a planned presentation to a group of patients and their caregivers, or informal such as teaching a patient about medications prior to giving them.

Learning is the act of a person acquiring knowledge, skills, or attitudes that may result in a permanent change.[4] Observation of this change is an indication that learning has occurred. However, learning may not result in any observable change. A patient who understands the instruction and is fully informed may choose not to change behavior.

Although learning may occur without teaching, a teacher helps to organize information and skills to make learning more efficient. In patient teaching, the teaching-learning process involves the patient, the patient's caregiver(s), and you.

Adult Learner
Adult Learning Principles. Understanding how and why adults learn is important for you to effectively teach patients and their

caregivers. Many theories of adult learning have evolved from the work of Malcolm Knowles. He identified 6 principles of *andragogy* (adult learning) that are important for you to consider when teaching adults (Table 4.1).[5]

Models to Promote Health. Patients and their caregivers may progress through a series of steps before they are willing or able to accept a change in health behaviors. Prochaska and Velicer proposed 6 stages of change in their *Transtheoretical Model of Health Behavior Change* (Table 4.2).[6] This model is often used for planning to help patients stop smoking, manage diabetes, and lose weight.

Motivational interviewing uses nonconfrontational interpersonal communication techniques to motivate patients to change behavior.[7] This strategy includes interventions that enhance the patient's motivation for change (Table 4.3). The techniques used in motivational interviewing are linked to the stages of change identified by Prochaska and Velicer.

During the process of change, relapse and recycling through the stages are expected. Sometimes patients do not change behaviors, or they return to previous behaviors after a period of change. This may mean that the interventions used did not consider the patient's stage of change. Identify the patient's current stage of readiness for change and the stage to which the patient is moving. Patients who are in the early stages of change need and use different kinds of motivational support than patients at later stages of change.

For example, a hospitalized patient who smokes cigarettes may be in the *precontemplation* or *contemplation* stage of change. In the precontemplation stage, patients are not concerned about

TABLE 4.1   Adult Learning Principles Applied to Patient and Caregiver Teaching

Principles	Teaching Implications for Nurse	Examples
Need to know	• Patients need to know why they should learn something, what they need to learn, and how it will help them. • Ask the patient questions such as, "What do you think you need to learn about this topic?"	Your patient and his caregiver ask what they need to know about exercise guidelines after a heart attack.
Readiness to learn	• Readiness and motivation to learn are high when facing new tasks. • Health crises provide opportunities for patients to learn and change behavior. • Stress and anxiety may interfere with learning, thus requiring frequent reinforcement of content.	While recovering from a transient ischemic attack, your patient tells you that she is ready to learn about the changes she needs to take to reduce her risk for stroke.
Prior experiences	• Motivation is increased when one already knows something about the subject from past experiences. • Identification of past knowledge and experiences can help find familiar ground to increase patients' confidence.	Your patient needs to begin injections of enoxaparin. She tells you that she gives her father insulin injections and is ready to learn how to give this medication.
Motivation to learn	• Patients prefer to apply learning at once. • Long-term goals may have less appeal than short-term goals. • Focus teaching on information that the patient views as needed right now.	Your patient is scheduled for discharge in the morning. Both she and her caregiver have received instruction on wound care and have watched the procedure. The caregiver tells you that he wants to perform the wound care today.
Orientation to learning	• Patients seek out various resources for specific learning and prefer choices. • When the patient does not recognize the relevancy of the teaching, offer explanations of the value of the learning. • Teaching should target the specific problem or circumstance.	Your patient, who is newly diagnosed with diabetes mellitus, tells you that he is worried about the diet changes he will need to make. Share several options with him to learn about diet changes (e.g., cooking classes, Web-based tutorials, mobile applications, individual sessions with the dietitian, brochures).
Self-concept	• Patients need control and self-direction (sense of autonomy) to maintain their sense of self-worth. • Patients do not learn when we treat them like children and tell them what they must do.	Your patient has a temporary colostomy. She says she is not ready to look at the stoma. Work out a schedule with her for learning colostomy care that meets her need for control and prepares her for self-care.

TABLE 4.2 Stages of Change in Transtheoretical Model

Stage	Patient Behavior	Nursing Implications
1. Precontemplation	Is not considering a change. Is not ready to learn	Provide support, increase awareness of condition. Describe benefits of change and risks of not changing
2. Contemplation	Thinks about a change. May state recognition of need to change. Says "I know I should," but identifies barriers	Introduce what is involved in changing the behavior. Reinforce the stated need to change
3. Preparation	Starts planning the change, gathers information, sets a date to start change, shares decision to change with others	Reinforce the positive outcomes of change, give information and encouragement, develop a plan, help set priorities, and identify sources of support
4. Action	Begins to change behavior through practice. Tentative and may experience relapses	Reinforce behavior with reward, encourage self-reward, discuss choices to help minimize relapses and regain focus. Help patient plan to deal with potential relapses
5. Maintenance	Practices the behavior regularly. Able to sustain the change	Continue to reinforce behavior. Provide more teaching on the need to maintain change.
6. Termination	Change has become part of lifestyle. Behavior no longer considered a change	Evaluate effectiveness of the new behavior. No further intervention needed.

Adapted from Prochaska J, Velicer W: The transtheoretical model of health behavior change, *Am J Health Promot* 12:38, 1997. (Classic).

TABLE 4.3 Key Aspects of Motivational Interviewing

- Listen rather than tell.
- Adjust to, rather than oppose, patient resistance.
- Express empathy through reflective listening.
- Focus on the positive. Do not criticize the patient.
- Gently persuade with the understanding that change is up to the patient.
- Focus on the patient's strengths to support the hope needed to make changes.
- Avoid argument and direct confrontation, which can cause defensiveness and a power struggle.
- Help the patient recognize the "gap" between where he or she is and where he or she hopes to be.

their cigarette smoking and are not considering changing their behavior. During this stage, it is important to help the patient increase awareness of risks and problems related to smoking and create doubt about using cigarettes. Ask the patient what he or she thinks could happen if the behavior is continued. Give evidence of the problem (e.g., x-ray changes), and share facts about the risks of smoking. Although patients may not be ready to change behavior while experiencing an acute health problem, the seeds of doubt are sown. In other cases, such as when a patient has a life-threatening condition (e.g., heart attack), there may be an immediate awareness of the problem and motivation to change.

A patient in the *contemplation* stage of change often is ambivalent. The patient understands that the behavior is a problem and that change is necessary. However, he or she believes that change is too hard or that the pleasures of the behavior are worth the risks. This is seen in the patient who says, "I know that I have to stop smoking. This heart attack really scared me. I know I need to lose weight and start exercising, but I can't change everything all at once. Smoking helps me control my eating; I can't stop until I lose some weight." During this stage of change, help the patient consider the positive and negative aspects of his or her behavior (e.g., tobacco use), gently trying to tip the balance in favor of positive behavior. Helping the

patient discover internal motivators in addition to those external motivators (e.g., second heart attack, lung disease) that push the patient toward change can move the patient from contemplating change to preparation and action. Throughout this process, emphasize the patient's personal choices and responsibilities for change.

As the patient moves from contemplation to *preparation,* we can help strengthen the commitment to change by helping the patient develop **self-efficacy**. This is the belief that one can succeed in a given situation. In this case, it is the patient's belief that they can change tobacco-use behaviors. Support even the smallest effort to change. Movement through action and maintenance stages of change requires continued support to increase the patient's involvement and participation in treatment. You can find a comprehensive discussion of motivational interviewing in the Treatment Improvement Protocols available at *www. ncbi.nlm.nih.gov/books/NBK14856.*

The resolution of acute health problems or discharge from the hospital often occurs before the patient moves to the preparation and action stages of change. As the patient develops readiness in the contemplative stage of change, continue to support him or her with referral to appropriate community and outpatient resources.

Nurse as Teacher
Required Competencies
Knowledge of Subject Matter. Although it is impossible to be an expert in all subject areas, develop confidence as a teacher by becoming knowledgeable about the topic. For example, if you are teaching patients about managing hypertension, you must be able to explain what hypertension is and why treating it is important. Teach patients what they need to know about exercise, diet, medication side effects, monitoring BP, and situations that must be reported to the health care provider (HCP). Last, provide the patient with resources such as credible websites, brochures, and information about support organizations (e.g., American Heart Association).

Sometimes you will not be able to answer patients' or caregivers' questions. Clarify the questions to be sure of what they are asking. When you do not know the answer, tell this to the patient and caregiver. Seek help from co-workers, patient educators, and other reliable sources to answer the question.

Communication Skills. Patient teaching depends on effective communication between you and the patient or caregiver. Medical jargon can be intimidating and frightening. Introduce medical words and define their meanings. Limit the use of acronyms (e.g., CABG for coronary artery bypass graft) and abbreviations (e.g., IV) when talking with patients. Have the patient and caregiver clarify their understandings of the disease process. Ask them to explain what they know in their own words. For example, if we tell a patient he has leukopenia, define this term in words that mean something to him. Explain that *leuko-* refers to a leukocyte, a white blood cell that fights infections, and that *penia* refers to a shortage. To enhance learning, use a brief explanation such as, "You have a shortage of white blood cells, the cells that fight infection."

Nonverbal communication is critical when teaching. Cultural practices often guide nonverbal communication. For example, in Western culture, sitting in an open, relaxed position facing the patient with eyes at the same level delivers a positive nonverbal message (Fig. 4.1). Raise the patient's bed or sit in a chair at the bedside. Open body gestures communicate interest and a willingness to share. Patients from Eastern cultures may prefer that you avoid direct eye contact and give health information to a family spokesperson rather than directly to the patient.

Develop the art of *active listening* by paying attention to what the patient says, observing the patient's nonverbal cues, and not interrupting. Nod in response to the patient's statements and restate what the patient is saying to help clarify communication.

Empathy is the courage to enter the world of another in a manner that does not judge or correct but tries to understand. Empathy means putting aside your own self and stepping into the patient's shoes. Active listening, combined with empathy, is a powerful way to communicate caring and prepare the patient to learn.

Challenges to Nurse-Teacher Effectiveness. Teaching patients and caregivers has many challenges, including (1) lack of time, (2) your own feelings as a teacher, (3) nurse-patient differences in learning goals, and (4) rapid or early discharge from the health care system.

Lack of time can be a barrier to effective teaching. For example, the patient's physical needs may compete for time that you could use for teaching. To make the most of limited time, it is critical to set learning priorities with the patient. Tell the patient at the beginning of the interaction how much time you can devote to the session. Deliver or reinforce teaching during every contact with the patient or caregiver. For example, when giving medications, explain the purpose and side effects of each. Reinforcing small pieces of information over time is an effective teaching strategy, especially if information is new or complex.

Other barriers are your *own feelings as a teacher* and insecurity about your own knowledge and skill. Teaching is a skill that will take time to master. Become familiar with the resources for patient teaching available at your agency. Consult with nurse educators or experienced co-workers for further help with developing your teaching skills.

Sometimes disagreements arise among the patient, the caregiver, and you about the expectations or outcomes of teaching. Having realistic discussions about discharge plans, timelines,

FIG. 4.1 Open, relaxed positioning of patient, spouse, and nurse at eye level promotes communication in teaching and learning. (© Jupiterimages/Photos.com/Thinkstock.)

and home care options can emphasize the need for learning. For example, after a diagnosis of heart failure due to aortic valve insufficiency and subsequent emergent valve surgery, the patient and caregiver may reject teaching efforts until they realize and accept the seriousness of the patient's health problem.

Another important challenge to patient teaching relates to patients having early and quick discharges from the health care system. Shortened lengths of hospital stays have resulted in patients having only basic teaching plans implemented; thus it is important to begin teaching patients soon after admission to the health care system.

Caregiver Support in the Teaching-Learning Process

The teaching and learning process applies to the caregiver as well as the patient. **Caregivers** are people who care for those who cannot care for themselves. Most caregivers are family members or significant others who (1) give or help with direct patient care; (2) provide emotional, social, spiritual, and possibly financial support for the patient; and (3) manage and coordinate health care services.

About 1 in 4 American adults serves as a caregiver to a person with a long-term disability or illness.[8] We often categorize caregivers by their relationship to the patient. The most common caregivers are spouses, adult children, parents, grandparents, and life partners. Identify the key caregiver(s) and assess their roles and relationships to the patient. Because the patient's health problem affects family roles and functions, it is important to identify the needs of caregivers. If the caregiver's needs are unmet, this may interfere with the ability to assist the patient (Table 4.4).

Consider cultural differences when assessing the caregiver. In some cultures, a male family member may be the designated spokesperson to receive and communicate information among family members and the patient. In this type of situation, the caregivers who will actually provide care for the patient and the family spokesperson should be included in discharge planning (see Chapter 2 for more information on culturally competent care).

When possible, teach the caregiver along with the patient. Explain the goals of the teaching plan. Caregivers may need

TABLE 4.4	Assessment of Caregiver Needs

Ask caregivers the following questions:
1. How are you coping with your caregiver role?
2. Do you have any problems performing your caregiver responsibilities?
3. How much support do you get from outside sources (e.g., other family members, friends)?
4. Are you aware of and do you use community resources (e.g., disease-specific professional organizations [such as Alzheimer's Association, American Heart Association], adult day care centers, church, synagogue)?
5. Do you know about resources that are available for respite (someone caring for your loved one while you have time to yourself)?
6. What kind of help or services do you need now and in the near future?
7. How can I or other health care providers help you in your caregiving role?

TABLE 4.5	The Joint Commission's Speak Up Initiative

Speak up if you have questions or concerns. If you still do not understand, ask again. It is your body and you have a right to know.

Pay attention to the care you get. Always make sure you are getting the right treatments and medicines by the right health care professionals. Do not assume anything.

Educate yourself about your illness. Learn about the medical tests you get and your treatment plan.

Ask a trusted family member or friend to be your advocate (advisor or supporter).

Know what medicines you take and why you take them. Medicine errors are the most common health care mistakes.

Use a hospital, clinic, surgery center, or other type of health care organization that has been carefully checked out.

Participate in all decisions about your treatment. You are the center of the health care team.

Source: The Joint Commission: To prevent health care errors, patients are urged to Speak Up (poster). Retrieved from *www.jointcommission.org/assets/1/18/SpeakUp_Poster.pdf.*

help to learn the physical and technical requirements of care, find resources for home care, find equipment and supplies, and rearrange the home to accommodate the patient. Sources of support for the transition from hospital to home include community-based agencies, Medicare and Medicaid offices, and case managers at the hospital and insurance companies.

Patients and caregivers may have different teaching needs. For example, the priority of an older patient with a diabetic leg ulcer may be to learn how to transfer from a bed to a chair in the least painful manner. On the other hand, the caregiver may be most concerned about learning the technique for dressing changes. Both the patient's and caregiver's learning needs are important. The patient and caregiver may also have differing or conflicting views of the illness and treatment options. Developing a successful teaching plan requires you to view the patient's needs within the context of the caregiver's needs. For instance, you may teach a patient with right-sided *paresis* (weakness) self-feeding techniques with special tools, but at a home visit you find the caregiver feeding the patient. On questioning, the caregiver reveals that it is too hard to watch the patient struggle with feeding, it takes too long, and it is messy. As a result, the caregiver decided that it is easier to feed the patient. This is an example of a situation in which the patient and caregiver need more teaching about goals for self-care.

Discuss the potential that support groups, family and friends, and community resources have for providing ongoing resources. Support groups help by people sharing experiences and information, offering understanding and acceptance, and suggesting solutions to common problems and concerns.

Regulatory Mandates for Patient Teaching

Several important agencies have specific mandates related to teaching hospitalized patients. The Joint Commission's (TJC's) accreditation standards, National Patient Safety Goals,[9] and the American Hospital Association's Patient Care Partnership[10] state that patients have a fundamental right to receive information about their care. This information includes their diagnosis, treatment, and prognosis in terms that they can understand. For example, this means that written materials must be at the patient's reading level. One program started by TJC, Speak Up, was developed to encourage patients to become more involved and informed about their plan of care (Table 4.5).[11] Another program implemented by the Institute for Healthcare Improvement's National Patient

Safety Foundation is Ask Me 3.[12] Both programs encourage patients to ask specific questions about their care.

PROCESS OF PATIENT TEACHING

We use many different approaches in the process of patient teaching. However, the approach used most often by nurses parallels the nursing process. The **teaching process** and the nursing process involve the development of a plan that includes assessment, goal setting, implementation, and evaluation. The teaching process, like the nursing process, may not always flow in linear order, but the steps serve as checkpoints.

Assessment

During the general nursing assessment, gather data to determine if the patient has learning needs. For example, what does the patient know about the health problem? How does he or she perceive the problem? If you identify a learning need, you need a more detailed assessment, and address that problem with the teaching plan. Include caregivers in the assessment as you determine their role and ability to care for the patient at home. Key questions to use in the assessment are outlined in Table 4.6.

Physical Factors. The patient's age is a factor to consider in the teaching plan. Age affects the patient's experiences and rate of learning. Some effects of increased age on learning may be obvious, but the inexperience of younger people can also affect learning. For example, a man in his twenties who has never thought about his own mortality may be unable to accept the long-term health implications of diabetes mellitus.

Sensory impairments (e.g., hearing or vision loss) decrease sensory input and can alter learning. Cognition may be affected by disorders of the nervous system (e.g., stroke, head trauma) and by other diseases (e.g., liver impairment, heart failure). Patients with altered cognition may have a hard time learning and need more caregiver involvement in the teaching process. You need manual dexterity to perform skills such as giving injections or BP monitoring.

Pain, fatigue, and certain drugs influence the patient's ability to learn. No one can learn effectively when in pain.

TABLE 4.6 Assessment of Factors Affecting Patient Teaching

Key Factors and Questions

Physical
- What is the patient's age?
- Is the patient acutely ill?
- Is the patient fatigued or in pain?
- What is the primary diagnosis?
- Are there other medical problems?
- What is the patient's current mental status?
- What is the patient's hearing ability? Visual ability? Motor ability?
- What drugs does the patient take that may affect learning?

Psychologic
- Does the patient appear anxious, afraid, depressed, defensive?
- Is the patient in a state of denial?
- What is the patient's level of motivation? Self-efficacy?

Sociocultural
- What are the patient's beliefs about his or her illness or treatment?
- Is the proposed teaching consistent with the patient's cultural values?
- What is the patient's educational experience, reading ability, primary language?
- What is the patient's present or past occupation?
- How does the patient describe his or her financial status?
- What is the patient's living arrangement?
- Does the patient have family or close friends?

Learner
- What does the patient already know about his or her health problem?
- What does the patient think is most important to learn?
- What prior learning experiences could act as a frame of reference for current learning needs?
- Is the patient ready to learn? Change behavior?
- How does the patient learn best (e.g., reading, listening, looking at pictures, doing, playing games)?
- In what kind of environment does the patient learn best? Formal classroom? Computer/Web-based setting? Informal setting, such as home? Alone or in a group?
- In what way should the caregiver(s) be involved in patient teaching?

Provide teaching after the patient's pain is controlled. A tired, weak patient cannot learn effectively because of the inability to concentrate. Sleep disruption is common during hospitalization, and patients are often sleep deprived at the time of discharge. Drugs that cause central nervous system depression, such as opioids and sedatives, decrease mental alertness and can affect the patient's ability to learn new information. Adjust the teaching plan by setting high-priority goals based on need-to-know information and realistic expectations. Patients often need a referral for follow-up so that teaching continues and learning is confirmed after discharge.

Psychologic Factors. Psychologic factors have a major influence on the patient's ability to learn. Anxiety and depression are common reactions to illness. Although mild anxiety increases the learner's perceptual and learning abilities, moderate or severe anxiety limits learning. Anxiety and depression can negatively affect the patient's motivation and readiness to learn. For instance, the patient newly diagnosed with diabetes who is depressed about the diagnosis may not listen or respond to instructions about glucose testing. Discussions with the patient about these concerns or referrals to an appropriate support

group may help the patient to learn that management of diabetes is possible.

Patients respond to the stress of illness with a variety of defense mechanisms, such as denial, rationalization, or even humor. A patient who denies having cancer will not be receptive to information related to treatment options. Similarly, a caregiver may have a hard time accepting a terminal diagnosis. A patient using rationalization will imagine any number of reasons for avoiding change or for rejecting teaching. For example, a patient with heart disease who does not want to change dietary habits will relate stories of people who have eaten bacon and eggs every day and lived to be 100. Some patients use humor to filter reality or decrease anxiety. They may use laughter to escape from the experience of facing threatening situations. Humor in the teaching process is important and useful but notice when humor is used excessively or inappropriately to avoid reality.

One important factor in successful adoption of new behaviors is the patient's sense of self-efficacy. There is a strong relationship between self-efficacy and outcomes of illness management. Self-efficacy increases when a person gains new skills in managing a threatening situation. It decreases if the person has repeated failure, especially early in the course of events. Plan easily achievable goals early in the teaching sessions. Proceed from simple to more complex content to support a feeling of success.

Sociocultural Factors

Health Literacy. Literacy is the ability to use printed and written information to function in society. **Health literacy** is the degree to which a person can obtain and understand basic health information needed to make appropriate health decisions.[13] As many as 50% of U.S. adults have limited literacy skills, and almost 90% have limited health literacy skills.[14]

Improving health literacy will advance population health. Currently, only 64% of adults report receiving easy-to-understand instructions from their HCPs and only 24% report that a HCP asked them to describe how they will follow the instructions provided.[15] Patients with low levels of health literacy have trouble understanding and acting on health information, placing them at greater risk for hospital readmissions.[16] Even patients with high levels of health literacy may have a hard time understanding complex health information if they are sick or stressed. Health illiteracy results in poor patient outcomes, not following treatment plans, limited self-management skills, and increased health disparities.[16]

It is challenging to assess health literacy, because patients may be embarrassed to admit that they are having trouble understanding health information. Health professionals often over-estimate the health literacy of patients, so it is important to routinely assess health literacy level. Easy-to-use assessment tools are available. The Single-Item Literacy Screener (SILS) uses 1 question to identify adults who need help with reading.[17] The question is, "How often do you need to have someone help you when you read instructions, pamphlets, or other written material from your doctor or pharmacy?"

Another approach is to implement health literacy universal precautions. These are the steps to take when we assume that all patients may have difficulty understanding important health

FIG. 4.2 Nurse communicating with a non–English-speaking patient using a translation phone service. (Courtesy Linda Bucher, RN, PhD, CEN, CNE, Staff Nurse, Virtua Memorial Hospital, Mt. Holly, N.J.)

information and accessing health services. These include using simple communications about health information and verifying patient understanding.[14]

TJC states that we must tailor patient teaching to the patient's literacy needs. For example, teach patients and give them written materials in their primary language. Teaching materials are available in multiple languages. It is preferable to use medical interpreters instead of family members or friends, to protect patient privacy (Fig. 4.2). Medical interpreters are discussed in Chapter 2 in Table 2.10. Choose patient teaching materials written at the fifth-grade or lower reading level. Other interventions to help patients with low levels of health literacy include using the teach-back method, highlighting key text, and teaching content in small increments.

Cultural Considerations. The wider culture to which a patient belongs influences learning. Cultural traditions influence our health practices, beliefs, and behavior. These traditions, which can affect patient teaching, can be identified in a cultural assessment (see Table 2.3). TJC requires that patient teaching be tailored to the patient's cultural needs.[18] Ask patients to describe their beliefs about health and illness.

One cultural element that specifically affects the teaching-learning process is a conflict between the patient's cultural beliefs and values and the behaviors promoted by the health care team. For example, you can teach a patient who values a trim figure to use diet and exercise to keep that figure while at the same time improving BP control. However, being heavier may be valued in another patient's culture. This patient may have more difficulty accepting the need for diet and exercise in BP control.

Assess the patient's use of cultural remedies and healing practices (see the Complementary & Alternative Therapies Box: Assessment of Use of Herbs and Dietary Supplements in Chapter 3, p. 35). Consider the cultural remedies that may interfere with or are contraindicated by the treatment plan.

Last, it is important to know who has authority in the patient's culture. The patient may defer to the authority, such as an elder or a spiritual leader, for decisions. In this case, identify and work with the patient and the decision makers in the

patient's cultural group. See Chapter 2 for more information on cultural competence.

Socioeconomic Considerations. Consider a variety of socioeconomic factors when preparing to teach patients. Knowing the patient's present or past occupation may help you determine the vocabulary to use during teaching. For example, an auto mechanic may understand the volume overload associated with heart failure as flooding an engine. An engineer may understand the principles of physics associated with gravity and pressures when discussing vascular problems.

Ask the patient about living arrangements. Whether the patient lives alone, with friends, or with family influences who you include in the teaching process. You may need to change the teaching plan if the patient does not have access to electricity or phones. If the patient has unmet learning needs by the time of discharge, arrange for ongoing teaching after discharge.

Learner Factors. Last, assess learner factors, including the patient's learning needs, readiness to learn, and learning style.

Learning Needs. Learning needs are the new knowledge and skills that a person must have to meet a goal. The assessment of learning needs determines what the patient already knows and any past experiences with health problems. Patients with long-standing health problems may have different learning needs from those patients with newly diagnosed health problems.

What patients should learn about managing an illness or what behaviors promote health may seem obvious to you. However, what you think is important may be different from what patients want to know. Remember, adults learn best when the teaching gives information that they view as being needed at once (Table 4.1). Ask patients to prioritize what they see as the most critical information. Start by giving the patient a list of the recommended topics and then ask the patient to identify other topics not on the list. Having patients prioritize their own learning needs lets you begin with the patient's most important needs. Explain why critical information is "need to know."

Readiness to Learn. Readiness to learn and motivation depend on multiple factors, such as perceived need, attitudes, and beliefs. When teaching adults, identify what information the person values. Readiness to learn is increased if the patient perceives a need for information, has a belief that a behavior change has value, or perceives the learning activities as new and stimulating.[5]

Before implementing the teaching plan, determine where the patient is in the stages of change (Table 4.2). If the patient is in the precontemplation stage, provide support and increase the patient's awareness of the problem until the patient is ready to consider a change in behavior. Nurses in outpatient settings and home health care can continue to assess the patient's readiness to learn and implement the teaching plan as the patient moves through the stages of change. Reinforcement throughout the change process is a strong motivational factor for achieving a desired behavior. Positive reinforcement involves rewarding the target behavior with positive feedback or other rewards to maintain the behavior.[6]

Learning Style. Each person has a distinct style of learning. The 3 general learning styles are (1) *visual* (reading, pictures), (2) *auditory* (listening), and (3) *physical* (doing things). People often use more than 1 learning style to gain new knowledge or skills. To assess a patient's preferred learning style, ask how the patient likes to learn and has learned effectively in the past.

When assessing the patient's learning style, identify the patient who does not read or who has low health literacy. For example, the patient may tell you that he or she does not read much but likes to learn from television. In addition, assess the patient's *ehealth literacy*. This refers to the degree that patients use digital information (e.g., webinars, online health management tools) and communication technologies (e.g., online communication with HCP, online support groups) to improve their health (Fig. 4.3).[19] When possible, use the patient's or caregiver's preferred learning style.

FIG. 4.3 Older couple accessing the Web for health information. (© monkeybusinessimages/iStock/Thinkstock.)

Planning

Prioritize the patient's learning needs and agree on learning goals. If the patient's physical or psychologic condition interferes with participation, involve the patient's caregiver(s) in the planning phase.

Setting Goals. It is important to have clear and measurable learning goals or outcomes (Table 4.7). Learning goals relate to the intended outcome of the learning process, guide the choice of teaching strategies, and help evaluate the patient's progress. Learning goals are parallel to patient outcomes in the nursing care plan (NCP). Most settings have standardized NCPs with preset goals and interventions for specific learning needs. You will modify these NCPs based on the patient's unique sociocultural and learner characteristics.

Choosing Teaching Strategies. Three factors that influence the choice of teaching strategies are (1) patient characteristics (e.g., learning style, educational background, culture, language skills), (2) subject matter, and (3) available resources. Table 4.8 summarizes learner characteristics and recommends teaching approaches based on the generation of the patient or caregiver.

Consider various strategies (Table 4.9) in the teaching plan. We often use multiple teaching strategies to improve learning (Fig. 4.4). Discussion is the most common type of interaction used in teaching patients and caregivers. A type of group teaching involves *peer teaching,* as occurs in support groups. Patients dealing with common problems such as cancer, alcoholism, and eating disorders can receive help from peer teaching.

Adapt your teaching methods when teaching patients with a disability how to care for themselves or how to take part in

TABLE 4.7 Writing Learning Goals

Elements of Learning Goals

Learning goals (also called outcomes or objectives) are written statements that define exactly how patients demonstrate their knowledge of the content. Goals address the following 4 questions:

1. Who Will Perform the Activity or Acquire the Desired Behavior?
Examples:
I (the patient) will
I (the caregiver) will
We (patient's family/caregivers) will

2. What Is the Actual Behavior That the Learner Will Exhibit to Show Mastery of the Goal?
Examples:
List the symptoms.
Self-administer an insulin injection.
Choose from a hospital menu.

3. What Are the Conditions Under Which the Behavior Is to Be Demonstrated?
Examples:
In front of the nurse
From a random list
Using sterile technique

4. What Are the Specific Criteria That Will Be Used to Measure the Patient's Success, Such as Time and Degree of Accuracy?
Examples:
With 100% accuracy
Over the next week
Before discharge

Verbs in Learning Goals

Avoid vague, ambiguous verbs that are hard to measure:	*Use verbs that have precise descriptions with few interpretations:*
• Appreciate	• Identify
• Learn	• List
• Understand	• Describe
• Enjoy	• Demonstrate
• Feel	• Perform
• Value	• Choose

Poorly and Well-Written Learning Goals

Example of Poorly Written Learning Goal	Examples of Well-Written Learning Goals
• The patient will understand the importance of managing his own colostomy. *Analysis*: It is not clear how the patient will show that he "understands" the importance of managing his colostomy, when and to whom he will demonstrate this behavior, or what criteria will be used to determine whether the goal has been met.	• The patient will describe to the nurse the basic steps for changing the colostomy pouch and skin barrier by 2/14/21. • Using correct technique, the patient will empty his colostomy pouch when one-third full. • The patient's caregiver will perform colostomy care, including changing the pouch and skin barrier. • Given a list of signs and symptoms related to complications of a colostomy, the patient and caregiver will identify signs and symptoms to report to a health care provider before discharge. *Analysis*: When learning goals are clear and specific and documented in the patient's record, all members of the health care team can work together to achieve the same outcomes.

TABLE 4.8 Learner Characteristics and Teaching Strategies by Generation

Birth Year	Learner Characteristics	Recommended Teaching Strategies
Millennials (Generation Y, Yers, Nexters, Digital Natives)		
1981–2000	• Multitaskers • Prefer interactive and virtual environments • Technologically focused • Need flexibility • Short attention span • Team players • Prefer more structured learning compared to Xers • Accustomed to learning whatever, wherever, whenever	• Integrate technology and media in teaching • Discuss reliable health-related mobile apps and websites • Download health information to smart phones, tablets, or similar devices • Consider group teaching • Consider active learning approaches
Generation X (Xers, Digital Natives)		
1965–1980	• Self-directed or self-paced learning • Self-reliant • Consumers of education • Short attention span	• Integrate technology and media in teaching • Discuss reliable websites • Consider health-related mobile applications • Give Web-based education materials • Provide education materials that are brief and easy to read • Encourage questions
Baby Boomers (Digital Immigrants)		
1946–1964	• Emphasis on self-knowledge • Solve problems by action • Acquisition of knowledge from authoritative sources • Receptive to feedback • Prefer text over graphics • Process (step-by-step) oriented	• Assess ehealth literacy and consider strategies as appropriate • Consider lecture or lecture-discussion (e.g., PowerPoint presentation) • Use patient education TV channels • Provide printed materials
Veterans (Traditionalists, Digital Immigrants)		
Born before 1946	• Emphasis on rote learning • Memorization of knowledge • Follow rules	• Assess ehealth literacy and consider strategies as appropriate • Consider lecture or lecture-discussion • Use pictures and printed materials such as books

Compiled from Bradshaw M, Lowenstein A: *Innovative teaching strategies in nursing*, ed 7, Burlington, Mass, 2017, Jones & Bartlett Learning; and Hart S: Today's learners and educators: bridging the generational gaps, *Teach Learn Nurs* 12:253, 2017.

their own care. It is essential to know how to modify teaching methods to meet the needs of patients with cognitive impairment, hearing loss, limited manual dexterity, or vision loss. Magnifying glasses, bright lighting, and materials printed in a large font may help the patient with impaired vision read teaching materials. More visual stimuli can help people with hearing loss. Using adaptive equipment may help those with problems performing manual skills. Table 4.10 presents strategies for teaching patients with disabilities.

Learning Materials. Use learning materials in multiple formats. Learn what resources are available in your agency and from support services and professional groups. The use of CDs/DVDs and online videos is helpful, particularly when teaching visual content such as the steps of a procedure (e.g., suctioning a tracheostomy). The health care agency's television system may show high-quality, professionally produced patient teaching programs on demand or on a rotating schedule (Fig. 4.4).

Printed materials are useful for teaching patients and caregivers, especially for those whose preferred learning style is reading. Some health-related organizations, such as the American Cancer Society and the American Heart Association provide quality patient education materials free of charge. Some governmental organizations, such as the National Institutes of Health and the Centers for Disease Control and Prevention, have learning materials for patients and caregivers. These materials can be used in combination with other teaching strategies. For instance, after a discussion on the effects of smoking on health, you may use material from the American Cancer Society to reinforce the information.

When writing teaching materials, use several techniques to keep the reading level at a fifth-grade level. These include (1) organize the content logically; (2) highlight or place key information in bold or italics; (3) use short, common words of 1 or 2 syllables; (4) define medical words in simple language; (5) keep sentences short, between 10 and 15 words; (6) use pictures or drawings; and (7) use active voice in the same manner in which you would normally speak.[20] Whenever possible, appraise written materials for readability level using word processing (e.g., Microsoft Word) or Web-based (e.g., *www.wordscount.info*) programs.

Using Technology. Patients may use the Internet and other digital technology (e.g., smart phones) to obtain information and manage their health. Patients can quickly do a Web search or open a software application for access to information about diseases, drugs, treatments, and surgeries. Your job is to help patients sift through the information and determine if it is valid, reliable, and usable. Encourage patients to use websites established by the government, universities, or reputable health-related organizations (e.g., American Diabetes Association, American Heart Association, National Institutes of Health, U.S. Food and Drug Administration). Understanding the principles of Web searching for health information and teaching patients how to find valid information are critical skills. The presence of Internet connections in many patient rooms provides an opportunity for you to teach patients about their illness and how to use the Web to find related information.

Overall, the digital health divide for older adults has narrowed. However, adults older than 75 years of age, those with less than a high school education, and those with very low income are less likely to access the Internet for health-related Internet use.[21] Organizations dedicated to improving the quality of life for older adults promote the development of user-friendly websites (e.g., *www.nlm.nih.gov/pubs/checklist.pdf*) and publish guides to help evaluate Web-based health information (e.g., *www.mlanet.org/resources/userguide.html*).

The quantity and complexity of digital health care technology available to you and your patients will continue to increase. *Telehealth,* a broad term that refers to the delivery of

TABLE 4.9   Comparison of Teaching Strategies

Description	Advantages	Limitations
Discussion ("Teach Back") • Purpose is to exchange points of view about a topic or to arrive at a decision or conclusion • Can be done with patient, with patient and caregiver, or with group • *Example:* Weight loss	• Allows for an active exchange of information and previous experiences among participants • Good choice when patients have previous experience with subject and have information to share • Nonthreatening format • Can use peers (patients with common problems) to teach	• May need more time depending on topic and number of participants
Lecture-Discussion • Useful when group of patients and caregivers can benefit from basic information • Lecture portion is short (i.e., 15–20 min) • Discussion ("teach back") follows lecture • *Example:* Basic principles of cardiac rehabilitation (e.g., exercise, nutrition)	• Combines short lecture to present basic information with time for discussion • Provision of printed material related to lecture content is useful and recommended	• Need to limit number of lecture topics to 3 to 5 • May need more time depending on topic and number of participants
Demonstration/Return Demonstration ("Show Back") • Purpose is to teach patient and caregiver to perform a skill • Return demonstration ("show back") can show patient's ability to perform skill (see Fig. 4.5) • *Examples:* Dressing change, injection	• Provides for learning and practice of physical skills • Dividing skill into series of smaller steps helps mastery and provides reinforcement	• May need more time for practice needed to master skill • Patients with limited manual dexterity may have difficulty
Use of Teaching Resources • Audiovisual aids to supplement teaching • Printed materials (e.g., brochures) • CDs/DVDs • Hospital-based TV (see Fig. 4.4) • Digital and communication technologies (e.g., mobile applications, Web-based patient education programs, game-based education, online support groups) • Telehealth	• Enhances the presentation through visual and/or auditory stimulation • Best used in combination with other teaching strategies • Use of digital and communication technologies for health information is the preferred choice for many • Web access in patient rooms is standard in most health care agencies • Health information can be given and reinforced to patients remotely	• Review materials for accuracy, reading level, completeness, etc., before using • Evaluate websites, games, applications, programs, etc., for validity of information • May not be appropriate for all learners (e.g., lack of interest, decreased mental capacity) • Finances (e.g., equipment purchase, Internet service) may be a limiting factor to using digital technology

FIG. 4.4 Effective teaching using a variety of strategies (written materials, computer-based patient education programs). (Courtesy Linda Bucher, RN, PhD, CEN, CNE, Staff Nurse, Virtua Memorial Hospital, Mt. Holly, N.J.)

health-related services and information via telecommunications technologies, allows for (1) remote HCP-patient consultations *(telemedicine)*; (2) monitoring of vital signs, weight, heart rhythm, blood glucose, etc.; and (3) ongoing patient teaching.

Learn about these technologies and determine how useful they may be when teaching patients.

Implementation

During the implementation phase, use the planned strategies to present information and teach new skills (Table 4.10). Incorporate verbal and nonverbal communication skills, active listening, and empathy into the process. Based on the assessment of the patient's physical, psychologic, sociocultural, and learner characteristics, determine how much the patient can participate. Whenever possible and appropriate, involve the patient's caregiver(s) in the teaching-learning process.

Remember the principles and characteristics of the adult learner. Although reinforcement and reward are important, phrases such as, "Aren't you doing well!" in a tone one would use with a child can be condescending to adult learners.

Evaluation

Evaluation, the last step in the learning process, is a measure of the degree to which the patient has achieved the learning goals. You can use various evaluation techniques (Table 4.11). Use techniques such as "teach back" to determine the knowledge and skill levels of the patient and/or caregiver throughout the teaching and learning process (Fig. 4.5). If goals are not reached, reassess the patient and revise the teaching plan as needed.

TABLE 4.10 Teaching Patients With Disabilities

Hearing Loss[22]
- Sit in front of the patient at eye level with the light shining on your face
- Use assistive listening devices to amplify sound
- Speak slowly and clearly, using short, simple sentences
- Create a quiet environment that eliminates or minimizes background noises
- Assess patient's preferred communication method (sign language or lip reading)
- If patient prefers to use sign language:
  - Leave as much freedom as possible for their dominant hand to allow for signing
  - Use a sign language interpreter to preserve patient privacy and confidentiality
  - If using a sign language interpreter, speak to the patient, not the interpreter
- If the patient prefers lip-reading:
  - Make sure the patient can see your lips
  - Face the patient and maintain eye contact
  - Ensure there is good lighting on your lips
  - Speak in a normal rhythm and tone
  - Use facial expressions to help convey meaning

Limited Manual Dexterity
- Provide assistive (ease of use) devices to help the patient perform necessary tasks to perform a skill

Mild Cognitive Impairment[23]
- Explain what you will be doing
- Use simple wording
- Present 1 instruction at a time
- Ask yes/no questions
- Avoid open-ended questions
- Be patient
- Answer repeated questions as if it were the first time the question was asked
- Reinforce instructions often
- Create a quiet environment and minimize distractions

Vision Loss[24,25]
- Use low-vision aids, such as magnifiers, high-power reading glasses, or handheld or mounted telescopes
- Use technology, such as screen readers that read text on the computer screen using a speech synthesizer or convert text to braille
- Use electronic tablets or smart phones with adjustable text size
- Use large print publications
- Ensure that there is good lighting in the environment
- Minimize distractions and eliminate background noise
- Give educational materials available in braille
- Provide verbal or tactile instruction instead of written instruction

TABLE 4.11 Evaluating Patient and Caregiver Learning

Technique	Strategy and Examples

Observe patient or caregiver directly	• Ask person to show you how to change the dressing
	• Return demonstration ("show back") determines whether:
	  • Skill has been mastered
	  • Further instruction is needed
	  • Patient and caregiver are ready for new or more content

Observe verbal and nonverbal cues	• Teaching may have to be delayed, more teaching needed, or different strategy used if patient or caregiver:
	  • Asks you to repeat instructions
	  • Loses eye contact
	  • Begins to doze in chair or bed
	  • Becomes restless or fidgety
	  • Does not speak English

Ask open-ended questions ("teach back")	• Open-ended questions provide more information about understanding than closed-ended questions, which need only a "yes" or "no"
	• Ask questions such as:
	  • "How often do you need to change the dressing?"
	  • "What will you do if you develop chest pain at home?"

Talk with caregiver ("teach back")	• Involve caregiver in the evaluation process
	• Ask questions such as:
	  • "What medications is she taking?"
	  • "When does he use his oxygen?"

Seek the patient's self-evaluation of progress	• Ask patient's opinion about his or her progress • Assess what evidence the patient has that the goals are being met • Assess if the patient is ready to learn new material

Documentation is an essential part in the teaching-learning process. Record everything from the assessment through plans for evaluation and follow-up. Because members of the health care team use these records in different settings and for various reasons, the teaching goals, strategies, and evaluation results need to be clear, complete, and available to the team members.

❓ CHECK YOUR PRACTICE

Your patient is a 53-yr-old man with type 1 diabetes who entered the hospital with a blood glucose level of 550 mg/dL (30.53 mmol/L). He is now stable and soon will be discharged.

You prepare his insulin and plan to give him the syringe to let him do his own injection. Before you go to his room, your preceptor suggests that you observe his technique of preparing the insulin as well as the injection. This comment puzzles you because he has had diabetes for 32 years and should know how to do it.

When you go to his room, you ask him to prepare the insulin injection ("show back"). You notice that he filled the syringe with 30 units of insulin and 10 units of air, instead of 40 units of insulin. After correcting the dose and questioning the patient more fully ("teach back"), you wonder what happened.

What are possible reasons that he did not draw up the correct amount of insulin?

The patient may not have been giving himself enough insulin for some time. The patient's vision had declined, and he now needs special equipment to correctly draw up the insulin. The lesson here is that assumptions about a patient's knowledge and skills are dangerous. Confirm prior knowledge even as you are teaching new skills.

Long-term evaluation of learning goals often requires follow-up after discharge. Provide a written schedule of visits and other appropriate referrals before the patient leaves the hospital or clinic. It is important to share this information with the patient's caregiver(s) so that everyone involved in the patient's long-term progress has the same information.

CASE STUDY

Patient and Caregiver Teaching

Patient Profile
M.L., a 60-yr-old Asian woman, is admitted to the hospital with a diagnosis of exacerbation of chronic obstructive pulmonary disease (COPD).

(© Thomas M Perkins/
Shutterstock.)

Subjective Data

- History of COPD for 10 years. Admitted twice in the past 8 months for exacerbations of COPD. Reports a chronic cough but denies any recent change in sputum color. States: "I stopped smoking last year, but my son-in-law smokes in the house."
- Past medical history: Gastroesophageal reflux disease; macular degeneration in right eye.
- Social history: Widowed 5 years ago. Lives with daughter and son-in-law, who work full time. Cares for 2 young grandchildren after school. English is M.L.'s second language.

Objective Data

Physical Examination

- Alert, cognitively intact, anxious, thin woman with dyspnea on minimal exertion. Speaks in short phrases. States: "I have no energy."
- Oxygen via nasal cannula at 2 L/min
- Weight 100 lb, height 5 ft 2 in

Diagnostic Studies

- Chest x-ray negative for acute infection
- Arterial blood gases on room air: pH 7.35, $PaCO_2$ 47 mm Hg, PaO_2 75 mm Hg, HCO_3^- 30 mEq/L
- O_2 saturation (via pulse oximetry) during 6-minute walk test on room air = 83%
- Forced expiratory volume in 1 second of expiration (FEV_1) = 60% of predicted

Interprofessional Care

- Medications: bronchodilator therapy (inpatient nebulizer therapy, inhalers at home), oral corticosteroids
- Continuous home O_2 therapy 2 L/min via nasal cannula
- Pulmonary rehabilitation: inpatient and outpatient

Discussion Questions

1. *Priority Decision:* What are M.L.'s priority learning needs?
2. *Patient-Centered Care:* What factors (e.g., sociocultural, physical, psychologic) noted in the assessment may influence M.L.'s response to teaching?
3. *Patient-Centered Care:* What potential challenges might you expect when planning to teach M.L.? How would you manage them?
4. *Priority Decision:* Choose 2 of M.L.'s priority learning needs. Develop a teaching plan for M.L. for each of these needs.

Answers available at *http://evolve.elsevier.com/Lewis/medsurg.*

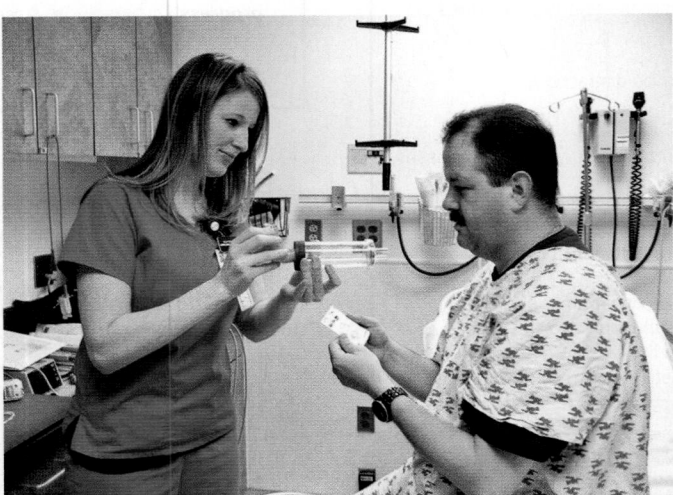

FIG. 4.5 Teaching using discussion ("teach back") and demonstration/return demonstration ("show back") increases successful learning by the patient. (Courtesy Linda Bucher, RN, PhD, CEN, CNE, Staff Nurse, Virtua Memorial Hospital, Mt. Holly, NJ.)

BRIDGE TO NCLEX EXAMINATION

The number of the question corresponds to the same-numbered outcome at the beginning of the chapter.

1. Which technique is *most* appropriate when using motivational interviewing with a patient who tells you that he is ready to start a weight-loss program?
   a. Confirm that the patient is serious about losing weight.
   b. Insist that the patient consider an organized group weight-loss program.
   c. Focus on the patient's strengths to support his optimism that he can successfully lose weight.
   d. Ask a prescribed set of questions to increase the patient's awareness of his dietary behaviors.

2. Which is the *priority* patient teaching strategy when limited time is available?
   a. Setting realistic goals that have high priority for the patient
   b. Referring the patient to a nurse educator in private practice
   c. Observing more experienced nurse-teachers to learn how to teach faster and more efficiently
   d. Providing reading materials for the patient instead of discussing information the patient needs to learn

3. The nurse needs to include caregivers in patient teaching primarily because *(select all that apply)*
   a. caregivers provide all the care for patients after discharge.
   b. they might feel rejected if they are not included in the teaching.
   c. patients have better outcomes when their caregivers are involved.
   d. the patient may be too ill or too stressed to fully understand the teaching.
   e. caregivers are responsible for the overall management of the patient's care.

4. Which patient characteristic enhances the teaching-learning process?
   a. Moderate anxiety
   b. High self-efficacy
   c. Being in the precontemplative stage of change
   d. Being able to laugh about the current health problem

5. What would be the *priority* teaching goal for a middle-aged Hispanic woman about methods to relieve symptoms of menopause?
   a. Prevent the development of future disease.
   b. Maintain the patient's current state of health.
   c. Provide information on possible treatment options.
   d. Change the patient's beliefs about herbal supplements.

6. A patient tells the nurse that she enjoys talking with others and sharing experiences but often falls asleep when reading. Which teaching strategy would be *most* effective with this patient?
   a. Formal lecture
   b. Journal writing
   c. Web-based program
   d. Small group discussion

7. The nurse has taught a family caregiver how to administer insulin. Evaluation of the caregiver's learning would include
   a. monitoring the patient's glucose readings.
   b. arranging for follow-up with a home care nurse.
   c. asking the caregiver to "show back" the ability to administer insulin.
   d. asking the caregiver what was helpful about the teaching experience.

1. c, 2. a, 3. c, d, 4. b, 5. c, 6. d, 7. c.

For rationales to these answers and even more NCLEX review questions, visit *http://evolve.elsevier.com/Lewis/medsurg*.

ⓔ EVOLVE WEBSITE/RESOURCES LIST

http://evolve.elsevier.com/Lewis/medsurg
Review Questions (Online Only)
Key Points
Answer Keys for Questions
- Rationales for Bridge to NCLEX Examination Questions
- Answer Guidelines for Case Study on p. 56
Conceptual Care Map Creator
Audio Glossary
Content Updates

REFERENCES

1. Centers for Disease Control and Prevention: Chronic disease prevention and health promotion. Retrieved from *www.cdc.gov/chronicdisease/index.htm*.
*2. Jenq GY, Doyle MM, Belton BM, Herrin J, Horwitz LI, et al: Quasi-experimental evaluation of the effectiveness of a large-scale readmission reduction program, *JAMA Intern Med* 176:681, 2016.
3. American Nurses Association: *Nursing scope and standards of practice*, ed 3, Washington, DC, 2015, The Association. (Classic)
4. Oermann M, Shellenbarger T, Gaberson K: *Clinical teaching strategies in nursing*, ed 5, New York, 2018, Springer.
5. Knowles MS, Holton EF, Swanson RA: *The adult learner: the definitive classic in adult education and human resource development*, ed 7, St Louis, 2011, Mosby. (Classic)
*6. Prochaska J, Velicer W. The transtheoretical model of health behavior change. *Am J Health Promotion* 12:38, 1997. (Classic)

7. Rollnick S, Miller WR, Yahne CE: *Motivational interviewing in health care: Helping patients change behavior*, New York, 2008, Guilford Press. (Classic)
8. Centers for Disease Control and Prevention: Healthy aging, Caregiving. Retrieved from *www.cdc.gov/aging/caregiving/index.htm*.
9. The Joint Commission: National patient safety goals. Retrieved from *www.jointcommission.org/standards_information/npsgs.aspx*.
10. American Hospital Association: The patient care partnership. Retrieved from *www.aha.org/advocacy-issues/communicatingpts/pt-care-partnership.shtml*.
11. The Joint Commission: Speak Up initiatives, 2016. Retrieved from *www.jointcommission.org/facts_about_speak_up/*.
12. Institute for Healthcare Improvement, National Patient Safety Foundation: Ask Me 3. Retrieved from *http://www.npsf.org/?page=askme3*.
13. National Institutes of Health: Health literacy. Retrieved from *www.nih.gov/institutes-nih/nih-office-director/office-communications-public-liaison/clear-communication/health-literacy*.
14. Agency for Healthcare Research and Quality: Health literacy universal precautions toolkit. Retrieved from *www.ahrq.gov/professionals/quality-patient-safety/quality-resources/tools/literacy-toolkit/index.html*.
15. Office of Disease Prevention and Health Promotion: Health communication and health information technology. Retrieved from *www.healthypeople.gov/2020/topics-objectives/topic/health-communication-and-health-information-technology*.
*16. Sand-Jecklin K, Daniels CS, Lucke-Wold N: Incorporating health literacy screening into patients' health assessment, *Clinical Nurs Res* 26:176, 2017.
*17. Morris NS, MacLean CD, Chew LD, et al: The single item literacy screener: Evaluation of a brief instrument to identify limited reading ability, *BMC Fam Pract* 7:21, 2006. (Classic)
18. The Joint Commission: Health equity. Retrieved from *www.jointcommission.org/assets/1/6/HLCOneSizeFinal.pdf*.

19. Oh H, Rizo C, Enkin M, et al What is e-health: A systematic review of published definitions, *J Med Internet Res* 7:1, 2005. (Classic)
20. Medline Plus: How to write easy-to-read health materials. Retrieved from *www.nlm.nih.gov/medlineplus/etr.html.*
*21. Hong YA, Cho J: Has the digital health divide widened? Trends of health-related internet use among older adults from 2003 to 2011. *J Gerontol* 72:856, 2017.
22. National Institutes of Health, National Institute on Deafness and Other Communication Disorders: Hearing loss and older adults. Retrieved from *www.nidcd.nih.gov/health/hearing-loss-older-adults.*
23. National Institute on Aging: Communicating with a confused patient. Retrieved from *www.nia.nih.gov/health/communicating-confused-patient.*
24. U.S. National Library of Medicine, Medline Plus: Living with vision loss. Retrieved from *www.medlineplus.gov/ency/patientinstructions/000526.htm.*
25. American Foundation for the Blind: Technology resources for people with vision loss. Retrieved from *www.afb.org/info/living-with-vision-loss/using-technology/12.*

*Evidence-based information for clinical practice.

5

Chronic Illness and Older Adults

Sherry A. Greenberg

Helping one person might not change the whole world,
but it could change the world for the one person.

Unknown

(e) http://evolve.elsevier.com/Lewis/medsurg/

CONCEPTUAL FOCUS

Cognition

Family Dynamics

Functional Ability

Mobility

Nutrition

Sensory Perception

LEARNING OUTCOMES

1. Describe the prevention and major causes of chronic illness.
2. Explain the characteristics of a chronic illness.
3. Describe the demographics of aging.
4. Explain the needs of special populations of older adults.
5. Describe nursing interventions to assist older adults with chronic illnesses.

6. Describe common problems of older adults related to hospitalization and acute illness and the nurse's role in assisting them.
7. Differentiate among care alternatives to meet needs of older adults.
8. Describe the nurse's role in health promotion and managing the special needs of older adults.

KEY TERMS

ageism, p. 63

elder mistreatment (EM), p. 65

ethnogeriatric, p. 65

frail older adult, p. 62

gerontologic nursing, p. 68

Medicaid, p. 67

Medicare, p. 67

old-old adult, p. 62

young-old adult, p. 62

This chapter discusses issues related to chronic illness and aging. The population of older adults is growing rapidly. You need to consider their multiple, complex health care conditions and needs when planning and providing comprehensive nursing care. Functional ability in those with chronic illness and older adults is interrelated with several concepts, including mobility, perfusion, nutrition, cognition, and sensory perception. Family dynamics and caregiving shape the care provided to those who need help to meet their needs.

CHRONIC ILLNESS

Illness can be categorized as either acute or chronic (Table 5.1). The U.S. health care system faces a growing burden of chronic illness as the population ages. Chronic illnesses account for 70% of all deaths in the United States. Chronic illness results in limitations in physical functioning, work productivity, and quality of life for nearly 1 out

of 10 Americans. Many older adults live with more than 1 chronic illness, some live with 6 or more. A sizable portion of U.S. health care dollars goes toward treating chronic illnesses.[1] Managing a chronic illness greatly affects the lives of the older adult, family, and caregiver. Table 5.2 presents the impact of some chronic illnesses.

In addition to people living longer, other societal changes have contributed to the increase in chronic illnesses. These include insufficient physical activity, lack of access to fresh fruits and vegetables, and tobacco and alcohol use.[1]

Trajectory of Chronic Illness

The person with a chronic illness can move from a level of optimum functioning, with the illness well controlled, to a period of physical instability. Corbin and Strauss proposed a view of chronic illness as a trajectory (Fig. 5.1) with overlapping phases[2] (Table 5.3). This trajectory characterizes the common course of most chronic conditions. In addition, Corbin and Strauss identified the 7 tasks of those who are chronically ill (Table 5.4). These tasks are discussed in the following sections.

Preventing and Managing a Crisis. Most chronic illnesses have the potential for an acute exacerbation of symptoms, which may result in further disability or death. Examples include the patient with heart disease who has another myocardial infarction or the patient with asthma who has a severe attack. A major task for the patient and caregiver is to learn to prevent or manage the crisis. First, the patient and caregiver need to understand the potential for the crisis to occur. Second, they need to know ways to prevent or modify the threat. This often involves adhering to a prescribed medical plan. Patients need to know the signs and symptoms of the onset of a crisis or exacerbation. Depending on the chronic illness, signs and symptoms may occur suddenly (e.g., bleeding in a patient with inflammatory bowel disease) or slowly (e.g., heart failure in a person with untreated hypertension). It is important for the patient and caregiver to develop a plan to manage a crisis that is likely to occur.

Carrying Out Prescribed Treatment Plan. Treatment plans vary in degree of difficulty and the impact they have on the person's lifestyle. Treatment plans may be challenging or time consuming, such as changing a dressing multiple times a day or following a toileting program. However, they generally save time and prevent complications.

Controlling Symptoms. An important task for those with chronic illnesses is to learn to control symptoms so that they can continue desired activities. Some redesign their lifestyle by learning to plan ahead. People with heart failure adjust the time they take diuretics when going out for the day to avoid needing to rush to a bathroom. Encourage independence in decision making and collaborating with the health care provider (HCP) about treatment plans to avoid an exacerbation of the illness. Others may redesign their living space. Patients and their families and/or caregivers need to learn about the pattern of symptoms, such as typical onset, duration, and severity, so that lifestyle may be changed accordingly, while maintaining safety.

Reordering Time. People with chronic illness often report having too much or too little time. Treatment plans that require large amounts of time for the person, as well as caregivers, may require changing schedules or eliminating other activities. For example, the patient with a new ileostomy needs to plan for increased time in the bathroom to change the drainage bag.

TABLE 5.1 Characteristics of Acute and Chronic Illness

Description	Characteristics
Acute Illness	
Diseases that have a rapid onset and short duration *Examples:* colds, influenza, acute gastroenteritis	• Usually self-limiting • Responds readily to treatment • Complications infrequent • After illness, return to previous level of functioning
Chronic Illness	
Diseases that are prolonged, do not resolve spontaneously, and are rarely cured completely *Examples:* Table 5.2	• Permanent impairments or deviations from normal • Irreversible pathologic changes • Residual disability • Special rehabilitation needed • Need for long-term medical and/or nursing management

---

TABLE 5.2 Impact of Chronic Illnesses

Chronic Illness	Impact	Chapter	Page
Alzheimer's disease	• Affects 5.5 million people • Sixth leading cause of death among all adults; fifth leading cause of death among those age 65 and above	59	1386
Arthritis	• Affects 1 in 5 people • One of most common chronic illnesses • Leading cause of disability	64	1499
Cancer	• Second leading cause of death • Risk increases with age	15	232
Cardiovascular disease, including heart disease and stroke	• Affects about 17 million adults • Account for 31% of U.S. deaths annually • Heart disease is leading cause of death in United States • Heart failure is a common cause of hospitalization and rehospitalization • Stroke is fifth leading cause of death • Stroke is a common cause of serious disability	33	698
Chronic obstructive pulmonary disease (COPD)	• Affects many older adults • Third leading cause of death	28	560
Diabetes	• Affects >29 million Americans • 25% of adults in United States do not know they have diabetes • Seventh leading cause of death	48	1108
Human immunodeficiency virus (HIV)	• 45% of those living with HIV in the United States are over 50 years old • Older adults more likely to receive diagnosis of HIV infection later in course of disease	14	216
Obesity	• Affects about 1 in 3 adults • Major contributor to other health problems and chronic diseases	40	869

CONTENT IN BOOK spans the Chapter and Page columns.

Data from Centers for Disease Control and Prevention: CDC's chronic disease press releases. Retrieved from *www.cdc.gov/chronicdisease/resources/publications/aag.htm* and *www.cdc.gov/hiv/group/age/olderamericans/index.html.*

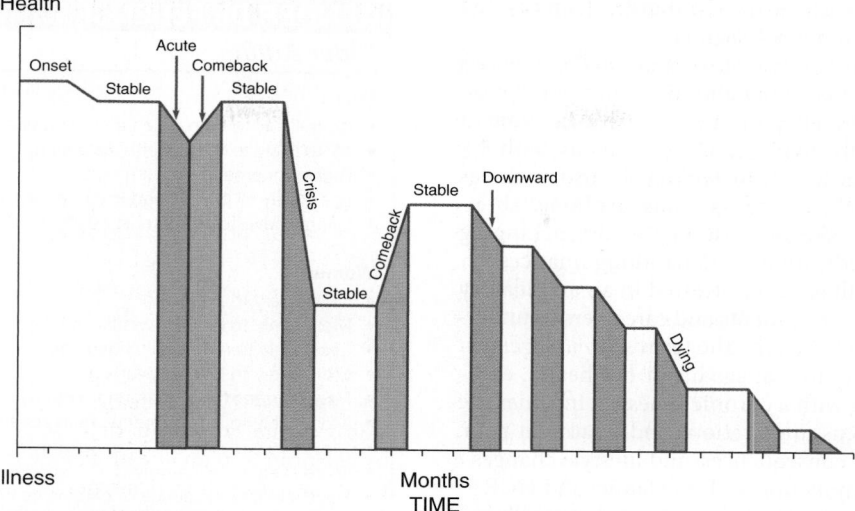

FIG. 5.1 The Chronic Illness Trajectory is a theoretical model of chronic illness. The trajectory model of chronic illness recognizes that chronic illness will have many phases (Table 5.3). (From Woog P: *The chronic illness trajectory framework: The Corbin and Strauss nursing model,* New York, 1992, Springer.)

TABLE 5.3 Chronic Illness Trajectory

Phases	Description
Onset	• Signs and symptoms are present • Disease diagnosed
Stable	• Illness course and symptoms controlled by treatment plan • Person maintains everyday activities
Acute	• Active illness with severe and unrelieved symptoms or complications • Hospitalization may be needed for management
Comeback	• Gradual return to an acceptable way of life
Crisis	• Life-threatening situation occurs • Emergency services are necessary
Unstable	• Unable to keep symptoms or disease course under control • Life becomes disrupted while patient works to regain stability • Hospitalization not required
Downward	• Gradual and progressive deterioration in physical or mental status • Accompanied by increasing disability and symptoms • Continuous changes in everyday life activities
Dying	• Patient has to relinquish everyday life interests and activities, let go, and die peacefully • Immediate weeks, days, hours preceding death

Source: Woog P: *The chronic illness trajectory framework: The Corbin and Strauss nursing model,* New York, 1992, Springer.

TABLE 5.4 7 Tasks of People With Chronic Illness

1. Prevent and manage a crisis
2. Carry out prescribed treatment plan
3. Control symptoms
4. Reorder time
5. Adjust to changes in course of disease
6. Prevent social isolation
7. Attempt to normalize interactions with others

Source: Corbin JM, Strauss A: A nursing model for chronic illness management based upon the trajectory framework, *Sch Inq Nurs Pract* 5:155, 1991.

Adjusting to Changes in the Course of Disease. Some diseases, such as multiple sclerosis, have unpredictable courses that make planning activities difficult. Part of the person's task is to develop a personal identity that includes the chronic illness and to adjust to the necessary lifestyle changes. For example, a person taking warfarin due to a mechanical heart valve may need to avoid extreme physical sports that have a high potential for injury.

Preventing Social Isolation. Social isolation may occur with chronic illness. The person may choose to withdraw from social activities or others withdraw from the chronically ill person. For example, a woman who has aphasia secondary to a stroke may not want to go out in public because of embarrassment related to communication issues.

Attempting to Normalize Interactions With Others. Most persons with chronic illness try to manage symptoms so that they can hide their disabilities or disfigurement. This may involve wearing a prosthesis or showing that they can function the same as a person without a disability or chronic illness. An example of this is the woman with heart failure who stops walking to catch her breath but appears to be inspecting a plant or looking in a store window.

Prevention of Chronic Illness

Chronic illnesses are often preventable. *Primary prevention* refers to measures such as eating a healthy diet, getting proper exercise, and receiving immunizations that prevent a specific disease. Appropriate immunizations for older adults include influenza, pneumococcal, herpes zoster, tetanus/diphtheria/pertussis (Td/Tdap), and hepatitis A and B. *Secondary prevention* refers to actions aimed at health screening and early detection of disease. This can lead to interventions to prevent disease progression, such as colon cancer screening or breast cancer screening. *Tertiary prevention* refers to activities that limit disease progression such as rehabilitation.

❖NURSING MANAGEMENT: CHRONIC ILLNESS

Diagnosis and treatment of the acute phase or acute exacerbations of a chronic illness sometimes take place in a hospital. Other phases of a chronic illness are regularly assessed and managed in an ambulatory care setting, at home, in an assisted living facility, or in a skilled nursing facility.

An assessment of health status, at least annually, includes a person's level of daily functioning and his or her perception of relative health, function, and/or illness. Health assessment includes activities of daily living (ADLs), such as bathing, dressing, eating, toileting, and transferring. It also includes instrumental ADLs (IADLs), such as using a phone, shopping, preparing food, housekeeping, doing laundry, arranging transportation, taking medications, and handling finances.[3]

Because most chronic illnesses are treated in an ambulatory care setting, it is important for patients and caregivers to understand and manage their own health. The term *self-management* refers to the person's ability to manage his or her health, especially in response to living with a chronic illness. It includes the ability to manage symptoms, medications and treatment plan, physical and psychosocial consequences, and lifestyle changes.[4] Self-management is in conjunction with the family and HCP.

You play a key role in managing patients with chronic illness. This includes conducting a comprehensive history and physical assessment, teaching the patient and caregiver about the treatment plan, implementing strategies for symptom management, and evaluating patient outcomes.

Family caregivers (e.g., spouses, partners, adult children) often have important roles in the life of the chronically ill person. The ideal situation is 1 in which family caregivers work together with the patient to manage the chronic condition(s). This collaboration begins under the direction of the health care team at the time of diagnosis. When the caregiver is a spouse or partner who is also older, he or she may have a chronic illness or multiple chronic conditions as well. This may add a level of complexity to the coordination of care.[5]

OLDER ADULTS

DEMOGRAPHICS OF AGING

The older adult population (those 65 years of age and older) continues to outpace the rest of the population. Nearly 1 in 7 U.S. residents, more than 47.8 million people, or 14.9% of the population, were age 65 or older in 2016.[6] This is projected to more than double to 98 million in 2060. The U.S. Census Bureau predicts life expectancy to continue to increase for both men and women. Those reaching 65 years have an average life expectancy of an added 19.4 years, specifically 20.6 years for females and 18 years for males.[6] Whether this gender difference is due to differences in health behaviors (e.g., smoking, alcohol use) or occupation is not known.

The fastest-growing segment of older Americans is people ages 85 or older. The 85 and older population is projected to increase from 6.3 million in 2015 to 14.6 million in 2040.[6] The increase in life span is due to declining infant mortality, new drug therapies, mechanical devices, and improved surgical interventions. A greater emphasis on health promotion, disease prevention, and earlier detection as well as better care management has led to more Americans living past 85 years.

In 2016, 22% of the U.S. population age 65 years or older were of racial or ethnic minority populations, including 9% black; 4% Asian or Pacific Islanders; and 0.5% Native American. People of Hispanic ethnicity (who may be of any race) represented 8% of the older population.[6] The number of older adults of racial or ethnicity populations in the United States is projected to increase from 10.6 million in 2015 (22% of older adults) to 21.1 million in 2030 (28% of older adults).[6]

<table>
<tr><td colspan="2" style="background:black;color:white;">**GENDER DIFFERENCES**</td></tr>
<tr><td colspan="2">*Older Adults*</td></tr>
<tr><td colspan="2">

Men
- More likely to be married and living with spouse or partner
- More likely to have health insurance
- Higher income after retirement
- Less likely to be involved in caregiving activities
- Overall have fewer chronic health conditions

Women
- More likely to live alone
- More likely to be widowed
- Less likely to have health insurance
- More likely to live in poverty
- Poverty rates highest among minority women
- More likely to lack formal work experience, leading to lower income
- More likely to rely on Social Security as major source of income
- More likely to be caregiver of ill spouse or partner
- Have a higher incidence of chronic health conditions such as arthritis, hypertension, stroke, and diabetes

</td></tr>
</table>

Upcoming cohorts of older adults will likely have increased access to higher education, employment, technology, and resources than previous cohorts. Between 1970 and 2015, the percent of older adults who had completed high school rose from 28% to 85%.[6] In 2016, about 28% of the population 65 and older have earned a bachelor's degree or higher.[6]

The terms **young-old adult** (65–74 years of age) and **old-old adult** (85 years of age and older) describe 2 groups of older adults with distinct characteristics, needs, and living arrangements. The number of older adults age 65 living in nursing homes increases with age; 1% of those age 65 to 74, 3% of those age 75 to 84, and 9% of those 85 and older live in nursing homes. The old-old adult is often a widowed, divorced, or single woman dependent on family for support or care. Many old-old adults have outlived children, spouses or partners, and siblings.

The **frail older adult** is usually over age 75 with multiple physical, cognitive, and/or mental conditions. These often interfere with self-management and the ability to perform daily activities independently. Frail older adults are discussed later in this chapter on page 64.

ATTITUDES TOWARD AGING

Who is old? The answer to this question often depends on the respondent's age and attitude. Your "real" age is set by a date in time. Many factors influence how "old" you feel. These include emotional and physical health, developmental stage, socioeconomic status, culture, and ethnicity. We all age. As we do, we are exposed to new and different life experiences. The accumulation of these differences makes older adults more diverse than any other age-group.

As you assess older adults, consider and value their diversity and life history. Assess their feelings of what it means to be an older adult. Most older adults report having good-to-excellent health despite having a chronic condition. However, those with poor health often report a higher perceived age and lower sense of well-being when compared with healthy older adults. Age is important, but it may not be the most relevant factor in determining the appropriate care of an individual older adult.

Myths and stereotypes about aging are often supported by media reports of older adults who are "problematic." These misconceptions may lead to omissions or errors in assessment and unnecessary limitations or interventions. For example, if you think that all older people are rigid in their thinking, you may not present new ideas to a patient.[7]

Ageism is a negative attitude based on age. Ageism leads to discrimination and disparities in the care given to older adults. If you have negative attitudes, it may be because you fear your own aging process. Or, you are not knowledgeable about aging and the health care needs of the older adult.

BIOLOGIC AGING

From a biologic view, *aging* reflects the changes that occur over time. Biologic aging is a multifactorial process involving genetics, diet, and environment.[8] In part, we view biologic aging as a balance of positive and negative factors (Fig. 5.2). Research is directed at increasing the average life span, functional status, and quality of life of older adults. The hope is that we can develop new antiaging therapies to slow down or reverse age-related changes that result in chronic illness and disability.

AGE-RELATED PHYSIOLOGIC CHANGES

Age-related changes affect every body system. These changes are normal and occur as people age. However, the age at which specific changes occur differs from person to person and within the same person. For instance, a person who has gray hair at age 45 may have relatively unwrinkled skin at age 80. As a nurse, you will assess for age-related changes. Table 5.5 shows where you can find tables outlining specific age-related assessment findings throughout the book.

SPECIAL OLDER ADULT POPULATIONS

Chronically Ill Older Adults

Daily living with chronic illness is a reality for many older adults. The incidence of chronic illness triples after age 45. Most people 65 years of age and older have at least 1 chronic condition, and many have multiple conditions.[1] The most common chronic conditions in older adults are hypertension, heart failure, coronary artery disease, chronic obstructive pulmonary disease (COPD),

cancer, diabetes, and osteoarthritis. Other common chronic conditions include Alzheimer's disease, vision and hearing deficits, osteoporosis, stroke, Parkinson's disease, and depression.

Cognitively Impaired Older Adults

Most healthy older adults have no noticeable decline in cognitive abilities (Table 5.6). Older adults may have a mild decline in memory and may need more time to recall events or new information. This differs from cognitive impairment. New learning may be slower. Refer older adults with memory loss to their HCP for an evaluation. Teach them to use memory aids, attempt recall in a calm and quiet environment, and actively engage in enhancing memory. Memory aids include clocks, calendars, notes, marked pillboxes, safety alarms on stoves, and identification necklaces or bracelets. Memory techniques include word association, mental imaging, and mnemonics.

Dementia, delirium, and depression can occur and may coexist in older adults. Declining physical health and acute illness are important factors that may influence cognition. For example, an older adult who undergoes surgery may have an acute change in mental status known as *delirium*.[9] Delirium superimposed on dementia may signify an acute or emergent condition such as heart failure. Hence, it is important to distinguish signs

TABLE 5.5 Gerontologic Assessment Differences

Summary of Tables

Body System	Table Number	Page
Visual	20-1	352
Auditory	21-1	378
Integumentary	22-1	398
Respiratory	25-2	460
Hematologic	29-3	591
Cardiovascular	31-1	661
Gastrointestinal	38-5	835
Urinary	44-2	1012
Endocrine	47-3	1095
Reproductive	50-3	1178
Nervous	55-2	1287
Musculoskeletal	61-1	1434

TABLE 5.6 Gerontologic Assessment Differences

Cognitive Function

Effect of Aging	Cognitive Function
Improves with aging	• Vocabulary and verbal reasoning • Crystallized intelligence (ability to use skills, knowledge, and experience)
Declines during middle age	• Mental performance speed • Synthesis of new information • Fluid intelligence (ability to think logically and solve problems in new situations)
Declines during old age	• Short-term recall memory
Constant (no changes with aging)	• Long-term recall memory

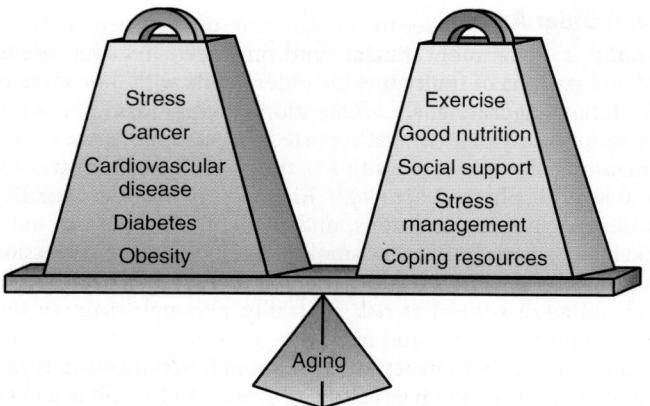

FIG. 5.2 The aging process can be viewed as a balance between negative and positive factors.

and symptoms of each. Cognitive impairment, delirium, and dementia are discussed in Chapter 59.

Rural Older Adults

Key barriers to health care access for rural older adults are transportation, limited supply of health care workers and facilities, lack of quality health care, social isolation, and financial limitations. Particularly vulnerable are older adults of racial or ethnic minority living in rural areas, who have even less access to HCPs. Older adults who live in rural areas may be less likely to engage in health-promoting activities.

When you work with older adults in rural areas, recognize lifestyle values and practices of rural life (Fig. 5.3). In planning care, be aware that transportation is the number 1 barrier to health care for rural older adults. Alternative service approaches such as computer-based Internet sources, DVDs, radio, community centers, and church social events may be used to promote healthy practices or to conduct health screening (Fig. 5.4).

The use of telehealth devices for monitoring patients in their home environments has enhanced the ability to provide care, including to those more isolated.[10] We must continue to develop innovative models of nursing practice to help the rural older adult. Older adults are increasingly using technology in their daily lives. Most older adults use the Internet and own a cell phone.[10]

FIG. 5.3 Older adults living in rural areas often enjoy outside activities, such as gardening. (© iStockphoto/Thinkstock.)

INFORMATICS IN PRACTICE

Older Adults and Internet Use

- Sixty-seven percent of older adults use the Internet, as of 2016.
- Older adults may use the Internet to look for health information.
- Many track their weight, diet, and exercise using apps.
- Older adults are more likely to accept as true what they read on the Internet.
- Teach those who use the Internet as a source of information how to assess the credibility of a website.
- Suggest the use of websites and apps that include senior-friendly design elements.

Source: *www.pewinternet.org/2017/05/17/technology-use-among-seniors/*.

Homeless Older Adults

The number of older adults who are homeless is increasing. Key factors associated with homelessness include (1) having a low income, (2) having reduced cognitive capacity, (3) living alone, and (4) living in a community that lacks affordable housing. Homeless older adults may be chronically homeless or recently homeless because of a crisis in either health, economic, or social status.

Mortality rates for homeless older adults are higher than for older adults who have housing. Older homeless adults are at higher risk for more health problems because many aging network services are not designed to reach out to homeless people. They are less likely to use shelters or meal site services than younger homeless people. This may be due to fear of institutionalization. Care for homeless older adults requires an interprofessional approach (including nurses, physicians, social workers, clerical workers, and transporters) that links shelters with outreach, primary care clinics, Medicare and Medicaid offices, pharmacies, senior centers, and Area Agencies on Aging. Long-term care placement is often an alternative to homelessness, especially when the person is cognitively impaired.

FIG. 5.4 Older adults are using computers more often and accessing health care information on the Internet. (© iStockphoto/Thinkstock.)

Frail Older Adults

Frailty is a common clinical syndrome seen in older adults. Manifestations of frailty include older adults with 3 or more of the following criteria: (1) unintentional weight loss (10 pounds or more in a year); (2) self-reported exhaustion; (3) weakness (measured by grip strength); (4) slow walking speed; and (5) low level of physical activity.[11] Risk factors include disability, multiple chronic conditions, and dementia. People are more likely to become frail if they smoke, have a history of depression or long-term medical health problems, or are underweight. The old-old adult is most at risk for frailty, although many in this age-group are healthy and robust.

Older frail adults experience declining function and decreasing daily energy. When stressful life events (e.g., death of a close friend) and daily strain (e.g., caring for an ill spouse) occur, frail older adults often have ineffective coping mechanisms and, as a result, may become ill. Common health problems of frail older

TABLE 5.7 SCALES: Nutritional Assessment of Older Adults

The acronym SCALES can remind you to assess important nutritional indicators:

Sadness, or mood change
Cholesterol, high
Albumin, low
Loss or gain of weight
Eating problems (e.g., mechanical problems, such as impaired swallowing, poor dentition)
Shopping and food preparation problems

adults include mobility limitations, sensory impairment, cognitive decline, and falls.

Frail older adults may tire easily, have little physical reserve, and are at risk for physical dependence and institutionalization. They are especially at risk for malnutrition and dehydration. These are related to factors such as living alone, depression, and low socioeconomic status. Other factors, such as dementia, inadequate dental care, sensory deficits, fatigue, and limited mobility increase the risk for malnutrition and dehydration. Monitor frail older adults for adequate calorie, protein, iron, calcium, vitamin D, and fluid intake. Use the SCALES tool to assess the risk factors for poor nutritional status in older adults (Table 5.7). Once you identify an older adult's nutritional needs, common interventions include home-delivered meals, dietary supplements, Supplemental Nutrition Assistance Program (SNAP), dental referrals, and vitamin supplements.[12] Because medications may affect appetite or interact with nutrients, perform a thorough medication review, including prescription drugs, over-the-counter (OTC) drugs, vitamins, minerals, supplements, herbs, and cultural remedies. Nutrition is discussed in Chapter 39.

Culturally Competent Care: Older Adults

The term ethnogeriatric describes the specialty area of providing culturally competent care to older adults.[13] As American society changes, ethnic institutions and neighborhoods may also change. For the older adult with strong ethnic and cultural roots, there may be a loss of friends who speak the native language, a loss of the religious institution that supports social ethnic activities, and a loss of stores that carry desired ethnic foods. This sense of loss is increased when children and others deny or ignore ethnic and cultural practices. Support for older adults of racial or ethnic minority is most often found in the family, religious practices, and isolated geographic or community ethnic clusters.

Ethnic populations of older adults face unique situations. Older adults may live in neighborhoods where physical security and personal safety related to crime may be a concern. Those who identify with particular ethnic groups often have disproportionately lower incomes and may not be able to afford Medicare deductibles or drugs needed to treat chronic illnesses. Older adults from minority populations such as Hispanics use health care services less often when compared to nonminority groups.[13]

Assess each older adult's ethnic and cultural background. Assume that ethnicity and culture are important and of value to older adults and their families unless they tell you otherwise during an assessment. For you to be effective with the ethnic older adult, a sense of respect and clear communication are critical. Nursing interventions to help meet the needs of ethnic populations are described in Table 2.9.[14] Culturally competent care is discussed in Chapter 2.

SOCIAL SUPPORT FOR OLDER ADULTS

Social support for older adults occurs at 3 levels. First, family members are the primary and preferred providers of social support. Second, semiformal support is found in clubs, religious (faith-based) organizations, neighborhoods, adult day care, and senior centers. Third, older adults may be linked to formal systems of social welfare agencies, health facilities, and government support. Generally, you, as a nurse, are part of the formal support system.

Family Caregivers

Many older adults need caregiving by family members. This includes those with multiple chronic conditions, those needing help with ADLs and IADLs, and older adults with dementia. The most common caregivers are spouses, adult children, parents, grandparents, and life partners. Older adult women, age 65 or older, are the most common family caregivers.[15] Other examples include husbands who care for wives with Alzheimer's disease, adult children who care for a parent with a stroke, grandparents who care for a grandchild with a developmental disorder, and parents who care for an adult child with a spinal cord injury. Many family caregivers are caring for themselves, their aging parents, and their children and grandchildren.

The caregiver usually takes on responsibilities gradually. For example, a caregiver may initially need only to adjust work schedules to accommodate a patient's health care appointments. Later, as the patient's needs become greater, the caregiver may have to reduce work hours and provide more help with ADLs.

Caregiving is an experience for which most people are not prepared. It is common for caregivers to become physically, emotionally, and economically overwhelmed by the responsibilities and demands of caring for a loved one. The stress of caregiving may lead to emotional problems such as depression, anger, and resentment. Signs of caregiver stress include irritability, inability to concentrate, fatigue, and sleeplessness. The caregiver often experiences decreased social interactions and may be at risk for social isolation. Multiple commitments, fatigue, and, at times, the patient's socially inappropriate behaviors contribute to the caregiver's social isolation. Stress can progress to burnout and result in negligence and abuse of the patient by the caregiver. Consider collaborating with a social worker if caregiver stress or strain is present and caregivers need respite.

Encourage caregivers to take care of themselves. Suggest journaling or joining a support group to help them share feelings that may be hard to express. Remind caregivers that getting regular exercise and sleep and eating balanced meals will enhance their well-being. Encourage contact with others to give emotional support. Finally, humor is important. Sometimes its use by caregivers can provide distraction and relieve stress-filled situations.

Elder Mistreatment

Elder mistreatment (EM) describes intentional acts of omission or commission by a caregiver or "trusted other" that cause harm or serious risk for harm to a vulnerable older adult. EM may occur in community (home or assisted living facility) or long-term care (institutional) settings.

Between 2 and 10% of community-dwelling older adults in the United States are abused, neglected, or exploited by trusted others.[16] The prevalence of EM in institutional settings is unknown, but it is thought to be widespread. Although EM rates are similar in women and men, most victims are women because of the predominance of women in older age cohorts. Victims of EM have a mortality risk that is 3 times higher than that of nonmistreated peers. The higher mortality risk is not due to the abuse or neglect itself but may be due to stress-related illnesses associated with prolonged mistreatment.[16]

EM is a hidden problem. For every reported case in the community setting, more than 5 cases go unreported. Underreporting may be higher based on immigration status, ethnic background, or sexual orientation. Victims are unlikely to report mistreatment by "trusted others" because of isolation; impaired cognitive or physical function; feelings of shame, guilt, or self-blame; fear of reprisal; pressure from family members; fear of long-term care; or cultural norms. HCPs also underreport EM, possibly from a failure to suspect or recognize EM, perceived inability to successfully intervene, desire to avoid responsibility for further action, or ageism.

Family members are responsible for up to 90% of domestic EM.[16] Adult children who abuse, neglect, or exploit their parents are usually dependent on their parent(s) for housing and financial support, have a history of violence, are unemployed, and/or are disabled from substance use or mental illness. Abusive spouses or partners may either begin intimate partner violence in older age or continue a lifelong pattern of abuse.

Many factors put community-dwelling older adults at risk for domestic EM. These include (1) physical or cognitive dysfunction that leads to an inability to perform ADLs (and therefore produces dependence on others for care), (2) any psychiatric diagnoses, including dementia and depression, (3) alcohol misuse and abuse, (4) decreased social support; (5) living with a large number of household members other than a spouse and (6) low income.[17] In long-term care settings the same factors that lead to institutionalization are risk factors for mistreatment by staff, visitors, and others. These include dependence on others for care because of physical or cognitive limitations.

Types of EM, characteristics, and manifestations are shown in Table 5.8. In institutional settings, EM includes the types described in Table 5.8 as well as failure to follow the plan of care, unauthorized use of physical or chemical restraints, overuse or underuse of medication, or isolation as punishment.

Follow your organization's protocols for EM screening and interventions. Perform a thorough history and physical examination that includes screening for mistreatment. It is important that you interview people alone. If mistreatment is occurring, they may not disclose it in the presence of the person who is with them, especially if that person is the abuser. Be especially attentive to explanations about injuries that are not consistent with what you observe, contradictory explanations between the patient and the caregiver, or behavioral clues that suggest the patient is being threatened or intimidated. Other nursing assessments and interventions are listed in Table 5.9. In most states, health care workers are among those mandated to report suspected or actual EM to Adult Protective Services (APS) and/or law enforcement. Know your legal responsibilities by checking the laws in your state.

Self-Neglect

Most referrals made to APS are for self-neglect. Older adults who self-neglect are often unable to meet their basic needs and refuse help; have multiple, untreated medical or psychiatric conditions; and live alone and often in squalor. Older community-dwelling adults who self-neglect face a higher risk for mortality than peers who do not self-neglect.[18] Nursing interventions include assessment for possible self-neglect, referrals for long-term interprofessional case management, and referral to APS.

TABLE 5.8 Types of Elder Mistreatment

Characteristics	Manifestations
Abandonment	
Desertion of an older person by a person who has assumed responsibility for providing care or by a person with physical custody.	Older adult's reports of being abandoned; deserting an older adult at a hospital or skilled nursing facility, shopping center, or other public place.
Financial Abuse	
Denying access to personal resources, stealing money or possessions. Coercing to sign contracts or durable power of attorney. Making changes in will or trust.	Living situation below level of personal resources. Sudden change in personal finances, sudden transfer of assets.
Neglect	
Failure or refusal to provide basic life needs, including food, water, medications, clothing, hygiene. Failure to provide physical aids such as dentures, eyeglasses, hearing aid. Failure to ensure safety.	Older adult's report of being neglected. Untreated or infected pressure injuries on sacral area, heels. Weight loss, malnutrition. Laboratory values showing dehydration. Poor personal hygiene. Lack of adherence with medical treatment.
Failure to provide social stimulation. Leaving alone for long periods. Failure to provide companionship.	Depression, withdrawn behavior, agitation. Ambivalent attitude toward caregiver or family member.
Physical Abuse	
Slapping, striking, restraining, incorrect position-ing. Oversedation with medications.	Bruises, bilateral injuries (upper arms, ankles, wrists), repeated injuries in various stages of healing, burn marks, oversedation. Use of several emergency departments.
Psychologic Abuse	
Berating verbally, harassment, intimidation, threats of punishment, or deprivation. Childlike treatment, isolation.	Depression, withdrawn behavior, agitation. Ambivalent attitude toward caregiver or family member.
Sexual Abuse	
Nonconsensual sexual contact, including touching inappropriately. Forced sexual contact.	Older adult's report of sexual abuse. Unexplained vaginal or anal bleeding, bruised breasts, unexplained sexually transmitted or genital infections.
Violation of Personal Rights	
Denying right to privacy or right to make decisions about health care or living environment. Forcible eviction.	Sudden inexplicable changes in living situation, confusion.

SOCIAL SERVICES FOR OLDER ADULTS

A network of services supports older adults in the community and health care facilities. In the United States, most older adults are the beneficiaries of at least 1 social or governmental service. To understand the older adult's situation, learn about government structures that fund and regulate programs for older adults. The

TABLE 5.9 Nursing Management

Elder Mistreatment

When elder mistreatment is suspected, it is important to do the following:

- Screen for possible elder mistreatment, including domestic violence.
- Conduct a thorough history and head-to-toe physical assessment. Document your findings, including any statements made by the older adult or accompanying adult.
- If the older adult appears to be in immediate danger, develop and implement a safety plan in collaboration with the interprofessional team involved in the person's care.
- Identify, collect, and preserve physical evidence (e.g., dirty or bloody clothing dressing sheets).
- After obtaining consent, take photographs to document physical findings of suspected abuse or neglect. If possible and appropriate, do this before treating or bathing the alleged victim.
- If you suspect that mistreatment is occurring, report your findings to the state agency and/or law enforcement as mandated by the laws in your state.
- Initiate appropriate consultations with social work, forensic nursing, and adult protective services.

FIG. 5.5 Senior centers offer places for older adults who live independently to meet and gather with friends. (© Jupiterimages/Comstock/Thinkstock.)

Administration on Aging (AoA), which is part of the Department of Health and Human Services, is the federal agency responsible for many older adult programs. Funding from the AoA is given to state and local Area Agencies on Aging (AAAs).

MEDICARE AND MEDICAID

Medicare is a federally funded health insurance program for people ages 65 years or older. It also covers people under age 65 with certain disabilities and people of any age with end-stage renal disease (ESRD) requiring dialysis or a kidney transplant.

Medicare has 4 options for coverage: A, B, C, and D. Part A covers inpatient hospital care and partially covers skilled nursing facility care, hospice, and home health care. Part A coverage is "free" because workers support Medicare through payroll taxes. Medicare Part B partially covers outpatient care, physicians' or primary care providers' services, and home health care. It also covers some preventive services, such as mammograms. Medicare Part B is voluntary and has a monthly premium and an annual deductible before payment begins. Medicare Advantage Plans, sometimes called "Part C" or "MA Plans," are offered by private companies approved by Medicare to provide Part A and Part B benefits. Part D is available to Medicare enrollees and provides a prescription drug benefit. Members pay a yearly deductible, monthly premium, and copayment. People with lower incomes and limited assets may qualify for extra help to pay for prescriptions.

Medicare does not cover long-term care, custodial ADLs or IADLs care, dental care or dentures, hearing aids, or eyeglasses. (More information is available at *www.medicare.gov*.) Out-of-pocket expenditures for people on Medicare continue to rise. The costs increase with age, functional disabilities, number of chronic conditions, and number of hospitalizations.[19]

Medicaid is a state-administered, needs-based program to help eligible low-income people, including Medicare beneficiaries, with certain medical expenses. Those who qualify for both Medicare and Medicaid are referred to as *dual-eligible*. Eligibility and coverage vary by state. For qualified Medicare beneficiaries, Medicaid pays Medicare premiums, deductibles, and co-insurance, as well as long-term care and home health expenses. In the United States most long-term care is paid for by Medicaid or private pay. (More information is available at *www.medicaid.gov*.)

CARE ALTERNATIVES FOR OLDER ADULTS

Older adults with special care needs include people who are homeless, in need of help with ADLs, cognitively impaired, homebound, or no longer able to live at home. Older adults may be served by adult day care, adult day health care, home health care, and long-term care. Continuing care retirement communities, congregate housing, and assisted living facilities are housing options for older adults.

Adult Day Care and Adult Day Health Care

Adult day care centers provide social, recreational, and health-related services to people in a safe, community-based environment (Fig. 5.5). This includes daily supervision, social activities, opportunities for social interaction, and ADLs help for 2 groups of adults: (1) those who are cognitively impaired and (2) those who have problems independently performing ADLs. Adult day care programs provide individualized services based on need. Programs designed for adults who are cognitively impaired offer therapeutic recreation, support for family, family counseling, and social involvement.

Adult day health care centers are like adult day care but provide care to meet the needs of older adults and people with disabilities who need a higher level of care. This might include health monitoring, therapeutic activities, 1-on-1 ADLs training, and personal services.

Adult day care centers and adult day health care centers may offer respite to allow continued employment for the caregiver and delay institutionalization of older adults. States set standards and regulate centers. Medicare does not cover costs. Adult day health care is tax deductible as dependent care. Appropriate placement in adult care programs that match participants' needs is important. You can help by knowing the available centers in your area and assessing the needs of older adults and their families. You will then be able to help them make good decisions about their care.

Home Health Care

Home health care (HHC) can be a cost-effective care alternative for older adults who are homebound, have health needs that are intermittent or acute, and have supportive caregiver involvement. HHC is not an alternative for adults in need of 24-hour help with ADLs or continuous safety supervision. Private duty care may be an alternative in these situations. HHC services require physician orders and skilled nursing care for Medicare reimbursement. Unless one meets these requirements, Medicare will not pay for home health aides for ADLs management or a homemaker for IADLs management.

In addition to HHC, caregivers often seek homemaker services and respite and personal care through organizations that provide nonmedical assistance. These services help older adults stay at home.

Long-Term Care Facilities

Three factors appear to precipitate placement in a long-term care facility: (1) rapid patient deterioration, (2) caregiver inability to continue care because of stress and burnout, and (3) a change in or loss of the family support system. Progressive dementia, urinary incontinence, or a major health event (e.g., stroke) can hasten long-term care placement.

The conflicts and fears faced by older adults and their families make placement a difficult transition. Common caregiver concerns include: (1) Will the older adult resist the admission process? (2) Will the level of care given by staff be insufficient? (3) Will the resident be lonely? and (4) Will nursing care be affordable?

The physical relocation of the older adult may lead to adverse health effects. *Relocation stress syndrome* is associated with the disruption, confusion, and challenges that older adults face when moving to a new environment. Older adults may have anxiety, depression, and disorientation. Appropriate interventions can reduce the effects of relocation. Whenever possible, involve older adults in the decision to move and fully inform them about the location. Caregivers can share information, pictures, or a video recording of the new location. Staff members at the institution can send a welcome message. On arrival, they can greet new residents and provide orientation. To bridge the relocation, new residents can be "buddied" with seasoned residents (Fig. 5.6).

Programs for All-Inclusive Care for the Elderly (PACE)

Programs for All-Inclusive Care for the Elderly (PACE) provide care for adults age 55 and older. PACE services include primary care including prescription medications and wound care; physical, occupational, recreational, and speech therapy; adult day care; dental; podiatry; social services; and home health care.

FIG. 5.6 Social interaction and acceptance are important for older adults. (©Hemera/Thinkstock.)

Respite care, hospitalization, short-term rehabilitation, and long-term care are provided as needed.[20]

A person who has Medicaid will not have to pay a monthly premium for the long-term portion of the PACE benefit. A person who does not qualify for Medicaid but has Medicare must pay a monthly premium to cover the long-term care portion.

LEGAL AND ETHICAL ISSUES

Legal guidance and assistance is needed by many older adults. Legal issues include advance directives, estate planning, taxation issues, appeals for denied services (e.g., disability), financial decisions, or exploitation by strangers or "trusted others."

Advance directives are written statements of a person's wishes about medical care. A health care proxy may be appointed to make medical decisions if a person is unable to make his or her own medical decisions. These documents allow people to direct their own care at end of life. Advance directives are discussed in detail in Chapter 9 and Table 9.6.

When working with older adults, you may find several ethical issues that influence practice, such as the assessment of older adults' ability to make decisions. Other ethical issues related to end-of-life care include decisions about resuscitation, treatment of infections, nutrition and hydration, and transfer to more intensive treatment units and the hospital. These situations are often complex, especially during emotionally difficult times. You can assist the older adult, family, and other health care workers by (1) keeping current on the ethical issues, (2) acknowledging when an ethical dilemma is present, and (3) advocating for an institutional ethics committee to help provide guidance in the decision-making process and assist when differences of opinion occur.

❖ NURSING MANAGEMENT: OLDER ADULTS

Gerontologic nursing is the care of older adults based on the specialty body of knowledge of gerontology and nursing. These specialty nurses provide care for older adults using a whole-person (physical, psychologic, functional, developmental, socioeconomic, cultural) perspective. Care of older adults is complex and presents challenges that require skilled assessment and creative nursing interventions tailored to this population.

Diseases and conditions in older adults may be hard to accurately assess and diagnose. Older adults may underreport symptoms and try to manage these symptoms by changing their functional status. For example, a woman having loss of feeling in her feet because of neuropathy may start using a walker to get around, while not reporting the symptom to her HCP. The older adult may attribute a new symptom to "aging" and ignore it. The older adult may eat less, sleep more, or "wait it out."

In older adults, disease symptoms are often atypical. For example, confusion may be a sign of an infection. A patient being treated for a urinary tract infection may be diagnosed with asymptomatic heart disease. Pathologic conditions with similar symptoms can be confused. For example, depression may be misdiagnosed and treated as dementia. The most common atypical illness presentations are "delirium" or "acute change in mental status" and change in functional status. A caregiver may say that a relative "is acting differently," "doesn't appear as him/herself," or is no longer taking part in usual activities or self-care.

In older adults a *cascade disease pattern* may occur. For example, a person who has insomnia treats the condition with a sleeping medication becomes lethargic and delirious and falls, sustaining a hip fracture. This decreases activity and mobility, leading to pneumonia and/or pressure injuries. Nurses play a vital role in preventing this downward trajectory.

For older adults, the stress of an illness may lead to fear and anxiety. They may view health care personnel as helpful but perceive institutions as negative and potentially harmful places. Communicate a sense of concern and care by use of direct and simple statements, appropriate eye contact, direct touch, and gentle humor. These actions help the older adult relax in this stressful situation.

◆ Nursing Assessment

Prior to assessment, attend to the person's primary needs. For example, ensure that older adults are comfortable and ask if they need to use the bathroom. If older adults normally use eyeglasses and hearing aids, ask them to use these during the assessment. Place all assistive devices, such as walkers, within reach. Assess your patient's level of fatigue and pause the interview if necessary. Allow adequate time to offer information and time for the person to respond to questions. Interview both the older adult and his or her family or caregivers. You can do this separately, unless the patient is cognitively impaired or specifically requests the caregiver's presence. Although the health history may be lengthy, it is important to obtain. Review medical records and determine what information is most relevant or needs more detail.

The focus of a comprehensive geriatric assessment is to determine appropriate interventions to support and enhance the health, quality of life, function, and independence of older adults. At a minimum, it includes the medical history, functional assessment, medication review, cognitive and mood evaluation, social resources, and physical examination followed by recommended diagnostic tests. Comprehensive geriatric assessment is often conducted by an interprofessional geriatric assessment team. This team minimally includes a staff nurse, an HCP such as a physician or adult-geriatric nurse practitioner, and a social worker. It may also include a physical and/or occupational therapist, dietitian, podiatrist, ophthalmologist, dentist, and pastoral care representative. After the assessment is complete, the interprofessional team meets with the patient and family to present the team's findings and recommendations.

Specific elements in a comprehensive nursing assessment include a thorough history, mood assessment, functional assessment including ADLs and IADLs, mental status evaluation, social-environmental assessment, and physical assessment. Evaluation of mental status is particularly important for older adults because these results often determine the potential for independent living. *SPICES,* an effective tool for obtaining assessment data in older adults, may be used as an initial nursing assessment in any setting (Fig. 5.7). Multiple evidence-based geriatric assessment tools and best practice approaches to nursing care for older adults are available from the *Try This* Series at the Hartford Institute for Geriatric Nursing (available at *www.consultgeri.org/tools*).

A comprehensive geriatric assessment includes fall risk, fear of falling, cause(s) of past falls, and post-fall assessment. Those at increased risk for falls have a history of falls or a fear of falling. Many factors increase the risk for falls, including prescription and nonprescription medications; infection; orthostatic hypotension; dehydration; electrolyte imbalance or other laboratory abnormalities; arthritis; changes in gait, balance,

and mobility; neurologic impairment (e.g., stroke, Parkinson's disease); decreased muscle strength; and decreased visual acuity. Assess for symptoms of dizziness or lightheadedness upon standing. Other risk factors include environmental hazards, feet abnormalities, poor footwear, clutter, throw rugs, incorrect use of an assistive device such as a walker or cane, shiny or waxy floors, slippery floors, poor lighting, bed in an incorrect position such as too high, and uneven pavement.

Evaluation of the results of a comprehensive nursing assessment helps determine the service and potential long-term placement needs of older adults. Collect data about community resources that will help older adults and their caregivers in supporting maximal function. The goal is to plan and implement actions that help older adults stay as functionally independent as possible and to promote their quality of life.

◆ Planning

When setting goals with older adults, identify their strengths and abilities. Include caregivers in planning. Priority goals may include gaining a sense of control, feeling safe, and reducing stress.

◆ Nursing Implementation

When carrying out a plan of action for older adults, adjust your approach and actions based on their physical, functional, and mental status. The small body size common in frail older adults may require the use of pediatric equipment (e.g., BP cuff). Safety is a primary concern when caring for an older adult. Those with bone and joint changes often need transfer assistance, altered positioning, and use of gait belts and lift devices. Older adults with declining energy reserves may need extra time to complete tasks. A slower approach and the use of other adaptive equipment may be needed. Cognitive impairment, if present, requires that you offer careful explanations and a calm approach to avoid producing anxiety and resistance. Depression can result in apathy and poor cooperation with the treatment plan.

◆ **Health Promotion.** Health promotion and prevention of health problems for older adults focus on 3 areas: (1) increased participation in health promotion and disease prevention activities (Fig. 5.8), (2) reduction in diseases and health-related issues, and (3) increased use of services that reduce health hazards. Programs exist for screening for chronic health conditions, tobacco cessation, geriatric foot care, vision and hearing screening, stress reduction, exercise

Patient name:		Date:	
		EVIDENCE	
	SPICES	Yes	No
Sleep disorders			
Problems with eating or feeding			
Incontinence			
Confusion			
Evidence of falls			
Skin breakdown			

FIG. 5.7 SPICES. (Adapted from Fulmer T: The geriatric nurse specialist role: a new model. *Nurs Manag* 22:91, 1991. © Lippincott Williams & Wilkins, *www.lww.com.*)

FIG. 5.8 Water aerobics is an example of a health promotion activity for older adults. (© Purestock/Thinkstock.)

programs, fall prevention programs, drug usage, crime prevention, elder mistreatment, and home safety assessment.[3] Teach older adults about the need for specific preventive services and available programs.

 PROMOTING POPULATION HEALTH

Promoting Health in Older Adults

- Get influenza, pneumococcal, shingles, and tetanus vaccines as needed.
- Create a living environment free of hazards to reduce the risk for falling.
- Drink plenty of liquids. Limit drinks with lots of added sugar or salt.
- Be physically active 3 to 5 days each week.
- Maintain an appropriate weight based on a nutrient-rich diet.
- Use medications, herbs, and supplements according to your HCP's direction.

Include health promotion and disease prevention in nursing interventions and plans at any setting or level of care in which nurses and older adults interact. You can use health promotion activities to increase personal responsibility for health and independent functioning. Teaching and reinforcement are important tools for you to use to enhance self-care practices by older adults. Patient teaching is discussed in Chapter 4.

◆ **Acute and Ambulatory Care.** The hospital may be the first point of contact for older adults with the health care system. Conditions that often result in hospitalization include falls, dysrhythmias, heart failure, stroke, fluid and electrolyte imbalances (e.g., hyponatremia, dehydration), pneumonia, urosepsis, and hip fractures. Hospitalized older adults often have multiple problems.

When older adults are being cared for in the acute care setting, both patients and caregivers need help with a variety of functions (Table 5.10). The outcome of hospitalization for older adults varies. Of special concern are patients undergoing high-risk surgical procedures (e.g., hip replacement) and those who have delirium while hospitalized.

Care Transitions. The time of a care transition to another setting (e.g., acute care hospital to rehabilitation) is challenging for many older adults. While in the hospital, patients and caregivers are counseled on how to prepare for posthospital care. Those with multiple health conditions have a particularly high risk for rehospitalization.

Medicare regulations require a registered nurse, social worker, or qualified person to develop a care transition plan for patient discharge. Safe and effective care transitions are most

---

TABLE 5.10 Nursing Management

Care of the Hospitalized Older Adult

Give special consideration to the following nursing interventions when caring for hospitalized older adult:

- Identify older adults at risk for consequences of medical and/or surgical treatments).
- Consider discharge and postacute needs early in the hospital stay, especially assistance with activities of daily living and medications.
- Encourage the development and use of interprofessional teams, special care units, and providers who focus on the special needs of older patients.
- Implement standard protocols to screen for at-risk conditions common in the hospitalized older adult, such as urinary tract infection and delirium.
- Implement mobility and exercise programs to prevent functional decline.
- Monitor for and prevent skin integrity changes.
- Implement measures focused on safety (e.g., fall prevention).
- Refer patients to the appropriate community-based services.

likely to occur when interprofessional team members work together with the patient and family to coordinate care.

The Transitional Care Model (TCM) is an evidence-based, innovative approach to care coordination and management of the complex needs of older adults.[21] In this model a transitional care nurse delivers and coordinates care by nurses and other team members throughout potential and acute episodes of illness. Those most likely to benefit from transitional care nursing include those of older age and those with functional deficits, behavioral or psychiatric issues, multiple chronic conditions, polypharmacy, a recent hospitalization, lack of a support system, low health literacy, and history of non-adherence to treatment.[21]

Rehabilitation. The goal of rehabilitation is to help older adults adapt to or recover from disability or an acute functional decline. Rehabilitation may occur in acute inpatient rehabilitation, subacute rehabilitation, or long-term care settings. With proper training, assistive equipment, and attendant personal care, people with functional deficits may live independently. Older adults, primarily through Medicare reimbursement, can receive rehabilitative assistance through acute inpatient rehabilitation (limited days) and home health care programs (Fig. 5.9).

Older adults with chronic conditions, such as arthritis, have increased risk for functional decline. Decreased function or disabilities lead to increased self-care deficits, increased rates of institutionalization, decreased quality of life, and higher mortality rates.

Several factors influence the rehabilitation of older adults. First, preexisting conditions associated with decreased reaction time, visual acuity, fine motor ability, physical strength, and cognitive function affect the short- and long-term rehabilitation potential. Older adults may have anxiety, fear, or concern about falling. Poor nutrition and financial issues may limit the rehabilitation process. Encouragement, support, and acceptance from the interdisciplinary team members as well as their caregivers can help older adults remain motivated for potentially physically challenging rehabilitation.

Second, older adults often lose function because of inactivity and immobility. This deconditioning can occur because of unstable acute medical conditions, lack of assistive devices, and a lack of motivation to stay fit. The effect of inactivity leads to "use it or lose it" consequences. Older adults can improve flexibility, strength, and aerobic capacity even into very old

FIG. 5.9 The nurse assists a patient in a geriatric rehabilitation facility. (© KeithBrofsky/Photodisc/Thinkstock.)

age. Passive and active range-of-motion exercises are used with all older adults to preserve muscle tone and strength and prevent deconditioning and subsequent functional decline.

Last, the goal of rehabilitation is to strive for maximal function and physical capabilities considering the person's current health and functional status. For example, on admission to an acute or long-term care facility and home health services, assess for fall risk as well as the person's fear of falling. Initiate appropriate fall prevention interventions and assess for ongoing risk. Conduct comprehensive foot and peripheral vascular assessments for all older adults, especially those with diabetes, and arrange appropriate follow-up care.

Assistive Devices. Consider the use of assistive devices as interventions for older adults. Using appropriate assistive devices such as dentures, glasses, hearing aids, walkers, wheelchairs, adaptive utensils, elevated toilet seats, and skin protective devices can increase function. Include these tools and devices in the older adult's care plan when needed and teach the proper use of the devices. For example, using a cane correctly may decrease fall risk.

Technology can help with rehabilitation and living with functional impairments. For example, we can use electronic monitoring equipment to monitor heart rhythm and BP. Monitoring can locate a person with dementia who has wandered away from home or a long-term care facility. Computerized assistive devices may help patients with speech difficulties after a stroke. Small electronic devices can serve as memory aids.

Safety. Safety is crucial in the health maintenance of older adults. When compared to younger adults, older adults are at higher risk for accidents due to normal sensory changes, slowed reaction time, decreased thermal and pain sensitivity, changes in gait and balance, and medication effects. Most accidents occur in or around the home. Falls, motor vehicle accidents, and fires are common causes of accidental death in older adults. Declining thermoregulation impairs the older person's ability to adapt to extremes in environmental temperatures. The bodies of older adults can neither conserve nor dissipate heat as efficiently as those of younger adults. Therefore both hypothermia and hyperthermia occur more readily. The older adult age-group accounts for most deaths during severe cold spells and heat waves.

You can review environmental changes that can improve safety for older adults. Measures such as colored step strips, tub

and toilet grab bars, and stairway handrails can be effective in "safety-proofing" the living spaces of older adults. Uncluttered floor space (e.g., removal of throw rugs), railings, and increased lighting and night-lights are some of the easiest and most practical adaptations. Social workers may help older adults implement these environmental changes. You can advocate for home fire and security alarms.

Other interventions to decrease the risk for falling include exercise, physical therapy, and management of foot and footwear issues. Encourage the patient's use of glasses and hearing aids as ordered. Fear of falling can affect the older adults' decisions about the activities that they engage in and how active they remain.

Older adults who are new to inpatient or long-term care settings need a thorough orientation to the environment. Reassure the older adult that he or she is safe. Answer all questions and refer to interprofessional team members and specialists as needed. Foster orientation by displaying large-print clocks, keeping wall designs simple, clearly designating doors and exits, and using simple bed and nurse or family-call controls. Provide diffuse lighting while avoiding glare.

Medication Use. Medication use in older adults requires thorough and regular assessment, care planning, and evaluation. Nonadherence to medication plans by older adults is common. Many older adults are unable to read prescription drug labels and understand the health information that we provide them.

Age-related changes alter the pharmacodynamics and pharmacokinetics of drugs. Drug-drug, drug-nutrient, and drug-disease interactions influence the absorption, distribution, metabolism, and excretion of drugs. The most dramatic changes with aging are related to drug metabolism (Fig. 5.10). Hepatic blood flow and the enzymes responsible for drug metabolism decrease markedly with aging. These increase drug half-life in older adults and lead to greater risk for drug toxicity and adverse drug events. Overall, by age 75 to 80, there is a 50% decline in the renal clearance of drugs. Older adults with altered renal function may need a lower dose and/or decreased frequency of administration of a drug excreted by the kidney. When drug level monitoring is available (e.g., digoxin), identify toxic levels by serum monitoring at regular intervals, especially when there is a change of dose and/or frequency of administration.

Older adults may have difficulty managing medication due to cognitive impairment, altered sensory perception, and limited hand mobility or dexterity. Table 5.11 lists common reasons for drug errors made by older adults.

Polypharmacy (the use of multiple medications by a person who has more than 1 health problem), overdose, and addiction to prescription drugs are major causes of illness in older adults.[22] Potential medication errors include the (1) taking both brand and generic medications, (2) refilling medications too soon or too late (resulting in taking the medication incorrectly), and (3) drug-drug interactions. These errors can be prevented by having a pharmacist review medications regularly. Suggest the use of 1 pharmacy for filling all prescription medications.

The effects of medications in older adults with multiple health problems are particularly challenging to assess and manage. As 1 disease is treated, another may be affected. For example, the use of a drug such as oxybutynin, which is given to treat overactive bladder, may cause confusion. To accurately assess medication knowledge and use, ask older adults to bring all medications (OTC drugs, prescription drugs, vitamins and supplements, laxatives, sleep aids, and herbal remedies) that they take regularly or

Drug-receptor interaction
- Brain receptors become more sensitive, making psychoactive drugs very potent.

Metabolism
- Liver mass shrinks.
- Hepatic blood flow and enzyme activity decline.
- Metabolism drops to $1/2$ to $2/3$ the rate of young adults.
- Enzymes lose ability to process some drugs, thus prolonging drug half-life.

Absorption
- Gastric emptying rate and gastrointestinal motility slow.
- Absorption capacity of cells and active transport mechanism decline.

Circulation
- Vascular nerve control is less stable.
- Antihypertensives, for example, may overshoot, dropping BP too low.
- Digoxin, for example, may slow the heart rate too much.

Excretion
- In kidneys, renal blood flow, glomerular filtration rate, renal tubular secretion and reabsorption, and number of functional nephrons decline.
- Age-related changes increase half-life for renally excreted drugs.
- Oral antidiabetic drugs, among others, stay in the body longer.

Distribution
- Lean body mass falls.
- Adipose stores increase.
- Total body water declines, raising the concentration of water-soluble drugs, such as digoxin, which can cause heart dysfunction.
- Plasma protein levels decrease, reducing sites available for protein-bound drugs and raising blood levels of free drug.

FIG. 5.10 The effects of aging on drug metabolism.

TABLE 5.11 Drug Therapy
Causes of Medication Errors by Older Adults

- Decreased vision
- Forgetting to take drugs
- Use of nonprescription over-the-counter drugs
- Use of medications prescribed for someone else
- Lack of financial resources to obtain prescribed medication
- Refusal to take medication because of undesirable side effects
- Failure to understand instructions or importance of drug treatment

TABLE 5.12 Drug Therapy
Safe Medication Use by Older Adults

When older adults are using medications, it is important to take the following measures to prevent medication errors:
- Assess cognitive function and monitor for changes.
- Try to reduce medication use that is not essential by consulting the HCP and pharmacist.
- Assess ability to self-administer medication and overall medication use, including prescription drugs; OTC drugs; pain treatments; antihistamines; cough syrups; vitamins, minerals, and supplements; sleep remedies; and herbal remedies.
- Assess alcohol and illicit drug use.
- Encourage the use of written or electronic medication-reminder systems.
- Encourage the use of 1 pharmacy.
- Work with HCPs and pharmacists to set up routine drug profiles on all older adult patients.
- Advocate for low-income prescription support services.

occasionally to their health care appointment. You will then be able to accurately assess all medications that the patient is taking, including drugs that the person may have omitted or thought unimportant. The American Geriatrics Society (AGS) Beers Criteria are designed to reduce problems with medications in older adults.[22] Table 5.12 describes other nursing interventions to help older adults follow a safe medication routine.

Depression. Depression is not a normal part of aging. However, it is often an underrecognized problem in older adults. Around 15% of older adults living in their homes have manifestations of depression. Rates of depressive symptoms in older adults in institutional settings are higher. The second highest rate of suicide occurs in those over 75.

Depression is associated with female gender, being divorced or separated, low socioeconomic status, poor social support, and a recent adverse and unexpected event. Depression

in older adults tends to arise from a loss of self-esteem and may be related to life situations, such as retirement or loss of a spouse or partner. Problems such as pain, insomnia, lethargy, agitation, weight loss, and dementia are associated with depression.

Late-life depression often occurs together with medical conditions, such as heart disease, stroke, diabetes, and cancer.

Depression can worsen medical conditions by affecting adherence to diet, exercise, or drug regimens. It is important that your assessment include physical examination and interpretation of laboratory results for physical disorders that may have symptoms similar to those of depression (e.g., thyroid disorders, vitamin deficiencies).

Encourage older adults who have depressive symptoms to seek treatment. Because older adults with depression may feel unworthy, withdrawn, and isolated, the support of the family or others in encouraging older adults to seek treatment is important. Assist older adult caregivers who have depressive symptoms to seek medical attention, and help them in secure respite services and support for their caregiving role.

Restraint Use. Physical restraints are devices, materials, and equipment that physically prevent persons from moving freely, such as walking, standing, lying, transferring, or sitting. *Chemical restraints* are drugs used to restrict a patient's freedom of movement or in some cases to sedate a patient. The current standard is to provide safe care without using restraints of any form, whether physical or chemical. Restraints are a last resort in the care of older adults. Only use restraints to ensure the person's safety or the safety of others.

Before considering the use of any restraint, completely assess the perceived need for the restraint and document the assessment. Behavioral symptoms, such as crying and shouting, may arise from co-morbidities, pain, medication effects, unmet needs, and/or environmental factors. When behavioral manifestations are present, ask the following questions to better understand the patient's behavior: Is the person able to say what she or he needs and wants? People with dementia may respond by speaking, gesturing, nodding, or making eye contact. Questions that use "yes" or "no" answers are better than open-ended questions for gathering assessment information. Ask family, friends, or staff members from previous care settings about the patient's (1) history; (2) usual communication style and cues to indicate pain, fatigue, hunger, or a need to urinate or defecate; (3) abilities in ADLs; and (4) daily routines (e.g., "Is he often awake at night or an early riser?" "Does she prefer breakfast before dressing? Take an afternoon nap? Have a routine for dressing?").

Evaluate whether disruptive behaviors signal unmet physiologic or psychosocial needs. For example, a patient who tries to get out of bed without help may be trying to reach the toilet.

A toileting schedule will help to curtail such attempts and prevent incontinence.

Long-term care regulations and The Joint Commission set standards for restraint use. These include time limit, observation and care, mandating use of least restrictive measures (e.g., mittens), and alternatives to restraint use. Restraint alternatives include low beds, body props, and electronic devices (such as bed and chair alarm signaling). Such approaches support the development of a "restraint-free," safe environment. Alternatives to restraints require vigilant, creative, and sensitive nursing care.

All restraints require an order from an HCP. Carefully document restraint use and the reason for use. It is not appropriate to use restraints to prevent falls, avoid interference with medical devices, or reduce irritating behaviors, such as calling out. Frequent scheduled reviews of the ongoing need for the restraint are done with consideration of when to discontinue the restraint.

Sleep. Adequacy of sleep is often a concern for older adults because of altered sleep patterns. Older people have a marked decrease in deep sleep and are easily aroused. Many older adults report difficulty going to sleep and staying sleep. They may feel "unrefreshed" after sleep. See Chapter 7 for more about the sleep problems of older adults.

◆ Evaluation

The evaluation phase of the nursing process is similar for all patients. The results of evaluation direct you to continue the plan of care or revise as needed. When evaluating nursing care with older adults, focus on functional improvement and quality of life. Useful questions to consider when evaluating the plan of care for older adults are outlined in Table 5.13.

TABLE 5.13 Evaluating Nursing Care for Older Adults
Use the following questions to evaluate the effectiveness of care for older adults:
• Is there an identifiable change in function, mental status, or signs and symptoms of exacerbation of chronic condition(s)?
• Does the person consider his or her health state to be improved?
• Does the person think the plan is helpful?
• Do the person and caregiver think the care is worth the time and cost?
• Can you document positive changes that support the interventions?

CASE STUDY
Older Adults

(© azndc/iStock/
Thinkstock.)

Patient Profile

C.L., a 73-yr-old Taiwanese woman, was admitted through the emergency department with shortness of breath. She was diagnosed with community-acquired pneumonia. Her medical history includes COPD, hypertension, diabetes, mild cognitive impairment, depression, macular degeneration, and significant hearing loss.

Subjective Data

- A stroke 5 years ago and has right-sided weakness
- A 100 pack-year history of tobacco use but quit smoking after her stroke
- Not seen primary care physician in 1 year
- In past year has had an unplanned weight loss of 15 pounds
- Spends her days either in bed or in a recliner watching television
- Shortness of breath for past 5 days

Psychosocial Data

- Came to the United States 15 years ago from Taiwan
- Speaks Mandarin Chinese with limited English proficiency
- Lives with her unemployed adult son who provides help with ADLs and IADLs
- Has 3 daughters who live within a 2-hour drive
- Limited financial resources but has Medicare and Medicaid benefits
- Daughters raise concerns about their mother's care and safety at home, given their brother's history of anger issues and a gambling addiction
- When daughters ask their brother about how he is caring for his mother, he says, "I'm doing the best I can. She refuses help. She refuses to go to the doctor. What do you want me to do? She's old. She's crazy. She's going to die anyway!"
- Daughters state their mother does not want to go to a nursing home

Objective Data

Physical Examination

- Unwashed, matted hair, poor oral hygiene, overgrown toenails
- 2 Stage 3 sacral pressure injuries
- Unstageable right heel pressure injury
- Multiple small bruises on her forearms and shins
- 5- × 10-cm bruise in the middle of her back

Diagnostic Tests

- Serum albumin 2.4 g/dL
- X-ray reveals consolidation in lower left and right lung lobes

Discussion Questions

1. What other information do you need to assess C.L.'s condition? How should you address questions about potential elder mistreatment?
2. Define ageism, and explain how it may be manifested in this case.
3. Identify the stage of Corbin and Strauss chronic illness trajectory that describe C.L.'s current status. Which stage is the goal of your nursing care?
4. *Patient-Centered Care:* What is your assessment of C.L.'s ability to manage her chronic illnesses? What will you include in your care planning to optimize her self-care ability?
5. *Priority Decision:* Based on your assessment of C.L., what are the priority nursing diagnoses?
6. *Safety:* To ensure C.L.'s safety, what nursing interventions are necessary during her hospitalization?
7. *Collaboration:* How would you use unlicensed assistive personnel (UAP) on the hospital unit to carry out the priorities that you identified in question 4?
8. What risk factors does C.L. have for developing frailty? Which factors are modifiable?
9. Based on your knowledge of care alternatives for older adults, what setting would be most appropriate for C.L. upon hospital discharge?
10. *Collaboration:* Because she has an expressed desire to return home, what referrals would be indicated if this were the plan?
11. What risk factors does C.L. have for becoming a victim of elder mistreatment? List and provide the rationale for nursing interventions and legal and ethical responsibilities in this case.

Answers available at *http://evolve.elsevier.com/Lewis/medsurg.*

■ BRIDGE TO NCLEX EXAMINATION

The number of the question corresponds to the same-numbered outcome at the beginning of the chapter.

1. Examples of primary prevention strategies include
   a. colonoscopy at age 50.
   b. avoidance of tobacco products.
   c. teaching the importance of exercise to a patient with hypertension.
   d. intake of a diet low in saturated fat in a patient with high cholesterol.

2. A characteristic of a chronic illness is that it *(select all that apply)*
   a. has reversible pathologic changes.
   b. has a consistent, predictable clinical course.
   c. results in permanent deviation from normal.
   d. is associated with many stable and unstable phases.
   e. always starts with an acute illness and then progresses slowly.

3. Among older Americans in the United States
   a. more than 30% live in nursing homes.
   b. women are less likely to live in poverty.
   c. the number of those who completed college is lower than in previous decades.
   d. those 85 years or older account for the fastest growing segment of the population.

4. An ethnic older adult may feel a loss of self-worth when the nurse *(select all that apply)*
   a. prohibits visits from a faith healer.
   b. informs the patient about ethnic support services.
   c. allows a patient to rely on ethnic health beliefs and practices.
   d. emphasizes that a therapeutic diet does not allow ethnic foods.
   e. uses a medical interpreter to provide explanations and teaching.

5. An important nursing action to help a chronically ill older adult is to
   a. avoid discussing future lifestyle changes.
   b. ensure the patient that the condition is stable.
   c. treat the patient as a competent manager of the disease.
   d. encourage the patient to "fight" the disease as long as possible.

6. Older adults who become ill are more likely than younger adults to
   a. report symptoms to their health care providers.
   b. refuse to carry out lifestyle changes to promote recovery.
   c. seek medical attention because of limitations on their lifestyle.
   d. alter their daily living activities to accommodate new symptoms.

7. An appropriate care choice for an older adult who lives with an employed daughter but needs help with activities of daily living is
   a. adult day care.
   b. long-term care.
   c. a retirement center.
   d. an assisted living facility.

8. Nursing interventions directed at health promotion in the older adult are primarily focused on
   a. disease management.
   b. controlling symptoms of illness.
   c. teaching positive health behaviors.
   d. teaching about nutrition to enhance longevity.

1. b, 2. c, 3. d, 4. a, 5. c, 6. d, 7. a, 8. c.

For rationales to these answers and even more NCLEX review questions, visit *http://evolve.elsevier.com/Lewis/medsurg*.

ⓔ EVOLVE WEBSITE/RESOURCES LIST

http://evolve.elsevier.com/Lewis/medsurg
Review Questions (Online Only)
Key Points
Answer Keys for Questions
- Rationales for Bridge to NCLEX Examination Questions
- Answer Guidelines for Case Study on p. 74
Conceptual Care Map Creator
Audio Glossary
Content Updates

REFERENCES

1. Centers for Disease Control and Prevention: Chronic diseases and health promotion. Retrieved from *www.cdc.gov/chronicdisease*.
2. Corbin JM, Strauss A: A nursing model for chronic illness management based upon the Trajectory Framework, *Sch Inq Nurs Pract* 5:155, 1991. (Classic)
3. Hartford Institute for Geriatric Nursing: Try This: Series. Retrieved from *www.consultgeri.org/tools/try-this-series*.
4. Department of Health and Human Services: Self-management for health in chronic conditions. Retrieved from *www.grants.nih.gov/grants/guide/pa-files/PA-14-344.html*.
5. Schulz R, Beach SR, Friedman EM, et al: Changing structures and processes to support family caregivers of seriously ill patients. *J Palliat Med*. 2018;21:S36.
6. Administration on Aging: A profile of older Americans: 2016. Retrieved from *www.acl.gov/sites/default/files/Aging%20and%20Disability%20in%20America/2016-Profile.pdf*.
*7. Wilson DM, Nam MA, Murphy J, et al: A critical review of published research literature reviews on nursing and healthcare ageism, *J Clin Nurs* 26:23, 2017.
*8. Cellerino A, Terzibasi ET: Biology of aging: New models, new methods, *Semin Cell Dev Biol* 70:98, 2017.
9. Denny DL, Lindseth G: Preoperative risk factors for subsyndromal delirium in older adults who undergo joint replacement surgery, *Ortho Nurs* 36:402, 2017.
10. Czaja S: The potential role of technology in supporting older adults, *Public Policy & Aging Report*, 27:44, 2017.
11. Li G, Thabane L, Papaioannou A, et al: An overview of osteoporosis and frailty in the elderly, *BMC Musculoskelet Disord*, 18:46, 2017.
12. U.S. Department of Agriculture Food and Nutrition Service: Supplemental Nutrition Assistance Program. Retrieved from *www.fns.usda.gov/snap/snap-special-rules-elderly-or-disabled*.
13. Manuel JI: Racial/ethnic and gender disparities in health care use and access, *Health Serv Res* 53:1407, 2018.
14. Stanford Medicine Geriatric Education Center: A national resource center in ethnogeriatrics. Retrieved from *http://sgec.stanford.edu/*.
15. Administration on Aging Family Caregiver Alliance: Selected caregiver statistics. Retrieved from *https://www.caregiver.org/caregiver-statistics-demographics*.
16. National Center for Elder Abuse: What we do. Retrieved from *https://ncea.acl.gov/*.
17. National Center for Elder Abuse: Preventing elder abuse and neglect in older adults: Tools and tips. Retrieved from *https://ncea.acl.gov/resources/publications.html*.
*18. Dong X: Elder self-neglect: Research and practice, *Clin Interv Aging* 12:949, 2017.
19. Kaiser Family Foundation: How much is enough? Out-of-pocket spending among Medicare beneficiaries. Retrieved from *www.kff.org/medicare/report/how-much-is-enough-out-of-pocket-spending-among-medicare-beneficiaries-a-chartbook/*.
20. National PACE Association: Eligibility requirements. Retrieved from *www.npaonline.org/*.
21. Penn Nursing Science: Transitional care model. Retrieved from *www.nursing.upenn.edu/ncth/transitional-care-model/*.
*22. Levy HB: Polypharmacy reduction strategies, *Clin Geriatr Med* 33:241, 2017.

*Evidence-based information for clinical practice.

6

Stress Management

Margaret R. Rateau

You may not be able to change the stressors in your life, but you can change your reaction or response to them.

Florence Nightingale

http://evolve.elsevier.com/Lewis/medsurg/

CONCEPTUAL FOCUS

Coping   Stress

LEARNING OUTCOMES

1. Distinguish between the terms *stressor* and *stress*.
2. Describe the role of the nervous and endocrine systems in the stress process.
3. Describe the effects of stress on the immune system.
4. Discuss the effects of stress on health.

5. Explain the role of coping in managing stress.
6. Select coping and relaxation strategies that you, a patient, or a caregiver experiencing stress can use.
7. Describe the nursing assessment and management of a patient experiencing stress.

KEY TERMS

biofeedback, p. 83
coping, p. 81
emotion-focused coping, p. 81
imagery, p. 83

massage, p. 84
meditation, p. 83
mind-body-spirit connection, p. 80
problem-focused coping, p. 81

psychoneuroimmunology (PNI), p. 79
relaxation breathing, p. 82
stress, p. 76
stressors, p. 77

All people experience stress. Stress has a powerful effect on the mind and therefore a significant effect on one's health and well-being. The concept of stress directly relates to multiple other concepts. Chronic stress is a major factor in causing and worsening chronic health conditions. This in turn is a major driver of escalating health care costs.

High levels of stress are common among patients and caregivers. How they deal with their stress is critical to their well-being. As a nurse, you play a key role in helping them recognize stress and manage stressful events. This chapter focuses on how stress can affect the mind, body, and spirit and how a person can effectively cope with stress.

WHAT IS STRESS?

Stress is the inability to cope with perceived (real or imagined) demands or threats to one's mental, emotional, or spiritual

well-being.[1] What 1 person perceives as stressful may not be perceived as stressful to someone else. Responses to the same stressor vary greatly. Stress might be more prevalent in women than men, although it may be that women are more willing to admit they are experiencing stress.[2] *Perception* of the potential stressor influences the way a person responds to that stressor. This is shown in the following examples:

- B.J., a 43-yr-old woman, becomes depressed after a laparoscopic hysterectomy for fibroids. She is unwilling to take part in normal self-care activities. You are surprised by her response. You think she had a simple surgery and should get on with her life. After further assessment, you discover that removing her uterus is a great psychologic stressor because she perceives it as a loss of her womanhood and femininity.
- K.R., a 52-yr-old woman, has just been told by her health care provider (HCP) of her new diagnosis of type 2 diabetes. After the HCP's visit with her, you are prepared to provide emotional

Stressors

Physiologic
- Pain
- Excessive noise
- Starvation
- Infection

Emotional/Psychologic
- Diagnosis of cancer
- Death of spouse
- Caring for disabled child
- Marital problems

Perception → **Stress**

FIG. 6.1 Stressors can be physiologic or emotional/psychologic. Your perception of these stressors will determine whether they cause stress. Events or circumstances become stressful when you perceive them to be.

FIG. 6.2 During stressful situations, the demands seem to exceed the resources. (© iStock.com/AntonioGuillem.)

support. However, you are puzzled when she is smiling and feeling relieved. You think that this diagnosis should be stressful. However, K.R. tells you that she is so relieved because for weeks she was worried that her symptoms were caused by cancer.

Many different events or factors can be **stressors**. They can be physiologic or emotional/psychologic (Fig. 6.1). The emotional/psychologic stressors can be positive or negative. For example, the birth of a baby is usually a positive stressor. Marital discord is a negative stressor.

Is Stress Bad or Good?

We tend to think of stress as bad or a threat. Actually, any event or situation that is out of the ordinary can be a stressor. This includes events that we normally consider happy or enjoyable (e.g., getting married, going on a vacation).

Stress can be helpful. A little stress can motivate you. Stress can actually inspire you to achieve a goal and become more confident or stronger physically.

The body does not distinguish between bad stress and good stress or real or imaginary stress. It responds to the stressor with the same stress response. This stress response is the way our bodies react both physically and emotionally to any change, be it good, bad, real, or imagined.

For you as a nursing student, a test can be a stressful situation. A little bit of stress related to the upcoming test makes you study and become better prepared. If you feel mildly stressed during the test, it may help your test performance as a little stress heightens your awareness and increases your mental acuity. However, if you are overly stressed, it causes mental blocks, lack of concentration, and inability to remember things.

Stress is a key for survival, but too much stress can be detrimental. That is why it is important for you and your patients to learn to cope more effectively with the stressors in life.

Factors Affecting Response to Stress

Why do people respond so differently to stress? Why do some people cope better with stress than others? Interestingly, some people experience significant adverse life events but do not succumb to the effects of stress.

Differences in the responses to a stressor can be based on the duration of a stressor (acute or chronic) and intensity of a stressor (mild, moderate, or severe). For example, a person dealing with the chronic stress of caring for a loved one may be exposed to many acute stressors (e.g., car accident, influenza). The type, duration, and intensity of a stressor are important variables that can influence a person's response (Fig. 6.2).

TABLE 6.1 **Factors Affecting Response to Stress**
Internal
• Age
• Attitude
• Genetic background
• Hardiness
• Health status
• Nutritional status
• Optimistic outlook
• Personality characteristics
• Previous experience with stressors
• Resilience
• Sleep status
External
• Cultural and ethnic influences
• Number of stressors already experiencing
• Religious or spiritual influences
• Socioeconomic status
• Social support
• Timing of stressors

Factors that affect a person's response to stress include internal and external influences (Table 6.1). These factors show the importance of using a holistic approach when assessing the impact of stress on a person. Key personal characteristics that buffer the effects of stress are attitude, hardiness, being optimistic, and resilience.

Resilience is being resourceful and flexible and having good problem-solving skills. People who have a high degree of resilience are not as likely to perceive an event as stressful.

Hardiness is a combination of 3 characteristics: commitment, control, and openness to change. Together they give the courage and motivation needed to turn stressful circumstances from potential calamities into opportunities for personal growth.[3]

Attitude can influence the effect of stress on a person. People with positive attitudes view situations differently from those with negative attitudes. A person's attitude also influences how he or she manages stress. To some extent, positive emotional attitudes can prevent disease and prolong life.[4]

PATHOPHYSIOLOGY MAP

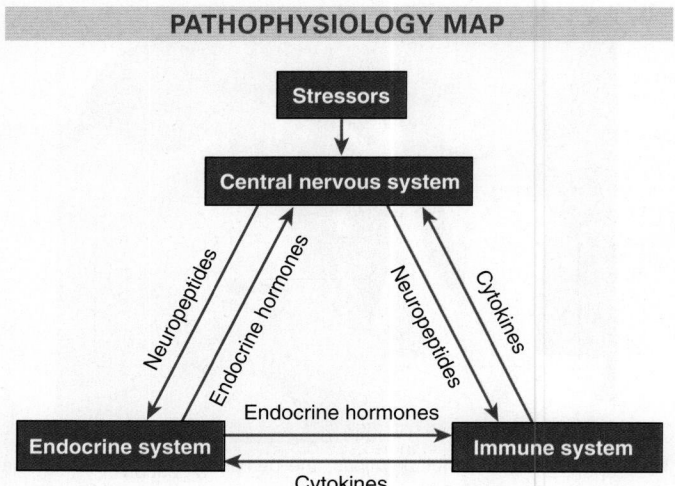

FIG. 6.3 Neurochemical links among the nervous, endocrine, and immune systems. The communication among the systems is bidirectional.

Being optimistic can help you cope more effectively with stress. Optimism also reduces a person's chances of developing stress-related illnesses. When optimistic people do become ill, they tend to recover more quickly. Pessimists are likely to deny the problem, distance themselves from the stressful event, focus on stressful feelings, or allow the stressor to interfere with achieving a goal. People with a more pessimistic attitude tend to report poorer health than people with optimistic attitudes.[4]

In addition to personal characteristics, external factors play a vital role in one's ability to cope with stress. Being surrounded by a strong social support system and receiving positive support from friends and family have a large impact on a person's ability to cope with stressors.

PHYSIOLOGIC RESPONSE TO STRESS

The nervous, endocrine, and immune systems are primarily involved in the stress response. These systems are interrelated, and that interrelationship is reflected in a person's physiologic response to stress (Fig. 6.3). Further, stress activation of these systems affects other body systems, such as the cardiovascular, respiratory, gastrointestinal, renal, and reproductive systems. A person's response to a stressor (real or imagined and physiologic or emotional/psychologic) determines the impact that stress will have on the body.

Nervous System
Cerebral Cortex. The areas of the cerebral cortex, or cerebrum, involved in the control of cognition, affect, and movement influence how we perceive stressors. We evaluate the stressor in light of past experiences and future consequences. This gives us some control over our response to stress. The motor areas also send signals to the adrenal medulla that directly relate to how stressors are managed.[5]
Limbic System. The *limbic system* lies in the inner midportion of the brain near the base of the brain. The limbic system is an important mediator of emotions and behavior. When the limbic system is stimulated, emotions, feelings, and behaviors can occur that ensure survival and self-preservation.
Reticular Formation. The *reticular formation* is located between the lower end of the brainstem and thalamus. It contains the *reticular activating system* (RAS), which sends impulses

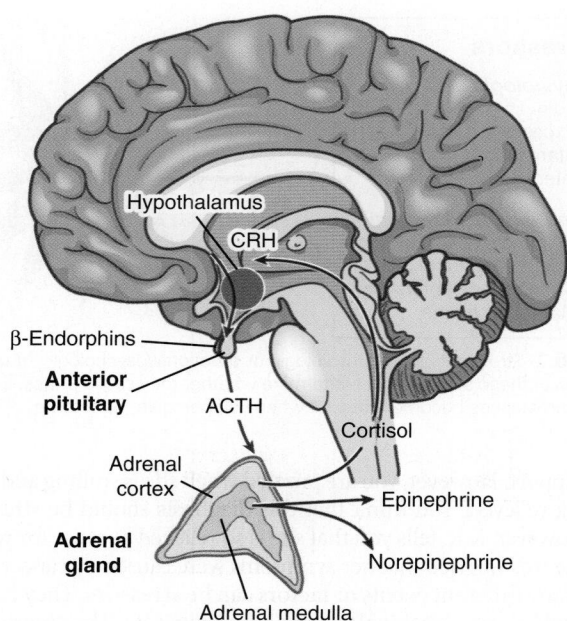

FIG. 6.4 Hypothalamic-pituitary-adrenal axis. *ACTH,* Adrenocorticotropic hormone; *CRH,* corticotropin-releasing hormone.

contributing to alertness to the limbic system and cerebral cortex. When the RAS is stimulated, it increases its output of impulses, leading to wakefulness. Stress usually increases the degree of wakefulness and can lead to sleep disturbances.
Hypothalamus. The hypothalamus, which lies at the base of the brain just above the pituitary gland, has many functions that aid in adaptation to stress. Stress activates the limbic system, which in turn stimulates the hypothalamus. Because the hypothalamus secretes neuropeptides that regulate the release of hormones by the anterior pituitary, it is central to the connection between the nervous and endocrine systems in responding to stress (Fig. 6.4).

The hypothalamus plays a primary role in the stress response by regulating the function of both the sympathetic and parasympathetic branches of the autonomic nervous system. When a person perceives a stressor, the hypothalamus sends signals that initiate both the nervous and endocrine responses to the stressor. It does this primarily by sending signals via nerve fibers to stimulate the sympathetic nervous system (SNS) and by releasing corticotropin-releasing hormone (CRH), which stimulates the pituitary to release adrenocorticotropic hormone (ACTH) (see Chapter 47).

Endocrine System
Once the hypothalamus is activated in response to stress, the endocrine system becomes involved. The SNS stimulates the adrenal medulla to release epinephrine and norepinephrine (catecholamines). The effect of catecholamines and the activation of the SNS, including the response of the adrenal medulla, is referred to as the *sympathoadrenal response.* Epinephrine and norepinephrine prepare the body for the *fight-or-flight response* (Fig. 6.5).

Stress activates the hypothalamic-pituitary-adrenal (HPA) axis. In response to stress, the hypothalamus releases CRH, which stimulates the anterior pituitary to release proopiomelanocortin (POMC). Both ACTH (a hormone) and β-endorphin (a neuropeptide) are derived from POMC.

PATHOPHYSIOLOGY MAP

FIG. 6.5 "Fight-or-flight" reaction. Alarm reaction responses resulting from increased sympathetic nervous system *(SNS)* activity.

Endorphins have analgesic-like effects and blunt pain perception during stress situations involving pain stimuli. ACTH in turn stimulates the adrenal cortex to synthesize and secrete corticosteroids (e.g., cortisol) and, to a lesser degree, aldosterone.

Corticosteroids are essential for the stress response. Cortisol produces several physiologic effects, such as increasing blood glucose levels, intensifying the action of catecholamines on blood vessels, and inhibiting the inflammatory response. Corticosteroids play an important role in "turning off" or blunting the stress response, which, if uncontrolled, can become self-destructive. This is shown by their ability to suppress the release of proinflammatory mediators, such as the cytokines tumor necrosis factor (TNF) and interleukin-1 (IL-1). The persistent release of such mediators is believed to initiate organ dysfunction in conditions such as sepsis or autoimmune disease. Thus corticosteroids act not only to support the body's adaptive response to a stressor but also to suppress an overzealous and potentially self-destructive response.

The stress response involves increases in (1) cardiac output (resulting from the increased heart rate and increased stroke volume), (2) blood glucose levels, (3) oxygen consumption, and (4) metabolic rate (Fig. 6.5). In addition, dilation of skeletal muscle blood vessels increases blood supply to the large muscles and supports quick movement. Increased cerebral blood flow increases mental alertness. For example, in the case of stressful situations (e.g., blood loss from trauma), the increased blood volume (from increased extracellular fluid and the shunting of blood away from the gastrointestinal system) helps to maintain adequate circulation to vital organs.

Summary of Stress Response

In summary, the fight-or-flight response is an important and necessary adaptive mechanism of the body to acute stress. We activate this response to stressors whether they are physiologic

(e.g., acute pain) or emotional/psychologic (e.g., death of a child, loss of a home through fire, fear).

Acute stress leads to physiologic changes that are important to a person's survival. This is your "alarm system." It puts you on high alert. The acute stress response is a state of physiologic and psychologic arousal characterized by increased SNS activity that leads to increased heart and respiratory rate, increased BP, increased muscle tension, increased brain activity, and decreased skin temperature.

Immune System

Stress has an impact on the immune system. **Psychoneuroimmunology (PNI)** is an interdisciplinary science that studies the interactions among psychologic, neurologic, and immune responses. Because neuroanatomic and neuroendocrine pathways connect the brain to the immune system, stressors have the potential to lead to changes in immune function (Fig. 6.6).

Nerve fibers extend from the nervous system and synapse on cells and tissues of the immune system (i.e., spleen, lymph nodes). In turn, the cells of the immune system have receptors for many neuropeptides and hormones. This allows them to respond to nervous and neuroendocrine signals. As a result, the mediation of stress by the central nervous system leads to corresponding changes in immune cell activity.

Both acute and chronic stress can cause immunosuppression. Stress affects immune function by (1) decreasing the number and function of natural killer cells; (2) decreasing lymphocyte proliferation; (3) altering production of *cytokines* (soluble factors secreted by white blood cells and other cells, e.g., interferon, interleukins); and (4) decreasing phagocytosis by neutrophils and monocytes. This stress-induced immunosuppression may worsen or increase the risk for progression of immune-related diseases such as multiple sclerosis, asthma, rheumatoid arthritis, and cancer.[6] Natural killer cells, lymphocytes, and cytokines are discussed in Chapter 13.

PATHOPHYSIOLOGY MAP

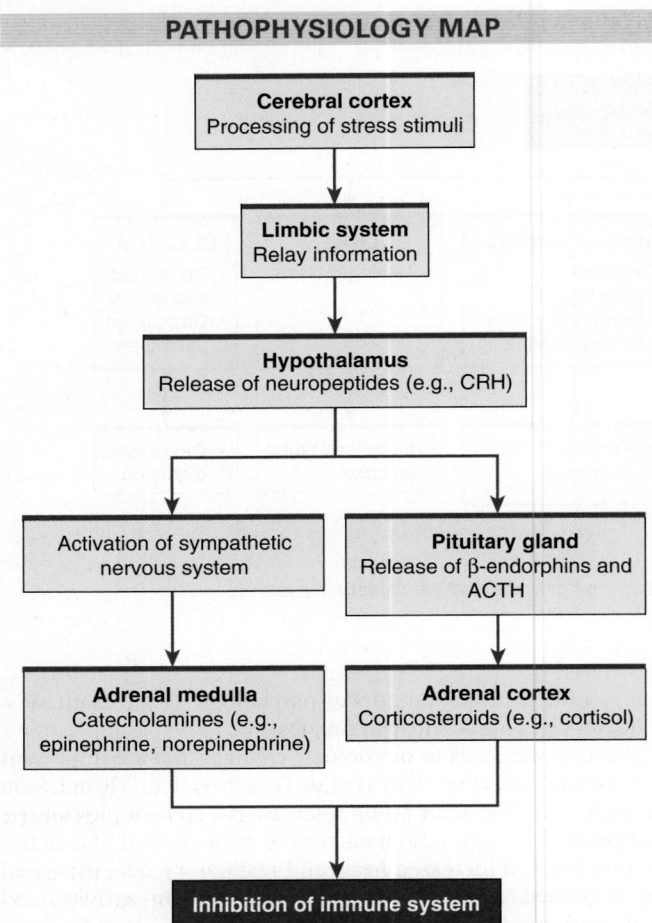

FIG. 6.6 The cerebral cortex processes stressful stimuli and relays the information via the limbic system to the hypothalamus. Corticotropin-releasing hormone *(CRH)* stimulates the release of adrenocorticotropic hormone *(ACTH)* from the pituitary gland. ACTH stimulates the adrenal cortex to release corticosteroids. Sympathetic nervous system stimulation results in the release of epinephrine and norepinephrine from the adrenal medulla. The result is the inhibition of the immune system.

Importantly, the network that links the brain and immune system is bidirectional (Fig. 6.3). Signals from these systems travel back and forth, allowing for communication among these systems. Consequently, not only do emotions influence the immune response, but products of immune cells send signals back to the brain and alter its activity. Many of the communication signals sent from the immune system to the brain are mediated by cytokines, which are central to the coordination of the immune response. For example, IL-1 (a cytokine made by monocytes) acts on the temperature regulatory center of the hypothalamus and initiates the febrile response to infectious pathogens (see Fig. 11.4).

Many questions about stress and the immune response are unanswered. For example, it is not known how much stress (intensity or chronicity) is needed to cause changes or how much of a change in the immune system is necessary before disease susceptibility occurs.

MIND-BODY-SPIRIT CONNECTION

The **mind-body-spirit connection** shows the relationship and interconnectedness among the parts that make up a person:

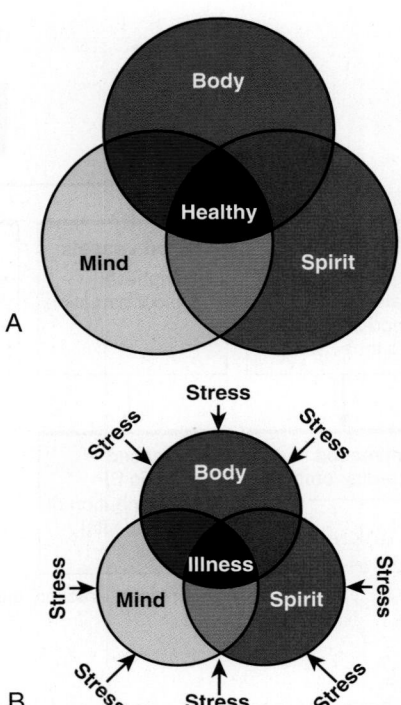

FIG. 6.7 The connections among the mind, body, and spirit can lead to a person being healthy (**A**) or the effects of stress on the mind, body, and spirit connections can lead to illness (**B**).

mind, body, and spirit (Fig. 6.7). All 3 parts are important in your life and in determining who you are. What goes on in your mind influences every part of the body. Your mind is 1 of the most powerful weapons you have to deal with and conquer stress. You have a choice in how you respond to a crisis or a difficult time. Even if the outcome of the situation is not what a person desired, one can emerge with a winning attitude.

How you deal with difficult situations or stressful times greatly influences your overall well-being: your mind, body, and spirit. When your mind is healthy, your body can resist illness better. When your body is healthy, your feelings are more positive. Your spirit is renewed and energized.

As a nurse, stress can have a significant effect on you. A primary source of stress for a nurse can be the work environment, which includes extreme physical demands and the potential for violence.[7] The mind-body-spirit connection also influences your ability to provide nursing care. Your ability to maintain the mind-body-spirit balance is important in providing proper care to your patients and in maintaining a healthy and meaningful life for yourself.

EFFECTS OF STRESS ON HEALTH

As previously mentioned, the acute stress response is your alarm system and puts you on alert. However, your body was not meant to be on high alert all the time. If stress is excessive or prolonged, these same "helpful" physiologic responses can lead to harm and disease. When a person sustains chronic, unrelieved stress, the body's defenses can no longer keep up with the demands. Therefore stress plays a role in the development and/or progression of diseases of adaptation, or stress-related illnesses (Table 6.2).

TABLE 6.2 Common Disorders With a Stress Component

- Depression
- Dyspepsia
- Eating disorders
- Erectile dysfunction
- Fatigue
- Fibromyalgia
- Headaches
- Hypertension
- Insomnia
- Irritable bowel syndrome
- Low back pain
- Menstrual irregularities
- Peptic ulcer disease
- Sexual dysfunction

Stress is linked to leading causes of death, including cancer, accidents, and suicides. Stress can have effects on cognitive function, including poor concentration, memory problems, distressing dreams, sleep disturbances, and impaired decision making. It can also cause a wide variety of changes in behavior. These include people withdrawing from others, becoming quiet or unusually talkative, changing eating habits, drinking alcohol excessively, or becoming irritable.[8] Long-term exposure to catecholamines resulting from excessive SNS activation may increase the risk for cardiovascular diseases such as atherosclerosis and hypertension.[9] Other conditions that are precipitated or worsened by stress include migraine headaches, irritable bowel syndrome, and peptic ulcers.[10] Stress affects the control of metabolic conditions, such as diabetes mellitus. Behavioral interventions aimed at stress reduction and relaxation have helped manage these diseases in conjunction with standard medical therapy.[11]

Stressful life events can make a person more susceptible to infection. For example, psychologic stress may increase one's risk for developing the common cold. In a landmark study, researchers intranasally inoculated healthy people with low doses of upper respiratory tract viruses. The people underwent psychologic testing to measure the occurrence of stressful events in their lives and their reactions to such stresses. The results showed that the rates of both viral infection and clinical colds increased with the degree of psychologic stress. In this study, social support buffered the harmful effects of stress.[12]

At the cellular level, stress may promote earlier onset of age-related diseases. There is a link between stress and telomere length. Telomeres are the protective end caps on chromosomes. Their diminishing size is a sign of age. Telomeres are highly susceptible to stress and depression. Telomeres are shorter in people who are stressed and depressed than in healthy people. Thus chronic stress can have a long-term effect on our overall health by changing our DNA and accelerating the rate at which our cells age.[13]

COPING STRATEGIES

Coping is a person's efforts to manage stressors.[14] *Coping strategies* are what you do (your behaviors and actions) to help deal with stress. Coping can be either positive or negative. Positive coping includes activities such as exercise and spending time with friends and family. Healthy coping helps you handle your stressors so that they do not overwhelm you. Negative coping may include substance use and denial.

Unfortunately, some coping strategies make the stress worse. Sometimes coping strategies temporarily relieve the stress, but in the long run they increase the stress. For example, you may really enjoy watching a favorite TV show as a form of coping. However, if you become fixated on several reality shows, then TV becomes an addiction and an escape from dealing with your real stressors.

> You cannot always choose your destiny in life, but you can choose how you cope with it.
>
> **Norman Vincent Peale**

We can use a number of coping strategies to cope with stress. Table 6.3 has examples of coping strategies that you can use in your life and teach to your patients and caregivers. Coping strategies can be divided into 2 broad categories: emotion-focused coping and problem-focused coping. Emotion-focused coping involves managing the emotions that a person feels when a stressful event occurs. When a situation is unchangeable or uncontrollable, emotion-focused coping may predominate. The primary purpose of emotion-focused coping is to help decrease negative emotions and create a feeling of well-being. Examples include discussing feelings with a friend or taking a hot bath.

Problem-focused coping involves attempts to resolve the problems causing the stress. If you can change or control a problem, this strategy is the most helpful. Problem-focused coping strategies allow a person to look at a challenge objectively, act to address the problem, and thereby reduce the stress. Setting priorities, collecting information, and seeking advice are examples of problem-focused coping.

We often use a combination of strategies to cope with the same stressor. Table 6.4 gives examples of emotion- and problem-focused coping when applied to the same stressful situation.

RELAXATION STRATEGIES

The *relaxation response* is a state of physiologic and psychologic rest. It is opposite of the stress response. The relaxation response is characterized by decreased SNS activity, which leads to decreased heart and respiratory rate, decreased BP, decreased muscle tension, decreased brain activity, and increased skin temperature.

We can use a variety of relaxation strategies to elicit the relaxation response (Table 6.5). Regular elicitation of the relaxation response is an effective treatment for a wide range of stress-related disorders, including chronic pain, insomnia, and hypertension. People who regularly engage in relaxation strategies better cope with their stressors, increase their sense of control over stressors, and reduce their tension.[15]

Relaxation Breathing

The way one breathes affects every aspect of one's life. When a person is stressed, muscles tense and breathing becomes shallow

TABLE 6.3 Coping Strategies

Strategy	Description	How to Implement
Aromatherapy	• Use of essential oils (fragrant molecules from plants) for inhalation or topical application • Variety of essential oils, including lavender, peppermint, rosemary, eucalyptus, sandalwood, etc.	• Place 5–8 drops in a full bath and agitate water before bathing. • Place a few drops on a tissue or in diffuser or vaporizer.
Art therapy	• Allows a person to nonverbally express and communicate feelings, emotions, and thoughts • Can reduce stress, promote relaxation, and help process experiences • Based on the belief that the creative process is healing and life enhancing	• Close your eyes and draw a line on a piece of paper. Open your eyes. Continue to build on that line and draw whatever comes to mind. • Get a piece of paper and doodle. Do not edit. • Get a coloring book and crayons and just start coloring. • Walk, swim, garden, bicycle, dance, climb stairs, take part in group exercises.
Exercise	• Any form of movement, especially aerobic movement • Can be viewed as meditation in motion	

Strategy	Description	How to Implement
Humor	• Can take the form of laughter, cartoons, funny movies, videos, riddles, comic books, and joke books	• Keep a "tickler" scrapbook with funny photos, cartoons, etc. • Humor carts can be set up in many clinical settings for patient and family use.
Journaling	• Allows a person to express self in writing • Enhances personal development and awareness through self-reflection	• Use a journaling notebook or computer to write down thoughts, feelings, memories, and perceptions.
Pet therapy (animal-assisted therapy) (Fig. 6.8)	• Use of animals as a form of treatment • Improves a patient's social, emotional, or cognitive functioning	• Pet therapist or family member or friend brings a pet with which patient can socialize.
Social support	• Relationships with family and friends • Self-help groups and professional help	• Get together with family and friends on a regular basis. • Join a support group that specifically helps to meet needs (e.g., grief support group).

COMPLEMENTARY & ALTERNATIVE THERAPIES

Yoga

Yoga is an ancient system of relaxation, exercise, and healing with origins in Indian philosophy. The goal of yoga is physical and mental well-being achieved using stretching, postures, breathing practices, and meditation.

Scientific Evidence

Yoga can be used to treat hypertension and reduce stress and anxiety in cancer patients.[16]

Nursing Implications

• Deep abdominal relaxation breathing is a main component of all types of yoga. It helps one to focus on the inner self and promote the relaxation response.
• Yoga is used to promote relaxation, decrease stress, improve flexibility, and enhance overall health.
• Yoga is considered safe. Patients with certain medical conditions or illnesses should avoid some postures.

TABLE 6.4 Problem- and Emotion-Focused Coping

Stressor	Problem-Focused Coping	Emotion-Focused Coping
Failing an examination	Obtaining a tutor	Going for a run
Being diagnosed with diabetes	Attending education classes about diabetes	Getting a massage
Receiving questionable mammogram results	Scheduling follow-up testing for ultrasound	Expressing feelings of anxiety to friends and nurse

TABLE 6.5 Common Relaxation Strategies

• Biofeedback
• Imagery
• Massage
• Meditation
• Muscle relaxation
• Music
• Qigong
• Relaxing breathing
• Tai Chi
• Yoga

and rapid. Therefore 1 of the simplest and most effective ways to stop the stress response is to breathe deeply and slowly. It is hard to stay tense when breathing in a slow, deep, and relaxed pattern. Relaxation breathing forms the basis for most relaxation strategies. It is especially useful during a stressful or anxious situation to reduce stress. You can do relaxation breathing while sitting, standing, or lying down. It is natural for newborns and sleeping adults.

FIG. 6.8 Pet therapy can be used in a variety of settings including rehabilitation. (© RonChappleStudios/Hemera/Thinkstock.)

Before practicing relaxation breathing, it is important to assess one's normal breathing pattern (Table 6.6). Chest breathing, which involves the upper chest and shoulders, is inefficient. We often use it during times of anxiety and distress.

Relaxation breathing is a more efficient type of breathing. It involves the primary use of the diaphragm and less use of the upper chest and shoulders to help in each breath. In this type of breathing, the abdomen gently moves in and out during exhalation and inhalation. The breaths should be slow, steady, and deep.

One basic technique for relaxation breathing is as follows: (1) Inhale slowly and deeply, pushing the abdomen out. Think about breathing in peace. (2) Exhale slowly, letting the abdomen come in and all the muscles relax. Think about breathing out tension. (3) Repeat these deep breaths 10 times without interruption. As with any breathing exercise, if a light-headed feeling arises, stop for 30 seconds, and then start again.

Other methods used to teach relaxation breathing are the 4 × 4 technique and relaxation sigh. Breathing techniques are discussed in the Stress-Busting Kit for Nursing Students available on the website for this book.

Initially, relaxation breathing may feel unusual. With practice it becomes easier, and its relaxing benefits are soon obvious. You should personally learn to use relaxation breathing before teaching it to patients and their caregivers. Once learned, you can easily teach relaxation breathing to patients in a variety of settings, particularly when they are undergoing stressful and painful procedures.

Biofeedback

Biofeedback helps a person become more aware of involuntary body responses such as breathing, heart rate, and muscle activity. Electrodes attached to the skin or, in some cases, hand-held sensors measure these processes and display them on a monitor. This feedback allows the person to learn to control their responses. This gives a person the power to use thoughts to control the body, often to improve a health condition or physical performance.[15]

TABLE 6.6 Relaxation Breathing Techniques

Breathing Assessment

1. Begin by placing 1 hand gently on your abdomen below your waistline.
2. Place the other hand on the center of your chest on the sternum.
3. Without changing the normal breathing pattern, take several breaths. During inhalation notice which hand rises the most.
4. When relaxation breathing is done properly, the hand on the abdomen should rise more than the hand on the chest.

4 × 4 Technique

1. Sit up straight with your back flush to the support of the chair and your feet flat on the floor.
2. Rest your arms on your lap, thighs, or arms of the chair.
3. Take in a deep breath through your nose to a count of 4 (1 ... 2 ... 3 ... 4).
4. Hold your breath to a count of 4 (1 ... 2 ... 3 ... 4).
5. Release your breath through your mouth to a count of 4 (1 ... 2 ... 3 ... 4).
6. Rest for a count of 4 (1 ... 2 ... 3 ... 4).
7. Repeat the cycle 4 times.

Relaxing Sigh

1. Sit up straight with your back against the support of the chair and your feet flat on floor.
2. Inhale a natural breath and then sigh deeply. Let out a sound of relief as the air rushes out of your lungs.
3. Do not think about inhaling at the end of the sigh; just let the air come in naturally as you breathe deeply.
4. Repeat this sigh about 4 to 6 times very slowly.
5. You can repeat this exercise whenever you need it.

Meditation

Meditation is a practice of concentrated focus on a sound, object, visualization, the breath, or movement. The purpose of meditation is to increase awareness, reduce stress, promote relaxation, and enhance personal and spiritual growth.

It is best to practice meditation in a quiet place, free of distractions. Table 6.7 gives some basic guidelines on how to meditate. Meditation is often practiced while seated, and it is important to maintain a comfortable posture. Meditation can be done while walking and focusing on a single action such as the movement of the feet. In the beginning, you typically start with just 5 to 10 minutes of meditation at a time. Increase the time as the practice becomes more comfortable. Meditation exercises are available in the Stress-Busting Kit for Nursing Students on the website for this book.

Imagery

Imagery is the use of one's mind to generate images that have a calming effect on the body. It involves focusing the mind and incorporates all the senses to create physiologic and emotional changes. It is a simple relaxation technique that needs no equipment other than an active imagination. *Guided imagery* is a variation of imagery in which another person (either live or through technology) suggests the images to you.

You can use imagery in your own life or use guided imagery with your patients. One of the uses of imagery is to create a special place for a mental retreat. Table 6.8 describes the steps involved in creating a special place. More imagery exercises are available in the Stress-Busting Kit for Nursing Students on the website for this book.

TABLE 6.7 Guide to Meditation

You can teach yourself the basics of meditation by following a few simple steps:

1. Find a quiet place.
2. Make sure there are no distractions.
3. Sit in a comfortable position.
4. Close your eyes.
5. Shut out the world so that your brain can stop processing information coming from your senses.
6. Pick a focus word, short phrase, song verse (melody), or prayer that is firmly rooted in your belief system, such as *one, peace, The Lord is my shepherd, Hail Mary full of grace,* or *shalom.*
7. Breathe slowly and practice relaxation breathing. Say your focus word, short phrase, song verse, or prayer silently to yourself as you exhale.
8. Say the word or phrase again and again.
9. Try saying the word or phrase silently to yourself with every exhalation. The monotony will help you focus.
10. Relax your muscles, progressing from your feet to your calves, thighs, abdomen, shoulders, head, and neck.
11. Do not be concerned when other thoughts come to mind. Just acknowledge them and return calmly to your word or phrase.
12. Continue for 10 to 20 minutes, but even 5 minutes can leave you feeling calm and refreshed. Rise slowly.
13. Practice once or twice daily.

TABLE 6.8 Imagery

Creating Your Special Place

1. Begin by closing your eyes and taking several slow, deep breaths.
2. Imagine a place where you feel completely comfortable and peaceful. It may be a real place or 1 you imagine: 1 from your past or a place you have always wanted to go.
3. Allow this special place to take form, slowly. As it takes form, look around to your left, to your right. Enjoy the scenery: the colors, the texture, the shapes.
4. Listen carefully to the sounds of your place. What do you hear?
5. Is there a gentle breeze or sunshine warming your face? Pick up or touch some favorite objects from your special place.
6. Take in a deep breath through your nose and notice the rich smells around you. Perhaps your favorite flower is in bloom, or you smell the scents of the ocean.
7. Take another deep breath and relax. Enjoy the peace, comfort, and safety of your special place.
8. This is your special place. You relax and feel thankful that you are here, in your special place.
9. You can return to this place any time that you wish.

It is best to perform imagery in a comfortable position. Take slow, deep breaths. Focus should involve all senses (sight, hearing, touch, smell). For example, you can use an image, such as Fig. 6.9, engaging all the senses as you focus on the image.

Imagery can be used in many clinical settings for stress reduction and pain relief. Benefits of imagery include anxiety reduction, decreased muscle tension, improved comfort during medical procedures, enhanced immune function, decreased recovery time after surgery, and reduction in sleeping problems. It can specifically target a disease, problem, or stressor. Table 6.9 describes some suggestions for using imagery in specific diseases or disorders.

A person can use imagery to enhance performance or process stressful or difficult tasks. For example, an athlete or musician can use imagery to achieve greater success. Imagery allows one to mentally rehearse the difficult or challenging situation.

FIG. 6.9 In imagery, special places are created involving all the senses, such as a place where one can hear rustling water, smell flowers, feel the wind, and see a colorful landscape. (© iStockphoto/Thinkstock.)

TABLE 6.9 Examples of Imagery

Imagery can be used to relieve stress and promote health and healing in conjunction with regular medical care. Special images can be created to ease symptoms or treat diseases or disorders. The image should be strong and vivid for the person, using many senses to create the image. Below are some examples that some people have found useful.

Disease or Disorder	Images
Asthma	• Tiny elastic rubber bands that constrict the airways pop open
Cancer	• Shark gobbles up cancer cells • Radiation or chemotherapy treatments enter the body like healing rays of light; they destroy cancer cells
Coronary artery disease	• Water flows freely through a wide, open river
Depression	• Attach troubles and feelings of sadness to big colorful helium balloons that float off into a clear blue sky
Infection	• White blood cells with flashing red sirens arrest and imprison harmful germs
Pain	• Wash away pain by a cool calm river flowing through the entire body
Weakened immune system	• White blood cells rapidly multiply like millions of seeds bursting from a ripe seed pod

Adapted from Sobel DS, Ornstein R: *Healthy mind, healthy body,* New York, 1996, Patient Education Materials, Time Life.

Imagery can help a fearful nurse start an IV line or perform a difficult procedure. It can be used with a patient who is afraid to have a stressful or painful procedure (e.g., bone marrow biopsy).

Massage

Massage includes a range of techniques that manipulate the soft tissues and joints of the body. Involving touch and movement, massage is typically delivered with the hands. It reduces muscle tension and positively affects mental and emotional states.

Massage is an important form of touch. It is a form of caring, communication, and comfort. Your role related to massage differs from that of the registered massage therapist. A massage therapist can provide more comprehensive massage therapies. As a nurse, you can use specific massage techniques as part of nursing care. For example, you can give a back massage to help promote sleep. For a bedridden patient, gentle massage can stimulate circulation and help prevent skin breakdown. A simple hand massage can have a calming and relaxing effect, especially for patients who are anxious or agitated. During end-of-life care, hospice nurses may include massage into their nursing care as the massaging touch can lessen pain and restlessness.

When you identify that massage may be useful, first assess the patient's preference about touch and massage. Consider cultural and social beliefs and discuss potential benefits with the patient. You can teach family members to massage their loved one, giving a way for family members to take part in patient care. This can be therapeutic for the patient and family, even when the loved one is cognitively impaired or unresponsive.

Music

Music can help achieve relaxation and bring about healthy changes in emotional or physical states. Listening to relaxing music can divert one's focus from a stressful situation.

Music can be used in many clinical settings. It is noninvasive, safe, inexpensive, and easy to use. Music decreases anxiety and elicits the relaxation response. Music helps people with insomnia go to sleep. It can decrease muscle tension, pain sensation, and emotional stress.[17]

Each person considers different types of music to be relaxing. Music that has 60 to 80 beats/min is considered soothing. Many find low-pitched tones and music without words best for relaxation. Mozart's music is popular for relaxation. On the other hand, fast-tempo music can stimulate and uplift a person. Assess each patient's interest and preference in music, and find music that best matches the person's needs and circumstance. Create a listening environment by helping the patient find a comfortable position and minimizing interruptions. Evaluate patients' responses to the music, asking them how it sounds and how it makes them feel.

Prayer

Prayer can be a form of meditation. It is a spiritual communion with God or an object of worship. Many people find deep comfort in their faith. Religious services, conversations with clergy, and personal worship and prayer may help to ease a person's stress and give 1 greater perspective, strength, and inspiration.

❖ NURSING MANAGEMENT: STRESS

◆ Nursing Assessment

Patients and caregivers face many potential stressors that can have health consequences. As a nurse, you are in a key position to (1) assess stress in patients and their caregivers, (2) help them identify high-risk periods for stress, and (3) implement stress management strategies that can prevent the negative consequences of stress on their health (Fig. 6.10).

The first step in managing stress is to become aware of its presence. This includes identifying what the stressors are and the person's response to them. Be aware of situations that are likely to result in stress. Assess the number of stressors, duration of these stressors, and prior experience with similar demands.

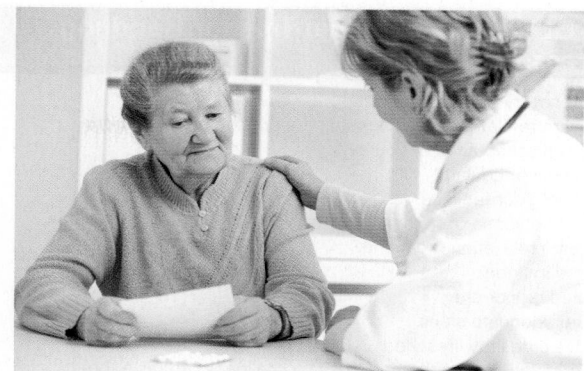

FIG. 6.10 As a nurse, you have a key role in helping patients deal with stress. (© AlexRaths/iStock/Thinkstock.)

Assess the personal meaning attached to the stressful situation to provide useful insight for planning stress management strategies with the patient.

Be specific with your questions: Have you experienced this stressor before? How did you handle it? What worked well and what did not? Although the manifestations of stress may vary from person to person, assess the patient for the signs and symptoms of the stress response, including an increased heart rate and BP, hyperventilation, sweating, headache, musculoskeletal pain, gastrointestinal upset, loss of appetite, insomnia, and fatigue. In addition, the patient may show stress-related illness (Table 6.2).

Behavioral manifestations of stress may include an inability to concentrate, accident proneness, impaired speech, anxiety, crying, frustration, and irritability. Work-related responses to stress may include absenteeism or tardiness at work, decreased productivity, and job dissatisfaction. Cognitive responses include self-reports about the inability to make decisions and forgetfulness. Some of these responses may be apparent to significant others.

Consider the caregivers' responses to the stressors. A patient's illness often causes stress for the caregiver and other family members. Assess what aspects of the illness are the most stressful for the patient and caregiver. These may include the patient's physical health, job responsibilities, finances, and children. This information is valuable because it helps you to understand the patient's perspective of the stressors. Knowledge of stressors, the feelings these stressors evoke, and the psychologic effects they can produce will help you recognize potential and actual sources of stress and their effect on the patient.

Nursing Implementation

Your role is to facilitate and enhance the patient's coping and adaptation. Nursing interventions depend on the severity of the stress experience. For example, a patient with multiple trauma expends energy to physically survive. As a nurse, you direct efforts toward life-supporting interventions and approaches aimed at reducing added stressors for the patient. The patient is much less likely to adapt or recover if faced with more stressors, such as sleep deprivation or an infection. You can assume a primary role in implementing stress management strategies. Some personal tips for handling stress are shown in Table 6.10. These tips will help you personally and enhance your own level of health and wellness. It is essential that you first care for yourself before you can help the patients who need your care.

TABLE 6.10 Personal Tips for Handling Stress

- Do not try to be superhuman.
- Learn to "let go" of things that are outside of your control.
- Learn acceptance of yourself.
- Exercise regularly.
- Share your feelings.
- Keep a sense of humor; laugh often.
- Learn relaxation breathing.
- Use imagery.
- Meditate or pray.
- Get adequate sleep.
- Live a healthy lifestyle.
- Try to look at change as a positive challenge, not as a threat.
- Solve the little problems, since this can help you gain a feeling of control.
- Work to resolve conflicts with other people.
- If needed, get professional counseling.

TABLE 6.11 How to Implement Stress Management in Practice

1. Learn relaxation breathing. It is the easiest method of relaxation to use.
2. Practice teaching relaxation breathing with peers, then patients.
3. Pick coping strategies (Table 6.4) and relaxation strategies that are appropriate for your clinical area.
4. Practice using the strategy yourself. It becomes easier with time.
5. Take advantage of opportunities to teach coping and relaxation strategies to patients.
6. If you have setbacks, think about what went wrong. Do NOT quit!
7. Attend seminars and workshops on stress management to learn more.

Many professional organizations, such as the American Nurses Association, offer resources to help you manage stress (*www. nursingworld.org*). Once you included these strategies into your life, you can share them with patients and caregivers.

Ideas for how to include stress management strategies into nursing practice are described in Table 6.11. Although some require additional training, many stress management strategies are within the scope of nursing practice. These include relaxation breathing, imagery, music, exercise, massage, meditation, art therapy, and journaling. More resources are in the Stress-Busting Kit for Nursing Students on the website for this book.

Coping strategies used should be helpful and not a source of added stress for the patient. You can teach most coping and relaxation strategies to patients in 10 to 15 minutes. Choose a coping or relaxation strategy to best suit the patient and situation. Effective stress management provides a sense of control of the stressful situation. As stress management practices become part of daily activities, the person can increase his or her confidence and self-reliance and limit the emotional response to the stressful circumstances. Having a sense of control can prevent the harmful effects of a stress response.

As a nurse, you are in an ideal situation to integrate stress management in clinical practice. You are well equipped to develop and test the effectiveness of new ways to manage stress and promote positive health outcomes. However, it is very important to recognize when you need to refer the patient or caregiver to a professional with advanced training in counseling.

CASE STUDY

Stress-Induced Illness

Patient Profile

K.F., a 48-yr-old woman, recently moved to the United States from Romania with her 2 teenage children. She has no family in the country and was recently divorced. She has taken a job as a waitress in a hectic restaurant and works as a seamstress out of her home in the evenings.

(© JackF/ iStock/ Thinkstock.)

She has developed some unusual symptoms and comes to see the nurse practitioner at a community clinic. Although she says that she was in good health when she left Romania, she now presents with fatigue, inability to sleep, and aches all over her body. Even when she gets some extra sleep, she still feels exhausted. Her co-worker told her she has fibromyalgia.

Discussion Questions

1. Consider K.F.'s situation and describe the stressors with which she is dealing. Describe the possible effects of these stressors on her health.
2. *Priority Decision:* What are the priority coping strategies that you should include in K.F.'s plan of care?
3. What limitations should you consider when discussing specific coping strategies?
4. *Patient-Centered Care:* What cultural considerations should you include in the plan of care?

Answers available at *http://evolve.elsevier.com/Lewis/medsurg.*

BRIDGE TO NCLEX EXAMINATION

The number of the question corresponds to the same-numbered outcome at the beginning of the chapter.

1. Determination of whether an event is a stressor is based on a person's
   a. tolerance.
   b. perception.
   c. adaptation.
   d. stubbornness.

2. The nurse would expect which finding in a patient because of the physiologic effect of stress on the reticular formation?
   a. An episode of diarrhea while awaiting painful dressing changes
   b. Refusal to communicate with nurses while awaiting a cardiac catheterization
   c. Inability to sleep the night before beginning to self-administer insulin injections
   d. Increased blood pressure, decreased urine output, and hyperglycemia after a car accident

3. The nurse uses knowledge of the effects of stress on the immune system by encouraging patients to
   a. sleep for 10 to 12 hours per day.
   b. avoid exposure to upper respiratory tract infections.
   c. receive regular immunizations when they are stressed.
   d. use emotion-focused rather than problem-focused coping strategies.

4. The nurse recognizes that a person who has chronic stress could be at higher risk for *(select all that apply)*
   a. osteoporosis.
   b. fibromyalgia.
   c. colds and flu.
   d. high blood pressure.
   e. high serum cholesterol.

5. The nurse recognizes that a patient with newly diagnosed breast cancer is using an emotion-focused coping process when she
   a. joins a support group for women with breast cancer.
   b. considers the pros and cons of the various treatment options.
   c. delays treatment until her family can take a weekend trip together.
   d. tells the nurse that she has a good prognosis because the tumor is small.

6. During a stressful circumstance that is unchangeable, which type of coping strategy is the *most* effective?
   a. Avoidance
   b. Coping flexibility
   c. Emotion-focused coping
   d. Problem-focused coping

7. An appropriate nursing intervention for a hospitalized patient who says she cannot cope with her illness is
   a. controlling the environment to prevent sensory overload and promote sleep.
   b. encouraging the patient's family to offer emotional support by frequent visiting.
   c. arranging for the patient to phone family and friends to maintain emotional bonds.
   d. asking the patient to describe previous stressful situations and how she managed to resolve them.

1. b, 2. c, 3. b, 4. b, c, d, 5. a, 6. c, 7. d.

For rationales to these answers and even more NCLEX review questions, visit *http://evolve.elsevier.com/Lewis/medsurg.*

ⓔ EVOLVE WEBSITE/RESOURCES LIST

http://evolve.elsevier.com/Lewis/medsurg
Review Questions (Online Only)
Key Points
Answer Keys for Questions
- Rationales for Bridge to NCLEX Examination Questions
Answer Guidelines for Case Study on p. 86
Conceptual Care Map Creator
Stress-Busting Kit for Nursing Students
Audio Glossary
Content Updates

REFERENCES

1. Seward BL: *Managing stress: Principles and strategies for health and well-being,* 9th ed, Burlington, MA, 2017, Jones & Bartlett.
2. The Physiological Society: Stress in modern Britain: Making sense of stress, our 2017 theme. Retrieved from *www.physoc.org/sites/default/files/press-release/4042-stress-modern-britain.pdf.*
*3. Maddi SR: Hardiness: The courage to grow from stresses, J Pos Psych, 1:160, 2006. (Classic)
4. Mayo Clinic: Positive thinking. Retrieved from *www.mayoclinic.org/healthy-living/stress-management/in-depth/positive-thinking/art-20043950.*
*5. Dum RP, Levinthal DJ, Strick PL: Motor, cognitive, and affective areas of the cerebral cortex influence the adrenal medulla, *PNAS* 113:9922, 2016.
6. American Institute of Stress: Effects of stress. Retrieved from *www.stress.org.*
7. Yoder L: Nursing: The balance of mind, body, and spirit, *MEDSURG Nursing* 26:75, 2017.
8. Bergland C: Chronic stress can damage brain structure and connectivity. Retrieved from *www.psychologytoday.com/blog/the-athletes-way/201402/chronic-stress-can-damage-brain-structure-and-connectivity.*
9. American Heart Association: Stress and heart health. Retrieved from *www.heart.org/HEARTORG/Conditions/More/MyHeartandStrokeNews/Stress-and-Heart-Health_UCM_437370_Article.jsp.*
10. U.S. Department of Health and Human Services: Stress and migraines. Retrieved from *www.womenshealth.gov/publications/our-publications/fact-sheet/migraine.html.*
11. National Institutes of Health: Feeling stressed? Stress relief might help your health. Retrieved from *http://newsinhealth.nih.gov/issue/Dec2014/Feature1.*
*12. Cohen S, Tyrrell DA, Smith AP: Psychological stress and susceptibility to the common cold, *N Engl J Med* 325:606, 1991. (Classic)
13. American Psychological Association: Stress in America: Our health at risk. Retrieved from *www.apa.org/news/press/releases/stress.*
14. Lazarus R, Folkman S: Stress, appraisal, and coping, New York, 1984, Springer. (Classic)
15. National Center for Complementary and Integrative Health: Relaxation techniques for health. Retrieved from *https://nccih.nih.gov/health/stress/relaxation.htm.*
16. Mayo Clinic: Alternative cancer treatments. Retrieved from *www.mayoclinic.org/diseases-conditions/cancer/in-depth/cancer-treatment/art-20047246.*
*17. Collingwood J: The power of music to reduce stress. Retrieved from *http://psychcentral.com/lib/the-power-of-music-to-reduce-stress/000930.*

*Evidence-based information for clinical practice.

7

Sleep and Sleep Disorders

Diana Taibi Buchanan

I slept and dreamt that life was joy. I awoke and saw that life was service. I acted and behold, service was joy.

Rabindranath Tagore

http://evolve.elsevier.com/Lewis/medsurg/

CONCEPTUAL FOCUS

Functional Ability
Mood and Affect

Sleep

LEARNING OUTCOMES

1. Define sleep.
2. Describe the stages of sleep.
3. Explain the relationship of various diseases/disorders and sleep disorders.
4. Describe the etiology, clinical manifestations, and interprofessional and nursing management of insomnia.

5. Describe the etiology, clinical manifestations, and interprofessional and nursing management of obstructive sleep apnea.
6. Describe clinical manifestations and interprofessional management of narcolepsy, parasomnias, and circadian rhythm disorders.
7. Select strategies for managing sleep problems associated with shift work sleep disorder.

KEY TERMS

circadian rhythms, p. 89
continuous positive airway pressure (CPAP), p. 96
insomnia, p. 91
jet lag disorder, p. 97
narcolepsy, p. 98

obstructive sleep apnea (OSA), p. 95
parasomnias, p. 98
periodic limb movement disorder (PLMD), p. 97
shift work sleep disorder, p. 99
sleep, p. 88

sleep-disordered breathing (SDB), p. 95
sleep disorders, p. 88
sleep disturbance, p. 88
sleep hygiene, p. 92
wake behavior, p. 89

SLEEP

Sleep is a state in which a person lacks conscious awareness of environmental surroundings but can be easily aroused. Sleep is distinct from unconscious states such as coma, in which the person cannot be aroused. Sleep is a basic, dynamic, highly organized, and complex behavior that is essential for healthy functioning and survival. Over a life span of 80 years, a person who sleeps 7 hours each night will spend around 24 years sleeping. Sleep influences mood, behavior, and physical functioning. Some physical functions affected by sleep are memory, mood, hormone secretion, glucose metabolism, immune function, and body temperature.

Most adults need 7 to 8 hours of sleep within a 24-hour period.[1] Adequate sleep is defined as the amount of sleep one needs to be fully awake and alert the next day. *Insufficient sleep* means getting less than the recommended amount of sleep. *Fragmented sleep* means a person wakes up or almost wakes (called an arousal), interrupting continuous sleep. *Nonrestorative sleep* means that a person sleeps the recommended amount but does not feel refreshed and alert the next day.

Sleep disturbance is a broad term that refers to poor sleep quality from various causes. Sleep disturbance may be related to environmental factors such as noise or light. It can be caused by health-related factors such as pain or by **sleep disorders**, which are problems unique to sleep. Sleep disorders discussed in this chapter include insomnia, obstructive sleep apnea syndrome, periodic limb movement disorder, circadian sleep disorders, narcolepsy, and parasomnias.

Sleep disturbances and sleep disorders can result in insufficient sleep. Many people get insufficient sleep because they simply are not in bed long enough to allow for an adequate amount of sleep. About 35% of Americans get less than the recommended 7 hours of sleep per night. An estimated 50 to 70 million people in the United States have a sleep disorder.[2] Many are unaware that they have a problem (Fig. 7.1). People with chronic illnesses have the greatest risk for sleep disturbances.

Untreated sleep disorders cause considerable health, safety, and economic consequences. Daytime sleepiness can be so severe that it interferes with work and social functioning. Driving while drowsy is related to 100,000 accidents

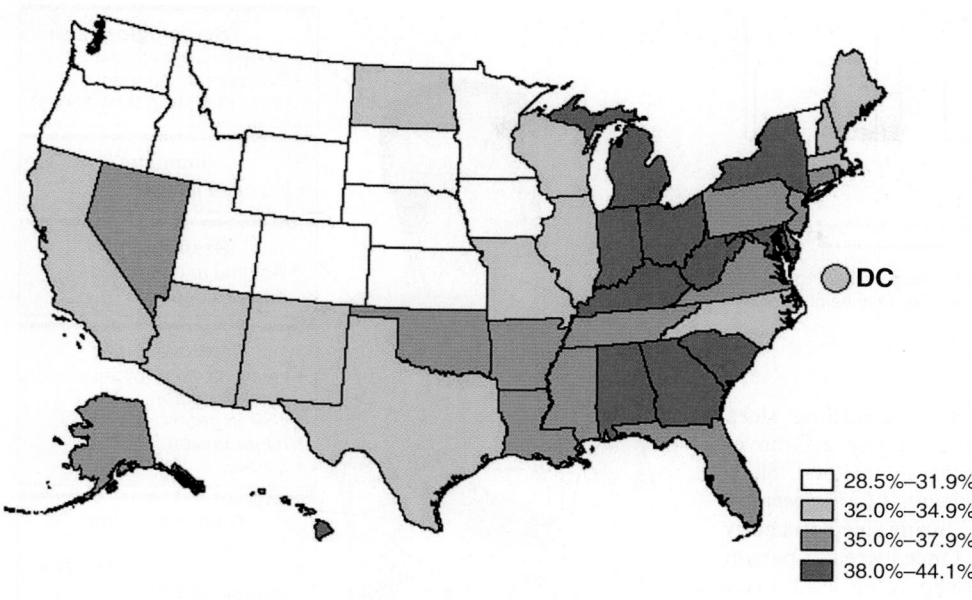

FIG. 7.1 Prevalence among U.S. adults of obtaining less than 7 hours of sleep each night. (Modified from *www.cdc.gov/sleep/data_statistics.html.*)

Legend:
- 28.5%–31.9%
- 32.0%–34.9%
- 35.0%–37.9%
- 38.0%–44.1%

and 1500 traffic fatalities per year.[3] Sleep disorders, sleep loss, and excessive daytime sleepiness cost the United States billions of dollars each year from the cost of health care, work-related accidents, and lost productivity.[4] Opportunities to address sleep problems are often missed because health care providers (HCPs) do not ask and patients do not readily talk about them.

PHYSIOLOGIC SLEEP MECHANISMS

Sleep-Wake Cycle

The brain controls the cyclic changes between sleep and waking. Complex networks in the areas of the forebrain (cerebral cortex, hypothalamus, thalamus) and brainstem interact to regulate the sleep-wake cycle.

Wake Behavior. Wake behavior is maintained by an integrated network of arousal systems from the brainstem and forebrain. A cluster of neuron structures in the brainstem, called the *ascending reticular activating system (ARAS)*, promote general activation of the cerebral cortex, which is responsible for higher brain functions. This activation gives rise to typical wake behaviors such as alertness and attention. Various neurotransmitters (glutamate, acetylcholine, norepinephrine, dopamine, histamine, serotonin) promote wake behavior.[5]

People with Alzheimer's disease lose cholinergic neurons in the forebrain, which results in sleep disturbances. In Parkinson's disease, dopamine neurons in the ARAS degenerate, which causes excessive daytime sleepiness. Histamine neurons in the hypothalamus stimulate cortical activation and wake behavior.[6] The sedating properties of many over-the-counter (OTC) medications (e.g., diphenhydramine) result from inhibiting histamine-related arousal systems.[7]

Orexin (also called hypocretin) is a neuropeptide found in the hypothalamus. Orexin is involved in regulating the sleep-wake cycle. It plays an important role in keeping people awake. Decreased levels of orexin or its receptors lead to difficulties staying awake, which is a syndrome called *narcolepsy*.[8] Narcolepsy is discussed later in this chapter on p. 98.

Sleep Behavior. An area in the hypothalamus just above the optic chiasm contains many sleep-promoting neurons. These neurons inhibit the ARAS and promote sleep.[5] Sleep is stimulated by a variety of sleep-promoting neurotransmitters and peptides, including γ-aminobutyric acid (GABA), galanin, melatonin, adenosine, somatostatin, growth hormone–releasing hormone (GHRH), delta-sleep–inducing peptide, prostaglandins, and proinflammatory cytokines. When a person has an infection, proinflammatory cytokines (interleukin-1, tumor necrosis factor, interleukin-6) contribute to sleepiness and lethargy. Peptides released by the gastrointestinal tract after food ingestion (e.g., cholecystokinin) may mediate sleepiness after eating (called *postprandial sleepiness*).

Melatonin is a hormone made by the pineal gland in the brain. Melatonin secretion is linked to the environmental light-dark cycle. Release of the hormone signals the time for sleep by "turning off" the mechanisms that promote wakefulness. Under normal day-night conditions, we release melatonin in the evening as it gets dark. Light exposure at night can suppress melatonin secretion.[7]

Circadian Rhythms. Many biologic rhythms of behavior and physiology fluctuate within a 24-hour period. These 24-hour patterns are called circadian (*circadian,* about a day) rhythms. The suprachiasmatic nucleus (SCN) in the hypothalamus is the master clock of the body. The SCN synchronizes the genetic clocks within individual cells and regulates the 24-hour sleep-wake cycle. Circadian rhythm timing is synchronized to the environmental light and dark periods through specific light detectors in the retina. Pathways from the retina reach the SCN, and pathways from the SCN innervate brain regions controlling wake and sleep behavior.[7]

Light is the strongest time cue for the sleep-wake rhythm. Thus we can use light as a therapy to shift the timing of the sleep-wake rhythm. For example, bright light used early in the morning will cause the sleep-wake rhythm to move to an earlier time; bright light used in the evening will cause the sleep-wake rhythm to move to a later time. For some people, being outside in daylight (without sunglasses) may be helpful. Others need light therapy, which is given through a device that makes very bright light.

FIG. 7.2 Sleep stages graphed across a complete sleep cycle. (From Goldman L, Schafer AI: *Goldman's Cecil medicine*, ed 25, Philadelphia, 2016, Saunders.)

Sleep Architecture

Sleep architecture refers to the pattern of nighttime sleep recorded from physiologic measures of brain waves, eye movements, and muscle tone called *polysomnography* (PSG). Sleep consists of 2 basic states: *rapid eye movement (REM) sleep* and *non–rapid eye movement (NREM) sleep*. During sleep, the body cycles between NREM and REM sleep. Once asleep, a person goes through 4 to 6 NREM and REM sleep cycles, each cycle lasting 60 to 110 minutes (Fig. 7.2).

NREM Sleep. Healthy adults spend about 75% to 80% of sleep time in NREM sleep. NREM sleep is subdivided into 3 stages.[9] However, you may see the older version of sleep staging that used 4 stages. The newer, 3-stage approach combines the old stages 3 and 4 into N3.

N1 is the stage that occurs at the beginning of sleep. It is characterized by slow eye movements and is a transition phase from wakefulness to sleep. During this period the person can be easily awakened.

N2 is the stage that takes up most of the night's sleep. The heart rate slows down and body temperature drops. N2 is associated with specific brain wave forms measured by electroencephalograph (EEG) that represent sleep-maintaining neural activity.

N3 is the deepest stage of sleep. It is called slow-wave sleep (SWS) because large, low-frequency EEG waves are characteristic. N3 is associated with large EEG waveforms, called delta waves. They are a measure of sleep intensity. SWS declines as people age. Most adults over 60 years of age have little NREM stage 3 sleep.

REM Sleep. REM sleep accounts for 20% to 25% of sleep. REM sleep follows NREM sleep in a sleep cycle. In this stage, brain waves resemble wakefulness and postural muscles are inhibited, leading to greatly reduced skeletal muscle tone. During REM sleep a person cannot initiate muscle movement (e.g., cannot stand up). REM sleep is the period when the most vivid dreaming occurs.

INSUFFICIENT SLEEP AND SLEEP DISTURBANCES

Insufficient sleep is associated with changes in body function (Fig. 7.3) and health problems (Table 7.1). Impaired cognitive function and impaired performance on simple behavioral tasks occur within 24 hours of sleep loss. The effects of sleep loss are cumulative.[10] Those who report less than 6 hours of sleep a night are more likely to be obese. The risk for developing glucose intolerance and diabetes is higher in those with a history of insufficient sleep. Chronic loss of sleep places people at risk for depression, impaired daytime functioning, social isolation, and overall reduction in quality of life.[11]

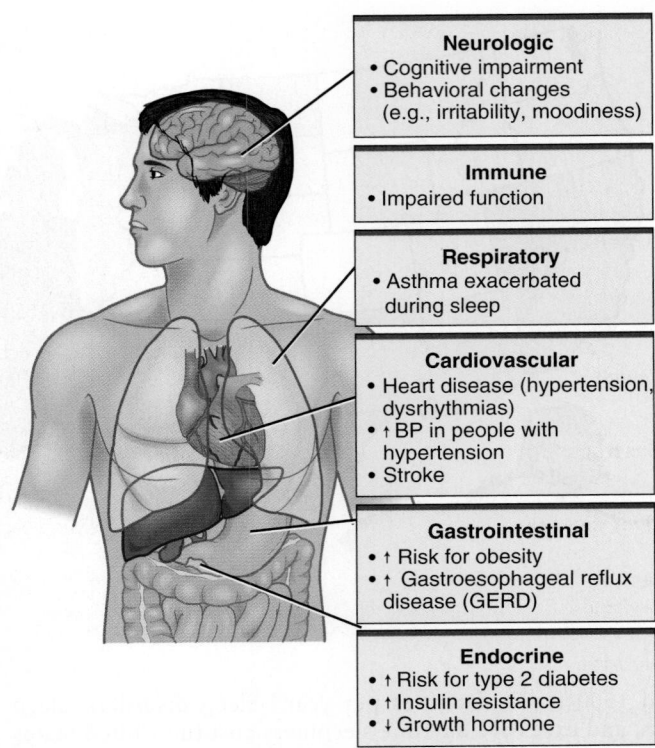

Neurologic
- Cognitive impairment
- Behavioral changes (e.g., irritability, moodiness)

Immune
- Impaired function

Respiratory
- Asthma exacerbated during sleep

Cardiovascular
- Heart disease (hypertension, dysrhythmias)
- ↑ BP in people with hypertension
- Stroke

Gastrointestinal
- ↑ Risk for obesity
- ↑ Gastroesophageal reflux disease (GERD)

Endocrine
- ↑ Risk for type 2 diabetes
- ↑ Insulin resistance
- ↓ Growth hormone

FIG. 7.3 Effects of sleep deprivation and sleep disorders on the body.

SLEEP DISTURBANCES IN THE HOSPITAL

Hospitalized patients, especially in the intensive care unit (ICU), may have decreased total sleep time, disrupted normal sleep stages, and disrupted circadian rhythms.[12] In the hospital, environmental sleep-disruptive factors, psychoactive medications, and acute and critical illness contribute to poor sleep. Contributing environmental factors include around-the-clock noise, light, and patient care activities. Hospital and ICU noise often persists both day and night from sources such as staff paging system, ventilator alarms, bedside monitors, infusion alarms, and staff conversations near patients (e.g., in hallways). Bright lights during the night disrupt sleep and reduce melatonin levels. Patient care activities including dressing changes, blood draws, vital sign monitoring, and medication administration often disrupt patients' ability to get sound, continuous sleep. This includes when we provide care to a patient's roommate in a shared room. Inactivity, boredom, and napping during the day and evening that can affect nighttime sleep. Patient symptoms, including pain, dyspnea, and nausea, can contribute to sleep loss in the acutely ill patient. Commonly used medications can further contribute to sleep loss. Preexisting sleep disorders may be worsened or triggered in those who are hospitalized.

Decreased sleep duration and sleep loss cause patients to be more sensitive to pain and less able to tolerate pain.[13] Adequate pain management may improve total sleep time, but many medications used to relieve pain, especially opioids, alter sleep quality and place a person at risk for sleep-disordered breathing.

You play a key role in creating an environment conducive to sleep. This includes the scheduling of medications and procedures, including those performed by unlicensed assistive personnel (UAP). Reducing light and noise levels can promote opportunities for sleep. Hypnotic sleep-aid medications are often available on an as-needed basis or can be discussed with the HCP.

TABLE 7.1 Relationship of Sleep Disturbances to Diseases and Disorders

Disease or Disorder	Sleep Disturbance
Cardiovascular (CV)	
Coronary artery disease	• People with sleep apnea or sleep disorders are at increased risk for CV disorders, including hypertension, dysrhythmias, and coronary artery disease
Heart failure (HF)	• Sleep problems (insomnia, PLMD, SDB) are common • Cheyne-Stokes breathing and central apnea are signs of HF exacerbation related to fluid overload
Hypertension	• Inadequate sleep in people with hypertension can lead to further elevations in BP
Endocrine	
Diabetes	• Insufficient sleep linked to increased risk for type 2 diabetes • Sleep deprivation in healthy people increases insulin resistance
Gastrointestinal	
Obesity	• Short sleep duration may result in metabolic changes that are linked to obesity • Higher body mass index (BMI) in those who sleep <6 hours compared with those who sleep >8 hours • Risk factor for SDB
Gastroesophageal reflux disease (GERD)	• Reflux of gastric contents into the esophagus occurs during sleep because of incompetent lower esophageal sphincter • Swallowing is depressed during sleep
Liver disease	• Associated with excessive sleepiness, nocturnal arousal, and RLS
Immune Disorders	
Human immunodeficiency virus (HIV)	• Sleep problems and fatigue highly prevalent and associated with increased morbidity and mortality
Musculoskeletal	
Arthritis	• Increased rates of RLS and SDB • Disease activity linked to sleep complaints
Fibromyalgia	• Co-morbid insomnia, especially complaint of nonrestorative sleep • Increased rates of PLMD and RLS • Lower levels of sleep-dependent hormones (growth hormone, prolactin)
Systemic exertion intolerance disease (chronic fatigue syndrome)	• Co-morbid insomnia • Increased rates of SDB
Neurologic	
Alzheimer's disease	• Many have SDB (frequently sleep apnea) • Circadian rhythm changes with nocturnal wandering, daytime sleepiness, and sleep disruption and awakening
Cancer	• Higher rates of insomnia • Chemotherapy for cancer treatment associated with fragmented sleep and fatigue
Pain (acute and chronic)	• Decreases quantity and quality of sleep • Poor sleep can intensify pain
Parkinson's disease	• Associated with difficulty initiating or maintaining sleep, parasomnias, and excessive daytime sleepiness
Renal	
End-stage renal disease (ESRD)	• Disrupted nocturnal sleep with excessive daytime sleepiness • Patients on dialysis have a high incidence of SDB and RLS, which are both significant predictors of mortality
Respiratory	
Asthma	• Worse during sleep
Chronic obstructive pulmonary disease (COPD)	• Associated with poor sleep quality, nocturnal oxygen desaturation, and coexisting sleep apnea
Obstructive sleep apnea (OSA)	• Linked with heart disease (hypertension, stroke, heart failure, coronary artery disease, dysrhythmias) • Results in impaired glucose control like that which occurs in type 2 diabetes

Source: National Center on Sleep Disorders and National Heart, Lung, and Blood Institute: National Sleep Disorders Research Plan: Section 4: Sleep and health. Retrieved from *www.cdc.gov/sleep/about_sleep/chronic_disease.html.*
PLMD, Periodic limb movement disorder; *RLS*, restless legs syndrome; *SDB*, sleep-disordered breathing.

SLEEP DISORDERS

INSOMNIA

The most common sleep disorder is insomnia. It affects 1 in 3 adults. Insomnia is characterized by difficulty falling asleep, difficulty staying asleep, waking up too early, or waking up feeling unrefreshed. The main problem people with insomnia report is overall dissatisfaction with sleep quality and quantity.

Acute insomnia refers to difficulties falling or remaining asleep at least 3 nights per week for less than a month. *Chronic insomnia* is defined by the same symptoms and a daytime problem related to poor sleep (e.g., fatigue, poor concentration, interference with social or family activities) that persist for 3 months or longer. Chronic insomnia occurs in 10% to 15% of Americans. It is more common in women than men. Insomnia is more common in people who are divorced, widowed, and separated than in those who are married. It is more prevalent in people with low socioeconomic status and less education.[14]

Etiology and Pathophysiology

Behaviors, lifestyle, diet, physical and mental conditions, and medications may contribute to insomnia. Insomnia is worsened or perpetuated by behaviors such as keeping irregular sleep-wake schedules (varying one's bedtime and rise time), taking long naps in the afternoon, spending time awake in bed trying to sleep, sleeping late in the morning, and exercising near bedtime. Lifestyle factors can contribute to insomnia. Although the sedative effects of alcohol help people fall asleep, it suppresses REM sleep and causes restlessness and awakenings later in the night. Use of various stimulants, including nicotine in tobacco products, caffeine, or methamphetamine, can cause restlessness and sleep disruption, worsening insomnia. Insomnia is a common side effect of many medications (e.g., antidepressants, antihypertensives, corticosteroids, psychostimulants, analgesics).

The physiologic and psychologic causes of chronic insomnia may be related to varied factors. Often people report that the onset occurred after a stressful life event, such as losing a job or the death of a loved one. In other cases, psychiatric illnesses, medical conditions, medications, or substance use may precipitate insomnia. Patients with psychiatric or medical conditions are more likely to have insomnia than those without these conditions. Once insomnia becomes chronic, symptoms are likely to persist over time.

Clinical Manifestations

Manifestations of insomnia include 1 or more of the following symptoms: (1) difficulty falling asleep *(long sleep latency)*, (2) frequent awakenings *(fragmented sleep)*, (3) prolonged nighttime awakenings or awakening too early and not being able to fall back to sleep *(difficulty maintaining sleep)*, and (4) awakening feeling unrefreshed *(nonrestorative sleep)*.[14] Daytime or functional consequences of insomnia include fatigue, having trouble concentrating at work or school, and having an altered mood. Behavioral manifestations of poor sleep include irritability, sleepiness during the day, forgetfulness, and attention and concentration problems.

Diagnostic Studies

Self-Report. The diagnosis of insomnia is made based on subjective complaints and an evaluation of a 1- or 2-week sleep diary completed by the patient. A diary or log usually includes the number and times of naps, times of going to bed, awakening, and getting up, number of awakenings, and overall sleep quality ratings.

In ambulatory care settings, the evaluation of insomnia requires a comprehensive sleep history. This establishes the type of insomnia and screens for possible psychiatric, medical, or other sleep disorders that would require specific treatment. Questionnaires, such as Pittsburgh Quality Sleep Index, Insomnia Severity Index, and Epworth Daytime Sleepiness, are often used to assess sleep quality and negative daytime symptoms related to insomnia.

Actigraphy. *Actigraphy* is a relatively noninvasive method of monitoring rest and activity cycles. An actigraph is a device that measures overall motor activity. It is worn on the wrist like commercially available activity monitors. Actigraphs used for sleep medicine and research are more accurate and sensitive than consumer-based devices. The unit continuously records the patient's movements, producing data that are downloaded to a computer and analyzed. Activity corresponds to time spent awake, and continuous inactivity corresponds to time spent asleep. Actigraphy is not necessary for diagnosing insomnia, but it is useful for confirming patient's sleep self-reports and monitoring the effects of treatments.

Polysomnography. A polysomnography (PSG) study is not recommended to diagnose insomnia. A PSG study is done only if there are symptoms or signs of another sleep disorder, such as sleep-disordered breathing (discussed later in the chapter). In a PSG study, electrodes simultaneously record physiologic measures that define the main stages of sleep and wakefulness. These measures include (1) muscle tone recorded using an electromyogram (EMG), (2) eye movements recorded with an electrooculogram (EOG), and (3) brain activity recorded through EEG. To determine additional characteristics of specific sleep disorders, other measures made during PSG include airflow at the nose and mouth, respiratory effort around the chest and abdomen, heart rate, noninvasive oxygen saturation, and EMG of the anterior tibialis muscles (used to detect periodic leg movements). Finally, cameras and microphones continuously monitor a patient's gross body movements.

Interprofessional Care

Insomnia treatments are directed toward changing behaviors that perpetuate insomnia and managing symptoms (Table 7.2). The goal is to (1) prevent acute insomnia from becoming chronic and (2) treat chronic insomnia. An important first step is to provide teaching about sleep along with behavioral strategies. **Sleep hygiene** is a variety of different practices that are important to have normal, quality nighttime sleep and daytime alertness (Table 7.3). Patients often have some familiarity with sleep hygiene principles, but they may still benefit from coaching on how to use these principles effectively.

Cognitive-Behavioral Therapy for Insomnia. Although teaching about sleep hygiene practices is useful, those with chronic insomnia need more in-depth *cognitive-behavioral therapy for insomnia (CBT-I)*.[14] CBT-I is based on structured treatment plans that include cognitive and behavioral components. The cognitive part of CBT-I may include stress management techniques (e.g., relaxation breathing, imagery) or cognitive strategies to address misconceptions about sleep. The specific approach used varies based on the patient's need. The behavioral

TABLE 7.2 **Interprofessional Care**	
Insomnia	
Diagnostic Assessment **History**	**Drug Therapy (Table 7.4)**
• Self-report sleep log or diary • Sleep assessment (Table 7.5) • Pittsburgh Sleep Quality Index • Insomnia Severity Index • Epworth Sleepiness Scale	• Benzodiazepines • Benzodiazepine-receptor–like agents • Orexin-receptor antagonist • Melatonin-receptor agonist • Antidepressants
Management **Nondrug Therapy**	**Complementary and Alternative Therapy**
• Sleep hygiene (Table 7.3) • Cognitive-behavioral therapies for insomnia (CBT-I)	• Melatonin

TABLE 7.3 Patient Teaching

Sleep Hygiene

Include the following instructions when teaching a patient who has a sleep disturbance or disorder.
- Do not go to bed unless you are sleepy.
- If you are not asleep after 20 minutes, get out of bed and do a non-stimulating activity. Return to bed only when you are sleepy.
- Adopt a regular pattern in terms of bedtime and awakening.
- Begin rituals (e.g., warm bath, light snack, reading) that help you relax each night before bed.
- Get a full night's sleep on a regular basis.
- Make your bedroom quiet, dark, and a little bit cool.
- Do not read, write, eat, watch TV, talk on the phone, or use technologies such as smart phones and tablet computers in bed.
- Avoid caffeine, nicotine, and alcohol at least 4–6 hours before bedtime.
- Do not go to bed hungry, but do not eat a big meal near bedtime either.
- Avoid strenuous exercise within 6 hours of your bedtime.
- Avoid sleeping pills, or use them cautiously.
- Practice relaxation techniques (e.g., relaxation breathing) to help you cope with stress.

Adapted from American Academy of Sleep Medicine: Healthy sleep habits, 2017. Retrieved from *www.sleepeducation.org/treatment-therapy/healthy-sleep-habits/*.

TABLE 7.4 Drug Therapy

Insomnia

Benzodiazepines
- Temazepam (Restoril)
- Triazolam (Halcion)

Benzodiazepine-Receptor–Like Agents
- Eszopiclone (Lunesta)
- Zaleplon (Sonata)
- Zolpidem (Ambien, Ambien CR, Edluar, Intermezzo, ZolpiMist)

Orexin-Receptor Antagonist
- Suvorexant (Belsomra)

Melatonin-Receptor Agonist
- Ramelteon (Rozerem)

Antidepressants
- Amitriptyline
- Doxepin

Source: U.S. Food and Drug Administration: Sleep disorder (sedative-hypnotic) drug information, 2017. Retrieved from *www.fda.gov/Drugs/DrugSafety/PostmarketDrugSafetyInformationforPatientsandProviders/ucm101557.htm*.

part of CBT-I includes instructions to (1) limit the amount of time a person can stay in bed, (2) set a scheduled time to get up in the morning, (3) go to bed only when feeling sleepy, and (4) get out of bed when unable to sleep. CBT-I includes focused teaching and coaching on how to effectively use sleep hygiene practices (Table 7.3). CBT-I requires people to change behavior, which can be hard.

Although full CBT-I treatment should be delivered by trained HCPs, you can apply many of the principles to help patients. Teach the person with insomnia to avoid naps. Older adults may have difficulty fully avoiding naps. You can teach them that naps are less likely to affect nighttime sleep if they are limited to 15 to 20 minutes, once per day, and scheduled no later than 7 to 9 hours after waking in the morning. Regular exercise may enhance sleep quality but should not be done within several hours of bedtime.

Drug Therapy. Most medications for insomnia work by producing sleepiness to promote the onset or maintenance of sleep. Based on the characteristics (onset, half-life, and mechanism of action), certain medications may be recommended for specific patterns of insomnia but not for others. They can treat problems falling asleep (sleep onset), waking during the night and having trouble falling back asleep (sleep maintenance), or both. Medications that treat insomnia can cause next-day drowsiness and impair driving and other activities that require alertness. People can be impaired even when they feel fully awake. Many people become used to taking OTC or prescription medications to treat insomnia and risk becoming dependent on them, psychologically and physically. *Rebound insomnia* is worsening of sleep that may occur when one abruptly stops certain sleep medications.

Medications are generally recommended for short-term treatment of insomnia. There is little evidence to support the use of medications for chronic insomnia. In 2017 the American Academy of Sleep Medicine (AASM) published new guidelines for pharmacologic treatment of chronic insomnia.[15] Drug classes used to treat insomnia include benzodiazepines, benzodiazepine-receptor agonists, orexin-receptor antagonist,

melatonin-receptor agonist, antidepressants, and antihistamines (Table 7.4).[16] Use of hypnotic medications in older adults is controversial due to side effects and safety concerns, such as fall risk.[17]

Benzodiazepine Hypnotics. Benzodiazepines activate GABA receptors to promote sleep. These agents are no longer recommended as first-line therapy for insomnia. Only 2 benzodiazepines are included in the 2017 AASM guidelines: triazolam (Halcion) is recommended for sleep onset insomnia, and temazepam (Restoril) is recommended for both sleep onset and sleep maintenance insomnia.[15] Some benzodiazepines are recommended for treating anxiety but not insomnia (e.g., diazepam, alprazolam). However, you may still encounter patients who are prescribed these medications for insomnia. Other benzodiazepines (estazolam, flurazepam, oxazepam) lack enough research to support clinical recommendations. The prolonged half-life of some of these drugs can result in daytime sleepiness, amnesia, dizziness, and rebound insomnia. Tolerance develops, and there is a risk for dependence and the potential for misuse. They should be used for only 2 to 3 weeks. In addition, they interact with alcohol and other central nervous system (CNS) depressants.

Non-Benzodiazepine Hypnotics. Non-benzodiazepine hypnotics act at GABA receptors but have more selective action than benzodiazepines, resulting in better safety.[16] These agents are considered first-line for pharmacologic treatment of insomnia. The 2017 AASM guidelines recommend zaleplon (Sonata) for sleep onset insomnia and zolpidem (Ambien) and eszopiclone (Lunesta) for sleep onset and sleep maintenance insomnia.[15] These drugs are effective and safe for use from 3 months to a year.[16] Food has the potential to delay onset of action and should not be taken with these agents. These agents have short half-lives, making their duration of action short and reducing the risk for daytime sedation. Newer formulations have improved specific therapeutic uses. A controlled-release formulation of zolpidem (Ambien CR) lengthens the action of the medication, improving its use for sleep maintenance insomnia. Zolpidem (Intermezzo) is available in a quick-acting sublingual tablet that may be taken for middle-of-the-night awakenings. A dissolvable tablet form of zolpidem (Edluar) and an oral spray formulation (ZolpiMist) may be used with those who have difficulty swallowing pills or are on restricted oral fluid intake.

Orexin-Receptor Antagonist. Suvorexant (Belsomra) is the first approved orexin-receptor antagonist. It promotes sleep by blocking the effects of orexin. Suvorexant should be taken no more than once per night, within 30 minutes of going to bed, with at least 7 hours remaining before the planned time of waking. It is recommended only for sleep maintenance insomnia.[15] The most common side effect is drowsiness.

Melatonin-Receptor Agonist. Ramelteon (Rozerem) is a melatonin-receptor agonist. It has a rapid onset that is effective for sleep onset. Ramelteon does not cause tolerance, but it is not always effective in improving sleep quality. Ramelteon is recommended for insomnia with sleep onset difficulty, not for sleep maintenance problems.[15]

Antidepressants. Certain tricyclic antidepressants (e.g., doxepin, amitriptyline) are used as sleep aids due to their side effects of sedation. The insomnia dose is much lower than the antidepressant dose. The AASM recommends doxepin for sleep maintenance insomnia.[15] Doxepin improves sleep without next-day drowsiness in older and middle-aged adults with chronic primary insomnia.

Trazodone, an atypical antidepressant, is 1 of the most common agents prescribed to treat insomnia, especially in older adults. Giving this drug to older adults is controversial. Daytime sleepiness is a common side effect. Tolerance can develop within a few weeks. The AASM recommends against using trazodone because there is not enough research to determine if the benefit outweighs risks for side effects.[15]

Antihistamines. Many people self-medicate with OTC sleep aids. These include doxylamine (Unisom) and several agents that contain diphenhydramine. Diphenhydramine is in many "nighttime" pain medicines. The AASM guidelines do not recommend diphenhydramine for insomnia because research does not show that it effectively improves sleep. It should not be used by older adults. Antihistamines have anticholinergic side effects, including daytime sleepiness, impaired cognitive function, blurred vision, urinary retention, constipation, and risk for increased intraocular pressure. The AASM guidelines do not mention doxylamine.[15]

Complementary and Alternative Therapy. Many types of complementary and alternative therapies are used as sleep aids (see Complementary & Alternative Therapies: Melatonin box). Melatonin is not recommended for treatment of insomnia,[15] but it may be effective for improving sleep disturbance associated with jet lag.[18] It also helps night shift workers sleep during the daytime. Valerian is an herb that has been used for many years as a sleep aid and to relieve anxiety. Although valerian is safe, it is not effective in treating insomnia. Other sleep aids include white noise devices or relaxation strategies.

🌿 COMPLEMENTARY & ALTERNATIVE THERAPIES
Melatonin

Scientific Evidence

Overall, the scientific evidence suggests melatonin may help people who take it for jet lag. It may also decrease the time it takes to fall asleep (sleep latency).

Nursing Implications

- Regarded as safe in recommended doses for short-term use.
- Avoid in patients using warfarin (Coumadin).
- Avoid in patients using central nervous system depressants.
- Common side effects are headache, nausea, dizziness, and drowsiness.

Source: Based on a systematic review of scientific literature. Retrieved from *www.naturalmedicines.therapeuticresearch.com.*

TABLE 7.5 Nursing Assessment
Sleep

Use the following questions to do an initial sleep assessment.
1. What time do you normally go to bed at night? What time do you normally wake up in the morning?
2. Do you often have trouble falling asleep at night?
3. About how many times do you wake up at night?
4. If you do wake up during the night, do you usually have trouble falling back asleep?
5. Does your bed partner say or are you aware that you frequently snore, gasp for air, or stop breathing?
6. Does your bed partner say or are you aware that you kick or thrash about while asleep?
7. Are you aware that you ever walk, eat, punch, kick, or scream during sleep?
8. Are you sleepy or tired during much of the day?
9. Do you usually take 1 or more naps during the day?
10. Do you usually doze off without planning to during the day?
11. How much sleep do you need to feel alert and function well?
12. Are you currently taking any type of medication or other preparation to help you sleep?

❖ NURSING MANAGEMENT: INSOMNIA

◆ Nursing Assessment

As a nurse, you are in a key position to assess sleep problems in patients and their caregivers. Sleep assessment is important in helping patients identify personal habits and environmental factors that contribute to poor sleep. Family caregivers may have sleep disruptions from the need to provide care to patients in the home. These sleep disruptions can increase the burden of caregiving.

Self-report and objective data are used to assess sleep duration and quality. Many patients do not tell their HCP about their sleep problems. Make sure to ask patients about their sleep and problems with sleep. A sleep history includes characteristics of sleep such as sleep duration, the pattern of sleep, and daytime alertness (Table 7.5). Healthy adults should have 7 to 8 hours of sleep a night. Occasional difficulty getting to sleep or awakening during the night is not unusual. However, sleep disturbances longer than 1 month are problematic. Assess the diet and caffeine intake.

Ask the patient about sleep aids. This includes OTC and prescription medications. Note the drug dose, frequency of use, and any side effects (e.g., daytime drowsiness, dry mouth). Ask about alcohol consumption and whether it is used as a sleep aid. Many people consume herbal or dietary supplements that they believe will improve sleep. Common supplements include valerian, melatonin, hops, passion flower, kava, and skullcap. Tell the patient that many of these products are sold as dietary supplements and do not have U.S. Food and Drug Administration (FDA) approval or regulatory oversight. The exact components and concentrations of herbs and supplements often are unknown. Patients may have adverse effects or herb-drug interactions. Certain agents such as kava are associated with liver toxicity.

Encourage the patient to keep a sleep diary for 1 to 2 weeks. A free sleep diary is available from the National Sleep Foundation (*www.sleepfoundation.org/sites/default/files/SleepDiaryv6.pdf*). You can help the patient choose 1 of the many sleep diary smartphone applications that track information about sleep. Commercially available activity monitors can track sleep, but these vary in accuracy. Encourage people with sleep problems to share this information with their HCP to help identify sleep patterns.

The patient's medical history can provide important information about factors that contribute to poor sleep. For example, a man with benign prostatic hyperplasia may report frequent awakenings during the night for voiding. Psychiatric problems (e.g., depression, anxiety, posttraumatic stress disorder [PTSD], drug use) are associated with sleep disturbances. Some patients being seen for sleep problems may complete short questionnaires to screen for mood disturbances. Sleep disturbances often develop as a result or complication of a chronic or terminal condition (e.g., heart disease, dementia, cancer). Painful conditions such as arthritis may contribute to nighttime awakenings.

Ask about work schedules and cross-country and international travel. Shift work contributes to reduced or poor-quality sleep. Work-related behaviors resulting from poor sleep may include poor performance, decreased productivity, and job absenteeism.

◆ Nursing Diagnoses

Nursing diagnoses related to sleep include sleep deprivation and impaired sleep pattern.

◆ Nursing Implementation

Nursing care depends on the severity and duration of the sleep problem. Although teaching about sleep hygiene practices (Table 7.3) is beneficial, patients with chronic insomnia need more in-depth intervention using CBT-I strategies. An important part of sleep hygiene is reducing dietary intake of caffeine-containing substances (Table 7.6). Caffeine has a half-life of about 6 hours and possibly as long as 9 hours in older adults. Patients should avoid consuming caffeinated beverages after 12 noon.

Suggest and implement changes in home and institutional environments to enhance sleep. Reducing light and noise levels enhances sleep. Awareness of time passing and watching the clock adds to anxiety about not falling asleep or returning to sleep. Keeping the bedroom dark and cool is conducive to good sleep.

Teach patients about sleeping medications. With the benzodiazepines, non-benzodiazepine hypnotics, and melatonin-receptor agonists, teach the patient to take the drug right before bedtime and be prepared to get a full night's sleep of at least 6 to 8 hours. Tell patients not to plan activities the next morning that require highly skilled psychomotor coordination. Advise patients not to take these medications with high-fat food (delays absorption), alcohol, or other CNS depressants. Patient follow-up about medications is important. Ask about daytime sleepiness, nightmares, and any difficulties in activities of daily living.

OBSTRUCTIVE SLEEP APNEA

The term **sleep-disordered breathing (SDB)** describes abnormal respiratory patterns associated with sleep. These include snoring, apnea (temporary cessation of respiration), and hypopnea (temporary restriction of respiration without full cessation) with increased respiratory effort leading to frequent arousals. SDB results in frequent sleep disruptions and changes in sleep stages. Obstructive sleep apnea is the most commonly diagnosed SDB problem.

Obstructive sleep apnea (OSA), also called *obstructive sleep apnea–hypopnea syndrome* (OSAHS), is characterized by partial or complete upper airway obstruction during sleep. *Apnea* is the cessation of respiratory airflow (90% or greater

TABLE 7.6	**Caffeine Content of Select Beverages**	
Food or Beverage	**Caffeine (mg)**
Coffee, brewed (8 oz)	95–165
Coffee, instant (8 oz)	7.63
Coffee, espresso (1 oz)	47.64
Coffee, decaffeinated	2–5
Cola (8 oz)	24–46
Energy drink (8 oz)	27.164
Energy shot (1 oz)	40–100
Hot chocolate (8 oz)	5
Root beer, most brands (8 oz)	0
Sprite, 7up (12 oz)	0
Tea, black (8 oz)	25–48
Tea, green (8 oz)	25–297

Source: Mayo Clinic: Caffeine content for coffee, tea, soda and more, 2017. Retrieved from *www.mayoclinic.org/healthy-lifestyle/nutrition-and-healthy-eating/in-depth/caffeine/art-20049372*.

reduction) lasting longer than 10 seconds. *Hypopnea* is a condition characterized by shallow respirations (30%–90% reduction in airflow).[9] Airflow obstruction in OSA occurs because of (1) narrowing of the air passages with relaxation of muscle tone during sleep and/or (2) the tongue and soft palate falling backward to partially or completely obstruct the pharynx (Fig. 7.4). Each obstruction may last from 10 to 90 seconds. During the apneic period the patient can have *hypoxemia* (decreased PaO_2 or SpO_2) and *hypercapnia* (increased $PaCO_2$). These changes are ventilatory stimulants and cause brief arousals, but the patient may not fully awaken.

The patient has a generalized startle response, snorts, and gasps, which cause the tongue and soft palate to move forward and the airway to open. Apnea and arousal cycles occur repeatedly throughout the night. Apneic episodes occur most often during REM sleep, when airway muscle tone is lowest.

There is no single cause for OSA. The condition is related to multiple factors that influence airway patency and the tone of airway musculature. Risk factors include obesity (body mass index [BMI] greater than 30 kg/m²), age older than 65 years, neck circumference greater than 17 inches, craniofacial abnormalities that affect the upper airway, and acromegaly (acromegaly is discussed in Chapter 49). Smokers are more likely to have OSA. OSA is more common in men than in women until after menopause, when the prevalence of the disorder is equal.[19] Women with OSA have higher mortality rates than men with OSA. OSA patients with excessive daytime sleepiness have increased mortality.

Clinical Manifestations

Clinical manifestations of sleep apnea include frequent arousals during sleep, insomnia, excessive daytime sleepiness, and witnessed apneic episodes. The patient's bed partner may complain about the patient's loud snoring. Other symptoms include morning headaches (from hypercapnia or increased BP that causes vasodilation of cerebral blood vessels), personality changes, and irritability.

A major risk of OSA is cardiovascular complications. Apnea during sleep causes hypoxia, nocturnal arousals, and increased pressure in the thoracic cavity. These events can lead to negative physiologic consequences, including overactivation of the sympathetic nervous system, increased

FIG. 7.4 How sleep apnea occurs. A, The patient predisposed to obstructive sleep apnea (OSA) has a small pharyngeal airway. B, During sleep, the pharyngeal muscles relax, allowing the airway to close. Lack of airflow results in repeated apneic episodes. C, Continuous positive airway pressure (CPAP) splints the airway open, preventing airflow obstruction. (Modified from LaFleur Brooks M: *Exploring medical language: A student-directed approach*, ed 8, St Louis, 2012, Mosby.)

vascular resistance, and reduced oxygenation of the heart muscle. Long-term effects include hypertension, cardiac dysrhythmias, arteriosclerosis, heart failure, and cardiovascular-related mortality.[20]

Chronic sleep loss predisposes the person to diminished ability to concentrate, impaired memory, failure to complete daily tasks, and interpersonal difficulties. Men may have impotence. Hypercapnia and arousals contribute to daytime sleepiness in people with OSA. Driving accidents may occur due to excessive daytime sleepiness. Family life and the patient's ability to maintain employment are often compromised. As a result, the patient may become depressed. Cessation of breathing reported by the bed partner is usually a source of great anxiety because of the fear that breathing may not resume.

Diagnostic Studies

Assessment of the patient with OSA includes a thorough sleep and medical history. Tools used to screen for OSA are the Berlin questionnaire and the STOP-BANG questionnaire, which assesses for clinical manifestations highly suspicious of OSA.[19]

Typically, OSA is diagnosed by PSG done in a clinical sleep laboratory. The patient's chest and abdominal movement, oral and nasal airflow, SpO_2, eye movement, and heart rate and rhythm are monitored. In some instances, portable sleep studies are done in the home setting. Overnight pulse oximetry assessment may be done to determine whether nocturnal oxygen supplementation is needed.

A diagnosis of sleep apnea requires documentation of apneic events or hypopneas of at least 10 seconds' duration. OSA is defined as more than 5 apnea/hypopnea events per hour with a 3% to 4% decrease in oxygen saturation. Severe apnea can be associated with apneic events of more than 30 to 50 per hour of sleep.[9]

INFORMATICS IN PRACTICE

Sleep Apnea Diagnosis and Monitoring

- Home respiratory monitoring is a cost-effective alternative to diagnose and manage SDB that allows patients the convenience of sleeping in their own home.
- It is used as part of a comprehensive sleep evaluation and in patients likely to have moderate to severe OSA but without heart failure, obstructive lung disease, or neuromuscular disease.
- Home respiratory monitoring is used to monitor the effectiveness of non-CPAP therapies for patients with sleep-related breathing disorders.
- Wireless monitors can detect changes in vital signs and pulse oximetry, raising an alarm if values fall outside of set parameters.

❖ NURSING AND INTERPROFESSIONAL MANAGEMENT: SLEEP APNEA

◆ Conservative Treatment

Mild sleep apnea (5–10 apnea/hypopnea events per hour) may respond to simple measures. Conservative treatment at home begins with sleeping on one's side rather than on the back (called *positional therapy*), which reduces the effects of gravity on the airway. Elevating the head of the bed may eliminate OSA in some patients.

Medications that relax airway muscle tone often make OSA worse. Teach the patient to avoid taking sedatives or consuming alcoholic beverages for 3 to 4 hours before sleep. Sleep medications often make OSA worse. Excess weight worsens sleep apnea as the pressure of adipose tissue in the neck and on the chest restricts ventilation. Referral to a weight loss program may be needed. Bariatric surgery may also reduce OSA.[19] Teach the patient the dangers of driving or using heavy equipment due to the profound sleepiness that is common in people with OSA. Insomnia is common in people with OSA. They may need specific treatment for the insomnia (such as CBT-I).

Symptoms may resolve in up to half of patients with OSA who use a special mouth guard, also called an oral appliance, during sleep to prevent airflow obstruction. Oral appliances bring the mandible and tongue forward to enlarge the airway space, thereby preventing airway occlusion.[19] Some find a support group helpful, because they can express concerns and feelings and discuss strategies for resolving problems.

In patients with more severe symptoms (>15 apnea/hypopnea events/hour), **continuous positive airway pressure (CPAP)** by mask is the treatment of choice. With CPAP, the patient applies a nasal mask that is attached to a high-flow blower (Fig. 7.5). The blower is adjusted to maintain enough positive pressure (5–25 cm H_2O) in the airway during inspiration and expiration to prevent airway collapse.

Some patients cannot adjust to wearing a mask over the nose or mouth or to exhaling against the high pressure. A technologically more sophisticated therapy, bilevel positive airway pressure (BiPAP), can deliver a higher inspiration pressure and a lower pressure during expiration. With BiPAP, the apnea can be relieved with a lower mean pressure and may be better tolerated.

CPAP reduces apnea episodes, daytime sleepiness, and fatigue. It improves quality of life ratings and returns cognitive functioning to normal. Benefits of CPAP are dose-dependent

FIG. 7.5 Examples of positive airway pressure devices for sleep apnea. **A,** Patient wearing a nasal mask and headgear (positive pressure only through nose). **B,** Patient wearing nasal pillows (positive pressure only through nose). **C,** Patient wearing a full face mask (positive pressure to nose and mouth). (From Goldman L, Schafer AI: *Goldman's Cecil medicine,* ed 24, Philadelphia, 2012, Saunders.)

based on how long the device is used during the night. It must be used a minimum of 4 hours each night to reduce/reverse the negative cardiovascular effects of OSA.[20] Although CPAP is a highly effective treatment, patients have problems with using it every day. About two-thirds of those using CPAP report side effects such as nasal stuffiness.

First, assess the patient's knowledge about OSA and CPAP. Involve the bed partner in teaching. Assess the patient for nasal resistance. To ensure successful adherence to CPAP treatment, patients need to be involved in choosing the mask and device before the start of therapy. Patient-centered care may improve patient outcomes given that OSA treatment requires behavioral and lifestyle changes. You can facilitate goal-setting discussions between patients and HCPs to arrive at treatment plans that are feasible and mutually agreed upon.

When patients with a history of OSA are hospitalized, be aware that giving opioid analgesics and sedating medications (benzodiazepines, hypnotics) may worsen OSA symptoms by depressing respirations. Check with the HCP in charge of the patient's care to determine if a patient who uses home CPAP or BiPAP should continue this therapy in the hospital. If so, it is important for these patients to wear the device when resting or sleeping. Many patients can use their own equipment but check hospital policy to be certain it can be used.

◆ Surgical Treatment

If other measures fail, OSA can be managed surgically. The goal of OSA surgery is to reduce collapsibility and increase patency of the upper airway, including oral, nasal, and pharyngeal passages. The most common procedures are uvulopalatopharyngoplasty (UPPP or UP3) and genioglossal advancement and hyoid myotomy (GAHM). UPPP involves excision of the tonsillar pillars, uvula, and posterior soft palate to remove the obstructing tissue. GAHM involves advancing the attachment of the muscular part of the tongue on the mandible. When GAHM is performed, UPPP is generally done as well. Depending on the site of the obstruction, symptoms are relieved in up to 80% of patients.

Radiofrequency ablation (RFA) of obstructive tissues alone or in combination with other surgical techniques is also used. RFA is the least invasive surgical intervention. New treatments involve surgically implanted neurostimulators. One type

stimulates the hypoglossal nerve to increase the tone of airway muscles. This treatment for OSA is still being tested for effectiveness and safety.[19]

After surgery, complications of airway obstruction or hemorrhage occur most often in the immediate postoperative period. Patients are usually discharged home within 1 day after the procedure. Before going home, teach the patient what to expect during the postoperative recovery period. Tell patients that their throat will be sore. They may have a foul breath odor that may be reduced by rinsing with diluted mouthwash and then salt water for several days. Snoring may persist until the inflammation has subsided. Follow-up after surgery is important. A repeat PSG is done 3 to 4 months after surgery.

PERIODIC LIMB MOVEMENT DISORDER

Periodic limb movement disorder (PLMD) is characterized by *periodic limb movements in sleep* (PLMS): involuntary, repetitive movement of the limbs that affects people only during sleep.[21] PLMD usually involves the legs and rarely involves the arms. Sometimes abdominal, oral, and nasal movement accompanies PLMD. Movements typically occur for 0.5 to 10 seconds, in intervals separated by 5 to 90 seconds. PLMD causes poor-quality sleep and excessive daytime sleepiness. The causes of PLMD are not fully understood. Iron deficiency and dopamine dysfunction in the CNS have been implicated.[21]

PLMS can occur with medical disorders (e.g., sleep apnea, narcolepsy) and certain medications. For a diagnosis of PLMD, the occurrence of PLMS must not be due to another disorder. PLMS affects many people with restless legs syndrome (RLS). RLS is discussed in Chapter 58.

PLMD is diagnosed using a detailed history from the patient and/or bed partner and doing PSG. PLMD is treated by medications aimed at reducing or eliminating the limb movements or the arousals. Clonazepam, a benzodiazepine, is used to treat PLMD. It likely helps patients by improving sleep quality rather than reducing limb movements. Other medications shown to be effective are valproic acid, an antiseizure drug that reduces muscle activity, and selegiline, a dopaminergic agent. Dopamine agonists (pramipexole, ropinirole) are used to treat RLS, but there is little research on their efficacy for PLMD. However, it is common practice for HCPs to prescribe these drugs treat PLMD.

CIRCADIAN RHYTHM DISORDERS

Circadian rhythm disorders can occur when the circadian time-keeping system loses synchrony with the environment. Lack of synchrony between the circadian time-keeping system and environment disrupts the sleep-wake cycle and affects the patient's ability to have quality sleep. The common symptoms are insomnia and excessive sleepiness. Jet lag disorder and shift work sleep disorder (see Special Sleep Needs of Nurses section on p. 99) are the most common types of circadian rhythm disorders.

Jet lag disorder occurs when a person travels across multiple time zones. The result is your body's time is not synchronized with environmental time. Most persons crossing at least 3 time zones get jet lag. The number of time zones crossed affects the severity of symptoms and the time it takes to recover. Resynchronization of the body's clock occurs at a rate of about

1 hr/day when traveling eastward and 1.5 hr/day when traveling westward. Melatonin and exposure to daylight help to synchronize the body's rhythm.

Several strategies may help to reduce the risk for developing jet lag. Before travel the person can start to get in harmony with the time schedule of the destination. When time at destination is brief (i.e., 2 days or less), keeping home-based sleep hours rather than adopting destination sleep hours may reduce sleepiness and jet lag symptoms.

NARCOLEPSY

Narcolepsy is a chronic neurologic disorder caused by the brain's inability to regulate sleep-wake cycles normally. At various times throughout the day, people with narcolepsy have uncontrollable urges to sleep. Patients with narcolepsy often go directly into REM sleep from wakefulness.[21] This does not occur in normal sleep and is a unique feature of narcolepsy. Patients with narcolepsy also have fragmented and disturbed nighttime sleep. There are 2 types of narcolepsy: with cataplexy (type 1) and without cataplexy (type 2).[21] Cataplexy is a brief and sudden loss of skeletal muscle tone. It can manifest as a brief episode of muscle weakness or complete postural collapse and falling. Laughter, anger, or surprise often triggers episodes.

The onset of narcolepsy typically occurs in adolescence or early in the third decade. Head trauma, a sudden change in sleep-wake habits, and infection may trigger the onset of narcolepsy symptoms. The cause of narcolepsy is unknown. It is associated with destruction of neurons that make orexin. The resulting deficiency of orexin causes instability of wake and transitions from wake to sleep that occur unpredictably. The loss of neurons may be due to an autoimmune process.[22]

Narcolepsy is diagnosed based on a history of sleepiness, PSG, and daytime *multiple sleep latency tests* (MSLTs).[21] For the MSLT, patients undergo an overnight PSG evaluation followed by 4 or 5 naps scheduled every 2 hours during the next day. Short sleep latencies and onset of REM sleep in more than 2 MSLTs are diagnostic signs of narcolepsy.

Narcolepsy cannot be cured. Management is focused management of common symptoms: excessive daytime sleepiness, nighttime sleep disturbance, and cataplexy (Table 7.3). Provide teaching about sleep and sleep hygiene. Advise the patient to take 3 or more short (15-minute) naps throughout the day and to avoid large or heavy meals and alcohol.[22] You can play a key role in ensuring patient safety by teaching safety behaviors and encouraging adherence to the prescribed medication regimen. Safety precautions, especially when driving, are critically important for patients with narcolepsy. The behavioral therapies for insomnia are also used to address the sleep disturbances. Stimulants are used to counter daytime sleepiness.

Modafinil (Provigil) and armodafinil (Nuvigil) are nonamphetamine wake-promotion drugs that are considered a first-line drug therapy. Sodium oxybate (Xyrem), a metabolite of GABA, is another wake-promoting medication that is effective for treating both daytime sleepiness and cataplexy. Antidepressants are used to treat cataplexy. Tricyclic antidepressants used to be commonly used, but selective serotonin reuptake inhibitors (SSRIs) (e.g., fluoxetine [Prozac], venlafaxine) are becoming favored for the management of cataplexy.[22]

PARASOMNIAS

Parasomnias are unusual and often undesirable behaviors that occur while falling asleep, transitioning between sleep stages, or arousing from sleep.[21] They are due to CNS activation and often involve complex behaviors. The parasomnia is generally goal directed, although the person is not aware or conscious of the act. Parasomnias may result in fragmented sleep and fatigue.

Sleepwalking and sleep terrors are arousal parasomnias that occur during NREM sleep. *Sleepwalking* behaviors can range from sitting up in bed, moving objects, and walking around the room to driving a car. During a sleepwalking event the person may not speak and may have limited or no awareness of the event. On awakening, the person does not remember the event. In the ICU, a parasomnia may be misinterpreted as ICU psychosis. Sedated ICU patients can have manifestations of a parasomnia.

Sleep terrors (night terrors) are characterized by a sudden awakening from sleep along with a loud cry and signs of panic. The person has marked increases in heart rate and respiration and diaphoresis. Factors in the ICU such as sleep disruption and deprivation, fever, stress, and exposure to noise and light can contribute to sleep terrors.

Nightmares are a parasomnia characterized by recurrent awakening with recall of a frightful or disturbing dream. These normally occur during REM sleep during the final third of sleep. In critically ill patients, nightmares are common and likely due to medications. Drug classes most likely to cause nightmares are sedative-hypnotics, β-adrenergic antagonists, dopamine agonists, and amphetamines.

🧍 Gerontologic Considerations: Sleep

Older age is associated with overall shorter total sleep time, decreased sleep efficiency, and more awakenings (Fig. 7.6). A common misconception is that older people need less sleep than younger people. In fact, the amount of sleep needed as a person ages stays relatively constant. Other sleep disorders (e.g., sleep-disordered breathing) increase with age and may manifest with symptoms of insomnia. Some older adults have a shift in their circadian sleep timing so that they get sleepy earlier in the evening and awaken early in the morning.[23]

Multiple factors impair older adults' ability to obtain quality sleep. Insomnia symptoms in older adults often occur with depression, cardiovascular disease, pain, and cognitive problems. Chronic conditions that are common in older adults (chronic obstructive pulmonary disease [COPD], diabetes, dementia, chronic pain, cancer) can affect sleep quality. Medications used to treat these conditions can contribute to sleep problems. OTC medications can lead to sleep problems. Stimulating OTC medications include cough and cold medications, especially those containing pseudoephedrine; caffeine-containing drugs; and drugs containing nicotine (e.g., nicotine gum, transdermal patches).

Awakening and getting out of bed during the night (e.g., to use the bathroom) increase the risk for falls. Older adults may use OTC medications or alcohol as a sleep aid. This practice can further increase the risk for falls at night. Chronic disturbed sleep in older adults can result in disorientation, delirium, impaired intellect, disturbed cognition, and increased risk for accidents and injury.

FIG. 7.6 Many older people have sleep problems. (© Studio-Annika/iStock/Thinkstock.)

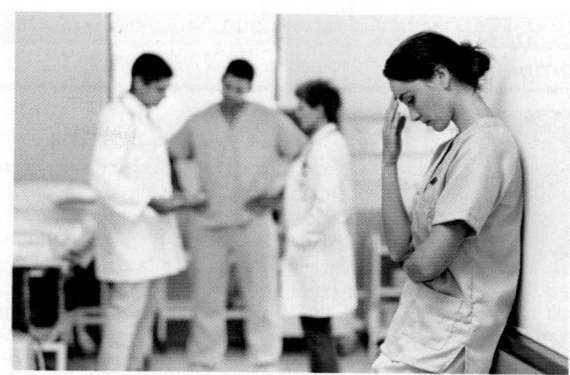

FIG. 7.7 Sleep disturbances are common among nurses. (© iStock.com/kupicoo.)

Because older adults may attribute their disturbed sleep to normal aging, they may fail to report symptoms of sleep disorders to their HCPs. Use a sleeping assessment (Table 7.5) to detect sleep disturbances in older adults.

Sleep medications should be used with great caution in older adults. Diphenhydramine, alone or in combination with other drugs, is sedating with anticholinergic effects. Any OTC medication labeled "PM" probably has diphenhydramine and should be used cautiously by older adults. Metabolism of most hypnotic drugs decreases with aging. Older adults have increased sensitivity to hypnotic and sedative medications. Thus drug therapies for sleep disturbances are started at lower doses and monitored carefully.[17] Whenever possible, long-acting benzodiazepines should be avoided. Older adults receiving benzodiazepines are at increased risk of daytime sedation, falls, and cognitive and psychomotor impairment.

❖ SPECIAL SLEEP NEEDS OF NURSES

Nursing is 1 of several professions that needs night shift and rotating shift schedules. In many settings, nurses work a variety of day and night shifts, often alternating and rotating them. Unfortunately, nurses who do shift work often report less job satisfaction and more job-related stress.[24]

Nurses on permanent night or rapidly rotating shifts are at increased risk for experiencing shift work sleep disorder. It is characterized by insomnia, sleepiness, and fatigue. Nurses on rotating shifts get the least amount of sleep. With repeated periods of inadequate sleep, the sleep debt grows. Chronic fatigue

in nurses doing shift work poses challenges for the individual nurse's health and for patient safety (Fig. 7.7).[24]

Shift work alters the synchrony between circadian rhythms and the environment, leading to sleep disruption. Nurses working the night shift are often too sleepy to be fully alert at work and too alert to sleep soundly the next day. Sustained changes in circadian rhythms such as those imposed by rotating shift work are linked to increased morbidity and mortality risks associated with cardiovascular problems. Mood disorders such as anxiety are higher in nurses who work rotating shifts.

From a safety perspective, disturbed sleep and subsequent fatigue can result in errors and accidents for nurses as well as for their patients. Fatigue diminishes or distorts perceptual skills, judgment, and decision-making capabilities. Lack of sleep reduces the ability to cope and handle stress and may result in physical, mental, and emotional exhaustion.

The problem of sleep disruption is critically important to nursing. Several strategies may help reduce the distress associated with rotating shift work. These include brief periods of on-site napping. Maintaining a consistent sleep-wake schedule even on days off is best but somewhat unrealistic. For night shift work, scheduling the sleep period just before going to work increases alertness and vigilance, improves reaction times, and decreases accidents during night shift work. Nurses who have control over their work schedules appear to have less sleep disruption than those whose schedule is imposed. As a nurse, you need to manage the impact of sleep disruption by using sleep hygiene practices.

CASE STUDY

Insomnia

(© JackF/ iStock/ Thinkstock.)

Patient Profile

G.P., a 49-yr-old black woman, is seen in the primary care clinic for chronic fatigue and disturbed sleep. She is postmenopausal based on self-report. In the past year, since the end of her periods, she has had daily hot flashes and sleep problems. She denies any other health problems. On a usual workday she drinks 2 cups of hot tea in the morning and a can of diet cola in the late afternoon. Currently she is taking OTC diphenhydramine for sleep. Her partner, who has accompanied her to the clinic, states that her snoring has gotten worse, and it is interfering with his sleep.

Subjective Data

- Reports hot flashes and nighttime sweating
- Reports daytime tiredness and fatigue
- States she has trouble getting to sleep and staying asleep

Objective Data

Physical Examination

- Laboratory evaluations within normal limits
- Height 5′6″
- Weight 190 lb

Diagnostic Studies

- Nighttime PSG study reveals episodes of obstructive sleep apnea

Interprofessional Care

- CPAP nightly
- Referred for weight reduction counseling
- Education about sleep hygiene

Discussion Questions

1. What are G.P.'s risk factors for sleep apnea?
2. What are the major health risks for G.P. from sleep apnea?
3. *Priority Decision:* Based on the assessment data provided, what are the priority nursing diagnoses?
4. How does CPAP work?
5. *Priority Decision:* Based on your assessment of G.P., what are the priority nursing interventions for her?
6. *Collaboration:* For the interventions that you identified in the previous question, which can you delegate to unlicensed assistive personnel (UAP)?
7. *Patient-Centered Care:* What specific sleep hygiene practices could G.P. use to improve the quality of her sleep?
8. *Collaboration:* What referrals may be indicated for G.P.?

Answers available at *http://evolve.elsevier.com/Lewis/medsurg.*

■ BRIDGE TO NCLEX EXAMINATION

The number of the question corresponds to the same-numbered outcome at the beginning of the chapter.

1. Sleep is *best* described as a
   a. loosely organized state similar to coma.
   b. quiet state in which there is little brain activity.
   c. state in which a person has reduced sensitivity to pain.
   d. state in which a person lacks conscious awareness of the environment.

2. Which statements are true about rapid eye movement (REM) sleep (*select all that apply*)?
   a. The EEG pattern is quiescent.
   b. Muscle tone is greatly reduced.
   c. It occurs only once in the night.
   d. It is physiologically similar to NREM sleep.
   e. The most vivid dreaming occurs during this phase.

3. Insufficient sleep is associated with (*select all that apply*)
   a. increased body mass index.
   b. increased insulin resistance.
   c. impaired cognitive functioning.
   d. improved immune responsiveness.
   e. increased daytime body temperature.

4. When teaching the patient with primary insomnia about sleep hygiene, the nurse should emphasize
   a. the importance of daytime naps.
   b. the need for long-term use of hypnotics.
   c. the need to exercise about 1 hour before bedtime.
   d. the importance of avoiding caffeine 6 to 9 hours before bedtime.

5. An overweight patient with sleep apnea would like to avoid using a nasal CPAP device. To help him reach this goal, the nurse suggests that the patient
   a. lose excess weight.
   b. take a nap during the day.
   c. eat a high-protein snack at bedtime.
   d. use mild sedatives or alcohol at bedtime.

6. While caring for a patient with a history of narcolepsy with cataplexy, the nurse can delegate which activity to the unlicensed assistive personnel (UAP)?
   a. Teaching about the timing of medications
   b. Walking the patient to and from the bathroom
   c. Developing a plan of care with a family member
   d. Planning an appropriate diet that avoids caffeine-containing foods

7. Strategies to reduce sleepiness during nighttime working include
   a. exercising before work.
   b. taking melatonin before working the night shift.
   c. sleeping for at least 2 hours immediately before work time.
   d. walking for 10 minutes every 4 hours during the night shift.

1. d, 2. b, e, 3. a, b, c, 4. d, 5. a, 6. b, 7. c

For rationales to these answers and even more NCLEX review questions, visit *http://evolve.elsevier.com/Lewis/medsurg.*

Ⓔ EVOLVE WEBSITE/RESOURCES LIST

http://evolve.elsevier.com/Lewis/medsurg
Review Questions (Online Only)
Key Points
Answer Keys for Questions
- Rationales for Bridge to NCLEX Examination Questions
- Answer Guidelines for Case Study on p. 100

Conceptual Care Map Creator
Audio Glossary
Content Updates

REFERENCES

1. National Heart, Lung, and Blood Institute: How much sleep is enough? Retrieved from *www.nhlbi.nih.gov/health-topics/sleep-deprivation-and-deficiency.*
2. Centers for Disease Control and Prevention: Short sleep duration among U.S. adults. Retrieved from *www.cdc.gov/sleep/data_statistics.html.*
3. National Sleep Foundation: Facts and stats. Retrieved from *www.drowsy-driving.org/about/facts-and-stats/.*
4. Centers for Disease Control and Prevention: Insufficient sleep is a public health problem. Retrieved from *www.cdc.gov/features/dssleep/.*
*5. Saper CB, Fuller PM: Wake-sleep circuitry: An overview, *Curr Opin Neurobiol* 44:186, 2017.
6. Bhat S, Chokroverty S: Hypersomnia in neurodegenerative diseases, *Sleep Med Clin* 12:443, 2017.
7. Equihua-Benitez AC, Guzman-Vasquez K, Drucker-Colin R: Understanding sleep-wake mechanisms and drug discovery, *Expert Opin Drug Discov* 12:643, 2017.
8. Chow M, Cao M: The hypocretin/orexin system in sleep disorders: Preclinical insights and clinical progress, *Nat Sci Sleep* 8:81, 2016.
9. Berry RB, Brooks R, Gamaldo C, et al: *The American Academy of Sleep Medicine: The AASM manual for the scoring of sleep and associated events,* Westchester, IL, 2017, American Academy of Sleep Medicine.
*10. Lowe CJ, Safati A, Hall PA: The neurocognitive consequences of sleep restriction: A meta-analytic review, *Neurosci Biobehav Rev* 80:58, 2017.
*11. Hossin MZ: From habitual sleep hours to morbidity and mortality: Existing evidence, potential mechanisms, and future agenda, *Sleep Health* 2:146, 2016.
*12. Boyko Y, Jennum P, Nikolic M, et al: Sleep in intensive care unit: The role of environment, *J Crit Care* 37:99, 2017.
*13. Simpson NS, Scott-Sutherland J, Gautam S, et al : Chronic exposure to insufficient sleep alters processes of pain habituation and sensitization. *Pain* 159:33, 2018.
*14. Sorscher AJ: Insomnia: Getting to the cause, facilitating relief, *J Fam Pract* 66:216, 2017.
*15. Sateia MJ, Buysse DJ, Krystal AD, et al: Clinical practice guideline for the pharmacologic treatment of chronic insomnia in adults: An AASM clinical practice guideline, *J Clin Sleep Med* 13:307, 2017.
*16. Asnis GM, Thomas M, Henderson MA: Pharmacotherapy treatment options for insomnia: A primer for clinicians, *Int J Mol Sci* 17:50, 2016.
*17. Markota M, Rummans TA, Bostwick JM, et al: Benzodiazepine use in older adults: Dangers, management, and alternative therapies, *Mayo Clin Proc* 91:1632, 2016.
*18. Noyek S, Yaremchuk K, Rotenberg B: Does melatonin have a meaningful role as a sleep aid for jet lag recovery? *Laryngoscope* 126:1719, 2016.
*19. Semelka M, Wilson J, Floyd R. Diagnosis and treatment of obstructive sleep apnea in adults. *Am Fam Physician.* 2016; 94:355.
*20. Abuzaid AS, Al Ashry HS, Elbadawi A, et al: Meta-analysis of cardiovascular outcomes with continuous positive airway pressure therapy in patients with obstructive sleep apnea, *Am J Cardiol* 120:693, 2017.
21. American Academy of Sleep Medicine: *International classification of sleep disorders,* Darien, IL, 2014, American Academy of Sleep Medicine. (Classic)
*22. Bhattarai J, Sumerall S: Current and future treatment options for narcolepsy: A review, *Sleep Sci* 10:19, 2017.
23. National Sleep Foundation: Aging and sleep. Retrieved from *www.sleepfoundation.org/sleep-topics/aging-and-sleep.*
*24. Tahghighi M, Rees CS, Brown JA, et al: What is the impact of shift work on the psychological functioning and resilience of nurses? An integrative review, *J Adv Nurs* 73:2065, 2017.

*Evidence-based information for clinical practice.

8

Pain

Debra Miller-Saultz

One word frees us of all the weight and pain of life. That word is love.

Sophocles

http://evolve.elsevier.com/Lewis/medsurg/

CONCEPTUAL FOCUS

Coping

Functional Ability

Pain

LEARNING OUTCOMES

1. Define pain.
2. Describe the neural mechanisms of pain and pain modulation.
3. Distinguish between nociceptive and neuropathic types of pain.
4. Explain the physical and psychologic effects of unrelieved pain.
5. Interpret the subjective and objective data that are obtained from a comprehensive pain assessment.
6. Describe effective interprofessional pain management techniques.
7. Describe drug and nondrug methods of pain relief.
8. Explain your role and responsibility in pain management.
9. Discuss ethical and legal issues related to pain and pain management.
10. Evaluate the influence of one's own knowledge, beliefs, and attitudes about pain assessment and management.

KEY TERMS

analgesic ceiling, p. 111
breakthrough pain (BTP), p. 108
central sensitization, p. 105
complex regional pain syndrome (CRPS), p. 107
equianalgesic dose, p. 117
modulation, p. 106

multimodal analgesia, p. 110
neuropathic pain, p. 106
nociception, p. 103
nociceptive pain, p. 106
pain, p. 102
patient-controlled analgesia (PCA), p. 119

patient-controlled epidural analgesia (PCEA), p. 119
peripheral sensitization, p. 104
transduction, p. 104
transmission, p. 104
trigger point, p. 120

Pain is a complex, multidimensional experience that can cause suffering and decreased quality of life. Pain is 1 of the major reasons that people seek health care. To effectively assess and manage patients with pain, you need to understand the physiologic and psychosocial dimensions of pain. Pain is interrelated with many concepts. Culture and spirituality influence the expression of pain. Acute pain adversely affects mobility and sleep, leading to fatigue. Having pain is a stressor that can lead to depression. Those with severe or chronic pain are more likely to describe their health as poor and have increased mortality. This chapter presents evidence-based information to help you assess and safely manage pain in collaboration with other interprofessional team members.

MAGNITUDE OF PAIN PROBLEM

Millions of people suffer from pain. Each year in the United States, at least 25 million people have acute pain because of

injury or surgery. Common chronic pain conditions, such as arthritis, migraine headache, and back pain, affect more than 1 million American adults.[1] Of the 1.7 million people diagnosed with cancer each year, about 60% have pain during treatment.[2] Despite the high prevalence and costs of acute and chronic pain, inadequate pain management occurs. Consequences of unrelieved acute pain are shown in Table 8.1.

DEFINITIONS AND DIMENSIONS OF PAIN

In 1968 Margo McCaffery, a nurse and pioneer in pain management, defined **pain** as "whatever the person experiencing the pain says it is, existing whenever the person says it does."[3] The International Association for the Study of Pain (IASP) defines *pain* as "an unpleasant sensory and emotional experience associated with actual or potential tissue damage, or described in terms of such damage."[1]

TABLE 8.1 Negative Consequences of Unrelieved Acute Pain

Response	Possible Consequences
Cardiovascular	
↑ Heart rate	Hypertension
↑ Cardiac output	Unstable angina
↑ Peripheral vascular resistance	Myocardial infarction
↑ Myocardial oxygen consumption	Deep vein thrombosis
↑ Coagulation	
Endocrine and Metabolic	
↑ Adrenocorticotropic hormone (ACTH)	Weight loss (from ↑ catabolism)
↑ Cortisol	↑ Respiratory rate
↑ Antidiuretic hormone (ADH)	↑ Heart rate
↑ Epinephrine and norepinephrine	Shock
↑ Renin, ↑ aldosterone	Glucose intolerance
↓ Insulin	Hyperglycemia
Gluconeogenesis	Fluid overload
Glycogenolysis	Hypertension
Muscle protein catabolism	Urinary retention, ↓ urine output
Gastrointestinal	
↓ Gastric and intestinal motility	Constipation
	Anorexia
	Paralytic ileus
Immunologic	
↓ Immune response	Infection
Musculoskeletal	
Muscle spasm	Immobility
Impaired muscle function	Weakness and fatigue
Neurologic	
Impaired cognitive function	Confusion
	Impaired ability to think, reason, and make decisions
Renal and Urologic	
↓ Urine output	Fluid imbalance
Urinary retention	Electrolyte disturbance
Respiratory	
↓ Tidal volume	Atelectasis
Hypoxemia	Pneumonia
↓ Cough, sputum retention	

TABLE 8.2 Dimensions of Pain

Dimension	Description
Affective	• Emotional responses to pain include anger, fear, depression, and anxiety • Negative emotions impair patient's quality of life
Behavioral	• Observable actions (e.g., grimacing, irritability, coping skills) are used to express or control pain • People unable to communicate may have behavioral changes (e.g., agitation, combativeness)
Cognitive	• Beliefs, attitudes, memories, and meaning attributed to pain influence the ways in which a person responds to pain
Physiologic	• Genetic, anatomic, and physical determinants of pain influence how painful stimuli are processed, recognized, and described
Sociocultural	• Age and gender influence nociceptive processes and responses to opioids • Families and caregivers influence patient's response to pain through their beliefs, behaviors, and support • Culture affects pain expression, medication use, pain-related beliefs, and coping methods

GENDER DIFFERENCES

Pain

Men
- Are less likely to report pain than women
- Report more control over pain
- Are less likely to use alternative treatments for pain

Women
- More often have migraine headache, back pain, arthritis, fibromyalgia, irritable bowel syndrome, neuropathic pain, abdominal pain, and foot ache
- Are more likely to be diagnosed with a nonspecific, somatic disorder
- Are less likely to receive analgesics for symptoms of chest and abdominal pain

These definitions emphasize the subjective nature of pain, in which the patient's self-report is the most valid means of assessment. Although understanding the patient's experience and relying on his or her self-report is essential, this view is problematic for many patients. For example, patients who are comatose or who have dementia, patients who are mentally disabled or challenged, and patients with expressive aphasia have varying abilities to report pain. In these instances, you must include nonverbal information, such as observed behaviors, into your pain assessment.

The emotional distress of pain can cause *suffering*, which is the state of distress associated with loss. Suffering can result in a sense of insecurity, lack of control, and spiritual distress. It is important to assess the ways in which a person's spirituality influences and is influenced by pain.[4]

The meaning of the pain to the person is important. For example, a woman in labor may have severe pain but can manage it without analgesics because for her it is associated with a joyful event. Moreover, she may feel control over her pain because of the training she received in prenatal classes and the knowledge that the pain is time-limited. In contrast, a woman with chronic, undefined musculoskeletal pain may be stressed by thoughts that her pain is "not real," is uncontrollable, or is caused by her own actions. Perceptions influence the ways in which a person responds to pain and must be included in a comprehensive treatment plan.

Some people cope with pain by distracting themselves. Others convince themselves that the pain is permanent, untreatable, and overwhelming. People who believe their pain is uncontrollable and overwhelming are more likely to have poor outcomes.[5] The biopsychosocial model of pain includes the physiologic, affective, cognitive, behavioral, and sociocultural dimensions of pain (Table 8.2).

Families and caregivers influence the patient's response to pain through their beliefs and behaviors. For example, families may discourage the patient from taking opioids because they have preconceived notions and fears that the patient may become addicted. Understanding these beliefs helps you address them through patient and family teaching.

Pain Mechanisms

Nociception is the physiologic process by which information about tissue damage is communicated to the central nervous system (CNS). It involves 4 processes: (1) transduction, (2) transmission, (3) perception, and (4) modulation (Fig. 8.1).

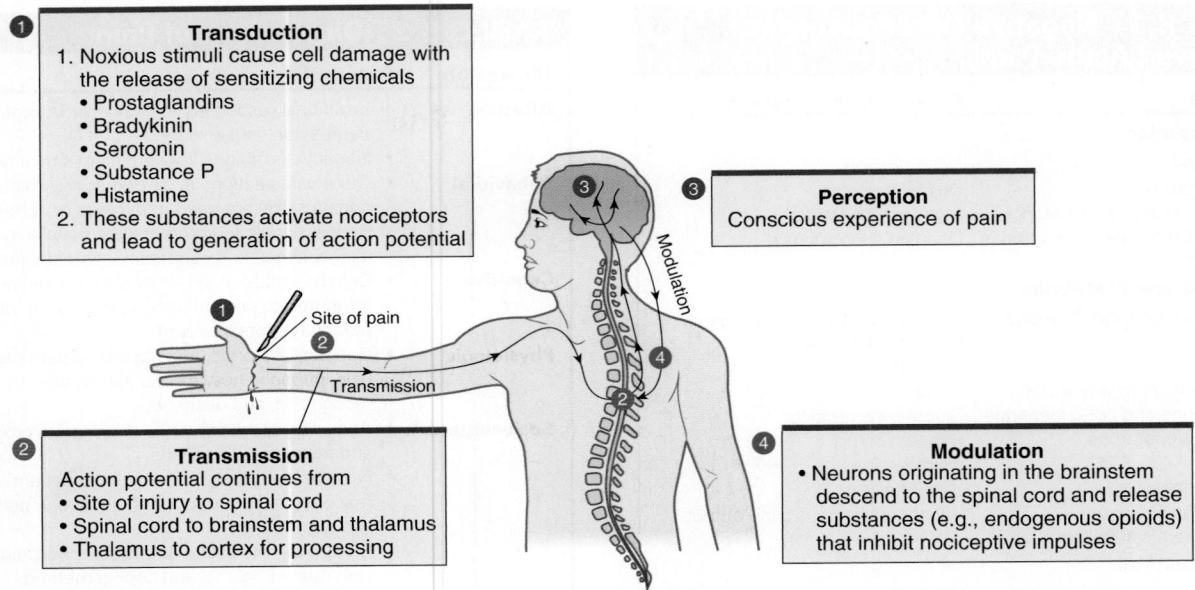

FIG. 8.1 Nociceptive pain originates when the tissue is injured. 1, Transduction occurs when there is release of chemical mediators. 2, Transmission involves the conduct of the action potential from the periphery (injury site) to the spinal cord and then to the brainstem, thalamus, and cerebral cortex. 3, Perception is the conscious awareness of pain. 4, Modulation involves signals from the brain going back down the spinal cord to modify incoming impulses. (Developed by McCaffery M, Pasero C, Paice JA. Modified from McCaffery M, Pasero C: *Pain: Clinical manual*, ed 2, St Louis, 1999, Mosby.)

Transduction. Transduction involves the conversion of a noxious mechanical, thermal, or chemical stimulus into an electrical signal called an action potential. Noxious (tissue-damaging) stimuli, including thermal (e.g., sunburn), mechanical (e.g., surgical incision), or chemical (e.g., toxic substances) stimuli, cause the release of chemicals, such as substance P and adenosine triphosphate (ATP), into the damaged tissues. Other chemicals are released from mast cells (e.g., serotonin, histamine, prostaglandins) and macrophages (e.g., cytokines). These chemicals activate nociceptors, which are specialized receptors, or free nerve endings, which respond to painful stimuli. Activation of nociceptors results in an action potential that is carried from the nociceptors to the spinal cord primarily by small, rapidly conducting, myelinated A-delta fibers and slowly conducting unmyelinated C fibers.

In addition to stimulating nociceptors, inflammation and the subsequent release of chemical mediators lower nociceptor thresholds. As a result, nociceptors may fire in response to stimuli that previously were insufficient to elicit a response. They may also fire in response to non-noxious stimuli, such as light touch. We call this increased susceptibility to nociceptor activation **peripheral sensitization**. Leukotrienes, prostaglandins, cytokines, and substance P are involved in peripheral sensitization. Cyclooxygenase (COX), produced in the inflammatory response, also plays a key role in peripheral sensitization. A clinical example of this process is sunburn. This thermal injury causes inflammation that results in a sensation of pain when the affected skin is lightly touched. Peripheral sensitization amplifies signal transmission, which in turn contributes to central sensitization (discussed under Dorsal Horn Processing). The pain from activation of peripheral nociceptors is called nociceptive pain (described later in the chapter on p. 106).

Therapies that change either the local environment or sensitivity of the peripheral nociceptors can prevent transduction and initiation of an action potential. Decreasing the effects of chemicals released at the periphery is the basis of several drug approaches to pain relief. For example, nonsteroidal antiinflammatory drugs (NSAIDs), such as ibuprofen (Advil), exert their analgesic effects by blocking the action of COX (see Fig. 11.4).

Transmission. Transmission is the process by which pain signals are relayed from the periphery to the spinal cord and then to the brain. Nerves that carry pain impulses from the periphery to the spinal cord are called *primary afferent fibers*. These include A-delta and C fibers. Each is responsible for a different pain sensation. A-delta fibers conduct pain rapidly and are responsible for the initial, sharp pain that accompanies tissue injury. C fibers transmit painful stimuli more slowly and produce pain that is typically aching or throbbing. Primary afferent fibers end in the dorsal horn of the spinal cord. Activity in the dorsal horn integrates and modulates pain inputs from the periphery.

The movement of pain impulses from the site of transduction to the brain is shown in Fig. 8.1. Three segments are involved in nociceptive signal transmission: (1) transmission along the peripheral nerve fibers to the spinal cord, (2) dorsal horn processing, and (3) transmission to the thalamus and cerebral cortex.

Drugs that stabilize the neuronal membrane act on peripheral sodium channels to inhibit movement of nerve impulses. These medications include local anesthetics (e.g., injectable or topical lidocaine, bupivacaine [Sensorcaine]) and antiseizure drugs (e.g., gabapentin [Neurontin]).

Transmission to Spinal Cord. The *first-order neuron* extends the entire distance from the periphery to the dorsal horn with no synapses. For example, an afferent fiber from the great toe travels from the toe through the fifth lumbar nerve root into

FIG. 8.2 Sequence of mechanisms leading to peripheral and central sensitization. Increased susceptibility to nociceptor activation is called *peripheral sensitization.* Increased sensitivity and hyperexcitability of neurons in the CNS is called *central sensitization.*

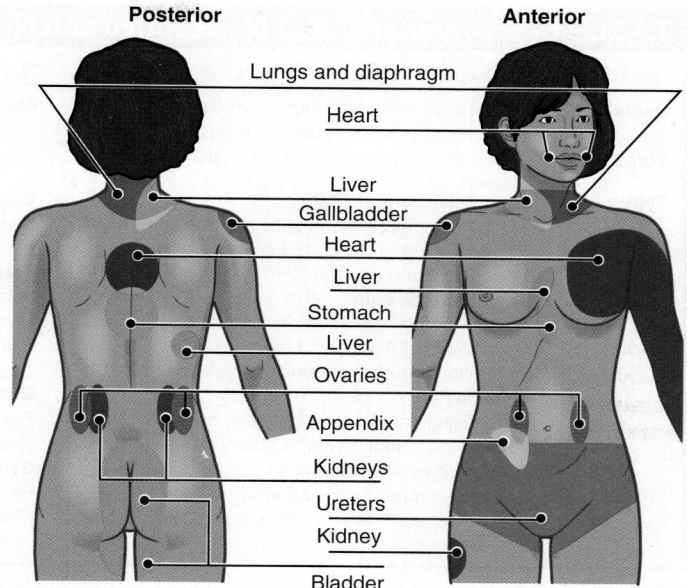

FIG. 8.3 Typical areas of referred pain.

the spinal cord; it is 1 cell. Once generated, an action potential travels all the way to the spinal cord unless it is blocked by a sodium channel inhibitor (e.g., local anesthetic) or disrupted by a lesion, such as a dorsal root entry zone lesion.

The way nerve fibers enter the spinal cord is central to the notion of spinal dermatomes. *Dermatomes* are areas on the skin that are innervated primarily by a single spinal cord segment. The distinct pattern of the rash caused by herpes zoster (shingles) across the back and trunk is determined by dermatomes (see Fig. 23.7). Different dermatomes and their innervations are shown in Fig. 55.7.

Dorsal Horn Processing. Once a nociceptive signal arrives in the spinal cord, it is processed within the dorsal horn. Neurotransmitters released from the afferent fiber bind to receptors on nearby cells. Some of these neurotransmitters (e.g., glutamate, substance P) produce activation. Others (e.g., γ-aminobutyric acid [GABA], serotonin) inhibit activation of nearby cells. In this area, exogenous and endogenous opioids (e.g., encephalin, β-endorphin) play a vital role by binding to opioid receptors and blocking the release of neurotransmitters, especially substance P. They produce analgesic effects similar to those of exogenous opioids, such as morphine. The neurons that project to the thalamus are called *second-order neurons.*

Increased sensitivity and hyperexcitability of neurons in the CNS is called central sensitization. With central sensitization, the central processing circuits are altered. Peripheral tissue damage or nerve injury can cause central sensitization. Continued nociceptive input from the periphery maintains it (Fig. 8.2). In some cases, central sensitization can be long-lasting due to multiple changes that occur in the periphery and CNS.[6]

Because of the increased excitability of CNS neurons, normal sensory inputs cause abnormal sensing and responses to painful and other stimuli. This explains why some people have significant pain from touch or tactile stimulation in and around the areas of tissue or nerve injury. We call this *allodynia,* pain from a stimulus that is not typically painful. It also explains why some people have *hyperalgesia,* an exaggerated or increased pain response to noxious stimuli.

With ongoing stimulation of slowly conducting unmyelinated C-fiber nociceptors, firing of specialized dorsal horn neurons gradually increases. These inputs can lead to the sprouting of wide dynamic range (WDR) neuron dendrites and

the induction of glutamate-dependent *N*-methyl-ᴅ-aspartate (NMDA) receptors. This results in an increased capacity to transmit a broader range of stimuli-producing signals, which are then passed up the spinal cord and to the brain. This process is known as *wind-up.*[7] Activation of NMDA receptors also plays a role in wind-up. NMDA receptor antagonists, such as ketamine (Ketalar), potentially interrupt or block mechanisms that lead to or sustain central sensitization. Wind-up is like central sensitization and hyperalgesia in that it occurs in response to C-fiber inputs. Wind-up is different, however, in that it can be short-lasting, while central sensitization and hyperalgesia persist over time.

It is important for you to understand that acute, unrelieved pain leads to chronic pain through central sensitization. Even brief intervals of acute pain can induce long-term neuronal remodeling and sensitization *(plasticity),* chronic pain, and lasting psychologic distress.

Neuroplasticity refers to processes that allow neurons in the brain to compensate for injury and adjust their responses to new situations or changes in their environment.[8] Neuroplasticity contributes to adaptive mechanisms for reducing pain but can result in maladaptive mechanisms that enhance pain sensitivity.

Genetic variability may play a key role in changes that occur in the CNS and the response to different analgesic therapies to treat pain. Understanding this phenomenon helps explain individual differences in response to pain and why some patients develop chronic pain conditions and others do not.[9] *Referred pain* must be considered when interpreting the location of pain reported by the person with an injury or a disease involving visceral organs. The location of a stimulus may be distant from the pain location reported by the patient (Fig. 8.3). For example, pain from liver disease often occurs in the right upper abdominal quadrant. It also can be referred to the anterior and posterior neck region, shoulder area, and posterior flank area. If we do not consider referred pain when evaluating a pain location report, diagnostic tests and therapy could be misdirected.

TABLE 8.3	Comparison of Nociceptive and Neuropathic Pain	
	Nociceptive Pain	**Neuropathic Pain***
Definition	Normal processing of stimulus that damages normal tissue or has the potential to do so if prolonged	Abnormal processing of sensory input by the peripheral or central nervous system
Treatment	Usually responsive to nonopioid and/or opioid drugs	Usually includes adjuvant analgesics
Types	**Superficial Somatic Pain** Pain arising from skin, mucous membranes, subcutaneous tissue. Tends to be well localized *Examples:* Sunburn, skin contusions **Deep Somatic Pain** Pain arising from muscles, fasciae, bones, tendons. Localized or diffuse and radiating *Examples:* Arthritis, tendonitis, myofascial pain **Visceral Pain** Pain arising from visceral organs, such as the GI tract and bladder. Well or poorly localized. Often referred to cutaneous sites *Examples:* Appendicitis, pancreatitis, cancer affecting internal organs, irritable bowel and bladder syndromes	**Central Pain** Caused by primary lesion or dysfunction in the CNS *Examples:* Poststroke pain, pain associated with multiple sclerosis **Peripheral Neuropathies** Pain felt along the distribution of 1 or many peripheral nerves caused by damage to the nerve *Examples:* Diabetic neuropathy, alcohol-nutritional neuropathy, trigeminal neuralgia, postherpetic neuralgia **Deafferentation Pain** Pain resulting from a loss of or altered afferent input *Examples:* Phantom limb pain, postmastectomy pain, spinal cord injury pain **Sympathetically Maintained Pain** Pain that persists secondary to autonomic nervous system dysfunction *Examples:* Phantom limb pain, complex regional pain syndrome

*Some types of neuropathic pain (e.g., postherpetic neuralgia) are caused by more than 1 neuropathologic mechanism.

Transmission to Thalamus and Cortex. From the dorsal horn, nociceptive stimuli are communicated to the *third-order neuron,* primarily in the thalamus. Fibers of dorsal horn projection cells enter the brain through several pathways, including the spinothalamic tract and spinoreticular tract. Distinct thalamic nuclei receive nociceptive input from the spinal cord and have projections to several regions in the cerebral cortex, where the perception of pain is presumed to occur.

Therapeutic approaches that target pain transmission include opioid analgesics that bind to opioid receptors on primary afferent and dorsal horn neurons. These agents mimic the inhibitory effects of endogenous opioids. Another medication, baclofen (Lioresal), inhibits pain transmission by binding to GABA receptors, thus mimicking the inhibitory effects of GABA.

Perception. *Perception* occurs when pain is recognized, defined, and assigned meaning by the person experiencing the pain. In the brain, nociceptive input is perceived as pain. There is no single, precise location where pain perception occurs. Instead, pain perception involves several brain structures. For example, it is thought that the reticular activating system is responsible for warning the person to attend to the pain stimulus; the somatosensory system is responsible for localization and characterization of pain; and the limbic system is responsible for the emotional and behavioral responses to pain.

Cortical structures are crucial to constructing the meaning of the pain. Therefore behavioral strategies, such as distraction and relaxation, are effective pain-reducing therapies for many people. Meditation and imagery can affect pain perception. By directing attention away from the pain sensation, patients can reduce the sensory and affective components of pain.

Modulation. Modulation involves the activation of descending pathways that exert inhibitory or facilitatory effects on the transmission of pain (Fig. 8.1). Depending on the type and degree of modulation, nociceptive stimuli may or may not be perceived as pain. Modulation of pain signals can occur at the level of the periphery, spinal cord, brainstem, and cerebral cortex. Descending modulatory fibers release chemicals, such as serotonin, norepinephrine, GABA, and endogenous opioids, which can inhibit pain transmission.

Several antidepressants exert their effects through the modulatory systems. For example, tricyclic antidepressants (e.g., amitriptyline) and serotonin norepinephrine reuptake inhibitors (SNRIs) (e.g., venlafaxine) are used to manage chronic noncancer and cancer pain. These agents interfere with the reuptake of serotonin and norepinephrine, thereby increasing their availability to inhibit noxious stimuli.

CLASSIFICATION OF PAIN

We categorize pain in several ways. Most often, pain is categorized as nociceptive or neuropathic based on underlying pathology (Table 8.3). Another useful scheme is to classify pain as acute or chronic (Table 8.4).

Nociceptive Pain

Nociceptive pain is caused by damage to somatic or visceral tissue. *Somatic pain* often is further categorized as superficial or deep. *Superficial pain* arises from skin, mucous membranes, and subcutaneous tissues. It is often described as sharp, burning, or prickly. *Deep pain* is often described as aching or throbbing. It originates in bone, joint, muscle, skin, or connective tissue.

Visceral pain comes from the activation of nociceptors in the internal organs and lining of the body cavities, such as the thoracic and abdominal cavities. Visceral nociceptors respond to inflammation, stretching, and ischemia. Stretching of hollow viscera in the intestines and bladder that occurs from tumor involvement or obstruction can produce intense cramping pain. Examples of visceral nociceptive pain include pain from a surgical incision, pancreatitis, and inflammatory bowel disease.

Neuropathic Pain

Neuropathic pain is caused by damage to peripheral nerves or structures in the CNS. Although neuropathic pain is often associated with diabetic neuropathy and other neuropathic pain syndromes, around 8% of the general population has pain with neuropathic characteristics.[9] Typically described as numbing, hot, burning, shooting, stabbing, sharp, or electric shock–like,

TABLE 8.4 Differences Between Acute and Chronic Pain

	Acute Pain	Chronic Pain
Onset	Sudden	Gradual or sudden
Duration	<3 mo or as long as it takes for normal healing to occur	>3 mo. May start as acute injury or event but continues past the normal time for recovery
Severity	Mild to severe	Mild to severe
Cause of pain	Usually can identify a precipitating event (e.g., illness, surgery)	May not be known. Original cause of pain may differ from mechanisms that maintain the pain.
Course of pain	Decreases over time and goes away as recovery occurs	Typically pain does not go away. Characterized by periods of increasing and decreasing pain
Typical physical and behavioral manifestations	Manifestations vary but can reflect sympathetic nervous system activation: • ↑ Heart rate, respiratory rate, BP • Diaphoresis, pallor • Anxiety, agitation, confusion • Urine retention	Common behavioral manifestations: • Flat affect • ↓ Physical activity • Fatigue • Withdrawal from social interaction
Usual goals of treatment	Pain control with ability to take part in recovery activities. Minimize side effects of treatment	Pain control to the extent possible. Focus on enhancing function and quality of life

neuropathic pain can be sudden, intense, short lived, or lingering. Paroxysmal firing of injured nerves is responsible for shooting and electric shock-like sensations. Common causes of neuropathic pain include trauma, inflammation, metabolic diseases (e.g., diabetes), alcoholism, nervous system infections (e.g., herpes zoster, human immunodeficiency virus), tumors, toxins, and neurologic diseases (e.g., multiple sclerosis). Examples of neuropathic pain conditions include phantom limb sensation, diabetic neuropathy, and trigeminal neuralgia. No single sign or symptom is diagnostic for neuropathic pain.

CNS lesions or dysfunction cause *central pain*. *Deafferentation pain* results from loss of or altered afferent input secondary to either peripheral nerve injury (e.g., amputation) or CNS damage, including a spinal cord injury. Painful peripheral polyneuropathies (pain felt along the distribution of multiple peripheral nerves) and painful mononeuropathies (pain felt along the distribution of a damaged nerve) arise from damage to peripheral nerves. They generate pain that people may describe as burning, paroxysmal, or shock-like. The patient may have positive or negative motor and sensory signs, including numbness, allodynia, or change in reflexes and motor strength.

Sympathetically maintained pain is associated with a group of conditions that have a degree of changes in autonomic nervous system. One particularly debilitating type is **complex regional pain syndrome (CRPS)**. Typical features include dramatic changes in the color and temperature of the skin over the affected limb or body part, accompanied by intense burning pain, skin sensitivity,

sweating, and swelling. CRPS type I is often triggered by tissue injury, surgery, or a vascular event, such as stroke.[10] CRPS type II includes all these features and a peripheral nerve lesion.

Neuropathic pain is often not well controlled by opioid analgesics alone. Treatment often requires a multimodal approach combining various adjuvant analgesics from different drug classes. These include tricyclic antidepressants (e.g., amitriptyline), SNRIs (e.g., bupropion [Wellbutrin, Zyban]), antiseizure drugs (e.g., pregabalin [Lyrica]), transdermal lidocaine, and α_2-adrenergic agonists (e.g., clonidine). NMDA receptor antagonists, such as ketamine, have shown promise in alleviating neuropathic pain refractory to other drugs.

Acute and Chronic Pain

Acute pain and chronic pain differ in their cause, course, manifestations, and treatment (Table 8.4). Examples of *acute pain* include postoperative pain, labor pain, pain from trauma (e.g., lacerations, fractures, sprains), pain from infection (e.g., dysuria from cystitis), and pain from acute ischemia. For acute pain, treatment includes analgesics for symptom control and treatment of the underlying cause (e.g., splinting for a fracture, antibiotic therapy for an infection). Normally, acute pain decreases over time as healing occurs. However, acute pain that persists can lead to disabling chronic pain states. For example, pain associated with herpes zoster subsides as the acute infection resolves, usually within a month. However, sometimes the pain persists and develops into a chronic pain state called *postherpetic neuralgia*. Because of the connection between inadequately treated acute pain and chronic pain, it is important to treat acute pain aggressively.

Chronic pain, or *persistent pain*, lasts for longer periods, often defined as longer than 3 months or past the time when an expected acute pain or acute injury should subside. The severity and functional impact of chronic pain often are disproportionate to objective findings because of changes in the nervous system not detectable with standard tests. Although acute pain functions as a signal, warning the person of potential or actual tissue damage, chronic pain does not appear to have an adaptive role. Chronic pain can be disabling and often is accompanied by anxiety and depression.

PAIN ASSESSMENT

Assessment is an essential, although often overlooked, step in pain management. Regularly screen all patients for pain and, when present, perform a more thorough pain assessment. The key to accurate and effective pain assessment is to consider the principles of pain assessment (Table 8.5).

The goals of a nursing pain assessment are to (1) describe the patient's pain experience to identify and implement appropriate pain management techniques and (2) identify the patient's goal for therapy and resources for self-management.

Elements of a Pain Assessment

Most components of a pain assessment involve direct interview or observation of the patient. Diagnostic studies and physical examination findings complete the initial assessment. Although the assessment differs according to the clinical setting, patient population, and point of care (i.e., whether the assessment is part of an initial workup or a reassessment of pain following therapy), the evaluation of pain should always be multidimensional (Table 8.6).

Before beginning any assessment, recognize that patients may use words other than "pain." For example, older adults may deny that they have pain but respond positively when asked

TABLE 8.5 Principles of Pain Assessment

Principles	Nursing Implications
1. Patients have the right to appropriate assessment and management of pain.	• Assess pain in *all* patients.
2. Pain is always subjective.	• Patient's self-report of pain is the single most reliable indicator of pain. • Accept and respect this self-report unless there are clear reasons for doubt.
3. Physiologic and behavioral signs of pain (e.g., tachycardia, grimacing) are not reliable or specific for pain.	• Do not rely primarily on observations and objective signs of pain unless the patient is unable to self-report pain.
4. Pain is an unpleasant sensory and emotional experience.	• Address physical and psychologic aspects of pain when assessing pain.
5. Assessment approaches, including tools, must be appropriate for the patient population.	• Special considerations are needed for assessing pain in patients with difficulty communicating. • Include family members in the assessment process (when appropriate).
6. Pain can exist even when no physical cause can be found.	• Do not attribute pain that does not have an identifiable cause to psychologic causes.
7. Different patients have different levels of pain in response to comparable stimuli.	• A uniform pain threshold does not exist.
8. Patients with chronic pain may be more sensitive to pain and other stimuli.	• Pain tolerance varies among and within persons depending on several factors (e.g., genetics, energy level, coping skills, prior experience with pain).
9. Unrelieved pain has adverse consequences. Acute pain that is not adequately controlled can result in physiologic changes that increase the chance of developing persistent pain.	• Encourage patients to report pain, especially patients who are reluctant to discuss pain, deny pain when it is probably present, or fail to follow through on prescribed treatments.

if they have soreness or aching. Document the specific words that the patient uses to describe pain. Then consistently ask the patient about pain using those words.

Pain Pattern. Assessing pain *onset* involves determining when the pain started. Patients with acute pain resulting from injury, acute illness, or treatment (e.g., surgery) typically know exactly when their pain began. Those with chronic pain may be less able to relate when the pain started. Establish the *duration* of the pain (how long it has lasted). This information helps to determine whether the pain is acute or chronic and helps identify the cause of the pain. For example, a patient with advanced cancer who has chronic low back pain from spinal stenosis reports a sudden, severe pain in the back that began 2 days ago. Knowing the onset and duration can lead to a diagnostic workup that may reveal new metastatic disease in the spine.

The pain pattern gives clues about the cause of the pain and directs its treatment. Many types of chronic pain (e.g., arthritis pain) can increase and decrease over time. A patient may have pain all the time (around-the-clock pain), as well as discrete periods of intermittent pain.

Breakthrough pain (BTP) is transient, moderate to severe pain that occurs in patients whose baseline persistent pain is otherwise mild to moderate and fairly well controlled. The average peak of BTP can be 3 to 5 minutes and can last up to 30 minutes or even longer. BTP can be either predictable or unpredictable. Patients can have 1 to many episodes per day. Several transmucosal fentanyl products are used specifically to treat BTP.

End-of-dose failure is pain that occurs before the expected duration of a specific analgesic. It should not be confused with BTP. Pain that occurs at the end of the duration of an analgesic often leads to a prolonged increase in the baseline persistent pain. For example, in a patient on transdermal fentanyl (Duragesic patches) the typical duration of action is 72 hours. An increase in pain after 48 hours on the drug would be an end-of-dose failure. End-of-dose failure signals the need for changes in the dose or scheduling of the analgesic. Episodic, procedural, or *incident pain* is a transient increase in pain that is caused by a specific activity or event that precipitates pain. Examples include dressing changes, movement, position changes, and procedures, such as catheterization.

TABLE 8.6 Nursing Assessment
Pain

Subjective Data
Important Health Information

Health history: Pain history includes onset, location, intensity, quality, patterns, aggravating and alleviating factors, and expression of pain. Coping strategies. Past treatments and their effectiveness. Review health care use related to the pain problem (e.g., emergency department visits, treatment at pain clinics, visits to primary HCPs and specialists)

Medications: Use of any prescription or over-the-counter, illicit, or herbal products for pain relief. Alcohol use

Nondrug measures: Use of therapies, such as massage, heat or ice, Reiki, aromatherapy, acupuncture, hypnosis, yoga, or meditation

Functional Health Patterns

Health perception–health management: Social and work history, mental health history, smoking history. Effects of pain on emotions, relationships, sleep, and activities. Interviews with family members. Records from psychologic/psychiatric treatment related to the pain

Elimination: Constipation related to opioid drug use, other medication use, or pain related to elimination

Activity-exercise: Fatigue, limitations in ability to perform activities of daily living (ADLs), instrumental activities of daily living (IADLs), and pain related to use of muscles

Sexuality-reproductive: Decreased libido

Coping–stress tolerance: Psychologic evaluation using standardized measures to examine coping style, depression, anxiety

Objective Data

Physical examination, including evaluation of functional limitations
Psychosocial evaluation, including mood

Location. Determining the *location* of pain helps us identify possible causes and treatment. Some patients may be able to specify the precise location(s) of their pain. Others may describe general areas or comment that they "hurt all over." The location of the pain may be referred from its origin to another site (Fig. 8.3). For example, myocardial infarction can result in pain in the left shoulder. Pain can radiate from its origin to another site. For example, angina pectoris can radiate from the chest to the jaw or down the left arm. We refer to this as radiating pain. *Sciatica* is pain that follows the course of the sciatic nerve. It may originate

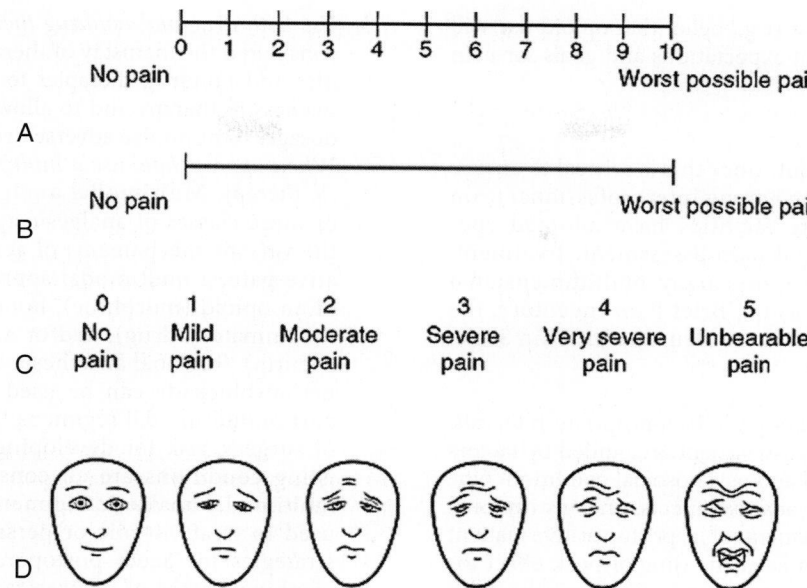

FIG. 8.4 Pain intensity scales. A, 0 to 10 numeric scale. B, Visual analog scale. C, Descriptive scale. D, Faces Pain Scale. (Modified from Baird M: *Manual of critical care nursing: Nursing interventions and collaborative management,* ed 2, St Louis, 2015, Elsevier.)

from joints or muscles around the back or from compression or damage to the sciatic nerve. The pain is projected along the course of the peripheral nerve, causing painful shooting sensations down the back of the thigh and inside of the leg to the foot.

Obtain information about the location of pain by asking the patient to (1) describe the site(s) of pain, (2) point to painful areas on the body, or (3) mark painful areas on a pain map. Because many patients have more than 1 site of pain, make certain that the patient describes every location.

Intensity. Assessing the severity, or *intensity,* of pain provides a reliable measure to determine the type of treatment and its effectiveness. Pain scales help the patient communicate pain intensity. Base your choice of a scale on the patient's developmental needs and cognitive status (Fig. 8.4). Most adults can rate the intensity of their pain using a numeric rating scale (e.g., 0 = no pain, 10 = the worst pain). Patients who wish to have word choices to quantify pain may prefer a verbal descriptor scale (e.g., none, mild, moderate, severe). For those oriented to vertical representations, the Pain Thermometer Scale is an option. Other visual pain measures, such as the Wong-Baker FACES pain tool, are useful for patients with cognitive or language barriers to describe their pain.[11] Pain assessment measures for cognitively impaired adults and nonverbal adults are addressed later in this chapter.

Although intensity is an important factor in determining analgesic approaches, do not dose patients with opioids solely based on reported pain scores.[12] Opioid "dosing by numbers" without considering a patient's sedation level and respiratory status can lead to unsafe practices and serious adverse events. Safer analgesic administration can be achieved by balancing an amount of pain relief with analgesic side effects and using a multimodal approach. (Multimodal approach is described later in this chapter.) Adjustments in therapy can be made to promote better pain control and minimize adverse outcomes.

Quality. The pain *quality* refers to the nature or characteristics of the pain. For example, patients often describe neuropathic pain as burning, numbing, shooting, stabbing, electric shock–like, or itchy. Nociceptive pain may be described as sharp, aching, throbbing, dull, and cramping. Since the quality of pain relates to a degree to the classification of pain (e.g., neuropathic, nociceptive), these descriptors can help to guide treatment options that best address the specific mechanism of pain.

Associated Symptoms. *Associated symptoms,* such as anxiety, fatigue, and depression, may worsen or be worsened by pain. Patients with pain often report poor sleep and subsequent daytime sleepiness. Poor sleep can further increase pain perception. Ask about aggravating factors that increase pain as well as activities and situations that alleviate pain. For example, musculoskeletal pain may be increased or decreased with movement and ambulation. Resting or immobilizing a painful body part can decrease pain. Knowing what makes pain better or worse can help characterize the type of pain and be helpful in selecting treatments.

Management Strategies. As people experience and live with pain, they may cope differently and be more or less willing to try different strategies to manage it. Some strategies are successful, while others are not. To maximize the effectiveness of the pain treatment plan, ask patients what they are using now to control pain, what they have used in the past, and the outcomes of these methods. Strategies include prescription and nonprescription drugs and nondrug therapies, such as hot and cold applications, complementary and alternative therapies (e.g., acupuncture), and relaxation strategies (e.g., imagery). It is important to document both those that work and those that are ineffective.

Impact of Pain. Pain can have a profound influence on a patient's quality of life and functioning. Assess the effect of the pain on the patient's ability to sleep, enjoy life, interact with others, perform work and household duties, and engage in physical and social activities. Assess the impact of pain on the patient's mood.

In an acute care setting, time limitations may dictate a shortened assessment. At a minimum, assess the effects of the pain on the patient's sleep and daily activities, relationships with others, physical activity, and emotional well-being. Include the ways in which the patient describes the pain and strategies used to cope with and control the pain.

Patient's Beliefs, Expectations, and Goals. Patient and family beliefs, attitudes, and expectations influence responses to pain and pain treatment. Assess for attitudes and beliefs that may hinder effective treatment (e.g., belief that opioid use will result in addiction). Ask about expectations and goals for pain management.

Documentation

Document the pain assessment, since this is critical to ensure safe, effective communication among interprofessional team members. Many health care facilities have adopted specific tools to record an initial pain assessment, treatment, and reassessment. There also are many multidimensional pain assessment tools, such as the Brief Pain Inventory, the McGill Pain Questionnaire, and the Neuropathic Pain Scale.

Reassessment

It is critical for you to reassess pain at appropriate intervals. The frequency and scope of reassessment are guided by factors such as pain severity, physical and psychosocial condition, type of intervention and risks for adverse effects, and institutional policy. For example, reassessment of a postoperative patient may be done frequently, such as at the time of peak effect for each analgesic dose. In a long-term care facility, residents with chronic pain are reassessed at least quarterly or with a change in condition or functional status.

PAIN TREATMENT

Basic Principles

All pain treatment plans are based on the following 10 principles and practice standards:

1. *Follow the principles of pain assessment* (Table 8.5). Remember that pain is a subjective experience. The patient is not only the best judge of his or her own pain but also the expert on the effectiveness of each pain treatment.
2. *Use a holistic approach to pain management.* The pain experience affects all aspects of a person's life. Thus a holistic approach to assessment, treatment, and evaluation is required.
3. *Every patient deserves adequate pain management.* Many patient populations, including ethnic minorities, cognitively impaired adults, and people with past or current substance abuse, are at risk for inadequate pain management. Be aware of your own biases and ensure that all patients are treated respectfully.
4. *Base the treatment plan on the patient's goals.* Discuss with the patient realistic goals for pain relief during the initial pain assessment. Although goals can be described in terms of pain intensity (e.g., the desire for average pain to decrease from "8/10" to "3/10"), with chronic pain conditions, encourage functional goal setting (e.g., a goal of performing certain daily activities, such as socializing and recreational activities). Encourage functional activities for the patient with acute pain as well. For example, the pain must be at a level that allows the patient to use the incentive spirometer, get out of bed, and ambulate. Over time, reassess these goals and progress made toward meeting them. The patient, in collaboration with the interprofessional team, determines new goals. If the patient has unrealistic goals for therapy, such as wanting to be completely rid of all chronic arthritis pain or be completely pain free after a major surgery, work with the patient to establish a more realistic goal.
5. *Use both drug and nondrug therapies.* Although drugs are considered the mainstay of therapy, include self-care activities and nondrug therapies to increase the overall effectiveness of therapy and to allow for the reduction of drug dosages to minimize adverse drug effects.
6. *When appropriate, use a multimodal approach to analgesic therapy.* **Multimodal analgesia** employs the use of 2 or more classes of analgesic agents to take advantage of the various mechanisms of action. For acute, postoperative pain, a multimodal approach may include the use of an opioid (morphine), nonopioid (nonsteroidal antiinflammatory drug), and/or antiseizure drug (e.g., gabapentin). Regional anesthesia and continuous peripheral neural blockade can be used with local anesthetics as part of multimodal regimens.[13] Factors such as age, type of surgery, risk for developing chronic pain, and coexisting conditions are all considered when designing a multimodal analgesic regimen. Multimodal analgesia is used to treat chronic or persistent pain. Similar to the strategies for acute postoperative pain, the goal is to combine classes of analgesics for the maximum benefit of relieving pain with minimum doses to achieve relief and reduce adverse events from analgesics. Multimodal regimens achieve superior pain relief, enhance patient satisfaction, and decrease adverse effects of individual drugs.[14]
7. *Address pain using an interprofessional approach.* The expertise and perspectives of an interprofessional team are often necessary to provide effective assessment and therapies for patients with both acute and chronic pain. For hospitalized patients or those with complex acute or chronic pain issues, anesthesiology-based pain services may be available to manage patients with technology-supported pain care (e.g., patient-controlled analgesia or regional analgesia). Team members for these services can include pain management nurses, nurse practitioners, clinical nurse specialists, anesthesiologists, and clinical pharmacists. These teams help to establish realistic goals with patients and families to facilitate recovery and discharge. Many outpatient pain management centers or clinics are available. Some provide comprehensive pain care and employ multiple providers, including anesthesiologists, rehabilitation physicians, nurses, psychologists, physical and occupational therapists, and social workers. Services may focus on medication management, pain interventional therapies, psychologic counseling, cognitive and behavioral therapies, rehabilitative therapies (physical and occupational therapy), and social services. Specialized pain treatment centers may also offer more holistic therapies, such as massage, music and art therapy, and acupuncture. Advise patients seeking specialized pain care from outpatient treatment centers to check about services that are provided.
8. *Evaluate the effectiveness of all therapies to ensure that they are meeting the patient's goals.* Achievement of an effective treatment plan often requires trial and error. Adjustments in drug, dosage, or route are common to achieve maximal benefits while minimizing adverse effects. This trial-and-error process can become frustrating for the patient and caregivers. Reassure them that pain relief, if not pain cessation, is possible and that the interprofessional team will continue to work with them to achieve adequate pain relief.

TABLE 8.7 Drug Therapy
Managing Side Effects of Pain Medications

Side effects can be managed by 1 or more of the following methods:
- Decreasing the dose of analgesic by 10% to 15%
- Changing to a different medication in the same class
- Adding a drug to counteract the adverse effect of the analgesic (e.g., using a stool softener for patients experiencing opioid-induced constipation)
- Using an administration route that minimizes drug concentrations (e.g., intraspinal administration of opioids used to minimize high drug levels that produce sedation, nausea, and vomiting)

9. *Prevent and/or manage medication side effects.* Side effects or adverse events are a major reason for treatment failure and nonadherence. Side effects are managed in 1 of several ways, as described in Table 8.7. You play a key role in monitoring for and treating side effects and in teaching patients and caregivers how to minimize these effects.

10. *Include patient and caregiver teaching throughout assessment and treatment.* Content should include information about the causes of the pain, pain assessment methods, treatment goals and options, expectations of pain management, proper use of drugs, side effect management, and nondrug and self-help pain relief measures. Document the teaching and include evaluation of patient and caregiver comprehension.

Drug Therapy for Pain

Pain medications generally are divided into 3 categories: nonopioids, opioids, and adjuvant drugs. Patient-centered treatment regimens may include medications from 1 or more of these groups. Mild pain often can be relieved using nonopioids alone. Moderate to severe pain usually requires an opioid. Certain types of pain, such as neuropathic pain, typically require adjuvant drug therapy alone or in combination with an opioid or another class of analgesics. Pain caused by cancer may be treated with chemotherapy or radiation therapy, as well as pain medications.

Nonopioids. Nonopioid analgesics include acetaminophen, aspirin and other salicylates, and NSAIDs (Table 8.8). These agents are characterized by (1) their analgesic properties have an **analgesic ceiling**; that is, increasing the dose beyond an upper limit provides no greater analgesia; (2) they do not produce tolerance or physical dependence; and (3) many are available without a prescription. To provide safe care, monitor over-the-counter (OTC) analgesic use to avoid serious problems related to drug interactions, side effects, and overdose.

Nonopioids are effective for mild to moderate pain. They are often used in conjunction with opioids because they allow for effective pain relief using lower opioid doses (thereby causing fewer opioid side effects). This phenomenon is called the *opioid-sparing effect.*

Aspirin is effective for mild pain, but its use is limited by its common side effects, including increased risk for bleeding, especially gastrointestinal (GI) bleeding. Other salicylates, such as choline magnesium trisalicylate (Trilisate), cause fewer GI problems and bleeding abnormalities. Similar to aspirin, acetaminophen (Tylenol) has analgesic and antipyretic effects. Unlike aspirin, it has no antiplatelet or antiinflammatory effects. Acetaminophen is well tolerated. It is metabolized by the liver.

TABLE 8.8 Drug Therapy
Selected Nonopioid Analgesics

Drug	Nursing Considerations
Nonsalicylate acetaminophen (Tylenol)	• Chronic overdose: Liver toxicity • Sustained release, rectal suppository, and injectable forms (OFIRMEV) available • Maximum daily dose of 3 g • Oral doses of >3 g may cause hepatotoxicity • Acute overdose: Acute liver failure • Chronic overdose: Liver toxicity • Maximum daily IV dose should not exceed 4 g/day for adults ≥50 kg
Nonsteroidal Antiinflammatory Drugs (NSAIDs)	
celecoxib (Celebrex)	• Causes fewer GI side effects (e.g., bleeding) than other NSAIDs, but risk still present • More costly than other NSAIDs • May increase risk for serious cardiovascular thrombotic events, myocardial infarction, and stroke • Risks may increase with duration of use, preexisting cardiovascular disease, or risk factors for cardiovascular disease
diclofenac K	• Use lowest effective dose for shortest possible duration • Available in oral, ophthalmic, topical preparations
ibuprofen (Advil)	• Use lowest effective dose for shortest possible duration • Increased risk for serious GI adverse events (bleeding, ulceration, perforation), especially in older adults • May increase risk for serious cardiovascular thrombotic events, myocardial infarction, and stroke • May increase risk for hypertension and renal insufficiency
ketorolac	• Limit treatment to 5 days • May precipitate renal failure in dehydrated patients
naproxen (Naprosyn, Aleve)	• Use lowest effective dose for shortest possible duration • Increased risk for serious GI adverse events (bleeding, ulceration, perforation), especially in older adults • Contraindicated for the treatment of perioperative pain in setting of coronary artery bypass graft (CABG) surgery
Salicylates	
aspirin	• Rectal suppository and sustained-release preparations available • Chance of upper GI bleeding • Used more often in low doses as a cardioprotective measure than for its analgesic properties
choline magnesium trisalicylate (Trilisate)	• Unlike aspirin and NSAIDs, does not increase bleeding time

Hepatotoxicity may result from chronic dosing of more than 3 g/day, acute overdose, or use by patients with severe preexisting liver disease.[15] Adding acetaminophen to opioid therapy produces an opioid-sparing effect, lower pain scores, and fewer side effects. This is the reason for opioid-acetaminophen combinations.

FIG. 8.5 Arachidonic acid is oxidized by 2 different pathways: lipoxygenase and cyclooxygenase. The cyclooxygenase pathway leads to 2 forms of the enzyme cyclooxygenase: COX-1 and COX-2. COX-1 is known as *constitutive* (always present), and COX-2 is known as *inducible* (its expression varies markedly depending on the stimulus). Nonsteroidal antiinflammatory drugs (NSAIDs) differ in their actions, with some having more effects on COX-1 and others more on COX-2. Indomethacin acts primarily on COX-1. Ibuprofen is equipotent on COX-1 and COX-2. Celecoxib primarily inhibits COX-2.

IV acetaminophen (Ofirmev) is used alone for the treatment of acute mild to moderate pain and as an adjunct to opioid analgesics or part of a multimodal analgesic regimen for moderate to severe pain. It must be given over 15 minutes and has a short duration of action. The daily dose should not exceed 4 g/day.

NSAIDs represent a broad class of drugs with varying efficacy and side effects. All NSAIDs inhibit COX, the enzyme that converts arachidonic acid into prostaglandins and related compounds. The enzyme has 2 forms: COX-1 and COX-2. COX-1 is found in almost all tissues. It is responsible for several protective physiologic functions. In contrast, COX-2 is made mainly at the sites of tissue injury, where it mediates inflammation (Fig. 8.5). Inhibition of COX-1 causes many of the untoward effects of NSAIDs, such as impairment of renal function, bleeding tendencies, GI irritation, and ulceration. COX-2 inhibition is associated with the therapeutic, antiinflammatory effects of NSAIDs. (Celecoxib [Celebrex] is a COX-2 inhibitor.) Older NSAIDs, such as ibuprofen, inhibit both forms of COX. We refer to them as nonselective NSAIDs.

Patients vary greatly in their responses to a specific NSAID. So, when 1 NSAID does not provide relief, another should be tried. NSAIDs are associated with many side effects, including GI problems ranging from dyspepsia to life-threatening ulceration and hemorrhage. NSAIDs can cause cognitive impairment and hypersensitivity reactions with asthma-like symptoms.

Patients at risk for NSAID-associated GI toxicity include those who have a recent history of peptic ulcer disease, patients who are older than 65, and those concurrently using corticosteroids or anticoagulants. If NSAIDs are used in patients at risk for GI bleeding, they should have concomitant therapy with misoprostol (Cytotec) or a proton pump inhibitor, such as omeprazole. NSAIDs should not be given concurrently with aspirin since this increases the risk for GI bleeding.

💊 DRUG ALERT   Nonsteroidal Antiinflammatory Drugs (NSAIDs)

- NSAIDs, except aspirin, have been linked to a higher risk for cardiovascular events, such as myocardial infarction, stroke, and heart failure.
- Patients who have just had heart surgery should not take NSAIDs.

Opioids. Opioids (Table 8.9) produce their effects by binding to receptors in the CNS. This results in (1) inhibition of the transmission of nociceptive input from the periphery to the spinal cord, (2) altered limbic system activity, and (3) activation of the descending inhibitory pathways that modulate transmission in the spinal cord. Thus opioids act on several nociceptive processes.

Types of Opioids. Opioids are categorized according to their physiologic action (i.e., agonist, antagonist) and binding at specific opioid receptors (e.g., mu, kappa, delta). The most commonly given subclass of opioids is the pure opioid agonists, or morphine-like opioids, which bind to mu receptors.

Opioid agonists are used for acute and chronic pain. Although nociceptive pain seems to be more responsive to opioids than neuropathic pain, opioids may be used to treat both types of pain. In the treatment of neuropathic pain, antineuropathic pain drugs, such as antidepressants and antiseizure drugs, are recommended as first-line agents. Pure opioid agonists include morphine, oxycodone (OxyContin), hydrocodone, codeine, methadone, hydromorphone (Dilaudid), and levorphanol (Table 8.9). These drugs are effective for moderate to severe pain because they are potent, theoretically have no analgesic ceiling, and can be given by several routes. When opioids are prescribed for moderate pain, they are usually combined with a nonopioid analgesic, such as acetaminophen with codeine or hydrocodone plus acetaminophen or ibuprofen. Adding acetaminophen limits the total daily dose that we can give.

💊 DRUG ALERT   Morphine

- Morphine may cause respiratory depression.
- If respirations are 12 or fewer breaths per minute, withhold medication and contact the health care provider (HCP).

Methadone has a unique mechanism of action as an NMDA receptor antagonist and mu opioid receptor agonist. It is used primarily in the treatment of chronic pain but can be used for acute pain. It produces analgesic effects independent of its action as an opioid.[16]

💊 DRUG ALERT   Methadone (Dolophine)

- Methadone may cause respiratory depression.
- Methadone can cause cardiac toxicity, specifically QT prolongation.

Mixed agonist-antagonists (e.g., pentazocine [Talwin], butorphanol) bind as agonists on kappa receptors and as weak antagonists or partial agonists on mu receptors. Because of this difference in binding, mixed agonist-antagonists produce less respiratory depression than drugs that act only at mu receptors. These drugs cause more dysphoria and agitation. In addition, opioid agonist-antagonists have an analgesic ceiling and can precipitate withdrawal if used by a patient who is physically dependent on mu agonist drugs. Partial opioid agonists (e.g.,

TABLE 8.9 Drug Therapy

Opioid Analgesics

Drug	Routes of Administration	Nursing Considerations
Mu Agonists		
codeine oral (with acetaminophen [Tylenol #3]), codeine injectable	PO, subcutaneous	• Associated with higher incidence of nausea and constipation than other mu agonists • Many codeine preparations are combined with acetaminophen • 5%–10% of European Americans lack the enzyme to metabolize codeine to morphine
fentanyl (Sublimaze [IV]), Duragesic [transdermal], Actiq [transmucosal], Fentora [buccal tablet], Abstral [sublingual], Lazanda [nasal spray]	IV, epidural, intrathecal, transmucosal, transdermal	• Immediate onset after IV route, 7–8 min after IM route, 5–15 min after transmucosal route, up to 6 hr after transdermal route • For procedures, IV fentanyl often combined with benzodiazepines for analgesia and sedation • Very potent; dosage is in micrograms (mcg) • Transdermal fentanyl used only for chronic pain and should not be given to opioid-naive patients
hydrocodone with acetaminophen (Norco), hydrocodone with bitartrate (Hysingla, Zohydro ER), hydrocodone with ibuprofen (Reprexain)	PO (short-acting and long-acting)	• Used for moderate or moderately severe pain • For short-term management of acute pain (e.g., trauma, musculoskeletal)
hydromorphone (Dilaudid)	PO (short-acting and long-acting forms), rectal, IV, subcutaneous, epidural, intrathecal	• Slightly shorter duration than morphine • For moderate to severe pain • Tablets for sustained-release preparations are to be swallowed whole and must not be broken, chewed, dissolved, or crushed • Preparations for neuraxial administration must be preservative free
levorphanol	PO, IV, IM, subcutaneous	• Accumulates with repeated dosing
methadone (Dolophine)	PO, IV, IM	• High oral and rectal bioavailability • Accumulates with repeated dosing • Use with caution in older adults • Risk for QT interval prolongation
morphine (MS Contin, Kadian, Duramorph, Embeda)	PO (short-acting and sustained-release forms), rectal, IV, subcutaneous, epidural, intrathecal, sublingual, intranasal	• Standard of comparison for opioid analgesics (Table 8.12) • For moderate to severe pain • Can stimulate histamine release, leading to pruritus, with systemic administration • Tablets for sustained-release preparations are to be swallowed whole and must not be broken, chewed, dissolved, or crushed • Preparations for neuraxial administration must be preservative free
oxycodone (Roxicodone) oxycodone extended-release (OxyContin) oxycodone plus acetaminophen (Percocet) oxycodone plus aspirin (Percodan)	PO (short-acting and extended-release forms)	• Available as single entity and in combination with a nonopioid • Used similarly to oral morphine for moderate to severe pain • Often combined with a nonopioid for acute, moderate pain • Extended-release indicated for chronic pain
tapentadol (Nucynta)	PO (short-acting and extended release)	• Dual mechanism of action: Mu opioid agonist and blocks reuptake of norepinephrine and serotonin
tramadol (Ultram)	PO (short-acting and extended release)	• Dual mechanism of action: Mu opioid agonist and blocks reuptake of norepinephrine and serotonin • Used for moderate pain
Mu Mixed Agonist-Antagonists		
butorphanol	Nasal spray, injectable form Not available orally	• Psychotomimetic effects lower than with pentazocine • May precipitate withdrawal in opioid-dependent patients • Injectable used for acute pain • Nasal spray given for migraine headaches
pentazocine (Talwin)	IM, IV, subcutaneous	• May cause psychotomimetic effects (e.g., hallucinations) and may precipitate withdrawal in opioid-dependent patients • Not recommended for treatment of chronic pain and rarely for acute pain
Partial Agonists		
buprenorphine buprenorphine plus naloxone sublingual (Suboxone)	Sublingual, injectable, implant	• Sublingual form should not be chewed or swallowed • Lower abuse potential than morphine • Does not produce psychotomimetic effects • May precipitate withdrawal in opioid-dependent patients. Not readily reversed by naloxone • Buprenorphine plus naloxone used as a sublingual preparation to treat opioid dependence for easier withdrawal when necessary to taper from opioids

buprenorphine [Buprenex]) can produce some pain relief but bind tightly to mu receptors and can block the effect of other drugs. Agonist-antagonists and partial agonists currently have limited clinical application in pain management.

Dual-Mechanism Agents. Some analgesics have 2 distinct actions, or dual mechanisms. Tramadol (Ultram) is a weak mu agonist and inhibits the reuptake of norepinephrine and serotonin. It is effective in low back pain, osteoarthritis, fibromyalgia, diabetic peripheral neuropathic pain, polyneuropathy, and postherpetic neuralgia. The most common side effects are like those of other opioids, including nausea, constipation, dizziness, and sedation. As with other medications that increase serotonin and norepinephrine, avoid this drug in patients with a history of seizures because it lowers seizure threshold.

Tapentadol (Nucynta) is a centrally acting analgesic that works at mu receptors and inhibits norepinephrine reuptake. It is approved for management of moderate to severe acute pain. For chronic moderate to severe pain, an extended-release formula is available. The side effects are like those of conventional opioids, except that this drug is associated with less nausea and constipation.

Opioids to Avoid. Some opioids should be avoided for pain relief because of limited efficacy and/or toxicities. Meperidine (Demerol), or pethidine, is associated with neurotoxicity (e.g., seizures) caused by accumulation of its metabolite, normeperidine. Its use is limited for very short-term (i.e., less than 48 hours) treatment of acute pain when other opioid agonists are contraindicated.

 DRUG ALERT   Meperidine (Demerol)

> The American Pain Society does not recommend the use of meperidine as an analgesic.

Side Effects of Opioids. Common side effects of opioids include constipation, nausea and vomiting, sedation, respiratory depression, and pruritus. With continued use, many side effects diminish; the exception is constipation. Less common side effects include urinary retention, myoclonus, dizziness, confusion, and hallucinations. *Constipation* is the most common side effect of opioids. Left untreated, it may increase the person's pain and can lead to fecal impaction and paralytic ileus.

Because tolerance to opioid-induced constipation does not develop, a bowel regimen should be started at the beginning of opioid therapy and continued for as long as the person takes opioids. Although dietary fiber, fluids, and exercise should be encouraged, these measures alone may not be enough. Most patients should use a gentle stimulant laxative (e.g., senna) plus a stool softener (e.g., docusate sodium [Colace]). Other agents (e.g., Milk of Magnesia, bisacodyl, polyethylene glycol, lactulose) can be added if needed. Methylnaltrexone (Relistor), naldemedine (Symproic), and naloxegol (Movantik) are peripheral opioid receptor antagonists used for opioid-induced constipation when the response to traditional laxative and stool softener therapy is insufficient.

Nausea is often a problem in opioid-naive patients. The use of an antiemetic, such as ondansetron (Zofran), metoclopramide (Reglan), transdermal scopolamine, or hydroxyzine (Vistaril), can prevent or minimize nausea and vomiting until tolerance develops, usually within 1 week. Opioids delay gastric emptying (patient relates gastric fullness). Metoclopramide can reduce this effect. If nausea and vomiting are severe and persistent, changing to a different opioid may be needed.

Sedation is usually seen in opioid-naive patients being treated for acute pain. Regularly monitor patients receiving opioid analgesics for acute pain, especially in the first few days (e.g., after surgery). Be aware that the risk for unintended sedation in postoperative patients is greatest within 4 hours after leaving the postanesthesia care unit. Opioid-induced sedation resolves with the development of tolerance. Persistent sedation with chronic opioid use can be effectively treated with psychostimulants, such as caffeine, dextroamphetamine (Dexedrine), methylphenidate (Ritalin), or the anticataleptic drug modafinil (Provigil).

The risk for *respiratory depression* is higher in opioid-naive, hospitalized patients who are treated for acute pain. Clinically significant respiratory depression is rare in opioid-tolerant patients and when opioids are titrated to analgesic effect. Patients most at risk for respiratory depression include those who are age 65 or older, have a history of snoring or witnessed apneic episodes, report excessive daytime sleepiness, have underlying heart or lung disease, are obese (body mass index greater than 30 kg/m^2), have a history of smoking (more than 20 pack-years), or are receiving other CNS depressants (e.g., sedatives, benzodiazepines, antihistamines). For postoperative patients the greatest risk for opioid-related respiratory adverse events is within the first 24 hours after surgery. Clinically significant respiratory depression cannot occur in patients who are fully awake.

? CHECK YOUR PRACTICE

A 74-yr-old male patient returned to the clinical unit after surgery for a hip replacement. You are having difficulty arousing him with either verbal or physical stimulation. His wife tells you to just let him sleep. His respiratory rate ranges from 8 to 10 breaths/min.
• What should you do?

Frequently monitor both the sedation level and respiratory rate in patients receiving opioid analgesics.[17] A sedation scale can be used for monitoring and providing appropriate interventions based on the level of sedation (Table 8.10).

! SAFETY ALERT   Sedation and Respiratory Depression

• If the patient's respiratory rate falls below 8 or 10 breaths/min and the sedation level is 3 or greater, you should vigorously stimulate the patient and try to keep the patient awake.
• If the patient becomes oversedated, apply oxygen.
• In this situation, the opioid dose should be reduced.

For patients who are excessively sedated or unresponsive, we can give naloxone, an opioid antagonist that rapidly reverses the effects of opioids. Naloxone can be given IV, subcutaneously, or intranasally. Evzio (hand-held autoinjector containing naloxone) can be used by a caregiver or family member to treat a person known or suspected to have had an opioid overdose.

If the patient has been taking opioids regularly for more than a few days, use naloxone carefully because it can precipitate severe, agonizing pain; profound withdrawal symptoms; hypertension; and pulmonary edema. Because naloxone's half-life is shorter than that of most opioids, frequently monitor the patient.

Pruritus (itching) is another common side effect of opioids. It occurs most often when opioids are given by neuraxial (i.e., epidural, intrathecal) routes. Managing opioid-induced pruritus in noncancer patients may include low-dose infusions of naloxone.

TABLE 8.10 Pasero Opioid-Induced Sedation Scale (POSS) With Interventions

Level of Sedation	Nursing Intervention
S = Sleep, easy to arouse	• Acceptable • No action necessary • May increase opioid dose if needed
1. Awake and alert	• Acceptable • No action necessary • May increase opioid dose if needed
2. Slightly drowsy, easily aroused	• Acceptable • No action necessary • May increase opioid dose if needed
3. Frequently drowsy, arousable, drifts off to sleep during conversation	• Unacceptable • Monitor respiratory status and sedation level closely until sedation level is stable at <3 and respiratory status is satisfactory • Decrease opioid dose 25%–50% or notify HCP or anesthesiologist for orders • Consider giving a nonsedating, opioid-sparing nonopioid, such as acetaminophen or an NSAID, if not contraindicated
4. Somnolent, minimal or no response to verbal or physical stimulation	• Unacceptable • Stop opioid • Consider giving naloxone • Notify HCP or anesthesiologist • Monitor respiratory status and sedation level closely until sedation level is stable at <3 and respiratory status is satisfactory

Adapted from Pasero C: Assessment of sedation during opioid administration for pain management, *J PeriAnesthesia Nurs* 24:186, 2009.

A rare but concerning problem with long-term and even short-term use of high-dose opioids is *opioid-induced hyperalgesia* (OIH). OIH is a state of nociceptive sensitization caused by exposure to opioids. It is characterized by a paradoxical response in which patients become more sensitive to certain painful stimuli and report increased pain with opioid use. The exact mechanism is not clearly understood, but it may be due to neuroplasticity changes. This may explain why opioids tend to lose their effectiveness in certain patients over time.

Adjuvant Analgesic Therapy. Analgesic adjuvants are drugs that can be used alone or in conjunction with opioid and nonopioid analgesics (Table 8.11). Generally, these agents were developed for other purposes (e.g., antiseizure drugs, antidepressants) and found to be effective for treating pain.

α₂-Adrenergic Agonists. We think clonidine and tizanidine (Zanaflex), the most widely used α_2-adrenergic agonists, work on the central inhibitory α-adrenergic receptors. These agents may also decrease norepinephrine release peripherally. They are given for chronic headache and neuropathic pain.

Antidepressants. Tricyclic antidepressants (TCAs) enhance the descending inhibitory system by preventing the cellular reuptake of serotonin and norepinephrine. Higher levels of serotonin and norepinephrine in the synapse inhibit the transmission of nociceptive signals in the CNS. Other potential beneficial actions of TCAs include sodium channel modulation, α_1-adrenergic antagonist effects, and a weak NMDA receptor modulation. They are effective for a variety of pain syndromes, especially neuropathic pain syndromes. However, side effects, such as sedation, dry mouth, blurred vision, and weight gain, limit their usefulness. Antidepressants that selectively inhibit reuptake of serotonin and norepinephrine (SNRIs) are effective for many neuropathic pain syndromes and have fewer side effects than the TCAs. These agents include venlafaxine, desvenlafaxine (Pristiq), milnacipran (Savella), and bupropion.

Antiseizure Drugs. Antiseizure drugs affect peripheral nerves and the CNS in several ways, including sodium channel modulation, central calcium channel modulation, and changes in excitatory amino acids and other receptors. Agents such as gabapentin, lamotrigine, and pregabalin are valuable adjuvant agents in chronic pain therapy and are being used more in the treatment of acute pain.

GABA-Receptor Agonist. Baclofen, an agonist at GABA receptors, can interfere with the transmission of nociceptive impulses. It is used for muscle spasms and neuropathic pain. It crosses the blood-brain barrier poorly and is much more effective for spasticity when delivered intrathecally.

Corticosteroids. Corticosteroids include dexamethasone, prednisone, and methylprednisolone (Medrol). They are used for managing acute and chronic cancer pain, pain secondary to spinal cord compression, and inflammatory joint pain syndromes. Mechanisms of action may be related to the ability of corticosteroids to decrease edema and inflammation.

Corticosteroids have many side effects, especially when given chronically in high doses. These include hyperglycemia, fluid retention, dyspepsia and GI bleeding, impaired healing, muscle wasting, osteoporosis, adrenal suppression, and susceptibility to infection. Because they act through the same final pathway as NSAIDs, do not give corticosteroids at the same time as NSAIDs.

Local Anesthetics. For acute pain from surgery or trauma, local anesthetics, such as bupivacaine and ropivacaine, can be given epidurally by continuous infusion or by intermittent or continuous infusion with regional nerve blocks. Systemic lidocaine given in an IV infusion is sometimes used for neuropathic and postoperative visceral pain. Topical applications are used to interrupt transmission of pain signals to the brain. For example, 5% lidocaine patch (Lidoderm) is a first-line agent for the treatment of several types of neuropathic pain. In the treatment of chronic severe neuropathic pain that is refractory to other analgesics, oral therapy with mexiletine (Mexitil) may be tried.

Cannabinoids. Cannabinoid-derived medications show promise in the treatment of neuropathic pain, certain pain syndromes, and some symptoms. However, these preparations have sparked considerable controversy and confusion, mostly because cannabinoids are related to the cannabis plant, also known as marijuana. Synthetic cannabinoids (e.g., dronabinol [Marinol]) have been approved for medical use. Smoking marijuana or cannabis rapidly increases plasma levels of tetrahydrocannabinol (THC). The increase depends on composition of the marijuana cigarette and inhalation technique. As a result, this form of use is associated with variable pain relief. With commercially available oral preparations, the absorption and bioavailability are more reliable and predictable.

Cannabinoids exert their analgesic effects primarily through the cannabinoid-1 (CB1) and CB2 receptors. Activation of cannabinoid receptors modulates neurotransmission in the serotoninergic, dopaminergic, and glutamatergic systems, as well as other systems. Cannabinoids also enhance the endogenous opioid system. Other beneficial effects include alleviating nausea and increased appetite. They may have opioid-sparing effects, possibly reducing opioid tolerance and symptoms of opioid withdrawal.[18]

TABLE 8.11   Drug Therapy

Adjuvant Drugs Used for Pain

Drug	Specific Indication	Nursing Considerations
α₂-Adrenergic Agonists		
clonidine (Duraclon)	Particularly useful for neuropathic pain when given intrathecally	• Side effects include sedation, orthostatic hypotension, dry mouth • Often combined with anesthetics (e.g., bupivacaine)
tizanidine (Zanaflex)		
Anesthetics: Local		
capsaicin (active compound of chili peppers)	Pain associated with arthritis, postherpetic neuralgia, diabetic neuropathy	• Apply very sparingly onto affected area. • Use gloves or wash hands with soap and water after application • Monitor for side effects: Skin irritation (burning, stinging) at application site and cough when inhaled
lidocaine (L-M-X)	Topical local anesthetic cream applied to intact skin before venipuncture or lumbar puncture. May be effective for postherpetic neuralgia	• Apply bubble layer to intact skin and wait at least 20–30 min before wiping and performing painful procedure • Duration is around 60 min after wiped from skin • Available without prescription
lidocaine 2.5% + prilocaine 2.5% (topical eutectic mixture of local anesthetics [EMLA])	Longer time to take effect than L-M-X	• Apply under an occlusive dressing (e.g., Tegaderm, Duo-Derm) or on an anesthetic disk • Side effects include mild erythema, edema, skin blanching
Anesthetics: Oral or Systemic		
5% lidocaine-impregnated transdermal patch (Lidoderm patch)	Postherpetic neuralgia	• Local skin reactions (e.g., change in color, colored spots, irritation, itching, rash, burning) occur at the site of application; typically mild
mexiletine	Diabetic neuropathy Neuropathic pain	• Monitor for side effects: High incidence of nausea, dizziness, perioral numbness, paresthesias, tremor, seizures (at high doses), dysrhythmias, and myocardial depression • Avoid in patients with preexisting heart disease
Antidepressants		
Tricyclic Antidepressants		
amitriptyline	Neuropathic pain	• Side-effect profile differs for each agent and is often dose-dependent • Common side effects include anticholinergic effects (e.g., dry mouth) and sedation • Monitor for anticholinergic side effects • Titrate slowly over days to weeks to reach optimal therapeutic doses
desipramine (Norpramin)		
doxepin		
imipramine (Tofranil)		
nortriptyline (Pamelor)		
Serotonin Norepinephrine Reuptake Inhibitor (SNRI) Antidepressants		
duloxetine (Cymbalta)	Neuropathic pain	• Side effects vary with each agent • Decreased arousal and desire for sex
milnacipran (Savella)	Multimodal therapy for acute pain (venlafaxine)	
venlafaxine (Effexor)	Fibromyalgia (duloxetine, milnacipran)	
Other Antidepressants		
bupropion (Wellbutrin)	Neuropathic pain Headaches	• Low risk for sexual problems and sedation • Distinguished from TCAs and SNRIs as an inhibitor of norepinephrine and dopamine uptake
Antiseizure Drugs		
First generation: carbamazepine (Tegretol) phenytoin (Dilantin) Second generation: gabapentin (Neurontin) lamotrigine (Lamictal) pregabalin (Lyrica)	Neuropathic pain Multimodal therapy for acute pain (gabapentin, pregabalin) Fibromyalgia (pregabalin)	• Start with low doses, increase slowly • Side effects vary with each agent
Cannabinoids		
dronabinol (Marinol)	Neuropathic pain Certain pain syndromes	• May relieve nausea and increase appetite • May have opioid-sparing effects, possibly reducing opioid tolerance and symptoms of opioid withdrawal
Corticosteroids		
dexamethasone (Decadron)	Inflammation	• Avoid high doses for long-term use
GABA-Receptor Agonist		
baclofen (Lioresal)	Neuropathic pain Muscle spasms	• Monitor for weakness, urinary dysfunction • Avoid abrupt discontinuation because of CNS irritability

Adapted from Pasero C, Polomano RC, McCaffery M, etal: Adjuvant analgesics. In Pasero C, McCaffery M, editors: *Pain: Assessment and pharmacological management*, New York, 2011, Mosby.

Administration

Scheduling. Appropriate analgesic scheduling focuses on preventing or controlling pain, rather than providing analgesics only after the patient's pain has become severe. Premedicate a patient before procedures and activities that will likely produce pain. Similarly, a patient with constant pain should receive analgesics around the clock rather than on an "as needed" (PRN) basis. These strategies control pain before it starts and usually result in lower analgesic requirements. Use fast-acting drugs for incident or breakthrough pain, while long-acting analgesics are more effective for constant pain. Examples of fast-acting and sustained-release analgesics are described later in this section.

Titration. Analgesic titration is dose adjustment based on assessment of the adequacy of analgesic effect versus the side effects produced. The amount of analgesic needed to manage pain varies widely, and titration is an important strategy in addressing this variability. An analgesic can be titrated upward or downward, depending on the situation. For example, in a postoperative patient the dose of analgesic decreases over time as the acute pain resolves. On the other hand, opioids for chronic, severe cancer pain may be titrated upward many times over the course of therapy to maintain adequate pain control. The goal of titration is to use the smallest dose of analgesic that provides effective pain control with the fewest side effects.

Equianalgesic Dosing. The term equianalgesic dose refers to a dose of 1 analgesic that is equivalent in pain-relieving effects to a given dose of another analgesic (Table 8.12). This equivalence helps guide opioid dosing when changing routes or opioids when a specific drug is ineffective or causes intolerable side effects. Equianalgesic charts and conversion programs are widely available in clinical guidelines, in health care facility pain protocols, and on the Internet. They are useful tools, but you need to understand their limitations since these doses are estimates. To ensure safety, all changes in opioid therapy must be carefully monitored and adjusted for the individual patient.

Administration Routes. We can deliver opioids and other analgesic agents by many routes. This flexibility allows the HCP to (1) target a particular anatomic source of the pain, (2) achieve therapeutic blood levels rapidly when necessary, (3) avoid certain side effects through localized administration, and (4) provide analgesia when patients are unable to swallow. The following discussion highlights the uses and nursing considerations for analgesic agents delivered through a variety of routes.

TABLE 8.12 Opioid Equianalgesic Doses*

Drug	DOSE EQUAL TO PARENTERAL MORPHINE 10 mg	
	Oral (mg)	Parenteral (IM, IV, Subcutaneous) (mg)
Codeine	200	120–130
Fentanyl	NA	0.1 (100 mcg)
Hydrocodone	30	NA
Hydromorphone	7.5	1.5
Levorphanol	4	2
Meperidine	300	75
Morphine	30	10
Oxycodone	15–30	NA

*All equivalencies are approximations. These amounts can be affected by many factors, including interpatient variability, type of pain, and tolerance. Monitor patients for effectiveness and adverse reactions and adjust the dose accordingly.

Oral. Generally, oral administration is the route of choice for the person with a functioning GI system. Most pain medications are available in oral preparations, such as liquid and tablet. For opioids, larger oral doses are needed to achieve the equivalent analgesia of doses given IM or IV (Table 8.12). For example, 10 mg of parenteral morphine is equivalent to around 30 mg of oral morphine. The reason larger doses are needed is related to the *first-pass effect* of hepatic metabolism. This means that oral opioids are absorbed from the GI tract into the portal circulation and shunted to the liver. Partial metabolism in the liver occurs before the drug enters the systemic circulation and becomes available to peripheral receptors or can cross the blood-brain barrier and access CNS opioid receptors, which is needed to produce analgesia. Oral opioids are as effective as parenteral opioids if the dose is large enough to compensate for the first-pass metabolism.

Many opioids are available in short-acting (immediate-release) and long-acting (sustained-release or extended-release) oral preparations. Immediate-release products are effective in providing rapid, short-term pain relief. Sustained-release or extended-release preparations generally are given every 8 to 12 hours, although some preparations (e.g., Kadian, Exalgo) may be dosed every 24 hours.

> **! SAFETY ALERT Sustained-Release or Extended-Release Preparations**
> - These should not be crushed, broken, dissolved, or chewed. These drugs are to be swallowed whole.
> - If all the medicine is released into a person at once, serious side effects can occur, including death from overdose.

Transmucosal and buccal routes. Although morphine has historically been given sublingually to people with cancer pain who have difficulty swallowing, little of the drug is absorbed from the sublingual tissue. Instead, most of the drug dissolves in saliva and is swallowed, making its absorption similar to that of oral morphine.

Several transmucosal fentanyl products are used for the treatment of breakthrough pain. These include (1) oral transmucosal fentanyl citrate (OTFC) (Actiq), with the fentanyl embedded in a flavored lozenge on a stick that is absorbed by the buccal mucosa after being rubbed actively over it when given as the lozenge (not sucked as a lollipop); (2) fentanyl buccal tablet (FBT) (Fentora) in the form of a buccal tablet that disintegrates; and (3) fentanyl sublingual (Abstral). Transmucosal absorption allows the drug to enter the bloodstream and travel directly to the CNS. Pain relief typically occurs 5 to 7 minutes after administration. These formulations should be used only for patients who are already receiving and are tolerant to opioid therapy.[19]

Intranasal route. Intranasal administration allows delivery of medication to highly vascular mucosa and avoids the first-pass effect. Butorphanol is given for acute headache and other intense, recurrent types of pain. A transmucosal fentanyl nasal spray (Lazanda) is available for the treatment of breakthrough pain.

Rectal. The rectal route is often overlooked but is particularly useful when the patient cannot take an analgesic by mouth, such as with severe nausea and vomiting. Analgesics that are available as rectal suppositories include hydromorphone, oxymorphone, morphine, and acetaminophen. If rectal preparations are not available, many oral formulations can be given rectally if the patient is unable to take medications by mouth.

Transdermal route. Transdermal patches are designed for systemic drug delivery (e.g., Duragesic) or for topical or local delivery (e.g., Lidoderm). Fentanyl (Duragesic) is useful for the patient who cannot tolerate oral analgesic drugs. Absorption from the patch is slow. It takes 12 to 17 hours to reach full effect with the first application. Therefore transdermal fentanyl is not suitable for rapid dose titration but can be effective if the patient's pain is stable and the dose needed to control it is known. Patches may have to be changed every 48 hours rather than the recommended 72 hours based on individual patient responses. Patches are applied to intact, nonhairy skin. Rashes caused by the patch's adhesive may be reduced by preparing the skin 1 hour before placement with a weak corticosteroid cream. Bioocclusive dressings are available if the patch keeps falling off because of sweating. A transdermal patient-controlled analgesia (PCA) system (iontophoretic transdermal system [ITS]) is available.

> 💊 **DRUG ALERT   Fentanyl Patches**
> - Fentanyl patches (Duragesic) may cause death from overdose.
> - Signs of overdose include trouble breathing or shallow respirations; tiredness, extreme sleepiness, or sedation; inability to think, talk, or walk normally; and faintness, dizziness, or confusion.

A 5% lidocaine-impregnated transdermal patch (Lidoderm patch) is used for postherpetic neuralgia. The patch is placed directly on the intact, nonhairy skin in the area of postherpetic pain and left in place for up to 12 hours. There are few systemic side effects, even with chronic use.

Creams and lotions containing 10% trolamine salicylate (Aspercreme, Myoflex Creme) are available for joint and muscle pain. This aspirin-like substance is absorbed locally. This route avoids GI irritation but not the other side effects of high-dose salicylates. Topical diclofenac solution and a diclofenac patch (Flector) are effective for osteoarthritic pain of the knee.

Other topical analgesic agents, such as capsaicin (e.g., Zostrix) and lidocaine (L-M-X cream), also provide analgesia. Derived from red chili pepper, capsaicin acts on C-fiber heat receptors. If used 3 or 4 times a day for 4 to 6 weeks, it will cause the C nociceptor fibers to become inactive. The result is neuronal resistance to painful stimuli. Capsaicin may control pain associated with diabetic neuropathy, arthritis, and postherpetic neuralgia. L-M-X cream is useful for control of pain associated with venipunctures. Cover the targeted area of intact skin with a layer of L-M-X for at least 20 to 30 minutes, then wipe it off prior to beginning a painful procedure.

Parenteral routes. The parenteral routes include IV and subcutaneous administration. Single, repeated, or continuous dosing (IV or subcutaneous) is possible with parenteral routes. IV administration is the best route when immediate analgesia and rapid titration are needed. Continuous IV infusions provide excellent steady-state analgesia through stable blood levels.

Onset of analgesia after subcutaneous administration is slow, and thus the subcutaneous route is rarely used for acute pain management. However, continuous subcutaneous infusions are effective for pain management at the end of life. This route is especially helpful for people with abnormal GI function and limited venous access.

The IM route is not recommended because injections cause significant pain and result in unreliable absorption. With chronic use, IM injections can result in abscesses and fibrosis.

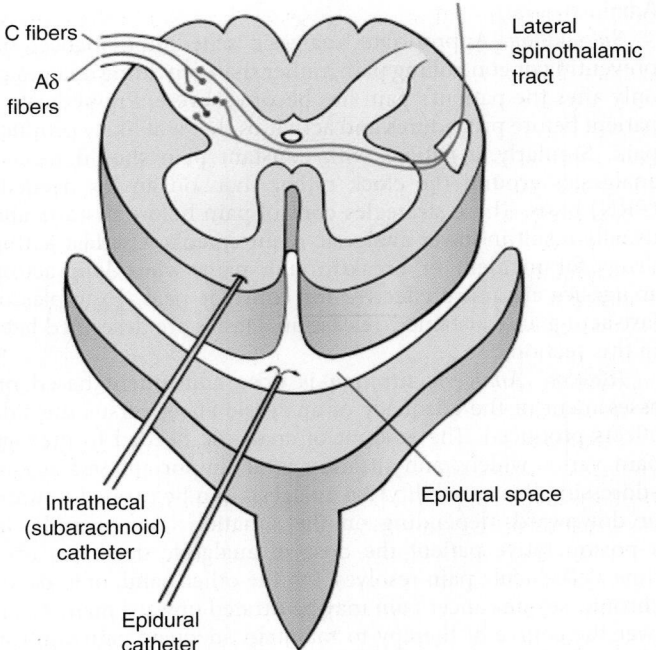

FIG. 8.6 Cross section of spinal cord with placement of catheters into the subarachnoid space (intrathecal delivery) and the epidural space (epidural delivery). (From Urden LD, Stacy KM, Lough ME: *Critical care nursing: Diagnosis and management*, ed 8, St Louis, 2018, Elsevier.)

Intraspinal delivery. Intraspinal or neuraxial opioid therapy involves inserting a catheter into the subarachnoid space *(intrathecal delivery)* or the epidural space *(epidural delivery)* (Fig. 8.6). Analgesics are injected either by intermittent bolus doses or continuous infusion.

Percutaneously placed temporary catheters are used for short-term therapy (2 to 4 days), and surgically implanted catheters are used for long-term therapy. Although the lumbar region is the most common site of placement, epidural catheters may be placed at any point along the spinal column (cervical, thoracic, lumbar, or caudal). The tip of the epidural catheter is placed as close to the nerve supplying the painful dermatome as possible. For example, a thoracic catheter is placed for upper abdominal surgery, and a high lumbar catheter is used for lower abdominal surgery. Fluoroscopy ensures correct placement of the catheter.

Intraspinal analgesics are highly potent because they are delivered close to the receptors in the spinal cord dorsal horn. Smaller doses of analgesics are needed than with other routes, including IV. For example, 1 mg of intrathecal morphine equals 10 mg of epidural morphine, 100 mg of IV morphine, and 300 mg of oral morphine. Drugs delivered intraspinally include morphine, fentanyl, sufentanil (Sufenta), alfentanil (Alfenta), hydromorphone, clonidine, and ziconotide, a calcium channel receptor modulator for use in neuropathic pain syndromes. Nausea, itching, and urinary retention are common side effects of intraspinal opioids.

Complications of intraspinal analgesia include catheter displacement and migration, accidental infusions of neurotoxic agents, epidural hematomas, and infection. Clinical manifestations of catheter displacement or migration depend on catheter location and the drug being infused. A catheter that migrates out of the intrathecal or epidural space causes a decrease in pain relief with no improvement with more boluses or increases in the infusion rate. If an epidural catheter migrates into the subarachnoid space, increased side effects become quickly apparent. Somnolence, confusion, and increased anesthesia (if the infusate contains an anesthetic) occur. Check with institutional policy before aspirating cerebrospinal fluid to determine intrathecal catheter placement. Migration of a catheter into a blood vessel may cause an increase in side effects because of systemic drug distribution.

Many drugs and chemicals are highly neurotoxic when given intraspinally. These include antibiotics, chemotherapy agents, potassium, parenteral nutrition, and many preservatives, such as alcohol and phenol. To avoid inadvertent injection of IV drugs into an intraspinal catheter, the catheter should be clearly marked as an intraspinal access device. Only preservative-free drugs should be used.

Infection is a rare but serious complication of intraspinal analgesia. Assess the skin around the exit site for inflammation, drainage, or pain. Manifestations of an intraspinal infection include diffuse back pain, pain or paresthesia during bolus injection, and unexplained sensory or motor deficits in the lower limbs. Fever may or may not be present. Acute bacterial infection (meningitis) is manifested by photophobia, neck stiffness, fever, headache, and altered mental status. Regular, meticulous wound care and using sterile technique when caring for the catheter and injecting drugs reduces infection risk.

Long-term epidural catheters may be placed for terminal cancer patients or patients with certain pain syndromes that are unresponsive to other treatments. If a long-term indwelling epidural catheter is used, bacterial filters are recommended.

Implantable pumps. Intraspinal catheters can be surgically implanted for long-term pain relief. The surgical placement of an intrathecal catheter to a subcutaneously placed pump and reservoir allows for the delivery of drugs directly into the intrathecal space. The pump, which is normally placed in a pocket made in the subcutaneous tissue of the abdomen, may be programmable or fixed.

We make changes reprogramming the pump, changing the mixture, or concentration of drug in the reservoir. The pump is refilled every 30 to 90 days depending on flow rate, mixture, and reservoir size.

Patient-controlled analgesia. Patient-controlled analgesia (PCA) (demand analgesia) is a method that allows the patient to self-administer preset doses of an analgesic within a prescribed time period by activating an infusion pump. Routes of administration include oral, IV, epidural, inhaled, nasal, and transcutaneous. In acute care, PCA often refers to an electronically controlled infusion pump that delivers the medication by an IV or epidural route (patient-controlled epidural analgesia [PCEA]). PCEA often combines an opioid and local anesthetic. PCA also can be adapted for oral administration. With PCA/PCEA, a dose of opioid is delivered when the patient decides a dose is needed. PCA/PCEA uses an infusion system in which the patient pushes a button to receive a bolus infusion of an analgesic. PCA/PCEA is used widely for the management of acute pain, including postoperative pain and cancer pain.

Opioids, such as morphine and hydromorphone, are often given via PCA therapy for acute and chronic pain. Sometimes IV PCA is given with a continuous or background infusion called a *basal rate*, depending on the patient's opioid requirement. Adding a basal rate in opioid-naive patients and those at risk for adverse respiratory outcomes (e.g., older age, obstructive sleep apnea, lung disease) may lead to serious respiratory events. Basal rates are often used with epidural catheter pain management. Because the medication is delivered directly into the epidural space, the amount of opioid is 10 times less than is needed by IV route. This lessens the risk for respiratory depression but does not eliminate it.

Patient teaching is very important with the use of PCA/PCEA. Help the patient understand the mechanics of getting a drug dose and how to titrate the drug to achieve good pain relief. Teach the patient to self-administer the analgesic before pain is severe. Assure the patient that he or she cannot "overdose" because the pump is programmed to deliver a maximum number of doses per hour. The patient will not receive more analgesic once the maximum dose has been reached. If the maximum dose is inadequate to relieve pain, the pump can be reprogrammed to increase the amount or frequency of dosing. In addition, you can give bolus doses if they are part of the HCP's orders. To make a smooth transition from infusion PCA to oral drugs, the patient should receive increasing doses of oral drug as the PCA analgesic is tapered.

Patient-controlled delivery systems are intended for use by the patient. An *authorized agent controlled analgesia (AACA)* is a method of delivery performed by a consistently available and competent person for patients who are unable to independently activate PCA devices.[20] This authorized agent must be carefully selected, taught the principles of PCA, and capable of recognizing pain and the appropriate times to give medication via the PCA device. Understand your institution's policies about PCA and AACA.

Interventional Therapy

Therapeutic Nerve Blocks. Nerve blocks involve 1-time or continuous infusion of local anesthetics into a particular area to produce pain relief. These techniques are also called *regional anesthesia*. Nerve blocks interrupt all afferent and efferent transmission to the area and thus are not specific to nociceptive pathways. They include local infiltration of anesthetics into a surgical area (e.g., chest incisions, inguinal hernia) and injection of anesthetic into a specific nerve (e.g., occipital, pudendal nerve) or nerve plexus (e.g., brachial, celiac plexus). Nerve blocks can be used during and after surgery to manage pain. For longer term relief of chronic pain syndromes, local anesthetics can be given by a continuous infusion.

Adverse effects of nerve blocks are similar to those for local anesthetics delivered by other systemic routes. Effects include systemic toxicity resulting in dysrhythmias, confusion, nausea and vomiting, blurred vision, tinnitus, and metallic taste. Temporary nerve blocks affect motor function and sensation and typically last 2 to 24 hours, depending on the agent and the site of injection. Motor ability generally returns before sensation.

Neuroablative Techniques. Neuroablative interventions are done for severe pain that is unresponsive to all other therapies. They involve destroying nerves, thereby interrupting pain transmission. Destruction is by surgical resection or thermocoagulation, including radiofrequency coagulation. Neuroablative interventions that destroy the sensory division of a peripheral or spinal nerve are classified as *neurectomies, rhizotomies,* and *sympathectomies.* Neurosurgical procedures that ablate the lateral spinothalamic tract are classified as *cordotomies* if the tract is interrupted in the spinal cord or *tractotomies* if the interruption is in the medulla or midbrain of the brainstem (Fig. 8.7). Cordotomy and tractotomy can

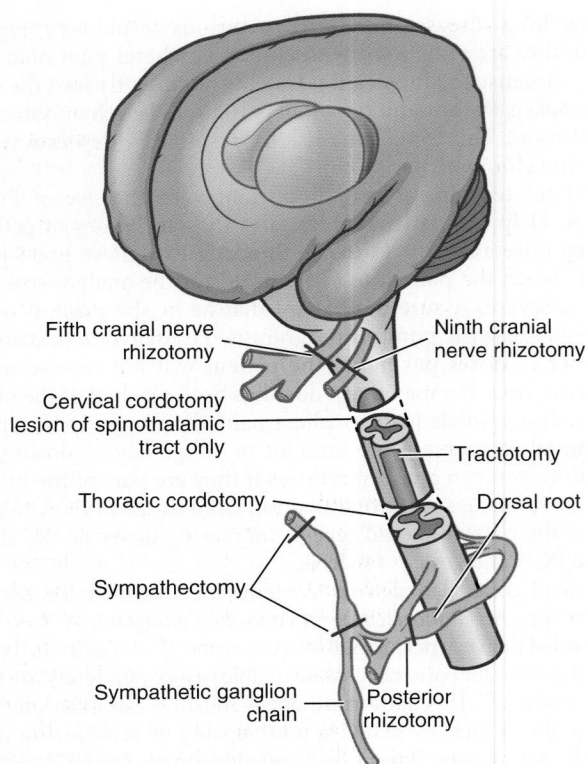

Fifth cranial nerve rhizotomy

Ninth cranial nerve rhizotomy

Cervical cordotomy lesion of spinothalamic tract only

Tractotomy

Thoracic cordotomy

Dorsal root

Sympathectomy

Sympathetic ganglion chain

Posterior rhizotomy

FIG. 8.7 Sites of neurosurgical procedures for pain relief.

be done with the aid of local anesthesia by a percutaneous technique under fluoroscopy.

Neuroaugmentation. *Neuroaugmentation* involves electrical stimulation of the brain and spinal cord. Spinal cord stimulation (SCS) is done much more often than brain stimulation. The most common use of SCS is for chronic back pain secondary to nerve damage that is unresponsive to other therapies. Other uses include CRPS, spinal cord injury pain, and interstitial cystitis. Potential complications include those related to the surgery (bleeding and infection), migration of the generator (which usually is implanted in the subcutaneous tissues of the upper gluteal or pectoralis area), and nerve damage.

Nondrug Therapies for Pain

Nondrug strategies play an important role in pain management (Table 8.13). They can reduce the dose of an analgesic needed to relieve pain and thereby minimize side effects of drug therapy. Moreover, they increase the patient's sense of personal control about managing pain and increase coping skills. Some strategies are thought to alter ascending nociceptive input or stimulate descending pain modulation mechanisms. These nondrug therapies are useful for both acute and chronic pain.

Physical Pain Relief Strategies

Massage. Massage is useful for acute and chronic pain. Many different massage techniques exist, including moving the hands or fingers over the skin slowly or briskly with long strokes or in circles (superficial massage) or applying firm pressure to the skin to maintain contact while massaging the underlying tissues (deep massage). Another type is trigger point massage. A **trigger point** is a circumscribed hypersensitive area within a tight band of muscle. It is caused by acute or chronic muscle strain. It feels like a tight knot under the skin. Trigger point massage is done

TABLE 8.13 **Nondrug Therapies for Pain**
Physical Therapies
• Acupuncture
• Application of heat and cold (Table 8.14)
• Exercise
• Massage
• Transcutaneous electrical nerve stimulation (TENS)
Cognitive Therapies
• Distraction
• Hypnosis
• Imagery
• Relaxation strategies (see Chapter 6)
• Art therapy
• Imagery
• Meditation
• Music therapy
• Relaxation breathing

FIG. 8.8 Treatment of pain with transcutaneous electrical nerve stimulation (TENS) treatment after shoulder surgery. (© Noel Moore/Hemera/Thinkstock.)

by applying strong, sustained digital pressure; deep massage; or gentler massage with ice followed by muscle heating. Massage is discussed in Chapter 6.

Exercise. Exercise is an essential part of the treatment plan for patients with chronic pain, particularly those with musculoskeletal pain. Many patients become physically deconditioned from their pain, which in turn leads to more pain. Exercise acts via many mechanisms to relieve pain. It enhances circulation and cardiovascular fitness, reduces edema, increases muscle strength and flexibility, and enhances physical and psychosocial functioning. Tailor an exercise program to the patient's physical needs and lifestyle. It may include aerobic exercise, stretching, and strengthening exercises. Trained personnel (e.g., physical therapist) should supervise the program.

Transcutaneous Electrical Nerve Stimulation. *Transcutaneous electrical nerve stimulation* (TENS) involves the delivery of an electric current through electrodes applied to the skin surface over the painful region, at trigger points, or over a peripheral nerve. A TENS system consists of 2 or more electrodes connected by lead wires to a small, battery-operated stimulator (Fig. 8.8). Usually a physical therapist is responsible for delivering TENS therapy, although nurses can be trained in the technique.

TENS may be used for acute pain, including postoperative pain and pain associated with physical trauma. The effects of TENS on chronic pain are less clear, but it may be effective in these cases.[21]

TABLE 8.14 Patient & Caregiver Teaching

Heat and Cold Therapy

Include the following instructions when teaching the patient and caregiver about superficial heat or cold techniques:

Heat Therapy

- Do not use heat on an area that is being treated with radiation therapy, is bleeding, has decreased sensation, or has been injured in the past 24 hours.
- Do not use any menthol-containing products (e.g., Ben-Gay, Vicks, Icy Hot) with heat applications because this may cause burns.
- Cover the heat source with a towel or cloth before applying to the skin to prevent burns.

Cold Therapy

- Cover the cold source with a cloth or towel before applying to the skin to prevent tissue damage.
- Do not apply cold to areas that are being treated with radiation therapy, have open wounds, or have poor circulation.
- If it is not possible to apply the cold directly to the painful site, try applying it right above or below the painful site or on the opposite side of the body on the corresponding site (e.g., left elbow if the right elbow hurts).

Acupuncture. Acupuncture is a technique of Traditional Chinese Medicine in which very thin needles are inserted into the body at designated points. Acupuncture is used for many kinds of pain. Acupuncture is described in Chapter 6.

Heat Therapy. Heat therapy is the application of either moist or dry heat to the skin. Heat therapy can be either superficial or deep. We can apply superficial heat using an electric heating pad (dry or moist), a hot pack, hot moist compresses, warm wax (paraffin), or a hot water bottle. To expose large areas of the body, patients can immerse themselves in a hot bath, shower, or whirlpool. Physical therapy departments provide deep-heat therapy through techniques such as short-wave diathermy, microwave diathermy, and ultrasound therapy. Patient and caregiver teaching about heat therapy is described in Table 8.14.

Cold Therapy. Cold therapy involves the application of either moist or dry cold to the skin. Dry cold can be applied by using an ice bag, moist cold by using towels soaked in ice water, cold hydrocollator packs, or immersion in a bath or under running cold water. Icing with ice cubes or blocks of ice made to resemble Popsicles is another technique used for pain relief. Cold therapy is thought to be more effective than heat for a variety of painful conditions, including acute pain from trauma or surgery, acute flare-ups of arthritis, muscle spasms, and headache. Patient and caregiver teaching about cold therapy is described in Table 8.14.

Cognitive Therapies. Techniques to alter the affective, cognitive, and behavioral components of pain include a variety of cognitive strategies and behavioral approaches. For example, patients can identify and challenge negative pain-related thoughts and replace them with more positive coping thoughts. Some techniques need little training and often are adopted independently by the patient. For others, a trained therapist is needed.

Distraction. Distraction involves redirection of attention away from the pain and onto something else. It is a simple but powerful strategy to relieve pain. Distraction involves engaging the patient in any activity that can hold his or her attention (e.g., watching TV or a movie, conversing, listening to music). It is

important to match the activity with the patient's energy level and ability to concentrate.

Hypnosis. Hypnotherapy is a structured technique that enables a patient to achieve a state of heightened awareness and focused concentration that can be used to alter the patient's pain perception. Hypnosis should be delivered and monitored only by specially trained clinicians.

Relaxation Strategies. Relaxation strategies reduce stress, decrease acute anxiety, distract from pain, ease muscle tension, combat fatigue, promote sleep, and enhance the effectiveness of other pain relief measures.[22] Relaxation strategies include relaxation breathing, music, imagery, meditation, muscle relaxation, and art (see Chapter 6).

❖ NURSING AND INTERPROFESSIONAL MANAGEMENT: PAIN

You are an important member of the interprofessional pain management team. You provide input into the assessment and reassessment of pain. You help in planning and implementing treatments, including teaching, advocacy, and support of the patient, caregiver, and family. Because patients in any care setting can have pain, you must be knowledgeable about current therapies and flexible in trying new approaches to pain management.

Together with the patient, develop a written agreement or treatment plan that describes the pain management. The plan should ensure that pain will be treated based on the patient's perception and report of pain. When appropriate, the plan outlines the gradual tapering of the analgesic dose, with eventual substitution of parenteral analgesics with long-acting oral preparations and possibly cessation of opioids.

Many nursing roles are described earlier in this chapter, including assessing pain, giving treatment, monitoring for side effects, and teaching patients and caregivers. However, the success of these actions depends on your ability to establish a trusting relationship with the patient and caregiver and to address their concerns about pain and its treatment.

◆ Effective Communication

Because pain is a subjective experience, patients need to feel confident that their reporting of pain will be believed and will not be perceived as "complaining." The patient and caregiver need to know that you consider the pain significant and understand that pain may profoundly disrupt a person's life. Communicate concern and commit to helping the patient obtain pain relief and cope with any unrelieved pain. Support the patient and caregiver through the period of trial and error that may be necessary to implement an effective therapeutic plan. It is important to clarify responsibilities in pain relief. Help the patient understand the role of the interprofessional team members, as well as the patient's roles and expectations.

In addition to addressing specific aspects of pain assessment and treatment, evaluate the impact that the pain has on the lives of the patient and caregiver. Table 8.15 addresses teaching needs of patients and caregivers related to pain management.

◆ Challenges to Effective Pain Management

Common challenges to effective pain management include misunderstandings about tolerance, physical dependence, and addiction. It is important for you to understand and be able to explain these concepts. Table 8.16 lists barriers to pain management and strategies to address them.

NURSING MANAGEMENT

Pain Management

- Assess pain characteristics (pattern and onset, area or location, intensity, quality, associated symptoms, and management strategies).
- Develop treatment plan for patient's pain (including drug and nondrug therapies).
- Give ordered pain medications.
- Evaluate whether current treatment plan is effective.
- Teach patient and caregiver about treatment plan.
- Implement discharge teaching about pain management.
- Provide effective supervision of UAP:
  - Help with screening for pain and notify RN if patient expresses pain.
  - Take and report vital signs before and after pain medications are given.
  - Note and report if patient is refusing to take part in ordered activities, such as ambulation (since this may indicate inadequate pain management).

TABLE 8.15   Patient & Caregiver Teaching

Pain Management

Include the following information in the teaching plan for the patient with pain and caregiver:
- Self-management techniques
- Realistic goals for pain control
- Negative consequences of unrelieved pain
- Need to maintain a record of pain level and effectiveness of treatment
- Treat pain with drugs and/or nondrug therapies before it becomes severe
- Medication may stop working after it is taken for a period of time, and dosages may have to be adjusted
- Potential side effects and complications associated with pain therapies can include nausea and vomiting, constipation, sedation and drowsiness, itching, urinary retention, and sweating.
- Need to report when pain is not relieved to tolerable levels

◆ **Tolerance.** *Tolerance* occurs with chronic exposure to a variety of drugs. In the case of opioids, tolerance to analgesia is characterized by the need for an increased opioid dose to maintain the same degree of analgesia. Although the development of tolerance to side effects (except constipation) is more predictable, the incidence of clinically significant analgesic opioid tolerance in chronic pain patients is unknown, since dosage needs may increase as the disease (e.g., cancer) progresses. It is essential to assess for increased analgesic needs in patients on long-term therapy. The interprofessional team must evaluate and rule out other causes of increased analgesic needs, such as disease progression or infection.

If significant tolerance to opioids develops and the opioid is losing its effectiveness, or intolerable side effects are associated with escalation of doses, the practice of *opioid rotation* may be considered. This involves switching from 1 opioid to another, assuming that the new opioid will be more effective at lower equianalgesic doses. However, very high opioid doses can result in OIH rather than pain relief. This means that increases in the dose can lead to higher pain levels. (OIH is discussed on p. 115.)

◆ **Physical Dependence.** Like tolerance, physical dependence is a normal physiologic response to ongoing exposure to drugs. It is manifested by a withdrawal syndrome when the drug is abruptly decreased. Manifestations of opioid withdrawal are listed in Table 8.17. When opioids are no longer needed to provide pain relief, a tapering schedule should be used in conjunction with careful monitoring. A typical tapering schedule may involve reducing the dose by 20% to 50% per day. The goal is to reduce the amount of medication and at the same time minimize adverse and withdrawal effects.

◆ **Pseudoaddiction.** Inadequate treatment of pain can lead to a phenomenon called *pseudoaddiction*. This occurs when patients show behaviors associated with addiction (e.g., frequent requests for analgesic refills or higher dosages), but the behaviors resolve with adequate treatment of the patient's pain. These patients are often labeled as drug seeking, which can result in mistrust between the patient and HCP. This problem can be avoided by effective communication strategies and optimal pain management.

◆ **Addiction.** *Addiction* is a complex neurobiologic condition characterized by aberrant behaviors arising from a drive to obtain and take substances for reasons other than the prescribed therapeutic value (see Chapter 10). Tolerance and physical dependence are not indicators of addiction. Rather, they are normal physiologic responses to chronic exposure to certain drugs, including opioids. Addiction rarely occurs in patients who receive opioids for pain control. If addiction is suspected, it must be investigated and appropriately diagnosed. It should not be implied without evidence because this interferes with pain management. The hallmarks of addiction include (1) compulsive use, (2) loss of control of use, and (3) continued use despite risk of harm.

◆ **Risk Monitoring.** Several opioid risk assessments are available to help clinicians assess patients for abuse, misuse, and addiction. A controlled substance agreement for those at risk for addiction may be used. Addiction risk assessment tools, such as the Opioid Risk Tool (*www.drugabuse.gov/sites/default/files/files/OpioidRiskTool.pdf*) and the Screener and Opioid Assessment for Patient Pain (*www.nhms.org/sites/default/files/Pdfs/SOAPP-14.pdf*) are available. Patient monitoring with urine drug screens and access to state prescription monitoring programs to track prescriptions are effective in detecting misuse of drugs. The risk for addiction should not prevent HCPs from using opioids to effectively treat moderate to severe acute and chronic pain.

INSTITUTIONALIZING PAIN EDUCATION AND MANAGEMENT

Besides patient and caregiver barriers, other barriers to effective and safe pain management include inadequate HCP education and lack of institutional support. Traditionally, medical and nursing school curricula have spent little time teaching future physicians and nurses about pain and symptom management. The lack of emphasis on pain has contributed to inadequate training of HCPs.

We have made progress overcoming these barriers. Medical and nursing schools devote more time to addressing pain. Numerous professional organizations have published evidence-based guidelines for assessing and managing pain in many patient populations and clinical settings.

Institutional commitment and practices are changing clinical practice. One major step in institutionalizing pain management is the development and adoption of The Joint Commission (TJC) guideline on pain.[23] TJC is the accrediting body for most health care facilities (hospitals, nursing homes, and health care clinics). Under these standards, health care facilities are required to (1) recognize the patient's right to appropriate assessment and management of pain; (2) identify pain in patients during their initial assessment and as needed, during ongoing, periodic reassessments; (3) teach HCPs about pain assessment and management and ensure competency; and (4) teach patients and their families about pain management.

TABLE 8.16 Patient & Caregiver Teaching

Reducing Barriers to Pain Management

When teaching the patient and caregiver about pain management discuss the following barriers:

Barrier	Nursing Considerations
Fear of addiction	• Explain that addiction is uncommon in patients taking opioids as directed by the HCP for pain.
Fear of tolerance	• Teach that tolerance is a normal physiologic response to chronic opioid therapy. If tolerance does develop, the drug may have to be changed (e.g., morphine in place of oxycodone).
	• Teach that there is no absolute upper limit to pure opioid agonists (e.g., morphine). Dosages can be increased, and patient should not save drugs for when the pain is worse.
	• Teach that tolerance develops more slowly to analgesic effects of opioids than to side effects (e.g., sedation, respiratory depression). Tolerance does not develop to constipation; thus a regular bowel program should be started early.
Concern about side effects	• Teach methods to prevent and to treat common side effects.
	• Stress that side effects, such as sedation and nausea, decrease with time.
	• Explain that different drugs have unique side effects, and other pain drugs can be tried to reduce the specific side effect.
Fear of injections	• Explain that oral medicines are preferred.
	• Stress that even if oral route becomes unusable, transdermal or indwelling parenteral routes can be used rather than injections.
Desire to be "good" patient	• Discuss that patients are partners in their care and that partnership requires open communication by both patient and nurse.
	• Stress to patients that they have a responsibility to keep you informed about their pain.
Desire to be stoic	• Explain that although stoicism is a valued behavior in many cultures, failure to report pain can result in undertreatment and severe, unrelieved pain.
Forgetting to take analgesic	• Provide and teach use of pill containers.
	• Provide methods of record keeping for drug use.
	• Recruit caregivers to help with the analgesic regimen.
Concern that pain indicates disease progression	• Explain that increased pain or the need for analgesics may reflect tolerance.
	• Stress that new pain may come from a non–life-threatening source (e.g., muscle spasm, urinary tract infection).
	• Use drug and nondrug strategies to reduce anxiety.
	• Ensure that patient and caregivers have current, accurate, comprehensive information about the disease and prognosis.
	• Provide psychologic support.
Sense of fatalism	• Explain that pain can be managed in most patients.
	• Explain that most therapies require a period of trial and error.
	• Stress that side effects can be managed.
Ineffective medication	• Teach that there are multiple options within each category of medication (e.g., opioids, NSAIDs), and another medication from the same category may provide better relief.
	• Discuss that finding the best treatment regimen may require trial and error.
	• Include nondrug approaches in treatment plan.

TABLE 8.17 Manifestations of Opioid Withdrawal Syndrome

	Early Response (6–12 hr)	Late Response (48–72 hr)
Psychosocial	• Anxiety	• Excitation
Secretions	• Lacrimation	• Diarrhea
	• Rhinorrhea	
	• Diaphoresis	
Other	• Yawning	• Restlessness
	• Piloerection	• Fever
	• Shaking, chills	• Nausea and vomiting
	• Dilated pupils	• Abdominal cramping pain
	• Anorexia	• Hypertension
	• Tremor	• Tachycardia
		• Insomnia

ETHICAL ISSUES IN PAIN MANAGEMENT

Fear of Hastening Death by Giving Analgesics

A common concern of health care professionals and caregivers is that giving a sufficient amount of drug to relieve pain will hasten or precipitate death of a terminally ill person. However, there is no scientific evidence that opioids can hasten death, even among patients at the very end of life. Moreover, you have a moral obligation to provide comfort and pain relief at the end of life. Even if there is a concern about the possibility of hastening death, the rule of double effect provides ethical justification. This rule states that if an unwanted consequence (i.e., hastened death) occurs because of an action taken to achieve a moral good (i.e., pain relief), the action is justified if the nurse's intent is to relieve pain and not to hasten death.

Requests for Assisted Suicide

Unrelieved pain is 1 of the reasons that patients make requests for assisted suicide. Aggressive and adequate pain management may decrease the number of such requests. Assisted suicide is a complex issue that extends beyond pain and pain management. Physician-assisted suicide is legal in some states (e.g., Oregon, Washington). To address the legal and ethical issues about this situation, the International Association for Hospice and Palliative Care prepared a position paper on this topic.[24]

Use of Placebos in Pain Assessment and Treatment

Placebos are still sometimes used to assess and treat pain. Using a placebo involves deceiving patients by making them think they are receiving an analgesic when they are receiving an inert substance, such as saline. Many professional organizations condemn the use of placebos to assess or treat pain.

Gerontologic Considerations: Pain

Persistent pain is a common problem in older adults and is often associated with physical disability and psychosocial problems.

The prevalence of chronic pain among community-dwelling older adults exceeds 50% and among older nursing home patients is around 80%. The most common painful conditions among older adults are musculoskeletal conditions, such as osteoarthritis and low back pain. Chronic pain often results in depression, sleep problems, decreased mobility, increased health care use, and physical and social role dysfunction. Despite its high prevalence, pain in older adults is often inadequately assessed and treated.

Several barriers to pain assessment in the older patient exist. Older adults and their HCPs often believe that pain is a normal, inevitable part of aging and that nothing can be done to relieve the pain. Older adults may not report pain for fear of being a "burden" or a "complainer." They may fear taking opioids. In addition, older patients are more likely to use words such as "aching," "soreness," or "discomfort" rather than "pain." Be persistent in asking older adults about pain. Carry out the assessment in an unhurried, supportive manner.

Another barrier is the increased prevalence of cognitive, sensory-perceptual, and motor problems that interfere with a person's ability to process information and communicate. Examples include dementia and delirium, poststroke aphasia, and other communication barriers. Hearing and vision deficits may complicate assessment. Therefore pain assessment tools may have to be adapted for older adults. For example, you many need to use a large-print pain intensity scale. Most older adults, even those with mild to moderate cognitive impairment, can use quantitative scales accurately and reliably.

In older patients with chronic pain, perform a thorough physical examination and history to identify causes of pain, possible therapies, and potential problems. Assess for depression and functional impairments, because they are also common among older adults with pain.

Treatment of pain in older adults is complicated by several factors. First, older adults metabolize drugs more slowly than younger people and thus are at greater risk for higher blood levels and adverse effects. The adage "start low and go slow" must be applied to analgesic therapy in this age group. Second, the use of NSAIDs in older adults is associated with a high frequency of GI bleeding. Third, older adults often are taking many drugs for 1 or more chronic conditions. The addition of analgesics can result in dangerous drug interactions and increased side effects. Fourth, cognitive impairment and ataxia can be worsened by analgesics, such as opioids, antidepressants, and antiseizure drugs. This requires that HCPs titrate drugs slowly and monitor carefully for side effects.

Treatment regimens for older adults must include nondrug modalities. Exercise and patient teaching are important nondrug interventions for older adults with chronic pain. Include family and caregivers in the treatment plan (Tables 8.15 and 8.16).

MANAGING PAIN IN SPECIAL POPULATIONS

Patients Unable to Self-Report Pain

Although the patient's self-report is the gold standard of pain assessment, many illnesses and conditions affect a patient's ability to report pain. These diagnoses and conditions include dementia and delirium. For these people, behavioral and physiologic changes may be the only indicators of pain. You must be astute at recognizing behavioral symptoms of pain.

TABLE 8.18	Assessing Pain in Nonverbal Patients

The following assessment techniques are recommended:
- Obtain a self-report when possible.
- Never assume a nonverbal person is unable to communicate pain; blinking, writing, hand gestures, or nodding can be ways to express pain or the absence of pain.
- Investigate potential causes of pain.
- Observe patient behaviors that indicate pain (e.g., grimacing, frowning, rubbing a painful area, groaning, restlessness).
- Obtain surrogate reports of pain from professional and family caregivers.
- Try to use analgesics and reassess the patient to observe for a decrease in pain-related behaviors.

Modified from Herr K, Coyne PJ, McCaffery M, et al: Position statement from the American Society for Pain Management Nursing (ASPMN): Pain assessment in the patient unable to self-report—Position statement with clinical practice recommendations, *Pain Manag Nurs* 12:230, 2011.

A guide for assessing pain in nonverbal patients is outlined in Table 8.18. Several scales are available to assess pain-related behaviors in nonverbal patients, particularly those with advanced dementia and the critically ill. Links to several pain assessment tools are available at the City of Hope Pain and Palliative Care Resource Center website *(http://prc.coh.org)*.

Patients With Substance Use Problems

HCPs are often reluctant to give opioids to patients at risk for addiction or those with substance-abuse disorders for fear of promoting or worsening addictions. However, there is no evidence that providing opioid analgesia to these patients in any way worsens their addictive disease. In fact, the stress of unrelieved pain may contribute to relapse in the recovering patient or increased drug use in the patient who is actively abusing drugs.

❓	**CHECK YOUR PRACTICE**

A 36-yr-old male patient is recovering from abdominal surgery to remove his spleen after an automobile accident. He is a known drug user. You are taking care of him, and he is very irritable because he is not getting enough pain medication. You are reluctant to give him his PRN morphine for fear that you will contribute to his addiction problem.
- What should you do?

Guidelines for pain management in patients with addictive disease have been established by the American Society for Pain Management Nursing (ASPMN). These guidelines reflect your role in a team approach in which patients with addictive disease and pain have the right to be treated with dignity, respect, and the same quality of pain assessment and management as all other patients.

If the patient acknowledges substance use, determine the types and amounts of drugs used. Avoid exposing the patient to the misused drug. Effective equianalgesic doses of other opioids may be determined if daily drug doses are known. If a history of drug use is unknown or if the patient does not acknowledge substance use, be suspect when normal doses of analgesics do not relieve the patient's pain.

Aggressive behavior patterns and signs of withdrawal may occur. Withdrawal symptoms can worsen pain and lead to drug-seeking behavior or illicit drug use. Toxicology screens may be helpful in determining recently used drugs. Discussing these findings with the patient may help gain the patient's cooperation in pain control.

Severe pain should be treated with opioids and at much higher doses than those used with drug-naive patients. The use of a single opioid is preferred. Avoid using a mixed opioid agonist-antagonist (e.g., butorphanol) or a partial agonist (e.g., buprenorphine) because these drugs may precipitate withdrawal symptoms. Nonopioid and adjuvant analgesics and nondrug pain relief measures may be used as needed. To maintain opioid blood levels and prevent withdrawal symptoms, provide analgesics around the clock. Use supplemental doses to treat breakthrough pain. IV or PCA infusions may be considered for acute pain management.

Pain management for people with addiction is challenging and needs an interprofessional team approach. When possible, the team includes pain management and addiction specialists. Team members need to be aware of their own attitudes about people with substance use problems, which may result in undertreatment of pain.

CASE STUDY

Pain

(© iStock.com/XiXinXing.)

Patient Profile

K.C. is a 280-lb (127-kg) 68-yr-old black man with diabetes, peripheral neuropathy, hypertension, and gout, who was admitted for an incision and drainage of a right abdominal abscess. He is being discharged on his second postoperative day. His daughter will perform dressing changes at home.

Subjective Data

- Lives alone
- Desires 0 pain but will accept 1 or 2 on a scale of 0 to 10
- Reports incision area pain as a 2 or 3 between dressing changes and as a 6 during dressing changes
- States sharp pain persists 1 to 2 hours after dressing change
- Reports pain between dressing changes controlled by 2 oxycodone tablets
- Has history of peripheral neuropathy and describes chronic pain in his feet

Objective Data

- Needs dressing changes 4 times per day after discharge
- For discharge, oxycodone (2 tablets q4hr for pain PRN) is prescribed.

Discussion Questions

1. Describe the assessment data that are important for determining whether K.C. has adequate pain management.
2. *Priority Decision:* Based on the data presented, what are the priority nursing diagnoses? Are there any collaborative problems?
3. *Priority Decision:* What are the priority nursing interventions for K.C.?
4. How long should the daughter wait after the oxycodone is given to begin the dressing change?
5. *Patient-Centered Care:* What other pain therapies might you plan to help K.C. through the dressing change?
6. *Safety:* What side effects might he have because of his pain medication? How can these be safely managed?
7. *Collaboration:* To whom can you delegate teaching K.C. and his daughter the plan of care at home?
8. *Evidence-Based Practice:* K.C.'s daughter asks you if any other strategies could be used to help decrease her father's incisional pain and his peripheral neuropathy pain.

Answers available at *www.evolve.elsevier.com/Lewis/medsurg.*

BRIDGE TO NCLEX EXAMINATION

The number of the question corresponds to the same-numbered outcome at the beginning of the chapter.

1. Pain is *best* described as
   a. a creation of a person's imagination.
   b. an unpleasant, subjective experience.
   c. a maladaptive response to a stimulus.
   d. a neurologic event resulting from activation of nociceptors.

2. A patient is receiving a PCA infusion after surgery to repair a hip fracture. She is sleeping soundly but awakens when the nurse speaks to her in a normal tone of voice. Her respirations are 8 breaths/min. The *most* appropriate nursing action in this situation is to
   a. stop the PCA infusion.
   b. obtain an oxygen saturation level.
   c. continue to closely monitor the patient.
   d. administer naloxone and contact the provider.

3. Which words are *most* likely to be used to describe neuropathic pain *(select all that apply)*?
   a. Dull
   b. Itching
   c. Burning
   d. Shooting

   e. Shock-like

4. Unrelieved pain is
   a. not expected after major surgery.
   b. expected in a person with cancer.
   c. dangerous and can lead to many physical and psychologic complications.
   d. an annoying sensation, but it is not as important as other physical care needs.

5. A cancer patient who reports ongoing, constant moderate pain with short periods of severe pain during dressing changes is
   a. probably exaggerating his pain.
   b. in need of a referral for surgical treatment of his pain.
   c. best treated by receiving a long-acting and a short-acting opioid.
   d. best treated by regularly scheduled short-acting opioids plus acetaminophen.

6. An example of distraction to provide pain relief is
   a. TENS.
   b. music.
   c. exercise.
   d. biofeedback.

7. Appropriate nonopioid analgesics for mild pain include *(select all that apply)*
   a. oxycodone.
   b. ibuprofen (Advil).
   c. lorazepam (Ativan).
   d. acetaminophen (Tylenol).
   e. codeine with acetaminophen (Tylenol #3).
8. An *important* nursing responsibility related to pain is to
   a. leave the patient alone to rest.
   b. help the patient appear to not be in pain.
   c. believe what the patient says about the pain.
   d. assume responsibility for eliminating the patient's pain.
9. Giving opioids to an actively dying patient who has moderate to severe pain
   a. may cause addiction.
   b. will likely be ineffective.
   c. is an appropriate nursing action.
   d. will likely hasten the person's death.

10. A nurse believes that patients with the same type of tissue injury should have the same amount of pain. This statement reflects
    a. a belief that will contribute to appropriate pain management.
    b. an accurate statement about pain mechanisms and expected goals of pain therapy.
    c. a belief that will not have any effect on the type of care provided to people in pain.
    d. a lack of knowledge about pain mechanisms, which is likely to contribute to poor pain management.

1. b, 2. c, 3. b, 4. e, 5. c, 6. b, 7. b, d, 8. c, 9. c, 10. d.

For rationales to these answers and even more NCLEX review questions, visit *http://evolve.elsevier.com/Lewis/medsurg*.

EVOLVE WEBSITE/RESOURCES LIST

http://evolve.elsevier.com/Lewis/medsurg
Review Questions (Online Only)
Key Points
Answer Keys for Questions
- Rationales for Bridge to NCLEX Examination Questions
- Answer Guidelines for Case Study on p. 125
Student Case Study
- Patient With Pain
Conceptual Care Map Creator
Audio Glossary
Content Updates

REFERENCES

1. Centers for Disease Control and Prevention. Guideline for prescribing opioids for chronic pain. Retrieved from *www.cdc.gov/drugoverdose/prescribing/guideline.html*.
*2. Van den Beuken-Van Everdingen MH, Hochstenbach LM, Joosten EA, et al: Update on prevalence of pain in patients with cancer: Systematic review and meta-analysis, *J Pain Symptom Manage* 51:6, 2016.
3. McCaffery M. *Nursing practice theories related to cognition, bodily pain and man-environmental interactions*, Los Angeles, 1968, UCLA Students Store. (Classic)
*4. Goncalves JPB, Lucchetti G, Menezes PR, et al: Complimentary religious and spiritual interventions in physical health and quality of life: A systematic review of randomized controlled clinical trials, *PLoS One* 12:10, 2017.
5. Jensen MP, Tomé-Pires C, de la Vega C, et al: What determines whether a pain is rated as mild, moderate, or severe? *Clin J Pain* 33:414, 2017.
6. Nix WA: *Muscles, nerves, and pain*. Berlin, 2017, Springer.
*7. Tesarz J, Eich W, Treede RD, et al: Altered pressure pain thresholds and increased wind-up in adult patients with chronic back pain with a history of childhood maltreatment: A quantitative sensory testing study, *Pain* 157:1799, 2016.
*8. Parker RS, Lewis, GN, Rice DA, et al: Is motor cortical excitability altered in people with chronic pain? A systematic review and meta-analysis, *Brain Stimul* 9:4, 2016.
*9. Blyth FM: The global burden of neuropathic pain, *Pain* 159:614, 2018.

*10. Kuttikat A, Maliha S, Oomatia A, et al: Novel signs and their clinical utility in diagnosing complex regional pain syndrome: A prospective observational cohort study, *Clin J Pain* 33:496, 2017.
11. Hale D, Marshall K. Assessing and treating pain in the cognitively impaired geriatric home care patient, *Home Health Now* 25:116, 2017.
*12. Gordon DB, Dahl J, Phillips P, et al: The use of "as-needed" range orders for opioid analgesic in the management of acute pain: A consensus statement of the American Society of Pain Management Nurses and the American Pain Society, *Pain Manag Nurs* 5:53, 2004. (Classic)
*13. Kumar K, Kirksey MA, Duong S, et al: A review of opioid-sparing modalities in perioperative pain management: methods to decrease opioid use postoperatively, *Anesth Analg* 125:1749, 2017.
14. Tawfic Q, Kumar K, Pirani Z, et al: Prevention of chronic post-surgical pain: The importance of early identification of risk factors, *J Anesth* 31:424, 2017.
15. Yoon E, Barbar A, Choudhary M, et al: Acetaminophen-induced hepatotoxicity: A comprehensive update, *J Clin Transl Hepatol* 4:131, 2016.
16. Kharasch ED: Current concepts in methadone metabolism and transport, *Clin Pharmacol Drug Dev* 6:125, 2017.
*17. Gupta K, Prasad A, Nagappa M, et al: Risk factors for opioid-induced respiratory depression and failure to rescue, *Curr Opin Anaesthesiol* 31:110, 2018.
*18. Mu A, Weinberg E, Moulin DE, et al: Pharmacologic management of chronic neuropathic pain: Review of the Canadian Pain Society consensus statement, *Can Fam Physician* 63:844, 2017.
19. Janknegt R, van den Beuken M, Schiere S, et al: Rapid acting fentanyl formulations in breakthrough pain in cancer: Drug selection by means of the System of Objectified Judgement Analysis. *Eur J Hosp Pharm Sci Pract*, 25:e2, 2018.
20. Webb RJ, Shelton CP: The benefits of authorized agent controlled analgesia (AACA) to control pain and other symptoms at the end of life, *J Pain Symptom Manage* 50:371, 2015.
21. Coutaux A. Non-pharmacological treatments for pain relief: TENS and acupuncture, *Joint Bone Spine* 84:657, 2017.
*22. Felix MM, Ferreira MB, da Cruz LF, et al: Relaxation therapy with guided imagery for postoperative pain management: An integrative review, *Pain Manag Nurs* 35:342, 2017.
23. The Joint Commission: Revised standard on pain assessment and management, 2018. Retrieved from *www.jointcommission.org*.
24. De Lima L, Woodruff R, Pettus K, et al: International Association for Hospice and Palliative Care position statement: Euthanasia and physician-assisted suicide, *J Palliat Med* 20:8, 2017.

*Evidence-based information for clinical practice.

9

Palliative and End-of-Life Care

Denise M. McEnroe-Petitte

> *Those who have the strength and the love to sit with a dying patient in the silence that goes beyond words will know that this moment is neither frightening nor painful, but a peaceful cessation.*
>
> ***Elisabeth Kübler-Ross***

e http://evolve.elsevier.com/Lewis/medsurg/

CONCEPTUAL FOCUS

Coping

Ethics

Family Dynamics

Health Care Organizations

Palliation

Spirituality

LEARNING OUTCOMES

1. Distinguish the purpose of palliative care at the end of life and hospice care.
2. Describe the physical and psychologic manifestations at the end of life.
3. Explain the process of grief and bereavement at the end of life.
4. Examine the cultural and spiritual issues related to end-of-life care.
5. Discuss ethical and legal issues in end-of-life care.

6. Describe the nursing management of the dying patient.
7. Explore the special needs of family caregivers in end-of-life care.
8. Discuss the special needs of the nurse who cares for dying patients and their families.

KEY TERMS

advance directives, p. 133
bereavement, p. 131
brain death, p. 129
Cheyne-Stokes respiration, p. 130

death, p. 129
death rattle, p. 130
end of life, p. 129
grief, p. 131

hospice, p. 128
palliative care, p. 127
spirituality, p. 132

PALLIATIVE CARE

Palliative care is any form of care or treatment that focuses on reducing the severity of disease symptoms. The overall goals of palliative care are to (1) prevent and relieve suffering and (2) improve quality of life for patients with serious life-limiting illnesses[1] (Fig. 9.1). Specific goals of palliative care are listed in Table 9.1.

Ideally, all patients receiving curative or restorative health care should receive palliative care at the same time. Palliative care extends into the period of end-of-life (EOL) care and offers patient and family support while planning for EOL needs.[2] Bereavement care follows the patient's death (Fig. 9.2).

Palliative care originated as EOL care in the 1960s. Initially, this care focused on providing symptom relief and emotional support to the patient, family, and significant others during the terminal phases of a serious life-limiting disease. We now call that phase of palliative care *palliative care at the end of life*, which is the focus of this chapter.

The role of palliative care at the EOL is increasing in our current health care environment. Demographic changes are increasing the demand for palliative care. A growing number of Baby Boomers are turning 65. Improvements in health care technology have led to longer life expectancies and an increased number of older adults. The growing number of people with conditions such as diabetes and heart disease contribute to the increased use of palliative care.[2]

Older adults often have multiple chronic illnesses resulting in increased health care use.[3] Palliative care has been shown to (1) improve quality of life for those with chronic illness, (2) decrease the associated economic costs for their health care, and (3) ease caregiver burden for those with chronic and terminal illnesses.

FIG. 9.1 One goal of palliative care is to improve the quality of the patient's remaining life. (Courtesy Kathleen A. Pollard, RN, MSN, CHPN, Phoenix, AZ.)

FIG. 9.3 Relationship of palliative care and end-of-life care/hospice. (From Rosenberg M, Lamba S, Misra S: Palliative medicine and geriatric emergency care: Challenges, opportunities, and basic principles, *Clin Geriatr Med* 29:1, 2013.)

TABLE 9.1   **Goals of Palliative Care**
• Regard dying as a normal process
• Provide relief from symptoms, including pain
• Affirm life and neither hasten nor postpone death
• Support holistic patient care and enhance quality of life
• Offer support to patients to live as actively as possible until death
• Offer support to the family during the patient's illness and in their own bereavement

Adapted from World Health Organization: WHO definition of palliative care. Retrieved from *www.who.int/cancer/palliative/definition/en.*

FIG. 9.4 Hospice care is designed to provide compassion, concern, and support for the dying. (From Rick Brady, Riva, MD.)

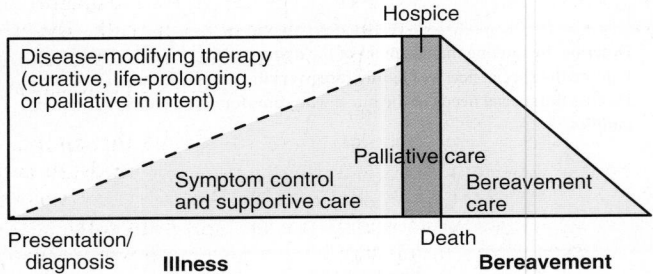

FIG. 9.2 Continuum-of-care model showing integration of curative care, palliative and end-of-life/hospice care, and bereavement care. (Redrawn from Robert Wood Johnson Foundation: *The EPEC Project: Elements and models of end-of-life care,* 1999.)

To optimize the benefits of palliative care, it should be started after a person receives a diagnosis of a life-limiting illness, such as cancer, heart failure, chronic obstructive pulmonary disease, dementia, or end-stage kidney disease. The palliative care team is an interprofessional collaboration involving physicians, nurses, social workers, pharmacists, chaplains, and other health care professionals. Communication among the patient, family, and interprofessional palliative team is important to provide optimal care.

Patients may receive palliative care services in multiple settings, including the home, long-term and acute care, mental health facilities, rehabilitation centers, and prisons. Many institutions have established interprofessional palliative and hospice care teams.[1]

HOSPICE CARE

Palliative care often includes hospice care before or at the EOL (Fig. 9.3). **Hospice** is a concept of care that provides compassion,

concern, and support for persons in the last phases of a terminal disease (Fig. 9.4). The main goals of hospice care are to assist the patient to live as fully and comfortably as possible while dying with dignity. Hospice programs provide care with an emphasis on symptom management, advance care planning, spiritual care, and family support.

The major difference between palliative care and hospice care is that palliative care allows a person to simultaneously receive curative and palliative treatments. Hospice care is an option when the physician determines a person has 6 months or less to live and that person or health care proxy decides to forgo curative treatments. Hospice is often underused, as many assume the person must be actively dying before hospice is necessary. On the contrary, it is important that the person be referred to hospice as soon as possible to ease the physical, emotional, and spiritual distress so common at the EOL.

Almost half of the patients who die in the United States are under the care of a hospice program.[4] More than three-quarters of persons in hospice programs are over the age of 65 years, and the majority are white. Most patients have cancer, dementia, stroke, or heart or respiratory conditions.[4]

Hospice programs are organized under a variety of models. Some are hospital-based programs, others are part of existing home health care agencies, and others are freestanding or community-based programs.

Like palliative care, hospice care is provided in a variety of locations, including the home, inpatient settings, acute and long-term care facilities, and rehabilitation centers. Hospice services are available 24 hours a day, 7 days a week to help

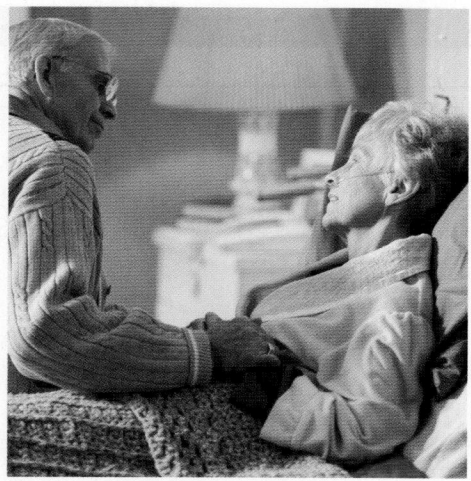

FIG. 9.5 Inpatient hospice settings are designed to make the atmosphere as relaxed and homelike as possible. (© Photodisc/Thinkstock.)

patients and families in their homes. Inpatient hospice settings often have a relaxed and homelike atmosphere (Fig. 9.5). Staff and volunteers are available for the patient and family.

A medically supervised interprofessional team and volunteers provide holistic hospice services. The hospice nurse plays a pivotal role in coordination of the hospice team.[5] Hospice nurses work with other interprofessional team members to provide care and support to the patient and family. Hospice nurses focus on pain control and symptom management, spiritual assessment, and assessment and management of family needs. To meet patient and family needs, the hospice nurse needs excellent teaching skills, compassion, flexibility, cultural competence, and adaptability.

The decision to begin hospice care is hard for several reasons. Many patients, families, physicians, and other health care providers (HCPs) lack information about hospice care. Some cultural/ethnic groups may not use hospice because of a lack of awareness of hospice services, a desire to continue with potentially curative therapies, and concerns about lack of minority hospice workers. Physicians may be reluctant to give referrals because they sometimes view a patient's decline as their personal failure. Some patients or family members see hospice care as "giving up" or receiving second-rate care.

It is important to consider potential barriers to hospice care in vulnerable populations. These may include veterans, homeless, immigrants, impoverished, disabled, or institutionalized persons. In these populations, besides the hospice team, you may need to collaborate with community partners to facilitate support services to meet the needs of the patient and family.[5]

Medicare, Medicaid, and many private insurance agencies cover hospice services. Admission to a hospice program has 2 criteria. The first criterion is that the patient must want the services and agree in writing to use only hospice care, not curative care, to treat the terminal illness. The second criterion is that the patient must be medically eligible for hospice. Medicare, Medicaid, and other insurers require that 2 physicians certify that the patient's prognosis is terminal, with less than 6 months to live. After this initial certification, only 1 physician (e.g., the hospice medical director) is needed to recertify the patient. It is important to realize that the physician who certified that a hospice patient is terminal does not "guarantee" death within

6 months. If a patient in hospice survives beyond 6 months, Medicare and other reimbursement organizations will continue to reimburse for an extended period if the patient still meets enrolment criteria.

Hospice patients can receive care for other health problems that are not related to the terminal illness. However, the hospice, Medicare, Medicaid, or patient's insurance company may not cover those services.[6] They can voluntarily withdraw from the program at any time. Occasionally, a patient's condition stabilizes, and the patient may be discharged from hospice care. This decision is made after review of the current treatment plan and input from members of the interprofessional hospice team.

DEATH

Death occurs when all vital organs and body systems cease to function. It is the irreversible cessation of cardiovascular, respiratory, and brain function.

Brain death is an irreversible loss of all brain functions, including those of the brainstem. Brain death is a clinical diagnosis. It occurs when the cerebral cortex stops functioning or is irreversibly destroyed.

With the growing use of technology that assists in supporting life, controversies have arisen over the exact definition of death. Questions and discussions have focused on whether brain death occurs when the whole brain (cortex and brainstem) ceases activity or when function of the cortex alone stops. The American Academy of Neurology developed the diagnostic criteria guidelines for clinical diagnosis of brain death. The criteria include coma or unresponsiveness, absence of brainstem reflexes, and apnea. Physicians must perform specific assessments to confirm each of the criteria.[7]

Currently, legal and medical standards require that all brain function must cease to be able to pronounce brain death and disconnect life support. Diagnosing brain death is of special importance when organ donation is an option. In some states and under specific circumstances, a registered nurse is legally allowed to pronounce death. Policies and procedures may vary from state to state and among health care institutions.

END-OF-LIFE CARE

End of life generally refers to the final phase of a patient's illness when death is imminent. The time from diagnosis of a terminal illness to death varies depending on the patient's diagnosis and extent of disease.

The National Academy of Medicine defines *end of life* as the period during which a person copes with declining health from a terminal illness or from the frailties associated with advanced age, even if death is not clearly imminent.[8] In some cases it is obvious to HCPs that the patient is at the EOL. In other cases, they may be uncertain if the EOL is near. This uncertainty adds to the challenge of answering the common question asked by the patient and family, "How much time is left?"

End-of-life care (EOL care) is the term used for issues and services related to death and dying. EOL care focuses on physical and psychosocial needs for the patient and family. The goals for EOL care are to (1) provide comfort and supportive care during the dying process, (2) improve the quality of the patient's remaining life, (3) help ensure a dignified death, and (4) provide emotional support to the family.

TABLE 9.2   Physical Manifestations at End of Life

System	Manifestations
Cardiovascular system	• Increased heart rate; later slowing and weakening of pulse • Irregular rhythm • Decreased BP • Delayed absorption of drugs given IM or subcutaneously
Gastrointestinal system	• Slowing or cessation of GI function (may be enhanced by pain-relieving drugs) • Gas accumulation • Distention and nausea • Loss of sphincter control, producing incontinence • Bowel movement before imminent death or at time of death
Integumentary system	• Mottling on hands, feet, arms, and legs • Cold, clammy skin • Cyanosis of nose, nail beds, knees • "Waxlike" skin when very near death
Musculoskeletal system	• Gradual loss of ability to move • Sagging of jaw resulting from loss of facial muscle tone • Difficulty speaking • Swallowing becoming more difficult • Difficulty maintaining body posture and alignment • Loss of gag reflex • Jerking seen in patients on high doses of opioids
Respiratory system	• Increased respiratory rate • Cheyne-Stokes respiration • Inability to cough or clear secretions resulting in grunting, gurgling, or noisy congested breathing (death rattle or terminal secretions) • Irregular breathing, gradually slowing down to terminal gasps (may be described as guppy breathing)
Sensory system Hearing Sight Taste and smell Touch	 • Usually last sense to disappear • Blurring of vision • Sinking and glazing of eyes • Blink reflex absent • Eyelids stay half-open • Decreased with disease progression • Decreased sensation • Decreased sense of pain and touch
Urinary system	• Gradual decrease in urine output • Incontinence of urine • Inability to urinate

Physical Manifestations at End of Life

As death approaches, metabolism reduces and the body gradually slows down until all functions end. Respiratory changes are common. Respirations may be rapid or slow, shallow, and irregular. Breath sounds may become wet and noisy, both audibly and on auscultation. Mouth breathing and accumulation of mucus in the airways cause noisy, wet-sounding respirations, termed the **death rattle** or terminal secretions. **Cheyne-Stokes respiration** is a pattern of breathing characterized by alternating periods of apnea and deep, rapid breathing. When respirations cease, the heart stops beating within a few minutes. The physical manifestations of approaching death are listed in Table 9.2.

Psychosocial Manifestations at End of Life

A variety of feelings and emotions can affect the dying patient and family at the EOL (Table 9.3). Most patients and families struggle with a terminal diagnosis and the realization that there is no cure. The patient and family may feel overwhelmed, fearful, powerless, and fatigued. The family's response depends in part on the type and length of the illness and their relationship with the person.

The patient's needs and wishes must be respected. Patients need time to think and express their feelings. Response time

TABLE 9.3   Psychosocial Manifestations at End of Life

- Altered decision making
- Anxiety about unfinished business
- Decreased socialization
- Fear of loneliness
- Fear of meaninglessness of one's life
- Fear of pain
- Helplessness
- Life review
- Peacefulness
- Restlessness
- Saying goodbyes
- Unusual communication
- Vision-like experiences
- Withdrawal

to questions may be sluggish because of fatigue, weakness, and confusion.

Bereavement and Grief

Although we often use the terms interchangeably, *bereavement* refers to the state of loss and *grief* refers to the reaction to loss.

TABLE 9.4   Kübler-Ross Model of Grief

Stage	What Person May Say	Characteristics
Denial	No, not me. It cannot be true.	Denies the loss has taken place and may withdraw. This response may last minutes to months
Anger	Why me?	May be angry at the person who inflicted the hurt (even after death) or at the world for letting it happen. May be angry with self for letting an event (e.g., car accident) take place, even if nothing could have stopped it
Bargaining	Yes me, but . . .	May make bargains with God, asking, "If I do this, will you take away the loss?"
Depression	Yes me, and I am sad.	Feels numb, although anger and sadness may remain underneath
Acceptance	Yes me, but it is okay.	Anger, sadness, and mourning have tapered off. Accepts the reality of the loss

Adapted from Kübler-Ross E: *On death and dying,* New York, 1969, Macmillan. (Classic)

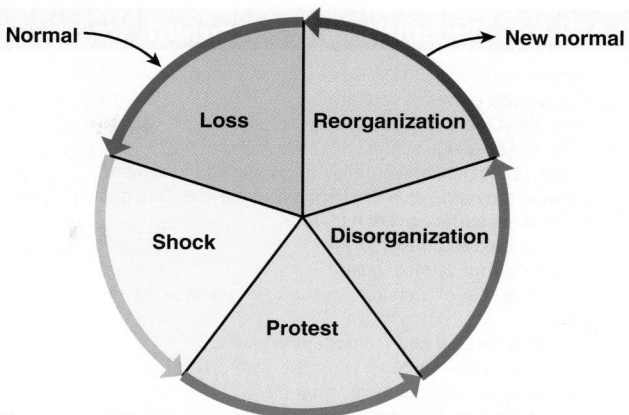

FIG. 9.6 The grief wheel model begins with the normal state at the bottom. After a person goes through the grief process, eventually the grief will resolve. However, because of the loss, the normal state is different from before. The challenge is to accept the "new normal."

Bereavement is the period after the death of a loved one during which we experience grief and mourning occurs. The time spent in bereavement depends on several factors, including how attached one was to the person who died and how much time one spent expecting the loss.

Grief is a normal reaction to loss. Grief occurs in response to the real loss of a loved one and the loss of what might have been. Grief is dynamic and includes both psychologic and physiologic responses after a loss. Psychologic responses include anger, guilt, anxiety, sadness, depression, and despair. Physiologic reactions include sleeping problems, changes in appetite, physical problems, and illness.

Grief is a powerful emotional state that affects all aspects of a person's life. It is a complex and intense emotional experience. In the Kübler-Ross model of grief, there are 5 stages[9] (Table 9.4). Not every person experiences all the stages of grieving, and they are not always progressive. It is common to reach a stage and then go backward. For example, a person may have reached the stage of bargaining and then revert to the denial or anger stage.

Another model of grief is the grief wheel (Fig. 9.6). After a person has a loss, he or she feels *shock* (numbness, denial, inability to think straight). Next is the *protest* stage, in which a person may have anger, guilt, sadness, fear, and searching. Then comes the *disorganization* stage, in which a person feels despair, apathy, anxiety, and confusion. The next stage is *reorganization,* in which a person gradually returns to normal functioning, but he or she feels different. The last stage is the *new normal.* Eventually the destabilization experienced in grief resolves and a normal state can begin. However, because of the loss, the normal state is different from before. The challenge is to accept the new normal. Trying to go back to the "old" normal (which is not there anymore) is what causes a great deal of anxiety and stress.

The way a person grieves depends on factors such as the relationship with the person who has died (e.g., spouse, parent), physical and emotional coping resources, concurrent life stresses, cultural beliefs, and personality. Other factors that affect the grief response include mental and physical health, economic resources, religious influences or spiritual beliefs, family relationships, social support, and time spent preparing for the death. Issues that occurred before the death (e.g., marital problems) may affect the grief response.[10]

The grief experience for the caregiver of the patient with a chronic illness often begins long before the actual death event. This is called *anticipatory grief.* Patients at the EOL also can have anticipatory grief.

Working in a positive way through the grief process helps to adapt to the loss. Grief that helps the person accept the reality of death is called *adaptive grief.* It is a healthy response. It may be associated with grieving before death occurs or when the inevitability of the death is known. Indicators of adaptive grief include the ability to see some good resulting from the death and positive memories of the deceased person.

Dysfunctional reactions to loss can occur, and the physical and psychologic impact of the loved one's death may persist for years. *Prolonged grief disorder,* formerly called *complicated grief,* is a term used to describe prolonged and intense mourning. Prolonged grief disorder can include symptoms such as recurrent and severe distressing emotions and intrusive thoughts related to the loss of a loved one, self-neglect, and denial of the loss for longer than 6 months. About 1 in 5 bereaved persons has prolonged grief disorder. Those with prolonged grief disorder have a higher risk for illness and may have work and social impairments.

Bereavement and grief counseling are core parts of patient- and family-centered palliative care. The goal of a bereavement program is to provide support and to help survivors in the transition to a life without the deceased person. Incorporate grief support into the plan of care for the family and significant others during the patient's illness and after the death.

TABLE 9.5	**Spiritual Assessment**

1. Who or what provides you strength and hope?
2. Do you use prayer in your life?
3. How do you express spirituality?
4. How would you describe your philosophy of life?
5. What type of spiritual or religious support do you wish?
6. What is the name of your clergy, minister, chaplain, pastor, rabbi?
7. What does suffering mean to you?
8. What does dying mean to you?
9. What are your spiritual goals?
10. Is there a role of a church, synagogue, mosque, or temple in your life?
11. Has belief in God been important in your life?
12. How does your faith help you cope with illness?
13. How do you keep going day after day?
14. What helps you get through this health care experience?
15. How has illness affected you and your family?

© The Joint Commission. Adapted with permission.

FIG. 9.7 Spiritual needs are an important consideration in end-of-life care. (© Photodisc/Thinkstock.)

Priority interventions for grief focus on providing an environment that allows the patient and family to express their feelings, such as anger, fear, and guilt. Discussing feelings helps the patient and family work toward resolution of the grief process. Respect for the patient's privacy and need or desire to talk (or not to talk) is important. Honesty in answering questions and giving information is essential.

Spiritual Needs

Assessment of spiritual needs in EOL care is a key consideration (Table 9.5). **Spirituality** is a broad concept that encompasses beliefs, values, and purpose that relate to the search for existential meaning and purpose.[11] Some define spirituality as a relationship with a supreme being that directs beliefs and practices. Spiritual needs do not necessarily equate to religion or belief in a higher power. A person may not be part of a particular religion but have a deep spirituality. Assess the patient's and family's preferences related to spiritual guidance or pastoral care services and make appropriate referrals.

Deep-seated spiritual beliefs may surface for some patients when they deal with their terminal diagnosis and related issues. Patients may question their beliefs about a higher power, their journey through life, religion, and an afterlife (Fig. 9.7). Spiritual distress may occur.[11] Characteristics of spiritual distress include anger toward God or a higher being, change in behavior and mood, desire for spiritual assistance, or displaced anger toward clergy.

Spirituality has been associated with decreased despair in patients at EOL. Some dying patients are secure in their faith about the future. It is common to see patients relinquish material possessions of life and focus on values that they believe will lead them on to another place. Many turn to religion because it gives order to the world even in the presence of physical decline, social losses, suffering, and impending death. Religion may offer an existential meaning that offers a sense of peace and recognition of one's place in the broader cosmic context.[11]

 Culturally Competent Care: End of Life

Culture and ethnicity are important considerations for patients who are receiving palliative and EOL care and their families. Cultural beliefs affect a person's understanding of and reaction to death or loss. In some cultural/ethnic groups, death and dying are private matters shared only with significant others. Often feelings are repressed or internalized. People who believe in "toughing it out" or "being strong" may not express themselves when they are experiencing a loss. Some cultural groups, such as blacks and Hispanic/Latinos, may easily express their feelings and emotions. Kinship tends to be strong in the Hispanic culture, and immediate and extended family provide support for one another. Expressing feelings of loss is encouraged and accepted easily.

Culture and ethnicity affect decision making about life support, withholding and withdrawing treatments, and using palliative or hospice care.[12] In some cultures, such as the Filipino American culture, it may be appropriate to first discuss a terminal diagnosis with the family before informing the patient. For Hispanics, often spouses and daughters are involved in decisions about palliative care and hospice. Blacks and Asian Americans use hospice care less often, with blacks being more likely to prefer aggressive treatment.

Rituals associated with dying are part of all cultures. In certain cultures, the family may want to keep constant vigil in the room of a dying patient or in the waiting area. For example, some Jewish Americans believe that the spirit should not be alone when it leaves the body at the time of death. Therefore someone who is terminally ill should never be alone. The Jewish culture believes all body tissues must be buried with the person. Once a death has occurred, some cultures, such as the Puerto Rican American culture, may want to kiss and touch the body to say goodbye. In the Islamic cultures, the traditional rites of washing, shrouding, funeral prayers, and burial are done as soon as possible.

Cultural variations exist in symptom expression (e.g., pain expression) and use of health care services. Providing culturally competent care requires assessment of nonverbal cues, such as grimaces, body position, and decreased or guarded movements. See Chapter 8 for issues related to pain assessment and management.

Many differences exist among cultural beliefs and values in relation to death and dying. Assess beliefs and preferences on an individual basis to avoid stereotyping patients with different cultural belief systems. Assess and document the patient's cultural background, concerns, health practices, and attitudes about suffering. Ask the patient and family to describe their desires for care before death and care of the body after death. Use this assessment to guide the patient's plan of care and evaluation. You can suggest or plan grief and bereavement counseling for the family.

Make accommodations related to the patient's language, diet, and cultural beliefs and practices. Families with non–English-speaking members are at risk for receiving less information about their family member's critical illness and prognosis.[13] When appropriate, access medical interpreter services so that the patient's wishes are known. Culturally competent care is discussed in Chapter 2.

LEGAL AND ETHICAL ISSUES AFFECTING END-OF-LIFE CARE

Patients and families struggle with many decisions during the terminal illness and dying experience. Many people decide that the outcomes related to their care should be based on their own wishes and values. It is important to provide information to help patients with these decisions. The decisions may involve the choice for (1) organ and tissue donations, (2) advance directives (e.g., medical power of attorney, living wills), (3) resuscitation, (4) mechanical ventilation, and (5) feeding tube placement.

Decisional capacity refers to the ability to consent to or refuse care. It means that the person has an understanding and appreciation of the information received and has the capacity to engage in the reasoning process.

Organ and Tissue Donation

Persons who are legally competent may choose organ donation. You can donate any body part or the entire body. The decision to donate organs or to provide anatomic gifts may be made by a person before death or by immediate family after death. Family permission must be obtained at the time of donation.[14]

Some people carry donor cards. Some states mark organ donation wishes on drivers' licenses. The names of agencies that handle organ donation vary by state and community. Common names for such an agency may be the organ bank, organ-sharing network, and organ-sharing alliance. Organ and tissue donations follow specific legal guidelines. Follow those requirements and facility policies for organ or tissue donation. Notify the proper personnel at once when organ donation is intended, because some tissues must be used within hours after death.

Advance Care Planning and Advance Directives

Advance care planning is a process that involves having patients (1) think through their values and goals for treatment, (2) talk about their values and goals with others, and (3) document them. Advance directives are the written documents that provide information about the patient's wishes and his or her designated spokesperson (Table 9.6).

The first advance directive was known by laypersons as a *living will*. Most states have replaced the idea of living wills with *natural death acts,* which may include *directive to physicians* (DTPs), *durable power of attorney for health care* (DPAHC), *medical power of attorney* (MPOA), and *power of attorney for health care* (POAH). Under the natural death acts, a person can tell the HCP exactly what treatment is or is not desired. Each state has its own unique requirements. Patients often change their minds about desired treatments as their disease state progresses. It is important to reassess a patient's advance directives. For cognitively impaired older adults, consider the person's values and manner of life to make health care decisions consistent with decisions they made when they were cognitively intact.

People can get copies of state-specific forms from local medical associations and on the Internet. However, a person may

write his or her wishes without special forms. Verbal directives can be given to the attending physician in the presence of 2 witnesses. The physician may use a Physician Order for Life-Sustaining Treatment (POLST) or Medical Order for Life-Sustaining Treatment (MOLST) to outline current treatment options that honor the person's desire for treatment (Table 9.6).

The person should keep a copy of the order to use in case of an emergency in which the primary physician is not available for consultation. Attorneys and notaries may not be needed to develop these directives. If the person is not capable of communicating his or her wishes, the surrogate decision maker (most often family or significant other) decides the measures that will or will not be taken. In this case, the physician and nurse can discuss the available options with the family. Then it is important to document the family's decision. This is important because often nurses and other medical professionals do not know who can legally make EOL decisions for patients when they no longer have decisional capacity.

Resuscitation

Cardiopulmonary resuscitation (CPR) is common practice in health care. Patients who have respiratory or cardiac arrest receive CPR unless the physician gives a *do-not-resuscitate (DNR) order*. A DNR order is a written medical order that documents a patient's wishes about resuscitation and, more important, the patient's desire to avoid CPR.[15]

There are several types of CPR decisions. Complete and total heroic measures, which may include CPR, drugs, and mechanical ventilation, can be referred to as a *full code*. Some people choose variations of the full code. A *chemical code* involves the use of drugs for resuscitation without the use of CPR. A "no code," or a DNR order, allows the person to die with comfort measures only and without the interference of technology. Some states have implemented a form called *out-of-hospital DNR* for use by terminally ill patients who wish to have no heroic measures used to prolong life after they leave an acute care facility.

Allow natural death (AND) is a term being used to replace "no code" or DNR. This term more accurately conveys our actions. It is sometimes referred to as *"comfort measures only"* status. The patient receives all comfort measures associated with pain control and symptom management, but the natural physiologic progression to death is not delayed or interrupted. The use of this type of language means that we do not withhold care, but care is supportive while allowing nature to take its course. It is meant to promote comfort and dignity at the EOL.

An advance directive includes whether to withhold or withdraw certain treatments. The directive must clearly state what is to be done and what is not to be done. The American Nurses Association (ANA) states that the decision to withhold artificial nutrition and hydration should be made by the patient or surrogate together with the interprofessional team. It is important we continue to provide expert nursing care for patients who are no longer receiving artificial nutrition and hydration.

You need to be aware of legal issues and have a primary role in supporting the patient's wishes. Advance directives and organ donor information should be in the medical record and identified on the patient's record and/or the nursing care plan. All caregivers responsible for the patient need to know the patient's wishes. Additionally, you need to be familiar with state, local, and agency procedures in EOL care documentation.

TABLE 9.6   Common Documents Used in End-of-Life Care

Document	Description	Special Considerations
Advance directive	General term used to describe documents that give instructions about future medical care and treatments and who should make the decisions in the event the person is unable to communicate	• Should adhere to guidelines established by state of residence
Allow natural death (AND)	Written order acknowledging that comfort measures only are being provided to patient. Used in many palliative care and hospice settings to indicate that patient wants to die naturally with dignity and comfort	• In many settings, may be used in conjunction with DNR terminology to ensure patient/family wishes for advance directives are followed (DNR/AND)
Directive to physicians (DTP)	Written document specifying the patient's wish to be allowed to die without heroic or extraordinary measures	• Indicates specific measures to be used or withheld
Do not resuscitate (DNR)	Written physician's order instructing HCPs not to attempt CPR. DNR order often requested by family	• Must indicate any specific measures to be used or withheld • Must be signed by a physician to be valid
Living will	Lay term used to describe any documents that give instructions about future medical care and treatments or the wish to be allowed to die without heroic or extraordinary measures should the patient be unable to communicate for self	• Must identify specific treatments that a person wants or does not want at end of life
Medical power of attorney (MPOA)	Term used by some states to describe a document used for listing the person(s) to make health care decisions should a patient become unable to make informed decisions for self	• May be the same as durable power of attorney for health care, health care proxy, or appointment of a health care agent or surrogate • Specifies measures to be used or withheld • Person appointed may be called a health care agent, surrogate, attorney-in-fact, or proxy
Physician Order for Life-Sustaining Treatment (POLST) or Medical Order for Life-Sustaining Treatment (MOLST)	A standardized physician order guided by the patient's medical condition and based upon personal preferences stated by patient or expressed in advance directive	• Only for those whose illness may limit life to <12 mo • Guides current treatments. Differs from advance directive, which guides future treatments • Physician completes form based on discussion with patient or authorized representative, or in review of advance directive • Signed by physician, patient, or patient representative • Printed on bright pink paper
Power of attorney for health care (POAH)	Term used by some states to describe a document used for listing the person(s) to make health care decisions should a patient become unable to make informed decisions for self	• May be the same as medical power of attorney • Indicates specific measures to be used or withheld

Euthanasia is the deliberate act of hastening death. The ANA statement on active euthanasia states that the nurse should not take part in active euthanasia, because such an act is in direct violation of the Code for Nurses, ethical traditions and goals of the profession, and its covenant with society.

Physician-assisted suicide is legal in some states. In this case, the physician provides the means and/or information about how the patient can commit suicide. As a nurse, you have an obligation to provide prompt, humane, comprehensive, and compassionate EOL care. Some confuse euthanasia with *palliative sedation,* which is the use of medications to intentionally produce sedation to relieve intractable symptoms and distress in a patient who is imminently dying. The intent of palliative sedation is to relieve pain and suffering and not to shorten life or to hasten death, as is the case with euthanasia.

The use of opioids for symptom management at the EOL is often misunderstood and feared by patients, families, and HCPs. For this reason, many patients refuse to take opioids, which leads to physical and emotional suffering due to uncontrolled pain and symptoms. Your ethical obligation is to relieve suffering. This includes giving medications that have the potential of producing harm, such as with opioids. The *principle of double effect* refers to a principle that regards it morally permissible to give a medication that has the potential for harm if it is given with the intent of relieving pain and suffering and not intended to hasten death.

As a nurse, your role is to teach the patient and family about addiction and tolerance to and dependence on medications. The person with terminal illness should not be concerned with addiction when the goal of treatment is comfort. Pain management is discussed in Chapter 8.

ETHICAL/LEGAL DILEMMAS
End-of-Life Care

Situation

A.P. is a terminally ill 50-yr-old woman with metastatic breast cancer who is hospitalized with severe bone pain. She moans at rest and shows severe pain with any movement to reposition her. The present dose of IV morphine is not controlling her pain. At the team conference, the nurses discuss the need for more effective pain control but are concerned that more pain medicine could hasten her death.

Ethical/Legal Points for Consideration

- Adequate pain relief is an important outcome for all patients, especially patients who are terminally ill.
- The *Code of Ethics for Nurses* addresses the responsibility of the nurse to relieve suffering and have conversations with patients and families about pain and symptom management.[1]
- The *principle of beneficence* means that we provide care to benefit patients. The goal of adequate pain control in the terminally ill to ease suffering is based on the *principle of nonmaleficence* (preventing or reducing harm to the patient). The secondary effect of hastening the patient's death is ethically justified and known as the *double effect*.
- Legally, the *standard of care* is used to define the nursing acts that are required for safe and competent nursing practice. When the actual nursing care falls below the standard of care, it is considered negligent and unsafe, and the nurse is at risk for being found incompetent.
- In a court of law, the standard of care in nursing is determined by nursing experts and evidence-based practices. The increasing use of technology to access the latest scientific findings is changing the standard of nursing care to a national, if not global, standard defined by research findings and nationally recognized expert testimony. Standards for providing expert nursing care and counseling at EOL are available.[1]
- In A.P.'s situation the standard of care is that the patient will have pain relief. Failure of the nurse to act assertively to achieve pain relief for the patient and failure to effectively use resources to obtain that pain relief will be considered below the standard of care and unsafe and incompetent practice.

Discussion Questions

1. What types of discussions need to occur among the health care team, patient, and family as the terminally ill patient approaches this phase of care?
2. Distinguish between promotion of comfort and relief of pain in dying patients and between assisted suicide and euthanasia.

Reference

1. ANA: Code of ethics for nursing. Retrieved from *www.nursingworld. org/DocumentVault/Ethics-1/Code-of-Ethics-for-Nurses.html.*

❖ NURSING MANAGEMENT: END OF LIFE

Nurses spend more time with patients near the EOL than any other health care professionals. Nursing care of terminally ill and dying patients is holistic and encompasses all psychosocial and physical needs. Respect, dignity, and comfort are important for the patient and family. Although there is no cure for the person's disease, the treatment plan still consists of assessment, planning, implementation, and evaluation. The main difference is that the focus of care is on the management of the symptoms of the disease, not necessarily the disease itself. Nurses who care for the dying need to recognize their own needs when dealing with grief and dying.

◆ Nursing Assessment

Assessment of the terminally ill or dying patient varies with the patient's condition. Be sensitive and do not impose repeated, unnecessary assessments on the dying patient. When possible, use health history data that are available in the medical record rather than tiring the patient with an interview.

Document the specific event or change that brought the patient into the health care setting. Record the patient's medical diagnoses, medication profile, and allergies.

If the patient is alert, do a brief review of the body systems. Assess for discomfort, pain, nausea, and dyspnea so that you can implement interventions using evidence-based tools for symptom assessment. These include numeric scales or visual analog scales for pain rating. Evaluate and manage co-morbidities or acute episodes of problems, such as diabetes mellitus or headache. Elicit information about the patient's abilities, food and fluid intake, patterns of sleep and rest, and response to the stress of terminal illness. Assess the patient's ability to cope with the diagnosis and prognosis of the illness. Determine the family's ability to manage the needed care and to cope with the illness and its consequences.

The physical assessment is abbreviated and focuses on changes that accompany terminal illness and the specific disease process. Pay attention to patients who are nonverbal for subtle changes in their condition.[16] The frequency of assessment depends on the patient's stability. Assessment is done at least every 8 hours in the institutional setting. For patients cared for in their homes by hospice programs, assessment may occur weekly. As changes occur, you may have to complete assessment and documentation more often. If the patient is in the final hours of life, we may limit the physical assessment to essential data.

Key elements of a social assessment include determining the relationships and patterns of communication among the family. If multiple family members are present, listen to concerns from different members. Differences in expectations and interpersonal conflict can produce disruptions during the dying process and after the death of the loved one. Social assessment also includes evaluating the goals of the patient and family.

As death approaches, monitor the patient for multiple systems that often are failing during the EOL period. This requires vigilance and attention to often subtle physical changes. Neurologic assessment is especially important and includes level of consciousness, presence of reflexes, and pupil responses. Evaluation of vital signs, skin color, and temperature shows changes in circulation. Monitor and describe respiratory status, character and pattern of respirations, and characteristics of breath sounds. Assess nutritional and fluid intake, urine output, and bowel function, since this gives data about renal and gastrointestinal functioning. Assess skin condition on an ongoing basis, because skin becomes fragile and may easily break down.

In the last hours of life, limit assessments to only those that you need to determine patient comfort. Assessment of pain and respiratory status may be the most important during this time. It may be more peaceful and comforting to the patient and family to refrain from overstimulation that may occur from certain types of assessments, such as measuring BP or checking for pupillary response. As death approaches, your efforts may be better spent providing emotional support to the patient and family rather than performing tasks that will have no impact on the patient's physical care.

◆ Planning

The patient and family need to be involved in planning and coordinating EOL care. In some cases, a family conference may be helpful to develop a coordinated plan of care.

Develop a comprehensive plan to support, teach, and evaluate patients and families. Nursing care goals during the last stages of life involve comfort and safety measures and care of the patient's emotional and physical needs. These goals may include determining where the patient would like to die and whether this is possible. For example, the patient may want to die at home, but the family may object. Many factors contribute to the patient and family's decision. Interprofessional EOL care that includes the physician, social worker, chaplain, and other members of the palliative and/or hospice care team is important. Advocate for the patient so that their wishes are met as much as possible.

The last hours or days of the patient experiencing brain death (e.g., from trauma) are often spent in the ICU. Planning for EOL care may be particularly challenging in the ICU environment. At this time, some families are approached about organ donation. Consultation from palliative care specialists may help the family plan and cope with EOL issues.

◆ Nursing Implementation

Psychosocial care and physical care are interrelated for both the dying patient and family. Teaching them is an important part of EOL care. Families need ongoing information on the disease, the dying process, and any care you will be providing. They need information on how to cope with the many issues during this period of their lives. Denial and grieving may be barriers to learning and understanding at the EOL for both the patient and family.

◆ **Psychosocial Care.** As death approaches, respond appropriately to the patient's psychosocial manifestations at the EOL (Table 9.7).

Anxiety and Depression. Patients often show signs of anxiety and depression during the EOL period. Causes of anxiety and depression may include uncontrolled pain and dyspnea, psychosocial factors related to the disease process or impending death, altered physiologic states, and drugs used in high dosages. Anxiety is often related to fear. Encouragement, support, and teaching decrease some of the anxiety and depression. Management of anxiety and depression may include both medications and nonpharmacologic interventions. Relaxation strategies, such as relaxation breathing, muscle relaxation, music, and imagery, may be useful (see Chapter 6).

Anger. Anger is a common and normal response to grief. A grieving person cannot be forced to accept the loss. The surviving family members may be angry with the dying loved one who is leaving them. Encourage the expression of feelings, but at the same time realize how hard it is to come to terms with loss. As a nurse, you may be the target of the anger. You need to understand what is happening and not react on a personal level.

Hopelessness and Powerlessness. Feelings of hopelessness and powerlessness are common during the EOL period. Encourage realistic hope within the limits of the situation. Allow the patient and family to deal with what is within their control and help them recognize what is beyond their control. When possible, support the patient's involvement in decision making about care to foster a sense of control and autonomy.

TABLE 9.7 Nursing Management

Psychosocial Care at End of Life

Manifestations	Nursing Management
Saying Goodbyes	
It is important for the patient and family to acknowledge their sadness, mutually forgive one another, and say goodbye.	Encourage the dying person and family to share their feelings of sadness, loss, forgiveness and to touch, hug, cry. Allow the patient and family privacy to express their feelings and comfort one another.
Spiritual Needs	
Patient or family may request spiritual support, such as the presence of a chaplain.	Assess spiritual needs. Allow patient to express his or her spiritual needs. Encourage visit by appropriate spiritual care service provider, chaplain, or family member.
Unusual Communication	
This may indicate that an unresolved issue is preventing the dying person from letting go. Patient may become restless and agitated or perform repetitive tasks (may also indicate terminal delirium).	Encourage the family to talk with and reassure the dying person.
Vision-Like Experiences	
Patient may talk to persons who are not there or see places and objects not visible. Vision-like experiences help the dying person in coming to terms with meaning in life and transition from it.	Affirm the dying person's experience as a part of transition from this life.
Withdrawal	
Patient near death may seem withdrawn from the physical environment, maintaining the ability to hear but unable to respond	Converse as though the patient were alert, using a soft voice and gentle touch.

Fear. Fear is a typical feeling associated with dying. Specific fears associated with dying are fear of pain, fear of shortness of breath, fear of loneliness and abandonment, and fear of meaninglessness.

Fear of pain. Many people assume that pain always accompanies death. Physiologically, there is no absolute indication that death is always painful. Psychologically, pain may occur based on the anxieties and separations related to dying. Patients can take part in their own pain relief by discussing pain relief measures and their effects. Most patients want their pain relieved without the side effects of grogginess or sleepiness. Pain relief measures do not have to deprive the patient of the ability to interact with others.

Patients with physical pain should have pain-relieving drugs available. Assure the patient and family that drugs will be given promptly when needed and that side effects of drugs can and will be managed. As many EOL patients are unable to swallow, other routes, such as patches, sublingual, and rectal routes, may be used.[17] Consider alternative methods like massage, music, aromatherapy, and mindfulness.

Fear of shortness of breath. Respiratory distress and dyspnea are common near the EOL. The sensation of air hunger results in anxiety for the patient and family. Current therapies

FIG. 9.8 Dying patients typically want someone whom they know and trust to stay with them. (© iStockphoto/Thinkstock.)

include opioids, bronchodilators, and oxygen, depending on the cause of the dyspnea. Anxiety-reducing agents (e.g., anxiolytics) may help produce relaxation.

Fear of loneliness and abandonment. Most terminally ill and dying people fear loneliness and do not want to be alone. Many dying patients are afraid that loved ones who are unable to cope with the patient's imminent death will abandon them. Simply being present offers support and comfort (Fig. 9.8). Holding hands, touching, and listening are important nursing interventions. Providing companionship allows the dying person a sense of security.

Fear of meaninglessness. Fear of meaninglessness leads people to review their lives. They review their intentions during life, examining actions and expressing regrets about what might have been. *Life review* helps patients recognize the value of their lives. Assist patients and their families to identify the positive qualities of the patient's life. Practical ways of helping may include looking at photo albums or collections of important mementos. Sharing thoughts and feelings may enhance spirituality and provide comfort. Respect and accept the practices and rituals associated with the patient's life review while staying nonjudgmental.

Communication. Communication among the interprofessional team, patient, and family is essential at the EOL. Empathy and active listening are essential parts of communication in care. *Empathy* is the identification with and understanding of another's situation, feelings, or motives. *Active listening* is paying attention to what is said, observing the patient's nonverbal cues, and not interrupting.

There may be silence. Often silence is related to the overwhelming feelings experienced at the EOL. Silence can also allow time to gather thoughts. Listening to the silence sends a message of acceptance and comfort. Communication must be respectful of the patient's ethnic, cultural, and religious backgrounds.

Patients and family members may have difficulties expressing themselves emotionally. Allow time for them to express their feelings and thoughts. Make time to listen and interact in a sensitive way to enhance the relationship among you, the patient, and the family. A family conference is 1 way to create a good environment for communication.

Prepare family members for changes in emotional and cognitive function that occur as death nears. Unusual communication by the patient may take place. The patient's speech may become confused, disoriented, or garbled. Patients may speak to or about family members or others who have predeceased them

or give instructions to those who will survive them. Active, careful listening allows for the identification of specific patterns in the dying person's communication and decreases the risk for inappropriate labeling of behaviors.

◆ **Physical Care.** Nursing management related to physical care at the EOL focuses on symptom management and comfort rather than treatment for curing a disease or disorder (Table 9.8). The priority is meeting the patient's physiologic and safety needs. Physical care focuses on the needs for oxygen, nutrition, pain relief, mobility, elimination, and skin care. People who are dying deserve and require the same physical care as people who are expected to recover. If possible, it is important to discuss with the patient and family the goals of care before treatment begins. An advance directive should be completed so that the patient and family wishes are followed.

Postmortem Care. After the patient is pronounced dead, prepare or delegate preparing the patient's body for immediate viewing by the family with consideration for cultural customs and in accord with state law and agency policies and procedures (Table 9.9). In some cultures and in some types of death, it may be important to allow the family to prepare or help in caring for the patient's body. When the death is unexpected, preparing the patient's body for viewing or release to a funeral home depends on state law and agency policies and procedures.

Care of and discussion related to the person should continue to be respectful even after death. Allow the family privacy and as much time as they need with the deceased person. Never refer to the deceased person as "the body."

SPECIAL NEEDS OF CAREGIVERS AND NURSES IN END-OF-LIFE CARE

Special Needs of Family Caregivers

Family caregivers are important in meeting the patient's physical and psychosocial needs. Their role includes working and communicating with the patient and other family members, supporting the patient's concerns, and helping the patient resolve any unfinished business. Families often face emotional, physical, and economic consequences from caring for a family member who is dying. The caregiver's responsibilities do not end when the patient is admitted to an acute care, inpatient hospice, or long-term care facility.[18]

An understanding of the grieving process as it affects both the patient and family is important. Being present during a family member's dying process can be highly stressful. Recognize signs and behaviors among family members who may be at risk for abnormal grief reactions and be prepared to intervene if needed. Warning signs may include dependency and negative feelings about the dying person, inability to express feelings, sleep disturbances, a history of depression, difficult reactions to previous losses, perceived lack of social or family support, low self-esteem, multiple previous bereavements, alcoholism, or substance abuse. Caregivers with concurrent life crises (e.g., divorce) are especially at risk.

Family caregivers and other family members need encouragement to continue their usual activities as much as possible. They need to discuss their activities and maintain some control over their lives. Inform caregivers about resources for support, including respite care. Community counseling and local support may help some people in working through their grief.

Encourage caregivers to build a support system of extended family, friends, faith community, and clergy. The caregivers

TABLE 9.8   Nursing Management

Physical Care at End of Life

Manifestation	Nursing Management
Anorexia, Nausea, and Vomiting • May be caused by complications of disease process • Drugs contribute to nausea • Constipation, impaction, and bowel obstruction can cause anorexia, nausea, and vomiting	• Assess the patient for nausea or vomiting • Assess possible contributing causes of nausea or vomiting • Provide antiemetics before meals if ordered • Offer and provide frequent meals with small portions of favorite foods • Offer culturally appropriate foods • Provide frequent mouth care, especially after vomiting • Ensure uninterrupted mealtimes • If ordered, give drugs (e.g., megestrol, corticosteroids) to increase appetite • Teach family that appetite naturally decreases at end of life and hunger is rare • Do not force the patient to eat
Bowel Patterns • Immobility, opioid medication use, depression, lack of fiber in the diet, and dehydration can cause constipation • Diarrhea may occur as muscles relax or from a fecal impaction related to the use of opioids and immobility	• Assess bowel function • Assess for and remove fecal impactions • Encourage movement and physical activities as tolerated • Encourage fiber in the diet if appropriate • Encourage fluids if appropriate • Use suppositories, stool softeners, laxatives, or enemas if ordered • Assess for confusion, agitation, restlessness, and pain, which may be signs of constipation
Candidiasis • White, cottage cheese–like oral plaques • Fungal overgrowth in the mouth due to chemotherapy and/or immunosuppression	• If ordered, give oral antifungal nystatin • Clean dentures and other dental appliances to prevent reinfection • Provide oral hygiene and use soft toothbrush
Dehydration • May occur during the last days of life • Hunger and thirst are rare in the last days of life • As the end of life approaches, patients tend to take in less food and fluid	• Assess mucous membranes often for dryness, which can lead to discomfort • Maintain complete, regular oral care to provide for comfort and hydration of mucous membranes • Encourage consumption of ice chips and sips of fluids or use moist cloths to provide moisture to the mouth • Use moist cloths and swabs for unconscious patients to avoid aspiration • Apply lubricant to the lips and oral mucous membranes as needed • Do not force the patient to drink • Teach family that thirst is rare in the last days of life • Reassure family that cessation of food and fluid intake is a natural part of the process of dying
Delirium • A state characterized by confusion, disorientation, restlessness, clouding of consciousness, incoherence, fear, anxiety, excitement, and often hallucinations • May be misidentified as depression, psychosis, anger, or anxiety • May be caused by using opioids or corticosteroids • Underlying disease process may contribute to delirium • Considered a reversible process	• Perform a thorough assessment for reversible causes of delirium, including pain, constipation, and urinary retention • Provide a room that is quiet, well lit, and familiar to reduce the effects of delirium • Reorient the dying person to person, place, and time with each encounter • Give ordered benzodiazepines and sedatives as needed • Stay physically close to frightened patient Reassure in a calm, soft voice with touch and slow strokes of the skin • Provide family with emotional support and encouragement in their efforts to cope with the behaviors associated with delirium
Dysphagia • May occur because of extreme weakness and changes in level of consciousness • Difficulty swallowing • Aspiration of liquids and/or solids • Drooling/inability to swallow secretions	• Identify the least invasive alternative routes of administering drugs needed for symptom management • Suction orally as needed • Modify diet as tolerated/desired • Hand feed small meals • Elevate the head for meals and at least 30 minutes after • If necessary, use alternative (rectal, buccal, transdermal) medication routes • Discontinue nonessential medications • Discuss risk for aspiration
Dyspnea • Subjective symptom • Accompanied by fear of suffocation and anxiety • Underlying disease process can worsen dyspnea • Coughing and expectorating secretions become difficult	• Assess respiratory status regularly • Elevate the head and/or position patient on side to improve chest expansion • Use a fan or air conditioner to help movement of cool air • Teach and encourage the use of pursed-lip breathing • Give supplemental oxygen as ordered • Suction PRN to remove accumulation of mucus from the airways. Suction cautiously in the terminal phase • Give an expectorant as ordered

TABLE 9.8   Nursing Management—cont'd

Physical Care at End of Life

Manifestation	Nursing Management
Myoclonus	
• Mild to severe jerking or twitching sometimes associated with use of high dose of opioids • Patient may have involuntary twitching of extremities	• Assess for initial onset, duration, and any discomfort or distress • If myoclonus is distressing or becoming more severe, discuss possible drug therapy modifications with the HCP • Changes in opioid medication may decrease myoclonus
Pain	
• May be a major symptom associated with terminal illness and the 1 most feared • Can be acute or chronic • Bone pain can be caused by metastases, fractures, arthritis, immobility • Physical and emotional stressors can worsen pain	• Assess pain thoroughly and regularly to determine the quality, intensity, location, and contributing and alleviating factors • Minimize irritants, such as skin irritations from wetness, heat or cold, pressure • Give medications around the clock, in a timely manner, and on a regular basis to provide constant relief rather than waiting until the pain is unbearable and then trying to relieve it • Provide complementary and alternative therapies, such as guided imagery, massage, and relaxation techniques as needed (see Chapter 6) • Evaluate effectiveness of pain relief measures frequently to ensure that the patient is on a correct, adequate drug regimen • Do not delay or deny pain relief measures to a terminally ill patient
Restlessness	
• May occur as death approaches and cerebral metabolism slows • May occur with tachypnea, dyspnea, sweating	• Assess for previous anxiety disorder • Assess for spiritual distress and/or concerns related to death as causes of restlessness and agitation • Assess for urinary retention and stool impaction • Do not restrain • Use soothing music and slow, soft touch and voice • Limit the number of persons at the bedside
Skin Breakdown	
• Skin integrity is hard to maintain at the end of life • Immobility, urinary and bowel incontinence, dry skin, nutritional deficits, anemia, friction, and shearing forces lead to a high risk for skin breakdown • Disease and other processes may impair skin integrity • As death approaches, circulation to the extremities decreases and they become cool, mottled, and cyanotic	• Assess skin for signs of breakdown • Implement protocols to prevent skin breakdown by controlling drainage and odor and keeping the skin and any wound areas clean • Perform wound assessments as needed • Follow appropriate nursing management protocol for dressing wounds • Follow appropriate nursing management protocol for a patient who is immobile, but consider realistic outcomes of skin integrity vs. maintenance of comfort • Follow appropriate nursing management to prevent skin irritations and breakdown from urinary and bowel incontinence • Use blankets to cover for warmth. Never apply heat
Urinary Incontinence	
• May result from disease progression or changes in the level of consciousness • As death becomes imminent, the perineal muscles relax	• Assess urinary function • Use absorbent pads for urinary incontinence • Follow appropriate nursing protocol for the consideration and use of indwelling or external catheters • Follow appropriate nursing management to prevent skin irritations and breakdown from urinary incontinence
Weakness and Fatigue	
• Expected at the end of life • Metabolic demands related to disease process contribute to weakness and fatigue	• Assess the patient's tolerance for activities • Time nursing interventions to conserve energy • Help the patient identify and complete valued or desired activities • Provide support as needed to maintain positions in bed or chair • Give frequent rest periods

 TABLE 9.9   Nursing Management

Postmortem Care

- Close the patient's eyes and jaw.
- Replace dentures; remove jewelry and eyeglasses.
- Wash the body as needed then apply a clean gown and bed linen.
- Place a waterproof pad or incontinence brief to absorb urine and feces.
- Comb and arrange the hair neatly.
- Remove tubes and dressings (if appropriate).
- Straighten the body, placing the arms at their sides or across the abdomen with palms down.
- Place a pillow under the head.

should have people to call on at any time to express any feelings they are experiencing.

Special Needs of Nurses

Many nurses who care for dying patients do so because they are passionate about providing high-quality EOL care. Caring for patients and their families at the EOL is challenging and rewarding but also intense and emotionally charged. A bond or connection may develop between you and the patient or family. Be aware of how grief personally affects you. When you provide care for terminally ill or dying patients, you are not immune to feelings of loss. It is common to feel helpless and powerless when dealing with death. Express feelings of sorrow, guilt, and frustration. It is important to recognize your own values, attitudes, and feelings about death. Common ethical concerns include lack of adequate communication, lack of effective decision making, when to stop life-prolonging interventions, and concerns with symptom treatment, especially with use of opioids.

Interventions are available that may help ease your physical and emotional stress. Be aware of what you can and cannot control. Recognizing personal feelings allows openness in exchanging feelings with the patient and family. Realizing that it is okay to cry with the patient or family during the EOL may be important for your well-being.

To meet your personal needs, focus on interventions that will help decrease your stress. Get involved in hobbies or other interests, schedule time for yourself, ensure time for sleep, maintain a peer support system, and develop a support system beyond the workplace. Many hospice agencies offer support groups and discussion sessions that can help you cope.

CASE STUDY

Spiritual Distress at End of Life

(© Mocker_bat/iStock/Thinkstock.)

Patient Profile

G.M. is a 42-yr-old Orthodox Jewish man. He is being seen by the hospice nurse for increasing abdominal pain, nausea, vomiting, lack of appetite, and constipation. He was diagnosed 6 months ago with pancreatic cancer that has metastasized to the liver and lungs. He quit work 1 month later. Two weeks ago, he ended the drug trial he was on for 5 months and enrolled in hospice. Currently, he is taking oral opioids for pain, ondansetron for nausea and vomiting, sertraline for depression, and megestrol for appetite. His wife is worried that he will become addicted to the pain medication.

Subjective Data

- States that he is angry at God for giving him this illness
- Reports fatigue and lack of appetite
- Reports pain at 7 (0–10 point scale) not relieved by medication
- States he is worried about the loss of his health benefits and what will happen to his young family, including a son age 3, when he is gone

Objective Data

Physical Examination

- Underweight (20% less than ideal body weight for height)
- Skin is jaundiced
- Yellow sclera

Interprofessional Care

- Review pain medications for dosage adjustment.
- Hospice social worker to review medical benefits and disability application
- Ensure that advance directives are in place.

Discussion Questions

1. What are G.M.'s risk factors for spiritual distress?
2. Based on the data given, what are the major health problems for G.M.?
3. ***Patient-Centered Care:*** What specific palliative care needs does G.M. have?
4. ***Priority Decision:*** Based on your assessment of G.M., what are the priority nursing interventions for him?
5. ***Collaboration:*** For the interventions that you identified in the previous question, which personnel could be responsible for implementing them: RN, LPN/VN, unlicensed assistive personnel (UAP)?
6. ***Collaboration:*** What referrals may be indicated?

Answers available at *http://evolve.elsevier.com/Lewis/medsurg.*

▮ BRIDGE TO NCLEX EXAMINATION

The number of the question corresponds to the same-numbered outcome at the beginning of the chapter.

1. An 80-yr-old female patient is receiving palliative care for heart failure. The *primary* purpose(s) of her receiving palliative care is (are) to (*select all that apply*)
   a. improve her quality of life.
   b. assess her coping ability with disease.
   c. have time to teach patient and family about disease.
   d. focus on reducing the severity of disease symptoms.
   e. provide care that the family is unwilling or unable to give.

2. A 67-yr-old woman was recently diagnosed with inoperable pancreatic cancer. Before the diagnosis, she was very active in her neighborhood association. Her husband is concerned because his wife is staying at home and missing her usual community activities. Which common EOL psychologic manifestation is she *most* likely demonstrating?
   a. Peacefulness
   b. Decreased socialization
   c. Decreased decision making
   d. Anxiety about unfinished business

3. For the past 5 years, Tom has repeatedly asked his mother to donate his deceased father's belongings to charity, but his mother has refused. She sits in the bedroom closet, crying and talking to her long-dead husband. What type of grief is Tom's mother experiencing?
   a. Adaptive grief
   b. Disruptive grief
   c. Anticipatory grief
   d. Prolonged grief disorder

4. While caring for his dying wife, the husband states that his wife is a devout Roman Catholic, but he is a Baptist. Who is considered the *most* reliable source for spiritual preferences concerning EOL care for the dying wife?
   a. A priest
   b. Dying wife
   c. Hospice staff
   d. Husband of dying wife

5. The family attorney informed a patient's adult children and wife that the patient did not have an advance directive after he suffered a serious stroke. Who is responsible for making the decision about EOL measures when the patient cannot communicate his or her specific wishes?
   a. Notary and attorney
   b. Physician and family
   c. Wife and adult children
   d. Physician and nursing staff

6. The home health nurse visits a 40-yr-old patient with metastatic breast cancer who is receiving palliative care. The patient has pain at a level of 7 (0–10 point scale). In prioritizing activities for the visit, what should the nurse do *first*?
   a. Auscultate for breath sounds.
   b. Give as needed pain medication.
   c. Check pressure points for skin breakdown.
   d. Ask family about patient's food and fluid intake.

7. The children caregivers of an older patient whose death is imminent have not left the bedside for the past 36 hours. In the nurse's assessment of the family, what findings indicate the potential for an abnormal grief reaction to occur *(select all that apply)*?
   a. Family cannot express their feelings to one another.
   b. Dying patient is becoming more restless and agitated.
   c. A family member is going through a difficult divorce.
   d. Family talks with and reassures the patient at frequent intervals.
   e. Siblings who were estranged from each other have now reunited.

8. A nurse has been working full-time with terminally ill patients for 3 years. He has been experiencing irritability and mixed emotions when expressing sadness since 4 of his patients died on the same day. To optimize the quality of his nursing care, he should examine his own
   a. full-time work schedule.
   b. past feelings toward death.
   c. patterns for dealing with grief.
   d. demands for involvement in patient care.

1. a, d, 2. b, 3. d, 4. b, 5. c, 6. b, 7. a, c, 8. c.

For rationales to these answers and even more NCLEX review questions, visit *http://evolve.elsevier.com/Lewis/medsurg*.

ⓔ EVOLVE WEBSITE/RESOURCES LIST

http://evolve.elsevier.com/Lewis/medsurg
Review Questions (Online Only)
Key Points
Answer Keys for Questions
- Rationales for Bridge to NCLEX Examination Questions
- Answer Guidelines for Case Study on p. 140
Student Case Study
- Patient With Chronic Myelogenous Leukemia Including End-of-Life Care
Conceptual Care Map Creator
Audio Glossary
Content Updates

REFERENCES

1. National Coalition for Hospice and Palliative Care: Clinical practice guidelines for quality palliative care. Retrieved from *www.nationalcoalitionhpc.org/ncp/*.
*2. Cleary A: Integrating palliative care into primary care for patients with chronic, life-limiting conditions, *TNP* 41:42, 2016.
3. Centers for Disease Control and Prevention: *Healthy aging*. Retrieved from *www.cdc.gov/aging*.
4. National Hospice and Palliative Care Organization: Facts on hospice and palliative care. Retrieved from *www.nhpco.org/hospice-statistics-research-press-room/facts-hospice-and-palliative-care*.
5. Hospice and Palliative Nurses Association: *HPNA position statements*. Retrieved from *https://advancingexpertcare.org/HPNA/Leadership/Position_Statements/HPNA/Leadership_Advocacy/Position_Statements.aspx?hkey=a794c17f-c88f-42d9-a09f-caf413e42aa3*.
6. National Hospice and Palliative Care Organization: Palliative care costs and benefits. Retrieved from *www.caringinfo.org/i4a/pages/index.cfm?pageid=3297*.

7. Lungu M, Lupu MN, Voinescu CD: The neurologist's responsibilities in declaring the time of brain death and organ donation, *Acta Medica* 22:15, 2017.
8. Field M, Cassel C: *Approaching death: Improving care at the end of life*, Washington, DC, 1997, National Academy Press. (Classic)
9. Kübler-Ross E: *On death and dying*, New York, 1969, Macmillan. (Classic).
10. National Cancer Institute: PDQ: Grief, bereavement, and coping with loss. Retrieved from *www.cancer.gov/cancertopics/pdq/supportivecare/bereavement/HealthProfessional*.
11. O'Brien ME: *Spirituality in nursing*, 3rd ed, Burlington, MA, 2017, Jones & Bartlett Learning.
*12. LoPresti MA, Dement F, Gold HT: End-of-life care for people from ethnic minority groups: A systematic review, *Am J Hosp Palliat Care* 33:291, 2016.
*13. Hagerty TA, Velázquez Á, Schmidt JM, et al: Assessment of satisfaction with care and decision-making among English and Spanish-speaking family members of neuroscience ICU patients, *App Nurs Res*. 29:262, 2016.
14. U.S. Department of Health and Human Services: U.S. government information on organ donation and transplantation. Retrieved from *www.organdonor.gov/index.html*.
*15. Robinson EM, Cadge W, Zollfrank AA, et al: After the DNR: Surrogates who persist in requesting cardiopulmonary resuscitation, *Hastings Center Report* 47:10, 2017.
*16. Davies P: Pharmacologic pain management at the end of life, *TNP* 41:26, 2016.
*17. Paez K, Gregg M, Massion C, et al: A new intervention for rapid end-of-life symptom control in the home setting, *JHPN* 18:498, 2016.
18. Marrelli T: Caregivers and caregiving: An important part of the healthcare team, *Home Healthcare Now* 35:427, 2017.

*Evidence-based information for clinical practice.

10

Substance Use Disorders

Mariann M. Harding

You can accomplish with kindness what you cannot by force.

Publilius Syrus

ⓔ http://evolve.elsevier.com/Lewis/medsurg/

CONCEPTUAL FOCUS

Addiction   Motivation
Coping

LEARNING OUTCOMES

1. Relate the effects of substance use to its resulting major health complications.
2. Distinguish among the effects of the use of stimulants, depressants, and cannabis.
3. Explain your role in promoting the cessation of smoking and tobacco use.
4. Summarize the nursing and interprofessional management of patients who experience toxicity or withdrawal from stimulants and depressants.

5. Apply the Screening, Brief Intervention, and Referral to Treatment approach in clinical situations.
6. Describe the incidence and effects of substance use in the older adult.

KEY TERMS

acute alcohol toxicity, p. 147
alcohol use disorder (AUD), p. 145
alcohol withdrawal syndrome (AWS), p. 147
binge drinking, p. 145

electronic cigarettes, p. 143
Screening, Brief Intervention, and Referral to Treatment (SBIRT), p. 150

substance use disorder (SUD), Table 10.1, p. 143
tobacco use disorder (TUD), p. 142

Substance use is a serious problem affecting society and the health care system. Substance-related disorders involve several types of substances, ranging from widely used and accepted tobacco and alcohol to illegal, brain-altering drugs such as heroin and cocaine. The *Diagnostic and Statistical Manual of Mental Disorders V (DSM-V)* outlines criteria used to identify the presence of substance use disorder (SUD)[1] (Table 10.1).

Whether SUD is mild, moderate, or severe depends on the person's pattern of use and the functional impact of use on the person's daily life. Knowing the severity of substance use allows the health care team to tailor treatment according to a patient's needs. For example, a person who binge drinks may not have alcohol SUD but is at increased risk for it. On the other hand, a person who uses heroin or cocaine is likely to have severe SUD because these substances are highly addictive.

Many patients with substance use problems receive acute care for problems associated with substance use. SUD does not exist in isolation. There are many interrelated concepts depending on the patient situation. Every drug associated with SUD harms some tissue or organ. Substance use causes specific health problems, such as liver damage related to alcohol use or lung cancer related to smoking. Other problems result from injuries associated with substance

use, such as falls or motor vehicle accidents. Common health problems related to substance use are outlined in Table 10.2.

This chapter focuses on the role of the medical-surgical nurse in identifying and managing the patient with SUD in the acute care setting. A hospitalized patient who uses substances can develop withdrawal when substance use abruptly stops. You need to be able to recognize substance use and its effects on health problems and manage withdrawal. The health care setting offers an opportunity for screening and providing teaching about substance use. It is your responsibility to motivate the patient to change behavior and refer the patient to programs that offer treatment.

DRUGS ASSOCIATED WITH SUBSTANCE USE DISORDER

NICOTINE

You are most likely to encounter people with **tobacco use disorder (TUD)**. People with TUD are dependent on the drug nicotine due to using tobacco products. Several products contain

TABLE 10.1 Criteria for Substance Use Disorder

The following criteria (clustered in 4 groups) can be used to identify substance use disorder (SUD). The severity of SUD can be classified as mild (2-3 criteria), moderate (4-5 criteria), or severe (6 or more criteria).

Impaired Control
- Taking more or for longer than intended
- Not quitting use despite multiple times of trying to do so
- Spending a great deal of time obtaining, using, or recovering from use
- Craving the substance

Social Impairment
- Missing school, work, or other responsibilities due to use
- Continuing use despite problems caused or worsened by use
- Giving up or reducing important activities because of use

Risky Use
- Recurrent use in hazardous situations
- Continued use despite causing or worsening problems

Pharmacologic Dependence
- Physical tolerance to effects of the substance
- Presence of withdrawal symptoms when not using or using less

Source: American Psychiatric Association: *The diagnostic and statistical manual of mental disorders*, ed 5, Arlington, VA, 2013, The Association.

TABLE 10.2 Health Problems Related to Substance Use

Substance	Health Problems*
Amphetamines	• Cardiac dysrhythmias, myocardial ischemia and infarction • Liver, lung, kidney damage • Mood disturbances, violent behavior, psychoses
Cannabis	• Bronchitis, chronic cough • Depression, anxiety, schizophrenia • Memory impairment
Cocaine	• Cardiac dysrhythmias, myocardial ischemia and infarction • Seizures, stroke • Psychosis
Inhalants	• Cognitive and motor impairment • Acute and chronic kidney injury
Opioids	• Sexual dysfunction • Gastric ulcers • Glomerulonephritis
Sedative-hypnotics	• Memory impairment • Personality changes, depression
Behaviors	
Injecting drugs	• Blood clots, phlebitis, skin infections • Hepatitis B and C • HIV/AIDS • Other infections: endocarditis, tuberculosis, pneumonia, meningitis, tetanus, bone and joint infections, lung abscesses
Personal neglect	• Malnutrition, impaired immunity • Accidental injuries
Risky sexual behavior	• HIV/AIDS • Hepatitis B and C • Sexually transmitted infections
Snorting drugs	• Nasal sores, septal necrosis or perforation • Chronic sinusitis

Adapted from National Institute on Drug Abuse: Medical consequence of drug abuse. Retrieved from *www.drugabuse.gov/related-topics/medical-consequences-drug-abuse.*
*Health problems related to SUD are discussed in the appropriate chapters throughout the text where they are identified as risk factors for these problems.

nicotine, including smoked tobacco (cigarettes, cigars, pipes), smokeless tobacco (chew, snuff, dip), and some electronic cigarettes. Cigarette smoking is the main form of tobacco use in the United States.

Effects of Use and Complications

Nicotine is a central nervous system stimulant. Within seconds of entering the body, nicotine reaches the brain, causing the release of adrenaline and creating feelings of a "high" or a "buzz." The effects last about 1 to 2 hours before withdrawal symptoms occur, leaving the person feeling tired, irritable, and anxious. The need to have the "high" or "buzz" feelings again makes the person crave more nicotine, leading to addiction.

Smoked tobacco is the most harmful method of nicotine use. Smoking harms nearly every organ in the body and reduces the general health of smokers. More than 14 million persons in the United States have a smoking related disease.[2] Smoking causes lung disease, cardiovascular disease, and lung and other cancers and is a major factor in many other conditions (Fig. 10.1).

Although those who use smokeless tobacco have less risk for lung disease, use can cause serious health problems. Holding tobacco in the mouth is associated with periodontal disease and cancer of the mouth, cheek, tongue, throat, and esophagus. Smokeless tobacco users experience the systemic effects of nicotine on the cardiovascular system, increasing the risk for heart attack and stroke.[3]

The use of electronic cigarettes, or e-cigs, continues to increase. E-cigs have a similar look and feel of traditional cigarettes. These battery-operated devices turn nicotine and other chemicals, including propylene glycol and flavorings, into an aerosol. Emerging information shows e-cigs can be harmful. E-cigs may affect the respiratory and immune systems. Those containing nicotine may increase the risk for cardiovascular problems and influence brain development in adolescents and pregnant users.[4] Other problems, such as poisonings and facial burns from device explosions, have occurred. Although some believe using an e-cig

may aid in smoking cessation, no e-cigs are FDA approved. Do not recommend them as a smoking cessation aid.

❖ NURSING AND INTERPROFESSIONAL MANAGEMENT: TOBACCO USE DISORDER

◆ Tobacco Cessation

As a nurse, you have a professional responsibility to help people stop smoking or using tobacco. The Joint Commission mandates that every health professional must identify tobacco users and provide them with information on ways to stop using tobacco. Patients who receive even brief advice and intervention from you are more likely to quit than those who receive no intervention.

With each patient encounter, encourage the patient to quit and offer specific smoking cessation interventions. The Agency for Healthcare Research and Quality has issued clinical practice guidelines for clinicians, including nurses, to use to motivate users to quit[5] (Tables 10.3 and 10.4). Use these brief clinical interventions, called the "5 As," with each patient encounter. These interventions will help you identify tobacco users, encourage

Cancers   **Chronic diseases**

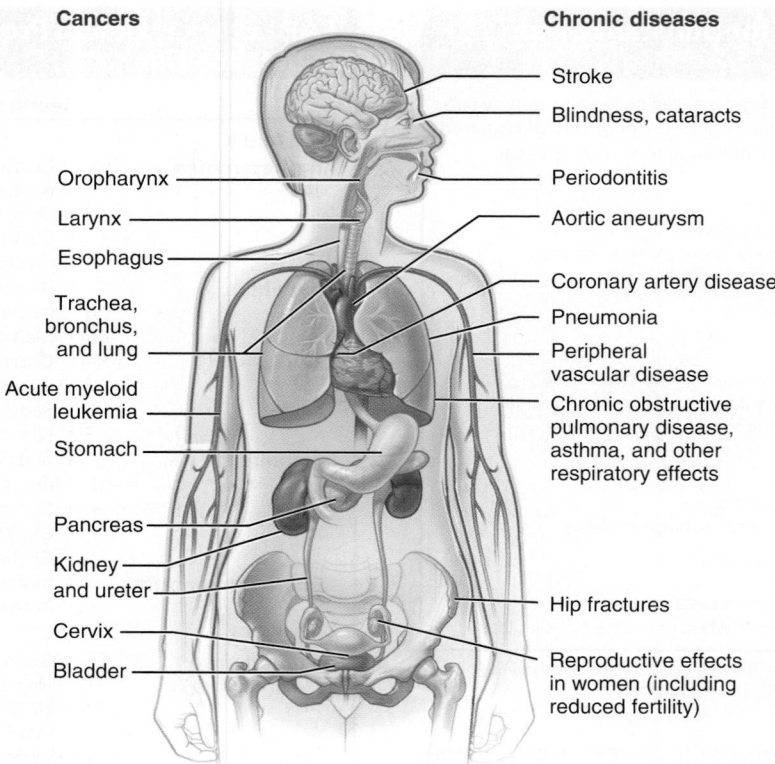

— Stroke

— Blindness, cataracts

Oropharynx — — Periodontitis

Larynx — — Aortic aneurysm

Esophagus — — Coronary artery disease

Trachea, — Pneumonia
bronchus,
and lung — — Peripheral
vascular disease

Acute myeloid — Chronic obstructive
leukemia — pulmonary disease,
asthma, and other
Stomach — respiratory effects

Pancreas —

Kidney —
and ureter —

Cervix — — Hip fractures

Bladder — — Reproductive effects
in women (including
reduced fertility)

FIG 10.1 Health effects of smoking. (From Samet JM: Tobacco smoking, *Thorac Surg Clin* 23[2]:103, 2013.)

TABLE 10.3 Clinical Practice Guideline

Treating Tobacco Use Disorder

The 5 *A*s for Users Who Want to Quit	The 5 *R*s for Users Unwilling to Quit
1. **Ask:** Identify all tobacco users at every contact.	1. **Relevance:** Ask the patient to say why quitting is personally relevant (e.g., health).
2. **Advise:** Strongly urge all tobacco users to quit.	2. **Risks:** Ask the patient to identify his or her potential risks/consequences of tobacco use.
3. **Assess:** Determine willingness to make a quit attempt.	3. **Rewards:** Ask the patient to relate potential benefits of stopping tobacco use.
4. **Assist:** Develop a plan with the patient to help the patient quit (e.g., counseling, medication).	4. **Roadblocks:** Ask patient to identify barriers or impediments to quitting.
5. **Arrange:** Schedule follow-up contact.	5. **Repetition:** Repeat process every clinic visit.

Source: Agency for Healthcare Research and Quality: *AHCPR supported clinical practice guideline: Treating tobacco use and dependence—2008 update,* Washington, DC, 2008, U.S. Public Health Service.

TABLE 10.4 Inpatient Tobacco Cessation Interventions

Take the following steps for every hospitalized patient:
- Ask each patient on admission if he or she uses tobacco and document tobacco use status.
- For current tobacco users, list tobacco use status on the admission problem list and as a discharge diagnosis.
- Use counseling and medication to help all tobacco users stay abstinent and to treat withdrawal symptoms.
- Give advice and assistance on how to quit during hospitalization and stay abstinent after discharge.
- Arrange for follow-up about smoking status. Provide supportive contact for at least a month after discharge.

Source: Agency for Healthcare Research and Quality: *AHCPR supported clinical practice guideline: Treating tobacco use and dependence: 2008 update,* Washington, DC, 2008, U.S. Public Health Service.

them to quit, determine their willingness to quit, assist them in quitting, and arrange for follow-up. A patient teaching guide (Table 10.5) expands on the fourth strategy, *Assist,* to help you aid the user willing to quit. If a tobacco user is unwilling to quit, using the "5 *R*s" may motivate the user to quit in the future.

A variety of smoking cessation products are available to help support users in quitting. These include prescription medicines as well as over-the-counter (OTC) products such as skin patches, lozenges, and gum. Nicotine replacement products are 1 type of smoking cessation product. These products reduce the craving and withdrawal symptoms associated with cessation by supplying the body with smaller amounts of nicotine (Table 10.6).

Because most health care facilities are tobacco-free environments, admitted patients who are addicted to nicotine may experience withdrawal symptoms since they are unable to smoke. These symptoms are the same as for the person who stops using tobacco "cold turkey." Offering nicotine replacement therapy to every patient who wants to quit will help control withdrawal symptoms during hospitalization and promote continued cessation after discharge.

Non-nicotine products also play a role in helping users quit. Varenicline (Chantix) is a drug used to aid smoking cessation. Varenicline is unique in that it has both agonist and antagonist

TABLE 10.5 Patient Teaching
Smoking and Tobacco Use Cessation

The following interventions are methods that work for quitting tobacco use. Tobacco users have the best chance of quitting if they use more than 1 method.

Develop a Quit Plan
- Set a quit date, ideally within 2 weeks.
- Talk to your HCP about getting help to quit.
- Tell family, friends, and co-workers about quitting and request understanding and support.
- Expect withdrawal symptoms and challenges when quitting.
- Before quitting, avoid smoking in places where you spend a lot of time (work, car, home).
- Throw away all tobacco products from your home, car, and work.
- Have support options in place by your quit date.

Use Approved Nicotine Replacement Systems
- Use a nicotine replacement agent unless you are a pregnant or nursing woman (Table 10.6).
- Do not use other forms of tobacco when using nicotine replacement systems.

Support and Encouragement
- Joining a quit-tobacco support group will increase your chances of stopping permanently.
- If you get the urge for tobacco, call someone to help talk you out of it—preferably an ex-user.
- Be proud every time you reach a quit milestone and reward yourself.
- Do not be afraid to talk about how you feel while quitting, especially fears of not being able to quit for good. Ask your spouse or partner, friends, and co-workers to support you. Self-help materials, mobile phone applications, and hot lines are available:
  - American Lung Association: 800-586-4872; *www.lung.org*
  - American Cancer Society: 800-227-2345; *www.cancer.org*
  - National Cancer Institute: LiveHelp; *www.smokefree.gov*

Dealing With Urges to Use Tobacco
- Identify situations that may cause you to want to smoke or use other tobacco, such as being around other smokers, being under time pressure, feeling sad or frustrated, and drinking alcohol.
- Avoid difficult situations while you are trying to quit. Try to lower your stress level.
- Exercise can help, such as walking, jogging, or bicycling.
- Distract yourself from thoughts of smoking and the urge to use tobacco by talking to someone, going to a movie, getting busy with a task, or having a game night with friends.
- Drink a lot of water.
- Keep your hands busy with a pen or toothpick.

Avoiding Relapse
Most relapses occur within the first 3 months after quitting. Do not be discouraged if you start using tobacco again. Remember, most people try several times before they finally quit. Explore different ways to break habits. You may have to deal with some of the following triggers that cause relapse.
- *Change your environment.* Get rid of cigarettes, tobacco (in any form), and ashtrays in your home, car, and place of work. Get rid of the smell of cigarettes in your car and home.
- *Alcohol.* Consider limiting or stopping alcohol use while you are quitting tobacco.
- *Other smokers at home.* Encourage housemates to quit with you. Work out a plan to cope with others who smoke and avoid being around them.
- *Weight gain.* Tackle 1 problem at a time. Work on quitting tobacco first. You will not necessarily gain weight, and increased appetite is often temporary. Eat healthy and exercise.
- *Negative mood or depression.* If these symptoms persist, talk to your HCP. You may need treatment for depression.
- *Withdrawal symptoms.* Your body will go through many changes when you quit tobacco. You may have a dry mouth, cough, or scratchy throat, and you may feel irritable. The nicotine patch or gum may help with cravings (Table 10.6).
- *Focus on the benefits of quitting:*
  - Your BP and heart rate will lower almost at once.
  - Your risk for a heart attack declines within 24 hours. The blood will become less likely to clot, making dangerous blood clots less likely.
  - Within a few weeks, you will be less short of breath, cough less, and have more energy. Your ability to smell and taste should improve.
  - Your immune system will be stronger, so you will be less likely to be sick.
  - Quitting will improve your night vision and help preserve your overall vision.

Adapted from National Cancer Institute: 18 ways smoking affects your health. Retrieved from *www.smokefree.gov/health-effects.*

actions. Its agonist activity at 1 subtype of nicotinic receptors provides some nicotine effects to ease withdrawal symptoms. If the person does resume smoking, its antagonist action blocks the effects of nicotine at another subtype of nicotinic receptor, making smoking less enjoyable. Bupropion (Zyban), an antidepressant drug, reduces the urge to smoke, reduces some symptoms of withdrawal, and helps prevent weight gain associated with smoking cessation.

DRUG ALERT   Varenicline (Chantix) and Bupropion (Zyban)
- Serious neuropsychiatric symptoms such as changes in behavior, hostility, agitation, depressed mood, suicidal thoughts and behavior, and attempted suicide can occur.
- Tell patients to stop taking these drugs and contact the HCP at once if they have any of these manifestations.

Along with using a smoking cessation product, users who wish to quit are more likely to succeed if they take part in a tobacco cessation program. You should be aware of available community resources. Cessation programs may involve hypnosis, acupuncture, behavioral interventions, aversion therapy, group support programs, individual therapy, and self-help options. Many of these programs teach users to avoid high-risk situations for smoking relapse (e.g., those that promote cue-induced craving) and help them develop coping skills, such as cigarette refusal skills, assertiveness, alternative activities, and peer support systems.

ALCOHOL

Of Americans ages 18 and older, 70% consume alcohol. Most people use alcohol in moderation.[6] *Risky drinking* is consuming more alcohol than the amounts in guidelines established by the National Institute on Alcohol Abuse and Alcoholism (Fig. 10.2). Risky drinking can have negative physical, emotional, and social consequences. **Alcohol use disorder (AUD)**, or alcoholism, affects about 6.2% of U.S. adults.[6] A higher percent engages in periodic excess alcohol use. **Binge drinking** is consuming 5 or more alcoholic drinks for males or 4 or more alcoholic drinks for females on the same occasion at least once per month.

TABLE 10.6 Drug Therapy
Smoking Cessation*

Agents	Common Side Effects	Considerations
Nicotine Replacement Agents		
Nicotine Gum (OTC) Nicorette 2 mg, 4 mg • Use up to 12 wk • Use 1 piece q1–2hr for 6 wk then q2–4hr for 3 wk • Maximum dose: 24 pieces/day	Hiccups, mouth/jaw pain, mouth ulcers, indigestion, throat irritation, nausea	Specific 30-min chewing regimen with periods of holding the gum between cheek and teeth. Take only water 15 min before and during use. Hard to use with dentures.
Nicotine Lozenge (OTC) Commit 2 mg, 4 mg • Use 8–12 wk • Use 1 lozenge q1–2hr tapering to 1 lozenge q4–8hr in 12 wk	Insomnia, nausea, sore throat, hiccups, cough, heartburn, headache	Dissolves in mouth in 20–30 min. Do not chew or swallow. Avoid food and drink during use. Occasionally rotate around the mouth.
Nicotine Patch (OTC) NicoDerm CQ, Habitrol, Nicotine transdermal system • 18- or 24-hr doses • Use ≥8 wk	Local skin irritation, insomnia, nausea, headache	Provides steady level of nicotine and is easy to use. Cannot be used by those with adhesive allergies. Rotate site to diminish skin irritation.
Nicotine Nasal Spray Nicotrol NS • 1–2 doses (2 sprays)/hr • Use ≥6 mo	Nose and throat irritation, sneezing, rhinitis, headache, cough	Requires a prescription. Provides fastest nicotine delivery. Do not sniff or inhale while dosing. Tilt head back slightly for best results.
Nicotine Inhaler Nicotrol nicotine inhalation system • Use 1 cartridge q1–2hr • Use 3–6 mo	Cough, mouth and throat irritation, headache, nausea, hiccups	Requires a prescription. Simulates smoking with mouthpiece and nicotine cartridge. May not be advisable for those with asthma or pulmonary disease
Non-Nicotine Agents		
bupropion (Zyban) • 150 mg/day for 3 days, then 150 mg bid • Use 12 wk; can use up to 6 mo	Insomnia, dry mouth, irritability, rash, tremors, anorexia	Contraindicated with history of seizures or eating disorders. Promotes weight loss. First choice for smokers with depression
varenicline (Chantix)† • 0.5 mg/day for 3 days, 0.5 mg bid for 4 days, then 1 mg bid • Use 12 wk; additional 12 wk may be used in select patients	Nausea, sleep disturbances, constipation, flatulence, vomiting, headache	If taken concurrently with nicotine replacement therapy, incidence of nausea, headache, vomiting, dizziness, dyspepsia, and fatigue is increased, but nicotine pharmacokinetics not affected.

*OTC nicotine replacement agents are also available in generic forms. More information and patient instructions are available from the American Lung Association at *www.lungusa.org*.
†See the Drug Alert for varenicline on p. 145.

| 12 fl oz of regular beer | = | 8-9 fl oz of malt liquor (shown in a 12 oz glass) | = | 5 fl oz of table wine | = | 1.5 fl oz shot of 80-proof spirits ("hard liquor" — whiskey, gin, rum, vodka, tequila, etc.) |

| About 5% alcohol | About 7% alcohol | About 12% alcohol | About 40% alcohol |

The percent of "pure" alcohol, expressed here as alcohol by volume (alc/vol), varies by beverage.

FIG 10.2 U.S. standard drink equivalents. The National Institute on Alcohol Abuse and Alcoholism (NIAAA) guidelines for alcohol use state that healthy men younger than 65 should consume no more than 14 standard drinks per week or 4 drinks per drinking occasion. Healthy, nonpregnant women and adults older than 65 should consume no more than 7 standard drinks per week or 3 drinks per drinking occasion. (From NIAAA: *What's a standard drink?* Retrieved from *www.niaaa.nih.gov*.)

Effects of Use and Complications

Alcohol affects almost all cells of the body. It changes levels of neurotransmitters in the central nervous system (CNS), affecting all areas and functions of the CNS. These include centers that control our impulses, mood, and behavior; coordinate motor activity; and promote respiratory and cardiac function. The immediate effects of alcohol depend on a person's susceptibility to alcohol and the blood alcohol concentration (BAC).

For the person who is not dependent on alcohol, the BAC generally predicts alcohol's effects. The relationship between BAC and behavior is different in a person who has developed tolerance to alcohol and its effects. The *tolerant person* is usually able to drink large amounts without obvious impairment and perform complex tasks without problems at BAC levels much higher than levels that would produce obvious impairment in the *nontolerant drinker*. Women have higher blood alcohol levels than men do after the same amount of alcohol intake.

Alcohol use is linked to many health problems (Table 10.7), which are often the reason that people seek health care. Long-term alcohol use can lead to hypertension, heart disease, stroke, liver disease, and digestive problems. Short-term, excess alcohol

TABLE 10.7 Effects of Chronic Alcohol Use

BODY SYSTEM	EFFECTS
Cardiac	Hypertension, atrial fibrillation, cardiomyopathy, stroke, coronary artery disease, sudden cardiac death
Gastrointestinal	Gastritis, gastroesophageal reflux disease (GERD), peptic ulcer, esophagitis, esophageal varices, gastrointestinal bleeding, pancreatitis, oropharyngeal cancer, colorectal cancer
Hematologic	Bone marrow depression, anemia, leukopenia, thrombocytopenia, blood clotting abnormalities
Hepatic	Alcoholic hepatitis, cirrhosis, liver cancer
Integumentary	Palmar erythema, spider angiomas, rosacea, rhinophyma
Musculoskeletal	Myopathy, osteoporosis, gout
Neurologic	Alcoholic dementia, Wernicke-Korsakoff syndrome, impaired cognitive function, psychomotor skills, abstract thinking, and memory. Depression, anxiety, attention deficit, labile moods, seizures, insomnia, peripheral neuropathy, chronic headache
Nutrition	Diabetes, anorexia, malnutrition, vitamin deficiencies (especially thiamine)
Reproductive	Breast cancer, testicular atrophy, decreased beard growth, decreased libido, decreased sperm count, gynecomastia
Urinary	Diuretic effect from inhibition of antidiuretic hormone

use increases the risk for injury from motor vehicle crashes, falls, firearms, assault, drowning, and burns. Patients with AUD undergoing surgery have increased in-hospital death rates and longer lengths of stay.

Complications may arise from the interaction of alcohol with commonly prescribed or OTC medications. Those that interact with alcohol in an additive manner include antihypertensives, antihistamines, and antianginals. Alcohol taken with aspirin may cause or worsen GI bleeding. Alcohol taken with acetaminophen may increase the risk for liver damage. Taking a CNS depressant with alcohol can increase, or potentiate, the effect of both. An alcohol-dependent person may have cross-tolerance, needing higher doses of CNS depressants to achieve the desired effect.

❖ NURSING AND INTERPROFESSIONAL MANAGEMENT: ALCOHOL USE DISORDER

◆ Alcohol Toxicity

Acute alcohol toxicity occurs when a person has a high level of alcohol in the blood, generally after ingesting a large amount of alcohol. This leads to behavior changes and alcohol-induced CNS depression, resulting in respiratory and circulatory

failure. Unconsciousness, coma, and death can occur. Other common effects include hypokalemia, hypomagnesemia, and hypoglycemia.

Obtain as accurate a health history as possible and assess for injuries, diseases, and hypoglycemia. No antidote for alcohol is available. Implement supportive care measures to maintain airway, breathing, and circulation (the ABCs) until the alcohol metabolizes. Frequently monitor vital signs and level of consciousness. Treat alcohol-induced hypotension with IV fluids.

Patients with hypoglycemia may receive glucose-containing IV solutions. IV thiamine may be given before or with IV glucose solutions to prevent *Wernicke-Korsakoff syndrome*, which can cause seizures and brain damage.[7] Many patients have low serum magnesium levels and other signs of malnutrition, so HCPs often add multivitamins and magnesium to the IV fluids.

Agitation and anxiety are common. Stay with the patient as much as possible, orienting as necessary. Assess the patient for increasing belligerence and a potential for violence. Since the patient is at risk for injury because of lack of coordination and impaired judgment, use protective measures.

◆ Alcohol Withdrawal Syndrome

Alcohol withdrawal syndrome (AWS) can develop in a hospitalized patient when the use of alcohol abruptly stops. The onset of AWS is variable depending on the quantity, frequency, pattern, and duration of alcohol use. The early signs usually develop within a few hours after the last drink. They peak after 24 to 48 hours and then disappear unless the withdrawal progresses to alcohol withdrawal delirium.

Alcohol withdrawal delirium is a serious complication that can occur from 2 to 3 days after the last drink and last 2 to 3 days. The greater the patient's dependence on alcohol, the greater the risk for alcohol withdrawal delirium. Death may result from multiorgan dysfunction, dysrhythmias, or peripheral vascular collapse.[8]

Management begins with identifying at-risk persons. Use a symptom assessment tool, such as the Clinical Institute Withdrawal Assessment of Alcohol Scale, Revised (CIWA-Ar), to determine treatment[7] (Table 10.8). Table 10.9 presents the clinical manifestations and suggested treatment for AWS. A nursing care plan (eNursing Care Plan 10.1) for a patient with AWS is available on the website at *http://evolve.elsevier.com/Lewis/medsurg.*

👤 CHECK YOUR PRACTICE

A 34-yr-old male patient was admitted for multiple trauma following a car accident. His girlfriend tells you that he always drinks too much and she knew he would get in trouble someday.
- What signs and symptoms would alert you to the presence of AWS?
- What measures would you use to protect his safety?
- How would you involve members of the interprofessional team in planning patient care?

USE OF OTHER SUBSTANCES

STIMULANTS

Amphetamine-related stimulants are highly addictive substances. While the use of crack cocaine and methamphetamine is illegal, amphetamines have a role in treating narcolepsy, obesity, and attention deficit disorder. Though most people responsibly use

TABLE 10.8 Clinical Institute Withdrawal Assessment of Alcohol Scale, Revised (CIWA-Ar)

CIWA-AR CATEGORIES	SCORE RANGE IN EACH CATEGORY
Agitation	0–7
Anxiety	0–7
Auditory disturbances	0–7
Headache	0–7
Clouding of sensorium	0–4
Paroxysmal sweats	0–7
Tactile disturbances	0–7
Tremor	0–7
Visual disturbances	0–7

Source: University of Maryland School of Medicine. Available at www.umem.org/files/uploads/1104212257_CIWA-Ar.pdf.

TABLE 10.9 Manifestations and Treatment of Alcohol Withdrawal

Manifestations	Interprofessional Care
Alcohol Withdrawal Syndrome	
• Agitation • Anxiety • ↑ Heart rate • ↑ BP • Sweating • Nausea • Tremors • Insomnia • Hyperactivity	• Benzodiazepines (e.g., lorazepam, diazepam) to prevent seizures and delirium • Thiamine to prevent Wernicke-Korsakoff syndrome • Multivitamins (e.g., folic acid, B vitamins) • Magnesium sulfate to treat low serum magnesium • IV glucose solution to treat hypoglycemia • β-Blockers (e.g., atenolol) or α_2-agonists (e.g., clonidine) to stabilize vital signs • Respiratory support
Alcohol Withdrawal Delirium	
• Disorientation • Visual, tactile, or auditory hallucinations • Seizures	• Continued use of benzodiazepines • Valproic acid or gabapentin to treat seizures • Antipsychotic agents (haloperidol [Haldol]) • Chlordiazepoxide if psychosis persists after benzodiazepine administration

TABLE 10.10 Emergency Management
Stimulant Toxicity

ASSESSMENT FINDINGS	INTERVENTIONS
Cardiovascular • Palpitations • Tachycardia • ↑ BP • Dysrhythmias • Myocardial ischemia • Chest pain **Central Nervous System** • Agitation • Euphoria • Insomnia • Combativeness • Seizures • Hallucinations • Confusion • Paranoia • Fever	• Ensure patent airway. • Establish IV access and start appropriate fluid replacement. • Obtain a 12-lead ECG and start ECG monitoring. • Treat ventricular dysrhythmias as needed. • Treat hypertension and chest pain with nitrates or calcium channel blockers. • Aspirin may be given to lower the risk for myocardial infarction. • Give IV diazepam or lorazepam for seizures. • Give IV antipsychotic drugs for psychosis and hallucinations. • Monitor vital signs and level of consciousness. • Begin cooling measures for hyperthermia. • Treat insomnia with trazodone, hydroxyzine, or diphenhydramine at bedtime. • Start gastric lavage in cases of recent ingestion.

seizures, confusion, and diaphoresis. Death may occur from stroke, dysrhythmias, or myocardial infarction.[1]

The emergency management depends on the clinical manifestations at the time of treatment (Table 10.10). A specific antidote for stimulant toxicity is not available. Treatment focuses on supportive care measures.

◆ Withdrawal

Stimulant withdrawal is usually not an emergency. Abrupt cessation can lead to a "crash." The patient may be depressed and experience fatigue, disturbed sleep, vivid dreams, general aching, irritability, increased appetite, and mood swings.[9] Craving for the drug is intense during the first hours to days of drug cessation and may continue for weeks. Supportive care includes providing a safe, quiet environment and allowing the patient to sleep and eat as desired. If a patient has severe depression, initiate suicide precautions and refer for further treatment.

DEPRESSANTS

Commonly used depressants include sedative-hypnotics and opioids. Depressants have a rapid development of tolerance and dependence. Their use is associated with many medical emergencies involving toxicity and withdrawal. The majority of drug overdose deaths involve an opioid, either alone or in combination with another depressant (e.g., opioid and benzodiazepine).[10] Common health problems resulting from depressant use are outlined in Table 10.2.

Sedative-Hypnotics

Common sedative-hypnotic agents include barbiturates, benzodiazepines, and barbiturate-like drugs. Sedative-hypnotic drugs depress the CNS, causing sedation at low doses and sleep

prescribed stimulants, prescription stimulants are often misused. All stimulants increase cardiac activity and excite the CNS by increasing levels of norepinephrine, serotonin, and dopamine. People use these drugs to produce feelings of euphoria, increase alertness, and boost their energy. Health problems associated with using stimulants are outlined in Table 10.2.

❖ NURSING AND INTERPROFESSIONAL MANAGEMENT: STIMULANT USE

◆ Toxicity

Patients with stimulant toxicity present with *sympathetic overdrive* (increased stimulation of the sympathetic nervous system). The patient has restlessness, agitation, delirium, impaired judgment, and paranoia with psychotic symptoms. Physical effects include hypertension, tachycardia, fever, pupil dilation, at high doses. Their use produces a euphoria and intoxication that resembles that of alcohol. Tolerance develops rapidly to the effects of these drugs, requiring higher doses to achieve euphoria. However, tolerance may not develop to the brainstem-depressant effects. As a result, an increased dose may trigger hypotension and respiratory depression, resulting in death.

Opioids

Opioids include substances directly derived from the opium poppy (e.g., morphine), semisynthetics (e.g., heroin, hydromorphone), and synthetic compounds (e.g., fentanyl). Persons dependent on opioids include those who use illegal drugs sold on the street and those who misuse prescription opioids. Opioids act on opiate receptors and neurotransmitter systems in the CNS, causing sedation and analgesia. The person taking an opioid experiences euphoria, mood changes, mental clouding, drowsiness, and pain reduction. While this makes prescription opioids useful in treating a number of medical conditions, their pleasurable effects promote misuse. Misusing oxycodone or fentanyl can result in the same harmful consequences as abusing heroin.

❖ NURSING AND INTERPROFESSIONAL MANAGEMENT: DEPRESSANT USE

◆ Toxicity

Overdoses can occur when a person purposefully misuses a depressant or takes 1 prescribed for someone else. Unintentional overdose often occurs, especially when depressants are used with alcohol or other drugs. Depressant toxicity can cause death from respiratory and CNS depression. The priority of care is always the patient's ABCs. Supporting respiratory and cardiovascular function and continuous monitoring of neurologic status is critical until the patient is stable. The emergency management depends on the substance used and the clinical manifestations (Table 10.11).

TABLE 10.11 Emergency Management
Depressant Toxicity

Assessment Findings	Interventions
• Aggressive behavior	• Ensure patent airway.
• Agitation	• Expect intubation if respiratory distress present.
• Confusion	• Establish IV access.
• Lethargy	• Obtain temperature.
• Stupor	
• Hallucinations	• Obtain 12-lead ECG and start continuous ECG monitoring.
• Depression	• Obtain information about substance (name, route, when taken, amount).
• Slurred speech	
• Pinpoint pupils	
• Nystagmus	
• Seizures	• Obtain specific drug levels or comprehensive toxicology screen.
• Cold, clammy skin	
• Rapid, weak pulse	• Obtain a health history, including drug use and allergies.
• Slow or rapid shallow respirations	• Give the right antidotes.
• Decreased O₂ saturation	• Perform gastric lavage if necessary.
• Hypotension	
• Dysrhythmias	• Give activated charcoal and cathartics as needed.
• ECG changes	
• Cardiac or respiratory arrest	• Monitor vital signs, level of consciousness, and O₂ saturation.

◆ **Sedative-Hypnotics.** On occasion, a patient with a benzodiazepine overdose may receive flumazenil, a specific benzodiazepine antagonist. Because flumazenil may have a shorter duration of action than some benzodiazepines, repeated doses may be needed until the benzodiazepine is metabolized. Place the patient on safety precautions as flumazenil can cause seizures.

There are no antagonists for barbiturates or other sedative-hypnotic drugs. The patient receives supportive care, including passive rewarming, hydration, and vasopressors, along with treatments to promote drug elimination. If the airway can be maintained, activated charcoal is an option. Dialysis can be used in certain situations.

◆ **Opioids.** Overdose in the inpatient setting may occur when a patient inadvertently receives an incorrect dose, or when opioids are aggressively dosed, given to patients with new kidney or liver impairment, or given with drugs that potentiate respiratory depression.[11] Treatment includes supporting respiratory function and giving the opioid antagonist naloxone. Naloxone reverses respiratory depression and other manifestations of toxicity. Monitor the patient closely because naloxone has a shorter duration of action than most opioids. Repeated doses or IV infusion of naloxone may be needed until the opioid is metabolized.

Overdose in the community setting can occur when a person deliberately misuses an illegal or prescription opioid, takes an opioid in combination with other depressants, or takes an opioid prescribed for someone else. In many areas, naloxone is publicly available. This allows police, first responders, family members, and friends to give someone naloxone in emergencies, thus reversing the effects of an overdose sooner. As a result, you may see more patients requiring postreversal care.

◆ Withdrawal

◆ **Sedative-Hypnotics.** Withdrawal from sedative-hypnotics can be life threatening. The manifestations and treatment are similar to those of AWS. Early, the patient may have tremors, anxiety, insomnia, fever, orthostatic hypotension, and disorientation. Since the patient may experience delirium, seizures, and respiratory and cardiac arrest within 24 hours after the last dose, closely monitor the patient. Treatment consists of giving a long-acting benzodiazepine in a tapered dose. IV diazepam is an option for severe manifestations. Supportive care includes implementing patient safety and comfort measures, frequently assessing neurologic status and vital signs, and providing reassurance and orientation.

◆ **Opioids.** Opioid withdrawal symptoms depend on the opioid used, route of administration, and duration of use. It is usually not life threatening but can be extremely uncomfortable. Manifestations include intense drug craving, diaphoresis, gastrointestinal distress, restlessness, fever, insomnia, watery eyes, tremors, muscle aches, runny nose, and anxiety.[1] With shorter acting drugs, withdrawal may begin 4 to 6 hours after the last dose, peak in 36 to 72 hours, and last 7 to 10 days. With longer acting drugs, manifestations may begin 24 to 48 hours after last dose and peak in 3 to 4 days.[11]

Treatment focuses on relieving symptoms and often requires drug therapy. Substituting a long-acting opioid (e.g., methadone, buprenorphine) at low doses or α₂-adrenergic agonists (e.g., clonidine) decreases withdrawal symptoms. Other therapies include medications for GI distress (e.g., loperamide, ondansetron), acetaminophen or nonsteroidal antiinflammatory agents for muscle aches and fever, and antihistamines for acute anxiety and sleep disturbances.

INHALANTS

Persons with inhalant use disorder inhale hydrocarbon-based fumes, such as those found in glues or paints, to change their mental state.[1] Inhalants are rapidly absorbed and reach the CNS quickly. Most are depressants with effects like those of alcohol. They cause a brief period of euphoria, followed by drowsiness and lightheadedness. Long-term use can result in neurologic problems, including damage to parts of the brain that control cognition, movement, vision, and hearing (Table 10.2).

The patient with inhalant toxicity may have lethargy, dizziness, slurred speech, blurry vision, tremors, and impaired coordination.[1] The effects usually resolve within minutes to a few hours. Inhalant toxicity is managed with supportive care. However, in some cases, users need emergency treatment for dysrhythmias, heart failure, or CNS hyperactivity (e.g., seizures). Using some inhalants (e.g., toluene) can result in nephrotoxicity; so, you must monitor renal function. Withdrawal is rare as most inhaled substances have a very short duration. Any manifestations that may occur require supportive care.

CANNABIS

The use of cannabis, also called marijuana or weed, continues to increase in the United States. Cannabis is available in forms that can be smoked, vaporized, or ingested. The main ingredient is tetrahydrocannabinol (THC). At low to moderate doses, THC produces euphoria, reduced anxiety, and improved appetite. Adverse effects include impaired memory, impaired motor coordination, altered judgment, and, in high doses, paranoia and psychosis. Long-term use is associated with a wide range of effects, particularly on cardiopulmonary and mental health (Table 10.2).

Legalizing cannabis for recreational and medical use is controversial. Sales for recreational use continue to grow. More than half of the states have legalized its use for specific medical reasons. If an HCP in 1 of those states determines a patient has a disorder that qualifies for medical cannabis use, the HCP can give the patient an *authorization for use*. This form allows the patient to buy cannabis at special dispensaries or have a limited number of cannabis plants. THC-based medications, dronabinol (Marinol) and nabilone (Cesamet), are available to control nausea and vomiting from cancer chemotherapy. Dronabinol is also used to stimulate appetite in patients with acquired immunodeficiency syndrome (AIDS). Illegal synthetic cannabinoid drugs (e.g., K2, Spice) have some of the same properties as THC. They contain varying amounts of different ingredients. The result is that these products have unpredictable effects and are more toxic. Sometimes, death has occurred with 1 use.

Patients with *acute marijuana toxicity* can present with acute psychotic episodes, especially if the patient used a synthetic derivative. Cannabis can induce tachycardia and hypertension, triggering dysrhythmias and myocardial infarction. Support the patient's ABCs. Panic and flashbacks are managed by maintaining a quiet environment and reassuring the patient. Benzodiazepines give symptom relief. [12]

Withdrawal can occur in a hospitalized patient who uses cannabis. The patient may have irritability, insomnia, anorexia, cramping, mild agitation, and nausea.[13] This peaks about 48 hours after cessation and may be more severe in women. There

is no specific drug therapy for treating withdrawal. Supportive care includes measures to promote sleep, safety, and patient comfort, including analgesics and hydration.

CAFFEINE

Caffeine is the most widely used psychoactive substance in the world. It is very weak when compared with the other stimulants. Most people use it to promote wakefulness. Other uses include promoting motor activity and treating headaches. Its use is safe in most people. Problems from high doses of caffeine have occurred in association with specialized drinks. A large caffeine intake can cause cardiac dysrhythmias, hypertension, disturbed sleep, seizures, and anxiety. Treatment consists of seizure control with benzodiazepines and supportive care until the effects wear off. In a hospitalized patient, caffeine withdrawal can result in muscle pain or stiffness, drowsiness, irritability, and headaches after general anesthesia or during restrictions on usual caffeine intake.[1]

❖ NURSING MANAGEMENT: SUBSTANCE USE

◆ Nursing Assessment

You need to be able to determine if patients use substances in a way that places them at risk or if SUD is present. Screening is a simple, effective way to identify patients who need further assessment. Use the Screening, Brief Intervention, and Referral to Treatment (SBIRT) approach (Fig. 10.3). SBIRT consists of 3 parts: (1) screening to quickly identify and assess the severity of any substance use problems, (2) providing a brief intervention or teaching patients about the consequences of substance use, and (3) referring those who screen positive for further treatment.[14]

Screening is the first part of SBIRT. Use screening tools to identify those who may have problems with substance use. As a baseline, ask every patient about the use of all substances, including prescribed medications, OTC medications, caffeine, tobacco, and recreational drugs. Use simple 1 or 2 question screening tests to detect alcohol, tobacco, and/or other substance use problems (Table 10.12). If a patient has a positive screen, follow up with a detailed assessment to identify specific problems. A screening tool for AUD, the Alcohol Use Disorders

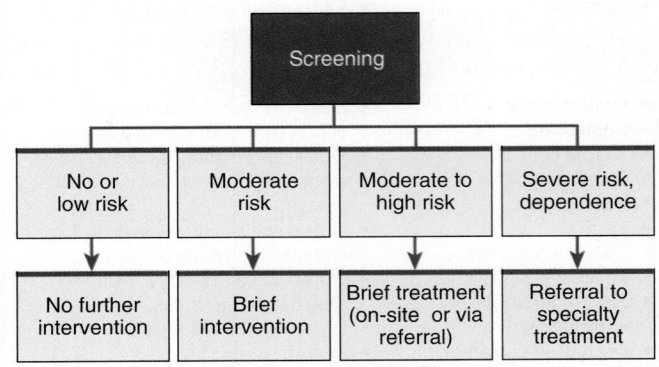

FIG 10.3 Screening, Brief Intervention, and Referral to Treatment approach. (From Substance Abuse and Mental Health Services Administration [SAMHSA]: Systems-level implementation of screening, brief intervention, and referral to treatment, Technical Assistance Publication [TAP] Series 33. HHS Publication No. 13-4741, Rockville, MD, 2013, SAMHSA. Retrieved from *www.integration.samhsa.gov/SBIRT/tap33.pdf*.)

TABLE 10.12 Brief Screening Tools for Substance Use

Single Question Tests

Use 1 of the following questions to screen for the presence of alcohol, drug, or tobacco use.

- How often in the past year have you had 5 (men) or 4 (women) or more drinks in a day?
- How many times in the past year have you used illegal drugs or prescription medications for nonmedical reasons?
- In the past year, how often have you used tobacco products?

2-Question Tests

Use the following 2 questions to screen for alcohol or drug use.

- In the past year, have you ever drunk or used drugs more than you meant to?
- Have you felt you wanted or needed to cut down on your drinking or drug use in the past year?

Adapted from Strobbe S: Prevention and screening, brief intervention, and referral to treatment for substance use in primary care, *Prim Care Clin Office Pract* 41:185, 2014.

TABLE 10.13 Alcohol Use Disorders Identification Test (AUDIT)

Please answer each question by checking 1 of the circles in the second column.

Question	Response	Score
1. How often do you have a drink containing alcohol?	Never	(0)
	Monthly or less	(1)
	2 to 4 times per month	(2)
	2 to 4 times per week	(3)
	4+ times per week	(4)
2. How many drinks containing alcohol do you have on a typical day when you are drinking?	1 or 2	(0)
	3 or 4	(1)
	5 or 6	(2)
	7 to 9	(3)
	10 or more	(4)
3. How often do you have 6 or more drinks on 1 occasion?	Never	(0)
	Less than monthly	(1)
	Monthly	(2)
	Weekly	(3)
	Daily or almost daily	(4)
4. How often during the last year have you found that you were not able to stop drinking once you had started?	Never	(0)
	Less than monthly	(1)
	Monthly	(2)
	Weekly	(3)
	Daily or almost daily	(4)
5. How often in the last year have you failed to do what was normally expected of you because you were drinking?	Never	(0)
	Less than monthly	(1)
	Monthly	(2)
	Weekly	(3)
	Daily or almost daily	(4)
6. How often during the last year have you needed a first drink in the morning to get yourself going after a heavy drinking session?	Never	(0)
	Less than monthly	(1)
	Monthly	(2)
	Weekly	(3)
	Daily or almost daily	(4)
7. How often during the last year have you had a feeling of guilt or remorse about drinking?	Never	(0)
	Less than monthly	(1)
	Monthly	(2)
	Weekly	(3)
	Daily or almost daily	(4)
8. How often during the last year have you been unable to remember what happened the night before because you had been drinking?	Never	(0)
	Less than monthly	(1)
	Monthly	(2)
	Weekly	(3)
	Daily or almost daily	(4)
9. Have you or someone else been injured as a result of your drinking?	No	(0)
	Yes, but not in the last year	(2)
	Yes, during the last year	(4)
10. Has a relative, friend, or other health worker been concerned about your drinking or suggested that you cut down?	No	(0)
	Yes, but not in the last year	(2)
	Yes, during the last year	(4)

Scoring for AUDIT: Questions 1 through 8 are scored 0, 1, 2, 3, or 4. Questions 9 and 10 are scored 0, 2, or 4 only. The minimum score (nondrinkers) is 0 and the maximum possible score is 40. A score of 9 or more indicates hazardous or harmful alcohol consumption.
Source: Babor TF, Higgins-Biddle JC, Saunders JB, Monteiro M: *The alcohol use disorders identification test,* ed 2, Geneva, Switzerland, 2001, WHO Press.

Identification Test, is shown in Table 10.13. A score of 8 points or more in men or 7 or more in women is concerning. Another useful tool is the Drug Abuse Screening Test (DAST-10), shown in Table 10.14.

If there is any sign of substance use, figure out when the patient last used the substance. Knowing this information will let you know when to expect the onset of withdrawal and help you anticipate drug interactions. Assess for factors that influence the onset of withdrawal, including the substance used, dose taken, method of intake, and length of time the patient has used the substance. You may discover that the patient is dealing with *polysubstance use,* or the use of more than 1 substance. Alert the HCP as these patients need care tailored to the combination of substances used.

You may find problems associated with substance use during your physical assessment. Assess the patient's general appearance and nutritional status. Examine the abdomen, skin, and cardiovascular, respiratory, and neurologic systems. The presence of a mental health disorder, such as anxiety, bipolar disorder, or depression, increases the risk for SUD. Serum and urine drug screens can identify the type and amounts of drugs present in the body. A complete blood count, serum electrolytes, blood urea nitrogen, creatinine, and liver function tests evaluate for electrolyte imbalances and cardiac, kidney, or liver dysfunction.

During your assessment, look for patient behaviors such as denial, avoidance, underreporting or minimizing substance use, or giving inaccurate information. Behaviors and physical manifestations suggesting substance use are outlined in Table 10.15. However, these behaviors are not all inclusive.

◆ Nursing Diagnoses

Nursing diagnoses for the patient with substance use disorder include:

- Substance abuse, drug, alcohol and/or tobacco
- Risk for injury
- Acute confusion
- Altered perception

◆ Planning

Nursing care focuses on the priority problems of reducing the risk for injury and managing acute confusion. The overall goals are that the patient with a substance use problem will (1) have normal physiologic functioning, (2) acknowledge a substance use problem, (3) explain the psychologic and physiologic effects of substance use, (4) abstain from substance use, and (5) cooperate with a proposed treatment plan.

TABLE 10.14 Drug Abuse Screening Test (DAST-10)

In the last 12 months:

1.	Have you used drugs other than those required for medical reasons?	No	Yes
2.	Do you abuse more than 1 drug at a time?	No	Yes
3.	Are you always able to stop using drugs when you want to?	No	Yes
4.	Have you had "blackouts" or "flashbacks" as a result of drug use?	No	Yes
5.	Do you ever feel bad or guilty about your drug use?	No	Yes
6.	Does your spouse (or parents) ever complain about your involvement with drugs?	No	Yes
7.	Have you neglected your family because of your use of drugs?	No	Yes
8.	Have you engaged in illicit activities in order to obtain drugs?	No	Yes
9.	Have you ever experienced withdrawal symptoms or felt sick when you stopped taking drugs?	No	Yes
10.	Have you had medical problems as a result of your drug use?	No	Yes

© 1982 by Harvey A. Skinner, PhD, and the Centre for Addiction and Mental Health, Toronto, Canada. You may reproduce this instrument for noncommercial use (clinical, research, training purposes) as long as you credit the author, Dr. Harvey A. Skinner, Dean, Faculty of Health, York University, Toronto, Canada.

TABLE 10.15 Findings Suggesting Substance Use

Physiologic
- Fatigue
- Insomnia
- Headaches
- Seizure disorder
- Changes in mood
- Anorexia, weight loss
- Vague physical complaints
- Appearing older than stated age, unkempt appearance
- Sexual dysfunction, decreased libido, erectile dysfunction
- Failure of standard doses of sedatives to have a therapeutic effect

Behavioral
- Overuse of mouthwash or toiletries
- Citations for driving while intoxicated or impaired
- Leisure activities that involve alcohol and/or other drugs
- Trauma secondary to falls, auto accidents, fights, or burns
- Financial problems, including those related to spending for substances
- Defensive or evasive answers to questions about substance use and its importance in the person's life
- Problems in areas of life function (e.g., frequent job changes; marital conflict, separation, or divorce; work-related accidents, tardiness, absenteeism; legal problems; social isolation, estranged from friends or family)

◆ Nursing Implementation

Health Promotion. Your role in health promotion includes prevention and early detection of substance use. Prevention measures include abstaining from harmful substances and limiting alcohol use. These measures decrease the risk for substance-related injury or illness. You can help prevent substance use problems by (1) teaching about the effects and negative outcomes of substance use and (2) providing support. Through screening, you have an opportunity to prevent patients from becoming dependent on alcohol and drugs. You can do this by using brief interventional techniques and helping patients access appropriate care through referral to treatment if they show risky behaviors or are already dependent.

Acute Intervention. The immediate result of overconsumption is acute toxicity or overdose. The patient may also present with trauma or injuries. The priority of care is supporting the patient's ABCs, especially respiratory status. In addition to treating injuries, provide supportive care until detoxification can occur. Nursing care includes frequently assessing neurologic status and vital signs, giving IV fluids to prevent dehydration, orienting to time and place, and implementing patient safety measures.

Sometimes, uncertainty exists as to what substances are involved. If the patient used multiple substances, a complex clinical picture can result. For example, a patient presents with toxicity and the health care team does not know what substances are involved. Although blood and urine tests will help identify the substances, treatment is started while waiting for the test results. The patient in this situation would usually receive naloxone. If the substance used is a barbiturate or another CNS depressant, naloxone will not help the patient, but it will not hurt the patient either. If the patient does not respond to a total dose of 10 mg of naloxone, it is unlikely opioids are involved.

Once acute health issues are resolved, provide a brief intervention to teach patients about the consequences of substance use and support behavioral change. When patients have a substance use problem, it is critical to motivate the patient to engage in long-term treatment. You are in a unique position to facilitate behavior change. When a patient seeks care for health problems related to substance use or when hospitalization interferes with the usual pattern of use, the patient's awareness of any substance use problem increases. Intervention at this time can promote behavior change. Take an active role in performing motivational interviewing and providing counseling aimed at cessation. (Motivational interviewing is discussed in Chapter 4.) Discuss the risks associated with substance use and provide feedback and advice. If the patient agrees, assist with referral to counseling or behavioral therapy.

⬛ Gerontologic Considerations: Substance Use

Substance use in older adults is a fast-growing and often hard to recognize problem. Older adults do not fit the image of users. For example, older users are less likely to binge drink and use different substances than younger users. The effects of alcohol and drugs can be mistaken for medical conditions common among older adults (e.g., hypertension, dementia). So, we may attribute substance use problems to another cause and not offer treatment. Some use alcohol or drugs to cope with grief and loss issues, such as the death of a spouse.[15]

Because of the higher rate of coexisting medical problems, older adults are at greater risk for medical problems associated with substance use. Common problems include liver damage and cardiovascular, GI, and endocrine problems. Substance use may cause confusion, delirium, memory loss, and neuromuscular impairment. Physiologic changes may lead to toxicity at levels that may not have been a problem at a younger age. Withdrawal symptoms may be more severe than in younger persons.

FIG 10.4 Older adults are often unaware of their substance use problems. (© Ned White/iStock/Thinkstock.)

It is important to screen older adults for substance use. Family members are important sources of information (Fig. 10.4). Other potential sources include friends, home health aides, meal delivery personnel, and staff members at senior citizen centers and long-term care facilities. It is important for you to discuss drug and alcohol use with older adult patients, including OTC and herbal drug use. Assess the patient's knowledge of currently used drugs. Common screening questionnaires may not identify an older adult with a substance use problem. The Short Michigan Alcoholism Screening Test–Geriatric version (SMAST-G) is a short-form alcoholism screening instrument for older adults *(www.consultgerirn.org)* that can identify older adults with potential AUD.

Smoking and other tobacco use is another issue. Those who have smoked for decades may feel unable to stop or believe there is no benefit to stopping at an advanced age. However, smoking contributes to and worsens many chronic illnesses found in the older adult population. Smoking cessation at any age is beneficial. The information about smoking cessation discussed earlier is appropriate for helping older adults with smoking cessation (Tables 10.3 to 10.6).

Patient teaching for the older adult includes teaching about the desired effects, possible side effects, and proper use of prescribed and OTC drugs. When you suspect alcohol or substance use, refer the patient for treatment. It is a mistaken belief that older people have little to gain from alcohol and drug dependence treatment. The rewards of treatment can lead to greater quality and quantity of life for older adults.

CASE STUDY

Substance Use Disorder

(©JPC-PROD/ iStock/Think- stock.)

Patient Profile

C.M., a 78-yr-old woman, is admitted to the emergency department after falling and injuring her right hip. She has been widowed for 4 years and lives alone. Recently her best friend died. Her only family is a daughter who lives out of town. When contacted by phone, the daughter tells the nurse that her mother has appeared more disoriented and confused over the past few months when she has talked to her on the phone.

Subjective Data

- Describing severe pain in her right hip
- Admits she had some wine in the late afternoon to stimulate her appetite
- Has experienced several falls in the past 2 months
- Reports that she fell after taking a prescribed sleeping pill because she does not sleep well
- Speech is hesitant and slurred
- Says she smokes about a half pack of cigarettes a day

Objective Data

Physical Examination

- Oriented to person and place, but not time
- BP 162/94, pulse 92, respirations 24
- Severe pain and tenderness in the right hip region
- Bilateral hand tremors

Diagnostic Tests

- X-ray reveals a subtrochanteric fracture of the right femur requiring surgical repair
- Blood alcohol concentration (BAC) 120 mg/dL (0.12%)
- Complete blood count: Hemoglobin 10.6 g/dL, hematocrit 33%

Discussion Questions

1. What other information is needed to assess C.M.'s condition?
2. How should you address questions about these areas?
3. What factors may contribute to C.M.'s substance use?
4. ***Priority Decision:*** Based on the assessment data given, what are the priority nursing diagnoses? Are there any collaborative problems?
5. ***Priority Decision:*** What are the priority nursing interventions during C.M.'s preoperative period?
6. What possible complications and injury risks may occur during C.M.'s postoperative recovery?
7. ***Safety:*** To ensure C.M.'s safety, what nursing interventions are necessary after surgery?
8. ***Delegation Decision:*** How would you use the unlicensed assistive personnel (UAP) on the postoperative unit to carry out the interventions that you identified in question 5?
9. ***Collaboration:*** What referrals are indicated?

Answers available at *http://evolve.elsevier.com/Lewis/medsurg.*

■ BRIDGE TO NCLEX EXAMINATION

The number of the question corresponds to the same-numbered outcome at the beginning of the chapter.

1. When admitting a patient, the nurse must assess the patient for substance use based on the knowledge that long-term use of addictive substances leads to
   a. the development of coexisting psychiatric illnesses.
   b. a higher risk for complications from underlying health problems.
   c. potentiation of effects of similar drugs taken when the person is drug free.
   d. increased availability of dopamine, resulting in decreased sleep requirements.

2. The nurse would suspect cocaine toxicity in the patient who is experiencing
   a. agitation, dysrhythmias, and seizures.
   b. blurred vision, restlessness, and irritability.
   c. diarrhea, nausea and vomiting, and confusion.
   d. slow, shallow respirations; bradycardia; and hypotension.

3. The *most* appropriate nursing intervention for a patient who is being treated for an acute exacerbation of chronic obstructive pulmonary disease who is not interested in quitting smoking is to
   a. accept the patient's decision and not intervene until the patient expresses a desire to quit.
   b. ask the patient to identify the risks and benefits of quitting and what barriers to quitting are present.
   c. realize that some smokers never quit, and trying to assist them increases the patient's frustration.
   d. motivate the patient to quit by describing how continued smoking will worsen the breathing problems.

4. While caring for a patient who is experiencing alcohol withdrawal, the nurse should *(select all that apply)*
   a. monitor neurologic status on a routine basis.
   b. provide a quiet, nonstimulating, dimly lit environment.
   c. pad the side rails and place suction equipment at the bedside.
   d. orient the patient to environment and person with each contact.
   e. give antiseizure drugs and sedatives to relieve withdrawal symptoms.

5. A patient admitted for scheduled surgery has a positive brief screening test result for an alcohol use disorder. Which initial action is *most* appropriate?
   a. Notify the health care provider.
   b. Complete a detailed alcohol use assessment.
   c. Initiate a referral to a specialty treatment center.
   d. Provide patient teaching on postoperative health risks.

6. Substance use problems in older adults are usually related to
   a. use of drugs and alcohol as a social activity.
   b. continuing the use of illegal drugs started during middle age.
   c. misuse of prescribed and over-the-counter medications and alcohol.
   d. a pattern of binge drinking for weeks or months with periods of sobriety.

1. b, 2. a, 3. b, 4. a, c, d, e, 5. b, 6. c

For rationales to these answers and even more NCLEX review questions, visit *http://evolve.elsevier.com/Lewis/medsurg.*

ⓔ EVOLVE WEBSITE/RESOURCES LIST

http://evolve.elsevier.com/Lewis/medsurg
Review Questions (Online Only)
Key Points
Answer Keys for Questions
- Rationales for Bridge to NCLEX Examination Questions
- Answer Guidelines for Case Study on p. 153
- Answer Guidelines for Managing Care of Multiple Patients Case Study (Section 2) on p. 155

Nursing Care Plan
- eNursing Care Plan 10.1: Patient in Alcohol Withdrawal

Conceptual Care Map Creator
Audio Glossary
Content Updates

REFERENCES

1. American Psychiatric Association: *The diagnostic and statistical manual of mental disorders*, 5th ed, Arlington, VA, 2013, The Association. (Classic)
2. Centers for Disease Control and Prevention: Adult cigarette smoking in the U.S. Retrieved from *www.cdc.gov/tobacco/data_statistics/fact_sheets/adult_data/cig_smoking.*
3. Centers for Disease Control and Prevention: Health effects of cigarette smoking. Retrieved from *www.cdc.gov/tobacco/data_statistics/fact_sheets/health_effects/effects_cig_smoking/#overview.*

*4. Breland A, Soule E, Lopez A, et al: Electronic cigarettes: What are they and what do they do? *Ann NY Acad Sci* 1394:5, 2017.
5. Agency for Healthcare Research and Quality: Treating tobacco use and dependence: 2008 update. Retrieved from *www.ahrq.gov/professionals/clinicians-providers/guidelines-recommendations/tobacco/index.html.*
6. Alcohol facts and statistics. Retrieved from *www.niaaa.nih.gov/alcohol-health/overview-alcohol-consumption/alcohol-facts-and-statistics.*
*7. Gortney JS, Raub JN, Patel P, et al: Alcohol withdrawal syndrome in medical patients, *Cleve Clin J Med* 83:67, 2016.
*8. Sutton LJ, Jutel A: Alcohol withdrawal syndrome in critically ill patients: Identification, assessment, and management, *Crit Care Nurse* 36:28, 2016.
*9. Rasimas JJ, Sinclair CM: Assessment and management of toxidromes in the critical care unit, *Crit Care Clin* 33:521, 2017.
10. Centers for Disease Control and Prevention: Understanding the epidemic. Retrieved from *www.cdc.gov/drugoverdose/epidemic/index.html.*
*11. Donroe JH, Holt SR, Tetrault JM: Caring for patients with opioid use disorder in the hospital, *CMAJ* 188:17, 2016.
*12. Phillips J, Lim F, Hsu R: Synthetic cannabinoid poisoning: A growing health concern, *Nursing* 46:34, 2016.
*13. Bonnet U, Preuss UW: Cannabis withdrawal syndrome: Current insights, *Subst Abuse Rehabil* 8:9, 2017.
14. SAMSA-HRSA Center for Integrated Health Solutions: SBIRT. Retrieved from *www.samhsa.gov/sbirt.*
*15. Masferrer L, Garre-Olmo J, Caparrós B: Is complicated grief a risk factor for substance use? *Addict Research Theory* 9:1, 2017.

*Evidence-based information for clinical practice.

CASE STUDY

Managing Care of Multiple Patients

You are assigned to care for the following 5 patients on a medical-surgical unit. Your team consists of yourself, a new LPN still on orientation, and a UAP.

Patients

(© Luevanos/ iStock/Thinkstock.)

M.S. is an 81-yr-old woman who came to the United States from India 4 years ago with her daughter, son-in-law, and their 4 children. She speaks minimal English, relying on her oldest granddaughter to translate. M.S., who has a history of diabetes, was admitted to the hospital yesterday with a diagnosis of heart failure.

(© Thomas M Perkins/ Shutterstock.)

M.L. is a 60-yr-old Asian woman who was admitted to the hospital with a diagnosis of exacerbation of chronic obstructive pulmonary disease (COPD). She is receiving O_2 at 2 L/min via nasal cannula. Her condition is currently stable.

(© azndc/iStock/ Thinkstock.)

C.L. is a 73-yr-old Taiwanese woman who was brought to the ED by her son. Her chief complaint is shortness of breath. She has a history of COPD, hypertension, and diabetes. She was diagnosed with community-acquired pneumonia, which is being treated with IV antibiotics.

(© azndc/iStock/ Thinkstock.)

K.C. is a 280-lb (127-kg) 68-yr-old black man with diabetes who was admitted for incision and drainage of a right abdominal abscess. He is being discharged on his second postoperative day. His daughter will assist with dressing changes at home.

(© JPC-PROD/ iStock/Thinkstock.)

C.M. is a 78-yr-old woman who was admitted from the ED after falling and fracturing her right hip. She is in Buck's traction and is scheduled to undergo surgical repair later this morning. She has a history of substance use, and her blood alcohol content (BAC) was 120 mg/dL (0.12 %) on admission. The night nurse reports that she has been confused and restless overnight.

Discussion Questions

1. ***Priority Decision:*** After receiving report, which patient should you see first? Provide rationale.
2. ***Collaboration:*** Which morning task(s) could you delegate to the LPN *(select all that apply)*?
   a. Obtain a capillary blood glucose reading on K.C.
   b. Assess C.L.'s IV site for signs of phlebitis or infiltration.
   c. Access the hospital's available translation services for M.S.
   d. Provide discharge teaching on wound care for K.C. and her daughter.
   e. Titrate M.L.'s O_2 to obtain a pulse oximetry reading of 95% (as ordered by the HCP).
3. ***Priority and Collaboration:*** When you and the LPN enter M.S.'s room, you find her sitting up in bed with labored respirations. Although you cannot understand what she is saying, you note that she is unable to say more than a few words without stopping for a breath. Which initial action would be the most appropriate?
   a. Give M.S.'s cardiac and respiratory medications and reassess her in 30 minutes.
   b. Ask the LPN to stay with M.S. while you go to the nurse's station to call the HCP.
   c. Have the LPN find M.S.'s granddaughter so that she can translate what M.S. is trying to tell you.
   d. Ask the LPN to obtain an O_2 saturation and vital signs while you perform a respiratory assessment.

Case Study Progression

M.S.'s assessment reveals bibasilar crackles, 2+ dependent pitting edema, BP 175/84, pulse 116, RR 32, temp 36.8°C, and pulse oximetry 88% on room air. You apply O_2 at 4 L/min via nasal cannula and obtain an order from M.S.'s HCP for furosemide 40 mg IV stat. After giving the diuretic, M.S.'s granddaughter arrives and you discuss her grandmother's condition. She tells you that her grandmother asked her to bring in potato chips and soda yesterday. She did not think her grandmother should be eating salt, but M.S. insisted that the dietitian said that she could eat them.

4. On further investigation, the dietitian tells you that an interpreter (translator) was not available when she saw M.S. yesterday. Because the dietitian did not understand what the patient was saying, she could not respond to her questions. She planned to visit M.S. today when the granddaughter is present. Being a culturally competent nurse, you realize that M.S. most likely interpreted the dietitian's silence as
   a. agreement with what A.Z. was asking.
   b. demonstrating a lack of respect for A.Z.'s wishes.
   c. a lack of understanding by the dietitian as to what she was asking.
   d. a need for the dietitian to get more information before answering her questions.
5. Which assessment findings may suggest elder mistreatment by C.L.'s son with whom she lives *(select all that apply)*?
   a. 2 sacral ulcers
   b. Asking when her son is coming to visit
   c. Multiple small bruises on her forearms and shins
   d. Matted hair, poor oral hygiene, overgrown toenails
   e. C.L. becomes totally silent when her son comes to visit
6. Knowing that C.M.'s confusion and restlessness overnight may indicate acute alcohol withdrawal, you perform a more thorough assessment. Your assessment reveals a score of 11 on the Clinical Institute Withdrawal Assessment for Alcohol Scale. To prevent alcohol delirium, you plan to give which medication per the HCP's order?
   a. morphine
   b. naloxone
   c. lorazepam
   d. IV thiamine
7. ***Priority Decision:*** You assess C.M. and find her trying to pull out the IV line and remove the Buck's traction. What action should you do *first*?
   a. Have the UAP stay with C.M.
   b. Ask C.M.'s daughter to stay with her.
   c. Obtain a restraint order from the HCP.
   d. Move C.M. to a room closer to the nurse's station.
8. ***Management Decision:*** The UAP informs you that the LPN is not following C.L.'s fall risk protocol. What is your most appropriate action?
   a. Notify the unit manager as soon as possible.
   b. Ask the UAP to explain hospital protocol to the LPN.
   c. Write up the LPN's actions so they will be included in her evaluation.
   d. Talk to the LPN about the importance of following protocol to prevent C.L. from sustaining a fall-related injury.

11

Inflammation and Healing

Catherine R. Ratliff

A kind gesture can reach a wound only compassion can heal.

Steve Maraboli

http://evolve.elsevier.com/Lewis/medsurg/

CONCEPTUAL FOCUS

Health Promotion	Pain	Tissue Integrity
Inflammation	Perfusion	
Nutrition	Sensory Perception	

LEARNING OUTCOMES

1. Describe the inflammatory response, including vascular and cellular responses and exudate formation.
2. Explain local and systemic manifestations of inflammation and their physiologic bases.
3. Describe the drug therapy, nutrition therapy, and nursing management of inflammation.
4. Distinguish among healing by primary, secondary, and tertiary intention.
5. Describe the factors that delay wound healing and common complications of wound healing.
6. Describe the nursing and interprofessional management of wound healing.
7. Explain the etiology and clinical manifestations of pressure injuries.
8. Apply a patient risk assessment for pressure injuries to measures used to prevent the development of pressure injuries.
9. Discuss nursing and interprofessional management of a patient with pressure injuries.

KEY TERMS

This chapter focuses on inflammation, wound healing, and pressure injury prevention and management. Maintaining skin and tissue integrity is a key nursing role. Multiple concepts are closely related to tissue integrity. Adequate nutrition and perfusion are essential so that the body has the necessary factors to promote healing when injury occurs. Impaired mobility and sensory perception increase the risk for injury. When injury does occur, pain and problems regulating temperature and fluid and electrolyte balance are common.

INFLAMMATORY RESPONSE

The **inflammatory response** is a sequential reaction to cell injury. It neutralizes and dilutes the inflammatory agent, removes necrotic materials, and establishes an environment suitable for healing and repair. The term *inflammation* is often incorrectly used as a synonym for *infection*. Inflammation is always present with infection, but infection is not always present with inflammation. However, a person who is neutropenic may not be able to mount an inflammatory response. An infection involves invasion of tissues or cells by microorganisms, such as bacteria, fungi, and viruses. In contrast, heat, radiation, trauma, chemicals, allergens, and an autoimmune reaction also can cause inflammation.

The mechanism of inflammation is basically the same regardless of the injuring agent. The intensity of the response depends on the extent and severity of injury and on the injured person's reactive capacity. The inflammatory response can be

PATHOPHYSIOLOGY MAP

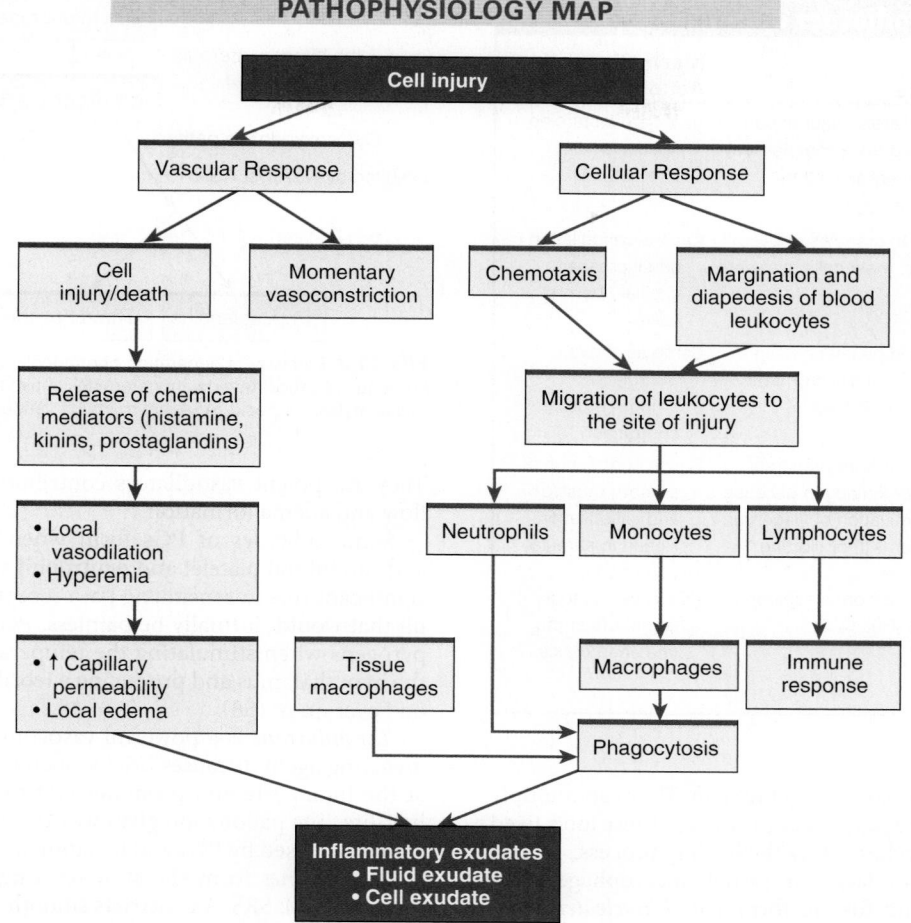

FIG 11.1 Vascular and cellular responses to tissue injury.

divided into a vascular response, cellular response, formation of exudate, and healing. Fig. 11.1 shows the vascular and cellular response to injury.

Vascular Response

After cell injury, local arterioles briefly undergo transient vasoconstriction. After release of histamine and other chemicals by the injured cells, the vessels dilate. Chemical mediators cause increased capillary permeability and facilitate fluid movement from capillaries into tissue spaces. At first this inflammatory exudate is made up of serous fluid. Later, it contains plasma proteins, primarily albumin. These proteins exert oncotic pressure that further draws fluid from blood vessels. Both vasodilation and increased capillary permeability are responsible for redness, heat, and swelling at the site of injury and the surrounding area.

As the plasma protein fibrinogen leaves the blood, it is activated to fibrin by the products of the injured cells. Fibrin strengthens a blood clot formed by platelets. In tissues, the clot functions to trap bacteria, prevent their spread, and serve as a framework for the healing process. Platelets release growth factors that start the healing process.

Cellular Response

Neutrophils and monocytes move from circulation to the site of injury (Fig. 11.1). *Chemotaxis* is the directional migration of

white blood cells (WBCs) to the site of injury, resulting in an accumulation of neutrophils and monocytes at the site.

Neutrophils. Neutrophils are the first WBCs to arrive at the injury site (usually within 6 to 12 hours). They phagocytize (engulf) bacteria, other foreign material, and damaged cells. With their short life span (24 to 48 hours), dead neutrophils soon accumulate. In time, a mixture of dead neutrophils, digested bacteria, and other cell debris accumulates as a creamy substance called *pus*.

To keep up with the demand for neutrophils, the bone marrow releases more neutrophils into circulation. This results in a high WBC count, especially the neutrophil count. Mature neutrophils are called *segmented neutrophils*. Sometimes the demand for neutrophils increases to the extent that the bone marrow releases immature forms of neutrophils *(bands)* into circulation. We call an increased number of band neutrophils in circulation a *shift to the left*. It is common in patients with acute bacterial infections. (See Chapter 29 for a discussion of neutrophils.)

Monocytes. Monocytes are the second type of phagocytic cells that migrate from circulating blood. They usually arrive at the site within 3 to 7 days after the onset of inflammation. On entering the tissue spaces, monocytes transform into macrophages. Together with the tissue macrophages, these newly arrived macrophages help in phagocytosis of the inflammatory debris. The macrophage role is important in cleaning the area before healing

TABLE 11.1 Mediators of Inflammation

Mediator	Source	Mechanisms of Action
Complement components (C3a, C4a, C5a)	Anaphylatoxic agents generated from complement pathway activation	Stimulate histamine release and chemotaxis
Cytokines	See Table 13.3	
Histamine	Stored in granules of basophils, mast cells, platelets	Causes vasodilation and increased capillary permeability
Serotonin	Stored in platelets, mast cells, enterochromaffin cells of GI tract	Same as above. Stimulates smooth muscle contraction
Kinins (e.g., bradykinin)	Produced from precursor factor kininogen because of activation of Hageman factor (XII) of clotting system	Cause contraction of smooth muscle and vasodilation. Result in stimulation of pain
Prostaglandins (PGs) **and leukotrienes** (LTs)	Produced from arachidonic acid (Fig. 11.2)	PGs cause vasodilation. LTs stimulate chemotaxis

FIG 11.2 Pathway of generation of prostaglandins, thromboxane, and leukotrienes. Corticosteroids, nonsteroidal antiinflammatory drugs *(NSAIDs)*, and acetylsalicylic acid *(ASA)* act to inhibit various steps in this pathway.

can occur. Macrophages have a long life span. They can multiply and may stay in the damaged tissues for weeks. These long-lived cells are important in orchestrating the healing process.

When particles are too large for a single macrophage, macrophages accumulate and fuse to form a *multinucleated giant cell.* Collagen encapsulates this giant cell, leading to the formation of a granuloma. A classic example of this process occurs in tuberculosis of the lung. While the *Mycobacterium* bacillus is walled off, a chronic state of inflammation exists. The granuloma formed is a cavity of necrotic tissue.

Lymphocytes. Lymphocytes arrive later at the site of injury. Their primary role is related to humoral and cell-mediated immunity (see Chapter 13).

Chemical Mediators

Mediators of the inflammatory response are outlined in Table 11.1.

Complement System. The complement system is an enzyme cascade (C1 to C9) consisting of pathways to mediate inflammation and destroy invading pathogens. Major functions of the complement system are enhanced phagocytosis, increased vascular permeability, chemotaxis, and cellular lysis. All these activities are important mediators of the inflammatory response and healing.

Cell lysis occurs when the final components create holes in the cell membranes and cause targeted cell death by membrane rupture. In autoimmune disorders, complement activation and the resulting inflammatory response can damage healthy tissue. Examples of this include rheumatoid arthritis and systemic lupus erythematosus.

Prostaglandins and Leukotrienes. When cells are activated by injury, the arachidonic acid in the cell membrane is rapidly converted to produce prostaglandins (PGs), thromboxane, and leukotrienes (Fig. 11.2). PGs are considered proinflammatory.

They are potent vasodilators contributing to increased blood flow and edema formation.

Some subtypes of PGs form when platelets are activated and can inhibit platelet and neutrophil aggregation. PGs have a significant role in sensitizing pain receptors to arousal by stimuli that would normally be painless. PGs have a pivotal role as pyrogens when stimulating the temperature-regulating area of the hypothalamus and producing a febrile response (see section on Fever on p. 158).

Thromboxane is a powerful vasoconstrictor and platelet-aggregating agent. It causes brief vasoconstriction and skin pallor at the injury site and promotes clot formation. It has a short half-life. The pallor soon gives way to vasodilation and redness, which is caused by PGs and histamine.

Leukotrienes form the slow-reacting substance of anaphylaxis (SRS-A). SRS-A constricts smooth muscles of the bronchi, causing narrowing of the airway, and increases capillary permeability, leading to airway edema.

Exudate Formation

Exudate consists of fluid and WBCs that move from the circulation to the site of injury. The nature and quantity of exudate depend on the type and severity of the injury and tissues involved (Table 11.2).

Clinical Manifestations

The *local* manifestations of inflammation include redness, heat, pain, swelling, and loss of function (Table 11.3 and Fig. 11.3). *Systemic* manifestations include an increased WBC count with a shift to the left, malaise, nausea and anorexia, increased pulse and respiratory rate, and fever.

Leukocytosis results from the increased release of WBCs from the bone marrow. The causes of other systemic manifestations may be related to complement activation and the release of *cytokines* (soluble factors secreted by WBCs and other types of cells that act as intercellular and intracellular messengers). Some cytokines (e.g., interleukins [ILs], tumor necrosis factor [TNF]) are important in causing fever and other systemic manifestations of inflammation. An increase in pulse and respiration follows the rise in metabolism because of an increase in body temperature. (Cytokines are discussed in Chapter 13.)

Fever. The release of cytokines triggers the onset of fever. Cytokines cause fever by initiating metabolic changes in the temperature-regulating center in the hypothalamus (Fig. 11.4). The synthesis of PGs is the most critical metabolic change. PGs

TABLE 11.2 Types of Inflammatory Exudate

Type	Description	Examples
Catarrhal	Found in tissues where cells produce mucus Inflammatory response accelerates mucus production	Runny nose associated with upper respiratory tract infection
Fibrinous	Occurs with increasing vascular permeability and fibrinogen leakage into interstitial spaces Excessive amounts of fibrin that coats tissue surfaces may cause them to adhere	Adhesions, gelatinous ribbons seen in surgical drain tubing Frequently covers fluid-exuding wounds, such as venous injuries
Hemorrhagic	Results from rupture or necrosis of blood vessel walls	Hematoma, bleeding after surgery or tissue trauma
Purulent (pus)	Consists of WBCs, microorganisms (dead and alive), liquefied dead cells, and other debris	Furuncle (boil), abscess, cellulitis (diffuse inflammation in connective tissue)
Serosanguinous	Found during the midpoint in healing after surgery or tissue injury Composed of RBCs and serous fluid, which is semiclear pink and may have red streaks	Surgical drain fluid
Serous	Results from outpouring of fluid. Seen in early stages of inflammation or when injury is mild	Skin blisters, pleural effusion

TABLE 11.3 Local Manifestations of Inflammation

Manifestations	Cause
Heat	Increased metabolism at inflammatory site
Loss of function	Swelling and pain
Pain	Change in pH. Nerve stimulation by chemicals (e.g., histamine, prostaglandins). Pressure from fluid exudate
Redness	Hyperemia from vasodilation
Swelling	Fluid shift to interstitial spaces. Fluid exudate accumulation

FIG 11.3 Inflammation secondary to postoperative deep wound infection after wrist surgery. (From Hayden RJ, Jebson PJL: Wrist arthrodesis, *Hand Clin* 21[4]:631, 2005.)

FIG 11.4 Production of fever. When monocytes/macrophages are activated, they secrete cytokines such as interleukin-1 *(IL-1)*, interleukin-6 *(IL-6)*, and tumor necrosis factor *(TNF)*, which reach the hypothalamic temperature-regulating center. These cytokines promote the synthesis and secretion of prostaglandin E_2 *(PGE$_2$)* in the anterior hypothalamus. PGE$_2$ increases the thermostatic set point, and the autonomic nervous system is stimulated, resulting in shivering, muscle contraction, and peripheral vasoconstriction.

act directly to increase the thermostatic set point. The hypothalamus then activates the autonomic nervous system to stimulate increased muscle tone and shivering and decreased perspiration and blood flow to the periphery. Epinephrine released from the adrenal medulla increases the metabolic rate. The net result is fever.

With the physiologic thermostat raised to a higher-than-normal temperature, the body increases heat production and conservation until the temperature reaches that new set point. At this point, the person feels chilled and shivers. The shivering response is the body's method of raising the body's temperature to the new set point.[1] This seeming paradox is dramatic: the body is hot, yet the person piles on blankets and may go to bed to get warm. When the body temperature reaches the set point, the chills and warmth-seeking behavior cease.

The released cytokines and the fever that they trigger activate the body's defense mechanisms. Beneficial aspects of fever include increased killing of microorganisms, increased phagocytosis by neutrophils, and increased proliferation of T cells. Higher body temperatures may enhance the activity of interferon, the body's natural virus-fighting substance (see Chapter 13).

Types of Inflammation

The basic types of inflammation are acute, subacute, and chronic. In *acute inflammation,* the healing occurs in 2 to 3 weeks and usually leaves no residual damage. Neutrophils are the predominant cell type at the site of inflammation. A *subacute inflammation* has the features of the acute process but lasts longer. For example, infective endocarditis is a smoldering infection with acute inflammation, but it lasts for weeks or months (see Chapter 36).

Chronic inflammation lasts for weeks, months, or even years. The injurious agent persists or repeatedly injures tissue. The predominant cell types present at the site of inflammation are lymphocytes and macrophages. Examples of chronic inflammation include rheumatoid arthritis and osteomyelitis. The prolongation and chronicity of any inflammation may be the result of an alteration in the immune response (e.g., autoimmune disease) and can lead to physical deterioration.

❖ NURSING AND INTERPROFESSIONAL MANAGEMENT: INFLAMMATION

◆ Nursing Implementation

◆ **Health Promotion.** The best management of inflammation is the prevention of infection, trauma, surgery, and contact with potentially harmful agents. This is not always possible. A simple mosquito bite causes an inflammatory response. Because occasional injury is inevitable, concerted efforts to minimize inflammation and infection are needed.

Adequate nutrition is essential so that the body has the necessary factors to promote healing when injury occurs. A high fluid intake will replace fluid loss from perspiration. There is a 7% increase in metabolism for every 1°F increase in temperature above 100°F (37.8°C), or a 13% increase for every 1°C increase. The increased metabolic rate increases a patient's need for calories.

Early recognition of inflammation is essential so that appropriate treatment can begin. This may be rest, drug therapy, or specific treatment of the injured site. Immediate treatment may prevent the extension and complications of inflammation.

◆ Acute Care

Observation and Vital Signs. The ability to recognize the manifestations of inflammation is important. In the immunosuppressed person (e.g., taking corticosteroids, receiving chemotherapy), the classic manifestations of inflammation may be masked. The early symptoms of inflammation may be malaise or "just not feeling well."

Vital signs are important to note with any inflammation, especially when an infectious process is present. With infection, the temperature may rise, and pulse and respiration rates may increase.

Fever. An important aspect of fever management is determining its cause. Although many regard fever as harmful, an increase in body temperature is an important host defense mechanism. In the seventeenth century, Thomas Sydenham noted that "fever is a mighty engine which nature brings into the world for the conquest of her enemies."[2]

Steps are often taken to lower body temperature to relieve anxiety of the patient and health care professionals. Because mild to moderate fever usually does little harm, imposes no great discomfort, and may help host defense mechanisms, antipyretic drugs are rarely essential to patient welfare. Moderate fevers (up to 103°F [39.4°C]) usually produce few problems in most patients. However, if the patient is very young or very old, is extremely uncomfortable, or has a significant medical problem (e.g., severe heart or lung disease, brain injury), antipyretic use should be considered. Fever in the immunosuppressed patient should be treated immediately with antibiotic therapy because infections can rapidly progress to septicemia. (Neutropenia is discussed in Chapter 30 on pp. 631.)

Fever, especially if greater than 104°F (40°C), can damage body cells, and delirium and seizures can occur. At temperatures

TABLE 11.4   Drug Therapy

Inflammation and Healing

Drug	Mechanism of Action
Antipyretic Drugs	
Acetaminophen (Tylenol)	Inhibits synthesis of prostaglandins (PGs). Lowers temperature by action on heat-regulating center in hypothalamus
NSAIDs (e.g., ibuprofen [Advil])	Inhibit synthesis of PGs
Salicylates (aspirin)	Inhibit synthesis of PGs (Fig. 11.2). Lower temperature by action on heat-regulating center in hypothalamus, resulting in peripheral vasodilation and heat loss
Antiinflammatory Drugs	
Corticosteroids (e.g., prednisone)	Interfere with tissue granulation, induce immunosuppressive effects (decreased lymphocyte synthesis), prevent liberation of lysosomes
NSAIDs (e.g., ibuprofen, piroxicam [Feldene])	Inhibit synthesis of PGs
Salicylates (aspirin)	Inhibit synthesis of PGs, reduce capillary permeability
Vitamins	
Vitamin A	Accelerates epithelialization
Vitamin B complex	Acts as coenzymes
Vitamin C	Aids in synthesis of collagen and new capillaries
Vitamin D	Facilitates calcium absorption

greater than 105.8°F (41°C), the hypothalamic temperature control center becomes impaired. Damage can occur to many cells, including those in the brain.

Older adults have a blunted febrile response to infection. The body temperature may not rise to the level expected for a younger adult, or there may be a delay in the onset of the rise. The blunted response can delay diagnosis and treatment. By the time fever (as defined for younger adults) is present, the illness may be more severe. Patients who are taking nonsteroidal antiinflammatory drugs (NSAIDs) on a regular basis (e.g., for rheumatoid arthritis) may have a blunted febrile response.

Although sponge baths increase evaporative heat loss, they may not decrease the body temperature unless the person received antipyretic drugs to lower the set point. Otherwise, the body will initiate compensatory mechanisms (e.g., shivering) to restore body heat. The same principle applies to the use of cooling blankets. They are most effective in lowering body temperature after the set point has been lowered.

A nursing care plan for the patient with a fever (eNursing Care Plan 11.1) is available on the website for this chapter at *http://evolve.elsevier.com/Lewis/medsurg.*

Drug Therapy. Drugs can decrease the inflammatory response and lower the body temperature (Table 11.4). Aspirin blocks PG synthesis in the hypothalamus and elsewhere in the body. Acetaminophen acts on the heat-regulating center in the hypothalamus. Some NSAIDs (e.g., ibuprofen [Motrin, Advil]) have antipyretic effects. Corticosteroids are antipyretic through the dual actions of preventing cytokine production and PG synthesis. This results in dilation of superficial blood vessels, increased skin temperature, and sweating.

❓ CHECK YOUR PRACTICE

A 76-yr-old female patient has acute osteomyelitis after a fractured femur. You are checking her temperature every 2 hours and giving acetaminophen when it is higher than 102° F. However, you notice that her temperature is fluctuating from 96° to 103° F.
• What should you do?

Antipyretics cause a sharp decrease in temperature. They should be given around the clock to prevent acute swings in temperature. Giving them intermittently can induce or perpetuate chills. When the antipyretic wears off, the body may initiate a compensatory involuntary muscular contraction (i.e., chill) to raise the body temperature back up to its previous level. We can prevent this unpleasant side effect by giving them regularly at 2- to 4-hour intervals.

Antihistamine drugs may be used to inhibit the action of histamine. Antihistamines are discussed in Chapters 13 and 26.

RICE. **R**est, **i**ce, **c**ompression, and **e**levation (RICE) is a key concept in treating soft tissue injuries and related inflammation.

Rest. Rest helps the body use its nutrients and O_2 for the healing process. The repair process is facilitated by allowing fibrin and collagen to form across the wound edges with little disruption.

Cold and heat. Cold application is usually appropriate at the time of the initial trauma. Use promotes vasoconstriction and decreases swelling, pain, and congestion from increased metabolism in the area of inflammation. Heat may be used later (e.g., after 24 to 48 hours) to promote healing by increasing the circulation to the inflamed site and subsequent removal of debris. Heat is used to localize the inflammatory agents. Warm, moist heat may help debride the wound site if necrotic material is present.

Compression and immobilization. Compression counters the vasodilation effects and development of edema. Compression by direct pressure over a laceration occludes blood vessels and stops bleeding. Compression bandages support injured joints when tendons and muscles are unable to provide support on their own. Assess distal pulses and capillary refill before and after application of compression to evaluate whether compression has compromised circulation (e.g., pale color of skin, loss of feeling).

Immobilization of the inflamed or injured area promotes healing by decreasing the tissues' metabolic needs. Immobilization with a cast or splint supports fractured bones and prevents further tissue injury from sharp bone fragments that could sever nerves or blood vessels, causing hemorrhage. As with compression, evaluate the patient's circulation after application and at regular intervals. Swelling can occur within the closed space of a cast and compromise circulation.

Elevation. Elevating the injured extremity above the level of the heart reduces the edema at the inflammatory site by increasing venous and lymphatic return. Elevation helps reduce pain associated with blood engorgement at the injury site. Elevation may be contraindicated in patients with significantly reduced arterial circulation.

TABLE 11.5	**Regenerative Ability of Different Types of Tissues**	
Tissues	**Cell Type**	**Description**
Skin, lymphoid organs, bone marrow, and mucous membranes	Labile cells	Cells divide constantly. Injury to these organs is followed by rapid regeneration.
Liver, pancreas, kidney, and bone cells	Stable cells	Retain their ability to regenerate but do so only if the organ is injured. Regeneration is slow.
Neurons of the central nervous system (CNS) and skeletal and cardiac muscle cells	Permanent cells	Do not divide. Damage to CNS neurons or skeletal or heart muscle can lead to permanent loss. Healing of skeletal and cardiac muscle will occur by repair with scar tissue. If neurons in the CNS are destroyed, the tissue is generally replaced by glial cells. Neurogenesis may occur from stem cells (see Chapter 55).

HEALING PROCESS

The last phase of the inflammatory response is healing. Healing includes 2 major components: regeneration and repair.

Regeneration

Regeneration is the replacement of lost cells and tissues with cells of the same type. The ability of cells to regenerate depends on the cell type (Table 11.5).

Repair

Repair is healing, with connective tissue replacing lost cells. Repair is the more common type of healing and usually results in scar formation. Repair is a more complex process than regeneration. Most injuries heal by connective tissue repair. Repair healing occurs by primary, secondary, or tertiary intention (Fig. 11.5).

Primary Intention. Primary intention healing takes place when wound margins are neatly approximated, as in a surgical incision or a paper cut. A continuum of processes is associated with primary healing (Table 11.6). These processes include 3 phases.

Initial Phase. In the *initial* (inflammatory) phase, the edges of the incision are aligned and sutured (or stapled) in place. The incision area fills with blood from the cut blood vessels, blood clots form, and platelets release growth factors to begin the healing process. This forms a matrix for WBC migration. An acute inflammatory reaction occurs.

The area of injury is composed of fibrin clots, erythrocytes, neutrophils (dead and dying), and other debris. Macrophages ingest and digest cellular debris, fibrin fragments, and red blood cells (RBCs). Extracellular enzymes derived from macrophages and neutrophils help digest fibrin. As the wound debris is removed, the fibrin clot serves as a meshwork for future capillary growth and migration of epithelial cells.

Granulation Phase. The *granulation* phase is the second step. The components of granulation tissue include proliferating

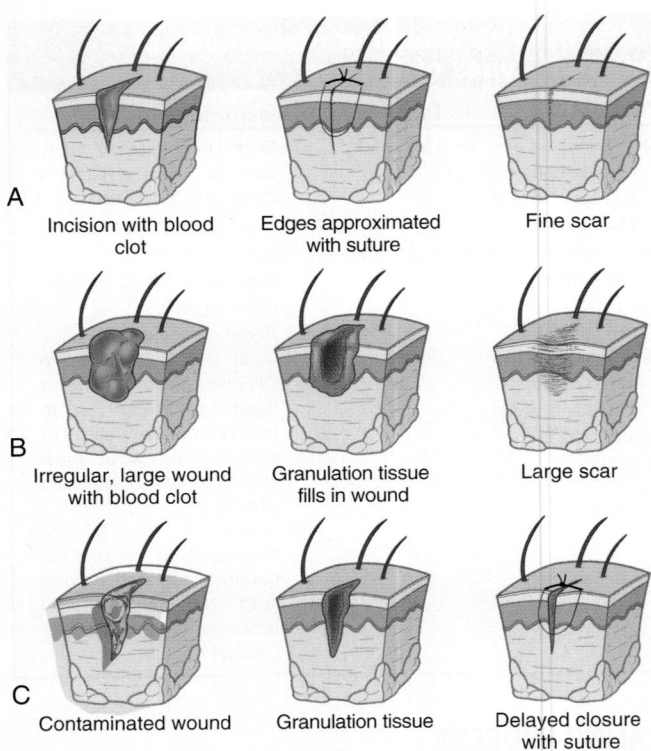

A
Incision with blood clot | Edges approximated with suture | Fine scar

B
Irregular, large wound with blood clot | Granulation tissue fills in wound | Large scar

C
Contaminated wound | Granulation tissue | Delayed closure with suture

FIG 11.5 Types of wound healing. **A**, Primary intention. **B**, Secondary intention. **C**, Tertiary intention.

TABLE 11.6	**Phases in Primary Intention Healing**	
Phase	**Duration**	**Description**
Initial	3 to 5 days	Approximation of incision edges. Migration of epithelial cells. Clot serving as meshwork for starting capillary growth
Granulation	5 days to 4 weeks	Migration of fibroblasts. Secretion of collagen. Abundance of capillary buds. Wound fragile
Maturation and scar contraction	7 days to several months	Remodeling of collagen. Strengthening of scar

fibroblasts; proliferating capillary sprouts *(angioblasts)*; various WBCs; exudate; and loose, semifluid, ground substance.

Fibroblasts are immature connective tissue cells that migrate into the healing site and secrete collagen. In time, the collagen is organized and restructured to strengthen the healing site. At this stage, it is called *fibrous* or *scar tissue*.

During the granulation phase, the wound is pink and vascular. Numerous red granules (young budding capillaries) are present. At this point, the wound is friable, at risk for dehiscence (Fig. 11.6), and resistant to infection.

Surface epithelium at the wound edges begins to regenerate. In a few days, a thin layer of epithelium migrates across the wound surface in a 1-cell-thick layer until it contacts cells spreading from

FIG 11.6 Dehiscence after a cholecystectomy. (From Bale S, Jones V: *Wound care nursing: A patient-centered approach,* ed 2, St Louis, 2006, Mosby.)

the opposite direction. The epithelium thickens and begins to mature, and the wound now closely resembles the adjacent skin. In a superficial wound, re-epithelialization may take 3 to 5 days.

Maturation Phase and Scar Contraction. The *maturation* phase, during which scar contraction occurs, overlaps with the granulation phase. It may begin 7 days after the injury and continue for several months or years. This is the reason abdominal surgery discharge instructions limit lifting for up to 6 weeks.

Collagen fibers are further organized, and the remodeling process occurs. Fibroblasts disappear as the wound becomes stronger. The active movement of the myofibroblasts causes contraction of the healing area, helping to close the defect and bring the skin edges closer together. A mature scar is then formed. In contrast to granulation tissue, a mature scar is virtually avascular and pale. The scar may be more painful at this phase than in the granulation phase.

Secondary Intention. Wounds that occur from trauma, injury, and infection have large amounts of exudate and wide, irregular wound margins with extensive tissue loss. These wounds may have edges that cannot be *approximated* (brought together). The inflammatory reaction may be greater than in primary healing. This results in more debris, cells, and exudate. We may have to clear the debris away *(debride)* before healing can take place.

The process of healing by secondary intention is essentially the same as healing by primary intention. The major differences are the greater defect and the gaping wound edges. Healing and granulation take place from the edges inward and from the bottom of the wound upward until the wound is filled. There is more granulation tissue, and the result is a much larger scar.

Tertiary Intention. *Tertiary intention* (delayed primary intention) healing occurs with delayed suturing of a wound in which 2 layers of granulation tissue are sutured together. This occurs when a contaminated wound is left open and sutured closed after the infection is controlled. It also occurs when a primary wound becomes infected, is opened, allowed to granulate, and then sutured. Tertiary intention usually results in a larger and deeper scar than primary or secondary intention.

Wound Classification

A *wound* is a break or opening into the skin. Wounds often occur because of accidents or injuries. Types of wounds can range from minor scrapes to deep wounds involving bones, blood vessels, and nerves.

Identifying the cause of a wound is essential to classifying the wound properly. Wounds can be classified by their cause (surgical or nonsurgical; acute or chronic) or the depth of tissue affected (superficial, partial thickness, or full thickness). A *superficial wound* involves only the epidermis. *Partial-thickness* wounds extend into the dermis. *Full-thickness* wounds have the deepest layer of tissue destruction. They involve the subcutaneous tissue and sometimes extend into the fascia and underlying structures, including muscle, tendon, or bone.

A *skin tear* is a wound caused by shear, friction, and/or blunt force resulting in separation of skin layers. A skin tear can be partial thickness or full thickness. This type of wound is common, especially in older adults and critically or chronically ill adults.[3]

Complications of Healing

Certain factors can interfere with wound healing and lead to complications (Table 11.7).

TABLE 11.7 Complications of Wound Healing

Adhesions
- Bands of scar tissue that form between or around organs
- May occur in the abdominal cavity or between the lungs and the pleura
- Those in the abdomen may cause an intestinal obstruction.

Contractions
- Wound contraction is a normal part of healing.
- Complications occur when excessive contraction results in deformity.
- Shortening of muscle or scar tissue, especially over joints, results from excessive fibrous tissue formation.

Dehiscence
- Separation and disruption of previously joined wound edges (Fig. 11.6)
- Usually occurs when a primary healing site bursts open
- May be caused by:
  - Infection causing an inflammatory process
  - Granulation tissue not strong enough to withstand forces imposed on wound
  - Obesity, because adipose tissue has less blood supply and may slow healing
  - Pocket of fluid (seroma, hematoma) developing between tissue layers and preventing the edges of the wound from coming together

Evisceration
- Occurs when wound edges separate to the extent that intestines protrude through wound
- Usually needs immediate surgical treatment

Excess Granulation Tissue ("Proud Flesh")
- Excess granulation tissue may protrude above surface of healing wound.

- If the tissue is cauterized or cut off, healing continues in normal manner.

Fistula Formation
- An abnormal passage between organs or a hollow organ and skin (abdominal or perianal fistula)

Infection (Fig. 11.3)
- ↑ Risk for infection when wound contains necrotic tissue or blood supply is ↓, patient's immune function is ↓ (e.g., from immunosuppressive drugs), undernutrition, multiple stressors, and hyperglycemia in diabetes.

Hemorrhage
- Abnormal internal or external blood loss may be caused by suture failure, clotting abnormalities, dislodged clot, infection, or erosion of a blood vessel by a foreign object (tubing, drains) or infection process.

Hypertrophic Scars
- Inappropriately large, raised red and hard scars (Fig. 11.7)

- Occur when an overabundance of collagen is made during healing

Keloid Formation
- Great protrusion of scar tissue that extends beyond wound edges and may form tumor-like masses of scar tissue (Fig. 11.8)

- Permanent without any tendency to subside
- Patients often have tenderness, pain, and hyperparesthesia, especially in early stages.
- Thought to be a hereditary condition occurring most often in dark-skinned people.

FIG 11.7 Hypertrophic scarring. (Reproduced with kind permission from Dr. C. Lawrence, Wound Healing Research Unit, Cardiff. In Bale S, Jones V, eds: *Wound care nursing: A patient-centered approach*, ed 2, St Louis, 2006, Mosby.)

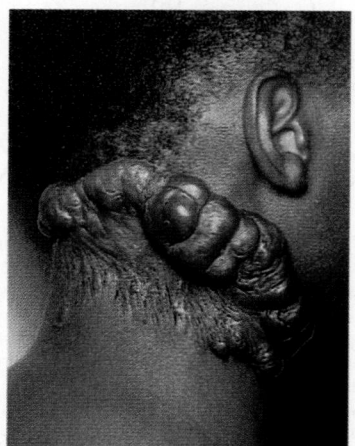

FIG 11.8 Keloid scarring. (Reproduced with kind permission from Dr. C. Lawrence, Wound Healing Research Unit, Cardiff. In Bale S, Jones V, editors: *Wound care nursing: A patient-centered approach*, ed 2, St Louis, 2006, Mosby.)

❖ NURSING AND INTERPROFESSIONAL MANAGEMENT: WOUND HEALING

◆ Nursing Assessment

The first step in wound care is to carefully assess and document the characteristics of the wound and surrounding area. This includes the location, size (longest length and widest width), depth, undermining and tunneling, wound margin (e.g., normal, macerated, erythema), and wound base (e.g., eschar, slough, exudate). There are several ways to measure a wound. One way is shown in Fig. 11.9. Record the consistency, color, and odor of any drainage and report if abnormal for the situation. *Staphylococcus* and *Pseudomonas* are common organisms that cause purulent, draining wounds.

Thoroughly assess the wound on admission, or first clinic visit, and on a regular basis thereafter. In healthy people, wounds heal at a normal, predictable rate. Assess for factors that may delay wound healing and contribute to chronic nonhealing wounds (Table 11.8). If deterioration in the wound occurs, you need to assess and document changes more often.[4]

Chronic wounds are those that do not heal within the normal time (around 3 months). If a wound does not heal as expected, assess and identify factors that may delay healing. Refer the patient to an HCP specializing in wound management. Time does not heal all wounds. While caring for patients during the healing process, you need to continually assess for complications (e.g., infection) associated with healing (Table 11.7).

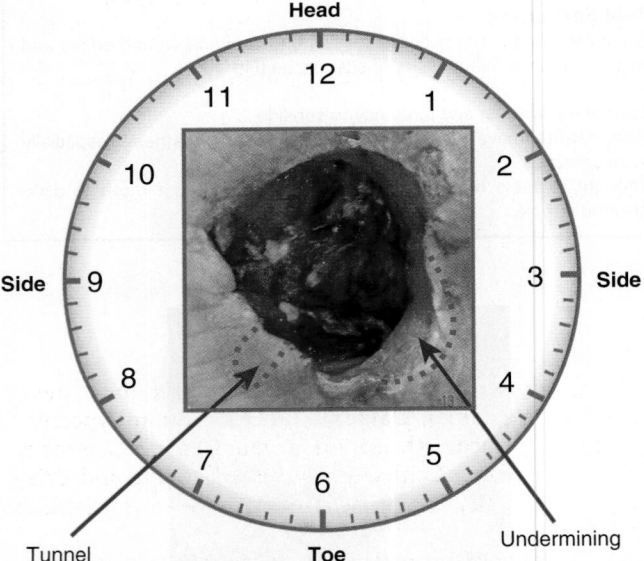

FIG 11.9 Wound measurements are made in centimeters. The first measurement is oriented from head to toe, the second is from side to side, and the third is the depth (if any). If there is any tunneling (when cotton-tipped applicator is placed in wound, there is movement) or undermining (when cotton-tipped applicator is placed in wound, there is a "lip" around the wound), this is charted in respect to a clock, with 12 o'clock being toward the patient's head. This wound would be charted as a full-thickness, red wound, 7 × 5 × 3 cm, with a 3-cm tunnel at 7 o'clock and 2 cm undermining from 3 o'clock to 5 o'clock. (Courtesy Robert B. Babiak, RN, BSN, CWOCN, San Antonio, TX.)

◆ Nursing Implementation

The type of wound management and dressings needed depend on the type, extent, and characteristics of the wound and the phase of healing. The purposes of wound management include (1) protecting a clean wound from trauma so that it can heal normally, (2) cleaning a wound to remove any dirt and debris from the wound bed, and (3) treating infection to prepare the wound for healing.

Clean Wounds. Superficial skin injuries may only need cleansing. Material used to close wounds include adhesive strips (e.g., Steri-Strips, butterflies), sutures (stitches), staples, and tissue adhesives (fibrin sealants). We use adhesive strips instead of *sutures* for some injuries because they decrease scarring and it is easier to care for them. Sutures are used to close wounds because suture material provides the mechanical support needed to sustain closure. A wide variety of suturing materials are available. Tissue adhesives are a biologic adhesive that can be applied alone or with sutures or tape.

A dressing material that keeps the wound surface clean and slightly moist is best to promote epithelialization. For wounds that heal by primary intention, it is common to cover the wound or incision with a dry, sterile dressing. It is removed as soon as

TABLE 11.8	**Factors Delaying Wound Healing**
Factor	**Effect on Wound Healing**
Advanced age	Slows collagen synthesis by fibroblasts, impairs circulation, needs longer time for epithelialization of skin, alters phagocytic and immune responses
Anemia	Supplies less O_2 at tissue level
Corticosteroid drugs	Impair phagocytosis by WBCs, inhibit fibroblast proliferation and function, depress formation of granulation tissue, inhibit wound contraction
Diabetes	Decreases collagen synthesis, delays capillary growth, impairs phagocytosis (result of hyperglycemia), reduces supply of O_2 and nutrients secondary to vascular disease
Inadequate blood supply	Decreases supply of nutrients to injured area, decreases removal of exudative debris, inhibits inflammatory response
Infection	Increases inflammatory response and tissue destruction
Mechanical friction on wound	Destroys granulation tissue, prevents apposition of wound edges
Nutritional deficiencies	
Vitamin C	Delays formation of collagen fibers and capillary development
Protein	Decreases supply of amino acids for tissue repair
Zinc	Impairs epithelialization
Obesity	Decreases blood supply in fatty tissue
Poor general health	Causes generalized absence of factors necessary to promote wound healing
Smoking	Nicotine, a potent vasoconstrictor, impedes blood flow to healing areas

TABLE 11.9 Types of Wound Dressings

Type of Dressing	Description	Uses	Examples
Alginates	Derived from processed seaweed or kelp. Form a nonstick gel on contact with draining wound. Highly absorbent. Easy to use over irregular-shaped wounds. Require a secondary dressing	Wounds with moderate to heavy exudates (e.g., pressure injuries, infected wounds)	Algisite, CalciCare, Kalginate, Melgisorb
Antimicrobials	Alter the wound bed bioburden. Often contain silver, iodine, chlorhexidine, honey, or polyhexamethylene biguanide (PHMB). Available as sponges, impregnated woven gauzes, film dressings, absorptive products, nylon fabric, nonadherent barriers, or a combination of materials		Aquacel, Acticoat, Curity AMD, Iodoflex, Medihoney, SilverSorb, Silvercel
Foams	Film-coated gel or polyurethane. Absorption of minimal to heavy exudate, nonadherent. May need to be affixed with a secondary dressing	Primary dressing for absorption, secondary dressing for wounds with packing. Used for prevention of sacral pressure injuries	Allevyn, Cutimed, Hydro-cell, Lyofoam, Mepilex, PolyMem
Gauze	Made of woven or nonwoven material. Absorb exudates. Most often combined with another kind of dressing	Can be used on almost any kind of wound. Cleansing, packing, and covering a variety of wounds	Numerous products available (e.g., Curity, Kerlix)
Hydrocolloids	Gelatin, pectin, or carboxymethylcellulose bonded to a film or sheet. Produce a flat occlusive dressing that forms a gel on wound surface. Occlusion does not interfere with wound healing. Support autolytic debridement and prevent secondary infections	Wounds with light to moderate drainage	Bursamed, Comfeel, Duo-Derm, Primacol
Hydrogels	Available in gels, gel-covered gauze, or sheets. Give moisture to a dry wound and maintain a moist environment. Can rehydrate wound tissue. Debridement (autolytic) because of moisturizing effects. Require a secondary dressing	Dry wounds. Wounds with minimal drainage. Necrotic wounds. May have a cooling effect to help decrease pain	Aquasite, Curasol, IntraSite, Purilon, Solosite
Nonadherent	Woven or nonwoven dressings. May be impregnated with saline, petrolatum, or antimicrobials. Minimally absorbent	Minor wounds or as a second dressing	Adaptic, Vaseline gauze, Xeroform
Transparent films	Generally composed of polyurethane. Transparency allows visualization of the wound. Minimally absorbent. Use with caution over superficial wounds. Can result in further tissue loss in fragile wounds (e.g., skin tears). In other wounds, can draw in moisture, increasing risk for infection	Dry, uninfected wounds or wounds with minimal drainage	Bioclusive, OpSite, Suresite, Tegaderm, Transeal

For more information, see *www.woundsource.com/product-category/dressings*.

the drainage stops or in 2 to 3 days. Medicated sprays that form a transparent film on the skin may be used for dressings on a clean incision or injury. Transparent film or adhesive semipermeable dressings (e.g., OpSite, Tegaderm) are occlusive dressings that are permeable to oxygen. The wound is then usually covered with a sterile dressing. Sometimes an HCP will leave a surgical wound uncovered or remove the dressing within 48 hours after surgery.[5] Examples of types of wound dressings are described in Table 11.9.

Clean wounds that are granulating and re-epithelializing should be kept slightly moist and protected from further trauma until they heal naturally.[6] Do not let a wound that has the potential to heal dry out. Dryness is an enemy of wound healing. "Airing out" a wound is a great mistake. Wounds need a moist environment to heal. Unnecessary manipulation during dressing changes may destroy new granulation tissue and break down fibrin formation.

Topical antimicrobials and antibactericidals (e.g., povidone-iodine [Betadine], Dakin's solution [sodium hypochlorite]), should be used with caution in wound care because they can damage the new epithelium of healing tissue and delay healing. They should never be used in a clean granulating wound.

Sometimes drains are inserted into the wound to help remove fluid. The Jackson-Pratt drain is a suction drainage device consisting of a flexible plastic bulb connected to an internal plastic drainage tube (Fig. 11.10).

Contaminated Wounds. If the wound is contaminated, it must be converted into a clean wound before healing can occur normally. Debridement of a wound that has debris or dead tissue may be needed. Another option is absorptive dressings. They can be used to absorb exudate and clean the wound surface. These dressings work by drawing excess drainage from the wound surface. The amount of wound secretions determines the number of dressing changes.

In hydrocolloid dressings, such as DuoDerm, the inner part of the dressing interacts with the exudate, forming a hydrated gel over the wound. When the dressing is removed, the gel separates and stays over the wound. The wound must be cleansed gently to prevent damage to newly formed tissue. We can leave these dressings in place for up to 7 days or until leakage occurs around the dressing.

Debridement is done to remove dead tissue.[7] The debridement method used depends on the amount of debris and the condition of the wound tissue (Table 11.10).

◆ **Negative-Pressure Wound Therapy.** Negative-pressure wound therapy (NPWT) is used to treat acute and chronic wounds. A vacuum source creates continuous or intermittent negative pressure inside the wound to remove fluid, exudates, and infectious materials to prepare the wound for healing and closure. We do not know exactly how NPWT promotes healing. It is thought that NPWT pulls excess fluid from the wound, reduces bacterial load, and encourages blood flow into the wound base.

NPWT systems consist of a vacuum pump, drainage tubing, a foam or gauze wound dressing, and an adhesive film dressing

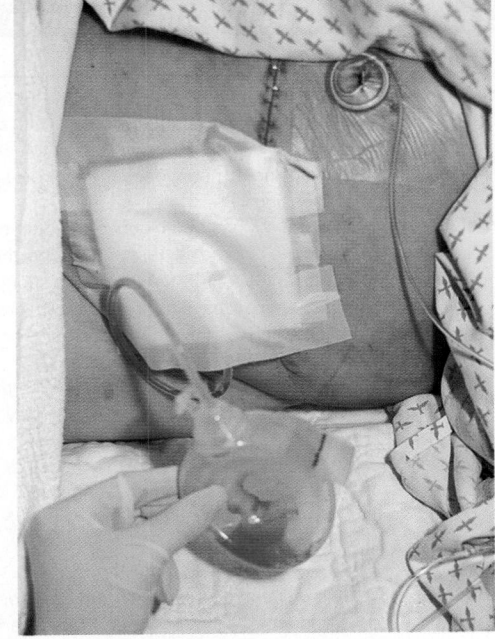

FIG 11.10 Jackson-Pratt drainage device. (From Perry AG, Potter PA, Elkin MK: *Nursing interventions and clinical skills,* ed 5, St Louis, 2012, Mosby.)

NURSING MANAGEMENT

Wound Care

In general, the registered nurse (RN) manages wound care for complex or nonhealing wounds. Wound, ostomy, and continence (WOC) nurses may treat and manage pressure injuries, traumatic and draining wounds, surgical incisions, and tubes and fistulas. State nurse practice acts vary in the wound care actions allowed by licensed practical/vocational nurses (LPNs/VNs). In general, the role of the RN includes:

- Assess all patients at risk for pressure injury at time of first hospital and/or home visit or whenever the patient's condition changes. Thereafter, assess at regular intervals based on care setting (every 24 hours for acute care or every visit in home care).
- Assess patients for factors that may delay wound healing and develop a plan of care to address these factors.
- Assess and document initial wound appearance, including wound size, depth, color, and drainage.
- Develop a plan of care to prevent the development of pressure injuries.
- Plan nursing actions to aid with wound healing, including wound care, positioning, and nutritional interventions.
- Choose dressings and therapies for wound treatment (in conjunction with the HCP and/or wound care specialist).
- Implement wound care for complex or new wounds, including negative-pressure wound therapy and hyperbaric O_2 therapy.
- Evaluate whether wound care is effective in promoting wound healing.
- Provide teaching to patient and caregivers about home wound care and pressure injury prevention.
- Oversee LPN/VN:
  - Perform sterile dressing changes on acute and chronic wounds.
  - Apply ordered topical antimicrobials and antibactericidals to wounds.
  - Apply prescribed dressings or medications for wound debridement.
  - Collect and record data about wound appearance.
- Collaborate with dietitian to:
  - Assess and monitor patient's nutritional status.
  - Outline diet to support proper wound healing.

TABLE 11.10	Types of Debridement
Type	**Description**
Autolytic debridement	• Moisture-retentive semiocclusive or occlusive dressings (e.g., hydrocolloids, transparent films, hydrogels) (Table 11.9) that soften dry eschar by autolysis • Must assess area around wound for maceration
Biologic debridement (larval therapy)	• Application of sterile fly larvae to dead tissue
Conservative sharp	• Use of scalpels, curettes, scissors to remove nonviable tissue • Ensure adequate vascular blood supply
Enzymatic debridement	• Drug applied topically to dissolve necrotic tissue and then covered with moist dressing (e.g., saline-moistened gauze) • Process can be slow, and thick eschar may have to be scored with scalpel

Mechanical debridement	• Methods:
	  • *Wet-to-dry dressings,* in which open-mesh gauze is moistened with normal saline, lightly packed into wound surface, and outer layer allowed to dry. Wound debris adheres to dressing and then dressing is removed
	  • *Wound irrigation.* Make certain bacteria are not accidentally driven into wound with high irrigation pressure
	• Noncontact low-frequency ultrasound and ultrasonic mist

Surgical/sharp debridement	• Quick method of debridement to prevent, control, or remove infection • Used when large amounts of nonviable tissue are present • Prepares wound bed for healing, skin grafting, or flaps

FIG 11.11 Negative-pressure wound therapy in woman with history of IV drug abuse. **A,** The completely destroyed femoral artery was reconstructed with a homograft. **B,** A black open-pore polyurethane foam was directly applied to the vascular reconstruction and negative pressure applied to wound. **C,** Wound site 16 days after surgery. **D,** Healed wound at 28 months without reinfection. (Reprinted from Mayer D, Hasse B, Koelliker J, et al: Long-term results of vascular graft and artery preserving treatment with negative pressure wound therapy in Szilagyi grade III infections justify a paradigm shift, *Ann Surg* 254:754, 2011. © Southeastern Surgical Congress.)

that covers and seals the wound.[8] In NPWT, the wound is cleansed and a gauze or foam dressing is cut to the dimensions of the wound. A large occlusive dressing is applied, with a small hole made over the gauze or foam dressing where the tubing is attached (Fig. 11.11). The tubing is connected to a pump, which creates a negative pressure in the wound bed.

Monitor the patient's serum protein levels and fluid and electrolyte balance because of losses from the wound. Also, monitor the patient's coagulation studies (platelet count, prothrombin time [PT], partial thromboplastin time [PTT]).

◆ **Hyperbaric Oxygen Therapy.** Hyperbaric O_2 therapy (HBOT) is the delivery of O_2 at increased atmospheric pressures. It can be given topically by creating a chamber around the injured limb. It also can be given systemically with the patient in an enclosed chamber, receiving 100% O_2 at 1.5 to 3 times the normal atmospheric pressure.

HBOT allows O_2 to diffuse into the serum, rather than RBCs, and be transported to the tissues. By increasing the O_2 content in the serum, HBOT moves the O_2 past narrowed arteries and capillaries where RBCs cannot go.

In addition, high O_2 levels stimulate *angiogenesis* (production of new blood vessels), kill anaerobic bacteria, and increase the killing power of WBCs and certain antibiotics (e.g., fluoroquinolones, aminoglycosides). HBOT accelerates granulation tissue formation and wound healing.

Most systemic treatments last from 90 to 120 minutes. The number of treatments is highly variable (from 10 to 60), depending on the condition being treated.

◆ **Drug Therapy.** Platelet-derived growth factor is released from the platelets and stimulates cell proliferation and migration. Becaplermin (Regranex), a recombinant human platelet–derived growth factor gel, actively stimulates wound healing. It is used to treat foot injuries in patients with diabetes (see Chapter 48). Becaplermin should be used only when the wound

is free of dead tissue and infection. It should not be used if cancer is suspected in the wound.

◆ **Nutritional Therapy.** Special nutritional measures promote wound healing. A high fluid intake is needed to replace fluid loss from perspiration and exudate formation. An increased metabolic rate intensifies water loss. Persons at risk for wound healing problems are those with malabsorption problems (e.g., Crohn's disease, GI surgery, liver disease), deficient intake or high energy demands (e.g., cancer, major trauma or surgery, sepsis, fever), and diabetes.

Undernutrition puts a person at risk for poor healing. A diet high in protein, carbohydrate, and vitamins with moderate fat intake is necessary to promote healing. Protein is needed to correct the negative nitrogen balance resulting from the increased metabolic rate. It is also needed for the synthesis of immune factors, WBCs, fibroblasts, and collagen, which are the building blocks for healing. Carbohydrates are needed to meet the increased metabolic energy required for healing. If there is a carbohydrate deficit, the body will break down protein for the needed energy. Fats help in the synthesis of fatty acids and triglycerides, which are part of the cellular membrane.[9]

Vitamin C is needed for capillary synthesis and collagen production by fibroblasts. The B-complex vitamins are necessary as coenzymes for many metabolic reactions. If a vitamin B deficiency develops, a disruption of protein, fat, and carbohydrate metabolism will occur. Vitamin A aids in epithelialization. It increases collagen synthesis and tensile strength of the healing wound.

If the patient is unable to eat, enteral feedings and supplements should be the first choice if the GI tract is functional. Parenteral nutrition is indicated when enteral feedings are contraindicated or not tolerated. (Enteral and parenteral nutrition are discussed in Chapter 39.)

◆ **Infection Prevention and Control.** You and the patient must scrupulously follow aseptic procedures, including hand washing, for keeping the wound free from infection. Do not allow the patient to touch a recently injured area. The patient's environment should be as free as possible from contamination from items introduced by roommates and visitors. Some patients may receive prophylactic antibiotics.

If an infection develops, a culture and sensitivity test is done to determine the organism and the most effective antibiotic for that specific organism. Obtain the culture before the first dose of antibiotic is given. We can obtain cultures by needle aspiration, tissue culture, or swab technique. HCPs perform needle and tissue punch biopsies.

As a nurse, you can obtain cultures using the swab technique. This is done using Levine's technique, which involves rotating a culture swab over a cleansed 1-cm^2 area near the center of the wound. Use enough pressure to extract wound fluid from deep tissue layers. Take a culture of the clean tissue because exudate and necrotic tissue will not provide an accurate sample.[10] The sample must be sent to the laboratory within 1 hour.

◆ **Psychologic Implications.** The patient may be distressed at the thought or sight of an incision or wound because of fear of scarring or disfigurement. Drainage and odor from a wound often cause alarm. The patient needs to understand the healing process and normal changes that occur as the wound heals.

When changing a dressing, avoid inappropriate facial expressions that may alert the patient to problems with the wound or raise doubts about your ability to care for it. Wrinkling your nose may convey disgust to the patient. Be careful not to focus on the wound to the extent that you are not treating the patient as a total person.

◆ **Patient Teaching.** Because patients are being discharged earlier after surgery and many have surgery as outpatients, it is important that the patient and caregiver know how to care for the wound and perform dressing changes. Wound healing may not be complete for 4 to 6 weeks or longer. Emphasize the importance of adequate rest and good nutrition throughout this time. Physical and emotional stress should be minimal. Observing the wound for complications, such as contractures, adhesions, and secondary infection, is important. Teach the patient and caregiver the signs and symptoms of infection. Have them note changes in the wound color and amount of drainage. Teach the patient to notify the HCP of any signs of abnormal wound healing.

Drugs may be given for a time after recovery from the acute infection. Review drug-specific side effects and adverse effects with the patient and caregiver, as well as methods to prevent side effects (e.g., taking with food). Teach the patient to contact the HCP if any of these effects occur. Discuss the need to complete the entire course of therapy. For example, a patient who needed to take an antibiotic for 10 days decides to stop taking the drug after 5 days because of absent symptoms. However, the organism was not entirely eliminated. It becomes resistant to the antibiotic, and the patient develops a more severe infection.

PRESSURE INJURIES

Etiology and Pathophysiology

A **pressure injury** is localized damage to the skin and/or underlying soft tissue. It usually occurs over a bony prominence or is related to a medical or other device. The injury occurs because of intense and/or prolonged pressure or pressure in combination with shear. The most common site for pressure injuries is the sacrum, with heels being second.

TABLE 11.11	Risk Factors for Pressure Injuries

- Advanced age
- Anemia
- Contractures
- Critically ill, cared for in critical care setting
- Diabetes
- Fever
- Friction (rubbing of surfaces together)
- Hip fracture
- Immobility
- Incontinence
- Long and/or extensive surgical procedure
- Low diastolic blood pressure (<60 mm Hg)
- Major trauma
- Mental deterioration
- Neurologic disorders
- Pain
- Peripheral vascular disease
- Spinal cord injury

Factors that influence the development of pressure injuries include the amount of pressure (intensity), length of time the pressure is exerted on the skin (duration), and ability of the patient's tissue to tolerate the externally applied pressure. Other factors that contribute to pressure injury formation include shear (pressure exerted on the skin when it adheres to the bed and the skin layers slide in the direction of body movement [e.g., when pulling the patient up in bed]) and *excessive moisture* (increases risk for skin breakdown). The tolerance of soft tissue for pressure and shear are affected by microclimate, nutrition, perfusion, co-morbidities, and condition of the soft tissue.[11]

Factors that put a patient at risk for developing a pressure injury are outlined in Table 11.11. Patients at risk include those who are older, incontinent, unable to reposition or unaware of the need to reposition (e.g., spinal cord injury), and bed- or wheelchair-bound.

Clinical Manifestations

The manifestations of pressure injuries depend on the extent of the tissue involved. The injury can present as intact skin or an open injury and may be painful. We stage pressure injuries based on the visible or palpable tissue in the injury bed. Table 11.12 shows the pressure injury stages based on the National Pressure Injury Advisory Panel (NPUAP).[11]

If the pressure injury becomes infected, the patient may have signs of infection (e.g., leukocytosis, fever). The pressure injury may increase in size, odor, and drainage; have necrotic tissue; and be indurated, warm, and painful. Untreated pressure injuries may lead to *cellulitis* (spreading of inflammation to subcutaneous or connective tissue), chronic infection, sepsis, and possibly death. The most common complication of a pressure injury is recurrence. Therefore it is important to note the location of previously healed pressure injuries on a patient's admission assessment.

◆ NURSING AND INTERPROFESSIONAL MANAGEMENT: PRESSURE INJURIES

In 1859, Florence Nightingale wrote, "If he has a bedsore, it is generally not the fault of the disease, but of the nursing."[12] Her comment emphasizes the critical role that nurses have in prevention and treatment of pressure injuries.

TABLE 11.12 Pressure Injuries

Pressure Injuries

Stage 1 Pressure Injury: Non-Blanchable Erythema of Intact Skin

Intact skin with a localized area of non-blanchable erythema, which may appear differently in dark skin. Blanchable erythema or changes in sensation, temperature, or firmness may precede visual changes.

Stage 2 Pressure Injury: Partial-Thickness Skin Loss With Exposed Dermis

Partial-thickness loss of skin with exposed dermis. The wound bed is viable, pink or red, and moist. May present as an intact or ruptured serum-filled blister. Adipose and deeper tissues are not visible. Often result from adverse microclimate and shear in the skin over the pelvis and shear in the heel.

Stage 3 Pressure Injury: Full-Thickness Skin Loss

Full-thickness loss of skin, in which adipose is visible in the injury. Granulation tissue and epibole (rolled wound edges) are often present. Slough and/or eschar (types of dead tissue) may be visible. The depth of tissue damage varies by anatomical location; areas of significant adiposity can develop deep wounds. Undermining and tunneling may occur.

Stage 4 Pressure Injury: Full-Thickness Skin and Tissue Loss

Full-thickness skin and tissue loss with exposed or directly palpable fascia, muscle, tendon, ligament, cartilage, or bone in the injury. Slough and/or eschar may be visible. Epibole, undermining, and/or tunneling often occur. Depth varies by anatomical location.

Unstageable Pressure Injury: Obscured Full-Thickness Skin and Tissue Loss

Full-thickness skin and tissue loss in which the extent of tissue damage within the injury cannot be confirmed because it is obscured by slough or eschar. A Stage 3 or Stage 4 pressure injury is present after removing slough or eschar. Stable eschar (i.e., dry, adherent, intact without erythema or fluctuance) on the heel or ischemic limb should not be softened or removed.

Deep Tissue Pressure Injury (DTPI): Persistent Non-Blanchable Deep Red, Maroon, or Purple Discoloration

Intact or non-intact skin with localized area of persistent non-blanchable deep red, maroon, purple discoloration, or epidermal separation revealing a dark wound bed or blood-filled blister. Pain and temperature change often precede skin color changes. Discoloration may appear differently in dark skin. Results from intense and/or prolonged pressure and shear forces at the bone-muscle interface. May evolve rapidly to reveal the actual extent of tissue injury or may resolve without tissue loss. Visible necrotic tissue, subcutaneous tissue, granulation tissue, fascia, muscle, or other underlying structures indicates a full-thickness pressure injury (Unstageable, Stage 3 or Stage 4). Do not use DTPI to describe vascular, traumatic, neuropathic, or dermatologic conditions.

TABLE 11.12   Pressure Injuries—cont'd

Pressure Injuries

Medical Device–Related Pressure Injury	**Mucosal Membrane Pressure Injury**
Results from the use of devices designed and applied for diagnostic or therapeutic purposes. The resultant injury generally conforms to the pattern or shape of the device. Stage the injury using the staging system.	Found on mucous membranes with a history of a medical device in use at the site of the injury. These injuries cannot be staged due to the anatomic location.

Photos used with permission of the National Pressure Injury Advisory Panel. Retrieved from *www.npuap.org/resources/educational-and-clinical-resources/pressure-injury-staging-illustrations/*.

TABLE 11.13   Assessing Patients With Dark Skin

- Look for changes in skin color, such as skin that is darker (purplish, brownish, bluish) than surrounding skin.
- Use natural or halogen light source to accurately assess the skin color. Fluorescent light casts blue color, which can make skin assessment difficult.
- Assess the area for the skin temperature using your hand. The area may feel initially warm, then cooler.
- Touch the skin to feel its consistency. Boggy or edematous feel may indicate a Stage 1 pressure injury.
- Ask the patient if he or she has any pain or itchy sensation.

❗ SAFETY ALERT   Pressure Injuries

- Stage 3 or 4 (full skin–thickness injury) pressure injury acquired after admission to a health care setting is considered a serious reportable event (SRE) (never event).[13] (SREs are discussed in Chapter 1.)

Nursing and interprofessional management are discussed together because the activities are interrelated. In addition to the nurse, other members of the health team, such as the wound care specialist, plastic surgeon, dietitian, physical therapist, and occupational therapist, can provide valuable input into the complex treatment necessary to prevent and treat pressure injuries.

◆ Nursing Assessment

Assess patients for pressure injury risk initially on admission and at periodic intervals based on the patient's condition. Conduct a thorough head-to-toe assessment on admission to identify and document any pressure injuries. After admission, conduct periodic reassessments of the skin and wounds.

❗ SAFETY ALERT   Assessing for Pressure Injuries

- In acute care, reassess patients for pressure injuries every 24 hours.
- In long-term care, reassess residents weekly for the first 4 weeks after admission and then at least monthly or quarterly.
- In home care, reassess patients at every nurse visit.

To do a risk assessment, use a validated assessment tool, such as the Braden Scale (available at www.bradenscale.com). Knowing the level of risk can help determine how aggressive preventive measures should be.

Identification of skin changes may be hard in patients with dark skin. Table 11.13 presents techniques to help assess darker skin.

TABLE 11.14   Nursing Assessment

Pressure Injuries

Subjective Data

Important Health Information

Past health history: Stroke, spinal cord injury; prolonged bed rest or immobility; circulatory impairment; poor nutrition; altered level of consciousness; prior history of pressure injury; immunologic abnormalities; advanced age; diabetes; anemia; trauma

Medications: Use of opioids, hypnotics, systemic corticosteroids

Surgery or other treatments: Recent surgery

Functional Health Patterns

Nutritional-metabolic: Obesity, emaciation; decreased fluid, calorie, or protein intake; vitamin or mineral deficiencies; clinically significant malnutrition as shown by low serum albumin, decreased total lymphocyte count, and decreased body weight (15% less than ideal body weight)

Elimination: Incontinence of urine, feces, or both

Activity-exercise: Weakness, debilitation, inability to turn and position body; contractures

Cognitive-perceptual: Pain or altered cutaneous sensation in pressure injury area; decreased awareness of pressure on body areas; capacity to follow treatment plan

Objective Data

General

Fever

Integumentary

Diaphoresis, edema, and discoloration, especially over bony areas, such as sacrum, hips, elbows, heels, knees, ankles, shoulders, and ear rims, progressing to increased tissue damage characteristic of injury stages

Possible Diagnostic Findings

Leukocytosis, positive cultures for microorganisms from pressure injury

Subjective and objective data that should be obtained from a person with or at risk for a pressure injury are outlined in Table 11.14.

◆ Nursing Diagnoses

Nursing diagnoses for the patient with a pressure injury may include:

- Impaired tissue integrity
- Risk for infection

◆ Planning

The overall goals are that the patient with a pressure injury will (1) have no deterioration of the wound, (2) not develop an infection in the pressure injury, (3) have healing of pressure injuries, and (4) have no recurrence.

◆ **Nursing Implementation**

◆ **Health Promotion.** The primary nursing responsibilities are (1) identifying patients at risk for developing pressure injuries (Tables 11.11 and 11.14) and (2) implementing pressure injury prevention strategies for those who are at risk. Prevention is the best treatment for pressure injuries. Implementing evidence-based pressure injury prevention programs can reduce the occurrence of health care–acquired pressure injuries.[14,15]

EVIDENCE-BASED PRACTICE

Repositioning and Pressure Injuries

You are doing discharge planning with L.H., an obese 76-yr-old woman with a history of diabetes, hypertension, and macular degeneration. L.H. has spent most of her time while hospitalized in a bed or wheelchair and now has a stage 1 pressure injury on her sacrum. You explain the importance of skin care with her son, who is her primary caregiver.

Making Clinical Decisions

Best Available Evidence. Repositioning is the primary method of reducing the risk for pressure injury. Pressure relief schedules should be developed. Pressure-reducing devices (e.g., foam mattress, padded commode, wheelchair seats) may be used but are not be a substitute for repositioning. In addition, develop a nutrition care plan based on the patient's nutritional and hydration needs, feeding route, and care goals.

Clinician Expertise. You know patients with pressure injury should be repositioned at least every 2 hours while in bed and every hour when in a chair.

Caregiver Preferences and Values. L.H.'s caregiver states he will reposition his mother during the day and have the home health care aide reposition her more often at night.

Implications for Nursing Practice

1. In addition to repositioning, what information is important to discuss with L.H.'s son to prevent further skin injury?
2. What are the risk factors for L.H. to develop worsening pressure injury?
3. What is important for the home health care nurse to monitor on her visits to L.H. related to pressure injuries and healing?

References for Evidence

Edsberg LE, Black JM, Goldberg M, et al: Revised National Pressure Advisory Panel Pressure Injury Staging System, *J Wound Ostomy Continence Nurs* 43(585), 2016. National Pressure Injury Advisory Panel. Retrieved from *www.npuap.org/wp-content/uploads/2014/08/Updated-10-16-14-Quick-Reference-Guide-DIGITAL-NPUAP-EPUAP-PPPIA-16Oct2014.pdf*.

⚠ **SAFETY ALERT   Preventing Pressure Injuries**

- Use devices to reduce pressure and shear (e.g., low-air-loss mattresses, foam mattresses, wheelchair cushions, padded commode seats, boots [foam, air], lift sheets) as appropriate. These devices do not replace the need for frequent repositioning.
- Reposition patients often to prevent pressure injuries.

In the past, the "standard" was to turn and reposition patients every 2 hours. However, this "policy" is not evidence-based. Individualize time schedules and frequency based on risk factors, patient's overall condition, and type of mattress and support surface. For example, some high-risk patients may need to be turned and repositioned every hour, while others at lower risk may need to be turned and repositioned only every 3 to 4 hours.[11,14]

◆ **Acute Care.** Care of a patient with a pressure injury requires wound care and support measures of the whole person, including adequate nutrition, pain management, control of other medical conditions, and redistributing pressure. Both conservative and surgical strategies are used in the treatment of pressure injuries, depending on the stage and condition of the injury.

Once a pressure injury has developed, initiate interventions based on the injury characteristics (e.g., stage, size, location, amount of exudate, type of wound, presence of infection or pain) and the patient's general status (e.g., nutritional state, age, cardiovascular status, level of mobility). Carefully document the size of the pressure injury. A wound-measuring card or tape can be used to note the injury's maximum length and width in centimeters. To find the depth of the injury, take a sterile cotton-tipped applicator and soak it with saline. Gently place it into the deepest part of the injury, and then measure the length of the part of the applicator that probed the injury. Documentation of the healing wound can be done using several available pressure injury healing tools, such as the NPUAP Pressure Injury Scale for Healing (PUSH) tool (available at *www.npuap.org/wp-content/uploads/2012/03/push3.pdf*).

Some agencies require that pictures of the pressure injury be taken initially and at regular intervals during treatment. The Informatics box has suggestions for digital imaging.

INFORMATICS IN PRACTICE

Digital Images

To monitor wound progress, use digital photography. For the best images:

- Include a ruler with date, length, width, and depth of the wound in each photo.
- Position the patient the same way for each photo.
- Take the photo from the same angle each time. Pointing perpendicularly at the wound is best.
- Use natural light, without flash, whenever possible.
- Show the wound on a solid background, avoiding shiny underpads.
- Avoid patient identifiers, such as jewelry, tattoos, or visible family members.

Pressure injuries generally fall under the category of healing by secondary intention. Care may involve debridement, wound cleaning, application of a dressing, and offloading pressure. It is important to choose the right pressure-redistributing techniques (e.g., mattress replacement, mattress overlay, integrated bed system, seat cushion, seat cushion overlay) to move pressure off areas of pressure injury. Whenever possible, do not turn the patient onto a body surface that has blanchable erythema. Massage is contraindicated in the presence of acute inflammation and where there is the possibility of damaged blood vessels or fragile skin.

Sliding down in bed causes shear. Encourage patients to reposition themselves by lifting rather than sliding and to use a trapeze if needed. Use lift sheets to move patients up in bed or to transfer them.

A pressure injury that has necrotic tissue or eschar (except for dry, stable necrotic feet or heels) should have the tissue removed by surgical, mechanical, enzymatic, or autolytic debridement methods. Once the pressure injury has been successfully debrided and has a clean granulating base, the goal is to provide a wound environment that supports moist wound healing and prevents disruption of the newly formed granulation tissue. Reconstruction of the pressure injury site by surgical repair, including skin grafting, skin flaps, musculocutaneous flaps, or free flaps, may be necessary.

Clean pressure injuries with noncytotoxic solutions (e.g., normal saline) that do not kill or damage cells, especially fibroblasts. Cytotoxicity is a concern when applying a topical agent to a pressure injury. However, if there is a delay in healing due to infection, then antimicrobial use (e.g., sodium hypochlorite [Dakin's solution], povidone-iodine, cadexomer iodine) overrides the toxicity concern. Hydrogen peroxide is cytotoxic and should not be used. It is important to use enough irrigation pressure (4 to 15 psi) to adequately clean the pressure injury without causing trauma or damage to the wound. You can achieve this pressure using a 30-mL syringe and a 19-gauge needle.

After the pressure injury has been cleansed, cover it with an appropriate dressing. Keep a pressure injury slightly moist, rather than dry, to enhance re-epithelialization. Some factors to consider when choosing a dressing are maintaining a moist environment, preventing the wound from drying out, ability to absorb the wound drainage, location of the wound, amount of caregiver time required to change the dressing, cost of the dressing, presence of infection, clean versus sterile dressings, and care delivery setting. Dressings are described in Table 11.9.

Stages 2 through 4 pressure injuries are considered contaminated or colonized with bacteria. Remember that in people who have chronic wounds or are immunocompromised, the signs and symptoms of infection (purulent exudate, odor, erythema, warmth, tenderness, edema, pain, fever, high WBC count) may not be present even when the pressure injury is infected.

Maintaining adequate nutrition is an important nursing responsibility for the patient with a pressure injury. Often the patient is debilitated and has a poor appetite secondary to inactivity. Oral feedings must be adequate to meet the patient's nutritional requirements. The caloric intake needed to correct and maintain nutritional balance may be 30 to 35 calories/kg/day and 1.25 to 1.50 g of protein/kg/day.

Enteral feedings can supplement oral feedings. When oral and enteral feedings are inadequate, parenteral nutrition consisting of amino acid and glucose solutions is used. Parenteral and enteral nutrition are discussed in Chapter 39.

◆ **Ambulatory Care.** Pressure injuries affect the quality of life of patients and their caregivers. Because pressure injuries often recur, teaching prevention techniques to the patient and caregiver is extremely important (Table 11.15). A sixth-grade level

TABLE 11.15	**Patient & Caregiver Teaching**

Pressure Injury

When teaching the patient and caregiver to prevent and care for pressure injuries, do the following:
1. Identify and explain risk factors and cause of pressure injuries.
2. Teach the caregiver techniques for incontinence. If incontinence occurs, cleanse skin at time of soiling and use absorbent pads or briefs.
3. Demonstrate correct positioning to decrease risk for skin breakdown. NEVER position the patient directly on the pressure injury if possible.
4. Teach caregiver to reposition a bed-bound patient at least every 2 hours and a chair-bound patient every hour.
5. Review the available resources (i.e., caregiver's availability and skill, finances, equipment) of patients who need pressure injury care at home.
6. Teach patient and/or caregiver to place clean dressings over sterile dressings using "no touch" technique when changing dressings. Review the disposal of contaminated dressings.
7. Teach patient and caregiver to inspect skin daily. Tell them to report any significant changes to the HCP.
8. Teach patient and caregiver the importance of good nutrition to enhance injury healing.
9. Evaluate program effectiveness.

version of the patient guide to pressure injury prevention is available for use in patient teaching at *www.npuap.org/wp-content/uploads/2016/04/Pressure-Injury-Prevention-Points-2016.pdf.*

The caregiver needs to know the cause of pressure injuries, prevention techniques, early signs, nutritional support, and care techniques for actual pressure injuries. Because the patient with a pressure injury often needs extensive care for other health problems, it is important that the nurse support the caregiver with the added responsibility for pressure injury treatment. eNursing Care Plan 11.2 (available on the website for this chapter at *http://evolve.elsevier.com/Lewis/medsurg*) outlines the care for the patient with a pressure injury.

◆ **Evaluation**

The expected outcomes are that the patient with a pressure injury will have
• Healing of pressure injury(s)
• Intact skin with no further breakdown

CASE STUDY

Inflammation and Infection

(© iStockphoto/Thinkstock.)

Patient Profile
G.N., a 65-yr-old black man, was admitted to the hospital emergency department with partial-thickness burns that involved his face, neck, and upper trunk. He also had a lacerated right leg. His injuries occurred about 36 hours earlier when he fell out of a tree onto his lit gas grill while trimming tree branches.

Subjective Data
• Reports a slightly hoarse voice and irritated throat
• States that he tried to treat himself because he does not have health insurance
• Has been coughing up sooty sputum
• Describes severe pain in left hip

Objective Data
Physical Examination
• Leg wound is gaping and has drainage: temperature 101.1°F (38.4°C)
• X-rays reveal a fractured right tibia and fractured left hip

Laboratory Studies
• WBC count 26,400/μL (26.4 × 10⁹/L) with 80% neutrophils (10% bands)

Interprofessional Care
• Surgery was done to repair the left hip.

Continued

CASE STUDY—cont'd

Inflammation and Infection

Discussion Questions

1. What manifestations of inflammation did G.N. exhibit, and what are their pathophysiologic mechanisms?
2. What type of exudate formation did he develop?
3. What is the basis for the development of the temperature?
4. What is the significance of his WBC count and differential?
5. Because his wound was gaping, primary tissue healing was not possible. How would you expect healing to take place? What complications could he develop?
6. What risk factors does G.N. have to develop a pressure injury?
7. **Priority Decision:** Based on the assessment data provided, what are the priority nursing diagnoses? Are there any collaborative problems?
8. **Collaboration:** What nursing activities related to wound care can be delegated to unlicensed assistive personnel (UAP)?
9. **Quality Improvement:** What outcomes would indicate that interprofessional care was effective?

Answers available at *http://evolve.elsevier.com/Lewis/medsurg*.

■ BRIDGE TO NCLEX EXAMINATION

The number of the question corresponds to the same-numbered outcome at the beginning of the chapter.

1. A patient 1 day postoperative after abdominal surgery has incisional pain, 99.5°F temperature, slight erythema at the incision margins, and 30 mL serosanguinous drainage in the Jackson-Pratt drain. Based on this assessment, what conclusion would the nurse make?
   a. The patient has a normal inflammatory response.
   b. The abdominal incision shows signs of an infection.
   c. The abdominal incision shows signs of impending dehiscence.
   d. The patient's health care provider must be notified about her condition.

2. The nurse assessing a patient with a chronic leg wound finds local signs of erythema, and the patient reports pain at the wound site. What would the nurse expect to be ordered to assess the patient's systemic response?
   a. Serum protein analysis
   b. WBC count and differential
   c. Punch biopsy of center of wound
   d. Culture and sensitivity of the wound

3. A patient in the unit has a 103.7°F temperature. Which intervention would be *most* effective in restoring normal body temperature?
   a. Using a cooling blanket while the patient is febrile
   b. Giving antipyretics on an around-the-clock schedule
   c. Providing increased fluids and have the UAP give sponge baths
   d. Giving prescribed antibiotics and placing warm blankets for comfort

4. A nurse is caring for a patient who has a pressure injury that is treated with debridement, irrigations, and moist gauze dressings. How would the nurse expect healing to occur?
   a. Cell regeneration
   b. Tertiary intention
   c. Secondary intention
   d. Remodeling of tissues

5. Which patient has the *greatest* risk for experiencing delayed wound healing?
   a. A 65-yr-old woman with stress incontinence
   b. A 52-yr-old obese woman with type 2 diabetes
   c. A 78-yr-old man who has a history of hypertension
   d. A 30-yr-old man who drinks 2 alcoholic beverages per day

6. Which order should a nurse question in the plan of care for an older adult, immobile stroke patient with a pink, clean stage 3 pressure injury?
   a. Pack the wound with foam dressing.
   b. Turn and position the patient every hour.
   c. Clean the wound every shift with Dakin's solution.
   d. Assess for pain and medicate before dressing change.

7. An 85-yr-old patient has a score of 16 on the Braden Scale. What should the nurse include in the plan of care?
   a. Implementing a 1-hour turning schedule with skin assessment.
   b. Elevating the head of bed to 90 degrees when the patient is supine.
   c. Continuing with weekly skin assessments with no special precautions.
   d. Placing a silicone foam dressing on the patient's sacrum to prevent breakdown.

8. Which patients are at *most* risk for pressure injuries? *Select all that apply.*
   a. A patient with right sided-paralysis and fecal incontinence
   b. An older adult who is alert and needs assistance to ambulate
   c. A young adult patient with paraplegia after a gunshot wound
   d. A morbidly obese patient who has an open abdominal wound
   e. An ambulatory patient who has occasional stress incontinence
   f. A young adult with a tibial fracture from a motor vehicle accident

9. An 82year-old man is being cared for at home by his family. A pressure injury on his right buttock measures $1 \times 2 \times 0.8$ cm in depth, and pink subcutaneous tissue is completely visible on the wound bed. Which stage would the nurse document on the wound assessment form?
   a. Stage 1
   b. Stage 2
   c. Stage 3
   d. Stage 4

1. a, 2. b, 3. b, 4. c, 5. b, 6. c, 7. a, 8. a, c, d, 9. c

For rationales to these answers and even more NCLEX review questions, visit *http://evolve.elsevier.com/Lewis/medsurg*.

ⓔ EVOLVE WEBSITE/RESOURCES LIST

REFERENCES

*1. Schieber AM, Ayres JS: Thermoregulation as a disease tolerance defense strategy, *Pathogens and Disease* 1:74, 2016.
 2. Atkins E: Fever: Its history, cause, and function, *Yale J Biol Med* 55:283, 1982. (Classic)
*3. LeBlanc K, Baranoski S, Christensen D, et al: The art of dressing selection: A consensus statement on skin tears and best practice, *Adv Skin Wound Care* 29:32, 2016.

 4. Nix DP: *Acute and chronic wounds: Current management concepts*, 5th ed, St Louis, 2016, Mosby.
 5. Whitney JD: Surgical wounds and incision care. In *Acute and chronic wounds: Current management concepts*, 5th ed, St Louis, 2016, Mosby.
*6. Sibbald RG, Elliott JA, Verma L, et al: Topical antimicrobial agents for chronic wounds, *Adv Skin Wound Care* 30:438, 2017.
*7. International Wound Infection Institute: Wound infection in clinical practice. Retrieved from *www.woundinfection-institute.com/wp-content/uploads/2017/07/IWII-Consensus_Final-2017.pdf.*
*8. Driver VR, Eckert KA, Carter MJ, et al: Cost-effectiveness of negative pressure wound therapy in patients with many comorbidities and severe wounds of various etiology, *Wound Repair Regen* 24:1041, 2016.
*9. Molnar JA, Vlad LG, Gumus T, et al: Nutrition and chronic wounds: Improving clinical outcomes, *Plast Reconstr Surg* 138:71S, 2016.
*10. Stallard Y: When and how to perform cultures on chronic wounds? *J Wound Ostomy Continence Nurs* 45:179, 2018.
*11. National Pressure Injury Advisory Panel: Prevention and treatment of pressure ulcers. Retrieved from *www.npuap.org/resources/educational-and-clinical-resources/.*
 12. Nightingale F: Notes on nursing, Philadelphia, 1859, Lippincott. (Classic)
*13. Elsabrout K, Orbacz E, McMahon LA, et al: Large-scale hospital mattress switch-out leads to reduction hospital-acquired pressure injuries: Operationalization of a multidisciplinary task force, *Worldviews Evid Based Nurs* 15:161, 2018.
*14. Jocelyn CH, Thiara E, Lopez V, et al: Turning frequency in adult bedridden patients to prevent hospital-acquired pressure injury: A scoping review, *Int Wound J* 15:225, 2018.
*15. Pickham D, Berte N, Pihulic M, et al: Effect of a wearable patient sensor on care delivery for preventing pressure injuries in acutely ill adults: A pragmatic randomized clinical trial, *Int J Nurs Stud* 80:12, 2018.

*Evidence-based information for clinical practice.

12

Genetics

Janice Smolowitz

*The things you do for yourself are gone when you are gone,
but the things you do for others remain as your legacy.*

Kalu Ndukwe Kalu

Ⓔ http://evolve.elsevier.com/Lewis/medsurg/

CONCEPTUAL FOCUS

Cellular Regulation

Ethics

LEARNING OUTCOMES

1. Describe common terms related to genetics and genetic disorders: autosomal, carrier, heterozygous, homozygous, mutation, recessive, and X-linked gene.
2. Distinguish between the 2 common causes of genetic mutations.
3. Compare and contrast the 3 most common inheritance patterns of genetic disorders.
4. Describe the most common classifications of genetic disorders.

5. Explore the complex ethical and social implications of genetic testing.
6. Analyze the role of pharmacogenomics and pharmacogenetics in developing personalized drug therapy.
7. Discuss your role in assisting the patient and family in dealing with genetic and genomic issues.

KEY TERMS

epigenetics, p. 180
genes, p. 175
genetics, p. 175
genome, p. 175

genomics, p. 175
hereditary, Table 12.1, p. 176
heterozygous, Table 12.1, p. 176
homozygous, Table 12.1, p. 176

mutation, p. 178
pharmacogenetics, p. 183
pharmacogenomics, p. 183

GENETICS AND GENOMICS

Genes are the basic units of heredity. They are composed of sequences of DNA found along a person's chromosomes. Genes are passed from 1 generation to the next. The **genome** is the complete set of DNA. It includes all the organism's genes. An organism's genome has all the information it needs to build and maintain itself.[1]

Genetics is the study of genes and their role in inheritance. Genetics determines the way that certain traits or conditions are passed down through genes. A person's genes can have a profound impact on health and disease. More than 4000 diseases are thought to be related to altered genes.

Genomics is the study of all a person's genes (the *genome*), including interactions of these genes with each other and with the person's environment. Genomics includes the study of complex diseases, such as heart disease, diabetes, and cancer, because these diseases are typically caused by a combination of genetic and environmental factors rather than by a single gene.

Genomics may help us understand why some people who eat healthy diets and exercise regularly die at a young age of cancer, and some people eat unhealthy diets and never exercise and yet live to an old age. Common terms used in genetics and genomics are defined in Table 12.1.

Important advances in genetic and genomic research and technology have affected the delivery of health care services.[2] In response to these scientific developments, nursing organizations have established practice standards that provide a framework for applying the nursing process to the care of persons with genetic and genomic concerns. Other standards outline competencies and education in relation to professional practice and genetics.

The identification of a genetic basis for many diseases has the potential to strongly influence the care of patients at risk for or diagnosed with a disease that has a genetic link. You need to know the basic principles of genetics, be familiar with the impact that genetics and genomics have on health and disease and be prepared to aid the patient and family with genetic issues.

TABLE 12.1 **Glossary of Genetic and Genomic Terms**

Term	Definition
Allele	One of a series of alternative forms (genotypes) at a specific region (locus) of a chromosome
Autosome	A chromosome other than X or Y. The human genome has 44 autosomes (22 pairs of autosomes)
Carrier	A person who is heterozygous for a gene variant that causes autosomal recessive or X-linked recessive disease. Used to describe heterozygotes for risk alleles of complex traits with variable penetrance, regardless of inheritance type
Carrier rate	Frequency of carriers in a population
Carrier testing	Clinical method used to identify at-risk family members of populations, who are usually asymptomatic but may have a pathogenic variant for an autosomal recessive or X-linked disorder
Chromosome	Microscopic structures in the cell nucleus composed of chromatin, which contain genetic information. Each cell normally has 46 chromosomes in 23 pairs (22 autosome pairs and 2 sex chromosomes)
Codominance	Expression of each pair of alleles when present in the heterozygous state (e.g., AB blood type)
Congenital	Present at birth
Consanguineous	Reproduction between 2 persons from the same bloodline, such as first or second cousins. Consanguineous parentage increases the probability of a rare recessive disease
Dominant allele	Gene that is expressed in the phenotype of a heterozygous person
Familial disorder	A trait that appears with higher frequency among close relatives than in the general population
Gene	Functional unit of heredity. A gene is a unit of DNA sequence that encodes for a specific functional product, such as RNA
Genetic risk	Probability that a trait will occur or recur in a family, based on knowledge of its genetic pattern of transmission
Genetics	Study of genes and their role in inheritance
Genome	All the DNA contained in a person. A person's genetic constitution
Genome-wide association study (GWAS)	A type of genetic mapping study design that involves scanning complete sets of DNA (genomes) of many people to find genetic variations associated with a particular disease
Genomics	Study of how genes interact and influence people's biologic and physical characteristics
Genotype	Genetic identity of a person, comprised of the entire complex of genes inherited from both parents
Haploid	Cells or organisms that have 1 copy of each autosomal chromosome and 1 copy of each sex chromosome. Ova and sperm are haploid. Fertilization results in an embryo with 1 set of chromosomes from each parent (diploid embryo)
Hereditary	Transmission of a disease, condition, or trait from parent to children
Heterozygous	Having 2 different alleles for 1 given gene, 1 inherited from each parent
Homozygous	Having 2 identical alleles for 1 given gene, 1 inherited from each parent
Locus	Position of a gene on a chromosome
Mutation	A change in a gene that affects function. Types include nonsense, missense silent, and frameshift. A mutation associated with a disease is called a *pathogenic variant*. Sometimes mutations are passed from parent to children.
Oncogene	Gene that contributes to the conversion of normal cells to cancer cells. Usually dominant
Pedigree	A graphic representation that shows family relationships, gender, age, and presence of diseases for each family member
Pharmacogenetics	Study of variability of drug metabolism related to variations in single genes
Pharmacogenomics	Study of variability of drug metabolism in relation to variations in and interactions of multiple genes or the person's genome
Phenotype	Observable characteristics of a person. Can be measured categorically or quantitatively
Protooncogene	Genes that can be turned into oncogenes by a dominant activating mutation. Oncogenes synthesize structurally altered proteins that result in cancer
Recessive allele	Allele that has no noticeable effect on the phenotype in a heterozygous person
Trait	Physical characteristic that one inherits, such as hair or eye color
X-linked gene	Gene found on the X chromosome rather than an autosome. In general, sex-linked disorders are seen in males

Basic Principles of Genetics

Genes. We think there are around 30,000 genes in each person's genome. Genes carry the instructions (encode) for making proteins that direct the activities of cells. Genes control how a cell functions, including how quickly it grows, how often it divides, and how long it lives. To control these functions, genes make proteins that perform specific tasks and act as messengers for the cell. It is essential that each gene have the correct instructions, or "code," for making its protein so that the protein can perform the proper function for the cell.

Genes are arranged in a specific linear formation along a chromosome (Fig. 12.1). Each gene has a specific location on a chromosome, termed a *locus*. An *allele* is 1 of 2 or more alternative forms of a gene that occupy corresponding loci on *homologous chromosomes* (a pair of chromosomes having corresponding deoxyribonucleic acid [DNA] sequences, with 1 coming from the mother and the other from the father). Each allele codes for a specific inherited characteristic.

When there are 2 different alleles, the allele that is fully expressed is the *dominant allele*. The other allele that lacks the ability to express itself in the presence of a dominant allele is the *recessive allele*. The actual genetic makeup of the person is called the *genotype*. Physical traits expressed by a person are called the *phenotype*.

Chromosomes. *Chromosomes* are found in the cell nucleus. They occur in pairs. Humans have 23 pairs of chromosomes. Twenty-two of the 23 pairs of chromosomes are *homologous* and are termed *autosomes*. Autosomes are the same in both

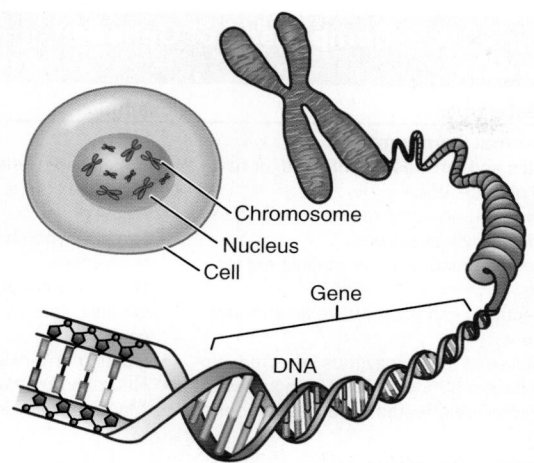

FIG. 12.1 The long, stringy DNA that makes up genes is spooled within chromosomes inside the nucleus of a cell. (Note that a gene would be a much longer stretch of DNA than what is shown here.) (Adapted from *The new genetics*, Bethesda, MD, 2010, National Institute of General Medical Science, National Institutes of Health, U.S. Department of Health and Human Services.)

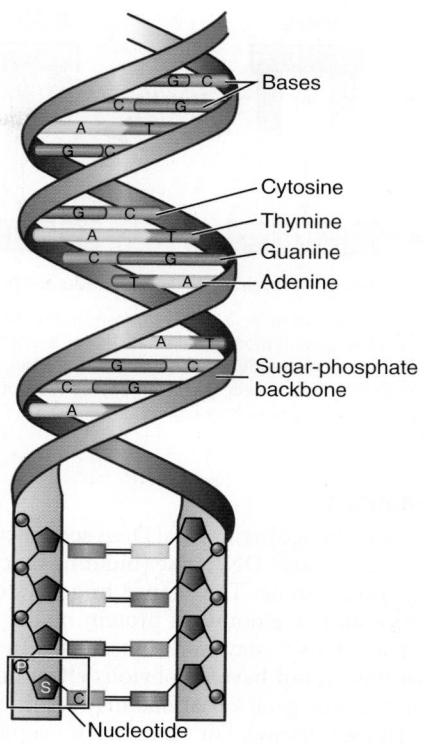

FIG. 12.2 DNA consists of 2 long, twisted chains made up of nucleotides. Each nucleotide contains a base, a phosphate molecule (P), and the sugar molecule deoxyribose (S). The bases in DNA nucleotides are adenine (A), thymine (T), cytosine (C), and guanine (G). (Adapted from *The new genetics*, Bethesda, MD, 2010, National Institute of General Medical Science, National Institutes of Health, U.S. Department of Health and Human Services.)

males and females. The sex chromosomes make up the twenty-third pair of chromosomes. A female has 2 X chromosomes, and a male has 1 X and 1 Y chromosome. One chromosome of each pair is inherited from the mother and one from the father. Half of each child's chromosomes (and therefore the genetic makeup) comes from his or her father and half from his or her mother.

DNA. Genes are made up of a nucleic acid called *deoxyribonucleic acid* (DNA). DNA stores genetic information and encodes the instructions for synthesizing specific proteins needed to maintain life. DNA also dictates the rate at which proteins are made. Every somatic cell in a person's body has the same DNA.

The information in DNA is stored as a code made up of 4 nitrogenous bases: adenine (A), guanine (G), cytosine (C), and thymine (T). Human DNA consists of about 3 billion bases, and more than 99% of those bases are the same in all people. The order, or sequence, of these bases determines the information for building and maintaining an organism. This is similar to the way we use letters of the alphabet to create words and sentences.

DNA bases pair up with each other, A with T and C with G, to form units called *base pairs*. Each base is attached to a sugar molecule and a phosphate molecule (Fig. 12.2). Together, a base, sugar, and phosphate are called a *nucleotide*. Nucleotides are arranged in 2 long strands that form a spiral called a *double helix*. The structure of the double helix is like a ladder, with the base pairs forming the ladder's rungs and the sugar and phosphate molecules forming the ladder's vertical sidepieces.

DNA can *replicate* or make copies of itself. Each strand of DNA in the double helix can serve as a pattern for duplicating the sequence of bases. When cells divide, each new cell must have an exact copy of the DNA that was in the parent (original) cell.

If you uncoiled the chromosomes in a cell and placed it end to end, the DNA would be about 6 feet long. If all the DNA in your body were connected, it would stretch about 67 billion miles.[2]

RNA. *Ribonucleic acid* (RNA) is similar to DNA but with some significant differences. RNA contains the nitrogenous bases adenine, guanine, and cytosine, but it contains uracil instead of thymine. RNA is single, not double, stranded. It contains ribose instead of deoxyribose sugar. RNA transfers the genetic information obtained from DNA to the proper location for protein synthesis.

Protein Synthesis. Protein synthesis, or the making of proteins, occurs in 2 steps: *transcription* and *translation*. Transcription is the process by which messenger RNA (mRNA) is made from single-stranded DNA. The mRNA becomes attached to a ribosome, where translation occurs. At this point another specialized type of RNA, transfer RNA (tRNA), arranges the amino acids in the correct sequence to assemble the protein. Once the protein is complete, it is released from the ribosome and able to perform its specific function in the cell.

Mitosis. *Mitosis* is a type of cell division that results in the formation of genetically identical daughter cells. Before cell division, the chromosomes duplicate, and each new cell (called *daughter cells*) receives an exact replica of the chromosomes from the original cell (called the *parent cell*).

Meiosis. Meiosis occurs only in germline, or sexual reproductive, cells. Two consecutive nuclear divisions, meiosis I and meiosis II, occur without chromosomes replicating in between. This results in the production of 4 haploid sex cells. Each has a single copy of each chromosome.

FIG. 12.3 In sickle cell disease, a single gene mutation leads to mutant (incorrect) protein. The substitution of valine *(VAL)* for glutamic acid on the β-globin chain of hemoglobin produces abnormal hemoglobin, hemoglobin S *(Hb S)*. In response to low O₂ levels, the erythrocytes with Hb S stiffen and elongate, taking on a sickle shape (see Fig. 30.3).

Genetic Mutations

A **mutation** is any change in the usual DNA sequence. Mutations range in size from a single DNA base (building block) to a large segment of a chromosome. The change in gene structure may change the type and/or amount of protein made. The protein may not work at all, or it may work incorrectly. In some cases, genetic mutations do not have an obvious effect on the people who have them. Some gene variations may result in disease or an increased risk for disease. For example, in people with sickle cell disease, a substitution of a single base (adenine is replaced by thymine) in a single gene (β-globin gene) causes the disease (Fig. 12.3).

Types of Mutations. Genetic mutations occur in 2 ways. They can be inherited from a parent (germline mutation) or acquired (somatic mutation) during a person's lifetime.

Germline mutations are passed from parent to child. These mutations are present in the oocyte and sperm cells. This type of mutation is present throughout a person's life in virtually every cell in the body.

Acquired (somatic) mutations occur in the DNA of a cell at some time during a person's life. An acquired mutation is passed on to all cells that develop from that single cell. These mutations in somatic cells cannot be passed on to the next generation. Acquired mutations can occur if (1) a mistake is made as DNA replicates during cell division or (2) environmental factors alter the DNA.

Mutations can occur when a cell is dividing. During replication, occasionally mistakes, such as deletions, insertions, or duplication of DNA material, can occur. Although DNA repair enzymes can correct replication errors, mistakes can go uncorrected.

DNA damage can also occur from environmental factors. For example, ultraviolet (UV) radiation can cause DNA damage, leading to skin cancer. Toxins in cigarettes can lead to lung cancer. Many chemotherapy drugs used to treat cancer target the DNA of cancer cells and healthy cells. In the process, these drugs increase a person's risk for developing secondary cancers (see Chapter 15).

Cells have built-in mechanisms that catch and repair most of the changes that occur during DNA replication or from environmental damage. However, as we age, our DNA repair does not work as effectively and we accumulate changes in our DNA.

Inheritance Patterns

Genetic conditions can be inherited in several ways, including autosomal dominant, autosomal recessive, X- linked, and

TABLE 12.2	**Comparison of Genetic Disorders**
Characteristics	**Examples**
Autosomal Dominant	
• Males and females are affected, or have the disease, equally • More common than recessive disorders and usually less severe • Affected persons show variable expression • Affected persons may have an affected parent • Children of a heterozygous (affected) parent have a 50% chance of being affected • Persons are affected in successive generations	• Breast and ovarian cancer related to *BRCA* genes • Familial hypercholesterolemia • Hereditary nonpolyposis colorectal cancer • Huntington's disease • Neurofibromatosis • Marfan's syndrome
Autosomal Recessive	
• Males and females are affected equally • Heterozygotes are carriers and usually asymptomatic • Affected persons may have unaffected parents who are heterozygous for trait • Children of 2 heterozygous parents have a 25% chance of being affected and a 50% chance of being carriers (Fig. 12.9) • Often no family history of disease	• Cystic fibrosis • Phenylketonuria • Sickle cell disease • Tay-Sachs disease • Thalassemia
X-Linked Recessive	
• Most affected persons have unaffected parents • Affected persons are usually male • Daughters of affected males are carriers • Sons of affected males are unaffected (unless mother is a carrier)	• Duchenne muscular dystrophy • Hemophilia • Wiskott-Aldrich syndrome

Y-linked disorders. If the mutant gene is found on an autosome, the genetic disorder is called *autosomal*. If the mutant gene is on the X chromosome, the genetic disorder is called *X-linked*. These patterns are considered mendelian patterns of inheritance. They occur less often than multifactorial or complex traits and disorders. Table 12.2 compares characteristics of autosomal dominant, autosomal recessive, and X-linked recessive conditions. Family pedigrees for autosomal recessive and dominant disorders and X-linked recessive disorders are shown in Figs. 12.4 and 12.5. These diagrams will be discussed later in this chapter in the context of documenting a pedigree and family history.

Autosomal dominant disorders are caused by a mutation of a single gene pair (heterozygous) on a chromosome. A dominant allele prevails over a normal allele. *Penetrance* describes the chance that a carrier of a dominant mutation will show signs of the disorder. *Incomplete penetrance* occurs when a person with a genetic mutation does not have signs of the disorder. It explains why a parent who has a genetic disorder may not have signs of the disorder, but the child does. Autosomal dominant disorders show variable expressivity. *Expressivity* describes the way the phenotype manifests. This accounts for how symptoms of a disorder vary from person to person, even though they have the same mutated gene. Symptoms are also influenced by other, usually unknown, genetic factors, gene-environment interactions, and chance events.

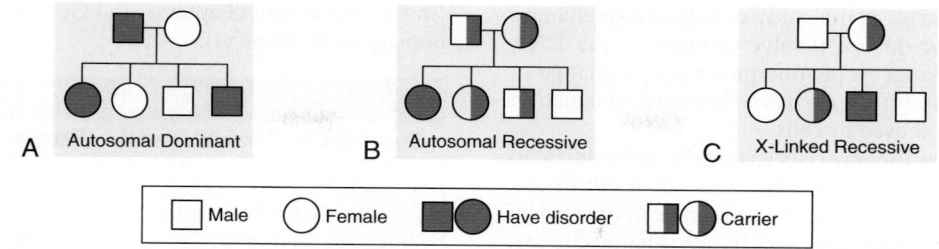

FIG. 12.4 Examples of family pedigrees showing inheritance of (**A**) autosomal dominant, (**B**) autosomal recessive, and (**C**) X-linked recessive disorders.

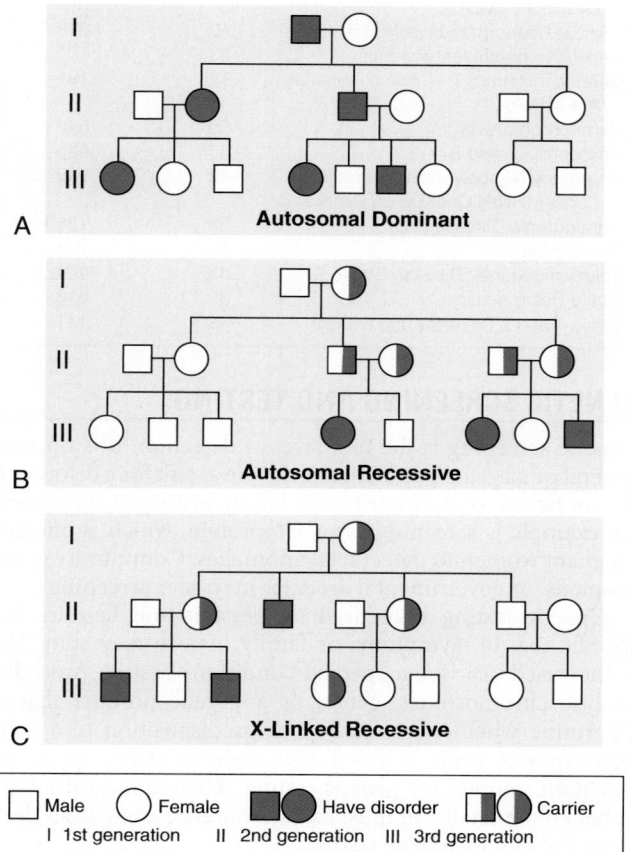

FIG. 12.5 Family pedigrees showing 3 generations. **A,** Family pedigree suggestive of an autosomal dominant disorder. **B,** Family pedigree suggestive of an autosomal recessive disorder. **C,** Family pedigree suggestive of an X-linked recessive disorder.

Autosomal recessive disorders are caused by mutations of 2 gene pairs (homozygous) on a chromosome. A person who inherits 1 copy of the recessive allele does not develop the disease because the normal allele predominates.[3] However, this person is a *carrier*. Several children of 1 couple may be affected. Males and females are affected with equal frequency and severity. These disorders occur in 1 generation and more often among children of parents who are blood relatives, such as first cousins.

X-linked recessive disorders are caused by a mutation on the X chromosome. Men can be severely affected because they have only 1 X chromosome. Women who carry the mutated gene on 1 X chromosome have another X chromosome to compensate

for the mutation. Women who carry the mutated gene can transmit it to their offspring.

Y chromosomal inheritance occurs for genes that are only on the Y chromosome. An affected father transmits the disorder to all his sons. Only men are affected.

Human Genome Project

The Human Genome Project (HGP), which was completed in 2003, mapped the entire human genome.[4] Analysis of the data will continue for many years. The knowledge gained through the HGP will (1) help improve the diagnosis of diseases, (2) allow for earlier detection of genetic predisposition to diseases, and (3) play a critical role in determining risk assessment for genetic-related diseases. In addition, the results of the HGP help match organ donors with transplant recipients.

GENETIC DISORDERS

A *genetic disorder* is caused in whole or in part by a change in the DNA sequence. They can be inherited (person born with altered genetic code) or they can be acquired (e.g., replication errors, damage to DNA from toxins).[3] Genetic disorders can be caused by (1) a mutation in 1 gene (single gene disorder); (2) mutations in multiple genes (multifactorial inheritance disorder), which are often related to environmental factors; or (3) damage to chromosomes (changes in the number or structure of chromosomes).

Classification of Genetic Disorders

Single Gene Disorders. Some genetic disorders result from a single gene mutation (Fig. 12.6, *A*). Examples include cystic fibrosis, sickle cell disease, and polycystic kidney disease. The pattern of inheritance for single gene disorders can be autosomal dominant, autosomal recessive, or X-linked. Single gene disorders are relatively rare compared with more commonly occurring multifactorial genetic disorders.

Multifactorial Inherited Conditions. *Multifactorial inherited conditions* are complex diseases that result from inherited variations in genes acting together with environmental factors (Fig. 12.6, *B*). These disorders run in families but do not show the same inherited characteristics as the single gene mutation conditions. Heart disease, diabetes, and most cancers are examples of such disorders.[5]

Many diseases can also be caused by rare hereditary mutations in a single gene. In these cases, genetic mutations that cause or strongly predispose a person to these diseases run in a family. These mutations can significantly increase each family member's risk for developing the disease. One example is breast cancer, in which inheritance of a mutated *BRCA1* or *BRCA2* gene confers significant risk for developing the disease.

Epigenetics. Epigenetics is the study of inheritable changes in gene expression that do not involve changes in the DNA sequence. There is a change in phenotype without a change in genotype. Epigenetic modifications define how the information in genes is expressed and used by cells.

Epigenetics influences the way cells terminally differentiate to become different types of cells (e.g., skin, liver) or result in disease. Epigenetic changes occur regularly and can be influenced by age, the environment, exercise, diet, and disease. Identical twins, who have the same genetic makeup, do not always develop the same diseases or at the same rate. Twins share the same genes, but their environments become different as they age. This unique aspect of twins makes them an excellent model for understanding how genes and the environment contribute to certain traits, especially complex behaviors and diseases.[6]

Chromosome Disorders. *Chromosome disorders* are caused by structural changes within chromosomes or by an excess or deficiency of the genes that are found on chromosomes. For example, an extra copy of chromosome 21 causes Down syndrome (called *trisomy 21*), so there are 3 copies of this chromosome instead of 2. In Down syndrome, there is no individual abnormal gene on the chromosome.

Chronic myelocytic leukemia can be caused by a chromosomal translocation, in which portions of 2 chromosomes (chromosomes 9 and 22) are exchanged. This translocation is called the *Philadelphia chromosome.*

Throughout the book, genetic disorders are highlighted in Genetics in Clinical Practice boxes, Genetic Risk Alert boxes

(in the assessment chapters), and Genetic Links content (in the management chapters).

🧬 GENETICS IN CLINICAL PRACTICE

Genetics in Clinical Practice Boxes Throughout Book

Genetic Disorder	Chapter	Page
α_1-Antitrypsin (AAT) Deficiency	28	561
Alzheimer's Disease (AD)	59	1387
Ankylosing Spondylitis	64	1517
Breast Cancer	51	1195
Cystic Fibrosis (CF)	28	577
Duchenne and Becker Muscular Dystrophy (MD)	63	1484
Familial Adenomatous Polyposis (FAP)	42	948
Familial Hypercholesterolemia	33	701
Genetic Information Nondiscrimination Act (GINA)	12	181
Hemochromatosis	30	620
Hemophilia A and B	30	626
Hereditary Nonpolyposis Colorectal Cancer (HNPCC) or Lynch Syndrome	42	949
Huntington's Disease (HD)	58	1380
Ovarian Cancer	53	1244
Polycystic Kidney Disease (PKD)	45	1042
Sickle Cell Disease	30	616
Types 1 and 2 Diabetes and MODY	48	1110

GENETIC SCREENING AND TESTING

Genetic screening is the first level of detection. It is offered to general or targeted populations who are at risk for a disorder but do not have symptoms or have a family history of the disorder. An example is screening for α-fetoprotein, which is offered to pregnant women to detect fetal anomalies. Community groups, hospitals, or governmental agencies may offer screenings.

Genetic testing is focused on persons and families for a specific reason. Symptoms or family history may show there is increased risk for a specific condition. Testing procedures analyze chromosomes, genes, or any gene product that can determine whether a mutation or predisposition to a condition exists. A person's blood, skin, hair, or saliva can be used to obtain samples for genetic testing. Tissues and cells can be obtained prenatally. In most cases, insurance companies do not cover the cost of genetic testing.

Genetic testing has been very useful in health care (Table 12.3). Genetic tests have been developed for more than 2000 diseases. Most tests assess single genes and are used to diagnose genetic disorders, such as cystic fibrosis or Duchenne muscular dystrophy.[7] Some genetic tests look at rare inherited mutations of otherwise protective genes, such as *BRCA1* and *BRCA2*, which are responsible for some types of hereditary breast and ovarian cancers.[8]

Test results are used to assess risk or diagnose a disorder, an important step in providing ongoing care for the person and family. It is important to identify people at high risk for conditions that may be preventable. For example, persons who have inherited a gene for familial adenomatous polyposis (FAP) need ongoing monitoring.[8] FAP is discussed in Chapter 42 on p. 948.

Genetic testing may raise ethical questions. People considering genetic testing should receive counseling about the various issues. They should be aware that test results in their medical

A   **Mutation in a single gene**

1 2 3 4 5 6 7 8 9 10 11 12

13 14 15 16 17 18 19 20 21 22 23

B   **Mutations in multiple genes**

FIG. 12.6 **A,** Genetic disorders can be caused by a mutation in a single gene (e.g., sickle cell disease, cystic fibrosis, hemophilia). **B,** Most genetic disorders are multifactorial genetic disorders caused by a combination of mutations in multiple genes, often interacting with environmental factors. Examples include cancer, diabetes, obesity, and hypertension.

records might not be private and there is the potential for discrimination by employers and insurance companies. To protect people from discrimination by employers and health insurance companies, the federal government passed the Genetic Information Nondiscrimination Act (GINA) in 2008.

GENETICS IN CLINICAL PRACTICE

Genetic Information Nondiscrimination Act (GINA)

The Genetic Information Nondiscrimination Act (GINA) is a federal law that prohibits discrimination in health care coverage and employment based on genetic information. Genetic information is any data about a person's genetic tests, family members' genetic tests, and family history of a genetic disease or disorder.

- Addresses concerns about discrimination that might prevent people from seeking genetic tests
- Enables people to take part in research studies without fear that their DNA information may be used against them in the workplace or prevent them from getting health insurance
- Prevents health insurers from denying health insurance coverage and discriminating against a person based solely on genetic or family history information
- Prevents health insurers from asking that a person have a genetic test
- Prohibits most employers from using genetic information for hiring, firing, or promotion decisions and for any decisions about terms of employment
- Protection does not extend to life insurance, disability insurance, and long-term care insurance

For more information see:
- www.genome.gov/Pages/PolicyEthics/GeneticDiscrimination/GINAInfoDoc.pdf.
- Frequently Asked Questions about GINA at *www.dol.gov/sites/default/files/ebsa/about-ebsa/our-activities/resource-center/faqs/gina.pdf.*

If a person has genetic testing, it may uncover information that may affect a family member who was not tested. These persons may not have taken part in the decision-making process to undergo testing. Similarly, if a whole family is tested, the results may show that a biologic relationship is not what the family believed it to be. For more information about genetic testing, see www.cdc.gov/genomics/gtesting/index.htm.

Interpreting Genetic Test Results

The results of genetic tests are not always straightforward, which often makes them challenging to interpret and explain. When interpreting test results, HCPs need to consider the reason the test was done, pretest counseling provided, the person's medical history, the family history, and the type of genetic test.[8]

A *positive test* result means that the laboratory found a change in a particular gene, chromosome, or protein that was being tested. Depending on the purpose of the test, this result may confirm a diagnosis (e.g., Huntington's disease), show that a person is a carrier of a particular genetic mutation (e.g., cystic fibrosis), identify an increased risk for developing a disease (e.g., breast cancer), or suggest a need for further testing. A positive result of a predictive or presymptomatic genetic test usually cannot establish the absolute risk for developing a disorder. A positive test also cannot predict the course or severity of a condition.

In some situations, it is difficult to interpret a positive result because some people who have the genetic mutation never develop the disease. For example, having the *apolipoprotein E-4 (Apo E-4)* allele increases the risk for developing Alzheimer's disease. However, many people who test positive for *Apo E-4* never develop Alzheimer's disease (see Chapter 59).

A *negative test* result means that the laboratory did not find an altered form of the gene, chromosome, or protein under consideration. This result generally means a person is not affected by a particular disorder, is not a carrier of a specific genetic mutation, or does not have increased risk for developing a certain disease. It is possible that the test missed a disease-causing genetic alteration. Many tests cannot detect all the genetic changes that cause a particular disorder. Further testing may be needed to confirm a negative result.

Direct-to-Consumer Genetic Tests

Direct-to-consumer genetic tests are marketed directly to people (consumers) via television, print advertisements, or the Internet. The test kit is mailed to the person instead of being ordered through an HCP's office. The test typically involves collecting a DNA sample at home, often by swabbing the inside of the cheek, and mailing the sample back to the laboratory. In some cases, the person must visit a health clinic to have blood drawn. People are notified of their results by mail, over the telephone, or online. In some cases, a genetics counselor or other HCP is available to explain the results and answer questions.

ETHICAL/LEGAL DILEMMAS

Genetic Testing

Situation

A 30-yr-old woman informs you that she is 3 months pregnant. She has 2 children with her current husband. This pregnancy was unplanned, and her youngest child has cystic fibrosis (CF). She expresses concern about the chance of having another child with CF. She mentions that she would like to have genetic testing on her fetus. Her husband asks you what the chance is of having another child with CF.

Ethical/Legal Points for Consideration

- With genetic testing, the patient and her family can find out whether their child will have CF. The woman and her husband can then make an informed decision.
- Genetic counseling is recommended before and after genetic testing because of the complexity of the information and the emotional issues involved with implications and options.
- Knowing that CF is an autosomal recessive condition, you can use Punnett squares (Fig. 12.9) or a family pedigree (Figs. 12.4 and 12.5) to show the woman and her husband the probability of having another child with CF.
- Be mindful of the privacy and confidentiality of genetic information and the potential conflict between 1 person's right to privacy and another person's right to information.

Discussion Questions

1. What information would you give the patient and her husband about genetic testing for them to make an informed decision?
2. What options are available for this couple?
3. How would you help this couple as they are considering ending the pregnancy if the results of the genetic testing reveal that the fetus will have CF?

TABLE 12.3 **Use of Genetic Tests**

Type of Test	Description	Examples
Carrier screening	• Can be used to identify unaffected persons who carry 1 copy of a gene • Offered to persons who have a family history of a genetic disorder and to those in ethnic groups with an increased risk for specific genetic conditions • If both parents are tested, the test can provide information about a couple's risk for having a child with a genetic condition	• Cystic fibrosis • Sickle cell disease • Hemophilia
Diagnostic testing	• Used to diagnose, rule out, or confirm a specific genetic or chromosomal condition • Used to confirm findings when patient's signs and symptoms suggest a genetic disorder • Can be done at any time during a person's life but is not available for all genes or all genetic conditions	• Cystic fibrosis • Sickle cell disease • Polycystic kidney disease • Hemophilia • Familial hypercholesterolemia
Forensic testing	• Done to identify a person for legal purposes	• Identify crime or victims in catastrophic situations • Rule out or implicate a crime suspect
Newborn screening	• Most widespread use of genetic testing • Early intervention to treat these disorders can eliminate or reduce symptoms that may otherwise cause a lifetime of disability	• Phenylketonuria • Congenital hypothyroidism • Cystic fibrosis
Parental testing	• Establish biologic relationships between people	• Paternity testing
Pharmacogenomic testing	• Identifies genetic variations that influence a person's response to drugs • Results provide information to help choose drug therapy that is best for the person	• Warfarin (Coumadin) dose
Predictive testing	• Can identify mutations that increase a person's risk for developing disorders • If results are positive, person can have prophylactic measures (e.g., mastectomy, oophorectomy) to prevent development of cancer	• Breast cancer • Ovarian cancer
Preimplantation genetic diagnosis (PGD)	• Fertilized embryos tested before implantation and pregnancy • Allows embryos free of particular disorders to be placed into the uterus • Embryos that test positive for genetic disorders can be destroyed	• For persons known to have or be a carrier for a genetic mutation (e.g., Huntington's disease)
Prenatal diagnostic testing	• Fluid obtained from amniocentesis or tissue from chorionic villus used to obtain fetal cells. Can obtain fetal samples from mother's blood • Used to detect changes in genes or chromosomes of fetus before birth • Type of testing offered to a couple with an increased risk for having a baby with a genetic or chromosomal disorder • Can decrease a couple's uncertainty or help them decide whether to end a pregnancy	• Down syndrome • Other genetic alterations in fetuses
Presymptomatic testing	• Used to detect genetic mutations associated with disorders that appear later in life • Can be helpful to people who have a family member with a genetic disorder but who have no features of the disorder themselves at the time of testing • Results can provide information about a person's risk for developing a specific disorder and help with making decisions about treatment	• Huntington's disease • Adult polycystic kidney disease • Hemochromatosis • Familial adenomatous polyposis • Hereditary nonpolyposis colorectal cancer syndrome

Direct-to-consumer genetic tests have significant risks and limitations. People may want their genetic information, but they may not understand what it means. They are vulnerable to being misled by the results of unproven or invalid tests. Without guidance from an HCP, they may make important decisions about disease treatment or prevention based on inaccurate, incomplete, or misunderstood information about their health. People may experience an invasion of genetic privacy if testing companies use their genetic information in an unauthorized way. When people are considering using these kinds of genetic tests, nurses should provide education and suggest they discuss the issue with their HCP or a genetics counselor. Teaching related to genetic testing is outlined in Table 12.4.

Genetic Technology

DNA Fingerprinting. DNA (genetic) fingerprinting begins by extracting DNA from the cells in a sample of blood, saliva, semen, or other appropriate fluid or tissue. *Polymerase chain reaction* (*PCR*) is a quick, easy method to provide unlimited copies of a DNA or RNA sequence using only a small amount of sample. PCR involves the artificial replication of a DNA or RNA sequence. The DNA or RNA strands can be separated to form new templates that are used for replication.

PCR is a key element in *genetic fingerprinting*. It is an essential technique to finding mutations in genes. It is used in forensic medicine to identify the DNA of criminal suspects by using samples from blood, hair, saliva, and semen. It has been used to free persons who are wrongly incarcerated. PCR is used in paternity testing and as a confirmatory test in human immunodeficiency virus (HIV) testing. This is especially important when an infant of a mother who is HIV-antibody positive tests HIV positive. In this situation, PCR will determine if the baby is infected with HIV or if the antibodies are from the mother.

DNA Microarray (DNA Chip). Although all a person's somatic cells have identical genetic material, the same genes are not active in every cell. Studying which genes are active and which

TABLE 12.4 Patient & Family Teaching

Genetic Testing

Genetic Counselors

- People who are considering genetic testing should meet with a genetics counselor who is specially trained in medical genetics and counseling.
- Counseling is advised to help you understand the purpose of genetic testing, considerations before testing, and the emotional and medical impact of the test results.
- Genetics counseling can help you understand the pros and cons of genetic testing before making a decision to undergo a genetic test.

General Information

The following includes some important general information about genetic testing:

- Genetic testing can be expensive and may not be included in your medical insurance policy.
- Genetic testing may determine whether you are predisposed to developing an inherited disease.
- A particular genetic test will only tell you whether there is a specific genetic variant or mutation. Positive tests do not mean you will develop that disease or disorder. Neither can the results tell you when you will develop the disease.
- If a genetic test shows a genetic predisposition to an inherited disorder, the news can be depressing.
- Knowledge of a genetic predisposition to a disease may give you the motivation to take preventive measures (e.g., taking drugs for familial hypercholesterolemia) or make lifestyle changes to lower the risk for a disease (e.g., exercising to decrease the risk for type 2 diabetes).
- If a genetic test reveals you are at risk for a specific genetic disorder, there is the chance that other family members may be at risk.
- If a genetic test reveals you are at risk for developing an inherited disease, whether you decide to share that information with family members is a personal and an ethical decision that you will have to make.
- Genetic testing may provide important information that you can use when making decisions about having children.

are inactive in different cell types helps to understand (1) how these cells function normally and (2) how they are affected when various genes do not perform properly.

Gene expression profiling uses a technology called *DNA microarrays* (DNA chips). DNA chips can identify changes in gene sequences or if certain genes are turned off in cells and tissues. It can serve as a diagnostic test or determine if certain medications might have a better therapeutic effect for certain people. The chip is a small glass plate enclosed in plastic. The surface of each chip has thousands of short, synthetic, single-stranded DNA sequences. Together they represent the normal gene, as well as known variations of the gene.

To determine if a mutation is present for a specific disease, a sample of DNA from the blood of the person with suspected disease and a control sample, which does not have a mutation in the gene, are obtained. The DNA in the samples is separated into single-stranded molecules and then cut into small fragments. The fragments are labeled using fluorescent dye. Different colors are used to identify the control and test samples. Both sets are inserted into the chip, where they bind to the synthetic DNA on the chip. If the person does not have a mutation for the gene, both samples will bind to the normal sequences on the chip. If a mutation is present, the person's DNA will bind to the sequence on the chip that represents the mutated DNA.

Genome-Wide Association Study (GWAS)

Genome-wide association study (GWAS) is an approach that involves rapidly scanning complete sets of DNA, or genomes, of many people to find genetic variations associated with the development or progression of a particular disease.

Until recently, researchers looked at single genes and the proteins that they encoded. With GWAS, researchers study large numbers of genes and proteins, including how they act and interact. This gives a more complete picture of what goes on in a person. After the genetic associations are found, researchers may be able to learn how to stop or jump-start genes on demand, change the course of a disease, or prevent it from ever happening. GWAS is particularly useful in finding genetic variations that contribute to multifactorial inherited disorders, such as cancer and heart disease.

To carry out a GWAS, researchers use 2 groups of people: those with the disease and similar people without the disease. Each person's complete set of DNA, or genome, is purified from the blood or cells, placed on tiny chips, and scanned on automated laboratory machines. The machines quickly survey each person's genome for strategically selected markers of genetic variation.

If certain genetic variations are significantly more common in people with the disease compared to people without the disease, the variations are said to be "associated" with the disease. The associated genetic variations can serve as powerful pointers to the region of the human genome where the disease-causing problem exists.

The potential impact of GWAS is substantial, since it lays the groundwork for personalized medicine. This changes the "1-size-fits-all" approach to health care. It provides a mechanism for providing more individualized plans of care. The information will help the HCP tailor prevention programs.

PHARMACOGENOMICS AND PHARMACOGENETICS

Patients vary widely in their response to drugs. Although the reasons for this are complex, genetic factors may account for a large percentage of individual variability. **Pharmacogenomics** looks at how drugs affect and interact with the genome and output expression. Pharmacogenomics allows for the identification of variations in multiple genes that affect drug response. **Pharmacogenetics** is the study of variable drug responses, including adverse events from differences in inheritable genes. These terms are often used interchangeably when describing the relationship between pharmacology and genetic variability in determining a person's response to drugs. Pharmacogenetics has a narrower focus than pharmacogenomics.[9]

Pharmacogenetic and pharmacogenomic studies could lead to the development of drugs that can be tailor-made or adapted to each person's particular genetic makeup. This will make it possible to have personalized medicine by choosing the right drug and the right dose for the right person.[8] HCPs are starting to use pharmacogenomic information to prescribe drugs. Examples are shown in Table 12.5.

One important area of study has focused on the hepatic cytochrome P450 (CYP450) enzyme system, which is responsible for oxidizing many drugs and chemicals.[8] The enzymes in this system share certain amino acid sequences. Each is coded by a separate gene. People with a less active form of the enzyme (who metabolize the drug slowly) may get too much of the drug. People with a more active form of the enzyme (who metabolize

TABLE 12.5 **Examples of Pharmacogenetics**

Drug	Role of Pharmacogenetics
abacavir (Ziagen)	• Some people are at greater risk for serious allergic reactions when first starting treatment with this drug. • Genetic testing for *HLA-B*5701* before taking the drug can identify those who carry a genetic marker that is associated with life-threatening hypersensitivity reactions.
clopidogrel (Plavix)	• For clopidogrel to work, cytochrome P450 enzymes in the liver (particularly CYP2C19) must convert the drug to its active form. • About 2% to 14% of the population are poor metabolizers of the drug. These patients may not receive the full benefits of the drug. • Genetic tests are available to identify genetic differences in CYP2C19 function.
crizotinib (Xalkori)	• Used to treat patients with late-stage, non–small cell lung cancers (NSCLCs) who express the abnormal anaplastic lymphoma kinase *(ALK)* gene. • *ALK* gene abnormality causes cancer development and growth. • Blocks certain proteins called *kinases,* including the protein made by the abnormal *ALK* gene. • Drug was approved for use with a companion genetic diagnostic test that determines whether a patient with NSCLC has the abnormal *ALK* gene.
trastuzumab (Herceptin)	• In breast cancer, drug works only for women whose tumors have genes that lead to the overproduction of a protein called HER-2. • Drug is a monoclonal antibody to HER-2. After the antibody attaches to the antigen, it kills the cells. • Genetic testing provides information on which women are good candidates for treatment with drug. • Drug does not work for women whose tumor genes do not express HER-2.
vemurafenib (Zelboraf)	• Approved for patients with late-stage (metastatic) or unresectable melanoma. • Indicated for the treatment of patients with melanoma whose tumors express a gene mutation called *BRAF V600E.* • To be considered for treatment, patients must first have genetic testing to determine whether melanoma cells have the *BRAF V600E* mutation.
warfarin (Coumadin) (see Fig. 12.7)	• Genetic variants in the genes *VKORC1* and cytochrome P450 2C9 *(CYP2C9)* have a significant impact on people's sensitivity to warfarin (Fig. 12.7). • Persons with particular variations in these genes need a lower warfarin dose to maintain therapeutic levels of anticoagulation. • Persons with other variations need higher doses. • Together, these genetic variations explain about 50% of the required dose difference between persons. • Testing for *CYP2C9* and *VKORC1* genotype information can assist in choosing the starting dose.

Metabolism of Drug	Genetic Variants of Cytochrome P450	Drug Dose Based on Genetic Testing of Cytochrome P450
Normal metabolism		Normal dose
Some people metabolize the drug quickly (fast metabolizers) and need higher doses		Higher dose
Some people metabolize the drug slowly (slow metabolizers) and need lower doses		Lower dose

FIG. 12.7 People respond differently to the drug warfarin (Coumadin). The diversity of responses is partially due to genetic variants in 1 of the cytochrome *P450* genes.

the drug quickly) may get too little of the drug. It may appear that the medication is not effective. These persons may need more frequent dosing. So, pharmacogenomic testing can help HCPs in prescribing the right dose of medicine based on a patient's particular genetic makeup (Fig. 12.7).

GENE THERAPY

Gene therapy is an investigational technique used to treat the underlying cause of a disease. Gene therapy may be used to supply a missing gene, avoid the missing gene's role, or enhance treatment of a disease. The goal is to provide a normally functioning gene to a person with a pathogenic gene variant. A carrier molecule called a *vector* must be used to deliver the therapeutic gene to the person's target cells.[10] Currently, the most common vector is a virus that has been genetically altered to carry normal human DNA.[11] The vector can be injected or given intravenously directly into specific tissue. The vector unloads its genetic material containing the therapeutic human gene into the target cell. If the treatment is successful, the new gene will make a functional protein and restore the target cell to a normal state. A diagram of gene therapy is shown in Fig. 12.8.

Although gene therapy is a promising treatment for a number of diseases (including inherited disorders, some types of cancer, certain viral infections), the technique is still under study. In 2017 the FDA approved the first 2 gene therapies. Tisagenlecleucel (Kymriah) is used to treat certain pediatric and young adult patients with a form of acute lymphoblastic leukemia. The other gene therapy treats vision loss from a congenital retinal degenerative disorder. The cost of that 1-time gene therapy is currently $850,000.[12]

STEM CELL THERAPY

Stem cells are the subject of much discussion because they may offer treatment for many diseases.[8] The use of stem cells may

In Vitro Manipulation

Viral vector

Proliferation

Dysfunctional ADA gene

Therapeutic ADA gene

Self-replication

Corrected Cell

FIG. 12.8 Gene therapy for adenosine deaminase *(ADA)* deficiency tries to correct this immunodeficiency state. The viral vector containing the therapeutic ADA gene is inserted into the patient's lymphocytes. These cells can then make the ADA enzyme.

allow for the regeneration of lost tissue and restoration of function in various diseases.

Stem cells are unspecialized cells in the body that have the ability to (1) remain in their unspecialized state and divide or (2) differentiate and develop into specialized cells. Stem cells can be derived from human embryos or adult somatic tissues. Stem cells can be totipotent, pluripotent, multipotent, or unipotent. Totipotent cells can produce all the cell types of the developing organism. Pluripotent cells can make any body cell because they make all cells of the embryo. Multipotent cells only make cells within a specific germ layer. Unipotent cells make a single cell type.

Adult stem cells are undifferentiated cells that are found in small numbers in many organs and tissues, including brain, bone marrow, peripheral blood, blood vessels, skeletal muscle, skin, teeth, heart, GI tract, liver, ovarian epithelium, and testes. The primary roles of adult stem cells are to maintain and repair the tissues in which they are found. They are usually thought of as multipotent cells, giving rise to a closely related family of cells within the tissue. For example, skin stem cells produce new skin cells. Hematopoietic stem cells found within the bone marrow can form all the various blood cells. These cells are prolific by design.

Stems cells are used to treat persons with many different disorders, including severe burns and orthopedic conditions that require bone grafting. For the past 20 years, hematopoietic stem cell transplantation has been a standard for treatment for hematologic cancers and bone marrow failure (see Chapter 15). Medical researchers are investigating the use of stem cells to repair or replace damaged body tissues, similar to whole organ transplants.

❖ NURSING MANAGEMENT: GENETICS AND GENOMICS

You need to understand genetics and genomics to assist persons and families seeking information and making decisions related

to genetic issues.[13] By understanding the profound influence that genetics has on health and illness, you can aid the patient and family in making critical decisions related to genetic issues, such as genetic testing. You can facilitate access to resources and provide education in response to questions.

You will collaborate with other health care team members, including genetics nurses and genetics counselors. A genetics nurse is a licensed professional nurse with specialized education and training in genetics. Nurses with *GCN* after their names are baccalaureate-prepared licensed registered nurses who have received specialty credentialing as a Genetic Clinical Nurse (GCN). Nurses with *APNG* after their names are registered nurses with a master's degree who have received specialty credentialing as an Advanced Practice Nurse in Genetics (APNG).

The specialized knowledge and counseling skills of a genetics nurse or genetics counselor are often important when genetic testing is considered. Genetic testing may raise many emotional issues. Knowledge of carrier status of a genetic disorder may influence a person's career, marriage, and childbearing decisions. It may also affect family members, as they contemplate potentially serious life and health care issues.

For example, how should a wife deal with a husband who has tested positive for Huntington's disease and shows early signs of cognitive impairment? Should their children be tested for the disease? Consider the situation of a woman who has a family history of breast cancer and is now diagnosed with breast cancer. She asks whether she and her teenage daughters should have *BRCA* testing. What do you tell her?

Genetic testing raises ethical questions. Who should know the results of a genetic test? Who should protect the privacy of test results and prevent persons from discrimination? People may be reluctant to share or disclose information about family history or genetic test results. They fear they are vulnerable to discrimination based on their DNA. As a nurse, you need to understand how different health care policies relate to genetic testing. Discuss how the Genetic Information Nondiscrimination Act (GINA) protects persons from discrimination by employers and health care insurance companies (see Genetics in Clinical Practice Box on p. 181).[14]

◆ Nursing Assessment: Family History

As a nurse, it is very important that you ask persons about their family history and identify and assess inheritance patterns by constructing a family pedigree (Figs. 12.4 and 12.5). The family health history is a written or graphic record of the diseases and health conditions present in one's family (see Chapter 3). A pedigree is a graphic representation of the family history. The family history and pedigree should include a minimum of 3 generations.

To help people record information about their family history, the Centers for Disease Control and Prevention (CDC) has collaborated with the U.S. Surgeon General and other federal agencies to develop a Web-based tool called My Family Health Portrait (*https://phgkb.cdc.gov/FHH/html/index.html*). Other Web-based programs are available to help create pedigree diagrams based on the information entered. Or, you can draw a pedigree by hand.

When constructing the pedigree, start with the proband, or person being interviewed. Identify that person with an arrow. For each family member, document date of birth, any medical illnesses or health conditions and the age when diagnosed, and age and cause of death, if the person is deceased. Comment on ancestors' racial and ethnic information, information that is unknown, and presence of consanguinity. After recording the family history or pedigree, review the information to identify key features that may increase a person's risk for genetic-related diseases. These include:

- Disease in more than 1 close relative
- Disease that does not usually affect a certain gender (e.g., breast cancer in a male)
- Disease that occurs at an earlier age than expected (e.g., myocardial infarction before age 35)
- Certain combinations of diseases within a family (e.g., breast and ovarian cancer, heart disease, and diabetes)

If 1 or more of these features are identified, the family history may hold important clues about a person's risk for a genetic disease. These persons may benefit from further clinical investigation, screening, and diagnostic testing. As a nurse, you may refer these persons to a specialist for information about the benefits and risks of genetic screening and testing.

Genetic Risk Alert boxes in the assessment chapters of this book highlight persons' risks related to genetic diseases and disorders. You can use the information in these boxes to assess the family history.

As a nurse, you can support the person and family by providing education and reinforcing the information they receive throughout the process. You can use the family history, pedigree, and Punnett squares (Fig. 12.9) to explain the risk for inheritable disease. When a diagnosis is confirmed, you can discuss health promotion activities. People with multifactorial disorders may benefit from lifestyle modification that addresses unhealthy behaviors (e.g., smoking, poor eating habits). You can help the person and family understand how evidence-based guidelines are used for monitoring, screening, and ongoing follow-up. For example, it is important to monitor cholesterol levels in a person with a family history of familial hypercholesterolemia. Throughout this process, maintain the person's confidentiality and respect his or her values and beliefs.

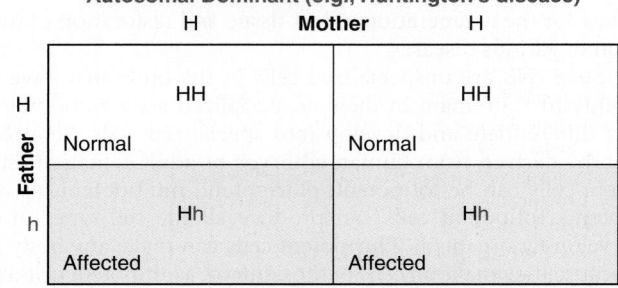

FIG. 12.9 Punnett squares illustrate inheritance possibilities. **A,** If the mother and father are both carriers for cystic fibrosis, there is a 25% chance that offspring will have cystic fibrosis. **B,** If the mother is a carrier for the hemophilia gene and the father has a normal genotype, there is a 50% chance that any male offspring will have hemophilia. There is a 50% chance that any female offspring will be a carrier. **C,** If the mother has a normal genotype and the father has Huntington's disease, there is a 50% chance that offspring will have the disease.

BRIDGE TO NCLEX EXAMINATION

The number of the question corresponds to the same-numbered outcome at the beginning of the chapter.

1. If a person is heterozygous for a given gene, it means that the person
   a. is a carrier for a genetic disorder.
   b. is affected by the genetic disorder.
   c. has 2 identical alleles for the gene.
   d. has 2 different alleles for the gene.
2. Common causes of genetic mutations include *(select all that apply)*
   a. DNA damage from toxins.
   b. DNA damage from UV radiation.
   c. inheritance of altered genes from father.
   d. inheritance of altered genes from mother.
   e. inheritance of somatic mutations from either parent.
3. A father who has an X-linked recessive disorder and a wife with a normal genotype will
   a. pass the carrier state to all his children.
   b. pass the carrier state to his male children.
   c. pass the carrier state to his female children.
   d. not pass on the genetic mutation to any of his children.
4. What characterizes multifactorial genetic disorders?
   a. Often caused by single gene alterations
   b. Genetic testing available for most disorders
   c. Many family members report having the disorder
   d. Caused by complex interactions of genetic and environmental factors

5. If a person tests positive for a genetic mutation, it means (select all that apply)
   a. the laboratory found an alteration in a gene.
   b. the person is predisposed to develop a genetic disease.
   c. there is the chance other family members may be at risk.
   d. the person will develop the disease at some point in time.
   e. the person should not have any children or any more children.

6. What role does pharmacogenomics have in health care?
   a. It can assess individual variability to many drugs.
   b. It can be used to assess the effectiveness of a drug.
   c. It provides important assessment data for gene therapy.
   d. It can assess the variability of drug responses due to single genes.

7. A couple who recently had a son with hemophilia A is consulting with a nurse. They want to know if their next child will have hemophilia A. The nurse can tell the parents that if their child is a
   a. boy, he will have hemophilia A.
   b. boy, he will be a carrier of hemophilia A.
   c. girl, she will be a carrier of hemophilia A.
   d. girl, there is a 50% chance she will be a carrier of hemophilia A.

1. d, 2. a, b, c, d, 3. c, 4. d, 5. a, c, 6. d, 7. d

For rationales to these answers and even more NCLEX review questions, visit *http://evolve.elsevier.com/Lewis/medsurg.*

ⓔ EVOLVE WEBSITE/RESOURCES LIST

http://evolve.elsevier.com/Lewis/medsurg
Review Questions (Online Only)
Key Points
Answer Key for Questions
  • Rationales for Bridge to NCLEX Examination Questions
Conceptual Care Map Creator
Audio Glossary
Content Updates

REFERENCES

1. National Human Genome Research Institute: Your guide to understanding genetic conditions. Retrieved from *www.ghr.nlm.nih.gov/primer/hgp/genome.*
2. National Human Genome Research Institute: An animation of the interactive timeline found on genome. Retrieved from *www.unlockinglifescode.org/timeline?tid=4.*
3. U.S. National Library of Medicine: Different ways genetic conditions can be inherited. Retrieved from *www.ghr.nlm.nih.gov/primer/inheritance/inheritancepatterns.*
4. U.S. Department of Energy: Human Genome Project information. Retrieved from *www.ornl.gov.*
5. National Center for Biotechnology Information: Genes and diseases. Retrieved from *www.ncbi.nlm.nih.gov/books/NBK22183.*
6. Schwab TL, Hogenson TL: Effect of epigenetic differences in identical twins, *Handbook of Nutrition, Diet, and Epigenetics,* 1, 2017.
7. National Center for Biotechnology Information: Gene tests. Retrieved from *www.ncbi.nlm.nih.gov/sites/GeneTests.*
8. Kasper CE, Schneidereith TA, Lashley FR: *Lashley's essentials of clinical genetics in nursing practice,* ed 2, New York, 2017, Springer.
9. Singh DB: Pharmacogenomics: Clinical perspective, strategies, and challenges. In *Translational bioinformatics and its application,* Dordrecht, 2017, Springer.
10. U.S. National Library of Medicine: Gene therapy. Retrieved from *www.ghr.nlm.nih.gov/handbook/therapy/genetherapy.*
*11. Lee CS, Bishop ES, Zhang R, et al: Adenovirus-mediated gene delivery: Potential applications for gene and cell-based therapies in the new era of personalized medicine, *Genes Dis* 4:43, 2017.
12. Food and Drug Administration News Release (2017). FDA approves novel gene therapy to treat patients with a rare form of inherited vision loss. Retrieved from *www.fda.gov/NewsEvents/Newsroom/PressAnnouncements/UCM589467.htm?utm_campaign=12192017_PR_FDA%20approves%20first%20gene%20therapy%20treatment&utm_medium=email&utm_source=Eloqua.*
*13. Montgomery S, Brouwer WA, Everett PC, et al Genetics in the clinical setting, *American Nurse Today* 12:10, 2017.
14. International Society of Nurses in Genetics: Position statements: Privacy and confidentiality of genetic information. Retrieved from *www.isong.org/resources/Documents/PS_Privacy_Confidentiality.pdf.*

*Evidence-based information for clinical practice.

Immune Responses and Transplantation

Haley Hoy and Yeow Chye Ng

Compassion is the ultimate expression of your highest self.

Russell Simmons

http://evolve.elsevier.com/Lewis/medsurg/

CONCEPTUAL FOCUS

Functional Ability
Immunity
Infection

Inflammation
Tissue Integrity

LEARNING OUTCOMES

1. Describe the components and functions of the immune system.
2. Characterize the 5 types of immunoglobulins.
3. Distinguish among the 4 types of hypersensitivity reactions in terms of immunologic mechanisms and resulting alterations.
4. Outline the clinical manifestations and emergency management of a systemic anaphylactic reaction.
5. Describe the assessment and interprofessional care of a patient with chronic allergies.

6. Describe the etiologic factors, clinical manifestations, and treatment modalities of autoimmune diseases.
7. Describe the etiologic factors and categories of immunodeficiency disorders.
8. Explain the relationship between the human leukocyte antigen system and certain diseases.
9. Distinguish among the types of rejections after transplantation.
10. Identify the types and side effects of immunosuppressive therapy.

KEY TERMS

anergy, p. 193
antigen, p. 189
autoimmunity, p. 202
cell-mediated immunity, p. 193

cytokines, p. 191
human leukocyte antigen (HLA), p. 204
humoral immunity, p. 193
hypersensitivity reactions, p. 194

immunocompetence, p. 193
immunodeficiency, p. 203
immunosuppressive therapy, p. 206

Our bodies have several defense mechanisms for protecting ourselves. One of the most complex is the immune response. Immune processes must be functioning properly for the body to defend itself against the presence of foreign substances. This response is critical to maintaining health. Thus many problems occur when the immune response is altered. These problems are closely related to the concepts of inflammation, infection, and tissue integrity. You will find that the care of patients with immune disorders discussed in this chapter will be similar to the care of patients with inflammation (Chapter 11), neutropenia (Chapter 30), and general infection (Chapter 14).

NORMAL IMMUNE RESPONSE

Immunity is the body's ability to resist disease. Immune responses serve the following 3 functions:
1. *Defense:* The body protects against invasions by microorganisms and prevents the development of infection by attacking foreign antigens and pathogens.
2. *Homeostasis:* Damaged cellular substances are digested and removed. Through this mechanism, the body's different cell types stay uniform and unchanged.
3. *Surveillance:* Mutations continually arise but are recognized as foreign cells and destroyed.

TABLE 13.1 Types of Acquired Specific Immunity

Type	Natural	Artificial
Active	Natural contact with antigen through actual infection (e.g., chicken-pox, measles, mumps)	Immunization with antigen (e.g., vaccines for chicken-pox, measles, mumps)
Passive	Transplacental and colostrum transfer from mother to child (e.g., maternal immunoglobulins passed to baby)	Injection of serum with antibodies from 1 person (e.g., injection of hepatitis B immune globulin) to another person who does not have antibodies

Antigens

An antigen is a substance that elicits an immune response. Most antigens are composed of protein. However, other substances such as large polysaccharides, lipoproteins, and nucleic acids can act as antigens. All the body's cells have antigens on their surface that are unique to that person and enable the body to recognize itself. The immune system normally becomes "tolerant" to the body's own molecules. Therefore it is nonresponsive to "self" antigens.

Types of Immunity

We classify immunity as innate or acquired.

Innate Immunity. *Innate immunity* is present at birth. Its primary role is first-line defense against pathogens. This type of immunity involves a nonspecific response, and neutrophils and monocytes are the primary white blood cells (WBCs) involved. Innate immunity is not antigen specific. So, it can respond within minutes to an invading microorganism without prior exposure to that organism.

Acquired Immunity. *Acquired immunity* is the development of immunity, either actively or passively (Table 13.1).

Active Acquired Immunity. *Active acquired immunity* results from the invasion of the body by foreign substances such as microorganisms and the subsequent development of antibodies and sensitized lymphocytes. With each reinvasion of the microorganisms, the body responds more rapidly and vigorously to fight off the invader. Active acquired immunity may result naturally from a disease or artificially through immunization. Because the body makes antibodies, immunity takes time to develop but is long lasting.

Passive Acquired Immunity. In *passive acquired immunity,* the host receives antibodies to an antigen rather than making them. This may take place naturally through the transfer of immunoglobulins across the placental membrane from mother to fetus. Artificial passive acquired immunity occurs through injection with gamma globulin (serum antibodies). The benefit of this immunity is its immediate effect. Unfortunately, passive immunity is short lived because the person does not make the antibodies and memory cells for the antigen.

Lymphoid Organs

The lymphoid system is composed of central (or primary) and peripheral lymphoid organs. The *central lymphoid organs* are the thymus gland and bone marrow. The *peripheral lymphoid organs* are the lymph nodes; tonsils; spleen; and gut-, genital-, bronchial-, and skin-associated lymphoid tissues (Fig. 13.1).

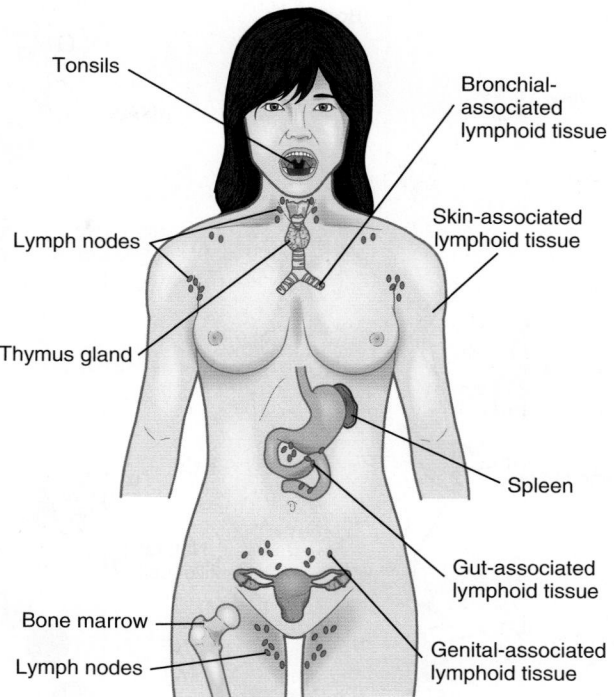

FIG. 13.1 Organs of the immune system.

Lymphocytes are made in the bone marrow. They eventually migrate to the peripheral organs. The thymus is involved in the differentiation and maturation of T lymphocytes and is therefore essential for a cell-mediated immune response. The thymus is its largest during childhood. After puberty, the thymus starts to slowly shrink and become replaced by fat. By age 75, the thymus is little more than fatty tissue and produces few T lymphocytes.

When antigens enter the body, they may be carried by the bloodstream or lymph channels to regional lymph nodes. The antigens interact with B and T lymphocytes and macrophages in the lymph nodes. The 2 major functions of lymph nodes are (1) filtration of foreign material brought to the site and (2) circulation of lymphocytes.

The tonsils are an example of lymphoid tissue. The spleen, a peripheral lymph organ, is important as the primary site for filtering foreign antigens from the blood. Lymphoid tissue is found in the submucosa of the GI (gut-associated), genitourinary (genital-associated), and respiratory (bronchial-associated) tracts. This tissue protects the body from external microorganisms.

The skin-associated lymph tissue consists primarily of lymphocytes and Langerhans' cells (type of dendritic cell) found in the epidermis of skin. When Langerhans' cells are depleted, the skin cannot initiate an immune response. Therefore a delayed hypersensitivity reaction (as determined by skin testing with injected antigens) does not occur.

Cells Involved in Immune Response

Mononuclear Phagocytes. The *mononuclear phagocyte system* includes monocytes in the blood and macrophages found throughout the body. Mononuclear phagocytes have a critical role in the immune system. They are responsible for capturing, processing, and presenting the antigen to the

FIG. 13.2 The immune response to a virus. **A,** A virus invades the body through a break in the skin or another portal of entry. The virus must make its way inside a cell to replicate itself. **B,** A macrophage recognizes the antigens on the surface of the virus. The macrophage digests the virus and displays pieces of the virus (antigens) on its surface. **C,** T helper cell recognizes the antigen displayed and binds to the macrophage. This binding stimulates the production of cytokines (interleukin-1 *[IL-1]* and tumor necrosis factor *[TNF]*) by the macrophage and interleukin-2 *(IL-2)* and γ-interferon *(γ-IFN)* by the T cell. These cytokines are intracellular messengers that provide communication among the cells. **D,** IL-2 instructs other T helper cells and T cytotoxic cells to proliferate (multiply). T helper cells release cytokines, causing B cells to multiply and make antibodies. **E,** T cytotoxic cells and natural killer cells destroy infected body cells. **F,** The antibodies bind to the virus and mark it for macrophage destruction. **G,** Memory B and T cells stay behind to respond quickly if the same virus attacks again.

lymphocytes. This stimulates a humoral or cell-mediated immune response. Capturing is accomplished through phagocytosis. The macrophage-bound antigen, which is highly immunogenic, is presented to circulating T or B lymphocytes and thus triggers an immune response (Fig. 13.2).

Lymphocytes. Lymphocytes are made in the bone marrow (Fig. 13.3). They then differentiate into B and T lymphocytes.

B Lymphocytes. In the early research on *B lymphocytes* (bursa-equivalent lymphocytes) in birds, we discovered that they mature under the influence of the bursa of Fabricius, hence the name *B cells*. However, this lymphoid organ does not exist in humans. The bursa-equivalent tissue in humans is the bone marrow. B cells differentiate into *plasma cells* when activated. Plasma cells make antibodies (immunoglobulins) (Table 13.2).

T Lymphocytes. Cells that migrate from the bone marrow to the thymus differentiate into *T lymphocytes* (thymus-dependent cells). The thymus secretes hormones, including thymosin, that stimulate the maturation and differentiation of T lymphocytes. T cells make up 70% to 80% of the circulating lymphocytes. They are primarily responsible for immunity to intracellular viruses, tumor cells, and fungi. T cells can live from a few months to the life span of a person. They account for long-term immunity.

T lymphocytes can be categorized into T cytotoxic and T helper cells. Antigenic characteristics of WBCs can be classified using monoclonal antibodies. These antigens are classified as *clusters of differentiation,* or *CD antigens.* We refer to many types of WBCs, especially lymphocytes, by their CD designations. All mature T cells have the CD3 antigen.

T cytotoxic cells. T cytotoxic (CD8) cells are involved in attacking antigens on the cell membrane of foreign pathogens and releasing cytolytic substances that destroy the pathogen. These cells have antigen specificity and are sensitized by exposure to the antigen. Much like B cells, some sensitized T cells do not attack the antigen but remain as memory T cells. As in the humoral immune response, a second exposure to the antigen results in a more intense and rapid cell-mediated immune response.

T helper cells. T helper (CD4) cells are involved in the regulation of cell-mediated immunity and the humoral antibody response. T helper cells differentiate into subsets of cells that make distinct types of cytokines (discussed in a later section). These subsets are called T_H1 cells and T_H2 cells. T_H1 cells stimulate phagocyte-mediated ingestion and killing of microbes, the key component of cell-mediated immunity. T_H2 cells stimulate eosinophil-mediated immunity, which is effective against parasites and is involved in allergic responses.

Natural Killer Cells. Natural killer (NK) cells are involved in cell-mediated immunity. These cells are not T or B cells but are large lymphocytes with many granules in the cytoplasm. NK cells do not need prior sensitization for their generation. These cells are involved in recognition and killing of virus-infected

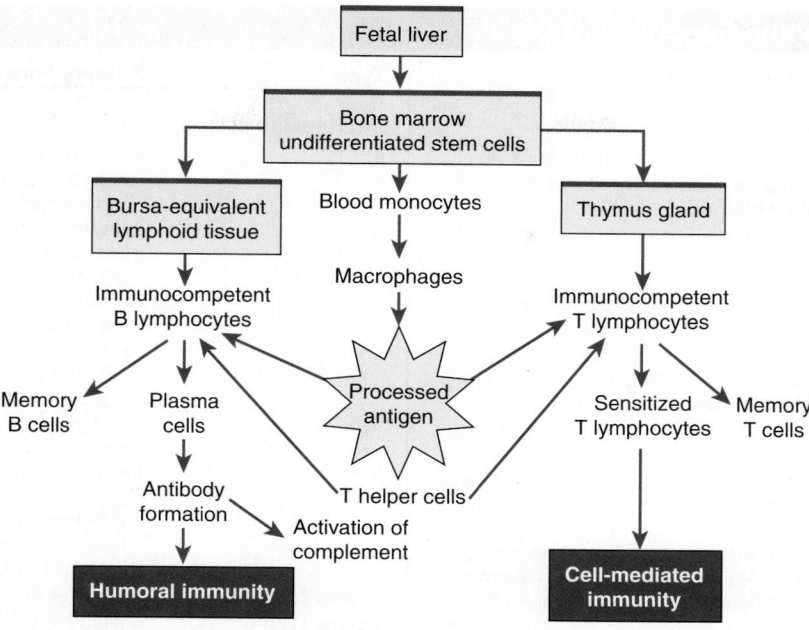

FIG. 13.3 Relationships and functions of macrophages, B lymphocytes, and T lymphocytes in an immune response.

TABLE 13.2   Characteristics of Immunoglobulins

Class	Serum Concentration (%)	Location	Characteristics
IgG	76	Plasma, interstitial fluid	Only immunoglobulin that crosses placenta. Responsible for secondary immune response
IgA	15	Body secretions, including tears, saliva, breast milk, colostrum	Lines mucous membranes and protects body surfaces
IgM	8	Plasma	Responsible for primary immune response. Forms antibodies to ABO blood antigens
IgD	1	Plasma	Present on lymphocyte surface. Aids in the differentiation of B lymphocytes
IgE	0.002	Plasma, interstitial fluids	Causes symptoms of allergic reactions. Fixes to mast cells and basophils. Aids in defense against parasitic infections

cells, tumor cells, and transplanted grafts. NK cells have a vital role in immune surveillance for malignant cell changes. We do not fully understand the mechanism of recognition.

T Dendritic Cells. *Dendritic cells* make up a system of cells that is important to the immune system, especially the cell-mediated immune response. They have an atypical shape with extensive dendritic processes that form and retract. They are found in many places in the body, including the skin (where they are called *Langerhans' cells*) and the lining of the nose, lungs,

stomach, and intestine. There are many immature dendritic cells in the blood.[1]

Dendritic cells function primarily to capture antigens at sites of contact with the external environment (e.g., skin, mucous membranes) and then transport the antigen until it meets a T cell with specificity for that antigen. In this role, they have an important function in activating the immune response.

Cytokines

The immune response involves complex interactions of T cells, B cells, monocytes, and neutrophils. These interactions depend on **cytokines** (soluble factors secreted by WBCs and a variety of other cells in the body) that act as messengers among the cell types. Cytokines instruct cells to alter their proliferation, differentiation, secretion, or activity.

Currently, we know of more than 100 different cytokines. They can be classified into distinct categories. Some of these cytokines are listed in Table 13.3. In general, the interleukins (ILs) act as immunomodulatory factors. Colony-stimulating factors act as growth-regulating factors for hematopoietic cells. Interferons are antiviral and immunomodulatory.

The net effect of an inflammatory response is determined by a balance between proinflammatory and antiinflammatory mediators. We can sometimes classify cytokines as proinflammatory or antiinflammatory. However, it is not that clear-cut, since many other factors (e.g., target cells, environment) influence the inflammatory response to a given injury or insult.

Cytokines have a beneficial role in hematopoiesis and immune function. They can have detrimental effects such as those seen in chronic inflammation, autoimmune diseases, and sepsis. Cytokines such as colony-stimulating factors, interferons, and IL-2 have clinical uses (Table 13.4).

Interferon helps the body's natural defenses attack tumors and viruses. We know of 3 types of interferon (Table 13.3). Interferon is not directly antiviral but produces an antiviral

TABLE 13.3   Types and Functions of Cytokines

Type	Primary Functions	Type	Primary Functions
Colony-Stimulating Factors (CSFs)		**Interleukins (ILs)**	
Granulocyte colony-stimulating factor (G-CSF)	Stimulates proliferation and differentiation of neutrophils, enhances functional activity of mature PMNs	IL-1	Proinflammatory mediator. Promotes proliferation of B cells. Activates T cells, NK cells, and macrophages
Granulocyte-macrophage colony-stimulating factor (GM-CSF)	Stimulates proliferation and differentiation of PMNs and monocytes	IL-2	Activates T cells, NK cells, and macrophages. Stimulates release of other cytokines (α-IFN, TNF, IL-1, IL-6)
Macrophage colony-stimulating factor (M-CSF)	Promotes proliferation, differentiation, and activation of monocytes and macrophages	IL-3	Hematopoietic growth factor for hematopoietic precursor cells
Erythropoietin	Stimulates erythroid progenitor cells in bone marrow to make red blood cells	IL-4	Antiinflammatory mediator. B cell growth and differentiation. Induces differentiation into T_H2 cells. Stimulates growth of mast cells
		IL-5	B-cell growth and differentiation. Promotes growth and differentiation of eosinophils
Interferons (IFNs)		IL-6	Proinflammatory mediator. T- and B-cell growth factor, promotes differentiation of B cells into plasma cells and stimulates antibody secretion. Induces fever. Synergistic effects with IL-1 and TNF
α-IFN β-IFN	Inhibits viral replication, activates NK cells and macrophages, antiproliferative effects on tumor cells		
γ-IFN	Proinflammatory mediator. Activates macrophages, neutrophils, and NK cells. Promotes B cell differentiation. Inhibits viral replication	**Tumor Necrosis Factor (TNF)**	Proinflammatory mediator. Activates macrophages and granulocytes. Promotes immune and inflammatory responses. Kills tumor cells. Responsible for weight loss associated with chronic inflammation and cancer

NK, Natural killer; *PMNs,* polymorphonuclear neutrophils.

TABLE 13.4   Clinical Uses of Cytokines

Cytokine	Clinical Uses
Colony-Stimulating Factors	
G-CSF filgrastim (Neupogen) pegfilgrastim (Neulasta)	Chemotherapy-induced neutropenia
GM-CSF sargramostim (Leukine)	Neutropenia, myeloid recovery after bone marrow transplantation
Erythropoietin epoetin alfa (Epogen, Procrit), darbepoetin alfa (Aranesp)	Anemia related to chronic kidney disease, cancer, and chemotherapy
IL-1 Receptor Antagonist anakinra (Kineret)	Rheumatoid arthritis
Interferons	
α-**Interferon** (Roferon-A, Intron A)	Hairy cell leukemia, chronic myelogenous leukemia, malignant melanoma, renal cell cancer, ovarian cancer, multiple myeloma, Kaposi sarcoma, hepatitis B and C
β-**Interferon** (Betaseron, Avonex, Rebif)	Multiple sclerosis
Interleukins	
Interleukin-2 aldesleukin (Proleukin)	Metastatic renal cell cancer, metastatic melanoma
Interleukin 11 (platelet growth factor) oprelvekin (Neumega)	Thrombocytopenia related to chemotherapy
Soluble TNF Receptor etanercept (Enbrel)	Rheumatoid arthritis

G-CSF, Granulocyte colony-stimulating factor; *GM-CSF,* granulocyte-macrophage colony-stimulating factor; *TNF,* tumor necrosis factor.

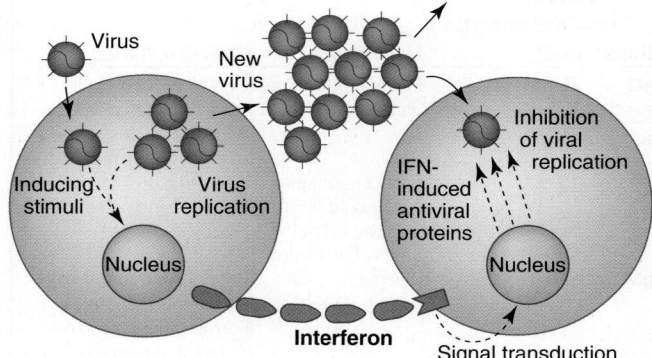

FIG. 13.4 Mechanism of action of interferon *(IFN)*. When a virus attacks a cell, the cell begins to make viral DNA and IFN. IFN serves as an intercellular messenger and induces the production of antiviral proteins. Then the virus is not able to replicate in the cell.

effect in cells by reacting with them and inducing the formation of a second protein termed *antiviral protein* (Fig. 13.4). This protein mediates the antiviral action of interferon by changing the cell's protein synthesis and preventing new viruses from becoming assembled.

Comparison of Humoral and Cell-Mediated Immunity

Humans need both humoral and cell-mediated immunity to remain healthy. Each type of immunity has unique properties, different methods of action, and reactions against particular antigens. Table 13.5 compares humoral and cell-mediated immunity.

TABLE 13.5 Comparison of Humoral and Cell-Mediated Immunity

Characteristics	Humoral Immunity	Cell-Mediated Immunity
Cells involved	B lymphocytes	T lymphocytes, macrophages
Products	Antibodies	Sensitized T cells, cytokines
Memory cells	Present	Present
Protection	Bacteria	Fungus
	Viruses (extracellular)	Viruses (intracellular)
	Respiratory and GI pathogens	Chronic infectious agents
		Tumor cells
Examples	Anaphylactic shock	Tuberculosis
	Atopic diseases	Fungal infections
	Transfusion reaction	Contact dermatitis
	Bacterial infections	Graft rejection
		Destruction of cancer cells

FIG. 13.5 Primary and secondary immune responses. The introduction of antigen induces a response dominated by 2 classes of immunoglobulins, IgM and IgG. IgM predominates in the primary response, with some IgG appearing later. After the host's immune system is primed, another challenge with the same antigen induces the secondary response, in which some IgM and large amounts of IgG are made.

Humoral Immunity. Humoral immunity consists of antibody-mediated immunity. The term *humoral* comes from the Greek word *humor*, which means body fluid. Since antibodies are made by plasma cells (differentiated B cells) and found in plasma, the term *humoral immunity* is used. Antibody production is an essential part of the humoral immune response. Each of the 5 classes of immunoglobulins (Igs) (IgG, IgA, IgM, IgD, IgE) has specific characteristics (Table 13.2).

When a pathogen (especially bacteria) enters the body, it may encounter a B cell that is specific for antigens found on that bacterial cell wall. In addition, a monocyte or macrophage may phagocytize the bacteria and present its antigens to a B cell. The B cell recognizes the antigen because it has receptors on its cell surface specific for that antigen. When the antigen comes in contact with the cell surface receptor, the B cell becomes activated, and most B cells differentiate into plasma cells (Fig. 13.3). The mature plasma cell secretes immunoglobulins. Some stimulated B cells remain as memory cells.

The primary immune response becomes evident 4 to 8 days after the first exposure to the antigen (Fig. 13.5). IgM is the first type of antibody formed. Because of the large size of the IgM molecule, IgM is confined to the intravascular space. As the immune response progresses, we make IgG. IgG can move from intravascular to extravascular spaces.

When a person is exposed to the antigen the second time, a secondary antibody response occurs. This response occurs faster (1 to 3 days), is stronger, and lasts for a longer time than a primary response. Memory cells account for the memory of the first exposure to the antigen and the more rapid production of antibodies. IgG is the primary antibody found in a secondary immune response.

IgG crosses the placental membrane. It provides the newborn with passive acquired immunity for at least 3 months. Infants may get some passive immunity from IgA in breast milk and colostrum.

Cell-Mediated Immunity. Immune responses that are initiated through specific antigen recognition by T cells are termed cell-mediated immunity. Several cell types and factors are involved in cell-mediated immunity. These include T cells, macrophages, and NK cells. Cell-mediated immunity is of primary importance in (1) immunity against pathogens that survive inside of cells, including viruses and some bacteria (e.g., mycobacteria); (2) fungal infections; (3) rejection of transplanted tissues; (4) contact hypersensitivity reactions; and (5) tumor immunity.

Gerontologic Considerations: Effects of Aging on the Immune System

With advancing age, there is a decline in the function of the immune response (Table 13.6). The main evidence of *immunosenescence* is the high incidence of cancer in older adults. Older people are also more susceptible to infections (e.g., influenza, pneumonia) from pathogens that they were more immunocompetent against earlier in life. Bacterial pneumonia is the leading cause of death from infections in older adults. The antibody response to immunizations (e.g., flu vaccine) in older adults is considerably lower than in younger adults.[1]

The bone marrow is unaffected by increasing age. Immunoglobulin levels decrease with age, leading to a suppressed humoral immune response in older adults. The thymus shrinks with age, along with decreased numbers of T cells. These changes in the thymus gland are a primary cause of immunosenescence. Both T and B cells show deficiencies in activation, transit time through the cell cycle, and subsequent differentiation. However, the most significant changes involve T cells. As thymic output of T cells diminishes, the differentiation of T cells increases. Consequently, there is an accumulation of memory cells rather than new precursor cells responsive to previously unencountered antigens.

The delayed hypersensitivity reaction, as determined by skin testing with injected antigens, is often decreased or absent in older adults. This altered response reflects anergy (an immunodeficient condition characterized by lack of or diminished reaction to an antigen or a group of antigens).

ALTERED IMMUNE RESPONSE

Immunocompetence exists when the body's immune system can identify and inactivate or destroy foreign substances. When the immune system is incompetent or underresponsive, severe infections, cancers, and immunodeficiency diseases may occur. When the immune system overreacts, hypersensitivity disorders such as allergies and autoimmune diseases may develop.

Hypersensitivity Reactions

Sometimes the immune response is overreactive against foreign antigens or reacts against its own tissue, resulting in tissue damage. These responses are termed hypersensitivity reactions. *Autoimmune disease,* a type of hypersensitivity response, occurs when the body does not recognize self-proteins and reacts against self-antigens.

We can classify hypersensitivity reactions by the source of the antigen, time sequence (immediate or delayed), or immunologic mechanisms causing the injury. Four types of hypersensitivity reactions exist (Table 13.7). Types I, II, and III are immediate and are examples of humoral immunity. Type IV is a delayed hypersensitivity reaction and is related to cell-mediated immunity.

TABLE 13.6 Gerontologic Assessment Differences

Effects of Aging on the Immune System

- Thymic shrinkage
- ↓ Cell-mediated immunity
- ↓ Delayed hypersensitivity reaction
- ↓ IL-1 and IL-2 synthesis
- ↓ Expression of IL-2 receptors
- ↓ Proliferative response of T and B cells
- ↓ Primary and secondary antibody responses
- ↑ Autoantibodies

IL, Interleukin.

Type I: IgE-Mediated Reactions. *Anaphylactic reactions* are type I reactions that occur only in susceptible people who are highly sensitized to specific allergens. IgE antibodies, made in response to the allergen, have a characteristic property of attaching to mast cells and basophils (Fig. 13.6; see Fig. 28.2). Within these cells are granules containing potent chemical mediators (histamine, serotonin, leukotrienes, eosinophil chemotactic factor of anaphylaxis [ECF-A], kinins, and bradykinin). Chemical mediators of inflammation are discussed in Chapter 11 and Table 11.1.

On the first exposure to the allergen, IgE antibodies are made and bind to mast cells and basophils. On any subsequent exposures, the allergen links with the IgE bound to mast cells or basophils and triggers degranulation of the cells and the release of chemical mediators from the granules. In this process, the mediators that are released attack target tissues, causing clinical symptoms of an allergic response. These effects include smooth muscle contraction, increased vascular permeability, vasodilation, hypotension, increased secretion of mucus, and itching. Fortunately, the mediators are short acting and their effects are reversible. The mediators are listed in Table 13.8.

A genetic predisposition to the development of allergic diseases exists. The capacity to become sensitized to an allergen, rather than the specific allergic disorder, appears to be the inherited trait. For example, a father with asthma may have a son who has allergic rhinitis.

The manifestations of an anaphylactic reaction depend on whether the mediators remain localized or become systemic or whether they affect specific organs. When the mediators are localized, a cutaneous response termed the *wheal-and-flare reaction* occurs. This reaction is characterized by a pale wheal containing edematous fluid surrounded by a red flare from the hyperemia. The reaction occurs in minutes or hours and is usually not dangerous. A classic example of a wheal-and-flare reaction is the mosquito bite. The wheal-and-flare reaction serves a

TABLE 13.7   Types of Hypersensitivity Reactions

Type I: IgE-Mediated	Type II: Cytotoxic	Type III: Immune-Complex	Type IV: Delayed Hypersensitivity
Antigen			
Pollen, food, drugs, dust	Cell surface of RBCs Cell basement membrane	Extracellular fungal, viral, bacterial	Intracellular or extracellular
Rate of Development			
Immediate	Minutes to hours	Hours to days	Several days
Complement Involved			
No	Yes	Yes	No
Mediators of Injury			
Histamine	Complement lysis	Neutrophils	Cytokines
Mast cells	Macrophages in tissues	Complement lysis	T cytotoxic cells
Leukotrienes		Monocytes, macrophages	
Prostaglandins		Lysosomal enzymes	
Examples			
Allergic rhinitis	Transfusion reaction	SLE	Contact dermatitis (e.g., to poison ivy)
Asthma	Goodpasture syndrome	Rheumatoid arthritis	
Atopic dermatitis	Immune thrombocytopenic purpura	Acute glomerulonephritis	
Urticaria	Graves' disease		
Angioedema			
Skin Test			
Wheal and flare	None	Erythema and edema in 3–8 hr	Erythema and edema in 24–48 hr (e.g., TB test)

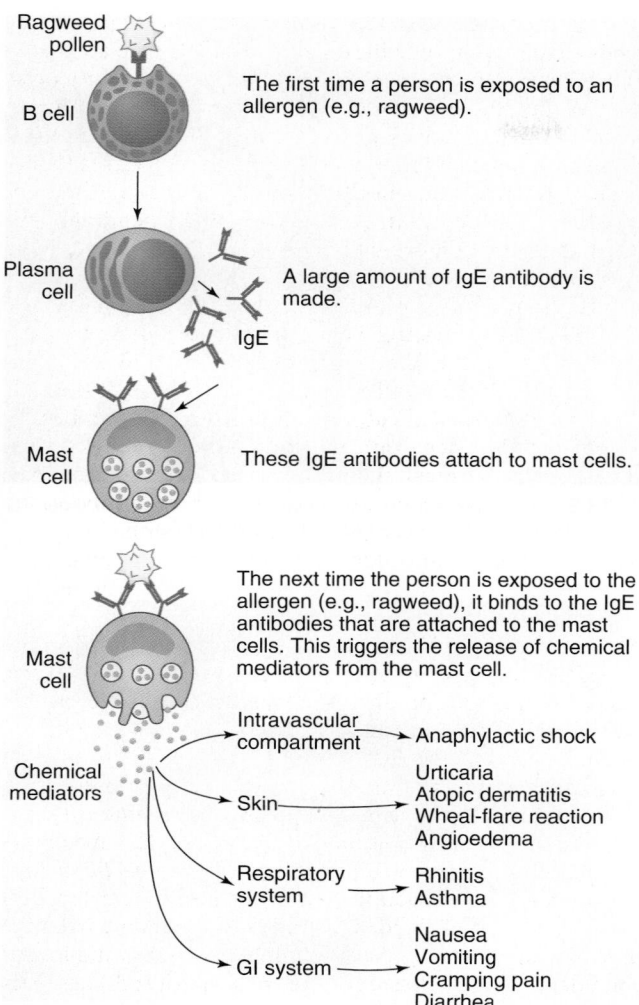

Ragweed pollen

B cell — The first time a person is exposed to an allergen (e.g., ragweed).

Plasma cell — A large amount of IgE antibody is made.

IgE

Mast cell — These IgE antibodies attach to mast cells.

Mast cell — The next time the person is exposed to the allergen (e.g., ragweed), it binds to the IgE antibodies that are attached to the mast cells. This triggers the release of chemical mediators from the mast cell.

Chemical mediators

Intravascular compartment → Anaphylactic shock

Skin → Urticaria / Atopic dermatitis / Wheal-flare reaction / Angioedema

Respiratory system → Rhinitis / Asthma

GI system → Nausea / Vomiting / Cramping pain / Diarrhea

FIG. 13.6 Steps in a type I allergic reaction.

TABLE 13.8 Mediators of Allergic Response

- Anaphylatoxins (C3a, C4a, C5a from complement activation)
- Histamine
- Kinins
- Leukotrienes
- Platelet-activating factor
- Prostaglandins
- Serotonin

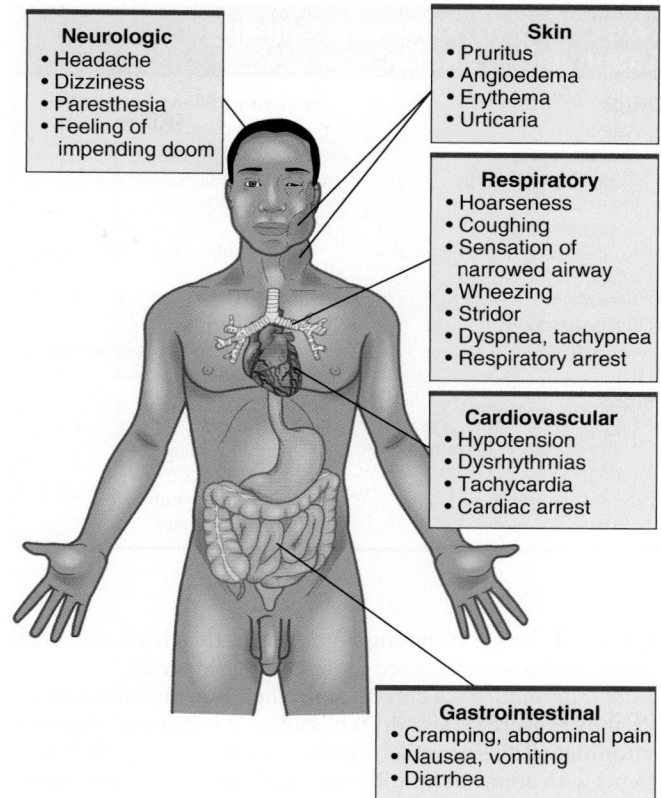

Neurologic
- Headache
- Dizziness
- Paresthesia
- Feeling of impending doom

Skin
- Pruritus
- Angioedema
- Erythema
- Urticaria

Respiratory
- Hoarseness
- Coughing
- Sensation of narrowed airway
- Wheezing
- Stridor
- Dyspnea, tachypnea
- Respiratory arrest

Cardiovascular
- Hypotension
- Dysrhythmias
- Tachycardia
- Cardiac arrest

Gastrointestinal
- Cramping, abdominal pain
- Nausea, vomiting
- Diarrhea

FIG. 13.7 Manifestations of a systemic anaphylactic reaction.

diagnostic purpose as a means of showing allergic reactions to specific allergens during skin tests.

Common allergic reactions include anaphylaxis and atopic reactions.

Anaphylaxis. *Anaphylaxis* can occur when mediators are released systemically (e.g., after injection of a drug, after an insect sting). The reaction occurs within minutes and can be life threatening because of bronchial constriction and subsequent airway obstruction and vascular collapse. The target organs affected are shown in Fig. 13.7. Initial symptoms include edema and itching at the site of exposure to the allergen. Shock can occur rapidly and is manifested by rapid, weak pulse;

hypotension; dilated pupils; dyspnea; and possibly cyanosis. Bronchial edema and angioedema can compound shock. Death will occur without emergency treatment. Some of the important allergens that can cause anaphylactic shock in hypersensitive people are listed in Table 13.9. Drugs are the leading cause of anaphylaxis-related deaths.[2]

Atopic Reactions. Around 20% of the population is *atopic,* having an inherited tendency to become sensitive to environmental allergens. The atopic diseases that can result are allergic rhinitis, asthma, atopic dermatitis, urticaria, and angioedema.

Allergic rhinitis, or hay fever, is the most common type I hypersensitivity reaction. It may occur year-round (perennial allergic rhinitis), or it may be seasonal (seasonal allergic rhinitis). Airborne substances such as pollens, dust, and molds are the primary causes of allergic rhinitis. Dust, molds, and animal dander often cause perennial allergic rhinitis. Seasonal allergic rhinitis is often caused by pollens from trees, weeds, or grasses. The target areas affected are the conjunctiva of the eyes and the mucosa of the upper respiratory tract. Symptoms include nasal discharge; sneezing; tearing; mucosal swelling with airway obstruction; and pruritus around the eyes, nose, throat, and mouth. Treatment of allergic rhinitis is discussed in Chapter 26 on p. 480.

Many patients with *asthma* have an allergic component to their disease. These patients often have a history of atopic disorders (e.g., infantile eczema, allergic rhinitis, food intolerances). Inflammatory mediators produce bronchial smooth muscle constriction, excess secretion of thick mucus, edema of the mucous membranes of the bronchi, and decreased lung compliance. Because of these physiologic changes, patients have

TABLE 13.9   Allergens Causing Anaphylactic Shock

Drugs
- Aspirin
- Cephalosporins
- Chemotherapy drugs
- Insulins
- Local anesthetics
- Nonsteroidal antiinflammatory drugs
- Penicillins
- Sulfonamides
- Tetracycline

Foods
- Eggs, milk, nuts, peanuts, shellfish, fish, chocolate, strawberries

Treatment Measures
- Allergenic extracts used in immunotherapy
- Blood products (whole blood and components)
- Iodine-contrast media for CT scan or other radiologic procedures

Insect Venoms
- Wasps, hornets, yellow jackets, bumblebees, ants

Animal Sera
- Diphtheria antitoxin
- Rabies antitoxin
- Snake venom antitoxin
- Tetanus antitoxin

FIG. 13.8 Atopic dermatitis of the hands. (From James W, Berger TG: *Andrews' diseases of the skin,* ed 12, St Louis, 2016, Elsevier.)

FIG. 13.9 Allergic reaction with angioedema of the lip. (From Habif TP: *Clinical dermatology,* ed 6, Philadelphia, 2016, Saunders.)

dyspnea, wheezing, coughing, tightness in the chest, and thick sputum. Asthma is discussed in depth in Chapter 28.

Atopic dermatitis is a chronic, inherited skin disorder characterized by exacerbations and remissions. It is caused by several environmental allergens that are often hard to identify. Although patients with atopic dermatitis have high IgE levels and positive skin tests, the histopathologic features do not represent the typical, localized wheal-and-flare type I reactions. The skin lesions are more generalized and involve vasodilation of blood vessels, resulting in interstitial edema with vesicle formation (Fig. 13.8). Dermatitis is discussed in Chapter 23.

Urticaria (hives) is a cutaneous reaction against systemic allergens occurring in atopic people. It is characterized by transient wheals (pink, raised, edematous, pruritic areas) that vary in size and shape and may occur all over the body. Urticaria develops rapidly after exposure to an allergen and may last minutes or hours. Histamine causes localized vasodilation (erythema), transudation of fluid (wheal), and flaring. Flaring is due to dilated blood vessels on the edge of the wheal. Histamine is responsible for the pruritus associated with the lesions. Urticaria is discussed in Chapter 23.

Angioedema is a localized cutaneous lesion similar to urticaria but involving deeper layers of the skin and submucosa. The principal areas of involvement include the eyelids, lips, tongue, larynx, hands, feet, GI tract, and genitalia (Fig. 13.9). Swelling usually begins in the face and then progresses to the airways and other parts of the body. Dilation and engorgement of the capillaries secondary to the release of histamine cause the diffuse swelling. Welts are not present as in urticaria. The outer skin appears normal or has a reddish hue. The lesions may burn, sting, or itch and can cause acute abdominal pain if in the GI tract. The swelling may occur suddenly or over several hours and usually lasts for 24 hours.

Type II: Cytotoxic and Cytolytic Reactions. Cytotoxic and cytolytic reactions are type II hypersensitivity reactions involving the direct binding of IgG or IgM antibodies to an antigen on the cell surface. Antigen-antibody complexes activate the complement system, which mediates the reaction. Cellular tissue is destroyed by either (1) activation of the complement system resulting in cytolysis or (2) enhanced phagocytosis.

Target cells often destroyed in type II reactions are erythrocytes, platelets, and leukocytes. The tissue damage usually occurs rapidly. Some of the antigens involved are the ABO blood group, Rh factor, and drugs. Pathophysiologic disorders characteristic of type II reactions include ABO incompatibility transfusion reaction, Rh incompatibility transfusion reaction, autoimmune and drug-related hemolytic anemias, leukopenias, thrombocytopenias, erythroblastosis fetalis (hemolytic disease of the newborn), and Goodpasture syndrome.

Hemolytic Transfusion Reactions. A classic type II reaction occurs when a recipient receives ABO-incompatible blood from a donor. Naturally acquired antibodies to antigens of the ABO blood group are in the recipient's serum but are not present on the erythrocyte membranes (see Table 29.9). For example, a person with type A blood has anti-B antibodies, a person with type B blood has anti-A antibodies, a person with type AB blood has no antibodies, and a person with type O blood has anti-A and anti-B antibodies.

If the recipient is transfused with incompatible blood, antibodies immediately coat the foreign erythrocytes, causing *agglutination* (clumping). The clumping of cells blocks small blood vessels in the body, uses existing clotting factors, and depletes them, leading to bleeding. Within hours, neutrophils and macrophages phagocytize the agglutinated cells. The complement system is activated. Cell lysis occurs, which causes the release of hemoglobin into the urine and plasma. Acute kidney injury can result from the hemoglobinuria. Blood transfusions are discussed in Chapter 30.

Goodpasture Syndrome. Goodpasture syndrome is a disorder involving the lungs and kidneys. An antibody-mediated autoimmune reaction occurs involving the glomerular and alveolar basement membranes. The circulating antibodies combine with tissue antigen to activate the complement system, which causes deposits of IgG to form along the cell basement membranes of the lungs or kidneys. This reaction may result in pulmonary hemorrhage and glomerulonephritis. Goodpasture syndrome is discussed in Chapter 45.

Type III: Immune-Complex Reactions.
Tissue damage in immune-complex reactions, which are type III reactions, occurs secondary to antigen-antibody complexes. Soluble antigens combine with IgG and IgM to form complexes that are too small to be effectively removed by the mononuclear phagocyte system. Therefore the complexes deposit in tissue or small blood vessels. They cause activation of the complement system and release of chemotactic factors that lead to inflammation and destruction of the involved tissue.

Type III reactions may be local or systemic and immediate or delayed. The manifestations depend on the number of complexes and the location in the body. Common sites for deposit are the kidneys, skin, joints, blood vessels, and lungs. Severe type III reactions are associated with autoimmune disorders such as systemic lupus erythematosus (SLE), acute glomerulonephritis, and rheumatoid arthritis. SLE and rheumatoid arthritis are discussed in Chapter 64. Acute glomerulonephritis is discussed in Chapter 45.

Type IV: Delayed Hypersensitivity Reactions.
A *delayed hypersensitivity reaction*—a type IV reaction—is a *cell-mediated immune response*. Although cell-mediated responses are usually protective mechanisms, tissue damage occurs in delayed hypersensitivity reactions.

The tissue damage in a type IV reaction does not occur in the presence of antibodies or complement. Rather, sensitized T cells attack antigens or release cytokines. Some of these cytokines attract macrophages into the area. The macrophages and enzymes released by them are responsible for most of the tissue destruction. In the delayed hypersensitivity reaction, it takes 24 to 48 hours for a response to occur.

Examples of delayed hypersensitivity reactions include contact dermatitis (Fig. 13.10); hypersensitivity reactions to bacterial, fungal, and viral infections; and transplant rejections. Some drug sensitivity reactions also fit this category.

Contact Dermatitis. Allergic contact dermatitis is an example of a delayed hypersensitivity reaction involving the skin. The reaction occurs when the skin is exposed to substances that easily penetrate the skin to combine with epidermal proteins. The substance then becomes antigenic. Over a period of 7 to 14 days, memory cells form to the antigen. On subsequent exposure to the substance, a sensitized person develops eczematous skin lesions within 48 hours. The most common antigenic substances are metal compounds (e.g., those containing nickel or mercury); rubber compounds; poison ivy, poison oak, and poison sumac; cosmetics; and some dyes.

In acute contact dermatitis, the skin lesions appear erythematous and edematous and are covered with papules, vesicles, and bullae. The involved area is pruritic but may burn or sting. When

FIG. 13.10 Contact dermatitis to rubber. (From Morison MJ: *Nursing management of chronic wounds,* Edinburgh, 2001, Mosby.)

contact dermatitis becomes chronic, the lesions resemble atopic dermatitis because they are thickened, scaly, and lichenified. The main difference between contact dermatitis and atopic dermatitis is that contact dermatitis is localized and restricted to the area exposed to the allergens. Atopic dermatitis is usually widespread.

Microbial Hypersensitivity Reactions. The classic example of a microbial cell-mediated immune reaction is the body's defense against the tubercle bacillus. Tuberculosis results from invasion of lung tissue by the highly resistant tubercle bacillus. The organism itself does not directly damage the lung tissue. However, antigenic material released from the tubercle bacilli reacts with T cells, initiating a cell-mediated immune response. The resulting response causes extensive caseous necrosis of the lung.

After the first cell-mediated reaction, memory cells persist, so subsequent contact with the tubercle bacillus or an extract of purified protein from the organism causes a delayed hypersensitivity reaction. This is the basis for the purified protein derivative (PPD) tuberculosis skin test, which we read 48 to 72 hours after injecting the PPD intradermally. Tuberculosis is discussed in Chapter 27.

ALLERGIC DISORDERS

Assessment

For a thorough assessment of a patient with allergies, obtain a complete history and perform a comprehensive physical examination, diagnostic workup, and skin testing for allergens. Obtain information from the patient about family allergies, past and present allergies, and social and environmental factors.

Family history, including information about atopic reactions in relatives, is especially important in identifying at-risk patients. Note past and present allergies. Obtain information about the manifestations and course of allergic reaction. The time of year when an allergic reaction occurs can be a clue to a seasonal allergen. Ask about any over-the-counter or prescription medications used to treat the allergies.

Social and environmental factors, especially the physical environment, are important. Ask about pets, trees and plants on the property, pollutants in the air, floor coverings, houseplants, and cooling and heating systems in the home and workplace. Note any reactions to medication. A daily or weekly food diary with a description of any untoward reactions may be useful.[3] Ask about the patient's lifestyle and stress level in connection with the allergic symptoms.

TABLE 13.10 Nursing Assessment

Allergies

Subjective Data

Important Health Information

Past health history: Recurrent respiratory problems, seasonal exacerbations. Unusual reactions to insect bites or stings; past and present allergies

Medications: Unusual reactions to any medications; use of over-the-counter drugs or medications for allergies

Functional Health Patterns

Health perception–health management: Family history of allergies; malaise

Nutritional-metabolic: Food intolerances, vomiting

Elimination: Abdominal cramps, diarrhea

Activity-exercise: Fatigue; hoarseness, cough, dyspnea

Cognitive-perceptual: Itching, burning, stinging of eyes, nose, throat, or skin; chest tightness

Role-relationship: Altered home and work environment, presence of pets

Objective Data

Integumentary

Rashes, including urticaria, wheal and flare, papules, vesicles, bullae; dryness, scaliness, scratches, irritation

Eyes, Ears, Nose, and Throat

Eyes: Conjunctivitis, lacrimation, rubbing or excessive blinking, dark circles under the eyes ("allergic shiner")

Ears: Diminished hearing, immobile or scarred tympanic membranes, recurrent ear infections

Nose: Nasal polyps, nasal voice, nose twitching, itchy nose, rhinitis; pale, boggy mucous membranes; sniffling, repeated sneezing; swollen nasal passages; recurrent, unexplained nosebleeds; crease across the bridge of nose ("allergic salute")

Throat: Continual throat clearing, swollen lips or tongue, red throat, palpable neck lymph nodes

Respiratory

Wheezing, stridor; thick sputum

Possible Diagnostic Findings

Eosinophilia of serum, sputum, or nasal and bronchial secretions; increased serum IgE levels; positive skin tests; abnormal chest and sinus x-rays

---

Table 13.10 outlines subjective and objective data to obtain. During the physical examination, focus attention on the site of the allergic manifestations.

Diagnostic Studies

Various immunologic techniques are used to detect abnormalities of lymphocytes, eosinophils, and immunoglobulins. A complete blood count (CBC) with WBC differential is done, with an absolute lymphocyte count and eosinophil count. Immunodeficiency is diagnosed if the lymphocyte count is below 1200/μL (1.2×10^9/L). T cell and B cell quantification is used to diagnose specific immunodeficiency syndromes. The eosinophil count is high in type I hypersensitivity reactions involving IgE. The serum IgE level is also generally high in type I hypersensitivity reactions and serves as a diagnostic indicator of atopic diseases.

We can test sputum and nasal and bronchial secretions for the presence of eosinophils. Pulmonary function tests, especially for forced expiratory volume, are helpful for patients with asthma.

Skin testing for allergens is the preferred method. Sometimes skin testing is contraindicated and blood allergy testing is used. Allergy blood testing is recommended if a person (1) is using a drug that interferes with skin test results (e.g., antihistamines, corticosteroids) and cannot stop taking it for a few days, (2) cannot tolerate the many needle scratches needed for skin testing, or (3) has a skin disorder (e.g., severe eczema, dermatitis, psoriasis).

Skin Tests. Skin testing is used to identify the specific allergens that are causing the allergy symptoms. With the use of empiric allergy medications as the treatment of choice for most allergic rhinitis, it has become common practice to omit skin testing for specific allergens in these patients. However, diagnosing an allergy to a specific antigen allows the patient to avoid an allergen and makes him or her a candidate for immunotherapy. Unfortunately, we cannot do skin testing on patients who cannot stop taking drugs that suppress the histamine response or patients with food allergies.

Procedure. We can do skin testing by 3 different methods: (1) a scratch or prick test, (2) an intradermal test, or (3) a patch test. The areas of the body usually used in skin testing are the arms and back. Allergen extracts are applied to the skin in rows with a corresponding control site opposite the test site. Saline or another diluent is applied to the control site. In the *scratch test* a drop of allergen is placed on the skin, and then a pricking device is used so that the allergen can enter the skin. In the *intradermal test* the allergen extract is injected under the skin, similar to a PPD test for TB. In the *patch test* an allergen is applied to a patch that is placed on the skin.

Results. In the scratch and intradermal tests, the reaction occurs in 5 to 10 minutes. In the patch test the patches must be worn for 48 to 72 hours. If the person is hypersensitive to the allergen, a positive reaction will occur within minutes after insertion in the skin and may last for 8 to 12 hours. We will see a local wheal-and-flare response with a positive reaction.

The size of the positive reaction does not always correlate with the severity of allergy symptoms. False-positive and false-negative results may occur. Negative results from skin testing do not always mean the person does not have an allergic disorder. Positive results do not always mean that the allergen was causing the manifestations. Positive results imply that the person is sensitized to that allergen. Therefore correlating skin test results with the patient's history is important.

Precautions. A highly sensitive person is always at risk for developing an anaphylactic reaction to skin tests. Therefore never leave a patient during the testing period. If a severe reaction does occur with a skin test, the extract is immediately removed and antiinflammatory topical cream is applied to the site. For intradermal testing, the arm is best so that a tourniquet can be applied during a severe reaction. A subcutaneous injection of epinephrine may be needed.

Interprofessional and Nursing Management

After an allergic disorder is diagnosed, treatment is aimed at reducing exposure to the offending allergen, treating the symptoms, and, if needed, desensitizing the person through immunotherapy.

✚ TABLE 13.11   Emergency Management
Anaphylactic Shock

Etiology
- Injection of, inhalation of, ingestion of, or topical exposure to substance that produces profound allergic response (Table 13.9)

Assessment Findings
- See Fig. 13.7

Interventions

Initial
- Ensure patent airway. Intubation if evidence of impending obstruction
- Remove insect stinger if present
- Establish IV access
- Epinephrine (1 mg/mL preparation): Give 0.3–0.5 mg IM preferably in the mid-outer thigh. Can repeat every 5–15 min.
- Give high-flow O_2 (8–10 L/min) via face mask. Can give up to 100% as needed
- Nebulized albuterol for bronchospasm resistant to epinephrine
- Diphenhydramine IV for urticaria and itching
- Corticosteroids: Methylprednisolone IV

Hypotension
- Place recumbent and elevate legs
- IV normal saline rapid bolus of 1–2 L
- Maintain BP with fluids, volume expanders, vasopressors (e.g., dopamine)

Ongoing Monitoring
- Monitor vital signs, respiratory effort, O_2 saturation, level of consciousness, cardiac rhythm, and urine output
- Anticipate intubation with severe respiratory distress
- Anticipate cricothyrotomy or tracheostomy with severe laryngeal edema

Anaphylaxis. Anaphylactic reactions occur suddenly in hypersensitive patients after exposure to the offending allergen. They may occur after parenteral injection of drugs (especially antibiotics) or blood products and after insect stings. The cardinal principle in management is speed in (1) recognizing signs and symptoms of an anaphylactic reaction, (2) maintaining a patent airway, (3) giving drugs, and (4) treating for shock. Table 13.11 outlines the emergency treatment of anaphylactic shock.

Epinephrine is the drug of choice to treat an anaphylactic reaction. It must be given parenterally (IM, IV). Patients receiving β-blockers may be resistant to treatment with epinephrine and can develop refractory hypotension and bradycardia. Glucagon should be given to these patients because it has inotropic and chronotropic effects that are not mediated through β-receptors. Severe cases of anaphylaxis may result in hypovolemic shock because of the loss of intravascular fluid into interstitial spaces that occurs due to increased capillary permeability.[4] Peripheral vasoconstriction and stimulation of the sympathetic nervous system occur to compensate for the fluid shift. However, unless shock is treated early, the body will no longer be able to compensate and irreversible tissue damage will occur, leading to death. (Hypovolemic shock is discussed in Chapter 66.)

❓ CHECK YOUR PRACTICE

You are caring for a patient who has been receiving IV antibiotic therapy for 2 days. Several minutes after starting the latest infusion, the patient states that his chest feels tight and begins coughing. You take his BP and it is 100/64 and his pulse is 124.
- What should you do?

All health care workers must be prepared for the rare but life-threatening anaphylactic reaction, which requires immediate medical and nursing interventions. It is extremely important to list all the patient's allergies on the chart, nursing care plan, and medication record.

Chronic Allergies. Most allergic reactions are chronic. They are characterized by remissions and exacerbations of symptoms. Treatment focuses on identification and control of allergens, relief of symptoms through drug therapy, and hyposensitization of a patient to an offending allergen.

Allergen Recognition and Control. You play a key role in helping the patient make lifestyle adjustments so that there is minimal exposure to offending allergens. Reinforce that, even with drug therapy and immunotherapy, the patient will never be totally desensitized or completely symptom free. Help the patient use various preventive measures to control the allergic symptoms.

Of primary importance is the need to identify the offending allergen. Sometimes this is done through skin testing. In the case of food allergies an elimination diet is sometimes valuable. If an allergic reaction occurs, all foods eaten shortly before the reaction should be eliminated and gradually reintroduced 1 at a time until the offending food is detected.

Many allergic reactions, especially asthma and urticaria, may be worsened by fatigue and emotional stress. Help the patient plan a stress management program. Have the patient practice relaxation techniques when coming in for frequent immunotherapy treatments.

Sometimes control of allergic symptoms requires environmental control, including changing an occupation, moving to a different climate, or giving up a favorite pet. In the case of airborne allergens, sleeping in an air-conditioned room, damp dusting daily, covering mattresses and pillows with hypoallergenic covers, and wearing a mask outdoors may be helpful.

If the allergen is a drug, have the patient avoid the drug. The patient has the responsibility to make any drug allergies known to all health care team members. The patient should wear a Medic Alert bracelet listing the drug allergy and have the drug allergy listed on all medical and dental records.

For a patient allergic to insect stings, commercial kits containing automatic injectable epinephrine are available. Teach the patient and family how to use the injector and have them practice assembling and using the non–drug containing training device (Table 13.12). This patient should wear a Medic Alert bracelet and carry an insect-sting kit whenever going outdoors.

Drug Therapy. The major categories of drugs used for symptomatic relief of chronic allergic disorders include antihistamines, sympathomimetic/decongestant drugs, corticosteroids, antipruritic drugs, and mast cell–stabilizing drugs. Many of these drugs can be bought OTC and are often misused by patients.

TABLE 13.12 Patient and Caregiver Teaching

Automatic Epinephrine Injectors

Include the following information when teaching the patient and caregiver how to use an automatic epinephrine injector.

1. Fill the prescription at once and keep at least 2 doses available.
2. Always keep at least 1 autoinjector with you.
3. Keep an autoinjector in a place where others can easily find it in case of an emergency. Tell family and friends where it is stored.
4. Keep the autoinjector in the original case, at room temperature, away from extremes of cold and heat.
5. Mark on your calendar when the autoinjector expires, although an expired autoinjector may be used if there is no alternative. Replace solutions that are discolored or contain particles.
6. Use the device if you have any sign of anaphylaxis, such as trouble breathing or feeling tightness in the throat or lightheaded.
7. When needed:
   - Inject the drug into the top of the thigh, slightly to the outside, at a 90-degree angle. Hold in place for at least 2 to 3 seconds.
   - You can inject the drug through clothes. Avoid pockets and seams where the fabric is thick.
   - After use, call 911 and get to the nearest hospital for monitoring. Take the autoinjector with you.

Antihistamines. Antihistamines are the best drugs for treatment of allergic rhinitis and urticaria (see Chapter 26, Table 26.2). They are less effective for severe allergic reactions. They act by competing with histamine for H_1-receptor sites, thus blocking the effect of histamine. Results are best if they are taken as soon as allergy symptoms appear. Antihistamines can be used effectively to treat edema and pruritus. They are ineffective in preventing bronchoconstriction. With seasonal rhinitis, antihistamines should be taken during peak pollen seasons.

Sympathomimetic/Decongestant Drugs. The major sympathomimetic drug is epinephrine (Adrenalin). Epinephrine is made by the adrenal medulla and stimulates α- and β-adrenergic receptors. Stimulation of the α-adrenergic receptors causes vasoconstriction of peripheral blood vessels. β-Receptor stimulation relaxes bronchial smooth muscles. Epinephrine also acts directly on mast cells to stabilize them against further degranulation. The action of epinephrine lasts only a few minutes.

Minor sympathomimetic drugs differ from epinephrine because they are taken orally or nasally and last for several hours. Included in this category are drugs containing phenylephrine and pseudoephedrine. The minor sympathomimetic drugs are used mainly to treat allergic rhinitis (see Chapter 26 and Table 26.2).

Corticosteroids. Nasal corticosteroid sprays are effective in relieving the symptoms of allergic rhinitis (see Chapter 26 and Table 26.2). Occasionally patients have such severe manifestations of allergies that they are truly incapacitated. In these situations, a brief course of oral corticosteroids can be used.

Antipruritic Drugs. Topically applied antipruritic drugs are most effective when the skin is intact. These drugs protect the skin and provide relief from itching. Common OTC drugs include calamine lotion, coal tar solutions, and camphor. Menthol and phenol may be added to other lotions to produce an antipruritic effect.

Mast Cell–Stabilizing Drugs. Cromolyn is a mast cell–stabilizing agent that inhibits the release of histamines, leukotrienes, and other agents from the mast cell after antigen-IgE interaction. It is available as an inhalant nebulizer solution or a nasal spray. Cromolyn is used in the management of allergic rhinitis (see Chapter 26).

Leukotriene Receptor Antagonists. Leukotriene receptor antagonists (LTRAs) block leukotriene, 1 of the major mediators of the allergic inflammatory process (see Table 26.2). These medications can be taken orally. They are used to treat allergic rhinitis and asthma.

Immunotherapy. Immunotherapy is the recommended treatment for control of allergic symptoms when the allergen cannot be avoided and drug therapy is not effective. Few patients with allergies have symptoms so intolerable that they need allergy immunotherapy. Immunotherapy is definitively indicated for those with anaphylactic reactions to insect venom.

Immunotherapy involves giving small titers of an allergen extract in increasing strengths until hyposensitivity to the specific allergen is achieved. For best results, teach the patient to avoid the offending allergen whenever possible because complete desensitization is impossible. Unfortunately, not all allergy-related conditions respond to immunotherapy. Food allergies cannot be safely treated with this therapy. Eczema may worsen with immunotherapy.

Mechanism of Action. The IgE level is high in atopic people. When IgE combines with an allergen in a hypersensitive person, a reaction occurs, releasing histamine in various body tissues. Allergens more readily combine with IgG than with other immunoglobulins. Therefore immunotherapy involves injecting allergen extracts that will stimulate increased IgG levels. The goal of long-term immunotherapy is to keep "blocking" IgG levels high. By increasing IgG levels, IgE is blocked from binding to the allergen. This prevents mast cell degranulation. In addition, allergen-specific T suppressor cells develop in those receiving immunotherapy.

Method of Administration. The allergens included in immunotherapy are chosen based on the results of skin testing with a panel of allergens. Results are best when immunotherapy is given throughout the year.

Subcutaneous immunotherapy. Subcutaneous immunotherapy (SCIT) involves the subcutaneous injection of titrated amounts of allergen extracts biweekly or weekly. The dose is small at first and then increased slowly until a maintenance dosage is reached. Generally, it takes 1 to 2 years of immunotherapy to reach the maximal therapeutic effect. Therapy may continue for about 5 years. After that, some patients may stop therapy. Many have a sustained decrease in symptoms after the treatment is stopped. Those with severe allergies or sensitivity to insect stings may continue maintenance therapy indefinitely.

Sublingual immunotherapy. Sublingual immunotherapy (SLIT) involves allergen extracts taken under the tongue. SLIT has been used in Europe for decades. Recently the first sublingual products have become available in the United States. These include a 5-grass pollen tablet (Oralair), a single grass pollen tablet (Grastek), and a ragweed pollen tablet (Ragwitek).[5]

Patients usually take SLIT once daily at home. The first dose is usually given under medical supervision. Some patients have local application site reactions (e.g., oral pruritus, throat irritation, tongue swelling). Local reactions subside in many patients within a few days to a week. Systemic allergic reactions are markedly fewer than with SCIT.

SLIT has the advantage of being a convenient, self-administered oral therapy. Its primary disadvantage is that the patient must consistently adhere to the therapy.[6]

❖ NURSING MANAGEMENT: IMMUNOTHERAPY

You will often be the person responsible for giving SCIT. Immunotherapy always carries the risk for a severe anaphylactic reaction. Therefore an HCP, emergency equipment, and essential drugs should be available whenever injections are given. Always anticipate adverse reactions, especially when using a new dose strength, after a previous reaction, or after a missed dose. Early manifestations of a systemic reaction include pruritus, urticaria, sneezing, laryngeal edema, and hypotension. If these occur, initiate emergency measures for anaphylactic shock at once.

Describe any local reaction according to the degree of redness and swelling at the injection site. If the area is greater than the size of a quarter in an adult, report the reaction to the HCP so that the allergen dosage may be decreased.

Record keeping must be accurate and can help prevent an adverse reaction to the allergen extract. Before giving an injection, check the patient's name against the name on the vial. Next, determine the vial strength, amount of last dose, date of last dose, and any reaction information.

Always give the allergen extract in an extremity away from a joint so that a tourniquet can be applied for a severe reaction. Rotate the site for each injection. After giving the injection, carefully observe the patient for 20 to 30 minutes, since systemic reactions are most likely to occur immediately. However, warn the patient that a delayed reaction can occur as long as 24 hours later.

Latex Allergies

Allergies to latex products have become an increasing problem, affecting patients and health care workers. The increase in allergic reactions has coincided with the sharp increase in glove use. The more frequent and prolonged the exposure to latex, the greater the risk for developing a latex allergy.[7]

Besides gloves, we use many other latex-containing products in health care. These include BP cuffs, stethoscopes, tourniquets, IV tubing, syringes, electrode pads, O_2 masks, tracheal tubes, colostomy and ileostomy pouches, urinary catheters, anesthetic masks, and adhesive tape. Latex proteins can become aerosolized through powder on gloves and can result in serious reactions when inhaled by sensitized persons. All health care facilities should use powder-free gloves to avoid respiratory exposure to latex proteins.[8]

Types of Latex Allergies. Two types of latex allergies can occur: type IV allergic contact dermatitis and type I allergic reactions. *Type IV contact dermatitis* is caused by the chemicals used in the manufacturing process of latex gloves. It is a delayed reaction that occurs within 6 to 48 hours. Typically, the person first has dryness, pruritus, fissuring, and cracking of the skin, followed by redness, swelling, and crusting at 24 to 48 hours. Chronic exposure can lead to lichenification, scaling, and hyperpigmentation. The dermatitis may extend beyond the area of physical contact with the allergen.

A *type I allergic reaction* is a response to the natural rubber latex proteins and occurs within minutes of contact with the proteins. The manifestations of type I reactions can vary from skin redness, urticaria, rhinitis, conjunctivitis, or asthma to full-blown anaphylactic shock. Systemic reactions to latex may result from exposure to latex protein via various routes, including the skin, mucous membranes, inhalation, and blood.

Latex-Food Syndrome. Because some proteins in rubber are similar to food proteins, some foods may cause an allergic reaction in people who are allergic to latex. This is called *latex-food*

TABLE 13.13 Guidelines for Preventing Allergic Latex Reactions

- Use nonlatex gloves for activities that are not likely to involve contact with infectious materials (e.g., food preparation, housekeeping).
- Use appropriate barrier protection when handling infectious materials.
- If you choose latex gloves, use powder-free gloves with reduced protein content.
- Do not use oil-based hand creams or lotions when wearing latex gloves.
- Frequently clean work areas that are contaminated with latex-containing dust (e.g., carpets, ventilation ducts).
- Learn to recognize the symptoms of latex allergy: Skin rash; hives; flushing; itching; nasal, eye, or sinus symptoms; asthma; and shock.
- If symptoms of latex allergy develop, avoid direct contact with latex gloves and products.
- Wear a Medic Alert bracelet and carry an epinephrine pen (e.g., EpiPen, Symjepi).

Source: National Institute for Occupational Safety and Health (NIOSH). Retrieved from *www.cdc.gov/niosh.*

---

syndrome. The most common of these foods are banana, avocado, chestnut, kiwi, tomato, water chestnut, guava, hazelnut, potato, peach, grape, and apricot. Most people with latex allergy have a positive allergy test to at least 1 related food.

❖ NURSING AND INTERPROFESSIONAL MANAGEMENT: LATEX ALLERGIES

Identifying patients and health care workers sensitive to latex is crucial to prevent adverse reactions. Obtain a thorough health history and history of any allergies, especially for patients with any history of latex contact symptoms. We cannot identify all latex-sensitive people, even with a careful and thorough history. The greatest risk factor is long-term multiple exposures to latex products (e.g., health care personnel, those who have had multiple surgeries, rubber industry workers). Other risk factors include a patient history of allergic rhinitis, asthma, and allergies to certain foods (listed earlier).

Use latex precaution protocols for those patients with a positive latex allergy test or a history of signs and symptoms related to latex exposure. Many health care facilities have created latex-free product carts to use with patients with latex allergies. The National Institute for Occupational Safety and Health (NIOSH) has published recommendations for preventing allergic reactions to latex in the workplace (Table 13.13).

Because of the potential for severe symptoms of food allergy, teach patients to avoid those foods. Other recommendations for people with latex and food allergies include wearing a Medic Alert bracelet or necklace and carrying an injectable epinephrine pen.

Multiple Chemical Sensitivity

Multiple chemical sensitivity (MCS) is a subjective illness marked by recurrent, vague, nonspecific symptoms attributed to low levels of chemical, biologic, or physical agents.

Commonly accused substances include smoke, pesticides, plastics, synthetic fabrics, scented products, petroleum products, and paint fumes. Women between the ages of 30 and 50 are more likely to develop the symptoms. MCS is a controversial diagnosis. It is not recognized as an illness by the American Medical Association or other authorities.[9]

The symptoms that people report are wide-ranging and not specific. They include headache, fatigue, dizziness, nausea, congestion, itching, sneezing, sore throat, chest pain, breathing problems, muscle pain or stiffness, skin rash, diarrhea, bloating, gas, confusion, difficulty concentrating, memory problems, and mood changes. These symptoms are usually subjective, with no evidence of a pathologic condition or physiologic dysfunction.

Diagnosis is usually made based on a patient's health history. There is no established test to diagnose MCS. The most effective treatment for MCS is to avoid the chemicals that may trigger the symptoms and create a chemical-free and odor-free home and workplace.

Psychotherapy is the recommended treatment. In patients who are unwilling to undergo psychotherapy but willing to accept medications, antidepressants, including selective serotonin reuptake inhibitors (SSRIs) (e.g., citalopram [Celexa]), are options. Drugs for anxiety and sleep also have been used.

AUTOIMMUNITY

Autoimmunity is an immune response against self in which the immune system no longer differentiates self from nonself. For some unknown reason, immune cells that are normally unresponsive (tolerant to self-antigens) are activated. In autoimmunity, autoantibodies and autosensitized T cells cause pathophysiologic tissue damage.

The cause of autoimmune diseases is still unknown. Age may play some role because the number of circulating autoantibodies increases in people over age 50. However, the principal factors in the development of autoimmunity are (1) the inheritance of susceptibility genes, which may contribute to the failure of self-tolerance, and (2) initiation of autoreactivity by triggers, such as infections, which may activate self-reactive lymphocytes.

Autoimmune diseases tend to cluster. A given person may have more than 1 autoimmune disease (e.g., rheumatoid arthritis, Addison's disease), or the same or related autoimmune diseases may be found in other members of the same family. This observation has led to the concept of genetic predisposition to autoimmune disease. Most of the genetic research in this area correlates certain human leukocyte antigen (HLA) types with an autoimmune condition. (HLAs and disease association are discussed later in this chapter on p. 204.)

Even in a genetically predisposed person, some trigger is needed to initiate autoreactivity. This may include infectious agents such as a virus. Viral infections can change cells or tissues that are not normally antigenic. The virally induced changes make the cells or tissues antigenic. Viruses may be involved in the development of diseases such as type 1 diabetes. Rheumatic fever and rheumatic heart disease are autoimmune responses triggered by streptococcal infection and mediated by antibodies against group A β-hemolytic streptococci that cross-react with heart muscles and valves and synovial membranes.

Drugs can be precipitating factors in autoimmune disease. Hemolytic anemia can result from methyldopa administration. Procainamide can induce the formation of antinuclear antibodies and cause a lupus-like syndrome.

Gender and hormones have a role in autoimmune disease. More women than men have autoimmune disease. During pregnancy, many autoimmune diseases get better. After delivery, the woman with an autoimmune disease often has an exacerbation.

Autoimmune Diseases

Generally, autoimmune diseases are grouped according to organ-specific and systemic diseases (Table 13.14). SLE is a classic

TABLE 13.14	Examples of Autoimmune Diseases
Systemic Diseases • Rheumatoid arthritis • Scleroderma (systemic sclerosis) • Systemic lupus erythematosus **Organ-Specific Diseases** **Blood** • Autoimmune hemolytic anemia • Hemochromatosis • Immune thrombocytopenic purpura (ITP) **Central Nervous System** • Guillain-Barré syndrome • Multiple sclerosis **Endocrine System** • Addison's disease • Graves' disease • Hypothyroidism • Thyroiditis • Type 1 diabetes	**Eye** • Uveitis **Gastrointestinal System** • Celiac disease • Inflammatory bowel disease • Pernicious anemia **Heart** • Rheumatic fever **Kidney** • Glomerulonephritis • Goodpasture syndrome **Liver** • Autoimmune hepatitis • Primary biliary cirrhosis **Muscle** • Myasthenia gravis

example of a systemic autoimmune disease characterized by damage to multiple organs. The cause is unknown, but there appears to be a loss of self-tolerance for the body's own DNA antigens.

In SLE, tissue injury appears to be the result of the formation of antinuclear antibodies. For some reason (possibly a viral infection), the cell membrane is damaged and DNA is released into the systemic circulation, where it is viewed as nonself. This DNA is normally sequestered inside the nucleus of cells. On release into the circulation, the DNA antigen reacts with an antibody. Some antibodies are involved in immune complex formation, and others may cause damage directly. Once the complexes are deposited, the complement system is activated and further damages the tissue, especially the renal glomerulus. SLE is discussed in Chapter 64.

Apheresis

Apheresis is a procedure to separate components of the blood followed by the removal of 1 or more of these components. It is an effective treatment for several autoimmune diseases and other diseases and disorders. Compound words are often used to describe a specific apheresis procedure, depending on the blood components being collected. *Plateletpheresis* is the removal of platelets, usually for collection from normal persons to infuse into patients with low platelet counts (e.g., patients taking chemotherapy who develop thrombocytopenia). *Leukocytapheresis* is a general term indicating the removal of WBCs. It is used in chronic myelogenous leukemia to remove high numbers of leukemic cells.

Apheresis is used in hematopoietic stem cell transplantation to collect stem cells from peripheral blood. These stem cells can then be used to repopulate a person's bone marrow after high-dose chemotherapy (see Chapter 15 for more on hematopoietic stem cell transplants).

Plasmapheresis. *Plasmapheresis* is the removal of plasma containing components causing or thought to cause disease. It can be used to get plasma from healthy donors to give to patients as replacement therapy.

Plasmapheresis involves the removal of whole blood through an IV device, and then the blood circulates through the apheresis machine. Inside the machine the blood is divided into plasma and its cellular components by centrifugation or membrane filtration. The plasma is generally replaced with normal saline, lactated Ringer's solution, fresh-frozen plasma, plasma protein fractions, or albumin. When we manually remove blood, we can only take 500 mL at 1 time. However, with the use of apheresis procedures, more than 4 L of plasma can be pheresed in 2 to 3 hours.

Plasmapheresis has been used to treat autoimmune diseases such as SLE, glomerulonephritis, Goodpasture syndrome, myasthenia gravis, rheumatoid arthritis, and Guillain-Barré syndrome. Many of these disorders have circulating autoantibodies (usually of the IgG class) and antigen-antibody complexes. The reason for performing therapeutic plasmapheresis in autoimmune disorders is to remove pathologic substances present in plasma. Immunosuppressive therapy has been used to prevent recovery of IgG production, and plasmapheresis to prevent antibody rebound.

Plasmapheresis may remove inflammatory mediators (e.g., complement) that are responsible for tissue damage. In the treatment of SLE, plasmapheresis is usually reserved for the patient having an acute attack who is unresponsive to conventional therapy.

You need to be aware of side effects associated with plasmapheresis. The most common complications are hypotension and citrate toxicity. Hypotension is usually the result of a vasovagal reaction or transient volume changes. Citrate, used as an anticoagulant, may cause hypocalcemia, which may cause headache, paresthesias, and dizziness.

IMMUNODEFICIENCY DISORDERS

When the immune system does not adequately protect the body, immunodeficiency exists. Immunodeficiency disorders involve an impairment of 1 or more immune mechanisms, which include (1) phagocytosis, (2) humoral response, (3) cell-mediated response, (4) complement, and (5) a combined humoral and cell-mediated deficiency. Immunodeficiency disorders are *primary* if the immune cells are improperly developed or absent and *secondary* if an illness or treatment causes the deficiency. Primary immunodeficiency disorders are rare and often serious. Secondary disorders are more common and less severe.

Primary Immunodeficiency Disorders
The basic categories of primary immunodeficiency disorders are (1) phagocytic defects, (2) B-cell deficiency, (3) T-cell deficiency, and (4) a combined B-cell and T-cell deficiency (Table 13.15).

Secondary Immunodeficiency Disorders
Key factors that may cause secondary immunodeficiency disorders are listed in Table 13.16. Drug-induced immunosuppression is the most common. Immunosuppressive therapy is prescribed for patients to treat autoimmune disorders and to prevent transplant rejection. Immunosuppression is a serious side effect of drugs used in cancer chemotherapy. Generalized leukopenia often results, leading to a decreased humoral and cell-mediated response. Therefore secondary infections are common in immunosuppressed patients.

Malnutrition alters cell-mediated immune responses. When protein is deficient over a prolonged period, the thymus gland atrophies and lymphoid tissue decreases. In addition, an increased susceptibility to infections always exists.

TABLE 13.15 Primary Immunodeficiency Disorders

Disorder	Affected Cells	Genetic Basis
Ataxia-telangiectasia	B, T	Autosomal recessive
Bruton's X-linked agammaglobulinemia	B	X-linked
Chronic granulomatous disease	PMNs, monocytes	X-linked
Common variable hypogammaglobulinemia	B	—
DiGeorge syndrome (thymic hypoplasia)	T	—
Graft-versus-host disease	B, T	—
Job syndrome	PMNs, monocytes	—
Severe combined immunodeficiency disease	Stem, B, T	X-linked or autosomal recessive
Selective IgA, IgM, or IgG deficiency	B	Some X-linked
Wiskott-Aldrich syndrome	B, T	X-linked

Ig, Immunoglobulin; *PMNs,* Polymorphonuclear neutrophils.

TABLE 13.16 Causes of Secondary Immunodeficiency

Age
- Infants
- Older adults

Diseases or Disorders
- Acquired immunodeficiency syndrome (AIDS)
- Burns
- Cancers
- Chronic kidney disease
- Cirrhosis
- Diabetes
- Hodgkin's lymphoma
- Severe infection
- Systemic lupus erythematosus
- Trauma

Drug-Induced Immunodeficiency
- Chemotherapy drugs
- Corticosteroids

Malnutrition
- Cachexia
- Dietary deficiency

Stress
- Chronic stress
- Trauma (physical or emotional)

Therapies
- Anesthesia
- Radiation
- Surgery

Hodgkin's lymphoma impairs the cell-mediated immune response, and patients may die from severe viral or fungal infections (see Chapter 30). Viruses, especially rubella, may cause immunodeficiency by direct cytotoxic damage to lymphoid cells. Systemic infections can place such a demand on the immune system that resistance to a secondary or another infection is impaired.

Radiation can destroy lymphocytes either directly or through depletion of stem cells. As the radiation dose is increased, more bone marrow atrophies, leading to severe pancytopenia and suppression of immune function. Splenectomy in children is especially dangerous. They may develop sepsis from a simple respiratory tract infection.

Stress may alter the immune response. This response involves interrelationships among the nervous, endocrine, and immune systems (see Chapter 6).

FIG. 13.11 Patterns of human leukocyte antigen (HLA) inheritance. **A,** HLA genes are found on chromosome 6. **B,** The 2 haplotypes of the father are labeled P^1 and P^2, and the haplotypes of the mother are labeled M^1 and M^2. Each child inherits 2 haplotypes, one from each parent. **C,** Therefore only 4 combinations—P^1M^1, P^1M^2, P^2M^1, and P^2M^2—are possible, and 25% of the offspring will have identical HLA haplotypes.

HUMAN LEUKOCYTE ANTIGEN SYSTEM

The antigens responsible for rejection of genetically unlike tissues are called the *major histocompatibility antigens*. These antigens are products of histocompatibility genes. In humans, they are called the **human leukocyte antigen (HLA)** system. The genes for the HLA antigens are linked and occur together on the sixth chromosome. HLAs are present on all nucleated cells and platelets. We primarily use the HLA system in matching organs and tissues for transplantation.

An important characteristic of HLA genes is that they are highly *polymorphic* (variable). Each HLA locus can have many different possible alleles, and thus many combinations exist. Each person has 2 alleles for each locus, 1 inherited from each parent. Both alleles of a locus are expressed independently (i.e., they are codominant). The proteins encoded by certain genes are known as *antigens*.

The entire set of A, B, C, D, and DR genes (the HLA genes) on 1 chromosome is termed a *haplotype*. A complete set is inherited as a unit (haplotype). One haplotype is inherited from each parent (Fig. 13.11). This means that a person has HLA genes that are half identical to those of each parent. The HLA genes of 1 person have a 25% chance of being identical to the HLA genes of a sibling.

In organ transplantation A, B, and DR are primarily used for compatibility matching. The specific allele at each locus is identified by a number. For example, a person could have an HLA of A2, A6, B7, B27, DR4, and DR7. Currently more than 8000 HLA alleles have been identified for the various HLA genes.

Human Leukocyte Antigen and Disease Associations

The early interest in HLAs was stimulated by the role of HLAs in matching donors and recipients of organ transplants. Since that time, the interest in the association between HLAs and disease

has grown. Several diseases show significant associations with specific HLA alleles. People who have these alleles are much more likely to develop the associated disease than those who do not have the alleles. However, having a particular HLA allele does not mean that the person will necessarily develop the associated disease—only that the relative risk is greater than in the general population.

Most of the HLA-associated diseases are classified as autoimmune disorders. Examples of HLA types and disease associations include (1) HLA-B27 and ankylosing spondylitis; (2) HLA-DR2, HLA-DR3, and SLE; (3) HLA-DR3, HLA-DR4, and diabetes; and (4) HLA-DR2 and narcolepsy.

The discovery of HLA associations with certain diseases was a major breakthrough in understanding the genetic bases of these diseases. It is now known that at least part of the genetic bases of HLA-associated diseases lies in the HLA region, but the actual mechanisms involved in these associations are still unknown. However, most people who inherit a specific HLA type (e.g., HLA-DR3) that is associated with a disease will never develop that disease.

Currently the association between HLAs and certain diseases is of minimal practical clinical importance. Nevertheless, there is promise for the development of clinical applications in the future. For example, with certain autoimmune diseases, it may be possible to identify members of a family at greatest risk for developing the same or a related autoimmune disease. These people would need close medical supervision, implementation of preventive measures (if possible), and early diagnosis and treatment to prevent chronic complications.

ORGAN TRANSPLANTATION

Transplantation success has improved with advances in surgical technique, advances in histocompatibility testing, and more effective immunosuppressant drugs. Common tissue transplants include corneas, skin, bone marrow, heart valves, bone, and connective tissues (Fig. 13.12). Cornea transplants can prevent or correct blindness. Skin grafts are used in managing burn patients. Donated bone marrow can help patients with leukemias and other cancers.

Transplanted organs currently come from many different body systems. These organs include the heart, lung, liver, kidney, pancreas, and intestine. Multiple organs can be transplanted together, such as kidney and pancreas, kidney and liver, kidney and heart, or the complete intestinal tract. For example, some patients with diabetes who receive a pancreas transplant also receive a kidney transplant because the diabetes has not only impaired the pancreas but also led to renal failure.

Some organs can be transplanted in parts or segments instead of transplanting an entire organ. Liver and lung lobes (rather than the whole organ) may be transplanted, or an intestine may be used in segments, thus allowing for 1 person's organ donation to help many recipients. This technique enables living donors to donate part of an organ or 1 of their organs, in the case of kidneys.

Organ donations come from either deceased (cadaver) or living donors. Most organs and tissues currently come from deceased donors. However, because of the shortage of organs from deceased donors, the use of related and living unrelated donor organs is increasing.

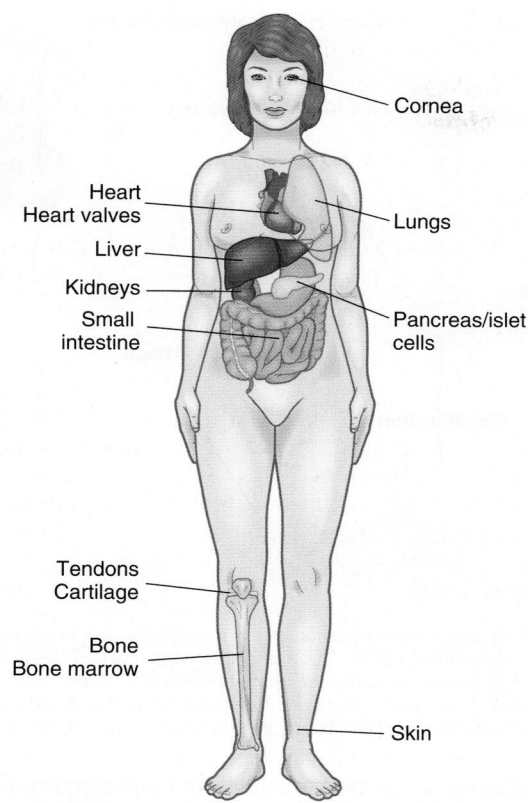

FIG. 13.12 Tissues and organs that can be transplanted.

People can indicate their wish to become a donor when they sign a donor card or driver's license or join a donor registry (depending on the state). However, on their death or imminent death, the person's legal next of kin may need to consent to the donation. Legal requirements and the facility's policy for a donor's legal next of kin to consent regardless of whether the donor's wishes varies from state to state and from facility to facility.

Currently more than 116,000 people are on the organ procurement and transplantation network's national waiting list. This list is maintained by the United Network for Organ Sharing (UNOS). However, fewer than 35,000 people receive transplants annually. The organs in highest demand are kidneys, hearts, and livers. These are also the most often transplanted organs.[10] The Uniform Anatomical Gift Act regulates organ and tissue donations to allow for fair and consistent transplantation laws among all states.[11] Patients are matched to available donors based on a number of factors: ABO blood and HLA typing, medical urgency, time on the waiting list, and geographic location.

Tissue Typing

The recipient usually receives a transplant from an ABO blood group–compatible donor (see Table 29.9). The donor and recipient do not need to share the same Rh factor.

HLA Typing. HLA typing is done on potential donors and recipients. Currently we think only the A, B, and DR antigens are clinically significant for transplantation. Because each locus has 2 alleles that encode for antigens, a total of 6 antigens is identified. In transplantation we try to match as many antigens as possible between the HLA-A, HLA-B, and HLA-DR loci. Antigen matches of 5 and 6 antigens and some 4-antigen matches have

better clinical outcomes (i.e., the patient is less likely to reject the transplanted organ), especially in kidney and bone marrow transplants.

The degree of HLA matching needed or suitable for successful solid organ transplantation depends on the type of organ and degree of acceptable risk. Certain organ and tissue transplants need a closer histocompatibility match than other organs. For example, a cornea transplant can be accepted by nearly anyone because corneas are avascular and therefore no antibodies reach the cornea to cause rejection. In kidney and bone marrow transplantation, HLA matching is very important, since these transplants are at high risk for graft rejection. On the other hand, for liver transplants, HLA mismatches have little impact on graft survival. Heart and lung transplants fall somewhere in between but minimizing HLA mismatches significantly improves survival. For liver, lung, and heart transplants, few donors are available and it is hard to get good HLA matches.

Transporting and storing donated organs can take time. The "best" match may live many miles from the "ideal" recipient. The need to have the "best" matches must be balanced against the time it takes to procure and transport a donated organ and then transplant it.

Panel of Reactive Antibodies. A *panel of reactive antibodies (PRA)* shows the recipient's sensitivity to various HLAs before receiving a transplant. To detect preformed antibodies to HLA, the recipient's serum is mixed with a randomly selected panel of donor lymphocytes to determine reactivity. The potential recipient may have been exposed to HLA antigens by previous blood transfusions, pregnancy, or a previous organ transplant.

PRA allows for the determination of whether a recipient is of high or low reactivity to potential donors. The results for the PRA are calculated in percentages. A high PRA indicates that the person has a large number of cytotoxic antibodies and is highly sensitized, which means there is a poor chance of finding a crossmatch-negative donor. In patients awaiting transplantation, a PRA panel is usually done on a regular basis. In highly sensitized patients (high PRA), plasmapheresis and IV immunoglobulin (IVIG) can be used to lower the number of antibodies.

Crossmatch. A crossmatch is done to determine the existence of antibodies against the potential donor. A crossmatch uses serum from the recipient mixed with donor lymphocytes to test for any preformed anti-HLA antibodies to the potential donor organ. The crossmatch can be used as a screening test when possible living donors are being considered or once a cadaver donor is chosen.

A negative crossmatch means that no preformed antibodies are present, and it is safe to go ahead with transplantation. A positive crossmatch means that the recipient has cytotoxic antibodies to the donor, which is an absolute contraindication in living donor transplants. Live donor transplants may be done for patients with a positive crossmatch if no other live donors (with a negative crossmatch) exist. In this situation, plasmapheresis or IVIG can be done to remove antibodies.

It is not always possible to complete a crossmatch prior to transplantation. If a retrospective crossmatch is done, the results will have implications for immunosuppression protocols after the transplant. A prospective crossmatch is especially important for kidney transplants. It may not be done for lung, liver, and heart transplants.

Transplant Rejection

Rejection is 1 of the major problems after organ transplantation. Organ rejection occurs as a normal immune response to foreign tissue. The risk for rejection is reduced by using immunosuppression therapy, performing ABO and HLA matching, and ensuring that the crossmatch is negative. Unfortunately, many different HLAs exist. A perfect match is nearly impossible unless the tissue is from one's self, an identical twin, or in some cases a sibling. Rejection can be hyperacute, acute, or chronic. Prevention, early diagnosis, and treatment of rejection are essential for long-term graft function.

Hyperacute Rejection. *Hyperacute rejection* occurs within 24 hours after transplantation because the blood vessels are rapidly destroyed. It occurs because the person had preexisting antibodies against the transplanted tissue or organ. There is no treatment for hyperacute rejection, and we must remove the transplanted organ. Fortunately, hyperacute rejection is a rare event because of improved immunosuppression medications and because the final testing prior to transplantation usually determines whether the recipient is sensitized to any of the donor HLAs.

Acute Rejection. *Acute rejection* most often occurs in the first 6 months after transplantation. This type of rejection is usually a cell-mediated immune response by the recipient's lymphocytes, which have been activated against the donated (foreign) tissue or organ (Fig. 13.13). In addition to cell-mediated rejection, another type of acute rejection occurs when the recipient develops antibodies to the transplanted organ (humoral rejection).

It is common to have at least 1 rejection episode, especially with organs from deceased donors. These episodes are usually reversible with additional immunosuppressive therapy. This may include increased corticosteroid doses or polyclonal or monoclonal antibodies. Unfortunately, immunosuppressants increase the risk for infection. To combat acute rejection, all patients with transplants need long-term use of immunosuppressants, putting them at a high risk for infection, especially in the first few months after transplant when the immunosuppressive doses are highest.

Chronic Rejection. *Chronic rejection* is a process that occurs over months or years and is irreversible. Chronic rejection can occur for unknown reasons or from repeated episodes of acute rejection. Large numbers of T and B cells infiltrate the transplanted organ, indicating ongoing, low-grade, immune-mediated injury. Chronic rejection results in fibrosis and scarring. In heart transplants it manifests as accelerated coronary artery disease. In lung transplants it manifests as bronchiolitis obliterans. In liver transplants, we see a loss of bile ducts. In kidney transplants it manifests as fibrosis and glomerulopathy.

There is no definitive therapy for this type of rejection. Treatment is primarily supportive. This type of rejection is hard to manage and is not associated with the optimistic prognosis of acute rejection.

Immunosuppressive Therapy

Immunosuppressive therapy requires a lifelong balance between rejection and infection. On 1 hand, the immune response must be suppressed to prevent rejection of the transplanted organ. On the other hand, an adequate immune response must be maintained to prevent overwhelming infection and the development of cancers.[12]

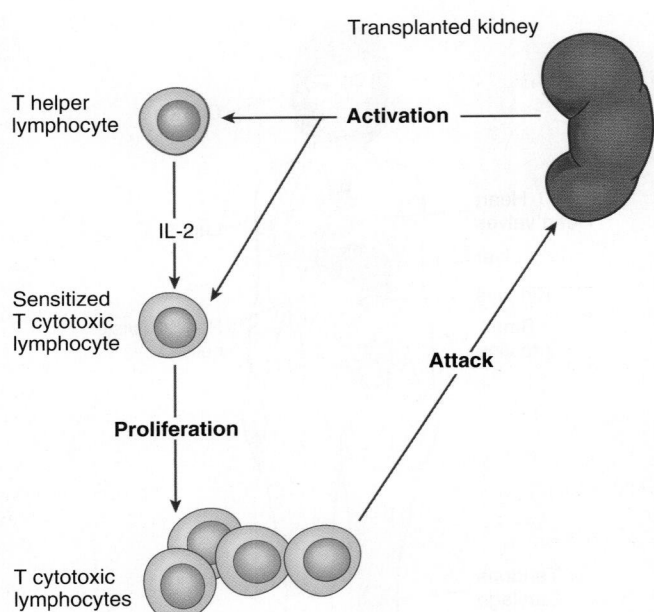

FIG. 13.13 Mechanism of action of T cytotoxic lymphocyte activation and attack of transplanted tissue. The transplanted organ (e.g., kidney) is recognized as foreign and activates the immune system. T helper cells are activated to make interleukin-2 *(IL-2)*, and T cytotoxic lymphocytes are sensitized. After the T cytotoxic cells proliferate, they attack the transplanted organ.

Many of the drugs used to achieve immunosuppression have significant side effects. Because transplant recipients must take immunosuppressants for life, the risk for toxicity continues for the rest of their lives.

Immunosuppressant drugs are listed in Table 13.17. With the use of a combination of agents that work during different phases of the immune response (Fig. 13.13), we can give lower doses of each drug to produce effective immunosuppression while minimizing side effects.

The major immunosuppressive agents are (1) calcineurin inhibitors; (2) corticosteroids (prednisone, methylprednisolone); (3) purine synthesis antagonists, including mycophenolate mofetil (CellCept, Myfortic) and azathioprine (Imuran); and (4) sirolimus. Muromonab-CD3 (Orthoclone OKT3) and either horse antithymocyte globulin (Atgam) or rabbit antithymocyte globulin (ATG) are IV medications used for short periods to prevent early rejection or reverse acute rejection.

Immunosuppression protocols are highly variable among transplant centers, with different combinations of medications being used. Most patients are initially on triple therapy. The standard triple therapy usually includes a calcineurin inhibitor, a corticosteroid, and mycophenolate mofetil.

The doses of immunosuppressant drugs are reduced over time after the transplant. The trend in many transplant centers is to follow an immunosuppression protocol that uses minimal corticosteroids because of their many side effects. Patients taking corticosteroids may be weaned off after a few years.

Calcineurin Inhibitors. This group of drugs, including tacrolimus (Prograf) and cyclosporine (Sandimmune), is the foundation of most immunosuppression regimens. As the most effective immunosuppressants, these drugs prevent a cell-mediated attack against the transplanted organ (Fig. 13.14). They are generally used in combination with corticosteroids, mycophenolate mofetil, and sirolimus. Tacrolimus is the most widely used calcineurin inhibitor. Cyclosporine is being used less often.

TABLE 13.17 Drug Therapy

Immunosuppressive Therapy

Agent	Route	Mechanism of Action	Side Effects
Calcineurin Inhibitors			
cyclosporine (Sandimmune, Neoral, Gengraf)	PO, IV	Acts on T helper cells to prevent production and release of IL-2 Inhibits proliferation of T and B cells	Nephrotoxicity, ↑ risk for infection, neurotoxicity (tremors, seizures), hepatotoxicity, lymphoma, hypertension, tremors, hirsutism, leukopenia, gingival hyperplasia
tacrolimus (Prograf)	PO, IV	Same as cyclosporine but more effective	Same as cyclosporine
Corticosteroids			
prednisone, methylprednisolone	PO, IV	Suppress inflammatory response Inhibit cytokine production (IL-1, IL-6, TNF) and T-cell activation and proliferation	Peptic ulcers, hypertension, osteoporosis, Na$^+$ and H$_2$O retention, muscle weakness, easy bruising, delayed healing, hyperglycemia, ↑ risk for infection
Cytotoxic (Antiproliferative) Drugs			
azathioprine (Imuran)	PO, IV	Inhibits purine synthesis Suppresses proliferation of T and B cells	Bone marrow suppression (neutropenia, anemia, thrombocytopenia)
cyclophosphamide	PO, IV	Cross-links DNA, leading to cell injury and death. Results in decrease in number and activity of T and B cells	Neutropenia, hemorrhagic cystitis
everolimus (Zortress)	PO	Binds to mechanistic target of rapamycin (mTOR), thereby suppressing T-cell activation and proliferation	Peripheral edema, constipation, hypertension, nausea, anemia, urinary tract infection, hyperlipidemia
mycophenolate mofetil (CellCept, Myfortic)	PO, IV	Inhibits purine synthesis Suppresses proliferation of T and B cells	Diarrhea, nausea and vomiting, neutropenia, thrombocytopenia, ↑ risk for infection, ↑ incidence of cancer
sirolimus (Rapamune)	PO	Same as everolimus	↑ Risk for infection, leukopenia, anemia, thrombocytopenia, hyperlipidemia, hypercholesterolemia, arthralgias, diarrhea. ↑ incidence of cancer
Monoclonal Antibodies			
alemtuzumab (Campath)	IV	Monoclonal antibody that targets the CD52 antigen on T and B cells, monocytes, and macrophages Causes prolonged T cell depletion	Fever, chills, dyspnea, chest pain, nausea, vomiting. Neutropenia, anemia, thrombocytopenia Increased risk for opportunistic infections
basiliximab (Simulect)	IV	Monoclonal antibody that targets IL-2 receptor and inhibits T cell activation and proliferation	Can cause acute hypersensitivity reaction, including anaphylaxis
daclizumab (Zenapax)	IV	Same as basiliximab	Same as basiliximab
muromonab-CD3 (Orthoclone OKT3)	IV push	Monoclonal antibody that binds to CD3 receptors on T cells, causing cell lysis. Inhibits function of T cells	Fever, chills, dyspnea, chest pain, nausea, vomiting Anaphylactic reactions include pulmonary edema, cardiac or respiratory arrest
Other			
belatacept (Nulojix)	IV	Prevents the activation of T cells	Anemia, diarrhea, constipation, urinary tract infection, peripheral edema
Polyclonal Antibodies			
Horse antithymocyte globulin (Atgam) Rabbit antithymocyte globulin (Thymoglobulin, ATG)	IV	Prepared by immunizing horse or rabbit with human thymocytes or T cells. Polyclonal antibodies directed against T cells, thus depleting them	Fever, chills, dyspnea, myalgia, chest pain, nausea and vomiting, anaphylaxis, leukopenia, thrombocytopenia, rash, ↑ risk for infection

They do not cause bone marrow suppression or change the normal inflammatory response. Many of the side effects are dose related. These drugs are potentially nephrotoxic. We monitor drug levels closely to prevent toxicity.

DRUG ALERT Tacrolimus and Cyclosporine

- A substance in grapefruit and grapefruit juice prevents metabolism of these drugs.
- Consuming grapefruit or grapefruit juice while using these drugs can increase their toxicity.

Mycophenolate Mofetil. Mycophenolate mofetil inhibits purine synthesis with suppressive effects on T and B cells. The major limitation of this drug is GI toxicity, including nausea, vomiting, and diarrhea. In many cases the side effects can be lessened by lowering the dose or giving smaller doses more often.

DRUG ALERT Mycophenolate Mofetil

- When given IV, it can only be reconstituted in D$_5$W.
- Do not give as IV bolus. Give over 2 or more hours.

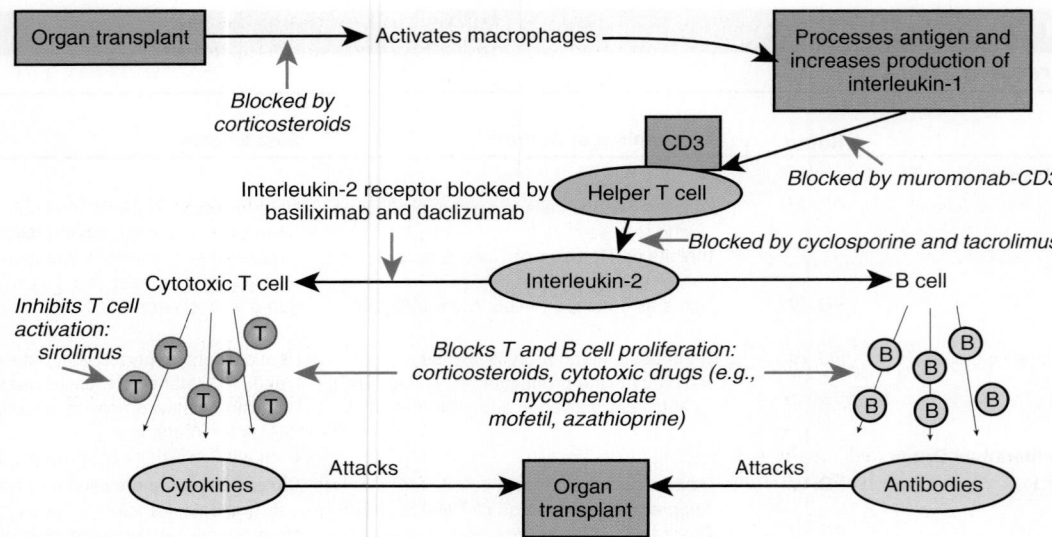

FIG. 13.14 Sites of action for immunosuppressive agents. (Adapted from McKenry L, Tessier E, Hogan M: *Mosby's pharmacology in nursing,* St Louis, 2006, Mosby.)

Sirolimus. Sirolimus (Rapamune) suppresses T-cell activation and proliferation. It is used in combination with corticosteroids, cyclosporine, and/or tacrolimus.

Monoclonal Antibodies. Monoclonal antibodies are used to prevent and treat acute rejection episodes. Muromonab-CD3 was the first of these monoclonal antibodies to be used in clinical transplantation. It is a mouse monoclonal antibody that binds with the CD3 antigen found on the surface of human thymocytes and mature T cells. It interferes with the function of T cells, the pivotal cells involved in rejection. All T cells are affected, rather than just the subset active in graft rejection. It is given by IV bolus. Within minutes after the first infusion of muromonab-CD3, the number of circulating T cells decreases significantly.

A flu-like syndrome occurs during the first few days of treatment because of cytokine release. Side effects include fever, rigors, headache, myalgias, and various GI disturbances. To reduce the expected side effects of muromonab-CD3, give patients acetaminophen, diphenhydramine, and IV methylprednisolone beforehand.

Newer generation monoclonal antibodies are a hybrid of mouse and human antibodies and have fewer side effects than muromonab-CD3 because they have been "humanized." These include daclizumab (Zenapax) and basiliximab (Simulect), which target the IL-2 receptor and impair lymphocyte proliferation. Another monoclonal antibody is alemtuzumab (Campath), which targets the CD52 antigen found on T and B cells, monocytes, and macrophages. It can cause prolonged T-cell depletion.

Polyclonal Antibodies. Polyclonal antibodies to T cells include horse antithymocyte globulin (Atgam) and rabbit antithymocyte globulin (thymoglobulin, ATG). These agents are derived by injecting animals (rabbit or horse) with human lymphoid cells, then procuring and purifying the resultant antibody. They are often used for induction immunosuppression and treatment of acute rejection.

Allergic reactions to the foreign proteins from the host animal, manifested by fever, arthralgias, and tachycardia, are common but usually not severe enough to prevent use. These side effects can be decreased by giving the preparation slowly, over 4 to 6 hours, and premedicating patients with acetaminophen, diphenhydramine, and methylprednisolone. The main toxicities of polyclonal antibodies are leukopenia and thrombocytopenia. They are caused by antibody contaminants that are not completely removed during preparation of the antibodies.

GRAFT-VERSUS-HOST DISEASE

Graft-versus-host disease (GVHD) occurs when an immunoincompetent (immunodeficient) patient receives immunocompetent cells. A GVHD response is most common in hematopoietic stem cell transplants. In most transplantation situations, the biggest concern is the patient's (host's) rejection of the organ or transplant. However, in GVHD disease, the graft (donated tissue) rejects the host (recipient) tissue.[12]

The GVHD response may begin 7 to 30 days after transplantation. Once the reaction is started, little can be done to change its course. The exact mechanism involved in this reaction is not completely understood. However, it involves donor T cells attacking and destroying vulnerable host (recipient) cells.

The target organs for the GVHD phenomenon are the skin, liver, and GI tract. The skin disease may be a maculopapular rash, which may be pruritic or painful. It initially involves the palms and soles of the feet but can progress to a generalized erythema with bullous formation and desquamation (shedding of the outer layer of skin). The liver disease may range from mild jaundice with high liver enzymes to hepatic coma. GI manifestations may include mild to severe diarrhea, severe abdominal pain, GI bleeding, and malabsorption.

The biggest problem with GVHD is infection, with different types of infections seen in different periods. Bacterial and fungal infections predominate right after transplantation when granulocytopenia exists. The development of interstitial pneumonitis is the primary concern later.

There is no adequate treatment of GVHD once it is established. Although corticosteroids are often used, they enhance the susceptibility to infection. The use of immunosuppressive agents (e.g., methotrexate, cyclosporine) has been most effective as a preventive rather than a treatment measure. Radiating blood products before they are given is another way to prevent T-cell replication. Ibrutinib (Imbruvica), a kinase inhibitor that is used to treat several forms of leukemia and lymphoma, is an option for some patients with chronic GVHD.[13]

BRIDGE TO NCLEX EXAMINATION

The number of the question corresponds to the same-numbered outcome at the beginning of the chapter.

1. The function of monocytes in immunity is related to their ability to
   a. stimulate the production of T and B lymphocytes.
   b. make antibodies after exposure to foreign substances.
   c. bind antigens and stimulate natural killer cell activation.
   d. capture antigens by phagocytosis and present them to lymphocytes.

2. The reason newborns are protected for the first 3 months of life from bacterial infections is because of the maternal transmission of
   a. IgA.
   b. IgE.
   c. IgG.
   d. IgM.

3. In a type I hypersensitivity reaction the primary immunologic disorder appears to be
   a. binding of IgG to an antigen on a cell surface.
   b. deposit of antigen-antibody complexes in small vessels.
   c. release of cytokines used to interact with specific antigens.
   d. release of chemical mediators from IgE-bound mast cells and basophils.

4. The nurse is alerted to possible anaphylactic shock immediately after a patient has received IM penicillin by the development of
   a. edema and itching at the injection site.
   b. sneezing and itching of the nose and eyes.
   c. a wheal-and-flare reaction at the injection site.
   d. chest tightness and production of thick sputum.

5. The nurse tells a friend who asks him to administer his allergy shots that
   a. it is illegal for nurses to administer injections outside of a medical setting.
   b. he is qualified to do it if the friend has epinephrine in an injectable syringe provided with his extract.
   c. avoiding the allergens is a more effective way of controlling allergies, and allergy shots are not usually effective.
   d. immunotherapy should only be administered in a setting where emergency equipment and drugs are available.

6. A patient is undergoing plasmapheresis for treatment of systemic lupus erythematosus. The nurse explains that plasmapheresis is used in treatment to
   a. remove T lymphocytes in her blood that are producing antinuclear antibodies.
   b. remove normal particles in her blood that are being damaged by autoantibodies.
   c. exchange her plasma that contains antinuclear antibodies with a substitute fluid.
   d. replace viral-damaged cellular components of her blood with replacement whole blood.

7. The *most* common cause of secondary immunodeficiencies is
   a. drugs.
   b. stress.
   c. malnutrition.
   d. human immunodeficiency virus.

8. Association between HLA antigens and diseases is *most* commonly found in what disease conditions?
   a. Cancers
   b. Infectious diseases
   c. Neurologic diseases
   d. Autoimmune disorders

9. What accurately describes rejection after transplantation?
   a. Hyperacute rejection can be treated with OKT3.
   b. Acute rejection can be treated with sirolimus or tacrolimus.
   c. Chronic rejection can be treated with tacrolimus or cyclosporine.
   d. Hyperacute reaction can be avoided if crossmatching is done before transplantation.

10. In a person having an acute rejection of a transplanted kidney, what would help the nurse understand the course of events (*select all that apply*)?
    a. A new transplant should be considered.
    b. Acute rejection can be treated with OKT3.
    c. Repeated episodes of acute rejection can lead to chronic rejection.
    d. Corticosteroids are the most successful drugs used to treat acute rejection.
    e. Acute rejection is common after a transplant and can be treated with drug therapy.

1. d, 2. c, 3. d, 4. a, 5. d, 6. c, 7. a, 8. d, 9. d, 10. b, c, e

For rationales to these answers and even more NCLEX review questions, visit *http://evolve.elsevier.com/Lewis/medsurg.*

ⓔ EVOLVE WEBSITE/RESOURCES LIST

http://evolve.elsevier.com/Lewis/medsurg
Review Questions (Online Only)
Key Points
Answer Key for Questions
- Rationales for Bridge to NCLEX Examination Questions

Conceptual Care Map Creator
Audio Glossary
Supporting Media
- Animations
- Antibodies and Antigens
- Vaccination

Content Updates

REFERENCES

1. Banasik, Jacquelyn L: *Pathophysiology*, 6th ed, St. Louis, 2018, Elsevier.
*2. Lee SE: Management of anaphylaxis, *Otolaryng Clin N Amer* 50:1175, 2017.
3. American Academy of Allergy, Asthma & Immunology: Food allergy. Retrieved from *www.aaaai.org/conditions-and-treatments/allergies/food-allergies.*
4. American Academy of Allergy, Asthma & Immunology: Anaphylaxis. Retrieved from *www.aaaai.org/conditions-and-treatments/allergies/anaphylaxis.*
5. American Academy of Allergy, Asthma & Immunology: SLIT treatment for allergic rhinitis. Retrieved from *www.aaaai.org/conditions-and-treatments/library/allergy-library/sublingual-immunotherapy-for-allergic-rhinitis.*
6. American Academy of Allergy, Asthma & Immunology: Practice parameters and other guidelines. Retrieved from *www.aaaai.org/practice-resources/statements-and-practice-parameters/practice-parameter-guidelines.*
7. Asthma and Allergy Foundation of America: Allergies. Retrieved from *www.aafa.org/page/latex-allergy.aspx.*
8. Centers for Disease Control and Prevention: Preventing allergic reactions to natural rubber latex in the workplace. Retrieved from *www.cdc.gov/niosh/docs/97-135/pdfs/97-135.pdf.*
9. U.S. Department of Labor: Multiple chemical sensitivities. Retrieved from *www.osha.gov/SLTC/multiplechemicalsensitivities/.*
10. United Network of Organ Sharing (UNOS). Retrieved from *www.unos.org.*
11. U.S. Department Health and Human Services: Organ procurement and transplantation network. Retrieved from *https://optn.transplant.hrsa.gov/.*
12. Cupples SA, Lerret S, McCalmont V, et al: *Core curriculum for transplant nurses*, 2nd ed, Philadelphia, 2017, Wolters Kluwer.
13. Voelker R: Relief for graft-vs-host disease, *JAMA* 318:996, 2017.

14

Infection

Jeffrey Kwong

Always be kind, for everyone you meet is fighting a harder battle.

Plato

http://evolve.elsevier.com/Lewis/medsurg/

CONCEPTUAL FOCUS

Adherence	Functional Ability	Inflammation
Coping	Immunity	Nutrition
Fatigue	Infection	

LEARNING OUTCOMES

1. Evaluate the impact of emerging and reemerging infections on health care.
2. Identify interventions to reduce health care–associated infections.
3. Explain the transmission of human immunodeficiency virus (HIV) and factors that affect transmission.
4. Describe the pathophysiology of HIV infection.
5. Apply the diagnostic criteria for acquired immunodeficiency syndrome (AIDS).
6. Describe methods used to test for HIV infection.
7. Discuss the role of HIV antiretroviral therapy.
8. Summarize the characteristics of opportunistic diseases associated with AIDS.
9. Describe the potential complications associated with long-term treatment of HIV infection.
10. Compare and contrast HIV prevention methods.
11. Describe the nursing management of HIV-infected patients and HIV-at-risk patients.

KEY TERMS

acquired immunodeficiency syndrome (AIDS), p. 219
antiretroviral therapy (ART), p. 217
emerging infection, p. 213
health care–associated infections (HAIs), p. 214

human immunodeficiency virus (HIV), p. 216
opportunistic diseases, p. 218
postexposure prophylaxis (PEP), p. 225
preexposure prophylaxis (PrEP) p. 222
standard precautions, p. 216

transmission-based precautions, p. 216
viral load, p. 218
window period, p. 219

This chapter presents a brief overview of the concept of emerging and health care–associated infections (HAIs). This includes identifying persons most at risk, recognizing signs and symptoms of infection, and understanding ways to treat or manage infection. Infection, immunity, and inflammation are closely related. Infection stimulates an inflammatory response and affects thermoregulation. The patient may have fatigue and pain. Maintaining adequate nutrition and rest is important to combating infection and supporting immune function. The chapter closes with a comprehensive discussion of human immunodeficiency virus (HIV) infection, focusing on transmission, pathophysiology, and interprofessional and nursing management.

INFECTIONS

Infections, such as lower respiratory tract infections, malaria, HIV, and tuberculosis (TB), are responsible for a significant number of deaths worldwide. Infection occurs when a *pathogen* (a microorganism that causes disease) invades the body, multiplies, and produces disease, usually causing harm to the host. The signs and symptoms of infection are a result of specific pathogen activity, which triggers inflammation and other immune responses.

We categorize infections as localized, disseminated, or systemic. A *localized* infection is limited to a small area. A *disseminated* infection has spread to areas of the body beyond the initial site of infection. *Systemic* infections have spread extensively throughout the body, often via the blood.

TYPES OF PATHOGENS

The many kinds of pathogens are classified into several groups, including bacteria, viruses, fungi, protozoa, and prions. *Bacteria* are one-celled organisms that are common throughout nature.

Many bacteria are normal flora. They live harmoniously in or on the human body without causing disease under normal circumstances. Normal flora protect the human body by preventing the overgrowth of other microorganisms. For example, *Escherichia coli* is part of the normal flora in the large intestine.

Bacteria cause disease in 2 ways: by entering the body and growing inside human cells (e.g., TB) or by secreting toxins that damage cells (e.g., *Staphylococcus aureus*). Bacteria are classified based on the shape of their cells. *Cocci*, such as streptococci and staphylococci, are round. *Bacilli* are rod shaped and include tetanus and TB. *Curved rods* include *Vibrio* bacteria, one of which causes cholera. *Spirochetes* are spiral shaped. They include the organisms that cause leprosy and syphilis. Table 14.1 lists common bacteria that cause disease.

Viruses, unlike bacteria, do not have a cellular structure. They are simple infectious particles that consist of a small amount of genetic material (either ribonucleic acid [RNA] or deoxyribonucleic acid [DNA]) and a protein envelope. Viruses can reproduce only after releasing their genetic material into the cell of another living organism. Examples of diseases caused by viruses are shown in Table 14.2.

Fungi are organisms similar to plants, but they lack chlorophyll. *Mycosis* is any disease caused by a fungus. Pathogenic fungi cause infections that are usually localized but can become disseminated in an immunocompromised person. Tinea pedis (athlete's foot) and tinea corporis (ringworm) are common mycotic infections. Some fungi are normal flora in the body, but when overgrowth occurs, disease can result. Overgrowth of *Candida albicans*, for example, can cause candidiasis in the mouth (thrush), esophagus, intestines, and vagina. Table 14.3 lists other fungi and their respective mycotic infections.

Protozoa are single-cell, animal-like microorganisms. Protozoa normally live in soil and bodies of water. When

TABLE 14.1 Disease-Causing Bacteria

Bacteria	Diseases Caused
Chlamydia trachomatis	Chlamydia, lymphogranuloma venereum
Clostridia	
• *Clostridium botulinum*	Food poisoning with progressive muscle paralysis
• *Clostridium tetani*	Tetanus (lockjaw)
Corynebacterium diphtheriae	Diphtheria
Escherichia coli	UTIs, peritonitis, hemolytic-uremic syndrome
Haemophilus	
• *Haemophilus influenzae*	Nasopharyngitis, meningitis, pneumonia
• *Haemophilus pertussis*	Pertussis (whooping cough)
Helicobacter pylori	Peptic ulcers, gastritis
Klebsiella-Enterobacter organisms	UTIs, peritonitis, pneumonia
Legionella pneumophila	Pneumonia (Legionnaires' disease)
Mycobacteria	
• *Mycobacterium leprae*	Hansen's disease (leprosy)
• *Mycobacterium tuberculosis*	Tuberculosis
Neisseriae	
• *Neisseria gonorrhoeae*	Gonorrhea, pelvic inflammatory disease, proctitis
• *Neisseria meningitidis*	Meningococcemia, meningitis
Proteus species	UTIs, peritonitis
Pseudomonas aeruginosa	UTIs, meningitis
Salmonella	
• *Salmonella typhi*	Typhoid fever
• Other *Salmonella* organisms	Food poisoning, gastroenteritis
Shigella	Shigellosis; diarrhea, abdominal pain, and fever (dysentery)
Staphylococcus aureus	Skin infections, pneumonia, UTIs, acute osteomyelitis, toxic shock syndrome
Streptococci	
• *Streptococcus faecalis*	Genitourinary infection, infection of surgical wounds
• *Streptococcus pneumoniae*	Pneumococcal pneumonia
• *Streptococcus pyogenes* (group A β-hemolytic streptococci)	Pharyngitis, scarlet fever, rheumatic fever, acute glomerulonephritis, erysipelas, pneumonia
• *S. pyogenes* (group B β-hemolytic streptococci)	UTIs
• *Streptococcus viridans*	Bacterial endocarditis
Treponema pallidum	Syphilis

TABLE 14.2 Disease-Causing Viruses

Virus	Diseases Caused
Adenoviruses	Upper respiratory tract infection, pneumonia
Arbovirus	Syndrome of fever, malaise, headache, myalgia; aseptic meningitis; encephalitis
Coronavirus	Upper respiratory tract infection
Coxsackieviruses A and B	Upper respiratory tract infection, gastroenteritis, acute myocarditis, aseptic meningitis
Ebola	Hemorrhagic fever
Echoviruses	Upper respiratory tract infection, gastroenteritis, aseptic meningitis
Hepatitis A, B, C	Viral hepatitis
Herpesviruses	
• Cytomegalovirus CMV)	Gastroenteritis; pneumonia and retinal damage in immunosuppressed persons, infectious mononucleosis-like syndrome
• Epstein-Barr	Mononucleosis, Burkitt's lymphoma (possibly)
• Herpes simplex type 1	Herpes labialis ("fever blisters"), genital herpes infection
• Herpes simplex type 2	Genital herpes infection
• Varicella-zoster	Chickenpox, shingles
Human immunodeficiency virus (HIV)	HIV infection, AIDS
Influenza A and B	Upper respiratory tract infection, H1N1 (swine) flu, H5N1 avian (bird) flu
Mumps	Parotitis, orchitis in postpubertal males
Papillomavirus	Genital warts, cervical and anal cancer
Parainfluenza 1-4	Upper respiratory tract infection
Parvovirus	Gastroenteritis
Poliovirus	Poliomyelitis
Pox viruses	Smallpox, Molluscum contagiosum
Reoviruses 1, 2, 3	Upper respiratory tract infection
Respiratory syncytial virus	Gastroenteritis, respiratory tract infection
Rhabdovirus	Rabies
Rhinovirus	Upper respiratory tract infection, pneumonia
Rotaviruses	Gastroenteritis
Rubella	German measles
Rubeola	Measles
West Nile virus	Flu-like symptoms, meningitis, encephalitis
Zika virus	Flu-like symptoms, fetal microcephaly

TABLE 14.3 Disease-Causing Fungi

Fungi	Diseases Caused	Organs Affected
Aspergillus fumigatus	Aspergillosis	Lungs*
	Otomycosis	Ears
Blastomyces derma-titidis	Blastomycosis	Lungs,* various organs
Candida albicans	Candidiasis	Intestines
	Vaginitis	Vagina
	Thrush	Skin,† mouth
Coccidioides immitis	Coccidioidomycosis	Lungs*
Epidermophyton	Tinea corporis	Skin†
Microsporum	Tinea capitis	Skin†
Pneumocystis jiroveci	Pneumocystis pneu-monia (PCP)	Lungs*
Sporothrix schenckii	Sporotrichosis	Skin, lymph vessels
Trichophyton	Tinea pedis	Skin†

*See Table 27.14: Fungal Infections of the Lung.
†See Table 23.8, Common Fungal Infections of the Skin.

TABLE 14.4 Emerging Infections

Microorganism	Related Disease
Bacteria	
Borrelia burgdorferi	Lyme disease
Campylobacter jejuni	Diarrhea
Escherichia coli O157:H7	Hemorrhagic colitis, hemolytic-uremic syndrome
Helicobacter pylori	Peptic ulcer disease
Legionella pneumophila	Pneumonia (Legionnaires' disease)
Vibrio cholerae O139	New strain associated with epidemic cholera
Virus	
Chikungunya	Fever, muscle aches, rash
Ebola virus	Ebola hemorrhagic fever
H1N1	H1N1 (swine) flu
Hantavirus	Hemorrhagic fever associated with severe pulmonary syndrome
Hepatitis C virus	Parenterally transmitted hepatitis
Hepatitis E virus	Enterically transmitted hepatitis
Human immunodeficiency virus (HIV)	HIV infection and AIDS
Human herpesvirus 6 (HHV-6)	Roseola subitum
Human herpesvirus 8 (HHV-8)	Associated with Kaposi sarcoma in immunosuppressed patients, including people with HIV infection
West Nile virus	West Nile fever
Zika virus	Fever, rash, muscle aches; microcephaly in children born to infected mothers
Parasite	
Cryptosporidium parvum	Acute and chronic diarrhea

introduced into the human body, they can cause infection. Protozoal parasites cause amoebic dysentery and giardiasis. A sporozoan called *Plasmodium malariae* causes malaria.

Prions are infectious particles that have abnormally shaped proteins. Not all prions cause disease. Those that do typically affect the nervous system. They can cause a group of illnesses called *transmissible spongiform encephalopathies (TSEs)*. Examples of TSEs are Creutzfeldt-Jakob disease and bovine spongiform encephalopathy in cattle (also known as mad cow disease).

EMERGING INFECTIONS

An **emerging infection** is an infectious disease that has recently increased in incidence or that threatens to increase in the immediate future.[1] Table 14.4 lists examples of emerging infections. Emerging infectious diseases can originate from unknown sources or from contact with animals, changes in known diseases, or biologic warfare. For example, severe acute respiratory syndrome (SARS) and the Ebola virus come from animal sources. Others emerged when a previously treatable organism developed resistance to antibiotics.

The battle against infection is not new, but modern technologies have changed the rules of the game. Global travel, population density, encroachment into new environments, misuse of antibiotics, and bioterrorism have increased the risk for widespread distribution of emerging infections.

Additionally, some diseases thought to be under control, such as TB, measles, and pertussis, have reemerged. Newer infections include Middle Eastern respiratory syndrome (MERS), severe acute respiratory syndrome (SARS), Zika virus, and zoonotic influenza viruses (e.g., H1N1, H5N1).

Studies in *zoonosis* (science of transmission of diseases from animals to humans) have shown that many known infectious diseases come from animal and insect vectors. The SARS outbreak in China in 2003, for instance, was linked to the civet cat, a small carnivorous mammal found throughout much of Asia and Africa. SARS is discussed in Chapter 67.

West Nile virus is carried and transmitted by mosquitoes. Mosquitoes acquire the virus as they draw blood from infected animals and humans. The virus does not cause illness in the mosquito. The mosquito transfers the virus to uninfected animals and humans when it feeds. Bird deaths are an early warning sign of a West Nile virus outbreak, which can spread quickly if action is not taken promptly. West Nile virus is discussed in Chapter 56.

Influenza viruses are examples of how disease can spread between animals and humans. Variants of influenza A viruses are responsible for many influenza epidemics. We traced the 2009 influenza A (H1N1) outbreak back to pigs, hence the name *swine flu*. In 1997 and 2003, outbreaks of the influenza A (H5N1) strain of avian flu resulted from transmission of influenza virus from chickens to humans.

Ebola virus has been an ongoing public health challenge since it was first seen in 1976. In 2014, rates of Ebola increased significantly in East Africa and the first cases of Ebola occurred in the United States. These initial cases were primarily from travelers or medical aid workers who were working in Africa. Ebola virus can cause severe hemorrhagic fever and is usually lethal. Therapeutic and preventive measures are limited. The natural reservoir and path of transmission are unknown, which makes it impossible to effectively combat Ebola virus and the disease it causes.

Reemerging Infections

Advances in the development of medications and vaccines has led to the near eradication of some infections (e.g., smallpox, polio), but infective agents can reemerge under the right conditions. Table 14.5 presents some diseases that have shown resurgence in recent decades. For example, infections such as measles and pertussis have had sporadic resurgences.[2] This is in part due to people not receiving recommended vaccines.

TABLE 14.5 Reemerging Infections

Microorganism	Infection	Description
Bacteria		
Corynebacterium diphtheriae	Diphtheria	Localized infection of mucous membranes or skin
Bordetella pertussis	Pertussis	Acute, highly contagious respiratory disease characterized by loud whooping inspiration. Also known as whooping cough
Mycobacterium tuberculosis	Tuberculosis	Chronic infection transmitted by inhalation of infected droplets (see Chapter 27)
Virus		
Dengue viruses (flaviviruses)	Dengue fever	Acute infection transmitted by mosquitoes. Occurs mainly in tropical and subtropical regions
Rubeola	Measles	Fever, malaise, cough, and maculopapular rash
Parasite		
Giardia	Giardiasis	Diarrheal illness that usually originates in water contaminated with fecal matter. Also known as traveler's diarrhea

TABLE 14.6 Common Antibiotic-Resistant Organisms and Treatment

Bacteria	Resistant to	Preferred Treatment
Enterococcus faecalis	vancomycin streptomycin gentamicin	daptomycin (Cubicin) linezolid (Zyvox) oritavancin (Orbactiv) tigecycline (Tygacil)
Enterococcus faecium	vancomycin streptomycin gentamicin	daptomycin (Cubicin) linezolid (Zyvox) tigecycline (Tygacil)
Klebsiella pneumoniae	carbapenems (e.g., imipenem, meropenem)	ceftazidime and avibactam (Avycaz)
Staphylococcus aureus	methicillin*	vancomycin
Staphylococcus epidermidis	methicillin*	vancomycin
Streptococcus pneumoniae	penicillin G	ceftriaxone cefotaxime

*This drug is no longer available in the United States.

International travel has created a new obstacle for the local eradication of diseases. For example, measles is no longer endemic in the United States but is still a leading cause of death in developing countries. Domestic outbreaks have typically occurred in areas with low vaccination rates. Some cases occurred in people who have recently traveled to measles-endemic areas outside the United States.[3]

Antimicrobial-Resistant Organisms

Resistance occurs when pathogenic organisms change in ways that decrease the ability of a drug (or a family of drugs) to treat disease.[4] Microorganisms can become resistant to classic treatments (e.g., penicillin) as well as to newer antibiotics and antiviral agents. Microorganisms are highly adaptable. They have evolved genetic and biochemical mechanisms to defend against antimicrobials. Genetic mechanisms include mutation and acquisition of new DNA or RNA. Biochemically, bacteria can resist antibiotics by producing enzymes that destroy or inactivate the drugs. Drug target sites are then altered so that the antibiotic cannot bind to or enter the bacteria. If the drug cannot enter the cell, it cannot kill the bacteria. Table 14.6 describes common antibiotic-resistant bacteria.

Methicillin-resistant *S. aureus* (MRSA), vancomycin-resistant enterococci (VRE), vancomycin-resistant *S. aureus* (VRSA), carbapenem-resistant Enterobacteriaceae (CRE), and penicillin-resistant *Streptococcus pneumoniae* are examples of emerging strains of antibiotic-resistant organisms. These drug-resistant bacteria were first seen in health care settings but are becoming more prevalent in the community. For example, we initially considered MRSA, a form of *S. aureus* that does not respond to methicillin- or penicillin-based therapies, a health care–associated infection (HA-MRSA). However, a variant strain of MRSA that is primarily acquired in the community (community-acquired MRSA [CA-MRSA]) has emerged.[5] This strain of MRSA is more *virulent* (able to cause disease or infection) compared with HA-MRSA. CA-MRSA can cause rapidly forming skin infections and systemic diseases, including pneumonia and sepsis. VRE infection is another concern for patients and health care workers. VRE are more virulent than MRSA and can survive on environmental surfaces for weeks. Although antibiotic-resistant bacteria can infect anyone, hospitalized patients and those with a suppressed immune system are more likely to be exposed to these bacteria and to develop infection.

HCPs have contributed to the development of drug-resistant microorganisms by (1) giving antibiotics for viral infections, (2) succumbing to patient pressure to prescribe unnecessary antibiotic therapy, (3) using inadequate drug regimens to treat infections, or (4) using broad-spectrum or combination agents for infections that should be treated with first-line medications.

Patients can contribute to resistance development by (1) skipping doses, (2) not taking antibiotics for the full duration of prescribed therapy, or (3) saving unused antibiotics "in case I need them later." In addition, limited resources and access to medications make it hard for some patients to get adequate treatment for infections. Teaching patients and their families the proper use of antibiotics (Table 14.7) is crucial to treatment success and prevention of drug-resistant pathogens. The Centers for Disease Control and Prevention (CDC), the Infectious Diseases Society of America (IDSA), and many health care organizations campaign for greater vigilance in minimizing the misuse of antibiotics in reaction to this growing concern.

Although antibiotics are a class of drugs that we typically think of when discussing drug-resistant organisms, any organism (virus, fungi, parasite) can develop drug resistance to agents typically used to treat them. Hence, we now use the term *antimicrobial resistance* to describe the phenomena of resistance across different classes of organisms.

HEALTH CARE–ASSOCIATED INFECTIONS

Health care–associated infections (HAIs) are infections that are acquired because of exposure to microorganisms in a health care setting.[6] About 722,000 HAIs occur annually, and nearly 1 in every 25 hospitalized patients has at least 1 HAI.

TABLE 14.7 Patient & Caregiver Teaching
Decrease Risk for Antibiotic-Resistant Infection

Include the following instructions when teaching patients or their care-givers how to decrease the risk for antibiotic-resistant infection.

1. Only Take Antibiotics Prescribed for You
- This decreases your risk for developing resistant infection.
- You may need antibiotics before certain surgeries and dental work or in the presence of immune dysfunction.

2. Wash Your Hands Frequently
- Hand washing is the single most important thing you can do to prevent infection.

3. Follow Directions When Taking Antibiotics
- Not taking your antibiotic as prescribed or skipping doses can allow antibiotic-resistant bacteria to develop.

4. Do Not Request an Antibiotic for Flu or Colds
- If your HCP says that you do not need an antibiotic, chances are you do not.
- Antibiotics are effective against bacterial infections but not viruses, which cause colds and flu.

5. Finish Your Antibiotic
- Do not stop taking your antibiotic when you feel better.
- If you stop taking your antibiotic early, the hardiest bacteria survive and multiply.
- Eventually you could develop an infection resistant to any antibiotics. You should never have leftover antibiotics.

6. Do Not Take Leftover Antibiotics
- Do not save unfinished antibiotics for later use or borrow leftover drugs from family or friends.
- This is dangerous because (1) the leftover antibiotic may not be appropriate for you, (2) your illness may not be a bacterial infection, (3) old antibiotics can lose their effectiveness and, in some cases, can be fatal, and (4) there will not be enough doses in a leftover bottle to provide full treatment.

TABLE 14.8 OSHA Requirements for Personal Protective Equipment

The following equipment minimizes exposure to blood-borne pathogens.

Equipment	Indications for Use
Gloves	- Must be used when the employee can reasonably expect having contact with blood or other potentially infectious materials, when performing vascular access procedures, and when handling or touching contaminated items or surfaces.
	- Gloves must be replaced if torn, punctured, or contaminated or their ability to function as a barrier is compromised.
Clothing (gowns, aprons, caps, boots)	- Must be used when occupational exposure is expected.
	- The type and characteristics depend on the task and degree of exposure expected.
Face protection (mask and glasses with solid side shields or a chin-length face shield)	- Must be used when splashes, sprays, spatters, or droplets of blood or other potentially infectious materials pose a hazard to the eyes, nose, or mouth.

Source: Occupational Safety and Health Administration (OSHA): Bloodborne pathogens and needlestick prevention. Retrieved from *www.osha.gov/SLTC/bloodbornepathogens.*

Improvements in infection control have resulted in fewer infections in recent years.[7] We have seen decreases in several of the major types of HAIs, including central line–associated bloodstream infections, surgical site infections, *Clostridium difficile* infections, and methicillin-resistant *S. aureus* bacteremia. Any organism can cause HAIs, but certain bacteria, including *E. coli, S. aureus, Enterobacter aerogenes,* and various types of streptococci, are the more common culprits. Some bacteria that do not normally cause disease can cause infections in high-risk patients because of illness or treatment of illness. Surgical and immunocompromised patients are at highest risk.

Around one-third of HAIs are preventable. HCPs often transmit HAIs from patient to patient through direct contact. First lines of defense to prevent the spread of HAIs include hand washing (or using an alcohol-based hand sanitizer) before and after patient contact or procedures, appropriate use of personal protective equipment such as gloves, and decontamination of equipment used for patient care.[8] Isolated infections also can be caused when bacteria that normally stay in one area of the body are introduced into another area. Therefore you must take care to change gloves and wash hands when moving from one task to another, even when working with the same patient. Most facilities have developed and implemented guidelines on reducing

and controlling the spread of disease in health care settings, especially of antimicrobial-resistant organisms (Table 14.8).[9] Nurses and all HCPs have the responsibility of using appropriate measures, including transmission-based precautions, to help protect patients from HAIs.

 Gerontologic Considerations: Infections in Older Adults

For older adults, the rate of HAIs is 2 to 3 times higher compared to younger patients. Persons in long-term care facilities are at higher risk for HAI. Age-related changes (e.g., impaired immune function) and co-morbidities, such as diabetes and physical disabilities, contribute to higher infection rates in older adults.[10]

Infections common in older adults include pneumonia, urinary tract infections (UTIs), skin infections, and TB. UTIs are more common in those who live in long-term care facilities. Patients with indwelling catheters are at particular risk.

❓ CHECK YOUR PRACTICE

You are working in a long-term care facility. One of your residents, a 76-yr-old man who is recovering from a stroke, seems very confused today. You discuss your concerns with the unlicensed assistive personnel (UAP). You explain that he seemed so alert yesterday and wonder if he may have an infection, such as pneumonia or a UTI. The UAP says, "I just took his temperature and it is normal. I don't think he has an infection."
- How should you follow up with the resident and the UAP?

Infections in older adults often have atypical manifestations, such as cognitive and behavioral changes, before the emergence of fever, pain, or changes in laboratory values. Do not rely on the presence of fever to indicate infection in older adults because many have lower core body temperatures and decreased immune responses. Suspicion of disease should typically begin if a patient shows changes in the ability to perform daily activities or in cognitive function. In addition, underlying diseases, increased frequency of drug reactions, and institutionalization can complicate the management of an older adult with infection.

INFECTION PREVENTION AND CONTROL

Occupational Safety and Health Administration (OSHA) Guidelines

OSHA is a federal agency that protects workers from injury and illness in places of employment and supports activities that minimize or eliminate exposure to infectious materials in the workplace. OSHA mandates that any employer whose employees could be exposed to potentially infectious materials implement standard policies and procedures to protect those employees. Employees must be provided with appropriate personal protective equipment (PPE) and safety equipment at no cost to the employee.[11] These include gloves, gowns, facial protection, and disposal systems for sharps (Table 14.8). PPE also must be provided in the right sizes. Hypoallergenic gloves or similar alternatives must be made available to those who have an allergic sensitivity to gloves. Appropriate PPE varies depending on the situation. You need to use sound judgment when deciding when and how to use protective equipment.

Infection Precautions

The CDC has established guidelines with 2 levels of precautions: (1) **standard precautions**, designed for the care of all patients in hospitals and health care facilities and (2) **transmission-based precautions**, designed for specific diseases.[12] The purpose of these precautions is to prevent the transmission of organisms from patients to HCPs, from HCPs to patients, from patients to other patients, and from health care personnel and patients to people outside of the hospital (Table 14.9).

The *standard precautions* system applies to (1) blood; (2) all body fluids, secretions, and excretions; (3) non-intact skin; and (4) mucous membranes. Standard precautions are designed to reduce the risk for transmission of microorganisms in hospitals. Standard precautions should be applied to *all* patients regardless of diagnosis or presumed infection status. The CDC's standard precautions incorporate all the OSHA blood-borne pathogens standard requirements.

Transmission-based precautions are used for patients known to be or suspected of being infected with highly transmissible or epidemiologically important pathogens that require additional precautions to interrupt transmission and prevent infection. Transmission-based precautions include airborne precautions, droplet precautions, and contact precautions. *Airborne precautions* are used if the organism can cause infection over long distances when suspended in the air (e.g., TB, rubeola). *Droplet precautions* minimize contact with pathogens that spread through the air at close contact and that affect the respiratory system or mucous membranes (e.g., influenza, pertussis). *Contact precautions* minimize the spread of pathogens that are acquired from direct or indirect contact, especially multidrug-resistant organisms (e.g., MRSA, VRE, CRE). Transmission-based precautions may be combined for diseases that have multiple routes of transmission. Whether used alone or in combination, transmission-based precautions should always be used in conjunction with standard precautions.

HUMAN IMMUNODEFICIENCY VIRUS INFECTION

Human immunodeficiency virus (HIV) is a retrovirus that causes immunosuppression. Persons with HIV are more susceptible to infections that people normally control through immune responses. The terms *HIV disease* and *HIV infection* are used interchangeably. With advances in treatment, we view HIV as a chronic disease since people with the disease are living longer.

More than 1 million people are currently living with HIV in the United States, with about 37,600 new infections occurring each year.[13] With the availability of effective HIV treatment, there has been a dramatic drop in the number of deaths attributable to HIV. In North America HIV is most prevalent among men who have sex with men (MSM).

Transmission of HIV

HIV can be transmitted through contact with infected blood, semen, vaginal secretions, or breast milk.[14] HIV transmission occurs through sexual intercourse with an infected partner; exposure to HIV-infected blood or blood products; and perinatal transmission during pregnancy, at delivery, or through breastfeeding. HIV is not spread casually. The virus cannot be transmitted through hugging, dry kissing, shaking hands, sharing eating utensils, using toilet seats, or casual encounters in any setting. It is not spread by tears, saliva, urine, emesis, sputum, feces, sweat, respiratory droplets, or enteric routes. Health care personnel have a low risk for acquiring HIV at work, even after a needle-stick injury.[15]

Sexual Transmission. The most common mode of HIV transmission is unprotected sexual contact with an HIV-infected partner. Sexual activity involves contact with semen, vaginal secretions, and/or blood, all of which have lymphocytes that may contain HIV. During any form of sexual intercourse (anal, vaginal, oral), the risk for infection is greater for the partner who receives the semen. This is because the receiver has prolonged contact with infected fluids. It helps explain why it is easier to infect women than men during heterosexual intercourse. Sexual activities that cause trauma to local tissues can increase

---

TABLE 14.9 Types of Isolation Precautions Used in Health Care Settings

Type	Examples
Standard Precautions	
• Used for care of all patients, regardless of their diagnosis or presumed infection status	Includes the use of hand washing and appropriate personal protective equipment
Transmission-Based Precautions	
• Recommended to provide additional precautions beyond standard precautions to prevent transmission of pathogens • Can be used for patients known or suspected to be infected or colonized with pathogens that can be transmitted by airborne or droplet transmission, or by contact with dry skin or contaminated surfaces • These precautions should be used in addition to standard precautions	**Airborne precautions:** Used for infections spread in small particles in the air, such as chickenpox (varicella), measles, and TB **Droplet precautions:** Used for infections spread in large droplets by coughing, talking, or sneezing, such as influenza and bacterial meningitis **Contact precautions:** Used for infections spread by skin-to-skin contact or contact with other surfaces, such as *C. difficile*, MRSA, and VRE

the risk for transmission. In addition, genital lesions from other sexually transmitted infections (e.g., herpes, syphilis) significantly increase the chance of transmission.

Contact With Blood and Blood Products. HIV can be transmitted from exposure to blood when sharing drug-using paraphernalia. Needles, syringes, straws, and other equipment may be contaminated with HIV or other blood-borne organisms. Sharing this equipment can result in disease transmission.

Routine screening of blood donors to identify at-risk persons and testing donated blood for the presence of HIV have

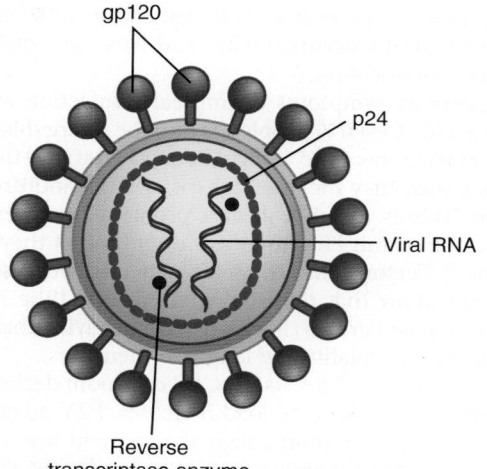

FIG. 14.1 HIV is surrounded by an envelope made up of proteins (including gp120) and a core of viral RNA and proteins.

improved the safety of the blood supply. In countries that routinely test donated blood, HIV infection because of blood transfusions or hemophilia clotting factors is unlikely.

Puncture wounds are the most common means of work-related HIV transmission. The risk for infection after a needle-stick exposure to HIV-infected blood is 0.3% to 0.4% (or 3 or 4 out of 1000).[15] The risk is higher if the exposure involves blood from a patient with a high level of circulating HIV, a deep puncture wound, a needle with a hollow bore and visible blood, or a device used for venous or arterial access. Splash exposures of blood on skin with an open lesion present some risk, but it is much lower than from a puncture wound.

Perinatal Transmission. Perinatal transmission from an HIV-infected mother to her infant can occur during pregnancy, delivery, or breastfeeding. On average, 25% of infants born to women with untreated HIV infection are born with HIV. Fortunately, the risk for transmission is less than 2% in settings in which pregnant women are routinely tested for HIV infection and, if found to be infected, treated with **antiretroviral therapy (ART)**, a combination of medications used to control and suppress HIV replication.[16]

Pathophysiology

HIV is an RNA virus. RNA viruses are called *retroviruses* because they replicate in a "backward" manner (going from RNA to DNA). Like all viruses, HIV cannot replicate unless it is inside a living cell.[17] The *CD4+ T cell (CD4 cell)*, a type of lymphocyte, is the target cell for HIV. HIV enters the CD4 cell by binding to protein receptors on the outside of the cell (Fig. 14.1). This process is known as *fusion* (Fig. 14.2).

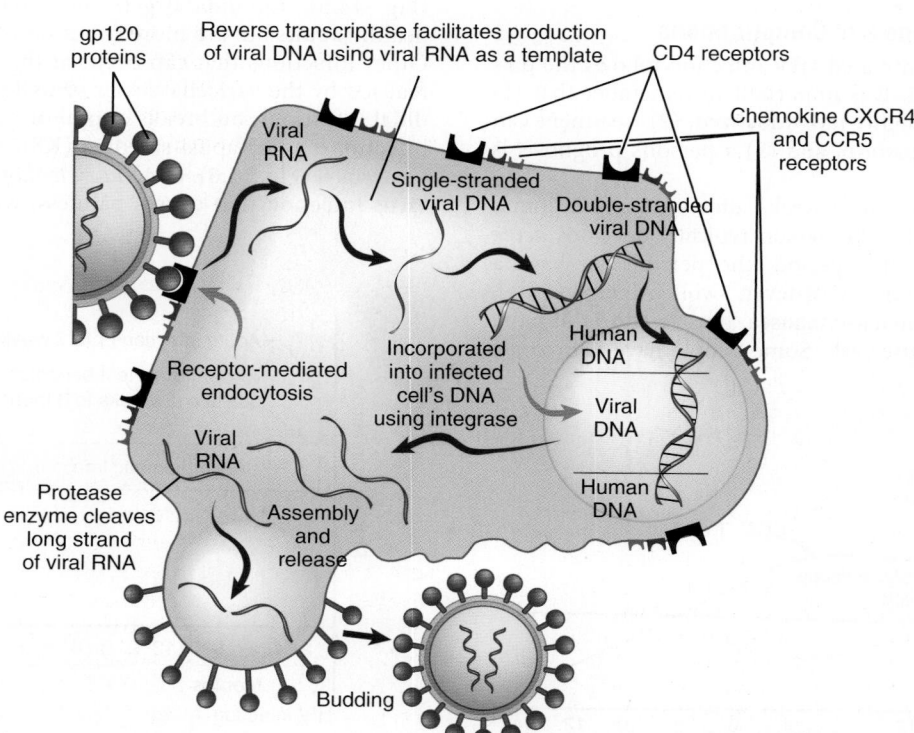

FIG. 14.2 HIV has gp120 glycoproteins that attach to CD4 and chemokine CXCR4 and CCR5 receptors on the surface of CD4 cells. Viral RNA then enters the cell, produces viral DNA in the presence of reverse transcriptase, and incorporates itself into the cellular genome in the presence of integrase, causing permanent cellular infection and the production of new virions. New viral RNA develops initially in long strands that are cut in the presence of protease and leave the cell through a budding process that contributes to cellular destruction.

Once HIV is attached and fused with the CD4 cell, HIV RNA enters the CD4 cell. This triggers the release of *reverse transcriptase,* an enzyme that transforms HIV RNA into a single strand of DNA. This strand copies itself, becoming double-stranded viral DNA. Another enzyme, called *integrase,* allows the newly formed double-stranded DNA to integrate itself into the host' genetic structure. This action has 2 consequences: (1) because all genetic material is replicated during cell division, all daughter cells are infected and (2) viral DNA in the genome directs the cell to make new HIV.

Protease, another enzyme involved in the replication process, cleaves the newly formed strands of HIV genetic material into smaller pieces. New HIV virions are then formed and released. The CD4 cell is then destroyed after the HIV virions are released.[17]

HIV destroys about 1 billion CD4 cells every day. For many years, the body can make new CD4 cells to replace the destroyed cells. However, over time the ability of HIV to destroy CD4 cells exceeds the body's ability to replace the cells. The decline in the CD4 cell count impairs immune function. Generally, the immune system remains healthy with more than 500 CD4 cells/μL. Immune problems begin to occur when the count drops below 500 CD4 cells/μL. Severe problems develop with fewer than 200 CD4 cells/μL.

With HIV, a point is eventually reached at which so many CD4 cells have been destroyed that not enough are left to regulate immune responses (Fig. 14.3). This allows **opportunistic diseases** (infections and cancers that occur in immunosuppressed patients) to develop. Opportunistic diseases are the main cause of disease, disability, and death in patients with HIV infection.

Clinical Manifestations and Complications

The typical course of untreated HIV infection follows the pattern shown in Fig. 14.4. It is important to remember that (1) disease progression is highly individualized, (2) treatment can significantly alter this pattern, and (3) a person's prognosis is unpredictable.

Acute Infection. About 2 to 4 weeks after someone becomes newly infected with HIV, the person typically develops *acute HIV infection.* During this period, the person can have a mononucleosis-like syndrome of fever, swollen lymph nodes, sore throat, headache, malaise, nausea, muscle and joint pain, diarrhea, and/or a diffuse rash. Some people have neurologic

complications, such as aseptic meningitis, peripheral neuropathy, facial palsy, or Guillain-Barré syndrome.[18] During this time, there is a high **viral load**, the amount of HIV circulating in the blood. CD4 cell counts fall temporarily but quickly return to baseline or near-baseline levels (Fig. 14.3). Many people, including HCPs, mistake acute HIV symptoms for a bad case of the flu. People are most infectious during the acute infection stage because of the high amounts of circulating HIV.

Chronic HIV Infection

Asymptomatic Infection. The time between initial HIV infection and a diagnosis of AIDS is about 10 years in untreated infection. During the first several years after initial infection, people are typically asymptomatic and have no symptoms or limited signs of infection.

Because most symptoms during early infection are vague and nonspecific for HIV, people may not be aware that they are infected. During this time, infected people continue their usual activities, which may include high-risk sexual and drug-using behaviors. This is a public health problem because infected persons can transmit HIV to others even though they have no symptoms.[19] Personal health is also affected because people who do not know that they are infected have little reason to seek treatment and are less likely to make behavior changes that could improve the quality and length of their lives.

Symptomatic Infection. As the CD4 cell count declines closer to 200 cells/μL and the viral load increases, HIV advances to a more active stage. Symptoms such as persistent fever, frequent night sweats, chronic diarrhea, recurrent headaches, and severe fatigue may develop.

One of the more common infections associated with this phase of HIV infection is oropharyngeal candidiasis (thrush) (Fig. 14.5). *Candida* organisms rarely cause problems in healthy adults but are more common in HIV-infected people. Other infections that can occur at this time include shingles (caused by the varicella-zoster virus); persistent vaginal candidal infections; outbreaks of oral or genital herpes; bacterial infections; and Kaposi sarcoma (KS), caused by human herpesvirus 8 (Fig. 14.6). *Oral hairy leukoplakia,* an Epstein-Barr virus infection that causes painless, white, raised lesions on

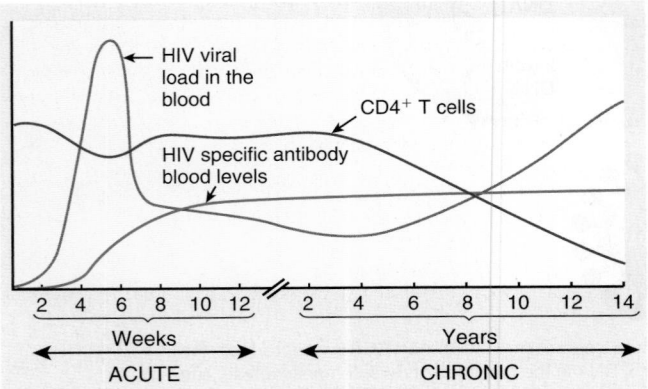

FIG. 14.3 Viral load in the blood in relationship to number of CD4 cells over the spectrum of untreated HIV infection.

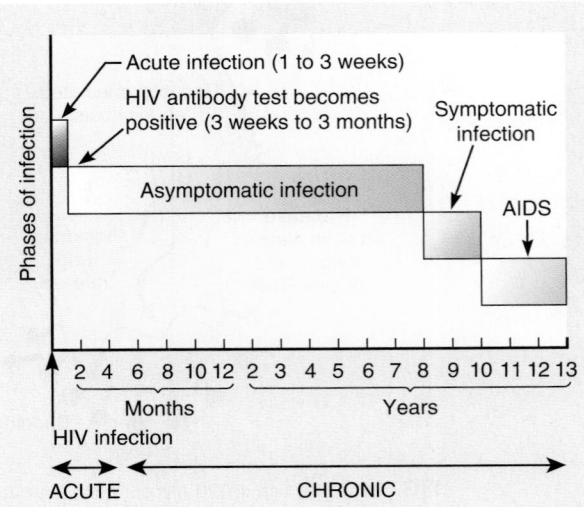

FIG. 14.4 Timeline for the spectrum of untreated HIV infection. The timeline represents the course of untreated illness from the time of infection to clinical manifestations of disease.

the lateral aspect of the tongue (Fig. 14.7), is another sign of disease progression.

AIDS. A diagnosis of acquired immunodeficiency syndrome (AIDS) is made when an HIV-infected patient meets criteria established by the CDC.[20] This occurs when the immune system becomes severely compromised (Table 14.10). Opportunistic diseases generally do not occur in the presence of a functioning immune system. Many infections, a variety of cancers, wasting, and HIV-related cognitive changes can occur in patients with immune impairment (Table 14.11). Organisms that do not cause severe disease in people with functioning immune systems can cause debilitating, life-threatening infections during this stage. Several opportunistic diseases may occur at the same time, increasing the difficulties of diagnosis and treatment. Advances in HIV treatment have decreased the occurrence of opportunistic diseases.

Diagnostic Studies

Diagnosis of HIV Infection. Diagnosis of HIV infection is made by testing for HIV antibodies and/or antigens.[21] HIV screening tests can be done using blood or saliva. Typically it takes several weeks after infection before a screening test can detect evidence of HIV (Fig. 14.3). This delay is known as the window period. The typical window period for most tests to detect HIV infection is about 3 weeks (Table 14.12). If a newly infected person is tested during the window period, the test may not be able to detect infection and they will have a false negative result.

Laboratory Studies in HIV Infection. Two laboratory tests are used for monitoring HIV progression: CD4 cell count and viral load. The CD4 cell count is a marker of immune function. As the disease progresses, the number of CD4 cells usually decreases (Fig. 14.3). The normal range for CD4 cells is 800 to 1200 cells/μL. Laboratory tests that measure viral levels provide an assessment of disease progression. The lower the viral load, the less active the disease. In HIV, viral loads are reported as

FIG. 14.5 Oral thrush involving hard and soft palate. (From Emond R, Welsby P, Rowland H: *Colour atlas of infectious diseases,* ed 4, Edinburgh, 2003, Mosby.)

FIG. 14.6 Kaposi sarcoma (KS). KS lesions can appear anywhere on the skin surface or on internal organs. Lesions vary in size from pinpoint to large and may appear in a variety of shades. (From Friedman-Kien AE: Color atlas of AIDS, Philadelphia, 1989, Saunders.)

FIG. 14.7 Oral hairy leukoplakia on the lateral aspect of the tongue. (Set of slides published in 1992 by Jon Fuller, MD, and Howard Libman, MD, at Boston University School of Medicine, Boston, MA.)

TABLE 14.10 **Diagnostic Criteria for AIDS**
AIDS is diagnosed when a person with HIV develops at least one of the following conditions:
1. CD4+ T cell count drops below 200 cells/μL.
2. One of the following opportunistic infections (OIs):
• *Bacterial: Mycobacterium tuberculosis* (any site); any disseminated or extrapulmonary mycobacteria, including *Mycobacterium avium* complex (MAC) or *Mycobacterium kansasii;* recurrent pneumonia; recurrent *Salmonella* septicemia
• *Fungal:* Candidiasis of bronchi, trachea, lungs, or esophagus; *Pneumocystis jiroveci* pneumonia (PCP); disseminated or extrapulmonary coccidioidomycosis; disseminated or extrapulmonary histoplasmosis
• *Protozoal:* Toxoplasmosis of the brain, chronic intestinal isosporiasis, chronic intestinal cryptosporidiosis
• *Viral:* Cytomegalovirus (CMV) disease other than liver, spleen, or nodes; CMV retinitis (with loss of vision); herpes simplex with chronic ulcer(s) or bronchitis, pneumonitis, or esophagitis; progressive multifocal leukoencephalopathy (PML); extrapulmonary cryptococcosis
3. One of the following opportunistic cancers:
• Burkitt's lymphoma
• Immunoblastic lymphoma
• Invasive cervical cancer
• Kaposi sarcoma (KS)
• Primary lymphoma of the brain
4. Wasting syndrome. *Wasting* is defined as a loss of 10% or more of ideal body mass.

Modified from Centers for Disease Control and Prevention: 1993 Revised classification system for HIV infection and expanded surveillance case definition for AIDS among adolescents and adults, 1993. Retrieved from *www.cdc.gov/mmwr/preview/mmwrhtml/rr5710a1.htm?s_cid=rr5710a1_e.*

TABLE 14.11 Common Opportunistic Diseases Associated With HIV Infection

Organism or Disease	Clinical Manifestations
Candida albicans	Thrush (Fig. 14.5), esophagitis, vaginitis. Whitish yellow patches in mouth, esophagus, GI tract, vagina
Coccidioides immitis	Pneumonia and fever, weight loss, cough
CNS lymphoma	Cognitive dysfunction, motor impairment, aphasia, seizures, personality changes, headache
Cryptococcus neoformans	Meningitis, cognitive impairment, motor dysfunction, fever, seizures, headache
Cryptosporidium muris	Gastroenteritis, watery diarrhea, abdominal pain, weight loss
Cytomegalovirus (CMV)	*Retinitis:* retinal lesions, blurred vision, loss of vision
	Esophagitis, stomatitis: difficulty swallowing, colitis or gastritis: bloody diarrhea, pain, weight loss
	Pneumonitis: respiratory symptoms
	Neurologic disease: central nervous system (CNS) manifestations
Hepatitis B virus (HBV)	Jaundice, fatigue, abdominal pain, loss of appetite, nausea, vomiting, joint pain. Some have no signs or symptoms
Hepatitis C virus (HCV)	Jaundice, fatigue, abdominal pain, loss of appetite, nausea, vomiting, dark urine. Many have no signs or symptoms
Herpes simplex virus (HSV)	*HSV-1 (type 1):* orolabial and mucocutaneous vesicular and ulcerative lesions. Keratitis, visual changes, encephalitis, CNS manifestations
	HSV-2 (type 2): genital and perianal vesicular and ulcerative lesions
Histoplasma capsulatum	*Pneumonia:* fever, cough, weight loss
	Meningitis: CNS manifestations, disseminated disease
JC papovavirus	Progressive multifocal leukoencephalopathy (PML), CNS manifestations, mental and motor declines
Kaposi sarcoma (KS) caused by human herpesvirus 8 (HHV-8)	Vascular lesions on the skin (Fig. 14.6), mucous membranes, and viscera with wide range of presentation: firm, flat, raised, or nodular; pinpoint to several cm in size; hyperpigmented, multicentric. Can cause lymphedema and disfigurement. Usually not serious unless occurring in the respiratory or GI system
Mycobacterium avium complex (MAC)	Gastroenteritis, watery diarrhea, weight loss
Mycobacterium tuberculosis (MTB, TB)	Respiratory and disseminated disease. Productive cough, fever, night sweats, weight loss
Pneumocystis jiroveci pneumonia (PCP)	Pneumonia, nonproductive cough, hypoxemia, progressive shortness of breath, fever, night sweats, fatigue
Toxoplasma gondii	Encephalitis, cognitive dysfunction, motor impairment, fever, altered mental status, headache, seizures, sensory abnormalities
Varicella-zoster virus (VZV)	*Shingles:* erythematous maculopapular rash along dermatomal planes, pain, pruritus
	Ocular: progressive outer retinal necrosis (PORN)

TABLE 14.12 HIV Testing

HIV-Antibody/Antigen Testing

A highly sensitive test detects antibodies and antigens associated with HIV. Blood samples that are negative for HIV infection are reported as negative. The antigen/antibody testing algorithm includes confirmation with HIV viral load testing for any indeterminate results.

- If the patient has a negative HIV antibody/antigen test, but reports recent risky behaviors, encourage retesting in 4 to 6 weeks. Persons at ongoing risk should be assessed or counseled for risk reduction interventions, including preexposure prophylaxis (PrEP).
- If the results are positive and consistent with HIV infection, assist the patient in getting appropriate counseling, support, and follow-up HIV primary care.

Rapid HIV-Antibody Testing

1. The Centers for Disease Control and Prevention strongly recommends rapid testing. Results are highly accurate. It can be done in a variety of settings (mobile health units, HCP offices, privacy of a person's home). Results are typically available within 20 minutes.
2. In-home HIV test kits are available. Testing is done on saliva.
3. Follow a negative rapid test with a risk assessment to determine the need for repeat tests.
4. Positive rapid tests can be disclosed to the patient but must be confirmed with a standard HIV assay. This step necessitates a blood draw and a return appointment to get results.

the virus has been eliminated from the body or that the person no longer has HIV infection. Rather, it refers to the fact that the amount of circulating HIV in the blood is below the level of detection of the test. Studies show that an undetectable viral load prevents sexual transmission to others.

Abnormal blood test results are common in HIV infection. They may be caused by HIV, opportunistic diseases, or complications of therapy. Decreased white blood cell (WBC) counts, especially below-normal numbers of lymphocytes (lymphopenia) and neutrophils (neutropenia), often occur. HIV, antiplatelet antibodies, or drug therapy can cause low platelet counts (thrombocytopenia). Anemia is associated with the chronic disease process and adverse effects of ART. Altered liver function, caused by HIV infection, drug therapy, or co-infection with a hepatitis virus, is common. Early identification of co-infection with hepatitis B virus (HBV) or hepatitis C virus (HCV) is extremely important. These infections have a more serious course in patients with HIV, may limit options for ART, and can cause liver-related morbidity and mortality.[22]

Resistance tests can determine if a patient's HIV is resistant to drugs used for ART. *Genotype* and *phenotype* assays help HCPs know which medications can best control a patient's infection. These tests are similar to culture and sensitivity testing used for antibiotic selection.

Interprofessional Care

Interprofessional care of the HIV-infected patient focuses on (1) monitoring HIV disease progression and immune function, (2) initiating and monitoring ART, (3) preventing the development of opportunistic diseases, (4) detecting and

real numbers (e.g., 1260 copies/μL). The goal of treatment is to suppress the viral load to the lowest level possible, which is below the level of detection on a commercial assay. This is often referred to as "undetectable." "Undetectable" does *not* mean that

TABLE 14.13 Drug Therapy

HIV Infection

Drug Classification	Mechanism of Action	Drug Names
Attachment Inhibitors	Interrupts the ability of HIV to attach to the CD4 cell.	ibalizumab-uiyk (Trogarzo)
Entry Inhibitors	Prevent binding of HIV to cells, thus preventing entry of HIV into cells where replication would occur	enfuvirtide (Fuzeon) maraviroc (Selzentry)
Integrase Inhibitors	Bind with integrase enzyme and prevent HIV from incorporating its genetic material into the host cell	bictegravir* dolutegravir (Tivicay) elvitegravir* raltegravir (Isentress)
Protease Inhibitors (PIs)	Prevent the protease enzyme from cutting HIV proteins into the proper lengths needed to allow viable virions to assemble and bud out from the cell membrane	atazanavir (Reyataz) darunavir (Prezista) fosamprenavir (Lexiva) indinavir (Crixivan) lopinavir + ritonavir (Kaletra) nelfinavir (Viracept) ritonavir (Norvir)† saquinavir (Fortovase, Invirase) tipranavir (Aptivus)
Reverse Transcriptase Inhibitors		
Nonnucleoside Reverse Transcriptase Inhibitors (NNRTIs)	Inhibit the action of reverse transcriptase	efavirenz (Sustiva) etravirine (Intelence) delavirdine (Rescriptor) nevirapine (Viramune XR) rilpivirine (Edurant)
Nucleoside Reverse Transcriptase Inhibitors (NRTIs)	Insert a piece of DNA into the developing HIV DNA chain, blocking further development of the chain and leaving the production of the new strand of HIV DNA incomplete	abacavir (Ziagen) didanosine (Videx, Videx-EC) doravarine (Pifeltro) emtricitabine (Emtriva) lamivudine (Epivir) stavudine (Zerit) zidovudine (Retrovir)
Nucleotide Reverse Transcriptase Inhibitor (NtRTI)	Combines with reverse transcriptase enzyme to block the process needed to convert HIV RNA into HIV DNA	tenofovir (Viread)

*Elvitegravir and bictegravir are integrase inhibitors that are available only in fixed-dose combinations with tenofovir AF and emtricitabine (Table 14.14).
†Most often used in low doses with other PIs to boost effect.

treating opportunistic diseases, (5) managing symptoms, (6) preventing or decreasing complications of treatment, and (7) preventing further transmission of HIV. To achieve these goals, ongoing assessment, clinician-patient interactions, and patient teaching and support are needed.

The first patient visit provides an opportunity to gather baseline data and start establishing rapport. A complete history and physical examination, including an immunization history and psychosocial and dietary evaluations, should be done. Findings from the history, assessment, and laboratory tests help determine patient needs. This is a good time to complete the case reports required by the state health department. Initiate patient teaching about the spectrum of HIV disease, treatment, prevention of transmission to others, improvements in health, and family planning at this meeting. Use patient input to develop a plan of care and determine the need for referrals. Remember that a newly diagnosed patient may not be able to retain or understand information. Be prepared to repeat and clarify information over the course of several months.

Drug Therapy for HIV Infection. The goals of drug therapy in HIV infection are to (1) decrease the viral load, (2) maintain or increase CD4 cell counts, (3) prevent HIV-related symptoms and opportunistic diseases, (4) delay disease progression, and

(5) prevent HIV transmission. HIV cannot be cured, but ART can delay disease progression by decreasing viral replication.[23] When taken consistently and correctly, ART can reduce viral loads by 90% to 99%. This makes adherence to treatment regimens extremely important.

Drugs used to treat HIV work at various points in the HIV replication cycle (Tables 14.13 and 14.14). The major advantage of using drugs from different classes is that combination therapy can inhibit viral replication in different ways. This makes it more difficult for the virus to recover and decreases the chance of drug resistance. A major problem with most drugs used in ART is that resistance develops rapidly when they are used alone (monotherapy) or taken in inadequate doses. This is why patients receive combinations of 3 or more drugs.

⚠ SAFETY ALERT Interaction of ART With Other Drugs

- Significant interactions with ARTs occur with over-the-counter (OTC) drugs, including antacids, proton pump inhibitors, and certain supplements.
- Many ARTs have interactions with other commonly used drugs and herbal therapies (e.g., St. John's wort).
- Be sure to ask patients about prescribed and OTC drugs as well as herbal products and supplements.

TABLE 14.14 Fixed-Dose Drug Combination Products

HIV Infection

Mechanism of Action
More than one drug combined into a single tablet. Drugs may be from the same or different classes.

Examples
Atripla (tenofovir DF + emtricitabine + efavirenz)
Biktarvy (tenofovir AF + emtricitabine + bictegravir)
Combivir (lamivudine + zidovudine)
Complera (tenofovir DF + emtricitabine + rilpivirine)
Delstrigo (tenofovir DF + lamivudine + doravarine)
Descovy (tenofovir AF + emtricitabine)
Epzicom (abacavir + lamivudine)

Evotaz (atazanavir + cobicistat†)
Genvoya (tenofovir AF + emtricitabine + elvitegravir + cobicistat†)
Juluca (dolutegravir + rilpivirine)
Odefsey (tenofovir AF + emtricitabine + rilpivirine)
Prezcobix (darunavir + cobicistat†)
Temixys (tenofovir DF + lamivudine)
Triumeq (abacavir + lamivudine + dolutegravir)
Trizivir (abacavir + lamivudine + zidovudine)
Truvada (tenofovir DF + emtricitabine)
Stribild (tenofovir DF + emtricitabine + elvitegravir + cobicistat†)
Symtuza (tenofovir AF + emtricitabine + darunavir + cobicistat†)

†Cobicistat is a pharmacologic booster that enhances the potency of some HIV antiretrovirals. It has no direct effects against HIV.
AF, Alafenamide. *DF*, disoproxil fumarate.

Drug Therapy for Opportunistic Diseases. Management of HIV is complicated by the many opportunistic diseases that can develop as the immune system deteriorates (Table 14.11). Prevention is the preferred approach to opportunistic diseases. Several opportunistic diseases associated with HIV can be delayed or prevented with adequate ART, vaccines (including hepatitis B, influenza, pneumococcal), and disease-specific prevention measures.[24] Although it is usually not possible to eradicate opportunistic diseases once they occur, prophylactic medications can significantly decrease morbidity and mortality rates. Advances in the prevention, diagnosis, and treatment of opportunistic diseases have contributed significantly to increased life expectancy.

Preventing Transmission of HIV. Preexposure prophylaxis (PrEP) is a comprehensive HIV prevention strategy to reduce the risk for sexually acquired HIV infection in adults at high risk.[25] PrEP should be used in conjunction with other proven prevention interventions such as condoms, risk reduction counseling, and regular HIV testing.

Currently, certain antiretrovirals are approved for both treatment of HIV in persons living with HIV, as well as prevention of HIV infection in persons without HIV infection. Various formulations have been studied for PrEP. The first medications approved for PrEP were tenofovir disoproxil fumarate (Tenofovir DF) in combination with emtricitabine. Other medications, including injectable options, will soon be available. As PrEP, these medications reduce the risk for HIV infection in uninfected people who are at significant risk for acquiring HIV. Tenofovir and emtricitabine are also used in combination with other antiretroviral agents for the treatment of HIV-infected people.

❖ NURSING MANAGEMENT: HIV INFECTION

◆ Nursing Assessment

Nursing assessment of people not known to have HIV infection should focus on behaviors that put the person at risk for HIV and other sexually transmitted and blood-borne infections. Assess patients for risky behaviors on a regular basis. Do not assume that someone is without risk because he or she is too old, too young, heterosexual, or married.

Assess risk by asking some basic questions: (1) Have you ever had a blood transfusion or used clotting factors? If so, was it before 1985? (2) Have you ever shared drug-using equipment with another person? (3) Have you ever had a sexual experience in which your penis, vagina, rectum, or mouth came into contact with another person's penis, vagina, rectum, or mouth? (4) Have you ever had a sexually transmitted infection? (5) Have you ever had sexual contact with someone known to have HIV? These questions provide the minimum information needed to initiate a risk assessment. Follow up a positive response to any of these questions with an in-depth exploration of issues related to the identified risk.

A person who has HIV infection needs specific, ongoing assessment. Subjective and objective data are outlined in Table 14.15. Repeated nursing assessments over time are essential because people's circumstances change. Early recognition and treatment can slow the progression of HIV infection and prevent new infections. A complete history and thorough systems review can help identify and address problems in a timely manner.

◆ Nursing Diagnoses

Nursing diagnoses for the patient with HIV disease may include:
- Risk for infection
- Lack of knowledge
- Difficulty coping
- Impaired nutritional status

◆ Planning

Nursing interventions can help the patient (1) adhere to drug regimens; (2) adopt a healthy lifestyle that includes avoiding exposure to other sexually transmitted infections and blood-borne diseases; (3) protect others from HIV; (4) maintain or develop healthy and supportive relationships; (5) maintain activities and productivity; (6) explore spiritual issues; (7) come to terms with issues related to disease, disability, and death; and (8) cope with symptoms caused by HIV and its treatments.

❖ Nursing Implementation

The complexity of HIV disease is related to its chronic nature. As with most chronic and infectious diseases, primary prevention and health promotion are the most effective health care strategies. When prevention fails, disease results. Table 14.15 shows a summary of nursing goals, assessments, and interventions throughout the course of HIV infection.

◆ Health Promotion.
Even with recent successes in HIV treatment, prevention is key in controlling the epidemic. In addition, health promotion encourages early detection of the disease so that, if primary prevention has failed, early intervention can be initiated.

TABLE 14.15 Nursing Assessment
HIV-Infected Patient

Subjective Data

Important Health Information

Past health history: Route of infection. Hepatitis, other sexually transmitted infections, tuberculosis. Frequent viral, fungal, and/or bacterial infections
Medications: Use of immunosuppressive drugs

Functional Health Patterns

Health perception–health management: Perception of illness. Alcohol and drug use. Malaise
Nutritional-metabolic: Weight loss, anorexia, nausea, vomiting. Lesions, bleeding, or ulcerations of lips, mouth, gums, tongue, or throat. Sensitivity to acidic, salty, or spicy foods. Difficulty swallowing, abdominal cramping. Skin rashes, lesions, or color changes
Elimination: Persistent diarrhea, change in character of stools. Painful urination, low back pain
Activity-exercise: Chronic fatigue, muscle weakness, difficulty walking. Cough, shortness of breath
Sleep-rest: Insomnia, night sweats, fatigue
Cognitive-perceptual: Headaches, stiff neck, chest pain, rectal pain, retrosternal pain. Blurred vision, photophobia, diplopia, loss of vision. Hearing impairment. Confusion, forgetfulness, attention deficit, changes in mental status, memory loss, personality changes. Paresthesias, hypersensitivity in feet, pruritus
Role-relationship: Support system(s), career or job, financial resources
Sexuality-reproductive: Lesions on genitalia or anus (internal or external), pruritus or burning in vagina, penis, or anus. Painful sexual intercourse, rectal pain or bleeding, changes in menstruation, vaginal or penile discharge. Use of birth control measures, pregnancies, desire for future children
Coping–stress tolerance: Stress levels, previous losses, coping patterns, self-concept; social withdrawal

Objective Data

General

Lethargy, persistent fever, lymphadenopathy, peripheral wasting, fat deposits in truncal areas and upper back

Eyes

Presence of exudates, retinal lesions or hemorrhage, papilledema

Integumentary

Decreased skin turgor, dry skin, diaphoresis. Pallor, cyanosis. Lesions, eruptions, discolorations, bruises of skin or mucous membranes. Vaginal or perianal excoriation. Alopecia. Delayed wound healing

Respiratory

Tachypnea, dyspnea, intercostal retractions. Crackles, wheezing, productive or nonproductive cough

Cardiovascular

Pericardial friction rub, murmur, bradycardia, tachycardia

Gastrointestinal

Mouth lesions, including blisters (HSV), white-gray patches (*Candida* infection), painless white lesions on the side of the tongue (hairy leukoplakia), discolorations (Kaposi sarcoma). Gingivitis, tooth decay or loosening. Redness or white patchy lesions of throat. Vomiting, diarrhea, incontinence, rectal lesions, hyperactive bowel sounds, abdominal masses, hepatosplenomegaly

Musculoskeletal

Muscle wasting, weakness

Neurologic

Ataxia, tremors, lack of coordination. Sensory loss, slurred speech, aphasia. Memory loss, peripheral neuropathy, apathy, agitation, depression, inappropriate behavior. Decreasing levels of consciousness, seizures, paralysis, coma

Reproductive

Genital lesions or discharge, abdominal tenderness secondary to pelvic inflammatory disease (PID)

Possible Diagnostic Findings

Positive HIV antibody/antigen assay. Detectable viral load. ↓ CD4 cell count, ↓ WBC count, lymphopenia, anemia, thrombocytopenia. Electrolyte imbalances, abnormal liver function tests. ↑ cholesterol, triglycerides, and blood glucose

ETHICAL/LEGAL DILEMMAS
Individual vs. Public Health Protection

Situation

A nurse in a community clinic is having a follow-up visit with V.T., a 38-yr-old woman who was diagnosed with HIV infection during her annual examination 2 weeks ago. During the visit, V.T. discloses that her partner verbally and physically abuses her. V.T. says she had not yet told her partner about the HIV diagnosis because she is afraid that he will hurt her. She has not used any protection during sex with him since she learned of her test results because she suspects he infected her.

Ethical/Legal Points for Consideration

- You face a conflict between preventing further harm to V.T. (possible increase in intimate partner violence), providing care to her partner (his need for an HIV test, diagnosis, and treatment), and protecting the public health (potential spread of HIV infection to her partner or from her partner to others in the community). Patient teaching and support are essential because your primary obligation is to the patient.
- Because relevant law varies from state to state, your first step is to be familiar with your state law concerning mandated reporting for domestic partner abuse and infectious diseases.
- Federal laws about protection of privacy in HIV testing apply everywhere.
- In many states, reporting domestic abuse is mandatory only when the reporter actually witnesses the abuse or when the immediate effects of the abuse (e.g., wounds, contusions, broken bones) are witnessed.[1]

- You should be familiar with crisis counseling services for V.T. and offer her the following advice: Collect and stash a set of car keys or taxi money in a safe place, keep a bag packed and hidden or even stored in a locker somewhere accessible, develop a code phrase to use with a friend or family member to call for help, keep a cell phone charged, and have money hidden in a safe place.

Discussion Questions

1. Within the parameters of your state's requirements for reportable conditions, how can you protect the patient's confidentiality to prevent further intimate partner violence?
2. What services does your state offer to notify a partner without disclosing the source patient's name? How would V.T. access those services in your state?
3. How can you protect the partner from possible infection while also protecting V.T. from further violence?
4. How can you best address the issue of intimate partner violence? What resources would V.T. have in your community?
5. Discuss the benefits of universal, voluntary testing in light of V.T.'s case.

Reference

National Coalition Against Domestic Violence. Retrieved from *www.ncadv.com*.

Prevention of HIV Infection. HIV infection is preventable. Avoiding or modifying risky behaviors is the most effective prevention tool. Nursing interventions to prevent disease transmission are based on an assessment of the person's risk behaviors. Provide culturally sensitive, language-appropriate, and age-specific teaching and behavior change counseling. Nurses who are comfortable with and know how to talk about sensitive topics such as sexuality and drug use are best prepared to provide prevention education.

♥ PROMOTING POPULATION HEALTH

Prevention and Early Detection of HIV

* Increase safer sexual practices, including condom use
* Decrease equipment sharing among IV drug users
* Increase clinician skills to assess for risk factors for HIV infection, recommend HIV testing, and provide counseling for behavior change
* Make voluntary HIV testing a routine part of health care
* Increase access to new HIV testing technologies, especially rapid testing
* Increase access to HIV testing facilities in traditional health care settings and alternative sites, such as drug and alcohol treatment facilities and community-based organizations
* Increase risk assessment and individualized behavior change messages to people with HIV to prevent new infections
* Decrease perinatal HIV infection by offering voluntary HIV testing as a part of routine prenatal care
* Provide counseling and appropriate HIV therapy to those who are infected

A wide variety of activities can reduce the risk for HIV infection.[26] Help people choose the methods that best fit their needs and circumstances. Prevention techniques are divided into *safe sexual activities* (those that eliminate risk) and *risk-reducing sexual activities* (those that decrease, but do not eliminate, risk).

The goal is to develop safer, healthier, and less risky behaviors. The more consistently and correctly one uses prevention methods, the more effective they are in preventing HIV infection. It is a good idea to use a combination of prevention methods (e.g., using condoms, decreasing the number of sex partners) to increase the prevention effect.

Decreasing risks related to sexual intercourse. *Safe sexual activities* eliminate the risk for exposure to HIV in semen and vaginal secretions. Abstaining from all sexual activity is an effective way to achieve this goal, but there are safe options for those who cannot or do not wish to abstain. Limiting sexual behavior to activities in which the mouth, penis, vagina, or rectum does not come into contact with a partner's mouth, penis, vagina, or rectum eliminates contact with blood, semen, or vaginal secretions. Safe activities include masturbation, mutual masturbation ("hand job"), and other activities that meet the "no contact" requirements. *Insertive sex* between partners who are not infected with HIV and not at risk of becoming infected with HIV is considered safe.

Risk-reducing sexual activities decrease the risk of contact with HIV through the use of barriers. Barriers should be used when engaging in insertive sexual activity (oral, vaginal, anal) with a partner who has HIV or whose HIV status is not known. The most commonly used barrier is the male condom. Male condoms offer protection during anal, vaginal, and oral intercourse. Female condoms are an alternative to male condoms. Squares of latex (known as dental dams) can be used as a barrier during oral sexual activity.

Decreasing risks related to drug use. Drug use, including alcohol and tobacco, can cause immunosuppression, poor nutrition, and a host of psychosocial problems. However, drug use does not cause HIV infection. The major risk for HIV related to using drugs involves sharing equipment or having unsafe sexual experiences while under the influence of drugs. Basic risk reduction rules are (1) do not use drugs; (2) if you use drugs, do not share equipment; and (3) do not have sexual intercourse when under the influence of any drug, including alcohol, that impairs decision making.[27]

The safest method is to abstain from drugs, but this may not be a practical option for users who are not prepared to quit or have no access to drug treatment services. The risk for HIV infection for these persons is eliminated if they do not share equipment. Injecting equipment ("works") includes needles, syringes, cookers (spoons or bottle caps used to mix the drug), cotton, and rinse water. Blood can contaminate equipment used to snort (straws) or smoke (pipes) drugs and should not be shared.

Access to sterile equipment is an important risk elimination tactic. Some communities have needle and syringe exchange programs (NSEPs) that provide sterile equipment in exchange for used equipment. Opposition to these programs is related to the fear that access to injecting supplies will increase drug use. However, studies have shown that in communities with NSEPs, drug use does not increase, rates of HIV and other blood-borne

EVIDENCE-BASED PRACTICE

Condom Use and HIV

As a nurse in an HIV clinic, you are counseling M.J., a 27-yr-old gay man and his partner. M.J. is on antiretroviral therapy (ART). His viral load is very low, and his CD4 cell count is normal. He tells you that since the drugs are working, he and his partner (who is HIV-negative) are considering not using condoms in the future.

Making Clinical Decisions

Best Available Evidence. One of the best ways to prevent HIV transmission from an infected person to an uninfected person continues to be the consistent and correct use of latex condoms. Those with HIV who take ART and get and keep an undetectable viral load (<200 copies/mL) have effectively no risk for transmitting HIV to their HIV-negative sexual partners. Behavior change programs provided by HCPs, peers, and others can significantly reduce risk behaviors among those with HIV and the transmission of the virus to others.

Clinician Expertise. You know that risk-reducing sexual activities in this situation include the continued use of condoms. However, you also know that other strategies can also reduce the risk of HIV transmission.

Patient Preferences and Values. M.J. tells you that he and his partner are in a committed relationship, have no other partners, and do not like using condoms.

Implications for Practice

1. What information would you discuss with M.J. related to HIV transmission, ART and viral load, and the risks of unprotected sexual activity?
2. What measures besides condom use would you discuss with M.J. to reduce the risk for HIV transmission?

References for Evidence

Centers for Diseases Control and Prevention. Evidence of HIV treatment and viral suppression in preventing the sexual transmission of HIV. Retrieved from *www.cdc.gov/hiv/pdf/risk/art/cdc-hiv-art-viral-suppression.pdf.*
Centers for Diseases Control and Prevention. Proven HIV prevention methods. Retrieved from *www.cdc.gov/nchhstp/newsroom/docs/factsheets/hiv-proven-prevention-methods-508.pdf.*

infections are controlled, and an overall cost benefit results.[28] Appropriately cleaning equipment before use can reduce risk by decreasing the chance of blood contact.

Providing support for patients with substance use and referring them to professionals who can assist with managing the psychologic aspects of substance use is important. Other self-help programs (e.g., Narcotics Anonymous, Alcoholics Anonymous) may be helpful.

Decreasing risks of perinatal transmission. The best way to prevent HIV infection in infants is to prevent HIV infection in women. Women infected with HIV should be asked about their reproductive desires. Those who choose not to have children need to have family planning methods discussed in detail. Should they become pregnant, we need to discuss their options, including the possibility of maintaining the pregnancy and using ART to decrease the risk for transmission or having an abortion.

If HIV-infected pregnant women are appropriately treated during pregnancy, the rate of perinatal transmission decreases from 25% to less than 2%. ART has significantly decreased the risk for infants born to HIV-infected women, and more of these women are now becoming mothers. The current standard of care is for all women who are pregnant or contemplating pregnancy to receive HIV counseling, be offered access to voluntary HIV-antibody testing, and, if infected, offered optimal ART.[29]

Decreasing risks at work. The risk for infection from occupational exposure to HIV is small but real. OSHA requires employers to protect workers from exposure to blood and other potentially infectious materials (Table 14.8). Precautions and safety devices decrease the risk for direct contact with blood and body fluids. Should exposure to HIV-infected fluids occur, **postexposure prophylaxis (PEP)** with combination ART can significantly decrease the risk for infection.[15] The need for timely treatment and counseling makes it critical for nurses to report all blood exposures.

HIV Testing. An estimated 14% of people living with HIV in the United States are not aware that they are infected. People who do not know they are infected are more likely to transmit the infection to others. Current guidelines recommend universal, voluntary testing as part of routine medical care.[30,31] The goal is to normalize the test, decrease the stigma related to HIV testing, find hidden cases, get infected persons into care, and prevent new cases of infection.

◆ **Acute Care**

Early Intervention. Early intervention after detection of HIV infection can promote health and limit disability. The nursing assessment in HIV disease should focus on early detection of symptoms, opportunistic diseases, and psychosocial problems (Table 14.16).

Initial response to diagnosis of HIV. Reactions to an HIV diagnosis are similar to the reactions of people who are diagnosed with any life-threatening, debilitating, or chronic illness. These reactions include anxiety, panic, fear, depression, denial, hopelessness, anger, and guilt.[32] Unfortunately, all these emotions are overlaid with the stigma and discrimination that continue to infuse societal reactions to HIV. The patient's family members, friends, and caregivers experience many of the same reactions. As time passes, patients and their loved ones will be confronted with complex treatment decisions; feelings of loss, anger, powerlessness, depression, and grief; social isolation; the possibility of death; and/or thoughts of suicide.

Antiretroviral therapy. ART can significantly slow the progression of HIV. However, treatment regimens can be complex, the drugs have side effects, ART does not work for everyone, and it is expensive. These factors can contribute to problems with adherence to treatment, a dangerous situation because of the high risk for developing drug resistance.

CHECK YOUR PRACTICE

You are working in an outpatient HIV clinic, and one of the patients, a 34-yr-old single parent with HIV infection, tells you, "I've been feeling well lately. I've been so busy taking care of my kids and working, I have not been taking my HIV meds."
• How would you respond to this patient?

Interventions include teaching about (1) advantages and disadvantages of new treatments, (2) dangers of poor adherence to therapeutic regimens, (3) how and when to take each drug, (4) drug interactions to avoid, and (5) side effects to report to the HCP. Table 14.17 outlines patient and caregiver teaching on HIV treatment and initial follow-up.

Clinical guidelines provide information on initial drug regimens.[23] However, one of the most important considerations for initiating therapy is patient readiness for treatment. Adherence to ART is a critical part of successful drug therapy for people with HIV infection. Nurses are uniquely prepared to provide assistance with adherence to the drug regimen (Table 14.18). Taking drugs as prescribed (right dose and time) is important for all drug therapy, but with HIV infection, missing even a few doses can lead to drug resistance. We can help patients adhere to difficult treatment regimens with electronic reminders, beepers, timers on pillboxes, and calendars. Group support and individual counseling can help. The best approach is to learn about the patient's life and assist with problem solving related to taking medications within the confines of that life.

INFORMATICS IN PRACTICE
Use of Internet and Mobile Devices to Manage HIV

• The Internet offers resources and support for patients that can help them cope with their illness and teach them about signs and symptoms of serious illness.
• By monitoring their health and quickly spotting warning signs of serious illnesses, patients are able to alert their HCPs and receive earlier treatment.
• These systems can help the patient manage antiretroviral therapy by sending medication reminders by text or e-mail.

Delaying disease progression. Promoting a healthy immune system, whether the patient chooses to take ART or not, may delay the progression of HIV disease. Useful interventions for HIV-infected patients include (1) getting nutritional support to maintain lean body mass and ensure appropriate levels of vitamins and micronutrients; (2) moderating or eliminating alcohol, tobacco, and drug use; (3) keeping up to date with recommended vaccines; (4) getting adequate rest and exercise; (5) reducing stress; (6) avoiding exposure to new infectious agents; (7) accessing counseling; (8) getting involved in support groups and community activities; and (9) developing a consistent relationship with HCPs, including attending regular appointments.

TABLE 14.16 Nursing Management

HIV Infection

Nursing Care and Goals	Assessment	Interventions
Health Promotion **Prevent HIV infection**	*Risk factors:* What behaviors or social, physical, emotional, pathogenic, or immune factors place the patient at risk?	• Education, including knowledge, attitudes, and behaviors, with emphasis on risk reduction to the following: • *General population:* Cover general information • *Pregnant women:* General information and information specific to HIV infection and pregnancy • *Individual patient:* Specific to assessed need • Empower patients to take control of prevention measures.
Detect HIV infection early	Does the patient need to be tested for HIV?	• Provide HIV antibody/antigen testing with appropriate counseling.
Acute Care **Promote health and limit disability**	*Physical health:* Is the patient experiencing problems? *Mental health:* How is the patient coping? *Resources:* Does the patient have family or social support? Is the patient accessing community services? Is money or insurance a problem? Does the patient have access to spiritual support as desired?	• Provide case management or refer to interprofessional team, including social work. • Teach about HIV, the spectrum of infection, options for care, signs and symptoms to report, treatment options, immune enhancement, risk reduction, and ways to adhere to treatment regimens. • Establish long-term, trusting relationship with patient, family, and significant others. • Provide emotional and spiritual support. • Develop resources for legal needs: discrimination prevention, wills and advance directives, child care wishes. • Empower the patient to identify needs, direct care, and seek services.
Manage problems caused by HIV infection	*Physical health:* Has the patient had an acute exacerbation of problems related to immunodeficiency, opportunistic disease, or risk factors (e.g., substance use)? *Mental health status:* Has the patient's ability to cope with psychosocial issues deteriorated?	• Provide care during acute exacerbations: recognition of life-threatening developments, life support, rapid intervention with treatments and drugs, comfort, and hygiene needs. • Support patient and family during crisis. • Assist the patient with mental health issues and provide referral to mental health specialist as needed.
Ambulatory Care **Maximize quality of life**	*Physical health:* Are new symptoms developing? Is the patient experiencing drug side effects or interactions?	• Continue case management. • Teach about changing treatment options and continued adherence. • Empower patient to continue to direct care and to make desires known to family members and significant others.
Resolve life and death issues	*Mental health:* How is the patient coping? What adjustments have been made? *Finances:* Can the patient maintain health care and basic standards of living? *Family, social, and community support:* Are these available? Is the patient using support in an effective manner? Do family or significant others need teaching, encouragement, or stress relief? *Spirituality issues:* Does the patient desire support from a religious organization or spiritual counselor? What assistance does the patient desire?	• Continue physical care for chronic disease process: treatments, drugs, comfort, and hygiene needs. • Encourage health promotion measures (as above). • Refer the patient to resources to support finances. • Support patient and family or significant others in a trusting relationship. • Assist with end-of-life issues: resuscitation orders, comfort measures, funeral plans, estate planning, child care, etc. • Assess desires and refer to resources that will help in meeting spiritual needs.

Teach patients to recognize symptoms that may indicate disease progression and/or drug side effects so that prompt medical care can be initiated. Table 14.19 gives an overview of symptoms that patients should report.

Acute Exacerbations. Acute exacerbations of recurring problems characterize chronic disease. This is especially true in HIV disease in which infections, cancers, debility, and psychosocial or economic issues may interact to overwhelm the patient's ability to cope. Nursing care becomes more complex as the patient's immune system declines and new problems arise to compound existing difficulties. When opportunistic diseases or difficult treatment side effects develop, the patient needs symptom management, teaching, and emotional support.

Nursing care can help prevent the many opportunistic diseases associated with HIV infection. The best way to prevent opportunistic disease is to ensure that the patient is adhering to an effective ART regimen and, if appropriate, taking prophylactic medications for opportunistic infections. Should an opportunistic disease occur, nursing care is an essential part of helping the patient adhere to medications and providing supportive care specific to the opportunistic disease. For example, if the patient has *Pneumocystis jiroveci* pneumonia (PCP) (Fig. 14.8), nursing interventions can ensure adequate oxygenation. If the patient has cryptococcal meningitis, an important nursing concern is maintaining a safe environment for a confused patient.

TABLE 14.17 Patient & Caregiver Teaching
Antiretroviral Drugs

Resistance to antiretroviral drugs is a major problem in treating HIV infection. Include the following instructions when teaching the patient and/or caregiver to decrease the risk for developing resistance.

1. Discuss options with your HCP to find the best regimen for you.
2. Know the drugs you are taking and how to take them (some have to be taken with food, some must be taken on an empty stomach, some cannot be taken together). If you do not understand, ask. Have your nurse write the instructions for you.
3. Take the full dose prescribed and take it on schedule. If you cannot take the drug because of side effects or other problems, report it to your HCP immediately.
4. Take all your medications as prescribed. Do not quit taking one drug while continuing the others. If you cannot tolerate even one of your drugs, talk to your HCP, who will recommend a way to deal with the side effects or a new set of drugs.
5. Many antiretroviral drugs interact with other drugs, including many common drugs you can buy without a prescription. Be sure your HCP and pharmacist know all the drugs that you are taking. Do not take any new drugs without checking for possible interactions.
6. The goals of antiretroviral therapy are to decrease the amount of virus in your blood (your viral load) and to keep your CD4 cell count high. The best results reduce your viral load below detectable levels and keep your CD4 cell count high. Most HCPs do routine laboratory work every 3 to 6 months whether you are taking antiretroviral drugs or not.
7. At 2 to 4 weeks after you start on drug therapy or change your therapy, your HCP will test your viral load to find out how the drugs are working.
   - Your viral load is reported in absolute numbers. All you need to know is that you want to see the viral load drop.
   - Your CD4 cell count is reported in absolute numbers or percentages. It is best for your CD4 cell count to be above 500 cells/μL. If reported in percentages, you would like your CD4 cell value to be above 14%.
8. An undetectable viral load means that the amount of virus is extremely low, and HIV cannot be found in the blood using current testing technology. It does not mean that the virus is gone because the virus can be in lymph nodes and organs that blood tests cannot detect. An undetectable viral load prevents sexual transmission to others.

TABLE 14.18 Patient & Caregiver Teaching
Improving Adherence to Antiretroviral Therapy

The following are strategies that you can use to improve a patient's adherence to using antiretroviral therapy:

1. Determine whether the patient understands the importance of adherence and is ready to start therapy.
2. Provide teaching on medication dosing.
3. Review potential side effects of drugs.
4. Assure the patient that side effects can be treated. If not, medication regimens can be changed.
5. Use teaching and memory aids, including pictures, pillboxes, and calendars.
6. Engage family and friends in the teaching process. Solicit their support to help the patient take treatment.
7. Simplify regimens, dosing, and food requirements as much as possible.
8. Use a team of nurses, HCPs, pharmacists, case managers, and mental health and peer counselors to support the patient.
9. Help the patient integrate the medication regimen into his or her typical life activities and work schedules.

Modified from Centers for Disease Control and Prevention: Guidelines for the use of antiretroviral agents in HIV-1-infected adults and adolescents, 2015. Retrieved from *www.aidsinfo.nih.gov*.

TABLE 14.19 Patient & Caregiver Teaching
Signs and Symptoms HIV-Infected Patients Need to Report

Teach the patient with HIV infection and the caregiver to report the following signs and symptoms.

Report Immediately
- Any change in level of consciousness: lethargic, hard to arouse, unable to be aroused, unresponsive, unconscious
- Headache accompanied by nausea and vomiting, changes in vision, changes in ability to perform coordinated activities, or after any head trauma
- Vision changes: blurry or black areas in vision field, new floaters, double vision
- Persistent shortness of breath related to activity and not relieved by a short rest period
- Nausea and vomiting accompanied by abdominal pain
- Vomiting blood
- Dehydration: unable to eat or drink because of nausea or mouth lesions; severe diarrhea or vomiting; dizziness when standing
- Yellow discoloration of the skin
- Any bleeding from the rectum that is not related to hemorrhoids or trauma (e.g., from anal sexual intercourse)
- Pain in the flank with fever and inability to urinate for more than 6 hours
- Blood in the urine
- New onset of weakness in any part of the body, new onset of numbness that is not obviously related to pressure, new onset of difficulty speaking
- Chest pain not obviously related to cough
- Seizures
- New rash accompanied by fever
- New oral lesions accompanied by fever
- Severe depression, anxiety, hallucinations, delusions, or thoughts of causing danger to self or others

Report the Following Signs and Symptoms Within 24 Hours
- New or different headache; constant headache not relieved by over-the-counter medication
- Headache accompanied by fever, nasal congestion, or cough
- Burning, itching, or discharge from the eyes
- New or productive cough
- Vomiting 2 or 3 times a day
- Vomiting accompanied by fever
- New, significant, or watery diarrhea (more than 6 times a day)
- Painful urination, bloody urine, urethral discharge
- Significant new rash (widespread; painful; or following a path down the leg or arm, around the chest, or on the face)
- Difficulty eating or drinking because of mouth lesions
- Vaginal discharge, pain, or itching

◆ **Ambulatory Care.** HIV infection has no cure, continues for life, causes physical disability, and contributes to impaired health. In many cases it can lead to death. HIV infection affects the entire range of a person's life from physical health to social, emotional, economic, and spiritual well-being. As a nurse, you are often the person who works most closely with patients who are trying to cope with living with HIV.

Stigma of HIV. HIV-infected patients share problems experienced by all those with chronic diseases, but these problems are worsened by negative social attitudes and beliefs surrounding HIV. HIV-infected people may be thought to lack control over urges to have sex or use IV drugs. Some people conclude that people with HIV brought the disease

FIG. 14.8 Chest x-ray showing interstitial infiltrates as the result of *Pneumocystis jiroveci* pneumonia. (From the Centers for Disease Control and Prevention. Courtesy Jonathan W. M. Gold, MD, New York, NY.)

FIG. 14.9 Lipodystrophy manifestations. (From James WD, Berger T, Elston D: *Andrews' diseases of the skin: Clinical dermatology*, ed 11, St Louis, 2011, Saunders.)

on themselves and deserve to be sick. Some view behaviors associated with HIV infection as immoral (e.g., homosexuality, promiscuity). Other behaviors are sometimes illegal (e.g., using drugs, sex work). The fact that infected people can transmit HIV to others creates fear, which leads to stigma and discrimination in all areas of life.[33]

In the United States, HIV-infected people have lost jobs, homes, and insurance, although the Americans with Disabilities Act (ADA) prohibits these forms of discrimination. HIV-related stigma is a global problem that is often more severe for women. Discrimination can lead to social isolation, dependence, frustration, low self-image, loss of control, and economic pressures.

Disease and Drug Side Effects. Physical problems related to HIV or its treatment can interfere with the patient's ability to maintain a desired lifestyle. HIV-infected patients often have anxiety, fear, depression, diarrhea, peripheral neuropathy, pain, nausea, vomiting, and fatigue. Nursing interventions for these symptoms are similar to what they would be for the patient who does not have HIV infection. For example, nursing management of diarrhea includes helping patients collect specimens, recommending diet changes, encouraging fluid and electrolyte replacement, teaching the patient about skin care, and managing skin breakdown around the perianal area. Nursing approaches for fatigue in HIV include teaching patients to assess fatigue patterns; determine contributing factors; set activity priorities; conserve energy; schedule rest periods; exercise regularly; and avoid substances such as caffeine, nicotine, alcohol, and other drugs that may disturb sleep.

Some HIV-infected patients, especially those who have been infected and on ART for a long time, may develop a set of metabolic disorders. These include (1) lipodystrophy (changes in body shape caused by a redistribution of fat in the abdomen, upper back, and breasts along with fat loss in the arms, legs, and face) (Fig. 14.9); (2) hyperlipidemia (high triglycerides, high low-density lipoproteins, and decreased high-density lipoproteins); (3) insulin resistance; (4) hyperglycemia; (5) bone disease (osteoporosis, osteopenia, avascular necrosis); (6) lactic acidosis; (7) renal disease; and (8) cardiovascular disease.[34]

It is still not clear why these disorders develop, but it is likely a combination of factors such as long-term infection with HIV, side effects of ART, genetic predisposition, and chronic stress. Management of metabolic disorders focuses on detecting problems early, dealing with symptoms, and helping the patient cope with emerging problems and changes to treatment regimens. It is important to recognize and treat these problems early, especially because cardiovascular disease and lactic acidosis are potentially fatal complications.

A frequent first intervention is to change ART medications because some drugs are more often associated with these disorders. Lipid abnormalities are generally treated with lipid-lowering drugs (see Table 33.6), diet changes, and exercise. Insulin resistance is treated with hypoglycemic drugs and weight loss. Exercise, diet changes, and calcium and vitamin D supplements may improve bone disease.

End-of-Life Care. Despite new developments in the treatment of HIV infection, many patients eventually have disease progression, disability, and death. Sometimes these occur because treatments do not work for the patient. Sometimes the patient's HIV becomes resistant to all available drug therapies. In addition, ART is now allowing people living with HIV to live longer and to develop diseases of aging, such as cardiovascular and endocrine problems that lead to death.

Nursing care during the terminal phase of any disease should focus on keeping the patient comfortable, facilitating emotional and spiritual acceptance of the finite nature of life, helping the patient's significant others deal with grief and loss, and maintaining a safe environment.[35] As a nurse, you are the pivotal care provider during this phase of illness, whether at home, through hospice, or in a health care facility. End-of-life care is discussed in Chapter 9.

◆ Evaluation

The expected outcomes are that the patient at risk for HIV infection will:

- Develop and implement a personal plan to decrease personal risk factors
- Have testing for HIV

The expected outcomes are that the patient with HIV infection will:

- Adhere to treatment for HIV disease
- Work with the health care team to achieve optimal health
- Prevent transmission of HIV to others

 Gerontologic Considerations: HIV Infection

The number of older adults who have HIV disease is increasing because (1) HIV treatment has been effective in reducing the number of deaths from HIV-related opportunistic infections and (2) people 60 and older are being infected at increasing rates. The number of people over the age of 60 living with HIV is expected to grow.

Remember that older people living with HIV are susceptible to the same diseases as non–HIV-infected older people. These include heart disease, cancer, diabetes, bone disease, arthritis, hypertension, kidney disease, and cognitive impairment. However, people with HIV infection may develop these diseases at an earlier age (compared with non–HIV-infected people) and be at higher risk for co-morbidities related to ART.[36] For example, some HIV medications are associated with increased lipids and altered insulin metabolism. Focusing nursing care on early identification of these complications, and helping patients reduce their risk for heart disease, diabetes, or other chronic disease, are critical aspects of caring for the older HIV patient.

The impact of polypharmacy is another consideration with the aging HIV population. In general, older adults take multiple medications to manage various chronic diseases. Some medications may interact with or be potentiated by HIV medications. Therefore careful monitoring and assessment of possible drug interactions is important when providing care to this population.

Older adults may be ashamed and hesitate to tell anyone that they have an HIV infection. This may make it hard for them to get the appropriate health care and support. As a nurse, you need to recognize that HIV will affect an increasing number of older adults and be prepared to help the older person who is living with HIV infection.

CASE STUDY
HIV Infection

(© iStock.com/ Cecilie_Arcurs.)

Patient Profile

J.N., a 69-yr-old black male with HIV, chronic hepatitis B, and hypertension, was admitted 2 days ago with *Pneumocystis jiroveci* pneumonia (PCP).

Subjective Data
- Diagnosed with HIV infection at age 56 after his male partner was diagnosed with Kaposi's sarcoma
- Has had issues taking ART consistently, "Too many side effects"
- Has fatigue and frequent oral candidiasis outbreaks
- Expresses concern about his future, "I don't know who will take care of me. I don't have any family around"

Objective Data

Physical Examination
- 5 ft 10 in tall, 150 lb, temperature 100.4° F (38° C), O_2 saturation 92% on 3 L of O_2 via nasal cannula

Laboratory Studies
- CD4 cell count 185 cells/μL
- Viral load 155,328 copies/μL

Interprofessional Care
- Trimethoprim/sulfamethoxazole
- Combination antiretroviral therapy: tenofovir alafenamide and emtricitabine (Descovy), with dolutegravir (Tivicay)

Discussion Questions
1. Why was trimethoprim/sulfamethoxazole ordered, and what are its common side effects?
2. ***Priority Decision:*** What priority teaching needs should be covered before J.N. is discharged from the hospital to return home?
3. How can J.N. be helped to adhere to his medication schedule?
4. ***Priority Decision:*** What are the priority nursing interventions? What nursing care will he need after discharge?
5. ***Collaboration:*** Older lesbian, gay, bisexual, transgender (LGBT) adults often lack familial social support as they age. What barriers could this cause for J.N.'s treatment? How could the interprofessional team assist in addressing these issues? What referrals may be made?
6. ***Safety:*** The nurse needs to start an IV for fluid replacement on J.N. Before inserting the IV what type of personal protective equipment is recommended for this situation?

Answers available at *http://evolve.elsevier.com/Lewis/medsurg.*

BRIDGE TO NCLEX EXAMINATION

The number of the question corresponds to the same-numbered outcome at the beginning of the chapter.

1. Emerging and reemerging infections affect health care by (select all that apply)
   a. reevaluating vaccine practices.
   b. revealing antimicrobial resistance.
   c. limiting antibiotics to those with life-threatening infection.
   d. challenging researchers to discover new antimicrobial therapies.

2. Interventions to prevent health care–associated infections include (select all that apply)
   a. following hand-washing protocols.
   b. limiting visitors to persons over age 18.
   c. placing high-risk patients in private rooms.
   d. decontaminating equipment used for patient care.
   e. appropriately using personal protective equipment.

3. Transmission of HIV from an infected person to another most often occurs because of
   a. unprotected anal or vaginal sexual intercourse.
   b. low levels of virus in the blood and high levels of CD4+ T cells.
   c. transmission from mother to infant during labor and delivery and breastfeeding.
   d. sharing eating utensils, dry kissing, hugging, using toilet seats, or shaking hands.

4. During HIV infection
   a. reverse transcriptase helps HIV fuse with the CD4+ T cell.
   b. HIV RNA uses the CD4+ T cell's mitochondria to replicate.
   c. the immune system is impaired predominantly by the eventual widespread destruction of CD4+ T cells.
   d. a long period of dormancy develops during which HIV cannot be found in the blood and there is little viral replication.

5. A diagnosis of AIDS is made when an HIV-infected patient has
   a. a CD4+ T cell count below 200/μL.
   b. a high level of HIV in the blood and saliva.
   c. lipodystrophy with metabolic abnormalities.
   d. oral hairy leukoplakia, an infection caused by Epstein-Barr virus.

6. Screening for HIV infection generally involves
   a. detecting CD8+ cytotoxic T cells in saliva.
   b. laboratory analysis of saliva to detect CD4+ T cells.
   c. analysis of lymph tissues for the presence of HIV RNA.
   d. laboratory analysis of blood to detect HIV antigen and/or antibody.

7. HIV antiretroviral drugs are used to
   a. cure acute HIV infection.
   b. decrease viral RNA levels.
   c. treat opportunistic diseases.
   d. decrease symptoms in terminal disease.

8. Opportunistic diseases in HIV infection
   a. are usually benign.
   b. are generally slow to develop and progress.
   c. occur in the presence of immunosuppression.
   d. are curable with appropriate drug interventions.

9. Which statements about metabolic side effects of ART are true (select all that apply)?
   a. These are annoying symptoms that are ultimately harmless.
   b. ART-related body changes include fat redistribution and peripheral wasting.
   c. Lipid problems include increases in triglycerides and decreases in high-density cholesterol.
   d. Insulin resistance and hyperlipidemia can be treated with drugs to control glucose and cholesterol.
   e. Compared to uninfected people, insulin resistance and hyperlipidemia are harder to treat in HIV-infected patients.

10. Which strategy can the nurse teach the patient to eliminate the risk for HIV transmission?
    a. Using sterile equipment to inject drugs
    b. Cleaning equipment used to inject drugs
    c. Taking lamivudine (Epivir) during pregnancy
    d. Using latex or polyurethane barriers to cover genitalia during sexual contact

11. What is the most appropriate nursing intervention to help an HIV-infected patient adhere to a treatment regimen?
    a. Set up a drug pillbox for the patient every week.
    b. Give the patient a video and a brochure to view and read at home.
    c. Tell the patient that side effects of ART are bad but that they go away.
    d. Assess the patient's routines and find adherence cues that fit into the patient's life circumstances.

1. a, b, d, 2. a, d, e, 3. a, 4. c, 5. a, 6. d, 7. b, 8. c, 9. b, c, d, 10. a, 11. d

For rationales to these answers and even more NCLEX review questions, visit http://evolve.elsevier.com/Lewis/medsurg.

EVOLVE WEBSITE/RESOURCES LIST

http://evolve.elsevier.com/Lewis/medsurg
Review Questions (Online Only)
Key Points
Answer Keys for Questions
  • Rationales for Bridge to NCLEX Examination Questions
  • Answer Guidelines for Case Study on p. 229.
Student Case Study
  • Patient With Human Immunodeficiency Virus (HIV) Infection and Acquired Immunodeficiency Syndrome (AIDS)
Conceptual Care Map Creator
Audio Glossary
Content Updates

REFERENCES

1. Centers for Disease Control and Prevention: National Center for Emerging and Zoonotic Infectious Diseases (NCEZID). Retrieved from www.cdc.gov/ncezid.
2. Hall V, Banerjee E, Kenyon C, et al: Measles outbreak—Minnesota April–May 2017, MMWR 66:713, 2017.
3. Grobusch MP, Rodriguez-Morales AJ, Wilson ME: Measles on the move, Travel Med Infect Dis 18:1, 2017.
4. Infectious Disease Society of America: Antimicrobial resistance. Retrieved from www.idsociety.org/topic_antimicrobial_resistance.
*5. Ray SM: Preventing methicillin-resistant Staphylococcus aureus (MRSA) disease in urban US hospitals-now for the hard part: More evidence pointing to the community as the source of MRSA acquisition, JID 215:1631, 2017.

6. Centers for Disease Control and Prevention: Healthcare-associated infections. Retrieved from *www.cdc.gov/HAI*.

7. Centers for Disease Control and Prevention: Healthcare-associated infections (HAI) progress report. Retrieved from *www.cdc.gov/hai/surveillance/progress-report/index.html*.

*8. Dunne CP, Kingston L, Slevin B, et al: Hand hygiene and compliance behaviors are the under-appreciated human factors pivotal to reducing hospital-acquired infections, *J Hosp Infect* 98:4, 2018.

9. Office of Disease Prevention and Health Promotion: Health care-associated infections. Retrieved from *www.health.gov/hcq/prevent-hai.asp*.

10. Katz MJ, Roghmann MC: Healthcare-associated infections in the elders: What's new, *Curr Opin Infect Dis* 29:388, 2016.

11. U.S. Food and Drug Administration: Personal protective equipment for infection control. Retrieved from *www.fda.gov/MedicalDevices/ProductsandMedicalProcedures/GeneralHospitalDevicesandSupplies/PersonalProtectiveEquipment/default.htm*.

*12. Centers for Disease Control and Prevention: Transmission-based precautions. Retrieved from *www.cdc.gov/infectioncontrol/basics/transmission-based-precautions.html*.

13. Centers for Disease Control and Prevention: HIV in the United States: At a glance. Retrieved from *www.cdc.gov/hiv/statistics/overview/ataglance.html*.

14. Centers for Disease Control and Prevention: HIV transmission. Retrieved from *www.cdc.gov/hiv/basics/transmission.html*.

15. Centers for Disease Control and Prevention: Occupational HIV transmission and prevention among health care workers. Retrieved from *www.cdc.gov/hiv/workplace/healthcareworkers.html*.

*16. Beste S, Essajee S, Siberry G, et al: Optimal antiretroviral prophylaxis in infants at high risk of acquiring HIV: A systematic review, *Pediatr Infect Dis J* 37:169, 2018.

17. US Department of Health and Human Services: The HIV life cycle. Retrieved from *www.aidsinfo.nih.gov/understanding-hiv-aids/fact-sheets/19/73/the-hiv-life-cycle*.

*18. Hoenigl M, Green N, Camacho M, et al: Signs or symptoms of acute HIV infection in a cohort undergoing community-based screening, *Emerg Infect Dis* 22:532, 2016.

*19. Rutstein SE, Ananworanich J, Fidler S, et al: Clinical and public health implications of acute and early HIV detection and treatment: A scoping review, *J Int AIDS Soc* 20:21579, 2017.

20. US Department of Health and Human Services: AIDS case definition. Retrieved from *www.aidsinfo.nih.gov/understanding-hiv-aids/glossary/2925/aids-case-definition*.

21. Centers for Disease Control and Prevention: 2018 Quick reference guide: Recommended laboratory HIV testing algorithm for serum or plasma specimens. Retrieved from *https://stacks.cdc.gov/view/cdc/50872*.

22. Centers for Disease Control and Prevention: HIV/AIDS and viral hepatitis. Retrieved from *www.cdc.gov/hepatitis/populations/hiv.htm*.

*23. Panel on Antiretroviral Guidelines for Adults and Adolescents: Guidelines for the use of antiretroviral agents in adults and adolescents living with HIV. Retrieved from *www.aidsinfo.nih.gov/guidelines/html/1/adult-and-adolescent-treatment-guidelines/0*.

*24. Panel on Opportunistic Infections in HIV-Infected Adults and Adolescents: Guidelines for the prevention and treatment of opportunistic infections in HIV-infected adults and adolescents. Retrieved from *www.aidsinfo.nih.gov/guidelines/html/4/adult-and-adolescent-opportunistic-infection/0*.

*25. Smith DK, Koenig LJ, Martin M, et al: Preexposure prophylaxis for the prevention of HIV infection: A clinical practice guideline. Retrieved from *www./stacks.cdc.gov/view/cdc/23109*.

26. Corey L, Gray GE: Preventing acquisition of HIV is the only path to an AIDS-free generation, *Proc Natl Acad Sci USA* 114:3798, 2017.

27. US Department of Health and Human Services: Alcohol and drug use and HIV risk. Retrieved from *www.hiv.gov/hiv-basics/hiv-prevention/reducing-risk-from-alcohol-and-drug-use/alcohol-and-drug-use-and-hiv.risk*.

*28. Mackesy-Amiti ME, Boodram B, Spiller MW, et al: Injection-related risk behavior and engagement in outreach, intervention and prevention services across 20 US cities, *J Acquir Immune Defic Syndr* S3:S316, 2017.

*29. Panel on Treatment of Pregnant Women with HIV Infection and Prevention of Perinatal Transmission: Recommendations for use of antiretroviral drugs in transmission in the United States. Retrieved from *www.aidsinfo.nih.gov/guidelines/html/3/perinatal/0*.

30. Centers for Disease Control and Prevention: Revised guidelines for HIV testing of adults, adolescents, and pregnant women in health-care settings. Retrieved from *www.cdc.gov/mmwr/preview/mmwrhtml/rr5514a1.htm*.

31. US Preventive Services Task Force: Human immunodeficiency virus (HIV) infection: Screening. Retrieved from *www.uspreventiveservicestaskforce.org/Page/Document/UpdateSummaryFinal/human-immunodeficiency-virus-hiv-infection-screening*.

32. University of California San Francisco HIV InSite: Coping with HIV/AIDS: Mental health. Retrieved from *http://hivinsite.ucsf.edu/insite?page=pb-daily-mental*.

*33. Davtyan M, Olshansky EF, Lakon C: Addressing HIV stigma in health care, *Am J Nurs* 118:11, 2018.

34. Mirza FS, Luthra P, Chirch : Endocrinological aspects of HIV infection, *J Endocrinol Invest* 41:881-899, 2018.

35. Goodkin K, Kompella S, Kendell SF: End-of-life care and bereavement issues in human immunodeficiency virus–AIDS, *Nurs Clin North Am* 53:123, 2018.

*36. The HIV and Aging Consensus Project: Clinical recommendations. Retrieved from *www.hiv-age.org/clinical-recommendations/*.

*Evidence-based information for clinical practice.

15

Cancer

Marisa Cortese

So long as you can sweeten another's pain, life is not in vain.

Helen Keller

http://evolve.elsevier.com/Lewis/medsurg/

CONCEPTUAL FOCUS

Cellular Regulation
Coping

Health Promotion

LEARNING OUTCOMES

1. Describe the incidence, survival, and mortality rates of cancer in the United States.
2. Describe the processes involved in the biology of cancer.
3. Outline the stages of cancer development.
4. Describe the role of the immune system related to cancer.
5. Discuss the role of the nurse in the prevention, detection, and diagnosis of cancer.
6. Explain the use of surgery, chemotherapy, radiation therapy, immunotherapy, targeted therapy, and hormone therapy in the treatment of cancer.
7. Identify the classifications of chemotherapy agents and methods of administration.

8. Distinguish between external beam radiation and brachytherapy.
9. Describe the effects of radiation therapy and chemotherapy on normal tissues.
10. Identify the types and effects of immunotherapy and targeted therapy.
11. Describe the nursing management of patients receiving chemotherapy, radiation therapy, immunotherapy, and targeted therapy.
12. Describe nutritional therapy for patients with cancer.
13. Identify complications associated with advanced cancer.
14. Describe support interventions for cancer patients, cancer survivors, and their caregivers.

KEY TERMS

brachytherapy, p. 247
cancer, p. 232
carcinogens, p. 235
carcinoma in situ (CIS), p. 239
chemotherapy, p. 243
external beam radiation, p. 247
hematopoietic stem cell transplantation (HSCT), p. 258
histologic grading, p. 238

immunologic surveillance, p. 237
immunotherapy, p. 255
malignant neoplasms, p. 238
metastasis, p. 235
oncogenes, p. 234
peripheral stem cell transplantation (PSCT), p. 258
protooncogenes, p. 234
staging, p. 238

targeted therapy, p. 255
tumor angiogenesis, p. 236
vesicants, p. 245

Cancer is a group of diseases characterized by uncontrolled and unregulated growth of cells. The resulting problems may be directly related to the cancer, a consequence of treating the cancer, or a combination of both. The combined physiologic, psychologic, and social impact of cancer on patients and their caregivers is considerable. Despite advances in treatment and care, a great deal of anxiety and fear continue to be associated with a diagnosis of cancer.

Educating health care professionals and the public is essential to promote realistic attitudes about cancer and cancer treatment. You are in a strategic position to lead efforts for changing attitudes about cancer. You can (1) help people decrease their risk for cancer development, (2) increase rates of cancer screening, (3) help patients adhere to cancer management plans, and (4) support patients and caregivers as they cope with the effects of cancer and related treatment. You need to be knowledgeable about specific types of cancer, treatment options, management of side effects of therapy, and supportive therapies for cancer.

Cancer is often considered a disease of aging, with most cases diagnosed in those over age 55 years. However, it occurs in people of all ages. An estimated 1.7 million people in the United States are diagnosed annually with invasive cancer (excluding basal and squamous cell skin cancers).[1]

Overall both the incidence and mortality rates of cancer have been declining.[2] The incidence of many cancers, such as colorectal, lung, breast, and oropharyngeal cancers, have declined largely because of preventive efforts. However, the incidence of other types of cancers, such as kidney, thyroid, pancreas, liver, uterus, skin melanoma, multiple myeloma, and non-Hodgkin's lymphoma, is increasing.[3]

Overall cancer incidence is higher in men than women. Gender differences in incidence and death rates for specific cancers are shown in the Gender Differences box and Tables 15.1 and 15.2.

GENDER DIFFERENCES

Cancer

Men
- More men than women die from cancer-related deaths each year.
- Mortality rate from lung cancer is higher in men.
- Cancer with the highest incidence among men is prostate cancer.
- Men are more likely to develop liver cancer.
- Head and neck cancers occur more often in men.

Women
- Cancer with the highest death rate among women is lung cancer.
- Cancer with the highest incidence among women is breast cancer.
- Thyroid cancer is more prevalent in women.
- Women are less likely to have colon cancer screenings.

TABLE 15.1 Cancer Incidence by Site and Gender*

MALE		FEMALE	
Type	%	Type	%
Prostate	19	Breast	30
Lung	14	Lung	13
Colon/rectum	9	Colon/rectum	7
Urinary bladder	7	Uterus	7
Melanoma of the skin	5	Thyroid	5
Kidney and renal pelvis	5	Melanoma of the skin	4
Non-Hodgkin's lymphoma	5	Non-Hodgkin's lymphoma	4
Oral cavity and pharynx	4	Pancreas	3
Leukemia	4	Leukemia	3
Liver and intrahepatic bile duct	4	Kidney and renal pelvis	3

Source: American Cancer Society: *Cancer facts & figures 2018*, Atlanta, 2018, American Cancer Society.

*Numbers are estimates and exclude basal and squamous cell skin cancers and carcinoma in situ.

TABLE 15.2 Cancer Deaths by Site and Gender

MALE		FEMALE	
Type	%	Type	%
Lung and bronchus	26	Lung and bronchus	25
Prostate	9	Breast	14
Colon/rectum	8	Colon/rectum	8
Pancreas	7	Pancreas	7
Liver and intrahepatic bile ducts	6	Ovary	5
Leukemia	4	Leukemia	4
Esophagus	4	Uterus	4
Urinary bladder	4	Non-Hodgkin's lymphoma	3
Non-Hodgkin's lymphoma	4	Liver and intrahepatic bile ducts	3
Kidney and renal pelvis	3	Brain and other nervous system	3

Source: American Cancer Society: *Cancer facts & figures 2018*, Atlanta, 2018, American Cancer Society.

Although mortality rates from all cancers combined are on the decline, it is still the second most common cause of death in the United States. Cancer is the leading cause of death of people 40 to 79 years of age. Each year about 609,640 Americans are expected to die because of cancer, which is more than 1600 people per day.[1,2]

Considerable progress has been made in controlling cancer for long periods. More than 15.5 million Americans are alive today who have a history of cancer. This includes those who have cancer and are undergoing treatment, are disease free, or are in remission.[2] Cancer survivors are discussed later on pp. 264-265.

BIOLOGY OF CANCER

Two major dysfunctions present in the process of cancer development are defective cell proliferation (growth) and defective cell differentiation.

Defect in Cell Proliferation

Normally, most tissues have a population of undifferentiated cells known as stem cells. These stem cells ultimately differentiate and become mature, functioning cells of a specific tissue.

Cell proliferation starts in the stem cell and begins when the stem cell enters the cell cycle (Fig. 15.1). The time from when a cell enters the cell cycle to when the cell divides into 2 identical cells is called the *generation time* of the cell. A mature cell continues to function until it degenerates and dies.

All the body's cells are controlled by an intracellular mechanism that determines when cell proliferation is necessary. Under normal conditions, there is a state of dynamic equilibrium. This means cell proliferation equals cell degeneration or death. Normally, the process of cell division and proliferation is activated only in the presence of cell degeneration or death (*apoptosis*). Cell proliferation also occurs if the body has a physiologic need for more cells. For example, a normal increase in white blood cell (WBC) count occurs with infection.

Another means of proliferation control in normal cells is *contact inhibition*. Normal cells respect the boundaries and territory of the cells surrounding them. They will not invade a territory that is not their own. We think the neighboring cells inhibit cell growth through the physical contact of the surrounding cell membranes. Cancer cells grown in tissue culture have a loss of contact inhibition. They have no regard for cell boundaries and grow on top of one another and on top of or between normal cells.

The rate of normal cell proliferation (from the time of cell birth to the time of cell death) differs in each body tissue. In some tissues, such as bone marrow, hair follicles, and epithelial lining of the gastrointestinal (GI) tract, the rate of cell proliferation is rapid. In other tissues, such as myocardium and cartilage, cell proliferation does not occur or is slow.

Cancer cells proliferate at the same rate as the normal cells of the tissue from which they arise. However, cancer cells respond differently from normal cells to the intracellular signals that regulate cell proliferation and death. The result is that the proliferation of the cancer cells is indiscriminate and continuous. Sometimes they produce more than 2 cells at the time of mitosis. In this way, there is continuous growth of a tumor mass: $1 \times 2 \times 4 \times 8 \times 16$ and so on. This is termed the *pyramid effect*. The time needed for a tumor mass to double in size is known as its *doubling time*.

FIG. 15.1 Cell life cycle and metabolic activity. Generation time is the period from *M* phase to *M* phase. Cells not in the cycle but capable of division are in the resting phase *(G₀).* (Adapted from Kumar V, Abbas AK, Fausto N, et al: *Robbins and Cotran pathologic basis of disease,* ed 8, Philadelphia, 2010, Saunders.)

Defect in Cell Differentiation

Cell differentiation is normally an orderly process that progresses from a state of immaturity to a state of maturity. Because all body cells are derived from the fertilized ova, all cells have the potential to perform all body functions. As cells differentiate, this potential is repressed, and the mature cell can perform only specific functions. With cell differentiation, there is a stable and orderly phasing out of cell potential. Under normal conditions, the differentiated cell is stable and will not *dedifferentiate,* or return to its previous undifferentiated state.

Genetic Link

Cancer involves the malfunction of genes that control differentiation and proliferation. Two types of normal genes that can be affected by mutation are *protooncogenes* and *tumor suppressor genes*. **Protooncogenes** are normal cell genes that are important regulators of normal cell processes. Protooncogenes promote growth. Tumor suppressor genes suppress growth. Mutations that change the expression of protooncogenes can cause them to function as **oncogenes** (tumor-inducing genes).

The protooncogene has been described as the genetic lock that keeps the cell in its mature functioning state. When this lock is "unlocked," as may occur through exposure to *carcinogens* (agents that cause cancer) or oncogenic viruses, genetic alterations and mutations occur. The abilities and properties that the cell had in fetal development are again expressed. Oncogenes can change a normal cell to a malignant one. This cell regains a fetal appearance and function. For example, some cancer cells make new proteins characteristic of the embryonic and fetal periods of life. These proteins, found on the cell membrane, include carcinoembryonic antigen (CEA) and α-fetoprotein (AFP). They can be found in the blood by laboratory studies. Other cancer cells, such as small cell cancer of the lung, make hormones that are usually made by cells arising from the same embryonic cells as the tumor cells. See Complications of Cancer later in this chapter on pp. 260-263.

Tumor suppressor genes regulate cell growth. They prevent cells from going through the cell cycle. Mutations can change tumor suppressor genes and make them inactive. This results in a loss of their tumor-suppressing action. Examples of tumor suppressor genes are *BRCA1* and *BRCA2*. Alterations in these genes increase a person's risk for breast and ovarian cancer. Another tumor suppressor gene is the *APC* gene. Mutations in this gene increase a person's risk for familial adenomatous polyposis, a precursor for colorectal cancer (see Chapter 42). Mutations in the *p53* tumor suppressor gene have been found in many cancers, including bladder, breast, colorectal, esophageal, liver, lung, and ovarian cancers.

Development of Cancer

The following is a theoretical model of cancer development. The cause and development of each type of cancer are likely to be multifactorial. A common misbelief is that cancer development is a rapid, haphazard event. However, cancer is usually an orderly process that occurs over time. It has 3 stages: initiation, promotion, and progression (Fig. 15.2).

Initiation. Cancer cells arise from normal cells because of changes in genes. The first stage, *initiation*, involves a mutation in the cell's genetic structure. A *mutation* is any change in the usual DNA sequence.

Genetic Link

Gene mutations can occur in 2 ways: *inherited* from a parent (passed from one generation to the next) or *acquired* during a person's lifetime. (Mutations are discussed in Chapter 12.)

The genetic predisposition to cancer is thought to play a role in about 5 to 10% of all cancers. These genetic alterations lead to a high risk for developing a specific type of cancer. However, most cancers do not result from inherited genes. They are acquired from damage to genes occurring during one's lifetime. An acquired mutation is passed on to all cells that develop from that single cell. The damaged cell may die or repair itself. However, if cell death or repair does not occur before cell

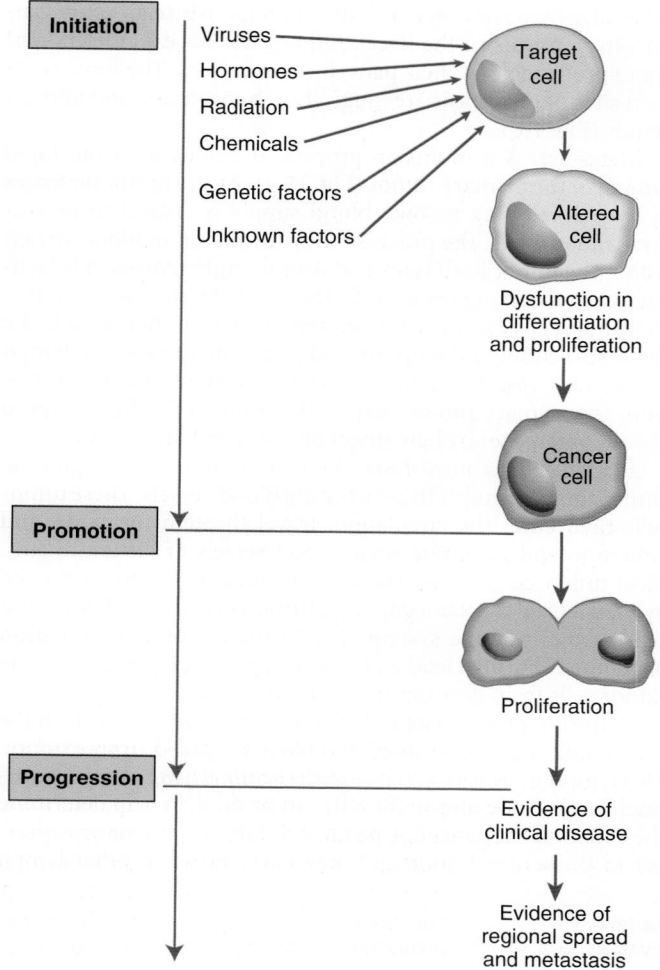

FIG. 15.2 Process of cancer development.

division, the cell will replicate into daughter cells, each with the same genetic alteration.

Carcinogens. Many carcinogens (cancer-causing agents capable of producing cell alterations) are detoxified by protective enzymes and harmlessly excreted. If this protective mechanism fails, carcinogens can enter the cell's nucleus and alter deoxyribonucleic acid (DNA). Carcinogens may be chemical, radiation, or viral.

Chemical carcinogens. Chemicals were identified as cancer-causing agents in the latter part of the 18th century. Percival Pott noted that chimney sweeps had a higher incidence of cancer of the scrotum associated with exposure to soot residue in chimneys. As the years passed, we have found many chemicals that are carcinogens (e.g., benzene, arsenic, formaldehyde). People exposed to these chemicals over time have a greater incidence of certain cancers than others. The long latency period from the time of exposure to the development of cancer makes it hard to identify cancer-causing chemicals.

Radiation. Radiation can cause cancer in almost any body tissue. When cells are exposed to a source of radiation, damage occurs to DNA. Certain cancers are correlated with radiation as a carcinogenic agent:

- The incidence of leukemia, lymphoma, and thyroid cancer increased in the general population of Hiroshima and Nagasaki after the atomic bomb explosions.

- A higher incidence of bone cancer occurs in people exposed to radiation in certain occupations, such as radiologists, radiation chemists, and uranium miners.

Ultraviolet (UV) radiation has long been associated with melanoma and squamous and basal cell skin cancers. Skin cancer is the most common type of cancer among whites in the United States. Sunlight exposure is the main source of UV exposure, giving off UVA and UVB rays. UV radiation from tanning beds also causes skin cancer.[4]

Viral carcinogens. Certain DNA and ribonucleic acid (RNA) viruses, termed *oncogenic,* can alter the cells they infect and induce malignant transformation. These viruses have been identified as causative agents of cancer in animals and humans. Burkitt's lymphoma is associated with Epstein-Barr virus (EBV).[5] People with acquired immunodeficiency syndrome (AIDS), which is caused by human immunodeficiency virus (HIV), have a high incidence of Kaposi sarcoma (see Chapter 14). Other viruses linked to cancer development include hepatitis B virus, which is associated with hepatocellular cancer, and human papillomavirus (HPV). HPV is thought to cause lesions that progress to squamous cell cancers, such as cervical, anal, and head and neck cancers.

Promotion. A single alteration of the genetic structure of the cell is not enough to cause cancer. However, the odds of cancer development are increased with the presence of promoting agents. *Promotion,* the second stage in cancer development, is characterized by the reversible proliferation of the altered cells. An increase in the altered cell population further increases the likelihood of more mutations.

An important distinction between initiation and promotion is that the activity of promoters is reversible. This is a key concept in cancer prevention. Promoting factors include agents such as dietary fat, obesity, cigarette smoking, and alcohol use. Changing a person's lifestyle to modify these risk factors can reduce the chance of cancer development. Around one third of cancer-related deaths in the United States are related to tobacco use, unhealthy diet, physical inactivity, and obesity.[1]

Several promoting agents have activity against specific types of body tissues. So, these agents tend to promote specific kinds of cancer. For example, cigarette smoke is a promoting agent in lung cancer. In conjunction with alcohol use, it promotes esophageal and bladder cancers.

Some carcinogens, termed *complete carcinogens,* are capable of both initiating and promoting cancer development. Cigarette smoke is an example of a complete carcinogen.

A period of time elapses between the first genetic alteration and the actual clinical evidence of cancer. This period, called the *latent* period, includes both the initiation and promotion stages in the natural history of cancer. The variation in the length of time that elapses before the cancer becomes clinically evident is related to the mitotic rate of the tissue of origin and environmental factors. In most cancers, this process is years or even decades in length.

For the disease process to become clinically evident, the cells must reach a critical mass. A tumor that is 1.0 cm (0.4 inch) (the size usually detectable by palpation) has 1 billion cancer cells. A 0.5-cm tumor is the smallest that can be detected by current diagnostic measures, such as MRI.

Progression. *Progression* is the last stage in the natural history of a cancer. This stage is characterized by increased growth rate of the tumor, increased invasiveness, and metastasis (spread of the cancer to a distant site). Certain cancers have an affinity for a

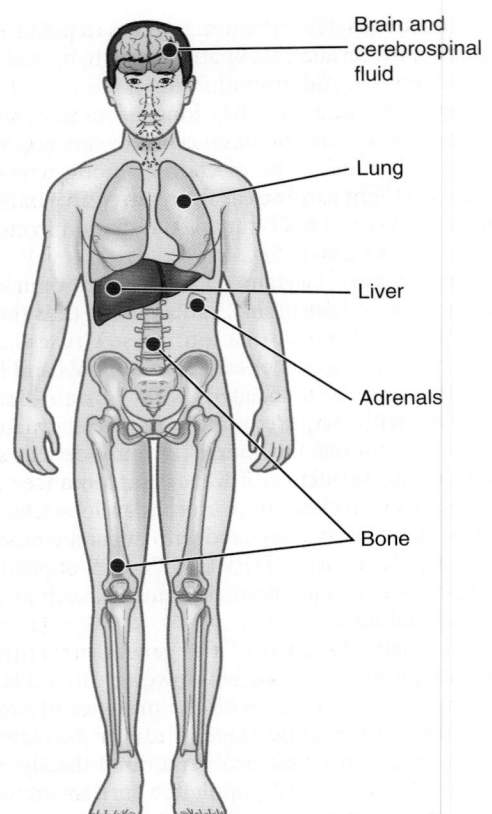

FIG. 15.3 Main sites of metastasis. (Adapted from Stevens A, Lowe J: *Pathology: An illustrated review in colour*, ed 2, London, 2000, Mosby.)

particular tissue or organ as a site of metastasis (e.g., colon cancer often spreads to the liver). Other cancers (e.g., melanoma) are unpredictable in their pattern of metastasis. The most common sites of metastasis are lungs, liver, bone, brain, and adrenal glands (Fig. 15.3).

Metastasis is a multistep process. It begins with the rapid growth of the primary tumor (Fig. 15.4). As the tumor increases in size, developing its own blood supply is critical to its survival and growth. The process of the formation of blood vessels within the tumor itself is termed **tumor angiogenesis**. It is facilitated by tumor angiogenesis factors made by the cancer cells.

Tumor cells can detach from the primary tumor, invade the tissue surrounding the tumor, and penetrate the walls of lymph or vascular vessels for metastasis to a distant site. Once free from the primary tumor, metastatic tumor cells often travel to distant organ sites by hematogenous or lymphatic routes.

Hematogenous metastasis involves several steps beginning with primary tumor cells penetrating blood vessels. These tumor cells then enter the circulation, travel through the body, and adhere to and penetrate small blood vessels of distant organs. Most tumor cells do not survive this process and are destroyed by mechanical mechanisms (e.g., turbulence of blood flow) and cells of the immune system. The formation of a combination of tumor cells, platelets, and fibrin deposits may protect some tumor cells from destruction in blood vessels.

In the lymphatic system, tumor cells may be "trapped" in the first lymph node confronted and likely to spread from a tumor. This lymph node is referred to as the *sentinel lymph node*. A sentinel lymph node biopsy (SLNB) can be done to help determine the extent of the cancer. A positive SLNB means cancer is present in the sentinel node and may have spread to other lymph

FIG. 15.4 The pathogenesis of cancer metastasis. To produce metastases, tumor cells must detach from the primary tumor and enter the circulation, survive in the circulation to rest in the capillary bed, adhere to capillary basement membrane, gain entrance into the organ parenchyma, respond to growth factors, proliferate, induce angiogenesis, and evade host defenses. (Adapted from Fidler IT: The pathogenesis of cancer metastasis: The "seed and soil" hypothesis revisited, *Nat Rev Cancer* 3:453, 2003.)

nodes and organs. Sometimes, the tumor cells may bypass local lymph nodes and travel to distant lymph nodes, a phenomenon termed *skip metastasis*.

Tumor cells that survive the process of metastasis must create an environment in the distant organ site that promotes their growth and development. Growth and development are facilitated by the tumor cells' ability to evade cells of the immune system and produce a vascular supply within the metastatic site like that of the primary tumor site. Vascularization is critical to the supply of nutrients to the metastatic tumor and the removal of waste products.

Role of the Immune System

This section is limited to a discussion of the role of the immune system in the recognition and destruction of tumor cells. For a detailed discussion of immune system function, see Chapter 13.

The immune system has the potential to tell normal (self) cells from abnormal (nonself) cells. For example, cells of transplanted organs can be recognized by the immune system as *nonself* and thus elicit an immune response. This response can result in organ rejection. Similarly, cancer cells can be perceived as nonself. This can elicit an immune response, resulting in their rejection and destruction. However, unlike transplanted cells, cancer cells arise from normal human cells and, although they are mutated and thus different, the immune response that is mounted against cancer cells may be inadequate to effectively kill them.

Cancer cells may have altered cell-surface antigens because of malignant transformation. These antigens are termed *tumor-associated antigens (TAAs)* (Fig. 15.5). We think that the immune system responds to TAAs through a process termed immunologic surveillance. In this process, lymphocytes continuously check cell-surface antigens. They detect and destroy cells with abnormal or altered antigenic determinants. Under most circumstances, immune surveillance prevents transformed cells from developing into clinically detectable tumors.

Immune response to cancer cells involves cytotoxic T cells, natural killer (NK) cells, macrophages, and B cells. *Cytotoxic T cells* play a dominant role in resisting tumor growth. These cells can kill tumor cells. T cells are important in the production of cytokines (e.g., interleukin-2 [IL-2], γ-interferon), which stimulate T cells, NK cells, B cells, and macrophages.

Natural killer (NK) cells can directly lyse tumor cells spontaneously without any prior sensitization. γ-Interferon (made by T cells) and IL-2 (released from T cells) stimulate NK cells, resulting in increased cytotoxic activity.

Monocytes and *macrophages* have several important roles in tumor immunity. γ-Interferon can activate macrophages

to become nonspecifically lytic for tumor cells. Macrophages secrete cytokines, including IL-1, tumor necrosis factor (TNF), and colony-stimulating factors (CSFs). The release of IL-1, coupled with the presentation of the processed antigen, stimulates T-cell activation and production. α-Interferon augments the killing ability of NK cells. TNF causes hemorrhagic necrosis of tumors and exerts cytocidal or cytostatic actions against tumor cells. CSFs regulate the production of various blood cells in the bone marrow and stimulate the function of various WBCs.

B cells can make specific antibodies that bind to tumor cells. These antibodies are often detectable in the patient's serum and saliva.

Escape Mechanisms From Immunologic Surveillance. The process by which cancer cells evade the immune system is termed *immunologic escape*. Possible mechanisms by which cancer cells escape immunologic surveillance include (1) suppression of factors that stimulate T cells to react to cancer cells; (2) weak surface antigens allowing cancer cells to "sneak through" immunologic surveillance; (3) development of tolerance of the immune system to some tumor antigens; (4) suppression of the immune response by products secreted by cancer cells; (5) induction of suppressor T cells by the tumor; and (6) blocking antibodies that bind TAAs, thus preventing their recognition by T cells (Fig. 15.6).

Oncofetal Antigens and Tumor Markers. *Oncofetal antigens* are a type of tumor antigen. They are found on the surfaces and the inside of cancer cells and fetal cells. These antigens are an expression of the shift of cancerous cells to a more immature metabolic pathway. This expression is usually associated with embryonic or fetal periods of life. The reappearance of fetal antigens in cancer is not well understood. We think it is the result of the cell regaining its embryonic capability to differentiate into many different cell types.

Examples of oncofetal antigens are CEA and AFP. CEA is found on the surfaces of cancer cells from the GI tract and normal cells from the fetal gut, liver, and pancreas. Normally, CEA disappears during the last 3 months of fetal life. CEA was originally isolated from colorectal cancer cells. However, high CEA levels can be found in nonmalignant conditions (e.g., cirrhosis of the liver, ulcerative colitis, heavy smoking).

Oncofetal antigens can be used as *tumor markers* that may be clinically useful to monitor the effect of therapy and indicate tumor recurrence. However, they are not 100% specific for tumor recurrence. Tumor markers are affected by various factors that

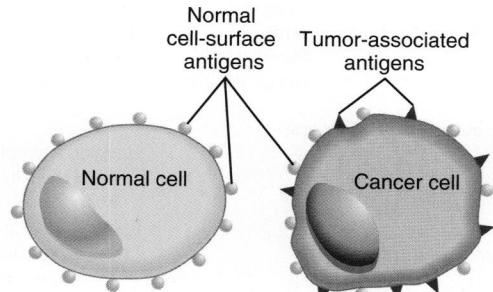

FIG. 15.5 Tumor-associated antigens appear on the cell surface of cancer cells.

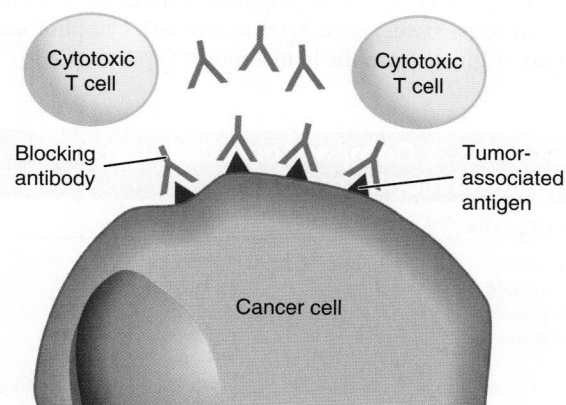

FIG. 15.6 Blocking antibodies prevent T cells from interacting with tumor-associated antigens and from destroying the cancer cell.

must be accounted for when reviewing these results. For example, the persistence of high preoperative CEA titers after surgery means that the tumor is not completely removed. A rise in CEA levels after chemotherapy may mean recurrence or spread of the cancer. Or, it may be due to chronic lung disease and smoking.

AFP is made by malignant liver cells and fetal liver cells. AFP has diagnostic value in primary liver cancer (hepatocellular cancer). It is also made when metastatic liver growth occurs. This makes AFP valuable in tumor detection and determination of tumor progression. AFP levels are also high in some cases of testicular cancer and viral hepatitis.

Other examples of oncofetal antigens are CA-125 (ovarian cancer), CA-19-9 (pancreatic and gallbladder cancer), prostate-specific antigen (PSA) (prostate cancer), and CA-15.3 and CA-27-29 (breast cancer). Molecular markers for specific tumors include kRAS (expression of oncogene in colon cancer), epidermal growth factor receptor (EGFR) often overexpressed in lung cancer, and human epidermal growth factor receptor-2 (HER-2) expression in breast cancer.

BENIGN VERSUS MALIGNANT NEOPLASMS

Tumors can be classified as benign or malignant. In general, *benign neoplasms* are well differentiated. Malignant neoplasms range from well differentiated to undifferentiated. The ability of malignant tumor cells to invade and metastasize is the major difference between benign and malignant neoplasms. Other differences are outlined in Table 15.3.

CLASSIFICATION OF CANCER

Tumors can be classified according to anatomic site, histology (grading), and extent of disease (staging). Tumor classification systems provide a standardized way to (1) communicate the status of the cancer to all members of the interprofessional care team, (2) assist in determining the most effective treatment plan, (3) evaluate the treatment plan, (4) predict prognosis, and (5) compare groups for statistical purposes.

Anatomic Site Classification

In the *anatomic classification* of tumors, the tumor is identified by the tissue of origin, anatomic site, and behavior of the tumor (e.g., benign or malignant) (Table 15.4). *Carcinomas* originate from embryonal *ectoderm* (skin and glands) and *endoderm* (mucous membrane linings of the respiratory tract, GI tract, and genitourinary [GU] tract). *Sarcomas* originate from embryonal *mesoderm* (connective tissue, muscle, bone, and fat). Lymphomas and leukemias originate from the hematopoietic system.

Histologic Classification

In **histologic grading** of tumors, the appearance of cells and degree of differentiation are evaluated pathologically. For many tumor types, 4 grades are used to evaluate abnormal cells based on the degree to which the cells resemble the tissue of origin. Tumors that are poorly differentiated (undifferentiated) have a poorer prognosis than those that are closer in appearance to the normal tissue of origin (well differentiated):

Grade I: Cells differ slightly from normal cells (mild dysplasia) and are well differentiated (low grade).

Grade II: Cells are more abnormal (moderate dysplasia) and moderately differentiated (intermediate grade).

Grade III: Cells are very abnormal (severe dysplasia) and poorly differentiated (high grade).

Grade IV: Cells are immature, primitive *(anaplasia)*, and undifferentiated; cell of origin is hard to determine (high grade).

Grade X: Grade cannot be assessed.

Extent of Disease Classification

Classifying the extent and spread of disease is termed **staging**. Staging is based on the anatomic extent of disease. Although there are similarities in the staging of various cancers, there are many differences for specific types of cancer.

Clinical Staging. The clinical staging classification system determines the anatomic extent of the malignant disease process by stages:

Stage 0: Cancer in situ

Stage I: Tumor limited to the tissue of origin; localized tumor growth

Stage II: Limited local spread

Stage III: Extensive local and regional spread

Stage IV: Metastasis

Clinical staging has been used as a basis for staging a variety of tumor types, including colorectal cancer (see Fig. 42.7) and Hodgkin's lymphoma (see Fig. 30.15). Other cancers (e.g., leukemia) do not use this staging approach.

TABLE 15.3 Comparison of Benign and Malignant Neoplasms

Characteristic	Benign	Malignant
Encapsulated	Usually	Rarely
Differentiated	Normally	Poorly
Metastasis	Absent	Capable
Recurrence	Rare	Possible
Vascularity	Slight	Moderate to marked
Mode of growth	Expansive	Infiltrative and expansive
Cell characteristics	Fairly normal, like parent cells	Cells abnormal, become more unlike parent cells

TABLE 15.4 Anatomic Classification of Tumors

Site	Benign	Malignant
Epithelial Tissue Tumors*	**-oma**	**-carcinoma**
Surface epithelium	Papilloma	Carcinoma
Glandular epithelium	Adenoma	Adenocarcinoma
Connective Tissue Tumors[†]	**-oma**	**-sarcoma**
Fibrous tissue	Fibroma	Fibrosarcoma
Cartilage	Chondroma	Chondrosarcoma
Striated muscle	Rhabdomyoma	Rhabdomyosarcoma
Bone	Osteoma	Osteosarcoma
Nervous Tissue Tumors	**-oma**	**-oma**
Meninges	Meningioma	Meningeal sarcoma
Nerve cells	Ganglioneuroma	Neuroblastoma
Hematopoietic Tissue Tumors		
Lymphoid tissue	—	Hodgkin's lymphoma, non-Hodgkin's lymphoma
Plasma cells	—	Multiple myeloma
Bone marrow	—	Lymphocytic and myelogenous leukemia

*Body surfaces, lining of body cavities, and glandular structures.
[†]Supporting tissue, fibrotic tissue, and blood vessels.

TNM Classification System. The *TNM classification system* (Table 15.5) is used to determine the anatomic extent of the disease involvement according to 3 parameters: tumor size and invasiveness (T), presence or absence of regional spread to the lymph nodes (N), and metastasis to distant organ sites (M). Examples of the TNM classification system can be found in Tables 27.17 and 51.6. TNM staging cannot be applied to all cancers. For example, leukemias are not solid tumors and cannot be staged using these guidelines.

The latest cancer staging guidelines for some cancers add nonanatomic factors when making the final determination of stage. Staging is still based on the TNM classification, but it now adds grade and hormone receptor expression. When appropriate, it also includes genomic profile results (e.g., Oncotype DX, Mammaprint). This information should allow a more accurate determination of prognosis and better guide therapy.

Carcinoma in situ (CIS) refers to a cancer whose cells are localized and show no tendency to invade or metastasize to other tissues. CIS has its own designation in the system (T_{is}) because it has all the histologic characteristics of cancer except invasion—a key feature of the TNM staging system.

Staging of the disease can be done initially and at several points. Clinical staging is done at the completion of the diagnostic workup to guide treatment selection. Examples of diagnostic studies that may be done to assess for extent of disease include bone and liver scans, ultrasonography, and CT, MRI, and positron emission tomography (PET) scans.

Surgical staging refers to the extent of the disease as determined by surgical excision, exploration, and/or lymph node sampling. For example, a laparotomy and splenectomy may be done to stage Hodgkin's lymphoma. During a staging laparotomy, lymph node biopsies may be done, and margins of any masses may be marked with metal clips for use during radiation therapy. Exploratory surgical staging is being used less often as noninvasive diagnostic technology becomes more sophisticated.

After the extent of the disease is determined, the stage classification is set. The original description of the extent of the tumor stays part of the record. If more treatment is needed, or if treatment fails, retreatment staging is done to determine the extent of the disease before retreatment. "Restaging" classification (rTNM) is differentiated from the stage at diagnosis, since the clinical significance may be different. Staging can never

decrease, but the stage can increase. For example, a patient may initially be a stage 3. After treatment failure, the tumor metastasizes, and now the patient is a stage 4.

In addition to tumor classification systems, other rating scales can be used to describe and document the status of patients with cancer at the time of diagnosis, treatment, and retreatment and at each follow-up examination. For example, the Karnofsky Performance Scale and Katz Index of Independence in Activities of Daily Living describe patient's functional performance.

PREVENTION AND EARLY DETECTION OF CANCER

We can reduce the incidence of cancer through a stronger emphasis on prevention through promoting healthy lifestyles. As a nurse, you have an essential role in the prevention and early detection of cancer. Reducing risk factors reduces the incidence of cancer. For example, rates of smoking-related cancers (e.g., lung and head and neck cancers) have declined with a reduction in smoking rates.[1]

Early detection and prompt treatment are responsible for increased survival rates in patients with cancer. Colonoscopy is important in reducing colon cancer mortality both by early detection of colon cancers and prevention (e.g., excision of adenomatous polyps).

The goals of public education are to (1) motivate people to recognize and change behaviors that may negatively affect health and (2) encourage awareness of and participation in health-promoting behaviors. When you teach about cancer, try to minimize the fear that surrounds the diagnosis.

Teach people to be familiar with their bodies. Review how to perform self-examinations and the 7 warning signs of cancer (Table 15.6). Encourage them to seek immediate medical care if they notice a change in what is normal for them or if cancer is suspected. Following recommended cancer screening guidelines for breast, colon, cervical, and prostate cancer from the American Cancer Society (ACS) is important.[6]

❤ PROMOTING POPULATION HEALTH

Prevention and Early Detection of Cancer

Teach patients and the public about cancer prevention and early detection, including:

- Limit alcohol use.
- Get regular physical activity (e.g., 30 minutes or more of moderate physical activity 5 times weekly).
- Maintain a normal body weight.
- Have regular physical examinations.
- Obtain regular colorectal screenings.
- Avoid cigarette smoking and other tobacco use.
- Get regular mammography screening and Pap tests.
- Be familiar with your own family history and risk factors for cancer.
- Obtain adequate, consistent periods of rest (at least 6 to 8 hours per night).
- Use sunscreen with a sun protection factor of 15 or higher. Avoid the use of tanning beds.
- Eliminate, reduce, or change the perception of stressors and enhance the ability to effectively cope with stress (see Chapter 6).
- Eat a balanced diet that includes vegetables and fresh fruits, whole grains, and adequate amounts of fiber. Reduce dietary fat and preservatives, including smoked and salt-cured meats with high nitrite concentrations.

TABLE 15.5 TNM Classification System

Primary Tumor (T)

T_0	No evidence of primary tumor
T_{is}	Carcinoma in situ
T_{1-4}	Ascending degrees of increase in tumor size and involvement
T_x	Tumor cannot be measured or found

Regional Lymph Nodes (N)

N_0	No evidence of disease in lymph nodes
N_{1-4}	Ascending degrees of nodal involvement
N_x	Regional lymph nodes unable to be assessed clinically

Distant Metastases (M)

M_0	No evidence of distant metastases
M_{1-4}	Ascending degrees of metastatic involvement, including distant nodes
M_x	Cannot be determined

Diagnosis of Cancer

When a patient has a possible diagnosis of cancer, it is a stressful time for the patient and caregivers. Patients may undergo several days to weeks of diagnostic studies. During this time, fear of the unknown may be more stressful than the actual diagnosis of cancer. Patients may be overwhelmed or confused by the need for multiple diagnostic studies and consultations. Help coordinate care between multiple specialists. Explain the purpose of required tests and any special preparation needed for them.

Some facilities have comprehensive oncology teams and services that are all housed in the same building to help coordinate care among the cancer specialists. These centers combine appointments to make the experience convenient and comfortable for patients and their caregivers.

While patients are waiting for the results of diagnostic studies, be available to actively listen to their concerns. Their anxiety may arise from myths and misconceptions about cancer (e.g., cancer is a "death sentence," cancer treatment is worse than the illness). Correcting those misconceptions can help to minimize their anxiety.

Learn to recognize your own discomfort during difficult conversations. Avoid communication patterns that may hinder exploration of feelings and meaning. These include providing false reassurances (e.g., "It's probably nothing"), redirecting the discussion (e.g., "Let's discuss that later"), generalizing (e.g., "Everyone feels this way"), and using overly technical language. These self-protective strategies deny patients the opportunity to share the meaning of their experience. They can jeopardize your ability to build a trusting relationship with your patients.

During this time of high anxiety, the patient may need repeated explanations of the diagnostic workup. Include as much information as needed by the patient and caregivers. Give clear, understandable explanations and reinforce them as needed. Written information is helpful to reinforce verbal information.

A diagnostic plan for the person suspected of having cancer includes the health history (including a history of present illness), identifying risk factors, the physical examination, and specific diagnostic studies. For many people, cancer is diagnosed after the findings of an abnormal screening test (e.g., mass on mammogram). For others, they are alerted to the presence of cancer by a presenting symptom or cluster of symptoms (e.g., cough and hemoptysis, anorexia and weight loss).

Concentrate on risk factors for cancer. Obtain information about any family and personal history of cancer and any exposure to or use of known carcinogens (e.g., cigarette smoking, occupational pollutants or chemicals, radiation exposure). Review the medical history for diseases characterized by chronic inflammation or immunosuppression (e.g., ulcerative colitis) and treatments (e.g., hormone therapy, previous anticancer therapies). Assess factors that may call for additional supportive care during therapy, including alcohol or drug use, living situation, social support, and coping strategies for perceived stressors.

Diagnostic studies depend on the suspected primary or metastatic site(s) of the cancer. (Specific procedures as they relate to each body system are discussed in the respective assessment chapters.) Examples of diagnostic studies include:

- Cytology studies (e.g., Pap test, bronchial washings)
- Tissue biopsy
- Chest x-ray
- Complete blood count (CBC), chemistry profile
- Liver function studies (e.g., aspartate aminotransferase [AST])
- Endoscopic examination: upper GI, sigmoidoscopy, or colonoscopy (including guaiac test for occult blood)
- Radiographic studies (e.g., mammography, ultrasound, CT scan, MRI)
- Radioisotope scans (e.g., bone, lung, liver, brain)
- PET scan (Fig. 15.7)
- Tumor markers (e.g., CEA, AFP, PSA, CA-125)
- Genetic markers (e.g., *BRCA1, BRCA2*)
- Molecular receptor status (e.g., estrogen and progesterone receptors)
- Bone marrow examination (if a hematolymphoid malignancy is suspected or to document metastatic disease)

Biopsy. A *biopsy* is the removal of a tissue sample for pathologic analysis. Various methods are used to obtain a biopsy depending on the location and size of the suspected tumor. *Percutaneous biopsy* is often done for tissue that can be safely reached through the skin. *Endoscopic biopsy* may be used for lung or other intraluminal lesions (esophageal, colon, bladder).

TABLE 15.6	**7 Warning Signs of Cancer**

Change in bowel or bladder habits
A sore that does not heal
Unusual bleeding or discharge from any body orifice
Thickening or a lump in the breast or elsewhere
Indigestion or difficulty in swallowing
Obvious change in a wart or mole
Nagging cough or hoarseness

FIG. 15.7 PET scan before treatment (**A**) showing metastasis throughout the body. PET scan after treatment (**B**) shows the effects of therapy. More radioactive material accumulates in areas that have higher levels of activity. This often corresponds to areas of disease and shows up as brighter spots on the PET scan. (From Shimizu N, Masuda H, Yamanaka H, et al: Fluorodeoxyglucose PET scan of prostate cancer bone metastases with flare reaction after endocrine therapy, *J Urol* 151:609, 1999.)

When a tumor is not easily accessible, a *surgical procedure* (laparotomy, thoracotomy, craniotomy) is often needed to obtain a piece of the tumor tissue. Many radiographic techniques may be used in conjunction with the biopsy procedure (e.g., CT, MRI, ultrasound-guided biopsy, stereotactic biopsy) to improve tissue localization.

Various types and sizes of biopsy needles are available and chosen according to the type of tissue to be sampled. *Fine-needle aspiration* (FNA) may be done with a small-gauge aspiration needle that provides cells from the mass for cytologic examination. *Large-core biopsy* cutting needles deliver an actual piece of tissue (core) that can be analyzed. An advantage is that it preserves the histologic architecture of the tissue specimen. *Excisional biopsy* involves the surgical removal of the entire lesion, lymph node, nodule, or mass. So, it is therapeutic as well as diagnostic. If an excisional biopsy is not feasible, an *incisional biopsy* (partial excision) may be done with a scalpel or dermal punch.

Pathologic evaluation of a tissue sample is the only definitive way to diagnose cancer. The pathologist examines the tissue to determine (1) whether it is benign or malignant, (2) the anatomic tissue from which the tumor arises *(histology),* and (3) the degree of cell differentiation *(histologic grade).* Other information that can be obtained includes the extent of malignant involvement (size of tumor and depth), evidence of invasiveness (extracapsular, lymphatic), adequacy of surgical excision (positive or negative surgical margin status), and nuclear grade (mitotic rate). Special staining techniques may give insight into responsiveness of the tumor to treatment or disease behavior (receptor status, tumor markers).

INTERPROFESSIONAL CARE

TREATMENT GOALS

The goals of cancer treatment are cure, control, and palliation (Fig. 15.8). When caring for the patient with cancer, knowing the treatment goals will help you appropriately communicate with, teach, and support the patient. The main factors that determine what therapy is used are the tumor histology and staging outcomes. Other crucial factors are the patient's physiologic status (e.g., presence of co-morbid illnesses), psychologic status, and personal desires (e.g., active treatment versus palliation).

These factors influence (1) the modalities chosen for treatment (e.g., surgery, radiation therapy, chemotherapy, immunotherapy, targeted therapy, hormone therapy), (2) how therapies are sequenced, and (3) the length of time the treatment is prescribed. Each type of therapy can be used alone or in any combination during initial treatment, as maintenance therapy, and in retreatment if the disease does not respond or recurs after remission.

For many cancers, 2 or more of the treatment modalities (known as *multimodality therapy* or *combined modality therapy*) are used to achieve the goal of cure or control for a long time. Multimodality therapy has the benefit of being more effective (because it takes advantage of more than one mechanism of action), but often at the expense of greater toxicity.

Cure

When *cure* is the goal, treatment is expected to have the greatest chance of eradicating the cancer. Curative cancer therapy

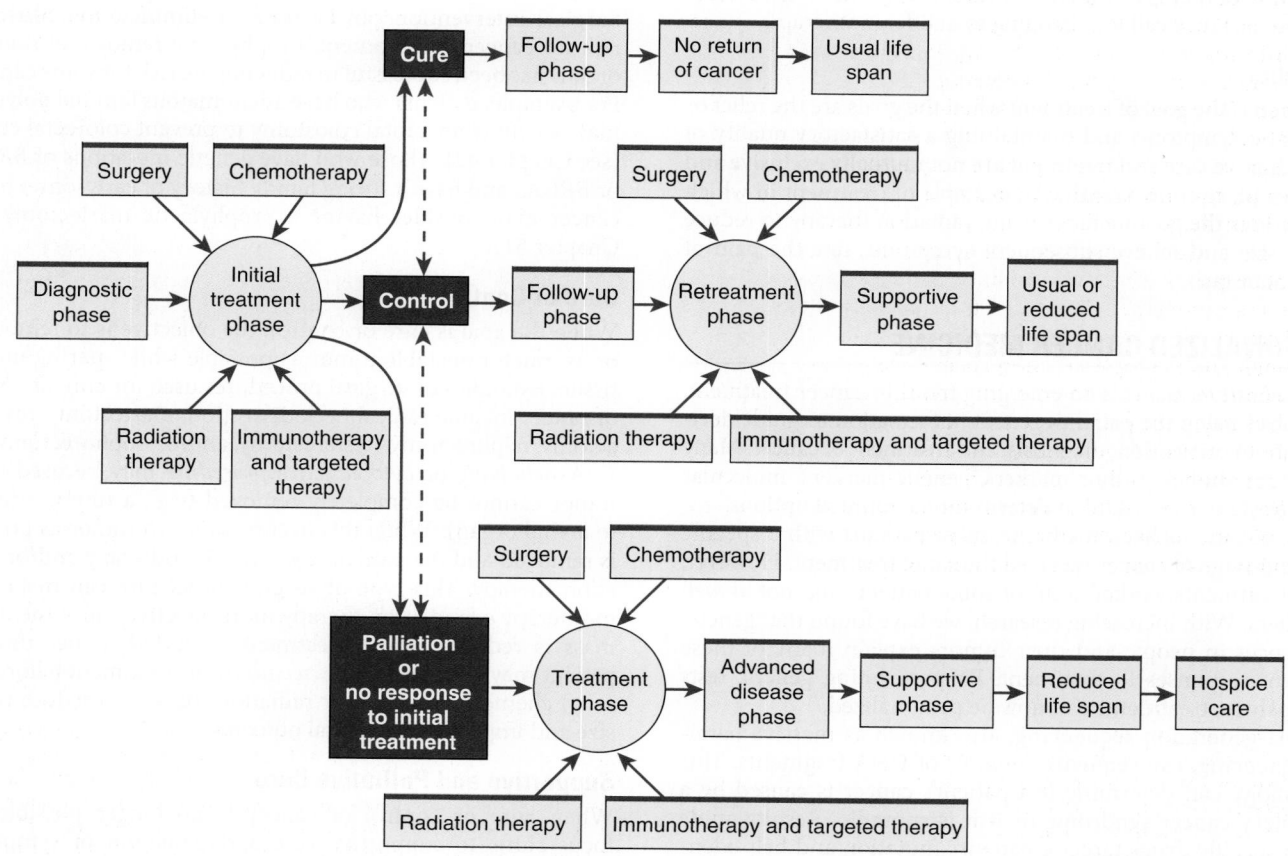

FIG. 15.8 Goals of cancer treatment.

differs according to the cancer being treated. It may involve local therapies (e.g., surgery or radiation) alone or in combination, with or without periods of adjunctive systemic therapy (e.g., chemotherapy).

For example, basal cell skin cancer is usually cured by surgical removal of the lesion and several weeks of radiation therapy. In the treatment plan for acute promyelocytic leukemia (which has curative potential), several chemotherapy drugs are given on a scheduled basis over many months to several years. Testicular cancer can be cured with a combination of surgery, chemotherapy, and radiation.

There is no benchmark that ensures "cure" for most cancers. In general, the risk for recurrent disease is highest after treatment completion. It gradually decreases the longer the patient is disease free after treatment. Cancers with a higher mitotic rate (e.g., testicular cancer) are more likely to recur than cancers with slower mitotic rates (e.g., postmenopausal breast cancer). So, the timeframe to consider a person "cured" may differ according to the tumor and its characteristics.

Control

Control is the goal of treatment for cancers that cannot be completely eradicated but are responsive to anticancer therapies. As with other chronic illnesses (e.g., diabetes, heart failure), cancer can be controlled for long periods with therapy. Examples include multiple myeloma and chronic lymphocytic leukemia (see Chapter 30). Patients may undergo an initial course of treatment followed by maintenance therapy for as long as the disease is responding. Patients are monitored closely for early signs and symptoms of disease recurrence or progression and the cumulative effects of therapy. Evidence of tumor resistance (e.g., disease progression) may call for changing to a different therapy.

Palliation

Palliation is the goal of treatment when the goals are the relief or control of symptoms and maintaining a satisfactory quality of life. Palliative care and treatment are not mutually exclusive and can take place concurrently. An example of treatment in which palliation is the goal includes using radiation therapy to reduce tumor size and relieve subsequent symptoms, like the pain of bone metastasis.

PERSONALIZED CANCER MEDICINE

Personalized medicine is an emerging trend in cancer treatment. It involves using the patient's genetic information to guide decisions about prevention, diagnosis, and treatment of cancer. Many diagnostic studies (tumor markers, genetic markers, molecular receptor status) are useful in determining treatment options.

Before personalized medicine, most patients with a specific type and stage of cancer received the same treatment. However, some treatments worked well for some patients and not as well for others. With increasing research, we have found that genetic differences in people and their tumors explain many of these different responses to treatment. By performing genetic tests and analysis, treatments can now be personalized.[7]

Next-generation sequencing, also known as massive parallel sequencing, can sequence millions of DNA fragments. This technology can determine if a patient's cancer is caused by a hereditary cancer syndrome or if it is sporadic. Results guide which specific drugs target a patient's mutation and help identify clinical trials specific to the genetic mutation.[8]

Targeted therapy (Table 15.13) targets a cancer's specific genes or proteins that contribute to cancer growth and survival. Treatment with a targeted therapy depends on assessing whether the tumor has the specific target. This is usually done by testing a sample of the tumor obtained through a biopsy.

Pharmacogenomics and *pharmacogenetics* is the study of genomic variation associated with drug responses.[9] Examples of how the results of genetic testing can be applied to the use of cancer drugs are shown in Table 12.5. For example, vemurafenib (Zelboraf) is used to treat patients with metastatic melanoma. However, it is indicated only for the treatment of patients with melanoma whose tumors express a gene mutation called *BRAF V600E*.

Despite the promises of personalized cancer treatments, not all types of cancer have personalized treatment options. Genetic testing may be costly and time consuming. Many insurance plans do not cover the costs of these tests. Some personalized treatments, such as targeted treatments, can be expensive.[7]

SURGICAL THERAPY

Surgery is the oldest form of cancer treatment. The treatment of choice for many years was to remove the cancer and as much of the surrounding normal tissue as possible. What this approach did not fully consider was the ability of cancer cells to travel from the original tumor site to other locations, making surgical cure possible only when the tumor was localized and relatively small. Today surgery is used to meet a variety of goals (Fig. 15.9). The trend is toward less radical surgeries.

Prevention

Surgical intervention can be used to eliminate or reduce the risk for cancer development. Prophylactic removal of nonvital organs has been successful in reducing the risk for some cancers. For example, patients who have adenomatous familial polyposis may benefit from a total colostomy to prevent colorectal cancer (see Chapter 42). Those who have genetic mutations of *BRCA1* or *BRCA2* and have a strong family history of early-onset breast cancer may consider having a prophylactic mastectomy (see Chapter 51).

Cure or Control

When the goal is cure or control, the objective is to remove all or as much resectable tumor as possible while sparing normal tissue. Examples of surgical procedures used for cure or control of cancer include radical neck dissection, mastectomy, thyroidectomy, nephrectomy, hysterectomy, and/or oophorectomy.

A *debulking* or *cytoreductive procedure* may be used if the tumor cannot be completely removed (e.g., a tumor attached to a vital organ). When this occurs, as much tumor as possible is removed and the patient is given chemotherapy and/or radiation therapy. This type of surgical procedure can make chemotherapy or radiation therapy more effective, since the tumor mass is reduced before treatment is started. Other times, a patient may need to receive *neoadjuvant* (treatment before surgery) chemotherapy and/or radiation therapy to reduce tumor size and improve the surgical outcome.

Supportive and Palliative Care

When cure or control of cancer is no longer possible, the focus shifts to supportive care and palliation of symptoms. Surgical procedures may be used to provide supportive care

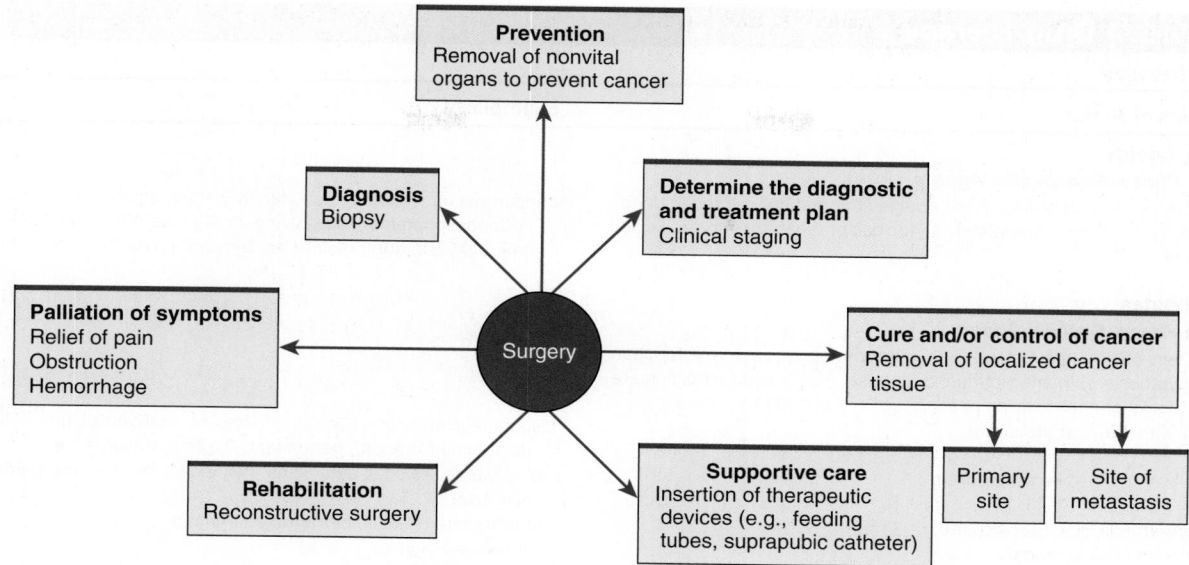

FIG. 15.9 Role of surgery in the treatment of cancer.

that maximizes bodily function or facilitates cancer treatment. Examples of supportive surgical procedures include:

- Insertion of a feeding tube to maintain nutrition during head and neck cancer treatment
- Placement of a central venous access device to deliver chemotherapy agents
- Prophylactic surgical fixation of bones at risk for pathologic fracture

Effects of treatment or symptoms from metastatic cancer may require surgical intervention for palliation. Examples include (1) tumor debulking to relieve pain or pressure, (2) colostomy for the relief of a bowel obstruction (see Chapter 42), and (3) laminectomy for the relief of a spinal cord compression (see Chapter 60).

CHEMOTHERAPY

Chemotherapy (antineoplastic therapy) is the use of chemicals as a systemic therapy for cancer. In the 1970s, chemotherapy was proven an effective treatment for cancer. Chemotherapy is now a mainstay of cancer treatment for most solid tumors and hematologic cancers (e.g., leukemias, lymphomas). Chemotherapy can offer cure for some cancers, control other cancers for long periods, and in some cases, offer palliative relief of symptoms when cure or control is no longer possible (Fig. 15.10).

Effect on Cells

The goal of chemotherapy is to eliminate or reduce the number of cancer cells in the primary and metastatic tumor site(s). All cells (cancer cells and normal cells) enter the cell cycle for replication and proliferation (Fig. 15.1). The effects of the chemotherapy drugs are described in relation to the cell cycle.

The 2 major categories of chemotherapy drugs are cell cycle phase–nonspecific and cell cycle phase–specific drugs. *Cell cycle phase–nonspecific chemotherapy drugs* have their effect on the cells during all phases of the cell cycle. This includes the process of cell replication and proliferation and the resting phase (G_0). *Cell cycle phase–specific chemotherapy drugs* have their greatest effects during specific phases of the cell cycle (e.g., when cells

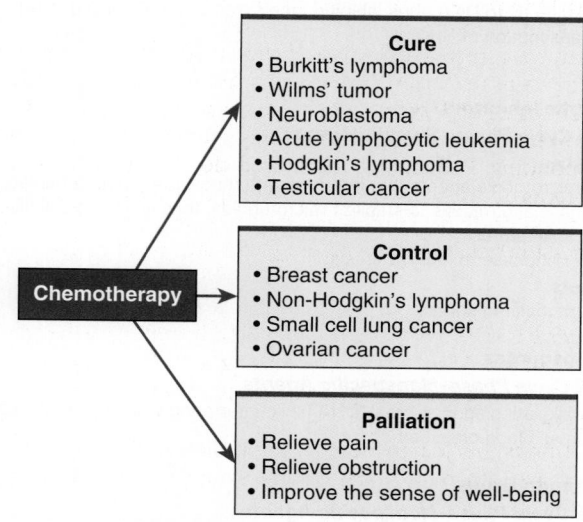

FIG. 15.10 Goals of chemotherapy.

are in the process of replication or proliferation during G_1, S, G_2, or M). Cell cycle phase–specific and cell cycle phase–nonspecific agents are often given together to maximize effectiveness by using agents that function in different ways and throughout the cell cycle.

When cancer first begins to develop, most of the cells are actively dividing. As the tumor increases in size, more cells become inactive and convert to a resting state (G_0). Because most chemotherapy agents are effective against dividing cells, cells can escape death by staying in the G_0 phase. A major challenge is to overcome the effect of resistant resting and noncycling cells.

Classification of Chemotherapy Drugs

Chemotherapy drugs are classified in general groups according to their molecular structure and mechanisms of action (Table 15.7). Each drug in a particular class has many similarities. However, there are major differences in how the drugs work and the unique side effects associated with drugs in each class.

TABLE 15.7 Drug Therapy

Chemotherapy

Mechanisms of Action	Examples
Alkylating Agents	
Cell Cycle Phase–Nonspecific Agents	
Damage DNA by causing breaks in the double-stranded helix. If repair does not occur, cells will die immediately (cytocidal) or when they try to divide (cytostatic).	bendamustine (Treanda), busulfan (Myleran), chlorambucil (Leukeran), cyclophosphamide, dacarbazine, ifosfamide (Ifex), mechlorethamine (Mustargen), melphalan, temozolomide (Temodar), thiotepa
Antimetabolites	
Cell Cycle Phase–Specific Agents	
Mimic naturally occurring substances, thus interfering with enzyme function or DNA synthesis. Primarily act during S phase. Purine and pyrimidine are building blocks of nucleic acids needed for DNA and RNA synthesis.	
• Interfere with purine metabolism	cladribine, clofarabine (Clolar), fludarabine, mercaptopurine (Purixan), nelarabine (Arranon), pentostatin (Nipent), thioguanine
• Interfere with pyrimidine metabolism	capecitabine (Xeloda); cytarabine, floxuridine, fluorouracil, gemcitabine (Gemzar)
• Interfere with folic acid metabolism	methotrexate (Trexall), pemetrexed (Alimta)
• Interfere with DNA synthesis	hydroxyurea (Hydrea, Droxia)
Antitumor Antibiotics	
Cell Cycle Phase–Nonspecific Agents	
Bind directly to DNA, thus inhibiting the synthesis of DNA and interfering with transcription of RNA.	bleomycin, dactinomycin (Cosmegen), daunorubicin, doxorubicin (Doxil), epirubicin (Ellence), idarubicin, mitomycin, mitoxantrone, valrubicin (Valstar)
Mitotic Inhibitors	
Cell Cycle Phase–Specific Agents	
Taxanes	
Antimicrotubule agents that interfere with mitosis. Act during the late G_2 phase and mitosis to stabilize microtubules, thus inhibiting cell division.	albumin-bound paclitaxel (Abraxane), docetaxel (Taxotere), paclitaxel (Taxol)
Vinca Alkaloids	
Act in M phase to inhibit mitosis.	vinblastine, vincristine, vinorelbine (Navelbine)
Others	
Microtubular inhibitors.	estramustine (Emcyt), ixabepilone (Ixempra), eribulin (Halaven)
Nitrosoureas	
Cell Cycle Phase–Nonspecific Agents	
Like alkylating agents, break DNA helix, interfering with DNA replication. Cross blood-brain barrier.	carmustine (BiCNU, Gliadel), lomustine (Gleostine), streptozocin (Zanosar)
Platinum Drugs	
Cell Cycle Phase–Nonspecific Agents	
Bind to DNA and RNA, miscoding information and/or inhibiting DNA replication, and cells die.	carboplatin, cisplatin, oxaliplatin
Topoisomerase Inhibitors	
Cell Cycle Phase–Specific Agents	
Inhibit topoisomerases (normal enzymes) that function to make reversible breaks and repairs in DNA that allow for flexibility of DNA in replication.	etoposide, irinotecan (Camptosar), topotecan (Hycamtin)

Preparation of Chemotherapy

Only persons specifically trained in chemotherapy handling techniques should be involved with the preparation and administration of cancer drugs.[10] They may pose an occupational hazard to health care professionals who do not follow safe handling guidelines. A person preparing, transporting, or giving chemotherapy may absorb the drug through inhalation of particles when reconstituting a powder or through skin contact from exposure to droplets or powder. There may be some risk in handling the body fluids and excretions of people during the first 48 hours after they receive chemotherapy. Guidelines for the safe handling of chemotherapy agents have been developed by the National Institute for Occupational Safety and Health (OSHA) and the Oncology Nursing Society (ONS).[11]

Methods of Administration

Chemotherapy can be given by multiple routes (Table 15.8). With advances in drug formulation techniques, more oral chemotherapy agents are available. With oral agents, the patient will need to be taught about storage and side effects.

The IV route is the most common method of giving chemotherapy. Major concerns associated with IV chemotherapy administration include venous access problems, device- or catheter-related infection, and *extravasation*.[10] It is the infiltration of

TABLE 15.8 Drug Therapy Methods of Chemotherapy Administration

Method	Examples
Oral	cyclophosphamide, capecitabine (Xeloda), temozolomide (Temodar)
Intramuscular	bleomycin
Intravenous	doxorubicin, vincristine, cisplatin, fluorouracil, paclitaxel (Taxol)
Intraarterial	dacarbazine, fluorouracil, methotrexate
Intracavitary (pleural, peritoneal)	Radioisotopes, alkylating agents, methotrexate
Intrathecal	methotrexate (preservative free), cytarabine
Perfusion	Alkylating agents
Subcutaneous	cytarabine, bortezomib
Topical	fluorouracil

FIG. 15.11 Extravasation injury from infiltration of chemotherapy drug. (From Weinzweig N, Weinzweig J: *The mutilated hand*, Philadelphia, 2005, Mosby.)

drugs into tissues surrounding the infusion site, causing local tissue damage (Fig. 15.11).

Many chemotherapy drugs are either irritants or vesicants. *Irritants* will damage the intima of the vein, causing phlebitis and sclerosis and limiting future peripheral venous access. They will not cause tissue damage if infiltrated. However, vesicants, if inadvertently infiltrated into the skin, may cause severe local tissue breakdown and necrosis. It is extremely important to monitor for and promptly take action if extravasation of a vesicant occurs. To minimize discomfort, emotional distress, and risks of infection and infiltration, IV chemotherapy can be given through a *central venous access device* (CVAD). CVADs are placed in large blood vessels and allow frequent, continuous, or intermittent administration of chemotherapy, immunotherapy, and targeted therapy, and other products, thus avoiding multiple venipunctures for vascular access. (CVADs are discussed in Chapter 16.)

Regional Chemotherapy Administration

Regional treatment with chemotherapy involves delivery of the drug directly to the tumor site. The advantage of this method is that higher concentrations of the drug can be delivered to the tumor with less systemic toxicity. Several regional delivery methods have been developed. These include intraarterial, intraperitoneal, intrathecal, intraventricular, and intravesical bladder chemotherapy.

Intraarterial Chemotherapy. Intraarterial chemotherapy delivers the drug to the tumor through the arteries supplying the tumor. This method has been used for the treatment of osteogenic sarcoma; cancers of the head and neck, bladder, and cervix; melanoma; primary liver cancer; and metastatic liver disease. One method of intraarterial drug delivery involves the surgical placement of a catheter that is connected to an external or implanted infusion pump for infusion of the chemotherapy agent.

Intraperitoneal Chemotherapy. Intraperitoneal chemotherapy involves the delivery of chemotherapy to the peritoneal cavity. It is a treatment for peritoneal metastases from primary colorectal and ovarian cancers and malignant ascites. Temporary Silastic catheters (Tenckhoff, Hickman, Groshong) are percutaneously or surgically placed into the peritoneal cavity for short-term administration of chemotherapy. An implanted port also can be used to give chemotherapy intraperitoneally. Chemotherapy is generally infused into the peritoneum in 1 to 2 L of fluid and allowed to *dwell* in the peritoneum for 1 to 4 hours. After the *dwell time,* the fluid is drained from the peritoneum.

Intrathecal or Intraventricular Chemotherapy. Cancers that metastasize to the central nervous system (CNS) are hard to treat because the blood-brain barrier often prevents distribution of chemotherapy to this area. One method used to treat metastasis to the CNS is intrathecal chemotherapy. This method involves a lumbar puncture and injection of chemotherapy into the subarachnoid space. To reduce the need for repeated lumbar punctures, patients may have an Ommaya reservoir inserted. An Ommaya reservoir is a Silastic, dome-shaped disk with an extension catheter that is surgically implanted through the cranium into a lateral ventricle.

Intravesical Bladder Chemotherapy. *Intravesical bladder chemotherapy* involves instilling chemotherapy into the bladder. This is done through a urinary catheter. The solution is retained for 1 to 3 hours.

Effects of Chemotherapy on Normal Tissues

Chemotherapy agents cannot selectively distinguish between normal cells and cancer cells. Chemotherapy-induced side effects are the result of the destruction of normal cells, especially those that are rapidly proliferating. These include those in the bone marrow, lining of the GI system, and integument (skin, hair, nails) (Table 15.9). The general and drug-specific adverse effects of these drugs are classified as acute, delayed, or chronic.

Acute toxicity occurs during and right after drug administration. It includes anaphylactic and hypersensitivity reactions, extravasation or a flare reaction, anticipatory nausea and vomiting, and dysrhythmias.

Delayed effects are numerous. They include delayed nausea and vomiting, mucositis, alopecia, skin rashes, bone marrow suppression, altered bowel function (diarrhea, constipation), and a variety of cumulative neurotoxicities.

Chronic toxicities involve damage to organs, such as the heart, liver, kidneys, and lungs. Chronic toxicities can be either long-term effects that develop during or right after treatment and persist or late effects that are absent during treatment and manifest later.

Some side effects fall into more than 1 category. For example, nausea and vomiting can be both acute and delayed.

Treatment Plan

Although single-drug chemotherapy is sometimes prescribed, the most common modality is combining agents in multidrug regimens. Multidrug treatment targets more than one signaling

TABLE 15.9 Cells With Rapid Rate of Proliferation

Cells	Generation Time	Effect of Cell Destruction
Bone marrow stem cell	6–24 hr	Myelosuppression (infection, bleeding, anemia)
Epithelial cells lining the GI tract	12–24 hr	Anorexia, mucositis (including stomatitis, esophagitis), nausea, vomiting, diarrhea
Hair follicle cells	24 hr	Alopecia
Neutrophils	12 hr	Leukopenia, infection
Ova or testes	24–36 hr	Reproductive problems

pathway and is more effective in managing most cancers. The regimens involve drugs with different mechanisms of action and varying toxicity profiles. However, when chemotherapy agents are used in combination, patients can have an increase in toxicities.

Drug regimens are chosen based on evidence supporting their use in specific cancers. Sometimes they are customized to meet the needs of an individual patient. Chemotherapy is most effective when the tumor burden is low, therapy is not interrupted, and the patient receives the intended dose. The dose of each drug is based on the person's body weight and height using the body surface area calculation.

Mutation of cancer cells within the tumor can result in cells that are resistant to chemotherapy. With multiple drugs working at different places in the cell cycle, cancer cells can be more effectively killed. Thus mutation and resistance of cancer cells can be decreased.

INFORMATICS IN PRACTICE

Managing Cancer Patients' Symptoms

- Patients arriving at some clinics are handed a tablet computer. While in the waiting room or chemotherapy infusion unit, with the touch of a finger they select the symptoms that they are having.
- Health care team members can review the information and provide care aimed at managing the patient's specific symptoms.
- After the visit, the notes are stored in the patient's electronic health record. This system can help determine if standards of care were followed.

RADIATION THERAPY

Along with surgery, radiation therapy is one of the oldest methods of cancer treatment. It was first used to treat a woman with breast cancer in 1896. Although the patient responded locally, she died later of metastatic disease. It was not until the 1960s that advances in equipment and treatment planning facilitated the delivery of adequate radiation doses to tumors and tolerable doses to normal tissues. Today many cancer patients receive radiation therapy at some point in their treatment.

Effects of Radiation

Radiation is energy that is emitted from a source and travels through space or some material. Delivery of high-energy beams, when absorbed into tissue, produces ionization of atomic particles. The energy in ionizing radiation acts to break the chemical bonds in DNA. The DNA is damaged, causing cell death.

Different types of ionizing radiation are used to treat cancer, including *electromagnetic radiation* (e.g., x-rays, gamma rays) and *particulate radiation* (e.g., alpha particles, electrons, neutrons, protons). High-energy x-rays (photons) are generated by an electric machine, such as a linear accelerator.

Technologic advances have expanded and refined the sources and methods of delivering radiation therapy. This allows for more accurate and less invasive treatment options. Most radiation centers in the United States use megavoltage linear accelerator technology. Larger facilities may offer a combination of machines that give patients more options at that site.

Principles of Radiobiology

As the radiation beam passes through the treatment field, energy is deposited. *Low-energy beams* (e.g., electrons) expend energy quickly on impact with matter, so they penetrate only a short distance. They are clinically useful in treating superficial skin lesions. *High-energy beams* (e.g., photons) have greater depth of penetration, not reaching full intensity until they reach a certain depth. This makes them suitable for delivering optimal doses to internal targets while sparing the skin.

Technically, all cancer cells could be killed with radiation given in high enough doses. However, to avoid serious toxicity and long-term complications of treatment, radiation to surrounding healthy tissue must be limited to the *maximal tolerated dose* for that specific tissue. Advances in planning and in delivery technology (e.g., *intensity-modulated radiation therapy [IMRT]* and *image-guided radiation therapy [IGRT]*) have greatly improved the ability to deliver maximal doses while sparing critical structures (e.g., spinal cord, carotid arteries, optic chiasm) as much as possible.

Historically, the radiation dose was expressed in units called *rads* (radiation absorbed doses). Now we use *gray* (Gy) or centigray (cGy). A *centigray* is equal to 1 rad; 100 centigray equals 1 gray. Once the total dose to be delivered is determined, that dose is divided into daily *fractions*. Doses between 180 and 200 cGy/day are considered *standard fractionation*. They are typically delivered once a day Monday through Friday for a period of 2 to 8 weeks, depending on the desired total dose.

Certain cancers are more responsive to the effects of radiation than others (Table 15.10). Radiosensitivity is the relative responsiveness of cells and tissues to the effects of radiation. In highly responsive tumors (such as lymphomas), even a large tumor is affected by radiation therapy. In less responsive tumors, there may be a slower or incomplete response. Localized prostate cancer responds very slowly to radiation (several months after treatment is completed).

Simulation and Treatment Planning

Simulation is a process by which the radiation treatment fields are defined, filmed, and marked out on the skin. The radiation oncologist specifies the dose and volume of area to be treated. Treatment volumes include the (1) *gross target v*olume (GTV), which is the gross extent of the tumor identified by examination or imaging; (2) the *clinical target* volume (CTV), which is the GTV plus additional margin to encompass any potential microscopic or subclinical disease; and (3) the *planning target* volume (PTV), which is the GTV/CTV plus additional margin to allow for organ motion or variance in daily set-up position.

During the simulation, the patient is positioned on a simulator. It is a diagnostic x-ray machine that re-creates the actions of the linear accelerator. The radiation fields are marked on the

TABLE 15.10 Tumor Radiosensitivity

High Radiosensitivity
- Hodgkin's lymphoma
- Neuroblastoma
- Non-Hodgkin's lymphoma
- Ovarian dysgerminoma
- Testicular seminoma
- Wilms' tumor

Moderate Radiosensitivity
- Bladder carcinoma
- Breast adenocarcinoma
- Esophageal carcinoma
- Oropharyngeal carcinoma
- Prostate carcinoma
- Uterine and cervical carcinoma

Mild Radiosensitivity
- Colon adenocarcinoma
- Gastric adenocarcinoma
- Renal adenocarcinoma
- Soft tissue sarcomas (e.g., chondrosarcoma)

Poor Radiosensitivity
- Osteosarcoma
- Malignant glioma
- Melanoma
- Testicular nonseminoma

FIG. 15.12 Immobilization device. A head holder and an immobilization mask may be used to ensure accurate positioning for daily treatment of head and neck cancer. (Courtesy Jormain Cady, Virginia Mason Medical Center, Seattle, WA.)

FIG. 15.13 Linear accelerator. Varian Clinac EX linear accelerator with multiple photon and electron energies available for use according to the treatment plan. Patient is positioned on radiation treatment table for treatment of head and neck cancer. (Courtesy Jormain Cady, Virginia Mason Medical Center, Seattle, WA.)

patient's skin. Immobilization devices (e.g., casts, bite blocks, thermoplastic face masks) are typically used to help the patient keep a stable position (Fig. 15.12).

The target is defined using a variety of imaging techniques (e.g., x-rays; CT, MRI, PET scans), physical examination, and surgical reports. Small tattoos may be placed to ensure the patient position is precisely reproduced each treatment.

Treatment

Radiation is used to treat a carefully defined area of the body. Since radiation affects only tissues within the treatment field, it is not appropriate as the main treatment for systemic disease. However, radiation may be used by itself, in combination with chemotherapy or surgery to treat primary tumors, or for palliation of metastatic lesions.

External Radiation. Radiation can be delivered externally (*external beam radiation therapy*) or internally (*brachytherapy*). External beam radiation is the most common form of radiation treatment delivery. With this technique, the patient is exposed to radiation from a megavoltage treatment machine. The beam passes through the external tissues to reach the internal target. A linear accelerator, which generates ionizing radiation from electricity and can have multiple energies, is the most commonly used machine for delivering external beam radiation (Fig. 15.13). *Gamma knife technology* (used to deliver highly accurate stereotactic treatment to a localized treatment volume) uses a cobalt source.

Internal Radiation. Radiation can be delivered as brachytherapy, which means "close" or internal radiation treatment. It consists of the implantation or insertion of radioactive materials directly into the tumor (interstitial) or near the tumor (intracavitary or intraluminal). This allows for direct delivery of radiation to the target with minimal exposure to surrounding healthy tissues. It is often used in combination with external radiation as a supplemental "boost" treatment. It may be a primary or adjuvant therapy.

Sources of radiation for brachytherapy include temporary sealed sources (e.g., iridium-192, cesium-137) and permanent sealed sources (e.g., iodine-125, gold-198, palladium-103). These are supplied in the form of seeds or ribbons. With a temporary implant, the source may be placed into a special catheter or metal tube that has been inserted into the tumor area. It is left in place until the prescribed dose of radiation has been reached in the calculated number of hours.

Brachytherapy may be delivered as high-dose-rate (HDR) treatment (e.g., several doses given at varying intervals over a few minutes each time) or low-dose-rate (LDR) treatment (e.g., continuous treatment over several hours or days). A remote "afterloading" technique (e.g., the source is inserted after the applicator is in place) is designed to enhance HCP and patient safety. It is used for HDR brachytherapy with iridium-192. These methods are often used for head and neck, lung, breast, and gynecologic cancers.

Permanent implants, such as for prostate brachytherapy, involve the insertion of radioactive seeds directly into the tumor tissue, where they stay permanently. As interstitial seeds used for treatment emit low energies with limited tissue penetration, patients are not considered radioactive. However, some initial radiation precautions may be recommended because of a small risk of seed dislodgement. Over time, the isotopes that are used decay and are no longer radioactive. The timeframe for side effects induced by treatment can be predicted based on the rate of decay for the specific isotope used.

Radioactive drugs, or radiopharmaceuticals, are used to treat some cancers systemically. They may be given orally as a capsule or drink (e.g., iodine-131 for thyroid cancer), or IV as with yttrium-90 given for resistant lymphomas or samarium-153 used to treat bone metastases. The drug is sometimes bound to monoclonal antibodies. The antibodies attach to the cancer cell, directly delivering the radiation. This may minimize the effects of the radiation on healthy cells.

Caring for the person undergoing brachytherapy or receiving radioactive drugs requires that you be aware when the patient is emitting radioactivity. Patients with temporary implants are radioactive only while the source is in place. In those with permanent implants, because the sources have short half-lives and are weak emitters, the radioactive exposure to the outside and to others is low. These patients may be discharged with minimal precautions.

The principles of *ALARA (as low as reasonably achievable)* and *time, distance,* and *shielding* are vital to our safety when caring for the person with a source of internal radiation. Organize care to limit the time spent in direct contact with the patient. To minimize anxiety and confusion, tell the patient the reason for time and distance limitations before the procedure.

The radiation safety officer will say how much time at a specific distance can be spent with the patient. This is determined by the dose delivered by the implant. Because the source is non-penetrating, small differences in distance are critical. Only care that must be delivered near the source, such as checking placement of the implant, is done in close proximity. Use shielding, if available. Do not deliver care without wearing a film badge (dosimeter) showing cumulative radiation exposure. Do not share the film badge. Do not wear it anywhere but at work and return it according to the agency's protocol.

❖ NURSING MANAGEMENT: CHEMOTHERAPY AND RADIATION THERAPY

You play a key role in helping patients deal with the side effects of chemotherapy and radiation therapy. Before starting teaching, assess the patient's ability to process information. Customize teaching to meet the patient's and caregiver's learning needs.

Common side effects of chemotherapy and radiation are outlined in Table 15.11. Bone marrow suppression, fatigue, GI disturbances, skin and mucosal reactions, and pulmonary and reproductive effects are discussed in this section.

◆ Nursing Implementation
◆ **Bone Marrow Suppression.** Myelosuppression is one of the most common effects of chemotherapy. To a lesser extent, it can occur with radiation. Treatment-induced myelosuppression can result in life-threatening and distressing effects. These include infection, hemorrhage, and overwhelming fatigue. The major

difference in manifestations between radiation therapy and chemotherapy is that radiation (a local therapy) only affects bone marrow within the treatment field. Chemotherapy (a systemic therapy) affects bone marrow function throughout the body. When the therapies are combined, the risk for myelosuppression greatly increases.

In general, the onset of bone marrow suppression is related to the life span of the type of blood cell. WBCs (especially neutrophils) are affected first (within 1 to 2 weeks), platelets in 2 to 3 weeks, and red blood cells (RBCs), with a longer life span of 120 days, later. The severity of myelosuppression depends on the chemotherapy drugs used, drug dosages, and the radiation treatment field. Radiation to large marrow-containing regions of the body produces the most clinically significant myelosuppression. In the adult, most of the active marrow is in the pelvis and thoracic and lumbar vertebrae.

Monitor the CBC, especially the neutrophil, platelet, and RBC counts, in patients receiving chemotherapy or radiation. Patients often have the lowest blood cell counts (called the *nadir*) between 7 and 10 days after starting therapy. However, the exact onset depends on the drug regimen.

Neutropenia is more common in patients receiving chemotherapy than radiation therapy. It is a serious risk factor for life-threatening infection and sepsis. Significant neutropenia will prompt treatment delay or adjustments (e.g., lower dosages). Take every measure to prevent infections in these patients. Hand hygiene is the mainstay of patient protection. Patients and their contacts, including health care team members, should follow hand-washing guidelines.

Monitor temperature routinely. Any sign of infection should be treated promptly, since fever in the presence of neutropenia is a medical emergency. WBC growth factors (e.g., filgrastim [Neupogen], pegfilgrastim [Neulasta]) are routinely used to reduce the duration of chemotherapy-induced neutropenia. They are used as a prophylactic measure to prevent neutropenia when highly myelosuppressive chemotherapy drugs are used.[12] (Neutropenia is discussed in Chapter 30. See the patient teaching guide in Table 30.23 and eNursing Care Plan 30.3 on the website for that chapter.)

Thrombocytopenia can result in spontaneous bleeding or major hemorrhage. Avoid invasive procedures. Teach patients to avoid activities that place them at risk for injury or bleeding (including excessive straining). Risk for serious bleeding is generally not present until the platelet count falls below 50,000/µL. Platelet transfusions may be necessary and are usually given when platelet counts fall below 20,000/µL. (Thrombocytopenia is discussed in Chapter 30. See the patient teaching guide in Table 30.15 and eNursing Care Plan 30.2 on the website for that chapter.)

Anemia is common in patients undergoing either radiation therapy or chemotherapy. It generally has a later onset (about 3 to 4 months after starting treatment). For patients with low hemoglobin levels, RBC growth factors (e.g., darbepoetin [Aranesp], epoetin [Procrit]) may be given according to clinical guidelines. In extreme circumstances (e.g., symptomatic anemia), RBC transfusions may be needed. However, in general, RBC transfusions are avoided. (Hematopoietic growth factors are discussed later in this chapter and in Table 15.15.)

◆ **Fatigue.** *Fatigue* is the persistent subjective sense of tiredness that interferes with usual day-to-day functioning. Fatigue is a nearly universal symptom affecting most patients with cancer. It is often reported by patients as the most distressful of

TABLE 15.11 Nursing Management

Problems Caused by Chemotherapy and Radiation Therapy

Etiology	Nursing Management
Biochemical	
Hyperuricemia	
Increased uric acid levels due to chemotherapy-induced cell destruction. Can cause secondary gout and obstructive uropathy.	• Monitor uric acid levels. • Allopurinol may be given as a prophylactic measure. • Maintain increased fluid intake.
Cardiovascular	
Cardiotoxicity	
Some chemotherapy drugs (e.g., anthracyclines, taxanes) can cause ECG changes and rapidly progressive heart failure.	• Monitor heart with ECG and cardiac ejection fractions. • Drug therapy may need to be changed for symptoms or deteriorating cardiac function studies. • Administer antidysrhythmic drugs as ordered.
Pericarditis and Myocarditis	
Inflammation from radiation injury. Complication from chest wall radiation. May occur up to 1 year after treatment. Side effect of some chemotherapy drugs.	• Monitor for manifestations of these disorders (e.g., dyspnea).
Comfort	
Fatigue	
Anabolic processes result in accumulation of metabolites from cell breakdown.	• Assess for reversible causes of fatigue and address them as indicated. • Reassure patient that fatigue is a common side effect of therapy. • Encourage patient to rest when fatigued, to maintain usual lifestyle patterns, as much as possible, and to pace activities in accordance with energy level. • Encourage moderate exercise as tolerated.
Gastrointestinal System	
Anorexia	
Release of TNF and IL-1 from macrophages has appetite-suppressant effect. Therapy-induced GI effects (mucositis, nausea, vomiting, bowel problems) and anxiety reduce appetite.	• Monitor weight. • Encourage patient to eat small, frequent meals of high-protein, high-calorie foods. • Gently encourage patient to eat, but do not nag. • Recommend keeping a food diary to track daily calories and fluids. • Serve food in pleasant environment.
Constipation	
Autonomic nervous system dysfunction decreases intestinal motility. Caused by neurotoxic effects of plant alkaloids (vincristine, vinblastine).	• Teach patients to take stool softeners as needed, eat high-fiber foods, and increase fluid intake. • Teach patients to increase activity (e.g., walking) if tolerated.
Diarrhea	
From denuding of epithelial lining of intestines. Side effect of chemotherapy. Follows radiation to abdomen, pelvis, lumbosacral areas.	• Give antidiarrheal drugs as needed. • Encourage low-fiber, low-residue diet. • Encourage fluid intake of at least 3 L/day.
Hepatotoxicity	
Toxic effects from chemotherapy drugs (usually transient and resolve when drug is stopped).	• Monitor liver function tests.
Nausea and Vomiting	
Release of intracellular breakdown products stimulates vomiting center in brain. Drugs stimulate vomiting center in brain (see Fig. 41.1). Radiation and chemotherapy destroy lining of GI tract.	• Encourage patient to eat and drink when not nauseated. • Give prophylactic antiemetics before chemotherapy and on as-needed basis. • Teach patients to take antiemetics on a scheduled basis for 2–3 days after highly emetogenic chemotherapy. • Use diversional activities (if appropriate).

Continued

TABLE 15.11 Nursing Management—cont'd

Problems Caused by Chemotherapy and Radiation Therapy

Etiology	Nursing Management
Stomatitis, Mucositis, and Esophagitis Epithelial cells are destroyed by chemotherapy or radiation treatment when located in field (e.g., head and neck, stomach, esophagus). Rapid cell destruction causes inflammation and ulceration.	• Assess oral mucosa daily and teach patient to do this. • Encourage nutritional supplements (e.g., Ensure, Carnation Instant Breakfast) if intake is decreasing. • Be aware that eating, swallowing, and talking may be difficult and patient may need analgesics. • Teach avoidance of irritating spicy or acidic foods or too hot or too cold food (extremes in temperature). • Teach how to choose moist, bland, and softer foods. • Encourage patient to keep oral cavity clean and moist by frequent oral rinses with saline or salt and soda solution. • Encourage patient to use artificial saliva to manage dryness (radiation). • Discourage use of irritants, such as tobacco and alcohol. • Apply topical anesthetics (e.g., viscous lidocaine, oxethazaine).
Genitourinary Tract **Hemorrhagic Cystitis** Chemotherapy (e.g., cyclophosphamide, ifosfamide) destroys cells lining the bladder Side effect of radiation when in the treatment field.	• Encourage increased fluid intake 24–72 hr after treatment as tolerated. • Monitor for urgency, frequency, and hematuria. • Give cytoprotectant agent (mesna [Mesnex]) and hydration. • Give supportive care agents to manage symptoms (e.g., flavoxate).
Nephrotoxicity Exposure to nephrotoxic agents (cisplatin and high-dose methotrexate) directly damages renal cells. Precipitation of metabolites of cell breakdown (tumor lysis syndrome [TLS]).	• Monitor BUN and serum creatinine levels. • Avoid potentiating drugs. • Alkalinize the urine by adding sodium bicarbonate to IV infusion • Give allopurinol or rasburicase for TLS prevention.
Reproductive Problems Therapy damages cells of testes or ova.	• Discuss possibility with patients before treatment initiation. • Offer opportunity for sperm and ova banking before treatment for patients of childbearing age.
Hematologic System **Anemia** Therapy causes bone marrow depression. Malignant infiltration of bone marrow by cancer.	• Monitor hemoglobin and hematocrit levels. • Give iron supplements and erythropoietin. • Encourage intake of foods that promote RBC production (see Table 30.5).
Leukopenia Chemotherapy or radiation therapy causes bone marrow depression. Infection most frequent cause of morbidity and death in cancer patients. Respiratory and genitourinary system are usual sites of infection.	• Monitor WBC count, especially neutrophils. • Tell patient to report temperature elevation and any other manifestations of infection. • Teach patient to avoid large crowds and people with infections. • Give WBC growth factors (Table 15.15). • For patient teaching, see Table 30.23.
Thrombocytopenia Chemotherapy causes bone marrow depression. Malignant infiltration of bone marrow crowds out normal marrow. Spontaneous bleeding can occur with platelet counts ≤20,000/µL.	• Observe for signs of bleeding (e.g., petechiae, ecchymosis). • Monitor platelet counts. • For patient teaching, see Table 30.15.
Integumentary System **Alopecia** Chemotherapy or radiation to scalp destroys hair follicles. Hair loss usually is temporary with chemotherapy, but usually permanent in response to radiation.	• Suggest ways to cope with hair loss (e.g., hair pieces, scarves, wigs). • Cut long hair before therapy. • Avoid excessive shampooing, brushing, and combing of hair. • Avoid use of electric hair dryers, curlers, and curling rods. • Discuss impact of hair loss on self-image.

TABLE 15.11 Nursing Management—cont'd
Problems Caused by Chemotherapy and Radiation Therapy

Etiology	Nursing Management
Chemotherapy-Induced Skin Changes Acneiform eruptions. Acral erythema. Hyperpigmentation. Photosensitivity. Telangiectasia.	• Alert patient to potential skin changes. • Encourage patient to avoid sun exposure. • Implement symptomatic management as needed depending on specific skin effect (e.g., application of lotions, corticosteroid creams).
Radiation Skin Changes (dry to moist desquamation) Radiation damages skin.	• See Table 15.12 for patient management details.

Nervous System
Cognitive Changes ("chemo brain")
Occur during and after treatment (especially with chemotherapy).
Problems with concentration, memory lapses, trouble remembering details, taking longer to finish tasks.
May happen quickly and last a short time. Some people have mild long-term effects.
	• Teach patients to:
	  • Use detailed daily planner.
	  • Get enough sleep and rest.
	  • Exercise brain (learn something new, do word puzzles).
	  • Focus on one thing (no multitasking).

Intracranial Pressure May result from radiation edema in central nervous system.	• Monitor neurologic status. • May be controlled with corticosteroids.
Peripheral Neuropathy Paresthesias, areflexia, skeletal muscle weakness, and smooth muscle dysfunction can occur as a side effect of plant alkaloids, taxanes, and cisplatin.	• Monitor for manifestations in patients on these drugs. • Consider temporary chemotherapy dose interruption or reduction until symptoms improve. • Antiseizure drugs (e.g., gabapentin [Neurontin]) may be considered.
Respiratory System **Pneumonitis** Radiation pneumonitis develops 2–3 mo after start of treatment. After 6–12 mo, fibrosis occurs and is evident on x-ray. Side effect of some chemotherapy and immunotherapy drugs.	• Monitor for dry, hacking cough; fever; and dyspnea with exertion. • Encourage activity and respiratory exercises.

treatment-related side effects. Fatigue may persist long after treatment has ended.

Anemia is one cause of fatigue. Other causes may be related to the (1) accumulation of toxic substances that are left in the body after cells are killed by cancer treatment, (2) need for extra energy to repair and heal body tissue damaged by treatment, and (3) lack of sleep caused by some chemotherapy drugs. Assess for reversible causes of fatigue, such as anemia, hypothyroidism, depression, anxiety, insomnia, dehydration, or infection.

Help patients recognize that fatigue is a common side effect of therapy. Teach them energy conservation strategies. Help patients identify days or times during the day when they typically feel better. Encourage them to be more active during that period.

Resting before activity and having others help with work or home tasks may be necessary. Ignoring the fatigue or overstressing the body when fatigue is tolerable may lead to an increase in symptoms. Maintaining exercise and activity within tolerable limits is often helpful in managing fatigue. Walking programs are a way for most patients to keep active without overtaxing themselves. Staying active helps improve mood and avoid the debilitating cycle of fatigue-depression-fatigue that can occur in patients with cancer. Guidelines for the evaluation and management of cancer-related fatigue are available.[13]

CHECK YOUR PRACTICE

Your 56-yr-old female patient with breast cancer has just completed 4 cycles of a chemotherapy regimen of CAF (cyclophosphamide, doxorubicin, fluorouracil). At her clinic visit today, she reports being so tired that she "can barely get out of bed." She then becomes tearful, sharing "who knows what my future holds, and now I am missing so many things with my grandchildren."
• How would you respond?

◆ **Gastrointestinal Effects.** The cells of the mucosal lining of the GI tract are highly proliferative. The epithelial cells are replaced every 2 to 6 days. The intestinal mucosa is one of the most sensitive tissues to radiation and chemotherapy. The cause of GI reactions is related to a variety of mechanisms. These include (1) the release of serotonin from the GI tract, which then stimulates the chemoreceptor trigger zone (CTZ) and the vomiting center in the brain and (2) cell death and resulting damage to GI mucosa. Radiation to treatment fields that contain GI structures (e.g., abdominopelvic, lumbosacral, lower thoracic areas) and selected chemotherapy agents cause direct injury to GI epithelial cells. These injuries cause a variety of GI effects, including nausea and vomiting, diarrhea, mucositis, and anorexia. These problems can significantly affect the patient's hydration and nutritional status and sense of well-being.

Nausea and Vomiting. Nausea and vomiting are common effects of chemotherapy and sometimes radiation therapy. Chemotherapy-induced nausea and vomiting (CINV) may occur within 1 hour of chemotherapy administration. Vomiting may start a few hours after radiation therapy to the chest or abdomen. It may persist for 24 hours or more. Several antiemetic drugs are available (see Table 41.1).

Serotonin (5-HT$_3$) receptor antagonists (ondansetron [Zofran], granisetron, palonosetron [Aloxi]) and neurokinin-1 receptor antagonists (NK$_1$RA), (e.g., aprepitant [Emend], netupitant, rolapitant [Varubi]) can reduce CINV. Dexamethasone is given with other antiemetics to manage acute and delayed CINV. Akynzeo is a fixed combination of palonosetron (a 5-HT$_3$ receptor antagonist) and netupitant (a NK$_1$RA antagonist).

Anticipatory nausea and vomiting can develop if a patient has poorly controlled nausea and vomiting after chemotherapy administration. In this phenomenon, encountering the cues even without receiving treatment may precipitate nausea and vomiting. Aggressive emesis control, including giving prophylactic antiemetic and antianxiety medication 1 hour before treatment, is recommended. The patient may find that eating a light meal of nonirritating food before treatment is helpful.

Delayed nausea and vomiting can develop 24 hours to a week after treatment. Assess patients who have nausea and vomiting for signs and symptoms of dehydration and metabolic alkalosis. Nausea and vomiting can be successfully managed with antiemetic drugs, diet adjustments, and other nondrug interventions (e.g., relaxation breathing).

Diarrhea. Diarrhea is a reaction of the bowel mucosa to radiation and some chemotherapy drugs. It is characterized by an increase in frequency and liquidity of stool. The small bowel is extremely sensitive and does not tolerate significant radiation doses. With pelvic radiation, patients may be treated with a full bladder. This moves the small bowel out of the treatment field. Both radiation- and chemotherapy-induced diarrhea are best managed with diet adjustments, antidiarrheals, antimotility agents, and antispasmodics (see Table 42.2).

Recommend a diet low in fiber and residue before chemotherapy known to cause diarrhea. This includes limiting foods high in roughage (e.g., fresh fruits, vegetables, seeds, nuts). To prevent diarrhea, other foods to avoid include fried, fatty, or highly seasoned foods and foods that are gas producing. Bowel mucosal injury from radiation may cause temporary lactose intolerance. So, avoiding milk products is helpful for some patients during and right after treatment.

Depending on the severity of the diarrhea, hydration and electrolyte supplementation are recommended. Lukewarm sitz baths may ease discomfort and cleanse the rectal area if significant rectal irritation has developed. The rectal area must be kept clean and dry to maintain skin integrity. Inspect the perianal area for evidence of skin breakdown. Systemic analgesia may be used for painful skin irritations. Note the number, volume, consistency, and character of stools per day. Have patients keep a diary or log to record episodes and aggravating and alleviating factors.

Mucositis. Mucositis is irritation, inflammation, and/or ulceration of the mucosa. Chemotherapy or radiation therapy can cause mucositis. Patients diagnosed with head and neck cancer who receive radiation are at high risk. Like the bowel mucosa, the mucosal linings of the oral cavity, oropharynx, and esophagus are extremely sensitive to the effects of radiation and chemotherapy.

Certain factors can compound the problem. For example, patients undergoing head and neck radiation may face the added challenge of radiation-induced parotid gland dysfunction. This may result in decreased salivary flow, causing acute or chronic *xerostomia* (dry mouth). Dryness or thick saliva compromises the protective salivary functions of assisting with cleansing teeth, moistening food, and swallowing. Meticulous oral care during and for a long time after treatment reduces the risk for cavities, which may occur due to decreased saliva. Teach patients to continue regular dental follow-up every 6 months. They should use fluoride supplements as recommended by their dentist. Saliva substitutes may be offered to patients with xerostomia. Many patients find that drinking small amounts of water frequently has a similar effect.

Dysgeusia (taste loss) may develop during therapy. By the end of treatment, patients often report that all food has lost its flavor. Ultimately, nutritional status may be compromised. *Dysphagia* (difficulty swallowing), which marks pharyngeal and/or esophageal involvement, further impedes eating. Patients may report feeling that they have a "lump" as they swallow and that "foods get stuck." The patient with *odynophagia* (painful swallowing) caused by oropharyngeal or esophageal irritation and ulceration may need analgesics before meals.

Oral assessment and meticulous intervention to keep the oral cavity moist, clean, and free of debris are essential to prevent infection and promote nutritional intake. Implementing standard oral care protocols that address prevention and management of mucositis promotes routine assessment, patient and caregiver teaching, and intervention.

Routinely assess the oral cavity, mucous membranes, characteristics of saliva, and ability to swallow. Having a dentist perform all necessary dental work before starting treatment is recommended. Teach the patient to self-examine the oral cavity and how to perform oral care. Oral care should be done at least before and after each meal, at bedtime, and as needed through the day. A saline solution of 1 tsp of salt in 1 L of water is an effective cleansing agent; 1 tsp of sodium bicarbonate may be added to the oral care solution to decrease odor, ease pain, and dissolve mucin. Have the patient use a soft bristled toothbrush.

Mucositis or pain in the throat can be eased by systemic and/or topical analgesics and antibiotics if infection is present. Monitor and get prompt treatment for oral candidiasis (which often occurs with mucositis). Frequent cleansing with saline and water and topical application of anesthetic gels directly to the lesions are standard care.

Anorexia. Anorexia (loss of appetite) is a common occurrence in patients with cancer. It is a side effect of the cancer as well as of cancer treatment. Anorexia may be related to an inflamed mouth or esophagus, which creates difficulty chewing or swallowing, or to emotions, such as anxiety or depression. It is important to have a dietitian involved in patient care before cancer treatment starts.

Patients with nausea and vomiting, bowel problems, mucositis, and taste changes typically have little desire to eat. Anorexia seems to peak at about 4 weeks of treatment. It resolves more quickly than fatigue when treatment ends.

Monitor patients with anorexia during and after treatment to ensure that weight loss does not become excessive. Observe for dehydration. Small, frequent meals of high-protein, high-calorie foods are better tolerated than large meals. Nutritional supplements can be helpful, too. Enteral or parenteral nutrition may be needed if the patient is severely malnourished, if symptoms are expected to interfere with nutrition for a time, or if the bowel is being rested. Monitor for and manage other symptoms that may interfere with appetite (e.g., nausea, vomiting, pain, depression).

◆ Skin Reactions

Radiation Skin Changes. With radiation therapy, skin effects are local, occurring only in the treatment field. Radiation-induced skin changes can be acute or chronic depending on the area irradiated, dosage, and technique. The skin-sparing ability of modern radiation equipment limits the severity of these reactions.

Erythema may develop 1 to 24 hours after a single treatment. It generally occurs progressively as the treatment dose accumulates. It is an acute response followed by dry desquamation (Fig. 15.14). If the rate of cell sloughing is faster than the ability of the new epidermal cells to replace dead cells, a wet desquamation occurs with exposure of the dermis and weeping of serous fluid (Fig. 15.15). Skin reactions are especially evident in areas of skinfolds or where skin is subjected to pressure. This includes behind the ear; in gluteal folds; on the perineum, breast, or collar line; and bony prominences.

Although skin care protocols vary, basic skin care principles apply. The goal is to prevent infection and promote wound healing. Protect radiated skin from temperature extremes. Do not use heating pads, ice packs, and hot water bottles in the treatment field. Avoid constricting garments, rubbing, harsh chemicals, and deodorants, since they may traumatize the skin. Dry reactions are uncomfortable and result in pruritus. Lubricate

FIG. 15.14 Dry desquamation.

FIG. 15.15 Wet desquamation.

dry skin with a nonirritating lotion emollient that contains no metal, alcohol, perfume, or additives. These can be irritating. Calendula ointment and topical hyaluronic acid cream are effective for managing radiation dermatitis. Aloe vera gel is useful for preventing skin problems.

Wet desquamation of tissues generally causes pain, drainage, and increased risk for infection. Skin care to manage moist desquamation includes keeping tissues clean with normal saline compresses or modified Burow's solution soaks. Protect the skin from further damage with moisture vapor–permeable dressings or Vaseline petrolatum gauze. Because protocols vary widely, you should verify the guidelines in Table 15.12 with your agency' s radiation oncology department.

Chemotherapy Skin Changes. Chemotherapy causes a wide range of skin toxicities. These can range from mild erythema and hyperpigmentation to more distressing effects, such as acral erythema and *erythrodysesthesia syndrome* (also called palmar-plantar erythrodysesthesia or hand-foot syndrome).

TABLE 15.12 Patient & Caregiver Teaching

Radiation Skin Reactions

Include the following instructions when teaching the patient and caregiver to clean and protect the skin in a radiation treatment area:

1. Gently cleanse the skin in the treatment field using a mild soap (Ivory, Dove), tepid water, a soft cloth, and a gentle patting motion. Rinse thoroughly and pat dry.
2. Apply nonmedicated, nonperfumed, moisturizing lotion or cream, such as calendula ointment, aloe gel, Aquaphor, or Biafine cream, to alleviate dry skin. Some substances must be gently cleansed from the treatment field before each treatment and reapplied. Over-the-counter hydrocortisone cream 1% may reduce itching.
3. Rinse the area with saline solution. Expose the area to air as often as possible. If copious drainage is present, use astringent compresses (such as Domeboro solution) and nonadhesive absorbent dressings. Change dressings as soon as they become wet.
4. Observe the area daily for signs of infection.
5. Avoid wearing tight-fitting clothing, including brassieres and belts, over the treatment field.
6. Avoid wearing harsh fabrics, such as wool and corduroy. A lightweight cotton garment is best. If possible, expose the treatment field to air.
7. Use gentle detergents (e.g., Dreft, Ivory Snow) to wash clothing that will come in contact with the treatment field.
8. Avoid direct exposure to the sun. If the treatment field is in an area that is exposed to the sun, wear protective clothing, such as a wide-brimmed hat, when out in the sun and apply sunscreen lotion.
9. Avoid all sources of excessive heat (hot water bottles, heating pads, sunlamps) on the treatment field.
10. Avoid exposing the treatment field to cold temperatures (ice bags or cold weather).
11. Avoid swimming in saltwater or in chlorinated pools during the time of treatment.
12. Avoid the use of potential irritants (e.g., perfumes, powders, or cosmetics) on the skin in the treatment field. Review the use of other topical medications or lotions with your HCP during treatment. Avoid tape, dressings, and adhesive bandages unless allowed by the radiation therapist.
12. Continue to protect sensitive skin after the treatment is completed. Do the following:
    - Avoid direct exposure to the sun. A sunscreen agent and protective clothing must be worn if the potential of exposure to the sun is present.
    - Use an electric razor if shaving is needed in the treatment field.

Erythrodysesthesia syndrome can cause mild symptoms of redness and tingling of the palms of the hands and soles of the feet. It may also cause severe symptoms of painful moist desquamation, ulceration, blistering, and pain.

Alopecia is an easily recognizable effect of cancer treatment. Hair loss associated with radiation is local. Chemotherapy affects hair throughout the body. The degree and duration of hair loss depends on the type and dose of the chemotherapy agent. Scalp cooling during chemotherapy may reduce alopecia. Cold caps are placed on the head before, during, and after chemotherapy treatment. Common side effects are headache and cold sensation.[14]

Alopecia caused by chemotherapy agents is usually reversible. Usually the hair does not grow back until 3 to 4 weeks after the end of therapy. Often the new hair is a different color and texture than the hair that was lost.

Patients have a range of emotions at the prospect of losing their hair and when hair loss occurs. These may include anger, grief, embarrassment, or fear. Hair loss is a visible reminder of their cancer and the challenges of treatment. For some people, the hair loss is one of the most stressful events experienced during treatment. The ACS's "Look Good, Feel Better" program is an excellent support and resource for people with hair loss and body image changes.

◆ **Pulmonary Effects.** Both chemotherapy and radiation have the potential to cause irreversible and progressive lung damage. Distinguishing between the complications of treatment and those related to disease is challenging. The effects of radiation on the lung include both acute and late reactions. Acute effects can be alarming to patients because they may mimic symptoms (e.g., cough, dyspnea) that precipitated the cancer diagnosis.

Pneumonitis is a delayed acute inflammatory reaction that may occur within 1 to 3 months after completing thoracic radiation. This reaction is often asymptomatic, although an increase in cough, fever, and night sweats may occur. Some patients may develop pulmonary fibrosis (with or without prior pneumonitis), which is a late effect of therapy.

The most common toxicities associated with chemotherapy include pulmonary edema (noncardiogenic) related to capillary leak syndrome or fluid retention, hypersensitivity pneumonitis, interstitial fibrosis, and pneumonitis due to an inflammatory reaction or destruction of alveolar-capillary endothelium.

◆ **Cardiovascular Effects.** Radiation to the thorax can damage the pericardium, myocardium, valves, and coronary blood vessels. The pericardium is most often involved. Pericardial effusion and pericarditis are key problems. Patients with preexisting coronary artery disease are especially at risk.

Anthracyclines (e.g., doxorubicin, daunorubicin) cause cardiotoxicity. Acute cardiotoxicities may cause electrocardiographic (ECG) changes. Late effects cause left ventricular dysfunction and heart failure. Baseline and periodic echocardiograms to monitor left ventricular function during treatment are usually done.

◆ **Cognitive Effects.** Cognitive effects can happen at any time during cancer, especially after treatment. This change in mental function, often described by patients as mental cloudiness or fog, is commonly called *chemo brain*.[15] Patients can have thinking and memory problems. Although the brain will usually recover over time, the effects can last a short time or for years. The effects can be so severe that patients may be unable to be involved in any activities that need mental effort, including school, work, or social activities.

◆ **Reproductive Effects.** Reproductive problems from radiation and chemotherapy vary according to the radiation treatment field and dosage, the chemotherapy agent and dosage, and host factors (e.g., age). Treatment can cause temporary or permanent gonadal failure. Reproductive problems occur most often when reproductive organs are included in the radiation treatment field and when alkylating agents are used.

The testes are highly sensitive to radiation. They should be protected with a testicular shield whenever possible. Pretreatment status may be a significant factor. A low sperm count and loss of motility are seen in those with testicular cancer and Hodgkin's lymphoma before any therapy is begun. Combined modality treatment or prior chemotherapy with alkylating agents enhances and prolongs the effects of radiation on the testes. When radiation is used alone with conventional doses and appropriate shielding, testicular recovery often occurs. Men may have erectile dysfunction after pelvic radiation.

The radiation dose that induces ovarian failure changes with age. Unlike the testes, there is no way to repair ovarian function. When radiation therapy is given, the ovaries are shielded whenever possible. Other factors that influence reproductive or sexual functioning in women include reactions in the cervix and endometrium. These tissues withstand a high radiation dose with minimal sequelae. This accounts for the ability to treat endometrial and cervical cancer with high external and brachytherapy doses. Acute reactions, such as tenderness, irritation, and loss of lubrication, compromise sexual activity. Late effects of combined internal and external radiation therapy include vaginal shortening related to fibrosis and loss of elasticity and lubrication.

The patient and partner need information about the expected effects of treatment related to reproductive and sexual issues. Fertility preservation should be addressed before starting cancer treatment. Pretreatment harvesting of sperm, ova, or ovarian tissue may be considered.[16]

Potential infertility can be a significant consequence, and counseling may be needed. However, in no case should the patient think that conception is not possible during treatment. Specific suggestions that have an impact on sexual function include using a water-soluble vaginal lubricant and a vaginal dilator after pelvic irradiation. Encourage discussion of issues related to reproduction and sexuality, offer specific suggestions, and make referrals for ongoing counseling when needed.

LATE EFFECTS OF RADIATION AND CHEMOTHERAPY

Cancer survivors are achieving long-term remission and survival with advancements in treatment modalities. However, therapy (especially radiation therapy and chemotherapy) may cause long-term effects *(late effects)* that occur months to years after therapy.[17] Every body system can be affected to some extent by radiation therapy or chemotherapy.

Acute radiation effects generally manifest as transient inflammatory changes in highly proliferative cells (e.g., epithelial tissues). In contrast, late radiation effects occur most often in post-mitotic cells (e.g., liver, kidney, lung, heart, muscle, bone, connective tissues). Once they occur, the late effects may be progressive and generally are permanent. Examples range from skin telangiectasias to strictures, fistulas, or radiation necrosis.

Alteration of the lymphatic channels (e.g., axillary lymph node dissection) may contribute to lymphedema.

Long-term effects of chemotherapy include cardiac toxicity, cataracts, arthralgia, endocrine problems, renal insufficiency, hepatitis, osteoporosis, neurocognitive problems, or other effects depending on the agents. The additive effects of multiagent chemotherapy before, during, or after a course of radiation therapy can significantly increase the resulting late effects.

The cancer survivor may be at risk for secondary cancers, including leukemia, angiosarcoma, and skin cancer. Patients treated with alkylating agents and those treated with high-dose radiation have an increased risk. The potential risk for developing a secondary cancer does not contraindicate the use of cancer treatment.

IMMUNOTHERAPY AND TARGETED THERAPY

Immunotherapy uses the immune system, the body's main defense against infection and disease, to fight cancer. Some types of immunotherapy are called *biologic therapy*. Immunotherapy can (1) boost or manipulate the immune system and create an environment that is not conducive for cancer cells to grow or (2) attack cancer cells directly. Types of immunotherapy include cytokines, vaccines, and monoclonal antibodies (Table 15.13). Antibodies are proteins made by the immune system that bind to a target antigen on the cell surface. Monoclonal antibodies (drugs ending in -mab) are the most successful immunotherapy. Because each antibody is specific to an antigen, that mechanism is used to develop specific drugs to treat cancer. Many of the monoclonal antibodies are targeted therapies.

Targeted therapy interferes with cancer growth by targeting specific cell receptors and pathways that are important in tumor growth.[18,19] Targeted therapies work at sites that are on the cell surface, at the intracellular level, or in the extracellular domain (Fig. 15.16 and Table 15.13). Targeted therapies are more selective for specific molecular targets than chemotherapy drugs. Thus they act on specific targets that are associated with cancer. A major advantage of targeted therapy is that it does less damage to normal cells.

As we identify more oncogene targets, agents are being developed that target those specific oncogenes. Targeted therapies provide personalized treatment based on the biology of the tumor. Examples of some targeted therapies are discussed in the next few paragraphs.

A major class of targeted therapy is tyrosine kinase inhibitors (Table 15.13). Tyrosine kinases are enzymes responsible for activating many proteins by signal transduction cascades. EGFR is a transmembrane molecule that works by activating intracellular tyrosine kinase (TK). Overexpression of EGFR is associated with unregulated cell growth and a poor prognosis. Drugs that inhibit EGFR suppress cell proliferation and promote *apoptosis* (programmed cell death).

EGFRs belong to the same receptor family as human epidermal growth factor receptor-2 (HER-2). It is the target for trastuzumab (Herceptin), a drug mainly used to treat breast cancer. HER-2 is overexpressed in certain cancers (especially breast cancers). It is associated with more aggressive disease and decreased survival. Trastuzumab is a monoclonal antibody (MoAb) that binds to HER-2. It is given IV to inhibit the growth of breast cancer cells that overexpress the HER-2 protein. Lapatinib (Tykerb) is an oral agent used for breast cancer that overexpresses HER-2.

Chronic myeloid leukemia (CML) cells make an abnormal active enzyme called BCR-ABL tyrosine kinase. Drugs, such as imatinib (Gleevec), that inhibit this enzyme suppress proliferation of CML cells and promote cell death.

Angiogenesis inhibitors work by preventing the mechanisms and pathways necessary for vascularization of tumors. Bevacizumab (Avastin), a recombinant human MoAb, binds with vascular endothelial growth factor (VEGF), a compound that stimulates blood vessel growth. When bevacizumab binds with VEGF, it prevents VEGF from binding with its receptors on vascular endothelial cells and promoting new vessel formation. As a result, further tumor growth is inhibited.

Proteasomes are intracellular multienzyme complexes that degrade proteins. In cancer cells, proteasome inhibitors (e.g., bortezomib [Velcade]) promote accumulation of proteins that leads to cell death.

Cancer cells can become resistant to targeted therapies. This can occur because the (1) target changes through mutation and the therapy no longer interacts with it and (2) tumor finds a new growth pathway and no longer depends on the target. Because of the possibility of resistance, targeted therapies work best in combination or in combination with a chemotherapy drug.

Side Effects of Immunotherapy and Targeted Therapy

The administration of one type of immunotherapy usually induces the endogenous release of other agents. The release and action of these agents result in systemic immune and inflammatory responses. The toxicities and side effects are related to dose and schedule.

Common side effects include flu-like symptoms, including headache, fever, chills, myalgias, fatigue, malaise, weakness, photosensitivity, anorexia, and nausea. Those receiving interferon therapy almost always have flu-like symptoms. Their severity generally decreases over time. Acetaminophen given every 4 hours, as prescribed, and large amounts of fluids often reduce the severity of the flu-like syndrome. The patient is often premedicated with acetaminophen to try to prevent or decrease the intensity of these symptoms.

Tachycardia and orthostatic hypotension are common. IL-2 and MoAbs can cause *capillary leak syndrome,* which can result in pulmonary edema. Other toxic and side effects may involve the CNS, renal and hepatic systems, and cardiovascular system. These effects are found with interferons and IL-2.

A wide range of neurologic problems can occur with interferon and IL-2 therapy. The nature and extent of these problems are not yet completely understood. They are frightening to the patient and caregivers. Teach them to observe for neurologic problems (e.g., confusion, memory loss, difficulty making decisions, insomnia), report their occurrence, and institute safety and support measures.

MoAbs are given by infusion. Patients may have infusion-related symptoms, including fever, chills, urticaria, mucosal congestion, nausea, diarrhea, and myalgias.

Skin rashes are common in patients receiving EGFR inhibitors. They manifest generally as erythema and acneiform-like rash that can cover a large part of the upper body. Angiogenesis inhibitors can cause arterial thrombi, hemorrhage, hypertension, impaired wound healing, and proteinuria. Other toxicities of MoAbs include hepatotoxicity, bone marrow depression, and CNS effects.

TABLE 15.13 Drug Therapy

Select Immunotherapies and Targeted Therapies

Mechanism of Action	Examples
Angiogenesis Inhibitors	
Bind vascular endothelial growth factor (VEGF), thereby inhibiting angiogenesis.	bevacizumab (Avastin) pazopanib (Votrient) ramucirumab (Cyramza)
CD20 Monoclonal Antibodies	
Bind CD20 antigen, causing cytotoxicity and radiation injury. Bind CD20 antigen, causing cytotoxicity.	ibritumomab tiuxetan/yttrium-90 (Zevalin) ofatumumab (Arzerra) rituximab (Rituxan)
CD52 Monoclonal Antibody	
Bind CD52 antigen (found on T and B cells, monocytes, natural killer [NK] cells, neutrophils).	alemtuzumab (Campath)
Cytokines (see Table 13.4)	
Inhibit DNA and protein synthesis. Suppress cell proliferation. Increase cytotoxic effects of NK cells. Stimulate proliferation of T and B cells. Activate NK cells.	α-interferon (Intron A) interleukin-2 (aldesleukin [Proleukin])
Human Epidermal Growth Factor Receptor-2 (HER-2)	
Monoclonal antibody to HER-2 that attaches to the antigen. It is taken into the cells and eventually kills them. Trastuzumab connected to a chemotherapy drug called DM1.	pertuzumab (Perjeta) trastuzumab (Herceptin) ado-trastuzumab emtansine (Kadcyla)
Immunomodulatory Drugs (IMiDs)	
Inhibit production of TNF, IL-6, and VEGF (which leads to its antiangiogenic effects). Stimulate T and NK cells and increase γ-interferon and IL-2 production.	apremilast (Otezla) lenalidomide (Revlimid) pomalidomide (Pomalyst) thalidomide (Thalomid)
Kinase Inhibitors	
Anaplastic Lymphoma Kinase (ALK) Inhibitors	
Inhibit anaplastic lymphoma kinase (ALK).	ceritinib (Zykadia) crizotinib (Xalkori)
BCR-ABL Tyrosine Kinase Inhibitors	
Inhibit BCR-ABL TK. Primarily used in chronic myeloid leukemia.	bosutinib (Bosulif) dasatinib (Sprycel) imatinib (Gleevec) nilotinib (Tasigna)
BRAF and MEK Kinase Inhibitors	
Inhibit BRAF and MEK enzymes.	dabrafenib (Tafinlar) trametinib (Mekinist) vemurafenib (Zelboraf) cobimetinib (Cotellic)
EGFR Tyrosine Kinase (TK) Inhibitors	
Inhibit epidermal growth factor receptor (EGFR) TK.	cetuximab (Erbitux) erlotinib (Tarceva) gefitinib (Iressa) panitumumab (Vectibix)
Inhibit EGFR-TK and binds HER-2.	lapatinib (Tykerb)
Multi-Tyrosine Kinase Inhibitors	
Inhibit multiple TKs.	axitinib (Inlyta) cabozantinib (Cometriq) pazopanib (Votrient) regorafenib (Stivarga) sorafenib (Nexavar) sunitinib (Sutent) vandetanib (Caprelsa)
mTOR Kinase Inhibitors	
Inhibit a specific protein known as the mechanistic target of rapamycin (mTOR).	everolimus (Afinitor) temsirolimus (Torisel)

TABLE 15.13 Drug Therapy—cont'd

Select Immunotherapies and Targeted Therapies

Mechanism of Action	Examples
Programmed Death Receptor (PD)-1 Blockers	
Block PD-1, a protein on T cells that normally helps keep these cells from attacking other cells. This boosts immune response against cancer cells.	nivolumab (Opdivo) pembrolizumab (Keytruda)
Proteasome Inhibitors	
Inhibit proteasome activity, which functions to regulate cell growth.	bortezomib (Velcade) carfilzomib (Kyprolis)
Vaccines	
Live attenuated strain of *Mycobacterium bovis* induces immune response. Used intravesically to treat bladder cancer (see Chapter 45).	BCG vaccine
Vaccine against prostate cancer that stimulates the immune system against the cancer (see Chapter 54).	sipuleucel-T (Provenge)

FIG. 15.16 Sites of action of targeted therapy. Examples of targeted therapy drugs that work at the specific site of action are shown in colored, italicized font. *EGFR*, Epidermal growth factor receptor; *HER-2*, human epidermal growth factor receptor-2; *VEGF*, vascular endothelial growth factor.

❖ NURSING MANAGEMENT: IMMUNOTHERAPY AND TARGETED THERAPY

Some problems experienced by the patient receiving immunotherapy and targeted therapy are different from those seen with more traditional forms of cancer treatment. These effects occur more acutely and are dose limited (e.g., effects resolve when therapy is over). Patients may be hesitant to inform the HCP of intolerable side effects. Some may be afraid to discuss side effects because they may think that the drug will be stopped. Or, they decide to stop the drug because of side effects. Assess and evaluate the patient's side effects and tolerance. Appropriate proactive nursing care can prevent these problems because you are able to intervene.

Capillary leak syndrome and pulmonary edema are problems that require critical care nursing. Bone marrow depression is generally more transient and less severe than that seen with chemotherapy. Fatigue associated with immunotherapy and targeted therapy can be so severe that it is a dose-limiting toxicity. When these agents are combined with chemotherapy, the spectrum of therapy-related effects expands.

Nursing interventions for flu-like syndrome include giving acetaminophen before treatment and every 4 hours after treatment. IV meperidine (Demerol) has been used to control the severe chills or rigors associated with some agents. Other nursing measures include monitoring vital signs and temperature, planning for periods of rest for the patient, assisting with activities of daily living (ADLs), and monitoring for adequate oral intake.

HORMONE THERAPY

Hormones are substances that are made in endocrine glands and function as chemical messengers in the body. The hormones estrogen and progesterone can enhance the growth of some breast cancers. Androgen (testosterone) can enhance the growth of some prostate cancers. When given as a cancer treatment, drugs (hormone therapy) can block the effects of the hormone and stop the growth of cancer cells (Table 15.14).

Corticosteroids are used in combination with many drug regimens for cancer. They are antiinflammatory agents that reduce swelling and inflammation, which may be contributing to cancer pain. They may be used with other drugs, such as ondansetron and aprepitant, to control and prevent nausea and vomiting caused by chemotherapy.

In addition to drug manipulation of hormones, surgical interventions (oophorectomy, castration) can be used to remove the effects of the hormone on cancer growth.

HEMATOPOIETIC GROWTH FACTORS

Hematopoietic growth factors are used to support patients through their cancer treatment (Table 15.15). Colony-stimulating factors (CSFs) are a family of glycoproteins made by various cells. CSFs stimulate production, maturation, regulation, and activation of cells of the hematologic system. The name of the CSF is based on the specific cell line it affects.

Erythropoiesis-stimulating agents (ESAs) should be used only when treating anemia specifically caused by chemotherapy. ESA use is avoided in patients receiving chemotherapy with the intent to cure the disease. Their use has raised safety concerns. They can cause potential harm (thromboembolic events, shorter survival) and increase the risk for death and serious cardiovascular events when given to achieve a target hemoglobin of greater than 12 g/dL. Thus the lowest dose should be used that will gradually increase hemoglobin to the lowest level sufficient to avoid the need for blood transfusion. Monitor the hemoglobin level regularly.

TABLE 15.14 Drug Therapy

Hormone Therapy

Androgen Receptor Blockers
Selectively attach to androgen receptors, blocking androgen from binding. Inhibits tumor growth.

flutamide, bicalutamide (Casodex), enzalutamide (Xtandi)

Aromatase Inhibitors
Inhibit aromatase, thus preventing the production of estrogen.

anastrozole (Arimidex), exemestane (Aromasin), letrozole (Femara)

Corticosteroids
Disrupt the cell membrane and inhibit synthesis of protein. Decrease circulating lymphocytes, inhibit mitosis, depress immune system, increase sense of well-being.

cortisone, dexamethasone, hydrocortisone, methylprednisolone, prednisone

Estrogens
Interfere with the effect of testosterone.

estradiol, estramustine (Emcyt), estrogen (Menest)

Estrogen Receptor Blockers
Selectively attach to estrogen receptors, blocking estrogen from binding. Inhibits tumor growth.

fulvestrant (Faslodex), tamoxifen, toremifene (Fareston)

Estrogen Receptor Modulator
Has both estrogen-agonistic effects on bone and estrogen-antagonistic effects on breast tissue.

raloxifene (Evista)

TABLE 15.15 Drug Therapy

Hematopoietic Growth Factors Used in Cancer Treatment

Growth Factor	Drug Name	Indications	Side Effects
Erythropoietin	epoetin alfa (Epogen, Procrit)	Anemia of chronic cancer	Hypertension, thrombosis, headache
	darbepoetin alfa (Aranesp)	Anemia related to chemotherapy	Hypertension, thrombosis, headache
Granulocyte colony-stimulating factor (G-CSF)	filgrastim (Neupogen) filgrastim-sndz (Zarxio) pegfilgrastim (Neulasta) tbo-filgrastim (Granix)	Chemotherapy-induced neutropenia	Bone pain, nausea, vomiting
Granulocyte-macrophage colony-stimulating factor (GM-CSF)	sargramostim (Leukine)	Myeloid cell recovery after bone marrow transplantation	Nausea, vomiting, diarrhea, fever, chills, myalgia, headache, fatigue
Interleukin-11 (platelet growth factor)	oprelvekin (Neumega)	Thrombocytopenia related to chemotherapy	Fluid retention, peripheral edema, dyspnea, tachycardia, nausea, mouth sores

HEMATOPOIETIC STEM CELL TRANSPLANTATION

Hematopoietic stem cell transplantation (HSCT) and **peripheral stem cell transplantation (PSCT)** are effective, lifesaving procedures for the treatment of several malignant and nonmalignant diseases (Table 15.16). Both allow for the safe use of very high doses of chemotherapy agents and/or radiation therapy in patients whose tumors have developed resistance (refractory) or did not respond to standard doses of chemotherapy and radiation. Although these procedures are lifesaving, patients may have long-term or delayed complications that can affect their quality of life.

This therapeutic approach was referred to as bone marrow transplant because the bone marrow was the original source of stem cells when the procedure was first developed. However, advances in harvesting and cryopreservation technologies have opened new pathways to the collection of stem cells from the peripheral blood.[20] Consequently, the terminology has changed. Overall cure rates are steadily increasing. Even when cure is not achieved, transplantation can result in a period of remission.

The approach in HSCT is to eradicate diseased tumor cells and/or clear the bone marrow of its components to make way for engraftment of the transplanted, healthy stem cells. This is done by giving higher than usual dosages of chemotherapy with or without radiation therapy. Life-threatening consequences

TABLE 15.16 Indications for Hematopoietic Stem Cell Transplantation

Malignant Diseases
- Acute and chronic lymphocytic leukemia
- Acute and chronic myelogenous leukemia
- Hodgkin's lymphoma
- Multiple myeloma
- Myelodysplastic syndrome
- Non-Hodgkin's lymphoma

Nonmalignant Diseases
- Aplastic anemia
- Chronic granulomatous disease
- Fanconi's anemia
- Hematologic diseases
- Immunodeficiency diseases
- Severe combined immunodeficiency disease (SCID)
- Sickle cell disease (severe)
- Thalassemia
- Wiskott-Aldrich syndrome

associated with pancytopenia and other adverse effects can result from this procedure. After chemotherapy and radiation therapy are over, healthy stem cells are infused. These healthy stem cells "rescue" the damaged bone marrow through subsequent proliferation and differentiation of the donated stem cells in the recipient.

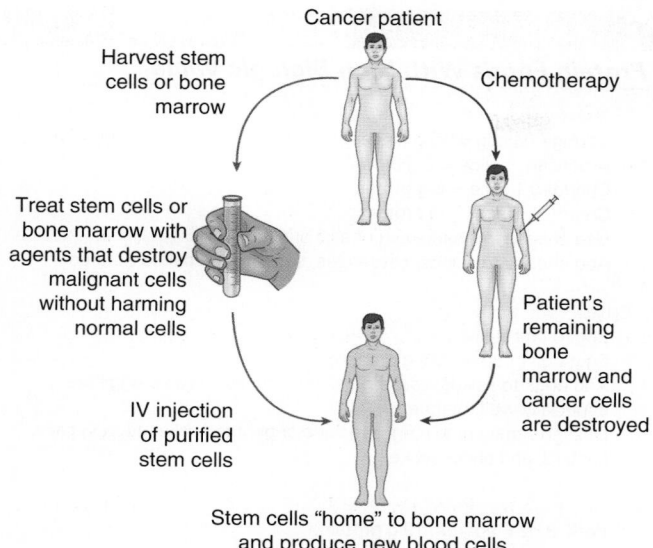

FIG. 15.17 Autologous stem cell transplant.

HSCT is an intensive procedure with many risks. Some patients die from treatment-related complications or from recurrence of the original disease. Because it is a highly toxic therapy, the patient must weigh the significant risks for treatment-related death or treatment failure (relapse) against the hope of cure.

Types of Hematopoietic Stem Cell Transplants

HSCTs are categorized as allogeneic, syngeneic, or autologous. The sources of stem cells include the bone marrow, peripheral circulating blood, and umbilical cord blood. In *allogeneic transplantation*, stem cells are acquired from a donor (graft) who, through human leukocyte antigen (HLA) tissue typing, has been determined to be HLA matched to the recipient (host). HLA typing involves testing WBCs to identify genetically inherited antigens common to both donor and recipient that are important in compatibility of transplanted tissue. (HLA tissue typing is discussed in Chapter 13.) The donor is often a family member. It may be an unrelated donor found through a national or international bone marrow registry (e.g., National Marrow Donor Program). These are known as matched unrelated donor (MUD) transplants. Increased risks and toxicities may be associated with a MUD. Common indications for allogeneic transplant are certain leukemias, multiple myeloma, and lymphoma.

Syngeneic transplantation is a type of allogeneic transplant that involves obtaining stem cells from one identical twin and infusing them into the other. Identical twins have identical HLA types and are a perfect match

In *autologous transplantation*, patients receive their own stem cells back after *myeloablative* (destroying bone marrow) chemotherapy (Fig. 15.17). The aim of this approach is purely "rescue." It allows patients to receive intensive chemotherapy and/or radiation by supporting them with their previously harvested stem cells until their marrow generates blood cells again on its own. Restoration usually takes about 4 to 6 weeks.

The newer, nonmyeloablative or reduced intensity transplant uses lower doses of radiation or chemotherapy that result in less toxicity and myelosuppression. HSCT continues to be investigated in managing some solid tumors resistant to treatment.

Procedures

Harvest Procedures. Hematopoietic stem cells are *harvested* from a donor (for allogeneic transplantation) or from the recipient (for autologous transplantation) via 2 methods. The procedure used for harvesting stem cells from bone marrow is done in the operating room using general or spinal anesthesia. Multiple bone marrow aspirations (usually from the iliac crest, but sometimes from the sternum) are carried out to obtain stem cells. The harvested marrow is processed to strain out bone fragments. The entire bone marrow harvest procedure takes about 1 to 2 hours. The patient can be discharged after recovery. Postharvest, the donor may have pain at the collection site that lasts up to 7 days. It can be treated with mild analgesics. The donor's body will replenish the removed bone marrow in a few weeks.

In the other procedure, peripheral stem cell transplants are obtained from the peripheral blood in an outpatient procedure. It is done using cell separator equipment that automatically separates the stem cells from the blood circulating through the machine and returns the remaining blood components to the donor. The process averages about 2 to 4 hours. Sometimes it takes longer depending on donor factors and the quality of the venous access. Often it takes more than one procedure to obtain enough stem cells. Because the blood has fewer stem cells than the bone marrow, "mobilization" of stem cells from the bone marrow into the peripheral blood can be achieved with chemotherapy and/or hematopoietic growth factors.

To increase stem cell production for collection, common growth factors that are used are granulocyte-macrophage colony-stimulating factor (GM-CSF) and granulocyte colony-stimulating factor (G-CSF) (see Table 15.15). When patients are given growth factors for mobilization, stem cells are harvested 4 or 5 days after growth factor injections.

After collection, the marrow or peripheral stem cells are used immediately or bagged with preservative for cryopreservation and storage until they are needed. Since they come from the patient, autologous stem cells are sometimes treated (purged) to remove undetected cancer cells. Many different pharmacologic, immunologic, physical, and chemical agents are used for this purpose.

Umbilical cord blood is rich in hematopoietic stem cells. Successful allogeneic transplants have been done using this source. Cord blood can be HLA-typed and cryopreserved. A disadvantage of cord blood is the possibility of insufficient numbers of stem cells to allow transplant to adults. Considerable research is currently ongoing to define the optimal use of this technology.

Preparative Regimens and Stem Cell Infusions. Patients receive myeloablative dosages of chemotherapy with or without adjunctive radiation to treat the underlying disease. Total-body irradiation (TBI) can be used for immunosuppression or to treat the disease. These preparative therapies are known as the *conditioning regimen.*

Stem cell infusions are given IV. They can be injected via the slow bolus method or infused much like a blood transfusion (using tubing without a filter). The infused stem cells reconstitute the bone marrow elements, "rescuing" the recipient's hematopoietic system. It usually takes 2 to 4 weeks for the transplanted marrow to start making hematopoietic blood cells. During this period the patient has pancytopenia. The patient must be protected from exposure to infectious agents and supported with electrolyte supplements, nutrition, and blood component transfusions (as needed) to maintain adequate levels of circulating RBCs and platelets.

Complications. Bacterial, viral, and fungal infections are common after HSCT. Prophylactic therapies are used to reduce their incidence. A potentially serious complication of allogeneic transplant is graft-versus-host disease. This occurs when the T cells from the donated marrow (graft) recognize the recipient (host) as foreign and begin to attack certain organs, such as the skin, liver, and GI tract. (Graft-versus-host disease is discussed in Chapter 13.)

The occurrence and severity of posttransplant complications depend on the drugs used (some are more toxic than others) and the stem cell source. Because stem cells in the peripheral blood are more mature than those harvested from the marrow, the hematologic recovery period in PSCT is shorter, and fewer, less severe complications are seen.

GENE THERAPY

Gene therapy is an experimental therapy that involves introducing genetic material into a person's cells to fight disease. At this time, the use of gene therapy is investigational. (Gene therapy is discussed in Chapter 12.)

COMPLICATIONS OF CANCER

The patient may develop complications related to the continual growth of the cancer into normal tissue or to the side effects of treatment.

NUTRITIONAL PROBLEMS

Malnutrition

The patient with cancer may have protein and calorie malnutrition characterized by fat and muscle depletion. The assessment of malnutrition is discussed in Chapter 39.

Soft, nonirritating high-protein and high-calorie foods should be eaten throughout the day. Foods suggested for increasing the protein intake are shown in Table 15.17. High-calorie foods that provide energy and minimize weight loss are shown in Table 15.18. Foods in a high-calorie, high-protein diet are outlined in Table 39.10.

Teach the patient to avoid extremes of temperature, tobacco, alcohol, spicy or rough foods, and other irritants. Encourage nutritional supplements (e.g., Ensure) as an adjunct to meals and fluid intake. Weigh the patient at least twice each week to monitor for weight loss.

Suggest a referral for nutritional counseling to the patient or HCP as soon as a 5% weight loss is noted or if the patient has the potential for protein and calorie malnutrition. Monitor albumin and prealbumin levels. Once a 10-lb (4.5-kg) weight loss occurs, it may be hard to maintain the patient's nutritional status.

Teach the patient to use nutritional supplements in place of milk when cooking or baking. Foods to which nutritional supplements can be easily added include scrambled eggs, pudding, custard, mashed potatoes, cereal, and cream sauces. Packages of instant breakfast can be used as indicated or sprinkled on cereals, desserts, and casseroles.

Caregivers are an integral part of the health care team. As symptom severity increases, the caregiver's role in helping the patient eat becomes increasingly critical.

If the malnutrition cannot be treated with dietary intake, it may be necessary to use enteral or parenteral nutrition. (Enteral and parenteral nutrition are discussed in Chapter 39.)

TABLE 15.17 Nutritional Therapy

Protein Foods With High Biologic Value

Cheese
- Cottage: ½ cup = 15 g protein.
- American: 1 slice = 3 g protein.
- Cheddar: 1 slice = 6 g protein.
- Cream: 1 Tbsp = 1 g protein.
- Use cheese in a sandwich or as a snack.
- Add cheese to salads, casseroles, sauces, and baked potatoes.

Eggs
- Egg: 6 g protein.
- Eggnog: 1 cup = 15.5 g protein.
- Add eggs to salads, casseroles, and sauces. Deviled eggs are especially well tolerated.
- Desserts that contain eggs include angel food cake, sponge cake, custard, and cheesecake.

Meat, Poultry, Fish
- Pork: 3 oz = approx. 19 g protein.
- Chicken: ½ breast = approx. 26 g protein.
- Fish: 3 oz = approx. 30 g protein.
- Tuna fish: 6½ oz = approx. 44.5 g protein.
- Add meat, poultry, and fish to salads, casseroles, and sandwiches.
- Add strained and junior baby meats to soups and casseroles.

Milk
- Whole milk: 1 cup = 9 g protein.
- Double-strength milk (1 quart of whole milk plus 1 cup of dried skim milk blended and chilled): 1 cup = 14 g protein.
- Milk shake (1 cup of ice cream plus 1 cup of milk): 15 g protein, 415 cal.
- Use evaporated milk, double-strength milk, or half-and-half to make casseroles, hot cereals, sauces, gravies, puddings, milk shakes, and soups.
- Yogurt (regular and frozen): Select brands with high protein content: 1 cup = 10 g protein

---

TABLE 15.18 Nutritional Therapy

High-Calorie Foods

Mayonnaise	1 Tbsp	=	101 cal
Butter or margarine	1 tsp	=	35 cal
Sour cream	1 Tbsp	=	72 cal
Peanut butter	1 Tbsp	=	94 cal
Whipped cream	1 Tbsp	=	53 cal
Corn oil	1 Tbsp	=	119 cal
Jelly	1 Tbsp	=	49 cal
Ice cream	1 cup	=	256 cal
Honey	1 Tbsp	=	64 cal

Altered Taste Sensation (Dysgeusia)

Cancer cells may release substances that stimulate the bitter taste buds. The patient may have changes in the sweet, sour, and salty taste sensations. Meat may taste bitter or bland. We do not know the cause of these taste changes.

Teach patients with altered taste problems to avoid foods that they dislike. Often, the patient may feel compelled to eat certain foods that are believed to be beneficial. Tell the patient to try different ways to mask the taste changes. Some find stronger seasonings and spices effective. Others find it better to avoid strong flavors and eat more bland foods. Avoiding strong smells, drinking more water with food, oral care before eating, eating smaller amounts more often, and using plastic utensils may help.[21]

Cancer Cachexia

Cancer cachexia (wasting syndrome) is a complex, multifactorial syndrome characterized by anorexia and/or unintended loss of weight and appetite. It is accompanied by generalized tissue wasting, skeletal muscle atrophy, immune dysfunction, and metabolic problems. The weight loss cannot be reversed nutritionally. Patients with upper GI and pancreatic cancers are prone to cachexia. As cancer progresses, cachexia can affect many cancer patients. It is associated with increased morbidity.[22]

The best management of cancer cachexia is to effectively treat the cancer. Unfortunately, this is not a realistic goal for patients with advanced cancer. A second option is to increase nutritional intake, but this does not completely reverse the wasting associated with cachexia. A third option is to use megestrol acetate (Megace). It is a synthetic form of the hormone progesterone, which stimulates appetite in patients with cachexia.

INFECTION

Infection is a leading cause of death in the patient with cancer. The usual sites of infection include the lungs, GU system, mouth, rectum, peritoneal cavity, and blood (septicemia). Infection occurs because of the ulceration and necrosis caused by the tumor, the tumor compressing vital organs, and neutropenia from the cancer or cancer treatment.

Teach patients at risk for neutropenia to call their HCP if they have a temperature of 100.4° F (38° C) or greater. Assessment often includes signs and symptoms of fever, determination of possible cause (e.g., sinuses, mucous membranes, respiratory, GI, urinary, sites of any tubes or lines), and CBC.

Many patients are neutropenic when an infection develops. In these persons, infection may cause significant morbidity. It may be rapidly fatal if not treated promptly. The classic manifestations of infection are often subtle or absent in a patient with neutropenia and a depressed immune system. (Neutropenia was discussed earlier in this chapter on p. 248. It is also discussed in Chapter 30.)

ONCOLOGIC EMERGENCIES

Oncologic emergencies are life-threatening emergencies that can occur because of cancer or cancer treatment. These emergencies can be obstructive, metabolic, or infiltrative (Table 15.19).

Obstructive Emergencies

Obstructive emergencies are mainly caused by tumor obstruction of an organ or blood vessel. They include superior vena cava syndrome (Fig. 15.18), spinal cord compression syndrome, third space syndrome, and intestinal obstruction.

Metabolic Emergencies

Metabolic emergencies are caused by the production of ectopic hormones directly from the tumor or from metabolic problems caused by the cancer or cancer treatment. Ectopic hormones arise from tissues that do not normally make these hormones. Cancer cells return to a more embryonic form, thus allowing the cells' stored potential to become evident.

Metabolic emergencies include syndrome of inappropriate antidiuretic hormone secretion (Chapter 49), hypercalcemia (Chapter 16), tumor lysis syndrome, septic shock (Chapter 66), and disseminated intravascular coagulation (Chapter 30).

Infiltrative Emergencies

Infiltrative emergencies occur when cancer infiltrates major organs or from cancer treatment. The most common infiltrative emergencies are cardiac tamponade and carotid artery rupture.

CANCER PAIN

Moderate to severe pain occurs in around 50% of patients who are receiving active treatment for their cancer and in 80% to 90% of patients with advanced cancer.[23] What is concerning is that these statistics have not changed in the past 30 years. Undertreatment of cancer pain is common. It causes needless suffering, decreases quality of life, and increases the burden on caregivers.

Pain Assessment

Inadequate pain assessment is the single greatest barrier to effective pain management. Data, such as vital signs and patient behaviors, are not reliable indicators of pain, especially long-standing, chronic pain. It is important to know if pain is persistent or episodic, positional, or breakthrough pain. It is essential that a comprehensive pain assessment include a detailed history to elicit the characteristics of pain. This includes the quality, location, intensity, duration, and precipitating and alleviating factors. Distinguishing between types of pain (e.g., visceral, bone, neuropathic) is important in developing an effective pain management plan.

Assess pain on an ongoing basis to determine the effectiveness of the treatment plan. Obtain data and document at regular intervals the location and intensity of the pain, what it feels like, and how it is relieved. Assess change in pain (e.g., a change in the intensity, character, worsening, or location of pain) to determine the cause (e.g., progression of disease).

Always believe the patient's report and accept it as the primary source of assessment data. Table 15.20 presents assessment questions that may facilitate data collection. Have patients keep a pain management diary.[23]

Pain Management

Pain management for the cancer patient must address both persistent and breakthrough components of pain if they are present. Adjuvant therapies need to be delivered specific to the type or nature of the pain.

Drug therapy, including NSAIDs (e.g., ibuprofen), opioids (e.g., morphine), and adjuvant pain medications, should be used and selected based on the character and/or cause of the pain. Opioids normally are prescribed for the treatment of moderate to severe cancer pain. Drug dosages are adjusted to control pain with the fewest side effects. Analgesic medications (e.g., morphine, fentanyl) should be given on a regular schedule (around the clock) with more doses available as needed for breakthrough pain. In general, oral administration is preferred. Other routes (e.g., transdermal, transmucosal) are options.

Treatment plans should be developed that balance analgesia and side effects to maintain optimal functional status. It is important for you to pay attention to common side effects of pain medications (e.g., constipation) to ensure the patient's well-being and adherence with the pain management program. NSAIDs often serve as helpful adjuncts to opioid therapy, especially for bone pain. Antidepressant and antiseizure drugs may be helpful in managing neuropathic pain, which is often resistant to opioids.

TABLE 15.19 Oncologic Emergencies

Description	Manifestations	Management
Obstructive Emergencies		
Spinal Cord Compression		
• Neurologic emergency caused by cancer in epidural space of spinal cord. • Common causes are breast, lung, prostate, GI, renal cancers, melanoma. • Lymphomas can invade epidural space.	• Intense, localized, and persistent back pain with vertebral tenderness. • Motor weakness, sensory paresthesia and loss. • Autonomic dysfunction (e.g., change in bowel or bladder function).	• Radiation therapy, corticosteroids. • Surgical decompressive laminectomy. • Activity limitations and pain management.
Superior Vena Cava Syndrome (SVCS)		
• Results from obstruction of superior vena cava by tumor or thrombosis. • Common causes are lung cancer, non-Hodgkin's lymphoma, metastatic breast cancer. • Presence of central venous catheter and previous mediastinal radiation increase risk.	• Facial edema, periorbital edema. • Distention of veins of head, neck, and chest (Fig. 15.18). • Headache, seizures. • Mediastinal mass on chest x-ray.	• Considered a serious medical problem. • Radiation therapy to site of obstruction. • Chemotherapy for tumors more sensitive to this therapy.
Third Space Syndrome		
• Shifting of fluid from vascular space to interstitial space. • Occurs due to extensive surgical procedures, immunotherapy, septic shock.	• Signs of hypovolemia: hypotension, tachycardia, low central venous pressure, decreased urine output.	• Fluid, electrolyte, plasma protein replacement. • During recovery hypervolemia can occur, causing hypertension, increased central venous pressure, weight gain, shortness of breath.
Metabolic Emergencies		
Hypercalcemia		
• Occurs in metastatic disease of bone or multiple myeloma, or when a parathyroid hormone–like substance is secreted by cancer cells. • Immobility and dehydration can contribute to or worsen hypercalcemia.	• Serum calcium higher than 12 mg/dL (3 mmol/L) often produces symptoms. • Apathy, depression, fatigue, muscle weakness, ECG changes, polyuria and nocturia, anorexia, nausea, vomiting. • High calcium elevations can be life threatening. • Chronic hypercalcemia can result in nephrocalcinosis and irreversible renal failure.	• Treat primary disease. • Hydration (3 L/day) and bisphosphonate therapy. • Diuretics (especially loop diuretics) used to prevent heart failure or edema. • Infusion of bisphosphonate zoledronate (Zometa) or pamidronate (Aredia).
Syndrome of Inappropriate Antidiuretic Hormone (SIADH)		
• Tumor cells can produce abnormal or sustained production of antidiuretic hormone (ADH). • Many chemotherapy agents may contribute to ectopic ADH production or potentiate ADH effects.	• Water retention and hyponatremia (hypotonic hyponatremia) (see Chapter 49). • Weight gain without edema, weakness, anorexia, nausea, vomiting, personality changes, seizures, oliguria, decrease in reflexes, coma.	• Treat underlying cancer. • Take measures to correct sodium-water imbalance, including fluid restriction, oral salt tablets or isotonic (0.9%) saline administration, and IV 3% sodium chloride solution (severe cases). • Furosemide (Lasix) used in early phases. • Monitor sodium level. Correcting SIADH quickly may cause seizures or death.
Tumor Lysis Syndrome (TLS)		
• Metabolic complication characterized by rapid release of intracellular components in response to chemotherapy and radiation therapy (less often). • Massive cell destruction releases intracellular components (potassium, phosphate, DNA, RNA) that are metabolized to uric acid by liver.	• *Hallmark signs*: hyperuricemia, hyperphosphatemia, hyperkalemia, hypocalcemia. • Weakness, muscle cramps, diarrhea, nausea, vomiting. • Occurs within 24–48 hr after starting chemotherapy. • May last 5–7 days. • Metabolic abnormalities and concentrated uric acid (which crystallizes in distal tubules of kidneys) can lead to acute kidney injury.	• Identify patients at risk. • Increase urine production using hydration therapy. • Decrease uric acid concentrations using allopurinol. • Use IV sodium bicarbonate to counter effects of acidic properties that are released.
Infiltrative Emergencies		
Cardiac Tamponade		
• Fluid accumulation in pericardium. • Caused by constriction of pericardium by tumor or pericarditis from radiation therapy to the chest.	• Heavy feeling over chest, shortness of breath, tachycardia, cough, dysphagia, hiccups, hoarseness. • Nausea, vomiting, excessive perspiration. • Decreased level of consciousness, distant or muted heart sounds. • Extreme anxiety.	• Decrease fluid around heart using (1) surgery to create a pericardial window or an (2) indwelling pericardial catheter. • Administer O_2 therapy, IV hydration, and vasopressor therapy.
Carotid Artery Rupture		
• Invasion of arterial wall by tumor or erosion following surgery or radiation therapy. • Occurs most often in patients with head and neck cancer.	• Bleeding: ranges from minor oozing to spurting of blood in the case of a "blowout" of artery.	• Give IV fluids and blood products. • Surgery: ligation of carotid artery above and below rupture site and reduction of local tumor.

FIG. 15.18 Superior vena caval obstruction in bronchial cancer. Note the swelling of the face and neck and the development of collateral circulation in the veins. (From Forbes CD, Jackson WF: *Colour atlas and text of clinical medicine*, ed 3, London, 2003, Mosby.)

TABLE 15.20 Pain Assessment in Cancer Patients

Characteristic	Questions to Ask
Location	• Where is the pain? • Is the pain in more than one place? Is the pain in a new location? • Does location of pain correlate with known diagnosis?
Intensity	• How bad is the pain? • Rate the pain on a scale of 0 to 10. (See Chapter 8 for rating scales.)
Quality	• What does the pain feel like—sharp, dull, burning, shooting, aching, or other? (See Chapter 8 for descriptors.)
Pattern	• Has the pain changed? • Is the pain getting better, worse, or unchanged? • What makes the pain better or worse?
Relief measures	• What do you do to control your pain? • Do you use medications? • Do the relief measures help much? How much?

TABLE 15.21 Factors Affecting How Patients Cope With Cancer

Factor	Description
Ability to cope with stressful events in the past	How patients coped with previous stressful events (e.g., loss of job, major disappointment, significant traumatic event) affects how they cope with diagnosis of cancer.
Ability to express feelings and concerns	Patients who express feelings and needs and ask for help cope better than those who internalize feelings and needs.
Age at the time of diagnosis	Age determines coping strategies to a great degree. For example, a young mother with cancer may have different concerns than a 70-yr-old woman with cancer.
Attitude associated with the cancer	Patients who feel in control and have a positive attitude about cancer and cancer treatment cope better with the diagnosis and treatment of cancer than those who feel hopeless, helpless, and out of control.
Availability of significant others	Patients who have effective support systems cope better than those who do not.
Disruption of body image	Disruption of the body image (e.g., radical neck dissection, alopecia, mastectomy) may intensify the psychologic impact of cancer.
Extent of disease	Cure or control of the disease process is usually easier to cope with than the reality of terminal illness.
Past experience with cancer	Negative experiences with cancer (personal or in others) influence perceptions about the current situation.
Symptoms	Symptoms such as fatigue, nausea, diarrhea, and pain may intensify the psychologic impact of cancer.

Radioactive drugs (e.g., samarium-153) may help patients with diffuse bone pain, especially if no further chemotherapy is planned. Patients may have an initial pain *flare* after administration. Nerve blocks or epidural or intrathecal analgesia may be used to treat patients with unrelieved pain or to minimize the use of opioids.

Discuss the goals of analgesic therapy with patients, especially those needing large or chronic doses of opioids. You need to assess the patient for risk factors for opioid misuse. Patient teaching should clarify myths and misconceptions and reassure patients and caregivers that cancer pain can be effectively relieved. Fear of addiction is not warranted. However, it must be addressed as part of patient teaching. It is a significant barrier for patients and nurses in appropriate pain management. Stress that addiction and tolerance are not problems associated with effective cancer pain management. Nondrug interventions, including relaxation therapy and imagery, can be effectively used to manage pain (see Chapter 6). Other strategies to relieve pain are discussed in Chapter 8.

COPING WITH CANCER AND TREATMENT

You have a key role in assisting patients in coping with the psychosocial issues associated with cancer and cancer treatment. The patient may have a variety of concerns, including fears of dependency, loss of control, family and relationship stress, financial burden, and fear of death. Anxiety and fear may occur throughout the cancer continuum, including at diagnosis, during or after treatment, and in association with long-term follow-up.

Repetitive office visits or hospitalizations, continuing medications, and frequent laboratory testing force the patient to confront the cancer on a daily basis. Treatment-related uncertainties and fears are often most evident at the beginning of therapy. However, anxiety and fear may be present throughout treatment and when therapy is completed (e.g., fear of recurrence, less available support).

Adaptation and coping with a cancer diagnosis may be influenced by a variety of patient factors. These include demographics, prior coping skills and strategies, social support, and religious and spiritual beliefs (Table 15.21). You are in a key position to assess the patient's and caregiver's responses and support positive coping strategies. To promote effective coping and to support them during the various stages of cancer, you should:
- Be available and continue to be available, especially during difficult times.
- Exhibit a caring attitude.
- Listen actively to fears and concerns.
- Help provide relief from distressing symptoms.
- Provide accurate, essential information about cancer and cancer care.

- Help establish realistic expectations about what the patient will experience.
- Maintain a relationship based on trust and confidence. Be open, honest, and caring in the approach.
- Use touch to show caring. A squeeze of the hand or a hug may at times be more effective than words.
- Help the patient in setting realistic, reachable short-term and long-term goals.
- Help the patient maintain usual lifestyle patterns.
- Maintain hope, which is the key to effective cancer care.

Hope varies, depending on the patient's status—hope that the symptoms are not serious, hope that the treatment is curative, hope for independence, hope for relief of pain, hope for a longer life, hope to achieve meaningful goals, or hope for a peaceful death. Hope provides control over what is occurring and is the basis of a positive attitude toward cancer and cancer care.

Tell patients that they will be followed, and reassure them that support is ongoing. Give information and support to help minimize the negative impact of cancer treatment on quality of life. Patient teaching and symptom management help patients to self-manage their illness (e.g., adjusting treatment schedules to allow patients to work when possible, making referrals to support groups). Work with the oncology nurse navigators, who serve as the liaison between the patient and members of the interprofessional care team.

Arrange for patients to meet with people who have successfully completed therapy. This can increase their hopefulness and confidence. Make regular supportive telephone contacts between office visits. Assist with planning for transportation, nutrition, and emotional support.

Do not forget the caregivers. They need education and support throughout the trajectory of diagnosis, treatment, and follow-up. Patients and caregivers may benefit from a variety of psychosocial interventions. These include supportive listening, stress management techniques, individual or group counseling, and cognitive-behavioral therapy. Assess the psychosocial concerns and emotional responses of patients, caregivers, and families so you can connect them with appropriate supportive care resources. Use the available resources in the community, such as the ACS, Cancer Lifeline, churches, and other community resources.

Gerontologic Considerations: Cancer

Cancer is usually a disease of aging, with 78% of cancers occurring in people 55 years or older.[1] Cancer mortality rates are exceedingly high in older adults. Of all deaths due to cancer, 70% occur in those over age 65. This is especially important since the normal life span is increasing and the proportion of the population who are older than 65 years is increasing.

Manifestations of cancer in older adults may be mistakenly attributed to age-related changes and ignored by the person.[24] Older adults are especially at risk for complications of both cancer and cancer treatment. This is due to their decline in physiologic functioning, social and emotional resources, and cognitive function.

The older adult's functional status should be taken into consideration when developing a treatment plan. Age alone is not a good predictor of tolerance or response to treatment. Advances in cancer treatment are making cancer therapies beneficial to more older adults, including those with suboptimal health.

ETHICAL/LEGAL DILEMMAS
Medical Futility

Situation

D.M., a 65-yr-old Asian woman, has breast cancer with metastasis to the liver and bone. The family asks you why their mother is not receiving chemotherapy. They want to make sure that she will be resuscitated should her heart stop. They are aware of her diagnosis and that she only has a few months to live. In morning rounds, you were told that D.M. does not want any more treatment that would prolong her life.

Ethical/Legal Points for Consideration

- Although court decisions have varied, legally there is substantial consensus about the right to privacy (a constitutional right), right to informed consent and refusal of treatment, and rights about end-of-life decision making. The *Code of Ethics for Nurses* addresses the key components in the informed consent process that nurses must address.[1]
- A patient who is an adult and is competent (defined as capable of understanding and interpreting information, making choices, and communicating those choices) solely retains the right to make personal health care decisions.
- The Patient Self-Determination Act requires that the patient be asked on admission whether they have an advance directive. If available, it is placed in the medical record. If the patient does not have an advance directive, it must be documented.
- The National POLST Paradigm is an approach to end-of-life planning that emphasizes patients' wishes about the care they receive. The POLST Paradigm is an approach to end-of-life planning emphasizing the medical orders and includes coverage regardless of location (e.g., hospital, home, assisted living).[2]
- Often families have difficulty accepting the finality of a terminal diagnosis.
- Sometimes family members have conflicting interests (e.g., finances, property, inheritance rights) that influence their decision-making abilities.

Discussion Questions

1. How can you help D.M. communicate her wishes to her family?
2. How can you and the interprofessional team help the family in planning end-of-life care that incorporates their mother's wishes?
3. What are the cultural issues in D.M.'s case?

References

1. Code of Ethics for Nurses. Retrieved from. *www.nursingworld.org/practice-policy/nursing-excellence/ethics/code-of-ethics-for-nurses/*.
2. Physician Orders for Life Sustaining Treatment (POLST) Paradigm. Retrieved from. *www.polst.org*.

Assess the patient at the time of diagnosis to identify important issues that may affect decisions about treatment options. Issues to assess include projected life expectancy, estimate of morbidity from cancer, co-morbidities that would affect treatment, and patient decision-making capacity and wishes.

Some important questions to consider when an older adult is diagnosed with cancer include: Will the treatment provide more benefits than harm? Will they be able to tolerate the treatment safely? Is there a need to treat co-morbidities or nutritional or functional status before starting treatment? What are the patient's preferences and wishes?

CANCER SURVIVORSHIP

As the overall death rate from cancer decreases, the number of cancer survivors continues to increase. It is estimated that there are currently more than 14.5 million cancer survivors in the

TABLE 15.22 Patient Teaching

Cancer Survivors

You can help cancer survivors by doing the following:

1. Provide all cancer patients with a treatment summary and care plan outlining treatment exposures, risk for late effects, preventive care recommendations, and follow-up surveillance plan after completion of treatment.
   - Care plans should clearly identify all members of the interprofessional team and their responsibilities for follow-up care.
   - Include referrals to appropriate supportive care and community resources that would help the patient in recovery or ongoing care.
2. Coordinate care among the oncology team, primary HCP, and other specialists.
3. Teach HCPs about the needs of cancer survivors, including long-term effects of cancer and cancer treatments.
4. Teach cancer survivors to look for and report any ongoing symptoms resulting from treatment, including late effects of radiation therapy and chemotherapy.
5. Teach cancer survivors healthy behaviors:
   - *Prevention:* good nutrition, exercise, smoking avoidance, maintaining proper weight, cardiac risk reduction, bone health.
   - *Early detection:* routine health screenings (e.g., breast, colon), cholesterol, diabetes, osteoporosis screening as recommended.
6. Encourage cancer survivors to have regular follow-up examinations with their HCP.
7. Assess for psychologic, financial, health insurance, or vocational problems related to cancer. Assist patients in getting appropriate help if necessary.

TABLE 15.23 Resources for Cancer Survivors

Organization	Purpose
ACS Cancer Survivors Network	Provides survivorship information and resources and online forum for connecting with others affected by cancer. (*https://csn.cancer.org/*)
CancerCare	Provides a variety of free support services delivered by professional oncology social workers for patients and anyone else affected by cancer. (*www.cancer-care.org*)
Cancer.Net	American Society of Clinical Oncology (ASCO) patient support site that includes extensive information and resources for cancer survivors. (*www.cancer.net*)
National Cancer Institute Office of Cancer Survivorship	Supports research into the short- and long-term physical, social, emotional, and economic effects of cancer survivorship. Offers educational and support resources for cancer survivors, caregivers, and advocates. (*www.cancercontrol.cancer.gov/ocs/*)
National Coalition for Cancer Survivorship	Advocates for quality cancer care. Seeks to teach patients and advocates about issues that affect the quality of life of cancer survivors. (*www.canceradvocacy.org*)

United States. Some of these persons are cancer free. Others still have evidence of cancer and may be receiving treatment. The increase in survivorship is attributed to the aging and growth of the population and improvements in early detection and treatment. Survival statistics vary by the type and stage of cancer.[1,25]

The rapid increase in cancer survivors has been accompanied by a greater awareness of the long-term health and quality-of-life issues that a cancer diagnosis imposes. Cancer survivors have a variety of long-term and late effects after treatment. You need to be aware of the effects of the various treatments so that you can teach patients and their caregivers.

The impact of cancer and its treatment confers greater risk for non–cancer-related death and co-morbidities (e.g., heart disease, diabetes, metabolic syndrome, endocrine dysfunction, osteoporosis) among cancer survivors. Cancer survivors may continue to have symptoms or functional impairment related to treatment for years after treatment.

The impact of a cancer diagnosis can affect many aspects of a patient's life. Cancer survivors often report financial, vocational, marital, and spiritual concerns long after treatment is over. Psychosocial and emotional issues can play a profound role in a patient's life after cancer. Many find living in uncertainty challenging.

Some patients may wish to return to their normal lives as soon as possible. They may not go to scheduled follow-up appointments. Others become cancer advocates or active members of a cancer support group. Still others allow their lives to revolve around the cancer and may even resist giving up the illness role.

Tips to help cancer survivors are described in Table 15.22. Connecting cancer survivors to online support and resources is a strategy to enhance positive health outcomes (Table 15.23).

Culturally Competent Care: Cancer

Cancer incidence and death rates are disproportionately higher in blacks than in whites and other minority groups. Although overall racial disparities in cancer death rates have been declining, death rates continue to be higher among blacks than whites. Blacks are more likely to have later stage disease at the time of diagnosis than whites.[1]

PROMOTING HEALTH EQUITY

Cancer

- Cancer incidence and death rates for men are highest among blacks, followed by whites, Hispanics, and Asians/Pacific Islanders.
- Cancer incidence rates for women are highest among whites, followed by blacks, Hispanics, and Asians/Pacific Islanders.
- Cancer death rates for women are highest among blacks, followed by whites, Hispanics, and Asians/Pacific Islanders.

Differences in survival rates from cancer are attributed to a combination of factors. These include poverty, difficult access to and poorer quality of health care, more co-morbid conditions, and differences in tumor biology. Disparities in cancer care exist throughout the continuum from cancer prevention and screening to end-of-life care and survivorship. The disparity in prevention and screening results in cancer being in advanced stages at the time of diagnosis.[1,2]

Culturally competent care in oncology is needed to meet the needs of diverse groups. It involves awareness of personal background, how culture affects care delivery, and how to adapt to meet cultural needs. Nurses need to actively seek to understand cultural differences to meet the patient's needs. Culture is discussed in Chapter 2. Culturally competent care related to specific cancers is in the chapters in which the cancer is discussed.

BRIDGE TO NCLEX EXAMINATION

The number of the question corresponds to the same-numbered outcome at the beginning of the chapter.

1. Trends in the incidence and death rates of cancer include the fact that
   a. a higher percent of women than men have lung cancer.
   b. lung cancer is the most common type of cancer in men.
   c. blacks have a higher death rate from cancer than whites.
   d. breast cancer is the leading cause of cancer deaths in women.

2. What features of cancer cells distinguish them from normal cells *(select all that apply)*?
   a. Cells lack contact inhibition.
   b. Cells undergo rapid proliferation.
   c. Cells return to a previous undifferentiated state.
   d. Proliferation occurs when there is a need for more cells.
   e. New proteins characteristic of embryonic stage emerge on cell membrane.

3. A characteristic of the stage of progression in cancer development is
   a. oncogenic viral transformation of target cells.
   b. a reversible steady growth facilitated by carcinogens.
   c. a period of latency before clinical detection of cancer.
   d. proliferation of cancer cells despite host control mechanisms.

4. The primary protective role of the immune system related to malignant cells is
   a. surveillance for cells with tumor-associated antigens.
   b. binding with free antigens released by all cancer cells.
   c. producing blocking factors that immobilize cancer cells.
   d. reacting to a new set of antigenic determinants on cancer cells.

5. The nurse is caring for a 59-year-old woman who had surgery 1 day ago to remove an ovarian cancer mass. The patient is awaiting the pathology report. She is tearful and says that she is scared to die. The *most* effective nursing intervention at this point is to use this opportunity to
   a. motivate change in an unhealthy lifestyle.
   b. teach her about the 7 warning signs of cancer.
   c. discuss healthy stress relief and coping practices.
   d. let her communicate about the meaning of this experience.

6. The goals of cancer treatment are based on the principle that
   a. surgery is the single most effective treatment for cancer.
   b. initial treatment is always directed toward cure of the cancer.
   c. a combination of treatment modalities is effective for controlling many cancers.
   d. although cancer cure is rare, quality of life can be increased with treatment modalities.

7. The *most* effective method of administering a chemotherapy agent that is a vesicant is to
   a. give it orally.
   b. give it intraarterially.
   c. use an Ommaya reservoir.
   d. use a central venous access device.

8. The nurse explains to a patient undergoing brachytherapy of the cervix that she
   a. must undergo simulation to locate the treatment area.
   b. requires the use of radioactive precautions during nursing care.
   c. may have desquamation of the skin on the abdomen and upper legs.
   d. requires shielding of the ovaries during treatment to prevent ovarian damage.

9. A patient on chemotherapy and radiation for head and neck cancer has a WBC count of $1.9 \times 10^3/\mu L$, hemoglobin of 10.8 g/dL, and a platelet count of $99 \times 10^3/\mu L$. Based on the CBC results, what is the *most* serious clinical finding?
   a. Cough, rhinitis, and sore throat
   b. Fatigue, nausea, and skin redness at site of radiation
   c. Temperature of 101.9° F, fatigue, and shortness of breath
   d. Skin redness at site of radiation, headache, and constipation

10. To prevent fever and shivering during an infusion of rituximab (Rituxan), the nurse should premedicate the patient with
    a. aspirin.
    b. acetaminophen.
    c. sodium bicarbonate.
    d. meperidine (Demerol).

11. The nurse counsels the patient receiving radiation therapy or chemotherapy that
    a. effective birth control methods should be used for the rest of the patient's life.
    b. after successful treatment, patients can expect a return to their previous level of function.
    c. the cycle of fatigue-depression-fatigue that may occur during treatment may be reduced by restricting activity.
    d. nausea and vomiting can usually be managed with antiemetic drugs, diet modification, and other interventions.

12. A patient on chemotherapy for 10 weeks started at a weight of 121 lb. She now weighs 118 lb and has no sense of taste. Which nursing intervention would be a *priority*?
    a. Discuss with the provider the need for parenteral nutrition.
    b. Teach the patient to eat foods that are fatty, fried, or high in calories.
    c. Tell the patient to drink a nutritional supplement beverage three times a day.
    d. Have the patient try various spices and seasonings to enhance the flavor of food.

13. A 70-year-old male patient has multiple myeloma. His wife calls to report that he sleeps most of the day, is confused when awake, and reports nausea and constipation. Which complication of cancer is this *most* likely caused by?
    a. Hypercalcemia
    b. Tumor lysis syndrome
    c. Spinal cord compression
    d. Superior vena cava syndrome

14. A patient has recently been diagnosed with early stages of breast cancer. What is *most* appropriate for the nurse to focus on?
    a. Maintaining the patient's hope
    b. Preparing a will and advance directives
    c. Discussing replacement child care for the patient's children
    d. Discussing the patient's past experiences with her grandmother's cancer

1. c, 2. a, c, e, 3. d, 4. a, 5. d, 6. c, 7. d, 8. b, 9. c, 10. b, 11. d, 12. d, 13. a, 14. a

For rationales to these answers and even more NCLEX review questions, visit *http://evolve.elsevier.com/Lewis/medsurg*.

ⓔ EVOLVE WEBSITE/RESOURCES LIST

http://evolve.elsevier.com/Lewis/medsurg
Review Questions (Online Only)
Key Points
Answer Keys for Questions
- Rationales for Bridge to NCLEX Examination Questions
Conceptual Care Map Creator
Supporting Media
- Animations
  - Chemotherapy
  - Radiation Therapy
Audio Glossary
Content Updates

REFERENCES

1. American Cancer Society: Cancer facts & figures 2018. Retrieved from *www.cancer.org/research/cancer-facts-statistics/all-cancer-facts-figures/cancer-facts-figures-2018.html*.
*2. Siegel RL, Miller KD, Jemal A: Cancer statistics 2018, *CA Cancer J Clin* 68:7, 2018.
3. National Cancer Institute: Cancer trends progress report. Retrieved from *www.progressreport.cancer.gov*.
4. Centers for Disease Control and Prevention: Skin cancer. Retrieved from *www.cdc.gov/cancer/skin/*.
5. Kanabar AH, Sacher RA, Besa EC: Burkitt lymphoma and Burkitt-like lymphoma. Retrieved from *https://emedicine.medscape.com/article/1447602-overview*.
*6. American Cancer Society: Cancer screening guidelines. Retrieved from *www.cancer.org/healthy/find-cancer-early/cancer-screening-guidelines.html*.
7. American Society of Clinical Oncology: What is personalized cancer medicine? Retrieved from *www.cancer.net/navigating-cancer-care/how-cancer-treated/personalized-and-targeted-therapies/what-personalized-cancer-medicine*.
*8. Kamps R, Brandao RD, van den Bosch BJ, et al: Next-generation sequencing in oncology: genetic diagnosis, risk prediction and cancer classification, *Int J Mol Sci* 18:1, 2017.
9. Patel JN: Cancer pharmacogenomics, challenges in implementation and patient focused perspectives. Retrieved from *www.ncbi.nlm.nih.gov/pmc/articles/PMC4948716/*.
10. Polovich M, Olsen M, LeFebvre K: *Chemotherapy and biotherapy guidelines and recommendations for practice*, ed 4, Pittsburgh, 2014, Oncology Nursing Society.
11. National Institute for Occupational Safety and Health: Safe handling of chemotherapy agents. Retrieved from *www.cdc.gov/niosh/topics/antineoplastic*.
*12. Mhaskar R, Clark OA, Lyman G, et al: Colony-stimulating factors for chemotherapy-induced febrile neutropenia, *Cochrane Database Syst Rev* 10:CD003039, 2014. (Classic)
13. National Cancer Institute: Fatigue (PDQ^R)—Health professional version. Retrieved from *www.cancer.gov/about-cancer/treatment/side-effects/fatigue/fatigue-hp-pdq*.
*14. Rugo HS, Voight J: Scalp hypothermia for preventing alopecia during chemotherapy: a systematic review and meta-analysis of randomized controlled trials, *Clin Breast Cancer* 18:19, 2018.
*15. Loh KP, Janelsins MC, Mohile SG, et al: Chemotherapy-related cognitive impairment, *J Geriatr Oncol* 7:270, 2016.
*16. Oktay K, Harvey BE, Partridge AH, et al: Fertility preservation in patients with cancer: ASCO clinical practice guideline update, *J Clin Oncol* 36:1994, 2018.
*17. Langer T, Grabow D, Steinmann D, et al: Late effects and long-term follow-up after cancer in childhood, *Oncol Res Treatment* 40:746, 2017.
18. American Cancer Society (ACS): What is targeted cancer therapy? Retrieved from *www.cancer.org/treatment/treatments-and-side-effects/treatment-types/targeted-therapy/what-is.html*.
19. National Cancer Institute: Targeted cancer therapies. Retrieved from *www.cancer.gov/about-cancer/treatment/types/targeted-therapies/targeted-therapies-fact-sheet*.
20. Gratwohl A: Global perspectives on hematopoietic stem cell transplants. In *Establishing a hematopoietic stem cell transplantation unit*, New York, 2018, Springer.
*21. Munankarmi D: Management of dysgeusia related to cancer, *JLMC* 5:3, 2017.
*22. Arends J, Baracos V, Bertz H, et al: ESPEN expert group recommendations for action against cancer-related malnutrition, *Clin Nutr* 36:1187, 2017.
23. National Comprehensive Cancer Network: *National clinical practice guidelines in oncology: Adult cancer pain*, version 1, 2018. Retrieved from www.nccn.org/.
24. National Institute on Aging: Global health and aging. Retrieved from *www.nia.nih.gov/sites/default/files/2017-06/global_health_aging.pdf*.
*25. Miller KD, Siegel RL, Lin CC, et al: Cancer treatment and survivorship statistics, 2016, *CA Cancer J Clin* 66:271, 2016.

*Evidence-based information for clinical practice.

16

Fluid, Electrolyte, and Acid-Base Imbalances

Margaret R. Rateau

Even the smallest act of caring for another person is like a drop of water. It will make ripples throughout the entire pond.

Jessy Mateo

http://evolve.elsevier.com/Lewis/medsurg/

CONCEPTUAL FOCUS

Acid-Base Balance
Fluids and Electrolytes

Nutrition

LEARNING OUTCOMES

1. Describe the composition of the major body fluid compartments.
2. Define processes involved in regulating the movement of water and electrolytes between the body fluid compartments.
3. Describe the etiology, laboratory diagnostic findings, clinical manifestations, and nursing and interprofessional management of the following disorders:
   a. Extracellular fluid volume imbalances: fluid volume deficit and fluid volume excess
   b. Sodium imbalances: hypernatremia and hyponatremia
   c. Potassium imbalances: hyperkalemia and hypokalemia
   d. Magnesium imbalances: hypermagnesemia and hypomagnesemia

   e. Calcium imbalances: hypercalcemia and hypocalcemia
   f. Phosphate imbalances: hyperphosphatemia and hypophosphatemia
4. Identify the processes involved in maintaining acid-base balance.
5. Discuss the etiology, diagnostic findings, clinical manifestations, and nursing and interprofessional management of the following acid-base imbalances: metabolic acidosis, metabolic alkalosis, respiratory acidosis, and respiratory alkalosis.
6. Describe the composition of and indications for common IV fluid solutions.
7. Discuss the types and nursing management of commonly used central venous access devices.

KEY TERMS

acidosis, p. 285
alkalosis, p. 285
anions, p. 269
buffers, p. 285
cations, p. 269
central venous access devices (CVADs), p. 292

electrolytes, p. 269
fluid spacing, p. 272
hydrostatic pressure, p. 271
hypernatremia, p. 276
hypertonic, p. 271
hyponatremia, p. 278

hypotonic, p. 271
isotonic, p. 271
oncotic pressure, p. 271
osmolality, p. 271
osmotic pressure, p. 270

HOMEOSTASIS

Body fluids and electrolytes play an important role in maintaining *homeostasis,* the body's stable internal environment. Body fluids are in constant motion transporting nutrients, electrolytes, and oxygen to cells and carrying waste products away from cells. The body uses many adaptive responses to keep the composition and volume of fluids and electrolytes within narrow limits to maintain homeostasis and promote health.

Many diseases and their treatments affect fluid and electrolyte balance. Conceptually, these imbalances are often reflected by changes in perfusion, gas exchange, mobility, and cognition. For example, a patient with metastatic colon cancer may develop hypercalcemia because of bone destruction from tumor invasion and have severe muscle weakness and confusion. Chemotherapy used to treat the cancer may result in nausea and vomiting, which causes dehydration and acid-base imbalances.

When correcting dehydration with IV fluids, the patient needs close monitoring to prevent fluid overload.

It is important to anticipate the potential for fluid and electrolyte imbalances associated with certain disorders and medical therapies, recognize the signs and symptoms of imbalances, and intervene with the appropriate action. This chapter describes the (1) normal control of fluids, electrolytes, and acid-base balance; (2) conditions that disrupt homeostasis and resulting manifestations; and (3) actions that the health care provider and you can take to manage fluid, electrolyte, and acid-base imbalances and restore homeostasis.

WATER CONTENT OF THE BODY

The body is composed primarily of water. It accounts for about 50% to 60% of body weight in the adult. Water content varies with body mass, gender, and age (Fig. 16.1). Lean body mass has

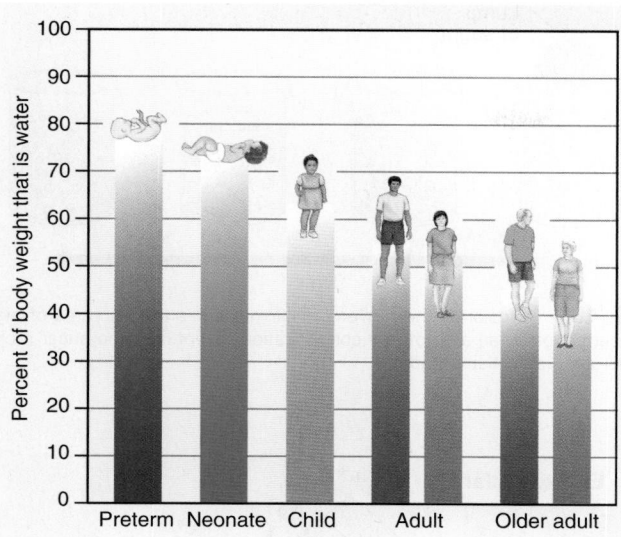

FIG. 16.1 Body water over the life span.

FIG. 16.2 Relative volumes of 3 body fluids. Values represent fluid distribution in a young male adult.

a higher percentage of water, while adipose tissue has a lesser percentage of water. So, the more fat present in the body, the less the total water content. Women generally have a lower percentage of body water because they tend to have less lean body mass than men. Older adults also tend to have less lean body mass, resulting in a lower percentage of body water when compared to younger adults. In older adults, body water content averages 45% to 50% of body weight. This places them at a higher risk for fluid-related problems than young adults.

Body Fluid Compartments

The 2 fluid compartments in the body are the *intracellular space* (inside the cells) and the *extracellular space* (outside the cells) (Fig. 16.2). About two thirds of body water is found within cells and is termed *intracellular fluid* (ICF). ICF makes up about 40% of body weight of an adult. This means a 70-kg young man would have about 42 L of water, with about 28 L of that water within his cells.

The fluid in the extracellular space is *extracellular fluid* (ECF). The 2 main compartments containing ECF are the *interstitial fluid,* or the fluid in the spaces between cells, and the intravascular fluid or *plasma,* the liquid part of blood. Other ECF compartments include lymph and *transcellular fluids.* Transcellular fluids include cerebrospinal fluid; fluid in the gastrointestinal (GI) tract and joint spaces; and pleural, peritoneal, intraocular, and pericardial fluid. ECF makes up about one third of the body water; this amounts to about 14 L in a 70-kg man. About one third of ECF is in the intravascular space as plasma (3 L in a 70-kg man), and two thirds is in the interstitial space (10 L in a 70-kg man). The fluid in the transcellular spaces totals about 1 L at any given time.

Calculation of Fluid Gain or Loss

One liter of water weighs 2.2 lb. (1 kg). Body weight change, especially sudden change, is an excellent indicator of overall fluid volume loss or gain. For example, if a patient drinks 240 mL (8 oz) of fluid, weight gain will be 0.5 lb (0.23 kg). A patient receiving diuretic therapy who loses 4.4 lb (2 kg) in 24 hours has a fluid loss of about 2 L. An adult patient who is fasting may

lose 1 to 2 lb/day. A weight loss exceeding this is likely due to loss of body fluid.

ELECTROLYTES

Electrolytes are substances whose molecules dissociate, or split, into ions when placed in water. *Ions* are electrically charged particles. **Cations** are positively charged ions. Examples include sodium (Na^+), potassium (K^+), calcium (Ca^{2+}), and magnesium (Mg^{2+}) ions. **Anions** are negatively charged ions. Examples include bicarbonate (HCO_3^-), chloride (Cl^-), and phosphate (PO_4^{3-}) ions. Most proteins bear a negative charge and thus are anions.

Measurement of Electrolytes

The concentration of electrolytes in body fluids is expressed in milliequivalents (mEq) per liter. Since electrolytes are active chemicals, it is useful to express their concentration according to their chemical activity, or the number of electrolytes able to combine chemically. Ions combine milliequivalent for milliequivalent. For example, 1 mEq (1 mmol) of sodium combines with 1 mEq (1 mmol) of chloride.

Electrolyte Composition of Fluid Compartments

Electrolyte composition varies between ECF and ICF. The overall concentration of electrolytes is nearly the same in the ECF and ICF. However, concentrations of specific ions differ greatly (Fig. 16.3). In ECF the main cation is sodium, with small amounts of potassium, calcium, and magnesium. The primary ECF anion is chloride, with small amounts of bicarbonate, sulfate, and phosphate anions.

In ICF the prevalent cation is potassium, with small amounts of magnesium and sodium. The prevalent ICF anion is phosphate, with some protein and a small amount of bicarbonate. Table 16.1 lists normal serum electrolyte values.

MECHANISMS CONTROLLING FLUID AND ELECTROLYTE MOVEMENT

The movement of electrolytes and water between ICF and ECF to maintain homeostasis involves many different processes, including simple diffusion, facilitated diffusion, and active transport. Water moves as driven by 2 forces: hydrostatic pressure and osmotic pressure.

PLASMA | INTRACELLULAR

FIG. 16.3 The relative concentrations of the major cations and anions in the intracellular space and the plasma.

TABLE 16.1 Normal Serum Electrolyte Values

Electrolyte	Reference Interval
Anions	
Bicarbonate (HCO$_3^-$)	22–26 mEq/L (22–26 mmol/L)
Chloride (Cl$^-$)	98–106 mEq/L (98–106 mmol/L)
Phosphate (PO$_4^{3-}$)	3.0–4.5 mg/dL (0.97–1.45 mmol/L)
Cations	
Calcium (Ca^{2+}) (total)	9.0–10.5 mg/dL (2.25–2.62 mmol/L)
Calcium (ionized)	4.5–5.6 mg/dL (1.05–1.3 mmol/L)
Magnesium (Mg^{2+})	1.3–2.1 mEq/L (0.65–1.05 mmol/L)
Potassium (K$^+$)	3.5–5.0 mEq/L (3.5–5.0 mmol/L)
Sodium (Na$^+$)	136–145 mEq/L (136–145 mmol/L)

Diffusion

Diffusion is the movement of molecules from an area of high concentration to low concentration (Fig. 16.4). Net movement of molecules stops when the concentrations are equal in both areas. It occurs in liquids, gases, and solids. Simple diffusion requires no external energy.

Facilitated Diffusion

Facilitated diffusion involves the use of a protein carrier in the cell membrane. The protein carrier combines with a molecule, especially one too large to pass easily through the cell membrane, and helps move the molecule across the membrane from an area of high to low concentration. Like simple diffusion, facilitated diffusion is passive and requires no energy. An example of facilitated diffusion is glucose transport into the cell. The large glucose molecule must combine with a carrier molecule to be able to cross the cell membrane and enter most cells.

Active Transport

Active transport is a process in which molecules move against the concentration gradient. External energy is needed for this

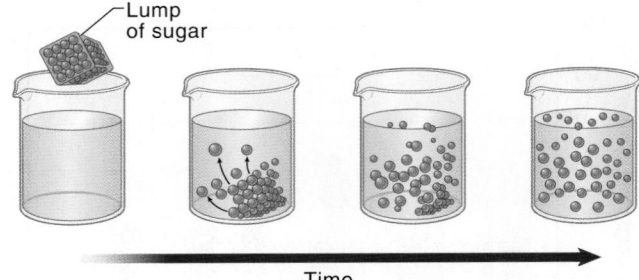

FIG. 16.4 Diffusion is the movement of molecules from an area of high concentration to an area of low concentration. Eventually, the sugar molecules are evenly distributed.

FIG. 16.5 Sodium-potassium pump. As sodium *(Na$^+$)* diffuses into the cell and potassium *(K$^+$)* diffuses out of the cell, an active transport system supplied with energy delivers Na$^+$ back to the extracellular compartment and K$^+$ to the intracellular compartment. *ATP,* Adenosine triphosphate.

process. An example is the sodium-potassium pump. The concentrations of sodium and potassium differ greatly intracellularly and extracellularly (Fig. 16.3). To maintain this concentration difference, the cell uses active transport to move sodium out of the cell and potassium into the cell (Fig. 16.5). The energy source for this movement is adenosine triphosphate (ATP), which is made in the cell mitochondria.

Osmosis

Osmosis is the movement of water "down" a concentration gradient, that is, from a region of low solute concentration to one of high solute concentration, across a semipermeable membrane. Osmosis requires no outside energy sources. It stops when the concentration differences disappear or when hydrostatic pressure builds and opposes any further movement of water. Imagine a chamber with 2 compartments separated by a semipermeable membrane, one that allows only the movement of water (Fig. 16.6). If you add albumin to one side, water will move from the less concentrated side (has more water) to the more concentrated side of the chamber (has less water) until the concentrations are equal.

Whenever dissolved substances are contained in a space with a semipermeable membrane, they can pull water into the space by osmosis. The concentration of the solution determines the strength of the osmotic pull. The higher the concentration, the greater a solution's pull, or **osmotic pressure**. Osmotic pressure is measured in milliosmoles (mOsm). It may be expressed as

FIG. 16.6 Osmosis is the process of water movement through a semipermeable membrane from an area of low solute concentration to an area of high solute concentration.

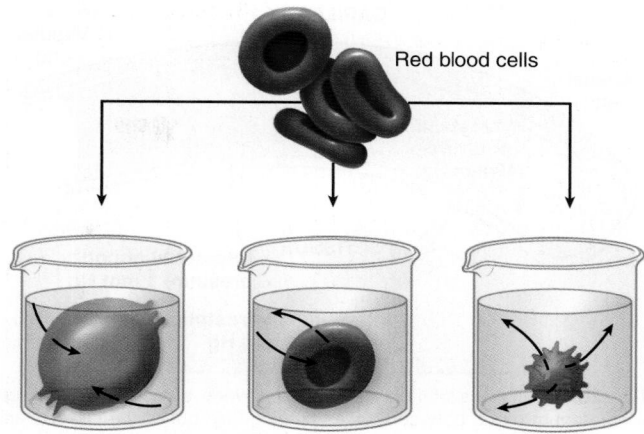

A Hypotonic solution **B** Isotonic solution **C** Hypertonic solution

FIG. 16.7 Effects of water status on red blood cells. **A,** Hypotonic solution (H_2O excess) results in cellular swelling. **B,** Isotonic solution (normal H_2O balance) results in no change. **C,** Hypertonic solution (H_2O deficit) results in cellular shrinking.

either fluid osmolarity or fluid osmolality. Although you will often see the terms *osmolarity* and *osmolality* used interchangeably, they are different measurements. *Osmolarity* measures the total milliosmoles per liter of solution, or the concentration of molecules per volume of solution (mOsm/L). Osmolality measures the number of milliosmoles per kilogram of water, or the concentration of molecules per weight of water. Osmolality is the preferred measure to evaluate the concentration of plasma, urine, and other body fluids, as changes in the ECF osmolality can significantly influence changes in the ICF osmolality. These changes can affect normal cell function.[1]

Measurement of Osmolality. Osmolality is nearly the same in the various body fluid spaces. Therefore measuring or estimating plasma osmolality is a useful way to assess the state of the body's water balance. Calculate the plasma osmolality using the following formula.[2]

Plasma osmolality = $(2 \times Na) + (BUN/2.8) + (Glucose/18)$

Normal plasma osmolality is between 280 and 295 mOsm/kg. A value greater than 295 mOsm/kg indicates that the concentration of solute is too great, or the water content is too little. This condition is termed *water deficit*. A value less than 275 mOsm/kg indicates too little solute for the amount of water or too much water for the amount of solute. This condition is termed *water excess*. Both conditions are clinically significant.

Urine osmolality can range from 100 to 1300 mOsm/kg. It depends on fluid intake, the amount of antidiuretic hormone (ADH) in circulation, and the renal response to ADH.

Osmotic Movement of Fluids. The osmolality of the fluid surrounding cells affects them. Fluids with the same osmolality as the cell interior are isotonic. Normally, ECF and ICF are isotonic to one another, so no net movement of water occurs.

Changes in the osmolality of ECF change the volume of cells. Solutions in which the solutes are less concentrated than in the cells are hypotonic (hypoosmolar). If a cell is surrounded by hypotonic fluid, water moves into the cell, causing it to swell and possibly burst. Fluids with solutes more concentrated than in cells, or an increased osmolality, are hypertonic (hyperosmolar). If hypertonic fluid surrounds a cell, water leaves the cell to dilute ECF. The cell shrinks and may eventually die (Fig. 16.7).

Hydrostatic Pressure

Hydrostatic pressure is the force of fluid in a compartment pushing against a cell membrane or vessel wall. In the blood vessels, hydrostatic pressure is the BP generated by the heart's contraction. Hydrostatic pressure in the vascular system

gradually decreases as the blood moves through the arteries until it is about 30 mm Hg in the capillary bed. At the capillary level, hydrostatic pressure is the major force that pushes water out of the vascular system and into the interstitial space.

Oncotic Pressure

Oncotic pressure (colloidal osmotic pressure) is the osmotic pressure caused by plasma colloids (large molecules) in solution. The major colloids in the vascular system contributing to osmotic pressure are proteins, such as albumin. Plasma has large amounts of protein, while the interstitial space has very little. Plasma protein molecules attract water, pulling fluid from the tissue space to the vascular space. Under normal conditions, plasma oncotic pressure is about 25 mm Hg. The small amount of protein found in the interstitial space exerts an oncotic pressure of about 1 mm Hg.

FLUID MOVEMENT IN CAPILLARIES

As plasma flows through the capillary bed, 4 factors determine if fluid moves out of the capillary and into the interstitial space or if fluid moves back into the capillary from the interstitial space. The amount and direction of movement are determined by the interaction of (1) capillary hydrostatic pressure, (2) plasma oncotic pressure, (3) interstitial hydrostatic pressure, and (4) interstitial oncotic pressure.

Capillary hydrostatic pressure and interstitial oncotic pressure move water out of the capillaries. Plasma oncotic pressure and interstitial hydrostatic pressure move fluid into the capillaries. At the arterial end of the capillary, capillary hydrostatic pressure exceeds plasma oncotic pressure, and fluid moves into the interstitial space. At the venous end of the capillary, the capillary hydrostatic pressure is lower than plasma oncotic pressure, drawing fluid back into the capillary by the oncotic pressure created by plasma proteins (Fig. 16.8).

Fluid Shifts

If capillary or interstitial pressures change, fluid may abnormally shift from one compartment to another, resulting in edema or dehydration.

FIG. 16.8 Dynamics of fluid exchange between a capillary and tissue. An equilibrium exists between forces filtering fluid out of the capillary and forces absorbing fluid back into the capillary. Note that the hydrostatic pressure is greater at the arterial end of the capillary than at the venous end. The net effect of pressures at the arterial end of the capillary causes a movement of fluid into the tissue. At the venous end of the capillary, there is net movement of fluid back into the capillary.

TABLE 16.2 Normal Fluid Balance in the Adult	
Intake	
Fluids	1200 mL
Solid food	1000 mL
Water from oxidation	300 mL
Total	2500 mL
Output	
Insensible loss (skin and lungs)	900 mL
In feces	100 mL
Urine	1500 mL
Total	2500 mL

Shifts of Plasma to Interstitial Fluid. *Edema,* an accumulation of fluid in the interstitial space, occurs if venous hydrostatic pressure rises, plasma oncotic pressure decreases, or interstitial oncotic pressure rises. Edema may also develop if an obstruction of lymphatic outflow causes a decrease in the removal of interstitial fluid.

Elevation of Venous Hydrostatic Pressure. Increasing the pressure at the venous end of the capillary inhibits fluid movement back into the capillary, which results in edema. Causes of increased venous pressure include fluid overload, heart failure, liver failure, obstruction of venous return to the heart (e.g., tourniquets, restrictive clothing, venous thrombosis), and venous insufficiency (e.g., varicose veins).

Decrease in Plasma Oncotic Pressure. Fluid stays in the interstitial space if the plasma oncotic pressure is too low to draw fluid back into the capillary. Low plasma protein content decreases oncotic pressure. This can result from excess protein loss (renal disorders), deficient protein synthesis (liver disease), and deficient protein intake (malnutrition).

Elevation of Interstitial Oncotic Pressure. Trauma, burns, and inflammation can damage capillary walls and allow plasma proteins to accumulate in the interstitial space. This increases interstitial oncotic pressure, draws fluid into the interstitial space, and holds it there.

Shifts of Interstitial Fluid to Plasma. An increase in the plasma osmotic or oncotic pressure draws fluid into the plasma from the interstitial space. This could happen when we give colloids, dextran, mannitol, or hypertonic solutions. Increasing the tissue hydrostatic pressure is another way of causing a shift of fluid into plasma. Wearing elastic compression gradient stockings or hose to decrease peripheral edema is a therapeutic application of this effect.

FLUID SPACING

Fluid spacing is a term used to describe the distribution of body water. *First spacing* describes the normal distribution of fluid in ICF and ECF compartments. *Second spacing* refers to an abnormal accumulation of interstitial fluid (i.e., edema). *Third spacing* occurs when excess fluid collects in the nonfunctional area between cells. This fluid is trapped where it is difficult or impossible for it to move back into the cells or blood vessels. Third spacing occurs with ascites; fluid leaking into the abdominal cavity with peritonitis or pancreatitis; and edema associated with burns, trauma, or sepsis.

REGULATION OF WATER BALANCE

Many factors are involved in maintaining the finely tuned balance among water intake, use, and excretion. For proper fluid balance, an average healthy adult needs a daily water intake between 2000 and 3000 mL (Table 16.2). This amount replaces what the body loses in urinary output and insensible losses. Oral fluid intake accounts for most of the water intake. Water intake also includes water from food metabolism and water present in solid foods.

Insensible water loss, which is invisible vaporization from the lungs and skin, helps regulate body temperature. Accelerated body metabolism, which occurs with increased body temperature and exercise, increases the amount of water lost and may result in the need for additional water replacement.

Do not confuse water loss through the skin with the vaporization of water excreted by sweat glands. Insensible perspiration causes only water loss. Excess sweating *(sensible perspiration)* caused by exercise, fever, or high environmental temperatures may lead to large losses of water and electrolytes.

Hypothalamic-Pituitary Regulation

Water ingestion equals water loss in the person who has free access to water, intact thirst and ADH mechanism, and normally functioning kidneys. A body fluid deficit or increase in plasma osmolality activates osmoreceptors in the hypothalamus. This stimulates thirst and the release of ADH from the posterior pituitary gland. ADH acts on the distal tubules and collecting ducts in the kidney by making them more permeable to water. The result is increased water reabsorption from the tubular filtrate into the blood and decreased excretion in the urine. Because ADH is only able to regulate how much water the body holds onto, an intact thirst mechanism is our main protection against developing dehydration or hyperosmolality. Thirst causes us to increase the amount of water we drink. Together these result in increased free water in the body, decreasing plasma osmolality and restoring fluid volume.

Many factors influence ADH secretion and thirst. Decreased BP, nausea, pain, hypoglycemia, and hypoxemia stimulate ADH release. In the postoperative patient, the stress response to surgery and receiving analgesics and anesthesia cause ADH release and decreased osmolality. The unconscious or cognitively

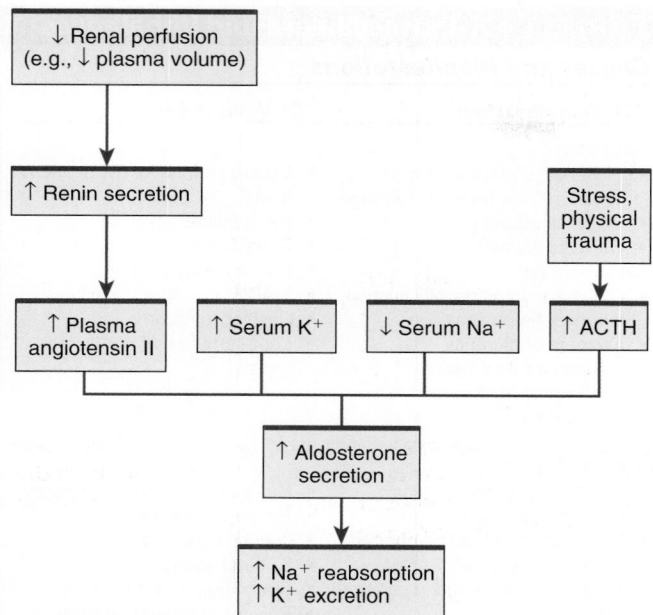

FIG. 16.9 Factors affecting aldosterone secretion. *ACTH,* Adrenocorticotropic hormone.

impaired patient is at increased risk for fluid deficit and hyperosmolality because of an inability to express thirst and act on it. A dry mouth will cause a person to drink, even when there is no body water deficit.

Renal Regulation

The primary function of the kidneys is to regulate fluid and electrolyte balance by adjusting urine volume and the excretion of most electrolytes (see Chapter 44). The kidneys filter the total plasma volume many times each day. In the average adult, the kidneys reabsorb 99% of this filtrate, producing around 1.5 L of urine per day. Under the influence of ADH, aldosterone, and other hormones, selective reabsorption and secretion of water and electrolytes in the renal tubules result in urine that is different in composition and concentration from plasma. This process helps maintain normal plasma osmolality, electrolyte balance, blood volume, and acid-base balance.

With severely impaired renal function, the kidneys cannot maintain fluid and electrolyte balance. This condition results in edema, potassium and phosphate retention, acidosis, and other electrolyte imbalances (see Chapter 46).

Adrenal Cortical Regulation

Glucocorticoids and mineralocorticoids secreted by the adrenal cortex help regulate water and electrolyte balance. The glucocorticoids (e.g., cortisol) primarily have an antiinflammatory effect and increase serum glucose levels. The mineralocorticoids (e.g., aldosterone) enhance sodium retention and potassium excretion (Fig. 16.9). When sodium is reabsorbed, water follows because of osmotic changes.

Aldosterone is a mineralocorticoid with strong sodium-retaining and potassium-excreting capabilities. Decreased renal perfusion or decreased sodium in the distal part of the renal tubule activates the renin-angiotensin-aldosterone system (RAAS), resulting in aldosterone secretion. In addition to the RAAS, increased serum potassium, decreased serum sodium, and adrenocorticotropic hormone (ACTH) stimulate

FIG. 16.10 Effects of stress on fluid and electrolyte balance. *ACTH,* Adrenocorticotropic hormone; *ADH,* antidiuretic hormone; *CRH,* corticotropin-releasing hormone.

aldosterone secretion. Aldosterone increases sodium and water reabsorption in the renal distal tubules, decreasing plasma osmolality and restoring fluid volume.

Cortisol is the most abundant glucocorticoid. In large doses, cortisol has both glucocorticoid (glucose-elevating and antiinflammatory) and mineralocorticoid (sodium-retention) effects. Normally cortisol secretion is in a diurnal or circadian pattern. Increased cortisol secretion occurs in response to physical and psychologic stress. This affects many body functions, including fluid and electrolyte balance (Fig. 16.10).

Cardiac Regulation

Natriuretic peptides, including atrial natriuretic peptide (ANP) and b-type natriuretic peptide (BNP), are hormones made by cardiomyocytes. They are made in response to increased atrial pressure (increased volume, such as occurs in heart failure) and high serum sodium levels. They are natural antagonists to the RAAS and suppress secretion of aldosterone, renin, and ADH, and the action of angiotensin II. In the renal tubules, peptides promote excretion of sodium and water, decreasing blood volume and BP.

Gastrointestinal Regulation

In addition to oral intake, the GI tract normally secretes around 8000 mL of digestive fluids each day. The GI tract normally reabsorbs most of this fluid, with only a small amount eliminated in feces. This is why diarrhea and vomiting, which prevent GI reabsorption of secreted fluid, can lead to significant fluid and electrolyte loss.

Gerontologic Considerations: Fluid and Electrolytes

The older adult has normal physiologic changes that increase susceptibility to fluid and electrolyte imbalances. Structural changes to the kidneys and a decrease in the renal blood flow lead to decreased glomerular filtration rate and loss of the ability to concentrate urine and conserve water. Hormonal changes include a decrease in renin and aldosterone and an increase in ADH and ANP. Subcutaneous tissue loss and thinning of the dermis lead to increased moisture lost through the skin and an inability to respond quickly to heat or cold.

Do not automatically attribute older patients' fluid and electrolyte problems to the natural processes of aging. Throughout this chapter are suggestions for adapting your assessment and nursing interventions when caring for the older adult.

FLUID VOLUME IMBALANCES

Fluid and electrolyte imbalances occur in most patients with a major illness or injury because illness disrupts normal homeostatic mechanisms. Illness or disease directly causes some fluid and electrolyte imbalances (e.g., burns, heart failure). Other times, therapeutic measures (e.g., colonoscopy preparation, diuretics) cause or contribute to imbalances. Perioperative patients are at risk for developing fluid and electrolyte imbalances because of fluid restrictions, blood or fluid loss, and the stress of surgery.

Fluid and electrolyte imbalances are commonly classified as *deficits* or *excesses*. ECF volume deficit *(hypovolemia)* and ECF volume excess *(hypervolemia)* are common clinical conditions. ECF volume imbalances are usually accompanied by one or more electrolyte imbalances, particularly changes in the serum sodium level.

Although each imbalance is discussed separately in this chapter, it is common for more than one imbalance to occur in the same patient. For example, a patient with prolonged nasogastric (NG) suction will lose sodium, potassium, hydrogen, and chloride ions. This may result in sodium and potassium deficiencies, a fluid volume deficit, and metabolic alkalosis caused by the loss of HCl acid.

FLUID VOLUME DEFICIT

Fluid volume deficit can occur with abnormal loss of body fluids (e.g., diarrhea, vomiting, hemorrhage, polyuria), inadequate fluid intake, or a shift from plasma to interstitial fluid. Though often used interchangeably, *fluid volume deficit* and *dehydration* are not the same. *Dehydration* refers to loss of pure water alone without a corresponding loss of sodium. Table 16.3 lists causes and manifestations of fluid volume deficit.

Interprofessional Care

Managing fluid volume deficit involves correcting the underlying cause and replacing both water and any needed electrolytes. Replacement therapy depends on the severity and type of volume loss. In mild losses, we can use oral rehydration. If the deficit is more severe, we replace volume with blood products or balanced IV solutions, such as isotonic (0.9%) sodium chloride or lactated Ringer's solution. The choice of fluid depends on the cause and patient's electrolyte status. For rapid volume replacement, 0.9% sodium chloride is preferred. Blood is given when volume loss is due to blood loss.

TABLE 16.3 Extracellular Fluid Imbalances
Causes and Manifestations

ECF Volume Deficit	ECF Volume Excess
Causes	
• ↑ Insensible water loss or perspiration (high fever, heatstroke)	• Excess isotonic or hypotonic IV fluids
• Diabetes insipidus	• Heart failure
• Osmotic diuresis	• Renal failure
• Hemorrhage	• Primary polydipsia
• GI losses: vomiting, NG suction, diarrhea, fistula drainage	• SIADH
• Overuse of diuretics	• Cushing syndrome
• Inadequate fluid intake	• Long-term use of corticosteroids
• Third-space fluid shifts: burns, pancreatitis	
Manifestations	
• Restlessness, drowsiness, lethargy, confusion	• Headache, confusion, lethargy
• Thirst, dry mucous membranes	• Peripheral edema
• Cold clammy skin	• Jugular venous distention
• Decreased skin turgor, ↓ capillary refill	• S_3 heart sound
• Postural hypotension, ↑ pulse, ↓ CVP	• Bounding pulse, ↑ BP, ↑ CVP
• ↓ Urine output, concentrated urine	• Polyuria (with normal renal function)
• ↑ Respiratory rate	• Dyspnea, crackles, pulmonary edema
• Weakness, dizziness	• Muscle spasms
• Weight loss	• Weight gain
• Seizures, coma	• Seizures, coma

FLUID VOLUME EXCESS

Fluid volume excess may result from excess intake of fluids, abnormal retention of fluids (e.g., heart failure, renal failure), or a shift of fluid from interstitial fluid into plasma fluid. Weight gain is the most consistent manifestation of fluid volume excess. Table 16.3 lists causes and manifestations of fluid volume excess.

Interprofessional Care

Managing fluid volume excess involves treating the underlying cause and removing fluid without producing abnormal changes in the electrolyte composition or osmolality of ECF. Diuretics and fluid restriction are the primary forms of therapy. Some patients also need sodium restrictions. If the fluid excess leads to ascites or pleural effusion, an abdominal paracentesis or thoracentesis may be needed.

❖ NURSING MANAGEMENT: FLUID VOLUME IMBALANCES

◆ Nursing Diagnoses

Nursing diagnoses and collaborative problems for the patient with a fluid imbalance include:
ECF volume deficit:
• Fluid imbalance
• Impaired cardiac output
• Acute confusion
• Potential complication: hypovolemic shock
ECF volume excess:
• Fluid imbalance
• Impaired gas exchange

- Impaired tissue integrity
- Activity intolerance
- Disturbed body image
- Potential complications: pulmonary edema, ascites

◆ **Nursing Implementation**

◆ **Daily Weights.** Daily weights are the most accurate measure of volume status. An increase of 1 kg (2.2 lb) is equal to 1000 mL (1 L) of fluid retention, provided the person has maintained usual dietary intake or has not been on NPO status. Obtain the weight under standardized conditions. Weigh the patient at the same time every day, wearing the same clothes and on the same carefully calibrated scale. Remove excess bedding and empty all drainage bags before the weighing. If items are present that are not there every day, such as bulky dressings or tubes, note this along with the weight.

◆ **Intake and Output.** Intake and output records give valuable information about fluid and electrolyte problems. An accurately recorded intake and output will identify sources of excess intake or fluid losses. Intake should include oral and IV fluids, tube feedings, and retained irrigation solutions. Output includes urine, excess perspiration, wound or tube drainage, vomitus, and diarrhea. Estimate fluid loss from wounds and perspiration. Note the amount and color of the urine and measure the urine specific gravity. Readings greater than 1.025 mean urine is concentrated, while readings less than 1.010 mean urine is dilute.

◆ **Laboratory Findings.** Monitor laboratory results when available and calculate the serum osmolality. The patient with a fluid volume deficit often has increased blood urea nitrogen (BUN), sodium, and hematocrit levels with increased plasma and urine osmolality. With fluid volume excess, the patient will have decreased BUN, sodium, and hematocrit levels, with decreased plasma and urine osmolality.

⬛ NURSING MANAGEMENT

Fluid Volume Changes

- Assess patient for manifestations of fluid imbalances.
- Give IV fluids and medications as ordered.
- Give O_2 therapy as ordered.
- Implement fall precautions.
- Monitor patient for effectiveness of therapy.
- Oversee UAP:
  - Obtain daily weights and vital signs.
  - Offer frequent oral care.
  - Record accurate intake and output.
  - Perform skin care and frequent position changes.
  - Elevate edematous extremities.
  - Encourage oral fluids as appropriate.

◆ **Cardiovascular Care.** Monitor vital signs and perform a thorough cardiovascular assessment as needed. Changes in BP, central venous pressure, pulse force, and jugular venous distention reflect ECF volume imbalances. In fluid volume excess, the pulse is full, bounding, and not easily obliterated. Increased volume causes distended neck veins (jugular venous distention), increased central venous pressure, and high BP. Auscultate heart sounds, being alert for the presence of an S_3.

In mild to moderate fluid volume deficit, sympathetic nervous system compensation increases the heart rate and results in peripheral vasoconstriction to try to keep BP within normal limits. Pulses may be weak and thready. Assess for orthostatic

FIG. 16.11 Assessment of skin turgor. **A** and **B**, When normal skin is pinched, it resumes shape in seconds. **C**, If the skin stays wrinkled for 20 to 30 seconds, the patient has poor skin turgor.

changes. A change in position from lying to sitting or standing may decrease BP or further increase the heart rate (orthostatic hypotension). In more severe deficits, hypotension may be present.
Respiratory Care. Monitor pulse oximetry and auscultate lung sounds as needed. ECF excess can cause pulmonary congestion and pulmonary edema, as increased hydrostatic pressure in the pulmonary vessels forces fluid into the alveoli. The patient will have shortness of breath and moist crackles on auscultation. The patient with ECF deficit will have an increased respiratory rate because of decreased tissue perfusion and resultant hypoxia. Give O_2 as ordered.
Patient Safety. The patient with fluid volume deficit is at risk for falls because of orthostatic hypotension, muscle weakness, and changes in level of consciousness. Assess level of consciousness, gait, and muscle strength. Implement fall precautions. If orthostatic hypotension is present, teach the patient to change positions slowly when rising from a bed or chair. Place alarm monitors on patients who are confused and try to get out of bed without help.
Skin Care. Assess the skin for turgor and mobility. Normally, a fold of skin, when pinched, will readily move and, on release, rapidly return to its former position. In ECF volume deficit, there is diminished skin turgor with tenting, or a lag in the pinched skinfold's return to its original state. Skin areas over the sternum, abdomen, and anterior forearm are the usual sites we use to assess turgor (Fig. 16.11). In older people, decreased skin turgor is less predictive of fluid deficit because of the loss of tissue elasticity.

In mild fluid deficits, the skin may appear warm, dry, and wrinkled. These signs may be hard to assess in the older adult because the person's skin may be normally dry, wrinkled, and non-elastic. In more severe deficits, the skin may be cool and moist if there is vasoconstriction to compensate for the decreased fluid volume. Oral mucous membranes will be dry, the tongue may be furrowed, and the person often is thirsty. Routine oral care is critical for the comfort of a patient who is dehydrated or on a fluid restriction.

Edematous skin may feel cool because of fluid accumulation and a decrease in blood flow secondary to the pressure of the

FIG. 16.12 Differential assessment of extracellular fluid (ECF) volume.

fluid. The fluid can stretch the skin, causing it to feel taut and hard. Assess edema by pressing with a thumb or forefinger over the edematous area. Use a grading scale to standardize the description if an indentation (ranging from 1+ [slight edema; 2-mm indentation] to 4+ [pitting edema; 8-mm indentation]) remains when pressure is released. Assess for edema in areas where soft tissues overlie a bone, particularly the tibia, fibula, and sacrum.

Good skin care is important. Protect tissues from extremes of heat and cold, prolonged pressure, and trauma. Frequent skin care and changes in position will prevent skin breakdown. Elevate edematous extremities to promote venous return and fluid reabsorption. Dehydrated skin needs frequent care without the use of soap. Applying moisturizing creams or oils increases moisture retention and stimulates circulation.

◆ **Fluid Therapy.** Give IV fluids as ordered. Carefully monitor the rates of infusion of IV fluid solutions, especially when you are giving large volumes of fluid. This is especially true in patients with heart, renal, or neurologic problems.

In the presence of fluid volume deficit, you can use several interventions to maintain adequate oral intake. Assess the patient's ability to obtain adequate fluids independently, express thirst, and swallow effectively. Fluids should be easily accessible. Provide a variety of fluids that the patient likes.[3] Serve fluids at a temperature preferred by the patient. Offer fluids every 1 to 2 hours and at select times, such as when giving medications. Remind the patient to finish all drinks.

If the patient is choosing to limit intake to decrease nocturia or incontinence, make it easier for the patient to reach the toilet when needed.[3] Help those with physical limitations, such as arthritis, to open and hold containers. Involve the dietitian, speech therapist, or occupational therapist for help with patients with dysphagia or physical limitations.

SODIUM IMBALANCES

Sodium, the main cation of ECF, plays a major role in maintaining the concentration and volume of ECF and influencing water distribution between ECF and ICF. Sodium is important in generating and transmitting nerve impulses, muscle contractility, and regulating acid-base balance.

The serum sodium level reflects the ratio of sodium to water, not necessarily the amount of sodium in the body. Changes in the serum sodium level can reflect a primary water imbalance, primary sodium imbalance, or combination of the two. Sodium imbalances are typically associated with imbalances in ECF volume (Figs. 16.12 and 16.13). Because sodium is the primary determinant of ECF osmolality, sodium imbalances are typically associated with parallel changes in osmolality.

The GI tract absorbs sodium from foods. Typically, daily intake of sodium far exceeds the body's daily requirements. Sodium leaves the body through urine, sweat, and feces. The kidneys primarily regulate sodium balance. The kidneys control ECF sodium concentration by excreting or retaining water under the influence of ADH. Aldosterone plays a smaller role in sodium regulation by promoting sodium reabsorption from the renal tubules.

HYPERNATREMIA

Hypernatremia (high serum sodium) may occur with inadequate water intake, excess water loss, or, rarely, sodium gain. Because sodium is the major determinant of ECF osmolality, hypernatremia causes hyperosmolality. ECF hyperosmolality causes water to move out of the cells to restore equilibrium, leading to cellular dehydration. As discussed earlier, the primary protection against the development of hyperosmolality is thirst. Hypernatremia is not a problem in an alert person who has access to water, can sense thirst, and is able to swallow. Hypernatremia from water deficiency is often the result of an impaired level of consciousness or inability to obtain fluids.

Several clinical states can produce hypernatremia from water loss (Table 16.4). A deficiency in the synthesis or release of ADH from the posterior pituitary gland (central diabetes insipidus) or a decrease in kidney responsiveness to ADH (nephrogenic diabetes insipidus) can result in profound diuresis, producing a water deficit and hypernatremia. Hyperosmolality with osmotic diuresis can result from hyperglycemia associated with uncontrolled diabetes or giving concentrated hyperosmolar tube feedings.

Excess sodium intake with inadequate water intake can also lead to hypernatremia. Examples of sodium gain include IV administration of hypertonic saline or sodium bicarbonate, use of sodium-containing drugs, excess oral intake of sodium (e.g., ingesting seawater), and *primary aldosteronism* (excess aldosterone secretion) caused by a tumor of the adrenal glands.

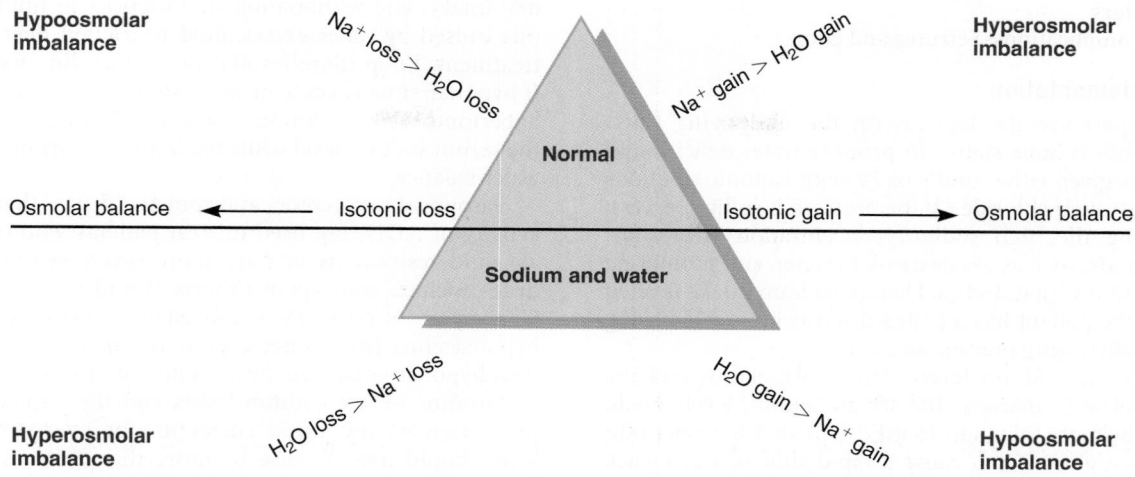

FIG. 16.13 Isotonic gains and losses affect mainly the extracellular fluid (ECF) compartment, with little or no water movement into the cells. Hypertonic imbalances cause water to move from inside the cell into the ECF to dilute the concentrated sodium, causing cell shrinkage. Hypotonic imbalances cause water to move into the cell, causing cell swelling.

TABLE 16.4 Sodium Imbalances

Causes and Manifestations

Hypernatremia (Na⁺ >145 mEq/L [mmol/L])	Hyponatremia (Na⁺ <136 mEq/L [mmol/L])
Causes	**Causes**
Excess Sodium Intake	***Excess Sodium Loss***
• IV fluids: hypertonic NaCl, excess isotonic NaCl, IV sodium bicarbonate	• *GI losses:* diarrhea, vomiting, fistulas, NG suction
• Hypertonic tube feedings without water supplements	• *Renal losses:* diuretics, adrenal insufficiency, Na⁺ wasting renal disease
• Near-drowning in salt water	• *Skin losses:* burns, wound drainage
Inadequate Water Intake	***Inadequate Sodium Intake***
• Unconscious or cognitively impaired persons	• Fasting diets
Excess Water Loss (↑ sodium concentration)	***Excess Water Gain (↓ sodium dilution)***
• ↑ Insensible water loss (high fever, heatstroke, prolonged hyperventilation)	• Excess hypotonic IV fluids
• Osmotic diuretic therapy	• Primary polydipsia
• Diarrhea	
Diseases	***Diseases***
• Diabetes insipidus	• SIADH
• Primary hyperaldosteronism	• Heart failure
• Cushing syndrome	• Primary hypoaldosteronism
• Uncontrolled diabetes	• Cirrhosis
Manifestations	
With Decreased ECF Volume	***With Decreased ECF Volume***
• Restlessness, agitation, lethargy, seizures, coma	• Irritability, apprehension, confusion, dizziness, personality changes, tremors, seizures, coma
• Intense thirst, dry swollen tongue, sticky mucous membranes	• Dry mucous membranes
• Postural hypotension, ↓ CVP, weight loss, ↑ pulse	• Postural hypotension, ↓ CVP, ↓ jugular venous filling, ↑ pulse, thready pulse
• Weakness, muscle cramps	• Cold and clammy skin
With Normal or Increased ECF Volume	***With Normal or Increased ECF Volume***
• Restlessness, agitation, twitching, seizures, coma	• Headache, apathy, confusion, muscle spasms, seizures, coma
• Intense thirst, flushed skin	• Nausea, vomiting, diarrhea, abdominal cramps
• Weight gain, peripheral and pulmonary edema, ↑ BP, ↑ CVP	• Weight gain, ↑ BP, ↑ CVP

Clinical Manifestations

The manifestations of hypernatremia are primarily the result of water shifting out of cells into ECF with resultant dehydration and shrinkage of cells (Table 16.4). Dehydration of brain cells results in changes in mental status, ranging from drowsiness, restlessness, confusion, and lethargy to seizures and coma.[4] If there is an accompanying ECF volume deficit, manifestations such as postural hypotension, tachycardia, and weakness occur.

❖ NURSING AND INTERPROFESSIONAL MANAGEMENT: HYPERNATREMIA

◆ Nursing Diagnoses

Nursing diagnoses and collaborative problems for the patient with hypernatremia include:
• Electrolyte imbalance
• Fluid imbalance

- Risk for injury
- Potential complications: Seizures and coma

◆ Nursing Implementation

Managing hypernatremia depends on the underlying cause and the patient's volume status. In primary water deficit, fluid replacement is given either orally or IV with isotonic solutions such as 0.9% sodium chloride.[2] If the problem is sodium excess, expect diluting the high sodium concentration with sodium-free IV fluids, such as 5% dextrose in water, and promoting sodium excretion with diuretics. Dietary sodium intake is often restricted. If the patient has an altered sensorium or is having seizures, initiate seizure precautions.

Monitor serum sodium levels, serum osmolality, and the patient's response to therapy. The serum sodium level should not decrease by more than 8 to 15 mEq/L in an 8-hour period.[2] Quickly reducing levels can cause a rapid shift of water back into the cells, causing cerebral edema and neurologic complications. This risk is greatest in the patient who developed hypernatremia over several days or longer.

HYPONATREMIA

Hyponatremia (low serum sodium) may result from a loss of sodium-containing fluids, water excess in relation to the amount of sodium (dilutional hyponatremia), or a combination of both (Table 16.4). Hyponatremia is usually associated with ECF hypoosmolality from the excess water. To restore balance, fluid shifts out of the ECF and into the cells, leading to cellular edema.

Common causes of hyponatremia from loss of sodium-rich body fluids include draining wounds, diarrhea, vomiting, and primary adrenal insufficiency. Inappropriate use of sodium-free or hypotonic IV fluids causes hyponatremia from water excess. This may occur in patients after surgery or major trauma, or if we give fluids to patients with renal failure. Patients with psychiatric disorders may have an excess water intake. Syndrome of inappropriate antidiuretic hormone secretion (SIADH) results in dilutional hyponatremia caused by abnormal retention of water (see Chapter 49).

Clinical Manifestations

The manifestations are due to cellular swelling and first appear in the central nervous system (CNS). Mild hyponatremia has minor, nonspecific neurologic symptoms, including headache, irritability, and difficulty concentrating. More severe hyponatremia can cause confusion, vomiting, seizures, and even coma. If hyponatremia is severe and develops rapidly, irreversible neurologic damage or death from brain herniation can occur.

❖ NURSING AND INTERPROFESSIONAL MANAGEMENT: HYPONATREMIA

◆ Nursing Diagnoses

Nursing diagnoses and collaborative problems for the patient with hyponatremia include:

- Electrolyte imbalance
- Risk for injury
- Acute confusion
- Potential complication: seizures and coma

◆ Nursing Implementation

Managing hyponatremia from fluid loss includes replacing fluid using isotonic sodium-containing solutions, encouraging oral intake, and withholding all diuretics.[2] In mild hyponatremia caused by water excess, fluid restriction may be the only treatment. Loop diuretics and demeclocycline may be given. If hyponatremia is acute or more serious, small amounts of IV hypertonic saline solution (3% sodium chloride) can restore the serum sodium level while the body is returning to a normal water balance.[5]

Vasopressor receptor antagonists (drugs that block the activity of ADH) are used to treat patients who cannot tolerate fluid restrictions or have more severe symptoms.[6] These drugs include conivaptan (Vaprisol) and tolvaptan (Samsca). Conivaptan is given IV to hospitalized patients with severe hyponatremia from water excess. Tolvaptan is given orally to treat hyponatremia from heart failure or SIADH.

Monitor serum sodium levels and the patient's response to therapy. Avoid rapid correction or overcorrection. The level should not increase by more than 6 to 12 mEq/L per hour in the first 24 hours and 18 mEq/L or less per hour within 48 hours.[6] Quickly increasing sodium levels can cause osmotic demyelination syndrome with permanent damage to nerve cells in the brain. An accurate urine output record is essential. The patient may need a urinary catheter placed if unable to help with monitoring output. If the patient has an altered sensorium or is having seizures, initiate seizure precautions.

▎ POTASSIUM IMBALANCES

Potassium is the major ICF cation, with 98% of the body potassium being in cells. For example, potassium concentration within muscle cells is around 140 mEq/L; potassium concentration in ECF is 3.5 to 5.0 mEq/L. The sodium-potassium pump in cell membranes maintains this concentration difference by pumping potassium into the cell and sodium out. Insulin helps by stimulating the sodium-potassium pump.

Because the ratio of ECF potassium to ICF potassium is the major factor in the resting membrane potential of nerve and muscle cells, potassium imbalances often affect neuromuscular and cardiac function. Potassium is involved with regulating intracellular osmolality and promoting cellular growth. It is required for glycogen to be deposited in muscle and liver cells. It also plays a role in acid-base balance (discussed in the section on Acid-Base Regulation later in this chapter).

Diet is the main source for potassium. The typical Western diet contains roughly 50 to 100 mEq of potassium daily, mainly from protein-rich foods and various fruits and vegetables. Many salt substitutes used in low-sodium diets have substantial potassium. Patients may receive potassium from parenteral sources, including IV fluids; transfusions of stored, hemolyzed blood; and certain medications (e.g., potassium penicillin).

The kidneys are the primary route for potassium loss, eliminating about 90% of the daily potassium intake. Potassium excretion depends on the serum potassium level, urine output, and renal function. When serum potassium is high, urine potassium excretion increases, and when serum levels are low, excretion decreases. Large urine output can cause excess potassium loss. Impaired kidney function can cause potassium retention. There is an inverse relationship between sodium and potassium reabsorption in the kidneys. Factors that cause sodium retention (e.g., low blood volume, hyponatremia, aldosterone secretion) cause potassium excretion.

HYPERKALEMIA

Hyperkalemia (high serum potassium) may result from impaired renal excretion, a shift of potassium from ICF to ECF, a massive intake of potassium, or a combination of these factors (Table 16.5). The most common cause of hyperkalemia is renal failure. Adrenal insufficiency with subsequent aldosterone deficiency leads to potassium retention. Factors that cause potassium to move from ICF to ECF include acidosis, massive cell destruction (as in burn or crush injury, tumor lysis, severe infections), and intense exercise. In metabolic acidosis, potassium ions shift from ICF to ECF in exchange for hydrogen ions moving into the cell.

Digoxin-like drugs and β-adrenergic blockers (e.g., propranolol) can impair entry of potassium into cells, resulting in higher ECF potassium concentrations. Several drugs, such as NSAIDs, potassium-sparing diuretics, angiotensin II receptor blockers (e.g., losartan), and angiotensin-converting enzyme (ACE) inhibitors (e.g., lisinopril), can contribute to hyperkalemia by reducing the kidney's ability to excrete potassium.[7]

Clinical Manifestations

The increased potassium concentration outside the cell changes the normal ECF and ICF ratio. This results in increased cell excitability and changes in impulse transmission to the nerves and muscles. The most clinically significant problems are the changes in cardiac conduction. The initial finding is tall, peaked T waves. As potassium increases, cardiac depolarization decreases, leading to loss of P waves, a prolonged PR interval, ST segment depression, and widening QRS complex (Fig. 16.14). Heart block, ventricular fibrillation, or cardiac standstill may occur.[7]

The patient may have fatigue, confusion, tetany, muscle cramps, paresthesias, and weakness. As potassium increases, loss of muscle tone and weakness or paralysis of other skeletal muscles, including the respiratory muscles, can occur, leading to respiratory arrest. Abdominal cramping, vomiting, and diarrhea occur from hyperactivity of GI smooth muscles.

❖ NURSING AND INTERPROFESSIONAL MANAGEMENT: HYPERKALEMIA

◆ Nursing Diagnoses

Nursing diagnoses and collaborative problems for the patient with hyperkalemia include:

- Electrolyte imbalance
- Activity intolerance
- Impaired cardiac output
- Potential complication: dysrhythmias

TABLE 16.5 Potassium Imbalances

Causes and Manifestations

Hyperkalemia (K⁺ >5.0 mEq/L [mmol/L])	Hypokalemia (K⁺ <3.5 mEq/L [mmol/L])
Causes	
Excess Potassium Intake	***Potassium Loss***
• Excess or rapid parenteral administration	• *GI losses:* diarrhea, vomiting, fistulas, NG suction, ileostomy drainage
• Potassium-containing drugs (e.g., potassium penicillin)	• *Renal losses:* diuretics, hyperaldosteronism, magnesium depletion
• Potassium-containing salt substitute	• *Skin losses:* diaphoresis
	• Dialysis
Shift of Potassium Out of Cells	***Shift of Potassium Into Cells***
• Acidosis	• Increased insulin release (e.g., IV dextrose load)
• Tissue catabolism (e.g., fever, crush injury, sepsis, burns)	• Insulin therapy (e.g., with diabetic ketoacidosis)
• Intense exercise	• Alkalosis
• Tumor lysis syndrome	• ↑ Epinephrine (e.g., stress)
Failure to Eliminate Potassium	***Lack of Potassium Intake***
• Renal disease	• Starvation
• Adrenal insufficiency	• Diet low in potassium
• *Medications:* Angiotensin II receptor blockers, ACE inhibitors, heparin, potassium-sparing diuretics, NSAIDs	• Failure to include potassium in parenteral fluids if NPO
Clinical Manifestations	
• Fatigue, irritability	
• Muscle weakness, cramps	• Fatigue
• Loss of muscle tone	• Muscle weakness, leg cramps
• Paresthesias, decreased reflexes	• Soft, flabby muscles
• Abdominal cramping, diarrhea, vomiting	• Paresthesias, decreased reflexes
• Confusion	• Constipation, nausea, paralytic ileus
• Irregular pulse	• Shallow respirations
• Tetany	• Weak, irregular pulse
	• Hyperglycemia
ECG Changes	***ECG Changes***
• Tall, peaked T wave	• Flattened T wave
• Prolonged PR interval	• Presence of U wave
• ST segment depression	• ST segment depression
• Widening QRS	• Prolonged QRS
• Loss of P wave	• Peaked P wave
• Ventricular fibrillation	• Ventricular dysrhythmias
• Ventricular standstill	• First- and second-degree heart block

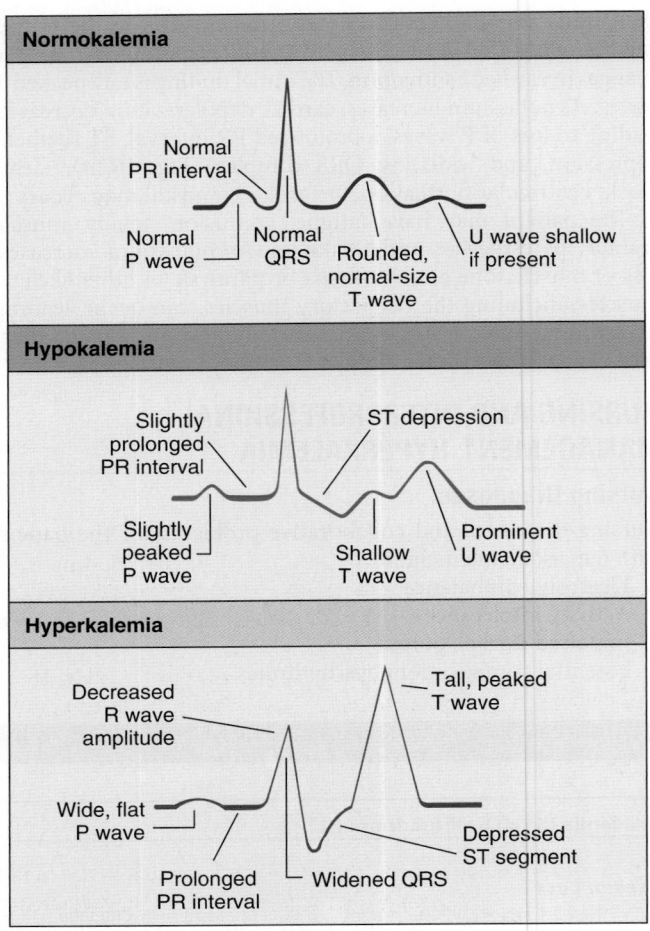

FIG. 16.14 ECG changes associated with changes in potassium levels.

TABLE 16.6 Nutritional Therapy

High-Potassium Foods

Fruits	Vegetables	Other Foods
• Apricot, raw (medium)	• Baked beans	• Bran or bran products
• Avocado (¼ whole)	• Butternut squash	• Chocolate (1.5–2 oz)
• Banana (¼ whole)	• Refried beans	• Granola
• Cantaloupe	• Black beans	• Milk, all types (1 cup)
• Dried fruits	• Broccoli, cooked	• Nutritional supple-
• Grapefruit juice	• Carrots, raw	ments (use only
• Honeydew	• Greens, except kale	under the direction
• Orange (medium)	• Mushrooms, canned	of physician or dietitian)
• Orange juice	• Potatoes, white and sweet	• Nuts and seeds (1 oz)
• Prunes	• Spinach, cooked	• Peanut butter (2 Tbsp)
• Raisins	• Tomatoes or tomato products	• Salt substitutes, Lite Salt
	• Vegetable juices	• Salt-free broth
		• Yogurt

When the potassium elevation is mild and the kidneys are functioning, it may be enough to (1) withhold potassium from the diet and IV sources and (2) increase renal potassium excretion by giving fluids and loop or thiazide diuretics. Patients with severe hyperkalemia or symptomatic patients should receive treatment to force potassium into cells.

Use continuous ECG monitoring for all patients with clinically significant hyperkalemia to detect dysrhythmias and monitor the effects of therapy. The patient with dangerous dysrhythmias should receive IV calcium immediately. Monitor BP because giving calcium rapidly can cause hypotension. When giving insulin, monitor for hypoglycemia and give glucose as needed. Monitor serum potassium levels as appropriate.

HYPOKALEMIA

Hypokalemia (low serum potassium) can result from an increased loss of potassium, an increased shift of potassium from ECF to ICF, or, rarely, from deficient dietary potassium intake. The most common causes are abnormal losses from either the kidneys or GI tract. GI tract losses are associated with diarrhea, laxative misuse, vomiting, and ileostomy drainage. Renal losses occur when a patient is diuresing or has a low magnesium level. Low magnesium levels stimulate renin and aldosterone release, resulting in potassium excretion.

Among the factors causing potassium to move from ECF to ICF are insulin therapy, especially in conjunction with diabetic ketoacidosis, and β-adrenergic stimulation (catecholamine release in stress, coronary ischemia). Alkalosis can cause a shift of potassium into cells in exchange for hydrogen, lowering potassium in ECF and causing symptomatic hypokalemia.

Clinical Manifestations

Hypokalemia alters the resting membrane potential, resulting in hyperpolarization (an increased negative charge within the cell) and impaired muscle contraction. Therefore the manifestations of hypokalemia involve changes in cardiac and muscle function (Table 16.5).

◆ Nursing Implementation

Management of hyperkalemia consists of the following:
1. Stop oral and parenteral potassium intake (Table 16.6).
2. Increase potassium excretion. This may be done with loop or thiazide diuretics, dialysis, patiromer (Veltassa), and/or sodium polystyrene sulfonate (Kayexalate). Kayexalate, given orally or rectally, is used acutely to bind potassium in the bowel. Each gram of the drug removes roughly 1 mEq of potassium. Patients with renal failure need hemodialysis.[7] Patiromer, given orally, also binds potassium in the GI tract. It takes several hours to days to work and is best for patients with chronic hyperkalemia. Patiromer binds with many other oral drugs and reduces their effectiveness. You should not give it within 6 hours of other drugs.
3. Force potassium from ECF to ICF. A combination of IV regular insulin with dextrose and a β-adrenergic agonist stimulates the sodium-potassium pump, shifting potassium into cells. Using these drugs together is more effective than using either alone. Both metered-dose inhalers and nebulized β-adrenergic agonists (e.g., nebulized albuterol) are equally effective. IV sodium bicarbonate is an option if the patient is acidotic.[7]
4. Stabilize cardiac membranes. IV calcium chloride or calcium gluconate does not lower the potassium but serves as an antagonist to reverse the toxic effects on the cardiac cell membrane. This protects the patient from life-threatening dysrhythmias.[7]

The most serious clinical problems are cardiac changes, including impaired repolarization, resulting in a flattened T wave, depressed ST segment, and the presence of a U wave. The P waves peak and the QRS complex is prolonged (Fig. 16.14). There is an increased incidence of heart block and potentially lethal ventricular dysrhythmias.

As with hyperkalemia, skeletal muscle weakness and paresthesias may occur. Severe hypokalemia can cause paralysis. This usually involves the extremities but can involve the respiratory muscles, leading to shallow respirations and respiratory arrest. Changes in smooth muscle function may lead to decreased GI motility (e.g., constipation, paralytic ileus). Finally, hypokalemia impairs insulin secretion, leading to glucose intolerance and hyperglycemia.

❖ NURSING AND INTERPROFESSIONAL MANAGEMENT: HYPOKALEMIA

◆ Nursing Diagnoses

Nursing diagnoses and collaborative problems for the patient with hypokalemia include:
- Electrolyte imbalance
- Activity intolerance
- Impaired cardiac output
- Potential complication: dysrhythmias

Nursing Implementation

Managing hypokalemia consists of oral or IV potassium chloride (KCl) supplements and increased dietary intake of potassium. Consuming potassium-rich foods can usually correct mild hypokalemia. See Table 16.6 for foods that are high in potassium. Clinically significant hypokalemia requires giving oral or IV KCl.

⚠ SAFETY ALERT IV KCl
- Always dilute IV KCl and do not give in concentrated amounts.
- Never give KCl via IV push or as a bolus.
- Invert IV bags containing KCl several times to ensure even distribution in the bag.
- Do not add KCl to a hanging IV bag to prevent giving a bolus dose.

IV KCl infusion rates should not exceed 10 mEq/hr unless the patient is in a critical care setting with continuous ECG monitoring and central line access for administration.[5] IV KCl must be given by infusion pump to ensure correct administration rate. Because KCl is irritating to the vein, assess IV sites at least hourly for phlebitis and infiltration. Infiltration can cause necrosis and sloughing of the surrounding tissue.

Patients who are critically ill and those at risk for hypokalemia should have continuous ECG monitoring to detect cardiac changes. Monitor serum potassium levels and urine output as appropriate.

❓ CHECK YOUR PRACTICE

You are taking care of a 78-yr-old female patient with heart failure. She is taking furosemide (Lasix) and digitalis.
- What should you be alert for in a patient who takes both drugs?

KCl is usually given only if the urine output is at least 0.5 mL/kg of body weight per hour. Because patients on digoxin therapy have an increased risk for toxicity if their serum potassium

---

TABLE 16.7 Patient & Caregiver Teaching

Prevention of Hypokalemia

Include the following instructions when teaching at-risk patients how to prevent hypokalemia:
1. For all patients at risk:
   - Report the signs and symptoms of hypokalemia (Table 16.5) to the HCP.
   - Have serum potassium levels checked regularly.
   - Regularly include foods high in potassium in your diet (Table 16.6).
   - Consume alcohol in moderation only.
   - Avoid consuming large amounts of licorice.
2. For patients taking oral potassium supplements:
   - Take the medication as prescribed to prevent overdosing.
   - Take the supplement with a full glass of water. Do not crush or chew tablets.

---

level is low, monitor the patient for digitalis toxicity. Patients who have confusion, lethargy, or GI problems, including nausea/vomiting or poor appetite, may have digitalis toxicity. Visual problems, including blurred vision and changes in color vision, may be seen in digitalis toxicity.[8]

Teach patients ways to prevent hypokalemia (Table 16.7). Patients at risk should have regular monitoring of serum potassium levels. Teach the patient taking digitalis to report signs and symptoms of digoxin toxicity at once to the HCP.

▌ CALCIUM IMBALANCES

Calcium has a role in many metabolic processes. It is the major cation in bones and teeth. Calcium plays a role in blood clotting, transmission of nerve impulses, myocardial contractions, and muscle contractions. The major source for calcium is dietary intake. Calcium absorption requires the active form of vitamin D. Vitamin D is obtained from foods or made in the skin by the action of sunlight on cholesterol.

The total body content of calcium is about 1200 g. The bones contain 99% of the body' calcium; the rest is in plasma and body cells. Of the calcium in plasma, 50% is bound to plasma proteins, primarily albumin; 40% is in a free or ionized form, and the rest is found bound with phosphate, citrate, or carbonate. The ionized or free calcium is biologically active. The serum pH influences how much calcium is ionized or bound to albumin. A decreased plasma pH (acidosis) decreases calcium binding to albumin, leading to more ionized calcium. An increased plasma pH (alkalosis) increases calcium binding, leading to decreased ionized calcium.

Serum calcium levels reflect the total level of all forms of plasma calcium. Serum albumin levels affect the interpretation of total calcium levels. Total calcium values increase or decrease directly with serum albumin levels. Ionized calcium levels are measured using special laboratory techniques or calculated using a formula. Albumin levels do not affect ionized calcium levels.

Parathyroid hormone (PTH) and calcitonin regulate calcium levels. Since the bones serve as a readily available store of calcium, the body can usually keep calcium levels normal by regulating the movement of calcium into or out of the bone. Low serum calcium levels stimulate the parathyroid glands to make and release PTH. PTH increases bone resorption (movement of calcium out of bones), increases GI absorption of calcium, and increases renal

TABLE 16.8 Calcium Imbalances

Causes and Manifestations

Hypercalcemia (Ca^{2+} >10.5 mg/dL [2.62 mmol/L])	Hypocalcemia (Ca^{2+} <9.0 mg/dL [2.25 mmol/L])
Causes	
Increased Total Calcium	*Decreased Total Calcium*
• Hyperparathyroidism	• Primary hypoparathyroidism
• Hematologic cancer	• Renal insufficiency
• Cancers with bone metastasis	• Acute pancreatitis
• Prolonged immobilization	• High phosphate level
• Vitamin A or D overdose	• Vitamin D deficiency, malnutrition
• Paget's disease	• Low magnesium level
• Adrenal insufficiency	• Bisphosphonates
• Thyrotoxicosis	• Tumor lysis syndrome
• Thiazide diuretics	• Loop diuretics
• Excess dairy intake	• Chronic alcohol use
• Calcium-containing antacids	• Diarrhea
• *Mycobacterium* infection	• ↓ Serum albumin
Increased Ionized Calcium	*Decreased Ionized Calcium*
• Acidosis	• Alkalosis
	• Receiving excess citrated blood
Manifestations	
• Lethargy, weakness, fatigue	• Weakness, fatigue
• Decreased memory	• Depression, irritability, confusion
• Depressed reflexes	• Hyperreflexia, muscle cramps
• ↑ BP	• ↓ BP
• Confusion, psychosis	• Numbness and tingling in extremities and region around mouth
• Anorexia, nausea, vomiting	• Chvostek's sign
• Bone pain, fractures	• Trousseau's sign
• Polyuria, dehydration	• Laryngeal and bronchial spasms
• Nephrolithiasis	• Tetany, seizures
• Seizures, coma	
ECG Changes	*ECG Changes*
• Shortened ST segment	• Elongation of ST segment
• Shortened QT interval	• Prolonged QT interval
• Ventricular dysrhythmias	• Ventricular tachycardia
• Increased digitalis effect	

tubule reabsorption of calcium. High serum calcium levels stimulate the release of calcitonin from the thyroid gland. Calcitonin has the opposite effect of PTH. It lowers the serum calcium level by increasing calcium deposition into bone, increasing renal calcium excretion, and decreasing GI absorption.

HYPERCALCEMIA

Hypercalcemia (high serum calcium) is caused by hyperparathyroidism in about two thirds of persons. Cancers, especially hematologic, breast, and lung cancers, cause the remaining third. Cancers lead to hypercalcemia through tumor-producing factors that prompt osteoclastic activity and bone resorption.[9] More rare causes include thiazide diuretic use, prolonged immobilization, and increased calcium intake (e.g., use of calcium-containing antacids).

Excess calcium acts like a sedative, leading to reduced excitability of muscles and nerves. Neurologic manifestations begin with fatigue, lethargy, weakness, and confusion and progress to hallucinations, seizures, and coma. Changes in cardiac conduction can lead to dysrhythmias, including heart block and ventricular tachycardia. Table 16.8 lists the causes and manifestations of hypercalcemia.

❖ NURSING AND INTERPROFESSIONAL MANAGEMENT: HYPERCALCEMIA

◆ Nursing Diagnoses

Nursing diagnoses and collaborative problems for the patient with hypercalcemia include:

- Electrolyte imbalance
- Acute confusion
- Impaired physical mobility
- Potential complication: dysrhythmias

◆ Nursing Implementation

Management depends on the degree of hypercalcemia, patient's condition, and underlying cause. Patients with mild hypercalcemia should stop any medications related to hypercalcemia, start a diet low in calcium, increase weight-bearing activity, and maintain adequate hydration. The patient must drink 3000 to 4000 mL of fluid daily to promote the renal excretion of calcium and decrease the chance of kidney stone formation. Fluids that promote urine acidity (cranberry or prune juice) will help to prevent formation of stones.

Managing severe hypercalcemia includes giving IV isotonic saline, a bisphosphonate, and calcitonin. IV saline therapy requires careful monitoring. Fluid overload can occur in patients who cannot excrete the excess sodium because of impaired renal function. Bisphosphonates (e.g., pamidronate, zoledronic acid) are the gold standard in treating hypercalcemia, particularly when caused by cancer. They interfere with the activity of osteoclasts, cells that break down bone. Because it takes 2 to 4 days for them to achieve maximum effect, patients receive calcitonin injections for an immediate effect. Calcitonin rapidly increases renal calcium excretion. However, therapy is effective for only a few days and may cause tachycardia. For patients who do not respond to bisphosphonates or have renal impairment, denosumab (Prolia) may be used as an alternative treatment.[9] Dialysis is an option in life-threatening situations.

HYPOCALCEMIA

Hypocalcemia (low serum calcium) can result from any condition associated with PTH deficiency. This may occur with surgical removal of part of, or injury to, the parathyroid glands during thyroid or neck surgery or with neck radiation. The patient who receives multiple blood transfusions can develop hypocalcemia because citrate, used as an anticoagulant in blood bags, binds with calcium, decreasing ionized calcium levels. Sudden alkalosis may result in symptomatic hypocalcemia despite a normal total serum calcium level. The high pH increases calcium binding to protein, decreasing the amount of ionized calcium. Table 16.8 lists causes and manifestations of hypocalcemia.

Low ionized calcium levels decrease the threshold for activating the sodium channels that cause cell membrane depolarization. This results in increased nerve excitability and sustained muscle contraction, or *tetany*. Clinical signs of tetany include Chvostek's sign and Trousseau's sign. *Chvostek's sign* is contraction of facial muscles in response to a tap over the facial nerve in front of the ear (Fig. 16.15, *A*). *Trousseau's sign* refers to carpal spasms induced by inflating a BP cuff on the arm (Fig. 16.15, *B* and *C*). When you inflate the cuff above the systolic pressure, carpal spasms occur within 3 minutes if hypocalcemia is

FIG. 16.15 Tests for hypocalcemia. **A,** Chvostek's sign is contraction of facial muscles in response to a light tap over the facial nerve in front of the ear. **B,** Trousseau's sign is a carpal spasm induced by **(C)** inflating a BP cuff above the systolic pressure for a few minutes.

present. Other manifestations of tetany are laryngeal stridor, dysphagia, paresthesia, and numbness and tingling around the mouth or in the extremities. Cardiac effects include decreased cardiac contractility and ECG changes. A prolonged QT interval may develop into ventricular tachycardia.

❖ NURSING AND INTERPROFESSIONAL MANAGEMENT: HYPOCALCEMIA

◆ Nursing Diagnoses

Nursing diagnoses and collaborative problems for the patient with hypocalcemia include:
- Electrolyte imbalance
- Impaired breathing
- Activity intolerance
- Potential complications: fracture, respiratory arrest

◆ Nursing Implementation

Managing hypocalcemia depends on the underlying cause and the presence of symptoms. Treating mild or asymptomatic hypocalcemia involves a diet high in calcium-rich foods and calcium and vitamin D supplementation. Symptomatic hypocalcemia is treated with IV calcium gluconate.[10] Measures to promote CO_2 retention, such as breathing into a paper bag or sedating the patient, can control muscle spasm and other symptoms of tetany until the calcium level is corrected. Patients taking loop diuretics may need to change to thiazide diuretics to decrease urinary calcium excretion. Closely assess any patient who had thyroid or neck surgery in the immediate postoperative period for manifestations of hypocalcemia because of the proximity of the surgery to the parathyroid glands. Adequately treat pain and anxiety because hyperventilation-induced respiratory alkalosis can precipitate hypocalcemic symptoms.

PHOSPHATE IMBALANCES

Phosphorus is the primary anion in ICF and the second most abundant element in the body after calcium. Most phosphorus is in bones and teeth as calcium phosphate. The remaining phosphorus is metabolically active in the form of phosphate salts. Thus, we use the terms *phosphorus* and *phosphate* interchangeably in this text. Phosphate is essential to the function of muscle, red blood cells, and the nervous system. It is involved in the acid-base buffering system; the mitochondrial formation of ATP; cellular uptake and use of glucose; and carbohydrate, protein, and fat metabolism.

PTH maintains serum phosphate levels and balance. Proper phosphate balance requires adequate renal functioning because the kidneys are the major route of phosphate excretion. When the phosphate level in the glomerular filtrate falls below normal or PTH levels are low, the kidneys reabsorb more phosphate. A reciprocal relationship exists between phosphate and calcium. This means a low serum calcium level will result in a high phosphate level and vice-versa.[10]

HYPERPHOSPHATEMIA

Hyperphosphatemia (high serum phosphate) is common in patients with acute kidney injury or chronic kidney disease, which alter the kidney's ability to excrete phosphate. Other causes include excess phosphate intake from the use of phosphate-containing laxatives or enemas or a shift of phosphate from ICF to ECF. This may occur in patients with tumor lysis syndrome or rhabdomyolysis. Hypoparathyroidism and vitamin D intoxication cause increased kidney phosphate reabsorption. Table 16.9 describes causes and manifestations of hyperphosphatemia.

Hyperphosphatemia can be asymptomatic unless calcium binds with phosphate, leading to manifestations of hypocalcemia. These include tetany, muscle cramps, paresthesias, hypotension, dysrhythmias, and seizures.[10] Long-term, increased phosphate levels result in the development of calcified deposits outside of the bones. These calcium deposits can be found in soft tissues, such as joints, arteries, skin, corneas, and kidneys, and cause organ dysfunction, notably renal failure.

Managing hyperphosphatemia involves identifying and treating the underlying cause. Restrict the intake of foods and fluids high in phosphorus (e.g., dairy products). Oral phosphate-binding agents (e.g., calcium carbonate) limit intestinal phosphate absorption and increase phosphate secretion in the intestine. With severe hyperphosphatemia, hemodialysis may be used to rapidly decrease levels. Volume expansion and forced diuresis with a loop diuretic may increase phosphate excretion. If hypocalcemia is present, institute measures to correct calcium levels. See Chapter 46 for more information about treating hyperphosphatemia associated with kidney disease.

HYPOPHOSPHATEMIA

Hypophosphatemia (low serum phosphate) can result from decreased intestinal absorption, increased urinary excretion, or ECF to ICF shifts. Malabsorption, diarrhea, and phosphate-binding antacids lead to decreased absorption. Phosphate shifts occur in respiratory alkalosis, treatment of diabetic ketoacidosis, and refeeding syndrome (reinstitution of nutrition to patients who are severely malnourished). Hypophosphatemia

TABLE 16.9 Phosphate Imbalances

Causes and Manifestations

Hyperphosphatemia (PO_4^{3-} >4.5 mg/dL [1.45 mmol/L])	Hypophosphatemia (PO_4^{3-} <3.0 mg/dL [0.97 mmol/L])
Causes	
• Renal failure	• Malabsorption syndromes
• Phosphate enemas (e.g., Fleet Enema)	• Chronic diarrhea
• Excess ingestion (e.g., phosphate-containing laxatives)	• Malnutrition, vitamin D deficiency
• Rhabdomyolysis	• Parenteral nutrition
• Tumor lysis syndrome	• Chronic alcohol use
• Thyrotoxicosis	• Phosphate-binding antacids
• Hypoparathyroidism	• Diabetic ketoacidosis
• Sickle cell anemia, hemolytic anemia	• Hyperparathyroidism
• Hyperthermia	• Refeeding syndrome
	• Respiratory alkalosis
Manifestations	
• Hypocalcemia	• CNS depression (confusion, coma)
• Numbness and tingling in extremities and region around mouth	• Muscle weakness, including respiratory muscle weakness
• Hyperreflexia, muscle cramps	• Polyneuropathy, seizures
• Tetany, seizures	• Heart problems (dysrhythmias, heart failure)
• Calcium-phosphate precipitates in skin, soft tissue, cornea, viscera, blood vessels	• Osteomalacia, rickets
	• Rhabdomyolysis

TABLE 16.10 Magnesium Imbalances

Causes and Manifestations

Hypermagnesemia (Mg^+ >2.1 mEq/L [1.05 mmol/L])	Hypomagnesemia (Mg^+ <1.3 mEq/L [0.65 mmol/L])
Causes	
• Renal failure	• GI tract fluid losses (e.g., diarrhea, NG suction)
• IV administration of magnesium, especially for treatment of eclampsia	• Chronic alcohol use
• Tumor lysis syndrome	• Malabsorption syndromes
• Hypothyroidism	• Prolonged malnutrition
• Metastatic bone disease	• Acute pancreatitis
• Adrenal insufficiency	• ↑ Urine output
• Antacids, laxatives	• Hyperglycemia
	• Proton pump inhibitor therapy
Manifestations	
• Lethargy, drowsiness	• Confusion
• Muscle weakness	• Muscle cramps
• Urinary retention	• Tremors, seizures
• Nausea, vomiting	• Vertigo
• Diminished deep tendon reflexes	• Hyperactive deep tendon reflexes
• Flushed, warm skin, especially facial	• Chvostek's and Trousseau's signs
• ↓ Pulse, ↓ BP	• ↑ Pulse, ↑ BP, dysrhythmias

may occur in those who are malnourished or receive parenteral nutrition with inadequate phosphorus replacement. Table 16.9 lists causes and manifestations of hypophosphatemia.

Most of the manifestations of hypophosphatemia result from impaired cellular energy and O_2 delivery due to low levels of cellular ATP and 2,3-diphosphoglycerate (2,3-DPG), an enzyme in RBCs that facilitates O_2 delivery to the tissues. Mild to moderate hypophosphatemia is often asymptomatic. Severe hypophosphatemia may be fatal because of decreased cellular function. Acute manifestations include CNS depression, muscle weakness and pain, respiratory failure, and heart failure. Chronic hypophosphatemia alters bone metabolism, resulting in rickets and osteomalacia.

Managing mild phosphate deficiency involves increasing oral intake with dairy products or phosphate supplements. Dairy products are better tolerated because phosphate supplements are often associated with adverse GI effects, including diarrhea and bloating.[11] Symptomatic hypophosphatemia can be fatal and usually requires IV administration of sodium phosphate or potassium phosphate. During IV replacement, monitor serum calcium and phosphate levels every 6 to 12 hours.[11] Perform frequent assessment during IV therapy, as complications include hypocalcemia, hyperkalemia, hypotension, and dysrhythmias.

MAGNESIUM IMBALANCES

Magnesium, the second most abundant intracellular cation, plays a key role in essential cellular processes. It is a cofactor in many enzyme systems, including those responsible for carbohydrate metabolism, DNA and protein synthesis, blood glucose control, and BP regulation. Magnesium is needed for the production and use of ATP, the energy source for the sodium-potassium pump. Muscle contraction and relaxation,

normal neurologic function, and neurotransmitter release depend on magnesium.

About 50% to 60% of the body's magnesium is stored in muscle and bone; 30% is in cells, with only 1% in ECF. The kidneys and GI system regulate serum magnesium by controlling the amount of magnesium reabsorbed in the ascending loop of Henle and distal tubules and absorption in the small intestine. GI absorption and renal reabsorption increase when magnesium levels are low.

HYPERMAGNESEMIA

Hypermagnesemia (high serum magnesium level) usually occurs only with increased magnesium intake accompanied by renal insufficiency or failure. A patient with chronic kidney disease who ingests products containing magnesium (e.g., Maalox, Milk of Magnesia) will have a problem with excess magnesium. Magnesium excess could develop in a pregnant woman receiving magnesium sulfate for the treatment of eclampsia or in patients taking laxatives and antacids that contain magnesium. Table 16.10 lists the causes and manifestations of hypermagnesemia.

Excess magnesium inhibits acetylcholine release at the myoneural junction and calcium movement into cells, impairing nerve and muscle function. Initial manifestations include hypotension, facial flushing, lethargy, urinary retention, nausea, and vomiting. As the serum magnesium level increases, deep tendon reflexes are lost, followed by muscle paralysis and coma. Respiratory and cardiac arrest can occur.

Management begins with avoiding magnesium-containing drugs and limiting dietary intake of magnesium-containing foods (e.g., green vegetables, nuts, bananas, oranges, peanut butter, chocolate). If renal function is adequate, increased fluids and diuretics promote urinary excretion of magnesium. The patient with impaired renal function may need dialysis. If hypermagnesemia is symptomatic, giving IV calcium gluconate will oppose the effects of the excess magnesium on cardiac muscle.[12]

HYPOMAGNESEMIA

Hypomagnesemia (low serum magnesium level) occurs in patients with limited magnesium intake or increased GI or renal losses. Causes of hypomagnesemia from insufficient food intake include prolonged fasting or starvation and chronic alcohol use. Another potential cause is prolonged parenteral nutrition without magnesium supplementation. Fluid loss from the GI tract, acute pancreatitis, and poorly controlled diabetes may contribute to hypomagnesemia. Diuretics, proton-pump inhibitors, and certain antibiotics may lead to magnesium loss.[12] Table 16.10 lists the causes and manifestations of hypomagnesemia.

Clinically, hypomagnesemia resembles hypocalcemia. Neuromuscular manifestations are common, such as muscle cramps, tremors, hyperactive deep tendon reflexes, Chvostek's sign, and Trousseau's sign. Neurologic manifestations include confusion, vertigo, and seizures. Dysrhythmias, such as torsades de pointes and ventricular fibrillation, can occur.

Management depends on the underlying cause and the patient's symptoms. Mild magnesium deficiency involves oral supplements and increased dietary intake of foods high in magnesium. If the deficiency is severe or if hypocalcemia is present, IV magnesium (e.g., magnesium sulfate) is given. Monitor vital signs and use an infusion pump, since rapid administration can lead to hypotension and cardiac or respiratory arrest.

ACID-BASE IMBALANCES

The body normally maintains a steady balance between the acids continually produced during normal metabolism and the bases that neutralize and promote the excretion of the acids. Because these acids alter the body's internal environment, their regulation is necessary to maintain homeostasis and acid-base balance. Many health problems may lead to acid-base imbalances. Patients with diabetes, chronic obstructive pulmonary disease (COPD), and kidney disease often develop acid-base imbalances.

Remember that an acid-base imbalance is not a disease but a symptom of an underlying health problem. Always consider the possibility of acid-base imbalance in patients with serious illnesses.

pH AND HYDROGEN ION CONCENTRATION

The acidity or alkalinity of a solution depends on its hydrogen ion (H^+) concentration. An increase in H^+ concentration leads to acidity; a decrease leads to alkalinity. H^+ concentration is usually expressed as a negative logarithm (symbolized as *pH*). The use of the negative logarithm means that the lower the pH, the higher is the H^+ concentration.

The pH of a chemical solution may range from 1 to 14. A solution with a pH of 7 is considered neutral. An acid solution has a pH less than 7, and an alkaline solution has a pH greater than 7. Blood is slightly alkaline and has a normal arterial pH of 7.35 to 7.45. Medically, if the pH drops below 7.35, a person has acidosis. If the blood pH is greater than 7.45, the person has alkalosis (Fig. 16.16).

ACID-BASE REGULATION

The body uses 3 mechanisms to regulate acid-base balance and keep the pH between 7.35 and 7.45. These are the buffer systems, respiratory system, and renal system. Each mechanism reacts at different speeds. Buffers are the fastest, reacting immediately.

FIG. 16.16 The normal range of plasma pH is 7.35 to 7.45. A normal pH is maintained by a ratio of 1 part carbonic acid to 20 parts bicarbonate.

The respiratory system responds in minutes and reaches maximum effectiveness in hours. The renal response occurs hours to days after a change in pH. The kidneys can maintain balance indefinitely in patients with chronic imbalances. But, if the person has impaired kidney function, the kidneys will not be effective in maintaining acid-base balance.

Buffer System

Buffering is the primary regulator of acid-base balance. **Buffers** act chemically to change strong acids into weaker ones or bind acids to neutralize them. This minimizes the effect of acids on blood pH until they can be excreted from the body. Buffers can maintain pH only if the respiratory and renal systems function adequately.

All body fluids contain buffers. The major buffer in ECF is the carbonic acid–bicarbonate system (H_2CO_3/HCO_3^-). Other buffer systems include phosphate, protein, and hemoglobin. The cell can act as a buffer by shifting H^+ in and out of the cell. When ECF levels of H^+ are increased, H^+ enters the cell in exchange for potassium. This may result in hyperkalemia as potassium moves into the ECF. Conversely, with decreased H^+ levels, H^+ enters plasma in exchange for potassium. This is why a patient with alkalosis can develop hypokalemia.

A buffer consists of a weak acid, which releases H^+ when fluid is too alkaline, or a base and its salt, which takes up H^+ when fluid is too acidic. The carbonic acid–bicarbonate buffer system neutralizes hydrochloric acid (HCl), a strong acid, by combining it with a strong base. This prevents the acid from making a large decrease in pH.

$$\underset{\text{Strong Acid}}{HCL} + \underset{\text{Strong Base}}{Na_2CO_3} \rightarrow \underset{\text{Salt}}{NaCl} + \underset{\text{Weak Acid}}{H_2CO_3}$$

The carbonic acid is broken down into H_2O and CO_2. The lungs excrete CO_2, either combined with insensible H_2O as carbonic acid or alone as CO_2.

The phosphate, protein, and hemoglobin buffer systems act in the same way as the bicarbonate system. The main components of the phosphate system are monohydrogen phosphate (HPO_4^{2-}) and dihydrogen phosphate ($H_2PO_4^-$). A phosphate, combined with sodium, can neutralize a strong acid, such as HCl, by forming sodium chloride (NaCl) and sodium biphosphate (NaH_2PO_4), a weak acid. If a strong base, such as sodium hydroxide (NaOH), is present, sodium biphosphate (NaH_2PO_4) neutralizes it to a weaker base (Na_2HPO_4) and H_2O.

Intracellular and extracellular proteins can act as an acid or base. Because the chemical structure of amino acids has an acid and a base, they can accept H^+ if pH decreases or release H^+ if fluid is too alkaline. Some amino acids have basic radicals (NH_3OH [ammonium hydroxide]) that can dissociate into NH_3^+ (ammonia) and OH^- (hydroxide). The OH^- can combine with H^+ to form H_2O.

Hemoglobin can bind with both H^+, forming a weak acid, and CO_2, forming carbaminohemoglobin ($HbCO_2$). $HbCO_2$ dissociates in the lungs, releasing CO_2 for exhalation. Because H^+ can combine only with hemoglobin that has released its O_2, venous blood is a better buffer than arterial blood, which contains saturated hemoglobin. Hemoglobin also aids in controlling pH by shifting chloride in and out of RBCs in exchange for bicarbonate.

The buffer system maintains a 20:1 ratio between HCO_3^- and carbonic acid in ECF. The body's ability to keep this ratio is important in controlling pH. For example, excess carbonic acid increases the ratio and decreases pH, resulting in acidosis. In response, the body can increase HCO_3^- levels to keep the ratio 20:1 and keep the pH near normal, a state called *compensation*. For example, a ratio of 40:2 is present in compensated acid-base balance.

Respiratory System

The lungs help maintain a normal pH by excreting CO_2 and water, which are by-products of cellular metabolism. When released into the circulation, CO_2 enters RBCs and combines with H_2O to form H_2CO_3. Carbonic acid dissociates into H^+ and HCO_3^-. Hemoglobin buffers the free H^+, and the HCO_3^- diffuses into the plasma. This process is reversed in the pulmonary capillaries, forming CO_2 that is excreted by the lungs.

The amount of CO_2 in the blood directly relates to carbonic acid and H^+ concentration. With increased respirations, more CO_2 is expelled and less stays in the blood. This leads to less carbonic acid and less H^+. With decreased respirations, more CO_2 stays in the blood. This leads to increased carbonic acid and more H^+.

The respiratory center in the medulla controls the rate of excretion of CO_2. If increased amounts of CO_2 or H^+ are present, the respiratory center stimulates an increased rate and depth of breathing to "blow off" CO_2 through hyperventilation. If the center senses low H^+ or CO_2 levels, respirations are reduced and CO_2 retained. The older adult has an impaired compensatory ability due to decreased respiratory function.

Renal System

Under normal conditions, the body depends on the kidneys to reabsorb and conserve all the HCO_3^- they filter and excrete some of the acid produced by cellular metabolism. The 3 mechanisms of acid excretion include (1) secreting small amounts of free hydrogen into the renal tubule, (2) combining H^+ with ammonia (NH_3) to form ammonium (NH_4^+), and (3) excreting weak acids.

The kidneys normally excrete acidic urine (average pH is 6). As a compensatory mechanism, the pH of the urine can decrease to 4 or increase to 8. To compensate for acidosis, the kidneys can reabsorb more HCO_3^- and excrete excess H^+. This increases the blood pH and decreases the urine pH. In the older adult, the kidneys are less able to compensate for acid load.

ALTERATIONS IN ACID-BASE BALANCE

An acid-base imbalance results when there is a change in the ratio of 20:1 between base and acid content. This occurs when a disease or process alters one side of the ratio (e.g., CO_2 retention in pulmonary disease) and the compensatory processes that maintain the other side of the ratio (e.g., increased renal HCO_3^- reabsorption) either fail or are inadequate. The compensatory process may be inadequate because either the pathophysiologic activity is overwhelming or there is not enough time for the compensatory process to work.

Acid-base imbalances are classified as respiratory or metabolic. *Respiratory imbalances* result from changes in carbonic acid concentration. *Metabolic imbalances* affect the base HCO_3^-. Acidosis occurs with an increase in carbonic acid (respiratory acidosis) or decrease in HCO_3^- (metabolic acidosis). Alkalosis occurs with a decrease in carbonic acid (respiratory alkalosis) or increase in HCO_3^- (metabolic alkalosis). Imbalances are further classified as acute or chronic. Chronic imbalances allow greater time for compensatory changes.

Respiratory Acidosis

Respiratory acidosis (carbonic acid excess) occurs when a person has hypoventilation (Table 16.11). Hypoventilation leads to a buildup of CO_2, resulting in an accumulation of carbonic acid in the blood. Carbonic acid dissociates, releasing H^+ and decreasing pH. If CO_2 is not eliminated from the blood, acidosis results from the accumulation of carbonic acid (Fig. 16.17, *A*).

During acute respiratory acidosis, the renal compensatory mechanisms begin to work within 24 hours. The kidneys conserve HCO_3^- and secrete increased H^+ into the urine. Until the renal mechanisms have an effect, the serum HCO_3^- level will usually be normal and then increase.

Respiratory Alkalosis

Respiratory alkalosis (carbonic acid deficit) occurs with hyperventilation, or an increase in respiratory rate or volume (Table 16.11). The primary cause of respiratory alkalosis is hypoxemia from acute pulmonary disorders (e.g., pneumonia, pulmonary embolus). Hyperventilation can occur as a physiologic response to metabolic acidosis and increased metabolic demands (e.g., fever). Pain, anxiety, and some CNS disorders can increase respirations without a physiologic need. The decrease in the arterial CO_2 level leads to decreased carbonic acid concentration in the blood and an increased pH (Fig. 16.17, *A*).

Compensated respiratory alkalosis is rare. In acute respiratory alkalosis, aggressive treatment of the cause of hypoxemia is essential and usually does not allow time for compensation to occur. If the respiratory alkalosis is caused by significant pain, anxiety, or panic, breathing into a closed system to rebreathe eliminated CO_2 can aid in the compensatory process. Some buffering may occur with shifting of HCO_3^- into cells in exchange for chloride ions (Cl^-). In chronic respiratory alkalosis that occurs with pulmonary fibrosis or CNS disorders, compensation may include renal excretion of HCO_3^-.

Metabolic Acidosis

Metabolic acidosis (base bicarbonate deficit) occurs when an acid other than carbonic acid accumulates in the body or when bicarbonate is lost in body fluids (Table 16.11 and Fig. 16.17, *B*). Ketoacid accumulation in diabetic ketoacidosis and lactic acid accumulation with shock are examples of acid accumulation. Severe diarrhea resulting in loss of HCO_3^- is an example of a base deficit. In renal disease, the kidneys lose their ability to reabsorb HCO_3^- and secrete H^+. To compensate for metabolic acidosis, the kidneys try to excrete extra acid and the lungs

TABLE 16.11 Acid-Base Imbalances

Causes	Pathophysiology	Laboratory Findings
Respiratory Acidosis		
• Chronic respiratory disease (e.g., COPD) • Barbiturate or sedative overdose • Chest wall abnormality • Severe pneumonia • Atelectasis • Respiratory muscle weakness • Mechanical hypoventilation • Pulmonary edema	• ↑ CO_2 retention from hypoventilation • Compensatory response is ↑ HCO_3^- retention by kidney	↓ Plasma pH ↑ $PaCO_2$ HCO_3^- normal (uncompensated) ↑ HCO_3^- (compensated) *Sample ABG* Uncompensated: 　pH 7.31 　$PaCO_2$ 54 mm Hg 　HCO_3^- 25 mEq/L
Respiratory Alkalosis		
• Hyperventilation (e.g., hypoxia, anxiety, fear, pain, exercise, fever) • Stimulated respiratory center (e.g., septicemia, stroke, meningitis, encephalitis, brain injury, salicylate poisoning) • Liver failure • Mechanical hyperventilation	↑ CO_2 excretion from hyperventilation Compensatory response is ↑ HCO_3^- excretion by kidney	↑ Plasma pH ↓ $PaCO_2$ HCO_3^- normal (uncompensated) ↓ HCO_3^- (compensated) *Sample ABG* Uncompensated: 　pH 7.52 　$PaCO_2$ 27 mm Hg 　HCO_3^- 24 mEq/L
Metabolic Acidosis		
• Diabetic ketoacidosis • Lactic acidosis • Starvation • Diarrhea • Renal tubular acidosis • Renal failure • GI fistulas • Shock	• Gain of fixed acid, inability to excrete acid or loss of base • Compensatory response is ↑ CO_2 excretion by lungs	↓ Plasma pH $PaCO_2$ normal (uncompensated) ↓ $PaCO_2$ (compensated) ↓ HCO_3^- *Sample ABG* Uncompensated: 　pH 7.29 　$PaCO_2$ 38 mm Hg 　HCO_3^- 18 mEq/L
Metabolic Alkalosis		
• Vomiting • NG suctioning • Diuretic therapy • Hypokalemia • Excess $NaHCO_3$ intake • Mineralocorticoid use	• Loss of strong acid or gain of base • Compensatory response is ↑ CO_2 retention by lungs	↑ Plasma pH $PaCO_2$ normal (uncompensated) ↑ $PaCO_2$ (compensated) ↑ HCO_3^- *Sample ABG* Uncompensated: 　pH 7.50 　$PaCO_2$ 40 mm Hg 　HCO_3^- 34 mEq/L

increase CO_2 excretion. The patient often develops *Kussmaul respirations* (deep, rapid breathing) when trying to compensate for metabolic acidosis.

If metabolic acidosis is present, calculating the anion gap helps determine the source of the acidosis. The *anion gap* is the difference between the measured serum cations and anions in ECF.

$$\text{Anion gap} = Na^+ - (HCO_3^- + Cl^-)$$

A normal anion gap is 8 to 12 mmol/L. The anion gap increases in metabolic acidosis associated with acid gain (e.g., lactic acidosis, diabetic ketoacidosis) but is normal in metabolic acidosis caused by bicarbonate loss (e.g., diarrhea).

Metabolic Alkalosis

Metabolic alkalosis (base bicarbonate excess) occurs when a loss of acid (e.g., from prolonged vomiting or gastric suction) or a gain in HCO_3^- (e.g., from ingestion of baking soda) occurs (Table 16.11 and Fig. 16.17, *B*). Renal excretion of HCO_3^- occurs in response to metabolic alkalosis. The lung's compensatory response is limited. The respiratory rate decreases to retain plasma CO_2. However, once hypoxemia occurs or plasma CO_2 reaches a certain level, stimulation of chemoreceptors will increase respirations.

Mixed Acid-Base Disorders

A mixed acid-base disorder occurs when 2 or more disorders are present at the same time. The pH depends on the type, severity, and acuity of each disorder involved and any compensatory mechanisms at work. Respiratory acidosis combined with metabolic alkalosis (e.g., a patient with atelectasis and NG suction) may result in a near-normal pH. Respiratory acidosis combined with metabolic acidosis causes a greater decrease in pH than either disorder alone. An example of a mixed acidosis is a patient in severe shock with poor perfusion and hypoventilation. Mixed alkalosis can occur in a patient hyperventilating because of postoperative pain who is losing acid from NG suctioning.

CLINICAL MANIFESTATIONS OF ACID-BASE IMBALANCES

The manifestations of acidosis and alkalosis are outlined in Tables 16.12 and 16.13. In both respiratory and metabolic acidosis, the

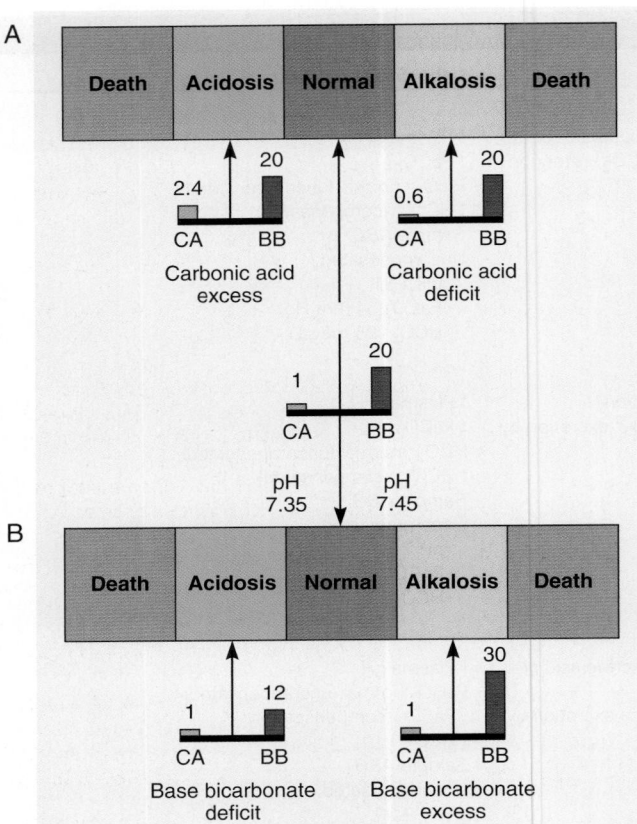

FIG. 16.17 Kinds of acid-base imbalances. A, Respiratory imbalances caused by carbonic acid *(CA)* excess and carbonic acid deficit. B, Metabolic imbalances caused by base bicarbonate *(BB)* deficit and base bicarbonate excess.

TABLE 16.12 Manifestations of Acidosis

Respiratory (↑ $PaCO_2$)	Metabolic (↓ HCO_3^-)
Neurologic	
Lethargy	Lethargy
Confusion	Confusion
Dizziness	Dizziness
Headache	Headache
Coma	Coma
Cardiovascular	
↓ BP	↓ BP
Ventricular fibrillation (related to hyperkalemia from compensation)	Dysrhythmias (related to hyperkalemia from compensation)
Warm, flushed skin	Cold, clammy skin
Gastrointestinal	
No significant findings	Nausea, vomiting, diarrhea, abdominal pain
Neuromuscular	
Seizures	Muscle weakness
Respiratory	
Hypoventilation with hypoxia	Deep, rapid respirations

CNS is depressed. Headache, lethargy, weakness, and confusion develop, leading eventually to coma and death. Compensatory mechanisms also produce specific manifestations. For example, the deep, rapid (Kussmaul) respirations of a patient with metabolic acidosis occur with respiratory compensation.

TABLE 16.13 Manifestations of Alkalosis

Respiratory (↓ $PaCO_2$)	Metabolic (↑ HCO_3^-)
Neurologic	
Dizziness	Irritability
Light-headedness	Lethargy
Confusion	Confusion
Headache	Headache
Cardiovascular	
Tachycardia	Tachycardia
Dysrhythmias (related to hypokalemia from compensation)	Dysrhythmias (related to hypokalemia from compensation)
Gastrointestinal	
Nausea, vomiting, diarrhea	Nausea, vomiting
Epigastric pain	Anorexia
Neuromuscular	
Tetany	Tetany
Numbness	Tremors
Tingling of extremities	Tingling of fingers and toes
Hyperreflexia	Muscle cramps, hypertonic muscles
Seizures	Seizures
Respiratory	
Hyperventilation (lungs are unable to compensate if there is a respiratory problem)	Hypoventilation (compensatory action by lungs)

TABLE 16.14 Normal Arterial Blood Gas Values

Parameter	Reference Interval
pH	7.35–7.45
$PaCO_2$	35–45 mm Hg
Bicarbonate (HCO_3^-)	22–26 mEq/L (mmol/L)
PaO_2*	80–100 mm Hg
SaO_2	>95%
Base excess	±2.0 mEq/L

*Decreases above sea level and with increasing age.

In both types of alkalosis, symptoms usually result from an accompanying electrolyte abnormality rather than the alkalosis. Hypocalcemia occurs due to increased calcium binding with albumin, lowering the amount of ionized, active calcium. Therefore muscle cramping and symptoms of CNS excitability, including tingling and numbness of the fingers and tetany, occur. If left untreated, respiratory alkalosis can be life-threatening.[13]

Blood Gas Values

Arterial blood gas (ABG) values give objective information about a patient's acid-base status, the underlying cause of an imbalance, and the body's ability to regulate pH. Knowing the patient's clinical situation and the extent of renal and respiratory compensation allows you to identify acid-base disorders and the patient's ability to compensate. Blood gas analysis also shows the partial pressure of arterial O_2 (PaO_2) and O_2 saturation. Table 16.14 lists normal blood gas values. These values help you evaluate the patient's overall oxygenation status and identify hypoxemia. Table 16.15 shows *ROME*, a quick memory device for understanding acid-base imbalances.

TABLE 16.15 ROME

Memory Device for Acid-Base Imbalances

For acid-base imbalances, use this quick memory device (mnemonic).

In **Respiratory** conditions, the pH and the $PaCO_2$ go in **Opposite** directions.
- In respiratory alkalosis, the pH is ↑ and the $PaCO_2$ is ↓.
- In respiratory acidosis, the pH is ↓ and the $PaCO_2$ is ↑.

In **Metabolic** conditions, the pH and the HCO_3^- go in the same direction **(Equal)**. The $PaCO_2$ may also go in the same direction.
- In metabolic alkalosis, pH and HCO_3^- are ↑ and the $PaCO_2$ is ↑ or normal.
- In metabolic acidosis, pH and HCO_3^- are ↓ and the $PaCO_2$ is ↓ or normal.

To interpret the results of an ABG, perform the following 5 steps:

1. Look at each of the values. If the pH is between 7.35 and 7.45, and the CO_2, HCO_3^-, and PaO_2 are within normal limits, the ABGs are normal. If any value is out of normal, then continue.

2. Look at the pH first. Values less than 7.35 indicate acidosis and values greater than 7.45 indicate alkalosis. A normal pH means there is normal acid-base status, compensation is occurring, or a mixed disorder is present.

3. Use ROME (Table 16.15) to figure out if the origin is respiratory or metabolic. Remember respiratory opposite and metabolic equal.

4. Once the metabolic or respiratory origin is determined, look at the remaining value, either the CO_2 or HCO_3^-, to figure the level of compensation. If the value is moving in the opposite direction, the body is trying to compensate. If the remaining value moving to compensate is abnormal and the pH is higher or lower than normal, *partial compensation* has occurred. If the pH is within normal limits, *full compensation* has occurred.

5. Assess the PaO_2 and O_2 saturation. If these values are abnormal, hypoxemia is present.

Table 16.16 explains how to analyze ABG results. The laboratory findings section of Table 16.11 shows ABG findings of the 4 major acid-base imbalances. See Chapter 25 for further discussion of ABGs.

ASSESSMENT OF FLUID, ELECTROLYTE, AND ACID-BASE IMBALANCES

Assessing patients for fluid, electrolyte, and acid-base imbalances is an important part of your nursing practice. In addition to assessing for the manifestations discussed earlier in this chapter, obtain subjective and objective data from any patient with suspected fluid, electrolyte, or acid-base imbalances.

Subjective Data

Important Health Information

Past Health History. Question the patient about any history of problems involving the kidneys, heart, GI system, or lungs that could affect the present fluid, electrolyte, and acid-base balance. Ask about specific diseases such as diabetes, diabetes insipidus, COPD, renal failure, ulcerative colitis, and Crohn's disease. Assess for any prior fluid, electrolyte, or acid-base disorders.

Medications. Assess the patient's current and past use of medications. The ingredients in many drugs, especially over-the-counter drugs, are often hidden sources of sodium, potassium,

TABLE 16.16 Applying Arterial Blood Gas (ABG) Analysis

Sample ABG Values	Analysis
pH 7.32 $PaCO_2$ 30 HCO_3^- 16 PaO_2 95	1. Look at each of the values. If the pH is between 7.35 and 7.45, and the CO_2, HCO_3^-, and PaO_2 are within normal limits, the ABGs are normal. If any value is out of normal, then continue. *The pH, CO_2, HCO_3^- are all abnormally low. Continue with analysis.* 2. Look at the pH first. Values less than 7.35 indicate acidosis and values greater than 7.45. *The pH is below 7.35, indicating acidosis.* 3. Use ROME to figure out if the origin is respiratory or metabolic. Remember respiratory opposite and metabolic equal. *Using ROME, the pH and CO_2 are not going in the opposite direction (the disorder is not respiratory in origin). The pH and HCO_3^- are moving in the same or equal direction, so the disorder is metabolic in origin.* 4. Once the metabolic or respiratory origin is determined, look at the remaining laboratory value (either CO_2 or HCO_3^-) to figure the level of compensation. *Since the disorder is metabolic in origin, review the remaining laboratory value (in this case the CO_2) The CO_2 is low, meaning the lungs are trying to compensate by lowering acid levels.* 5. Assess the PaO_2 and O_2 saturation. If these values are abnormal, hypoxemia is present. *The PaO_2 is normal and does not indicate hypoxemia.*

Interpretation

This ABG is interpreted as metabolic acidosis with partial compensation. Partial compensation is occurring because the pH remains abnormal. Full compensation would occur after the pH returns within normal limits.

calcium, magnesium, and other electrolytes. Many prescription drugs, including diuretics, corticosteroids, and electrolyte supplements, can cause fluid and electrolyte imbalances.

Surgery or Other Treatments. Ask the patient about past or present renal dialysis, kidney surgery, or bowel surgery resulting in a temporary or permanent external collecting system, such as an ileostomy.

Functional Health Patterns

Health Perception–Health Management Pattern. If the patient currently has a problem related to fluid, electrolyte, and acid-base balance, obtain a careful description of the illness, including onset, course, and treatment. Ask the patient about any recent changes in body weight.

Nutritional-Metabolic Pattern. Ask the patient about diet and any special dietary practices. Weight reduction diets, fad diets, or any eating disorders, such as anorexia or bulimia, can lead to fluid and electrolyte problems. If the patient is on a special diet, such as low sodium or high potassium, assess the ability to adhere to the dietary prescription.

Elimination Pattern. Make note of the patient's usual bowel and bladder habits. Carefully document any deviations from the expected elimination pattern, such as diarrhea, oliguria, polyuria, or incontinence.

Activity-Exercise Pattern. Ask about the patient's exercise pattern and any excess perspiration. Determine if the patient is exposed to extremely high temperatures during leisure or work activity. Ask the patient what he or she does to replace fluid and electrolytes lost through excess perspiration. Assess the patient's activity level to determine any functional problems that could lead to lack of ability to obtain food or fluids.

Cognitive-Perceptual Pattern. Ask about any changes in sensations, such as numbness, tingling, or muscle weakness, which could indicate a fluid and electrolyte problem. Ask the patient and caregiver if there have been any changes in mentation or alertness, such as confusion, memory impairment, or lethargy.

Objective Data

Physical Examination. Perform a complete physical examination because fluid, electrolyte, and acid-base balance affects all body systems. As you assess each system, check for manifestations that you would expect with an imbalance. Common abnormal assessment findings of major body systems offer clues to possible imbalances (Table 16.17).

TABLE 16.17 Assessment Abnormalities

Fluid and Electrolyte Imbalances

Finding	Possible Cause
Blood Pressure	
Hypotension	Fluid volume deficit, low Ca^{2+}, high Mg^{2+}
Hypertension	Fluid volume excess, high Ca^{2+}, low Mg^{2+}
Muscular	
Chvostek's sign	Low Ca^{2+}, high PO_4^{3-}, low Mg^{2+}
Muscle cramping	High K^+, low Ca^{2+}, high PO_4^{3-}, low Mg^{2+}
Muscle weakness	High or low K^+, high Ca^{2+}, low PO_4^{3-}, high Mg^{2+}
Trousseau's sign	Low Ca^{2+}, high PO_4^{3-}, low Mg^{2+}
Neurologic	
Confusion	Fluid volume excess, high or low Na^+, high or low K^+, low Ca^{2+}, high or low Mg^{2+}, low PO_4^{3-}
Decreased level of consciousness	Fluid volume deficit or excess, high or low Na^+, low PO_4^{3-}
Fatigue	Fluid volume deficit, low K^+, high Ca^{2+}
Irritability	Low Na^+, high K^+, low Ca^{2+}, high PO_4^{3-}
Tremors, seizures	High Na^+, low K^+, low Ca^{2+}, high PO_4^{3-}, low Mg^{2+}
Respirations	
Crackles	Fluid volume excess
Dyspnea	Fluid volume excess
Rapid respirations	Fluid volume deficit
Restricted airway	Low Ca^{2+}, high PO_4^{3-}
Pulse	
Bounding pulse	Fluid volume excess
Rapid, weak, thready pulse	Fluid volume deficit
Weak, irregular, rapid pulse	Severe low K^+, low Mg^{2+}
Weak, irregular, slow pulse	Severe high K^+, high Mg^{2+}
Skin	
Cold, clammy skin	Fluid volume deficit, low Na^+
Flushed, dry skin	High Na^+, High Mg^{2+}
Pitting edema	Fluid volume excess
Poor skin turgor	Fluid volume deficit

Laboratory Values. Assessing serum electrolyte values is a good starting point for evaluating fluid and electrolyte balance (Table 16.1). Serum electrolytes can also provide important information about a patient's acid-base balance. Changes in the serum HCO_3^- (often reported as total CO_2 or CO_2 content on an electrolyte panel) indicate metabolic acidosis (low HCO_3^- level) or alkalosis (high HCO_3^- level).

SAFETY ALERT Managing Critical Test Results
- Promptly report critical laboratory values to the HCP.
- Assess the patient and take appropriate actions (e.g., ECG monitoring).

Remember that serum electrolyte values often provide limited information. They reflect the concentration of that electrolyte in ECF but not necessarily in ICF. For example, most potassium is found in the cells. Changes in serum potassium values may be the result of a true deficit or excess of potassium or reflect the movement of potassium into or out of the cell during acid-base imbalances. An abnormal serum sodium level may reflect a sodium problem or, more likely, a water problem.

Other useful laboratory tests include serum and urine osmolality, serum glucose, blood urea nitrogen, serum creatinine, venous blood gas sampling, urine specific gravity, and urine electrolytes.

ORAL FLUID AND ELECTROLYTE REPLACEMENT

In all cases of fluid, electrolyte, and acid-base imbalances, the primary treatment involves correcting the underlying cause. Oral rehydration solutions containing water, potassium, sodium, and glucose may be used to correct mild fluid and electrolyte deficits. Glucose not only provides calories but also promotes sodium and water absorption in the small intestine. Commercial oral rehydration solutions are now available for home use. Avoid cola drinks because they do not contain adequate electrolyte replacement, and the sugar content may lead to osmotic diuresis.

IV. FLUID AND ELECTROLYTE REPLACEMENT

IV fluid and electrolyte therapy are necessary to treat many different fluid and electrolyte imbalances. Many patients need maintenance IV fluid therapy when they cannot take oral fluids (e.g., during and after surgery). Other patients need corrective or replacement therapy for losses that are ongoing or have already occurred. The amount and type of solution is determined by the normal daily maintenance requirements and by imbalances identified by laboratory results. We classify IV replacement solutions by their concentration or tonicity (Table 16.18). Tonicity is a key factor in determining the appropriate solution to correct imbalances.

Solutions

Hypotonic. A hypotonic solution has a lower osmolality when compared to plasma.[14] Infusing a hypotonic solution dilutes ECF, lowering serum osmolality. Osmosis then produces a movement of water from ECF to interstitial spaces and cells, causing cells to swell. After achieving equilibrium, ICF and ECF have the same osmolality. Hypotonic solutions (e.g., 0.45% NaCl) are useful in treating patients with hypernatremia. They are a good maintenance fluid because normal daily losses are hypotonic. They are not good for replacement because they can deplete ECF and lower BP. Because hypotonic solutions have the potential to cause cellular swelling, monitor patients for changes in mentation that may indicate cerebral edema.

Although 5% dextrose in water is technically an isotonic solution, the dextrose quickly metabolizes. The net result is the administration of hypotonic free water with equal expansion of ECF and ICF. One liter of a 5% dextrose solution provides 50 g of dextrose, or 170 calories. While this amount of dextrose is not enough to meet caloric requirements, it helps prevent ketosis associated with starvation.

Isotonic. An isotonic solution has an osmolality similar to plasma.[14] Because of this similarity, giving an isotonic solution expands only ECF and the fluid does not move into cells. This makes isotonic solutions the ideal fluid replacement for patients with ECF volume deficits. Examples of isotonic solutions include 0.9% NaCl and lactated Ringer's solution.

Isotonic saline (0.9% NaCl), or *normal saline,* has a sodium concentration (154 mEq/L) slightly higher than that of plasma (135 to 145 mEq/L) and a chloride concentration (154 mEq/L) significantly higher than the plasma chloride level (96 to 106 mEq/L). Therefore giving too much isotonic saline has the potential to increase sodium and chloride levels. Isotonic saline is used when a patient has had both fluid and sodium losses (e.g., diarrhea, vomiting).

Lactated Ringer's solution contains sodium, potassium, chloride, calcium, and lactate (the precursor of bicarbonate) in about the same concentrations as ECF. This makes it the ideal fluid in certain situations, such as surgery, burns, or GI fluid losses. Patients with liver dysfunction, hyperkalemia, and severe hypovolemia should not receive lactated Ringer's because they have a decreased ability to convert the lactate to bicarbonate.

Hypertonic. A hypertonic solution has a higher osmolality than plasma.[14] The higher osmotic pressure draws water out of the cells into ECF. It is useful in the treatment of hyponatremia and trauma patients with head injury. Those receiving hypertonic

---

TABLE 16.18 Common Crystalloid Solutions

Solution	Tonicity	mOsm/kg	Contents	Indications and Considerations
Dextrose in Water				
5%	Isotonic, but physiologically hypotonic	278	50 g/L dextrose	• Contains free water only, no electrolytes • Provides 170 cal/L • Used to replace water losses and treat hypernatremia
10%	Hypertonic	556	100 g/L dextrose	• Contains free water only, no electrolytes • Provides 340 cal/L • Used with parenteral nutrition
Saline				
0.45%	Hypotonic	154	77 mEq/L Na$^+$ 77 mEq/L Cl$^-$	• Contains free water, Na$^+$, and Cl$^-$, no calories • Used to treat hypernatremia and uncontrolled hyperglycemia • Used as a maintenance solution
0.9%	Isotonic	308	154 mEq/L Na$^+$ 154 mEq/L Cl$^-$	• Contains Na$^+$ and Cl$^-$ in excess of plasma levels • Does not contain free water or calories • Used to expand intravascular volume and replace extracellular fluid losses • Only solution given with blood products • May cause volume overload in patients with heart or kidney disease
3.0%	Hypertonic	1026	513 mEq/L Na$^+$ 513 mEq/L Cl$^-$	• Contains Na$^+$ and Cl$^-$ in excess of plasma levels • Used to treat symptomatic hyponatremia and trauma patients with head injury • Give slowly because it may cause volume overload and pulmonary edema
Dextrose in Saline				
5% in 0.25%	Isotonic	355	50 g/L dextrose 34 mEq/L Na$^+$ 34 mEq/L Cl$^-$	• Provides Na$^+$, Cl$^-$, and free water • Used to replace hypotonic losses and treat hypernatremia • Provides 170 cal/L
5% in 0.45%	Hypertonic	432	50 g/L dextrose 77 mEq/L Na$^+$ 77 mEq/L Cl$^-$	• Provides Na$^+$, Cl$^-$, and free water • Used as a maintenance solution
5% in 0.9%	Hypertonic	586	50 g/L dextrose 154 mEq/L Na$^+$ 154 mEq/L Cl$^-$	• Contains Na$^+$ and Cl$^-$ in excess of plasma levels • Used to treat metabolic alkalosis and volume deficits in patients with hyponatremia
Multiple Electrolyte Solutions				
Ringer's solution	Isotonic	309	147 mEq/L Na$^+$ 156 mEq/L Cl$^-$ 4 mEq/L K$^+$ 4 mEq/L Ca^{2+}	• Similar in composition to plasma except that it has excess Cl$^-$, no Mg^{2+}, no HCO$_3^-$ • Does not provide free water or calories • Used to expand the intravascular volume and replace extracellular fluid losses
Lactated Ringer's (Hartmann's) solution	Isotonic	273	130 mEq/L Na$^+$ 109 mEq/L Cl$^-$ 4 mEq/L K$^+$ 3 mEq/L Ca^{2+} 28 mmol/L lactate	• Similar in composition to normal plasma except does not contain Mg^{2+} • Does not provide free water or calories • Used to treat hypovolemia, burns, and GI fluid losses • Cannot be used in patients with alkalosis or lactic acidosis

solutions need frequent monitoring of BP, lung sounds, and serum sodium levels because of the risk for intravascular fluid volume excess.

Although concentrated dextrose and water solutions (10% dextrose or greater) are hypertonic solutions, once the dextrose is metabolized, the net result is the administration of water. This free water ultimately expands ECF and ICF. The primary use of these solutions is providing calories as part of parenteral nutrition (see Chapter 39). You may give solutions containing 10% dextrose or less through a peripheral line. You must use a central line to give solutions with dextrose concentrations greater than 10%.

IV Additives. Additives in basic IV solutions replace specific losses. KCl, $CaCl_2$, $MgSO_4$, and HCO_3^- are common additives. The use of each was described earlier in the discussion of the specific electrolyte deficiencies. Many premixed IV solutions containing specific additives are available. Using these solutions reduces error as the solution contains the correct amount of the electrolyte in the proper volume and type of IV solution.

Colloids. Colloid solutions contain large molecules that increase oncotic pressure and pull fluid into the blood vessels. Because this action restores blood volume, colloids are also called *volume expanders* or *plasma expanders*. Colloids include human plasma products (albumin, fresh frozen plasma, blood) and semisynthetic solutions (dextran, starches).

Albumin is available in 5% and 25% solutions. The 5% solution has an albumin concentration similar to that of plasma and results in plasma volume expansion equal to the volume infused. This makes it ideal for treating hypovolemic patients. In contrast, 25% albumin solution is hypertonic and draws fluid from the interstitial space. This makes it useful in treating patients with burns, hepatic failure, and ascites.

Dextran solutions are synthetic complex sugar solutions. There are 2 types: low-molecular-weight dextran (dextran 40) and high-molecular-weight dextran (dextran 70). Because dextran metabolizes slowly, it stays in the vascular system for a prolonged period. It pulls fluid into the intravascular space, expanding it by more volume than what is infused. Hydroxyethyl starches (e.g., Hespan) are synthetic colloids that work similarly to dextran to expand plasma volume.

Colloids can lead to circulatory overload because they pull fluid into ECF. Monitor vital signs and urine output frequently and assess for signs and symptoms of fluid volume excess. All colloids affect blood coagulation, with dextran and starches having the strongest anticoagulation effect.[14] Monitor coagulation times and implement any necessary precautions. Fatal anaphylactic reactions have occurred with Hespan and dextran. Monitor the patient closely for a hypersensitivity reaction and stop an infusion at once if a reaction occurs.

If the patient has lost blood, whole blood or packed RBCs are given. Packed RBCs have the advantage of giving the patient primarily RBCs rather than RBCs and fluid volume. Although packed RBCs have a decreased plasma volume, they increase the oncotic pressure and pull fluid into the intravascular space. The use of whole blood, with its added fluid volume, may cause circulatory overload, particularly in patients who are susceptible to complications from excess circulating volume (e.g., heart failure). To prevent fluid volume excess, loop diuretics may be given with blood and colloids. See Chapter 30 for more information on giving blood and blood products.

NURSING MANAGEMENT

IV Therapy

- Assess patient for manifestations of fluid and electrolyte imbalances.
- Determine if ordered IV therapies are appropriate.
- Choose and insert appropriate IV catheters and infusion devices.
- Give IV fluids and medications.
- Monitor for adverse reactions to IV fluids or medications.
- Assess for manifestations of fluid overload or hypovolemia and initiate appropriate changes in IV fluids.
- Evaluate if IV therapies are addressing patient's fluid and electrolyte needs.
- Collaborate with the pharmacist to:
  - Determine appropriateness of IV therapies and need for dose adjustments.
  - Prepare IV infusions and medications.
  - Screen for potential problems, such as compatibility issues.
  - Monitor response to therapy.

CENTRAL VENOUS ACCESS DEVICES

Central venous access devices (CVADs) are catheters placed in large blood vessels (e.g., subclavian vein, jugular vein) of people who need frequent or special access to the vascular system. There are 3 main types of CVADs: centrally inserted catheters, peripherally inserted central catheters (PICCs), and implanted ports.

Advantages of CVADs include immediate access to the central venous system, a reduced need for multiple venipunctures, and decreased risk for extravasation injury. CVADs permit frequent, continuous, rapid, or intermittent administration of fluids and medications. They allow for the administration of drugs that are potential *vesicants* (agents that can cause tissue damage), blood and blood products, and parenteral nutrition. CVADs can provide a means to perform hemodynamic monitoring and obtain venous blood samples. They are useful with patients who have limited peripheral vascular access or who have a projected need for long-term vascular access. CVADs also can be used to inject radiopaque contrast media. Table 16.19 gives examples of when CVADs are used.

The major disadvantages of CVADs are an increased risk for systemic infection and the invasiveness of the procedure. Extravasation (leakage of fluid) can still occur if there is displacement of or damage to the device.

Centrally Inserted Catheters

The tip of centrally inserted catheters (also called central venous catheters [CVCs]) rests in the distal end of the superior vena cava near its junction with the right atrium (Fig. 16.18). The other end of the catheter exits through a separate incision on the chest or abdominal wall. *Nontunneled catheters* are usually placed in the subclavian or internal jugular vein, more rarely in the femoral vein. They are best for patients with short-term needs in an acute care setting. *Surgically placed tunneled catheters* (e.g., Hickman, Broviac, Groshong) are suitable for long-term needs. Tunneling of the catheter through subcutaneous tissue and the synthetic cuff used to anchor the catheter provide stability and decrease infection risk. After the site heals, the catheter does not need a dressing, making it easier for the patient to maintain the site at home.

CVCs are available with single-, double-, or triple-lumens. Multilumen catheters are useful in the critically ill patient

TABLE 16.19 Common Indications for Central Venous Access Devices (CVADs)

Condition	Indications for Use
Autoimmune disorders	Perform plasmapheresis
Blood sampling	Multiple blood draws for diagnostic tests over time
Blood transfusions	Infusion of blood or blood products
Heart failure	Perform ultrafiltration
Hemodynamic monitoring	Used to measure central venous pressure to assess fluid balance
Medication administration	
• Cancer	Chemotherapy, infusion of irritating or vesicant medications
• Contrast media	Inject radiopaque contrast media for diagnostic testing
• Infection	Long-term administration of antibiotics
• Pain	Long-term administration of pain medication
• Drugs at risk for causing phlebitis	Epoprostenol (Flolan) Calcium chloride Potassium chloride Amiodarone
Nutritional replacement	Infusion of parenteral nutrition Infusion of high percentage dextrose solutions
Renal failure	Perform hemodialysis (especially on an acute basis) or continuous renal replacement therapy
Shock, burns	Infusion of high volumes of fluid and electrolyte replacement

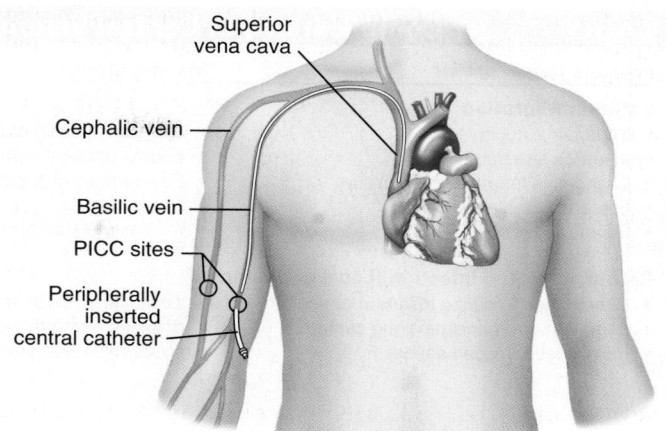

FIG. 16.19 Peripherally inserted central catheter (PICC) can be inserted using the basilic or cephalic vein.

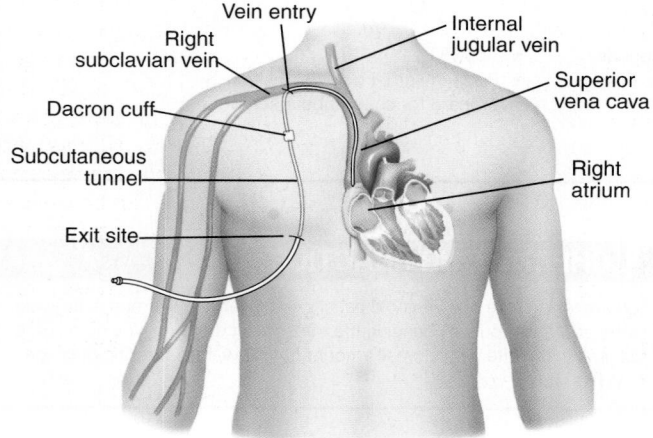

FIG. 16.18 Tunneled central venous catheter. Note tip of the catheter in the superior vena cava.

because each lumen can be used simultaneously to provide a different therapy. For example, incompatible drugs infuse in separate lumens without mixing while a third lumen gives access for blood sampling.

Peripherally Inserted Central Catheters

Peripherally inserted central catheters (PICCs) are CVCs inserted into a vein in the arm. The basilic vein is best because of its large diameter (Fig. 16.19). The cephalic, median cubital, or brachial veins are other options. Single-, double-, or triple-lumens are available. Double lumens are preferred because they allow for simultaneous uses. PICCs are used with patients who need vascular access for 1 week to 6 months, but they can be in place for longer periods.

Advantages of a PICC over a CVC are lower infection rate, fewer insertion-related complications, decreased cost, and ability to insert at the bedside or in an outpatient area. PICCs, however, are associated with an increased risk for deep vein thrombosis and phlebitis (Table 16.20). If phlebitis occurs, it usually happens within 7 to 10 days after insertion. Do not use the arm with the PICC to take a BP reading or draw blood. When the BP cuff is inflated, the PICC can touch the vein wall, increasing the risk for vein damage and thrombosis.

Implanted Infusion Ports

An implanted infusion port consists of a surgically implanted CVC connected to a reservoir or port (Fig. 16.20, A). The catheter tip lies in the desired vein. The port lies in a surgically created subcutaneous pocket on the upper chest or arm. It consists of a titanium or plastic reservoir covered with a self-sealing silicone septum. You access the port by using a special noncoring needle with a deflected tip. This prevents damage to the septum that could make the port useless (Fig. 16.20, B).

Drugs are placed in the reservoir either by a direct injection or through injection into an established IV line. The reservoir then slowly releases the medicine into the bloodstream. Implanted ports are good for long-term therapy and have a low risk for infection. The hidden port offers the patient cosmetic advantages and overall has less maintenance than other types of CVADs. Monitor accessed ports for infiltration that can occur if the needle is not in place or dislodges.

Midline Catheters

Midline catheters technically are peripheral catheters because they do not enter a central vein. However, their use and care are similar to a PICC. A specially trained nurse can insert a midline catheter. A catheter can be from 3 to 8 inches long and have single or double lumens. They are inserted in the antecubital area through either the basilic or cephalic vein, often under ultrasound guidance. The basilic vein is best since it has a larger diameter. The tip rests right below the axilla, staying below the shoulder joint to reduce the risk for vein irritation from moving the shoulder. These lines can stay in place for up to 4 weeks.

TABLE 16.20 Complications of Central Venous Access Devices (CVADs)

Possible Cause	Manifestations	Management
Catheter Migration		
• Improper suturing	• Sluggish infusion or aspiration	• Prepare for fluoroscopy to verify position
• Insertion site trauma	• Edema of chest or neck during infusion	• Assist with removal and new CVAD placement
• Changes in intrathoracic pressure	• Patient reports gurgling sound in ear	
• Forceful catheter flushing	• Dysrhythmias	
• Spontaneous	• Increased external catheter length	
Catheter-Related Infection (Local or Systemic)		
• Contamination during insertion or use	• *Local:* redness, tenderness, purulent drainage, warmth, edema	Local
• Migration of organisms along catheter	• *Systemic:* fever, chills, malaise	• Culture drainage from site
• Immunosuppressed patient		• Apply warm, moist compresses
		• Remove catheter if needed
		Systemic
		• Take blood cultures
		• Give antibiotic therapy
		• Give antipyretic therapy
		• Remove catheter if needed
Catheter Occlusion		
• Clamped or kinked catheter	• Sluggish infusion or aspiration	• Have patient change position, raise arm, and cough
• Tip against wall of vessel	• Inability to infuse and/or aspirate	• Assess and alleviate any clamping or kinking
• Thrombosis		• Flush with normal saline using a 10-mL syringe. Do not force flush
• Precipitate buildup in lumen		• Instill anticoagulant or thrombolytic agent
Embolism		
• Catheter breaking	• Chest pain	• Apply O$_2$
• Dislodgment of thrombus	• Respiratory distress (dyspnea, tachypnea, hypoxia, cyanosis)	• Clamp catheter
• Entry of air into circulation	• Hypotension	• Place patient on left side with head down (air emboli)
	• Tachycardia	• Notify provider
Pneumothorax		
• Perforation of visceral pleura during insertion	• Decreased or absent breath sounds	• Apply O$_2$
	• Respiratory distress (cyanosis, dyspnea, tachypnea)	• Place in semi-Fowler's position
	• Chest pain	• Prepare for chest tube insertion
	• Distended unilateral chest	

Complications

CVADs always have a potential for complications. Careful monitoring and assessment will help you to identify potential complications early. Table 16.19 lists common complications, potential causes, manifestations, and interventions.

❖ NURSING MANAGEMENT: CENTRAL VENOUS ACCESS DEVICES

Nursing management of CVADs includes assessment, dressing changes and cleansing, injection cap changes, and maintenance of catheter patency. The exact frequency and procedures for these requirements vary by type of CVAD and facility, so it is important to follow your facility's policies and procedures. The following section discusses some general guidelines.

Catheter and insertion site assessment includes inspecting the site for redness, edema, warmth, drainage, tenderness, or pain. Observing the catheter for misplacement or slippage is important. Perform a comprehensive pain assessment, particularly noting any reports of chest or neck discomfort, arm pain, or pain at the insertion site. Do not use a newly placed CVAD until the tip position is verified with a chest x-ray.

> ### ❓ CHECK YOUR PRACTICE
>
> You are taking care of a 74-yr-old patient with a left triple-lumen subclavian catheter. When you are changing the transparent dressing, you note some redness at the site with a small amount of yellow, foul-smelling drainage.
> • What should you do?

Before manipulating a catheter for any reason, perform hand hygiene. Perform dressing changes and cleanse the catheter insertion site using strict sterile technique. Typical dressings include transparent semipermeable dressings or gauze and tape. If the site is bleeding, a gauze dressing may be preferable. Otherwise, transparent dressings are best. They allow observation of the site without having to remove the dressing. Transparent dressings may be left in place for up to 1 week. Change any dressing at once if it becomes damp, loose, or soiled.

Cleanse the skin around the catheter insertion site according to facility policy. A chlorhexidine-based preparation is the cleansing agent of choice. Its effects last longer than either povidone-iodine or alcohol, offering improved killing of bacteria.[15] When using chlorhexidine, cleansing the skin with friction is critical to preventing infection. When applying a new dressing, allow the area to air dry completely. Secure the lumen ports to

FIG. 16.20 **A,** Cross section of implantable port displaying access of the port with the Huber-point needle. Note the deflected point of the Huber-point needle, which prevents coring of the port's septum. **B,** 2 Huber-point needles used to enter the implanted port. The 90-degree needle is used for top-entry ports for continuous infusion.

the skin above the dressing site. Document the date and time of the dressing change and initial the dressing.

Disinfect catheter hubs, needleless connectors, and injection ports before accessing the catheter. Use an alcoholic chlorhexidine preparation, 70% alcohol, or povidone-iodine. Change injection caps at regular intervals according to facility policy, or if they have damage from excess punctures. Use strict sterile technique.

Teach the patient to turn the head to the opposite side of the insertion site during cap change. If you cannot clamp the catheter, have the patient lie flat in bed and perform the Valsalva maneuver whenever the catheter is open to air to prevent an air embolism.

Flushing is one of the most effective ways to maintain catheter patency. It also keeps incompatible drugs or fluids from mixing. Use a normal saline solution in a syringe that has a barrel capacity of 10 mL or more to avoid excess pressure on the catheter. If you feel resistance, do not apply force. This could result in a ruptured catheter or create an embolism if a thrombus is present. Because of the risk for contamination and infection, use solution from prefilled syringes or single-dose vials rather than multiple-dose vials when flushing catheters. If you are not using a positive-pressure valve cap, clamp any unused lines after flushing.

Use the push-pause technique when flushing all catheters. Push-pause creates turbulence within the catheter lumen, promoting the removal of debris that adheres to the catheter lumen and decreasing the chance of occlusion. This technique involves injecting saline with a rapid alternating push-pause motion, instilling 1 to 2 mL with each push on the syringe plunger. If you are using a negative-pressure cap or neutral pressure cap, clamp the catheter while maintaining positive pressure while instilling the last 1 mL of saline. This prevents reflux of blood back into the catheter. If a positive-pressure valve cap is present, it works to prevent the reflux of blood and resultant catheter lumen occlusion. Remove the syringe before clamping the catheter to allow the positive pressure valve to work correctly.

CVAD Removal

Removing a CVAD is done according to agency policy and the nurse's scope of practice. In many agencies, nurses with demonstrated competency can remove PICCs and nontunneled central venous catheters. The procedure involves removing any sutures and then gently withdrawing the catheter. Have the patient perform the Valsalva maneuver as the last 5 to 10 cm of the catheter is withdrawn. Immediately apply pressure to the site with sterile gauze to prevent air from entering and to control bleeding. Inspect the catheter tip to determine that it is intact. After bleeding has stopped, apply an antiseptic ointment and sterile dressing to the site.

CASE STUDY

Fluid and Electrolyte Imbalance

Patient Profile

S.S., a 63-yr-old white woman with acute lymphocytic leukemia, has been receiving chemotherapy on an outpatient basis. She completed her third treatment 5 days ago and has had nausea and vomiting for 2 days despite using ondansetron (Zofran). S.S.'s daughter brings her to the hospital, where she is admitted to the medical unit. As the admitting nurse, you perform a thorough assessment.

(© Kevin Peterson/Photodisc/Thinkstock.)

Subjective Data

- Reports lethargy, weakness, dizziness, and dry mouth
- States she has been too nauseated to eat or drink anything for 2 days

Objective Data

- Heart rate 110 beats/min, pulse thready
- BP 100/65
- Weight loss of 5 lb since she received her chemotherapy treatment 5 days ago
- Dry oral mucous membranes

Discussion Questions

1. Based on her manifestations, what fluid imbalance does S.S. have?
2. What additional assessment data should you obtain?
3. What are her risk factors for fluid and electrolyte imbalances?
4. You draw blood for a serum chemistry evaluation. What electrolyte imbalances are likely and why?
5. S.S. is at risk for which acid-base imbalance? Describe the changes that would occur in S.S.'s ABGs with this acid-base imbalance. How would the body compensate?
6. **Priority Decision:** What are the priority nursing interventions for S.S.?
7. **Collaboration:** Who should be the primary members of the interprofessional team in caring for S.S.? What is the interprofessional team's priority at this time for S.S.?
8. The provider orders dextrose 5% in 0.45% saline to infuse at 100 mL/hr. What type of solution is this, and how will it help S.S.'s fluid imbalance?
9. **Evidence-Based Practice:** S.S. has a double-lumen PICC in her left arm. One lumen is connected to the IV infusion; the other is unused. What is the recommended practice for maintaining the patency of the unused lumen?
10. **Quality Improvement:** What outcomes will indicate that interprofessional care was effective?

Answers available at *http://evolve.elsevier.com/Lewis/medsurg*.

BRIDGE TO NCLEX EXAMINATION

The number of the question corresponds to the same-numbered outcome at the beginning of the chapter.

1. During the postoperative care of a 76-year-old patient, the nurse monitors the patient's intake and output carefully, knowing that the patient is at risk for fluid and electrolyte imbalances primarily because
   a. older adults have an impaired thirst mechanism and need reminding to drink fluids.
   b. water accounts for a greater percentage of body weight in the older adult than in younger adults.
   c. older adults are more likely than younger adults to lose extracellular fluid during surgical procedures.
   d. small losses of fluid are significant because body fluids account for 45% to 50% of body weight in older adults.

2. During administration of a hypertonic IV solution, the mechanism involved in equalizing the fluid concentration between ECF and the cells is
   a. osmosis.
   b. diffusion.
   c. active transport.
   d. facilitated diffusion.

3a. An older woman is admitted to the medical unit with GI bleeding. Assessment findings that indicate fluid volume deficit include (*select all that apply*)
   a. weight loss.
   b. dry oral mucosa.
   c. full bounding pulse.
   d. engorged neck veins.
   e. decreased central venous pressure.

3b. The nursing care for a patient with hyponatremia and fluid volume excess includes
   a. fluid restriction.
   b. administration of hypotonic IV fluids.
   c. administration of a cation-exchange resin.
   d. placement of an indwelling urinary catheter.

3c. The nurse should be alert for which manifestations in a patient receiving a loop diuretic?
   a. Restlessness and agitation
   b. Paresthesias and irritability
   c. Weak, irregular pulse and poor muscle tone
   d. Increased blood pressure and muscle spasms

3d. Which patient is at *greatest* risk for developing hypermagnesemia?
   a. 83-year-old man with lung cancer and hypertension
   b. 65-year-old woman with hypertension taking β-adrenergic blockers
   c. 42-year-old woman with systemic lupus erythematosus and renal failure
   d. 50-year-old man with benign prostatic hyperplasia and a urinary tract infection

3e. It is important for the nurse to assess for which manifestation(s) in a patient who has just undergone a total thyroidectomy (*select all that apply*)?
   a. Confusion
   b. Weight gain
   c. Depressed reflexes
   d. Circumoral numbness
   e. Positive Chvostek's sign

3f. The nurse expects the long-term treatment of a patient with hyperphosphatemia from renal failure will include
   a. fluid restriction.
   b. calcium supplements.
   c. magnesium supplements.
   d. increased intake of dairy products.

4. The lungs act as an acid-base buffer by
   a. increasing respiratory rate and depth when CO_2 levels in the blood are high, reducing acid load.
   b. increasing respiratory rate and depth when CO_2 levels in the blood are low, reducing base load.
   c. decreasing respiratory rate and depth when CO_2 levels in the blood are high, reducing acid load.
   d. decreasing respiratory rate and depth when CO_2 levels in the blood are low, increasing acid load.

5. A patient has the following arterial blood gas results: pH 7.52, $PaCO_2$ 30 mm Hg, HCO_3^- 24 mEq/L. The nurse determines that these results indicate
   a. metabolic acidosis.
   b. metabolic alkalosis.
   c. respiratory acidosis.
   d. respiratory alkalosis.

6. The typical fluid replacement for the patient with a fluid volume deficit is
   a. dextran.
   b. 0.45% saline.
   c. lactated Ringer's solution.
   d. 5% dextrose in 0.45% saline.

7. The nurse is unable to flush a central venous access device and suspects occlusion. The *best* nursing intervention would be to
   a. apply warm moist compresses to the insertion site.
   b. try to force 10 mL of normal saline into the device.
   c. place the patient on the left side with the head down.
   d. have the patient change positions, raise arm, and cough.

1. d, 2. a, 3a. a, b, e, 3b. a, 3c. c, 3d. c, 3e. a, d, e, 3f. b, 4. a, 5. d, 6. c, 7. d

For rationales to these answers and even more NCLEX review questions, visit *http://evolve.elsevier.com/Lewis/medsurg*.

---

e EVOLVE WEBSITE/RESOURCES LIST

http://evolve.elsevier.com/Lewis/medsurg
Review Questions (Online Only)
Key Points
Answer Keys for Questions
   • Answer Guidelines for Case Study on p. 295
   • Rationales for Bridge to NCLEX Examination Questions
   • Answer Guidelines for Managing Care of Multiple Patients Case Study (Section 3) on p. 298

Student Case Study
   • Patient With Hyponatremia/Fluid Volume Imbalance
Conceptual Care Map Creator
Audio Glossary
Fluids and Electrolytes Tutorial
Content Updates

REFERENCES

1. Henderson R: Osmolality, osmolarity, and fluid homeostasis. Retrieved from *www.patient.info/doctor/osmolality-osmolarity-and-fluid-homeostasis.*

2. Reddi AS: *Fluid, electrolyte and acid-base disorders*, ed 2, New York, 2018, Springer.

*3. Oates LL, Price CI: Clinical assessments and care interventions to promote oral hydration amongst older patients: A narrative systematic review, *BMC Nurs* 16:4, 2017.

4. Hew-Butler T, Weisz K: Focus the secret stories of sodium: hypernatremia, *Clin Lab Sci* 29:3, 2016.

*5. Hoorn EJ, Zietse R: Diagnosis and treatment of hyponatremia: compilation of the guidelines, *J Am Soc Nephrol* 28:1340, 2017.

6. Rafiq MF: Hyponatremia still remains largely undiagnosed and untreated, *Anaesth Pain Intensive Care* 21:1, 2017.

*7. Douglas M, Rizzolo D, Kruger D: Hyperkalemia in adults: Review of a common electrolyte imbalance, *Clin Rev* 3:40, 2017.

8. Pincus M: Management of digoxin toxicity, *Austr Prescr* 39:1, 2016.

9. Body JJ, Niepel D, Tonini G: Hypercalcemia and hypocalcemia: Finding the balance, *Support Care Cancer* 25:5, 2017.

10. Walker M: Fluid and electrolyte imbalance: interpretation and assessment, *J Infusion Nurs* 39:6, 2016.

11. Boyle SM, Goldfarb S: *Phosphate deficiency and the phosphate-depletion syndrome: Pathophysiology, diagnosis, and treatment*, New York, 2017, Springer.

12. Hiner A: Electrolyte series: magnesium, *Nursing2018 Crit Care* 13:15, 2018.

13. Perkins A: Alkalosis in brief, *Nursing Made Incredibly Easy* 14:13, 2016.

14. Naisbitt C, Buckley H, Kishen R: Crystalloids, colloids, blood products, and blood substitutes, *Anaesth Intensive Care* 17:308, 2016.

*15. Septimus EJ, Moody J: Prevention of device-related healthcare-associated infections, *F1000Res* 14:5, 2016.

*Evidence-based information for clinical practice.

CASE STUDY

Managing Care of Multiple Patients

You and another RN are assigned to care for the following 3 patients in the intensive care unit. There is also an unlicensed assistive personnel (UAP) on duty.

Patients

(© Stockphoto/ Thinkstock.)

G.N., a 65-yr-old black man, was admitted to the ICU after falling into a lit gas grill. He has partial-thickness burns on his face, neck, and upper trunk. He has undergone surgical repair of right tibia and left hip fractures and debridement of a severely lacerated right leg. His voice is slightly hoarse, and he is coughing up sooty sputum. He is receiving O_2 at 4 L/min via nasal cannula, and his O_2 saturation is 93%. His WBC count is 26,400/μL (26.4 × 10^9/L) with 80% neutrophils (10% bands).

(© iStock.com/ Cecilie_Arcurs.)

J.N., a 65-yr-old black man, was transferred to the ICU from the clinical unit last evening with acute respiratory failure. He was diagnosed 2 days ago with AIDS and *Pneumocystis jiroveci* pneumonia (PCP). Prior to this hospital admission he was started on oral trimethoprim/sulfamethoxazole (Bactrim) and combination antiretroviral therapy. However, his respiratory distress worsened, and he was transferred to the ICU for intubation and mechanical ventilation. He is now receiving IV Bactrim.

(© Kevin Peterson/ Photodisc/ Thinkstock.)

S.S., a 63-yr-old white woman with acute lymphocytic leukemia, has been receiving chemotherapy on an outpatient basis. She completed her third treatment 5 days ago and has been experiencing nausea and vomiting for 2 days despite using ondansetron (Zofran). She was initially admitted to the clinical unit but was transferred to the ICU for close monitoring after becoming severely hypotensive overnight. Her most recent blood pressure was 98/50, HR 82 and regular, O_2 saturation 95% on 2 L via nasal cannula, RR 22 and regular.

Discussion Questions

1. ***Priority Decision:*** After receiving report, which patient should you see first? Provide your rationale.
2. ***Collaboration:*** Which morning tasks should you delegate to the UAP *(select all that apply)*?
   a. Take BP readings on S.S.
   b. Perform respiratory assessment on G.N.
   c. Document strict intake and output on S.S.
   d. Provide oral care around the endotracheal tube for J.N.
   e. Titrate S.S.'s IV infusion rate based on her BP reading.
3. ***Priority Decision and Collaboration:*** When you enter J.N.'s room, the ventilator alarms are going off. The UAP had just finished providing oral care, and she tells you that J.N. has become increasingly agitated within the last 5 minutes. Which *initial* action would be *most* appropriate?
   a. Suction J.N.'s endotracheal tube.
   b. Have the UAP stay with J.N. while you obtain IV sedation for him.
   c. Ask the UAP to describe exactly what she did when she was providing oral care.
   d. Assess the ventilator to identify what alarm is going off and to make sure all connections are secure.

Case Study Progression

J.N.'s ventilator tubing became disconnected. You quickly reconnect his tubing, and as he settles down his oxygenation improves. You ask the UAP to obtain vital signs on your other patients while you begin a more thorough assessment of J.N.

4. During your assessment of J.N., you note gray-white patches on the inside of his mouth. You recognize these as *most* likely caused by
   a. *Candida albicans.*
   b. poor oral hygiene.
   c. *Coccidioides immitis.*
   d. irritation from recent mouth care.
5. G.N.'s family asks you why surgery was performed on his leg wound. Your response is based on the knowledge that debridement *(select all that apply)*
   a. is used to remove infected tissue.
   b. is used to remove nonviable tissue.
   c. prepares the wound bed for healing.
   d. can be accomplished only in surgery.
   e. is necessary in any burn wound involving the skin.
6. S.S.'s morning laboratory results reveal a serum potassium level of 2.8 mEq/L. You notify the health care provider and obtain an order for IV potassium. During infusion of the potassium replacement, you prioritize assessment of S.S.'s
   a. bowel function.
   b. cardiac rhythm.
   c. muscle strength.
   d. level of consciousness.
7. ***Priority Decision:*** As the day continues, you find that you are getting busy. Which nursing task should be your priority?
   a. Changing the sterile dressings on G.N.'s leg wounds
   b. Performing routine suctioning of J.N.'s endotracheal tube
   c. Starting a 500-mL fluid bolus to S.S., whose most recent BP is 76/42
   d. Calling the hospital chaplain to speak with S.S., who is upset over her condition
8. ***Priority Decision:*** Which medication should you administer first?
   a. Daily subcutaneous enoxaparin to G.N.
   b. IV Bactrim, ordered twice daily, to J.N.
   c. IV proton pump inhibitor, ordered twice daily, to S.S.
   d. As needed IV morphine to G.N., who reports pain at a level 9 (1 to 10 scale)
9. ***Management Decision:*** While sitting at the computer charting your patients' morning assessments, you overhear the UAP telling a nursing student that J.N. deserves what he got because HIV is God's way of punishing those who sin. Your *most* appropriate response would be to
   a. report the UAP's actions to the supervisor.
   b. ask the UAP to keep her opinions to herself.
   c. ignore the conversation because it does not affect patient care.
   d. talk to the UAP and student about keeping personal feelings separate from patient care.

Answers available at *http://evolve.elsevier.com/Lewis/medsurg.*

17

Preoperative Care

Janice A. Neil

From caring comes courage.

Lao Tzu

ℯ http://evolve.elsevier.com/Lewis/medsurg/

CONCEPTUAL FOCUS

Anxiety
Patient Education

Safety

LEARNING OUTCOMES

1. Distinguish the common purposes and settings of surgery.
2. Apply knowledge of the purpose and components of a preoperative nursing assessment.
3. Interpret the significance of data related to the preoperative patient's health status and operative risk.
4. Analyze the components and purpose of the patient's informed consent for surgery.

5. Examine the nursing role in the physical, psychological, and educational preparation of the surgical patient.
6. Prioritize the nursing responsibilities related to day-of-surgery preparation for the surgical patient.
7. Discern the purposes and types of common preoperative medications.
8. Apply knowledge of the special considerations of preoperative preparation for the older adult surgical patient.

KEY TERMS

ambulatory surgery, p. 300
elective surgery, p. 300

emergency surgery, p. 300
informed consent, p. 307

same-day admission, p. 300
surgery, p. 299

Surgery is the art and science of treating diseases, injuries, and deformities by operation and instrumentation. The total surgical episode is called the *perioperative period*. This period includes the time before surgery (preoperative period), the time spent during the actual surgical procedure (intraoperative period), and the period after the surgery is over (postoperative period).

The surgical experience involves an interprofessional team, including the patient, surgeon, anesthesia care provider (ACP), nurse, and other health care team members. Preparing patients for surgery is an important nursing role. This chapter discusses preoperative care that applies to all surgical patients. Preparation measures for specific surgical procedures (e.g., abdominal, thoracic, or orthopedic surgery) are discussed in the appropriate chapters of this book.

Surgery is performed for many reasons. These include:

- *Diagnosis:* Determine the presence and extent of a pathologic condition (e.g., lymph node biopsy, bronchoscopy).

- *Cure:* Eliminate or repair a pathologic condition (e.g., removal of ruptured appendix or benign ovarian cyst).
- *Palliation:* Alleviate symptoms without cure (e.g., cutting a nerve root [rhizotomy] to reduce pain, creating a colostomy to bypass an inoperable bowel obstruction).
- *Prevention:* Reduce risk of developing a condition (e.g., removal of a mole before it becomes malignant, removal of the colon in a patient with familial polyposis to prevent cancer).
- *Cosmetic improvement*: Alter physical appearance (e.g., repairing a burn scar, breast reconstruction after a mastectomy).
- *Exploration:* Determine the nature or extent of a disease (e.g., laparotomy). With the use of advanced diagnostic tests, exploration is less common because we can identify many problems noninvasively.

Surgical procedures are usually described by combining specific suffixes with a body part or organ (Table 17.1).

TABLE 17.1	Suffixes Describing Surgical Procedures	
Suffix	**Meaning**	**Example**
-ectomy	Excision or removal of	Appendectomy
-lysis	Destruction of	Electrolysis
-orrhaphy	Repair or suture of	Herniorrhaphy
-oscopy	Looking into	Endoscopy
-ostomy	Creation of opening into	Colostomy
-otomy	Cutting into or incision of	Tracheotomy
-plasty	Repair or reconstruction of	Mammoplasty

SURGICAL SETTINGS

Surgery may be a carefully planned event (elective surgery) or may arise with unexpected urgency (emergency surgery). Both elective and emergency surgeries are done in a variety of settings. The type of surgery, potential complications, and the patient's health status influence the setting where a patient can safely undergo a surgical procedure

For inpatient surgery, patients who are going to be admitted to the hospital are usually admitted on the day of surgery (same-day admission). Patients who are in the hospital before surgery are usually there because of acute or chronic medical conditions.

Most surgical procedures are performed as ambulatory surgery (also called *same-day* or *outpatient surgery*). Many of these surgeries use minimally invasive techniques (e.g., laparoscopic techniques). Ambulatory surgery often occurs in endoscopy clinics, physicians' offices, freestanding surgical clinics, and outpatient surgery units in hospitals. These procedures can involve the use of general, regional, or local anesthetic. Patients require less than a 24-hour stay after surgery. Many go home with a caregiver within hours of surgery.

Patients and HCPs often prefer ambulatory surgery. Generally, it requires fewer laboratory tests and medications and reduces the patient's risk for health care–associated infections. Patients like the convenience of recovering at home. HCPs prefer the flexibility in scheduling. The costs are usually less for the patient and the insurer.

You play an essential role in preparing the patient for surgery, caring for the patient during surgery, and aiding the patient's recovery after surgery. To perform these functions effectively, first know the reason the patient is undergoing surgery and any co-morbidities. Second, identify the individual patient's response to the stress of surgery. Third, know the results of preoperative diagnostic tests. Last, identify potential risks and complications associated with the surgical procedure and any special considerations that should be addressed in the plan of care. The nurse caring for the patient before surgery is likely to be different from the nurse in the operating room (OR), postanesthesia care unit (PACU), surgical intensive care unit (SICU), or surgical unit. Communication and documentation of important preoperative assessment findings are essential for quality care.

PATIENT INTERVIEW

One of the most important nursing actions is the preoperative interview. The nurse who works in the physician's office, ambulatory surgery center, or hospital may do the interview.

The preoperative interview can occur in advance or on the day of surgery. The primary purposes of the patient interview are to (1) obtain the patient's health information, including drug and food allergies; (2) provide and clarify information about the planned surgery, including anesthesia; and (3) assess the patient's emotional state and readiness for surgery, including his or her expectations about the surgical outcomes. The interview gives the patient and caregiver an opportunity to ask questions about the surgery, anesthesia, and postoperative care. Often patients ask about taking their routine drugs, such as insulin, anticoagulants, or heart medications, and if they will have pain. By being aware of the patient's and caregiver's needs, you can provide the information and support needed during the perioperative period.

NURSING ASSESSMENT OF PREOPERATIVE PATIENT

The overall goal of the preoperative assessment is to identify risk factors and plan care to ensure patient safety throughout the surgical experience. To achieve this, you will need to do the following:

- Establish baseline data for comparison in the intraoperative and postoperative period.
- Determine the patient's psychologic status to reinforce the use of coping strategies during the surgical experience.
- Determine physiologic factors directly or indirectly related to the surgical procedure that may contribute to operative risk factors.
- Participate in the identification and documentation of the surgical site according to agency protocol.
- Identify prescription drugs, over-the-counter (OTC) drugs, and herbs taken by the patient that may result in drug interactions affecting the surgical outcome.
- Review the results of all preoperative diagnostic studies in the patient's record and share this information with the appropriate HCPs.
- Identify cultural and ethnic factors that may affect the surgical experience.
- Determine if the patient received adequate information from the surgeon to make an informed decision to have surgery and that the consent form is signed and witnessed.

Subjective Data

Psychosocial Assessment. Surgery is a stressful event, even when the procedure is minor. The psychologic and physiologic reactions to surgery may elicit the stress response (e.g., elevated BP and heart rate). The stress response enables the body to meet the demands in the perioperative period. If stressors or the responses to the stressors are excessive, the stress response can be magnified and may affect recovery. Many factors influence the patient's reaction to stress, including age, past experiences with illness and pain, current health, and socioeconomic status.

The use of common language and avoidance of medical jargon are essential. Use words and language that are familiar to the patient to help the patient understand the surgery. Familiar language also helps reduce anxiety.

Your role in psychologically preparing the patient for surgery is to assess the patient for potential or actual stressors that could negatively affect surgery (Table 17.2). Communicate all concerns to the appropriate surgical team member, especially if the concern requires intervention later in the surgical experience.

TABLE 17.2 Psychosocial Assessment of Preoperative Patient

Situational Changes
- Define current degree of personal control, decision making, and independence
- Determine the presence of hope and anticipation of positive results
- Consider the impact of surgery and hospitalization and possible effects on lifestyle
- Identify support systems, including family, other caregivers, and religious and spiritual groups

Concerns With the Unknown
- Identify degree of anxiety and fears related to the surgery (e.g., pain)
- Identify expectations of surgery, changes in current health status, effects on daily living, and sexual activity (if appropriate)

Concerns With Body Image
- Identify current roles or relationships and view of self
- Determine perceived or potential changes in roles or relationships and their impact on body image

Past Experiences
- Review previous surgical experiences, hospitalizations, and treatments
- Determine responses to those experiences (positive and/or negative)
- Identify current perceptions of surgical procedure in relation to the above and information from others (e.g., a friend's view of a personal surgical experience)

Lack of Knowledge
- Determine the amount and type of information the patient wants
- Assess understanding of surgical procedure, including preparation, care, interventions, preoperative activities, restrictions, and expected outcomes
- Review the accuracy of information the patient has received from others, including health care team, family, friends, and media

EVIDENCE-BASED PRACTICE
Music and Preoperative Anxiety

You are taking care of D.G., a 67-yr-old woman scheduled for a renal mass biopsy to rule out metastatic disease. She was admitted early this morning to the preoperative unit. Unfortunately, an emergency surgery has resulted in at least a 4-hour delay of her procedure. You note that she has a high level of anxiety.

Making Clinical Decisions

Best Available Evidence. Complementary and alternative therapies include a variety of interventions, such as mental imagery, aromatherapy, acupuncture, and music. Music intervention in the preoperative period, including listening to pre-recorded music or individually tailored music given by a trained therapist, can help reduce anxiety. While sedatives and antianxiety drugs are often given before surgery, these drugs can have negative side effects, especially in the older adult.

Clinician Expertise. Anxiety can increase BP and pulse rate and may lengthen postoperative recovery. Excessive anxiety can even result in surgery being canceled.

Patient Preference and Values. D.G. tells you that she cannot relax and would like "a strong pill" to help her calm down. D.G.'s family mentioned to you earlier that she enjoys listening to classical music at home.

Implications for Practice

1. What information would you share with D.G. related to the use of drugs to reduce her anxiety?
2. How would you respond to D.G. when she asks how music could possibly help in reducing her anxiety?

Reference for Evidence

Bradt J, Dileo C, Shim M: Music interventions for preoperative anxiety, *Cochrane Database Syst Rev* 6:CD006908, 2013. (Classic)

Because many patients are admitted directly into the preoperative area from their homes, you must be skilled in assessing important psychologic factors in a short time. The most common psychologic factors are anxiety, fear, and hope.

Anxiety. Most people are anxious when facing surgery because of the unknown. This is normal and is an inborn survival mechanism. However, a high anxiety level can impair cognition, decision making, and coping abilities.

Anxiety can arise from lack of knowledge. This can range from not knowing what to expect to uncertainty about the outcome and may result from past experiences or stories heard through friends or the media. You can decrease some anxiety for the patient by giving information about what to expect. This is often done through classes or Web-based or audiovisual teaching materials before surgery. Inform the surgeon if the patient needs more information or has excessive anxiety.

Patients may have anxiety when surgery conflicts with their religious or cultural beliefs. Identify, record, and communicate patient decisions about the possibility of blood transfusions. For example, Jehovah's Witnesses may choose to refuse blood or blood products.[1]

Common Fears. Patients fear surgery for many reasons. The most common fear is the risk for death or permanent disability resulting from surgery. Sometimes the fear comes after hearing or reading about the risks during the informed consent process. Other fears are related to pain, change in body image, or results of diagnostic procedures.

Fear of death can be extremely harmful. Notify the HCP if the patient has a strong fear of death. A patient's strong fear of impending death may prompt the HCP to delay the surgery because the emotional state influences the stress response and thus the surgical outcome.

Fear of pain and discomfort during and after surgery is common. If the fear is extreme, notify the ACP or the surgeon. Reassure the patient that drugs are available for anesthesia and analgesia during surgery. For pain after surgery, tell patients to ask for pain medication before pain becomes severe. Teach the patient how to use a pain intensity scale (e.g., 0 to 10, FACES). See Chapter 8 for more on pain scales.

The patient may receive drugs that provide an amnesic effect so that the patient will not remember what occurs during surgery. Tell the patient that helps decrease anxiety after surgery.

Fear of mutilation or an *altered body image* can occur whether the surgery is radical, such as amputation, or minor, such as a breast biopsy. Even a small scar on the body can upset some, and others fear keloid development (overgrowth of a scar). Listen to and assess the patient's concern about this fear with an accepting attitude.

Fear of anesthesia may arise from the unknown, personal experience, or tales of others' bad experiences. These concerns can also result from information about the risks of anesthesia (e.g., brain damage, paralysis). Many patients fear losing control while under anesthesia. If you identify any of these fears, inform the ACP at once so that he or she can talk further with the patient.

Fear of disruption of life functioning may be present in varying degrees. It can range from fear of permanent disability to concern about not being able to engage in activities of daily living for a few weeks. You may find concerns about loss of role function, separation from family, and how the family will manage. Financial concerns include dealing with an expected loss of income and the costs of surgery.

If you find any of these fears, a consult with the patient's caregiver, a social worker, a spiritual advisor, or a psychologist may be appropriate. Financial advisors at the hospital may be able to give information about financial support.

❓ CHECK YOUR PRACTICE

Your 19-yr-old male patient is in the holding area. He is scheduled for an orchiectomy for testicular cancer. He is visibly sweating and agitated. When you ask him how he is doing, he responds, "I am scared. Wouldn't you be?"
- What can you do to reduce his fear?

Hope. Although many psychologic factors related to surgery seem to be negative, hope is a positive attribute. Hope may be the patient's strongest method of coping. To deny or minimize hope may negate the positive mental attitude necessary for a quick and full recovery. Some patients hopefully anticipate surgery. These can be the surgeries that repair (e.g., plastic surgery for burn scars), rebuild (e.g., total joint replacement to reduce pain and improve function), or save and extend life (e.g., repair of aneurysm, organ transplant). Assess and support the presence of hope and the patient's anticipation of positive results.

Past Health History. Ask the patient about any previous health problems and surgeries. Determine if the patient understands the need for surgery. For example, the patient scheduled for a total knee replacement may say that increasing pain and immobility are the reasons for the surgery.

Record the reason for any past hospitalizations, including previous surgeries and the dates. Identify any problems with previous surgeries. For example, the patient may have had a wound infection or a reaction to a drug.

Ask women about their menstrual and obstetric history. This includes the date of their last menstrual period, the number of pregnancies, and any history of cesarean section.

When obtaining a family health history, ask the patient and caregiver about any inherited traits, since they may contribute to the surgical outcome. Record any family history of heart and endocrine diseases. For example, if a patient reports a parent with hypertension, sudden cardiac death, or myocardial infarction, this should alert you to the possibility that the patient may have a similar predisposition or condition. Obtain information about the patient's family history of adverse reactions to or problems with anesthesia. For example, malignant hyperthermia has a genetic predisposition. If present, measures will be taken to decrease complications associated with this condition (see Chapter 18).

Medications. Document all current medication use, including OTC drugs and herbs. Many surgery centers ask patients to bring their medications with them when reporting for surgery.

This helps to accurately assess and document the name and dosage of medications.

The interaction of the patient's current drugs and anesthetics can increase or decrease the desired physiologic effect of anesthetics. Consider the effects of opioids and prescribed drugs for chronic health conditions (e.g., heart disease, hypertension, depression, seizure disorder, diabetes). For example, certain antidepressants can potentiate the effect of opioid agents used for anesthesia or pain control. Antihypertensive drugs may predispose the patient to shock from the combined effect of the drug and the vasodilator effect of some anesthetic agents. Insulin or oral hypoglycemic drugs may need adjustments during the perioperative period because of increased body metabolism, decreased oral intake, stress, and anesthesia. Antiplatelet drugs (e.g., aspirin, clopidogrel [Plavix]) and nonsteroidal antiinflammatory drugs (NSAIDs) inhibit platelet aggregation and may contribute to postoperative bleeding.

HCPs may have patients withhold medications before surgery. Specific timeframes for withholding medications depend on the medication and the patient. Patients on long-term anticoagulation therapy (e.g., warfarin [Coumadin], rivaroxaban [Xarelto], dabigatran [Pradaxa], apixaban [Eliquis]) present a unique challenge. The options for these patients include (1) continuing therapy, (2) withholding therapy for a time before and after surgery, or (3) withholding the therapy and starting subcutaneous or IV heparin therapy during the perioperative period. The management strategy selected is based on the patient history and the nature of the surgery.[2]

Ask about the use of herbs and dietary supplements because their use is so common. Many patients do not think to include supplements in their list of medications. They believe that herbal and dietary supplements are "natural" and do not pose a surgical risk.[3] Excess use of vitamins and herbs can cause harmful effects in patients undergoing surgery. In those taking anticoagulants or antiplatelets, herbal supplements can produce excess postoperative bleeding that may require a return to the OR.[3] The Complementary & Alternative Therapies box lists the effects of specific herbs that are of concern during the perioperative period.

🌿 COMPLEMENTARY & ALTERNATIVE THERAPIES
Herbal Products and Surgery

Use the following as a guide for patient teaching:
- Notify your HCP of all vitamins, herbs, and dietary supplements that you are taking.
- Avoid astragalus and ginseng, since they can increase BP before and during surgery.
- Avoid garlic, vitamin E, ginkgo, and fish oils because they can increase bleeding.
- Avoid kava and valerian because they can cause excessive sedation.
- In general, stop taking all herbs 2 to 3 weeks before any surgical procedure. Consult your HCP for specific instructions.
- Take multivitamins until the day before surgery. Taking them on the day of surgery on an empty stomach may contribute to nausea and vomiting after surgery.

Ask the patient about any substance use. The most likely used substances include tobacco, alcohol, opioids, marijuana, cocaine, and amphetamines. Ask questions about use in a frank manner. Stress that substance use may affect the type and amount of anesthesia the patient will need. When patients become aware of the potential interactions of these substances with anesthetics, most patients respond honestly about using them.

Chronic alcohol use can place the patient at risk because of lung, GI, or liver damage. Decreased liver function prolongs the metabolism of anesthetic agents, alters nutritional status, and increases the potential for postoperative complications. Alcohol withdrawal can occur during lengthy surgery or in the postoperative period. Proper planning and management are needed to avoid this life-threatening event (see Chapter 10).

Record and share all findings of the drug history with the perioperative health care team. The ACP will decide the best schedule and dose of the patient's routine drugs before and after surgery. Ensure that you identify all the patient's drugs, implement any changes in the medication plan, and monitor the patient for potential interactions and complications.

Allergies. Ask the patient about drug intolerances and drug allergies. Drug intolerance usually results in side effects that are unpleasant for the patient but are not life threatening. These effects can include nausea, constipation, diarrhea, or *idiosyncratic* (opposite than expected) reactions. A true drug allergy produces hives and/or an anaphylactic reaction, causing cardiopulmonary compromise (e.g., hypotension, tachycardia, bronchospasm). Being aware of drug intolerances and drug allergies helps the health care team maintain patient comfort and safety.

Record all drug intolerances and allergies and, if needed, place an allergy identification band on the patient on the day of surgery.

> **! SAFETY ALERT Allergies**
> • Some local anesthetic agents contain bisulfite preservatives.
> • Notify the ACP if the patient reports an allergy to sulfur-containing drugs.

Ask about nondrug allergies, specifically food and environmental (e.g., latex, pollen, animals) allergies. The patient with a history of any allergic reactions has a greater potential for hypersensitivity reactions to drugs given during anesthesia. Screen all patients for latex allergies by gathering data about:
- Risk factors
- Contact dermatitis
- Contact urticaria (e.g., hives)
- Aerosol reactions
- History of reactions that suggest an allergy to latex

Risk factors for latex allergy include long-term, multiple exposures to latex products, such as those experienced by health care and rubber industry workers. Other risk factors include a history of hay fever, asthma, and allergies to certain foods (e.g., eggs, avocados, bananas, chestnuts, potatoes, peaches).[4] Latex allergies are discussed in Chapter 13.

Review of Systems. The last part of the patient history is the body systems review. Ask specific questions to confirm the presence or absence of any diseases. Current health problems can alert you to areas that you will need to examine in the preoperative physical examination. The combined review of systems and patient history provide essential data to determine the specific preoperative tests that the patient needs.

Cardiovascular System. Evaluate cardiovascular (CV) function to determine preexisting disease or problems (e.g., coronary artery disease, prosthetic heart valve). In reviewing the CV system, you may find a history of hypertension, angina, dysrhythmias, heart failure, or myocardial infarction (MI). Ask about the patient's current treatment for any CV condition (e.g., drugs) and the level of functioning. A cardiology consult is often needed before surgery if the patient has a significant CV history (e.g., recent MI, valvular heart disease, implantable cardioverter-defibrillator).

If indicated, the patient should have a 12-lead electrocardiogram (ECG) and coagulation studies and the results should be on the chart before surgery. The CV assessment provides data on what other measures the patient needs. For example, the patient who is on diuretic therapy needs to have a serum potassium level drawn before surgery. If the patient has hypertension, the ACP may give vasoactive drugs to maintain adequate BP during surgery. The patient with a prosthetic heart valve may receive antibiotic prophylaxis before surgery to decrease the risk for infective endocarditis (see Chapter 36).

Venous thromboembolism (VTE), a condition that includes deep vein thrombosis and pulmonary embolism, is a concern for any surgical patient. Patients at high risk for VTE include those with a history of previous thrombosis, blood-clotting disorders, cancer, varicosities, obesity, tobacco use, heart failure, or chronic obstructive pulmonary disease (COPD).[5] People are also at risk for developing a VTE because of immobility and positioning during the operative procedure. Intermittent pneumatic compression devices (IPCs) may be applied in the preoperative holding area.

Respiratory System. Ask the patient about any recent or chronic respiratory disease or infections. Elective surgery may be postponed if the person has an upper respiratory tract infection. Upper airway infections may increase the risk for bronchospasm, laryngospasm, decreased O_2 saturation, and problems with respiratory secretions. Report a patient's history of dyspnea at rest or with exertion, coughing (dry or productive), or hemoptysis (coughing blood) to the ACP and surgeon.

If a patient has a history of asthma, ask about the use of inhaled or oral corticosteroids and bronchodilators, as well as the frequency and triggers of asthma attacks. The patient with a history of COPD is at high risk for pulmonary complications, including hypoxemia and atelectasis.

Gather information about the patient's tobacco use. The HCP and you should encourage the patient to stop smoking at least 6 weeks before surgery. Smoking increases the risk for pulmonary complications during and after surgery. Report conditions likely to affect respiratory function such as sleep apnea, obesity, and spinal, chest, and airway deformities. For example, patients are often asked to bring their sleep apnea devices with them to the hospital or surgical center. Depending on the patient's history and physical examination, baseline pulmonary function tests and arterial blood gases may be done before surgery.

Neurologic System. Evaluation of neurologic functioning includes assessing the patient's ability to respond to questions, follow commands, and maintain orderly thought patterns. Changes in the patient's hearing and vision may affect responses and the ability to follow directions throughout the perioperative assessment and evaluation. Record the patient's ability to pay attention, concentrate, and respond appropriately to establish a baseline for postoperative comparison.

If you note deficits in cognitive function, determine the extent of the problems and whether they can be corrected before surgery. If the problems cannot be corrected, it is important to involve a legal guardian or person with durable power of attorney for health care to aid the patient and provide informed consent for surgery.

Preoperative assessment of the older person's baseline cognitive function is especially crucial for comparison during and after surgery. The older adult may have intact mental abilities before surgery but is more prone to adverse outcomes during and after surgery than the younger adult. This is due to the added stressors of the surgical procedure, dehydration, hypothermia, and anesthesia and adjunctive drugs. These factors may contribute to the development of *emergence delirium,* a condition that may be falsely labeled as senility or dementia.

In the review of the neurologic system, obtain about any history of strokes, transient ischemic attacks, or spinal cord injury. Ask about neurologic diseases, such as myasthenia gravis, Parkinson's disease, and multiple sclerosis, and any treatments used.

Genitourinary System. Assess for a history of renal or urinary tract diseases, such as chronic kidney disease or repeated urinary tract infections. Record the present disease state and current treatment. Renal dysfunction is associated with several problems, including fluid and electrolyte imbalances, coagulopathies, increased risk for infection, and impaired wound healing. Because the kidneys metabolize and excrete many drugs, a decrease in renal function can lead to an altered response to drugs and unpredictable drug elimination. Renal function tests (e.g., serum creatinine, blood urea nitrogen [BUN]) are often done before surgery.

Record and share with the perioperative team if the patient has problems voiding (e.g., incontinence, hesitancy). Older male patients may have an enlarged prostate that can interfere with the insertion of a bladder catheter or impair voiding after surgery.

For a woman of childbearing age, determine if she is pregnant or thinks she could be pregnant. Most agencies perform a pregnancy test for all women of childbearing age before surgery.[6] Immediately tell the surgeon if the patient states that she may be pregnant. Maternal and fetal exposure to anesthetics should be avoided during the first trimester.

Hepatic System. The liver is involved in glucose homeostasis, fat metabolism, protein synthesis, drug and hormone metabolism, and bilirubin formation and excretion. The liver detoxifies many anesthetics and adjunctive drugs. The patient with hepatic dysfunction may have an increased perioperative risk for clotting abnormalities and adverse responses to drugs. Consider the presence of liver disease if there is a history of jaundice, hepatitis, alcohol abuse, or obesity.

Integumentary System. Ask about a history of skin problems. Assess the current condition of the skin, especially at the incision site, for rashes, breakdown, or other skin conditions. A patient with a history of pressure injuries may need extra padding during surgery. Skin problems can affect wound healing.

Body art such as tattoos and piercings are increasingly common. When possible, select pigment-free areas for injections, IV sites, and laboratory draws.

Musculoskeletal System. Note any musculoskeletal and mobility problems, especially in the older adult. If the patient has arthritis, identify all affected joints. Mobility restrictions may influence intraoperative and postoperative positioning and ambulation. Spinal anesthesia may be difficult if the patient cannot flex the lumbar spine enough to allow easy needle insertion. If the neck is affected, intubation and airway management may be difficult. Any mobility aids (e.g., cane, walker) should be with the patient on the day of surgery.

Endocrine System. The patient with diabetes is especially at risk for adverse effects of anesthesia and surgery. Hypoglycemia, hyperglycemia, delayed wound healing, and infection are common complications of diabetes during the perioperative period. Clarify with the surgeon or ACP whether the patient should take the usual dose of insulin or oral hypoglycemic agents on the day of surgery. ACPs may vary the usual insulin dose based on the patient's status and history of glucose control. Measure serum or capillary glucose levels the morning of surgery to establish baseline levels. Assess the patient's glucose levels regularly and, if necessary, manage according to agency protocol.

Determine if the patient has a history of thyroid dysfunction. Hyperthyroidism or hypothyroidism can place the patient at surgical risk because of changes in metabolic rate. If the patient takes a thyroid replacement drug, check with the ACP about administering the drug on the day of surgery. If the patient has a history of thyroid dysfunction, laboratory tests may be done to determine current levels of thyroid function.

The patient with Addison's disease needs special consideration during surgery. Addisonian crisis or shock can occur if a patient abruptly stops taking replacement corticosteroids. The patient may need additional IV corticosteroid therapy from the stress of surgery[7] (see Chapter 49).

Immune System. Note if the patient has a history of a compromised immune system or takes immunosuppressive drugs. Corticosteroids used in immunosuppressive doses may be tapered before surgery. Impairment of the immune system can lead to delayed wound healing and increased risk for infections.[8] Elective surgery may be cancelled if the patient has an acute infection (e.g., sinusitis, influenza). Patients with active chronic infections such as hepatitis B or C, acquired immunodeficiency syndrome, or tuberculosis may have surgery if needed. However, when preparing the patient for surgery, remember to take infection control precautions for the protection of the patient and staff. Infection control guidelines are discussed in Chapter 14.

Fluid and Electrolyte Status. Ask the patient about any recent conditions that increase the risk for fluid and electrolyte imbalances, such as vomiting, diarrhea, or completing a bowel prep. Identify drugs that change fluid and electrolyte status, such as diuretics. Serum electrolyte levels are often assessed before surgery. Many patients may have restricted fluids for a specific period of time before surgery. They could develop dehydration if surgery is delayed. A patient with or at risk for dehydration may need more fluids and electrolytes before or during surgery.

Complete a preoperative fluid balance history for all patients. This is especially critical for older adults. Their reduced adaptive capacity leaves a narrow margin of safety between overhydration and underhydration.

Nutritional Status. Nutritional problems include overnutrition and undernutrition, both of which need considerable time to correct. However, knowing that a patient has a nutritional problem can help the health care team provide more customized care. For example, if the patient is thin, place more padding than usual on the OR table. Notify the team if a patient is severely obese (body mass index [BMI] greater than 40 kg/m^2) to allow time to obtain special equipment needed for the patient's care (e.g., longer instruments for abdominal surgery).

Obesity stresses the heart and lung systems and makes access to the surgical site and anesthesia administration more difficult.[9] It predisposes the patient to wound dehiscence, wound infection, and incisional herniation after surgery. Adipose tissue is less vascular than other types of tissue. The patient may be slower to recover from anesthesia because adipose tissue absorbs and stores inhalation agents, so they leave the body more slowly. See Chapter 40 for the special needs of obese patients undergoing surgery.

Nutritional problems impair the ability to recover from surgery. Remember that the obese patient or the very thin patient can be protein and vitamin deficient. If the problem is severe, surgery may be postponed. Protein and vitamins A, C, and B complex deficiencies are particularly important because these substances are essential for wound healing.[10] Patients who are malnourished may receive supplemental nutrition during the perioperative period. The older adult is often at risk for malnutrition and fluid volume deficits.

Identify patients who consume large quantities of coffee or caffeinated soft drinks. In many cases, withholding caffeinated beverages before surgery or for some time after surgery can lead to severe withdrawal headaches.[11] These headaches can be confused with spinal headaches if the preoperative data are not recorded. Giving caffeinated beverages after surgery, when possible, may prevent these headaches.

Objective Data

Physical Examination. The Joint Commission requires that all patients admitted to the OR have a documented history and physical examination (H&P) in their chart.[12] This may be done in advance of surgery or on the day of surgery. Any qualified HCP, including advanced practice nurses, physicians, physician assistants, or ACPs, may perform the H&P. Findings from the H&P enable the ACP to assign the patient a physical status rating for anesthesia administration (Table 17.3). This rating is an indicator of the patient's perioperative risk and may influence perioperative decisions. It uses a scale of P1 to P6. A rating of P6 is reserved for a brain-dead patient undergoing organ procurement. Patients undergoing surgery in ambulatory or outpatient settings generally have ratings of P1, P2, or P3. Other designations can be added to the ASA status (e.g., "E" to designate an "emergent" procedure).

Complete a physical examination of the patient before surgery (Table 17.4). Review the documentation already present in the patient's chart, including the H&P, to better proceed with

TABLE 17.3 American Society of Anesthesiologists' (ASA) Physical Classification System

Rating	Definition
P1 (ASA I)	Normal healthy person
P2 (ASA II)	Patient with mild systemic disease
P3 (ASA III)	Patient with severe systemic disease
P4 (ASA IV)	Patient with severe systemic disease that is a constant threat to life
P5 (ASA V)	Moribund patient who is not expected to survive without surgery
P6 (ASA VI)	Declared brain-dead patient whose organs are being removed for donor purposes

Source: American Society of Anesthesiologists: ASA physical status classification system, 2014. Retrieved from www.asahq.org/resources/clinical-information/asa-physical-status-classification-system.

TABLE 17.4 Health Assessment and Physical Examination of Preoperative Patient*

Cardiovascular System
- Identify acute or chronic problems. Note presence of angina, hypertension, heart failure, recent myocardial infarction.
- Identify any drugs (e.g., aspirin) or herbs (e.g., ginkgo) that may affect coagulation.
- Identify patients with prosthetic heart valves, pacemakers, or implantable cardioverter-defibrillators.
- Assess for edema (including dependent areas), noting location and severity.
- Inspect neck veins for distention.
- Obtain bilateral baseline BPs.
- Assess capillary refill and pulses for rate, rhythm, and quality: apical, radial, and pedal.

Gastrointestinal System
- Determine patterns of food and fluid intake and any recent changes in weight.
- Review usual pattern of bowel movements, including date of last bowel movement.
- Assess for presence of dentures and bridges (loose dentures or teeth may be dislodged during intubation).
- Weigh patient.
- Auscultate abdomen for presence of bowel sounds.

Genitourinary System
- Identify any infection or preexisting disease.
- Determine ability to void.
- Note color, amount, and characteristics of urine.
- Determine pregnancy status (if appropriate).

Hepatic System
- Review any substance use, especially alcohol and IV drug use.
- Inspect skin color and sclera of eyes for any signs of jaundice.

Immune System
- Note any immunodeficiency or autoimmune disorders.
- Assess for use of corticosteroids or other immunosuppressant drugs.

Integumentary System
- Determine skin status. Note any current or previous skin problems (e.g., pressure injuries, eczema, bruising).
- Inspect skin for rashes, boils, or infection, especially around the planned surgical site.
- Inspect mucous membranes and skin turgor for signs of dehydration.
- Assess skin moisture and temperature.

Musculoskeletal System
- Examine skin around bone pressure points.
- Assess for limitations in joint range of motion and muscle strength.
- Assess for joint or muscle pain.
- Assess mobility, gait, and balance.

Neurologic System
- Determine orientation to person, place, and time.
- Assess baseline mental status. Note any confusion, disorderly thinking, or inability to follow commands.
- Identify any history of strokes, transient ischemic attacks, or neurologic diseases (e.g., Parkinson's disease, multiple sclerosis).

Respiratory System
- Identify acute or chronic problems. Note presence of infection, chronic obstructive pulmonary disease, or asthma.
- Note use of continuous positive airway pressure (CPAP) machine.
- Assess tobacco history, including date/time of last cigarette and number of pack-years.
- Determine baseline O_2 saturation and respiratory rate and rhythm.
- Observe for cough, dyspnea, and use of accessory muscles of respiration.
- Auscultate lungs for normal and adventitious breath sounds.

*See specific body system chapters for more detailed assessments and related laboratory studies.

TABLE 17.5 Common Preoperative Diagnostic Studies

Test	Assessment
ABGs, pulse oximetry	Respiratory and metabolic function, oxygenation status
Blood glucose	Metabolic status, diabetes
Blood urea nitrogen, creatinine	Renal function
Chest x-ray	Lung disorders, cardiac enlargement, heart failure
CBC: RBCs, Hgb, Hct, WBCs	Anemia, immune status, infection
Electrocardiogram	Heart disease, dysrhythmias
Electrolytes	Metabolic status, renal function, diuretic side effects
hCG	Pregnancy status
Liver function tests	Liver status
PT, PTT, INR, platelet count	Coagulation status
Pulmonary function studies	Pulmonary status
Serum albumin	Nutritional status
Type and crossmatch	Blood available for replacement (elective surgery patients may have own blood available)
Urinalysis	Renal status, hydration, urinary tract infection

CBC, Complete blood count; *hCG,* human chorionic gonadotropin; *Hct,* hematocrit; *Hgb,* hemoglobin; *INR,* international normalized ratio; *PT,* prothrombin time; *PTT,* partial thromboplastin time.

your examination. Record all findings and share any relevant findings at once with the surgeon or ACP.

Diagnostic Studies. Obtain and assess the results of diagnostic studies ordered before surgery (Table 17.5). For example, a patient taking an antiplatelet drug (e.g., aspirin) may have a coagulation profile done or a patient on diuretic therapy may have a potassium level checked. A woman of childbearing age may receive a pregnancy test. An ECG is done for many who take drugs for dysrhythmias or have high blood pressure. Patients with diabetes undergo blood glucose monitoring. In many settings, patients are tested for methicillin-resistant *Staphylococcus aureus.* Those with positive results are prescribed antibiotics for several days before surgery.[13]

Ideally, preoperative tests are ordered based on the patient's H&P. However, many agencies and insurers have protocols for preoperative tests, which may not include all those in Table 17.5. In addition, some tests may be done days before surgery. Ensure that all laboratory and diagnostic reports are in the patient's chart. Missing reports may result in a delay or cancellation of the surgery.

❖ NURSING MANAGEMENT: PREOPERATIVE PATIENT

Base the preoperative nursing interventions on the nursing assessment, depending on the patient's specific needs. The pending surgery and routines of the surgery setting guide the patient's physical preparation. Preoperative teaching may be minimal or extensive. The Association of periOperative Registered Nurses (AORN) provides standards and recommended practices to guide nursing interventions in all perioperative settings.[5]

◆ Preoperative Teaching

The patient has a right to know what to expect and how to take part effectively during the surgical experience. Preoperative teaching increases patient satisfaction and can reduce postoperative fear, anxiety, and stress.[14] Teaching may decrease the

development of complications, length of hospitalization, and recovery time after discharge.

In most surgical settings, patients often arrive only a short time before their surgery. Preoperative teaching for these patients generally occurs in the surgeon's office or a preadmission surgical clinic and is reinforced on the day of surgery. After ambulatory surgery, the patient usually goes home several hours after recovery, depending on the patient's progress and procedure-specific needs. Teaching must include information that focuses on the patient's safety. Give written materials for patients and caregivers to use for review and reinforcement at home. Discharge teaching is required for all patients (see Chapter 19).

When delivering teaching, find a balance between explaining so much that the patient is overwhelmed and telling so little that the patient is unprepared. If you observe and listen carefully to the patient, you can usually figure out how much information is enough. Remember that anxiety and fear may limit learning ability. Assess what the patient wants to know and give priority to those concerns.

Generally, preoperative teaching includes 3 types of information: sensory, process, and procedural. Different patients, with varying cultures, backgrounds, and experience, may want different types of information. See Table 4.6 for factors affecting patient teaching.

With *sensory information,* patients find out what they will see, hear, smell, and feel during the surgery. For example, you may tell them that the OR will be cold, but they can ask for a warm blanket; the lights in the OR are bright; or many unfamiliar sounds and specific smells will be present.

Patients wanting *process information* may not want specific details but just the general flow of what is going to happen. This information would include the patient's transfer to the holding area, visits by the nurse and the ACP before transfer to the OR, and waking up in the PACU.

With *procedural information,* patients desire details that are more specific. For example, this information would include saying an IV line will be started while the patient is in the holding area and the surgeon will mark the operative area with an indelible marker to verify the surgical site.[5]

Share the preoperative teaching given to the patient with the nurses providing postoperative care to evaluate learning and avoid duplication of teaching. Because there is limited time for teaching, a team approach is often used. For example, teaching may start in the outpatient setting. Your responsibility is to assess the patient's understanding of this teaching and fill in the gaps at this point in the surgical process.

Record all teaching in the patient's chart. A guide for preoperative patient and caregiver teaching is outlined in Table 17.6. See Chapter 4 for more on patient and caregiver teaching.

◆ General Surgery Information.
Unless it is contraindicated (e.g., after craniotomy, tonsillectomy), all patients should receive instruction about deep breathing, coughing, and early ambulation postoperatively. This is essential because patients may not want to do these activities after surgery unless they know the reason for them and practice them before surgery. Tell patients and caregivers if tubes, drains, monitoring devices, or special equipment will be used after surgery. Explain that these devices help you to safely care for the patient. Examples of specific teaching may include how to use incentive spirometers or patient-controlled analgesia pumps. Patients should have a clear understanding of how to rate their pain and how their pain will be managed[10] (see Chapter 8).

TABLE 17.6 Patient & Caregiver Teaching

Preoperative Preparation

Include the following information in the preoperative teaching plan for the patient and caregiver.

Sensory Information

- Preoperative holding area may be noisy
- Drugs and cleaning solutions may be odorous
- Operating room (OR) can be cold. Forced air warming devices may be used. Warm blankets are available
- Talking may be heard but may be distorted because of masks. Ask questions if something is not understood
- OR bed will be narrow. A safety strap will be applied over the thighs
- Lights in the OR may be bright
- Monitoring machines may be heard (e.g., beeping noises) when awake

Procedural Information

- What to bring and what type of clothing to wear to the surgery center
- Any changes in time of surgery
- Fluid and food restrictions
- Physical preparation needed (e.g., shower, bowel, or skin preparation)
- Purpose of frequent vital signs assessment
- Pain control and other comfort measures
- Why turning, deep breathing, and coughing after surgery are important. Do practice sessions
- Insertion of IV lines
- Procedure for anesthesia administration
- Surgical site may be marked with indelible ink or marker

Process Information

Information About General Flow of Surgery

- Admission area
- Preoperative holding area, OR, and postanesthesia care unit (PACU)
- Caregivers can usually stay in preoperative holding area until surgery
- Caregivers will be able to see patient after discharge from the PACU or possibly in PACU once the patient is awake
- Identification of any technology that may be present on awakening, such as monitors, central lines, intermittent pneumatic compression devices

Where Caregivers Can Wait During Surgery

- Encourage caregivers to ask questions and express any concerns
- OR staff will update caregivers during surgery and when surgery is over
- Surgeon will usually talk with caregivers after surgery

TABLE 17.7 Preoperative Fasting Recommendations

Liquid and Food Intake	Minimum Fasting Period (hr)
Clear liquids (e.g., water, clear tea, black coffee, carbonated beverages, fruit juice without pulp)	2
Breast milk	4
Nonhuman milk, including infant formula	6
Light meal (e.g., toast and clear liquids)	6
Regular meal (may include fried or fatty food, meat)	8 or more

Source: Practice guidelines for preoperative fasting and the use of pharmacologic agents to reduce the risk of pulmonary aspiration: Application to healthy patients undergoing elective procedures, *Anesthesiology* 126:376, 2017.

before surgery. Evidence-based guidelines for healthy patients of all ages undergoing elective surgery (except women in labor) from the American Society of Anesthesiologists are less strict[15] (Table 17.7). Restricting fluids and food is designed to reduce the risk for pulmonary aspiration and nausea and vomiting. Protocols may vary for patients having local anesthesia or surgery scheduled late in the day. Follow the NPO protocol of each surgical setting. The patient who has not followed the NPO instructions may have surgery delayed or cancelled. It is critical that the patient understands the reason for and follows all restrictions.

◆ Legal Preparation for Surgery

Legal preparation for surgery consists of checking that all required forms have been correctly signed and are present in the patient's chart and that the patient and caregiver clearly understand what is going to happen. Standard consent forms include those for the surgical procedure and blood transfusions. Other forms may include advance directives and durable power of attorney for health care (see Chapter 9).

◆ **Consent for Surgery.** Before nonemergency surgery can be legally performed, the patient must voluntarily sign an informed consent form in the presence of a witness. **Informed consent** is an active, shared decision-making process between the HCP and recipient of care. Three conditions must be met for consent to be valid. First, there must be *adequate disclosure* of the (1) diagnosis; (2) nature and purpose of the proposed treatment; (3) risks and consequences of the proposed treatment; (4) probability of a successful outcome; (5) availability, benefits, and risks of alternative treatments; and (6) prognosis if treatment is not instituted. Second, the patient must show a clear *understanding* of the information before receiving sedating preoperative drugs. If a patient is sedated prior to signing the consent, surgery may be cancelled or delayed. Third, the recipient of care must *give consent voluntarily*. The patient must not be persuaded or coerced in any way by anyone to undergo the procedure.

The surgeon is ultimately responsible for obtaining the patient's consent for surgical treatment. You may be asked to witness the patient's signature on the consent form. At this time, you must be a patient advocate, verifying that the patient understands the information in the consent and the implications of consent, and that consent for surgery is truly voluntary. If the patient is unclear about the surgical plans, contact the surgeon about the patient's need for more information. The patient

The patient should also receive surgery-specific information. For example, a patient having a total joint replacement may have an immobilizer after surgery. Tell a patient having open heart surgery about waking up in the intensive care unit.

◆ **Ambulatory Surgery Information.** The ambulatory surgery patient or the patient admitted to the hospital the day of surgery needs to receive information before admission. Some ambulatory surgical centers telephone patients several days before the procedure to obtain health information, give instructions, and answer questions. Each center has policies and procedures for communicating this information.

In addition to specifics on the procedure, patients need information on day-of-surgery events such as arrival time, registration, parking, what to wear, what to bring, and the need to have a responsible adult present for transportation home after surgery.

Traditionally, we tell patients having elective surgery to have nothing by mouth (NPO) starting at midnight on the night should be aware that consent, even when signed, can be withdrawn at any time.

If the patient is a minor, unconscious, or mentally incompetent to sign the permit, a legally appointed representative or responsible family member may give written permission. An *emancipated minor* is one who is younger than the legal age of consent but is recognized as having the legal capacity to provide consent.[10] Procedures for obtaining consent vary among states and agencies. Follow your state's nurse practice act and agency policies that apply to a specific situation.

ETHICAL/LEGAL DILEMMAS
Informed Consent

Situation
J.S., a 72-yr-old woman, is waiting in the preoperative holding area. You are discussing her impending surgery when you realize that this competent adult does not fully understand her surgery and was not informed of the alternatives to this surgery. Although she has previously signed a consent form, your assessment is that she was not fully informed about her treatment options or does not recall them.

Ethical/Legal Points for Consideration
- Informed consent requires that patients have complete information about the proposed treatment, as well as alternative treatments, risks and benefits of each treatment option, and possible consequences of the surgical procedure. The person (usually the surgeon) performing the procedure usually has this responsibility.
- An opportunity to have questions answered about the various treatment options and their possible outcomes is a crucial element of informed consent.
- A patient can revoke the consent at any time, even at the very last minute. It is essential that you report any circumstance that suggests that the patient does not understand the information or is revoking the informed consent to the person who obtained the consent.
- In most states, the registered nurse's legal role is to witness the signing of the document. This means that as a nurse, you attest to the fact that the patient's signature was valid.

Discussion Questions
1. What do you think you should do next?
2. What is your role as a patient advocate in the informed consent process?
3. What should you do if the patient states that she does not want to know about the surgical procedure or alternatives to surgery?

A true medical emergency may override the need to obtain consent.[10] The next of kin may give consent when immediate medical treatment is necessary to preserve life or prevent serious impairment to life or limb and the patient is incapable of giving consent. If reaching the next of kin is not possible, the HCP may begin treatment without written consent. A note in the chart must document the medical necessity of the procedure. In the case of an emergency in which consent cannot be obtained, you will usually need to complete an event report because it is an occurrence that is inconsistent with routine agency practices.

◆ Day-of-Surgery Preparation
◆ **Nursing Role.** Day-of-surgery preparation varies a great deal depending on whether the patient is an inpatient or an ambulatory surgical patient. Your responsibilities immediately before surgery include final preoperative teaching, assessment, and communication of pertinent findings. In addition, ensure that all preoperative orders are done and that the chart is complete

FIG. 17.1 The nurse performs a safety check by verifying that the patient has an identification band (wristband) as part of the preoperative preparations before she goes to surgery. (Courtesy Susan R. Volk, RN, MSN, CCRN, CPAN, Staff Development Specialist, Christiana Care Health System, Newark, DE.)

and goes with the patient to the OR. It is especially important to verify the presence of a signed informed consent form, results of laboratory and diagnostic studies, an H&P, a record of any consultations, baseline vital signs, proper skin preparation, and completed nursing notes. The surgical site is identified and marked with an indelible marker by the surgeon and documented to show that the patient agrees.[5]

Hospitals often require that a patient wear a hospital gown with no underclothes. Surgical centers may allow the patient to wear underwear, depending on the procedure. The patient should remove any cosmetics, since observation of skin color is important. Remove nail polish and artificial nails so you can assess capillary refill and pulse oximetry. Place an identification band on the patient and, if applicable, an allergy band (Fig. 17.1). Return all patient valuables to a caregiver or secure according to agency policy. All prostheses, including dentures, contact lenses, and glasses, are generally removed to prevent loss or damage. If electrocautery devices will be used during surgery, jewelry in piercings must be removed as a safety measure. Leave hearing aids in place to allow the patient to better follow instructions. Return glasses to the patient as soon as possible after surgery.

Encourage the patient to void before you give preoperative drugs and before transfer to the OR. An empty bladder prevents involuntary elimination under anesthesia and reduces the risk for urinary retention during the early postoperative recovery.

Many preoperative drugs interfere with balance and increase the risk for a fall during ambulation. Carefully assess each patient for responses to drugs given and adjust the plan of care as needed.

🔲 CHECK YOUR PRACTICE

You are caring for an older female patient who received a dose of alprazolam (Xanax) for preoperative anxiety. One hour later, she requests to use the bathroom. You ask her if she can walk and she replies "yes." When helping her to stand, she becomes dizzy and almost falls. You return her to bed.
- Instead of trying to help this patient ambulate to the bathroom, what should have you done?

TABLE 17.8 Drug Therapy
Commonly Used Preoperative Medications

Class	Drug	Purpose
Antibiotics	cefazolin	Prevent postoperative infection
Anticholinergics	atropine glycopyrrolate	↓ Oral and respiratory secretions
	scopolamine (Transderm Scop)	Prevent nausea and vomiting
		Provide sedation
Antidiabetics	insulin (Humulin R)	Stabilize blood glucose
Antiemetics	metoclopramide (Reglan)	↑ Gastric emptying
	ondansetron (Zofran)	Prevent nausea and vomiting
Benzodiazepines	diazepam (Valium)	↓ Anxiety, induce sedation, amnesic effects
	lorazepam (Ativan)	
	midazolam	
β-Blockers	labetalol	Manage hypertension
Histamine (H₂)-receptor antagonists	famotidine	↓ HCl acid secretion, ↑ pH, ↓ gastric volume
	ranitidine	
Opioids	fentanyl	Relieve pain during preoperative procedures
	morphine	

◆ **Preoperative Medications** . Preoperative medications are used for a variety of reasons (Table 17.8). A patient may receive a single drug or a combination of drugs. Benzodiazepines are used for their sedative and amnesic properties. Anticholinergics are sometimes given to reduce secretions. Opioids may be given to decrease pain and anesthetic requirements during surgery. Antiemetics can decrease nausea and vomiting.

Other drugs that may be given before surgery include antibiotics, eyedrops, and routine prescription drugs. Antibiotics may be given throughout the perioperative period for patients with a history of prosthetic heart valve to prevent infective endocarditis and for patients with previous joint replacement. They also may be given when wound contamination is a potential risk (e.g., GI surgery). Antibiotics are most often given IV. We often give a single or first dose within 30 to 60 minutes of the surgical incision.

INFORMATICS IN PRACTICE
Computer-Based Timing for Antibiotic Administration

- A patient who receives the appropriate preoperative antibiotic has a decreased risk for a health care–associated infection.
- Using a computer to time antibiotic administration can decrease the incidence of wound infections.
- Computer-based timing systems aid with quality of care by tracking patient outcomes.
- You can look at the time patients received antibiotics and compare the rate of wound infections for those who did and did not receive timely treatment.

People with known hypertension or coronary artery disease may receive β-adrenergic blockers (β-blockers) to control BP or reduce the chances of MI and cardiac arrest.[16] Those with diabetes are carefully monitored and may receive insulin in the preoperative period.[10] Eyedrops are often given prior for the patient undergoing cataract and other eye surgery. Many times, the patient will need multiple sets of eyedrops given at 5-minute intervals. It is important to give these drugs as ordered and on time to adequately prepare the eye for surgery.

Patients may or may not receive drugs they routinely take on the day of surgery. To aid patient teaching and remove confusion about which drugs patients are taking, carefully check written preoperative orders and clarify the orders with the surgeon and/or ACP if there is any question.

Preoperative drugs may be given by mouth (PO), IV, or subcutaneously. Provide PO drugs with a small sip of water 60 to 90 minutes before the patient goes to the OR unless otherwise ordered. Subcutaneous injections (e.g., insulin) and IV drugs are usually given to the patient after arrival in the preoperative holding area. Teach the patient about the expected effects of the drugs (e.g., drowsiness).

> **⚠ SAFETY ALERT Preoperative Checklist**
> - Use a preoperative checklist (Table 17.9) to make sure you have completed all required preparations.
> - This is especially important to do before the patient receives any sedating drugs.

◆ Transportation to the Operating Room

For inpatients, transport staff move the patient by stretcher to the OR. Help the patient in moving from the bed to the stretcher and raise the side rails. Ensure that the completed chart and any needed equipment goes with the patient. In many agencies, the caregiver may go with the patient to the holding area.

In an ambulatory surgical center, the patient may go to the OR by stretcher or wheelchair. If no sedatives have been given, the patient may even walk with someone to the OR. In all cases, it is important to ensure patient safety during transport. Record the method of transportation and the person who transports the patient to the OR. Provide the hand-off communication to the nurse receiving the patient. This allows each of you to ensure you have shared all pertinent information about the patient. To avoid adverse events related to miscommunication, AORN recommends the use of the Situation-Background-Assessment-Recommendation (SBAR) model for the hand-off process in this setting[5] (see Table 1.4).

Show the caregiver where to wait for the patient during surgery. Many hospitals have a surgical waiting room where OR staff communicate the patient's status to the caregiver(s) and let them know when the surgery is complete. The surgeon can find the caregiver in this room after surgery to discuss the outcome. Some hospitals give pagers to caregivers so that they may eat or do errands during the surgery.

TABLE 17.9 Preoperative Checklist

Preoperative Data	Initials
Height _____ Weight _____	
Isolation Y or N Type _____	
Allergies noted on chart Y or N	
Vital signs (baseline) T _____ P _____ R _____ BP _____ Pulse Ox _____	
Chart Review	
H&P on chart	
H&P within 30 days? Y or N	
Signed and witnessed informed consent form on chart Y or N	
Signed consent for blood administration Y or NA	
Blood type and crossmatch Y or NA	
Diagnostic Results	
Hgb/Hct _____ / _____ NA	
PT/INR/PTT _____ / _____ / _____ NA	
CXR _____ NA	
ECG _____ NA hCG _____ Negative _____ Positive _____ NA	
Other labs:	
Final Chart Review	
Additional forms attached:	

Day of Surgery	Initials
Surgical site marked Y or NA	
ID band on patient Y or N	
Allergy band on patient Y or NA	
Vital signs Time _____ T _____ P _____ R _____ BP _____ Pulse Ox _____	
Procedures	
NPO since _____	
Capillary blood glucose Time _____ Result: _____ NA	
Voided/catheter Time _____	
Preoperative drugs given Time _____ NA	
Preoperative antibiotics given Time _____ NA	
Preoperative skin prep Y or NA Shower _____ Scrub _____ Clip _____	
Makeup, nail polish, false fingernails, and false eye- lashes removed Y or NA	
Hospital gown applied Y or NA	
Valuables	
Dentures Y or N	
Wig or hairpiece Y or N	
Eyeglasses Y or N	
Contact lenses Y or N	
Hearing aid Y or N	
Prosthesis Y or N	
Jewelry Y or N Piercings with jewelry Y or N	
Clothing Y or N	
Disposition of valuables: Hearing aid in place Y or NA	

Time to OR _____ Date _____
Transported to OR by _____
Final check by _____ RN _____

Culturally Competent Care: Preoperative Patient

Include cultural considerations when assessing and implementing care for the patient's preoperative needs. For example, culture often determines one's expression of pain, family expectations, and ability to verbally express needs. One's culture may require that the family be included in any decision making. For example, many older Hispanic women may defer to their family for the decision whether to have surgery. Respect these decisions. If the patient or caregiver does not speak English, you must use a qualified interpreter (translates orally) or translator (interprets written text) communication system.[17] See more on culturally competent care in Chapter 2.

Gerontologic Considerations: Preoperative Patient

Many patients older than 65 years of age undergo surgery. Surgery on older adults requires careful evaluation. Frequently performed procedures in older adults include cataract extraction, coronary and vascular procedures, prostate surgery, cholecystectomy, and joint repair or replacement. Communication is important. The patient's primary HCP is usually not the surgeon. Often several HCPs are involved in the patient's care.

Be particularly alert when assessing and caring for the older adult surgical patient. An event that has little effect on a younger adult may be overwhelming to the older patient. Hospitalization may represent a physical decline and loss of health, mobility, and independence. The older adult may view the hospital as a place to die or as a stepping-stone to a nursing home. Help to decrease anxieties and fears while maintaining the self-esteem of the older adult during the surgical experience.

The risks associated with anesthesia and surgery increase in the older patient. In general, the older the patient, the greater are the risks for complications after surgery. In planning care, consider the patient's physiologic status, not only the chronologic age. The surgical risk in the older adult relates to normal physiologic aging and changes that compromise organ function, reduce reserve capacity, and limit the body's ability to adapt to stress. This decreased ability to cope with stress, often compounded by the burden of one or more chronic illnesses, and the surgery itself increase the risk for complications.

Confirm and document the patient's goals and treatment preferences. In those with advance directives, discuss any new risks associated with the surgical procedure. Make sure the approach for treating any potential problems is consistent with the patient's preferences.[18]

Older adults may have some sensory deficits. Bright lights may bother those with eye problems. They can have reduced vision and hearing. Thought processes and cognitive abilities may be slowed or impaired. Assess and record baseline sensory and cognitive function. Physical reactions are often slowed because of mobility and balance problems. Because of these changes, the older adult may need more time to complete preoperative testing and understand preoperative instructions.

These changes also require you to pay more attention to promote patient safety and prevent injury.

When older adults live in a long-term care or assisted living facility, you may need to coordinate transportation from these facilities so that timely arrival allows for surgery preparation. A legal representative of the patient must be present to provide consent for surgery if the patient cannot sign for himself or herself.

Finally, determine the presence of or need for caregiver support for the older adult undergoing surgery. With the increase in outpatient surgical procedures and shorter length of stays after surgery, caregiver support is critical in the continuity of care for this population.

CASE STUDY

Preoperative Patient

(© Ryan McVay/ Photodisc/ Thinkstock.)

Patient Profile

F.D., a 72-yr-old Hispanic retired librarian, is admitted to the hospital with compromised circulation of the right lower leg and a necrotic right foot. She has diabetes and takes insulin to maintain appropriate blood glucose levels. She has been NPO since midnight. It is now 10 AM on the morning of the surgery.

Subjective Data

- History of type 2 diabetes for 30 years; states, "My blood sugar is hard to control" and "I just started taking insulin"
- History of hypertension and peripheral vascular disease
- History of stage 2 chronic kidney disease
- History of macular degeneration in right eye; reports poor vision
- Surgical history: cesarean section at age 30, cholecystectomy at age 65; reports poor wound healing after last surgery
- States her Social Security checks barely cover her living expenses
- States she often runs out of her drugs and cannot always afford to refill them right away
- Reports chronic burning pain in both legs and has trouble sleeping at night
- Lives alone but has family who want her to move in with them after surgery
- Uses herbs to control blood glucose levels and often skips her insulin

Objective Data

Physical Examination

- Alert, cognitively intact, anxious, older woman with numbness and lack of feeling in right leg
- Weight 190 lb, height 5 ft 3 in
- BP 180/94, pulse 84 and slightly irregular
- Wears glasses for close work and reading

Diagnostic Studies

- Admission serum blood glucose level 272 mg/dL (15.2 mmol/L), glycosylated hemoglobin (Hb A1C) 14%
- Morning capillary blood glucose level 198 mg/dL (11 mmol/L)
- Doppler pulses for right lower leg weak, absent in right foot
- Doppler pulses in left lower leg present, weak in left foot
- Serum creatinine 2.0 mg/dL (176 mmol/L)

Interprofessional Care

- Scheduled for a below-the-knee amputation of the right leg at 1 PM today

Discussion Questions

1. What factors may influence F.D.'s response to hospitalization and surgery?
2. *Priority Decision:* Given F.D.'s history, what priority preoperative nursing assessments would you want to complete and why?
3. What potential perioperative complications may you expect for F.D.?
4. *Priority Decision:* What priority topics would you include in F.D.'s preoperative teaching plan?
5. *Priority Decision:* Based on the assessment data presented, identify the priority nursing diagnoses and related interventions. Are there any collaborative problems?
6. *Collaboration:* Identify appropriate interventions that could be delegated to unlicensed assistive personnel (UAP).
7. *Safety:* To ensure F.D.'s safety, what preoperative nursing interventions are essential?
8. *Evidence-Based Practice:* F.D. asks you why she received insulin this morning when she has not eaten anything since midnight. How would you respond to her?

Answers available at *http://evolve.elsevier.com/Lewis/medsurg.*

■ BRIDGE TO NCLEX EXAMINATION

The number of the question corresponds to the same-numbered outcome at the beginning of the chapter.

1. An overweight patient (BMI 28.1 kg/m²) is scheduled for a laparoscopic cholecystectomy at an outpatient surgery setting. The nurse knows that
   a. surgery will involve multiple small incisions.
   b. this setting is not appropriate for this procedure.
   c. surgery will involve removing a part of the liver.
   d. the patient will need special preparation because of obesity.

2. The patient tells the nurse in the preoperative setting that she has noticed she has a reaction when wearing rubber gloves. What is the *most* appropriate action?
   a. Notify the surgeon so that the surgery can be cancelled.
   b. Ask additional questions to assess for a possible latex allergy.
   c. Notify the OR staff at once so they can use latex-free supplies.
   d. No action is needed because the patient's rubber sensitivity has no bearing on surgery.

3. A 59-yr-old man scheduled for a herniorrhaphy in 2 days reports that he takes ginkgo daily. What is the *priority* intervention?
   a. Inform the surgeon, since the procedure may have to be rescheduled.
   b. Notify the anesthesia care provider, since this herb interferes with anesthetics.
   c. Ask the patient if he has noticed any side effects from taking this herbal supplement.
   d. Tell the patient to continue to take the herbal supplement up to the day before surgery.

4. A 17-yr-old patient with a leg fracture who is scheduled for surgery is an emancipated minor. She has a statement from the court for verification. Which intervention is *most* appropriate?
   a. Witness the permit after the surgeon obtains consent.
   b. Call a parent or legal guardian to sign the permit since the patient is under 18.
   c. Notify the hospital attorney that an emancipated minor is consenting for surgery.
   d. Obtain verbal consent since written consent is not necessary for emancipated minors.

5. A *priority* nursing intervention to aid a preoperative patient in coping with fear of postoperative pain would be to
   a. inform the patient that pain medication will be available.
   b. teach the patient to use guided imagery to help manage pain.
   c. describe the type of pain expected with the patient's particular surgery.
   d. explain the pain management plan, including the use of a pain rating scale.

6. A patient is scheduled for surgery requiring general anesthesia at an ambulatory surgical center. The nurse asks him when he ate last. He replies that he had a light breakfast a couple of hours before coming to the surgery center. What should the nurse do *first*?
   a. Tell the patient to come back tomorrow, since he ate a meal.
   b. Have the patient void before giving any preoperative medications.
   c. Proceed with the preoperative checklist, including site identification.
   d. Notify the anesthesia care provider of when and what the patient last ate.

7. A patient who normally takes 40 units of glargine insulin (long acting) at bedtime asks the nurse what to do about her dose the night before surgery. The *best* response would be to have her
   a. skip her insulin altogether the night before surgery.
   b. get instructions from her surgeon or HCP on any insulin adjustments.
   c. take her usual dose at bedtime and eat a light breakfast in the morning.
   d. eat a moderate meal before bedtime and then take half her usual insulin dose.

8. Preoperative considerations for older adults include *(select all that apply)*
   a. using only large-print educational materials.
   b. speaking louder for patients with hearing aids.
   c. recognizing that sensory deficits may be present.
   d. providing warm blankets to prevent hypothermia.
   e. teaching important information early in the morning.

1. a, 2. b, 3. a, 4. a, 5. d, 6. d, 7. b, 8. c, d

For rationales to these answers and even more NCLEX review questions, visit *http://evolve.elsevier.com/Lewis/medsurg*.

ⓔ EVOLVE WEBSITE/RESOURCES LIST

http://evolve.elsevier.com/Lewis/medsurg
- Review Questions (Online Only)
- Key Points
- Answer Keys for Review Questions
  - Rationales for Bridge to NCLEX Examination Questions
  - Answer Guidelines for Case Study on p. 311
- Conceptual Care Map Creator
- Audio Glossary
- Content Updates

REFERENCES

1. Jehovah's Witnesses: Why don't Jehovah's Witnesses accept blood transfusions? Retrieved from *www.jw.org/en/jehovahs-witnesses/faq/jehovahs-witnesses-why-no-blood-transfusions/*.
*2. Ebner M, Birschmann I, Peter A, et al: Point-of-care testing for emergency assessment of coagulation in patients treated with direct oral anticoagulants, *Critical Care* 21:32, 2017.
3. Society of Gastroenterology Nurses and Associates: Patient safety issues with use of herbal supplements. Retrieved from *www.sgna.org/Practice/GI-Nurse-Sedation/Patient-Care-Safety*.
4. American College of Allergy, Asthma, and Immunology: Latex allergy. Retrieved from *https://acaai.org/allergies/types/latex-allergy*.
5. Association of periOperative Registered Nurses: *Guidelines for perioperative practice*. Denver, 2017, AORN.
*6. Bock M, Fritsch G, Hepner D: Preoperative laboratory testing, *Anesthesiol Clin* 34:43, 2016.
*7. Troy HK, Stikkelbroeck NM, Smans LC, et al: Adrenal crisis: Still a deadly event in the 21st century, *AJM* 129:339, 2016.

8. Wound Care Centers: How diabetes affects wound healing. Retrieved from *www.woundcarecenters.org/article/living-with-wounds/how-diabetes-affects-wound-healing*.
*9. Prabhaker A, Helander E, Chopra N, et al: Preoperative assessment for ambulatory surgery, *Curr Pain Headache Rep* 21:43, 2017.
10. Rotruck JC: *Alexander's care of the patient in surgery*, ed 16, St Louis, 2018, Elsevier.
*11. Martin VT, Vij B: Diet and headache, *Headache* 56:1543, 2016.
12. The Joint Commission: History and physical content. Retrieved from *www.jointcommission.org/standards_information/jcfaqdetails.aspx?StandardsFaqId=1851&ProgramId=46*.
*13. Torres EG, Lindmair JM, Langan JW, et al: Is preoperative nasal povidone-iodine as efficient and cost-effective as standard MRSA screening protocol in total joint arthroplasty? *J Arthroplasty* 31:215, 2016.
*14. Wilson RA, Watt-Watson J, Hodnett E, et al: A randomized controlled trial of an individualized preoperative education intervention for symptom management after total knee arthroplasty, *Orthopaedic Nursing* 35:20, 2016.
*15. Practice guidelines for preoperative fasting and the use of pharmacologic agents to reduce the risk of pulmonary aspiration: Application to healthy patients undergoing elective procedures, *Anesthesiology* 126:376, 2017.
16. Smeltz A, Kumar P: Angiotensin axis blocking drugs in the perioperative period, *Anesthesiol News*, 2016. Retrieved from *www.anesthesiologynews.com/Review-Articles/Article/02-16/Angiotensin-Axis-Blocking-Drugs-In-the-Perioperative-Period/35357/ses=ogst*.
17. The Joint Commission: Standard FAQ details. Retrieved from *www.jointcommission.org/standards_information/jcfaqdetails.aspx?StandardsFaqId=1490&ProgramId=46*.
*18. Mohanty S, Rosenthal RA, Russell MM, et al: Optimal perioperative management of the geriatric patient: A best practices guideline from the American College of Surgeons NSQIP and the American Geriatrics Society, *JACS* 222:930, 2016.

*Evidence-based information for clinical practice.

18

Intraoperative Care

Mark Karasin

Unless someone like you cares a whole awful lot,
nothing is going to get better, it's not.

Dr. Seuss

ⓔ http://evolve.elsevier.com/Lewis/medsurg/

CONCEPTUAL FOCUS

Gas Exchange	Perfusion	Tissue Integrity
Pain	Safety	

LEARNING OUTCOMES

1. Distinguish various areas of perioperative department and appropriate attire.
2. Outline the roles and responsibilities of interprofessional surgical team members.
3. Prioritize needs of patients undergoing surgery.
4. Analyze role of a perioperative nurse in the management of patients undergoing surgery.

5. Apply basic principles of infection prevention and aseptic technique in the operating room.
6. Recognize operating room safety measures related to patients, equipment, and anesthesia.
7. Distinguish various anesthesia techniques and common anesthesia drugs.

KEY TERMS

anesthesia care provider (ACP), p. 315
anesthesiology, p. 315
epidural block, p. 325

general anesthesia, p. 320
local anesthesia, p. 324
malignant hyperthermia (MH), p. 325

nurse anesthetist, p. 315
regional anesthesia, p. 324
spinal anesthesia, p. 324

Historically, surgery took place in the traditional environment of the hospital operating room (OR). Now, many surgical procedures are done as ambulatory surgery (outpatient surgery). In addition, the use of *minimally invasive surgery* (MIS) is rapidly increasing. More procedures use endoscopes, robotics, and other advanced technologies that lead to decreased blood loss, incision size, pain, recovery time, and hospital length of stay. Hybrid ORs, which allow for MIS, such as endovascular procedures, and the traditional open incision approach within the same room, are becoming more common. This chapter discusses the basics of intraoperative care that apply to all surgical patients regardless of where or how the surgery is done.

PHYSICAL ENVIRONMENT OF THE OPERATING ROOM

Department Layout

The surgery department is a controlled environment designed to minimize the spread of pathogens and allow a smooth flow of patients, staff, and equipment needed to give safe surgical patient care. The department is divided into 3 distinct zones: (1) unrestricted, (2) semirestricted, and (3) restricted (Fig. 18.1). The *unrestricted zone* is where people in street clothes interact with those in scrub attire. These areas typically include the points of entry for patients (e.g., holding area), staff (e.g., locker rooms), and information (e.g., nursing station or control desk). The *semirestricted zone* includes the surrounding support areas and corridors. Only authorized staff are allowed access to semirestricted areas. All staff in the semirestricted area should wear clean surgical attire. This includes scrub attire that was laundered in an accredited laundry facility, long-sleeved jacket, shoes dedicated for surgery use or shoe covers, surgical head cover and mask that covers all head and facial hair, and any appropriate personal protective equipment (e.g., face shield). The *restricted zone* is found within the semirestricted area. It includes the surgical suite (OR) where the invasive procedure takes place and the sterile core (Fig. 18.2). Masks should be worn and traffic minimized whenever sterile supplies are open in the restricted area.[1]

The physical layout is designed to reduce cross-contamination. The flow of clean and sterile supplies and equipment is separate from contaminated supplies, equipment, and waste by space, time, and traffic patterns. Staff members move supplies from clean areas, such as the sterile core, through the OR for surgery, and on to the instrument decontamination and sterilization area (e.g., central processing department [CPD]).

FIG. 18.1 Perioperative department layout.

FIG. 18.2 Typical OR. (© iStock.com/windslegend.)

Holding Area

The *holding area,* often called the *preoperative holding area,* is an unrestricted zone where patient identification and assessment take place. The size can range from a large centralize area that handles many patients to a small designated area right outside of the OR.

In some settings, the holding area is called the *admission, observation, and discharge* (AOD) unit. An AOD unit is designed to allow early morning admission for outpatient surgery, same-day admission, and inpatient holding before surgery. The patient is identified and assessed before and after surgery, before being discharged home or transferred to an inpatient room. The AOD unit is important in outpatient surgery and prevents unnecessary overnight stays in the inpatient setting.

Operating Room

The traditional OR is a unique setting separate from other clinical units. This restricted zone is controlled geographically, environmentally, and aseptically (Fig. 18.1). It is best to have the OR next to the postanesthesia care unit (PACU) and the surgical intensive care unit. This allows for quick transport of the patient after surgery and close proximity to anesthesia staff if complications occur.

We use several methods to prevent the transmission of infection in the OR. Filters and controlled airflow in the ventilating systems provide dust control. Positive air pressure in the rooms prevents air from entering the OR from the halls and corridors. ORs are kept within a narrow range of temperature and humidity to prevent bacteria growth. ORs follow strict protocols for cleaning between cases and terminal cleaning at the end of the day. The use of ultraviolet lighting reduces the number of microorganisms in the air.[2]

Using OR furniture that is adjustable, easy to clean, and easy to move promotes safety and comfort. All equipment is checked frequently to ensure proper functioning and electrical safety. The lighting is designed to give a low- to high-intensity range for a precise view of the surgical site. A communication system offers a way to deliver routine and emergency messages.[3]

SURGICAL TEAM

Registered Nurse

The *perioperative nurse* is a registered nurse (RN) who collaborates with the rest of the surgical team and implements the patient's plan of care during perioperative period. Depending on the size of the OR department, this role may include three domains: (1) preoperative RN, (2) OR RN, and (3) PACU RN. As an OR RN, you are the patient's advocate during surgery. This includes (1) maintaining the patient's safety, dignity, and confidentiality; (2) communicating with the patient, the surgical team, and other departments (e.g., CPD, PACU, laboratory); and (3) providing nursing care discussed in the Nursing Management section of this chapter.

TABLE 18.1 Intraoperative Nursing Activities

Circulating, Nonsterile Activities

- Helps prepare room, ensuring that supplies and equipment are available, in working order, and sterile
- Maintains aseptic technique in all required activities
- Monitors practices of aseptic technique in self and others
- Checks mechanical and electrical equipment and environmental factors
- Conducts a preprocedure verification process
- Assesses patient's physical and emotional status
- Confirms and implements facility protocols and safety measures
- Plans and coordinates intraoperative nursing care
- Checks chart and relates pertinent data to team members
- Helps with applying monitoring devices and insertion of invasive lines and other devices
- Assists with and ensures patient safety in transferring and positioning patient
- Aids with anesthesia induction
- Monitors draping
- Takes part in surgical time-out
- Records intraoperative care
- Prepares, records, labels, and sends blood, pathology, and any anatomic specimens to proper locations
- Measures blood, urine output, and other fluid loss
- Confirms, dispenses, and records drugs used, including local anesthetics
- Coordinates all intraoperative activities with team members and other staff and departments
- Works with scrubbed personnel to keep correct count of sponges, needles, instruments, and medical devices
- Facilitates patient transfer to PACU
- Gives hand-off report to PACU nurse with information relevant to care of patient

Scrubbed, Sterile Activities

- Helps prepare the OR
- Completes surgical hand antisepsis and gowns and gloves self and other members of surgical team
- Prepares instrument table and arranges sterile equipment for functional use
- Assists with draping
- Takes part in surgical time-out procedure
- Passes instruments to surgeon and assistants by anticipating their needs
- Keeps correct count of sponges, needles, instruments, and medical devices that could be retained in the patient
- Monitors practices of aseptic technique in self and others
- Keeps track of irrigation solutions used for calculation of blood loss
- Accepts, verifies, and reports drugs used by surgeon and/or ACP, including local anesthetics

During surgery, the OR RN assumes functions that involve either sterile or unsterile activities (Table 18.1). The *scrub nurse* (sterile) follows the designated surgical hand antisepsis and glove and gown sterile attire and prepares and manages the sterile field and instrumentation. The *circulating nurse* stays in the unsterile field, facilitates the progress of the procedure, and keeps documentation.[4] Examples of nursing activities that occur during each phase of the surgical experience are outlined in Table 18.2.

After meeting specific criteria (e.g., 2 years of experience), perioperative RNs can obtain OR certification (CNOR). CNOR certification is an objective measure (written test) that validates a nurse has essential knowledge and skills in perioperative nursing.[5]

Licensed Practical/Vocational Nurse and Surgical Technologist

Depending on the state's nurse practice act, an LPN/VN or a surgical technologist may fill the role of the circulating or scrub nurse. Surgical technologists attend an associate degree program or a vocational, hospital, or military training program. The Association of Surgical Technologists sets the standards for education, provides continuing education opportunities, and offers certification for surgical technologists.[6]

If the circulating nurse is not an RN, the LPN/VN or surgical technologist must always have access to an RN. As an OR RN, you take on responsibility for supervising an LPN/VN or surgical technologist performing delegated nursing tasks.[7]

Surgeon and Assistant

The *surgeon* is the physician who does the surgical procedure. The surgeon is primarily responsible for:

- Preoperative medical history and physical assessment, directing preoperative testing, and postoperative management Obtaining informed consent
- Leading the surgical team and directing the course of a procedure

The *surgeon's assistant* can be another physician, registered nurse first assistant (RNFA), physician's assistant, surgical resident or fellow, medical student, or a certified surgical first assistant. The assistant usually holds retractors to expose surgical areas and helps with hemostasis and suturing. In some agencies, especially in educational settings, the assistant may perform some portions of the surgery under the surgeon's direct supervision.

Registered Nurse First Assistant

The *registered nurse first assistant* (RNFA) works with the surgeon to achieve an optimal surgical outcome for the patient. The Association of periOperative Registered Nurses (AORN) states that you must have formal education for this role and work collaboratively with the surgeon, patient, and surgical team.[8] CNOR nurses or nurse practitioners can complete RNFA program to assume this expanded role. RNFAs can obtain certification (C-RNFA).

Anesthesia Care Provider

Anesthesiology is a medical specialty that focuses on clinical management of the patient in the perioperative period, pain management, critical care, trauma, airway management, and cardiopulmonary resuscitation. The **anesthesia care provider (ACP)** is the person responsible for administering anesthetic agents and managing vital life functions (e.g., breathing, BP) during the perioperative period.[9] This can be an anesthesiologist, nurse anesthetist, or anesthesiologist assistant (AA).

A **nurse anesthetist** is a master's or a doctorate prepared RN who has graduated from an accredited nurse anesthesia program and completed a national certification examination to become a certified registered nurse anesthetist (CRNA).

The CRNA's scope of practice includes:[10]

- Performing and documenting a preanesthetic assessment and evaluation
- Developing and implementing a plan for delivering anesthesia
- Choosing, obtaining, and administering anesthesia, adjuvant drugs, and fluids
- Choosing, applying, and inserting appropriate monitoring devices
- Managing a patient's airway and pulmonary status
- Managing emergence and recovery from anesthesia
- Releasing or discharging patients from a PACU
- Ordering, starting, or modifying pain relief therapy
- Responding to emergency situations by providing airway management

TABLE 18.2 Common Perioperative Nursing Activities

Before Surgery	During Surgery	After Surgery
Home, Clinic, Holding Area • Starts preoperative assessment • Plans teaching appropriate to patient's needs • Involves caregiver	**Safety Maintenance** • Ensures integrity of sterile field • Ensures that sponge, needle, instrument, and medical device counts are correct • Positions patient to ensure correct alignment, exposure of surgical site, and prevention of injury • Prevents chemical injury from prepping solutions, drugs, etc. • Ensures safe use of electrical equipment • Safely gives ordered drugs	**Postanesthesia, Discharge Area** • Determines patient's response to surgical intervention • Monitors ABCs, vital signs, level of consciousness • Safely gives ordered drugs
Surgical Unit • Completes preoperative assessment • Coordinates patient teaching with staff • Develops a plan of care that reflects patient's level of function and ability • Safely gives ordered drugs		**Clinical Unit** • Evaluates effectiveness of nursing care in OR using patient outcome criteria • Determines patient's level of satisfaction with care given • Assesses patient's psychologic status • Helps with discharge planning
Surgical Suite • Conducts preprocedure verification • Assesses patient's level of consciousness, skin integrity, mobility, emotional status, and functional limitations • Reviews chart • Ensures all supplies and equipment needed are available, functioning, and sterile, if appropriate	**Monitoring Physical Status** • Monitors and reports changes in patient's vital signs • Monitors blood loss and urine output **Monitoring Psychologic Status** • Gives emotional support to patient • Ensures patient's right to privacy • Communicates patient' emotional status to health care team	**Home, Clinic** • Seeks patient's perception of surgery in terms of effects of anesthetic agents, impact on body image, immobilization • Determines caregiver's perceptions of surgery

An AA is a master's-prepared health professional who serves under the direction of an anesthesiologist. AAs have completed an accredited program and passed a national certification examination. They take part in all types of anesthesia. This includes giving drugs, obtaining vascular access, applying and interpreting monitors, maintaining airways, and helping with preoperative assessment.

❖ NURSING MANAGEMENT: PATIENT BEFORE SURGERY

The preoperative assessment of the surgical patient provides baseline data for intraoperative and postoperative care and is used to plan intraoperative care. Preoperative care of the patient is discussed in Chapter 17.

Provide physical and emotional comfort for the patient and caregivers along with teaching about the upcoming surgery. This is particularly important in the same-day surgery settings, where caregivers must assume greater responsibility for postoperative care.

◆ Psychosocial Assessment

Knowing about the activities that occur when a patient moves into the OR allows you to provide teaching and comfort, especially to the anxious patient. You can usually answer general questions about surgery and anesthesia, such as, "When will I go to sleep?" "Who will be in the room?" "When will my surgeon arrive?" "How much of my body will be exposed?" "Will I be cold?" "When will I wake up?" Refer specific questions about the details of the surgery and anesthesia to the surgeon or ACP. For patients who do not speak English, use a qualified interpreter (see Table 2.10).

Separation from caregivers just before surgery can produce anxiety for the patient. Allowing the caregiver to wait with the patient in the holding area until we transfer the patient to the OR can reduce anxiety.

◆ Physical Assessment

Perform a thorough physical assessment during the preoperative preparation of the patient (see Chapter 17).

◆ Chart Review

Required chart data vary with agencies, patient conditions, and surgical procedures. Tables 17.2 and 17.4 provide examples of data we obtain during the preoperative assessment. This information gives an understanding of past and present medical history and an opportunity to anticipate and prepare for potential needs during surgery, such as obtaining equipment or drugs. You can discuss any abnormal findings or concerns for infection and other complications with the surgeon or ACP.

❓ CHECK YOUR PRACTICE

Your patient has arrived in the holding area. As you review the chart, you realize the patient has not signed the consent for blood. You see the patient has Alzheimer's disease and is not mentally competent to give consent.
• How would you proceed?

◆ Admitting the Patient

Agency policy guides the protocol you follow when admitting the patient to the holding area and OR. A general routine includes initial greeting, proper identification, and offer of human contact and warmth.

The admitting process continues with reassessment of the patient and time for last-minute questions. Determine if any other tasks need to be done. Complete the chart review for the previously mentioned data and note any problems or changes. Ask the patient about valuables, prostheses, and last intake of food and fluid. Confirm that any ordered preoperative drugs were given. Provide a pillow or adjust the patient's position if requested. Most agencies require the patient's hair to be covered just before transfer to the OR suite to reduce potential shedding.

You may offer complementary and alternative therapies, such as aromatherapy, music therapy, guided imagery, and distraction (see the Complementary & Alternative Therapies box).

These therapies may decrease anxiety, promote relaxation, and reduce pain.[11] Some agencies start these therapies before the patient is admitted to the OR. In others, such as ambulatory settings, they may start after the patient arrives in the holding area.

COMPLEMENTARY & ALTERNATIVE THERAPIES

Music Therapy

Music is an ancient healing tool recognized in the writings of Plato.

Scientific Evidence

Strong evidence supports using music therapy to reduce stress and anxiety and enhance mood.

Nursing Implications

- To be effective, the music used must be appropriate for the situation. Music can have many different physiologic effects.
- Listening to calming music can result in slower, deeper breathing and a decrease in heart rate and BP. Both indicate relaxation.
- Music with a faster pace can energize a person and promote mental alertness.
- Music therapy is safe in combination with other treatment approaches.

Source: Daniel E: Music used as anti-anxiety intervention for patients during outpatient procedures: a review of the literature, *Complement Ther Clin Pract* 22:21, 2016.

❖ NURSING MANAGEMENT: PATIENT DURING SURGERY

Patient care in the surgical setting is dynamic and depends on the knowledge, skills, and judgment of the RN.[4] The circulating nurse is responsible for implementing the intraoperative plan of care and serving as the patient's advocate. The circulating nurse focuses on the whole patient. This involves ongoing assessment, reassessment, and adjusting the care plan to promote the best surgical outcomes.

◆ Room Preparation

Before transferring the patient into the OR, prepare the room to ensure privacy, prevention of infection, and safety. Individualized preparation is essential to achieve the expected patient outcomes.

When a patient is severely obese, extra staff and special equipment may be needed to safely position and transfer the patient to and from the OR bed. During surgery, special equipment (e.g., extra-long instrumentation, bariatric OR bed) may be used.

❓ CHECK YOUR PRACTICE

You are assigned to observe in the OR. A severely obese patient is admitted to the holding area. The circulating nurse tells you that the team will address the unique needs of the patient for a safe surgical experience.

- What special considerations are needed for this patient?

All people entering the OR wear surgical attire (Fig. 18.3). All electrical and mechanical equipment is checked for proper functioning. Each surgical item is opened and placed on the instrument table using aseptic technique. Sponges, needles, instruments, and small medical devices (e.g., surgical clip

FIG. 18.3 All surgical personnel wear surgical attire. (© iStock.com/Ridofranz.)

cartridges, universal adapters) are counted according to strict processes to ensure accurate retrieval at the end of the procedure. Any retained surgical supplies, devices, or instruments are sentinel events (never events) or serious reportable events (SREs) that can result in negative outcomes for the patient.[1,4] (Sentinel events and SREs are discussed in Chapter 1.)

During room preparation and the surgical procedure, the scrub person does surgical hand antisepsis, dons sterile gown and gloves, and touches only items in the sterile field. The circulating nurse stays in the unsterile field and does those activities that involve contact with all unsterile items and the patient. This coordinated effort allows for smooth functioning throughout the procedure.

◆ Transferring Patient

The patient is moved into the OR after the preoperative assessment is complete and the surgical suite is ready. Always maintain privacy during transfers through public areas by covering the patient with a gown and/or blanket. Each time a patient is transferred between beds, the wheels of each must be locked. Enough staff members using ergonomic tools for safe patient handling and movement should be available to lift, guide, and prevent accidental falling or injury to staff and the patient. Once the patient is on the OR bed, ensure that there is always someone on both sides of the patient until a safety strap is secured to prevent falls. The monitor leads (e.g., ECG leads), BP cuff, and pulse oximeter are usually applied after the patient is safe on the OR bed.

◆ Scrubbing, Gowning, and Gloving

Surgical hand antisepsis is required of all sterile members of the surgical team (scrub nurse, surgeon, assistant). When wet scrubbing is the chosen method for surgical hand antisepsis, your finger nails are cleaned first, followed by scrubbing each plane of individual fingers, palms, and forearms in the distal to proximal fashion. The hands should always be held away from surgical attire and higher than the elbows. This prevents contamination from clothing or detergent suds and water from draining from the unclean area above the elbows to the clean and previously scrubbed areas of the hands and fingers.

Waterless, alcohol-based agents are replacing soap and water in many agencies. When using an alcohol-based surgical hand-scrub product, prewash hands and forearms with soap and dry completely before applying the alcohol-based product. After applying the alcohol-based product, rub hands and forearms thoroughly until dry before donning sterile attire.[1,4]

Once surgical hand antisepsis is completed, the team members enter the OR to put on sterile gowns and 2 pairs of gloves. This protects patients and themselves from the transmission of microorganisms.[1,4] Because the gowns and gloves are sterile, those who have scrubbed can manipulate and organize all sterile items for use during the procedure.

◆ Basic Aseptic Technique

Aseptic technique is practiced in the OR to prevent infection. This is done through the creation and maintenance of a sterile field. The center of the sterile field is the site of the surgical incision. Items used in the sterile field, including surgical instruments and equipment, have been sterilized by appropriate sterilization methods.

Team members must understand specific principles to practice aseptic technique (Table 18.3). If these principles are not followed, the patient's safety is compromised and the risk for infection is increased.[1,4]

The surgical team is also responsible for following the guidelines established by the U.S. Occupational Safety and Health Administration (OSHA) and the AORN to protect the patient and the team from exposure to blood-borne pathogens.[12] These guidelines emphasize (1) standard and transmission-based precautions, (2) engineering and work practice controls, and (3) the use of personal protective equipment, such as gloves, gowns, caps, face shields, masks, and protective eyewear. This is especially important in the OR because of the high potential for exposure to blood-borne pathogens.

◆ Assisting Anesthesia Care Provider

While you check the OR to complete the final preparations, the ACP prepares the patient for receiving anesthesia. You need to

---

TABLE 18.3 Principles of Aseptic Technique in Operating Room

- All materials that enter the sterile field must be sterile.
- If a sterile item comes in contact with an unsterile item, it is contaminated.
- Contaminated items are removed at once from the sterile field. If the unsterile item is small (e.g., unopened suture), once it is removed, the area is marked off (i.e., covered with a sterile drape). If the entire field is contaminated, it should be set up again with all new materials.
- The surgical team working in the operative field must wear sterile gowns and gloves. Once dressed for procedure, they must recognize that the only parts of the gown considered sterile are the front from chest to table level and sleeves to 2 inches above elbow.
- A wide margin of safety is maintained between sterile and unsterile fields.
- Tables are sterile only at tabletop level. Items extending beneath this level are contaminated.
- The edges of a sterile package are contaminated once the package has been opened. If a sterile package (e.g., package of sutures) is placed on the sterile field, that entire package stays sterile even when opened.
- Microorganisms travel on airborne particles and will enter the sterile field with excessive air movements and currents.
- Microorganisms travel by capillary action through moist fabrics, resulting in contamination.
- Microorganisms on the patient's and team members' hair, skin, and respiratory tracts must be confined by proper attire.

---

understand the effects of the anesthetic agents and know the location of all emergency drugs and equipment.

If you are the circulating nurse, you may be involved in placing monitoring devices used during the procedure (e.g., ECG leads). If the patient is having general anesthesia, stay at the patient's side to ensure safety and aid the ACP. These responsibilities may include measuring BP and helping maintain the patient's airway. During the procedure, you are a vital communication link for the ACP to other departments, such as the laboratory or blood bank.

◆ Positioning Patient

The surgical team carefully plans the patient's positioning and monitors the patient throughout the procedure. Positioning is a critical part of every procedure and usually follows induction of anesthesia. The ACP says when to begin positioning. The patient's position should allow for accessibility to the operative site, administering and monitoring of anesthetic agents, and maintaining the patient's airway. We use a variety of surgical positions, including supine, prone, lateral, lithotomy, or sitting. The supine is the most common position. It allows operating on most body systems, including the abdomen, heart, chest, or head. The prone position is often used in spine surgery (e.g., laminectomy). The lithotomy position is used for various gynecological, genitourinary, and colon procedures.

With any position, take great care to prevent injury to the patient. Take care to (1) provide correct musculoskeletal alignment; (2) prevent undue pressure on nerves, skin over bony prominences, earlobes, and eyes; (3) provide for adequate thoracic excursion; (4) prevent occlusion of arteries and veins; (5) provide modesty in exposure; and (6) recognize and respect individual needs, such as previously assessed pains or deformities. It is your responsibility to secure the extremities, provide adequate padding and support, and have physical or mechanical help to avoid unnecessary straining of the staff and patient.

Because anesthesia blocks the sensory nerve impulses, the patient will not feel pain, discomfort, or stress placed on nerves, muscles, bones, and skin. General anesthesia causes peripheral vessels to dilate. Position changes affect where the pooling of blood occurs. If the head of the OR bed is raised, the lower torso will have increased blood volume and the upper torso may become compromised. Hypovolemia and cardiovascular disease can further compromise the patient's status. Improper positioning can potentially result in muscle strain, joint damage, pressure injuries, nerve damage, and other untoward effects.

◆ Electrosurgery and Smoke

Care must be taken to correctly place the grounding pad and all electrosurgical equipment to prevent injury from burns or fire. When an electrosurgical unit is in use, the patient must be properly grounded to prevent unintended injury (Fig. 18.4). Excess hair, adipose tissue, bony prominences, fluid (edema), adhesive failure, and scar tissue can compromise safety. Fire in the OR can have devastating consequences for the patient. Fortunately, we can prevent surgical fires with awareness of the hazards and emphasis on safe practices.[13]

◆ Preparing Surgical Site

The purpose of skin preparation, or "prepping," is to reduce the number of microorganisms available to migrate to the surgical wound. The circulating nurse, surgeon, or surgical assistant completes the task of prepping before surgery.

FIG. 18.4 A well-vascularized muscle mass is the best site for grounding. (Courtesy Covidien, Mansfield, MA.)

The skin is prepared by mechanically scrubbing or cleansing the surgical site with an antimicrobial agent specific to the procedure. Follow manufacturer's instructions for proper application of the prepping agent. The principle of scrubbing from the clean area (site of the incision) to the dirty area (distal to the incision) is always followed.

Antiseptic agents used for skin preparation may contain alcohol and therefore are flammable. Skin injury can occur if these agents pool under the patient. Care must be taken to ensure that these agents are properly confined and allowed to fully dry. After the skin is prepped and the fumes are allowed to dispel to reduce the risk for fire, the sterile members of the surgical team drape the area. Only the site to be incised is left exposed.

◆ Safety Considerations

All surgical procedures put the patient at risk for injury. These injuries include infections, physical trauma from positioning or equipment used, or physiologic effects of surgery itself. Although technical skills, such as operating equipment or proper instrument handling, are a critical part of OR RN competency, there is strong research supporting that nontechnical skills (NTS) also have a high impact on outcomes. These include proper and clear communication, teamwork, situational awareness (e.g., anticipatory cognitive skills), and stress and fatigue management.[14] Considering the importance of NTS skills, especially in crisis events, some agencies use special training programs to develop these skills. There are standard approaches, such as a variety of communication tools, that promote safe patient care and minimize the potential negative effects of human factors.

◆ Communication.
Many team members care for patients as they move through the perioperative continuum. Chances for error arise whenever team members share information. The Joint Commission requires that all health care providers use a standardized approach to hand-off communication. As a RN, use SBAR (see Table 1.4) to ensure that a complete and accurate hand-off is done every time patient care is transferred to

another provider (e.g. change of shift, surgeon to nurse, OR RN to PACU RN).

◆ Surgical Care Improvement Project.
The *Surgical Care Improvement Project* (SCIP) is a national quality partnership of organizations focused on improving surgical care by significantly reducing the number of complications from surgery.[2] Specific SCIP measures include (1) a prophylactic antibiotic started within 30 to 60 minutes before the surgical incision to decrease risk for infection, (2) applying a warming blanket to prevent unintended hypothermia, and (3) applying intermittent pneumatic compression devices (IPCs) to minimize the risk for VTE.

◆ Time Out and Surgical Checklist.
The National Patient Safety Goals (NPSGs) require a preprocedure verification process. This includes verification of relevant documentation (e.g., history and physical examination, signed consent forms, nursing and preanesthetic assessment) and the results of any diagnostic studies (e.g., x-rays, biopsy reports). Any needed blood products, implants, devices, and special equipment must be available.

The *Universal Protocol,* one of the NPSGs, is followed to prevent wrong site, wrong procedure, and wrong patient. Wrong surgical procedure and surgery on the wrong body part or wrong patient are *sentinel events (never events)* or *SREs* (described in Chapter 1). The AORN has a position statement about correct site surgery and guidelines for implementing the Universal Protocol.[15] The surgeon marks the procedure site. If possible, the marking is done with the patient's involvement.[3]

A patient safety checklist for ORs is the cornerstone of a major focus to make surgery safer. Using the World Health Organization (WHO) Surgical Safety Checklist has improved compliance with standards and decreased complications from surgery (Fig. 18.5). In addition, OR staff complete a fire risk assessment to identify and reduce the potential for a fire.

> **! SAFETY ALERT   Surgical Time-Out**
> • Before anesthesia induction, ask the patient to confirm name, birthdate, procedure and site, and consent.
> • All members of the surgical team stop what they are doing just before the procedure starts to verify patient identification, procedure, and surgical site.

❖ NURSING MANAGEMENT: PATIENT AFTER SURGERY

Through constant observation of the surgical process, the ACP anticipates the end of the procedure. The ACP gives proper types and doses of anesthetic agents so that their effects will be minimal at the end of the surgery. This allows greater physiologic control of the patient during the transfer to the PACU.

The ACP and you or another member of the surgical team go with the patient to the PACU. The hand-off, including the patient's status and the procedure done, is communicated to the nurse receiving the patient in the PACU to promote safe, ongoing care.

▌ANESTHESIA

The American Society of Anesthesiologists (ASA) defines anesthesia according to the effect that it has on the patient's sensorium and pain perception. These definitions include minimal

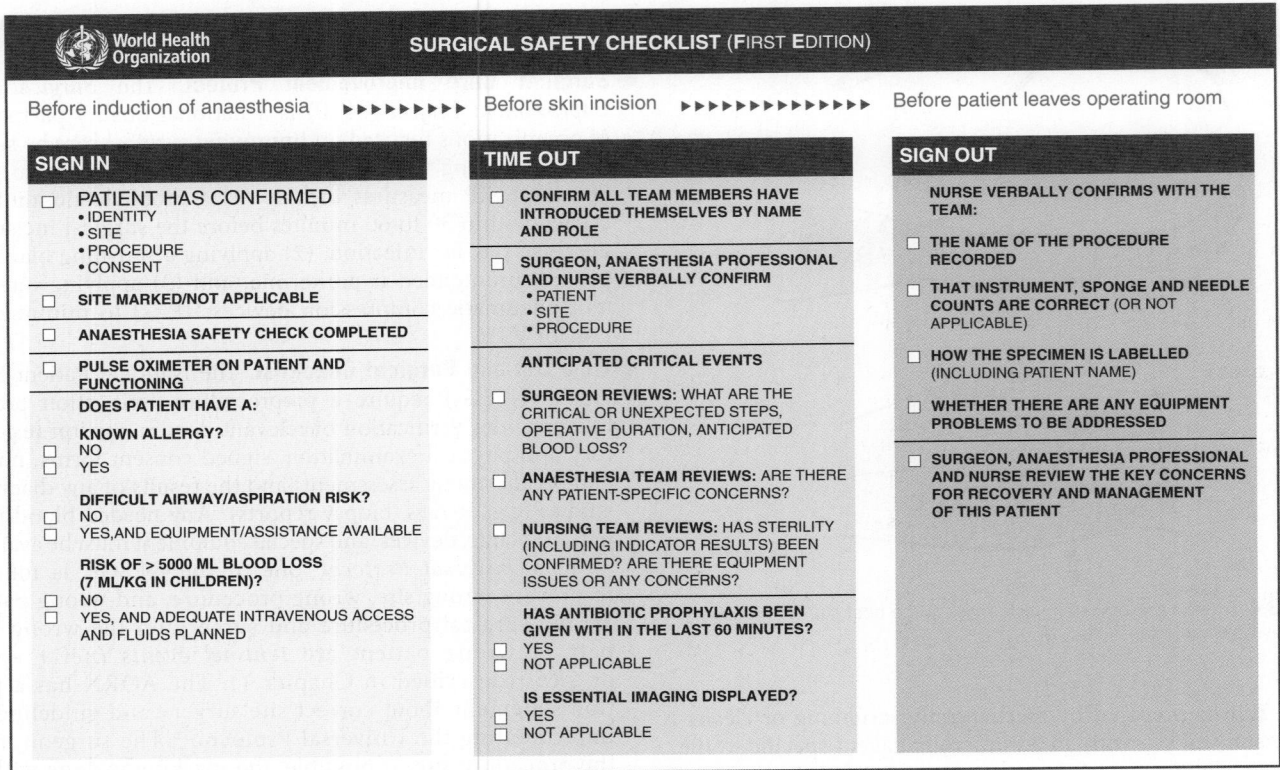

FIG. 18.5 WHO Surgical Safety Checklist.

sedation (e.g., anxiolysis), moderate sedation/analgesia, deep sedation/analgesia, and general anesthesia. The science of providing anesthesia continues to evolve. For example, noninvasive electroencephalogram-based technology allows ACPs to track the level of patient awareness (i.e., *awareness monitoring*) during surgery and adjust anesthesia as needed.

The anesthetic technique and agents are chosen by the ACP in collaboration with the surgeon and patient. The ACP has ultimate responsibility for the choice of anesthesia. Contributing factors include the patient's current physical and mental status, age, allergies, pain history, expertise of the ACP, and factors related to the procedure (e.g., length, site, discharge plans). An absolute contraindication to any anesthetic technique or agent is patient refusal.

The ACP obtains anesthesia consent, writes orders for preoperative and postoperative drugs, and assigns the patient an anesthesia classification. The ASA physical status classification system is based on the patient's physiologic status. It uses a scale of P1 to P6 (see Table 17.3). An intraoperative complication is more likely to develop with a higher classification number.

ANESTHESIA TECHNIQUES

Types of anesthesia techniques include moderate to deep sedation, monitored anesthesia care (MAC), general anesthesia, and local and regional anesthesia (Table 18.4).

Moderate to Deep Sedation

Moderate to deep sedation is used for procedures done outside of the OR (e.g., reduction of dislocated joints in the emergency department). The presence of an ACP is not needed. Trained

RNs who are allowed by agency protocols and state nurse practice acts can provide this type of anesthesia.[16] It is given by the nurse under the direct supervision of a physician.

Monitored Anesthesia Care

Monitored anesthesia care (MAC) is used for diagnostic or therapeutic procedures done in or outside of the OR (e.g., endoscopy clinic). It includes varying levels of sedation, analgesia, and anxiolysis. A critical part of MAC is the assessment and management of any physiologic problems that may develop. The provider of MAC must be an ACP since it may be necessary to change to general anesthesia during the procedure.

General Anesthesia

The goals of anesthesiology include the (1) control of excessive biologic responses induced by a variety of stressors and (2) protection of patients from stress-induced complications. To this end, *total intravenous anesthesia (TIVA)* and newer inhalation agents have a fast onset, fast elimination, and fewer undesirable side effects than earlier agents. These factors promote early discharge from the PACU and ambulatory surgery centers.

General anesthesia is the technique of choice for patients who are having surgical procedures that are of significant duration, need skeletal muscle relaxation, require uncomfortable operative positions because of the location of the incision site, or require control of ventilation. Other reasons include patient refusal of local or regional techniques, contraindications to other techniques, and uncooperative patients. Patients may be uncooperative due to intoxication, emotional lability, head injury, impaired cognition, or inability to remain immobile for any length of time. Phases of general anesthesia are outlined in Table 18.5.

TABLE 18.4 Anesthesia Techniques and Effects

Technique	Patient Effects
General anesthesia	• Loss of sensation with loss of consciousness • Combination of hypnosis, analgesia, and amnesia • Usually involves use of inhalation agents • Skeletal muscle relaxation • Elimination of coughing, gagging, vomiting, and sympathetic nervous system responsiveness • Requires advanced airway management
Local anesthesia	• Loss of sensation without loss of consciousness • Induced topically or via infiltration, intracutaneously, or subcutaneously • Topical applications may be aerosolized or nebulized
Moderate sedation/analgesia (formerly called *conscious sedation*)	• Sedative, anxiolytic, and/or analgesic drugs used • Does not include use of inhalation agents • Patient responsive and breathes without assistance • Not expected to induce level of sedation that would impair patients' ability to protect their airway • Most often used for minor therapeutic procedures (e.g., fracture realignment in the emergency department)
Monitored anesthesia care (MAC)	• Sedative, anxiolytic, and/or analgesic drugs used • Does not usually involve inhalation agents • Patient less responsive and may need airway management • Gives greatest flexibility to match sedation level to patient needs and procedural requirements • Often used in conjunction with regional or local anesthesia • Often used for minor therapeutic and diagnostic procedures (e.g., eye surgery, colonoscopy)
Regional anesthesia	• Loss of sensation to a region of body without loss of consciousness • Involves blocking a specific nerve or group of nerves by administering a local anesthetic • Includes spinal, caudal, and epidural anesthesia and IV and peripheral nerve blocks (e.g., interscalene, axillary, infra-/supra-clavicular, popliteal, femoral, sciatic)

Source: American Society of Anesthesiologists: *Distinguishing monitored anesthesia care ("MAC") from moderate sedation/analgesia (conscious sedation),* Schaumburg, Ill, 2013, The Society.

TABLE 18.5 Phases of General Anesthesia

Preinduction	Induction	Maintenance	Emergence
Description			
• Period starting with initiation of IV or arterial access, application of monitors (e.g., ECG), administration of preoperative drugs	• Initiation of drugs that make patient unconscious • Airway secured with airway assist devices	• Period during which procedure is done • Patient stays in an unconscious state with measures to ensure airway safety	• Period when procedure is completed • Patient is prepared for return to consciousness and removal of airway assist devices
Role of Anesthesia Care Provider			
• Determine anesthetic care plan • Insert and monitor IV or arterial access • Confirm antibiotic prophylaxis • Give drugs for anxiety, aspiration prophylaxis	• Give appropriate drugs • Secure airway • Position patient appropriately for procedure	• Monitor patient's physiologic status • Give drugs and titrate fluids as appropriate	• Reverse residual neuromuscular blocking agents • Assess for return of all protective reflexes • Remove airway assist devices • Assess pain
Role of Perioperative Nurse			
• Complete preoperative assessment • Check and confirm signed informed consent • Complete surgical time-out	• Help with application of monitors (noninvasive and invasive) • Assist with airway management	• Adjust patient position as needed • Monitor patient safety	• Help place dressing • Protect patient during return of reflexes • Prepare patient to move to PACU
Classes of Drugs Used (Tables 17.8, 18.6, and 18.7)			

• Benzodiazepines
• Opioids
• Antibiotics
• Aspiration prophylaxis:
  • H_2 receptor blockers (e.g., ranitidine)
  • Gastric motility agents (e.g., metoclopramide)
  • Anticholinergics (e.g., scopolamine)
	• Benzodiazepines
	• Opioids
	• Barbiturates
	• Hypnotics
	• Volatile gases
		• Benzodiazepines
		• Opioids
		• Barbiturates
		• Hypnotics
		• Volatile gases
		• Neuromuscular blocking agents
			• Reversal agents (PRN):
			  • Anticholinesterases (e.g., neostigmine)
			  • Opioid antagonists (e.g., naloxone)
			  • Benzodiazepine antagonists (e.g., flumazenil)
			  • Neuromuscular block reversal of rocuronium [Zemuron] and vecuronium [Norcuron] (e.g., sugammadex [Bridion])
			• Supplemental opioids (PRN)
			• Antiemetics (PRN)

General anesthesia may be induced by IV or inhalation and maintained by either or a combination of the two (Table 18.6). A *balanced technique,* using adjunctive drugs to complement the induction, is the most common approach used for general anesthesia.

IV Agents. All routine general anesthetics begin with an IV induction agent, whether it is a hypnotic, an anxiolytic, or a dissociative agent. When used during the initial period of anesthesia, these agents induce sleep with a rapid onset of action. A single dose lasts only a few minutes. This is long enough for placement of a laryngeal mask airway (LMA) or an endotracheal (ET) tube. Once this is done, the ACP gives the inhalation and IV agent(s).

Recent advances in IV hypnotics (e.g., dexmedetomidine [Precedex]) and opioids (e.g., remifentanil [Ultiva]) have led to the more frequent use of TIVA. However, the patient may still need advanced airway management (e.g., LMA, ET tube) to receive oxygen/air mixtures.

Inhalation Agents. Inhalation agents are the cornerstone of general anesthesia. They may be volatile liquids or gases. Volatile liquids are given through a specially designed vaporizer after being mixed with oxygen as a carrier gas. This gas mixture is then delivered to the patient through the anesthesia circuit. Waste gases are removed using negative evacuation pressure venting to the outside of the agency.

TABLE 18.6 Drug Therapy

General Anesthesia

Drugs	Advantages	Adverse Effects	Nursing Interventions
IV Agents **Barbiturates** methohexital (Brevital)	Rapid induction, duration of action <5 min.	Cardiac effects (e.g., myocardial depression), hypotension, respiratory depression, excitation, involuntary movement.	Usually have minimal effects after surgery because of short duration of action. Increased incidence of nausea in patients with barbiturate sensitivity, histamine-triggered nausea, vomiting.
Nonbarbiturate Hypnotics etomidate (Amidate)	Has little effect on cardiovascular function. Useful for hemodynamically unstable patients. Only minor respiratory depression. No histamine release.	Myoclonia, nausea and vomiting, hiccups, adrenocortical inhibition.	Observe for myoclonia, nausea and vomiting, hiccups, hypotension, hypoglycemia.
propofol (Diprivan)	Ideal for short outpatient procedures because of rapid onset of action, metabolic clearance. May be used for induction and maintenance of anesthesia.	Bradycardia and other dysrhythmias, hypotension, apnea, transient phlebitis, nausea and vomiting, hiccups. May cause hypertriglyceridemia.	Monitor for hypotension, bradycardia. Monitor serum triglycerides q24hr when sedated >24 hr.
Inhalation Agents **Gaseous Agents** nitrous oxide	Potentiates volatile agents, thus speeding induction and reducing total dosage and side effects. Weak anesthetic, rarely used alone. Good analgesic potency.	Little or no toxicity at therapeutic concentrations.	Avoid in patients with bone marrow depression. Must be given with O_2 to prevent hypoxemia. Avoid in patients with strong history of nausea and vomiting.
Volatile Liquids desflurane (Suprane) isoflurane (Forane) sevoflurane (Ultane)	All cause skeletal muscle relaxation. *desflurane:* Fastest onset and emergence, widely used in ambulatory settings. Least postoperative cognitive dysfunction. Potential airway irritant. *isoflurane:* No increase in ventricular irritability. Does not cause liver or renal toxicity. Resistant to metabolic breakdown. *sevoflurane:* Predictable effects on cardiovascular and respiratory systems, rapid acting. Preferred for inhalation induction as nonirritating to respiratory tract.	All cause respiratory depression, hypotension, myocardial depression. *desflurane and isoflurane:* May be unsuitable for patients with coronary artery disease. *sevoflurane:* May be associated with emergence delirium (see Chapter 19) and atypical seizure-like activity.	Assess and treat pain during early anesthesia recovery. Assess for adverse reactions such as cardiopulmonary depression with hypotension and prolonged respiratory depression. Monitor for nausea and vomiting.
Dissociative Anesthetic ketamine (Ketalar)	Given IV or IM. Potent analgesic and amnesic.	May cause hallucinations and nightmares, ↑ intracranial and intraocular pressure, ↑ heart rate, ↑ BP.	Anticipate use of a benzodiazepine if agitation and hallucinations occur. Calm, quiet environment is essential in postoperative care.

Inhalation agents enter the body through the alveoli in the lungs. Ease of administration and rapid excretion by ventilation make them desirable agents. One undesirable trait is the irritating effect some inhalation agents (e.g., desflurane [Suprane]) have on the respiratory tract. Complications include coughing, laryngospasm, and increased secretions.

Once the patient has been induced with an IV agent, the choice for delivering inhalation agents is usually through an ET tube or LMA. The ET tube allows control of ventilation and protects the airway from aspiration. LMAs are currently an important option for patients with difficult airways, but they do not provide access to the trachea or airway protection with the same certainty as ETs. Complications of ET tube or LMA use are

primarily related to insertion and removal. These include failure to intubate, damage to teeth and lips, laryngospasm, laryngeal edema, sore throat, and hoarseness caused by injury or irritation of the vocal cords or surrounding tissues.

Adjuncts to General Anesthesia. General anesthesia is rarely limited to a single agent. Drugs added to an inhalation anesthetic (other than an IV induction drug) are termed *adjuncts*. Adjuncts are added to the anesthetic regimen to achieve unconsciousness, analgesia, amnesia, muscle relaxation, or autonomic nervous system control. They include opioids, benzodiazepines, neuromuscular blocking agents (muscle relaxants), and antiemetics (Table 18.7). It is important to know that we often give these drugs in combination and they may have synergistic or

TABLE 18.7 Drug Therapy

Adjuncts to General Anesthesia

Agents	Intended Effect	Adverse Effects	Nursing Interventions
Antiemetics (See Table 41.1) aprepitant (Emend) granisetronmetoclopramide (Reglan) ondansetron (Zofran) palonosetron prochlorperazine promethazine rolapitant (Varubi)	Counteract emetic effects of inhalation agents and opioids. Prophylactic prevention of nausea and vomiting related to histamine release, vagal stimulation, vestibular disturbance, procedure (e.g., abdominal laparoscopy).	Headache, dizziness, IV irritation, dysrhythmias, dysphoria, dystonia, dry mouth, central nervous system sedation.	• Monitor heart rhythm, cardiopulmonary status, level of central nervous system excitation or sedation, ability to move limbs, presence of nausea or vomiting.
Benzodiazepines diazepam (Valium) lorazepam (Ativan) midazolam (Versed)	Reduce anxiety, induce and maintain anesthesia, induce amnesia, treat emergence delirium. Supplement sedation in local and regional anesthesia and MAC.	Synergistic effect with opioids, increasing potential for respiratory depression. Hypotension and tachycardia. Prolonged sedation or confusion.	• Monitor level of consciousness. Assess for respiratory depression, hypotension, and tachycardia. • Reverse severe benzodiazepine-induced respiratory depression with flumazenil (Romazicon).
Neuromuscular Blocking Agents *Depolarizing agent:* succinylcholine (Anectine) *Nondepolarizing agents:* • atracurium • cisatracurium (Nimbex) • pancuronium • rocuronium	Promote endotracheal intubation, promote skeletal muscle relaxation (paralysis) to enhance access to surgical sites. Effects of nondepolarizing agents are usually reversed toward end of surgery by giving anticholinesterase agents (e.g., neostigmine).	Apnea related to paralysis of respiratory muscles. Duration of action of nondepolarizing agents may be longer than surgery. Reversal agents may not completely eliminate effects. Confusion and nausea. Recurrence of muscle weakness with correction of hypothermia.	• If intubated, monitor return of muscle strength, level of consciousness, and ventilation. • Maintain patent airway. Monitor respiratory rate and rhythm until patient able to cough and return to previous levels of muscle strength. Ensure availability of nondepolarizing reversal agents (e.g., neostigmine) and emergency respiratory support equipment. • Monitor temperature and levels of muscle strength with temperature changes.
Opioids alfentanil (Alfenta) fentanyl (Sublimaze) hydromorphone (Dilaudid) morphine sulfate remifentanil (Ultiva) sufentanil (Sufenta)	Induce and maintain anesthesia, reduce stimuli from sensory nerve endings, provide analgesia during surgery and recovery in PACU.	Respiratory depression, vomiting, bradycardia, peripheral vasodilation (when combined with anesthetics). High risk for pruritus with both regional and IV administration.	• Assess respiratory rate and rhythm, monitor pulse oximetry, protect airway in anticipation of vomiting. • Use standing orders for antipruritics and antiemetics. • Reverse opioid-induced respiratory depression with naloxone. If used, reversal of analgesic effects also occurs.
Other Agents dexmedetomidine (Precedex)	Induces and maintains sedation in nonintubated patients prior to and/or during surgery.	Hypotension, bradycardia, sinus arrest, transient hypertension during administration of loading dose.	• Monitor heart rate and rhythm, and BP for side effects.

antagonistic effects. You may see deeper levels of sedation or more drug-related side effects beyond those seen with inhalation anesthetics alone. If needed, drugs are available to reverse the effects of some of these adjuncts.

Dissociative Anesthesia. *Dissociative anesthesia* interrupts associative brain pathways while blocking sensory pathways. The patient may appear catatonic, is amnesic, and has profound analgesia that lasts into the postoperative period. Ketamine (Ketalar) (given IV or IM) is a common dissociative anesthetic. It is a potent analgesic and amnesic. Ketamine is given to asthmatic patients because it promotes bronchodilation. In trauma patients, it increases heart rate and helps maintain cardiac output. Because ketamine is a phenyl cyclohexyl piperidine (PCP) derivative, the drug may cause hallucinations and nightmares, limiting its usefulness. Concurrent use of midazolam (Versed) can reduce or eliminate the hallucinations. Providing a quiet, unhurried environment in the PACU is especially important for all patients receiving dissociative anesthesia.

Local and Regional Anesthesia

Local anesthesia interrupts the generation of nerve impulses by changing the flow of sodium into nerve cells. The result is autonomic nervous system blockade, anesthesia, and skeletal muscle flaccidity or paralysis. Local anesthetics are topical, ophthalmic, nebulized, or injected. A local anesthetic is applied to a specific area of the body by the surgeon or ACP. It does not involve sedation or loss of consciousness.

Regional anesthesia (or block) using a local anesthetic is always injected. It involves a central nerve (e.g., spinal) or group of nerves (e.g., plexus) that innervate a site remote to the point of injection. Administration of a local or regional anesthetic may involve concurrent use of MAC or moderate to deep sedation (Table 18.4), either preinjection or intraoperatively. Regional blocks are used as preoperative analgesia, during surgery to manage surgical pain, and after surgery to control pain. Indwelling catheters that deliver local anesthetic to the surgical site through a pump implanted during surgery can give continuous pain relief up to 72 hours after surgery.

Advantages of local and regional anesthesia include rapid recovery and discharge with continued postoperative analgesia without any accompanying cognitive dysfunction. They can be safely used in patients who have co-morbidities that prevent the use of general anesthesia.

Disadvantages include the potential for technical problems, discomfort at the injection site, and the inability to precisely match the agent's duration of action to the duration of the procedure. Another disadvantage is the risk for inadvertent vascular injection leading to local anesthetic systemic toxicity (LAST). LAST first presents as confusion, metallic taste, oral numbness, and dizziness.[17] Without treatment, seizures, coma, and dysrhythmias may occur.

The topical applications of creams, ointments, aerosols, and liquids are standard methods to administer local anesthesia. The drug is applied directly to the skin, mucous membranes, or open surface. Eutectic mixture of local anesthetics (EMLA cream, a combination of prilocaine and lidocaine) is an example. It is applied to the site 30 to 60 minutes before a procedure. The success of injected local anesthetics may be limited by prolonged duration of procedure or infection at the injection site that interferes with drug absorption.

In ambulatory or outpatient procedures, you may aid the ACP in administering a peripheral or regional block. You must be familiar with the drugs, including the methods of administration and adverse and toxic effects. Initial assessment of the patient should include the patient's history with the use of local anesthetics and any adverse events associated with their use by the patient or blood relatives.

Many patients report "allergies" to local anesthetics. Although true allergies to local anesthetics occur, they are rare. Allergies are likely to be a result of additives or preservatives in the preparation. Some local anesthetics are combined with epinephrine to provide localized vasoconstriction. This decreases absorption and extends the action of the agent. However, if the local anesthetic is absorbed in the tissues or inadvertently injected IV and enters the general circulation, the patient may have tachycardia, hypertension, and a general feeling of panic.

Examples of common regional nerve blocks include brachial plexus block; IV regional anesthesia (IVRA) or Bier block anesthesia; and femoral, axillary, cervical, sciatic, ankle, and retrobulbar blocks. For IVRA or Bier block, the patient has a double-cuff tourniquet applied as a safety measure.

You can promote the success of regional anesthesia by properly positioning the patient, monitoring vital signs during block delivery, applying oxygen therapy, and using supporting devices (at the direction of the ACP) that contribute to the anesthesia (e.g., ultrasound imaging, nerve stimulator, tourniquets). When a patient is receiving regional anesthesia, airway equipment, emergency drugs, and a cardiac monitor/defibrillator should be available to provide advanced airway and cardiopulmonary support if needed.

Spinal and Epidural Anesthesia. Spinal anesthesia and epidural anesthesia are also types of regional anesthesia. **Spinal anesthesia** involves the injection of a local anesthetic into the cerebrospinal fluid in the subarachnoid space, usually below the level of L2 (Fig. 18.6, *A*). The local anesthetic mixes with cerebrospinal fluid. Depending on the extent of its spread, various levels of anesthesia are achieved. Because the local anesthetic is given directly into the cerebrospinal fluid, a spinal anesthetic produces an autonomic, sensory, and motor blockade. Patients develop vasodilation and may become hypotensive from the autonomic block. They feel no pain because of the sensory block. They cannot move because of the motor block. The duration of action of the spinal anesthetic depends on the drug used and the dose

Sagittal section

FIG. 18.6 Location of needle point and injected anesthetic relative to dura and spinal cord. A, Spinal anesthesia. B, Single-injection epidural. C, Epidural catheter. (Interspaces most often used are L2-3, L4-5, L3-4.)

given. A spinal anesthetic may be used for procedures involving the extremities (e.g., joint replacements) and lower gastrointestinal, prostate, and gynecologic surgeries.

An *epidural block* involves injection of a local anesthetic into the epidural space via a thoracic or lumbar approach (Fig. 18.6, *B*). The anesthetic agent does not enter the cerebrospinal fluid but binds to nerve roots as they enter and exit the spinal cord. With the use of a low concentration of local anesthetic, sensory pathways are blocked but motor fibers are still intact. In higher doses, sensory and motor fibers are blocked. Epidural anesthesia may be the sole anesthetic for a surgical procedure. In addition, a catheter may be placed to allow for intraoperative use and continued analgesia in the postoperative period (Fig. 18.6, *C*). For postoperative analgesia, lower doses of epidural local anesthetic, usually in combination with an opioid, are used. Epidural anesthesia is often used for analgesia or in combination with MAC or general anesthesia, in obstetrics, vascular procedures involving the lower extremities, lung resections, and renal and midabdominal surgeries. The desirable effects of vasodilation and analgesia contribute to better surgical outcomes.

With spinal or epidural anesthesia, the patient can stay fully conscious, receive MAC, or choose general anesthesia. The onset of spinal anesthesia is more rapid than that of epidural anesthesia. Both may be extended in duration using indwelling catheters, thus allowing for more doses of anesthetic.

With either anesthesia, closely observe the patient for manifestations of autonomic nervous system blockade. These include hypotension, bradycardia, nausea, and vomiting. There is less autonomic nervous system blockade with epidural anesthesia than with spinal anesthesia. Should "too high" a block be present, the patient may have tingling in the arms and hands or inadequate breathing and apnea. Other complications include postdural puncture headache, back pain, isolated nerve injury, and meningitis.

Gerontologic Considerations: Patient During Surgery

Although anesthetic agents have become safer and more predictable, the aging process affects the absorption, distribution, and metabolism of drugs. This results in changes in their onset, peak, and duration independent of the route of administration. Because of this, anesthetic drugs need to be carefully titrated when given to older adults. Physiologic changes in aging may also change the patient's response to blood and fluid loss and replacement, hypothermia, pain, and tolerance of the procedure and positioning. Carefully monitor the older adult's response to all anesthetic agents. Postoperative delirium is a common complication in this population and associated with adverse surgical outcomes.[18] Assess the postoperative recovery from anesthesia before the patient is transferred out of the PACU.

Some older adults may have a hard time communicating and following directions because of problems with hearing or vision. These factors increase the need for clear and concise communication in the OR, especially when preoperative sedation is combined with already existing sensory deficits. Because of decreased ability to perceive discomfort or pressure on vulnerable areas and a loss of skin elasticity, the older adult's skin is at risk for injury from tape, electrodes, warming and cooling blankets, and certain types of dressings. Pooling of solutions used to prepare the skin in dependent areas can quickly create skin burns or abrasions.

Care and vigilance are needed in preparing and positioning the older patient. The older adult often has osteoporosis and/or osteoarthritis. Misalignment, pressure, or other insults to arthritic joints desensitized from an anesthetic may create long-term injury and disability. Older adults are at a greater risk for perioperative hypothermia. Consider using warming devices and carefully monitor them when used.

PERIOPERATIVE CRISIS EVENTS

Although the incidence of crisis events has significantly decreased with scientific advancements, there is an inherent risk with surgery for an adverse outcome, which may be of critical nature. Some events may be expected (e.g., cardiac arrest in an unstable patient, massive blood loss during trauma surgery). Others may occur without warning (e.g., air embolism, hypoxia), demanding immediate intervention by all members of the OR team. More rare events include anaphylactic reactions and malignant hyperthermia.

Anaphylactic Reactions

Anaphylaxis is the most severe form of an allergic reaction, manifesting with life-threatening pulmonary and circulatory complications. ACPs give patients a variety of drugs, including anesthetics, antibiotics, and blood products. Anesthetic agents, antibiotics, and latex cause many allergic reactions. Vigilance and rapid intervention are essential. Anesthesia may mask the initial manifestations of anaphylaxis. An anaphylactic reaction causes hypotension, tachycardia, bronchospasm, and pulmonary edema. Anaphylaxis is discussed in Chapter 13.

Latex allergy has become a concern in the surgical setting. Gloves, catheters, and many devices contain natural rubber latex. Latex allergy protocols should be set up in each agency to provide a latex-safe environment for susceptible patients.[19] Latex allergies are discussed in Chapter 13.

Malignant Hyperthermia

Malignant hyperthermia (MH) is a rare disorder characterized by hyperthermia with skeletal muscle rigidity. It can result in death. MH occurs in susceptible people when they are exposed to certain anesthetic agents. Succinylcholine (Anectine), especially when given with volatile inhalation agents, is the primary trigger of MH. Other factors include stress, trauma, and heat. When MH does occur, it is usually during general anesthesia. It may occur in the recovery period, too.[20]

MH is an autosomal dominant trait. It is variable in its genetic manifestation, so predictions based on family history are important but not reliable. The fundamental defect is hypermetabolism of skeletal muscle resulting from altered control of intracellular calcium. This leads to muscle contracture, hyperthermia, hypoxemia, lactic acidosis, and hemodynamic and cardiac problems. Tachycardia, tachypnea, hypercarbia, and ventricular dysrhythmias may occur but are nonspecific to MH.

MH is diagnosed after ruling out other causes of the hypermetabolism. The rise in body temperature is not an early sign of MH. Unless promptly detected and treated, MH can result in cardiac arrest and death. The definitive treatment of MH is prompt administration of dantrolene (Dantrium, Ryanodex).[20] Dantrolene slows metabolism, reduces muscle contraction, and mediates the catabolic processes associated with MH.

To prevent MH, take a careful family history and be alert to the development of MH perioperatively. The patient known or suspected to be at risk for this disorder can receive anesthesia with minimal risks if proper precautions are taken. Patients with MH need to be aware of the condition so that family members may be genetically tested.

CASE STUDY

Intraoperative Patient

(© shironosov/
iStock/Thinkstock.)

Patient Profile

G.S., a 63-yr-old retired accountant, was admitted to the hospital for severe pain from acute cholecystitis. G.S.'s medical history includes hypertension and type 2 diabetes. His pain has been managed with hydromorphone (Dilaudid) using patient-controlled analgesia. Intractable nausea and vomiting required the placement of a NG tube. He is scheduled for a laparoscopic cholecystectomy. The surgery will be done under general anesthesia.

Subjective Data

- G.S. is awake and able to identify himself, his birth date, procedure, and surgical site
- Rates pain as a 4 on a 0- to 10 scale on arrival to the holding area

Objective Data

- Admitted to the holding area with an NG tube in place and one peripheral IV catheter
- Capillary blood glucose 1 hour ago was 125 mg/dL
- Oxygen saturation 96% on room air

Interprofessional Care

- Vital signs per holding area routine
- 0.9 normal saline solution at 100 mL/hr
- Titrate O_2 therapy to keep O_2 saturation >90%
- NG tube connected to low, intermittent suction

Discussion Questions

1. What are the potential intraoperative problems that you may expect with G.S.?
2. **Priority Decision:** What priority nursing interventions would be appropriate to prevent these complications from occurring?
3. **Collaboration:** What are the interprofessional team's priorities for G.S.?
4. **Evidence-Based Practice:** G.S. tells you that he is cold despite a blanket in place. Why is it important that G.S. stays warm?
5. **Safety:** Identify 2 areas of risk for injury to G.S. What actions can be taken to ensure patient safety?

Answers available at *http://evolve.elsevier.com/Lewis/medsurg.*

BRIDGE TO NCLEX EXAMINATION

The number of the question corresponds to the same-numbered outcome at the beginning of the chapter.

1. Proper attire for the semirestricted area of the surgery department is
   a. street clothing.
   b. surgical attire and head cover.
   c. scrub attire, head cover, shoe covers.
   d. street clothing with the addition of shoe covers.

2. Activities that the nurse might perform in the role of a scrub nurse during surgery include (*select all that apply*)
   a. checking electrical equipment.
   b. preparing the instrument table.
   c. assisting with draping the patient.
   d. passing instruments to the surgeon and assistants.
   e. documenting activities occurring in the operating room.

3. The nurse is caring for a patient undergoing surgery for a knee replacement. What is critical to the patient's safety during the procedure (*select all that apply*)?
   a. Universal protocol is followed.
   b. The ACP is an anesthesiologist.
   c. The patient has adequate health insurance.
   d. The patient's family is in the surgery waiting area.
   e. The patient's allergies are conveyed to the surgical team.

4. The nurse's *primary* responsibility for the care of the patient undergoing surgery is
   a. developing an individualized plan of nursing care for the patient.
   b. carrying out specific tasks related to surgical policies and procedures.
   c. ensuring that the patient has been assessed for safe administration of anesthesia.
   d. performing a preoperative history and physical assessment to identify patient needs.

5. When scrubbing at the scrub sink, the nurse should
   a. scrub from elbows to hands.
   b. scrub without mechanical friction.
   c. scrub for a minimum of 10 minutes.
   d. hold the hands higher than the elbows.

6. When positioning a patient in preparation for surgery, the nurse understands that injury to the patient can occur because of (*select all that apply*)
   a. loss of pain perception.
   b. incorrect musculoskeletal alignment.
   c. vasoconstriction of the peripheral vessels.
   d. hypovolemia contributing to decreased perfusion.
   e. inability to sense pressure over bony prominences.

7. IV induction for general anesthesia is the method of choice for *most* patients because
   a. the patient is not intubated.
   b. the agents are nonexplosive.
   c. induction is rapid and controlled.
   d. emergence is longer but with fewer complications.

1. c, 2. b, c, d, 3. a, e, 4. a, 5. d, 6. a, b, d, e, 7. c

For rationales to these answers and even more NCLEX review questions, visit *http://evolve.elsevier.com/Lewis/medsurg.*

ⓔ EVOLVE WEBSITE/RESOURCES LIST

http://evolve.elsevier.com/Lewis/medsurg
Review Questions (Online Only)
Key Points
Answer Keys for Questions
- Rationales for Bridge to NCLEX Examination Questions
- Answer Guidelines for Case Study on p. 326

Conceptual Care Map Creator
Audio Glossary
Content Updates

REFERENCES

*1. Association of periOperative Registered Nurses: *2018 Guidelines for perioperative practice.* Denver, 2018, AORN.

2. The Joint Commission: Surgical care improvement project core measure set. Retrieved from *www.jointcommission.org/assets/1/6/Surgical%20 Care%20Improvement%20Project.pdf.*

3. The Joint Commission: National patient safety goals. Retrieved from *www.jointcommission.org/standards_information/npsgs.aspx.*

4. Rothrock JC: *Alexander's care of the patient in surgery,* ed 16, St Louis, 2018, Mosby.

5. Competency and Credentialing Institute: CNOR certification. Retrieved from *www.cc-institute.org/cnor/about.*

6. Association of Surgical Technologists: About the profession. Retrieved from *www.ast.org/AboutUs/About_AST.*

*7. Association of periOperative Registered Nurses: AORN position statement on allied health care providers and support personnel in the perioperative practice setting. Retrieved from *www.aorn.org/-/media/aorn/guidelines/ position-statements/posstat-personnel-allied-health-care.pdf.*

*8. Association of periOperative Registered Nurses: AORN position statement on RN first assistants. Retrieved from *www.aorn.org/-/media/aorn/ guidelines/position-statements/posstat-rnfa.pdf.*

9. American Society of Anesthesiologists: Types of careers in anesthesia. Retrieved from *https://www.asahq.org/education-and-career/career-resources/anesthesia-as-a-career/types-of-careers-in-anesthesia.*

10. American Association of Nurse Anesthetists. *Scope of nurse anesthesia practice.* Retrieved from *www.aana.com/docs/default-source/practice-aana-com-web-documents-(all)/scope-of-nurse-anesthesia-practice. pdf?sfvrsn=250049b1_2.*

*11. Hudson BF, Ogden J: Exploring the impact of intraoperative interventions for pain and anxiety management during local anesthetic surgery: A systematic review and meta-analysis, *J PeriAnesthesia Nurs* 31:118, 2016.

12. Occupational Safety and Health Administration: Occupational safety and health standards, toxic and hazardous substances: Bloodborne pathogens. Retrieved from *www.osha.gov/pls/oshaweb/owadisp.show_document?p_ id=10051&p_table=STANDARDS.*

13. Spruce L: Back to basics: Surgical fire prevention, *AORN J* 104:217, 2017.

14. Sanchez JA, Barach P, Johnson J: *Surgical patient care: Improving safety, quality and value,* New York, 2017, Springer.

*15. Association of periOperative Registered Nurses: Prevention of sentinel events. Retrieved from *www.aorn.org/education/staff-development/ prevention-of-sentinel-events* .

16. American Association of Nurse Anesthetists: *Non anesthesia provider procedural sedation and analgesia.* Retrieved from *www.aana.com/docs/ default-source/practice-aana-com-web-documents-(all)/non-anesthesia-provider-procedural-sedation-and-analgesia.pdf?sfvrsn=670049b1_2.*

17. Wadlund DL: Local anesthetic systemic toxicity, *AORN J* 106:367, 2017.

*18. Mohanty S, Rosenthal R, Russell M, et al: Optimal perioperative management of the geriatric patient: A best practices guideline from the American College of Surgeons NSQIP and the American Geriatrics Society, *JACS* 222:930, 2016.

19. Seifert P: Crisis management of anaphylaxis in the OR, *AORN J* 105:219, 2017.

20. Malignant Hyperthermia Association of the United States: Emergency treatment for an acute MH event. Retrieved from *www.mhaus.org/ healthcare-professionals/managing-a-crisis.*

*Evidence-based information for clinical practice.

Postoperative Care

Diane M. Rudolphi

Three things in human life are important. The first is to be kind. The second is to be kind. And the third is to be kind.

Henry James

ⓔ http://evolve.elsevier.com/Lewis/medsurg/

CONCEPTUAL FOCUS

Gas Exchange	Pain	Tissue Integrity
Fluids and Electrolytes	Perfusion	
Infection	Safety	

LEARNING OUTCOMES

1. Prioritize nursing responsibilities related to managing patients in the postanesthesia care unit (PACU).
2. Prioritize nursing responsibilities to maintain patient safety and prevent postoperative complications in the PACU and clinical unit.
3. Apply data from the initial nursing assessment to the management of the patient after transfer from the PACU to the clinical unit.
4. Select nursing interventions to manage potential problems during the postoperative period.
5. Distinguish discharge criteria from Phase I and Phase II postanesthesia care.

KEY TERMS

airway obstruction, p. 332	delayed emergence, p. 337	patient-controlled analgesia (PCA), p. 338
atelectasis, p. 332	emergence delirium, p. 337	postoperative ileus (POI), p. 340

The postoperative period begins immediately after surgery and continues until the patient is discharged from medical care. This chapter focuses on the multiple concepts central to postoperative nursing. Nursing plays a vital role in supporting ventilation and perfusion, maintaining fluid and electrolyte balance, promoting comfort, reducing infection, and promoting safety. Specific surgical procedures and related postoperative care are discussed in the appropriate chapters of this text.

POSTOPERATIVE CARE OF SURGICAL PATIENT

The patient's immediate recovery period is managed in a *postanesthesia care unit* (*PACU*). It is usually next to the operating room (OR). This location limits transportation of the patient right after surgery and gives ready access to anesthesia and OR staff. The goals of PACU care are to maintain patient safety during recovery from anesthesia and identify actual and potential patient problems that may occur because of anesthesia and surgery and intervene appropriately.

Postanesthesia Care Unit Admission

The patient's admission to the PACU is a joint effort among the anesthesia care provider (ACP), OR nurse, and PACU nurse. This collaboration fosters a smooth transfer of care to the PACU and helps determine which phase we assign the patient.

PACU Progression. There are 3 phases of postanesthesia care. During each phase, we provide different levels of care depending on the patient's needs[1] (Table 19.1). How patients move through the phases of care is determined by their condition and the type of anesthesia they received. If a patient assigned to Phase I care on admission to the PACU is stable and recovering well, the patient may rapidly progress through Phase I to either Phase II care or an inpatient unit. This accelerated progress is called rapid postanesthesia care unit progression (RPP). Another accelerated system of care is fast-tracking, which involves admitting ambulatory surgery patients directly to Phase II care. Although RPP and fast-tracking can result in time and cost savings, the patient's safety is the primary factor determining where and at what level we provide postoperative care.

TABLE 19.1 Phases of Postanesthesia Care

Phase I
- Care during the immediate postanesthesia period
- ECG and more intense monitoring (e.g., arterial BP monitoring, mechanical ventilation)

Goal: Prepare patient for transfer to Phase II level of care, an inpatient unit, or intensive care setting

Phase II
- Ambulatory surgery patients
- Fast-tracking (i.e., patients who have bypassed Phase I level of care)

Goal: Prepare patient for transfer to extended observation, home, or extended care facility

Extended Observation
- Extended care or observation after transfer/discharge from Phase I or Phase II levels of care

Goal: Prepare patient for self-care

Blended Levels of Care
- Various levels of care offered in the same environment

Source: American Society of PeriAnesthesia Nurses: *2015-2017 Perianesthesia nursing standards, practice recommendations and interpretive statements,* Cherry Hill, NJ, 2015, The Society.

TABLE 19.2 PACU Hand-Off Report

General Information
- Patient name and age
- Surgeon and anesthesia care provider
- Surgical procedure
- Presence of tubes, drains, catheters, and IV lines
- Type of anesthesia (e.g., general, regional, monitored anesthesia care)
- Use of any reversal agents
- Airway status (artificial airway and/or interventions to maintain adequate oxygenation)
- Pain management interventions
- NPO status and postoperative orders that need started

Patient History
- Indication for surgery
- Medical history, medications, allergies
- Preoperative or baseline vital signs, laboratory and diagnostic findings
- Level of consciousness, orientation
- Specific patient characteristics (e.g., hearing loss, vision impairment, mobility limitations)
- Patient preferences (e.g., cultural, personal beliefs/restrictions)
- Patient emotional status on arrival to OR

Intraoperative Management
- Anesthetic agents
- Other drugs received preoperatively or intraoperatively
- Last dose of opioid administration/pain management plan
- Total fluid replacements, including blood transfusions
- Total fluid losses (e.g., blood, nasogastric drainage)
- Urine output

Intraoperative Course
- Unexpected anesthetic events or reactions
- Unexpected surgical events
- Most recent vital signs and monitoring trends
- Results of laboratory tests and x-rays

Phase I Initial Assessment. On admission of the patient to the PACU, the ACP gives you a postanesthesia hand-off report (Table 19.2). Hand-off reports should be standardized and interactive, allowing you to ask questions and clarify information.[2] The ACP should stay in the PACU until you accept responsibility for the care of the patient. Potential problems in the postoperative period are shown in Fig. 19.1. Table 19.3 describes key parts of a PACU assessment.

Begin your initial assessment by evaluating the patient's airway, breathing, and circulation (ABC) status. Residual neuromuscular blockade, opioid use, and patient characteristics such as sleep-disordered breathing (e.g., obstructive sleep apnea [OSA], abnormal airway anatomy) affect oxygenation and ventilation. Be alert for signs of inadequate oxygenation and ventilation (Table 19.4). Any sign of respiratory distress needs prompt intervention.

Pulse oximetry monitoring is a noninvasive means of assessing oxygenation and can provide an early warning of hypoxemia. *Transcutaneous carbon dioxide ($PtcCO_2$)* and *end-tidal CO_2 ($PetCO_2$) (capnography) monitoring* are used to detect respiratory depression in high-risk patients.[3] Volumetric capnography and acoustic respiratory rate monitoring can help you detect respiratory distress early.[4] Pulse oximetry, capnography, $PtcCO_2$, and $PetCO_2$ are discussed in Chapter 25.

Note and assess changes in ECG findings from the preoperative baseline. Measure the BP and compare it with baseline readings. Invasive monitoring (e.g., arterial BP) may be needed. Assess body temperature, peripheral pulses, capillary refill, and skin condition (e.g., color, moisture). Any signs of inadequate tissue perfusion need prompt intervention.

Focus the initial neurologic assessment on level of consciousness; orientation; sensory and motor status; and size, equality, and reactivity of the pupils. The patient may be awake, drowsy but arousable, or asleep. Because hearing is the first sense to return in the unconscious patient, explain all activities to the patient from the time of admission to the PACU. If the patient received a regional anesthetic (e.g., spinal, epidural), sensory and motor blockade may still be present and you should assess dermatome levels (Fig. 19.2). During recovery from regional anesthesia, sensory and motor function first returns distal to the site where the anesthetic was given. This means the areas near the site of injections are the last to recover.

> **! SAFETY ALERT Regional Anesthesia**
> - Monitor for complications of regional anesthesia.
> - Be alert for respiratory distress, hypotension, dysrhythmias, changes in heart rate, bleeding or hematoma at site, headache, neurologic deficit or prolonged block, urinary retention, nausea, and pruritis.
> - Implement treatment protocols and notify the health care provider (HCP) as needed.

Assess the urinary system by measuring intake and output and determining fluid balance. Intraoperative fluid totals are part of the ACP report. Note the presence of all IV lines; all irrigation solutions and infusions; and all output devices, including catheters and wound drains. Assess the surgical site. Note the condition of any dressings and the type and amount of any drainage. Implement orders related to incision care.

The rest of this chapter discusses the nursing management of select problems. You can apply this information to patients in both the PACU and clinical unit.

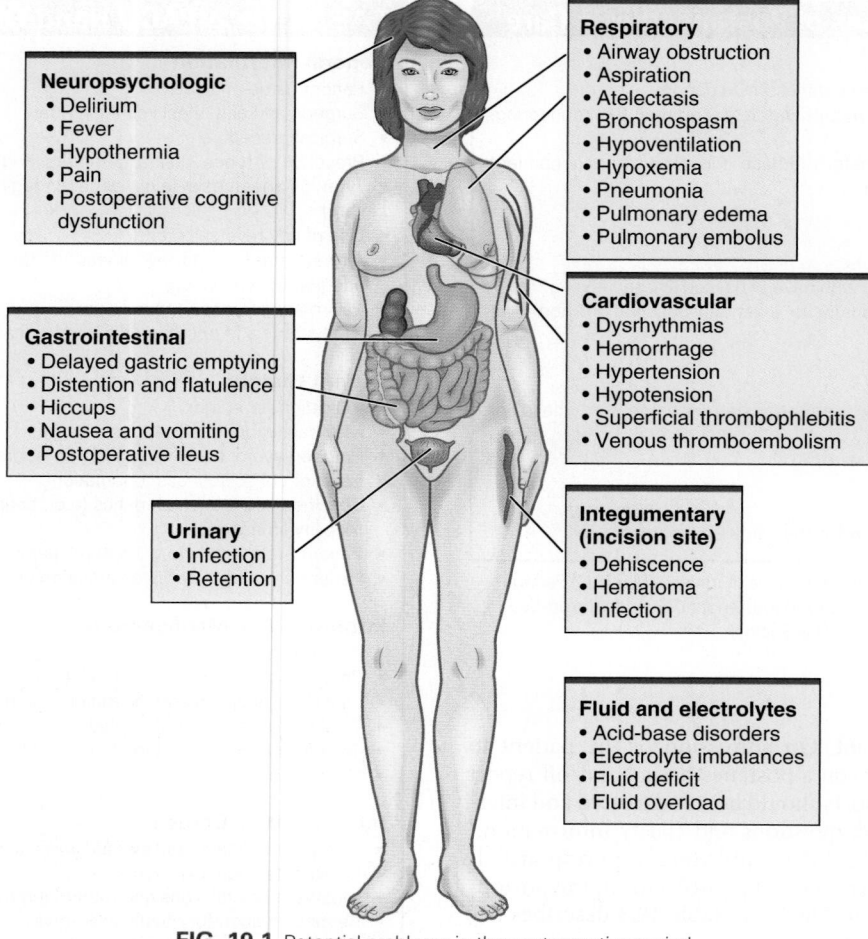

Neuropsychologic
- Delirium
- Fever
- Hypothermia
- Pain
- Postoperative cognitive dysfunction

Respiratory
- Airway obstruction
- Aspiration
- Atelectasis
- Bronchospasm
- Hypoventilation
- Hypoxemia
- Pneumonia
- Pulmonary edema
- Pulmonary embolus

Gastrointestinal
- Delayed gastric emptying
- Distention and flatulence
- Hiccups
- Nausea and vomiting
- Postoperative ileus

Cardiovascular
- Dysrhythmias
- Hemorrhage
- Hypertension
- Hypotension
- Superficial thrombophlebitis
- Venous thromboembolism

Urinary
- Infection
- Retention

Integumentary (incision site)
- Dehiscence
- Hematoma
- Infection

Fluid and electrolytes
- Acid-base disorders
- Electrolyte imbalances
- Fluid deficit
- Fluid overload

FIG. 19.1 Potential problems in the postoperative period.

TABLE 19.3 **Initial PACU Assessment**

Airway
- Patency
- Oral or nasal airway
- Laryngeal mask airway
- Endotracheal tube with ventilator settings

Breathing
- Respiratory rate and quality
- Auscultated breath sounds
- Pulse oximetry
- Capnography or other technology-supported monitoring if indicated
- Supplemental O_2

Circulation
- ECG monitoring: rate and rhythm
- BP: noninvasive or arterial line
- Hemodynamic pressure readings (if applicable)
- Temperature
- Capillary refill
- Color, temperature, moisture of skin
- Apical and peripheral pulses

Neurologic
- Level of consciousness
- Orientation
- Sensory and motor status
- Pupil size and reaction

Surgical Site
- Dressings and visible incisions
- Drains: type, patency, and drainage
- IV assessment: location and condition of sites, solutions infusing

Genitourinary
- Urine output

Gastrointestinal
- Nausea, vomiting
- Intake (fluids, irrigations)
- Output (vomitus)
- Bowel sounds

Pain
- Incision
- Other

Patient Safety Needs
- Patient position
- Fall risk assessment

TABLE 19.4 Signs of Inadequate Oxygenation

Cardiovascular System
- Hypertension
- Hypotension
- Tachycardia
- Bradycardia
- Dysrhythmias
- Delayed capillary refill
- Weak peripheral pulses
- Decreased O_2 saturation

Central Nervous System
- Restlessness
- Agitation
- Confusion
- Muscle twitching
- Seizures
- Coma

Integumentary System
- Flushed, cool, or moist skin
- Cyanosis

Renal System
- Urine output <0.5 mL/kg/hr

Respiratory System
- Increased to absent respiratory effort
- Use of accessory muscles
- Abnormal breath sounds
- Abnormal arterial blood gas values

NURSING MANAGEMENT

Caring for the Postoperative Patient

In the PACU, patients need frequent assessment and intervention by RNs. On the clinical units, the RN is responsible for assessment, developing an individualized plan of care, implementing and evaluating the plan of care, and discharge teaching. The RN can delegate much of the care to LPNs/VNs and UAP. Respiratory and physical therapy may have a role in the patient's care, depending on the type of surgery and the patient's past medical history.

PACU

- Assess patient's initial airway, breathing, and circulation status.
- Evaluate for the return to consciousness, ability to maintain airway and breathing.
- Perform ongoing assessments for postoperative problems (e.g., airway obstruction, hypoventilation, hypotension or hypertension, dysrhythmias, emergence delirium).
- Administer and titrate O_2 based on agency protocols.
- Give analgesics and IV fluids.
- Evaluate patient's readiness for transfer to clinical unit or discharge from ambulatory surgery.
- Give hand-off report to RN about patient status when transferring patient to clinical unit.
- Provide discharge teaching for patient and caregiver after ambulatory surgery.
- Oversee UAP:
  - Assist with positioning of patients in the lateral recovery position.
  - Obtain vital signs, pulse oximetry and capillary blood glucose levels (per agency policy). Report abnormal levels to RN.
  - Aid patient with elimination needs.

Clinical Unit

- Assess patient on initial admission to the unit.
- Assess for complications (e.g., atelectasis, hemodynamic instability, cognitive dysfunction, pain, fluid and electrolyte imbalance, fever or hypothermia, nausea and vomiting, urinary retention, wound infection).
- Develop and implement an individualized plan of care based on identification of patient risk factors and potential complications.
- Titrate O_2 administration according to prescribed parameters.
- Monitor pain level and give prescribed analgesics.
- Give medications.
- Provide wound care, including dressing changes.
- Insert urinary catheter as prescribed for urinary retention.
- Develop and implement individualized patient and caregiver education, including discharge teaching.
- Oversee UAP:
  - Record oral intake and output.
  - Obtain vital signs, pulse oximetry and capillary blood glucose levels (per agency policy). Report abnormal levels to RN.
  - Aid patient with nutrition, elimination, and hygienic needs.
  - Reposition and ambulate patient as instructed.
  - Help patient with deep breathing and coughing exercises.

Collaborate With Interprofessional Team

Respiratory Therapist

- Provide respiratory care modalities that support patient recovery from anesthesia (e.g., O_2 therapy, nebulizer treatments, pulmonary drainage procedures, mechanical ventilation, and airway support).
- Institute extubation protocols.
- Monitor pulse oximetry, capnography, or other technology-assisted means of assessing hypoxemia or hypoventilation.
- Assist with O_2 and/or ventilation management during patient transport.
- Perform arterial blood gas sampling in the absence of an arterial line.

- Institute rapid intubation protocols if needed in the absence of ACP.
- Provide respiratory care modalities (e.g., O_2 therapy, nebulizer treatments, pulmonary drainage procedures).
- Assist with O_2 and/or ventilation support during patient transport.
- Monitor pulse oximetry and capnography and titrate O_2 as needed.
- Perform arterial blood gas sampling as needed.

Physical Therapist

- Perform initial assessment to determine normal functioning level if surgery was emergent.
- Support patient motion and joint mobility.

- Support patient motion and joint mobility.
- Support patient return to baseline functional mobility following surgery.
- Support nursing staff on best measures for joint positioning, transferring from bed to chair, and/or ambulation.

Sensory level anesthesia necessary for surgical procedures	
Sensory level	**Type of surgery**
S2-S5	Hemorrhoidectomy
L2-L3 (knee)	Foot surgery
L1-L3 (inguinal ligament)	Lower extremity surgery
T10 (umbilicus)	Hip surgery Transurethral resection of the prostate Vaginal delivery
T6-T7 (xiphoid process)	Lower abdominal surgery Appendectomy
T4 (nipple)	Upper abdominal surgery Cesarean section

FIG. 19.2 Sensory innervation by spinal nerves and sensory level required for various surgical procedures. (From Pardo M, Miller R: *Basics of anesthesia,* ed 7, St Louis, 2018, Elsevier.)

RESPIRATORY PROBLEMS

Etiology

PACU. In the immediate postanesthesia period the most common causes of airway compromise include obstruction, hypoxemia, and hypoventilation (Table 19.5). Patients at high risk include those who (1) have had general anesthesia; (2) are older than 55 years of age; (3) have a history of tobacco use; (4) have preexisting lung disease and/or sleep-disordered breathing; (5) are obese; (6) have co-morbidities (e.g., renal disease, diabetes, hypertension); or (7) have undergone airway, thoracic, or abdominal surgery. Pulmonary complications pose the greatest risk to patients in the postanesthesia period and in the immediate postoperative period. High-risk patients should be monitored in a critical care or postanesthesia care unit.[5]

Airway obstruction is often caused by the patient's tongue blocking the airway (Fig. 19.3). The base of the tongue falls backward against the soft palate and occludes the pharynx. It is most pronounced in the supine position and in the patient who is extremely sleepy after surgery.

Hypoxemia, a partial pressure of arterial oxygen (PaO_2) less than 60 mm Hg, is characterized by a variety of nonspecific clinical signs and symptoms, ranging from agitation to somnolence, hypertension to hypotension, and tachycardia to bradycardia. Pulse oximetry will show low O_2 saturation (less than 92%).

The most common cause of hypoxemia after surgery is atelectasis. **Atelectasis** (alveolar collapse) may be the result of bronchial obstruction caused by retained secretions, decreased respiratory excursion, or general anesthesia. Atelectasis occurs when mucus blocks bronchioles or there is not enough alveolar surfactant (substance that holds the alveoli open) (Fig. 19.4). As air becomes trapped beyond the plug and is absorbed, the alveoli collapse. Atelectasis may affect a part of or an entire lobe of the lung.

Other causes of hypoxemia include pulmonary edema, pulmonary embolism (PE), aspiration, and bronchospasm. An accumulation of fluid in the alveoli can cause *pulmonary edema.* It may be the result of fluid overload, heart failure, prolonged airway obstruction, sepsis, or aspiration.

After surgery patients are at risk for *aspiration* of gastric contents into the lungs. This can occur because anesthesia depresses the respiratory protective airway reflexes. Gastric aspiration is a potentially serious emergency. It may result in laryngospasm, pneumonia, and pulmonary edema. Because of the grave consequences of aspiration of gastric fluids, prevention is the goal.

Bronchospasm is the result of an increase in bronchial smooth muscle tone with resulting closure of small airways. Airway edema develops, causing secretions to build up in the airway. The patient will have wheezing, dyspnea, use of accessory muscles, hypoxemia, and tachypnea. Bronchospasm may be due to aspiration, endotracheal intubation, pharyngeal suctioning, or an allergic response. (Allergic responses are discussed in Chapter 13.) Bronchospasm may occur in any patient. It occurs more often in patients with a history of smoking, asthma, and chronic obstructive pulmonary disease (COPD).

Hypoventilation, a common complication in the PACU, is characterized by a decreased respiratory rate or effort, hypoxemia, and increasing hypercapnia (increasing $PaCO_2$). It may result from depression of the central respiratory drive (from anesthesia or use of opioids), poor respiratory muscle tone (from neuromuscular blockade or disease), or a combination of both.

> ⚠ **SAFETY ALERT Hypoventilation**
> - Always assess for respiratory depression when giving opioids.
> - Use a sedation assessment scale (e.g., Richmond Agitation and Sedation Scale, available at *www.icudelirium.org/docs/RASS.pdf*) to assess for levels of sedation and promote patient safety when giving opioids in the PACU.
> - Begin emergency management protocols if hypoventilation is present.

Clinical Unit. Common causes of respiratory problems are atelectasis and pneumonia, especially in patients with co-morbidities (e.g., OSA, COPD, heart failure) and after abdominal and thoracic surgery.[6,7] The development of mucous plugs and decreased surfactant production is directly related to hypoventilation, immobility and bed rest, ineffective coughing, and history of tobacco use. Increased bronchial secretions occur when the respiratory passages have been irritated by heavy smoking, COPD, pulmonary infection, or dry mucous membranes that occurs with intubation, inhalation anesthesia, and dehydration. Without intervention, atelectasis can progress to pneumonia.

TABLE 19.5 Postoperative Respiratory Complications

Complications	Mechanisms	Manifestations	Interventions
Airway Obstruction			
Laryngeal edema	Allergic drug reaction Mechanical irritation from intubation Fluid overload	Similar to laryngospasm	O_2 therapy Antihistamines Corticosteroids Sedatives Possible intubation
Laryngospasm	Irritation from endotracheal tube, anesthetic gases, or gastric aspiration Most likely to occur after removal of endotracheal tube	Inspiratory stridor (crowing respirations) Sternal retraction Acute respiratory distress	O_2 therapy Positive pressure ventilation IV muscle relaxant Lidocaine Corticosteroids
Retained thick secretions	Secretion stimulation by anesthetic agents Dehydration of secretions	Noisy respirations Coarse crackles	Suctioning Deep breathing and coughing IV hydration Chest PT
Tongue falling back	Muscular flaccidity associated with ↓ consciousness and muscle relaxants	Use of accessory muscles Snoring respirations ↓ Air movement	Patient stimulation Head tilt, jaw thrust (Fig. 19.3) Artificial airway
Hypoxemia			
Aspiration	Inhalation of gastric contents into lungs	Unexplained tachypnea Bronchospasm ↓ O_2 saturation Atelectasis Interstitial edema Alveolar hemorrhage Respiratory failure	O_2 therapy Cardiopulmonary support Antibiotics
Atelectasis	Bronchial obstruction caused by retained secretions or ↓ lung volumes	↓ Breath sounds ↓ O_2 saturation	Humidified O_2 therapy Deep breathing Incentive spirometry Early mobilization
Bronchospasm	↑ Smooth muscle tone with closure of small airways	Wheezing Dyspnea Tachypnea ↓ O_2 saturation	O_2 therapy Bronchodilators
Pulmonary edema	Fluid overload ↑ Hydrostatic pressure ↓ Interstitial pressure ↑ Capillary permeability	↓ O_2 saturation Crackles Infiltrates on chest x-ray	O_2 therapy Diuretics Fluid restriction
Pulmonary embolism	Thrombus dislodged from peripheral venous system and lodged in pulmonary arterial system	Acute tachypnea Dyspnea Tachycardia Hypotension ↓ O_2 saturation Bronchospasm	O_2 therapy Cardiopulmonary support Anticoagulant therapy
Hypoventilation			
Depressed central respiratory drive	Medullary depression from anesthetics, opioids, sedatives	Shallow respirations ↓ Respiratory rate, apnea ↓ PaO_2 ↑ $PaCO_2$	Start capnography or other technology-supported respiratory monitoring Stimulation Reversal of opioids or benzodiazepines Mechanical ventilation
Mechanical restriction	Tight casts, dressings, abdominal binders Positioning and obesity preventing lung expansion	As above	Elevate head of bed Repositioning Loosen dressings
Pain	Shallow breathing to prevent incisional pain	↑ Respiratory rate Hypotension Hypertension ↓ $PaCO_2$ ↓ PaO_2 Reports of pain Guarding behavior	Opioid analgesic drug therapy Nonsteroidal antiinflammatory drug therapy Complementary and alternative therapies (e.g., music, imagery)
Poor respiratory muscle tone	Neuromuscular blockade Neuromuscular disease	As above	Reversal of paralysis Mechanical ventilation

Tongue

Tongue occluding airway

Manually elevate the jaw
while tilting the head back

Tongue

Airway cleared

FIG. 19.3 Etiology and relief of airway obstruction.

❖ NURSING MANAGEMENT: RESPIRATORY PROBLEMS

◆ Nursing Assessment

Respiratory assessment requires evaluation of airway patency; chest symmetry; and depth, rate, and character of respirations. Impaired ventilation may first be seen as slowed breathing or reduced chest and abdominal movement during breathing. Abdominal or accessory muscle use may occur with respiratory distress. Auscultating breath sounds will alert you to decreased or absent breath sounds. These findings may mean airflow is diminished or obstructed. Arouse patients with poor respiratory effort, noisy respirations, or other signs of respiratory distress at once and have them take deep breaths.

Regular monitoring of vital signs, including pulse oximetry, capnography, or other technology-supported monitoring (e.g., acoustic monitoring), and a thorough respiratory assessment allow you to recognize early signs of respiratory problems. Manifestations of hypoxemia include tachypnea, gasping, anxiety, restlessness, confusion, and a rapid or thready pulse.

Note and record the characteristics of sputum or mucus. Mucus from the trachea and throat is normally colorless and thin in consistency. Sputum from the lungs and bronchi is normally thick with a pale, yellow tinge. Changes in sputum (e.g., color) may indicate a respiratory infection.

◆ Nursing Diagnoses

Nursing diagnoses and collaborative problems related to respiratory problems include:
- Impaired airway clearance
- Impaired breathing
- Impaired gas exchange
- Risk for aspiration
- Potential complications: pneumonia, atelectasis

FIG. 19.4 Postoperative atelectasis. **A,** Normal bronchiole and alveoli. **B,** Mucous plug in bronchiole. **C,** Collapse of alveoli resulting from atelectasis after absorption of air.

◆ Nursing Implementation

In the PACU, nursing interventions are aimed at preventing and treating respiratory problems. Proper positioning of the patient aids breathing and protects the airway.

> **⚠ SAFETY ALERT Postoperative Patient Positioning**
> • Position the unconscious patient in a lateral "recovery" position (Fig. 19.5).
> • This position keeps the airway open and reduces the risk for aspiration if vomiting occurs.

Once conscious, place the patient in a supine position with the head of the bed elevated. This position maximizes expansion of the thorax by decreasing the pressure of the abdominal contents on the diaphragm.

Start O_2 therapy via nasal cannula or face mask if ordered. O_2 helps to eliminate anesthetic gases and meet the increased demand for O_2 resulting from decreased blood volume or increased metabolism.

All postoperative patients are at risk for atelectasis. Encourage deep breathing to aid gas exchange and promote the return to consciousness. Once the patient is more awake, deep breathing, coughing, and use of an incentive spirometer help prevent alveolar collapse and move respiratory secretions to larger airway passages for expectoration. One technique, known as *sustained maximal inspiration,* requires the patient to inhale as deeply as possible and, at the peak of inspiration, hold the breath for a few seconds, and then exhale. This is followed by another deep breath and cough.

The use of an incentive spirometer helps by giving visual feedback of respiratory effort (Fig. 19.6). Diaphragmatic or abdominal breathing involves inhaling slowly and deeply through the nose, holding the breath for a few seconds, and then exhaling slowly and completely through the mouth. Place the patient's hands lightly over the lower ribs and upper abdomen so that the patient can feel the abdomen rise during inspiration and fall during expiration. Unless contraindicated, have the patient perform these maneuvers 10 times every hour while awake.

Effective coughing is essential in mobilizing secretions. If secretions are in the respiratory tract, deep breathing often moves them up and stimulates the cough reflex. Splinting an abdominal incision with a pillow or a rolled blanket supports the incision and aids in coughing and expectorating secretions (Fig. 19.7).

Change the patient's position every 1 to 2 hours to allow full chest expansion and increase perfusion of both lungs. Help the patient sit in a chair and ambulate as soon as ordered. Provide adequate and regular pain medication. Incisional pain often is the greatest barrier to patient participation in effective breathing exercises and ambulation. Reassure the patient that these activities will not cause the incision to open. Adequate hydration, either parenteral or oral, is essential to maintain the integrity of mucous membranes and to keep secretions thin and loose for easy expectoration.

Other nursing interventions for specific respiratory problems are detailed in Table 19.5. A nursing care plan for the postoperative patient (eNursing Care Plan 19.1) is available on the website for this chapter.

INFORMATICS IN PRACTICE
Respiratory Monitoring

- Continuous monitoring of respiratory rate is important for those receiving patient-controlled analgesia (PCA) for pain management, as opioids can cause respiratory depression and place patients at risk for serious injury or death.
- Acoustic respiration rate (RRa) is a new measurement that allows for the noninvasive and continuous assessment of patients' breathing. RRa uses a sensor with an acoustic transducer that is placed on the patient's neck.
- The respiratory signal is displayed as a continuous respiration rate.

CARDIOVASCULAR PROBLEMS

Etiology

PACU. In the immediate postanesthesia period the most common cardiovascular problems include hypotension, hypertension, and dysrhythmias. Patients at greatest risk for altered

FIG. 19.5 Position of patient during recovery from general anesthesia.

FIG. 19.6 Proper use of an incentive spirometer. (Courtesy Christine R. Hoch, MSN, RN, ACNS-BC, Nursing Instructor, University of Delaware, Newark, DE.)

FIG. 19.7 Techniques for splinting incision when coughing.

cardiovascular function include those with altered respiratory function, those with a history of cardiovascular disease, older adults, the debilitated, and the critically ill.

Hypotension can cause hypoperfusion to the vital organs, especially the brain, heart, and kidneys. Clinical signs of disorientation, loss of consciousness, chest pain, and oliguria reflect hypoperfusion, hypoxemia, and the loss of physiologic compensation. Intervention must be prompt to prevent the devastating complications of cardiac ischemia or infarction, cerebral ischemia, renal ischemia, and bowel infarction.

The most common cause of hypotension in the PACU is fluid and blood loss, which may lead to hypovolemic shock. Hemorrhage is always a risk of surgery. Marked blood loss is possible when cauterization or sutures fail. Hemorrhage most often occurs internally. Assess for changes in level of consciousness and vital signs. If detected, treatment is aimed toward restoring circulating volume. If there is no response to fluid administration, heart dysfunction may be the cause of hypotension.

Primary heart dysfunction, which may occur in myocardial infarction, cardiac tamponade, or PE, results in an acute drop in cardiac output. Secondary heart dysfunction occurs because of the negative *chronotropic* (rate of heart contraction) and negative *inotropic* (force of heart contraction) effects of drugs, such as β-adrenergic blockers, digoxin, or opioids. Other causes of hypotension include decreased systemic vascular resistance and dysrhythmias.

Hypertension most often occurs from sympathetic nervous system stimulation. This may be the result of pain, anxiety, bladder distention, or respiratory distress. Hypertension may be related to hypothermia and preexisting hypertension.

Many problems can cause dysrhythmias. These include hypoxemia, hypercapnia, electrolyte and acid-base imbalances, circulatory instability, preexisting heart disease, hypothermia, pain, surgical stress, and many anesthetic agents.

Clinical Unit. On the clinical unit, postoperative fluid and electrolyte imbalances are contributing factors to heart problems. Such imbalances may result from a combination of the body's normal response to the stress of surgery, excessive fluid losses, and IV fluid replacement. The body's fluid status directly affects cardiac output.

Fluid retention during postoperative days 1 to 3 can result from the stress response, which maintains both blood volume and BP. Fluid retention results from the release of antidiuretic hormone (ADH) and adrenocorticotropic hormone (ACTH) and activation of the renin-angiotensin-aldosterone system (RAAS). ADH release leads to increased water reabsorption and decreased urine output, increasing blood volume. ACTH stimulates the adrenal cortex to secrete cortisol and, to a lesser degree, aldosterone (see Figs. 16.9 and 16.10). Fluid losses resulting from surgery decrease kidney perfusion, stimulating the RAAS and causing marked release of aldosterone. Both mechanisms that increase aldosterone lead to significant sodium and fluid retention, thus increasing blood volume.

Fluid overload may occur during this period of fluid retention if we infuse IV fluids too rapidly, when chronic disease (e.g., heart, kidney) exists, or when the patient is an older adult. Fluid deficits from untreated preoperative dehydration, blood loss during surgery, or slow or inadequate fluid replacement can decrease cardiac output and tissue perfusion. Losses from vomiting, bleeding, wound drainage, or suctioning can contribute to fluid deficits.

Hypokalemia can result from urinary and gastrointestinal (GI) tract losses. Low serum potassium levels directly affect the

heart's contractility and may contribute to decreases in cardiac output and tissue perfusion. The patient can receive potassium replacement, usually 40 mEq/day, if renal function is adequate. A urine output of at least 0.5 mL/kg/hr and a normal serum creatinine are considered indicative of adequate renal function.

The state of tissue perfusion or blood flow affects cardiovascular status. The stress response contributes to an increase in clotting tendencies by increasing platelet production. A *venous thromboembolism (VTE)* may form in leg veins because of venous stasis, vein injury, or a hypercoagulable state. VTE is especially common in older adults, obese persons, immobilized patients, and patients with a history of PE or predisposition to clotting. It is a potentially life-threatening complication because it may lead to PE and infarction. Suspect PE in any patient with tachypnea, chest pain, hypotension, agitation, tachycardia, and dyspnea, especially when the patient is already receiving O_2 therapy. Superficial thrombophlebitis is an uncomfortable but less serious complication. It may develop in a leg vein because of venous stasis or in the arm veins because of irritation from IV catheters or solutions. (PE and VTE are discussed in Chapters 27 and 37, respectively.)

Syncope (fainting) may result from decreased cardiac output, fluid deficits, or defects in cerebral perfusion. Syncope often occurs because of postural hypotension when the patient ambulates. It is more common in the older adult or in the patient who has been immobile for long periods. Normally when the patient stands up quickly, the arterial baroreceptors respond to the accompanying fall in BP with sympathetic nervous system stimulation. This produces vasoconstriction and maintains BP. These sympathetic and vasomotor functions may be diminished in the older adult, immobile, or postanesthesia patient.

❖ NURSING MANAGEMENT: CARDIOVASCULAR PROBLEMS

◆ Nursing Assessment

The most important aspect of the cardiovascular assessment is frequent vital sign monitoring. Plan to obtain vital signs every 15 minutes in Phase I, or more often until stabilized and then less often in Phase II. Compare postoperative vital signs with preoperative and intraoperative findings to determine when the signs are returning to baseline. Notify the ACP or HCP if any of the following occurs:

- Systolic BP <90 mm Hg or >160 mm Hg
- Pulse rate <60 beats/min or >120 beats/min
- Pulse pressure (difference between systolic and diastolic BP) narrows
- BP trends gradually decrease or increase over several consecutive readings
- Change in heart rhythm

Hypotension accompanied by a normal pulse and warm, dry, pink skin is usually from the residual vasodilating effects of anesthesia and suggests only a need for continued observation. Hypotension accompanied by a rapid or weak pulse and cold, clammy, pale skin may indicate impending hypovolemic shock and needs immediate treatment.

ECG monitoring is recommended for patients who have a history of heart disease and for all older patients who have undergone major surgery, regardless of whether they have heart problems. Assess the apical-radial pulse carefully and report any deficits or irregularities. Assess peripheral pulses and skin color, temperature, and moisture for valuable information about tissue perfusion.

◆ Nursing Diagnoses

Nursing diagnoses and collaborative problems related to cardiovascular problems include:

- Altered blood pressure
- Impaired cardiac output
- Risk for bleeding
- Potential complications: hypovolemic shock, VTE

◆ Nursing Implementation

◆ **PACU.** Begin treatment of hypotension with O_2 therapy to promote oxygenation of hypoperfused organs. Because the most common cause of hypotension is fluid loss, give IV fluid boluses to normalize BP. Inspect the surgical incision to determine if excess bleeding is the cause of volume loss. Primary heart dysfunction may require drug intervention. Peripheral vasodilation and hypotension may require vasoconstrictive drugs to increase systemic vascular resistance.

Treatment of hypertension centers on removing the cause of sympathetic nervous system stimulation. This may include giving analgesics, assisting with voiding, and correcting respiratory problems. Rewarming corrects hypothermia-induced hypertension. The patient with preexisting hypertension or who has undergone heart or vascular surgery usually needs drug therapy to reduce BP.

Since most dysrhythmias seen in the PACU have identifiable causes, treatment is directed toward removing the cause. Correcting the cause usually corrects the dysrhythmias. With life-threatening dysrhythmias (e.g., ventricular tachycardia), follow your agency's protocol for advanced cardiac life support.

◆ **Clinical Unit.** Continue to monitor vital signs. Keep an accurate intake and output record, monitor laboratory findings (e.g., electrolytes, hematocrit), and manage IV therapy after surgery.

Early ambulation is the most significant general nursing measure to prevent complications. The exercise associated with walking (1) increases muscle tone; (2) stimulates circulation, which prevents venous stasis and VTE, and speeds wound healing; and (3) increases vital capacity and supports normal respiratory function. Begin progression to ambulation by first raising the head of the patient's bed for 1 to 2 minutes. Then help the patient to sit, with legs dangling, while monitoring the pulse rate. If you do not note changes or problems, start ambulation with ongoing monitoring of the pulse. If you note changes in the pulse or dizziness occurs, sit the patient in a nearby chair. The patient should stay in this location until the BP and pulse are stable. Then help the patient back to the bed. If dizziness occurs, it is often frightening for the patient. Injury can result from a fall, so take measures to ensure patient and staff safety.

❓ CHECK YOUR PRACTICE

You are caring for an older, obese male patient who is 1 day post colon resection with activity orders for moving out of the bed to a chair. While he is in bed, you help him to a sitting position with his legs dangling. He tells you that he feels dizzy. You take his BP and it is 108/64 and his pulse is 124.

- What should you do?

NEUROLOGIC AND PSYCHOLOGIC PROBLEMS

Etiology

PACU. Postoperatively, **emergence delirium** is a short-term neurologic change manifested by behaviors such as restlessness, agitation, disorientation, thrashing, and shouting. If delirium occurs, first suspect hypoxia. Other causes include anesthetic agents, bladder distention, pain, long duration of preoperative fasting, residual neuromuscular blockade, or the presence of an endotracheal tube.

Delayed emergence can be a problem after surgery. Patients with delayed emergence spend longer periods in the PACU and have prolonged hospital courses. Identifying the causative factors is critical for determining appropriate interventions.[8] The most common cause of delayed emergence after anesthesia is drug-related. This includes anesthetic agents as well as drugs used during the perioperative period. Contributory nonpharmacologic causes include metabolic disorders, electrolyte imbalances, hypertension, liver disease, uremia, central anticholinergic syndrome, and hypothyroidism. Other causes can include hypoxia, hypercapnia, hemorrhage, and embolism.

Clinical Unit. Two types of cognitive impairments seen in surgical patients are *postoperative cognitive dysfunction (POCD)* and *delirium*. POCD is a decline in the patient's cognitive function (e.g., memory, ability to concentrate) for weeks or months after surgery. POCD occurs primarily in the older surgical patient. Preexisting cognitive impairment, duration of anesthesia, complications during surgery, and infection contribute to the development of POCD. Quickly and thoroughly investigate any changes in mental status as the causes may be life threatening.

Postoperative delirium is more common in the older patient, but it can occur in patients of any age. Delirium may be the result of severe pain, fluid and electrolyte imbalances, hypoxemia, drug effects, sleep deprivation, and sensory deprivation or overload. Signs include cognitive dysfunction, varying levels of consciousness, altered psychomotor activity, and a disturbed sleep/wake cycle. See Chapter 59 for more about delirium.

Anxiety and depression may occur and correlate with an increased likelihood for complications.[9] These responses may be part of grieving for lost body parts or altered body function or for loss of independence during recovery and rehabilitation.

Alcohol withdrawal delirium results from the patient undergoing alcohol withdrawal. It is characterized by restlessness, insomnia, nightmares, irritability, and auditory or visual hallucinations. Chapter 10 discusses the identification and management of alcohol withdrawal delirium.

❖ NURSING MANAGEMENT: NEUROLOGIC AND PSYCHOLOGIC PROBLEMS

◆ Nursing Assessment

Assess the patient's level of consciousness, orientation, memory, and ability to follow commands. Determine the size, reactivity, and equality of the pupils. Assess the patient's sleep/wake cycle and sensory and motor status. Determine the possible cause if the patient has an altered neurologic status. If the patient was mentally alert before surgery and becomes cognitively impaired after surgery, you need to do further assessment to rule out hypoxia, delirium, or POCD.

◆ Nursing Diagnoses

Nursing diagnoses related to neurologic and psychologic problems include:

- Confusion
- Disturbed body image
- Sleep deprivation

◆ Nursing Implementation

◆ **PACU.** The most common cause of agitation in the PACU is hypoxemia. So, you need to focus attention on evaluating respiratory function. Once you have ruled out hypoxemia or other known causes of postoperative delirium, sedation may be beneficial in controlling agitation. Because the most common cause of delayed emergence is prolonged drug action, delays in awakening usually spontaneously resolve with time. If necessary, antagonists can reverse the effects of benzodiazepines and opioids.

Interventions to prevent perioperative delirium, other than reducing the depth of anesthesia, have not significantly reduced the incidence of emergence delirium [10] Until the patient is awake and able to communicate effectively, you are responsible for patient safety. This includes monitoring physiologic status, having the side rails up and the call bell available, securing equipment (e.g., IV lines, artificial airways), using 2 patient identifiers before giving drugs or completing treatments, and verifying allergies.

◆ **Clinical Unit.** To prevent or manage postoperative delirium or POCD, address any potential contributing factors. Maintain normal physiologic function by achieving fluid and electrolyte balance, adequate nutrition and sleep, pain management, proper bowel and bladder function, and early mobilization. To help orient the patient, use specific aids, such as clocks, calendars, and photos.

To prevent or limit psychologic problems, provide adequate support for the patient. This includes listening to and talking with the patient, offering explanations and reassurance, and encouraging the presence and aid of the patient's caregiver(s). Evaluate the patient's behavior to distinguish a normal reaction to a stressful situation from one that is becoming abnormal or excessive. Recognizing alcohol withdrawal delirium can be a challenge. Record and report any unusual or disturbed behavior so that a diagnosis can be made and treatment started.

PAIN AND DISCOMFORT

Etiology

Despite the availability of pain-relieving drugs and techniques, pain is a common problem and a significant fear for patients. Pain is caused by the interaction of several physiologic and psychologic factors. The incision and retraction during surgery traumatize the skin and underlying tissues. In addition, there may be reflex muscle spasms around the incision. Anxiety and fear, sometimes related to the anticipation of pain, create tension and further increase muscle tone and spasm. Positioning during surgery and the use of internal devices such as an endotracheal tube or catheters may also cause discomfort. The effort and movement associated with deep breathing, coughing, and ambulating may worsen pain by creating tension on the incision area. Other sources of discomfort include nausea and vomiting, environmental noises, noxious odors, and shivering.

The patient does not feel pain when the internal viscera are cut. Pain, does, however, come from pressure in the internal viscera. This means deep visceral pain may signal a complication such as intestinal distention, bleeding, or abscess formation. Pain increases the risk for atelectasis and impaired respiratory function.

❖ NURSING MANAGEMENT: PAIN

◆ Nursing Assessment

Assess the patient on arrival to the PACU and at frequent intervals. The patient's self-report is the single most reliable indicator of pain. Use a pain scale, such as a numeric or FACES pain scale, to assess the severity or intensity of pain. (Pain scales are discussed in Chapter 8.) Assess pain levels at rest and during activities. Since verbalization of pain is not always possible in the PACU, assess the patient for other indications of pain (e.g., restlessness, grimacing, changes in vital signs). You need to identify the location of the pain. Expect that patients will have incisional pain, especially with movement, and with certain procedures (e.g., removal of drains). Other causes of pain, such as a full bladder, may be present.

Always involve patients in the assessment and management of their pain. Assessing patients from different cultures or who do not speak English may be challenging. Take extra time to explore the pain experience with these patients. Adapt care as needed to meet the patient's unique needs and expectations for pain control.

◆ Nursing Implementation

Begin before surgery to develop a plan for pain control that includes behavioral modalities and control of anxiety. Evaluate any adjustments to or continuation of drugs used to treat any chronic pain during the preoperative phase. During this time, teach patients to report pain and how it will be managed after surgery. Share pain management plans during the hand-off report.

The acute pain of surgery almost always requires the use of analgesics. Organizational approaches can reduce pain intensity with fewer side effects associated with the analgesic use. These approaches include using procedure-specific pain management guidelines with titration of analgesia based on specific patient needs.[11]

Pain control techniques include the use of single modalities (e.g., opioid drugs, PCA, regional analgesic [local anesthetic infiltration]), or multimodal analgesia. *Multimodal analgesia,* or the use of 2 or more analgesics with different mechanisms of action (e.g., an opioid and a nonsteroidal antiinflammatory drug [NSAID]), is recommended. Multimodal analgesia reduces pain, opioid use, and opioid-related adverse effects. It also enhances recovery and increases patient satisfaction.[12] These drugs may be given via the same or different routes. The choice of modalities should be procedure and patient specific.

The HCP often writes orders for pain medication and other comfort measures on an as-needed (PRN) basis. Time giving analgesics to ensure that they are in effect during activities that may be painful, such as walking. Although opioid analgesics are often essential for the patient's comfort, there are undesirable side effects. The most common include constipation, nausea and vomiting, respiratory and cough depression, and hypotension.

Before giving any analgesic, first assess the patient's pain, including location, quality, and intensity; vital signs; and level of consciousness. Treat incisional pain as ordered. If the patient reports chest or leg pain, analgesics may mask a complication (e.g., VTE). If it is gas pain, opioids can worsen it. If the analgesic either does not relieve the pain or makes the patient lethargic or somnolent, notify the HCP and request a change in the order.

Patient-controlled analgesia (PCA) allows the self-administration of predetermined doses of analgesia by the patient. The goals of PCA are to provide immediate analgesia and maintain an acceptable level of pain control. Continuous infusions allow for a steady blood level of analgesia with additional patient doses used prior to painful events (e.g., walking, deep breathing, and coughing) or for breakthrough pain. Opioid-tolerant patients may need patient-administered boluses. The route of delivery may be IV, oral, epidural, or transdermal. The transdermal route is for short-term pain management and may offer advantages over the IV route (e.g., needleless, low infection risk, decreased drug errors associated with pump malfunction or inaccurate programming). Some advantages of PCA are early ambulation, better pain management than with as-needed analgesia, and greater patient satisfaction. (PCA is discussed in Chapter 8.)

⚠ SAFETY ALERT Patient-Controlled Analgesia (PCA)
- Carefully check the HCP's order and properly program the pump for IV or epidural PCA to deliver the ordered dose of analgesic (e.g., continuous rate, bolus dose, maximum dose).
- A patient's death or serious injury associated with a drug error (e.g., wrong drug, wrong dose, wrong patient, wrong rate) is a serious reportable event (never event).

Epidural analgesia is the infusion of opioid analgesics through a catheter placed into the epidural space surrounding the spinal cord. The goal of epidural analgesia is delivery of the drug directly to opiate receptors in the spinal cord. Administration methods include intermittent bolus dosing, continuous infusion, and epidural PCA. This technique results in a constant circulating level and a reduced total dose of medication. The use of epidural analgesia for managing pain after surgery is increasing.

Perineural local anesthesia, the infiltration of a nonopioid drug into the surgical site, is another way to manage postoperative pain. A disposable or mechanical infusion pump delivers the local anesthetic via a catheter directly to the surgical incision site. A single dose of bupivacaine liposome injectable suspension (Exparel) provides pain relief with reduced opioid needs for up to 72 hours.

Complementary and alternative therapies such as music therapy, guided imagery, relaxation exercises, and aromatherapy are effective adjuncts in pain management. Nondrug approaches such as repositioning, massage, and distraction can enhance pain management.

❓ CHECK YOUR PRACTICE

Although PCA is infusing as ordered, your postoperative patient reports ongoing pain that is rated 8 on a 0 to 10 scale.
- What steps would you take next to manage this patient's pain more effectively?

TEMPERATURE CHANGES

Etiology

Knowing the patient's temperature in the postoperative period is valuable (Table 19.6). We are giving increased attention to the importance of maintaining a normal body temperature.

Perioperative temperature management is a quality measure by the Surgical Care Improvement Project (SCIP), a national partnership of organizations whose goal is to reduce surgical site infections (SSIs).[13]

Hypothermia. Perioperative *hypothermia* is a core body temperature less than 96.8°F (36°C). Hypothermia occurs when heat loss exceeds heat production. Heat loss may occur due to skin exposure, use of cold irrigants, skin preparations, and unwarmed inhaled gases. Although all patients are at risk for postoperative hypothermia, patients with low preoperative core body temperatures, those with systolic BP less than 140 mm Hg, older patients, female patients, and patients who receive epidural or spinal anesthesia are at a higher risk.[1] Long surgical procedures, open cavity procedures (e.g., abdominal or thoracic) and prolonged anesthetic administration lead to redistribution of body heat from the core to the periphery. This places the patient at an increased risk for hypothermia and complications.[14]

Complications associated with hypothermia can include vasoconstriction with resulting hypertension, compromised immune function, bleeding, untoward cardiac events, SSIs, altered drug metabolism, increased pain, and shivering. Shivering can increase resting energy expenditure and O_2 consumption up to 500%, which can lead to hypoxemia and myocardial ischemia (angina). Shivering can also increase carbon dioxide production; increase heart rate, BP, and intracranial pressure; and significantly affect the patient's comfort level.[1]

Fever. Fever may occur at any time after surgery (Table 19.6). SSI, particularly from aerobic organisms, is often accompanied by a fever that spikes in the afternoon or evening and returns to near-normal levels in the morning. The respiratory tract may be infected from stasis of secretions in areas of atelectasis. Urinary tract infections (UTIs) may occur from catheterization. Superficial thrombophlebitis may occur at the IV site. VTE in the leg veins may raise temperature.

Surgical patients who receive antibiotic therapy are at risk for *Clostridium difficile* infections. Manifestations of *C. difficile* may include fever, diarrhea, and abdominal pain.

Intermittent high fever accompanied by shaking chills and diaphoresis suggests septicemia. This may occur at any time after surgery. It can result from microorganisms being introduced into the bloodstream during surgery, especially in GI or genitourinary (GU) procedures. Septicemia may occur later from a wound or UTI.

Malignant hyperthermia (MH) is a muscle metabolism disorder that is triggered by general anesthetic agents. Although often a late sign, it is characterized by a rapid rise in core body temperature and severe muscle rigidity. Other signs of MH include tachycardia, hypercarbia, metabolic and respiratory acidosis, myoglobinuria, and elevated creatine kinase levels. MH is a life-threatening complication. While most cases of MH occur during general anesthesia, the 1-hour period right after surgery (e.g., in the PACU) is a critical time.[1]

TABLE 19.6 Postoperative Temperature Changes

Time After Surgery	Temperature	Possible Causes
Up to 12 hr	Hypothermia: ≤96.8°F (36°C)	Effects of anesthesia, body heat loss during surgical procedure
First 48 hr (postoperative days 1 and 2)	Mild elevation: ≤100.4°F (38°C)	Inflammatory response to surgical stress
	Moderate elevation: >100.4°F (38°C)	Lung congestion, dehydration
After first 48 hr (postoperative day 3 and later)	Elevation >100°F (37.8°C)	Infection (e.g., wound, urinary, respiratory)

❖ NURSING MANAGEMENT: TEMPERATURE CHANGES

◆ Nursing Assessment

Take the patient's temperature on arrival to the PACU and every hour if the patient stays normothermic. If the patient is hypothermic, take the temperature every 15 minutes until normothermia is reached. Use the same route of measuring temperature during the patient's stay in the PACU.

Assess the color and temperature of the skin. Communicate risk factors for hypothermia or MH to all members of the perioperative team. Observe the patient for early signs of inflammation and infection that may precede a fever so that any complications can be treated promptly.

◆ Nursing Diagnoses

Nursing diagnoses related to altered temperature include:
- Hypothermia
- Hyperthermia

◆ Nursing Implementation

Passive warming measures include the use of warmed cotton blankets, socks, and reflective blankets and limiting skin exposure. *Active warming measures* involve the application of external warming devices, including forced air warmers; heated water mattresses; radiant warmers; heated, humidified O_2; and warmed IV fluids. When using any external warming device, record body temperature and the patient's comfort level at 15-minute intervals. In addition, take care to prevent skin injuries.

Apply O_2 therapy via nasal cannula or mask to treat the increased demand for O_2 caused by shivering. Shivering can be treated with opioids (e.g., meperidine). Keep the supplies readily available to manage MH. Treatment for MH includes the administration of dantrolene (Dantrium), measures to cool the patient (e.g., ice packs), and correcting acid-base imbalances.

Use meticulous asepsis with wound and IV site care. Encourage airway clearance with deep breathing, coughing, and use of the incentive spirometer. If fever develops, chest x-rays may be taken, and antipyretic drugs given. Depending on the suspected cause of the fever, obtain cultures of the wound, sputum, urine, or blood. If a bacterial infection is the source of the fever, start antibiotics as soon as you obtain cultures. If the fever rises above 103° F (39.4° C), you may use body-cooling measures.

GASTROINTESTINAL PROBLEMS

Etiology

Postoperative nausea and vomiting (PONV) are the most common complications affecting as many as 80% of high-risk patients. Risk factors include younger age (under 50 years of age), gender (female), history of motion sickness or previous PONV, nonsmoking status, action of anesthetics or opioids, and duration and type of surgery.[2] Delayed gastric emptying and slowed peristalsis that result from handling of the bowel during abdominal surgery contribute to PONV, as does starting oral intake too soon after surgery.

Constipation may occur after surgery. It can be due to anesthetics used during surgery that may paralyze the intestine; immobility; changes in diet and fluid intake; and the use of opioids for pain relief. Opioids contribute to constipation by decreasing peristalsis and slowing fecal transport through the intestinal tract. They may also decrease a patient's urge to defecate.

Postoperative ileus (POI) is the temporary impairment of gastric and bowel motility after surgery. It results from the handling or reconstruction of the intestine during surgery and limited dietary intake before and after surgery. POI is normal after abdominal surgery and may occur after nonabdominal surgery. After abdominal surgery, motility in the large intestine may be reduced for 2 to 7 days. Motility in the small intestine resumes within several hours after surgery.

Risk factors for POI include the use of opioids, immobility, older age, prior abdominal surgery, and early postoperative feeding. Use of opioid analgesia may prolong the duration of POI. Abdominal cramps, increasing abdominal distention, constipation, nausea, vomiting, and dehydration often accompany POI.[15]

Hiccups (singultus) are intermittent spasms of the diaphragm caused by irritation of the phrenic nerve, which innervates the diaphragm. The phrenic nerve may be irritated after surgery by gastric distention, intestinal obstruction, intraabdominal bleeding, or a subphrenic abscess. Indirect irritation of the phrenic nerve may occur with acid-base and electrolyte imbalances. Reflex irritation may come from drinking hot or cold liquids or from the presence of a nasogastric (NG) tube. Hiccups usually last a short time and stop spontaneously.

❖ NURSING MANAGEMENT: GASTROINTESTINAL PROBLEMS

◆ Nursing Assessment

Ask the patient about feelings of nausea. If nausea is present, assess the severity using a verbal descriptor or numeric scale. If vomiting occurs, determine the quantity, characteristics, and color of the vomitus. Assess the abdomen for distention and presence of bowel sounds. Because bowel sounds are often absent or diminished right after surgery, auscultate all 4 quadrants to determine the presence, frequency, and characteristics of the sounds. The return of normal bowel motility is usually accompanied by passing gas or stool and the ability to tolerate oral intake without nausea or vomiting.

◆ Nursing Diagnoses

Nursing diagnoses and collaborative problems related to GI problems include:
- Nausea and vomiting
- Electrolyte imbalance
- Fluid imbalance
- Potential complications: POI, hiccups

◆ Nursing Implementation

When the patient is NPO, give IV fluids to maintain fluid and electrolyte balance. Begin oral fluids as ordered and tolerated. Depending on the type of the surgery, the patient may begin oral intake as soon as the gag reflex returns. When starting oral intake, offer clear liquids first and continue the IV fluids, usually at a reduced rate. If the patient tolerates oral intake, the IV fluids are stopped.

Be alert to prevent aspiration if the patient vomits while still sleepy from anesthesia. Position the patient in the lateral recovery position and have suction equipment available. Interventions for PONV include monitoring fluid status and giving antiemetic drugs (see Table 41.1). Consider prophylactic antiemetic drugs for patients at high risk for PONV.[16] Complementary and alternative therapy interventions for PONV (e.g., imagery, music, aromatherapy, acupressure) may help.

Constipation may be prevented using bowel protocols that include the use of a stool softener and laxative. Assess the patient regularly to detect the return of peristalsis. Encourage the patient to expel gas. Gas pains tend to become pronounced on the second or third postoperative day. Ambulation and frequent repositioning may provide relief. Positioning the patient on the right side permits gas to rise along the transverse colon and aids its release. Bisacodyl (Dulcolax) suppositories may be given to stimulate colonic peristalsis and expulsion of gas and stool. Resuming a normal diet after bowel sounds have returned also aids the return of normal peristalsis.

The goal of treatment for POI is the relief of associated symptoms and return of normal GI function. Management includes bowel rest or the withholding of solid foods with a gradual reintroduction of food starting with clear liquids. Advance the diet to solid food with an ongoing assessment of tolerance to oral intake.

An NG tube may be needed to decompress the stomach to prevent nausea, vomiting, and abdominal distention. Oral care is critical for comfort and stimulation of salivary glands when the patient is NPO or has an NG tube.

URINARY PROBLEMS

Etiology

Low urine output (800 to 1500 mL) in the first 24 hours after surgery may be expected regardless of fluid intake. Causes include increased aldosterone and ADH secretion resulting from the stress of surgery; fluid restriction before surgery; and fluid loss through surgery, drainage, and diaphoresis. By the second or third day, after fluid has been mobilized and the immediate stress reaction subsides, the patient will begin to have increasing urine output.

Acute urinary retention can occur for a variety of reasons. Anesthesia depresses the nervous system, including the micturition reflex arc and the higher centers that influence it. This allows the bladder to fill more completely than normal before the patient feels the urge to void. Anesthesia also impedes voluntary micturition. Anticholinergic and opioid drugs interfere with the ability to start voiding or to empty the bladder completely.

Urinary retention is more likely to occur after lower abdominal or pelvic surgery because spasms or guarding of the abdominal and pelvic muscles interferes with their normal function in micturition. Pain may alter perception and interfere with the patient's awareness of bladder filling. Immobility and bed rest impair voiding ability. The supine position reduces the ability to relax the perineal muscles and external sphincter.

Oliguria (diminished output of urine) can be a sign of renal failure and is a less common, although more serious, problem after surgery. It may result from renal ischemia caused by inadequate renal perfusion.

❖ NURSING MANAGEMENT: URINARY PROBLEMS

◆ Nursing Assessment

Examine the urine for both quantity and quality. Note the color, amount, and odor of the urine. Assess indwelling catheters for patency. Urine output should be at least 0.5 mL/kg/hr. To decrease the risk for catheter-associated urinary tract infection (CAUTI), remove the catheter as soon as possible or within 24 hours, unless there is a reason to continue its use. Most patients void within 6 to 8 hours after surgery. If no voiding occurs, scan or percuss the suprapubic area for signs of bladder fullness or distention.

◆ Nursing Diagnoses

Nursing diagnoses and collaborative problems related to urinary problems include:
• Urinary retention
• Potential complication: CAUTI, acute kidney injury

◆ Nursing Implementation

Reassure the patient about the ability to void. You can promote voiding by helping the patient into a normal position. Other helpful techniques include providing privacy, running water, offering water for the patient to drink, or pouring warm water over the perineum. Walking, preferably to the bathroom, and the use of a bedside commode are other measures to help with voiding.

The HCP often leaves an order to catheterize the patient in 6 to 8 hours if voiding has not occurred. Because of the risk for CAUTI, first confirm that the bladder is full. Consider fluid intake during and after surgery and determine bladder fullness (e.g., discomfort with bladder palpation). Scan the bladder with a portable ultrasound to assess volume of urine in the bladder and avoid unnecessary catheterization. If catheterization is needed, a straight catheterization, as compared to an indwelling catheter, is preferred to limit the risk for CAUTI.

INTEGUMENTARY PROBLEMS

Etiology

Surgery generally involves an incision through the skin and underlying tissues, disrupting the protective skin barrier. Wound healing is a major concern after surgery. One of the greatest risks during the perioperative period is SSI. SSIs account for 14% to 16% of hospital-acquired infections and are associated with prolonged hospitalizations, increased costs, and poor patient outcomes.[17] Many are preventable with using evidence-based strategies (e.g., hand hygiene; selection, timing, and duration of prophylactic antibiotics; surgical site skin preparation; maintaining perioperative normothermia).[18] Adhering to these strategies can reduce the incidence of SSIs, a major goal of the SCIP initiative.[14]

SSIs may result from wound contamination from 3 major sources: (1) exogenous flora present in the environment and on the skin, (2) oral flora, and (3) intestinal flora. The incidence of SSI is higher in patients who are malnourished, immunosuppressed, or older, or who have had a long hospital stay or a lengthy surgical procedure (more than 3 hours). Patients post bowel surgery, particularly after a traumatic injury, are at high risk. SSI may involve the entire incision and may extend downward through deeper tissues. An abscess may form locally, or it may spread throughout entire body cavities, as in peritonitis.

Evidence of SSI usually does not become clear before the third to fifth postoperative day. Local manifestations include redness, swelling, and increasing pain and tenderness at the site. Systemic manifestations are fever and leukocytosis.

An accumulation of fluid in a wound may create pressure, impair circulation and wound healing, and predispose the patient to infection. To allow for drainage, the HCP may place a drain in the incision or make a stab wound next to the incision. Drains may be of soft rubber and drain into a dressing, or firm catheters attached to a Hemovac or other source of gentle suction.

Adequate nutrition is essential for wound healing. The patient who is well nourished before surgery can tolerate the lack of nutritional intake for several days. However, the patient with preexisting nutritional deficits that occur with chronic diseases (e.g., diabetes, ulcerative colitis, alcoholism) is more prone to problems of wound healing. The patient who cannot meet nutritional needs may need enteral or parenteral nutrition to promote healing.

❖ NURSING MANAGEMENT: SURGICAL WOUNDS

◆ Nursing Assessment

Assessment of the wound and dressing requires knowledge of the type of wound, the drains inserted, and expected drainage related to the specific type of surgery. Immediately after surgery, check the wound every 15 to 30 minutes or as ordered. When drainage appears on the dressing, record the type, amount, color, and odor of drainage. Assess the effect of position changes on drainage. A small amount of serous drainage is common from any type of wound. If a drain is in place, assess the amount of drainage and compare to what is expected. Expected drainage from tubes is outlined in Table 19.7. An abdominal incision with an accompanying drain will likely have a moderate amount of serosanguineous drainage in the first 24 hours. In contrast, an inguinal herniorrhaphy should have only minimal serous drainage.

In general, expect the drainage to change from sanguineous (red) to serosanguineous (pink) to serous (clear yellow). Purulent drainage may occur with an SSI. The drainage should decrease over hours or days, depending on the type of surgery. *Wound dehiscence* (separation and disruption of previously joined wound edges) may be preceded by a sudden discharge of brown, pink, or clear drainage. (Wound dehiscence is discussed in Chapter 11.) Notify the HCP of any excess or abnormal drainage or significant changes in vital signs.

◆ Nursing Diagnoses

Nursing diagnoses related to surgical wounds include:
- Surgical wound
- Risk for infection

◆ Nursing Implementation

The incision may be covered with a dressing right after surgery. Many HCPs prefer to change the first postoperative dressing. If the initial operative dressing is saturated, follow agency policy as to whether you should change or simply reinforce the dressing. Skin graft dressings may stay in place for 3 to 5 days to avoid disturbing the graft site and promote graft acceptance. Specially trained nurses may change these dressings. (Skin grafts are discussed in Chapter 23.)

TABLE 19.7 Output From Tubes, Drains, and Catheters

Substance	Daily Amount	Color	Odor	Consistency
Indwelling Catheter				
Urine	800–1500 mL for first 24 hr Minimum expected output: 0.5 mL/kg/hr	Clear, yellow	Ammonia	Watery
Nasogastric Tube or Gastrostomy Tube				
Gastric contents	<1500 mL/day	Pale, yellow-green Bloody after GI surgery	Sour	Watery
Open Drains (e.g., Penrose)				
Wound drainage	Varies with procedure May decrease over hours or days	Varies with procedure Initially may be sanguineous or serosanguineous, changing to serous	Same as wound dressing Foul odor may indicate infection	Thin, watery
Closed Suction Drains (e.g., Hemovac, Jackson-Pratt)				
Wound drainage	Varies with procedure May decrease over hours or days	Varies with procedure Initially may be sanguineous or serosanguineous, changing to serous	Little to no odor Foul odor may indicate infection	Thin, watery
T-Tube				
Bile	500 mL	Bright yellow to dark green	Acid	Thick
Mediastinal Chest Tube				
Wound drainage post cardiothoracic surgery	Varies with procedure Should decrease over several hours after surgery	Sanguineous or serosanguineous	N/A	Thin
Pleural Chest Tube				
Fluid that has collected in the pleural space	Varies with procedure Decreases over hours or days>100 mL/hr is considered excessive	Varies with indication for insertion and fluid collected in the pleural spaces	N/A	Varies with indication for insertion

When you change a dressing, note the number and type of drains present and avoid dislodging the drains. Inspect the incision site carefully. The area around the sutures may be slightly reddened and swollen, which is an expected inflammatory response. However, the skin around the incision should be of normal color and temperature. If the wound is healing by primary intention, has little or no drainage, or has no drains in place, a single-layer dressing or no dressing is sufficient. Use a multilayer dressing when drains are in place, moderate to heavy drainage is occurring, or healing occurs other than by primary intention. (Wound healing and care are discussed in Chapter 11.)

DISCHARGE FROM THE PACU

The choice of discharge site is based on patient acuity, access to follow-up care, and the potential for complications. The decision to discharge the patient from the PACU is based on written discharge criteria approved by the agency's anesthesiology and medical staff[1] (Table 19.8). Standardized scoring systems (e.g., *Modified Aldrete Scoring System*) are often used to determine the patient's general condition and readiness for discharge from the PACU.

Discharge to Clinical Unit

Before discharging the patient from the PACU to the clinical unit, give a hand-off report about the patient to the receiving nurse. The report summarizes the operative and postanesthesia period. It should include information as to where the patient's caregivers are waiting. Nurse-to-nurse communication must be accurate and allow for questions. The use of a standardized communication tool, such as SBAR *(Situation-Background-Assessment-Recommendation),* provides a complete report and enhances a safe transfer of the patient from PACU to the clinical unit (Table 19.9).

When you receive the patient on the clinical unit, assist the PACU transport staff to safely move the patient from the stretcher to the bed. Take care to protect IV lines, drains, and traction devices. Obtain vital signs and compare the patient status with the report provided by the PACU nurse. After this, perform a more focused assessment and initiate postoperative orders and nursing care (Table 19.10).

TABLE 19.8 Surgery Discharge Criteria

PACU Discharge Criteria (Phase I)
- Patient awake, easily arousable (or baseline)
- Vital signs at baseline or stable
- No excess bleeding or drainage
- No respiratory depression
- O_2 saturation >90%
- Pain controlled or acceptable
- Nausea and vomiting controlled
- Report given

Ambulatory Surgery Discharge Criteria (Phase II or Extended Observation)
- All PACU discharge criteria (Phase I) met
- No IV opioid drugs for last 30 minutes
- Voided if appropriate to surgical procedure or orders
- Able to ambulate if not contraindicated
- Responsible adult present to accompany and drive patient home
- Written discharge instructions given and patient and caregiver understanding confirmed

---

TABLE 19.9 Postoperative SBAR Hand-Off Communication

Situation
Patient _____ Date of birth _____
Transferring to Room # _____ Surgeon _____
ACP _____ Type of Anesthesia _____
Procedure _____
Surgical site(s) _____
Past medical history _____
Code status _____ Isolation precautions _____

Background
Allergies _____
Medications received in PACU _____
IV site/fluids _____
Dressings and/or drains _____
Significant OR events _____

Assessment
PACU vital signs T _____ P _____ RR _____ BP _____ O_2 Sat _____
O_2 source _____ FIO_2 _____
Pain rating at discharge _____
Method of pain management _____
Last dose of pain medication _____
Mental status _____
Nausea/vomiting at discharge _____
Intake _____ Output _____
Laboratory tests _____
Recovery comments _____

Recommendations
Equipment needed _____
Orders to be completed _____
Family _____
Other notes _____
Transferring RN _____ Phone # for questions _____
Receiving RN _____

TABLE 19.10 Nursing Assessment

Care of Patient on Admission to Clinical Unit
1. Record time of patient's return to unit and assess airway, breathing, and circulation.
2. Obtain baseline vital signs, including O_2 saturation.
3. Assess neurologic status, including level of consciousness and movement of extremities.
4. Assess level of pain:
   - Last dose and type of pain control
   - Current pain rating
5. Assess wound, dressing, and drainage tubes:
   - Type and amount of drainage
   - Tubing connected to gravity or suction drainage (per orders)
6. Assess color, temperature, and appearance of skin.
7. Position for airway maintenance, comfort, and safety (bed in low position, side rails up).
8. Check IV infusion:
   - Type of solution
   - Amount of fluid remaining
   - Patency and flow rate
   - Condition of insertion site and size of catheter
9. Assess urinary status:
   - Time of voiding
   - Presence of catheter, patency, and total output
   - Bladder distention or urge to void
10. Assess for any nausea or vomiting.
    - Availability of emesis basin and tissues
11. Position call bell within reach, and orient patient to use of call bell.
12. Determine emotional state and provide support as needed.
13. Check for presence of caregiver.
    - Patient and caregiver oriented to immediate environment
14. Check and carry out postoperative orders.

AMBULATORY SURGERY

Phase II and Extended Observation

Advances in minimally invasive and noninvasive procedures, anesthesia, and analgesia have resulted in an increase in ambulatory surgical procedures. Ambulatory surgery patients include those patients receiving Phase II and extended observation postoperative care (Table 19.1). PONV and pain are common problems after ambulatory surgery. These can lead to delirium, prolonged PACU stay, delayed discharge, readmission, delayed resumption of usual activities, and decreased patient satisfaction.

Ambulatory Surgery Discharge

The patient leaving an ambulatory surgery setting must be hemodynamically stable, mobile, alert, and able to provide a degree of self-care when discharged to home (Table 19.8). PONV and pain must be under control. Overall, the patient must be stable and near the level of preoperative functioning for discharge from the unit. The patient may not drive and must be accompanied by an adult at the time of discharge. Carefully assess the patient's readiness for discharge and home care needs. Determine availability of caregivers (e.g., family, friends) and access to (1) a pharmacy for prescriptions, (2) a phone in the case of an emergency, and (3) follow-up care.

INFORMATICS IN PRACTICE

Discharge Teaching

- When discharging a patient who needs a complex dressing change and the written instructions are not adequate, consider using a video. This may be available on the hospital's television system or the Internet (e.g., YouTube).
- If using a video from the Internet, check to ensure that the procedure is properly performed.
- The patient and caregiver can view the video or pictures at home as a reference when performing the procedure.
- Have the patient and/or caregiver provide teach back information and/or demonstration.

Planning for Discharge and Follow-up Care

Preparation for the patient's discharge is an ongoing process that begins before surgery. Include the patient and caregiver in discharge planning and provide them with the information and support to make informed decisions about ongoing care. The informed patient is prepared as events unfold and gradually assumes more responsibility for self-care during the postoperative period.

As discharge approaches, be sure that the patient and caregiver(s) have the following information:

- Symptoms to report (e.g., fever, increased incisional drainage, unrelieved incisional pain, discomfort in other parts of the body)
- When and how to take prescribed drugs and possible side effects
- Care of incision and any dressings, including bathing recommendations
- Activities allowed and prohibited, when various activities can be resumed safely (e.g., driving, return to work, sexual intercourse, leisure activities)
- Dietary restrictions or modifications

- Where and when to return for follow-up appointment
- Answers to any questions or concerns

Common reasons patients seek help after discharge include unrelieved pain, need for advice about drugs, and wound issues (e.g., drainage). Attention to complete discharge instructions may prevent needless distress for the patient and caregiver. Standardized, preprinted discharge instructions that are surgery specific and easy to read ensure that information is complete.

Record the discharge teaching in the chart. For the patient, the postoperative phase of care continues and extends into the recuperative period. Assessment and evaluation of the patient after discharge may be done with a follow-up call or by a visit from a home health nurse, who can address any specific questions and concerns.

Increasingly, patients are discharged from the hospital with many care needs. They may be transferred to transitional care facilities, to long-term care facilities, or directly to their homes. When discharged directly to home, the patient is expected to continue self-care, with help from caregivers or home health care personnel (e.g., nurses, physical therapists). The care may include dressing changes, wound care, catheter or drain care, home antibiotics, or continued physical therapy. Working together with the discharge planner or case manager, ensure the patient's safe transition from hospital-based care to community- or home-based care.

Gerontologic Considerations: Postoperative Patient

The older surgical patient deserves special consideration. The older adult has decreased respiratory function, including decreased ability to cough and decreased thoracic compliance. These changes lead to an increase in the work of breathing and a decreased ability to eliminate drugs. Carefully monitor reactions to anesthetic drugs. Pneumonia is a common complication in older adults.

Altered vascular function in the older adult is due to atherosclerosis and decreased elasticity in the blood vessels. Cardiac function is often compromised with limited compensatory responses to changes in BP and volume. Circulating blood volume decreases. Hypertension is common. Cardiovascular status needs to be monitored closely throughout surgery and the postoperative period.

Drug toxicity is a potential problem in the older adult. Renal perfusion normally decreases, along with a reduced ability to remove drugs that the kidneys excrete. Decreased liver function leads to reduced drug metabolism and increased drug activity. Carefully assess renal and liver function to prevent drug overdose and toxicity.

Observing for changes in mental status is an important part of postoperative care in older adults. Factors such as age, history of alcohol abuse, poor baseline cognition, hypoxia, metabolic imbalances, hypotension, and polypharmacy can contribute to postoperative delirium. Anesthetics, especially anticholinergic and benzodiazepine drugs, increase the risk for delirium.

Pain control in the older patient is challenging because of possible preexisting cognitive deficits, impaired communication, and physiologic changes that affect drug metabolism. Patients may hesitate to ask for pain medication because they believe pain is inevitable with surgery. Some older patients may fear addiction or be nervous about using PCA machines. Thoroughly assess pain in a surgical patient who does not report any pain. Encourage the use of analgesics. Explain to the patient and caregiver that untreated pain has a negative effect on recovery.

CASE STUDY
Postoperative Patient

(© BananaStock/
BananaStock/
Thinkstock.)

Patient Profile

E.G., a 74-yr-old retired college professor, has just undergone surgery for a fractured hip. He fell off a ladder while painting his house. E.G.'s medical history includes type 2 diabetes and COPD. The surgery, done while he was under general anesthesia, lasted 3 hours.

Subjective Data

- Active walker in his home community
- Smokes 1 pack of cigarettes per day × 58 years
- Always had problems sleeping
- Difficulty hearing, wears hearing aid
- Upset with injury and its impact on life
- Is a widower and has no relatives nearby or friends to assist with care
- Reports pain is 8 on a 0 to 10 scale on arrival to PACU

Objective Data

- Admitted to PACU with abduction pillow between his legs, one peripheral IV catheter, a self-suction drain from the hip dressing, an indwelling urinary catheter
- O_2 saturation 91% on 40% O_2 face mask

Interprofessional Care
Postoperative Orders

- Vital signs per PACU routine
- Capillary blood glucose level on arrival and every 4 hours. Call for blood glucose level <70 mg/dL or >250 mg/dL. Follow agency guidelines for management of hypoglycemia.
- 0.45 normal saline at 100 mL/hr
- Morphine via patient-controlled analgesia 1 mg q10min (20 mg max in 4 hr) for pain
- Advance diet as tolerated
- Incentive spirometry q1hr × 10 while awake
- O_2 therapy to keep O_2 saturation >90%

- Respiratory: albuterol 2.5 mg via nebulizer every 4 hours PRN for wheezing
- Neurovascular checks q1hr × 4 hr
- Empty and measure self-suction drain every shift
- Strict intake and output

Discussion Questions

1. What are the potential postanesthesia problems you may expect with E.G.?
2. *Priority Decision:* What priority nursing interventions would be appropriate to prevent these problems from occurring?
3. *Collaboration:* Which interventions could you delegate to unlicensed assistive personnel (UAP)?
4. What factors predispose E.G. to the following problems: atelectasis, SSI, and VTE?
5. How would you determine E.G. is sufficiently recovered from general anesthesia to be discharged to the clinical unit?
6. What potential postoperative problems on the clinical unit might you expect?
7. What are risk factors for his developing postoperative delirium? What are the signs and symptoms of delirium?
8. Why is drug toxicity a potential problem for E.G.?
9. *Priority Decision:* Based on the assessment data, identify 3 priority nursing diagnoses. Are there any collaborative problems?
10. *Evidence-Based Practice:* E.G. tells you he does not want the "catheter" out because he does not want anyone to help him to the bathroom. How would you respond to this request?
11. *Patient-Centered Care:* What teaching will you provide so that E.G. can successfully self-manage his care?
12. *Collaboration:* What referrals may be indicated based on E.G.'s medical history?
13. *Safety:* Identify 2 areas of risk for injury to E.G. What actions can you take to ensure patient safety?
14. *Quality Improvement:* What outcomes would indicate that interprofessional care with respiratory therapy was effective?

Answers available at *http://evolve.elsevier.com/Lewis/medsurg.*

BRIDGE TO NCLEX EXAMINATION

The number of the question corresponds to the same-numbered outcome at the beginning of the chapter.

1. What are the *priority* interventions the nurse performs when admitting a patient to the PACU?
   a. Assess the surgical site, noting presence and character of drainage.
   b. Assess the amount of urine output and the presence of bladder distention.
   c. Assess for airway patency and quality of respirations and obtain vital signs.
   d. Review results of intraoperative laboratory values and medications received.

2. A patient is admitted to the PACU after major abdominal surgery. During the initial assessment the patient tells the nurse he thinks he is going to "throw up." A *priority* nursing intervention is to
   a. increase the rate of the IV fluids.
   b. give antiemetic medication as ordered.
   c. obtain vital signs, including O_2 saturation.
   d. position patient in lateral recovery position.

3. After admitting a postoperative patient to the clinical unit, which assessment data require the *most* immediate attention?
   a. O_2 saturation of 85%
   b. Respiratory rate of 13/min
   c. Temperature of 100.4° F (38° C)
   d. Blood pressure of 90/60 mm Hg

4. A 70-kg postoperative patient has an average urine output of 25 mL/hr during the first 8 hours. The *priority* nursing intervention(s) given this assessment would be to
   a. notify the surgeon and expect obtaining blood work to evaluate renal function.
   b. perform a straight catheterization to measure the amount of urine in the bladder.
   c. continue to monitor the patient because this is a normal finding during this time period.
   d. evaluate the patient's fluid volume status since surgery and obtain a bladder ultrasound.

5. Discharge criteria for the Phase II patient include (*select all that apply*)
   a. no nausea or vomiting.
   b. ability to drive self home.
   c. no respiratory depression.
   d. written discharge instructions understood.
   e. opioid pain medication given 45 minutes ago.

1. c, 2. d, 3. a, 4. d, 5. c, d, e

For rationales to these answers and even more NCLEX review questions, visit *http://evolve.elsevier.com/Lewis/medsurg.*

REFERENCES

1. Schick L, Windle P: *Perianesthesia nursing core curriculum: Preprocedure, phase i and phase II PACU nursing,* ed 3, St Louis, 2016, Elsevier.
2. Odom-Forren J: *Drain's perianesthesia nursing: A critical care approach,* ed 7, St Louis, 2018, Elsevier.
*3. Smallwood CD, Walsh BK: Noninvasive monitoring of oxygen and ventilation, *Respir Care* 62:6, 2017.
*4. Patino M, Kalin M, Griffin A, et al: Comparison of postoperative respiratory monitoring by acoustic and transthoracic impedance technologies in pediatric patients at risk of respiratory depression, *Anesthes Analg* 124:6, 2017.
*5. Gillies M, Sander M, Shaw A, et al: Current research priorities in perioperative intensive care medicine, *Intensive Care Med* 43:9, 2017.
*6. Auffret V, Becerra Munoz V, Loirat A, et al: Transcatheter aortic valve implantation versus surgical aortic valve replacement in lower surgical risk patients with chronic obstructive pulmonary disease, *Am J Cardiol* 120:10, 2017.
*7. Feng B, Lin J, Jin J et al: Thirty–day postoperative complications following primary total knee replacement arthroplasty: A retrospective study of incidence and risk factors at a single center in China, *Chin Med J* 130:21, 2017.
*8. Misal U, Joshi S, Shaikh M: Delayed recovery from anesthesia: A postgraduate educational review, *Anesth Essays Res* 10:2, 2016.
*9. Takagi H, Ando T, Umemoto T: Perioperative depression or anxiety and postoperative mortality in cardiac surgery: A systematic review and meta-analysis, *Heart Vessels* 32:12, 2017.
*10. Oh E, Fong, T, Hsheih T, et al: Delirium in older persons advances in diagnosis and treatment, *JAMA* 318:12, 2017.
*11. Singh K, Bohl D, Ahn J, et al: Multimodal analgesia versus intravenous patient-controlled analgesia for minimally invasive transforaminal lumbar interbody fusion procedures, *Spine* 42:15, 2017.
12. Polomano R, Fillman M, Giordano N et al: Multimodal analgesia for acute postoperative and trauma-related pain, *AJN* 117:3, 2017.
13. The Joint Commission: Specifications manual for national hospital inpatient quality measures. Retrieved from *www.jointcommission.org/specifications_manual_for_national_hospital_inpatient_quality_measures.aspx.*
*14. Ziolkowski N, Rogers A, Xiong W, et al: The impact of operative time and hypothermia in acute burn surgery, *Burns* 43:1673, 2017.
*15. Venara A, Neunlist M, Slim K et al: Postoperative ileus: Pathophysiology, incidence, and prevention, *J Visc Surg* 153:6, 2016.
*16. Cao X, White, P, Ma, H: An update on the management of postoperative nausea and vomiting, *J Anesthes* 31:617, 2017.
17. Rothrock J: *Alexander's care of the patient in surgery,* ed 15, 2015, St Louis.
18. Berrios-Torres S, Umscheid C, Bratzler D, et al: Centers for Disease Control and Prevention guidelines for the prevention of surgical site infection, *JAMA Surg* 152:784, 2017.

*Evidence-based information for clinical practice.

CASE STUDY
Managing Care of Multiple Patients

You have been called into work at 10:00 AM to cover patients for a nurse who had a family emergency. You take over care for the following 3 patients on a surgical unit. You have 1 UAP available who is assigned to help you. Two other RNs are on the unit.

Patients

(© Ryan McVay/ Photodisc/Think-stock.)

F.D., a 72-yr-old woman, was admitted to the hospital with compromised circulation of the right lower leg and a necrotic right foot as a complication of her diabetes. She is scheduled for a below-the-knee amputation of the right leg at 1:00 PM today. She has been NPO since midnight. Her morning capillary blood glucose level was 198 mg/dL. She received 4 units of regular insulin at 8 AM. She has an IV of normal saline infusing at 125 mL/hr.

(© shironosov/ iStock/Thinkstock.)

G.S., a 63-yr-old man, was admitted to the hospital for severe pain and intractable vomiting from acute cholecystitis. G.S.'s medical history includes hypertension and type 2 diabetes. He had a laparoscopic cholecystectomy yesterday afternoon. His capillary blood glucose 1 hour ago was 135 mg/dL.

(© BananaStock/ BananaStock/ Thinkstock.)

E.G., a 74-yr-old man, had surgery for a fractured hip yesterday. He is currently receiving dextrose 5% in 0.45 normal saline at 100 mL/hr, morphine via patient-controlled analgesia at 1 mg q10min (20 mg max in 4 hr) for pain, heparin 5000 units subcutaneously every 12 hours, and O_2 to keep O_2 saturation >93%. He has a self-suction drain in place at the surgical site. He has good respiratory effort when using his incentive spirometer.

Discussion Questions

1. **Priority Decision:** After receiving report, which patient should you see first? Provide a rationale for your decision.
2. **Collaboration:** Which tasks should you delegate to the UAP? *(select all that apply)*
   a. Explain discharge instructions to G.S.
   b. Obtain noon vital signs on E.G. and F.D.
   c. Measure capillary blood glucose levels on F.D. and G.S.
   d. Confirm E.G.'s understanding of how to use the PCA pump.
   e. Remind E.G. and G.S. to use their incentive spirometers every hour.
3. **Priority Decision and Collaboration:** When you enter F.D.'s room, you find her somewhat withdrawn and lethargic. Her face is cool and slightly clammy. What initial action would be most appropriate?
   a. Give 1 ampule of D_{50} IV stat.
   b. Increase F.D.'s IV rate to 150 mL/hr.
   c. Obtain a stat capillary blood glucose level.
   d. Ask the UAP to give F.D. a glass of orange juice.

Case Study Progression

F.D.'s capillary blood glucose reading was 52 mg/dL. You notify her HCP and give 1 ampule of D_{50} IV dextrose as ordered. You then change her IV infusion to D_5 ½NS. You check her capillary blood glucose within 15 minutes and then monitor her blood glucose levels each hour.

4. A preoperative checklist for F.D. is used to ensure completion of *(select all that apply)*
   a. removal of nail polish and jewelry.
   b. signed and witnessed informed consent.
   c. patient understanding of sensory information.
   d. identification of surgical site with surgical skin marker.
   e. notification of family of where to wait during the surgery.
5. F.D. tells you that she is afraid they may amputate the wrong leg. She tells you she has read stories of that happening at other hospitals. Your *best* response to F.D. would be to
   a. ask her if she would like a sedative to calm her fears.
   b. reassure her that it has never happened in this hospital.
   c. explain the "time-out" procedure for preventing such errors.
   d. offer to go to the operating room with her to ensure the correct leg is amputated.
6. **Priority Decision:** The laboratory calls to report that E.G.'s aPTT (activated partial thromboplastin time) is 84 seconds. You assess him and find that the hip dressing is saturated with serosanguinous drainage. The next dose of heparin is due at 2100 this evening; the last dose was at 0900 this morning. His blood pressure is 92/54 with a heart rate of 110 bpm. Respiratory rate is 30 breaths/min, and O_2 saturation is 98% on 2 L of O_2. The nursing *priority* for this patient would be to
   a. notify physical therapy that his session today will have to be postponed until evening.
   b. notify the previous RN that a medication error occurred with the patient's heparin dose at 0900.
   c. send an order to the laboratory for stat CBC and type and screen for 4 units of packed red blood cells.
   d. notify the provider of the aPTT result and anticipate orders for reversal agent, such as protamine.
7. **Collaboration:** Which instructions should you give to the UAP who will be helping E.G. with ADLs? *(Select all that apply.)*
   a. Use a soft toothbrush for oral care.
   b. Provide an emery board for nail care.
   c. Avoid overinflating blood pressure cuffs.
   d. Use an electric razor to shave the patient.
   e. Offer mouthwash with alcohol for rinsing.
8. **Management Decision:** When providing discharge instructions to G.S., he tells you that the UAP told him that he could do whatever activity he was comfortable doing—to let pain guide his progress. Your *initial* reaction to this statement should be to
   a. ask the UAP to clarify what was said to G.S.
   b. report the UAP's actions to the nurse manager.
   c. teach G.S. about the reason for activity restrictions.
   d. clarify the discharge instructions with the health care provider.

Answers available at *http://evolve.elsevier.com/Lewis/med-surg.*

20

Assessment and Management: Visual Problems

Jonel L. Gomez

Be the beacon of light in someone's darkness.

Randi Fine

ⓔ http://evolve.elsevier.com/Lewis/medsurg/

CONCEPTUAL FOCUS

Coping

Functional Ability

Infection

Sensory Perception

LEARNING OUTCOMES

1. Describe the structures and functions of the visual system.
2. Explain the physiologic processes involved in normal vision.
3. Obtain significant subjective and objective assessment data related to the visual system.
4. Perform a physical assessment of the visual system using the appropriate techniques.
5. Distinguish normal from common abnormal findings of a physical assessment of the visual system.
6. Link the age-related changes in the visual system to differences in assessment findings.
7. Describe the purpose, significance of results, and nursing responsibilities related to diagnostic studies of the visual system.
8. Compare and contrast the types of refractive errors and appropriate corrections.
9. Describe the common causes and assistive measures for severe visual impairment.
10. Discuss nursing measures that promote eye health.
11. Explain the pathophysiology, clinical manifestations, and interprofessional and nursing management of the patient with ocular disorders.
12. Discuss the general preoperative and postoperative care of patients undergoing surgery of the eye.

KEY TERMS

age-related macular degeneration (AMD), p. 369

astigmatism, p. 359

cataract, p. 364

conjunctivitis, p. 362

enucleation, p. 373

glaucoma, p. 369

hordeolum, p. 361

hyperopia, p. 358

keratitis, p. 362

myopia, p. 358

presbyopia, p. 358

retinal detachment, p. 367

retinopathy, p. 367

strabismus, p. 363

VISUAL SYSTEM

For people to be as independent as possible and take part in fulfilling activities, it is important that the visual system is as functional as possible. The impact of poor vision or blindness can be devastating to activities of daily living (ADLs) and independence. The psychosocial consequences can include decreased quality of life, social isolation, depression, and loss of self-esteem. Vision loss also takes a huge toll on caregivers. This makes our being involved in vision-loss prevention, detection, and treatment strategies important.

STRUCTURES AND FUNCTIONS OF VISUAL SYSTEM

The visual system is part of the central nervous system (CNS). It consists of 2 main parts, the eyes, which contain the image receptors, and the brain. The brain functions to process and interpret the information transmitted from the receptors into images. Anatomically, the visual system is made up of the orbit, the ocular adnexa (external tissues and structures surrounding the eye), the eye, and the visual pathway (optic nerve, optic chiasm, lateral geniculate nucleus, and visual cortex). The entire visual system is important for visual function.

Periocular Structures

Orbit. The orbits, or eye sockets, are the bony structures that house the eyeballs. Seven bones form the orbit: frontal, zygoma, maxilla, ethmoid, sphenoid, lacrimal, and palatine (Fig. 20.1). The average orbit is 35 mm high and 40 mm wide. In addition to the eye, the orbits contain the associated muscles, nerves, blood vessels, and fat.[1]

Within the orbit are 3 main orbital openings, or *fissures,* the optic canal, the superior orbital fissure, and the inferior orbital fissure. They are all important conduits for arteries, veins, and nerves. The optic canal is located at the top of the socket. It provides an entry point for the optic nerve (CN II). The superior orbital fissure is a small slit in the posterior orbit. It is the main entry point for several other cranial nerves to enter the orbit from the brain. These include the oculomotor nerve (CN III),

trochlear nerve (CN IV), trigeminal nerve (CN V), and abducens nerve (CN VI). The inferior orbital fissure is in the floor of the orbit. It holds the zygomatic branch of the maxillary nerve.

There are 6 extraocular muscles: (1) superior and inferior rectus muscles, (2) medial and lateral rectus muscles, and (3) superior and inferior oblique muscles. They emerge from the apex of the orbit and attach to the eye to stabilize and move it (Fig. 20.2). Neuromuscular coordination produces simultaneous movement of the eyes in the same direction.

Ocular Adnexa. The ocular adnexa include the eyebrows, eyelids, eyelashes, and lacrimal system. Eyebrows, eyelids, and eyelashes are vital in protecting the eye. They are a physical barrier to dust and foreign particles. Blinking protects the eye from injury, distributes tears over the anterior surface of the eyeball, and supplies necessary nourishment to surface cells.

The upper and lower eyelids join at the medial and lateral canthi. Eyelid skin is the thinnest skin in the human body, measuring less than 1 mm thick. The upper eyelids contain the levator palpebrae superioris muscle, innervated by the superior division of CN III. This muscle elevates and retracts the upper eyelid. The eyelids close through the action of the orbicularis muscle, which is innervated by CN VII.

Lacrimal System. The lacrimal system includes the structures needed for tear production and drainage. The main lacrimal gland and accessory lacrimal glands make tears. The lacrimal glands, in the superotemporal orbit, are exocrine glands. They make and secrete the aqueous layer of tear film and are responsible for reflex tear production. The tear film moistens the eye and supplies oxygen to the cornea. The accessory lacrimal glands, the *glands of Wolfring* and *glands of Krause,* are found within the conjunctiva of the upper eyelid. They are responsible for baseline tear production. Tears pass over the surface of the eye and then enter the nasolacrimal system. The nasolacrimal drainage system includes the puncta, canaliculi, lacrimal sac, and nasolacrimal duct (Fig. 20.3).

Eyeball. The eyeball, or globe, is composed of 3 layers (Fig 20.4). The tough outer layer is composed of the cornea, conjunctiva, and sclera. The middle layer consists of the uveal tract (iris, choroid

FIG. 20.1 Bones that form the orbit, or eye socket. (From Lampignano J, Kendrick L: *Bontrager's textbook of radiographic positioning and related anatomy,* ed 9, St Louis, 2018, Mosby.)

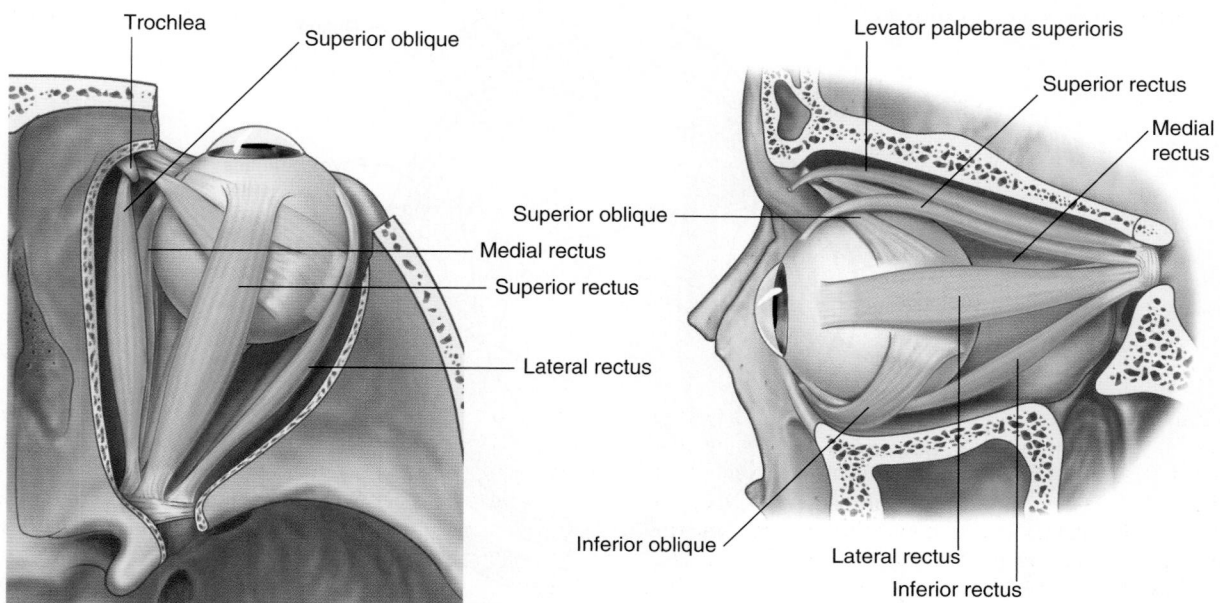

FIG. 20.2 The 6 extraocular muscles. (From Drake R, Vogl AW, Mitchell AWM: *Gray's anatomy for students,* ed 3, Philadelphia, 2015, Churchill Livingstone.)

and ciliary body), and the innermost layer, the retina. The *anterior cavity* is divided into the anterior and posterior chambers. The anterior chamber lies between the iris and posterior surface of the cornea. The posterior chamber lies between the anterior surface of the lens and posterior surface of the iris. The *posterior cavity* lies in the large space behind the lens and in front of the retina.

External Ocular Structures

The conjunctiva is a transparent mucous membrane that covers the inner surfaces of the eyelids and extends over the sclera. Glands in the conjunctiva secrete mucus and tears. Tenon's capsule, also called the fascia bulbi, is a thin layer of fascia that encases the eyeball behind the conjunctiva. The capsule extends posteriorly, ultimately fusing with the optic nerve.

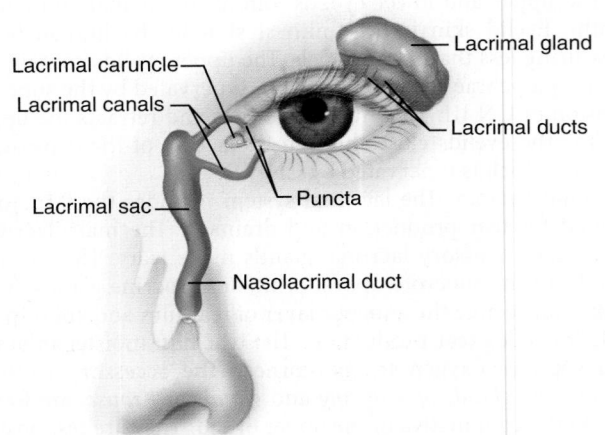

FIG. 20.3 External eye and lacrimal apparatus. Tears made in the lacrimal gland pass over the surface of the eye and enter the lacrimal canal. From there the tears are carried through the nasolacrimal duct to the nasal cavity. (Modified from Patton KT, Thibodeau GA: *Anatomy and physiology*, ed 8, St Louis, 2013, Mosby.)

The cornea allows light to enter the eye. It is transparent and avascular. Its curved shape refracts or bends incoming light rays to help focus them on the retina. The cornea has 6 layers: epithelium, Bowman's layer, stroma, Descemet's membrane, Dua's layer, and endothelium.

The sclera, the white part of the eye, is a fibrous connective tissue layer that protects the eye and helps the eye maintain its shape and structure. The sclera extends from the cornea to the optic nerve. We call the junction of the sclera and cornea the limbus.

Middle Ocular Structures

The iris gives the eye its color. It has a small round opening in the center, the *pupil*, which allows light to enter the eye. The pupil constricts by action of the iris sphincter muscle (under parasympathetic control) and dilates by action of the iris dilator muscle (under sympathetic control). This controls the amount of light that enters the eye.

The ciliary body contains the ciliary muscle and ciliary processes. It is behind the iris. The ciliary muscle helps us focus by changing the shape of the lens to refract light onto the retina. The ciliary processes make aqueous humor for both the anterior and posterior chamber. The choroid is a highly vascular structure that nourishes the ciliary body, iris, and outer part of the retina. It lies inside and parallel to the sclera.

Internal Structures

Aqueous Humor. Aqueous humor fills the anterior chamber of the eye. It is a clear watery fluid composed of electrolytes, growth factors, and proteins. It nourishes the nonvascular structures of the anterior chamber, such as the lens. Aqueous humor is made from capillary blood in the ciliary body. It is secreted into the posterior chamber and flows through the pupil to enter the anterior chamber. Aqueous humor exits the eye through the *trabecular meshwork* and into the *canal of Schlemm* and venous circulation or through the ciliary muscle. Balanced secretion and excretion of aqueous humor is important. Excess production or

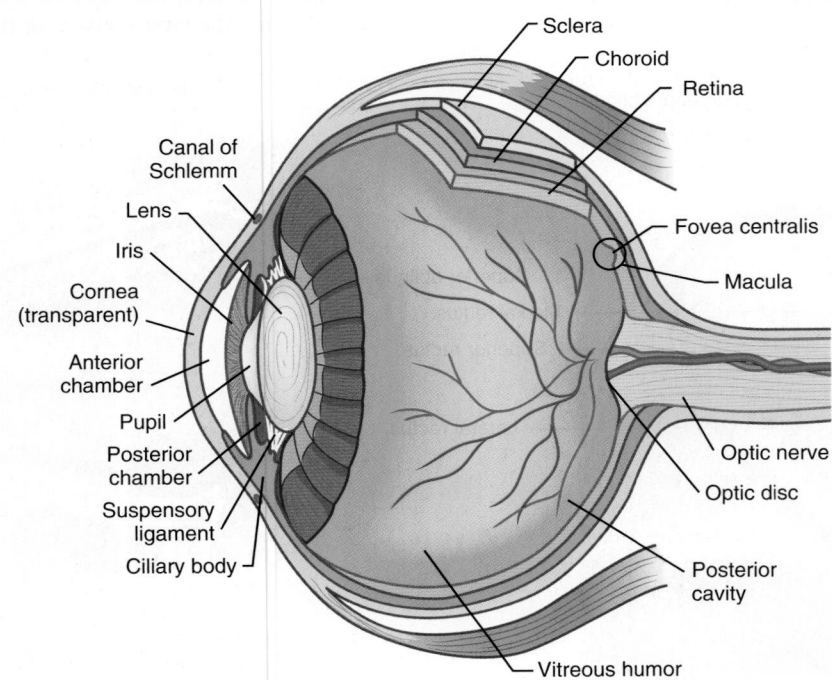

FIG. 20.4 The human eye. (Modified from Patton KT, Thibodeau GA: *Anatomy and physiology*, ed 8, St Louis, 2013, Mosby.)

decreased outflow can increase intraocular pressure (IOP) above the normal 10 to 21 mm Hg, a condition termed *glaucoma*.

Lens. The lens is a biconvex structure behind the iris. It is kept in place by small fibers collectively called the suspensory ligament, or the zonule. The ligament is a series of microscopic wire-like threads that connect the lens to the ciliary body. The primary function of the lens is to change shape to alter the focal distance of the eye. It works with the cornea to refract, or bend light. The lens shape is changed by action of the ciliary body as part of accommodation, a process that allows a person to focus. An example of accommodation is the ability to focus on near objects, such as when reading.

Vitreous Humor. The retina lines the back of the eye, extending from the area of the optic nerve to the ciliary body (Fig. 20.4). Neurons make up most of the retina. Therefore retinal cells are unable to regenerate if destroyed. The retina converts images into a form that the brain can understand and process as vision.

The retina has 2 main parts, the peripheral retina and central retina. The central retina contains the macula and fovea. The macula is about 6 mm in diameter. It is responsible for the central visual field. The fovea is at the center of the macula. This area provides the sharpest visual acuity, which we need for activities in which detail is important, like reading and driving.

The retina contains light-sensitive structures called photoreceptor cells. There are 2 types of photoreceptors, rods and cones. Rods and cones convert light to neural signals, which the nervous system translates into vision. Rods are mostly found in the peripheral retina. They are responsible for most of our peripheral vision and night vision. Rods only perceive light and dark and do not contribute to color vision. Cones are in the central retina, condensed mostly in the fovea. They are responsible for central vision and color vision. There are 3 types of cone cells, red, green, and blue. They all work together to create the full color spectrum.

The retina receives oxygen and nutrients from the choroid and the retinal vasculature. The central retinal artery carries blood and nutrients into the retina. The central retinal vein carries blood away from the retina.

Optic Nerve. The optic nerve, or CN II, transmits visual information from the retina to the brain. The optic nerve begins at the optic disc, which is the region of the retina where the optic nerve and vessels leave the retina. Because there are no photoreceptor cells over the optic disc, there is an anatomic blind spot in this area. In the center of the optic disc is a white, cup-shaped area called the optic cup.

VISUAL PATHWAY

For light to reach the retina, it must pass through many structures: the cornea, aqueous humor, lens, and vitreous humor. These structures must be clear for light to reach the retina and stimulate the photoreceptor cells. Once the image travels through the refractive media, it is focused on the retina (Fig. 20.5). From the retina, the impulses travel through the optic nerve to the optic chiasm, where the nasal fibers of each eye cross over to the other side. Fibers from the left field of both eyes form the left optic tract and travel to the left occipital cortex. The fibers from the right field of both eyes form the right optic tract and travel to the right occipital cortex.

Gerontologic Considerations: Effects of Aging on the Visual System

Every structure of the visual system is subject to changes as a person ages. While many of these changes are relatively benign,

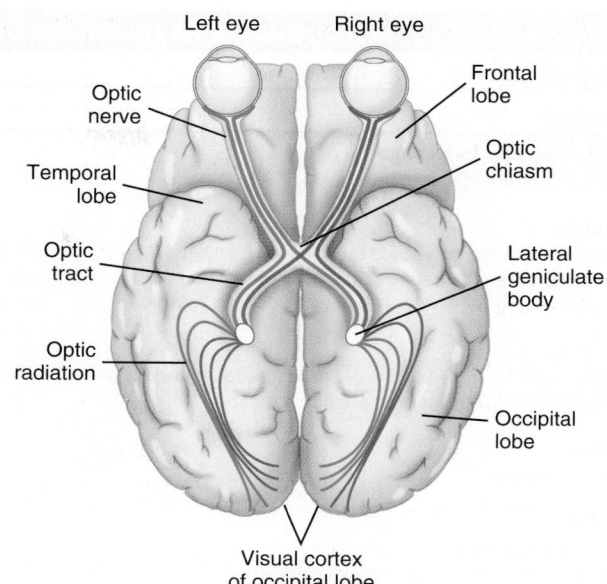

FIG. 20.5 The visual pathway. Fibers from the nasal portion of each retina cross over to the opposite side of the optic chiasma, ending in the lateral geniculate body of the opposite side. Location of a lesion in the visual pathway determines the resulting visual defect.

others may result in severely compromised visual acuity in the older adult. Age-related changes in the visual system and differences in assessment findings are shown in Table 20.1.

ASSESSMENT OF VISUAL SYSTEM

Assessment of the visual system may be as simple as determining a patient's visual acuity or as complex as collecting complete subjective and objective data pertinent to the visual system. The patient in a clinic or office setting is often seeking routine eye care or a change in the prescription of eyewear. However, the patient may have some underlying concerns that he or she does not mention or even recognize. To perform an appropriate visual evaluation, assess what is necessary for the specific patient. While many of these assessments are within your scope of practice, some require special training.

CASE STUDY
Patient Introduction

(© Jack Hollingsworth/ Photodisc/ Thinkstock.)

F.M. is an 81-yr-old Hispanic woman who comes to the emergency department with visual changes. F.M. states that her vision "looks like everything is covered with a spider web." She reports seeing periodic light flashes and small white spots "floating" in the air.

Discussion Questions

1. What are the possible causes of F.M.'s vision problems?
2. What type of assessment would be most appropriate for F.M.: comprehensive, focused, or emergency?
3. What assessment questions will you ask her?

You will learn more about F.M. and her condition as you read through this assessment chapter.

(See p. 354 for more information on F.M.)

Answers available at *http://evolve.elsevier.com/Lewis/medsurg.*

🔹 TABLE 20.1   Gerontologic Assessment Differences

Visual System

Changes	Differences in Assessment Findings
Eyebrows and Eyelashes	
Loss of pigment in hair	Graying of eyebrows, eyelashes
Eyelids	
Loss of orbital fat, decreased muscle tone	Entropion, ectropion
Tissue atrophy and stretching, prolapse of fat into eyelid tissue, loosening of the levator palpebrae superioris muscle	Dermatochalasis (excess upper lid skin), ptosis
Conjunctiva	
Tissue damage related to chronic exposure to ultraviolet light or to other chronic environmental exposure	Pinguecula (small yellowish spot usually on medial aspect of conjunctiva)
Sclera	
Lipid deposition	Scleral color yellowish as opposed to bluish
Cornea	
Cholesterol deposits in peripheral cornea	Arcus senilis (milky white-gray ring encircling periphery of cornea) (Fig. 20.6)
Tissue damage related to chronic exposure	Pterygium (thickened, triangular bit of pale tissue that extends from inner canthus of eye to nasal border of cornea)
Decrease in water content, atrophy of nerve fibers	Decreased corneal sensitivity and corneal reflex
Epithelial changes	Loss of corneal luster
Accumulation of lipid deposits	Blurring of vision
Lacrimal Apparatus	
Decreased tear secretion	Dryness
Malposition of eyelid and punctal eversion resulting in tears overflowing lid margins instead of draining through puncta	Tearing, irritated eyes
Iris	
Increased rigidity of iris	Decreased pupil size
Dilator muscle atrophy or weakness	Slower recovery of pupil size after light stimulation
Loss of pigment	Change of iris color
Ciliary muscle becoming smaller, stiffer	Decrease in near vision and accommodation
Lens	
Biochemical changes in lens proteins, oxidative damage, chronic exposure to ultraviolet light	Cataracts
Increased rigidity of lens	Presbyopia
Opacities in lens (also may be related to opacities in cornea and vitreous)	Reports of glare, night vision impaired
Accumulation of yellow substances	Yellow color of lens
Retina	
Retinal vascular changes related to atherosclerosis and hypertension	Narrowed, pale, straighter arterioles. Acute branching
Decrease in number of cones	Changes in color perception, especially blue and violet
Loss of photoreceptor cells, retinal pigment, epithelial cells, and melanin	Decreased visual acuity
Age-related macular degeneration because of vascular changes	Loss of central vision, presence of yellow deposits, atrophy of macular retinal pigment
Vitreous	
Liquefaction and detachment of vitreous	Increased "floaters"

Subjective Data

Important Health Information

Past Health History. Take information about the patient's past health history, including the ocular and nonocular history. The patient's nonocular history can be significant in assessing and treating an eye condition. Ask the patient about systemic diseases that may have ocular manifestations. These include diabetes, hypertension, cancer, rheumatoid arthritis, syphilis and other sexually transmitted infections (STIs), acquired immunodeficiency syndrome (AIDS), muscular dystrophy, myasthenia gravis, multiple sclerosis, inflammatory bowel disease, and hypothyroidism or hyperthyroidism. Include any history of stroke or neurologic problems as these have the potential to result in visual field defects.

Obtain a history of tests for visual acuity, including the date of the last examination and change in glasses or contact lenses. Ask the patient about a history of strabismus, amblyopia, cataracts, retinal detachment, refractive surgery, or glaucoma. Note any trauma to the eye, its treatment, and sequelae.

Obtain information about allergies. Allergies often cause eye symptoms, such as itching, burning, watering, drainage, and blurred vision.

FIG. 20.6 Arcus senilis, or age-related degeneration of the cornea. (From Kanski JJ: *Clinical ophthalmology: A synopsis*, ed 2, New York, 2009, Butterworth-Heinemann.)

Medications. Obtain a complete medication history, including dosage and frequency of over-the-counter (OTC) medicines, eyedrops, herbal therapies, and dietary supplements. Many of these drugs have ocular effects. For example, many cold preparations contain a form of epinephrine (e.g., pseudoephedrine) that can dilate the pupil. Note the use of any antihistamine or decongestant, since these drugs can cause ocular dryness. Ask whether the patient uses any prescription drugs, such as corticosteroids, thyroid medications, or oral hypoglycemics and insulin. Long-term use of corticosteroid preparations can contribute to the development of glaucoma or cataracts.[2] Note whether the patient is taking any β-blockers, since β-blockers used to treat glaucoma can potentiate their effects. Hydroxychloroquine, which is used to treat rheumatoid arthritis and other autoimmune diseases, has the potential to result in retinal toxicity. It is important that these patients have annual comprehensive eye examinations.

Surgery or Other Treatments. Obtain a comprehensive history of both ocular and nonocular surgeries. Include laser-based surgery and invasive treatments, such as retinal injections.

Functional Health Patterns. The focus of the functional health pattern assessment depends on the presence or absence of vision loss and whether the loss is permanent or temporary. Table 20.2 lists suggested health history questions related to the functional health patterns.

Health Perception–Health Management Pattern. Patient characteristics, such as gender, ethnicity, and age, are important in assessing eye problems. Men are more likely than women to have color blindness. The leading cause of blindness among blacks is glaucoma.[3]

The patient's visual health can affect activities at home or at work. It is important to know how the patient perceives the current health problem. As outlined in Table 20.2, guide the patient in describing the current problem. Assess the patient's ability to perform self-care, especially any eye care related to the patient's eye problem.

The patient may not recognize the importance of eye-safety practices, like wearing protective eyewear during potentially hazardous activities or avoiding noxious fumes and other eye irritants. Ask about the use of sunglasses in bright light. Prolonged exposure to ultraviolet (UV) light can affect the retina. Ask about night driving habits and any problems encountered. Today, millions of people wear contact lenses, but many do not care for them properly. The type of contact lenses used and the patient's wearing and care habits may provide an opportunity for teaching.

Hereditary systemic diseases (e.g., sickle cell anemia) can significantly affect eye health. In addition, many refractive

errors and other eye problems are hereditary. Ask whether the patient has a family history of arteriosclerosis, diabetes, thyroid disease, hypertension, arthritis, or cancer. Determine whether the patient has a family history of eye problems, including cataracts, tumors, glaucoma, refractive errors (especially myopia, hyperopia), and retinal degenerative conditions (e.g., macular degeneration, retinal detachment).

 TABLE 20.2 Health History

Visual System

Health Perception–Health Management
- Describe the change in your vision. Describe how this affects your daily life.
- Do you wear protective eyewear (sunglasses, safety goggles, hats)?*
- Do you wear contact lenses? If so, how do you take care of them?
- If you use eyedrops, how do you instill them?
- Do you have any allergies that cause eye symptoms?*
- Do you have a family history of cataracts, glaucoma, or macular degeneration?*

Nutritional-Metabolic
- Do you take any nutritional supplements?*
- Does your visual problem affect your ability to obtain and prepare food?*

Elimination
- Do you have to strain to void or defecate?*

Activity-Exercise
- Are your activities limited in any way by your eye problem?*
- Do you take part in any leisure activities that have the potential for eye injury?*

Sleep-Rest
- Is your vision affected by the amount of sleep you get?*
- Does your eye problem affect your sleeping patterns?*

Cognitive-Perceptual
- Does your eye problem affect your ability to read?*
- Do you have any eye pain?*
- Do you have any eye itching, burning, or foreign body sensation?*

Self-Perception–Self-Concept
- How does your eye problem make you feel about yourself?

Role-Relationship
- Do you have any problems at work or home because of your eyes?*
- Have you made any changes in your social activities because of your eyes?*

Sexuality-Reproductive
- Has your eye problem caused a change in your sex life?*
- For women: Are you pregnant? Do you use birth control pills?*
- For men: Do you use any erectile dysfunction drugs? Any vision problems with their use?*

Coping–Stress Tolerance
- Do you feel able to cope with your eye problem?*
- How do you feel that your eye problem has affected your life, and how do you cope with these changes?*

Value-Belief
- Do you have any conflicts about the treatment of your eye problem?*

* If yes, describe.

Nutritional-Metabolic Pattern. High doses of vitamins containing antioxidant, carotenoids, and omega-3 fatty acids (vitamins C and E, beta-carotene, zinc) may be important to ocular health. Some patients with age-related macular degeneration (AMD) may benefit from supplements of these vitamins.

Elimination Pattern. Straining to defecate (Valsalva maneuver) can raise IOP. After patients have eye surgery, many HCPs do not want them to strain. Assess the patient's usual pattern of elimination and determine whether there is the potential for constipation in the patient who has had eye surgery.

Activity-Exercise Pattern. The patient's usual level of activity or exercise may be affected by reduced vision, symptoms accompanying an eye problem, or activity restrictions after surgery. Ask about leisure activities during which the patient may incur an eye injury. For example, gardening, woodworking, and other craft activities can result in corneal or conjunctival foreign bodies or even penetrating injuries of the globe. Sports activities, such as racquetball, baseball, and tennis, carry risks for blunt trauma to the eyes. People should wear protection goggles for these sports.

Sleep-Rest Pattern. In the otherwise healthy person, lack of sleep may cause ocular irritation, especially if the patient wears contact lenses. Painful eye problems, such as corneal abrasions, may disrupt normal sleep patterns.

Cognitive-Perceptual Pattern. Assess for other cognitive or perceptual problems. For example, the functional ability of a patient with a visual deficit will be further compromised if the patient also has hearing problems. The patient who cannot see to read may find it harder to follow discharge instructions if he or she also has trouble hearing or remembering verbal instructions. Eye pain is always an important symptom to assess. If eye pain is present, ask the patient about treatment and response.

Self-Perception–Self-Concept Pattern. The loss of independence that can follow a partial or complete loss of vision, even if the condition is temporary, can have devastating effects on the patient's self-concept. Evaluate the potential effect of vision loss on the patient's self-image. For instance, disabling glare from a cataract may prevent nighttime driving. In today's highly mobile society, losing the ability to drive can represent a significant loss of independence and self-esteem.

Role-Relationship Pattern. Eye problems can negatively affect the patient's ability to take part in roles and responsibilities in the home, work, and social environments. For example, with decreased visual acuity, the patient may no longer adequately function at work. Many occupations place workers in conditions in which eye injury may occur. For example, factory workers may be at risk from flying metal debris. Eye-safety practices, such as the use of goggles or safety glasses, are now a legal requirement in some workplaces. The patient with diabetes may not be able to see well enough to self-administer insulin. This patient may resent dependence on a caregiver who takes over this function. Sensitively ask if the problem has affected the patient's preferred roles and responsibilities.

Sexuality-Reproductive Pattern. The patient with severe vision loss may develop such a poor self-image that the ability to be sexually intimate is lost. Assure the patient that low vision or blindness does not affect a person's ability to be sexually expressive. Often touch is more important than vision.

Coping–Stress Tolerance Pattern. The patient with temporary or permanent visual problems may have emotional stress. Assess the patient's coping strategies and availability of support systems.

Value-Belief Pattern. Be sensitive to each patient's individual values and spiritual beliefs as these may guide decisions about eye care. It can be hard to understand why a patient refuses treatment that has potential benefit or wants treatment that may have limited potential benefit.

CASE STUDY
Subjective Data

(© Jack Hollingsworth/ Photodisc/ Thinkstock.)

A focused subjective assessment of F.M. revealed the following information:
* **PMH:** Extraocular extraction of cataract on right eye (OD) with implantation of intraocular lens 2 mo ago. Type 2 diabetes, hypothyroidism, and hypertension.
* **Medications:** Glucophage 500 mg twice daily, levothyroxine 100 mcg daily, metoprolol 50 mg daily.
* **Health Perception–Health Management:** States she used antibiotic and corticosteroid eyedrops after surgery as directed and followed-up with surgeon. Recovery was uneventful. Eyedrops were stopped 2 wk ago. Does not have allergies. Had excellent eyesight until today.
* **Elimination:** Has had problems moving bowels with increased straining. Trying prune juice to help.
* **Activity-Exercise:** Walks in the mall at least ½ mile 3 times a week. No resistance or isotonic exercises.
* **Cognitive-Perceptual:** Denies eye pain, itching, or tearing. Having difficulty reading.
* **Coping–Stress Tolerance:** Afraid she is having a stroke.

Discussion Questions
1. Which subjective assessment findings are of most concern to you?
2. What should be included in the physical assessment? For what would you be looking?
3. How will you individualize the assessment based on her age, ethnic/cultural background, and condition?

You will learn more about the physical assessment of the visual system in the next section.

(See p. 358 for more information on F.M.)

Objective Data

Physical Examination. Physical examination of the visual system includes inspecting the ocular structures and determining the status of their respective functions. Physiologic functional assessment includes (1) assessing the patient's visual acuity, ability to judge closeness and distance, and extraocular muscle function; (2) evaluating visual fields; (3) checking pupil function; and (4) measuring IOP. Assessment of ocular structures should include examining the ocular adnexa, external eye, and internal structures. Some structures, such as the retina, blood vessels, and optic disc, must be assessed with an ophthalmoscope.

TABLE 20.3 Normal Physical Assessment of Visual System

- Visual acuity 20/20 OU. No diplopia
- External eye structures symmetric and without lesions or deformities
- Lacrimal apparatus nontender and without drainage
- Conjunctiva clear. Sclera white
- PERRLA (pupils equal, round, reactive to light and accommodation)
- Lens clear
- EOMs intact (extraocular movements intact)
- Optic disc margins sharp
- Retinal vessels without hemorrhages or spots

FOCUSED ASSESSMENT
Visual System

Use this checklist to make sure the key assessment steps have been done.

Subjective

Ask the patient about any of the following and note responses.

Changes in vision (e.g., acuity, blurred)	Y	N
Eye redness, itching, discomfort	Y	N
Drainage from eyes	Y	N

Objective: Physical Examination

Inspect

Eyes for any discoloration or drainage	✓
Conjunctiva and sclera for color and vascularity	✓
Lens for clarity	✓
Eyelid for ptosis	✓

Assess

Vision based on patient looking at nurse or Snellen chart	✓
Extraocular movements (EOMs)	✓
Peripheral vision	✓
PERRLA	✓

PERRLA, Pupils equal, round, reactive to light and accommodation.

Normal physical assessment of the visual system is outlined in Table 20.3. Assessment techniques related to vision are described in Table 20.4. Table 20.5 shows select assessment abnormalities.

A *focused assessment* is used to evaluate the status of previously identified visual problems and to monitor for signs of new problems. A focused assessment of the visual system is shown in the box above.

Initial Observation. Your initial observation of the patient can provide information that will help focus the assessment. A patient dressed in clothing with unusual color combinations may have a color-vision deficit. Note an unusual head position. The patient with diplopia may hold the head in a skewed position to try to see a single image. The patient with a corneal abrasion or photophobia will cover the eyes with the hands to try to block out room light. Make a crude estimate of depth perception by extending a hand for the patient to shake.

During the initial observation, observe the patient's overall facial and eye appearance. The eyes should be symmetric and normally placed on the face. The globes should not have a bulging or sunken appearance.

TABLE 20.4 Nursing Assessment
Assessment Techniques: Visual System

Description	Purpose
Color Vision Testing In the Ishihara test, a patient identifies numbers or paths formed by pattern of dots in series of color plates.	Determines ability to distinguish colors
Confrontation Visual Field Test Patient faces examiner, covers one eye, fixates on examiner's face, and counts number of fingers that examiner brings into patient's field of vision.	Determines if patient has a full field of vision, without obvious blind spots or vision loss
Intraocular Pressure Testing: Tonometry Covered end of probe is gently touched several times to anesthetized corneal surface. Examiner records several readings to obtain a mean IOP.	Measures IOP. Normal pressure is 10–21 mm Hg
Keratometry Examiner aligns projection and notes readings of corneal curvature. Often done before fitting contact lenses, before refractive surgery, or after corneal transplantation.	Measures corneal curvature
Ophthalmoscopy Examiner holds ophthalmoscope close to patient's eye, shining light into back of eye and looking through aperture on ophthalmoscope. Examiner adjusts dial to choose the ophthalmoscope lens that produces desired amount of magnification to inspect retina.	Provides magnified view of retina and optic nerve (Fig. 20.7)
Pupil Function Testing Examiner shines light into patient's pupil and checks pupillary response. Each pupil is examined independently. Examiner also checks for consensual and accommodative response.	Determines if patient has normal pupillary response
Visual Acuity Testing Patient reads from Snellen chart at 20 ft (distance vision test) or Jaeger chart at 14 in (near vision test). Examiner notes smallest print patient can read on each chart.	Determines distance and near visual acuity

Assessing Functional Status

Visual acuity. Always record the patient's visual acuity for medical and legal reasons. When doing a physical examination of the eyes, assess the right eye first and then the left eye. Use the abbreviations right eye "OD," left eye "OS," and both eyes "OU." Record the patient's visual acuity before the patient receives any eye care.

To assess visual acuity, position the person on a mark exactly 20 ft (6 m) from the Snellen eye chart. If the person wears glasses or contacts, leave them on. Using an occlude, cover one eye at a time during the test. Ask the person to read down the lines of the chart to the smallest line of letters and numbers possible. Record the result using the numeric fraction at the end of the last successful line read. Indicate whether any letters

TABLE 20.5 Assessment Abnormalities

Visual System

Finding	Description	Possible Etiology and Significance
Subjective Data		
Blurred vision	Gradual or sudden inability to see clearly	Refractive errors, corneal opacities, cataracts, migraine aura, retinal changes (detachment, macular degeneration)
Diplopia	Double vision	Abnormal extraocular muscle action related to muscle or cranial nerve pathologic condition
Dryness	Discomfort, sandy, gritty, irritation, or burning	Decreased tear formation or changes in tear composition because of aging or various systemic diseases
Pain	Foreign body sensation	Superficial corneal erosion or abrasion. Can result from contact lens wear or trauma. Conjunctival or corneal foreign body
	Severe, deep, throbbing	Anterior uveitis, acute glaucoma, infection. Acute glaucoma also associated with nausea, vomiting
Photophobia	Persistent abnormal intolerance to light	Inflammation or infection of cornea or anterior uveal tract (iris and ciliary body)
Spots, floaters	Patient describes seeing spots, "spider webs," "curtain," or floaters within the field of vision	Most common cause is vitreous liquefaction (benign phenomenon). Other causes include hemorrhage into the vitreous humor, retinal holes or tears
Objective Data		
Eyelids		
Allergic reactions	Redness, excessive tearing, and itching of lid margins	Many possible allergens. Associated eye trauma can occur from rubbing itchy eyelids
Blepharitis	Redness, swelling, and crusting along lid margins	Bacterial invasion of lid margins. Often chronic
Dermatochalasis	Excess eyelid skin	May eventually obstruct superior and peripheral vision
Ectropion	Outward turning of lower lid margin	Age-related tissue changes, posttraumatic changes, facial paralysis
Entropion	Inward turning of upper or lower lid margin, unilateral or bilateral	Age-related tissue changes, posttraumatic changes, facial paralysis
Hordeolum (sty) (Fig. 20.8)	Small, superficial white nodule along lid margin	Infection of meibomian gland of eyelid. Causative organism is usually bacterial (most often *Staphylococcus aureus*)
Ptosis	Drooping of upper eyelid, unilateral or bilateral	Myasthenia gravis, congenital, or mechanical causes from eyelid tumors or excess skin
Conjunctiva		
Conjunctivitis	Redness, swelling of conjunctiva. May be itchy	Bacterial or viral infection. May be allergic response or inflammatory response to chemical exposure
Subconjunctival hemorrhage	Appearance of blood spot on sclera. May be small or can affect entire sclera	Conjunctival blood vessels rupture, leaking blood into the subconjunctival space.
Cornea		
Corneal abrasion	Localized painful disruption of the epithelial layer of cornea. Can be seen with fluorescein dye	Trauma. Overwear or improper fit of contact lenses
Globe		
Exophthalmos (Fig. 20.9)	Protrusion of globe beyond its normal position within bony orbit. Sclera often visible above iris when eyelids are open	Intraocular or periorbital tumors Hyperthyroidism
Pupil		
Abnormal response to light or accommodation	Pupils respond asymmetrically or abnormally to light stimulus or accommodation	CNS disorders, general anesthesia
Anisocoria	Pupils unequal (constricted)	CNS disorders. Slight difference in pupil size is normal in some people
Extraocular Muscles		
Strabismus	Deviation of eye position in one or more directions	Overaction or underaction of one or more extraocular muscles
Lens		
Cataract	Opacification of lens. Pupil can appear cloudy or white when opacity is visible behind pupil opening.	Aging, trauma, diabetes, long-term systemic corticosteroid therapy
Visual Field Defect		
Central	Loss of central vision	Macular disease
Peripheral	Partial or complete loss of peripheral vision	Glaucoma. Interruption of visual pathway (e.g., tumor). Migraine headache

were missed and if corrective lenses were worn (e.g., "Right eye, 20/30-2, with contacts"). Next ask the patient to cover the other eye and repeat the process. Normal visual acuity is 20/20. The first number indicates the distance the person is standing or sitting from the chart. The second number gives the distance at which a normal eye can read the particular line. *Legal blindness* is defined as the best-corrected vision in the better eye of 20/200 or less.

If the patient reports near vision difficulty or is 40 years of age or older, use a hand-held vision screener with varying print sizes (e.g., a Jaeger chart). Hold the card at 14 in (35 cm) from the eye in good light to assess near vision. Examine each eye separately, with glasses on if worn. A normal result is "14/14" in each eye, read without hesitancy and without the patient moving the card. If you must assess near visual acuity without access to a Jaeger eye chart, you can still make an accurate assessment using newsprint or the label on a container. Record the acuity as "reads newspaper headline at X inches." If the patient is unable to read any of the lines on both the near and distant visual acuity charts, the next step is to assess whether they can see hand motion and light perception.

Extraocular muscle functions. Assess the corneal light reflex to evaluate for weakness or imbalance of the extraocular muscles. In a darkened room, ask the patient to look straight ahead while shining a penlight directly on the cornea. The light reflection should be in the center of both corneas as the patient faces the light source.

To assess eye movement, hold a finger or an object within 10 to 12 inches of the patient's nose. Ask the patient to follow with eyes only the movement of the object or finger in the 6 cardinal positions of gaze. This test can indicate weakness or paralysis in the extraocular muscles and cranial nerves (CN III, CN IV, and CN VI).

Pupil function and intraocular pressure. Pupil function is determined by inspecting the pupils and their reactions to light. The normal finding is often abbreviated as PERRL (pupils are equal [in size], round, and reactive to light). The pupils should react to light directly (pupil constricts when a light shines into the eye) and consensually (pupil constricts when a light shines into the opposite eye). In a small number of people, the pupils are normally unequal in size (*anisocoria*).

To test for accommodation, ask the person to focus on a distant object. This process dilates the eyes. Then have the person shift the focus to a near object (e.g., your finger held about 3 inches from the person's nose). A normal response is constriction of the eyes and convergence (inward movement of both eyes toward each other). When accommodation is assessed with the pupillary light reflex, a normal response is *PERRLA* (pupils are equal, round, and reactive to light and accommodation).

IOP (Table 20.4) is measured by a variety of methods, including tonometry. Normal IOP ranges from 10 to 21 mm Hg.

Assessing Structures. We assess the visual system structures primarily by inspection. The visual system is unique because we can inspect not only the external structures but also many of the internal structures. The iris, lens, vitreous, retina, and optic nerve can be seen directly through the clear cornea and pupil opening.

This direct inspection requires special observation equipment, such as the slit lamp microscope or ophthalmoscope. These permit examination of the conjunctiva, sclera, cornea, anterior chamber, iris, lens, vitreous, and retina under magnification. The *ophthalmoscope* is a hand-held instrument with

a light source and magnifying lenses that is held close to the patient's eye to visualize the posterior part of the eye. Little pain or discomfort is associated with these examinations.

Eyebrows, eyelashes, and eyelids. All structures should be present and symmetric, without deformities, redness, or swelling. Eyelashes extend outward from the lid margins. In normal closing, the upper and lower eyelid margins just touch. The lacrimal puncta should be open and positioned properly against the globe.

Conjunctiva and sclera. The conjunctiva and sclera are easily examined at the same time. Assess the color, smoothness, and presence of lesions or foreign bodies. The conjunctiva covering the sclera is normally clear, with fine blood vessels visible. These blood vessels are more common in the periphery.

The sclera is normally white. A slight yellow cast may be found in some dark-skinned people, such as blacks and Native Americans, or in the older adult from lipid deposition. A pale blue cast caused by scleral thinning can be normal in older adults.

Cornea. The cornea should be clear, transparent, and shiny. The iris should appear flat and not bulge toward the cornea. The area between the cornea and iris should be clear, with no blood or purulent material visible in the anterior chamber.

Iris. Both irises should be of similar color and shape. However, a color difference between the irises occurs normally in a small number of people.

Retina and optic nerve. We can get vital information about the vascular system and CNS through direct visualization with an ophthalmoscope. It is used to magnify the retina and optic nerves and bring them into crisp focus (Fig. 20.7). Skilled use of this instrument takes practice.

Examine the optic nerve or disc for size, color, and abnormalities. The optic disc is creamy yellow with distinct margins. A central depression in the disc, called the *physiologic cup,* may be seen. This area is the exit site for the optic nerve. The cup should be less than half the diameter of the disc. Normally, no hemorrhages or exudates are present in the fundus (retinal background). Careful inspection of the fundus can reveal retinal holes, tears, detachments, or lesions. Small hemorrhages can be associated with diabetes or hypertension and can appear in various shapes, such as dots or flames. Finally, examine the macula for shape and appearance. This area is normally devoid of any blood vessels.

FIG. 20.7 Magnified view of retina through the ophthalmoscope. (From Newell FW: *Ophthalmology: Principles and concepts,* ed 7, St Louis, 1992, Mosby.)

Special Assessment Techniques

Color Vision. Testing the patient's ability to distinguish colors is an important part of the overall assessment. Some occupations require accurate color discrimination. The Ishihara color test determines the patient's ability to distinguish a pattern of color in a series of color plates.

Stereopsis. Stereoscopic vision allows a patient to see objects in 3 dimensions. An event that causes a patient to have monocular vision (e.g., enucleation, patching) results in the loss of stereoscopic vision. Without stereopsis, the person's ability to judge distances or the height of a step is impaired. This can have profound consequences if the person trips over a step when walking or follows too closely behind another vehicle when driving.

CASE STUDY

Objective Data: Physical Examination and Diagnostic Studies

(© Jack Hollingsworth/ Photodisc/ Thinkstock.)

Physical examination findings of F.M. were as follows:
- PERRL. No abnormalities noted on visual examination of external eye structures. EOMs intact and symmetric.

The HCP performs an ophthalmoscopic examination and finds a partial retinal detachment. Ultrasonography confirms the diagnosis.

Discussion Questions
1. Are these the diagnostic studies that you expected to be ordered?
2. Which diagnostic study results are of most concern to you?

Answers available at *http://evolve.elsevier.com/Lewis/medsurg.*

DIAGNOSTIC STUDIES OF VISUAL SYSTEM

Diagnostic studies of the visual system provide vital information in monitoring the patient's condition and planning appropriate interventions. These studies are considered objective data. Table 20.6 presents common diagnostic studies of the visual system.

VISUAL PROBLEMS

REFRACTIVE ERRORS

Refraction is the eye's ability to bend light rays so that they fall on the retina. In the normal eye, parallel light rays are focused through the lens into a sharp image on the retina. When the light does not focus properly, it is called a refractive error. This defect prevents light rays from converging into a single focus on the retina. Defects are a result of irregularities of the corneal curvature, focusing power of the lens, or length of the eye.

Refractive errors are the most common visual problem. Blurred vision is the major symptom. In some cases, the patient may have eye discomfort, eyestrain, or headaches. Most refractive errors can be corrected using eyeglasses or contact lenses, refractive eye laser surgery, or surgical implantation of an artificial lens.

Myopia (nearsightedness) is an inability to accommodate for objects at a distance. It causes light rays to be focused in front of the retina. This means the person can see near objects but objects in the distance are blurry. Myopia may occur because of excessive light refraction by the cornea or lens or because of

TABLE 20.6 Diagnostic Studies

Visual System

Study	Description, Purpose, and Nursing Responsibility
Amsler Grid test	Self-administered test using a hand-held card printed with a grid of lines (like graph paper) (Fig. 20.15). Using one eye at a time, patient fixates on center dot and records any abnormalities of grid lines, such as wavy, missing, or distorted areas. Used to monitor macular problems.
Fluorescein angiography	Fluorescein injected IV into peripheral vein followed by serial photographs (over 10-min period) of retina through dilated pupils Provides diagnostic information about flow of blood through retinal vessels. If extravasation occurs, fluorescein is toxic to tissue. Tell patient that dye can sometimes cause transient nausea or vomiting. Yellow-orange discoloration of urine and skin may occur.
Perimetry (visual field) testing	Can detect changes in central and peripheral vision, which may be caused by various conditions, including glaucoma, stroke, brain tumors, or other neurologic deficits. Person sits and looks inside a bowl-shaped instrument called a *perimeter*. While staring at the center of bowl, a light flashes, and the person presses a button each time flash is seen. A computer records the results, and a printout shows if there are areas where flashes of light are not seen.
Refractometry	Measure of refractive error. Patient sits looking through apertures at Snellen acuity chart and lenses are changed. Patient chooses lenses that make acuity sharpest. Dilation of eyes may help visualize retina and optic nerves. Procedure is painless. Pupil dilation, which may last 3–4 hr, makes it difficult to focus on near objects.
Ultrasonography	*A-scan* determines the right power of a lens implant before cataract surgery. *B-scan* used to diagnose ocular pathologic conditions, including intraocular foreign bodies or tumors, vitreous opacities, retinal detachments.

an abnormally long eye. Myopia is the most common refractive error. About 30% of Americans have this disorder.[4] There is strong evidence that many people inherit myopia, or at least the tendency to develop myopia.[4]

Hyperopia (farsightedness) is an inability to accommodate for near objects. It causes the light rays to focus behind the retina and requires the person to use accommodation to focus the light rays on the retina for near objects. The person with hyperopia can see distant objects clearly. This type of error occurs when the cornea or lens does not have adequate focusing power or when the eyeball is too short.

Presbyopia is the loss of accommodation associated with age. One usually begins to notice this condition in the early to mid-40s. As the eye ages, the lens becomes larger, firmer, and less elastic. These changes, which progress with aging, result in an inability to focus on near objects.

Astigmatism is an uneven or irregular curvature of the cornea. The irregularity causes the incoming light rays to be bent unequally. Thus, the light rays do not come to a single point of focus on the retina, which results in visual distortion. Astigmatism can occur in conjunction with any of the other refractive errors.

Aphakia is the absence of the lens. Rarely, the lens may be absent congenitally, or it may be removed during cataract surgery. A lens that is traumatically injured is removed and replaced with an intraocular lens (IOL) implant. The absence of the lens results in a significant refractive error. Without the focusing ability of the lens, images are projected behind the retina.

Nonsurgical Corrections

Corrective Glasses. The right corrective lenses can enhance vision in those with myopia, hyperopia, presbyopia, and astigmatism. Glasses for presbyopia are often called "reading glasses" because they are usually worn only for close work. Presbyopic correction may be combined with a correction for another refractive error, such as myopia or astigmatism. In these combined glasses, the presbyopic correction is in the lower part of the spectacle lens. A traditional bifocal or trifocal has visible lines. However, most lenses today that correct vision at various distances do not have visible lines. The prescription varies throughout the lens, allowing distance focusing in the top two thirds and near focus in the bottom one third of the lens.

Contact Lenses. Contact lenses are another way to correct refractive errors. Contact lenses are made from various plastic and silicone substances. They are highly permeable to oxygen and have a high water content. These features allow for increased wearing time with greater comfort. If the oxygen supply to the cornea is decreased, it becomes swollen, visual acuity decreases, and the patient has severe discomfort.

In general, you need to know whether the patient wears contact lenses, the pattern of wear (daily versus extended), and care practices. Shining a light obliquely on the eyeball can help visualize a contact lens. Contact lenses are associated with microbial keratitis, a severe sight-threatening complication. Risk factors for keratitis include poor hand cleaning, poor lens case hygiene, and inadequate lens cleaning. Teach the patient the importance of following recommended cleaning practices and reporting redness, sensitivity, vision problems, and pain to the eye care provider. Teach the patient to remove contact lenses at once if any of these problems occur.

Surgical Therapy

Surgery can eliminate or reduce the need for eyeglasses or contact lenses and correct refractive errors by changing the focus of the eye. Surgical management for refractive errors includes laser surgery and IOL implantation.

Laser. *Laser-assisted in situ keratomileusis* (LASIK) may be considered for patients with low to moderately high amounts of myopia or hyperopia, with or without astigmatism. The procedure first involves using a laser or surgical blade to create a flap in the cornea. The flap is folded back, exposing the middle section (stroma) of the cornea. Pulses from a computer-controlled laser vaporize a part of the stroma. The flap is then repositioned, adhering on its own without sutures in a few minutes.[5]

Photorefractive keratectomy (PRK) is indicated for low to moderate amounts of myopia or hyperopia, with or without astigmatism. It is a good option for a patient with insufficient corneal thickness for a LASIK flap. In PRK, the epithelium is removed and the laser sculpts the cornea to correct the refractive error. *Laser-assisted subepithelial keratomileusis* (LASEK) is similar to PRK, except that the epithelium is replaced after surgery.

Implant. *Refractive intraocular lens* (refractive IOL) implantation is an option for patients with a high degree of myopia or hyperopia. Like cataract surgery, it involves removing the patient's natural lens and implanting an IOL. The IOL implant used is a special lens designed to correct the patient's refractive error. Refractive IOLs can correct both myopia and presbyopia.

Phakic intraocular lenses (phakic IOLs) are sometimes called *implantable contact lenses*. They are implanted into the eye without removing the eye's natural lens. They are used for patients with high degrees of myopia or hyperopia. Unlike refractive IOLs, the phakic IOL is placed in front of the eye's natural lens. Leaving the natural lens preserves the eye's ability to focus for reading vision.

🌐 PROMOTING HEALTH EQUITY

Visual Problems

- Glaucoma has an increased incidence and severity among blacks compared with whites.
- Hispanic Americans have an increased incidence of diabetic retinopathy.
- Whites have a higher incidence of macular degeneration than Hispanics, blacks, and Asian Americans.

VISUAL IMPAIRMENT

Visual impairment describes vision that cannot be fully corrected by corrective lenses, medical treatment, or surgery. The term *visual impairment* includes conditions ranging from low vision to the absence of all vision (total blindness). Many terms are used when people refer to visual impairment, including:

- *Low vision* refers to impaired vision that cannot be improved by conventional eyeglasses, contact lenses, medications, or surgery in which some good usable vision remains.
- *Severe visual impairment* describes visual impairment in people who are unable to read ordinary newsprint even with correction. People with a severe visual impairment may or may not be legally blind.
- *Legal blindness* refers to central visual acuity of 20/200 or less in the better eye with correction or a peripheral visual field of 20 degrees or less.[6]

Most blindness in the United States is the result of common eye diseases, including cataracts, glaucoma, age-related macular degeneration, and diabetic retinopathy.

❖ NURSING MANAGEMENT: VISUAL IMPAIRMENT

◆ Nursing Assessment

It is important to assess how long the patient has had a visual impairment. Recent loss of vision has different implications for nursing care. Determine how the patient's visual impairment affects normal functioning. Ask the patient about the level of difficulty involved in doing certain tasks. For example, how hard is it for the patient to read, write a check, move from one room to the next, or view the television? Other questions can help determine the personal meaning that the patient attaches to the visual impairment. Ask how the vision loss has affected specific aspects of the patient's life, whether the patient has lost a job, or what activities the patient does not engage in because of the visual impairment.

Determine the patient's emotional reactions, coping strategies, and support systems. The patient may attach many negative meanings to the impairment because of societal views of blindness. For example, the patient may view the impairment as punishment or view themselves as useless and burdensome.

◆ Planning

The overall goals are that the patient with impaired vision will (1) make a successful adjustment to the impairment, (2) discuss feelings related to the loss, (3) identify personal strengths and support systems, and (4) use appropriate coping strategies. If the patient has been functioning at an appropriate or acceptable level, the goal is to maintain the current level of function.

◆ Nursing Implementation

◆ **Health Promotion.** Encourage the patient with preventable causes of further visual impairment to seek appropriate health care. For example, the patient with vision loss from glaucoma may be able to prevent further visual loss by with prescribed therapies and eye examinations.

◆ **Acute Care.** Provide emotional support and direct care to the patient with recent visual impairment. Allow the patient to express fear, anger, and grief. Help the patient identify positive coping strategies. Caregivers are intimately involved in the experiences that occur with vision loss. With the patient's knowledge and permission, include caregivers in discussions and encourage them to express their concerns.

Many people are uncomfortable around a person with visual impairment because they are not sure what behaviors are appropriate. Being sensitive to the patient's feelings without being overly worried or smothering the patient's independence is vital in creating a therapeutic nursing presence. Always communicate in a normal conversational tone and manner with the patient and address the patient, not the caregiver. Common courtesy dictates introducing yourself and any other people who approach the patient. It is important to say good-bye when leaving the patient's presence. Making eye contact with the patient achieves several goals. It ensures that you are speaking while facing the patient so that the patient has no difficulty hearing. Your head position confirms that you are attentive to the patient. In addition, establishing eye contact ensures that you can observe the patient's facial expressions and reactions.

Help the patient using a *sighted-guide technique.* Stand slightly in front and to one side of the patient and offer an elbow for the patient to hold. Serve as the sighted guide, walking slightly ahead of the patient with the patient holding the back of your arm. As you walk, describe the environment to help orient the patient. For example, "We're going through an open doorway and approaching 2 steps down." Help the patient sit by placing one of his or her hands on the seat of the chair.

◆ **Ambulatory Care.** In working with the patient who is visually impaired, remember that a person classified as legally blind may have some useful vision. Rehabilitation after partial or total loss of vision can foster independence, self-esteem, and productivity. Know what services and devices are available and make appropriate referrals. For the legally blind patient the primary resource for services is the state agency for rehabilitation of the blind. Legally blind persons are often eligible for federal and state assistance and income tax benefits. A list of agencies that serve the partially sighted or blind patient is available from the American Foundation for the Blind (*www.afb.org*).

Braille or audio books for reading and a cane or guide dog for ambulation are examples of vision substitution techniques. These are usually best for the patient with no functional vision. For most patients who have some remaining vision, vision enhancement techniques can help in learning to ambulate, read printed material, and perform ADLs.

Optical Devices for Vision Enhancement. A wide range of newer technologies are available to help people with low vision. These devices include desktop video magnification/closed circuit units, electronic hand-held magnifiers, text-to-speech scanners (material read aloud to you), E-readers, and computer tablets (material read aloud, magnification, image zooming, brighter screen, voice recognition). Many of these devices require some training by an assistive technology professional. Encourage patients to practice with the technologic device to ensure they can use it successfully.

Nonoptical Methods for Vision Enhancement. Approach magnification is a simple way to enhance the patient's residual vision. Recommend that the patient sit closer to the television or hold books closer to the eyes. Contrast enhancement techniques include watching television in black and white, using a black felt-tip marker, and using contrasting colors (e.g., a red stripe at the edge of steps or curbs). Increased lighting can be provided by halogen lamps, direct sunlight, or gooseneck lamps that are aimed directly at the reading material or other near objects. Large type is often helpful, especially when used with other vision enhancements.

Non–24-Hour Sleep/Wake Disorder. A common problem that can occur in blind people, especially those who are totally blind, is *non–24-hour sleep/wake disorder (Non-24).* It is a circadian rhythm sleep disorder in which a person's biologic clock does not synchronize to a 24-hour day.[7] It is caused by lack of light input to the circadian clock.

People with Non-24 have problems falling asleep or staying asleep at night. During the day, they may have an uncontrollable urge to sleep. This can result in severe sleep issues, including insomnia, excessive sleepiness, changing patterns of when a person sleeps, and social and work consequences.

Taking melatonin can shift the circadian clock earlier (an advance) or later (a delay). Tasimelteon (Hetlioz), a melatonin receptor agonist, also can be used for treatment. It works by targeting receptors in the brain that control the timing of the sleep/wake cycle.

◆ Evaluation

The overall expected outcomes are that the patient with visual impairment will:

- Follow treatment plan to prevent further loss of vision
- Be able to use adaptive coping strategies
- Maintain self-esteem and take part in social interactions
- Function safely within her or his own environment

♥ PROMOTING POPULATION HEALTH
Responsible Eye Care

- Regular hand washing prevents the spread of disease from one eye to the other.
- Seeking appropriate health care can lead to early detection of disease and prevent further loss of vision in patients with certain types of partial vision loss.
- Wearing sunglasses and practicing proper nutrition may help prevent cataract development and age-related macular degeneration.
- Wearing eye protection during potentially hazardous work, hobby, and sport activities reduces the risk for eye injuries.

Gerontologic Considerations: Visual Impairment

The older adult is at an increased risk for vision loss caused by eye disease. They may have other deficits, such as cognitive impairment or limited mobility, that further affect the ability to function in usual ways. Societal devaluation of older adults may compound the self-esteem or isolation issues associated with visual impairment. Financial resources may be inadequate to secure vision services or assistive devices.

The older patient may become increasingly confused or disoriented when visually compromised. The combination of decreased vision and confusion increases the risk for falls, which can have serious consequences. Decreased vision may compromise the older patient's ability to function, resulting in concerns about independence and a diminished self-image. Decreased manual dexterity may make instilling prescribed eyedrops hard. Those with low vision are more likely to make medication errors that are potentially dangerous, such as taking too much insulin or mistaking one drug for another.

EYE TRAUMA

Although the eyes are well protected by the bony orbit and fat pads, everyday activities can result in eye trauma. The most common eye injuries in the United States are due to falls and fights. Injuries at home may be caused by cleaning, gardening, power tool use, and home repair work. Sport- and work-related injuries are other causes of eye trauma.[8]

? CHECK YOUR PRACTICE

You are working in your garden when your neighbor comes running into your yard. She is screaming and waving her arms. Her husband was using a chain saw to cut down a tree when a piece of wood chip flew into his eye. When you go to your neighbor's yard, the husband is on the ground crying in pain and you assess that the wood chip is embedded in his eye.
- What should you do next?

Table 20.7 outlines the emergency management of the patient with an eye injury. Chemical burns can be devastating to the eye and need immediate attention. Alkaline chemicals with a pH greater than 7 are the most harmful. They can penetrate the eye and damage the inner components. Acidic chemicals with a pH of less than 7 are unable to penetrate the eye but can damage the cornea. Both types of injury have the potential to result in blindness.

A *Morgan lens* may be used to provide continuous irrigation of an injured eye. It consists of a sterile plastic device resembling a contact lens that floats over the eye (never physically touches it) and allows copious irrigation of the eye. The device is connected to tubing that delivers irrigating solution. The Morgan lens provides relief for chemical or thermal burns and removes nonembedded foreign materials in the eye.

Trauma is often a preventable cause of visual impairment. Many eye injuries could be prevented by wearing protective eyewear. Your role in individual and community education is extremely important in reducing the incidence of eye trauma.

EXTRAOCULAR DISORDERS

INFLAMMATION AND INFECTION

One of the most common eye conditions is inflammation or infection of the external eye. Many external irritants or microorganisms can affect the eye, conjunctiva, and avascular cornea.

An external hordeolum (or a *sty*) is an infection of the meibomian glands in the lid margin (Fig. 20.8). The most common bacterial infective agent is *Staphylococcus aureus*. A red, swollen, circumscribed, and acutely tender area develops rapidly. Have the patient apply warm, moist compresses at least 4 times a day until it improves. This may be the only treatment needed. If it tends to recur, teach the patient to do lid scrubs daily. On occasion, antibiotic ointments or drops may be needed.

A *chalazion* is a chronic inflammatory granuloma of the meibomian glands in the lid. It may evolve from a hordeolum or

✚ TABLE 20.7 Emergency Management

Eye Injury

Etiology	Assessment Findings	Interventions
Chemical Burn • Acid • Alkaline **Foreign Bodies** • Ceramics • Glass • Metal • Plastic • Wood **Thermal Burn** • Direct burn from hot surface • Indirect burn from UV light (e.g., welding torch, looking directly at sun) **Trauma** • Blunt (e.g., fist) • Penetrating (e.g., glass, metal, or wood fragments; knife, stick, other object)	• Pain • Photophobia • Redness—diffuse or localized • Swelling • Bruising • Tearing • Blood in the anterior chamber • Absent eye movements • Fluid drainage from eye (e.g., blood, aqueous humor) • Abnormal or decreased vision • Visible foreign body • Prolapsed globe • Abnormal IOP • Visual field defect	**Initial** • Determine mechanism of injury. • Ensure airway, breathing, and circulation. • Assess for other injuries. • Assess for chemical exposure. • Begin ocular irrigation *immediately* in case of chemical exposure. Do not stop until emergency personnel arrive to continue irrigation. Use sterile saline or water if saline is unavailable. • Assess visual acuity. • Do not put pressure on the eye. • Tell patient not to blow nose. • Do not try to treat the injury (except as noted above for chemical exposure). • Stabilize foreign objects. • Cover the eye(s) with dry, sterile patches and a protective shield. • Do not give the patient food or fluids. • Elevate head of bed 45 degrees. • Give proper analgesia. **Ongoing Monitoring** • Reassure the patient. • Monitor pain. • Anticipate surgical repair for penetrating injury, globe rupture, or globe avulsion.

FIG. 20.8 Hordeolum (sty) on the upper eyelid caused by staphylococcal infection. (Courtesy Stephen J. Laquis, MD, FACS Ophthalmic Facial Plastic Surgery Specialists, Fort Myers, FL.)

occur in response to the material released into the lid when a blocked gland ruptures. The chalazion usually appears on the upper lid as a swollen, tender, reddened area that may be painful. Initial treatment is like that for a hordeolum. If warm, moist compresses are ineffective in promoting spontaneous drainage, the HCP may drain the lesion or inject it with corticosteroids.

Blepharitis is a common chronic bilateral inflammation of the lid margins. The lids are red rimmed with many scales or crusts on the lid margins and lashes. The patient mainly has itching but may also have burning, irritation, and photophobia.

If a staphylococcal infection caused blepharitis, an eye antibiotic ointment must be used. Often blepharitis is caused by both staphylococcal and seborrheal microorganisms. The treatment must be more vigorous to avoid hordeolum, *keratitis* (inflammation of the cornea), and other eye infections. Emphasize thorough cleaning practices of the skin and scalp. Gentle cleansing of the lid margins with baby shampoo or lid scrubs can effectively soften and remove crusting.

Conjunctivitis

Conjunctivitis is an infection or inflammation of the conjunctiva. Infections may be bacterial or viral. Conjunctival inflammation may result from exposure to allergens or chemical irritants. Careful hand washing and use of individual or disposable towels help prevent spreading the condition.

Bacterial Infections. Acute bacterial conjunctivitis *(pinkeye)* is a common infection. Although it occurs in every age group, epidemics are common among children. *S. aureus* is the most common cause. The patient with bacterial conjunctivitis may have discomfort, pruritus, redness, and a mucopurulent drainage. Although it typically occurs initially in one eye, it generally spreads to the unaffected eye. It is usually self-limiting, but treatment with antibiotic drops shortens the course of the disorder. Teach patients the importance of hand washing and avoiding contact with an infected person.

Viral Infections. Many different viruses cause conjunctival infections. The patient with viral conjunctivitis may have tearing, foreign body sensation, redness, and mild photophobia. This condition is usually mild and self-limiting. However, it can be severe, with increased discomfort and subconjunctival hemorrhaging. Adenovirus conjunctivitis may be contracted in contaminated swimming pools and through direct contact with an infected patient.

Epidemic keratoconjunctivitis (EKC) is the most serious ocular adenoviral disease. EKC is spread by direct contact. In the medical setting, contaminated hands and instruments can be the source of spread. The patient may have tearing, redness, photophobia, and foreign body sensation. In most patients, the disease involves only one eye. Treatment is primarily palliative and includes ice packs and dark glasses. Therapy for severe cases can include mild topical corticosteroids to temporarily relieve symptoms and topical antibiotic ointment. Teach the patient the importance of good hygiene practices to avoid spreading the disease.

Chlamydial Infections. *Trachoma* is a chronic conjunctivitis caused by *Chlamydia trachomatis* (serotypes A through C). It is a major cause of blindness worldwide. Trachoma is most often seen in underdeveloped countries. It is transmitted mainly by the hands and by flies. Adult inclusion conjunctivitis (AIC) is caused by *C. trachomatis* (serotypes D through K). AIC is becoming more prevalent in the United States because of the increase in sexually transmitted chlamydial infection.[9]

Manifestations of both trachoma and AIC are mucopurulent eye discharge, irritation, redness, and lid swelling. For unknown reasons, AIC does not carry the long-term consequences of trachoma. Antibiotic therapy is usually effective for trachoma and AIC. Patients with AIC have a high risk for concurrent chlamydial genital infection and STIs that may need treatment.

Allergic Conjunctivitis. Conjunctivitis caused by exposure to an allergen can be mild and transitory, or it can be severe enough to cause significant swelling. The defining symptom of allergic conjunctivitis is itching. The patient may have burning, redness, and tearing. The patient may develop allergic conjunctivitis in response to pollens, animal dander, ocular solutions, and medications. Teach the patient to avoid known allergens if possible. Artificial tears can be effective in diluting the allergen and washing it from the eye. Topical medications include antihistamines and corticosteroids.

Keratitis

Keratitis is an inflammation or infection of the cornea. It is caused by a variety of microorganisms or by other factors. The condition may involve the conjunctiva and/or the cornea. When it involves both, the disorder is termed *keratoconjunctivitis*.

Bacterial Infections. The cornea can become infected by a variety of bacteria. Risk factors include mechanical or chemical corneal epithelial damage, contact lens wear, nutritional deficiencies, immunosuppressed states, and contaminated products (e.g., lens care solutions and cases, topical medications, cosmetics). Treatment includes topical antibiotics. In some cases, the patient may need subconjunctival antibiotic injection or, in severe cases, IV antibiotics.

Viral Infections. Herpes simplex virus (HSV) keratitis is the most common infectious cause of corneal blindness in the Western hemisphere. It is a growing problem, especially with immunosuppressed patients. The corneal ulcer has a characteristic dendritic (tree-branching) appearance. Pain and photophobia are common.

Current treatment for HSK includes acyclovir, ganciclovir, trifluorothymidine, penciclovir, and valacyclovir.[10] Therapy may also involve corneal debridement. Topical corticosteroids are usually contraindicated because they contribute to a longer course and possible deeper ulceration of the cornea.

The varicella-zoster virus (VZV) causes both chickenpox and herpes zoster ophthalmicus (HZO). HZO may occur by reactivation of an endogenous infection that has persisted in a latent form after an earlier attack of varicella or by contact with a patient with chickenpox or herpes zoster. It occurs most often in the older adult and immunosuppressed patient. Care of the patient with acute HZO may include analgesics for pain, topical corticosteroids to reduce inflammation, antiviral agents to reduce viral replication, mydriatic agents to dilate the pupil and relieve pain, and topical antibiotics to combat secondary infection. The patient may apply warm compresses and povidone-iodine gel to the affected skin.

Other Causes of Keratitis. Keratitis may be caused by fungi, such as *Aspergillus*, *Candida*, and *Fusarium* species. This is especially true in the case of eye trauma in an outdoor setting where fungi are prevalent in the soil and moist organic matter.

Acanthamoeba keratitis is caused by a parasite that is associated with contact lens wear, usually from contaminated lens care solutions or cases. Homemade saline solution is particularly susceptible to *Acanthamoeba* contamination. Teach the patient who wears contact lenses about good lens care practices. The treatment of *Acanthamoeba* keratitis is difficult since the organism is resistant to most drugs. Antifungal agents (e.g., ketoconazole) may be given. If antimicrobial therapy fails, the patient may need a corneal transplant.

Exposure keratitis occurs when the eyelids cannot adequately close. The patient with *exophthalmos* (protruding eyeball) from thyroid eye disease or masses posterior to the globe is susceptible to exposure keratitis (Fig. 20.9).

Corneal Ulcer. Tissue loss caused by a corneal infection produces a *corneal ulcer* (infectious keratitis) (Fig. 20.10). The infection can be due to bacteria, viruses, or fungi. Corneal ulcers are often painful. The patient may feel as if there is a foreign body in the eye. Other symptoms can include tearing, purulent or watery discharge, redness, and photophobia. Treatment is aggressive to avoid permanent vision loss. Antibiotic, antiviral, or antifungal eyedrops may be given as often as every hour for the first 24 hours. An untreated corneal ulcer can result in corneal scarring and perforation, or hole in the cornea. A corneal transplant may be needed.

❖ NURSING MANAGEMENT: INFLAMMATION AND INFECTION

Assess ocular changes, such as edema, redness, decreased visual acuity, feelings that a foreign body is present, or discomfort. Record the findings in the patient's record. Consider the psychosocial aspects of the patient's condition, especially when vision is impaired.

The patient's primary need is for information about prescribed care and how to perform that care. Careful asepsis and frequent, thorough hand washing are essential to prevent spreading organisms from one eye to the other, to other patients, to caregivers, and to health care team members. Teach the patient and caregivers how to avoid sources of ocular irritation or infection and to respond appropriately if an eye problem occurs. The patient with infective disorders that may have a sexual mode of transmission needs specific information about those disorders.

Apply warm or cool compresses as needed. Darkening the room and giving an analgesic are other comfort measures. If the patient's visual acuity is decreased, modify the environment and activities for safety. Suggest alternative ways to perform daily activities and self-care.

The patient may need eyedrops as often as every hour. If the patient receives 2 or more different drops, stagger the eye drops to promote maximum absorption. For example, if 2 different eyedrops are ordered hourly, give 1 drop on the hour and 1 drop on the half hour (unless otherwise prescribed). The patient who needs to instill eyedrops frequently may have sleep deprivation. Review the proper technique for eye drop instillation.

Review the use and care of lenses and lens care products. Teach the patient who wears contact lenses and develops infections to discard all opened or used lens care products and cosmetics. This will decrease the risk for reinfection from contaminated products.

DRY EYE DISORDERS

Keratoconjunctivitis sicca (dry eyes) is a common problem, especially in older adults and people with certain systemic autoimmune diseases, such as scleroderma, systemic lupus erythematosus, and Sjögren's. It is caused by a decrease in the quality or quantity of the tear film. Patients with dry eyes report irritation or "sand in my eye." The sensation typically worsens through the day.

Treatment is aimed at the underlying cause. With decreased tear secretion, the patient may use artificial tears or ointments. Cyclosporine ophthalmic emulsion (Restasis) helps to increase the eyes' natural ability to make tears. In severe cases, closure of the lacrimal puncta may be done.

STRABISMUS

Strabismus is a condition in which a person cannot consistently focus both eyes simultaneously on the same object. One eye may deviate in *(esotropia)*, out *(exotropia)*, up *(hypertropia)*, or down

FIG. 20.9 Exophthalmos. (Courtesy Stephen J. Laquis, MD, FACS Ophthalmic Facial Plastic Surgery Specialists, Fort Myers, FL.)

FIG. 20.10 Corneal ulcer. Infection associated with poor contact lens care. (Courtesy Cory J. Bosanko, OD, FAAO, Eye Centers of Tennessee, Crossville, TN.)

(hypotropia). Strabismus in an adult may be caused by thyroid disease, neuromuscular problems of the eye muscles, retinal detachment repair, or cerebral lesions. The primary problem is double vision.

CORNEAL DISORDERS

Corneal Scars

Any wound (e.g., trauma, infection) to the cornea can cause it to become scarred and opacified, thus decreasing the normal transparency. The treatment is a corneal transplant.

Keratoconus

Keratoconus is a noninflammatory, usually bilateral disease with a familial tendency. Keratoconus usually appears during adolescence and slowly progresses between ages 20 and 60 years. The anterior cornea thins and protrudes forward, taking on a cone shape. The only symptom is blurred vision. The astigmatism may be corrected with glasses or rigid contact lenses.

Intacs inserts are generally used to delay the need for a corneal transplant when contact lenses or glasses no longer help a patient achieve adequate vision. They are clear plastic lenses surgically inserted on the cornea perimeter to reduce astigmatism and myopia.

Sometimes, the cornea can perforate as central corneal thinning progresses. In these cases, a corneal transplant is done before the cornea can perforate.

Corneal Transplant. Around 46,000 corneal transplants are done in the United States each year. The surgery is one of the fastest and safest of all tissue or organ transplant surgeries.[11] Indications for corneal transplants (keratoplasty) are corneal scarring and keratoconus. Types include penetrating (full thickness) corneal transplant and lamellar corneal transplant.

Penetrating (full thickness) cornea transplant involves transplanting all the layers of the cornea using a donor cornea. In this procedure, the HCP removes the full thickness of the patient's cornea and replaces it with a donor cornea that is sutured into place (Fig. 20.11). Vision may not be restored for up to 12 months.

During a *lamellar cornea transplant,* only some layers of the cornea are replaced with the transplant. This can include the deepest layer, called the *endothelium* (posterior lamellar cornea transplant). Versions of this procedure include Descemet's stripping endothelial keratoplasty (DSEK) or Descemet's membrane endothelial keratoplasty (DMEK). Lamellar transplants may be better than full penetrating transplants when the disease process is limited to only part of the cornea.

FIG. 20.11 Sutures on a donated cornea after penetrating keratoplasty (corneal transplant). (Courtesy Cory J. Bosanko, OD, FAAO, Eye Centers of Tennessee, Crossville, TN.)

The time between the donor's death and the removal of the tissue should be as short as possible. Eye banks test donors for human immunodeficiency virus (HIV) and hepatitis B and C. The tissue is preserved in a special nutritive solution. Improved methods of tissue procurement and preservation, postoperative topical corticosteroids, and careful follow-up have decreased graft rejection. Matching the blood type of the donor and recipient improves the success rate.

INTRAOCULAR DISORDERS

CATARACT

A **cataract** is an opacity within the lens. The patient may have a cataract in one or both eyes. If cataracts are present in both eyes, one may affect the patient's vision more than the other. Cataract removal is the most common surgery in the United States.[12]

Etiology and Pathophysiology

Although most cataracts are age related *(senile cataracts),* they can be associated with other factors. These include blunt or penetrating trauma, smoking, alcohol use, radiation or UV light exposure, certain drugs (e.g., steroids), and ocular inflammation. The rate of cataract development varies from patient to patient. The patient with diabetes tends to develop cataracts at a younger age.[13]

In senile cataract formation, altered metabolic processes within the lens cause an accumulation of water and changes in the lens fiber structure. These changes affect lens transparency, causing vision changes.

Clinical Manifestations and Diagnostic Studies

The patient with cataracts may have a decrease in vision, abnormal color perception, and glare. Glare is due to light scatter caused by the lens opacities. It may be significantly worse at night when the pupil dilates. The visual decline is gradual.

Diagnosis is based on decreased visual acuity or other visual problem. The opacity is directly observable by ophthalmoscopic or slit lamp microscopic examination. A totally opaque lens creates the appearance of a white pupil. Table 20.6 lists other diagnostic studies that may be helpful in evaluating a cataract.

Interprofessional Care

The presence of a cataract does not necessarily indicate a need for surgery. For many patients the diagnosis is made long before they decide to have surgery. Interprofessional care for cataracts is outlined in Table 20.8.

Nonsurgical Therapy. Currently, no treatment is available to "cure" cataracts other than surgical removal. Often changing the patient's eyewear prescription can improve visual acuity, at least temporarily. Other visual aids, such as strong reading glasses or magnifiers, may help the patient with near vision. Increasing the amount of light to read or do other near-vision tasks is useful. The patient may be willing to adjust his or her lifestyle to adjust to visual decline. For example, if glare makes it hard to drive at night, a patient may choose to drive only during daylight hours or to have a someone else drive at night. Sometimes, informing and reassuring the patient about the disease process makes the patient comfortable about choosing nonsurgical measures, at least temporarily.

Surgical Therapy. When palliative measures no longer provide an acceptable level of visual function, the patient is a

⚛ TABLE 20.8 Interprofessional Care

Cataract

Diagnostic Assessment

- History and physical examination
- Visual acuity measurement
- Ophthalmoscopy (direct and indirect)
- Slit lamp microscopy
- Glare testing, potential acuity testing in selected patients
- Keratometry and A-scan ultrasound (if surgery is planned)
- Other tests (e.g., visual field perimetry) to determine cause of visual loss

Management

Nonsurgical

- Change in glasses prescription
- Strong reading glasses or magnifiers
- Increased lighting
- Lifestyle adjustment

Acute Care: Surgical Therapy

Preoperative

- Mydriatic, cycloplegic agents
- Nonsteroidal antiinflammatory drugs
- Topical antibiotics
- Antianxiety medications

Surgery

- Removal of lens
- Phacoemulsification
- Extracapsular extraction
- Correction of surgical aphakia
- Intraocular lens implantation (most frequent type of correction)
- Contact lenses

Postoperative

- Topical antibiotic
- Topical corticosteroid or other antiinflammatory agent
- Mild analgesia, if necessary
- Eye patch or shield and activity as prescribed

FIG. 20.12 Intraocular lens implant after cataract surgery. (Courtesy Cory J. Bosanko, OD, FAAO, Eye Centers of Tennessee, Crossville, TN.)

candidate for surgery. The patient's occupational needs and lifestyle changes are also factors affecting the decision to have surgery. In some instances, factors other than the patient's visual needs may influence the need for surgery. Lens-induced problems, such as increased IOP, may require lens removal. Opacities may prevent the HCP from getting a clear view of the retina in the patient with diabetic retinopathy or other sight-threatening pathologic conditions. In those cases, the cataract is removed to allow visualization of the retina and adequate management of the problem.

Preoperative Phase. Before surgery, obtain an appropriate history and physical examination. Because most patients have local anesthesia, they do not need extensive preoperative physical assessment. However, most patients with cataracts are older adults who may have several medical problems that should be evaluated and controlled before surgery. Most patients are admitted on an outpatient basis. The patient normally presents several hours before surgery to allow time for preoperative procedures.

The patient receives a nonsteroidal antiinflammatory eyedrop to reduce inflammation and dilating drops. One type of drug used for dilation is a *mydriatic,* an α-adrenergic agonist that produces pupillary dilation by contracting the iris dilator

muscle. Another type of drug is a *cycloplegic,* such as tropicamide (Mydriacyl), which are anticholinergic agents. They block the effects of acetylcholine on the ciliary body muscles. This produces paralysis of accommodation (cycloplegia), and on the iris sphincter muscle, pupillary dilation (mydriasis). The patient may receive antianxiety medication before surgery.

 DRUG ALERT Cycloplegics and Mydriatics

- Teach the patient to wear dark glasses to minimize photophobia.
- Monitor for signs of systemic toxicity (e.g., tachycardia, CNS effects).

Intraoperative Phase. The most common form of cataract surgery is *phacoemulsification.* In this procedure, a very small incision is made in the surface of the eye in or near the cornea. A thin ultrasound probe is inserted into the eye and ultrasonic vibrations are used to dissolve the clouded lens into fragments. These pieces are then suctioned out through the same ultrasound probe. The small incisions are self-sealing and usually do not need sutures.

An *extracapsular cataract extraction procedure* is used for very advanced cataracts where the lens is too dense to dissolve into fragments. This technique requires a larger incision so that the cataract can be removed in one piece without being fragmented inside the eye. Sutures are needed to close the larger wound, and visual recovery is often slower.

Most patients have an IOL implanted at the time of cataract extraction surgery (Fig. 20.12). The lens of choice is a posterior chamber lens that is placed in the capsular bag behind the iris. At the end of the procedure, other drugs, such as antibiotics and corticosteroids, may be given.

Postoperative Phase. Unless complications occur, the patient is usually ready to go home as soon as the effects of sedative agents have worn off. Postoperative medications usually include antibiotic drops to prevent infection and corticosteroid drops to decrease the inflammatory response. The eyedrops are gradually reduced in frequency and then stopped when the eye has healed.

Recommendations for activity restrictions and nighttime eye shielding vary based on the HCP's preference. Many prefer that the patient avoid activities that increase the IOP, such as bending or stooping, coughing, or lifting.

During each postoperative examination, the HCP measures the patient's visual acuity, checks anterior chamber depth, assesses corneal clarity, and measures IOP. Even on the operative day, the patient's uncorrected visual acuity in the operative eye may be good. However, it is not unusual if the patient's visual acuity is reduced right after surgery. Multifocal IOL can correct for both near and far vision. Some patients may still need glasses or contact lenses to achieve their best visual acuity.

❖ NURSING MANAGEMENT: CATARACTS

◆ Nursing Assessment

Assess the patient's distance and near visual acuity. If the patient is going to have surgery, especially note the visual acuity in the patient's unoperated eye. Use this information to determine how visually compromised the patient may be while the operative eye is healing. Assess the psychosocial impact of the visual disability and the level of knowledge about the disease process and therapeutic options. After surgery, assess the patient's level of comfort and ability to follow the discharge plan.

◆ Planning

Preoperatively, the overall goals are that the patient with a cataract will (1) make informed decisions about therapeutic options and (2) have minimal anxiety. Postoperatively, the overall goals are that the patient with a cataract will (1) understand and follow discharge instructions, (2) maintain an acceptable level of physical and emotional comfort, and (3) remain free of infection and other complications.

◆ Nursing Implementation

◆ **Health Promotion.** There are no proven measures to prevent cataract development. However, it is wise to suggest that the patient wear sunglasses, avoid unnecessary radiation, and maintain appropriate intake of antioxidant vitamins (e.g., vitamins C, E) and good nutrition. Provide information about vision enhancement techniques for the patient who chooses not to have surgery.

◆ **Acute Care.** Before surgery, the patient with cataracts needs accurate information about the disease process and treatment options, since cataract surgery is considered an elective procedure. Be available to the patient and caregiver to help them make an informed decision about treatment. For the patient having surgery, provide information, support, and reassurance about the surgical and postoperative experience to reduce anxiety.

Photophobia is common when receiving pupil dilation medications. Therefore decreasing the room lighting is helpful. These medications produce transient stinging and burning.

After cataract surgery the patient usually has little or no pain but may have some scratchiness or blurriness in the operative eye. Mild analgesics are usually enough to relieve any pain. If the pain is intense, the patient should notify the HCP because this may indicate hemorrhage, infection, or increased IOP. A nursing care plan for the patient after eye surgery (eNursing Care Plan 20.1) is available on the website for this chapter.

◆ **Ambulatory Care.** Patients with cataracts who have surgery remain in the surgical facility for only a few hours. The patient and caregiver are responsible for almost all postoperative care. Give them written and verbal instructions before discharge. Include the caregiver in the instructions because some patients may have difficulty with self-care activities, especially if the vision in the unoperated eye is poor. Table 20.9 outlines patient and caregiver teaching after eye surgery.

Most patients have little visual impairment after surgery. IOL implants provide immediate visual improvement. Many

TABLE 20.9 Patient & Caregiver Teaching

After Eye Surgery

Include the following information in the teaching plan for the patient and caregiver after eye surgery:

- Proper hygiene and eye care techniques to ensure that medications, dressings, and/or surgical wound is not contaminated during eye care
- Signs and symptoms of infection (e.g., increased or purulent drainage, increased redness, any decrease in visual acuity) and when and how to report these to allow for early recognition and treatment of possible infection
- Importance of following restrictions on head positioning, bending, coughing, and Valsalva maneuver to optimize visual outcomes and prevent increased IOP
- How to instill eye medications using aseptic techniques and adherence with prescribed eye medication routine to prevent infection
- How to take pain medication and report pain not relieved by medication
- Importance of continued follow-up as recommended to maximize potential visual outcomes

patients achieve a usable level of visual acuity within a few days after surgery.

A few patients may have significant visual impairment after surgery. These include patients who do not have an IOL implanted at the time of surgery, those who need several weeks to achieve a usable level of visual acuity after surgery, or those with poor vision in their unoperated eye. For those patients, the time between surgery and receiving glasses or contacts can be a period of significant visual disability. Suggest ways the patient and caregiver can modify activities and the environment to maintain an adequate level of safe functioning. Suggestions may include getting help with steps, removing area rugs and other potential obstacles, preparing meals for freezing before surgery, or obtaining audio books for diversion until visual acuity improves.

If a patch is used, tell patients that they will not have depth perception until the patch is removed. This makes special measures to avoid falls or other injuries necessary. The patient with significant visual impairment in the unoperated eye needs more help while the operative eye is patched. Some patients may need 1 or 2 weeks for the visual acuity in the operated eye to reach an adequate level for most visual needs. These patients need special assistance until the vision improves.

◆ Evaluation

The overall expected outcomes are that the patient after cataract surgery will:
- Have improved vision
- Be better able to take care of self
- Have minimal to no pain
- Be optimistic about expected outcomes

👤 Gerontologic Considerations: Cataracts

Most patients with cataracts are older. When the older patient is visually impaired, even temporarily, the patient may have a loss of independence, lack of control over her or his life, and a significant change in self-perception. Societal devaluation of the older adult complicates these experiences. The older patient often needs emotional support and encouragement, as well as specific suggestions to allow a maximum level of independent function. Assure the older patient that cataract surgery can be done safely and comfortably with minimal sedation.

RETINOPATHY

Retinopathy is a process of microvascular damage to the retina. It can develop slowly or rapidly and lead to blurred vision and progressive vision loss. Retinopathy occurs most often in adults with diabetes or hypertension.

Diabetic retinopathy is a common complication of diabetes, especially in patients with long-standing uncontrolled disease.[13] *Nonproliferative retinopathy* is the most common form of diabetic retinopathy. It is characterized by capillary microaneurysms, retinal swelling, and hard exudates. Macular edema represents a worsening of the retinopathy as plasma leaks from macular blood vessels. As capillary walls weaken, they can rupture, leading to intraretinal "dot or blot" hemorrhaging (Fig. 20.13). A severe loss in central vision can result. As the disease advances, *proliferative retinopathy* may occur. New blood vessels grow, but they are abnormal, fragile, and predisposed to leak, thus causing severe vision loss. (Diagnosis and treatment of diabetic retinopathy are discussed in Chapter 48.)

Hypertensive retinopathy is caused by blockages in retinal blood vessels from hypertension. (Hypertension is discussed in Chapter 32.) These changes may not initially affect a person's vision. On a routine eye examination, retinal hemorrhages, anoxic cotton-wool spots, and macular swelling can be seen. Sustained, severe hypertension can cause sudden visual loss from swelling of the optic disc and nerve *(papilledema)*. Treatment, which may be an emergency, focuses on lowering the BP. Normal vision is usually restored by treating hypertension.

RETINAL DETACHMENT

A **retinal detachment** is a separation of the sensory retina and the underlying pigment epithelium, with fluid accumulation between the 2 layers. In the patient with no other risk factors who has had a retinal detachment in one eye, the risk for detachment in the second eye is as high as 25%.[14] Most patients with an untreated, symptomatic retinal detachment become blind in the involved eye.

Etiology and Pathophysiology

Retinal detachment has many causes. The most common is a retinal break. *Retinal breaks* are an interruption in the full thickness of the retinal tissue. They can be classified as tears or holes. *Retinal holes* are atrophic retinal breaks that occur spontaneously. *Retinal tears* can occur as the vitreous humor shrinks during aging and pulls on the retina. The retina tears when the traction force exceeds the strength of the retina. Once the retina has a break, liquid vitreous can enter the subretinal space between the sensory layer and the retinal pigment epithelium layer, causing a *rhegmatogenous* retinal detachment. Risk factors for retinal detachment are listed in Table 20.10.

Clinical Manifestations and Diagnostic Studies

Patients with a detaching retina describe symptoms that include *photopsia* (light flashes), floaters, and a "cobweb," "hairnet," or ring in the field of vision. Once the retina has detached, the patient describes a painless loss of peripheral or central vision, "like a curtain" coming across the field of vision.

The area of visual loss corresponds inversely to the area of detachment. For example, if the retinal detachment involves the superior retina, the defect is seen in the inferior visual field. If the detachment is small or develops slowly, the patient may not be aware of a visual problem.

Visual acuity measurements should be the first diagnostic procedure with any report of vision loss (Table 20.11). The HCP

TABLE 20.10 Risk Factors for Retinal Detachment

- Age
- Cataract surgery
- Eye trauma
- Family or personal history of retinal detachment
- Severe myopia

Source: National Eye Institute, National Institutes of Health: Retinal detachment. Retrieved from *www.nei.nih.gov/health/retinaldetach.*

TABLE 20.11 Interprofessional Care

Retinal Detachment

Diagnostic Assessment

- History and physical examination
- Visual acuity measurement
- Ophthalmoscopy (direct and indirect)
- Slit lamp microscopy
- Ultrasound if cornea, lens, or vitreous is hazy or opaque

Management
Preoperative

- Mydriatic, cycloplegic agents
- Photocoagulation of retinal break that has not progressed to detachment

Surgery

- Laser photocoagulation
- Cryopexy
- Scleral buckling procedure
- Vitrectomy
- Intravitreal bubble

Postoperative

- Topical antibiotic
- Topical corticosteroid
- Analgesia
- Mydriatics
- Positioning and activity as prescribed

FIG. 20.13 Diabetic retinopathy. Intraretinal dot or blot hemorrhages. (Courtesy Cory J. Bosanko, OD, FAAO, Eye Centers of Tennessee, Crossville, TN.)

can see a retinal detachment using direct and indirect ophthalmoscopy or slit lamp microscopy in conjunction with a special lens to view the far periphery of the retina. Ultrasound may be useful in finding a retinal detachment if the retina cannot be directly visualized (e.g., when the cornea, lens, or vitreous is hazy or opaque).

Interprofessional Care

Some retinal breaks are not likely to progress to detachment. In these situations, the HCP simply monitors the patient and teaches the patient to seek immediate evaluation if warning signs and symptoms of impending detachment occur. The goals of treatment are to re-attach the retina and seal any retinal breaks. Several techniques are used to meet these goals.

Surgical Therapy

Laser Photocoagulation and Cryopexy. These techniques seal retinal breaks by creating an inflammatory reaction that causes a chorioretinal adhesion or scar. *Laser photocoagulation* involves using an intense, precisely focused light beam to create an inflammatory reaction. The light is directed at the area of the retinal break. *Cryopexy* involves freezing (cryotherapy) the retinal break by placing a probe on the ocular surface at the location of the break. The probe is activated with compressed nitrous oxide gas that temporarily freezes the break. The freeze thaw reaction creates scarring in the area that will seal the break.

For retinal breaks accompanied by significant detachment, photocoagulation or cryopexy may be used intraoperatively in conjunction with scleral buckling. Tears or holes without accompanying retinal detachment may be treated prophylactically with laser photocoagulation or cryopexy if there is a high risk for progression to a retinal detachment. When used alone, laser photocoagulation and cryopexy therapy are outpatient procedures. They usually require topical anesthesia. The patient may have minimal adverse symptoms during or after the procedure.

Scleral Buckling. Scleral buckling is an extraocular surgical procedure that involves placing a band around the globe to move the pigment epithelium, choroid, and sclera toward the detached retina. A silicone implant is sutured against the sclera, causing the sclera to buckle inward. An encircling band may be placed over the implant if there are multiple retinal breaks, if suspected breaks cannot be found, or if there is widespread inward traction on the retina (Fig. 20.14). If present, subretinal fluid may be drained using a small-gauge needle. This promotes contact between the retina and buckled sclera. Scleral buckling is usually done as an outpatient procedure.

Intraocular Procedures. Intraocular procedures are used on occasion. *Pneumatic retinopexy* is the intravitreal injection of a gas to form a temporary bubble in the vitreous that closes retinal breaks and provides apposition of the separated retinal layers. Because the intravitreal bubble is temporary, this technique is combined with laser photocoagulation or cryopexy. The patient with an intravitreal bubble must position the head so that the bubble is in contact with the retinal break. The patient may need to maintain this position as much as possible for up to several weeks.

Vitrectomy (surgical removal of the vitreous) may relieve traction on the retina, especially when the traction results from proliferative diabetic retinopathy. Vitrectomy may be combined with scleral buckling to provide a dual effect in relieving traction.

Postoperative Considerations. Visual prognosis varies, depending on the extent, length, and area of detachment. After surgery, the patient may be on bed rest and need special positioning to maintain proper position of an intravitreal bubble. The level of activity restriction after retinal detachment surgery varies. Verify the prescribed level of activity with the HCP and help the patient plan for any help needed related to activity restrictions.

The patient may need multiple topical medications, including antibiotics, antiinflammatory agents, or dilating agents. Give prescribed pain medications and teach the patient to take the medication as prescribed after discharge.

In most cases, retinal detachment is an urgent situation, and the patient is suddenly confronted with the need for surgery. The patient needs emotional support, especially during the immediate preoperative period when preparations for surgery can lead to more anxiety.

The patient may go home within a few hours of surgery or may remain in the hospital for several days, depending on the surgeon and type of repair. Discharge planning and teaching are important and should begin early. Patient and caregiver teaching after eye surgery is discussed in Table 20.11. Because the patient is at increased risk for retinal detachment in the other eye, teach the patient the signs and symptoms of retinal detachment. Promote the use of proper protective eyewear to help avoid damage related to trauma.

FIG. 20.14 Retinal break with detachment and surgical repair by scleral buckling technique.

AGE-RELATED MACULAR DEGENERATION

Age-related macular degeneration (AMD) is the most common cause of irreversible central vision loss in people over age 60 in the United States. AMD is classified as dry (nonexudative) or wet (exudative). *Dry AMD* is the more common form, accounting for 90% of all cases. Those with dry AMD often notice that close vision tasks become harder. In dry AMD, the macular cells start to atrophy. This leads to a slowly progressive and painless vision loss.

Wet AMD is the more severe form. It accounts for most cases of AMD-related blindness. Wet AMD has a more rapid onset of vision loss. With wet AMD there is the development of abnormal blood vessels in or near the macula. Many patients with wet AMD have dry AMD first.

Etiology and Pathophysiology

AMD is related to retinal aging. Genetic factors also play a major role, and family history is a major risk factor for AMD.[15] Other risk factors include light-colored irises, high C-reactive protein levels, smoking, and hypertension.

Dry AMD starts with the abnormal accumulation of yellowish extracellular deposits called *drusen* in the retinal pigment epithelium. Over time atrophy and degeneration of macular cells occur. In wet AMD, vascular endothelial growth factor (VEGF) promotes the growth of new blood vessels in an abnormal location in the retinal epithelium. As the new blood vessels grow, they leak fluid and can bleed, causing scar tissue to gradually form.

Clinical Manifestations and Diagnostic Studies

Acute vision loss may occur from either the dry or wet forms of AMD. The patient may have blurred and darkened vision, *scotomas* (blind spots in the visual field), and *metamorphopsia* (distortion of vision). If only one eye is affected, the patient may not notice early changes in vision.

In addition to visual acuity measurement, the primary diagnostic procedure is ophthalmoscopy. The HCP looks for drusen and other fundus changes associated with AMD. The Amsler grid test may help define the involved area. It provides a baseline for future comparison (Fig. 20.15). Fundus photography and IV angiography with fluorescein and/or indocyanine green dyes may help to further determine the extent and type of AMD. Retinal anatomy can be analyzed using optical coherence tomography (OCT) or scanning laser ophthalmoscopy.

Interprofessional Care

Visual prognosis varies greatly. Limited treatment options for patients with wet AMD include medications that are injected directly into the vitreous cavity. Ranibizumab (Lucentis), bevacizumab (Avastin), aflibercept (Eylea), and pegaptanib (Macugen) inhibit VEGF. This helps slow vision loss by stopping new vessels from forming.[15] Side effects can include blurred vision, eye irritation, eye pain, and photosensitivity. Injections are given at 4- to 6-week intervals, depending on treatment response. Disease stability is determined by OCT, which looks at pathology in the macula. The findings determine the need for continued intravitreal injections.

Photodynamic therapy (PDT) uses verteporfin (Visudyne) IV and a "cold" laser to excite the dye. The PDT procedure is used in wet AMD to damage the abnormal blood vessels. Verteporfin is a photosensitizing drug that becomes active when exposed to the low-level laser light wave. Until the drug is completely excreted by the body, it can be activated by exposure to sunlight or other high-intensity light, such as halogen. Have patients avoid direct exposure to sunlight and other intense forms of light for 5 days after treatment. Exposure of the skin to sunlight could activate the drug in that area, causing a chemical burn.

Nutritional factors may play a role in the progression of AMD. Dietary supplements of vitamin C, vitamin E, beta-carotene, and zinc decrease the progression of AMD. Lutein/zeaxanthin supplements may help some patients. Teach the patient to eat dark green, leafy vegetables containing lutein (e.g., kale and spinach) and fatty fish at least twice a week.[16] Smoking cessation may help in halting the progression of dry AMD to a more advanced stage.

The management of the patient with visual impairment discussed on p. 359 is appropriate for the patient with AMD. Many patients with low-vision assistive devices can continue reading and keep a license to drive during the daytime and at lowered speeds. The permanent loss of central vision has significant psychosocial implications for nursing care. Avoid giving the impression that "nothing can be done" about the problem when caring for the patient with AMD. Although therapy may not recover lost vision, much can be done to augment the remaining vision.

GLAUCOMA

Glaucoma is a group of disorders characterized by increased IOP and its' consequences, optic nerve atrophy, and peripheral visual field loss. Glaucoma is the second leading cause of permanent blindness in the United States and the leading cause of blindness among blacks.[3,17] Many people with glaucoma are unaware of their condition. The incidence of glaucoma increases with age. Blindness from glaucoma is largely preventable with early detection and proper treatment. Genetic factors play a role in some types of glaucoma.[17]

Etiology and Pathophysiology

A proper balance between the rate of aqueous production (*inflow*) and the rate of aqueous reabsorption (*outflow*) is essential to maintain the IOP within normal limits. We call the place where the outflow occurs the *angle* because it is the angle where the iris meets the cornea. When the rate of inflow is greater than the rate of outflow, IOP can increase above the normal limits. If IOP stays increased, permanent vision loss may occur.

Primary open-angle glaucoma (POAG) is the most common type of glaucoma. In POAG the outflow of aqueous humor is decreased in the trabecular meshwork. The drainage channels become clogged, like a clogged kitchen sink. Damage to the optic nerve can then result.

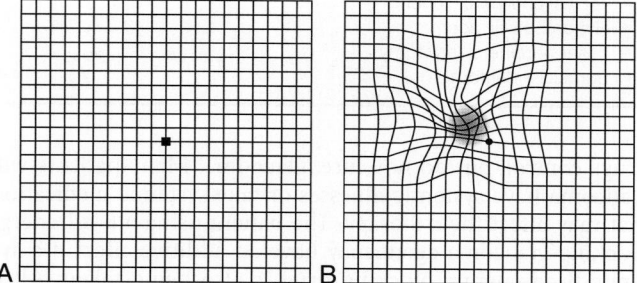

FIG. 20.15 Amsler grid. **A,** Normal grid. **B,** Abnormal grid as seen by person with macular degeneration.

Angle-closure glaucoma (ACG) is due to a reduction in the outflow of aqueous humor that results from angle closure. Usually, this is caused by the lens bulging forward because of the aging process. Angle closure may also occur because of pupil dilation in the patient with anatomically narrow angles. Acute angle-closure glaucoma (AACG) may be precipitated by situations in which the pupil stays partially dilated long enough to cause an acute and significant rise in the IOP. This may occur because of drug-induced mydriasis, emotional excitement, or darkness. Drug-induced mydriasis may occur from topical eye preparations or many systemic medications (both prescription and OTC). Check medication records before giving medications to the patient with ACG. Teach the patient not to take any mydriatic medications.

Clinical Manifestations

POAG develops slowly and without symptoms of pain or pressure. The patient usually does not notice the gradual visual field loss until peripheral vision has been severely compromised. Eventually, the patient with untreated glaucoma has "tunnel vision," with only a small center visual field. All peripheral vision is absent.

AACG causes definite symptoms, including sudden, severe pain in or around the eye. The patient often has nausea and vomiting. Visual symptoms include seeing colored halos around lights, blurred vision, and ocular redness.

Manifestations of subacute or chronic ACG appear more gradually. The patient who had a previous, unrecognized episode of subacute ACG may report blurred vision, seeing colored halos around lights, ocular redness, or eye or brow pain.

Diagnostic Studies

IOP is usually increased in glaucoma (normal is 10 to 21 mm Hg). In the patient with increased pressures, the measurements are repeated over time to verify the elevation. In POAG, IOP is usually between 22- and 32-mm Hg. In AACG, IOP may be more than 50 mm Hg.

In POAG, slit lamp microscopy reveals a normal angle. In ACG, there may be a markedly narrow or flat anterior chamber angle, an edematous cornea, a fixed and moderately dilated pupil, and ciliary injection (hyperemia of the ciliary blood vessels produces a red color).

Measures of peripheral and central vision provide more diagnostic information. While central acuity may remain 20/20 even in the presence of severe peripheral visual field loss, visual field perimetry may reveal subtle changes in the peripheral vision early in the disease process, long before actual scotomas develop. In ACG, central visual acuity is reduced if the patient has corneal edema, and the visual fields may be markedly decreased. As glaucoma progresses, *optic disc cupping* may be one of the first signs of chronic POAG. The optic disc becomes wider, deeper, and paler (light gray or white), which is visible with direct or indirect ophthalmoscopy (Fig. 20.16).

Interprofessional Care

The primary focus of glaucoma therapy is to keep the IOP low enough to prevent the patient from developing optic nerve damage. Therapy varies with the type of glaucoma. The diagnostic and interprofessional care of glaucoma is outlined in Table 20.12.
Chronic Open-Angle Glaucoma. Drug therapy is the initial treatment in POAG (Table 20.13). The patient must understand that continued treatment and supervision are needed because the

FIG. 20.16 A, In the normal eye the optic cup is pink with little cupping. B, In glaucoma the optic cup is bleached and optic cupping is present. (Note the appearance of the retinal vessels, which travel over the edge of the optic cup and appear to dip into it.)

TABLE 20.12 Interprofessional Care

Glaucoma

Diagnostic Assessment
- History and physical examination
- Visual acuity measurement
- Tonometry
- Ophthalmoscopy (direct and indirect)
- Slit lamp microscopy
- Gonioscopy
- Visual field perimetry

Management
Chronic Open-Angle Glaucoma
Drug Therapy (Table 20.13)
- β-Adrenergic blockers
- α-Adrenergic agonists
- Cholinergic agents (miotics)
- Carbonic anhydrase inhibitors

Surgical Therapy
- Argon laser trabeculoplasty (ALT)
- Trabeculectomy with or without filtering implant

Acute Angle-Closure Glaucoma
- Topical cholinergic agent
- Hyperosmotic agent
- Laser peripheral iridotomy
- Surgical iridectomy

drugs control, but do not cure, glaucoma. Many patients with glaucoma have systemic illnesses or take systemic medications that may affect their therapy. The patient using a β-adrenergic blocking glaucoma agent may have an additive effect if a systemic β-adrenergic blocking drug is also being taken. All β-adrenergic blocking glaucoma agents are contraindicated in the patient with bradycardia, heart block greater than first-degree

TABLE 20.13 Drug Therapy

Acute and Chronic Glaucoma

Drug	Action	Side Effects	Nursing Considerations
α-Adrenergic Agonists			
apraclonidine (Iopidine), brimonidine (Alphagan)	↓ Aqueous humor production	Ocular redness, irregular heart rate	Topical drops Used to control or prevent acute postlaser IOP rise (used before and immediately after ALT and iridotomy, Nd:YAG laser capsulotomy) Teach patient at risk for systemic reactions to occlude puncta
α- and β-Adrenergic Agonists			
dipivefrin (Propine)	Converted to epinephrine inside the eye aqueous humor production, enhances outflow facility	Ocular discomfort and redness, tachycardia, hypertension	Topical drops Contraindicated in patient with narrow-angle glaucoma Teach punctal occlusion if patient at risk for systemic reactions
epinephrine	Same as dipivefrin	Same as dipivefrin, but can be more pronounced	Topical drops Same as dipivefrin
β-Adrenergic Blockers			
betaxolol (Betoptic)	β₁ cardioselective ↓ IOP, ↓ aqueous humor production	Transient discomfort Systemic reactions rarely reported but include bradycardia, heart block, pulmonary distress, headache, depression	Topical drugs Contraindicated in patient with bradycardia, cardiogenic shock, or heart failure Systemic absorption can have additive effect with systemic β₁-blocking agents
levobunolol (Betagan) timolol maleate (Timoptic, Istalol)	β₁ and β₂ noncardioselective blockers ↓ IOP, ↓ aqueous humor production	Transient ocular discomfort, blurred vision, photophobia, bradycardia, decreased BP, bronchospasm, headache, depression	Topical drops Same as betaxolol Contraindicated in patients with asthma or COPD
Carbonic Anhydrase Inhibitors			
Systemic			
acetazolamide (Diamox) dichlorphenamide (Daranide) methazolamide	↓ Aqueous humor production	Paresthesias, especially "tingling" in extremities, hearing problems or tinnitus, loss of appetite, taste changes, GI problems, drowsiness, confusion	Oral nonbacteriostatic sulfonamides Anaphylaxis and other sulfa-type allergic reactions may occur in patient allergic to sulfa Diuretic effect can ↓ electrolyte levels Do not give to patient on high-dose aspirin therapy
Topical			
brinzolamide (Azopt) dorzolamide (Trusopt)	↓ Aqueous humor production	Transient stinging, blurred vision, redness	Anaphylaxis and other sulfa-type allergic reactions may occur in patient allergic to sulfa
Cholinergic Agents (Miotics)			
carbachol (Miostat, Isopto Carbachol)	Parasympathomimetic Stimulates iris sphincter contraction, causing miosis and opening of trabecular meshwork, facilitating aqueous outflow Partially inhibits cholinesterase	Transient ocular discomfort, headache, blurred vision, decreased adaptation to the dark, syncope, salivation, dysrhythmias, vomiting, diarrhea, hypotension	Topical drops Caution patient about ↓ visual acuity caused by miosis, particularly in dim light
pilocarpine (Isopto Carpine, Pilocar)	Parasympathomimetic Stimulates iris sphincter contraction, causing miosis and opening of trabecular meshwork, facilitating aqueous humor outflow	Same as carbachol	Topical drops Same as carbachol
Prostaglandin Agonists			
bimatoprost (Lumigan) latanoprost (Xalatan) tafluprost (Zioptan) travoprost	↓ Outflow of aqueous humor between the uvea and sclera and the usual exit through the trabecular meshwork	Increased brown iris pigmentation, ocular discomfort and redness, dryness, itching, and foreign body sensation	Topical drops Teach patient to only administer 1 drop per day Have patient remove contact lens 15 min before instilling

ALT, Argon laser trabeculoplasty; *Nd:YAG,* neodymium-doped yttrium aluminum garnet (laser).

heart block, cardiogenic shock, and heart failure. The noncardioselective β-adrenergic blocking glaucoma agents are contraindicated in the patient with chronic obstructive pulmonary disease (COPD) or asthma. The hyperosmolar agents may precipitate heart failure or pulmonary edema in the susceptible patient. The patient on high-dose aspirin therapy should not take carbonic anhydrase inhibitors. The α-adrenergic agonists can cause tachycardia or hypertension. This may have profound consequences in the older patient.

Argon laser trabeculoplasty (ALT) is a noninvasive way to lower IOP when medications are not successful or when the patient either cannot or will not use the drug therapy as recommended. ALT is an outpatient procedure that uses topical anesthetic. The laser stimulates scarring and contraction of the trabecular meshwork, which opens the outflow channels. ALT reduces IOP most of the time. The patient uses topical corticosteroids for 3 to 5 days after the procedure. The most common complication is an acute rise in IOP. The HCP examines the patient at 1 week and again at 4 to 6 weeks after surgery.

Filtration surgery, also called a *trabeculectomy,* may be used if medical management and laser therapy are not successful.

Acute Angle-Closure Glaucoma. AACG is an ocular emergency that needs immediate intervention. Miotics (Table 20.13) and oral or IV hyperosmotic agents, including glycerin liquid (Ophthalgan), isosorbide solution (Ismotic), and mannitol solution (Osmitrol), are usually successful in immediately lowering IOP. A laser peripheral iridotomy or surgical iridectomy is necessary for long-term treatment and prevention of more episodes. These procedures allow the aqueous humor to flow through a newly created opening in the iris and into normal outflow channels. A procedure may be done on the other eye as a precaution because many patients often have an acute attack in the other eye.

 DRUG ALERT Miotics

• Warn patients about decreased visual acuity, especially in dim light.

❖ NURSING MANAGEMENT: GLAUCOMA

◆ Nursing Assessment

Because glaucoma is a chronic condition requiring long-term management, assess the patient's ability to understand and adhere to the therapy plan. Assess the patient's psychologic reaction to the diagnosis of a potentially sight-threatening chronic disorder. Include the patient's caregiver in the assessment process because the chronic nature of this disorder affects them too. For example, caregivers may become the eyedrop administrator if the patient is unwilling or unable.

◆ Nursing Diagnoses

Nursing diagnoses for the patient with glaucoma include:
• Risk for injury
• Acute pain

◆ Planning

The overall goals are that the patient with glaucoma will (1) have no progression of visual impairment, (2) follow the treatment plan, and (3) have no complications.

◆ Nursing Implementation

◆ **Health Promotion.** Loss of vision because of glaucoma is a preventable problem. Teach the patient and caregiver about the risk for glaucoma and that it increases with age. Stress the importance of early detection and treatment in preventing visual impairment. A comprehensive eye examination is important in identifying people with glaucoma or those at risk for developing glaucoma. The current recommendation is for an eye examination every 2 to 4 years for people between ages 40 and 64 years, and every 1 to 2 years for people age 65 years or older. Blacks in every age category should have one more often because of the increased incidence and more aggressive course of glaucoma.[17]

◆ **Acute Care.** Acute nursing interventions are directed primarily toward the patient with AACG and the surgical patient. The patient with AACG needs medication immediately to lower the IOP. Most surgeries for glaucoma are outpatient procedures. Provide care to relieve any discomfort related to the procedure. Patient and caregiver teaching after eye surgery is discussed in Table 20.9.

◆ **Ambulatory Care.** Because of the chronic nature of glaucoma, teach the patient to follow the therapy plan and follow-up recommendations prescribed by the HCP. Provide accurate information about the disease process and treatment options, including the reason for each option. In addition, the patient needs information about the purpose, frequency, and technique for administering antiglaucoma drugs. Encourage adherence by helping the patient set up a medication administration schedule and advocating a change in therapy if the patient reports unacceptable side effects.

◆ Evaluation

The overall expected outcomes are that the patient with glaucoma will:
• Have no further loss of vision
• Adhere to the recommended therapy
• Safely function within own environment
• Have relief from pain associated with the disease and surgery

INTRAOCULAR INFLAMMATION AND INFECTION

The term *uveitis* is used to describe inflammation of the uveal tract, retina, vitreous body, or optic nerve. Inflammation may be caused by bacteria, viruses, fungi, or parasites. *Cytomegalovirus retinitis* (CMV retinitis) is an opportunistic infection that occurs in patients with acquired immunodeficiency syndrome (AIDS) and in other immunosuppressed patients. The cause of sterile intraocular inflammation includes autoimmune disorders, AIDS, cancer, or disorders associated with systemic diseases, such as inflammatory bowel disease. Pain and photophobia are common symptoms.

Endophthalmitis is an extensive intraocular inflammation of the vitreous cavity. Bacteria, viruses, fungi, or parasites can induce this serious inflammatory response. The mechanism of infection may be endogenous, in which the infecting agent arrives at the eye through the bloodstream, or exogenous, in which the infecting agent is introduced through a surgical wound or a penetrating injury. Although rare, endophthalmitis is a devastating complication of intraocular surgery or penetrating ocular injury. It can lead to irreversible blindness within hours or days. Manifestations include ocular pain, photophobia, decreased visual acuity, headaches, reddened and swollen conjunctiva, and corneal edema.

Treatment depends on the underlying cause. Intraocular infections require antimicrobial agents. They may be delivered topically, subconjunctivally, intravitreally, systemically, or in some combination. Inflammatory responses require antiinflammatory medications (e.g., corticosteroids). The patient with intraocular inflammation is usually uncomfortable and may be noticeably anxious and frightened. Provide accurate information and emotional support to the patient and caregiver. In severe cases, enucleation may be needed. When the patient has lost visual function or even the entire eye, the patient will grieve the loss. Your role includes helping the patient through the grieving process.

OCULAR TUMORS

Benign and cancerous tumors can occur in many areas of the eye, including the conjunctiva, retina, and orbit.[18] Eyelid cancers include basal cell and squamous cell cancers (see Chapter 23).

Uveal melanoma is a cancer of the iris, choroid, or ciliary body. It more often occurs in light-skinned people with light eye color, who are over age 60, and have chronic UV exposure.[19] Uveal melanoma can arise from preexisting nevi in the eye. Tumors may be asymptomatic or associated with vision loss. This depends on their size and location and presence of hemorrhage and retinal detachment. As with other cancers, cancer stage and cell type are important variables in the prognosis. Diagnostic testing may include ultrasound, MRI, and fine-needle aspiration biopsy. Uveal melanoma often appears as a dome-shaped, well-circumscribed, solid brown to golden pigment in the iris, choroid, or ciliary body (Fig. 20.17).

Depending on the status of the involved eye, treatment options can include enucleation, radiation therapy (brachytherapy), external beam radiation, transpupillary photocoagulation, eye wall resection, and eye removal. Many patients do not lose their eye. Some may have good vision after treatment in the affected eye.

ENUCLEATION

Enucleation is the removal of the eye. The primary reason for enucleation is a blind, painful eye. This may result from glaucoma, infection, or trauma. Enucleation may be used to treat ocular cancer. The surgical procedure includes severing the extraocular muscles close to their insertion on the globe, inserting an implant to maintain the intraorbital anatomy, and suturing the ends of the muscles over the implant. The conjunctiva covers the joined muscles, and a clear conformer is placed over the conjunctiva until the permanent prosthesis is fitted. A pressure dressing helps prevent bleeding.

FIG. 20.17 Uveal melanoma. A large tumor in the choroid, the most common location in the eye for melanoma. (Courtesy Cory J. Bosanko, OD, FAAO, Eye Centers of Tennessee, Crossville, TN.)

After surgery, observe the patient for signs of complications, including excess bleeding or swelling, increased pain, displacement of the implant, and fever. Patient teaching should include the instillation of topical ointments or drops and wound cleansing. Teach the patient how to insert the conformer into the socket in case it falls out. The loss of an eye is often devastating, even when enucleation occurs after a lengthy period of painful blindness. Recognize the patient's emotional response and provide support to the patient and caregivers.

About 6 weeks after surgery, the wound is sufficiently healed for the permanent prosthesis. An ocularist fits the prosthesis and designs it to match the remaining eye. Teach the patient how to remove, cleanse, and insert the prosthesis. Special polishing is needed periodically to remove dried protein secretions.

OCULAR MANIFESTATIONS OF SYSTEMIC DISEASES

Many systemic diseases have significant ocular manifestations. Ocular signs and symptoms may be the first finding or complaint in the patient with a systemic disease. One example is the patient with undiagnosed diabetes who seeks eye care for blurred vision. A careful history and examination can reveal that the underlying cause of the blurred vision is lens swelling from hyperglycemia. Another example is the patient who seeks care for a conjunctival lesion. AIDS may be diagnosed based on the presence of a conjunctival Kaposi sarcoma (KS).

CASE STUDY

Glaucoma and Diabetic Retinopathy

(© Kevin Peterson/Stockbyte/Thinkstock.)

Patient Profile

J.K. is a 68-yr-old black woman with a history of osteoarthritis and type 2 diabetes for the past 15 years. She now has diabetic retinopathy. She returns to the eye clinic with her daughter for continued care of primary open-angle glaucoma (POAG) and reexamination for changes in diabetic retinopathy. Her current drug therapy for POAG includes topical timolol maleate 0.5% extended (Timoptic-XE) once daily in both eyes (OU) and latanoprost (Xalatan) 0.005% OU daily at bedtime. At her last examination, she had microaneurysms and hard exudates of the retina.

Subjective Data

• She can no longer read the newspaper and reports that medication labels are difficult to read.
• States she is not always successful in getting the eyedrops instilled because her hands are gnarled and painful from osteoarthritis.

Objective Data

• Distant and near visual acuity are stable at 20/60 (OD) and 20/50 (OS). This is a reduction from 20/40 (OU) at her last visit.
• Intraocular pressure (IOP) stable at 20 mm Hg (OU).
• There is a new scotoma on visual field testing in the OS.
• Fluorescein angiography reveals diabetic macular edema OU.

Continued

CASE STUDY

Glaucoma and Diabetic Retinopathy—cont'd

Interprofessional Care

- Brimonidine 0.15% (OS) 15 min before and immediately after argon laser trabeculoplasty (ALT)
- Argon laser (OU) to seal leaking microaneurysms from macular edema
- Check IOP 1 hr after ALT
- Continue previous glaucoma drop regimen
- Follow-up examination for in 2 wk for possible ALT of OD

Discussion Questions

1. Explain the cause of the new scotoma.
2. Why is ALT an appropriate therapy for J.K.?

3. What is the purpose of the eyedrops before and immediately after ALT?
4. What is the cause of the vision loss from diabetic retinopathy?
5. Priority Decision: Based on the assessment data, what are the priority nursing diagnoses? Are there any collaborative problems?
6. ***Priority Decision:*** What are the priority nursing interventions for J.K.?
7. ***Patient-Centered Care:*** What are the priority topics that should be discussed in discharge teaching with J.K.?
8. ***Evidence-Based Practice:*** J.K. wants to know if her glaucoma is related to her diabetes. How would you respond to her question?

Answers available at *http://evolve.elsevier.com/Lewis/medsurg.*

■ BRIDGE TO NCLEX EXAMINATION

The number of the question corresponds to the same-numbered outcome at the beginning of the chapter.

1. In a patient who has a hemorrhage in the posterior cavity of the eye, the nurse knows that blood is accumulating
   a. in the aqueous humor.
   b. between the lens and retina.
   c. between the cornea and lens.
   d. in the space between the iris and lens.
2. Increased intraocular pressure may occur because of
   a. edema of the corneal stroma.
   b. dilation of the retinal arterioles.
   c. blockage of the lacrimal canals and ducts.
   d. increased aqueous humor production by the ciliary process.
3. Ask patients using eyedrops to treat their glaucoma about
   a. use of corrective lenses.
   b. their usual sleep pattern.
   c. a history of heart or lung disease.
   d. sensitivity to opioids or depressants.
4. Always assess the patient with an eye problem for
   a. visual acuity.
   b. pupillary reactions.
   c. intraocular pressure.
   d. confrontation visual fields.
5. When examining the patient's eyes, which finding would be of *most* concern to the nurse?
   a. Intraocular pressure of 16 mm/Hg
   b. Slightly yellowish cast of the sclera
   c. Outward turning of the lower lid margin
   d. Small, white nodule on the upper lid margin
6. Presbyopia occurs in older people because
   a. the eyeball elongates.
   b. the lens becomes inflexible.
   c. the corneal curvature becomes irregular.
   d. light rays are focusing in front of the retina.
7. Before injecting fluorescein for angiography, it is important for the nurse to *(select all that apply)*
   a. obtain an emesis basin.
   b. ask if the patient is fatigued.
   c. administer a topical anesthetic.
   d. inform patient that skin may turn yellow.
   e. assess for allergies to iodine-based contrast media.

8. A patient says she was diagnosed with astigmatism. When she asks what that is, what is the best explanation the nurse can give to the patient?
   a. "It happens because the lens of the eye is absent."
   b. "People with astigmatism have abnormally long eyeballs."
   c. "The cornea of the eye is uneven or irregular with astigmatism."
   d. "Astigmatism occurs because the eye muscles weaken with age."
9. Which intervention would be part of the plan of care for a patient who has new vision loss?
   a. Allow the patient to express feelings of grief and anger.
   b. Have the UAP perform all self-care activities for the patient.
   c. Address any family present first when discussing care concerns.
   d. Speak loudly and clearly, addressing the patient with each contact.
10. Which patient behaviors would the nurse promote for healthy eyes *(select all that apply)*?
    a. Protective sunglasses when bicycling
    b. Taking part in a smoking cessation program
    c. Supplementing diet intake of vitamin C and beta-carotene
    d. Washing hands thoroughly before putting in or taking out contact lenses
    e. A woman avoiding pregnancy for 4 weeks after receiving MMR immunization
11. The *most* important intervention for the patient with epidemic keratoconjunctivitis is
    a. cleansing the affected area with baby shampoo.
    b. monitoring spread of infection to the opposing eye.
    c. regular instillation of artificial tears to the affected eye.
    d. teaching the patient and caregivers good hygiene techniques.
12. What should be included in the discharge teaching for the patient who had cataract surgery *(select all that apply)*?
    a. Eye discomfort is often relieved with mild analgesics.
    b. A decline in visual acuity is common for the first week.
    c. Stay on bed rest and limit activity for the first few days.
    d. Notify the provider if an increase in redness or drainage occurs.
    e. Following activity restrictions is essential to reduce intraocular pressure.

1. b, 2. d, 3. c, 4. a, 5. d, 6. b, 7. a, d, 8. c, 9. a, 10. a, b, c, d, 11. d, 12. a, d, e

For rationales to these answers and even more NCLEX review questions, visit *http://evolve.elsevier.com/Lewis/medsurg.*

⊖ EVOLVE WEBSITE/RESOURCES LIST

http://evolve.elsevier.com/Lewis/medsurg

Review Questions (Online Only)

Key Points

Answer Keys for Questions

- Rationales for Bridge to NCLEX Examination Questions
- Answer Guidelines for Case Study on pp. 351, 354, 358, and 373

Student Case Study

- Patient Undergoing Cataract Surgery

eNursing Care Plan

- eNursing Care Plan 20.1: Patient After Eye Surgery

Conceptual Care Map Creator

Audio Glossary

Supporting Media

- Animations
- Cataract Removal
- LASIK
- Myringotomy
- Scleral Buckling

Content Updates

REFERENCES

1. Lampignano J, Kendrick L: *Bontrager's textbook of radiographic positioning and related anatomy*, ed 9, St Louis, 2018, Elsevier.
*2. Martin E, Patrianakos T, Giovingo M: Medication induced glaucoma, *Disease-a-Month* 63:54, 2017.
3. National Eye Institute: Statistics and data. Retrieved from *www.nei.nih. gov/eyedata*.
4. American Optometric Association: Myopia. Retrieved from *www.aoa. org/patients-and-public/eye-and-vision-problems/glossary-of-eye-and-vision-conditions/myopia?sso=y*.
5. US Food and Drug Administration: LASIK. Retrieved from *www.fda.gov/ medicaldevices/productsandmedicalprocedures/surgeryandlifesupport/lasik/ default.htm*.
6. American Optometric Association: Low vision. Retrieved from *www.aoa. org/patients-and-public/caring-for-your-vision/low-vision*.
*7. Salva MA, Hartley S, Léger D, et al : Non-24-hour sleep–wake rhythm disorder in the totally blind: Diagnosis and management., *Front Neurol* 8:686, 2017.
8. American Academy of Ophthalmology: Preventing eye injuries. Retrieved from *www.aao.org/eye-health/diseases/preventing-injuries*.
*9. Satpathy G, Behera HS, Ahmed NH: Chlamydial eye infections: Current perspectives, *Indian J Ophthalmol* 65:97, 2017.
*10. Azher TN, Yin XT, Tajfirouz D, et al: Herpes simplex keratitis: Challenges in diagnosis and clinical management, *Clin Ophthalmol* 11:185, 2017.
11. Saving Sight: Important information about saving sight. Retrieved from *www.saving-sight.org/cornea-donation-facts*.
12. Date RC, Al-Mohtaseb ZN: Advances in preoperative testing for cataract surgery, *Internat Ophthalmol Clin* 57:99, 2017.
13. American Diabetes Association: Standards of medical care in diabetes—2018, *Diabetes Care* 1:S105, 2018.
14. Schachat AP, Sadda SR, Hinton DR, et al: *Ryan's retina: Principles and practice*, ed 6, St Louis, 2018, Elsevier.
15. American Macular Degeneration Foundation: About macular degeneration. Retrieved from *www.macular.org/about-macular-degeneration*.
*16. Carneiro Â, Andrade JP: Nutritional and lifestyle interventions for age-related macular degeneration: A review, *Oxid Med Cell Longev*, 2017.
17. Glaucoma Research Foundation: Glaucoma. Retrieved from *www. glaucoma.org/glaucoma/*.
18. International Society of Ocular Oncology: Eye tumors. Retrieved from *www.isoo.org/tumors*.
*19. Pandiani C, Béranger GE, Leclerc J, et al : Focus on cutaneous and uveal melanoma specificities, *Genes Dev* 31:724, 2017.

*Evidence-based information for clinical practice.

21

Assessment and Management: Auditory Problems

Mariann M. Harding

Kindness is a language which the deaf can hear and the blind can see.

Mark Twain

http://evolve.elsevier.com/Lewis/medsurg/

CONCEPTUAL FOCUS

Coping
Functional Ability

Infection
Sensory Perception

LEARNING OUTCOMES

1. Describe the structures and functions of the auditory system.
2. Obtain significant subjective and objective assessment data related to the auditory system from a patient.
3. Perform a physical assessment of the auditory system using the appropriate techniques.
4. Distinguish normal from common abnormal findings of a physical assessment of the auditory system.
5. Link the age-related changes in the auditory system to differences in assessment findings.
6. Describe the purpose, significance of results, and nursing responsibilities related to diagnostic studies of the auditory system.

7. Explain the pathophysiology, clinical manifestations, and nursing and interprofessional management of common ear problems.
8. Compare the common causes, management, and rehabilitative potential of conductive and sensorineural hearing loss.
9. Explain the use, care, and patient teaching related to assistive devices for ear problems.
10. Describe measures used to assist the patient in adapting to decreased hearing.

KEY TERMS

acoustic neuroma, p. 387
benign paroxysmal positional vertigo (BPPV),
    p. 387
external otitis, p. 383

Ménière's disease, p. 386
nystagmus, p. 378
otosclerosis, p. 385
presbycusis, p. 378

tinnitus, p. 378
vertigo, p. 378

AUDITORY SYSTEM

Hearing is a complex process that allows us to interact with the environment. It is the basis for social interaction and communication. Having a hearing impairment can lead to major challenges that can negatively affect well-being. In the adult, difficulties with related concepts, including functional ability and cognition, may be present with hearing loss. This chapter presents an overview of auditory function and discusses care when problems occur.

STRUCTURES AND FUNCTIONS OF AUDITORY SYSTEM

The auditory system is composed of the peripheral auditory system and central auditory system. The peripheral auditory system includes the structures of the ear itself: external, middle, and inner ear (Fig. 21.1). This system is involved with the reception and perception of sound. The inner ear functions in hearing and balance.

The central auditory system integrates and assigns meaning to what one hears. This system includes the vestibulocochlear nerve (cranial nerve [CN] VIII) and auditory cortex of the brain. The brain and its pathways transmit and process sound and sensations that maintain a person's equilibrium.

The role of the external and middle part of the ear is to conduct and amplify sound waves from the environment. This part of sound conduction is termed *air conduction.* Problems in these two parts of the ear may cause *conductive hearing loss,* resulting in a decrease in sound intensity and/or a distortion in sound.[1]

Disturbances in equilibrium can impair coordination, balance, and orientation. Damage to or an abnormality of the inner ear or along the nerve pathways results in *sensorineural hearing loss.* In addition to causing distortion or faintness of sound, sensorineural hearing loss may affect the ability to understand speech or cause complete hearing loss. Impairment within the auditory pathways of the brain causes *central hearing loss.* This type of hearing loss causes difficulty in understanding the meaning of words the person heard. Types of hearing loss are discussed later in this chapter on pp. 387-389.

External Ear

The external ear consists of the *auricle* (pinna), external auditory canal, and *tympanic membrane (TM).* The auricle is composed of cartilage and connective tissue covered with epithelium, which also lines the external auditory canal (Fig. 21.1). The external auditory canal is a slightly S-shaped tube about 1 inch (2.5 cm) in length in the adult. The lining of the proximal one third of the canal contains fine hairs (cilia), sebaceous (oil) glands, and ceruminous (wax) glands. The oil and wax lubricate the ear canal, keep it free from debris, and kill bacteria. Thin epithelium lines the distal two thirds of the canal. It is over bone and very sensitive.

The function of the external ear and canal is to collect and transmit sound waves to the TM, or eardrum. The TM is a shiny, translucent, pearl-gray membrane. It is made up of epithelial cells, connective tissue, and mucous membrane. It serves as a partition and transmits sounds between the external auditory canal and middle ear.

Middle Ear

The middle ear cavity is an air space in the temporal bone. Mucous membrane lines the middle ear and is continuous from the nasal pharynx via the eustachian (auditory) tube. The eustachian tube equalizes atmospheric air pressure between the middle ear and throat. This allows the TM to move freely. It is normally closed, opening only with yawning, swallowing, and chewing. Blockage of the tube can occur with allergies, nasopharyngeal infections, or enlarged adenoids. A tube that stays open is called *patulous.* When this occurs, *autophony,* or hearing your own voice, may be present.

The middle ear contains the *ossicles,* the 3 smallest bones in the body: *malleus, incus,* and *stapes.* Vibrations of the TM cause the ossicles to move and transmit sound waves to the oval window. The superior part of the middle ear is the *epitympanum,* or the attic. It also communicates with air cells within the mastoid bone. The mastoid is the posterior part of the temporal bone. The facial nerve (CN VII) traverses above the oval window of the middle ear. The thin, bony covering of the facial nerve can become damaged by chronic ear infection, skull fracture, or trauma during ear surgery. Problems may occur related to voluntary facial movements, eyelid closure, and taste discrimination. Permanent damage to the facial nerve can result.

Inner Ear

The inner ear consists of 3 spaces in the temporal bone, assembled in a system called the bony labyrinth. The space is filled with watery fluid called perilymph. Within the perilymph is the membranous labyrinth. It follows the shape of the bony labyrinth and holds a thicker fluid called *endolymph.*

The inner ear holds the functional organs for hearing and balance. The receptor organ for hearing is the *cochlea,* a coiled structure that contains the *organ of Corti.* Its tiny hair cells respond to stimulation of select portions of the basilar membrane according to pitch. This stimulus is converted into an electrochemical impulse. It is transmitted by the acoustic part

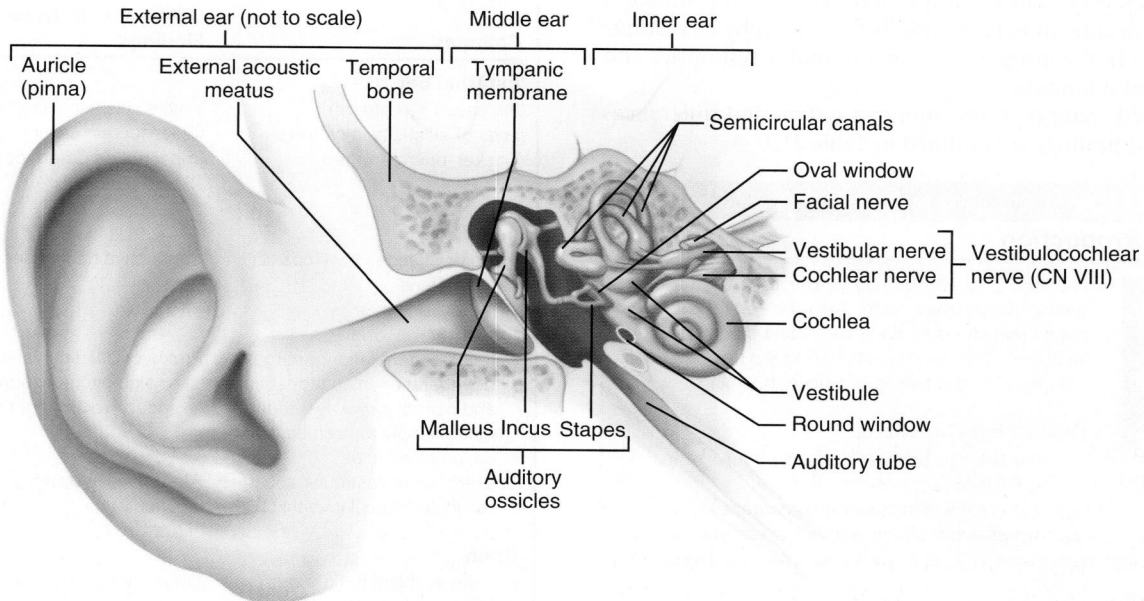

FIG. 21.1 External, middle, and inner ear. (Modified from Patton KT, Thibodeau GA: *Anatomy and physiology,* ed 8, St Louis, 2013, Mosby.)

of the vestibulocochlear nerve (CN VIII) to the temporal lobe of the brain to process and interpret the sound.

Three *semicircular canals* and the *vestibule* make up the organ of balance. The semicircular canals sit at right angles to each other. Structures in each canal and the vestibule generate nerve impulses in response to our movements. The vestibule is beside the oval window between the semicircular canals and the cochlea. Nerves from receptors in the vestibule join those from the semicircular canals to form the vestibular nerve, which joins with the cochlear nerve to form the *vestibulocochlear nerve,* or CN VIII.

Transmission of Sound

Sound waves travel by air (air conduction) and are picked up by the auricles and auditory canal. Sound waves strike the TM, causing it to vibrate. The central part of the TM is connected to the malleus, which then starts to vibrate. The malleus transmits the vibration to the incus and then the stapes. As the stapes moves back and forth, it pushes the membrane of the oval window in and out. Movement of the oval window makes waves in the perilymph.

Once sound waves are transmitted to the liquid medium of the inner ear, the vibration is picked up by the tiny sensory hair cells of the cochlea, which initiate nerve impulses. These impulses are carried by nerve fibers to the main branch of the acoustic portion of CN VIII and then to the brain. The bones of the skull can also transmit sound directly to the inner ear (bone conduction).

Gerontologic Considerations: Effects of Aging on Auditory System

Presbycusis, or hearing loss due to aging, is the third most common health issue in older adults, after arthritis and heart disease.[2] Sound transmission is diminished by calcification of the ossicles. **Tinnitus,** or ringing in the ears, may accompany the hearing loss that results from the aging process. Cerumen glands atrophy, causing cerumen (earwax) to be much drier. The hair in the ear becomes thicker and coarser, entrapping the hard, dry cerumen in the canal. Accumulation of dry cerumen in the external canal can interfere with the transmission of sound. A decline in balance results from atrophy of vestibular structures in the inner ear, slowing of motor responses, and musculoskeletal limitations.

Age-related changes in the auditory system and differences in assessment findings are outlined in Table 21.1.

CASE STUDY

Patient Introduction

(© iStock.com/ EyeMark.)

R.S. is a 57-yr-old woman who comes to the emergency department with extreme dizziness. R.S. states that she is so dizzy she "can't do anything but lie down." She also reports feeling like her right ear is "plugged" and is having ringing in that ear.

Discussion Questions
1. What are the possible causes of R.M.'s hearing and balance problems?
2. Is her condition stable or an emergency?
3. What assessment questions will you ask her?

You will learn more about R.S. and her condition as you read this chapter.

(See p. 380 for more information on R.S.)

ASSESSMENT OF AUDITORY SYSTEM

Assessment of the auditory system should include assessment of hearing and equilibrium because the auditory and *vestibular* (balance) systems are closely related. It is often hard to separate symptoms related to these two systems. Help the patient describe symptoms and problems to determine the source of the problems. Health history questions to ask a patient with an auditory problem are listed in Table 21.2.

Problems with balance may manifest as vertigo or nystagmus. **Vertigo** is a sense that the person or objects around the person are moving or spinning. It is usually stimulated by head movement. *Dizziness* is a sensation of being off-balance that occurs when standing or walking. **Nystagmus** is an abnormal eye movement that may be seen as a twitching of the eyeball or described by the patient as a blurring of vision with head or eye movement.

At first, try to determine symptoms that are related to balance and separate them from those related to hearing loss or tinnitus. The symptoms can be combined later in the assessment to help make a diagnosis and care plan for the patient.

Subjective Data
Important Health Information

Past Health History. Many ear problems result from childhood illnesses or problems of adjacent organs. This makes a careful assessment of past health problems is important.

Ask the patient about previous ear problems, especially during childhood. Record the (1) frequency of acute middle ear infections (otitis media); (2) surgical procedures (e.g., myringotomy); (3) perforations of the eardrum; (4) drainage; and (5) history of mumps, measles, or scarlet fever. Assess for systemic

 TABLE 21.1 Gerontologic Assessment Differences

Auditory System

Changes	Differences in Assessment Findings
External Ear	
Increased hair growth	Visible hair, especially in men
Loss of elasticity in cartilage	Collapsed ear canal
Thicker, drier cerumen	Impacted cerumen, potential hearing loss
Middle Ear	
Atrophic changes of tympanic membrane	Conductive hearing loss
Inner Ear	
Hair cell degeneration, neuron degeneration in auditory nerve and central pathways, reduced blood supply to cochlea, calcification of ossicles	Presbycusis, diminished sensitivity to high-pitched sounds, impaired speech reception, tinnitus
Less effective vestibular apparatus in semicircular canals	Alterations in balance and body orientation
Brain	
Decline in ability to filter out unwanted and unnecessary sound	Difficulty hearing in a noisy environment, heightened sensitivity to loud sounds

conditions, including hypertension, rheumatoid arthritis, and inflammatory bowel disease, that are associated with hearing loss.[3] Document head injury because it may result in hearing loss. Information about food and environmental allergies is important because they can cause the eustachian tube to become edematous and prevent aeration of the middle ear.

Record symptoms such as vertigo, tinnitus, and hearing loss in the patient's words. Ask for specific details of the sensations and situations that may cause them or make them worse. Information about family members with hearing loss and type of hearing loss is important. Some congenital hearing loss is hereditary. The age of onset of presbycusis also follows a familial pattern.

Medications. Obtain information about present or past use of ototoxic drugs (cause damage to CN VIII). These include aspirin, some antibiotics (aminoglycosides, erythromycin, vancomycin), loop diuretics, nonsteroidal antiinflammatory drugs (NSAIDs), antimalarial agents, and certain chemotherapy drugs (e.g., bleomycin, cyclophosphamide, cisplatin). Ask about hearing and balance problems, such as hearing loss, tinnitus, and vertigo, in patients receiving these drugs. For many, the hearing loss may be reversible if treatment is stopped. Chemicals used in industry (e.g., toluene, carbon disulfide, mercury) may damage the inner ear.

Surgery or Other Treatments. Document previous hospitalizations for ear surgery, including myringotomy (ventilation holes placed in the TM with or without tubes), tympanoplasty (surgical repair of TM), tonsillectomy, and adenoidectomy. Record the use of and satisfaction with a hearing aid. Note any problems with impacted cerumen.

Functional Health Patterns. Hearing and balance problems can affect all aspects of a person's life. To assess the impact of hearing loss, ask health history questions based on a functional health patterns approach (Table 21.2).

Health Perception–Health Management Pattern. Note the onset of hearing loss, whether sudden or gradual, and who noted the onset (e.g., patient, family, significant others). Gradual hearing losses are often noted by those who communicate with the patient. Sudden losses and those worsened by other condition are often reported by the patient.

Assess the patient for personal measures used to preserve hearing. The use of protective ear covers or earplugs is good practice for people in high-noise environments. Document if the patient is a swimmer and the frequency and duration of swimming and use of ear protection. Note the type of water (pool, lake, ocean) in which the swimming takes place to help identify contact with contaminated water. Assess for the placement of any item in the ear, including hearing aids, which can cause trauma to the canal and TM.

Nutritional-Metabolic Pattern. Alcohol, sodium, and dietary supplements affect the amount of endolymph in the inner ear system. Patients with Ménière's disease may notice some

---

TABLE 21.2 Health History

Auditory System

Health Perception–Health Management

Hearing
- Have you had a change in your hearing?* If yes, how does this change affect your daily life?
- Do you use any devices to improve your hearing (e.g., hearing aid, special volume control, headphones for television or stereo)?*
- How do you protect your hearing?
- Do you have any allergies that result in ear problems?*

Equilibrium
- When did the dizziness or spinning sensation first occur?
- Does this sensation occur when you first stand up, when you are lying down, or both?
- Have you ever fallen because of the dizziness?*
- Can you drive or walk alone? If no, elaborate.
- Are there any times of the day when your symptoms are worse?*

Tinnitus
- How long have you experienced ringing in your ears? Has it changed?* Describe the ringing (e.g., buzzing, ringing, roaring). Do you also have a feeling of fullness or pressure?*
- When does it bother you the most?
- What things have you tried that help or have not helped?
- What medications are you taking?

Nutritional-Metabolic
- Do you notice any differences in symptoms with changes in diet?*
- Does your ear problem cause nausea that interferes with your food intake?*
- Does chewing or swallowing cause you any ear discomfort?*

Elimination
- Does straining during a bowel movement cause ear pain?*

Activity-Exercise
- Do you need help with certain activities (e.g., lifting, bending, climbing stairs, driving, speaking) because of symptoms?*

Sleep-Rest
- Is your sleep disturbed by noises or ringing in the ears or by a sensation of spinning?*

Cognitive-Perceptual
- Do you experience ear pain?* What relieves the pain? What makes it worse? Does the pain affect your hearing or balance?
- Have you noticed any problem with communicating or understanding what people are saying?*

Self-Perception–Self-Concept
- Have changes in your hearing affected how you feel about yourself or your feeling of independence?*

Role-Relationship
- What effect has your ear problem had on your work, family, or social life?
- Are you able to recognize the effects of your ear problems on your life?*

Sexuality-Reproductive
- Has your ear problem caused a change in your sex life?*

Coping–Stress Tolerance
- Do you consider your ear problem a source of stress?*
- How do you cope when you are experiencing symptoms?

Value-Belief
- Do you have a conflict between what your health care provider would like you to do and what you believe you should do?

*If yes, describe.

improvement in their symptoms with alcohol restriction and a low-sodium diet. Note changes in symptoms with food intake. Ask the patient about any ear pain (otalgia) or discomfort associated with chewing or swallowing. These symptoms are often associated with middle ear problems.

Assessment of clenching or grinding of the teeth helps distinguish problems of the ear from referred pain of the temporomandibular joint (TMJ). Ask about dental problems and dentures.

Elimination Pattern. Elimination patterns are of interest in the patient with perilymph fistula and after surgical procedures. Frequent constipation or straining with bowel or bladder elimination may interfere with healing or repair of a perilymph fistula. After middle ear surgery (stapedectomy) the patient needs to prevent increased intracranial (and consequent inner ear) pressure associated with straining during bowel movements. Stool softeners may be needed after surgery for the patient who reports chronic problems with constipation.

Activity-Exercise Pattern. A review of the patient's activity-exercise pattern is essential when assessing for balance problems. Ask the patient about the onset, duration, and frequency of symptoms. Identify activities that relieve or worsen symptoms and how they relate to the time of the day. For example, patients with Ménière's disease are less able to compensate for environmental input as the day progresses.

Sleep-Rest Pattern. Ask the patient with chronic tinnitus about sleep problems. Find out if the patient has tried anything to minimize the tinnitus (e.g., having fan on, using white noise devices). Assess for snoring. It can be caused by swelling or hypertrophy of tissue in the nasopharynx. This excess tissue can impair eustachian tube function and cause the sensation of ear fullness or pain.

Cognitive-Perceptual Pattern. Pain is associated with some ear problems, particularly those involving the middle ear and auditory canal. If pain is present, ask the patient to describe the pain, presence of drainage *(otorrhea)*, history of teeth grinding, and treatments used for relief. Note the effect on the pain level when you move the auricle or palpate the tragus.

Note the patient's ability to pay attention and follow directions. Problems with these tasks may be an early indicator of hearing loss. The patient may not recognize a gradual hearing loss. Ask caregivers if they have noted any change in the patient's hearing.

Self-Perception–Self-Concept Pattern. Ask the patient to describe how the ear problem has affected his or her personal life and feelings about himself or herself. Hearing loss and chronic vertigo are particularly distressing for the patient. Hearing loss can result in embarrassing social situations that affect the patient's self-concept. People may think a patient with chronic vertigo is intoxicated. Sensitively question the patient about such situations. Clarify the symptom history with the patient and consider an evaluation with a hearing specialist.

Role-Relationship Pattern. Ask the patient about the effect that an ear problem or vertigo has had on family life, work responsibilities, and social relationships. Hearing loss can result in strained relationships and misunderstandings.

Ask about employment or contact with environments that have excessive noise levels, such as work with jet engines and machinery and electronically amplified music. Document the use of preventive devices worn in noisy environments. Many jobs rely on the ability to hear accurately and respond appropriately. If a hearing loss is present, gather detailed information

on the effect this has on the patient's job. The unpredictability of vertigo attacks can have devastating effects on all aspects of life. Ordinary activities, such as driving, cooking, and work, that require balance all have an element of danger.

Sexuality-Reproductive Pattern. Determine whether hearing loss or vertigo has interfered with having a satisfactory sex life. Although intimacy does not depend on the ability to hear, hearing loss can interfere with establishing or maintaining a relationship.

Coping–Stress Tolerance Pattern. Ask the patient about his or her usual coping style, stress management strategies, and available support. If the patient seems unable to manage the situation, outside intervention may be needed. Denial is a common response to a hearing problem and should be assessed.

Value-Belief Pattern. Ask the patient about any conflicts produced by the problem or treatment related to values or beliefs. Make every effort to resolve the problem so that the patient does not have added stress. Ask about the use of home remedies such as hot oil in the ear.

CASE STUDY
Subjective Data

(© iStock.com/ EyeMark.)

A focused subjective assessment of R.S. revealed the following information:
- *PMH:* History of mild osteoarthritis. Hysterectomy 5 years ago. Last saw health care provider 6 months ago.
- *Medications:* Multivitamin 1 PO daily, ASA 81 mg PO daily, ibuprofen 200 mg PO every 6 hours as needed.
- *Health Perception–Health Management:* She says last night she felt like she had the start of a cold. The symptoms were present this morning when she woke up. She tried to clear her ear by blowing her nose and could not use that ear to talk on the phone. Had excellent hearing until today. Denies any syncope. Does not have allergies.
- *Nutritional-Metabolic:* States she is nauseous but has not vomited. Has only had a few sips of water since the symptoms started.
- *Activity-Exercise:* Dizziness worse when standing. It is still present when lying down but is less. Her husband drove her to the emergency room since she was unable to drive. Normally walks 1 to 2 miles 5 times a week and attends yoga class 2 times a week.
- *Cognitive-Perceptual:* Denies any ear pain, headache.
- *Coping–Stress Tolerance:* Concerned she is having a stroke.

Discussion Questions
1. Which subjective assessment findings concern you most?
2. Based on the subjective assessment findings, what should you include in the physical assessment? For what would you be looking?

You will learn more about the physical assessment of the auditory system in the next section.
(See p. 381 for more information on R.S.)

Answers available at *http://evolve.elsevier.com/Lewis/medsurg.*

Objective Data

Physical Examination. During the interview to obtain a health history, obtain objective data about the patient's ability to hear. Look for cues that a patient cannot hear (Table 21.3). Record these observations. This is important because the patient is often unaware of hearing loss or does not admit to changes in hearing until moderate losses have occurred.

A normal assessment of the auditory system is shown in Table 21.4. Age-related changes of the auditory system and differences in assessment findings are found in Table 21.1.

TABLE 21.3 Indicators of Possible Hearing Loss

- Does not respond to or understand oral communication
- Has excessively loud or soft speech
- Answers questions inappropriately
- Tilts head, leans forward when listening
- Constantly needs to clarify conversation
- States other people mumble all the time
- Increases the volume of radio or TV
- Difficulty hearing over the phone

TABLE 21.4 Normal Physical Assessment of Auditory System

- Ears symmetric in location and shape
- Auricles and tragus nontender, without lesions
- Canal clear, tympanic membrane intact, landmarks and light reflex intact
- Able to hear low whisper at 30 cm. Weber test results, no lateralization. Rinne test results AC > BC

AC, Air conduction; *BC,* bone conduction.

A *focused assessment* is used to evaluate the status of previously identified auditory problems and monitor for signs of new problems. A focused assessment of the auditory system is presented in the box below.

FOCUSED ASSESSMENT
Auditory System

Use this checklist to make sure the key assessment steps have been done.

Subjective
Ask the patient about any of the following and note responses.

Changes in hearing	Y	N
Ear pain	Y	N
Ear drainage	Y	N
Tinnitus	Y	N

Objective: Physical Examination
Inspect

Alignment and position of ears on head	✓
Size, shape, symmetry, color, and skin intactness	✓
External auditory meatus for discharge or lesions	✓

Assess

Hearing based on ability to respond to conversation, respond to a whisper, or hear a ticking watch	✓

External Ear. Inspect and palpate the external ear before examining the external canal and tympanum. Observe the auricle, preauricular area, and mastoid area for symmetry, color of skin, swelling, redness, and lesions. Then palpate the auricle and mastoid areas for tenderness and nodules. Grasping the auricle or pressing on the tragus may cause pain, especially if the external ear or canal is inflamed.

External Auditory Canal and Tympanum. Before inserting an otoscope, inspect the canal opening for patency, palpate the tragus, and gently move the auricle to check for discomfort. Select

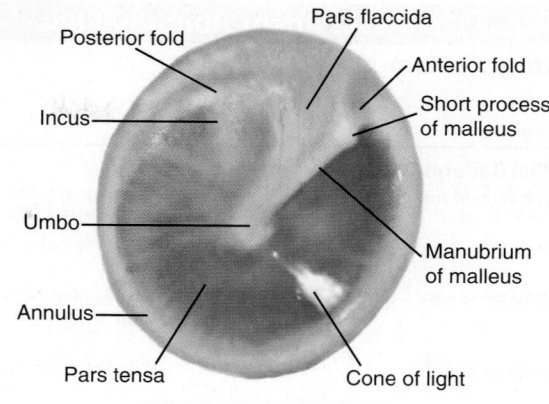

FIG. 21.2 Normal tympanic membrane. (From Jarvis C: *Physical examination and health assessment,* ed 7, St Louis, 2015, Elsevier.)

a speculum slightly smaller than the size of the ear canal. Tip the patient's head to the opposite shoulder. Grasp the top of the auricle and gently pull up and backward to straighten the canal. Hold the otoscope while stabilizing it with your fingers on the patient's cheek, and then insert it slowly. A pneumatic otoscope creates negative pressure to pull at the TM and is helpful in confirming TM retraction or fluid behind the membrane. A tight seal of the speculum is essential during this step of the examination. Observe the canal for size and shape and the color, amount, and type of cerumen. Be careful when clearing the canal of cerumen. Damage can occur to the middle ear if the TM is perforated.

Inspect the TM for color, fluid behind the membrane, landmarks, contour, and intactness (Fig. 21.2). The TM is normally pearl gray, white, or pink; shiny; and translucent. The handle (manubrium) of the malleus and its short process (umbo) should be visible through the membrane. The position and dome (concave) shape of the TM cause the light from the otoscope to reflect in a cone shape with crisp edges. If the TM is bulging or retracted, the edges of the light reflex will be fuzzy (diffuse) and may spread over the TM. The middle and inner ear cannot be examined with the otoscope.

Table 21.5 summarizes assessment abnormalities of the auditory system.

CASE STUDY
Objective Data: Physical Examination

(© iStock.com/ EyeMark.)

Physical examination findings of R.S. were as follows:
- Neurologic and otoscopic examinations normal
- Unable to hear whisper on the right at 30 cm
- Vision normal. PERRLA without nystagmus
- Gait unsteady. No motor weakness
- Skin pale, warm, and dry
- Heart rate 84 beats/min, temperature 97.4° F (36.3° C)

Discussion Questions

1. What physical assessment findings concern you most?
2. What diagnostic studies might you expect to be ordered?

As you continue to read this chapter, consider diagnostic studies that you would expect being performed for R.S.
(See p. 382 for more information on R.S.)

Answers available *at http://evolve.elsevier.com/Lewis/medsurg.*

TABLE 21.5 Assessment Abnormalities

Auditory System

Finding	Description	Possible Etiology and Significance
External Ear and Canal		
Sebaceous cyst behind ear	Usually within skin, possible presence of black dot (opening to sebaceous gland)	Removal or incision and drainage if painful
Tophi	Hard nodules in the helix or antihelix consisting of uric acid crystals	Associated with gout, metabolic disorder. Further diagnosis needed
Impacted cerumen	Wax that has not normally been excreted from the ear. No visualization of eardrum	Decreased hearing possible, pain, sensation of fullness in auditory canal, removal necessary before otoscopic examination
Discharge in canal	Infection of external ear, usually painful	Swimmer's ear, infection of external ear. Possibly caused by ruptured eardrum and otitis media
Swelling of pinna, pain	Infection of glands of skin, hematoma caused by trauma	Aspiration (for hematoma)
Scaling or lesions	Change in usual appearance of skin	Seborrheic dermatitis, actinic keratosis, basal or squamous cell carcinoma
Exostosis	Bony growth extending into canal causing narrowing of canal	Possible interference with visualizing tympanum. Usually asymptomatic
Tympanum		
Retracted eardrum	Appearance of shorter, more horizontal malleus. Absent or bent cone of light	Vacuum in middle ear, blockage of eustachian tube, negative pressure in middle ear
Hairline fluid level, yellow-amber bubbles above fluid level	Caused by transudate of blood and serum, meniscus of fluid producing hairline appearance	Serous otitis media
Bulging red or blue eardrum, lack of landmarks	Fluid-filled middle ear, pus, blood	Acute otitis media, perforation possible
Perforation of eardrum (Fig. 21.3)	Previous perforations of the eardrum that have failed to heal. Thin, transparent layer of epithelium surrounding eardrum	Chronic otitis media, mastoiditis, drainage
Recruitment	Perception that sounds are getting too loud too fast	Sensorineural hearing loss. Hearing aid hard to use

DIAGNOSTIC STUDIES OF AUDITORY SYSTEM

Table 21.6 describes common diagnostic studies used to assess the auditory system.

Audiometry

Audiometry is beneficial as a screening test for hearing acuity and as a diagnostic test to determine the degree and type of hearing loss. The most common test performed by the audiologist is pure-tone audiometry. The audiometer produces pure tones at varying intensities to which the patient can respond. Sound is characterized by the number of vibrations or cycles that occur each second. Hertz (Hz) is the unit of measurement used to classify the frequency of a tone. The higher the frequency is, the higher the pitch.

Hearing loss can affect certain sound frequencies. The specific pattern produced on the audiogram by these losses can help in diagnosing the type of hearing loss. The intensity or strength of a sound wave is expressed in terms of decibels (dB), ranging from 0 to 110 dB. The intensity of a sound needed to make any frequency barely audible to the average normal ear is 0 dB. Threshold refers to the signal level at which pure tones are detected (pure-tone thresholds) or the signal level at which the patient correctly hears 50% of the signals (speech detection thresholds).

Normal speech is around 40 to 65 dB; a soft whisper is 20 dB. Normally, a child and a young adult can hear frequencies from about 16 to 20,000 Hz, but hearing is most sensitive between 500 and 4000 Hz. This is similar to normal speech frequencies.

A 40- to 45-dB loss in these frequencies causes moderate difficulty in hearing normal speech. A hearing aid may be helpful because it makes sound information louder but not clearer. A hearing aid may not be helpful to the patient who has problems with discrimination of sounds or sound information because the consonants are still not heard well enough to make speech understandable.

Specialized Tests

More sophisticated tests are available to determine the cause of certain hearing losses (Table 21.6). CT scan and MRI can detect lesions such as a tumor of the auditory nerve.

CASE STUDY

Objective Data: Diagnostic Studies

(© iStock.com/ EyeMark.)

The Weber's test shows lateralization to the left. An audiogram confirms low-frequency, sensorineural hearing loss with normal speech discrimination. An MRI of the head is normal.

Discussion Questions

1. Are these the diagnostic studies that you expected to be ordered?
2. Which diagnostic study results are of most concern to you?

(See p. 393 for more information on R.S.)

Answers available at *http://evolve.elsevier.com/Lewis/medsurg.*

TABLE 21.6 Diagnostic Studies

Auditory System

Study	Description, Purpose, and Nursing Responsibility
Auditory	
Audiometry	*Pure-tone audiometry* quantifies hearing loss. Sounds are presented through earphones in soundproof room. Patient responds when sound is heard. Response is recorded on an audiogram. Purpose is to determine patient's hearing range in terms of decibels (dB) and Hertz (Hz) for diagnosing hearing loss. Tinnitus can cause inconsistent results. *Speech audiometry* includes speech reception threshold (measure of intensity at which speech is recognized) and word recognition score (ability to discriminate among various speech sounds).
Auditory brainstem response (ABR)	Study measures electrical peaks along auditory pathway of inner ear to brain and provides diagnostic information related to acoustic neuromas, brainstem problems, and stroke.
Auditory evoked potential (AEP)	Procedure is like an electroencephalogram (see Chapter 55 and Table 55.10). Electrodes are placed typically at vertex, mastoid process, and forehead. A computer is used to isolate auditory from other electrical activity of brain. Patient should avoid loud noises for 24 hours before the test.
Electrocochleography	Test records electrical activity in cochlea and auditory nerve. Electrode placed on or through the eardrum. Used to assess and monitor patients with dizziness.
Tympanometry	Used to check middle ear and mobility of eardrum. A probe is placed snugly into external ear canal, and positive and negative pressures are applied. Measurements are made of movement of eardrum.
Tuning Fork Tests	
Rinne test	Compares hearing by bone conduction (BC) and air conduction (AC). Stem of vibrating tuning fork held against mastoid bone (for BC of sound) and time noted. When the sound is no longer perceived behind the ear (BC of sound), time is noted once again and the still-vibrating fork is moved close to the pinna (AC of sound). Have the patient report when the sound next to the ear canal (AC) is no longer heard and note time. Normally, sound is heard twice as long in front of the ear as it is on the bone. With conductive hearing loss, the relationship is reversed; BC is longer than AC. With sensorineural hearing loss, both AC and BC are reduced, but AC remains longer.
Weber test	Stem of vibrating tuning fork is placed on midline of skull or forehead. Patient asked to indicate where the sound is heard best. In normal auditory function, the patient perceives a midline tone and the sound is heard equally in both ears. If a patient has conductive hearing loss in one ear, the sound will be heard louder (lateralizes) in that ear. If sensorineural loss is present, the sound is louder (lateralizes) in the normal (unaffected) ear.
Vestibular Tests	
Electronystagmography (ENG)	Used to diagnose diseases of vestibular system such as dizziness and balance disorders. Electrodes are placed near patient's eyes, and eye movement (nystagmus) is recorded on graph during specific eye movements and when ear is irrigated. Caloric test may be part of testing to measure responses to warm and cold water circulated into the ear canal. Have patient eat a light meal before test to avoid nausea. Observe patient for vomiting. Ensure patient safety.
Posturography	Balance test that can isolate one semicircular canal from others to determine site of lesion. Test is done in a boxlike device in which floor moves in response to a correction in balance by patient. Tell patient that test may be uncomfortable. Test can be stopped at any time at patient's request.
Rotary chair testing	Evaluates peripheral vestibular system. Patient is seated in a chair driven by a motor under computer control. Test is usually done in the dark. Tell patient to eat light meal before test to avoid nausea. Observe patient for vomiting. Ensure patient safety.

AUDITORY PROBLEMS: EXTERNAL EAR AND CANAL

EXTERNAL OTITIS

The skin of the external ear and canal is subject to the same problems as skin anywhere on the body. **External otitis** involves inflammation or infection of the epithelium of the auricle and ear canal. Swimming may change the flora of the external canal because of chemicals and contaminated water. This can result in an infection often referred to as "swimmer's ear." Trauma from picking the ear or using sharp objects (e.g., hairpins) often causes the initial break in the skin. Piercing of cartilage in the upper part of the auricle also places the patient at higher risk for infection.

Infections and skin conditions may cause external otitis. Bacteria or fungi may be the cause. *Pseudomonas aeruginosa* is the most common bacterial cause. Fungi, especially *Candida albicans* and *Aspergillus*, thrive in warm, moist climates. The warm, dark environment of the ear canal provides a good growth medium for microorganisms.

Malignant external otitis is a serious infection caused by *P. aeruginosa*. It occurs mainly in older patients with diabetes. The infection, which can spread from the external ear to the parotid gland and temporal bone (osteomyelitis), is usually treated with antibiotics.

Ear pain *(otalgia)* is one of the first signs of external otitis. Even in mild cases, the patient may have significant discomfort with chewing, moving the auricle, or pressing on the tragus. Swelling of the ear canal can muffle hearing. There may be serosanguineous (blood-tinged fluid) or purulent (white to green thick fluid) drainage. Fever occurs when the infection spreads to surrounding tissue.

❖ NURSING AND INTERPROFESSIONAL MANAGEMENT: EXTERNAL OTITIS

External otitis is diagnosed by otoscopic examination of the ear canal. Take care to avoid pain when pulling on the pinna to straighten out the canal or when inserting the otoscope speculum. The eardrum may be hard to see due to swelling in the

TABLE 21.7 Patient & Caregiver Teaching

Prevention of External Otitis

Include the following instructions when teaching the patient and caregiver:

1. Do not put anything in your ear canal unless requested by your health care provider.
2. Report itching if it becomes a problem.
3. Earwax is normal.
   - It lubricates and protects the canal.
   - Report chronic excess cerumen if it impairs your hearing.
4. Keep your ears as dry as possible.
   - Use earplugs if you are prone to swimmer's ear.
   - Turn your head to each side for 30 seconds at a time to help water run out of the ears.
   - Do not dry with cotton-tipped applicators.
   - A hair dryer set to low and held at least 6 inches from the ear can speed water evaporation.

canal. Culture and sensitivity studies of the drainage may be done. Moist heat, mild analgesics, and topical anesthetic drops usually control the pain. Topical treatments may include antibiotics for infection and corticosteroids for inflammation. If the surrounding tissue is involved, systemic antibiotics are used. Improvement should occur in 48 hours. The patient needs to adhere to the prescribed therapy for 7 to 14 days for complete resolution.

Wash hands before and after applying eardrops (otic drops). The drops should be at room temperature. Cold drops can cause vertigo due to stimulation of the semicircular canals, and heated drops can burn the tympanum. The tip of the dropper should not touch the ear during application to prevent contamination of the entire bottle of drops. Position the ear so that the drops can run into the canal. The patient should stay in this position for 2 minutes to allow the drops to spread. Sometimes you can place the drops onto a wick of cotton, then place the wick in the canal. Tell the patient not to push the cotton farther into the ear. Careful handling and disposal of material saturated with drainage are important. Teach the patient ways to reduce the risk for external otitis (Table 21.7).

CERUMEN AND FOREIGN BODIES IN EXTERNAL EAR CANAL

Impacted cerumen (earwax) can cause discomfort and decreased hearing. Other symptoms include tinnitus and vertigo. Remove an impaction by irrigating the canal with body-temperature solutions to soften the earwax. Special syringes may be used. These vary from a simple bulb syringe to special irrigating equipment. Place the patient in a sitting position with an emesis basin under the ear. Pull the auricle up and back, and direct the flow of solution above or below the impaction. Do not completely occlude the ear canal with the syringe tip. If irrigation does not remove the wax, use mild lubricant drops to soften the earwax. The HCP may need to remove severe impactions.

Attempts to remove a foreign object from the ear may result in pushing it farther into the canal. Vegetable matter in the ear tends to swell. This can create a secondary inflammation, making removal more difficult. Mineral oil or lidocaine drops can be used to kill an insect before removal under microscope guidance. The HCP should remove impacted objects.

Cleanse ears with a washcloth and finger. Avoid using cotton-tipped applicators. Penetration of the middle ear by a cotton-tipped applicator can cause serious injury to the TM and ossicles. Their use can also cause earwax to become impacted against the TM and impair hearing.

TRAUMA

Trauma to the external ear can cause injury to the subcutaneous tissue and result in a hematoma. If a hematoma is not aspirated, inflammation of the membranes of the ear cartilage (perichondritis) can result. Blows to the ear can cause conductive hearing loss if the ossicles in the middle ear are damaged or the TM is perforated. Head trauma that injures the temporal lobe of the cerebral cortex can impair the ability to understand the meaning of sounds.

MALIGNANCY OF EXTERNAL EAR

Skin cancers are the only common cancers of the ear. Precancerous actinic keratoses, rough sandpaper-like lesions on the upper border of the auricle, are associated with chronic sun exposure. They are often treated with liquid nitrogen. Cancers in the external ear canal include basal cell carcinoma in the pinna and squamous cell carcinoma in the ear canal. If left untreated, they can invade underlying tissue. Teach the patient about the dangers of sun exposure and the importance of using hats and sunscreen when outdoors. See Chapter 23 for more about skin cancer.

MIDDLE EAR AND MASTOID

OTITIS MEDIA

Acute Otitis Media

Acute otitis media is an infection of the tympanum, ossicles, and space of the middle ear. Swelling of the auditory tube from colds or allergies can trap bacteria, causing a middle ear infection. Pressure from the inflammation pushes on the TM, causing it to become red, bulging, and painful. Acute otitis media is usually a childhood disease. In children the auditory tube that normally drains fluid and mucus from the middle ear is shorter and narrower, and its position is flatter than in adults. Infection can be due to viruses or bacteria. Pain, fever, malaise, drainage, and reduced hearing are signs and symptoms of infection. Referred pain from the TMJ, teeth, gums, sinuses, or throat can also cause ear pain.

Oral antibiotics and eardrops are used if an infection is present. Surgical intervention is reserved for the patient who does not respond to medical treatment. A *myringotomy* involves an incision in the tympanum to release the increased pressure and exudate from the middle ear. A tympanostomy tube may be used short- or long-term for ventilation of the ear. Prompt treatment of an episode of acute otitis media can help prevent spontaneous perforation of the TM. If allergies are a causative factor, the patient may receive antihistamines and a nasal corticosteroid spray.

Otitis Media With Effusion

Otitis media with effusion is an inflammation of the middle ear with a collection of fluid in the middle ear space. The fluid

FIG. 21.3 Perforation of the tympanic membrane (TM). (From Flint P, Haughey B, Lund V, Niparko JK, eds: *Cummings otolaryngology: Head and neck surgery*, ed 5, St Louis, 2010, Mosby.)

TABLE 21.8 **Interprofessional Care**
Chronic Otitis Media

Diagnostic Assessment
 • History and physical examination
 • Otoscopic examination
 • Culture and sensitivity of middle ear drainage
 • Mastoid x-ray
 	
 Management
 • Ear irrigations
 • Otic, oral, or parenteral antibiotics
 • Analgesics
 • Antiemetics
 • Surgery
   • Tympanoplasty
   • Mastoidectomy

TABLE 21.9 **Patient & Caregiver Teaching**
After Ear Surgery
Include the following information in the teaching plan for the patient and caregiver after ear surgery.   1. Sleep on your back or the unoperated ear for 1 week.   2. Avoid air travel and sun exposure for 6 weeks.   3. If you need to cough or sneeze, keep your mouth open.   4. Blow your nose gently, without blocking either nostril.   5. Do not shampoo your hair for 5 days. Wear a shower cap when bathing.   6. No swimming. Keep your ear dry for 6 weeks.   7. You may resume strenuous activity and contact sports in 1 month.   8. Change your ear dressing daily as prescribed.   9. Report excess drainage or severe dizziness to the health care provider.

may be thin, mucoid, or purulent. If the auditory tube does not open and allow equalization of atmospheric pressure, negative pressure within the middle ear pulls fluid from surrounding tissues. This problem commonly follows upper respiratory tract or chronic sinus infections, barotrauma (caused by pressure change), or otitis media.

Symptoms include a feeling of fullness of the ear, a "plugged" feeling or popping, and decreased hearing. The patient does not have pain, fever, or discharge from the ear. It is common to have otitis media with effusion for weeks to months after an episode of acute otitis media. It usually resolves without treatment but may recur.

Chronic Otitis Media and Mastoiditis

Repeated attacks of otitis media may lead to chronic otitis media, especially in adults who have a history of recurrent otitis media in childhood. Because the mucous membrane of the middle ear is continuous with the air cells of the mastoid bone, both can be involved in the chronic infectious process.

Chronic otitis media is characterized by a purulent exudate and inflammation that can involve the ossicles, auditory tube, and mastoid bone. It is often painless. Hearing loss, nausea, and episodes of dizziness can occur. Hearing loss is a complication from inflammatory destruction of the ossicles, a TM perforation, or accumulation of fluid in the middle ear space. A mass of epithelial cells and cholesterol in the middle ear (*cholesteatoma*) may develop. The cholesteatoma enlarges and can destroy the adjacent bones. Unless removed surgically, it can cause extensive damage to the ossicles and impair hearing.

Otoscopic examination of the TM may reveal changes in color and mobility or a perforation (Fig. 21.3). Culture and sensitivity tests of the drainage are necessary to identify the organisms involved so the patient may receive the appropriate antibiotic therapy. The audiogram may show a hearing loss as great as 50 to 60 dB if the ossicles have been damaged or separated. Sinus x-rays, MRI, or a CT scan of the temporal bone can assess for bone destruction and the presence of a mass.

❖ NURSING AND INTERPROFESSIONAL MANAGEMENT: CHRONIC OTITIS MEDIA

The goals of treatment are to clear the middle ear of infection, repair any perforations, and preserve hearing (Table 21.8). Otic

and systemic (oral and IV) antibiotic therapy is started based on the culture and sensitivity results. In many cases of chronic otitis media, antibiotic resistance is present. The patient may need to have frequent evacuation of drainage and debris in an outpatient setting.

Often chronic TM perforations do not heal with conservative treatment, and surgery is necessary. *Tympanoplasty (myringoplasty)* involves reconstruction of the TM and/or the ossicles. A *mastoidectomy* is often performed with a tympanoplasty to remove infected portions of the mastoid bone. Removal of tissue stops at the middle ear structures that appear capable of conducting sound. Sudden pressure changes in the ear and postoperative infections can disrupt healing or cause facial nerve paralysis.

Expect impaired hearing during the postoperative period if there is packing in the ear. A cotton ball dressing is used if an incision was made through the external auditory canal. Teach the patient to change the cotton packing as needed (Table 21.9). If a postauricular (behind the ear) incision was used and a drain is in place, place a dressing over that area. Then, place a soft outer dressing over the top of that dressing. This will prevent putting pressure on the auricle. Monitor the tightness of the outer dressing to prevent tissue necrosis and assess the amount and type of drainage. Keep the suture line dry.

OTOSCLEROSIS

Otosclerosis is a hereditary autosomal dominant disease. It is the most common cause of hearing loss in young adults. Spongy

TABLE 21.10 Interprofessional Care

Otosclerosis

Diagnostic Assessment
- History and physical examination
- Otoscopic examination
- Rinne test
- Weber test
- Audiometry
- Tympanometry

Management
- Hearing aid
- Surgery (stapedectomy or stapes prosthesis)
- Drug therapy
  - Calcium carbonate
  - Sodium fluoride with vitamin D

bone develops from the bony labyrinth, preventing movement of the footplate of the stapes in the oval window. This reduces the transmission of vibrations to the inner ear fluids and results in conductive hearing loss. Although otosclerosis is typically bilateral, one ear may show faster progression of hearing loss. The patient is often unaware of the problem until the loss becomes so severe that communication is difficult.

Otoscopic examination may reveal a reddish blush of the tympanum (Schwartz's sign) caused by the vascular and bony changes within the middle ear. Tuning fork tests (e.g., Rinne) and an audiogram show good hearing by bone conduction with poor hearing by air conduction (air-bone gap) (Table 21.6). Usually a difference of at least 20 to 25 dB between air and bone conduction levels of hearing occurs with otosclerosis.

The hearing loss associated with otosclerosis may be stabilized by giving oral sodium fluoride with vitamin D and calcium carbonate. These medications slow bone resorption and promote the calcification of bony lesions. Amplifying sound with a hearing aid can be effective because inner ear function is normal.

Interprofessional care of otosclerosis is outlined in Table 21.10. Microdrill or laser surgical treatment involves opening the footplate (stapedotomy) or replacing the stapes with a metal or Teflon substitute (prosthesis). These procedures are usually done with the patient under conscious sedation. The ear with poorer hearing is repaired first. The other ear may be operated on within a year. Immediately after surgery the patient often reports a significant improvement in hearing in the operative ear. Because blood and fluid accumulates in the middle ear during the postoperative period, the hearing level decreases initially, but it improves gradually with healing.

Nursing management of the patient undergoing surgery to correct otosclerosis is like that of the patient having a tympanoplasty. Place a cotton ball in the ear canal and cover the ear with a small dressing. The patient may have dizziness, nausea, and vomiting because of stimulation of the labyrinth during surgery. Disturbing the perilymph fluid can cause nystagmus. Teach the patient to avoid sudden movements that may bring on or worsen vertigo and actions that increase inner ear pressure, such as coughing, sneezing, lifting, bending, and straining during bowel movements.

INNER EAR PROBLEMS

Three manifestations that indicate disease of the inner ear are vertigo, sensorineural hearing loss, and tinnitus. Symptoms of vertigo arise from the vestibular labyrinth, while hearing loss and tinnitus arise from the auditory labyrinth. There is an overlap between manifestations of inner ear problems and central nervous system (CNS) disorders.

MÉNIÈRE'S DISEASE

Ménière's disease is a progressive disorder leading to an accumulation of endolymph in the membranous labyrinth. Although it usually affects only one ear, it can affect both. The cause is unknown. Genetic and environmental factors may play a role. Symptoms usually begin between 30 and 60 years of age. Women are more likely to be affected.[4]

The excess fluid and resulting pressure lead to hearing and balance problems, including episodic vertigo, tinnitus, and ear pressure or fullness. Progressive hearing loss occurs over time. The patient has significant disability because of sudden, severe attacks of vertigo with nausea, vomiting, and sweating. A sense of fullness in the ear, increasing tinnitus, and muffled hearing may precede an attack. The patient may have the feeling of being pulled to the ground ("drop attacks"). Some patients report feeling like they are whirling in space. Attacks may last hours or days and may occur several times a year. The clinical course of the disease is highly variable.

❖ NURSING AND INTERPROFESSIONAL MANAGEMENT: MÉNIÈRE'S DISEASE

Interprofessional care of Ménière's disease (Table 21.11) includes diagnostic tests to rule out other causes of the symptoms, including CNS disease. Results that suggest Ménière's disease include low-frequency sensorineural hearing loss on audiogram, 2 or more spontaneous episodes of vertigo, and abnormal vestibular tests.[5] A glycerol test may aid in diagnosis. The patient receives an oral dose of glycerol, followed by serial audiograms over 3 hours. Improvement in hearing or speech discrimination supports a diagnosis of Ménière's disease. This is attributed to the osmotic effect of glycerol pulling fluid from the inner ear.

No cure exists for Ménière's disease. Treatments aim to reduce the number and severity of vertigo attacks. During an acute attack, corticosteroids, antihistamines (e.g., diphenhydramine), anticholinergics (e.g., atropine), and benzodiazepines (e.g., lorazepam [Ativan]) can decrease the abnormal sensation and lessen nausea and vomiting.[4] Acute vertigo is treated symptomatically with bed rest, sedation, and antiemetics (e.g., prochlorperazine) or antivertigo drugs (e.g., meclizine) for motion sickness. Management between attacks may include diuretics, corticosteroids, a low-sodium diet, and stress reduction. Over time, most patients respond to the medications but must learn to live with the unpredictability of the attacks and the loss of hearing.

Frequent and incapacitating attacks are indications for surgical intervention. Decompression of the endolymphatic sac and shunting can reduce the pressure on the cochlear hair cells and prevent further damage and hearing loss. If relief is not achieved, a vestibular nerve section (cutting the nerve) may be done. When involvement is unilateral, surgical ablation of the labyrinth, resulting in the loss of vestibular and hearing cochlear function, is an option. Some patients with severe attacks of vertigo have shown improvement with the injection of gentamicin through the TM. This results in inner ear damage and a reduction in endolymph production.

TABLE 21.11 Interprofessional Care

Ménière's Disease

Diagnostic Assessment
- History and physical examination
- Studies (including speech discrimination, tone decay)
- Vestibular tests (including caloric test, positional test)
- Electronystagmography
- Glycerol test

Management
Acute Care
Drug Therapy
- Anticholinergics
- Antihistamines
- Antiemetics
- Benzodiazepines
- Corticosteroids

Surgical Therapy
- Endolymphatic sac decompression
- Endolymphatic shunt
- Labyrinthectomy
- Vestibular nerve section

Ambulatory Care
- Diuretics
- Corticosteroids
- Dietary restriction of sodium, caffeine, nicotine, and alcohol
- Stress reduction techniques

Plan nursing interventions to minimize vertigo and provide patient safety. During an acute attack, keep the patient in a quiet, darkened room in a comfortable position. Teach the patient to avoid sudden head movements and position changes and to close the eyes until vertigo stops. Avoid fluorescent or flickering lights and television as they may worsen symptoms. Make an emesis basin available because vomiting is common. To minimize the risk for falling, keep the side rails up and the bed in a low position when the patient is in bed. Teach the patient to call for help when getting out of bed. Give medications and fluids parenterally. Monitor intake and output. When the attack subsides, help the patient with ambulation because unsteadiness may remain.

Discharge teaching should emphasize ways to protect the patient from injury between attacks. Review with the patient the need to sit or lie down at the onset of any dizziness. Discuss home safety and measures to decrease fall risk. Teach the need to avoid swimming under water, using ladders, and being on high places until vertigo is under control. Encourage the patient to practice any balance therapy exercises daily.

BENIGN PAROXYSMAL POSITIONAL VERTIGO

Benign paroxysmal positional vertigo (BPPV) is a common cause of vertigo. About 50% of the cases of vertigo may be due to BPPV. In BPPV, free-floating debris in the semicircular canal causes vertigo with specific head movements, such as getting out of bed, rolling over in bed, and sitting up from lying down. The debris ("ear rocks") is composed of small crystals of calcium carbonate that come from the utricle in the inner ear. The utricle may have been injured by head trauma, infection, or degeneration from the aging process. However, for many patients, we do not know the cause.

Symptoms of BPPV include nystagmus, vertigo, light-headedness, loss of balance, and nausea. There is no hearing loss, and symptoms tend to be intermittent. The symptoms of BPPV may be confused with those of Ménière's disease. Diagnosis is based on the results of auditory and vestibular tests.

Although BPPV is bothersome, it is rarely serious unless a person falls. The Epley maneuver, or canalith repositioning procedure, is effective in providing symptom relief for many patients. This maneuver moves ear debris from areas in the inner ear that cause symptoms and into less sensitive areas where they do not cause these problems. It does not change the presence of debris but changes the location. A trained HCP can teach the patient how to perform the maneuver (Fig. 21.4).

ACOUSTIC NEUROMA

An acoustic neuroma is a unilateral benign tumor that occurs where the vestibulocochlear nerve (CN VIII) enters the internal auditory canal. Early diagnosis is important because the tumor can compress the trigeminal and facial nerves and arteries within the internal auditory canal. Symptoms usually begin between 40 and 60 years of age.

Early symptoms are associated with CN VIII compression and destruction. They include unilateral, progressive, sensorineural hearing loss; reduced touch sensation in the posterior ear canal; unilateral tinnitus; and mild, intermittent vertigo. Diagnostic tests include neurologic, audiometric, and vestibular tests; CT scans; and MRI.

Surgery to remove small tumors can preserve hearing and vestibular function. Large tumors (larger than 3 cm) and the surgery to remove them can leave the patient with permanent hearing loss and facial paralysis. Stereotactic radiosurgery may slow tumor growth and preserve the facial nerve. Teach the patient to report any clear, colorless discharge from the nose. This may be cerebrospinal fluid (CSF), which increases the risk for infection. Follow-up care after surgery is important to monitor hearing and for tumor recurrence.

HEARING LOSS AND DEAFNESS

Hearing disorders are a common cause of disability. Age is the strongest predictor of hearing impairment. In the United States, about 25% of those 65 to 74 and 50% of those 75 and older have hearing loss.[6] Causes of hearing loss are shown in Fig. 21.5.

Types of Hearing Loss

Conductive Hearing Loss. *Conductive hearing loss* occurs when conditions in the outer or middle ear impair the transmission of sound through air to the inner ear. Common causes of conductive hearing loss in adults include impacted cerumen, otitis media with effusion, TM perforation, otosclerosis, and narrowing of the external auditory canal.[1]

The audiogram shows better hearing through bone than through air (air-bone gap). The patient often speaks softly because hearing his or her own voice (which is conducted by bone) seems loud. This patient hears better in a noisy environment. The first step is to identify and treat the cause if possible. If correction of the cause is not possible, a hearing aid may help if the loss is greater than 40 to 50 dB.

FIG. 21.4 Epley maneuver.

FIG. 21.5 Causes of hearing loss.

External ear	Middle ear	Inner ear
• Impacted cerumen	• Otitis media	• Ménière's disease
• Foreign bodies	• Serous otitis	• Noise-induced
• External otitis	• Otosclerosis	hearing loss
	• Tympanic	• Presbycusis
	membrane	• Ototoxicity
	trauma	
	• Cholesteatoma	
	• Acoustic neuroma	

Sensorineural Hearing Loss. *Sensorineural hearing loss* is caused by impairment of function of the inner ear or the vestibulo-cochlear nerve (CN VIII). Congenital and hereditary factors, noise exposure, aging (presbycusis), Ménière's disease, trauma, and ototoxicity can cause sensorineural hearing loss. The main problems are the ability to hear sound but not to understand speech and the lack of understanding of the problem by others. The ability to hear high-pitched sounds (including consonants) diminishes. Sounds become muffled and hard to understand. An audiogram shows a loss in decibel levels of the 4000-Hz range and eventually the 2000-Hz range. A hearing aid may help some patients, but it only makes sounds and speech louder, not clearer.

Mixed Hearing Loss. Mixed hearing loss occurs due to a combination of conductive and sensorineural causes. Careful evaluation is needed if corrective surgery for conductive loss is planned because the sensorineural hearing loss will still be present.

Central and Functional Hearing Loss. Central hearing loss involves an inability to interpret sound, including speech, because of a problem in the brain (CNS). A careful history is helpful because there are usually cases of deafness in the family. Refer the patient to a qualified hearing and speech service if indicated.

An emotional or a psychologic factor can cause functional hearing loss. The patient does not seem to hear or respond to pure-tone subjective hearing tests, but no physical reason for hearing loss can be found. Psychologic counseling may help.

Genetic Link

Heredity hearing loss is labeled non-syndromic or syndromic. Most persons have *non-syndromic hearing impairment,* in which hearing loss is the only primary problem. *GJB2* gene mutations are one of the most common causes of non-syndromic hearing loss. These result in changes in the production of the protein Connexin 26, which has a role in the cochlear function. Other genetic mutations increase the risk for ototoxicity or result in malformations of structures in the middle and/or inner ear. *Syndromic hearing impairment* is associated with other clinical abnormalities, such as malformations of the external ear or problems involving other organs. There are more than 400 syndromes that include hearing loss.

Classification of Hearing Loss. Hearing loss can be classified by the decibel level or loss as recorded on the audiogram. Normal hearing is in the 0- to 15-dB range. Most people with a hearing loss of 90 decibels or greater have been deaf since birth (congenitally deaf). Table 21.12 describes the levels of hearing loss.

Clinical Manifestations

Common early signs of hearing loss are answering questions inappropriately and not responding when not looking at the speaker (Table 21.3). Other behaviors that suggest hearing loss include straining to hear, cupping the hand around the ear, reading lips, and an increased sensitivity to slight increases in noise level. Often the patient is unaware of minimal hearing loss. Family and friends who get tired of repeating or talking loudly are often the first to notice the hearing loss. Pressure exerted by significant others is a significant factor in whether the patient seeks help for hearing impairment.

Sudden hearing loss, or sudden deafness, occurs as an unexplained, rapid loss of hearing (usually in one ear) either at once or over several days. It is a medical emergency, and the patient should see an HCP at once.

Tinnitus and Hearing Loss. *Tinnitus* is the perception of *sound* in the ears where no external source is present. It is "ringing in the ears" or "head noise" (see www.ata.org). Tinnitus is sometimes the first symptom of hearing loss, especially in older adults. It may be soft or loud, high pitched or low pitched.

Often, tinnitus occurs because of noise exposure. It also can be a drug side effect. More than 200 drugs are known to cause tinnitus.

❖ NURSING AND INTERPROFESSIONAL MANAGEMENT: HEARING LOSS AND DEAFNESS

Deafness is often called the "unseen handicap" because you may not realize the difficulty in communication with a deaf person until you begin a conversation with that person. You need to confirm a deaf person's understanding of health teaching. Descriptive visual aids can be helpful. If the significantly hearing-impaired person uses sign language to communicate, the Americans with Disabilities Act requires providing an interpreter when presenting significant information, such as for patient consent or discharge teaching.[7]

Interference in communication and interaction with others can be the source of many problems for the patient and caregiver. Often the patient refuses to admit or may be unaware of impaired hearing. Irritability is common because the patient must concentrate so hard to understand speech. The loss of clarity of speech in the patient with sensorineural hearing loss is most frustrating. The patient may hear what is said but not understand it. Withdrawal, depression, and accelerated cognitive decline are often associated with advancing hearing loss.[8]

? CHECK YOUR PRACTICE

Your newly assigned 68-yr-old female patient is being discharged today following a hip replacement. Before going to her room, you prepared the materials and information for her discharge. You sit down by her bed and start talking with her. She shakes her head and says, "No, no." You are perplexed until she flashes a bracelet that says *I am deaf.*

• How will you proceed?

◆ Health Promotion

◆ **Environmental Noise Control.** Noise is the most preventable cause of hearing loss. Fig. 21.6 lists the levels of environmental noise generated by common indoor and outdoor sounds. Sudden severe loud noise (acoustic trauma) and chronic exposure to loud noise (noise-induced hearing loss) can damage hearing. Acoustic trauma causes hearing loss by destroying the hair cells of the organ of Corti. Sensorineural hearing loss from increased and prolonged environmental noise, such as amplified sound, is occurring in young adults at an increasing rate. Amplified music (e.g., on smartphones) should not exceed 50% of maximum volume. Ear protection should be worn when firing a gun and during other recreational pursuits with high noise levels. Health teaching about avoiding continued exposure to noise levels greater than 70 dB is essential.

In work environments known to have high noise levels (more than 85 dB), people should wear ear protection. Occupational Safety and Health Administration (OSHA) standards mandate ear protection for workers in environments where the noise levels consistently exceed 85 dB. Periodic audiometric screening should be part of the health maintenance policies of industry. This provides baseline data on hearing to measure subsequent hearing loss.

Employees should take part in hearing conservation programs in work environments. Such programs should include noise exposure analysis, provision for control of noise exposure (hearing protectors), measurements of hearing, and employee-employer notification and education. Encourage young adults to keep amplified music at a reasonable level and limit their exposure time. Hearing loss caused by noise is not reversible

TABLE 21.12 Classification of Hearing Loss	
Decibel (dB) Loss	**Meaning**
0–15	Normal hearing
16–25	Slight hearing loss
26–40	Mild impairment
41–55	Moderate impairment
56–70	Moderately severe impairment
71–90	Severe impairment
>90	Profound deafness

PROMOTING POPULATION HEALTH

Promoting Healthy Hearing

- Wear ear protection during recreational and work activities involving high noise levels.
- Monitor your audio level and how long you use personal listening devices.
- Avoid exposure to excessively loud noise whenever possible.
- Undergo audiometric screening to detect hearing loss before it progresses.
- Avoid injury from cotton-tipped applicators and other cleaning materials.

FIG. 21.6 Range of common environmental sounds.

Immunizations. Various viruses can cause deafness because of fetal damage and malformations affecting the ear. Promote childhood and adult immunizations, including the measles, mumps, and rubella (MMR) vaccine. Rubella infection during the first 8 weeks of pregnancy is associated with a high incidence of congenital rubella syndrome, which causes sensorineural deafness. Women of childbearing age should be tested for antibodies to these viral diseases. Women should avoid pregnancy for at least 3 months after being immunized. Immunization must be delayed if a woman is pregnant. Women who are susceptible to rubella can be vaccinated safely during the postpartum period.

Ototoxic Substances. Monitor the patient who is receiving ototoxic drugs or exposed to ototoxic agents for signs and symptoms of ototoxicity, including tinnitus, diminished hearing, and balance problems. If these symptoms develop, stopping the drug may prevent further damage and allow the symptoms to disappear.

Assistive Devices and Techniques

Hearing Aids. The patient with a suspected hearing loss should have a hearing assessment by a qualified audiologist. If a hearing aid is needed, it should be fitted by an audiologist or a speech and hearing specialist. Many types of hearing aids are available, each with advantages and disadvantages (Table 21.13). The conventional hearing aid serves as a simple amplifier. For the patient with bilateral hearing impairment, binaural hearing aids offer the best sound lateralization and speech discrimination.

The goal of hearing aid therapy is improved hearing with consistent use. Patients who are motivated and optimistic about using a hearing aid are more successful users. Determine the patient's readiness for hearing aid therapy, including acknowledgment of a hearing problem, the patient's feelings about wearing a hearing aid, the degree to which the hearing loss affects life, and any difficulties the patient has manipulating small objects such as putting a battery in a hearing aid.

Initially, use of a hearing aid should be restricted to quiet situations in the home. The patient must first adjust to voices (including the patient's own voice) and household sounds. The patient should try increasing and decreasing the volume as situations require. As the patient adjusts to the increase in sounds and background noise, they can progress to situations in which several people will be talking at once. Next, the environment is expanded to the outdoors and then a shopping mall or grocery store. Adjustment to different environments occurs gradually, depending on the patient.

When a hearing aid is not being worn, it should be placed in a dry, cool area where it will not be inadvertently damaged or lost. The battery should be disconnected or removed when not in use. Battery life averages 1 week, depending on the hearing

TABLE 21.13 Types of Hearing Aids

Type	Advantages	Disadvantages
Completely in the canal (mild to moderate hearing loss)	Smallest and least visible aid. Protected from sounds such as wind noise	Costly. No space for add-ons such as directional microphones or volume controls. Small, short-lived batteries
In the canal (mild to severe hearing loss)	More powerful than aids completely in the canal. Has adjustable features such as noise reduction	Small size of aid with added features may be hard to use for patients with visual loss or arthritis

Type	Advantages	Disadvantages
In the ear (mild to severe hearing loss)	Powerful amplification. Inserts and adjusts easily. Longer lasting batteries	Visible. May pick up wind noise readily
Behind the ear (all types of hearing loss)	Most powerful aid. Adjusts easily. Longest battery life	Largest, most visible aid. Newer models may be smaller and less obvious

aid, battery, and amount of use. Advise patients to buy only a month's supply at a time. Ear molds should be cleaned weekly or as needed. Toothpicks or pipe cleaners can easily clear a clogged ear tip.

An *implantable hearing device* or aid is available to patients who cannot or will not use traditional hearing aids or cochlear implants. Implanted hearing devices amplify sound and transmit the sound vibrations through the ear. The device does not have visible external components. There are 2 types of implantable hearing devices: fully implantable and partially implantable. Fully implantable devices are placed surgically, and nothing is visible externally. Partially implanted devices have an internal device that is implanted surgically and an external device that is worn behind or in the ear.

Speech Reading. *Speech reading,* or *lip reading,* can be helpful in increasing communication. It allows for about 40% understanding of the spoken word. The patient uses visual cues associated with speech, such as gestures and facial expressions, to help clarify the spoken message. In speech reading, many words look alike to the patient (e.g., rabbit, woman). Help the patient by using and teaching verbal and nonverbal communication techniques as described in Table 21.14.

TABLE 21.14 Communicating With Patients With Hearing Impairment

Nonverbal Aids
- Draw attention with hand movements.
- Have speaker's face in good light.
- Avoid light behind the speaker.
- Maintain eye contact.
- Avoid covering mouth or face with hands.
- Avoid chewing, eating, smoking while talking.
- Remove background noise.
- Move close to better ear.

Verbal Aids
- Speak normally and slowly. Do not shout.
- Do not exaggerate facial expressions.
- Do not overenunciate.
- Use simple sentences.
- Rephrase sentence. Use different words.
- Write name or difficult words.
- Speak in normal voice directly into better ear.

Sign Language. *Sign language* is a form of communication for people with profound hearing impairment. It involves gestures and facial features such as eyebrow motion and lip-mouth movements. Sign language is not universal. American Sign

FIG. 21.7 Cochlear implant.

TABLE 21.15 **Classification of Presbycusis**	
Type	**Hearing Change and Prognosis**
Cochlear Stiffening of basilar membrane, which interferes with sound transmission in the cochlea	Hearing loss increases from low to high frequencies. Speech discrimination affected with higher frequency losses. Helped by appropriate forms of amplification
Metabolic Atrophy of blood vessels in wall of cochlea with interruption of essential nutrient supply	Uniform loss for all frequencies accompanied by recruitment. Good response to hearing aid
Neural Degenerative changes in cochlea and spinal ganglion	Loss of speech discrimination. Amplification alone not sufficient
Sensory Atrophy of auditory nerve. Loss of sensory hair cells	Loss of high-pitched sounds. Little effect on speech understanding. Good response to sound amplification

Language (ASL) is used in the United States and the English-speaking parts of Canada.

Cochlear Implant. A *cochlear implant* may be used for some people with severe to profound sensorineural hearing loss in one or both ears.[9] The implant bypasses damaged or missing portions of the ear and directly activates cranial nerve VIII. The ideal candidate is one who has become deaf after acquiring speech and language. The system consists of (1) an external microphone placed behind the ear, (2) a speech processor, (3) a transmitter implanted under the skin that changes sounds into electrical impulses, and (4) electrodes placed within the cochlea that stimulate the auditory nerves in the ear (Fig. 21.7). The electrodes are inserted as far as possible into the cochlea. Cochlear implants send information that covers the entire range of sound frequencies. For patients with conductive and mixed hearing loss, the cochlear Baha system may be surgically implanted. The system works through direct bone conduction and integrates with the skull bone over time.

Extensive training and rehabilitation are essential to receive the most benefit from these implants. Besides providing sound to a person who heard none, cochlear implants improve lip-reading ability, allow self-monitoring of the loudness of speech, improve the sense of security, and decrease feelings of isolation.

Assistive Listening Devices. Many devices are available to help the hearing-impaired person. Direct amplification devices, amplified telephone receivers, alerting systems that flash when activated by sound, an infrared system for amplifying the sound of the television, and a combination FM receiver and hearing aid may be options based on patient needs. People with profound deafness may be aided by text-telephone alerting systems that flash when activated by sound, closed captioning on television, and a specially trained dog. The dogs are trained to alert their owners to specific sounds within the environment, thus increasing the person's safety and independence.

 Gerontologic Considerations: Hearing Loss

Presbycusis, hearing loss associated with aging, includes the loss of peripheral auditory sensitivity, a decline in word recognition ability, and associated psychologic and communication issues. Because consonants (high-frequency sounds) help us recognize spoken words, the older person with presbycusis has a decreased ability to understand speech. Vowels are heard, but one cannot distinguish consonants in the high-frequency range. This may lead to confusion and embarrassment because of the difference in what was said and what was heard.

Degenerative changes in the inner ear cause presbycusis. Noise exposure is thought to be a common factor. Table 21.15 describes the classification of specific causes and associated hearing changes of presbycusis. Often a person may have more than one type of presbycusis. The prognosis for hearing depends on the cause of the loss. Sound amplification with the right device is often helpful in improving the understanding of speech. In other situations, an audiologic rehabilitation program can be valuable.

The older adult is often reluctant to use a hearing aid for sound amplification. Reasons cited most often include cost, appearance, insufficient knowledge about hearing aids, amplification of competing noise, and unrealistic expectations. Most hearing aids and batteries are small, and neuromuscular changes such as stiff fingers, enlarged joints, and decreased sensory perception often make the care and handling of a hearing aid frustrating for an older person. Some older adults may also tend to accept their losses as part of getting older and believe there is no need for improvement.

CASE STUDY

Ménière's Disease

(© iStock.com/ EyeMark.)

Patient Profile

While R.S. is in the emergency department, she starts violently vomiting. She tells you that any movement is making her feel like she is "spinning like crazy." The HCP decides to admit her under observation with plans to administer an intratympanic injection of dexamethasone.

Objective Data

- Skin pale, extremely diaphoretic
- Heart rate 112 beats/min, respirations 22 breaths/ min, BP 100/64

Interprofessional Care

- 1000 mg sodium diet as tolerated
- Ondansetron 2 mg IV now
- Lorazepam 1 mg IV every 6 hours
- Meclizine 25 mg PO every 6 hours

- Electronystagmogram and glycerol test
- Dextrose 5% with 0.45% NaCl at 75 mL/hr

Discussion Questions

1. Explain the etiology of Ménière's disease.
2. What clinical manifestations of Ménière's disease does R.S. exhibit?
3. Give the rationale for each treatment measure ordered.
4. ***Priority Decision:*** Based on the assessment data, what are the priority nursing diagnoses?
5. ***Priority Decision:*** What are the priority nursing interventions for R.S.?
6. ***Delegation Decision:*** Identify interventions for R.S. that can be delegated to unlicensed assistive personnel (UAP).
7. ***Safety:*** Identify an area of risk for injury to R.S. What actions will you take to ensure patient safety?
8. ***Patient-Centered Care:*** What teaching will you provide so R.S. can successfully self-manage her condition after discharge?
9. ***Quality Improvement:*** What outcomes would indicate interprofessional care was effective?

Answers available at *http://evolve.elsevier.com/Lewis/medsurg.*

▌ BRIDGE TO NCLEX EXAMINATION

The number of the question corresponds to the same-numbered outcome at the beginning of the chapter.

1. In a patient with vertigo, the parts of the ear most likely involved are the *(select all that apply)*
   a. cochlea.
   b. ossicles.
   c. vestibule.
   d. semicircular canals.
   e. tympanic membrane.

2. A patient reports tinnitus and balance problems. The medication that may be responsible is
   a. digoxin.
   b. warfarin.
   c. furosemide.
   d. acetaminophen.

3. What assessment technique should the nurse use to assess an adult patient's tympanic membrane?
   a. Have the patient tilt the head toward the nurse.
   b. Stabilize the otoscope with your fingers on the patient's cheek.
   c. Pull the auricle down and back to straighten the auditory canal.
   d. Use a speculum slightly larger than the size of the patient's ear canal.

4. A normal finding the nurse would expect when assessing hearing would be
   a. absent cone of light.
   b. bluish purple tympanic membrane.
   c. fluid level at hairline in the tympanum.
   d. midline tone heard equally in both ears.

5. Common age-related changes in the auditory system include *(select all that apply)*
   a. drier cerumen.
   b. tinnitus in both ears.
   c. auditory nerve degeneration.
   d. atrophy of the tympanic membrane.
   e. greater ability to hear high-pitched sounds.

6. The nurse teaches a patient scheduled for an electronystagmography that the test involves
   a. measuring ear drum movement in response to pressure.

   b. recording eye movements associated with ear irrigation.
   c. placing an electrode on the eardrum and assessing for dizziness.
   d. wearing headphones and determining which sounds can be heard.

7. Care of the patient experiencing an acute attack of Ménière's disease includes *(select all that apply)*
   a. giving antiemetics as needed.
   b. implementing fall precautions.
   c. keeping the room dark and quiet.
   d. placing the patient on NPO status.
   e. ambulating in the hall independently.

8. The patient who has a conductive hearing loss
   a. hears better in a noisy environment.
   b. hears sound but does not understand speech.
   c. often speaks loudly because his or her own voice seems low.
   d. has clearer sound with a hearing aid if the loss is less than 30 dB.

9. Teach the patient who is newly fitted with bilateral hearing aids to *(select all that apply)*
   a. replace the batteries monthly.
   b. clean the ear molds weekly or as needed.
   c. clean ears with cotton-tipped applicators daily.
   d. disconnect or remove the batteries when not in use.
   e. initially restrict usage to quiet listening in the home.

10. Which strategies would *best* aid the nurse communicate with a patient who has a hearing loss *(select all that apply)*?
    a. Overenunciate speech.
    b. Speak normally and slowly.
    c. Exaggerate facial expressions.
    d. Raise the voice to a higher pitch.
    e. Write out names or difficult words.

1. c, d, 2. c, 3. b, 4. d, 5. a, b, c, d, 6. b, 7. a, b, c, 8. a, c, 9. b, d, e, 10. b, e

For rationales to these answers and even more NCLEX review questions, visit http://evolve.elsevier.com/Lewis/medsurg.

EVOLVE WEBSITE/RESOURCES LIST

http://evolve.elsevier.com/Lewis/medsurg

Review Questions (Online Only)

Key Points

Answer Keys for Questions

- Rationales for Bridge to NCLEX Examination Questions
- Answer Guidelines for Case Study on pp. 378, 380, 381, 382, and 393

Conceptual Care Map Creator

Audio Glossary

Content Updates

REFERENCES

1. Eggermont J: *Hearing loss: Causes, prevention, and treatment*, Cambridge, 2017, Academic Press.
2. Hearing Loss Association of America Retrieved from *http://hearingloss.org*.
3. Popelka G, Moore B, Fay R, Popper A, eds: *Hearing aids*, Switzerland, 2016, Springer International Publishing.
4. Patel H, Isildak H: Ménière's disease, *Oper Tech Otolaryngol Head Neck Surg* 27:184, 2016.
5. Pullen R: Navigating the challenges of Ménière's disease, *Nursing* 47:38, 2017.
6. Quick statistics about hearing. Retrieved from *www.nidcd.nih.gov/health/statistics/quick-statistics-hearing*.
7. Communicating with people who are deaf or hard of hearing in hospital settings. Retrieved from *www.ada.gov/hospcombr.htm*.
8. Tremblay KL: Why is hearing loss a public health concern, *Hear J* 70:14, 2017.
9. National Institute on Deafness and Other Communication Disorders: Cochlear implants. Retrieved from *www.nidcd.nih.gov*.

*Evidence-based information for clinical practice.

22

Assessment: Integumentary System

Mariann M. Harding

The greatest gift you can give another is the purity of your attention.

Richard Moss

http://evolve.elsevier.com/Lewis/medsurg/

LEARNING OUTCOMES

1. Describe the structures and functions of the integumentary system.
2. Link the age-related changes in the integumentary system to differences in assessment findings.
3. Obtain significant subjective and objective data related to the integumentary system from a patient.
4. Compare the critical components for describing primary and secondary lesions.
5. Perform a physical assessment of the integumentary system using appropriate techniques.

6. Specify the structural and assessment differences in light- and dark-skinned persons.
7. Distinguish normal from common abnormal findings of a physical assessment of the integumentary system.
8. Describe the purpose, significance of results, and nursing responsibilities related to diagnostic studies of the integumentary system.

KEY TERMS

alopecia, Table 22.8, p. 404
dermis, p. 396
epidermis, p. 395
erythema, Table 22.8, p. 404

hirsutism, Table 22.8, p. 404
intertriginous, p. 401
keloid, p. 404
keratinocytes, p. 395

melanocytes, p. 395
mole (nevus), Table 22.8, p. 404
pruritus, p. 401
sebaceous glands, p. 397

The integumentary system is the largest organ of the body. It is composed of the skin, hair, nails, and certain glands. The skin has 2 major layers: epidermis (outer layer) and dermis (inner layer). The subcutaneous tissue (layer) lies under the dermis (Fig. 22.1). The skin is as complex as any organ, but, unlike the others, it is readily visible. Being able to see and touch the skin helps you assess your patients. You can see abnormalities, understand their significance, and intervene early.

STRUCTURES AND FUNCTIONS OF SKIN AND APPENDAGES

Structures

Epidermis. The **epidermis**, the outer layer of the skin, is relatively thin, ranging from 0.05 mm on the eyelids to 0.1 mm on the soles.[1] There are no lymphatic or vascular structures in the epidermis. It is supported by passive circulation from the dermis.

The epidermis is divided into 5 distinct but interrelated layers. Two of the layers are the stratum corneum (the surface layer) and the stratum germinativum (deepest, basal layer) (Fig. 22.1).

Most epithelial cells are keratinocytes (90%). The remaining cells are melanocytes, Langerhans' cells, and Merkel cells.

Keratinocytes form in the basal layer. Initially, they are undifferentiated and shaped like columns. As they mature (keratinize), they move to the surface, where they flatten and die to form the outer skin layer (stratum corneum). Keratinocytes make a fibrous protein, keratin, which is vital to the skin's protective barrier function. The upward movement of keratinocytes from the basal layer to the outermost levels of the stratum corneum takes about 14 days. The keratinocytes stay there for another 14 days, allowing the epidermis to regenerate every 28 days. Thus each month you have a new layer of skin.

Many skin problems result from changes in this cell cycle. If dead cells slough off too rapidly, the skin appears thin and eroded. If new cells form faster than you shed old cells, the skin becomes scaly and thickened. Failure of the epidermis to function normally occurs with skin cancer and psoriasis (discussed in Chapter 23).

Melanocytes are found in the deep, basal layer. They contain melanin, a pigment that gives color to the skin and hair and protects the body from damaging ultraviolet (UV) sunlight.

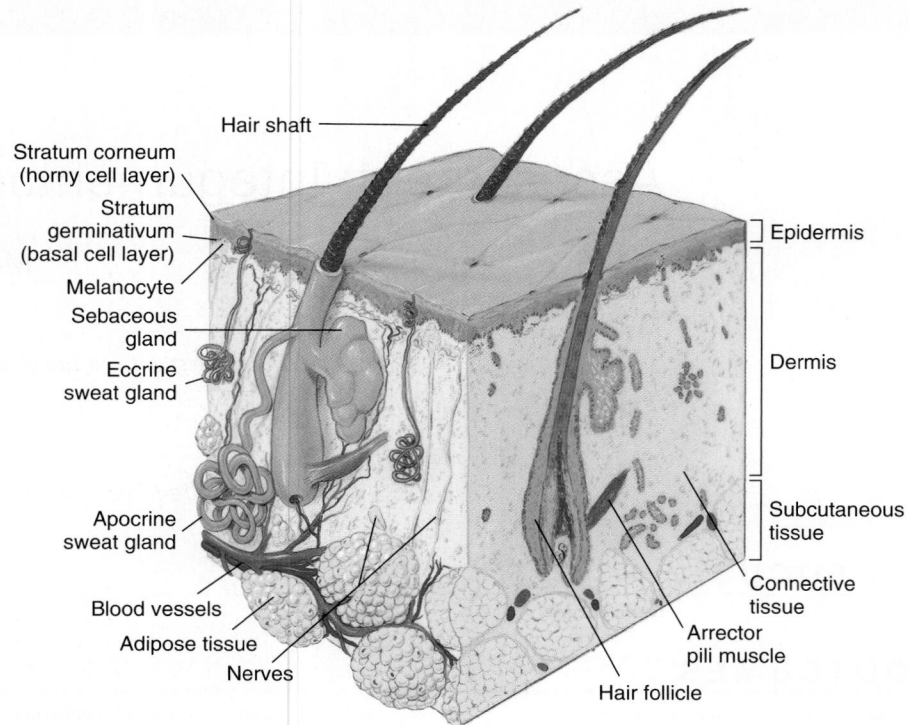

Hair shaft

Stratum corneum
(horny cell layer)

Stratum
germinativum
(basal cell layer)

Melanocyte

Sebaceous
gland

Eccrine
sweat gland

Apocrine
sweat gland

Blood vessels

Adipose tissue

Nerves

Epidermis

Dermis

Subcutaneous
tissue

Connective
tissue

Arrector
pili muscle

Hair follicle

FIG. 22.1 Microscopic view of the skin in longitudinal section. (From Jarvis C: *Physical examination and health assessment,* ed 6, St Louis, 2012, Saunders.)

Sunlight and hormones stimulate the melanosome (within the melanocyte) to increase the production of melanin. People of all races have similar numbers of melanocytes. In darker skin, the melanosomes are larger and more numerous, thus producing more melanin.[2] This increased melanin forms a natural sun shield for dark skin and results in a decreased incidence of skin cancer. The distribution of melanocytes varies from one area of the body to another. For example, the face has more melanocytes than the abdomen.

Langerhans' cells are a type of dendritic cell (discussed in Chapter 13 on p. 191). They are immunocompetent cells that recognize antigens. When they are depleted, the skin cannot initiate an immune response. The Langerhans' cells in bioengineered skin grafts have been removed to prevent graft rejection. In skin diseases such as psoriasis and sarcoidosis, there are decreased numbers of Langerhans' cells. *Merkel cells* are found in the basal layer and are involved in the sensation of light touch. We use them when feeling the texture of an object and figuring out what it is.

The basement membrane zone is between the epidermis and dermis. This structure provides for the (1) exchange of fluids between the epidermis and dermis and (2) structural support for the epidermis. The basement membrane helps to secure the two layers together. Inflammation and separation of the epidermal and dermal layers result in the blisters seen with problems such as burns, full-thickness wounds, and mechanical trauma.

Dermis. The dermis is the connective tissue below the epidermis. Dermal thickness ranges from 0.3 mm on the eyelid to 3.0 mm on the back.[1] The dermis is very vascular, containing many blood vessels. It also contains nerves, lymphatic vessels, hair follicles, sebaceous glands, and specialized cells such as mast cells and macrophages that protect the body from external stimuli.

The dermis is made of 3 types of connective tissue: collagen, elastic fibers, and reticular fibers. Collagen forms the greatest part of the dermis. It gives the skin toughness and strength. The primary cell type in the dermis is the *fibroblast,* which makes collagen and elastin. Collagen is critical in wound healing.

The dermis has 2 layers: upper thin papillary layer and a deeper, thicker reticular layer. The papillary layer is arranged haphazardly in ridges, or papillae, which extend into the outer epidermal layer. These elevated surface ridges form fingerprints and footprints. The reticular layer forms the bulk of the dermis. It is made up of thick collagen bundles arranged parallel to the skin's surface.

Subcutaneous Tissue. The subcutaneous tissue lies below the dermis. It is made of loose connective tissue and fat cells that provide insulation, cushioning, temperature regulation, and energy storage. The subcutaneous tissue attaches the skin to underlying tissues, such as muscle and bone. The distribution pattern of subcutaneous tissue varies with gender, heredity, age, and nutritional status.

Skin Appendages. *Skin appendages* include the hair, nails, and glands (sebaceous, apocrine, and eccrine). These appendages are epidermal extensions that have their roots in the dermis. These structures receive nutrients, electrolytes, and fluids from the dermis. Hair and nails form from specialized keratin. Systemic diseases can affect the condition and health of both hair and nails.

Hair grows on most of the body except for the lips, palms of the hands, interdigital spaces, portions of the genitalia, and soles of the feet. The density and pattern of distribution varies depending on age, sex, and race. Hair color is a result of heredity and determined by the type and amount of melanin in the hair shaft. Hair grows about 1 cm per month. People lose about

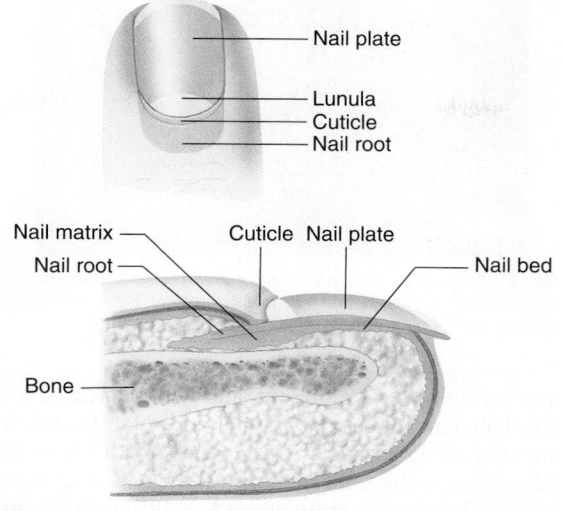

FIG. 22.2 Structure of a nail. (From Patton KT, Thibodeau GA, Douglas M: *Essentials of anatomy and physiology,* St Louis, 2014, Mosby.)

FIG. 22.3 Pigmented nail bands normally seen with dark skin color. (From Ball J, Dains J, Flynn J, et al: *Seidel's guide to physical examination,* ed 8, St Louis, 2014, Mosby.)

100 hairs each day.[3] Baldness, or *alopecia,* results when we do not replace lost hair.

Nails are made of heavily keratinized cells. The part of the nail that you can see is the nail body. The rest is the nail root. A fold of skin hides most of the nail root. The cuticle borders this skinfold. Nail growth begins in the nail root. The part of the nail root you can see is the *lunula.* This white, crescent-shaped area is the site of mitosis and nail growth (Fig. 22.2). Under the nail is an area of epidermis called the *nail bed.* The nail bed has many blood vessels. Nails grow slowly, but continuously. Fingernails grow much faster than toenails, at a rate of 0.5 to 2 mm per week.[1] It takes 3 to 6 months to replace a fingernail. A toenail may take 12 months or longer to replace. Nail color ranges from pink to yellow or brown depending on skin color. Color and texture variations in nails may be normal or represent an abnormal condition. Pigmented longitudinal bands *(melanonychia striata)* occur in the nail bed in 90% or more of people with dark skin[4] (Fig. 22.3).

There are 2 major types of glands in the skin: sebaceous and sweat (apocrine and eccrine) glands. Sebaceous glands secrete *sebum,* which is emptied into the hair follicles. Sebum waterproofs and lubricates the skin and promotes the absorption of fat-soluble substances. Sebum is somewhat bacteriostatic and fungistatic. These glands depend on sex hormones, particularly testosterone, to regulate sebum secretion and production. Actual production varies depending on age, sex, and testosterone and estrogen levels. Sebaceous glands are present on all areas of the skin except the palms and soles and dorsum of the feet. These glands are most abundant on the face, scalp, upper chest, and back.

The *apocrine sweat glands* are mainly found in the axillary, genital, and breast areas. They are always connected to a hair follicle. These glands enlarge and become active at puberty because of reproductive hormones. They secrete a thick milky substance that is naturally odorless. Odor occurs when skin surface bacteria alter the secretions.

The *eccrine sweat glands* are found on most of the body, except the lips, ear canals, nail beds, labia minora, glans penis, and prepuce. One square inch of skin has about 3000 eccrine sweat glands. Their main function is to cool the body by evaporation,

excrete waste products, and moisturize surface cells. Sweat is a transparent watery solution composed of salts, ammonia, urea, and other wastes. In extreme situations, the body can make 2 to 4 L of sweat per hour or up to 12 liters in 24 hours. Heat, certain mental stimuli, and ingestion of hot, spicy foods stimulate sweat secretion.

Functions of Integumentary System

The skin's main function is to protect the underlying body tissues by serving as a barrier to the external environment. The skin acts as a barrier against invasion by bacteria and viruses and prevents excess water loss. The fat in the subcutaneous layer insulates the body and provides protection from trauma. Melanin screens and absorbs UV radiation.

The skin with its nerve endings and special receptors collects sensory information from environmental stimuli. These highly specialized nerve endings give information to the brain related to pain, heat and cold, touch, pressure, and vibration.

The skin controls heat regulation by responding to changes in internal and external temperature with vasoconstriction or vasodilation. The skin's excretory function and heat regulation are related. We lose between 600 and 900 mL of water daily through insensible water loss (invisible vaporization from the lungs and skin), which helps regulate body temperature. Sebum and sweat lubricate the skin surface. Endogenous synthesis of vitamin D, which is critical to calcium and phosphorus balance, occurs in the epidermis. Vitamin D is made in the epidermis when UV light acts on vitamin D precursor cells.

Gerontologic Considerations: Effects of Aging on Integumentary System

Many skin changes are associated with aging. Depending on a person's view of self, the normal, visible effects of aging on the skin and hair may have a profound psychologic effect. Having a youthful look may affect a person's self-image. The appearance of the signs of aging can be a threat to self-concept. Other changes in skin structure related to normal changes with aging can pose serious risk. Age-related changes of the integumentary system and differences in assessment findings are listed in Table 22.1.

Chronic UV exposure is the major contributor to the photoaging and wrinkling of skin.[5] Sun damage to the skin is

TABLE 22.1 Gerontologic Assessment Differences

Integumentary System

Changes	Differences in Assessment Findings
Skin	
Decreased subcutaneous fat, muscle laxity, degeneration of elastic fibers, collagen stiffening	Increased wrinkling, sagging breasts and abdomen, redundant flesh around eyes, slowness of skin to flatten when pinched (tenting)
Decreased extracellular water, surface lipids, and sebaceous gland activity	Dry, flaking skin with possible signs of excoriation caused by scratching
Decreased activity of apocrine and sebaceous glands	Dry skin with minimal to no perspiration, skin color uneven
Increased capillary fragility and permeability	Bruising
Increased focal melanocytes in basal layer with pigment accumulation	Solar lentigines on face and back of hands
Diminished blood supply	Decrease in rosy appearance of skin and mucous membranes. Skin cool to touch. Diminished awareness of pain, touch, temperature, peripheral vibration
Decreased proliferative capacity	Delayed wound healing
Decreased immunocompetence	Increase in neoplasms
Hair	
Decreased melanin and melanocytes	Gray or white hair
Decreased oil	Dry, coarse hair. Scaly scalp
Decreased hair density	Thinning and hair loss
Cumulative androgen effect; decreasing estrogen levels	Facial hirsutism, baldness
Nails	
Decreased peripheral blood supply	Thick, brittle nails with diminished growth
Increased keratin	Longitudinal ridging
Decreased circulation	Prolonged return of blood to nails on blanching

FIG. 22.4 Photoaging. Irregular pigmentation and keratoses occur on sun-damaged skin on forehead. (From Gawkrodger D, Ardern-Jones MR: *Dermatology*, ed 5, Edinburgh, 2012, Churchill Livingstone.)

Fewer melanocytes are present, and with decreased levels of melanin, hair color fades. Hormonal and vitamin deficiencies can cause dry, thin hair and alopecia. The growth rate of the hair and nails decreases because of atrophy. The nail plate thins, and nails become brittle and more prone to splitting and yellowing. Nails, especially the toenails, may thicken with age. With aging, the apocrine and eccrine sweat glands atrophy, causing dry skin and decreased body odor.

Benign neoplasms related to the aging process can occur. These growths include seborrheic keratoses, vascular lesions such as cherry angiomas, and skin tags. *Actinic keratoses* appear on areas of chronic sun exposure, especially in the person who has a fair complexion and light eyes (blue, green, or hazel). These premalignant cutaneous lesions place a person at increased risk for squamous cell and basal cell carcinomas.

ASSESSMENT OF INTEGUMENTARY SYSTEM

The general skin assessment begins with your first contact with the patient and continues throughout the examination. As you are meeting your patient for the first time, take a moment to note the overall condition of the patient's skin and hair. You will assess specific areas of the skin when examining other body systems, unless the chief complaint is a skin problem. Record a general statement about the skin's physical condition (Table 22.2). In addition, ask the health history questions presented in Table 22.3 when you note a skin problem.

cumulative (Fig. 22.4). The wrinkling of sun-exposed areas such as the face and hands is more marked than that of a sun-shielded area, such as the buttocks. A photoaged person is more susceptible to skin cancers because UV exposure decreases the ability to repair cellular damage. Chronic UV exposure from tanning beds causes the same damage as UV from the sun. Other factors that influence skin aging include diabetes, smoking, and alcohol use.

The junction between the dermis and epidermis flattens. This causes the two layers to lose their tight bond. Skin tears and other trauma become common as the epidermis slides separately from the dermis. Collagen fibers stiffen, elastic fibers degenerate, and the amount of subcutaneous tissue decreases. These changes, with the added effects of gravity, lead to wrinkling. Fewer free fatty acids in the epidermis results in dry, scaly, itchy skin. Dryness, combined with trauma caused by scratching, increases the risk for fissures (cracks) in the skin and secondary infections. Decreased subcutaneous fat increases the risk for traumatic injury, hypothermia, and skin shearing, which may lead to pressure ulcers.

CASE STUDY

Patient Introduction

(© iStockphoto/ Thinkstock.)

D.A. is a 74-yr-old woman who comes to the medical clinic with concerns related to various "spots" on her face. She says they have been there for a while and she thought they were just "age spots." She became concerned after her friend was diagnosed with a malignant melanoma.

Discussion Questions

1. Which type of assessment should you perform: comprehensive, focused, or emergency?
2. What are the possible causes of D.A.'s facial lesions?
3. What questions would you ask D.A. to determine the possible causes?

You will learn more about D.A. and her condition as you read this chapter.

(See p. 401 for more information on D.A.)

Answers available at *http://evolve.elsevier.com/Lewis/medsurg*.

TABLE 22.2 Normal Physical Assessment of Integumentary System

Skin	• Evenly pigmented. No petechiae, purpura, lesions, or excoriations • Warm, good turgor
Nails	• Pink, oval, adhere to nail bed with 160-degree angle
Hair	• Shiny and full; amount and distribution appropriate for age and gender • No flaking of scalp, forehead, or pinna

Subjective Data

Perform the interview using a sensitive and nonjudgmental attitude. The problem may be the result of poor hygiene or unhealthful behaviors. Some problems are highly visible and affect the patient's body image and self-concept. A thorough health history yields information about possible causes and the effect of the problem on the person's life.

Important Health Information

Past Health History. Past health history reveals previous trauma, surgery, or disease that involves the skin. Many diseases have skin manifestations (Table 22.4). Determine if the patient has noticed any problems such as jaundice (liver disease), delayed wound healing (diabetes), cyanosis (respiratory, cardiovascular disorder), or pallor (anemia). Obtain specific information related to food sensitivities, pet or drug allergies, and skin reactions to insect bites and stings. Note any history of chronic or unprotected exposure to UV light, including tanning bed use and radiation treatments.

Medications. A thorough medication history is important. Ask the patient about skin-related problems that occurred because of taking a medication. Many hormones, antibiotics, corticosteroids, and antimetabolites have side effects that manifest in the skin. Medications may contain fragrances and preservatives that can cause skin reactions. Document the use of medications specifically used to treat a primary skin problem, such as acne, or a secondary skin problem, such as itching. Record the drug's name, length of use, method of application, and effectiveness.

Surgery or Other Treatments. Determine if any surgical procedures, including cosmetic surgery, were done on the skin. Record any biopsy results. Note any treatments specific for a skin problem (e.g., phototherapy) or for a health problem (e.g., radiation therapy). Document any treatments undergone primarily for cosmetic purposes, such as tanning booth use, laser resurfacing, or cosmetic "peels."

Functional Health Patterns

Health Perception–Health Management Pattern. Ask the patient about health practices, such as self-care habits related to daily hygiene. Document the frequency of use and sun protection factor (SPF) of sunscreen products. Assess the use of personal care products (e.g., shampoos, moisturizing agents, cosmetics), including brand name, quantity, and frequency. Record a description of any current skin problem, including onset, symptoms, course, and treatment. Note any medications used for treating hair loss.

Obtain information about the family history of any skin diseases, including congenital and familial diseases (e.g., alopecia, psoriasis) and systemic diseases with skin manifestations (e.g., diabetes, thyroid disease, cardiovascular diseases, immune disorders). Note any family and personal history of skin cancer, particularly melanoma.

TABLE 22.3 Health History
Integumentary System

Health Perception–Health Management
• Describe your daily hygiene practices.
• What skin products are you now using?
• Describe any current skin condition, including onset, course, and treatment (if any).

Nutritional-Metabolic
• Describe any changes in the condition of your skin, hair, nails, and mucous membranes.
• Have you noticed any recent changes in the way sores or wounds heal?*
• Have you had any weight loss or dietary changes?*

Elimination
• Have you noticed recent changes in your skin related to excess sweating, dryness, or swelling?*

Activity-Exercise
• Do your leisure or work activities involve using any chemicals that might irritate your skin?*
• Do you do anything to protect yourself from the sun?*

Sleep-Rest
• Does your skin condition keep you awake or awaken you from sleep?*

Cognitive-Perceptual
• Do you have any unusual sensations of heat, cold, or touch?*
• Do you have any pain associated with your skin condition?*
• Do you have any joint pain?*

Self-Perception–Self-Concept
• How does your skin condition make you feel about yourself?

Role-Relationship
• Has your skin condition changed your relationships with others?*
• Have you changed your lifestyle because of your skin condition?*

Sexuality-Reproductive
• Has your skin condition changed your intimate relationships with others?*
• Has your birth control method (if used) caused a skin problem?*

Coping–Stress Tolerance
• Are you aware of any situation or stressor that changes your skin condition?*
• Do you think that stress plays a role in your skin condition?*
• How do you handle stress?

Value-Belief
• Are there any cultural beliefs that influence your thinking or feelings about your skin condition?*
• Are there any treatment options that you would be opposed to using?

*If yes, describe.

GENETIC RISK ALERT

• The primary risk factor leading to skin cancer and melanoma is environmental exposure to UV radiation. UV radiation damages DNA, causing an error in the genetic code and resulting in abnormal skin cells.[6]
• Inherited genetic factors can increase skin cancer risk. A person has an increased risk for developing melanoma if they have a first-degree relative (e.g., parent, full sibling) who had a melanoma.
• People with a fair complexion (light-colored skin that easily freckles, red or blond hair, and blue or light-colored eyes) have an increased risk for skin cancer.

TABLE 22.4 Diseases With Skin Manifestations

Systemic Problem	Skin Manifestations
Endocrine	
Addison's disease	Loss of body hair (especially axillary), generalized hyperpigmentation (accentuated in folds)
Androgen deficiency	Development of sparse hair. Marked reduction in sebum production
Androgen excess	Enlarged facial pores, male sex characteristics, acne, acceleration of coarse hair growth
Diabetes	Erythematous plaques of shins, delayed wound healing, neuropathy, acanthosis nigricans (velvety, dark skin on the neck and in skin folds)
Glucocorticoid excess (Cushing syndrome)	Atrophy, striae, epidermal thinning, telangiectasia, acne. Decreased subcutaneous fat over extremities. Thin, loose dermis. Impaired wound healing. Increased vascular fragility. Mild hirsutism. Excess collection of fat over clavicles, back of neck, abdomen, and face
Hypoparathyroidism	Opaque, brittle nails with transverse ridges. Coarse, sparse hair with patchy alopecia
Hypothyroidism	Cold, dry, pale to yellow skin. Generalized nonpitting edema. Dry, coarse, brittle hair. Brittle, slow-growing nails
Hyperpituitarism (acromegaly)	Coarsened skin, deepened lines. Increased oiliness and sweating, acne. Increased number of nevi, hyperpigmentation; hypertrichosis (excess hair growth)
Hyperthyroidism	Increased sweating, warm skin with persistent flush, thin nails, alopecia. Fine, soft hair
Reproductive Organs	
Paget's disease	Eczematous patch of nipple and areola
Primary syphilis	Chancre
Secondary syphilis	Generalized skin lesions, alopecia
Tertiary syphilis	Gummas
Gastrointestinal	
Cystic fibrosis	Abnormal sweat gland function
Deficiency of essential fatty acids	Scaly skin
Inflammatory bowel disease	Mouth ulcers, erythema nodosum
Liver disease and biliary tract obstruction	Jaundice, itching, pigmentary abnormalities, changes in nails and hair, spider angiomas, telangiectasia
Malabsorption syndrome	Acquired ichthyosis (dry, scaly skin)
Musculoskeletal and Connective Tissue	
Dermatomyositis	Edema; purplish-red upper eyelids; scaly, macular erythema over knuckles
Scleroderma	Leathery hardening and stiffness of skin
Systemic lupus erythematosus	Discoid lesions, maculopapular semiconfluent rash (butterfly rash), alopecia, mouth ulcers
Metabolic	
Nicotinic acid (niacin) deficiency	Redness of exposed areas of skin of hand or foot, face, or neck; infected dermatitis
Vitamin B$_1$ (thiamine) deficiency	Edema, redness of soles of feet
Vitamin B$_2$ (riboflavin) deficiency	Red fissures at corner of mouth, glossitis
Vitamin C deficiency	Petechiae, purpura, bleeding gums
Immune	
HIV infection	Kaposi sarcoma, eosinophilic folliculitis
Hodgkin's lymphoma	Pruritus, sensitive skin
Non-Hodgkin's lymphoma	Papules, nodules, plaques, pruritus
Cardiovascular	
Rheumatic heart disease	Petechiae, urticaria, nodules, erythema
Peripheral vascular disease	Loss of hair on hands and feet. Delayed capillary filling. Dependent rubor (redness), pain
Thromboangiitis obliterans (Buerger's disease)	Pallor or cyanosis, gangrene, ulceration
Venous ulcers	Leathery, brownish skin on lower leg; pruritus, concave lesion with edema. Scar tissue with healing
Respiratory	
Inadequate oxygenation due to respiratory disease	Cyanosis
Hematologic	
Anemia	Pallor, hyperpigmentation, pale mucous membranes, hair loss, nail dystrophy
Clotting disorders	Purpura, petechiae, ecchymosis
Renal	
Chronic kidney disease	Dry skin, pruritus, uremic frost, pallor, bruises
Neurologic	
Chronic sensory polyneuropathies Spinal cord trauma	Trophic changes in skin resulting from sensory denervation, pressure ulcers, anesthesia, paresthesias

Nutritional-Metabolic Pattern. Ask the patient about the condition of skin, hair, nails, and mucous membranes and whether they notice any changes related to diet. A diet history reveals the adequacy of nutrients essential to healthy skin and wound healing such as vitamins A, D, E, and C; dietary fat; and protein. Note any food allergies that cause a skin reaction. Ask obese patients if they have areas of chafing or a rash in intertriginous areas, where skin surfaces overlap and rub on each other (e.g., below the breasts, axillae, and groin). Skin in these areas is predisposed to skin tags *(acrochordons)* and candidiasis (yeast), intertrigo (bacteria, fungi, yeast), and erythrasma (bacteria) infections. Note any excess or absent sweating. Ask the patient about poor or delayed wound healing.

Elimination Pattern. Ask the patient about skin conditions, such as dehydration, edema, and pruritus (itching), which can indicate changes in fluid balance. If urinary or fecal incontinence is a problem, ask about the condition of the skin in the anal and perineal areas.

Activity-Exercise Pattern. Obtain information about environmental hazards in relation to hobbies and recreational activities, including exposure to known carcinogens, chemical irritants, and allergens. Ask the patient if any changes occur in the skin during exercise or other activities.

Sleep-Rest Pattern. Ask the patient about changes in sleep patterns caused by a skin condition. For example, pruritus can be distressing and interfere with normal sleep. Poor sleep and resulting tiredness can be reflected in a patient's face by dark circles under the eyes and a decreased firmness in the facial skin.

Cognitive-Perceptual Pattern. Determine the patient's perception of the sensations of heat, cold, pain, and touch. Note any discomfort associated with a skin condition, especially when observed in intact skin, or any reports of unusual skin sensations. Patients with neuropathy may describe numbness, tingling, or crawling sensations in their arms or legs. Ask about joint pain. Assess the mobility of the joints, since the patient's skin condition may cause changes in mobility.

Self-Perception–Self-Concept Pattern. Assess any feelings related to the patient's skin condition such as sadness, anxiety, despair, or altered body image. These feelings can occur with classic signs of aging or visible skin problems such as acne, rosacea, and psoriasis, which alter physical appearance.

Role-Relationship Pattern. Determine how the patient's skin condition affects relationships with family members, peers, and work associates. Ask the patient about the effect of environmental factors on the skin, such as occupational exposure to irritants, sun, and unusually cold or unhygienic conditions. Contact dermatitis caused by allergens and irritants is a common problem associated with occupation.

Sexuality-Reproductive Pattern. Tactfully assess the effect of the patient's skin condition on sexual activity. Note the reproductive status of the female patient relative to possible therapeutic interventions. For example, isotretinoin, used to treat acne, and topical fluorouracil, used to treat actinic keratoses, are teratogenic drugs that may cause abnormal fetal development. Pregnant women or women who could become pregnant should not use them.

Coping–Stress Tolerance Pattern. Assess the role that stress may play in creating or worsening the skin condition. Ask the patient what coping strategies are used to manage the skin condition.

Value-Belief Pattern. Ask about cultural or religious beliefs that could influence the patient's self-image as related to the skin condition. Assess values and beliefs that may influence or limit the choice of treatment options.

CASE STUDY

Subjective Data

(© iStockphoto/ Thinkstock.)

A focused subjective assessment of D.A. reveals the following:

- *PMH:* Negative except for an appendectomy at age 16.
- *Medications:* None at present. NKA.
- *Health Perception–Health Management:* Washes her face with a skin cleanser in the morning and nighttime. After cleansing, she applies a moisturizer with SPF 15. She has used these facial products for the past 3 years since she first started noticing small age spots appearing. Before that, she just used soap and water.
- *Nutritional:* D.A. reports that her skin seems to be drier as she ages but otherwise no changes besides the "age spots" or "whatever they are." Denies any changes in the way cuts or sores heal. No weight loss. Does not take any supplemental vitamins or minerals.
- *Elimination:* Although skin is a little dry, D.A. does not perceive it to be excessively dry. Denies excess sweating or any swelling.
- *Activity-Exercise:* Loves to garden and go for walks outdoors. Reports a history of frequent, sometimes severe, sunburns as a child. No use of sunscreen growing up but does remember her mother making her wear T-shirts over her bathing suits to help prevent sunburn. Has used sunscreen for the past 20 years when outdoors. Reapplies as needed.
- *Cognitive-Perceptual:* Denies any pain or discomfort associated with skin lesions.
- *Coping–Stress Tolerance:* Fearful that she might have skin cancer.

Discussion Questions

1. Which subjective assessment findings are of most concern to you?
2. What should you include in the physical assessment? What specific characteristics of the skin lesions would you be looking for?

You will learn more about the physical examination of the skin in the next section.

(See p. 406 for more information on D.A.)

Answers available at *http://evolve.elsevier.com/Lewis/medsurg.*

Objective Data

Physical Examination. A physical examination of the skin begins with a systematic, general inspection and then a more specific assessment of problem areas. A normal range of differences exists in the skin, hair, and nails. Your assessment should note normal skin changes related to age, genetic factors, and environmental exposures from other changes. Look for changes in the color of the skin, turgor, temperature, dryness, thickness, and vascularity. General principles when assessing the skin are:

- Have a private examination room of moderate temperature with good lighting; a room with exposure to daylight is preferred.
- Ensure that the patient is comfortable and in a dressing gown that allows easy access to all skin areas.
- Perform a general inspection and then a lesion-specific examination.
- Use the metric system when taking measurements.
- Use the right terminology when reporting or documenting.

Clinical Photography. Photographs are an adjunct to documentation and promote communication among the interprofessional team. They are used to assess and monitor skin conditions and determine if the condition has improved or declined with treatment. They can be used to track moles and precancerous lesions and detect any changes early. Follow clinical agency protocol for obtaining a patient's consent to photograph lesions.

Inspection. Inspect the skin for general color and pigmentation, vascularity, bruising, and lesions or discolorations. The critical factor in assessment of skin color is change. A skin color that is normal for one patient can be a sign of a pathologic condition in another patient. The skin color depends on the amount of melanin (brown), carotene (yellow), oxyhemoglobin (red), and reduced hemoglobin (bluish red) present at a particular time. The most reliable areas to assess erythema, cyanosis, pallor, and jaundice are the areas of least pigmentation, such as the sclera, conjunctivae, nail beds, lips, and buccal mucosa. The true skin color is best seen in photo-protected areas such as the buttocks. Activity, sun (UV) exposure, emotions, cigarette smoking, and edema, as well as respiratory, renal, cardiovascular, and hepatic disorders, can all directly affect skin color.

In your general inspection, note the presence of body art such as piercings and tattoos. The nose, ears, eyebrows, lips, navel, and nipples are common sites of piercing. Examine tattoos and needle-track marks and note the location and characteristics of the surrounding skin area. Tattoo pigments deposited in the skin may cause itching, pain, and sensitivity for several weeks after the tattoo is placed.

Examine the skin for problems related to vascularity, including bruising and vascular and purpuric lesions such as *angioma* (benign tumor of blood or lymph vessels), *petechiae* (tiny, flat, purplish red pinpoint lesions on skin), *ecchymosis* (bruise larger than petechiae), or *purpura* (purple colored spots and patches characterized by ecchymosis or other small hemorrhages). Note the reaction to direct pressure on the lesion. If a lesion blanches on direct pressure and then refills, the redness is due to dilated blood vessels. If the discoloration stays, it is the result of subcutaneous or intradermal bleeding or a nonvascular lesion. Note any pattern of bruising such as discoloration in the shape of the hand or fingers or bruises at different stages of resolution. These may indicate other health problems or abuse and need further investigation.

Record the color, size, height, distribution, location, and shape of any lesions. Lesions may be primary or secondary lesions. *Primary skin lesions* develop on previously unaltered skin. The common characteristics of primary skin lesions are shown in Table 22.5. *Secondary skin lesions* are lesions that change with time or occur because of scratching or infection. Secondary skin lesions are shown in Table 22.6.

Skin lesions are usually described in terms related to the lesions' configuration (solitary or pattern in relation to other lesions) and distribution (arrangement of lesions over an area of skin) (Table 22.7). Note any unusual odors. Skin sites with lesions, such as rashes, may be colonized with yeast or bacteria, which can be associated with distinctive odors in areas where skin rubs together (Fig. 22.5).

Inspect all body hair. Note the distribution, texture, and quantity of hair. Changes in the normal distribution of body hair and growth may indicate an endocrine or vascular disorder. Carefully inspect the nails, including nail shape, thickness, curvature, and surface. Note any grooves, pitting, ridges, or detachment from nail bed. Changes in nail smoothness or thickness can occur with anemia, psoriasis, thyroid problems, decreased vascular circulation, and some infections.

Palpation. Palpate the skin to obtain information about temperature, turgor, moisture, and texture. Use the back of your hand to gauge skin temperature. The skin should be warm, not hot. Skin temperature increases when blood flow to the dermis increases. A localized temperature increase occurs with burns

and local inflammation. A generalized increase occurs when a person has a fever. A decreased body temperature may occur when shock or other circulatory problems, chilling, or infection are present.

Turgor refers to the elasticity of the skin. Assess turgor by gently pinching an area of skin under the clavicle or on the back of the hand. Skin with good turgor should move easily when

TABLE 22.5 Primary Skin Lesions

Lesion	Description
Macule	Circumscribed, flat discoloration that is blue, red, brown, or hypopigmented. <0.5 cm in diameter. If lesion >0.5 cm, it is a patch *Examples:* freckles, petechiae, measles, flat mole (nevus), café-au-lait spots, vitiligo (complete depigmentation)
Papule	Elevated, solid lesion. <0.5 cm in diameter. Color varies. If lesion is >0.5 cm in diameter, it is a nodule *Examples:* wart (verruca), elevated moles, lipoma, basal cell carcinoma
Plaque	Circumscribed, elevated, superficial, solid lesion. >0.5 cm in diameter *Examples:* psoriasis, seborrheic and actinic keratoses
Pustule	Elevated, superficial lesion filled with purulent fluid *Examples:* acne, impetigo
Vesicle	Circumscribed, superficial collection of serous fluid. <0.5 cm in diameter. If lesion >0.5 cm, it is a bulla *Examples:* varicella (chickenpox), herpes zoster (shingles), second-degree burn
Wheal	Firm, edematous, irregularly shaped area. Size varies. May last only a few hours *Examples:* insect bite, urticaria, angioedema

TABLE 22.6 Secondary Skin Lesions

Lesion	Description
Atrophy	Depression in skin resulting from thinning of the epidermis or dermis *Examples:* aged skin, striae
Excoriation	Area in which epidermis is missing, exposing the dermis *Examples:* abrasion, scratch
Fissure	Linear crack or break from the epidermis to the dermis. Dry or moist *Examples:* athlete's foot, chapping, eczema
Scale	Excess, dead epidermal cells made by abnormal keratinization and shedding *Examples:* flaking of skin after a drug reaction or sunburn
Scar	Abnormal formation of connective tissue that replaces normal skin *Examples:* surgical incision, healed wound
Ulcer	Loss of the epidermis and dermis. Crater-like, irregular shape. Heals with scarring *Examples:* pressure ulcer, chancre

TABLE 22.7 Lesion Distribution Terminology

Term	Description
Annular	Circular, begins in center and spreads to periphery (e.g., tinea corporis [ringworm])
Asymmetric	Unilateral distribution
Confluent	Merging together (e.g., urticaria [hives])
Discrete	Distinct individual lesions that are separate (e.g., acne)
Gyrate	Twisted, coiled spiral, snakelike
Grouped	Clusters of lesions (e.g., vesicles of contact dermatitis)
Localized	Clearly defined, limited areas of involvement (confined to one area)
Polycyclic	Annular lesions grow together (e.g., psoriasis)
Solitary	Single lesion
Symmetric	Bilateral distribution
Zosteriform	Linear arrangement along a dermatome area (e.g., herpes zoster)

flaking, scaling, or cracking. Skin generally becomes drier with increasing age.

Texture refers to the fineness or coarseness of the skin. The skin should feel smooth and firm with the surface evenly thin in most areas. Thickened callus areas are normal on the soles and palms and relate to weight bearing. Increased skin thickness is often work related and the result of excess pressure. Excess calluses on the soles of patients with neuropathy or diabetes predispose them to developing lesions.

Use a *focused assessment* to evaluate the status of previously identified skin problems and to monitor for signs of new problems. A focused assessment of the skin is presented in the following box. Assessment abnormalities of the skin are described in Table 22.8.

FOCUSED ASSESSMENT
Integumentary System

Use this checklist to make sure the key assessment steps have been done.

Subjective
Ask the patient about any of the following and note responses.

Hair loss (unusual or rapid)	Y	N
Changes in skin (e.g., lesions, bruising)	Y	N
Nail discoloration	Y	N

Objective: Diagnostic
Check the following for results and critical values.

Biopsy results	✓
Albumin	✓

Objective: Physical Examination
Inspect

Skin for color, integrity, scars, lesions, signs of breakdown	✓
Facial and body hair for distribution, color, quantity, hygiene	✓
Nails for shape, contour, color, thickness, cleanliness	✓
Dressings, if present	✓

Palpate

Skin for temperature, texture, moisture, thickness, turgor, mobility	✓

lifted and immediately return to its original position when released. In patients with dehydration and aging, a loss of turgor occurs and can cause tenting of the skin.

Skin moisture (dampness or dryness of the skin) increases in areas where skin rubs together. Skin moisture varies with environmental temperature, muscular activity, body weight, and body temperature. The skin should be intact with no

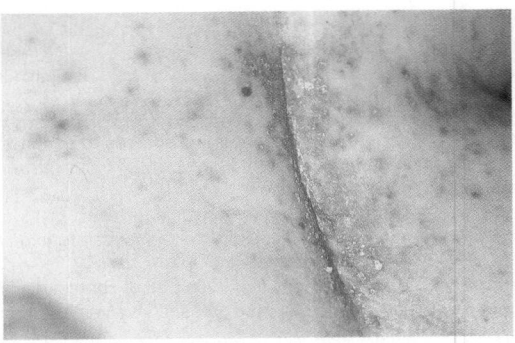

FIG. 22.5 Intertrigo. Rash in body folds with *Candida* infection. (From Graham-Brown R, Bourke J, Cunliffe T: *Dermatology: Fundamentals of practice,* Edinburgh, 2008, Mosby.)

Assessment of Dark Skin

The structures of dark skin are no different from those of lighter skin, but they are often harder to assess (Table 22.9). Color is easiest to assess in areas where the epidermis is thin, and pigmentation is not influenced by sun exposure, such as the lips, mucous membranes, nail beds, and protected areas (e.g., buttocks). Palmar and plantar surfaces are lighter than other skin areas in darker skinned persons. Rashes are often harder to see and may have to be palpated. Wrinkling is less apparent in those with dark skin.

Persons with dark skin are predisposed to certain skin and hair conditions. Keloid is an overgrowth of collagenous tissue at the site of a skin injury (e.g., ear piercing) (Fig. 22.6). *Vitiligo* is total loss of pigment in the affected area (Fig. 22.7). In *dermatosis papulosa nigra*, the person has small, pigmented wart-like

---

TABLE 22.8 Assessment Abnormalities

Integumentary System

Finding	Description	Possible Etiology and Significance
Alopecia	Loss of hair (localized or general)	Heredity, friction, rubbing, traction, trauma, stress, infection, inflammation, chemotherapy, pregnancy, emotional shock, tinea capitis, immunologic factors
Angioma	Tumor consisting of blood or lymph vessels	Normal increase in incidence with aging, liver disease, pregnancy, varicose veins
Carotenemia (carotenosis)	Yellow discoloration of skin, no yellowing of sclerae, most noticeable on palms and soles	Vegetables containing carotene (e.g., carrots, squash), hypothyroidism
Comedo (acne lesion)	Enlarged hair follicle plugged with sebum, bacteria, and skin cells; can be open (blackhead) or closed (whitehead)	Heredity, certain drugs, hormonal changes with puberty and pregnancy
Cyanosis	Slightly bluish gray or dark purple discoloration of the skin and mucous membranes caused by excess amounts of reduced hemoglobin in capillaries	Cardiorespiratory problems, vasoconstriction, asphyxiation, anemia, leukemia, and cancers
Cyst	Sac containing fluid or semisolid material	Obstruction of a duct or gland, parasitic infection
Ecchymosis	Large, bruise-like lesion caused by collection of extravascular blood in dermis and subcutaneous tissue	Trauma, bleeding disorders
Erythema	Redness occurring in patches of variable size and shape	Heat, certain drugs, alcohol, ultraviolet rays, any problem that causes dilation of blood vessels in the skin
Hematoma	Extravasation of blood of enough size to cause visible swelling	Trauma, bleeding disorders
Hirsutism	Male distribution of hair in women	Abnormality of ovaries or adrenal glands, decrease in estrogen level, familial trait
Hypopigmentation	Loss of pigmentation resulting in lighter patches than the normal skin	Chemical agents, nutritional factors, burns, inflammation, infection
Intertrigo	Dermatitis of overlying surfaces of the skin (Fig. 22.5)	Moisture, irritation, obesity; may be complicated by *Candida* infection
Jaundice	Yellow (in white patients) or yellowish brown (in dark-skinned patients) discoloration of the skin, best seen in the sclera, secondary to increased bilirubin in the blood	Liver disease, red blood cell hemolysis, pancreatic cancer, common bile duct obstruction
Keloid	Hypertrophied scar beyond wound margins (Fig. 22.6)	Predisposition more common in dark-skinned persons
Lichenification	Thickening of the skin with accentuated normal skin markings	Repeated scratching, rubbing, and irritation usually because of pruritus or neurosis
Mole (nevus)	Benign overgrowth of melanocytes	Defects of development; excess numbers and large, irregular moles; often familial
Petechiae	Pinpoint, discrete deposits of blood <1–2 mm in the extravascular tissues and visible through the skin or mucous membrane	Inflammation, marked vasodilation, blood vessel trauma, blood dyscrasia that results in bleeding tendencies (e.g., thrombocytopenia)
Telangiectasia	Visibly dilated, superficial, cutaneous small blood vessels, commonly found on face and thighs	Aging, acne, sun exposure, alcohol, liver failure, corticosteroids, radiation, certain systemic diseases, skin tumors
Tenting	Failure of skin to return immediately to normal position after gentle pinching	Aging, dehydration, cachexia
Varicosity	Increased prominence of superficial veins	Interruption of venous return (e.g., from tumor, incompetent valves, inflammation), commonly found on lower legs with aging
Vitiligo	Complete absence of melanin (pigment) resulting in chalky white patch (Fig. 22.7)	Autoimmune, familial, thyroid disease

TABLE 22.9 Nursing Assessment
Assessment Variations in Light- and Dark-Skinned Persons

Light Skin	Dark Skin
Cyanosis	
Grayish blue tone, especially in nail beds, earlobes, lips, mucous membranes, palms, and soles	Ashen or gray color most easily seen in the conjunctiva of the eye, mucous membranes, and nail beds
Ecchymosis	
Dark red, purple, yellow, or green color, depending on age of bruise	Purple to brownish black. Hard to see unless occurring in an area of light pigmentation
Erythema	
Reddish tone, possibly accompanied by increased skin temperature secondary to localized inflammation	Deeper brown or purple skin tone with evidence of increased skin temperature secondary to inflammation
Jaundice	
Yellowish color of skin, sclera, fingernails, palms, and oral mucosa	Yellowish green color most obviously seen in sclera of eye (do not confuse with yellow eye pigmentation, which may be seen in dark-skinned patients), palms, and soles
Pallor	
Pale skin color that may appear white or ashen; also seen on lips, nail beds, and mucous membranes	Lack of underlying red tone in brown or black skin. In lighter dark-skinned persons, yellowish brown skin. In darker dark-skinned persons, ashen or gray skin
Petechiae	
Lesions appearing as small, reddish purple pinpoints, best seen on abdomen and buttocks	Hard to see. May be seen in the buccal mucosa of the mouth or conjunctiva of the eye
Rash	
May be seen and felt with light palpation	Not easily seen. May be felt with light palpation
Scar	
Generally heals, showing narrow scar line	Higher incidence of keloid development, resulting in a thickened, raised scar (Fig. 22.6)

papules, often on the face (Fig. 22.8). *Nevus of Ota* is a slate-gray or blue-gray birthmark found on the forehead and face around the eye area. It may involve the sclera. *Traction alopecia* may be the result of trauma from hair rollers or from tight braiding of the hair (Fig. 22.9). The hair loss may be temporary or

FIG. 22.7 Vitiligo. Total loss of pigment in the affected area. (From Graham-Brown R, Bourke J, Cunliffe T: *Dermatology: Fundamentals of practice*, Edinburgh, 2008, Mosby.)

FIG. 22.8 Dermatosis papulosa nigra. Small, pigmented wart-like papules, often on the face. (From James W, Berger T, Elston D: *Andrews' diseases of the skin*, ed 12, Edinburgh, 2016, Elsevier.)

FIG. 22.9 Traction alopecia. Hair loss in scalp because of prolonged tension from hair rollers, braiding, or straightening combs. (From Ahanogbe I, Gavino A: Evaluation and management of the hair loss patient in the primary care setting, *Prim Care* 42:569, 2015.)

FIG. 22.6 Keloid. Hypertrophic scarring after skin injury, which is more common in dark-skinned persons. (From Kliegman RM et al: *Nelson textbook of pediatrics*, Philadelphia, 2011, Saunders.)

permanent. *Pseudofolliculitis* is an inflammatory response to ingrown hairs that occurs after shaving too closely in the beard area. The ingrown hairs result in pustules and papules.

Because of the darkness of the skin in some people, color may not be a reliable indicator of systemic conditions (e.g., flushed skin with fever). Cyanosis may be hard to detect because a normal bluish hue occurs in dark-skinned people. Dark skin rarely shows a blanch response, making it harder to identify pressure injuries.

CASE STUDY

Objective Data: Physical Examination

(© iStockphoto/ Thinkstock.)

- Physical examination findings of D.A.'s skin are as follows:
  - Complexion fair. Wrinkles around eyes, above upper lip, and on sides of cheeks bilaterally. Normal skin temperature and turgor.
  - Lesions: on upper right forehead measuring 2 × 3 mm; on left forehead near hairline measuring 1 × 2 mm; and on left lower cheek measuring 2 × 2.5 mm.

(Cheek lesion. From Bolognia JL, Schaffer JV, Duncan KO, et al: Dermatology essentials, Philadelphia, 2014, Saunders.)

- The lesions are slightly erythematous but do not blanch with direct pressure. Borders are distinct. The lesions on the forehead have minimal elevation noted on palpation. The lesion on the cheek is slightly elevated.
- No other skin lesions noted on rest of body.

Discussion Questions

1. Which physical assessment findings are of most concern to you?
2. What diagnostic studies do you think may be ordered for D.A.?

You will learn more about diagnostic studies related to the skin in the next section.
(See p. 407 for more information on D.A.)

Answers available at *http://evolve.elsevier.com/Lewis/medsurg.*

DIAGNOSTIC STUDIES OF INTEGUMENTARY SYSTEM

Table 22.10 presents common diagnostic studies used for the integumentary system. The main diagnostic techniques related to skin problems are inspection of an individual lesion and a careful history related to the problem. If a definitive diagnosis cannot be made by these techniques, other tests may be needed. With *dermatoscopy*, the HCP uses a lighted instrument with optical magnification to see skin structures and colors not visible with the naked eye.[7] These hand-held screening devices (e.g., MelaFind) can help the HCP determine if a lesion should be biopsied.

Biopsy is one of the most common diagnostic tests used to evaluate a skin lesion. A biopsy is needed when cancer is suspected or a specific diagnosis is questionable. Techniques include punch, incisional, excisional, and shave biopsies. The method used depends on factors such as the site of the biopsy, cosmetic result desired, and type of tissue needed.

Other diagnostic procedures include stains and cultures for fungal, bacterial, and viral infections. Direct immunofluorescence is a special diagnostic technique used on biopsy specimens. It may be needed in certain conditions such as bullous diseases and systemic lupus erythematosus. Indirect immunofluorescence is done on blood samples.

CASE STUDY

Objective Data: Diagnostic Studies

(© iStockphoto/ Thinkstock.)

The HCP examines the lesion via dermatoscopy and uses a Wood's lamp to rule out a fungal infection. The HCP suspects basal cell carcinoma.

Discussion Questions

1. Are these the diagnostic tests you expected the HCP to perform?
2. What, if any, other diagnostic studies would you expect to be ordered for D.A.?
3. What are the interprofessional team's priorities for D.A. at this time?

Answers available at *http://evolve.elsevier.com/Lewis/medsurg.*

TABLE 22.10 Diagnostic Studies Integumentary System

Study	Description and Purpose	Nursing Responsibility
Biopsy		
Excisional	Used when good cosmetic results and/or entire lesion removal desired. Skin closed with subcutaneous and skin sutures.	*Before:* Verify that consent form is signed (if needed).
Incisional	Wedge-shaped incision made in lesion too large for excisional biopsy. Useful when specimen needed is larger than shave or punch biopsy.	*During:* Help with site preparation, anesthesia, procedure, and hemostasis. Properly identify specimen.
Punch	Special punch biopsy instrument of appropriate size used. Instrument rotated to appropriate level to include dermis and some fat. Suturing depends on size and site. Provides full-thickness skin for diagnostic purposes.	*After:* Apply dressing, give postprocedure instructions to patient.
Shave	Single-edged razor blade used to shave off superficial lesions or small sample of a large lesion. Provides thin specimen for diagnostic purposes.	

TABLE 22.10 Diagnostic Studies Integumentary System—cont'd

Study	Description and Purpose	Nursing Responsibility
Microscopic Tests		
Culture	Test identifies fungal, bacterial, and viral organisms. For *fungi*, scraping or swab of skin performed. For *bacteria*, material obtained from intact pustules, bullae, or abscesses. For *viruses*, vesicle or bulla and exudate taken from base of lesion.	*Before:* Teach patient the purpose of test. *During:* Properly identify specimen. Follow instructions for storing specimen if not immediately sent to laboratory.
Immunofluorescence studies	Some skin diseases have specific, abnormal antibody proteins that can be identified by fluorescence studies. Can examine both skin tissue and serum.	*Before:* Teach patient the purpose of test. *During:* Help obtain specimen. For punch biopsy, place specimen in special fixative (e.g., Michel's) and not formalin.
Mineral oil slides	To check for infestations, place scrapings on slide with mineral oil and view microscopically.	*Before:* Teach patient the purpose of test. *During:* Prepare slide.
Potassium hydroxide (KOH)	Hair, scales, or nails examined for superficial fungal infection. Put specimen on glass slide and add 10%–20% concentration of KOH.	*Before:* Teach patient the purpose of test. *During:* Prepare slide.
Tzanck test (Wright's and Giemsa's stain)	Fluid and cells from vesicles examined. Used to diagnose herpes infections. Specimen put on slide, stained, and examined microscopically.	*Before:* Teach patient the purpose of test. *During:* Use sterile technique for collecting fluid.
Miscellaneous		
Patch test (Fig. 22.10)	Used to assess for allergic dermatitis and photoallergic reactions. Application of allergens to the patient's skin (usually on the back) for 48 hr. Test sites examined 48 hr later for a reaction, characterized by the presence of erythema, papules, and/or vesicles. May do additional readings beyond 48 hr.	*Before:* Teach patient the purpose of test and procedure. *After:* Tell patient to leave patches in place for 48 hr. During this time it is important not to wash the area or play vigorous sports because if the adhesive tape peels off, the process will need to be repeated. Do not expose the patches to sunlight or other sources of ultraviolet (UV) light.
Wood's lamp (black light)	Examination of skin with long-wave ultraviolet light causes specific substances to fluoresce (e.g., *Pseudomonas* organisms, fungal infections, vitiligo).	*Before:* Teach patient the purpose of test and procedure. Inform patient it is not painful. *During:* Darken room.

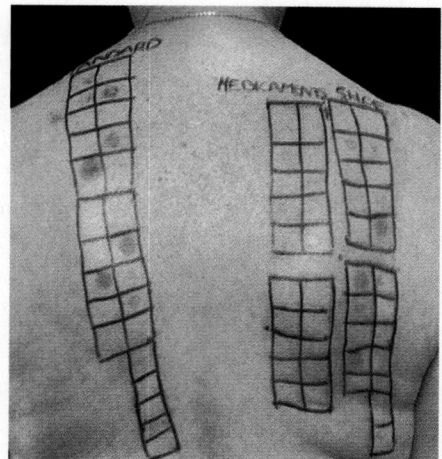

FIG. 22.10 Patch test. Results from applying possible allergens to the skin shows positive reactions in the sites labeled "standard" and "shoe." (From Graham-Brown R, Bourke J, Cunliffe T: *Dermatology: Fundamentals of practice,* Edinburgh, 2008, Mosby.)

■ BRIDGE TO NCLEX EXAMINATION

The number of the question corresponds to the same-numbered outcome at the beginning of the chapter.

1. The primary function of the skin is
   a. insulation.
   b. protection.
   c. sensation.
   d. absorption.

2. Age-related changes in the hair and nails include *(select all that apply)*
   a. oily scalp.
   b. scaly scalp.
   c. thinner nails.
   d. thicker, brittle nails.
   e. longitudinal nail ridging.

3. When assessing the nutritional-metabolic pattern in relation to the skin, the nurse asks the patient about
   a. joint pain.
   b. the use of moisturizing shampoo.
   c. recent changes in wound healing.
   d. self-care habits related to daily hygiene.

4. The nurse assessed the patient's skin lesions as firm, edematous, irregularly shaped with a variable diameter. They would be called
   a. wheals.
   b. papules.
   c. pustules.
   d. plaques.

5. During the physical examination of a patient's skin, the nurse would
   a. use a flashlight in a poorly lit room.
   b. note cool, moist skin as a normal finding.
   c. pinch up a fold of skin to assess for turgor.
   d. perform a lesion-specific examination first and then a general inspection.

6. Persons with dark skin are more likely to develop
   a. keloids.
   b. wrinkles.
   c. skin rashes.
   d. skin cancer.

7. On inspection of a patient's dark skin, the nurse notes a blue-gray birthmark on the forehead and eye area. This assessment finding is called
   a. vitiligo.
   b. intertrigo.
   c. Nevus of Ota.
   d. telangiectasia.

8. Diagnostic testing is recommended for skin lesions when
   a. a health history cannot be obtained.
   b. a more definitive diagnosis is needed.
   c. percussion reveals an abnormal finding.
   d. treatment with prescribed medication has failed.

1. b, 2. b, d, e, 3. c, 4. a, 5. c, 6. a, 7. c, 8. b

For rationales to these answers and even more NCLEX review questions, visit *http://evolve.elsevier.com/Lewis/medsurg*.

ⓔ EVOLVE WEBSITE/RESOURCES LIST

http://evolve.elsevier.com/Lewis/medsurg
Review Questions (Online Only)
Key Points
Answer Keys for Questions
  • Rationales for Bridge to NCLEX Examination Questions
  • Answer Guidelines for Case Study on pp. 398, 401, and 406
Conceptual Care Map Creator
Audio Glossary
Content Updates

REFERENCES

1. Habif TP: *Clinical dermatology*, ed 6, St Louis, 2015, Mosby.
2. Gawkrodger D, Ardern-Jones M: *Dermatology*, ed 6, St Louis, 2016, Mosby.
3. Alikhan A, Hocker TL: *Review of dermatology*, St. Louis, 2016, Elsevier Health Sciences.
4. Bishop BE, Tosti A: *Melanonychias*, New York, 2017, Springer International Publishing.
*5. Tobin DJ: Introduction to skin aging, *J Tissue Viability* 26:37, 2017.
*6. Coit DG, Thompson JA, Algazi A, et al: Melanoma, *JNCCN* 14:450, 2016.
*7. Russo T, Piccolo V, Lallas A, Argenziano G: Recent advances in dermoscopy, *F1000Research* 5:184, 2016.

*Evidence-based information for clinical practice

23

Integumentary Problems

Mariann M. Harding

The world is not dangerous because of those who do harm, but because of those who look at it without doing anything.

Albert Einstein

http://evolve.elsevier.com/Lewis/medsurg/

CONCEPTUAL FOCUS

Cellular Regulation	Infection	Tissue Integrity
Coping	Pain	

LEARNING OUTCOMES

1. Specify health promotion practices related to environmental hazards.
2. Explain the etiology, clinical manifestations, and interprofessional and nursing management of skin cancers.
3. Relate the etiology, clinical manifestations, and interprofessional and nursing management of bacterial, viral, and fungal skin infections.
4. Describe the etiology, clinical manifestations, and interprofessional and nursing management of infestations and insect bites.
5. Discuss the etiology, clinical manifestations, and interprofessional and nursing management of allergic skin disorders.

6. Explain the etiology, clinical manifestations, and interprofessional and nursing management related to benign skin disorders.
7. Select appropriate nursing interventions to manage the patient with a skin problem.
8. Explain the indications and nursing management related to common cosmetic procedures and skin grafts.

KEY TERMS

acne vulgaris, Table 23.10, p. 421
actinic keratosis, p. 411
basal cell carcinoma (BCC), p. 413
cellulitis, Table 23.5, p. 415
cryosurgery, p. 424

curettage, p. 423
dysplastic nevi (DN), p. 414
herpes zoster, Table 23.6, p. 417
impetigo, Table 23.5, p. 415
lichenification, p. 425

melanoma, p. 413
psoriasis, p. 419
squamous cell carcinoma (SCC), p. 413
sun protection factor (SPF), p. 410

This chapter discusses common skin conditions and skin cancer. Impaired skin integrity affects many body functions. The skin reflects both physical and psychologic well-being. Having a small abrasion or cancerous lesion leaves underlying tissues unprotected from infection and chemical dangers. Lesions can be painful because the skin has many sensory nerve endings. Skin conditions are often highly visible, potentially affecting body image and causing distress.

ENVIRONMENTAL HAZARDS

Sun exposure comes with serious risk and results in permanent sun damage. Sunlight is made up of visible light and ultraviolet (UV) light. There are two types of UV light: UVA and UVB. Specific wavelengths (Table 23.1) have different effects on the skin. UVA light is responsible for tanning, UVB for sunburn. The damage caused by UV rays is cumulative. It results in degenerative changes in the dermis and premature aging (e.g., loss of

elasticity, thinning, wrinkling, abnormal dryness). Prolonged and repeated sun exposure increases risk for actinic keratosis, basal and squamous cell cancers, and melanoma.

Patient teaching on sun protection is important. People often do not understand the serious risks of sun exposure. Following sun safety guidelines beginning early in life can help avoid the damaging effects of the sun and prevent the formation of skin cancer later in life. Fair-skinned persons and those with light-colored eyes should be especially cautious about excess sun exposure. They have less melanin and thus less natural protection.

Teach the patient ways to avoid the damaging effects of the sun. This includes wearing protective clothing, including sunglasses, a large-brimmed hat, and a darker colored, long-sleeved shirt of a tightly woven fabric or carrying an umbrella. The greatest risk is with midday sun, between the hours of 10:00 am and 2:00 pm, regardless of the latitude. This is when 80% of UV rays occur. Even on overcast days, serious sunburn can occur because up to 80% of the sun's UV rays can penetrate the clouds.

Warn people of the dangers of tanning booths and sun lamps, which emit UVA. Tanning booths increase the risk for sunburn, cataracts, and skin cancer.[1]

Sunscreens can filter both UVA and UVB wavelengths. The two types of topical sunscreens are chemical and physical. Chemical sunscreens are light creams or lotions designed to absorb or filter UV light, resulting in decreased UV light penetration. Physical sunscreens are thick, opaque, heavy creams that reflect UV radiation. Regular sunscreen use decreases the risk for developing melanoma.

The U.S. Food and Drug Administration (FDA) rates sunscreen products on their sun protection factor (SPF). The SPF measures the effectiveness of a sunscreen in filtering and absorbing UV radiation. All sunscreen labels in the United States must say which rays they protect against. Products labeled with "broad spectrum" block both UVA and UVB.[2] Sunscreens with broad spectrum labeling must have an SPF of at least 15. Sunscreens with an SPF of 15 or more filter 92% of the UVB rays and make sunburn unlikely when applied appropriately.

People need to select the right sunscreen for their needs. The general recommendation is that everyone should use daily sunscreen with a minimum SPF of 15. Teach patients to look for the term *broad spectrum* on sunscreen packaging. Those who have a history of skin cancer or problems with sun sensitivity should use a product with an SPF of at least 30. Sunscreens should be applied 20 to 30 minutes before going outdoors, even in cloudy weather. The SPF value of all sunscreens decreases with time. Sunscreen should be reapplied every 2 hours. You should apply 1 ounce per total body application. The ears, toes, and lips also need sunscreen. Sunscreens are not "waterproof" and must be reapplied after swimming.

TABLE 23.1 Wavelengths of Sun and Effects on Skin

Wavelength	Effect
Long (ultraviolet A [UVA])	Can produce elastic tissue damage and actinic skin damage Contributes to formation of skin cancer
Middle (ultraviolet B [UVB])	Causes sunburn and cumulative effect of sun damage Major factor in development of skin cancer
Short (ultraviolet C [UVC])	Blocked by the atmosphere and does not reach earth

TABLE 23.2 Drug Therapy
Drugs That May Cause Photosensitivity

Categories	Examples
Antidepressants	amitriptyline, doxepin, venlafaxine
Antidysrhythmics	quinidine, amiodarone (Cordarone)
Antihistamines	diphenhydramine, chlorpheniramine, clemastine, cetirizine (Zyrtec)
Antimicrobials	tetracycline, sulfamethoxazole, azithromycin (Zithromax), ciprofloxacin (Cipro)
Antifungals	griseofulvin, ketoconazole
Antipsychotics	chlorpromazine, haloperidol
Chemotherapy	methotrexate, dacarbazine, fluorouracil
Diuretics	furosemide (Lasix), hydrochlorothiazide
Hypoglycemics	tolbutamide, glipizide (Glucotrol), glyburide
Nonsteroidal antiinflammatory drugs	diclofenac (Voltaren), piroxicam (Feldene), sulindac

EVIDENCE-BASED PRACTICE
Tanning Booths and Skin Cancer

You are a nurse working in a dermatology clinic. D.F., a 30-yr-old woman with fair skin and blue eyes, is completing her health history before her annual skin screening. She says she regularly visits an indoor tanning salon every other week. She tells you that being tan makes her feel "healthier and prettier."

Making Clinical Decisions

Best Available Evidence. There is a strong link between exposure to UVA from indoor tanning booth use and increased risk for skin cancer (melanoma and nonmelanoma). Melanoma causes less than 5% of skin cancers yet accounts for almost 75% of skin cancer deaths. Melanoma risk increases with the number of years, hours, and sessions of indoor tanning independent of outdoor exposure.

Clinician Expertise. You note that D.F. has the following skin cancer risk factors: fair skin, blue eyes, frequent use of tanning booths.

Patient Preferences and Values. After listening, D.F. tells you that she will consider reducing the frequency of her visits—going only when she has an important event to attend.

Implications for Nursing Practice

1. How would you respond to D.F. given the information that she has provided to you?
2. What resources can help address her view that a "tan looks healthy?"
3. What sun safety guidelines should she follow when outdoors to prevent skin cancer?

Reference for Evidence

Gershenwald JE, Halpern AC, Sondak VK: Melanoma prevention: avoiding indoor tanning and minimizing overexposure to the sun, *JAMA* 316(18):1913, 2016.

Tripp MK, Watson M, Balk SJ, et al.: State of the science on prevention and screening to reduce melanoma incidence and mortality, *CA Can J Clin* 66:460, 2016.

Certain drugs potentiate the sun's effects, even with brief exposure. The chemicals in these drugs absorb light when exposed to natural sunlight and release energy that harms cells and tissues. Common photosensitizing drugs are shown in Table 23.2. The manifestations of drug-induced photosensitivity (Fig. 23.1) are like those of a sunburn. These include swelling, erythema, vesicles, and papular, plaquelike lesions. Assess the photosensitivity of each individual drug. Teach patients who are taking these drugs about their photosensitizing effect and the need to protect the skin from photosensitivity reactions by using sunscreen products.

Teach patients to self-examine their skin monthly. They should have a periodic professional assessment of areas that are hard to see. The cornerstone of skin examination is the ABCDE rule. Examine skin lesions for *Asymmetry, Border* irregularity, *Color* change and variation, *Diameter* of 6 mm or more, and *Evolving* in appearance (Fig. 23.2). Emphasize that a persistent skin lesion that does not heal and lesions once flat and now raised, once small and recently growing, or changing in appearance are warning signs. Patients should consult their HCP at once if any lesions or moles show any clinical signs (ABCDEs).

SKIN CANCER

Skin cancer is the most commonly diagnosed cancer.[3] Skin cancers are either nonmelanoma or melanoma. The fact that

FIG. 23.1 Intense eruption in areas exposed to sunlight after patient started on hydrochlorothiazide. (From Habif TP: Clin*ical dermatology: A color guide to diagnosis and therapy*, ed 5, St Louis, 2011, Mosby.)

FIG. 23.2 The ABCDEs of melanoma. **A,** Asymmetry: one half unlike the other half. **B,** Border irregularity: edges are ragged, notched, or blurred. **C,** Color: varied pigmentation; shades of tan, brown, and black. **D,** Diameter: greater than 6 mm (diameter of a pencil eraser). **E,** (not pictured) Evolving; changing appearance (change in shape, size, color, or other characteristic noted over time). (From The Skin Cancer Foundation, New York, NY.)

skin lesions are so visible increases the chance of early detection and diagnosis. This can often lead to a highly favorable prognosis.

Risk Factors

Risk factors for skin cancer include (1) having fair skin, blond or red hair with blue eye color; (2) history of outdoor sunbathing; (3) living near the equator or at high altitudes; (4) family or personal history of skin cancer; (5) having an outdoor occupation; (6) spending a lot of time in outdoor recreation activities; and (7) indoor tanning.[4] The Fitzpatrick Classification of Skin Type can help you determine a person's skin complexion and how likely the person is to get skin cancer (Table 23.3). Patients treated with oral methoxsalen (psoralen) and psoralen plus ultraviolet A radiation (PUVA) have a higher risk.

TABLE 23.3 Fitzpatrick Classification of Skin Type

Skin Type	Skin Color	Characteristics
I	White, freckles, very fair. Red or blond hair. Blue eyes	Always burns, never tans
II	White, fair. Red or blond hair. Blue, hazel, or green eyes	Usually burns, tans with difficulty
III	Cream white, fair. Any eye or hair color	Sometimes mild burn, gradually tan
IV	Brown, typical Mediterranean skin	Rarely burns, tans with ease
V	Deep brown, Middle Eastern skin types	Very rarely burns, tans very easily
VI	Black	Never burns, tans very easily

⊕ PROMOTING HEALTH EQUITY
Skin Problems

- Blacks, Asians, and Hispanics have a lower incidence of skin cancer than whites.
- Melanoma can occur in dark-skinned persons but often goes unrecognized until the advanced stages.
- Blacks and Asians are more likely to develop a keloid at the site of an injury.
- Skin cancer outcomes are poorer for ethnic minorities, those of low socioeconomic status, and the uninsured.

Dark-skinned persons are less susceptible to skin cancer because of their increased melanin, which acts like a sunscreen. However, there is still a risk, and they need to wear sunscreen. They often have melanomas on areas with less melanin, such as the palms, soles, mucous membranes, and under the nails. Since it is common for people with dark skin to have pigmented, longitudinal bands on their nails, assess and follow any nail discoloration.

NONMELANOMA SKIN CANCER

Nonmelanoma skin cancers (basal cell and squamous cell cancers) are the most common forms of skin cancer. More than 5.4 million new cases are diagnosed each year.[3] Nonmelanoma skin cancers do not develop from melanocytes. They develop in the basement membrane of the skin. Although there are few deaths from nonmelanoma skin cancer, they have the potential for severe local destruction, permanent disfigurement, and disability.

Nonmelanoma skin cancers usually develop in sun-exposed areas, such as the face, head, neck, back of the hands, and arms. The most common causative factor is sun exposure. There are some differences between basal and squamous cell cancers. Squamous cell cancers usually occur on the head and neck where there is the highest degree of UV radiation. Basal cell cancers do not follow that pattern and may occur in sun-protected areas.

Actinic Keratosis

Actinic keratosis (AK), also known as *solar keratosis,* is the most common precancerous skin lesion. They affect most of the older white population. Sun exposure is a key factor. AKs appear most often on skin that has been exposed to the sun or to artificial UV light. They may spontaneously resolve if a person reduces exposure to sunlight.

The clinical appearance of AK can be highly varied. The typical lesion is an irregularly shaped, flat, slightly erythematous papule with indistinct borders and an overlying hard keratotic scale or horn (Table 23.4). Because AK is impossible to distinguish from squamous cell cancer, treatment should be aggressive. Nonsurgical procedures are the first-line treatment. Any lesion that persists should be evaluated for a biopsy.

TABLE 23.4 Premalignant and Malignant Conditions of the Skin

Etiology and Pathophysiology	Clinical Manifestations	Treatment and Prognosis
Actinic Keratosis • Actinic (sun) damage • Premalignant skin lesions • Common in older whites • Increase in number with age	• Flat or elevated, dry, hyperkeratotic scaly papule. Often multiple • May be rough or wartlike • Rough adherent scale on red base, which returns when removed • Often on erythematous sun-exposed area	• Cryosurgery. Topical application of fluorouracil, imiquimod (Aldara) or diclofenac (Solaraze), chemical peels, laser resurfacing, photodynamic therapy • Recurrence possible even with adequate treatment
Atypical or Dysplastic Nevi • Morphologically between common acquired nevi and melanoma • May be precursor of melanoma	• Often >5 mm. Irregular border, possibly notched. Frequently multiple • Varying colors of tan, brown, black, red, or pink within single mole • Central part often raised with flat edges • Most common site on back, but possible in uncommon mole sites such as scalp or buttocks (Fig. 23.5)	• Increased risk for melanoma • Careful monitoring of those with a familial tendency to melanoma or dysplastic nevi • Excisional biopsy for suspicious lesions
Basal Cell Carcinoma • Change in basal cells. No maturation or normal keratinization • Continuing division of basal cells and formation of enlarging mass • Related to excessive sun exposure, genetic skin type, x-ray radiation, scars, and some types of nevi	*Nodular and ulcerative:* • Small, slowly enlarging papule • Borders semitranslucent or "pearly" with overlying telangiectasia • Erosion, ulceration, and depression of center • Normal skin markings lost (Fig. 23.3) *Superficial:* • Erythematous, pearly, sharply defined, barely elevated plaques	• Surgical excision, electrodessication and curettage, cryosurgery, radiation therapy, laser therapy, and photodynamic therapy • Vismodegib (Erivedge) or sonidegib (Odomzo) for metastatic or recurrent locally invasive lesions • Fluorouracil and imiquimod for superficial lesions • Slow-growing tumor that invades local tissue • Metastasis rare, 90% cure rate with primary lesions
Cutaneous T-Cell Lymphoma • Origins in skin. Localized chronic, slowly progressing disease • Possibly related to environmental toxins and chemical exposure • Mycosis fungoides (MF) is most common form • Sézary syndrome is an advanced form of MF • Prevalence twice as high in men as in women	• Classic presentation involves 3 stages: patch (early), plaque, and tumor (advanced) • History of persistent macular eruption followed by gradual appearance of indurated erythematous plaques on trunk • Appears similar to psoriasis • Pruritus, lymphadenopathy	• Treatment usually controls symptoms but is not curative • Skin-directed treatment includes phototherapy with ultraviolet light, radiation therapy, corticosteroids, and topical nitrogen mustard, imiquimod, or retinoids • Interferon, systemic chemotherapy, extracorporeal photopheresis, romidepsin (Istodax), denileukin diftitox (Ontak), and vorinostat (Zolinza) for progressive disease • Disease course is unpredictable. 10% will have progressive disease
Melanoma • Neoplastic growth of melanocytes anywhere on skin, eyes, or mucous membranes • Classification according to major histologic mode of spread • Potential invasion and widespread metastases	• Irregular color, surface, and border • Variegated color, including red, white, blue, black, gray, brown • Flat or elevated. Eroded or ulcerated • Often <1 cm in size • Most common sites in males are back, then chest. In females are legs, then back (Fig. 23.2)	• Surgical excision and possible sentinel lymph node evaluation • Adjuvant therapy after surgery if lesion >1.5 mm in depth • Correlation between survival rate and depth of invasion • Poor prognosis unless diagnosed and treated early • Spreading by local extension, regional lymphatic vessels, and bloodstream
Squamous Cell Carcinoma • Frequent occurrence on previously damaged skin (e.g., from sun, radiation, scar) • Malignant tumor of squamous cell of epidermis. Invasion of dermis, surrounding skin	• Most common on sun-exposed areas such as face and hands • *Superficial:* Thin, scaly erythematous plaque without invasion into the dermis • *Early:* Firm nodules with indistinct borders, scaling, and ulceration • *Late:* Covering of lesion with scale or horn from keratinization, ulceration	• Surgical excision, cryosurgery, radiation therapy, electrosurgery, laser therapy, and photodynamic therapy • Untreated lesion may metastasize to regional lymph nodes and distant organs • Fluorouracil and imiquimod for noninvasive SCC • Chemotherapy for metastatic lesions • High cure rate with early detection and treatment

Basal Cell Carcinoma

Basal cell carcinoma (BCC) is a locally invasive cancer arising from epidermal basal cells. It is the most common type of skin cancer but the least deadly. BCC usually occurs in middle-aged to older adults. Most BCCs occur in the head and neck area (e.g., sun-exposed), followed by the trunk and extremities.[5]

Manifestations are described in Table 23.4. Some BCCs are pigmented, with curled borders and an opaque appearance. They may be hard to distinguish from melanoma. A tissue biopsy is needed to confirm the diagnosis. BCCs rarely metastasize (Fig. 23.3). However, untreated BCC may result in massive tissue destruction. Treatment depends on the tumor location and histologic type, size, history of recurrence, and patient characteristics (Table 23.4).

Squamous Cell Carcinoma

Squamous cell carcinoma (SCC) is a cancer arising from keratinizing epidermal cells. SCC can be aggressive and has the potential to metastasize. It may lead to death if not treated early and correctly. SCC often occurs at the base of an actinic keratosis or another lesion. The main risk factors are sun exposure and immunosuppression after organ transplantation.[6] Pipe, cigar, and cigarette smoking contribute to the formation of SCC on the mouth and lips. The manifestations of SCC are described in Table 23.4. A biopsy should always be done when a lesion is suspected to be SCC.

MELANOMA

Melanoma is a tumor arising from melanocytes, the cells that make melanin. It causes most skin cancer deaths. Unlike most cancers whose incidence is stable or decreasing, the incidence of melanoma is steadily rising.[1] More than 87,000 new cases are diagnosed every year in the United States and almost 10,000 people will die from the disease.[3] Melanoma can metastasize to any organ, including the brain and heart.

A combination of environmental and genetic factors is likely involved in the development of melanoma. UV radiation from the sun is the main cause of melanoma. Artificial sources of UV radiation, such as sunlamps and tanning booths, also play a role. UV radiation damages the deoxyribonucleic acid (DNA) in skin cells, causing "misspellings" (mutations) in their genetic code. This alters the cells. Although anyone can develop melanoma, the risk is greatest for people who have red or blond hair, blue or light-colored eyes, and light-colored skin that freckles easily. These people have less melanin and thus less protection from UV radiation. The use of immunosuppressive drugs and a history of dysplastic nevi also increase risk.

A person may have a genetic predisposition toward getting melanoma. Of those with melanoma, 5% to 10% have a first-degree relative (e.g., parent, full sibling) who had melanoma.[4] This risk increases significantly if multiple relatives have had melanoma. Mutated genes have been found in some families who have a high familial incidence of melanoma.

Cutaneous melanoma begins in the skin. There are 4 subtypes of melanoma: (1) superficial spreading melanoma, (2) nodular melanoma, (3) lentigo maligna melanoma, and (4) acral lentiginous melanoma.

Clinical Manifestations

Melanoma often occurs on the lower legs in women and on the trunk and head in men. About one fourth of melanomas occur in existing nevi or moles. About 20% occur in dysplastic nevi. Rarely, it occurs in the mouth, intestines, and eyes.

The cornerstone of skin examination is the ABCDE rule (Fig. 23.2). Because most melanoma cells continue to produce melanin, melanoma tumors are often deep brown or black (Table 23.4). Lesions showing any sudden or progressive change in the ABCDE rule need evaluated.

Interprofessional Care

One of the first steps in diagnosing a suspicious lesion is dermoscopic examination. Dermoscopy can help the HCP decide if a lesion should be biopsied. Biopsy is a critical tool for determining the type of lesion. A biopsy should be done using an excisional biopsy technique. Shave biopsy, shave excision, or electrocauterization should not be done because these techniques do not measure the depth of the lesion.

The most important prognostic factor is tumor thickness at the time of diagnosis. We use 2 methods to determine thickness. The *Breslow measurement* indicates the depth of the tumor in millimeters (Fig. 23.4). The *Clark level* indicates the depth of invasion of the tumor; the higher the number, the deeper the melanoma.

Treatment depends on the site of the original tumor and the stage of the cancer. Melanoma staging (stages 0 to IV) is based on tumor size (thickness), nodal involvement, and metastasis. In stage 0, melanoma is confined to one place (in situ) in the epidermis. Melanoma is nearly 100% curable by excision if diagnosed at stage 0. Unfortunately, those with deep tumors or disease that has already spread to lymph nodes often develop metastases. The 5-year survival rate for those with advanced disease is less than 10%.[7]

The initial treatment of melanoma is wide surgical excision. Melanoma that has spread to the lymph nodes or nearby sites usually requires additional (adjuvant) therapy with combinations of immunotherapy, targeted therapy, chemotherapy, and/or radiation therapy.

Immunotherapy can include cytokines (α-interferon, interleukin-2), PD-1 inhibitors, and CTLA-4 inhibitors. Cytokines enhance the production of many immune system cells, including T cells and B cells. Drugs that block PD-1 or CTLA-4 boost the immune response against melanoma cells.[7] PD-1 inhibitors include nivolumab (Opdivo) and pembrolizumab (Keytruda). They block PD-1, a protein on T cells that keeps T cells from attacking other cells in the body. Ipilimumab (Yervoy) blocks

FIG. 23.3 Basal cell carcinoma. Rolled, well-defined border and central erosion. (From Goldman L, Schafer A: *Goldman-Cecil medicine*, ed 25, Philadelphia, 2016, Saunders.)

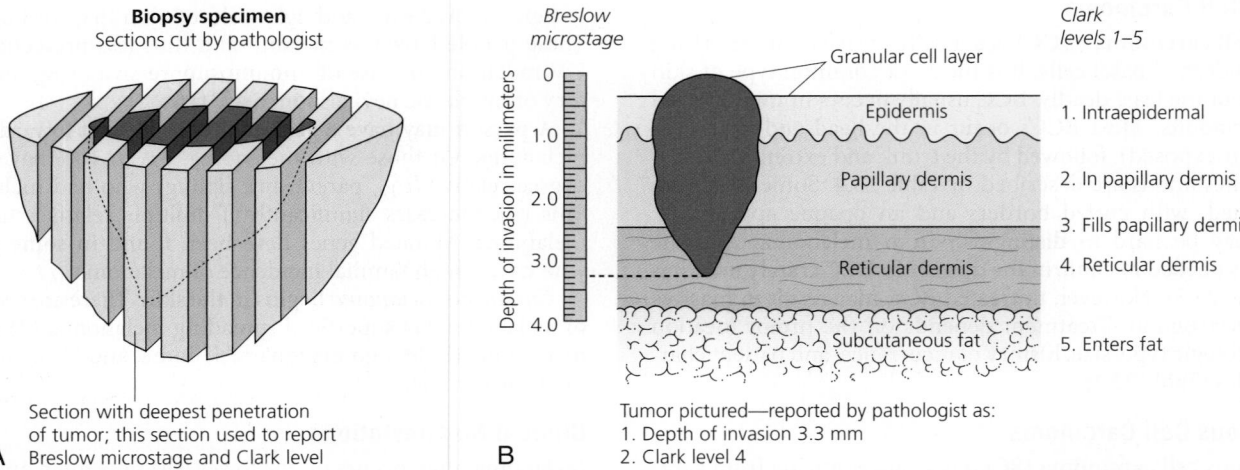

FIG. 23.4 A, Breslow measurement of tumor thickness. B, Clark level, showing tumor invasion. (From Habif TP: *Clinical dermatology: A color guide to diagnosis and therapy,* ed 6, St Louis, 2016, Mosby.)

FIG. 23.5 Dysplastic nevus. Irregular border and color. (From Graham-Brown R, Bourke J, Cunliffe T: *Dermatology: Fundamentals of practice,* Edinburgh, 2008, Mosby.)

the action of CTLA-4, another protein that normally suppresses the action of T cells.

Targeted therapy for melanoma includes BRAF and MEK inhibitors. About half of all melanomas have mutations in the *BRAF* gene, which makes an altered BRAF protein that signals melanoma cells to proliferate. Vemurafenib (Zelboraf), dabrafenib (Tafinlar), trametinib (Mekinist), and cobimetinib (Cotellic) are drugs that target BRAF mutations.[7]

Chemotherapy is not as effective for melanoma as it is for most other cancers. It is usually used only with advanced disease. Drugs used includes dacarbazine, temozolomide, cisplatin, paclitaxel, carboplatin, and vincristine.[3] Radiation therapy has a role in treating lymph node and brain metastases.

Atypical or Dysplastic Nevus

Dysplastic nevi (DN), or atypical moles, are nevi that are larger than usual (greater than 5 mm across) with irregular borders and various shades of color (Fig. 23.5). DN may have the same ABCDE characteristics as melanoma, but they are less pronounced. About 5% of the white population have DN.[8] Those with DN have an increased risk for developing melanoma in a mole or elsewhere on the body. The more DN a person has, the higher the risk. Those with 10 or more DN have 12 times the risk for developing melanoma.

SKIN INFECTIONS AND INFESTATIONS

Bacterial Infections

The skin provides an ideal environment for bacterial growth with an abundant supply of nutrients, water, and warm temperature. Bacterial infection occurs when the balance between the host and microorganisms is changed. This can occur as a primary infection after a break in the skin. Or, a secondary infection can occur in already damaged skin or as a sign of a systemic disease (Table 23.5). Predisposing factors include the presence of excess moisture, obesity, having atopic dermatitis, systemic corticosteroid and antibiotic use, and having a chronic disease, such as diabetes.

Staphylococcus aureus and group A β-hemolytic streptococci are the major types of bacteria responsible for primary and secondary skin infections. Streptococci cause impetigo, erysipelas, cellulitis, and lymphangitis. *S. aureus* causes impetigo, folliculitis, cellulitis, and furuncles (Fig. 23.6). When an infection is present, the resulting drainage is infectious. Good skin hygiene and infection control practices are necessary to prevent the spread of the infection.

Viral Infections

Like viral infections anywhere in the body, viral infections of the skin are hard to treat. When a virus infects a cell, a skin lesion may develop. Lesions can also result from an inflammatory response to viral infections. Herpes simplex, herpes zoster (Fig. 23.7), and warts (Fig. 23.8) are the most common viral infections affecting the skin (Table 23.6).

TABLE 23.5 Common Bacterial Infections of the Skin

Etiology and Pathophysiology	Clinical Manifestations	Treatment and Prognosis
Carbuncle • Multiple, interconnecting furuncles	• Many pustules appearing in erythematous area • Most common at nape of neck	• Incision and drainage (possibly with packing), antibiotics, meticulous care of involved skin, frequent application of warm, moist compresses • Heal slowly with scar formation
Cellulitis • Inflammation of subcutaneous tissues • May be a primary infection or secondary complication • Often following break in skin • *Staphylococcus aureus* and streptococci usual causative agents • Deep inflammation of subcutaneous tissue from enzymes produced by bacteria	• Hot, tender, erythematous, and edematous area with diffuse borders • Chills, malaise, and fever (Fig. 23.6)	*Topical:* • Moist heat, immobilization, and elevation *Systemic:* • Systemic antibiotic therapy • Hospitalization if severe for IV antibiotic therapy (vancomycin, linezolid, ceftaroline fosamil, daptomycin) based on culture and sensitivity • Progression to gangrene possible if untreated
Erysipelas • Superficial cellulitis primarily involving the dermis • Group A β-hemolytic streptococci	• Red, hot, sharply demarcated plaque that is indurated and painful • Bacteremia possible • Most common on face and extremities • Toxic signs: fever, ↑ WBC count, headache, malaise	• Systemic antibiotics, usually penicillin • Hospitalization often needed
Folliculitis • Usually staphylococci • Present in areas subjected to friction, moisture, rubbing, or oil • Increased incidence in patients with diabetes mellitus	• Small pustule at hair follicle opening with minimal erythema • Development of crusting • Most common on scalp, beard, extremities in men • Tender to touch	• Antistaphylococcal soap (e.g., Hibiclens, Lever 2000, Dial) and water cleansing • Topical antibiotics (e.g., mupirocin) • Warm compresses of water or aluminum acetate solution • Usually heals without scarring • If lesions extensive and deep, possible scarring, loss of involved hair follicles, and treatment with systemic antibiotics
Furuncle • Deep infection with staphylococci around hair follicle • Often associated with severe acne or seborrheic dermatitis	• Tender erythematous area around hair follicle that is painful • Draining pus and core of necrotic debris on rupture • Most common on face, back of neck, axillae, breasts, buttocks, perineum, thighs	• Treatment is the same as for carbuncles
Furunculosis • Increased incidence in patients who are obese, diabetic, chronically ill, or regularly exposed to moisture, pressure	• Lesions as above • Malaise, regional adenopathy, elevated body temperature	*Topical:* • Incision and drainage of painful nodules • Warm, moist compresses to erythematous plaques • Measures to reduce surface staphylococci include antimicrobial cream to nares, armpits, and groin and antiseptic to entire skin • Meticulous personal hygiene *Systemic:* • Systemic antibiotic effective against MRSA pending culture and sensitivity results • Often recurrent with scarring
Impetigo • Group A β-hemolytic streptococci, staphylococci, or combination of both • Associated with poor hygiene • Primary or secondary infection. Contagious	• Vesiculopustular lesions that develop thick, honey-colored crust surrounded by erythema • Pruritic • Most common on face as primary infection	*Topical:* • Wound care with warm saline or aluminum acetate soaks followed by soap-and-water removal of crusts and application of topical antibiotic cream or ointment (mupirocin, retapamulin [Altabax]) • Meticulous hygiene essential *Systemic:* • Systemic antibiotics (e.g., cephalosporins, erythromycin, amoxicillin, clindamycin) for widespread infections or systemic manifestations

MRSA, Methicillin-resistant *S. aureus.*

FIG. 23.6 Cellulitis with characteristic redness, tenderness, and edema. (From Habif TP: *Clinical dermatology: A color guide to diagnosis and therapy,* ed 5, St Louis, 2011, Mosby.)

FIG. 23.7 Herpes zoster (shingles) on the anterior chest, classic dermatomal distribution. (From James WD, Berger T, Elston DMD: *Andrews' diseases of the skin,* ed 11, Philadelphia, 2011, Saunders.)

FIG. 23.8 Plantar wart. **A,** Keratotic lesion. **B,** After excision. (From Swartz MH: *Textbook of physical diagnosis: History and examination,* ed 6, Philadelphia, 2010, Saunders.)

Infestations and Insect Bites

There are many opportunities for exposure to *infestations* (harboring insects or worms) and insect bites (Table 23.7). In many instances, an allergy to the venom plays a key role in the reaction. In other cases, the clinical manifestations are a reaction to the eggs, feces, or body parts of the invading organism. Some

people react with a severe hypersensitivity (anaphylaxis), which can be life threatening. Anaphylaxis is discussed in Chapter 13.

Preventing insect bites by avoidance or using repellents is somewhat effective. Meticulous hygiene related to personal articles, clothing, bedding, and examination and care of pets, as well as careful choice of sexual partners, can reduce the incidence of infestations. Prompt, routine skin inspection is necessary in geographic areas where there is a risk for tick bite. Lyme disease, which is caused by a tick, is discussed in Chapter 64.

Fungal Infections

Because of the large number of fungi that are present everywhere, exposure to some pathologic varieties may occur. Skin, hair, and nails can become infected with fungi, including candidiasis and tinea unguium. Common fungal infections of the skin are described in Table 23.8. Most infections are harmless in healthy adults, but they can cause embarrassment and distress.

Fungal infections are easy to diagnose. A microscopic examination showing the appearance of hyphae (threadlike structures) in a skin scraping mounted in 10% to 20% potassium hydroxide (KOH) indicates a fungal infection. A Wood's light examination of hair infected with certain fungi will fluoresce blue to green.

ALLERGIC SKIN PROBLEMS

Patients often seek treatment for irritant or allergic dermatitis, two common types of contact dermatitis. *Irritant contact dermatitis* results from direct chemical injury to the skin. *Allergic contact dermatitis* is an antigen-specific, type IV delayed hypersensitivity response. The pathophysiology of allergic and contact dermatitis is discussed in Chapter 13. Skin problems associated with allergies and hypersensitivity reactions may present a challenge to the clinician (Table 23.9). A careful family history and discussion of exposure to possible offending agents can provide valuable data. Patch testing can help determine possible causative agents (see Fig. 22.10). The best treatment of allergic dermatitis is to avoid known irritants. The extreme pruritus and its potential for chronicity make it a frustrating problem for you and the patient, especially if we cannot determine the offending agent.

Cutaneous Drug Reactions

Stevens Johnson syndrome (SJS) and *toxic epidermal necrolysis* (TEN) are rare, life-threatening diseases. They are violent immune responses that often occur as a severe adverse reaction to either a medication or, more rarely, an infection. The result is the acute destruction of the epithelium of the skin and mucous membranes. SJS, SJS-TEN overlap, and TEN represent a spectrum of disease severity. SJS involves less than 10% of total body surface area, TEN involves more than 30% of total body surface area, and SJS-TEN overlap involves 10% to 29% of total body surface area.[8]

SJS/TEN typically occur 4 to 21 days after starting use of the offending drug. Systemic symptoms, including fever, cough, headache, anorexia, myalgia, and nausea, precede skin and mucous membrane findings by 1 to 3 days. Skin involvement starts as an erythematous, macular rash with purpuric centers. Over a period of hours to days, the rash merges to form blisters with sheet-like epidermal detachment (Fig. 23.9). The lesions usually start on the palms, soles, and trunk, then spread to the

TABLE 23.6 Common Viral Infections of the Skin

Etiology and Pathophysiology	Clinical Manifestations	Treatment and Prognosis
Herpes Simplex Virus (HSV) Types 1 and 2 • Oral or genital HSV infections serotyped as either HSV-1 or HSV-2 • Both are recurrent lifelong viral infections • Worsened by sunlight, trauma, menses, stress, and systemic infection • Contagious to those not previously infected • Transmitted by respiratory droplets or virus-containing fluid (e.g., saliva, cervical secretions) • Infection in one area readily transmitted to another site by contact	*First episode:* • Symptoms occurring 2 days to 2 weeks after contact • Painful local reaction • Single or grouped vesicles on erythematous base • Systemic symptoms (e.g., fever, malaise) possible or no symptoms possible *Recurrent:* • Recurrence in similar spot • Characteristic grouped vesicles on erythematous base	• Symptomatic • Soothing, moist compresses. Petroleum jelly to lesions • Scarring not usual result • Antiviral agents such as acyclovir (Zovirax), famciclovir (Famvir), and valacyclovir (Valtrex) • Vaccine not currently available, but is being researched, for HSV-1 or HSV-2
Herpes Zoster (Shingles) • Activation of the varicella-zoster virus • Incidence increases with age • Potentially contagious to anyone who has not had varicella or who is immunosuppressed	• Linear distribution along a dermatome of grouped vesicles and pustules on erythematous base resembling chickenpox (Fig. 23.7) • Usually unilateral on trunk, face, and lumbosacral areas • Burning, pain, and neuralgia preceding outbreak • Mild to severe pain during outbreak	*Topical:* • Wet compresses, silver sulfadiazine (Silvadene) to ruptured vesicles *Systemic:* • Antiviral agents (e.g., acyclovir, famciclovir, valacyclovir) within 72 hr to prevent postherpetic neuralgia • Analgesia. Mild sedation at bedtime • Gabapentin (Neurontin) to treat postherpetic neuralgia • Usually heals without complications, but scarring and postherpetic neuralgia possible • Vaccine (Zostavax) to prevent shingles one-time dose for adults ≥60 yr
Plantar Warts • Caused by human papillomavirus (HPV)	• Wart on bottom surface of foot, growing inward because of pressure of walking or standing (Fig. 23.8) • Painful when pressure applied • Interrupted skin markings • Cone shaped with black dots (thrombosed vessels) when wart removed	• Topical immunotherapy (imiquimod), cryosurgery, salicylic acid, duct tape
Verruca Vulgaris • Caused by HPV • May disappear spontaneously in 1-2 yr • Mildly contagious by autoinoculation • Specific response dependent on body part affected • Prevalence greater in youth and immunosuppressed	• Circumscribed, hypertrophic, flesh-colored papule limited to epidermis • Painful on lateral compression	• Multiple treatments, including surgery using blunt dissection with scissors or curette • Liquid nitrogen therapy • Blistering agent (cantharidin) • Keratolytic agent (salicylic acid) • CO_2 laser destruction

TABLE 23.7 Common Infestations and Insect Bites

Etiology and Pathophysiology	Clinical Manifestations	Treatment and Prognosis
Bedbugs • Cimicidae species • Feeding periodic, usually at night • Present in furniture, walls during day	• Wheal surrounded by vivid flare • Firm urticaria transforming into persistent lesion • Severe pruritus • Often grouped in threes appearing on uncovered parts of body	• Lesions usually require no treatment • Severe itching may require use of antihistamines or topical corticosteroids
Bees and Wasps • Hymenoptera species	• Intense, burning, local pain • Swelling and itching • Severe hypersensitivity may lead to anaphylaxis	• Cool compresses • Local application of antipruritic lotion • Antihistamines if indicated • Usually uneventful recovery

Continued

TABLE 23.7 **Common Infestations and Insect Bites—cont'd**

Etiology and Pathophysiology	Clinical Manifestations	Treatment and Prognosis
Pediculosis (Head Lice, Body Lice, Pubic Lice)		
• *Pediculus humanus* var. capitis, *Pediculus humanus* var. corporis, *Phthirus pubis* • Obligate parasites that suck blood, leave excrement and eggs on skin and hair, live in seams of clothing (if body lice) and in hair as nits. Transmission of pubic lice often by sexual contact	• Minute, red, noninflammatory • Points flush with skin. Progression to papular wheal-like lesions • Pruritus • Secondary excoriation, especially parallel linear excoriations in intrascapular region • Nits and eggs are firmly attached to hair shaft in head and body	• γ-Benzene hexachloride or pyrethrins to treat various parts of body • Spinosad (Natroba) topical suspension 0.9% to treat scalp and hair • Screen and treat close contacts (e.g., bed partners and playmates) as needed • Do not share head gear
Scabies		
• *Sarcoptes scabiei* • Mite penetrates stratum corneum, deposits eggs • Allergic reaction to eggs, feces, mite parts • Transmission by direct physical contact, sometimes by shared personal items • Rarely seen in dark-skinned people	• Severe itching, especially at night, usually not on face • Presence of burrows, especially in interdigital webs, flexor surface of wrists, genitalia, and anterior axillary folds • Erythematous papules (may be crusted), possible vesiculation, interdigital web crusting	• 5% permethrin topical lotion, 1 overnight application with second application 1 wk later, may yield 95% eradication • Treat all family members, treat environment with plastic covering for 5 days, launder all clothes and linen with bleach • Treat sexual partner • Antibiotics, if secondary infections present • Possible residual pruritus up to 4 wk after treatment • Recurrence possible if inadequately treated
Ticks		
• *Borrelia burgdorferi* (spirochete transmitted by ticks in certain areas) causes Lyme disease • Endemic areas include Northeast, Mid-Atlantic states, parts of Midwest and West (see Chapter 64)	• Spreading, ringlike rash 3–4 wk after bite (see Fig. 64.7) • Rash common in groin, buttocks, axillae, trunk, and upper arms and legs • Warm, itchy, or painful rash • Flu-like symptoms • Cardiac, arthritic, and neurologic manifestations possible • Unreliable laboratory test	• Oral antibiotics, such as doxycycline • IV antibiotics for arthritic, neurologic, and cardiac symptoms • Rest and healthy diet • Most patients recover

TABLE 23.8 **Common Fungal Infections of the Skin and Nails**

Etiology and Pathophysiology	Clinical Manifestations	Treatment and Prognosis
Candidiasis		
• Caused by *Candida albicans* • Also known as moniliasis • 50% of adults symptom-free carriers • Appears in warm, moist areas such as groin area, oral mucosa, and submammary folds • Immunosuppression (e.g., from HIV infection, chemotherapy, radiation, and organ transplantation) allows yeast to become pathogenic	*Mouth:* White, cheesy plaque, resembles milk curds *Vagina:* Vaginitis with red, edematous, painful vaginal wall, white patches. Vaginal discharge. Pruritus. Pain on urination and intercourse *Skin:* Diffuse papular erythematous rash with pinpoint satellite lesions around edges of affected area	• Azole antifungals (e.g., fluconazole, ketoconazole) or other specific medication such as vaginal suppository or oral lozenge • Sexual abstinence or use of condom • Skin hygiene to keep area clean and dry • Powder is effective on nonmucosal surfaces of skin to prevent recurrence
Tinea Corporis		
• Various dermatophytes, commonly called *ringworm*	• Typical annular (ringlike) scaly appearance, well-defined margins • Erythematous	• Cool compresses • Topical antifungals for isolated patches. Creams or solutions of miconazole, ketoconazole, clotrimazole, butenafine
Tinea Cruris		
• Various dermatophytes • Commonly called *jock itch*	• Well-defined scaly plaque in groin area • Does not affect mucous membranes	• Topical antifungal cream or solution
Tinea Pedis		
• Various dermatophytes • Commonly called *athlete's foot*	• Interdigital scaling and maceration • Scaly plantar surfaces sometimes with erythema and blistering • May be pruritic and painful	• Topical antifungal cream, gel, solution, spray, or powder
Tinea Unguium (Onychomycosis)		
• Various dermatophytes • Incidence increases with age	• Only few nails on one hand may be affected. Toenails more commonly affected • Scaliness under distal nail plate • Brittle, thickened, broken, or crumbling nails with yellowish discoloration	• Oral antifungal (terbinafine [Lamisil], itraconazole [Sporanox]) • Topical antifungal cream or solution (minimal effectiveness) if unable to tolerate systemic treatment • Thinning of toenails if needed • Nail avulsion (removal) is an option

TABLE 23.9 Common Allergic Conditions of the Skin

Etiology and Pathophysiology	Clinical Manifestations	Treatment and Prognosis
Allergic Contact Dermatitis • Type IV delayed hypersensitivity response (see Chapter 13) • Absorbed agent acts as antigen • Sensitization occurs after one or more exposures • Appearance of lesions 2–7 days after contact with allergen	• Red papules and plaques • Sharply circumscribed with occasional vesicles (see Fig. 13.10) • Usually pruritic • Area of dermatitis often takes shape of causative agent (e.g., metal allergy and bandlike dermatitis on ring finger).	• Topical or oral corticosteroids, antihistamines • Skin lubrication • Elimination of contact allergen • Avoidance of irritating affected area • Systemic corticosteroids if sensitivity severe
Atopic Dermatitis • Type 1 hypersensitivity response (see Chapter 13) • Genetically influenced, chronic, relapsing disease • Exaggerated by a skin response to environmental allergens • Associated with allergic rhinitis and asthma	• Multiple presentations, including acute, subacute, and chronic stages. All are pruritic • *Acute stage:* Bright erythema, oozing vesicles, with extreme pruritus (see Fig. 13.8) • *Subacute stage:* Scaly, light red to red-brown plaques • *Chronic stage:* Thickened skin with accentuation of skin markings (lichenification), possible hypopigmentation, or hyperpigmentation. Dry skin. Common in antecubital and popliteal space	• Lubrication of dry skin • Topical immunomodulators (pimecrolimus [Elidel], tacrolimus [Protopic]) • Reduction of stress reduces flares • Corticosteroids, phototherapy for severe inflammation and pruritus • Antibiotics for secondary infection as needed
Drug Reaction • May be caused by any drug that acts as antigen and causes hypersensitivity reaction • Certain drugs (e.g., penicillin) more likely to cause reactions • Not all reactions are allergic, some are intolerance (e.g., gastric upset)	• Rash of any morphology • Often red, macular and papular, semiconfluent, generalized rash with abrupt onset • Appearance as late as 14 days after cessation of drug. May be pruritic • Some reactions may be life threatening requiring immediate and intensive care	• Withdrawal of drug if possible • Antihistamines, topical or systemic corticosteroids may be necessary depending on severity of symptoms
Urticaria • Usually allergic phenomenon • Erythema and edema in upper dermis resulting from a local increase in permeability of capillaries (usually from histamine release)	• Spontaneously occurring, raised or irregularly shaped wheals, varying size, usually multiple • A single lesion usually resolves in 24 hr • Can occur anywhere on the body	• Removal of triggering agent, if known • Oral antihistamine therapy • Possibly systemic corticosteroids

face and extremities. They are extremely painful. Most people have mucosal lesions in the eye, mouth, and genital areas.

Identifying and stopping the offending drug(s) is the most important action in caring for a patient with SJS/TEN. The most common drugs involved include sulfonamides, carbamazepine, nonsteroidal antiinflammatory drugs, lamotrigine, allopurinol, phenytoin, and phenobarbital.[8] Immunotherapy may play a role in slowing disease progression and promoting skin repair.

The patient receives supportive care, often in an intensive care unit. Interventions focus on airway management, preserving renal function, maintaining fluid and electrolyte balance, and pain control. Fluid replacement is given to maintain urine output. Proper wound care helps prevent infection and promote healing. Dressing with petrolatum gauze or other nonadhesive material provides a barrier and offers moisture to help the skin repair. Because of painful oral lesions, most patients need parenteral or enteral nutrition to meet nutrition and caloric demands. Apply eyedrops, lubricating ointment, and antibiotic drops to those with conjunctivitis.

BENIGN SKIN PROBLEMS

Although the list of benign skin problems is extensive, some of the most commonly seen and distressing ones include acne vulgaris (Fig. 23.10), psoriasis, and seborrheic keratoses. Benign problems are outlined in Table 23.10.

Psoriasis is a chronic autoimmune disease. It is fairly common, affecting about 7.5 million Americans.[9] Men and women develop psoriasis at equal rates. The rate is highest in whites (3.6%).[10] It usually develops in those 15 to 35 years old. One third of people with psoriasis have at least one relative with the disease. It is associated with metabolic syndrome, heart disease, and type 2 diabetes. Up to 40% of people with psoriasis also have psoriatic arthritis. Psoriatic arthritis is discussed in Chapter 64.

The diagnosis of plaque psoriasis, the most common form, is based on the skin's appearance (Fig. 23.11). Lesions are distinct and appear as red, scaling papules that merge to form plaques. The affected area is normally rounded, with adherent silver scales that bleed easily when removed. Plaques are common on the knees, elbows, scalp, hands, feet, and lower back.[9] They are often pruritic and may be painful. Clinical presentation varies. While most have mild disease, some have psoriasis on much of their skin surface.

Treatment is tailored to meet a person's needs. This varies depending on the location of lesions, severity, patient preferences, and comorbidities. Goals range from improved quality of life to complete disease resolution. Psoriasis for most is more emotionally than physically disabling. It erodes the self-image. The person may be self-conscious and withdraws from social contacts.[8] Quality of life can diminish as people avoid activities. Depression is common.

FIG. 23.9 Toxic epidermal necrolysis. (From *Ferri's clinical advisor 2018*. Dabiri, Ganary, MD, PhD; Rüenger, Thomas M., MD, PhD. Published January 1, 2018. Pages 1282.e2-1282.e3. © 2018.)

FIG. 23.10 Acne vulgaris. Papules and pustules. (From James WD, Berger T, Elston DMD: *Andrews' diseases of the skin*, ed 11, Philadelphia, 2011, Saunders.)

DRUG ALERT Isotretinoin (Accutane)

- Used to treat acne (Table 23.10)
- Can cause serious damage to fetus
- Contraindicated in women who are pregnant or want to become pregnant
- Cannot donate blood during treatment and for 1 month after treatment ends
- May cause depression and suicidal ideation

INTERPROFESSIONAL CARE: SKIN PROBLEMS

Diagnostic Studies

A careful history is of prime importance in diagnosing skin problems. The HCP must be skilled at detecting any evidence that could lead to the cause of many different skin problems. After a careful history and physical examination, inspect individual lesions. The history, physical examination, and diagnostic test results guide therapy.

Interprofessional Therapy

Many different treatment methods are used in dermatology. Advances in this field have brought relief to many previously chronic, untreatable conditions. Many of the specific therapeutic treatments require specialized equipment. They are usually used by a dermatologist or specially trained nurse.

Phototherapy. Ultraviolet light (UVL) therapy is a part of treating many skin problems, including psoriasis, cutaneous T-cell lymphoma, atopic dermatitis, vitiligo, and pruritus. Light sources available include broadband UVB, narrowband UVB, and long-wave UV (UVA1). One form of phototherapy combines the use of the photosensitizing drug methoxsalen with UVA light (PUVA). With PUVA, patients receive methoxsalen and then are exposed to UVA.

Treatments are generally given 2 to 3 times a week. Side effects include nausea, itching, and erythema. Taking methoxsalen with food and milk may reduce nausea. Caution patients about the hazards of using methoxsalen and concurrent exposure to UV rays from sunlight or artificial UVL during therapy. Because of the risk for cataracts, patients receiving PUVA need to wear prescription goggles that block 100% of UVL. Teach patients to wear the eyewear for 24 hours after taking the medication when outdoors or near a bright window because UVA penetrates glass. Perform frequent skin assessments on all patients receiving phototherapy. The immunosuppressive effects of PUVA increase the risk for SCC, BCC, and melanoma.

Photodynamic therapy is a special type of phototherapy used to treat actinic keratosis and some skin cancers. This therapy uses a photosensitizing agent in a different way than other phototherapy treatments. The patient receives the photosensitizing agent IV or topically, depending on the area treated. Time is allowed for the drug to be absorbed by the target cells. Light is then applied to the area, causing the drug to react with oxygen. This starts a reaction that kills the cells.[11]

❓ CHECK YOUR PRACTICE

You are working in a dermatology clinic preparing a 64-yr-old woman for phototherapy to treat multiple actinic keratoses on her nose and both cheeks. She says the first lesion appeared a few years ago. She then started to worry about all the time she spent in her garden without sunscreen. She thought the lesions were just "age spots" and was unconcerned until a few started to grow and periodically bleed.

- What teaching will you do to get her ready for the procedure and to take care of herself after the procedure?

Radiation Therapy. The use of radiation therapy to treat BCC and SCC varies. The best candidates are those with lesions in challenging locations, such as the ear, nose, scalp, neck, and shin; those who may have trouble with wound healing; or those with medical comorbidities who cannot undergo surgery.[12]

TABLE 23.10 Common Benign Conditions of the Skin

Etiology and Pathophysiology	Clinical Manifestations	Treatment and Prognosis
Acne Vulgaris • Inflammatory disorder of sebaceous glands • More common in teenagers • May begin and persist into adulthood • Flare can occur with use of corticosteroids and androgen-dominant birth control pills and before menses.	• Noninflammatory lesions, including open comedones (blackheads) and closed comedones (whiteheads) • Inflammatory lesions, including papules and pustules • Most common on face, neck, and upper back (Fig. 23.10)	*Topical:* • Mechanical removal of multiple lesions with comedo extractor • Topical benzoyl peroxide, retinoids, or antimicrobials (clindamycin, erythromycin) *Systemic:* • Systemic antibiotics • Use of isotretinoin (Accutane) for severe nodulocystic acne may provide lasting remission. Pregnancy tests, monitor liver function, cholesterol, triglycerides, and for depression • Aim of treatment to suppress new lesions and minimize scarring • Spontaneous remission possible • Often improvement with exposure to sun
Acrochordons (Skin Tags) • Common after midlife • Appearance on neck, axillae, and upper trunk secondary to mechanical friction or redundant skin (associated with obesity)	• Small, skin-colored, soft, pedunculated papules • May become irritated	• No treatment medically necessary • Surgical removal when needed. Usually just snipping without anesthesia
Lentigo • Increased number of normal melanocytes in basal layer of epidermis from sun exposure and aging • Also called "liver spots" or "age spots"	• Hyperpigmented, brown to black macule or patch (flat lesion) on sun-exposed areas	• Evaluate carefully for progression • Treatment only for cosmetic purposes: liquid nitrogen, laser resurfacing • May recur • Biopsy when suspicious of melanoma
Lipoma • Benign tumor of adipose tissue, often encapsulated • Most common in 40- to 60-yr-old age group	• Rubbery, compressible, round mass of adipose tissue • Single or multiple • Variable in size, may be extremely large • Most common on trunk, back of neck, and forearms	• Usually no treatment • Biopsy to distinguish from liposarcoma • Excision usual treatment (when indicated)
Nevi (Moles) • Grouping of normal cells derived from melanocyte-like precursor cells	• Hyperpigmented areas that vary in form and color • Flat, slightly elevated, verrucoid, polypoid, dome-shaped, sessile, or papillomatous • Preservation of normal skin markings • Hair growth possible	• No treatment necessary except for cosmetic reasons • Skin biopsy for suspicious nevi
Psoriasis • Autoimmune chronic dermatitis that involves extremely rapid turnover of epidermal cells • Family predisposition • Usually develops before age 40	• Sharply demarcated silvery scaling plaques on reddish skin often on the scalp, elbows, knees, palms, soles, and fingernails (Fig. 23.11) • Itching, burning, pain • Localized or general, intermittent or continuous • Symptoms vary in intensity from mild to severe	• Goal to reduce inflammation and suppress rapid turnover of epidermal cells. No cure, but control is possible *Topical treatments:* • Corticosteroids, tazarotene, calcipotriene, anthralin, calcineurin inhibitors (tacrolimus) • Intralesional injection of corticosteroids for chronic plaques *Systemic treatments:* • Natural or artificial UVB. PUVA (UVA with topical or systemic photosensitizer [psoralen]) • Traditional and oral therapies: antimetabolite (methotrexate), retinoid (acitretin), apremilast (Otezla), immunosuppressant (cyclosporine) • Biologic therapies: adalimumab (Humira), etanercept (Enbrel), infliximab (Remicade), ustekinumab (Stelara), brodalumab (Siliq), certolizumab pegol (Cimzia), secukinumab (Cosentyx), golimumab (Simponi), guselkumab (Tremfya), ixekizumab (Taltz) for moderate to severe plaque disease
Seborrheic Keratoses • Benign, familial, exact etiology unknown • Usually occur after age 40, increase in number with age	• Irregularly round or oval, often verrucous papules or plaques • Well-defined shape, appearance of being stuck on • Increase in pigmentation with time • Usually multiple, may be itchy	• Removal by curettage or cryosurgery for cosmetic reasons or to eliminate source of irritation • Biopsy if unable to distinguish from melanoma

PUVA, Psoralen ultraviolet A; *UVA,* ultraviolet A; *UVB,* ultraviolet B.

FIG. 23.11 Psoriasis. Characteristic inflammation and scaling. (From Habif TP: *Clinical dermatology: A color guide to diagnosis and therapy*, ed 5, St Louis, 2011, Mosby.)

TABLE 23.11 Skin Conditions Treated by Laser

- Acne scars
- Hair removal
- Hemangiomas
- Leg veins
- Pigment discoloration in epidermis
- Pigmented nevi
- Port wine stain
- Psoriasis
- Resurfacing of skin
- Rosacea
- Skin lesions
- Tattoo removal
- Vascular lesions
- Warts
- Wrinkles

Use is limited in those with melanoma to palliative pain control or treating brain metastases.

Radiation therapy requires multiple visits to a radiology department. It can produce permanent hair loss *(alopecia)* of the irradiated areas. Other adverse effects, depending on anatomic location and dose of radiation delivered, include telangiectasia, atrophy, hyperpigmentation, depigmentation, ulceration, hearing loss, ocular damage, atrophy, and mucositis. Careful shielding is necessary to prevent ocular lens damage if the irradiated area is around the eyes. See Chapter 15 for more on radiation therapy.

Total-body skin irradiation is one treatment for cutaneous T-cell lymphoma. Treatment follows a lengthy course and causes premature aging of the skin. Patients have varying degrees of permanent alopecia and radiation dermatitis with a transient loss of sweat gland function.

Laser Technology. Laser treatment is expanding rapidly as an efficient surgical tool for many types of skin problems (Table 23.11). Depending on the type of laser and the wavelength, lasers serve a wide variety of functions. Lasers can make measurable, repeatable, consistent zones of tissue damage. They can cut, coagulate, and vaporize tissue to some degree. Laser light does not accumulate in body cells and cannot cause cumulative cellular changes or damage. With less damage to surrounding tissue, there is a decreased risk for scarring.

The surgical use of laser energy requires a focusing device to produce a small, high-density spot of energy. Several types of lasers are available. The CO_2 laser, the most common, has many applications as a vaporizing and cutting tool for most tissues. The argon laser emits light that is primarily absorbed by hemoglobin. It helps in the treatment of vascular and other pigmented lesions. Other, less common lasers include copper and gold vapors and neodymium:yttrium-aluminum-garnet (Nd:YAG). Those who work with laser equipment must be familiar with facility policies and procedures on laser safety.

Drug Therapy

Antibiotics. Several topical and systemic antibiotics are used to treat skin problems. Sometimes they are used concurrently. Many common systemic antibiotics are not used topically because of the danger of allergic contact dermatitis. Common OTC topical antibiotics include bacitracin-neomycin-polymyxin (Neosporin), bacitracin, and polymyxin B. Some HCPs do not recommend Neosporin because of the risk for allergic contact dermatitis. Prescription topical antibiotics include (1) mupirocin (for superficial *Staphylococcus* infections such as impetigo), (2) gentamicin (used for *Staphylococcus* and many gram-negative organisms), and (3) erythromycin (used for gram-positive cocci [staphylococci and streptococci] and gram-negative cocci and bacilli). Metronidazole is a common therapy for rosacea. Topical erythromycin and clindamycin are options for acne vulgaris.

Systemic infections require systemic antibiotics. They have a role in treating acne vulgaris and bacterial infections, such as erysipelas, cellulitis, abscesses, and certain wound infections. Frequently used oral drugs include penicillin, erythromycin, doxycycline, clindamycin, and linezolid. Vancomycin is the drug of choice for severe infections.[13] Give patients drug-specific instructions on the proper technique of taking or applying antibiotics.

Corticosteroids. Corticosteroids are effective in treating a wide variety of skin problems. They can be used topically, intralesionally, or systemically. Topical corticosteroids have local antiinflammatory and antipruritic effects. Since corticosteroids may alter the manifestations, try to diagnose a skin problem before applying a corticosteroid preparation.

The potency of a preparation depends on the concentration of active drug. With prolonged use, high-potency corticosteroids can cause adrenal suppression, especially if a large surface area is covered and occlusive dressings are used. Other side effects include skin atrophy from impaired cell mitosis, capillary fragility, rosacea eruptions, severe exacerbations of acne vulgaris, and bruising. In general, atrophy does not occur until a corticosteroid has been in use for 2 to 3 weeks. If drug use is stopped at the first sign of atrophy, recovery usually occurs in several weeks. Rebound dermatitis can occur when therapy is stopped. Tapering the use of high-potency topical corticosteroids when improvement is noted reduces the risk.

Low-potency corticosteroids such as hydrocortisone act more slowly. However, they can be used for a longer time without producing serious side effects. Low-potency corticosteroids are safe to use on the face and areas where skin may touch or rub together, such as the axillae and groin.

The most potent delivery system for a topical corticosteroid is an ointment form. Apply creams and ointments in thin layers and slowly massage into the site 1 to 3 times a day.

Intralesional corticosteroids are injected directly into or just beneath the lesion. This method provides a reservoir of medication with an effect lasting several weeks to months. Intralesional injection is common in the treatment of psoriasis, alopecia areata (patchy hair loss), cystic acne, hypertrophic scars, and keloids. Triamcinolone acetonide (Kenalog) is the most common drug used for intralesional injection.

Systemic corticosteroids can have remarkable results in the treatment of skin conditions. However, they often have undesirable systemic effects (see Chapter 49). Corticosteroids are helpful in short-term therapy for acute conditions such as contact dermatitis caused by poison ivy. Long-term therapy is reserved for those with severe disease such as bullous (blistering) disorders.

Antihistamines. Oral antihistamines are helpful in treating urticaria, angioedema, and pruritus that can occur in problems such as atopic dermatitis, allergic dermatitis, and other allergic cutaneous reactions. Several antihistamines may be tried before getting an acceptable effect. Antihistamines with sedative effects, such as hydroxyzine and diphenhydramine, may be better for pruritic conditions because the tranquilizing and sedative effects offer symptomatic relief. Warn the patient about sedative effects, a problem when driving or using heavy machinery. Antihistamines, such as loratadine (Claritin), fexofenadine (Allegra), and cetirizine (Zyrtec), bind to peripheral histamine receptors, giving antihistamine action without sedation. They are not effective for controlling pruritus. Use any antihistamines with caution in older adults because of their long half-life and anticholinergic effects.

Topical Fluorouracil. Fluorouracil is a topical cytotoxic agent with selective toxicity for sun-damaged cells. It is used to treat precancerous lesions (especially AK) and some skin cancers. Patient adherence is a consideration in the use of fluorouracil. The medication produces erythema, burning, and pruritus within 3 to 5 days. Painful, eroded areas over the damaged skin occur within 1 to 3 weeks, depending on skin thickness at the site. Reduce redness and pruritus by applying a low-potency topical corticosteroid 20 minutes after. There are 5 strengths (0.5%, 1%, 2%, 4%, and 5%). Treatment must continue with applications 1 or 2 times a day for 2 to 4 weeks. Healing may take up to 4 weeks after the medication is stopped.[8]

Adherence to therapy depends on your teaching. Tell the patient that they will look worse before they look better. Teach about the effect of the medication. Because fluorouracil is a photosensitizing drug, tell the patient to avoid sunlight during treatment. After treatment, skin should be smooth and free of AK. AK may recur in treated areas, and multiple courses of therapy may be necessary over the years for those with severely sun-damaged skin.

Immunomodulators. Topical immunomodulators, such as pimecrolimus (Elidel) and tacrolimus (Protopic), are used to treat atopic dermatitis, psoriasis, and rosacea.[14] They work by suppressing an overreactive immune system. The side effects are minimal and may include a transient burning or feeling of heat at the application site. Use may increase the risk for skin cancer and precancerous lesions.

The topical immunomodulator imiquimod (Aldara) is used to treat external genital warts, AK, and superficial BCC. It stimulates the production of α-interferon and other cytokines to enhance cell-mediated immunity. It boosts the immune response only where applied and is safe for transplant patients. Most patients using this cream experience skin reactions, including redness, swelling, blistering, peeling, itching, and burning. Dosing varies depending on the type of lesion treated and the strength of medication prescribed.[8]

Diagnostic and Surgical Therapy

Skin Scraping. Scraping with a scalpel blade can yield a sample of surface cells (stratum corneum) for microscopic inspection and diagnosis. The most common tests of skin scrapings are mineral oil examination for scabies and 10% to 20% potassium hydroxide (KOH) for fungus.

Electrodessication and Electrocoagulation. Electrical energy can be converted to heat with the tip of an electrode. The heat burns and destroys tissue. The major uses of these therapies are coagulation of bleeding vessels to obtain hemostasis and destruction of small *telangiectasias* (dilation of groups of superficial capillaries and venules). *Electrodessication* usually involves more superficial destruction. It uses a monopolar electrode. *Electrocoagulation* uses a bipolar electrode. It has a deeper effect, with better hemostasis, but an increased chance of scarring. While minor electrosurgery on patients with a pacemaker poses minimal risk, the electrical energy can affect both pacemakers and internal defibrillators.

Curettage. Curettage is the removal and scooping away of tissue using an instrument called a *curette*. A curette looks like a small spoon with very sharp edges. Although a curette is not usually strong enough to cut normal skin, it can remove many types of small, soft skin tumors and superficial lesions, such as warts, AK, seborrheic keratosis, and small BCCs and SCCs. The area to be curetted is anesthetized before the procedure. The HCP removes the lesion and then cauterizes the skin. The removed tissue is usually sent for biopsy. A dressing may be applied, and you will need to teach the patient wound care. A small scar and hypopigmentation can result.

Punch Biopsy. Punch biopsy is a common procedure used to obtain a tissue sample for histologic study or to remove small lesions (Fig. 23.12). The procedure is simple. The HCP marks the biopsy area and then anesthetizes it so that the anesthetic will not obscure the landmarks. The HCP rotates the punch into the skin and removes a small cylinder of skin. Hemostasis is

FIG. 23.12 Punch biopsy. **A,** Removal of skin for diagnostic purposes. **B,** Specimen obtained. (From Graham-Brown R, Bourke J, Cunliffe T: *Dermatology: Fundamentals of practice,* Edinburgh, 2008, Mosby.)

achieved with pressure or absorbable gelatin (Gelfoam) packing. Sites of 4 mm or larger are usually closed with sutures. Punch biopsies are not done below the knee if other sites are available. Circulatory changes can make evaluating the tissue sample more difficult.

Cryosurgery. Cryosurgery is the use of subfreezing temperatures to destroy epidermal lesions. Cryosurgery is used to treat common and genital warts, cutaneous tags, thin seborrheic keratoses, lentigines, AK, BCC, and SCC. Topical liquid nitrogen is the agent most commonly used for cryosurgery.[12] Damage occurs in treated tissue because of intracellular ice formation. It causes the cell to rupture during thaw, leading to cell death and necrosis. The degree of damage depends on the rate of cooling and the minimum temperature achieved.

Liquid nitrogen is applied topically (directly onto the lesion) with a direct spray or contact probe. Tell patients that they will feel a painful, stinging cold sensation. The lesion first becomes swollen and red, and it may blister. A scab forms and falls off in 1 to 3 weeks. The skin lesion sloughs along with the scab. Growth of new skin follows.

The size of an affected area may limit the use of cryotherapy. Other disadvantages include the potential for harming adjacent healthy tissue and the low temperature of liquid nitrogen destroying melanocytes, leaving an area of hypopigmentation resembling a scar.

Excision. Excision is an option if the lesion involves the dermis. Complete closure of the excised area usually results in a good cosmetic result.

A specific type of excision is *Mohs surgery,* which is the microscopically controlled removal of a skin cancer. In this procedure, the HCP removes tissue sections in thin horizontal layers. All the specimen's margins are examined to see if any cancer cells remain (Fig. 23.13). Any residual tumor not removed by the first surgical excision is removed in serial excisions performed the same day. Benefits of Mohs surgery are that it preserves normal tissue, produces the smallest possible wound, and can completely remove the cancer. Although it can be a lengthy procedure, it is done in an outpatient setting using local anesthesia.

❖ NURSING MANAGEMENT: SKIN PROBLEMS

◆ Ambulatory Care

Skin problems are not usually a primary reason for hospitalization. Nevertheless, many hospitalized patients have skin problems that need nursing intervention and patient education. Nursing interventions for skin conditions fall into broad categories. They apply to many problems in both inpatient and outpatient settings. A nursing care plan for the patient with chronic skin lesions (eNursing Care Plan 23.1) is available on the website for this chapter.

In your general teaching with the patient, stress the duration of the treatment and the need to follow package directions. Skin problems may be slow to resolve. Tell the patient to follow package directions when using OTC drugs. If the package insert says its use should not exceed 7 days, patients should heed this warning. Teach the patient to stop self-care and seek the help of an HCP if any systemic signs of inflammation or extensions of the skin problem (e.g., an increasing number of lesions, increased erythema, increased swelling) develop.

◆ **Wet Compresses.** For superficial skin problems that involve inflammation, itching, and infection, wet compresses are commonly used. They are appropriate for damaged, oozing skin. Wet compresses are a good way to remove crusts and scabs that are adhering to the wound surface. They provide comfort and treatment of conditions such as poison ivy, insect bites, and skin infections.

It is important to understand how to do a wet compress correctly. Unless there is a concern about water quality, tap water at room temperature is the best choice. If drinkable water is not available, use filtered, bottled, or sterile water. Depending on the problem, additives may be used. Common solutions include (1) saline, (2) Burow's solution (Domeboro powder [aluminum acetate; calcium acetate]), (3) acetic acid (vinegar), and (4) silver nitrate.[8] The temperature of the fluid should be tepid. However, when an anti-inflammatory effect is desired, the fluid should be cool.

The material you select for the compress should be 4 to 8 layers thick and slightly larger than the area that you are treating. Use gauze or any clean material (e.g., thin cotton sheeting, thermal underwear, tube socks). Ingenuity is sometimes needed when covering odd-shaped body parts. Do not use gauze sponges with fillers (abdominal pads). They will retain too much solution, and fibers can be left in the wound if the skin is open. Place the prescribed compress material into fresh solution and squeeze out excess fluid. Your goal is a wet compress—not damp but not dripping.

Wet compresses are applied continuously or intermittently. When used continuously, remove the compress and replace with a new one as needed. Do not add solution to a compress. This can change the fluid's concentration and damage the skin. They can be placed intermittently, for 10 to 30 minutes, several times a day. Careful monitoring of the skin is important. If the skin appears *macerated* (softens and turns white), stop the compresses for 2 to 3 days. Change and wash daily any material used repeatedly throughout the day. Protect the patient from discomfort and chilling. A water-resistant pad will help protect the mattress, linens, and furniture.

◆ **Baths.** Baths are an appropriate intervention when large areas of the body need treatment. Baths may be relaxing and will help decrease itching. Agents such as colloidal oatmeal (Aveeno) and

FIG. 23.13 **A,** Removal of melanoma by Mohs surgery. **B,** After plastic surgery using a skin flap to repair defect. (Courtesy Peter Bonner, Placitas, NM.)

sodium bicarbonate can be added directly to bath water. Fill the tub with tepid water to cover the affected areas. Depending on the severity of the problem and the patient's discomfort, have the patient soak for 15 to 20 minutes 3 or 4 times a day. Stress to the patient not to rub the skin dry with a towel but gently pat to prevent increased irritation and inflammation. Avoid adding oils as their use increases the risk for falls. To sustain the hydrating effect, apply cream, ointment emollients (moisturizers), or other prescribed topical agents after the bath. This helps seal the moisture in the hydrated cells and increases the absorption of any topical agents.

◆ **Hygienic Practices.** The patient's skin type, lifestyle, culture, age, and gender influence hygienic practices. The normal acidity of the skin and perspiration protect against bacterial overgrowth. Most soaps are alkaline and neutralize the skin surface, leading to a loss of protection. Using mild, moisturizing soaps and lipid-free cleansers and avoiding hot water and vigorous scrubbing can noticeably decrease local skin irritation and inflammation. Skin piercings in which jewelry has been inserted can be cared for with antibacterial soaps that do not contain sulfites.

In general, skin and hair must be washed often enough to remove excess oil and excretions and to prevent odor. Older persons should avoid harsh soaps and shampoos and frequent bathing because of the dryness of their skin and scalp. Using moisturizers right after a bath or shower (while the skin is still damp) seals in the moisture.

◆ **Topical Medications.** Topical medications are commonly used to treat skin problems. The effectiveness of topical therapy depends on which base the medication is prepared in. Table 23.12 summarizes the common agents used as bases for topical preparations and their therapeutic considerations. The base selected depends on the properties needed.

Creams are very versatile and most commonly prescribed. Ointments are more lubricating than creams and offer enhanced potency of the active ingredient. They may be too occlusive for conditions with lots of exudate or in body creases. Gels work well on the scalp, where other compounds may mat the hair, and for acute exudative conditions such as poison ivy. Lotions are also fine for the scalp but may cause stinging and drying when used in skinfolds. Pastes are good for protecting the skin but are messy. A limited number of foams are available.

TABLE 23.12 Drug Therapy
Common Bases for Topical Medications

Agent	Therapeutic Considerations
Cream	Emulsions of oil and water. Most common base for topical medications. Lubrication and protection
Gel	Nongreasy combination of propylene glycol and water. May contain alcohol
Lotion	Emulsions of water, alcohol, and/or oil. Cooling and drying. Some leave residual powder film after evaporation of water. Useful in subacute pruritic eruptions
Ointment	Oil with differing amounts of water added in suspension. Lubrication and prevention of dehydration. Petrolatum most common
Paste	Mixture of powder and ointment, used when drying effect necessary because moisture is absorbed
Powder	Promotion of dryness. Lubricates skinfold areas to prevent irritation. Base for antifungal preparations. Protect patient from inhaling

Apply topical medications as directed. Proper administration will yield best results and avoid waste. Some are very costly. As a rule, apply topical medication in a thin film to clean skin and spread evenly in a downward motion in the direction of hair growth. Thick creams will spread easier if the skin is still damp. If you are using a secondary dressing, you can apply the medication directly onto a dressing. Teach the patient and caregiver proper dosing, application technique, expected results, and common reactions.

Occlusion with a plastic wrap is an effective way to increase the absorption of topical corticosteroids or simple emollients. The plastic wrap traps perspiration against the outer layer of the epidermis. Applying preparations to moist skin increases absorption 10-fold. Use tape or stretch wraps to keep the plastic wrap in place. For conditions on the feet or lower legs, the patient can wear socks over the plastic wrap. Wraps applied multiple times daily are kept in place for 2 to 8 hours. Some patients choose to use the occlusion technique at bedtime. Occlusion is not appropriate in areas prone to infection, such as skin creases.

◆ **Control of Pruritus.** Many conditions cause *pruritus* (itching). This includes dry skin, almost any physical or chemical stimulus to the skin (such as drugs or insects), and any scaling skin disorder. The itch sensation is carried by the same nonmyelinated nerve fibers as pain and temperature. The patient will have pain rather than an itch if the epidermis is damaged or absent. It is important to figure out if itching preceded a skin lesion. Itching can lead to scratching that results in an excoriated and inflamed lesion.

Certain circumstances make itching worse. Teach the patient ways to help break the itch/scratch cycle. A cool environment may cause vasoconstriction and decrease itching. Hydration, wet compresses, and moisturizers (including antipruritic lotions) are normally helpful. Apply wet compresses for 30 to 60 minutes, pat the skin dry, and apply a lubricant or medication. Topical and injectable corticosteroids are sometimes used. Topically applied menthol, camphor, or phenol numb itch receptors. Systemic antihistamines may give relief. The main side effect of most antihistamines is sedation. This may be desirable because pruritus is often worse at night and can interfere with sleep. Adequate rest increases the patient's ability to tolerate itching, thereby decreasing skin damage from the resultant scratching. Have the patient avoid anything that causes vasodilation, such as heat or rubbing. Dry skin lowers the itch threshold and increases the itch sensation.

Lichenification is a thickening of epidermis with exaggerated markings resembling a washboard. It is caused by chronic scratching or rubbing of the skin. Lichenification is often associated with atopic dermatoses and other pruritic conditions. Although any area of the body may be affected, the hands, forearms, shins, and nape of the neck are common sites. Scratching may become a habit. Persistent scratching can cause excoriations. Treating the cause of the itching is the key to preventing lichenification.

◆ **Prevention of Spread.** Although most skin problems are not contagious, infection control precautions indicate wearing gloves when working with any open wounds or lesions with drainage. Not all infected drainage is purulent. Careful hand washing and properly disposing of soiled dressings are the best means of preventing the spread of infections or infestations. The most common contagious lesions include impetigo, streptococcal infections, staphylococcal infections (e.g., methicillin-resistant *S. aureus* [MRSA]), fungal infections, primary chancre, scabies, and pediculosis.

◆ **Prevention of Secondary Infections.** Open skin lesions are susceptible to invasion by other viral, bacterial, or fungal organisms. Meticulous hygiene, hand washing, and dressing changes are important to minimize the potential for secondary infections. Warn the patient about scratching lesions, which can cause excoriations and create a portal of entry for pathogens. Trim the patient's nails short to minimize trauma from scratching.

◆ **Specific Skin Care.** You are often in a position to teach patients skin care after simple surgical procedures, such as skin biopsy, excision, and cryosurgery. In general, your teaching should include dressing changes, use of topical antibiotics, and the signs and symptoms of infection. After a skin procedure, cleanse any oozing wound with a saline solution twice daily or as ordered by the HCP. Potable (safe, drinking water) is a safe alternative in some situations. Apply antibiotic or plain petrolatum ointment with a secondary dressing that is both absorbent and nonadherent.

Wounds that are kept moist and covered heal more rapidly and with less scarring. The initial crust that forms should be left undisturbed as a protective coating for the damaged skin beneath it. Healing crusts that have been moisturized and protected will separate naturally from healed epidermis.

A sutured wound may be covered with a variety of dressings. Sutures are generally removed in 4 to 14 days, depending on the placement site. Sometimes alternating sutures are removed after the third day. Incision lines may need daily cleansing, usually with plain water. If necessary, a topical antibiotic is applied and the wound either is covered with a dry dressing or left open to air. The patient may have some swelling and discomfort in the first 24 hours. Intermittent application of cold (ice packs) over the surgical dressing may reduce edema. Mild analgesics, such as acetaminophen, should control discomfort. Teach the patient how to distinguish normal inflammation from an infection. A slight red border during the first few days after a procedure is normal. Signs and symptoms of infection include redness that persists longer than a week or extends beyond a 1-cm border, a fever above 101° F, increased pain, pronounced swelling, and purulent drainage. If these occur, they should be reported to the HCP at once.

■ NURSING MANAGEMENT

Skin Conditions

- Assess patient's skin for acute and chronic skin problems.
- Assess patient's risk factors for skin problems.
- Document skin condition and risk factor assessment and develop a plan of care.
- Determine whether patient is taking drugs that increase photosensitivity.
- Teach about risks associated with sun exposure and methods for decreasing exposure to the sun.
- Administer prescribed therapies such as dressings and oral or topical medications.
- Teach about therapies used for skin disorders, including dressings, baths, and oral or topical medications used on an outpatient basis.
- Evaluate treatment for effectiveness and any adverse effects.

◆ **Psychologic Effects of Chronic Skin Problems.** Emotional stress can occur for those who suffer from chronic skin problems, such as psoriasis, atopic dermatitis, or acne. The sequelae of chronic skin problems could result in social and employment problems with subsequent financial implications, a poor self-image, problems with sexuality, and increasing and progressive frustration. The usual lack of systemic illness coupled with the visibility of the skin lesions often presents a real problem to the patient.

Help the patient follow the prescribed regimen. Allow the patient to verbalize the "Why me?" question, even though there is no ready answer. Refer the patient to dermatology support groups. Many are listed on the American Academy of Dermatology website (*www.aad.org*). These groups are extremely helpful with patient support and education.

The location of lesions and scars is the determining factor with respect to their cosmetic implications. Facial scars are the most damaging psychologically because they are so visible. Creative use of cosmetics can do much to mask lesions and scarring. Consider individual sensitivity to product ingredients when selecting cosmetics. Oil-free, hypoallergenic cosmetics are available and may be beneficial for the allergic patient. Rehabilitative cosmetics are available to help camouflage and deemphasize such lesions as *vitiligo* (loss of pigmentation), *melasma* (tan to brown patches on the face), or healed postoperative wound sites. These commercially available products are opaque, smudge resistant, and water resistant.

COSMETIC PROCEDURES

A vast array of cosmetic procedures is available, including chemical peels, toxin injections, fillers, laser surgery, breast enlargement and reduction (see Chapter 51), face-lift, eyelid-lift, and liposuction. Common cosmetic topical procedures are outlined in Table 23.13. Other types of cosmetic procedures include the injection of botulinum toxin (Botox), deoxycholic acid (Kybella), calcium hydroxylapatite (Radiesse), collagen (Zyplast), and hyaluronic acid fillers (e.g., Restylane, Perlane, Juvéderm).[15] Transitory side effects may occur, such as mild redness, pain, swelling, and bruising. Uncommon side effects from cosmetic procedures include allergic reaction, infection, grayish skin discoloration, or lumps at the injection sites. Tell the patient that the procedure will need repeating at prescribed intervals to maintain the desired appearance.

The reasons for undergoing these procedures are as varied as the techniques. The most common reason that people incur the discomfort and financial expense (most are not covered by health insurance) of a cosmetic procedure is to improve their body image. If they feel better about themselves after having cosmetic procedures, they often act more confident and self-assured. Often social position and economic considerations are part of the decision. Increased longevity is providing a larger population to whom cosmetic procedures are appealing.

Regardless of the patient's reasons for seeking a cosmetic procedure, maintain a supportive, nonjudgmental attitude. If the patient wishes to change or enhance a body feature perceived as unattractive and has realistic expectations about the outcome, you should support this decision.

Elective Surgery

Laser Surgery. Laser surgery is used to treat congenital and acquired vascular lesions (cherry angiomas, spider leg veins, hemangiomas, port wine stains, and tattoo removal) and for skin resurfacing and hair removal. Lasers can reduce scarring and fine wrinkles around the lips or eyes and remove facial lesions (Table 23.11). Swelling, redness, and bruising are common after treatment. The treated areas usually are kept moist

TABLE 23.13 Common Cosmetic Topical Procedures

Tretinoin (Retin-A, Renova)	Chemical Peels (e.g., Beta-Hydroxy Acid, Jessner's Peel, TCA)	Microdermabrasion	α-Hydroxy Acids (e.g., Glycolic Acid, Lactic Acid)
Indications			
Improves appearance of photodamaged skin, especially fine wrinkling. Reduces actinic keratoses	Improves appearance of photodamaged skin, acne scarring, actinic and seborrheic keratoses	Smoothes appearance of photodamaged and wrinkled skin, acne scarring	Smoothes appearance of photodamaged and wrinkled skin, acne scarring
Description			
Initially applied every 2–3 days. Treatment stopped if severe inflammation occurs. Maximum response in 8–12 mo	Solution applied in varying amounts to the skin, causing a controlled burn with a loss of melanin	Epidermis and top dermal layer removed by applying aluminum oxide or baking soda crystals. Re-epithelialization of abraded surface then occurs	Low concentrations (<10%) in many skin care products consumers can apply to the skin. Higher concentrations (50%–70%) applied only by an HCP
Side Effects			
Erythema, swelling, flaking, pigmentation changes. Teratogenic. Increases phototoxicity if taking other photosensitive drugs	Moderate swelling and crusting for 1 wk. Redness for 6–8 wk. Pink tone possible for several mo. Photosensitivity	Light pink tone that resolves within 24 hr. Photosensitivity	Photosensitivity, slight irritation at lower concentrations, severe redness, oozing, and flaking skin possible with higher concentrations
Patient Teaching			
Apply at night since preparation is inactivated by light. Apply emollients, use sunscreen, use sun avoidance measures, avoid using abrasive or drying facial cleansers for severe sensitivity (e.g., excess irritation)	Use sunscreen. Avoid sun for 6 mo to prevent hyperpigmentation	Generous application of emollients and sunscreen	Use sunscreen and sun avoidance measures

FIG. 23.14 Face-lift. A, Preoperative. B, Postoperative. (From Cuzalina A, Copty TV, Khan H: *Current therapy in oral and maxillofacial surgery*, St Louis, 2012, Elsevier.)

with ointment or occlusive dressings for the first few days. The patient must protect treated skin from the sun.

Face-Lift. A face-lift *(rhytidectomy)* is the lifting and repositioning of the lower two thirds of the face and neck to improve appearance (Fig. 23.14). Indications for this procedure include:

- Redundant soft tissue or scarring resulting from disease (e.g., acne scarring)
- Asymmetric redundancy of soft tissues (e.g., facial palsy)
- Redundant soft tissue resulting from trauma
- Preauricular lesions
- Redundant soft tissues resulting from *solar elastosis* (sagging of the skin from sun damage), changes in body weight, and the effects of gravity
- Restoration of body image

The surgical approach and lines of incisions vary according to the desired correction and the position of the hairline. Eyelid-lifts *(blepharoplasty)* can remove redundant tissue and possibly improve the field of vision. Preventing hematoma formation is the most important postoperative consideration. Ice packs are usually applied for the first 24 to 48 hours to reduce swelling and decrease the possibility of hematoma formation. Usually the pain is minimal. Antibiotics are used at the HCP's discretion. Complications can occur if the person smokes or is involved in vigorous exercise.

Liposuction. Liposuction is a technique for removing subcutaneous fat to improve facial and body contours. Although not a substitute for diet and exercise, it can be successful in removing areas of fat from almost any body area that is resistant to other techniques.

Liposuction is relatively free of complications. Possible contraindications include the use of anticoagulants, uncontrolled hypertension, diabetes, and poor cardiovascular status. Those under 40 years of age with good skin elasticity are the best candidates. However, patients over 40 can be treated successfully.

The procedure is usually done on an outpatient basis under local anesthesia. One or more sessions may be needed, depending on the size of the area. The HCP inserts a blunt-tipped cannula through a small incision and pushes into the fat to break it loose from the fibrous stroma. Multiple repeated thrusts disrupt the fat and create tunnels. The loosened fat is removed with a powerful suction. Afterward, firm pressure is applied to the wounds until drainage stops.[16] It may take several months for the results to be evident.

❖ NURSING MANAGEMENT: COSMETIC SURGERY

Many cosmetic surgical procedures are done in well-equipped day-surgery units or in dermatologist or plastic surgeon in-office surgery suites.

◆ Preoperative Management

A major consideration before surgery relates to informed consent and realistic expectations of what cosmetic surgery can accomplish. Although the HCP should provide this information, reinforce it and answer questions and concerns. For instance, a face-lift has little or no effect on deep wrinkling of the forehead and temples, deep nasolabial grooves, or vertical lip wrinkles. Before-and-after treatment photographs of similar cases are often useful in helping the patient to set realistic expectations.

Your teaching plan should include the timeframe for healing. Explain the oozing, crusting stage of an abrasive procedure so the patient can plan time off from work if necessary. Since wound healing may not be complete for 1 year, the patient should not expect complete results at once. The final result is affected by the patient's age, general state of health, and skin type and the extent (severity) of the condition being treated. Efforts should be made to correct or control any existing health problem before the procedure.

◆ Postoperative Management

Most cosmetic procedures are not extremely painful. Usually, mild analgesics are enough to keep the patient comfortable. Although infection is not a common problem after cosmetic surgery, assess the sites for signs of infection. Teach the patient signs and symptoms of infection. Stress that it is important to report them at once so that treatment can be started.

If the surgery involved a change in the skin's circulation, as in a face-lift, carefully monitor for adequate circulation. Warm, pink skin that blanches on pressure shows that adequate circulation is present in the surgical area. Supportive, compressive dressings and ice packs may be necessary early in the postoperative period.

SKIN GRAFTS

Uses

Skin grafts may be necessary to protect underlying structures or to reconstruct areas for cosmetic or functional purposes. They may be used to facilitate rapid closure and minimize complications. Ideally, wounds heal by primary intention. However,

large wounds, surgically created wounds, trauma, and chronic wounds can result in extensive tissue destruction, making healing by primary intention impossible. In these cases, skin grafting may be necessary to close the defect. Improved surgical techniques make it possible to graft skin, bone, cartilage, fat, fascia, muscles, and nerves. For cosmetically pleasing results, the color, thickness, texture, and hair-growing nature of skin used for grafting should match the recipient site. See Chapter 24 for a discussion of skin grafting for patients with burn injuries.

Types

The two types of traditional skin grafts are free grafts and skin flaps. Free grafts are classified according to how they supply blood to the grafted skin. One method is to transfer the graft (epidermis and part or all the dermis) to the recipient site from the donor site. The *autograft* (from the patient's own body) or *isograft* (from an identical twin) revascularizes and becomes fixed to the new site. The other method of free skin grafting is by *reconstructive microsurgery.* With the use of an operating microscope, the HCP establishes circulation immediately in the graft by connecting blood vessels in the skin flap to vessels in the recipient site.

Skin flaps involve moving a section of skin and subcutaneous tissue from one part of the body to another without terminating the vascular attachment *(pedicle).* Skin flaps are used to cover wounds with a poor vascular bed, provide padding when needed, and cover wounds over cartilage and bone. The patient may need intermediate flap placement if the recipient site is far removed from the donor site. For instance, a skin flap from the thigh to the head would require an intermediate graft. The flap is advanced to the recipient site when circulation is well established at the intermediate site. The patient's needs and the type of defect determine the type of flap and the route of transfer.

Soft tissue expansion is a technique for providing skin (1) for resurfacing of a defect, such as a burn scar; (2) for removal of a disfiguring mark (e.g., a tattoo); or (3) as a preliminary step in breast reconstruction. A subcutaneous tissue expander of a proper size and shape is placed under the skin, usually as an outpatient procedure. Weekly expansion with saline solution can be done in a health care setting or by the patient at home. This expansion procedure is repeated until the skin reaches the size needed for the repair. This may take from several weeks to 3 to 4 months. Once enough skin is available, the old incision is opened, the expander is removed, and the soft tissue is ready to be used as an advancement flap. The tissue expander next to a defect has the primary tissue characteristics, such as color and texture.

Engineered skin substitutes (e.g., Apligraf, Dermagraft, Integra) are gaining popularity. There are several available, each with its own indications and benefits. Some are two-layered membranes with both dermal and epidermal components. Others are only one layer. The skin is engineered from neonatal foreskins and cadavers. Skin substitutes do not contain structures such as blood vessels, hair follicles, sweat glands, or cells such as melanocytes, Langerhans cells, macrophages, and lymphocytes.[17] Engineered skin grafts have an extended shelf life. Some are cryopreserved, others shipped overnight as they are needed. Advantages include ready availability, the avoidance of a donor site, application in outpatient settings, minimal scarring, and less pain.

CASE STUDY

Melanoma and Dysplastic Nevi

(© Dimedrol68/ iStock/Think stock.)

Patient Profile

G.L. is a 48-yr-old white, fair-skinned man who is a long-distance truck driver. In his leisure time, he enjoys swimming. He comes to the clinic because of a changing lesion on his left arm.

Subjective Data

- History of a basal cell cancer (BCC) on his left ear in the last 4 years
- Father treated for metastatic melanoma in the last 2 years
- First noted the lesion 1 month ago when it started changing size
- Anxious that removing the lesion will require extensive, disfiguring surgery

Objective Data

Physical Examination

- Has a 4-mm lesion, deep brown, scalloped with vaguely defined borders
- 5 dysplastic nevi found on back

Diagnostic Studies

- Excisional biopsy confirmed superficial spreading melanoma.
- Sentinel node biopsy results were negative.
- Diagnostic tests indicate melanoma stage I.

Discussion Questions

1. What risk factors for melanoma does he have?
2. What are the usual clinical manifestations associated with melanoma?
3. What is the prognosis for a patient with this stage of melanoma?
4. What treatment options are available for him?
5. *Priority Decision:* Based on the assessment data presented, what are the priority nursing diagnoses?
6. *Patient-Centered Care:* How would you help G.L. deal with his anxiety over the treatment outcomes?
7. *Priority Decision:* What is the priority of care for G.L.?
8. *Safety:* What would you include in his patient teaching plan to address future sun exposure?
9. *Evidence-Based Practice:* G.L. wants to know whether regularly applying sunscreen will reduce his risk for developing a second melanoma. How would you reply?

Answers available at *http://evolve.elsevier.com/Lewis/medsurg.*

▌BRIDGE TO NCLEX EXAMINATION

The number of the question corresponds to the same-numbered outcome at the beginning of the chapter.

1. Which safe sun practices would the nurse include in the teaching plan for a patient who has photosensitivity *(select all that apply)*?
   a. Wear protective clothing.
   b. Apply sunscreen liberally and often.
   c. Emphasize the short-term use of a tanning booth.
   d. Avoid exposure to the sun, especially during midday.
   e. Wear any sunscreen as long as it is bought at a drugstore.

2. When teaching a patient with melanoma about this disorder, the nurse recognizes that the patient's prognosis is *most* dependent on
   a. the thickness of the lesion.
   b. the degree of asymmetry in the lesion.
   c. the amount of ulceration in the lesion.
   d. how much the lesion has spread superficially.

3. The nurse determines that a patient with which disorder is *most* at risk for spreading the disease?
   a. Tinea pedis
   b. Impetigo on the face
   c. Candidiasis of the nails
   d. Psoriasis on the palms and soles

4. A mother and her two children have been diagnosed with pediculosis corporis at a health care center. An appropriate measure to treat this condition is
   a. applying pyrethrins to the body.
   b. topical application of griseofulvin.
   c. moist compresses applied frequently.
   d. administration of systemic antibiotics.

5. A common site for the lesions associated with atopic dermatitis is the
   a. buttocks.
   b. temporal area.
   c. antecubital space.
   d. plantar surface of the feet.

6. During the assessment of a patient, you note an area of red, sharply defined plaques covered with silvery scales that are mildly itchy on the patient's knees and elbows. You would describe this finding as
   a. lentigo.
   b. psoriasis.
   c. actinic keratosis.
   d. seborrheic keratosis.

7. In teaching a patient who is using topical corticosteroids to treat acute dermatitis, the nurse should tell the patient that *(select all that apply)*
   a. the cream form is the most efficient system of delivery.
   b. short-term use of topical corticosteroids usually does not cause systemic side effects.
   c. use a glove to apply small amounts of creams or ointments to prevent further infection.
   d. abruptly stopping the use of topical corticosteroids may cause the dermatitis to reappear.
   e. systemic side effects from topical corticosteroids are likely if the patient is malnourished.

8. Important patient teaching after a chemical peel includes
   a. avoidance of sun exposure.
   b. application of firm bandages.
   c. limitation of vigorous exercise.
   d. use of moist heat to relieve discomfort.

1. a, b, d. 2. a. 3. b. 4. a. 5. c. 6. b. 7. b, d. 8. a.

For rationales to these answers and even more NCLEX review questions, visit *http://evolve.elsevier.com/Lewis/medsurg.*

ⓔ EVOLVE WEBSITE/RESOURCE LIST

http://evolve.elsevier.com/Lewis/medsurg
Review Questions (Online Only)
Key Points
Answer Keys for Questions
- Rationales for Bridge to NCLEX Examination Questions
- Answer Guidelines for Case Study on p. 429
Nursing Care Plan
- eNursing Care Plan 23.1: Patient With Chronic Skin Lesions
Conceptual Care Map Creator
Audio Glossary
Supporting Media
- Animation
- Mohs Surgery
Content Updates

REFERENCES

*1. Tripp MK, Watson M, Balk SJ, et al: State of the science on prevention and screening to reduce melanoma incidence and mortality, *CA Can J Clin* 66:460, 2016.
2. US Food and Drug Administration: Sunscreen Innovation Act. Retrieved from *www.fda.gov/drugs/guidancecomplianceregulatoryinformation/ucm434782.htm.*
3. American Cancer Society: Skin cancer facts. Retrieved from *www.cancer.org/cancer/skin-cancer.html.*
4. Canavan T, Cantrell W: Recognizing melanoma: Diagnosis and treatment options, *TNP* 41:24, 2016.
*5. Verkouteren JA, Ramdas KH, Wakkee M, et al: Epidemiology of basal cell carcinoma: Scholarly review, *Br J Dermatol* 177:359, 2017.
*6. Green AC, Olsen CM: Cutaneous squamous cell carcinoma: An epidemiological review, *Br J Dermatol* 177:373, 2017.
*7. Coit DG, Thompson JA, Algazi A, et al: Melanoma, version 2.2016, NCCN clinical practice guidelines in oncology, *JCCN* 14:450, 2016.
8. Habif TP: *Clinical dermatology*, ed 6, St Louis, 2016, Saunders.
9. American Academy of Dermatology: Psoriasis. Retrieved from *www.aad.org/public/diseases/scaly-skin/psoriasis.*
*10. Cantrell W: Psoriasis and psoriatic therapies, *TNP* 42:35, 2017.
*11. Abrahamse H, Hamblin MR: New photosensitizers for photodynamic therapy, *Biochem J* 473:347, 2016.
*12. Stegman L: Electronic brachytherapy for nonmelanoma skin cancer, *Oncology Times* 39:38, 2017.
*13. Russo A, Concia E, Cristini F, et al: Current and future trends in antibiotic therapy of acute bacterial skin and skin-structure infections, *Clin Microbiol Infect* 22:S27, 2016.
14. Luger TA, McDonald I, Steinhoff M: *Clinical and basic immunodermatology*, New York, 2017, Springer.
*15. Costa CR, Kordestani R, Small KH, et al: Advances and refinement in hyaluronic acid facial fillers, *PRS* 138:233, 2016.
*16. Chia CT, Neinstein RM, Theodorou SJ: Evidence-based medicine: Liposuction, *PRS* 139:267, 2017.
17. Bryant R, Nix D: *Acute and chronic wound*, ed 5, St Louis, 2016, Mosby.

*Evidence-based information for clinical practice.

24

Burns

Cecilia Bidigare

Every life deserves a certain amount of dignity, no matter how poor or damaged the shell that carries it.

Rick Bragg

http://evolve.elsevier.com/Lewis/medsurg/

CONCEPTUAL FOCUS

Coping

Fluids and Electrolytes

Infection

Nutrition

Pain

Perfusion

Tissue Integrity

LEARNING OUTCOMES

1. Relate the causes of burns to the prevention strategies for burn injuries.
2. Distinguish between partial-thickness and full-thickness burns.
3. Apply tools used to determine the severity of burns.
4. Compare the pathophysiology, clinical manifestations, complications, and interprofessional care throughout the 3 burn phases.
5. Compare the fluid and electrolyte shifts during the emergent and acute burn phases.
6. Outline the nutritional needs of the burn patient throughout the 3 burn phases.
7. Compare the various burn wound care techniques and surgical options for partial-thickness and full-thickness burn wounds.
8. Prioritize nursing interventions in the management of the burn patient's physiologic and psychosocial needs.
9. Examine the various physiologic and psychosocial aspects of burn rehabilitation.
10. Develop a plan of care to prepare the burn patient and caregiver for discharge.

KEY TERMS

burn, p. 431

carboxyhemoglobin, p. 433

chemical burns, p. 432

contracture, p. 448

cultured epithelial autograft (CEA), p. 447

debridement, p. 442

electrical burns, p. 433

escharotomy, p. 439

excision and grafting, p. 446

full-thickness burns, p. 434

partial-thickness burns, p. 434

smoke and inhalation injuries, p. 432

thermal burns, p. 432

The focus of this chapter is the care of patients who have a burn injury. A **burn** is an injury to the skin or other tissues of the body caused by heat, chemicals, electric current, or radiation. The resulting effects on tissue integrity are influenced by the temperature and type of burning agent, duration of contact, and type of tissue that is injured. The location of the injury, associated injuries, and age and general health of the patient influence the seriousness of the injury.

The patient with a burn injury may have a multitude of problems. There may be difficulty maintaining an airway and adequate circulation, affecting perfusion. Fluid and electrolyte imbalances are common. We must give attention to preventing malnutrition and infection. The patient often has fear, anger, guilt, and depression. The patient may have body image concerns, especially with facial and hand burns; anxiety about future therapy and surgery; and frustrations with ongoing pain.

An estimated 486,000 Americans seek medical care each year for burns.[1] Around 40,000 people are hospitalized, 60% receiving care in specialized burn centers. About 3275 Americans die annually as a direct result of their injuries. The highest fatality rates occur in children ages 4 years and younger and adults over age 65. Worldwide, over 11 million people need medical attention annually for burn injuries and about 180,000 die.[2] Although burn incidence in the United States has decreased over the past 20 years, international burn injuries still occur too often, mainly to those living in low- and middle-income counties. Most burn accidents are preventable. The focus of burn prevention has shifted from blaming victims to educating people in vulnerable communities to identify hazards and provide first aid.

Coordinated national prevention programs in higher income countries have focused on child-resistant lighters, tap water anti-scald devices, stricter building codes, having smoke detectors, and fire and burn safety education curriculums for schools.[3] As a nurse, you can advocate for and teach about burn risk-reduction strategies in the home and at work (Tables 24.1 and 24.2).

TABLE 24.1 Common Sources of Burn Injury

Home Hazards

Bathroom and Kitchen
- Hot water heaters set at 120° F (60° C) or higher
- Microwaved food
- Steam, hot grease or liquids from cooking

General Household
- Carelessness with cigarettes, matches, candles
- Heat lamps
- Fireplaces (e.g., gas, wood)
- Flammables (e.g., starter fluid, gasoline, kerosene)
- Frayed or defective wiring
- Multiple extension cords per outlet
- Open space heaters
- Outdoor grills (e.g., propane, charcoal)
- Radiators (e.g., home, automobile)

Occupational Hazards
- Cement
- Chemicals
- Combustible fuels
- Electricity from power lines
- Fertilizers, pesticides
- Hot metals
- Sparks from live electric sources
- Steam pipes
- Tar

 ## TABLE 24.2 Promoting Population Health

Strategies to Reduce Burn Injury

Chemical
- Store chemicals safely in approved containers and label clearly.
- Ensure safety of workers handling chemicals (education, protective eyewear, gloves, masks, clothing).

Electrical
- Avoid or repair frayed wiring.
- Avoid outdoor activities during electrical (i.e., lightning) storms.
- Ensure electrical power source is shut off before beginning repairs.
- Wear protective eyewear and gloves when making electrical repairs.

Flame or Contact
- Never smoke in bed.
- Use "child-resistant" lighters.
- Hold regular home fire exit drills.
- Never leave hot oil unattended while cooking.
- Never use gasoline or other flammable liquids to start a fire.
- Never leave candles unattended or near open windows or curtains.
- Consider a flame-retardant smoking apron for older or "at-risk" people.
- Exercise caution when microwaving food and beverages as they can get very hot.

Inhalation
- Install smoke and carbon monoxide detectors and change batteries annually (if appropriate).

Scald
- Use "anti-scald" devices with showerhead or faucet fixtures.
- Lower hot water temperature to the "lowest point" or 120° F (49° C).
- After running bath water, check temperature with back of hand or bath thermometer.
- Supervise bathing with small children, older adults, or anyone with impaired physical movement, physical sensation, or judgment.

TYPES OF BURN INJURY

Thermal Burns

Thermal burns, caused by flame, flash, scald, or contact with hot objects, are the most common type of burn injury (Fig. 24.1). The severity of the injury depends on the temperature of the burning agent and duration of contact time. Scald injuries often occur in bathrooms and kitchens. Flash, flame, or contact burns can occur while cooking, smoking, or burning leaves in the backyard.

Chemical Burns

Chemical burns are the result of contact with acids, alkalis, and organic compounds. In addition to skin damage, eyes can be injured if splashed. Acids are found in the home and at work. They include hydrochloric, oxalic, and hydrofluoric acid. Alkali burns can be more difficult to manage than acid burns since alkalis adhere to tissue, causing protein hydrolysis and melting. Alkalis are found in cement, oven and drain cleaners, and heavy industrial cleansers.[4] Organic compounds, including phenols (chemical disinfectants) and petroleum products (creosote and gasoline), produce contact burns and systemic toxicity.

Smoke and Inhalation Injury

Smoke and inhalation injuries from breathing noxious chemicals or hot air can damage the respiratory tract. Three types of smoke and inhalation injuries can occur: upper airway injury,

FIG. 24.1 Types of burn injury. **A,** Superficial, partial-thickness scald burn to thigh. **B,** Deep, partial-thickness flame burn to hand. **C,** Full-thickness flame burn to posterior chest and arm. (Courtesy Judy Knighton, Toronto, Canada.)

lower airway injury, and metabolic asphyxiation. Smoke inhalation injuries are a major predictor of mortality in burn patients. Rapid initial and ongoing assessment is critical. Airway compromise and pulmonary edema can quickly develop within hours of injury.[5]

Metabolic Asphyxiation. Most deaths at a fire scene are the result of inhaling certain smoke elements, primarily carbon monoxide (CO) or hydrogen cyanide. Oxygen delivery to or consumption by tissues is impaired, resulting in hypoxia. Death may occur if carboxyhemoglobin (i.e., hemoglobin combined with CO) blood levels are greater than 20%. CO and hydrogen cyanide poisoning may occur in the absence of burn injury to the skin.

Upper Airway Injury. Upper airway injury results from an inhalation injury to the mouth, oropharynx, and/or larynx. The injury may be caused by thermal burns or the inhalation of hot air, steam, or smoke. Mucosal burns of the oropharynx and larynx are manifested by redness, blistering, and edema (Table 24.3). The swelling can be massive and the onset rapid. Burns to the neck and chest may make breathing more difficult because of the burn eschar, which becomes tight and constricting. Edema from facial and neck burns can be lethal, as can internal pressure from edema narrowing the airway. Obstruction can occur quickly, presenting a true airway emergency.

Lower Airway Injury. An inhalation injury to the trachea, bronchioles, and alveoli is usually caused by breathing in toxic chemicals or smoke. Tissue damage is related to the duration of exposure to toxic fumes or smoke. Manifestations of lower airway lung injury are outlined in Table 24.3. Carefully assess the patient for facial burns, singed nasal hair, hoarseness, painful swallowing, darkened oral and nasal membranes, carbonaceous sputum, history of being burned in an enclosed space, and clothing burns around the neck and chest. Pulmonary edema may not appear until 12 to 48 hours after the burn. Then it may manifest as acute respiratory distress syndrome (ARDS) (see Chapter 67).

Electrical Burns

Electrical burns result from intense heat generated from an electric current. Direct damage to nerves and vessels, causing tissue anoxia and death, can occur. The severity of an electrical injury depends on the amount of voltage, tissue resistance,

current pathways, surface area in contact with the current, and length of time that the current flow was sustained (Fig. 24.2). Tissue densities offer various amounts of resistance to electric current. For example, fat and bone offer the most resistance. Nerves and blood vessels offer the least resistance. Current that passes through vital organs (e.g., brain, heart, kidneys) produces more life-threatening sequelae than that which passes through other tissues. In addition, electric sparks may ignite the patient's clothing, causing a flash injury.

As with inhalation injury, perform a rapid assessment of the patient with an electrical injury. Transfer to a burn center is indicated. The severity of an electrical injury can be hard to determine since most of the damage is below the skin.

Determining the electric current contact points and history of the injury may help reveal the likely path of the current and potential areas of injury. Contact with electric current can cause muscle contractions strong enough to fracture the long bones and vertebrae. Another reason to suspect long bone or spinal fractures is a fall resulting from the electrical injury. For this reason, consider cervical spine injury for all patients with electrical burns. Continue cervical spine immobilization during transport and diagnostic testing until injury is ruled out.

Electrical injury puts the patient at risk for dysrhythmias or cardiac arrest, severe metabolic acidosis, and myoglobinuria.[6] The electric shock can cause immediate heart standstill or ventricular fibrillation. Delayed dysrhythmias or arrest can occur without warning during the first 24 hours after injury. Whenever massive muscle and blood vessel damage occurs, myoglobin from injured muscle and hemoglobin from damaged red blood cells (RBCs) are released into the circulation. The myoglobin travels to the kidneys and can block the renal tubules. This can result in acute tubular necrosis (ATN) and acute kidney injury (see Chapter 46).

TABLE 24.3 **Manifestations of Burn-Related Lung Injury**
Upper Airway
• Blisters, edema
• Copious secretions
• Difficulty swallowing
• Hoarseness
• Stridor
• Substernal and intercostal retractions
• Total airway obstruction
Lower Airway
• High degree of suspicion if patient was trapped in a fire in an enclosed space or clothing caught fire
• Altered mental status
• Carbonaceous sputum
• Dyspnea
• Facial burns or singed nasal or facial hair
• Hoarseness
• Wheezing

FIG. 24.2 Electrical injury produces heat coagulation of blood supply and contact area as electric current passes through the skin. **A,** Back and buttock *(arrows)*. **B,** Leg *(arrow)*. (Courtesy Judy Knighton, Toronto, Canada.)

Cold Thermal Injury

Cold thermal injury, or frostbite, is discussed in Chapter 68.

CLASSIFICATION OF BURN INJURY

The treatment of burns is related to the severity of the injury.[7] Severity is determined by (1) depth of burn, (2) extent of burn calculated in percent of total body surface area (TBSA), (3) location of burn, and (4) age of the patient, preburn medical history, and circumstances or complicating factors. The American Burn Association (ABA) uses referral criteria to determine which burn injuries should be treated in burn centers (Table 24.4).[8] Patients with minor burn injuries can be managed in community hospitals.

TABLE 24.4 **Burn Center Referral Criteria**
Burn injuries that should be referred to a burn center include the following:
1. Partial thickness burns greater than 10% total body surface area (TBSA)
2. Burns that involve the face, hands, feet, genitalia, perineum, or major joints
3. Third-degree burns in any age-group
4. Electrical burns, including lightning injury
5. Chemical burns
6. Inhalation injury
7. Injury in patients with preexisting medical disorders that could complicate management, prolong recovery, or affect mortality
8. Any patient with burns and concomitant trauma (e.g., fractures) in which the burn injury poses the greatest risk for morbidity or mortality. In such cases, if the trauma poses the greater immediate risk, the patient may be initially stabilized in a trauma center before being transferred to a burn unit. Physician judgment will be necessary in such situations and should be in concert with the regional medical control plan and triage protocols
9. Burned children in hospitals without qualified personnel or equipment for the care of children
10. Burn injury in patients who will need special social, emotional, or rehabilitative intervention

Source: American Burn Association: Guidelines for the operation of burn centers. Retrieved from *http://ameriburn.org/wp-content/uploads/2017/05/burncenterreferralcriteria.pdf.*

Depth of Burn

Burn injury involves the destruction of the integumentary system. Table 24.5 compares the various burn classifications according to the depth of the burn injury. One system defines an injury by degrees as first, second, third, or fourth degree. The ABA recommends a more precise definition and classifies burns according to depth of skin destruction: partial-thickness burns and full-thickness burns (Fig. 24.3). If significant damage occurs to the dermis (i.e., a full-thickness burn), not enough skin cells remain to regenerate new skin. A permanent, alternative source of skin must be found.

Extent of Burn

Two common tools for determining the TBSA affected or the extent of a burn wound are the *Lund-Browder chart* (Fig. 24.4, *A*) and the *Rule of Nines* (Fig. 24.4, *B*). First-degree burns, equivalent to a sunburn, are not included when calculating TBSA. The Lund-Browder chart is considered more accurate because it considers the patient's age in proportion to relative body-area size. The Rule of Nines is often used for initial assessment of a burn patient because it is easy to remember. For irregular- or odd-shaped burns, the patient's hand (including the fingers) is 1% TBSA. Other tools include the *Sage Burn Diagram*, a free, Web-based tool for estimating TBSA burned (*www.sagediagram.com*). There are mobile applications (e.g., 3D Burn Report, Mersey Burns) that can estimate the percent of burn and fluid resuscitation needs.[9]

Location of Burn

The location of the burn injury influences the severity. Burns to the face and neck and circumferential burns to the chest or back may interfere with breathing because of obstruction from edema or leathery, devitalized burn tissue *(eschar).* These burns may indicate possible smoke or inhalation injury.

Burns to the hands, feet, joints, and eyes are of concern because they make self-care difficult and may jeopardize future function. Burns to the hands and feet are challenging to manage because of superficial vascular and nerve supply systems that must be protected while the burn wounds are healing.

Burns of the ears and nose are at risk for infection as the skin is very thin and the underlying cartilage may be exposed. Burns

TABLE 24.5 **Classification of Burn Injury Depth**			
Classification	**Appearance**	**Possible Cause**	**Structures Involved**
Partial-Thickness Skin Destruction			
Superficial (first-degree) burn	Erythema, blanching on pressure, pain and mild swelling, no vesicles or blisters (although after 24 hr skin may blister and peel)	Quick heat flash Superficial sunburn	Superficial epidermal damage with hyperemia. Tactile and pain sensation intact
Deep (second-degree) burn	Fluid-filled vesicles that are red, shiny, wet (if vesicles have ruptured). Severe pain caused by nerve injury. Mild to moderate edema	Chemicals Contact burns Electric current Flame Flash Scald Tar, cement	Epidermis and dermis involved to varying depths. Skin elements, from which epithelial regeneration occurs, remain viable
Full-Thickness Skin Destruction			
Third- and fourth-degree burns	Dry, waxy white, leathery, or hard skin. Visible thrombosed vessels. Insensitivity to pain because of nerve destruction. Possible involvement of muscles, tendons, and bones	Chemical Electric current Flame Scald Tar, cement	All skin elements and local nerve endings destroyed. Coagulation necrosis present. Surgical intervention required for healing

to the buttocks or perineum are at high risk for infection from urine or feces contamination. Circumferential burns to the extremities can cause circulation problems distal to the burn, with possible nerve damage to the affected extremity. Patients may develop compartment syndrome (see Chapter 62) from deep damage to muscles.

Patient Risk Factors

Any patient with preexisting heart, lung, or kidney disease has a poorer prognosis for recovery because of the increased demands placed on the body by a burn injury. The patient with diabetes or peripheral vascular disease is at high risk for delayed healing, especially with foot and leg burns.[10] General physical weakness from any chronic disease, including alcohol or drug use and malnutrition, makes it challenging for the patient to fully recover from a burn injury. The burn patient who has fractures, head injuries, or other trauma has a more difficult recovery.

PREHOSPITAL AND EMERGENCY CARE

At the scene of the injury, priority is given to removing the person from the source of the burn and stopping the burning process. Rescuers must protect themselves from being injured. In the case of electrical and chemical injuries, initial care involves removing the patient from contact with the electrical or chemical source.

Small thermal burns (10% or less of TBSA) should be covered with a clean, cool, tap water–dampened towel for the patient's comfort and protection until medical care is available. Cooling of the injured area (if small) within 1 minute helps minimize the depth of the injury. If the burn is large (greater than 10% TBSA) or an electrical or inhalation burn is suspected, and the patient is unresponsive, first focus your attention on CAB:
- *Circulation:* Check for presence of pulses and elevate the burned limb(s) above the heart to decrease pain and swelling.
- *Airway:* Check for patency, soot around nares and on the tongue, singed nasal hair, darkened oral or nasal membranes.
- *Breathing:* Check for adequacy of ventilation.

If the patient is responsive, your priorities would follow the order of the ABCs: airway, breathing, and circulation.

To prevent hypothermia, cool large burns for no more than 10 minutes. Do not immerse the burned body part in cool water because it may cause extensive heat loss. Never cover a burn with ice, since this can cause hypothermia and vasoconstriction of blood vessels, thus further reducing blood flow to the injury. Gently remove as much burned clothing as possible to prevent further tissue damage. Leave adherent clothing in place until the patient is transferred to a hospital. Wrap the patient in a dry, clean sheet or blanket to prevent further contamination of the wound and provide warmth.

Chemical burns are best treated by quickly removing any chemical particles or powder from the skin. Remove all clothing

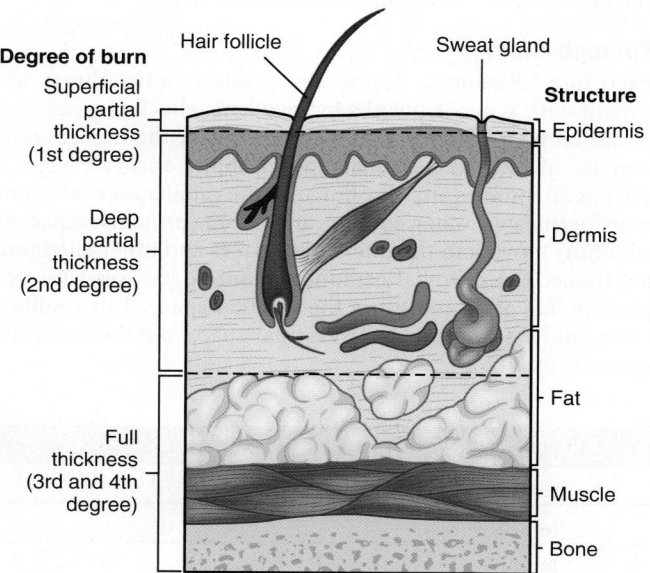

FIG. 24.3 Cross section of skin showing the depth of burn and structures involved.

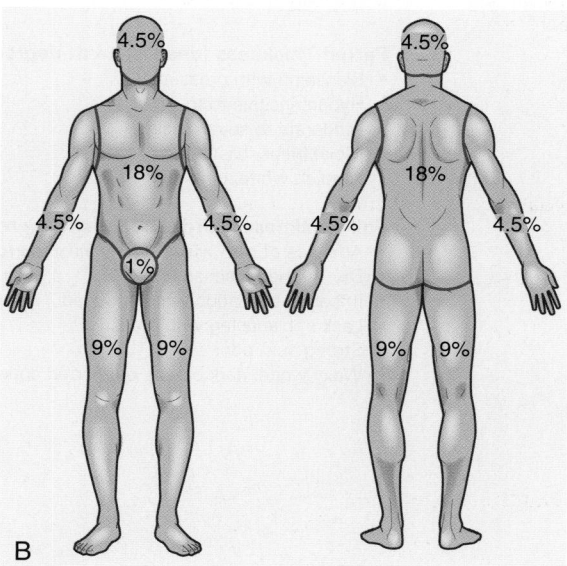

FIG. 24.4 A, Lund-Browder chart. By convention, areas of partial-thickness injury are colored in *blue* and areas of full-thickness injury in *red*. Superficial partial-thickness burns are not calculated. B, Rule of Nines chart.

containing the chemical because the burning process continues while the chemical is in contact with the skin. Flush the affected area with copious amounts of water to irrigate the skin from 20 minutes to 2 hours after exposure. Tap water is acceptable for flushing eyes exposed to chemicals. Tissue destruction may continue for up to 72 hours after contact with some chemicals.

Watch patients with inhalation injuries closely for signs of respiratory distress. These patients need to be treated quickly and efficiently if they are to survive. If CO poisoning is suspected, treat the patient with 100% humidified O_2. Patients who have both burns and an inhalation injury must be transferred to the nearest burn center.

Always remember that the burn patient may have sustained other injuries that could take priority over the burn itself. Persons involved in the prehospital phase of burn care must fully share the circumstances of the injury to emergency department (ED) staff. This is especially important if the patient was trapped in a closed space, exposed to hazardous chemicals or electricity, or had a possible traumatic injury (e.g., fall).

Prehospital and emergency care are outlined in tables that describe thermal burns (Table 24.6), inhalation injury (Table 24.7), electrical burns (Table 24.8), and chemical burns (Table 24.9).

PHASES OF BURN MANAGEMENT

Burn management can be organized chronologically into 3 phases: emergent (resuscitative), acute (wound healing), and rehabilitative (restorative). Overlap in care does exist.

For example, the emergent phase begins at the time of the burn injury, and care often begins prehospital or in the ED. Wound care is the primary focus of the acute phase, but wound care takes place in both the emergent and rehabilitation phases. Planning for rehabilitation begins on the day of the burn injury or admission to the burn center. Formal rehabilitation begins as soon as functional assessments can be done.

EMERGENT PHASE

The *emergent (resuscitative) phase* is the time needed to resolve the immediate, life-threatening problems resulting from the burn injury. This phase usually lasts up to 72 hours from the time the burn occurred. The main concerns are the onset of hypovolemic shock and edema formation. The emergent phase ends when fluid mobilization and diuresis begin.

Pathophysiology

Fluid and Electrolyte Shifts. The greatest initial threat to a patient with a major burn is hypovolemic shock (Fig. 24.5). It is caused by a massive shift of fluids out of the blood vessels because of increased capillary permeability and can begin as early as 20 minutes after the burn. As the capillary walls become more permeable, water, sodium, and plasma proteins (especially albumin) move into the interstitial spaces and other surrounding tissue. The colloidal osmotic pressure decreases with progressive loss of protein from the vascular space. This results in more fluid shifting out of the vascular space into the interstitial spaces (Fig. 24.6).

✚ TABLE 24.6 Emergency Management

Thermal Burns

Etiology	Assessment Findings	Interventions
• Flash flame • Hot liquids or solids • Hot surface • Open flame • Steam • Ultraviolet rays	**Partial-Thickness (superficial; first-degree) Burn** • Blanching with pressure • Minimal edema • Moderate to severe tenderness • Pain • Redness **Partial-Thickness (deep; second-degree) Burn** • Blanching with pressure • Hypersensitive to touch or air • Moderate to severe pain • Moist blebs, blisters • Mottled white, pink to cherry-red **Full-Thickness (third- and fourth-degree) Burns** • Absence of pain with severe pain in surrounding tissues • Dry, leathery eschar • Impaired sensation when touched • Lack of blanching with pressure • Strong burn odor • Waxy white, dark brown, or charred appearance	**Initial** • If unresponsive, assess circulation, airway, and breathing. • If responsive, monitor airway, breathing, and circulation. • Assess for inhalation injury. • Provide supplemental O_2 as needed. • Anticipate endotracheal intubation and mechanical ventilation with circumferential full-thickness burns to the neck and chest or large TBSA burns. • Monitor vital signs, level of consciousness, respiratory status, O_2 saturation, and heart rhythm. • Remove nonadherent clothing, shoes, watches, jewelry, glasses or contact lenses (if face was exposed). • Cover any concurrent thermal burns with dry dressings or clean sheet. • Establish IV access with 2 large-bore catheters if burn >15% TBSA. • Begin fluid replacement. • Insert indwelling urinary catheter if burn >15% TBSA. • Elevate burned limbs above heart to decrease edema. • Give IV analgesia and assess effectiveness frequently. • Identify and treat other associated injuries (e.g., fractures, head injury). **Ongoing Monitoring** • Monitor airway, breathing, and circulation. • Monitor vital signs, O_2 saturation, heart rhythm, and level of consciousness. • Monitor pain level. • Monitor urine output.

TBSA, Total body surface area.

✚ TABLE 24.7 Emergency Management

Inhalation Injury

Etiology	Assessment Findings	Interventions
• Exposure of respiratory tract to intense heat or flames • Inhalation of noxious chemicals, smoke, or CO • Occurs with being trapped in an enclosed space, being in an explosion, or having clothing catch fire	• Altered mental status, including confusion, coma • Carbonaceous sputum • Cherry-red skin color (CO levels >20%) • Coughing • Darkened oral or nasal membranes • Decreased O_2 saturation • Difficulty swallowing • Dysrhythmias • Increasing hoarseness • Irritation of upper airways or burning pain in throat or chest • Productive cough with black, gray, or bloody sputum • Rapid, shallow respirations • Restlessness, anxiety • Singed nasal or facial hair • Smoky breath	**Initial** • If unresponsive, assess circulation, airway, and breathing. • If responsive, monitor airway, breathing, and circulation. • Assess for concurrent thermal burn. • Provide 100% humidified O_2. • Anticipate endotracheal intubation and mechanical ventilation with significant inhalation injury. • Monitor vital signs, level of consciousness, O_2 saturation, and heart rhythm. • Obtain arterial blood gas, carboxyhemoglobin levels, and chest x-ray. • Remove nonadherent clothing, jewelry, glasses, or contact lenses (if face was exposed). • Establish IV access with 2 large-bore catheters if burn >15% TBSA. • Begin fluid replacement. • Insert indwelling urinary catheter if burn >15% TBSA. • Elevate burned limb(s) above heart to decrease edema. • Give IV analgesia and assess effectiveness frequently. • Identify and treat other associated injuries (e.g., fractures, pneumothorax, head injury). • Cover concurrent burned areas with dry dressings or clean sheet. • Anticipate need for fiberoptic bronchoscopy or intubation. **Ongoing Monitoring** • Monitor airway, breathing, and circulation. • Monitor vital signs, O_2 saturation, heart rhythm, and level of consciousness. • Monitor pain level. • Monitor urine output.

CO, Carbon monoxide; *TBSA,* total body surface area.

✚ TABLE 24.8 Emergency Management

Electrical Burns

Etiology	Assessment Findings	Interventions
• Defibrillator • Electric wires • Lightning • Utility wires	• Burn odor • Cardiac arrest • Depth and extent of wound difficult to see • Assume injury greater than what is seen • Decreased peripheral circulation in injured extremity • Dysrhythmias • Fractures or dislocations from force of current • Impaired touch sensation • Leathery, white, or charred skin • Location of contact points • Loss of consciousness • Minimal or absent pain • Neck or head injury if fall occurred • Thermal burns if clothing ignites	**Initial** • Remove patient from electrical source while protecting rescuer. • If unresponsive, assess circulation, airway, and breathing. • If responsive, monitor airway, breathing, and circulation. • Provide supplemental O_2 as needed. • Monitor vital signs, heart rhythm, level of consciousness, respiratory status, and O_2 saturation. • Remove nonadherent clothing, shoes, watches, jewelry, glasses or contact lenses (if face was exposed). • Cover burned areas with dry dressings or clean sheet. • Establish IV access with 2 large-bore catheters if burn >15% TBSA. • Begin fluid replacement. • Identify entrance and exit wounds. • Obtain arterial blood gas to assess acid-base balance. • Insert indwelling urinary catheter if burn >15% TBSA. • Elevate burned limb(s) above heart to decrease edema. • Give IV analgesia and assess effectiveness frequently. • Identify and treat other associated injuries (e.g., fractures, head injury, thermal burns). **Ongoing Monitoring** • Monitor airway, breathing, and circulation. • Monitor vital signs, O_2 saturation, heart rhythm, level of consciousness, and neurovascular status of injured limbs. • Monitor pain level. • Monitor urine output. • Monitor urine for development of myoglobinuria from muscle breakdown and hemoglobinuria from RBC breakdown. • Anticipate possible administration of $NaHCO_3$ to alkalinize the urine and maintain serum pH >6.0.

$NaHCO_3$, Sodium bicarbonate; *TBSA,* total body surface area.

✚ TABLE 24.9 **Emergency Management**

Chemical Burns

Etiology	Assessment Findings	Interventions
• Acids • Alkalis • Organic compounds	• Burning • Decreased muscle coordination (if organo-phosphate) • Discoloration of injured skin • Edema of surrounding tissue • Localized pain • Paralysis, redness, swelling of injured tissue • Respiratory distress if chemical inhaled • Tissue destruction continuing for up to 72 hr	**Initial** • If unresponsive, assess circulation, airway, and breathing before decontamination procedures. • If responsive, monitor airway, breathing, and circulation. • Provide supplemental O_2 as needed. • Brush dry chemical from skin before irrigation. • Remove nonadherent clothing, shoes, watches, jewelry, glasses or contact lenses (if face was exposed). • Flush chemical from wound and surrounding area with copious amounts of saline solution or water. • For chemical burn of the eye(s), flush from inner to outer corner of eye with water or lactated Ringer's (if available). • Cover burned areas with dry dressings or clean sheet. • Establish IV access with 2 large-bore catheters if burn >15% TBSA. • Begin fluid replacement. • Insert indwelling urinary catheter if burn >15% TBSA. • Elevate burned limb(s) above heart to decrease edema. • Give IV analgesia and assess effectiveness frequently. • Contact poison control center. **Ongoing Monitoring** • Monitor airway if exposed to chemicals. • Monitor pain level. • Monitor urine output. • Consider systemic impact of identified chemical. Monitor and treat accordingly. • Monitor pH of eye if exposed to chemicals.

TBSA, Total body surface area.

PATHOPHYSIOLOGY MAP

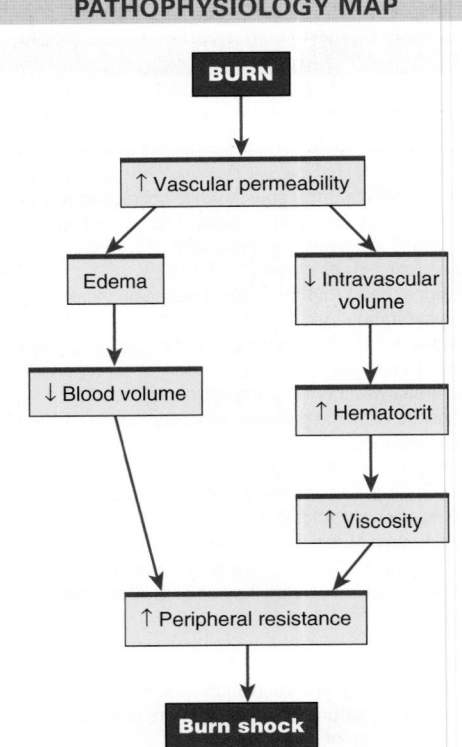

FIG. 24.5 At the time of major burn injury, there is increased capillary permeability. All fluid components of the blood begin to leak into the interstitium, causing edema and a decreased blood volume. Hematocrit increases, and the blood becomes more viscous. The combination of decreased blood volume and increased viscosity produces increased peripheral resistance. Burn shock, a type of hypovolemic shock, rapidly ensues and, if not corrected, can result in death.

FIG. 24.6 A, Facial edema before fluid resuscitation. B, Facial edema after 24 hours. (Courtesy Judy Knighton, Toronto, Canada.)

Fluid moves to areas that normally have minimal to no fluid, a phenomenon termed *third spacing*. Examples of third spacing in burn injury are exudate and blister formation, as well as edema in unburned areas.

Other sources of fluid loss are insensible losses by evaporation from large, denuded body surfaces and the lungs. The normal insensible loss of 30 to 50 mL/hr is higher in the severely burned patient. The net result of the fluid shifts and losses is termed *intravascular volume depletion*. Signs of hypovolemic shock include decreased BP and increased heart rate. If hypovolemic shock is not corrected, refractory shock and death may result. (Shock is discussed in Chapter 66.)

The circulatory system is affected by the hemolysis of RBCs from circulating factors (e.g., oxygen free radicals) released at the time of the burn and the direct insult of the burn injury. Thrombosis in the capillaries of burned tissue causes loss of more circulating RBCs. A high hematocrit is often caused by hemoconcentration due to fluid loss. After fluid balance is restored, the hematocrit levels return to normal.

Major electrolyte shifts of sodium and potassium occur during this phase. A potassium shift develops first because injured cells and hemolyzed RBCs release potassium into the circulation. Sodium rapidly moves to the interstitial spaces and stays there until edema formation ends (Fig. 24.7).

Toward the end of the emergent phase, capillary membrane permeability is restored if fluid replacement is adequate. Interstitial fluid gradually returns to the vascular space (Fig. 24.7). Diuresis occurs, and the urine has a low specific gravity.

Inflammation and Healing. Burn injury to tissues and vessels causes coagulation necrosis. Neutrophils and monocytes accumulate at the site of injury. Fibroblasts and newly formed collagen fibrils appear and begin wound repair within the first 6 to 12 hours after injury. (The inflammatory response is discussed in Chapter 11.)

Immunologic Changes. A burn injury challenges the body's immune system. The skin barrier to invading organisms is destroyed. Bone marrow depression occurs and circulating levels of immunoglobulins decrease. Defects occur in the function of white blood cells (WBCs). The inflammatory cytokine cascade, triggered by tissue damage, impairs the function of lymphocytes, monocytes, and neutrophils. Thus the patient is at a greater risk for infection.

Clinical Manifestations

The patient with severe burns is likely to be in shock from hypovolemia. Often the areas of full-thickness and deep partial-thickness burns are at first painless because the nerve endings have been destroyed. Superficial to moderate partial-thickness burns are very painful. Blisters, filled with fluid and protein, are common in partial-thickness burns. The patient with a larger burn may develop a paralytic ileus, with absent or decreased bowel sounds. Shivering may occur because of chilling that is caused by heat loss, anxiety, or pain.

The patient may be alert and able to answer questions shortly after admission or until intubated (if there is respiratory compromise). Patients are often frightened and need your calm reassurances. Give simple explanations of what to expect as you provide care. Unconsciousness or altered mental status in a burn patient usually results from hypoxia associated with smoke inhalation. Other possibilities include head trauma, substance use, or excess amounts of sedation or pain medication.

Complications

The three major organ systems most susceptible to complications during the emergent phase of burn injury are the cardiovascular, respiratory, and urinary systems.

Cardiovascular System. Cardiovascular complications include dysrhythmias and hypovolemic shock. These, if untreated, may progress to irreversible shock. Circulation to the extremities can be severely impaired by deep circumferential burns and subsequent edema formation, which act like a tourniquet. If untreated, ischemia, paresthesia, and necrosis can occur. An escharotomy (an incision through the full-thickness eschar) is often done to restore circulation to compromised extremities or improve chest expansion (Fig. 24.8).

Initially, blood viscosity increases because of the fluid loss. Microcirculation is impaired because of the damage to skin structures that contain small capillary systems. This results in a phenomenon termed *sludging*. Sludging is corrected by adequate fluid replacement.

Burn patients are at an increased risk for venous thromboembolism (VTE) if 1 or more of the following conditions are present: advanced age, obesity, extensive or lower extremity burns, concomitant lower extremity trauma, and prolonged immobility. VTE prophylaxis with anticoagulant drugs should be started, unless contraindicated.[11]

Respiratory System. The respiratory system is vulnerable to 2 types of injury: (1) upper airway burns and (2) lower airway

FIG. 24.7 The effects of burn shock are shown above the *purple line.* As the capillary seal is lost, interstitial edema develops. Cellular integrity is altered, with sodium *(Na)* moving into the cell in abnormal amounts and potassium *(K)* leaving the cell. The shifts after the resolution of burn shock are shown below the *blue line.* The water and sodium move back into the circulating volume through the capillary. Albumin stays in the interstitium. Potassium is transported into the cell and sodium is transported out as the cellular integrity returns.

FIG. 24.8 Escharotomies of the anterior and lateral chest and arm (indicated by *arrows*). (Courtesy Judy Knighton, Toronto, Canada.)

injury (Table 24.3). Upper airway distress may occur with or without smoke inhalation, and airway injury at either level may occur in the absence of burn injury to the skin. (Smoke and inhalation injuries are discussed earlier in this chapter on pp. 432-433.)

The patient may need a fiberoptic bronchoscopy and carboxyhemoglobin blood levels to confirm a suspected inhalation injury. Look in the prehospital and ED notes to see if the patient was exposed to smoke or fumes. Examine any sputum for carbon. Watch for signs of respiratory distress, such as increased agitation, anxiety, restlessness, or a change in the rate or character of the patient's breathing, as symptoms may not be present at first.

In general, there is no correlation between the percentage TBSA burn (% TBSA) and the severity of inhalation injury. In a patient with inhalation injury, a chest x-ray may appear normal on admission, but changes can occur over the next 24 to 48 hours. Arterial blood gas (ABG) values may be within the normal range on admission and change over time.

Other Cardiopulmonary Problems. Patients with preexisting heart disease (e.g., myocardial infarction) or lung disease (e.g., chronic obstructive pulmonary disease [COPD]) are at an increased risk for complications. If fluid replacement is too vigorous, watch for early signs of heart failure or pulmonary edema. Invasive measures (e.g., hemodynamic monitoring) may be needed to monitor fluid resuscitation.

Patients with preexisting lung disease are more likely to develop a respiratory infection. Pneumonia, a common complication of major burns, is the leading cause of death in patients with an inhalation injury.[12]

Urinary System. The most common complication of the urinary system in the emergent phase is ATN. If your patient becomes hypovolemic, blood flow to the kidneys is decreased, causing renal ischemia. If this continues, acute kidney injury may develop.

With full-thickness and major electrical burns, myoglobin (from muscle cell breakdown) and hemoglobin (from RBC breakdown) are released into the bloodstream and block renal tubules. Carefully monitor the adequacy of fluid replacement because this can reverse the obstruction of the tubules.

❖ NURSING AND INTERPROFESSIONAL MANAGEMENT: EMERGENT PHASE

In the emergent phase, the patient's survival depends on rapid and thorough assessment and appropriate interventions. Usually the HCP and you make an initial assessment of the depth and extent of the burn and coordinate the actions of others on the health care team. In a community hospital, determine whether the patient needs inpatient or outpatient care. In the case of inpatient care, decide whether the patient stays at the hospital or must be transferred to a burn center (Table 24.4). Care mainly focuses on airway management, fluid therapy, and wound care (Table 24.10). Patients can improve or worsen, unpredictably.

Although physical therapy (PT) and occupational therapy (OT) are important in both the acute and rehabilitation phases, proper positioning and splinting begin on the day of admission. Emotional support and teaching of patients and caregivers begin on admission. A nursing care plan for the patient with burn injury (eNursing Care Plan 24.1) is available on the website for this chapter.

◆ Airway Management

Airway management often involves early endotracheal (preferably orotracheal) intubation.[14] Early intubation removes the need for emergency tracheostomy after respiratory problems have become apparent. In general, the patient with burns to the face and neck needs intubation within 1 to 2 hours after injury. Intubation is discussed in Chapter 65.

After intubation, the patient is placed on ventilatory support, with settings based on ABG results. Extubation may occur when the edema resolves. This is usually 3 to 6 days after burn injury unless severe inhalation injury exists. Chest escharotomy may be needed to relieve respiratory distress with circumferential, full-thickness burns of the neck and chest (Fig. 24.8).

A fiberoptic bronchoscopy should be done to assess the lower airway within 6 to 12 hours after injury if smoke inhalation is suspected. When intubation is not done, treatment of inhalation injury includes giving 100% humidified O_2. Place the patient in a high Fowler's position, unless contraindicated (e.g., spinal injury). Encourage deep breathing and coughing every hour. Reposition the patient every 1 to 2 hours. Provide suctioning and chest physiotherapy.

If severe respiratory distress (e.g., hoarseness, shortness of breath) develops, intubation and mechanical ventilation are started. Positive end-expiratory pressure (PEEP) may be used to prevent collapse of the alveoli and progressive respiratory failure (see Chapters 65 and 67). Bronchodilators may be given to treat severe bronchospasm. CO poisoning is treated by giving 100% O_2 until carboxyhemoglobin levels return to normal.

> **⚠ SAFETY ALERT   Pulse CO Oximetry Monitoring**
> - Standard pulse oximetry (SpO_2) does not distinguish oxyhemoglobin from carboxyhemoglobin.
> - A patient with CO poisoning will have normal SpO_2 readings despite high carboxyhemoglobin levels.
> - For patients with suspected or confirmed CO poisoning, use a pulse CO oximetry (SpCO) device.

◆ Fluid Therapy

Obtaining IV access is critical for fluid resuscitation and drug administration. At least 2 large-bore IVs must be in place for patients with burns that are 15% TBSA or more. It is critical to obtain IV access that can handle large volumes of fluid. For patients with burns greater than 30% TBSA, consider a central line for fluid and drug administration and blood sampling (central lines are discussed in Chapter 16). An arterial line is often placed if frequent ABGs or invasive BP monitoring is needed.

Assess the extent of the burn wound using a standardized tool (Fig. 24.4). Then use a standardized formula to estimate the patient's fluid resuscitation needs. Fluid replacement is achieved with crystalloid solutions (usually lactated Ringer's), colloids (albumin), or a combination of the two. IV saline is usually started during the prehospital phase.

TABLE 24.10 Interprofessional Care

Burn Injury

Emergent Phase	Acute Phase	Rehabilitation Phase
Fluid Therapy (Table 24.11) • Assess fluid needs. • Begin IV fluid replacement. • Insert indwelling urinary catheter. • Monitor urine output.	**Fluid Therapy** • Continue to replace fluids, depending on patient's clinical response.	• Continue to teach patient and caregiver about wound care. • Continue to encourage and aid patient in resuming self-care. • Continue to prevent or minimize contractures. • Assess risk for scarring (surgery, physical and occupational therapy, splinting, pressure garments). • Discuss possible reconstructive surgery. • Prepare for discharge home or transfer to rehabilitation hospital. • Discuss possible need for home care nursing.
Wound Care • Start daily shower and wound care. • Debride as needed. • Assess extent and depth of burns. • Give tetanus toxoid or tetanus antitoxin.	**Wound Care** • Continue daily shower and wound care. • Continue debridement (if needed). • Assess wound daily and adjust dressing protocols as needed. • Observe for complications (e.g., infection).	
Pain and Anxiety • Assess and manage pain and anxiety.	**Early Excision and Grafting** • Provide temporary allografts. • Provide permanent autografts. • Care for donor sites.	
Physical and Occupational Therapy • Place patient in position that prevents contracture formation and reduces edema. • Assess need for splints.	**Pain and Anxiety** • Continue to assess for and treat pain and anxiety.	
Nutritional Therapy • Assess nutritional needs and begin feeding patient by most appropriate route as soon as possible.	**Physical and Occupational Therapy** • Begin daily therapy program for maintenance of range of motion. • Assess need for splints and anticontracture positioning. • Encourage and aid patient with self-care as possible.	
Respiratory Therapy • Assess oxygenation needs. • Provide supplemental O_2 as needed. • Intubate if needed. • Monitor respiratory status.	**Nutritional Therapy** • Continue to assess diet to support wound healing.	
Psychosocial Care • Provide support to patient and caregiver during initial crisis phase.	**Respiratory Therapy** • Continue to assess oxygenation needs. • Continue to monitor respiratory status. • Monitor for signs of complications (e.g., pneumonia).	
	Psychosocial Care • Provide ongoing support, counseling, and teaching to patient and caregiver about physical and emotional aspects of care and recovery. • Begin discharge planning.	
	Drug Therapy (Table 24.13) • Assess need for drugs (e.g., antibiotics). • Continue to monitor effectiveness and adjust dosage as needed.	

The Parkland (Baxter) formula for fluid replacement is the most common formula used (Table 24.11 or *www.mdcalc.com/parkland-formula-for-burns*). Remember that all formulas are estimates. Fluids are titrated based on the patient's response (e.g., hourly urine output, vital signs). Patients with an electrical injury have greater than normal fluid needs. They generally require an osmotic diuretic (mannitol [Osmitrol]) to increase their urine output and overcome high levels of hemoglobin and myoglobin in the urine. Too much fluid and overestimation of TBSA contribute to over-resuscitation of fluids or "fluid creep."[15] For the first 24 hours, the recommendation is 2 to 4 mL lactated Ringer's/kg/%TBSA burned.[16] Colloidal solutions (e.g., 5% albumin) may be given. However, they are often not started until 12 to 24 hours postburn when capillary permeability returns to normal or near normal. After this time, the plasma stays in the vascular space and expands the circulating volume. The replacement volume is calculated based on the patient's body weight and TBSA burned (e.g., 0.3 to 0.5 mL/kg/%TBSA burned).

Assess for the adequacy of fluid resuscitation hourly using clinical parameters. Urine output, the most often used parameter, and cardiac parameters are defined as follows:

• *Urine output:* 0.5 to 1 mL/kg/hr; 75 to 100 mL/hr for electrical burn patient with evidence of hemoglobinuria or myoglobinuria.
• *Cardiac parameters:* Mean arterial pressure (MAP) greater than 65 mm Hg, systolic BP greater than 90 mm Hg, heart rate less than 120 beats/min. MAP and BP are best measured by an arterial line. Manual BP measurement is often invalid because of edema and vasoconstriction.

CHECK YOUR PRACTICE

You are admitting a new burn patient who weighs 72 kg and has 45% TBSA burn.
• Outline the patient's fluid requirements over the first 24 hours.

TABLE 24.11 **Fluid Resuscitation Formulas**
Parkland (Baxter)*
4 mL lactated Ringer's solution per kilogram (kg) of body weight per percent of total body surface area (% TBSA) burned = Total fluid requirements for first 24 hr after burn
Application
½ of total in first 8 hr
¼ of total in second 8 hr
¼ of total in third 8 hr
Example
For a 70-kg patient with a 50% TBSA burn:
$4\text{ mL} \times 70\text{ kg} \times 50\ (\%TBSA)\text{ burned} = 14,000\text{ mL in 24 hr}$
½ of total in first 8 hr = 7000 mL (875 mL/hr)
¼ of total in second 8 hr = 3500 mL (437 mL/hr)
¼ of total in third 8 hr = 3500 mL (437 mL/hr)
American Burn Association Consensus Fluid Resuscitation
2–4 mL lactated Ringer's solution per kilogram (kg) of body weight per percent of total body surface area (% TBSA) burned = Total fluid requirements for first 24 hr after burn

FIG. 24.9 Shower cart. Showering presents an opportunity for PT and wound care. (Courtesy Judy Knighton, Toronto, Canada.)

◆ **Wound Care**

Once a patent airway, effective circulation, and adequate fluid replacement have been achieved, priority is given to care of the burn wound. Partial-thickness burn wounds appear pink to cherry-red and are wet and shiny with serous exudate. These wounds may or may not have intact blisters; are painful when touched; and have only minor, localized sensation because nerve endings may have been destroyed in the burned dermis.

You can perform cleansing and gentle debridement (using scissors and forceps) on a shower cart (Fig. 24.9), in a regular shower, or on a patient's bed or stretcher. Extensive, surgical debridement is done in the operating room (OR) (Fig. 24.10). During debridement, necrotic skin is removed. Releasing escharotomies and fasciotomies are done in the emergent phase, usually in burn centers by physicians.

Patients find the first wound care to be both physically and mentally demanding. Provide emotional support and begin to build trust during this activity. A once-daily shower and dressing change in the morning, with an evening dressing change in the patient's room, are part of the routine in many burn centers. Others opt to shower the patient on admission and then perform all other dressing changes in the patient's room. Some of the newer antimicrobial dressings can be left in place from 3 to 14 days, reducing the frequency of dressing changes.

Infection can cause further tissue injury and possible sepsis. The source of infection in burn wounds is likely the patient's own flora, mostly from the skin, respiratory, and gastrointestinal (GI) systems.

Two approaches to burn wound treatment are (1) the open method and (2) the use of multiple dressing changes (closed method). In the *open method* the patient's burn is covered with a topical antimicrobial and has no dressing over the wound. This approach is usually limited to the care of facial burns. In the *multiple dressing change,* or *closed method,* sterile gauze dressings are impregnated with or laid over a topical antimicrobial (Fig. 24.11). These dressings are changed from every 12 hours to once every 14 days depending on the product. Most burn centers use the closed technique.

FIG. 24.10 Surgical debridement of full-thickness burns is necessary to prepare the wound for grafting. (Courtesy Judy Knighton, Toronto, Canada.)

FIG. 24.11 Application of silver sulfadiazine cream to saline-moistened gauze. (Courtesy Judy Knighton, Toronto, Canada.)

When the patient's open burn wounds are exposed, always wear personal protective equipment (PPE) (e.g., disposable hats, masks, gowns, gloves). When removing contaminated dressings and washing wounds, use nonsterile, disposable gloves. Use sterile gloves when applying ointments and sterile dressings.

TABLE 24.12 Skin Grafts Used for Burn Injury

Graft Type	Source and Description	Coverage
Allograft (or homograft) (same species)	Cadaveric skin	Temporary (3 days to 2 wk)
Autografts		
Autograft	Patient's own skin	Permanent
Cultured epithelial autograft (CEA)–Epicel	Patient's own skin cell cultures	Permanent
Dermal Substitutes		
AlloDerm	Acellular dermal matrix derived from donated human skin	Permanent
Apligraf	Donated neonatal foreskin fibroblasts and keratinocytes in bovine collagen gel	Permanent
Biobrane	Semipermeable silicone membrane bonded to nylon fabric	Temporary (10–21 days)
Integra	Biodegradable dermal layer made of bovine collagen and glycosaminoglycan bonded to silicone membrane	Permanent
Matriderm	Bovine collagen and elastin matrix	Permanent
OrCel	Donated neonatal foreskin fibroblasts and keratinocytes in bovine collagen sponge	Permanent
Xenograft (or heterograft) (different species)	Porcine skin	Temporary (3 days to 2 wk)

In addition, prevent shivering by keeping the room warm (around 85°F [29.4°C]). Before leaving one patient, remove your PPE and wash your hands. Don new PPE before you treat another patient.

Permanent skin coverage is the primary goal for burn wound care. There is rarely enough unburned skin in the major (greater than 50% TBSA) burn patient for immediate skin grafting. In this situation, temporary wound closure methods are needed. *Allograft (homograft) skin* (from skin donor cadavers) is used, along with newer biosynthetic options. Treatment approaches vary among burn centers (Table 24.12).

◆ Other Care Measures

Certain parts of the body (e.g., face, eyes, hands, arms, ears, perineum) need vigilant nursing care. The face is highly vascular and can become very swollen. It is often covered with ointments and gauze but not wrapped to limit pressure on delicate facial structures. An eye exam should occur soon after admission for all patients with facial burns. Periorbital edema can temporarily prevent eye opening and is often frightening for the patient. Always check that the patient's eyelashes are not turned inward toward the eyeball. Provide assurance that the swelling is not permanent. Instill methylcellulose drops or artificial tears into the eyes for moisture and comfort. Apply antibiotic eye ointment for corneal burns or edema as ordered.

Keep the ears free from pressure because of their poor vascularization and tendency to become infected. Do not use pillows for the patient with ear burns. The pressure on the cartilage may cause chondritis. Also, the ear may stick to the pillowcase, causing pain and bleeding. Raise the patient's head using a rolled towel placed under the shoulders, being careful to avoid pressure necrosis. Follow the same strategy for the patient with neck burns to hyperextend the neck and prevent neck contracture.

Extend burned hands and arms and raise them on pillows or plastic-covered foam wedges to reduce edema. Ask the physical therapist (PT) and the HCP if splints should be applied to burned hands and feet to keep them in positions of function. Remove the splints often and inspect the skin and bony prominences to avoid areas of pressure from inappropriate or prolonged application. Elastic wraps may reduce edema.

Keep your patient's perineum as clean and dry as possible after each voiding or bowel movement. In addition to monitoring hourly urine outputs, an indwelling catheter prevents urine contamination of the perineal area. Regular once- or twice-daily perineal care is essential. Assess the need for an indwelling urinary catheter daily. Remove when it is no longer needed to limit the risk for a urinary tract infection. If your patient has frequent, loose stools, consider using a fecal diversion device.

Perform laboratory tests to monitor fluid and electrolyte balance. Draw ABGs to assess adequacy of ventilation and oxygenation in patients with suspected or confirmed inhalation or electrical injury.

Work with PT to perform range-of-motion (ROM) exercises during dressing changes and throughout the day. Movement aids the shift of the interstitial fluid back into the vascular bed. Active and passive exercise also maintains function and prevents skin and joint contractures. It may reassure the patient that movement is still possible.

❖ Drug Therapy

◆ Analgesics and Sedatives.
Promote the use of analgesics for the patient's comfort. Early in the postburn period, IV pain medications should be given because (1) onset of action is fastest with this route; (2) oral drugs have a slower onset of action and are not as effective when GI function is slowed or impaired because of shock or paralytic ileus; and (3) IM injections are not absorbed well in burned or edematous areas, causing pooling of drugs in the tissues. Consequently, when fluid mobilization starts, the patient could be inadvertently overdosed from the interstitial accumulation of previous IM drugs.

Common drugs used for pain control are listed in Table 24.13. Opioids are the drug of choice for severe pain. When given appropriately, these drugs should provide adequate pain relief. Evaluate the pain management plan often since the patient's needs may change and tolerance to drugs may develop over time. Remember that the patient's pain level may not directly correlate with the extent and depth of burn. Analgesic needs vary from one patient to another. Consider a multimodal approach to pain control. Sedatives/hypnotics and antidepressants can be given with analgesics to control the anxiety, insomnia, or depression that patients may have (Table 24.13).

◆ Tetanus Immunization.
All burn patients routinely receive tetanus toxoid because of the risk for anaerobic burn wound contamination. If the patient has not received an active immunization within 10 years before the burn injury, tetanus immunoglobulin should be considered. (Tetanus immunization is discussed in Table 68.6.)

TABLE 24.13 Drug Therapy

Burns

Drugs	Purpose
Analgesics	
morphine	Relieve pain
sustained-release morphine (MS Contin)	
hydromorphone (Dilaudid)	
sustained-release hydromorphone (Dilaudid CR)	
fentanyl (Sublimaze)	
oxycodone and acetaminophen (Percocet)	
nonsteroidal antiinflammatory (e.g., ketorolac)	
adjuvant analgesics (e.g., gabapentin [Neurontin])	
Anticoagulants	
enoxaparin (Lovenox)	Prevent venous thromboembolism
heparin	
Antidepressants	
citalopram (Celexa)	Reduce depression, improve mood
sertraline (Zoloft)	
Gastrointestinal Support	
aluminum hydroxide and magnesium hydroxide (Maalox)	Neutralize stomach acid
calcium carbonate and magnesium carbonate (Mylanta)	
esomeprazole (Nexium)	Decrease stomach acid and risk for Curling's ulcer
ranitidine (Zantac)	
nystatin	Prevent overgrowth of Candida albicans in oral mucosa
Nutritional Support	
Minerals: zinc, iron (ferrous sulfate)	Promote cell integrity and hemoglobin formation
Vitamins A, C, E, and multivitamins	Promote wound healing
Sedatives/Hypnotics	
lorazepam (Ativan)	Reduce anxiety
midazolam (Versed)	Provide short-acting amnesic effects
zolpidem (Ambien)	Promote sleep

◆ **Antimicrobial Agents**. After the wound is cleansed, topical antimicrobial agents may be applied (Fig. 24.11) and covered with a light dressing. Systemic antibiotics are not routinely used to control burn wound flora because the burn eschar has little or no blood supply, so little antibiotic is delivered to the wound. In addition, the routine use of systemic antibiotics increases the chance of developing multidrug-resistant organisms. Some topical burn agents penetrate the eschar and inhibit bacterial invasion of the wound. Silver-impregnated dressings can be left in place from 3 to 14 days, depending on the patient's clinical situation and the product. Silver sulfadiazine (Silvadene) and mafenide acetate (Sulfamylon) creams are also used.[17]

⚠ **SAFETY ALERT**   Drug Allergy Check
• Check the patient for any allergies to sulfa since many burn antimicrobial creams contain sulfa.

Sepsis is a leading cause of death in the patient with major burns and may lead to multiple organ dysfunction syndrome

(see Chapter 66). Systemic antibiotic therapy is started when the diagnosis of sepsis is made or when some other source of infection is identified (e.g., pneumonia).

Fungal infections may develop in the patient's mucous membranes (mouth and genitalia) because of systemic antibiotic therapy and low resistance. The offending organism is usually *Candida albicans*. Oral infection is treated with nystatin (Mycostatin) mouthwash. When a normal diet is resumed, yogurt or *Lactobacillus* (Lactinex) may be given to reintroduce the normal intestinal flora that was destroyed by antibiotic therapy.

◆ **Venous Thromboembolism Prophylaxis.** Burn patients are at risk for VTE. If there are no contraindications, it is recommended that low-molecular-weight heparin (enoxaparin) or low-dose unfractionated heparin be started as soon as it is considered safe. For burn patients who have a high bleeding risk, VTE prophylaxis with intermittent pneumatic compression devices and/or graduated compression stockings is used until the bleeding risk decreases and heparin can be started (Table 24.13). (VTE prophylaxis is discussed in Chapter 37.)

◆ **Nutritional Therapy**

Once fluid replacement needs have been addressed, nutrition takes priority in the initial emergent phase. Early and aggressive nutritional support within several hours of the burn injury can decrease complications and mortality, optimize burn wound healing, and minimize the negative effects of hypermetabolism and catabolism.[18] Nonintubated patients with a burn of less than 20% TBSA will usually be able to eat enough to meet their nutritional needs.

Intubated patients and those with larger burns need more support. Enteral feedings have almost entirely replaced parenteral feeding. Early enteral feeding, usually with smaller bore tubes, preserves GI function, increases intestinal blood flow, and promotes optimal conditions for wound healing. In general, begin the feedings slowly at a rate of 20 to 40 mL/hr and increase to the goal rate within 24 to 48 hours. If a large nasogastric tube is used, gastric residuals should be checked to rule out delayed gastric emptying. Assess bowel sounds every 8 hours.

A *hypermetabolic state* proportional to the size of the wound occurs after a major burn injury. Resting metabolic expenditure may be increased by 50% to 100% above normal in patients with major burns. Core temperature is increased. Catecholamines, which stimulate catabolism and heat production, are increased. Massive catabolism can occur and is characterized by protein breakdown and increased gluconeogenesis.

Failure to supply adequate calories and protein leads to malnutrition and delayed healing. Calorie-containing nutritional supplements are often given to meet the caloric needs.[19] Protein powder can be added to food and liquids. Supplemental vitamins may be started in the emergent phase, with iron supplements often given in the acute phase (Table 24.13).

ACUTE PHASE

The *acute phase* of burn care begins with the mobilization of extracellular fluid and subsequent diuresis. It ends when partial-thickness wounds are healed or full-thickness burns are covered by skin grafts. This may take weeks or months.

Pathophysiology

A healing burn injury causes many pathophysiologic changes in the body. Diuresis from fluid mobilization occurs, and the patient is less edematous. Bowel sounds return. The depth of the burn wounds may be more apparent as they "declare" themselves as partial or full thickness. The patient may now become more aware of the enormity of the situation and will benefit from emotional support and information.

Some healing begins as WBCs surround the burn wound and phagocytosis occurs. Necrotic tissue begins to slough. Fibroblasts lay down matrices of the collagen precursors that eventually form granulation tissue. A partial-thickness burn will heal, from both the wound edges and the dermal bed below, if kept free from infection and *desiccation* (dryness). However, full-thickness burn wounds, unless extremely small, must have the burn eschar surgically removed (excised) and skin grafts applied to heal. In some cases, healing time and length of hospitalization are decreased by early excision and grafting.

Clinical Manifestations

Partial-thickness wounds form eschar, which begins separating soon after injury. Once the eschar is removed, re-epithelialization begins at the wound margins and appears as red or pink scar tissue. Epithelial buds, from the hair follicles and glands in the dermal bed, eventually close the wound. Healing is spontaneous and usually occurs within 10 to 21 days.

Margins of full-thickness eschar take longer to separate. As a result, full-thickness burn wounds require surgical debridement and skin grafting to heal.

Laboratory Values

Because the body is trying to reestablish fluid and electrolyte balance in the initial acute phase, it is important to follow serum electrolyte levels closely.

Sodium. *Hyponatremia* can develop from excess GI suction and diarrhea. Manifestations include headache, irritability, confusion, vomiting, seizures, and even coma. The patient may develop, *dilutional hyponatremia,* called *water intoxication,* from excess water intake. To avoid this condition, offer the patient fluids other than water, such as juice or nutritional supplements.

Hypernatremia may occur after successful fluid resuscitation if large amounts of hypertonic solutions were used. Hypernatremia also may be caused by tube feedings or inappropriate fluid administration. Manifestations include changes in mental status, ranging from drowsiness, restlessness, confusion, and lethargy to seizures and coma. Sodium restrictions may be applied to IV fluids and enteral or oral feedings until levels return to safe limits.

Potassium. *Hyperkalemia* may occur if the patient has renal failure, adrenocortical insufficiency, or massive deep muscle injury (e.g., electrical burn). Large amounts of potassium are released from damaged cells. Dysrhythmias and arrest can occur with high potassium levels. The patient may have confusion, tetany, muscle cramps, paresthesias, and weakness.

Hypokalemia occurs with vomiting, diarrhea, prolonged GI suction, and IV therapy without potassium supplementation. Potassium is also lost through the patient's burn wounds. Besides dysrhythmias, the patient may have muscle weakness, paresthesia, decreased GI motility, and decreased reflexes (see Chapter 16).

Complications

Infection. A burn injury destroys the body's first line of defense, the skin. The burn wound is now colonized with the person's own organisms that were on the skin before the burn. The WBCs

have functional defects, and the patient is immunosuppressed for many months after the burn injury.

If the levels of bacteria between the eschar and viable wound bed rise to greater than 10^5 per gram of tissue, the patient has a burn wound infection. Infection can convert partial-thickness burns to full-thickness wounds. Wound infections may be treated with systemic and local antibiotics based on wound culture and sensitivity results.

Localized inflammation, induration, and sometimes pus can be seen at the burn wound margins. Watch for signs and symptoms of infection, including hypothermia or hyperthermia, increased heart and respiratory rate, decreased BP, and decreased urine output. The patient may have mild confusion, chills, malaise, and loss of appetite. The WBC count is between $10,000/\mu L$ ($10 \times 10^9/L$) and $20,000/\mu L$ ($20 \times 10^9/L$).

The causative organisms of sepsis are usually gram-negative bacteria (e.g., *Pseudomonas, Proteus*), putting the patient at further risk for septic shock. If sepsis is suspected, obtain cultures from all possible sources, including the burn wound, blood, urine, sputum, oropharynx and perineal regions, and IV site. A lactate level is collected. Treatment begins with a bolus of normal saline IV and antibiotics.[20] Antibiotic therapy may be continued or changed based on the culture and sensitivity results. At this stage, the patient's condition is considered critical. Close monitoring of vital signs and mental status is needed.

Cardiovascular and Respiratory Systems. The same cardiovascular and respiratory complications present in the emergent phase continue into the acute phase of care. In addition, new problems might arise, requiring prompt intervention.

Neurologic System. Neurologically, the patient probably has no physical symptoms, unless severe hypoxia from respiratory injuries or complications from electrical injuries occur. Probable causes of neurologic complications include electrolyte imbalance, stress, cerebral edema, sepsis, sleep problems, and the use of analgesics and antianxiety drugs.

Some patients may have certain behaviors that are not completely understood. The patient may become extremely disoriented, withdraw or become combative, hallucinate, or have frequent nightmare-like episodes. Delirium is more acute at night and occurs more often in the older patient. Start appropriate nursing interventions to prevent delirium and use a screening tool to diagnose delirium (see Table 59.18). Orient and reassure a patient who is confused or agitated. This state is usually transient, lasting from a day or two to several weeks, but complications and sequelae can last for years and be serious.

Musculoskeletal System. The musculoskeletal system is particularly prone to complications during the acute phase. The involvement of both PT and OT is vitally important. As the burns begin to heal and scar tissue forms, the skin is less supple and pliant. ROM may be limited, and skin and joint contractures can occur. Because of pain, the patient prefers a flexed position for comfort. Have the patient stretch and move the burned body parts as much as possible. Consult with PT or OT about proper positioning and splinting to prevent or reduce contracture formation.

Gastrointestinal System. The GI system may develop complications during this phase. Sepsis can cause paralytic ileus. Diarrhea may result from the use of enteral feedings or antibiotics. Constipation can occur as a side effect of opioids, decreased mobility, and a low-fiber diet. *Curling's ulcer* is a type of gastroduodenal ulcer characterized by diffuse superficial lesions (including mucosal erosion). It is caused by a generalized stress response to decreased blood flow to the GI tract. The patient has increased gastric acid secretion.

Aim to prevent Curling's ulcer by feeding the patient as soon as possible after the burn injury. Antacids, H_2-histamine blockers (e.g., ranitidine), and proton pump inhibitors (e.g., omeprazole) are used prophylactically to neutralize stomach acids and inhibit histamine and the secretion of hydrochloric acid (Table 24.13). Patients with major burns may have occult blood in their stools during the acute phase and require close monitoring for bleeding.

Endocrine System. Watch for transient increases in the patient's blood glucose levels because of stress-mediated cortisol and catecholamine release. There is an increased mobilization of glycogen stores and gluconeogenesis. Subsequently, glucose is produced, along with an increase in insulin production. However, insulin's effectiveness is decreased because of relative insulin insensitivity. This results in a high blood glucose level. Hyperglycemia also may be caused by the increased caloric intake needed to meet some patients' metabolic requirements. When hyperglycemia occurs, check blood glucose levels and give insulin as ordered. Point-of-care testing of glucose can be done, but serum glucose testing is more accurate. As the patient's metabolic demands are met and less stress is placed on the entire system, this stress-induced condition is reversed.

❖ NURSING AND INTERPROFESSIONAL MANAGEMENT: ACUTE PHASE

The major therapeutic interventions in the acute phase are (1) wound care, (2) excision and grafting, (3) pain management, (4) PT and OT, and (5) nutritional therapy.

◆ Wound Care

The goals of wound care are to (1) prevent infection by cleansing and debriding the area of necrotic tissue that would promote bacterial growth and (2) promote wound re-epithelialization and/or successful skin grafting.

Wound care consists of ongoing observation, assessment, cleansing, debridement, and dressing reapplication. Nonsurgical debridement, dressing changes, topical antimicrobial therapy, graft care, and donor site care are done as often as needed, depending on the topical cream or dressing ordered. Enzymatic debriding agents made of natural ingredients, such as collagenase, may be used for *enzymatic debridement* of burn wounds, which speeds up the removal of dead tissue from the healthy wound bed.

Cleanse wounds with soap and water or normal saline-moistened gauze to gently remove the old antimicrobial agent and any loose necrotic tissue, scabs, or dried blood. During the debridement phase, cover the wound with topical antimicrobial creams (e.g., silver sulfadiazine) or silver-impregnated dressings. When the partial-thickness burn wounds have been fully debrided, a protective, coarse or fine-meshed, greasy-based (paraffin, petrolatum) gauze dressing is applied to protect the re-epithelializing keratinocytes as they resurface and close the open wound bed.

If grafting is done, protect the skin graft (discussed later) with the same greasy gauze dressings next to the graft, followed by saline-moistened middle dressing and dry gauze outer dressings. With facial grafts, the unmeshed sheet graft is left open, so it is possible for *blebs* (serosanguineous exudate) to form between the graft and recipient bed. Blebs prevent the graft from permanently attaching to the wound bed. The evacuation of blebs is best done by aspiration with a tuberculin syringe and only by those trained in this specialized skill. (Dressings are discussed in Table 11.9.)

◆ Excision and Grafting

Management of full-thickness burn wounds involves early removal (surgical excision) of the necrotic tissue, followed by application of split-thickness autograft skin.[21] This approach has improved the management and survival rate of burn patients. In the past, patients with major burns had low rates of survival because healing and wound coverage took so long that the patient usually died of sepsis or malnutrition.

Many patients, especially those with major burns, are taken to the OR for wound excision on day 1 or 2 (emergent phase). The wounds are covered with a biologic dressing or allograft for temporary coverage until permanent grafting can occur (Table 24.12).

During the procedure of excision and grafting, devitalized tissue (eschar) is excised down to the subcutaneous tissue or fascia, depending on the degree of injury. Surgical excision can result in massive blood loss. To decrease surgical blood loss, topical application of epinephrine or thrombin, injection of saline and epinephrine, application of extremity tourniquets, or application of a fibrin sealant (Artiss) is used.

Once hemostasis has been achieved, a graft is then placed on clean, viable tissue to achieve good adherence. Whenever possible, the freshly excised wound is covered with *autograft* (the person's own) skin (Table 24.12). Recently, fibrin sealant has been used to attach skin grafts to the wound bed. Grafts also can be stapled or sutured into place (Fig. 24.12, *A*). Negative pressure wound therapy dressings are often placed on top of skin grafts to optimize adherence of the graft to the excised wound bed.[22] A temporary allograft can be used to test the suitability of the recipient site to accept a graft. The allograft is then removed several days later in the OR and an autograft applied.

With early excision, function is restored, and scar tissue formation is minimized. Clots between the graft and wound keep the graft from adhering to the wound. Outer occlusive dressings apply just enough pressure to promote adherence of the graft to the wound bed and help control bleeding. Protect the grafted area from shearing, friction, and pressure. Facial, neck, and hand burns require skilled nursing care to identify and manage clots quickly for the best functional and aesthetic outcomes.

Donor skin is taken from the patient for grafting by means of a *dermatome*, which removes a thin split-thickness layer of skin from an unburned site (Fig. 24.12, *B*). The donor skin can be meshed to allow for greater wound coverage, or it may be applied as an unmeshed sheet for a better cosmetic result when grafting the face, neck, and hands. The donor site now becomes a new open wound.

The goals of donor site care are to promote rapid, moist wound healing; decrease pain at the site; and prevent infection. The choices of dressings for donor sites include transparent dressings (e.g., OpSite), xenograft, silver sulfadiazine, silver-impregnated dressings, calcium alginate, and hydrophilic foam dressings (Fig. 24.12, *C*). Nursing care of the donor site is specific to the dressing used. Several of the newer dressings decrease healing time, which allows earlier reharvesting of skin at the same site. The average healing time for a donor site is 10 to 14 days (Fig. 24.12, *D*).

◆ Cultured Epithelial Autografts.

In the patient with large body burns, only a limited amount of unburned skin may be available

FIG. 24.12 A, Freshly applied split-thickness sheet skin graft to the hand. B, Split-thickness skin graft is harvested from a patient's thigh using a dermatome. C, Donor site is covered with a hydrophilic foam dressing after harvesting. D, Healed donor site. (Courtesy Judy Knighton, Toronto, Canada.)

FIG. 24.13 Patient with cultured epithelial autograft (CEA). A, Intraoperative application of CEA. B, Appearance of healed CEA.

as donor sites for grafting, and some of that skin may not be suitable for harvesting. **Cultured epithelial autograft (CEA)** is a method of getting permanent skin from a person with limited skin available for harvesting. CEA is grown from biopsy samples obtained from the patient's unburned skin. This procedure is done in suitable patients in some burn centers as soon as possible. The specimens are sent to a commercial laboratory, where the biopsied keratinocytes are grown in a culture medium containing epidermal growth factor. After about 18 to 25 days, the keratinocytes have expanded up to 10,000 times and form sheets that we can use as skin grafts. The cultured skin is returned to the burn center, where it is placed on the patient's excised burn wounds (Fig. 24.13, A). CEA grafts generally form a seamless, smooth replacement skin tissue (Fig. 24.13, B). Problems related to CEA include a poor graft take because of thin epidermal skin, graft loss during healing, infection, and contracture development.

◆ **Dermal Substitutes.** Dermal substitutes act as a synthetic dermis and are covered by skin graft.[23] The Integra artificial skin

dermal regeneration template is an example of a skin replacement system. As with CEA, it is used in the treatment of life-threatening full-thickness or deep partial-thickness burn wounds when a conventional autograft is not available or advisable, as in older or high anesthetic-risk patients. It also has been successfully used in reconstructive burn surgery procedures. It must be applied within a few days postburn for greatest success.

Integra artificial skin has a bilayer membrane composed of acellular dermis and silicone. The wound is excised, the bilayer membrane is placed dermal layer down, and the wound is wrapped with dressings in the OR. The dermal layer functions as a biodegradable template that induces organized regeneration of new dermis by the body. The silicone layer stays intact for 3 weeks as the dermal layer degrades, and epidermal autografts become available. At this point, the silicone is removed during a second surgery and replaced by the patient's own epidermal autografts.

Another dermal replacement is AlloDerm, a cryopreserved allogenic dermis. Human allograft dermis, harvested from cadavers, is decellularized to make it immunogenic and then freeze-dried. Once thawed, AlloDerm is rehydrated in normal saline immediately before placement on a freshly excised wound.

◆ Pain Management

Many aspects of burn care cause pain. Eliminating all pain is difficult, but most patients will have acceptable levels of relative comfort if they receive adequate analgesia. To provide effective pain management, you must understand both the physiologic and psychologic aspects of pain. Pain management is discussed in Chapter 8.

Burn patients have 2 kinds of pain: (1) *continuous, background pain* that might be present throughout the day and night; and (2) *treatment-induced pain* associated with dressing changes, ambulation, and rehabilitation activities. The first line of pain treatment is drugs (Table 24.13). With background pain, frequent IV administration of an opioid (e.g., hydromorphone [Dilaudid]) provides a steady, therapeutic level of the drug. If tolerating food, slow-release, twice-daily opioids (e.g., morphine [MS Contin]) can be used. Patient-controlled analgesia (PCA) is used in some burn centers, with varying degrees of success. Anxiolytics (e.g., lorazepam [Ativan], midazolam) and adjuvant analgesics (e.g., gabapentin [Neurontin], pregabalin [Lyrica]), can enhance opioids. The use of these drugs can help reduce the opioid dosage and undesirable side effects.

Breakthrough doses of analgesia must be available regardless of the regimen used. Additional doses of opioids are usually given. For treatment-induced pain, premedicate with an analgesic, and possibly an anxiolytic, via the IV or oral route. For patients with an IV, a short-acting analgesic is often used.

ⓘ CHECK YOUR PRACTICE

Your patient with a burn injury is ordered fentanyl (Sublimaze) before a dressing change. The patient has multiple IV lines, and you are not sure which line to use to insert the drug. You know that mixing up IV lines can lead to serious drug errors.
• How would you determine which IV line to use to give the drug?

Some pain can be managed using nondrug strategies. Relaxation breathing, guided imagery, hypnosis, biofeedback, computerized gaming, and music therapy can help patients cope with pain (see Chapter 6).[24]

Remember, the more control the patient has in managing pain, the more successful the chosen strategies will be. Active participation in asking for time-outs and scheduling treatments and rest periods can help the patient manage feelings of anticipatory pain.

◆ Physical and Occupational Therapy

Continuous PT throughout burn recovery is imperative if the patient is to regain and maintain muscle strength and optimal joint function. A good time for exercise is during dressing changes, when bulky dressings are removed and patients are medicated for pain. Passive and active ROM should be performed on all joints. PT and OT may join the nurse and patient during dressing changes. Ensure that the patient with neck burns continues to sleep without pillows or with the head hanging slightly over the top of the mattress to encourage hyperextension.

Maintain the OT schedule for wearing custom-fitted splints, which are designed to keep joints in functional position. Check the splints often to ensure an optimal fit, with no undue pressure that may lead to skin breakdown or nerve damage.

◆ Nutritional Therapy

The goal of nutritional therapy during the acute burn phase is to provide adequate calories and protein to promote healing. When the wounds are still open, the burn patient is in a hypermetabolic and catabolic state.

The patient may benefit from an antioxidant protocol, which includes selenium, vitamin E, acetylcysteine, ascorbic acid, zinc, and a multivitamin. Meeting daily caloric requirements is crucial and should start within the first 1 to 2 days postburn. The daily estimated caloric needs must be regularly calculated by a dietitian and readjusted as the patient's condition changes (e.g., wound healing improves, sepsis develops). Monitor laboratory values (e.g., albumin, prealbumin, total protein, transferrin) on a regular basis.

If the patient is on mechanical ventilation or unable to eat enough calories by mouth, a small-bore feeding tube is placed, and enteral feedings are started. When the patient is extubated, contact the speech pathologist for a swallowing assessment before an oral diet is started. Encourage the patient to eat high-protein, high-carbohydrate foods to meet caloric goals. Ask caregivers to bring in favorite foods from home. Appetite is usually reduced, and you will need to reinforce whatever steps are taken to achieve adequate intake. Ideally, weight loss should not be more than 10% of preburn weight. Record the patient's daily caloric intake using calorie count sheets, which are reviewed by the dietitian. Weigh your patient weekly to evaluate progress.

REHABILITATION PHASE

The formal *rehabilitation phase* begins when the patient's wounds have nearly healed and they are engaging in some level of self-care. This may happen as early as 2 weeks or as long as 7 to 8 months after a major burn injury. Goals for the patient now are to (1) work toward resuming a functional role in society and (2) rehabilitate from any functional and cosmetic postburn reconstructive surgery that may be needed.

Pathophysiologic Changes and Clinical Manifestations

Burn wounds heal by either spontaneous re-epithelialization or skin grafting. Layers of keratinocytes begin rebuilding the tissue structure destroyed by the burn injury. Collagen fibers, present in the new scar tissue, help with healing and add strength to weakened areas. The new skin appears flat and pink. In about 4 to 6 weeks, the area becomes raised and hyperemic. If adequate ROM is not started, the new tissue will shorten, causing a **contracture**. Mature healing is reached in about 12 months, when suppleness has returned and the pink or red color has faded to a slightly lighter hue than the surrounding unburned tissue.

Tell patients who have more heavily pigmented skin that it will take longer for it to regain its color because many of the melanocytes have been destroyed. Often, the skin does not regain its original color, though this is impossible to predict. Provide teaching and emotional support to help the patient with grieving about these changes to his or her body. Cosmetic camouflage, the implantation of pigment within the skin, can help even out unequal skin tones and improve the patient's overall appearance and self-image.

Scarring has 2 characteristics: discoloration and contour. The discoloration of scars fades somewhat with time. However, scar tissue tends to develop altered contours. That is, it is no longer flat or slightly raised but becomes elevated and enlarged above the original burned area. Some burn care providers think that pressure can eventually help keep a scar flat. Gentle pressure is maintained on the healed burn with custom-fitted pressure garments and clear, thermoplastic face masks. Pressure garments and masks should never be worn over unhealed wounds. Once a wearing schedule has been set, they are removed only for short periods while bathing. Pressure garments are worn up to 23 hours a day for as long as 12 to 18 months.

The patient typically reports discomfort from itching where healing is occurring. Teach your patient about the application of water-based moisturizers and selective, short-term use of oral antihistamines (e.g., hydroxyzine [Atarax]) to help reduce the itching. Massage, cooling, emollients, gabapentin, antidepressants, and anesthetic creams also may help.[25]

As "old" epithelium is replaced by new cells, flaking occurs. The newly formed skin is extremely sensitive to trauma. Blisters and skin tears are likely to develop from slight pressure or friction. These newly healed areas can be hypersensitive or hyposensitive to cold, heat, and touch. Grafted areas are more likely to be hyposensitive until peripheral nerve regeneration occurs. Have patients protect healed burn areas from direct sunlight for about 3 months to prevent hyperpigmentation and sunburn injury. Tell them to always wear sunscreen when outside.

Complications

The most common complications during the rehabilitation phase are skin and joint contractures and hypertrophic scarring.[26] A *joint contracture* (an abnormal condition of a joint characterized by flexion and fixation) develops because of the shortening of scar tissue in the flexor tissues of a joint. Areas that are most susceptible to skin and joint contractures include the anterior and lateral neck areas, axillae, antecubital fossae, fingers, groin areas, popliteal fossae, knees, and ankles (Fig. 24.14). Some areas encompass major joints. Not only does the skin over these areas develop contractures, but the underlying tissues, such as the ligaments and tendons, tend to shorten during the healing process.

Carefully watch the patient for these potential problems. Encourage proper positioning, splinting, and exercise to minimize this complication. Tell the patient to continue with these strategies until the skin matures at around 1-year post healing. Rehabilitative therapy is aimed at the extension of body parts because the flexors are stronger than the extensors. Burned legs first may be wrapped with elastic (e.g., tensor, ACE) bandages to assist with circulation to leg-graft and donor sites before ambulation. Burned arms can be wrapped with a layer of tubular elastic gauze (e.g., Tubigrip). This interim pressure prevents blister formation, promotes venous return, and decreases pain and itchiness. Once the skin is completely healed and less fragile, custom-fitted pressure garments replace the elastic bandages and tubular gauze.

❖ NURSING AND INTERPROFESSIONAL MANAGEMENT: REHABILITATION PHASE

During the rehabilitation phase, encourage both the patient and caregiver to take part in care. Since the patient may go home with unhealed wounds, teach your patient and caregiver the skills for wound care. Before discharge, have them show you the proper dressing change. In addition, make sure they know when to contact the burn team (e.g., signs of infection, increased pain) and the need to keep outpatient visits to ensure good wound healing.

If needed, arrange home care nursing to assist with care. The newly discharged patient will need to know how to gently remove the dressings in the shower once daily, if a nonadherent, greasy gauze dressing is used or twice daily if a topical, antimicrobial cream is ordered. Teach that showering, not bathing, with mild soap and warm water keeps the wounds clean.

Give advice on scar management, moisturizing, and sun protection. Suggest using water-based creams that penetrate the dermis (e.g., Vaseline Intensive Rescue) on healed areas to keep the skin supple and moisturized. This will decrease itching and flaking. Sometimes antihistamines are used at bedtime if itching persists.

Base ongoing pain management and nutritional needs on individual patient status. Continue to encourage the patient to perform the PT and OT routines. Encourage and reassure the patient to maintain morale, particularly once the patient realizes that recovery can be slow. Rehabilitation may have to be a primary focus for at least the next 6 to 12 months.

Postburn reconstructive surgery is often done after a major burn. The need for further surgery is reviewed at the outpatient burn clinic appointments after discharge.

🧑 Gerontologic Considerations: Burns

The older patient presents many challenges for the burn team.[27] The normal aging process puts the patient at risk for injury because of unsteady gait, limited eyesight, and decreased hearing. As people age, skin becomes drier and more wrinkled. Older adults have thinning of the dermal layer, a loss of elastic fibers, a reduction in subcutaneous adipose tissue, and a decrease in vascularity. As a result, the thinner dermis, with reduced blood flow, sustains deeper burns with poorer rates of healing.

Once injured, the older adult has more complications in the emergent and acute phases of burn resuscitation because of preexisting co-morbidities. For example, older patients with diabetes, heart failure, or COPD have morbidity and mortality rates exceeding those of healthy, younger patients. In older patients, pneumonia is a frequent complication, burn wounds and donor sites take longer to heal, and surgical procedures are not well tolerated. Weaning from a ventilator can be a challenge. Although usually self-limiting, delirium, if it develops, may be

FIG. 24.14 Neck contracture. (Courtesy Linda Bucher, RN, PhD, CEN, CNE, Staff Nurse, Virtua Memorial Hospital, Mt. Holly, NJ.)

distressing.[28] It usually takes longer for these patients to rehabilitate to the point at which they can safely return home. For some, a return home to independent living may not be possible. As the population ages, developing strategies to prevent burn injuries in older adults is a priority.

EMOTIONAL/PSYCHOLOGIC NEEDS OF PATIENTS AND CAREGIVERS

Patients and caregivers have many emotional/psychologic needs during the often lengthy, unpredictable, and complex course of care. You have an important supportive and counseling role as patients struggle to get their lives back on track.

To manage the enormous range of emotional responses that the burn patient may have, assess the circumstances of the burn (e.g., cause, people involved), family relationships, and previous ways of coping with stress. At any time, the patient may have a variety of emotions, such as fear, anxiety, anger, guilt, and depression (Table 24.14).

Burn survivors often have thoughts and feelings that are frightening and disturbing, such as guilt about the burn incident, reliving the burn experience, fear of dying, concern about future therapy and surgery, frustrations with ongoing discomfort and treatment, and hopelessness about the future. During recovery, as more independence is expected from the patient, new fears may occur: "Can I really do this?" "Am I a desirable person?" "How can I go outside looking like this?" These challenges confront patients throughout their recovery and often for years to come.

A burn injury may adversely affect the person's self-esteem. Some may fear the loss of relationships because of perceived or actual physical disfigurement. In a society that values physical beauty, changes in body image can result in psychologic distress.

Open and frequent communication among the patient, caregivers, close friends, and burn team members is essential. Because of the tremendous psychologic impact of a burn injury, be particularly sensitive to the patient's emotions and concerns. Encourage the patient to discuss fears about loss of life as they once knew it, loss of function, temporary or permanent deformity and disfigurement, return to work and home life, and financial burdens resulting from a long and costly hospitalization and rehabilitation.[29]

Encourage appropriate independence and an eventual return to preburn activities, such as school or work. Peer counseling and informal interactions with other burn survivors may bring comfort and help to restore confidence. Reassure patients that their feelings during this period of adjustment are a normal reaction to an extraordinary life event. Their frustration and impatience are to be expected as they work to establish a new life. Help patients in adapting to a realistic, yet positive appraisal of their specific situation, emphasizing what they *can* do instead of what they *cannot* do.

Caregivers may share some or all these challenges and feelings. At times, they may feel helpless or too exhausted to help their loved one. Continued support from trusted and familiar burn team members is essential. Helping caregivers assist with aspects of the patient's care helps them to reconnect with their loved one and eases the transition home. Many burn survivors and their caregivers remark on the powerful learning experience of the burn and a renewed appreciation of life, despite the ongoing challenges of a prolonged recovery. You must acknowledge that their feelings are real and common. Most burn survivors speak of a real satisfaction with their postburn life and are more empowered as time goes on.

It is important to address individual spiritual and cultural needs because both have a role in treatment decisions and recovery. Pastoral care may be a helpful resource for the patient and caregiver. The need for support, information, and family involvement may vary among cultures. Identify what is important to your patient and caregiver and communicate that information in the patient's plan of care. Encourage the burn care team to be culturally aware of and sensitive to the patient's and caregiver's cultural needs.

The difficult issue of sexuality must be met with honesty. Acceptance of any changes in physical appearance is difficult at first for the patient and significant other. The nature of skin injury in itself can cause modifications in processing sexual stimuli.[30] Touch is an important part of sexuality, and immature scar tissue may make the sensation of touch unpleasant or may dull it. This may be only transient, but the patient and partner need to know that it is normal and receive anticipatory guidance from the burn team to avoid undue emotional strain.

Burn survivors may have preexisting mental health or substance use issues, any of which may have contributed to the burn incident.[31] The stress of the burn injury can precipitate a psychologic crisis. Assessment by a psychiatrist who can prescribe appropriate drugs, if needed, and offer counseling is often helpful. Early psychiatric intervention is essential if the patient has been previously treated for a psychiatric illness or if the injury was a suicide attempt. Many burn patients have posttraumatic stress disorder. A history of mental health issues can influence the length of hospitalization and time needed to prepare for discharge.[31] However, it has been noted that distress and trauma symptoms can act as a catalyst for positive posttraumatic growth. Coping styles and social support assist in these positive changes postburn.[32]

Psychologic care typically begins in the hospital, but links to community resources must be made before discharge to ensure continuity of treatment. A referral to a psychiatrist, psychologist, psychiatric advanced practice nurse (APN), mental health counselor, or social worker should be discussed if concerns are raised at burn clinic follow-up.

Caregiver and patient support groups may be beneficial in meeting the patient's and caregiver's emotional needs at any phase of the recovery process. Speaking with others who have had burn trauma can be beneficial, both in terms of confirming that the patient's feelings are normal and in sharing helpful

TABLE 24.14 **Common Emotional Responses**	
Emotion	**Possible Verbal Expression**
Anger	• Why did this happen to me? • The nurses enjoy hurting me. • I hope the person who did this to me dies.
Anxiety	• I feel out of control. • What's going to happen to me? • When will I look normal again?
Depression	• It is no use going on like this. • I do not care what happens to me. • I wish people would leave me alone.
Fear	• Will I die? • What will happen next? • Will I be disfigured? • Will my family and friends still love me?
Guilt	• If only I had been more careful. • I'm being punished because I did something wrong.
Hopefulness	• What do I need to do to survive this injury emotionally and return to my life/family/friends? • What am I meant to learn from this injury?

advice. The Phoenix Society (*www.phoenix-society.org*) is an international, highly respected burn survivors' support group. For many years the society has offered valuable support and resources (e.g., annual World Burn Congress conference) to burn survivors, caregivers, and burn team staff.

SPECIAL NEEDS OF NURSES

Warm, trusting, and mutually satisfying relationships often develop between burn patients and nursing staff during hospitalization and the long-term rehabilitation period. Sometimes the bond can be so strong that the patient has difficulty separating from the hospital and staff. The frequency and intensity of family contact can be rewarding as well as draining to you. You may find it difficult to cope with the deformities caused by the burn injury, odors, unpleasant sight of the wound, and reality of the pain that accompanies the burn and its treatment.

Do not hesitate to seek help from co-workers, a manager, or the employee assistance program should you feel the need.

In time, you will come to know that the specialized burn care you provide makes a critical difference in helping patients not only survive but also cope with and triumph over an intense and complex injury.

Ongoing support services or critical incident stress debriefings led by a psychiatrist, psychologist, psychiatric APN, or social worker may be helpful. Peer support groups (e.g., ABA, International Society for Burn Injuries) can serve a similar purpose by helping you cope with difficult feelings experienced when caring for burn patients. Because burn nursing is physically, psychologically, and intellectually demanding, it has many challenges and inherent rewards. Attention to your own self-care is important to maintain a positive attitude and healthy work-life balance. Time with family and friends and rest and relaxation at home are essential parts of self-care and a balanced life with purpose and meaning.

CASE STUDY

Burn Injury

(© Comstock/ Thinkstock.)

Patient Profile

G.M., a 52-yr-old married white man, arrives at the ED with burns to his face, neck, chest, right arm and hand, and right foot. He was burning brush on his farm when the fire went out of control. He has an 18-gauge IV with NSS running at 100 mL/hr, and he is receiving 100% humidified O$_2$ by mask.

Subjective Data

- Reports blurry vision and trouble swallowing
- States his burns are painful and that he is scared
- States he is a "diabetic" and has "high blood pressure"

Objective Data

Physical Examination

- Is awake, alert, and oriented, but in some distress
- Eyes are red, irritated
- Voice is hoarse; nasal hair is singed
- Face is reddened with blisters noted on the nose and forehead
- Right arm, right hand, anterior chest, neck, and right foot have shiny, bright red, wet wounds
- Is shivering

Discussion Questions

1. *Priority Decision:* What are the priorities of care in the prehospital setting and ED? How should his airway, breathing, and circulation be managed?

2. *Priority Decision:* What factors place G.M. at high risk for an inhalation injury? What priority interventions can be anticipated?

3. *Patient-Centered Care:* What pain medications might be considered to relieve his pain?

4. Which of the criteria for burn center referral does G.M. meet for admission to the hospital burn unit?

5. What metabolic disturbances would be expected soon after G.M.'s admission? Explain the physiologic basis for these changes.

6. How might G.M.'s co-morbidities affect his burn care and rehabilitation?

7. *Patient-Centered Care:* What measures should be taken to support G.M.'s caregivers?

8. *Priority Decision:* Based on the assessment data presented, what are the priority nursing diagnoses?

9. *Evidence-Based Practice:* What are the most effective wound care strategies to manage G.M.'s burn wounds?

10. *Patient-Centered Care:* Prior to discharge what teaching should be provided to G.M. and his family so they can successfully manage his care at home?

11. *Safety:* To ensure G.M.'s safety at home, what interventions are necessary prior to discharge?

12. *Quality Improvement:* What outcomes will indicate that interprofessional care was effective?

Answers available at *http://evolve.elsevier.com/Lewis/medsurg.*

▌ BRIDGE TO NCLEX EXAMINATION

The number of the question corresponds to the same-numbered outcome at the beginning of the chapter.

1. Which prevention strategy would the nurse include when teaching about home fire safety?
   a. Set hot water temperature at 140° F.
   b. Use only hardwired smoke detectors.
   c. Encourage regular home fire exit drills.
   d. Do not allow older adults to cook unattended.

2. The injury that is *least* likely to result in a full-thickness burn is
   a. sunburn.
   b. scald injury.
   c. chemical burn.
   d. electrical injury.

3. When assessing a patient with a partial-thickness burn, the nurse would expect to find (*select all that apply*)
   a. blisters.
   b. exposed fascia.
   c. exposed muscles.
   d. intact nerve endings.
   e. red, shiny, wet appearance.

4. A patient is admitted to the burn center with burns to his head, neck, and anterior and posterior chest after an explosion in his garage. On assessment, the nurse auscultates wheezes throughout the lung fields. On reassessment, the wheezes are gone, and the breath sounds are greatly decreased. Which action is the *most* appropriate for the nurse to take *next*?
   a. Encourage the patient to cough and auscultate the lungs again.
   b. Obtain vital signs, oxygen saturation, and a STAT arterial blood gas.
   c. Document the findings and continue to monitor the patient's breathing.
   d. Anticipate the need for endotracheal intubation and notify the provider.

5. Fluid and electrolyte shifts that occur during the early emergent phase of a burn injury include
   a. adherence of albumin to vascular walls.
   b. movement of potassium into the vascular space.
   c. movement of sodium and water into the interstitial space.
   d. hemolysis of red blood cells from large volumes of rapidly administered fluid.

6. To maintain a positive nitrogen balance in a major burn, the patient must
   a. eat a high-protein, high-carbohydrate diet.
   b. increase normal caloric intake by about four times.
   c. eat at least 1500 calories/day in small, frequent meals.
   d. eat a gluten-free diet for the chemical effect on nitrogen balance.

7. A patient has 25% TBSA burn from a car fire. His wounds have been debrided and covered with a silver-impregnated dressing. The nurse's *priority* intervention for wound care would be to
   a. reapply a new dressing without disturbing the wound bed.
   b. observe the wound for signs of infection during dressing changes.
   c. apply cool compresses for pain relief in between dressing changes.
   d. wash the wound aggressively with soap and water three times a day.

8. Pain management for the burn patient is *most* effective when (*select all that apply*)
   a. a pain rating tool is used to monitor the patient's level of pain.
   b. painful dressing changes are delayed until the patient's pain is completely relieved.
   c. the patient is informed about and has some control over the management of the pain.
   d. a multimodal approach is used (e.g., sustained-release and short-acting opioids, NSAIDs, adjuvant analgesics).
   e. nonpharmacologic therapies (e.g., music therapy, distraction) replace opioids in the rehabilitation phase of a burn injury.

9. A therapeutic measure used to prevent hypertrophic scarring during the rehabilitation phase of burn recovery is
   a. applying pressure garments.
   b. repositioning the patient every 2 hours.
   c. performing active ROM at least every 4 hours.
   d. massaging the new tissue with water-based moisturizers.

10. A patient is recovering from second- and third-degree burns over 30% of his body, and the burn care team is planning for discharge. The *first* action the nurse should take when meeting with the patient would be to
    a. arrange a return-to-clinic appointment and prescription for pain medications.
    b. teach the patient and the caregiver proper wound care to be performed at home.
    c. review the patient's current health care status and readiness for discharge to home.
    d. give the patient written information and websites for information for burn survivors.

1. c, 2, a, 3, a, d, 4, d, 5, c, 6, a, 7, b, 8, a, c, d, 9, a, 10, c

For rationales to these answers and even more NCLEX review questions, visit *http://evolve.elsevier.com/Lewis/medsurg*.

⊕ EVOLVE WEBSITE/RESOURCES LIST

http://evolve.elsevier.com/Lewis/medsurg
Review Questions (Online Only)
Key Points
Answer Keys for Questions
   • Rationales for Bridge to NCLEX Examination Questions
   • Answer Guidelines for Case Study on p. 451
   • Answer Guidelines for Managing Care of Multiple Patients Case Study (Section 5) on p. 454
Student Case Study
   • Patient With Burns
Nursing Care Plan
   • eNursing Care Plan 24.1: Patient With a Thermal Burn Injury
Conceptual Care Map Creator
Audio Glossary
Content Updates

REFERENCES

1. American Burn Association: *Burn incidence and treatment in the US: 2016 fact sheet*. Retrieved from *http://ameriburn.org/who-we-are/media/burn-incidence-fact-sheet/*.
2. WHO International: *Burns fact sheet March 2018*. Retrieved from *www.who.int/news-room/fact-sheets/detail/burns*.
3. Grant EJ: Burn injuries: Prevention, advocacy, and legislation, *Clin Plast Surg* 44:451, 2017.
4. Roberts JR, Custalow CB, Thomsen TW: *Roberts and Hedges' clinical procedures in emergency medicine and acute care*, ed 7, Philadelphia, 2019, Elsevier.
5. Gupta K, Mehrotra M, Kumar P, et al: Smoke inhalation injury: Pathogenesis, diagnosis, and management, *Indian J Crit Care* Med 22:180, 2018.
6. Greenhalgh DG: *Burn care for general surgeons and general practitioners*, Wiesbaden, Germany, 2016, Springer.
7. Understanding burn care. Retrieved from *http://understandingburncare.org/burn-severity.html*.
8. American Burn Association Burn Center referral criteria. Retrieved from *www.ameriburn.org/wp-content/uploads/2017/05/burncenterreferral criteria.pdf*
9*. Wallis L, Fleming J, Hasselberg M, et al: A smartphone app and cloud-based consultation system for burn injury, *Emerg Care* 11:1, 2016.
10*. Sorg H, Tilkorn D, Hager S, et al: Skin wound healing: An update on the current knowledge and concepts, *European Surgical Res* 58:81, 2017.
11*. Pannucci C, Obi A, Timmins B, et al: Venous thromboembolism in patients with thermal injury: A review of risk assessment tools and current knowledge on the effectiveness and risks of mechanical and chemical prophylaxis, *Clin Plastic Surg* 44:573, 2017.
12*. Sutton T, Lenk I, Conrad P, et al: Severity of inhalation injury is predictive of alterations in gas exchange and worsened clinical outcomes, *J Burn Care Res* 38:390, 2017.
13. Alves dos Santos C, Souza-Junior V, Ferreira Lanza F, et al: Serious games in virtual environments for health teaching and learning, *Northeast Netw Nurs J* 18:702, 2017.
14. Deutsch C, Tan A, Smailes S, et al: The diagnosis and management of inhalation injury: An evidence-based approach, *Burns* 44:1040-1051, 2018.

15. Cartotto R, Greenhalgh D, Cancio C, et al: Burn state of the science: Fluid resuscitation, *J Burn Care Res* 38:e596-e604, 2017.

16. Ahuja R, Gibran N, Greenhalgh D, et al: ISBI practice guidelines for burn care, *Burns* 42:953, 2016.

17. Herndon DN: *Total burn care*, Edinburgh, 2018, Elsevier.

18. Berger M, Pantet O: Nutrition in burn injury: Any recent changes? *Curr Opin Crit Care* 22:285, 2016.

19. Clark A, Imran J, Madni T, et al : Nutrition and metabolism in burn patients, *Burns Trauma* 5:1, 2017.

20. Dellinger R, Schorr C, Levy M: A users guide to the 2016 surviving sepsis guidelines, *Crit Care Med* 45:381, 2017.

21. Ahuja R, Gibran N, Greenhalgh D, et al: ISBI practice guidelines for burn care, *Burns* 42:953, 2016.

22. Mushin O, Bogue J, Esquenazi M, et al: Use of a home vacuum-assisted closure device in the burn population is both cost-effective and efficacious, *Burns* 43:490, 2017.

23. Hussain A: Surgical treatment of acute burns, *Wounds UK* 14:30, 2018.

24. Najafi Ghezeljeh T, Mohades Ardebili F, Rafii F: The effects of massage and music on pain, anxiety and relaxation in burn patients, *Burns* 43:1034, 2017.

25. Parnell L: Itching for knowledge about wound and scar pruritus, *Wounds* 30:17, 2018.

26. Oosterwijk A, Mouton L, Schouten H, et al: Prevalence of scar contractures after burn: A systematic review, *Burns* 43:41, 2017.

27. Gregg D, Patil S, Singh K, et al: Clinical outcomes after burns in elderly patients over 70 years: A 17-year retrospective analysis, *Burns* 44:65, 2018.

28. Holmes E, Laughon S, Jones S: Retrospective analysis of neurocognitive impairment in older patients with burn injuries, *Psychosomatics* 58:386, 2017.

29. Jonathan B, Pius A, Richcane A: Study on acute burn injury survivors and the associated issues, *J Acute Dis* 3:206, 2016.

30. Kornhaber R, Haik J, Sayers J, et al: People with borderline personality disorder and burns: Some considerations for health professionals, *Issues Mental Health Nurs* 38:767, 2017.

31. Li F, Coombs D: Mental health history: A contributing factor for poorer outcomes in burn survivors, *Burns Trauma* 6:1, 2018.

32. Kruithof N, Traa M, Karabatzakis M, et al: Perceived changes in quality of life in trauma patients: A focus group study, *J Trauma Nurs* 25:177, 2018.

*Evidence-based information for clinical practice.

CASE STUDY
Managing Care of Multiple Patients

You are working the day shift on a medical-surgical unit and have been assigned to care for the following 5 patients. You have 1 UAP who is assigned to work with you. There are 15 other patients on the unit being cared for by an additional 3 RNs and 3 UAP.

Patients

(© Jack Hollingsworth/ Photodisc/Thinkstock.)

F.M., an 81-yr-old Hispanic woman, had pneumatic retinopexy surgery yesterday to repair a partial detached retina. She has a history of type 2 diabetes, hypothyroidism, and hypertension. She is scheduled to be discharged today, but the night nurse is concerned because her BP is elevated at 150/94 mm Hg.

(© iStock.com/EyeMark.)

R.S., a 57-yr-old woman, is under observation with Ménière's disease. She continues to have extreme dizziness, tinnitus, and nausea. The HCP plans to administer an intratympanic injection of dexamethasone today.

(© Stockphoto/ Thinkstock.)

D.A., a 74-yr-old woman, is admitted to the hospital with complaints of chest tightness and shortness of breath. Her past medical history is negative except for a recent diagnosis of basal cell carcinoma (BCC) on her face. She was scheduled to have the BCC surgically removed tomorrow. The HCP suspects D.A.'s symptoms are caused by anxiety but first needs to rule out any coronary artery disease before surgery.

G.L., a 48-yr-old white man, just arrived for admission. He is scheduled for surgical removal of melanoma lesions on his face at 1200. He is worried that the surgery will be disfiguring.

(© Dimedrol68/iStock/ Thinkstock.)

(© Stockphoto/ Thinkstock.)

D.B., a 74-yr-old white man, was admitted 3 hours ago from the ED with partial thickness burns on his chest and arms (estimated to be 6% TBSA). He was burning leaves and branches using gasoline. The pile exploded and his clothes caught fire.

Discussion Questions

1. ***Priority Decision:*** After receiving report, which patient should you see first? Provide rationale.
2. ***Collaboration:*** Which tasks could you delegate to the UAP *(select all that apply)*?
   a. Obtain vital signs on F.M.
   b. Take a blood pressure reading on D.B.
   c. Perform an admission assessment on G.L.
   d. Explain planned diagnostic testing to R.S.
   e. Obtain a 12-lead electrocardiograph on D.A.

3. ***Priority Decision and Collaboration:*** When you enter D.B.'s room, he tells you he is not feeling well. He says he has a headache and his legs are "cramping up." He is also somewhat confused as he is unaware that he is in the hospital. What initial action would be *most* appropriate?
   a. Administer acetaminophen for headache relief.
   b. Have the UAP obtain a STAT capillary blood glucose reading.
   c. Notify D.B.'s health care provider of his altered level of consciousness.
   d. Ask the UAP to obtain vital signs on D.B. while you review recent laboratory results.

Case Study Progression

D.B.'s vital signs are BP 154/88 mm Hg, heart rate is 112 bpm, respirations are 18 breaths/min, and temperature is 98°F (36.8°C). His most recent laboratory results reveal a serum sodium level of 128 mEq/L (128 mmol/L). You notify his HCP, who orders a normal saline IV to infuse at 100 mL/hr.

4. D.B. complains of thirst and asks for something to drink. Which fluids would be appropriate to give him *(select all that apply)*?
   a. Gatorade
   b. Tap water
   c. Cola soda
   d. Apple juice
   e. Orange juice
5. In addition to teaching F.M. how to administer postoperative eyedrops, you will also explain
   a. position and activity restrictions.
   b. how to change the dressing on her eye.
   c. the necessity for restricting fluid intake.
   d. that protective eyewear will no longer be required.
6. When giving report to your UAP regarding your assigned patients, you are asked by the UAP if there is a significant difference between D.A. and G.L.'s skin cancers. You reply based on knowledge that
   a. basal cell carcinoma is the deadliest form of skin cancer.
   b. melanoma typically appears as red, rough patches on the skin.
   c. melanoma can metastasize to any organ, including the brain and heart.
   d. basal cell carcinoma often occurs during the second and third decades of life.
7. ***Management Decision:*** Another RN offers to help you by providing care for F.M. Which observed action by the RN would require your immediate intervention?
   a. The RN assists F.M. to lie flat on her back.
   b. The RN gives F.M. oral medication for pain.
   c. The RN assures F.M. that retinal reattachment is usually successful.
   d. The RN explains to F.M. that she is at risk for detachment in the other eye.
8. ***Priority Decision:*** Which intervention has the *highest* priority for R.S.?
   a. Keeping the room dark and quiet.
   b. Placing an emesis basin at the bedside.
   c. Elevating the head of the bed to the height desired.
   d. Raising the side rails and having the bed in low position.

Answers available at *http://evolve.elsevier.com/Lewis/medsurg.*

Assessment: Respiratory System

Eugene Mondor

Do your little bit of good where you are; it's those little bits of good put together that overwhelm the world.

Desmond TuTu

ⓔ http://evolve.elsevier.com/Lewis/medsurg/

CONCEPTUAL FOCUS

Functional Ability   Gas Exchange

LEARNING OUTCOMES

1. Distinguish the structures and functions of the upper respiratory tract, lower respiratory tract, and chest wall.
2. Describe the process that initiates and controls inspiration and expiration.
3. Describe the process of oxygenation and ventilation.
4. Identify the respiratory defense mechanisms.
5. Describe the significance of arterial blood gas values in relation to respiratory function.
6. Relate the signs and symptoms of inadequate oxygenation to physical assessment findings.
7. Link age-related changes of the respiratory system to key differences in assessment findings.

8. Obtain significant subjective and objective assessment data related to the respiratory system.
9. Perform a physical assessment of the respiratory system using the appropriate techniques.
10. Distinguish normal from common abnormal findings in a physical assessment of a patient's respiratory system.
11. Describe the purpose, significance of results, and nursing responsibilities related to diagnostic studies of the respiratory system.

KEY TERMS

adventitious breath sounds, p. 467
chemoreceptor, p. 459
compliance, p. 458
crackles, Table 25.6, p. 468
dyspnea, p. 458

elastic recoil, p. 458
fremitus, p. 465
mechanical receptors, p. 459
oxygenation, p. 458
resistance, p. 458

surfactant, p. 457
tidal volume (V_T), p. 457
ventilation, p. 458
wheezes, Table 25.6, p. 468

The primary purpose of the respiratory system is gas exchange. This involves the transfer of oxygen (O_2) and carbon dioxide (CO_2) between the atmosphere and blood. While adequate perfusion is needed to distribute O_2 to the body tissues, adequate oxygenation depends on a healthy, functioning respiratory system.

STRUCTURES AND FUNCTIONS OF RESPIRATORY SYSTEM

The respiratory system is divided into 2 parts: the upper respiratory tract and the lower respiratory tract (Fig. 25.1).

Upper Respiratory Tract

The *upper respiratory tract* includes the nose, mouth, pharynx, epiglottis, larynx, and trachea. Air enters the respiratory tract through the nose. The nose is made of bone and cartilage. It is divided into 2 nares by the nasal septum. The inside of the nose is shaped into 3 passages by projections called *turbinates*. The turbinates increase the surface area of the nasal mucosa that warms and moistens the air as it enters the nose. The internal nose opens directly into the sinuses. The nasal cavity connects with the pharynx. It is a tubular passageway that is subdivided into 3 parts: the *nasopharynx, oropharynx,* and *laryngopharynx.*

455

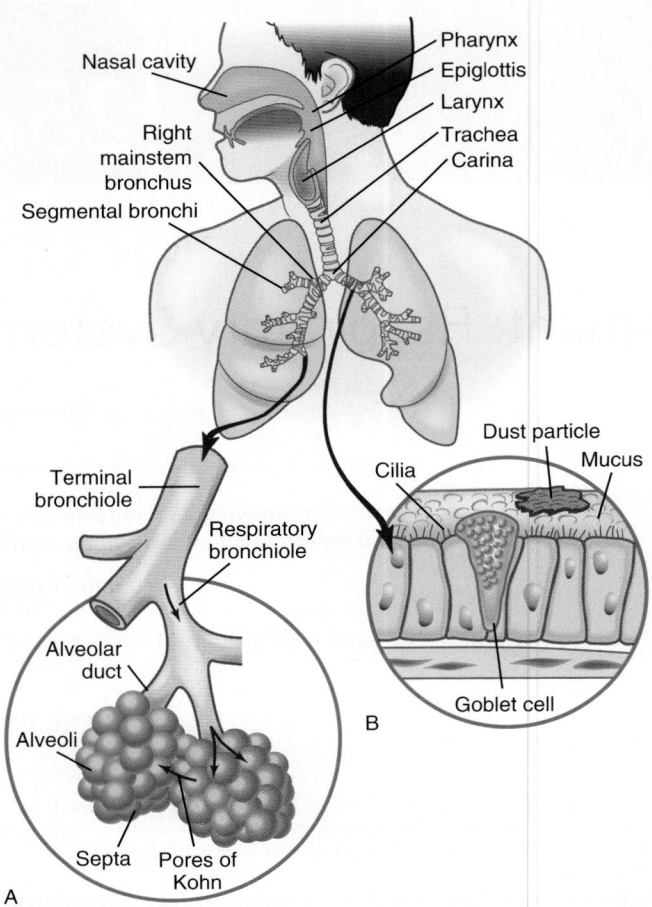

FIG. 25.1 Structures of the respiratory tract. **A,** Pulmonary functional unit. **B,** Ciliated mucous membrane. (Redrawn from Price SA, Wilson LM: *Pathophysiology: Clinical concepts of disease processes,* ed 6, St Louis, 2003, Mosby.)

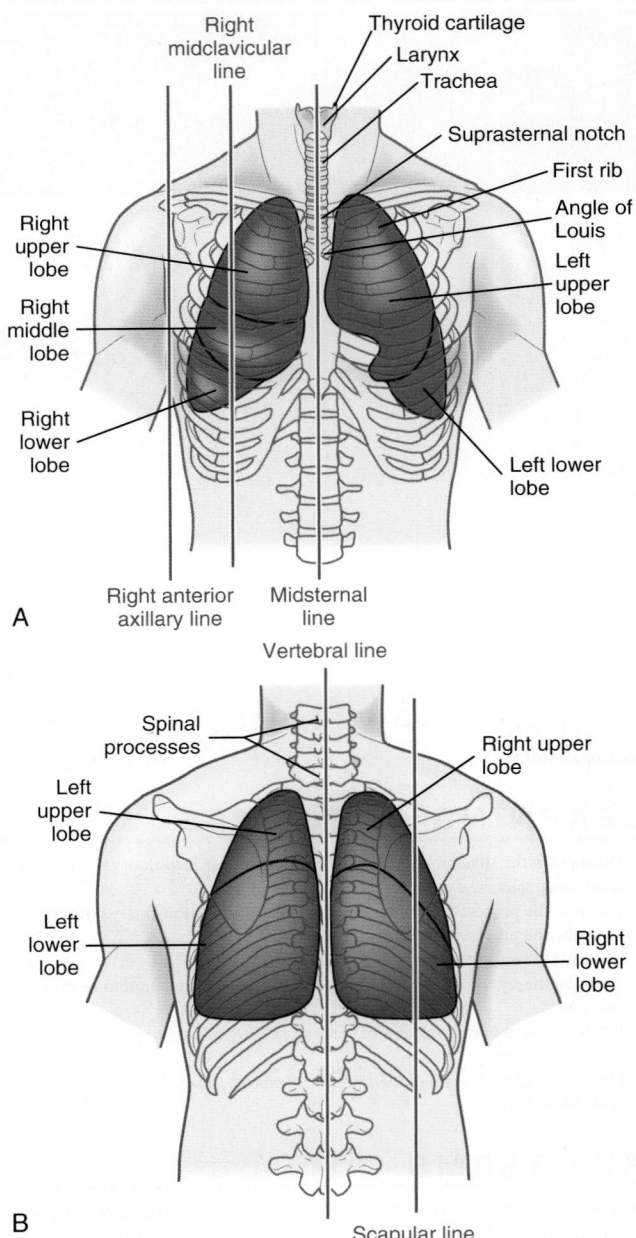

FIG. 25.2 Landmarks and structures of the chest wall. **A,** Anterior view. **B,** Posterior view. (Redrawn from Thompson JM, McFarland GK, Hirsch JE, et al: *Mosby's clinical nursing,* ed 5, St Louis, 2002, Mosby.)

The nose functions to protect the lower airway by warming and humidifying air and filtering small particles before air enters the lungs. The olfactory nerve, found within the mucosa of the upper part of the nasal cavity, is responsible for the sense of smell.[1]

Air moves through the oropharynx to the laryngopharynx. It then travels through the epiglottis to the larynx before moving into the trachea. The *epiglottis* is a small flap behind the tongue that closes over the larynx during swallowing. This prevents solids and liquids from entering the lungs. The vocal cords are in the larynx. Air passes through the glottis (the opening between the vocal cords) and into the trachea.

The trachea is a cylindrical tube about 5 in (10 to 12 cm) long and 1 in (1.5 to 2.5 cm) in diameter. U-Shaped cartilages keep the trachea open but allow the adjacent esophagus to expand for swallowing. The trachea bifurcates into the right and left mainstem bronchi at a point called the *carina.* The carina is located at the *angle of Louis,* which is at the level of the 4th and 5th thoracic vertebrae.[2] The carina is highly sensitive. Stimulation of this area during suctioning causes vigorous coughing.

Lower Respiratory Tract

Once air passes the carina, it is in the lower respiratory tract. The *lower respiratory tract* consists of the bronchi, bronchioles, alveolar ducts, and alveoli. Except for the right and left mainstem bronchi, all lower airway structures are found within the lungs. The right lung is divided into 3 lobes (upper, middle, and lower) and the left lung into 2 lobes (upper and lower) (Fig. 25.2).

The mainstem bronchi, pulmonary vessels, and nerves enter the lungs through a slit called the *hilus.* The right mainstem bronchus is shorter, wider, and straighter than the left mainstem bronchus. That is why aspiration is more likely to occur in the right lung than in the left lung.

The mainstem bronchi subdivide several times to form the lobar, segmental, and subsegmental bronchi. Further divisions form the bronchioles. The most distant bronchioles are the respiratory bronchioles. The bronchioles are encircled by smooth muscles that constrict and dilate in response to various stimuli.

Conducting airways					Respiratory unit	
Trachea	Bronchi, segmental bronchi	Sub-segmental bronchi	Bronchioles		Alveolar ducts, alveoli	
			Non-respiratory	Respiratory		
Branchings	8	15	21-22	24	28	

FIG. 25.3 Structures of lower airways. (Redrawn from Thompson JM, McFarland GK, Hirsch JE, et al: *Mosby's clinical nursing,* ed 5, St Louis, 2002, Mosby.)

Exhaled
PaO₂ 127 mm Hg
PaCO₂ 28 mm Hg

Inhaled
PaO₂ 159 mm Hg
PaCO₂ 0.3 mm Hg

Alveolus
PaO₂ 100 mm Hg
PaCO₂ 40 mm Hg

Venous blood
PaO₂ 40 mm Hg
PaCO₂ 46 mm Hg

Arterial blood
PaO₂ 100 mm Hg
PaCO₂ 40 mm Hg

FIG. 25.4 Partial pressure of respiratory gases in normal respiration. The pressures are shown in inhaled and exhaled air from the lungs and at the level of the alveoli and pulmonary venous and arterial blood vessels.

The terms *bronchoconstriction* and *bronchodilation* refer to a decrease or increase in the diameter of the airways caused by contraction or relaxation of these muscles. Beyond the bronchioles lie the alveolar ducts and alveoli (Fig. 25.3).

The trachea and bronchi act as a pathway to conduct gases to and from the alveoli. The volume of air in the trachea and bronchi is called the *anatomic dead space* (V_D).[3] This air does not take part in gas exchange. In adults, a normal tidal volume (V_T), or volume of air exchanged with each breath, is about 500 mL (in a 150-lb man). Of each 500 mL inhaled, about 150 mL is V_D.

The alveoli are the terminal part of the respiratory tract (Fig. 25.3). *Alveoli* are small sacs in the lungs that are the primary site of gas exchange for O_2 and CO_2. The adult lung has over 300 million alveoli, each 0.3 mm in diameter. The alveoli are interconnected by pores of Kohn.[4] They allow movement of air from alveolus to alveolus (Fig. 25.1). Deep breathing promotes air movement through these pores and helps move mucus out of the respiratory bronchioles. Bacteria can also move through these pores, spreading infection to previously uninfected areas. Alveoli have a total volume of about 2500 mL with a surface area for gas exchange that is about the size of a tennis court.

Gases are exchanged across the alveolar-capillary membrane, where the alveoli come in contact with pulmonary capillaries (Fig. 25.4). In conditions such as pulmonary edema, excess fluid fills the interstitial space and alveoli, markedly reducing gas exchange.

Surfactant. Because alveoli are unstable, they have a natural tendency to collapse. Alveolar cells secrete surfactant. Surfactant is a lipoprotein that lowers the surface tension in the alveoli.[5] It reduces the amount of pressure needed to inflate the alveoli and makes them less likely to collapse. Normally, each person takes a slightly larger breath, termed a *sigh,* after every 5 or 6 breaths. This sigh stretches the alveoli and promotes surfactant secretion.

When there is not enough surfactant, the alveoli collapse. The term *atelectasis* refers to collapsed, airless alveoli. The postoperative patient is at risk for atelectasis because of the effects of anesthesia, decreased mobility, and pain, which can alter breathing and lung expansion. In acute respiratory distress syndrome (ARDS), lack of surfactant contributes to widespread atelectasis and collapse of lung tissue (see Chapter 67).

Blood Supply. The lungs have 2 different types of circulation: pulmonary and bronchial. Pulmonary circulation provides the lungs with blood that takes part in gas exchange. The pulmonary artery receives deoxygenated blood from the right ventricle of the heart and delivers it to pulmonary capillaries that lie directly alongside the alveoli. O_2–CO_2 exchange occurs at this point. The pulmonary veins return oxygenated blood to the left atrium, which then delivers it to the left ventricle, and into systemic circulation. Venous blood is collected from capillary networks of the body and returned to the right atrium by way of the superior and inferior vena cava.

Bronchial circulation starts with the bronchial arteries, which arise from the thoracic aorta. Bronchial circulation does not take part in gas exchange but provides O_2 to the bronchi and other lung tissues. Deoxygenated blood returns from the bronchial circulation through the azygos vein into the superior vena cava.[1]

Chest Wall

The chest wall is shaped, supported, and protected by 24 ribs (12 on each side). The thoracic cage, which consists of the ribs and sternum, protect the lungs and the heart from injury. The *mediastinum* is the space in the middle of the thoracic cavity. It contains the major organs of the chest, including the heart, aorta, and esophagus. The mediastinum physically separates the right and left lungs into 2 separate compartments.

The chest cavity is lined with a membrane called the *parietal pleura.* The lungs are lined with a membrane called the *visceral pleura.* The parietal and visceral pleurae join to form one continuous membrane. The visceral pleura does not have any sensory (pain) fibers or nerve endings. The parietal pleura has pain fibers. This is why irritation or inflammation of the parietal pleura can cause pain with each breath.

The *intrapleural space* is the space between the pleural layers. Normally this space contains 20 to 25 mL of fluid. This fluid serves 2 purposes: (1) it provides lubrication, allowing the pleural layers to slide over each other during breathing and (2) it increases unity between the pleural layers. This promotes expansion of the pleurae and lungs during inspiration.

Fluid drains from the pleural space via lymphatic circulation. Several pathologic conditions may cause the accumulation of greater amounts of fluid, termed a *pleural effusion.* Pleural fluid may accumulate because of blockage of lymphatic drainage (e.g., from cancer) or because of an imbalance between intravascular and oncotic fluid pressures, as in heart failure. Purulent pleural fluid with bacterial infection is called *empyema*.

The *diaphragm* is the major muscle of respiration. During inspiration the diaphragm contracts, moves downward, and increases intrathoracic volume. At the same time, the internal intercostals relax and the external intercostal muscles contract. This increases the lateral and anteroposterior (AP) dimension of the chest.[6] The scalene muscles also contract on inspiration, raising the first and second ribs. This causes the size of the thoracic cavity to increase and intrathoracic pressure to decrease, pulling air into the lungs.

The diaphragm is made up of 2 hemidiaphragms, each innervated by the right and left phrenic nerves. The phrenic nerves arise from the spinal cord between C3 and C5, the 3rd and 5th cervical vertebrae. Injury to the phrenic nerve results in hemidiaphragm paralysis on the side of the injury. Complete spinal cord injuries above the level of C3 result in total diaphragm paralysis and dependence on a mechanical ventilator.

Physiology of Respiration

Oxygenation. Oxygenation refers to the process of obtaining O_2 from the atmospheric air and making it available to the organs and tissues of the body. The lungs' ability to oxygenate arterial blood adequately is evaluated by partial pressure of O_2 in arterial blood (PaO_2), arterial O_2 saturation (SaO_2), and patient assessment (Table 25.1).

O_2 is carried in the blood in 2 forms: dissolved O_2 and hemoglobin-bound O_2. The PaO_2 represents the amount of O_2 dissolved in the plasma. It is expressed in millimeters of mercury (mm Hg). The SaO_2 is the amount of O_2 bound to hemoglobin in comparison with the amount of O_2 the hemoglobin can carry. The SaO_2 is expressed as a percent. For example, if the SaO_2 is 90%, this means that 90% of hemoglobin attachments for O_2 have O_2 bound to them.

O_2 and CO_2 move back and forth across the alveolar-capillary membrane by diffusion. The overall direction of movement is from the area of higher concentration to the area of lower concentration. Thus O_2 moves from alveolar gas (atmospheric air) into the arterial blood and CO_2 from the arterial blood into the alveolar gas. Diffusion continues until equilibrium is reached.

Ventilation. Ventilation involves *inspiration*, or inhalation (movement of air into the lungs), and *expiration*, or exhalation (movement of air out of the lungs). Air moves in and out of the lungs because intrathoracic pressure changes in relation to pressure at the airway opening. Contraction of the diaphragm and external intercostal and scalene muscles increases chest dimensions, thus decreasing intrathoracic pressure. Gas flows from an area of higher pressure (atmospheric) to one of lower pressure (intrathoracic). When dyspnea (shortness of breath) occurs, neck and shoulder muscles, as well as other accessory muscles of respiration, can aid the effort. Some conditions (e.g., phrenic nerve paralysis, rib fractures, neuromuscular disease) may limit diaphragm or chest wall movement. This causes the patient to breathe with smaller tidal volumes. As a result, the lungs do not fully inflate and gas exchange may be impaired.

In contrast to inspiration, expiration is passive. Elastic recoil is the tendency for the lungs to return to their original size after being stretched or expanded. The elasticity of lung tissue is due to the elastin fibers found in the alveolar walls and surrounding the bronchioles and capillaries. The elastic recoil of the chest wall and lungs allows the chest to passively decrease in size (volume). When intrathoracic pressure rises, air moves out of the lungs.

Exacerbations of asthma or chronic obstructive pulmonary disease (COPD) cause expiration to become an active, labored process (see Chapter 28). Abdominal, intercostal, and accessory muscles (e.g., scalene, trapezius) help expel air during labored breathing.

Compliance and Resistance. Compliance (distensibility) is a measure of the ease of expansion of the lungs. This is a product of the elasticity of the lungs and elastic recoil of the chest wall.[6] When compliance is decreased, it is harder for the lungs to inflate. This occurs with conditions that increase fluid in the lungs (e.g., pulmonary edema, ARDS, pneumonia), make lung tissue less elastic or distensible (e.g., pulmonary fibrosis, sarcoidosis), or restrict lung movement (e.g., pleural effusion). Compliance increases when there is destruction of alveolar walls and loss of tissue elasticity, as in COPD.

On the other hand, resistance refers to any obstacle to airflow during inspiration and/or expiration. The main factor affecting airway resistance is changes in the diameter (size) of the airways. For example, a patient with an acute asthma attack has narrowed airways, resulting in increased resistance. The presence of secretions in the bronchi also increases resistance. Secretions can partially occlude airways, making airways narrower. This makes it harder for patients to get air into their lungs. Giving bronchodilators decreases resistance by increasing the diameter of the bronchi, promoting air entry.

Changes in compliance and/or resistance can seriously affect both oxygenation and ventilation.

TABLE 25.1 Manifestations of Inadequate Oxygenation

Manifestations	ONSET Early	ONSET Late
Central Nervous System		
Unexplained apprehension	X	
Unexplained restlessness or irritability	X	
Unexplained confusion or lethargy	X	X
Combativeness		X
Coma		X
Respiratory		
Tachypnea	X	
Dyspnea on exertion	X	
Dyspnea at rest		X
Use of accessory muscles		X
Retraction of intercostal spaces on inspiration		X
Pause for breath between sentences, words		X
Cardiovascular		
Tachycardia	X	
Mild hypertension	X	
Dysrhythmias	X	X
Hypotension		X
Cyanosis		X
Cool, clammy skin		X
Other		
Diaphoresis	X	X
Decreased urine output	X	X
Unexplained fatigue	X	X

Control of Respiration

Located in the brainstem, the respiratory center (the medulla) responds to chemical and mechanical signals. The medulla sends impulses to the respiratory muscles through the spinal cord and phrenic nerves.

Chemoreceptors. A chemoreceptor is a receptor that responds to a change in the chemical composition ($PaCO_2$ and pH) of the fluid around it. Central chemoreceptors are found in the medulla. They respond to changes in the hydrogen ion (H^+) concentration.[7] An increase in the H^+ concentration *(acidosis)* causes the medulla to increase the respiratory rate and V_T. A decrease in H^+ concentration *(alkalosis)* has the opposite effect. Changes in $PaCO_2$ regulate ventilation primarily by their effect on the pH of the cerebrospinal fluid. When the $PaCO_2$ level is increased, more CO_2 is available to combine with H_2O and form carbonic acid (H_2CO_3). This lowers the cerebrospinal fluid pH and stimulates an increase in respiratory rate. The opposite process occurs with a decrease in $PaCO_2$ level.

Peripheral chemoreceptors are found in the carotid bodies at the bifurcation of the common carotid arteries and in the aortic bodies above and below the aortic arch.[8] The peripheral chemoreceptors respond to decreases in PaO_2 and pH and to increases in $PaCO_2$. These changes also stimulate the respiratory center.

In a healthy person, an increase in $PaCO_2$ or a decrease in pH causes an immediate increase in the respiratory rate. The $PaCO_2$ does not vary more than about 3 mm Hg if lung function is normal. Conditions such as COPD change lung function and may result in chronically elevated $PaCO_2$ levels. In these instances, the patient is not sensitive to further increases in $PaCO_2$ as a stimulus to breathe and may be maintaining ventilation largely because of a hypoxic drive from the peripheral chemoreceptors (see Chapter 28).

Mechanical Receptors. Mechanical receptors are found in the conducting upper airways, chest wall, diaphragm, and capillaries of the alveoli. They are stimulated by a variety of physiologic factors, such as irritants, muscle stretching, and alveolar wall distortion. The 3 major types of mechanical receptors are irritant, stretch, and juxtacapillary (J) receptors.[9]

Irritant receptors are found in the conducting airways. These receptors are sensitive to inhaled particles and aerosols and, when stimulated, initiate the cough reflex. Signals from stretch receptors, in the smooth muscle of the airways, aid in the control of respiration. As the lungs inflate, stretch receptors activate the inspiratory center to inhibit further lung expansion. This is called the *Hering-Breuer reflex,* and it prevents overdistention of the lungs. Stimulation of J receptors, found in the capillaries of the alveoli, occurs with increased pulmonary capillary pressure. This causes rapid, shallow respiration (tachypnea) seen in pulmonary edema.

Respiratory Defense Mechanisms

Respiratory defense mechanisms are efficient in protecting the lungs from inhaled particles, microorganisms, and toxic gases. The defense mechanisms include air filtration, mucociliary clearance system, cough reflex, reflex bronchoconstriction, and alveolar macrophages.

Filtration of Air. Nasal hairs filter inspired air. In addition, the abrupt changes in direction of airflow that occur as air moves through the nasopharynx and larynx increase air turbulence. This causes particles and bacteria to contact the mucosa lining these structures. Most large particles (greater than 5 μm) are less dangerous because they are removed in the nasopharynx or bronchi and do not reach the alveoli.

The velocity of airflow slows greatly after it passes the larynx, facilitating the deposition of smaller particles (1 to 5 μm). They settle out the way that sand does in a river, a process termed *sedimentation*. Particles less than 1 μm in size are too small to settle in this manner and are deposited in the alveoli. An example of small particles that can build up is coal dust, which can lead to pneumoconiosis (see Chapter 27).

Mucociliary Clearance System. Below the larynx, the mucociliary clearance system, also called the *mucociliary escalator*, is responsible for the movement of mucus. Goblet cells and submucosal glands continually secrete mucus at a rate of about 100 mL/day. This mucus forms a blanket that contains the impacted particles and debris from distal lung areas (Fig. 25.1). Secretory immunoglobulin A (IgA) in the mucus helps protect against bacteria and viruses.

Cilia cover the airways from the level of the trachea to the respiratory bronchioles (Fig. 25.1). Each ciliated cell has about 200 cilia. They beat rhythmically about 1000 times per minute in the large airways, moving mucus toward the mouth. We normally swallow the mucus without noticing.

The ciliary beat is slower further down the tracheobronchial tree. As a result, we remove particles that penetrate more deeply into the airways less rapidly. Dehydration, smoking, inhalation of high O_2 concentrations, infection, and drugs, such as atropine, anesthetics, alcohol, or cocaine, impair ciliary action. Patients with COPD and cystic fibrosis often have repeated lower respiratory tract infections. These conditions are associated with destroyed cilia, resulting in impaired secretion clearance, a chronic productive cough, and chronic colonization by bacteria. These lead to frequent respiratory tract infections.

Cough Reflex. The cough is a protective reflex that clears the airway by a high-pressure, high-velocity flow of air. It is a backup for mucociliary clearance, especially when this clearance mechanism is overwhelmed or ineffective. Coughing is effective in removing secretions only above the subsegmental level (large or main airways). Secretions below this level must be moved upward by the mucociliary mechanism before we can remove them by coughing.

Reflex Bronchoconstriction. *Reflex bronchoconstriction* is another defense mechanism. In response to the inhalation of large amounts of irritating substances (e.g., dusts, aerosols), the bronchi constrict to prevent entry of the irritants. A person with hyperreactive airways, such as a person with asthma, may have bronchoconstriction after inhalation of triggers, such as cold air, perfume, or other strong odors.

Alveolar Macrophages. Because there are no ciliated cells below the level of the respiratory bronchioles, the primary defense mechanism at the alveolar level is alveolar macrophages. *Alveolar macrophages* rapidly phagocytize inhaled foreign particles, such as bacteria. The debris is moved to the level of the bronchioles for removal by the cilia or removed from the lungs by the lymphatic system. Particles (e.g., coal dust, silica) that cannot be adequately phagocytized tend to remain in the lungs for indefinite periods and can stimulate inflammatory responses (see Chapter 27). Because alveolar macrophage activity is impaired by cigarette smoke, the smoker who is employed in an occupation with heavy dust exposure (e.g., mining, foundries) is at an especially high risk for lung disease.

🕴 Gerontologic Considerations: Effects of Aging on Respiratory System

Age-related changes in the respiratory system can be divided into alterations in structure, defense mechanisms, and respiratory

TABLE 25.2 Gerontologic Assessment Differences

Respiratory System

Changes	Differences in Assessment Findings
Structures	
Chest wall stiffening	Barrel chest appearance, kyphotic posture, ↓ chest wall movement, ↓ deep breathing, ↓ cough effectiveness
Costal cartilage calcification	
↑ Anteroposterior diameter	
↓ Elastic recoil	↓ Vital capacity, ↑ residual volume, ↑ functional residual capacity
↓ Chest wall compliance	
↓ Functioning alveoli	Decreased breath sounds, particularly at lung bases
↓ Respiratory muscle strength	
	↓ PaO_2 and SaO_2, normal pH and $PaCO_2$
Defense Mechanisms	
↓ Cell-mediated immunity	↓ Cough effectiveness, ↓ secretion clearance, thickened mucus
↓ Specific antibodies	
↓ Cilia function	↑ Risk for upper respiratory aspiration, infection, influenza, pneumonia
↓ Cough force	
↓ Alveolar macrophage function	Respiratory infections may be more severe and last longer
↓ Sensation in pharynx	
Respiratory Control	
↓ Response to hypoxemia	Slight ↓ PaO_2 and ↑ $PaCO_2$ before respiratory rate changes
↓ Response to hypercapnia	
	↓ Ability to maintain acid-base balance
	Significant hypoxemia or hypercapnia may develop from relatively small incidents
	Retained secretions, excessive sedation, or positioning that impairs chest expansion may substantially change PaO_2 or SpO_2 values

control (Table 25.2). Structural changes include calcification of the costal cartilages, which can interfere with chest expansion. The outward curvature of the spine is marked, especially with osteoporosis, and the lumbar curve flattens. Therefore the chest may appear barrel shaped, and the older person may need to use accessory muscles to breathe. Respiratory muscle strength progressively declines after age 50. Overall, the lungs in the older adult are harder to inflate.

Within the lung, the number of functional alveoli decreases and they become less elastic. Small airways in the lung bases close earlier in expiration. Therefore more inspired air is distributed to the lung apices and ventilation is less well matched to perfusion, lowering the PaO_2. As a result, older adults have less tolerance for exertion and dyspnea can occur if their activity exceeds their normal exercise.

In older adults, *respiratory defense mechanisms* are less effective because of a decline in both cell-mediated and humoral immunity (ability to produce antibodies). The alveolar macrophages are less effective at phagocytosis. An older patient has a less forceful cough and fewer and less functional cilia. Mucous membranes tend to be drier. Retained mucus predisposes the older adult to respiratory tract infections. Formation of secretory IgA, an important defense mechanism, is decreased. Swallowing is slower because of transit time in the pharyngeal area, and there is reduced sensation in the pharynx. Consequently, the older adult is at greater risk for aspiration.

The aging process alters respiratory control, resulting in a more gradual response to changes in blood O_2 or CO_2 level. The

PaO_2 may drop to a slightly lower than normal level, and the $PaCO_2$ may rise to a level slightly higher than normal before the respiratory rate changes.

The extent of these changes in people of the same age varies greatly. For example, the older adult who has a significant smoking history, is obese, and has a chronic illness is at greater risk for adverse outcomes.

ASSESSMENT OF RESPIRATORY SYSTEM

Determining a patient's needs related to the respiratory system requires an accurate health history and a thorough physical examination. A respiratory assessment can be done as part of a comprehensive physical examination or as a focused respiratory examination. Use judgment in determining whether all or part of the history and physical examination will be completed, based on your immediate assessment of the patient's degree of respiratory distress. If respiratory distress is severe, only obtain pertinent information and defer a thorough assessment until the patient's condition stabilizes.

CASE STUDY
Patient Introduction

(© Fuse/Thinkstock.)

F.T. is a 70-yr-old black man who comes to the emergency department (ED) with nausea, fatigue, and increased shortness of breath, which started 3 days ago. He says that he started using his albuterol inhaler every 4 hours 2 days ago, and while it worked initially, it is no longer helping. He can walk only a few feet in his apartment before he becomes short of breath. He sleeps in a recliner in the living room. He has noticed some swelling to his hands and feet and has been having trouble urinating.

Discussion Questions
1. What are the possible causes of F.T.'s shortness of breath?
2. Does F.T. need to be admitted to the hospital or is his condition stable and he can be seen by an HCP in a few hours?
3. What questions would be a priority during the subjective assessment?

You will learn more about F.T. and his condition as you read through this assessment chapter.
(See p. 464 for more information on F.T.)

Answers available at *http://evolve.elsevier.com/Lewis/medsurg.*

Subjective Data
Important Health Information

Past Health History. It is important to determine the frequency of upper respiratory problems (e.g., colds, sore throats, sinus problems, allergies) and whether seasonal changes influence these problems. Ask about a history of lower respiratory problems, such as asthma, COPD, pneumonia, and tuberculosis (TB).

Ask the patient with allergies about possible precipitating factors or triggers, such as medications, pollen, smoke, mold, or pet exposure. Record the characteristics and severity of the allergic reaction, such as runny nose, wheezing, scratchy throat, or chest tightness. Determine the frequency of asthma exacerbations.

Because respiratory symptoms are often manifestations of problems that involve other body systems, it is important to ask about a history of other health problems. For example, the patient with heart problems may have dyspnea (shortness of breath) because of heart failure. The patient with

TABLE 25.3 Health History

Respiratory System

Health Perception–Health Management

- Describe your daily activities. Have breathing problems prevented you from doing activities that you used to be able to do?* Are your breathing problems better, worse, or about the same compared with 6 months ago?
- How do your breathing problems affect your self-care abilities?
- Have you ever smoked? Do you smoke now? If so, what have you smoked? Cigarettes? Cigars? Pipes? Electronic cigarettes?
- If yes, how many cigarettes each day and for how long? Are you interested in stopping smoking? Are there aids we can tell you about that would assist your quitting? Would you be willing to come back for a visit so that we can explore your quitting? If you stopped smoking, did you do so because of your health?* How did you stop?
- Have you ever used chewing tobacco?
- Have you ever smoked street drugs?*
- Do you get the flu shot yearly? When was your last flu shot? Have you had a Pneumovax vaccination?
- What equipment helps you manage your respiratory problems? How often do you use it? Does it help? Cause problems?
- Do you feel that your respiratory problem is getting better or worse?

Nutritional-Metabolic

- Have you recently lost weight because of trouble eating related to your respiratory problem? How much weight have you lost? Have you lost this weight voluntarily?
- Do any foods affect your breathing?* Sputum production?*

Elimination

- Does your breathing problem make it hard for you to get to the toilet?*
- Are you inactive because of shortness of breath to the point that you have incontinence?* Constipation?*

Activity-Exercise

- Are you ever short of breath during exercise?* At rest?*
- Do you get too short of breath to do the things you want to do?*
- Is your home 1 story? 2 stories? How many steps from the street to your door?
- Can you walk up a flight of steps without stopping?
- Are you able to maintain your typical activities of daily living? If not, what are you able to do independently? What do you need help with? What have you had to give up?
- What do you do when you get short of breath? Does this help? How long does it take you to recover after you have been short of breath?

Sleep-Rest

- Do breathing problems cause you to wake up during the night?*
- Can you lie flat at night? If not, how many pillows do you use?

- Do you need to sleep upright in a chair?*
- Are you or your partner aware of any snoring?
- Do you awaken in the morning feeling rested?
- Do you ever wake up in the morning with a headache?*
- Do you fall asleep easily during the day?*

Cognitive-Perceptual

- Do you have any pain associated with breathing?* On a scale from 0 to 10, with 0 being "no pain" and 10 being "the worst pain you can imagine," where would you rate your pain? Does it hurt more on inspiration?* Expiration?* Or both?*
- If you are having pain with breathing, describe the pain.
- Has the pain gotten better, worse, or stayed about the same over the past 6 months?
- Do you ever feel restless, irritable, or confused without a reason?*
- Do you have difficulty remembering things?*

Self-Perception–Self-Concept

- Describe how your respiratory problems have changed your life.
- If you use O_2, do you ever go out without bringing it with you? How often does this occur? Why?

Role-Relationship

- Has your respiratory problem caused any problems in your work, family, or social relationships?*

Sexuality-Reproductive

- Has your respiratory problem caused a change in your sexual activity?*
- Have you and your partner talked about ways to minimize your breathing problems during sexual activity?

Coping–Stress Tolerance

- On a daily/weekly basis, how often do you leave your home?
- Do you feel under any stress right now?
- Does stress influence your breathing?*
- Do you notice if your emotions have any effect on your respiratory problems?
- Are you aware of any respiratory support groups in your area?

Value-Belief

- What do you think causes/has caused your respiratory problem(s)?
- How are you feeling right now?
- Do you think the things you have been told to do for your respiratory problems help? If not, why?
- What are you looking for/expecting from the HCP today, in terms of your breathing problem(s)?

*If answer is "yes" to any of the above questions, ask the patient to describe.

human immunodeficiency virus (HIV) infection may have frequent respiratory tract infections because of compromised immune function.

Medications. Take a thorough medication history, including the names of prescription and over-the-counter (OTC) medications and nonprescription (illicit) substances. Ask about the dose (if known), frequency, length of time taken, any side effects, and the reason for taking the medication. Assess for overuse of short-term bronchodilators as a key indicator of symptom control. Cough is a common side effect of angiotensin-converting enzyme (ACE) inhibitors. Encourage the patient to bring all medication bottles and any inhalers to each visit with an HCP.

If the patient is using O_2 for a breathing problem, record the fraction of inspired O_2 concentration (FIO_2), flow rate (liters per minute), method of administration, number of hours used

per day, and effectiveness of the therapy. Assess safety practices, including the patient's cognitive and physical ability related to using O_2 and any metered-dose inhalers.

Surgery or Other Treatments. Find out if the patient has been hospitalized for a respiratory problem. Note the dates, therapy (including surgery), and status of the problem. Determine if the patient has ever been intubated because of a respiratory problem. Ask about the use of and response to respiratory treatments, such as a nebulizer, humidifier, airway clearance modalities (see Chapter 28), high-frequency chest wall oscillation, postural drainage, and percussion.

Functional Health Patterns. Health history questions to ask a patient with a respiratory problem are outlined in Table 25.3.

Health Perception–Health Management Pattern. Ask the patient if there has been a perceived change in health status within the last several days, months, or years. In COPD, lung function declines slowly over many years. The patient may not notice this decline because they have been altering activity to accommodate reduced tolerance. If an upper respiratory tract infection is superimposed on a chronic problem, dyspnea and decreased exercise tolerance may occur very quickly. In asthma, symptoms may occur or worsen during exercise, in the presence of mold, or with changes in temperature or air pollution.

Explore common manifestations of respiratory problems (e.g., cough, dyspnea). Describe the course of the patient's illness, including when it began, type of symptoms, and factors that worsen or relieve these symptoms. Because of the chronic nature of respiratory problems, the patient may relate a change in symptoms (rather than the onset of new symptoms) when describing the present illness. For example, increased shortness of breath or increased purulence of sputum may suggest an acute exacerbation of COPD.

If a cough is present, assess its quality. For example, a loose-sounding cough occurs with secretions. A dry, hacking cough may mean an airway irritation or obstruction. A harsh, barky cough suggests upper airway obstruction from inhibited vocal cord movement due to subglottic edema. Assess whether the cough is strong enough to clear secretions. Note whether it is productive or nonproductive of secretions. Determine if the cough is acute or chronic (longer than 3 weeks in duration) or if it first began with an upper respiratory tract infection. The pattern and cause of the cough are determined by asking questions such as: What has been the pattern of coughing? Has it been regular or paroxysmal (i.e., sudden, periodic onset) or related to a time of day, the weather, certain activities, talking, or deep breathing? Any change over time? Do you clear your throat a lot? What have you tried to relieve the coughing? Did you try any prescription or OTC drugs?

If the patient has a productive cough, evaluate the following characteristics of sputum: amount, color, consistency, and odor. Quantify the amount of sputum per day. Note any recent increases or decreases in the amount. Sputum is normally clear or slightly whitish. If a patient is a cigarette smoker, the sputum is usually clear to gray with occasional specks of brown. The patient with COPD may have clear, whitish, or slightly yellow sputum, especially in the morning on rising. If the patient reports any change from baseline color, suspect pulmonary complications. Note any changes in consistency of sputum to thick, thin, or frothy and pink tinged. These changes may indicate dehydration, postnasal drip or sinus drainage, or possible pulmonary edema. Normally sputum should be odorless. A foul odor or exceptionally bad breath or taste in the mouth suggests an infectious process. Ask the patient if sputum production increases or decreases with changes in position (e.g., increased with lying down) or activity.

When assessing phlegm, determine if the patient has a history of spitting or coughing up blood (*hemoptysis*). Hemoptysis can range from a slight streaking of blood in the sputum to massive coughing up of blood. The patient may not be able to tell between hemoptysis and *hematemesis* (vomiting blood). Hemoptysis occurs with a variety of conditions such as pneumonia, TB, lung cancer, and severe bronchiectasis.

Assess for a history of any difficulty breathing. For example, *wheezes* are musical sounds that can be audible. Wheezing indicates some degree of airway obstruction, such as asthma, foreign body aspiration, and emphysema. Assess for any history of family exposure to *Mycobacterium tuberculosis*.

GENETIC RISK ALERT

- Respiratory problems that have a strong genetic link include cystic fibrosis, COPD from α_1-antitrypsin deficiency, and asthma.
- If people have a family history of these respiratory problems, they have a greater risk for developing them.
- Although cigarette smoking is a major risk factor for COPD, only a minority of cigarette smokers develop symptomatic disease. The risk for COPD related to cigarette smoking is genetically related.
- Determine if there is a family history of any respiratory problems that may have genetic or familial tendencies.

Smoking is the most important risk factor for COPD and lung cancer. Ask about cigarette use and find out about the use of any tobacco products. This includes cigars, pipes, chewing tobacco, electronic cigarettes (e-cigarettes), and hookah (instrument for vaporizing and smoking flavored tobacco). Find out about exposure to secondhand smoke. Determine if the patient has tried to quit using tobacco products, including using prescription, OTC, and herbal remedies.

Discuss current and past smoking habits. Quantify smoking habits in *pack-years*. Do this by multiplying the number of cigarettes smoked per day by the number of years smoked. For example, a person who smoked 20 cigarettes per day for 15 years has a 15 pack-year history.

Assess if the patient received immunizations for influenza (flu) and pneumococcal pneumonia. Patients should receive an influenza vaccine yearly in the fall. Recommendations for pneumococcal vaccines are shown in Table 27.5.

Ask where the patient has lived and traveled. Risk factors for TB include prior residence in China, India, Africa, the former Soviet Republics, Latin America, or any developing country. Other TB risk factors include exposure to people with high rates of TB transmission, such as the homeless, injection drug users, and people with HIV infection. Risk factors for fungal lung infections include those exposed to bird and rodent feces or polluted water, those working closely with the soil, and immunocompromised patients. Ask the patient about the use of equipment to manage respiratory symptoms (e.g., home O_2 equipment, inhalers, devices for sleep apnea). Find out the type of equipment used, cleaning of the device, frequency of use, its effect, and any side effects. Have patients show you the use of their inhalers. Many patients do not use these devices correctly (see Chapter 28).

Nutritional-Metabolic Pattern. Weight loss can be a symptom of respiratory disease. Determine if weight loss was intentional, and, if not, if food intake is changed by anorexia (from medications), fatigue (from hypoxemia, increased work of breathing), or feeling full quickly (from lung hyperinflation). Anorexia, weight loss, and chronic malnutrition are common in patients with COPD, lung cancer, TB, and chronic severe infection (bronchiectasis). Assess fluid intake. Dehydration can cause sputum to thicken and obstruct the airway. Rapid weight gain from fluid retention may impair gas exchange.

Elimination Pattern. Healthy elimination habits depend on a healthy balance between activity and rest. Activity intolerance secondary to dyspnea could result in incontinence, when unable to reach a toilet when needed. Dyspnea can be the cause of limited mobility, which can cause constipation. Ask the patient with dyspnea about frequency, urgency, and elimination patterns (e.g., day vs night). People with a chronic cough, especially women, may have urinary incontinence during paroxysms of coughing.

TABLE 25.4 Dyspnea Rating Scale

Modified Borg Rating Scale for Perceived Dyspnea

Rate	Description
0	Nothing at all
0.5	Very, very slight shortness of breath
1	Very mild shortness of breath
2	Mild shortness of breath
3	Mild shortness of breath or breathing difficulty
4	Somewhat severe
5	Strong or hard breathing
6	
7	Severe shortness of breath or very hard breathing
8	
9	Extremely severe
10	Shortness of breath so severe you need to stop

From Hillegass E: *Essentials of cardiopulmonary physical therapy*, ed 4, Philadelphia, 2017, Saunders.

Activity-Exercise Pattern. Determine if dyspnea limits activity. Assess whether the patient's residence (e.g., number of steps, levels) poses any problems. Ask the patient about the perceived degree of the dyspnea (Table 25.4). For example, can the patient walk up 1 flight of stairs without stopping because of dyspnea? Is dyspnea associated with any activity better, worse, or about the same in the last few days? Months? Determine if the patient has difficulty breathing in a certain position, or if dyspnea is relieved by assuming a different position (e.g., tripod position in COPD).

Discuss whether the patient can carry out activities of daily living without dyspnea or other respiratory symptoms. If unable, record the amount and type of care the patient needs. Immobility and sedentary habits are risk factors for hypoventilation leading to atelectasis or pneumonia.

Sleep-Rest Pattern. Determine if the patient wakes up at night because of pulmonary problems. The patient with asthma or COPD may awaken with chest tightness, wheezing, or coughing. This suggests a need for adjunct therapy or other medication changes. The patient with heart disease (e.g., heart failure) may sleep with the head elevated on several pillows to avoid respiratory problems brought on by lying flat *(orthopnea)*. Excess weight interferes with normal ventilation and may cause sleep apnea (see Chapter 7). Extremely obese persons may hypoventilate while awake or asleep. Manifestations of sleep apnea include snoring, insomnia, abrupt awakenings, daytime drowsiness, and early morning headaches. Night sweats may be a sign of TB.

Cognitive-Perceptual Pattern. Because hypoxia can cause neurologic symptoms, ask the patient about apprehension, restlessness, irritability, and memory changes. These can indicate inadequate cerebral oxygenation (Table 25.1). Assess the patient's cognitive ability to cooperate with treatment. Hypoxemia interferes with the ability to learn and retain information. Failure or inability to take part in needed therapy may result in worsening of respiratory problems. For this reason, teaching may be more effective if the caregiver is present during teaching sessions to provide reinforcement later.

Ask about any discomfort or pain with breathing. Explore reports of chest pain carefully to rule out heart involvement. Problems such as pleurisy, fractured ribs, and costochondritis cause chest pain. Careful assessment of the patient having pain with breathing, such as onset, exact location of the pain, and factors that make the pain better or worse, can help establish a diagnosis.

Self-Perception–Self-Concept Pattern. Dyspnea limits activity, impairs ability to fulfill normal roles, and often alters self-esteem. A patient may be reluctant to appear in public with a highly visible nasal cannula and O_2 equipment. A barrel chest, clubbed fingers, pursed-lip breathing, and frequent expectoration of sputum or throat clearing can be embarrassing and can lead to social isolation. Explore with the patient any body image concerns. Referral to a support group or pulmonary rehabilitation program may be beneficial in developing a support system and coping strategies.

Role-Relationship Pattern. Acute and chronic respiratory problems can seriously affect performance in work or other activities. Discuss the impact of medications, O_2 therapy, and special routines (e.g., pulmonary hygiene for cystic fibrosis) on the patient's family, job, and social life.

Review the nature of the patient's work and frequency and intensity of exposure to fumes, toxins, asbestos, coal, fibers, or silica. Ask whether symptoms are worse in specific situations (e.g., home vs. work environments). Hobbies, such as woodworking (sawdust) or pottery (silica), and animal exposure (allergies) can cause respiratory problems. Because of hyperreactive airways, exposure to fumes, smoke, and other chemicals may trigger an attack in the patient with asthma.

Sexuality-Reproductive Pattern. Most patients can continue to have satisfactory sexual relationships despite marked physical limitations. In a tactful manner, ask whether breathing difficulties have caused changes in sexual activity. If so, discuss positions that decrease dyspnea during sexual activity and alternative strategies for sexual fulfillment. For example, patients may need to perform good pulmonary hygiene (bronchodilators, coughing, deep breathing) before intimacy. They may need to use O_2 therapy equipment during intercourse just like they would with any strenuous physical activity.

Coping–Stress Tolerance Pattern. Dyspnea causes anxiety, and anxiety worsens dyspnea. The result is a vicious cycle—the patient avoids activities that cause dyspnea, becoming more deconditioned and more dyspneic. The outcome is often physical and leads to social isolation. Assess how often the patient leaves home and interacts with others. Referral to a support group or pulmonary rehabilitation program may be helpful.

The chronic nature of many respiratory problems, such as COPD and asthma, can cause prolonged stress. Ask about the patient's coping strategies to manage this stress.

Value-Belief Pattern. Determine the patient's adherence to his or her treatment program. Explore possible reasons for lack of adherence, including conflict with cultural beliefs, financial constraints (e.g., costs of prescriptions), or failure to understand benefit. Correct misinformation and provide up-to-date information about respiratory conditions and medication management. Including the patient and caregiver in the planning of care can improve adherence.

Objective Data

Physical Examination. Vital signs are important data to collect before examining the respiratory system.

Nose. Inspect the nose for patency, inflammation, deformities, symmetry, and discharge. Check each nare for air patency with respiration while briefly occluding the other nare. Tilt the patient's head backward and push the tip of the nose upward

CASE STUDY
Subjective Data

(© Fuse/
Thinkstock.)

A focused subjective assessment of F.T. revealed the following information:

PMH: COPD, hypertension, heart failure, benign prostatic hyperplasia. No history of allergies.

Medications: Metoprolol (Toprol XL) 50 mg daily PO, furosemide 20 mg PO daily, finasteride (Proscar) 5 mg/day PO, Advair inhaler (fluticasone and salmeterol) 2 puffs twice daily, and albuterol inhaler 2 puffs every 4hr PRN. Uses O_2 @ 3L/min via nasal cannula at home for the past 10 years.

Health Perception–Health Management: States he usually manages his COPD well with the Advair inhaler and occasional use of the albuterol inhaler. He thinks he caught a cold from his granddaughter last week. Increasing difficulty breathing, even with albuterol. Has a history of 30 pack-years of smoking, quitting 5 years ago.

Nutritional-Metabolic Pattern: Eating and drinking very little over past 2 to 3 days.

Elimination: Voiding small amounts of dark, concentrated urine (mostly at night).

Activity-Exercise: At present, cannot walk 100 feet without feeling short of breath. Cannot walk up 1 flight of stairs (21 steps) to get in or out of his apartment without stopping to catch his breath.

Sleep-Rest: Difficulty sleeping. Last night he slept upright in his recliner.

Cognitive-Perceptual: Denies any pain associated with shortness of breath. Feels slightly irritable because of lack of sleep.

Coping–Stress Tolerance: Does not know how he will manage to get groceries or clean his apartment. His daughter lives an hour away and has 3 children in school.

Discussion Questions

1. Of the information provided, which subjective assessment findings are of most concern to you?
2. From the information provided from F.T., what other information would you ask him about his condition (time permitting)?
3. What type of assessment would be most appropriate for F.T.: comprehensive, focused, or emergency?
4. F.T. cannot use his inhaler appropriately while he is talking with you. Is this a good time to teach him about the proper use of his inhaler?
5. What will you include in the physical assessment? What would you think will be priorities in your physical assessment?

You will learn about the physical assessment of the respiratory system in the next section.

(See p. 467 for more information on F.T.)

Answers available at *http://evolve.elsevier.com/Lewis/medsurg.*

gently. With a nasal speculum and a good light, inspect the interior of the nose. The mucous membrane should be pink and moist, with no evidence of edema (bogginess), exudate, or bleeding. Inspect the nasal septum for deviation, perforations, and bleeding. Some septal deviation is normal in an adult. Inspect the turbinates for polyps, which are abnormal, finger-like projections of swollen nasal mucosa. Polyps may result from long-term irritation of the mucosa (e.g., from allergies). Assess any discharge for color and consistency. Purulent and malodorous discharge could occur with a foreign body. Watery discharge could be related to allergies or from cerebrospinal fluid. Bloody discharge could be from trauma or dryness. Thick mucosal discharge could mean an infection.

Mouth and Pharynx. Using a good light source, inspect the interior of the mouth for color, lesions, masses, gum retraction, bleeding, and poor dentition. Inspect the tongue for symmetry

and lesions. Observe the pharynx by pressing a tongue blade gently against the middle of the back of the tongue. If the oropharynx is tight, have the patient yawn, since this usually allows more structures to be visible. The pharynx should be smooth and moist, with no evidence of exudate, ulcerations, swelling, or postnasal drip. Note the color, symmetry, and any enlargement of the tonsils. Stimulate the gag reflex by placing a tongue blade along the side of the pharynx, at the back of the tongue. A normal response (gagging) means that cranial nerves IX (glossopharyngeal) and X (vagus) are intact and that the airway is protected.

Neck. Inspect the neck for symmetry and tender or swollen areas. Palpate the lymph nodes while the patient is sitting erect with the neck slightly flexed. Progression of palpation is from the nodes around the ears, to the nodes at the base of the skull, and then to those under the angles of the mandible to the midline. The patient may have small, mobile, nontender nodes *(shotty nodes),* which are not a sign of a pathologic condition. Tender, hard, or fixed nodes may indicate disease. Describe the location and characteristics of any palpable nodes.

Thorax and Lungs. Picture imaginary lines on the chest to help identify abnormalities (Fig. 25.2). Describe abnormalities in terms of their location relative to these lines (e.g., 2 cm lateral from the right midclavicular line).

Chest examination is best done in a well-lit, warm room with measures taken to ensure the patient's privacy. Expose the patient's chest. Perform all physical assessment maneuvers (inspection, palpation, percussion, auscultation) on either the anterior or the posterior chest first rather than moving from anterior to posterior or vice versa with each maneuver. It is best to begin on the posterior chest, particularly with female patients, since you can obtain more information without interference from breast tissue. If the patient tires or you are interrupted, you will obtain baseline data with the most information from examining the posterior chest.

When assessing the *posterior chest,* ask the patient to lean forward with arms folded. This position moves the scapulae away from the spine, exposing more of the area you need to examine. When assessing the *anterior chest,* have the patient sit upright or position the patient supine with the head of the bed elevated to 30 degrees (semi-Fowler's position). The patient may need to lean forward for support on the bedside table to facilitate breathing.

Inspection. First, observe the patient's appearance and note any evidence of respiratory distress, such as tachypnea or use of accessory muscles. Next, determine the shape and symmetry of the chest. Chest movement should be equal on both sides, and the anterior-posterior (AP) diameter should be less than the side-to-side or transverse diameter. Normal AP ratio is 1:2. An increase in AP diameter (e.g., barrel chest) may be due to normal aging or result from lung hyperinflation. Look for abnormalities in the sternum (e.g., *pectus carinatum* [a prominent protrusion of the sternum]) and *pectus excavatum* (an indentation of the lower sternum above the xiphoid process). Note any spinal curvature. Spinal curvatures that affect breathing include kyphosis, scoliosis, and kyphoscoliosis.

Observe the respiratory rate, depth, and rhythm. The normal adult respiratory rate is 12 to 20 breaths/min. Inspiration (I) should take half as long as expiration (E) (I/E ratio = 1:2). Observe for abnormal breathing patterns, such as *Kussmaul* (rapid, deep breathing), *Cheyne-Stokes* (abnormal respirations characterized by alternating periods of apnea and deep, rapid breathing), or *Biot's* (irregular breathing with apnea every 4 to 5 cycles) respirations.

Skin color provides clues to respiratory status. Cyanosis, a late sign of hypoxemia, is best seen in light-skinned patients as a bluish tinge to the mucous membranes, lips, and palms of the hands. In dark-skinned persons, cyanosis may be seen as a gray or white discoloration in the conjunctivae or around the mouth. Causes of cyanosis include hypoxemia or decreased cardiac output. Inspect the fingers for evidence of long-standing hypoxemia, known as *clubbing*. It is an increase in the angle between the base of the nail and the fingernail to 180 degrees or more. Clubbing usually accompanied by an increase in the depth, bulk, and sponginess of the end of the finger.

Palpation. Determine tracheal position by gently placing the index fingers on either side of the trachea just above the suprasternal notch and gently pressing backward. Normal tracheal position is midline; deviation to the left or right is abnormal. Tracheal deviation occurs away from the side of a tension pneumothorax or a neck mass, but toward the side of a pneumonectomy or lobar atelectasis.

Symmetry of chest expansion and extent of movement are determined at the level of the diaphragm. Place your hands over the lower anterior chest wall along the costal margin and move them inward until the thumbs meet at midline. Ask the patient to breathe deeply. Observe the movement of the thumbs away from each other. Normal expansion is 1 in (2.5 cm). Hand placement on the posterior side of the chest is at the level of the tenth rib. Move the thumbs until they meet over the spine (Fig. 25.5). You can check expansion anteriorly or posteriorly. It is not necessary to check both.

Normal chest movement is equal. Unequal expansion occurs when air entry is limited by conditions involving the lung (e.g., atelectasis, pneumothorax) or the chest wall (e.g., incisional pain). Equal but decreased expansion occurs in conditions that produce a hyperinflated or barrel chest or in neuromuscular diseases (e.g., amyotrophic lateral sclerosis, spinal cord lesions). Movement may be absent or unequal over a pleural effusion, an atelectasis, or a pneumothorax.

Fremitus is the vibration of the chest wall made by vocalization. You can feel tactile fremitus by placing the palmar surface of your hands against the patient's chest with the fingers hyperextended. Ask the patient to repeat a phrase, such as "boy-oh-boy," "toy boat," or "blue balloons," in a deeper, louder-than-normal voice. At the same time, move your hands from top to bottom on the patient's chest (Fig. 25.6). As you palpate, simultaneously compare vibrations (right side vs. left side, from top to bottom). Tactile fremitus is most intense by the sternum and between the scapulae because these areas are closest to the major bronchi. Fremitus is less intense farther away from these areas.

Note any increase, decrease, or absence of fremitus. Increased fremitus occurs when the lung becomes filled with fluid or is denser. As the patient's voice moves through a dense tissue or fluid, you can feel that the vibration is increased. This happens with pneumonia, lung tumors, thick bronchial secretions, and above a pleural effusion (the lung is compressed upward). Fremitus is decreased if the hand is farther from the lung (e.g., pleural effusion) or the lung is hyperinflated (e.g., barrel chest). Absent fremitus may occur with pneumothorax or atelectasis. The anterior of the chest is harder to palpate for fremitus because of the large muscles and breast tissue.

Percussion. Percussion is used to assess the density or aeration of the lungs. Percussion sounds are described in Table 25.5. (The technique for percussion is described in Chapter 3 and Fig. 3.3.)

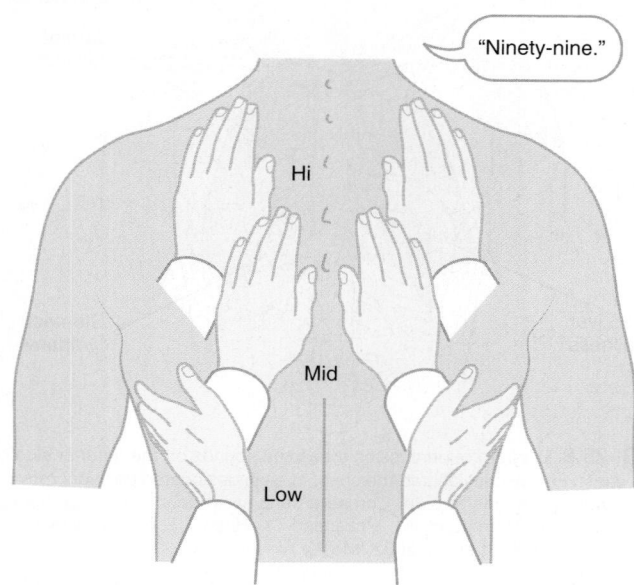

FIG. 25.6 Hand position for tactile fremitus. Place the palms of the hands in the position designated as "*low*" on the right and left sides of the chest. Compare the intensity of vibrations. Continue for all positions in each sequence.

FIG. 25.5 Estimation of thoracic expansion. **A,** Exhalation. **B,** Maximal inhalation.

TABLE 25.5 **Percussion Sounds**	
Sound	**Description**
Dull	Sound with medium-intensity pitch and duration heard over areas of "mixed" solid and lung tissue, such as top area of liver, partially consolidated lung tissue (pneumonia), or fluid-filled pleural space
Flat	Soft, high-pitched sound of short duration heard over very dense tissue where air is not present, such as posterior chest below level of diaphragm
Hyperresonance	Loud, lower pitched sound than normal resonance heard over hyperinflated lungs, such as in chronic obstructive pulmonary disease and acute asthma
Resonance	Low-pitched sound heard over normal lungs
Tympany	Drum-like, loud, empty quality sound heard over pneumothorax

FIG. 25.7 Sequence for auscultation of the chest. **A,** Anterior sequence. **B,** Lateral sequence. **C,** Posterior sequence. Place the stethoscope at each position and listen to at least 1 complete inspiratory and expiratory cycle. Keep in mind that with a female patient the breast tissue will modify the completeness of the anterior examination.

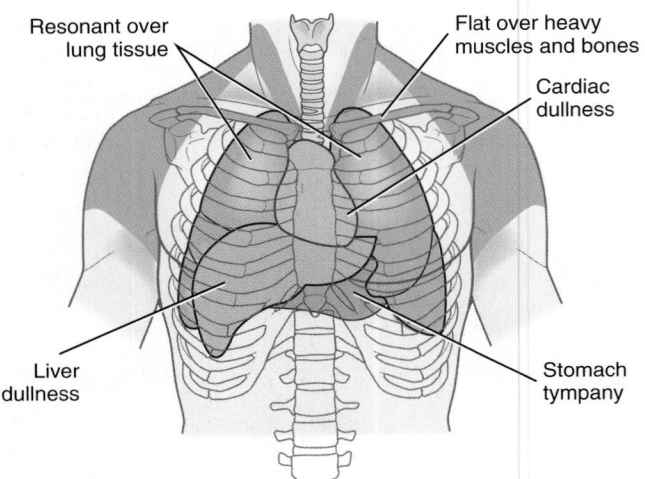

FIG. 25.8 Diagram of percussion areas and sounds on the anterior side of the chest. For percussion, tap the chest at each designated position, moving downward from side to side. Compare percussion sounds at all positions. (Redrawn from Thompson JM, McFarland GK, Hirsch JE, et al: *Mosby's clinical nursing,* ed 5, St Louis, 2002, Mosby.)

FIG. 25.9 Diagram of percussion areas and sounds on the posterior side of the chest. Percussion proceeds from the lung apices to the lung bases while comparing sounds in opposite areas of the chest. (Redrawn from Thompson JM, McFarland GK, Hirsch JE, et al: *Mosby's clinical nursing,* ed 5, St Louis, 2002, Mosby.)

The anterior chest is percussed with the patient in a semi-sitting or supine position. Starting above the clavicles, percuss downward, intercostal space by intercostal space (Fig. 25.7). The area over lung tissue should be resonant, except for the area of cardiac dullness (Fig. 25.8). To percuss the posterior chest, have the patient sit leaning forward with arms folded. The posterior chest should be resonant over lung tissue to the level of the diaphragm (Fig. 25.9).

Auscultation. During chest auscultation, have the patient breathe slowly and a little more deeply than normal through the mouth. Auscultation should proceed from the lung apices to the bases, comparing opposite areas of the chest. If the patient is in mild respiratory distress or you think the patient will tire easily, start at the bases. Place the stethoscope over lung tissue, not over bony prominences. At each placement of the stethoscope, listen to at least 1 cycle of inspiration and expiration. Visualize the location of normal breath sounds by using a lung model (Fig. 25.10).

Lung sounds are heard anteriorly from a line drawn perpendicular from the sternum lateral to the midclavicular line.

From the xiphoid process, palpate inferiorly (down) 2 ribs in the midaxillary line and around to the posterior chest. This gives you a fairly accurate and easy way to locate the lung fields. When recording the location of lung sounds, divide the anterior and posterior right lung into thirds (upper, middle, and lower) and the left lung into upper and lower areas. With practice, you will be able to identify which lobes of the lung has particular lung sounds.

The 3 normal breath sounds are bronchial, bronchovesicular, and vesicular. *Bronchial sounds* are loud, high-pitched sounds that resemble air blowing through a hollow pipe. Bronchial sounds have an inspiratory to expiratory (I/E) ratio of 2:3, with a gap between inspiration and expiration. To hear bronchial breath sounds, place the stethoscope next to the trachea in the neck. *Bronchovesicular sounds* have a medium pitch and intensity. They are best heard anteriorly between the first and second intercostal space and posteriorly between the scapulae. Bronchovesicular sounds have a 1:1 ratio, with inspiration equal to expiration. *Vesicular sounds* are relatively soft, low-pitched, gentle, rustling sounds. They are heard over all lung areas except

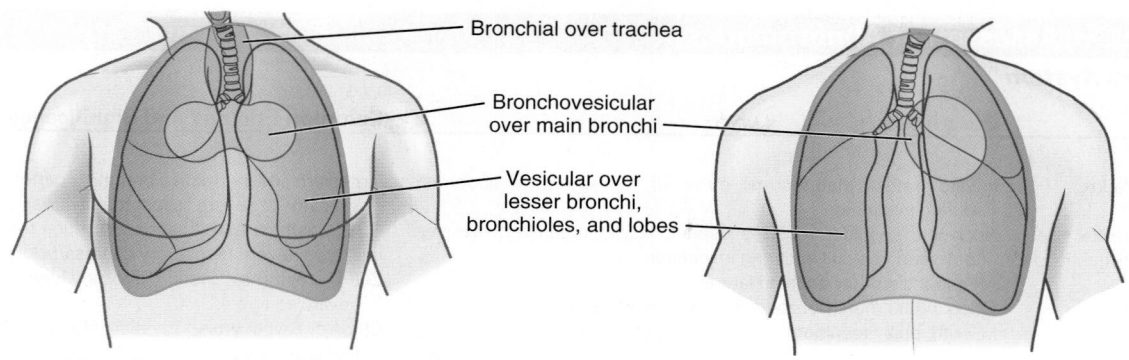

FIG. 25.10 Normal auscultatory sounds. (Redrawn from Beare PG, Myers JL: *Adult health nursing,* ed 3, St Louis, 1998, Mosby.)

the major bronchi. Vesicular sounds have a 3:1 ratio, with inspiration 3 times longer than expiration.

We classify breath sounds into 2 main categories: normal and abnormal (adventitious). There are a variety of terms that have been inconsistently used to describe abnormal breath sounds. Adventitious breath sounds include crackles (fine and coarse), wheezes, stridor, and pleural friction rub (Table 25.6). A *focused assessment* is used to evaluate the status of previously identified respiratory problems and to monitor for signs of new problems. A focused assessment of the respiratory system is shown in the box on this page.

As you begin your assessment of lung sounds, first note the air entry, which may be adequate, slightly decreased, or decreased. Absent air entry in any part of the lung is an assessment finding that you should report at once. Next, listen for the breath sounds and the presence of normal and adventitious sounds. Are the normal breath sounds where you would expect to hear them? Focus your assessment on the characteristics of

any abnormal sound, including the location, pitch (e.g., high, low), duration of sound, and whether the sound is heard on inspiration, expiration, or both.

Assessment abnormalities of the thorax and lungs are outlined in Table 25.6. A record of the normal physical assessment of the respiratory system is shown in Table 25.7. Chest examination findings in common pulmonary problems are described in Table 25.8. Age-related changes in the respiratory system and assessment findings are outlined in Table 25.2.

CASE STUDY

Objective Data: Physical Examination

(© Fuse/Thinkstock.)

Physical examination findings of F.T. are as follows: Temperature: 38°C (100.4°F), apical pulse 110 (irregular), respiratory rate 30 (regular, shallow, slightly labored), BP 170/90. Sitting on edge of bed with arms resting on bedside table. Skin color normal for race with no signs of cyanosis. Using accessory muscles in neck and shoulders. Trachea midline. Barrel-shaped chest; chest expansion minimal but equal. Prolonged expiration. Slight clubbing noted. Edema: 3+ pitting edema of both lower legs and feet, bilaterally. Lungs: adequate air entry at apices bilaterally with fine crackles; decreased air entry to right middle lobe and both bases with coarse crackles. Slight expiratory wheeze heard throughout all lung fields. Cough: moist, productive, with yellow-tinged sputum.

You decide to check F.T.'s O$_2$ saturation (SpO$_2$). His SpO$_2$ is 87% on room air.

Discussion Questions

1. What physical assessment findings are of most concern to you?
2. Identify 3 interventions that may be implemented immediately.
3. With F.T.'s physical assessment information, what diagnostic studies would you expect to be ordered?
(See p. 475 for more information on F.T.)

FOCUSED ASSESSMENT
Respiratory System

Use this checklist to make sure the key assessment steps have been done.

Subjective
Ask the patient about any of the following and note responses.

Shortness of breath	Y	N
Pain with breathing	Y	N
Cough	Y	N
Sputum production (color, quantity)	Y	N
Wheezing	Y	N

Objective: Physical Examination
Observe
Respirations: Rate, quality, and pattern
Accessory muscle use
Mouth or nose breathing

Inspect
Neck for position of trachea
Shape, symmetry, and movement of chest wall
Skin and nails for integrity and color

Palpate
Chest and back for abnormalities (i.e. masses)

Auscultate
Lung sounds (anterior and posterior)

Objective: Diagnostic
Check the following diagnostic tests for abnormal results.
Arterial blood gases
Chest x-ray
Hemoglobin
Hematocrit

TABLE 25.6 Assessment Abnormalities

Respiratory System

Finding	Description	Common Etiology and Significance
Inspection		
Abdominal paradox	Inward (rather than normal outward) movement of abdomen during inspiration	Inefficient and ineffective breathing pattern. Nonspecific indicator of severe respiratory distress
Accessory muscle use. Intercostal retractions	Neck and shoulder muscles used to assist breathing; muscles between ribs pull in during inspiration	COPD, asthma exacerbation, secretion retention Indicates severe respiratory distress/failure, hypoxemia
↑ AP diameter	AP chest diameter equal to lateral. Slope of ribs more horizontal (90 degrees) to spine	COPD, asthma, cystic fibrosis, lung hyperinflation, advanced age
Clubbing	↑ Depth, bulk, sponginess of distal part of finger	Chronic hypoxemia, cystic fibrosis, lung cancer, bronchiectasis
Cyanosis	Bluish color of skin best seen in lips and on the palpebral conjunctiva (inside the lower eyelid)	Reflects 5–6 g of hemoglobin not bound with O_2. ↓ O_2 transfer in lungs, ↓ cardiac output. Nonspecific, unreliable indicator
Kussmaul respirations	Regular, rapid, and deep respirations Fruity odor to breath	Metabolic acidosis. Increases CO_2 excretion
Pursed-lip breathing	Exhalation through mouth with lips pursed together to slow exhalation	COPD, asthma. Suggests ↑ breathlessness Strategy taught to slow expiration, ↓ dyspnea
Splinting	Voluntary ↓ in tidal volume to ↓ pain on chest expansion	Thoracic or abdominal incision, chest trauma, pleurisy
Tachypnea	Rate >20 breaths/min	Fever, anxiety, hypoxemia, restrictive lung disease Magnitude of ↑ above normal rate reflects increased work of breathing
Tripod position. Inability to lie flat	Leaning forward with arms and elbows supported on overbed table	COPD, asthma exacerbation, pulmonary edema Indicates moderate to severe respiratory distress
Palpation		
Altered chest movement	Unequal or equal but decreased movement of 2 sides of chest with inspiration	Unequal movement caused by atelectasis, pneumothorax, pleural effusion, splinting Equal but decreased movement caused by barrel chest, restrictive disease, neuromuscular disease
Altered tactile fremitus	Increase or decrease in vibrations	↑ In pneumonia, pulmonary edema. ↓ in pleural effusion, lung hyperinflation. Absent in pneumothorax, atelectasis
Tracheal deviation	Leftward or rightward movement of trachea from normal midline position	Nonspecific indicator of change in position of mediastinal structures. Medical emergency if caused by tension pneumothorax (trachea deviates to side opposite collapsed lung)
Percussion		
Dullness	Medium-pitched sound over areas that normally make a resonant sound	↑ Density (pneumonia, large atelectasis), ↑ fluid in pleural space (pleural effusion)
Hyperresonance	Loud, lower pitched sound over areas that normally make a resonant sound	Lung hyperinflation (COPD), lung collapse (pneumothorax), air trapping (asthma)
Auscultation		
Absent breath sounds	No sound heard over entire lung or area of lung	Pneumothorax, pleural effusion, mainstem bronchi obstruction, large atelectasis, pneumonectomy, lobectomy
Bronchophony, whispered pectoriloquy	Spoken or whispered syllable more distinct than normal on auscultation	Pneumonia
Coarse **crackles**	Louder, discontinuous, low-pitched sounds caused by air passing through airway intermittently occluded by mucus, unstable bronchial wall. May be heard on inspiration, expiration, or both. Similar sound to blowing through straw under water	Excess fluid within the lungs, heart failure, pulmonary edema, pneumonia with severe congestion, COPD
Egophony	Spoken "E" similar to "A" on auscultation because of altered transmission of voice sounds	Pneumonia, pleural effusion
Fine crackles	Short, discontinuous, high-pitched sounds heard just before the end of inspiration. Result of rapid equalization of gas pressure when collapsed alveoli or terminal bronchioles suddenly snap open. Similar sound to that made by rolling hair between fingers	Interstitial edema (early pulmonary edema), alveolar filling (pneumonia), loss of lung volume (atelectasis), early phase of heart failure, idiopathic pulmonary fibrosis
Pleural friction rub	Creaking or grating sound from roughened, inflamed pleural surfaces rubbing together. Evident during inspiration, expiration, or both. No change with coughing. Often uncomfortable, especially on deep inspiration	Pleurisy, pneumonia, pulmonary infarct
Stridor	Continuous musical or crowing sound of constant pitch. Result of partial obstruction of larynx or trachea	Croup, epiglottitis, vocal cord edema after extubation, foreign body
Wheezes	Continuous high-pitched squeaking or musical sound caused by rapid vibration of bronchial walls. First evident on expiration but possibly evident on inspiration as obstruction of airway increases. May be audible without stethoscope	Bronchospasm (caused by asthma), airway obstruction (caused by foreign body, tumor), COPD

DIAGNOSTIC STUDIES OF RESPIRATORY SYSTEM

Numerous diagnostic studies are available to assess the respiratory system. Tables 25.9 through 25.17 describe common studies. Select studies are described in more detail here.

Two methods are used to assess the efficiency of gas transfer in the lung and tissue oxygenation: (1) pulse oximetry and (2) analysis of *arterial blood gases* (ABGs) (Table 25.9). These are primarily used to assess for hypoxia. For the patient with normal or near-normal cardiac function, assessing PaO_2 or SaO_2 is usually enough to determine the level of oxygenation. With either one, we can also use CO_2 monitoring to assess for hypercapnia to determine patient's oxygenation and ventilatory status. The patient with impaired cardiac output or hemodynamic instability (e.g., altered level of consciousness, changes in heart rate and rhythm, low BP) may have inadequate tissue O_2 delivery and/or abnormal O_2 consumption. For these patients, we can evaluate a mixed venous blood gas.

Oximetry

Arterial O_2 saturation can be monitored noninvasively and continuously using a *pulse oximetry* probe on the finger, toe, ear, forehead, or bridge of the nose. The abbreviation SpO_2 is used to indicate the O_2 saturation of hemoglobin as measured by pulse oximetry. SpO_2 and heart rate are displayed on the monitor as digital readings. Normal SpO_2 values are 94% to 99% (Table 25.10).

In many inpatient areas, SpO_2 is assessed with each routine vital sign check. Oximetry is also used during exercise testing and when adjusting flow rates during O_2 therapy. Pulse oximetry is especially valuable in perioperative and critical care situations, in which anesthesia, sedation, or decreased consciousness may mask hypoxia. Changes in SpO_2 can be detected and treated quickly (Table 25.9).

Values obtained by pulse oximetry are less accurate if the SpO_2 is less than 70%.[10] At this level the oximeter may display a value that is ±4% of the actual value. For example, if the SpO_2 reading is 70%, the actual value can range from 66% to 74%. Pulse oximetry is inaccurate if hemoglobin variants (e.g., carboxyhemoglobin, methemoglobin) are present. Other factors that can alter the accuracy of pulse oximetry include motion, low perfusion, anemia, cold extremities, bright fluorescent lights, intravascular dyes, thick acrylic nails, and dark skin color. If there is doubt about the accuracy of the SpO_2 reading, obtain an ABG analysis to verify the values.

Arterial Blood Gases

ABGs are obtained to determine oxygenation status and acid-base balance. ABG analysis includes measurement of the PaO_2, $PaCO_2$ (the partial pressure of CO_2 in arterial blood), acidity (pH), bicarbonate (HCO_3^-), and SaO_2. Normal values for ABGs are shown in Table 25.11.

Blood for ABG analysis can be obtained by arterial puncture or from an arterial catheter, which is usually inserted into the radial or femoral artery. Both techniques allow only intermittent analysis, but an arterial catheter permits ABG sampling without repeated arterial punctures. The normal PaO_2 decreases with advancing age. It varies in relation to the distance above sea level. At higher altitudes, the barometric pressure is lower, resulting in a lower inspired O_2 pressure and a lower PaO_2.

TABLE 25.7 Normal Physical Assessment of the Respiratory System

Nose	• Symmetric with no deformities • Nasal mucosa pink, moist with no edema, exudate, blood, or polyps • Nasal septum straight (slight nasal deviation possible) • Nares patent bilaterally
Oral mucosa	• Light pink, moist, no exudate or ulcerations
Pharynx	• Smooth, moist, and pink
Neck	• Trachea midline
Chest	• AP diameter 1:2 • Respirations nonlabored at 12–20 breaths/min • Breath sounds vesicular without crackles or wheezes • Excursion equal bilaterally with no increase in tactile fremitus

---

TABLE 25.8 Chest Examination Findings in Respiratory Problems

Problem	Inspection	Palpation	Percussion	Auscultation
Asthma exacerbation	Prolonged expiration, tripod position, pursed lips	↓ Movement	Hyperresonance	Wheezes, ↓ breath sounds ominous sign (severely decreased air movement)
Atelectasis	No change unless involves entire segment, lobe	If small, no change If large, ↓ movement, ↓ fremitus	Dull over affected area	Fine crackles (may disappear with deep breaths) Absent sounds if large
COPD	Barrel chest, cyanosis, tripod position, use of accessory muscles	↓ Movement	Hyperresonant or dull if consolidation	Crackles, wheezes, distant breath sounds
Pleural effusion	Tachypnea, use of accessory muscles	↑ Movement ↑ Fremitus above effusion Absent fremitus over effusion	Dull	Decreased or absent over effusion, egophony above effusion
Pneumonia	Tachypnea, use of accessory muscles, duskiness or cyanosis	↑ Fremitus over affected area	Dull over affected areas	*Early:* Bronchial sounds *Later:* Fine and/or coarse crackles, egophony, whispered pectoriloquy
Pulmonary edema	Tachypnea, labored respirations, cyanosis, pink-tinged sputum	↓ Movement or normal movement	Dull or normal depending on amount of fluid	Fine or coarse crackles
Pulmonary fibrosis	Tachypnea	↓ Movement	Normal	Crackles or sounds like Velcro being pulled apart

TABLE 25.9 Diagnostic Studies: Oxygenation

Study	Description and Purpose	Nursing Responsibility
Arterial blood gases (ABGs)	Arterial blood is obtained through puncture of radial or femoral artery or through arterial catheter. Done to assess acid-base balance, oxygenation/ventilation status, need for and/or change in O_2 therapy, or change in ventilator settings. See Table 25.11 for reference values.	*Before:* Indicate whether patient is using O_2 (flow rate in L/min). Avoid change in O_2 therapy or interventions (e.g., suctioning, position change) for 15 min before obtaining sample. *During:* Assist with positioning (e.g., palm up, wrist slightly hyperextended if radial artery is used). Collect blood in heparinized syringe. To ensure accurate results, expel all air bubbles. *After:* Apply pressure to radial artery for at least 5 min after specimen is obtained to prevent hematoma at the arterial puncture site. Send sample to lab promptly for analysis.
O_2 Monitoring **Oximetry**	Monitors arterial or venous O_2 saturation. Probe attaches to finger, toe, earlobe, bridge of the nose for SpO_2 monitoring or is in a pulmonary artery catheter for SvO_2 monitoring. Used for intermittent or continuous monitoring and exercise testing. *Normal SpO_2:* 94%–100% *Normal SvO_2:* 60%–80%	*During:* Apply probe. When interpreting SpO_2 and SvO_2 values, first assess patient status and presence of factors that can alter accuracy of pulse oximeter reading. For SpO_2, these include motion, low perfusion, cold extremities, bright lights, acrylic nails, dark skin color, carbon monoxide, and anemia. For SvO_2, these include change in O_2 delivery or O_2 consumption.
CO_2 Monitoring **End-tidal CO_2 ($PetCO_2$)** **(capnography)**	Assesses the level of CO_2 in exhaled air. Graphically displays partial pressure of CO_2. Expired gases are sampled from patient's airway and analyzed by a CO_2 sensor to measure exhaled CO_2. Sensor may be attached to an adaptor on endotracheal or tracheostomy tube. A nasal cannula with a sidestream capnometer can be used in patients without an artificial airway. Can be a diagnostic measure to detect lung disease and for monitoring patients. Normal difference between $PaCO_2$ and $PetCO_2$ is 2–5 mm Hg ($PaCO_2$: 35–45 mm Hg; $PetCO_2$: 40–50 mm Hg).	*Before:* Teach patient and caregiver about purpose of capnography monitoring, emphasizing the benefit of continuous monitoring. *During:* Make sure that sensor is properly attached. Record data per agency policy.

SvO_2, venous O_2 saturation.

TABLE 25.10 Normal and Critical Values for PaO_2 and SpO_2

PaO_2 (mm Hg)	SpO_2 (%)	Significance	Manifestations	Management
80–100	≥94	Normal value	Asymptomatic	• Routine assessment of patient
60–79	90	Mild hypoxemia	Restlessness, tachycardia, dysrhythmias, dyspnea, hypertension	• Assess patient condition as needed • Supplemental O_2 may be needed
40–59	88	Moderate hypoxemia	Confusion, lethargy, dysrhythmias, hypotension, respiratory distress, accessory muscle use	• O_2 required • Escalate level of care. Obtain critical care consult • Monitor frequently for sudden deterioration in condition
<40	75	Severe hypoxemia	Cyanosis, coma, respiratory and/or cardiac arrest possible	• High FIO_2, intubation, mechanical ventilation • Continuous patient assessment and evaluation

TABLE 25.11 Normal Arterial Blood Gas Values

Laboratory Value	Sea Level BP 760 mm Hg	1 Mile Above Sea Level BP 629 mm Hg
pH	7.35–7.45	7.35–7.45
PaO_2†	80–100 mm Hg	65–75 mm Hg
SaO_2†	>95%	>95%
$PaCO_2$	35–45 mm Hg	35–45 mm Hg
HCO_3^-	22–26 mEq/L (mmol/L)	22–26 mEq/L (mmol/L)

BP, Barometric pressure; HCO_3^-, bicarbonate; *PaO_2*, partial pressure of O_2 in arterial blood; *$PaCO_2$*, partial pressure of arterial CO_2; *SaO_2*, arterial O_2 saturation.

TABLE 25.12 Normal Venous Blood Gas Values

Venous Blood Gases *Mixed Venous Blood Gases*	
pH	7.31–7.41
PvO_2	38–42 mm Hg
SvO_2	60%–80%‡
$PvCO_2$	38–55 mm Hg
HCO_3^-	22–26 mEq/L (mmol/L)

$PvCO_2$, Partial pressure of CO_2 in venous blood; *PvO_2*, partial pressure of O_2 in venous blood; *SvO_2*, venous O_2 saturation.

TABLE 25.13 Sputum Studies

Study	Description and Purpose	Nursing Responsibility
Acid-fast bacteria (AFB) smear and culture	2 different tests used to assess sputum for acid-fast bacilli (e.g., *Mycobacterium tuberculosis*). In AFB smear (a rapid test), sputum sample spread thinly on glass slide, treated with a fluorochrome stain, and examined under a microscope for AFB. Culture for AFB may take up to 6 wk.	*During:* Obtain specimen in early morning after mouth care because secretions collect during night. Have patient expectorate sputum into container after coughing deeply. If unsuccessful, try increasing oral fluid intake unless fluids are restricted. Can collect sputum in sterile container (sputum trap) during suctioning via endotracheal tube or by aspirating secretions from the trachea. If patient cannot produce specimen, bronchoscopy may be needed (Fig. 25.11). *After:* Send specimen to laboratory promptly for analysis.
Culture and sensitivity	Diagnose bacterial infection, select antibiotic, and evaluate treatment. Sputum specimen collected in a sterile container. Takes 48–72 hr for results.	
Cytology	Determines presence of abnormal cells that may indicate cancer. Single sputum specimen collected in special container with fixative solution.	
Gram stain	Sputum staining allows for classification of bacteria into gram-negative and gram-positive types. Results guide therapy until culture and sensitivity results are complete.	

TABLE 25.14 Interpreting Tuberculin Skin Testing

Types of Responses	Consider Positive in the Following Groups
Positive Reactions	
≥5-mm induration	• HIV-infected people • People who had recent contact with a person with TB disease • People with fibrotic lesions on chest x-ray consistent with prior TB • Patients with organ transplants • Immunosuppressed persons (e.g., taking the equivalent of ≥15 mg/day of prednisone for ≥1 mo)
≥10-mm induration	• Recent immigrants (<5 yr) from high-prevalence countries • Injecting drug users • Residents and employees of high-risk congregate settings • Mycobacteriology laboratory personnel • People with clinical conditions (e.g., diabetes mellitus, end-stage kidney disease) that place them at high risk
≥15-mm induration	• Any person (including those with no known risk factors for TB)
False Reactions	**Possible Causes**
False-negative reactions (do not react even though infected)	• Anergy, immunosuppression • Recent TB infection (within 8–10 wk of exposure) • Overwhelming TB infection • Very old TB infection (many years) • Recent live virus vaccination (e.g., measles, chickenpox)
False-positive reactions (react even though not infected)	• Nontuberculous mycobacteria (e.g., *Mycobacterium avium-intracellulare* [MAI] or *Mycobacterium avium* complex [MAC]) • Previous BCG vaccine

Source: Centers for Disease Control and Prevention: Tuberculosis (TB) fact sheet: Tuberculin skin testing. Retrieved from *www.cdc.gov/tb/publications/factsheets/testing/skintesting.htm*.

CO₂ Monitoring

CO_2 can be monitored using transcutaneous CO_2 ($PtCO_2$) and end-tidal CO_2 ($PetCO_2$) capnography. Transcutaneous measurement of CO_2 is a noninvasive method of estimating arterial pressure of CO_2 ($PaCO_2$) using an electrode placed on the skin.[11]

$PetCO_2$ is the noninvasive measurement of alveolar CO_2 during exhalation when CO_2 concentration is at its peak. It is used to monitor and assess trends in the patient's ventilatory status. Expired gases are sampled from the patient's airway and are analyzed by a CO_2 sensor that uses infrared light to measure exhaled CO_2. The sensor may be attached to an adaptor on the endotracheal tube or the tracheostomy tube. A nasal cannula with a sidestream capnometer can be used in patients without an artificial airway. Capnography is usually presented as a graph of expiratory CO_2 plotted against time.[12]

In the past, capnography was mainly used during and after surgery and in critical care units. Today's $PetCO_2$ monitors are portable and practical for use in emergency departments and on inpatient units.

Mixed Venous Blood Gases

The pulmonary artery (PA) catheter is a flow-directed catheter. When it is positioned correctly, the tip of the catheter lies in the pulmonary artery. Blood drawn from a PA catheter is called a mixed venous blood gas (SvO_2), because (1) it consists of venous blood that has returned to the right side of the heart from all parts of the body and (2) it samples blood just before blood enters the lungs to be oxygenated. Normal SvO_2 is 60% to 80%. Other normal mixed venous values are given in Table 25.12.

SvO_2 can be monitored intermittently by obtaining a blood sample from the PA catheter or continuously via a fiberoptic sensor as part of a specific central line with SpO_2 monitoring capability. Changes in SvO_2 provide an early warning of a change in cardiac output or tissue O_2 delivery. A decrease in SvO_2 suggests that less O_2 is being delivered to the tissues or that more O_2 is being consumed.

Sputum Studies

Observe the patient's sputum for color, volume, viscosity, and presence or absence of blood. We can obtain a sputum sample by expectoration, tracheal suction, or bronchoscopy. When the patient is unable to expectorate spontaneously, sputum may be collected by inhaling an irritating aerosol, usually hypertonic saline. This is called *sputum induction*.

Specimens may be examined for culture and sensitivity to identify an infecting organism (e.g., *Mycobacterium*) or to confirm a diagnosis (e.g., cancer). Table 25.13 describes common sputum tests and specific responsibilities when obtaining samples.

TABLE 25.15 Diagnostic Studies

Respiratory System

Study	Description and Purpose	Nursing Responsibility
Radiology		
Chest x-ray	Used to screen, diagnose, and evaluate changes in respiratory system. Most common views are anteroposterior (AP) and lateral.	*Before:* Have patient undress to waist, put on gown, and remove any metal between neck and waist.
Computed tomography (CT) scan	Diagnose suspicious lesions difficult to assess (e.g., mediastinum, hilum, pleura) by conventional x-ray. Common types are helical or spiral CT (contrast medium usually used) and high-resolution CT scan (contrast medium not used). Spiral CT used to diagnose a pulmonary embolism.	*Before:* Before contrast medium used, evaluate renal function. Assess if patient is allergic to shellfish, since the contrast is iodine based. Patient may need to be NPO 4 hr prior to study. *During:* Warn patient that contrast injection may cause a feeling of being warm and flushed. Patient must lie completely still during scan. *After:* Encourage patient to drink fluids to avoid renal problems with any contrast.
Magnetic resonance imaging (MRI)	Used for in-depth diagnosis of lesions difficult to assess by CT scan (e.g., lung apex) and for differentiating vascular from nonvascular structures. An IV contrast agent (gadolinium) may be given.	*Before:* Oral and/or IV contrast injection may be used. Check for pregnancy, allergies, and renal function before test. Have patient remove all metal objects. Remove metallic foil patches. Contraindicated for persons with implanted metallic devices or other metal fragments unless noted to be MRI safe. Ask about any history of surgical insertion of staples, plates, dental bridges, or other metal appliances. Patient may need to be fasting. Assess for claustrophobia and the need for antianxiety medication. *During:* Patient must lie completely still during scan.
Positron emission tomography (PET) scan	Glucose-containing nuclear tracer substance injected and taken up by metabolically active cells. Follow-up scan shows different-colored tissues based on metabolic rate. Because cancer cells have an increased uptake of glucose, "hot spots" reflecting increased glucose consumption indicate the presence of active cancer. Used to distinguish benign and cancerous lung nodules.	*Before:* Obtain IV access to inject the tracer substance. Patients should be NPO, except for water and medications, for at least 4 hr prior. Hold glucose-containing IV solutions and change to normal saline. Check blood glucose levels. The glucose level must be between 60-140 mg/dL (3.3–7.8 μmol/L) for accurate glucose metabolic activity. *During:* Patient must lie completely still during scan. *After:* Encourage fluids to excrete radioactive substance.
Pulmonary angiogram	Visualize pulmonary vasculature and locate obstruction or pathologic conditions (e.g., pulmonary embolus). Contrast medium injected through a catheter threaded into pulmonary artery or right side of heart. Series of x-rays taken after contrast medium is injected into pulmonary artery.	*Before:* Assess for allergies, especially to contrast dye. Have patient fast 6–12 hours before. Give sedative and other drugs, as ordered. *After:* Check pressure dressing site after procedure. Monitor BP, pulse, and circulation distal to injection site. Place compression device over site. Maintain IV and/or oral fluid intake.
Ventilation-perfusion (V/Q) scan	Assesses ventilation and perfusion of lungs. IV radioisotope given to assess perfusion. To assess ventilation, patient inhales a radioactive gas (xenon or krypton) that outlines alveoli. Normal scans show homogeneous radioactivity. Decreased or absent radioactivity suggests lack of perfusion or airflow. Ventilation without perfusion suggests a pulmonary embolus.	Same as for chest x-ray. *After:* No precautions needed afterward because the gas and isotope transmit radioactivity for only a brief interval.
Endoscopy		
Bronchoscopy (Fig. 25.11)	Flexible fiberoptic scope used for diagnosis, biopsy, specimen collection, or assessment of changes. It may be done to suction mucous plugs, lavage lungs, or remove foreign objects.	*Before:* Obtain signed consent. Have patient be NPO for 6–12 hr before the test. Give sedative as ordered. *After:* Keep patient NPO until gag reflex returns. Monitor for recovery from sedation. Blood-tinged mucus is not abnormal. If biopsy was done, monitor for hemorrhage and pneumothorax.
Lung biopsy	Specimens may be obtained by transbronchial or percutaneous biopsy or via transthoracic needle aspiration (TTNA), video-assisted thoracoscopic surgery (VATS), or open lung biopsy. Transbronchial biopsy and VATS can be done in the bronchoscopy suite. TTNA is done under CT guidance in radiology department. Open lung and VATS are done in the OR. Tests used to obtain specimens for laboratory analysis.	*Before:* Obtain signed consent. Same as bronchoscopy if procedure done with bronchoscope, and same as thoracotomy if open lung biopsy done. *After TTNA:* Check breath sounds q4hr for 24 hr and report any respiratory distress. Check incision site for bleeding. A chest x-ray should be done after TTNA or transbronchial biopsy to check for pneumothorax. *After VATS:* A chest tube may be placed postprocedure until lung has reexpanded. Monitor breath sounds to follow chest reexpansion. Encourage deep breathing for lung reinflation.
Mediastinoscopy	Scope inserted through a small incision in suprasternal notch and advanced into mediastinum to inspect and biopsy lymph nodes. Used to diagnose lung cancer, non-Hodgkin's lymphoma, granulomatous infections, and sarcoidosis.	*Before:* Obtain signed consent. Prepare patient for surgical intervention. Performed in OR using a general anesthetic. *After:* Monitor as for bronchoscopy.

TABLE 25.15 Diagnostic Studies—cont'd

Respiratory System

Study	Description and Purpose	Nursing Responsibility
Thoracentesis (Fig. 25.12)	Used to obtain specimen of pleural fluid for diagnosis, remove pleural fluid, or instill medication. Obtain chest x-ray after procedure to check for pneumothorax.	*Before:* Explain procedure and obtain signed consent. *During:* Usually done in patient's room. Position patient upright with elbows on an overbed table and feet supported. Tell patient not to talk or cough during procedure. *After:* Observe for signs of hypoxia and pneumothorax, and verify breath sounds in all fields. Encourage deep breaths to expand lungs. Send labeled specimens to laboratory promptly for analysis.
Pulmonary Function Tests	Used to evaluate lung function. Involves use of spirometer to assess air movement as patient performs prescribed respiratory maneuvers (Tables 25.16 and 25.17).	*Before:* Avoid scheduling immediately after mealtime. Avoid administration of inhaled bronchodilator 6 hr before. Assess for respiratory distress. *During:* Assess for respiratory distress. *After:* Assess for respiratory distress. Provide rest after procedure.
Exercise Testing	Used to diagnose and determine exercise capacity. A *complete test* involves walking on a treadmill while monitoring expired O_2 and CO_2, respiratory rate, heart rate, and heart rhythm. In a *modified test* (desaturation test), only SpO_2 is monitored.	*Before:* Have patient wear comfortable shoes. *During:* Encourage patient to hold handlebars on treadmill and walk as quickly as possible.
6-Min walk test	Used to measure functional capacity and response to treatment in patients with heart or lung disease. Pulse oximetry usually monitored during walk. Distance walked measured and used to monitor progression of disease or improvement after rehabilitation.	*During:* Patient walks as far as possible during 6 min, stopping when short of breath and continuing when able. Continually assess and observe patient tolerance to test.

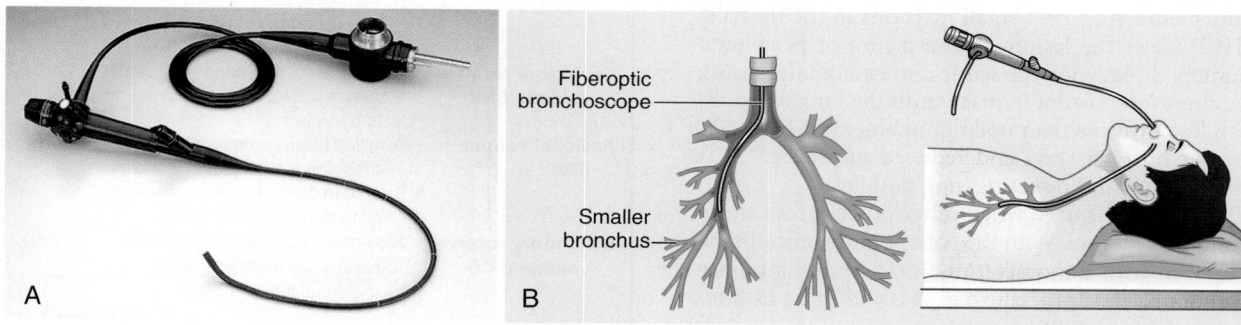

FIG. 25.11 Fiberoptic bronchoscope. **A,** The transbronchoscopic balloon-tipped catheter and the flexible fiberoptic bronchoscope. **B,** The catheter is introduced into a small airway and the balloon inflated with 1.5 to 2 mL of air to occlude the airway. Bronchoalveolar lavage is done by injecting and withdrawing 30-mL aliquots of sterile saline solution, gently aspirating after each instillation. Specimens are sent to the laboratory for analysis. (*A,* Courtesy Olympus America Inc, Melville, NY.)

Skin Tests

Skin tests may be done to test for allergic reactions (see Chapter 13) or exposure to TB bacilli or fungi. Skin tests involve the intradermal injection of an antigen. Table 25.14 discusses how to interpret tuberculin skin testing. For example, a positive result on a TB skin test means that the patient has been exposed to the antigen. It does not mean that the patient has TB. A negative result means either no exposure or a depression of cell-mediated immunity, which occurs in HIV infection.

Our responsibilities are similar for all skin tests. First, to prevent a false-negative reaction, be sure that the injection is intradermal and not subcutaneous. After the injection, circle the site(s) and tell the patient not to remove the marks. When charting administration of the antigen, draw a diagram of the forearm and hand, and label the injection site. The diagram is especially helpful when the patient receives more than 1 test.

When reading test results, use a good light. If an induration is present, use a marking pen to indicate the periphery on all 4 sides of the induration. As the pen touches the raised area, make a mark. Then determine the diameter of the induration in millimeters. Do not measure reddened, flat areas.

Endoscopy

Bronchoscopy. *Bronchoscopy* is a procedure in which the bronchi are visualized through a fiberoptic tube (Fig. 25.11). Bronchoscopy may be used for diagnostic purposes (obtain biopsy specimens) and for treatment (e.g., to remove mucous plugs, foreign bodies). Laser therapy, electrocautery, cryotherapy, and stents may be placed through a bronchoscope to achieve patency of an airway that has been partially or nearly fully obstructed by tumors (Table 25.15).

Bronchoscopy can be done in an outpatient procedure room, in a surgical suite, or at the bedside in the critical care unit or on a medical-surgical unit. The patient may be positioned supine, in low-Fowler's, or even be seated. The HCP inserts the bronchoscope through the nose or mouth. Depending on the approach, the nasopharynx or oropharynx is anesthetized with local anesthetic spray. The bronchoscope is coated with water-soluble lubricant and inserted down into the airways. Small amounts (30 mL) of sterile saline may be injected through the scope and withdrawn and examined for cells, a technique termed *bronchoalveolar lavage* (BAL). Bronchoscopy can be done through the endotracheal tube of a mechanically ventilated patient.

Lung Biopsy

Lung biopsy may be done (1) transbronchially, (2) percutaneously or via transthoracic needle aspiration (TTNA), (3) by video-assisted thoracic surgery (VATS), or (4) as an open lung biopsy (Table 25.15). The purpose of a lung biopsy is to obtain tissue, cells, and/or fluid for evaluation. Specimens can be cultured or examined for cancer cells.

Transbronchial biopsy involves passing a forceps or needle through the bronchoscope for a specimen. A combination of transbronchial lung biopsy and BAL is used to distinguish infection and rejection in lung transplant recipients. A percutaneous or TTNA biopsy involves inserting a needle through the chest wall, usually under bedside ultrasound or CT guidance. Because of the risk for a pneumothorax, a chest x-ray is done after TTNA.

In VATS, a rigid scope with a lens is passed through a trocar placed into the pleura via 1 or 2 small incisions in the thoracic cavity. The HCP views the lesions in the pleura or peripheral lung on a monitor directly via the scope and can obtain biopsy specimens. A chest tube is kept in place until the lung expands. VATS is much less invasive than open lung biopsy. It is associated with shorter hospital stays and reduced mortality.[13] It is ideal for pleural biopsy and resecting lung nodules.

An open lung biopsy is used when other procedures cannot diagnose pulmonary disease. With the patient under anesthesia, the chest is opened with a thoracotomy incision and a biopsy specimen is obtained. Postprocedure care is the same as after thoracotomy (see Chapter 27).

Thoracentesis

Thoracentesis is the insertion of a large-bore needle through the chest wall into the pleural space to obtain specimens for diagnostic evaluation, remove pleural fluid, or instill medication (Fig. 25.12). The patient is positioned sitting upright, leaning on an overbed table with feet supported. The skin is cleansed and a local anesthetic (lidocaine) is injected subcutaneously. A percutaneous catheter may be left in to allow further drainage of fluid (Table 25.15).

Pulmonary Function Tests

Pulmonary function tests (PFTs) measure lung volumes and airflow. The results of PFTs can diagnose pulmonary disease, monitor disease progression, assess response to bronchodilators, and evaluate disability. Airflow measurement is obtained by trained personnel using a spirometer. The patient inserts a mouthpiece, takes as deep a breath as possible, and exhales as hard, as fast, and for as long as possible. Verbal coaching is given to ensure that the patient continues blowing out until exhalation is complete.

Computer software calculates the patient's percent of predicted values, that is, how well the performance compares with

FIG. 25.12 Thoracentesis. A catheter is positioned in the pleural space to remove accumulated fluid.

TABLE 25.16 **Lung Volumes and Capacities**		
Parameter	**Definitions**	**Normal Value***
Volumes		
Tidal volume (V$_T$)	Volume of air inhaled and exhaled with each breath. Only a small proportion of total capacity of lungs	0.5 L
Expiratory reserve volume (ERV)	Additional air that can be forcefully exhaled after normal exhalation is complete	1.0 L
Residual volume (RV)	Amount of air remaining in lungs after forced expiration. Air available in lungs for gas exchange between breaths	1.5 L
Inspiratory reserve volume (IRV)	Maximum volume of air that can be inhaled forcefully after normal inhalation	3.0 L
Capacities		
Total lung capacity (TLC)	Maximum volume of air that lungs can contain (TLC = IRV + V$_T$ + ERV + RV)	6.0 L
Functional residual capacity (FRC)	Volume of air remaining in lungs at end of normal exhalation (FRC = ERV + RV). Increase or decrease possible with lung disease	2.5 L
Vital capacity (VC)	Maximum volume of air that can be exhaled after maximum inspiration (VC = IRV + V$_T$ + ERV). Higher VC for men (generally)	4.5 L
Inspiratory capacity (IC)	Maximum volume of air that can be inhaled after normal expiration (IC = V$_T$ + IRV)	3.5 L

*Normal values vary with patient's height, weight, age, race, and gender.

an average based on age, gender, race, and height.[14] Normal values are 80% to 120% of the predicted value. Normal values for PFTs are shown in Tables 25.16 and 25.17.

Spirometry may be done before and after giving a bronchodilator to determine the patient's response. This helps gauge the reversibility of airway obstruction (e.g., asthma). A positive

TABLE 25.17 Pulmonary Function Airflow

Measure	Description	Normal Value*
Forced vital capacity (FVC)	Amount of air that can be quickly and forcefully exhaled after maximum inspiration	>80% of predicted
Forced expiratory volume in first second of expiration (FEV_1)	Amount of air exhaled in first second of FVC. Grades severity of airway obstruction	>80% of predicted
FEV_1/FVC ratio	Dividing value for FEV_1 by value for FVC. Useful in differentiating obstructive and restrictive pulmonary dysfunction	*Age <50:* ≥75% of predicted *Age ≥50:* ≥70% of predicted
Forced midexpiratory flow rate ($FEF_{25\%-75\%}$)	Measurement of airflow rate in middle half of forced expiration. Early indicator of disease of small airways	*Age <50:* ≥75% of predicted *Age ≥50:* ≥70% of predicted
Maximal voluntary ventilation (MVV)	Deep breathing as rapidly as possible for specified period. Fairly nonspecific test that gives information about exercise capacity. Used in conjunction with exercise stress test	About 170 L/min
Peak expiratory flow rate (PEFR)	Maximum airflow rate during forced expiration. Aids in monitoring bronchoconstriction in asthma. Can be measured with peak flow meter	Up to 600 L/min

*Normal values vary with patient's height, age, race, and gender.

bronchodilator response is an increase of greater than 200 mL or 12% in FEV_1 after administering a bronchodilator.

Home spirometry may be used to monitor lung function in people with asthma, cystic fibrosis, or COPD, as well as before and after lung transplantation or other thoracic surgeries. A peak flow meter is the hand-held instrument used at home. The person blows through it forcefully and quickly after taking a deep breath. Spirometry changes can warn of early lung transplant rejection or infection. Data from a peak flow meter provide important feedback to patients with asthma so that they can learn to change activities and medications in response to changes in peak expiratory flow rates.

More specific pulmonary function parameters can be directly assessed at the bedside in a high-acuity or critical care unit to determine the need for or weaning and extubation from mechanical ventilation (see Table 65.13).

CASE STUDY

Objective Data: Diagnostic Studies

(© Fuse/Thinkstock.)

The HCP orders the following diagnostic studies for F.T.:
- Pulse oximetry
- Chest x-ray
- 12-lead electrocardiogram (ECG)
- CBC, basic metabolic panel (electrolytes, BUN, creatinine)
- ABGs
- Sputum for culture and sensitivity

F.T.'s SpO_2 is 87% on O_2 @ 3/L min via nasal cannula. The chest x-ray shows a slightly enlarged heart and bilateral consolidation to both lower lobes. The 12-lead ECG reveals sinus tachycardia, rate 110, with no ST segment elevation or depression and no T-wave inversion. The ABGs show compensated respiratory alkalosis with hypoxemia. The WBC is 17,350/μL and potassium 2.9 mEq/L. Sputum results are pending. F.T. is admitted to the medical nursing unit.

Discussion Questions
1. Of the diagnostic test results, is anything abnormal?
2. Which results concern you most?
3. What do you think is the cause of F.T.'s problems?
4. What patient teaching can you do with F.T. as he is waiting to be admitted to the hospital unit?
5. What is the interprofessional team's top priority for F.T. at this time?

You will learn more about the upper and lower respiratory problems and chronic obstructive pulmonary disease (COPD) in the next 3 chapters.

Answers available at *http://evolve.elsevier.com/Lewis/medsurg.*

BRIDGE TO NCLEX EXAMINATION

The number of the question corresponds to the same-numbered learning outcome identified at the beginning of this chapter.

1. The key anatomic landmark that separates the upper respiratory tract from the lower respiratory tract is the
   a. carina.
   b. larynx.
   c. trachea.
   d. epiglottis.
2. A patient asks, "How does air get into my lungs?" The nurse bases her answer on knowledge that air moves into the lungs because of
   a. positive intrathoracic pressure.
   b. contraction of the accessory abdominal muscles.
   c. stimulation of the respiratory muscles by the chemoreceptors.
   d. a decrease in intrathoracic pressure from an increase in thoracic cavity size.
3. The nurse can *best* determine adequate arterial oxygenation of the blood by assessing
   a. heart rate.
   b. hemoglobin level.
   c. arterial oxygen partial pressure.
   d. arterial carbon dioxide partial pressure.
4. Defense mechanisms that help protect the lung from inhaled particles and microorganisms include the (*select all that apply*)
   a. cough reflex.
   b. mucociliary escalator.
   c. alveolar macrophages.
   d. reflex bronchoconstriction.
   e. alveolar capillary membrane.

5. A student nurse asks the RN what can be measured by arterial blood gas (ABG). The RN tells the student that the ABG can measure *(select all that apply)*
   a. acid-base balance.
   b. oxygenation status.
   c. acidity of the blood.
   d. bicarbonate (HCO_3^-).
   e. compliance and resistance.
6. To detect early signs or symptoms of inadequate oxygenation, the nurse would examine the patient for
   a. dyspnea and hypotension.
   b. apprehension and restlessness.
   c. cyanosis and cool, clammy skin.
   d. increased urine output and diaphoresis.
7. During the respiratory assessment of an older adult, the nurse would expect to find *(select all that apply)*
   a. a vigorous reflex cough.
   b. increased chest expansion.
   c. increased residual volume.
   d. decreased lung sounds at base of lungs.
   e. increased anteroposterior (AP) chest diameter.
8. When assessing subjective data related to the respiratory health of a patient with emphysema, the nurse asks about *(select all that apply)*
   a. date of last chest x-ray.
   b. dyspnea during rest or exercise.
   c. pulmonary function test results.
   d. ability to sleep through the entire night.
   e. prescription and over-the-counter medication.
9. When auscultating the chest of an older patient in mild respiratory distress, it is *best* to
   a. begin listening at the apices.
   b. begin listening at the lung bases.
   c. begin listening on the anterior chest.
   d. Ask the patient to breathe through the nose with the mouth closed.
10. Which respiratory assessment finding does the nurse interpret as abnormal?
    a. Inspiratory chest expansion of 1 inch
    b. Symmetric chest expansion and contraction
    c. Resonance (to percussion) over the lung bases
    d. Bronchial breath sounds in the lower lung fields
11. The nurse is preparing the patient for a diagnostic procedure to remove pleural fluid for analysis. The nurse would prepare the patient for which test?
    a. Thoracentesis
    b. Bronchoscopy
    c. Pulmonary angiography
    d. Sputum culture and sensitivity

1.a, 2.d, 3.c, 4.a, b, c, d, 5.a, b, c, d, 6.b, 7.c, d, e, 8.b, d, e, 9.b, 10.d, 11.a

For rationales to these answers and even more NCLEX review questions, visit *http://evolve.elsevier.com/Lewis/medsurg.*

EVOLVE WEBSITE/RESOURCES LIST

http://evolve.elsevier.com/Lewis/medsurg
Review Questions (Online Only)
Key Points
Answer Keys for Questions
- Rationales for Bridge to NCLEX Examination Questions
- Answer Guidelines for Case Study on pp. 460, 464, 467, and 475

Conceptual Care Map Creator
Audio Glossary
Supporting Media
- Animations
  - Inhalation
  - Oxygenation
  - Pulse Oximetry
  - Respiration Cycle
  - Respiratory System Overview
- Audio
  - Bronchial Breath Sounds
  - Bronchovesicular Breath Sounds
  - High-Pitched Crackles
  - High-Pitched Wheeze
  - Low-Pitched Crackles
  - Low-Pitched Wheeze
  - Pleural Friction Rub
  - Stridor
  - Vesicular Breath Sounds
Content Updates

REFERENCES

1. Patton KT, Thibodeau GA: *Essentials of anatomy and physiology*, ed 9, St Louis, 2016, Mosby.
2. Tatco V, Smith D: Carina. Retrieved from *https://radiopaedia.org/articles/carina.*
3. Meriam-Webster Dictionary: Anatomic dead space. Retrieved from: *www.merriam-webster.com/medical/anatomical%20dead%20space.*
4. Goel A, Gaillard F: Pores of Kohn. Retrieved from *https://radiopaedia.org/articles/pores-of-kohn.*
5. Stacy KM: Pulmonary anatomy and physiology. In: Urden LD, Stacy KM, Lough ME (ed): *Critical care nursing: Diagnosis and management*, ed 8, St Louis, 2018, Mosby.
6. DeWit SC, Stromberg HK, Dallred CV: *Medical-surgical nursing: Concepts and practice*, ed 3, St Louis, 2017, Mosby.
*7. Whitten C: Don't withhold oxygen from that CO_2 retainer. Retrieved from *https://airwayjedi.com/2016/01/09/dont-withhold-oxygen-from-that-co2-retainer/.*
8. Rhoades RA, Bell DR: *Medical physiology: Principles for clinical medicine*, ed 5, Philadelphia, 2018, Wolters-Kluwer.
9. Pathway Medicine: J receptors. Retrieved from *www.pathwaymedicine.org/j-receptors.*
10. Wilson SF, Giddens JF: *Health assessment for nursing practice*, ed 6, St Louis, 2017, Mosby.
*11. Horvath CM, Brutsche MH, Baty F, et al: Transcutaneous versus blood carbon dioxide monitoring during acute noninvasive ventilation in the emergency department, *Swiss Med Wkly* 146:w14373, 2016.
12. Luehrs P: Continuous end-tidal carbon dioxide monitoring. In Wiegand, DL (ed): *AACN procedure manual for high acuity, progressive, and critical care*, ed 7, St Louis, 2017, Saunders.
13. Jarrar D: Video-assisted thoracic surgery (VATS). Retrieved from *https://emedicine.medscape.com/article/1970013-overview.*
14. Mottram CD: *Ruppel's manual of pulmonary function testing*, ed 11, St Louis, 2017, Mosby.

*Evidence-based information for clinical practice.

26

Upper Respiratory Problems

Eugene Mondor

You really can change the world if you care enough.

Marian Wright Edelman

ⓔ http://evolve.elsevier.com/Lewis/medsurg/

CONCEPTUAL FOCUS

Cellular Regulation	Gas Exchange	Infection
Functional Ability	Immunity	Sensory Perception

LEARNING OUTCOMES

1. Describe the clinical manifestations and nursing and interprofessional management of problems of the nose.
2. Discuss the clinical manifestations and nursing and interprofessional management of problems of the paranasal sinuses.
3. Describe the clinical manifestations and nursing and interprofessional management of problems of the pharynx and larynx.
4. Relate the nursing and interprofessional management of the patient who has a tracheostomy.
5. Identify the steps involved in performing tracheostomy care and suctioning a patient with a tracheostomy.
6. Outline the risk factors for and clinical manifestations of head and neck cancer.
7. Discuss the nursing and interprofessional management of patients requiring surgery for head and neck cancer.
8. Explain essential components of discharge teaching for the patient going home with a permanent tracheostomy after total laryngectomy for cancer.

KEY TERMS

allergic rhinitis, p. 480	laryngectomy, p. 494	rhinoplasty, p. 478
decannulation, p. 493	laryngitis, p. 487	sinusitis, p. 485
deviated septum, p. 477	nasal polyps, p. 486	surgical cricothyroidotomy, p. 488
epistaxis, p. 478	pharyngitis, p. 486	tracheostomy, p. 488

Disorders of the upper respiratory system, including the nose, sinuses, pharynx, and larynx, and the care of those undergoing surgery for head and neck cancers are the focus of this chapter. The primary concern with these problems is the impact on ventilation and oxygen (O_2) availability. Upper airway problems can negatively affect sleep and impair the ability to obtain and maintain nutrition. Sinus and upper respiratory tract infections, allergies, and oral problems can change the senses of both smell and taste. The patient with head and neck cancer often has depression and changes in body image and sexuality.

PROBLEMS OF NOSE AND PARANASAL SINUSES

DEVIATED SEPTUM

Deviated septum is a deflection of the normally straight nasal septum. Although up to 80% of adults may have septa that are slightly off center, the diagnosis of deviated septum is generally reserved for those whose septa are severely shifted.[1] Trauma to the nose, either at birth or later in life, is the most common cause

of deviated septum.[2] Deviated septum can interfere with both airflow and sinus drainage through the narrowed passageway.

Symptoms vary depending on the degree of deviation. Minor septal deviations can range from asymptomatic to nasal congestion and frequent sinus infections. Manifestations of severe septal deviation include facial pain, nosebleeds *(epistaxis)*, and obstruction to nasal breathing.

The diagnosis of deviated septum is made during physical examination with a nasal speculum. The medical management of minor septal deviation focuses on symptom control. For nasal inflammation and congestion, use saline rinses and decongestants to clear nasal passages and analgesics for pain relief. For severe septal deviation, a nasal septoplasty, done under local or general anesthetic, reconstructs and properly aligns the deviated septum.

NASAL FRACTURE

Nasal fracture is the most common facial fracture and the third most common fracture of any bone.[3] They often occur from blunt trauma, including fights, automobile accidents, falls, and sports injuries. Using protective sports equipment and safeguarding against falls can prevent many nasal fractures.

There is no universally accepted classification system for nasal fractures. We can classify nasal fractures according to the fracture pattern (e.g., impacted, comminuted) or based on direction of injury (e.g., lateral, frontal). *Simple fractures* may be unilateral or bilateral and typically have little or no displacement. Powerful frontal blows can cause *complex fractures,* which may involve damage to adjacent facial structures, such as the teeth or eyes. Patients with complex nasal fractures should be evaluated for injury to the cervical spine, orbital bone, or mandible.[4] Complications include airway obstruction, nosebleeds, meningeal tears causing cerebrospinal fluid (CSF) leakage, septal hematoma, and cosmetic deformity.

Diagnosis of a nasal fracture is based on health history and physical assessment. Although facial deformity with a nasal fracture is common, a nosebleed may be the only manifestation. Other manifestations include localized pain, crepitus on palpation, swelling, difficulty breathing out of the nostrils, and bruising.

Assess the patient's ability to breathe through each side of the nose. Note the presence of edema, bleeding, or hematoma. Periorbital bruising involving both eyes is called *raccoon eyes.* It suggests a basilar skull fracture (see Chapter 56). Inspect the nose internally for evidence of septal deviation, clear drainage, edema, or bleeding.

Clear or pink-tinged persistent drainage after control of bleeding suggests a possible CSF leak. Checking this fluid for glucose at the bedside to help confirm the presence of CSF is not recommended because the result is highly unreliable. If needed, send a specimen to the laboratory to determine the fluid type.

Goals of nursing management are to maintain a patent airway, reduce edema and pain, prevent complications, and provide emotional support. The best way to maintain the airway is to keep the patient sitting upright. Apply ice to the face and nose in 10- to 20-minute intervals to help reduce edema and bleeding. Give analgesia as ordered to control pain. Acetaminophen is preferred over nonsteroidal antiinflammatory drugs (NSAIDs) or acetylsalicylic acid (ASA; aspirin) for the first 48 hours to avoid prolonging clotting time and increasing the risk for bleeding. Nasal stuffiness may be relieved with nasal decongestants, saline nasal sprays, and a humidifier. The patient should avoid hot showers and alcohol for the first 48 hours to prevent an increase in swelling. Encourage the patient to quit or decrease smoking to help tissue healing.

When a fracture is confirmed, the goals are to realign the fracture using closed or open reduction.[5] Simple fractures are often reduced with manual manipulation. With complex nasal fractures, considerable swelling of soft tissues occurs. It may be necessary to wait to repair the fracture until after the edema subsides, which may be 5 to 10 days. Antibiotics should be considered for any nasal fracture with disruption to the mucosa.

Surgical options include septoplasty and rhinoplasty. Septoplasty is done to correct a deviated septum. Patients have rhinoplasty for several reasons. Both procedures help maintain a patent airway, restore function of the nose, and help reestablish the patient's cosmetic appearance. The presence of septal hematoma increases the patient's risk for deformity and infection, which may require drainage and antibiotic therapy.

RHINOPLASTY

Rhinoplasty, surgical reconstruction of the nose, is done to improve airway function when trauma or developmental deformities result in nasal obstruction or for cosmetic reasons. When caring for rhinoplasty patients before surgery, assess the patient's expectations of the surgery. Actual or perceived changes in body image (e.g., deformed or enlarged nose) can affect self-esteem and interactions with others. The HCP can use digital photographs to show patients their projected appearance after surgery. These images can help patients decide whether to undergo rhinoplasty.

Most rhinoplasty is an outpatient procedure using regional or general anesthesia. Nasal tissue is added or removed, and the nose may be lengthened or shortened. Plastic implants are sometimes used to reshape the nose. Incisions are typically inside the nose and hidden. Sonic rhinoplasty incorporates the use of an ultrasonic device to gently aspirate bone, enabling a refined cosmetic result.[6]

After surgery, nasal packing may be inserted to apply pressure and prevent bleeding or septal hematoma formation. An external plastic splint protects and supports the new shape of the nose during the healing process. If present, nasal packing is usually removed 1 or 2 days after surgery. The splint may be left in place for 1 to 2 weeks.

❖ NURSING MANAGEMENT: NASAL SURGERY

Before surgery, teach patients to notify the HCP about any medications that they take at home. Aspirin-containing drugs and NSAIDs may need to be stopped for 5 days to 2 weeks preoperatively to reduce the risk for bleeding. Encourage smoking cessation to promote postoperative wound healing. During the immediate postoperative period, nursing interventions include (1) ensuring patency of the airway, (2) continuous assessment of respiratory status, (3) monitoring for airway obstruction, (4) pain management, and (5) observation of the surgical site for edema, bleeding, and signs and symptoms of infection.

Teaching is important because the patient must be able to detect complications at home. The patient typically has temporary nasal and/or facial edema and bruising. Cold compresses and elevation of the head can help minimize swelling and discomfort. Teach about activity restrictions aimed at preventing bleeding and injury (no nose blowing, swimming, heavy lifting, strenuous exercise). Sometimes swelling may be slow to resolve, delaying the achievement of a full cosmetic result for up to 1 year.

EPISTAXIS

Epistaxis (nosebleed) most often occurs in adults over age 50. Nosebleeds can be caused by trauma, hypertension, low humidity, upper respiratory tract infections, allergies, sinusitis, foreign bodies, chemical irritants (e.g., street drugs), overuse of decongestant nasal sprays, facial or nasal surgery, anatomic malformation, and tumors.[7] Conditions that prolong bleeding time or change platelet counts may predispose a patient to nosebleeds. Bleeding time may be prolonged if the patient takes aspirin, NSAIDs, warfarin, or other anticoagulant drugs.

About 90% of nosebleeds occur in the anterior part of the nasal cavity and are easily visualized. Anterior bleeding can be self-treated and usually stops spontaneously.

Posterior bleeding occurs more often with older adults secondary to other health problems (e.g., hypertension). Since posterior nosebleeds are closer to the throat, it is often hard to determine how much blood loss has occurred. Posterior bleeding may need medical treatment.

❖ Interprofessional and Nursing Care

Use simple first aid measures to control nosebleeds. These include (1) place the patient in a sitting position, leaning slightly forward with head tilted forward; (2) apply direct pressure by squeezing the entire soft lower part of the nose (nostrils) together for 5 to 15 minutes; and (3) reassure and calm the patient. If bleeding does not stop within 15 minutes, seek medical assistance.

Medical management involves trying to find the location of the bleed. For anterior bleeds, a pledget (nasal tampon) impregnated with anesthetic solution (lidocaine) and/or vasoconstrictive agents (epinephrine) may be placed into the nasal cavity. Absorbable materials, such as oxidized cellulose (surgical), gelatin foam (Gelfoam), or a gelatin-thrombin combination (Floseal), are another option. Packing for anterior bleeds can stay in place for 48 to 72 hours. Silver nitrate may be used to chemically cauterize a specific bleeding point. Thermal cauterization is reserved for more severe bleeding and may require the use of local or general anesthesia.[8]

It may be harder to find the location of a posterior bleed. Posterior bleeds often need packing. Packing with compressed nasal sponges (e.g., Merocel) or epistaxis balloons (e.g., Rapid Rhino) is preferred over the use of traditional Vaseline ribbon gauze because of the ease of placement. Packing is inserted into the nares and advanced along the floor of the nasal cavity. The sponge expands with moisture to fill the nasal cavity and tamponade bleeding. The epistaxis balloon is inflated with air to achieve the same pressure effect (Fig. 26.1). In the absence of a specific nasal device, a size 10F, 12F, or 14F Foley catheter with a 30-mL balloon may be used. A nasal sling (folded 2 × 2–inch gauze pad) may be gently taped under the nares to absorb drainage. If packing does not stop the bleeding, arterial embolization may be needed.

Nasal sponges, packing, and balloons can impair respiratory status. Closely monitor the level of consciousness, heart rate and rhythm, respiratory rate, and O_2 saturation (SpO_2) using pulse oximetry. Observe for any signs of difficulty breathing or swallowing. Because of the increased risk for complications due to location of the injury, all patients with posterior packing should be admitted to a monitored unit for close observation.

Nasal packing is painful because sufficient pressure must be applied to stop the bleeding. The patient should receive appropriate analgesia. Nasal packing predisposes patients to infection from bacteria (e.g., *Staphylococcus aureus*) present in the nasal cavity. Antibiotics effective against staphylococci may be prescribed.

Nasal packing for posterior bleeds may be left in place for 2 to 3 days. Before removal, pre-medicate the patient for pain because

FIG. 26.1 A, Epistaxis balloon. The balloon is inflated after insertion. (Courtesy Boston Medical, Westborough, Mass.) B, Epistaxis balloon in proper position in nares. (From Roberts JR, Hedges JR: *Clinical procedures in emergency medicine*, ed 5, Philadelphia, 2009, Saunders.) C, Method for placing posterior nasal pack. Catheter is passed through the bleeding side of the nose and pulled out through the mouth with a hemostat. Strings are tied to the catheter, and the pack is pulled up behind the soft palate and into the nasopharynx. D, Nasal pack in position in the posterior nasopharynx. Dental roll at the nose helps maintain correct position.

this procedure is uncomfortable. After packing removal, cleanse the nares gently and lubricate them with water-soluble jelly.

Before discharge teach the patient and caregiver about follow-up care. Review how to use saline nasal spray and/or a humidifier. Have the patient sneeze with the mouth open and avoid the use of aspirin-containing products or NSAIDs. Teach the patient to avoid vigorous nose blowing, engaging in strenuous activity, and lifting and straining for 4 to 6 weeks.

ALLERGIC RHINITIS

Allergic rhinitis is inflammation of the nasal mucosa, often in response to a specific allergen. Allergic rhinitis can be classified according to the causative allergen (seasonal or perennial) or the frequency of symptoms (episodic, intermittent, or persistent). *Episodic* refers to symptoms related to sporadic exposure to allergens not typically encountered in the patient's normal environment, such as exposure to animal dander when visiting another person's home. *Intermittent* means that the symptoms are present less than 4 days a week or less than 4 weeks per year. *Persistent* means that symptoms are present more than 4 days a week and for more than 4 weeks per year.

Seasonal rhinitis usually occurs in the spring and fall. It is caused by allergy to pollens from trees, flowers, grasses, or weeds. Attacks may last for several weeks during times when pollen counts are high; then it disappears and often recurs at the same time the next year. *Perennial rhinitis* occurs year-round from exposure to environmental allergens, such as animal dander, dust mites, cockroaches, fungi, and molds. Both seasonal and perennial rhinitis can be classified as episodic, intermittent, or persistent, depending on the duration and frequency of symptoms.

Sensitization to an allergen occurs with initial allergen exposure, which results in the production of antigen-specific immunoglobulin E (IgE) (see Fig. 13.6). After exposure, mast cells and basophils release histamine, cytokines, prostaglandins, and leukotrienes. These cause the early symptoms of sneezing, itching, rhinorrhea, and congestion.[9] 4 to 8 hours after exposure, inflammatory cells infiltrate the nasal tissues, causing and maintaining the inflammatory response. Because symptoms of rhinitis are like those of the common cold, the patient may think the condition is a continuous or repeated cold.

Clinical Manifestations

Manifestations of allergic rhinitis are sneezing; watery, itchy eyes and nose; decreased sense of smell; and thin, watery nasal discharge that can lead to a more sustained mucus production and nasal congestion. Nasal turbinates appear pale, boggy, and swollen. The turbinates may fill the air space and press against the nasal septum. The posterior ends of the turbinates can become so enlarged that they obstruct sinus aeration or drainage and result in sinusitis. With chronic exposure to allergens, the patient may develop a headache, stuffy nose, nasal congestion, and sinus pressure. Nasal polyps and postnasal drip are the most common causes of cough. The patient may report hoarseness and the need to frequently clear the throat.

❖ Interprofessional and Nursing Care

The key step to managing allergic rhinitis is identifying and avoiding triggers of allergic reactions (Table 26.1). Teach the patient to take note when allergic reactions occur and keep a

TABLE 26.1   Patient & Caregiver Teaching

Avoiding Allergens in Allergic Rhinitis

Include the following instructions when teaching a patient or caregiver about allergic rhinitis:

What to Avoid	Specific Approaches
House dust	• Focus on the bedroom. Remove carpeting. Limit furniture. • Put the pillows and mattress in airtight vinyl bags. • Limit clothing in the bedroom to items worn often. Place clothing in airtight, zipper-sealed vinyl clothes bags. • Install a high-efficiency particulate air (HEPA) filter. • Close the air-conditioning vent into room. • Use blinds rather than draperies.
House dust mites	• Wash bedding in hot water (140° F [60° C]). • Wear a mask when vacuuming. • Install a filter on the outlet port of vacuum cleaner. • Avoid sleeping or lying on upholstered furniture. • Keep house temperature and conditions cool and dry.
Mold spores	• The 3 Ds that promote growth of mold spores are darkness, dampness, and drafts. • Ventilate closed rooms and open doors. Consider adding windows to dark rooms and keeping a small light on in closets. • Basement light with a timer that provides light several hours a day may decrease mold growth. • Avoid places where humidity is high (e.g., basements, clothes hampers, greenhouses, barns). Dehumidifiers are rarely helpful.
Pet allergens	• Remove pets from interior of home. • Clean living area thoroughly. • Do not expect instant relief. Symptoms usually do not improve significantly for 1 to 2 months after pet removal.
Pollens	• Stay inside with doors and windows closed during high-pollen season. • Install an air conditioner with an air filter. Wash filters weekly during high-pollen season. • Use your car's air conditioner "recirculation" feature (circulates air inside the car, while shutting off air coming into the vehicle from the outside). • Avoid having plants, especially in the bedroom.
Smoke	• Encourage family and friends to refrain from smoking (if possible) or to go outdoors to smoke. • Presence of a smoker will sabotage any symptom reduction program.

diary of activities that precipitate the reaction. Patients are often more aware of intermittent exposure to an allergen, such as pets, than they are of a more persistent exposure to allergens, such as dust mites, cockroaches, or mold. Identifying triggers is the first step toward avoiding them.

The goal of drug therapy is to reduce inflammation associated with allergic rhinitis, reduce nasal symptoms, minimize associated complications, and maximize quality of life. Nasal corticosteroid sprays are the first-line and most effective treatment for allergic rhinitis.[10] Appropriate oral medication options include H_1-antihistamines, decongestants, and leukotriene receptor antagonists (LTRAs). Intranasal medications include antihistamines, anticholinergics, corticosteroids, cromolyn, and decongestants (Table 26.2).[11]

TABLE 26.2 Drug Therapy

Rhinitis and Sinusitis

Drug	Mechanism of Action	Side Effects	Nursing Actions
Anticholinergic *Nasal Spray* ipratropium bromide (Atrovent)	Blocks nasal cholinergic receptors, reducing nasal secretions in the common cold and nonallergic rhinitis.	Nasal dryness and irritation, nosebleeds may occur. Does not cause systemic side effects.	• May reduce the need for other rhinitis medications.
Antihistamines **First-Generation Agents (Oral)** brompheniramine chlorpheniramine (Chlor-Trimeton) clemastine (Tavist) dexchlorpheniramine diphenhydramine (Benadryl)	Bind with H_1 receptors on target cells, blocking histamine release. Relieve acute symptoms of allergic response (itching, sneezing, rhinorrhea).	Cross blood-brain barrier, often causing sedation and somnolence. Can cause paradoxic stimulation (restlessness, nervousness, insomnia). Anticholinergic side effects (e.g., palpitations, dry mouth, constipation, urinary hesitancy).	• Warn patient that operating machinery and driving may be dangerous because of sedative effect. • Teach patient to report palpitations, change in heart rate, change in bowel or bladder habits. • Teach patient not to use alcohol with antihistamines because of additive depressant effect. • Rapid onset of action, no drug tolerance with prolonged use.
Second-Generation Agents (Oral) cetirizine (Zyrtec) desloratadine (Clarinex) fexofenadine (Allegra) levocetirizine (Xyzal) loratadine (Claritin)	Same as above.	Limited affinity for brain H_1 receptors. Cause minimal sedation, few effects on psychomotor activities or bladder function.	• Teach patient to expect few, if any, side effects. • More expensive than traditional antihistamines. • Rapid onset of action, no drug tolerance with prolonged use.
Second-Generation Agents (Intranasal) azelastine (Astelin) olopatadine (Patanase)	Blocks histamine release and reduces nasal congestion.	Headache, bitter taste, somnolence, nasal irritation.	• Longer use increases risk for rebound vasodilation, which can increase congestion.
Corticosteroids **Nasal Spray** beclomethasone budesonide (Rhinocort) ciclesonide (Omnaris) flunisolide fluticasone (Flonase) fluticasone mometasone (Nasonex) triamcinolone	Inhibits inflammatory response of allergic rhinitis. Decreases mucosal inflammation and facilitates drainage of sinuses. Systemic effects may occur with higher than recommended doses.	At recommended dose, systemic side effects unlikely due to low systemic absorption. Mild transient nasal irritation, mucosal drying, nosebleeds. In rare instances, localized fungal infection with *Candida albicans*.	• Adherence important. Teach patient to use on regular basis and not PRN. • Teach patient to clear nasal passages before use. • Reinforce that spray acts to decrease inflammation and it may take several days or 1–2 wks to achieve maximum effects. • Stop use if nasal infection develops.
Decongestants **Oral** pseudoephedrine (Sudafed)	Stimulates adrenergic receptors and promotes vasoconstriction of superficial vessels in the nose and reduces nasal congestion.	CNS stimulation, causing insomnia, excitation, headache, irritability, increased blood and ocular pressure, dysuria, palpitations, tachycardia.	• Tolerance variable. • Advise patient of adverse reactions. • Patient to inform HCP if preexisting cardiovascular disease, hypertension, diabetes, glaucoma, benign prostatic hyperplasia, hepatic or renal disease present before starting therapy. • Rebound nasal congestion may occur with chronic overusage.
Intranasal (Nasal Spray) oxymetazoline phenylephrine	Same as above.	Same as above.	• Teach patient that these drugs should not be used for >3 days or >3 or 4 times/day. • Rebound nasal congestion may occur. • Addiction possible.
Leukotriene Receptor Antagonists (LTRAs) and Inhibitors **Antagonists** montelukast (Singulair) zafirlukast (Accolate) **Inhibitors** zileuton (Zyflo)	Suppress leukotriene activity, thereby inhibiting airway edema, bronchoconstriction, mucus production, and inflammation (see Fig. 11.2).	Well tolerated. May cause headaches, dizziness, rash, altered liver function, GI changes. *Zafirlukast and zileuton:* Monitor PT levels if patient is taking warfarin.	• Monitor liver function tests periodically while on therapy. Stop if elevated. • Give on empty stomach. • Do not stop therapy without consulting HCP. • Do not use for acute attacks.

Continued

TABLE 26.2 Drug Therapy—cont'd

Rhinitis and Sinusitis

Drug	Mechanism of Action	Side Effects	Nursing Actions
Mast Cell Stabilizer ***Nasal Spray*** cromolyn spray	Suppresses release of histamine and other inflammatory mediators from mast cells.	Minimal side effects. Occasional nasal irritation.	• Reinforce that spray prevents symptoms. • Begin 1 wk before pollen season starts and use throughout pollen season. • For isolated allergy, use prophylactically before exposure to allergen. • When used to treat chronic rhinitis, antihistamine and/or nasal decongestant may be used at the same time.
Combination Cold Medications hydrocodone, pseudo-ephedrine (Rezira oral solution) hydrocodone, chlorpheniramine, pseudo-ephedrine (Zutripro oral solution)	Hydrocodone suppresses cough. Mechanism of action of chlorpheniramine and pseudoephedrine discussed above.	See individual drugs above.	• Potential for misuse with repeated use. • Avoid in patients with head injury, increased ICP, acute abdominal conditions. • Do not use at the same time, or, within 14 days of MAOI drugs. • Increased risk for sedation when used with CNS depressants and/or benzodiazepines.

PT, prothrombin time; *ICP*, intracranial pressure; *MAOI*, monoamine oxidase inhibitor.

Second-generation antihistamines are used before first-generation antihistamines because of their nonsedating effects. Teach patients taking antihistamines to have adequate fluid intake to reduce adverse symptoms. Nasal corticosteroid sprays decrease inflammation with little absorption in the systemic circulation. Therefore systemic side effects are rare. If monotherapy does not relieve symptoms, a 2-drug combination, such as an oral H$_1$-antihistamine and an intranasal corticosteroid, may be helpful.

DRUG ALERT Antihistamines

• First-generation antihistamines (e.g., chlorpheniramine [Chlor-Trimeton]) can cause drowsiness and sedation.
• Warn patients that operating machinery and driving may be dangerous because of the sedative effect.

DRUG ALERT Pseudoephedrine (Sudafed)

• Large doses may cause tachycardia and palpitations, especially in patients with heart disease.
• Overdose in those over 60 years of age may result in central nervous system depression, seizures, and hallucinations.

Immunotherapy (allergy shots) may be used when a specific, unavoidable allergen is identified, and drugs are not tolerated or are ineffective in controlling symptoms. Immunotherapy involves controlled exposure to small amounts of the known allergen through frequent (at least weekly) injections with the goal of decreasing sensitivity. Sublingual or intranasal administration of allergen immunotherapy may an option for select patients. Immunotherapy is discussed in Chapter 13.

ACUTE VIRAL RHINOPHARYNGITIS

Acute viral rhinopharyngitis (nasopharyngitis, common cold) is an infection of the upper respiratory tract. It is the most prevalent infectious disease, with the average adult contracting 1 to 3 colds per year. More than 200 different viruses can cause a common cold. Most are caused by the coronavirus and are mild and self-limiting. Other viruses, such as human respiratory syncytial virus (RSV) and enterovirus, can cause a common cold.

The viruses are contagious. They spread by airborne droplets emitted by the infected person while breathing, talking, sneezing, or coughing. Because they can survive on inanimate objects for up to 3 days, transmission also occurs by direct hand contact. Frequency of the infection increases in winter months when people stay indoors and overcrowding is more common. Other factors that increase susceptibility include fatigue, physical and emotional stress, allergies affecting the nose and throat, and a compromised immune status. Exercise may reduce the number of upper respiratory tract infections.

Symptoms typically begin 2 or 3 days after infection. They may include runny nose, watery eyes, nasal congestion, sneezing, cough, sore throat, fever, headache, and fatigue. Patients are contagious 1 to 2 days before symptom onset and remain contagious until symptoms have subsided. Symptoms may last 2 to 14 days, with typical recovery in 7 to 10 days.

🌿 COMPLEMENTARY & ALTERNATIVE THERAPIES

Echinacea

Scientific Evidence
• Echinacea may slightly reduce the incidence of the common cold.
• Taking echinacea does not appear to reduce the duration of a common cold.

Nursing Implications
• Echinacea is considered safe when used on a short-term basis in recommended doses.
• Caution patients with autoimmune disorders or a tendency toward allergic reactions about using this herb.

Source: Retrieved from *www.nccih.nih.gov/health/echinacea/ataglance.htm*.

❖ Interprofessional and Nursing Care

Interventions are directed at relieving symptoms. Rest, oral fluids, antipyretics, and analgesics are recommended. Warm salt water gargles, ice chips, lozenges, or sprays may help ease a sore throat. Petroleum jelly soothes a raw nose. Saline nasal spray reduces nasal congestion. Antihistamine and decongestant therapy reduce postnasal drip and decreases the severity of cough, nasal obstruction, and nasal discharge. Caution patients to use intranasal decongestant sprays for no more than 3 days to prevent rebound congestion from occurring. Cough suppressants, for irritating, bothersome coughs, may be used, but may not be effective. Patients may ask about vitamin C, echinacea, and zinc products. There is inconclusive evidence to support treatment with these therapies.

Complications include acute bronchitis, sinusitis, otitis media, tonsillitis, and pneumonia. Antibiotics have no effect on viruses. They are an option only if complications are present. Refer to an HCP if there is no improvement in symptoms within 10 to 14 days.

Teach patients to recognize the manifestations of a secondary bacterial infection, such as a temperature higher than 103° F (39.4° C); tender, swollen glands; severe sinus or ear pain; or significantly worsening symptoms. Green, purulent nasal drainage during the later stages of a cold is not uncommon and not always indicative of bacterial infection. In the patient with lung disease, signs of infection include a change in consistency, color, or volume of the sputum. Because infection can progress rapidly, teach the patient with chronic respiratory disease to immediately report sputum changes, increased shortness of breath, and chest tightness.

During the cold season, teach patients with a chronic illness or a compromised immune system to avoid crowded situations and those with obvious cold symptoms. Frequent hand washing and avoiding hand-to-face contact can help prevent direct spread.

INFLUENZA

Influenza (flu) is a highly contagious respiratory illness that causes significant morbidity and mortality. Millions of Americans (about 5% to 20% of U.S. population) contract influenza each year. The flu season begins in September and continues through April of each year, peaking between December to February. More than 310,000 people were hospitalized for flu-related complications in 2016.[12] Although the exact number of flu-related deaths is not known, it is estimated that influenza is responsible for 3000 - 49,000 deaths annually, depending on the strain.[13] Vaccination of high-risk groups may help prevent many of these deaths.

Etiology and Pathophysiology

We classify influenza viruses into 4 serotypes (A, B, C, D). Only A and B cause significant illness in humans. Influenza A is subtyped based on the presence of 2 surface proteins: hemagglutinin (H) and neuraminidase (N). The H antigens enable the virus to enter the cell, and the N antigens facilitate cell-to-cell transmission. As a result, we name influenza A viruses according to their H and N type (e.g., H3N2).

Influenza A is the most common and most virulent flu virus. It can infect a variety of animals as well as humans. More than 100 types of influenza A are found in birds (avian flu), pigs (swine flu), horses, seals, and dogs. When the virus mutates (changes), this allows it to infect different species. When a new viral strain reaches humans, people do not have immunity and the virus can spread quickly around the globe, causing a *pandemic.* For example, type A H1N1 influenza (swine flu) emerged in 2009 and had never been seen in humans before, resulting in a worldwide pandemic. The reemergence of a viral strain that has not circulated for many years can also trigger a pandemic. *Epidemics* are more localized outbreaks, often occurring yearly, caused by variants of already circulating strains of the influenza virus.

Influenza B and C viruses only infect humans. They are not divided into subtypes. Outbreaks of influenza B can cause regional epidemics, but the disease it produces is milder than that caused by influenza A. Influenza C causes mild illness and does not cause epidemics or pandemics. Influenza D only occurs in animals.

Influenza is communicable between humans primarily through infected droplets, inhalation of aerosolized particles, and, to a lesser extent, through direct contact with contaminated surfaces. The virus has an incubation period of 1 to 4 days, with peak transmission risk starting 1 day before onset of symptoms and continuing for 5 to 7 days after a person first becomes sick.[14]

Clinical Manifestations

For some patients, it may be hard to tell between the common cold and flu (Table 26.3). The onset of flu is abrupt. There may be chills, fever, and generalized myalgia, often accompanied by a headache, cough, sore throat, and fatigue. Assessment findings are usually minimal, with normal breath sounds on chest auscultation. In uncomplicated cases, symptoms often subside within 7 days.

Common complications include pneumonia, which can be either primary influenza [viral] pneumonia or secondary bacterial pneumonia, and ear or sinus infections. Dyspnea and diffuse crackles are signs of pulmonary complications. Some patients, especially older adults, have weakness or lethargy that may last for weeks. The patient who develops secondary bacterial pneumonia usually has gradual improvement of influenza symptoms, then worsening cough and purulent sputum. Treatment with antibiotics is usually effective if started early.

Diagnostic Studies

Influenza is often diagnosed based on the patient's health history and physical assessment and the knowledge of other cases of influenza in the community.

TABLE 26.3 Comparison of Common Cold and Influenza

Manifestations and Treatment	Common Cold (Viral Rhinitis)	Influenza
Symptom onset	Appear gradually	Abrupt onset. Within 3–6 hr
Fever	Rare	Characteristically high 102–104° F (38.9–40° C]). Lasts 3–4 days
Headache	Uncommon, but may occur	Common (can be severe)
General aches and pains	Slight	Often severe myalgia
Fatigue and weakness	Sometimes. Usually mild	Usual. Starts early and can last up to 2–3 wks
Exhaustion	Uncommon	Usual at beginning of illness
Stuffy nose	Common	Sometimes
Sneezing	Common	Sometimes
Sore throat	Common	Sometimes
Chest discomfort, cough	Common. Mild to moderate hacking cough	Common
Complications	Sinus congestion. Earache	Bronchitis, pneumonia, acute respiratory failure, ARDS. Can be life-threatening
Prevention	Hand washing. Avoid close contact with anyone who has a cold	Hand washing. Annual vaccination. Antiviral drugs. Avoid close contact with anyone who has the flu
Treatment	Temporary relief of symptoms: rest, hydration, decongestants, acetaminophen or ibuprofen for headache, aches, and pains	Antiviral drugs if given within 24–48 hrs of onset. Rest, hydration, acetaminophen or ibuprofen for headache, aches, and pains

Adapted from CDC Centers for Disease Control and Prevention. Retrieved from *www.cdc.gov/flu/about/qa/coldflu.htm*.

TABLE 26.4 Types of Influenza Immunization

Trivalent (TIV) or Quadrivalent (QIV) Inactivated Influenza Vaccine	Live Attenuated Influenza Vaccine (LSIV)
Trivalent: Protects against 3 different types of influenza virus (2-type A; 1-type B)	Made from weakened influenza virus
Quadrivalent: Protects against 4 different types of influenza virus (2-type A; 2-type B)	
Given by injection	Given as an intranasal spray into both nostrils
Approved for use in people ≥6 mo of age	Approved for healthy people ages 2–49 yrs
	• Children 2–8 yrs and have not had influenza vaccine before need 2 doses (second dose 4 weeks after first dose)
	• Children >9 yrs need 1 dose
	Should NOT be used in:
Should NOT be used in:	• Children <2 yrs or adults >50 yrs
• Infants <6 mo in age	• Pregnant women or women who plan to become pregnant
• Serious allergy/reaction to previous influenza vaccine	
• Guillain-Barré syndrome diagnosed within previous 6 wks	
Can be used in people at increased risk:	Prior to receiving the vaccination, please inform your HCP if you or the person you are caring for have any of the following:
• People of any age with chronic medical conditions	• Immunodeficiency
• Residents of nursing homes and long-term care facilities	• Children or adolescents receiving aspirin or other salicylates
• People who are immunocompromised	• Medical conditions that increase the risk for complications from influenza (chronic heart, lung, liver, kidney, or CNS disorders) diabetes; hemoglobinopathies)
• Pregnant women	• HCPs of high-risk patients because of risk for viral transmission from vaccine (should not care for high-risk patients for 7 days after vaccination)
Most common side effects are injection site reactions, such as pain, redness, and swelling	Adverse effects are rare. When effects do occur, may resemble mild flu with runny nose, nasal congestion, cough, and headache

Viral cultures, once considered the gold standard for diagnosing influenza, have decreased in popularity with the emergence of other rapid testing methods. We can obtain a viral culture from a throat swab, nasopharyngeal swab, expectorated sputum, ET tube sample, or bronchoscopy (bronchial wash). A viral culture can identify which virus (A, B, or another respiratory virus) and which viral strains are present.

Rapid influenza diagnostic tests (RIDTs) can help in the diagnosis by detecting the virus in secretions from the respiratory tract. Depending on the method, the test may be completed in the HCP's office with results available in as little as 5 minutes. The test can help distinguish influenza from other viral and bacterial infections with similar manifestations that may be serious but are treated differently. RIDTs are best used within the first 48 hours of the onset of symptoms. The main disadvantages of the rapid flu test are that it will miss some cases or occasionally be positive when a person does not actually have the flu. Always evaluate test results considering the patient's clinical condition.

❖ Interprofessional and Nursing Care

The most effective strategy for managing influenza is prevention. Two types of flu vaccines are available: inactivated and live attenuated (Table 26.4). Receiving a flu vaccine results in the production of antibodies against the viruses in the vaccine.

The influenza vaccine is changed on a yearly basis, depending on the virus strains the Centers for Disease Control and

Prevention (CDC) determines as being most likely to cause illness in the upcoming flu season. The best time to receive the vaccine is in September or October (before flu exposure) because it takes 2 weeks for full protection to occur. However, the vaccine can be given at any time during the flu season.

> ⚠ **SAFETY ALERT Influenza Vaccination**
> - Advocate for vaccination of all people older than 6 months of age, especially those at high risk (e.g., health care workers, residents of long-term care facilities).
> - Give high priority to groups, such as health care workers, who can transmit influenza to high-risk persons.

Vaccinating healthy people decreases the incidence and risk for transmitting influenza to those who have less ability to cope with the effects of this illness. Many people do not get receive the vaccination despite the obvious benefits. Current vaccines are highly purified, and reactions are extremely rare. Soreness at the injection site is the most reported adverse effect. Contraindications are a history of severe allergic reactions to previous flu vaccine. Patients with anaphylactic hypersensitivity to eggs should discuss the vaccine with their HCP, as alternatives for vaccinating patients with egg allergies are now available.

The primary nursing goals are relief of symptoms and prevention of secondary infection. Unless the patient with influenza is at high risk or complications develop, supportive therapy is often all the patient needs. Rest, hydration, analgesics, and antipyretics can provide symptom relief. Older adults and those with a chronic illness may need hospitalization.

There are several antiviral medications we can use to treat shorten the duration of influenza symptoms and reduce the risk for complications. Zanamivir (Relenza), oseltamivir (Tamiflu), and peramivir (Rapivab) are neuraminidase inhibitors that prevent the virus from being released and spreading to other cells.[15] Zanamivir is given using an inhaler, oseltamivir is available as an oral capsule, and peramivir is given IV. The newest drug is baloxavir marboxil (Xofluza). It is a PA endonuclease inhibitor that works by inhibiting viral replication. Patients receive 1 oral dose. Do not give Xofluza with dairy products or calcium-fortified drinks.

Treatment with antiviral medication should be started as soon as possible in hospitalized patients with influenza, those with severe or complicated illness, or those at high risk for complications. For maximum benefit in the treatment of influenza, therapy should begin within 2 days of the onset of symptoms, but it can be started later based on clinical judgment.

SINUSITIS

Sinusitis affects 1 in every 7 adults. It develops when inflammation or swelling of the mucosa blocks the openings (ostia) in the sinuses, through which mucus drains into the nose (Fig. 26.2). *Rhinosinusitis,* which may accompany sinusitis, is concurrent inflammation or infection of the nasal mucosa. Nasal polyps, foreign bodies, deviated septa, or tumors can cause obstruction of mucus drainage. Secretions that accumulate behind the blocked ostia provide a rich medium for growth of bacteria, viruses, and fungi, all of which may cause infection.

Viral sinusitis may follow an upper respiratory tract infection in which the virus penetrates the mucous membrane and decreases ciliary function. Viral infections usually resolve without treatment in less than 14 days. If symptoms worsen

FIG. 26.2 Location of the sinuses.

after 3 to 5 days or last for longer than 10 days, a secondary bacterial infection may be present. Only 5% to 10% of patients with viral sinusitis develop a bacterial infection and need antibiotic therapy.

Streptococcus pneumoniae, Haemophilus influenzae, and *Moraxella catarrhalis* are the most common causes of bacterial sinusitis.[7] Fungal sinusitis is uncommon. It usually occurs in patients who are debilitated or immunocompromised.

Sinusitis can be classified as acute, subacute, or chronic.[16] *Acute sinusitis* typically begins within 1 week of an upper respiratory tract infection and lasts less than 4 weeks. *Subacute sinusitis* is present when symptoms progress over 4 to 12 weeks. *Chronic sinusitis* (lasting longer than 12 weeks) is a persistent infection usually associated with allergies and nasal polyps. Chronic sinusitis generally results from repeated episodes of acute sinusitis that result in irreversible loss of the normal ciliated epithelium lining the sinus cavity.

Clinical Manifestations

Acute sinusitis causes significant pain over the affected sinus, purulent nasal drainage, nasal obstruction, congestion, fever, and malaise. The patient may appear acutely ill. Inspect the nasal mucosa and palpate the paranasal sinuses for pain. Findings that indicate acute sinusitis include edematous mucosa, discolored purulent nasal drainage, enlarged turbinates, tenderness over the involved frontal and/or maxillary sinuses, and *halitosis* (bad breath). Recurrent headaches are common and may change in intensity with position changes or when secretions drain.

The symptoms of chronic sinusitis are often nonspecific. The patient is rarely febrile. The patient may have facial or dental pain, nasal congestion, and increased drainage. Severe pain and purulent drainage are often absent. Some symptoms mimic those seen with allergies. X-rays or CT scan of the sinuses may help confirm the diagnosis. CT scans may show the sinuses are filled with fluid or a thickened mucous membrane. Nasal endoscopy with a flexible scope may be used to examine the sinuses, obtain a specimen for culture, and restore normal drainage.

As many as 50% of patients with moderate to severe asthma have chronic sinusitis. The exact link between these diseases is unclear. Postnasal drip associated with sinusitis may trigger asthma by stimulating bronchoconstriction. Gastroesophageal reflux disease (GERD) and smoking may increase the risk for a person with asthma developing sinusitis. Appropriate treatment of sinusitis often causes a reduction in asthma symptoms.

❖ Interprofessional and Nursing Care

If allergies are the precipitating cause of sinusitis, teach the patient ways to reduce sinus inflammation and infection, including environmental control of allergens and appropriate drug therapy (see allergic rhinitis discussed earlier in this chapter).

Initial treatment for acute sinusitis focuses on symptom relief. Medications include oral or topical decongestants to promote drainage, intranasal corticosteroids to decrease inflammation, analgesics to relieve pain, and saline nasal spray to relieve congestion. Teach patients using topical decongestants to use the medication for no longer than 4 to 5 days to prevent rebound congestion caused by vasodilation. Saline irrigation of the nasal cavity can rinse nasal passages, promote drainage, and decrease inflammation. Saline nasal spray is available over the counter.

If symptoms worsen or last longer than 1 week, antibiotic therapy may be prescribed. Amoxicillin is the first-line drug of choice. It is taken for 10 to 14 days to prevent the formation of antibiotic-resistant organisms.[17] If symptoms do not resolve, the antibiotic should be changed to amoxicillin with clavulanate, a fluoroquinolone, or a 2nd or 3rd generation cephalosporin.

With chronic sinusitis, mixed bacterial flora is often present and infections are hard to eliminate. Broad-spectrum antibiotics may be used for 4 to 6 weeks. Patient and caregiver teaching for acute and chronic sinusitis is shown in Table 26.5.

Medical therapy may not relieve the symptoms of some patients with persistent, recurrent, or chronic sinus illnesses. These patients may need nasal endoscopic surgery to relieve blockage caused by hypertrophy or septal deviation. This is usually done as an outpatient procedure using local anesthesia. Propel, a self-expanding implant, can be placed directly in the sinus during surgery. Propel helps maintain patency to the sinus cavity after surgery and provide local corticosteroid delivery directly to the sinus lining before dissolving after 30 days.

OBSTRUCTION OF NOSE AND SINUSES

Nasal Polyps

Nasal polyps are soft, painless, benign (noncancerous) growths that form slowly in response to repeated inflammation of the sinus or nasal mucosa. They are most common in adults over age 40 and are twice as likely to occur in men than women.[18] Polyps, which appear as chronic yellow, gray, or pink semitransparent projections in the naris, can exceed the size of a grape.

Small polyps are typically asymptomatic. Manifestations of larger polyps include nasal obstruction, nasal discharge (usually clear mucus), and speech distortion. Topical and systemic corticosteroids are primary therapies used to shrink nasal polyps. Endoscopic or laser surgery can remove nasal polyps, but recurrence is common.

Foreign Bodies

A variety of foreign bodies may potentially lodge in the upper respiratory tract of adults, but these are rare occurrences. Some situations may be the result of trauma or found in patients with mental illness. Foreign bodies may be inorganic or organic. Inorganic foreign bodies, such as plastic or metal objects, may cause no symptoms and be incidentally discovered on routine examination. Organic foreign bodies, such as food, may cause a local inflammatory reaction and nasal discharge, which may become purulent and foul smelling if the object stays in the nasal cavity for an extended time. Foreign bodies can cause pain, difficulty breathing, and nasal bleeding.

Foreign bodies should be removed from the nose through the route of entry. Sneezing or blowing the nose with the opposite nostril closed may be effective in removing the foreign object. Avoid irrigating the nose or pushing the object backward, since these could cause aspiration and airway obstruction. If sneezing or blowing the nose does not remove the object, consult an HCP.

▎ PROBLEMS OF PHARYNX

ACUTE PHARYNGITIS

Acute *pharyngitis* is an acute inflammation of the pharyngeal walls. It may include the tonsils, palate, and uvula. It can be caused by a viral, bacterial, or fungal infection. Viral pharyngitis accounts for about 90% of cases. Bacterial pharyngitis ("strep throat") usually results from group A β-hemolytic streptococci and accounts for 5% to 10% of cases.

Fungal pharyngitis, such as candidiasis, can develop with the prolonged use of antibiotics or inhaled corticosteroids. It can also occur in immunosuppressed patients, especially those with human immunodeficiency virus (HIV) infection. Other causes of pharyngitis include dry air, smoking, GERD, allergy and postnasal drip, ET intubation, chemical fumes, and cancer.

Clinical Manifestations

Symptoms of acute pharyngitis range in severity from a "scratchy" throat to pain so severe that swallowing is difficult. Because both viral and streptococcal infections appear as a red and edematous pharynx (with or without patchy exudates), it may be hard to distinguish between them.

TABLE 26.5 Patient & Caregiver Teaching

Acute or Chronic Sinusitis

Include the following instructions when teaching the patient and caregiver about management of sinusitis:

1. Get plenty of rest to help body fight infection and promote recovery.
2. Keep well hydrated by drinking 6 to 8 glasses of water per day to loosen secretions.
3. Take hot showers. Use a steam inhaler (15-minute vaporization of boiled water), bedside humidifier, or nasal saline spray to promote secretion drainage.
4. Apply warm, damp towels around nose, cheeks, and eyes to ease facial pain.
5. Sleep with head elevated to help sinuses drain and reduce congestion.
6. Report a temperature of 100.4° F (38° C) or higher, which indicates infection.
7. Follow prescribed medication plan:
   • Take analgesics to relieve pain.
   • Take decongestants/expectorants to relieve swelling.
   • Take antibiotics (as prescribed) for infection. Be sure to take entire prescription and report continued symptoms or a change in symptoms.
   • Use nasal sprays to relieve congestion.
8. Perform nasal saline washes once or twice a day to wash sinuses.
9. Do not smoke and avoid exposure to smoke (will irritate and will worsen symptoms).
10. If allergies predispose to sinusitis, follow instructions about environmental control, drug therapy, and immunotherapy to reduce the inflammation and prevent sinus infection.

Four classic manifestations present in bacterial pharyngitis include: (1) fever greater than 100.4° F (38° C); (2) anterior cervical lymph node enlargement; (3) tonsillar or pharyngeal exudate; and (4) absence of cough.[19] However, appearance is not always diagnostic. When 2 or 3 of these criteria are present, a rapid antigen detection test and/or a throat culture can help establish the cause and direct treatment. White, irregular patches on the oropharynx suggest fungal infection with *Candida albicans*.

❖ Interprofessional and Nursing Care

The goals of nursing management are infection control, symptom relief, and prevention of secondary complications.

For viral pharyngitis, antibiotics are not recommended. For bacterial pharyngitis caused by group A β-hemolytic streptococci, penicillin is the drug of choice. This antibiotic must be taken several times a day for a full 10 days to prevent complications, such as rheumatic fever. For patients allergic to penicillin, erythromycin and clindamycin are appropriate substitutes.[20] Other antibiotics, such as azithromycin (Zithromax) or a 1st generation cephalosporin, are options. Most people with streptococcal infections are contagious until they have been on antibiotics for 24 to 48 hours. Repeat throat cultures after antibiotic therapy are not required.

Candida infections are treated with nystatin, an antifungal antibiotic. Teach patients to swish the preparation in their mouths for as long as possible before swallowing it. Treatment should continue until symptoms are gone. Patients taking inhaled corticosteroids are at risk for infection with *Candida* organisms. Thoroughly rinsing the mouth with water after using corticosteroids can prevent this infection.

Teach patients to use ibuprofen or acetaminophen for pain relief. Encourage the patient to increase fluid intake. For symptom relief, have patients to gargle with warm salt water (½ tsp of salt in 8 oz of water); drink warm or cold liquids; and suck on popsicles, hard candies, or throat lozenges. Cool, bland liquids and gelatin will not irritate the pharynx. Citrus juices are often irritating. Encourage the patient to use a cool mist vaporizer or humidifier.

PERITONSILLAR ABSCESS

Peritonsillar abscess is a complication of tonsillitis. It is most often caused by group A β-hemolytic streptococci. The abscess causes pain, swelling, and blockage of the throat (when severe), threatening airway patency. The patient may have a high fever, chills, leukocytosis, difficulty swallowing, and a muffled voice. Treatment consists of IV antibiotic therapy and needle aspiration or incision and drainage of the abscess. In some cases an emergency tonsillectomy is done or an elective tonsillectomy is scheduled after the infection has subsided.

▌ PROBLEMS OF LARYNX AND TRACHEA

LARYNGEAL POLYPS

Laryngeal polyps develop on the vocal cords from vocal abuse (e.g., excessive talking, singing) or irritation (e.g., intubation, cigarette smoking). The most common sign is hoarseness. Polyps are treated conservatively with voice rest and adequate hydration. Large polyps may cause dysphagia, dyspnea, and

stridor and may need surgically removed. Polyps are usually benign but may be removed because they can become cancerous.

ACUTE LARYNGITIS

Acute laryngitis is swelling and inflammation of the voice box (larynx). A virus (e.g., flu, common cold) is the most common cause. Other causes include inflammatory or infectious conditions of the upper respiratory tract (e.g., tonsillitis, acute bronchitis), overuse of one's voice (e.g., yelling loudly at a concert or a sporting event), exposure to smoke-filled environments, or chemical inhalation.

The classic hallmark signs of acute laryngitis include a tingling or burning sensation at the back of the throat, a persistent need to clear the throat, and hoarseness, which may be accompanied by complete loss of voice. The patient may have a low-grade fever, persistent cough, or feeling of fullness in the throat. Symptoms will appear suddenly, increase in severity over 2 to 3 days, then gradually subside over the next 7 to 10 days as the condition improves. It usually resolves within 21 days.

Diagnosis of acute laryngitis is made based on the history, clinical presentation, and changes in voice. Treatment for acute laryngitis is supportive. The patient is strongly encouraged to limit use of the larynx. This includes no talking or singing, which realistically is almost impossible to do. Patients will want to whisper when communicating but whispering places increased strain on the vocal cords that may worsen the pain. Acetaminophen, cough suppressants, throat lozenges, and use of a humidifier are helpful for throat discomfort.

Have the patient increase fluid intake. They should avoid caffeine and alcohol, which may worsen a sore throat. Encourage smoking cessation. If a bacterial cause is known, such as acute bronchitis or tonsillitis, antibiotics should help resolve the condition. If symptoms last longer than 3 weeks, patients should return to their HCP for further investigation and treatment.

AIRWAY OBSTRUCTION

Acute airway obstruction is a medical emergency. Airway obstruction can be caused by aspiration of food or a foreign body, allergic reactions, edema and inflammation caused by infections or burns, peritonsillar or retropharyngeal abscesses, cancer, laryngeal or tracheal stenosis, and trauma.

Airway obstruction may be partial or complete. The presentation of an airway obstruction often depends on the cause of the obstruction and/or location of the blockage. For example, objects lodged within the larynx may cause voice hoarseness or complete airway obstruction. Tracheal obstruction may produce wheezing. Objects lodged within the lower respiratory system (e.g., bronchus) may produce a cough or decreased air entry on the affected side.

Manifestations include choking, stridor, use of accessory muscles, suprasternal and intercostal retractions, flaring nostrils, wheezing, restlessness, tachycardia, cyanosis, and change in level of consciousness.[21] Prompt assessment and treatment are essential because partial obstruction may quickly progress to complete obstruction. Complete airway obstruction can result in permanent brain damage or death if not corrected within 3 to 5 minutes.

Your immediate priority is to ensure the patient has a patent airway. Interventions to reestablish a patent airway include the obstructed airway (Heimlich) maneuver (see Appendix A), cricothyroidotomy, ET intubation, or tracheostomy. Unexplained partial airway obstruction or recurrent symptoms indicate the need for more tests, including a chest x-ray, laryngoscopy, and rigid bronchoscopy.

TRACHEOSTOMY

A **tracheostomy** is a surgically created stoma (opening) in the anterior part of the trachea (Fig. 26.3, *A*). A tracheostomy may be done to (1) establish a patent airway, (2) bypass an upper airway obstruction, (3) facilitate removal of secretions, (4) permit long-term mechanical ventilation, and (5) assist with weaning from mechanical ventilation.[22]

The tracheostomy tube is shorter in length and slightly wider in diameter than an ET tube. This makes it easier to keep the tube clean and facilitates better oral and bronchial hygiene.

A

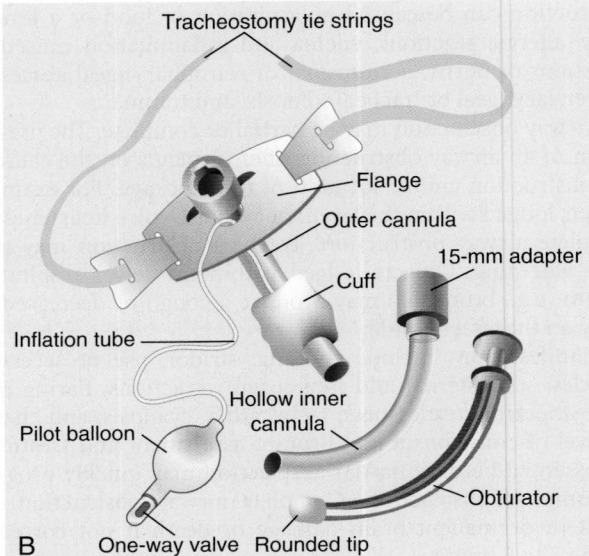

B

FIG. 26.3 Tracheostomy tube. **A,** Placement of a tracheostomy tube. **B,** Parts of a tracheostomy tube.

A tracheostomy (compared to an ET tube) may increase patient comfort because no tube is present in the mouth. There is also less risk for long-term damage to vocal cords.

A variety of tracheostomy tubes are available to meet specific patient needs (Table 26.6). All tracheostomy tubes have a faceplate, or *flange,* which rests against the neck, and an *obturator,* which is used to help insert the tube. Many tracheostomy tubes have an *outer cannula* (which keeps the airway patent), and an *inner cannula* (which can be disposable or nondisposable and removed for cleaning) (Fig. 26.3).

Cuffed and *uncuffed* tracheostomy tubes are available. A tracheostomy tube with an inflated cuff (balloon) is used the most, especially if the patient needs mechanical ventilation. The cuff, inflated via the *balloon inflation port* on the tracheostomy tube, ensures the patient receives the volume of air delivered by the ventilator, and helps decrease the risk for aspiration. Cuffless tubes are primarily used for patients with longer term tracheostomies, when mechanical ventilation is not required and the risk for aspiration has decreased. They make talking and eating easier.

The outer and/or inner cannula may be *fenestrated* or *non-fenestrated.* A *fenestrated tube* has an opening (a hole) on the dorsal surface of the tube. This tube promotes spontaneous breathing. For example, with the use of a cuffed, fenestrated tracheostomy tube, when the cuff is deflated and the inner cannula removed, air can pass from the lungs up through the opening in the tracheostomy tube through the vocal cords and larynx, into the upper airway, and out the mouth and nose. This allows the patient to breathe spontaneously and speak with the tracheostomy tube in place. When the cuff is reinflated and the inner cannula reinserted, air cannot pass from the lungs through the vocal cords.

Most patients who need mechanical ventilation first have an ET tube, because we can quickly insert one an emergency. Care of the patient with an ET tube is discussed in Chapter 65. When swelling, trauma, or upper airway obstruction prevents ET intubation, an emergent **surgical cricothyroidotomy** (also known as a cricothyrotomy) is needed. This procedure, which can be completed in minutes, involves making an incision through the skin and cricothyroid membrane on the anterior surface of the neck.

Most surgical tracheostomies are done in the operating room using general anesthesia. The HCP makes a horizontal incision on the anterior part of the trachea. After inserting the tracheostomy tube, the HCP sutures the incision and applies a sterile dressing.

A newer surgical technique is the *percutaneous tracheostomy.* Using local anesthesia, sedation, and under video-assisted guidance, the ET tube is withdrawn up to the level of the glottis. A needle is placed between the second and third tracheal rings, into the middle of the trachea. A dilator is then placed over the top of the needle. The HCP makes the opening progressively larger (with increasingly larger dilators) until the hole is big enough for insertion of the tracheostomy tube. Percutaneous tracheostomy approaches have less risk for bleeding and fewer postoperative complications.[23] Both surgical and percutaneous tracheostomies may be done at the patient's bedside in the emergency department or ICU.

❖ NURSING MANAGEMENT: TRACHEOSTOMY

◆ Acute Care

Before the tracheostomy procedure (and time permitting), explain the purpose of the procedure to both the patient and

TABLE 26.6 Nursing Management of Tracheostomies

Tube and Characteristics	Nursing Management

Tracheostomy tube with cuff and pilot balloon (Fig. 26.3, *B*)
 	
When properly inflated, low-pressure, high-volume cuff distributes cuff pressure over large area, minimizing pressure on tracheal wall.
	Procedure for cuff inflation
	• Mechanically ventilated patient:
	   • *Minimal occlusion volume (MOV) technique* recommended. Place stethoscope over lateral neck (beside trachea). Inflate cuff by slowly injecting air into the cuff until no leak (sound) is heard at peak inspiratory pressure (end of ventilator inspiration).
	   • *Minimal leak technique (MLT).* Involves inflating the cuff to minimal occlusion pressure and then withdrawing 0.1–0.5 mL of air. No longer recommended due to risk for silent aspiration.
	   • *Spontaneously breathing patient:* Inflate cuff by slowly injecting air into the cuff until no sound is heard after deep breath or during inhalation with bag-valve-mask. If using MLT, remove 0.1–0.5 mL of air while maintaining seal. MLT should not be used if there is risk for aspiration.
	   • *Immediately after cuff inflation (both groups):* Verify pressure is within accepted range (20–30 cm H_2O, 15–22 mmHg) with a manometer. Record cuff pressure and volume of air used for cuff inflation in chart.
	Care of patients with an inflated cuff:
	• Monitor and record cuff pressure q8hr. Cuff pressure should be 20–30 cm H_2O (15–22 mm Hg) to allow adequate tracheal capillary perfusion. If needed, remove or add air to the pilot tubing using a syringe and stopcock. Afterward, verify cuff pressure is within accepted range with manometer.
	• Report inability to keep the cuff inflated or need to use progressively larger volumes of air to keep cuff inflated. Potential causes include tracheal dilation at the cuff site or a crack or slow leak in the housing of the 1-way inflation valve. If the leak is due to tracheal dilation, the HCP may cannulate the patient with a larger tube.

Fenestrated tracheostomy tube (Shiley, Portex) with cuff, inner cannula, and decannulation plug (Fig. 26.6) When nonfenestrated inner cannula is removed, cuff deflated, and decannulation plug inserted, air flows around tube, through fenestration in outer cannula, and up over vocal cords. Patient can then speak. A fenestrated inner cannula can be used to facilitate cleaning.	• If possible, assess risk for aspiration before removing inner cannula. A speech pathologist may be able to assist if available. Deflate cuff. Note coughing. • *Never* insert decannulation plug in tracheostomy tube until cuff is deflated and nonfenestrated inner cannula removed. Otherwise, patient will be prevented from breathing (no air inflow). This will precipitate a respiratory arrest. • Assess for signs of dyspnea and/or respiratory distress when a fenestrated cannula is first used. If this occurs, remove the cap, insert a nonfenestrated inner cannula, reinflate the cuff, and notify the HCP. • A nonfenestrated inner cannula must be used to suction patient to prevent tracheal damage from suction catheter passing through fenestrated openings. • Cuff management as described above.
Talking tracheostomy tube (Portex with cuff, 2 external tubings) Has 2 tubings, one leading to cuff and second to opening above the cuff. When port is connected to air source, air flows out of opening and up over the vocal cords.	• Patient must be awake, alert, and hemodynamically stable. • Must be able to tolerate cuff deflation and exhale around the tracheostomy tube. • When patient desires to speak, deflate cuff, and connect port to compressed air (or O_2). Be certain to identify correct tubing. If gas enters the cuff, it will overinflate and rupture, requiring an emergency tube change. Use lowest flow (typically 4–6 L/min) that results in speech. Patient may not tolerate high flows. • Give O_2 via tracheal collar or O_2 adaptor on speaking valve. • Observe for any signs of dyspnea and/or respiratory distress. • Disconnect flow when patient does not want to speak to prevent mucosal dehydration. • Cuff management as described above.
Tracheostomy tube (Bivona Fome-Cuf) with foam-filled cuff Cuff is filled with plastic foam. Before insertion, cuff is deflated. After insertion, cuff self-inflates. Pilot tubing is not capped. Does not require cuff pressure monitoring. Patient cannot speak with this tube.	• Before insertion, withdraw all air from the cuff using a 20-mL syringe. Cap pilot balloon tubing to prevent reentry of air. • After tracheostomy is inserted, remove cap from pilot tubing, allowing cuff to passively reinflate. Cuff is always inflated on this tube. • Do not inject air into tubing or cap pilot balloon tubing while it is in patient. Air will flow in and out in response to pressure changes (head turning). Place tag on tubing to alert staff not to cap or inflate cuff. • Tube tends to collect moisture and secretions while patient is on the ventilator. • Deflate cuff daily via pilot balloon to evaluate integrity of cuff. Assess ability to easily deflate cuff. Difficulty deflating cuff indicates a need for tube change. If aspirate returns with air, cuff is no longer intact. • Tube can be used for up to 1 month in patients on home mechanical ventilation. • Good choice for patients who need an inflated cuff at home, since teaching about cuff pressure is simplified.

caregiver. If the patient is having the tracheostomy in the operating room, follow all hospital policies and procedures for preparing the patient for surgery (see care of the preoperative patient in Chapter 17).

If the procedure is being done at the patient's bedside, ensure all appropriate personnel, including respiratory therapist, are present. Emergency resuscitation equipment, including a bag-valve-mask (BVM), should be readily available and functional.

Record vital signs, including heart rate, respiratory rate and rhythm, BP, and SpO_2. Ensure an existing IV line is patent and that bedside suction is working. Help assemble and set up all necessary equipment. Position the patient supine. Give analgesia and sedation as ordered by the HCP, ensuring correct identification of times and dosages. Monitor patient response to analgesia and/or sedatives. Observe patient's tolerance to the procedure.

Immediately after the procedure, the tracheostomy cuff (balloon) is inflated. We use several different methods to confirm tracheostomy tube placement: (1) auscultation of the patient's chest for air entry, (2) end-tidal CO_2 capnography, and (3) passage of a suction catheter through the tracheostomy tube. After placement is confirmed, the ET tube (if present) is removed.

TABLE 26.7 Complications of Tracheostomy

Closely monitor patients with a tracheostomy for the following potential complications:
- Air leak
- Airway obstruction
- Altered body image
- Aspiration
- Bleeding
- Fistula formation
- Impaired cough
- Infection: wound or respiratory tract
- Subcutaneous emphysema
- Tracheal necrosis
- Tracheal stenosis
- Tube displacement

FIG. 26.4 Suctioning tracheostomy with closed system suction catheter. (From Potter PA, Perry AG: *Basic nursing: Essentials for practice*, ed 7, St Louis, 2011, Mosby.)

The tracheostomy tube is sutured and secured in place with cotton tracheostomy ties, tracheostomy tapes, or Velcro straps.

Monitor and record the patient's heart rate, respiratory rate, BP, and SpO$_2$. SpO$_2$ readings should remain stable. Note and record the mechanical ventilator settings, including mode, FIO$_2$, and positive end-expiratory pressure (PEEP). (Care of the patient receiving mechanical ventilation is discussed in Chapter 65.) Observe the amount of blood at the tracheostomy insertion site. Notify the HCP if bleeding persists. A chest x-ray should be obtained after the procedure. Many different complications can occur because of tracheostomy (Table 26.7). You must be aware of them, especially airway obstruction, bleeding, and infection.

There is considerable variation in the care of a patient with a new tracheostomy. In some places, it is the nurse who is primarily responsible; in others, it is a shared responsibility between nursing and respiratory therapy. You need to be familiar with your agency's policies and procedures. The following discussion highlights general guidelines when caring for a patient with a tracheostomy during the first few days after the procedure.

At a minimum, you must assess the tracheostomy site every shift. Confirm the patency of the tracheostomy tube. Observe the site for any redness, inflammation, edema, ulceration, or signs of infection. Sterile dressing changes should be done every 12 hours. Clean around the stoma with normal saline and apply a sterile pre-cut dressing around the tracheostomy tube site. You can complete dressing changes more often based on your assessment.

Because an inflated tracheostomy cuff exerts pressure on the tracheal mucosa, it is important to inflate the cuff with the least volume of air needed to obtain an airway seal. We can measure cuff inflation pressure with a hand-held cuff manometer. Monitor the pressure at least every 8 hours. Cuff inflation pressure should not exceed 20 to 25 cm H$_2$O. Higher pressures may compress tracheal capillaries, limit blood flow, and predispose the patient to tracheal necrosis. The minimal occlusion volume (MOV) is one way we often use to inflate the tracheostomy cuff (Table 26.6). Routine cuff deflation is not recommended.[24]

Suction the airway via the tracheostomy tube as needed (Fig. 26.4 and Table 26.8). Try to avoid suctioning through the newly created tracheostomy in the first few hours after the procedure, as this may aggravate discomfort and promote bleeding. Suctioning may be done using sterile glove and catheter technique, or an existing in-line suction catheter. Each time the patient is suctioned, note and record the amount, color, clarity,

and patient tolerance to the procedure. At first, patients should receive humidified air to compensate for the loss of the upper airway to warm and moisturize secretions. Humidification is essential to keep secretions thin and decrease formation of mucous plugs.

If the inner cannula is disposable, replace as per manufacturer and agency guidelines. Clean a nondisposable inner cannula at least every shift. Cleaning removes mucus from the inside of the tube to prevent airway obstruction (Table 26.9).

Change the tracheostomy tapes after the first 24 hours and then as needed (Fig. 26.5 and Table 26.9). A 2-person technique, 1 person to stabilize the tracheostomy and the other to change the tapes, is best practice to ensure that the tracheostomy does not become accidentally dislodged during the procedure. In some places, the HCP and/or respiratory therapist may complete this task. At the end of the procedure, place 2 fingers underneath the tapes to ensure they are not too tight around the neck.

When turning and repositioning the patient, take care not to dislodge the tracheostomy tube. Because tube replacement may be difficult in the immediate postoperative period, several precautions are required, including (1) keep a replacement tube of equal or smaller size at the bedside, readily available for emergency reinsertion; (2) do not change tracheostomy tapes for at least 24 hours after the surgical procedure; and (3) if needed, the HCP performs the first tube change usually no sooner than 7 days after the tracheostomy.

If the tube is accidentally dislodged, immediately call for help. While waiting for the HCP, a respiratory therapist, or other designated individual to arrive, several options may be used (depending on your nursing scope of practice and specific agency policies and procedures). It is essential that you know and understand your role and scope of practice for care of the patient with a tracheostomy.

Immediately call for help. Quickly assess the patient's level of consciousness, ability to breathe, and the presence or absence of any respiratory distress. If respiratory distress is present, you can quickly use a hemostat to spread the opening where the tube was displaced. Insert the obturator in the replacement (spare) tracheostomy tube, lubricate with saline, and insert the tube into the stoma. Once the tube is inserted, remove the obturator at once so that air can flow through the tube. Another option is to insert a suction catheter to allow passage of air and serve as a guide for insertion. Thread the tracheostomy tube over the

TABLE 26.8 Suctioning a Tracheostomy

Assess the need for suctioning hourly. Indications include visible coughing, coarse crackles or wheezes over large airways, moist cough, increase in peak inspiratory pressure on mechanical ventilator, and restlessness or agitation. Neurologic patients may not show any signs and/or symptoms of the need to be suctioned, so suctioning once per shift (at minimum) is recommended. Do not suction routinely.

1. If suctioning is indicated, explain procedure to patient.
2. Collect necessary sterile equipment: suction catheter (no larger than half the lumen of the tracheostomy tube), sterile water, cup, and personal protective equipment (PPE). If a closed tracheal suction system is used, the catheter is enclosed in a plastic sleeve and reused (Fig. 26.4). No other equipment is needed.
3. Check suction source and regulator. Adjust suction pressure to no greater than 125 mm Hg pressure with tubing occluded.
4. Assess heart rate and rhythm, respiratory rate and SpO_2 to provide baseline for detecting changes in patient condition during suctioning.
5. Wash hands and put on PPE.
6. Use sterile technique to open package, fill cup with sterile water, put on sterile gloves, and connect catheter to suction tubing. Designate one hand as contaminated for (1) connecting and disconnecting the tubing at the suction catheter, (2) using the manual bag-valve-mask (BVM), and (3) operating the suction control. Suction sterile water through the catheter to test the system.
7. Provide preoxygenation for a minimum of 30 seconds by (1) adjusting ventilator to deliver 100% O_2 or (2) using a reservoir-equipped BVM connected to 100% O_2. The method chosen depends on whether the patient is attached to a mechanical ventilator or has a tracheostomy tube in place but is spontaneously breathing and receiving supplemental O_2. The patient who has a long-term chronic tracheostomy and is not acutely ill may be able to tolerate suctioning without using a BVM.
8. Gently insert catheter *without suction* to the point at which the patient coughs. Do *not* insert the catheter until you meet resistance (this is the carina, and repeated trauma with suction catheter can promote bleeding). Apply suction as you slowly begin to withdraw the catheter.
9. Apply continuous suction for no more than 10 to 15 seconds.
10. Observe the patient during the suctioning procedure. Immediately stop suctioning and remove the suction catheter from the patient's trachea if the patient becomes bradycardic or hypotensive, a dysrhythmia occurs, or SpO_2 decreases to less than 90%. A vagal response may have occurred.
11. After each suction pass, wait at least 30 seconds before suctioning again. Always hyperoxygenate for at least 30 seconds (via mechanical ventilator or BVM with 5 or 6 breaths) in between each suctioning pass.
12. Repeat procedure until airway is clear. Limit insertion of suction catheter to as few times as possible. If airway is not clear after 3 suction passes, allow the patient to rest before additional suctioning.
13. Return O_2 concentration to prior setting.
14. Rinse catheter. If using the in-line suction catheter (via mechanical ventilation), ensure that normal saline used to flush out the suction catheter does not enter the patient's airway. For disposable suction catheters, dispose of catheter by wrapping it around fingers of gloved hand and pulling glove over catheter. Discard equipment in proper waste container.
15. Suction the oropharynx or use mouth suction.
16. Reassess heart rate and rhythm and SpO_2. Auscultate to assess changes in lung sounds.
17. Record time, amount, and character of secretions and patient response to suctioning.

TABLE 26.9 Tracheostomy Care

The following are general guidelines for basic tracheostomy care. Become familiar with the specific policies and/or procedures in your agency:

1. Explain procedure to patient.
2. Use tracheostomy care kit or collect necessary sterile equipment (e.g., suction catheter, 1 pair sterile gloves, 1 pair nonsterile gloves, water basin, tracheostomy ties, tube brush or pipe cleaners, 4 × 4–inch gauze pads, sterile water or normal saline, tracheostomy dressing [optional]). NOTE: Clean rather than sterile technique is used at home.
3. Place patient in semi-Fowler's position.
4. Assemble needed materials on bedside table next to patient.
5. Wash hands. Put on PPE.
6. Auscultate chest sounds. If wheezes or coarse crackles are present, suction the patient if unable to cough up secretions (Table 26.8). Remove soiled dressing and clean gloves.
7. Open sterile equipment, pour sterile H_2O or normal saline into 2 compartments of sterile container or 2 basins, and put on sterile gloves. NOTE: Hydrogen peroxide (3%) is only used if an infection is present. If it is used, rinse the inner cannula and skin with sterile H_2O or normal saline afterward to prevent trauma to tissue.
8. If present, unlock and remove inner cannula. Many tracheostomy tubes do not have inner cannulas. Care for these tubes includes all steps except for inner cannula care.
9. Replace a disposable inner cannula with a new cannula. With a non-disposable cannula:
   • Immerse inner cannula in sterile solution and clean inside and outside of cannula using tube brush or pipe cleaners.
   • Rinse cannula in sterile solution. Remove from solution and shake to dry.
   • Insert inner cannula into outer cannula with the curved part downward, and lock in place.
10. Remove dried secretions from stoma using 4 × 4–inch gauze pad soaked in sterile water or saline. Gently pat area around the stoma dry. Be sure to clean under the tracheostomy flange (faceplate), using cotton swabs to reach this area.
11. Place dressing around tube (Fig. 26.5). Use a pre-cut tracheostomy dressing or unlined gauze. Do not cut the gauze because threads may be inhaled or wrap around the tracheostomy tube. Change the dressing as needed. Wet dressings promote infection and stoma irritation.
12. Change tracheostomy tapes, using a 2-person change technique. Tie tracheostomy tapes securely with room for 2 fingers between tapes and skin (Fig. 26.5). To prevent accidental tube removal, secure the tracheostomy tube by gently applying pressure to the flange of the tube during the tape changes. *Do not change tracheostomy tapes for 24 hours after the tracheostomy procedure.*
13. Some patients prefer tracheostomy tapes made of Velcro, which are easier to adjust.
14. Repeat care 3 times/day and as needed.

Cover the stoma with a sterile dressing and provide ventilation with the BVM over the nose and mouth. If a patient has had a total laryngectomy, there will be complete separation between the upper airway and trachea. Ventilate this patient through the tracheostomy stoma. Severe dyspnea may progress to respiratory arrest.

? CHECK YOUR PRACTICE

You are caring for a patient who had a surgically created tracheostomy 6 hours ago. While suctioning the patient, he coughs, dislodging the tracheostomy tube.
• What should you do?

catheter and remove the suction catheter. Trying to reinsert will be easier if the stoma tract is mature or older than 1 week.

If the tube cannot be replaced because of tract immaturity (less than 1 week old) or other circumstances, immediately place the patient in semi-Fowler's position to decrease dyspnea.

FIG. 26.5 Changing tracheostomy tapes. **A,** A slit is cut about 1 in (2.5 cm) from the end. The slit end is put into the opening of the cannula. **B,** A loop is made with the other end of the tape. **C,** The tapes are tied together with a double knot on the side of the neck. **D,** A Velcro tracheostomy tube holder. (*D,* Courtesy Dale Medical Products.)

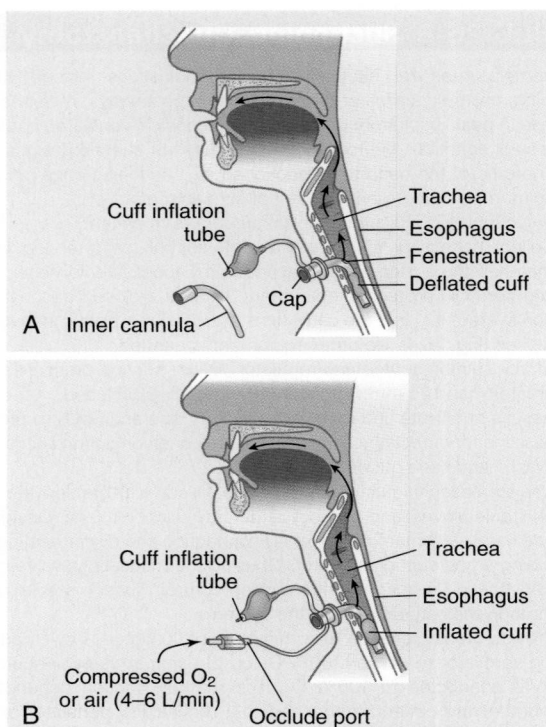

FIG. 26.6 Speaking tracheostomy tubes. **A,** Fenestrated tracheostomy tube with cuff deflated, inner cannula removed, and tracheostomy tube capped to allow air to pass over the vocal cords. **B,** Speaking tracheostomy tube. One tube is used for cuff inflation. The second tube is connected to a source of compressed air or O_2. When the port on the second tube is occluded, air flows up over the vocal cords, allowing speech with an inflated cuff.

◆ Chronic Care

Some patients will never be able to be weaned from mechanical ventilation and will need a tracheostomy for life. Care of the patient with a long-term tracheostomy includes all the same care as patients with a new tracheostomy. This includes observing the tracheostomy site, cleaning the inner cannula, suctioning, and changing tracheostomy tapes.

The tracheostomy tube should be changed around 1 month after the first tube change and every 1 to 3 months thereafter. When a tracheostomy has been in place for several months, the healed tract should be well formed. Changing the tracheostomy tube is important as it permits assessment of the stoma and cleaning of the tube. The patient may be taught to observe for signs and symptoms of infection and how to change the tube at home using a clean technique. Engaging patients to take part in their care may help decrease the incidence of complications, including infection, and promote an overall feeling of well-being.

◆ Swallowing Dysfunction

An inflated tracheostomy tube cuff may result in swallowing problems by interfering with the normal function of muscles used to swallow. Therefore, for long-term tracheostomy patients, it is important to evaluate the patient's swallowing ability and risk for aspiration.

A speech therapist is often the one who assesses the patient's ability to swallow. Using different consistencies of thickened fluids, the patient is evaluated for aspiration and/or microaspiration under videofluoroscopy or with a fiberoptic endoscopy. If the patient can swallow without aspiration when the cuff is deflated, the cuff may be left deflated or a cuffless tube

substituted. At this time, patients may be allowed varying levels of thickened fluids and soft foods.

◆ Speech With a Tracheostomy Tube

Several techniques promote speech in the patient with a tracheostomy. When the patient needs mechanical ventilation, provide the patient with a paper and pencil, a white board, or cellular phone for texting. A communication board with pictures of common needs is convenient for patients who may speak other languages. A visual alphabet for spelling words is useful for patients who are weak or have difficulty writing.

The spontaneously breathing patient may be able to talk with a tracheostomy. Several options are available depending upon the type of tracheostomy. For example, if the patient is at low risk for aspiration, (1) remove the inner cannula (if non-fenestrated), (2) deflate the cuff, and (3) place the cap on the tube (Fig. 26.6). When the tracheostomy cuff is deflated, exhaled air can flow upward over the vocal cords. When a fenestrated cannula is first used, frequently assess the patient for signs and symptoms of respiratory distress. If the patient is unable to tolerate the procedure, remove the cap, insert a non-fenestrated cannula, and reinflated the cuff. Monitor for improvement in patient condition.

The Passy-Muir valve is a simple device that attaches to the hub of the tracheostomy tube (Fig. 26.7). With the cuff deflated, the valve redirects airflow through the vocal cords. On inspiration, the valve on the device opens, allowing the patient to inhale. When the patient exhales, the valve closes and air flows

FIG. 26.7 Passy-Muir speaking tracheostomy valve. The valve is placed over the hub of the tracheostomy tube after the cuff is deflated. Multiple options are available and can be used for ventilated and nonventilated patients. The 1-way valve allows air to enter the lungs during inspiration and redirects air upward over the vocal cords into the mouth during expiration. (Courtesy Passy-Muir, Irvine, CA.)

upward around the tracheostomy and through the vocal cords. The patient exhales through the nose and mouth instead of through the tracheostomy, allowing speech. The patient may initially be able to tolerate only short periods of use until they become accustomed to exhaling through the mouth. Remove the valve immediately if there are any signs and symptoms of respiratory distress. Advocating for the use of speaking devices may help improve self-care and increase self-esteem for the patient with a long-term tracheostomy.

◆ Decannulation

Removal of the tracheostomy from the trachea is known as decannulation. Removal is possible when the primary condition for which the patient initially received a tracheostomy has been resolved. In addition, the patient needs to (1) be hemodynamically stable; (2) have a stable, intact respiratory drive; (3) be able to adequately exchange air, and (4) independently expectorate secretions.

Immediately prior to decannulation, explain to the patient what will occur. Monitor and record vital signs. Suction the patient prior to decannulation through the tracheostomy. Clear the mouth of any oral secretions. Loosen and/or cut the tracheostomy tapes, and remove any visible sutures holding the tracheostomy in place. Most importantly, ensure that the tracheostomy cuff is deflated. Pull the tracheostomy tube outward in one smooth motion. Stop if you meet any resistance and notify the appropriate personnel immediately.

After the tracheostomy tube is removed, care involves applying a sterile occlusive dressing and monitoring the site for bleeding. The dressing must be changed if it gets soiled or wet. If necessary, close the stoma with tape strips. Monitor the patient's respiratory status and O$_2$ saturation for any evidence of airway compromise or difficulty breathing. Apply an alternative method of O$_2$ delivery (e.g., nasal prongs) if needed. Teach the patient to splint the stoma with the fingers when coughing, swallowing, or speaking. Epithelial tissue begins to form in 24 to 48 hours, and the opening closes within 4 or 5 days. Surgical intervention to close the tracheostomy is usually not needed.

✦✦ NURSING MANAGEMENT
Suctioning and Tracheostomy Care

Suctioning and tracheostomy care are complex nursing activities. Every nurse who performs suctioning and tracheostomy care is responsible for knowing the scope of practice and policies and procedures of the agency in which they work for all health care personnel. Collaborate with respiratory therapy staff, who will play a key role in the patient's care.
  For unstable patients:
- Assess for the need for suctioning.
- Suction the ET or tracheostomy tube.
- Assess for adverse effects during suctioning, such as dysrhythmias.
- Evaluate the patient's respiratory status after suctioning.
- Maintain appropriate cuff inflation pressure at 20 to 25 cm H$_2$O or use minimal leak technique to maintain cuff pressure.
- Assess tracheostomy site at least once per shift for any signs of inflammation or infection.
- Replace the tracheostomy tube or ventilate the patient with a bag-valve-mask device after accidental tracheostomy dislodgment if needed.
- Assess swallowing ability and risk for aspiration.
- Develop plan to avoid aspiration in a patient with a tracheostomy.
- Teach patient and caregiver about home tracheostomy care.
- Delegate care of the stable patient to the licensed practical/vocational nurse (LPN/VN):
  - Determine the need for suctioning
  - Suction the tracheostomy
  - Evaluate patient status after suctioning
  - Provide tracheostomy care using sterile technique
  - Notify the RN of any changes in the patient's respiratory status
- Oversee the UAP in providing oral care to patient with a tracheostomy.
- Collaborate with the respiratory therapist:
  - Ensure proper equipment is available for suctioning and tracheotomy care
  - Measure tracheal cuff pressures
  - Replace tracheostomy tube after accidental dislodgement
  - Assist with bronchoscopy
  - Assist with decannulation

HEAD AND NECK CANCER

Head and neck cancer is classified according to the area where it occurs. These cancers may involve the nasal cavity and paranasal sinuses, nasopharynx, oropharynx, larynx, oral cavity, and/or salivary gland. (Cancer of the oral cavity is discussed in Chapter 41.) Most head and neck cancers arise from squamous cells that line the mucosal surfaces of the head and neck.

More than 52,000 new cases of head and neck cancer are diagnosed each year in the United States.[25] Tobacco use causes 85% of head and neck cancers. Excess alcohol consumption is another major risk factor. Head and neck cancer most often occurs in people over age 50 and twice as often in men compared to women. Head and neck cancers in those younger than 50 years are often associated with human papillomavirus (HPV) infection. Other risk factors include exposure to the sun, asbestos, industrial carcinogens, marijuana use, radiation therapy to the head and neck, and poor oral hygiene.[26]

Unfortunately, most patients have locally advanced disease at the time of diagnosis. Disability from both the disease and subsequent treatment is significant because of the potential loss of voice, adverse effects from chemotherapy and/or radiation, disfigurement, and social concerns.

Clinical Manifestations

The early manifestations of head and neck cancer vary with the location of the tumor. For example, patients with pharyngeal cancer may have what feels like a lump in the throat or a sore throat that does not get better with treatment. Some have white or red patches in the mouth or a change in the quality of the voice. Hoarseness that lasts more than 2 weeks may be a symptom of early laryngeal cancer.

Other manifestations may include ear pain or ringing in the ears, swelling or lumps in the neck, constant coughing, and coughing up blood. Swelling of the jaw can cause dentures to fit poorly or become uncomfortable. Unintentional weight loss and difficulty with chewing, swallowing, moving the tongue or jaw, and breathing are typically late symptoms. A partially or fully obstructed airway is often a late manifestation of head and neck cancer.

Diagnostic Studies

Early detection is key to patient survival. Physical assessment involves a focused assessment of the ears, nose, throat, mouth, and neck. Thoroughly examine the mouth, including the area under the tongue and dentures, with a flashlight. There may be thickening of the normally soft and pliable oral mucosa. Inspect the floor of the mouth and tongue. *Leukoplakia* (white patch) or *erythroplakia* (fiery red patch) may be present. Both leukoplakia and carcinoma in situ (localized to a defined area) may precede invasive carcinoma by many years. Palpate the lymph nodes in the neck.

If lesions are suspected, the HCP will examine upper airways may be examined using indirect pharyngoscopy and laryngoscopy (which involves using a laryngeal mirror). The larynx and vocal cords are visually inspected for lesions and tissue mobility. Typically, multiple biopsy specimens are obtained to help determine the extent of the disease. A CT scan or MRI may be done to detect local and regional spread. Positron emission tomography (PET) scanning is also used in diagnosis. The interprofessional care of head and neck cancer is outlined in Table 26.10.

TABLE 26.10 Interprofessional Care
Head and Neck Cancer

Diagnostic Assessment
- History and physical examination
- Indirect pharyngoscopy and laryngoscopy
- Endoscopy
- Biopsy
- Chest x-ray
- Barium swallow

Management
- Surgery
  - Vocal cord stripping
  - Laser surgery
  - Cordectomy
  - Partial or total laryngectomy
  - Pharyngectomy
  - Lymph node removal with neck dissection
  - Tracheostomy
  - Reconstructive procedures
- Radiation therapy
- Chemotherapy
- Targeted therapy
- Respiratory therapy
- Physical therapy
- Occupational therapy
- Speech therapy

Staging of Head and Neck Cancer

Head and neck cancer is staged based on the size of the tumor (T), number and location of involved lymph nodes (N), and extent of metastasis (M). This is referred to as *TNM staging*.[27] Staging is slightly different for each type of cancer. Generally, stage 0 is in situ, or confined to where it began, through stage 4, with more advanced disease. Oral cancer staging considers a patient's HPV status. TNM staging is discussed in Chapter 15.

Interprofessional Care

The choice of treatment for head and neck cancer is based on many factors. These include the location of tumor, TNM stage, patient's age and overall general health, urgency of treatment, cosmetic and functional considerations (e.g., ability to talk, swallow, chew), and patient choice. Treatment options include surgery, radiation therapy, chemotherapy, targeted therapy, or any combination of these modalities.[28]

Surgical Therapy. Surgery is often the first-line treatment option for head and neck cancers. Some patients may be treated with surgery alone. For other patients, combining surgery with radiation therapy and/or chemotherapy may be appropriate. Depending on the location and stage of cancer, surgical options include:

- *Vocal cord stripping:* Removal of outer layers of tissue on the vocal cords. This approach may be used for a biopsy or to treat some stage 0 cancers confined to the vocal cords. Vocal cord stripping rarely affects speech.
- *Laser surgery:* An endoscope with a laser is inserted down the throat, and the tumor can be vaporized or removed.
- *Cordectomy:* Removal of part or all the vocal cords. There may be changes in tone of voice. Removing part of a vocal cord may lead to a hoarse voice. If both vocal cords are removed, speech will no longer be possible.
- *Partial or total laryngectomy:* Removal of part or all the larynx. A total laryngectomy will change airflow in and out of the lungs and normal voice production will not be possible (Fig. 26.8).
- *Pharyngectomy:* Removal of part or all the throat.
- *Tracheostomy:* A tracheostomy is done to create an alternate pathway for breathing by creating a stoma in the trachea. *Lymph node removal:* Head and neck cancer sometimes spreads to the lymph nodes. The amount of tissue and number of lymph nodes that are removed depend on how far the cancer has spread.
- *Neck dissection surgery:* There are 3 main types:
  - *Radical neck dissection:* Removal of all the tissue on the side of the neck from the mandible to the clavicle. This includes the muscle, nerve, salivary gland, and major blood vessels.
  - *Modified radical neck dissection:* This is the most common type of neck dissection for cancer. All lymph nodes are removed. Less neck tissue is taken out than in radical dissection. This surgery may spare the nerves in the neck and, sometimes, the blood vessels or muscle.
  - *Selective neck dissection:* If cancer has not spread far, fewer lymph nodes are removed. The muscle, nerve, and blood vessels in the neck may be saved.

After extensive surgery to remove head and neck cancer, reconstructive operations can help restore both the structure and function of the affected areas.

Radiation Therapy. Radiation therapy can be delivered by either external-beam therapy or internal implants (brachytherapy). Brachytherapy is a concentrated and localized method of

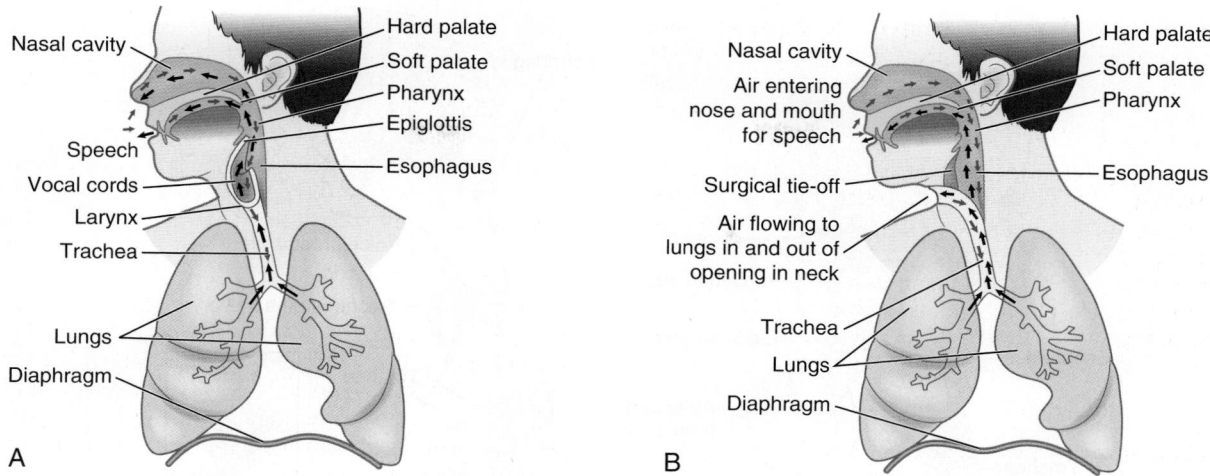

FIG. 26.8 Airflow in and out of the lungs after total laryngectomy. There is no anatomic connection between the nose, mouth, and throat. Inhaled and exhaled air enters the lungs through a surgically created stoma (hole) in the neck.

delivering radiation that involves placing a radioactive source near or into the tumor. The goal is to deliver high doses of radiation to the target area while limiting exposure of surrounding tissues. Thin, hollow, plastic needles are inserted into the tumor area, and radioactive seeds are placed in the needles. The seeds emit continuous radiation. Radiation therapy and brachytherapy are discussed in Chapter 15.

Radiation therapy is often preferred for patients with early head and neck cancer because it offers the patient good results with voice preservation. Some patients refuse surgical intervention for advanced lesions because of the extent of the procedure and potential risks involved. In this situation, radiation therapy is used as the sole treatment or in combination with chemotherapy. Other patients may opt for surgery and a combination of either radiation and/or chemotherapy treatments.

Chemotherapy and Targeted Therapy. Chemotherapy is used in combination with radiation therapy for patients with stage 3 or 4 head and neck cancers. Chemotherapy agents currently recommended include cisplatin, 5-fluorouracil, carboplatin, docetaxel (Taxotere), paclitaxel, methotrexate, and bleomycin.[29]

Cetuximab (Erbitux), a targeted therapy, is used with chemotherapy to treat patients with late-stage head and neck cancer. The drug targets epidermal growth factor receptor (EGFR), a specific protein within cancer cells, and stops the cells from growing. Targeted therapy is discussed in Chapter 15 and Table 15.13.

Nutritional Therapy. Many patients with head and neck cancer are malnourished even before treatment begins. Treatment modalities increase the risk for malnutrition. For example, after radical neck surgery, the patient may be unable to consume nutrients orally because of swelling, the location of sutures, or difficulty with swallowing. Side effects from chemotherapy and radiation therapy can impair the patient's ability to maintain adequate nutrition. Painful oral mucositis often leads to breaks in treatment if the patient is relying solely on oral intake for nutrition.

A thorough nutritional assessment and prophylactic placement of a gastrostomy tube in high-risk patients are vital to maintaining adequate nutrition. Enteral nutrition may be started before initiating treatment to obtain and maintain optimal nutritional status needed for tissue repair. (Enteral nutrition is described in Chapter 39.) Elevate the head of the bed while the patient is eating. Observe for feeding intolerance and adjust the amount, time, and/or formula if nausea, vomiting, diarrhea, or distention occurs. Teach the patient and caregiver about the enteral feedings.

Patients who are not candidates for or who refuse enteral feedings need to be monitored closely for weight loss. Antiemetics or analgesics given before meals can reduce nausea and mouth pain. Bland foods are easier for patients to tolerate. Patients can increase caloric intake by adding dry milk to foods during preparation, eating foods high in calories, and using oral supplements. It is helpful to add mild sauces and gravy to food. This adds calories and moistens food so that it is more easily swallowed. Expect swallowing problems when the patient resumes eating after surgery. The type and degree of difficulty varies depending on the surgical procedure. Videofluoroscopic swallowing studies may be used to evaluate the safety of swallowing postoperatively. When the patient can successfully swallow with low or no risk for aspiration, small amounts of thickened liquids or pureed foods may be given with the patient in high-Fowler's position. Avoid thin, watery fluids because they are hard to swallow and increase the risk for aspiration. Closely monitor and observe for any signs or symptoms of respiratory distress and/or choking when eating resumes. Oral suctioning may be done to prevent aspiration.

Physical Therapy. After surgery for head and neck cancer, the physical therapist will help teach the patient how to use the upper extremities to assist with support and movement of the head. In the immediate postoperative period, the patient should begin an exercise program to maintain strength and movement in the shoulders and neck. Without exercise, the patient could be left with a "frozen" shoulder and limited range of neck motion. The patient should continue the exercise program after discharge to prevent future functional disabilities.

Speech Therapy. Preoperatively, a speech therapist should meet with the patient and caregiver to discuss any effect that surgery will have on the voice and potential adaptations or voice restoration options. The International Association of Laryngectomees, an association of laryngectomy patients, focuses on helping patients reestablish speech. Local groups, such as "Lost Chord" or "New Voice," often have volunteers to visit patients before surgery.

FIG. 26.9 A, The sound waves created by the electrolarynx allow the person to speak. B, The Blom-Singer voice prosthesis and valve.

Three major approaches are used to restore oral communication: (1) electrolarynx, (2) tracheoesophageal puncture (TEP) voice restoration, and (3) esophageal speech. An *electrolarynx* is a hand-held, battery-powered device that creates speech with the use of sound waves (Fig. 26.9, *A*). This option allows for speech immediately after surgery. It needs little maintenance and is easy to learn. The primary disadvantage of the electrolarynx is the mechanical sound quality, which many patients find unacceptable.

In *transesophageal puncture (TEP)*, a fistula is created in the tracheoesophageal wall that diverts pulmonary air across the pharyngoesophageal mucosa for phonation when the tracheostoma is occluded. A 1-way prosthetic valve is placed in the tract. The valve prevents aspiration of food or saliva from the esophagus into the tracheostomy. To speak, the patient manually blocks the stoma with the finger. Air moves from the lungs, through the prosthesis, into the esophagus, and out the mouth. Speech is made by the air vibrating against the esophagus and is formed into words by moving the tongue and lips. A common voice prosthesis is the Blom-Singer prosthesis (Fig. 26.9, *B*). TEP offers the best speech quality with the highest degree of patient satisfaction.

Esophageal speech depends upon air that is introduced into the esophagus and then expelled past the pharyngoesophageal segment, the vibratory source for sound production. The primary disadvantages of developing esophageal speech are the length of time needed to learn the technique and the reduction in voice quality.

❖ NURSING MANAGEMENT: HEAD AND NECK CANCER

◆ Nursing Assessment

Table 26.11 presents subjective and objective data to obtain from a person with head and neck cancer.

◆ Nursing Diagnoses

Nursing diagnoses for the patient with head and neck cancer include:

- Impaired airway clearance
- Risk for aspiration
- Difficulty coping
- Impaired communication

More information on nursing diagnoses and the care of the patient with head and neck cancer is presented in eNursing Care Plan 26.2 on the website for this chapter.

TABLE 26.11 Nursing Assessment
Head and Neck Cancer

Subjective Data
Important Health Information

Past health history: Positive family history; prolonged tobacco use (cigarettes, pipes, cigars, chewing tobacco, smokeless tobacco); prolonged, heavy alcohol use; poor intake of fruits and vegetables
Medications: Prolonged use of over-the-counter medication for sore throat, decongestants

Functional Health Patterns

Health perception–health management: Does not take part in preventive health measures, long history of alcohol and tobacco use
Nutritional-metabolic: Mouth ulcer that does not heal, change in fit of dentures, change in appetite, sudden or unexplained weight loss, swallowing difficulty (e.g., sensation of lump in throat, pain with swallowing, aspiration when swallowing)
Activity-exercise: Fatigue with minimal exertion
Cognitive-perceptual: Sore throat, pain on swallowing, referred ear pain

Objective Data
Respiratory

Hoarseness, change in voice quality, chronic laryngitis, nasal voice, palpable neck mass and lymph nodes (tender, hard, fixed), tracheal deviation; dyspnea, stridor (late sign)

Gastrointestinal

White (leukoplakia) or red (erythroplakia) patches inside mouth, ulceration of mucosa, asymmetric tongue, exudate in mouth or pharynx, mass or thickening of mucosa

Possible Diagnostic Findings

Mass on direct or indirect laryngoscopy; tumor on soft tissue x-ray, CT scan, or MRI; positive biopsy

◆ Planning

The overall goals are that the patient will have (1) a patent airway, (2) an acceptable body image, (3) no complications related to therapy, (4) adequate nutritional intake, (5) minimal to no pain, and (6) the ability to communicate.

◆ Nursing Implementation

◆ **Health Promotion.** Most head and neck cancers can be prevented. The development of head and neck cancer is closely related to personal habits, mainly tobacco use and excess alcohol use. Poor oral hygiene and HPV infection are also risk factors for head and neck cancer.

Include information about risk factors in health teaching. Encourage good oral hygiene. Teach patients about safe sex practices to prevent HPV infection (e.g., use condoms, encourage monogamous relationships, choose a partner who has had no or few previous partners). If cancer has been diagnosed, tobacco and alcohol cessation are still important. The chance of a cure, by any treatment modality, for a patient with head and neck cancer who continues to smoke and use alcohol is decreased. Also, the risk for a second primary cancer is significantly increased. Give patients information about smoking cessation programs and techniques for success. If needed, refer to an alcohol treatment program. Smoking cessation and treatment of alcohol use are discussed in Chapter 10.

◆ **Acute Care.** Teach the patient and caregiver about the type of treatment to be performed, care needed, and reason for treatment and care. Help prepare them to deal with the psychological impact of the diagnosis of cancer, change in physical appearance, possible need for enteral feedings, and use of other communication methods because of loss of voice.

Care plans should include assessment of the patient's support system. The patient may not have someone to help after discharge or may have a job that cannot be continued, leaving the patient unemployed.

Surgical Therapy. Preoperatively assess the patient's physical and psychosocial needs. Physical preparation is the same as for any major surgery, with an emphasis on oral hygiene. Assess knowledge and understanding of the planned surgical procedure and clarify misinformation or misunderstanding as needed. When possible, include the caregiver in preoperative teaching.

Tailor teaching to the planned surgical procedure. For example, include information about expected changes in speech after a laryngectomy. Alphabet boards, writing materials, pictorial guides, laptops, and hand signals are useful methods for communicating. Programmable speech-generating devices allow use of recorded messages that are matched with a graphic representing each message. Integration of newer technology into patient care enhances the patient's ability to communicate basic needs after surgery.

INFORMATICS IN PRACTICE

Communication Devices for Patient With Laryngectomy

- Assisting with communication will improve a patient's quality of life after a laryngectomy.
- Use a tablet or smartphone and download a text-to-speech application. These applications allow the patient to type in text, and then a computer voice says the text aloud.
- You can teach the patient how to use a keyboard-based communication program. The patient types on a traditional keyboard and generates speech that is transmitted through hand-held speakers.

Immediately after surgery, nursing care priorities include airway management, wound care, nutrition, communication, and psychosocial issues related to body image changes. Maintaining a patent airway is essential. Inflammation in the surgical area may compress the trachea. Keep the patient in a semi-Fowler's position to decrease edema and limit tension on suture lines.

Give analgesic drugs as needed for pain control. Because patients may not be able to speak, have them nonverbally rate their pain (e.g., visual pain scale) to help assess the effectiveness of the medication. (Pain management is discussed in Chapter 8.) Monitor vital signs frequently. Be alert for hemorrhage, as many of the structures in the head and neck area are very vascular. Pay careful attention to heart rate, blood pressure, SpO_2, and the patient's hemoglobin value.

The patient with a laryngectomy needs frequent suctioning via the tracheostomy tube. Secretions typically change in amount and consistency over time. The patient may initially have a large amount of blood-tinged secretions that gradually diminish and thicken. Maintain adequate fluid intake (IV, enteral) and humidification of inspired gases to keep secretions liquid and mucous membranes moist. Encourage deep breathing and coughing.

Pressure dressings, packing, or drainage tubes may be present, depending on the type of surgical procedure. Do not change any dressing unless you have a specific order from the HCP. If skin flaps are used, dressings are typically not present. This allows better visualization of the flap and avoids excess pressure on tissue. Skin flaps must initially be checked hourly for color and any change in size or edema. Doppler ultrasound may be used to determine the presence of a pulse, depending upon the location of the skin flap. Hemovac, Jackson-Pratt, and Penrose drains are some of the drainage devices that may be used.

Drainage may initially be bloody, then serosanguineous, and gradually decrease in volume over 24 to 48 hours. Monitor patency of drainage tubes every hour in the first few hours after surgery, then every 4 hours to ensure proper functioning. If tubing becomes obstructed, fluid will accumulate under the skin flap and predispose the patient to formation of hematomas or seromas, impair wound healing, and increase the risk for infection. After drainage tubes are removed, closely monitor the area to detect any swelling. Closely monitor incision sites for signs of infection.

The patient may have a nasogastric tube inserted during surgery to remove gastric contents via intermittent suction for the first 24 to 48 hours until peristalsis returns. Because the nasogastric tube lies close to internal incision lines, do not manipulate or move the tube. When bowel sounds return, start enteral feedings slowly and advance to meet nutritional needs.

Radiation Therapy. Dry mouth (*xerostomia*), a frequent and annoying problem, typically occurs within a few weeks of treatment. The patient's saliva decreases in volume and becomes thick. This change may be temporary or permanent. Pilocarpine hydrochloride (Salagen) is often effective in increasing saliva production.

❓ CHECK YOUR PRACTICE

Your 64-yr-old male patient with oral cancer has been receiving radiation therapy for 3 weeks. He has developed xerostomia and oral mucositis. He asks if you have any suggestions to help relieve his symptoms.
- How would you respond?

Once patients can have foods or fluids by mouth, they can get symptom relief by increasing fluid intake, chewing sugarless gum or sugarless candy, using nonalcoholic mouth rinses (baking soda, glycerin solutions), and using artificial saliva. Teach patients to always carry a water bottle with them. Fluoride gels or treatments can help prevent dental deterioration caused by xerostomia.

Oral mucositis can cause irritation, ulceration, and pain. Teach the patient on oral care basics, including the use of a soft toothbrush and regular flossing. Empty fluoride gel trays, along with bite blocks, athletic mouth guards, or gauze pads, can be worn during radiation treatments. This prevents radiation scatter to the tongue and cheek from metal work in the mouth. Warm bland rinses, like those with salt and baking soda, 4 to 6 times daily may be helpful. Sucking on ice chips can also help with the pain. Patients should avoid commercial mouthwashes and hot, spicy, or acidic foods because they are irritating.

Skin over the irradiated area often becomes reddened and sensitive to touch. Teach patients to use only prescribed lotions and skin products while undergoing radiation therapy and to not use any lotions within 2 hours before treatment. Skin care for patients having radiation therapy is discussed in Chapter 15.

Fatigue is a common side effect of radiation therapy as well as chemotherapy. Encourage patients to walk 15 to 30 minutes each day since regular exercise can give them more energy. Teach patients to do activities that are most important to them and to rest during periods of low energy. Identify support systems and encourage patients to ask for help.

Stoma Care. Should the patient have a stoma after surgery, teach the patient proper care of the stoma. The patient should wash the area around the stoma daily with a moist cloth. A nasal wash spray (e.g., Alkalol) can be used every 1 to 2 hours to keep the stoma moist and prevent crusting. Dried secretions can be removed with tweezers. If a laryngectomy tube is in place, the patient must remove the entire tube at least daily and clean it in the same manner as a tracheostomy tube. The inner cannula may have to be removed and cleaned more often. A scarf or loose shirt can hide the stoma.

The patient should cover the stoma when coughing (because mucus may be expectorated) and during any activity (e.g., shaving, applying makeup) that may lead to inhalation of foreign materials. Because water can easily enter the stoma, the patient should wear a plastic collar when taking a shower. Swimming is contraindicated. Initially, humidification is given with mechanical ventilation or, after extubation, with a tracheostomy mask. After discharge, the patient can use a bedside humidifier.

Psychosocial Needs. Psychosocial care of the patient with head and neck cancer is of utmost importance. Issues concerning depression, change in body image, and sexuality are common. Although changes are discussed before surgery, the patient may not be psychologically prepared for the extent of these changes. If the patient has a significant other, this person's reaction to the patient's altered appearance is important. Acceptance by another person can promote an improved self-image.

Depression may occur for many reasons: inability to speak because of surgical procedure and/or presence of ET or tracheostomy tube, altered physical appearance due to the surgery and edema, loss of independence and reliance upon others, and feelings of helplessness and hopelessness. Depression also may be related to concern about the prognosis.

Allow the patient and caregiver to express their feelings and emotions. Convey acceptance to help patients regain positive feelings about their body image and self-concept. Encourage participation in support groups. Information about available groups can be obtained through the local branch of the American Cancer Society. A psychiatric referral may be needed for the patient who has prolonged or severe depression.

Surgery and surgical devices such as tracheostomy and gastrostomy tubes may dramatically affect body image. Xerostomia and fatigue can physically affect sexuality. It may be hard for the patient to talk about sexual problems because of changes in communication. Help the patient and partner by allowing them to talk about their sexuality and how surgery and treatment may affect their relationship. Helping the patient see that sexuality involves much more than appearance may relieve some anxiety.

◆ **Ambulatory Care.** The patient may be discharged with a tracheostomy and a nasogastric or gastrostomy feeding tube. Some patients initially need a home health care referral and assessment to evaluate the patient's or caregiver's ability to perform self-care activities. Both patient and caregiver need to learn how to manage tubes and whom to call if there are problems. Provide pictorial instructions for tracheostomy care, suctioning, stoma and skin care, and enteral feeding as appropriate. Encouraging the patient to take part in self-care is an important part of rehabilitation.

Teach the patient the importance of wearing a Medic Alert bracelet or other identification that alerts emergency personnel of the possible changes in breathing status because of surgery. Because the patient no longer breathes through the nose, the ability to smell smoke and taste food is often lost. Teach the patient to install smoke and carbon monoxide detectors in the home. Encourage preparation of food that is colorful, attractive, and nutritious because taste may be decreased due to the loss of smell and radiation therapy. Refer to a dietitian as needed.

The patient can resume exercise, recreation, and sexual activity when able. Most patients can return to work 1 to 2 months after surgery. However, many never return to full-time employment. The changes that follow a total laryngectomy can be upsetting. Loss of speech, loss of the ability to taste and smell, inability to produce audible sounds (including laughing and weeping), and the presence of a permanent tracheal stoma that produces undesirable mucus are often overwhelming to patients.

◆ **Evaluation**

Expected outcomes for the patient with head and neck cancer who is treated surgically are that the patient will:

- Have effective coughing and secretion clearance
- Swallow oral foods without aspiration
- Uses effective coping strategies
- Use techniques to effectively communicate

CASE STUDY

Laryngeal Cancer

(© iStockphoto/ Thinkstock.)

Patient Profile

M.R., a 69-yr-old retired baker, was admitted to the hospital for influenza. He told his HCP that he has "a cough that just won't go away," difficulty swallowing, and "a sore throat that really hasn't gotten better" over the past year. His wife passed away 6 years ago. He has 3 adult children; 1 daughter lives in the same city. He has a history of hypertension, smoking, alcohol use, gastroesophageal reflux disease (GERD), and type 2 diabetes.

Subjective Data

- States that his symptoms worsened in the past 3 months
- Has used various cough and cold remedies over the past 6 months to relieve symptoms without relief
- Has lost weight because of decrease in appetite and difficulty swallowing
- Has smoked 3 packs of cigarettes a day for the past 50 yrs
- Consumes 4 to 6 cans of beer a day

Objective Data

Physical Examination

- *Vital signs:* Temperature 102.4° F (39.1° C), heart rate 99 beats/min (pulse strong, regular), respiratory rate 24 breaths/min (short, shallow, slightly labored), BP 176/84 (cuff), SpO_2 87% on room air
- *Inspection:* Awake and alert, appears gray, malnourished, dehydrated. Small, irregular white patches on the sides of oral cavity
- *Palpation:* Enlarged cervical nodes bilaterally (nontender)
- *Auscultation:* Adequate and clear air entry to upper lung fields; slightly decreased air entry to bases with occasional fine crackles on expiration

Diagnostic Studies

- Chest x-ray: lung fields clear
- Laryngoscopy: mass in subglottic area (requires further evaluation)
- CT scan: subglottic lesion with lymph node involvement
- Diagnosis: laryngeal cancer

Interprofessional Care

- *Surgery:* suggests a total laryngectomy
- *Oncology:* suggests radiation and chemotherapy postoperatively

- *Gastroenterology:* percutaneous gastrostomy tube preoperatively for enteral feeding
- *Dietary:* explain nutritional options with/without ET tube/tracheostomy
- *Physical therapy:* visit pre-surgery to explain postoperative exercise routine
- *Social worker:* determine social supports available postoperatively

Discussion Questions

1. What assessment information suggests that M.R. is at risk for laryngeal cancer?
2. **Priority Decision:** What are your priority teaching strategies for M.R. before his total laryngectomy? Postoperative teaching priorities?
3. How would you explain the gastrostomy tube to M.R.?
4. Is there anything in his history that may affect wound healing after surgery?

Progression of Case

M.R. is transferred to the clinical unit after 24 hours in ICU. He is awake, alert, but slightly confused. Vital signs are stable. BP 168/94. Large surgical dressing on neck with 3 Jackson-Pratt drains. Tracheostomy tube in place. Receiving O_2 via tracheal mask. Enteral feeding at 30 mL/hr via gastrostomy tube. Foley catheter patent, draining a moderate amount of amber urine. M.R. is picking at his surgical drains, and when you try to reassure him, he just starts waving his hands at you.

5. **Collaboration:** What information would you want to know from the ICU nurse who has just transported M.R. to the clinical unit?
6. **Priority Decision:** Based on the assessment data presented, what are your priority nursing diagnoses? Are there any collaborative problems?
7. **Evidence-Based Practice:** How could you best meet M.R.'s communication needs during the first few postoperative days?
8. Four hours after transfer to the clinical unit, M.R. is tearful and is staring at the wall. What should you do?
9. **Patient-Centered Care:** What teaching is required to help him assume self-care after his surgery? What precautions should he take because of his stoma?

Answers available at *http://evolve.elsevier.com/Lewis/medsurg.*

▌BRIDGE TO NCLEX EXAMINATION

The number of the question corresponds to the same-numbered outcome at the beginning of the chapter.

1. A patient is seen in the clinic for a nosebleed, which is controlled by placement of anterior nasal packing. During discharge teaching, the nurse teaches the patient to
   a. use aspirin for pain relief.
   b. remove the packing later that day.
   c. avoid vigorous nose blowing and strenuous activity.
   d. insert more packing into the nose if rebleeding occurs.

2. A patient with allergic rhinitis reports severe nasal congestion; sneezing; and watery, itchy eyes and nose at various times of the year. When teaching the patient about how to control these symptoms, the nurse teaches the patient to
   a. avoid all intranasal sprays and oral antihistamines.
   b. limit the usage of nasal decongestant spray to 10 days.
   c. use oral decongestants at bedtime to prevent symptoms during the night.
   d. keep a diary of when the allergic reaction occurs and what precipitates it.

3. A patient is seen at the clinic with fever, muscle aches, sore throat with yellowish exudate, and headache. The nurse anticipates that the interprofessional management will include *(select all that apply)*
   a. antiviral agents to treat influenza.
   b. treatment with antibiotics starting ASAP.
   c. a throat culture or rapid strep antigen test.
   d. supportive care, including cool, bland liquids.
   e. comprehensive history to determine possible cause.

4. The *best* method for determining the risk for aspiration in a patient with a tracheostomy is to
   a. consult a speech therapist for swallowing assessment.
   b. have the patient drink plain water and assess for coughing.
   c. ask the patient to rate the perceived degree of swallowing difficulty.
   d. assess for sputum changes 48 hours after the patient drinks small amount of blue dye.

5. Which nursing action would be of *highest priority* when suctioning a patient with a tracheostomy?
   a. Auscultating lung sounds after suctioning is complete
   b. Giving antianxiety medications 30 minutes before suctioning
   c. Instilling 5 mL of normal saline into the tracheostomy tube before suctioning
   d. Assessing the patient's oxygen saturation before, during, and after suctioning

6. When planning health care teaching to prevent or detect early head and neck cancer, which people would be the *priority* to target *(select all that apply)*?
   a. 65-year-old man who has used chewing tobacco most of his life
   b. 45-year-old rancher who uses snuff to stay awake while driving his herds of cattle
   c. 21-year-old college student who drinks beer on weekends with his fraternity brothers
   d. 78-year-old woman who has been drinking liquor since her husband died 15 years ago
   e. 22-year-old woman who has been diagnosed with human papilloma virus of the cervix

7. While in the recovery room, a patient with a total laryngectomy is suctioned and has bloody mucus with some clots. Which nursing interventions would apply? *(select all that apply)*
   a. Notify the health care provider at once.
   b. Place the patient in semi-Fowler's position.
   c. Use a bag-valve-mask (BVM) and begin rescue breathing for the patient
   d. Instill 10 mL of normal saline into the tracheostomy tube to loosen secretions.
   e. Continue patient assessment, including O_2 saturation, respiratory rate, and breath sounds.

8. Appropriate discharge teaching for the patient with a permanent tracheostomy after a total laryngectomy for cancer would include *(select all that apply)*
   a. encouraging regular exercise such as swimming.
   b. washing around the stoma daily with a moist washcloth.
   c. encouraging participation in postlaryngectomy support group.
   d. providing pictures and "hands-on" instruction for tracheostomy care.
   e. teaching how to hold breath and trying to gag to promote swallowing reflex.

1. c, 2. d, 3. c, d, e, 4. a, 5. d, 6. a, b, d, e, 7. b, e, 8. b, c, d

For rationales to these answers and even more NCLEX review questions, visit *http://evolve.elsevier.com/Lewis/medsurg*.

Ⓔ EVOLVE WEBSITE/RESOURCES LIST

http://evolve.elsevier.com/Lewis/medsurg
Review Questions (Online Only)
Key Points
Answer Keys for Questions
- Rationales for Bridge to NCLEX Examination Questions
- Answer Guidelines for Case Study on p. 499
Student Case Study
- Patient With Head and Neck Cancer/Laryngectomy With Tracheostomy
Nursing Care Plans
- eNursing Care Plan 26.1: Patient With a Tracheostomy
- eNursing Care Plan 26.2: Patient Having Total Laryngectomy and/or Radical Neck Surgery
Conceptual Care Map Creator
Supporting Media
- Animation
- Tracheotomy
Audio Glossary
Content Updates

REFERENCES

1. American Academy of Otolaryngology: Deviated septum. Retrieved from *https://www.enthealth.org/nose-landing-page/*.
2. Paton KT, Thibodeau GA: *Anatomy and physiology*, ed 9, St Louis, 2016, Mosby.
3. Haraldson SJ: Nasal fracture. Retrieved from *https://emedicine.medscape.com/article/84829-overview*.
4. Good VS, Kirkwood PL: *Advanced critical care nursing*, ed 2, St Louis, 2018, Elsevier.
5. Rothrock JC: *Alexander's care of the patient in surgery*, ed 16, St Louis, 2019, Elsevier.
6. Shiffman MA, DiGiuseppe A: *Advanced aesthetic rhinoplasty: Art, science, and new clinical technologies*, New York, 2013, Springer (Classic).
7. DeWit SC, Stromberg HK, Dallred C: *Medical-surgical nursing: Concepts and practice*, ed 3, St Louis, 2017, Elsevier.
8. Nguyen QA: Epistaxis treatment and management. Retrieved from *https://emedicine.medscape.com/article/863220-treatment*.
9. Sheikh J: Allergic rhinitis. Retrieved from *https://emedicine.medscape.com/article/134825-overview#a5*.
*10. Scadding GK, Kariyawasam HH, Scadding G, et al: BSACI guideline for the diagnosis and management of allergic and non-allergic rhinitis, *Clin Exp Allergy*, 47:856, 2017.
11. American Academy of Asthma, Allergy and Immunology: Hay fever and allergy medications. Retrieved from *www.aaaai.org/conditions-and-treatments/library/allergy-library/hay-fever-medications*.
12. Centers for Disease Control and Prevention: Seasonal influenza-associated hospitalizations in the United States. Retrieved from *www.cdc.gov/flu/about/qa/hospital.htm*.
13. Centers for Disease Control and Prevention: Estimating seasonal influenza-associated deaths in the United States. Retrieved from *www.cdc.gov/flu/about/disease/us_flu-related_deaths.htm*.
14. University of California Irvine Health: How long is the flu contagious? Retrieved from *www.ucirvinehealth.org/blog/2017/02/flu-contagious*.
15. US Food and Drug Administration: Influenza (flu) antiviral drugs and related information. Retrieved from *www.fda.gov/drugs/drugsafety/informationbydrugclass/ucm100228.htm*.
*16. Hanson C, Lepule K: Management of acute and chronic sinusitis, *S Afr Pharm J* 84:45, 2017.
*17. Arina AM, Chan MM: Current concepts in adult acute rhinosinusitis, *Am Fam Physician* 94:97, 2016.
18. Newson L: Nasal polyps. Retrieved from *https://patient.info/health/nasal-polyps-leaflet*.
19. Hermann J: Say ahh: Acute pharyngitis diagnosis and management. Retrieved from *http://contemporaryclinic.pharmacytimes.com/journals/issue/2017/december2017/Say-Ahh-Acute-Pharyngitis-Diagnosis-and-Management*.
20. Carrillo-Marquez MA: Bacterial pharyngitis treatment and management. Retrieved from *https://emedicine.medscape.com/article/225243-treatment*.

*21. Lynch J, Crawley SM: Management of airway obstruction, *BJA Education* 18:46, 2018.

22. Urden LD, Stacy KM, Lough ME: *Critical care nursing: Diagnosis and management*, ed 8, St. Louis, 2018, Elsevier.

*23. Mehta C, Mehta Y: Percutaneous tracheostomy, *Ann Card Anaesth* 20:S19, 2017.

24. Salisbury NHS Foundation Trust: Tracheostomy cuffs—Management of. Retrieved from *www.icid.salisbury.nhs.uk/CLINICALMANAGEMENT/ENT/Pages/ThemanagementoftracheostomycuffsCPr.aspx*.

25. American Cancer Society: Key statistics for oral and oropharyngeal cancers. Retrieved from *www.cancer.org/cancer/oral-cavity-and-oropharyngeal-cancer/about/key-statistics.html*.

26. American Society of Clinical Oncology Cancer.Net: Head and neck cancer: Risk factors and prevention. Retrieved from *www.cancer.net/cancer-types/head-and-neck-cancer/risk-factors-and-prevention*.

27. Cancer Treatment Centers of America: TNM system for head and neck cancer. Retrieved from *www.cancercenter.com/head-and-neck-cancer/stages/*.

28. Australian Government Cancer Australia: Head and neck cancer treatment options. Retrieved from *https://head-neck-cancer.canceraustralia.gov.au/treatment*.

29. Cancer Treatment Centers of America: Head and neck cancer drug information. Retrieved from *www.cancercenter.com/head-and-neck-cancer/diagnostics-and-treatments/tab/drug-information/*.

*Evidence-based information for clinical practice.

27

Lower Respiratory Problems

Eugene Mondor

To know even one life has breathed easier because you have lived, that is to have succeeded.

Ralph Waldo Emerson

(e) http://evolve.elsevier.com/Lewis/medsurg/

CONCEPTUAL FOCUS

Cellular Regulation	**Functional Ability**	**Infection**
Clotting	**Gas Exchange**	

LEARNING OUTCOMES

1. Compare and contrast the clinical manifestations and nursing and interprofessional management of patients with acute bronchitis and pertussis.
2. Distinguish among the types of pneumonia and their etiology.
3. Describe the pathophysiology, clinical manifestations, diagnostic studies, and interprofessional and nursing management of patients with pneumonia.
4. Describe the pathogenesis, classification, clinical manifestations, complications, diagnostic abnormalities, and interprofessional and nursing management of patients with tuberculosis.
5. Describe the causes, clinical manifestations, and nursing and interprofessional management of patients with pulmonary fungal infections.
6. Explain the pathophysiology, clinical manifestations, and nursing and interprofessional management of a patient with a lung abscess.
7. Identify the causative factors, clinical manifestations, and nursing and interprofessional management of patients with environmental lung diseases.
8. Describe the etiology, risk factors, pathophysiology, clinical manifestations, and interprofessional and nursing management of lung cancer.
9. Compare and contrast the pathophysiology, clinical manifestations, and nursing and interprofessional management of fractured ribs, flail chest, and pneumothorax.
10. Describe the purpose, function, and nursing responsibilities related to chest tubes and chest drainage systems.
11. Explain the types of chest surgery and appropriate preoperative and postoperative care.
12. Describe the etiology, clinical manifestations, and nursing and interprofessional management of patients with restrictive lung disorders.
13. Describe the pathophysiology, clinical manifestations, and nursing and interprofessional management of pulmonary embolism, pulmonary hypertension, and cor pulmonale.
14. Discuss the use of lung transplantation as a treatment for pulmonary disorders, emphasizing nursing and interprofessional management of the postoperative lung transplant patient.

KEY TERMS

A variety of problems affect the lower respiratory system. This chapter discusses lower respiratory tract diseases that influence the concept of gas exchange. It focuses on infectious, environmental, oncologic, traumatic, restrictive, and vascular problems that impair gas exchange. Gas exchange is related with multiple concepts, as a problem has profound consequences because of the need of adequate oxygenation for life.

LOWER RESPIRATORY TRACT INFECTIONS

Lower respiratory tract infection is both a common and serious occurrence. It is the reason for thousands of clinic and emergency department (ED) visits and hospital admissions each year. In the United States, pneumonia and influenza cause more than 57,000 deaths annually.[1]

ACUTE BRONCHITIS

Acute bronchitis is a self-limiting inflammation of the bronchi in the lower respiratory tract. It is the reason for 10% of all clinic visits and 100 million ED visits per year.[2] Most acute bronchial infections are caused by viruses. Air pollution, dust, inhalation of chemicals, smoking, chronic sinusitis, and asthma are other triggers.

Cough, which is the most common symptom, may last for up to 3 weeks. It is the main reason for seeking medical care. Clear sputum is often present, although some patients have purulent sputum. The presence of colored (e.g., green) sputum is not a reliable indicator of bacterial infection. Other symptoms may include headache, fever, malaise, hoarseness, myalgias, dyspnea, and chest pain.

Diagnosis is based on the assessment. Assessment may reveal normal breath sounds or crackles or wheezes, usually on expiration and with exertion. *Consolidation* (which occurs when fluid accumulates in the lungs), suggestive of pneumonia, is absent with bronchitis. Chest x-rays are normal and not needed unless pneumonia or some other pulmonary disorder is suspected.

The goal of treatment is to relieve symptoms and prevent pneumonia. Treatment is supportive. It includes cough suppressants (e.g., dextromethorphan), encouraging oral fluid intake, and using a humidifier. Throat lozenges, hot tea, and honey may help relieve cough. β_2-Agonist (bronchodilator) inhalers are useful for patients with wheezes or underlying pulmonary conditions. Antibiotics are not prescribed for viral infections because they have side effects and promote antibiotic resistance. Antibiotics may be given to patients with underlying chronic conditions who have a prolonged infection associated with systemic symptoms.

Encourage patients not to smoke, to avoid secondhand smoke, and to wash their hands often. If the acute bronchitis is due to an influenza virus, treatment with antiviral drugs may be started. If patients with acute bronchitis develop a fever, have difficulty breathing, or have symptoms last longer than 4 weeks, they should see their HCP.

PERTUSSIS

Pertussis is a highly contagious infection of the respiratory tract caused by the gram-negative bacillus *Bordetella pertussis*. The bacteria attach to the cilia of the respiratory tract and release toxins that damage the cilia, causing inflammation and swelling. The incidence of pertussis has been steadily increasing in the United States since the 1980s. The largest increase is seen in adults. We think that immunity from childhood tetanus, diphtheria, and pertussis vaccine (Tdap) vaccination may decrease over time, allowing a milder (but still contagious) infection. The Centers for Disease Control and Prevention (CDC) currently recommends that all adolescents (11 years and older) and adults who have not received a dose of Tdap receive a one-time vaccination as soon as possible.[3]

Manifestations of pertussis occur in stages. The first stage, lasting 1 to 2 weeks, manifests as a mild upper respiratory tract infection (URI) with a low-grade or no fever, runny nose, watery eyes, generalized malaise, and mild, nonproductive cough. The second stage, from the second to tenth week of infection, is characterized by paroxysms of cough. The last stage lasts 2 to 3 weeks. It is characterized by a less severe cough and weakness.

♥ PROMOTING POPULATION HEALTH

Preventing Respiratory Diseases

- Wash hands often to prevent and avoid spreading infections.
- Avoid cigarette smoking and exposure to environmental smoke.
- Get a pneumococcal vaccine and yearly flu vaccine as directed by the HCP.
- Avoid exposure to allergens, indoor pollutants, and ambient air pollutants.
- Wear proper personal protective equipment when working in an occupation with prolonged exposure to dust, fumes, or gases.

The hallmark characteristic of pertussis is uncontrollable, violent coughing. Inspiration after each cough produces the typical "whooping" sound as the patient tries to breathe in air against an obstructed glottis. The "whoop" is often not present in teens and adults (especially those who have been vaccinated). Like acute bronchitis, the coughing is more frequent at night. Vomiting may occur with coughing. Unlike acute bronchitis, the cough with pertussis may last from 6 to 10 weeks.

In the community, diagnosis is primarily by history and examination. In the clinical setting, the CDC recommends nasopharyngeal cultures, polymerase chain reaction (PCR) of nasopharyngeal secretions, or serology testing.[4] The treatment is macrolide (erythromycin, azithromycin [Zithromax]) antibiotics to minimize symptoms and prevent spread of the disease. For the patient who cannot take macrolides, trimethoprim/sulfamethoxazole is used. The patient is infectious from the beginning of the first stage through the third week after onset of symptoms or until 5 days after antibiotic therapy has been started. Routine and droplet precautions are required for hospitalized patients. Patients should not use cough suppressants and antihistamines as they are ineffective and may induce coughing episodes. Corticosteroids and bronchodilators are also not helpful. The CDC recommends postexposure antibiotics to those who have had close contact with the patient.

PNEUMONIA

Pneumonia is an acute infection of the lung parenchyma. Despite remarkable progress in the development of antibiotics to treat pneumonia, pneumonia is still associated with significant morbidity and mortality. The CDC reports that pneumonia and influenza are the 8th leading cause of death in the United States.[5]

Etiology

Normally, various defense mechanisms protect the airway distal to the larynx from infection. Mechanisms that create a mechanical barrier to microorganisms entering the tracheobronchial tree include air filtration, epiglottis closure over the trachea, cough reflex, mucociliary escalator mechanism, and reflex bronchoconstriction (see Chapter 25). Immune defense mechanisms include secretion of immunoglobulins A and G and alveolar macrophages.

Pneumonia is more likely to occur when defense mechanisms become incompetent or are overwhelmed by the virulence or quantity of infectious agents. A weakened cough or epiglottal reflex may allow aspiration of oropharyngeal contents into the lungs. Tracheal intubation bypasses normal filtration processes and interferes with the cough reflex and mucociliary escalator mechanism. Air pollution, cigarette smoking, viral URIs, and normal changes that occur with aging can impair the mucociliary mechanism. Chronic diseases can suppress the immune system's ability to inhibit bacterial growth. The risk factors for pneumonia are listed in Table 27.1.

Pathogens that cause pneumonia reach the lung in 3 ways:
1. *Aspiration* of normal flora from the nasopharynx or oropharynx. Many organisms that cause pneumonia are normal inhabitants of the pharynx in healthy adults.
2. *Inhalation* of microbes present in the air. Examples include *Mycoplasma pneumoniae* and fungal pneumonias.
3. *Hematogenous spread* from a primary infection elsewhere in the body. Examples are streptococci and *Staphylococcus aureus* from infective endocarditis.

TABLE 27.1 Risk Factors for Pneumonia

- Abdominal or chest surgery
- Age >65 years
- Air pollution
- Altered consciousness: alcoholism, head injury, seizures, anesthesia, drug overdose, stroke
- Bed rest and prolonged immobility
- Chronic diseases: chronic lung and liver disease, diabetes, heart disease, cancer, chronic kidney disease
- Debilitating illness
- Exposure to bats, birds, rabbits, and farm animal droppings (excrement)
- Immunosuppressive disease and/or therapy (corticosteroids, cancer chemotherapy, HIV infection, immunosuppressive therapy after organ transplant)
- Inhalation or aspiration of noxious substances
- Intestinal and gastric feedings via nasogastric or nasointestinal tubes
- IV drug use
- Malnutrition
- Recent antibiotic therapy
- Resident of a long-term care facility
- Smoking
- Tracheal intubation (endotracheal intubation, tracheostomy)
- URI

Classifications of Pneumonia

There is no universally accepted classification system for pneumonia. Some suggest classifying pneumonia according to the causative pathogens (e.g., bacterial, viral, fungal, etc.), characteristics of the disease, or radiographic appearance on chest x-ray. The most widely recognized and effective way to classify pneumonia is as either *community-acquired* or *hospital-acquired* pneumonia. This classification helps the HCP identify the most likely cause (Table 27.2) and the choice of antimicrobial therapy.

Community-Acquired Pneumonia. Community-acquired pneumonia (CAP) is an acute infection of the lung occurring in patients who have not been hospitalized or lived in a long-term care facility within 14 days of the onset of symptoms. The decision to treat the patient at home or admit to hospital is based on several factors. These include the patient's age, vital signs, mental status, presence of co-morbid conditions, and current physiologic condition. We can use tools such as the expanded CURB-65 scale (Table 27.3) to supplement clinical judgment.

Hospital-Acquired Pneumonia. Hospital-acquired pneumonia (HAP), also known as *nosocomial pneumonia*, is pneumonia in a nonintubated patient that begins 48 hours or longer after admission to hospital and was not present at the time of admission. *Ventilator-associated pneumonia (VAP)*, a type of HAP, refers to pneumonia that occurs more than 48 hours after endotracheal intubation.[6] VAP is discussed in Chapter 65. Both HAP and VAP are associated with longer hospital stays, increased associated costs, sicker patients, and increased risk for morbidity and mortality.

Once the diagnosis of CAP, HAP, or VAP is made, treatment is started based on known risk factors, early versus late onset, presentation, underlying medical conditions, hemodynamic stability, and the likely causative pathogen. *Empiric antibiotic therapy,* the initiation of treatment before a definitive diagnosis or causative agent is confirmed, should be started as soon as pneumonia is suspected. Empiric antibiotic therapy is based on the knowledge of drugs known to be effective for the likely cause. Antibiotic therapy can be adjusted once the results of sputum cultures identify the exact pathogen.

TABLE 27.2 Organisms Causing Pneumonia

Community-Acquired Pneumonia

- *Chlamydophila pneumoniae*
- *Chlamydophila psittaci*
- *Coxiella burnettii*
- Gram-negative bacilli
- Fungi
- Influenzae
- Influenza A and B
- *Klebsiella pneumoniae*
- *Legionella pneumophila**
- MRSA*
- *Moraxella catarrhalis*
- *Mycobacterium tuberculosis*
- *Mycoplasma pneumoniae*
- Oral anaerobes (e.g., alcoholism, IV drug use)
- *Pseudomonas aeruginosa*
- Respiratory viruses
- *S. pneumoniae**

Hospital-Acquired Pneumonia

- *Acinetobacter* species[†]
- *Enterobacter* species
- *Escherichia coli*[†]
- *H. influenzae*
- *Klebsiella pneumoniae*[†]
- *Proteus* species
- *Pseudomonas aeruginosa*[†]
- *S. aureus*
- *S. pneumoniae*

*Most common cause of community-acquired pneumonia (CAP).
[†]Most common causes of hospital-acquired pneumonia (HAP).

TABLE 27.3 Assessing Pneumonia Severity Using Expanded CURB-65

The **Expanded CURB-65 scale** may be used as a supplement to clinical judgment to determine the severity of pneumonia and if patients need to be hospitalized.

Identifying the Level of Risk
Patients receive 1 point for each of the following indicators:
- **C:** Confusion (compared to baseline)
- **U:** BUN >20 mg/dL
- **R:** Respiratory rate ≥30 breaths/min
- **B:** Systolic blood pressure <90 mm Hg or diastolic blood pressure ≤60 mm Hg
- **65:** ≥Age 65 yr
- **LDH:** >230 µ/L
- **Albumin:** <3.5 g/dL
- **Platelet count:** <100 × 10^9/L

Scoring and Decision Making

Score	Perceived Risk	Location
0–2	Low	Outpatient
3–4	Intermediate	In patient
5–8	High	ICU

Source: Liu J, Xu F, Zhou H, et al: Expanded CURB-65: A new score system predicts severity of community-acquired pneumonia with superior efficiency, *Sci Rep* 6:22911, 2016.

Types of Pneumonia

There are several types of pneumonia. *Viral pneumonia* is the most common type of pneumonia. It occurs in one third of all pneumonia cases. It may be mild and self-limiting or cause potentially life-threatening problems, such as acute respiratory failure in influenza. Patients with *bacterial pneumonia* may be extremely unwell and need hospital admission. *Mycoplasma pneumonia*, which has traits of both bacteria and viruses, is often referred to as "atypical" pneumonia. It is mild and occurs in persons younger than 40 years of age. Aspiration, necrotizing, and opportunistic pneumonia deserve further attention.

Aspiration Pneumonia. *Aspiration pneumonia* results from the abnormal entry of material from the mouth or stomach into the trachea and lungs. Conditions that increase the risk for aspiration include decreased level of consciousness (e.g., seizure, anesthesia, head injury, stroke, alcohol intake), difficulty swallowing, and insertion of nasogastric (NG) tubes with or without enteral feeding. With loss of consciousness, the gag and cough reflexes are depressed and aspiration is more likely to occur.

The aspirated material (food, water, vomitus, oropharyngeal secretions) triggers an inflammatory response. The most common form of aspiration pneumonia is a primary bacterial infection. Typically, the sputum culture shows more than 1 organism, including aerobes and anaerobes, since they both make up the flora of the oropharynx.

Until cultures are done and results obtained, initial antibiotic therapy is based on an assessment of probable cause, severity of illness, and patient factors (e.g., malnutrition, current use of antibiotic therapy). For patients who aspirate in hospitals, antibiotic coverage should include both gram-negative organisms and methicillin-resistant *Staphylococcus aureus* (MRSA). Aspiration of acidic gastric contents causes *chemical (noninfectious) pneumonitis,* which may not need antibiotic therapy. However, secondary bacterial infection can occur 48 to 72 hours later.

Necrotizing Pneumonia. *Necrotizing pneumonia* is a rare complication of bacterial lung infection. It causes the lung tissue to turn into a thick, liquid mass. In some situations, cavitation occurs. This often happens with CAP. Although we do not know the exact pathophysiologic mechanisms involved, causative organisms include *Staphylococcus, Klebsiella,* and *Streptococcus.* Lung abscesses often occur. Signs and symptoms include immediate respiratory insufficiency and/or failure, leukopenia, and bleeding into the airways.[7] Treatment includes long-term antibiotic therapy and possible surgery.

Opportunistic Pneumonia. *Opportunistic pneumonia* is inflammation and infection of the lower respiratory tract in immunocompromised patients. Persons at risk include those with altered immune responses. This can include people with severe protein-calorie malnutrition or immunodeficiencies (e.g., human immunodeficiency virus [HIV] infection) and those receiving radiation therapy, chemotherapy, and any immunosuppressive therapy, including long-term corticosteroid therapy. In addition to the risk for bacterial and viral pneumonia, the immunocompromised person may develop an infection from organisms that do not normally cause disease, such as *Pneumocystis jiroveci* (formerly *carinii*) or cytomegalovirus (CMV).

P. jiroveci pneumonia (PJP) rarely occurs in the healthy person. It is the most common form of pneumonia in people with HIV disease. The onset is slow and subtle with symptoms of fever, tachypnea, tachycardia, dyspnea, nonproductive cough, and hypoxemia. The chest x-ray usually shows diffuse bilateral infiltrates. In widespread disease, the lungs have massive consolidation. PJP can be life-threatening, causing acute respiratory failure and death. Infection can spread to other organs, including the liver, bone marrow, lymph nodes, spleen, and thyroid. Bacterial and viral pneumonias first must be ruled out

FIG. 27.1 Pathophysiologic course of pneumonia.

because of the vague presentation of PJP. Although the causative agent is fungal, PJP does not respond to antifungal agents. Treatment consists of a course of trimethoprim/sulfamethoxazole (Bactrim, Septra) either IV or orally depending on the severity of disease and the patient's response.

CMV, a herpesvirus, can cause viral pneumonia. Most CMV infections are asymptomatic or mild. Severe disease can occur in people with an impaired immune response. CMV is one of the most important life-threatening infectious complications after hematopoietic stem cell transplantation.[8] Antiviral medications (e.g., ganciclovir [Cytovene], foscarnet [Foscavir], cidofovir) and high-dose immunoglobulin are used for treatment.

Pathophysiology

Specific pathophysiologic changes related to pneumonia vary according to the offending pathogen. Almost all pathogens trigger an inflammatory response in the lungs (Fig. 27.1). Inflammation, characterized by an increase in blood flow and vascular permeability, activates neutrophils to engulf and kill the offending pathogens. As a result, the inflammatory process attracts more neutrophils, edema of the airways occurs, and fluid leaks from the capillaries and tissues into alveoli. Normal O_2 transport is affected, leading to manifestations of hypoxia (e.g., tachypnea, dyspnea, tachycardia).

Atelectasis, the absence of gas or air in 1 or more areas of the lung, may occur with pneumonia. It rarely causes any adverse effects except shortness of breath (Fig. 27.2). On the other hand, *consolidation,* a feature typical of bacterial pneumonia, occurs when the normally air-filled alveoli become filled with water, fluid, and/or debris (Fig. 27.3). This can potentially obstruct airflow, impair gas exchange, and cause the signs and symptoms associated with bacterial infection. Over time and with appropriate antibiotic therapy, macrophages lyse and process the debris. This allows lung tissue to recover and gas exchange to return to normal.

Clinical Manifestations

The most common presenting symptoms of pneumonia are cough, fever, chills, dyspnea, tachypnea, and pleuritic chest

FIG. 27.2 Atelectasis. Scanning electron micrograph of lung parenchyma. **A,** Alveoli *(A)* and alveolar-capillary membrane *(arrow).* **B,** Effects of atelectasis. Alveoli *(A)* are partially or totally collapsed. (*A,* From Dantzker DR, Bone RC, George RB, eds: *Pulmonary and critical care medicine,* vol 1, St Louis, 1993, Mosby. *B,* From Albertine KH, Williams MC, Hyde DM: Anatomy of the lungs. In RJ Mason, VC Broaddus, JF Murray, et al, eds: *Murray and Nadel's textbook of respiratory medicine,* ed 4, Philadelphia, 2005, Saunders.)

FIG. 27.3 Chest x-ray examination of patient with acute bacterial pneumonia. (© *iStock*.com/stockdevil.)

pain. The cough may or may not be productive. Sputum may be green, yellow, or even rust colored (bloody). Viral pneumonia may initially be seen as influenza, with respiratory symptoms appearing and/or worsening 12 to 36 hours after onset.

The older or debilitated patient may not have classic symptoms of pneumonia. Confusion or stupor (possibly related to hypoxia) may be the only finding. Hypothermia, rather than fever, also may be seen in the older adult. Nonspecific manifestations include diaphoresis, anorexia, fatigue, myalgias, and headache.

On assessment, fine or coarse crackles may be auscultated over the affected region. If consolidation is present, bronchial breath sounds, egophony (an increase in the sound of the patient's voice), and increased fremitus (vibration of the chest wall made by vocalization) may be present. Patients with pleural effusion may have dullness to percussion over the affected area.

Complications

A major problem today is pneumonia caused by multidrug-resistant (MDR) pathogens. Common culprits include MRSA

and gram-negative bacilli. Risk factors for MDR pneumonia include advanced age, immunosuppression, history of antibiotic use, and prolonged mechanical ventilation. Antibiotic susceptibility tests can identify MDR pathogens. The virulence of these pathogens can severely limit the available and appropriate antimicrobial therapy. MDR pathogens increase the morbidity and mortality associated with pneumonia. (See Chapter 14 for more about MDR pathogens.)

Other complications from pneumonia develop more often in older adults and those with underlying chronic diseases. These include:

- *Atelectasis*
- *Pleurisy,* an inflammation of the pleura.
- *Pleural effusion,* or fluid in the pleural space. In most cases, the effusion is sterile and is reabsorbed in 1 to 2 weeks. Sometimes, effusions require aspiration by thoracentesis.
- *Bacteremia,* bacterial infection in the blood, is more likely to occur in infections with *Streptococcus pneumoniae* and *Haemophilus influenzae.*
- *Pneumothorax* can occur when air collects in the pleural space, causing the lungs to collapse.
- *Acute respiratory failure* is one of the leading causes of death in patients with severe pneumonia. Failure occurs when pneumonia damages the lungs' ability to exchange O_2 and CO_2 across the alveolar-capillary membrane.
- *Sepsis/septic shock* can occur when bacteria within alveoli enter the bloodstream. Severe sepsis can lead to shock and multisystem organ dysfunction syndrome (MODS) (see Chapter 66).

Lung abscess is not a common complication of pneumonia. However, it may occur with pneumonia caused by *S. aureus* and gram-negative organisms. *Empyema,* the accumulation of purulent exudate in the pleural cavity, occurs in less than 5% of cases. It requires antibiotic therapy and drainage of the exudate by a chest tube or open surgical drainage.[9] Pleurisy, pleural effusion, atelectasis, lung abscess, and pneumothorax are discussed later in this chapter.

Diagnostic Studies

The common diagnostic procedures for pneumonia are outlined in Table 27.4. History, physical examination, and chest x-ray often give enough information to make immediate decisions about early treatment. Chest x-ray often shows patterns characteristic of the infecting pathogen and is important in diagnosing pneumonia. X-ray may also show pleural effusions. A thoracentesis and/or bronchoscopy with washings may be used to obtain fluid samples from patients not responding to initial therapy.

Arterial blood gases (ABGs) may be obtained to assess for hypoxemia (partial pressure of O_2 in arterial blood [PaO_2] less than 80 mm Hg), hypercapnia (partial pressure of carbon dioxide in arterial blood [$PaCO_2$] greater than 45 mm Hg), and acidosis (pH less than 7.35). Leukocytosis occurs in most patients with bacterial pneumonia. The white blood cell (WBC) count is usually greater than 15,000/μL (15×10^9/L) with the presence of bands (immature neutrophils).

Ideally, a sputum specimen for culture and Gram stain to identify the organism is obtained before beginning antibiotic therapy. However, antibiotic administration should not be delayed if a specimen cannot be obtained. Delays in antibiotic therapy can increase the risk for morbidity and mortality. Blood cultures are done for patients who are seriously ill.

TABLE 27.4 Interprofessional Care

Pneumonia

Diagnostic Assessment
- History and physical examination
- Chest x-ray
- Sputum: Gram stain, culture and sensitivity test
- Pulse oximetry or arterial blood gases (if indicated)
- CBC, white blood cell differential, and routine blood chemistries (if indicated)
- Blood cultures (if indicated)

Management
- Increased fluid intake (at least 3 L/day), IV fluids
- Balance between activity and rest
- O_2 therapy
- Physiotherapy
- VTE prophylaxis
- Critical care management, with mechanical ventilation as needed

Drug Therapy
- Appropriate antibiotic therapy (Table 27.6)
- Antipyretics
- Analgesics
- Nonsteroidal antiinflammatory drugs (if no contraindications)

TABLE 27.5 Pneumococcal Vaccines

Vaccine*	Recommendations for Use
Pneumococcal conjugate vaccine (PCV13, Prevnar 13)[†]	• All children <2 yrs • All adults ≥65 yrs • Anyone 2–64 yrs old with certain medical conditions (e.g., sickle cell disease, asplenia, immunodeficiencies, HIV infection, chronic renal failure, leukemia, cancer, long-term immunosuppressive therapy, CSF leaks, cochlear implant[s])
Pneumococcal polysaccharide vaccine (PPSV23, Pneumovax 23)[†]	• All adults ≥65 yrs • Anyone 2–64 yrs old with certain long-term health problems (e.g., heart disease, lung disease, diabetes, alcoholism, cirrhosis, sickle cell disease, CSF leaks, cochlear implant) • Anyone 2–64 yrs with a disease or condition that weakens the immune system or taking drugs that lower the body's resistance to infection (e.g., HIV infection; lymphoma or leukemia; kidney failure; damaged or no spleen; multiple myeloma; receiving immunosuppressive chemotherapy, radiation therapy, or long-term corticosteroids; after organ or bone marrow transplantation) • Adults 19–64 yrs who smoke cigarettes or have asthma

*For more details on scheduling of pneumococcal vaccinations, see *www.cdc.gov/vaccines/vpd/pneumo/hcp/recommendations.html.*
[†]As their names imply, PCV13 and Prevnar 13 protect against 13 types of pneumococcal bacteria, and PPSV23 and Pneumovax 23 protect against 23 types of pneumococcal bacteria. The vaccinations have different mechanisms of action.

Serum levels of C-reactive protein (CRP), kallistatin, and procalcitonin are currently being explored as sources of information to help distinguish pneumonia from other types of heart and respiratory failure.[10]

Interprofessional Care

Pneumococcal vaccine is used to prevent *S. pneumoniae* infection (Table 27.5). Prompt treatment with the appropriate antibiotic is essential. Antibiotics are highly effective for both bacterial and mycoplasma pneumonia. In uncomplicated cases, the patient responds to drug therapy within 48 to 72 hours. Signs of improvement include decreased temperature, improved breathing, and reduced chest discomfort. Abnormal physical findings can last more than 7 days. A repeat chest x-ray may be done in 6 to 8 weeks to assess for resolution.

Supportive measures are tailored to the patient's needs. These may include O_2 therapy to treat hypoxemia, analgesics to relieve chest pain, and antipyretics (e.g., aspirin, acetaminophen) for fever. Although cough suppressants, mucolytics, bronchodilators, and corticosteroids are often prescribed as adjunctive therapy, the use of these drugs is debatable. However, they may be prescribed for patients with underlying chronic conditions.

Tailor rest and activity to each patient's tolerance. Benefits of mobility include improved diaphragm movement and chest expansion, mobilization of secretions, and prevention of venous stasis.

Currently, no definitive treatment exists for most viral pneumonias. Care is generally supportive. In most circumstances, viral pneumonia is self-limiting and will often resolve in 3 to 4 days. Antiviral therapy may be used to treat pneumonia caused by influenza (e.g., oseltamivir, zanamivir) or a few other viruses (e.g., acyclovir [Zovirax] for herpes simplex virus).[11]

Drug Therapy. Once the pneumonia is classified, the HCP selects empiric therapy based on the likely pathogen (Table 27.2). Table 27.6 presents the drug therapy for bacterial CAP.

For all types of pneumonia, empiric antibiotic therapy is based on whether the patient has risk factors for MDR pathogens. The prevalence and resistance patterns of MDR pathogens vary among localities and agencies. Therefore the antibiotic regimen must be adapted to local patterns of antibiotic resistance. Multiple regimens exist, but all should initially include antibiotics that are effective against both resistant gram-negative and resistant gram-positive organisms.

Clinical improvement usually occurs in 3 to 5 days. Patients who deteriorate or do not respond to therapy need aggressive reevaluation to assess for noninfectious causes, complications, coexisting infectious processes, or pneumonia caused by an MDR pathogen.

IV antibiotic therapy should be switched to oral therapy as soon as the patient is hemodynamically stable, is improving clinically, is able to ingest oral medication, and has a functioning gastrointestinal (GI) tract. Stable patients do not need to be observed in the hospital and can be discharged to home on oral antibiotics. Total treatment time for patients with CAP should be a minimum of 5 days. The patient should be afebrile for 48 to 72 hours before stopping treatment. However, you need to emphasize the importance of completing the full course of antibiotic treatment. Longer treatment time may be needed if initial therapy was not active against the identified pathogen or complications occur.

Nutritional Therapy. Hydration is important in the supportive treatment of pneumonia to prevent dehydration and to thin and loosen secretions. Carefully monitor fluid intake. If the patient is an older adult, has heart failure (HF), or has a known preexisting respiratory condition, IV administration of fluids and electrolytes may be needed.

Weight loss may occur in patients with pneumonia because of increased metabolic needs and difficulty eating due to shortness of breath or nonspecific abdominal symptoms. Small, frequent meals are easier for dyspneic patients to tolerate. Offer foods high in calories and nutrients.

TABLE 27.6 Drug Therapy

Bacterial Community-Acquired Pneumonia

Patient Variable	Treatment Options
Outpatient	
Previously healthy No recent antibiotic therapy in past 3 months and no risk for drug-resistant *Staphylococcus pneumoniae* (DRSP)	Macrolide *OR* doxycycline
Co-morbidities (e.g., COPD; diabetes; chronic heart, liver, lung, or renal disease; cancer; use of antibiotics in past 3 months)	Respiratory fluoroquinolone *OR* β-Lactam plus macrolide (doxycycline may be substituted for macrolide)
Regions with ≥25% macrolide-resistant *S. pneumoniae*	Respiratory fluoroquinolone *OR* β-Lactam plus macrolide
Inpatient	
Medical unit	Respiratory fluoroquinolone *OR* β-Lactam plus macrolide
ICU Acute respiratory failure, septic shock, intubation and mechanical ventilation	β-Lactam plus either azithromycin or respiratory fluoroquinolone
Special Considerations	
• Community-acquired methicillin-resistant *Staphylococcus aureus* (CA-MRSA)	Add vancomycin or linezolid (Zyvox)
• *Pseudomonas* infection	Antipneumococcal, antipseudomonal β-lactam plus either ciprofloxacin or levofloxacin *OR* Antipneumococcal, antipseudomonal β-lactam plus aminoglycoside and azithromycin *OR* Antipneumococcal, antipseudomonal β-lactam plus an aminoglycoside and an antipneumococcal fluoroquinolone
• *Pseudomonas* infection in patient with penicillin allergy	Substitute aztreonam for the above β-lactam
Types of Antibiotics	
Antipneumococcal, antipseudomonal β-lactams	imipenem/cilastatin, meropenem (Merrem), cefepime (Maxipime), piperacillin/tazobactam (Zosyn)
β-Lactams	High-dose amoxicillin, amoxicillin/clavulanate (Augmentin), cefpodoxime, ceftriaxone, cefuroxime (Ceftin)
Fluoroquinolones	moxifloxacin (Avelox, Vigamox), levofloxacin, gemifloxacin (Factive)
Macrolides	erythromycin, azithromycin (Zithromax), clarithromycin (Biaxin)

Source: Infectious Diseases Advisor: Community acquired pneumonia guidelines. Retrieved from *www.infectiousdiseaseadvisor.com/clinical-charts/community-acquired-pneumonia-guidelines/article/419038/*.

❖ NURSING MANAGEMENT: PNEUMONIA

◆ Nursing Assessment

Table 27.7 presents subjective and objective data to obtain from a patient with pneumonia.

◆ Nursing Diagnoses

Nursing diagnoses for the patient with pneumonia may include:
- Impaired gas exchange
- Impaired breathing
- Fluid imbalance
- Hyperthermia
- Activity intolerance

Additional information on nursing diagnoses and interventions for the patient with pneumonia is presented in eNursing Care Plan 27.1 on the website for this chapter.

TABLE 27.7 Nursing Assessment

Pneumonia

Subjective Data

Important Health Information

Past health history: Lung cancer, COPD, diabetes, chronic debilitating disease, malnutrition, altered consciousness, immunosuppression, exposure to chemical toxins, dust, or allergens

Medications: Antibiotics, corticosteroids, chemotherapy, or any immunosuppressants

Surgery or other treatments: Recent abdominal or chest surgery, splenectomy, endotracheal intubation, or any surgery with general anesthesia. Enteral feedings

Functional Health Patterns

Health perception–health management: Cigarette smoking, alcohol use; recent URI, malaise

Nutritional-metabolic: Anorexia, nausea, vomiting. Chills

Activity-exercise: Prolonged bed rest or immobility. Fatigue, weakness. Dyspnea, cough (productive or nonproductive). Nasal congestion

Cognitive-perceptual: Pain with breathing, chest pain, sore throat, headache, abdominal pain, muscle aches

Objective Data

General

Fever, restlessness, or lethargy. Splinting of affected area

Respiratory

Tachypnea, pharyngitis, asymmetric chest movements or retraction, decreased excursion, nasal flaring. Use of accessory muscles (neck, abdomen). Crackles, friction rub on auscultation, dullness on percussion over consolidated areas, increased tactile fremitus on palpation. Pink, rusty, purulent, green, yellow, or white sputum (amount may be scant to copious)

Cardiovascular

Tachycardia

Neurologic

Changes in mental status, ranging from confusion to delirium

Possible Diagnostic Findings

Leukocytosis. Abnormal ABGs with ↓ or normal PaO_2, ↓ or normal $PaCO_2$, and ↑ or normal pH initially, and later ↓ PaO_2, ↑ $PaCO_2$, and ↓ pH. Positive sputum on Gram stain and culture. Patchy or diffuse infiltrates, abscesses, pleural effusion, or pneumothorax on chest x-ray

❖ **Planning**

The overall goals are that the patient with pneumonia will have (1) clear breath sounds, (2) normal breathing patterns, (3) no signs of hypoxia, (4) normal chest x-ray, (5) normal WBC count, and (6) absence of complications related to pneumonia.

❖ **Nursing Implementation**

❖ **Health Promotion.** To reduce the risk for pneumonia, teach patients to practice good health habits, such as frequent hand washing, proper nutrition, adequate rest, regular exercise, and coughing or sneezing into the elbow rather than hands. Avoiding cigarette smoke is one of the most important health-promoting behaviors. If possible, avoid exposure to people with URIs. If a URI occurs, it requires prompt attention with supportive measures (e.g., rest, fluids). If symptoms persist for longer than 7 days, the person should seek medical care. Identifying patients at risk (Table 27.1) and taking measures to prevent pneumonia are priority interventions. Encourage those at risk for pneumonia (e.g., chronically ill, older adult) to obtain both influenza and pneumococcal vaccines (Table 27.5).

❖ **Acute Care.** Although many patients with pneumonia are treated on an outpatient basis, the nursing care plan for a patient with pneumonia (eNursing Care Plan 27.1) applies to both patients at home and hospitalized patients. Essential nursing care for patients with pneumonia includes monitoring physical assessment parameters, providing treatment, and monitoring the patient's response to treatment. Prompt collection of specimens and initiation of antibiotics are critical. O_2 therapy, hydration, nutritional support, breathing exercises, early ambulation, and therapeutic positioning are part of nursing care. Working with respiratory therapy to monitor the patient's condition and with physical therapy for postural drainage and chest percussion is essential.

Place the patient with altered consciousness in positions (e.g., side-lying, upright) that will prevent or minimize the risk for aspiration. Turn and reposition patients at least every 2 hours to promote adequate lung expansion and mobilization of secretions. Encourage and assist with ambulation and positioning into a chair. In the ICU, strict adherence to all aspects of the ventilator bundle (see Table 67.8), a group of interventions aimed at reducing the risk for VAP, significantly reduces VAP.

For the patient who has difficulty swallowing and needs aid in eating, drinking, and taking medication to prevent aspiration, elevate the patient's head-of-bed to at least 30 degrees and have the patient sit up for all meals. Assess for a gag reflex before giving food or fluids. Patients who have orogastric or NG tubes are at risk for aspiration pneumonia (see Chapter 39). Although feeding tubes are small, any interruption in the integrity of the lower esophageal sphincter can allow reflux of gastric contents. To prevent aspiration, elevate the head of the bed to at least 30 degrees (see Table 39.11).

Patients with impaired mobility from any cause need help with turning and moving as well as encouragement to breathe deeply at frequent intervals. Observe the patient's skin and all pressure points for any evidence of redness or breakdown, especially the sacrum and coccyx. Treat pain to a comfort level that permits the patient to deep breathe and cough yet remain awake and alert and achieve optimum mobility. Early mobilization, the use of an incentive spirometer, and twice-daily oral hygiene with chlorhexidine swabs significantly reduce the incidence of pneumonia in postoperative patients.[12]

Practice strict medical asepsis and adherence to infection control guidelines to reduce the incidence of health care–associated infection (HAI). Staff and visitors should wash their hands on entering and leaving the patient's room. Staff must wash or use sanitizing hand gel before and after providing care and on removing gloves. Use strict sterile aseptic technique when suctioning the patient's trachea, and use caution when handling ventilator circuits, tracheostomy tubing, and nebulizer circuits that can become contaminated from patient secretions. Avoid inappropriate use of antibiotics to prevent the development of MDR organisms.

❖ **Ambulatory Care.** Teach the patient about the importance of taking every dose of the prescribed antibiotic, any drug-drug and food-drug interactions for the prescribed antibiotic, and the need for adequate rest to promote recovery. Tell the patient to drink plenty of liquids (at least 6 to 10 glasses/day, unless contraindicated) and to avoid alcohol and smoking. A cool mist humidifier or warm bath may help the patient breathe easier. Tell patients that it may be several weeks before their usual vigor and sense of well-being return. Explain that a follow-up chest x-ray may be done in 6 to 8 weeks to evaluate resolution of pneumonia. The older adult or chronically ill patient may have a prolonged period of convalescence.

Teaching should include information about available influenza and pneumococcal vaccines. Patients can receive the pneumococcal vaccine and influenza vaccine at the same time but not in the exact same location. The vaccines cannot be mixed into 1 injection.

❖ **Evaluation**

The expected outcomes are that the patient with pneumonia will have:

• Effective respiratory rate, rhythm, and depth of respirations
• Lungs clear to auscultation
• Absence of infection

TUBERCULOSIS

Tuberculosis (TB) is an infectious disease caused by *Mycobacterium tuberculosis*. It usually involves the lungs, but can infect any organ, including the brain, kidneys, and bones. About one third of the world's population are infected with TB.[13] The incidence of TB worldwide declined until the mid-1980s. We are now seeing increasing rates of TB. This is attributed to HIV disease and the emergence of drug-resistant strains of *M. tuberculosis*. TB is the leading cause of mortality in patients with HIV infection. Though the prevalence of TB in the United States has steadily declined, we do not think it is currently possible to eradicate TB in the United States.[14]

TB occurs disproportionately in the poor, underserved, and minorities. People most at risk include the homeless, residents of inner-city neighborhoods, foreign-born people, those living or working in institutions (long-term care facilities, prisons, shelters, hospitals), IV injecting drug users, overcrowded living conditions, less than optimal sanitation, and those with poor access to health care. Immunosuppression from any cause (e.g., HIV infection, cancer, long-term corticosteroid use) increases the risk for active TB infection.

Once a strain of *M. tuberculosis* develops resistance to the most potent first-line antitubercular drugs (isoniazid [INH] and rifampin [Rifadin]), it is defined as *multidrug-resistant tuberculosis (MDR-TB)*.[15] Extensively drug-resistant TB (XDR-TB)

TABLE 27.8 Classification of Tuberculosis

Class	Exposure or Infection	Description
0	No TB exposure	No TB exposure, not infected (no history of exposure, negative tuberculin skin test)
1	TB exposure, no infection	TB exposure, no evidence of infection (history of exposure, negative tuberculin skin test)
2	Latent TB infection, no disease	TB infection without disease (positive reaction to tuberculin skin test, negative bacteriologic studies, no x-ray findings compatible with TB, no clinical evidence of TB)
3	TB, clinically active	TB infection with clinically active disease (positive bacteriologic studies or both a significant reaction to tuberculin skin test and clinical or x-ray evidence of current disease)
4	TB, but not clinically active	No current disease (history of previous episode of TB or abnormal, stable x-ray findings in a person with a positive reaction to tuberculin skin test. Negative bacteriologic studies if done. No clinical or x-ray evidence of current disease)
5	TB suspect	TB suspect (diagnosis pending). Person should not be in this classification for >3 mo

Source: American Thoracic Society.

occurs when the organism is also resistant to any of the fluoroquinolones plus any injectable antibiotic agent.[16] Resistance results from several problems, including incorrect prescribing, lack of public health case management, patient nonadherence to the prescribed regimen, and lack of funding for education and prevention.

Etiology and Pathophysiology

M. tuberculosis is a gram-positive, aerobic, acid-fast bacillus (AFB). It is usually spread from person to person by airborne droplets expectorated when breathing, talking, singing, sneezing, and coughing. A process of evaporation leaves small droplet nuclei, 1 to 5 µm in size, suspended in the air for minutes to hours. Another person then inhales the bacteria. Humans are the only known reservoir for TB. TB is not highly infectious, as transmission usually requires close contact and frequent or prolonged exposure. The disease cannot be spread by touching, sharing food utensils, kissing, or any other type of physical contact.

Factors that influence transmission include the (1) number of organisms expelled into the air, (2) concentration of organisms (small spaces with limited ventilation would mean higher concentration), (3) length of time of exposure, and (4) immune system of the exposed person. Once inhaled, these small droplets lodge in bronchioles and alveoli. A local inflammatory reaction occurs, and the focus of infection is established. This is called the *Ghon lesion* or *focus*. It represents a calcified TB granuloma, the hallmark of a primary TB infection.[17] The formation of a granuloma is a defense mechanism aimed at walling off the infection and preventing further spread. Replication of the bacillus is inhibited, and the infection is stopped.

Most immunocompetent adults infected with TB can completely kill the mycobacteria. Some people have the mycobacteria in a nonreplicating dormant state. Of these persons, 5% to 10% develop active TB infection when the bacteria begin to multiply months or years later. While *M. tuberculosis* is aerophilic (O_2 loving) and has an affinity for the lungs, the infection can spread through the lymphatic system and find favorable environments for growth in other organs. These include the cerebral cortex, spine, epiphyses of the bone, liver, kidneys, lymph nodes, and adrenal glands.

Classification

Several systems can be used to classify TB. The American Thoracic Society classifies TB based on development of the disease (Table 27.8). TB also can be classified according to (1) its

presentation (primary, latent, or reactivated) and (2) whether it is pulmonary or extrapulmonary.

Primary TB infection occurs when the bacteria are inhaled and start an inflammatory reaction. Most people mount effective immune responses to encapsulate these organisms for the rest of their lives, preventing the initial infection from progressing to disease. If the initial immune response is not adequate, the body cannot contain the organisms. As a result, the bacteria replicate and *active TB disease* results. When active disease develops within the first 2 years of infection, it is called *primary TB*. People co-infected with HIV are at greatest risk for developing active TB.

Post-primary TB, or *reactivation TB*, is defined as TB disease occurring 2 or more years after the initial infection. If the site of TB is pulmonary or laryngeal, the person is infectious and can transmit the disease to others.

Latent TB infection (LTBI) occurs in a person who does not have active TB disease (Table 27.9). People with LTBI have a positive skin test but are asymptomatic. They cannot transmit the TB bacteria to others but can develop active TB disease at some point. Immunosuppression, diabetes, poor nutrition, aging, pregnancy, stress, and chronic disease can reactivate the disease. Treatment of LTBI (discussed later in this chapter) is as important as primary TB.

Clinical Manifestations

Symptoms of pulmonary TB usually do not develop until 2 to 3 weeks after infection or reactivation. The primary manifestation is an initial dry cough that often becomes productive with mucoid or mucopurulent sputum. Active TB disease may initially present with constitutional symptoms (e.g., fatigue, malaise, anorexia, unexplained weight loss, low-grade fevers,

TABLE 27.9 Latent Tuberculosis Infection (LTBI) Compared to Tuberculosis Disease

LTBI	TB Disease
Has no symptoms	Has symptoms that may include: • Bad cough that lasts ≥3 wk • Pain in the chest • Coughing up blood or sputum • Weakness or fatigue • Weight loss, no appetite • Chills • Fever • Sweating at night
Does not feel sick	Usually feels sick
Cannot spread TB bacteria to others	May spread TB bacteria to others
Usually has a skin test or blood test result showing TB infection	Usually has a skin test or blood test result showing TB infection
Has a normal chest x-ray and a negative sputum smear	May have an abnormal chest x-ray or positive sputum smear or culture
Needs treatment for latent TB infection to prevent active TB disease	Needs treatment for active TB disease

Source: CDC: Latent TB infection and TB disease. Retrieved from *www.cdc.gov/tb/topic/basics/tbinfectiondisease.htm.*

night sweats). Dyspnea is a late symptom that may signify considerable pulmonary disease or a pleural effusion. Hemoptysis, which occurs in less than 10% of patients with TB, is also a late symptom.

Sometimes TB has a more acute, sudden presentation. The patient may have a high fever, chills, generalized flu-like symptoms, pleuritic pain, a productive cough, and acute respiratory failure. Auscultation of the lungs may be normal or reveal adventitious sounds, such as crackles.

Immunosuppressed (e.g., HIV-infected) people and older adults are less likely to have fever and other signs of an infection. In patients with HIV, classic manifestations of TB, such as fever, cough, and weight loss, may be wrongly attributed to PJP or other HIV-associated opportunistic diseases. Respiratory problems in patients with HIV must be carefully investigated to determine the cause. A change in cognitive function may be the only initial presenting sign of TB in an older person.

The manifestations of extrapulmonary TB depend on the organs infected. For example, renal TB can cause dysuria and hematuria. Bone and joint TB may cause severe pain. Headaches, vomiting, and lymphadenopathy may be present with TB meningitis.

Complications

Properly treated, pulmonary TB typically heals without complications, except for scarring and residual cavitation within the lung. Significant pulmonary damage, although rare, can occur in patients who are poorly treated or who do not respond to TB treatment.

Miliary TB is widespread dissemination of the mycobacterium. The bacteria spread through the bloodstream to several distant organs. The infection is characterized by a large amount of TB bacilli and may be fatal if untreated. It can occur with primary disease or reactivation of LTBI. Manifestations slowly progress over a period of days, weeks, or even months. Symptoms vary depending on the organs that are affected.

Fever, cough, and lymphadenopathy are present. Hepatomegaly and splenomegaly may occur.

Pleural TB, a specific type of extrapulmonary TB, can result from either primary disease or reactivation of a latent infection. Chest pain, fever, cough, and presence of a unilateral pleural effusion are common. A pleural effusion is caused by bacteria in the pleural space, which trigger an inflammatory reaction and a pleural exudate of protein-rich fluid. Empyema is less common than effusion but may occur from large numbers of tubercular organisms in the pleural space. Diagnosis is confirmed by AFB cultures and a pleural biopsy.

Because TB can infect organs throughout the body, various acute and long-term complications can result. TB in the spine (Pott's disease) can lead to destruction of the intervertebral disc and adjacent vertebrae. Central nervous system (CNS) TB can cause severe bacterial meningitis. Abdominal TB can lead to peritonitis, especially in HIV-positive patients. The kidneys, adrenal glands, lymph nodes, and urogenital tract can be affected.

❖ Diagnostic Studies

◆ **Tuberculin Skin Test.** The tuberculin skin test (TST) (Mantoux test) using purified protein derivative (PPD) is the standard method to screen people for *M. tuberculosis*. The test is given by injecting 0.1 mL of PPD intradermally on the ventral surface of the forearm. The test is read by inspection and palpation 48 to 72 hours later for the presence or absence of induration. Induration, a palpable, raised, hardened area or swelling (not redness) at the injection site means the person has been exposed to TB and has developed antibodies.[18] Antibody formation occurs 2 to 12 weeks after initial exposure to the bacteria. Any indurated area present is measured and recorded in millimeters. Based on the size of the induration and the risk factors, an interpretation is made according to CDC standards for determining a positive test reaction. Because the immunocompromised patient may have a decreased response to TST, smaller induration reactions (5 mm or larger) are considered positive. See Table 25.14 for guidelines in interpreting responses to the TST.

Two-step testing with the Mantoux TST should be used for baseline or initial screening. If the initial test is positive, the person needs further evaluation for active disease. If the first test is negative, a second TST is done 1 to 3 weeks later. Some people with LTBI or who were previously infected with TB may have a false negative result with the first TST. Repeating the TST may stimulate (boost) the body's ability to react to tuberculin in future tests.[18] A positive reaction to a subsequent test could be a new infection or the result of the boosted reaction to an old infection. Two-step testing is recommended for initial testing for health care workers and for those who have a decreased response to allergens. A previously negative 2-step TST ensures that any future positive results can be accurately interpreted as being caused by a new infection.

Interferon-γ Release Assays. Interferon-γ (INF-γ) release assays (IGRAs) are another screening tool for TB. IGRAs are blood tests that detect INF-γ release from T cells in response to *M. tuberculosis*.[19] Examples of IGRAs include QuantiFERON-TB Gold In-Tube test (QFT-GIT) and the T-SPOT.TB test. Test results are available in a few hours.

IGRAs offer several advantages over the TST in that they require only 1 patient visit, are not subject to reader bias, have no booster phenomenon, and are not affected by prior bacillus Calmette-Guérin (BCG) vaccination. The cost of an IGRA

TABLE 27.10 Interprofessional Care

Pulmonary Tuberculosis

Diagnostic Assessment

- History and physical examination
- Tuberculin skin test (TST)
- QuantiFERON-TB Gold In-Tube test (QFT-GIT) or T-SPOT.TB test
- Chest x-ray
- Bacteriologic studies
- Sputum smear for acid-fast bacilli (AFB)
- Sputum culture

Management

- Long-term treatment with antimicrobial drugs (Tables 27.11 and 27.12)
- Follow-up AFB smears, cultures, and chest x-rays
- Follow-up care, addressing needs and concerns of patient and close contacts, and involving community health care workers and social workers

TABLE 27.11 Drug Therapy

Tuberculosis

Drug	Common Side Effects
aminoglycosides	Hepatitis, GI toxicity
• amikacin	Prolongation of QT interval
• capreomycin (Capastat)	Ototoxicity, nephrotoxicity
bedaquiline (Sirturo)	Hepatotoxicity, nausea
ethambutol (Myambutol)	Headache, blurred vision, ocular toxicity (decreased red-green color discrimination)
fluoroquinolones	GI problems, neurologic effects (dizziness, headache), rash
• levofloxacin	
• moxifloxacin (Avelox, Vigamox)	
isoniazid	Hepatotoxicity, asymptomatic elevation of aminotransferases (ALT, AST)
	Vomiting, confusion, headaches
pyrazinamide	Hepatotoxicity, arthralgias, hyperuricemia
rifabutin (Mycobutin)	Hepatotoxicity, thrombocytopenia, neutropenia
	Orange discoloration of bodily fluids (sputum, urine, sweat, tears)
	Nausea, vomiting, loss of appetite
rifampin (Rifadin)	Hepatotoxicity, thrombocytopenia,
	Orange discoloration of bodily fluids (sputum, urine, sweat, tears)
	Anorexia, nausea, abdominal discomfort
rifapentine (Priftin)	Like those of rifampin
streptomycin	Ototoxicity, neurotoxicity, nephrotoxicity

ALT, Alanine transaminase; *AST,* aspartate aminotransferase; *MDR-TB,* multidrug resistant tuberculosis.

is much higher than the TST. Current guidelines suggest that both tests are viable options and that choice should be based on context and reasons for testing. Neither IGRAs nor TST can tell between LTBI and active TB infection. LTBI can only be diagnosed by excluding active TB.

Chest X-ray. Although the chest x-ray findings are important, it is not possible to make a diagnosis of TB solely on chest x-ray findings. The chest x-ray may appear normal in a patient with TB. Findings suggestive of TB include upper lobe infiltrates, cavitary infiltrates, lymph node involvement, and pleural and/or pericardial effusion. Other diseases, such as sarcoidosis, can mimic the appearance of TB.

Bacteriologic Studies. Culture is the gold standard for diagnosing TB. Three consecutive sputum specimens are needed, each collected at 8- to 24-hour intervals, with at least 1 early morning specimen. The initial test involves a microscopic examination of stained sputum smears for AFB. A definitive diagnosis of TB requires mycobacterial growth, which can take up to 6 weeks. Treatment is needed pending the culture results for patients in whom suspicion of TB is high. Samples for other suspected TB sites can be collected from gastric washings, cerebrospinal fluid (CSF), or fluid from an effusion or abscess.

Interprofessional Care

Most patients with TB are treated on an outpatient basis (Table 27.10). Many people can continue to work and maintain their lifestyles with few changes. Patients with sputum smear–positive TB are considered infectious for the first 2 weeks after starting treatment. Advise these patients to restrict visitors and avoid travel on public transportation and trips to public places. Teach them the importance of good hand washing and oral hygiene. Hospitalization may be needed for the severely ill or debilitated.

Drug Therapy

Active TB Disease. The mainstay of TB treatment is drug therapy (Table 27.11). Promoting and monitoring adherence are critical for treatment to be successful. Because of the growing prevalence of MDR-TB, it is important to manage the patient with active TB aggressively. Drug therapy is divided into 2 phases: initial and continuation (Table 27.12). In most circumstances the treatment regimen for patients with previously untreated TB consists of a 3-month initial phase with 4 drugs (isoniazid, rifampin, pyrazinamide, and ethambutol). If drug susceptibility test results show that the bacteria are

TABLE 27.12 Drug Therapy

Tuberculosis Treatment Regimens

Initial Phase	Continuation Phase
Option 1	
4-drug regimen consisting of isoniazid, rifampin, pyrazinamide, ethambutol Given daily for 56 doses (8 wk) *OR* 5 days/wk DOT for 40 doses (8 wk)	isoniazid, rifampin daily for 126 doses (18 wk) *OR* 5 days/wk DOT for 90 doses (18 wk)
Option 2	
4-drug regimen consisting of isoniazid, rifampin, pyrazinamide, ethambutol Given daily for 56 doses (8 wk) *OR* 5 days/wk DOT for 40 doses (8 wk)	isoniazid, rifampin 3 times weekly for 54 doses (18 wk)
Option 3	
4-drug regimen consisting of isoniazid, rifampin, pyrazinamide, ethambutol Given 3 times weekly for 24 doses (8 wk)	isoniazid, rifampin 3 times weekly for 54 doses (18 wk)
Option 4	
4-drug regimen consisting of isoniazid, rifampin, ethambutol, pyrazinamide Given daily for 14 doses (2 wk) then twice weekly for 12 doses	isoniazid, rifampin twice weekly for 36 doses (18 wk)

Source: Official American Thoracic Society/CDC/Infectious Diseases Society of America: Clinical practice guidelines: Treatment of drug susceptible tuberculosis. Retrieved from *www.cdc.gov/tb/topic/treatment/tbdisease.htm.* *DOT,* Directly observed therapy.

susceptible to all drugs, ethambutol may be stopped. If the patient develops a toxic reaction to the primary drugs, other drugs can be used, including rifabutin and rifapentine (Priftin). If pyrazinamide cannot be included in the initial phase (because of liver disease, pregnancy, etc.), the remaining 3 drugs are used for the initial phase.

 DRUG ALERT Isoniazid

- Alcohol may increase risk for hepatotoxicity.
- Teach patient to avoid drinking alcohol during treatment.
- Monitor for signs of hepatitis before and while taking drug.

Sensitivity testing guides the treatment for MDR-TB. MDR-TB therapy in the initial phase typically includes 5 drugs: 1or 2 first-line agents, a fluoroquinolone, an injectable antibiotic, and 1 or more second-line agents, for at least 6 months after sputum culture is negative. This is followed by at least 4 drugs, minus the injectable antibiotic, for 18 to 24 months. Two newer drugs, bedaquiline (Sirturo) and Delamanid (Deltyba), are used in combination with other drugs to treat MDR-TB and XDR-TB.

Directly observed therapy (DOT) involves providing the antitubercular drugs directly to patients and watching as they swallow the medications. To ensure adherence, it is the preferred strategy for all patients with TB, especially for those at risk for nonadherence.[20] Nonadherence is a major factor in the emergence of MDR-TB and treatment failures. Many people do not adhere to the treatment program despite understanding the disease process and value of treatment. DOT is an expensive but essential public health measure. The risk for reactivation of TB and MDR-TB is increased in patients who do not complete the full course of therapy. In many areas, the public health nurse administers DOT at a clinic site.

When DOT is not used, fixed-dose combination drugs may enhance adherence. Combinations of isoniazid and rifampin and of isoniazid, rifampin, and pyrazinamide are available to simplify therapy. The therapy for people with HIV follows the same therapy options outlined in Table 27.12. However, alternative regimens in any HIV-infected patient that include once-weekly isoniazid plus rifapentine continuation dosing or twice-weekly isoniazid plus rifampin or rifabutin, should not be used if CD4+ counts are less than 100/μL.

Teaching patients about the adverse effects of these drugs and when to seek prompt medical attention is critical. The major side effect of isoniazid, rifampin, and pyrazinamide is nonviral hepatitis. Baseline liver function tests (LFTs) are done at the start of treatment and monitored closely (e.g., every 2 to 4 weeks), especially if results are abnormal.

Latent Tuberculosis Infection. In people with LTBI, drug therapy helps prevent a TB infection from developing into active TB disease. Because a person with LTBI has fewer bacteria, treatment is much easier. Usually only 1 drug is needed. Drug therapy regimens for LTBI are outlined in Table 27.13.

The standard treatment regimen for LTBI is 9 months of daily isoniazid. It is an effective and inexpensive drug that the patient can take orally. While the 9-month regimen is more effective, adherence issues may make a 6-month regimen preferable. For patients with HIV and those with fibrotic lesions on chest x-ray, isoniazid is given for 9 months. An alternative 3-month regimen of isoniazid and rifapentine may be used for otherwise healthy patients who are not presumed to be infected with MDR bacilli. Four-month therapy with rifampin may be indicated if the patient is resistant to isoniazid. Because of severe liver injury

and deaths, the CDC does not recommend the combination of rifampin and pyrazinamide for treatment of LTBI.

Bacille Calmette-Guérin Vaccine. Bacille Calmette-Guérin (BCG) vaccine is a live, attenuated strain of *Mycobacterium*

ETHICAL/LEGAL DILEMMAS
Patient Adherence

Situation

While working at a health clinic at a homeless shelter, you discover that F.C., a 64-yr-old man with tuberculosis (TB), has not been taking his prescribed medications. He tells you that it is hard for him to get to the clinic to obtain the medication, much less to keep on a schedule. You are concerned not only about this patient, but about the risks for the other people at the shelter, in the park, and at the meal sites where he often visits.

Ethical/Legal Points for Consideration

- Adherence is a complex issue involving a person's culture, values, and beliefs, perceived risk for disease, availability of resources, access to treatment, and perceived consequences of failure to adhere to treatment.
- Advocacy for the patient and the community obliges you to involve other members of the health care team, such as social services, to aid in obtaining resources or support for the patient to complete a course of treatment.
- Some cities and states have a stepwise legal process for managing nonadherent TB patients.[1]
- Legally the constitutional right to control one's own body may be limited by state and federal obligation to protect public health and safety. Most of these laws have provisions for the protection of constitutional rights, such as right to counsel, right to least restrictive alternative in terms of confinement setting, and right to prompt judicial review.
- The federal government and many states have provisions for quarantine, detention, and treatment. With the threats of bioterrorism and the globalization of exposure to highly lethal infectious diseases, it seems unlikely that the government's power to detain will be removed.

Discussion Questions

1. What alternatives of care can we offer to F.C.?
2. Under what circumstances, if any, are HCPs justified in overriding a patient's autonomy or decision making?

Reference

California Department of Public Health: Plan for the detention of persistently non-adherent tuberculosis patients. Retrieved from *www.cdph.ca.gov/Programs/CID/DCDC/CDPH%20Document%20Library/TBCB-SPM-CD-Plan-for-Detention-of-Persistently-Non-Adherent-TB-Patients.pdf*

TABLE 27.13 Drug Therapy
Latent Tuberculosis Infection Regimens

Drugs	Duration (mo)	Interval	Minimum Doses
isoniazid	9	Daily	270
		Twice weekly*	76
isoniazid	6	Daily	180
		Twice weekly*	52
isoniazid and rifapentine	3	Once weekly*	12
rifampin	4	Daily	120

Source: Centers for Disease Control and Prevention: Treatment regimens for latent TB infection, 2017. Retrieved from *www.cdc.gov/tb/topic/treatment/ltbi.htm.*
*Use directly observed therapy (DOT).

bovis. The vaccine is given to infants in parts of the world with a high prevalence of TB. In the United States, it is typically not used because of the low risk for infection, the vaccine's variable effectiveness against adult pulmonary TB, and potential interference with TB skin test reactivity. The BCG vaccination can result in a false-positive TST. IGRA results are not affected. The BCG vaccine should be considered only for select persons who meet specific criteria (e.g., health care workers who are continually exposed to patients with MDR-TB and when infection control precautions are not successful).

❖ NURSING MANAGEMENT: TUBERCULOSIS

◆ Nursing Assessment
Ask the patient about a previous history of TB, chronic illness, or any immunosuppressive disease or medications. Obtain a social and occupational history to determine risk factors for transmission of TB. Assess the patient for productive cough, night sweats, fever, weight loss, pleuritic chest pain, and abnormal lung sounds. If the patient has a productive cough, early morning is the ideal time to collect sputum specimens for an AFB smear.

◆ Nursing Diagnoses
Nursing diagnoses for the patient with TB may include:
- Impaired breathing
- Impaired airway clearance
- Risk for infection
- Lack of knowledge

◆ Planning
The overall goals are that the patient with TB will (1) have normal pulmonary function, (2) adhere to the therapeutic regimen, (3) take appropriate measures to prevent the spread of the disease, and (4) have no recurrence of disease.

◆ Nursing Implementation
Health Promotion. The ultimate goal is to eradicate TB worldwide. Screening programs in known risk groups are of value in detecting persons with TB. Treatment of LTBI reduces the number of TB carriers in the community. The person with a positive TST should have a chest x-ray to assess for active TB disease. People with a diagnosis of TB must be reported to the public health authorities for identification and assessment of contacts and risk to the community.

Programs to address the social determinants of TB are needed to decrease transmission of TB. Reducing HIV infection, poverty, overcrowded living conditions, malnutrition, smoking, and drug and alcohol use can help minimize TB infection rates. Improving access to health care and education is important.

◆ **Acute Care.** Patients admitted to the ED or directly to the nursing unit with respiratory symptoms should always be assessed for the possibility of TB. Those strongly suspected of having TB should (1) be placed on airborne isolation; (2) receive a medical workup, including chest x-ray, sputum smear, and culture; and (3) receive appropriate drug therapy. Airborne infection isolation is needed for the patient with pulmonary or laryngeal TB until the patient is not infectious. *Airborne infection isolation* refers to isolation of patients infected with organisms spread by the airborne route. Patients are in a single-occupancy room with negative pressure and airflow of 6 to 12 exchanges per hour.

High-efficiency particulate air (HEPA) masks are worn whenever entering the patient's room. These masks are highly effective at protecting from small droplets 5 μm or less in diameter. Several types of HEPA masks are currently available. To ensure proper mask size, health care professionals should be "fit tested" with significant changes in weight gain or loss, with any facial and/or dental changes (e.g., Botox injections), and each time there is a new brand or model of mask. Otherwise, yearly mask "fit testing" is acceptable. To be effective, the mask must be molded to fit tightly around the nose and mouth.

Teach patients to cover the nose and mouth with paper tissues every time they cough, sneeze, or produce sputum. The tissues should be thrown into a paper bag and disposed of with the trash or flushed down the toilet. Emphasize careful hand washing after handling sputum and soiled tissues. If patients need to be out of the negative-pressure room, they must wear a standard isolation mask to prevent exposure to others. Minimize prolonged visitation to other parts of the hospital.

Identify and screen close contacts of the person with TB. Anyone testing positive for TB infection will need further evaluation and treatment for either LTBI or active TB disease.

◆ **Ambulatory Care.** Patients who respond clinically are discharged home (even with positive cultures) if their household contacts have already been exposed and the patient is not posing a risk to others. A sputum specimen for AFB smear and culture should be obtained at a minimum of monthly intervals until 2 consecutive specimens are negative on culture. More frequent AFB smears may be useful to assess the early response to treatment and provide an indication of infectiousness. Negative cultures are needed to declare the patient not infectious.

Teach the patient how to minimize exposure to close contacts and household members. Homes should be well ventilated, especially the areas where the infected person spends a lot of time. While still infectious, the patient should sleep alone, spend as much time as possible outdoors, and minimize time in congregate settings or on public transportation.

It is important to teach the patient and caregiver about adherence with the prescribed regimen. Most treatment failures occur because the patient does not take the drug, stops taking it too soon, or takes it irregularly. Strategies to improve adherence include teaching and counseling, reminder systems, incentives or rewards, contracts, and DOT.

Notifying the public health department is required. The public health nurse is responsible for follow-up on household contacts and assessment of the patient for adherence. If adherence is an issue, the public health agency may be responsible for DOT. Most patients can be considered adequately treated when the therapy regimen has been completed and there is evidence of negative cultures, overall improvement in patient condition, and improvement on chest x-ray.

Because about 5% of patients have relapses, teach the patient to recognize the symptoms that occur with recurrent TB. If these symptoms occur, the patient should seek immediate medical attention. Teach the patient about factors that could reactivate TB, such as immunosuppressive therapy, cancer, and prolonged debilitating illness. If the patient has any of these events, the HCP must be told so that TB can be closely monitored for reactivation. In some situations, it is necessary to put the patient on anti-TB therapy. Because smoking is associated with poor outcomes in TB, patients should be encouraged to quit. Provide patients with teaching and resources to help them stop smoking.

EVIDENCE-BASED PRACTICE
Adherence to Tuberculosis Treatment Program

You are a nurse working in an outpatient health clinic with C.J., a 42-yr-old man diagnosed 2 months ago with active TB. He is on DOT. You notice C.J. has started to miss or has been late for his clinic appointments. He tells you it is hard to make his appointments as a new job requires long work hours. He asks if he needs to continue with his visits to get his drugs. He says he is "feeling better" and will take the drugs on his own.

Making Clinical Decisions

Best Available Evidence. Guidelines for effective case management of patients with TB include patient education, field/home visits, patient reminders, and incentives. TB clinic attendance and treatment completion rates are higher when patients take part in DOT compared to self-administered therapy. When appointments are missed, phone calls, Web-based videos, or home visits will engage patients, resulting in improved clinic attendance and treatment completion.

Clinician Expertise. You know that patient-centered care includes being responsive to patients' changing needs. You know that patients may stop attending clinics and taking their drugs when feeling well again. This can lead to treatment failure, the need to restart therapy, and multidrug resistance.

Patient Preferences and Values. C.J. tells you he has a busy job and does not always remember his appointment dates. He would like to self-administer his drugs.

Implications for Nursing Practice

1. What information would you give C.J. about the importance of DOT?
2. Your clinic has interest in starting a reminder system for clinic appointments. What strategy would you recommend?
3. How will you know if C.J. is adhering to the prescribed drug treatment program?

References for Evidence

1. Centers for Disease Control and Prevention: Tuberculosis: General considerations for treatment of TB disease. Retrieved from *www.cdc.gov/tb/publications/factsheets/treatment/treatmenthivnegative.pdf*.
2. Nahid P, Dorman SE, Alipanah N: Official American Thoracic Society/CDC/Infectious Diseases Society of America clinical practice guidelines: Treatment of drug-susceptible tuberculosis, *Clin Infect Dis* 63:e147, 2016.

◆ **Evaluation**

The expected outcomes are that the patient with TB will have:
- Resolution of the disease
- Normal pulmonary function
- Absence of any complications
- No further transmission of TB

ATYPICAL MYCOBACTERIA

There are more than 30 varieties of acid-fast mycobacteria that do not cause TB but cause pulmonary disease, lymphadenitis, skin or soft tissue disease, or disseminated disease. Atypical mycobacteria are not airborne or transmitted by droplets. They can be found in tap water, soil, bird feces, and house dust.

Pulmonary symptoms include cough, shortness of breath, weight loss, fatigue, and blood-tinged sputum. People who are immunosuppressed (e.g., HIV/AIDS) or have chronic pulmonary disease are most susceptible. We cannot distinguish this type of pulmonary disease from TB clinically and radiologically. A culture is required. Treatment is similar to that for TB.

PULMONARY FUNGAL INFECTIONS

Pulmonary fungal pneumonia is an infectious process in the lungs caused by endemic (native and common) or opportunistic fungi (Table 27.14). *Endemic* fungal pathogens cause infection in healthy people and in immunocompromised people in certain geographic locations in the United States. For example, *Coccidioides,* which causes coccidioidomycosis, is a fungus found in the soil of dry, low-rainfall areas.[21] It is endemic in many areas of the southwestern United States. *Opportunistic* fungal infections occur in immunocompromised patients (e.g., those receiving chemotherapy, immunosuppressive drugs) and in patients with HIV and cystic fibrosis. These pulmonary fungal infections can be life-threatening.

Pulmonary fungal infections are acquired by inhaling spores. They are not transmitted from person to person. The patient does not have to be placed in isolation. The manifestations are like those of bacterial pneumonia. Skin testing, serology, and biopsy methods aid in identifying the infecting organism.

The choice of antifungal agent is made based on the pathogen identified on culture or most likely suspected. Amphotericin B is the standard therapy for treating serious systemic fungal infections. It must be given IV to achieve adequate blood and tissue levels because the GI tract does not absorb it well. Less serious infections can be treated with oral antifungals, such as ketoconazole, fluconazole (Diflucan), voriconazole (Vfend), and itraconazole (Sporanox). Effectiveness of therapy can be monitored with fungal serology titers.

LUNG ABSCESS
Etiology and Pathophysiology

A **lung abscess** is necrosis of lung tissue. It typically results from bacteria aspirated from the oral cavity in patients with periodontal disease. They can also result from IV drug use, cancer, pulmonary emboli, TB, and various parasitic and fungal diseases. The abscess usually develops slowly, beginning with an enlarging area of infection that becomes necrotic and eventually forms a cavity filled with purulent material. Abscesses usually contain more than 1 type of microbe, most often reflecting the anaerobic flora of the mouth.

The area of the lung most often affected due to aspiration is the posterior segment of the upper lobes. The abscess may erode into the bronchial system, causing the production of foul-smelling or sour-tasting sputum. It may grow toward the pleura and cause pleuritic pain. Multiple small abscesses, sometimes referred to as *necrotizing pneumonia,* can occur within the lung.

TABLE 27.14 Fungal Infections of the Lung

Infection	Organism
Endemic Fungal Infections	
Blastomycosis	*Blastomyces dermatitidis*
Coccidioidomycosis	*Coccidioides immitis*
Histoplasmosis	*Histoplasma capsulatum*
Opportunistic Fungal Infections	
Aspergillosis	*Aspergillus niger, Aspergillus fumigatus*
Candidiasis	*Candida albicans*
Cryptococcosis	*Cryptococcus neoformans*

Clinical Manifestations and Complications

Manifestations usually occur slowly over a period of weeks to months, especially if anaerobic organisms are the cause. Symptoms of abscess caused by aerobic bacteria develop more acutely and resemble bacterial pneumonia. The most common is cough-producing purulent sputum (often dark brown) that is foul smelling and foul tasting. Hemoptysis is common, especially when an abscess ruptures into a bronchus. Other manifestations include fever, chills, prostration, night sweats, pleuritic pain, dyspnea, anorexia, and weight loss.

Lung assessment reveals dullness to percussion and decreased breath sounds on auscultation over the involved segment of lung. Bronchial breath sounds may be transmitted to the periphery if the communicating bronchus becomes patent and the segment begins to drain. Crackles may be present in the later stages as the abscess drains.

The infection can spread through the bloodstream and cause several possible complications. Pulmonary abscess, bronchopleural fistula, bronchiectasis, and empyema from perforation of the abscess into the pleural cavity can occur.[22]

Diagnostic Studies

A chest x-ray is often the only test needed to diagnose a lung abscess. The presence of a single cavitary lesion with an air-fluid level and local infiltrate confirms the diagnosis. CT scanning may be helpful if the cavitation is not clear on chest x-ray. If there is drainage via the bronchus, sputum will contain the microorganisms that are present in the abscess. However, expectorated sputum samples are contaminated with oral flora, making it hard to determine the responsible organism(s).

Bronchoscopy may be used to (1) avoid oropharyngeal contamination, (2) collect a specimen if drainage is delayed, or (3) investigate for an underlying cancer. Pleural fluid and blood cultures may be useful to identify the offending organisms. Although nonspecific, an elevated neutrophil count from a complete blood count (CBC) may indicate an infectious process. Necrotic pulmonary lesions also can be caused by lung infarction, pulmonary embolism, and sarcoidosis.

❖ Interprofessional and Nursing Care

Monitor the patient's vital signs, level of consciousness, and respiratory status for any signs of hypoxemia. Note any signs and symptoms of respiratory distress. Apply O_2 as needed. IV antibiotic therapy should be started as soon as possible. Clindamycin is first-line therapy for its effectiveness against *Staphylococcus* and anaerobic organisms. Parenteral antibiotics are switched to oral antibiotics once the patient shows clinical and chest x-ray signs of improvement.

Because of the need for prolonged antibiotic therapy, the patient must be aware of the importance of continuing the medication for the prescribed period. To avoid the risk for a secondary or worsening infection, all antibiotics should be taken as directed for the entire prescribed period. Sometimes the patient is asked to return periodically during the course of antibiotic therapy for repeat cultures and sensitivity tests to ensure that the infecting organism is not becoming resistant to the antibiotic. When antibiotic therapy is complete, the patient is reevaluated.

Teach the patient how to cough effectively (see Table 28.21). Chest physiotherapy and postural drainage are not recommended because they may promote movement of microorganisms into other bronchi, extending infection. Rest, optimal nutrition, and adequate fluid intake are supportive measures to promote recovery. If dentition is poor and dental hygiene is not adequate, encourage the patient to obtain dental care. Collaborate with the social worker to evaluate available options for dental care if the patient has limited resources.

If the patient does not adequately respond to antibiotic treatment, percutaneous drainage of the abscess may be done. A small catheter, guided by CT or ultrasound, may be placed to drain the abscess. Surgery is sometimes done when reinfection of a large cavitary lesion occurs, when an empyema develops, or to establish a diagnosis when there is evidence of an underlying problem, such as cancer. The usual procedure in such cases is a lobectomy. A pneumonectomy may be needed for multiple abscesses.

ENVIRONMENTAL LUNG DISEASES

Environmental or occupational lung diseases result from inhaled dust or chemicals. The extent of lung damage is influenced by the toxicity of the inhaled substance, amount and duration of exposure, and individual susceptibility. Environmentally induced lung disease includes pneumoconiosis, chemical pneumonitis, and hypersensitivity pneumonitis.

Pneumoconiosis is a general term for a group of lung diseases caused by inhalation and retention of mineral or metal dust particles. The literal meaning of *pneumoconiosis* is "dust in the lungs." We classify these diseases according to the origin of the dust (e.g., silicosis, asbestosis, berylliosis). For example, silicosis occurs from inhaling silica from sand and rock. Coal worker's pneumoconiosis (CWP), also known as *black lung,* is caused by inhaling large amounts of coal dust. It is an occupational hazard for underground coal miners. The inhaled substance is ingested by macrophages, which releases substances that cause cell injury and death. Fibrosis occurs from tissue repair after inflammation. Breathing problems become evident after many years of repeated exposure, resulting in diffuse *pulmonary fibrosis* (excess connective tissue).

Asbestos is a group of minerals composed of microscopic fibers. For many years, asbestos was used for insulation and to help fireproof buildings. When disturbed, asbestos releases tiny filament particles into the air. Once inhaled, the tiny fibers become deposited within the lung. Asbestosis is chronic inflammation of the lung, and people with repeated exposure are at a greater risk for disease. Lung cancer, either squamous cell carcinoma or adenocarcinoma, is the most frequent cancer associated with asbestos exposure. There is a lapse of at least 15 to 19 years between first exposure and development of lung cancer. Mesothelioma, both pleural and peritoneal, is associated with asbestos exposure.

Chemical pneumonitis results from exposures to toxic chemical fumes. There are 2 types of chemical pneumonitis: acute and chronic. Acutely, there is diffuse lung injury characterized by pulmonary edema. Chronically, the clinical picture is that of *bronchiolitis obliterans* (obstruction of the bronchioles due to inflammation and fibrosis). It is usually associated with a normal chest x-ray or one that shows hyperinflation.

Hypersensitivity pneumonitis, or extrinsic allergic alveolitis, is a form of parenchymal lung disease seen when a person inhales antigens to which they are allergic. There are acute, subacute, and chronic forms. Examples include bird fancier's lung (exposure to particles in feathers and droppings of birds), and farmer's lung (inhalation of hay dust particles).

Clinical Manifestations

Symptoms of many environmental lung diseases may not occur until at least 10 to 15 years after the initial exposure to the inhaled irritant. Manifestations common to all pneumoconioses include dyspnea, cough, wheezing, and weight loss. Pulmonary function studies often show reduced vital capacity. A chest x-ray often reveals lung involvement specific to the primary problem. CT scans have been useful in detecting early lung involvement.

Cor pulmonale, a condition in which the right side of the heart fails, is a late complication, especially in conditions characterized by diffuse pulmonary fibrosis. COPD is the most common complication of environmental lung disease. Other associated disorders include acute pulmonary edema, lung cancer, mesothelioma, and TB. Appearance of these symptoms and complications are often the reason the patient seeks health care.

❖ Interprofessional and Nursing Care

The best approach to managing environmental lung diseases is to prevent or decrease environmental and occupational exposure. Teach those at risk about the use of appropriate personal protective equipment. Wearing masks and using well-designed, effective ventilation systems are appropriate for some occupations and household activities. Inhalation of smoke by nonsmokers has led to regulations requiring a smoke-free workplace. Periodic inspections and monitoring of workplaces by agencies such as the Occupational Safety and Health Administration (OSHA) and the National Institute for Occupational Safety and Health (NIOSH) reinforce employers' obligations to provide a safe work environment. NIOSH is responsible for workplace safety and health regulations in the United States.

Encourage regular medical check-ups. Early diagnosis is essential to halting the disease process. Strategies are directed toward preventing disease progression and monitoring, improving or controlling respiratory symptoms. They depend on the cause and severity of the condition. Strategies may include O_2 therapy, IV fluid, inhaled bronchodilators, corticosteroids, nonsteroidal antiinflammatory drugs (NSAIDs), intubation and mechanical ventilation, percussion therapy, and pulmonary rehabilitation. Patients should be immunized against pneumococcal pneumonia and influenza. Discontinuing exposure to the offending inhalant and smoking cessation may or may not be effective in stopping disease progression.

LUNG CANCER

Lung cancer is the leading cause of cancer-related deaths in the United States.[23] Lung cancer accounts for 26% of all cancer deaths, more than those caused by breast and colon cancer combined. In 2019, it is estimated that 234,000 new cases of lung cancer will be diagnosed, and 154,000 Americans will die. Although lung cancer is associated with a high mortality and low cure rate, advances in medical treatment are improving the response to treatment.

Etiology

Smoking causes 80% to 90% of all lung cancers.[24] There is no safe form of tobacco or tobacco product. Smokeless tobacco, pipes and cigars, hookah and waterpipe, bidis, and kreteks all pose significant risk for lung cancer to those who use them.[25]

Tobacco smoke contains over 7000 chemicals, of which 250 are harmful. Of the harmful substances in tobacco smoke, 69 interfere with normal cell development and are linked to lung cancer. Exposure to tobacco smoke causes changes in the bronchial epithelium, which usually returns to normal with smoking cessation. The risk for lung cancer gradually decreases with smoking cessation, reaching that of nonsmokers within 10 to 15 years of quitting.

The risk for developing lung cancer is directly related to total exposure to tobacco smoke. This is measured by total number of cigarettes smoked in a lifetime, age of smoking onset, depth of inhalation, tar and nicotine content, and the use of unfiltered cigarettes. Both smokers and nonsmokers can develop lung cancer. Sidestream smoke (smoke from burning cigarettes, cigars) has the same carcinogens found in mainstream smoke (smoke inhaled and exhaled by the smoker). This exposure to secondhand smoke creates a health risk for nonsmoking adults and children.

Other common causes of lung cancer include high levels of pollution, radiation (especially radon exposure), and asbestos. Heavy or prolonged exposure to industrial agents, such as ionizing radiation, coal dust, nickel, uranium, chromium, formaldehyde, and arsenic, can increase the risk for lung cancer, especially in smokers.[26]

Marked variations exist in a person's tendency to develop lung cancer. Differences in lung cancer incidence, risk factors, and survival exist between men and women (see Gender Differences box). Genetic, hormonal, and molecular influences may contribute to these differences.

GENDER DIFFERENCES
Lung Cancer

Men
- Have a 1 in 15 chance of developing lung cancer (smokers and nonsmokers)
- Diagnosed with lung cancer more than women
- Die from lung cancer more than women
- Male smokers are 10 times more likely to develop lung cancer than nonsmokers
- Lung cancer incidence and deaths are decreasing in men

Women
- Have a 1 in 17 chance of developing lung cancer (smokers and nonsmokers)
- Lung cancer incidence and deaths are increasing in women
- Develop lung cancer after fewer years of smoking than men
- Develop lung cancer at a younger age than men
- Nonsmoking women are at greater risk for developing lung cancer than nonsmoking men
- Women with lung cancer live, on the average, 12 months longer than men.

Lung Cancer

Blacks
- Have the highest incidence of lung cancer
- Are more likely to die from lung cancer than any other ethnic group
- Have a higher rate of lung cancer among men than in other ethnic groups

Whites
- Have the second-highest death rate from lung cancer
- Have a higher rate of lung cancer among women than in other ethnic groups

Asian/Pacific Islanders and Hispanics
- Have the lowest rates of lung cancer in both men and women

Other
- Regional variations among ethnic groups may be due to smoking prevalence or exposure to cancer-causing substances
- Cigarette use has decreased dramatically in developed countries, such as the United States and Canada
- Cigarette smoking is increasing in developing countries (e.g., nations in Africa, Asia, Latin America)

Source: Singh GK, Jemal A: Socioeconomic and racial/ethnic disparities in cancer mortality, incidence, and survival in the United States, 1950–2014, *J Environ Public Health*, 2017. Retrieved from www.doi.org/10.1155/2017/2819372.

Pathophysiology

Most primary lung tumors are believed to arise from mutated epithelial cells. The growth of mutations, which are caused by carcinogens, is influenced by various genetic factors. Once underway, tumor development is promoted by epidermal growth factor. These cells grow slowly, taking 8 to 10 years for a tumor to reach 1 cm in size, the smallest lesion detectable on x-ray. Lung cancers occur primarily in the segmental bronchi or beyond and usually occur in the upper lobes of the lungs (Fig. 27.4).

Primary lung cancers are categorized into 2 broad subtypes (Table 27.15): non–small cell lung cancer (NSCLC) (85%) and small cell lung cancer (SCLC) (15%).[27] Lung cancers metastasize primarily by direct extension and through the blood and lymph system. The common sites for metastasis are the lymph nodes, liver, brain, bones, and adrenal glands.

Paraneoplastic Syndrome. Lung cancers can cause *paraneoplastic syndrome*. Paraneoplastic syndrome may be caused by hormones, cytokines, enzymes (secreted by tumor cells) or antibodies (made by the body in response to the tumor) that destroy healthy cells. Sometimes the symptoms of paraneoplastic syndrome manifest even before the cancer is diagnosed.

Examples of paraneoplastic syndrome include hypercalcemia, syndrome of inappropriate antidiuretic hormone secretion (SIADH), adrenal hypersecretion, polycythemia, and Cushing syndrome. SCLCs are most often associated with paraneoplastic syndrome. These conditions may stabilize with treatment of the underlying cancer. SIADH, adrenal hypersecretion, and Cushing syndrome are discussed in Chapter 49.

FIG. 27.4 Lung cancer lesion. (© iStock.com/Sutthaburawonk.)

Clinical Manifestations

The manifestations of lung cancer are usually nonspecific and appear late in the disease process. Symptoms may be masked by a chronic cough attributed to smoking or smoking-related lung disease. Manifestations depend on the type of primary lung cancer, its location, and extent of metastatic spread. Lung cancer often presents as a lobar pneumonia that does not respond to treatment.

The most common symptom and often the one that is reported first is a persistent cough. The patient may report dyspnea or wheezing. Blood-tinged sputum may be present because of bleeding caused by the cancer. Chest pain, if present, may be localized or unilateral, ranging from mild to severe.

Later manifestations include nonspecific systemic symptoms, such as anorexia, nausea and vomiting, fatigue, and weight loss. Hoarseness may be present due to laryngeal nerve involvement. Dysphagia, unilateral paralysis of the diaphragm, and superior vena cava obstruction may occur because of intrathoracic spread of the cancer. Lymph nodes are often palpable in the neck or axillae. Mediastinal involvement may lead to pericardial effusion, cardiac tamponade, and dysrhythmias.

Diagnostic Studies

A chest x-ray is the first diagnostic test done for patients with suspected lung cancer. The x-ray may be normal or identify a lung mass or infiltrate (Fig. 27.4). Evidence of metastasis to the ribs or vertebrae and a pleural effusion may be seen on chest x-ray. CT scanning is used to further evaluate the lung mass. CT scans can identify the location and extent of masses in the chest, any mediastinal involvement, and lymph node enlargement.

Sputum cytologic studies can identify cancer cells, but sputum samples are rarely used in diagnosing lung cancer because cancer cells are not always present in the sputum. A definitive diagnosis requires a biopsy. Cells for biopsy can be obtained by CT-guided needle aspiration, bronchoscopy, mediastinoscopy, or video-assisted thoracoscopic surgery (VATS). If a

TABLE 27.15 Types of Primary Lung Cancer

Type	Growth Rate	Characteristics	Response to Therapy
Non–Small Cell Lung Cancer (NSCLC)			
Adenocarcinoma	Moderate	• Accounts for 40% of lung cancers • Most common lung cancer in United States • Most common cancer in people who have not smoked • Found in peripheral areas of lung • Often has no manifestations until widespread metastasis is present	• Surgical resection may be tried depending on staging • Does not respond well to chemotherapy
Large cell (undifferentiated) cancer	Rapid	• Accounts for 10% of lung cancers • Composed of large cells that are anaplastic • Often arise in bronchi • Is highly metastatic via lymphatics and blood	• Surgery is not usually done because of high rate of metastases • Tumor may be radiosensitive but often recurs
Squamous cell cancer	Slow	• Accounts for 25%–30% of lung cancers • Centrally located • Causes early symptoms of nonproductive cough and hemoptysis • Does not have a strong tendency to metastasize	• Surgical resection may be tried • Adjuvant chemotherapy and radiation • Depending on the staging, life expectancy is better than for SCLC
Small Cell Lung Cancer (SCLC)			
Small cell cancer	Very rapid	• Accounts for about 10%–15% of lung cancers • Very aggressive form of lung cancer • Spreads early via lymphatics and bloodstream • Frequent metastasis to brain • Associated with endocrine problems	• Chemotherapy mainstay of treatment; more responsive to chemotherapy than NSCLC • Radiation used as adjuvant therapy and palliative measure • Overall poor prognosis

TABLE 27.16 Interprofessional Care

Lung Cancer

Diagnostic Assessment
- History and physical examination
- Chest x-ray
- Bronchoscopy
- Cytologic study of bronchial washings or pleural space fluid
- Transbronchial or percutaneous fine-needle aspiration
- CT scan, MRI, PET
- Mediastinoscopy
- Video-assisted thoracoscopic surgery (VATS)

Management
- Surgery (segmental or wedge resection, lobectomy, pneumonectomy)
- Radiation therapy
- Chemotherapy
- Targeted therapy and immunotherapy
- Prophylactic cranial radiation
- Bronchoscopic laser therapy
- Photodynamic therapy
- Airway stenting
- Radiofrequency ablation

TABLE 27.17 Staging of Non–Small Cell Lung Cancer

Stages		Characteristics
0		Cells found in respiratory airway, alveoli
I		Tumor is small and localized to lung. No lymph node involvement
	A	Tumor <3 cm
	B	Tumor 3–4 cm and invading main airway, visceral pleura.
II		Increased tumor size, some lymph node involvement
	A	Tumor 4–5 cm with invasion of main airway, visceral pleura, lymph nodes on same side of chest
	B	Tumor 5–7 cm involving the bronchus and lymph nodes on same side of chest *OR* Tumor 5–7 cm with visceral and parietal pleura, diaphragm, phrenic nerve involvement
III		Increased spread of tumor
	A	Tumor ≤5 cm or smaller spread to the nearby structures (chest wall, pleura, pericardium) and regional lymph nodes
	B	Extensive tumor >5 cm involving heart, trachea, esophagus, mediastinum, malignant pleural effusion, contralateral lymph nodes, scalene or supraclavicular lymph nodes
	C	Tumor >5 cm and more than one tumor in a different lobe of the lung
IV		Distant metastasis

thoracentesis is done to relieve a pleural effusion, the fluid is analyzed for cancer cells.

Accurate assessment of lung cancer is critical for staging and determining appropriate treatment. Bone scans and CT scans of the brain, pelvis, and abdomen are used to determine if metastatic disease is present. A complete history and physical examination, CBC with differential, chemistry panel, liver function tests, and renal function tests are ordered. In some situations, pulmonary function tests will be done. MRI and/or positron emission tomography (PET) may be used to evaluate and stage lung cancer. Table 27.16 outlines the diagnostic assessment of lung cancer.

Staging. Staging of NSCLC is done using the TNM staging system (see Table 15.5). Under the TNM system, cancer is grouped into 4 stages with A or B subtypes. A simplified version of staging of NSCLC is shown in Table 27.17. Patients with stages I, II, and IIIA disease may be surgical candidates. However, stage IIIB or IV disease is usually inoperable and has a poor prognosis.

Staging of SCLC by TNM has not been useful because this cancer is aggressive and is always considered systemic. The stages of SCLC are *limited* and *extensive*. *Limited* means that the tumor is only on 1 side of the chest and regional lymph nodes. *Extensive* SCLC means that the cancer extends beyond the limited stage. Most patients with SCLC have extensive disease at time of diagnosis.

Screening for Lung Cancer. The American College of Chest Physicians recommends screening for high-risk patients.[28] Adults ages 55 to 77 with a history of smoking (30 pack-year smoking history or currently smoke) or who quit smoking but less than 15 years ago should have annual screening for lung cancer. Screening is done using low-dose CT. Several other groups have endorsed these guidelines, including the American Cancer Society.[29]

Interprofessional Care

Surgical Therapy. Surgical resection is the treatment of choice in NSCLC stages I to IIIA without mediastinal involvement. Resection gives the best chance for a cure. Factors that affect survival include the size of the primary tumor and preexisting co-morbidities. For other NSCLC stages, patients may have surgery in conjunction with radiation therapy, chemotherapy, and targeted therapy. Many NSCLCs are not resectable at the time of diagnosis.

Surgical procedures include segmental or wedge resection procedures, lobectomy (removal of 1 or more lobes of the lung), or pneumonectomy (removal of 1 entire lung). VATS may be used to treat lung cancers near the outside of the lung. Surgery is generally not done for SCLC because of its rapid growth and dissemination at the time of diagnosis.

When the tumor is considered operable, the patient's cardiopulmonary status must be evaluated to determine the ability to have surgery. Pulmonary function studies, ABGs, and anesthesia and critical care consults are often done before surgery to assess the patient's cardiopulmonary status.

Radiation Therapy. Radiation therapy may be used as treatment for both NSCLC and SCLC. Radiation therapy may be given as curative therapy, palliative therapy (to relieve symptoms), or adjuvant therapy in combination with surgery, chemotherapy, or targeted therapy.

Radiation therapy may be used as primary therapy in the person who is unable to tolerate surgical resection because of co-morbidities. Radiation therapy relieves symptoms of dyspnea and hemoptysis from bronchial obstructive tumors and treats superior vena cava syndrome. It can treat pain from metastatic bone lesions or brain metastasis. Radiation before surgery can reduce the tumor mass before surgical resection. Complications of radiation therapy include esophagitis, skin irritation, nausea and vomiting, anorexia, and radiation pneumonitis (see Chapter 15).

Stereotactic body radiotherapy (SBRT), also called *stereotactic radiosurgery (SRS),* is a newer lung cancer treatment. It is a type of radiation therapy that uses high doses of radiation delivered to tumors outside the CNS. SBRT uses special positioning procedures and radiology techniques to deliver a higher dose of radiation to the tumor and expose only a small part of healthy lung. It does not destroy the tumor, but damages tumor DNA. Therapy is given over 1 to 3 days. SBRT provides an option for patients with early-stage lung cancers who are not surgical candidates for other medical reasons.

Chemotherapy. Chemotherapy is the main treatment for SCLC. In NSCLC, chemotherapy may be used in the treatment of nonresectable tumors or as adjuvant therapy to surgery. We use a variety of chemotherapy drugs and multidrug protocols. Chemotherapy for lung cancer typically consists of combinations of 2 of the following drugs: etoposide (VP-16), carboplatin, cisplatin, paclitaxel (Taxol), vinorelbine (Navelbine), docetaxel (Taxotere), gemcitabine (Gemzar), and pemetrexed (Alimta).

Targeted Therapy. Targeted therapy uses drugs that block the growth of molecules involved in specific aspects of tumor growth (see Chapter 15). Because this type of therapy inhibits growth rather than directly killing cancer cells, targeted therapy may be less toxic than chemotherapy. One type of targeted therapy for patients with NSCLC inhibits tyrosine kinase, an enzyme associated with speeding up molecular reactions. Tyrosine kinase inhibitors, which block signals for growth in the cancer cells, include cetuximab (Erbitux), erlotinib (Tarceva), afatinib (Gilotrif), gefitinib (Iressa), osimertinib (Tagrisso), and necitumumab (Portrazza).

Another type of kinase inhibitor is used to treat patients with NSCLC who have an abnormal anaplastic lymphoma kinase *(ALK)* gene. Drugs in this class include crizotinib (Xalkori), brigatinib (Alunbrig), and ceritinib (Zykadia). These drugs directly inhibit the kinase protein made by the *ALK* gene that is responsible for cancer development and growth.

Another type of targeted therapy used to treat lung cancer inhibits the growth of new blood vessels (angiogenesis) by targeting vascular endothelial growth factor. Bevacizumab (Avastin) is an angiogenesis inhibitor.

Immunotherapy. Nivolumab (Opdivo), atezolizumab (Tecentriq), and pembrolizumab (Keytruda) are drugs that target PD-1, a protein on T cells that normally helps keep these cells from attacking other cells in the body. By blocking PD-1, these drugs boost the immune response against cancer cells. This can shrink some tumors or slow their growth. Nivolumab and pembrolizumab can be used in people with metastatic NSCLC whose cancer has progressed after other treatments and with tumors that express PD-1.

Other Therapies

Prophylactic Cranial Irradiation. Patients with SCLC have early metastases, especially to the CNS. Most chemotherapy does not penetrate the blood-brain barrier. As a result, after successful systemic treatment, the patient is at risk for brain metastases. Prophylactic radiation can decrease the incidence of brain metastases and may improve survival rates in patients with limited SCLC.[30]

Bronchoscopic Laser Therapy. Bronchoscopic laser therapy makes it possible to remove obstructing bronchial lesions. The laser's thermal energy is transmitted to the target tissue. It is a safe and effective treatment of endobronchial obstructions from tumors. Symptoms of airway obstruction are relieved due to thermal necrosis and shrinkage of the tumor. The procedure may be repeated as needed.

Photodynamic Therapy. Photodynamic therapy (PDT) is a form of treatment for early-stage lung cancers that uses a combination of a drug and a specific type of light. Cancer cells are killed when the drug, known as a photosynthesizer, is exposed to a specific wavelength of light. Porfimer (Photofrin) is the most used photosynthesizer. After an IV injection, it selectively concentrates in tumor cells in the esophagus and outer layers of the airways. After a set time (usually 48 hours), the tumor is exposed to laser light via bronchoscopy, activating the drug and causing cell death. Necrotic tissue is removed with bronchoscopy a few days later. This process can be repeated as needed. PDT can affect nutrient delivery to cancer cells and stimulate the immune system to attack the cancer cells.

Airway Stenting. Stents are used alone or in combination with other techniques for relief of dyspnea, cough, or respiratory insufficiency. The stent is inserted during a bronchoscopy. The advantage of an airway stent is that it supports the airway wall against collapse or external compression and can delay extension of tumor into the airway lumen. At this time, we do not know which patients will benefit most from airway stents.

Radiofrequency Ablation. Radiofrequency ablation therapy is used to treat small NSCLC lung tumors that are near the outer edge of the lungs. This therapy is an alternative to surgery in patients who cannot or elect not to have surgery. A thin, needle-like probe is inserted through the skin into the tumor. CT scans are used to guide placement. An electric current is then passed through the probe, which heats and destroys tumor cells. Local anesthesia is used for this outpatient procedure.

❖ NURSING MANAGEMENT: LUNG CANCER

◆ Nursing Assessment

It is important to determine the patient and caregiver's understanding of the current medical condition, diagnostic tests (those completed as well as those planned), diagnosis or potential diagnosis, treatment options, and prognosis. Assess the patient's level of anxiety and support provided by the patient's significant others. Subjective and objective data that should be obtained from a patient with lung cancer are described in Table 27.18.

◆ Nursing Diagnoses

Nursing diagnoses for the patient with lung cancer may include:
- Impaired airway clearance
- Impaired breathing
- Impaired gas exchange
- Anxiety

◆ Planning

The overall goals are that the patient with lung cancer will have (1) adequate airway clearance, (2) effective breathing patterns, (3) adequate oxygenation of tissues, (4) minimal to no discomfort, and (5) a realistic outlook about treatment and prognosis.

◆ Nursing Implementation

◆ **Health Promotion.** The best way to halt the epidemic of lung cancer is to prevent people from smoking, help smokers stop smoking, and decrease exposure to environmental pollutants. Because most smokers start in the teenage years, prevention of teen smoking has the most significant role in reducing the incidence of lung cancer. A wealth of material is available to the smoker who is interested in smoking cessation. (See Chapter 10.)

Modeling healthy behavior by not smoking, promoting smoking cessation programs, and actively supporting education and policy changes related to smoking are important nursing activities. Many changes have occurred because of the

TABLE 27.18 Nursing Assessment
Lung Cancer

Subjective Data
Important Health Information
Past health history: Exposure to secondhand smoke, airborne carcinogens (e.g., asbestos, radon, hydrocarbons), or other pollutants. Urban living environment. Chronic lung disease (e.g., TB, COPD, bronchiectasis). History of cancer.
Medications: Cough medicines, bronchodilators, expectorants, or other respiratory medications

Functional Health Patterns
Health perception–health management: Smoking history, including what was smoked, amount per day, and number of years. Family history of lung cancer. Frequent respiratory tract infections
Nutritional-metabolic: Anorexia, nausea, vomiting, weight loss, dysphagia (late). *Activity-exercise:* Fatigue. Persistent cough (productive or nonproductive). Dyspnea at rest or with exertion, hemoptysis (late symptom)
Cognitive-perceptual: Chest pain or tightness, shoulder and arm pain, headache, bone pain (late symptom)

Objective Data
General
Fever, nose and/or throat infection, neck and axillary lymphadenopathy, paraneoplastic syndrome (e.g., syndrome of inappropriate ADH secretion)

Integumentary
Edema of neck and face (superior vena cava syndrome), digital clubbing. Jaundice (liver metastasis).

Respiratory
Wheezing, hoarseness, stridor, dyspnea on exertion (unilateral diaphragm paralysis), pleural effusions (late signs)

Cardiovascular
Pericardial effusion, cardiac tamponade, dysrhythmias (late signs)

Neurologic
Confusion, disorientation, unsteady gait (brain metastasis)

Musculoskeletal
Pathologic fractures, muscle wasting (late)

Possible Diagnostic Findings
Observance of lesion on chest x-ray, CT scan, or PET scan. MRI findings of vertebral, spinal cord, or mediastinal invasion. Positive sputum or bronchial washings for cytologic studies. Positive fiberoptic bronchoscopy and biopsy findings

ADH, Antidiuretic hormone; *PET,* positron emission tomography.

recognition that secondhand smoke is a health hazard. Laws prohibit smoking in most public places and limit public smoking to designated areas. Most hospital environments are now completely smoke free, prohibiting smoking by employees and patients. A new trend is for hospitals to refuse employment to anyone testing positive for nicotine.

◆ **Acute Care.** Care of the patient with lung cancer initially involves support and reassurance during diagnostic evaluation. It is important to recognize the multiple stressors that occur when someone receives a lung cancer diagnosis. The stress response is a normal and adaptive response but can become detrimental when stress is overwhelming and intense.

Patients have the stress of their symptoms, including dyspnea and cough. Diagnostic and therapeutic interventions provide more stress by placing patients in unfamiliar environments with unusual and perhaps painful procedures. Emotional stressors include waiting for test results and awareness of the high mortality rate associated with lung cancer and the causal effect of cigarette smoking. Worries about role performance and ability to care for their family while undergoing cancer treatment provide further stress. Carefully assess the patient since each will have unique stressors. The insight gained will help the patient and caregiver cope with the stress of both illness and treatment.

Care of the patient undergoing chest surgery is discussed later in this chapter on pp. 529–530. Care of the patient undergoing radiation therapy and chemotherapy is discussed in Chapter 15. Individualized care depends on the plan for treatment. Assessment and intervention in symptom management are pivotal, as is teaching the patient to recognize signs and symptoms that may indicate progression or recurrence of disease. Teach signs and symptoms to report (e.g., hemoptysis, dysphagia, chest pain, hoarseness).

Provide patient comfort, teach methods to reduce pain, monitor for side effects of prescribed drugs, foster appropriate coping strategies for both the patient and caregiver, assess smoking cessation readiness, and help the patient access resources to deal with the illness.

❓ CHECK YOUR PRACTICE

You are completing discharge teaching with a 72-yr-old woman who had a lobectomy for NSCLC. She tells you, "I'm not going to give up smoking my cigarettes because I am just going to die anyhow. I might as well enjoy smoking while I still can."
• How would you respond?

◆ **Ambulatory Care.** Counseling patients on smoking cessation and prevention is essential in decreasing morbidity and mortality risks associated with lung cancer. Encourage the patient and family to provide a smoke-free environment. This may include smoking cessation for multiple family members. If the treatment plan includes home O_2, the teaching plan must include the safe use of O_2.

For many patients with lung cancer, little can be done to significantly prolong their lives. Radiation therapy and chemotherapy can provide palliative relief from distressing symptoms. Constant pain may become a major problem. Measures used to relieve pain are discussed in Chapter 8. Care of the patient with cancer is discussed in Chapter 15. The palliative care team should be involved as the patient and family move toward the end of life (see Chapter 9). The team can provide information about disability, financial planning, and community resources for end-of-life care, such as hospice and home care.

◆ **Evaluation**

The expected outcomes are that the patient with lung cancer will:
• Have adequate breathing patterns
• Maintain adequate oxygenation
• Have minimal to no pain
• Convey feelings openly and honestly, with a realistic attitude about prognosis

OTHER TYPES OF LUNG TUMORS

SCLC and NSCLC account for 95% of lung tumors. The other 5% include:
• *Hamartomas,* the most common benign tumor, is a slow-growing congenital tumor composed of fibrous tissue, fat, and blood vessels.
• *Mucous gland adenoma* is a benign tumor arising in the bronchi that consists of columnar cystic spaces.
• *Mesotheliomas* are either malignant or benign and start in the visceral pleura. Malignant mesotheliomas are associated with exposure to asbestos. Benign mesotheliomas are localized lesions.

Secondary metastases from other cancers can occur. Cancer cells from another part of the body reach the lungs through the pulmonary capillaries or lymphatic network. The main cancers that spread to the lungs often start in the breast, GI, or genitourinary tract.

▌CHEST TRAUMA AND THORACIC INJURIES

Traumatic injuries to the chest contribute to many deaths. Chest injuries range from simple rib fractures to cardiorespiratory arrest. We describe the primary mechanisms of injury responsible for chest trauma as either blunt trauma or penetrating trauma.

Blunt trauma occurs when the chest strikes or is struck by an object. The impact can cause shearing and compression of chest structures. The external injury may appear minor, but internally organs may have been severely damaged. Rib and sternal fractures can lacerate lung tissue. In a high-velocity impact, shearing forces can result in laceration or tearing of the aorta. Compression of the chest may result in contusion, crush injury, and organ rupture.

Penetrating trauma is an injury in which a foreign object impales or passes through the body tissues, creating an open wound. Examples include knife wounds, gunshot wounds, and injuries with other sharp objects. Emergency care of the patient with a chest injury is outlined in Table 27.19. The most common chest emergencies and their management are described in Table 27.20.

FRACTURED RIBS

Rib fractures are the most common type of chest injury from blunt trauma. Ribs 5 through 9 are most often fractured because they are the least protected by chest muscles. A fractured rib that is splintered or displaced can damage the pleura, lungs, heart, and other internal organs.

Manifestations of fractured ribs include pain at the site of injury, especially during inspiration and with coughing. The patient splints the affected area and takes shallow breaths to try to decrease the pain. Atelectasis and pneumonia may develop because of decreased chest wall movement and retained secretions.

The goal of treatment is to decrease pain so that the patient can breathe adequately and clear secretions. Strapping the chest with tape or using a thoracic binder is not recommended. These limit chest expansion and predispose the person to atelectasis. NSAIDs, opioids, and thoracic nerve blocks can be used to reduce pain and assist with deep breathing and coughing. Patient teaching should emphasize deep breathing, coughing, incentive spirometry, and appropriate use of pain medications.

TABLE 27.19 Emergency Management

Chest Trauma

Etiology	Assessment Findings	Interventions
Blunt • Assault with blunt object • Crush injury • Explosion • Fall • Motor vehicle collision • Pedestrian accident • Sports injury **Penetrating** • Arrow • Gunshot • Knife • Stick	**Respiratory** • Audible air escaping from chest wound • Cough with or without hemoptysis • Cyanosis of mouth, face, nail beds, mucous membranes • Decreased breath sounds on side of injury • Decreased O_2 saturation • Dyspnea, respiratory distress • Frothy secretions • Tracheal deviation **Cardiovascular** • Asymmetric BP values in arms • Chest pain • Decreased BP • Distended neck veins • Dysrhythmias • Muffled heart sounds • Narrowed pulse pressure • Rapid, thready pulse **Surface Findings** • Abrasions • Asymmetric chest movement • Bruising • Contusions • Lacerations • Open chest wound • Subcutaneous emphysema	**Initial** • If unresponsive, immediately assess circulation, airway, and breathing. • If responsive, monitor airway, breathing, and circulation. • Apply high-flow O_2 to keep SpO_2 >90%. • Establish IV access with 2 large-bore catheters. Begin IV fluid resuscitation as appropriate. • Remove clothing to assess injury. • Cover sucking chest wound with nonporous dressing taped on 3 sides (vent dressing). • Stabilize impaled objects with bulky dressings. *Do not remove object.* • Assess for life-threatening injuries and treat appropriately. • Place patient in a semi-Fowler's position if breathing is easier *after* cervical spine injury has been ruled out. • Give small amounts of analgesia as needed for pain and to help with breathing. • Prepare for emergency needle decompression if tension pneumothorax or cardiac tamponade present. **Ongoing Monitoring** • Monitor level of consciousness, vital signs, O_2 saturation, cardiac rhythm, respiratory status, and urine output. • Anticipate intubation for respiratory distress. • Release vent dressing if tension pneumothorax develops after sucking chest wound is covered.

 TABLE 27.20 Emergency Management

Chest Injuries

Injury and Description	Manifestations	Intervention
Cardiac Tamponade Blood rapidly collects in pericardial sac, compresses myocardium because pericardium does not stretch, and prevents ventricles from filling.	Muffled, distant heart sounds, hypotension, neck vein distention, increased central venous pressure	Medical emergency. Pericardiocentesis with surgical repair as appropriate.
Flail Chest Fracture of 2 or more adjacent ribs in 2 or more places with loss of chest wall stability (Fig. 27.5).	Paradoxical movement of chest wall, respiratory distress. May be associated hemothorax, pneumothorax, pulmonary contusion	O_2 as needed to maintain O_2 saturation, analgesia. Stabilize flail segment with positive pressure ventilation (intubation and mechanical ventilation as needed). Treat associated injuries. Possible surgical fixation.
Hemothorax Blood in the pleural space, may or may not occur in conjunction with pneumothorax.	Dyspnea, decreased or absent breath sounds, dullness to percussion, decreased Hgb, shock (depending on blood volume lost)	Chest tube insertion with chest drainage system. Autotransfusion of collected blood, treatment of hypovolemia as needed with IV fluid, packed red blood cells.
Pneumothorax Air in pleural space (Fig. 27.6).	Dyspnea, decreased movement of involved chest wall, decreased or absent breath sounds on the affected side, hyperresonance to percussion	Chest tube insertion with chest drainage system.
Tension Pneumothorax Air in pleural space that does not escape Increased air in the pleural space shifts organs and increases intrathoracic pressure (Fig. 27.6).	Cyanosis, air hunger, extreme agitation, subcutaneous emphysema, neck vein distention, hyperresonance to percussion, tracheal deviation away from affected side (late sign)	Medical emergency: needle decompression followed by chest tube insertion with chest drainage system.

FLAIL CHEST

Flail chest results from the fracture of 3 or more consecutive ribs, in 2 or more separate places, causing an unstable segment (Fig. 27.5). It also can be caused by fracture of the sternum and several consecutive ribs. The resulting instability of the chest wall causes paradoxical movement during breathing. The affected (flail) area moves in the opposite direction with respect to the intact part of the chest. During inspiration, the affected part is sucked in, and during expiration, it bulges out. This paradoxical chest movement prevents adequate ventilation and increases the work of breathing. The underlying injured lung may be contused, aggravating hypoxemia.

A flail chest is usually apparent on physical examination. The patient has rapid, shallow respirations and tachycardia. Movement of the thorax is asymmetric and uncoordinated. The patient may ventilate poorly and try to splint the chest to assist with breathing. Observation of abnormal chest cavity movement, palpation for crepitus near the rib fractures, and chest x-ray all assist in the diagnosis.

Initial therapy consists of ensuring adequate ventilation and supplemental O_2 therapy. The goal is to promote lung expansion and ensure adequate oxygenation. Analgesia can help promote adequate respiration. Although many patients can be managed without mechanical ventilation, intubation and ventilation may be needed. In cases of extreme chest trauma, surgical fixation of the flail segment may be done. The lung parenchyma and fractured ribs heal with time. Some patients continue to have intercostal pain several weeks after the flail chest has resolved.

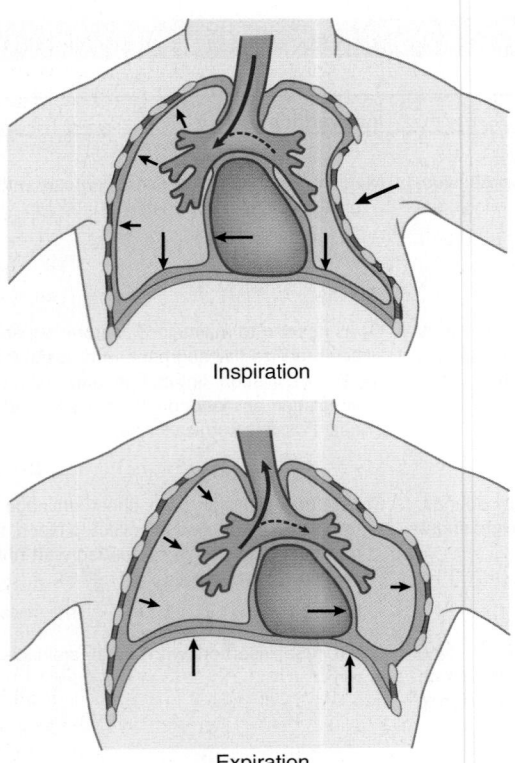

Inspiration

Expiration

FIG. 27.5 Flail chest causes paradoxical respiration. On inspiration, the flail section moves inward with mediastinal shift to the uninjured side. On expiration, the flail section bulges outward with mediastinal shift to the injured side.

PNEUMOTHORAX

A **pneumothorax** is caused by air entering the pleural cavity. Normally, negative (subatmospheric) pressure exists between the visceral pleura (surrounding the lung) and parietal pleura (lining the chest cavity), known as the *pleural space*. The pleural space has a few milliliters of lubricating fluid to reduce friction when the tissues move. When air enters this space, the change to positive pressure causes a partial or complete lung collapse (Fig. 27.6). As the volume of air in the pleural space increases, lung volume decreases.

Pneumothorax can be classified as *open* (air entering through an opening in the chest wall) or *closed* (no external wound). Penetrating trauma allows air to enter the pleural space through an opening in the chest wall (Fig. 27.6). A penetrating chest wound may be referred to as a *sucking chest wound,* since air enters the pleural space through the chest wall during inspiration. A pneumothorax should be suspected after any trauma to the chest wall.

If a pneumothorax is small, mild tachycardia and dyspnea may be the only manifestations. If the pneumothorax occupies a large area, respiratory distress may be present, including short, shallow, rapid respirations; dyspnea; air hunger; and O_2 desaturation. On auscultation, breath sounds are absent over the affected area. Time permitting, a chest x-ray will show air or fluid in the pleural space and reduction in lung volume.

Types of Pneumothorax

Spontaneous Pneumothorax. A spontaneous pneumothorax typically occurs due to the rupture of small blebs (air-filled sacs) on the surface of the lung. These blebs can occur in healthy, young people or from lung disease, such as COPD, asthma, cystic fibrosis, and pneumonia. Smoking increases the risk for bleb formation. Other risk factors include being tall and thin, male gender, family history, and previous spontaneous pneumothorax.

Iatrogenic Pneumothorax. *Iatrogenic pneumothorax* can occur due to laceration or puncture of the lung during medical procedures. For example, transthoracic needle aspiration, subclavian catheter insertion, pleural biopsy, and transbronchial lung biopsy all have the potential to injure the lung. Barotrauma from excessive ventilatory pressure during manual or mechanical ventilation can rupture alveoli, creating a pneumothorax. Esophageal procedures may result in a pneumothorax. For example, tearing of the esophageal wall during insertion of a gastric tube can allow air from the esophagus to enter the mediastinum and pleural space.

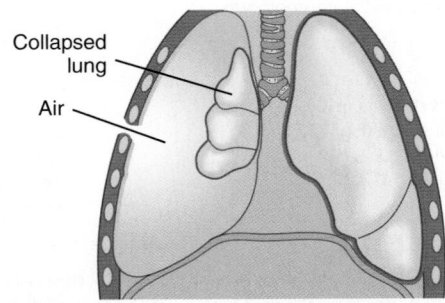

Collapsed lung

Air

FIG. 27.6 Open pneumothorax resulting from collapse of lung due to disruption of chest wall and outside air entering.

Tension Pneumothorax. Tension pneumothorax occurs when air enters the pleural space but cannot escape. The continued accumulation of air in the pleural space causes increasingly elevated intrapleural pressures. This results in compression of the lung on the affected side and pressure on the heart and great vessels, pushing them away from the affected side (Fig. 27.7). The mediastinum shifts toward the unaffected side, compressing the "good" lung, which further compromises oxygenation. As the pressure increases, venous return decreases and cardiac output falls.

Tension pneumothorax may result from either an open or a closed pneumothorax. In an open chest wound, a flap may act as a one-way valve. Thus air can enter on inspiration but cannot escape. Tension pneumothorax can occur with mechanical ventilation and resuscitative efforts. It can also occur if chest tubes are clamped or become blocked in a patient with a pneumothorax. Unclamping the tube or relieving the obstruction may correct this situation.

Tension pneumothorax is a medical emergency. It affects both the respiratory and cardiovascular systems. Manifestations include severe dyspnea, marked tachycardia, tracheal deviation, decreased or absent breath sounds on the affected side, neck vein distention, cyanosis, and profuse diaphoresis. If the tension in the pleural space is not relieved, the patient is likely to die from inadequate cardiac output or severe hypoxemia.

Hemothorax. Hemothorax is an accumulation of blood in the pleural space from injury to the chest wall, diaphragm, lung, blood vessels, or mediastinum. When it occurs with pneumothorax, it is called a *hemopneumothorax*. The patient with a traumatic hemothorax needs immediate insertion of a chest tube for evacuation of the blood. Recovered blood can be reinfused for a short time after the injury. (Autotransfusion is discussed in Chapter 30.)

Chylothorax. *Chylothorax* is the presence of lymphatic fluid in the pleural space. The thoracic duct is disrupted either traumatically or from cancer, allowing lymphatic fluid to fill the pleural space. This milky white fluid is high in lipids. Normal lymphatic flow through the thoracic duct is 1500 to 2500 mL/day. This amount can be increased up to 10-fold after ingestion of fats. Some cases heal with conservative treatment (chest drainage, bowel rest, dietary modifications). Octreotide may reduce the flow of lymphatic fluid. Surgery (thoracic duct ligation) and pleurodesis (the artificial production of adhesions between the parietal and visceral pleura) are options for refractory cases.

Interprofessional Care

Treatment of a pneumothorax depends on its severity, underlying cause, and hemodynamic stability of the patient. If the patient is stable and has minimal air and/or fluid accumulated in the intrapleural space, no treatment may be needed since the condition may resolve spontaneously.

Emergency treatment consists of covering the wound with an occlusive dressing that is secured on 3 sides (vent dressing). During inspiration, as negative pressure is created in the chest, the dressing pulls against the wound, preventing air from entering the pleural space. During expiration, as the pressure rises in the pleural space, the dressing is pushed out and air escapes through the wound and from under the dressing. If the object that caused the open chest wound is still in place, do not remove it. Stabilize the impaled object with a bulky dressing. Wait until an HCP is present or arrange transport to the nearest medical facility.

The most definitive and common treatment of pneumothorax and hemothorax is to insert a chest tube and connect it to water-seal drainage. Repeated spontaneous pneumothorax may need surgical treatment with a partial pleurectomy, stapling, or pleurodesis to promote adherence of the pleurae to one another. Tension pneumothorax is a medical emergency, requiring urgent needle decompression followed by chest tube insertion to water-seal drainage.

CHEST TUBES AND PLEURAL DRAINAGE

If enough fluid or air accumulates in the pleural space, the normally negative subatmospheric pressure becomes positive and the lungs collapse. Inserting a chest tube can drain the pleural space, reestablish negative pressure, and allow for proper lung expansion.

Chest tubes are about 20 in (51 cm) long and vary in size from 12F to 40F. The size inserted depends on the patient's condition. Large (36F to 40F) tubes are used to drain blood, medium (24F to 36F) tubes are used to drain fluid, and small (12F to 24F) tubes are used to drain air. Pigtail tubes are very small (10F to 14F) tubes with a curly end designed to keep them in place. Pigtail tubes are a safe and effective alternative to larger-bore chest tubes for treatment of pneumothorax.

Chest Tube Insertion

Insertion of a chest tube can take place in the ED, the operating room, or at the patient's bedside. Time permitting, a chest x-ray is used to confirm the affected side. The patient is positioned with the arm raised above the head on the affected side to expose the midaxillary area, the standard site for insertion. Elevate the patient's head 30 to 60 degrees, when possible, to lower the diaphragm and reduce the risk for injury.

The area is cleansed with an antiseptic solution. The HCP infiltrates the chest with a local anesthetic and makes a small incision over a rib. The chest tube is advanced up and over the top of the rib to avoid the intercostal nerves and blood vessels that are behind the rib inferiorly (Fig. 27.8). Once inserted, the HCP secures (sutures) the tube in place and closes the incision with sutures. The tube is connected to a pleural drainage system (Fig. 27.9). The wound is covered with an occlusive dressing. Most HCPs prefer

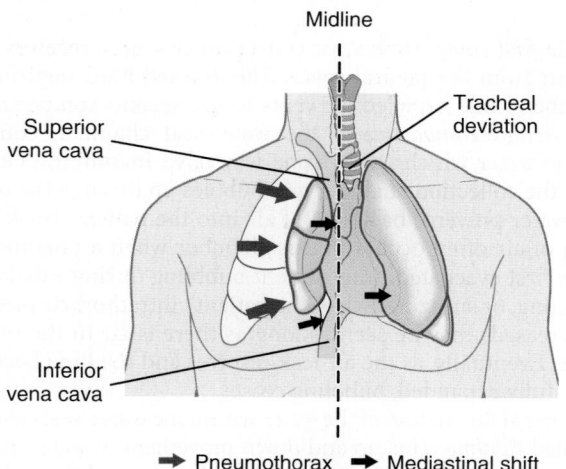

Midline

Superior
vena cava

Tracheal
deviation

Inferior
vena cava

➡ Pneumothorax ➡ Mediastinal shift

FIG. 27.7 Tension pneumothorax. As pleural pressure on the affected side increases, mediastinal displacement ensues, causing respiratory and cardiovascular compromise. Tracheal deviation is an external (but late) manifestation of the mediastinal shift.

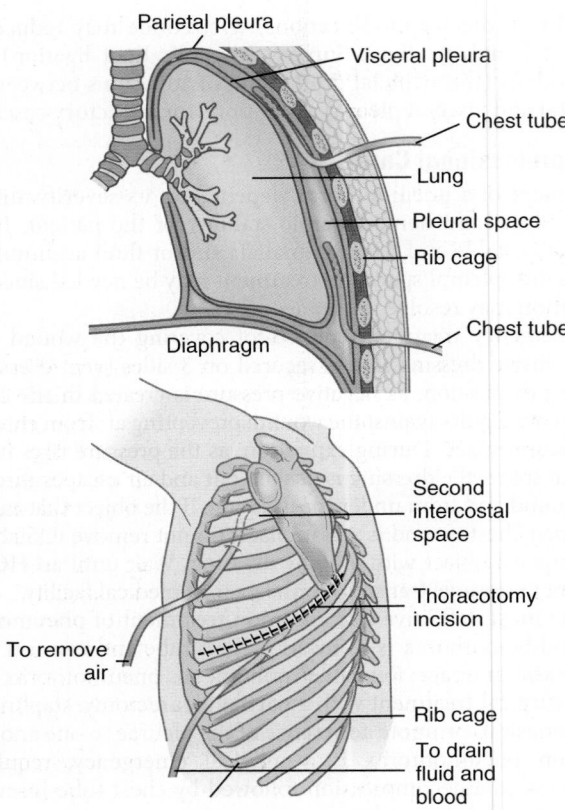

FIG. 27.8 Placement of chest tubes.

FIG. 27.9 Chest drainage unit. Both units have 3 chambers: (1) collection chamber; (2) water-seal chamber; and (3) suction control chamber. Suction control chamber requires a connection to a wall suction source that is dialed up higher than the prescribed suction for the suction to work. A, Water suction. This unit uses water in the suction control chamber to control the wall suction pressure. B, Dry suction. This unit controls wall suction by using a regulator control dial. (From Atrium Medical Corporation, Hudson, NH.)

to seal the wound around the chest tube with petroleum (airtight) gauze. Proper tube placement is confirmed by chest x-ray.

The insertion of a chest tube and its presence in the pleural space are painful. Monitor the patient's comfort frequently and use appropriate pain-relieving interventions.

Flutter or Heimlich Valve

A flutter valve (also called the *Heimlich valve*) is used to remove air from the pleural space (Fig. 27.10). This device consists of a one-way rubber valve within a rigid plastic tube. It is attached to the external end of the chest tube. It has 2 nozzles. The inlet nozzle allows the air to pass in the valve through the chest drainage tube attached to it. The outlet nozzle allows the air to pass to the environment or a collecting device during expiration. During inspiration, when pressure in the chest decreases, the valve closes. During expiration, when intrathoracic pressure increases, the valve closes.

The flutter valve can be used for small to moderate-sized pneumothorax. It also allows for patient mobility. The smaller drainage bag can be hidden under the clothes while the patient ambulates. Drainage bags attached to the flutter valve must have a vent to the atmosphere to prevent a tension pneumothorax. This is done by simply cutting a small slit in the top of any drainage bag that does not have a built-in vent. Patients may go home with a flutter valve in place.

Pleural Drainage

A chest tube is usually attached to a drainage device or chamber to collect fluid, air, and/or blood from the chest cavity. Several different disposable chest drainage units are currently available. All drainage units have 3 basic compartments (Fig. 27.9).

The *first compartment*, or collection chamber, receives fluid and air from the pleural space. The drained fluid stays in this chamber while expelled air vents to the second compartment. The *second compartment*, the water-seal chamber, contains 2 cm of water, which acts as a one-way valve. Incoming air enters from the collection chamber and bubbles up through the water. The water prevents backflow of air into the patient. Brisk bubbling of air often occurs in this chamber when a pneumothorax is first evacuated. Intermittent bubbling during exhalation, coughing, or sneezing (when the patient's intrathoracic pressure is increased) may be seen as long as there is air in the pleural space. Eventually, as the air leak resolves and the lung becomes more fully expanded, bubbling ceases.

Normal fluctuation of the water within the water-seal chamber is called *tidaling*. This up and down movement of water in concert with respiration reflects intrapleural pressure changes during inspiration and expiration. If tidaling stops suddenly, assess the chest tube as this may signify an occluded chest tube. As the lung reexpands, tidaling gradually slows then eventually stops.

FIG. 27.10 A, Heimlich chest drain valve is a specially designed flutter valve that is used in place of a chest drainage unit for small uncomplicated pneumothorax with little or no drainage and no need for suction. The valve allows for escape of air but prevents the reentry of air into the pleural space. B, Placement of valve between chest tube and vented drainage bag, which can be worn under a person's clothes. (A, Courtesy and © Becton, Dickinson and Company.)

The *third compartment,* the suction control chamber, applies suction to the chest drainage unit. There are 2 main types of suction control: water and dry. The water suction control chamber uses a column of water to control the amount of suction from the wall regulator.

The chamber is typically filled with 20 cm of water. The amount of suction applied to the chest drainage unit is regulated by the amount of water in this chamber and not by the amount of suction applied to the system. An increase in wall suction does not result in an increase in negative pressure to the system because any excess suction merely draws in air through the vent on top of the third chamber. The suction pressure is usually ordered to be −20 cm H_2O. Higher pressures (−40 cm H_2O) are sometimes needed to evacuate the pleural space. Lower pressure (−10 cm H_2O) may be used for frail and older patients at risk for tissue damage with higher pressures. When the negative pressure generated by the suction source exceeds the set −20 cm H_2O, air from the atmosphere enters the chamber through a vent on top of the chest drainage unit and the air bubbles up through the water, causing a suction-breaker effect. As a result, excess pressure is relieved.

To start suction, adjust (increase) the vacuum source until gentle bubbling is present in the third chamber. Excessive bubbling does not increase the amount of suction but does increase the rate of evaporation of the water and the amount of noise made by the device.

Dry suction chest drainage systems do not contain water. They often have a visual alert that shows if the suction is working. It uses either a restrictive device or a regulator to dial the desired negative pressure; this is internal in the chest drainage system. To increase the suction pressures, turn the dial on the drainage system. Increasing the vacuum source does not increase the pressure. When decreasing suction, depress the manual vent to reduce excess vacuum to the lower prescribed level.

A variety of disposable plastic chest drainage systems are available. Manufacturers include directions for set-up and use with each unit.

❖ NURSING MANAGEMENT: CHEST DRAINAGE

General guidelines for nursing care of the patient with chest tubes and water-seal drainage systems are shown in Table 27.21.

Clamping of chest tubes during transport or when the tube is accidentally disconnected is no longer advocated. The danger of rapid accumulation of air in the pleural space, causing tension pneumothorax, is far greater than that of a small amount of atmospheric air that enters the pleural space. If a chest tube becomes disconnected, the immediate priority is to reestablish the water-seal system. In some agencies, when disconnection occurs, the chest tube is immersed in sterile water to act as a water seal until a new system can be set up and chest drainage reestablished. It is important to know the unit protocol, the clinical situation (whether an air leak exists), and HCP preference before any chest tube clamping occurs.

Chest tubes may be momentarily clamped to change the drainage apparatus or to check for air leaks. Appearance of a new air leak warrants assessment of the drainage system to identify whether the air leak is coming from the patient or the system. Again, you must be familiar with the policies and procedures of your agency about specific clinical situations when you may clamp a chest tube.

Closely monitor the patient for complications associated with chest tube placement and drainage. If volumes from 1 to 1.5 L of fluid and/or blood are removed rapidly, reexpansion pulmonary edema or severe, symptomatic hypotension can occur. Subcutaneous emphysema can occur from air leaking into the tissue surrounding the chest tube insertion site. A "crackling" sensation will be felt when palpating the skin. A small amount of subcutaneous air is harmless and will be reabsorbed. However, severe subcutaneous emphysema can cause drastic swelling of the head and neck with potential airway compromise.

Meticulous sterile technique during dressing changes can reduce the incidence of infected chest tube insertion sites. Nursing care and patient teaching can minimize the risk for atelectasis and shoulder stiffness. Encourage coughing, deep breathing, incentive spirometer use, and range-of-motion exercises. Inspect the integrity of the chest tube system. Monitor the color and amount of drainage hourly in the first few hours after chest tube insertion. Drainage greater than 200 mL in the first hour, development of subcutaneous emphysema, or any signs and symptoms of respiratory distress should be reported to the HCP at once.

🌿 CHECK YOUR PRACTICE

You are caring for a 26-yr-old male patient who has chest injuries from a motorcycle accident. He has 2 chest tubes in place that are each attached to a chest drainage system. While turning him, you accidentally disconnect one of the chest tubes from the drainage system.
- What is your most immediate priority?

TABLE 27.21 Chest Tubes and Water-Seal Drainage

Set-Up and Insertion

1. Make sure patient is aware of the procedure and informed consent is obtained.
2. Gather equipment.
   - Thoracotomy or chest tube insertion tray
   - Chest drainage unit (CDU)
   - Chest tube
   - Bottle of sterile water
   - 1% lidocaine
   - Suction tubing and collection container
   - Occlusive dressing
3. Prepare CDU.
   - *Wet suction:* Add sterile water to 2-cm mark in water-seal chamber and to 20-cm mark (or as ordered) in suction control chamber.
   - *Dry suction:* Add sterile water to the fill line of the air leak meter. Attach suction tubing and increase suction until the bellows-like float moves across the display window.
4. Position and support the patient to minimize movement during procedure.

Drainage System

1. Keep all tubing loosely coiled below chest level. Tubing should drop straight from bed or chair to drainage unit. Do not let it be compressed.
2. Keep all connections between chest tubes, drainage tubing, and the drainage collector tight, and tape all connections.
3. Observe for air fluctuations (tidaling) and bubbling in the water-seal chamber.
   - If tidaling (rising with inspiration and falling with expiration in the spontaneously breathing patient) is not seen, the drainage system is blocked, the lungs are reexpanded, or the system is attached to suction.
   - If bubbling increases, there may be an air leak in the drainage system or a leak from the patient (bronchopleural leak).
4. If the chest tube is connected to suction, disconnect from wall suction to check for tidaling.
5. Suspect a system leak when bubbling is continuous.
   - Retape tubing connections.
   - Ensure that dressing is air occlusive.
   - If leak persists, briefly clamp the chest tube at the patient's chest. If the leak stops, the air is coming from the patient*
   - If the air leak persists, briefly and methodically move the clamps down the tubing away from the patient until the air leak stops. The leak will then be present between the last 2 clamp points. If the air leak persists all the way to the drainage unit, replace the unit.*
6. High fluid levels in the water seal indicate residual negative pressure.
   - The chest system may have to be vented by using the high-negativity release valve available on the drainage system to release residual pressure from the system.
   - Do not lower water-seal column when wall suction is not operating or when patient is on gravity drainage.

Patient's Clinical Status

1. Monitor the patient's clinical status. Assess vital signs, lung sounds, and pain.
2. Assess for reaccumulation of air and fluid in the chest (↓ or absent breath sounds), significant bleeding (>100 mL/hr), infection at chest tube insertion site (drainage, erythema, fever, ↑ WBCs), or poor wound healing. Notify HCP for management plan.

3. Evaluate for subcutaneous emphysema at chest tube site.
4. Encourage the patient to breathe deeply periodically to promote lung expansion and encourage range-of-motion exercises to the shoulder on the affected side. Encourage use of incentive spirometry every hour while awake to prevent atelectasis or pneumonia.

Chest Drainage

1. Never elevate the drainage system to the level of the patient's chest because this will cause fluid to drain back into the lungs. Change the unit if the collection chamber is full. Do not try to empty it.
2. Mark the time of measurement and the fluid level on the drainage unit according to the unit standards. Report any change in the quantity or characteristics of drainage (e.g., clear yellow to bloody) to the HCP and record the change. Notify HCP if >100 mL/hr drainage.
3. Check the position of the chest drainage container. If the drainage system is overturned and the water seal is disrupted, return it to an upright position and encourage the patient to take a few deep breaths, followed by forced exhalations and cough maneuvers.
4. If the drainage system breaks, place the distal end of the chest tubing connection in a sterile water container at a 2-cm level as an emergency water seal.
5. Position tubing so that drainage flows freely.

Monitoring Wet Versus Dry Suction Chest Drainage Systems
Suction Control Chamber in Wet Suction System

1. Keep the suction control chamber at the right water level by adding sterile water as needed to replace water lost to evaporation.
2. Keep the cover over the suction control chamber in place to prevent more rapid evaporation of water and to decrease the noise of the bubbling.
3. After filling the suction control chamber to the ordered suction amount (generally 20 cm H_2O suction), connect the suction tubing to the wall suction.
4. Dial the wall suction regulator until there is continuous gentle bubbling in the suction control chamber (generally 80 to 120 mm Hg). Vigorous bubbling is not necessary and will increase the rate of evaporation.
5. If there is no bubbling in the suction control chamber, (1) there is no suction, (2) suction is not high enough, or (3) the pleural air leak is so large that suction is not high enough to evacuate it.

Suction Control Chamber in Dry Suction System (see manufacturer's directions)

1. After connecting patient to system, turn the dial on the chest drainage system to amount ordered (generally −20 cm H_2O pressure), connect suction tubing to wall suction source, and increase the suction until the float appears in the window of the CDU.
2. If ordered to decrease suction, turn the dial down, depress the high-negativity vent, and assess for a rise in the water level of the water-seal chamber.

Chest Tube Dressings

1. Change dressing according to unit protocol and HCP preference.
2. Remove old dressing carefully. Assess the site for inflammation or infection and culture site as needed.
3. Cleanse the site according to protocol, maintaining strict sterile asepsis.
4. Redress with occlusive dressing. Some HCPs prefer the use of petroleum gauze dressing around the tube to prevent air leak. Date the dressing and document dressing change.

*As per agency policy and procedures.

◆ **Chest Tube Removal**

Chest tubes are removed when the lungs are reexpanded and fluid drainage has ceased or is minimal. In some centers, suction is discontinued, and the chest drain is allowed to drain by gravity for 24 hours before the tube is removed. Give the patient pain medication about 30 to 60 minutes before tube removal.

Gather dressing supplies, including petroleum jelly and dry gauze dressing. Explain the procedure to the patient. In most settings, the tube is removed by the HCP or an advanced practice nurse. The suture is cut, and with the patient holding his or her breath or bearing down (Valsalva maneuver), the tube is removed. The site is immediately covered with the airtight dressing to prevent air from entering the pleural space. The pleura will seal off, and the wound usually heals in a few days. A chest x-ray is done 30 to 60 minutes after chest tube removal to evaluate for pneumothorax or fluid accumulation. Observe the wound for drainage and reinforce the dressing if needed. Monitor and record vital signs. Assess the patient for respiratory distress, which may signify a recurrence of the original problem.

CHEST SURGERY

Chest surgery is done for various reasons, including lung, heart, vascular, and esophageal disorders. The most common types of chest surgery are described in Table 27.22.

Surgical Procedures

Thoracotomy. A *thoracotomy* is a surgical incision into the chest to gain access to the heart, lungs, esophagus, thoracic aorta, or anterior spine. Two common approaches to a thoracotomy are the median sternotomy and lateral thoracotomy. The median sternotomy involves splitting the sternum. It is primarily used for surgery involving the heart. The lateral thoracotomy incision can be done using a posterolateral or anterolateral incision. The *posterolateral incision* is used for most surgeries involving the lung. The incision is made from front to back at the level of the 4th, 5th, or 6th intercostal space. Strong mechanical retractors are used to separate the ribs and gain access to the lung. The

TABLE 27.22 **Chest Surgeries**		
Type	**Description**	**Indications**
Decortication Removal or stripping of thick, fibrous membrane from visceral pleura	• Need chest tubes postoperatively	Empyema or other inflammatory process unresponsive to conservative management
Exploratory Thoracotomy Incision into thorax to look for injured or bleeding tissues	• Need chest tubes postoperatively	Chest trauma
Lobectomy Removal of 1 lobe of lung	• Most common lung surgery • Lung tissue expands to fill up space left by resected lobe • Need chest tubes postoperatively	Lung cancer, bronchiectasis, TB, advanced emphysema, benign lung tumors, fungal infections
Lung Volume Reduction Surgery **Bronchoscopic procedure**	• Used to place one-way valves in airways leading to the diseased parts of the lung • Valves let air out, but not in, thus collapsing a certain segment of lungs	Advanced emphysema, α_1-antitrypsin emphysema
Open surgical procedure	• Involves reducing lung volume by multiple wedge excisions or VATS • Removes most diseased lung tissue	Emphysema, limited NSCLC
Pneumonectomy Removal of entire lung	• Done when lobectomy or segmental resection will not remove all diseased lung • Fluid will gradually fill space where lung was removed • May have chest tube postoperatively • Position patient on operative side to promote expansion of remaining lung	Lung cancer (most common)
Segmental Resection Removal of 1 or more lung segments	• Indicated for a patient unable to handle more extensive surgery • Remaining lung tissue expands to fill space • Need chest tubes postoperatively	Lung cancer, bronchiectasis
Thoracotomy (Not Involving Lungs) Incision into thorax for surgery on other organs	• Postoperative care related to thoracotomy and reason for surgical procedure • Need chest tubes postoperatively	Hiatal hernia repair, open heart surgery, esophageal surgery, tracheal resection, thoracic aorta repair
Video-Assisted Thoracic Surgery Video-assisted technique with a rigid scope with a distal lens inserted into pleura and image shown on a monitor screen	• Allows HCP to manipulate instruments passed into pleural space through separate small intercostal incisions • Done under general anesthesia in operating room • May need chest tube postoperatively	Lung biopsy, lobectomy, resection of nodules, repair of fistulas
Wedge Resection Removal of small, localized lesion that occupies only part of a segment	• Most conservative approach • Done to remove small peripheral nodules or for patients unable to handle more extensive surgery • Need chest tubes postoperatively	Lung biopsy, excision of small nodules

anterolateral incision is made in the 4th or 5th intercostal space from the sternal border to the midaxillary line. This procedure is often done for surgery or trauma victims, mediastinal operations, and wedge resections of the upper and middle lobes of the lung.

Video-Assisted Thoracic Surgery. *Video-assisted thoracoscopic surgery* (VATS) is a widely used, minimally invasive surgical approach. It provides a real-time 2-dimensional video image of the inside of the chest cavity. It is used for diagnosis and treatment of diseases of the pleura, pulmonary masses and nodules, mediastinal masses, and interstitial lung disease. Through incisions just large enough to insert the instruments, the HCP can inspect the chest cavity, biopsy suspicious areas, obtain samples of fluids for analysis, and remove tissue.

VATS is increasingly being used for patients with chest trauma. The HCP can examine, diagnose, and manage injuries in both blunt and penetrating trauma, including injuries to the diaphragm. A chest tube is placed in the pleural space through 1 or more of the incisions at the end of the procedure, secured with sutures, and connected to a drainage unit in the usual manner.

The advantages of VATS include less discomfort, faster return to normal activity level, reduced length of hospital stay, lower postoperative morbidity risk, and fewer complications.[31] Patients who have marginal respiratory reserve or are too debilitated to tolerate an open thoracotomy approach may benefit from the VATS procedure.

Preoperative Care

Assess the patient's cardiopulmonary status to determine their ability to tolerate the surgery and provide a baseline reference for postoperative care. Diagnostic studies may include chest x-ray, electrocardiogram (ECG), ABGs, pulmonary function studies, blood urea nitrogen (BUN), serum creatinine, blood glucose, serum electrolytes, prothrombin time/international normalized ratio (PT/INR), activated partial thromboplastin time (aPTT), and CBC. An anesthesia consult is usually completed.

The patient should be in the best possible health and, if applicable, stop smoking before elective surgery. Anxiety associated with anticipated surgery makes smoking cessation more difficult. Provide encouragement, support, and teaching about various methods to help stop smoking before surgery (see Chapter 10).

Teach the patient what to expect after surgery. Include the use of O_2, the chance of intubation, administration of blood and IV fluids, and the purpose and function of chest tubes. Reassure the patient that adequate medication will be used to reduce pain. Explain how to use patient-controlled analgesia (PCA), if planned. Preoperative teaching should always include exercises for effective deep breathing and use of incentive spirometry. If the patient practices these techniques before surgery, they will be easier to perform after surgery. Show the patient how to splint the incision with a pillow to promote deep breathing. Teach and have the patient provide a return demonstration of range-of-motion exercises on the surgical side (similar to those for the mastectomy patient [see Fig. 51.8]).

The thought of losing part of a vital organ is often frightening. Reassure the patient that the lungs have a large degree of functional reserve. Even after the removal of 1 lung, enough lung tissue is left to maintain adequate oxygenation. Be available to answer the patient and caregiver's questions. Answer questions openly and honestly. Encourage the expression of concerns, feelings, and questions.

Postoperative Care

The thoracotomy incision is the most painful surgical incision for patients and one of the most difficult for nurses to manage. Pain after a thoracotomy is typically intense because respiratory muscles are cut during surgery. For most chest surgeries, chest tubes are placed in the pleural space to allow for lung reexpansion. In a pneumonectomy, chest tubes may or may not be placed in the space from which the lung was removed. Adequate pain management is a priority to prevent respiratory compromise. The use of PCA, epidural infusions, and intercostal nerve blocks allows patients to breathe deeply, cough, and move the arm and shoulder on the operative side.

Nursing care priorities in the postoperative period include assessment of respiratory function, including observation of respiratory rate and effort, breath sounds, sputum volume and color, and chest tube function and drainage. Daily chest x-rays are often ordered. Assessment of pain, monitoring of temperature, and observation of the surgical site are similar to care provided for other postoperative patients (see Chapter 19). Care after thoracotomy is presented in eNursing Care Plan 27.2 (available on the website for this chapter).

Thoracentesis

Thoracentesis is aspiration of intrapleural fluid for diagnostic and therapeutic purposes. For a thoracentesis, the patient may sit on the edge of a bed and lean forward over a bedside table. A chest x-ray or ultrasound images are used to determine the optimal puncture site. The skin is cleansed with an antiseptic solution and injected with a local anesthetic. The thoracentesis needle is inserted into the intercostal space (see Fig. 25.12). Fluid is aspirated with a syringe, or tubing is connected to the needle to allow fluid to drain into a sterile container. After the fluid is removed, the needle is withdrawn, and a bandage is applied over the insertion site.

Usually no more than 1000 to 1200 mL of pleural fluid is removed at one time. Rapid removal of a large volume can result in hypotension, hypoxemia, or reexpansion pulmonary edema. A chest x-ray may be done after the procedure to assess for complications, such as pneumothorax. During and after the procedure, monitor vital signs and pulse oximetry. Observe the patient for respiratory distress.

RESTRICTIVE RESPIRATORY DISORDERS

Disorders that impair the ability of the chest wall and diaphragm to move with respiration are called *restrictive respiratory disorders*. There are 2 categories: *extrapulmonary conditions,* in which the lung tissue is normal, and *intrapulmonary conditions,* in which the cause is the lung or pleura. Examples of extrapulmonary and intrapulmonary conditions that alter respiratory functioning are listed in Table 27.23. These disorders are further described in their respective chapters.

Pulmonary function tests are the best means of distinguishing between restrictive and obstructive respiratory disorders. The hallmark characteristic of a restrictive lung disorder is a reduced total lung capacity (TLC). The hallmark characteristic of an obstructive disorder is reduced forced expiratory volume (FEV_1). Mixed obstructive and restrictive disorders sometimes occur together. For example, a patient may have both asthma (an obstructive problem) and pulmonary fibrosis (a restrictive problem).

TABLE 27.23 **Common Causes of Restrictive Lung Disease**
Intrapulmonary Causes
Pleural Disorders
• Pleural effusion
• Pleurisy (pleuritis)
• Pneumothorax
Parenchymal Disorders
• Acute respiratory distress syndrome (ARDS)
• Atelectasis
• Interstitial lung diseases
• Pneumonia
Extrapulmonary Causes
Central Nervous System
• Head injury, central nervous system lesion (e.g., tumor, stroke)
• Opioid and barbiturate overdose
Neuromuscular System
• Amyotrophic lateral sclerosis
• Guillain-Barré syndrome
• Muscular dystrophy
• Myasthenia gravis
Chest Wall
• Kyphoscoliosis
• Obesity-hypoventilation syndrome (Pickwickian syndrome)

ATELECTASIS

Atelectasis is a lung condition characterized by collapsed, airless alveoli. There may be decreased or absent breath sounds and dullness to percussion over the affected area. The most common cause of atelectasis is obstruction of the small airways with secretions. This is common in bedridden patients and in postoperative abdominal and chest surgery patients. Normally the pores of Kohn (see Fig. 25.1) provide collateral passage of air from one alveolus to another. Deep inspiration opens the pores effectively. For this reason, deep-breathing exercises, coughing, incentive spirometry, and early mobility are important to prevent atelectasis and treat the patient at risk. (The prevention and treatment of atelectasis are discussed in Chapter 19.)

PLEURISY

Pleurisy (pleuritis) is an inflammation of the pleura. It can be caused by infectious diseases, cancer, autoimmune disorders, chest trauma, GI disease, and certain medications. The inflammation usually subsides with adequate treatment of the primary disease. The pain of pleurisy is typically abrupt, sharp in onset, and worse with inspiration. The patient's breathing is shallow and rapid to avoid unnecessary movement of the pleura and chest wall. A pleural friction rub may occur. This is the sound heard over areas where inflamed visceral pleura and parietal pleura rub over one another during inspiration. This sound, like a squeaking door, is usually loudest at peak inspiration. It may be heard during exhalation as well.

Treatment of pleurisy is aimed at treating the underlying disease and providing pain relief. Teach the patient to splint the rib cage when coughing. If the pain is severe, intercostal nerve blocks may be considered.

PLEURAL EFFUSION

Types

The pleural space normally holds 5 to 15 mL of fluid that acts as a lubricant between the chest wall (parietal pleura) and lungs (visceral pleura). Pleural effusion is an abnormal collection of fluid in this space. It is not a disease but a sign of disease. A balance among hydrostatic pressure, oncotic pressure, and capillary membrane permeability governs movement of fluid in and out of the pleural space. Fluid accumulation can be due to increased pulmonary capillary pressure, decreased oncotic pressure, increased pleural membrane permeability, or obstruction of lymphatic flow.

We classify pleural effusions as transudative or exudative depending on the protein content. A *transudate* occurs primarily in noninflammatory conditions. It is an accumulation of protein-poor, cell-poor fluid. The fluid is clear, pale yellow. These effusions are caused by (1) increased hydrostatic pressure found in HF or (2) decreased oncotic pressure (from hypoalbuminemia) found in chronic liver or renal disease. An *exudative effusion* results from increased capillary permeability due to an inflammatory reaction. They most often occur with an infection or cancer (called a malignant effusion).

An empyema is the collection of purulent fluid in the pleural space. It is often caused by pneumonia, TB, lung abscess, and infected surgical wounds of the chest. Treatment options include antibiotic therapy (to eradicate the causative organism), percutaneous drainage, chest tube insertion, VATS, intrapleural fibrinolytic therapy (instilled through the chest tube) to dissolve fibrous adhesions, decortication, and open window thoracostomy.

Clinical Manifestations

Common manifestations of pleural effusion are dyspnea, cough, and occasional sharp, non-radiating chest pain that is worse on inhalation. Physical examination of the chest may show decreased movement of the chest on the affected side, dullness to percussion, and decreased breath sounds over the affected area. A chest x-ray and CT reveal the volume and location of the effusion. Indications of an empyema include the manifestations of pleural effusion as well as fever, night sweats, cough, and weight loss.

Interprofessional Care

The management of pleural effusions is to treat the underlying cause. For example, adequate treatment of HF with diuretics and sodium restriction may result in a decreased incidence of pleural effusion. The treatment of malignant effusions is more difficult. These effusions often reoccur and reaccumulate quickly after thoracentesis.

Chemical pleurodesis is done to obliterate the pleural space and prevent reaccumulation of effusion fluid. This procedure first requires chest tube drainage of the effusion. Once the fluid is drained, a chemical slurry is instilled into the pleural space. Talc is the most effective agent for pleurodesis. Other agents that can be used include doxycycline and bleomycin. The chest tube is clamped for 8 hours while the patient is turned in different positions to allow the chemical to contact the entire pleural space. After 8 hours the chest tube is unclamped and attached to a drainage unit. Chest tubes are left in place until fluid drainage is less than 150 mL/day and no air leaks are noted. Fever and chest pain are the most common side effects associated with pleurodesis.

INTERSTITIAL LUNG DISEASES

Interstitial lung disease (ILD), also called *diffuse parenchymal lung disease,* refers to more than 200 lung disorders in which the tissue between the air sacs of the lungs (the interstitium) is affected by inflammation or scarring (fibrosis).[32] Most ILDs are extremely rare. Many times, the cause is unknown. Two common ILDs of unknown cause are idiopathic pulmonary fibrosis and sarcoidosis. Other ILDs are caused by inhalation of occupational and environmental toxins, certain medications, radiation therapy, connective tissue disorders, cancer, and infection. Treatment is aimed at reducing exposure to the causative agent and/or treating the underlying disease process. Although scarring is irreversible, treatment with corticosteroids and immunosuppressant drugs can minimize progression. A lung transplant may be an option for some patients.

IDIOPATHIC PULMONARY FIBROSIS

Idiopathic pulmonary fibrosis (IPF) is a chronic, progressive disorder characterized by chronic inflammation and formation of scar tissue in the connective tissue. Risk factors include a history of cigarette smoking and exposure to wood and metal dust. IPF affects more men than women. It typically first appears between the ages of 50 and 70 years. There is no known cure for IPF.

Manifestations include exertional dyspnea; dry, nonproductive cough; clubbing of the fingers; and inspiratory crackles. Fatigue, weakness, anorexia, and weight loss may occur as the disease progresses. Chest x-ray findings are generally nonspecific. Pulmonary function tests may be abnormal, with evidence of restriction (reduced vital capacity) and impaired gas exchange. Open lung biopsy using VATS often helps to confirm the pathology and is considered the gold standard for diagnosis.

The course of IPF is variable and the prognosis is poor. The 5-year survival rate is 30% to 50% after diagnosis. Many people diagnosed with IPF are first treated with a corticosteroid (prednisone), sometimes in combination with other drugs that suppress the immune system (e.g., methotrexate, cyclosporine). Kinase inhibitor drugs, which block multiple pathways that involved with scarring, include nintedanib (Ofev) and pirfenidone (Esbriet).

O_2 therapy and pulmonary rehabilitation should be prescribed for all patients. Lung transplantation may be an option for those who meet the criteria. (Lung transplantation is discussed later in this chapter on p. 537.)

SARCOIDOSIS

Sarcoidosis is a chronic, multisystem granulomatous disease of unknown cause that primarily affects the lungs. The disease may also involve the skin, eyes, liver, kidney, heart, and lymph nodes. Those at higher risk include blacks and those with a family history of sarcoidosis.

Signs and symptoms vary depending on what organs are affected. Pulmonary symptoms include dyspnea, cough, and chest pain. Many patients do not have symptoms.

Staging and treatment decisions are based on pulmonary function and disease progression. Some patients have a spontaneous remission. Treatment is aimed at suppressing the inflammatory response. Patients are followed every 3 to 6 months with pulmonary function tests, chest x-ray, and CT scan to monitor disease progression.

TABLE 27.24 Causes of Pulmonary Edema

- Acute respiratory distress syndrome (ARDS)
- Altered capillary permeability of lungs: aspiration, inhaled toxins, inflammation (e.g., pneumonia), severe hypoxia, near-drowning
- Anaphylactic (allergic) reaction
- Hypoalbuminemia: nephrotic syndrome, liver disease, nutritional disorders
- Left ventricular (heart) failure
- Lymph system cancer (e.g., non-Hodgkin's lymphoma)
- Overhydration with IV fluids
- O_2 toxicity
- Unknown causes: neurogenic condition, opioid overdose, reexpansion pulmonary edema, high altitude

FIG. 27.11 Large embolus from the femoral vein lying in the main left and right pulmonary arteries. (From the teaching collection of the Department of Pathology, University of Texas Southwestern Medical School, Dallas, TX. In Kumar V, Abbas AK, Aster JC, Fausto N, eds: *Robbins and Cotran pathologic basis of disease,* ed 8, Philadelphia, 2010, Saunders.)

VASCULAR LUNG DISORDERS

PULMONARY EDEMA

Pulmonary edema is an abnormal accumulation of fluid in the alveoli and interstitial spaces of the lungs. It is a complication of various heart and lung diseases (Table 27.24). In severe cases, pulmonary edema can be a life-threatening medical emergency. The most common cause of pulmonary edema is left-sided HF. (HF is discussed in Chapter 34.)

PULMONARY EMBOLISM

Etiology and Pathophysiology

Pulmonary embolism (PE) is the blockage of 1 or more pulmonary arteries by a thrombus, fat or air embolus, or tumor tissue. The word *embolus* derives from a Greek word meaning "plug" or "stopper." *Emboli* are mobile clots that generally do not stop moving until they lodge at a narrowed part of the circulatory system. A PE consists of material that gains access to the venous system and then to the pulmonary circulation. The embolus travels with blood flow through ever-smaller blood vessels until it lodges and obstructs perfusion of the alveoli (Fig. 27.11). The lower lobes of the lung are most often affected.

Most PEs arise from deep vein thrombosis (DVT) in the deep veins of the legs. *Venous thromboembolism (VTE)* is the preferred term to describe the spectrum of pathologic conditions from DVT to PE (see Table 37.7). Other sites of origin of PE include femoral or iliac veins, right side of the heart (atrial fibrillation), and pelvic veins (especially after surgery or childbirth). Upper extremity DVT sometimes occurs in the presence of central venous catheters or arterial lines. These cases may resolve with the removal of the catheter. A *saddle embolus* refers to a large thrombus lodged at an arterial bifurcation.

Less common causes include fat emboli (from fractured long bones), air emboli (from improperly administered IV therapy), bacterial vegetation on heart valves, amniotic fluid, and cancer. Risk factors for PE include immobility or reduced mobility, surgery within the last 3 months (especially pelvic and lower extremity surgery), history of VTE, cancer, obesity, oral contraceptives, hormone therapy, cigarette smoking, prolonged air travel, HF, pregnancy, and clotting disorders.

Clinical Manifestations

The signs and symptoms of PE are varied and nonspecific, making diagnosis difficult. Manifestations depend on the type, size, and extent of emboli. Small emboli may go undetected or cause vague, transient symptoms. Symptoms may begin slowly or appear suddenly. Dyspnea is the most common presenting symptom, occurring in 85% of patients with PE. Mild to moderate hypoxemia may occur. Other manifestations include tachypnea, cough, chest pain, hemoptysis, crackles, wheezing, fever, accentuation of pulmonic heart sound, tachycardia, and syncope. Massive PE may cause a sudden change in mental status, hypotension, and feelings of impending doom.

Complications

About 10% of patients with massive PE die within the first hour. Treatment with anticoagulants significantly reduces mortality.

Complications include pulmonary infarction and pulmonary hypertension. *Pulmonary infarction* (death of lung tissue) is most likely when there is: (1) occlusion of a large or medium-sized pulmonary vessel (more than 2 mm in diameter), (2) insufficient collateral blood flow from the bronchial circulation, or (3) preexisting lung disease. Infarction results in alveolar necrosis and hemorrhage. Sometimes the necrotic tissue becomes infected and an abscess may develop. Concomitant pleural effusion is frequent.

Pulmonary hypertension results from hypoxemia or from involvement of more than 50% of the area of the normal pulmonary bed. As a single event, a PE rarely causes pulmonary hypertension. Recurrent PEs gradually reduce capillary bed blood flow and eventually cause pulmonary hypertension. Dilation and hypertrophy of the right ventricle can develop due to pulmonary hypertension. Depending on the degree of pulmonary hypertension and how quickly it develops, outcomes can vary, with some patients dying within months of the diagnosis and others living for decades.

Diagnostic Studies

D-dimer is a laboratory test that measures the amount of cross-linked fibrin fragments. These fragments are the result of clot degradation and are rarely found in healthy people. The disadvantage of D-dimer testing is that it is neither specific (many other conditions cause elevation) nor sensitive, because up to 50% of patients with a small PE have normal results. Patients with suspected PE and an elevated D-dimer level but normal venous ultrasound may need a spiral CT or lung scan.

A *spiral (helical) CT scan* (also known as CT angiography or CTA) is the most common test to diagnose PE. An IV injection of contrast media is needed to view the pulmonary blood vessels. The scanner continuously rotates around the patient while obtaining views (slices) of the pulmonary vasculature. This allows visualization of all anatomic regions of the lungs. Computer software reconstructs the data to give a 3-dimensional picture and assist in seeing PEs.

If a patient cannot have contrast media, a ventilation-perfusion (V/Q) scan is done. The V/Q scan has 2 parts. It is most accurate when both are done:
1. *Perfusion scanning* involves IV injection of a radioisotope. A scanning device images the pulmonary circulation.
2. *Ventilation scanning* involves inhalation of a radioactive gas, such as xenon. Scanning reflects the distribution of gas through the lung. The ventilation portion requires the patient's cooperation. It may not be possible to perform in the critically ill patient, especially if the patient is intubated.

ABG analysis is important but not diagnostic. The PaO_2 may be low because of inadequate oxygenation from occluded pulmonary vasculature preventing matching of perfusion to ventilation. The pH is often normal unless respiratory alkalosis develops because of prolonged hyperventilation or to compensate for lactic acidosis caused by shock. Abnormal findings may be seen on a chest x-ray (atelectasis, pleural effusion) and ECG (ST segment and T wave changes), but they are not diagnostic for PE. Serum troponin levels and b-type natriuretic peptide (BNP) levels are often increased but not diagnostic.

Interprofessional Care

To reduce mortality risk, treatment is started as soon as PE is suspected (Table 27.25). The goals are to (1) provide adequate tissue perfusion and respiratory function, (2) prevent further growth or extension of thrombi in the lower extremities, (3) prevent embolization from the upper or lower extremities to the pulmonary vascular system, and (4) prevent further recurrence of PE.

TABLE 27.25 Interprofessional Care

Acute Pulmonary Embolism

Diagnostic Assessment
- History and physical examination
- Chest x-ray
- Continuous ECG monitoring
- Arterial blood gases
- Spiral (helical) CT scan
- Ventilation-perfusion (V/Q) lung scan
- D-dimer level
- Troponin level, b-natriuretic peptide level

Management
- Supplemental O_2, intubation if needed
- Monitor hemoglobin, assess patient for bleeding
- Monitor activated partial thromboplastin time and international normalized ratio levels
- Balance activity and rest
- Inferior vena cava filter
- Pulmonary embolectomy in life-threatening situation

Drug Therapy
- Fibrinolytic agent
- Unfractionated heparin IV
- Low-molecular-weight heparin (e.g., enoxaparin [Lovenox])
- Warfarin (Coumadin) for long-term therapy
- Analgesia

Immediate assessment should focus on the patient's cardiopulmonary status, which can vary according to the size and location of the PE. O_2 should be given by mask or cannula when hypoxemia is present. The concentration of FIO_2 is titrated based on ABG analysis. In some situations, endotracheal intubation and mechanical ventilation are needed to maintain adequate oxygenation and ventilation. Respiratory measures, including turning, coughing, deep breathing, and incentive spirometry, are important to help prevent or treat atelectasis. If manifestations of shock are present, IV fluids and vasopressor agents are given as needed to support circulation (see Chapter 66). If HF is present, diuretics are used (see Chapter 34). Pain from pleural irritation or reduced coronary blood flow is treated with opioids.

Drug Therapy. Immediate anticoagulation is required for patients with PE. Subcutaneous administration of low-molecular-weight heparin (LMWH) (e.g., enoxaparin [Lovenox]) or fragmin [Dalteparin] or fondaparinux) is the recommended treatment for patients with acute PE. LMWH is safer and more effective than unfractionated heparin.[33] Advantages of LMWH over unfractionated heparin include greater bioavailability, subcutaneous administration, once daily dosing, and longer duration of therapeutic effect. Monitoring the aPTT is not necessary or useful with LMWH. Unfractionated IV heparin can be as effective but is hard to titrate to therapeutic levels.

Warfarin (Coumadin), an oral anticoagulant, should also be started at the time of diagnosis.[34] Warfarin should be given for at least 3 months and then reevaluated. Alternatives to warfarin include apixaban (Eliquis), dabigatran (Pradaxa), and edoxaban (Savaysa). Anticoagulant therapy may be contraindicated if the patient has complicating factors, such as liver problems causing changes in the clotting, overt bleeding, a history of hemorrhagic stroke, heparin-induced thrombocytopenia (HIT), or other blood dyscrasias.

Some HCPs use direct thrombin inhibitors (see Table 37.10) in the treatment of PE. Similarly, fibrinolytic agents, such as tissue plasminogen activator (tPA) or alteplase (Activase), may help dissolve the PE and the source of the thrombus in the pelvis or deep leg veins, thereby decreasing the risk for recurrent emboli. Fibrinolytic therapy is discussed in Chapter 33.

Surgical Therapy. Hemodynamically unstable patients with massive PE in whom thrombolytic therapy is contraindicated may be candidates for pulmonary embolectomy. Embolectomy, the removal of emboli, can be achieved through a diagnostic imaging (vascular catheter) or surgical approach. It can help decrease right ventricular afterload. Surgical outcomes have improved in recent years, in part due to rapid diagnosis and enhanced surgical procedures.

Percutaneous catheter embolectomy or endovascular ultrasound delivered thrombolysis are newer, moderately invasive procedures for PE. In patients who are at high risk and patients for whom anticoagulation is contraindicated, an inferior vena cava (IVC) filter may be the treatment of choice. This device, inserted percutaneously through the femoral vein, is placed at the level of the renal veins in the inferior vena cava. Once inserted, the filter expands and prevents migration of large clots into the pulmonary system. Complications associated with this device are rare but include misplacement, migration, and perforation.

❖ NURSING MANAGEMENT: PULMONARY EMBOLISM

Prevention of PE begins with prevention of DVT. Nursing measures aimed at prevention of PE are similar to those for prophylaxis of VTE (see Chapter 37). These include the use of intermittent pneumatic compression devices, early ambulation, and anticoagulant medications.

The prognosis of a patient with PE is good if therapy is started immediately. Keep the patient on bed rest in a semi-Fowler's position to facilitate breathing. Assess the patient's cardiopulmonary status with careful monitoring of vital signs, cardiac rhythm, pulse oximetry, ABGs, and lung sounds. Apply O_2 therapy as ordered. Maintain a patent IV line for medications and fluid therapy. Monitor laboratory results to ensure therapeutic ranges of INR (for warfarin) and aPTT (for IV heparin). Monitor platelet counts for thrombocytopenia and the development of HIT. Observe the patient for complications of anticoagulant and fibrinolytic therapy (e.g., bleeding, hematomas, bruising). Provide appropriate interventions related to immobility and fall precautions once the patient is permitted out of bed.

The patient may be anxious because of pain, inability to breathe, and fear of death. Carefully explain the situation and the medications. Provide emotional support and reassurance to help relieve the patient's anxiety.

Patient teaching about long-term anticoagulant therapy is essential. Anticoagulant therapy continues for at least 3 months. Patients with large or recurrent emboli may be treated indefinitely with anticoagulants. INR levels are drawn at intervals and warfarin dosage is adjusted. Some patients are monitored by nurses in an anticoagulation clinic.

Long-term management of PE is similar to that for the patient with VTE (see discussion of VTE in Chapter 37). Discharge planning is aimed at preventing worsening of the condition and avoiding complications and recurrence. Reinforce the need for the patient to return to the HCP for regular follow-up examinations.

PULMONARY HYPERTENSION

Pulmonary hypertension is characterized by elevated pulmonary artery pressure from an increase in resistance to blood flow through the pulmonary circulation. Normally the pulmonary circulation is characterized by low resistance and low pressure. In pulmonary hypertension the pulmonary pressures are high, with the mean pulmonary artery pressure greater than 25 mm Hg at rest (normal is 12 to 16 mm Hg) or greater than 30 mm Hg with exercise.

The World Health Organization (WHO) has identified 5 classes of pulmonary hypertension.[35] Each group is based on cause of the disorder.

Group 1: Attributed to medication, specific diseases, genetic (inherited) link, or idiopathic
Group 2: Related to left-sided HF
Group 3: Related to the lungs and hypoxemia
Group 4: Related to the cardiovascular system and thromboembolic occlusion
Group 5: Multifactorial (and often unclear) origins with hematologic or metabolic involvement

Pulmonary hypertension can occur as a primary disease *(idiopathic pulmonary arterial hypertension)* or as a secondary complication of a respiratory, heart, autoimmune, liver, or connective tissue disorder *(secondary pulmonary arterial hypertension).*

PATHOPHYSIOLOGY MAP

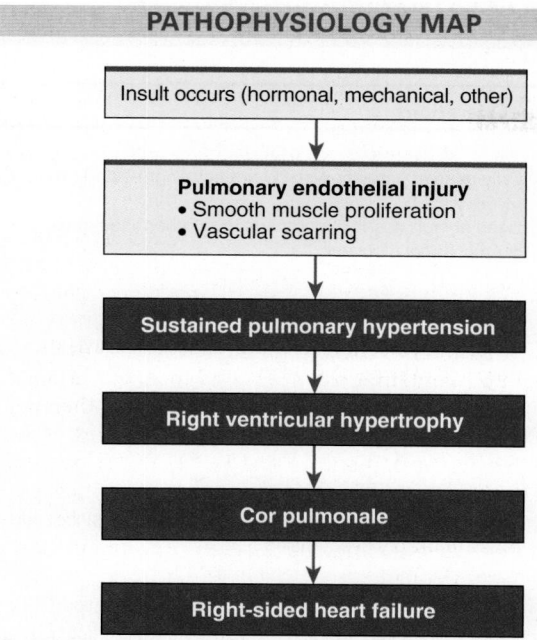

FIG. 27.12 Pathogenesis of pulmonary hypertension and cor pulmonale.

IDIOPATHIC PULMONARY ARTERIAL HYPERTENSION

Idiopathic pulmonary arterial hypertension (IPAH) is pulmonary hypertension that occurs without an apparent cause. It was previously known as *primary pulmonary hypertension* (PPH). If untreated, IPAH can rapidly progress, causing right-sided HF and death within a few years. Although new drug therapy has greatly improved survival, the disease is not curable.

Etiology and Pathophysiology

The cause of IPAH is unknown. It is related to connective tissue diseases, cirrhosis, and HIV. The exact relationship between these disorders and IPAH is unclear. Similarly, the pathophysiology of IPAH is poorly understood. We think that some type of insult (e.g., hormonal, mechanical) to the pulmonary endothelium may occur, causing a cascade of events leading to vascular scarring, endothelial dysfunction, and smooth muscle proliferation (Fig. 27.12). IPAH affects females more than males.

Clinical Manifestations and Diagnostic Studies

The classic symptoms are dyspnea on exertion and fatigue. Exertional chest pain, dizziness, and syncope may occur. These are related to the inability of cardiac output to increase in response to increased O_2 demand. Abnormal heart sounds may be heard, including an S_3. Eventually, as the disease progresses, dyspnea occurs at rest. Pulmonary hypertension increases the workload of the right ventricle and causes right ventricular hypertrophy (a condition called *cor pulmonale*) and eventually HF.

Right-sided cardiac catheterization is the definitive test to diagnose any type of pulmonary hypertension. It gives an accurate measurement of pulmonary artery pressures, cardiac output, and pulmonary vascular resistance. Confirmation of IPAH requires a thorough workup to exclude conditions that may cause secondary pulmonary hypertension. Diagnostic evaluation often includes ECG, chest x-ray, pulmonary function tests, echocardiogram, and CT scan.

The mean time between onset of symptoms and the diagnosis is about 2 years. By the time patients become symptomatic, the disease is already in the advanced stages and the pulmonary artery pressure is 2-3 times normal values.

❖ Interprofessional and Nursing Care

Early recognition is essential to interrupt the vicious cycle responsible for progression of the disease. Encourage patients to report unexplained shortness of breath, syncope, chest discomfort, and edema of the feet and ankles to their HCP.

Although IPAH has no cure, treatment can relieve symptoms, improve quality of life, and prolong life. Drug therapy consists of agents that promote vasodilation of the pulmonary blood vessels, reduce right ventricular overload, and reverse remodeling (Table 27.26). Diuretics are used to manage peripheral edema. Anticoagulants are beneficial in pulmonary complications related to thrombus formation. Because hypoxia is a potent pulmonary vasoconstrictor, low-flow O_2 gives symptomatic relief. The goal is to keep O_2 saturation 90% or greater.

Surgical interventions include pulmonary thromboendarterectomy (PTE), in which clots are removed from the pulmonary arteries. It is a technically demanding procedure and is done only at certain centers. Atrial septostomy (AS) is a palliative procedure that involves the creation of an intraatrial right-to-left shunt to decompress the right ventricle. It is used for a select group of patients awaiting lung transplantation. Lung transplantation is an option for patients who do not respond to drug therapy and progress to severe right-sided HF. Recurrence of the disease has not been reported in persons who had a transplant.

SECONDARY PULMONARY ARTERIAL HYPERTENSION

Secondary pulmonary arterial hypertension (SPAH) occurs when another disease causes a chronic increase in pulmonary artery pressures. The specific primary disease pathology can cause anatomic or vascular changes that cause the pulmonary hypertension. SPAH can develop due to parenchymal lung disease, left ventricular dysfunction, intracardiac shunts, chronic PE, or systemic connective tissue disease.

The symptoms can reflect the underlying disease, but some are directly attributable to SPAH, including dyspnea, fatigue, lethargy, and chest pain. The initial physical findings can include right ventricular hypertrophy and signs of right-sided HF (increased pulmonic heart sound, S_4 heart sound, peripheral edema, hepatomegaly).

Diagnosis of SPAH is like that of IPAH. Treatment of SPAH consists of treating the underlying primary disorder. When irreversible pulmonary vascular damage has occurred, therapies used for IPAH are started. A PTE may offer a cure for patients with chronic pulmonary hypertension caused by PE.

COR PULMONALE

Cor pulmonale is enlargement of the right ventricle caused by a primary disorder of the respiratory system. Almost any disorder that affects the respiratory system can cause cor pulmonale. The most common cause is COPD. Pulmonary hypertension is

TABLE 27.26 Drug Therapy

Pulmonary Hypertension

Drug	Mechanism of Action	Considerations
Calcium Channel Blockers diltiazem (Cardizem, Cardizem LA, Cartia XT, Tiazac) nifedipine (Procardia)	• Act on vascular smooth muscle, causing dilation • Lower pulmonary artery pressure	• Only used in patients who do not have right-sided heart failure (HF) • Used at high doses in comparison to other uses of calcium channel blockers
Endothelin Receptor Antagonists ambrisentan (Letairis) bosentan (Tracleer) macitentan (Opsumit)	• Binds to endothelin-1 receptors and blocks the constriction of pulmonary arteries • Promotes relaxation of pulmonary arteries and decrease pulmonary artery pressure	• Given orally • For patients with New York Heart Association (NYHA) class II to IV symptoms • Hepatotoxic • Monitor liver function tests monthly
Phosphodiesterase (Type 5) Enzyme Inhibitors sildenafil (Revatio) tadalafil (Adcirca)	• Promote selective smooth muscle relaxation in lung vasculature	• Given orally • Contraindicated in patients taking nitroglycerin, since may cause refractory hypotension
Vasodilators (Inhaled) iloprost (Ventavis) treprostinil (inhaled) (Tyvaso)	• Synthetic analogs of prostacyclin (PGI$_2$) • Dilate systemic and pulmonary arterial vasculature	• For patients with NYHA class III or IV HF • Given 6–9 times a day using a disk inserted into a nebulizer • Can cause orthostatic hypotension. Do not give to patients with systolic BP <85 mm Hg.
Vasodilators (Parenteral) adenosine (Adenocard) epoprostenol (Flolan, Veletri) treprostinil (Remodulin)	• Prostacyclin analog • Promote pulmonary vasodilation and reduce pulmonary vascular resistance	• Given IV to patients who do not respond to calcium channel blockers or have NYHA class III or IV right-sided HF • Given by continuous IV (central line) or continuous subcutaneous route • Half-life of epoprostenol is short. Potential clinical deterioration from abrupt withdrawal if infusion disrupted

usually a preexisting condition in the person with cor pulmonale. Overt HF may be present. Fig. 27.12 outlines the cause and pathogenesis of pulmonary hypertension and cor pulmonale.

Clinical Manifestations and Diagnostic Studies

Manifestations are subtle and often masked by symptoms of the pulmonary condition. Common symptoms include exertional dyspnea, tachypnea, cough, and fatigue. Physical signs include evidence of right ventricular hypertrophy on ECG and an increase in intensity of S$_2$. Chronic hypoxemia leads to polycythemia and increased total blood volume and viscosity of the blood. Polycythemia is often present in cor pulmonale from COPD.

If HF accompanies cor pulmonale, manifestations, including peripheral edema, weight gain, distended neck veins, full, bounding pulse, and enlarged liver, may occur. We use various laboratory tests and imaging studies to confirm the diagnosis of cor pulmonale (Table 27.27).

❖ Interprofessional and Nursing Care

Early identification is essential before changes to the heart occur that may be irreversible. Management is directed at determining the cause and treating the underlying problem (Table 27.27).

Long-term O$_2$ therapy, the mainstay of treatment to correct the hypoxemia, reduces vasoconstriction and pulmonary

TABLE 27.27 Interprofessional Care

Cor Pulmonale

Diagnostic Assessment
- History and physical examination
- Arterial blood gases, SpO$_2$
- Serum and urine electrolytes
- b-Type natriuretic peptide (BNP)
- ECG
- Chest x-ray
- Echocardiography
- CT scan, MRI
- Cardiac catheterization

Management
- O$_2$ therapy
- Low-sodium diet

Drug Therapy
- Bronchodilators
- Diuretics
- Vasodilators (if indicated)
- Calcium channel blockers (if indicated)
- Inotropic agents

hypertension. All other interventions are tailored for each patient. If fluid, electrolyte, and/or acid-base imbalances are present, they must be corrected. Diuretics may help decrease plasma volume and reduce the workload on the heart but must be used with extreme caution. In some cases, decreases in fluid volume from diuresis can worsen heart function. Bronchodilator therapy is needed if the underlying respiratory problem is due to an obstructive disorder.

Other treatments may include vasodilator therapy, calcium channel blockers, anticoagulants, digitalis, and phlebotomy. All have varying degrees of success. Chronic management of cor pulmonale from COPD is like that described for COPD (see Chapter 28).

LUNG TRANSPLANTATION

Lung transplantation has become an important alternative option for patients with end-stage lung disease. Unfortunately, the limiting factor for this therapy is the lack of donors. A variety of pulmonary disorders are potentially treatable with lung transplantation (Table 27.28). Better patient selection criteria, improvements in surgical techniques, enhanced methods of immunosuppression, and excellent postoperative care have resulted in improved survival rates.

Preoperative Care

Patients being considered for lung transplantation need to undergo extensive evaluation. Absolute contraindications for lung transplant include cancer within past 2 years (some types of skin cancer are excluded), chronic active hepatitis B or C, HIV, untreatable advanced dysfunction of another major organ system (e.g., liver or renal failure), current smoker, poor nutritional status, poor rehabilitation potential, and significant psychosocial problems. The patient and family must be able to cope with a complex postoperative regimen (e.g., strict adherence to immunosuppressive therapy, continuous monitoring for early signs of infection, prompt reporting of manifestations of infection). Many transplant centers require preoperative outpatient pulmonary rehabilitation to maximize physical conditioning.

In the United States, the United Network for Organ Sharing (UNOS) is a private, non-profit organization that works with the federal government to manage organ transplantation. UNOS designates recipients of donor lungs based on a lung allocation score (LAS). The LAS helps to prioritize waiting list recipients based on the urgency of need and expected posttransplant survival expectations.

Patients who are accepted as transplant candidates must always carry a pager in case a donor organ becomes available. They must be prepared to be at their transplant center at a moment's notice. Patients may be encouraged to limit their travel within a certain geographic region to facilitate rapid transportation to a transplant center.

TABLE 27.28 Common Indications for Lung Transplantation

- α_1-Antitrypsin deficiency
- Chronic obstructive pulmonary disease (COPD)
- Cystic fibrosis
- Idiopathic pulmonary arterial hypertension
- Idiopathic pulmonary fibrosis

Surgical Procedure

Four types of transplant procedures are available: single-lung transplantation, bilateral lung transplantation, heart-lung transplantation, and transplantation of lobes from a living-related donor.

Single-lung transplantation involves a thoracotomy incision on the side of the chest. The opposite lung is ventilated while the diseased lung is excised and the donor lung implanted. Three anastomoses are done: bronchus, pulmonary artery, and pulmonary veins. In *bilateral lung transplantation,* the incision is made across the sternum and the donor lungs are implanted separately. A median sternotomy incision is used for a *heart-lung transplant* procedure. *Lobar transplantation* from living donors is reserved for those who urgently need transplantation and are unlikely to survive until a donor becomes available. Most of these recipients are patients with cystic fibrosis, and donors are their parents or relatives. Once anastomosis is complete, the lung is gently reinflated, perfusion is reestablished, chest tubes are inserted, and the surgical incision is closed.

Postoperative Care

Early postoperative care often includes ventilatory support, hemodynamic management, IV fluid therapy, immunosuppression, nutritional support, detection of early rejection, and prevention or treatment of complications, including infection. Once hemodynamic stability has been achieved, the patient is often transferred from the ICU to a high-acuity observation or surgical unit. Maintaining accurate fluid balance is vital after surgery.

Lung transplant recipients are at high risk for multiple complications. Infections are the leading cause of death at all time points after lung transplant. Bacterial bronchitis and pneumonia are the most common infections. CMV, fungi, viruses, and mycobacteria are also causative agents. Noninfectious issues may include VTE, diaphragmatic dysfunction, and cancer.

Immunosuppressive therapy usually includes a 3-drug regimen of tacrolimus, mycophenolate mofetil (CellCept), and prednisone. The mechanisms of action of these drugs are discussed in Table 13.17 and Fig. 13.13.) Drug levels are monitored on a regular basis. Lung transplant recipients usually receive higher levels of immunosuppressive therapy than other organ recipients.

Acute rejection is fairly common in lung transplantation. It typically occurs in the first 5 to 10 days after surgery. Signs of rejection include low-grade fever, fatigue, dyspnea, dry cough, and O_2 desaturation. Accurate diagnosis of rejection is by transtracheal biopsy. Treatment consists of high doses of IV corticosteroids for 3 days, followed by high doses of oral prednisone. In patients with persistent or recurrent acute rejection, antilymphocyte therapy may be useful.

Bronchiolitis obliterans (BOS) is a manifestation of chronic rejection in lung transplant patients. BOS is characterized by airflow obstruction that progresses over time. The onset is often subacute, with gradual development of exertional dyspnea, nonproductive cough, wheezing, and/or low-grade fever. Airway obstruction is not responsive to bronchodilators and corticosteroid therapy. Although not proven effective, additional immunosuppressive agents may be used to treat chronic rejection. Because acute rejection is a major risk factor for BOS, preventing acute rejection is key to decreasing the incidence of chronic rejection.

Before discharge, the patient needs to be able to perform self-care activities, including medication management and activities of daily living, and to know when to call the transplant team. Patients are taught pulmonary clearance measures, including aerosolized bronchodilators, chest physiotherapy, and deep-breathing and coughing techniques, to help minimize complications. Home spirometry is useful in monitoring trends in lung function. Teach patients to keep medication logs, laboratory results, and spirometry records. Patients are placed in an outpatient rehabilitation program to improve physical endurance.

After discharge, the transplant team follows patients for transplant-related issues. Patients return to their HCP for health maintenance and routine illnesses. As transplant procedures become more frequent, transplant patients will return to hospitals for other routine procedures. Coordination of care among the transplant team, inpatient team, and primary care team is essential for ongoing successful management of these patients. (Organ transplantation, histocompatibility, rejection, and immunosuppressive therapy are discussed in Chapter 13.)

CASE STUDY

Pneumonia and Lung Cancer

(© iStockphoto/
Thinkstock.)

Patient Profile

J.H. is a 52-yr-old white man who comes to the ED with shortness of breath. He has not seen an HCP for many years.

Subjective Data

- Has a 38 pack-year history of cigarette smoking
- Has had 25-lb weight loss despite a normal appetite in the past few months
- Admits to a "smoker's cough" for the past 2 to 3 years; recently coughing up blood
- Is married and the father of 3 adult children

Objective Data

Physical Examination

- Thin, pale man who looks older than stated age
- Height 6 ft (182.9 cm); weight 135 lb (61.2 kg)
- Intermittently confused and anxious
- Lung auscultation reveals coarse crackles on left side that clear with cough; right side has decreased breath sounds
- Chest wall has limited excursion on right side
- Vital signs: temperature 102.6° F (39.2° C), heart rate 120, respiratory rate 36, BP 98/54; short, shallow respirations

Diagnostic Studies

- Arterial blood gases: pH 7.51, PaO$_2$ 62 mm Hg, PaCO$_2$ 30 mm Hg, HCO$_3$$^-$ 22 mEq/L, O$_2$ saturation 88% (room air)

- Chest x-ray: consolidation of the right lung, especially in the base with mass around right bronchus; pleural effusion on the right side
- Bronchoscopy with biopsy of mass: small cell lung cancer

Interprofessional Care

- Diagnosis: pneumonia with small cell lung cancer
- Follow-up with patient and family to consider treatment options

Discussion Questions

1. How would you classify J.H.'s pneumonia? Why is this important?
2. What is your analysis of J.H.'s arterial blood gas results?
3. *Priority Decision:* Based on the assessment data presented, what are the priority nursing diagnoses? Are there any collaborative problems?
4. *Priority Decision:* What are the priority nursing interventions for J.H.?
5. *Collaboration:* Identify activities that can be delegated to unlicensed assistive personnel (UAP).
6. *Patient-Centered Care:* You are planning a meeting with J.H. and his family to discuss their needs. The HCP tells you that J.H. is terminally ill. Who will you include in this meeting?
7. *Evidence-Based Practice:* J.H.'s children tell you that they are worried they will get lung cancer, since their father has it and they grew up around his secondhand smoke. They want to know what kind of screening is available for them. How will you respond?
- What is the goal if radiation therapy is used for J.H.?
- *Patient-Centered Care:* What issues should be addressed in your teaching of J.H. and his wife as you prepare him for discharge and care at home?

Answers available at *http://evolve.elsevier.com/Lewis/medsurg.*

▌ BRIDGE TO NCLEX EXAMINATION

The number of the question corresponds to the same-numbered outcome at the beginning of the chapter.

1. When caring for a patient with acute bronchitis, the nurse will *prioritize* interventions by
   a. auscultating lung sounds.
   b. encouraging fluid restriction.
   c. administering antibiotic therapy.
   d. teaching the patient to avoid cough suppressants.
2. Which patients have the greatest risk for aspiration pneumonia? *(select all that apply)*
   a. Patient with seizures
   b. Patient with head injury
   c. Patient who had thoracic surgery
   d. Patient who had a myocardial infarction
   e. Patient who is receiving nasogastric tube feeding

3. An appropriate nursing intervention to assist a patient with pneumonia manage thick secretions and fatigue would be to
   a. perform postural drainage every hour.
   b. provide analgesics as ordered to promote patient comfort.
   c. administer O$_2$ as prescribed to maintain optimal O$_2$ levels.
   d. teach the patient how to cough effectively and expectorate secretions.
4. A patient with TB has been admitted to the hospital and is placed on airborne precautions and in an isolation room. What should the nurse teach the patient? *(select all that apply)*
   a. Expect routine TB testing to evaluate the infection.
   b. No visitors will be allowed while in airborne isolation.
   c. Adherence to precautions includes coughing into a paper tissue.
   d. Take all medications for full length of time to prevent multidrug-resistant TB.
   e. Wear a standard isolation mask if leaving the airborne infection isolation room.

5. A patient has been receiving high-dose corticosteroids and broad-spectrum antibiotics for treatment of an infection after a traumatic injury. The nurse plans care for the patient knowing that the patient is most susceptible to
   a. candidiasis.
   b. cryptococcosis.
   c. histoplasmosis.
   d. coccidioidomycosis.
6. When caring for a patient with a lung abscess, what is the nurse's *priority* intervention?
   a. Postural drainage
   b. Antibiotic administration
   c. Obtaining a sputum specimen
   d. Patient teaching about home care
7. You are caring for patients exposed to a chlorine leak from a local factory. The nurse would closely monitor these patients for
   a. pulmonary edema.
   b. anaphylactic shock.
   c. respiratory alkalosis.
   d. acute tubular necrosis.
8. The nurse receives an order for a patient with lung cancer to receive influenza vaccine and pneumococcal vaccines. The nurse will
   a. call the health care provider to question the order.
   b. give both vaccines at the same time in different arms.
   c. give the pneumococcal vaccine and obtain a nasal influenza vaccine.
   d. give the flu shot and tell the patient to come back in 1 week to have the pneumococcal vaccine.
9. The nurse identifies a flail chest in a trauma patient when
   a. multiple rib fractures are determined by x-ray.
   b. a tracheal deviation to the unaffected side is present.
   c. paradoxical chest movement occurs during respiration.
   d. there is decreased movement of the involved chest wall.

10. The nurse notes tidaling of the water level in the water-seal chamber in a patient with closed chest tube drainage. The nurse should
    a. continue to monitor the patient.
    b. check all connections for a leak in the system.
    c. lower the drainage collector further from the chest.
    d. clamp the tubing at a distal point away from the patient.
11. After a pneumonectomy, an appropriate nursing intervention is
    a. monitoring chest tube drainage and functioning.
    b. positioning the patient on the unaffected side or back.
    c. doing range-of-motion exercises on the affected upper limb.
    d. auscultating frequently for lung sounds on the affected side.
12. A *priority* nursing intervention for a patient who has just undergone a chemical pleurodesis for recurrent pleural effusion is
    a. giving ordered analgesia.
    b. monitoring chest tube drainage.
    c. sending pleural fluid for laboratory analysis.
    d. monitoring the patient's level of consciousness.
13. When planning care for a patient at risk for pulmonary embolism, the nurse *prioritizes*
    a. maintaining the patient on bed rest.
    b. using intermittent pneumatic compression devices.
    c. encouraging the patient to cough and deep breathe.
    d. teaching the patient how to use the incentive spirometer.
14. Which statement(s) describe(s) the management of a patient following lung transplantation (*select all that apply*)?
    a. High doses of O_2 are administered around the clock.
    b. Using a home spirometer will help to monitor lung function.
    c. Immunosuppressant therapy usually involves a 3-drug regimen.
    d. Most patients have an acute rejection episode within the first 2 days.
    e. A lung biopsy is done using a transtracheal method if rejection is suspected.

13. b, 14. b, c, e
1. a, 2. a, e, 3. d, 4. c, d, e, 5. a, 6. b, 7. a, 8. b, 9. c, 10. a, 11. c, 12. a,

For rationales to these answers and even more NCLEX review questions, visit *http://evolve.elsevier.com/Lewis/medsurg*.

EVOLVE WEBSITE/RESOURCES LIST

http://evolve.elsevier.com/Lewis/medsurg
Review Questions (Online Only)
Key Points
Answer Keys for Questions
• Rationales for Bridge to NCLEX Examination Questions
• Answer Guidelines for Case Study on p. 538
Student Case Studies
• Patient With Lung Cancer
• Patient With Pulmonary Embolism and Respiratory Failure
Nursing Care Plans
• eNursing Care Plan 27.1: Patient With Pneumonia
• eNursing Care Plan 27.2: Patient After Thoracotomy
Conceptual Care Map Creator
Audio Glossary
Content Updates

REFERENCES

1. Centers for Disease Control and Prevention: *Deaths and mortality*. Retrieved from *www.cdc.gov/nchs/fastats/deaths.htm*.
*2. Harris AM, Hicks LA, Qaseem A: Appropriate antibiotic use for acute respiratory tract infection in adults: Advice for high-value care from the American College of Physicians and the CDC, *Ann Intern Med* 164:425, 2016.
*3. Centers for Disease Control and Prevention: Diphtheria, tetanus and pertussis vaccine recommendations. Retrieved from *www.cdc.gov/vaccines/vpd/dtap-tdap-td/hcp/recommendations.html*.
4. Centers for Disease Control and Prevention: Pertussis: diagnosis conformation. Retrieved from *www.cdc.gov/pertussis/clinical/diagnostic-testing/diagnosis-confirmation.html*.
5. Centers for Disease Control and Prevention: Leading causes of death. Retrieved from *www.cdc.gov/nchs/fastats/leading-causes-of-death.htm*.
6. Cunha BA: Hospital-acquired pneumonia and ventilator-associated pneumonia. Retrieved from *www.emedicine.medscape.com/article/234753-overview*.

7. Skidmore BD, Arteaga VA. Necrotizing pneumonia: diagnosis and treatment options, *Southwest J Pulm Crit Care* 15:274, 2017.

*8. Ljungman P, Lazarus HM: Optimal management approach to prevent cytomegalovirus infection in patients undergoing allogeneic hematopoietic cell transplantation, *The Hematologist* 15:4, 2018.

*9. Shen KR, Bribriesco A, Crabtree T, et al: The American Association for Thoracic Surgery consensus guidelines for the management of empyema, *J Cardiovasc Thorac Surg* 153:e129, 2016.

*10. Khan F, Martin-Loeches I: The significance of clinical scores and biological markers in disease severity, mortality prediction, and justifying hospital admissions in patients with community acquired pneumonia, *Community Acquir Infect* 3:36, 2016.

11. Mosenifar, Z: Viral pneumonia medication. Retrieved from *www.emedicine.medscape.com/article/300455-medication*.

12. Ruscic KJ, Grabitz SD, Rudolph MI, et al: Prevention of respiratory complications of the surgical patient, *Curr Opin Anaesthesiol* 30:399, 2017.

13. World Health Organization: Tuberculosis. Retrieved from *www.euro.who.int/en/health-topics/communicable-diseases/tuberculosis/tuberculosis-read-more*.

*14. CDC: Burden of TB in the United States. Retrieved from *www.cdc.gov/features/burden-tb-us/index.html*.

15. Lange C, Chesov D, Hevckendorf J, et al: Drug-resistant tuberculosis: an update on disease burden, diagnosis and treatment, *Respirology* 23:656, 2018.

16. Sloan DJ, Lewis JM: Management of multidrug resistant TB: Novel treatments and their expansion to low resource settings, *T Roy Soc Trop Med Hyg* 3:163, 2016.

17. Sharma R, Gaillard F: Ghon lesion. Retrieved from *www.radiopaedia.org/articles/ghon-lesion*.

18. Centers for Disease Control and Prevention: Tuberculin skin testing. Retrieved from *www.cdc.gov/tb/publications/factsheets/testing/skintesting.htm*.

*19. Lewinsohn DM, Leonard MK, LoBue PA, et al: Official American Thoracic Society/Infectious Diseases Society of America/CDC clinical practice guidelines: Diagnosis of tuberculosis in adults and children, *Clin Infect Dis* 64:111, 2017.

*20. World Health Organization Guidelines for treatment of drug-susceptible tuberculosis and patient care (2017 update). Retrieved from *www.who.int/tb/publications/2017/dstb_guidance_2017/en/*.

*21. Reyes-Montes MDR, Perez-Huitron MA, Ocana-Monroy JL, et al: The habitat of *Coccidioides* spp. and the role of animals as reservoirs and disseminators in nature, *BMC Infect Dis* 16:550, 2016.

22. Sethi S: Lung abscess. Retrieved from *www.merckmanuals.com/en-ca/professional/pulmonary-disorders/lung-abscess/lung-abscess*.

23. American Cancer Society: Key statistics for lung cancer. Retrieved from *www.cancer.org/cancer/non-small-cell-lung-cancer/about/key-statistics.html*.

24. American Lung Association: Lung cancer fact sheet. Retrieved from *www.lung.org/lung-health-and-diseases/lung-disease-lookup/lung-cancer/resource-library/lung-cancer-fact-sheet.html*.

25. National Cancer Institute: Harms of cigarette smoking and health benefits of quitting. Retrieved from *www.cancer.gov/about-cancer/causes-prevention/risk/tobacco/cessation-fact-sheet*.

26. Chandra AM: Cigarette smoking is the main cause of lung cancer. Retrieved from *www.healthxchange.sg/cancer/lung-cancer/cigarette-smoking-main-cause-lung-cancer*.

27. Lung Cancer.org: Types and staging of lung cancer. Retrieved from *www.lungcancer.org/find_information/publications/163-lung_cancer_101/268-types_and_staging*.

*28. Mazzone PJ, Silvestri GA, Patel S, et al: Screening for lung cancer: chest guideline and expert panel report, *Chest* 153:954, 2018.

*29. American Cancer Society: Lung cancer screening guidelines. Retrieved from *www.cancer.org/health-care-professionals/american-cancer-society-prevention-early-detection-guidelines/lung-cancer-screening-guidelines.html*.

*30. Groen HJM, Dingemans AMC, Belderbos J, et al: Prophylactic cranial irradiation versus observation in radically treated stage III non-small cell lung cancer, *J Clin Oncol* 35:s8502, 2017.

31. Simoglou C, Gymnopoulos D: Video-assisted thoracoscopic surgery, *Scientific Chronicles* 22:150, 2017.

32. Lee J: Overview of interstitial lung disease. Retrieved from *www.merckmanuals.com/en-ca/professional/pulmonary-disorders/interstitial-lung-diseases/overview-of-interstitial-lung-disease*.

33. Ryan J: Pulmonary embolism: New treatments for an old problem, *Emerg Medicine* 8:87, 2016.

34. Ouellette DR: Pulmonary embolism treatment and management. Retrieved from *https://emedicine.medscape.com/article/300901-treatment#d9*.

35. Pulmonary Hypertension Association: Types of pulmonary hypertension. Retrieved from *https://phassociation.org/patients/aboutph/types-of-ph/*.

*Evidence-based information for clinical practice.

28

Obstructive Pulmonary Diseases

Eugene Mondor

*Kindness is a breath of fresh air to someone who feels
they are suffocating.*

Franklin D. Roosevelt

http://evolve.elsevier.com/Lewis/medsurg/

CENCEPTUAL FOCUS

Fatigue
Functional Ability

Gas Exchange
Infection

Self-Management

LEARNING OUTCOMES

1. Describe the etiology, pathophysiology, and clinical manifestations of asthma.
2. Explain the difference between an acute asthma exacerbation and status asthmaticus.
3. Describe the interprofessional and nursing management of the patient with asthma.
4. Identify the classifications of drugs used in the treatment of asthma and chronic obstructive pulmonary disease (COPD).
5. Describe the etiology, pathophysiology, clinical manifestations, and interprofessional care of the patient with COPD.

6. Relate the indications for O_2 therapy, methods of delivery, and complications of O_2 administration.
7. Explain the nursing management of the patient with COPD.
8. Describe the pathophysiology, clinical manifestations, and interprofessional and nursing management of the patient with cystic fibrosis.
9. Describe the pathophysiology, clinical manifestations, and interprofessional and nursing management of the patient with bronchiectasis.

KEY TERMS

α_1-antitrypsin deficiency (AATD), p. 561
asthma, p. 542
bronchiectasis, p. 580
chest physiotherapy (CPT), p. 571
chronic bronchitis, p. 560

chronic obstructive pulmonary disease (COPD), p. 560
cor pulmonale, p. 563
cystic fibrosis (CF), p. 576
emphysema, p. 560

O_2 toxicity, p. 567
postural drainage, p. 571
pursed-lip breathing (PLB), p. 570
status asthmaticus, p. 545

Imagine needing to consciously think about every breath that you take each minute, each hour, and every day of your life. You are tired and weak and have not been sleeping well. Your appetite is poor. The stress of living with these symptoms makes you feel anxious and depressed. You have been absent from work and are having some financial problems. Many people with obstructive lung disease have this experience.

The obstructive pulmonary diseases are the most common chronic lung diseases. They are characterized by increased resistance to airflow because of airway obstruction or airway narrowing. There are 4 major types of obstructive lung disease: asthma, chronic obstructive pulmonary disease (COPD), cystic fibrosis (CF), and bronchiectasis.

Asthma causes inflammation with variable degrees of airflow obstruction. Between acute exacerbations, or attacks, the patient with asthma is often asymptomatic with normal lung function. On the other hand, in COPD there is progressive limitation in airflow that is not fully reversible. The limitation in expiratory airflow in COPD is generally more constant day-to-day and

worsens over time. Emphysema and chronic bronchitis are 2 related respiratory conditions often responsible for COPD.[1]

The pathophysiology of asthma and the response to therapy differs from COPD. However, patients with asthma who have less responsive airflow obstruction are hard to tell from COPD patients. In fact, some patients share features of both asthma and COPD. This is known as asthma-COPD overlap syndrome.[2] It is characterized by significantly worse respiratory signs and symptoms, an increased number of hospitalizations, and a much poorer quality of life than asthma or COPD alone.[3]

CF is an inherited genetic disorder. It produces airway obstruction because of changes in exocrine glandular secretions, resulting in increased mucus production. There are about 30,000 people in the United States living with CF, with 52.7% being adults.[4]

Bronchiectasis is characterized by dilated bronchioles, making it hard to clear secretions. It most often results from poorly treated or untreated pulmonary infections, immune system problems, or genetic factors.

541

Obstructive Pulmonary Diseases

Asthma
- Asthma prevalence rates are 38% higher among blacks than whites.
- Hispanics, especially those from Puerto Rico, have higher rates of asthma and age-adjusted death rates than all other racial and ethnic subgroups.
- Black females have the highest mortality rates from asthma.

COPD
- Whites have the highest incidence of COPD despite higher rates of smoking among other ethnic groups.
- Hispanics have lower death rates from COPD than other ethnic groups.

Cystic Fibrosis
- Whites have the highest incidence of CF.
- CF is uncommon among blacks, Hispanics, and Asian Americans.

ASTHMA

Asthma is a heterogenous disease characterized by bronchial hyperreactivity with reversible expiratory airflow limitation. Signs and symptoms can be variable. They often include episodes of wheezing, breathlessness, chest tightness, and cough, particularly at night or in the early morning. These episodes are associated with widespread, variable airflow obstruction that is usually reversible, either spontaneously or with treatment. The clinical course of asthma is unpredictable, ranging from periods of adequate control to attacks with poor control of symptoms.

Asthma affects around 20.4 million adult Americans.[5] It is a major public health concern, with more than 1.7 million emergency department (ED) visits each year.[5] After a long period of an increasing incidence of asthma, the mortality and use of health care services for asthma have decreased over the past 10 years. Unfortunately, more than 3600 people still die each year from asthma.[5]

GENDER DIFFERENCES
Asthma

Men
- Before puberty, more boys are affected than girls.

Women
- In adulthood, women are much more likely to be affected than men.
- Women who present to the ED are more likely to need hospitalization than men.
- Mortality is higher in women than in men.

Risk Factors for Asthma and Triggers of Asthma Attacks

Risk factors for asthma and triggers of asthma attacks can be related to the patient (e.g., genetic factors) or the environment (e.g., pollen) (Table 28.1). Important factors and triggers are discussed in this section.

Nose and Sinus Problems. Most patients with asthma have a history of allergic rhinitis. Treatment of allergic rhinitis usually improves the symptoms of asthma. Acute and chronic sinusitis, especially bacterial rhinosinusitis, may worsen asthma. Patients with asthma often have chronic sinus problems that cause inflammation of the mucous membranes and can trigger an

TABLE 28.1 Triggers of Asthma Attacks

Air Pollutants
- Aerosol sprays
- Cigarette smoke
- Exhaust fumes
- Oxidants
- Perfumes
- Sulfur dioxides

Allergen Inhalation
- Animal dander (e.g., cats, mice, guinea pigs)
- Cockroaches
- House dust mite
- Molds
- Pollens

Drugs
- Aspirin
- β-Adrenergic blockers
- Nonsteroidal antiinflammatory drugs

Food Additives
- Beer, wine, dried fruit, shrimp, processed potatoes
- Monosodium glutamate
- Sulfites (bisulfites and metabisulfites)
- Tartrazine

Occupational Exposure
- Agriculture, farming
- Industrial chemicals and plastics
- Laundry detergents
- Metal salts
- Paints, solvents
- Wood and vegetable dusts

Viral or Bacterial Infection
- Sinusitis, allergic rhinitis
- Viral URI

Other Factors
- Exercise and cold, dry air
- Gastroesophageal reflux disease (GERD)
- Hormones, menses
- Stress

asthma attack. Sinusitis must be treated and large nasal polyps removed for an asthma patient to have good control. (Sinusitis is discussed in Chapter 27.)

Respiratory Tract Infections. Respiratory tract infections are often a major trigger of an acute asthma attack. Acute infection can decrease the diameter of the airways and induce airway hyperresponsiveness. Viral-induced changes in epithelial cells, the accumulation of inflammatory cells, edema of airway walls, and exposure of airway nerve endings contribute to altered respiratory function. These changes may exacerbate asthma.

Allergens. Allergens cause varying degrees of allergic reactions in susceptible persons. Indoor and outdoor allergens, such as cockroaches, furry animals, fungi, pollen, and molds, can trigger asthma attacks. However, their role in the actual development of asthma is not as clear.[6]

Cigarette Smoke. The Centers for Disease Control and Prevention (CDC) estimates that 21% of asthma patients smoke.[7] In a person with asthma, smoking is associated with a faster decline of lung function, increased disease severity, more frequent visits to the HCP, and a decreased response to treatment. The smoke exhaled by a smoker, known as secondhand smoke, is also a risk factor.

Air Pollutants. Various air pollutants, such as wood smoke or vehicle exhaust, can trigger asthma attacks. In heavily industrialized or densely populated areas, climate conditions often lead to concentrated pollution in the atmosphere, especially with thermal inversions and stagnant air masses. News sources report ozone alert days. Patients with breathing problems should minimize outdoor activity during these times.

Occupational Factors. *Occupational asthma* is the most common job-related respiratory disorder. These irritants cause a change in the responsiveness of the airways. However, the development of symptoms may not occur until the patient has had months to years of exposure. These agents are diverse and include wood dusts, laundry detergents, metal salts, chemicals, paints, solvents, and plastics. Often, people with occupational asthma give a history of arriving at work feeling well but gradually develop symptoms, which may become progressively worse, by the end of the day.

Exercise. Asthma that is induced or worse during physical exertion is called exercise-induced asthma (EIA) or exercise-induced bronchospasm (EIB). Typically, symptoms of EIA are pronounced during activities in which there is exposure to cold, dry air. For example, swimming in an indoor heated pool is less likely to cause symptoms than downhill skiing. Airway obstruction may occur due to changes in the airway mucosa caused by hyperventilation during exercise, with either cooling or rewarming of air and capillary leakage in the airway wall. EIB occurs after vigorous exercise, not during it (e.g., jogging, aerobics, walking briskly, climbing stairs).

Drugs and Food Additives. Some people with asthma have what we call the *asthma triad*: nasal polyps, asthma, and sensitivity to aspirin and nonsteroidal antiinflammatory drugs (NSAIDs). Some persons with asthma who use salicylic acid (e.g., aspirin) or NSAIDs develop wheezing within 2 hours. In addition, there is usually profound rhinorrhea, congestion, tearing, and even angioedema. Avoiding salicylic acid and NSAIDs is required. Teach the patient to read labels. Salicylic acid is in many OTC drugs and some foods, beverages, and flavorings. Under the care of an allergist, daily administration of the drug can desensitize some patients.

β-Adrenergic blockers in oral form (e.g., metoprolol [Toprol-XL]) or topical eye drops (e.g., timolol [Timoptic]) may trigger an asthma attack because they can cause bronchospasm. Angiotensin-converting enzyme (ACE) inhibitors (e.g., lisinopril) may cause a dry, hacking cough in susceptible persons, making asthma symptoms worse. Asthma attacks can occur after the use of sulfite-containing preservatives found in topical ophthalmic solutions, IV corticosteroids, and some inhaled bronchodilator solutions.

Food and drug additives that may trigger asthma in the susceptible person are tartrazine (yellow dye no. 5) and sulfiting agents. They are widely used as preservatives and sanitizing agents. Sulfiting agents are in fruits, beer, and wine. They are used in salad bars to protect vegetables from oxidation. Food allergies triggering asthma reactions in adults are rare. Avoidance diets are not recommended until testing has proven an allergy is present.

Gastroesophageal Reflux Disease. Gastroesophageal reflux disease (GERD) is more common in people with asthma than in the general population. GERD can worsen asthma symptoms because reflux may trigger bronchoconstriction and cause aspiration. Asthma drugs may worsen GERD symptoms. β$_2$-Agonists used to treat asthma (especially when given orally) relax the lower esophageal sphincter. This allows stomach contents to reflux into the esophagus and be aspirated into the lungs. Effective treatment for GERD can improve nocturnal asthma control, improve quality of life, and prevent asthma symptoms in some patients. (GERD is discussed in Chapter 41.)

Genetics. Asthma has an inherited component, but the genetics are complex. Numerous genes may be involved in the development of asthma. They are likely responsible for varying responses among patients to different types of asthma drugs. Atopy, the genetic predisposition to develop an allergic (immunoglobulin E [IgE]–mediated) response to common allergens, is a major risk factor for asthma.

Immune Response. The *hygiene hypothesis* suggests that a newborn baby's immune system must be conditioned so that it will function properly during infancy and the rest of life. People who have a lower incidence of asthma were exposed to certain infections early in life, used fewer antibiotics, were around other children (e.g., siblings, day care), or lived in rural settings or with pets. People for whom these factors are not present in childhood have a higher incidence of asthma.

Psychological Factors. Asthma is not a psychosomatic disease. However, many people with asthma report that symptoms worsen with stress. An asthma attack caused by any triggering event can produce panic, stress, and anxiety. These emotions, and other psychological factors, can cause bronchoconstriction through stimulation of the cholinergic reflex pathways. Extreme behavioral expressions (e.g., crying, laughing, anger, fear) can lead to hyperventilation and hypocapnia, which can cause airway narrowing.

Pathophysiology

The main pathophysiologic process in asthma is persistent but variable inflammation of the airways. Airflow is limited because inflammation results in bronchoconstriction, airway hyperresponsiveness (hyperreactivity), and edema of the airways. Exposure to allergens or irritants initiates the inflammatory cascade (Fig. 28.1). A variety of inflammatory cells are involved, including mast cells, macrophages, eosinophils, neutrophils, T and B lymphocytes, and epithelial cells of the airways.

As the inflammatory process begins, mast cells (found beneath the basement membrane of the bronchial wall) degranulate and release multiple inflammatory mediators (Fig. 28.2). IgE antibodies are linked to mast cells, and the allergen cross-links the IgE. As a result, inflammatory mediators, such as leukotrienes, histamine, cytokines, prostaglandins, and nitric oxide, are released. Inflammatory mediators have effects on the (1) blood vessels, causing vasodilation and increasing capillary permeability (runny nose); (2) nerve cells, causing itching; (3) smooth muscle cells, causing bronchial spasms and airway narrowing; and (4) goblet cells, causing mucus production (Fig. 28.3). This whole process is sometimes referred to as the *early-phase response* in asthma. Clinically, it occurs within 30 to 60 minutes after exposure to an allergen or irritant.

Symptoms can recur 4 to 6 hours after the early response because of the influx of many inflammatory cells, which are set in motion by the initial response. At this later time, the patient may develop symptoms again or worsening of symptoms. This is called the *late-phase response*. It occurs in about 50% of people with asthma. In the late-phase response, more inflammatory cells are recruited and activated, with continuing inflammation of the airways. Thus bronchoconstriction with symptoms lasts for 24 hours or more. Corticosteroids are effective in treating inflammation in this phase.

Chronic inflammation may cause structural changes in the bronchial wall, known as *remodeling*. A progressive loss of lung function occurs that therapy cannot fully reverse. The changes in structure may include fibrosis of the subepithelium, hypertrophy of the smooth muscle of the airways, mucus hypersecretion, continued inflammation, and *angiogenesis* (proliferation of new blood vessels).[8] We think remodeling explains why some persons have persistent asthma and limited response to therapy.

PATHOPHYSIOLOGY MAP

FIG. 28.1 Pathophysiology of asthma. (Adapted from McCance KL, Huether SE, Brashers, VL, Rote, NS, editors: *Pathophysiology: The biologic basis for disease in adults and children,* ed 7, St Louis, 2015, Elsevier.)

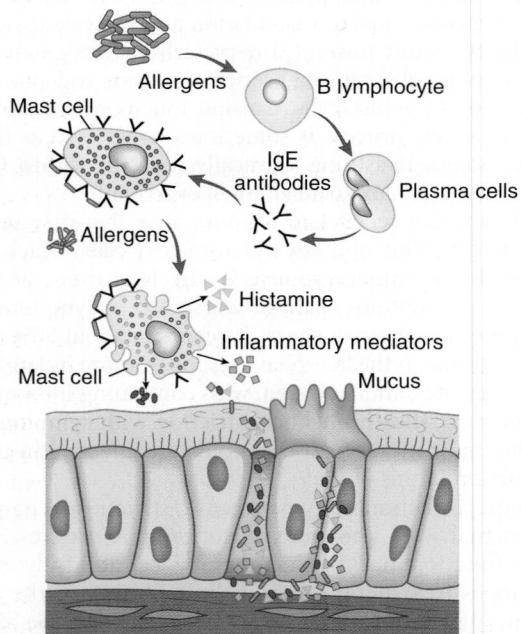

FIG. 28.2 Allergic asthma is triggered when an allergen cross-links *IgE* receptors on mast cells, which are then activated to release histamine and other inflammatory mediators (early-phase response). A late-phase response may occur due to further inflammation.

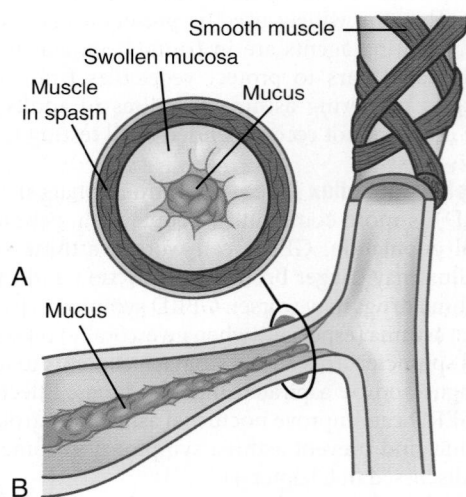

FIG. 28.3 Factors causing expiratory obstruction in asthma. A, Cross section of a bronchiole occluded by muscle spasm, swollen mucosa, and mucus in the lumen. B, Longitudinal section of a bronchiole. (Redrawn from Price SA, Wilson LM: *Pathophysiology: Clinical concepts of disease processes,* ed 6, St Louis, 2003, Mosby.)

Clinical Manifestations

The characteristic manifestations are wheezing, cough, dyspnea, and chest tightness after exposure to a risk factor or trigger. Normally the bronchioles constrict during expiration. However, in asthma, the airways become narrower than usual because of bronchospasm, edema, and mucus. As a result, it takes longer for the air to move out of the bronchioles (airflow obstruction). This causes the characteristic wheezing, air trapping, and hyperinflation of the lungs. As a result, expiration may be prolonged.

The most common finding during an acute asthmatic event is wheezing on auscultation. For wheezing to occur, the patient must be able to move enough air to make the sound. Wheezing usually occurs first on exhalation. As asthma progresses, the patient may wheeze during inspiration and expiration.

However, wheezing is an unreliable sign to gauge the severity of an attack. Many patients with minor attacks wheeze loudly. Others with severe attacks do not wheeze. The patient with a severe asthma attack may wheeze only during forced expiration or have no audible wheezing because of the marked reduction in airflow.

Decreased or absent breath sounds may signal a significant decrease in air movement resulting from exhaustion and an inability to generate enough muscle force to breathe. Severely decreased breath sounds, often referred to as the "silent chest," are an ominous sign. It means severe airway obstruction and impending respiratory failure.

⚠ SAFETY ALERT Silent Chest
- If the patient has been wheezing, then there is an absence of a wheeze (e.g., silent chest) and the patient is obviously struggling, this is a life-threatening situation. The patient may need mechanical ventilation.

Hyperventilation occurs during an asthma attack as lung receptors respond to increased lung volume from trapped air and airflow limitation. Decreased perfusion and ventilation of the alveoli and increased alveolar gas pressure lead to ventilation-perfusion abnormalities in the lungs. The patient is hypoxemic early on with decreased $PaCO_2$ and increased pH (respiratory alkalosis) because they are is hyperventilating. As the airflow limitation worsens with air trapping, the patient works much harder to breathe. The $PaCO_2$ normalizes as the patient tires, and then it increases to produce respiratory acidosis. This is an ominous sign of respiratory failure.

In some patients with asthma, cough is the only symptom. This is termed *cough variant asthma*. Bronchospasm is not present or may not be severe enough to cause airflow obstruction or wheezing, but it can increase bronchial tone and cause irritation with stimulation of the cough receptors. The cough may be nonproductive or with secretions. Sputum may be thick, tenacious, and gelatinous, which makes removal difficult.

The examination of the patient with asthma may be normal, especially between attacks. A runny nose, swollen nasal passages, and nasal polyps may be seen. The patient may have eczema and hives, which have been linked to asthma.

❓ CHECK YOUR PRACTICE

Your patient with a history of asthma was admitted to the ED in acute respiratory distress. He has been receiving therapy and seems to be responding. You notice he is no longer wheezing.
- Should you consider this finding a sign that he is doing better?

Asthma Classifications

There are several sets of guidelines for classifying asthma. Each set of guidelines has a slightly different perspective about asthma and how to classify the severity when attacks occur. Asthma severity is used to guide treatment decisions. Current guidelines focus on (1) assessing the severity of the disease at diagnosis and initial treatment and then (2) monitoring periodically to control the disease. All groups endorse the use of short-acting bronchodilators for an acute asthma attack and the importance of an "asthma action plan" to help prevent future attacks from occurring. They promote patient education and adherence to prescribed therapy. Many HCPs use the 2007 the National Heart, Lung, and Blood Institute classification of asthma severity (Table 28.2). It describes asthma as intermittent, mild persistent, moderate persistent, or severe persistent.

Complications

Asthma is characterized by an unpredictable and variable course. Asthma attacks range from minor interferences in breathing to life-threatening episodes. Depending on a person's response, asthma can rapidly progress from normal breathing to an acute, severe attack or a life-threatening medical emergency within a few minutes.

While asthma attacks may have an abrupt onset, most of the time, symptoms occur more gradually. Attacks may last for a few minutes to several hours. Between attacks, the patient may be asymptomatic with normal or near-normal spirometry, depending on the severity of disease. In some people, compromised pulmonary function (indicated by abnormal spirometry results) may lead to a state of continuous symptoms and chronic debilitation. Pneumonia, tension pneumothorax, status asthmaticus, and acute respiratory failure can occur.

Status Asthmaticus. A life-threatening medical emergency, status asthmaticus is the most extreme form of an acute asthma attack. It is characterized by hypoxia, hypercapnia, and acute respiratory failure.[9] The patient is unresponsive to treatment with bronchodilators and corticosteroids. The patient may have chest tightness, a severely marked increase in shortness of breath, or suddenly be unable to speak. Hypotension, bradycardia, and respiratory and/or cardiac arrest may occur if we do not recognize that the patient's condition is getting worse.

The patient must be immediately intubated, and mechanical ventilation started. Hemodynamic monitoring of the patient is critical. Analgesia and sedation are essential. Continuous analgesic infusions (e.g., ketamine, morphine) and sedation with drugs such as propofol (Diprivan) help decrease work of breathing (WOB) and facilitate patient synchrony with the ventilator. In some circumstances, neuromuscular blocking agents may be used. Inhaled anesthetics, such as isoflurane or halothane, are an option for those not responding to conventional treatment. IV magnesium sulfate, which has a bronchodilator effect, may be given to patients with a very low FEV_1 (forced expiratory volume in 1 second) or peak flow (less than 40% of predicted or personal best) or those who do not respond to initial treatment.

Diagnostic Studies

The tests we use to diagnose asthma are shown in Table 28.3. In general, the HCP should consider a diagnosis of asthma if various indicators (e.g., manifestations, health history, peak flow variability, spirometry) are positive.

Underdiagnosis of asthma is common. A detailed history is important to determine if a person has had similar attacks,

TABLE 28.2 Classification of Asthma Severity

Components of Severity	ASTHMA SEVERITY			
		PERSISTENT		
	Intermittent	Mild	Moderate	Severe
Impairment				
Symptoms	≤2 days/wk	>2 days/wk, not daily	Daily	Continuous
Nighttime awakenings	≤2/mos	3–4/mos	>1/wk, not nightly	Often 7/wk
SABA use for symptoms	≤2 days/wk	>2 days/wk, not daily	Daily	Several times per day
Interference with normal activity	None	Minor limitation	Some limitation	Extremely limited
Lung function*	Normal FEV_1 between attacks	FEV_1 >80% predicted	FEV_1 60%–80% predicted	FEV_1 <60% predicted
	FEV_1 >80%	FEV_1/FVC normal	FEV_1/FVC reduced by 5%	FEV_1/FVC reduced by 5%
	FEV_1/FVC normal			
Risk				
Attacks requiring oral corticosteroids	0–1/yr	≥2/yrs even in the absence of impairment		
	Consider severity and interval since last attack. ————————————————→			
	Frequency and severity may fluctuate over time. ————————————————→			
	Relative annual risk for exacerbation may be related to FEV_1. ————————→			
Recommended Step for Initiating Treatment	Step 1	Step 2	Step 3[†]	Step 4 or 5[†]
	Reevaluate asthma control in 2–6 wk and adjust therapy as needed			

Guidelines for Using Table
- Assign patients to the most severe step in which any feature occurs. Clinical features may overlap across steps. Determine level of severity by assessment of both impairment and risk. Assess impairment by patient's recall of previous 2–4 wk spirometry results.
- A person's classification should change over time with treatment. After treatment, the focus switches to the level of control, not the classification of severity.
- Patients at any level of severity of chronic asthma can have mild, moderate, or severe asthma attacks. Some patients with intermittent asthma have severe and life-threatening attacks separated by long periods of normal lung function and no symptoms.

Source: Adapted from National Asthma Education and Prevention Program, National Heart, Lung, and Blood Institute: *Expert Panel Report 3: Guidelines for the diagnosis and management of asthma,* NIH pub no 08-4051, Bethesda, MD, 2007, National Institutes of Health.
ercent predicted values for FEV_1 or ratio of FEV_1/FVC. Normal FEV_1/FVC: 8–19 yr, 85%; 20–39 yr, 80%; 40–59 yr, 75%; 60–80 yr, 70%.
[†]Consider short-term corticosteroid therapy.

TABLE 28.3 Interprofessional Care

Asthma

Diagnostic Assessment
- History and physical examination
- Spirometry, including response to bronchodilator therapy
- Peak expiratory flow rate (PEFR)
- Chest x-ray
- Measurement of oximetry
- Allergy skin testing (if indicated)
- Blood level of eosinophils and IgE (if indicated)

Management
- Identify and avoid or eliminate triggers
- Patient and caregiver teaching
- Drug therapy (Tables 28.6 and 28.7 and Figs. 28.4 and 28.5)
- Asthma action plan (Fig. 28.9)
- Desensitization (immunotherapy) if indicated
- Assess for control (e.g., Asthma Control Test [ACT])*

Acute Attacks
- SaO_2 monitoring
- ABGs
- Inhaled β_2-adrenergic agonists
- Inhaled anticholinergics
- O_2 by nasal cannula or mask
- IV or oral corticosteroids
- IV fluids
- IV magnesium
- Intubation and assisted ventilation

*See www.asthmacontroltest.com.

which are often precipitated by a known trigger. Because wheezing and cough occur with a variety of disorders (e.g., COPD, GERD, vocal cord problems, heart failure), it is important to determine if asthma or some other disease process is the cause of these problems. A comparison of asthma and COPD is shown in Table 28.4.

The peak expiratory flow rate (PEFR) measured by the peak flow meter (at home or in a health care setting) is a test of lung function (see Table 25.17). PEFR measurements can help predict an asthma attack or monitor the severity of disease. Test results depend on the patient's age, gender, and height. Since types of peak flow meters vary, PEFR should be compared with the patient's own previous best measurements using their own meter.

Spirometry is usually normal between asthma attacks if the patient has no other underlying pulmonary disease. However, the patient with asthma may show an obstructive pattern including a decrease in forced vital capacity (FVC), FEV_1, PEFR, and FEV_1 to FVC ratio (FEV_1/FVC) (see Table 25.16).

When spirometry is scheduled, the patient must stop taking any bronchodilator drugs for 6 to 12 hours before the test. Spirometry can be done before and after the administration of a bronchodilator to determine the degree of the response. This helps determine reversibility of airway obstruction, which is critical information for diagnosing asthma. A positive (favorable) response to the bronchodilator is an increase of more than 200 mL and an increase of more than 12% between preadministration and postadministration values.[10]

We can use a hand-held, point-of-care device to measure fractional exhaled nitric oxide (FENO). FENO levels are

TABLE 28.4 Comparison of Asthma and COPD*

	Asthma	COPD
Clinical Features		
Age	Usually <40 yr (onset)	Usually 40–50 yr (onset)
Smoking history	Not causal	Often long history (>10–20 pack-years)
Health and family history	Presence of allergy, rhinitis, eczema. Family history of asthma	Infrequent allergies. May have exposure to environmental pollutants. With α_1-antitrypsin deficiency, family history of lung or liver disease without smoking history
Clinical symptoms	Intermittent, vary day to day, worse at night or early morning	Slowly progressive and persistent
Dyspnea	Absent except in attacks or poor control	Dyspnea during exercise
Sputum	Infrequent	Often
Disease course	Stable (with attacks)	Progressive worsening (with exacerbations)
Diagnostic Study Results		
ABGs	Normal between or during attacks	Between exacerbations in advanced COPD • Often low-normal pH and PaO_2 • High-normal $PaCO_2$ with normal to high HCO_3^- (compensated respiratory acidosis)
pH	↑ Early in attack, then ↓ if prolonged or severe attack	N→↓
PaO_2	↓	N→↓
$PaCO_2$	↓ Early in attack, then ↑ if prolonged or severe attack	N→↑
Chest x-ray	May show hyperinflation	Hyperinflation. May have cardiac enlargement, flattened diaphragm
Lung volumes	Often normalizes	Never normalizes
• Total lung capacity	Increased	Increased
• Residual volume	Increased	Increased
• FEV_1	Decreased or normal	Decreased
• FEV_1/FVC	Normal to decreased	Decreased (<70%)

*Patients may have features of both asthma and COPD.

increased in people with asthma associated with eosinophilic-induced airway inflammation. FENO may be used to gauge loss of asthma control and attacks, assess a patient's adherence to therapy, or determine if more inhaled or oral antiinflammatory medication is needed.[11]

Increased serum eosinophil counts and IgE levels are highly suggestive of atopy. Allergy skin testing may be used to determine sensitivity to specific allergens. However, a positive skin test does not necessarily mean that the allergen is causing the asthma attack. On the other hand, a negative allergy test does not mean that the asthma event is not allergy related. (Allergy testing is discussed in Chapter 13.)

A chest x-ray in an asymptomatic patient with asthma is usually normal. A routine chest x-ray is usually not done unless other manifestations, such as fever, chills, or upper airway stridor, are present. It can show if something else is causing symptoms similar to those of asthma (e.g., pneumonia, foreign body in the airway.)

A sputum specimen for culture and sensitivity may be done to rule out bacterial infection, especially if the patient has purulent sputum, a history of upper respiratory tract infection (URI), a fever, or an increased white blood cell (WBC) count. However, most asthma attacks are viral, and sputum cultures are rarely done on an outpatient basis.

Interprofessional Care

The goal of care is to achieve and maintain control of the disease. Once the patient is diagnosed, guidelines provide direction about medications (based on steps) the patient needs (Fig. 28.4). The HCP will step up the medication therapy as asthma symptoms worsen and step down the medication as the patient achieves control (Table 28.5). The level of control is determined by the patient's medication use, symptoms, and PEFR or FEV_1.

During an acute attack, signs and symptoms, medication use, and PEFR or FEV_1 measurements can be used to help identify the severity of an asthma attack and guide us in providing the most appropriate treatment. The goal is to achieve rapid control of the symptoms and return the patient to their daily functioning at the best possible level. Management of acute asthma attacks is shown in Fig. 28.5.

Patients with mild or moderate asthma attacks are often seen in the community at an outpatient clinic. These attacks occur no more than twice per week, with minimal interference in day-to-day activity. The patient is alert, oriented, and speaks in sentences. The patient may describe chest tightness, varying degrees of difficulty breathing, and a slight increase in the use of asthma drugs. O_2 saturation is usually greater than 90% on room air and PEFR greater than 50% of predicted or personal best.

Inhaled bronchodilators and oral corticosteroids are the mainstays of treatment for mild to moderate asthma attacks. Monitor the patient's vital signs. Most improve within 60 minutes of starting therapy. Teach the patient the importance of a follow-up appointment with the HCP. Oral corticosteroids will be part of the discharge plan for a moderate attack and, based on the patient's history and HCP preference, sometimes for a mild attack. If the patient's condition is slow to respond, does not respond, or the HCP suspects that some other condition may be occurring or contributing to the acute attack, the patient should be transferred to an acute care facility.

In a severe attack the patient is still alert and oriented, but may be tachycardic, tachypneic, and focused on breathing. Respiratory rates greater than 30 breaths/min may be present. Accessory muscle use may be seen. The patient may be agitated from hypoxemia. If not immediately audible, auscultation of the lungs may reveal inspiratory or expiratory wheezing. The patient often sits forward to maximize diaphragmatic movement. Time permitting, percussion of the lungs indicates hyperresonance. PEFR is 50% or less of predicted or of personal best. Symptoms may re-occur, sometimes daily, and there is interference with activities of daily living (ADLs).

A severe acute attack is usually frightening enough for patients to go to the ED. In many cases, a severe attack will warrant hospital admission. Management of the patient with

FIG. 28.4 Stepwise approach to asthma treatment. (Modified from GINA evidence-based strategy document, 2018. Retrieved from *https://ginasthma.org.*)

TABLE 28.5 Components of Asthma Control

Components of Control	CLASSIFICATION OF ASTHMA CONTROL		
	Well Controlled	Not Well Controlled	Very Poorly Controlled
Impairment			
Symptoms	≤2 days/wk	>2 days/wk	Throughout the day
Nighttime Awakenings	≤2/mo	1–3/wks	≥4/wks
Interference with normal activity	None	Some limitation	Extremely limited
SABA use	≤2 days/wk	>2 days/wk	Several times/day
FEV_1 or PEFR	>80% predicted/personal best	60%–80% predicted/personal best	<60% predicted/personal best
Risk			
Attacks requiring oral corticosteroids	0–1/yr	≥2/yr	≥2/yr
Progressive loss of lung function	Consider severity and interval since last attack. ─────────────────────────────────→		
Treatment-related adverse effects	Evaluation requires long-term follow-up. ─────────────────────────────────→		
	Can vary in intensity from none to very troublesome and worrisome. Level of intensity does not correlate to specific levels of control but should be considered in the overall assessment of risk. ───────→		
Recommended Action for Treatment (based on assessment of control)	• Maintain current step. • Regular follow-up every 1–6 mos to maintain control. • Consider step down if well controlled for at least 3 mo.	• Step up one step. • Reevaluate in 2–6 wk. • For side effects, consider alternative treatment options.	• Consider oral corticosteroids. • Step up 1 or 2 steps and reevaluate in 2 wk. • For side effects, consider alternative treatment options.

Source: Adapted from National Asthma Education and Prevention Program, National Heart, Lung, and Blood Institute: *Expert Panel Report 3: Guidelines for the diagnosis and management of asthma,* NIH pub no 08-4051, Bethesda, MD, 2007, National Institutes of Health.

a severe attack focuses on correcting hypoxemia and continually observing and/or improving ventilation. Supplemental O_2 is given by nasal cannula or mask to achieve a PaO_2 of at least 60 mm Hg or O_2 saturation greater than 93%. O_2 monitoring should be continuous with pulse oximetry.

Bedside PEFR may be used to monitor airflow obstruction. Serial PEFR results, oximetry, and measurement of arterial blood gases (ABGs) give information about the severity of the attack and the response to therapy. Obtaining a PEFR during a severe asthma attack is usually not possible. However, if it can be obtained and is less than 200 L/min, it indicates severe obstruction in all but very small adults.

Careful monitoring of the patient's heart rate, respiratory rate and rhythm, and BP are essential. Bronchodilators and oral corticosteroids will be part of the treatment plan. The "silent chest" is an ominous clinical finding. It often signals impending respiratory failure. Immediate notification of the HCP is required.

Drug Therapy

Drug therapy for asthma can be complex and overwhelming for many practitioners, including you. It is important to understand the intended purpose, desired effect, side effects, and when to use different drugs. Asthma drugs are divided into 2 general

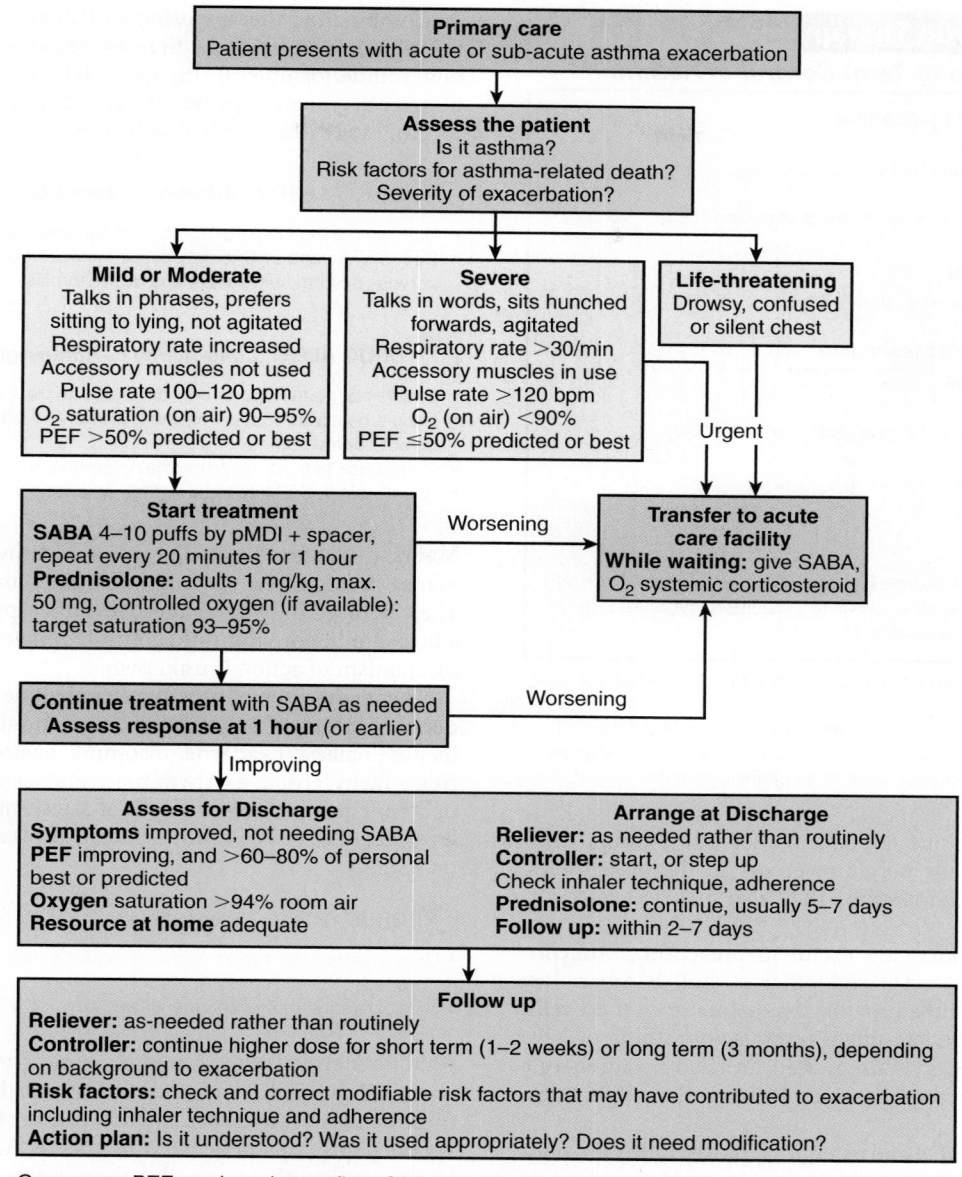

Primary care
Patient presents with acute or sub-acute asthma exacerbation

Assess the patient
Is it asthma?
Risk factors for asthma-related death?
Severity of exacerbation?

Mild or Moderate
Talks in phrases, prefers
sitting to lying, not agitated
Respiratory rate increased
Accessory muscles not used
Pulse rate 100–120 bpm
O_2 saturation (on air) 90–95%
PEF >50% predicted or best

Severe
Talks in words, sits hunched
forwards, agitated
Respiratory rate >30/min
Accessory muscles in use
Pulse rate >120 bpm
O_2 (on air) <90%
PEF ≤50% predicted or best

Life-threatening
Drowsy, confused
or silent chest

Urgent

Start treatment
SABA 4–10 puffs by pMDI + spacer,
repeat every 20 minutes for 1 hour
Prednisolone: adults 1 mg/kg, max.
50 mg, Controlled oxygen (if available):
target saturation 93–95%

Worsening

**Transfer to acute
care facility**
While waiting: give SABA,
O_2 systemic corticosteroid

Continue treatment with SABA as needed
Assess response at 1 hour (or earlier)

Worsening

Improving

Assess for Discharge
Symptoms improved, not needing SABA
PEF improving, and >60–80% of personal
best or predicted
Oxygen saturation >94% room air
Resource at home adequate

Arrange at Discharge
Reliever: as needed rather than routinely
Controller: start, or step up
Check inhaler technique, adherence
Prednisolone: continue, usually 5–7 days
Follow up: within 2–7 days

Follow up
Reliever: as-needed rather than routinely
Controller: continue higher dose for short term (1–2 weeks) or long term (3 months), depending
on background to exacerbation
Risk factors: check and correct modifiable risk factors that may have contributed to exacerbation
including inhaler technique and adherence
Action plan: Is it understood? Was it used appropriately? Does it need modification?

O_2: oxygen; PEF: peak expiratory flow; SABA: short-acting beta$_2$-agonist (doses are for salbutamol)

FIG. 28.5 Management of patient with acute asthma attack. (Modified from GINA evidence-based strategy document, 2018. Retrieved from *https://ginasthma.org*.)

types: (1) *quick relief,* or *rescue medications,* to treat attacks, and (2) long-term control medications (Table 28.6).

The patient's medical history, medication plan, and severity of attack helps the HCP determine which types of drugs are best suited to control asthma symptoms. Current guidelines all suggest a stepwise approach to drug therapy. Common drugs used in asthma therapy are discussed in Table 28.7.

The mainstay of asthma treatment is inhalation of short-acting β$_2$-adrenergic agonist (SABA) bronchodilators. All patients need a quick-relief or "rescue" medication. Short-acting SABAs, such as albuterol (ProAir HFA, Proventil HFA, Ventolin HFA), are the most effective rescue drugs for asthma.

In patients with a moderate to severe attack, inhaled ipratropium (Atrovent) is used in conjunction with a SABA. Combivent is a combination of both ipratropium and albuterol.

Oral and, in some situations, IV corticosteroids may be given to patients who do not initially respond to SABA alone.

Patients with asthma who have frequent attacks also must be on a long-term ("controller") medication. Inhaled corticosteroids (ICSs) (e.g., fluticasone [Flovent Diskus or HFA]) are the most effective long-term controllers to treat inflammation. Some ICSs are used in combination with long-acting bronchodilators (LABAs) to gain better asthma control.

Bronchodilators. The 3 classes of bronchodilator drugs used in asthma therapy are β$_2$-adrenergic agonists (also referred to as β$_2$-agonists), methylxanthines and derivatives, and anticholinergics.

β$_2$-Adrenergic Agonist Drugs. These drugs may be SABAs or LABAs. Because inhaled SABAs are the most effective drugs for relieving acute bronchospasm (as seen in an acute attack), they are known as *rescue medications.* These drugs have an onset of

TABLE 28.6 Drug Therapy

Quick Relief vs. Long-Term Control of Asthma

Quick-Relief ("Rescue") Medications
Bronchodilators
Short-acting inhaled β_2-adrenergic agonists (e.g., albuterol [Proventil HFA])
Anticholinergics (inhaled) (e.g., ipratropium [Atrovent HFA])*

Antiinflammatory Drugs
Corticosteroids (systemic) (e.g., prednisone)†

Long-Term ("Controller") Medications
Antiinflammatory Drugs
Corticosteroids
• Inhaled (e.g., fluticasone [Flovent Diskus or HFA])
• Oral (e.g., prednisone)
LTMAs (e.g., montelukast [Singulair])
Anti–IgE (omalizumab [Xolair])

Bronchodilators
Long-acting inhaled β_2-adrenergic agonists (e.g., salmeterol [Serevent])
Long-acting oral β_2-adrenergic agonists (e.g., albuterol [VoSpire ER])
Methylxanthines (e.g., theophylline [Theo-24])

*Used as alternative if patient has intolerable side effects to albuterol or in ED for severe attacks.
†Considered quick-relief drugs when used in a short burst (3–10 days) at the start of therapy or during a period of gradual deterioration. Corticosteroids are not used for immediate relief of an ongoing attack.

action within minutes and are effective for 4 to 8 hours. They act by stimulating β-adrenergic receptors in the bronchioles, thus producing bronchodilation. They also increase mucociliary clearance.

β_2-Adrenergic agonists are useful in preventing bronchospasm triggered by exercise and other stimuli because they prevent the release of inflammatory mediators from mast cells. They do not inhibit the late-phase response of asthma or have antiinflammatory effects. If used often, inhaled β_2-adrenergic agonists may cause tremors, anxiety, tachycardia, palpitations, and nausea.

Too frequent use of β_2-adrenergic agonists indicates poor asthma control, may mask asthma severity, and may lead to reduced drug effectiveness. The use of SABAs should be limited to less than 2 times weekly. SABA inhalers should last for months. SABAs are not to be used for long-term control. They should not be used alone for recurrent, repeated asthma attacks. Use of long-term bronchodilators with inhaled corticosteroids or other drugs can achieve this goal better if prescribed and used properly.

LABAs, including salmeterol (Serevent Diskus) and formoterol (Foradil), are effective for 12 hours. LABAs are added to a daily dose of ICSs for long-term control of moderate to severe persistent asthma and prevention of symptoms, particularly at night. When LABAs are added to a patient's daily regimen of corticosteroids, they decrease the need for SABAs and allow patients to achieve better asthma control with a lower dosage of ICSs.

LABAs should never be used alone as asthma therapy. They should only be used if the patient is on an ICS. Tell patients that these drugs should not be used to treat acute symptoms or to obtain quick relief from bronchospasm. Teach the patient that these drugs are used only once every 12 hours.

Combination therapy using an ICS and a LABA is available in several inhalers (e.g., fluticasone/salmeterol [Advair] and budesonide/formoterol [Symbicort]). The combinations are more convenient, improve adherence, and ensure that patients receive the LABA together with an ICS.

 DRUG ALERT *β_2-Adrenergic Agonists*

• Use with caution in patients with cardiac disorders.
• Both SABAs and LABAs may cause increased BP and heart rate, central nervous system stimulation, and dysrhythmias.

 DRUG ALERT *Long-Acting β_2-Adrenergic Agonists (LABAs)*

• Should not be the first or only drug used to treat asthma.
• Should be added to the treatment plan only if other controller medicines do not control asthma.
• Do not use to treat wheezing that is getting worse.
• Always use a SABA to treat sudden wheezing.

Methylxanthines. Sustained-release methylxanthine (theophylline) preparations are not a first-line controller medication. They are used only as an alternative therapy. Methylxanthine is a bronchodilator with mild antiinflammatory effects. The exact mechanism of action is unknown.

The main problems with theophylline are the high incidence of interaction with other drugs and the side effects. These include nausea, headache, insomnia, gastrointestinal (GI) distress, tachycardia, dysrhythmias, and seizures. Because theophylline has a narrow margin of safety, monitor serum blood levels regularly to determine if drug levels are within therapeutic range.

 DRUG ALERT *Theophylline*

• Teach patient to report signs of toxicity: nausea, vomiting, seizures, insomnia.
• Avoid caffeine to prevent intensifying adverse effects.

Anticholinergic Drugs. Anticholinergic drugs affect the muscles around the bronchi (large airways). When the lungs are irritated, these bands of muscle can tighten, causing bronchoconstriction via the parasympathetic nervous system. Anticholinergics work by preventing these muscles from tightening. Consequently, these drugs promote bronchodilation.

Anticholinergic drugs are less effective than equivalent doses of SABAs in asthma. However, they are more effective in COPD patients. Therefore short-acting anticholinergic drugs are not used in the routine management of asthma, except for in severe acute asthma attacks.

Antiinflammatory Drugs

Corticosteroids. Chronic inflammation is a key component of asthma. Corticosteroids are antiinflammatory drugs that reduce bronchial hyperresponsiveness, block the late-phase response, and inhibit migration of inflammatory cells. Corticosteroids are more effective in improving asthma control than any other long-term drug.

To gain prompt control in acute attacks, oral corticosteroids are used. ICSs must be used for 1 to 2 weeks before maximum therapeutic effects can be seen. Some ICSs (e.g., fluticasone, budesonide [Pulmicort Flexhaler]) begin to have a therapeutic effect in 24 hours. Long-term, maintenance doses of oral corticosteroids may be needed to control asthma in patients with severe chronic asthma. ICSs must be used on a fixed schedule.

TABLE 28.7 Drug Therapy
Asthma and Chronic Obstructive Pulmonary Disease (COPD)

Drug	Route of Administration	Comments
Anticholinergics		
Short Acting (SAMA)		
ipratropium (Atrovent HFA)	Nebulizer, MDI	Approved for COPD. May provide additive benefit to SABA in moderate to severe asthma attacks (used in ED with no benefit beyond that). Use in asthma as alternative for patients with intolerable side effects with SABA. Temporary blurred vision with eye contact. Use cautiously in patients with narrow-angle glaucoma or prostatic enlargement
Long Acting (LAMA)		
aclidinium bromide (Tudorza, Pressair)	DPI	Approved only for COPD. Do not give with other anticholinergics. Not for acute relief of bronchospasm. Dosed twice daily
revefenacin (Yupelri)	Nebulizer	Approved only for COPD. Dosed once daily as maintenance treatment. Do not give with other anticholinergics. Use cautiously in patients with narrow-angle glaucoma
tiotropium (Spiriva HandiHaler)	DPI	Approved only for COPD. Blurred vision if powder comes in contact with eyes. Must not use ipratropium while on tiotropium. Patients with COPD must use SABA or short-acting anticholinergics for quick-relief medication. Maximum effect 1 wk after starting drug. Dosed once daily
umeclidinium (Incruse Ellipta)	DPI	Approved only for COPD. Dosed once daily as maintenance treatment of airflow obstruction
β_2-Adrenergic Agonists		
Inhaled: Short Acting (SABA)		
albuterol (Proventil HFA, Ventolin HFA, Proair HFA, AccuNeb, VoSpire ER [oral only])	Nebulizer, MDI, oral tablets, including extended release NOTE: Oral tablets not for acute use, only long acting	Use with caution in patients with cardiac disorders because β-agonists may cause ↑ BP and heart rate, CNS stimulation/excitation, and ↑ risk for dysrhythmias. Has rapid onset of action (1–3 min). Duration of action is 4–8 hr. Ventolin HFA is the only albuterol MDI with a counter
levalbuterol (Xopenex, Xopenex HFA)	Nebulizer, MDI	Too frequent use can result in loss of effectiveness. Efficacy no better than other SABAs
Inhaled: Long Acting (LABA)	*In asthma:* Never use as monotherapy. Use in combination with ICSs. *In COPD:* Can be used as monotherapy. Not used for rapid relief of dyspnea	
arformoterol (Brovana)	Nebulizer	See formoterol. For chronic COPD use
formoterol (Foradil Aerolizer, Perforomist)	DPI, nebulizer (Perforomist)	Can affect blood glucose levels. Use with caution in patients with diabetes
indacaterol (Arcapta Neohaler)	DPI	Only once-daily LABA. For chronic COPD use. Not intended to treat asthma
olodaterol (Striverdi Respimat)	MDI	2 puffs daily. Less expensive than other LABAs
salmeterol (Serevent Diskus)	DPI	Not to exceed 2 puffs q12hr. Not used for acute attacks. Has a counter
Corticosteroids		
hydrocortisone (Solu-Cortef)	IV	Alternate-day therapy minimizes side effects. Oral dose should be taken in morning with food or milk. When given in high dosages, observe for GI distress. Long-term therapy requires vitamin D and calcium supplements to prevent osteoporosis. Discontinue gradually to prevent adrenal insufficiency. If symptoms recur during tapering, notify HCP
methylprednisolone (Medrol, Solu-Medrol)	Oral, IV	
prednisone	Oral	
Inhaled		
beclomethasone (Qvar)	MDI	Not recommended for acute asthma attack. May not see effects until after at least 2 weeks of regular treatment
budesonide (Pulmicort Flexhaler)	DPI	Same as above
ciclesonide (Alvesco)	MDI	Oral candidiasis and other localized oropharyngeal effects (e.g., hoarseness). Fewer side effects than other ICSs because of small particle size with minimal activation in oropharynx
fluticasone (Flovent HFA, Flovent Diskus, Arnuity Ellipta)	MDI, DPI	Not recommended for acute asthma attack. Rinse mouth with water or mouthwash after use to prevent oral fungal infections. Use of spacer device with MDI may decrease incidence of oral candidiasis. May not see effects until after at least 2 wks of regular treatment
mometasone (Asmanex Twisthaler)	DPI	Not recommended for acute asthma attack. May not see effects until after at least 2 wks of regular treatment
Leukotriene Modifiers		
Leukotriene Receptor Blocker		
montelukast (Singulair)	Oral tablets, chewable tablets, oral granules	Not used to treat acute asthma episodes
zafirlukast (Accolate)	Oral tablets	Take at least 1 hr before or 2 hrs after meals. Affects metabolism of erythromycin and theophylline. Not used to treat acute asthma episodes

Continued

TABLE 28.7 Drug Therapy

Asthma and Chronic Obstructive Pulmonary Disease (COPD)—cont'd

Drug	Route of Administration	Comments
Leukotriene Inhibitor zileuton (Zyflo, Zyflo CR)	Oral tablets	Monitor liver enzymes. May interfere with metabolism of warfarin and theophylline. Not used to treat acute asthma episodes
Methylxanthines *IV agent:* aminophylline (second-line therapy) *Oral:* theophylline	Oral tablets, IV, elixir, sustained-release tablets	Wide variety of response to drug metabolism exists. Half-life is ↓ by smoking and ↑ by heart failure and liver disease. Cimetidine, ciprofloxacin, erythromycin, and other drugs may rapidly ↑ theophylline levels. Taking drug with food or antacids may help GI effects. Use limited to situations in which other long-term bronchodilators not available or not affordable
Monoclonal Antibodies ***Anti-IgE*** omalizumab (Xolair)	Subcutaneous	Only for moderate to severe, persistent, allergic asthma with symptoms not adequately controlled by ICSs. Not for acute bronchospasm. Give only under direct medical supervision biweekly or monthly, depending on IgE levels and weight. Observe patient for a minimum of 2 hrs after giving because anaphylaxis can occur
Anti-Interleukin 5 mepolizumab (Nucala)	Subcutaneous	Only used for maintenance in patients with severe asthma attacks despite receiving current asthma medications. Given once every 4 wks by health care professional
reslizumab (Cinqair)	IV only	
Phosphodiesterase Inhibitor Type 4 (PDE-4) roflumilast (Daliresp)	Oral	Only used in severe COPD to reduce exacerbation frequency. Not to be used for acute bronchospasm. GI symptoms occur within 6 mos of starting therapy. Teach patients to report any psychiatric symptoms (e.g., anxiety, depression, suicidal thoughts). Do not use with theophylline
Combination Agents ***SAMA/SABA*** ipratropium/albuterol (Combivent Respimat, DuoNeb)	Nebulizer (DuoNeb), inhalation spray (Combivent Respimat)	Patients must be careful not to overuse. Respimat is an inhaler, but propellant free, unlike an MDI. Respimat is independent of inspiratory flow. Has dose indicator
ICS/LABA budesonide/formoterol (Symbicort)	MDI	Has a counter
fluticasone/salmeterol (Advair Diskus or HFA)	DPI, MDI	Has a counter. Comes in 3 strengths
fluticasone/vilanterol (Breo Ellipta)	DPI	Dose once daily
mometasone furoate/formoterol fumarate (Dulera)	MDI	Not for relief of acute bronchospasm
LAMA/LABA umeclidinium/vilanterol (Anoro Ellipta)	DPI	Anticholinergic/LABA for COPD. Not for relief of acute bronchospasm

When ICSs are used, asthma can usually be controlled without significant systemic side effects since little systemic drug absorption occurs from these drugs. However, ICSs at the highest dosage levels have been associated with side effects (e.g., easy bruising, decreased bone mineral density). Oropharyngeal candidiasis, hoarseness, and dry cough are local side effects caused by inhalation of corticosteroids. These problems can be reduced or prevented by using a spacer with the metered-dose inhaler (MDI) and by gargling with water or mouthwash after each use. Using a spacer or holding device can help get more medication into the lungs.

Women, especially postmenopausal women, who have asthma and use corticosteroids should take adequate amounts of calcium and vitamin D and take part in regular weight-bearing exercise. (Osteoporosis is discussed in Chapter 63.)

Leukotriene Modifiers. Leukotrienes are inflammatory mediators produced from arachidonic acid metabolism. They are potent bronchoconstrictors. Some leukotrienes cause airway edema and inflammation, contributing to the symptoms of asthma. Leukotriene modifying agents (LTMAs) block the release of some substances from mast cells and eosinophils, thereby producing both bronchodilator and antiinflammatory effects. LTMAs include leukotriene receptor blockers (zafirlukast [Accolate], montelukast [Singulair]) and leukotriene synthesis inhibitors (zileuton [Zyflo CR]). These drugs interfere with the synthesis or block the action of leukotrienes.

LTMAs do not reverse bronchospasm in acute asthma attacks. They are used only for prophylactic and maintenance therapy. One advantage of these drugs is that they are taken orally.

Anti-IgE. Omalizumab (Xolair) is a monoclonal antibody to IgE that decreases circulating free IgE levels. Omalizumab prevents IgE from attaching to mast cells, thus preventing the release of chemical mediators. This drug is indicated for patients with moderate to severe asthma, or those not controlled with ICSs alone. Omalizumab is given subcutaneously every 2 to 4 weeks. The drug has a risk for anaphylaxis, so patients must receive the medication in an HCP's office where this potential emergency can be treated.

Anti-Interleukin 5. Mepolizumab (Nucala) and reslizumab (Cinqair) are monoclonal antibodies to interleukin-5 (IL-5). IL-5 is a major cytokine involved in the inflammatory response in asthma by promoting eosinophil activity. By inhibiting IL-5, these drugs inhibit the production and survival of eosinophils. They are used for patients who have a history of severe asthma attacks despite using current asthma medication.

Nonprescription Combination Drugs. Several nonprescription combination drugs are available OTC. They are usually combinations of a bronchodilator (ephedrine) and an expectorant (guaifenesin). Often patients seek OTC drugs because they are less expensive than prescription medication. Many people consider these drugs safe because they can be obtained without a prescription. In general, they should be avoided due to their potential side effects.

Inhalers containing epinephrine may be available. These agents are advertised as drugs to relieve bronchospasm. Those containing ephedrine and epinephrine are potentially dangerous because they stimulate the central nervous and cardiovascular systems, causing nervousness, heart palpitations and dysrhythmias, tremors, insomnia, and increased BP. Many respiratory products containing ephedrine are behind the counter at pharmacies or need a prescription. This limited access is to prevent the diversion of ephedrine to the production of methamphetamine. Many OTC products have been reformulated with phenylephrine, instead of ephedrine, which works well topically but has modest effects in the oral form.

It is important to teach patients about the dangers associated with nonprescription combination drugs. These drugs are high risk and possibly unsafe to a patient with underlying heart problems because tachycardia and hypertension often occur. For the patient who insists on taking these drugs, caution them to read and follow the directions on the label.

Inhalation Devices for Drug Delivery. Many asthma drugs are given by inhalation because the onset of action is faster and systemic side effects are reduced. Inhalation devices include MDIs, dry powder inhalers (DPIs), and nebulizers.

Inhalers. MDIs are small, hand-held, pressurized devices that deliver a measured dose of drug with each activation. The dosing is usually 1 or 2 puffs. Depending on the specific MDI, a spacer or holding chamber (e.g., AeroChamber, InspirEase [Fig. 28.6]) is used to reduce the amount of drug delivered to the oropharynx and improve the amount of drug delivered to the lungs. Spacers also help people who have hand-breath coordination problems.

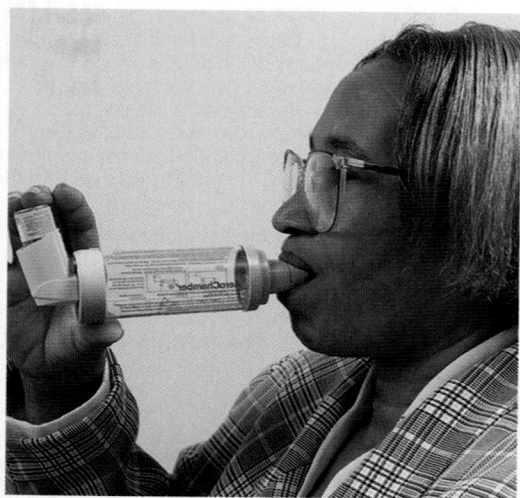

FIG. 28.6 Example of an AeroChamber spacer used with a metered-dose inhaler. (From Potter PA, Perry AG, Stockert P, et al: *Fundamentals of nursing,* ed 9, St Louis, 2017, Mosby.)

TABLE 28.8 Problems Using a Metered-Dose Inhaler (MDI)

- Not coordinating activation with inspiration
- Activating MDI in the mouth while breathing through nose
- Inspiring too rapidly
- Not holding the breath for 10 sec (or as close to 10 sec as possible)
- Holding MDI upside down or sideways
- Inhaling more than 1 puff with each inspiration
- Not shaking MDI before use (if indicated)
- Not waiting enough time between each puff
- Not opening mouth wide enough (if using open mouth technique), causing medication to bounce off teeth, tongue, or palate
- Not having adequate strength to activate MDI
- Not being able to understand and follow directions

International law mandates all MDIs have an ozone-friendly propellant that is a hydrofluoroalkane (HFA). This propellant is nontoxic, evaporates almost instantly once it forces medicine out of the MDI canister, and is not harmful to the patient. The number of times an MDI must be primed and the frequency of priming vary widely, so read the package insert with the patient.

The patient who needs to use several MDIs is often unclear about the order in which to take the medications. Historically it was recommended that SABAs be used first to open the airway and improve the delivery of subsequent medication. However, this recommendation is not evidence based. It is also a potential source of confusion to patients because SABAs are usually used on an as-needed basis.

One of the major problems with metered-dose drugs is the potential for overuse (more than 2 canisters per month) rather than seeking needed medical care (Table 28.8). As the patient has more asthmatic symptoms, they may use the β_2-adrenergic agonist MDI much more often. β_2-Adrenergic agonists help by relieving bronchospasm. They do not treat the inflammatory response. Therefore teach the patient the correct therapeutic use of these drugs.

Another problem is technique. Any MDI is effective only if taken properly. Review MDI technique during each visit as a standard part of care. The patient needs to know the correct way

Using an inhaler seems simple, but most patients do not use it the right way. When you use your inhaler the wrong way, less medicine gets to your lungs. (Your physician may give you other types of inhalers.)

For the next 2 weeks, read these steps aloud as you do them or ask someone to read them to you. Ask your physician or nurse to check how well you are using your inhaler.

Use your inhaler in one of the three ways pictured below (**A** or **B** is best, but **C** can be used if you have trouble with **A** or **B**).

Steps for Using Your Inhaler

Getting ready
1. Take off the cap and shake the inhaler.
2. Breathe out all the way.
3. Hold your inhaler the way your doctor said (**A, B,** or **C** below).

Breathe in slowly
4. As you start breathing in **slowly** through your mouth, press down on the inhaler **one** time. (If you use a holding chamber, first press down on the inhaler. Within 5 seconds, begin to breathe in slowly.)
5. Keep breathing in **slowly,** as deeply as you can.

Hold your breath
6. Hold your breath as you count to 10 slowly, if you can.
7. For inhaled quick-relief medicine (β_2-agonists), wait about 1 minute between puffs. There is no need to wait between puffs for other medicines.

A. Hold inhaler 1 to 2 inches in front of your mouth (about the width of two fingers).

B. Use a spacer/holding chamber. These come in many shapes and can be useful to any patient.

C. Put the inhaler in your mouth.

Clean Your Inhaler as Needed

Look at the hole where the medicine sprays out from your inhaler. If you see "powder" in or around the hole, clean the inhaler. Remove the metal canister from the L-shaped plastic mouthpiece. Rinse only the mouthpiece and cap in warm water. Let them dry overnight. In the morning, put the canister back inside. Put the cap on.

Know When to Replace Your Inhaler

For medicines you take each day (an example):
Say your new canister has 200 puffs (number of puffs is listed on canister) and you are told to take 8 puffs per day.

$$8 \text{ puffs per day} \overline{)} \begin{array}{c} 25 \text{ days} \\ \hline 200 \text{ puffs} \\ \text{in canister} \end{array}$$

So this canister will last 25 days. If you started using this inhaler on May 1, replace it on or before May 25. You can write the date on your canister.

For **quick-relief medicine take as needed** and count each puff.

Do not put your canister in water to see if it is empty as water may enter MDI and impair inhaler.

FIG. 28.7 How to use your metered-dose inhaler correctly.

to determine whether the MDI is empty and how to effectively clean and care for the device (Fig. 28.7).

DPIs are simpler to use than MDIs. The DPI contains dry, powdered medication and is breath activated (Fig. 28.8). No propellant is used. Instead, an aerosol is created when the patient inhales through a reservoir containing a dose of powder.

DPIs have several advantages over MDIs: (1) less manual dexterity is needed, (2) there is no need to coordinate device puffs with inhalation, and (3) no spacer is needed. Disadvantages are that some common drugs are not yet available in DPIs, and the medication may clump if exposed to humidity. Since the medicine is delivered only by the patient's inspiratory effort, patients with a low FEV_1 (less than 1 L) may not be able to inspire the medication. Table 28.9 describes how to effectively use a DPI.

Differences between MDIs and DPIs are described in Table 28.10. Aerosolized medication delivery systems, when used with comparable drug doses, provide equivalent efficacy. Therefore patients should use the device best suited to their needs.

Nebulizers. Nebulizers are small machines used to convert drug solutions into mists. The mist can be inhaled through a face mask or mouthpiece held between the teeth. Nebulizers are usually used for those who have severe asthma or difficulty with the MDI inhalation. They do not provide better delivery of medication than a spacer with an inhaler.

Nebulizers are usually powered by a compressed air or O_2 generator. At home, the patient may have an air-powered compressor. In the hospital, wall O_2 or compressed air powers the nebulizer.

Aerosolized medication orders must include the medication, dose, diluent, and whether it is to be nebulized with O_2 or compressed air. The advantage of nebulization therapy is that it is easy to use. Medications that are routinely nebulized include albuterol and ipratropium.

FIG. 28.8 Example of a dry powder inhaler (DPI). (From Potter PA, Perry AG, Stockert P, et al: *Fundamentals of nursing*, ed 9, St Louis, 2017, Mosby.)

TABLE 28.9 Patient Teaching

How to Use a Dry Powder Inhaler (DPI)

Include the following instructions when teaching a patient to use a DPI:
1. Remove mouthpiece cap or open the device according to manufacturer's instructions. Check for dust or dirt. If there is an external counter, note the number of doses left.
2. Load the medicine into the inhaler or engage the lever to allow the medicine to become available. Some DPIs re held upright while loading. Others are held sideways or in a horizontal position.
3. Do not shake your medicine.
4. Tilt your head back slightly and breathe out, getting as much air out of your lungs as you can. Do not breathe into your inhaler because this could affect the dose.
5. Close your lips tightly around the mouthpiece of the inhaler.
6. Breathe in deeply and quickly. This will ensure that the medicine moves down deeply into your lungs. You may not taste or sense the medicine going into your lungs.
7. Hold your breath for 10 seconds or as long as you can to disperse the medicine into your lungs.
8. If there is an external counter, note the number of doses left. It should be 1 less than the number in step 1 above.
9. Do not keep your DPI in a humid place, such as a shower room, because the medicine may clump.

The patient is placed in an upright position that allows for most efficient breathing to ensure adequate penetration and deposition of the aerosolized medication. The patient must breathe slowly and deeply through the mouth and hold each inspiration for 2 to 3 seconds. Deep diaphragmatic breathing helps ensure delivery of the medication. Tell the patient to breathe normally in between large, inhaled breaths. After treatment, have the patient cough effectively.

To reduce the potential for bacterial growth, review cleaning procedures for home respiratory equipment with the patient. An effective home-cleaning method is to wash the nebulizer daily in soap and water, rinse it with water, and soak it for 20 to 30 minutes in a 1:1 white vinegar–water solution, followed by a water rinse and air drying.

Patient Teaching Related to Drug Therapy. One of the major factors determining success in asthma management is the correct administration of drugs. The drug regimen can be

TABLE 28.10 Comparison of Metered-Dose and Dry Powder Inhalers

	Metered-Dose Inhaler (MDI)	Dry Powder Inhaler (DPI)
Shake before use	May be needed for some (e.g., albuterol), but not for others (Read package insert)	No
Inspiration	Slow	Rapid
Spacer	May be used with inhaled corticosteroids or for more effective delivery (Read package insert)	Not used
Counting device	Many have an external device, but some do not	Most preloaded forms include counter
Inhalations/dose	Often 2/dose	Often 1/dose
Cleaning	Use water for plastic case	Avoid moisture

confusing and complex. When teaching patients about their medications, include the name, purpose, dosage, method of administration, and when to use. It is essential that the patient understand the difference between rescue and controller medications, the importance of monitoring their response to therapy, and, most importantly, when to recognize that symptoms are not improving and help is required. Review side effects, appropriate action if side effects occur, and how to properly prime, use, and clean devices. Some patients may benefit from keeping a diary to record medication use, wheezing, or coughing, PEFR, side effects of drugs, and activity level. This information will help the HCP adjust the medication if needed.

Several factors can affect the correct use of inhalation devices. These include advanced age, changes in physical dexterity (e.g., arthritis in hands, coordination), psychologic state (e.g., cognition), affordability, convenience, and administration time and preference.

Poor adherence with medication therapy is a major challenge in the long-term management of chronic asthma. Lack of adherence often occurs when the patient is symptom free and does not use the long-term therapy (e.g., ICS) regularly because no immediate benefit is felt. The patient does not realize that ICSs are needed to treat the ongoing inflammatory process.

Explain the importance and purpose of taking the long-term therapy regularly, emphasizing that maximum improvement may take 1 week or longer. Tell the patient that without regular use, swelling in the airways may progress and asthma will likely worsen over time. Collaborate with social services to help lower income patients obtain medications.

Make sure that patients understand exactly how to use their inhaler device (Fig. 28.7). Give them printed instructions. At every clinic visit or hospitalization, reassess the patient's inhaler technique. If package inserts are available, you can review them before teaching the patient.

❖ NURSING MANAGEMENT: ASTHMA

◆ Nursing Assessment

If a patient is not in acute distress, obtain a detailed health history, including information about triggers and what has helped alleviate asthma attacks in the past. Subjective and objective data that should be obtained from a patient with asthma are outlined in Table 28.11.

TABLE 28.11 Nursing Assessment

Asthma

Subjective Data

Important Health Information

Past health history: Allergic rhinitis, sinusitis, or skin allergies. Previous asthma attack and hospitalization or intubation. Symptoms worsened by triggers in the environment. GERD. Occupational exposure to chemical irritants (e.g., paints, dust)

Medications: Adherence to medication, inhaler technique. Use of antibiotics. Pattern and amount of short-acting β_2-adrenergic agonist used per week. Medications that may trigger an attack in susceptible persons, such as aspirin, NSAIDs, β-adrenergic blockers

Functional Health Patterns

Health perception–health management: Family history of allergies or asthma. Recent URI or sinus infection

Activity-exercise: Fatigue, decreased or absent exercise tolerance. Dyspnea, cough (especially at night), productive cough with yellow or green sputum or sticky sputum. Chest tightness, feelings of suffocation, air hunger, talking in short sentences or words or phrases, sitting upright to breathe

Sleep-rest: Awakened from sleep because of cough or breathing difficulties, insomnia

Coping–stress tolerance: Emotional distress, stress in work environment or home

Objective Data

General

Restlessness or exhaustion, confusion, upright or forward-leaning body position

Integumentary

Diaphoresis, cyanosis (circumoral, nail bed), eczema

Respiratory

Nasal discharge, nasal polyps, mucosal swelling. Crackles, decreased or absent breath sounds, and wheezes (inspiratory, expiratory, or both) on auscultation. Hyperresonance on percussion. Sputum (thick, white, tenacious), ↑ work of breathing with use of accessory muscles. Intercostal and supraclavicular retractions. Tachypnea with hyperventilation. Prolonged expiration

Cardiovascular

Tachycardia, pulsus paradoxus, jugular venous distention, hypertension or hypotension, premature ventricular contractions

Possible Diagnostic Findings

Abnormal ABGs during attacks, ↓ O_2 saturation, serum and sputum eosinophilia, ↑ serum IgE, positive skin tests for allergens, chest x-ray showing hyperinflation with attacks, abnormal pulmonary function tests showing ↓ flow rates; FVC, FEV_1, PEFR, and FEV_1/FVC ratio that improve between attacks and with bronchodilators

◆ Nursing Diagnoses

Nursing diagnoses for the patient with asthma may include:
- Impaired breathing
- Activity intolerance
- Anxiety
- Lack of knowledge

Additional information on nursing diagnoses and interventions is presented in eNursing Care Plan 28.1 on the website for this chapter.

◆ Planning

The overall goals are that the patient with asthma will achieve asthma control, as evidenced by (1) minimal symptoms during the day and night, (2) acceptable activity levels (including exercise), (3) maintaining greater than 80% of personal best PEFR, (4) few or no adverse effects of therapy, (5) no acute attacks of asthma, and (6) adequate knowledge to carry out the plan of care.

◆ Nursing Implementation

◆ Health Promotion.
Your role in preventing asthma attacks or decreasing their severity focuses primarily on teaching both the patient and caregiver. Teach the patient to identify and avoid known personal triggers for asthma (e.g., cigarette smoke, pet dander) and irritants (e.g., cold air, aspirin, foods, cats, indoor air pollution) (Table 28.1). Washing bedclothes in hot water or cooler water with detergent and bleach has some effect on allergen levels. Avoiding furred animals is suggested, but pet allergens are impossible to avoid. Pet allergens can be found in many public areas for months even after removal of the animal. Many people are allergic to cockroach remains and the dried droppings, so measures to avoid or control cockroaches are partly effective in removing allergens.

When cold air cannot be avoided, dressing properly with scarves or using a mask helps reduce the risk for an asthma attack. Aspirin and NSAIDs should be avoided if they are known to trigger an attack. Many OTC drugs contain aspirin. Teach the patient to read the labels carefully. Nonselective β-blockers (e.g., propranolol [Inderal]) are contraindicated because they inhibit bronchodilation. Selective β-blockers (e.g., atenolol [Tenormin]) should be used with caution. Desensitization (immunotherapy) may be partially effective in decreasing the patient's sensitivity to known allergens (see Chapter 13).

Prompt diagnosis and treatment of URIs and sinusitis may prevent an asthma attack. If occupational irritants are involved, the patient may need to consider changing jobs. Those who are obese often find that weight loss improves asthma control. Encourage the patient to maintain a fluid intake of 2 to 3 L/day, adequate nutrition, and plenty of rest. If exercise is planned or if the patient has asthma only with exercise, the HCP can suggest a medication regimen for pretreatment or long-term control of symptoms to prevent bronchospasm.

◆ Acute Care.
A major goal in asthma care is to maximize the patient's ability to safely manage acute asthma using an asthma action plan developed in conjunction with the HCP (Fig. 28.9). Action plans are important for all people with asthma, especially those who have frequent, acute attacks. They are based on the patient's asthma symptoms and PEFR. The action plan dictates what symptoms or PEFR necessitates a change in asthma management to gain control.

The patient can take 2 to 4 puffs of a SABA every 20 minutes, up to 3 times, as a rescue plan. Depending on the response (e.g., alleviation of symptoms, improved PEFR), continued SABA use and/or oral corticosteroids may be a part of the home management plan. If symptoms persist or if the patient's PEFR is less than 50% of the personal best, the HCP or emergency medical services must be contacted at once.

When the patient is in the health care agency with an acute attack, it is important to monitor the patient's respiratory and cardiovascular systems. This includes (1) monitoring heart rate and rhythm, respiratory rate and WOB, and BP; (2) monitoring pulse oximetry, PEFR, and ABGs; and (3) auscultating lung sounds.

Asthma Action Plan

For:_____ Doctor:_____ Date:_____

Doctor's Phone Number _____ Hospital/Emergency Department Phone Number _____

GREEN ZONE

Doing Well

- No cough, wheeze, chest tightness, or shortness of breath during the day or night
- Can do usual activities

And, if a peak flow meter is used,

Peak flow: more than _____ (80 percent or more of my best peak flow)

My best peak flow is: _____

Take these long-term control medicines each day (include an antiinflammatory).

Medicine	How much to take	When to take it
_____	_____	_____
_____	_____	_____
_____	_____	_____
_____	_____	_____

Before exercise	❑ _____	❑ 2 or ❑ 4 puffs _____	5 minutes before exercise

YELLOW ZONE

Asthma Is Getting Worse

- Cough, wheeze, chest tightness, or shortness of breath, or
- Waking at night due to asthma, or
- Can do some, but not all, usual activities

-Or-

Peak flow: _____ to _____ (50 to 79 percent of my best peak flow)

First ➡ **Add: quick-relief medicine—and keep taking your GREEN ZONE medicine.**

_____ (short-acting beta₂-agonist) ❑ 2 or ❑ 4 puffs, every 20 minutes for up to 1 hour

❑ Nebulizer, once

Second ➡ **If your symptoms (and peak flow, if used) return to GREEN ZONE after 1 hour of above treatment:**

❑ Continue monitoring to be sure you stay in the green zone.

-Or- _____

If your symptoms (and peak flow, if used) do not return to GREEN ZONE after 1 hour of above treatment:

❑ Take:_____ ❑ 2 or ❑ 4 puffs or ❑ Nebulizer
(short-acting beta₂-agonist)

❑ Add: _____ mg per day For _____(3–10) days
(oral steroid)

❑ Call the doctor ❑ before/ ❑ within _____ hours after taking the oral steroid.

RED ZONE

Medical Alert!

- Very short of breath, or
- Quick-relief medicines have not helped, or
- Cannot do usual activities, or
- Symptoms are same or get worse after 24 hours in Yellow Zone

-Or-

Peak flow: less than _____ (50 percent of my best peak flow)

Take this medicine:

❑ _____ ❑ 4 or ❑ 6 puffs or ❑ Nebulizer
(short-acting beta₂-agonist)

❑ _____ mg
(oral steroid)

Then call your doctor NOW. Go to the hospital or call an ambulance if:

- You are still in the red zone after 15 minutes AND
- You have not reached your doctor.

DANGER SIGNS

- Trouble walking and talking due to shortness of breath
- Lips or fingernails are blue

➡ ■ Take ❑ 4 or ❑ 6 puffs of your quick-relief medicine AND

■ Go to the hospital or call for an ambulance _____ NOW!
(phone)

FIG. 28.9 Asthma action plan. (Source: National Heart, Lung, and Blood Institute, Bethesda, MD.)

Give drugs as ordered. Louder wheezing may actually occur in airways that are responding to therapy as airflow increases. As improvement continues and airflow increases, breath sounds increase and wheezing decreases. The disappearance of most bronchospasm, resolution of edema and cellular infiltration of airway mucosa, and the elimination of viscous mucous plugs may take several days to improve. As a result, therapy must be continued even after clinical improvement. Always evaluate the patient's response to therapy.

An important nursing goal during an acute attack is to decrease the patient's anxiety and sense of panic. Position the patient comfortably (usually sitting, in semi- to high-Fowler's position) to maximize chest expansion. A calm, quiet, reassuring attitude may help the patient relax. A technique called "talking

TABLE 28.12 Patient Teaching

Pursed-Lip Breathing (PLB)

Teach the patient how to do PLB using the following guidelines:
1. Use PLB before, during, and after any activity causing you to be short of breath.
2. Inhale slowly and deeply through the nose.
3. Exhale slowly through pursed lips, as if whistling.
4. Relax your facial muscles without puffing your cheeks—like whistling—while you are exhaling.
5. Make breathing out (exhalation) 3 times as long as breathing in (inhalation).
6. The following activities can help you get the "feel" of PLB:
   - Blow through a straw in a glass of water with the intent of forming small bubbles.
   - Blow a lit candle enough to bend the flame without blowing it out.
   - Steadily blow a table-tennis ball across a table.
   - Blow a tissue held in the hand until it gently flaps.
7. Practice 8-10 repetitions of PLB 3 or 4 times a day.

down" can help the patient remain calm. In talking down, you gain eye contact with the patient. In a firm, calm voice, coach the patient to use pursed-lip breathing. Pursed-lip breathing keeps the airways open by maintaining positive pressure (Table 28.12). Stay with the patient until the respiratory rate has slowed.

When the acute attack subsides, provide rest and a quiet, calm environment. When the patient is less exhausted, can breathe easier, and beginning to recover, try to obtain a health history and do a physical assessment. If caregivers are present, they may be able to provide information about the patient's health history. This information is important in planning and implementing an individualized nursing care plan.

◆ **Ambulatory Care.** Control of symptoms can be achieved by teaching the patient about drug therapy and monitoring. Review the written asthma action plan. As part of the plan, the patient must measure PEFR at least daily. PEFR monitoring, when done correctly, is a reliable, objective measurement of asthma control (Table 28.13). Some patients may not perceive changes in their

TABLE 28.13 Patient Teaching

How to Use Your Peak Flow Meter

Include the following instructions when teaching the patient to use a peak flow meter:

Why Use a Peak Flow Meter?
- Peak flow meters are used to check your asthma the way that BP cuffs are used to check BP. A peak flow meter is a device that measures how well air moves out of your lungs.
- During an asthma episode, the airways of the lungs usually begin to narrow slowly. The peak flow meter may tell you if there is narrowing in the airways hours, sometimes even days, before you have any asthma symptoms.
- By taking your medicines early (before symptoms), you may be able to stop the episode quickly and avoid a severe asthma episode.
- The peak flow meter is used to help you and your HCP:
- Learn what makes your asthma worse.
- Decide if your treatment plan is working well.
- Decide when to add or stop medicine.
- Decide when to seek emergency care.

How to Use Your Peak Flow Meter
Complete the following 5 steps with your peak flow meter:
1. Move the indicator to the bottom of the numbered scale.
2. Stand up.
3. Take a deep breath, filling your lungs completely.
4. Place the mouthpiece in your mouth and close your lips around it. Do not put your tongue inside the hole.
5. Blow out as hard and fast as you can in a single blow.
   - Write down the number you get. But if you cough or make a mistake, do not write down the number. Perform the action again.
   - Repeat steps 1 through 5 two more times. Write down the best of the 3 blows in your asthma diary.

Find Your Personal Best Peak Flow Number
- Your personal best peak flow number is the highest peak flow number you can achieve over a 2-week period when your asthma is under good control. Good control is when you feel good and do not have any asthma symptoms.
- Each patient's asthma is different. Your best peak expiratory flow rate (PEFR) may be higher or lower than the peak flow of someone of your height, weight, and gender. This means that it is important for you to find your own personal best peak flow number, which is the basis for your treatment plan.

- To find your personal best peak flow number, take peak flow readings:
  - At least twice a day for 2-3 weeks, between 12 noon and 2 PM when your peak flow is the highest
  - 15 to 20 minutes after taking inhaled short-acting β_2-agonist (SABA) for quick relief
  - As instructed by your HCP

The Peak Flow Zone System
Once you know your personal best peak flow number, your HCP will put the peak flow numbers into zones that are set up like a traffic light. This will help you know what to do when your peak flow number changes. For example:

  Green Zone (more than __ L/min [80% of your personal best number]) signals good control. No asthma symptoms are present. Take your medicines as usual.

  Yellow Zone (between __ and __ L/min [50% to <80% of your personal best number]) signals caution. If you stay in the yellow zone after several measures of peak flow, take an inhaled SABA. If you continue to register peak flow readings in the yellow zone, your asthma may not be under good control. Ask your HCP if you need to change or increase your daily medicines.

  Red Zone (<__ L/min [<50% of your personal best number]) signals a medical alert. Take an inhaled SABA (quick-relief medicine) right away. Call your HCP and ask what to do or go directly to the ED.

Use the Diary to Keep Track of Your Peak Flow
- Record your personal best peak flow number and peak flow zones in your asthma diary.
- Measure your peak flow when you wake up, *before* taking medicine. Write down your peak flow number in the diary every day, or as instructed by your HCP.

Actions to Take When Peak Flow Numbers Change
- PEFR goes between __ and __ L/min (50% to <80% of personal best, yellow zone).
  ACTION: Take an inhaled SABA (quick-relief medicine) as prescribed by your HCP.
- PEFR increases ≥20% when measured before and after taking an inhaled SABA (quick-relief medicine).
  ACTION: Talk to your HCP about adding more medicine to control your asthma better (e.g., an antiinflammatory medication).

Source: Adapted from National Asthma Education and Prevention Program, National Heart, Lung, and Blood Institute: *Expert Panel Report 3: guidelines for the diagnosis and management of asthma*, NIH pub no 08-4051, Bethesda, Md, 2007, National Institutes of Health.

breathing and may have a significant decrease in lung function without any symptoms other than a change in PEFR.

If a patient's PEFR is within the green zone (usually 80% to 100% of the patient's personal best), the patient should remain on their usual medications. A PEFR within the yellow zone (usually 50% to 80% of personal best) indicates caution. A PEFR in the red zone (50% or less of personal best) indicates a serious problem. In other words, something is triggering the patient's asthma (e.g., viral infection).

Consequently, the written asthma action plan needs to clearly identify the step-up increase in medications during the acute phase of an infection. For example, the patient can use different strategies, such as using the SABA more often. Although it may happen, it is unusual for a patient's PEFR to drop from the green zone to the red zone quickly. Usually the patient has time to make changes in medications, avoid triggers, and notify the HCP. The dose is stepped down once the symptoms subside.

? CHECK YOUR PRACTICE

A 32-yr-old man is admitted to the ED for an acute attack of asthma. It is his third admission in the past 2 months. He had been watching his 6-yr-old son play soccer when his attack started. He says to you, "I am just not a good father. My son is going to think I am just a 'sicky.' I can't play sports . . . can't . . . even . . . watch him . . . without something happening."
* How would you respond to this man?

It is important to involve the patient's caregivers. They should know where to find the patient's medications. Teach them how to decrease the patient's anxiety if an asthma attack occurs. When the patient is stabilized or controlled, the caregiver can gently remind the patient about monitoring daily PEFR by asking questions, such as "What zone are you in?" or "How's your peak flow today?" A patient and caregiver teaching guide for the patient with asthma is shown in Table 28.14.

Good nutrition is important. Physical exercise (e.g., swimming, walking, stationary cycling) within the patient's limit of tolerance is beneficial. It may require pretreatment with a SABA. Uninterrupted sleep is an important goal. If patients with asthma report lack of sleep because of asthma symptoms, their asthma is not under good control and their plan should be reevaluated.

INFORMATICS IN PRACTICE
Home Monitoring of Asthma

* To reduce the rate of hospital readmissions, the patient with asthma may be discharged with a home monitoring system. These systems provide an easy and inexpensive approach to remotely monitoring lung function.
* Asthma home monitoring usually consists of PEFR, pulse oximetry, vital signs, and lung sounds. This information is sent to the HCP so that problems are quickly detected.
* As part of your discharge planning, help the patient obtain a system and review its use.

Validated questionnaires (e.g., Asthma Control Test [ACT] available at *www.asthmacontroltest.com*) can be used to assess quality-of-life in asthma patients. Patients with asthma may have frequent absences from school or work and psychological issues, such as stress, anxiety, despair, and depression.

TABLE 28.14 Patient & Caregiver Teaching
Asthma

Include the following information in a teaching plan for the patient with asthma and the caregiver. It will help to improve the patient's quality of life and promote lifestyle changes that support successful living with asthma.

What Is Asthma?
* Basic anatomy and physiology of lung
* Pathophysiology of asthma
* Relationship of pathophysiology to signs and symptoms
* Measurement and correlation of spirometry and peak expiratory flow rate

What Is Good Asthma Control?
* Personal ideas of good control
* Use Asthma Control Test available at www.asthmacontroltest.com

Obstacles to Asthma Treatment and Control
* Discuss with patient and caregiver about possible obstacles (e.g., denial, poor perception of asthma severity by patient)

Environmental and Trigger Control
* Identify triggers and preventive measures (use trigger diary)
* Avoiding allergens and other triggers
* Need to maintain good hydration

Medications
* Types (include mechanism of action)
* Use of preventive and maintenance (e.g., antiinflammatory) agents
* Write out medication list and schedule
* Asthma Action Plan (Fig. 28.9)
* Correct use of inhalers, spacer, and nebulizer

Pursed-Lip Breathing (Table 28.12)
Correct Use of Peak Flow Meter (Table 28.13)
Asthma Action Plan (Fig. 28.9)
* Peak flow zones
* Individualize asthma action plan with HCP and patient
* Early recognition of infection
* Building a partnership with your HCP
* Questions patients may have about asthma, but patient cannot reach the HCP

For more information, visit the American Lung Association website at *www.lung.org/lung-disease/asthma*.

An increased number of older adults have asthma. This is a special concern because they have more complicated health issues than younger patients with asthma. Issues that face older adults are hypertension, heart disease, costly medications, and difficulty accessing the health care system. Keep these factors in mind when implementing a management plan for older adults.

Disparities in socioeconomic status and access to proper health care, as well as cultural beliefs about asthma may be part of the reason blacks and Hispanics have higher rates of poorly controlled asthma. Seek to explore and eliminate any potential barriers to health care. Use culturally appropriate resources and educational material in languages other than English to help improve knowledge about asthma and asthma control for these persons.

Relaxation therapies (e.g., yoga, meditation, relaxation techniques, breathing techniques) may help a patient relax respiratory muscles and decrease the respiratory rate. (Chapter 6 discusses relaxation breathing and other relaxation strategies.)

A healthy emotional outlook is also important in preventing asthma attacks. Asthma support groups are available online and around the country.

◆ **Evaluation**

The expected outcomes are that the patient with asthma will
- Maintain patent airway with removal of excessive secretions
- Have normal (for the patient) breath sounds and respiratory rate
- Report decreased anxiety with increased control of breathing
- Correctly use medications
- Express confidence in ability to manage asthma

CHRONIC OBSTRUCTIVE PULMONARY DISEASE

Chronic obstructive pulmonary disease (COPD) is a preventable, treatable, but often progressive disease characterized by persistent airflow limitation. COPD is associated with an enhanced chronic inflammatory response in the airways and lungs, primarily caused by cigarette smoking and other noxious particles and gases. COPD exacerbations and other coexisting illnesses or co-morbidities may contribute to the overall severity of the disease.

Previous definitions of COPD have included such terms as *chronic bronchitis* and *emphysema*. Neither term is part of the current definition of COPD. **Chronic bronchitis** is the presence of cough and sputum production for at least 3 months in each of 2 consecutive years. It is an independent disease that may precede or follow the development of airflow limitation. **Emphysema**, the destruction of alveoli without fibrosis, describes one of several structural abnormalities in COPD patients.

An estimated 16 million adults in the United States have COPD.[12] The number of people with COPD is greatly underestimated because the disease is usually not diagnosed until it is moderately advanced. COPD is the third leading cause of death in the United States, causing more than 120,000 deaths each year.[12]

GENDER DIFFERENCES
COPD

Men
- COPD is more common in men.
- The number of men with COPD is not increasing.
- Have a poorer response to O_2 therapy compared with women.

Women
- The number of women with COPD is increasing.
- The increase is likely due to more women smoking and increased susceptibility (e.g., smaller lungs and airways).
- More women die from COPD than men.
- Women with COPD have a lower quality of life, more exacerbations, and increased dyspnea, compared with men.

Risk Factors for COPD

Many factors affect the development and progression of COPD. The following discussion addresses the most common risk factors.

Cigarette Smoking. The major risk factor for developing COPD is cigarette smoking. COPD affects about 20% of smokers.[13] COPD should be considered in any person who is over the age of 40 with a smoking history of 10 or more pack-years.

TABLE 28.15 Effects of Tobacco Smoke on Respiratory System

Area of Defect	Acute Effects	Long-Term Effects
Respiratory mucosa		
• Nasopharyngeal	↓ Sense of smell	Cancer
• Tongue	↓ Sense of taste	Cancer
• Vocal cords	Hoarseness	Chronic cough, cancer
• Bronchus and bronchioles	Bronchospasm, cough	Chronic bronchitis, asthma, cancer
Cilia	Paralysis, sputum accumulation, cough	Chronic bronchitis, cancer
Mucous glands	↑ Secretions, ↑ cough	Hyperplasia and hypertrophy of glands, chronic bronchitis
Alveolar macrophages	↓ Function	↑ Incidence of infection
Elastin and collagen fibers	↑ Destruction by proteases ↓ Function of antiproteases (α_1-antitrypsin) ↓ Synthesis and repair of elastin	Emphysema

Cigarette smoke has several direct effects on the respiratory tract (Table 28.15). The irritating effect of smoke causes hyperplasia of cells, including goblet cells, thereby increasing mucus production. Hyperplasia reduces airway diameter and makes it harder to clear secretions. Smoking reduces the ciliary activity and may cause actual loss of cilia. Smoking causes abnormal dilation of the distal air space with destruction of alveolar walls. Many cells develop large, atypical nuclei, which are considered a precancerous condition. Smoking causes chronic, enhanced inflammation of various parts of the lung with structural changes and repair (called *remodeling*). The reasons for the inflammatory response are not clearly understood. Genetics may be involved since patients who have never smoked can develop COPD.

Cigarette smoking causes oxidative stress and an imbalance between proteases that break down connective tissue in the lung and antiproteases that protect the lungs. These changes increase with more severe disease and persist even after the patient has stopped smoking. (See Chapter 10 for more details about cigarette smoking.)

Passive smoking is the exposure of nonsmokers to cigarette smoke, also known as *environmental tobacco smoke* (ETS) or secondhand smoke. In adults, ETS is associated with decreased pulmonary function, increased respiratory symptoms, and severe lower respiratory tract infections (e.g., pneumonia). ETS is associated with increased risk for nasal sinus cancer and lung cancer.

Infection. Infections are a risk factor for developing COPD. Severe recurring respiratory tract infections in childhood have been associated with reduced lung function and increased respiratory symptoms in adulthood. It is unclear whether the development of COPD is related to recurrent infections in adults. People who smoke and have human immunodeficiency virus (HIV) infection have an accelerated development of COPD.[14] Tuberculosis is also a risk factor for COPD development.[15]

Asthma. Patients with COPD may have asthma. Asthma may be a risk factor for the development of COPD. There is a considerable pathologic and functional overlap between these disorders (Table 28.4), particularly among older adults, who may have components of both diseases. We call this *asthma-COPD overlap syndrome*.[3]

Air Pollution. High levels of urban air pollution are harmful to people with existing lung disease. However, the effect of outdoor air pollution as a risk factor for the development of COPD is unclear. Another risk factor is exposure to coal and other biomass fuels that are used for indoor heating and cooking. Many people who have never smoked have significant risk because of cooking with these fuels in poorly ventilated areas.

Occupational Chemicals and Dusts. If a person has intense or prolonged exposure to various dusts, vapors, irritants, or fumes in the workplace, symptoms of lung impairment consistent with COPD can develop. If a person has occupational exposure and smokes, the risk for COPD increases.

Aging. Although aging is often considered a risk factor for COPD, the evidence is unclear. Does the aging process lead to COPD, or is COPD a result of the cumulative exposures that occur over a lifetime? Normal aging results in loss of elastic recoil, stiffening of the chest wall, and decrease in exercise tolerance. The lungs gradually lose their elastic recoil. The thoracic cage becomes stiff and rigid, and the ribs are less mobile. The shape of the rib cage gradually changes because of the increased residual volume (RV), causing it to enlarge and become more rounded. Decreased chest compliance and elastic recoil of the lungs caused by aging affect the mechanical aspects of ventilation and increase the WOB. The number of functional alveoli decrease as peripheral airways lose supporting tissues. Over time, the surface area for gas exchange decreases, and the PaO_2 decreases. Changes in the elasticity of the lungs reduce the ventilatory reserve. These changes are similar to those seen in the patient with COPD.

Genetics. An intriguing question is why some smokers develop COPD and others do not. The fact that a small number of smokers get COPD strongly suggests genetic factors play a major role in who develops COPD. Because of the genetic-environmental interaction, 2 people may have the same smoking history, but only 1 develops COPD. To date, only 1 genetic factor has been clearly identified.

Alpha-1 Antitrypsin Deficiency (AATD). Alpha-1(α1) antitrypsin deficiency (AATD) is an autosomal recessive disorder that may affect the lungs or liver. AATD is a genetic risk factor for COPD.[16] α1-Antitrypsin (AAT) is a serum protein made by the liver and normally found in the lungs. The main function of AAT, an α_1-protease inhibitor, is to protect normal lung tissue from attack by proteases during inflammation related to smoking and infections. Severe AATD leads to premature bullous emphysema in the lungs. About 3% of all people diagnosed with COPD may have undetected AAT deficiency. Smoking hastens the disease process in these patients.

Pathophysiology

COPD is characterized by chronic inflammation of the airways, lung parenchyma (respiratory bronchioles and alveoli), and pulmonary blood vessels (Fig. 28.10). The pathogenesis of COPD is complex and involves many mechanisms. The defining feature of COPD is airflow limitation not fully reversible during forced exhalation. This is caused primarily by loss of elastic recoil and airflow obstruction, attributable to mucus hypersecretion, mucosal edema, and bronchospasm.

🧬 GENETICS IN CLINICAL PRACTICE

α_1-Antitrypsin Deficiency (AATD)

Genetic Basis
- Autosomal recessive disorder.
- Mutations in *SERPINA1* gene (found on chromosome 14) cause AAT deficiency.
- Gene provides instructions for the liver to make the protein AAT, which protects the lungs and liver from powerful proteolytic enzymes.
- Without enough functional AAT, proteolytic enzymes destroy alveoli and cause lung disease.

Incidence
- Occurs in 1 in 1700 to 3500 live births in the United States
- People of northern European descent most affected

Genetic Testing
- DNA testing is available.
- Screening of siblings is useful
- Serum assay is available to measure the amount of AAT

Clinical Implications
- AAT deficiency can cause lung and liver disease.
- Onset of disease is between ages 20 and 40 yrs.
- Treatment includes AAT replacement therapy.
- Disease predisposes to early-onset emphysema.

As the disease progresses, abnormalities in airflow limitation, air trapping, and gas exchange worsen. In severe COPD, pulmonary hypertension and systemic manifestations occur. COPD has an uneven distribution of pathologic changes. Severely impaired and/or destroyed areas of lung tissue exist alongside areas of relatively normal lung.

The inflammatory process most often starts with inhalation of noxious particles and gases (e.g., cigarette smoke). The abnormal inflammatory process causes tissue destruction and disrupts the normal defense mechanisms and repair process of the lung. We do not clearly understand the mechanisms for the enhanced inflammatory response. It may be genetically determined.

The predominant inflammatory cells in COPD are neutrophils, macrophages, and lymphocytes. This pattern of inflammatory cells is different from that in asthma, in which eosinophils, mast cells, neutrophils, lymphocytes, and macrophages are the main culprits. Inflammatory cells attract other inflammatory mediators (e.g., leukotrienes) and proinflammatory cytokines (e.g., tumor necrosis factor).

The inflammatory process may be magnified by oxidants, which are made by cigarette smoke and other inhaled particles and released from the inflammatory cells. Oxidants adversely affect the lungs as they inactivate antiproteases (which prevent the natural destruction of the lungs), stimulate mucus secretion, and increase fluid in the lungs. The result of the inflammatory process is structural changes in the lungs.

After the inhalation of oxidants in tobacco or air pollution, the activity of proteases (which break down the connective tissue of the lungs) increases and the antiproteases (which protect against the breakdown) are inhibited. Therefore the natural balance of protease/antiprotease is tipped in favor of destruction of the alveoli and loss of the lungs' elastic recoil.

Inability to expire air is a main characteristic of COPD. The main site of the airflow limitation is in the smaller airways. As the peripheral airways become obstructed, air is progressively

PATHOPHYSIOLOGY MAP

FIG. 28.10 Pathophysiology of chronic obstructive pulmonary disease *(COPD)*.

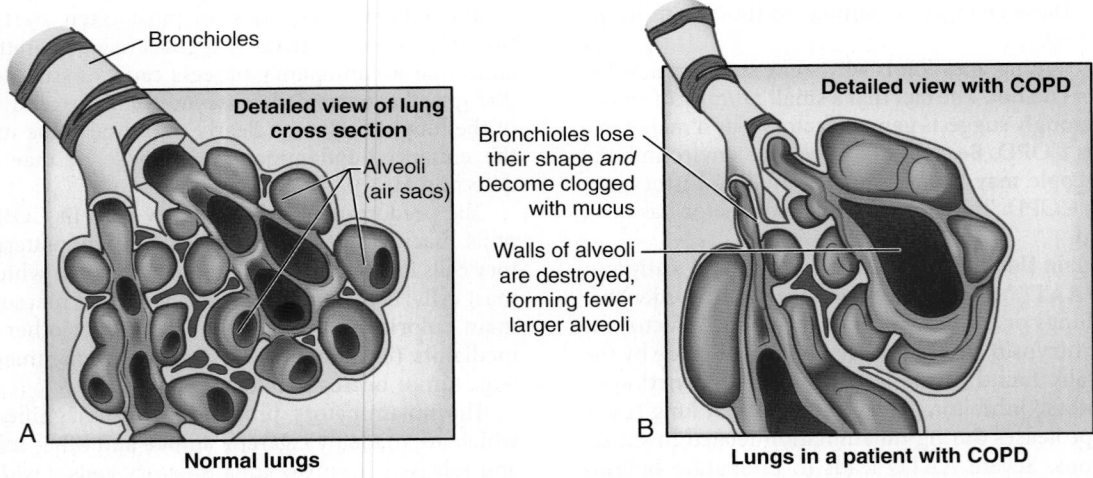

FIG. 28.11 A, Normal lungs showing bronchioles and alveoli. B, Changes in the bronchioles and alveoli in the lungs of a patient with chronic obstructive pulmonary disease *(COPD)*.

trapped during expiration. The volume of residual air becomes greatly increased in severe COPD as alveolar attachments (similar to rubber bands) to small airways are destroyed. As air is trapped in the lungs, the chest hyperexpands and becomes barrel shaped, because the respiratory muscles are not able to function effectively. Functional residual capacity (FRC) is increased. The residual air, combined with the loss of elastic recoil, makes passive expiration of air difficult. The patient is now trying to breathe in when the lungs are in an "overinflated" state. Thus, the patient becomes dyspneic with limited exercise capacity.

Typically, the patient does not have problems with hypoxemia at rest until late in the disease. Initially, hypoxemia may develop during exercise and the patient may benefit from supplemental O_2. Gas exchange abnormalities result in hypoxemia and hypercapnia (increased CO_2) as the disease worsens. As the air trapping increases, walls of alveoli are destroyed (Fig. 28.11). Bullae (large air spaces in the parenchyma) and blebs (air spaces next to pleurae) can form.

Bullae and blebs are not effective in gas exchange because they do not contain the capillary bed that normally surrounds each alveolus. Therefore a significant ventilation-perfusion (V/Q) mismatch and hypoxemia result. Peripheral airway obstruction also results in V/Q imbalance and, combined with respiratory muscle impairment, leads to CO_2 retention, particularly in severe forms of the disease.

Excess mucus production, resulting in a chronic productive cough, is a feature of persons with predominant chronic bronchitis. However, not all COPD patients have sputum production. When present, excess mucus production is multifactorial, including (1) an increased number of mucus-secreting goblet cells, (2) enlarged submucosal glands, (3) dysfunction of cilia, and (4) stimulation from inflammatory mediators.

In addition to lung disease, COPD is a systemic disease. Chronic inflammation is an underlying problem for many patients. Common systemic diseases, including osteoporosis, diabetes, and metabolic syndrome, have been seen with COPD. Cardiovascular diseases are common.

Pulmonary vascular changes resulting in mild to moderate pulmonary hypertension may occur late in the course of COPD. The small pulmonary arteries vasoconstrict due to hypoxia. As the disease advances, the structure of the pulmonary arteries changes, resulting in thickening of the vascular smooth muscle. Because of the loss of alveolar walls and the capillaries surrounding them, pressure in the pulmonary circulation increases. Pulmonary hypertension may progress and lead to hypertrophy of the right ventricle of the heart. The right ventricle dilates and may eventually lead to right-sided heart failure.

Classification of COPD

COPD can be classified as mild, moderate, severe, and very severe (Table 28.16). An FEV_1/FVC ratio of less than 70% establishes the diagnosis of COPD. The severity of obstruction (as shown by FEV_1) determines the stage of COPD. The management of COPD is based on the patient's symptoms, classification, and exacerbation history.

Clinical Manifestations

The manifestations of COPD typically develop slowly. A clinical diagnosis of COPD should be considered in any patient who has chronic cough or sputum production, dyspnea, and a history of exposure to risk factors for the disease (e.g., tobacco smoke, occupational dusts). It is sometimes hard to distinguish COPD from asthma, especially if the person has a history of cigarette smoking. However, some clinical features are different (Table 28.4).

A chronic intermittent cough, which is often the first symptom to develop, may be present as the disease becomes apparent to the patient. Patients often dismiss the cough as they associate it with smoking or environmental exposures. The cough may be productive. Significant airflow limitation may exist without cough or sputum. Typically, dyspnea is progressive, usually occurs with exertion, and is present every day.

Patients may report chest heaviness, not being able to take a deep breath, gasping, increased effort to breathe, and air hunger. Patients tend to ignore symptoms and rationalize that "I'm getting older" or "I'm out of shape." They change behaviors to avoid dyspnea, such as taking the elevator instead of the stairs. Patients will seek out medical care only when dyspnea is severe or when shortness of breath significantly impairs their ability to complete ADLs.

In late stages of COPD, dyspnea may be present at rest. As more alveoli become overdistended, increasing amounts of air

TABLE 28.16 Classification of COPD Severity*

Classification is based on postbronchodilator FEV_1

Classification	Level of Severity	FEV_1 Results
GOLD 1	Mild	FEV_1 ≥80% predicted
GOLD 2	Moderate	FEV_1 50%–80% predicted
GOLD 3	Severe	FEV_1 30%–50% predicted
GOLD 4	Very severe	FEV_1 <30% predicted

Adapted from Global Initiative for COPD: 2018 Global strategy for prevention, diagnosis, and management of COPD. Retrieved from *www.goldcopd.org*.
*A diagnosis of COPD is made when a patient has a FEV_1/FVC <70%.

are trapped. This causes the diaphragm to flatten, and the patient must work harder to breathe. Effective abdominal breathing is decreased because of the flattened diaphragm from overinflated lungs. The patient becomes more of a chest breather, relying on the intercostal and accessory muscles. However, chest breathing is not particularly efficient, especially over long periods.

Wheezing and chest tightness may be present but may vary by time of the day or from day to day, especially in patients with more severe disease. Chest tightness, which often follows activity, may feel similar to muscle contractions.

The person with advanced COPD often has fatigue, weight loss, and anorexia. Even with adequate caloric intake, the patient may still lose weight. Fatigue is a highly prevalent symptom that affects the patient's ADLs. During physical examination, a prolonged expiratory phase is observed. Decreased breath sounds and/or wheezes are auscultated in all lung fields. Because the anteroposterior diameter of the chest is increased ("barrel chest") from the chronic air trapping, the patient may need to breathe louder than normal for breath sounds to be heard with a stethoscope. The patient may sit upright with arms supported on a fixed surface, such as an overbed table (*tripod position*). The patient may naturally purse lips on expiration (pursed-lip breathing) and use accessory muscles, such as those in the neck, to aid with inspiration. Edema in the ankles may be the only clue to right-sided heart involvement (cor pulmonale).

Over time, hypoxemia (PaO_2 less than 60 mm Hg or O_2 saturation less than 88% on room air) may develop with hypercapnia ($PaCO_2$ over 45 mm Hg). The bluish-red color of the skin results from polycythemia and cyanosis. Polycythemia develops from increased production of red blood cells as the body tries to compensate for chronic hypoxemia. Hemoglobin concentrations may reach 20 g/dL (200 g/L) or more. However, the person may have lowered hemoglobin and hematocrit because of chronic anemia.

Complications

Primary complications that can occur in patients with COPD include pulmonary hypertension, cor pulmonale, acute exacerbations, and acute respiratory failure.

Pulmonary Hypertension and Cor Pulmonale. Cor pulmonale results from pulmonary hypertension, which is caused by diseases affecting the lungs or pulmonary blood vessels (Fig. 28.12). It is a late manifestation of COPD. Once the patient develops cor pulmonale, the prognosis worsens. Not all patients with COPD develop cor pulmonale.

PATHOPHYSIOLOGY MAP

FIG. 28.12 Mechanisms involved in the pathophysiology of pulmonary hypertension and cor pulmonale from COPD.

In COPD, pulmonary hypertension is caused primarily by constriction of the pulmonary vessels in response to alveolar hypoxia. Chronic hypoxia stimulates erythropoiesis, which causes polycythemia. This results in increased viscosity of the blood. These patients have increased pulmonary vascular resistance, and, as a result, develop pulmonary hypertension.

Normally the right ventricle and pulmonary circulatory system are low-pressure systems compared with the left ventricle and systemic circulation. When pulmonary hypertension (pressure within the lungs increases), the pressures on the right side of the heart must increase to push blood into the lungs. Eventually, because the pressure in the lungs is so high, right-sided heart failure develops.

Dyspnea is the most common symptom of chronic cor pulmonale. Lung sounds are normal, or crackles may be heard in the bases of the lungs bilaterally. Heart sound changes may include the presence of S_3 and S_4 and systolic murmurs.[17] Other manifestations of right-sided heart failure may develop. These include distended neck veins, hepatomegaly with right upper quadrant tenderness, peripheral edema, and weight gain.

Typically, the patient has large pulmonary vessels on chest x-ray and increased pressure on right-sided heart catheterization. Echocardiogram may show right-sided heart enlargement. b-Type natriuretic peptide (BNP) levels, which are used to diagnose heart failure, may be high. Normally BNP levels are used to distinguish cardiac from respiratory causes of dyspnea, but in cor pulmonale the cause of the heart failure is the lung disease.

Treatment of cor pulmonale is initially targeted at managing the underlying cause, including COPD. Continuous low-flow

long-term O_2 therapy is often part of care. Diuretics may be given if left heart failure or pulmonary edema are present but must be used with caution.[18] In some cases, decreases in fluid volume from diuresis can worsen heart function. Long-term anticoagulation therapy is started to help decrease the risk for venous thromboembolism (VTE). (Cor pulmonale is discussed in Chapter 27.)

Acute Exacerbations. An exacerbation of COPD is an acute event characterized by a worsening of the patient's respiratory symptoms. Exacerbations are signaled by an acute change in the patient's usual dyspnea, cough, and/or sputum (e.g., something different from the usual daily patterns). The main causes of exacerbations are bacterial or viral infections.[19] Exacerbations are common and increase in frequency (on average 1 or 2 per year) as the disease progresses. As the severity of COPD increases, COPD exacerbations are associated with poorer outcomes.

Assess patients for the classic manifestations of exacerbation, including increased dyspnea, increased sputum volume, or increased sputum purulence. They may have malaise, insomnia, fatigue, depression, confusion, decreased exercise tolerance, increased wheezing, or fever.

Exacerbations may be treated at home or in the hospital, depending on severity. The severity is determined by the patient's medical history leading up to the exacerbation, current symptoms, hemodynamic stability, O_2 requirements, WOB, ABGs, and the presence of coexisting diseases.

Your observations will help determine the severity of the exacerbation and whether the patient is treated as an inpatient or outpatient. Assess for new symptoms or worsening of usual symptoms. Be alert for signs of severity, such as use of accessory muscles, central cyanosis, edema in the lower extremities, unstable BP, right-sided heart failure, and altered alertness. Assess the patient's ABGs for respiratory acidosis and worsening hypoxemia, indicating an "acute-on-chronic" respiratory failure. Determine the number of exacerbations per year and if treatment occurred in the home or hospital. The presence of other co-morbid conditions often complicates exacerbations.

SABAs and oral systemic corticosteroids are the typical therapies for exacerbations. SABAs with short-acting anticholinergics are an option. Drug administration by MDI or nebulizer works equally well, although sicker patients often prefer the nebulizer. Antibiotics are given if the exacerbation was caused by a bacterial infection (e.g., pneumonia).

Therapies in the hospital are similar to home management, except supplemental O_2 therapy titrated by ABG measurement may be used. Attempts are made to use noninvasive mechanical methods (e.g., continuous positive airway pressure [CPAP] or bi-level positive airway pressure [Bi-PAP] to support ventilation rather than invasive ventilatory support [e.g., intubation and mechanical ventilation]). Small doses of diuretics maybe used for those with heart failure.

Teach the patient and caregiver early recognition of the 3 primary manifestations of exacerbations (increased dyspnea, increased sputum volume, or increased sputum purulence) to promote early treatment. This may prevent hospitalization and possible acute respiratory failure.

Acute Respiratory Failure. Patients with severe COPD who have severe exacerbations are at risk for acute respiratory failure. All too often, COPD patients wait too long to contact their HCP when they first develop symptoms suggestive of an exacerbation. Similarly, suddenly stopping a bronchodilator or corticosteroid medication may cause respiratory failure. (Respiratory failure is discussed in Chapter 67.)

Diagnostic Studies

A history and physical examination are extremely important in a diagnostic workup. Spirometry confirms the diagnosis in those suspected of having COPD. Spirometry confirms the presence of airflow obstruction and determines the severity of COPD.

In spirometry, the patient receives a SABA. Post-bronchodilator values are compared with a normal reference value. A diagnosis of COPD is made when the FEV_1/FVC ratio is less than 70%.[20] The value of FEV_1 provides a guideline for the degree of severity of COPD. The lower the FEV_1, the more obstructed are the airways.

Other diagnostic studies that may be done are outlined in Table 28.17. Chest x-rays are not diagnostic but often show a flat diaphragm because of hyperinflated lungs. Patients often have exercise-induced hypoxemia. A physical or respiratory therapist may do a 6-minute walk test. Pulse oximetry readings are taken when the patient is walking and at rest. If values of O_2 saturation are 88% or lower when at rest and the patient is breathing room air, they qualify for supplemental O_2.

Validated questionnaires such as the COPD Assessment Test (CAT) (www.catestonline.org) and Clinical COPD Questionnaire (CCQ) (www.ccq.nl) are recommended for a comprehensive assessment of symptoms.

ABGs are usually monitored in patients hospitalized with acute COPD exacerbations. ABGs alone are not diagnostic of COPD but help identify the severity of the exacerbation by assessing abnormalities in oxygenation and ventilation. In early

TABLE 28.17 Interprofessional Care
Chronic Obstructive Pulmonary Disease (COPD)

Diagnostic Assessment
- History and physical examination
- Spirometry
- Chest x-ray
- Serum α_1-antitrypsin levels
- ABGs
- 6-Minute walk test
- COPD Assessment Test (CAT)* or Clinical COPD Questionnaire (CCQ)†

Management
- Cessation of cigarette smoking
- Drug therapies (Tables 28.7 and 28.18)
- Airway clearance techniques
- Breathing exercises and retraining
- Hydration of 2 to 3 L/day (if not contraindicated)
- Immunizations:
  - Influenza yearly
  - Pneumococcal vaccine
- Long-term O_2 (if indicated)
- Progressive plan of exercise, especially walking and upper body strengthening
- Pulmonary rehabilitation program
- Nutritional supplementation
- Treatment of complications
  - Cor pulmonale
  - Acute exacerbations
  - Acute respiratory failure
- Surgical therapy
  - Lung volume reduction
  - Bullectomy
  - Lung transplantation

*See www.catestonline.org.
†See www.ccq.nl.

stages, there may be a normal or only slightly decreased PaO_2 and a normal $PaCO_2$. In the later stages of COPD, typical findings are a low-normal pH, high-normal or above-normal $PaCO_2$, and high-normal bicarbonate (HCO_3^-). This may indicate either partially or fully compensated respiratory acidosis. The patient has chronically retained CO_2 and the kidneys have conserved HCO_3^- to increase the pH to within the normal range.

An ECG may be normal or show signs of right heart failure. An echocardiogram or (MUGA) (cardiac blood pool) scan (see Table 31.7) can be used to evaluate heart function. Sputum for culture and sensitivity may be done if an infection, such as pneumonia, is suspected.

Interprofessional Care

Most patients with COPD are treated as outpatients. They are hospitalized for an acute exacerbation of COPD or complications, such as pneumonia, heart failure, or acute respiratory failure.

Evaluate the patient's exposure to environmental or occupational irritants and determine ways to control or avoid them. For example, teach the patient to avoid, if possible, smoke-filled rooms and air pollutants. The patient with COPD is extremely susceptible to lung infections. The patient with COPD should receive influenza immunization yearly. The pneumococcal vaccine is recommended for all smokers ages 19 or older and all patients with COPD. Guidelines for pneumococcal vaccine are outlined in Table 27.5.

Smoking Cessation. Stopping cigarette smoking in any person with COPD at any level of severity is the most important intervention that can affect the natural progression of COPD. After a person stops smoking, the accelerated decline in pulmonary function found with smoking slows to almost nonsmoking levels. The sooner the smoker stops, the less pulmonary function is lost and the sooner the symptoms decrease, especially cough and sputum production. Smoking cessation is discussed in Chapter 10 and in Tables 10.4 to 10.6.

Drug Therapy. Drugs for COPD can reduce symptoms, increase exercise capacity, improve overall health, and reduce the number and severity of exacerbations. Like asthma, they are given in a stepwise fashion according to the level of airflow obstruction determined from spirometry (FEV_1) and symptoms. Medications are stepped up but usually not stepped down, as in asthma, because in COPD continual symptoms are present (Table 28.18). The inhaled route of medication is preferred and used on a regular or as-needed basis.

Bronchodilator drug therapy relaxes smooth muscles in the airway and improves the ventilation of the lungs, thus reducing the degree of breathlessness. Patients with COPD do not respond as dramatically to bronchodilator therapy as those with asthma. However, bronchodilator therapy reduces dyspnea and increases FEV_1.

Bronchodilator drugs commonly used are β_2-adrenergic agonists, anticholinergic agents, and, to a much lesser extent, methylxanthines (Table 28.7). The choice of bronchodilator depends on the patient's response. They are given on a scheduled or as-needed basis. When the patient has mild COPD or fewer symptoms, a SABA is used. Albuterol or ipratropium may be used alone, but combining bronchodilators improves their effect and decreases the risk for adverse effects. Albuterol and ipratropium can be nebulized together (DuoNeb) or delivered by inhalation spray (Combivent Respimat).

In the moderate stage of COPD (FEV_1 less than 60%), a LABA is often part of the medication treatment plan. Unlike asthma, they can be used in COPD as monotherapy. Salmeterol and formoterol are widely used LABAs. A SABA may still be used as a "rescue" for dyspnea.

In COPD patients with FEV_1 of less than 60%, regular treatment with ICS is often prescribed with a LABA. Examples of combinations of ICSs with LABAs are fluticasone/salmeterol (Advair) and budesonide/formoterol (Symbicort).

Inhaled long-acting anticholinergics, LABAs, and ICSs all reduce COPD exacerbations. However, in COPD, unlike asthma, ICSs are not used as monotherapy because of the concerns about side effects. Some patients with COPD are on triple therapy with Advair and tiotropium. Oral corticosteroids should not be used for long-term therapy in COPD but are effective for short-term use to treat acute exacerbations.

The use of long-acting theophylline in the treatment of COPD is controversial because it interacts with many drugs. A low dose of theophylline with an ICS may help a few patients with COPD who do not respond to other inhaled medications.

Roflumilast (Daliresp) is an oral medication used to decrease the frequency of exacerbations in patients with severe COPD and chronic bronchitis. This drug is a phosphodiesterase inhibitor. It is an antiinflammatory drug that suppresses the release of cytokines and other inflammatory mediators and inhibits the production of reactive O_2 radicals.

New drug delivery devices are becoming available at a rapid pace. One example is Respimat. It is an easy-to-use, hand-held device that provides a high deposition of drug to the lungs and low mouth and throat deposition. Respimat simplifies coordination between activation of the medication and inhalation without propellant. It is independent of inspiratory flow. Combivent and Spiriva Respimats are examples.

Surgical Therapy. Various surgical procedures are used to help manage severe COPD. However, it is important to remember that not all patients with severe COPD are candidates for surgery.

One type of surgery is *lung volume reduction surgery* (LVRS). The goal of LVRS is to reduce the size of the lungs by removing some of the diseased lung tissue, so that the remaining healthy lung tissue can perform better. Reducing the diseased lung tissue by about 30% results in decreased airway obstruction and increased room for the remaining normal alveoli (small air sacs at the end of each bronchiole) to expand and function.[21] Besides improving lung and chest wall mechanics, LVRS can allow the diaphragm to return to its normal shape. This allows the patient to breathe more efficiently.

Another type of surgical procedure is *bronchoscopic lung volume reduction surgery*. It involves placing 1-way valves, by bronchoscopy, in the airways leading to the diseased parts of the lung. By completely occluding a specific lobe of the lung, this collapses a certain segment of the lung and produces a result similar to LVRS.[22] Pneumothorax is a common complication. An a *bullectomy*, 1 or more very large bullae are removed. Removal of bullae help decrease WOB.

A lung transplant benefits certain patients with advanced COPD. Although single-lung transplant is the most commonly used technique because of a shortage of donors, bilateral transplantation can be done. (Lung transplantation is discussed in Chapter 27.)

Interprofessional Care: Respiratory Care

Oxygen Therapy. O_2 therapy is often used in the treatment of COPD and other problems associated with hypoxemia. O_2 is a colorless, odorless, tasteless gas that constitutes 21% of the atmosphere. Giving supplemental O_2 increases the partial pressure of O_2 (PO_2) in inspired air. Used clinically, it is considered a prescribed medication. It is the only one that has been linked to improved survival of COPD patients.

TABLE 28.18　Drug Therapy

Medication Guidelines

The treatment guidelines are based on the FEV_1 results.

FEV_1 Results	Treatment Guidelines
FEV_1 60%–80% predicted (with respiratory symptoms)	Treatment with inhaled bronchodilators may be used
FEV_1 <60% predicted (with respiratory symptoms)	Treat with inhaled bronchodilators: anticholinergics or long-acting β_2-agonist
	OR
	Monotherapy with long-acting inhaled anticholinergics or long-acting β_2-agonist
	OR
	Combination therapy with long-acting inhaled anticholinergics, long-acting β_2-agonist, or inhaled corticosteroids

O_2 is usually given to treat hypoxemia caused by many other problems, such as shock, pneumonia, and pulmonary emboli. O_2 therapy must be tailored to meet each patient's unique circumstances and physiologic needs. For most patients, the goal of O_2 therapy is to keep the SaO_2 greater than 90% during rest, sleep, and exertion or the PaO_2 greater than 60 mm Hg. These goals may be modified for the patient with moderate to severe COPD. For example, based upon the patient's condition, the HCP may accept an SaO_2 an PaO_2 greater than 88%.

Methods of Administration. There are various methods of administering O_2 (Table 28.19). The device used depends on the patient's underlying condition, fraction of inspired O_2 (FIO_2) needed by the patient and delivered by the device, humidification requirements, patient cooperation, comfort, cost, and financial resources.

O_2 delivery systems are classified as low- or high-flow systems. Most methods of O_2 delivery are low-flow devices that provide O_2 in concentrations that vary with the person's respiratory pattern. Low-flow devices pull in a proportion of room air. This makes the range of FIO_2 known, but the exact FIO_2 hard to determine. Nasal prongs and non-rebreather masks are examples of low-flow O_2 systems. High-flow O_2 delivery devices deliver fixed concentrations of O_2 (e.g., 28%, 35%) independent of the patient's respiratory pattern. The Venturi mask and mechanical ventilators are examples of a high-flow O_2 delivery systems.

Humidification and Nebulization. O_2 obtained from O_2 cylinders or wall systems is dry. Dry O_2 has an irritating effect on mucous membranes and dries secretions. Therefore it is important that O_2 be humidified. Humidification involves the addition of sterile distilled water, attached to the O_2 delivery device, to prevent breathing dry air. For example, a common device used for humidification when the patient has a cannula or a mask is a small plastic jar filled with distilled water called a *bubble-through humidifier.* It is attached to the O_2 source by a flowmeter.

Complications of Oxygen Therapy

Combustion. O_2 supports combustion and increases the rate of burning, so it is important to prohibit smoking or have open flames in the area in which O_2 is being used. A "No Smoking" sign should be prominently displayed on the patient's door. Caution the patient against smoking cigarettes with an O_2 cannula in place as it can easily ignite and cause significant burns and life-threatening airway issues.

CO_2 narcosis. Chemoreceptors in the respiratory center that control the drive to breathe respond to CO_2 and O_2. Normally, an increase in CO_2 in the blood is a major stimulant of the respiratory center. Over time, some COPD patients with hypercapnia develop a tolerance for high CO_2 levels (the respiratory center loses its sensitivity to high CO_2 levels). For these people, a major "drive" to breathe is hypoxemia. As a result, there is concern about the dangers of giving O_2 to COPD patients and reducing their drive to breathe.

However, the "hypoxic drive" is complex and involves other factors, including ventilation and perfusion. Plus, not all patients with COPD retain CO_2. So, the thought is that it is better to give O_2 to a patient who needs it because the danger of not giving O_2 to a patient far outweighs the risk.

Pulse oximetry and/or ABGs are used as a guide to determine the FIO_2 needed by each patient. Safe administration of O_2 can be achieved by gradually increasing the concentration of O_2 with close monitoring of both PaO_2 and $PaCO_2$. High-flow O_2

devices may be used to have tighter regulation of the FIO_2. Once again, the goal is a pulse O_2 saturation (SpO_2) of at least 90% or a PaO_2 of at least 60 mm Hg. Always remember to assess the patient's mental status and vital signs before starting O_2 therapy and frequently thereafter.

O_2 toxicity. Pulmonary O_2 toxicity may result from prolonged exposure to a high level of O_2 (PaO_2). High concentrations of O_2 can result in a severe inflammatory response because of O_2 free radical damage to alveolar-capillary membranes. This causes severe pulmonary edema, shunting of blood, and hypoxemia. Although it is rare, patients can develop acute respiratory distress syndrome (ARDS) (see Chapter 67).

Preventing O_2 toxicity is important. The amount of O_2 applied should be enough to maintain the PaO_2 within a normal or acceptable range for that patient. Monitor ABGs often to evaluate the effectiveness of therapy and guide the tapering of supplemental O_2. The most important rule you can follow is to provide FIO_2 at the lowest possible level, while still maintaining acceptable SaO_2 and PaO_2 values for every patient.

NURSING MANAGEMENT
Oxygen Administration

- Assess need for adjustments in O_2 flow rate.
- Evaluate response to O_2 therapy.
- Monitor patient for signs of adverse effects of O_2 therapy.
- Teach patient and caregivers about home O_2 use.
- Oversee UAP:
  - Use pulse oximetry to measure O_2 saturation and report level to RN.
  - Assist patient with adjustment of O_2 delivery devices (e.g., nasal cannula, face mask).
  - Report to RN any change in patient condition.
- Collaborate with respiratory therapist:
  - Assist RN with choosing optimal O_2 delivery device (e.g., nasal cannula or simple face mask).
  - Make sure equipment is clean and replaced as needed.
  - Check accuracy of O_2 delivery and assess need for adjustments in O_2 flow rate.
- Evaluate patient response to O_2 therapy.

Infection. Infection can be a complication of O_2 administration. Heated nebulizers present the highest risk. The constant use of humidity supports bacterial growth. The most common organism is *Pseudomonas aeruginosa.* Disposable equipment that operates as a closed system, such as the Ballard closed suctioning system, should be used. Each agency has a policy on the frequency of equipment changes based on the type of O_2 equipment used.

Oxygen Therapy at Home. Short-term home O_2 therapy (up to 30 days) may be needed for the patient in whom hypoxemia persists after discharge from the hospital. For example, a patient with underlying COPD who develops a serious respiratory tract infection may need continued O_2 therapy to treat hypoxemia for several weeks after discharge from the hospital. Home health care personnel can measure the patient's oxygenation status after an acute episode to determine if the O_2 is still needed.

Patients may receive O_2 only during exercise and/or sleep. Evaluate the need for O_2 during these periods with a 6-minute walk test or overnight oximetry. Improved survival occurs in patients with COPD who receive long-term O_2 therapy (LTOT)

TABLE 28.19 Methods of Oxygen Administration

Description	Nursing Interventions
Low-Flow Delivery Devices	

Nasal Cannula

<table>
<tr><td>

- Most commonly used device.
- O_2 delivered via plastic nasal prongs.
- Safe and simple method
- Allows some freedom of movement. Patient can eat, talk, or cough while wearing device.
- Used for a patient requiring low O_2 concentrations.
- Obtains O_2 concentrations of 24% (at 1 L/min) to 44% (at 6 L/min).

</td><td>

- Stabilize nasal cannula when caring for a restless patient.
- Amount of O_2 inhaled depends on room air and patient's breathing pattern.
- Most patients with COPD can tolerate 2 L/min via cannula.
- Assess patient's nares and ears for skin breakdown. May need to pad cannula where it sits on ears.
- If flow rates are >5 L/min, nasal membranes may dry and place patient at risk for nose bleeding.

</td></tr>
</table>

Simple Face Mask

<table>
<tr><td>

- Covers patient's nose and mouth.
- Used only for short periods, especially when transporting patients.
- Longer use is typically not tolerated because of tight seal and heat generated around nose and mouth from mask.
- Achieves O_2 concentrations of 35%–50% with flow rates of 6–12 L/min.
- Mask provides adequate humidification of inspired air.

</td><td>

- Wash and dry under mask q4h and PRN.
- Mask must fit snugly.
- Nasal cannula may be used while patient is eating.
- Watch for pressure necrosis at top of ears from elastic straps if patient wears for a longer time. Gauze or other padding may alleviate this problem.

</td></tr>
</table>

Partial and Non-Rebreather Masks

<table>
<tr><td>

- Used for short-term (24 hr) therapy for patients needing higher O_2 concentrations (60%–90% at 10–15 L/min).
- O_2 flows into reservoir bag and mask during inhalation.
- Bag allows patient to rebreathe about first third of exhaled air (rich in O_2) in conjunction with flowing O_2.
- Vents stay open on partial mask only. Some agencies prefer this over non-rebreather as a safety issue.

</td><td>

- O_2 flow rate must be sufficient to keep bag from deflating during inspiration to avoid CO_2 buildup and rebreathing of CO_2.
- If deflation occurs, increase flowrate on flowmeter on wall to keep bag inflated.
- Mask should fit snugly.
- With non-rebreather masks, make sure valves are open during expiration and closed during inhalation to prevent decrease in FIO_2 or build-up in CO_2.
- Monitor patient closely, since more advanced interventions may be needed such as CPAP, BiPAP, or intubation with mechanical ventilation.

</td></tr>
</table>

Oxygen-Conserving Cannula

<table>
<tr><td>

- Generally indicated for long-term O_2 therapy at home (e.g., pulmonary fibrosis, pulmonary hypertension).
- Looks like a "moustache" (Oxymizer) or "pendant" type.
- Cannula has a built-in reservoir that ↑ O_2 concentration and allows patient to use lower flow, usually 30%–50%, which increases comfort, lowers cost, and can be increased with activities.
- Can deliver O_2 up to 8 L/min.

</td><td>

- May cause necrosis over tops of ears. Tubing can be padded.
- Cannula cannot be cleaned. Manufacturer recommends changing cannula every week.
- More expensive than standard cannulas and may need evaluation with ABGs and oximetry to determine correct flow for patient.
- Cannula is highly visible.

</td></tr>
</table>

Pendant-type O_2-conserving cannula.

TABLE 28.19 Methods of Oxygen Administration

Description	Nursing Interventions

High-Flow Delivery Devices

Tracheostomy Collar

- Collar attaches to neck with elastic strap and can deliver humidity and O_2 via tracheostomy.
- Some O_2 concentration is lost into atmosphere because collar does not fit tightly.
- Venturi device can be attached to flowmeter and thus can deliver exact amounts of O_2 via collar.

- Secretions collect inside collar and around tracheostomy. Remove collar and clean at least q4hr and PRN to prevent aspiration of fluid and infection.
- Because condensation occurs in tubing, periodically drain tubing distal to tracheostomy.

Tracheostomy T-Piece

- Almost identical to tracheostomy collar, but it has a T-connector attached to an O_2 blender.
- T-piece allows an inline catheter (e.g., Ballard catheter) to be connected for suctioning.
- Tight fit allows better O_2 and humidity delivery than tracheostomy collar.

- Because T-piece connectors can disconnect easily, monitor closely.
- T-piece connector may pull on a patient's tracheostomy tube, causing irritation and potential tissue damage. Monitor this closely.

Venturi Mask

- Mask can deliver precise, high-flow rates of O_2.
- Lightweight plastic, cone-shaped mask Masks are available for delivery of 24%, 28%, 31%, 35%, 40%, and 50% O_2.
- Method is especially helpful for giving low, constant O_2 concentrations to patients with COPD.
- Adaptors can increase humidification.

- Entrainment device on mask must be changed to deliver higher concentrations of O_2.
- Air entrainment ports must not be occluded.
- Uncomfortable.
- Must be removed when patient eats.
- Patient can talk but voice may be muffled.

Adjustable nose clip

Opening Exhaled air

Venturi barrel

Room air

High-Flow Nasal Cannula

- Blends O_2 with compressed air to generate FIO_2 up to 1.0 at flow rate of up to 60 L/min.
- Active heated humidifier capable of providing 100% body humidity.
- Soft and flexible nasal prongs.
- More comfortable than mask.

- Nasal cannula must be smaller than 50% of nares to allow flow during exhalation and flush out end-expiratory CO_2.
- Patients can eat and drink with device in place.
- Well tolerated.
- Patient may describe feeling of always having to blow nose ("rainout") due to humidification.

BiPAP, Biphasic positive airway pressure; *CPAP*, continuous positive airway pressure; *FIO₂*, Fraction of inspired O_2.

FIG. 28.13 A portable liquid O_2 unit can be refilled from a liquid O_2 reservoir unit. (Courtesy Nellcor Puritan Bennett, Pleasanton, CA.)

TABLE 28.20 Patient & Caregiver Teaching
Home Oxygen Use

The company that provides the prescribed O_2 therapy equipment will teach the patient about equipment care. The following are some general instructions that you may include when teaching the patient and caregiver about the use of home O_2:

Decreasing Risk for Infection

- Brush teeth or use mouthwash several times a day.
- Wash nasal cannula (prongs) with a liquid soap and thoroughly rinse once or twice a week.
- Replace cannula every 2 to 4 weeks.
- If you have a cold, replace the cannula after your symptoms pass.
- Always remove secretions that are coughed out.
- If you use an O_2 concentrator, daily unplug the unit and wipe down the cabinet with a damp cloth and dry it.
- Ask the company providing the equipment how often to change the filter.

Safety Issues

- Post "No Smoking" warning signs outside the home.
- O_2 will not "blow up," but it will increase the rate of burning, since it is combustible.
- Do not allow smoking in the home, and do not smoke yourself while wearing O_2. Nasal cannulas and masks can catch fire and cause serious burns to face and airways.
- Do not use flammable liquids such as paint thinners, cleaning fluids, gasoline, kerosene, oil-based paints, or aerosol sprays while using O_2.
- Do not use blankets or fabrics that carry a static charge, such as wool or synthetics.
- Inform the staff at your electric company if you are using a concentrator. In case of a power failure, they will know the medical urgency of restoring your power.

Adapted from *www.YourLungHealth.org.*

(more than 15 hr/day) to treat hypoxemia. Periodic reevaluations for the patient who is using LTOT is needed. The patient is reevaluated every 30 to 90 days during the first year of therapy and annually after that if the patient stays stable.

Nasal cannulas, including O_2 conservation systems, deliver O_2 from a central source in the home. The source may be a liquid O_2 storage system, compressed O_2 in tanks or cylinders, or an O_2 concentrator or extractor, depending on the patient's activity level, environment, insurance coverage, and proximity to an O_2 supply company. To increase mobility in the home, the patient can use extension tubing (up to 50 ft) with some devices without adversely affecting the O_2 flow delivery. Small, portable systems, such as liquid O_2, may be used with the patient who is active outside the home.

Home O_2 systems are usually rented from a company that sends a respiratory therapist to the patient's home (Fig. 28.13). The therapist teaches the patient and caregiver how to use the O_2 system, how to care for it, and how to recognize when the supply is running low and must be reordered. A patient and caregiver teaching guide for the use of O_2 at home is shown in Table 28.20.

Encourage the patient who uses home O_2 to remain active and travel normally. If travel is by car, arrangements can be made for O_2 to be available at the destination point. O_2 supply companies can often help with these arrangements. If a patient wishes to travel by bus, train, or airplane, the patient should inform the appropriate people when reservations are made that O_2 will be needed for travel. If there is a potential for the patient to become hypoxic, O_2 needs for flying can be determined by a pulmonary function test, a 6-minute walk test, hypoxic challenge test, or predictive formula.[23] Portable O_2 concentrators are a ready source of renewable O_2 and can be available by recharging at home or with a direct current (DC) (e.g., auto) power supply. Several are approved by airlines for in-flight use. The patient should contact the airline to determine accommodations and policies for in-flight O_2.

Breathing Retraining. The patient with COPD often has dyspnea with an increased respiratory rate. The accessory muscles of breathing in the neck and upper part of the chest are used excessively to promote chest wall movement. These muscles are not designed for long-term use and as a result the patient has increased fatigue.

Two main types of breathing retraining exercises are (1) pursed-lip breathing and (2) diaphragmatic breathing. The purpose of **pursed-lip breathing (PLB)** is to prolong exhalation, which prevents bronchiolar collapse and air trapping. PLB is simple, easy to teach and learn, and it gives the patient more control over breathing, especially during exercise and periods of dyspnea (Table 28.12). Patients should be taught to use "just enough" positive pressure with pursed lips because excessive resistance may increase the WOB.

Diaphragmatic (abdominal) breathing focuses on using the diaphragm instead of the accessory muscles of the chest to (1) achieve maximum inhalation and (2) slow the respiratory rate. However, the use of diaphragmatic breathing in patients with COPD may increase the WOB and dyspnea. Patients with moderate to severe COPD with marked hyperinflation may be poor candidates for diaphragmatic breathing.

PLB slows the respiratory rate and is easier to learn than diaphragmatic breathing. In the setting of extreme acute dyspnea, it is most important to focus on helping the patient slow the respiratory rate by using the principles of PLB. Other techniques, such as a calm demeanor, positive encouragement, and guided imagery, may be used to reduce dyspnea.

Airway Clearance Techniques. Many patients with COPD or other conditions who retain secretions (e.g., CF, bronchiectasis) need help to adequately clear their airways. Airway clearance techniques (ACTs) loosen mucus and secretions so they can be cleared by coughing. There are a variety of techniques. These include effective coughing, chest physiotherapy, airway clearance devices, and high-frequency chest ventilation. Respiratory therapists, physical therapists, and nurses can perform these techniques.

ACTs are especially beneficial in patients who have a COPD exacerbation. They are often used in conjunction with other treatments. Typically, the patient receives bronchodilator therapy through an inhaled device (e.g., nebulization) before ACT. Then the ACT is used, followed by effective coughing (e.g., huff coughing).

Effective Coughing. Many patients with COPD have developed ineffective coughing patterns that do not adequately clear the airways of sputum. They fear developing bronchospasm, or spastic coughing, resulting in increased dyspnea. Although other techniques (e.g., chest physiotherapy) are used to loosen secretions and mucus, the patient must cough effectively to bring the secretions to the central airways to expectorate them.

Huff coughing is an effective forced expiratory technique that you can easily teach the patient. Before starting, ensure that the patient is breathing deeply from the diaphragm. Place the patient's hands on the lower lateral chest wall and then ask the patient to breathe deeply through the nose. You should feel the patient's hands move outward, which represents a breath from the diaphragm. Guidelines for effective huff coughing are shown in Table 28.21.

Chest Physiotherapy. Chest physiotherapy (CPT) is mainly used for patients with excessive bronchial secretions who have difficulty clearing them (e.g., CF, bronchiectasis). CPT consists of postural drainage, percussion, and vibration. CPT should be done by a properly trained person. Complications associated with improperly performed CPT include fractured ribs, bruising, hypoxemia, and discomfort. CPT may be stressful for some patients. Some may develop hypoxemia and bronchospasms.

Postural drainage. Postural drainage is the use of positioning techniques that drain secretions from specific segments of the lungs and bronchi into the trachea. The postural drainage positions used depend on the areas of lung that are involved. This is determined by patient assessment, chest x-rays, chest auscultation, and, when possible, patient preference. For example, some patients with left lower lobe involvement need postural drainage of only the affected region. A person with CF may need postural drainage of all segments.

The purpose of various positions in postural drainage is to drain each segment toward the larger airways. The patient who cannot tolerate a head-down position may use a side-lying position. Aerosolized bronchodilators and hydration therapy are usually given before postural drainage. The chosen postural drainage position is maintained for about 5 minutes during percussion and vibration. A common order is 2 to 4 times a day. In acute situations, postural drainage may be done as often as every 4 hours. Schedule the procedure at least 1 hour before meals or 3 hours after meals.

Beds are available that can rotate and percuss in various postural drainage positions. These are quite effective. Some positions for postural drainage (e.g., Trendelenburg) should not be used on the patient with traumatic brain injury, chest trauma, hemoptysis, heart disease, pulmonary embolus, or any other situation in which the patient's condition is not stable.

Percussion. *Percussion* is performed in the appropriate postural drainage position with the hands in a cuplike position, with the fingers and thumbs closed (Fig. 28.14). The cupped

TABLE 28.21 Patient & Caregiver Teaching

Effective Huff Coughing

When teaching effective huff coughing:
1. Help the patient assume a sitting position with head slightly flexed, shoulders relaxed, knees flexed, forearms supported by pillow, and, if possible, feet on the floor.

Then teach the patient to:
2. Inhale slowly through the mouth while breathing deeply from the diaphragm.
3. Hold the breath for 2 to 3 seconds.
4. Forcefully exhale quickly as if one is fogging up a mirror with one's breath (thus creating a "huff"). This moves the secretions to larger airways.
5. Repeat the "huff" 1 or 2 more times while refraining from a "regular" cough.
6. Cough when mucus is felt in the breathing tubes.
7. Rest for 5 to 10 regular breaths.
8. Repeat the huffs (3 to 5 cycles) until you feel you have cleared mucus or you become tired.

FIG. 28.14 Cupped-hand position for percussion. The hand should be cupped as though scooping up water.

hand should create an air pocket between the patient's chest and the hand. Both hands are cupped and used in an alternating rhythmic fashion. If it is done correctly, a hollow sound should be heard. The air-cushion impact facilitates the movement of thick mucus. For patient comfort, place a thin towel over the area to be percussed. The patient may choose to wear a T-shirt or hospital gown.

Vibration. *Vibration* is accomplished by tensing the hand and arm muscles repeatedly and pressing mildly with the flat of the hand on the affected area while the patient slowly exhales a deep breath. Vibrations promote movement of secretions to larger airways. Commercially available mechanical chest vibrators are available for hospital and home use.

Airway Clearance Devices. Various *airway clearance devices* are available to help mobilize secretions. They are easier to tolerate than CPT and take less time than CPT sessions. These devices include the Flutter, Acapella, and TheraPEP Therapy System. These devices use positive expiratory pressure (PEP). They may provide greater benefit to patients with COPD than other ACTs.

The Flutter mucus clearance device is a hand-held device. It is shaped like a small, fat pipe. It provides PEP treatment for patients with mucus-producing conditions. The Flutter has a mouthpiece, a high-density stainless-steel ball, and a cone that holds the ball. When the patient exhales through the Flutter, the steel ball moves, which causes oscillations (vibrations) in the airways and loosens mucus to allow improved expectoration. The patient must be upright as the angle at which the Flutter is held is critical.

The Acapella is another small hand-held device that combines the benefits of both PEP and airway vibrations to mobilize

FIG. 28.15 Acapella airway clearance device. (Courtesy Smiths Medical North America.)

secretions (Fig. 28.15). It can be used in any setting, since patients are free to sit, stand, or recline.

TheraPEP Therapy System can provide sustained PEP and while delivering aerosols so that the patient can inhale and exhale through it. TheraPEP has a mouthpiece attached to tubing connected to a small cylindric resistor and a pressure indicator. The pressure indicator gives visual feedback about the pressure that the patient needs to hold in an exhalation to receive the PEP.

High-Frequency Chest Wall Oscillation. High-frequency chest wall oscillation uses an inflatable vest (e.g., the Vest Airway system or the SmartVest) with hoses connected to a high-frequency pulse generator. The pulse generator delivers air to the vest, which vibrates the chest. The high-frequency airwaves dislodge mucus from the airways, mobilize the mucus, and move it toward larger airways. The vest can be used without the aid of another person. The unit weighs 23 to 30 lb, is quiet, comes in a suitcase, and is portable.

Nutritional Therapy. Many COPD patients in the advanced stages are underweight with loss of muscle mass and cachexia. Weight loss is a predictor of a poor prognosis and increased frequency of COPD exacerbations.[23] Malnutrition is multifactorial, including increased inflammatory mediators, increased metabolic rate due to the ventilatory effort, and lack of appetite. Other factors that contribute to malnutrition include taste changes caused by chronic mouth breathing, excessive sputum, fatigue, anxiety, depression, increased energy needs, numerous infections, and side effects of multiple medications.

To decrease dyspnea and conserve energy, the patient should rest for at least 30 minutes before eating and use a bronchodilator before meals. Teach the patient to avoid exercise and treatments for at least 1 hour before and after eating. If a patient desaturates while eating, supplemental O_2 by nasal cannula may be helpful. Encourage activity, such as walking or getting out of bed during the day, to stimulate appetite. Sensations of bloating and feeling full after consuming small amounts can be attributed to swallowing air while eating, side effects of medication (especially corticosteroids and theophylline), and the abnormal position of the diaphragm relative to the stomach in association with hyperinflation of the lungs.

Getting the patient to eat adequate amounts of nutritionally sound foods may be difficult even though well-balanced meals are available. Give the patient or those responsible for meal preparation printed information that can make mealtime easier and more nutritious (Table 28.22).

Underweight patients with COPD need extra protein and calories. They may need 25 to 45 kcal/kg body weight and more than 1.5 g of protein/kg body weight to maintain their weight. The patient with malnutrition may need up to 2.5 g of protein/kg of body weight to begin restoring muscle mass.

TABLE 28.22 Nutritional Therapy

Maximizing Food Intake in COPD

Sometimes it is hard for patients with COPD to consume adequate amounts of nutrients. Teach the patients to make mealtimes easier and more nutritious by increasing calories and protein without increasing the amount of food eaten.

- Eat high-calorie foods first.
- Limit liquids at mealtimes.
- Rest before meals.
- Try more frequent meals and snacks.
- Increase calories by adding margarine, butter, mayonnaise, sauces, gravies, and peanut butter to foods.
- Keep favorite foods and snacks on hand.
- Try cold foods, which can make you feel less full than hot foods.
- Keep ready-prepared meals available for times when you have increased shortness of breath.
- Eat larger meals when you are not as tired.
- Avoid foods that you know cause gas (e.g., cabbage, beans, cauliflower).
- Add skim milk powder (2 Tbsp) to regular milk (8 oz) to add protein and calories.
- Use milk or half-and-half instead of water when making soups, cereals, instant puddings, cocoa, or canned soups.
- Add grated cheese to sauces, vegetables, soups, and casseroles.
- Choose dessert recipes that contain egg (e.g., sponge cake, angel food cake, egg custard, bread pudding, rice pudding).

Source: Grodner M, Escott-Stump S, Dorner S: *Nutritional foundations and clinical applications: A nursing approach,* ed 6, St Louis, 2016, Mosby.

A diet high in calories and protein, moderate in carbohydrate, and moderate to high in fat is recommended. It can be divided into 5 or 6 small meals a day.[24] Offer high-protein, high-calorie nutritional supplements between meals. The dietitian is an excellent resource to determine what combination of nutrients and what supplements are best for the patient. (Nutritional supplements are discussed in Chapter 39.)

Gerontologic Considerations: COPD

Older adults have physiologic changes, including reduced lean body mass, decreased respiratory muscle strength, increased dyspnea, and lower exercise tolerance that may increase the burden of disease from COPD. This may lead to a higher incidence of acute exacerbations, which require hospitalization. Smoking cessation is a key intervention but can be hard to achieve.

COPD is often complicated by the presence of co-morbidities, such as heart disease, serious infections, osteoporosis, psychological problems (depression, anxiety), impaired cognition, and lung cancer. The presence of co-morbidities can make it harder for patients to cope with the stress of an exacerbation. Assessment of co-morbidities can aid in ensuring comprehensive and safe management, especially during an exacerbation.

Older adults may have difficulty handling the increased secretions during an acute COPD exacerbation. Drugs used to manage the acute exacerbation can complicate disease management and increase the chance of adverse events. Assess for potential drug-drug interactions, especially in patients being treated for coexisting co-morbidities.

Some drugs used to treat common disorders, such as hypertension, can worsen COPD symptoms. If possible, nonspecific β-blockers should be avoided since they can block the β_2 receptors in the airway and cause bronchoconstriction. Similarly, ACE inhibitors may cause a dry cough or worsen a present cough. In some circumstances, it may not always be possible to eliminate these drugs.

Older adults may not be adherent to drug therapies due to cognitive impairment and complexity of the multiple medications at different times of the day. An attempt to simplify the medication regimen with written large-font action plans can be an important intervention in patients with poor memory and vision impairment. Arthritis in the hands can hinder the person from using proper technique for MDIs. Review MDI technique during clinic visits and have DPI or spacers prescribed (if possible) because they are easier to use. Long-term use of ICSs has the potential of causing local and systemic side effects, including cataracts, glaucoma, and osteoporosis. Monitoring of ocular pressures, bone densitometry, and using the lowest possible ICS dose is recommended.

Older patients with COPD generally have impaired quality of life. An important role for us is to focus on ways to improve quality of life. Psychologic and emotional support becomes imperative to help patients achieve successful outcomes. In the later stages of COPD, palliative and hospice care can help manage symptoms and improve the quality of the rest of their lives, which is important.

❖ NURSING MANAGEMENT: COPD

◆ Nursing Assessment

Subjective and objective data that should be obtained from a person with COPD are outlined in Table 28.23.

◆ Nursing Diagnoses

The nursing diagnoses for the patient with COPD may include:
- Impaired breathing
- Activity intolerance
- Impaired nutritional status
- Difficulty coping

Additional information on nursing diagnoses and interventions is presented in eNursing Care Plan 28.2 available on the website for this chapter.

◆ Planning

The overall goals are that the patient with COPD will have (1) relief from symptoms, (2) ability to perform ADLs and improved exercise tolerance, (3) no complications related to COPD, (4) knowledge and ability to implement a long-term treatment plan, (5) prevention of disease progression, and (6) overall improved quality of life.

◆ Nursing Implementation

◆ **Health Promotion.** The incidence of COPD would decrease dramatically if people would not begin smoking or would stop smoking. Counseling the patient in smoking cessation is vital. It is the only way to slow the progression of COPD. As health care professionals, nurses who smoke should reevaluate their own smoking behavior and its relationship to their health. Nurses and other HCPs who smoke should be aware that the odor of smoke is obvious on their clothes and hair. It can be offensive or tempting to patients.

Early diagnosis and treatment of respiratory tract infections and exacerbations of COPD help prevent progression of the disease. People with COPD should avoid others who are sick, practice good hand-washing techniques, take drugs as prescribed, exercise regularly, and maintain a healthy weight. Avoiding or

controlling exposure to occupational and environmental pollutants and irritants is another preventive measure to maintain healthy lungs. Patients with COPD should have influenza and pneumococcal pneumonia vaccines.

Families with a history of COPD, as well as AATD, should be aware of the genetic nature of the disease. They may want to consider consulting a pulmonologist about regular spirometry

---

TABLE 28.23 Nursing Assessment
Chronic Obstructive Pulmonary Disease

Subjective Data

Important Health Information

Past health history: Long-term exposure to chemical pollutants, respiratory irritants, occupational fumes, dust; recurrent respiratory tract infections; previous hospitalizations

Medications: Use of O_2 and duration of O_2 use, bronchodilators, corticosteroids, antibiotics, anticholinergics, OTC drugs, illicit substances

Functional Health Patterns

Health perception–health management: Smoking (pack-years, including passive smoking, willingness to stop smoking, and previous attempts); what was smoked (e.g., cigarettes, pipes, cigars, e-cigarettes, hookahs, etc.); family history of respiratory disease (especially α_1-antitrypsin deficiency)

Nutritional-metabolic: Anorexia, weight loss or gain

Activity-exercise: Increasing dyspnea and/or increase in sputum volume or purulence; fatigue, ability to perform ADLs; swelling of feet; progressive dyspnea, especially on exertion; ability to walk up 1 flight of stairs without stopping; wheezing; recurrent cough; sputum production (especially in the morning); orthopnea

Elimination: Constipation, gas, bloating

Sleep-rest: Insomnia; sitting up position for sleeping, paroxysmal nocturnal dyspnea

Cognitive-perceptual: Headache, chest or abdominal soreness

Coping–stress tolerance: Anxiety, depression

Objective Data

General

Debilitation, restlessness, assumption of upright position

Integumentary

Cyanosis (bronchitis), pallor or ruddy color, poor skin turgor, thin skin, digital clubbing, easy bruising; peripheral edema (cor pulmonale)

Respiratory

Rapid, shallow breathing; inability to speak; prolonged expiratory phase; pursed-lip breathing; wheezing; crackles, decreased or bronchial breath sounds; ↓ chest excursion and diaphragm movement; use of accessory muscles; hyperresonant or dull chest sounds on percussion

Cardiovascular

Tachycardia, dysrhythmias, jugular venous distention, distant heart tones, right-sided S_3 (cor pulmonale), edema (especially in feet)

Gastrointestinal

Ascites, hepatomegaly (cor pulmonale)

Musculoskeletal

Muscle atrophy, ↑ anteroposterior diameter (barrel chest)

Possible Diagnostic Findings

Abnormal ABGs (compensated respiratory acidosis, ↓ PaO_2 or SaO_2, ↑ $PaCO_2$), polycythemia, pulmonary function tests showing expiratory airflow obstruction (e.g., low FEV_1, low FEV_1/FVC, large RV), chest x-ray showing flattened diaphragm and hyperinflation or infiltrates screening, even if they do not have symptoms. Genetic counseling may be appropriate for the patient with AATD deficiency who is planning to have children.

◆ **Acute Care.** The patient with COPD needs hospitalization for acute exacerbations of COPD, brought on by pneumonia or heart failure and associated complications, such as cor pulmonale and respiratory failure. Once the crisis has been resolved, reassessment of the degree and severity of any underlying problems is needed. The information obtained will help in planning care going forward and may assist with changes in the treatment plan that will be needed after discharge.

◆ **Ambulatory Care.** The interprofessional team works together to individualize the treatment plan for COPD patients. By far the most important aspect in the long-term care of the patient with COPD is teaching. A large part of your role is to teach patients self-management of their disease. A patient and caregiver teaching guide is shown in Table 28.24.

Pulmonary Rehabilitation. Pulmonary rehabilitation can be done in an inpatient or outpatient setting or in the home. Components of pulmonary rehabilitation vary, but usually include exercise training, smoking cessation, nutrition counseling, and education. Physical therapists or nurses who have experience in respiratory care are often responsible for managing pulmonary rehabilitation centers. Pulmonary rehabilitation indicated for any degree of airway obstruction or GOLD classification. It works best if the patient starts when COPD is in a moderate stage, but even patients who have advanced COPD can benefit. Pulmonary rehabilitation relieves dyspnea and fatigue, improves emotional function, and enhances the sense of control that people have over their COPD.

Pulmonary rehabilitation may be inaccessible to some because of disability, transportation, geographic location, or cost. One alternative program to in-person pulmonary rehabilitation uses the Internet or gaming technology. However, the HCP must approve these types of programs to ensure safety.

INFORMATICS IN PRACTICE
E-Mail and Texting for COPD Patients

* Sometimes patients with COPD or those who use O_2 therapy have difficulty speaking because of shortness of breath.
* Encourage your patient to use typed messages, such as e-mail, to communicate.
* Texting and instant messaging family and friends are good alternatives to having phone conversations.

Activity Considerations. The patient with severe COPD typically uses upper thoracic and neck muscles to breathe rather than the diaphragm. Thus the patient has difficulty performing upper extremity activities, particularly those that require raising the arm above the head. Exercise training leads to energy conservation, which is an important part in COPD rehabilitation. Exercise training of the upper extremities may improve muscle function and help to reduce dyspnea.

Often the patient is already using some alternative energy-saving practices for ADLs. Explore alternative methods of hair care, shaving, showering, and reaching.

An occupational therapist may help with ideas in these areas. Assuming a tripod posture (elbows supported on a table, chest in fixed position) and placing a mirror on the table while using an electric razor or hair dryer conserves much more energy

TABLE 28.24 **Patient & Caregiver Teaching**
Chronic Obstructive Pulmonary Disease

Include the following information in the teaching plan to assist the patient with COPD and the caregiver to improve quality of life through promoting lifestyle practices that support successful living with COPD:

What Is COPD?
* Basic anatomy and physiology of lung
* Basic pathophysiology of COPD
* Signs and symptoms of COPD, exacerbation
* How to tell COPD from the common cold, flu, pneumonia
* Tests to assess breathing

Breathing and Airway Clearance Exercises
* Pursed-lip breathing (Table 28.12)
* Airway clearance technique: huff cough (Table 28.21)

Energy Conservation Techniques
* Daily activities (e.g., waking up, bathing, grooming, shopping, traveling)
* Consult with physical therapist and occupational therapist

Medications
Types (include mechanism of action and types of devices)
* Establishing medication schedule
* Correct use of inhalers, spacer, and nebulizer
* Reason for use of O_2 equipment
* Guide for home O_2 use and equipment

Psychosocial/Emotional Issues
Open discussion (sharing with patient and/or caregiver)
* Concerns about interpersonal relationships (e.g., intimacy)
* Problems with emotions (e.g., depression, anxiety, panic)
* Dependency
Treatment decisions and end-of-life issues
* Support and rehabilitation groups

COPD Management Plan
Nurse and patient develop and write up COPD management plan that meets individual needs.
* Focus on self-management
* Need to report changes
* Cause of acute exacerbations
* Recognition of signs and symptoms of respiratory infection, heart failure
* Reduce risk factors, especially smoking cessation
* Exercise program of walking and arm strengthening
* Yearly follow-up

Healthy Nutrition (Table 28.22)
* Ways to lose weight (if overweight)
* Ways to gain weight (if underweight)
* Consultation with dietitian

For more information, see American Lung Association at www.lung.org/lung-disease/copd.

than when the patient stands in front of a mirror to shave or blow-dry hair.

If the patient uses home O_2 therapy, O_2 should be used during hygiene because these tasks are energy consuming. Encourage the patient to make a schedule and plan daily and weekly activities, leaving plenty of time for rest periods. In severe COPD, the patient should try to sit as much as possible when performing activities. Another energy-saving tip is to exhale when pushing, pulling, or exerting effort during an activity and inhale during rest.

Regular physical exercise is important for patients with COPD. To ensure long-term adherence, the exercise plan must be individualized and easy to perform. Walking or other endurance exercises (e.g., cycling) combined with strength training are the best interventions to strengthen muscles and improve the patient's endurance. Teach the patient coordinated walking with slow, pursed-lip breathing. Many patients with moderate or severe COPD are anxious and fearful of walking or performing exercise. Both patients and their caregivers need support while they build the confidence they need to walk, perform daily exercises, or help with these activities.

Developing exercise endurance is very important. If it takes longer than 5 minutes to return to baseline, the patient has most likely "overdone it" and should proceed at a slower pace during the next exercise period. Keeping a diary or log of the exercise program may help. Stationary cycling can be used either alone or with walking. Cycles and treadmills are particularly good when weather prevents walking outside.

Fatigue, sleep problems, and dyspnea are common problems. Of these symptoms, dyspnea seems to be the one that most affects the patient's ability to carry out daily activities. Therefore focus your interventions on improving dyspnea, which should then improve the patient's overall functional performance.

Patients often ask whether moving to a warmer or drier climate will help. In general, such moves are generally not beneficial. Discourage moves to places with an elevation of 4000 ft or more because of the lower partial pressure of O_2 found in the air at higher elevations. A disadvantage of moving may be that a person leaves a job, friends, and familiar environment, which could be psychologically stressful. This may outweigh any advantage gained from being in a different climate.

EVIDENCE-BASED PRACTICE
Physical Activity and COPD

You are working as a nurse in a pulmonary clinic with R.P., a 71-yr-old man who was recently discharged from the hospital with a new diagnosis of COPD. He tells you he has been inactive for most of the past 8 months because his breathing seems to worsen with any type of physical activity.

Making Clinical Decisions

Best Available Evidence. Patients with COPD who take part in regular moderate physical activity (e.g., brisk walking) have fewer severe flare-ups and are less likely to be readmitted to the hospital. Physical activity improves lung function and lessens depressive symptoms. The season of the year and temperature can be barriers to outdoor exercise.

Clinician Expertise. Physical inactivity is common in patients with COPD. You are aware that inactivity may place R.P. at a greater risk for functional decline and readmission.

Patient Preference and Values. R.P. tells you that he misses taking walks every day with his wife and dog. He is wondering if he would be able to resume this activity at a slower pace.

Implications for Practice

1. What important factors will you discuss with R.P. about physical activity and COPD?
2. How would you assess R.P.'s willingness and motivation to engage in physical activity?
3. How would you involve the interprofessional team members to assist R.P. in regular physical activity?

Reference for Evidence

Kantorowski A, Wan ES, Homsy D, et al.: Determinants and outcomes of change in physical activity in COPD, *ERJ Open Res* 4:1, 2018.

Psychosocial Considerations. Coping is a challenge for the COPD patient and family. As the disease progresses, patients with COPD are often confronted with many lifestyle changes that may involve decreased ability to care for themselves, decreased energy for social activities, and loss or change in a job.

When a patient with COPD is first diagnosed or has complications that require hospitalization, expect a variety of emotional responses. Emotions often expressed include denial, anger, frustration from increased dependence, and loneliness from social isolation. Guilt may result if the disease was caused primarily by cigarette smoking.

Patients experience many losses as the disease progresses. Because many patients have depression and anxiety, assess for both. Ask patients if they "feel down or blue" most of the time. Do they appear anxious about being able to control their breathlessness or know what to do if they have an exacerbation? Are they showing concern over more difficulty in self-care activities, such as bathing? How is the family coping with the patient's disease? The patient with COPD may benefit from stress management techniques (e.g., massage, muscle relaxation).

It is important to convey a sense of understanding and caring to the patient. Teach patients about COPD and their treatment, which can provide a sense of control. It is important to include caregivers in the teaching so they can help the patient cope physically and emotionally. Support groups at local American Lung Association chapters (e.g., the Better Breathers Club), hospitals, and clinics can be helpful.

Consultation with a mental health therapist may be needed for proper screening and diagnosis of depression or other mental health problems. Cognitive and behavioral therapy along with COPD teaching may improve the quality of life. Drugs may be used to treat both depression and anxiety. Buspirone (BuSpar), used to treat anxiety, has few respiratory effects. Benzodiazepines should be avoided because they may depress the respiratory drive and may be habit forming. When the patient becomes anxious because of dyspnea, the use of pursed-lip breathing and SABAs may be appropriate.

Sexuality and Sexual Activity. Modifying sexual activity can contribute to healthy psychologic well-being. First, assess the patient's concerns related to sexuality and functioning. Ask open-ended questions to determine if the patient wants or is willing to discuss concerns. You could ask, "How has your breathing problem affected how you see yourself as a person?" Another question could be, "How does your shortness of breath affect your desire for intimacy with your partner?" These types of questions give the patient an opening to discuss concerns.

Dyspnea, the predominant symptom in COPD, should not be a major problem with success in sexual functioning, except for patients in severe late stages. If the patient can walk up 2 flights of stairs or walk briskly, they likely have enough energy for sexual activity. Using an inhaled bronchodilator before sexual activity can help ventilation. The patient may find these suggestions helpful: (1) plan sexual activity during the part of the day when breathing is best, which is usually late morning or early afternoon (plus older men often achieve an erection more easily in the morning); (2) use slow pursed-lip breathing; (3) refrain from sexual activity after eating or drinking alcohol; (4) choose less stressful positions during intercourse (missionary position for men is the worst); and (5) use O_2 if prescribed.

Most patients with COPD are older. Many of the sexual performance issues experienced by the patient with COPD are changes related to aging. You can teach the patient the "normalcy" of the changes. The patient with coexisting heart disease should obtain advice from an HCP related to appropriate levels of activity. Open communication between partners about their needs and expectations and any changes that may be needed is important.

Sleep. Adequate sleep is extremely important to maintain quality of life and productivity. Most patients with COPD have sleep problems. Hyperinflation of the lungs and reduction in ventilation can result in severe drops in O_2 saturation (down to 60% or less) during sleep. This leads to an increased workload on the heart. Hypercapnia may contribute to more frequent awakening. The net result is sleeping poorly and waking up unrefreshed and fatigued.

Current tobacco use, depression, and anxiety are all common in COPD and lead to more trouble sleeping. β_2-Agonists may cause restlessness and insomnia. Postnasal drip or nasal congestion may cause coughing and wheezing at night. Nasal saline sprays or rinses before sleep and in the morning may help. If the patient is prescribed O_2 therapy, using it at night may decrease insomnia. If the patient is a restless sleeper, snores, stops breathing while asleep, and tends to fall asleep during the day, the patient may need testing for sleep apnea (see Chapter 7).

End-of-Life Considerations. The trajectory of COPD is a gradual decline in health characterized by increasing exacerbations that are associated with an increased risk for death. In the later, severe stages of this disease, palliative, end-of-life, and hospice care are important components of care for the patient with advanced COPD.

Patients need to know that symptoms can be managed, but COPD cannot be cured. End-of-life issues and advance directives are important topics for discussion in the latter stages of COPD. This may be hard for the patient and family to consider because of the uncertainty of the disease.

◆ Evaluation

The expected outcomes are that the patient with COPD will
- Maintain a patent airway by effectively coughing
- Have an effective rate, rhythm, and depth of respirations
- Have clear breath sounds
- Return to pre-exacerbation baseline respiratory function
- Have $PaCO_2$ and PaO_2 values that return to normal for the patient

CYSTIC FIBROSIS

Cystic fibrosis (CF) is an autosomal recessive, multisystem disease characterized by altered transport of sodium and chloride ions in and out of epithelial cells. This defect primarily affects the lungs, GI tract (pancreas and biliary tract), and reproductive tract.

The first signs and symptoms typically occur in childhood, but some patients are not diagnosed until they are adults. The severity and progression of the disease vary. With early diagnosis and improvements in therapy, the prognosis of patients with CF has significantly improved. The median predicted survival in 1970 was 16 years of age. Today it has increased to more than 37.5 years.[25]

Etiology and Pathophysiology

Genetic Link. CF is an autosomal recessive disorder. The CF gene is found on chromosome 7, which makes a protein called *CF transmembrane conductance regulator (CFTR)*. The CFTR

ETHICAL/LEGAL DILEMMAS
Advance Directives

Situation

L.H., an 84-yr-old man with end-stage COPD, is admitted to the hospital in respiratory failure. He is intubated in the ED and placed on a ventilator. L.H. sometimes responds by opening his eyes. His advanced personal directive (AD) was drawn up 5 years ago, and copies were given to his wife and HCP at that time. His wife brings the documents to the critical care unit and tells you that the hospital must stop treating her husband, and as per his request, allow him to die. However, the patient's oldest son is threatening the hospital with a lawsuit if the staff does not provide full care to his father.

Ethical/Legal Points for Consideration

- A Living Will, one form of AD, permits persons to state their own preferences and refusals should the person become terminally ill or be in a situation in which there is no hope of recovery and the person is not able to speak for themselves.
- The Durable Power of Attorney for Health Care, another form of AD, permits persons to identify a proxy to make health care decisions in the event the person is incapacitated.
- The National POLST Paradigm is an approach to end-of-life planning that emphasizes documenting patients' wishes about the care they receive.[1]
- AD laws vary from state to state concerning the need for witnesses and designating the proxy.
- Some families are deeply divided about decisions for their loved ones, and conflicts often arise when feelings of remorse or guilt and money and/or property are involved. This situation requires you to notify the HCP, engage social work and spiritual care, and ask for a family conference. In some circumstances, a consult from the ethics committee may be needed.
- HCPs are obligated to follow the patient's ADs when a patient is no longer able to speak for himself or herself.
- In your scope of nursing practice, you need to (1) be informed about the decision-making laws and regulations in your state, (2) make AD documents available to patients, (3) teach patients and families about ADs, (4) determine if all involved HCPs are aware of the ADs, (5) assist the patient and family in communicating with the HCP when a "no code" or "DNR" (do not resuscitate) order is requested, and (6) assist the conflicted family in obtaining appropriate counseling when needed.

Discussion Questions

1. What should you do next with the information provided by L.H.'s wife?
2. The HCP has asked that you organize a family conference. How should you address the needs of each member of this family in L.H.'s plan of care?
3. What resources can you use to facilitate decision making in this situation?
4. What would be your approach to L.H.'s plan of care?

Reference

Physician Orders for Life Sustaining Treatment (POLST) Program. Retrieved from *www.polst.org*.

---

protein localizes to the epithelial surface of the airways, GI tract, and ducts of the liver, pancreas, and sweat glands. Under normal conditions, CFTR regulates sodium and chloride movement in and out of epithelial cells. However, mutations in the *CFTR* gene change this protein in such a way that the channels are blocked. As a result, cells that line the passageways of the lungs, pancreas, intestines, and other organs make secretions that are low in sodium chloride content (thus low in water content),

Normal CFTR channel moves the sodium and chloride ions to the outside of the cell.

Mutant CFTR channel does not move sodium and chloride ions, causing sticky mucus to build up on the outside of the cell.

FIG. 28.16 People with cystic fibrosis inherit a defective gene on chromosome 7 called *cystic fibrosis transmembrane conductance regulator (CFTR)*. The protein made by this gene normally helps sodium and chloride move in and out of cells. If the protein does not work correctly, the movement of sodium and chloride is blocked, and an abnormally thick sticky mucus is produced on the outside of the cell.

making mucus abnormally thick and sticky (Fig. 28.16). This mucus plugs up the ducts in these organs, causing scarring in the organs and resulting in organ failure. The high concentrations of sodium and chloride in the sweat of the patient with CF result from decreased chloride reabsorption in the sweat duct.

GENETICS IN CLINICAL PRACTICE

Cystic Fibrosis (CF)

Genetic Basis
- Autosomal recessive disorder
- Caused by mutations in CF transmembrane regulator *(CFTR)* gene on chromosome 7
- *CFTR* gene provides the instructions for making the protein that controls the channel that transports sodium and chloride
- There are more than 17,000 different mutations of the *CFTR* gene
- Mutations in the *CFTR* gene disrupt the function of the channels, preventing them from regulating the flow of sodium, chloride, and water across cell membranes

Incidence
- In the United States, 1 in 3000 white births
- Less common in other ethnic populations (1 in 15,000 blacks, 1 in 9200 Hispanics, 1 in 30,000 Asian Americans)
- One in 20 to 25 whites are carriers of the gene

Genetic Testing
- Blood-based DNA testing is available for disease and carrier states.
- All 50 states require CF screening for all newborns.
- Testing is usually done in children if CF is suspected or if parents are possible carriers.
- In parents who are known carriers, amniocentesis or chorionic villus sampling in pregnant women may be useful for prenatal testing.

Clinical Implications
- CF has a wide range of clinical expression of disease.
- Most people who have a child with CF are not aware of a family history of disease.
- CF screening should be offered to all people of reproductive age regardless of family history.

The hallmark of CF is its effect on the airways. CF can affect both upper and lower respiratory tracts. URI manifestations may include chronic sinusitis and nasal polyposis. CF progresses from being a disease of the small airways *(chronic bronchiolitis)* to involvement of the larger airways that causes destruction of lung tissue. The mucus lining the airways becomes dehydrated and tenacious due to defects in chloride secretion and sodium absorption. Cilia motility is decreased, allowing mucus to adhere to the airways. The bronchioles become obstructed with thick secretions, leading to scarring of the airways (bronchiectasis), air trapping, and hyperinflation of the lungs.

CF is characterized by a persistent, chronic airway infection that cannot be cured. *P. aeruginosa* is by far the most common organism in adults. Other organisms include *Staphylococcus aureus, H. influenzae,* and less often, but more seriously, *Burkholderia cepacia.* Antibiotic resistance develops after multiple exposure to antibiotics. Pulmonary inflammation is associated with the chronic infection and can cause a decrease in respiratory function, further narrowing the lumen of the airways. Inflammatory mediators (e.g., interleukins, oxidants, proteases released by neutrophils) are increased and contribute to disease progression.

Lung disorders that initially occur are chronic bronchiolitis and bronchiectasis (Fig. 28.17). Over a long period, pulmonary vascular remodeling occurs because of local hypoxia and arteriolar vasoconstriction. Pulmonary hypertension, enlarged pulmonary arteries, and cor pulmonale occur in the later phases of the disease. Blebs and large cysts in the lung are severe manifestations of lung destruction. Pneumothorax may occur. Hemoptysis is caused by proliferation of capillaries in response to chronic infection. During exacerbations, erosion of these capillaries occurs. Hemoptysis may range from scant streaking to major bleeding, which can be fatal.

Pancreatic insufficiency is caused by mucous plugging of the pancreatic exocrine ducts. This results in atrophy of the gland and progressive fibrotic cyst formation. The pancreas's exocrine function may be completely lost. Because of this dysfunction, pancreatic enzymes, such as lipase, amylase, and proteases (trypsin, chemotrypsin), are not made in sufficient amounts to allow for absorption of nutrients. Malabsorption of fat, protein, and fat-soluble vitamins (A, D, E, and K) occurs. Fat malabsorption results in steatorrhea. Protein malabsorption results in failure to grow and gain weight. Osteopenia and osteoporosis are common. They are related to malnutrition, malabsorption of vitamin D, insufficient testosterone levels, and chronically elevated inflammatory cytokines.[26]

We believe CF-related diabetes mellitus (CFRD) is caused by underdevelopment of pancreatic islet cells (in utero) and destruction of islet cells over the person's lifetime. CFRD is unique because it has characteristics of both type 1 and type 2 diabetes. The pancreas in people with CF makes insulin, but they make it too late to fully respond to carbohydrate intake.

Persons with CF often have other GI problems, including GERD, gallstones, and pancreatitis. The liver and gallbladder can be damaged by mucus deposits in the ducts. Liver enzymes may become chronically elevated, with cirrhosis developing over time. Portal hypertension can occur. Distal intestinal obstruction syndrome (DIOS) results from an intermittent obstruction, often in the terminal ileum at the point of the ileocecal junction. It is caused by thickened, dehydrated stool and mucus. The patient may appear to have a small bowel obstruction. DIOS develops because of chronic malabsorption related

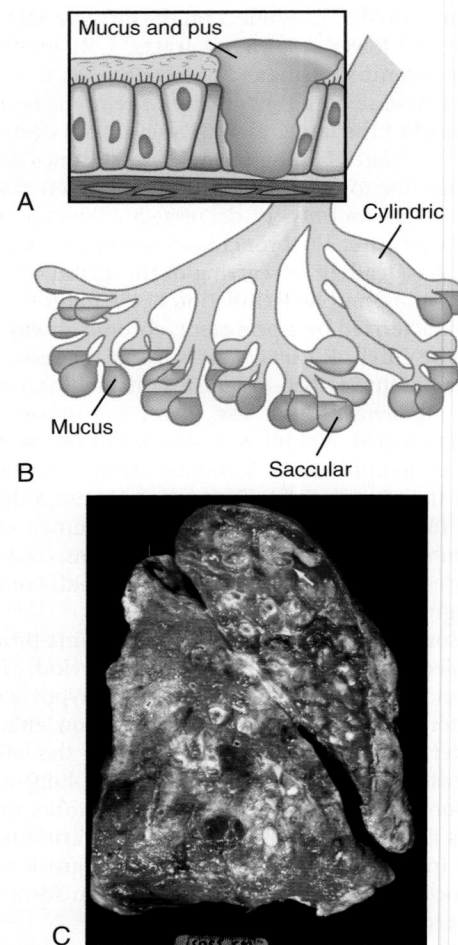

FIG. 28.17 Pathologic changes in bronchiectasis. **A**, Longitudinal section of bronchial wall where chronic infection has caused damage. **B**, Collection of purulent material in dilated bronchioles, leading to persistent infection. **C**, Bronchiectasis in a patient with cystic fibrosis who underwent lung transplantation. Cut surfaces of lung show markedly distended peripheral bronchi filled with mucopurulent secretions. (*C*, From Kumar V, Abbas AK, Aster JC, et al: *Robbins and Cotran pathologic basis of disease*, ed 8, Philadelphia, 2010, Saunders.)

to exocrine dysfunction, under- or over-dosing of pancreatic replacement enzyme supplementation, dehydration, and swallowing of mucus.

Clinical Manifestations

The manifestations vary depending on the severity of the disease. The disease severity may vary greatly, both within families and among different families. Mutations do not affect carriers.

The median age at diagnosis of CF is 6 to 8 months of age. Two thirds are diagnosed in the first year of life.[27] Currently every state has mandatory newborn screening for CF, which has allowed for early intervention. An initial finding of meconium ileus in the newborn infant prompts the diagnosis in 20% of people with CF. Other signs that suggest a CF diagnosis in childhood are acute or persistent respiratory symptoms (wheezing, coughing, frequent pneumonia), failure to thrive or malnutrition, steatorrhea (large, oily, frequent bowel movements), bronchiectasis, and family history. Without treatment, a large, protuberant abdomen may develop with an emaciated appearance of the extremities. Both males and females have delayed puberty.

In adults, patients often present with atypical symptoms, such as new-onset diabetes or infertility problems. One of the most common symptoms of CF in the adult is frequent cough. With time, the cough becomes persistent and produces viscous, purulent, often yellow or greenish sputum. The most common bacteria in the airways of adults is *Pseudomonas*. Other respiratory problems include recurring lung infections, such as bronchiolitis, bronchitis, and pneumonia. As the disease progresses, periods of clinical stability are interrupted by exacerbations characterized by increased cough, weight loss, increased sputum, and decreased pulmonary function. Over time, the exacerbations become more frequent, bronchiectasis worsens, and the recovery of lost lung function is less complete, which may ultimately lead to respiratory failure.

Patients who develop DIOS may have right lower quadrant pain (the area of the ileocecal valve), loss of appetite, nausea, emesis, and a palpable mass. Insufficient pancreatic enzyme release causes the typical pattern of protein and fat malabsorption with a person being thin with a low body mass index (BMI) and frequent bulky, foul-smelling stools.

Both males and females have delayed puberty. Some women with CF have difficulty conceiving. The cervical mucus may be thickened. During exacerbations, menstrual irregularities and secondary amenorrhea are common. Most women with CF can become pregnant. Most pregnancies result in viable infants.

Nearly all men with CF have reproductive issues because their vas deferens fails to develop in utero, so there is no transport of sperm from storage in the testes to the penile urethra. However, they make sperm normally, and with assisted reproductive technology, can father a child.

Complications

Complications in CF include CFRD and bone, sinus, and liver disease. With advanced lung disease, digital clubbing occurs. Respiratory failure and cor pulmonale caused by pulmonary hypertension are late complications of CF. Pneumothorax, a rare but serious complication, is caused by the formation of bullae and blebs. A small amount of blood in sputum is common in the CF patient because of chronic lung infection. Massive hemoptysis, though, is also rare but can be life-threatening.

Diagnostic Studies

The diagnostic criteria for CF include a combination of clinical presentation, family history, laboratory, and genetic testing. The sweat glands of CF patients secrete normal volumes of sweat, but sodium chloride cannot be absorbed from sweat as it moves through the sweat duct. As a result, 4 times the normal amount of sodium and chloride is excreted in sweat. This abnormality usually does not directly affect the person's general health, but helps confirm a diagnosis of CF.

The sweat chloride test is the gold standard for diagnosis of CF. It is done with the pilocarpine iontophoresis method.[28] Pilocarpine is placed on the skin and carried by a small electric current to stimulate sweat production. This part of the process takes about 5 minutes. The patient will feel a slight tingling or warmth. Next, the area (usually an arm) is wrapped in plastic to help facilitate sweating. The sweat is collected on filter paper or gauze and then analyzed for sweat chloride concentrations. The test takes about 1 hour. Sweat chloride values above 60 mmol/L are considered positive for the diagnosis of CF. A second sweat chloride test is done at the same time (1 test in each arm) to confirm the diagnosis.

Genetic testing is often used if the results from a sweat chloride test are uncertain. A blood sample or cells taken inside the cheek (buccal smear) are sent to a laboratory that specializes in genetic testing. Most laboratories test for only the most common mutations of the CF gene. Because more than 1700 mutations cause CF, screening for all mutations is hard and done only at a specialty laboratory.

Interprofessional Care

An interprofessional team should be involved in the care of a patient with CF. The Cystic Fibrosis Foundation provides funding for and accredits more than 120 CF care centers nationwide. The high quality of specialized care available throughout the care center network has led to the improved length and quality of life for people with CF. These care centers offer the best care, treatments, and support for those with CF. The teams at these care centers include a nurse, physician, respiratory therapist, physical therapist, dietitian, social worker, and often a nurse practitioner.

Management of pulmonary problems in CF aims at relieving airway obstruction and controlling infection. Drainage of thick bronchial mucus is assisted by aerosol and nebulization treatments of drugs used to dilate the airways, liquefy mucus, and promote clearance.

The abnormal viscosity of CF secretions is increased by concentrated deoxyribonucleic acid (DNA) from neutrophils involved in chronic infection. Agents that degrade the DNA in CF sputum (e.g., inhaled dornase alfa [Pulmozyme]) increase airflow and reduce the number of acute exacerbations. Inhaled hypertonic saline (7%) increases osmolality, allowing water to collect on airway surfaces. It is effective in clearing mucus and decreases the frequency of exacerbations. Some patients also need bronchodilators (e.g., β_2-adrenergic agonists) to control bronchospasm, but the long-term benefit is not known.

ACTs are critical since the normal ciliary motion in CF airways is impaired. CPT (including postural drainage with percussion and vibration) and high-frequency chest wall oscillation loosen mucus. Clearance is achieved by specialized expiratory techniques aimed at using airflow to remove the loosened secretions. Examples include PEP devices (Fig. 28.15), breathing exercises, pursed-lip breathing (Table 28.12), and huff coughing (Table 28.21). Persons with CF may prefer a certain technique or device that works well for them in a daily routine. No clear evidence exists that any ACT is better than the others.

Most patients with CF die of complications from lung infection. Standard treatment of infections includes antibiotics for exacerbations in conjunction with airway clearance. Early intervention with antibiotics is useful. Antibiotic choice should be based on sputum culture results. They may be given for 10 days to 3 weeks or longer. Some need chronic suppressive therapy. Prolonged high-dose therapy (larger doses, more frequent dosing) may be needed because many drugs are abnormally metabolized and rapidly excreted in the patient with CF.

If home support and resources are adequate, the CF patient and caregiver may be able to administer IV antibiotic therapy at home independently. The usual treatment is 2 antibiotics with different mechanisms of action (e.g., cephalosporin and an aminoglycoside). The patient with cor pulmonale or hypoxemia may need home O_2 therapy.

Oral agents used for mild exacerbations (e.g., increased cough and sputum) include a semisynthetic penicillin, trimethoprim/sulfamethoxazole (to treat *S. aureus*) or oral quinolones, especially ciprofloxacin (to treat *P. aeruginosa*). The quinolones are used with caution because of the rapid development of resistant strains.

Most patients have *Pseudomonas* infection, which can be hard to treat over time because the organism develops resistance to antibiotics. *Pseudomonas* can form a biofilm that protects the organism from antibiotics. One commonly used antibiotic to treat patients with chronic *Pseudomonas* infection is aerosolized tobramycin (TOBI). It is given twice a day, every day, every other month. Azithromycin used longer than 6 months decreases the frequency of pulmonary exacerbations, especially in those infected with *Pseudomonas*. It is also thought to act as an antiinflammatory.

Patients with a large pneumothorax need chest tube drainage, perhaps repeatedly. Sclerosing of the pleural space or partial pleural stripping and pleural abrasion may be done for recurrent episodes of pneumothorax. With massive hemoptysis, bronchial artery embolization is done. CF has become a leading reason for lung transplantation.

The management of pancreatic insufficiency includes pancreatic enzyme replacement of lipase, protease, and amylase (e.g., pancrelipase [Pancreaze, Creon, Zenpep]) taken before each meal and snack. Adequate intake of fat, calories, protein, and vitamins is important. Fat-soluble vitamins (A, D, E, and K) must be supplemented, since they are malabsorbed. Use of caloric supplements improves nutritional status. Dietary salt is indicated whenever sweating is excessive, such as during hot weather, when fever is present, or from intense physical activity. Hyperglycemia may need insulin treatment.

If the patient develops DIOS with partial or complete bowel obstruction, every attempt is made to manage the condition medically. Options include prokinetic agents (e.g., macrolide antibiotics, metoclopramide), mucolytics (oral N-acetylcysteine), stimulant laxatives, lactulose, and polyethylene glycol (PEG) electrolyte solution (MiraLAX, GoLYTELY).[29] Careful monitoring of bowel habits and patterns is essential for CF patients. If DIOS does not resolve with medical treatment, surgery may be done to prevent the development of ischemic bowel.

Ivacaftor (Kalydeco), a CFTR modulator, is used to treat patients who have mutations in a specific *CFTR* gene. It is not effective in patients with CF who have 2 copies (homozygous) of the *F508* mutation in the *CFTR* gene (the most common mutation that results in CF). If a patient's genotype is unknown, a CF mutation test should be done to detect the presence of a CFTR mutation. Combinations drugs, such as ivacaftor/lumacaftor (Orkambi), are used to treat CF patients with specific gene mutations. All patients diagnosed with CF should have CFTR genotyping. This will help determine if they carry a mutation that would be appropriate for CFTR modulator therapy.

❖ NURSING MANAGEMENT: CYSTIC FIBROSIS

◆ Nursing Assessment

Subjective and objective data that should be obtained from the patient with CF are presented in Table 28.25.

◆ Nursing Diagnoses

Nursing diagnoses for the patient with CF may include:
- Impaired airway clearance
- Impaired respiratory system function
- Impaired nutritional status
- Difficulty coping

TABLE 28.25   Nursing Assessment

Cystic Fibrosis

Subjective Data

Important Health Information

Past health history: Recurrent respiratory and sinus infections, persistent cough with excessive sputum production

Medications: Use of and compliance with bronchodilators, antibiotics

Functional Health Patterns

Health perception–health maintenance: Family history of cystic fibrosis, diagnosis of cystic fibrosis in childhood, genetic testing in offspring

Nutritional-metabolic: Dietary intolerances, voracious appetite, weight loss, heartburn

Elimination: Intestinal gas. Large, frequent bowel movements, constipation

Activity-exercise: Fatigue, ↓ exercise tolerance, amount and type of exercise. Dyspnea, cough, excessive mucus or sputum production, coughing up blood, airway clearance techniques

Cognitive-perceptual: Abdominal pain

Sexuality-reproductive: Delayed menarche, menstrual irregularities, problems conceiving or fathering a child

Coping–stress tolerance: Anxiety, depression, problems adapting to diagnosis

Objective Data

General

Restlessness; failure to thrive

Integumentary

Cyanosis (circumoral, nail bed), digital clubbing; salty skin

Eyes

Scleral icterus

Respiratory

Sinus congestion, postnasal drip, persistent runny nose. Decreased breath sounds, adventitious breath sounds (crackles, wheezes). Sputum (thick, light or dark, tenacious), ↑ WOB, use of accessory muscles of respiration, barrel chest, hemoptysis (rare)

Cardiovascular

Tachycardia

Gastrointestinal

Protuberant abdomen; abdominal distention; foul, fatty stools

Possible Diagnostic Findings

Abnormal ABGs and pulmonary function tests; abnormal sweat chloride test, chest x-ray, fecal fat analysis

◆ **Planning**

The overall goals are that the patient with CF will have (1) adequate airway clearance, (2) absence of respiratory infection, (3) adequate nutritional support to maintain appropriate BMI, (4) ability to perform ADLs, (5) recognition and treatment of complications related to CF, and (6) active participation in planning and implementing an achievable treatment plan.

◆ **Nursing Implementation**

Acute care for the patient with CF includes relief of bronchoconstriction, airway obstruction, and airflow limitation. Interventions include aggressive CPT, antibiotics, and O_2 therapy in severe disease. Good nutrition is important.

Aerobic exercise is effective in clearing the airways. Important needs to consider when planning an aerobic exercise program for the patient with CF are (1) meeting increased nutritional demands of exercise, (2) observing for dehydration, and (3) drinking large amounts of fluid and replacing salt losses.

As these persons continue into adulthood, you can help them in gaining independence by helping them assume responsibility for their care and life goals. An important issue to discuss is sexuality. Delayed development of secondary sex characteristics and irregular menses are common. The issue of marrying and having children is difficult. Genetic counseling is an appropriate suggestion for the couple considering having children. Another concern is the uncertainty surrounding the shortened life span of the parent with CF.

Other crises and life transitions that must be dealt with in the young adult include persisting with employment goals, developing motivation to achieve, learning to cope with the treatment program, and adjusting to the need for dependence if health fails. Disclosing the CF diagnosis to friends, potential spouses, or employers may pose significant emotional, social, psychological, and financial challenges.

CF imposes a significant emotional and financial burden on the patient and family. In many situations, the cost of drugs, special equipment, and health care poses considerable financial hardship. The burden of living with a chronic disease at a young age can be emotionally overwhelming. There is a higher incidence of depression among persons with CF than their unaffected peers. Issues related to costs of health care, burden of self-care, career choices, fertility, and decreased life expectancy, may lead to depression. Community resources are available to help patients and caregivers. The Cystic Fibrosis Foundation can be a source of information and support.

BRONCHIECTASIS

Etiology and Pathophysiology

Bronchiectasis is characterized by permanent, abnormal dilation of medium-sized bronchi. It is the result of inflammatory changes that destroy elastic and muscular structures supporting the bronchial wall. There is a continuing cycle of inflammation, airway damage, and remodeling, enhanced by the accumulation of neutrophils in the airways. Airways can become colonized with microorganisms (e.g., *Pseudomonas*), which causes the bronchial walls to weaken and pockets of infection to form (Fig. 28.17).

When the walls of the bronchial system are injured, the mucociliary mechanism is damaged, allowing bacteria and mucus to accumulate within the pockets. Bacteria attract neutrophils, which enhances inflammation and causes edema. Stasis of thickened mucus occurs due to impaired clearance of mucus by the cilia. This results in a reduced ability to clear mucus from the lungs and decreased expiratory airflow.

A variety of problems can result in bronchiectasis. CF is the main cause of bronchiectasis in children. In adults, the main cause is bacterial infections of the lungs. A wide variety of infectious agents initiate bronchiectasis. It can follow a single episode of severe pneumonia or infection that was either not treated or received delayed treatment. Other causes are obstruction of an airway with mucus plugs or generalized impairment of pulmonary defenses. Several systemic diseases, such as inflammatory bowel disease, rheumatoid arthritis, or immune disorders (e.g., acquired immunodeficiency syndrome [AIDS]) are associated with bronchiectasis.

Clinical Manifestations

The hallmark is persistent cough with consistent production of thick, tenacious, purulent sputum. In rare situations, some patients with severe disease and upper lobe involvement may have no sputum production and little cough. Recurrent infections injure blood vessels. Large connections (anastomoses) may develop between blood vessels in the lungs, and hemoptysis may occur. In severe cases the bleed can be life-threatening. Other manifestations are pleuritic chest pain, dyspnea, wheezing, clubbing of digits, weight loss, and anemia. On auscultation, adventitious sounds can be heard (e.g., crackles, wheezes).

Diagnostic Studies

A person who presents with a chronic productive cough with copious purulent sputum (which may be blood streaked) should be suspected of having bronchiectasis. A CT scan is the gold standard for diagnosing bronchiectasis.[30]

Chest x-rays may show nonspecific abnormalities. Spirometry usually shows an obstructive pattern, including a decrease in FEV_1 and FEV_1/FVC. Sputum may give information about the presence of active infection and the severity of impairment. Patients often have *H. influenzae, S. aureus,* or *P. aeruginosa,* with the latter leading to more frequent exacerbations and rapid decline in lung function. A complete blood cell count and AAT level may be done.

❖ INTERPROFESSIONAL AND NURSING MANAGEMENT: BRONCHIECTASIS

Bronchiectasis is hard to treat. Therapy is aimed at treating acute flare-ups and preventing a decline in lung function. Antibiotics are the mainstay of treatment. They are often given for a minimum of 14 days. Antibiotics may be given orally, IV, or inhaled (nebulizer). Choice of antibiotic primarily depends on culture results or most likely organism. The patient needs to understand the importance of taking prescribed drugs to obtain maximum effectiveness. Long-term antibiotic therapy is given to patients who have symptoms that recur a few days after stopping antibiotics. Concurrent bronchodilator therapy with SABAs, LABAs, or anticholinergics can prevent bronchospasm and stimulate mucus clearance. Some patients receive oral and inhaled corticosteroids.

One important goal is to promote drainage and removal of mucus. Various ACTs can be used to facilitate secretion removal. CPT with postural drainage is widely used. Direct hydration of the respiratory system may help with the expectoration of secretions. Hyperosmolar agents (e.g., hypertonic saline) given by nebulizer can liquefy secretions. At home, a steamy shower can be effective.

Teach the patient and caregiver manifestations to report to the HCP. These include increased sputum production, increasing dyspnea, fever, chills, and chest pain. Teach patients when to contact the HCP if hemoptysis occurs. Some patients may periodically expectorate a "spot" of blood that is usual for them and do not require urgent attention. However, if the patient expectorates a moderate to large amount of blood, they should contact the HCP at once. In the acute care setting, elevate the head of the bed, and place the patient in a side-lying position with the suspected bleeding side down. Closely monitor vital signs and respiratory status.

Maintaining hydration is important to liquefy secretions. Unless contraindicated, teach the patient to drink at least 2 to 3 L of fluid daily. To achieve this, tell the patient to increase intake by 1 glass per day until they reach that goal. Have the patient use low-sodium fluids, thereby avoiding systemic fluid retention. Rest is important to prevent overexertion.

Good nutrition is important but may be difficult to maintain because the patient is often anorexic. Oral hygiene to cleanse the mouth and remove dried sputum crusts may improve the patient's appetite. Offer foods that are appealing, in smaller quantities and more often since they may increase the patient's desire to eat.

Surgical resection of parts of the lungs, which was common in the past, has largely been replaced by more effective supportive and antibiotic therapy. For select patients who are disabled in spite of maximal therapy, lung transplantation may be an option. Massive hemoptysis may require surgical resection.

CASE STUDY

Chronic Obstructive Pulmonary Disease

(© iStockphoto/ Thinkstock.)

Patient Profile

H.M. is a 68-yr-old white, married, retired female police officer. She has been in the hospital for 6 days with an acute COPD exacerbation and will be discharged tomorrow.

Subjective Data

- Before admission, had 4 days of exceptional shortness of breath and increased volume of sputum, which turned greenish
- Increased Ventolin HFA use (at home) to 5 or 6 times a day for dyspnea
- Described having "jitters" and "racing heart"
- Had 3 or 4 COPD exacerbation in the past year that were managed at home
- 30 pack-year history of smoking; smokes half a pack per day now to "clear out lungs" in the morning
- Eats a regular diet but "gets full fast"
- Cannot climb 1 flight of stairs without stopping; walks down the flat driveway 10 yards without difficulty
- Awakens 2-3 times per night coughing and short of breath

Objective Data

Physical Examination

- Weight 129 lb, height 5 ft 8 in, BMI 20 kg/m²
- Temperature 37.8° C (100° F), pulse 86 (regular), respiratory rate 28 (shallow, slightly labored), BP 136/76 mm Hg
- Increased anteroposterior diameter of chest (barrel shaped)
- Slight use of accessory (neck) muscles with breathing
- Distant breath sounds with occasional expiratory wheezes
- 1+ non-pitting edema (ankles and feet bilaterally)

Diagnostic Studies

- Last spirometry: decreased FEV_1 (48%) and FEV_1/FVC (62%)
- ABG on admission: pH 7.34, $PaCO_2$ 59 mm Hg, HCO_3^- 27 mEq/L, PaO_2 68 mm Hg
- ABG (24 hours after admission): pH 7.30, $PaCO_2$ 63 mm Hg, HCO_3^- 29 mEq/L, PaO_2 64 mm Hg
- WBC: 14,000/μL on admission
- Chest x-ray: hyperinflation, flat diaphragm, no sign of pneumonia
- Sputum: negative (no organisms present)

Continued

CASE STUDY

Chronic Obstructive Pulmonary Disease—cont'd

Interprofessional Care

- GOLD 3 (severe) COPD with acute exacerbation
- O_2 2 L via nasal catheter while in hospital
- Prednisone 40 mg/day PO for 5 days
- Levofloxacin 750 mg/day PO for 10 days
- Ipratropium HFA MDI 2 puffs 4 times a day
- At discharge: Advair Diskus 250/50 one inhalation q12hr

Discussion Questions

1. What classic manifestations indicate the patient had a COPD exacerbation?
2. What are some likely causes of her COPD?
3. What symptoms in H.M. indicate the overuse of inhalers? Which drug would cause the symptoms described?

4. *Patient-Centered Care:* What is one suggestion you could make to H.M. that could halt the progression of her lung disease?
5. Why would H.M. "feel full fast" when eating? What could you do to minimize this issue?
6. Interpret the ABGs. What is your impression of each ABG? In comparing both ABGs, do you see a pattern?
7. *Priority Decision:* Based on the assessment data presented, what are the priority nursing diagnoses?
8. *Evidence-Based Practice:* H.M.'s son has been trying to convince his mother to quit smoking for many years without success. He asks you to tell his mother the results of her spirometry to convince her it is time to quit. Will this approach work?
9. *Priority Decision:* What are nursing priorities for discharge planning and teaching?
10. Develop a conceptual care map for H.M.

Answers available at *http://evolve.elsevier.com/Lewis/medsurg.*

▮ BRIDGE TO NCLEX EXAMINATION

The number of the question corresponds to the same-numbered outcome at the beginning of the chapter.

1. A patient is concerned that he may have asthma. Of the symptoms that he describes to the nurse, which ones suggest asthma or risk factors for asthma? *(select all that apply)*
   a. Allergic rhinitis
   b. Prolonged inhalation
   c. Cough, especially at night
   d. Gastric reflux or heartburn
   e. History of chronic sinusitis

2. Which findings indicate that a patient is developing status asthmaticus? *(select all that apply)*
   a. PEFR <300 L/min
   b. Positive sputum culture
   c. Unable to speak in complete sentences
   d. Lack of response to conventional treatment
   e. Chest x-ray shows hyperinflated lungs and a flattened diaphragm

3. Which statement indicates the patient with asthma requires further teaching about self-care?
   a. "I use my corticosteroid inhaler when I feel short of breath."
   b. "I get a flu shot every year and see my HCP if I have an upper respiratory tract infection."
   c. "I use my inhaler before I visit my aunt who has a cat, but I only visit for a few minutes because of my allergies."
   d. "I walk 30 minutes every day but sometimes I have to use my bronchodilator inhaler before walking to prevent me from getting short of breath."

4. Which medications would be *most* appropriate to administer to a patient experiencing an acute asthma attack? *(select all that apply)*
   a. montelukast (Singulair)
   b. inhaled hypertonic saline
   c. albuterol (Proventil HFA)
   d. ipratropium (Atrovent HFA)
   e. salmeterol (Serevent Diskus)

5. The plan of care for the patient with chronic obstructive pulmonary disease (COPD) should include *(select all that apply)*
   a. exercise such as walking.
   b. high flow rate of O_2 administration.
   c. low-dose chronic oral corticosteroid therapy.
   d. use of peak flow meter to monitor the progression of COPD.
   e. breathing exercises, such as pursed-lip breathing that focus on exhalation.

6. The major advantage of a Venturi mask is that it can
   a. deliver up to 80% O_2.
   b. provide continuous 100% humidity.
   c. deliver a precise concentration of O_2.
   d. be used while a patient eats and sleeps.

7. Which guideline should the nurse include when teaching a patient how to use a metered-dose inhaler (MDI)?
   a. After activating the MDI, breathe in as quickly as you can.
   b. Estimate the amount of remaining medicine in the MDI by floating the canister in water.
   c. Disassemble the plastic canister from the inhaler and rinse both pieces under running water every week.
   d. To determine how long the canister will last, divide the total number of puffs in the canister by the puffs needed per day.

8. Which treatments would the nurse expect to implement in the management plan of a patient with cystic fibrosis? *(select all that apply)*
   a. Sperm banking
   b. IV corticosteroids on a chronic basis
   c. Airway clearance techniques (e.g., Acapella)
   d. GoLYTELY given as needed for severe constipation
   e. Inhaled tobramycin to combat *Pseudomonas* infection

9. A patient who has bronchiectasis asks the nurse, "What conditions would warrant a call to the clinic?"
   a. Blood clots in the sputum
   b. Sticky sputum on a hot day
   c. Increased shortness of breath after eating a large meal
   d. Production of large amounts of sputum on a daily basis

1. a, c, d, e. 2. a, c, d. 3. a. 4. c, d. 5. a, d, e. 6. c. 7. d. 8. a, c, d, e. 9. a

For rationales to these answers and even more NCLEX review questions, visit *http://evolve.elsevier.com/Lewis/medsurg.*

EVOLVE WEBSITE/RESOURCES LIST

http://evolve.elsevier.com/Lewis/medsurg
Review Questions (Online Only)
Key Points
Answer Keys for Questions
- Rationales for Bridge to NCLEX Examination Questions
- Answer Guidelines for Case Study on p. 581
- Answer Guidelines for Managing Care of Multiple Patients Case Study (Section 6) on p. 584
Student Case Studies
- Patient With Asthma
- Patient With Chronic Obstructive Pulmonary Disease (COPD)
- Patient With Cystic Fibrosis
Nursing Care Plans
- eNursing Care Plan 28.1: Patient With Asthma
- eNursing Care Plan 28.2: Patient With Chronic Obstructive Pulmonary Disease
Conceptual Care Map Creator
- Conceptual Care Map for Case Study on p. 581
Audio Glossary
Content Updates

REFERENCES

1. Patton KT, Thibodeau GA: *Anatomy and physiology,* ed 9, St Louis, 2016, Elsevier.
*2. Leung JM, Sin DD: Asthma-COPD overlap syndrome: Pathogenesis, clinical features, and therapeutic targets, *BMJ* 358:j3772, 2017.
*3. Hines KL, Peebles RJ: Management of the asthma-COPD overlap syndrome: A review of the evidence, *Curr Allergy Asthma Rep* 17:15, 2017.
4. Cystic Fibrosis Foundation: 2016 Patient registry annual data report. Retrieved from *www.cff.org/Research/Researcher-Resources/Patient-Registry/2016-Patient-Registry-Annual-Data-Report.pdf.*
5. Centers for Disease Control and Prevention (CDC): Fast Facts: Asthma. Retrieved from *www.cdc.gov/nchs/fastats/asthma.htm.*
*6. Guibas GV, Matioudakis AG, Tsoumani M, et al: Relationship of allergy with asthma: There are more than the allergy "eggs" in the asthma "basket," *Front Pediatr* 5:92, 2017.
7. Centers for Disease Control and Prevention: Percentage of people with asthma who smoke. Retrieved from *www.cdc.gov/asthma/asthma_stats/people_who_smoke.htm.*
8. Fehrenbach H, Wagner C, Wegmann M: Airway remodeling in asthma: What really matters, *Cell Tissue Res* 367:551, 2017.
9. Saaden CK: Status asthmaticus. Retrieved from *https://emedicine.medscape.com/article/2129484-overview.*
10. Sim YS, Lee JH, Lee WY, et al: Spirometry and bronchodilator test, *Tuberc Respir Dis* 80:105, 2017.
*11. Sato S, Saito J, Fukuhara A, et al: The clinical role of fractional exhaled nitric oxide in asthma control, *Ann Allergy Asthma Immunol* 119:5421, 2017.
12. CDC: Chronic obstructive pulmonary disease. Retrieved from *www.cdc.gov/copd/index.html.*
*13. Terzikhan N, Verhamme KM, Hofman A, et al: Prevalence and incidence of COPD in smokers and non-smokers: The Rotterdam study, *Eur J Epidemiol* 31:785, 2016.
*14. Bigna JJ, Kenne AM, Asangbeh SL, et al: Prevalence of COPD in the global population with HIV: A systematic review and meta-analysis, *Lancet* 6:PE193, 2017.
15. Yakar HI, Gunen H, Pehlivan E, et al: The role of tuberculosis in COPD, *Int J Chron Obstruct Pulmon Dis* 12:323, 2017.
*16. Fahndrich S, Biertz F, Karch A, et al: Cardiovascular risk in patients with alpha-1-antitrypsin deficiency, *Respir Res* 18:171, 2017.
17. Leong D: Cor pulmonale: Overview of cor pulmonale management. Retrieved from *www.emedicine.medscape.com/article/154062-overview#a4.*
18. Shah SJ: Cor pulmonale. Retrieved from *www.merckmanuals.com/en-ca/professional/cardiovascular-disorders/heart-failure/cor-pulmonale.*
19. Viniol C, Vogelmeier CF: *Exacerbations of COPD, Eur Respir Rev* 27(147), 2018.
20. Lange P, Halpin DM, O'Donnell, et al: Diagnosis, assessment, and phenotyping of COPD: Beyond FEV_1, *Int J Chron Obstruct Pulmon Dis* 11:3, 2016.
21. American Lung Association: Surgery for COPD. Retrieved from *www.lung.org/lung-health-and-diseases/lung-disease-lookup/copd/diagnosing-and-treating/surgery.html.*
*22. Darwiche K, Karpf-Wissel R, Eisenmann S, et al: Bronchoscopic lung volume reduction with endobronchial valves in low-FEV 1 patients, *Respiration* 92:414, 2016.
23. Ergan B, Akgun M, Pacilli AMG, et al: Should I stay or should I go? COPD and Air Travel. Retrieved from *http://err.ersjournals.com/content/27/148/180030.*
*24. Hsieh MJ, Yang TM, Tsai YH: Nutritional supplementation in patients with chronic obstructive pulmonary disease, *JFMA* 115:595, 2016.
25. Henderson W: Life expectancy when you're living with cystic fibrosis. Retrieved from *https://cysticfibrosisnewstoday.com/2017/05/24/living-cf-life-expectancy/.*
26. Henderson W. Cystic fibrosis can lead to osteopenia and osteoporosis. Retrieved from: *https://cysticfibrosisnewstoday.com/2017/03/22/cystic-fibrosis-can-lead-osteopenia-osteoporosis/.*
27. Sharma GD: Cystic fibrosis clinical presentation. Retrieved from *https://emedicine.medscape.com/article/1001602-clinical.*
*28. Willems P, Weeks S, Meskal A, et al: Biological variation of chloride and sodium in sweat obtained by pilocarpine iontophoresis in adults: How sure are you about sweat test results? *Lung* 195:214, 2017.
*29. Green J, Gilchrist FJ, Carroll W: Interventions for treating distal intestinal obstruction syndrome (DIOS) in cystic fibrosis. Retrieved from *www.cochranelibrary.com/cdsr/doi/10.1002/14651858.CD012798/epdf/full.*
30. Smith MP: Diagnosis and management of bronchiectasis, *CMAJ* 189:E828, 2017.

*Evidence-based information for clinical practice.

CASE STUDY
Managing Care of Multiple Patients

You are assigned to care for the following 4 patients on a medical-surgical unit. You are sharing 1 UAP with another RN.

Patients

F.T. is a 70-yr-old man with a history of COPD who was admitted yesterday with bilateral lower lobe pneumonia. He is receiving O_2 at 2 L/min via nasal cannula and IV antibiotics. His last pulse oximetry reading was 92%.

(© Fuse/Thinkstock.)

M.R. is a 69-yr-old man who is 3 days postoperative following a total laryngectomy with tracheostomy for treatment of laryngeal cancer. He is receiving intermittent feeding via a percutaneous endoscopic gastrostomy (PEG) tube and last received pain medication 4 hours ago.

(© iStockphoto/Thinkstock.)

J.H. is a 52-yr-old man admitted with right lower lobe pneumonia. A bronchoscopy with biopsy showed small cell lung cancer. He is intermittently confused and anxious with rapid, shallow respirations. He and his family are currently considering his treatment options.

(© iStockphoto/Thinkstock.)

H.M. is a 68-yr-old woman admitted 6 days ago with a COPD exacerbation. She has not been able to ambulate much because of her shortness of breath. She is on oral prednisone and ipratropium. She is being discharged later today. She is to start Advair Diskus and chronic O_2 therapy at home after discharge.

(© iStockphoto/Thinkstock.)

Discussion Questions

1. **Priority Decision:** After receiving report, which patient should you see first? Provide a rationale for your decision.
2. **Collaboration:** Which morning tasks can you delegate to the UAP *(select all that apply)*?
   a. Take vital signs and a pulse oximetry reading on F.T.
   b. Assess M.R.'s pain level and show him how to administer his feeding.
   c. Assist H.M. with AM care and gather belongings in anticipation of discharge.
   d. Provide coffee for J.H.'s family as they await a family meeting with the HCP.
   e. Teach F.T. how to do pursed-lip breathing and titrate O_2 to obtain pulse oximetry >95%.

3. **Priority Decision and Collaboration:** While you are assessing J.H., the UAP tells you that H.M. is reporting chest pain and worsening shortness of breath. M.R. is requesting pain medication. What should you do *first*?
   a. Ask the UAP to get H.M.'s vital signs while you give M.R. pain medication.
   b. Ask the UAP to increase H.M.'s O_2 to 4 L/min while you assess M.R.'s pain.
   c. Ask the UAP to obtain a stat 12-lead ECG on H.M. while you perform a focused assessment.
   d. Ask the UAP to have another RN give M.R. his pain medication while you go directly to H.M.'s room.

Case Study Progression

After assessing H.M., you notify her HCP. A stat 12-lead ECG is done, and a blood sample is drawn to check cardiac enzymes. H.M.'s chest pain is not relieved by sublingual nitroglycerin. You then give 4 mg IV morphine. H.M. states that her pain is "a little better" but continues to report dyspnea. The 12-lead ECG and cardiac enzyme results are all within normal limits.

4. Because of H.M.'s reduced mobility, you recognize that she is at risk for developing _____ and anticipate the HCP will order which tests to determine the cause of her current symptoms?
   a. BNP and echocardiogram
   b. D-dimer and spiral CT scan
   c. CBC and abdominal flat-plate x-ray
   d. Serum electrolytes and renal ultrasound
5. While the charge nurse goes with H.M. to the radiology department, you turn your attention back to your remaining 3 patients. Before giving M.R.'s 8 AM enteral feeding, you find his PEG tube clogged. Which action should you take *next*?
   a. Flush the tube with warm water, using a back-and-forth motion.
   b. Obtain an x-ray to confirm the tube is still placed in the stomach.
   c. Notify the HCP so that surgery to insert new tube can be scheduled.
   d. Instill 30 mL of cranberry juice into the tube and recheck in 1 hour.
6. When preparing F.T.'s AM medications, you note that he is scheduled to receive the following antibiotics at 8 AM: levofloxacin 750 mg in 150 mL normal saline over 90 minutes (once daily) and cefazolin 1 gram in 100 mL normal saline over 30 minutes (every 8 hrs). He has only one IV site. Which action is *most* appropriate?
   a. Obtain a second peripheral IV site.
   b. Call the HCP to change the administration times.
   c. Check with pharmacy to see if they can be mixed together in the same IV bag.
   d. Administer the cefazolin first because it takes the least amount of time to infuse.
7. **Management Decision:** J.H.'s son calls you on the telephone to ask about his father's current condition and long-term prognosis. Which initial response would be *most* appropriate?
   a. Ask the person calling what the code word is to identify himself or herself as family.
   b. Tell the caller that you are not allowed to discuss any information over the telephone.
   c. Empathize with the son's need to know his father's long-term prognosis.
   d. Ask J.H.'s son what the HCP has told him to clarify his understanding of the situation.

Answers available at *http://evolve.elsevier.com/Lewis/medsurg.*

Assessment: Hematologic System

Sandra Irene Rome

We choose our destiny in the way we treat others.

Vivian, in "Wit"

ⓔ http://evolve.elsevier.com/Lewis/medsurg/

LEARNING OUTCOMES

1. Describe the structures and functions of the hematologic system.
2. Distinguish among the different types of blood cells and their functions.
3. Explain the process of hemostasis.
4. Link the age-related changes in the hematologic system to differences in findings of hematologic studies.
5. Obtain significant subjective and objective assessment data related to the hematologic system from a patient.
6. Perform a physical assessment of the hematologic system using the appropriate techniques.
7. Distinguish normal from common abnormal findings of a physical assessment of the hematologic system.
8. Describe the purpose, significance of results, and nursing responsibilities related to diagnostic studies of the hematologic system.

KEY TERMS

ecchymoses, p. 597	hemolysis, p. 587	petechiae, p. 597
erythropoiesis, p. 587	leukopenia, p. 602	reticulocyte, p. 587
fibrinolysis, p. 590	neutropenia, p. 602	thrombocytopenia, p. 603
hematopoiesis, p. 585	pancytopenia, p. 602	thrombocytosis, p. 603

Hematology is the study of blood and blood-forming tissues. This includes the bone marrow, blood, spleen, and lymph system. You need a basic knowledge of hematology to be able to evaluate several important concepts in the clinical setting. A functioning hematologic system is needed to support the patient's ability to transport oxygen (O_2) and carbon dioxide (CO_2), maintain intravascular volume, coagulate blood, and combat infections.

STRUCTURES AND FUNCTIONS OF HEMATOLOGIC SYSTEM

Bone Marrow

Blood cell production (hematopoiesis) occurs within the bone marrow. *Bone marrow* is the soft material that fills the central core of bones. There are 2 types of bone marrow, yellow (adipose) and red (hematopoietic). Red marrow actively makes blood cells. In adults, red marrow is found primarily in the flat and irregular bones, such as the ends of long bones, pelvic bones, vertebrae, sacrum, sternum, ribs, flat cranial bones, and scapulae.

All 3 types of blood cells (red blood cells [RBCs], white blood cells [WBCs], and platelets) develop from a common hematopoietic stem cell in the bone marrow. The hematopoietic *stem cell* is best described as an immature blood cell that can self-renew and differentiate into hematopoietic precursor cells. Several types of blood cells form as the cells mature and differentiate (Fig. 29.1).

The bone marrow responds by a negative feedback system to the need for specific blood cells by increasing that cell's production. Various factors or cytokines (e.g., erythropoietin, granulocyte colony-stimulating factor [G-CSF], stem cell factor, thrombopoietin) stimulate the bone marrow. This results in differentiation of the stem cells into one of the committed

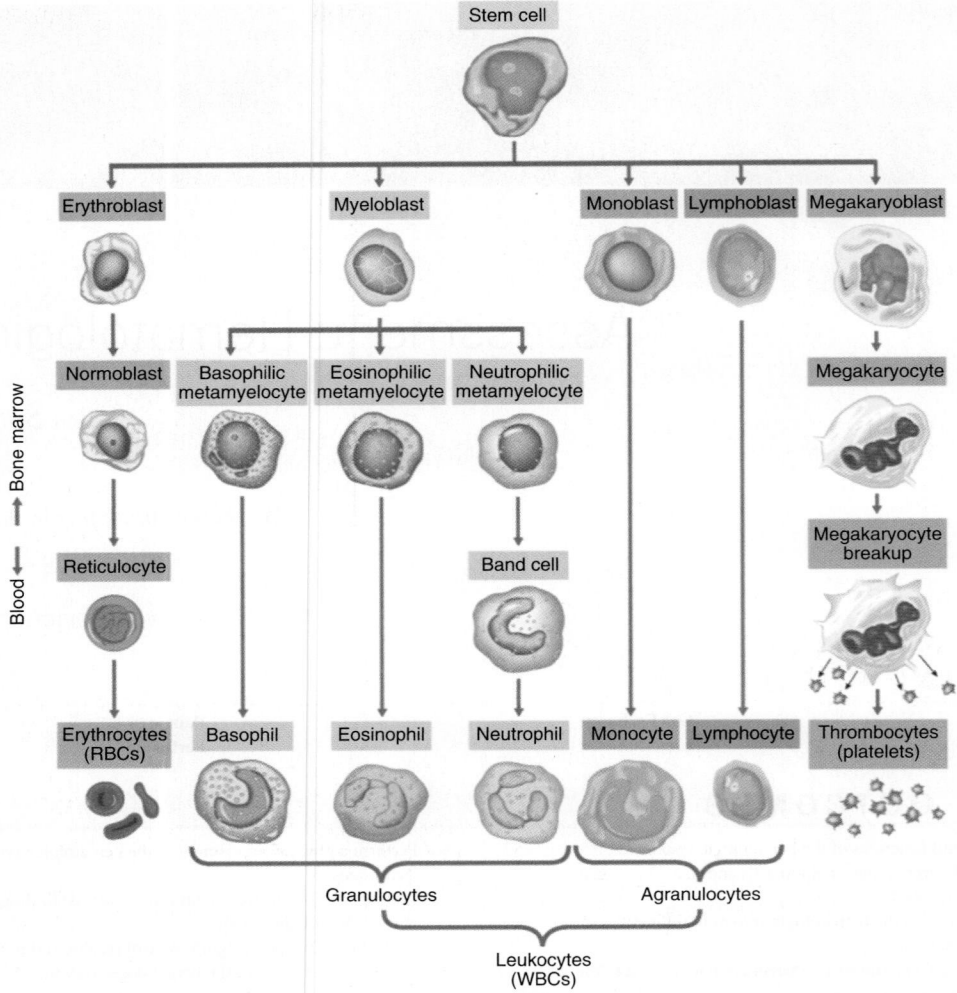

FIG. 29.1 Development of blood cells.

hematopoietic cells (e.g., RBC). For example, when tissue hypoxia occurs, the kidney secretes erythropoietin. It circulates to the bone marrow and causes proerythroblasts to differentiate in the bone marrow.[1]

Blood

Blood is a type of connective tissue that has 3 major functions: transportation, regulation, and protection (Table 29.1). Blood has 2 major components: plasma and blood cells. In an adult weighing between 150 and 180 lb, the volume of blood is usually between 4.7 and 5.5 L (5 to 6 quarts).

Plasma. About 55% of blood is plasma[1] (Fig. 29.2). Plasma is composed mainly of water. It also contains proteins, electrolytes, gases, nutrients (e.g., glucose, amino acids, lipids), and waste. The term *serum* refers to plasma minus its clotting factors. Plasma proteins include albumin, globulin, and clotting factors (mostly fibrinogen). Albumin is a protein that helps maintain oncotic pressure in the blood.[1] The liver makes most plasma proteins. The exception is antibodies (immunoglobulins). They are made by plasma cells.

Blood Cells. About 45% of the blood (Fig. 29.2) is composed of formed elements, or blood cells. The 3 types of blood cells are *erythrocytes* (RBCs), *leukocytes* (WBCs), and *thrombocytes*

TABLE 29.1	**Functions of Blood**
Function	**Examples**
Protection	• Maintaining homeostasis of blood coagulation
	• Combating invasion of pathogens and other foreign substances
Regulation	• Fluid and electrolyte balance
	• Acid-base balance
	• Body temperature
	• Maintaining intravascular oncotic pressure
Transportation	• O_2 from lungs to cells
	• Nutrients from GI tract to cells
	• Hormones from endocrine glands to tissues and cells
	• Metabolic waste products (e.g., CO_2, NH_3, urea) from cells to lungs, liver, and kidneys

(platelets). The primary function of RBCs is O_2 transportation. WBCs help protect the body from infection. Platelets promote blood coagulation.

Erythrocytes. The primary functions of RBCs include transport of gases (both O_2 and CO_2) and assistance in maintaining acid-base balance. RBCs are flexible cells with a unique

PLASMA (percentage by weight)
- Proteins 7%
- Water 91%
- Other solutes 2%

PROTEINS
- Albumins 57%
- Globulins 38%
- Fibrinogen 4%
- Prothrombin 1%

- Ions
- Nutrients
- Waste products
- Gases
- Regulatory substances

WHOLE BLOOD (percentage by volume)

Centrifuged sample of blood

Blood 8%

Other fluids and tissues 92%

Buffy coat

PLASMA 55%

FORMED ELEMENTS 45%

TOTAL BODY WEIGHT

Platelets 140,000–340,000

Leukocytes 5000–9000

Erythrocytes 4.2–6.2 million

LEUKOCYTES
- Neutrophils 60%–70%
- Lymphocytes 20%–25%
- Monocytes 3%–8%
- Eosinophils 2%–4%
- Basophils 0.5%–1%

FORMED ELEMENTS (number per cubic mm)

FIG. 29.2 Blood components in a healthy adult. Normally, 45% of the blood is composed of blood cells and 55% is composed of plasma. (From Patton KT, Thibodeau GA: Structure & function of the body, ed 15, St Louis, 2016, Mosby.)

biconcave shape. This flexibility allows the cell to change its shape so that it can easily pass through tiny capillaries. The cell membrane is thin to facilitate diffusion of gases.

RBCs are primarily composed of a large molecule called *hemoglobin*. Hemoglobin is a complex protein-iron compound composed of heme (an iron compound) and globin (a simple protein). It binds with O_2 and CO_2. As RBCs circulate through the capillaries surrounding alveoli within the lung, O_2 attaches to iron on the hemoglobin. We refer to this O_2-bound hemoglobin as *oxyhemoglobin*. It gives arterial blood its bright red appearance. As RBCs flow to body tissues, O_2 detaches from the hemoglobin and diffuses from the capillary into tissue cells. CO_2 diffuses from tissue cells into the capillary, attaches to the globin part of hemoglobin, and is transported to the lungs for removal. Hemoglobin also acts as a buffer and plays a role in maintaining acid-base balance. This buffering function is described in Chapter 16.

Erythropoiesis (the process of RBC production) is regulated by cellular O_2 requirements and general metabolic activity. Erythropoiesis is stimulated by hypoxia and controlled by *erythropoietin*, a glycoprotein growth factor made and released primarily by the kidney. Erythropoietin stimulates the bone marrow to increase RBC production. We make about 2.5 million RBCs per second. The normal life span of RBCs is about 120 days. The availability of nutrients influences erythropoiesis. Many essential nutrients are needed for erythropoiesis. These include protein, iron, folate (folic acid), cobalamin (vitamin B_{12}), riboflavin (vitamin B_2), pyridoxine (vitamin B_6), pantothenic acid, niacin, ascorbic acid (vitamin C), copper, and vitamin E. Endocrine hormones, such as thyroxine, corticosteroids, and testosterone, also affect RBC production. For example, hypothyroidism is often associated with anemia.[1]

Several distinct cell types evolve during RBC maturation (Fig. 29.1). The **reticulocyte** is an immature RBC. Reticulocytes can develop into mature RBCs within 48 hours of release into the circulation. A mature RBC lacks a nucleus and cannot undergo mitotic division. Assessing the number of reticulocytes is a useful way to evaluate the rate and adequacy of RBC production.[1]

Hemolysis (destruction of RBCs) by monocytes and macrophages removes abnormal, defective, damaged, and old RBCs from circulation. Hemolysis normally occurs in the bone marrow, liver, and spleen. Because one of the components of RBCs is bilirubin, hemolysis of these cells results in increased bilirubin the body must process. When hemolysis occurs by normal mechanisms, the liver conjugates and excretes all the bilirubin in bile.

Leukocytes. *Leukocytes* (WBCs) appear white when separated from blood. Like the RBCs, WBCs originate from stem cells within the bone marrow (Fig. 29.1). They may eventually reside in the thymus or secondary lymphoid tissues, such as the spleen, lymph nodes, and Peyer patches. There are several types of WBCs. Each has a different function. WBCs that have granules in the cytoplasm are *granulocytes* (also known as *polymorphonuclear leukocytes*). Granulocytes include neutrophils, basophils, and eosinophils.

WBCs that do not have granules in the cytoplasm are *agranulocytes*. They include lymphocytes, monocytes, and natural killer cells. Lymphocytes and monocytes are *mononuclear cells* because they have only one discrete nucleus. WBCs have a widely variable life span. Granulocytes may live for only hours. Some T lymphocytes may live for years.

Granulocytes. The primary function of the granulocytes is *phagocytosis,* a process by which WBCs engulf any unwanted organism and then digest and kill it. They can migrate through vessel walls and to the sites where they are needed. The *neutrophil* is the most common type of granulocyte, making up 60% to 70% of all WBCs. Neutrophils are the primary phagocytic cells involved in acute inflammatory responses. Once they engulf the pathogen, they die in 1 to 2 days.[1] Hematopoietic growth factors (e.g., G-CSF, granulocyte-macrophage colony-stimulating factor [GM-CSF]) stimulate neutrophil production and maturation (see Table 13.3).

We call a mature neutrophil a *segmented neutrophil,* or "seg" or "polysegmented neutrophil," because the nucleus is segmented into 2 to 5 lobes connected by strands. An immature neutrophil is a *band* (for the band appearance of the nucleus). Although band cells are sometimes found in the peripheral circulation of normal people and are capable of phagocytosis, the mature neutrophil is much more effective. An increase in neutrophils in the blood is a common indicator of infection and tissue injury.

Eosinophils make up only 2% to 4% of all WBCs. They have a similar but reduced ability for phagocytosis. One of their primary functions is to engulf antigen-antibody complexes formed during an allergic response. High eosinophil levels occur with some cancers, such as Hodgkin's lymphoma, in parasitic infections, and in various skin diseases and connective tissue disorders.[1]

Basophils make up less than 2% of all WBCs. They have cytoplasmic granules that contain chemical mediators, such as heparin and histamine. A basophil responds to stimulation by an antigen or by tissue injury by releasing substances from the granules. This is part of the response seen in allergic and inflammatory reactions. *Mast cells* are like basophils, but they reside in connective tissues. They play a key role in inflammation, permeability of blood vessels, and smooth muscle contraction.

Lymphocytes. Lymphocytes make up 20% to 25% of the WBCs in the blood.[1] They form the basis of the cellular and humoral immune responses. Two lymphocyte subtypes are B cells and T cells. T-cell precursors originate in the bone marrow. They migrate to the thymus gland for further differentiation into T cells. *Natural killer (NK) cells* are lymphocytes that kill virus-infected cells and activate T cells and phagocytes. They do not need prior exposure to antigens. Dendritic cells are the primary phagocytic cells in the peripheral organs and skin. Most lymphocytes briefly circulate in the blood and reside in lymphoid and other tissues. Details of lymphocyte function are discussed in Chapter 13.

Monocytes. Monocytes, the other type of agranular WBC, make up about 3% to 8% of the total WBCs.[1] Monocytes are potent phagocytic cells that ingest small or large masses of matter, such as bacteria, dead cells, tissue debris, and old or defective RBCs. These cells are present in the blood for only a brief time before they migrate into the tissues and become macrophages. In addition to macrophages that have differentiated from monocytes, tissues also have resident macrophages. These resident macrophages have special names (e.g., Kupffer cells in the liver, osteoclasts in the bone, alveolar macrophages in the lung). They protect the body from pathogens at these entry points and are more phagocytic than monocytes. Macrophages interact with lymphocytes to facilitate humoral and cellular immune responses.

Thrombocytes. The primary function of thrombocytes, or *platelets,* is to start the clotting process by producing an initial platelet plug at a site of injury. Platelets circulate suspended in plasma in an unactivated state. They must be available in enough numbers and be structurally and metabolically sound for blood clotting to occur. Platelet activation starts at the site of any capillary damage. Increasing numbers of platelets accumulate to form an initial platelet plug that is stabilized with clotting factors. About one third of the platelets in the body are stored in the spleen.

Platelets originate from stem cells within the bone marrow (Fig. 29.1). The stem cell undergoes differentiation by transforming into a *megakaryocyte,* which fragments into platelets. Platelet production is partly regulated by *thrombopoietin* (TPO), a growth factor that acts on bone marrow to stimulate platelet production. TPO is primarily made in the liver. During inflammation, interleukin 6 (IL-6) causes us to make more TPO, which increases production of platelets and potential thrombosis. Typically, platelets have a life span of only 8 to 11 days.

Normal Iron Metabolism

Our iron requirement is 25 mg daily. We get iron from food and dietary supplements. Our body absorbs only 1 mg of every 10 to 20 mg of iron we eat. The rest comes from the continued recycling of iron from RBCs.[1] As part of normal iron metabolism, iron is recycled after macrophages in the liver and spleen phagocytize, or ingest and destroy, old and damaged RBCs.

After dietary iron is absorbed in the duodenum and proximal jejunum, it is transported through the plasma by transferrin (Fig. 29.3). Transferrin is made in the liver. How much iron is bound to transferrin is a reliable indicator of the iron supply for developing RBCs.

About two thirds of total body iron is bound to heme in RBCs (hemoglobin) and muscle cells (myoglobin). The other one third of iron is stored as ferritin and hemosiderin (degraded form of ferritin) in the bone marrow, spleen, liver, and macrophages (Fig. 29.3). When we do not replace stored iron, hemoglobin production is reduced. Normally there is very little iron loss except from blood loss. We lose about 3% daily in urine, sweat, bile, and epithelial cells in the gastrointestinal (GI) tract.

Normal Clotting Mechanisms

Hemostasis describes the arrest of bleeding. This process is important in minimizing blood loss when various body structures are injured. The sequence of events includes (1) vascular injury and subendothelial exposure, (2) adhesion, (3) activation, (4) aggregation, (5) platelet plug formation, and (6) clot retraction and dissolution.

Vascular Injury and Subendothelial Exposure. When a blood vessel is injured, an immediate local vasoconstrictive response occurs. Vasoconstriction reduces the leakage of blood from the vessel by restricting the vessel size and pressing the endothelial surfaces together. The latter reaction enhances vessel wall stickiness and keeps the vessel closed after vasoconstriction subsides. Vascular spasm may last for 20 to 30 minutes. This allows time for the body to activate the platelet response and plasma clotting factors. The platelet response and plasma clotting factors are triggered by endothelial injury and the release of substances such as thromboxane A_2 (TXA_2). Platelets begin to fill endothelial gaps.[1]

Adhesion. The loss of endothelial cells exposes adhesive glycoproteins, such as collagen and von Willebrand factor (vWF), to which more platelets adhere. The stickiness is termed *adhesiveness.* The formation of clumps is termed *aggregation* or *agglutination.*

FIG. 29.3 Normal iron metabolism. Iron is ingested in the diet or from supplements. Macrophages break down ingested RBCs. Iron is returned to blood bound to transferrin or stored as ferritin or hemosiderin.

Activation. The interaction described previously causes the platelets to undergo an activation process. This leads to changes in platelet shape. The platelets then can bind adhesive proteins, including fibrinogen and vWF. Release of various platelet granules (including adenosine phosphate [ADP]) recruits and activates other platelets, clotting factors, and growth factors. As Fig. 29.4 shows, platelet lipoproteins stimulate necessary conversions in the clotting process.

Aggregation. Platelet aggregation is stimulated by TXA_2 and ADP, which induce fibrinogen receptors on the platelet. The formation of a visible fibrin clot on the platelet plug is the conclusion of a complex series of reactions involving different clotting (coagulation) factors. We label plasma clotting factors with both names and Roman numerals (Table 29.2).

Plasma proteins circulate in inactive forms until stimulated to start clotting through 1 of 2 pathways, intrinsic or extrinsic (Fig. 29.4). The *intrinsic pathway* is activated by collagen exposure from endothelial injury when the blood vessel is damaged. The *extrinsic pathway* is activated when tissue factor or tissue thromboplastin is released extravascularly from injured tissues.

Regardless of how we begin to clot, coagulation ultimately follows the same final common pathway of the clotting cascade. Thrombin, in the common pathway, is the most powerful enzyme in the coagulation process (Fig. 29.4). It converts fibrinogen to fibrin, which is an essential part of a blood clot.

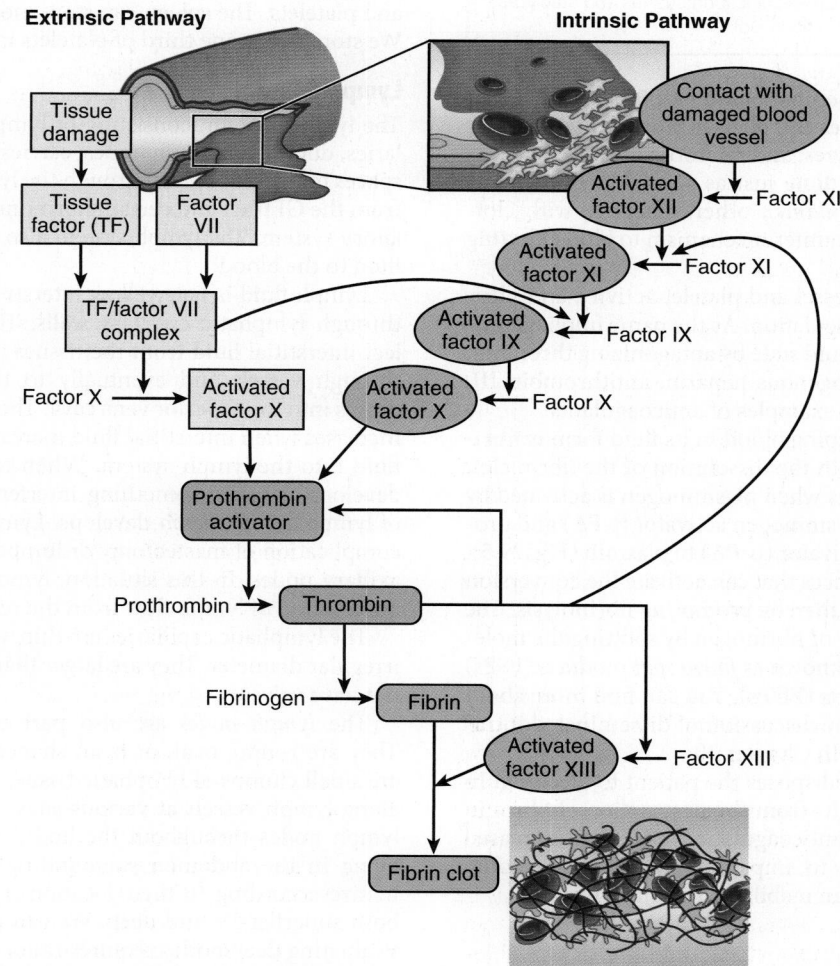

FIG. 29.4 Coagulation mechanism showing steps in the intrinsic pathway and extrinsic pathway as they would occur in the test tube.

TABLE 29.2 Coagulation Factors

Coagulation Factor	Action
I Fibrinogen	Source of fibrin to form a clot. Made in liver
II Prothrombin	Converted to thrombin, which then activates fibrinogen into fibrin as well as factors V, VII, VIII, XI, XIII, protein C, platelets
III Tissue factor, tissue thromboplastin	Released from damaged endothelial cells and activates the extrinsic pathway by reacting with factor VII
IV Calcium	Required cofactor at several points in the coagulation cascade
V Proaccelerin (labile) factor	Binds with factor X to activate prothrombin
VI	Not in use (obsolete)
VII Stable factor, proconvertin	Forms a complex with factor III and activates factors IX and X
VIII Antihemophilic factor	Works with factor IX and calcium to activate factor X
IX Christmas factor	Together with factor VIII, activates factor X
X Stuart factor	Activates conversion of factor II (prothrombin) to thrombin
XI Plasma thromboplastin antecedent	Activates factor IX when calcium is present
XII Hageman factor	Activates factor XI, which starts the intrinsic pathway
XIII Fibrin-stabilizing factor	Cross-links fibrin strands and stabilizes fibrin clot

FIG. 29.5 Fibrinolytic system.

Platelet Plug Formation. The final blood clot is a meshwork of protein strands that stabilizes the platelet plug and traps other cells, such as RBCs, phagocytes, and microorganisms.

Clot Retraction and Dissolution. Just as some blood elements foster coagulation *(procoagulants),* others interfere with clotting *(anticoagulants).* This counter mechanism to blood clotting keeps blood in its fluid state.

Antithrombin activity, vessel and platelet activity, and fibrinolysis contribute to anticoagulation. As the name implies, antithrombins keep blood in a fluid state by antagonizing thrombin, a powerful coagulant. Endogenous heparin, antithrombin III, protein C, and protein S are examples of anticoagulants.

The second means of keeping blood in its fluid form is **fibrinolysis**, a process resulting in the dissolution of the fibrin clot. The fibrinolytic system starts when plasminogen is activated by substances such as tissue plasminogen activator (t-PA) and urokinase-like plasminogen activator (u-PA) to plasmin (Fig. 29.5). Thrombin is 1 of the substances that can activate the conversion of plasminogen to plasmin, thereby promoting fibrinolysis. The plasmin attacks either fibrin or fibrinogen by splitting the molecules into smaller elements known as *fibrin split products* (FSPs) or *fibrin degradation products* (FDPs). You can find more about FSPs in Table 29.8 and in the discussion of disseminated intravascular coagulation (DIC) in Chapter 30.

Excessive fibrinolysis predisposes the patient to bleeding. In this situation, bleeding results from the destruction of fibrin in platelet plugs or from the anticoagulation effects of increased FSPs. Increased FSPs lead to impaired platelet aggregation, reduced prothrombin, and an inability to stabilize fibrin.

Spleen

The spleen is the largest lymphoid organ. It is found in the upper left quadrant of the abdomen. The spleen has 4 major

functions: hematopoietic, filtration, immunologic, and storage. The *hematopoietic function* is shown by the spleen's ability to make RBCs during fetal development. The *filtration function* is shown by the spleen's ability to remove old and defective RBCs from the circulation by the mononuclear phagocyte system. Filtration also involves the reuse of iron. The spleen can catabolize hemoglobin released by hemolysis and return the iron part of the hemoglobin to the bone marrow for reuse. The spleen plays a vital role in filtering circulating bacteria, especially encapsulated organisms such as gram-positive cocci. The spleen's rich supply of lymphocytes, monocytes, and stored immunoglobulins plays a role in *immunologic function.* The *storage function* is reflected in its role as a storage site for RBCs and platelets. The spleen can store more than 300 mL of blood. We store about one third of platelets in the spleen.

Lymph System

The lymph system, consisting of lymph fluid, lymphatic capillaries, ducts, and lymph nodes, carries fluid from the interstitial spaces to the blood. It is through the lymph that proteins and fat from the GI tract and certain hormones can return to the circulatory system. The lymph system also returns excess interstitial fluid to the blood.

Lymph fluid is pale yellow interstitial fluid that has diffused through lymphatic capillary walls. The lymphatic vessels collect interstitial fluid from the tissues and transport it as lymph through vessels and eventually to the thoracic duct, which drains into the superior vena cava. The formation of lymph fluid increases when interstitial fluid increases, thereby forcing more fluid into the lymph system. When too much interstitial fluid develops or when something interferes with the reabsorption of lymph, *lymphedema* develops. Lymphedema may occur as a complication of mastectomy or lumpectomy with dissection of axillary nodes. In this situation, lymphedema is caused by the obstruction of lymph flow from the removal of lymph nodes.

The lymphatic capillaries are thin-walled vessels that have an irregular diameter. They are larger than blood capillaries and do not have valves.

The *lymph nodes* are also part of the lymphatic system. They are round, oval, or bean shaped. Structurally, the nodes are small clumps of lymphatic tissue. They are found in groups along lymph vessels at various sites. There are more than 200 lymph nodes throughout the body, with the greatest number being in the abdomen surrounding the GI tract. They vary in size according to their location. Lymph nodes are situated both superficially and deep. We can palpate superficial nodes. Evaluating deep nodes requires radiologic examination.[2] A primary function of lymph nodes is filtration of pathogens and foreign particles that are carried by lymph to the nodes.

Liver

The liver has metabolic, secretory, vascular, and storage functions. It makes all the procoagulants that are essential to hemostasis and blood coagulation and secretes bilirubin and bile. It stores iron that exceeds tissue needs, which can occur with frequent blood transfusions or diseases that cause iron overload. *Hepcidin,* made by the liver, is a key regulator of iron balance. Iron overload or inflammation stimulates hepcidin synthesis. Hepcidin inhibits the release of stored iron from enterocytes (in the intestines) and macrophages. So, when iron is deficient, hepatocytes make less hepcidin. This results in the release of stored iron and an increase in dietary absorption. Other functions of the liver are described in Chapters 38 and 43.

 ## Gerontologic Considerations: Effects of Aging on Hematologic System

Aging leads to a decrease in bone marrow mass and cellularity and an increase in bone marrow fat.[3] 90% of the marrow space is occupied by hematopoietic tissue at birth. This is reduced to 50% at age 30 and 30% at age 70.[4] Although the older adult can still maintain adequate blood cell levels, the reduced reserve capacity leaves the older adult more vulnerable to possible problems with clotting, transporting O_2, and fighting infection, especially during periods of increased demand. This contributes to an older adult having a decreased ability to compensate for an acute or chronic illness.

Hemoglobin levels may begin to decrease in both men and women after middle age, with low-normal levels seen in most older people. Total serum iron, total iron-binding capacity, and intestinal iron absorption are all decreased in older adults. The RBC plasma membranes are more fragile. This may account for a slight increase in mean corpuscular volume (MCV) and a slight decrease in mean corpuscular hemoglobin concentration (MCHC) of RBCs in some older adults. While iron deficiency may cause low hemoglobin levels, other factors, such as GI bleeding, renal disease, testosterone deficiency, or bone marrow dysfunction, should be ruled out.[5] In 30% to 40% of cases, there is no specific cause of anemia. This is called "unexplained anemia in the elderly."[6] Cytokine levels may be high, but the amount of inflammation is not enough to increase hepcidin levels.[4] Healthy older patients are not able to make reticulocytes in response to hemorrhage or hypoxemia as well as younger adults. This is likely due to a blunted response to erythropoietin.[4]

Aging generally does not affect the total WBC count and differential. There may be a slight increase in neutrophils and a decrease in lymphocytes. However, the function of lymphocytes decreases, blunting the response to infection.[1] During an infection, the older adult may have only a minimal elevation in the total WBC count. This suggests decreased bone marrow reserve of granulocytes in older adults and reflects the possible impaired stimulation of hematopoiesis. Older adults are at higher risk for developing neutropenia from treatments.[6]

The number of platelets is unaffected by the aging process, but functionally they may have increased adhesiveness. Clotting factors increase with age. Thus aging is associated with an increased chance of clotting problems, such as venous thromboembolism.[3] Changes in vascular integrity related to aging can manifest as easy bruising.

Table 29.3 outlines the effects of aging on hematologic studies. Immune changes related to aging are detailed in Chapter 13.

 TABLE 29.3 Gerontologic Assessment Differences

Effects of Aging on Hematologic Studies

Study	Changes
CBC Studies	
Hemoglobin (Hgb)	Usually normal in women; possibly slight ↓ in men
Mean corpuscular hemoglobin concentration (MCHC)	May be slightly ↓
Mean corpuscular volume (MCV)	May be slightly ↑
Platelets	Unchanged; possible ↑ in adhesiveness
White blood cell (WBC) count	Decreased response to infection
Clotting Studies	
D-dimers	↑
Erythrocyte sedimentation rate (ESR)	↑ Significantly
Factors V, VII, IX	May be ↑
Fibrinogen	May be ↑
Partial thromboplastin time	May be ↓
Iron Studies	
Erythropoietin	May be ↑
Ferritin	↑
Serum iron	↓
Total iron-binding capacity	↓

ASSESSMENT OF HEMATOLOGIC SYSTEM

Much of the evaluation of the hematologic system is based on a thorough health history and presenting signs and symptoms.

Subjective Data
Important Health Information

Past Health History. Determine if the patient has had prior hematologic problems. Ask about problems with anemia, bleeding problems, and blood disorders. Ask about related medical conditions, such as malabsorption or liver (e.g., hepatitis, cirrhosis), kidney, or spleen problems. Patients may have received a solid organ transplant, may have lost a spleen to traumatic injury, or may have a history of IV drug or alcohol use that affects their risk for hematologic problems. A history of recent or recurrent infections or problems with blood clotting is important to note.

Medications. A complete medication history is an important part of a hematologic assessment. Ask about the use of vitamins, herbal products, or dietary supplements. Many medications may interfere with normal hematologic function.[3] Those on long-term anticoagulant therapy, such as warfarin, are at risk for bleeding problems. Chemotherapy drugs used to treat cancer (see Chapter 15) and antiretroviral agents used to treat human immunodeficiency virus (HIV) infection (see Chapter 14) may cause bone marrow depression. A patient previously treated with chemotherapy agents, particularly alkylating agents, has a higher risk for developing a secondary cancer of leukemia or lymphoma.

Surgery or Other Treatments. Ask the patient about specific surgical procedures. This includes splenectomy, tumor removal, prosthetic heart valve placement, surgical excision of the

CASE STUDY
Patient Introduction

(© Lisa F. Young/iStock.)

A.J. is a 63-yr-old white woman who is brought to the emergency department by her husband. He came home from work and found his wife at home, weak and lying in bed after she returned from work. She says she has been slowly getting more and more "cold and tired," but "that is what happens when you continue to work at this age." Her husband states that she has become more tired over the last couple of weeks and "her skin looks whiter." She has been having trouble working all day and even gets short of breath when doing simple errands. She also recently had a "bad cold and sinus infection" that only improved after 2 courses of antibiotics. A.J. says, "I've noticed I've had a lot of bruising lately."

Discussion Questions

1. What are the possible causes of A.J.'s weakness, pallor, and shortness of breath?
2. Is her condition stable or an emergency?
3. What type of assessment is most appropriate for A.J.: comprehensive, focused, or emergency? On what basis did you make that decision? What would be your priority?
4. What assessment questions would you ask A.J.?

You will learn more about A.J. and her condition as you read through this assessment chapter.
(See p. 594 for more information on A.J.)

duodenum (where iron absorption occurs), partial or total gastrectomy (which removes parietal cells, thus reducing intrinsic factor needed for the absorption of cobalamin [vitamin B_{12}]), gastric bypass (the duodenum may be bypassed and parietal cell surface area decreased), and ileal resection (where cobalamin absorption takes place). Assess how wound healing progressed postoperatively and if and when any bleeding problems occurred in relation to the surgery. Discuss wound healing and bleeding as responses to injuries (including minor trauma) and dental extractions. Determine the number of previous blood transfusions and any complications with administration. The risk for transfusion reactions and iron overload increases with the number of blood transfusions.

Functional Health Patterns. Key questions to ask a patient with a hematologic problem are outlined in Table 29.4.

Health Perception–Health Management Pattern. Ask the patient to describe the usual and present state of health. Gather complete demographic data, including age, gender, race, and ethnic background. Ask if there is any family history of hematologic problems.

🧬 GENETIC RISK ALERT

- Hematologic problems with a strong genetic link include sickle cell anemia, hemophilia, thalassemia, and hemochromatosis.
- People with a family history of these problems have a much greater risk for developing them.
- Leukemia, pernicious anemia, and clotting disorders may have a genetic predisposition.

When taking a family health history, ask about jaundice, anemia, cancer, RBC disorders, such as sickle cell disease, and bleeding disorders, such as hemophilia and clotting disorders.

Assess risk factors, such as alcohol and cigarette use, that may disrupt the hematologic system. Alcohol is caustic to the GI mucosa and can cause damage that results in GI bleeding,

esophageal varices, and decreased absorption of cobalamin and other nutrients.

Chronic alcohol users often have vitamin deficiencies. Alcohol exerts a damaging effect on platelet function and the liver, where we make clotting factors. Consequently, bleeding problems can develop and should be expected in cases of known chronic alcohol use. Illicit drug use is important to determine, since many of these drugs may affect hematopoiesis.

Cigarette smoking increases low-density lipoprotein (LDL) cholesterol and levels of CO_2, leading to hypoxia and changing the anticoagulant properties of the endothelium. Smoking increases platelet reactivity, plasma fibrinogen, hematocrit, and blood viscosity.

Nutritional-Metabolic Pattern. Obtain the patient's weight. Determine if the patient has had anorexia, nausea, vomiting, or oral discomfort. A dietary history may give clues about the cause of anemia. Iron, cobalamin, and folic acid are needed for the development of RBCs. Iron and folic acid deficiencies are associated with inadequate intake of foods such as meat, fish, eggs, leafy green vegetables, legumes, citrus fruits, and whole-grain and enriched breads, cereals, and rice. A diet with foods high in iron may offset folic acid deficiencies.[7]

Hematemesis (bright red, brown, or black vomitus) is a manifestation of an underlying problem and always needs investigating. Peptic ulcer disease is a common cause of hematemesis.

Explore any changes in the skin's texture, color, or temperature. Ask about bleeding gum tissue or bleeding from anywhere on the body. Ask about any lumps or swelling in the neck, armpits, or groin. Specifically, ask what the lumps feel like (i.e., hard or soft, tender or nontender) and if they are mobile or fixed. Primary lymph tumors are usually not painful. A nontender, consistently swollen lymph node may be a sign of a cancer, such as Hodgkin's or non-Hodgkin's lymphoma. Enlarged, tender lymph nodes are usually associated with an acute infection.[8] Explore any reports of fever. Determine if the patient currently has a fever, recurring fevers, chills, or night sweats.

Ask patients if they have a history of heart or lung diseases. Cardiovascular problems, such as valvular disease or hypertension, may predispose patients to hemolysis. Many medications used to treat cardiovascular disease can cause problems with hematopoietic cell production or coagulation. Lung problems that lead to hypoxemia may cause chronic stimulation of erythropoietin and result in *polycythemia* (excess RBCs).

Elimination Pattern. Ask if there has been blood in the urine or stool or if black, tarry stools have occurred. Ask the patient if they have had a recent stool tested for occult blood or colonoscopy.

Activity-Exercise Pattern. Because fatigue is a prominent symptom in many hematologic problems, ask about feelings of tiredness. Determine any weakness or feelings of heavy extremities. Assess for apathy, malaise, dyspnea, or palpitations. Note any change in the patient's ability to perform regular exercise and/or activities of daily living (ADLs), especially as they relate to a history of falling.

Sleep-Rest Pattern. Determine whether the patient feels rested after a night's sleep. Fatigue secondary to a hematologic problem often does not resolve after sleep.

Cognitive-Perceptual Pattern. Assess for any *arthralgia* (joint pain) that may be caused by a hematologic problem. Pain in the joint may occur with an autoimmune disorder, such as

TABLE 29.4 Health History

Hematologic System

Health Perception–Health Management
- Do you have any problem performing daily activities because of a lack of energy?*
- Do you smoke cigarettes or drink alcohol?*
- Do you take any prescribed or over-the-counter medications?*
- Are you taking any herbs?* Home remedies?*
- Have you in the past or are you currently consuming illegal drugs? What agents? What route? How often? When did you last use?
- Have you ever received a blood transfusion?*
- Is there any family history of anemia, cancer, bleeding, or clotting problems?*
- Have you had any surgeries?*

Nutritional-Metabolic
- Do you have any problems with eating, chewing, or swallowing?*
- Have you had any mouth sores, sore tongue, swollen or sore gums, oral bleeding?*
- What kind of diet do you follow? If a vegetarian, do you eat eggs, milk products, fish?
- How has your appetite been?
- Have you had any changes in your weight in the past year?*
- Do you take any vitamins, nutritional supplements, or iron?*
- Is nausea and vomiting a problem for you?*
- Have you ever had any unusual bleeding or bruising?*
- Have there been recent changes in the condition or color of your skin?*
- Have you had night sweats or cold intolerance?*
- Have you noticed any swelling in your armpits, neck, or groin?*

Elimination
- Have you had black or tarry stools?* Have you had light, clay-colored stools?*
- Have you noticed any blood or dark "tea color" in your urine?*
- Has your urine had a foul odor or cloudiness?
- Have you had any decrease in urine output?*
- Do you ever have diarrhea or change in bowel patterns?*

Activity-Exercise
- Do you have any shortness of breath at rest? With activity?*
- Do you have any limitations in joint motion?* Have any of your joints been swollen?*
- Do you have a problem with unsteady gait? Have you fallen recently?*
- Do you exercise regularly? What type and how often?*
- After activity, do you ever notice bleeding or bruising?*

Sleep-Rest
- Have you had excessive fatigue recently?*
- Are you more tired than usual?*
- Do you feel rested on awakening? If no, explain.

Cognitive-Perceptual
- Have you had any numbness or tingling?*
- Have you had any problems with your vision, hearing, or taste?*
- Have you noticed any changes in your mental function?*
- Do you have any pain, such as bone, joint, or abdominal pain, or abdominal fullness?*
- Do you have pain when moving your joints?*
- Have your muscles been sore or achy recently?*

Self-Perception–Self-Concept
- Does your health problem make you feel differently about yourself?*
- Do you have any physical changes that cause you distress?*

Role-Relationship
- Does your occupation bring you into contact with hazardous substances?*
- Has your present illness caused a change in your roles and relationships?*

Sexuality-Reproductive
- Has your hematologic problem caused any sexual or intimacy problems that concern you?*
- *Women:* When was your last menses? Do you consider your cycle normal? How long does your bleeding usually last? Have you had any increase in cramping or clotting?* Have there been any changes in the amount of flow?*
- *Men:* Do you ever have impotence?*
- Have you had unprotected sex in the past 6 months?* Was your partner someone new or a person with whom you have had a long-term sexual relationship?

Coping–Stress Tolerance
- Do you have a support system to help you when needed?
- What coping strategies do you use when your symptoms are worse?
- Do you have any specific symptoms when you feel stressed?*

Value-Belief
- Do you have any personal or religious objection to receiving blood or blood products?*
- Do you have any conflicts between your planned therapy and your value-belief system?*

*If yes, describe.

rheumatoid arthritis. It may occur with gout from increased uric acid production due to hematologic cancer or hemolytic anemia. Aching bones may result from pressure of expanding bone marrow with diseases such as leukemia. *Hemarthrosis* (blood in a joint) occurs in the patient with bleeding disorders and can be painful.

Note any paresthesias, numbness, and tingling as they may be related to a hematologic disorder. Assess for any changes in vision, hearing, taste, or mental status.

Self-Perception–Self-Concept Pattern. Determine the effect of the health problem on the patient's perception of self and personal abilities. Assess the effect of certain problems, such as bruising, petechiae, and lymph node swelling, on the patient's personal appearance.

Role-Relationship Pattern. Ask the patient about any past or present occupational or household exposures to radiation or chemicals. If such exposure has occurred, determine the type, amount, and duration of the exposure.

A person who has been exposed to radiation, as a treatment modality or by accident, has a higher incidence of certain hematologic problems. The same is true of a person who has been exposed to certain chemicals (e.g., benzene, lead, naphthalene, phenylbutazone). These chemicals are often used by potters, dry cleaners, and people in occupations that use adhesives. Ask the patient about a history in the military. Many Vietnam War veterans were exposed to a dioxin-containing defoliant (Agent Orange), which is linked with leukemia and lymphoma. Assess the effect of the present illness on the patient's usual roles and responsibilities.

Sexuality-Reproductive Pattern. Take a careful menstrual history from women, including the age at which menarche and menopause began, duration and amount of bleeding, incidence of clotting and cramping, and any associated problems. Ask men if they have any problems related to impotence or prolonged erections. Ask the patient about sexual behavior that may increase the risk for HIV infection.

Coping–Stress Tolerance Pattern. The patient with a hematologic problem often needs help with ADLs. Ask the patient if adequate support is available to meet daily needs. Determine the patient's usual methods of handling stress. In the patient with platelet disorders or hemophilia, the potential for hemorrhage can be so frightening that usual life patterns may be drastically curtailed, affecting the person's quality of life.

Value-Belief Pattern. Treatment for some hematologic problems involves blood transfusions or a bone marrow transplant. Determine if these treatments conflict with the patient's

CASE STUDY
Subjective Data

(© Lisa F. Young/iStock.)

A focused subjective assessment of A.J. revealed the following information:

Past Medical History: History of mild osteoarthritis. No surgical history. Prefers to take care of self with "natural therapy" and has not seen an HCP for 5 years, except for the recent sinus infection.

Medications: Metamucil 1 Tbsp/day PO; vitamins C, E, and D with calcium.

Health Perception–Health Management: A.J. denies family or personal history of anemia, cancer, or bleeding disorders. She believes she comes from a family with great genes for longevity because they "eat organic foods." She admits to drinking 1 glass of red wine with her evening meal "because it's good for your heart." She is a nonsmoker and cannot understand her gradual increase in shortness of breath with exertion. She says she really can't do anything anymore without having to stop and catch her breath. She says, "It's tough getting old."

Nutritional-Metabolic: A.J. and her husband eat a lot of pasta "because it is cheap." She uses a lot of garlic for flavoring and the "health benefit of it." Although not a vegetarian, she eats little meat.

Elimination: Denies black or tarry stool. Occasional constipation. No problems with urination. Urine without odor.

Activity-Exercise: A.J. is having a hard time performing ADLs without having to stop and catch her breath. Denies dyspnea at rest. States joints are stiff on arising in morning and after sitting but able to get around OK and work at her secretarial job. States her walking is steady but weak. No history of falling.

Sleep-Rest: Typically sleeps 8 to 9 hr/night with no trouble falling asleep. She still feels tired and needs to nap during her lunch break and during her days off.

Cognitive-Perceptual: Denies any numbness or tingling. Admits to being a little hard-of-hearing but can still see "pretty good."

Value-Belief: Prefers natural therapies over traditional medication.

Discussion Questions

1. What subjective assessment findings are of most concern to you?
2. Based on these subjective assessment findings, what type of physical assessment should you perform?
3. What should you include in the physical assessment? For what would you be looking?
4. How will you individualize the physical assessment based on the information from A.J. and her husband?

You will learn more about the physical examination of the hematologic system in the next section.
(See p. 598 for more information on A.J.)

value-belief system, including the patient's cultural and religious beliefs related to blood and blood transfusions. Notify the HCP if you identify any conflicts.

Objective Data

Physical Examination. A complete physical examination is needed to accurately examine all systems that affect or are affected by the hematologic system. A patient's presenting symptoms may not immediately point to a hematologic problem (Tables 29.5). For example, paresthesias of the lower extremities may not appear to be a hematologic problem, but when combined with other findings and risk factors, may indicate cobalamin deficiency and resulting pernicious anemia. Although you should perform a full physical examination on patients suspected of a hematologic disorder, certain aspects of that examination are specifically relevant. These include skin, lymph nodes, spleen, and liver.

Lymph Node Assessment. Assess lymph nodes symmetrically and take note of location, size (in centimeters), degree of fixation (e.g., movable, fixed), tenderness, and texture. Examine superficial lymph nodes with light palpation (Fig. 29.6). To assess superficial lymph nodes, lightly palpate the nodes using the pads of the fingers. Then gently roll the skin over the area and concentrate on feeling for lymph node enlargement. We cannot palpate deep lymph nodes. They are evaluated by radiologic examination.

Ordinarily, lymph nodes are not palpable in adults. If a node is palpable, it should be small (0.5 to 1 cm), mobile, firm, and nontender to be considered a normal finding. A node that is tender, hard, fixed, or enlarged (regardless if it is tender or not) is an abnormal finding and needs further investigation. Tender nodes are usually a result of inflammation. Hard or fixed nodes suggest cancer.[8]

Develop a sequence when examining the lymph nodes. A convenient sequence is to start at the head and neck. First, palpate the preauricular, posterior auricular, occipital, tonsillar, submandibular, submental, superficial cervical, posterior cervical chain, deep cervical chain, and supraclavicular nodes. Next, palpate the axillary lymph nodes and pectoral, subscapular, and lateral groups of nodes. Then examine the epitrochlear nodes, found in the antecubital fossa between the biceps and triceps muscles. Last, palpate the inguinal lymph nodes, found in the groin.

Palpation of Liver or Spleen. The liver and spleen are normally not detectable by palpating the abdomen. An enlarged liver or spleen may be detectable by percussion or palpation. Measure the degree of liver enlargement by the number of fingerbreadths it extends below the rib border. The spleen may be harder to detect because of its deep location in the left abdomen. Specific techniques for palpating the liver and spleen are described in Chapter 38.

Skin Assessment. Skin assessment may be a valuable source of information about the hematologic system. Examine the skin over the entire body in a systematic manner (e.g., starting with the face and oral cavity and moving downward over the body). In patients with RBC disorders, the skin may be pale or pasty or it may have a cyanotic tinge in severe anemia. Erythrocytosis often causes small vessel occlusions causing a purple, mottled appearance of the face, nose, fingers, or toes. Color changes in dark-skinned persons are best assessed in the sclera, conjunctiva, buccal mucosa, tongue, lips, nail beds, and palms.[8] *Clubbing of the fingers* (discussed in Chapter 25) can be seen with chronic anemia. Skin examination is discussed in Chapter 22.

TABLE 29.5 Assessment Abnormalities

Hematologic System

Finding	Description	Possible Etiology and Significance
Abdomen		
Distended abdomen	A larger than normal abdominal profile. May be soft or firm, tender or nontender, and accompanied by other symptoms, such as nausea, vomiting, or rebound tenderness	Lymphoma may manifest as abdominal adenopathy, mass(es), or bowel obstruction
Hepatomegaly	Palpable liver	Leukemia, cirrhosis, or fibrosis secondary to iron overload from sickle cell disease or thalassemia
Splenomegaly	Palpable spleen	Anemia, thrombocytopenia, leukemia, lymphomas, leukopenia, mononucleosis, malaria, cirrhosis, trauma, portal hypertension
Eyes		
Blurred vision, diplopia, visual field cuts	Decreased visual acuity or areas of blindness (field cuts)	Anemia, extreme leukocytosis, polycythemia, hyperviscosity may cause visual abnormalities. Thrombocytopenia may cause intraocular hemorrhage with visual abnormalities. Excessive clotting may cause thromboses in circulation to the brain that cause visual field cuts
Conjunctival pallor	Paleness. Decreased or absence of coloration in the conjunctiva	Low Hgb level (anemia)
Jaundiced sclera	Yellow appearance of sclera	Accumulation of bile pigment resulting from rapid or excessive hemolysis or liver disease or infiltration
Heart and Chest		
Altered blood pressure	*Hypertension:* >140/90 mm Hg *Hypotension:* <90 mm Hg systolic or >40 mm Hg drop from baseline *Orthostasis:* heart rate >20 beats/min increase or blood pressure >20 mm Hg decrease from baseline when moving from a lying position to either sitting or standing	May occur initially as a compensatory mechanism for anemia Infectious process, blood loss, compromised cardiovascular compensatory mechanisms Common with anemia, especially if also accompanied by low blood volume
Low O_2 saturation	O_2-carrying capacity as reflected by O_2 saturation by pulse oximetry	O_2 saturation may be decreased in cases of severe anemia
Palpitations	Feeling the heartbeat, flutter, or pound in chest	Anemia, fluid volume overload, hypotension with impending syncope, hypertension, dysrhythmias
Sternal tenderness	Abnormal sensitivity to touch or pressure on sternum	Leukemia resulting from increased bone marrow cellularity, causing increase in pressure and bone erosion. Multiple myeloma because of stretching of periosteum
Tachycardia	Heart rate >100 beats/min	Compensatory mechanism in anemia to increase cardiac output
Lymph Nodes		
Lymphadenopathy	Lymph nodes enlarged (>1 cm). May be tender to touch	Infection, foreign infiltrations, systemic disease such as leukemia, lymphoma, Hodgkin's lymphoma, metastatic cancer
Mouth		
Gingival and mucous membrane changes	Pallor, gingival and mucosal ulceration, swelling, or bleeding	Low Hgb level (anemia), neutropenia thrombocytopenia. Inability of impaired leukocytes to combat oral infections. Gingival hyperplasia may be present with some types of leukemia
Smooth tongue	Tongue surface smooth and shiny. Mucosa thin and red from decreased papillae	Pernicious anemia, iron-deficiency anemia
Musculoskeletal System		
Arthralgia	Joint pain	Sickle cell disease from hemarthrosis (bleeding into joints)
Bone pain	Pain in pelvis, ribs, spine, sternum	Multiple myeloma related to enlarged tumors that stretch periosteum. Bone invasion by leukemia cells, bone demineralization resulting from various cancers, sickle cell disease
Joint swelling	Fluid-filled spaces surrounding joints	Occurs with hemophilia and sickle cell anemia as hemarthrosis causes inflammation
Nervous System		
Headache, nuchal rigidity	Pain in the cranium, potentially involving one area or extending from frontal area to back of neck	Generalized headache is a common manifestation of mild to moderate anemia. Severe headache with or without visual changes may signal intracranial hemorrhage due to thrombocytopenia

Continued

TABLE 29.5 Assessment Abnormalities

Hematologic System—cont'd

Finding	Description	Possible Etiology and Significance
Paresthesias of feet and hands, ataxia	Numbness sensation and extreme sensitivity in central and peripheral nerves. Impaired muscle movement	Cobalamin (vitamin B_{12}) deficiency or folate deficiency
Weakness	Lacking physical strength or energy	Low Hgb level (anemia)
Nose		
Epistaxis	Spontaneous bleeding from nares	May occur with low platelet counts, especially if patient bends down for a long time, tries to lift a heavy item, or performs an intense Valsalva maneuver
Skin		
Chloroma	A tumor arising from myeloid tissue and containing a pale green pigment	Acute myelogenous leukemia that has infiltrated the skin
Cyanosis	Bluish discoloration of skin and mucous membranes	Anemia, excess concentration of deoxyhemoglobin in blood
Excoriation	Scratch or abrasion of skin	Scratching from intense pruritus
Flushing	Transient, episodic redness of skin (usually around face and neck)	Increase in Hgb (polycythemia), congestion of capillaries. Flushing of palms of hands or soles of feet sign of anemia
Jaundice	Yellow appearance of skin and mucous membranes	Accumulation of bile pigment caused by rapid or excessive hemolysis or liver damage
Leg ulcers	Prominent on the malleoli on the ankles	Sickle cell disease
Pallor of skin or nail beds	Paleness. Decreased or absence of skin coloration	Low Hgb level (anemia)
Plasmacytoma	Tumor arising from abnormal plasma cells	Multiple myeloma that has infiltrated tissue
Pruritus	Unpleasant cutaneous sensation that provokes the desire to rub or scratch skin	Hodgkin's lymphoma, cutaneous lymphomas, infiltrative leukemias, increased bilirubin

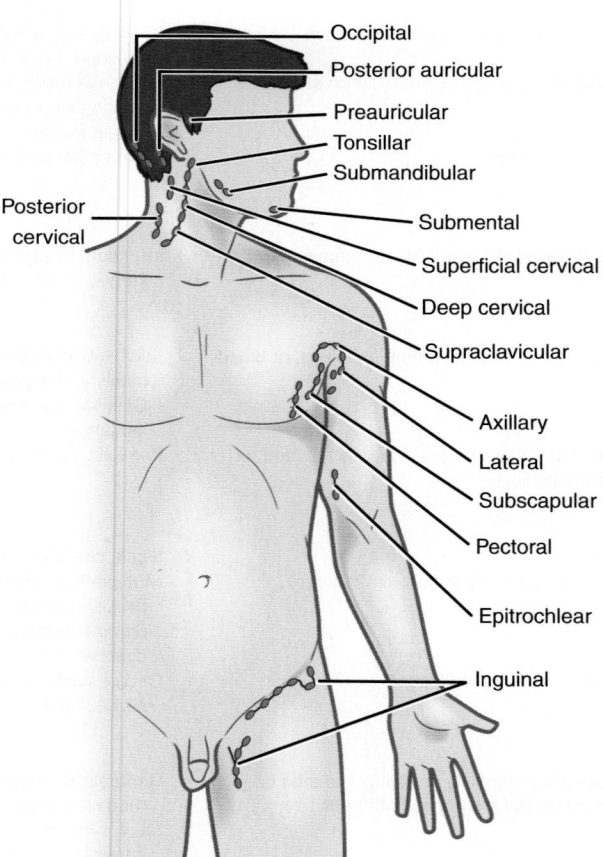

FIG. 29.6 Palpable superficial lymph nodes.

WBC disorders may cause infectious or cancerous skin lesions. These may occur anywhere and have a variable distribution pattern.

Look for findings that can indicate bleeding disorders. Assess for petechiae (small purplish red pinpoint lesions), ecchymoses (bruising), and *spider nevus* (a form of *telangiectasia*) (Table 29.6). The location of petechiae can indicate an accumulation of blood in the skin or mucous membranes. Small vessels leak under pressure, and the platelet numbers are not enough to stop the bleeding. Petechiae are more likely to occur where clothing constricts the circulation. In general, skin and mucosal bleeding means a platelet disorder, while spontaneous bleeding into joints or muscles means a coagulation factor problem.

A *focused assessment* is used to assess the status of previously identified hematologic problems and to monitor for signs of new problems. A focused assessment of the hematologic system is shown in the box on p. 598.

TABLE 29.6 Assessment Abnormalities

Vascular Skin Lesions

Finding	Description	Possible Etiology and Significance
Angioma	Benign tumor. Consists consisting of blood or lymph vessels	Most are congenital. May disappear spontaneously
Ecchymosis (bruise)	Hemorrhagic spots of varied size, Flat. Round or irregular	Decreased platelets or clotting factors resulting in hemorrhage into skin. Vascular abnormalities. Break in blood vessel walls from trauma
Petechiae	Pinpoint, flat, round area >2 mm. Purple, dark red, or brown	Same as above
Purpura	Flat purple or reddish discoloration. <5 mm. Do not blanche.	Same as above

Continued

TABLE 29.6 Assessment Abnormalities

Vascular Skin Lesions—cont'd

Finding	Description	Possible Etiology and Significance
Spider nevus (Spider angioma)	Has a round, red, central part and branching radiations resembling a spider's web. Usually found on face, neck, or chest	High estrogen levels as in pregnancy or liver disease
Telangiectasia	Fine, irregular red lines	Permanently dilated small blood vessels. Usually caused by sun damage or aging. May be seen with varicose veins, scleroderma, rosacea.

Figures from Ball JW, et al: *Seidel's guide to physical examination,* ed 9, St Louis, 2019, Mosby.

CASE STUDY

Objective Data: Physical Examination

(© Lisa F. Young/iStock.)

Physical examination findings of A.J. are as follows: BP 100/70 (lying), 88/60 (standing); apical pulse 110 (lying), 124 (standing), but regular in rhythm. Respiratory rate 26, temperature 96.8°F (36°C), O₂ saturation 90% on room air. No jugular venous distention. Weight 106 lb (48 kg). Height 5 ft 1 in. Skin pale and 2 ecchymoses on her arms and 1 on her left lower leg. A few scattered petechiae on both ankles. No jaundice noted. Conjunctivae pale. Tongue smooth and shiny. Lungs clear but diminished breath sounds in the bases bilaterally. No visible bleeding. No enlarged lymph nodes, spleen, or liver noted. General weakness with dyspnea on exertion. No numbness or tingling or peripheral edema.

Discussion Questions

1. Which physical assessment findings are of most concern to you?
2. Based on the results of the subjective and physical assessment findings, what diagnostic studies do you think may be ordered for A.J.?

You will learn more about diagnostic studies in relation to the hematologic system in the next section.
(See p. 604 for more information on A.J.)

Answers available at *http://evolve.elsevier.com/Lewis/medsurg.*

DIAGNOSTIC STUDIES OF HEMATOLOGIC SYSTEM

The most direct means of evaluating the hematologic system is through laboratory analysis (Tables 29.7, 29.8, 29.9, and 29.10) and other diagnostic studies (Table 29.11).[9]

Laboratory Studies

Complete Blood Count. The complete blood count (CBC) involves several laboratory tests (Table 29.7). In addition to the CBC, a *peripheral smear* may be done. The smear is used to look

FOCUSED ASSESSMENT

Hematologic System

Use this checklist to make sure the key assessment steps have been done.

Subjective
Ask the patient about any of the following and note responses.

Unusual bleeding or bruising	Y	N
Black, tarry stool	Y	N
Blood in vomitus	Y	N
Swelling in neck, armpits, or groin	Y	N
Dark-colored urine	Y	N
Fatigue	Y	N
Heart palpitations	Y	N

Objective: Diagnostic
Check the following laboratory results for critical values.

CBC	✓
WBC count with differential	✓
Clotting: PT, INR, aPTT, platelets	✓
Hgb, Hct	✓

Objective: Physical Examination
Inspect

Skin for lesions or color changes	✓

Auscultate

BP for change or orthostasis	✓

Palpate

Pulse for tachycardia	✓
Liver and spleen for enlargement	✓
Lymph nodes for lymphadenopathy	✓

aPTT, Activated partial thromboplastin time; *INR,* international normalized ratio; *PT,* prothrombin time.

TABLE 29.7 Diagnostic Studies

Complete Blood Count Studies

Study	Description and Purpose	Reference Intervals
Hemoglobin (Hgb)	Measures gas-carrying capacity of RBC	*Female:* 12–16 g/dL (120–160 g/L) *Male:* 14–18 g/dL (140–180 g/L)
Hematocrit (Hct)	Measure of packed cell volume of RBCs expressed as a percentage of the total blood volume	*Female:* 37%–47% (0.37–0.47) *Male:* 42%–52% (0.42–0.52)
Total RBC count (erythrocyte count)	Number of circulating RBCs per volume of blood	*Female:* $4.2\text{–}5.4 \times 10^6/\mu L$ ($4.2\text{-}5.4 \times 10^{12}/L$) *Male:* $4.7\text{–}6.1 \times 10^6/\mu L$ ($4.7\text{-}6.1 \times 10^{12}/L$)
Red cell indices		
Mean corpuscular volume (MCV) $MSV = \dfrac{Hct \times 10}{RBC \times 10^6}$	Determination of relative size of RBCs. Low MCV reflection of microcytosis. High MCV reflection of macrocytosis	80–95 fL
Mean corpuscular hemoglobin (MCH) $MCH = \dfrac{Hgb \times 10}{RBC \times 10^6}$	Measurement of average weight of Hgb/RBCs. Low MCH indicates microcytosis or hypochromia. High MCH indicates macrocytosis	27–31 pg
Mean corpuscular hemoglobin concentration (MCHC) $MCHC = \dfrac{Hgb \times 100}{Hct}$	Evaluates RBC saturation with Hgb. Low MCHC indicates hypochromia. High MCHC occurs with spherocytosis	32%–36% (0.32–0.36)
RBC morphology	Examination of shape and size of RBCs	No variation in RBC morphology
Reticulocyte count	Number of immature red blood cells released from the bone marrow into the blood	0.5%–2.0% of RBC
WBC count	Total number of WBCs	5000–10,000/μL ($5\text{–}10 \times 10^9/L$)
WBC differential	Determines whether each kind of WBC is present in proper proportion. Determine absolute value of each type of WBC by multiplying the percentage of cell type by total WBC count and dividing by 10	*Segmented neutrophils:* 55%–70% (0.55–0.70) *Banded neutrophils:* 0–8% (0–0.08) *Eosinophils:* 1%–4% (0.01–0.04) *Basophils:* 0.5%–1% (0.005–0.01) *Lymphocytes:* 20%–40% (0.20–0.40) *Monocytes:* 2%–8% (0.02–0.08)
Platelet count	Number of circulating platelets	$150,000\text{–}400,000 \times 10^3/L$ ($150\text{–}400 \times 10^9/L$)

TABLE 29. 8 Diagnostic Studies

Clotting Studies

Study	Description and Purpose	Reference Intervals
Activated clotting time (ACT)	Evaluates intrinsic coagulation status. More accurate than aPTT. Used during dialysis, coronary artery bypass procedure, arteriograms	70–120 sec
Activated partial thromboplastin time (aPTT)	Assesses intrinsic coagulation by measuring factors I, II, V, VIII, IX, X, XI, XII. Higher in patients receiving heparin	30–40 sec
Antithrombin (antithrombin III)	Naturally occurring protein made by liver that inhibits coagulation by inactivating thrombin and other factors. Lower in DIC and hypercoagulable disorders	17–30 mg/dL (170–300 mg/L) or 80%–120% of standard
Bleeding time	Duration of bleeding after a standardized superficial puncture wound of the skin measuring the integrity of the platelet plug	1–9 min
Capillary fragility test (tourniquet test, Rumpel-Leede test)	Reflects capillary integrity when pressure is applied to various areas of the body. Positive test indicates thrombocytopenia, toxic vascular reactions	<2 petechiae or negative
D-dimer	Assay to measure a fragment of fibrin that forms because of fibrin degradation and clot lysis. Used as an adjunctive measure in diagnosis of hypercoagulable conditions (e.g., DIC, pulmonary embolism)	<250 ng/mL (<250 mcg/L)
Fibrin split products (FSPs) or fibrin degradation products (FDPs)	Reflects degree of fibrinolysis and predisposition to bleed (if present). Screening test for DIC. High levels associated with DIC, advanced cancer, severe inflammation	<10 mcg/mL (<10 mg/L)
Fibrinogen (factor I)	Reflects level of fibrinogen. Increase is a possible sign of enhancement of fibrin formation, making patient hypercoagulable. Decrease means the patient may be predisposed to bleeding	200–400 mg/dL (2–4 g/L)
International normalized ratio (INR)	Standardized system of reporting prothrombin time (PT) based on a reference calibration model. Calculated by comparing patient's PT with a control value	0.8–1.1
Plasminogen	Assesses for deficiency of plasminogen in patients who have multiple thrombo-embolic episodes	2.4–4.4 units/mL
Platelet count	Number of circulating platelets	$150,000\text{–}400,000 \times 10^3/L$ ($150\text{–}400 \times 10^9/L$)
Prothrombin time (PT)	Assesses extrinsic coagulation by measuring factors I, II, V, VII, X	11–12.5 sec
Thrombin time	Reflects adequacy of thrombin and time to clot. Prolonged thrombin time means that coagulation is inadequate secondary to decreased thrombin activity	10–15 sec

DIC, Disseminated intravascular coagulation.

TABLE 29.9 ABO and Rh Blood Groups

Blood Type	ANTIGENS PRESENT ON RBC		ANTIBODIES POSSIBLY PRESENT IN PLASMA		Percent of General Population
	A or B	Rh (D)	A or B	Rh (D)	
O	—	—	A, B	Rh	35
O+	—	Rh	A, B	—	7
A	A	—	B	Rh	35
A+	A	Rh	B	—	7
B	B	—	A	Rh	8
B+	B	Rh	A	—	2
AB	A, B	—	—	Rh	4
AB+	A, B	Rh	—	—	2

TABLE 29.10 Diagnostic Studies

Miscellaneous Blood Studies

Study	Description and Purpose	Normal Values
Bilirubin	Measures degree of RBC hemolysis or liver's inability to excrete normal quantities of bilirubin. Increase in indirect bilirubin with hemolysis. Increase in direct bilirubin with obstructive problems (e.g., gallstones, liver tumor)	*Total:* 0.3–1.0 mg/dL (5.1–17.0 μmol/L) *Direct:* 0.1–0.3 mg/dL (1.7–5.1 μmol/L) *Indirect:* 0.2–0.8 mg/dL (3.4–12.0 μmol/L)
Blood smear (peripheral blood smear)	Reviews color, size, shape, quantity of cells in peripheral blood. Provides significant amount of information about problems affecting RBCs, WBCs, or platelets	Normal quantity of each cell type, normal size, shape and color of RBCs, normal WBC differential count and platelets
Coombs test	Differentiation among types of hemolytic anemias. Detection of immune antibodies and Rh factor	Negative
• Direct	Detects antibodies that are attached to RBCs	Negative
• Indirect	Detects circulating antibodies against red cells in serum	Negative
Cobalamin (vitamin B$_{12}$)	Level of cobalamin available for production of new RBCs	160–950 pg/mL (118–701 pmol/L)
Erythrocyte sedimentation rate (ESR)	Measures sedimentation or settling of RBCs in 1 hr. Inflammatory process cause a change in plasma proteins, resulting in aggregation of RBCs and making them heavier. The faster the sedimentation rate, the higher the ESR	<20 mm/hr (some gender variation)
Erythropoietin	Measures degree of hormonal stimulation to bone marrow to stimulate the release of RBCs	5–25 mU/mL (5–30 U/L)
Ferritin	Major iron storage protein. Is normally present in blood in concentrations directly related to iron storage	10–300 ng/mL (10–300 mcg/L)
Folic acid (folate)	Amount of folic acid (folate) available for RBC production	5–25 ng/mL (11–57 nmol/L)
Haptoglobin	A serum glycoprotein that binds to Hgb released into the bloodstream by hemolysis. Decreased with red cell hemolysis. Increased with infection, inflammation, cancer	50–220 mg/dL
Hemoglobin (Hgb) electrophoresis	Proteins involved in development of Hgb molecule have a definitive pattern of separation on electrophoresis. This pattern is changed with abnormal Hgb synthesis (e.g., thalassemia) or sickle cell anemia (where Hgb S is increased)	Normal Hb A1: >95% Hb A2: 2%–3% Hb F: 0.8%–2% Hb S: 0 Hb C: 0
Homocysteine	An intermediate amino acid formed during the metabolism of the essential amino acid methionine. Rapidly metabolized through pathways that require cobalamin (vitamin B$_{12}$) and folic acid. Increased in cobalamin and folic acid deficiency	*Normal:* 4–14 μmol/L
Iron		
• Iron total	Reflects amount of iron combined with proteins in serum. Accurate indicator of status of iron storage and use	*Male:* 80–180 mcg/dL (14–32 μmol/L) *Female:* 60–160 mcg/dL (11–29 μmol/L)
• (Total) iron-binding capacity (TIBC)	Measures all proteins available for binding iron. Transferrin represents the largest quantity of iron-binding proteins. Therefore TIBC is an indirect measure of transferrin, an evaluation of the amount of extra iron that can be carried	250–460 mcg/dL (45–82 μmol/L)
Lactic dehydrogenase (LDH)	Intracellular enzyme present in almost all body tissues. Levels rise in response to cell damage. Increased levels confirm diagnosis of injury or disease. Used as a nonspecific marker of hematologic cancer growth and response to treatment	100–190 U/L
Methylmalonic acid (MMA)	Indirect test for cobalamin (vitamin B$_{12}$). MMA metabolism requires cobalamin. Decreased levels with cobalamin deficiency. Helps distinguish cobalamin deficiency from folic acid deficiency	<3.6 μmol/mmol creatinine
Microglobulin (beta$_2$ microglobulin)	Protein found on the surface of all cells. Increased in cancers such as lymphoma, leukemia, or multiple myeloma. May be used as a tumor marker	*Blood:* 0.7–1.8 mcg/mL *Urine:* ≤300 mcg/L *Spinal fluid:* ≤2.4 mg/L
Serum protein electrophoresis (SPEP)	Separates proteins in blood on basis of electric charge. Helps detect hyperglobulinemic states, such as in multiple myeloma or some lymphomas	Normal banding pattern of albumin and globulins. Increase in any protein (*protein spike*) is abnormal
Transferrin	Largest of proteins that bind to iron. Increased in most people with iron-deficiency anemia	*Male:* 215–365 mg/dL (2.15–3.65 g/L) *Female:* 250–380 mg/dL (2.5–3.8 g/L)
Transferrin saturation (%)	Decreased in iron-deficiency anemia. Increased in hemolytic and megaloblastic anemia	*Male:* 20%–50% *Female:* 15%–50%

TABLE 29.11 Diagnostic Studies

Hematologic System

Study	Description and Purpose	Nursing Responsibility
Molecular, Cytogenetic, and Gene Analysis Studies		
Cancer genomics (genotyping) **Cell surface immunophenotyping (flow cytometry)** **Chromosomal karyotyping** **Fluorescence in situ hybridization (FISH)**	Assesses for genetic or chromosomal abnormalities of cancer cells. Uses peripheral blood (e.g., leukemia), biopsy specimen (bone marrow, lymph node, tissue), or CSF. Used to confirm diagnosis and determine treatment modalities and prognosis	*Before:* Explain purpose of testing to patient. HCP will provide specific significance.
Procedures		
Bone marrow biopsy (Fig. 29.7)	Technique involves removal of bone marrow through a locally anesthetized site to evaluate status of blood-forming tissue. Used to diagnose and monitor aplastic anemia, multiple myeloma, myelodysplastic syndromes, leukemia, and some lymphomas	*Before:* Explain procedure to patient. Obtain signed consent form. Perform a surgical time-out before procedure. Analgesics may be given to enhance patient comfort and cooperation. *After:* Apply pressure dressing. Assess biopsy site for bleeding and apply pressure as needed. Tenderness at the puncture site for a few days may be normal. Assess for infection.
Lumbar puncture (LP)	Done to obtain CSF for testing for cancer, infection, and degenerative brain diseases. May be used to give chemotherapy to the central nervous system	*During:* Help position patient and provide support. *After:* Watch site for bleeding and signs of infection. Spinal headaches may occur. Follow postprocedure orders for how long the patient should lie flat. Encourage the patient to drink fluids.
Lymph node biopsy	Used to obtain lymph tissue for histologic examination to determine diagnosis and therapy	*Before:* Explain procedure to patient. Obtain signed consent form.
• Closed (needle) or fine needle	Done at the bedside or in an outpatient area. An extremely small needle is used to reduce risk for tracking cancer cells through normal subcutaneous tissue	*After:* Watch site for bleeding and monitor vital signs, especially if platelet count is low. Change sterile dressing as ordered. Inspect wound for healing and infection.
• Open	Done in operating room or procedure area using either local or general anesthesia. After making an incision, the lymph node and surrounding tissue are excised whenever possible	
Radioisotope Studies		
Bone scan	Radioactive isotope is injected IV and taken up by the bones. Uniform uptake is normal. Increased uptake seen in osteomyelitis, certain fractures, and bone cancer	*Before:* Patient may be asked to drink 4–6 glasses of water and then void before imaging (to see pelvic bones). Obtain IV access for injection of isotope.
SPECT scan (single-photon emission computed tomography)	Radioactive isotope is injected IV. Images from radioactive emissions used to evaluate the structures, such as spleen, liver, bone, and possible tumors. Patient is not a source of radioactivity	*Before:* Obtain IV access for injection of isotope. *After:* Have the patient drink fluids to aid in the excretion of the isotope.
Radiologic Studies		
Computed tomography (CT) scan	Noninvasive radiologic examination using computer-assisted x-ray evaluates the lymph nodes. Contrast medium used in abdominal studies of liver or spleen. Spiral (helical) CT scans used to evaluate lymph nodes	*Before:* Assess for iodine sensitivity if contrast medium used. IV and/or oral contrast may be given prior to procedure, depending on the area being studied. Patient may need to be NPO for 4 hr. *After:* Have patient drink fluids to avoid renal problems with any contrast.
Liver, spleen, or abdominal ultrasound	Noninvasive probe is lubricated and slid across the abdomen to detect density and borders of the abdominal organs. Can detect irregular borders, masses, vascular structure, fluid collections, and biliary tree	*During:* Patients must be comfortable lying flat and having probe compress abdomen.
Magnetic resonance imaging (MRI)	Noninvasive procedure produces sensitive images of soft tissue (central nervous system, neck and back, bones and joints, heart, breasts). An IV contrast agent (gadolinium) may be given. Provides a better contrast between normal tissue and pathologic tissue than CT	*Before:* Oral and/or IV contrast injection may be used. Check for pregnancy, allergies, and renal function before test. Have patient remove all metal objects. Ask about any history of surgical insertion of staples, plates, dental bridges, or other metal appliances. Remove metallic foil patches. Patient may need to be fasting. Assess for claustrophobia and the need for antianxiety medication. *During:* Patient must lie completely still during scan.

Continued

TABLE 29.11 Diagnostic Studies

Hematologic System—cont'd

Study	Description and Purpose	Nursing Responsibility
Positron emission tomography (PET)	Glucose-containing nuclear tracer substance is injected and taken up by metabolically active cells. Follow-up scan shows different-colored tissues based on metabolic rate. Because cancer cells have an increased uptake of glucose, "hot spots" reflecting increased glucose consumption indicate the presence of active cancer. CT scanning may be done in conjunction or images fused.	*Before:* Obtain IV access to inject the tracer substance. Patients should be NPO, except for water and medications, for at least 4 hr prior. Hold glucose-containing IV solutions and change to normal saline. Check the blood glucose levels as high levels may interfere with test. May need bowel preparation depending on area being studied. *After:* Encourage fluids to excrete radioactive substance. No specific nursing responsibilities.
Skeletal x-ray	X-rays done as a bone survey to detect lytic lesions associated with multiple myeloma. Bone scans do not identify lesions in this condition because there is no uptake of radioactive isotopes due to lack of blood supply.	
Urine Studies Bence Jones protein (free kappa and lambda light chains)	An electrophoretic measurement used to detect Bence Jones protein, which is found in most cases of multiple myeloma. May be present in some other hematologic disorders and metastatic cancers. Negative finding is normal.	*During:* Obtain random urine specimen early in the morning. If a 24-hr urine collection is done, discard first specimen, and collect all urine voided during the 24 hr, keeping on ice or refrigerated. Remind patient not to put toilet paper in urine collection container.

at the *morphology* (shape and appearance) of the blood cells and may help with the diagnosis. For example, many immature *blast* WBCs may indicate acute leukemia.

Although the status of each cell type is important, diseases or treatment of diseases can disrupt the entire system. When the entire CBC is suppressed, a condition termed pancytopenia (marked decrease in the number of RBCs, WBCs, and platelets) exists.

Red Blood Cells. The total RBC count is reported as RBC × $10^6/\mu L$. However, the total RBC count is not fully reliable in determining the adequacy of RBC function. We must evaluate other data, such as hemoglobin, hematocrit, and RBC indices. Normal values of some RBC tests are different for men and women because normal values are based on body mass. Men usually have a larger body mass than women.

The *hemoglobin (Hgb) value* is reduced in cases of anemia, hemorrhage, and hemodilution, such as that occurring with excess fluid volume. Increased hemoglobin is found in polycythemia or in states of hemoconcentration, which can develop from volume depletion (dehydration). Reductions and elevations of the hematocrit value and RBC count occur with the same conditions that raise and lower the hemoglobin value.

The *hematocrit (Hct) value* is determined by spinning blood in a centrifuge. This causes RBCs and plasma to separate. The RBCs, being the heavier elements, settle to the bottom (Fig. 29.2). The hematocrit value is the percent of RBCs compared with the total blood volume. The hematocrit value generally is 3 times the hemoglobin value.

RBC indices are special indicators that reflect RBC volume, color, and hemoglobin saturation (Table 29.7).[9] These parameters give insight into the cause of anemia. The significance of these parameters is discussed more in Chapter 30.

White Blood Cells. The WBC count gives two different sets of information. The first is a total count of WBCs in 1 μL of peripheral blood. A WBC count over 10,000/μL is associated with infection, inflammation, tissue injury or death, and cancer

(e.g., leukemia, lymphoma). Although the degree of WBC elevation does not necessarily predict the severity of illness, it can give clues to the cause. Extremely high WBC counts (e.g., greater than 25,000/μL) occur with certain types of leukemia. A WBC count less than 5000/μL (leukopenia) is associated with bone marrow depression, severe or chronic illness, and other types of leukemia.

The second aspect of the WBC count, the *differential count,* measures the percent of each type of WBC. The WBC differential gives valuable clues in determining the cause of illness. When infections are severe, we release more granulocytes from the bone marrow as a compensatory mechanism. To meet the increased demand, many young, immature polymorphonuclear neutrophils *(bands)* are released into circulation. More mature neutrophils are called *polymorphonuclear segmented neutrophils (segs).* Together, bands and segs make up the *absolute neutrophil count* (ANC). The usual laboratory procedure is to report the WBCs in order of maturity, with the less mature forms on the left side of the written report. That is why we call the presence of many immature cells a *"shift to the left."*

The WBC differential is very important because it is possible for the total WBC count to be essentially normal despite a marked change in 1 type of WBC. For example, a patient may have a normal WBC count of 8800/μL, but the differential count may show that the proportion of lymphocytes is only 10%. This is an abnormal finding that needs further investigation.

When the bone marrow does not make enough neutrophils, neutropenia occurs. Neutropenia is a condition in which the ANC is less than 1000 cells/μL. Severe neutropenia is associated with an ANC of less than 500 cells/μL. You calculate the ANC by multiplying the total WBC count by the percentage of neutrophils. Neutropenia results from many disease processes, such as leukemia, or from bone marrow depression (see Chapter 30). It is associated with a high risk for infection and death from sepsis.

Platelet Count. The platelet count is the number of platelets per microliter of blood. Normal platelet counts are between 150,000 and 400,000/μL. Counts below 100,000/μL signify a condition termed thrombocytopenia. Bleeding may occur with thrombocytopenia. Spontaneous hemorrhage is possible once platelet counts fall below 10,000/μL, depending on the clinical situation.[6] A more extensive description of clotting studies is given in Table 29.8.

Thrombocytosis is defined as too many platelets. It occurs with inflammation and some cancers (see Chapter 30). The most likely complication of thrombocytosis is excessive clotting.

Blood Typing and Rh Factor. Blood group antigens (A and B) are found only on RBC membranes. They form the basis for the ABO blood typing system. The presence or absence of 1 or both of the 2 inherited antigens is the basis for the 4 blood groups: A, B, AB, and O. Blood group A has A antigens, group B has B antigens, group AB has both antigens, and group O has neither A nor B antigens. Each person has antibodies in the serum termed *anti-A* and *anti-B* that react with A or B antigens. These antibodies are found when the corresponding antigen is absent from the RBC surface. For example, B antibodies are found in the serum of people with blood group A (Table 29.9).

Blood reactions based on ABO incompatibilities result from intravascular hemolysis of the RBCs. RBCs *agglutinate* (or clump) when a serum antibody is present to react with the antigens on the RBC membrane. For example, agglutination would occur in the blood of a person with type A blood if he or she receives blood transfused from a person with B antigens (i.e., type B or AB). The anti-B antibodies in the type A blood would react with the B antigens, starting the process that results in RBC hemolysis. Blood component compatibilities for transfusions are outlined in Table 30.32.

The *Rh system* is based on a third antigen, D, which is also on the RBC membrane. Rh-positive people have the D antigen, while Rh-negative people do not. Rh-positive blood is indicated with a "+" after the ABO group (e.g., AB+). Rh status is determined by a Coombs test (Table 29.10).

Because of transfusion therapy or during childbirth, a Rh-negative person may be exposed to Rh-positive blood. After exposure during childbirth, a Rh-negative mother forms an antibody, anti-D, which acts against Rh antigens (Rh-positive people normally have no anti-D). In future pregnancies the mother's anti-D antibodies can cross the placenta and attack the RBCs of a Rh-positive fetus, causing hemolysis of the RBCs. A pregnant Rh-negative woman should receive Rho(D) immune globulin (RhoGAM) injections to prevent anti-D antibodies from forming.

Iron Metabolism. The laboratory tests used to evaluate iron metabolism include serum iron, total iron-binding capacity (TIBC), serum ferritin, and transferrin saturation. Tests for nutritional deficiencies leading to defective RBC production may be done (Table 29.10).[9]

Serum iron is a measurement of the amount of protein-bound iron circulating in the serum. TIBC gives a measurement of all proteins that act to bind or transport iron between the tissues and bone marrow. Although this indirect measurement is a general reflection of the amount of transferrin present in the circulation, it overestimates transferrin levels by 16% to 20% because it measures other proteins that can bind iron. These alternative proteins bind iron only when transferrin is more than half saturated. TIBC varies inversely with tissue iron stores. It is higher when iron stores are low and lower when iron stores are high.

Transferrin saturation is a better indicator of the availability of iron for erythropoiesis than serum iron. Unlike serum iron, the iron bound to transferrin is readily available for the body to use. You calculate transferrin saturation by dividing serum iron by TIBC and multiplying by 100. For example, a patient with a serum iron level of 100 mcg/dL and a TIBC of 300 mcg/dL would have a transferrin saturation of about 33%.

Under normal conditions, the serum ferritin concentration correlates closely with body iron stores. In normal patients, 1 ng/mL of ferritin corresponds to 8 to 10 mg of stored iron.

Biopsies

Biopsy procedures specific to hematologic assessment are bone marrow examination and lymph node biopsy. In general, these procedures are done when a peripheral blood smear is nonspecific. Furthermore, a biopsy provides information that is needed for diagnosis and treatment planning.

Bone Marrow Examination. Bone marrow examination is important in evaluating many hematologic problems. It may involve aspiration only or aspiration with biopsy (Table 29.11). The benefits gained from bone marrow examination are (1) a full evaluation of hematopoiesis and (2) the ability to get specimens for cytopathologic and chromosomal analysis. The preferred site for both aspiration and biopsy of bone marrow is the posterior iliac crest. A physician, nurse practitioner, or physician's assistant can perform a bone marrow aspiration and biopsy. The patient may receive local anesthesia and sedation to minimize anxiety and pain.

For bone marrow aspiration, the skin over the puncture site is cleansed with a bactericidal agent. The skin, subcutaneous tissue, and periosteum are injected with a local anesthetic agent. Once the area is anesthetized, a bone marrow needle is inserted through the cortex of the bone. The stylet of the needle is then removed, the hub is attached to a 10-mL syringe, and 0.2 to 0.5 mL of the fluid marrow is aspirated (Fig. 29.7). The patient will have pain when the periosteum is penetrated and with aspiration. Although the pain will last only a few seconds, it can be quite uncomfortable. After the marrow aspiration, the needle is removed. Pressure is applied over the aspiration site to ensure hemostasis, then the site is covered with a sterile pressure dressing.

Although complications of bone marrow aspiration are minimal, there is a chance of damaging underlying structures. Other complications include hemorrhage (if the patient is thrombocytopenic) and infection (if the patient is leukopenic).

Monitor the patient's vital signs until stable and assess the site for excess drainage or bleeding. If bleeding is present, have the patient lie on that side for 30 to 60 minutes to keep pressure on the site. If the bed is too soft, have the patient lie on a rolled towel to provide more pressure. You may give analgesics for postprocedure pain. Soreness over the puncture site for 3 to 4 days after the procedure is normal.

Lymph Node Biopsy. Lymph node biopsy involves obtaining lymph tissue for histologic examination to determine the diagnosis and help plan therapy. This may be done by either an open biopsy or a closed (needle) biopsy.

If the results from a needle biopsy are negative, it may only mean that the cancer cells were not part of the tissue in the biopsy specimen. However, a positive finding may be enough evidence for confirming a diagnosis. This technique is rarely used to confirm an initial diagnosis because larger specimens, such as excisional biopsies are usually needed to perform cytopathologic tests.

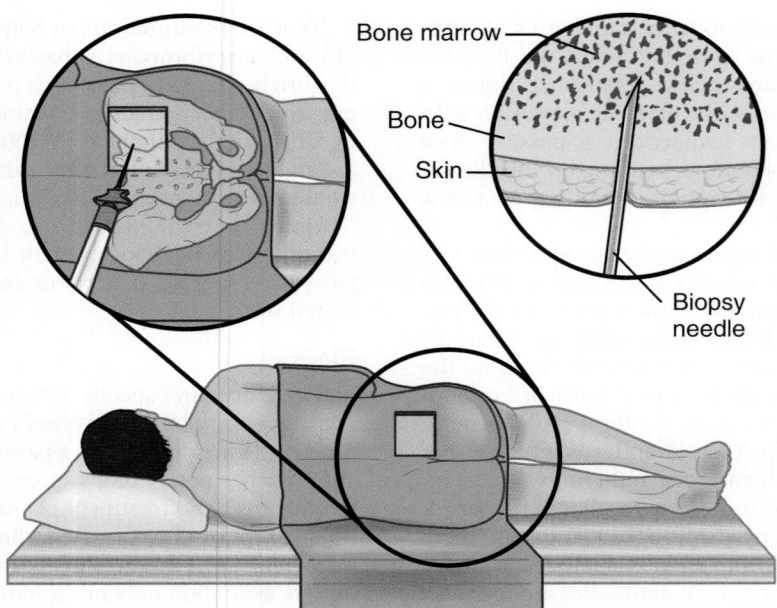

FIG. 29.7 Bone marrow aspiration from the posterior iliac crest.

Molecular Cytogenetics and Gene Analysis

Testing for specific genetic or chromosomal variations in hematologic conditions is often helpful in diagnosis and staging (Table 29.11). These results help determine treatment options and prognosis. If a large number of abnormal cells are circulating in the blood, such as in acute leukemia, these tests may be done on peripheral blood. However, testing is usually done on samples from bone marrow, lymph node biopsies, and sometimes cerebrospinal fluid (CSF).[9] For example, fluorescence in situ hybridization (FISH) identifies genetic defects using nucleic probes that are complementary to a targeted region of deoxyribonucleic acid (DNA). It can identify an abnormal extra chromosome 8, which is common in certain leukemias. Chromosomal karyotyping allows each set of chromosomes to be painted different colors. This helps identify normal from abnormal banding patterns.[9] It can be used to identify the translocation of chromosome 22 to 9 in the Philadelphia chromosome of chronic myelogenous leukemia. More information on genetics is available in Chapter 12.

CASE STUDY

Objective Data: Diagnostic Studies

(© Lisa F. Young/iStock.)

The HCP orders the following diagnostic studies for A.J.:
- CBC, basic metabolic panel (electrolytes, BUN, creatinine), PT/PTT
- Arterial blood gases
- Chest x-ray

A.J.'s CBC reveals an Hgb of 5.9 g/dL, Hct of 18.2%, WBC of 2600/μL (2.6 × 10⁹/L), platelet count of 72,000/μL, PT = 18 sec, aPTT = 37. The arterial blood gases and chest x-ray are normal. The HCP orders more blood work, including a WBC differential and RBC indices and admits her to the hospital for further evaluation.

Discussion Questions

1. Are these the diagnostic studies that you expected to be ordered?
2. Which diagnostic study results are abnormal?
3. Which diagnostic study results are of most concern to you? What other studies may be ordered on admission?

This case study is continued in Chapter 30 on p. 652.

Answers available at *http://evolve.elsevier.com/Lewis/medsurg*.

▌ BRIDGE TO NCLEX EXAMINATION

The number of the question corresponds to the same-numbered outcome at the beginning of the chapter.

1. A person who lives at a high altitude may normally have an increased Hgb and RBC count because
   a. high altitudes cause vascular fluid loss, leading to hemoconcentration.
   b. hypoxia caused by decreased atmospheric O₂ stimulates erythropoiesis.
   c. the function of the spleen in removing old RBCs is impaired at high altitudes.
   d. impaired production of platelets leads to proportionally higher red cell counts.

2. Cancer arising from granulocytic cells in the bone marrow will have the primary effect of causing
   a. risk for hemorrhage.
   b. altered oxygenation.
   c. decreased production of antibodies.
   d. decreased phagocytosis of bacteria.

3. An anticoagulant such as warfarin that interferes with prothrombin production will alter the clotting mechanism during
   a. platelet aggregation.
   b. activation of thrombin.
   c. the release of tissue thromboplastin.
   d. stimulation of factor activation complex.

4. When reviewing laboratory results of an older patient with an infection, the nurse would expect to find
   a. mild leukocytosis.
   b. decreased platelet count.
   c. increased hemoglobin and hematocrit levels.
   d. decreased erythrocyte sedimentation rate (ESR).

5. Significant information from the patient's health history that relates to the hematologic system includes
   a. jaundice.
   b. bladder surgery.
   c. early menopause.
   d. multiple pregnancies.

6. While assessing the lymph nodes, the nurse should
   a. apply gentle, firm pressure to deep lymph nodes.
   b. palpate the deep cervical and supraclavicular nodes last.
   c. lightly palpate superficial lymph nodes with the pads of the fingers.
   d. use the tips of the second, third, and fourth fingers to apply deep palpation.

7. If a lymph node is palpated, what is a normal finding?
   a. Hard, fixed nodes
   b. Firm, mobile nodes
   c. Enlarged, tender nodes
   d. Hard, nontender nodes

8. Nursing care for a patient immediately after a bone marrow biopsy and aspiration includes (select all that apply)
   a. giving analgesics as needed.
   b. preparing to start a blood transfusion.
   c. giving preprocedure and postprocedure antibiotic medications.
   d. having the patient lie still to keep the sterile pressure dressing intact.
   e. monitoring vital signs and assessing the site for excess drainage or bleeding.

9. You are taking care of a male patient who has the following laboratory values from his CBC: WBC $6.5 \times 10^3/\mu L$, Hgb 13.4 g/dL, Hct 40%, platelets $50 \times 10^3/\mu L$. What are you *most* concerned about?
   a. The patient is neutropenic.
   b. The patient has an infection.
   c. There is an increased risk for bleeding.
   d. Fall risk precautions are needed due to anemia.

1. b, 2. d, 3. b, 4. a, 5. a, 6. c, 7. b, 8. a, d, e, 9. c

For rationales to these answers and even more NCLEX review questions, visit *http://evolve.elsevier.com/Lewis/medsurg*.

EVOLVE WEBSITE/RESOURCES LIST

http://evolve.elsevier.com/Lewis/medsurg
Review Questions (Online Only)
Key Points
Answer Keys for Questions
- Rationales for Bridge to NCLEX Examination Questions
- Answer Guidelines for Case Studies on pp. 592, 594, 598, and 604

Conceptual Care Map Creator
Audio Glossary
Content Updates

REFERENCES

1. Huether SE, McCance KL: *Understanding pathophysiology*, ed 6, St Louis, 2017, Mosby.
2. Bickley LS, Szilagyi PG, Hoffman RM: *Bates' guide to physical examination and history taking*, ed 12, Philadelphia, 2017, Wolters Kluwer.
3. Lichtman MA, Kaushansky K, Prchal JT, et al: *Williams manual of hematology*, ed 9, New York, 2017, McGraw-Hill.
4. Kaushansky K, Lichtman MA, Prchal J, et al: *Williams hematology*, ed 9, New York, 2016, McGraw-Hill.
5. Bain BJ, Bates, I, Laffan MA: *Dacie and Lewis practical haematology*, ed 12, Philadelphia, 2017, Elsevier.
6. Hoffman R, Benz EJ, Silberstein LE, et al: *Hematology: Basic principles and practice*, ed 7, Philadelphia, 2018, Elsevier.
7. Academy of Nutrition and Dietetics: Food and nutrition topics. Retrieved from *www.eatright.org*.
8. Ball JW, Dains JE, Flynn JA, et al: *Seidel's guide to physical examination*, ed 9, St Louis, 2019, Mosby.
9. Pagana KD, Pagana TJ: *Mosby's manual of diagnostic and laboratory tests*, ed 6. St Louis, 2018, Mosby.

30

Hematologic Problems

Sandra Irene Rome

The capacity to care is what gives life its most deepest significance.

Pablo Casals

ⓔ http://evolve.elsevier.com/Lewis/medsurg/

CONCEPTUAL FOCUS

Cellular Regulation	**Functional Ability**	**Infection**
Clotting	**Gas Exchange**	**Pain**
Fatigue	**Immunity**	**Perfusion**

LEARNING OUTCOMES

1. Describe the general clinical manifestations and complications of anemia.
2. Distinguish the etiologies, clinical manifestations, diagnostic findings, and interprofessional and nursing management of iron-deficiency, megaloblastic, and aplastic anemias.
3. Explain the nursing management of anemia from blood loss.
4. Describe the pathophysiology, clinical manifestations, and interprofessional and nursing management of anemia caused by increased erythrocyte destruction.
5. Describe the pathophysiology and nursing and interprofessional management of polycythemia.
6. Explain the pathophysiology, clinical manifestations, and interprofessional and nursing management of various types of thrombocytopenia.
7. Describe the types, clinical manifestations, diagnostic findings, and interprofessional and nursing management of hemophilia and von Willebrand disease.
8. Explain the pathophysiology, diagnostic findings, and interprofessional and nursing management of disseminated intravascular coagulation.

9. Describe the etiology, clinical manifestations, and interprofessional and nursing management of neutropenia.
10. Describe the pathophysiology, clinical manifestations, and interprofessional and nursing management of myelodysplastic syndrome.
11. Compare and contrast the distinguishing clinical and laboratory findings of the major types of leukemia.
12. Explain the nursing and interprofessional management of acute and chronic leukemias.
13. Compare Hodgkin's lymphoma and non-Hodgkin's lymphomas in terms of clinical manifestations, staging, and interprofessional and nursing management.
14. Describe the pathophysiology, clinical manifestations, and interprofessional and nursing management of multiple myeloma.
15. Describe the spleen disorders and related interprofessional care.
16. Describe the nursing management of the patient receiving transfusions of blood and blood components.

KEY TERMS

anemia, p. 606
aplastic anemia, p. 614
disseminated intravascular coagulation (DIC), p. 628
hemochromatosis, p. 619
hemolytic anemia, p. 615
hemophilia, p. 626

Hodgkin's lymphoma, p. 640
iron-deficiency anemia, p. 609
leukemia, p. 634
lymphomas, p. 640
megaloblastic anemias, p. 612
multiple myeloma, p. 645
myelodysplastic syndrome (MDS), p. 634

neutropenia, p. 631
non-Hodgkin's lymphomas (NHLs), p. 642
pernicious anemia, p. 612
polycythemia, p. 620
sickle cell disease (SCD), p. 616
thalassemia, p. 611
thrombocytopenia, p. 622

There are a wide range of blood conditions and cancers. Because blood has so many essential functions, when hematologic problems occur the patient is affected in multiple ways. Patients with anemia and hematologic cancer may have to cope with fatigue. Compromised immunity and the risk for infection is a concern among patients with hematologic cancer and a common side effect of therapy. Pain is a common symptom associated with cancer and sickle cell disease. Clotting is an important protective mechanism that allows us to maintain homeostasis when injury occurs. Excessive clotting can impair perfusion, while inadequate clotting can lead to blood loss and fluid volume

deficits. This chapter will discuss the interprofessional and nursing care of common hematologic problems and their associated concepts.

ANEMIA

Definition and Classification

Anemia is a deficiency in the number of erythrocytes (red blood cells [RBCs]), the quantity or quality of hemoglobin, and/or volume of packed RBCs (hematocrit). It is a common condition

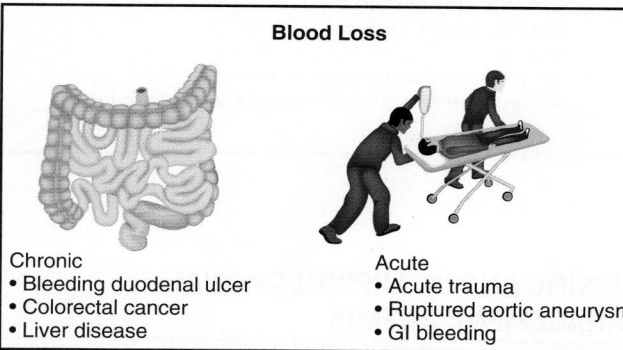

Decreased RBC Production

Deficient nutrients
• Iron
• Cobalamin
• Folic acid

Decreased erythropoietin

Decreased iron availability

Blood Loss

Chronic
• Bleeding duodenal ulcer
• Colorectal cancer
• Liver disease

Acute
• Acute trauma
• Ruptured aortic aneurysm
• GI bleeding

Increased RBC Destruction

Hemolysis
• Sickle cell disease
• Medication (e.g., methyldopa [Aldomet])
• Incompatible blood
• Trauma (e.g., cardiopulmonary bypass)

FIG. 30.1 Causes of anemia.

TABLE 30.1 Morphologic Classification of Anemia

Morphology	Etiology
Normocytic, normochromic (normal size and color) MCV 80–95 fL, MCH 27–31 pg	Acute blood loss, hemolysis, chronic kidney disease, chronic disease, cancers, endocrine disorders, starvation, aplastic anemia, sickle cell anemia, pregnancy
Microcytic, hypochromic (small size, pale color) MCV <80 fL, MCH <27 pg	Iron-deficiency anemia, vitamin B₆ deficiency, copper deficiency, thalassemia, lead poisoning
Macrocytic (megaloblastic), normochromic (large size, normal color) MCV >95 fL, MCH >31 pg	Cobalamin (vitamin B₁₂) deficiency, folic acid deficiency, liver disease (including effects of alcohol use)

MCH, Mean corpuscular hemoglobin; *MCV,* mean corpuscular volume.

with many diverse causes, such as blood loss, impaired production of RBCs, or increased destruction of RBCs (Fig. 30.1). Because RBCs transport O₂, RBC disorders can lead to tissue hypoxia. This hypoxia accounts for many of the signs and symptoms of anemia. Anemia is not a specific disease. It is a manifestation of a pathologic process.

TABLE 30.2 Etiologic Classification of Anemia

Decreased RBC Production
Decreased Hemoglobin Synthesis
• Iron deficiency
• Sideroblastic anemia (decreased porphyrin)
• Thalassemia (decreased globin synthesis)

Decreased Number of RBC Precursors
• Aplastic anemia and inherited disorders (e.g., Fanconi syndrome)
• Anemia of myeloproliferative diseases (e.g., leukemia) and myelodysplasia
• Chronic diseases or disorders
• Medications and chemicals (e.g., chemotherapy, lead)
• Radiation

Defective DNA Synthesis
• Cobalamin (vitamin B₁₂) deficiency
• Folic acid deficiency

Blood Loss
Acute
• Blood vessel rupture
• Splenic sequestration crisis
• Trauma

Chronic
• Gastritis
• Menstrual flow
• Hemorrhoids

Increased RBC Destruction (Hemolytic Anemias)
Acquired (Extrinsic)
• Antibodies against RBCs
• Infectious agents (e.g., malaria) and toxins
• Physical destruction
• Extracorporeal circulation
• Disseminated intravascular coagulopathy (DIC)
• HELLP syndrome (hemolysis, high liver enzymes, low platelets associated with pregnancy)
• Prosthetic heart valves
• Thrombotic thrombocytopenic purpura (TTP)
• Widespread cancer

Hereditary (Intrinsic)
• Abnormal hemoglobin (sickle cell disease)
• Enzyme deficiency (glucose-6-phosphate dehydrogenase [G6PD])
• Membrane abnormalities (paroxysmal nocturnal hemoglobinuria, hereditary spherocytosis)

We diagnose anemia based on a complete blood count (CBC), reticulocyte count, and peripheral blood smear. Once we identify anemia, further investigation is done to determine its specific cause.[1]

Anemia can result from primary hematologic problems or develop as a secondary consequence of diseases or disorders of other body systems. We classify the types of anemia according to either *morphology* (cellular characteristic) or *etiology* (cause). Morphologic classification is based on RBC size and color (Table 30.1). Etiologic classification is related to the clinical conditions causing the anemia (Table 30.2).[2] Although the morphologic system is the most accurate means of classifying anemias, it is easier to discuss patient care by focusing on the cause of the anemia.

🌐 PROMOTING HEALTH EQUITY
Hematologic Problems

• Sickle cell disease has a high incidence among African Americans.
• Thalassemia has a high incidence among blacks and people of Mediterranean origin.
• Tay-Sachs disease has the highest incidence in families of Eastern European Jewish origin, especially the Ashkenazi Jews.
• Pernicious anemia has a high incidence among Scandinavians and blacks.

TABLE 30.3 Manifestations of Anemia

Body System	Mild (Hgb 10–12 g/dL [100–120 g/L])	Moderate (Hgb 6–10 g/dL [60–100 g/L])	Severe (Hgb <6 g/dL [<60 g/L])
		SEVERITY OF ANEMI	
Cardiovascular	Palpitations	Increased palpitations, "bounding pulse"	Tachycardia, increased pulse pressure, systolic murmurs, intermittent claudication, angina, HF, myocardial infarction
Eyes	None	None	Icteric conjunctiva and sclera, retinal hemorrhage, blurred vision
Gastrointestinal	None	None	Anorexia, hepatomegaly, splenomegaly, difficulty swallowing, sore mouth
General	None or mild fatigue	Fatigue	Sensitivity to cold, weight loss, lethargy
Integument	None	None	Pallor, jaundice, pruritus
Mouth	None	None	Glossitis, smooth tongue
Musculoskeletal	None	None	Bone pain
Pulmonary	Exertional dyspnea	Dyspnea	Tachypnea, orthopnea, dyspnea at rest
Neurologic	None	"Roaring in the ears"	Headache, vertigo, irritability, depression, impaired thought processes

Clinical Manifestations

The manifestations of anemia are caused by the body's response to tissue hypoxia. Specific manifestations vary depending on how fast the anemia has evolved, its severity, and any coexisting disease. We often use hemoglobin (Hgb) levels to determine the severity of anemia.

Mild anemia (Hgb 10 to 12 g/dL [100 to 120 g/L]) may exist without causing symptoms. If symptoms develop, it is because the patient has an underlying disease or has a compensatory response to heavy exercise. Symptoms include palpitations, dyspnea, and mild fatigue.

In moderate anemia (Hgb 6 to 10 g/dL [60 to 100 g/L]), there is an increase in cardiopulmonary symptoms. The patient may have them while resting, as well as with activity.

In severe anemia (Hgb less than 6 g/dL [60 g/L]), the patient has many manifestations involving multiple body systems (Table 30.3).

Integumentary Manifestations. Skin manifestations include pallor, jaundice, and pruritus. Pallor results from reduced amounts of hemoglobin and reduced blood flow to the skin. Jaundice occurs when hemolysis of RBCs causes increased concentration of serum bilirubin. Hemolysis also causes pruritus because of increased serum and skin bile salt concentrations. Check the sclera of the eyes and mucous membranes for jaundice because they reflect skin changes more accurately, especially in a dark-skinned person.

Cardiopulmonary Manifestations. Cardiopulmonary manifestations of severe anemia result from the heart and lungs trying to provide adequate amounts of oxygen (O_2) to the tissues. Cardiac output is maintained by increasing the heart rate and stroke volume. The low viscosity of the blood contributes to the development of systolic murmurs and bruits. In extreme cases or when concomitant heart disease is present, angina pectoris and myocardial infarction (MI) may occur if myocardial O_2 needs cannot be met. Heart failure (HF), cardiomegaly, pulmonary and systemic congestion, ascites, and peripheral edema may develop if the heart is overworked for an extended period.

❖ NURSING AND INTERPROFESSIONAL MANAGEMENT: ANEMIA

This section discusses general management of anemia. Specific care related to various types of anemia is discussed later in this chapter. More information on the nursing care of the patient with anemia is presented in eNursing Care Plan 30.1.

◆ Nursing Assessment

Subjective and objective data you should obtain from a patient with anemia are outlined in Table 30.4. Assess the patient's knowledge about adequate nutritional intake and adherence to safety precautions to prevent cardiopulmonary stress, falls, and injury.

◆ Nursing Diagnoses

Nursing diagnoses for the patient with anemia include:
- Fatigue
- Impaired nutritional intake
- Ineffective tissue perfusion

◆ Planning

The overall goals are that the patient with anemia will (1) assume normal activities of daily living, (2) maintain adequate nutrition, and (3) develop no complications related to anemia.

◆ Nursing Implementation

Correcting the cause of the anemia is the goal of therapy. The many causes of anemia necessitate different nursing interventions specific to the patient's needs. Acute interventions may include blood transfusions, drug therapy (e.g., erythropoietin, vitamin supplements), and O_2 therapy to stabilize the patient. Dietary and lifestyle changes (described in sections on specific types of anemia) can reverse some anemias.

For the patient with fatigue, encourage alternate rest and activity periods. Help the patient prioritize activities to accommodate energy levels. Arrange physical activities (e.g., avoid activity right after meals) to reduce competition for O_2 supply to vital functions. Aid with regular physical activities (e.g.,

TABLE 30.4 Nursing Assessment
Anemia

Subjective Data	Objective Data
Important Health Information *Past health history:* Recent blood loss or trauma; chronic liver, endocrine, or renal disease (including dialysis); GI disease (malabsorption syndrome, ulcers, gastritis, or hemorrhoids); inflammatory disorders (especially Crohn's disease); smoking, exposure to radiation or chemical toxins (arsenic, lead, benzenes, copper); infectious diseases (HIV) or recent travel with possible exposure to infection; angina, myocardial infarction; history of falling *Medications:* Use of vitamin and iron supplements; aspirin, anticoagulants, oral contraceptives, phenobarbital, penicillins, nonsteroidal antiinflammatory drugs, omeprazole, phenacetin, phenytoin, sulfonamides, herbal products *Surgery or other treatments:* Recent surgery, small bowel resection, gastrectomy, prosthetic heart valves, chemotherapy, radiation therapy *Dietary history:* General dietary patterns, alcohol consumption **Functional Health Patterns** *Health perception–health management:* Family history of anemia; malaise *Nutritional-metabolic:* Nausea, vomiting, anorexia, weight loss; dysphagia, dyspepsia, heartburn; night sweats, cold intolerance *Elimination:* Hematuria, decreased urine output; diarrhea, constipation, flatulence, tarry stools, bloody stools *Activity-exercise:* Fatigue, muscle weakness and decreased strength; dyspnea, orthopnea, cough, hemoptysis; palpitations; shortness of breath with activity *Cognitive-perceptual:* Headache; abdominal, chest, and bone pain; painful tongue; paresthesias of feet and hands; pruritus; changes in vision, taste, or hearing; vertigo; hypersensitivity to cold; dizziness *Sexuality-reproductive:* Menorrhagia, metrorrhagia; recent or current pregnancy; male impotence	**General** Lethargy, apathy, general lymphadenopathy, fever **Integumentary** Pale skin and mucous membranes; blue, pale white, or icteric sclera; cheilitis (inflammation of the lips); poor skin turgor; brittle, spoon-shaped fingernails; jaundice; petechiae; ecchymoses; nose or gingival bleeding; poor healing; dry, brittle, thinning hair **Respiratory** Tachypnea **Cardiovascular** Tachycardia, systolic murmur, dysrhythmias; postural hypotension, widened pulse pressure, bruits (especially carotid); intermittent claudication, ankle edema **Gastrointestinal** Hepatosplenomegaly; glossitis; beefy, red tongue; stomatitis; abdominal distention; anorexia **Neurologic** Headache, roaring in the ears, confusion, impaired judgment, irritability, ataxia, unsteady gait, paralysis, loss of vibration sense **Possible Diagnostic Findings** ↓ RBCs, ↓ Hgb; ↓ Hct; ↑ or ↓ reticulocytes, ↑ or ↓ MCV; possible ↓ serum iron, ferritin, folate, or cobalamin (vitamin B_{12}); heme-positive stools; ↓ serum erythropoietin level; ↑ or ↓ LDH, bilirubin, transferrin (Table 30.6)

ambulation, transfers, personal care) to minimize fatigue and risk for injury from falls. Monitor the patient's cardiorespiratory response to activity (e.g., tachycardia, dysrhythmias, dyspnea, diaphoresis, pallor, respiratory rate).

Determine, in collaboration with the dietitian, the number of calories and type of nutrients needed to meet nutritional requirements. Provide information about nutritional needs and how to meet them to increase the patient's intake of essential nutrients. Encourage increased intake of foods listed in Table 30.5 that are high in the nutrients needed for erythropoiesis.[2,3]

Gerontologic Considerations: Anemia

Modest changes in RBC mass occur in older adults. Healthy older men have a modest decline in Hgb of about 1 g/dL after age 70, in part because of the decreased production of testosterone. Only a minimal decrease in Hgb (about 0.2 g/dL) occurs in healthy women older than age 70.[1]

Anemia is not a normal finding in older adults. However, the prevalence increases starting from the seventh decade of life. For many, anemia is related to an underlying cause, such as iron deficiency, bleeding, chronic disease/inflammation, renal insufficiency, or a hematologic problem. For those with no identifiable cause, it may be due to cytokine dysregulation with aging.[3]

Manifestations of anemia in older adults may include pallor, confusion, ataxia, fatigue, and worsening cardiovascular and respiratory problems. Unfortunately, anemia may go unrecognized in older adults because we mistake these manifestations for normal aging changes or overlook them because of another health problem. By recognizing signs of anemia, you can play a key role in the care of older adults with anemia.

ANEMIA CAUSED BY DECREASED ERYTHROCYTE PRODUCTION

Normally RBC production (termed *erythropoiesis*) is in equilibrium with RBC destruction and loss. This balance ensures that an adequate number of RBCs is always available. The normal life span of an RBC is 120 days. There are 3 problems that lead to decreased RBC production: (1) decreased hemoglobin synthesis from iron-deficiency anemia, thalassemia, and sideroblastic anemia; (2) defective deoxyribonucleic acid (DNA) synthesis in RBCs (e.g., cobalamin deficiency, folic acid deficiency) may lead to megaloblastic anemias; and (3) diminished availability of erythrocyte precursors may result in aplastic anemia and anemia of chronic disease (Table 30.2).

IRON-DEFICIENCY ANEMIA

Iron-deficiency anemia is the most common nutritional disorder in the world. Those most susceptible to iron-deficiency anemia are the very young, those on poor diets, and women in their reproductive years.[4] Normally, we lose 1 mg of iron daily in urine, bile, sweat, sloughing of epithelial cells from the skin and intestinal mucosa, and minor bleeding.[2]

Etiology

Iron-deficiency anemia may develop because of inadequate dietary intake, malabsorption, blood loss, or hemolysis. Normal dietary iron intake is usually enough to meet the needs of men and older women. It may be inadequate for people with higher iron needs (e.g., menstruating or pregnant women).

TABLE 30.5 Nutritional Therapy

Nutrients for Erythropoiesis

Role in Erythropoiesis	Food Sources
Amino Acids (Protein)	
Heme and plasma membrane synthesis and structure	Eggs, meat, milk and milk products (cheese, ice cream), poultry, fish, legumes, nuts, soy
Cobalamin (Vitamin B$_{12}$)	
Synthesis of DNA, RBC maturation, facilitates folate metabolism	Meat, eggs, enriched grain products, milk and dairy foods, fish (especially salmon)
Copper	
Mobilizes iron from tissues to plasma	Shellfish, whole grains, beans, nuts, potatoes, organ meats, dark leafy greens, dried fruits
Folic Acid	
Synthesis of DNA and RNA, RBC maturation	Green leafy vegetables, enriched grain products and breakfast cereals, orange juice, peanuts, avocado
Iron	
Hemoglobin synthesis	Lean beef, turkey, pork and chicken, fish, legumes, dark green leafy vegetables, whole-grain and enriched bread and cereals, beans
Niacin	
RBC maturation	Peanut butter, beef, poultry, fish, avocado; enriched and fortified grains
Pantothenic Acid (Vitamin B$_5$)	
Heme synthesis	Meats, vegetables, cereal grains, legumes, eggs, milk
Pyridoxine (Vitamin B$_6$)	
Heme synthesis	Beef, pork, chicken, fish, fortified cereals, potatoes, bananas, nuts, beans
Riboflavin (Vitamin B$_2$)	
Oxidative reactions	Milk and dairy foods, enriched bread and other grain products, lean meats, eggs, green leafy vegetables
Vitamin C (Ascorbic Acid)	
Maintains iron in its ferrous form, aids in iron absorption	Citrus fruits, green leafy vegetables, strawberries, potatoes, kiwi fruit, tomatoes, green and red bell peppers
Vitamin E	
Heme synthesis. Protection against oxidative damage to RBCs	Vegetable oils, salad dressings, margarine, wheat germ, whole-grain products, seeds, nuts, peanut butter

Iron malabsorption may occur after certain types of gastrointestinal (GI) surgery and in malabsorption syndromes. Iron absorption occurs in the duodenum. So, malabsorption may occur after a surgical procedure that involves removal or bypass of the duodenum. Or, it may occur if disease of the duodenum alters or destroys the absorption surface.

Blood loss is a major cause of iron deficiency in adults. The major sources of chronic blood loss are from the GI and genitourinary (GU) systems. GI bleeding is often not obvious. It may exist for a considerable time before the problem is identified.

Loss of 50 to 75 mL of blood from the upper GI tract is enough for stools to appear black *(melena)*. The black color results from the iron in the RBCs.

Common causes of GI blood loss are peptic ulcer, gastritis, esophagitis, diverticula, hemorrhoids, and cancer. GU blood loss occurs primarily from menstrual bleeding. The average monthly menstrual blood loss is about 45 mL and causes the loss of about 22 mg of iron. Postmenopausal bleeding can contribute to anemia in susceptible older women. In addition to anemia of chronic kidney disease, dialysis treatment may cause iron-deficiency anemia because of the blood lost in the dialysis equipment and frequent blood sampling.

Clinical Manifestations

In the early course of iron-deficiency anemia, the patient may not have any symptoms. As the disease becomes chronic, any of the general manifestations of anemia may develop (Table 30.3). In addition, specific manifestations may occur related to iron-deficiency anemia. Pallor is the most common finding. *Glossitis* (inflammation of the tongue) is the second most common. Another finding is *cheilitis* (inflammation of the lips). The patient may report headache, paresthesias, and a burning sensation of the tongue, all of which are caused by lack of iron in the tissues.

Diagnostic Studies

Laboratory abnormalities characteristic of iron-deficiency anemia are shown in Table 30.6. Other diagnostic studies (e.g., stool occult blood test) are done to determine the cause of the iron deficiency. Endoscopy and colonoscopy may detect GI bleeding. A bone marrow biopsy may be done if other tests are inconclusive.

Interprofessional and Nursing Management

The main goal is to treat the underlying problem that is causing iron loss or reduced intake (e.g., malnutrition, alcoholism) or poor absorption of iron. We also direct efforts toward replacing iron (Table 30.7). Teach the patient which foods are good sources of iron (Table 30.5). If nutrition is already adequate, increasing iron intake by dietary means may not be enough. The patient may need oral, or occasionally, parenteral iron supplements. If the iron deficiency is from acute blood loss, the patient may need a transfusion of packed RBCs.

Drug Therapy. Oral iron is a good option because it is inexpensive and convenient. Many iron preparations are available. When giving iron, consider the following factors:

1. Iron is absorbed best from the duodenum and proximal jejunum. So, enteric-coated or sustained-release capsules, which release iron farther down in the GI tract, are counterproductive and expensive.
2. The daily dose should provide 150 to 200 mg of elemental iron. This can be taken in 3 or 4 daily doses, with each tablet or capsule of the iron preparation containing between 50 and 100 mg of iron (e.g., a 325-mg tablet of ferrous sulfate contains 65 mg of elemental iron).[3]
3. Iron is best absorbed in an acidic environment. For this reason and to avoid binding the iron with food, iron should be taken about an hour before meals, when the duodenal mucosa is most acidic. Taking iron with vitamin C (ascorbic acid) or orange juice, which contains ascorbic acid, enhances iron absorption. Gastric side effects, however, may necessitate taking iron with meals.

TABLE 30.6 Laboratory Results in Anemia

Etiology of Anemia	Hgb/Hct	MCV	Reticulocytes	Serum Iron	TIBC	Transferrin	Ferritin	Bilirubin	Serum B$_{12}$	Folate
Acute blood loss	↓	N or ↓	N or ↑	N	N	N	N	N	N	N
Aplastic anemia	↓	N or slight ↑	↓	N or ↑	N or ↑	N	N	N	N	N
Chronic blood loss	↓	↓	N or ↑	↓	↑	N	N	N or ↓	N	N
Chronic disease	↓	N or ↓	N or ↓	N or ↓	↓	N or ↓	N or ↑	N	N	N
Cobalamin deficiency	↓	↑	N or ↓	N or ↑	N	Slight ↑	↑	N or slight ↑	↓	N
Folic acid deficiency	↓	↑	N or ↓	N or ↑	N	Slight ↑	↑	N or slight ↑	N	↓
Hemolytic anemia	↓	N or ↑	↑	N or ↑	N or ↓	N	N or ↑	↑	N	N
Iron deficiency	↓	↓	N or slight ↓ or ↑	↓	↑	N or ↑	↓	N or ↓	N	N
Sickle cell anemia	↓	N	↑	N or ↑	N or ↓	N	N	↑	N	↓
Thalassemia major	↓	N or ↓	↑	↑	↓	↓	N or ↑	↑	N	↓

MCV, Mean corpuscular volume; *N*, normal; *TIBC*, total iron-binding capacity.

TABLE 30.7 Interprofessional Care

Iron-Deficiency Anemia

Diagnostic Assessment

- History and physical examination
- Hgb and Hct (hematocrit) levels
- RBC count, including morphology
- Reticulocyte count
- Serum iron
- Serum ferritin
- Serum transferrin
- Total iron-binding capacity (TIBC)
- Stool examination for occult blood

Management

- Identification and treatment of underlying cause
- Drug therapy
- Oral: ferrous sulfate or ferrous gluconate
- IM or IV: iron dextran, sodium ferrous gluconate, iron sucrose
- Nutritional therapy (Table 30.5)
- Transfusion of packed RBCs

4. Undiluted liquid iron may stain the patient's teeth. Therefore it should be diluted and ingested through a straw.
5. GI side effects may occur, including heartburn, constipation, and diarrhea. Have the patient stay upright for 30 minutes after taking oral forms. If side effects develop, the dose and type of supplement may be adjusted. For example, many people who need supplemental iron cannot tolerate ferrous sulfate because of the effects of the sulfate base. However, ferrous gluconate may be a better substitute. Tell patients that iron preparations will cause their stools to become black because the GI tract excretes excess iron. Constipation is common. The patient should start on stool softeners and laxatives, if needed, when started on iron.

DRUG ALERT Iron

- Some IV iron preparations have a risk for an allergic reaction, so monitor the patient accordingly.
- Oral iron should be taken about 1 hr before meals.
- Vitamin C (ascorbic acid) enhances iron absorption.

In some situations, it may be necessary to give iron parenterally. Parenteral use of iron is indicated for malabsorption, intolerance of oral iron, a need for iron beyond oral limits, or poor patient adherence in taking the oral preparations of iron.

Parenteral iron can be given IM or IV. Sodium ferrous gluconate and iron sucrose are alternatives and may carry less risk for life-threatening anaphylaxis.[3]

Because IM iron solutions may stain the skin, use separate needles for withdrawing the solution and injecting the medication. Use a Z-track injection technique.

Reassess the Hgb and RBC count to evaluate the response to therapy. Stress adherence with dietary and drug therapy. To replenish the body's iron stores, the patient needs to take iron therapy for 2 to 3 months after the Hgb level returns to normal. Monitor patients who need lifelong iron supplementation for potential liver problems related to the iron storage.

THALASSEMIA

Etiology

Thalassemia is a group of diseases involving inadequate production of normal hemoglobin, which decreases RBC production. Thalassemia is due to an absent or reduced globulin protein. α-Globin chains are absent or reduced in α-thalassemia, and β-globin chains are absent or reduced in β-thalassemia. Hemolysis also occurs as most erythroblasts are destroyed by mononuclear phagocytes in the marrow.[2] Thalassemia is commonly found in members of ethnic groups whose origins are near the Mediterranean Sea and equatorial or near-equatorial regions of Southeastern Asia, the Middle East, India, Pakistan, China, Southern Russia, and Africa.[3]

Genetic Link. Thalassemia has an autosomal recessive genetic basis (see Fig. 12.4 and Table 12.2). A person with thalassemia may have a heterozygous or homozygous form of the disease. A person who is heterozygous has 1 thalassemic gene and 1 normal gene and has *thalassemia minor* (or thalassemic trait), which is a mild form of the disease. A homozygous person has 2 thalassemic genes, causing a severe condition known as *thalassemia major*.[3]

Clinical Manifestations

The patient with thalassemia minor is often asymptomatic. The patient has mild to moderate anemia with *microcytosis* (small cells) and *hypochromia* (pale cells), mild splenomegaly, bronzed color of the skin, and bone marrow hyperplasia.[2]

Thalassemia major is a life-threatening disease in which growth, both physical and mental, is often slowed. The person with thalassemia major is pale and displays other general symptoms of anemia (Table 30.3). The symptoms develop in childhood by 2 years of age and can cause growth and developmental deficits. Jaundice from the hemolysis of RBCs is prominent. There is pronounced splenomegaly, since the spleen continuously tries to remove the damaged red cells. Hepatomegaly and cardiomyopathy may occur from iron deposition.

INFORMATICS IN PRACTICE

Using the Internet to Access Information on Unfamiliar Diseases

- If you are assigned to take care of a patient with a disease or disorder that you are not familiar with, such as thalassemia, access a reputable source on the Internet, such as the National Institutes of Health, and do a quick search.
- Within minutes, you can learn the pathophysiology of thalassemia or other disease, treatment options, complications that you will need to monitor, and recommended medical and nursing interventions.
- Using this readily available information will help you deliver high-quality, evidence-based care.

As the bone marrow responds to the reduced O_2-carrying capacity of the blood, RBC production is stimulated. The marrow becomes packed with immature erythroid precursors that die. This stimulates further erythropoiesis, leading to chronic bone marrow hyperplasia and expansion of the marrow space. This may cause thickening of the cranium and maxillary cavity. Thrombocytosis after spleen dysfunction and/or removal may occur.

Cardiac complications from iron overload, lung disease, and hypertension also contribute to early death. Endocrine problems (diabetes, growth retardation, hypogonadism), osteoporosis, pulmonary hypertension, and thrombosis may be present.[1]

Interprofessional Care

The laboratory abnormalities of thalassemia major are outlined in Table 30.6. No specific drug or diet therapies are effective in treating thalassemia. Thalassemia minor does not need treatment because the body adapts to the reduction of normal hemoglobin.

Thalassemia major is managed with blood transfusions or exchange transfusions in conjunction with chelating agents that bind to iron. Transfusions are given to keep the Hgb level around 10 g/dL (100 g/L), depending on the manifestations.[1] Chelating agents reduce the iron overloading that occurs with chronic transfusion therapy. Drugs used include oral deferasirox (Exjade, JadeNu) or deferiprone (Ferriprox), or IV or subcutaneous deferoxamine (Desferal).[1] Ascorbic acid supplements may be needed during chelation therapy, since they increase urine excretion of iron. Ascorbic acid should only be taken with chelation therapy because it increases the absorption of dietary iron. It is given, along with folic acid, if there is evidence of hemolysis. Zinc supplements may be needed since zinc is reduced with chelation therapy. Iron supplements should not be given.

Because RBCs are sequestered in the enlarged spleen, the patient may need a splenectomy. Hepatic, heart, and lung function are monitored and treated as needed.

Although hematopoietic stem cell transplantation (HSCT) is the only cure for patients with thalassemia, the risk of this procedure may outweigh its benefits. With proper iron chelation therapy, patients are living longer.

TABLE 30.8 Causes of Megaloblastic Anemia

Cobalamin (Vitamin B_{12}) Deficiency
- Chronic alcoholism
- Dietary deficiency
- Deficiency of gastric intrinsic factor
  - Celiac disease
  - Gastrectomy
  - Gastric bypass
  - *Helicobacter pylori*
  - Pernicious anemia
- Increased requirement (pregnancy)
- Intestinal malabsorption

Folic Acid Deficiency
- Chronic alcoholism
- Chronic hemodialysis (folic acid lost during dialysis)
- Dietary deficiency (e.g., leafy green vegetables, citrus fruits)
- Drugs interfering with absorption or use of folic acid
  - Methotrexate
  - Antiseizure drugs (e.g., phenobarbital, phenytoin)
- Increased requirement (pregnancy)
- Malabsorption syndromes
  - Celiac disease
  - Crohn's disease
  - Small bowel resection

Drug-Induced Suppression of DNA Synthesis
- Alkylating agents
- Folate antagonists
- Metabolic inhibitors

Inborn Errors
- Defective folate metabolism
- Defective transport of cobalamin

Erythroleukemia

MEGALOBLASTIC ANEMIAS

Megaloblastic anemias are a group of disorders caused by impaired DNA synthesis and characterized by the presence of large RBCs. When DNA synthesis is impaired, defective RBC maturation results. The RBCs are large *(macrocytic)* and abnormal. We call them *megaloblasts.* Macrocytic RBCs are easily destroyed because they have fragile cell membranes. Most megaloblastic anemias result from cobalamin (vitamin B_{12}) and folic acid deficiencies. They can also occur from congenital disorders, suppression of DNA synthesis by drugs, inborn errors of cobalamin and folic acid metabolism, and *erythroleukemia* (malignant blood disorder characterized by a proliferation of erythropoietic cells in bone marrow) (Table 30.8).[5]

Cobalamin Deficiency

The most common cause of cobalamin deficiency is **pernicious anemia**. It is caused by an absence of *intrinsic factor* (IF). Pernicious anemia is a disease of insidious onset. It begins in middle age or later (usually after age 40), with 60 years being the most common age at diagnosis. Pernicious anemia occurs most often in persons of Northern European ancestry (particularly Scandinavians) and blacks.[1]

Etiology

Normally, the parietal cells of the gastric mucosa secrete a protein termed *IF.* IF is required for cobalamin (extrinsic factor) absorption. Cobalamin is normally absorbed in the distal ileum. Without IF, cobalamin will not be absorbed. In pernicious anemia, the gastric mucosa is not secreting IF because of either gastric mucosal atrophy or autoimmune destruction of parietal cells. In the autoimmune process, antibodies are directed against the gastric parietal cells and/or IF itself. Because parietal cells also secrete hydrochloric acid (HCl), in pernicious anemia there is a decrease in HCl in the stomach. An acid environment in the stomach is required for the secretion of IF.

Cobalamin deficiency can occur in patients who have had GI surgery (e.g., gastrectomy, gastric bypass); patients who have had a small bowel resection involving the ileum; and patients with Crohn's disease, ileitis, celiac disease, diverticula of the small intestine, or chronic atrophic gastritis (Table 30.8). In these cases, cobalamin deficiency results from the loss of IF-secreting gastric mucosal cells or impaired absorption of cobalamin in the distal ileum. Cobalamin deficiency also occurs with excess alcohol or hot tea ingestion, smoking, long-term users of H_2-histamine receptor blockers and proton pump inhibitors, and those who are strict vegetarians.[2]

There is a familial predisposition for pernicious anemia, so evaluate patients who have a positive family history of pernicious anemia for symptoms. Although the disease cannot be prevented, early detection and treatment can lead to reversal of symptoms.

Clinical Manifestations

General manifestations of anemia related to cobalamin deficiency develop because of tissue hypoxia (Table 30.3). GI manifestations include a sore, red, beefy, and shiny tongue; anorexia, nausea, and vomiting; and abdominal pain. Typical neuromuscular manifestations include weakness, paresthesias of the feet and hands, reduced vibratory and position senses, ataxia, muscle weakness, and impaired thought processes ranging from confusion to dementia. Because cobalamin deficiency–related anemia has an insidious onset, it may take several months for manifestations to develop.

Diagnostic Studies

Laboratory data reflective of cobalamin-deficiency anemia are outlined in Table 30.6. The RBCs appear large (macrocytic) and have abnormal shapes. This structure contributes to RBC destruction because the cell membrane is fragile. Serum cobalamin levels are low.

Serum folate levels are reviewed. If they are normal and cobalamin levels are low, it suggests that megaloblastic anemia is due to a cobalamin deficiency. A serum test for anti-IF antibodies may be done that is specific for pernicious anemia. Patients with pernicious anemia have an increased risk for gastric cancer. They may undergo an upper GI endoscopy and biopsy of the gastric mucosa at the time of diagnosis and at appropriate intervals afterward.

Testing of serum methylmalonic acid (MMA) (high in cobalamin deficiency) and serum homocysteine (high in both cobalamin and folic acid deficiencies) helps determine the cause of this type of anemia.

❖ Interprofessional and Nursing Management

If IF is lacking or if absorption in the ileum is impaired, the patient will not be able to absorb cobalamin regardless of how much they ingest. For this reason, increasing dietary cobalamin does not correct this anemia. Parenteral vitamin B_{12}

(cyanocobalamin, hydroxocobalamin) or intranasal cyanocobalamin (Nascobal) is needed. Without cobalamin administration, the patient will die in 1 to 3 years. A typical treatment schedule consists of 1000 mcg/day of cobalamin IM for 2 weeks and then weekly until the hemoglobin is normal and then monthly for life.

High-dose oral cobalamin and sublingual cobalamin are options for those in whom GI absorption is intact.

The nursing measures discussed in eNursing Care Plan 30.1 for the patient with anemia are appropriate for the patient with cobalamin-deficiency anemia. In addition to these measures, assess for neurologic difficulties that are not fully corrected by replacement therapy. Implement measures to reduce the risk for injury from the decreased sensitivity to heat and pain related to neurologic impairment. Protect the patient from falling, burns, and trauma. In some people, the neuromuscular complications may not be reversible and physical therapy may be needed.

Folic Acid Deficiency

Folic acid (folate) deficiency also causes megaloblastic anemia. Folic acid is needed for DNA synthesis leading to RBC formation and maturation. Common causes of folic acid deficiency are listed in Table 30.8.

The manifestations of folic acid deficiency are similar to those of cobalamin deficiency. The disease develops insidiously. The patient's symptoms may be attributed to other coexisting problems (e.g., cirrhosis, esophageal varices). GI problems may include stomatitis, cheilosis, dysphagia, flatulence, and diarrhea. Thiamine deficiency, which is often present with folate deficiency, can cause neurologic symptoms.[2]

The diagnostic findings for folic acid deficiency are shown in Table 30.6. The serum folate level is low (normal is 5 to 25 ng/mL [11 to 57 nmol/L]), with a normal serum cobalamin level.

We treat folic acid deficiency with replacement therapy. The usual dosage is 1 mg/day by mouth. The patient with malabsorption or chronic alcoholism may need up to 5 mg/day. The duration of treatment depends on the reason for the deficiency. Teach the patient to eat foods high in folic acid (Table 30.5). The nursing measures discussed in eNursing Care Plan 30.1 for the patient with anemia are appropriate for the patient with folic acid deficiency anemia.

ANEMIA OF CHRONIC DISEASE

Anemia of chronic disease (also called *anemia of inflammation*) can be caused by cancer, autoimmune and infectious disorders (human immunodeficiency virus [HIV], hepatitis, malaria), HF, or chronic inflammation. Bleeding episodes can contribute to anemia of chronic disease.

Anemia of chronic disease is associated with an underproduction of RBCs and mild shortening of RBC survival. The RBCs are usually normocytic, normochromic, and hypoproliferative. The anemia is usually mild. It can become more severe if the underlying disorder is not treated.

This type of anemia, which usually develops after 1 to 2 months of disease activity, has an immune basis. The cytokines released in these conditions, particularly interleukin-6 (IL-6), cause an increased uptake and retention of iron within macrophages (see Fig. 29.3). This leads to a diversion of iron from circulation into storage sites with subsequent limited iron available for erythropoiesis. There is reduced RBC life span, suppressed production of erythropoietin, and an ineffective bone marrow response to erythropoietin. We think cytokine dysregulation may be the cause of this type of anemia in elderly and obese patients when no other cause can be found.[6]

For any chronic disease, other factors may contribute to the anemia. For example, with renal disease, the primary factor causing anemia is decreased erythropoietin, a hormone made in the kidneys that stimulates erythropoiesis. With impaired renal function, erythropoietin production is decreased (see Chapter 46).

Anemia of chronic disease must first be recognized and distinguished from anemia of other causes. High serum ferritin and increased iron stores distinguish it from iron-deficiency anemia. Normal folate and cobalamin blood levels distinguish it from megaloblastic anemias from folate and cobalamin deficiencies.

The best treatment of anemia of chronic disease is to correct the underlying disorder. If the anemia is severe, blood transfusions may be needed, but they are not recommended for long-term treatment. Erythropoietin therapy is used for anemia related to renal disease (see Chapter 46) and cancer and its therapies (see Chapter 15). Its use is limited, though, because of the increased risk for thromboembolism and death in some patients.

APLASTIC ANEMIA

Aplastic anemia is a disease in which the patient has peripheral blood *pancytopenia* (decrease of all blood cell types—RBCs, white blood cells [WBCs], and platelets) and hypocellular bone marrow. The spectrum can range from a moderate condition managed with erythropoietin or blood transfusions to very severe with potentially fatal hemorrhage and sepsis. The incidence of aplastic anemia is rare, with an annual rate of 2 to 5 new cases per million per year.[3]

Etiology

About 70% of aplastic anemias are due to autoimmune activity by autoreactive T lymphocytes.[3] The cytotoxic T cells target and destroy the patient's own hematopoietic stem cells. Other anemias may be acquired from toxic injury to bone marrow stem cells or result from an inherited stem cell defect (Table 30.9).

Clinical Manifestations

Aplastic anemia can manifest abruptly (over days) or insidiously over weeks to months. It can vary from mild to very severe. The patient may have symptoms caused by suppression of any or all bone marrow elements. General manifestations of anemia, such as fatigue and dyspnea, as well as cardiovascular and cerebral

TABLE 30.9 Causes of Aplastic Anemia

- Chemical agents and toxins (e.g., benzene, insecticides, arsenic, alcohol)
- Drugs (e.g., alkylating agents, antiseizure drugs, antimetabolites, antimicrobials, gold, nonsteroidal antiinflammatory drugs, antithyroid medications, allopurinol)
- Immune suppression of stem cells by autoreactive T-lymphocytes
- Inherited stem cell defect (e.g., Fanconi anemia)
- Radiation
- Toxic injury to bone marrow stem cells
- Viral and bacterial infections

responses, may be seen (Table 30.3). The patient with neutropenia (low neutrophil count) is susceptible to infection and is at risk for septic shock and death. Thrombocytopenia is manifested by a predisposition to bleeding (e.g., petechiae, bruising, nosebleeds).

Diagnostic Studies

Laboratory studies confirm the diagnosis. Because aplastic anemia affects all marrow elements, hemoglobin, WBC, and platelet values are decreased. Other RBC indices are generally normal (Table 30.6). The condition is therefore classified as a normocytic, normochromic anemia. The reticulocyte count is low.

We can further evaluate aplastic anemia by assessing various iron studies. The serum iron and total iron-binding capacity (TIBC) may be high as initial signs of erythropoiesis suppression. Bone marrow biopsy, aspiration, and pathologic examination may be done. The marrow in aplastic anemia is hypocellular with increased yellow marrow (fat content).

❖ Interprofessional and Nursing Management

Management of aplastic anemia is based on identifying and removing the causative agent (when possible) and providing supportive care until the pancytopenia reverses. Nursing interventions appropriate for the patient with pancytopenia from aplastic anemia are discussed in eNursing Care Plan 30.1 for anemia, eNursing Care Plan 30.2 for thrombocytopenia, and eNursing Care Plan 30.3 for neutropenia (available on the website for this chapter). Nursing actions are directed at preventing complications from infection and hemorrhage.

The prognosis of severe untreated aplastic anemia is poor. However, advances in medical management, including HSCT and immunosuppressive therapy with antithymocyte globulin (ATG), steroids, and cyclosporine or cyclophosphamide, have improved outcomes significantly.[7] ATG is a horse serum that contains polyclonal antibodies against human T cells. ATG and cyclosporine are discussed in Chapter 13. Eltrombopag (Promacta), an oral thrombopoietin receptor agonist, can increase platelet counts. High-dose cyclophosphamide, alemtuzumab, or androgens may be helpful in select patients who do not respond to other therapies.[1]

The treatment of choice for adults younger than 55 years of age who do not respond to the immunosuppressive therapy and who have a human leukocyte antigen (HLA)–matched, half-matched, or unrelated donor, is an HSCT.[7] The best results occur in younger patients who have not had previous blood transfusions. Prior transfusions increase the risk for graft rejection. HSCT is discussed in Chapter 15.

For older adults without a donor, the treatment of choice is immunosuppression with ATG and cyclosporine, steroids, and eltrombopag.[3] Patients who need ongoing supportive blood transfusion should be on an iron-binding agent to prevent iron overload.

ANEMIA CAUSED BY BLOOD LOSS

An acute or chronic problem can cause anemia from blood loss.

ACUTE BLOOD LOSS

Acute blood loss occurs because of sudden hemorrhage. Causes of acute blood loss include trauma, complications of surgery, and conditions or diseases that disrupt vascular integrity. There

TABLE 30.10 Manifestations of Acute Blood Loss

VOLUME LOST*		
%	mL	Manifestations
10	500	None or rare vasovagal syncope
20	1000	No detectable signs or symptoms at rest. Tachycardia with exercise and slight postural hypotension
30	1500	Normal supine blood pressure and pulse at rest. Postural hypotension and tachycardia with exercise
40	2000	BP, central venous pressure, and cardiac output below normal at rest; air hunger; rapid, thready pulse and cold, clammy skin
50	2500	Shock, lactic acidosis, and potential death

*Based on an adult with a total blood volume of 5 L.

are 2 clinical concerns in such situations. First, a sudden reduction in the total blood volume can lead to hypovolemic shock. Second, if the acute loss is more gradual, the body maintains its blood volume by slowly increasing the plasma volume. Although this preserves circulating fluid volume, the number of RBCs available to carry O_2 is significantly decreased.

Clinical Manifestations

The manifestations of anemia from acute blood loss are caused by the body's attempts to maintain an adequate blood volume and meet O_2 requirements. Table 30.10 outlines the manifestations of patients with varying degrees of blood volume loss. It is essential to understand that the signs and symptoms the patient has are more important than the laboratory values. For example, an adult with a bleeding peptic ulcer who had a 750-mL hematemesis (15% of a normal total blood volume) within the past 30 minutes may have postural hypotension but have normal values for hemoglobin and hematocrit. Over the next 36 to 48 hours, most of the blood volume deficit will be replaced by the movement of fluid from the extravascular into the intravascular space. Only then will the hemoglobin and hematocrit reflect the blood loss.

Assess the patient's expression of pain. Internal hemorrhage may cause pain because of tissue distention, organ displacement, and nerve compression. Pain may be localized or referred. In the case of retroperitoneal bleeding, the patient may not have abdominal pain. Instead the patient may have numbness and pain in a lower extremity from compression of the lateral cutaneous nerve, which is in the region of the first to third lumbar vertebrae. The major complication of acute blood loss is shock (see Chapter 66).

Diagnostic Studies

When blood volume loss is sudden, plasma volume has not yet had a chance to increase. The loss of RBCs is not reflected in laboratory data, and values may seem normal or high for 2 to 3 days. However, once the plasma volume is replaced, the RBC mass is less concentrated. Then, RBC, hemoglobin, and hematocrit levels are low and reflect the actual blood loss.

❖ Interprofessional and Nursing Management

Interprofessional care is initially concerned with (1) replacing blood volume to prevent shock and (2) finding the source of the hemorrhage and stopping the blood loss. IV fluids used in emergencies include dextran, hetastarch, albumin, and crystalloid electrolyte solutions, such as lactated Ringer's solution. The amount of infusion varies with the solution used. Blood transfusions (packed RBCs) can be used depending on the volume lost. If a large volume of blood is lost, platelets, plasma, and cryoprecipitate may be needed because large volumes of RBCs dilutes the patient's own coagulation system. (See more on managing shock in Chapter 66.)

The body needs 2 to 5 days to make more RBCs in response to increased erythropoietin. The patient may need supplemental iron because the availability of iron affects the marrow production of RBCs. When anemia exists after acute blood loss, dietary sources of iron will probably not be enough to maintain iron stores. Therefore oral or parenteral iron preparations are given.

In the case of trauma, it may be impossible to prevent blood loss. For the postoperative patient, carefully monitor the blood loss from various drainage tubes and dressings and implement appropriate actions. The nursing care for the patient with anemia resulting from acute blood loss will likely include giving blood products (described at the end of this chapter on pp. 647–651).

The anemia should begin to correct itself once the source of hemorrhage is found, blood loss is controlled, and fluid and blood volumes are replaced. There should be no need for long-term treatment of this type of anemia.

CHRONIC BLOOD LOSS

The sources of chronic blood loss are similar to those of iron-deficiency anemia (e.g., bleeding ulcer, hemorrhoids, menstrual and postmenopausal blood loss). The effects of chronic blood loss are usually related to the depletion of iron stores and considered an iron-deficiency anemia. Management of chronic blood loss anemia involves identifying the source and stopping the bleeding. Supplemental iron may be needed.

ANEMIA CAUSED BY INCREASED ERYTHROCYTE DESTRUCTION

The third major cause of anemia is hemolytic anemia, a condition caused by the destruction or hemolysis of RBCs at a rate that exceeds production. Hemolysis can occur because of problems intrinsic or extrinsic to the RBCs. *Intrinsic hemolytic anemias,* which are usually hereditary, result from defects in the RBCs themselves (Table 30.2).

More common are the *acquired hemolytic anemias.* In this type of anemia, the RBCs are normal, but external factors are causing damage (Table 30.2). Macrophages, particularly those in the spleen, liver, and bone marrow, destroy RBCs that are old, defective, or moderately damaged. Fig. 30.2 shows the sequence of events involved in extravascular hemolysis.

The patient with hemolytic anemia has the general manifestations of anemia and specific manifestations related to this type of anemia (Table 30.3). Jaundice is likely because the increased destruction of RBCs causes an elevation in bilirubin levels. The spleen and liver may enlarge because of their hyperactivity, which is related to macrophage phagocytosis of the defective RBCs.

In all causes of hemolysis, a major focus of treatment is to maintain renal function. When RBCs are hemolyzed, the

FIG. 30.2 Sequence of events in extravascular hemolysis.

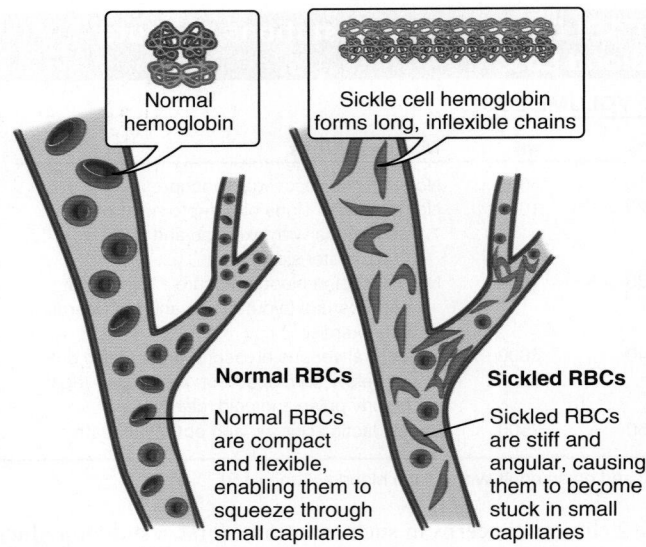

FIG. 30.3 In sickle cell, the hemoglobin forms long inflexible chains and alters the shape of the red blood cells (RBCs). The sickled RBCs can become stuck in the capillaries and occlude the blood flow.

hemoglobin molecule is released and filtered by the kidneys. The accumulation of hemoglobin molecules can obstruct the renal tubules and lead to acute tubular necrosis (see Chapter 46).

SICKLE CELL DISEASE

Sickle cell disease (SCD) is a group of inherited, autosomal recessive disorders characterized by an abnormal form of hemoglobin in the RBC. Because this is a genetic disorder, SCD is usually found during routine neonatal screening. Although median survival can now exceed 45 years old, the disease often results in irreversible damage of the lungs, kidneys, brain, retina, or bones that significantly affects patients' quality of life.[8]

Etiology and Pathophysiology

Genetic Link. In SCD, the abnormal hemoglobin, *hemoglobin S (Hgb S)*, results from the substitution of valine for glutamic acid on the β-globin chain of hemoglobin (see Fig. 12.3). Hgb S causes the RBC to stiffen and elongate, taking on a sickle shape in response to low O_2 levels (Fig. 30.3).

Types of SCD disorders include sickle cell anemia, sickle cell–thalassemia, sickle cell Hgb C disease, and sickle cell trait. *Sickle cell anemia* is the most severe of the SCD syndromes. It occurs when a person is homozygous for hemoglobin S (Hgb SS), meaning the person has inherited Hgb S from both parents. *Sickle cell–thalassemia* and *sickle cell Hgb C* occur when a person inherits Hgb S from one parent and another type of abnormal hemoglobin (such as thalassemia or Hgb C) from the other parent. Both these forms of SCD are less common and less severe than sickle cell anemia. *Sickle cell trait* occurs when a person is heterozygous for hemoglobin S (Hgb AS). This means the person has inherited hemoglobin S from one parent and normal hemoglobin (Hgb A) from the other parent. Sickle cell trait is typically a mild to asymptomatic condition.

🧬 GENETICS IN CLINICAL PRACTICE

Sickle Cell Disease[9]

Genetic Basis
- Autosomal recessive disorder
- Mutation in β-globin *(HBB)* gene found on chromosome 11
- Various versions of β-globin result from different mutations in the *HBB* gene
- Hgb S variant involves substitution of valine for glutamic acid in the β-globin gene

Incidence
- Most common inherited blood disorder in the United States
- Affects about 100,000 Americans
- Occurs in about 1 of every 365 African American births
- Occurs in about 1 of every 16,300 Hispanic American births
- Affects people of Mediterranean, Caribbean, Arabian, and East Indian descent
- 1 in 13 African American babies is born with sickle cell trait

Genetic Testing
- DNA testing is available
- Electrophoresis of hemoglobin and sickling screening test are most often used

Clinical Implications
- Sickle cell trait is the carrier state for SCD and is a mild type of SCD
- If both parents have the trait, there is a 1 in 4 chance that their baby will have SCD
- Genetic counseling is recommended for people with a family history of SCD so they can understand the risks for transmitting the genetic mutation

Sickling Episodes. The major pathophysiologic event of SCD is the sickling of RBCs (Fig. 30.3). Sickling episodes are most often triggered by low O_2 tension in the blood. Hypoxia or deoxygenation of the RBCs can be caused by viral or bacterial infection, high altitude, emotional or physical stress, surgery, and blood loss. Infection is the most common precipitating factor. Other events that can trigger or sustain a sickling episode include dehydration, increased hydrogen ion concentration (acidosis), increased plasma osmolality, decreased plasma volume, and low body temperature. A sickling episode can also occur without an obvious cause.

Sickled RBCs become rigid and take on an elongated, crescent shape (Fig. 30.3). Sickled cells cannot easily pass through capillaries or other small vessels and can cause vascular occlusion, leading to acute or chronic tissue injury. The resulting hemostasis promotes a self-perpetuating cycle of local hypoxia, deoxygenation of more RBCs, and more sickling. Circulating sickled cells are hemolyzed by the spleen, leading to anemia. At first, sickling is reversible with reoxygenation. It eventually becomes irreversible because of cell membrane damage from recurrent sickling. Vaso-occlusive phenomena and hemolysis are the clinical hallmarks of SCD.

Sickle cell crisis is a severe, painful, acute exacerbation of RBC sickling, causing a vaso-occlusive crisis. As sickled cells impair blood flow, vasospasm occurs, further restricting blood flow. Severe capillary hypoxia causes changes in membrane permeability, leading to plasma loss, hemoconcentration, thrombi, and further circulatory stagnation. Tissue ischemia, infarction, and necrosis eventually occur from lack of O_2. Shock is a possible life-threatening consequence of sickle cell crisis because of severe O_2 depletion of the tissues and a reduction of the circulating fluid volume. Sickle cell crisis can begin suddenly and persist for days to weeks.

The frequency, extent, and severity of sickling episodes are highly variable and unpredictable. They depend on the percent of Hgb S present. People with sickle cell anemia have the most severe form because the RBCs have a high percent of Hgb S.

Clinical Manifestations

The effects of SCD vary from person to person, the severity of which may be due to genetic variants. Many people with sickle cell anemia are in reasonably good health most of the time. However, they may have chronic health problems and pain because of organ tissue hypoxia and damage (e.g., involving the kidneys or liver).

The typical patient is anemic but asymptomatic except during sickling episodes. Because most people with sickle cell anemia have dark skin, pallor is easier to detect by examining the mucous membranes. The skin may have a grayish cast. Because of the hemolysis, jaundice is common, and patients are prone to gallstones (cholelithiasis).

The main symptom associated with sickling is pain. The pain severity can range from trivial to excruciating. During sickle cell crisis, the pain is severe because of ischemia of tissue. The episodes can affect any area of the body or several sites simultaneously. The back, chest, extremities, and abdomen are affected most often. Pain episodes are often accompanied by other manifestations, such as fever, swelling, tenderness, tachypnea, hypertension, nausea, and vomiting.

Complications

With repeated episodes of sickling, there is gradual involvement of all body systems, especially the spleen, lungs, kidneys, and brain. Organs that need large amounts of O_2 are most often affected and form the basis for many of the complications of SCD (Fig. 30.4). Infection is a major cause of morbidity and mortality in patients with SCD. One reason for this is the failure

of the spleen to phagocytize foreign substances as it becomes infarcted and dysfunctional (usually by 2 to 4 years of age) from the sickled RBCs. The spleen becomes small because of repeated scarring, a phenomenon termed *autosplenectomy.*

Pneumonia is the most common infection and often is of pneumococcal origin. Infections can be so severe that they cause an aplastic and hemolytic crisis and gallstones. *Aplastic crisis* can be so severe that it causes a temporary shutdown of RBC production in the bone marrow.

Acute chest syndrome is a term used to describe acute pulmonary complications that include pneumonia, tissue infarction, and fat embolism. It is characterized by fever, chest pain, cough, lung infiltrates, and dyspnea. Pulmonary infarctions may cause pulmonary hypertension, MI, and cor pulmonale. The heart may become ischemic and enlarged, leading to HF. Retinal vessel obstruction may result in hemorrhage, scarring, retinal detachment, and blindness. The increased blood viscosity and the lack of O_2 can injure the kidneys. Renal failure may occur. Pulmonary embolism or stroke can result from thrombosis and infarction of cerebral blood vessels. Bone changes may include osteoporosis and osteosclerosis after infarction. Chronic leg ulcers can result from the hypoxia and are especially prevalent around the ankles. *Priapism* (persistent penile erection) may occur if penile veins become occluded.

Diagnostic Studies

A peripheral blood smear may reveal sickled cells and increased, abnormal reticulocytes. Hemoglobin electrophoresis may be done to determine the amount of hemoglobin S and SCD from other variants.

Because of the accelerated RBC breakdown, the patient has characteristic findings of hemolysis (jaundice, high serum bilirubin levels) and abnormal laboratory test results (Table 30.6). Skeletal x-rays show bone and joint deformities and flattening. MRI can diagnose a stroke caused by blocked cerebral vessels from sickled cells. Doppler studies can assess for deep vein thromboses (DVT). A chest x-ray can diagnose infection or organ malfunction.

❖ Interprofessional and Nursing Management

Interprofessional care for a patient with SCD is directed toward (1) preventing sequelae from the disease; (2) alleviating the manifestations from the complications of the disease; (3) minimizing end-organ damage; and (4) continuously assessing for and promptly treating serious sequelae, such as acute chest syndrome, that can lead to immediate death.[8]

A patient in sickle cell crisis may need hospitalization. O_2 therapy treats hypoxia and controls sickling. Assess for any changes in respiratory status and encourage incentive spirometry. Rest can reduce metabolic requirements. DVT prophylaxis (using anticoagulants) should be prescribed. Fluids are given to reduce blood viscosity and maintain renal function. Priapism is managed with pain medication, fluids, and nifedipine (Procardia). If it does not resolve within a few hours, a urologist may be called.[10]

Transfusion therapy is indicated when an aplastic crisis occurs. Aggressive RBC exchange transfusion programs may be implemented for patients who have frequent crises or serious complications, such as acute chest syndrome. These patients, like those with thalassemia major, may need iron chelation therapy to reduce transfusion-produced iron overload.

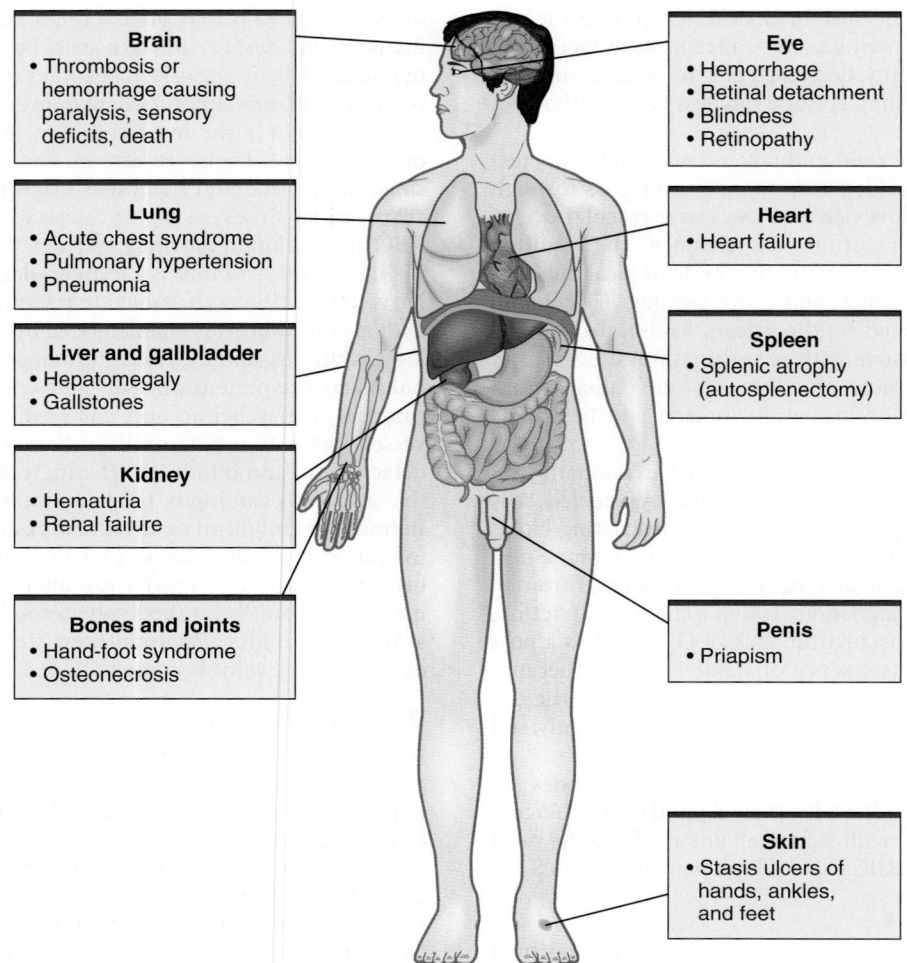

Brain
- Thrombosis or hemorrhage causing paralysis, sensory deficits, death

Lung
- Acute chest syndrome
- Pulmonary hypertension
- Pneumonia

Liver and gallbladder
- Hepatomegaly
- Gallstones

Kidney
- Hematuria
- Renal failure

Bones and joints
- Hand-foot syndrome
- Osteonecrosis

Eye
- Hemorrhage
- Retinal detachment
- Blindness
- Retinopathy

Heart
- Heart failure

Spleen
- Splenic atrophy (autosplenectomy)

Penis
- Priapism

Skin
- Stasis ulcers of hands, ankles, and feet

FIG. 30.4 Clinical manifestations and complications of sickle cell disease. (Modified from McCance KL, Huether SE: *Pathophysiology: The biologic basis for disease in adults and children*, ed 7, St Louis, 2014, Mosby.)

❓ CHECK YOUR PRACTICE

A 21-year-old African American woman was just admitted to the emergency department (ED) after a ski trip to Colorado. She is in excruciating pain in her chest and abdomen. She is short of breath and her O_2 saturation is 86%. Your examination reveals that her heart rate is 110 bpm and respiratory rate 28/minute. She has crackles in the lungs. She has had 6 previous ED admissions for sickle cell crises.
- What are your priorities for her nursing care?

Undertreatment of sickle cell pain is a major problem. Lack of understanding can lead HCPs to underestimate the severity of acute and chronic pain. SCD patients may develop tolerance, and larger doses of pain medication may be needed to reduce pain to a tolerable level. During an acute crisis, optimal pain control usually includes large doses of continuous (rather than as-needed) opioid analgesics, along with breakthrough analgesia, often in the form of patient-controlled analgesia (PCA). Morphine and hydromorphone are the drugs of choice.

Because patients may be having different types and sites of pain, as well as acute and chronic pain, a holistic approach should be used that addresses the pain and its impact on the patient's quality of life (see Chapter 8).[8] In addition to opioids, adjunctive measures, such as nonsteroidal antiinflammatory

agents, antineuropathic pain drugs (e.g., antidepressants, antiseizure drugs), local anesthetics, or nerve blocks may be used. Occupational and physical therapy can optimize functioning. Referral to social and chaplain services can help address social, emotional, and spiritual needs.

Infection is a frequent complication. Any febrile illness in a patient with SCD is an emergency. Infections, such as chronic leg ulcers, may be treated with rest, antibiotics, warm saline soaks, mechanical or enzyme debridement, and grafting, if needed. Patients with acute chest syndrome are treated with broad-spectrum antibiotics, O_2 therapy, fluid therapy, and possibly exchange transfusion. Blood transfusions are done sparingly between crises since patients develop antibodies to RBCs and iron overload. Because chronic hemolysis results in increased use of folic acid stores, the patient should take an oral folic acid supplement.

Hydroxyurea (Hydrea) is the only medication that is clinically beneficial. This drug increases the production of hemoglobin F (fetal hemoglobin) and alters the adhesion of sickled RBCs to the endothelium. The increase in Hgb F is accompanied by a reduction in hemolysis, an increase in hemoglobin concentration, and a decrease in sickled cells and painful crises.[10] Dietary supplementation with oral glutamine, an amino acid, can reduce the number and frequency of pain crises and hospitalizations.[11]

HSCT is the only available treatment that can cure some patients with SCD but is not widely available. The selection of appropriate recipients, scarcity of appropriate donors, risk, and cost-effectiveness limit its use. (HSCT is discussed in Chapter 15.) Gene therapy approaches are under investigation.[8]

Patient teaching and support are important in the long-term care of the patient with SCD. The patient and caregiver must understand the basis of the disease and the reasons for supportive care and ongoing pertinent screening tailored to SCD manifestations. Teach the patient ways to avoid crises. Review steps to avoid dehydration and hypoxia, such as avoiding high altitudes and seeking medical attention quickly to counteract problems, such as upper respiratory tract infections. Teach patients to maintain adequate fluid intake. Immunizations, such as pneumococcal, *H. influenzae,* influenza, and hepatitis, should be given. Screening for retinopathy should begin at age 10. Each person with SCD should have a reproductive life plan.[10] Teaching about pain control is needed because the pain during a crisis may be severe and often requires considerable analgesia. Minor pain episodes that are not associated with infection or other symptoms that need medical attention can sometimes be managed at home.

ACQUIRED HEMOLYTIC ANEMIA

Acquired hemolytic anemia results from hemolysis of RBCs from extrinsic factors. These factors include (1) physical destruction, (2) antibody reactions, and (3) infectious agents and toxins (Table 30.2).[3]

Physical destruction of RBCs results from the exertion of extreme force on the cells. Traumatic events causing disruption of the RBC membrane include hemodialysis, extracorporeal circulation used in cardiopulmonary bypass, and prosthetic heart valves. In addition, the force needed to push blood through abnormal vessels, such as those that have been burned, irradiated, or affected by vascular disease (e.g., diabetes), may physically damage RBCs.

RBCs can be fragmented and destroyed as they try to pass through abnormal arterial or venous microcirculation. The RBCs are sheared as they try to pass by excess platelet aggregation and/or fibrin polymer formation, such as is seen in thrombotic thrombocytopenic purpura (TTP) and disseminated intravascular coagulation (DIC) (discussed later in this chapter).

Antibodies may destroy RBCs by the mechanisms involved in antigen-antibody reactions. In blood transfusion reactions, the recipient's antibodies attack and hemolyze donor cells. Autoimmune antibody reactions occur when people develop antibodies against their own RBCs. This can be an idiopathic (no prior hemolytic history) or from other autoimmune diseases (e.g., systemic lupus erythematosus [SLE]), leukemia, lymphoma, or medications (penicillin, ibuprofen, metformin, chlorpromazine, procainamide).

Infectious agents cause hemolysis in 3 ways: (1) by invading the RBC and destroying its contents (e.g., parasites, such as in malaria), (2) by releasing hemolytic substances (e.g., *Clostridium perfringens*), and (3) by generating an antigen-antibody reaction (e.g., *Mycoplasma pneumoniae*). Various agents may be toxic to RBCs and cause hemolysis. These hemolytic toxins involve chemicals, such as oxidative drugs, arsenic, lead, copper, and bee stings or spider bites.

Laboratory findings in hemolytic anemia are shown in Table 30.6. Treatment and management of acquired hemolytic anemias involve general supportive care until the causative agent can be eliminated or at least made less injurious to the RBCs. Because a hemolytic crisis is a potential consequence, be ready to institute appropriate emergency therapy. This includes aggressive hydration and electrolyte replacement to reduce the risk for kidney injury caused by hemoglobin (from RBC lysis) clogging the kidney tubules and subsequent shock. Supportive care may include giving corticosteroids and blood products or removing the spleen.

The patient with chronic hemolytic anemia may need folate replacement. To suppress the RBC destruction, immunosuppressive agents may be used, such as glucocorticoids or rituximab (Rituxan), which is a monoclonal antibody to B-cell CD20. For severe cases associated with hemolysis, thrombocytopenia, and acute kidney injury, plasma exchange and eculizumab (Soliris), a monoclonal antibody to complement protein C5, are options.[12]

OTHER RED BLOOD CELL DISORDERS

HEMOCHROMATOSIS

Hemochromatosis is an iron overload disorder. Although a genetic defect is the most common cause, it may occur with diseases such as sideroblastic anemia. It also may be caused by liver disease and the chronic blood transfusions used to treat thalassemia and SCD.

Genetic Link

The genetic disorder *(hereditary hemochromatosis)* is an autosomal recessive disorder characterized by increased intestinal iron absorption and, as a result, increased tissue iron deposition.

GENETICS IN CLINICAL PRACTICE[13]

Hemochromatosis

Genetic Basis
- Autosomal recessive disorder
- Caused by mutations in the *HAMP, HFE, HFE2, SLC40A1,* and *TFR2* genes
- These genes play a key role in regulating the absorption, transport, and storage of iron
- Mutations in these genes impair the control of iron absorption during digestion and change the distribution of iron to other parts of the body, resulting in iron accumulation in tissues and organs

Incidence
- Most common genetic disease in people of European ancestry
- The C282Y mutation of the *HFE* gene is the most common
- About 4 to 5 of every 1000 whites carry 2 copies of the *HFE* gene; 1 of every 10 carries one copy
- Affects 1 in 200 to 500 in the United States
- Very low prevalence in other ethnic populations

Genetic Testing
- DNA testing is available and recommended for all first-degree relatives of people with the disease
- American Hemochromatosis Society recommends genetic testing regardless of family history

Clinical Implications
- Most Americans who have the gene mutation do not know it until diseases becomes apparent
- Clinical expression is variable and depends on dietary iron, blood loss, and other modifying factors
- Early treatment can prevent serious complications
- If untreated, progressive iron deposits can lead to multiple organ failure

The normal range for total body iron is 40 mg/kg in women and 50 mg/kg in men. People with hemochromatosis accumulate iron at an increased rate and may exceed total iron concentrations of 50 g.[1]

Symptoms usually do not develop until after age 40 years in men and after 50 years in women.[13] Early symptoms are nonspecific and include fatigue, arthralgia, impotence, abdominal pain, and weight loss. Later, the excess iron accumulates in the liver and causes liver enlargement and eventually cirrhosis. Excess iron is deposited in the liver, pancreas, heart, joints, and endocrine glands, resulting in diabetes, skin pigment changes (bronzing), heart problems (e.g., cardiomyopathy), arthritis, and testicular atrophy. Physical examination reveals an enlarged liver and spleen and pigmentation changes in the skin.

Laboratory values show a high serum iron, TIBC, and serum ferritin. Testing for known genetic mutations confirms the diagnosis. Liver biopsy can quantify the amount of iron and establish the degree of organ damage.

The goal of treatment is to remove excess iron from the body and minimize any symptoms the patient may have. Iron removal is achieved by removing 500 mL of blood each week for 2 to 3 years until the iron stores in the body are depleted. Then blood is removed less often to maintain iron levels within normal limits.

Iron chelating agents may be used. Deferoxamine, which chelates and removes accumulated iron via the kidneys, can be given IV or subcutaneously. Deferasirox and deferiprone are oral agents that chelate iron. Chelating agents form a complex with iron and promote its excretion from the body.[1] Iron accumulation can be reduced by dietary changes, such as avoiding vitamin C and iron supplements, uncooked seafood, and iron-rich foods.

Management of organ involvement (e.g., diabetes, HF) is the same as conventional treatment for these problems. The most common causes of death are cirrhosis, liver failure, liver cancer, and HF. With early diagnosis and treatment, life expectancy is normal. However, many cases go undetected and untreated.

POLYCYTHEMIA

Polycythemia is the production and presence of increased numbers of RBCs. The increase in RBCs can be so great that blood circulation is impaired because of the increased blood viscosity *(hyperviscosity)* and volume *(hypervolemia)*.

Etiology and Pathophysiology

The 2 types of polycythemia are primary polycythemia, or polycythemia vera, and secondary polycythemia (Fig. 30.5). Their causes and pathogenesis differ, although their complications and manifestations are similar.

Primary Polycythemia. *Polycythemia vera* is a chronic myeloproliferative disorder. It involves not only RBCs, but also WBCs and platelets, with an increased production of all these blood cells. This leads to enhanced blood viscosity and blood volume and congestion of organs and tissues with blood. Splenomegaly and hepatomegaly are common. Patients have hypercoagulopathies that predispose them to clotting. The disease develops insidiously and follows a chronic, vacillating course. The median age at diagnosis is 60 years old, with a slight male predominance.

Genetic Link. Polycythemia vera is associated with mutations in the Janus kinase-2 *(JAK2)* gene. The *JAK2* gene provides instructions for making a protein that promotes proliferation of cells, especially blood cells from hematopoietic stem cells. Polycythemia vera begins with 1 or more DNA mutations of a single hematopoietic stem cell. Most cases of polycythemia vera are not inherited. They are associated with genetic changes that are somatic, which means they are acquired during a person's lifetime and are present only in certain cells.

Secondary Polycythemia. *Secondary polycythemia* can be either hypoxia driven or hypoxia independent. In hypoxia-driven secondary polycythemia, hypoxia stimulates erythropoietin (EPO) production in the kidneys, which in turn stimulates RBC production. The need for O_2 may result from high altitude, lung disease, cardiovascular disease, alveolar hypoventilation, defective O_2 transport, or tissue hypoxia.

EPO levels may return to normal once the hemoglobin stabilizes at a higher level. In this situation, secondary polycythemia is a physiologic response in which the body tries to compensate for a problem, rather than a pathologic response. Hypoxia-driven secondary polycythemia is discussed in Chapter 28.

In hypoxia-independent secondary polycythemia, cancer or benign tumor tissue makes EPO. Serum EPO levels often stay increased in these situations. Splenomegaly does not occur with secondary polycythemia.

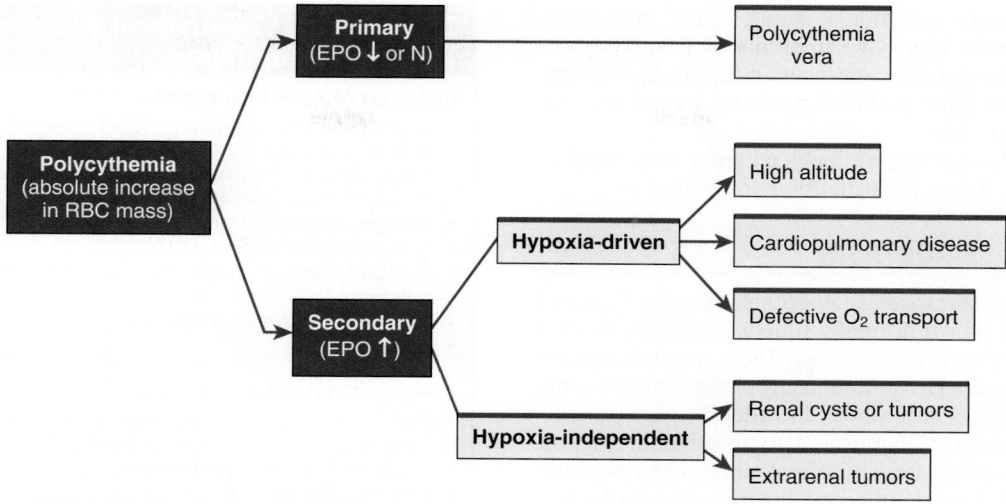

FIG. 30.5 Differentiating between primary and secondary polycythemia. *EPO,* Erythropoietin; *N,* normal.

Clinical Manifestations and Complications

Circulatory manifestations of polycythemia vera occur because of the hypertension caused by hypervolemia and hyperviscosity. They are often the first manifestations and include headache, vertigo, dizziness, tinnitus, and visual changes. Generalized pruritus (often exacerbated by a hot bath) may be a striking symptom and is related to histamine release from an increased number of basophils. Paresthesias and *erythromelalgia* (painful burning and redness of the hands and feet) may be present. The patient may have angina, HF, intermittent claudication, and thrombophlebitis, which may be complicated by embolization. These manifestations are caused by blood vessel distention, impaired blood flow, circulatory stasis, thrombosis, and tissue hypoxia from the hypervolemia and hyperviscosity. The most common serious acute complication is stroke from a thrombosis.

Hemorrhagic phenomena caused by either vessel rupture from overdistention or inadequate platelet function may result in petechiae, bruising, nosebleeds, or GI bleeding. Hemorrhage can be acute and catastrophic. Hepatomegaly and splenomegaly from organ engorgement may contribute to satiety and fullness. The patient may have pain from peptic ulcer caused either by increased gastric secretions or liver and spleen engorgement. *Plethora* (ruddy complexion) may be present. Uric acid is one of the products of RBC destruction. As RBC destruction increases, uric acid production increases, leading to hyperuricemia and gout.

Although the incidence is low, myelofibrosis and leukemia develop in some patients with polycythemia vera. These disorders may be caused by the chemotherapeutic drugs used to treat the disease, or they may be caused by a disorder in the stem cells that progresses to erythroleukemia. The major cause of morbidity and mortality from polycythemia vera is related to thrombosis (e.g., stroke).

Diagnostic Studies

The laboratory manifestations seen in a patient with polycythemia vera include (1) high hemoglobin and RBC count with microcytosis; (2) low to normal EPO level (secondary polycythemia has a high level); (3) high WBC count with basophilia and neutrophilia; (4) high platelet count (thrombocytosis) and platelet dysfunction; (5) high leukocyte alkaline phosphatase, uric acid, and cobalamin levels; and (6) high histamine levels.[3] Bone marrow examination in polycythemia vera shows hypercellularity of RBCs, WBCs, and platelets.

❖ Interprofessional and Nursing Management

Treatment is directed toward reducing blood volume and viscosity and bone marrow activity. Phlebotomy is the mainstay of treatment. The aim of phlebotomy is to reduce the hematocrit and keep it less than 45%.[14] Generally, at the time of diagnosis 300 to 500 mL of blood may be removed every few days until the hematocrit is reduced to acceptable levels.[14] Phlebotomy then may be needed every 2 to 3 months, reducing the blood volume by about 500 mL each time. A person managed with repeated phlebotomies eventually becomes deficient in iron, although this effect is rarely symptomatic. Avoid iron supplementation. Hydration therapy can reduce the blood's viscosity.

Myelosuppressive agents, such as hydroxyurea, busulfan (Myleran), and chlorambucil (Leukeran), may be given.[3] Ruxolitinib (Jakafi), which inhibits the expression of the *JAK2* mutation, is given to patients who have not responded to hydroxyurea.[14] Other therapies include anagrelide (Agrylin), which can reduce the platelet count and inhibit platelet aggregation. Low-dose aspirin is used to prevent clotting. α-Interferon (α-IFN) and pegylated interferon are given to women of childbearing age or those with intractable pruritus. Allopurinol (Zyloprim) may reduce the number of acute gouty attacks.[3]

When acute exacerbations of polycythemia vera develop, you have several nursing responsibilities. Depending on the agency's policies, you may either assist with or perform the phlebotomy. Assess fluid intake and output during hydration therapy to avoid fluid overload (which worsens circulatory congestion) or fluid deficit (which makes the blood even more viscous). If myelosuppressive agents are used, give the drugs as ordered, observe the patient, and teach the patient about the side effects of the drugs.

Assess the patient's nutritional status, since inadequate food intake can result from GI symptoms of fullness, pain, and dyspepsia. Begin activities and/or medications to decrease thrombus formation. Start active or passive leg exercises and ambulation when possible.

Because of its chronic nature, polycythemia vera requires ongoing evaluation. Assess the patient for complications.

PROBLEMS OF HEMOSTASIS

Hemostasis involves the vascular endothelium, platelets, and coagulation factors, which normally function together to stop hemorrhage and repair vascular injury. These mechanisms are described in Chapter 29. Disruption in any of these components may result in bleeding or thrombotic disorders.

Three major disorders of hemostasis discussed in this section are (1) thrombocytopenia (low platelet count), (2) hemophilia and von Willebrand disease (inherited disorders of specific clotting factors), and (3) DIC.

THROMBOCYTOPENIA

Etiology and Pathophysiology

Thrombocytopenia is a reduction of platelets below 150,000/μL (150×10^9/L). Acute, severe, or prolonged decreases from this normal range can result in abnormal hemostasis that presents as prolonged bleeding from minor trauma or spontaneous bleeding without injury.

Platelet disorders occur because of impaired production, increased destruction, or abnormal distribution (Table 30.11).[15] While they can be inherited (e.g., Wiskott-Aldrich syndrome), most are acquired. A common cause of acquired disorders is the ingestion of certain drugs.[1] Although some drugs are directly myelosuppressive (e.g., chemotherapy, ganciclovir), the usual mechanism of drug-related thrombocytopenia is accelerated platelet destruction caused by antibodies. Antibodies attack the platelets when the drug binds to the platelet surface.

Some drugs can affect platelet aggregation. Aspirin doses as low as 81 mg can alter platelet aggregation. Normal function is restored when new platelets are made.

Immune Thrombocytopenia. The most common acquired thrombocytopenia is a syndrome of abnormal destruction of circulating platelets termed *immune thrombocytopenia* (ITP). ITP is an acquired immune disorder in which the thrombocytopenia results from antiplatelet antibodies, impaired platelet production, and T-cell–mediated destruction of platelets.[16] In ITP, platelets are coated with antibodies. These platelets function normally; however, when they reach the spleen, these antibody-coated platelets are mistaken as foreign and destroyed by macrophages. Decreased platelet production contributes to ITP. Sometimes autoimmune disease (such as SLE) or infection, such as *Helicobacter pylori* or viral infection (HIV), contributes to this disorder.[16]

Platelets normally survive 8 to 10 days. However, in ITP, platelet survival is shortened. Generally, the syndrome presents as an acute condition in children and a chronic condition in adults.

Thrombotic Thrombocytopenic Purpura. *Thrombotic thrombocytopenic purpura* (TTP) is an uncommon syndrome characterized by hemolytic anemia, thrombocytopenia, neurologic abnormalities, fever (in the absence of infection),

TABLE 30.11 Causes of Acquired Thrombocytopenia

Impaired Platelet Production
- Cancers and other disorders
  - Aplastic anemia
  - Leukemia, lymphoma, myeloma, myelodysplastic disorders
  - Marrow metastases by solid tumors
- Drugs (chemotherapy, others)
- Immune thrombocytopenia (ITP)
- Infections, bacterial, fungal, or viral (hepatitis C virus, HIV, cytomegalovirus)
- Nutritional deficiencies, alcoholism
- Radiation

Increased Platelet Destruction
- Artificial surfaces (e.g., cardiopulmonary bypass, hemodialysis)
- Disseminated intravascular coagulation (DIC)
- Heparin-induced thrombocytopenia (HIT)
- Pregnancy-related
- Thrombotic microangiopathy
  - Thrombotic thrombocytopenic purpura (TTP)
  - Atypical Hemolytic Uremic Syndromes (aHUS)

Abnormal Platelet Distribution
- Dilution (massive blood transfusion, fluids)
- Splenic sequestration

and renal abnormalities. Not all features are present in all patients. Because it is almost always associated with hemolytic-uremic syndrome (HUS), TTP is often referred to as *TTP-HUS*. The disease is associated with enhanced aggregation of platelets, which form microthrombi that deposit in arterioles and capillaries.

In most cases, TTP is caused by the deficiency of a plasma enzyme (ADAMTS13) that breaks down the von Willebrand clotting factor (vWF) into normal size. vWF is the most important protein-mediating platelet adhesion to damaged endothelial cells. Without the enzyme, unusually large amounts of vWF attach to activated platelets, promoting platelet aggregation.

TTP occurs primarily in previously healthy adults, with a slight female predominance. The syndrome may be idiopathic (thought to be due to an autoimmune disorder against ADAMTS13) or due to certain drug toxicities (e.g., chemotherapy, cyclosporine, quinine, oral contraceptives, valacyclovir, clopidogrel [Plavix]), pregnancy or preeclampsia, infection, or a known autoimmune disorder, such as SLE or scleroderma.[3] TTP is a medical emergency because bleeding and clotting occur at the same time.

Heparin-Induced Thrombocytopenia. One of the risks associated with the use of heparin is the development of the life-threatening condition called *heparin-induced thrombocytopenia* (HIT), also called *heparin-induced thrombocytopenia and thrombosis syndrome* (HITTS). Typically, patients develop thrombocytopenia 5 to 10 days after the onset of heparin therapy. HIT should be suspected if the platelet count falls by more than 50% or falls to below 150,000/μL. As many as 5% of patients on heparin therapy develop HIT.[3,17]

Although the major problem of HIT is venous thrombosis, arterial thrombosis can occur. DVT and pulmonary emboli most often result as a complication of the thromboses. Other complications include arterial vascular infarcts, resulting in

FIG. 30.6 Acute immune thrombocytopenic purpura often presents with purpuric lesions. (From Forbes CD, Jackson WF: *Colour atlas and text of clinical medicine,* ed 3, London, 2003, Mosby.)

TABLE 30.12 Laboratory Results in Thrombocytopenia and DIC

Laboratory Test	ITP	TTP	HIT	DIC
Platelets	↓↓↓↓	↓↓↓	↓↓	↓↓↓
Hemolysis				
Haptoglobin	N	↓	N	↓
Hgb	N	↓↓	N	N or ↓
Indirect bilirubin	N	↑	N	N or ↑
LDH	N	↑↑↑	N	↑
Reticulo-cytes	N	↑	N	N or ↑
Schistocytes	N	↑↑↑	N or ↑	N or ↑
Coagulopathy				
PT	N	N	N	↑
aPTT	N	N	N	↑
D-dimer	N	N or ↑	↑	↑↑
Other tests	ITP IgG assay, platelet activation/ function assay, *Helicobacter pylori*, hepatitis C, HIV, bone marrow biopsy	ADAMTS13 Urinalysis (for proteinuria, hematuria), Creatinine	Platelet activation/ function assay, PF4-heparin complex (antigen assay)	

skin necrosis, stroke, and end-organ damage (e.g., kidneys). Symptoms of bleeding are unusual because the platelet count rarely drops below 20,000/µL.

In HIT, platelet destruction and vascular endothelial injury are the 2 major responses to an immune-mediated response to heparin. Platelet factor 4 (PF4) (protein made and released by platelets) binds to heparin. This PF4-heparin complex then binds to the platelet surface, leading to further platelet activation and release of more PF4, thus creating a positive feedback loop. Antibodies are created against the PF4-heparin-platelet complex. They are removed prematurely from circulation, leading to thrombocytopenia and platelet-fibrin thrombi.

Clinical Manifestations

Many patients with thrombocytopenia are asymptomatic. The most common symptom is bleeding, usually mucosal or cutaneous. Mucosal bleeding may manifest as nosebleeds and gingival bleeding. Large bullous hemorrhages may appear on the buccal mucosa because of the lack of vessel protection by the submucosal tissue.

Bleeding into the skin is seen as petechiae, purpura, or superficial ecchymoses. *Petechiae* are small, flat, red or reddish brown microhemorrhages (see Table 29.6). When the platelet count is low, RBCs may leak out of the blood vessels and into the skin to cause petechiae. When there are many petechiae, we call the resulting reddish skin *purpura* (Fig. 30.6). Purplish lesions caused by hemorrhage are termed *ecchymoses*. Pain and tenderness are sometimes present.

The major complication of thrombocytopenia is hemorrhage. The hemorrhage may be insidious or acute and internal or external. It may occur in any area of the body, including the joints, retina, and brain. Cerebral hemorrhage may be fatal. Insidious hemorrhage may be first detected by discovering the anemia that accompanies blood loss. Be aware of manifestations that reflect internal blood loss, including weakness, fainting, dizziness, tachycardia, abdominal pain, and hypotension. Prolonged bleeding after routine procedures, such as venipuncture or IM injection, may indicate thrombocytopenia.

Because thrombocytopenia can be accompanied by vascular thromboses, signs and symptoms of vascular ischemic problems may occur (see Chapter 37). For example, subtle confusion, headache, or even serious manifestations, such as seizures and coma due to TTP-related thrombosis, may occur. Because signs and symptoms may be subtle, astute and thorough assessment of the patient is essential.

Diagnostic Studies

The platelet count is decreased in thrombocytopenia. Any reduction below 150,000/µL (150 × 10⁹/L) may be termed *thrombocytopenia*. However, prolonged bleeding from trauma or injury does not usually occur until platelet counts are less than 50,000/µL (50 × 10⁹/L).[1] When the count drops below 20,000/µL (20 × 10⁹/L), spontaneous, life-threatening hemorrhages (e.g., intracranial bleeding) can occur. Platelet transfusions are generally not recommended until the count is below 10,000/µL (10 × 10⁹/L) unless the patient is actively bleeding.[3]

The patient's history and clinical examination, along with comparisons of laboratory parameters, help to determine the cause of the thrombocytopenia. Table 30.12 compares the types of thrombocytopenia.

Laboratory tests that assess secondary hemostasis or coagulation, such as the prothrombin time (PT) and aPTT, can be normal even in severe thrombocytopenia. If they are increased, this may point toward DIC.

Specific assays, such as ITP antigen-specific assay, platelet activation/function assay, or PF4-heparin complex for HIT, can be done to assist with the diagnosis. In TTP, testing for deficiency of ADAMTS13 is not always diagnostic, so an increase of lactate dehydrogenase (LDH) may help establish the diagnosis. When thrombocytopenia occurs with anemia characterized by altered RBC morphology, including *spherocytes* (small, globular, completely hemoglobinated RBCs), fragmented cells (schistocytes), and pronounced reticulocytosis, a diagnosis of TTP should be suspected. These findings are partially a result of intravascular fibrin deposition causing a "slicing" of RBCs. In TTP, thrombocytopenia may be severe, but coagulation studies are normal.

TABLE 30.13 Interprofessional Care

Thrombocytopenia

Diagnostic Assessment
- History and physical examination
- Bone marrow aspiration and biopsy
- CBC, including platelet count
- Specific laboratory studies (Table 30.12)

Management
Immune Thrombocytopenic Purpura
- Corticosteroids
- IV immunoglobulin (IVIG)
- Anti-Rh$_0$(D)
- Rituximab (Rituxan)
- Romiplostim (Nplate)
- Eltrombopag (Promacta)
- Splenectomy
- Immunosuppressives (e.g., cyclosporine)
- Platelet transfusions
- Epsilon-aminocaproic acid (Amicar)

Thrombotic Thrombocytopenic Purpura
- Identification and treatment of cause
- Plasmapheresis (plasma exchange)
- Corticosteroids
- Rituximab (Rituxan)
- Immunosuppressives (e.g., cyclophosphamide)
- Splenectomy

Heparin-Induced Thrombocytopenia
- Direct thrombin inhibitor (argatroban [Acova])
- Indirect thrombin inhibitor (fondaparinux [Arixtra])
- Synthetic thrombin inhibitor (bivalirudin)
- Plasmapheresis (plasma exchange)
- Warfarin (Coumadin)
- Thrombolytic agents

Decreased Platelet Production
- Identification and treatment or removal of cause
- Corticosteroids
- Platelet transfusions

Bone marrow examination may be done to rule out production problems as the cause of thrombocytopenia (e.g., leukemia, aplastic anemia, other myeloproliferative disorders) or when other tests are inconclusive. When destruction of circulating platelets is the cause, bone marrow analysis shows *megakaryocytes* (precursors of platelets) to be normal or increased, even though circulating platelets are reduced. The absence or decreased number of megakaryocytes on bone marrow biopsy is consistent with thrombocytopenia caused by decreased bone marrow production (e.g., aplastic anemia).

Interprofessional Care

Interprofessional care of thrombocytopenia differs based on the cause. Removal or treatment of the underlying cause or disorder is sometimes sufficient. The patient with thrombocytopenia should avoid aspirin and other drugs that affect platelet function or production. The following sections discuss management strategies for the different causes of thrombocytopenia (Table 30.13).

Immune Thrombocytopenic Purpura. Multiple therapies are used to manage the patient with ITP. If the patient is asymptomatic,

therapy may not be used unless the patient's platelet count is below 30,000/μL.[1] Corticosteroids (e.g., prednisone, methylprednisolone) are used initially to treat ITP because of their ability to suppress the phagocytic response of splenic macrophages. This alters the spleen's recognition of platelets and increases the life span of the platelets. Corticosteroids depress antibody formation and reduce capillary leakage.

High doses of IV immunoglobulin (IVIG) and a component of IVIG, anti-Rh$_0$(D) (anti-D, WinRho), may be used in the patient who is unresponsive to corticosteroids or splenectomy or for whom splenectomy is not an option. We think that one way these agents work is by competing with the antiplatelet antibodies for macrophage receptors in the spleen. Rituximab (Rituxan) may be used for its ability to lyse activated B cells, thus reducing the immune recognition of platelets. Romiplostim (Nplate) and eltrombopag (Promacta) are used for patients with chronic ITP who had an insufficient response to the other treatments. These drugs are thrombopoietin receptor agonists, thus increasing platelet production.[1]

Splenectomy may be needed if the patient does not respond to treatment. Two thirds of patients benefit from splenectomy, resulting in a sustained remission.[3] The effectiveness of splenectomy is based on 4 factors. First, the spleen has an abundance of the macrophages that sequester and destroy platelets. Second, structural features of the spleen enhance the interaction between antibody-coated platelets and macrophages. Third, some antibody synthesis occurs in the spleen, so antiplatelet antibodies decrease after splenectomy. Fourth, the spleen normally sequesters around one third of the platelets, so its removal increases the number of platelets in circulation.

Immunosuppressive therapy (e.g., cyclosporine) may be used in refractory cases (Table 30.13).[1] Platelet transfusions may increase platelet counts in cases of life-threatening hemorrhage. Platelets should not be given prophylactically because of the risk for antibody formation. The usual indication for giving platelets is for a platelet count less than 10,000/μL or if there is expected bleeding before a procedure. Epsilon-aminocaproic acid (EACA, Amicar), an antifibrinolytic agent, may treat severe bleeding.[3]

Thrombotic Thrombocytopenic Purpura. TTP may be treated in a variety of ways. The first step is to treat the underlying disorder (e.g., infection) or remove the causative agent, if known. If untreated, TTP usually results in irreversible renal failure and death. Plasma exchange (plasmapheresis) (see Chapter 13) can aggressively reverse platelet consumption by supplying the appropriate vWF and enzyme (ADAMTS13) and removing the large vWF molecules that bind with platelets. Treatment should be continued daily until the patient's platelet counts normalize and hemolysis has ceased. Corticosteroids may be given with this treatment.[3]

Rituximab is used for patients who are refractory to plasma exchange. It decreases the level of inhibitory ADAMTS13 IgG antibodies. Other immunosuppressants, such as cyclosporine or cyclophosphamide, are options. Splenectomy may be considered in patients who are refractory to plasma exchange or immunosuppression. Platelet administration is generally contraindicated because this may lead to new vWF-platelet complexes and increased clotting.[3]

Heparin-Induced Thrombocytopenia. All forms of heparin must be stopped when HIT is first recognized. This includes heparin flushes for vascular catheters.

To maintain anticoagulation, the patient should be started on a direct thrombin inhibitor, such as argatroban. Fondaparinux (Arixtra), a factor Xa inhibitor (indirect thrombin inhibitor), or bivalirudin (a synthetic thrombin inhibitor) may be used.[17] Warfarin should be started only when the platelet count has reached 150,000/μL. If the clotting is severe, the most commonly used treatment modalities are plasmapheresis to clear the platelet-aggregating IgG from the blood, protamine sulfate to interrupt the circulating heparin, thrombolytic agents to treat the thromboembolic events, and surgery to remove clots. Platelet transfusions are not effective because they may enhance thromboembolic events.[3]

Patients who have had HIT should never receive heparin or low-molecular-weight heparin (LMWH) again. This should be clearly marked in the patient's medical record.

Thrombocytopenia From Decreased Platelet Production. The management of acquired thrombocytopenia is based on finding the cause and treating the disease or removing the causative agent. If the precipitating factor is unknown, the patient may receive corticosteroids. Platelet transfusions are given if life-threatening hemorrhage develops.

Often acquired thrombocytopenia is caused by another underlying condition (e.g., aplastic anemia, leukemia) or therapy used to treat another problem. For example, in acute leukemia all blood cell types may be depressed. Plus, the patient may receive chemotherapeutic drugs that cause bone marrow suppression. If the patient can be supported throughout the course of chemotherapy-induced thrombocytopenia, the thrombocytopenia will also resolve.

❖ NURSING MANAGEMENT: THROMBOCYTOPENIA

◆ Nursing Assessment

Subjective and objective data that should be obtained from a patient with thrombocytopenia are outlined in Table 30.14.

◆ Nursing Diagnoses

The main nursing diagnosis for the patient with thrombocytopenia is risk for bleeding.

◆ Planning

The overall goals are that the patient with thrombocytopenia will (1) have no bleeding, (2) maintain vascular integrity, and (3) manage home care to prevent any complications related to an increased risk for bleeding.

◆ Nursing Implementation

◆ Health Promotion. Discourage the use of over-the-counter (OTC) medications known to be causes of acquired thrombocytopenia and reduced platelet function. Some have aspirin as an ingredient. Aspirin reduces platelet adhesiveness, thus contributing to bleeding.

Encourage persons to have a complete medical evaluation if manifestations of bleeding tendencies (e.g., prolonged nosebleeds, petechiae) develop. Observe for early signs of thrombocytopenia in the patient receiving cancer chemotherapy drugs.

◆ Acute Care. The goal during acute episodes of thrombocytopenia is to prevent or control hemorrhage (see eNursing Care Plan 30.2 on the website for this chapter). In the patient with thrombocytopenia, bleeding is usually from superficial sites. Deep bleeding (into muscles, joints, and abdomen) usually occurs only when clotting factors are decreased. Stress that a minor nosebleed or

---

TABLE 30.14 Nursing Assessment

Thrombocytopenia

Subjective Data

Important Health Information

Past health history: Recent hemorrhage, excessive bleeding, or viral illness; HIV infection; cancer (especially leukemia or lymphoma); aplastic anemia; SLE; cirrhosis; exposure to radiation or toxic chemicals; DIC

Medications: Many medications, including chemotherapy agents, valproic acid (Depakote), furosemide (Lasix), gold, nonsteroidal antiinflammatory drugs, penicillin

Functional Health Patterns

Health perception–health management: Family history of bleeding problems; malaise

Nutritional-metabolic: Bleeding gingiva; coffee-ground or bloody vomitus; easy bruising

Elimination: Hematuria, dark or bloody stools

Activity-exercise: Fatigue, weakness, fainting; nosebleeds, hemoptysis; dyspnea

Cognitive-perceptual: Pain and tenderness in bleeding areas (e.g., abdomen, head, extremities); headache

Sexuality-reproductive: Menorrhagia, metrorrhagia

Objective Data

General

Fever, lethargy

Integumentary

Petechiae, bruising, purpura

Gastrointestinal

Splenomegaly, abdominal distention; heme-positive stools

Possible Diagnostic Findings

Platelet count <150,000/μL (150 × 10⁹/L), prolonged bleeding time, ↓ hemoglobin and hematocrit; normal or ↑ megakaryocytes in bone marrow examination

---

new petechiae may indicate potential hemorrhage and to notify the HCP.

Bleeding from the posterior nasopharynx may be hard to detect because the blood may be swallowed. If you cannot avoid a subcutaneous injection, use a small-gauge needle and apply direct pressure for at least 5 to 10 minutes after the injection. An ice pack may be helpful. Avoid IM injections. Help the patient understand the importance of adhering to self-care measures that reduce the risk for bleeding (Table 30.15).

Note that many of these disorders may be accompanied by vascular clotting, and appropriate assessment and management should be taken (see Chapter 37). As bleeding occurs, RBCs and coagulation factors are consumed along with platelets. It is important to monitor all blood cell and coagulation studies.

In a woman with thrombocytopenia, menstrual blood loss may exceed the usual amount and duration. Counting sanitary napkins used during menses is another important intervention to detect excess blood loss. Blood loss of 50 mL will completely soak a sanitary napkin. Suppression of menses with hormonal agents may be needed during predictable periods of thrombocytopenia (e.g., during chemotherapy and HSCT) to reduce blood loss from menses.

Closely monitor the platelet count, coagulation studies, hemoglobin, and hematocrit. Together these give vital information about potential or actual bleeding.

TABLE 30.15 Patient & Caregiver Teaching

Thrombocytopenia

Include the following instructions when teaching a patient or caregiver the precautions to take when the platelet count is low.

1. Notify your HCP of any symptoms of bleeding. These include:
   - Black, tarry, or bloody bowel movements
   - Black or bloody vomit, sputum, or urine
   - Bleeding from the mouth or anywhere in the body
   - Bruising or small red or purple spots on the skin
   - Difficulty talking, sudden weakness of an arm or leg, confusion
   - Headache or changes in how well you can see
2. Ask your HCP about restrictions in your normal activities, such as vigorous exercise or lifting weights. Generally, walking is safe. Wear sturdy shoes or slippers. If you are weak and at risk for falling, get help or supervision when getting out of bed or chair.
3. Do not blow your nose forcefully; gently pat it with a tissue if needed. For a nosebleed, keep your head up and apply firm pressure to the nostrils and bridge of your nose. If bleeding continues, place an ice bag over the bridge of your nose and the nape of your neck. If you are unable to stop a nosebleed after 10 minutes, call your HCP.
4. Do not bend down with your head lower than your waist.
5. Prevent constipation by drinking plenty of fluids. Do not strain when having a bowel movement. Your HCP may prescribe a stool softener. Do not use a suppository, an enema, or a rectal thermometer without the permission of your HCP.
6. Shave only with an electric razor. Do not use blades.
7. Do not tweeze your eyebrows or other body hair.
8. Do not puncture your skin, such as getting tattoos or body piercing.
9. Do not use any medication that can prolong bleeding, such as aspirin. Other medications and herbs can have similar effects. If you are unsure about any medication, ask your HCP or pharmacist about it in relation to your thrombocytopenia.
10. Use a soft-bristle toothbrush to prevent injuring the gums. Flossing is usually safe if done gently using the thin tape floss. Do not use alcohol-based mouthwashes since they can dry your gums and increase bleeding.
11. Women who are menstruating should keep track of the number of pads that are used per day. When you start using more pads per day than usual or bleed more days, notify your HCP. Do not use tampons; only use sanitary pads.
12. Ask your HCP before you have any invasive procedures done, such as a dental cleaning, manicure, or pedicure.

The proper administration of platelet transfusions is an important nursing responsibility. This is discussed under Blood Component Therapy later in this chapter.

◆ **Ambulatory Care.** Monitor the patient with ITP who is receiving treatment for the response to therapy. Teach the person with acquired thrombocytopenia to avoid causative agents when possible (Table 30.11). If the patient cannot avoid causative agents (e.g., chemotherapy), teach them to avoid injury or trauma during these periods and to be aware of the signs and symptoms of bleeding caused by thrombocytopenia (Table 30.15).

Patients with either ITP or acquired thrombocytopenia should have planned periodic medical evaluations to assess and treat situations in which exacerbations and bleeding are likely to occur. Address the impact of either an acute or a chronic condition on the patient's quality of life.

◆ **Evaluation**

The expected outcomes are that the patient with thrombocytopenia will
- Have no evidence of bleeding or bruising
- State needed knowledge and skills to manage disease process

TABLE 30.16 Types of Hemophilia

Type	Inheritance Pattern
Hemophilia A Factor VIII	Recessive sex-linked (transmitted by female carriers, displayed almost exclusively in men)
Hemophilia B Factor IX	Recessive sex-linked (transmitted by female carriers, displayed almost exclusively in men)
von Willebrand Disease vWF, variable factor VIII deficiencies and platelet dysfunction	Autosomal dominant, seen in both genders Recessive (in severe forms of the disease)

vWF, von Willebrand factor.

HEMOPHILIA AND VON WILLEBRAND DISEASE

Hemophilia is an X-linked recessive genetic disorder caused by a defective or deficient coagulation factor. The 2 major types of hemophilia, which can occur in mild to severe forms, are *hemophilia A* (classic hemophilia, factor VIII deficiency) and *hemophilia B* (Christmas disease, factor IX deficiency). *von Willebrand disease* is a related disorder involving a deficiency of the von Willebrand coagulation protein. Factor VIII is made in the liver and circulates as a complex with vWF.

Hemophilia A is 4 times as common as hemophilia B.[18] Although rare, there are cases of *acquired hemophilia A*, which is due to the development of antibodies against the body's own factor VIII. von Willebrand disease is the most common congenital bleeding disorder.[19]

Genetic Link. The inheritance patterns of hemophilia and von Willebrand disease are compared in Table 30.16. (X-linked genetic disorders are discussed in Chapter 12 and Table 12.2.)

GENETICS IN CLINICAL PRACTICE[1,3]

Hemophilia A and B

Genetic Basis
- X-linked recessive disorder
- *Hemophilia A:* Caused by mutations in the *F8* gene that provides instructions for making coagulation factor VIII
- *Hemophilia B:* Caused by mutations in the *F9* gene that provides instructions for making coagulation factor IX
- Mutations in the *F8* or *F9* gene lead to the production of an abnormal version or reduced amounts of coagulation factors

Incidence
- *Hemophilia A:* 1 in 5000 to 10,000 male births
- *Hemophilia B:* 1 in 25,000 to 30,000 male births

Genetic Testing
- DNA testing is available

Clinical Implications
- Female carriers transmit the genetic defect to 50% of their sons, 50% of their daughters are carriers
- Males with hemophilia do not transmit the genetic defect to their sons, but all their daughters are carriers
- Though rare, female hemophilia can occur if a male with hemophilia mates with a female carrier
- Replacement therapy is available for factors VIII and IX

Clinical Manifestations and Complications

The manifestations of hemophilia A and B are similar. All manifestations relate to bleeding, and any bleeding episode in persons with hemophilia may lead to a life-threatening hemorrhage. Manifestations and complications related to hemophilia include (1) slow, persistent, prolonged bleeding from minor trauma and small cuts; (2) delayed bleeding after minor injuries (the delay may be several hours or days); (3) uncontrollable hemorrhage after dental extractions or irritation of the gingiva with a hard-bristle toothbrush; (4) nosebleeds, especially after a blow to the face; (5) GI bleeding from ulcers and gastritis; (6) hematuria and potential renal failure from GU trauma and splenic rupture resulting from falls or abdominal trauma; (7) bruising and subcutaneous hematomas (Fig. 30.7) and possible compartment syndrome; (8) neurologic signs, such as pain, anesthesia, and paralysis, which may develop from nerve compression caused by hematoma formation; and (9) hemarthrosis (bleeding into the joints) (Fig. 30.8), which may lead to joint injury and deformity severe enough to cause crippling (most often in knees, elbows, and ankles).[1]

In children, these manifestations may lead to the diagnosis. In adults, these may be the first sign of a newly diagnosed mild form of the disease that escaped detection through a childhood free of major injuries, dental procedures, or surgeries.

Diagnostic Studies

Laboratory studies are done to determine the type of hemophilia present. Any factor deficiency within the intrinsic system (factor VIII, IX, XI, or XII or vWF) will yield the laboratory results outlined in Table 30.17.

Interprofessional Care

The goals of interprofessional care are to prevent and treat bleeding. Care for persons with hemophilia or von Willebrand disease requires (1) preventive care, (2) the use of replacement therapy during acute bleeding episodes and as prophylaxis, and (3) the treatment of the complications of the disease and its therapy. Today, most patients can expect almost normal life spans free of bloodborne illnesses because of improved preparation of replacement products, improved screening of blood donor populations, and use of recombinant replacement factors.[1,3]

Replacement of deficient clotting factors is the primary means of supporting a patient with hemophilia. Replacement therapy may be given before surgery and dental care as a prophylactic measure. Table 30.18 lists examples of replacement therapy. Fresh frozen plasma, once commonly used for replacement therapy, is rarely used today.

For mild hemophilia A and certain subtypes of von Willebrand disease, desmopressin acetate (DDAVP), a synthetic

FIG. 30.7 Severe ecchymoses in a person with hemophilia after a fall. (Courtesy Peter Bonner.)

FIG. 30.8 Acute hemarthrosis of the knee is a common complication of hemophilia. (From Forbes CD, Jackson WF: *Colour atlas and text of clinical medicine*, ed 3, London, 2003, Mosby.)

TABLE 30.17 Laboratory Results in Hemophilia

Test	Results
Bleeding time	Prolonged in von Willebrand disease because of structurally defective platelets. Normal in hemophilia A and B because platelets not affected
Factor assays	Reductions of factor VIII in hemophilia A, factor IX in hemophilia B, vWF in von Willebrand disease
Partial thromboplastin time	Prolonged because of deficiency in intrinsic clotting system factor
Platelet count	Normal. Adequate platelet production
Prothrombin time	Normal. No involvement of extrinsic system
Thrombin time	Normal. No impairment of thrombin-fibrinogen reaction

vWF, von Willebrand factor.

TABLE 30.18 Drug Therapy

Replacement Factors for Hemophilia

Factor VIII	Factor IX	Von Willebrand	For Patients Who Have Inhibitors
Advate	Alphanine	Vonvendi	NovoSeven (factor VIIa)
Afstyla	Alprolix		Autoplex T
Alphanate	Bebulin VH		FEIBA (factor VIII inhibitor bypassing activity)
Eloctate	BeneFIX		
Hemofil M	Mononine		
Humate-P	Profilnine SD		
Koāte-DVI	Rixubis		
Kogenate FS			
Monoclate			
Obizur*			
Xyntha			

*For acquired hemophilia A.

analog of vasopressin, may be used to stimulate an increase in factor VIII and vWF. This drug acts on platelets and endothelial cells to cause the release of vWF, which then binds with factor VIII, thus increasing its concentration. It can be given IV, subcutaneously, or by intranasal spray. Beneficial effects (e.g., decreased bleeding time) of DDAVP when given IV are seen within 30 minutes and can last for more than 12 hours. Because the effect of DDAVP is short lived, the patient must be closely monitored and repeated doses may be needed. It is an appropriate therapy for minor bleeding episodes and dental procedures. The intranasal form may be used as home therapy for some patients with mild to moderate forms of the disease.

Antifibrinolytic therapy (tranexamic acid [Cyklokapron] and EACA) inhibits fibrinolysis by inhibiting plasminogen activation in the fibrin clot, thus enhancing clot stability. These agents stabilize clots in areas of increased fibrinolysis, such as the oral cavity, and in patients with difficult episodes of nosebleeds and menorrhagia. Topical thrombin and fibrin sealants may be used for mucosal bleeding.

Complications of the treatment of hemophilia include development of inhibitors to factors VIII or IX, transfusion-transmitted infectious disorders (hepatitis, HIV), allergic reactions, and thrombotic complications with the use of factor IX because it contains activated coagulation factors. Patients with vWF may develop antibodies against vWF concentrates, the infusion of which could cause life-threatening anaphylaxis. Thus replacement factors for these patients should not contain vWF.

The most common problems with acute management are starting factor replacement therapy too late and stopping it too soon. Minor bleeding episodes should be treated for at least 72 hours. Surgery and traumatic injuries may need longer therapy. Chronically, development of inhibitors to the factor products has occurred and needs individualized expert patient management. Designated treatment centers in the United States and many other countries provide interprofessional care of hemophilia and related disorders. Gene transfer therapy has been used on an experimental basis to treat hemophilia.[1]

❖ NURSING MANAGEMENT: HEMOPHILIA

◆ Nursing Implementation

◆ **Health Promotion.** Because of the hereditary nature of hemophilia, referral of affected persons for genetic counseling before reproduction is an important measure. This is especially important because many persons with hemophilia live into adulthood. Reproductive concerns and long-term effects are issues that you should include in the patient's care plan.

◆ **Acute Care.** Interventions are related primarily to controlling bleeding and include the following:
1. Stop the topical bleeding as quickly as possible. Apply direct pressure or ice, pack the area with Gelfoam or fibrin foam, and apply topical hemostatic agents, such as thrombin.
2. Give the specific coagulation factor to raise the patient's level of the deficient coagulation factor. Monitor the patient for signs and symptoms, such as hypersensitivity.
3. When joint bleeding occurs, in addition to giving replacement factors, it is important to use the "RICE" protocol. Rest the involved joint to prevent crippling deformities from hemarthrosis, ice the joint for 20 minutes every 3 to 4 hours, compress/wrap the joint, and elevate.[1] Give analgesics to reduce severe pain. Do not use aspirin and aspirin-containing compounds. As soon as bleeding ceases,

encourage mobilization of the affected area through range-of-motion exercises and physical therapy. Avoid weight bearing until all swelling has resolved and muscle strength has returned. Orthotics may be prescribed.
4. Manage any life-threatening complications that may develop because of hemorrhage or side effects from coagulation factors. Examples include nursing interventions to prevent or treat airway obstruction from hemorrhage into the neck and pharynx, recognition of compartment syndrome in an extremity, and early assessment and treatment of intracranial bleeding.

◆ **Ambulatory Care.** Home management is a primary consideration for the patient with hemophilia because the disease follows a progressive, chronic course. The quality and length of life may be significantly affected by the patient's knowledge of the illness and how to live with it. Refer the patient and caregiver to a local chapter of the National Hemophilia Foundation to encourage associations with others who are dealing with the problems of hemophilia.[18] Provide ongoing assessment of the patient's adaptation to the illness. Psychosocial support and assistance should be readily available as needed.

Most of the long-term care measures are related to patient teaching. Teach the patient to recognize disease-related problems and to learn which problems can be resolved at home and which require hospitalization. Immediate medical attention is needed for severe pain or swelling of a muscle or joint that restricts movement or inhibits sleep and for a head injury, swelling in the neck or mouth, abdominal pain, hematuria, melena, and skin wounds in need of suturing.

Teach the patient to perform daily oral hygiene without causing trauma. Understanding how to prevent injuries is another consideration. Teach the patient to take part only in noncontact sports (e.g., golf) and to wear gloves when doing household chores to prevent cuts or abrasions from knives, hammers, and other tools. The patient should wear a Medic Alert tag to ensure that HCPs know about the hemophilia in case of an accident. Many patients or their caregivers can be taught to self-administer the factor replacement therapies at home.

◆ Evaluation

The overall expected outcomes are similar to those for the patient with thrombocytopenia (see p. 626).

DISSEMINATED INTRAVASCULAR COAGULATION

Disseminated intravascular coagulation (DIC) is a serious bleeding and thrombotic disorder that results from abnormally initiated and accelerated clotting. Subsequent decreases in clotting factors and platelets ensue, which may lead to uncontrollable hemorrhage. The term DIC can be misleading because it suggests that blood is only clotting. However, there is profuse bleeding that results from the aggregation of platelets and clotting factors. DIC is always caused by an underlying disease or condition. That underlying problem must be treated for the DIC to resolve.

Etiology and Pathophysiology

DIC is not a disease. It is an abnormal response of the normal clotting cascade stimulated by a disease process or disorder.[2,3] The diseases and disorders known to predispose a patient to DIC are listed in Table 30.19. DIC can occur as an acute, catastrophic condition, or it may exist at a subacute or chronic level.

Each condition may have 1 or multiple triggering mechanisms to start the clotting cascade. For example, tumors and traumatized or necrotic tissue release tissue factors into circulation. Endotoxin from gram-negative bacteria activates several steps in the coagulation cascade.

Tissue factor is released at the site of tissue injury and by some cancers, such as leukemia, and enhances normal coagulation mechanisms. Abundant intravascular thrombin, the most powerful coagulant, is made (Fig. 30.9). It catalyzes the conversion of fibrinogen to fibrin and enhances platelet aggregation. There is widespread fibrin and platelet deposition in capillaries and arterioles, resulting in thrombosis. This process can lead to multiorgan failure.

In addition, clotting inhibitory mechanisms, such as antithrombin III (AT III) and protein C, are depressed. Excess clotting activates the fibrinolytic system, which in turn breaks down the newly formed clot, creating fibrin split products (FSPs). These products have anticoagulant properties and inhibit normal blood clotting. As FSPs accumulate and clotting factors are depleted, the blood loses its ability to clot. A stable clot cannot be formed at injury sites, which predisposes the patient to hemorrhage.

Chronic and subacute DIC is most often seen in patients with long-standing illnesses, such as cancer or autoimmune disease. Occasionally these patients have subclinical disease manifested only by laboratory abnormalities. However, the clinical spectrum ranges from easy bruising to hemorrhage, and from hypercoagulability to thrombosis.

Clinical Manifestations

DIC has both bleeding and thrombotic manifestations. Multiple factors cause bleeding manifestations of DIC (Fig. 30.9). They result from consumption and depletion of platelets and coagulation factors, as well as clot lysis and formation of FSPs that have anticoagulant properties. Bleeding in a person with no history or obvious cause should be questioned because it may be one of the first manifestations of acute DIC.

Bleeding manifestations include manifestations in the (1) skin, such as pallor, petechiae, purpura, oozing blood, venipuncture site bleeding, hematomas, and occult hemorrhage; (2) respiratory system (e.g., tachypnea, hemoptysis, and orthopnea); (3) cardiovascular system, such as tachycardia and hypotension; (4) GI tract, such as upper and lower GI bleeding, abdominal distention, and bloody stools; (5) urinary tract (e.g., hematuria); (6) neurologic system, such as vision changes, dizziness, headache, mental status changes, and irritability; and (7) musculoskeletal system (e.g., bone and joint pain).

Thrombotic manifestations are a result of fibrin or platelet deposition in the microvasculature (Fig. 30.9). These manifestations affect the (1) skin (e.g., cyanosis, ischemic tissue necrosis, hemorrhagic necrosis) (Fig. 30.10); (2) respiratory system (e.g., tachypnea, dyspnea, pulmonary emboli, and acute respiratory distress

TABLE 30.19	Risk Factors for DIC
Acute DIC Cancers • Acute leukemia • Metastatic solid tumors Hemolytic processes • Acute hemolysis from infection or immunologic disorders • Transfusion of mismatched blood Obstetric conditions • Abruptio placentae • Amniotic fluid embolism • HELLP syndrome • Septic abortion or pregnancy Septicemia (bacterial, viral, fungal, parasitic) Shock • Anaphylactic • Cardiogenic • Hemorrhagic Tissue damage • Acute anoxia (e.g., after cardiac arrest) • Extensive burns and trauma	• Fulminant hepatitis • Heatstroke • Postoperative damage, especially after extracorporeal membrane oxygenation • Prosthetic devices • Severe head injury • Snakebites • Transplant rejections • Vascular disorders (e.g., aortic aneurism) **Subacute DIC** Cancer • Metastatic cancer • Myeloproliferative/lymphoproliferative cancers Obstetric • Retained dead fetus **Chronic DIC** • Cancer • Liver disease • SLE

FIG. 30.9 Sequence of events that occur during DIC.

FIG. 30.10 Gangrene resulting from severe DIC. (From Howard MR, Hamilton PJ: *Haematology: An illustrated colour atlas,* ed 4, London, 2013, Churchill Livingstone.)

TABLE 30.20 Laboratory Results in Acute DIC	
Test	**Finding in Acute DIC**
Screening Tests	
Prothrombin time (PT)	Prolonged
Partial thromboplastin time (PTT)	Prolonged
Activated partial thromboplastin time (aPTT)	Prolonged
Fibrinogen	Reduced
Platelets	Reduced
Thrombin time	Prolonged
Special Tests	
Antithrombin III (AT III)	Reduced
D-dimers (cross-linked fibrin fragments)	Increased
Factor assays (prothrombin and factors V, VIII, X, XIII)	Reduced but may give misleading results, since V and VIII rise with inflammation
Fibrin split products (FSPs)	Increased
Peripheral blood smear	Schistocytes present
Plasminogen, tissue plasminogen activator	Reduced
Proteins C and S	Reduced

syndrome [ARDS]); (3) cardiovascular system (e.g., ECG changes, venous distention); (4) GI tract (e.g., abdominal pain, paralytic ileus); and (5) kidney damage and oliguria, leading to failure.

Diagnostic Studies

Tests to diagnose acute DIC are listed in Table 30.20. As more clots are made in the body, more breakdown products from fibrinogen and fibrin are formed. These are termed *fibrin split products* (FSPs), and they interfere with blood coagulation by (1) coating the platelets and interfering with platelet function; (2) interfering with thrombin and thus disrupting coagulation; and (3) attaching to fibrinogen, which interferes with the polymerization process necessary to form a stable clot. D-dimer, a polymer resulting from the breakdown of fibrin (and not fibrinogen), is a specific marker for the degree of fibrinolysis. In general, tests that measure raw materials needed for coagulation (e.g., platelets, fibrinogen) are reduced and values that measure clotting times are prolonged. Fragmented RBCs (schistocytes), indicative of partial occlusion of small vessels by fibrin thrombi, may be found on blood smears.

Interprofessional Care

It is important to diagnose DIC quickly, stabilize the patient (e.g., oxygenation, volume replacement), treat the underlying causative disease or problem, and control the ongoing thrombosis and bleeding. Depending on its severity, a variety of methods are used to manage DIC (Fig. 30.11). First, if chronic DIC is diagnosed in a patient who is not bleeding, no therapy for DIC is needed. Treatment of the underlying disease may be enough to reverse the DIC (e.g., chemotherapy when DIC is caused by cancer). Second, when the patient with DIC is bleeding, therapy is directed toward providing support with needed blood products while treating the primary disorder.

Blood products are given cautiously based on specific component deficiencies to patients who have serious bleeding, are at high risk for bleeding (e.g., surgery), or require invasive procedures. Blood product support with platelets, cryoprecipitate,

and fresh frozen plasma (FFP) is usually reserved for a patient with life-threatening hemorrhage.[20] Therapy stabilizes a patient, prevents exsanguination or massive thrombosis, and permits institution of definitive therapy to treat the underlying cause. Cryoprecipitate replaces factor VIII and fibrinogen and is given if the fibrinogen level is below 100 mg/dL (1 g/L).[1] FFP is given only to patients with significant bleeding and a prolonged PT and aPTT. It replaces all clotting factors except platelets and is a source of antithrombin.

A patient with thrombosis is often treated by anticoagulation with heparin or LMSH. Heparin is used in the treatment of DIC only when the benefit (reduce clotting) outweighs the risk (further bleeding). Antithrombin III (ATnativ) may be useful in fulminant DIC, although it increases the risk for bleeding. Chronic DIC does not respond to oral anticoagulants. It is controlled with long-term use of heparin.

❖ NURSING MANAGEMENT: DISSEMINATED INTRAVASCULAR COAGULATION

◆ Nursing Diagnoses

Nursing diagnoses for the patient with DIC may include the following:

- Risk for bleeding
- Ineffective tissue perfusion
- Acute pain
- Impaired cardiac output

◆ Nursing Implementation

Be alert to the development of DIC, especially with the precipitating factors listed in Table 30.19. Remember that because DIC is caused by an underlying disease, that problem must be managed while providing supportive care for the manifestations of DIC.

Appropriate nursing interventions are essential to the survival of a patient with acute DIC. Astute ongoing assessment, active attention to manifestations of DIC, and prompt administration of prescribed therapies are crucial. Table 30.14 and

FIG. 30.11 Sites of action for therapies in DIC. *AT III*, Antithrombin III; *FSPs*, fibrin split products.

eNursing Care Plan 30.2 (available on the website for this chapter) provide assessments and interventions appropriate for the patient with DIC.

Early detection of bleeding and clotting, both occult and overt, must be a primary goal. Assess for signs of external bleeding (e.g., petechiae, oozing at IV or injection sites), signs of internal bleeding (e.g., increased heart rate, changes in mental status, increasing abdominal girth, pain), and any signs that microthrombi may be causing clinically significant organ damage (e.g., decreased renal output). Minimize tissue damage and protect the patient from sources of bleeding. Give blood products and medications correctly. Blood product transfusion is discussed later in this chapter on pp. 647–651.

NEUTROPENIA

Leukopenia refers to a decrease in the total WBC count (granulocytes, monocytes, and lymphocytes). *Granulocytopenia* is a deficiency of granulocytes, which include neutrophils, eosinophils, and basophils. The neutrophilic granulocytes (neutrophils), which play a key role in phagocytizing pathogenic microbes, are closely monitored in clinical practice as an indicator of a patient's risk for infection. A reduction in neutrophils is termed **neutropenia**. Some clinicians use the terms granulocytopenia and neutropenia interchangeably because the largest constituent of granulocytes is the neutrophils.

The *absolute neutrophil count* (ANC) is determined by multiplying the total WBC count by the percent of neutrophils. *Neutropenia* is defined as ANC less than 1000 cells/μL (1 × 10^9/L). Normally, neutrophils range from 2200 to 7700 cells/μL. *Severe neutropenia* is defined as an ANC less than 500 cells/μL.[21]

In considering the clinical significance of neutropenia, it is important to know whether the decrease in the neutrophil count was gradual or rapid, the degree of neutropenia, and the duration. The faster the drop and the longer the duration, the greater the chance of life-threatening infection, sepsis, and death. Other factors and co-morbid conditions, such as immune disorders (e.g., HIV), being older than 60, having an existing infection, being in the hospital, and having chronic obstructive pulmonary disease, can increase the risk for a serious infection.[22]

Neutropenia is a clinical consequence that occurs with a variety of conditions or diseases (Table 30.21). It can be an expected effect, a side effect, or an unintentional effect of certain drugs. The most common cause of neutropenia is the use of chemotherapy and immunosuppressive therapy in the treatment of cancer and autoimmune disease. A term we use to describe the lowest point of neutropenia (and other blood cells) in a patient treated with chemotherapy is *nadir*.

Clinical Manifestations

The patient with neutropenia is predisposed to infection with opportunistic pathogens and nonpathogenic organisms from

TABLE 30.21 Common Causes of Neutropenia

Autoimmune Disorders
- Felty syndrome
- Systemic lupus erythematosus

Drugs
- Alkylating agents (busulfan)
- Antiinflammatory drugs (indomethacin)
- Antimetabolites (methotrexate, mercaptopurine, cytarabine)
- Antimicrobial agents (ganciclovir, penicillin G, trimethoprim/sulfamethoxazole)
- Antitumor antibiotics (daunorubicin, doxorubicin)
- Cardiovascular drugs (captopril, procainamide)
- Diuretics (hydrochlorothiazide)
- Miscellaneous (ticlopidine, penicillamine)

Hematologic Disorders
- Aplastic anemia
- Congenital (cyclic neutropenia)
- Fanconi syndrome
- Idiopathic neutropenia
- Leukemia
- Myelodysplastic syndrome

Infections
- Fulminant bacterial infection (e.g., typhoid fever, miliary tuberculosis)
- Parasitic
- Rickettsial
- Viral (e.g., hepatitis, influenza, HIV, measles)

Others
- Bone marrow infiltration (e.g., carcinoma, tuberculosis, lymphoma)
- Hemodialysis
- Hypersplenism (e.g., portal hypertension, storage diseases [e.g., Gaucher disease])
- Nutritional deficiencies (cobalamin, folic acid)
- Severe sepsis

TABLE 30.22 Interprofessional Care

Neutropenia

Diagnostic Assessment
- History and physical examination
- Risk assessment for severity and duration of neutropenia
- WBC count with differential count
- WBC morphology
- Hgb and Hct
- Reticulocyte and platelet count
- Bone marrow aspiration or biopsy
- Cultures of nose, throat, sputum, urine, stool, obvious lesions, blood (as indicated)
- Chest x-ray or other diagnostic tests

Management
- Identification and removal of cause of neutropenia (if possible)
- Identification of site of infection (if present) and causative organism
- Antimicrobial therapy (prophylactically or empiric)
- Blood cultures drawn STAT, before antibiotics
- Prophylactic hematopoietic myeloid growth factors after myelosuppressive chemotherapy
- Strict hand hygiene
- Patient hygiene (daily skin and frequent oral care; chlorhexidine bathing should be done in the inpatient setting if the patient has a central venous catheter)
- Single-patient room, positive-pressure or high-efficiency particulate air (HEPA) filtration, depending on risk
- Community isolation and home precautions (if outpatient)
- Nutritional therapy (dietary instruction) on foods to avoid and safe food handling
- Safe activity and ambulation to maintain physical and pulmonary function

G-CSF, Granulocyte colony-stimulating factor; *GM-CSF,* granulocyte-macrophage colony-stimulating factor.

the normal body flora. When the WBC count is low or immature WBCs are present, normal phagocytic mechanisms are impaired. The classic manifestations of inflammation—redness, heat, and swelling—may not occur. WBCs are the major component of pus. Therefore, in the patient with neutropenia, pus formation (e.g., as a visible skin lesion or as lung infiltrates on a chest x-ray) is absent.

> **! SAFETY ALERT Neutropenia**
> - A low-grade fever in neutropenic patients is of great significance because it may indicate infection and lead to septic shock and death unless treated promptly.
> - Neutropenic fever (≥100.4°F [38°C] and/or new signs or symptoms suggesting infection and a neutrophil count <500/μL) is a medical emergency.[22]
> - Blood cultures should be drawn STAT and antibiotics started within 1 hr.

When fever occurs in a neutropenic patient, it is assumed to be caused by infection and requires immediate attention. The immunocompromised, neutropenic patient has little or no ability to fight infection. So, minor infections can lead rapidly to sepsis and death. The mucous membranes of the throat and mouth, skin, perineal area, and pulmonary system are common entry points for pathogenic organisms in susceptible hosts.

Manifestations related to infection at these sites include sore throat and dysphagia, ulcerative lesions of the pharyngeal and buccal mucosa, diarrhea, rectal tenderness, vaginal itching or discharge, shortness of breath, and nonproductive cough. Any report of minor pain or any other symptom by the patient may be significant and should be reported to the HCP at once. These seemingly minor problems can progress to fever, chills, sepsis, septic shock, and death if not recognized and treated early.

Systemic infections caused by bacterial, fungal, and viral organisms are common in patients with neutropenia. The patient's own flora (normally nonpathogenic) contributes significantly to life-threatening infections. Organisms known to be common sources of infection include gram-positive coagulase-negative *Staphylococcus* and *Staphylococcus aureus* and gram-negative *E. coli, Klebsiella, Enterobacter,* and *Pseudomonas aeruginosa.*[22] Fungi involved include *Candida* (usually *C. albicans*) and *Aspergillus* organisms. Viral infections caused by reactivation of herpes simplex and zoster are common after prolonged periods of neutropenia, such as in HSCT patients.[23]

Diagnostic Studies

The primary diagnostic tests for assessing neutropenia are the peripheral WBC count and bone marrow aspiration and biopsy (Table 30.22). A total WBC count of less than 4000/μL (4 × 10^9/L) reflects leukopenia. However, only a differential count can confirm the presence of neutropenia (neutrophil count less than 1000/μL [1 × 10^9/L]). If the differential WBC count reflects an absolute neutropenia of 500 to 1000/μL (0.5 to 1.0 × 10^9/L), the patient is at moderate risk for a bacterial infection. An absolute neutropenia of less than 500/μL (0.5 × 10^9/L) places the patient at severe risk. Patients with acute leukemia who present with a high WBC may in fact have neutropenia, because most of the WBCs are ineffective leukemia blasts cells.

A peripheral blood smear assesses for immature forms of WBCs (e.g., bands). The hematocrit level, reticulocyte count, and platelet count are done to evaluate bone marrow function. Review the patient's recent past and current drug history. If the cause of neutropenia is unknown, a bone marrow aspiration and biopsy is done to examine cellularity and cell morphology. Other studies may be done to assess spleen and liver function.

❖ Interprofessional and Nursing Management

The nursing and interprofessional care of neutropenia includes (1) determining the cause of the neutropenia, (2) instituting antibiotic therapy promptly, (3) identifying the offending organisms if an infection has developed, (4) giving hematopoietic growth factors prophylactically after chemotherapy, and (5) implementing protective practices (e.g., strict hand washing, skin and oral hygiene) (Table 30.22).[24]

Sometimes, the cause of the neutropenia can be easily treated (e.g., nutritional deficiencies). However, neutropenia can be a side effect that must be tolerated as a necessary step in therapy (e.g., chemotherapy, radiation therapy). In some situations, the neutropenia resolves when the primary disease or disorder is treated.

🧑 NURSING MANAGEMENT
Caring for the Patient With Neutropenia

All members of the health care team have important roles in preventing infection in the patient with neutropenia. Careful hand washing is an important preventive measure. It should be done before, during, and after patient care by everyone caring for the patient.

- Determine the type of isolation precautions that need to be started, if any.
- Assess patient for signs and symptoms of infection.
- Screen visitors for infectious diseases.
- Place the patient on a neutropenic diet to protect them from bacteria found in some foods.
- Obtain cultures of sputum, throat, lesions, wounds, urine, and feces.
- Give antibiotics and hematopoietic growth factors.
- Teach patient and visitors about hand washing.
- Provide teaching about how to avoid infection, including the need for skin care and oral hygiene.
- Teach the patient and caregivers about signs and symptoms of infection and what to do if they occur.

Monitor the neutropenic patient for signs and symptoms of infection (e.g., any fever 100.4° F [38° C] or greater) and early septic shock. Early identification of a potentially infective organism depends on obtaining cultures from various sites. Serial blood cultures (at least 2) or 1 from a peripheral site and 1 from a venous access device should be done promptly and antibiotics started within 1 hour.

Giving broad-spectrum antibiotics is usually by the IV route because of the rapidly lethal effects of infection. However, some oral antibiotics are highly effective and routinely used for prophylaxis against infection in some neutropenic patients. The use of a third- or fourth-generation cephalosporin with broad microorganism coverage (e.g., cefepime, ceftazidime) or a carbapenem (e.g., imipenem/cilastatin [Primaxin]) will be started and augmented depending on the patient's response and/or results of the diagnostic tests.

Begin therapy promptly and observe the patient for side effects of antimicrobial agents. Ongoing febrile episodes or a change in the patient's assessment requires a call to the HCP for assessment, or more cultures, diagnostic tests, or antimicrobial therapies. The longer the neutropenia, the greater the risk is for a fungal infection. Antifungal therapy is started whenever a culture is positive, or in patients who do not become afebrile with broad-spectrum antibiotic coverage.

Cultures of sputum, throat, lesions, wounds, urine, and feces may part of patient surveillance. Depending on the clinical situation, it may be necessary to do CT scans, bronchoscopy with bronchial brushings, or lung biopsy to diagnose the cause of pneumonic infiltrates. Invasive diagnostic studies are often contraindicated because of the concern of introducing infection and the fact that these patients are also often thrombocytopenic. Despite these many tests, the causative organism is found in only 20% to 30% of neutropenic patients. Thus the priority is to obtain the blood cultures and begin the antibiotic at once. Ongoing monitoring is essential as early identification and appropriate management can prevent death from sepsis.[25]

Myeloid growth factors (see Table 15.15) can be used to prevent neutropenia or to reduce its severity and duration.[24] Once neutropenia has occurred, these agents are generally not as effective.

Keep the following care principles in mind: (1) the patient's normal flora is the most common source of microbial colonization and infection; (2) transmission of organisms from humans most often occurs by direct contact with the hands; (3) air, food, water, and equipment provide opportunities for infection transmission; and (4) HCPs, visitors, and other patients with infections also can be sources of infection transmission under certain conditions.

Hand washing is the single most important preventive measure to minimize the risk for infection in the neutropenic patient. Strict hand washing by staff and visitors using an antiseptic hand wash before and after contact is the major method to prevent transmission of harmful pathogens.

Separate immunocompromised patients from those who are infected or have conditions that increase the probability of transmitting infections (e.g., poor hygiene caused by lack of understanding or cognitive dysfunction). Often patients can be managed on an outpatient basis if the patient and caregiver can monitor for fever and other signs of infection and then report promptly to a nearby health care facility (Table 30.23).[1,21] If the patient is hospitalized, a private room should be used. High-efficiency particulate air (HEPA) filtration is an air-handling method with a high-flow filtering system that can reduce or eliminate the number of aerosolized pathogens in the environment used for hematopoietic stem cell transplant patients. Care routines in a HEPA environment are the same as care in any other private room. Neutropenic precaution guidelines may be used, such as prophylactic antibiotics and antifungals. Teach the patient and caregiver to avoid potentially hazardous foods, such as raw and undercooked meats and eggs and soft cheeses with molds.[1] The nursing measures discussed in eNursing Care Plan 30.3 (available on the website for this chapter) are important in the treatment of the patient with neutropenia.

Do not overlook quality-of-life issues for the patient with neutropenia. Fatigue, malaise, a decrease in functioning, and social isolation require coaching on safe activity.

TABLE 30.23   Patient & Caregiver Teaching

Neutropenia

Include the following instructions when teaching a patient or caregiver the precautions to take when the neutrophil count is low:

1. WASH YOUR HANDS frequently and make sure those around you wash their hands frequently, especially if they help with your care. You may also use an antibacterial hand gel.
2. Notify your nurse or HCP if you have any of the following:
   Fever ≥100.4° F (38° C)*
   Chills or feeling hot
   Redness, swelling, discharge, or new pain on or in your body
   Changes in urination or bowel movements
   Cough, sore throat, mouth sores, or blisters
3. If you are at home, take your temperature as directed and follow instructions on what to do if you have a fever.
4. Avoid crowds and people with colds, flu, or infections. If you are in a public area, wear a mask and use hand sanitizing gel frequently.
5. Avoid uncooked meats, seafood, or eggs and unwashed fruits and vegetables. Ask your HCP about specific dietary guidelines for you.
6. Bathe or shower daily. Use a moisturizer to prevent skin from drying and cracking.
7. Maintain some daily activity as instructed by your health care team. This may include walking and moderate exercise while avoiding crowds.
8. Brush your teeth with a soft toothbrush 4 times daily. You may floss once daily if it does not cause excessive pain or bleeding. Avoid alcohol-based mouthwashes.
9. Do not garden or clean up after pets. You may feed and pet your dog or cat if you wash your hands well after handling.

*Need to verify cut-off temperature with HCP.

MYELODYSPLASTIC SYNDROME

Myelodysplastic syndrome (MDS) is a group of related hematologic disorders characterized by peripheral blood cytopenias (from ineffective blood cell production) and changes in the cellularity of the bone marrow with dysplastic changes. In MDS, *hematopoiesis* is disorderly and ineffective. The estimated incidence is 4.9 per 100,000 people per year in the United States. Although it can occur in all age-groups, the highest prevalence is in people over 80 years of age, at which point the rate increases to 59.8 per 100,000.[26]

Etiology and Pathophysiology

The etiology of MDS is unknown. People who have received radiation therapy, had chemotherapy with alkylating agents (e.g., chlorambucil, cyclophosphamide, melphalan), or were exposed to industrial solvents (e.g., benzene) have a higher risk for developing MDS than people who have not had these exposures. About 50% of MDS patients have an overt chromosome abndormality.[1,3] Rarely, genetic disorders are responsible for the disease.

We refer to MDS as a *clonal disorder because* some bone marrow stem cells continue to function normally, while others do not. The abnormal clone of the stem cells is usually found in the bone marrow. Eventually, it may be found in the circulation.

Sometimes, one type of MDS transforms into another. Depending on the subtype, MDS may progress to acute myelogenous leukemia (AML).[26] In contrast to AML, in which the leukemic cells show little normal maturation, the clonal cells in MDS always display some degree of maturity. Disease progression is slower than in AML, and sometimes treatment is not needed.

Clinical Manifestations

Manifestations result from neoplastic transformation of the immature hematopoietic stem cells in the bone marrow. MDS often presents as infection and bleeding caused by inadequate numbers of ineffectively functioning circulating granulocytes or platelets. It may be found in the older adult during testing for the symptoms of anemia, thrombocytopenia, or neutropenia. It may be diagnosed incidentally from a routine CBC. During the advanced stage of MDS, life-threatening anemia, thrombocytopenia, and neutropenia occur.

Diagnostic Studies

Bone marrow biopsy with aspirate analysis is essential for both the diagnosis and classification of the specific type of MDS. The patient with MDS has peripheral cytopenia and changes in the bone marrow (hypocellular or hypercellular). Laboratory data and bone marrow studies help rule out other causes of the dysplasia, such as nonmalignant disorders, cobalamin and folate deficiencies, and infections.

❖ Interprofessional and Nursing Management

Treatment of MDS is based on the premise that the aggressiveness of treatment should match the aggressiveness of the disease. This is based on the amount and type of dysplasia in the bone marrow, specific genetic mutations, anticipated patient tolerance, and patient preference.[26] Supportive treatment consists of hematologic monitoring (serial bone marrow and peripheral blood examinations), antibiotic therapy, or transfusions with blood products along with iron chelators to prevent iron overload.

Low-risk patients often can be treated with EPO, myeloid growth factors, and thrombopoietin.[26] Some patients are treated with intensive chemotherapy and/or HSCT. Azacitidine (Vidaza) and decitabine (Dacogen) are drugs that help restore normal growth control and differentiation of hematopoietic cells and reduce the frequency of transformation of MDS to acute leukemia. Side effects include myelosuppression, nausea, vomiting, constipation or diarrhea, renal dysfunction, and injection site redness.

Other treatments for MDS include lenalidomide (Revlimid), cytarabine with or without antitumor antibiotics (anthracyclines), antithymocyte globulin, and cyclosporine.[25,26] Chemotherapy and allogeneic HSCT are used in appropriate patients with high-risk features to treat bone marrow dysfunction of MDS and restore it with normal hematopoiesis.

Nursing care of a patient with MDS is like that of a patient with manifestations of anemia, thrombocytopenia, and neutropenia. (See eNursing Care Plan 30.1 for the patient with anemia, eNursing Care Plan 30.2 for the patient with thrombocytopenia, and eNursing Care Plan 30.3 for the patient with neutropenia. The eNursing Care Plans are available on the website for this chapter.)

LEUKEMIA

Leukemia is the general term used to describe a group of cancers affecting the blood and blood-forming tissues of the bone marrow, lymph system, and spleen. Leukemia occurs in all age-groups. It results in an accumulation of dysfunctional cells because of a loss of regulation in cell division. An estimated 62,130 new cases are diagnosed each year. Leukemias account for 29% of all childhood cancers. Of those, 76% are lymphoid

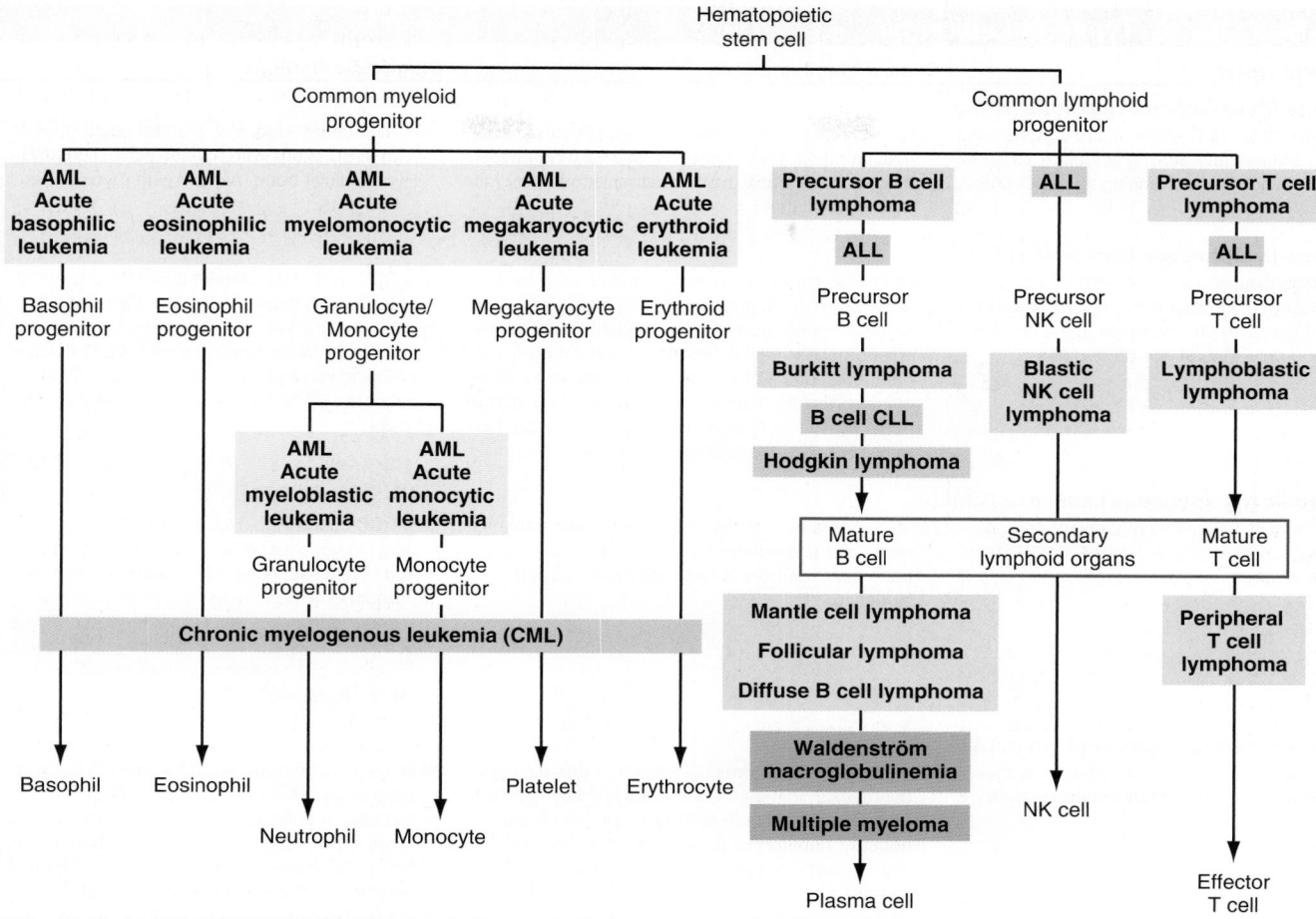

FIG. 30.12 Origins of leukemias, lymphomas, and myeloma. Differentiation pathways of blood-forming cells and the point at which the malignant clone originates. (Modified from Huether SE, McCance KL, editors: *Understanding pathophysiology*, ed 7, St Louis, 2017, Elsevier.)

leukemias.[27] Leukemia follows a progressive course that is eventually fatal if untreated. However, progress in successful cancer treatments has been most rapid for hematopoietic and lymphoid cancers in the past 3 decades.[27]

Etiology and Pathophysiology

Leukemia has no single cause. It is now known that all cancers, including leukemia, begin as a mutation in the DNA of certain cells. Most leukemias result from a combination of factors, including genetic and environmental influences. Abnormal genes *(oncogenes)* can cause many types of cancers, including leukemias (see Chapter 15). Chemical agents (e.g., benzene), chemotherapeutic agents (e.g., alkylating agents, topoisomerase II inhibitors), viruses, radiation, and immunologic deficiencies have all been associated with the development of leukemia. Depending on the type of leukemia, other potential causes are exposure to pesticides (farmworkers), smoking, and obesity.[3]

Although ribonucleic acid (RNA) retroviruses cause several leukemias in animals, a viral cause for a human leukemia has been established for only some patients with adult T-cell leukemia/lymphoma. This form of leukemia is endemic in southwestern Japan and parts of the Caribbean and is caused by the human T-cell leukemia virus, type 1 (HTLV-1).[28] Leukemia occurs more often in those with certain congenital or inherited abnormalities (e.g., Down syndrome). Chronic lymphocytic leukemia has a familial trend.[3]

Classification

Leukemia is classified based on acute versus chronic disease and on the type of WBC involved. The terms *acute* and *chronic* refer to cell maturity and nature of disease onset. Acute leukemia is characterized by the clonal proliferation of immature hematopoietic cells. The leukemia develops after malignant transformation of a single type of immature hematopoietic cell, followed by cellular replication and expansion of that malignant clone (Fig. 30.12). Chronic leukemias involve more mature forms of the WBC. The disease onset is more gradual.

Leukemia classified by the type of leukocyte involved is described as myelogenous or lymphocytic origin. By combining the acute and chronic categories with the cell type involved, one can identify 4 major types of leukemia: acute lymphocytic leukemia (ALL), acute myelogenous leukemia (AML), chronic myelogenous (granulocytic) leukemia (CML), and chronic lymphocytic leukemia (CLL). Other defining features of these leukemic subtypes are shown in Table 30.24.

Acute Myelogenous Leukemia. AML represents about one third of all leukemias, and it makes up about 80% of the acute leukemias in adults.[3,29] Its onset is often abrupt and dramatic.

TABLE 30.24 Types of Leukemia

Age of Onset	Clinical Manifestations	Diagnostic Findings
Acute Myelogenous Leukemia (AML) Accounts for 15%–20% of acute leukemia in children and 80% in adults. Increase in incidence with advancing age after 60 yr.	Fatigue and weakness, headache, mouth sores, anemia, bleeding, fever, infection, sternal tenderness, gingival hyperplasia, mild hepatosplenomegaly (one third of patients)	Low RBC count, Hgb, Hct, platelet count. Low to high WBC count with myeloblasts. High LDH. Hypercellular bone marrow with myeloblasts.
Acute Lymphocytic Leukemia (ALL) Median diagnosis is 15 yr with 57.2% diagnosed at younger than 20 yr. About 27% of cases are diagnosed at age 4 or older and only 11% at age 65 or older.	Fever, pallor, bleeding, anorexia, fatigue, and weakness. Bone, joint, and abdominal pain. Generalized lymphadenopathy, infections, weight loss, hepatosplenomegaly, headache, mouth sores, neurologic manifestations: CNS involvement, increased intracranial pressure (nausea, vomiting, lethargy, cranial nerve dysfunction) from meningeal infiltration. Men may have painless enlargement of the scrotum.	Low RBC, Hgb, Hct, platelet count. Low, normal, or high WBC count. High LDH. Hypercellular bone marrow with lymphoblasts. Lymphoblasts may be in cerebrospinal fluid. Presence of Philadelphia chromosome (up to 30% of patients). Up to 15% may have a mediastinal mass.
Chronic Myelogenous Leukemia (CML) Increase in incidence with advancing age, with median age at diagnosis of 67. Rare in children.	No symptoms early in disease. Fatigue and weakness, fever, sternal tenderness, weight loss, joint pain, bone pain, massive splenomegaly, increase in sweating.	Low RBC count, Hgb, Hct. High platelet count early, lower count later. ↑ Banded neutrophils and myeloblasts and often basophils, normal number of lymphocytes, and normal or low number of monocytes. Nucleated red cells are common. Low leukocyte alkaline phosphatase. Presence of Philadelphia chromosome in ≥90% of patients.
Chronic Lymphocytic Leukemia (CLL) Increase in incidence with advancing age after 65 yr, with predominance in men.	Frequently no symptoms. Detection of disease often during examination for unrelated condition, chronic fatigue, anorexia, splenomegaly and lymphadenopathy, hepatomegaly. May progress to fever, night sweats, weight loss, fatigue, and frequent infections.	Mild anemia and thrombocytopenia with disease progression. Total WBC count >100,000/μL. Increase in peripheral lymphocytes and lymphocytes in bone marrow. May have autoimmune hemolytic anemia, idiopathic thrombocytopenic purpura, and hypogammaglobulinemia.

A patient may have serious infections and abnormal bleeding from the onset of the disease.

AML is characterized by uncontrolled proliferation of myeloblasts, the precursors of granulocytes. There is hyperplasia of the bone marrow. The manifestations are usually related to replacement of normal hematopoietic cells in the marrow by leukemic myeloblasts and, to a lesser extent, to infiltration of other organs and tissue (Table 30.24).

Acute Lymphocytic Leukemia. ALL is the most common type of leukemia in children and accounts for about 20% of acute leukemia cases in adults.[3,30] In ALL, immature small lymphocytes proliferate in the bone marrow. Most are of B-cell origin. Most patients have fever at the time of diagnosis. Signs and symptoms may appear abruptly with bleeding or fever, or they may be insidious with progressive weakness, fatigue, bone and/or joint pain, and bleeding tendencies.

Central nervous system (CNS) manifestations are especially common in ALL and are a serious problem. Infiltration into other tissues and lymph nodes can occur.[3]

Chronic Myelogenous Leukemia. CML is caused by excessive development of neoplastic granulocytes in the bone marrow. These granulocytes are in all stages of development. They move into the peripheral blood in massive numbers and infiltrate the liver and spleen.[31]

The natural history of CML is a chronic stable phase followed by the development of a more acute, aggressive phase referred to as the *blastic phase*. The chronic phase of CML can last for several years. It usually can be well controlled with treatment.

Even with treatment, the chronic phase of the disease eventually progresses to the accelerated phase, ending in a blastic phase. Once CML transforms to an acute or blastic phase, it must be treated more aggressively, similar to an acute leukemia.

Genetic Link. The *Philadelphia chromosome* originates from the translocation between the *BCR* gene on chromosome 22 and the *ABL* gene on chromosome 9. The protein that is encoded by the newly created *BCR-ABL* gene on the Philadelphia chromosome interferes with normal cell cycle events, such as the regulation of cell proliferation.

The Philadelphia chromosome, which is present in about 90% or more of patients with CML, is a diagnostic hallmark of CML.[31] In addition, its presence is an important indicator of residual disease or relapse after treatment. However, the presence of the Philadelphia chromosome is not specific to diagnose CML. It is also found in ALL and occasionally in AML.

Chronic Lymphocytic Leukemia. CLL is the most common leukemia in adults in Western countries.[32] CLL is characterized by the production and accumulation of functionally inactive but long-lived, small, mature-appearing lymphocytes. B cells are usually involved. The lymphocytes infiltrate the bone marrow, spleen, and liver. Lymph node enlargement (lymphadenopathy) is present throughout the body.

Complications are rare in early-stage CLL but may develop as the disease advances. Pressure on nerves from enlarged lymph nodes causes pain and even paralysis. Mediastinal node enlargement leads to pulmonary symptoms. Because CLL is usually a disease of older adults, treatment decisions must be

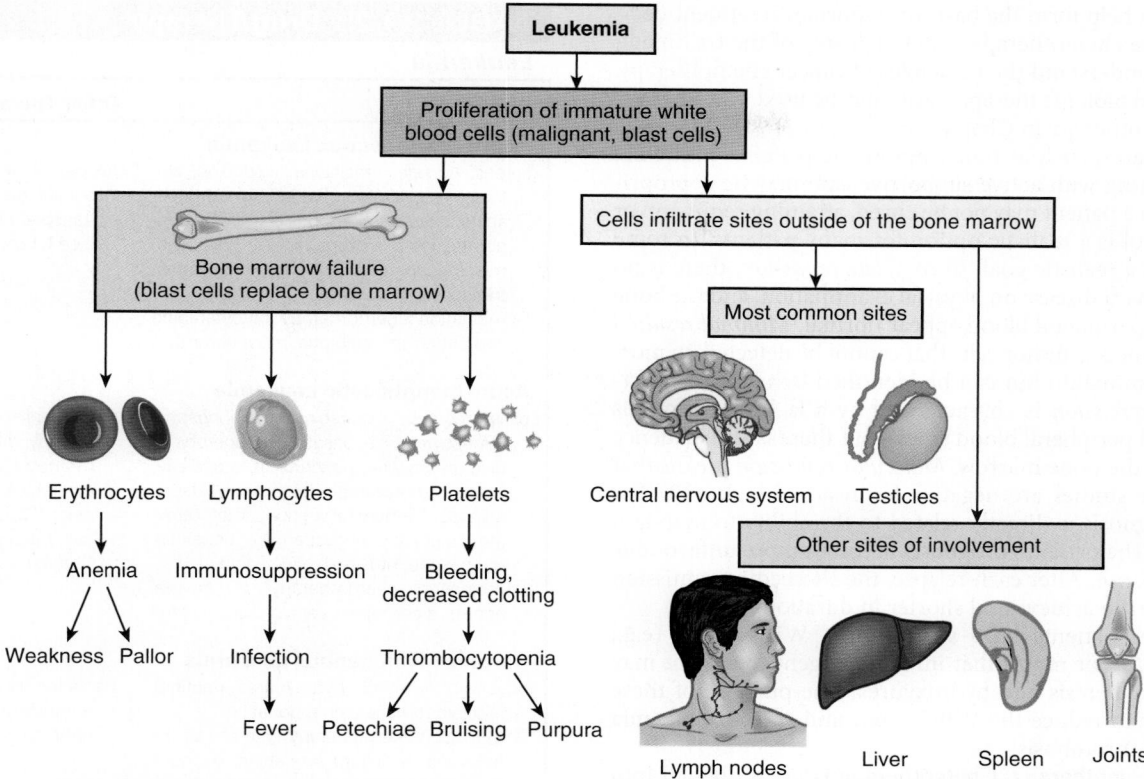

FIG. 30.13 Pathophysiology of leukemia. (Modified from McKinney ES, James SR, Murray SS, et al: *Maternal-child nursing*, Philadelphia, 2000, Saunders.)

made by considering the progression of the disease and the side effects of treatment. Many patients in the early stages of CLL do not need treatment. Others are followed closely and receive treatment only when the disease progresses. About one-third need immediate treatment at the time of diagnosis.

Other Leukemias. Occasionally the subtype of leukemia cannot be identified. The cancerous leukemic cells may have lymphoid, myeloid, or mixed characteristics. Often these patients do not respond to treatment and have a poor prognosis. Other rare types include hairy cell and biphenotypic (both abnormal myeloid and lymphoid clones) leukemias.

Overlap Between Leukemia and Lymphoma. Overlap exists between leukemia and non-Hodgkin's lymphoma (NHL) because both involve proliferation of lymphocytes or their precursors (Fig. 30.12). A leukemia-like picture with peripheral lymphocytosis and bone marrow involvement may be present in about 15% of adults with some types of NHL.[3] Patients with more extensive nodal involvement (especially mediastinal), fewer circulating abnormal cells, and fewer blast forms in the marrow are considered to have lymphoma. A prominent leukemic phase is less common in aggressive lymphomas, except Burkitt's, lymphoblastic lymphomas, and those classified as "double hit," meaning they have a double oncogene mutation.[3,33]

Clinical Manifestations

The manifestations of leukemia are varied (Table 30.24). They relate to problems caused by bone marrow failure and the formation of leukemic infiltrates (Fig. 30.13). Bone marrow failure results from (1) bone marrow overcrowding by abnormal cells and (2) inadequate production of normal marrow elements.

The patient is predisposed to anemia, thrombocytopenia, and decreased number and function of WBCs.

As leukemia progresses, fewer normal blood cells are made. The abnormal WBCs continue to accumulate because they do not go through the normal cell life cycle to death *(apoptosis).* The leukemic cells may infiltrate the patient's organs, leading to problems such as splenomegaly, hepatomegaly, lymphadenopathy, bone pain, meningeal irritation, and oral lesions. Solid masses resulting from collections of leukemic cells, called *chloromas,* can occur. A high leukemic white count in the peripheral blood (more than 100,000 cells/µL) can cause the blood to thicken and potentially block circulatory pathways. This is called *leukostasis.* It can be life threatening.

Diagnostic Studies

Peripheral blood evaluation and bone marrow examination are the primary methods of diagnosing and classifying the types of leukemia. Morphologic, histochemical, immunologic, and cytogenetic methods are used to identify leukemic cell types, stage of development, and significant genetic mutations. Knowing the type of leukemia is important because each type has a different prognosis and treatment options. For example, in CML, the finding of the Philadelphia chromosome is an important diagnostic indicator. It is also sometimes present in ALL and affects the treatment as well.[30,31] Other studies, such as lumbar puncture and PET/CT scans, can detect leukemic cells outside of the blood and bone marrow.

Interprofessional Care

Once a diagnosis of leukemia has been made, care focuses on the initial goal of attaining remission. Age and cytogenetic analysis often help form the basis of important treatment decisions. Because chemotherapy is the mainstay of the treatment, you need to understand the principles of cancer chemotherapy. Radiation and biologic therapies also may be used. (See the section on chemotherapy in Chapter 15.)

In some cases, such as nonsymptomatic patients with CLL, watchful waiting with active supportive care may be appropriate. Although a patient may not be cured, attaining remission or disease control is a realistic option for many patients. In some cases, cure is a realistic goal. In *complete remission,* there is no evidence of overt disease on physical examination, and the bone marrow and peripheral blood appear normal. *Minimal residual disease* is defined as tumor cells that cannot be detected by morphologic examination but can be identified by molecular testing. *Partial remission* is characterized by a lack of symptoms and a normal peripheral blood smear, but there is still evidence of disease in the bone marrow. *Molecular remission* means that all molecular studies are negative for residual leukemia. The patient's prognosis is directly related to the ability to maintain a remission. The patient's prognosis becomes more unfavorable with each relapse. After each relapse, the succeeding remission may be harder to achieve and shorter in duration.

Sometimes patients have such a high WBC count (e.g., 100,000 cells/μL or more) that initial emergent treatment may include leukapheresis and hydroxyurea. The purpose of these treatments is to reduce the WBC count and risk for leukemia cell–induced thrombosis.

Stages of Chemotherapy. Chemotherapy is often divided into 3 stages: induction, postinduction or postremission (consolidation), and maintenance.

Induction Therapy. The first stage, *induction therapy,* is the attempt to bring about a remission. Induction is aggressive treatment that seeks to destroy leukemic cells in the tissues, peripheral blood, and bone marrow to eventually restore normal hematopoiesis on bone marrow recovery. During induction therapy, a patient may become critically ill because the bone marrow is severely depressed by the chemotherapeutic agents. Nursing interventions focus on neutropenia, thrombocytopenia, and anemia. Common chemotherapy agents for induction of AML include cytarabine and an antitumor antibiotic (anthracycline), such as daunorubicin, idarubicin, or mitoxantrone.[29] After 1 course of induction therapy, around 70% of newly diagnosed patients younger than 60 achieve complete remission. It is assumed that leukemic cells persist undetected after induction therapy. This could lead to relapse within a few months without further therapy.[29]

Postinduction or Postremission Therapy. Terms used to describe postinduction or postremission chemotherapy include *intensification* and *consolidation. Intensification therapy,* or high-dose therapy, may be given immediately after induction therapy for several months. Other drugs that target the cell in a different way than those given during induction may be added.

Consolidation therapy is started after a remission is achieved. It may consist of 1 or 2 more courses of the same drugs given during induction or involve high-dose therapy (intensive consolidation). The purpose of consolidation therapy is to eliminate remaining leukemic cells that may not be clinically or pathologically evident.

Maintenance Therapy. Maintenance therapy may be used and involves treatment with lower doses of the same drugs used in induction or other drugs given every few weeks for a prolonged period. Like consolidation or intensification, the goal is to keep

TABLE 30.25 Drug Therapy

Leukemia

Drug Therapy	Other Therapy
Acute Myelogenous Leukemia	
arsenic trioxide, azacitidine, cladribine, clofarabine, cytarabine, daunorubicin, decitabine, enasidenib, etoposide, fludarabine, gemtuzumab ozogamicin, idarubicin, midostaurin, mitoxantrone, thioguanine, tretinoin, venetoclax Combination chemotherapy of cytarabine and antitumor antibiotic (most common)	Allogeneic hematopoietic stem cell transplant (HSCT) (see Chapter 15)
Acute Lymphocytic Leukemia	
blinatumomab, clofarabine, cyclophosphamide, cytarabine, dasatinib, daunorubicin, dexamethasone, doxorubicin, etoposide, imatinib, inotuzumab ozogamicin, L-asparaginase, 6-mercaptopurine, methotrexate, nelarabine, pegaspargase, ponatinib, prednisone, rituximab, vincristine Combination chemotherapy of several agents is common over a prolonged time	Cranial radiation therapy, intrathecal methotrexate or cytarabine, allogeneic HSCT, CAR-T cell therapy (see Chapter 15)
Chronic Myelogenous Leukemia	
bosutinib, dasatinib, hydroxyurea, imatinib, nilotinib, omacetaxine, ponatinib Combination chemotherapy with any of the following: busulfan, cytarabine, daunorubicin, etoposide, L-asparaginase, 6-mercaptopurine, methotrexate, mitoxantrone, prednisone, vincristine	Radiation, HSCT, α-interferon, leukapheresis
Chronic Lymphocytic Leukemia	
Alemtuzumab, chlorambucil, bendamustine, cyclophosphamide, fludarabine, ibrutinib, idelalisib, lenalidomide, obinutuzumab, ofatumumab, pentostatin, prednisone, rituximab, venetoclax, vincristine	Radiation, splenectomy, colony-stimulating factors, allogeneic HSCT

the body free of leukemic cells. This is often used with ALL and extends for several years.[30]

Drug Therapy Regimens. The therapeutic agents used to treat leukemia vary. Table 30.25 gives examples of treatment regimens used in various types of leukemia.

Combination therapy is the mainstay of treatment for leukemia. The 3 purposes for using multiple drugs are to (1) decrease drug resistance, (2) minimize the drug toxicity by using multiple drugs with varying toxicities, and (3) interrupt cell growth at multiple points in the cell cycle.

Some therapeutic drugs are aimed at small molecules that promote the growth and differentiation of leukemic cells. For example, all-*trans* retinoic acid, which treats acute promyelocytic leukemia (a type of AML), causes normal differentiation of the promyelocytes which has arrested in this type of leukemia by the translocation of the *PML* gene on chromosome 15 to the *RARA* gene on chromosome 17 (t15;17).[29] Midostaurin is a multikinase inhibitor that inhibits this growth pathway in AML patients with the *FLT3* mutation.[29] Imatinib (Gleevec) and other tyrosine-kinase inhibitors target the BCR-ABL protein that is present in nearly all patients with CML and some patients with ALL.[30,31] This drug kills only cancer cells, leaving healthy cells alone.

The use of specific targeted therapy in the form of mono-clonal antibodies is an important treatment modality in hema-topoietic cancers, but cures with these therapies alone are rare (see Table 15.13 and Fig. 15.16). Rituximab binds to the B-cell antigen (CD20) and is a treatment for CLL.[32] Alemtuzumab (Campath), a treatment for CLL, binds to CD52, a panlympho-cyte antigen present on both T and B cells.[32]

Other Treatments. In addition to chemotherapy, corticosteroids and radiation therapy have a role in the treatment of the patient with leukemia. Total body radiation may be used to prepare a patient for bone marrow transplantation. Radiation may be restricted to certain areas (fields,) such as the liver and spleen, or other organs affected by infiltrates. In ALL, prophylactic intrathecal methotrexate or cytarabine is given to decrease the chance of CNS involvement, which is common in this type of leukemia. When CNS leukemia does occur, cranial radiation is an option. Immunotherapy and targeted therapy, such as mono-clonal antibodies and chimeric antigen receptor (CAR) T cells, may be indicated for specific leukemias. (Immunotherapy and targeted therapy are discussed in Chapter 15.)

Hematopoietic Stem Cell Transplantation. HSCT is another type of therapy used for patients with different forms of leuke-mia. The goal of HSCT is to eliminate all leukemic cells from the body using combinations of chemotherapy with or without total body irradiation. This treatment eradicates the patient's hematopoietic stem cells, which are then replaced with those of an HLA-matched sibling, HLA-half-matched relative, volunteer donor *(allogeneic),* or identical twin *(syngeneic).* (HSCT is dis-cussed in Chapter 15.)

The primary complications for patients with allogeneic HSCT are graft-versus-host disease (GVHD), relapse of leu-kemia, and infection and sepsis. Because HSCT has serious associated risks, the patient must weigh the significant risks for treatment-related death or treatment failure (relapse) with the hope of cure.

❖ NURSING MANAGEMENT: LEUKEMIA

◆ Nursing Assessment
Subjective and objective data that should be obtained from a patient with leukemia are outlined in Table 30.26.

◆ Nursing Diagnoses
Nursing diagnoses for the patient with leukemia include those for anemia (see p. 608), thrombocytopenia (see p. 625), and neutropenia (see eNursing Care Plan 30.3, available on the website).

◆ Planning
The overall goals are that the patient with leukemia will (1) understand and adhere to the treatment plan; (2) have mini-mal side effects and complications associated with both the disease and its treatment; and (3) establish realistic hope and goals, feeling supported during periods of treatment, relapse, or remission.

◆ Nursing Implementation
◆ **Acute Care.** The nursing role during acute phases of leukemia is extremely challenging because the patient has many physical and psychosocial needs. As with other forms of cancer, the diagnosis of leukemia can evoke great fear and be equated with death. It may be viewed as a hopeless, horrible disease with many painful

---

TABLE 30.26 Nursing Assessment
Leukemia

Subjective Data
Important Health Information
Past health history: Exposure to chemical toxins (e.g., benzene, arse-nic), radiation, or viruses (HTLV-1); chromosome abnormalities (Down syndrome, Klinefelter syndrome, Fanconi syndrome), immunologic deficiencies; organ transplantation; frequent infections; bleeding ten-dencies
Medications: Chemotherapy
Surgery or other treatments: Radiation exposure; prior radiation and che-motherapy for cancer

Functional Health Patterns
Health perception–health management: Family history of leukemia; malaise
Nutritional-metabolic: Mouth sores, weight loss; chills, night sweats; nausea, vomiting, anorexia, dysphagia, early satiety; easy bruising
Elimination: Hematuria, decreased urine output; diarrhea, dark or bloody stools
Activity-exercise: Fatigue with progressive weakness; dyspnea, nose-bleeds, cough
Cognitive-perceptual: Headache; muscle cramps; sore throat; general-ized sternal tenderness, bone, joint, abdominal pain; paresthesias, numbness, tingling, visual changes
Sexuality-reproductive: Prolonged menses, menorrhagia, metrorrhagia, impotence

Objective Data
General
Fever, generalized lymphadenopathy, lethargy

Integumentary
Pallor or jaundice; petechiae, ecchymoses, purpura, reddish brown to purple cutaneous infiltrates, macules, and papules

Cardiovascular
Tachycardia, systolic murmurs

Gastrointestinal
Gingival bleeding and hyperplasia; oral ulcerations, herpes and *Candida* infections; perirectal irritation and infection; hepatomegaly, spleno-megaly

Neurologic
Seizures, disorientation, confusion, decreased coordination, cranial nerve palsies, papilledema

Musculoskeletal
Muscle wasting, bone pain, joint pain

Possible Diagnostic Findings
Low, normal, or high WBC count with shift to the left (↑ blast cells) and neutropenia; anemia, ↓ hematocrit and hemoglobin, thrombocytope-nia, specific chromosome abnormalities; hypercellular bone marrow aspirate or biopsy with myeloblasts, lymphoblasts, and markedly ↓ normal cells

HTLV-1, Human T-cell leukemia virus, type 1.

and undesirable consequences. The treatment and prognosis of each patient with leukemia are driven by many factors, such as age and type of leukemia. Therefore you must understand the patient's type of leukemia, prognosis, treatment plan, and goals. By doing this, you can help the patient realize that, although the future may be uncertain, one can have a meaningful quality of life while in remission or with disease control and that, in some cases, there is reasonable hope for cure.

The family needs help adjusting to the stress of this abrupt onset of serious illness and the losses imposed by the sick role (e.g., dependence, withdrawal, changes in role responsibilities, changes in body image). The diagnosis of leukemia often brings with it the need to make difficult decisions at a time of profound stress for the patient and family.

Patients may have co-morbid conditions that affect treatment decisions. Important nursing interventions include (1) maximizing the patient's physical functioning, (2) teaching patients that acute side effects of treatment are usually temporary, and (3) encouraging patients to discuss their quality-of-life issues.

You are an important advocate in helping the patient and family understand the complexities of treatment decisions and manage the side effects and toxicities. This may include making sure the HCP addresses fertility concerns. A patient may need a long hospitalization or may need to temporarily relocate to an appropriate treatment center. This situation can lead a patient to feel deserted and isolated at a time when support is most needed. You have contact with a patient many hours a day and can help reverse feelings of abandonment and loneliness by balancing the demanding technical needs with a humanistic, caring approach. The needs of the patient with leukemia are best met by an interprofessional team (e.g., psychiatric and oncology clinical nurse specialists, case managers, dietitians, chaplains, and social workers).

From a physical care perspective, you are challenged to make astute assessments and plan care to help the patient manage the severe side effects of chemotherapy. The life-threatening results of bone marrow suppression (neutropenia, thrombocytopenia, and anemia) require aggressive nursing interventions. Other critical aspects of care include anticipating, monitoring for, and helping to treat emergencies, such as DIC, tumor lysis syndrome, leukostasis, and cytokine release syndrome. Complications of chemotherapy may affect the patient's GI tract, nutritional status, skin and mucosa, cardiopulmonary status, liver, kidneys, and neurologic system. (Nursing interventions related to chemotherapy are discussed in Chapter 15.)

Review all drugs being given, including the mechanism of action, purpose, routes of administration, doses, potential side effects, safe handling considerations, and toxic effects. Assess laboratory data reflecting the effects of the drugs and sequelae of the disease. Unlike treatments for solid tumors, chemotherapy is given to patients with leukemia even if they have severe myelosuppression, since the underlying disorder is causing the problem and will not resolve unless treated. Quality nursing care significantly affects patient survival and comfort during aggressive chemotherapy.

◆ **Ambulatory Care.** Ongoing care for the patient with leukemia is necessary to monitor for signs and symptoms of disease control or relapse. For a patient receiving long-term or maintenance chemotherapy, the fatigue of long-term chronic disease management can become discouraging. Teach the patient and caregiver the importance of continued diligence in disease management and the need for follow-up care. Review the drugs, self-care measures, and when to seek medical attention.

The goals of rehabilitation for long-term survivors of leukemia are to manage the physical, psychologic, social, and spiritual consequences and delayed effects from the disease and its treatment. Assistance may be needed to reestablish the various relationships that are a part of the patient's life. Involving the patient in survivor networks and support groups or services may help the patient adapt to living after a life-threatening illness. Exploring national and community resources (e.g., American

TABLE 30.27 Comparison of Hodgkin's and Non-Hodgkin's Lymphoma

	Hodgkin's Lymphoma	Non-Hodgkin's Lymphoma
Cellular origin	B lymphocytes	B lymphocytes (88%) T or natural killer lymphocytes (12%)
Extent of disease	Localized to regional but may be more widespread. Spreads to adjacent tissues	Disseminated, can spread to other areas of the body
B symptoms (fever, drenching night sweats, weight loss)	Common	Uncommon
Extranodal involvement	Rare	Common

Cancer Society, Leukemia & Lymphoma Society) may reduce the financial burden and the feelings of dependence. Provide resources for spiritual support.

Vigilant follow-up care helps to ensure that we recognize and treat the cancer survivor's unique needs. Often these needs may need a referral or consultation. For example, physical therapy personnel may develop an exercise program to prevent post-treatment deficits caused by drug-induced peripheral neuropathy. Most patients should receive a pneumococcal vaccine and an annual influenza vaccine.

◆ Evaluation

The expected outcomes are that the patient with leukemia will
- Cope effectively with the diagnosis, treatment regimen, and prognosis
- Have no complications related to the disease or its treatment
- Feel supported throughout treatment

LYMPHOMAS

Lymphomas are cancers originating in the bone marrow and lymphatic structures resulting in the proliferation of lymphocytes. Lymphomas make up 4% to 5% of all cancers in the United States.[27] Two major types of lymphoma are Hodgkin's lymphoma and non-Hodgkin's lymphoma (NHL). A comparison of these 2 types of lymphoma is shown in Table 30.27.

HODGKIN'S LYMPHOMA

Hodgkin's lymphoma, also called *Hodgkin's disease,* makes up about 10% of all lymphomas. It is characterized by proliferation of abnormal giant, multinucleated cells, called *Reed-Sternberg cells,* or it's variant, *Hodgkin cells* (mononucleated), which proliferate in the lymph nodes.[3] The disease has a bimodal age-specific incidence, occurring most frequently in persons from 15 to 30 years of age and above 55 years of age.[34] Each year, about 8260 new cases of Hodgkin's lymphoma are diagnosed, with around 1070 deaths.[27] Long-term survival exceeds 80% for all stages.[34]

Etiology and Pathophysiology

Although the cause of Hodgkin's lymphoma is unknown, we think several key factors play a role in its development. The main

FIG. 30.14 Enlarged cervical lymph node in the neck of a man with Hodgkin lymphoma. (From Howard MR, Hamilton PJ: *Haematology: An illustrated colour atlas*, ed 4, London, 2013, Churchill Livingston.)

interacting factors include infection with Epstein-Barr virus (EBV), genetic predisposition, and exposure to occupational toxins. The incidence of Hodgkin's lymphoma is increased in those with HIV infection.[1]

The disease likely starts in a single location (it starts in cervical lymph nodes in 60% to 70% of patients) and then spreads along adjacent lymphatics.[3] However, in recurrent disease, it may spread more diffuse. It eventually infiltrates other organs, especially lungs, spleen, and liver. When the disease begins above the diaphragm, it stays confined to lymph nodes for a variable time. Disease originating below the diaphragm often spreads to extralymphoid sites, such as the liver. There are 5 histologic subtypes. Nodular sclerosis is the most common.[1]

Clinical Manifestations

The onset of symptoms in Hodgkin's lymphoma is usually gradual. The initial development is most often enlargement of cervical, axillary, or inguinal lymph nodes (Fig. 30.14). A mediastinal node mass is the second most common location. The nodes are movable and nontender. Enlarged nodes are not painful unless they exert pressure on adjacent nerves.

The patient may notice weight loss, fatigue, weakness, fever, chills, tachycardia, or night sweats. A group of initial findings, including fever (over 100.4°F [38°C]), drenching night sweats, and weight loss (exceeding 10% in 6 months), are termed *B symptoms*. They correlate with a worse prognosis. After having even small amounts of alcohol, patients with Hodgkin's lymphoma may have a rapid onset of pain at the site of disease. The cause for the alcohol-induced pain is unknown. Generalized pruritus without skin lesions may develop. Cough, dyspnea, stridor, and dysphagia may all reflect mediastinal node involvement.

In more advanced disease, there may be hepatomegaly and splenomegaly. Anemia results from increased destruction and decreased production of RBCs. Other physical signs vary depending on where the disease is located. For example, intrathoracic involvement may lead to superior vena cava syndrome. Enlarged retroperitoneal nodes may cause palpable abdominal masses or interfere with renal function. Jaundice may occur from liver involvement. Spinal cord compression leading to paraplegia may occur with extradural involvement. Bone pain occurs from bone involvement.

Diagnostic and Staging Studies

Peripheral blood analysis, excisional lymph node biopsy, bone marrow examination, and radiologic studies are important means of evaluating Hodgkin's lymphoma. Abnormalities in the CBC, such as a microcytic hypochromic anemia, are variable and not diagnostic. Leukopenia and thrombocytopenia may develop, but they are usually a consequence of treatment, advanced disease, or superimposed hypersplenism. Other blood studies may show increased erythrocyte sedimentation rate, high leukocyte alkaline phosphatase from liver and bone involvement, hypercalcemia from bone involvement, and hypoalbuminemia from liver involvement.

Radiologic evaluation can help define all sites and determine the clinical stage of the disease. PET and CT scans are used to stage and then assess the response to therapy and to distinguish residual tumor from fibrotic masses after treatment. These scans may show increased uptake (by PET) and masses, such as renal displacement caused by retroperitoneal node enlargement, abdominal or mediastinal lymph node enlargement, and liver, spleen, bone, and brain infiltration.

❖ Interprofessional and Nursing Management

Using all the information from the various diagnostic studies, HCPs determine a clinical stage of disease (Fig. 30.15).[34] The final staging is based on the clinical stage (extent of the disease), presence of B symptoms, and other unfavorable prognostic features. Treatment depends on the nature and extent of the disease. The terms used in staging involve an A or B classification, depending on whether systemic symptoms are present at diagnosis, and a Roman numeral (I to IV) that reflects the location and extent of the disease.[34]

Once the stage of Hodgkin's lymphoma is determined, management focuses on selecting a treatment plan. The standard for chemotherapy is the ABVD regimen: doxorubicin (**A**driamycin), **b**leomycin, **v**inblastine, and **d**acarbazine. Patients with favorable early-stage disease receive 2 to 4 cycles of chemotherapy.[3] Patients with early-stage disease but unfavorable prognostic features (e.g., B symptoms) or intermediate-stage disease receive 4 to 6 cycles of chemotherapy. Advanced-stage Hodgkin's lymphoma is treated more aggressively using 6 to 8 cycles of chemotherapy. A common regimen is BEACOPP (**b**leomycin, **e**toposide, doxorubicin [**A**driamycin], **c**yclophosphamide, vincristine [**O**ncovin], **p**rocarbazine, and **p**rednisone).[3,34] The role of involved-site radiation as a supplement to chemotherapy varies depending on the extent of disease and the presence of resistant disease after chemotherapy.[34] Response to therapy is determined by PET and CT scans and other diagnostic tests (e.g., bone marrow biopsy).

A variety of chemotherapy regimens and newer agents, such as brentuximab vedotin, nivolumab, bendamustine, and pembrolizumab are used to treat patients who have relapsed or refractory disease.[34] Ideally, once remission is obtained, a curative option may be intensive chemotherapy with the use of autologous or allogeneic HSCT.[34] HSCT has allowed patients to receive higher, potentially curative doses of chemotherapy while reducing life-threatening leukopenia (see Chapter 15). Combination chemotherapy works well because, as in leukemia, the drugs used have an additive antitumor effect without increasing side effects. As with

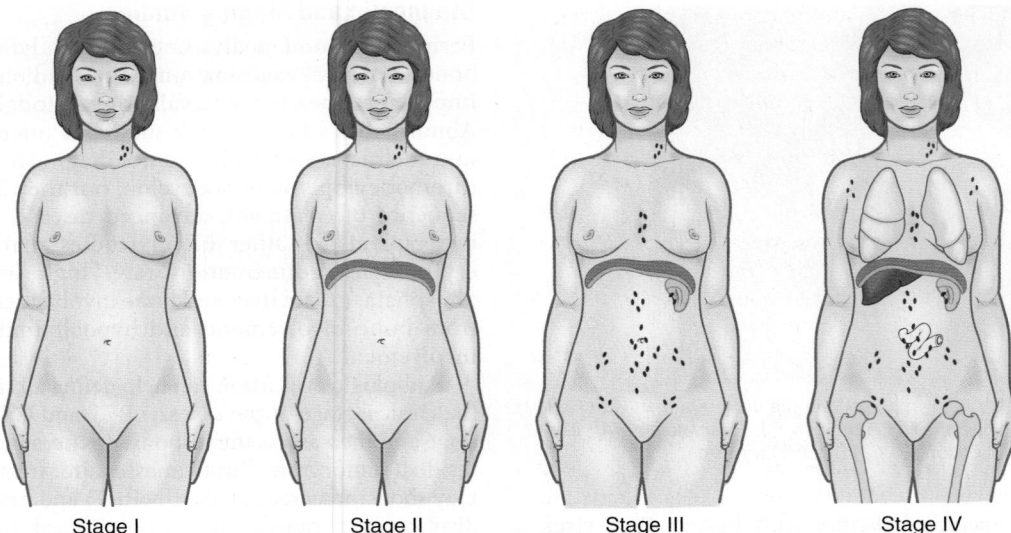

| Stage I | Stage II | Stage III | Stage IV |

FIG. 30.15 Staging system for Hodgkin's lymphoma and non-Hodgkin's lymphoma. *Stage I,* Involvement of single lymph node (e.g., cervical node). *Stage II,* Involvement of 2 or more lymph nodes on one side of diaphragm. *Stage III,* Lymph node involvement above and below the diaphragm. *Stage IV,* Involvement outside of diaphragm (e.g., liver, bone marrow). The stage is followed by the letter *A* (absence) or *B* (presence) to indicate significant systemic symptoms (e.g., fever, night sweats, weight loss).

leukemia, therapy must be aggressive. Potentially life-threatening problems are an issue in the attempt to achieve a remission.

Maintenance chemotherapy does not contribute to increased survival after achieving complete remission. Occasionally, single drugs may be given palliatively to those who cannot tolerate intensive combination therapy. A serious consequence of the treatment for Hodgkin's lymphoma is the later development of secondary cancers and potential long-term toxicities from the treatment, such as endocrine (hypothyroidism), heart, and lung dysfunction. Secondary solid tumor cancers may occur 10 years after treatment for Hodgkin's lymphoma.[34] The most common secondary cancers are lung and breast cancer, especially with radiation therapy. Patients should have close follow-up and screening for early detection of these problems.

The nursing care for Hodgkin's lymphoma is based on managing problems related to the disease (e.g., pain caused by a tumor, superior vena cava syndrome), pancytopenia, and other side effects of therapy. Because the survival of patients with Hodgkin's lymphoma depends on their response to treatment, supporting the patient through the consequences of treatment is extremely important.

Psychosocial considerations are as important as they are with leukemia. However, the prognosis for Hodgkin's lymphoma is better than that for many forms of cancer. Address the physical and spiritual consequences of the patient's disease. Fertility issues may be of concern because this disease is often seen in adolescents and young adults. Help to ensure that these issues are addressed soon after diagnosis. Evaluating patients for long-term effects of therapy is important because delayed consequences of disease and treatment may not be apparent for many years. Secondary cancers and delayed effects are discussed in Chapter 15.

EVIDENCE-BASED PRACTICE
Exercise and Hematologic Cancer

You are a nurse caring for G.R., a 59-yr-old male patient with non-Hodgkin's lymphoma who is receiving chemotherapy. Due to a decrease in red blood cells and platelets, he was told to rest and avoid the high level of physical exercise he once enjoyed. He misses his active lifestyle and now admits to you that he is "somewhat depressed."

Making Clinical Decisions

Best Available Evidence. Aerobic exercise, especially walking and stretching, to maintain mobility may improve physical functioning, fatigue, and depression in patients with hematologic cancers.

Clinician Expertise. You know recommendations to decrease intensive physical exercise may diminish quality of life for many patients, especially for people who are used to being physically active.

Patient Preferences and Values. G.R. is considering joining a neighborhood bicycling club so that he can "feel better."

Implications for Nursing Practice

1. Why is intensive exercise contraindicated in someone who is getting chemotherapy or acutely ill?
2. What precautions would you discuss with G.R. before he increases his exercise level?
3. How would you involve G.R. in monitoring his fatigue?
4. As G.R. seeks ways to improve his quality of life, how would you support him?

Reference for Evidence

Berger AM, Mooney K: Cancer-related fatigue, NCCN clinical practice guidelines, version 2,.2017. Retrieved from *www.nccn.org*.

NON-HODGKIN'S LYMPHOMA

Non-Hodgkin's lymphomas (NHLs) are a broad group of cancers of primarily B, T, natural killer (NK), histiocytic, and dendritic cells.[33] They affect persons of all ages. There are over 75 types. They are categorized by the level of differentiation (maturity), cell of origin, immunophenotype (cell surface markers), and genetic and clinical features.[33,35] The most common subtypes in the United States are diffuse large B-cell lymphoma, follicular lymphoma, marginal zone lymphoma, mantle cell lymphoma, and peripheral T-cell lymphoma not otherwise specified.[33] A simplified example of the classification system is shown in Table 30.28.[33,35]

A variety of presentations and courses occur, from indolent (slowly developing) to rapidly progressive disease. NHL is the most commonly occurring hematologic cancer. It causes 3% to 4% of cancer-related deaths. Each year about 72,240 new cases of NHL are diagnosed and 20,140 deaths occur.[27]

Etiology and Pathophysiology

As with Hodgkin's lymphoma, the cause of NHL is usually unknown. NHLs may result from chromosomal translocations, infections, environmental factors, and immunodeficiency states. Chromosomal translocations have a key role in the pathogenesis of many NHLs. Viruses and bacteria implicated in the pathogenesis of NHL, include HTLV-1, EBV, human herpesvirus 8, hepatitis B and C, *H. pylori, Chlamydophila psittaci, Campylobacter jejuni,* and *Borrelia burgdorferi.*[3] Environmental factors linked to the development of NHL include chemicals (e.g., pesticides, herbicides, solvents, organic chemicals, wood preservatives). NHL is more common in people who have inherited immunodeficiency syndromes, have used immunosuppressive agents (e.g., to prevent rejection after an organ transplant or to treat autoimmune disorders), or received chemotherapy or radiation therapy.

NHL does not have a hallmark feature that parallels the Hodgkin or Reed-Sternberg cell of Hodgkin's lymphoma. However, all NHLs involve lymphocytes arrested in various stages of development and may mimic a leukemia. For example, small lymphocytic lymphoma (SLL) and CLL result from malignant proliferation of small B lymphocytes, with most CLL disease within the bone marrow versus the lymph nodes. Some NHLs can begin outside the lymph nodes.

TABLE 30.28 Classification of Non-Hodgkin's Lymphoma*

B-Cell Lymphomas
- Burkitt's lymphoma
- Diffuse large B-cell lymphoma (DLBCL)
- Follicular lymphoma
- Mantle cell lymphoma
- Marginal zone B-cell lymphoma (MALT)
- Plasmablastic lymphoma
- Small lymphocytic lymphoma/chronic lymphocytic leukemia

T-Cell and NK-Cell Lymphomas
- Anaplastic large T-cell lymphoma
- Extranodal NK/T cell lymphoma
- Lymphoblastic lymphoma
- Mycosis fungoides and Sézary syndrome
- Peripheral T-cell lymphoma, not otherwise specified (NOS)

Posttransplant Lymphoproliferative Disorders (PTLD)
- Infectious mononucleosis-like PTLD

Histocytic and Dendritic Cell Tumors
- Langerhans cell histiocytosis

*This is only a partial list.

Diffuse large B-cell lymphoma, the most common aggressive lymphoma, starts in the lymph nodes, usually in the neck or abdomen. Burkitt's lymphoma is the most aggressive disease. We think it begins in B-cell blasts in the lymph nodes.

Clinical Manifestations

The method of spread can be unpredictable. Most patients have widespread disease at the time of diagnosis (Fig. 30.16). The primary manifestation is painless lymph node enlargement. The lymphadenopathy can wax and wane in indolent disease. Because the disease has usually spread, other symptoms are present depending on where the disease is present (e.g., hepatomegaly with liver involvement, neurologic symptoms with CNS disease). NHL can manifest in nonspecific ways, such as an airway obstruction, hyperuricemia and renal failure from tumor lysis syndrome, pericardial tamponade, and GI symptoms. Patients with high-grade lymphomas may have lymphadenopathy and B symptoms, such as fever, night sweats, and weight loss.

Diagnostic and Staging Studies

Diagnostic studies used for NHL resemble those used for Hodgkin's lymphoma. However, because NHL is more often in extranodal sites, more diagnostic studies may be done. These include an MRI or lumbar puncture to rule out CNS disease, a bone marrow biopsy to determine bone marrow infiltration, or a barium enema or upper endoscopy to look for GI involvement. Clinical staging, as described for Hodgkin's lymphoma, helps guide therapy (Fig. 30.15). Establishing the precise histologic subtype through biopsy is extremely important. NHL is classified based on morphologic, genetic, immunophenotypic (cell surface antigens, CD20, CD52), and clinical features. In early NHL, the CBC may be normal, but some lymphomas manifest in a "leukemic" phase.

Treatment is guided by the cell type, cytogenetic studies, and clinical behavior: *indolent* (low grade), *aggressive* (high grade), or *highly aggressive* (very high grade). Other factors, known as the International Prognostic Index (IPI), may be considered for each subtype. These include the clinical stage, number of extranodal sites, serum LDH, WBC count, and patient's age and performance status.[33,35] Immunologic, cytogenetic, and molecular studies are used for making therapeutic decisions and assessing prognosis. Other studies might include blood tests for tumor lysis; screening for hepatitis, HIV, and other infections; skin biopsies; bone marrow biopsies; and lumbar punctures. The prognosis for NHL is based on the histopathology.

FIG. 30.16 Non-Hodgkin's lymphoma involving the spleen. The presence of an isolated mass is typical. (From Cotran RS, Kumar V, Abbas AK: *Robbins pathologic basis of disease,* ed 6, Philadelphia, 1999, Saunders.)

❖ Interprofessional and Nursing Management

Treatment for NHL involves chemotherapy, biotherapy, radiation, and sometimes phototherapy and topical therapy (Table 30.29).[35] Ironically, more aggressive lymphomas (diffuse large B cell) are generally more responsive to treatment. In contrast, indolent lymphomas (e.g., follicular lymphomas) have a naturally long course but are hard to effectively treat.[33]

Patients with low-grade (indolent) lymphoma may live 10 years or more without treatment. However, some early therapies can be well tolerated and may reduce the time to progression of the disease. Those that have an infectious basis, such as *H. pylori* gastric lymphomas, may be treated with antibiotic or antiviral therapy. HSCT may help in certain subtypes of aggressive or refractory lymphomas. Chimeric antigen receptor (CAR) T-cell immunotherapy may be used.

Rituximab, a monoclonal antibody against the CD20 antigen on the surface of normal and malignant B cells, is used to treat NHL in combination with other agents. Once bound to the cells, rituximab causes lysis and cell death. Numerous chemotherapy combinations are used to try to overcome the resistant nature of this disease. Targeted therapies are becoming more prevalent (Table 30.29).

 DRUG ALERT Rituximab (Rituxan)
- Monitor patient for signs of severe hypersensitivity infusion reactions, especially with first infusion.
- Manifestations may include hypotension, bronchospasm, dysrhythmias, angioedema, and cardiogenic shock.
- Screen for history of hepatitis because the drug may reactivate hepatitis.

Another therapy for some types of NHL is the monoclonal antibody ibritumomab tiuxetan (Zevalin). It contains a radioactive particle that can kill cancer cells. The therapy targets the CD20 antigen, which is on the surface of mature B cells and B-cell tumors. Targeting allows for the delivery of the radiation directly to the cancer cells. Side effects include pancytopenia. Use radiation precautions in caring for these patients. Teach patients about safety issues and how to minimize the risk for radiation exposure to staff and others.

In general, T-cell lymphomas are harder to treat. They are often treated aggressively up front, often followed by an HSCT. Cutaneous T-cell lymphomas may be treated with topical corticosteroids or topical chemotherapy for limited-stage disease. For more diffuse disease, treatment may include methotrexate, α-interferon, brentuximab vedotin, or other drugs.[35]

The nursing care for NHL is similar to that for Hodgkin's lymphoma. It is based on managing problems related to the disease (e.g., pain caused by the tumor, spinal cord compression, tumor

TABLE 30.29 Treatment of Non-Hodgkin's Lymphoma *

Recommended Therapies	Common Chemotherapy Combinations
Indolent (Low Grade) Follicular Lymphoma, Marginal Zone B-Cell Lymphoma, Mucosa-Associated Lymphoid Tissue (MALT)	
• Observation until disease progression for asymptomatic patients with low-volume tumors and normal blood counts • External beam irradiation for local, limited disease • Single-agent rituximab, obinutuzumab • Single-agent chemotherapy (bendamustine, chlorambucil, cyclophosphamide, idelalisib) • Rituximab with another agent (bendamustine, fludarabine, lenalidomide) • Combination chemotherapy (R-CHOP or other) • Radioimmunotherapy • Hematopoietic stem cell transplant (HSCT)	**R-CHOP: r**ituximab, **c**yclophosphamide, doxorubicin **h**ydrochloride, vincristine (**O**ncovin), **p**rednisone **R-CVP: r**ituximab, **c**yclophosphamide, **v**incristine, **p**rednisone **RFND: r**ituximab, **f**ludarabine, mitoxantrone (**N**ovantrone), **d**examethasone ± rituximab
Aggressive (Intermediate or High Grade) Mantle Cell, Diffuse Large B-Cell, T-Cell, Natural Killer Cell Lymphomas	
• Combination chemotherapy with localized radiation if needed • Aggressive combination chemotherapy for 3–8 cycles with rituximab with local radiation if needed • Intrathecal chemotherapy if needed • Single agent or other combination treatment, depending on subtype and response (e.g., acalabrutinib, alemtuzumab, asparaginase, belinostat, bendamustine, bortezomib, brentuximab vedotin, cladribine, gemcitabine, ibrutinib, lenalidomide, oxaliplatin, romidepsin, venetoclax) • HSCT	**CHOP** ± rituximab (see above) **ICE** (or "RICE" with rituximab): **i**fosfamide, **c**yclophosphamide, **e**toposide **R-EPOCH: r**ituximab, **e**toposide, **p**rednisone, vincristine (**O**ncovin), **c**yclophosphamide, doxorubicin **h**ydrochloride **ESHAP ± R: e**toposide, methylprednisolone (**S**olu-Medrol), **h**igh-dose cytarabine (**A**ra-C), cisplatin (**P**latinol), with or without rituximab **Hyper-CVAD ± R:** hyperfractionated **c**yclophosphamide, **v**incristine, doxorubicin (**A**driamycin), **d**examethasone alternating with high-dose methotrexate and cytarabine with or without rituximab **DHAP ± R: d**examethasone, **h**igh-dose cytarabine (**A**ra-C), cisplatin (**P**latinol), with or without rituximab
Highly Aggressive (e.g., Burkitt's Lymphoma)	
• Aggressive combination chemotherapy for 3–8 cycles • HSCT	**R-EPOCH: r**ituximab, **e**toposide, **p**rednisone, vincristine (**O**ncovin), **c**yclophosphamide, doxorubicin **h**ydrochloride **Hyper-CVAD ± R** (see above) **CODOX-M: c**yclophosphamide, vincristine (**O**ncovin), **d**oxorubicin, high-dose **m**ethotrexate, with or without rituximab (includes intrathecal methotrexate)

*The acronym for some drug regimens use the trade name of chemotherapy agents. In some cases, the trade name drug has been discontinued, and the drug currently used is the generic version.

lysis syndrome), pancytopenia, and other side effects of therapy. However, because NHL can be more extensive and involve specific organs (e.g., CNS, spleen, liver, GI tract, bone marrow), it is important to understand the subtype and extent of the disease. For example, a patient with known involvement of the colon may report acute abdominal pain. The patient would likely have abdominal guarding and an enlarged and tympanic abdomen. This could indicate a bowel perforation and be considered a medical emergency. A patient with a Burkitt's NHL beginning chemotherapy would be at high risk for tumor lysis syndrome and would need frequent laboratory studies and monitoring, as well as strict documentation of intake and output. Cancer-related therapies and side effects are discussed in Chapter 15.

The patient undergoing external beam radiation therapy has special nursing needs. The skin in the radiation field needs special care. Concepts related to safety issues with radiation therapy are important to include in the plan of care (see Chapter 15).

Psychosocial considerations are important. Help the patient and family understand the disease, treatment, and expected and potential side effects. Some aggressive treatments need close follow-up and even inpatient admission. Fertility issues may be of concern in young patients. As in Hodgkin's lymphoma, evaluation of patients with NHL for long-term effects of therapy is important because the delayed consequences of disease and treatment may not become apparent for many years.

MULTIPLE MYELOMA

Multiple myeloma, or *plasma cell myeloma,* is a condition in which cancerous plasma cells proliferate in the bone marrow and destroy bone. Multiple myeloma accounts for about 1.8% of all cancers and for about 17% of all hematologic cancers.[27] The disease is more common in men than women and more common in blacks than whites.[3] It generally occurs between the ages of 65 and 74 years old, with an average onset age of 69 years.[36] Because of the variety of treatments that can be provided throughout the course of the disease, over 40% of patients have more than a 10-year survival rate.[1]

Etiology and Pathophysiology

The cause of multiple myeloma is unknown. It is possible that exposure to organic chemicals (such as benzene), herbicides, and insecticides may play a role. Viral infections, such as HIV, may influence the risk for developing multiple myeloma.[37]

The disease process involves excess production of plasma cells. Normal plasma cells are activated B cells, which make immunoglobulins (antibodies) that normally protect the body. In multiple myeloma, instead of a variety of plasma cells making antibodies to fight different infections, myeloma tumors make monoclonal antibodies. *Monoclonal* means they are all of one kind, making them ineffective and even harmful. Not only do they not fight infections, but they infiltrate the bone marrow. These monoclonal proteins (called *M proteins*) are made up of 2 light chains and 2 heavy chains. *Bence Jones proteins* are the light chain part of these monoclonal antibodies. They may show up in the urine in many patients with multiple myeloma.[1]

Furthermore, plasma cell production of excess, abnormal amounts of cytokines (interleukins [ILs]; IL-4, IL-5, and IL-6) plays a key role in the pathologic process of bone destruction. As myeloma protein increases, normal plasma cells are reduced. This further compromises the body's normal immune response.

Proliferation of cancerous plasma cells and the overproduction of immunoglobulin and proteins may result in the end-organ effects of myeloma on the bone marrow, bone, and kidneys and possibly the spleen, lymph nodes, liver, and even heart muscle.

Clinical Manifestations

Multiple myeloma develops slowly and insidiously. The patient often does not have symptoms until the disease is advanced. Skeletal pain is the major manifestation. Pain in the pelvis, spine, and ribs is particularly common and triggered by movement. Diffuse osteoporosis develops as the myeloma protein destroys bone. Osteolytic lesions are seen in the skull, vertebrae, long bones, and ribs. Vertebral destruction can lead to collapse of vertebrae with ensuing compression of the spinal cord. Loss of bone integrity can lead to the development of pathologic fractures.

Bony degeneration causes calcium loss from bones, eventually causing hypercalcemia. Hypercalcemia may cause renal, GI, or neurologic problems, such as polyuria, anorexia, confusion, and heart problems. A serum *hyperviscosity syndrome* leading to cerebral, lung, renal, and other organ dysfunction can occur in some patients. Even without hyperviscosity, high protein levels caused by the myeloma protein can result in renal tubular obstruction, interstitial nephritis, and renal failure. The patient may have anemia, thrombocytopenia, neutropenia, and immune dysfunction from the replacement of normal bone marrow with plasma cells. Neurologic problems may be caused by regional myeloma cell growth compressing the spinal cord or cranial nerves, or by perineuronal or perivascular deposition of the abnormal protein.[1,38]

Diagnostic Studies

Evaluating multiple myeloma involves laboratory, radiologic, and bone marrow examination. M protein is often found in the blood and urine. Possible findings include pancytopenia, hypercalcemia, Bence Jones protein in the urine, and a high serum creatinine.

Skeletal bone surveys, MRI, and/or PET and CT scans show distinct areas of destroyed bone; generalized thinning of the bones; or fractures, especially in the vertebrae, ribs, pelvis, and bones of the thigh and upper arms. Bone marrow analysis shows significantly increased numbers of plasma cells in the bone marrow. The simplest measure of staging and prognosis in multiple myeloma is based on blood levels of 2 markers: β_2-microglobulin and albumin. In general, higher levels of β_2-microglobulin and lower levels of albumin are associated with a poorer prognosis. Cytogenetic studies of the bone marrow plays a role in prognostic stratification. For example, deletion of chromosome 17p13 is considered a high risk (poor prognostic) feature.[36]

❖ Interprofessional and Nursing Management

Interprofessional care involves managing both the disease and its symptoms. The current treatment options include corticosteroids, chemotherapy, immunotherapy, targeted therapy, and HSCT.[36] Multiple myeloma is seldom cured. Treatment can relieve symptoms, produce remission, and prolong life. Control of pain and prevention of pathologic fractures are goals of management.

Bisphosphonates, such as pamidronate and zoledronic acid, inhibit bone breakdown and are used to treat skeletal pain and hypercalcemia. They inhibit bone resorption without inhibiting bone formation and mineralization. They are given monthly by IV infusion. A major focus of nursing care relates to patient safety due to the bone involvement and sequelae from bone breakdown. Because of the potential for pathologic fractures, use caution when moving and ambulating the patient. A slight twist or strain in the wrong area (e.g., a weak area in the patient's bones) may cause a fracture.

💊 DRUG ALERT Zoledronic Acid (Zometa)
- Make sure the patient is adequately hydrated before giving drug.
- Renal toxicity may occur if IV infusion of drug is given in less than 15 min.
- Patients should have a dental exam prior to first dose and ongoing monitoring for osteonecrosis of the jaw.[36]

Kyphoplasty is sometimes used to control spine vertebral disease. *Kyphoplasty* is a minimally invasive procedure (usually done in an interventional radiology area) that injects cement to stabilize the vertebral compression.

Chemotherapy includes a corticosteroid (dexamethasone or prednisone) plus 2 chemotherapy agents, such as bortezomib and lenalidomide or bortezomib and cyclophosphamide. The goal is to reduce the number of plasma cells. Initial treatment depends on whether the patient is a future bone marrow transplant candidate and predicted tolerance of therapy. High-dose chemotherapy followed by HSCT has evolved as the standard of care in eligible patients.[36]

Immunotherapy and targeted therapy are options. Immunomodulator drugs (described in Chapter 15) include thalidomide, lenalidomide, and pomalidomide. Proteosome inhibitors include bortezomib, carfilzomib, and ixazomib. Panobinostat is a drug that affects enzymes that promote cancer cell growth. Daratumumab is a monoclonal antibody against CD38, a protein which is found on the surface of myeloma cells.

Other drugs can treat some complications of multiple myeloma. For example, IV furosemide promotes renal excretion of calcium. Although tumor lysis is rare, once chemotherapy is started, allopurinol may be given to prevent any renal damage from uric acid accumulation (from cell breakdown). Because of the myeloma proteins, the patient is at risk for renal dysfunction and electrolyte and fluid imbalances.

Ambulation and adequate hydration are used to treat hypercalcemia, dehydration, and potential renal damage. Weight bearing helps the bones resorb some calcium. Maintaining adequate hydration helps minimize problems from hypercalcemia and prevent protein precipitates from causing renal tubular obstruction. IV fluids may be given to maintain a urine output of 1.5 to 2 L/day if the patient does not already have renal compromise.

In some patients, the levels of plasma proteins are so high that it causes a hyperviscosity of the blood leading to neurologic changes, renal insufficiency, and other problems related to lack of blood flow. In this instance plasmapheresis is used.

Pain management requires innovative and knowledgeable nursing interventions. Analgesics, such as nonsteroidal antiinflammatory drugs, acetaminophen, or an acetaminophen/opioid combination, may be more effective than opioids alone in diminishing bone pain. Braces, especially for the spine, may help control pain. As in any pain management situation, assess the patient and implement measures to control pain (see Chapter 8). Peripheral neuropathy is common with several therapies for multiple myeloma and can contribute to discomfort, the inability to do basic activities of daily living, and the risk for injury from falling.

Patients are at risk for DVT related to chemotherapy and immobility and should have preventive measures employed.[36]

Assessment and prompt treatment of infection are important in the care of patients with multiple myeloma. Recurrent infections may be due to a decrease in the production of normal immunoglobulins, the ineffectiveness of the overproduced and abnormal immunoglobulins, corticosteroids, and/or neutropenia because of the bone marrow infiltration or side effects of treatment.

The patient's psychosocial needs require sensitive, skilled management. Help the patient and significant others adapt to changes fostered by chronic illness and adjust to the losses related to the disease process, while helping to maximize functioning and quality of life. The patient with multiple myeloma may have remissions and exacerbations. Patients may be on dialysis because of myeloma-induced renal failure. Acute care is needed at various times during the illness.

The final, acute phase is unresponsive to treatment and usually short in duration. Help the patient and family navigate needed resources, such as palliative or hospice care, social services, and spiritual care, as appropriate.

DISORDERS OF THE SPLEEN

Many illnesses can affect the spleen. Most can cause some degree of *splenomegaly* (enlarged spleen) (Table 30.30).[2] However, an enlarged spleen may be present in some people without any evidence of disease. The term *hypersplenism* refers to the occurrence of splenomegaly and peripheral cytopenias (anemia, leukopenia, and thrombocytopenia).[2] The degree of splenic enlargement varies with the disease. For example, massive splenic enlargement may occur with infectious mononucleosis, chronic myelogenous leukemia, and thalassemia major.

TABLE 30.30 Common Causes of Splenomegaly

Congestion
- Acquired hemolytic anemia
- Cirrhosis of the liver
- HF (portal hypertension)
- Portal or splenic vein thrombosis
- Sickle cell disease
- Thalassemia

Infections and Inflammations
- Autoimmune diseases: systemic lupus erythematosus, rheumatoid arthritis
- Bacterial infections: endocarditis, splenic abscess, syphilis, tuberculosis, Rocky Mountain spotted fever, typhoid fever
- Fungal infections: histoplasmosis, systemic candidiasis
- Parasitic infections: malaria, trypanosomiasis, schistosomiasis, leishmaniasis
- Viral infections: human immunodeficiency virus, cytomegalovirus, mononucleosis

Infiltrative Diseases and Tumors or Cysts
- Acute and chronic leukemia
- Amyloidosis
- Gaucher disease
- Lymphomas
- Polycythemia vera
- Other primary or secondary tumors and cysts
- Sarcoidosis

Mild splenic enlargement occurs with HF and SLE. The normal spleen holds 350 mL of blood. About one third of the platelet mass is stored in the spleen.

When the spleen enlarges, its normal filtering and storage capacity increases. Consequently, there is often a reduction in the number of circulating blood cells as they engorge the spleen. In addition, there are unusual findings in the peripheral smear, such as pitted or pocked RBCs or Howell-Jolly bodies. These findings aid in diagnosing a malfunctioning spleen. A slight to moderate enlargement of the spleen is usually asymptomatic and found during routine examination of the abdomen. While massive splenomegaly can be well tolerated, the patient may have abdominal discomfort and early satiety. Other techniques to assess the size of the spleen include radionuclide colloid liver-spleen scan, CT or PET scan, MRI, and ultrasound scan.[3]

Occasionally a splenectomy is done as part of the evaluation or treatment of splenomegaly. Another major reason for splenectomy is splenic rupture. The spleen may rupture from trauma; inadvertent tearing during other surgical procedures; and diseases, such as mononucleosis, malaria, and lymphoid tumors. After a splenectomy, there can be a dramatic increase in peripheral RBC, WBC, and platelet counts.

Nursing responsibilities for patients with spleen disorders vary depending on the problem. Splenomegaly may be painful. The patient may need analgesics; care in moving, turning, and positioning; and evaluation of lung expansion because spleen enlargement may impair diaphragmatic excursion. If anemia, thrombocytopenia, or leukopenia develops from splenic enlargement, institute nursing measures to support the patient and prevent life-threatening complications. After a splenectomy, observe the patient for hemorrhage and shock.

After splenectomy, immunologic deficiencies may develop, such as low IgG levels. Patients have a lifelong risk for infection, especially from encapsulated organisms, such as *Pneumococcus* species. This risk is reduced by immunization with pneumococcal vaccine.[3]

BLOOD COMPONENT THERAPY

Blood component therapy is often used to manage hematologic diseases. Many therapeutic and surgical procedures depend on blood product support. However, blood component therapy only temporarily supports the patient until the underlying problem is resolved. Because transfusions are not free from hazards, they should be used only if needed.

Avoid developing a complacent attitude about this common but potentially dangerous therapy. Make sure that the HCP has discussed the risks, benefits, and alternatives with the patient and that this is recorded in the medical record.

Traditionally, the term *blood transfusion* meant the administration of whole blood. Blood transfusion now has a broader meaning because of the ability to give specific components of blood, such as platelets, packed RBCs, or plasma. Usually, a specific component is ordered. Whole blood is rarely used except in cases of massive hemorrhage, severe coagulopathy, shock, or in military settings (Table 30.31). [1]

Administration Procedure

Blood components may be given through a 22-gauge IV needle, cannula, or catheter. Smaller gauges, such as 25-gauge, may be used in neonates.[39] Larger sizes (e.g., 18- or 16-gauge) in adults may be preferred if rapid transfusions are given or if the

ETHICAL/LEGAL DILEMMAS
Religious Beliefs

Situation

W.D., an 81-yr-old woman with dementia, is transferred from a nursing home to a hospital because of GI bleeding from an unknown cause. Some of her family members tell you that she is a Jehovah's Witness and must not receive blood products. If she does not have exploratory surgery and transfusions, the surgeon believes that she will die.

Ethical/Legal Points for Consideration

- Competent adults have the right to make health care decisions, including the right to refuse treatment, based on their religious beliefs.
- If the patient is determined to be incompetent and a guardian has been appointed, the guardian has the legal right to make the consent or refusal.
- If the HCP believes that the treatment is essential to preserve life and health and there is no legal decision maker, a request is made for a legal determination of whether the patient is incapable of consent or refusal. If the judge agrees, the patient is made a ward of the court for this issue. Usually the HCP is directed to make a decision based on the patient's best interests.

Discussion Questions

1. What resources do you have available to consult about religious practices?
2. How could you determine if the family were acting in W.D.'s best interest or their own?
3. What nonblood alternatives are available for Jehovah's Witnesses?

infusion is sluggish. Smaller needles can be used for platelets, albumin, and clotting factor replacement. Verify the patency of the venous access before requesting the blood component from the blood bank. Most blood product administration tubing is of a "Y type" with a macroaggregate filter (170 to 260 microns; filters out particulate). One arm of the Y is for the isotonic saline solution and the other arm of the Y for the blood product. You may use infusion pumps or syringes approved for blood administration according to agency policy.[39]

! SAFETY ALERT Blood Transfusions

- Do not use dextrose solutions, lactated Ringer's solution, or any other solution other than 0.9% sodium chloride for giving blood because they will cause RBC hemolysis.
- Exceptions to the above restrictions may be appropriate, such as in trauma situations. These solutions, approved by the FDA, include ABO-compatible plasma and 5% albumin. Follow agency policy.[39]
- Do not give any additives, including medications, in the same tubing as the blood unless you first clear the tubing with saline solution.

After obtaining the blood or blood components from the blood bank, make a positive identification of the blood product and recipient. Improper product-to-patient identification is the most common cause of hemolytic transfusion reactions, thus placing a great responsibility on nurses to carry out the identification procedure appropriately. Follow the policy and procedures at your agency. Most have a dual-checking system with 2 licensed persons checking the patient identification with the labeled blood component. The blood bank is responsible for typing and crossmatching the donor's blood with the recipient's blood. The result of any needed compatibility testing should be on the product bag or tag.

Table 30.32 outlines blood component compatibilities for transfusions.[37,39] ABO compatibility is not a prerequisite for platelet transfusions. However, after multiple platelet

TABLE 30.31 **Common Blood Products**

Description	Special Considerations	Indications for Use
Albumin Prepared from plasma. Can be stored for 5 yr. Available in 5% or 25% solution. Heat treated and does not transmit viruses.	Albumin 25% expands the blood volume by about 3.5 times. Hyperosmolar solution acts by moving water from extravascular to intravascular space.	Hypovolemic shock, hypoalbuminemia, after large-volume paracentesis, replacement in plasmapheresis.
Cryoprecipitates and Commercial Concentrates Prepared from fresh frozen plasma. 10–15 mL/bag. Can be stored for 1 yr. Once thawed, must be used within 5 days.	See also Table 30.18.	Replacement for fibrinogen deficiency, usually due to DIC, severe liver disease, or massive transfusion. Has other clotting factors, especially factor VIII, factor XIII, and von Willebrand factor.
Fresh Frozen Plasma Liquid portion of whole blood is separated from cells and frozen. 1 unit contains about 250 mL. Rich in clotting factors but contains no platelets. Can be stored for up to 1 yr, depending on storage. Must be used within 24 hr after thawing.	Use in treating hemorrhagic shock is being replaced by pure preparations, such as albumin and plasma expanders.	Bleeding caused by deficiency in clotting factors (e.g., DIC, hemorrhage, massive transfusion, liver disease, vitamin K deficiency, excess warfarin).
Frozen RBCs Prepared from RBCs using glycerol for protection and frozen. Can be stored for 10 yr.	Must be used within 24 hr of thawing. Successive washings with saline solution remove most WBCs and plasma proteins.	Autotransfusion. Stockpiling or rare donors for patients with alloantibodies.
Packed RBCs Prepared from whole blood by sedimentation or centrifugation. 1 unit contains 250–350 mL. Can be stored up to 42 days depending on processing (anticoagulants and preservatives).	Use of RBCs for treatment allows remaining components of blood (e.g., platelets, albumin, plasma) to be used for other purposes. Less danger of fluid overload. Preferred RBC source because they are more component specific. Leukocyte depletion (leukoreduction) by filtration, washing, or freezing is frequently used. Decreases non-hemolytic febrile or mild allergic reactions in patients who receive frequent transfusions. Reduces transmission of cytomegalovirus.	Severe or symptomatic anemia, acute blood loss. 1 unit of RBCs can be expected to increase Hgb by 1 g/dL or Hct by 3% in a typical adult. 1 unit can replace a blood loss of 500 mL.
Platelets Prepared from fresh whole blood. An apheresed single donation is usually 200–400 mL in volume. May be pooled from multiple donors.	Can obtain multiple units from 1 donor by plateletpheresis. Can be kept at room temperature in the blood bank under gentle agitation for 1–5 days depending on type of collection and storage bag used. For patients who receive frequent transfusions and become refractory, may give leukocyte reduced, HLA, or type specific to prevent alloimmunization to HLA antigens.	Bleeding caused by thrombocytopenia. May be contraindicated in thrombotic thrombocytopenic purpura and HITT except in life-threatening hemorrhage. Average corrected count increment is 10×10^9/L. Failure to have an increase may be due to fever, sepsis, splenomegaly, or DIC or development of antibodies *(refractory)*.

DIC, Disseminated intravascular coagulation; *HITT,* heparin-induced thrombocytopenia and thrombosis; *HLA,* human leukocyte antigen.

TABLE 30.32 **Blood Component Compatibilities for Transfusions**

Recipient's Type	DONOR PRODUCT			
	Packed Red Blood Cells	Plasma	Platelets	Cryoprecipitate
O+	O+, O–	All groups	O, B, A, AB	Any group is safe to transfuse
O–	O–			
A+	A+, A–, O+, O–	A, AB	A, AB, B, O	
A–	A–, O–			
B+	B+, B–, O+, O–	B, AB	B, AB, A, O	
B–	B–, O–			
AB+	All groups	Only AB	Any group	
AB–	AB–, B–, A–, O–			

transfusions, a patient may develop anti-HLA antibodies to the transfused platelets. With the use of lymphocyte typing to match HLA types of the donor and recipient, multiple platelet transfusions can be given with fewer complications to those who develop antibodies to platelets. The patient may be premedicated with an antihistamine (e.g., diphenhydramine) and hydrocortisone to decrease the chance of reacting to platelet transfusions if there is a history of reactions.[39]

 NURSING MANAGEMENT

Blood Transfusions

Role of Nursing Personnel
Registered Nurse (RN)
- Complete a baseline physical assessment of the patient as a basis to assess changes during and after the transfusion.
- Ensure that the IV line has an appropriate needle, catheter, or cannula, and that it is patent.
- Double-check patient identification and blood product identification data with another licensed nurse (consider state nurse practice act and agency policy).
- Adjust infusion rate of transfusion according to patient needs, provider's order, and agency policy.
- Assess patient for signs of transfusion reactions.
- Delegate UAP to take vital signs as directed.
- Evaluate for therapeutic effect of blood product (improvement in CBC, increased blood pressure, decreased bleeding).
- Monitor for signs of circulatory overload (e.g., shortness of breath) if the transfusion is given rapidly.

Role of Other Team Members
Blood Bank Personnel
- Responsible for typing and crossmatching the donor's blood with the recipient's blood.
- Note the result of the compatibility testing on the product bag or tag.
- When handing off the blood or blood component to nursing personnel, ensure that a positive identification is made with product and patient's information.

Take the patient's vital signs before beginning the transfusion so that you have a baseline measure. If the patient has abnormal vital signs (e.g., high fever), call the HCP to clarify if you should give the blood component. Start the blood as soon as it is brought to the patient. Do not refrigerate it on the nursing unit. If the blood is not started within 30 minutes, return it to the blood bank for storage. During the first 15 minutes or 50 mL of blood infusion, stay with the patient. If there are any untoward reactions, they are most likely to occur during this time. The rate of infusion during this period should be no more than 2 mL/min. Do not infuse packed RBCs quickly except in an emergency. Rapid infusion of cold blood may cause the patient to become chilled. If rapid replacement of large amounts of blood is needed, a blood-warming device may be used. Other blood components, such as fresh frozen plasma and platelets, may be given over 15 to 30 minutes. Refer to your agency's policy and procedure.

After the first 15 minutes, vital signs are usually retaken. The rate of infusion is determined by the prescriber's orders, the patient's clinical condition, and the product being infused. Observe the patient periodically throughout the transfusion (e.g., every 30 minutes) and up to 1 hour after the transfusion. Most patients not in danger of fluid overload can tolerate the infusion of 1 unit of packed RBCs over 2 hours. The transfusion

should not take more than 4 hours to give because of the increased risk for bacterial growth in the product once it is out of refrigeration.

Blood Transfusion Reactions

A *blood transfusion reaction* is an adverse reaction to blood transfusion therapy. It can range in severity from mild symptoms to a life-threatening condition. Because complications of transfusion therapy may be significant, careful evaluation of the patient is needed. Common signs and symptoms are associated with more than 1 type of adverse reaction. Blood transfusion reactions can be classified as acute or delayed[1,39] (Tables 30.33 and 30.34).

CHECK YOUR PRACTICE

Your 82-yr-old male patient with severe iron-deficiency anemia is receiving his second unit of packed RBCs. He received his first transfusions without any problems. He is now reporting chills and feels like his heart is racing.
- What should you do?

If a transfusion reaction occurs, take the following steps: (1) stop the transfusion; (2) maintain a patent IV line with saline solution; (3) notify the blood bank and the HCP immediately; (4) recheck identifying tags and numbers; (5) monitor vital signs and urine output; (6) treat symptoms per HCP order; (7) save the blood bag and tubing and send them to the blood bank for examination; (8) collect required blood and urine specimens at intervals based on the hospital policy to evaluate for hemolysis; and (9) document on transfusion reaction form and patient chart. The blood bank and laboratory are responsible for identifying the type of reaction.

A transfusion reaction is a *serious reportable event* (SRE) and a *sentinel event*. These events are discussed in Chapter 1.

Acute Transfusion Reactions. The most common cause of hemolytic reactions is transfusion of ABO-incompatible blood (Table 30.33). This is an example of a type II cytotoxic hypersensitivity reaction (see Chapter 13). Severe hemolytic reactions are rare. Mislabeling specimens and giving blood to the wrong person cause most acute hemolytic reactions. This again points to the importance of using proper patient identifiers when drawing blood samples and when giving medications and blood products.

Delayed Transfusion Reactions. Delayed transfusion reactions include delayed hemolytic reactions (discussed previously), infections, and iron overload (Table 30.34).

Autotransfusion

Autotransfusion, or autologous transfusion, involves removing whole blood from a person and transfusing that blood back into the same person. This avoids problems of incompatibility, allergic reactions, and disease transmission. Methods of autotransfusion include:

- *Autologous donation* or *elective phlebotomy* (predeposit transfusion). A person donates blood before a planned surgical procedure. The blood can be frozen and stored for up to 10 years. Usually the blood is stored without being frozen and given to the person within a few weeks of donation. This technique is especially beneficial to the patient with a rare blood type or for any patient who may be expected to need limited blood product support during a major surgical procedure (e.g., elective orthopedic surgery).

TABLE 30.33 Acute Transfusion Reactions

Cause	Manifestations	Management	Prevention
Acute Hemolytic Reaction			
Infusion of ABO-incompatible whole blood, RBCs, or components containing as little as 10 mL of RBCs. Antibodies in the recipient's plasma attach to antigens on transfused RBCs, causing RBC destruction.	Reactions usually develop in first 15 min. Fever with or without chills; back, abdominal, chest or flank pain; infusion site pain, tachycardia, dyspnea, tachypnea, hypotension, hemoglobinuria, acute jaundice, dark urine, bleeding, acute kidney injury, shock, cardiac arrest, DIC, death.	• Treat shock and DIC if present. • Draw blood samples for serologic testing slowly to avoid hemolysis from the procedure. Send urine specimen to the laboratory. • Maintain BP with IV colloid solutions. Give diuretics as prescribed to maintain urine flow. • Insert indwelling urinary catheter or measure voided amounts to monitor hourly urine output. Dialysis may be needed if renal failure occurs. • Do not transfuse more RBC-containing components until blood bank has provided newly crossmatched units.	Verify and document patient identification from sample collection to component infusion (e.g., visually compare label on sample collection and blood component with patient identification).
Febrile, Nonhemolytic Reaction			
Sensitization to donor WBCs (most common), platelets, or plasma proteins.	Sudden chills, rigors, and fever (rise in temperature of >1°C), headache, vomiting.	Give antipyretics as prescribed (acetaminophen). Do not restart transfusion unless HCP orders.	Consider leukocyte-reduced blood products (filtered, washed, or frozen) for patients with a history of 2 or more such reactions. Give acetaminophen or diphenhydramine 30 min before transfusion.
Mild Allergic Reaction			
Sensitivity to foreign plasma proteins. More common in people with history of allergies.	Flushing, itching, pruritus, urticaria (hives).	• Give antihistamine, corticosteroid, epinephrine, as ordered. • If symptoms are mild and transient, transfusion may be restarted slowly with HCP's order. • Do not restart transfusion if fever or pulmonary symptoms develop.	Treat prophylactically with antihistamines or steroids. Consider washed RBCs and platelets.
Anaphylactic and Severe Allergic Reaction			
Sensitivity to donor plasma proteins. Infusion of IgA proteins to IgA-deficient recipient who has developed IgA antibody.	Anxiety, abdominal pain, urticaria, dyspnea, wheezing, progressing to cyanosis, bronchospasm, hypotension, shock, and possible cardiac arrest.	• Start CPR, if indicated. Administer O_2. • Have epinephrine ready for injection. • Antihistamines, corticosteroids, β_2-agonists may be given. • Do not restart transfusion.	Transfuse extensively washed RBC products from which all plasma has been removed. Use blood from IgA-deficient donor. Use autologous components.
Circulatory Overload Reaction			
Fluid given faster than the circulation can accommodate. People with cardiac or renal disease at risk.	Cough, dyspnea, pulmonary congestion, adventitious breath sounds, headache, hypertension, tachycardia, distended neck veins.	• Place patient upright with feet in dependent position. • Obtain chest x-ray STAT if ordered. • Administer prescribed diuretics, O_2, morphine.	Adjust transfusion volume and flow rate based on patient size and clinical status. Have blood bank divide future units into smaller aliquots for better spacing of fluid infused.
Sepsis			
Transfusion of bacterially infected blood components.	Rapid onset of chills, rigors, high fever, vomiting, diarrhea, marked hypotension, or shock.	• Obtain culture of patient's blood. • Treat septicemia as directed—antibiotics, IV fluids, vasopressors,	Collect, process, store, and transfuse blood products according to blood banking standards and complete the transfusion within 4 hr of starting time.
Transfusion-Related Acute Lung Injury (TRALI) Reaction			
Reaction between transfused antileukocyte antibodies and recipient's leukocytes, causing pulmonary inflammation and capillary leak.	Fever, chills, hypotension, tachypnea, frothy sputum, dyspnea, hypoxemia, respiratory failure. Noncardiogenic pulmonary edema. Leading cause of transfusion-related deaths. Arises within 1–6 hr of transfusion.	• Draw blood for arterial blood gases and HLA or antileukocyte antibodies. Obtain chest x-ray STAT. • Provide O_2 and administer corticosteroids (diuretics of no value) as ordered. • Start CPR if needed and provide ventilatory and BP support if needed.	Provide leukocyte-reduced products. Identify donors who are implicated in TRALI reactions and do not allow them to donate.

TABLE 30.33 Acute Transfusion Reactions—cont'd

Cause	Manifestations	Management	Prevention
Massive Blood Transfusion Reaction			
Can occur with replacement of 10 or more RBC units within 24 hr. RBC transfusions do not contain clotting factors, albumin, and platelets.	Hypothermia and cardiac dysrhythmias (from rapid infusion of large quantities of cold blood). Citrate toxicity and hypocalcemia (from the use of citrate as a storage solution). Hypocalcemia (citrate binds calcium). Hyperkalemia or hypokalemia.	• When patients receive massive transfusions of blood products, monitor clotting status and electrolyte levels.	Use blood-warming equipment. Infuse 10% calcium gluconate with citrated blood products. Because of dilution effect on coagulation due to massive RBC transfusion, platelets and plasma will also be given.

DIC, disseminated intravascular coagulation; *HLA*, human leukocyte antigen; *IgA*, immunoglobulin A.

TABLE 30.34 Delayed Transfusion Reactions

Manifestations	Prevention and Management
Delayed Hemolytic	
Fever, mild jaundice, decreased hemoglobin. Occurs as early as 3 days or as late as several months posttransfusion as the result of destruction of transfused RBCs by alloantibodies not detected during crossmatch.	Generally, no acute treatment is needed. Hemolysis may be severe enough to warrant further transfusions.
Hepatitis B*	
Increased liver enzymes (AST and ALT), anorexia, malaise, nausea and vomiting, fever, dark urine, jaundice. Usually resolves spontaneously within 4–6 wk. Chronic carrier state can develop and result in permanent damage to the liver.	Hepatitis B virus can be detected in donated blood by the presence of hepatitis B surface antigen (HBsAg). Treat symptomatically.
Hepatitis C*	
Similar to hepatitis B, but symptoms are usually less severe. Chronic liver disease and cirrhosis may develop.	Before testing of anti-HCV in donated blood, accounted for 90%–95% of all posttransfusion hepatitis. Treat with direct-acting antivirals and symptomatically.
Iron Overload	
Excess iron is deposited in heart, liver, pancreas, and joints, causing dysfunction. HF, dysrhythmias, impaired thyroid and gonadal function, diabetes, arthritis, cirrhosis. Occurs in patients receiving >20 units for chronic anemia (e.g., sickle cell anemia, β-thalassemia) over time.	May be prevented by deferoxamine, which chelates and removes accumulated iron via the kidneys, given IV or subcutaneously. Deferasirox and deferiprone, oral agents that chelate iron, may be used. Phlebotomy may be used.
Other	
Cytomegalovirus (CMV), HIV, human herpesvirus type 6 (HSV-6), Epstein-Barr virus (EBV), human T cell leukemia virus, HTLV-1, and malaria. Most recent threats have been agents that primarily affect animals but have been transmitted to the blood supply through the food supply, or vectors, such as mosquitoes or ticks. These include *Plasmodium* species (malaria), dengue fever virus, West Nile virus, *Trypanosoma cruzi* (Chagas' disease), *Babesia* species (babesiosis), human herpesvirus 8 (KS virus), and variant Creutzfeldt-Jakob disease ("mad cow disease").	Treatment based on the cause. Ways of detecting some agents are now used, such as the nucleic acid test for West Nile virus, Zika virus, HIV, and *T. cruzi*. Donor screening has been the only available method to reduce the risk for donor-contaminated blood for others. Leukocyte-reduced components may reduce virus transmission. Patients may be monitored serologically (e.g., CMV titers are followed for allogeneic stem cell transplant patients).

*New cases of transfusion-related hepatitis B and C are not common.
ALT, Alanine aminotransferase; *AST*, aspartate aminotransferase; *HCV*, hepatitis C virus; *CMV*, cytomegalovirus; *HTLV-1*, human T-cell leukemia virus, type 1; *KS*, Kaposi sarcoma.

- *Autotransfusion.* A method for replacing blood volume that involves safely and aseptically collecting, filtering, and returning the patient's own blood lost during a major surgical procedure or from a traumatic injury. It is an important way to safely replace volume and stabilize bleeding patients. Autotransfusion collection devices are most often used with surgery. Some allow blood to be automatically and continuously reinfused. Others require collecting the blood for a time (usually no longer than 4 hours) and then reinfusing it. Drainage after the first 24 hours or drainage that is suspected to contain pathogens is generally not reinfused. Anticoagulants may be added before reinfusion. Clots that develop after blood is filtered through the collection system can sometimes prevent reinfusion of the blood. Sometimes the collected blood is depleted of its normal coagulation factors. So, monitoring coagulation studies in the patient receiving an autotransfusion is important.[1]

CASE STUDY
Leukemia

(© Lisa F. Young/iStock.)

Patient Profile

A.J. is a 63-yr-old white woman who is brought to the ED by her husband (see the Chapter 29 case study). She has become progressively weaker and was admitted for further evaluation.

Subjective Data
- Progressive weakness over the last couple of weeks
- Has had a recent sinus infection that resolved after 2 courses of antibiotics
- Reports periodic shortness of breath
- Has noticed a lot of bruising lately

Objective Data
Physical Examination
- Has scattered petechiae on both ankles and 2 ecchymoses on her arms and 3 on her left lower leg
- Her skin is very pale
- BP 100/70 (lying), 88/60 (standing), temperature 96.8°F (36°C), respiratory rate 26/min, apical pulse 110/min (lying), 124/min (standing), O_2 saturation 90% on room air

Laboratory Results
- Hct 18.2%
- Hgb 5.9 g/dL, WBC count 2600/µL (2.6 × 10⁹/L)
- Platelet count 72,000/µL (72 × 10⁹/L)
- Peripheral blood smear shows that 80% of the WBCs are blasts
- PT 18 sec, aPTT 37 sec
- LDH 560 units/L

Bone Marrow Biopsy
- Multiple myeloblasts (>50%)

Interprofessional Care
- Consultation with a hematologist-oncologist
- 2 units of packed red blood cells
- *Diagnosis:* acute myelogenous leukemia

Discussion Questions
1. What components of the laboratory test results and bone marrow biopsy suggest acute leukemia?
2. How is acute myelogenous leukemia treated?
3. What is A.J.'s prognosis?
4. What are the life-threatening problems that can occur because of this disease and treatment? How can you anticipate and assess for these problems?
5. ***Priority Decision:*** Based on the assessment data presented, what are the priority nursing diagnoses? Are there any collaborative problems?
6. ***Priority Decision:*** What are the priority nursing interventions for A.J.?
7. ***Patient-Centered Care:*** What are the priorities for patient teaching with a newly diagnosed adult with leukemia?
8. Collaboration: What members of the interprofessional team are likely to be involved in A.J.'s care?
9. ***Evidence-Based Practice:*** A.J. becomes fatigued after starting chemotherapy. She wants to know if she can still work and do household chores even if she is so fatigued. What is your best advice for her?
10. Develop a conceptual care map for A.J.

Answers available at *http://evolve.elsevier.com/Lewis/medsurg.*

▋ B R I D G E   T O   N C L E X   E X A M I N A T I O N

The number of the question corresponds to the same-numbered outcome at the beginning of the chapter.

1. In a severely anemic patient, the nurse would expect to find
   a. cyanosis and cardiomegaly.
   b. pulmonary edema and fibrosis.
   c. dyspnea at rest and tachycardia.
   d. ventricular dysrhythmias and wheezing.

2. When obtaining assessment data from a patient with a microcytic, hypochromic anemia, the nurse would ask the patient about
   a. folic acid intake.
   b. dietary intake of iron.
   c. a history of gastric surgery.
   d. a history of sickle cell anemia.

3. Nursing interventions for a patient with severe anemia related to peptic ulcer disease include (*select all that apply*)
   a. instructions for high-iron diet.
   b. taking vital signs every 8 hours.
   c. monitoring stools for occult blood.
   d. teaching self-injection of erythropoietin.
   e. administration of cobalamin (vitamin B₁₂) injections.

4. The nursing management of a patient in sickle cell crisis includes (*select all that apply*)
   a. monitoring CBC.
   b. optimal pain management and O_2 therapy.
   c. blood transfusions if needed and iron chelation.
   d. rest as needed and deep vein thrombosis prophylaxis.
   e. administration of IV iron and diet high in iron content.

5. A complication of the hyperviscosity of polycythemia is
   a. thrombosis.
   b. cardiomyopathy.
   c. pulmonary edema.
   d. disseminated intravascular coagulation (DIC).

6. When caring for a patient with thrombocytopenia, the nurse instructs the patient to
   a. dab his or her nose instead of blowing.
   b. be careful when shaving with a safety razor.
   c. continue with physical activities to stimulate thrombopoiesis.
   d. avoid aspirin because it may mask the fever that occurs with thrombocytopenia.

7. The nurse would expect that a patient with von Willebrand disease undergoing surgery would be treated with administration of vWF and
   a. thrombin.
   b. factor VI.
   c. factor VII.
   d. factor VIII.

8. DIC is a disorder in which
   a. the coagulation pathway is genetically altered, leading to thrombus formation in all major blood vessels.
   b. an underlying disease depletes hemolytic factors in the blood, leading to diffuse thrombotic episodes and infarcts.
   c. a disease process stimulates coagulation processes with resultant thrombosis, as well as depletion of clotting factors, leading to diffuse clotting and hemorrhage.
   d. an inherited predisposition causes a deficiency of clotting factors that leads to overstimulation of coagulation processes in the vasculature.

9. Priority nursing actions when caring for a hospitalized patient with a new-onset temperature of 102.2°F (39°C) and severe neutropenia include *(select all that apply)*
   a. starting the prescribed antibiotic STAT.
   b. drawing peripheral and central line blood cultures.
   c. ongoing monitoring of the patient's vital signs for septic shock.
   d. taking a full set of vital signs and notifying the physician immediately.
   e. administering transfusions of WBCs treated to decrease immunogenicity.

10. Because myelodysplastic syndrome arises from the pluripotent hematopoietic stem cell in the bone marrow, laboratory results the nurse would expect to find include a(n)
    a. excess of T cells.
    b. excess of platelets.
    c. deficiency of granulocytes.
    d. deficiency of all cellular blood components.

11. The most common type of leukemia in adults in western countries is
    a. acute myelocytic leukemia.
    b. acute lymphocytic leukemia.
    c. chronic myelocytic leukemia.
    d. chronic lymphocytic leukemia.

12. Multiple drugs are often used in combinations to treat leukemia and lymphoma because
    a. there are fewer toxic and side effects.
    b. the chance that one drug will be effective is increased.
    c. the drugs are more effective without causing side effects.
    d. the drugs work by different mechanisms to maximize killing of cancer cells.

13. The nurse is aware that a major difference between Hodgkin's lymphoma and non-Hodgkin's lymphoma is that
    a. Hodgkin's lymphoma occurs only in young adults.
    b. Hodgkin's lymphoma is considered potentially curable.
    c. non-Hodgkin's lymphoma can manifest in multiple areas.
    d. non-Hodgkin's lymphoma is treated only with radiation therapy.

14. A patient with multiple myeloma becomes confused and lethargic. The nurse would expect that these clinical manifestations may be explained by diagnostic results that indicate
    a. hyperkalemia.
    b. hyperuricemia.
    c. hypercalcemia.
    d. CNS myeloma.

15. When reviewing a patient's hematologic laboratory values after a splenectomy, the nurse would expect to find
    a. RBC abnormalities.
    b. increased WBC count.
    c. decreased hemoglobin.
    d. decreased platelet count.

16. Complications of transfusions that can be decreased by using leukocyte depletion or reduction of RBC transfusion are
    a. chills and hemolysis.
    b. leukostasis and neutrophilia.
    c. fluid overload and pulmonary edema.
    d. transmission of cytomegalovirus and fever.

12. d, 13. c, 14. c, 15. b, 16. d
1. c, 2. b, 3. a, c, 4. a, b, c, d, 5. a, 6. a, 7. d, 8. c, 9. a, b, c, d, 10. d, 11. d,

For rationales to these answers and even more NCLEX review questions, visit *http://evolve.elsevier.com/Lewis/medsurg.*

EVOLVE WEBSITE/RESOURCES LIST

http://evolve.elsevier.com/Lewis/medsurg
Review Questions (Online Only)
Key Points
Answer Keys for Review Questions
- Rationales for Bridge to NCLEX Examination Questions
- Answer Guidelines for Case Study on p. 652
- Answer Guidelines for Managing Care of Multiple Patients Case Study (Section 7) on p. 655
Student Case Studies
- Patient With Chronic Myelogenous Leukemia Including End-of-life Care
- Patient With Sickle Cell Anemia
Nursing Care Plans
- eNursing Care Plan 30.1: Patient With Anemia
- eNursing Care Plan 30.2: Patient With Thrombocytopenia
- eNursing Care Plan 30.3: Patient With Neutropenia
Conceptual Care Map Creator
- Conceptual Care Map for Case Study on p. 652
Audio Glossary
Content Updates

REFERENCES

1. Hoffman R, Benz EJ, Silberstein LE, et al: *Hematology: Basic principles and practice*, ed 7, Philadelphia, 2018, Elsevier.
2. Huether SE, McCance KL: *Understanding pathophysiology*, ed 6, St Louis, 2017, Mosby.
3. Lichtman MA, Kaushansky K, Prchal JT, et al: *Williams manual of hematology*, ed 9, New York, 2017, McGraw-Hill.
4. World Health Organization. Anemia policy brief. Retrieved from *www.who.int/nutrition/topics/globaltargets_anaemia_policybrief.pdf.*
*5. Green R, Mitra AD: Megaloblastic anemias: Nutritional and other causes, *Med Clin N Am* 101:297, 2017.
*6. Fraenkel PG: Anemia of inflammation: A review, *Med Clin N Am* 101:285, 2017.
*7. Kumar R, Bonfim C, George B: Hematopoietic cell transplantation for aplastic anemia, *Curr Opin Hematol* 24:509, 2017.
*8. Thein MS, Igbineweka NE, Thein SL: Sickle cell disease in the older adult, *Pathology* 49:1, 2017.
9. Centers for Disease Control: Sickle cell disease. Retrieved from *www.cdc.gov/ncbddd/sicklecell/data.html.*
*10. National Heart, Lung, and Blood Institute. Evidence-based management of sickle cell disease: Expert panel report. Retrieved from: *www.nhlbi.nih.gov/health-topics/evidence-based-management-sickle-cell-disease.*
*11. Wilmore DW: FDA approval of glutamine for sickle cell disease, *J Parenter Enteral Nutr* 41:912, 2017.
*12. Zhang K, Lu Y, Harley KT, et al: Atypical hemolytic uremic syndrome: A brief review, *Hematol Reports* 9:7053, 2017.
13. The National Institute of Diabetes and Digestive and Kidney Diseases: Hemochromatosis. Retrieved from *www.niddk.nih.gov/health-information/liver-disease/hemochromatosis.*

*14. Mesa R, Jamieson C, Bhatia R, et al: Myeloproliferative neoplasms, NCCN clinical practice guidelines, version 2.2018. Retrieved from *www.nccn.org.*

*15. Sverdlin D, Peters-Watral B: Atypical hemolytic uremic syndrome, *Clin J Oncol Nurs* 21:481, 2017.

*16. Lambert MP, Gernsheimer TB: Clinical updates in adult immune thrombocytopenia, *Blood* 129:2829, 2017.

*17. Arepally GM: Heparin-induced thrombocytopenia, *Blood* 129:2864, 2017.

18. National Hemophila Foundation. Retrieved from *www.hemophilia.org.*

19. Castaman G, Linari S: Diagnosis and treatment of von Willebrand Disease and rare bleeding disorders, *J Clin Med* 6:45, 2017.

20. Squizzato A, Hunt BJ, Kinasewitz GT, et al: Supportive management strategies for disseminated intravascular coagulation, *Thromb Haemost* 115:896, 2016.

21. White L, Ybarra M: Neutropenic fever, *Hematol Oncol Clin N Am* 31:981, 2017.

*22. Freifeld AG, Bow EJ, Sepkowitz KA, et al: Clinical practice guideline for the use of antimicrobial agents in neutropenic patients with cancer: 2010 Update by the Infectious Diseases Society of America, *Clin Infect Dis* 52:e56, 2011. (Classic)

*23. Baden LR, Swaminathan S: Prevention and treatment of cancer-related infections, NCCN clinical practice guidelines, version 1.2018. Retrieved from *www.nccn.org.*

*24. Crawford J, Becker PS: Myeloid growth factors, NCCN clinical practice guidelines, version 2.2017. Retrieved from *www.nccn.org.*

*25. Rhodes A, Evans LE, Alhazzani W, et al: Surviving sepsis campaign: International guidelines for management of sepsis and septic shock: 2016, *Intensive Care Med* 43:304, 2017.

*26. Greenberg PL, Stone RM: Myelodysplastic syndromes, NCCN clinical practice guidelines, version 1.2018. Retrieved from *www.nccn.org.*

27. Siegel RL, Miller KD, Jemal A: Cancer statistics, 2017, *CA Cancer J Clin* 67:7, 2017.

28. The Lymphoma Research Foundation. Adult T-cell leukemia/lymphoma. Retrieved from *www.lymphoma.org.*

*29. O'Donnell MR, Tallman MS: Acute myeloid leukemia, NCCN clinical practice guidelines, version 3.2017. Retrieved from *www.nccn.org.*

*30. Brown PA: Acute lymphoblastic leukemia, NCCN clinical practice guidelines, version 5.2017. Retrieved from *www.nccn.org.*

*31. Radich JP, Deininger M: Chronic myeloid leukemia, NCCN clinical practice guidelines, version 2.2018. Retrieved from *www.nccn.org.*

*32. Wierda WG, Byrd JC: Chronic lymphocytic leukemia/small lymphocytic lymphoma, NCCN clinical practice guidelines, version 2.2018. Retrieved from *www.nccn.org.*

*33. Zelenetz AD, Gordon LI: B-cell lymphomas, NCCN clinical practice guidelines, version 7.2017. Retrieved from *www.nccn.org.*

*34. Hoppe RT, Advani RH: *Hodgkin lymphoma, NCCN clinical practice guidelines, version 1.2018.* Retrieved from *www.nccn.org.*

*35. Horwitz SM, Ansell S: *T-cell lymphomas, NCCN clinical practice guidelines, version 1.2018.* Retrieved from *www.nccn.org.*

*36. Kumar SK, Callander NS: *Multiple myeloma, NCCN clinical practice guidelines, version 3.2018.* Retrieved from *www.nccn.org.*

37. International Myeloma Foundation. Retrieved from *www.nccn.org.*

*38. Bertolotti P, Pierre A, Rome S, et al. Evidence-based guidelines for preventing and managing side effects of multiple myeloma, *Semin Oncol Nurs* 33:332, 2017.

39. Fung MK, Eder AF, Spitalnik SL, et al: *Technical manual: Standards for blood banks and transfusion services,* ed 19, Bethesda, MD, 2017, AABB.

*Evidence-based information for clinical practice.

CASE STUDY
Managing Care of Multiple Patients

You are working on the oncology unit and have been assigned to care for the following 4 patients. You have 1 UAP who is assigned to help you, and there are 2 other RNs on your clinical unit.

Patients

(© Lisa F. Young/iStock.)

A.J. is a 63-yr-old white woman admitted with severe anemia (Hgb 5.9 g/dL and Hct 18.2%). Her WBC count is 2600/μL and platelet count is 72,000/μL. She prefers to take care of herself with "natural therapy" and has not seen an HCP for 5 years. A.J. is having difficulty performing ADLs without having to stop and catch her breath. She received 2 units of RBCs. After a further workup, she is diagnosed with acute myelocytic leukemia (AML). She starts chemotherapy tomorrow.

(© g-stockstudio/ iStock/Thinkstock.)

J.J. is a 52-yr-old white man newly diagnosed with acute lymphocytic leukemia (ALL). His most recent vital signs are BP 100/70, temperature 102.2°F (39°C), respiratory rate 26/min, pulse 110. Laboratory results reveal Hgb 6.9 g/dL, Hct 20%, WBC count 120,000/μL (120 × 10^9/L), and platelet count 25,000/μL (25 × 10^9/L). He is admitted for blood transfusions and induction therapy.

(© Studio Grand Ouest/ iStock/Thinkstock.)

P.H. is a 45-yr-old woman who is currently receiving chemotherapy for treatment of ovarian cancer. She is admitted with fever and chills. Her WBC count is 2200/μL (2.2 × 10^9/L), with an absolute neutrophil count (ANC) of 400/μL (0.4 × 10^9/L). She will begin IV antibiotic therapy. Her most recent vital signs are BP 118/60, temperature 99.2°F (37.3°C), respiratory rate 20/min, pulse 98.

(© Ridofranz/ iStock.)

G.L. is a 67-yr-old man who came to the ED yesterday evening with abdominal pain. A CT scan of the abdomen revealed several masses in his lymphatic system. The HCP suspects non-Hodgkin's lymphoma and admits him for a diagnostic workup. He currently rates his pain as a 3 on a scale of 0 to 10.

Discussion Questions

1. **Priority Decision:** After receiving report, which patient should you see first? Provide a rationale for your decision.
2. **Collaboration:** Which tasks could you delegate to the UAP *(select all that apply)*?
   a. Assist A.J. to a chair after completing her AM care.
   b. Obtain the first unit of blood for J.J. from the blood bank.
   c. Explain the importance of isolation to P.H. and her family.
   d. Ask A.J. why she has not received regular medical care for 5 years.
   e. Assess G.L. for other clinical manifestations of non-Hodgkin's lymphoma.

3. **Priority and Delegation Decision:** When you enter J.J.'s room, you find him somewhat confused and lethargic. His family states he had just had a severe coughing episode. What initial action would be the *most* appropriate?
   a. Perform a focused neurologic examination.
   b. Call respiratory therapy to give him a breathing treatment.
   c. Have the UAP stay with J.J. while you page the HCP STAT.
   d. Ask his family members if they have a copy of his living will.

Case Study Progression

J.J.'s HCP orders a repeat CBC and an emergency CT scan of the head. Your supervisor makes arrangements for another RN to accompany J.J. to the CT scan while you prepare to administer the first unit of RBCs.

4. The HCP orders ferrous sulfate 325 mg TID for A.J. You teach A.J. to take her iron *(select all that apply)*
   a. at breakfast time in the morning.
   b. with orange juice to increase absorption.
   c. 1 hour before meals to facilitate absorption.
   d. 2 hours after eating to minimize side effects.
   e. whenever she feels tired or is short of breath with activity.
5. When teaching P.H.'s family about neutropenic precautions, you stress that the *most* important intervention to prevent infection is
   a. hand hygiene.
   b. wearing a mask.
   c. keeping P.H. in a private room.
   d. limiting the number of visitors in her room.
6. G.L. asks you to explain the diagnostic testing he can expect to undergo related to the suspected lymphoma. Which tests will you explain to him *(select all that apply)*?
   a. PET scan
   b. Bone marrow biopsy
   c. Peripheral blood smear
   d. Excisional lymph node biopsy
   e. Lymphangiography of internal lymph nodes
7. **Management Decision:** An RN from the float pool arrives to accompany J.J. to CT scan at the same time the UAP arrives with the first unit of packed RBCs. Which intervention would be *most* appropriate?
   a. Put the unit of RBCs in the refrigerator to start when J.J. returns to the floor.
   b. Ask the RN to verify the correct unit of RBCs with you and start the infusion.
   c. Give the RN an SBAR report and ask her to start the blood on the way to CT scan.
   d. Ask the RN if she would prefer to give the blood or hold it for J.J.'s return to the unit.

Answers available at *http://evolve.elsevier.com/Lewis/medsurg*.

31

Assessment: Cardiovascular System

Debra Hagler and Diana Rabbani Hagler

The purpose of human life is to serve, and to show compassion and the will to help others.

Albert Schweitzer

ℯ http://evolve.elsevier.com/Lewis/medsurg/

CONCEPTUAL FOCUS

Health Promotion
Nutrition

Perfusion

LEARNING OUTCOMES

1. Discern the anatomic location and function of the pericardial layers, atria, ventricles, and valves.
2. Relate the coronary circulation to the areas of heart muscle supplied by the major coronary arteries.
3. Distinguish the structure and function of arteries, veins, capillaries, and endothelium.
4. Describe the mechanisms involved in the regulation of blood pressure.
5. Relate the various waveforms on a normal electrocardiogram to the associated cardiac events.
6. Obtain significant subjective and objective assessment data related to the cardiovascular system from a patient and/or caregiver.
7. Perform a physical assessment of the cardiovascular system using the appropriate techniques.
8. Distinguish normal from abnormal findings of a physical assessment of the cardiovascular system.
9. Link the age-related changes of the cardiovascular system to the differences in assessment findings.
10. Describe the purpose, significance of results, and nursing responsibilities related to diagnostic studies of the cardiovascular system.

KEY TERMS

action potential, p. 657
afterload, p. 659
arterial blood pressure, p. 660
cardiac index (CI), p. 658
cardiac output (CO), p. 658
cardiac reserve, p. 659
coronary angiography, p. 675

diastole, p. 657
diastolic blood pressure (DBP), p. 660
ejection fraction (EF), p. 674
heaves, p. 666
Korotkoff sounds, p. 660
mean arterial pressure (MAP), p. 660
murmur, p. 661

point of maximal impulse (PMI), p. 666
preload, p. 659
pulse pressure, p. 660
systole, p. 658
systolic blood pressure (SBP), p. 660

STRUCTURES AND FUNCTIONS OF CARDIOVASCULAR SYSTEM

Heart

Structure. The heart is a 4-chambered hollow muscular organ normally about the size of a fist. It lies within the thorax in the mediastinal space that separates the right and left pleural cavities. The heart is composed of 3 layers: a thin inner lining, the *endocardium;* a layer of muscle, the *myocardium;* and an outer layer, the *epicardium.* The heart is covered by a fibroserous sac called the *pericardium.* This sac consists of 2 layers: the inner *(visceral)* layer of the pericardium (part of the epicardium) and the outer *(parietal)* layer. A small amount of pericardial fluid (around 10 to 15 mL) lubricates the space between the pericardial layers *(pericardial space)* and prevents friction between the surfaces as the heart contracts.

The septum vertically divides the heart. The interatrial septum creates a right and left atrium. The interventricular septum creates a right and left ventricle. The thickness of the wall of each chamber is different. The atrial myocardium is thinner than that

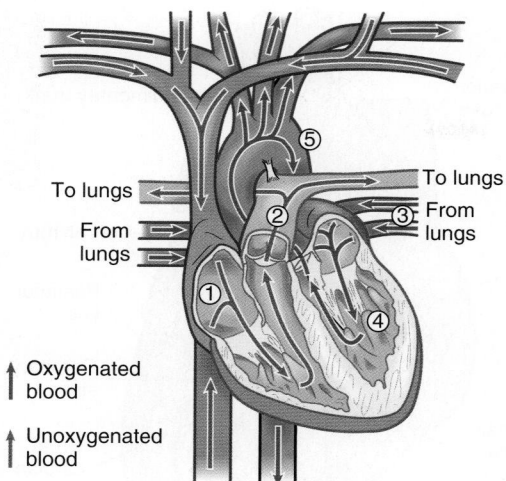

FIG. 31.1 Schematic representation of blood flow through the heart. *Arrows* show direction of flow. *1,* The right atrium receives venous blood from the inferior and superior venae cava and the coronary sinus. The blood then passes through the tricuspid valve into the right ventricle. *2,* With each contraction, the right ventricle pumps blood through the pulmonic valve into the pulmonary artery and to the lungs. *3,* Oxygenated blood flows from the lungs to the left atrium by way of the pulmonary veins. *4,* It then passes through the mitral valve and into the left ventricle. *5,* As the heart contracts, blood is ejected through the aortic valve into the aorta and thus enters the systemic circulation.

of the ventricles. The left ventricular wall is 2 to 3 times thicker than the right ventricular wall. The thickness of the left ventricle is needed to make the force needed to pump the blood into the systemic circulation.[1]

Blood Flow Through Heart. The blood flow through the heart is shown in Fig. 31.1.

Heart Valves. The 4 valves of the heart keep blood flowing in a forward direction. The cusps of the mitral and tricuspid valves are attached to thin strands of fibrous tissue called *chordae tendineae* (Fig. 31.2). Chordae are anchored in the papillary muscles of the ventricles. This support system prevents the eversion of the leaflets into the atria during ventricular contraction. The pulmonic and aortic valves (also known as *semilunar valves*) prevent blood from regurgitating into the ventricles at the end of each ventricular contraction.

Blood Supply to Myocardium. The myocardium has its own blood supply, the *coronary circulation* (Fig. 31.3). Blood flow into the 2 major coronary arteries occurs primarily during diastole (relaxation of the myocardium). The left coronary artery arises from the aorta and divides into 2 main branches: the left anterior descending artery and left circumflex artery. These arteries supply the left atrium, left ventricle, interventricular septum, and part of the right ventricle. The right coronary artery also arises from the aorta, and its branches supply the right atrium, right ventricle, and part of the posterior wall of the left ventricle. In 90% of people, the atrioventricular (AV) node and the bundle of His receive blood supply from the right coronary artery. For this reason, blockage of this artery often causes serious defects in cardiac conduction.

The divisions of coronary veins parallel the coronary arteries. Most of the blood from the coronary system drains into the coronary sinus (a large channel), which empties into the right atrium near the entrance of the inferior vena cava.[1]

Conduction System. The conduction system consists of specialized tissue responsible for creating and transporting the

FIG. 31.2 Anatomic structures of the heart and heart valves.

electrical impulse, or **action potential**. This impulse starts depolarization of the heart cells and leads to heart muscle contraction (Fig. 31.4, *A*). The electrical impulse normally begins in the sinoatrial (SA) node (pacemaker of the heart). Impulses from the SA node travel through interatrial pathways to depolarize the atria, resulting in a contraction.

The electrical impulse travels from the atria to the AV node through internodal pathways. The signal then moves through the bundle of His and the left and right bundle branches. The left bundle branch has 2 divisions: anterior and posterior. The action potential moves through the walls of both ventricles via *Purkinje fibers.* The ventricular conduction system delivers the impulse within 0.12 second. This triggers a synchronized right and left ventricular contraction and ejection of blood into the pulmonary and systemic circulations.

Last, repolarization occurs when the contractile and conduction pathway cells regain their resting polarized condition. Heart muscle cells have a compensatory mechanism that makes them unresponsive or refractory to restimulation during the action potential. During ventricular contraction, there is an *absolute refractory period* during which heart muscle does not respond to any stimuli. After this period, heart muscle gradually recovers its excitability, and a *relative refractory period* occurs by early diastole.

Electrocardiogram. The electrical activity of the heart can be detected on the body surface using electrodes. It is recorded on an electrocardiogram (ECG). We use the letters *P, QRS, T,* and *U* to name the separate waveforms (Fig. 31.4, *B*). The first waveform, the P wave, begins with the firing of the SA node. It represents depolarization of the atria. The QRS complex represents depolarization from the AV node throughout the ventricles. There is a delay of impulse transmission through the AV node that accounts for the time between the beginning of the P wave and the beginning of the QRS wave. The T wave represents repolarization of the ventricles. The U wave, if seen, may represent repolarization of the Purkinje fibers. A large U wave may occur with hypokalemia.[2]

Intervals between these waves (PR, QRS, and QT intervals) reflect the time it takes for the signal to travel from 1 area of the heart to another. We can measure these time intervals. Changes

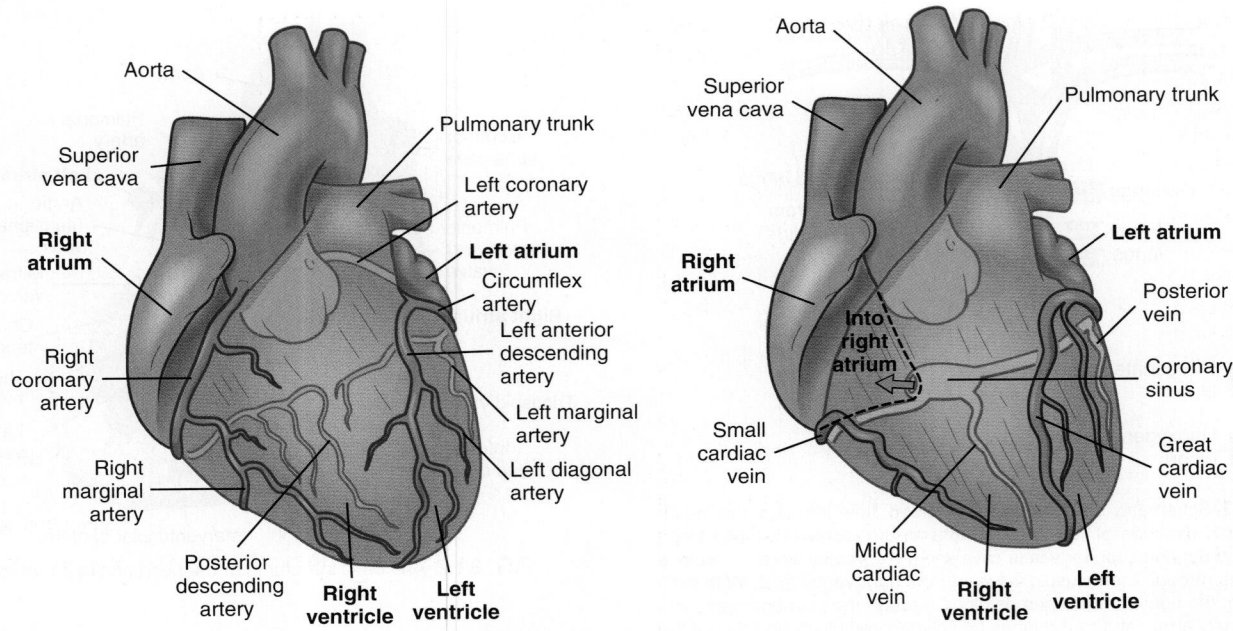

FIG. 31.3 Coronary arteries and veins.

FIG. 31.4 **A,** Conduction system of the heart. *AV,* Atrioventricular; *SA,* sinoatrial. **B,** The normal electrocardiogram (ECG) pattern. The P wave represents depolarization of the atria. The QRS complex indicates depolarization of the ventricles. The T wave represents repolarization of the ventricles. The U wave, if present, may represent repolarization of the Purkinje fibers, or it may be associated with hypokalemia. The PR, QRS, and QT intervals reflect the time it takes for the impulse to travel from one area of the heart to another.

from these time references often indicate pathologic conditions. See Chapter 35 for a complete discussion of ECG monitoring.

Mechanical System. *Depolarization* triggers mechanical activity. **Systole,** contraction of the heart muscle, results in ejection of blood from the ventricles. Relaxation of the heart muscle, *diastole,* allows for filling of the ventricles. **Cardiac output (CO)** is the amount of blood pumped by each ventricle in 1 minute. It is calculated by multiplying the amount of blood ejected from the ventricle with each heartbeat: *stroke volume* (SV) times heart rate (HR) per minute:

$$CO = SV \times HR$$

For the normal adult at rest, CO is maintained in the range of 4 to 8 L/min. **Cardiac index (CI)** is the CO divided by the body surface area (BSA). The CI reflects the relative CO for the body size. The normal CI is 2.8 to 4.2 L per minute per meter squared (L/min/m²).[3]

Factors Affecting Cardiac Output. Numerous factors can affect either the HR or SV and thus the CO. The HR, which is controlled primarily by the autonomic nervous system, can reach as high as 180 beats/min for short periods without harmful effects. With rapid HRs, there is less time for diastolic filling and perfusion of the coronary arteries. The factors affecting the SV are preload, contractility, and afterload. Increasing preload, contractility, and afterload increases the workload of the heart muscle, resulting in increased O_2 demand.

The Frank-Starling law states that, to a point, the more the myocardial fibers are stretched, the greater their force of contraction. The volume of blood stretching the ventricles at the end of diastole, before the next contraction, is called **preload**. Preload can be increased by conditions such as hypertension, aortic valve disease, and hypervolemia. Preload is decreased when a rapid HR or hypovolemia reduces ventricular filling during diastole. Contractility can be increased by epinephrine and norepinephrine released by the sympathetic nervous system. Increasing contractility raises the SV by increasing ventricular emptying. [3]

Afterload is the peripheral resistance against which the left ventricle must pump. Afterload depends on the size of the ventricle, wall tension, and arterial BP. If the arterial BP is elevated, the ventricles meet increased resistance to ejection of blood, increasing the work demand. Eventually this results in *ventricular hypertrophy,* an enlargement of the heart muscle without an increase in CO or the size of chambers. Although we often think of afterload as affecting left heart function, both right and left ventricles work against resistance. The right ventricle pumps against the afterload of pulmonary arterial resistance.

Cardiac Reserve. The cardiovascular system must respond to many situations in health and illness (e.g., exercise, stress, hypovolemia). The ability to respond to these demands by altering CO is termed **cardiac reserve**.

Vascular System

Blood Vessels. The 3 major types of blood vessels are the arteries, veins, and capillaries. Arteries, except for the pulmonary artery, carry oxygenated blood away from the heart. Veins, except for the pulmonary veins, carry deoxygenated blood toward the heart. Small branches of arteries and veins are arterioles and venules, respectively. Blood circulates from the left side of the heart into arteries, arterioles, capillaries, venules, and veins, and then back to the right side of the heart.

Arteries and Arterioles. The arterial system differs from the venous system by the amount and type of tissue that make up arterial walls (Fig. 31.5). The large arteries have thick walls composed mainly of elastic tissue. This elastic property cushions the impact of the pressure created by ventricular contraction and provides recoil that propels blood forward into the circulation. Large arteries contain some smooth muscle. Examples of large arteries are the aorta and pulmonary artery.

Arterioles have more smooth muscle and little elastic tissue. Arterioles serve as the major control of arterial BP and distribution of blood flow. They respond readily to local conditions such as low oxygen (O_2) and increasing levels of carbon dioxide (CO_2) by dilating or constricting.

The innermost lining of the arteries is the endothelium. The endothelium maintains hemostasis, promotes blood flow, and,

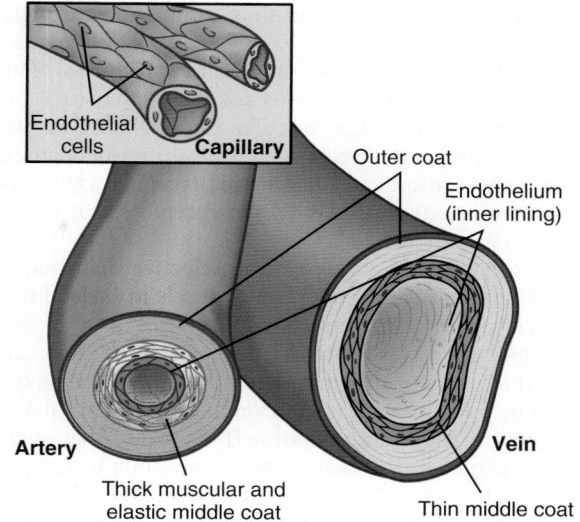

FIG. 31.5 Comparative thickness of layers of the artery, vein, and capillary.

under normal conditions, inhibits blood coagulation. When the endothelial surface is disrupted (e.g., rupture of an atherosclerotic plaque), the coagulation cascade is initiated and results in the formation of a fibrin clot.

Capillaries. The thin capillary wall, made up of endothelial cells, has no elastic or muscle tissue (Fig. 31.5). The exchange of cellular nutrients and metabolic end products takes place through these thin-walled vessels. Capillaries connect the arterioles and venules.

Veins and Venules. Veins are large-diameter, thin-walled vessels that return blood to the right atrium (Fig. 31.5). The venous system is a low-pressure, high-volume system. The larger veins have semilunar valves at intervals to maintain the blood flow toward the heart and to prevent backward flow. The amount of blood in the venous system is affected by several factors. These include arterial flow, compression of veins by skeletal muscles, changes in thoracic and abdominal pressures, and right atrial pressure.

The largest veins are the *superior vena cava,* which returns blood to the heart from the head, neck, and arms, and the *inferior vena cava,* which returns blood to the heart from the lower part of the body. Pressure in the right side of the heart affects these large vessels. Elevated right atrial pressure can cause distended neck veins or liver engorgement because of resistance to blood flow.

Venules are smaller vessels made up of a small amount of muscle and connective tissue. Venules collect blood from the capillary beds and channel it to the larger veins.

Regulation of Cardiovascular System

Autonomic Nervous System. The autonomic nervous system consists of the sympathetic nervous system and parasympathetic nervous system (see Chapter 55).

Effect on Heart. Stimulation of the sympathetic nervous system increases the HR, speed of impulse conduction through the AV node, and force of atrial and ventricular contractions. This effect is mediated by specific sites in the heart called *beta (β)-adrenergic receptors,* which are receptors for norepinephrine and epinephrine.

In contrast, stimulation of the parasympathetic system (mediated by the vagus nerve) slows the HR by decreasing the impulses from the SA node and thus conduction through the AV node.

Effect on Blood Vessels. The source of neural control of blood vessels is the sympathetic nervous system. Alpha$_1$ (α_1)-adrenergic receptors are found in vascular smooth muscles. Stimulation of α_1-adrenergic receptors results in vasoconstriction. Decreased stimulation to α_1-adrenergic receptors causes vasodilation. Sympathetic nervous system receptors that influence BP are described in Table 32.1.

The parasympathetic nerves have selective distribution in the blood vessels. For example, blood vessels in skeletal muscle do not receive parasympathetic input.

Baroreceptors. *Baroreceptors* in the aortic arch and carotid sinus (at the origin of the internal carotid artery) are sensitive to stretch or pressure within the arterial system. Stimulation of these receptors (e.g., volume overload) sends information to the vasomotor center in the brainstem. This results in temporary inhibition of the sympathetic nervous system and enhancement of the parasympathetic influence, causing a decreased HR and peripheral vasodilation. Decreased arterial pressure causes the opposite effect.

Chemoreceptors. *Chemoreceptors* are found in the aortic and carotid bodies and the medulla. They can cause changes in respiratory rate and BP in response to increased arterial CO_2 pressure (hypercapnia) and, to a lesser degree, decreased plasma pH (acidosis) and arterial O_2 pressure (hypoxia). Chemoreceptors in the medulla stimulate the vasomotor center to increase BP.[3]

Blood Pressure

The **arterial blood pressure** is a measure of the pressure exerted by blood against the walls of the arterial system. **The systolic blood pressure (SBP)** is the peak pressure exerted against the arteries when the heart contracts. The **diastolic blood pressure (DBP)** is the residual pressure in the arterial system during ventricular relaxation (or filling).

The main factors influencing BP are CO and *systemic vascular resistance* (SVR):

$$BP = CO \times SVR$$

SVR is the force opposing the movement of blood. This force is created primarily in small arteries and arterioles. Normal BP is SBP <120 mm Hg and DBP <80 mm Hg[4] (see Chapter 32).

Measurement of Arterial Blood Pressure. We can measure BP by using invasive and noninvasive techniques. The invasive technique consists of catheter insertion into an artery. The catheter is attached to a transducer, and the pressure is measured directly (see Chapter 65).

Noninvasive, indirect measurement of BP can be done with a sphygmomanometer and stethoscope. The sphygmomanometer consists of an inflatable cuff and a pressure gauge. The BP is measured by auscultating for sounds of turbulent blood flow through a compressed artery (termed **Korotkoff sounds**). The brachial artery is the recommended site for taking a BP.

After placing the right size cuff on the upper arm, inflate the cuff to a pressure 20 to 30 mm Hg above the SBP. This causes blood flow in the artery to cease. If the SBP is not known, estimate the pressure by palpating the brachial pulse and inflating the cuff until the pulse ceases. The pressure noted at this time is the estimated SBP. Inflate the BP cuff 20 to 30 mm Hg above this number.

As you lower the pressure in the cuff, listen to the artery for Korotkoff sounds. There are 5 phases of Korotkoff sounds. The first phase is a tapping sound caused by the spurt of blood into the constricted artery as the pressure in the cuff is gradually deflated. This sound is the SBP. The fifth phase occurs when the sound disappears, which is the DBP.[5]

BP is recorded as the ratio of SBP to DBP (e.g., 120/80 mm Hg). Sometimes, an *auscultatory gap* occurs, which is a loss of sound between the SBP and DBP. Proper BP technique (e.g., using the correct cuff size, positioning arm at heart level) is essential for correct readings (see Table 32.12).

Another noninvasive way to measure BP indirectly is an automated device that uses oscillometric measurements to assess BP. Though this method does not involve auscultation, the same attention to proper technique is essential for accuracy.

We can assess SBP and pulse using a Doppler ultrasonic flowmeter. The hand-held transducer is positioned over the artery (identified by audible, pulsatile sounds). The cuff is applied above the artery, inflated until the sounds disappear, and then inflated another 20 to 30 mm Hg beyond that point. The cuff is then slowly deflated. The point where sounds return is the SBP.

Pulse Pressure and Mean Arterial Pressure. **Pulse pressure** is the difference between the SBP and DBP. It is normally about one third of the SBP. If the BP is 120/80 mm Hg, the pulse pressure is 40 mm Hg. An increased pulse pressure due to an increased SBP may occur during exercise or in people with atherosclerosis of the larger arteries. A decreased pulse pressure may occur with heart failure (HF) or hypovolemia.

Another measurement related to BP is **mean arterial pressure (MAP)**. The MAP refers to the average pressure within the arterial system that is felt by organs in the body. It is not the average of the DBP and SBP, because the length of diastole exceeds that of systole at normal HRs. MAP is calculated as follows:

$$MAP = (SBP + 2\,DBP) \div 3$$

A person with a BP of 120/60 mm Hg has an estimated MAP of 80 mm Hg. A MAP greater than 60 mm Hg is needed to perfuse the vital organs of an average person under most conditions. When the MAP is low for a period of time, vital organs are underperfused and will become ischemic.

Gerontologic Considerations: Effects of Aging on the Cardiovascular System

One of the greatest risk factors for cardiovascular disease (CVD) is age. CVD is the leading cause of death in adults older than age 65. The most common cardiovascular problem is coronary artery disease (CAD) due to atherosclerosis. Many of the physiologic changes in the cardiovascular system of older adults are a result of the combined effects of the aging process, disease, environmental factors, and lifetime health behaviors rather than just age alone.[6]

Age-related changes in the cardiovascular system and differences in assessment findings are found in Table 31.1. With increased age, the amount of collagen in the heart increases and elastin decreases. These changes affect the heart muscle's ability to stretch and contract.[6] One of the major changes in the cardiovascular system is the response to physical or emotional stress. In times of increased stress, CO and SV decrease due to reduced contractility and HR response. Aging does not really affect the resting supine HR. When the patient changes positions (e.g., sits upright), the sympathetic nerve pathway results in a blunted (reduced) HR response.[7]

TABLE 31.1 Gerontologic Assessment Differences

Cardiovascular System

Changes	Differences in Assessment Findings
Chest Wall	
Kyphosis	Altered chest landmarks for palpation, percussion, and auscultation. Distant heart sounds
Heart	
Myocardial hypertrophy, ↑collagen and scarring, ↓elastin	↓ Cardiac reserve, HF. S₄ may be present
Downward displacement	Difficulty in isolating apical pulse.
↓ CO, HR, SV in response to exercise or stress	↓ Response to exercise and stress. Slowed recovery from activity
Cellular aging and fibrosis of conduction system	↓ Amplitude of QRS complex and slight lengthening of PR, QRS, and QT intervals. Irregular cardiac rhythms, ↓maximal HR, ↓ HR variability
Valvular rigidity from calcification, sclerosis, or fibrosis, impeding complete closure of valves	Systolic murmur (aortic or mitral) possible without a sign of cardiovascular disease
Blood Vessels	
Arterial stiffening caused by loss of elastin in arterial walls, thickening of intima of arteries, and progressive fibrosis of media	↑ In SBP and possible ↑ or ↓ in DBP. Possible widened pulse pressure. Pedal pulses diminished. Intermittent claudication
Venous tortuosity increased	Inflamed, painful, or cordlike varicosities. Dependent edema

Heart valves become thicker and stiffer from lipid accumulation, degeneration of collagen, and fibrosis. The aortic and mitral valves are most often affected. These changes result in either regurgitation of blood when the valve should be closed or narrowing of the orifice of the valve *(stenosis)* when the valve should be open. The turbulent blood flow across the affected valve results in a **murmur**.

Numbers of pacemaker cells in the SA node and conduction cells in the internodal tracts, bundle of His, and bundle branches decrease with age. These changes contribute to the development of sinus and atrial dysrhythmias and heart blocks. Many older adults have an abnormal resting ECG that shows increases in the PR, QRS, and/or QT intervals.[7]

The autonomic nervous system control of the cardiovascular system changes with aging. The number and function of β-adrenergic receptors in the heart decrease with age. So, the older adult not only has a decreased response to physical and emotional stress but also is less sensitive to β-adrenergic agonist drugs. Exercise results in a much smaller increase in CO for older adults than for younger adults.[7]

With age, arteries and veins thicken and become less elastic. Arteries increase their sensitivity to vasopressin (antidiuretic hormone). Both changes increase SBP with a decreased or unchanged DBP, increasing the pulse pressure. Valves in the large leg veins do not return the blood to the heart as effectively, often resulting in dependent edema.[6]

Orthostatic hypotension may be related to drugs and/or decreased baroreceptor function. *Postprandial hypotension*

(decrease in BP of at least 20 mm Hg that occurs within 75 minutes after eating) may occur in otherwise healthy older adults. Both orthostatic and postprandial hypotension may be related to falls in older adults. Despite the changes associated with aging, the heart can function adequately under most circumstances.

CASE STUDY

Patient Introduction

(© Jupiterimages/ Banana-Stock/ Thinkstock.)

L.P., a 63-yr-old Asian American man, is brought to the hospital by ambulance at 6 AM after reporting chest tightness, shortness of breath (SOB), and "heart pounding" (palpitations). The paramedics started an IV and O_2 at 2 L/min via nasal cannula. They obtained a 12-lead ECG and gave him 4 chewable baby ASA and a nitroglycerin tablet. L.P. is pain free on arrival to the emergency department, but still has palpitations.

Discussion Questions

1. Is L.P.'s condition stable or unstable?
2. What are the possible causes of L.P.'s chest tightness, SOB, and palpitations?
3. What type of assessment is most appropriate for L.P.: emergency, focused, or comprehensive? On what basis did you make that decision?
4. What assessment questions will you ask him?

You will learn more about L.P. and his condition as you read through this assessment chapter.
(See p. 664 for more information on L.P.)

Answers available at *http://evolve.elsevier.com/Lewis/medsurg.*

ASSESSMENT OF CARDIOVASCULAR SYSTEM

Subjective Data

A careful health history and physical examination will help you distinguish symptoms that reflect a cardiovascular problem from problems of other body systems. Explore and record all cues that alert you to the possibility of underlying CVD.

Important Health Information

History of Present Illness. Ask the patient what problem has brought him or her to seek health care. Fully explore all symptoms the patient reports.

Past Health History. Many illnesses affect the cardiovascular system directly or indirectly. Ask the patient about a history of angina, diabetes, alcohol and tobacco use, anemia, rheumatic fever, streptococcal throat infections, congenital heart disease, stroke, hypertension, thrombophlebitis, dysrhythmias, and varicosities. Fully explore any symptoms the patient may have. Ask about shortness of breath, fatigue, dizziness with position changes, syncope, edema, intermittent claudication, and palpitations.

Assess for allergies to drugs, food, or the environment. Determine whether the patient has ever had a drug reaction or an allergic or anaphylactic reaction. Ask specifically about any allergic reaction to contrast media.

Medications. Assess the patient's current and past use of medications. Include over-the-counter (OTC) and prescription drugs and herbal supplements. For example, aspirin prolongs the blood clotting time and is in some drugs used to treat cold symptoms. Record the dose and time last taken for each. Assess for noncardiac drugs that can adversely affect the cardiovascular system (Table 31.2).

TABLE 31.2 Potential Cardiovascular Effects of Select Noncardiac Drugs

Drug Classification	Examples	Cardiovascular Effects
Anticancer agents	daunorubicin doxorubicin	Dysrhythmias, cardiomyopathy
Antipsychotics	chlorpromazine haloperidol	Dysrhythmias, orthostatic hypotension
Corticosteroids	cortisone prednisone	Hypotension, edema, potassium depletion
Hormone therapy, oral contraceptives	estrogen + progestin (Prempro)	MI, thromboembolism, stroke, hypertension
Nonsteroidal antiinflammatory drugs (NSAIDs)	celecoxib (Celebrex) diclofenac ibuprofen	MI, stroke, hypertension, HF
Psychostimulants	amphetamines cocaine	Tachycardia, angina, MI, hypertension, dysrhythmias
Tricyclic antidepressants	amitriptyline doxepin (Silenor)	Dysrhythmias, orthostatic hypotension

Surgery or Other Treatments. Ask the patient about specific treatments, past surgeries, or hospital admissions related to cardiovascular problems. Explore any admissions or procedures performed for cardiovascular symptoms. Note whether a baseline ECG or a chest x-ray has been done.

Functional Health Patterns. The strong correlation between lifestyle and cardiovascular health supports the need to review each functional health pattern. Key questions to ask a person with a cardiovascular problem are listed in Table 31.3.

Health Perception–Health Management Pattern. Ask the patient about the presence of major cardiovascular risk factors. These include abnormal serum lipids, hypertension, sedentary lifestyle, diabetes, obesity, and tobacco use. Estimate the number of pack-years of tobacco use (number of packs smoked per day multiplied by the number of years the patient has smoked). Note the patient's attitude about tobacco use and attempts and methods used to stop. Record the type of alcohol used, amount, frequency, and any changes in the reaction to it. Note any use of habit-forming or recreational drugs.

GENETIC RISK ALERT

Coronary Artery Disease
- Specific genetic links, especially related to lipoprotein genes, have been found for some families with CAD.
- The clustering of CAD in families is strong if there is early age of onset affecting several relatives.

Cardiomyopathy
- Autosomal dominant mutations can cause hypertrophic cardiomyopathy.
- X-linked and autosomal dominant mutations can cause dilated cardiomyopathy.

Hypertension
- Hypertension results from a complex interplay between genetic and environmental factors.
- Lifestyle choices (e.g., smoking, lack of exercise) may trigger genetic tendencies to hypertension.

Genomic studies have found over 60 common genetic variants highly associated with CAD.[8] Confirmed illnesses of blood relatives can highlight any genetic or familial tendencies toward CAD, hypertension, varicosities, bleeding, diabetes, atherosclerosis, and stroke. Note any family members who had heart disease at an early age (<50 years of age for men; <55 years of age for women). Last, assess for family health history of noncardiac

problems such as lung, kidney, or liver disease and obesity, because they can affect the cardiovascular system.

Nutritional-Metabolic Pattern. Being underweight or overweight may indicate potential cardiovascular problems. Assess the patient's weight history (e.g., over the past year) in relation to height. Determine the amount of salt and saturated fats in the patient's typical diet. In addition to food habits, which may be influenced by culture, explore the patient's attitudes and plans about diet and weight management.

Elimination Pattern. The patient taking diuretics may report increased voiding and/or nocturia. Ask about any history of incontinence or constipation, including use of drugs (prescribed and OTC) for constipation. Teach patients with heart problems to avoid straining (*Valsalva maneuver*) during a bowel movement. Ask patients if they have swelling of the lower extremities and if it resolves when their feet are elevated.

Activity-Exercise Pattern. The benefit of exercise for cardiovascular health is clear, with aerobic exercise being most beneficial. Record the types, duration, intensity, and frequency of exercise. Ask about symptoms during exercise (e.g., chest pain, shortness of breath, claudication) that may indicate a cardiovascular problem.

Sleep-Rest Pattern. Cardiovascular problems often disrupt sleep. *Paroxysmal nocturnal dyspnea* (attacks of shortness of breath, especially at night that awaken the patient) and *Cheyne-Stokes respiration* (periods of very shallow breaths to alternating periods of apnea and deep, rapid breathing) are associated with HF. Note the number of pillows needed to sleep or the need to sleep upright in a chair (*orthopnea*) and whether this has changed recently.

Sleep apnea is associated with an increased risk for life-threatening dysrhythmias, especially in patients with HF. Nocturia, a common finding with cardiovascular patients, interrupts normal sleep patterns.

Cognitive-Perceptual Pattern. Ask both the patient and caregiver about cognitive-perceptual problems. Cardiovascular problems such as dysrhythmias, hypertension, and stroke may cause difficulties with syncope, language, and memory. Report pain associated with the cardiovascular system (e.g., chest pain, claudication).

Self-Perception–Self-Concept Pattern. Acute cardiovascular events may affect the patient's self-perception. Invasive diagnostic procedures often lead to body image concerns. When CVD is chronic, the patient may describe an inability to "keep up" previous levels of activity, affecting quality of life.

Role-Relationship Pattern. Gender, race, and age are all related to cardiovascular health. The patient's marital status, role

TABLE 31.3 Health History

Cardiovascular System

Health Perception–Health Management

- Do you practice any measures to decrease risk factors for heart disease?*
- Have you noticed an increase in heart symptoms such as chest pain or dyspnea?*
- Does your heart problem cause you to be less able to care for yourself?*
- Do you foresee any potential self-care problems because of your heart problem?*
- Have you ever used tobacco? If yes, in what form, how much, and for how long? Have you tried to quit? If yes, what methods have you tried? Are you interested in more information about quitting?
- How often and how much alcohol do you drink?

Nutritional-Metabolic

- Describe your usual daily diet, including salt, fat, and liquid intake.
- What is your present weight? What was your weight 1 year ago? If different, explain.
- Does eating cause fatigue or shortness of breath?*

Elimination

- Do your feet or ankles ever swell?* If yes, how far up your legs? Does it go away after sleeping all night?
- Have you ever taken drugs to help you get rid of excess fluid or to relieve constipation?*
- Are you having any problems related to urination?*
- Do you ever strain to have a bowel movement?

Activity-Exercise

- Are your daily activities or exercise limited because of your heart problem?*
- When were you last able to comfortably perform your usual activities or exercise?
- Do you have any discomfort or symptoms because of exercise or any activity?*
- Can you comfortably walk and talk at the same time?
- How often do you attend activities outside your home?
- What was your most strenuous activity in the last few weeks compared with 6 months ago?

Sleep-Rest

- How many pillows do you sleep on at night? Has this changed recently?*
- Do you ever wake up suddenly and feel as if you cannot catch your breath?*
- Do you have a history of sleep apnea?*

- Do you ever sleep in a chair at night? Is yes, how often?
- How many times a night do you awaken to urinate?

Cognitive-Perceptual

- Do you ever have dizziness or fainting?*
- Do you ever find it hard to express yourself or to remember things?*
- Do you have any pain (e.g., chest pain, leg pain with activity) because of your heart problem?*

Self-Perception–Self-Concept

- Have your perceptions of yourself changed since you were diagnosed with heart disease?*
- How has your heart disease affected the quality of your life?

Role-Relationship

- Has this illness affected any of the roles that you play in your daily life?*
- How has your heart disease affected your significant others?

Sexuality-Reproductive

- Has your heart disease caused a change in your sexual activity?*
- Do you have any heart-related symptoms during sexual activity?*
- Do any of your drugs affect your ability to take part in sexual activities?*
- *Females:* Are you currently taking oral contraceptives, hormonal therapy, or drug therapy for breast cancer?
- *Males:* Are you taking any drugs to treat erectile dysfunction?

Coping–Stress Tolerance

- Describe your normal coping mechanisms during times of stress or anxiety.
- To whom or where would you turn during a time of stress? Are these people or services helping you now?*
- Do you practice any stress reduction techniques?*
- Do you have a history of depression?*
- Do you feel capable of handling your present health situation?
- Do you have any heart symptoms (e.g., chest pain, palpitations) during times of stress or anger?*

Values-Beliefs

- What influence have your values or beliefs had during your illness?
- Do you feel any conflicts between your values or beliefs and the plan of care?*
- Describe any cultural or religious beliefs that may influence the management of your heart problem.

*If yes, describe.

---

in the household, employment status, number of children and their ages, living environment, and caregivers help you to identify strengths and support systems in the patient's life. Assess the patient's satisfaction with life roles, since this may alert you to possible areas of stress or conflict.

Sexuality-Reproductive Pattern. Ask the patient about the effect of the cardiovascular problem on sexual activity. Because some patients fear sudden death during sexual intercourse, they may change their sexual behavior. Fatigue, chest pain, or shortness of breath may limit sexual activity. Erectile dysfunction (ED) may be a symptom of peripheral vascular disease and/or a side effect of some drugs used to treat CVD (e.g., β-blockers, diuretics). Ask male patients about the use of drugs for ED (phosphodiesterase inhibitors, e.g., sildenafil [Viagra]). These drugs are contraindicated if the patient is taking a nitrate because the combination can cause significant hypotension.[9]

Ask female patients if they use oral contraceptives, hormone therapy (HT) for symptoms of menopause, or drug therapy for breast cancer. Women who smoke tobacco and use oral contraceptives are at increased risk for blood clots (e.g., venous thromboembolism). Similarly, there is an increased risk for CVD with the use of HT and selective estrogen-receptor modulators (e.g., tamoxifen).[9]

Coping–Stress Tolerance Pattern. Ask the patient to identify sources of stress and the usual methods of coping with stress. Potentially stressful areas include health concerns, marital relationships, family and friends, occupation, and finances.

Work-related stress, depression, and inadequate social support are risk factors for CVD and heart events. Ask the patient about each of these factors. Information about support systems such as family, extended family and friends, counselors, or religious groups can give vital insight when planning care.

Values-Belief Pattern. Individual values and beliefs, which are greatly affected by culture, may play a key role in the real or potential conflict that a patient faces when dealing with CVD. Some patients may attribute their illness to punishment from God; others may think that a "higher power" can help them. Information about a patient's values and beliefs will help you provide support during periods of crisis.

CASE STUDY
Subjective Data

(@ Jupiterimages/
Banana-Stock/
Thinkstock.)

A focused subjective assessment of L.P. revealed the following information:

- **Past Medical History:** History of hypertension, mitral valve prolapse with mild regurgitation, HF, and type 2 diabetes.
- **Oral Medications:** Lisinopril (Prinivil) 10 mg/day, metoprolol (Lopressor) 50 mg twice daily, ASA 81 mg/day , furosemide 40 mg/day, and glipizide (Glucotrol) 5 mg/day.
- **Health Perception–Health Management:** L.P. denies any history of chest pain or CAD. He reports feeling fine until this morning when he awoke and developed SOB, chest tightness, and palpitations while walking to the bathroom. He thought he was having a heart attack, so his wife called 911. Denies smoking or alcohol intake. SOB and chest tightness are now gone, but he continues to feel palpitations.
- **Elimination:** Denies edema or nocturia. States he takes Lasix in the morning and typically "passes urine until lunchtime."

Discussion Questions

1. Which subjective assessment findings are of most concern to you?
2. How will you individualize the assessment based on his age, ethnic/cultural background, and condition?
3. Is this an appropriate time to teach him about the proper use of nitroglycerin tablets? Why or why not?
4. What should you include in your physical assessment?

You will learn more about the physical examination of the cardiovascular system in the next section. (See p. 667 for more information on L.P.)

Answers available at *http://evolve.elsevier.com/Lewis/medsurg.*

Objective Data
Physical Examination

Vital Signs. Observe the patient's general appearance and obtain vital signs. Measure BP bilaterally. Readings can vary from 5 to 15 mm Hg between arms. Use the arm with the highest BP for later measurements. Obtain an orthostatic (postural) BP and HR while the patient is supine, sitting with legs dangling, and standing. SBP should not decrease more than 20 mm Hg from the supine to the standing position. HR should not increase more than 20 beats/min from the supine to the standing position.

Peripheral Vascular System

Inspection. Inspect the skin for color, hair distribution, and venous pattern. Check the extremities for edema, dependent rubor, clubbing of the nail beds, varicosities, and lesions such as stasis ulcers. Edema in the legs can be caused by gravity, varicosities, or right-sided HF.

Inspect the large neck veins (internal and external jugular) while gradually moving the patient from a supine position to an upright (30 to 45 degrees) position. Distention and prominent pulsations of the neck veins, referred to as *jugular venous distention,* can be caused by right-sided HF.

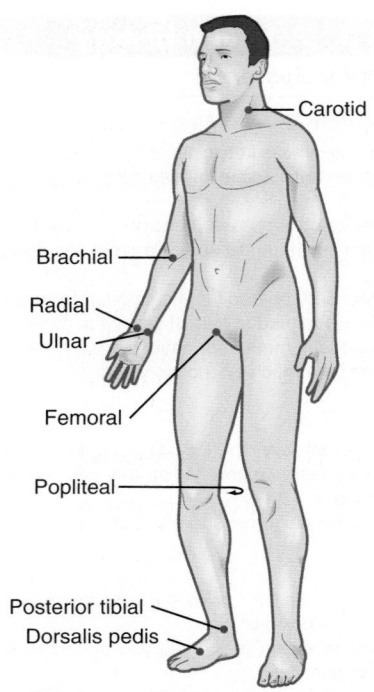

FIG. 31.6 Common sites for palpating arteries.

Palpation. Palpate the upper and lower extremities for temperature, moisture, pulses, and edema bilaterally to assess for symmetry. Look for edema by depressing the skin over the tibia or medial malleolus for 5 seconds. Normally, there is no depression after you release pressure. If pitting edema is present, grade it from 1+ (mild pitting, slight brief indentation) to 4+ (very deep pitting, indentation that lasts a long time).

Palpate the pulses in the neck and extremities for rhythm and force of arterial blood flow. Palpate each carotid pulse separately to avoid vagal stimulation and dysrhythmias. Compare the characteristics of the arteries in the right and left extremities simultaneously to determine symmetry.

When palpating the arteries identified in Fig. 31.6, rate the force of the pulse using the following scale:

0 = Absent
1+ = Weak
2+ = Normal
3+ = Increased, full, bounding

Note the rigidity (hardness) of the artery. The normal pulse feels like a tap, but a narrowed or bulging vessel wall vibrates. The term for a palpable vibration is *thrill.*

Capillary refill is used to assess arterial flow to the extremities. Position the patient's hands near the level of the heart and squeeze a nail bed briefly to produce blanching. Color should return to the nail bed in less than 2 seconds with normal tissue perfusion and CO.

Auscultation. An artery that is narrowed or has a bulging wall may create turbulent blood flow. This abnormal flow can cause a buzzing or humming termed a *bruit,* heard with the bell of the stethoscope over the vessel. Auscultate major arteries such as the carotid arteries, abdominal aorta, and femoral arteries as part of the initial cardiovascular assessment. Abnormalities of the peripheral vascular system are described in Table 31.4.

TABLE 31.4 Assessment Abnormalities

Cardiovascular System

Finding*	Description	Possible Etiology* and Significance
Inspection		
Central cyanosis	Bluish or purplish tinge in central areas such as tongue, conjunctivae, inner surface of lips	Inadequate O_2 saturation of arterial blood because of pulmonary or cardiac disorders (e.g., congenital defects)
Clubbing of nail beds	Obliteration of normal angle between base of nail and skin	Endocarditis, congenital defects, prolonged O_2 deficiency
Color changes in extremities with postural change	Pallor, cyanosis, mottling of skin after limb elevation. Dependent rubor (reddish blue discoloration). Glossy skin	Chronic decreased arterial perfusion
Jugular venous distention	Distended neck (jugular) veins with patient sitting at 30- to 45-degree angle	High right atrial pressure, right-sided HF
Peripheral cyanosis	Bluish or purplish tinge in extremities or in nose and ears	Reduced blood flow from HF, vasoconstriction, cold environment
Splinter hemorrhages	Small red to black streaks under fingernails	Infective endocarditis (infection of endocardium, usually in area of cardiac valves)
Ulcers	*Venous:* Necrotic crater-like lesion usually found on lower leg at medial malleolus. Characterized by slow wound healing	Poor venous return, varicose veins, incompetent venous valves
	Arterial: Pale ischemic base, well-defined edges usually found on toes, heels, lateral malleoli	Arteriosclerosis, diabetes
Varicose veins	Visible dilated, discolored, tortuous vessels in lower extremities	Incompetent valves in vein
Palpation		
Pulse		
<60 beats/min	Bradycardia	Rest or sleeping, SA or AV node damage, athletic conditioning, side effect of drugs (e.g., β-blockers), hypothyroidism
>100 beats/min	Tachycardia	Exercise, anxiety, shock, need for increased cardiac output, hyperthyroidism
Absent	Lack of pulse	Atherosclerosis, trauma, embolus
Bounding	Sharp, brisk, pounding pulse	Hyperkinetic states (e.g., anxiety, fever), anemia, hyperthyroidism
Displaced point of maximal impulse (apical pulse)	Palpate (or auscultate) the point of maximal impulse below the fifth ICS and to the left of the MCL	Cardiac enlargement because of coronary artery disease, HF, cardiomyopathy
Irregular	Regularly irregular or irregularly irregular. Skipped beats	Dysrhythmias
Pulsus alternans	Regular rhythm, but strength of pulse varies with each beat	HF, cardiac tamponade
Rigidity	Stiffness or inflexibility of vessel wall	Atherosclerosis
Thready	Weak, slowly rising pulse easily obliterated by pressure	Blood loss, decreased cardiac output, aortic valve disease, peripheral arterial disease
Thrill	Vibration of vessel or chest wall	Aneurysm, aortic regurgitation, arteriovenous fistula
Extremities		
Abnormal capillary refill	Blanching of nail bed for ≥2 sec after release of pressure	Possible reduced arterial capillary perfusion, anemia
Asymmetry in limb circumference	Measurable swelling of involved limb	Venous thromboembolism, varicose veins, lymphedema
Cold extremities	Hands and/or feet cold to touch. External covering needed for comfort	Intermittent claudication, peripheral arterial disease, low cardiac output, severe anemia
Pitting edema of lower extremities or sacral area	Visible finger indentation after application of firm pressure, weight gain, tightening of clothing (including shoes), marks or indentations from constricting garments	Interruption of venous return to heart, right-sided HF
Unusually warm extremities	Hands and feet warmer than normal	Thyrotoxicosis
Auscultation		
3rd heart sound (S_3)	Extra heart sound, low pitched, heard in early diastole. Similar to sound of a gallop	Left ventricular failure. Volume overload. Mitral, aortic, or tricuspid regurgitation. Hypertension (possible)
4th heart sound (S_4)	Extra heart sound, low pitched, heard in late diastole. Similar to sound of a gallop	Forceful atrial contraction from resistance to ventricular filling (e.g., in left ventricular hypertrophy, aortic stenosis, hypertension, coronary artery disease)
Arterial bruit	Turbulent flow sound in peripheral artery	Arterial obstruction or aneurysm
Heart murmurs	Turbulent sounds occurring between normal heart sounds. Characterized by loudness, pitch, shape, quality, duration, timing	Heart valve disorder, abnormal blood flow patterns
Pericardial friction rub	High-pitched, scratchy sound heard during S_1 and/or S_2 at the apex. Heard best with patient sitting and leaning forward, and while holding breath at the end of expiration	Pericarditis
Pulse deficit	Apical heart rate exceeding peripheral pulse rate	Dysrhythmias, most often atrial fibrillation/flutter or premature ventricular contractions

*Limited to common abnormal assessment findings and etiologic factors. (Further discussion of conditions listed may be found in Chapters 32 to 37, 65, and 66.)

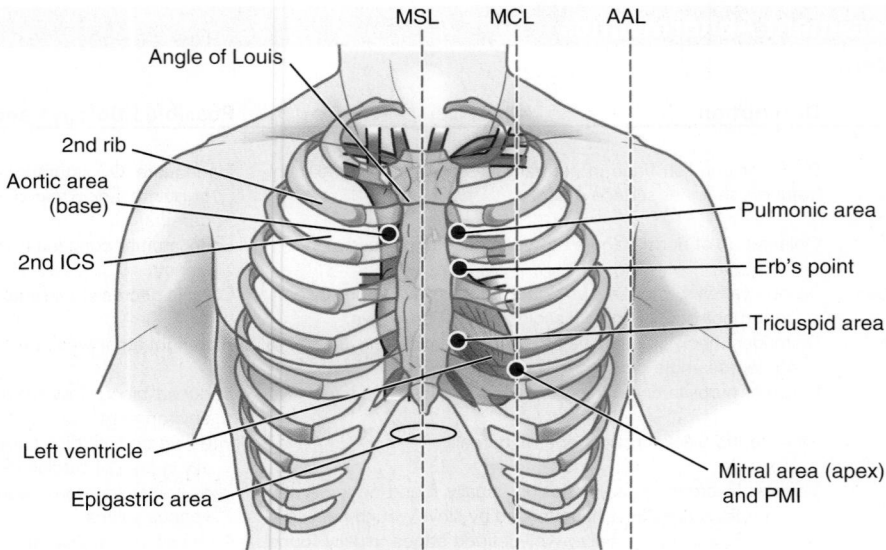

FIG. 31.7 Orientation of the heart within the thorax and cardiac auscultatory areas. *Red lines* indicate the midsternal line *(MSL)*, midclavicular line *(MCL)*, and anterior axillary line *(AAL)*. *ICS,* Intercostal space; *PMI,* point of maximal impulse.

Thorax

Inspection and palpation. Begin examining the thorax with a general inspection and palpation. Next, inspect and palpate the areas where the heart valves project their sounds by finding the intercostal spaces (ICSs). The raised notch, the *angle of Louis,* is where the manubrium and body of the sternum join at the level of the second rib. It is palpable in the midline of the sternum. Palpate for the 2nd ICS then count each ICSs to find specific auscultatory areas (Fig. 31.7).

Locate the following auscultatory areas: aortic area in the second ICS to the right of the sternum, pulmonic area in the second ICS to the left of the sternum, tricuspid area in the fifth left ICS close to the sternum, and mitral area in the left midclavicular line at the fifth ICS. A fifth auscultatory area is *Erb's point,* located at the third left ICS near the sternum. Normally, we cannot feel pulsations in these areas unless the patient has a thin chest wall.

A heart valve disorder may be present if you feel abnormal pulsations or thrills. Next, inspect and palpate the epigastric area on either side of the midline just below the xiphoid process. In a thin person, you may see pulsations from the abdominal aorta. Normally, you can palpate it here. Next, inspect the precordium, which is over the heart, for heaves. Heaves are sustained lifts of the chest wall in the precordial area that you can see or palpate. They may be caused by left ventricular hypertrophy. Normally no pulsations are seen or felt here.

When the patient is supine, palpate the mitral valve area for the **point of maximal impulse (PMI)** (also called the *apical pulse*). This reflects the pulsation of the apex of the heart. The PMI lies medial to the midclavicular line in the 4th or 5th ICS. If you can palpate the PMI, record its position in relation to the midclavicular line and ICSs. If the PMI is below the fifth ICS and left of the midclavicular line, the heart may be enlarged.

Auscultation. Normal heart sounds are made by the movement of blood through the heart valves. These sounds can be heard through a stethoscope placed on the chest wall. The first heart sound (S_1) is associated with closure of the tricuspid

FIG. 31.8 Relationship of electrocardiogram, cardiac cycle, and heart sounds.

and mitral valves. It has a soft lubb sound. The second heart sound (S_2) is associated with closure of the aortic and pulmonic valves. It has a sharp dupp sound. S_1 signals the beginning of systole. S_2 signals the beginning of diastole (Fig. 31.8). Listen to the auscultatory areas in sequence (Fig. 31.7).

S_1 and S_2 are heard best with the diaphragm of the stethoscope because they are high pitched. Extra heart sounds (S_3 or S_4), if present, are heard best with the bell of the stethoscope because they are low pitched. Have the patient lean forward while sitting to enhance the sounds from the second ICSs (aortic and pulmonic areas). Place the patient in a left side-lying position to enhance the sounds at the mitral area.

When auscultating the apical area, simultaneously palpate the radial pulse. Determine whether the rhythm is regular or irregular while listening and feeling. If the apical and radial pulses are not equivalent, count the apical pulse while a second person simultaneously counts the radial pulse for 1 full minute. A difference between the 2 numbers, called a *pulse deficit,* can indicate dysrhythmias.

Normally no sound is heard between S_1 and S_2. An exception to this is a normal splitting of S_2, which is best heard at the pulmonic area during inspiration. Splitting of S_2 can be abnormal if it is heard during expiration or if it is constant (fixed) during the respiratory cycle. Describe any sounds heard in addition to S_1 and S_2.

The S₃ heart sound is a low-intensity vibration of the ventricular walls usually associated with decreased compliance of the ventricles during filling. An S_3 heart sound may be normal (physiologic) in young adults. It is pathologic in patients with left-sided HF or mitral valve regurgitation. S_3 is heard closely after S_2 and is known as a *ventricular gallop*.

The S_4 heart sound is a low-frequency vibration caused by atrial contraction. It precedes S_1 of the next cycle and is known as an *atrial gallop*. An S_4 heart sound may be normal in older adults with no evidence of heart disease. It is pathologic in patients with CAD, cardiomyopathy, left ventricular hypertrophy, or aortic stenosis.

Murmurs, if heard, are graded on a 6-point Roman numeral scale based on loudness and recorded as a ratio. I/VI means a murmur that is barely audible with the stethoscope, heard only in a quiet room and then not easily. VI/VI means a murmur that we can hear with the stethoscope lifted just off the chest wall.

Pericardial friction rubs are sounds that occur when inflamed surfaces of the pericardium (pericarditis) move against each other. They are high-pitched, scratchy sounds that may be intermittent and may last several hours to days. Friction rubs are heard best at the apex with patients upright, leaning forward, and holding their breath after expiration.[5]

Record the characteristics of any abnormal sounds. This includes the timing (during systole or diastole), location (the anatomic site on the chest where it is heard the loudest), position (heard best when the patient is supine, sitting and leaning forward, or in the left side-lying position), and any other findings (irregular apical pulse or palpable chest wall heaves) associated with the sound.

Abnormal assessment findings are described in Table 31.4. A method of recording data from the cardiovascular assessment is shown in Table 31.5.

A *focused assessment* is used to evaluate the status of previously identified cardiovascular problems and to monitor for signs of new problems. A focused assessment of the cardiovascular system is outlined in the box on this page.

CASE STUDY

Objective Data: Physical Examination

(© Jupiterimages/ Banana-Stock/ Thinkstock.)

Physical examination findings of L.P. are as follows:
- BP 100/54, apical-radial pulse 154, pulse irregular, respiratory rate 20, temperature 98.2° F (36.8° C), O₂ saturation 94% on room air
- Awake, alert, and oriented ×3
- Lungs clear on auscultation; systolic murmur present
- Heart monitor shows atrial fibrillation with a rapid ventricular response
- +1 pedal pulses bilaterally
- No peripheral edema, jugular venous distention, or heaves noted

Discussion Questions
1. Which physical assessment findings are of most concern to you?
2. Based on the results of the subjective and physical assessment findings, what diagnostic studies do you think will be ordered for L.P.?

You will learn more about diagnostic studies related to the cardiovascular system in the next section.

(See p. 676 for more information on L.P.)

Answers available at *http://evolve.elsevier.com/Lewis/medsurg.*

TABLE 31.5 Normal Physical Assessment of Cardiovascular System

Inspection	No pallor or cyanosis. PMI not visible. No JVD with patient at 45-degree angle
Palpation	Skin warm. Capillary refill <2 sec. PMI palpable in 4th ICS at left MCL. No thrills or heaves. Slight palpable pulsations of abdominal aorta in epigastric area. Carotid and extremity pulses 2+ and equal bilaterally. No pedal or sacral edema
Auscultation	S_1 and S_2 heard. Apical-radial pulse rate equal, 72, and regular. No murmurs or extra heart sounds

ICS, Intercostal space; *JVD,* jugular venous distention; *MCL,* midclavicular line; *PMI,* point of maximal impulse.

FOCUSED ASSESSMENT
Cardiovascular System

Use this checklist to remind you of the key assessment steps.

Subjective
Ask the patient about the following and note responses.

Chest pain, discomfort	Y	N
Palpitations	Y	N
Shortness of breath (especially when lying down or at rest)	Y	N
Edema in legs or any part of body	Y	N
Leg pain during exercise	Y	N
Excess urination at night	Y	N

Objective: Diagnostic
Check the following for critical values or changes.

Cardiac biomarkers	✓
Hematocrit, hemoglobin, platelets	✓
Glucose, electrolytes, BUN, creatinine	✓
Electrocardiogram	✓
Chest x-ray	✓

Objective: Physical Examination
Inspect and Palpate

Anterior chest wall for pulsations and heaves	✓
Pulses for symmetry, quality, and rhythm	✓

Auscultate

Bilateral blood pressures	✓
Heart for rate, rhythm, and sounds	✓

DIAGNOSTIC STUDIES OF CARDIOVASCULAR SYSTEM

Numerous diagnostic tests are available to assess the cardiovascular system. Tables 31.6, 31.7, and 31.8 describe common serology studies, diagnostic studies, and interventional study procedures. Select studies are discussed in more detail next.

Blood Studies

Many blood studies provide information about the cardiovascular system. For example, some reflect the O₂-carrying capacity (red blood cell count and hemoglobin) and coagulation properties (clotting times) of the blood. See Chapter 29 and Tables 29.7, 29.8, and 29.10 about hematology studies.

Cardiac Biomarkers. When cells are injured, they release their contents, including enzymes and other proteins, into the

TABLE 31.6 Serology Studies

Cardiovascular System

Study	Reference Interval*	Description and Purpose
Biomarkers		
b-Type natriuretic peptide (BNP)	<100 pg/mL (100 pmol/L)	Peptide that causes natriuresis. High in HF. Levels increased after nesiritide (Natrecor) infusion and for 1 month after cardiac surgery.
CK-MB	Concentrations <4%–6% of total creatine kinase (CK)	Tests for myocardial cell injury. High levels highly indicative of MI. Serum levels increase within 3–6 hr after MI, peak after 12–24 hours, normalize within 48 hours. Explain purpose of serial sampling.
Copeptin	<10 pmol/L	Reflects arginine vasopressin (AVP) concentration. High levels highly indicative of MI. Higher in men, after exercise, and with stress. Influenced by fasting and water load.
C-reactive protein (CRP)	High-sensitivity (hs) CRP assay. *Lowest risk:* <1 mg/dL *Moderate risk:* 1–3 mg/dL *High risk:* >3 mg/dL	Marker of inflammation. May help predict risk for cardiac disease and cardiac events such as an acute MI. High in bacterial infections and inflammatory disorders.
Homocysteine	4–14 μmol/L Levels may increase with age	Amino acid made during protein catabolism. Risk factor for cardiovascular disease. Associated with vitamin B_{12} and folate deficiencies.
NT-Pro-BNP	*≤74 yr:* 124 pg/mL *>75 yr:* 449 pg/mL	Helps to assess severity of HF. Levels are higher in women and patients with renal insufficiency.
Troponin (cardiac)	*Troponin T (cTnT)* <0.1 ng/mL (<0.1 mcg/L) *Troponin I (cTnI)* *Negative:* <0.03 ng/mL (<0.03 mcg/L)	Contractile proteins released after an MI. Both troponin T and troponin I test for cardiac injury/ischemia. Serial sampling needed: draw 3 sets of troponins 3–6 hours apart.
Lipids		
Cholesterol	<200 mg/dL (<5.2 mmol/L) (varies with age and gender)	A blood lipid associated with arteriosclerosis. High level is a risk factor for cardiovascular heart disease. Can obtain in a nonfasting or fasting state.
Lipoprotein (a) (Lp[a])	<30 mg/dL (<0.3 g/L)	High levels indicate an increased risk for atherosclerosis, MI, and stroke. Can obtain in a nonfasting or fasting state.
Lipoprotein-associated phospholipase A₂ (Lp-PLA₂)	*Low risk:* ≤151 ng/mL *Moderate risk:* 152–194 ng/mL *High risk:* ≥195 ng/mL	Indicates inflammation and increased risk for CAD. Serum levels are measured by the PLAC test. Can obtain in a nonfasting or fasting state.
Lipoproteins (HDL, LDL)	HDL Recommended *Male:* >45 mg/dL *Female:* >55 mg/dL *Low risk for CAD:* ≥60 mg/dL *High risk for CAD:* <40 mg/dL LDL <130 mg/dL *Moderate risk for CAD:* 130–159 mg/dL *High risk for CAD:* >160 mg/dL	There are marked day-to-day fluctuations, so more than 1 level is needed for accurate diagnosis. Can be obtained in a nonfasting or fasting state. Assess risk for heart disease by dividing the total cholesterol level by the HDL level and obtaining a ratio. *Low risk:* Ratio <3 *Average risk:* Ratio 3–5 *Increased risk:* Ratio >5
Triglycerides	*Male:* 40–160 mg/dL *Female:* 35–135 mg/dL	Mixtures of fatty acids. Elevations are associated with cardiovascular disease and diabetes. Avoid alcohol for 24 hr before testing. Can obtain in a nonfasting or fasting state.

*Reference ranges for the laboratory tests vary by agency because of differences in equipment and reagents used.

circulation. These *biomarkers* are useful in the diagnosis of acute coronary syndrome (ACS) (Table 31.6). Interpreting biomarker level results requires you to consider the time elapsed from the onset of symptoms. Other data (patient symptoms, history, and ECG changes) complete the diagnostic picture for the patient with suspected ACS.

Cardiac-specific troponin is a heart muscle protein released into circulation after injury or infarction. Two subtypes, cardiac-specific troponin T (cTnT) and cardiac-specific troponin I (cTnI), are specific to heart muscle. Normally the level in the blood is very low, so a rise in level is diagnostic of myocardial infarction (MI) or injury. cTnT and cTnI are detectable within hours (on average 4 to 6 hours) of MI or injury, peak at 10 to 24 hours, and can be detected for up to 10 to 14 days. Troponin is the biomarker of choice in the diagnosis of ACS. High-sensitivity troponin (hs-cTnT, hs-cTnI) assays may provide even

earlier detection of a heart event.[10] Fig. 33.15 shows the changes in cardiac markers related to an MI.

Copeptin, a substitute marker for arginine vasopressin (AVP), can be detected immediately in patients with an acute MI. Considering both troponin and copeptin levels together may provide increased sensitivity for rapidly diagnosing acute MI.[10] High circulating copeptin levels are associated with increased mortality in patients with HF.[11]

Creatine kinase (CK) enzymes are found in a variety of organs and tissues and occur as 3 isoenzymes. These isoenzymes are specific to skeletal muscle (CK-MM), brain and nervous tissue (CK-BB), and the heart (CK-MB). CK-MB rise is specific for MI or injury. Levels begin to increase 3 to 6 hours after symptom onset, peak in 12 to 24 hours, and return to baseline within 12 to 48 hours after MI.[12] In some acute care settings, CK is no longer used for diagnosis of acute MI.[13]

TABLE 31.7 Diagnostic Studies

Cardiovascular System

Study	Description and Purpose	Nursing Responsibility
Electrocardiography (ECG)		
12-lead ECG	Electrodes are placed on the chest and extremities, allowing the ECG machine to record cardiac electrical activity from 12 different views. A resting 12-lead ECG can identify conduction problems, dysrhythmias, position of heart, cardiac hypertrophy, pericarditis, myocardial ischemia or infarction, pacemaker activity, and effectiveness of drug therapy at one point in time.	*Before:* Prepare skin and apply electrodes and leads. Place patient supine (or with head of bed elevated, if short of breath). Tell patient that no discomfort is involved and to lie still to decrease motion artifact. *During:* Ensure the patient lies still to decrease motion artifact.
ECG event monitor or loop recorder	Records rhythm changes that are not frequent enough to be recorded in 1 24-hr period. Can aid in diagnosing the cause of chest pain, palpitations, shortness of breath, and syncope. It allows more freedom than a regular Holter monitor. Some units have electrodes that attach to the chest and have a loop of memory that captures the onset and end of an event. Other types are placed directly on patient's wrist, chest, or fingers and have no loop of memory but record the patient's ECG in real time. Recordings may be transmitted over the phone to a receiving unit.	*Before:* Teach how to use equipment for recording and transmitting events. Teach patient about skin preparation for lead placement or steady skin contact to ensure quality tracings. Tell patient to start recording when symptoms begin or as soon after as possible.
ECG Holter monitoring	Recording of ECG rhythm for 24–48 hr to correlate with symptoms and activities recorded in diary. Encourage normal patient activity to simulate conditions that produce symptoms. Electrodes are placed on chest. A recorder stores information until it is recalled, printed, and analyzed for any rhythm changes.	*Before:* Prepare skin and apply electrodes and leads. Explain importance of keeping an accurate diary of activities and symptoms. Tell patient there is no bathing and showering during monitoring. Skin irritation may develop from electrodes. If device has an event marker, teach patient to push that button when experiencing symptoms.
Signal-averaged ECG (SAECG)	A high-resolution ECG that can identify electrical activity called late potentials, indicating a patient is at risk for developing ventricular dysrhythmias (e.g., ventricular tachycardia).	Same as for 12-lead ECG.
Functional		
6-minute walk test	Distance patient can walk on a flat surface in 6 min. Used to measure response to treatments and determine functional capacity for activities of daily living. Can help assess response to therapy for chronic cardiopulmonary conditions. Useful in those who are debilitated or unable to perform treadmill or exercise bike testing. May be a better measure of fitness for older adults than exercise testing.	*Before:* Tell patient to wear comfortable shoes. Inform patient to carry or pull O_2 if used routinely. *During:* Encourage patient to walk as quickly as possible.
Exercise or stress testing	Provides information on cardiac function and exercise tolerance. A common protocol uses 3-min stages at set speeds and elevation of treadmill belt. The patient can exercise to either predicted peak HR (calculated by subtracting the person's age from 220) or peak exercise tolerance, at which time the test is ended. The test is ended for chest discomfort, significant changes in vital signs from baseline, or significant ECG changes (e.g., ischemia, dysrhythmias). Vital signs and ECG are monitored. The ECG is monitored after exercise for ischemia and rhythm changes or, if ECG changes occurred with exercise, for return to baseline. Important in the diagnosis of CAD. An exercise bike may be used if the patient is unable to walk on the treadmill.	*Before:* Tell patient to wear comfortable clothes and shoes that can be worn for walking or running. Tell patient to report any symptoms. β-Blockers may be held 24 hr before the test because they blunt the HR and limit the patient's ability to achieve maximal HR. Caffeine is held for 24 hr. Patients must refrain from smoking and strenuous exercise for 3 hr before test. Obtain baseline vital signs and 12-lead-ECG. *During:* Monitor vital signs and ECG during each stage of exercise and after until all vital signs and ECG changes have returned to normal or baseline. Monitor patient's response throughout procedure for any signs of distress (e.g., angina, shortness of breath).
Noninvasive hemodynamic monitoring	Obtained using a continuous finger cuff or by thoracic bioreactance method. Possible to obtain repeated measurements of stroke volume, cardiac output, and systemic BP.	Minimal to no risk. Patients who need hemodynamic monitoring are likely to be in perioperative settings, critical care units, and emergency departments. See Chapter 65 for complete information on hemodynamic monitoring.
Imaging		
Chest x-ray	Patient is placed in 2 upright positions to examine lung fields and heart size. The 2 common positions are lateral and posteroanterior (PA) (Fig. 31.9). Helps with the diagnosis of HF and pulmonary edema and visualization of heart size and contour.	*Before:* Ask about frequency of recent x-rays and chance of pregnancy. Provide lead shielding to areas not being viewed. Remove jewelry or metal objects that may obstruct the view of heart and lungs.

Continued

TABLE 31.7 Diagnostic Studies—cont'd

Cardiovascular System

Study	Description and Purpose	Nursing Responsibility
Cardiac computed tomography (CT); electron beam CT (EBCT)	Cardiac CT is heart-specific imaging technology with or without IV contrast medium used to evaluate heart anatomy, coronary circulation, and blood vessels. EBCT, or ultrafast CT, uses a scanning electron beam to quantify calcification in coronary arteries and heart valves (Fig. 31.11). IV contrast may be used if calcium scoring is below threshold level. Primarily used for risk assessment in asymptomatic patients and to assess for heart disease in patients with atypical symptoms potentially related to cardiac causes.	*Before:* Assess for contrast allergy. Explain that patient may feel a warm sensation, salty taste after IV contrast injection, nausea. *During:* Patient must lie still during test.
Cardiovascular magnetic resonance imaging (CMRI)	Noninvasive imaging technique obtains information about heart tissue, EF, aneurysms, cardiac output, and patency of proximal coronary arteries. Measures regurgitant fraction that may determine valve repair or replacement. It does not involve ionizing radiation and is an extremely safe procedure. Provides images in multiple planes with uniformly good resolution.	*Before:* Check for pregnancy, allergies, and renal function before test. Have patient remove all metal objects. Remove metallic foil patches. Patient may need to be fasting. Assess for claustrophobia and the need for antianxiety medication Contraindicated for persons with implanted metallic devices or other metal fragments unless noted to be MRI safe. Ask about any history of surgical insertion of staples, plates, dental bridges, or other metal appliances. *During:* Patient must lie completely still during test.
Coronary CT angiography (CTA)	Use of CT with injected IV contrast medium to obtain images of coronary vessels and diagnose CAD. Used to evaluate chest pain and monitor the progression of coronary vascular disease.	*Before:* Assess for contrast allergy. Obtain IV access. Remove metal objects before test. The patient may need to fast for several hours prior. A β-blocker may be given before the test to control HR. *During:* Patients must have a regular heart rhythm for accurate testing.
Echocardiogram • Contrast • M-mode • 2-dimensional • Color-flow imaging (duplex) • Real-time 3-dimensional • Pharmacologic echocardiogram	Ultrasound transducer is placed in 4 positions on the chest to record sound waves bounced off the heart. Records direction and flow of blood through the heart and transforms it to audio and graphic data. Measures valve abnormalities, congenital heart defects, wall motion, EF, and heart function. IV contrast agent may be used to enhance images (Fig. 31.10). Pharmacologic Echocardiogram is a substitute for the exercise stress test in persons unable to exercise. IV adenosine, dobutamine, or dipyridamole is given over several minutes or regadenoson (Lexiscan) is given as a single bolus over 10 sec while echocardiogram is performed to detect wall motion abnormalities.	*Before:* Place patient in a left side-lying position. Tell patient about procedure and sensations (pressure and mechanical movement from head of transducer). May be difficult to obtain in patients with COPD due to large amount of air between heart and chest cavity. *Pharmacologic echocardiogram:* *Before:* Obtain baseline vital signs and IV access for injection of drugs. *During:* Monitor vital signs until baseline achieved. Monitor patient for signs and symptoms of distress or side effects (e.g., shortness of breath, dizziness, nausea). Aminophylline may be given to prevent or reverse side effects of dipyridamole.
Exercise (stress) nuclear imaging	Purpose of test is to identify cardiac symptoms and rhythm changes and simulate in a safe environment. Nuclear imaging images are taken at rest. Injection is given at maximum HR (usually 85% of age-predicted maximum) on bicycle or treadmill. Patient then continues exercise for 1 min to circulate the radioactive isotope. Scanning is done 15–60 min after exercise. A resting scan is done 60–90 min after initial infusion or 24 hr later.	*Before:* Tell patient to eat only a light meal between scans. Certain drugs may need to be held for 1–2 days before the scan. Patients should not have caffeine 12 hr prior. Obtain IV access. *During:* If targeted maximum HR is not achieved with exercise, test may be changed to pharmacologic imaging.
Magnetic resonance angiography (MRA)	Used for imaging vascular occlusive disease and abdominal aortic aneurysms. Same as MRI but with use of gadolinium as IV contrast medium.	*Before:* Contraindications include allergies to contrast medium and implanted metallic devices or other metal fragments unless noted to be MRA safe. Discuss any implants before scan. Obtain IV access.
Multigated acquisition (MUGA) (cardiac blood pool) scan	Small amount of the patient's blood is removed, mixed with a radioactive isotope (e.g., Technetium-99m (^{99m}Tc sestamibi), and reinjected IV. With the ECG used for timing, images are obtained during the cardiac cycle. Indicated for patients with MI, HF, or valve disease. Can evaluate the effect of various cardiac or cardiotoxic drugs on the heart and the cardiac EF.	*Before:* Explain procedure to patient. Obtain IV access for removal of blood sample and reinjection of isotope. Start ECG monitoring.
Nuclear imaging	Study involves IV injection of radioactive isotopes (^{99m}Tc sestamibi [Cardiolite]). Radioactive uptake is counted over the heart by scintillation camera. It supplies information about heart contractility, myocardial perfusion, and acute injury.	*Before:* Women must remove bras to decrease breast artifact. Obtain IV access for injection of isotopes. Explain that radioactive isotope used is a small, diagnostic amount and will lose most of its radioactivity in a few hours. Tell patient that they will be lying still on back with arms extended overhead for 20 min. *During:* Repeat scans are done within a few minutes to hours after the injection.

TABLE 31.7 Diagnostic Studies—cont'd

Cardiovascular System

Study	Description and Purpose	Nursing Responsibility
Pharmacologic nuclear imaging	Regadenoson, dipyridamole, or adenosine are given to produce vasodilation for patients unable to tolerate exercise. Vasodilation increases blood flow to well-perfused coronary arteries. Scanning procedure is same. Aminophylline may be given to prevent or reverse side effects of dipyridamole (e.g., shortness of breath, dizziness, nausea). Dobutamine is used if vasodilators are contraindicated.	*Before*: Tell patient to avoid caffeine products and theophylline (for regadenoson or dipyridamole testing) for 12 hr before procedure. Hold calcium channel blockers and β-blockers for 24 hr before the test. *During*: Observe patient for any side effects (e.g., shortness of breath, dizziness, nausea).
Positron emission tomography (PET)	Highly sensitive in distinguishing viable and nonviable heart tissue. Uses 2 radionuclides. Nitrogen-13-ammonia is injected IV first and scanned to evaluate myocardial perfusion. A second radioactive isotope, fluoro-18-deoxyglucose, is then injected and scanned to show myocardial metabolic function. In the normal heart, both scans match, but in an ischemic or damaged heart, they differ. The patient may or may not be stressed. A baseline resting scan is usually done for comparison.	*Before:* Obtain IV access to inject the tracer substance. Patients should be NPO, except for water and medications, for at least 4 hr prior. If exercise is part of testing, patient needs to fast and refrain from tobacco and caffeine for 24 hr before test. Hold glucose-containing IV solutions and change to normal saline. Check blood glucose levels. The glucose level must be between 60–140 mg/dL (3.3–7.8 μmol/L) for accurate glucose metabolic activity. *During*: Patient must lie completely still during scan. *After:* Encourage fluids to excrete radioactive substance.
Single-photon emission computed tomography (SPECT)	Used to determine size or risk for infarction and to determine infarction size. Small amounts of a radioactive isotope (e.g., ^{99m}Tc tetrofosmin [Myoview], thallium-201) are injected IV and recordings are made of the radioactivity emitted over a specific area of the body. Circulation of the isotope can detect coronary artery blood flow, intracardiac shunts, motion of ventricles, EF, and size of the heart chambers.	*Before:* Short fasting period may be needed. Obtain IV access for injection of isotope. Remove all jewelry from chest wall. Start ECG monitoring. *During*: Patient must lie completely still during scan. *After:* Encourage fluids to excrete radioactive substance.
Stress echocardiogram	Combination of exercise test and echocardiogram. Differences in left ventricular wall motion and thickening before and after exercise are evaluated with ultrasound. Postexercise images are taken within 1 min of stopping exercise.	*Before:* Prepare patient for treadmill or exercise bicycle. Tell patient of importance of timely return to examination table for imaging after exercise.
Transesophageal echocardiogram (TEE)	A probe with an ultrasound transducer at the tip is swallowed while the HCP controls angle and depth. As it passes down the esophagus, it sends back clear images of heart size, wall motion, valve abnormalities, endocarditis vegetation, and possible source of thrombi without interference from lungs or chest ribs. A contrast medium may be injected IV for evaluating direction of blood flow if an atrial or ventricular septal defect is suspected. Doppler ultrasound and color-flow imaging can be used concurrently.	*Before:* Tell patient to fast for at least 6 hr before test. Remove dentures. *During:* IV sedation is given and throat locally anesthetized. A bite block is placed in the mouth. Monitor vital signs, specifically O_2 saturation and BP. Perform suctioning as needed during procedure. *After:* Patient may not eat or drink until gag reflex returns. Monitor patient until sedation resolves. Sore throat is temporary. A designated driver is needed if test is done in the outpatient department.

C-Reactive Protein. C-reactive protein (CRP) is made by the liver during periods of acute inflammation. An increased level of CRP is linked with the presence of atherosclerosis and the first occurrence of a heart event. The CRP level may predict the risk for future heart events in patients with MI.[14]

Homocysteine. Homocysteine (Hcy) is an amino acid made during protein catabolism. High Hcy levels can be either hereditary or from dietary deficiencies of vitamin B_6, vitamin B_{12}, or folate. They are linked to a higher risk for CVD, peripheral vascular disease, and stroke. Hcy testing is recommended for patients with a familial predisposition for early CVD or a history of CVD in the absence of common risk factors.[14]

Cardiac Natriuretic Peptide Markers. There are 3 natriuretic peptides: (1) atrial natriuretic peptide (ANP) from the atrium, (2) b-type natriuretic peptide (BNP) from the ventricles, and (3) c-type natriuretic peptide from endothelial and renal epithelial cells. BNP is the marker of choice for distinguishing between a cardiac or respiratory cause of dyspnea. N-terminal pro-brain natriuretic peptide (NT-pro-BNP) is secreted in the ventricles and is more sensitive but less specific than BNP

as a diagnostic marker of HF.[12] When DBP increases (e.g., HF), BNP and NT-pro-BNP are released and increase natriuresis (excretion of sodium in the urine). ANP and BNP are also discussed in Chapter 32 on p. 680 and in Chapter 34 on p. 638.

Serum Lipids. Serum lipids consist of triglycerides, cholesterol, and phospholipids (Table 31.6). These *lipoproteins* circulate in the blood bound to protein. A lipid panel usually measures cholesterol, triglyceride, low-density lipoprotein (LDL), and high-density lipoprotein (HDL).

Triglycerides, the main storage form of lipids, make up about 95% of fatty tissue. Cholesterol, a structural part of cell membranes and plasma lipoproteins, is a precursor of corticosteroids, sex hormones, and bile salts. In addition to being absorbed from food in the gastrointestinal tract, cholesterol can be synthesized in the liver. Phospholipids contain glycerol, fatty acids, phosphates, and a nitrogenous compound. Although formed in most cells, phospholipids usually enter the circulation as lipoproteins synthesized by the liver. Apoproteins are water-soluble proteins that combine with most lipids to form lipoproteins.

TABLE 31.8 Interventional and Invasive Studies

Cardiovascular System

Study	Description and Purpose	Nursing Responsibility
Cardiac catheterization; coronary angiography	Involves insertion of catheter into heart via a vein (for right side of heart) and/or an artery (for left side of heart). Procedure is done to evaluate chest pain and obtain information about the aorta, inferior vena cava, pulmonary artery and veins. Measures pressures within the heart chambers. Contrast medium is injected to help see structures and motion of heart. With coronary angiography, contrast medium is injected directly into coronary arteries to evaluate patency and collateral circulation.	See Table 31.9.
Electrophysiology study (EPS)	Invasive study to record intracardiac electrical activity using catheters (with multiple electrodes) inserted via the femoral or jugular veins into right side of heart. Catheter electrodes record the electrical activity in different heart structures. Can induce and stop dysrhythmias. Insertion of a pacemaker or implantable cardioverter defibrillator (ICD) or ablation of a dysrhythmia pathway may be done during or right after the EPS. See Chapter 35 for more details.	*Before:* Antidysrhythmic drugs may be stopped several days before study. Keep patient NPO 6–8 hr before test. Give premedication to promote relaxation if ordered. Obtain IV access. IV sedation often used during procedure. *After:* Assess vital signs often. Monitor ECG continuously per agency protocol. Patient will be on bedrest for 6–8 hr after procedure.
Fractional flow reserve (FFR)	During cardiac catheterization, a specialized wire is inserted into coronary arteries to measure pressure and flow. Information is used to determine need for angioplasty or stenting on nonsignificant blockages.	Same as for cardiac catheterization.
Invasive hemodynamic monitoring	Invasive and minimally invasive bedside hemodynamic monitoring is done using intraarterial, pulmonary artery, and central vein catheters. Monitors arterial BP, stroke volume variation, pulmonary artery pressure, pulmonary artery wedge pressure, cardiac output, and central venous pressure. Used to evaluate cardiovascular status and response to treatment.	Patients who need invasive hemodynamic monitoring are critically ill and are monitored in critical care units. See Chapter 65 for complete information on hemodynamic monitoring.
Intravascular ultrasound (IVUS)	During cardiac catheterization a small ultrasound probe is introduced into coronary arteries. Used to assess blood vessel patency, size and consistency of plaque, arterial walls, and effectiveness of intracoronary artery treatment.	Same as for cardiac catheterization.
Peripheral arteriography and venography	Peripheral vessel blood flow is assessed by injecting contrast media into appropriate arteries or veins (arteriography and venography). Serial x-ray studies done to detect atherosclerotic plaques, occlusion, aneurysms, venous abnormalities, or traumatic injury. See Table 37.9 for more peripheral vascular diagnostic studies.	*Before:* Assess for contrast allergy. Explain that patient may feel a warm sensation, salty taste after contrast injection. Patient may have nausea. Give mild sedative, if ordered. *During:* Observe patient for allergic reaction to contrast media. *After:* Inspect insertion site for bleeding or swelling. Check extremity with puncture site for pulsation, warmth, color, and motion. Encourage fluids to excrete radioactive substance.

Different classes of lipoproteins contain varying amounts of the naturally occurring lipids. These include:

1. *Chylomicrons:* primarily exogenous triglycerides from dietary fat
2. *Low-density lipoproteins (LDLs):* mostly cholesterol with moderate amounts of phospholipids
3. *High-density lipoproteins (HDLs):* about 50% protein and 50% phospholipids and cholesterol
4. *Very-low-density lipoproteins (VLDLs):* primarily endogenous triglycerides with moderate amounts of phospholipids and cholesterol

Elevations in triglycerides and LDL are strongly associated with CAD. An increased HDL level is associated with a decreased risk of CAD. HDLs serve a protective role by mobilizing cholesterol from tissues.

Although a relationship exists between high serum cholesterol levels and CAD, a measure of total cholesterol alone is not enough for an assessment of CAD. A risk assessment is calculated by comparing the total cholesterol to HDL ratio over time. An increase in the ratio means increased risk. This provides more information than either value alone.

Plasma levels of apolipoprotein A-I (apo A-I) (the major HDL protein) and the ratio of apo A-I to apolipoprotein B (apo B) (the major LDL protein) are stronger predictors of CAD than the HDL cholesterol level alone. Measurements of these lipoproteins can be useful in identifying patients at risk for CAD.

Lipoprotein (a), or Lp(a), has been studied for its role as a risk factor for CAD. Increased levels of Lp(a), especially with increased levels of lactate dehydrogenase (LDH), have been linked with the progression of atherosclerosis, especially in women.

Lipoprotein-associated phospholipase A_2 (Lp-PLA$_2$) is an inflammatory enzyme expressed in atherosclerotic plaques. High levels of Lp-PLA$_2$ are related to an increased risk for CAD, especially in black women.[14]

TABLE 31.9 Nursing Management

Care of the Patient Undergoing Cardiac Catheterization

Preprocedure

- Assess for allergies, especially to contrast dye.
- Perform baseline assessment, including vital signs, pulse oximetry, heart and breath sounds, neurovascular assessment of extremities (e.g., distal pulses, skin temperature, skin color, sensation).
- Withhold food and fluids for 6–12 hours before.
- Assess baseline laboratory values (e.g., cardiac biomarkers, creatinine).
- Teach patient and caregiver about procedure and postprocedure care. Explain the use of local anesthesia at insertion site, placement of catheter, flushed feeling when dye is injected, and possible fluttering sensation of heart as catheter is passed.
- Give sedative and other drugs, as ordered.

Postprocedure

- Perform assessment and compare to baseline: vital signs, pulse oximetry, and heart and breath sounds. Note hypotension or hypertension and signs of pulmonary emboli (e.g., respiratory difficulty).
- Assess neurovascular status, including peripheral pulses, color, and sensation, of extremity per agency protocol.
- Place compression device over arterial site to achieve hemostasis, if indicated.
- Observe insertion site for hematoma and bleeding every 15 min for the first hour, then according to agency policy
- Monitor ECG for dysrhythmias or other changes (e.g., ST segment elevation).
- Monitor patient for chest pain and other sources of pain or discomfort.
- Maintain bedrest as ordered after femoral access.
- Maintain IV and/or oral fluid intake and monitor urine output.
- Teach patient and caregiver about discharge care, including signs and symptoms to report to HCP (e.g., site complications, return of chest pain), and any activity restrictions.

FIG. 31.9 Chest x-ray: standard posterior-anterior view. (From Drake RL, Vogl AW, Mitchell AWM: *Gray's anatomy for students,* ed 2, Philadelphia, 2010, Churchill Livingstone.)

Electrocardiography

Electrocardiogram. The basic P, QRS, and T waveforms (Fig. 31.4, *B*) are used to assess heart activity. Deviations from the normal sinus rhythm can indicate problems in heart function. There are many types of ECG monitoring, including a resting 12-lead ECG, ambulatory ECG monitoring, and exercise or stress testing (Table 31.7). Continuous ambulatory ECG (Holter monitoring) provides diagnostic information over a period of time. See Chapter 35 for a complete discussion of ECG monitoring.

Event Monitor or Loop Recorder. An event monitor or loop recorder is used to record less frequent ECG events. An event monitor is a portable unit that uses electrodes to store ECG data. There are 2 types, external and implantable. External loop recorders are worn for a month. They require electrodes continuously placed on the skin. They must be activated by the patient when symptoms occur. A disadvantage of external recorders is that, if symptoms occur for only a brief time, they may be over before the patient puts on the device and triggers it to record. Likewise, if patients are extremely symptomatic (e.g., syncopal), they may not be physically able to trigger the ECG recording. These devices can be perform a routine pacemaker check over the phone.

An implantable loop recorder is used for patients who may have serious yet infrequent dysrhythmias. This small recorder is implanted through a small incision into the chest wall. It continuously monitors heart activity. It keeps recordings if the patient uses a remote device when symptoms occur or automatically if the HR exceeds or goes below a set rate.

Functional Studies

Exercise or Stress Testing. Heart symptoms often occur only with activity because of the demand on the coronary arteries to supply more O_2. Exercise testing can evaluate the heart's response to physical stress. This helps to assess CVD and set limits for exercise programs. Exercise testing is used for persons who can walk unassisted or use a bicycle. It is also helpful for those with normal ECGs that limit diagnostic interpretation (e.g., pacemakers) (Table 31.7). ECG and BP are monitored throughout the exercise period for signs of cardiac stress.

6-Minute Walk Test. A general test of cardiac fitness, often used with older adults, is measuring the distance the patient can walk on a flat surface in 6 minutes. The test can provide a baseline for determining response to treatment and physical therapy.

Noninvasive Hemodynamic Monitoring. Noninvasive hemodynamic monitoring provides information about cardiovascular status changes without the risks of inserting and maintaining invasive devices. SV, CO, and systemic BP are measured using a continuous finger cuff or by thoracic bioreactance.[15] Monitoring stroke volume and CO during complex surgical procedures allows the anesthesia provider to titrate fluids and vasoactive drugs.

Imaging

Chest X-Ray. A radiographic picture of the chest can show heart shape and size and anatomic changes in individual chambers (Fig. 31.9). The chest x-ray records any displacement or enlargement of the heart, extra fluid around the heart (pericardial effusion), and pulmonary congestion (Table 31.7).

Echocardiography. The echocardiogram uses ultrasound (US) waves to record the movement of the structures of the heart. In the normal heart, US waves directed at the heart are reflected back in typical patterns. *Contrast echocardiography* involves the addition of an IV contrast agent (e.g., agitated saline) to help

FIG. 31.10 Long-axis images of the aortic and mitral valve with the depth adjusted to optimize evaluation of valve anatomy and motion. The 2-D images *(left)* in diastole *(top)* and systole *(bottom)* show normal aortic and mitral opening and closure. The color flow images *(right)* show normal left ventricular inflow with no aortic regurgitation in diastole *(top)* and normal antegrade flow in the left ventricular outflow tract and no mitral regurgitation in systole *(bottom)*. (From Otto C: *Textbook of clinical echocardiography,* ed 3, St Louis, 2004, Saunders.)

define the images, especially in technically difficult patients (e.g., obese).

The echocardiogram provides information about abnormalities of (1) valvular structures and motion, (2) heart chamber size and contents, (3) ventricular and septal motion and thickness, (4) pericardial sac, and (5) ascending aorta. The **ejection fraction (EF)**, or the percentage of end-diastolic blood volume that is ejected during systole, can be measured. The EF provides information about the function of the left ventricle during systole.

Two common types of echocardiograms are the *motion-mode (M-mode) echocardiogram* and the *two-dimensional (2-D) echocardiogram*. In the M-mode, a single US beam is directed toward the heart, recording the motion of the intracardiac structures and detecting wall thickness and chamber size. The 2-D echocardiogram sweeps the US beam through an arc, producing a cross-sectional view. This shows correct spatial relationships among the structures.

Doppler technology allows for sound evaluation of the flow or motion of the scanned object (heart valves, ventricular walls, blood flow). *Color-flow imaging (duplex)* is the combination of 2-D echocardiography and Doppler technology (Fig. 31.10). It uses color changes to show the speed and direction of blood flow. Pathologic conditions, such as valvular leaks and congenital defects, can be diagnosed more effectively.

Real-time three-dimensional (3-D) ultrasound is a technology that uses multiple 2-D echo images with computer technology to provide a reconstruction of the heart. This technique gives information about the structures of the heart and how these structures change during the cardiac cycle.

Stress echocardiography combines the information from a stress test with the information from an echocardiogram. A digital computer compares images before and after exercise, revealing wall motion and function. For those persons unable to exercise, IV drugs are used. These include dobutamine, which produces pharmacologic stress on the heart and dipyridamole (Persantine), which vasodilates healthy arteries. Unhealthy arteries do not respond as well, which is seen on the echocardiogram.

Transesophageal echocardiography (TEE) provides more precise echocardiography of the heart than surface 2-D echocardiography by removing interference from the chest wall and lungs (Table 31.7). The TEE uses a flexible endoscope with a US transducer in the tip for imaging of the heart and great vessels. The scope is passed into the esophagus to the level of the heart. M-mode, 2-D, Doppler, and color-flow imaging can be obtained.

TEE is used often in an outpatient setting for evaluation of mitral valve disease and for identification of endocarditis vegetation, thrombus before cardioversion, or the source of heart emboli. In addition, TEE is used in the operating room to assess intraoperative heart function and in the emergency department to detect suspected aortic dissection.

The risks of TEE are low. However, complications include perforation or tearing of the esophagus, hemorrhage, dysrhythmias, vasovagal reactions, and transient hypoxemia. TEE is contraindicated if the patient has a history of esophageal disorders, dysphagia, or radiation therapy to the chest wall. Patients need sedation during a TEE.

Cardiac Computed Tomography. Cardiac CT is a heart-imaging test that uses CT technology with or without IV contrast (dye) to see the heart anatomy, coronary circulation, and great blood vessels (e.g., aorta, pulmonary veins, artery). This technology is often called *multidetector CT (MDCT) scanning*. Types of CT scans used to diagnose heart disease include coronary CT angiography (CTA) and calcium-scoring CT scan (Table 31.7).

Coronary CTA is a noninvasive test. It can be done faster than a cardiac catheterization with less risk and discomfort to the patient. Patients must have a normal sinus rhythm for this test. Although the use of coronary CTA is increasing, cardiac catheterization is the gold standard to diagnose CAD. Further, when a cardiac catheterization is done, procedures (e.g., angioplasty, stent placement) can be done if coronary blockages are found. Last, the radiation exposure during a cardiac catheterization is less than the exposure during a CTA.

The calcium-scoring CT scan is used to find calcium deposits in plaque in the coronary arteries. The most common method used is the electron beam CT (EBCT) (Fig. 31.11). It can detect early coronary calcification before symptoms develop and confirm CAD in patients with suspected CAD. The amount of coronary calcium is a predictor of future cardiac events. The calcium score can be used in the risk analysis of patients without known CVD.

Cardiovascular Magnetic Resonance Imaging. Cardiovascular magnetic resonance imaging (CMRI) can detect and find areas of MI in a 3-D view. It is sensitive enough to find even small MIs that are not apparent with single-photon emission computed tomography (SPECT). CMRI aids in the final diagnosis of MI and the assessment of EF. It plays a role in prediction of recovery from MI and in the diagnosis of congenital heart and aortic disorders and CAD. One major advantage of CMRI is that it does not require any radiation to the patient.

Patients with coronary stents can undergo CMRI 6 weeks after stent placement. In patients with older model pacemakers

FIG. 31.11 Examples of coronary calcification of the left anterior descending coronary artery *(large arrow)* and left circumflex artery *(small arrow)* as seen on electron beam computed tomography. (From Libby P, Bonow R, Zipes D, et al: *Braunwald's heart disease: A textbook of cardiovascular medicine,* ed 8, St Louis, 2008, Saunders.)

and ICDs, CMRI is discouraged because the magnets can change the function of the devices. However, when there is a strong clinical need and the benefits outweigh the risks, CMRI can be done at centers experienced in this procedure. Many newer models of pacemakers and ICDs are approved for use with MRI.

Nuclear Cardiology. One of the most common nuclear imaging tests is the multigated acquisition (MUGA) or cardiac blood pool scan. This test provides information on wall motion during systole and diastole, heart valves, and EF (Table 31.7).

Perfusion imaging is used with exercise testing to determine whether the coronary blood flow changes with increased activity. Stress perfusion imaging may show an abnormality even when a resting image is normal. This procedure is used to diagnose CAD, make a prognosis in existing CAD, distinguish viable heart muscle from scar tissue, and determine the potential for success of various interventions (e.g., coronary artery bypass surgery, percutaneous coronary intervention) (see Chapter 33).

Exercise stress perfusion imaging is an option if a patient cannot exercise. IV regadenoson (Lexiscan), dipyridamole, or adenosine (Adenocard) can be given to dilate the coronary arteries and simulate the effect of exercise. After the drug takes effect, the isotope is injected, and the imaging is done.

SPECT uses technetium, thallium, or sestamibi as an imaging agent (isotope). Both obese patients and women with large breasts can have artifact, which can lead to false-positive results. Patients with severe multivessel coronary disease or blockages in their left main coronary artery may have false-negative results.

Positron emission tomography (PET) stress testing is increasingly being used due to its high sensitivity for revealing myocardial ischemia and viability. This type of myocardial perfusion imaging is often performed using rubidium-82. This agent allows for quicker studies with lower radiation exposure and better diagnostic quality.[16]

Interventional and Invasive Studies

Cardiac Catheterization. Cardiac catheterization is a common procedure. It provides information about CAD, coronary spasm, congenital and valvular heart disease, and ventricular function. Cardiac catheterization is also used to measure intracardiac pressures and O_2 levels, as well as CO and EF. With injection of contrast media and fluoroscopy, the coronary arteries can be seen, chambers of the heart can be outlined, and wall motion assessed (Table 31.8).

Cardiac catheterization is done by inserting a radiopaque catheter into the right and/or left side of the heart. For the right side of the heart, the HCP inserts a catheter into the femoral, internal jugular, subclavian, or antecubital vein. Pressures are recorded as the catheter is moved into the vena cava, right atrium, right ventricle, and pulmonary artery. The catheter is then moved until it is wedged or lodged in position. This blocks the blood flow and pressure from the right side of the heart and looks ahead through the pulmonary capillary bed to the pressure in the left side of the heart *(pulmonary artery wedge pressure)*. This pressure assesses the function of the left side of the heart.

Left-sided heart catheterization is done by inserting a catheter into a radial, femoral, or brachial artery. The catheter is passed in a retrograde manner up to the aorta, across the aortic valve, and into the left ventricle.

Coronary angiography is done with a left-sided heart catheterization. The catheter is positioned at the origin of the

FIG. 31.12 Angiogram showing a normal left coronary and circumflex artery. (From Drake RL, Vogl AW, Mitchell AWM: *Gray's anatomy for students*, ed 2, Philadelphia, 2010, Churchill Livingstone.)

coronary arteries (Fig. 31.3), and contrast medium is injected into the arteries. Patients often feel a temporary flushed sensation with dye injection. The images show the location and severity of any coronary blockages (see Figs. 31.12 and 33.7).

Complications of cardiac catheterization include bleeding or hematoma at the puncture site; allergic reactions to the contrast media; looping or kinking of the catheter; infection; thrombus formation; aortic dissection; dysrhythmias; MI; stroke; and puncture of the ventricles, septum, or lung tissue.

Intravascular Ultrasound. Intravascular ultrasound (IVUS), or intracoronary ultrasound (ICUS), is an invasive procedure done in the catheterization laboratory with coronary angiography. The 2-D or 3-D US images provide a cross-sectional view of the arterial walls of the coronary arteries. In IVUS, a miniature transducer attached to a small catheter is moved to the artery to be studied. Once it is in the artery, US images are obtained. The health of the arterial layers is assessed, including the composition, location, and thickness of any plaque. IVUS can evaluate vessel response to treatments such as stent placement and atherectomy, as well as any complications that

may have occurred during the procedure. Patients often have IVUS in addition to angiography or a coronary intervention. Thus nursing care after is similar to that of patient after a cardiac catheterization.

Electrophysiology Study. The electrophysiology study (EPS) records and manipulates the heart's electrical activity using electrodes placed inside the heart chambers. It provides information on SA node, AV node, and ventricular conduction. It is particularly helpful in determining the source and treatment of dysrhythmias. Patients with symptomatic tachydysrhythmias are at risk for sudden cardiac death. Information from an EPS helps to make a correct diagnosis and guides treatment decisions (Table 31.8). In EPS, catheters are inserted like a right-sided heart catheterization. Thus nursing care after EPS is similar to that of a patient after a cardiac catheterization.

CASE STUDY

Objective Data: Diagnostic Studies

(© Jupiterimages/ Banana-Stock/ Thinkstock.)

The HCP orders the following initial diagnostic studies for L.P.:
- 12-lead ECG
- CBC, basic metabolic panel (glucose, electrolytes, BUN, creatinine)
- PTT, PT, INR
- Pro-BNP
- Troponin, CK-MB
- TSH, free T_4
- Chest x-ray

The ECG shows atrial fibrillation with a rapid ventricular response. L.P.'s initial troponin and CK-MB levels are within normal limits. Chest x-ray, CBC, and coagulation studies are all within normal limits. The potassium level is 3.1 mEq/L and pro-BNP is high (1204 pg/mL). The HCP orders 250 mL NSS IV bolus; an oral dose of potassium, a loading dose of IV diltiazem followed by a continuous infusion, and weight-based heparin to be started in the emergency department. L.P. will be admitted to the progressive care unit and will have a consult with a cardiologist.

Discussion Questions

1. Are these the diagnostic studies that you expected to be ordered?
2. Which diagnostic study results are abnormal?
3. Which diagnostic study results are of most concern to you?

Answers available at *http://evolve.elsevier.com/Lewis/medsurg*.

■ BRIDGE TO NCLEX EXAMINATION

The number of the question corresponds to the same-numbered outcome at the beginning of the chapter.

1. A patient with a tricuspid valve disorder has impaired blood flow between the
   a. vena cava and right atrium.
   b. left atrium and left ventricle.
   c. right atrium and right ventricle.
   d. right ventricle and pulmonary artery.

2. A patient has a severe blockage in his right coronary artery. Which heart structures are *most* likely to be affected by this blockage *(select all that apply)*?
   a. AV node
   b. Left ventricle
   c. Coronary sinus
   d. Right ventricle
   e. Pulmonic valve

3. The part of the vascular system responsible for hemostasis is the
   a. thin capillary vessels.
   b. endothelial layer of the arteries.
   c. elastic middle layer of the veins.
   d. smooth muscle of the arterial wall.

4. When a person's blood pressure rises, the homeostatic mechanism to compensate for an elevation involves stimulation of
   a. baroreceptors that inhibit the sympathetic nervous system, causing vasodilation.
   b. chemoreceptors that inhibit the sympathetic nervous system, causing vasodilation.
   c. baroreceptors that inhibit the parasympathetic nervous system, causing vasodilation.
   d. chemoreceptors that stimulate the sympathetic nervous system, causing an increased heart rate.

5. A P wave on an ECG represents an impulse arising at the
   a. SA node and repolarizing the atria.
   b. SA node and depolarizing the atria.
   c. AV node and depolarizing the atria.
   d. AV node and spreading to the bundle of His.

6. Which subjective data related to the cardiovascular system should be obtained from the patient *(select all that apply)*?
   a. Annual income
   b. Smoking history
   c. Religious preference
   d. Number of pillows used to sleep
   e. Blood for basic laboratory studies

7. Which heart valve sound is heard best at the left midclavicular line at the level of the fifth ICS?
   a. Aortic
   b. Mitral
   c. Tricuspid
   d. Pulmonic

8. When assessing a patient, you note a pulse deficit of 23 beats. This finding may be caused by
   a. dysrhythmias.
   b. heart murmurs.
   c. gallop rhythms.
   d. pericardial friction rubs.

9. An expected finding in the assessment of an 81-year-old patient is
   a. a narrowed pulse pressure.
   b. diminished carotid artery pulses.
   c. difficulty isolating the apical pulse.
   d. an increased heart rate in response to stress.

10. Which nursing responsibilities are priorities when caring for a patient returning from a cardiac catheterization *(select all that apply)*?
    a. Monitoring vital signs and ECG
    b. Checking the catheter insertion site and distal pulses
    c. Helping the patient to ambulate to the bathroom to void
    d. Telling the patient that he will be sleepy from the general anesthesia
    e. Teaching the patient about the risks of the radioactive isotope injection

1. c, 2. a, b, 3. b, 4. a, 5. b, 6. b, c, d, 7. b, 8. a, 9. c, 10. a, b

For rationales to these answers and even more NCLEX review questions, visit *http://evolve.elsevier.com/Lewis/medsurg*.

ⓔ EVOLVE WEBSITE/RESOURCES LIST

http://evolve.elsevier.com/Lewis/medsurg
Review Questions (Online Only)
Key Points
Answer Keys for Questions
- Rationales for Bridge to NCLEX Examination Questions
- Answer Guidelines for Case Studies on pp. 661, 664, 667, and 676

Conceptual Care Map Creator
Audio Glossary
Supporting Media
- Animations
- Auscultation of Heart Valves
- Blood Flow: Circulatory System
- Cardiac Cycle During Systole and Diastole
- Pulse Variations
- Audio
- Diastolic Murmur
- Fourth Heart Sound (S_4)
- Murmurs: Blowing, Harsh or Rough, and Rumble
- Murmurs: High, Medium, and Low
- S_1 at Various Locations
- S_2 at Various Locations
- Single S_1
- Single S_2
- Systolic Murmur
- Third Heart Sound (S_3)

Content Updates

REFERENCES

1. Patton KT, Thibodeau GA: *The human body in health and disease*, ed 7, St Louis, 2018, Elsevier.
2. Wesley K: *Huszar' ECG and 12-lead interpretation*, ed 5, St Louis, 2017, Elsevier.
3. Huether S, McCance K: *Understanding pathophysiology*, ed 6, St Louis, 2017, Elsevier.
4. American Heart Association: Understanding blood pressure readings. Retrieved from *www.heart.org/HEARTORG/Conditions/HighBloodPressure/AboutHighBloodPressure/Understanding-Blood-Pressure-Readings_UCM_301764_Article.jsp*.
5. Wilson SF, Giddens JF: *Health assessment for nursing practice*, ed 6, St Louis, 2017, Elsevier.
*6. Parikh JD, Hollingsworth KG, Wallace D, et al: Left ventricular functional, structural and energetic effects of normal aging: Comparison with hypertension, *PLoS One* 12, 2017. Retrieved from *https://doi.org/10.1371/journal.pone.0177404*.
7. Fajemiroye JO, Cunha LC, Saavedra-Rodríguez R, et al: Aging-induced biological changes and cardiovascular diseases, *Biomed Res Int*, 2018. Retrieved from *www.hindawi.com/journals/bmri/2018/7156435/*.
8. Girelli D, Piubelli C, Martinelli N, et al: A decade of progress on the genetic basis of coronary artery disease, *Eur J Intern Med* 41:10, 2017.
9. Clayton BD, Willihnganz MJ: *Basic pharmacology for nurses*, ed 17, St Louis, 2017, Elsevier.
*10. Ricci F, Di Scala R, Massacesi C, et al: Ultra-sensitive copeptin and cardiac troponin in diagnosing non-ST-segment elevation acute coronary syndromes—The COPACS study, *AJM* 129:105, 2016.
*11. Zhang P, Wu X, Li G, et al: Prognostic role of copeptin with all-cause mortality after heart failure: A systematic review and meta-analysis, *Ther Clin Risk Manag* 13:49, 2017.
12. Pagana KD, Pagana TJ, Pagana TN: *Mosby's diagnostic and laboratory test reference*, ed 13, St Louis, 2017, Elsevier.
*13. Alvin MD, Jaffe AS, Ziegelstein RC, et al: Eliminating creatine kinase–myocardial band testing in suspected acute coronary syndrome, *JAMA Intern Med* 177:1508, 2017.
*14. Rusnak J, Fastner C, Behnes M, et al: Biomarkers in stable coronary artery disease, *Curr Pharm Biotechnol* 18:456, 2017.
15. Renner J, Grünewald M, Bein B: Monitoring high-risk patients: Minimally invasive and non-invasive possibilities, *Best Pract Res Clin Anaesthesiol* 30:201, 2016.
16. Waterstram-Rich KM, Gilmore DA: *Nuclear medicine and PET/CT: Technology and techniques*, ed 8, St Louis, 2017, Elsevier.

*Evidence-based information for clinical practice.

32

Hypertension

Pamela Wilkerson and Melissa Hutchinson

By doing what you love, you inspire and awaken the hearts of others.

Satsuki Shibuya

ⓔ http://evolve.elsevier.com/Lewis/medsurg/

CONCEPTUAL FOCUS

Adherence
Fluids and Electrolytes

Perfusion
Self-Management

LEARNING OUTCOMES

1. Relate the pathophysiologic mechanisms associated with primary hypertension to the clinical manifestations and complications.
2. Choose appropriate strategies for the prevention of primary hypertension.
3. Describe the interprofessional care for primary hypertension, including drug therapy and lifestyle modifications.

4. Explain the interprofessional care of the older adult with primary hypertension.
5. Prioritize the nursing management of the patient with primary hypertension.
6. Describe the nursing and interprofessional care of a patient with a hypertensive crisis.

KEY TERMS

blood pressure (BP), p. 678
hypertension, p. 678
hypertensive crisis, p. 695

orthostatic hypotension, p. 692
elevated blood pressure, p. 681
primary hypertension, p. 681

secondary hypertension, p. 681
systemic vascular resistance (SVR), p. 679

Hypertension, or high blood pressure (BP), is one of the most important modifiable risk factors that can lead to the development of cardiovascular disease (CVD). As BP increases so does the risk for myocardial infarction (MI), heart failure (HF), stroke, and renal disease. Hypertension-induced retinopathy can impair vision. This chapter discusses the nursing and interprofessional care of patients with or at risk for hypertension. Providing comprehensive care will require you to collaborate with many members of the health care team. Patient education is key to hypertension management. Proper nutrition and exercise are important health promotion behaviors.

Current guidelines reveal that around 46% of adults in the United States meet criteria for the general diagnosis of hypertension. Heart disease, often directly related to hypertension, accounts for 23.7% of all deaths each year in the United States.[1,2] The National Health and Nutrition Examination Survey (NHANES) tracks prevention, treatment, and control of hypertension.[3] Data from NHANES showed that 83% of people 20 years of age and older with hypertension were aware that they had high BP. Of those, 76% were receiving treatment; 48%, though, did not currently have their BP well controlled.[4]

The American College of Cardiology Foundation and the American Heart Association (AHA) provide performance measures for hypertension management that address the treatment and control of BP to target goals. Target goals have been updated with new information from the evidence-based Guideline for the Prevention, Detection, Evaluation, and Management of High Blood Pressure in Adults: A Report of the American College of Cardiology/AHA Task Force on Clinical Practice Guidelines and the Systolic Blood Pressure Intervention Trial (SPRINT). Target goals take age and comorbidities into consideration when recommending treatment options.[5]

National guidelines are designed to apply to all racial and ethnic groups. However, specific groups have a higher incidence of risk factors (see boxes on Promoting Health Equity and Gender Differences).[5,6]

NORMAL REGULATION OF BLOOD PRESSURE

Blood pressure (BP) is the force exerted by the blood against the walls of the blood vessel. It must be adequate to maintain tissue perfusion during activity and rest. Maintaining normal BP and tissue perfusion requires the integration of both systemic factors and local peripheral vascular effects. BP is mainly a function of cardiac output (CO) and systemic vascular resistance (Fig. 32.1).

All Ethnicities
- There are 3 factors associated with decreased prevalence of hypertension for all ethnicities: People born outside the United States, living in a household that does not speak English in the home, or living in a household with limited time living in the United States

Blacks
- Have the highest prevalence of hypertension in the world
- Are more likely to have resistant hypertension
- Develop hypertension at a younger age than other ethnicities with higher average blood pressure
- Have a higher incidence of hypertension among women than among men
- Have more nocturnal nondipping BP than whites, which is associated with an increase in CVD
- Hypertension is more aggressive and results in more severe end-organ damage
- Have the highest death rate resulting from hypertension
- Make less renin and do not respond well to renin-inhibiting drugs
- Have better BP control with calcium channel blockers and diuretics, especially with monotherapy
- Have a higher risk for angioedema with ACE inhibitors than whites

Hispanics
- Are less likely to receive treatment for hypertension than whites and blacks
- Have lower rates of BP control than whites and blacks
- Have lower levels of awareness of hypertension and its treatment than whites and blacks

GENDER DIFFERENCES
Hypertension

Men
- Before early middle age, hypertension is more common in men.

Women
- Hypertension is 2 to 3 times more common in women who take oral contraceptives than in women who do not.
- A history of preeclampsia may be an early sign of risk for CVD.
- After age 64, hypertension is more common in women. Part of the rise in BP in women is attributed to menopause-related factors, such as estrogen withdrawal, overproduction of pituitary hormones, and weight gain.
- It is harder to control hypertension in older women (ages 70 to 79) than in women ages 50 to 69, despite having similar rates of treatment.

CO is the total blood flow through the systemic or pulmonary circulation per minute. It is described as the stroke volume (SV) or the amount of blood pumped out of the left ventricle per beat (about 70 mL) multiplied by the heart rate (HR).

Systemic vascular resistance (SVR) is the force opposing the movement of blood within the blood vessels. The radius of the small arteries and arterioles is the principal factor determining SVR. As arteries narrow, resistance to blood flow increases. As arteries dilate, resistance to blood flow decreases. A small change in the radius of the arterioles creates a significant change in the SVR. If SVR is increased and CO stays constant or increases, arterial BP will increase.

The mechanisms that regulate BP can affect either CO or SVR or both. Regulation of BP is a complex process involving both short-term (seconds to hours) and long-term (days to weeks) mechanisms. Short-term mechanisms, including the sympathetic nervous system (SNS) and vascular endothelium, are active within a few seconds. Long-term mechanisms include renal and hormonal processes that regulate arteriolar resistance and blood volume. In a healthy person, these regulatory mechanisms work in response to the body's demands.

Sympathetic Nervous System
The nervous system, which reacts within seconds after a drop in BP, increases BP by activating the SNS. Increased SNS activity increases HR, and cardiac contractility produces widespread vasoconstriction in the peripheral arterioles and promotes the release of renin from the kidneys. The net effect of SNS activation is to increase BP by increasing both CO and SVR.

Specialized nerve cells called *baroreceptors* are found in the carotid arteries and arch of the aorta. These cells sense changes in BP and send this information to the vasomotor centers in the brainstem. The brainstem sends this information through complex networks of neurons that excite or inhibit efferent nerves. SNS efferent nerves innervate cardiac and vascular smooth muscle cells. Under normal conditions, a low level of continuous SNS activity maintains vascular tone. BP may be reduced by the withdrawal of SNS activity or by stimulation of the parasympathetic nervous system (PNS). The PNS decreases the HR (via the vagus nerve) and thereby decreases CO.

The neurotransmitter norepinephrine (NE) is released from SNS nerve endings. NE activates receptors in the sinoatrial

FIG. 32.1 Factors influencing BP. Hypertension develops when one or more of the BP-regulating mechanisms are defective.

TABLE 32.1 Sympathetic Nervous System Receptors Affecting BP

Receptor	Location	Response When Activated
α_1	Vascular smooth muscle	Vasoconstriction
	Heart	Increased contractility (positive inotropic effect)
α_2	Presynaptic nerve terminals	Inhibition of norepinephrine release
	Vascular smooth muscle	Vasoconstriction
β_1	Heart	Increased contractility (positive inotropic effect)
		Increased heart rate (positive chronotropic effect)
		Increased conduction (positive dromotropic effect)
	Juxtaglomerular cells of the kidney	Increased renin secretion
β_2	Smooth muscle of blood vessels in heart (e.g., coronary arteries), lungs (e.g., bronchi), and skeletal muscle	Vasodilation
Dopamine receptors	Primarily renal blood vessels	Vasodilation

node, myocardium, and vascular smooth muscle. The response to NE depends on the type of receptors present. SNS receptors are classified as α_1, α_2, β_1, and β_2 (Table 32.1). The smooth muscle of the blood vessels has α-adrenergic and β_2-adrenergic receptors. α-Adrenergic receptors found in the peripheral vasculature cause vasoconstriction when stimulated by NE. β_1-Adrenergic receptors in the heart respond to NE and epinephrine with increased HR (chronotropic), increased force of contraction (inotropic), and increased speed of conduction (dromotropic). β_2-Adrenergic receptors are activated mainly by epinephrine released from the adrenal medulla and cause vasodilation (Fig. 32.1).

The sympathetic vasomotor center interacts with many areas of the brain to maintain normal BP under various conditions. It is activated during times of pain, stress, and exercise. The SNS response causes an appropriate increase in CO and BP to adjust to the body's increased O_2 demands. During postural change from lying to standing, there is a transient decrease in BP. The vasomotor center is stimulated, and the SNS response causes peripheral vasoconstriction and increased venous return to the heart. If this reaction did not occur, blood flow to the brain would be inadequate, resulting in dizziness or syncope.

Baroreceptors. *Baroreceptors* have a vital role in maintaining BP stability during normal activities. They are sensitive to stretching and, when stimulated by an increase in BP, send inhibitory impulses to the sympathetic vasomotor center. SNS inhibition results in decreased HR, decreased force of contraction, and vasodilation in peripheral arterioles.

When baroreceptors sense a fall in BP, the SNS is activated. The result is constriction of the peripheral arterioles, increased HR, and increased contractility of the heart. In long-standing hypertension, the baroreceptors become adjusted to elevated BP levels and recognize this level as their new "normal."

Vascular Endothelium

The vascular endothelium is a single-cell layer that lines the blood vessels. The endothelium is very active and responsible for several critical functions. These include platelet adhesion, coagulation regulation, immune function, and regulating fluid control within the vessel and extravascular space. The endothelium can cause adhesion and aggregation of neutrophils and stimulate smooth muscle growth.

The endothelium is essential to the regulation and maintenance of vasodilating and vasoconstricting substances. Endothelium-derived vasoactive substances include *nitric oxide* (NO) and *prostacyclin*, which are both vasodilators. Another product of the endothelium is *endothelin* (ET), which is a potent vasoconstrictor (Fig. 32.1). Cardiovascular risk factors, such as smoking and diabetes, can reduce functional endothelial cells. This can cause arterial tone changes (through either excessive constriction or dilation), which is an early warning signal of CVD.

Renal System

The kidneys contribute to BP regulation by controlling sodium excretion and extracellular fluid (ECF) volume (see Chapter 44). Sodium retention results in water retention, which causes an increase in ECF volume. This action increases the venous return to the heart and SV. Together these increase CO and BP.

The renin-angiotensin-aldosterone system (RAAS) plays an essential role in BP regulation (Fig. 32.1). The juxtaglomerular apparatus in the kidney secretes renin in response to SNS stimulation, decreased blood flow through the kidneys, or decreased serum sodium concentration. Renin is an enzyme that converts angiotensinogen to angiotensin I. Angiotensin I is then converted to angiotensin II (A-II) by angiotensin-converting enzyme (ACE). A-II increases BP by 2 different mechanisms (see Fig. 44.4). First, A-II is a potent vasoconstrictor and increases SVR. This results in an immediate increase in BP. Second, over a period of hours or days, A-II increases BP indirectly by stimulating the adrenal cortex to secrete aldosterone.

A-II acts at a local level within the heart and blood vessels. These effects include vasoconstriction and tissue growth that result in remodeling of the vessel walls, which can be due to or caused by endothelial dysfunction. These changes are linked to the development of primary hypertension and the long-term effects of hypertension (e.g., atherosclerosis, renal disease, cardiac hypertrophy).

Prostaglandins (PGE_2 and PGI_2) secreted by the renal medulla have a vasodilator effect on the systemic circulation. This results in decreased SVR and lowering of BP. Heart cells secrete the natriuretic peptides (atrial natriuretic peptide [ANP] and b-type natriuretic peptide [BNP]). They oppose the effects of antidiuretic hormone (ADH) and aldosterone. This results in *natriuresis* (excretion of sodium in urine) and diuresis, resulting in reduced blood volume and BP.

Endocrine System

SNS stimulation results in the release of epinephrine along with a small fraction of NE by the adrenal medulla. Epinephrine increases CO by increasing HR and myocardial contractility. Epinephrine activates β_2-adrenergic receptors in peripheral arterioles of skeletal muscle, causing vasodilation. In peripheral arterioles with only α_1-adrenergic receptors (skin and kidneys), epinephrine causes vasoconstriction.

A-II stimulates the adrenal cortex to release aldosterone. Aldosterone stimulates the kidneys to retain sodium and water, which increases blood volume and CO (see Fig. 44.4).

Increased blood sodium and osmolarity levels stimulates the release of ADH from the posterior pituitary gland. ADH increases the ECF volume by promoting the reabsorption of water in the distal and collecting tubules of the kidneys. The resulting increase in blood volume causes an increase in CO and BP.

HYPERTENSION

Classification of Hypertension

Table 32.2 shows the BP classifications for people 18 years of age and older. Normal blood pressure is defined as a systolic BP (SBP) < 120 mm Hg and a diastolic BP (DBP < 80 mm Hg. Elevated blood pressure is defined as an SBP between 120-129 mm Hg and a DBP < 80 mm Hg. *Hypertension (stage 1)* is defined as an SBP between 130-139 mm Hg and a DBP between 80-89 mm Hg. *Hypertension (stage 2)* is defined as an SBP > 140 mm Hg and a DBP > 90 mm Hg.[5] If either the SBP or DBP is outside of a range, the higher measurement determines the classification. For example, 115/86 would be classified as hypertension stage 1 even though the SBP is within normal limits. SBP increases with age. DBP rises until around 55 years old and then declines. BP classification is based on 2 or more readings, accurately performed on both arms, on 2 separate occasions.

Etiology

Hypertension can result from either primary or secondary causes.

Primary Hypertension. Primary hypertension *(essential* or *idiopathic)* is elevated BP without an identified cause. It accounts for 90% to 95% of all cases of hypertension. Although the exact reason for primary hypertension is unknown, there are multiple contributing factors. These include changes in endothelial function related to either vasoconstricting or vasodilating agents, increased SNS activity, overproduction of sodium-retaining hormones, increased sodium intake, greater than ideal body weight, age, family history, ethnicity, diabetes, tobacco use, and excess alcohol intake.

Secondary Hypertension. Secondary hypertension is elevated BP with a specific cause that often can be identified and corrected (Table 32.3). Secondary hypertension can become resistant, causing cardiovascular complications if left untreated. This type of hypertension accounts for 5% to 10% of hypertension in adults. Secondary hypertension should be suspected in people who suddenly develop high BP, especially if it is severe. Findings that suggest secondary hypertension relate to the underlying cause. For example, an abdominal bruit heard over the renal arteries may indicate renal disease. It is often present in patients with obstructive sleep apnea. Treatment is aimed at removing or treating the underlying cause. Secondary hypertension is a contributing factor to hypertensive crisis (discussed later in this chapter).

Pathophysiology of Primary Hypertension

BP rises with any increase in CO or SVR. As hypertension progresses from elevated to stage 1, increases in both blood volume and CO are often present, leading to an increase in SVR. As hypertension progresses, SVR rises, and CO returns to normal. The hemodynamic hallmark of hypertension is a persistently increased SVR. This persistent elevation in SVR may occur in several ways. Table 32.4 shows factors that relate to the development of primary hypertension or contribute to its consequences. Abnormalities of any of the mechanisms involved in maintaining normal BP can result in hypertension (Fig. 32.1).

 ## Genetic Link

Different sets of genes may regulate BP at various times throughout the life span.[2] Genetic variations are associated with the development of hypertension. For example, genetic abnormalities have been associated with a rare form of hypertension characterized by excess levels of potassium. Several genetic variants of substances on the endothelium affect BP and the development of hypertension by influencing the body's sensitivity to salt. When endothelial surface proteins are activated, proinflammatory properties are stimulated, impairing the endothelial cells' ability to activate vasodilatory effects, which leads to hypertension.

Research is currently ongoing to understand the complicated role that endothelial dysfunction and genetics play in the formation and progression of hypertension. We currently recommend screening of children and siblings of persons with hypertension and strongly advising them to adopt healthy lifestyles to minimize their risk for developing hypertension.

Water and Sodium Retention. Excess sodium intake is linked to the development of hypertension. Although most people consume a high-sodium diet, only 1 in 3 will develop hypertension. When sodium is restricted in people with hypertension, their BP usually falls. This suggests that some degree of sodium sensitivity may exist for high sodium intake to trigger the development of hypertension. A high sodium intake may

---

TABLE 32.2 Classification of Hypertension

Category	SBP (mm Hg)		DBP (mm Hg)
Normal	<120	and	<80
Elevated	120–129	and	<80
Hypertension, stage 1	130–139	or	80–89
Hypertension, stage 2	≥140	or	≥90

Source: Whelton PK, Carey RM, Aronow WS, et al: 2017 ACC/AHA/AAPA/ABC/ACPM/AGS/APhA/ASH/ASPC/NMA/PCNA guideline for the prevention, detection, evaluation, and management of high blood pressure in adults: A report of the American College of Cardiology/AHA Task Force on Clinical Practice Guidelines, *Journal of the American College of Cardiology* 71:e127, 2018.
DBP, Diastolic blood pressure; *SBP,* systolic blood pressure.

TABLE 32.3 Common Causes of Secondary Hypertension

- Cirrhosis
- Coarctation or congenital narrowing of the aorta
- Drug-related: estrogen replacement therapy, oral contraceptives, corticosteroids, nonsteroidal antiinflammatory drugs (e.g., cyclooxygenase-2 inhibitors), SNS stimulants (e.g., cocaine, monoamine oxidase)
- Endocrine disorders (e.g., pheochromocytoma, Cushing syndrome, thyroid disease)
- Neurologic disorders (e.g., brain tumors, quadriplegia, traumatic brain injury)
- Pregnancy-induced hypertension
- Renal disease (e.g., renal artery stenosis, glomerulonephritis)
- Sleep apnea

activate a number of systemic mechanisms. Fig. 32.2 shows the relationships among salt intake, BP, and changes in the structure of the heart.

In clinical practice, there is not an easy or straightforward test to identify people whose BP will rise with even a small increase in salt intake *(salt sensitive)* versus those who can ingest large amounts of sodium without much change in BP *(salt resistant)*. The effect of sodium on BP has a strong genetic component. The effect of sodium is more significant in blacks and middle-aged and older adults. This can increase the potential of renal dysfunction, endothelial dysfunction, and HF in these persons.[7,8]

TABLE 32.4 Risk Factors for Primary Hypertension

Risk Factor	Description
Age	• Systolic BP rises progressively with age. • After age 50, SBP >140 mm Hg is a more important cardiovascular risk factor than diastolic BP
Alcohol	• Excess alcohol intake is strongly associated with hypertension • Moderate intake of alcohol has cardioprotective properties; males should limit their daily intake of alcohol to 2 drinks per day, and 1 drink per day for females
Diabetes	• Hypertension is more common in patients with diabetes • When hypertension and diabetes coexist, complications (e.g., target organ disease) are more severe
Elevated serum lipids	• ↑ Levels of cholesterol and triglycerides are primary risk factors for atherosclerosis • Hyperlipidemia is more common in people with hypertension
Ethnicity	• The incidence of hypertension is 2 times higher in blacks than in whites (See Promoting Health Equity box on p. 679.)

Excess dietary sodium	• High sodium intake can
	  • Contribute to hypertension in salt-sensitive patients
	  • Decrease the effectiveness of certain antihypertensive drugs

Family history	• History of a close blood relative (e.g., parents, sibling) with hypertension is associated with an ↑ risk for developing hypertension
Gender	• Hypertension is more prevalent in men in young adulthood and early middle age • After age 64, hypertension is more prevalent in women (See Gender Differences box on p. 679)
Obesity	• Weight gain is associated with ↑ frequency of hypertension • Risk increases with central abdominal obesity
Sedentary lifestyle	• Regular physical activity can help control weight and reduce cardiovascular risk • Physical activity may ↓ BP
Socioeconomic status	• Hypertension is more prevalent in lower socioeconomic groups and among the less educated
Stress	• People exposed to repeated stress may develop hypertension more often than others • People who develop hypertension may respond differently to stress than those who do not develop hypertension
Tobacco use	• Smoking tobacco greatly ↑ risk for CVD • People with hypertension who smoke tobacco are at even greater risk for CVD

Altered Renin-Angiotensin-Aldosterone Mechanism. High plasma renin activity (PRA) increases the conversion of angiotensinogen to angiotensin I (see Fig. 44.4). This change in the RAAS may contribute to the development of hypertension. Any rise in BP inhibits the release of renin from the renal juxtaglomerular cells. Based on this feedback loop, we would expect low levels of PRA in patients with primary hypertension. However, only about 30% have low PRA, 50% have normal levels, and 20% have high PRA. These normal or high PRA levels may be related to excess renin secretion from ischemic nephrons.

Stress and Increased Sympathetic Nervous System Activity. We have long recognized that factors such as anger, fear, and pain influence BP. Physiologic responses to stress, which are typically protective, may persist to a pathologic degree, resulting in a prolonged increase in SNS activity. Increased SNS stimulation produces increased vasoconstriction, increased HR, and increased renin release. Increased renin activates the RAAS, leading to elevated BP. People with high levels of repeated psychological stress develop hypertension more than those who have less stress.

Insulin Resistance and Hyperinsulinemia. Defects in glucose, insulin, and lipoprotein metabolism are common in primary hypertension. These defects are not present in secondary hypertension and do not improve when primary hypertension is treated. Insulin resistance is a risk factor in the development of hypertension and CVD. High insulin levels stimulate SNS activity and impair nitrous oxide–mediated vasodilation. Other pressor effects of insulin include vascular hypertrophy and increased renal sodium reabsorption.

Endothelial Dysfunction. Endothelial dysfunction is a marker for CVD, including primary hypertension. Hypertension can manifest as a prolonged vasoconstriction response or as a reduced vasodilator response. High levels of ET may cause prolonged vasoconstriction. Vasodilation effects can be altered by oxygen free radicals, which impair the bioavailability of NO. This leads to cellular dysfunction and an imbalance of the vasodilation and vasoconstriction mechanisms in the endothelium.

Clinical Manifestations

Hypertension is often called the "silent killer" because it is often asymptomatic until it becomes severe and target organ disease occurs. A patient with severe hypertension may have a variety of symptoms secondary to the effects on blood vessels in the various organs and tissues or to the increased workload of the heart. These secondary symptoms include fatigue, dizziness, palpitations, angina, and dyspnea.

In the past, we thought headaches and nosebleeds were symptoms of hypertension. Unless BP is very high, these symptoms are no more frequent in people with hypertension than in the general population. However, patients with hypertensive crisis (discussed later in the chapter) may have severe headaches, dyspnea, anxiety, and nosebleeds.[9]

Complications

The most common complications of hypertension are *target organ diseases* occurring in the heart (hypertensive heart disease), brain (cerebrovascular disease), peripheral vessels (peripheral vascular disease), kidneys (nephrosclerosis), and eyes (retinal damage) (Fig. 32.3).

Hypertensive Heart Disease

Coronary Artery Disease. Hypertension is a significant risk factor for coronary artery disease (CAD). The mechanisms

FIG. 32.2 Proposed link among salt intake, blood pressure, and changes in the heart. High dietary salt intake exerts hypertrophic effects on the left (and potentially also on the right) ventricle. Ventricular fibrosis can also result from the high salt intake through mechanisms mediated by the renin-angiotensin-aldosterone system (RAAS). Transforming growth factor-β1 (TGF-β1) is a multifunctional cytokine with fibrogenic properties. Overproduction of TGF-β1 (in part mediated by angiotensin II) results in fibrosis and ventricular dysfunction. (Modified from Frisoli TM, Schmieder RE, Grodzicki T, et al: Salt and hypertension: Is salt dietary reduction worth the effort? *Am J Med* 125:433, 2012.)

High dietary salt intake

↑ BP (afterload)

↑ Intravascular volume (preload)

Direct effects on protein synthesis of myocardial cells

↑ Aldosterone synthesis in myocardium

↑ Angiotensin receptors in myocardial cells

↑ Concentration of TGF-β1

Ventricular hypertrophy

Ventricular fibrosis

Eye
• Arteriovenous nicking
• Narrowing of retinal arterioles
• Hemorrhages or exudates
• Papilledema

Brain
• Stroke
• Transient ischemic attack

Heart
• CAD
• Heart failure
• Left ventricular hypertrophy

Kidney
• Microalbuminuria
• Proteinuria
• Serum creatinine ≥1.5 mg/dL

Abdominal
• Aneurysm
• Aortic dissection

Penis
• Erectile dysfunction

Peripheral Vascular
• Intermittent claudication
• Faint or absent peripheral pulses

FIG. 32.3 Common complications of hypertension.

by which hypertension contributes to the development of atherosclerosis are not fully known. The "response-to-injury" theory of atherogenesis suggests that hypertension disrupts the coronary artery endothelium (see Fig. 33.1). This results in a rigid arterial wall with a narrowed lumen and may account for the high rate of CAD, angina, and MI.

Left Ventricular Hypertrophy. Sustained high BP increases the cardiac workload and produces left ventricular hypertrophy (LVH) (Fig. 32.4). Initially, LVH is a compensatory mechanism that strengthens cardiac contraction and increases CO. However, increased contractility increases myocardial work and O_2 demand. Progressive LVH, especially in the presence of CAD, is associated with the development of HF.

Heart Failure. HF occurs when the heart's compensatory mechanisms are overwhelmed and the heart can no longer pump enough blood to meet the body's demands (see Chapter 34). Contractility is depressed, and SV and CO are decreased. The patient may have shortness of breath on exertion, paroxysmal nocturnal dyspnea, and fatigue.

Cerebrovascular Disease. Atherosclerosis is the most common cause of cerebrovascular disease. Hypertension is a significant risk factor for cerebral atherosclerosis and stroke. Even in mildly hypertensive people, the risk for stroke is 4 times higher than in normotensive people. Adequate BP control decreases the risk for stroke.

Atherosclerotic plaques are often found at the bifurcation of the common carotid artery and in the internal and external carotid arteries. Portions of the atherosclerotic plaque or the blood clot that forms with disruption of the plaque may break off and travel to cerebral vessels, producing a thromboembolism. The patient may have transient ischemic attacks or a stroke. These conditions are discussed in Chapter 57.

Hypertensive encephalopathy may occur after a marked rise in BP if autoregulation does not decrease the cerebral blood flow. *Autoregulation* is a physiologic process that keeps cerebral blood flow constant despite fluctuations in BP. Typically, as pressure in the cerebral blood vessels rises, the vessels constrict to maintain constant flow. When BP exceeds the body's ability to autoregulate, the cerebral vessels suddenly dilate, capillary permeability increases, and cerebral edema develops. This produces a rise in intracranial pressure. If left untreated, patients can die quickly from brain damage. Chapter 56 reviews cerebral blood flow and autoregulation.

Peripheral Vascular Disease. Hypertension speeds up the process of atherosclerosis in the peripheral blood vessels. This leads to peripheral vascular disease (PVD), aortic aneurysm, and aortic dissection (see Chapter 37). *Intermittent claudication* (ischemic leg pain precipitated by activity and relieved by rest) is a classic symptom of PVD.

Nephrosclerosis. Hypertension is one of the leading causes of chronic kidney disease (CKD), especially among blacks. Some degree of renal disease is usually present even with mild hypertension. Renal disease results from ischemia caused by the narrowing of the renal blood vessels. This leads to atrophy of the tubules, destruction of the glomeruli, and eventual death of nephrons. Initially intact nephrons can compensate, but these changes may eventually lead to renal failure. Laboratory signs of renal disease are albuminuria, proteinuria, microscopic hematuria, and high serum creatinine and blood urea nitrogen (BUN) levels. Nocturia is an early symptom of renal disease (see Chapter 46).

Retinal Damage. The appearance of the retina gives essential information about the severity and duration of hypertension. We can directly see the blood vessels of the retina with an ophthalmoscope. Damage to the retinal vessels indicates related vessel damage in the heart, brain, and kidneys. Manifestations of severe retinal damage include blurring of vision, retinal hemorrhage, and vision loss.

Diagnostic Studies

Measurement of BP is essential in assessing and monitoring hypertension. Chapter 31 and the Nursing Management section later in this chapter discuss BP measurement.

Some controversy exists over the diagnostic workup in the initial assessment of a person with hypertension. Most hypertension is classified as primary hypertension. Basic laboratory studies may be done to (1) identify or rule out causes of secondary hypertension, (2) evaluate target organ disease, (3) determine overall cardiovascular risk, or (4) establish baseline levels before starting therapy.

Table 32.5 lists diagnostic studies performed in a person with hypertension. Routine urinalysis, BUN, and serum creatinine levels are used to screen for renal involvement and provide baseline information about kidney function. Creatinine clearance reflects the glomerular filtration rate. Decreases in creatinine clearance indicate renal insufficiency. Chapter 44 discusses serum creatinine and creatinine clearance.

Measurement of serum electrolytes, especially potassium, is essential to detect hyperaldosteronism, a cause of secondary hypertension. Blood glucose levels aid in the diagnosis of diabetes. A lipid profile gives information about risk factors related to atherosclerosis and CVD. Uric acid levels establish a baseline since the levels often rise with diuretic therapy. An electrocardiogram (ECG) gives baseline information about heart status. It can identify the presence of LVH, cardiac ischemia, or previous MI. If LVH is suspected, echocardiography is often done. If the patient's age, history, physical examination, or severity of

FIG. 32.4 A, Massively enlarged heart caused by hypertrophy of the muscle in the left ventricle. B, Compare with the thickness of the normal left ventricle. The patient had from severe hypertension. (From Kumar V, Cotran RS, Robbins SL: *Robbins basic pathology,* ed 8, Philadelphia, 2007, Saunders.)

TABLE 32.5 Interprofessional Care

Hypertension

Diagnostic Assessment
- History and physical examination, including an ophthalmic examination
- Fasting blood glucose
- Routine urinalysis
- Basic metabolic panel with eGFR
- Complete blood count
- Serum lipid profile (total lipids, triglycerides, HDL and LDL cholesterol, total-to-HDL cholesterol ratio)
- Serum uric acid, calcium, and magnesium
- 12-Lead ECG

Optional
- 24-hour urinary creatinine clearance
- Echocardiography
- Liver function studies
- Serum thyroid-stimulating hormone (TSH)

Management
- Periodic BP monitoring
  - Home BP monitoring
  - Ambulatory BP monitoring
  - Every 3 to 6 months by an HCP once goal BP is achieved and stabilized
- Nutritional therapy
  - Restrict salt and sodium
  - Restrict cholesterol and saturated fats
  - Maintain adequate intake of potassium and calcium
  - Weight management
- Regular, moderate physical activity
- Tobacco cessation (see Tables 10.4 through 10.6)
- Moderation of alcohol intake
- Stress management techniques (see Chapter 6)
- Antihypertensive drugs (Tables 32.7, 32.8 and 32.9)
- Patient and caregiver teaching

eGFR, Estimated glomerular filtration rate.

EVIDENCE-BASED PRACTICE

Lifestyle Changes and Uncontrolled Hypertension

You are caring for F.H., a 43-yr-old black, female patient with a history of poorly controlled hypertension and CKD. She is taking 3 antihypertensive drugs and tells you she no longer can tolerate the side effects (e.g., fatigue, peripheral edema, dry mouth, frequent voiding). She wants to stop taking the drugs and control her hypertension by weight loss, exercise, and reducing her salt intake.

Making Clinical Decisions

Best Available Evidence. Nonpharmacologic interventions to reduce and control BP include weight loss (if appropriate), a DASH diet, and potassium supplementation; regular physical activity; and limiting women to no more than 1 alcohol drink per day. The potential impact of each lifestyle change is a 4-5 mm Hg decrease in SBP and 2-4 mm Hg decrease in DBP. A DASH diet may decrease SBP by about 11 mm Hg. Antihypertensive medications reduce the risk for cerebrovascular events, HF, and overall mortality in patients with concurrent risk for CVD (e.g., diabetes, kidney disease). Most hypertensive patients will need to take 2 or more medications on a long-term basis to achieve their goal BP, in addition to lifestyle changes.

Clinician Expertise. You know lifestyle changes can help reduce and control BP in some patients and should always be encouraged. However, patients with poorly controlled hypertension and target organ disease need medications to control BP and prevent further catastrophic complications (e.g., stroke).

Patient Preferences and Values. F.H. wants to stop her antihypertensive drugs because of unacceptable side effects.

Implications for Nursing Practice

1. What factors would you discuss with F.H. related to hypertension treatment and preventing further target organ disease?
2. Would you support F.H. in her desire to stop taking her prescribed drugs? Why or why not?
3. How can you help F.H. with her intentions to make lifestyle changes?

Reference for Evidence

Whelton PK, Carey RM, Aronow WS, et al.: 2017 ACC/AHA/AAPA/ABC/ACPM/AGS/APhA/ASH/ASPC/NMA/PCNA guideline for the prevention, detection, evaluation, and management of high blood pressure in adults: a report of the American College of Cardiology/AHA Task Force on Clinical Practice Guidelines, *Hypertension,* 2017.

---

hypertension points to a secondary cause, further diagnostic testing is needed.

Ambulatory Blood Pressure Monitoring. Some patients have elevated BP readings in a clinical setting and normal readings when BP is measured elsewhere. This phenomenon is referred to as *"white coat"* hypertension. Ambulatory BP monitoring (ABPM) is one method for diagnosing white coat hypertension. It is a noninvasive, fully automated system that measures BP at preset intervals over a 12- to 24-hour period. The equipment is worn continuously for 24 hours, and results are reviewed by the provider. The monitoring equipment includes a BP cuff and a microprocessing unit that fits into a pouch worn on a shoulder strap or belt. Tell patients to hold their arm still by their side when the device is taking a reading. Have them keep a diary of activities that may affect BP. Other potential applications for ABPM include suspected antihypertensive drug resistance, hypotensive symptoms with antihypertensive therapy, episodic hypertension, or SNS dysfunction.

BP has diurnal variability expressed as sleep-wakefulness difference. For day-active people, BP is highest in the early morning, decreases during the day, and is lowest at night. BP at night (during sleep) usually drops by 10% or more from daytime (awake) BP.[5] ABPM verifies the presence of diurnal variability.

Some patients with hypertension do not show a typical nocturnal dip in BP. They are referred to as "nondippers." Patients at highest risk for CVD are "reverse dippers." These patients have an increase in nighttime systolic BP. Current research is focused on using drugs to optimize cardioprotective effects and convert nondippers and reverse dippers to dippers.

Interprofessional Care

Table 32.5 summarizes the interprofessional care for a patient with hypertension. Goals include achieving and maintaining goal BP and reducing cardiovascular risk and target organ disease. Lifestyle modifications are a part of therapy for all patients with elevated blood pressure and hypertension.

Lifestyle Modifications. Lifestyle modifications are directed toward reducing the patient's BP and overall cardiovascular risk. The AHA's "Life's Simple 7" steps support ways to modify and improve health. These are (1) manage blood pressure, (2) control cholesterol, (3) reduce blood sugar, (4) get active, (5) eat better, (6) lose weight, and (7) stop smoking. Other modifications by the taskforce on hypertension address sodium restrictions and alcohol intake. Tools used by the AHA are available online at *www.heart.org/HEARTORG/Conditions/My-Life-Check---Lifes-Simple-7_UCM_471453_Article.jsp#.Wm1uaainHIU.*

Weight Reduction. Persons who are overweight have an increased incidence of hypertension and increased risk for CVD. Weight reduction has a significant effect on lowering BP in many people. The effect is seen with even moderate weight loss. A rule of thumb is for every 1 kg of weight lost, BP will decrease by 1 mm Hg. When a person decreases caloric intake, sodium and fat intake are usually also reduced. Although reducing the fat content of the diet has not shown any sustained benefits in BP control, it may slow the progress of atherosclerosis and reduce overall CVD risk (see Chapter 33). Weight reduction through a combination of calorie restriction and moderate physical activity is recommended for overweight patients with hypertension (see Chapter 40).

DASH Eating Plan. The DASH (Dietary Approaches to Stop Hypertension) eating plan stresses fruits, vegetables, fat-free or low-fat milk and milk products, whole grains, fish, poultry, beans, seeds, and nuts. Compared with the typical American diet, the plan has less red meat, salt, sweets, added sugars, and sugar-containing beverages. The DASH eating plan significantly lowers BP and reduces low-density lipoprotein (LDL) cholesterol.[7]

Dietary Sodium Reduction. Healthy adults should restrict sodium intake to 2300 mg/day or less. Blacks, people middle aged and older, and those with hypertension, diabetes, or CKD should restrict sodium to 1500 mg/day or less.[7] This involves avoiding foods known to be high in sodium. The AHA calls 6 food groups that are the highest sodium sources throughout the United States the "Salty Six." They recommend not adding salt and reducing intake of foods in these groups: bread products, lunch meat and cured meats, pizza, soup, sandwiches, and poultry (see Table 34.8).

Most adults exceed the recommended limits for sodium. Average sodium intake is around 4200 mg/day in men and 3300 mg/day in women.[8] The patient and caregiver, especially the person who prepares the meals, need to learn about low-sodium diets. Teaching should include reading labels of over-the-counter (OTC) drugs, prepared and packaged foods, and health products (e.g., toothpaste containing baking soda) to identify hidden sources of sodium. Review the patient's typical diet to identify foods high in sodium.

Sodium restriction may be enough to control BP in some patients. This may allow for lower drug dosages. Further, moderate sodium restriction lessens the risk for hypokalemia associated with diuretic therapy. However, the response differs between patients who are salt sensitive or salt resistant.

The significance of other dietary elements for the control of hypertension is not certain. Increased levels of dietary potassium and calcium are associated with lower BP in the general population and those with hypertension. People with hypertension should receive adequate intake of these from food sources. Calcium supplements are not recommended to lower BP.

Moderation of Alcohol Intake. Excess alcohol intake is strongly associated with hypertension. Drinking 3 or more alcoholic drinks a day is a risk factor for CVD and stroke. Men should limit their intake of alcohol to no more than 2 drinks per day and women and lighter weight men to no more than 1 drink per day; 1 drink is defined as 12 oz of regular beer, 5 oz of wine (12% alcohol), or 1.5 oz of 80-proof distilled spirits. Excess alcohol intake that results in cirrhosis is a frequent cause of secondary hypertension.

Physical Activity. A physically active lifestyle is essential to promote good health. The AHA and American College of Sports Medicine recommend that adults perform a moderate-intensity aerobic physical activity for at least 30 minutes most days (i.e., more than 5 days per week) with a goal of at least 150 minutes per week. Exercise goals can be achieved by performing shorter periods of exercise that last at least 10 minutes, several times during a day. Combinations of moderate and vigorous activity are acceptable (e.g., walking briskly for 30 minutes on 2 days of the week and jogging for 20 minutes on 2 other days).[10]

Differences in physical activity guidelines exist for adults age 18 to 65 years, adults over 65 years, and adults age 50 to 64 years with functional limitations. The differences relate to the definition of moderate and vigorous aerobic activity. For adults ages 18 to 65, walking briskly at a pace that noticeably increases the pulse defines moderate-intensity aerobic activity. Jogging at a pace that substantially increases the pulse and causes rapid breathing is an example of vigorous activity for this age group. For all other adults, individual fitness levels guide aerobic intensity.[10]

All adults should perform muscle-strengthening activities using the major muscles of the body at least twice a week. This helps to maintain or increase muscle strength and endurance. Flexibility and balance exercises are recommended at least twice a week for older adults, especially for those at risk for falls.[11] Moderate-intensity activities can lower BP, promote relaxation, and decrease or control body weight. Regular activity of this type can reduce SBP by 4 to 9 mm Hg.[5]

Physical activity is more likely to become a habit if it is safe and enjoyable, fits easily into one's daily schedule, and is inexpensive. Many shopping malls open early in the morning, offering a warm, safe, flat area for walking. Some health clubs offer special "off-peak" rates to encourage physical activity among older adults. Some health insurance carriers offer health club discounts as a benefit to encourage member fitness. Cardiac rehabilitation programs offer supervised exercise and education about cardiovascular risk factor reduction.

Help people with hypertension to increase their physical activity by explaining the need for physical activity, describing the types of physical activities, and aiding in starting an exercise plan. Advise sedentary people to increase activity levels gradually. Those with CVD or other serious health problems need a thorough examination and possibly a stress test before beginning an exercise program.

Avoiding Tobacco Products. Nicotine contained in tobacco causes vasoconstriction and increases BP, especially in people with hypertension. Smoking tobacco is a major risk factor for CVD. The cardiovascular benefits of stopping tobacco use are seen within a year in all age-groups. Strongly encourage everyone, especially patients with hypertension, to avoid tobacco use. Advise those who continue to use tobacco products to monitor their BP during use. Chapter 10 discusses tobacco use and smoking cessation.

Managing Risk Factors. Risk factors can be related to social determinants of health and psychosocial risk factors. These factors can contribute to the risk for developing CVD, and to a poorer prognosis and clinical course in patients with CVD. Social determinants of health are defined by the World Health Organization as "the conditions in which people are born, grow, live, work, and age, and the wider set of forces and systems shaping the conditions of daily life."[12] These factors include socioeconomic status, resources to meet daily needs, emotional and social support systems, stress at work and in family life, educational preparation, access to health care, safe housing, exposure to crime and violence, and negative emotions, such as depression and hostility. Often, these risk factors are clustered. For example, rates of depression tend to be higher in people with job stress or without access to safe housing.

These risk factors have direct effects on the cardiovascular system by activating the SNS and stress hormones. A wide variety of pathophysiologic responses can occur, including hypertension and tachycardia, inflammation, endothelial dysfunction, increased platelet aggregation, insulin resistance, and central obesity.[12]

Social determinants of health and psychosocial risk factors can contribute to CVD indirectly by their impact on lifestyle behaviors and choices. Screening for risk factors is essential so appropriate referrals can be given to help the patient and family. Referrals might include counseling, behavioral interventions, such as community or religious support systems, social work assistance for finding resources, such as fresh fruits and vegetables, or information on housing assistance. Once basic needs are met, options that can be beneficial might include relaxation training, stress management courses, support groups, and exercise training for people who are not in acute psychologic distress.[13]

Drug Therapy. The following are recommendations for antihypertensive drug therapy from the 2017 High Blood Pressure Clinical Practice Guidelines[5]:

- In patients 65 years or older with an average SBP of more than 130 mm Hg who are ambulatory and living in a community setting, rather than living in a care facility, treatment goals should be to obtain an SBP < 130 mmHg.
- In patients 65 years or older with an average SBP of more than 130 mm Hg who live in a care facility, and/or have multiple comorbidities or limited life expectancy, treatment should be based on patient preference, clinical experiences, and team input.
- In patients over 18 years old with hypertension, known CVD or other risk factors, a BP of 130/80 mm Hg is the goal of treatment.
- In all other patients without CVD or other risk factors, a BP of less than 130/80 mm Hg may be reasonable.

Drugs currently available for treating hypertension have 2 primary actions: (1) decrease the volume of circulating blood and (2) reduce SVR (Tables 32.6, 32.7, and 32.8).[5]

TABLE 32.6 Drug Therapy

Antihypertensive Agents

Drug	Mechanism of Action	Nursing Considerations
Adrenergic Inhibitors		
Central-Acting α-Adrenergic Agonist		
clonidine (Catapres) clonidine patch (Catapres-TTS)	Reduce sympathetic outflow from central nervous system Reduce peripheral sympathetic tone, produces vasodilation, decreases SVR and BP	Sudden discontinuation may cause withdrawal syndrome, including rebound hypertension, tachycardia, headache, tremors, apprehension, sweating Chewing gum or hard candy may relieve dry mouth Alcohol and sedatives increase sedation Transdermal patch may be related to fewer side effects and better adherence
guanabenz guanfacine (Tenex)	Same as clonidine	Same as clonidine, but not available in the transdermal formulation
methyldopa	Same as clonidine	Teach patient about daytime sedation and avoiding hazardous activities Taking a single daily dose at bedtime minimizes the sedative effect
α₁-Adrenergic Blockers		
doxazosin (Cardura) prazosin (Minipress) terazosin	Block α₁-adrenergic effects, producing peripheral vasodilation (decreases SVR and BP) Beneficial effects on lipid profile	Reduced resistance to the outflow of urine in benign prostatic hyperplasia Take at bedtime to reduce risk associated with orthostatic hypotension
phentolamine	Blocks α₁-adrenergic receptors, resulting in peripheral vasodilation (decreases SVR and BP)	Used in the short-term management of pheochromocytoma Used locally to prevent necrosis of skin and subcutaneous tissue after extravasation of adrenergic drug No oral formulation
β-Adrenergic Blockers		
Cardioselective Blockers		
acebutolol (Sectral) atenolol (Tenormin) betaxolol bisoprolol esmolol (Brevibloc) metoprolol (Lopressor)	Block β₁-adrenergic receptors (Table 32.1) Reduce BP by blocking β-adrenergic effects Decrease CO and reduce sympathetic vasoconstrictor tone Decrease renin secretion by kidneys	Monitor pulse and BP regularly Use with caution in patients with diabetes because may depress the tachycardia associated with hypoglycemia and adversely affect glucose metabolism Drug of choice for patients with a history of an MI or HF Less effective BP reduction in black patients Esmolol is for IV use only Lose cardioselectivity at higher doses
Non-Cardioselective Blockers		
nadolol (Corgard) pindolol propranolol (Inderal)	Block β₁- and β₂-adrenergic receptors (Table 32.1) Reduce BP by blocking β₁- and β₂-adrenergic effects	Same as cardioselective, except may cause bronchospasm, especially in patients with a history of asthma

TABLE 32.6 Drug Therapy

Antihypertensive Agents—cont'd

Drug	Mechanism of Action	Nursing Considerations
Mixed α- and β-Blockers		
carvedilol (Coreg) labetalol	α_1-, β_1-, and β_2-adrenergic blocking properties producing peripheral vasodilation and decreased heart rate (Table 32.1) Reduce CO, SVR, and BP	Same as β-blockers IV form is available for hypertensive crisis in hospitalized patients Keep patient supine during IV administration Assess patient tolerance of upright position (severe orthostatic hypotension) before allowing upright activities (e.g., commode)
Angiotensin Inhibitors		
Angiotensin-Converting Enzyme (ACE) Inhibitors		
benazepril (Lotensin) captopril enalapril (Vasotec) fosinopril lisinopril (Zestril) moexipril perindopril quinapril (Accupril) ramipril (Altace) trandolapril (Mavik)	Inhibit ACE, reduce conversion of angiotensin I to angiotensin II (A-II) Inhibit A-II–mediated vasoconstriction	Aspirin and NSAIDs may reduce effectiveness Adding a diuretic enhances effect, but should not be used with potassium-sparing diuretics Can cause an increase in serum creatinine Inhibit breakdown of bradykinin, which may cause a dry, hacking cough that can occur at any point during treatment, even years later Captopril may be given orally for hypertensive crisis
Angiotensin II Receptor Blockers (ARBs)		
azilsartan (Edarbi) candesartan (Atacand) eprosartan (Teveten) irbesartan (Avapro) losartan (Cozaar) olmesartan (Benicar) telmisartan (Micardis) valsartan (Diovan)	Prevent action of A-II and produce vasodilation and increased Na^+ and water excretion	Full effect on BP may not be seen for 3–6 wk Do not affect bradykinin levels, therefore an acceptable alternative to ACE inhibitors in people who develop a dry cough In patients with kidney disease, ACE inhibitors and ARBs should not be used together due to adverse renal effects
Calcium Channel Blockers		
Non-Dihydropyridines		
diltiazem extended release (Cardizem LA) verapamil intermediate release (Calan) verapamil timed-release (Verelan PM)	Inhibit movement of Ca^{++} across cell membrane, resulting in vasodilation Cardioselective resulting in a decrease in heart rate and slowing of AV conduction	Use with caution in patients with HF Grapefruit juice may increase serum concentrations and toxicity of certain calcium channel blockers; avoid concurrent use Used for supraventricular tachydysrhythmias Avoid in patients with second- or third-degree AV block or left ventricular systolic dysfunction
Dihydropyridines		
amlodipine (Norvasc) clevidipine (Cleviprex) felodipine isradipine nicardipine sustained release nifedipine long acting (Procardia XL) nisoldipine (Sular)	Cause vascular smooth muscle relaxation resulting in decreased SVR and arterial BP	More potent peripheral vasodilators Clevidipine is for IV use only; solution must be changed every 12 hrs Use of sublingual short-acting nifedipine in hypertensive emergencies is unsafe and not effective Serious adverse events (e.g., stroke, acute MI) have occurred IV nicardipine is available for hypertensive crisis in hospitalized patients; change peripheral IV infusion sites every 12 hrs
Direct Vasodilators		
fenoldopam (Corlopam)	Activates dopamine receptors, resulting in systemic and renal vasodilation	IV use only for hypertensive crisis in hospitalized patients Use cautiously in patients with glaucoma Patient should remain flat for 1 hr after administration
hydralazine	Reduces SVR and BP by direct arterial vasodilation	IV use for hypertensive crisis in hospitalized patients Twice-daily oral dosage Not used as monotherapy because of side effects Contraindicated in patients with CAD
minoxidil	Reduces SVR and BP by direct arterial vasodilation	Reserved for treatment of severe hypertension associated with renal failure and resistant to other therapy Once- or twice-daily dosage
nitroglycerin	Relaxes arterial and venous smooth muscle, reducing preload and SVR At a low dose, venous dilation predominates; at a higher dose, arterial dilation is present	IV use for hypertensive crisis in hospitalized patients with myocardial ischemia Given by continuous IV infusion with pump or control device
sodium nitroprusside	Direct arterial vasodilation reduces SVR and BP	IV use for hypertensive crisis in hospitalized patients Given by continuous IV infusion with pump or control device Arterial BP monitoring BP recommended Wrap IV solutions with an opaque material to protect from light Stable for 24 hrs then metabolized to cyanide, then thiocyanate Monitor thiocyanate levels with prolonged use (>3 days) or doses ≥4 mcg/kg/min

TABLE 32.7 Drug Therapy

Diuretic Agents

Drug	Mechanism of Action	Nursing Considerations
Aldosterone Receptor Blockers spironolactone (Aldactone) eplerenone (Inspra)	Inhibit the Na^+-retaining and K^+-excreting effects of aldosterone in the distal and collecting tubules	Monitor for orthostatic hypotension and hyperkalemia Do not combine with potassium-sparing diuretics or potassium supplements Use with caution in patients on ACE inhibitors or angiotensin II blockers Classified as potassium-sparing diuretics
Loop Diuretics bumetanide (Bumex) furosemide (Lasix) torsemide (Demadex)	Inhibit NaCl reabsorption in the ascending limb of the loop of Henle Increase excretion of Na^+ and Cl^- More potent diuretic effect than thiazides, but shorter duration of action	Monitor for orthostatic hypotension and electrolyte abnormalities Remain effective despite renal insufficiency Diuretic effect increases at higher doses Less effective for hypertension
Thiazide and Related Diuretics chlorothiazide chlorthalidone hydrochlorothiazide indapamide metolazone (Zaroxolyn)	Inhibit NaCl reabsorption in the distal convoluted tubule Increase excretion of Na^+ and Cl^- Initial decrease in ECF Sustained decrease in SVR Lower BP moderately in 2–4 wk	Monitor for orthostatic hypotension, hypokalemia, and alkalosis May potentiate cardiotoxicity of digoxin by producing hypokalemia Dietary sodium restriction reduces the risk for hypokalemia NSAIDs can decrease diuretic and antihypertensive effect and potentially cause renal impairment Teach patient to supplement with potassium-rich foods
Potassium-Sparing Diuretics amiloride (Midamor) triamterene (Dyrenium)	Reduce K^+ and Na^+ exchange in the distal and collecting tubules Reduce excretion of K^+, H^+, Ca^{++}, and Mg^{++}	Monitor for orthostatic hypotension and hyperkalemia Contraindicated in patients with renal failure Use with caution in patients on ACE inhibitors or angiotensin II blockers Avoid potassium supplements
Renin Inhibitors Aliskiren hemifumarate (Tekturna)	Directly inhibits renin, thus reducing the conversion of angiotensinogen to angiotensin I	May cause angioedema of the face, extremities, lips, tongue, glottis, and/or larynx Not to be used in pregnancy

ECF, extracellular fluid.

Fig. 32.5 shows the various sites and methods of action of antihypertensive agents. Drugs used in the treatment of hypertension include:

- *Adrenergic-inhibiting agents* act by decreasing the SNS effects that increase BP. Adrenergic inhibitors include drugs that work centrally on the vasomotor center and peripherally to inhibit norepinephrine release or to block the adrenergic receptors on blood vessels.
- *Angiotensin-converting enzyme (ACE) inhibitors* prevent the conversion of angiotensin I to angiotensin II and reduce angiotensin II (A-II)–mediated vasoconstriction and sodium and water retention.
- *A-II receptor blockers (ARBs)* prevent angiotensin II from binding to its receptors in the walls of the blood vessels.
- *Calcium channel blockers (CCB)* increase sodium excretion and cause arteriolar vasodilation by preventing the movement of extracellular calcium into cells.
- *Direct vasodilators* decrease the BP by relaxing the vascular smooth muscle and reducing SVR.
- *Diuretics* promote sodium and water excretion, reduce plasma volume, and reduce the vascular response to catecholamines.

 DRUG ALERT Doxazosin (Cardura)

- Use caution when giving the first dose. It is best to give the first dose at bedtime to reduce the first dose BP drop.
- Syncope occasionally occurs 30 to 90 min after the first dose, a too-rapid increase in dose, or addition of another antihypertensive agent to therapy.
- Drug interactions (severe low BP) can occur with patients taking phosphodiesterase inhibitors, such as sildenafil (Viagra) or tadalafil (Cialis).

The preferred first-line therapy for patients with stage 1 hypertension includes nonpharmacologic treatment and 1 first-line pharmacologic drug. The 3 preferred 3 first-line drugs are a thiazide diuretic, a calcium channel blocker, and an ACE inhibitor or ARB. For most patients, a diuretic should be the first drug ordered.[5] Patients with stage 2 hypertension will receive nonpharmacologic treatment and 2 antihypertensive agents from difference classifications. If a drug is not tolerated or is contraindicated, then a drug from another class is used.

Once antihypertensive therapy is started, patients should return for follow-up and dosage adjustments at monthly intervals until the goal BP is reached. More frequent visits are needed for patients with stage 2 hypertension or with co-morbidities.

TABLE 32.8 Drug Therapy

Combination Therapy for Hypertension

Combinations	Trade Names
Angiotensin-Converting Enzyme Inhibitors and Diuretics	
benazepril/hydrochlorothiazide	Lotensin HCT
enalapril/hydrochlorothiazide	Vaseretic
lisinopril/hydrochlorothiazide	Zestoretic
Angiotensin II Receptor Blockers and Calcium Channel Blockers	
olmesartan/amlodipine	Azor
telmisartan/amlodipine	Twynsta
valsartan/amlodipine	Exforge
Angiotensin II Receptor Blockers and Diuretics	
candesartan/hydrochlorothiazide	Atacand HCT
losartan/hydrochlorothiazide	Hyzaar
olmesartan medoxomil/hydrochlorothiazide	Benicar HCT
valsartan/hydrochlorothiazide	Diovan HCT
Angiotensin II Receptor Blocker, Diuretic, and Calcium Channel Blocker	
amlodipine/hydrochlorothiazide/valsartan	Exforge HCT
β-Blockers and Diuretics	
metoprolol/hydrochlorothiazide	Lopressor HCT
nadolol/bendroflumethiazide	Corzide
olmesartan medoxomil/amlodipine/hydrochlorothiazide	Tribenzor
Calcium Channel Blocker and Angiotensin-Converting Enzyme Inhibitor	
amlodipine/benazepril	Lotrel
Diuretics and Diuretics	
spironolactone/hydrochlorothiazide	Aldactazide
triamterene/hydrochlorothiazide	Dyazide, Maxzide

After BP is at goal and stable, follow-up visits can usually be at 3- to 6-month intervals. Comorbidities (e.g., HF), associated diseases (e.g., diabetes), and the need for ongoing monitoring (e.g., laboratory testing) influence the frequency of visits.

Patient and Caregiver Teaching Related to Drug Therapy. Side effects of antihypertensive therapy are common and may be so severe or undesirable that the patient does not adhere to the therapy.[5] Telling the patient about side effects that may reduce with time may help the person to continue with therapy. The number or severity of side effects may relate to the dose. It may be necessary to change the drug or decrease the dose. Advise the patient to report all side effects to the HCP.

A common side effect of several of the antihypertensive drugs is orthostatic hypotension. It results from a change in the autonomic nervous system's mechanisms for regulating BP, which are needed for position changes. Consequently, the patient may feel dizzy and faint when assuming an upright position after sitting or lying down. Table 32.12 (later in this chapter) presents specific measures to control or decrease orthostatic hypotension.

Sexual problems may occur with many antihypertensive drugs. This can be a significant reason that patients do not adhere to the treatment plan. Problems can range from reduced libido to erectile dysfunction. Rather than discussing a sexual problem with an HCP, the patient may decide just to stop therapy.

Approach the patient on this sensitive subject and encourage discussion of any sexual problems. The sexual problems may be easier for the patient to discuss once you explain that the drug may be the source of the problem.

Changing to another antihypertensive drug can decrease or relieve these side effects. Encourage the patient to discuss sexual issues with the HCP. If the patient is reluctant to do so, offer to alert the HCP to the side effects that the patient has. There are many options for treating hypertension, and a plan that is acceptable to the patient should be the goal.

Some unpleasant side effects result from a drug's therapeutic effect, but these can be decreased. For example, diuretics cause dry mouth and frequent voiding. Sugarless gum or hard candy may help ease the dry mouth. Taking diuretics earlier in the day may limit frequent voiding during the night and preserve sleep.

Resistant Hypertension. Carefully explore all reasons why a patient may not be at goal BP (Table 32.9). *Resistant hypertension* is the failure to reach goal BP in patients who are taking full doses of an appropriate 3-drug therapy regimen that includes a diuretic. Resistant hypertension carries a 2- to 6-fold increase in complications including MI and stroke over other hypertensive patients. Treatments focus on identifying potential factors that could contribute to hypertension, assessing adherence, and evaluating alternative drug combinations. Overactive renal nerves can be a cause of resistant hypertension. Percutaneous catheter-based radiofrequency ablation of the renal nerves (known as *renal denervation*) may help lower BP and SNS activity in patients with resistant hypertension. But, we need more evidence to support this treatment as a standard of care.

❖ NURSING MANAGEMENT: PRIMARY HYPERTENSION

◆ Nursing Assessment

Table 32.10 presents subjective and objective data to obtain from a patient with hypertension.

TABLE 32.9 Causes of Resistant Hypertension

- **Causes of pseudoresistant hypertension:**
  - Improper BP measurements (i.e., inappropriate BP cuff size)
  - Inadequate drug doses
  - Inappropriate drug therapy
  - Poor adherence to drug regimen (e.g., due to side effects, finances)
  - White coat syndrome
- **Volume overload**
  - Excess salt intake
  - Volume retention from kidney disease
  - Inadequate diuretic therapy
  - Drug-induced
  - Corticosteroids
  - Cyclosporine and tacrolimus (Prograf)
  - Erythropoietin
  - Illegal drugs (e.g., cocaine, amphetamines)
  - Licorice
  - Nonsteroidal antiinflammatory drugs
  - Oral contraceptives
  - OTC dietary or herbal supplements and drugs (e.g., ma huang, bitter orange)
  - Sympathomimetics (e.g., decongestants, diet pills)
- **Associated conditions**
  - Excess alcohol intake
  - Increasing obesity

Source: Brandani L: Resistant hypertension: A therapeutic challenge, *J Clin Hypertens* 20:76, 2018.

FIG. 32.5 Site and method of action of various antihypertensive drugs *(bold type)*. (From US Department of Health and Human Services: Seventh report of the Joint National Committee on Prevention, Detection, Evaluation, and Treatment of High Blood Pressure [JNC 7], Washington, DC, 2003, National Institutes of Health.)

◆ Nursing Diagnoses

Nursing diagnoses and collaborative problems for the patient with hypertension include:

- Altered blood pressure
- Ineffective tissue perfusion
- Impaired sexual function
- Potential complication: stroke, MI

◆ Planning

Nursing care focuses on the priority problems of maintaining BP at a level that decreases complications and supporting the patient to manage what may be a complicated drug regimen with many side effects. The overall goals for the patient with hypertension are that the patient will (1) achieve and maintain the goal BP; (2) have minimal side effects of therapy; and (3) manage and cope with this condition.

◆ Nursing Implementation

◆ **Health Promotion.** Primary prevention of hypertension is a cost-effective approach. Current recommendations for primary prevention include lifestyle modifications that prevent or delay the rise in BP in at-risk people. Following the DASH diet and reducing sodium can lower BP. This diet is recommended for primary prevention in the general population. Dietary changes

by the food industry (e.g., reducing the amount of salt in processed foods) may be useful.

The National Heart, Lung, and Blood Institute provides web-based educational materials in several languages for HCPs, patients, and the public to raise awareness about the dangers of high BP. Search available publications at *https://catalog.nhlbi. nih.gov/*.

Individual Patient Evaluation. Hypertension is usually discovered through routine screening for insurance, employment, and military physical examinations. You are in an ideal position to assess for the presence of hypertension, identify the risk factors for hypertension and CAD, and teach patients about these conditions. In addition to BP measurement, a health assessment should include such factors as age, gender, and race; diet history (including salt and alcohol intake); weight patterns; tobacco use; and family history of CVD, stroke, renal disease, and diabetes. Note all drugs taken, prescribed, OTC, and recreational. Last, ask the patient about a history of high BP and the results of any treatment.

Blood Pressure Measurement. Proper size and correct placement of the BP cuff are critical for accurate measurement (Table 32.11). Place the cuff snugly around the patient's bare upper arm with the midline of the bladder of the cuff (usually marked on the cuff by the manufacturer) placed in line with the brachial artery. Place the patient's arm at the level of the heart

TABLE 32.10 Nursing Assessment

Hypertension

Subjective Data

Important Health Information

- *Past health history:* Known duration and past workup of high BP; cardiovascular, cerebrovascular, renal, or thyroid disease; diabetes; pituitary disorders; obesity; dyslipidemia; menopause or hormone replacement status
- *Medications:* Use of any prescription, OTC, recreational, or herbal drugs or products; use of antihypertensive drug therapy

Functional Health Patterns

- *Health perception–health management:* Family history of hypertension or CVD; tobacco use, alcohol use; sedentary lifestyle; health literacy; readiness for change
- *Nutritional-metabolic:* Usual salt and fat intake; weight gain or loss
- *Elimination:* Nocturia
- *Activity-exercise:* Fatigue; dyspnea on exertion, palpitations, exertional chest pain; intermittent claudication, muscle cramps; usual pattern and type of exercise
- *Cognitive-perceptual:* Dizziness; blurred vision; paresthesias
- *Sexual-reproductive:* Erectile dysfunction, decreased libido
- *Coping–stress tolerance:* Stressful life events

Objective Data

Cardiovascular

- SBP consistently >130 mm Hg or DBP >80 mm Hg; orthostatic changes in BP and HR; bilateral BPs significantly different; abnormal heart sounds; laterally displaced apical pulse; decreased or absent peripheral pulses; carotid, renal, or femoral bruits; peripheral edema

Gastrointestinal

- Obesity (BMI ≥30 kg/m^2); abnormal waist-hip ratio

Neurologic

- Mental status changes

Possible Diagnostic Findings

- Abnormal serum electrolytes (especially potassium); ↑ BUN, creatinine, glucose, cholesterol, and triglyceride levels; proteinuria, albuminuria, microscopic hematuria; evidence of ischemic heart disease and left ventricular hypertrophy on ECG; evidence of structural heart disease and left ventricular hypertrophy on echocardiogram; evidence of arteriovenous nicking, retinal hemorrhages, and papilledema on funduscopic examination

TABLE 32.11 Blood Pressure Measurement

The patient should not have smoked, exercised, or ingested caffeine within 30 min before measurement.

1. Seat patient with legs uncrossed, feet on the floor, and back supported. Bare patient's arm and support it at heart level.
2. Begin measurement after the patient has rested quietly for 5 min. Ask patient to relax as much as possible and not to talk during the measurement.
3. Use the right cuff size, following instructions for fit and placement according to manufacturer's recommendations.
4. Measure and record BP in both arms initially and note any differences. There are conditions when an extremity should not be used for blood pressures. These exclusions include, but are not limited to, deep venous thrombosis, arteriovenous fistula or graft, peripherally inserted central line (PICC), lymphedema, and limb ischemia. Use the arm with the highest BP and verify the reference point is at the heart.
5. BP should preferably be taken with an oscillometric device, rather than manually. The accuracy of oscillometric devices may be limited if patients are hypertensive, hypotensive, or have heart dysrhythmias (e.g., atrial fibrillation).
6. Patients with atrial fibrillation may HR variations causing variations in BP, so it is recommended to take 3 different measurements over several minutes to confirm the BP.
7. For auscultatory measurement, estimate SBP by palpating the radial pulse and inflating the cuff until the pulse disappears. Inflate the cuff 20–30 mm Hg above this level.
8. Deflate the cuff at a rate of 2–3 mm Hg/sec.
9. Record the SBP and DBP. Note the SBP when the first of 2 or more Korotkoff sounds are heard and the DBP when sound disappears.
10. Provide the patient (verbally and in writing) with the BP reading, BP goal, and recommendations for follow-up.
11. Clean BP cuffs between patients according to the agencies policy for reusable medical equipment cleaning.

Source: Whelton PK, Carey RM, Aronow WS, et al: 2017 ACC/AHA/AAPA/ABC/ACPM/AGS/APhA/ASH/ASPC/NMA/PCNA guideline for the prevention, detection, evaluation, and management of high blood pressure in adults: A report of the American College of Cardiology/AHA Task Force on Clinical Practice Guidelines, *Journal of the American College of Cardiology* 71:e127, 2018.

> **!** **SAFETY ALERT Blood Pressure Measurement**
> - If using the forearm rather than the upper arm for BP measurement, document the site.
> - BP cuffs that are too small or too large will result in readings that are falsely high or low, respectively.
> - If bilateral BP measurements are not equal, record this finding and use the arm with the highest BP for all future measurements.

during BP measurement. For BP measurements taken in the sitting position, raise and support the arm at the level of the heart. For measurements taken in a supine position, raise and support (e.g., with a small pillow) the arm at heart level. If the arm is resting on the bed, it will be below heart level.

BP can be measured using the auscultatory (oscillatory) method.[14] Note any differences in measurements between each arm. Atherosclerosis in the subclavian artery can cause a falsely low reading on the side where the narrowing occurs.

If neither upper arm can be used to measure the BP (e.g., the presence of IV lines, fistula), or if a maximum size BP cuff does not fit the upper arm, use the forearm. In this case, position the proper size cuff midway between the elbow and the wrist. Auscultate Korotkoff sounds over the radial artery or use a Doppler device to note SBP. Use of an oscillometric device on the forearm is acceptable. Forearm and upper arm BPs are not interchangeable.[14]

Assess for orthostatic (or postural) changes in BP and HR in older adults, people taking antihypertensive drugs, and patients who report symptoms consistent with reduced BP on standing (e.g., light-headedness, dizziness, syncope). Measure serial BP and HR with the patient in the supine, sitting, and standing positions. First, have the patient lie down for 5 minutes then measure BP and HR. Help the patient to a standing position and measure the BP and HR both 1 minute and 3 minutes after standing. Record all 3 measurements, noting the patient's position and corresponding measurement. Usually, the SBP decreases slightly (less than 10 mm Hg) on standing, while the DBP and pulse increase slightly. Orthostatic hypotension occurs when a patient moves from a supine to standing position, and there is a decrease of 20 mm Hg or more in SBP, a decrease of 10 mm Hg or more in DBP, and/or an increase in the HR of 20 beats/min. Document any lightheadedness or dizziness during the procedure, which is considered an abnormal finding.[15] Common causes of orthostatic hypotension include dehydration and inadequate vasoconstrictor mechanisms related to disease or drug therapy.

Some people have a wide gap between the first Korotkoff sound and subsequent beats. This is called the *auscultatory gap.* Failure to inflate the cuff high enough may result in an inaccurate SBP, one that is too low for the patient.

In acute care settings, BP measurement is usually done to assess vital signs, volume status, and effects of drugs, rather than to diagnose hypertension. Trends in BP are more important than a single value. Inform the HCP of any patient with a persistent elevated BP. These patients should be evaluated for hypertension.[5]

Verifying how blood pressures are obtained at home is important when assessing for potential hypertension. Ensure that the home machine has been validated for accuracy and the patient records measurements to review later and measures the pressure at the same time of day for consistency. Confirming office BP readings with blood pressures obtained at home can help determine average BP.

Screening Programs. Screening programs in the community are widely used to identify persons who have a high BP. At the time of the BP measurement, give each person a written, numeric value of the reading. Explain why further evaluation is needed.

NURSING MANAGEMENT
Caring for the Patient With Hypertension

You will need to collaborate with many health care team members to deliver, delegate, and coordinate care based on the patient's status.
- Develop and conduct hypertension screening programs.
- Assess patients for hypertension risk factors and develop risk modification plans.
- Teach patients about lifestyle management and drug therapy.
- Monitor for adverse effects of antihypertensive drugs.
- Evaluate the effectiveness of lifestyle management and drug therapy in decreasing BP to acceptable levels.
- Teach about home BP monitoring, including the correct use of automatic BP monitors. Check that the device chosen by the patient meets the Association for the Advancement of Medical Instrumentation standards *(www.dableducational.org/sphygmomanometers/devices_1_clinical.html#ClinTable).*
- Make appropriate referrals to other HCPs, such as dietitians or stress management programs.
- Monitor for complications of hypertension, such as CAD, HF, cerebrovascular disease, PVD, and renal disease.
- Assess the patient with a hypertensive crisis for evidence of target organ disease (e.g., encephalopathy, renal insufficiency, cardiac decompensation).
- Manage the patient with hypertensive urgency or emergency, including giving drugs and evaluating for resolution of the crisis.
- Oversee UAP:
- Obtain accurate BP readings in outpatient and inpatient settings.
- Report high or low BP readings at once to RN.
- Check postural BPs as directed.

Collaborate With Other Team Members
Dietitian
- Obtain a diet history from the patient.
- Teach the components of the DASH diet.
- Provide instructions for dietary changes as needed.

Physical Therapist
- Assess patient's current level of fitness.
- Develop an exercise plan with the patient.

Focus efforts on (1) controlling BP in persons already identified as having hypertension; (2) identifying and controlling BP in at-risk groups, such as blacks, obese people, and blood relatives of people with hypertension; (3) screening those with limited access to health care; and (4) connecting persons with a HCP and/or health insurance if needed.

Cardiovascular Risk Factor Modification. Teaching about CVD risk factors is appropriate for all persons. Modifiable CVD risk factors include hypertension, obesity, diabetes, tobacco use, and physical inactivity. Discuss lifestyle modifications based on identified risk factors. Table 32.12 discusses general information and health-promoting behaviors for patients with hypertension.

◆ **Ambulatory Care.** Your primary role in the long-term management of hypertension is to assist the patient to reach the goal BP and adhere to the treatment plan. Your actions include

TABLE 32.12 Patient & Caregiver Teaching
Hypertension

When teaching the patient and/or caregiver about hypertension, include the following information:

General Instructions
- Give patient the BP reading and explain what it means (e.g., high, low, goal, borderline).
- Encourage patient to monitor BP at home and teach the patient to call the HCP if BP exceeds high or low limits set by HCP.
- Hypertension is usually asymptomatic, and symptoms (e.g., nosebleeds) do not reliably indicate BP levels.
- Long-term therapy and follow-up care are necessary to treat hypertension. Therapy involves lifestyle changes (e.g., weight management, sodium reduction, smoking cessation, regular physical activity) and, in most cases, drugs to regulate the BP.
- Therapy will not cure but should control, hypertension.
- Controlled hypertension usually results in an excellent prognosis.
- Explain the potential dangers of uncontrolled hypertension (e.g., stroke, heart attack).

Instructions Related to Medication Therapy
- Be specific about the names, actions, dosages, and side effects of prescribed drugs.
- Help the patient plan regular and convenient times for taking medications and measuring BP.
- Do not stop drugs abruptly since withdrawal may cause a severe hypertensive reaction.
- Do not double up on a dose when a dose is missed.
- If BP increases or decreases, do not change the dose of the drug without consulting the HCP.
- Do not take any drugs belonging to someone else.
- Supplement diet with foods high in potassium (e.g., citrus fruits, green leafy vegetables) if taking potassium-wasting diuretics.
- Avoid hot baths, excess amounts of alcohol, and strenuous exercise within 3 hours of taking drugs that promote vasodilation.
- Many drugs cause orthostatic hypotension. Reduce the effects of orthostatic hypotension by rising slowly from the bed, sitting on the side of the bed for a few minutes, standing slowly, and beginning to move if no symptoms develop (e.g., dizziness, lightheadedness). Do not stand still for prolonged periods, do leg exercises to increase venous return, or sleep with the head of the bed raised. Do lie or sit down when dizziness occurs.
- Some drugs cause sexual problems (e.g., erectile dysfunction, decreased libido). Consult with the HCP about changing drugs or dosages if sexual problems develop.
- Some side effects may decrease with time (e.g., fatigue, diarrhea).
- Be careful about taking potentially high-risk OTC drugs, such as high-sodium antacids, NSAIDs, appetite suppressants, and cold and sinus medications. Read warning labels and consult with a pharmacist.

evaluating therapeutic effectiveness, detecting and reporting any adverse treatment effects, assessing and enhancing adherence, and patient and caregiver teaching.

Home BP Monitoring. Most patients with known or suspected hypertension should monitor their BP at home. Home BP monitoring reduces the white coat effect. The readings are often lower than those taken in the office setting and are a better predictor of CVD risk. Home BP readings may help achieve patient adherence by reinforcing the need to remain on therapy. However, some patients become overly concerned with the BP readings. Provide information that will help patients understand what their goal or target BP is and why.

🔎 CHECK YOUR PRACTICE

You are making a home visit for a 78-yr-old woman who is recovering from a hip replacement after she fractured her femur. She currently takes a combination of lisinopril/hydrochlorothiazide. The patient's daughter (her caregiver) tells you that her BP that morning was 150/88 and then she took it 2 more times and it was the same. They are both worried and anxious that something is wrong because they heard that a BP over 120/80 is very bad.

• What should you do? What teaching would you provide?

Patient teaching is critical to ensure accuracy. Tell patients to buy an oscillometric BP monitor that uses a cuff for the upper arm or wrist. The patient should bring the BP monitor to the office to verify proper cuff size, the accuracy of the device, and the patient's technique.

Teach the patient to obtain a BP according to the steps in Table 32.11. Tell the patient to measure BP in the nondominant arm, or arm with the higher BP if there is a known difference between arms. Tell the patient to measure BP first thing in the morning (if possible, before taking any drugs) and at night before going to bed. Have the patient record all BP measurements and bring the record to office visits.

For clinical decision making (e.g., changes in dosage, starting a new drug), tell patients to take BP readings as described for 1 week. Stable, normotensive patients should measure morning and evening BP for at least 1 week every 3 months. Devices that have memory or printouts of the readings are convenient for reporting.[5]

INFORMATICS IN PRACTICE

Monitoring Blood Pressure

• Smartphone and computer applications can help patients manage their care, including BP self-monitoring, medication history, and appointment tracking. Patients can enter a variety of variables including SBP and DBP, HR, time of day, arm or wrist used, and position (e.g., lying, sitting).
• Remote BP monitoring using telehealth technology can be used with those who have limited access to health care services.
• Reports can be used to evaluate BP control.

Patient Adherence. A significant problem in the long-term management of the patient with hypertension is poor adherence to the treatment plan. The reasons for nonadherence are complicated and can include inadequate patient teaching, low health literacy, unpleasant drug side effects, the BP returns to normal range with the therapy, the high cost of drugs, and lack of insurance.

It is important to determine the reasons why a patient is not adhering to treatment. Assess the patient's diet, activity level,

and lifestyle as other indicators of adherence. Develop a plan with the patient and caregiver to improve adherence. The plan should be compatible with the patient's habits, cultural beliefs, and lifestyle. Active patient participation increases the chance of adherence to the plan. Measures include involving the patient in choosing drugs that are affordable and involving caregivers to help increase patient adherence.

Substituting combination drugs for multiple drugs once the BP is stable may promote adherence. They reduce the number of pills that the patient must take each day and may reduce costs. Combination drugs are shown in Table 32.8.

It is important to help the patient and caregiver understand that hypertension is a chronic illness that cannot be cured. Stress that it can be controlled with drug therapy, diet changes, physical activity, periodic follow-up, and other relevant lifestyle modifications.

◆ Evaluation

The overall expected outcomes are that the patient with hypertension will

• Achieve and maintain goal BP as defined for the person
• Understand, accept, and implement the treatment plan
• Report minimal side effects of drug therapy

👤 Gerontologic Considerations: Hypertension

The prevalence of hypertension increases with age. The lifetime risk for developing hypertension is around 90% for normotensive men and women over age 55. Older adults are more likely to have white coat hypertension.[5]

The pathophysiology of hypertension in the older adult involves several age-related physical changes: (1) loss of elasticity in large arteries from atherosclerosis, (2) increased collagen content and stiffness of the myocardium, (3) increased peripheral vascular resistance, (4) decreased adrenergic receptor sensitivity, (5) blunting of baroreceptor reflexes, (6) decreased renal function, and (7) decreased renin response to sodium and water depletion.

In the older adult who is taking antihypertensive drugs, absorption of some agents may be altered because of decreased blood flow to the gut. Metabolism and excretion may be prolonged.

Current recommendations for target BP goals in people older than 65 years of age who live independently are no different for other independent living adults under 65 years old. Care should be taken to assess for orthostatic hypotension and acute kidney injury in patients over 65 years old. Older adults who have multiple comorbidities and do not live independently (i.e., skilled facility) should have gradual titrations of antihypertensives to minimize complications.[5]

Orthostatic hypotension often occurs in older adults because of varying degrees of impaired baroreceptor reflexes. Orthostatic hypotension in this age group is often associated with volume depletion or chronic disease states, such as decreased renal and hepatic function or electrolyte imbalance.

Older adults may have postprandial drops in BP. The most significant decrease occurs about 1 hour after eating. BP returns to preprandial levels 3 to 4 hours after eating. Drugs should be started at low doses and increased slowly to reduce the chance of orthostatic hypotension. Measure BP and HR in the supine, sitting, and standing positions at every visit.

After CVD, arthritis is the second most prevalent disease in older adults. Older adults most often take prescription and OTC nonsteroidal antiinflammatory drugs (NSAIDs). Nonselective NSAIDs (e.g., ibuprofen) and selective NSAIDs (e.g., celecoxib) can cause loss of BP control and HF. There is the potential for adverse renal effects and/or hyperkalemia when NSAIDs are used with ACE inhibitors, ARBs, or aldosterone antagonists.

HYPERTENSIVE CRISIS

Hypertensive crisis is a term used to indicate either a hypertensive urgency or emergency. A hypertensive crisis occurs at systolic BP greater than 180 mm Hg and/or diastolic BP greater than 120 mm Hg. BPs often can be greater than 220/140 mm Hg. Difference between hypertensive urgency and emergency are the presence of target organ damage and the type of treatment the patient will receive.

Hypertensive emergencies have evidence of target organ disease. It most often requires hospitalization for immediate, controlled reduction of BP. Without prompt treatment, a hypertensive emergency can produce severe problems. These include encephalopathy, intracranial or subarachnoid hemorrhage, HF, MI, renal failure, dissecting aortic aneurysm, and retinopathy.[16] Untreated hypertensive emergencies have a 1-year mortality rate of more than 79%, so prompt recognition and treatment are essential to decrease the threat to organ function and life.

Hypertensive urgency has no clinical evidence of target organ disease. Hospitalization may not be needed to correct the BP. Hypertensive urgency is much more common than hypertensive emergency. It may be associated with chronic, stable complications such as stable angina, chronic HF, or prior MI or cerebrovascular accident with no threat of an acute event.

A hypertensive crisis occurs more often in patients with a history of hypertension who have not adhered to their medication regimens or who have been undermedicated. Rapidly increasing BP can cause shearing of the endothelial surface due to turbulent blood flow within the vessels leading to further vascular damage and the release of more vasoconstricting substances. A vicious cycle of BP elevation follows, leading to life-threatening damage to target organs.

Hypertensive crisis related to cocaine or crack use is a frequent problem. Other drugs, such as amphetamines, phencyclidine (PCP), and lysergic acid diethylamide (LSD), can cause a hypertensive crisis that may be complicated by drug-induced seizures, stroke, MI, or encephalopathy. Table 32.13 lists causes of hypertensive crisis.

Clinical Manifestations

A hypertensive emergency often presents as *hypertensive encephalopathy*, a syndrome in which a sudden rise in BP is associated with a severe headache, nausea, vomiting, seizures, confusion, and coma. The manifestations of encephalopathy are the result of increased cerebral capillary permeability, which can lead to cerebral edema and disruption in cerebral function. On retinal examination, exudates, hemorrhages, and/or papilledema are found (Fig. 32.6).

Renal insufficiency ranging from minor injury to complete renal failure can occur. Rapid cardiac decompensation ranging from unstable angina to MI and pulmonary edema is possible. Patients can have chest pain and dyspnea. Aortic dissection can develop and will cause sudden, severe chest and back pain with reduced or absent pulses in the extremities.

◆ Interprofessional and Nursing Management

Hypertensive emergencies require hospitalization, IV administration of antihypertensive drugs, and intensive monitoring. BP level alone is not the major factor in deciding the treatment for a hypertensive crisis. The link between elevated BP and signs of new or progressive target organ disease determines the seriousness of the situation.

When treating hypertensive emergencies, we often use the mean arterial pressure (MAP instead of BP readings to guide and evaluate therapy. Calculate the MAP as follows:

$$MAP = (SBP + 2\,DBP) \div 3$$

The initial goal is to decrease MAP by no more than 20% to 25% or to decrease MAP to 110 to 115 mm Hg. If the patient is clinically stable, drugs can be titrated to gradually lower BP over the next 24 hours. Lowering the BP too quickly or too much may decrease cerebral, coronary, or renal perfusion. A rapid decrease could cause a stroke, MI, or renal failure.

❓ CHECK YOUR PRACTICE

A 68-yr-old male patient presents to the emergency department with a BP 210/118 and reporting a severe headache and vomiting. You know that his BP is dangerously high and must be lowered.
- Calculate his MAP.
- What treatments would you expect to be ordered for this patient?

Patients with aortic dissection require special consideration. These patients should have their SBP lowered to less than 100 to 120 mm Hg as soon as possible (if tolerated). Another exception is patients with acute ischemic stroke. Their BP is lowered to allow the use of thrombolytic agents. Last, an elevated BP in the

---

TABLE 32.13 Causes of Hypertensive Crisis

- Acute aortic dissection
- Exacerbation of chronic hypertension
- Head injury
- Monoamine oxidase inhibitors are taken with tyramine-containing foods
- Pheochromocytoma
- Preeclampsia, eclampsia
- Rebound hypertension (from abrupt withdrawal of some antihypertensive drugs, such as clonidine or β-blockers)
  Recreational drug use (cocaine, amphetamines)
- Renovascular hypertension

FIG. 32.6 Massive retinal exudates (indicated by *arrows*) from hypertensive retinopathy. To see what a normal retina looks like on ophthalmoscopic examination, see Fig. 20.7. (From Kliegman RM, Behrman RE, Jenson HB, Stanton B: *Nelson textbook of pediatrics,* ed 18, Philadelphia, 2011, Saunders.)

immediate poststroke period may be a compensatory response to improve cerebral perfusion to ischemic brain tissue. There is no evidence supporting the use of antihypertensive drugs in these patients (see Chapter 57).[5]

IV agents used for hypertensive emergencies include vasodilators (e.g., sodium nitroprusside, fenoldopam, nicardipine), adrenergic inhibitors (e.g., phentolamine, labetalol, esmolol), and the calcium channel blocker clevidipine (Cleviprex). Sodium nitroprusside is the most effective IV drug to treat hypertensive emergencies. Oral agents may be given along with IV ones to help make an earlier transition to long-term therapy.

DRUG ALERT Labetalol

- Teach patient not to stop the drug abruptly.
- Abrupt cessation may precipitate angina or HF.

Antihypertensive drugs given IV have a rapid (within seconds to minutes) onset of action. Assess the patient's BP and HR every 2 to 3 minutes during their initial administration. Use an arterial line (see Chapter 65) or an automated, noninvasive BP machine to monitor the BP. Titrate the drug according to MAP or BP as ordered. Monitor the ECG for dysrhythmias and signs of ischemia or MI. Use extreme caution in treating the patient with CAD or cerebrovascular disease. Measure urine output hourly to assess renal perfusion. Patients receiving IV agents may be on bed rest. Getting up (e.g., to use the commode) may cause severe cerebral ischemia and fainting.

Ongoing assessment is essential to evaluate the effectiveness of and the patient's response to therapy. Monitor cardiac, lung, and renal systems for decompensation caused by the severe elevation in BP (e.g., angina, pulmonary edema, renal failure).

Frequent neurologic checks, including the level of consciousness, pupillary size and reaction, and movement of extremities, help detect any changes in the patient's condition. The neurologic changes are often like those of a stroke. However, a hypertensive crisis does not show focal or lateralizing signs often seen with a stroke. In a stroke, focal impairments affect a specific region of the body, such as weakness in the left arm or right leg. Lateralizing signs are restricted to one side of the body, such as weakness of an arm or leg.

Hypertensive urgencies usually do not need IV drugs but can be managed with oral agents. The patient with hypertensive urgency may not need hospitalization but will need follow-up. The initial decision for oral antihypertensive agents should be made based on the underlying cause of the hypertensive urgency, the patient characteristics, and comorbidities. Some of the most commonly used oral drugs are captopril, labetalol, clonidine (Catapres), and amlodipine (Norvasc) (Table 32.6).[16] The disadvantage of oral drugs is the inability to regulate the dosage moment to moment, as can be done with IV therapy. A patient with hypertensive urgency who is not hospitalized should have outpatient follow-up care within 24 hours.

Once the hypertensive crisis is resolved, it is essential to determine the cause. The patient will need appropriate management and teaching to avoid future crises.

DRUG ALERT Clonidine (Catapres)

- Teach patient to change positions slowly to limit orthostatic hypotension.
- Avoid hazardous activities since the drug may cause drowsiness.
- Do not stop abruptly as this may cause rebound hypertension.

Not every patient with an elevated BP and no target organ disease will need emergent drug therapy or hospitalization. Allowing the patient to sit for 20 or 30 minutes in a quiet environment may significantly reduce BP. Oral drugs may be started or adjusted. Other interventions include encouraging the patient to share any concerns or fears, answering questions about hypertension, and reducing any adverse stimuli (e.g., excess noise) in the environment.

CASE STUDY

Primary Hypertension

(© iStockphoto/ Thinkstock.)

Patient Profile

R.L. is a 45-yr-old black man with no history of hypertension. At a screening clinic 2 months ago, his BP was 150/95 mm Hg. His HCP has followed him for the past month. During this time, he has been taking hydrochlorothiazide 12.5 mg/day. He is here today for a follow-up visit.

Subjective Data

- Father died of stroke at age 60
- Mother is alive but has hypertension and a history of MI
- States that he feels fine and is not a "hyper" person
- Smokes 1 pack of cigarettes daily for the past 28 yrs
- Drinks "about 2" 6-packs of beer on most Friday and Saturday nights
- Has heard that BP drugs "make you impotent"

Objective Data

Physical Examination

- Mild retinopathy (retinal arteriolar narrowing on ophthalmoscopic examination)
- BP: 166/108 mm Hg (highest of 2 readings, 2 min apart)
- Sustained apical impulse palpable in the 4th intercostal space just lateral to the midclavicular line

Diagnostic Studies

- ECG: mild left ventricular hypertrophy
- Urinalysis: protein 30 mg/dL (0.3 g/L)
- Serum creatinine level: 1.6 mg/dL (141 mmol/L)

Interprofessional Care

- Low-sodium, DASH diet
- Hydrochlorothiazide 25 mg/day oral (dose increase)
- Nicardipine sustained-release 30 mg oral twice daily (second drug added)

Discussion Questions

1. What risk factors for hypertension does R.L. have?
2. What evidence of target organ disease is present?
3. ***Patient-Centered Care:*** What misconceptions about hypertension should be corrected?
4. ***Priority Decision:*** Based on the assessment data, what are the priority nursing diagnoses? What are the collaborative problems?
5. ***Evidence-Based Practice:*** R.L. wants to know the most effective nonpharmacologic strategies to lower his BP. What would you tell him?
6. ***Patient-Centered Care:*** What lifestyle preferences should be addressed in R.L.'s plan of care?
7. ***Collaboration:*** What referrals may be indicated?
8. ***Safety:*** What safety precautions should be considered when changing R.L.'s antihypertensive therapy?
9. ***Quality Improvement:*** What outcomes would indicate that interprofessional care was successful?

BRIDGE TO NCLEX EXAMINATION

The number of the question corresponds to the same-numbered outcome at the beginning of the chapter.

1. Which BP-regulating mechanism(s) can result in the development of hypertension if defective? *(select all that apply)*
   a. Release of norepinephrine
   b. Secretion of prostaglandins
   c. Stimulation of the sympathetic nervous system
   d. Stimulation of the parasympathetic nervous system
   e. Activation of the renin-angiotensin-aldosterone system

2. While obtaining subjective assessment data from a patient with hypertension, the nurse recognizes that a modifiable risk factor for the development of hypertension is
   a. A low-calcium diet.
   b. Excess alcohol intake.
   c. A family history of hypertension.
   d. Consumption of a high-protein diet.

3. In teaching a patient with hypertension about controlling the illness, the nurse recognizes that
   a. All patients with elevated BP need drug therapy.
   b. Obese persons must achieve a normal weight to lower BP.
   c. It is not necessary to limit salt in the diet if taking a diuretic.
   d. Lifestyle modifications are needed for all persons with elevated BP.

4. A *priority* consideration in the management of the older adult with hypertension is to
   a. Prevent primary hypertension from converting to secondary hypertension.
   b. Recognize that the older adult is less likely to adhere to the drug therapy regimen than a younger adult.
   c. Ensure that the patient receives larger initial doses of antihypertensive drugs because of impaired absorption.
   d. Use precise technique in assessing the BP of the patient because of the possible presence of an auscultatory gap.

5. A patient with newly discovered high BP has an average reading of 158/98 mm Hg after 3 months of exercise and diet modifications. Which management strategy will be a *priority* for this patient?
   a. Drug therapy will be needed because the BP is still not at goal.
   b. BP monitoring should continue for 3 months to confirm a diagnosis of hypertension.
   c. Lifestyle changes are less important since they were not effective, and drugs will be started.
   d. More changes in the patient's lifestyle are needed for a longer time before starting drug therapy.

6. A patient is admitted to the hospital in a hypertensive emergency (BP 244/142 mm Hg). Sodium nitroprusside is started to treat the elevated BP. Which management strategies would be *most* appropriate for this patient? *(select all that apply)*
   a. Measuring hourly urine output
   b. Continuous BP monitoring with an arterial line
   c. Decreasing the MAP by 50% within the first hour
   d. Maintaining bed rest and giving tranquilizers to lower the BP
   e. Assessing the patient for signs and symptoms of heart failure and changes in mental status

1. a, c, e, 2. b, 3. d, 4. d, 5. a, 6. a, b, e

For rationales to these answers and even more NCLEX review questions, visit *http://evolve.elsevier.com/Lewis/medsurg*.

ⓔ EVOLVE WEBSITE/RESOURCES LIST

http://evolve.elsevier.com/Lewis/medsurg
Review Questions (Online Only)
Key Points
Answer Keys for Questions
  • Rationales for Bridge to NCLEX Examination Questions
  • Answer Guidelines for Case Study on p. 696
Student Case Study
Patient With Hypertension and Stroke
Conceptual Care Map Creator
Audio Glossary
Content Updates

REFERENCES

1. Centers for Disease Control and Prevention: High blood pressure facts. Retrieved from *www.cdc.gov/bloodpressure/facts.htm*.
2. Benjamin EJ, Blaha MJ, Chiuve SE, et al: Heart disease and stroke statistics—2017 update: A report from the American Heart Association, *Circulation* 135:e146, 2017.
3. Centers for Disease Control and Prevention: National Health and Nutrition Examination Survey (NHANES). Retrieved from *www.cdc.gov/nchs/nhanes/index.htm*.
4. Merai R, Siegel C, Rakotz M, et al: CDC grand rounds: A public health approach to detect and control hypertension, *MMWR Morb Mortal Wkly Rep* 65:1261, 2016.
*5. Whelton PK, Carey RM, Aronow WS, et al: 2017 ACC/AHA/AAPA/ABC/ACPM/AGS/APhA/ASH/ASPC/NMA/PCNA guideline for the prevention, detection, evaluation, and management of high blood pressure in adults: A report of the American College of Cardiology/AHA Task Force on Clinical Practice Guidelines, *Journal of the American College of Cardiology* 71:e127, 2018.
*6. McKibben RA, Al Rifai M, Mathews LM, et al: Primary prevention of atherosclerotic cardiovascular disease in women, *Curr Cardiovascular Risk Reports* 10:1, 2016.
7. National Heart, Lung, and Blood Institute: DASH eating plan. Retrieved from *www.nhlbi.nih.gov/health-topics/dash-eating-plan*.
8. Kirabo A: A new paradigm of sodium regulation in inflammation and hypertension, *Am J Physiol Regul Integr Comp Physiol* 313:R706, 2017.
9. American Heart Association: What are the symptoms of high blood pressure? Retrieved from *http://www.heart.org/HEARTORG/Conditions/HighBloodPressure/SymptomsDiagnosisMonitoringofHighBloodPressure/What-are-the-Symptoms-of-High-Blood-Pressure_UCM_301871_Article.jsp*.
*10. Haskell WL, Lee I-M, Pate RR, et al: Physical activity and public health: Updated recommendations for adults from the American College of Sports Medicine and the American Heart Association, *Circulation* 116:1081, 2007. (Classic)
*11. Nelson ME, Rejeski WJ, Blair SN, et al: Physical activity and public health in older adults: Recommendation from the American College of Sports Medicine and the American Heart Association, *Circulation* 116:1094, 2007. (Classic)
12. International health constitution of the World Health Organization, *Bulletin of the World Health Organization* 80:983, 2002. (Classic)
13. Rozanski A, Blumenthal JA, Davidson KW, et al: The epidemiology, pathophysiology, and management of psychosocial risk factors in cardiac practice, *J Am Coll Cardiol* 45:637, 2005. (Classic)
*14. AACN Clinical Resources Task Force: AACN practice alert: Non-invasive blood pressure monitoring. Retrieved from *www.aacn.org/~/media/aacn-website/clincial-resources/practice-alerts/nibpadult2016pa.pdf*.
15. CDC's STEADI Tools and Resources: Measuring orthostatic changes. Retrieved from *www.cdc.gov/steadi/pdf/measuring_orthostatic_blood_pressure-a.pdf*.
16. Ipek E, Oktay AA, Krim SR: Hypertensive crisis: An update on clinical approach and management, *Curr Opin Cardiol* 32:397, 2017.

*Evidence-based information for clinical practice.

33

Coronary Artery Disease and Acute Coronary Syndrome

Rose Shaffer

I have witnessed the softening of the hardest hearts with a warm smile.

Goldie Hawn

http://evolve.elsevier.com/Lewis/medsurg/

CONCEPTUAL FOCUS

Adherence	Glucose Regulation	Sexuality
Clotting	Pain	
Fatigue	Perfusion	

LEARNING OUTCOMES

1. Relate the etiology and pathophysiology of coronary artery disease (CAD), chronic stable angina, and acute coronary syndrome (ACS) to the clinical manifestations of each disorder.
2. Describe the nursing role in the promotion of therapeutic lifestyle changes in patients at risk for CAD.
3. Distinguish the precipitating factors, clinical manifestations, and interprofessional and nursing care of the patient with CAD and chronic stable angina.
4. Explain the clinical manifestations, diagnostic studies, complications, and interprofessional and nursing care of the patient with ACS.
5. Outline drug therapy used to treat patients with CAD, chronic stable angina, and ACS.
6. Prioritize key components to include in the rehabilitation of patients recovering from ACS and coronary revascularization procedures.
7. Distinguish the precipitating factors, manifestations, and interprofessional and nursing care of patients who are at risk for or have had sudden cardiac death.

KEY TERMS

acute coronary syndrome (ACS), p. 717
angina, p. 708
atherosclerosis, p. 698
chronic stable angina, p. 708
collateral circulation, p. 699

coronary artery disease (CAD), p. 698
coronary revascularization, p. 714
metabolic equivalent (MET), p. 728
myocardial infarction (MI), p. 718
percutaneous coronary intervention (PCI), p. 714

Prinzmetal's angina, p. 709
silent ischemia, p. 708
stent, p. 714
sudden cardiac death (SCD), p. 730
unstable angina (UA), p. 717

Cardiovascular disease (CVD) is the leading cause of death both globally and in the United States.[1] Coronary artery disease (CAD) is the most common type of CVD. CAD was an underlying cause of death in about 1 of every 7 deaths.[2] Patients with CAD may be asymptomatic or develop chronic stable angina (chest pain). CAD may evolve to more serious conditions of unstable angina (UA) and myocardial infarction (MI), which are referred to as acute coronary syndrome (ACS).

Conceptually, CAD has a profound effect on perfusion. The process of perfusion is based on the heart's ability to generate enough cardiac output (CO) to distribute blood to all body tissues. CAD negatively affects cardiac function, resulting in impaired CO and decreased perfusion. This chapter discusses the care of patients with CAD, chronic stable angina, and ACS and measures to promote optimal perfusion.

CORONARY ARTERY DISEASE

Coronary artery disease (CAD) is a type of blood vessel disorder that we consider in the general category of atherosclerosis. The term atherosclerosis comes from 2 Greek words: *athere,* meaning "fatty mush," and *skleros,* meaning "hard."[3] This combination means that atherosclerosis begins as soft deposits of fat that harden with age. That is why many refer to atherosclerosis as "hardening of the arteries." It can occur in any artery in the body. When the *atheromas* (fatty deposits) form in the coronary arteries, the disease is called CAD. The terms *arteriosclerotic heart disease (ASHD), cardiovascular heart disease (CVHD), ischemic heart disease (IHD), coronary heart disease (CHD),* are other terms used to describe CAD. They are often used interchangeably.

Endothelium   Intima

Chronic Endothelial Injury
- Hypertension
- Tobacco use
- Hyperlipidemia
- Hyperhomocysteinemia
- Diabetes
- Infections
- Toxins

Damaged endothelium

A

Fatty Streak
- Lipids accumulate and migrate into smooth muscle cells

B

Fibrous Plaque
- Collagen covers the fatty streak
- Vessel lumen is narrowed
- Blood flow is reduced
- Fissures can develop

C

Complicated Lesion
- Plaque rupture
- Thrombus formation
- Further narrowing or total occlusion of vessel

D

FIG. 33.1 Pathogenesis of atherosclerosis. A, Damaged endothelium. B, Fatty streak and lipid core formation. C, Fibrous plaque covers the lipid core. D, Complicated lesion: Plaque rupture with thrombus formation.

A   B   C

FIG. 33.2 Vessel occlusion with collateral circulation. **A,** Open, functioning coronary artery. **B,** Partial coronary artery closure with collateral circulation being established. **C,** Total coronary artery occlusion with collateral circulation bypassing the occlusion to supply blood to the myocardium.

Etiology and Pathophysiology

Atherosclerosis is the major cause of CAD. It is characterized by lipid deposits within the intima of the artery. Endothelial injury and inflammation play a key role in the development of atherosclerosis.

The endothelium (inner lining of the vessel wall) is normally nonreactive to platelets and leukocytes, as well as coagulation, fibrinolytic, and complement factors. Damage to the endothelial lining can result from tobacco use, hyperlipidemia, hypertension, toxins, diabetes, high homocysteine levels, and infection causing a local inflammatory response (Fig. 33.1, A).[3]

C-reactive protein (CRP), a protein made by the liver, is a nonspecific marker of inflammation. CRP levels rise when there is systemic inflammation, such as rheumatoid arthritis or inflammatory bowel disease. CRP and levels of lipoprotein(a), which has proinflammatory properties, are increased in many patients with CAD (see Table 31.6). CRP and lipoprotein(a) are not a part of a routine risk assessment for CAD. They can be used in patients with an intermediate- or high-risk suspicion of CAD.[4]

Developmental Stages. CAD is a progressive disease that develops in stages over many years. When the patient becomes symptomatic, the disease process usually is well advanced. The stages of development in atherosclerosis are (1) fatty streak, (2) fibrous plaque, and (3) complicated lesion.

Fatty Streak. Fatty streaks, the earliest lesions of atherosclerosis, are lipid-filled smooth muscle cells. As streaks of fat develop within the smooth muscle cells, a yellow tinge appears. Fatty streaks can be seen in the coronary arteries by age 20. They involve an increasing amount of surface area as one ages. Treatment that lowers low-density lipoprotein (LDL) cholesterol may slow this process (Fig. 33.1, *B*).

Fibrous Plaque. The *fibrous plaque* stage is the beginning of progressive changes in the endothelium of the arterial wall. These changes can appear in the coronary arteries by age 30 and increase with age.

Normally, the endothelium repairs itself immediately. This does not occur in the person with CAD. LDLs and growth factors from platelets stimulate smooth muscle proliferation and thickening of the arterial wall. Once endothelial injury has taken place, lipoproteins (carrier proteins within the bloodstream) transport cholesterol and other lipids into the arterial intima. Collagen covers the fatty streak and forms a fibrous plaque with a grayish or whitish appearance. These plaques can form on one side of the artery or in a circular fashion involving the entire lumen. The borders can be smooth or irregular with rough, jagged edges. The result is a narrowing of the vessel lumen and reduced blood flow to the distal tissue (Fig. 33.1, *C*).

Complicated Lesion. The last stage in the development of the atherosclerotic lesion is the most dangerous. As the fibrous plaque grows, continued inflammation can result in plaque instability, ulceration, and rupture. Once the integrity of the artery's inner wall is compromised (plaque rupture), platelets accumulate in large numbers, leading to a thrombus (platelet aggregation and adhesion is the body's attempt to "heal" the ruptured area). The thrombus may adhere to the wall of the artery, leading to further narrowing or total occlusion of the artery. Activation of the exposed platelets causes expression of glycoprotein IIb/IIIa receptors that bind fibrinogen. This, in turn, leads to more platelet aggregation and adhesion, further enlarging the thrombus. At this stage, the plaque is referred to as a *complicated lesion* (Fig. 33.1, *D*).

Collateral Circulation. Normally, some arterial anastomoses or connections, called collateral circulation, exist within the coronary circulation. Two factors contribute to the growth and extent of collateral circulation: (1) inherited predisposition to develop new blood vessels *(angiogenesis)* and (2) presence of chronic ischemia (poor blood flow). When plaque blocks the normal flow of blood through a coronary artery and the resulting *ischemia* is chronic, increased collateral circulation may develop (Fig. 33.2). When blockages in coronary arteries occur

TABLE 33.1 Risk Factors for Coronary Artery Disease

Nonmodifiable Risk Factors	Modifiable Risk Factors

• Increasing age
• Gender (highest incidence of CAD is among middle-aged men, but for men over age 45 and women over age 55, the risk for CAD increases for both genders)
• Ethnicity (more common in white than black men)
• Genetic predisposition and family history of heart disease
	Major
	• Serum lipids:
	  • Total cholesterol >200 mg/dL
	  • Triglycerides ≥150 mg/dL*
	  • LDL cholesterol >130 mg/dL
	  • HDL cholesterol <40 mg/dL in men or <50 mg/dL in women*
	• BP >120/80 mm Hg*
	• Diabetes*
	• Tobacco use
	• Physical inactivity
	• Obesity: Waist circumference ≥102 cm (≥40 in) in men and ≥88 cm (≥35 in) in women*
	
	Contributing
	• Psychosocial risk factors (e.g., depression, hostility)
	• High homocysteine levels
	• Substance abuse

*3 or more of these risk factors meet the criteria for metabolic syndrome (discussed in Chapter 40).

slowly over a long time, there is a greater chance of collateral circulation developing, so the heart muscle may still receive an adequate amount of blood and oxygen (O_2) except during increased workload on the heart, such as exercise.

However, with rapid-onset CAD (e.g., familial hypercholesterolemia) or coronary spasm, there is not enough time to develop collateral circulation. When this happens, reduced blood flow results in more severe ischemia or infarction.

Risk Factors for Coronary Artery Disease

Many risk factors have been associated with CAD. We group them as nonmodifiable and modifiable (Table 33.1). *Nonmodifiable risk factors* are age, gender, ethnicity, family history, and genetics. *Modifiable risk factors* include high serum lipids, high BP, tobacco use, physical inactivity, obesity, diabetes, metabolic syndrome, psychologic states, and high homocysteine level.

Nonmodifiable Risk Factors

Age, Gender, Ethnicity, and Genetics. The incidence of CAD is highest among middle-aged men, however, the risk for CAD increases for men over age 45 and women over age 55.[4] Heart disease is often diagnosed about 10 years later in women than men. One possible reason for this may be the cardioprotective effects of estrogen. But, interestingly, hormone replacement therapy does not protect women after menopause and may be harmful.[4] Because women are older at the time of CAD diagnosis, they are more likely to have co-morbidities (e.g., hypertension, diabetes). Women are more likely than men to die after their first MI. CAD is present in black women at rates higher than their white or Hispanic counterparts.[4] (See Promoting Health Equity box for more differences in CAD among ethnic groups.)

Most women do not consider CAD their greatest health risk.[4] Despite efforts to increase awareness that more women die from heart disease than from breast cancer (e.g., the American Heart Association's Go Red for Women campaign), heart disease kills almost 10 times more women than breast cancer. It is the leading cause of death in women. When women present to the HCP,

their symptoms may be unrecognized as heart related because the symptoms are often atypical. These symptoms include fatigue, shortness of breath, upper back pain, indigestion, weakness, sleep problems, palpitations, and anxiety.[5] These atypical symptoms can relate to many different diseases and syndromes. This lack of recognition of symptoms as a cardiac problem leads to delays in women seeking treatment and HCPs recognizing the symptoms (see the Gender Differences box on p. 701).

🌐 PROMOTING HEALTH EQUITY
Coronary Artery Disease

Whites
• White men have the highest incidence of CAD.

Blacks
• Blacks have an early age of onset of CAD.
• Deaths from CVDs, including CAD and strokes, are higher for blacks than for the overall population in the United States.
• Black women have a higher incidence and death rate related to CAD than white and Hispanic women.

Native Americans
• Native Americans die from heart disease earlier than expected. Mortality rates for those under age 65 are twice as high as those of other Americans.
• Major modifiable CVD risk factors for Native Americans include tobacco use, hypertension, obesity, and diabetes.

Hispanics
• Hispanics have slightly lower rates of CAD than either non-Hispanic whites or blacks.
• Hispanics have lower death rates from CAD than non-Hispanic whites.

🧬 Genetic Link

Genetic predisposition is a key factor in the occurrence of CAD. Family history is a risk factor for CAD and MI. Often patients with angina or MI can name a parent or sibling who died of CAD.

The genetic basis of CAD/MI is complex and poorly understood. We estimate that the genetic contribution to CAD is as high as 40% to 60%. This proportion relates mainly to genes that control known risk factors (e.g., lipid metabolism).[6] (See Genetics in Clinical Practice box.)

Major Modifiable Risk Factors

High Serum Lipids. A high serum lipid level is a major risk factors for CAD (see Table 31.6). The risk for CAD is associated with a total serum cholesterol level greater than 200 mg/dL (5.2 mmol/L), an LDL greater than 130 mg/dL (3.4 mmol/L), a high-density lipoprotein (HDL) level less than 40 mg/dL (1.0 mmol/L) in men and less than 50 mg/dL (1.3 mmol/L) in women, and/or a fasting triglyceride level greater than 150 mg/dL (1.7 mmol/L).

For the body to be able to use and transport lipids, they must become soluble in blood by combining with proteins. Lipids combine with proteins to form lipoproteins. Lipoproteins are vehicles for fat mobilization and transport. They vary in composition. The 3 major lipoproteins are HDLs, LDLs, and very-low-density lipoproteins (VLDLs).[7]

HDLs contain more protein by weight and fewer lipids than any other lipoprotein. HDLs carry lipids away from arteries to the liver for metabolism. This process of HDL transport

GENDER DIFFERENCES

Coronary Artery Disease and Acute Coronary Syndrome

Men	Women
• First heart event is more often MI than angina.	• First heart event is more often UA than MI.
• Report more typical signs and symptoms of angina and MI.	• Fewer women have the "classic" signs and symptoms of UA or MI.
• Receive more evidence-based therapies (e.g., aspirin, statins, diagnostic catheterization, PCI) when acutely ill from CAD (e.g., MI).	• Fatigue is often the first symptom of ACS.
• Mortality rates from CAD have decreased more rapidly for men than women.	• Experience the onset of heart disease about 10 years later than men.
• Have larger diameter coronary arteries. Vessel diameter is inversely related to risk for restenosis after interventions.	• More women with MI die of sudden cardiac death before reaching the hospital.
• After age 55, the incidence of MI in men and women equalizes.	• Before menopause, have higher HDL cholesterol levels and lower LDL cholesterol levels. After menopause LDL levels and risk for MI increase.
• Develop more collateral circulation.	• Report more disability after a heart event.
• Standard screening for risk for sudden cardiac death is more predictive in men.	• Seek medical care later in the CAD process, most likely because of lack of recognition of atypical symptoms.
	• Have more "silent" MIs compared with men.
	• Those who have an MI are more likely to have a fatal heart event within 1 year than men.
	• Women who have coronary artery bypass graft surgery have a higher mortality rate and more complications after surgery.
	• Ae undertreated with guideline-based recommendations, leading to worse outcomes and increased rates of readmission, reinfarction, and death in the first year after MI.

GENETICS IN CLINICAL PRACTICE

Familial Hypercholesterolemia

Genetic Basis
- Autosomal dominant disorder
- Exists in both heterozygous (most common) and homozygous forms
- Mutation in low-density lipoprotein receptor (LDLR) gene
- Gene codes for low-density lipoprotein (LDL) receptor that binds to LDLs
- LDLs are the primary carriers of cholesterol in the blood. By removing LDLs from the bloodstream, the LDL receptors play a critical role in regulating cholesterol levels
- High cholesterol levels are a result of defective function of the LDL receptors
- Person has high serum LDLs throughout life

Incidence
- Heterozygotes: 1 in 500
- Homozygotes: rare

Genetic Testing
- DNA testing is available

Clinical Implications
- Develop severe atherosclerosis in early to middle years
- A serum lipid profile measures total cholesterol, triglycerides, LDLs, and high-density lipoproteins (HDLs)
- Homozygous familial hypercholesterolemia is much more severe. Cholesterol levels may exceed 600 mg/dL
- Develop xanthomas (fatty growths on the skin [e.g., around eyes, over joints])
- Treatment includes low-fat diet, exercise, and lipid-lowering drugs (e.g., PCSK9 inhibitors)

prevents lipid accumulation within the arterial walls.[7] Therefore high serum HDL levels are desirable and lower the risk for CAD. Premenopausal women usually have higher HDL levels than men. This may be related to the protective effects of natural estrogen. After menopause, women's HDL levels decrease to levels near those of men. In general, HDL levels are higher in women, decrease with age, and are low in those with CAD.

Physical activity, eating more healthy fats, losing excess weight, moderate alcohol intake, and quitting smoking help increase HDL levels.

LDLs contain more cholesterol than any of the lipoproteins and have an attraction for arterial walls. High LDL levels correlate closely with an increased incidence of atherosclerosis and CAD. This is why low serum LDL levels are desirable. We cannot routinely calculate LDL if the triglycerides are higher than 400 mg/dL (> 4.35 mmol/L). VLDLs have a higher concentration of triglycerides and can deposit cholesterol directly on the walls of arteries.

Triglycerides are the most common type of fat in the blood. A certain amount of triglycerides is needed for bodily function, but high triglyceride levels may increase the risk for CAD. Certain diseases (e.g., type 2 diabetes, chronic kidney disease [CKD]), drugs (e.g., corticosteroids, hormone therapy) and genetic disorders have been associated with high triglyceride levels. Lifestyle factors that can contribute to high levels include high alcohol intake, high intake of refined carbohydrates and simple sugars, and physical inactivity. When a high triglyceride level is combined with a high LDL level, a smaller, denser LDL particle is formed, which favors deposition on arterial walls. People with insulin resistance often have this pattern.

Guidelines for treating high LDL cholesterol are based on a person's 10-year and lifetime risk for having heart disease or stroke. The following data generate a risk score: (1) age, (2) gender, (3) race, (4) use of tobacco, (5) diabetes, (6) systolic BP, (7) diastolic BP, (8) use of BP drugs, (9) total cholesterol level, and (10) HDL cholesterol level. A 10-year risk calculator is available at *www.cvriskcalculator.com*.

The 2013 American College of Cardiology (ACC)/American Heart Association (AHA) Cholesterol Guideline[8] does not promote treating LDL to target goals as had been recommended in earlier guidelines. However, the 2017 American Association of Clinical Endocrinologists (AACE) guideline endorses treating LDL to specific target goals.[9] The AACE guideline states that those with no cardiac risk factors are considered at low risk for the development of CAD. Their LDL goal is <130 mg/dL. Those with 2 or less risk factors and a 10-year risk of < 10% (moderate risk) should be treated to an LDL target of < 100 mg/dL. Those at high risk (>2 risk factors and a 10-year risk of 10-20%; or diabetes or CKD stage 3 to 4 with no other risk factors) should be treated to an LDL of < 100 mg/dL. Those at very high risk for developing CAD (recent hospitalization for ACS, established CAD, carotid disease or peripheral vascular disease; diabetes, CKD stage 3 to 4 with 1 or more risk factors) should be treated to an LDL target of < 70 mg/dL.[9]

Hypertension. Hypertension increases the risk for CAD, stroke, peripheral vascular disease, heart failure (HF), and death. In postmenopausal women, hypertension is associated with a higher incidence of CAD than in men and premenopausal women.

According to the most recent published hypertension guidelines, a normal BP is defined as < 120 mm Hg/< 80 mm Hg. BP is classified as elevated (BP 120-129 mm Hg/< 80 mm Hg); stage 1 hypertension (BP 130-139 mmHg/80-89 mm Hg); or stage 2 hypertension (BP >140 mm Hg/ > 90 mm Hg).[10]

The cause of hypertension in 90% of those affected is unknown, but it is usually controllable with lifestyle changes and medications.[11] Lifestyle changes are a part of therapy for all people with elevated BP and hypertension. Those with stage 1 or 2 hypertension usually need drug therapy, often more than 1 drug, to reach therapeutic goals (see Table 32.6).[10] Teach patients the importance of achieving and maintaining target BP goals.

The shearing stress of an elevated BP causes endothelial injury that increases the rate of atherosclerosis. Atherosclerosis, in turn, causes narrowed, thickened arterial walls and decreases the distensibility and elasticity of vessels. More force is needed to pump blood through diseased arteries. This increased force is reflected in a higher BP. This added workload results in left ventricular (LV) hypertrophy and decreased stroke volume with each contraction. See Chapter 32 for a complete discussion of hypertension.

Tobacco Use. A third major risk factor in CAD is tobacco use. The risk for developing CAD is much higher in those who smoke tobacco or use smokeless tobacco than in those who do not. Further, tobacco smoking decreases estrogen levels, placing premenopausal women who smoke at greater risk for CAD.

Nicotine in tobacco smoke causes catecholamine (i.e., epinephrine, norepinephrine) release. These neurohormones cause an increased heart rate (HR), peripheral vasoconstriction, and increased BP. These changes increase the heart's workload. Tobacco smoke is related to an increase in LDL level, a decrease in HDL level, and release of toxic O_2 radicals. All of these add to vessel inflammation and thrombosis.

Carbon monoxide, found in tobacco smoke, affects the O_2-carrying capacity of hemoglobin by reducing the sites available for O_2 transport. Thus the effects of an increased cardiac workload and the O_2-depleting effect of carbon monoxide significantly decrease the O_2 available to the heart muscle. We also believe that carbon monoxide is a chemical irritant that injures the endothelium.

The benefits of smoking cessation are dramatic and almost immediate. CAD mortality rates drop to those of nonsmokers within 12 months. However, nicotine is highly addictive, and people usually need intensive intervention to quit. Individual and group counseling, nicotine replacement therapy, and smoking cessation drugs (e.g., bupropion, varenicline) are examples of smoking cessation strategies. (See Chapter 10, Tables 10.4 through 10.6 for information on smoking cessation.)

Nonsmokers exposed to secondhand tobacco smoke increase their risk for CAD by 25% to 30%.[1] People who live in the same house as the person who smokes should encourage that person to quit. This reinforces the person's effort and decreases the risk for ongoing exposure to environmental smoke. Pipe and cigar smokers, who often do not inhale, have an increased risk for CAD similar to those exposed to secondhand smoke. The few studies on electronic cigarettes suggest they increase HR and BP through systemic absorption of nicotine.[12]

Physical Inactivity. Physical inactivity is the fourth major modifiable risk factor for CAD. Physical inactivity implies a lack of adequate physical exercise on a regular basis. The ACC and the AHA recommend 30 to 60 minutes of exercise, such as brisk walking at least 5 days per week.[13]

How physical inactivity predisposes a person to CAD is still unclear. Physically active people have increased HDL levels. Exercise improves thrombolytic activity, thus reducing the risk for clot formation. Exercise may help with the development of collateral circulation in the heart.

Exercise training for those who are physically inactive reduces the risk for CAD through more efficient lipid metabolism, increased HDL production, and more efficient O_2 extraction by the muscles. This decreases the heart's workload. For people with CAD, regular physical activity may reduce symptoms, improve functional capacity, and improve other risk factors, such as insulin resistance and glucose intolerance.

Obesity. The death rate from CAD is higher in obese persons. Obesity is defined as a body mass index (BMI) of greater than 30 kg/m^2 and a waist circumference more than 40 inches for men and more than 35 inches for women. We calculate BMI by dividing a person's weight (in kilograms) by the square of the height in meters (see Fig. 40.6).

The increased risk for CAD is proportional to the degree of obesity. Obese persons may make increased levels of LDLs and triglycerides, which are strongly related to atherosclerosis. Obesity is often linked with hypertension and insulin resistance. People who tend to store fat in the abdomen (an "apple" figure) rather than in the hips and buttocks (a "pear" figure) have a higher incidence of CAD (see Table 40.6).

Contributing Modifiable Risk Factors

Diabetes Mellitus. The incidence of CAD is 2 to 4 times greater among people who have diabetes, even those with well-controlled blood glucose levels. The patient with diabetes manifests CAD more often and at an earlier age. There is no age difference between males or females with diabetes in the onset of symptoms of CAD.

Undiagnosed diabetes is often discovered when a person has an MI. The person with diabetes has an increased tendency toward endothelial dysfunction. This may account for the development of fatty streaks in the arteries. Patients with diabetes also have changes in lipid metabolism and tend to have high cholesterol and triglyceride levels. Management of diabetes should include lifestyle changes and drug therapy to achieve a glycosylated hemoglobin (A1C or Hb A1C) level of less than 7%.[13]

Metabolic Syndrome. Metabolic syndrome refers to a cluster of risk factors for CAD whose underlying pathophysiology may be related to insulin resistance. These risk factors include central obesity, hypertension, abnormal serum lipids, and a high fasting blood glucose (see Table 40.12). These interrelated risk factors appear to promote the development of CAD. Chapter 40 discusses metabolic syndrome.

Psychologic States. Certain behaviors and lifestyles may contribute to the development of CAD. One type of behavior, referred to as type A, includes perfectionism and a hardworking, driven personality. The type A personality often suppresses anger and hostility, has a sense of time urgency, is impatient, and creates stress and tension. This person may be more prone to MIs than one with a type B personality, who is more easygoing, takes upsets in stride, knows personal limitations, takes time to relax, and is not an overachiever. However, the relationship between behaviors and the risk for CAD/MI is controversial and complex.

Psychologic risk factors thought to increase the risk for CAD include depression, acute and chronic stress (e.g., poverty, serving as a caregiver), anxiety, hostility and anger, and lack of social support.[14] Stressful states contribute to the development and progression of CAD. Sympathetic nervous system (SNS) stimulation and its effect on the heart are the physiologic mechanisms by which stress predisposes a person to the development of CAD. SNS stimulation causes an increased release of catecholamines (i.e., epinephrine, norepinephrine), which may contribute to endothelial injury, inflammation, and platelet activation.[14] SNS stimulation also increases HR and the force of myocardial contraction, which increases myocardial O_2 demand. Stress-induced mechanisms can cause elevated lipid and glucose levels and changes in blood coagulation, which contribute to the development of atherosclerosis.

Homocysteine. High blood levels of homocysteine are linked to an increased risk for CAD and other CVDs.[13] Homocysteine is made by the breakdown of the essential amino acid methionine, which is found in dietary protein. High homocysteine levels may contribute to atherosclerosis by (1) damaging the inner lining of blood vessels, (2) promoting plaque buildup, and (3) changing the clotting mechanism to make clots more likely to occur. Although folic acid lowers homocysteine levels, research has not shown that reducing homocysteine levels lowers the risk of CAD.[15]

Substance Use. The use of illegal drugs, such as cocaine and methamphetamine, can produce coronary artery spasm resulting in myocardial ischemia and chest pain. Most patients with drug-induced chest pain initially cannot be distinguished from those with CAD. They often have sinus tachycardia, high BP, and chest pain. Chest pain occurs because of increased myocardial O_2 demand from the increased HR and contractility and coronary vasoconstriction.[16] An MI can occur because of coronary spasm. Serum cardiac biomarkers and an electrocardiogram (ECG) help determine if the patient is experiencing ACS. A drug screen may be helpful to identify what precipitated the cardiac event.

❖ INTERPROFESSIONAL AND NURSING CARE: CORONARY ARTERY DISEASE

◆ Health Promotion

Management of CAD risk factors may prevent, modify, or slow disease progression. In the United States, there has been a gradual decline in CAD-related deaths over the past 35 years. This relates to people's efforts to become healthier and advances in the treatment of CAD. Prevention and early treatment of heart disease must involve a multifaceted approach and must be ongoing throughout the life span. In fact, healthy lifestyle behaviors should begin in childhood.

◆ **Identifying High-Risk Persons.** Clinical signs of CAD are not apparent in the early stages of the disease. Therefore it is critical to identify people at risk for CAD. Risk screening involves obtaining a thorough health history. Ask the patient about a family history of heart disease in parents and siblings, especially a premature history of CAD (under age 55 for males and under age 65 for females).[13] Note the presence of any cardiovascular symptoms. Assess environmental factors, such as eating habits, type of diet, and level of exercise, to elicit lifestyle patterns. Include a psychosocial history to determine tobacco use, alcohol intake, recent stressful events (e.g., loss of a spouse), and psychologic state (e.g., anxiety, depression, anger). The place and type of employment provide vital information on the kind of activity performed, exposure to pollutants or toxins, and degree of stress associated with work.

Identify the patient's attitudes and beliefs about health and illness. This gives insight to how disease and lifestyle changes may affect the patient. It also can reveal misconceptions about heart disease. Knowing the patient's educational background and health literacy helps determine teaching needs. If the patient has prescribed drugs, it is important to know the names and dosages and if the patient adheres to the drug regimen.

◆ **Managing High-Risk Persons.** Recommend preventive measures for all persons at risk for CAD. The person with nonmodifiable risk factors (e.g., age, gender, ethnicity) can still reduce the risk for CAD by controlling the additive effects of modifiable risk factors. For example, a young person with a family history of heart disease can decrease the risk for CAD by maintaining an ideal body weight, getting adequate physical exercise, reducing intake of saturated fats, and avoiding tobacco and illicit drug use.

Encourage people who have modifiable risk factors to make lifestyle changes to reduce their risk for CAD. You can play a key role in teaching health-promoting behaviors (Table 33.2). For highly motivated persons, just knowing how to reduce their risk may be all the information they need to start.

For people who are less motivated to take charge of their health, the idea of reducing risk factors may be so remote that they are unable to perceive a threat of CAD. Few people want to make lifestyle changes, especially in the absence of symptoms. First, help them to clarify their personal values. Then, discuss risk factors and have them identify their individual risks. This can help them set realistic goals and choose which risk factor(s) to change first. Some people are reluctant to change until they begin to have symptoms or have an MI. Others, having had an MI, may find the idea of changing lifelong habits still unacceptable. Help them review options and respect their decisions.

◆ Physical Activity

A regular physical activity program should be designed and implemented to improve physical fitness by following the FITT formula (Table 33.3): Frequency (how often), Intensity (how hard), Type (isotonic), and Time (how long). Everyone should aim for at least 30 minutes of moderate physical activity on most days of the week. Examples of moderate physical activity include brisk walking, hiking, biking, and swimming. The AHA encourages people to increase their daily physical activity and lower the chance of developing heart disease simply by walking. Adding weight training to an exercise program 2 days a week can help treat metabolic syndrome and improve muscle strength. Regular physical activity helps with weight reduction, reduces systolic BP, and can help increase HDL cholesterol.

◆ Nutritional Therapy

Dietary recommendations focus on ways to lower LDL cholesterol. They emphasize a decrease in saturated fat and cholesterol and an increase in complex carbohydrates (e.g., whole grains,

TABLE 33.2 Patient & Caregiver Teaching
Reducing Risk Factors for Coronary Artery Disease

Include the following instructions when teaching risk reduction for coronary artery disease:

Risk Factor	Health-Promoting Behaviors	Risk Factor	Health-Promoting Behaviors
Hypertension	• Monitor home-based BP and obtain regular checkups. • Take prescribed drugs for BP control. • Reduce salt intake. • Stop tobacco use. Avoid exposure to environmental tobacco (secondhand) smoke. • Control or reduce weight. • Perform physical activity daily.	**Psychologic state**	• Increase awareness of behaviors that are harmful to health. • Change patterns that add to stress (e.g., get up 30 min earlier so that breakfast is not eaten on way to work). • Set realistic goals for self. • Reassess priorities in light of identified risk factors. • Learn effective stress management strategies (see Chapter 6). • Seek professional help if feeling depressed, angry, anxious, etc. • Plan time for adequate rest and sleep (see Chapter 7).
High serum lipids	• Reduce total fat intake. • Reduce saturated fat intake. • Take prescribed drugs for lipid reduction. • Adjust total caloric intake to achieve and maintain ideal body weight. • Engage in daily physical activity. • Increase amount of complex carbohydrates, fiber, and vegetable proteins in diet. • Follow-up with HCP for regular lipid panel assessments.	**Obesity use** (see Chapter 40)	• Change eating patterns and habits. • Reduce caloric intake to achieve body mass index of 18.5 to 24.9 kg/m^2. • Increase physical activity to increase caloric expenditure. • Avoid fad and crash diets, which are not effective over time. • Avoid large, heavy meals. Consider smaller, more frequent meals.
Tobacco use (see Chapter 10)	• Begin a tobacco cessation program. • Change daily routines associated with tobacco use to reduce desire to smoke. • Substitute other activities for smoking. • Ask caregivers to support efforts to stop smoking. • Avoid exposure to environmental tobacco smoke.	**Diabetes use** (see Chapter 48)	• Follow the recommended diet. • Control or reduce weight. • Take prescribed drugs for diabetes. • Monitor blood glucose levels regularly and follow up with HCP regularly.
Physical inactivity	• Develop and maintain at least 30 minutes of moderate physical activity daily (minimum 5 days a week). • Increase activities to a fitness level.		

TABLE 33.3 Patient & Caregiver Teaching
FITT Activity Guidelines for CAD, Chronic Stable Angina, and ACS

Include the following information in the teaching plan for the patient with chronic stable angina and acute coronary syndrome and the caregiver:

Warm-Up/Cool-Down
Perform mild stretching for 3–5 min before the physical activity and 5 min after the activity. Do not start or stop activity abruptly.

Frequency
Perform physical activity on most days of the week.

Intensity
The patient's HR determines the activity intensity. If an exercise stress test has not been performed, the HR of the patient recovering from an MI should not exceed 20 beats/min over the resting HR.

Type of Physical Activity
Select physical activity that is regular, rhythmic, and repetitive, using large muscles to build up endurance (e.g., walking, cycling, swimming, rowing).

Time
Physical activity sessions should be at least 30 min long. Begin slowly at personal tolerance (perhaps only 5–10 min) and build up to 30 min.

fruit, vegetables) and fiber (Tables 33.4 and 33.5). Fat intake should be about 25% to 35% of total calories, with most coming from monounsaturated and polyunsaturated fats. Red meat, egg yolks, and whole milk products are major sources of saturated fat and cholesterol. They should be reduced or eliminated from diets. With a high serum triglyceride level, alcohol and simple sugars should be reduced or eliminated.

Omega-3 fatty acids reduce triglyceride levels and can slow the progression of CAD. They do not affect LDL levels. The AHA recommends eating fatty fish twice a week. Examples of fatty fish include salmon, tuna, and mackerel. Other foods that contain omega-3 fatty acids include soybean oils, canola, walnuts, and flaxseed.[17] Omega-3 fatty acids can be hard to get by diet alone. The HCP may recommend dietary supplements.

◆ Lipid-Lowering Drug Therapy

An estimated 28.5 million American adults over age 20 have cholesterol levels of 240 mg/dL (6.2 mmol/L) or greater.[1] Treatment of high cholesterol focuses mostly on lowering LDL cholesterol. A complete lipid profile should be done every 5 years beginning at age 20.[9] Middle-aged adults should be screened every 1 to 2 years. If multiple risk factors are present, more frequent testing is recommended.[9] Guidelines recommend the following groups of people receive statin therapy: (1) patients with known CVD, (2) patients with primary elevations of LDL cholesterol levels of 190 mg/dL or greater (e.g., familial hypercholesterolemia), (3)

TABLE 33.4 Nutritional Therapy
Therapeutic Lifestyle Changes to Diet

Dietary Recommendations	Recommended Daily Intake

Combined total fat calories from:
• *Saturated fats:* Limit fats that are usually solid at room and refrigerator temperature (e.g., lard, butter, whole-milk products, fatty cuts of meat, bacon)
• *Trans fats:* Mainly in foods made with hydrogenated vegetable oils, such as many hard margarines and shortenings
• *Unsaturated fats:* In oils that are usually liquid at room and refrigerator temperature (e.g., olive, corn, sunflower, soybean). There are 2 types of unsaturated fats:
  • *Monounsaturated fats:* In greatest amounts in foods from plants, including olives, avocadoes, and canola, sunflower, and peanut oils.
  • *Polyunsaturated fats:* Found mostly in nuts, seeds, fish, seed oils, and oysters. Omega-3 fatty acid is a type of polyunsaturated fat that may help reduce the risk of CAD.
	25%–35% of total daily calories (including <7% from saturated fat)

Cholesterol	<200 mg
Plant stanols or sterols (e.g., margarines, nuts, seeds, legumes, vegetable oils)*	2 g
Dietary soluble fiber*	10–25 g of soluble fiber
Total calories	Only enough calories to reach or maintain a healthy weight

Physical Activity
In addition to diet, teach the patient to get at least 30 min of a moderate intensity physical activity, such as brisk walking, on most, and preferably all, days of the week.

*Diet options for additional lowering of low-density lipoprotein (LDL).

COMPLEMENTARY & ALTERNATIVE THERAPIES
Lipid-Lowering Agents

Agent	Evidence for Use
Berberine	Possibly effective for reducing total cholesterol, low-density lipoproteins (LDLs), triglycerides
Garlic	Conflicting evidence. Possibly effective for reducing total cholesterol and LDL over short periods
Green tea	Possibly effective for reducing total cholesterol
Flaxseed	Conflicting evidence on the efficacy for reducing total cholesterol
Omega-3 fatty acids (fish oil)	Effective for reducing cholesterol and triglyceride levels
Black psyllium	Possibly effective for reducing total cholesterol and LDL
Plant sterols	Likely effective for reducing total cholesterol and LDL
Red yeast rice	Likely effective for reducing total cholesterol, LDL, and triglycerides. Red yeast rice contains a chemical similar to statins.
Soy	Possibly effective for slight reduction in total cholesterol and LDL

Source: Sahebkar A, Serban MC, Gluba-Brzózka A, et al: Lipid-modifying effects of nutraceuticals: an evidence-based approach, *Nutrition* 32:1179, 2016; Siscovick DS, Barringer TA, Fretts AM, et al: Omega-3 polyunsaturated fatty acid (fish oil) supplementation and the prevention of clinical cardiovascular disease, *Circulation*, 2017.

TABLE 33.5 Nutritional Therapy
Tips to Make Diet and Lifestyle Changes

General Tips
1. Know your calorie needs to achieve and maintain a healthy weight.
2. Know the calorie content of the foods and beverages you eat.
3. Track your weight, physical activity, and calorie intake.
4. Prepare and eat smaller, more frequent meals.
5. Track your activities and, whenever possible, decrease sedentary activities (e.g., watching television, computer time).
6. Incorporate physical movement into daily activities (e.g., take stairs and extra steps whenever possible).
7. Do not smoke or use tobacco products.
8. If you drink alcohol, do so in moderation (i.e., no more than 1 drink for women or 2 drinks for men a day).

Tips Related to Food Choices and Preparation
1. Use the Nutrition Facts panel on food labels and ingredients list when choosing foods to buy.
2. Use fresh or frozen vegetables and fruits in place of canned vegetables and fruits.
3. Replace high-calorie foods with fresh fruits and vegetables.
4. Increase fiber intake by eating beans (legumes), whole-grain products, fruits, and vegetables.
5. Use liquid vegetable oils in place of solid fats.
6. Limit beverages and foods high in added sugars (e.g., sucrose, glucose, fructose, maltose, dextrose, corn syrups, concentrated fruit juice, honey).
7. Choose foods made with whole grains (e.g., whole wheat, oats, rye, barley, brown rice, wild rice, buckwheat).
8. Avoid pastries and high-calorie bakery products (e.g., muffins, doughnuts).
9. Select milk and dairy products that are either fat free or low fat.
10. Reduce salt intake by
    • Comparing the sodium content of similar products (e.g., different brands of tomato sauce) and choosing products with less sodium.
    • Choosing versions of processed foods with reduced salt, including cereals, canned products, and baked goods.
    • Limiting condiments (e.g., soy sauce, ketchup).
11. Use lean cuts of meat and remove skin from poultry before cooking or eating.
12. Avoid processed meats that are high in saturated fat and sodium (e.g., deli meats).
13. Grill, bake, or broil fish, meat, and poultry.
14. Incorporate plant-based meat substitutes into recipes (e.g., soy, tofu, quinoa).
15. Consume whole vegetables and fruits in place of juices.

Source: U.S. Department of Health and Human Services: Your guide to lowering your cholesterol with TLC. Retrieved from *www.nhlbi.nih.gov/files/docs/public/heart/chol_tlc.pdf.*

patients 40 to 75 years old with diabetes and LDL cholesterol levels between 70 and 189 mg/dL, and (4) patients 40 to 75 years old with LDL cholesterol levels between 70 and 189 mg/dL and a 10-year risk for CVD of at least 7.5%.[8,18]

Drug therapy should continue for a lifetime unless the patient becomes intolerant. In that case, the patient should switch to another drug. The patient must fully understand the rationale and goals of treatment, as well as the safety and side effects of lipid-lowering drugs.

Concurrent diet change is essential to reduce the need for drug therapy. Treatment also includes weight loss, if overweight, and increased physical activity. Serum lipid levels should be reassessed after 6 weeks of therapy. If they are still high, changes in drug therapy (Table 33.6) and more dietary options (see the Complementary & Alternative Therapies box) may be considered.

◆ Drugs That Restrict Lipoprotein Production

HMG-CoA Reductase Inhibitors (Statins). The statin drugs are the most widely used lipid-lowering drugs (Table 33.6). These drugs inhibit the synthesis of cholesterol in the liver. An unexplained result of inhibiting cholesterol synthesis is an increase in hepatic LDL receptors. This allows the liver to remove more LDL from the blood. In addition, statins cause a minor increase in HDL and lower CRP levels. The statins are not equal in reducing LDL levels. Rosuvastatin (Crestor) is the most potent statin currently available. Serious adverse effects of these drugs are rare and include liver damage and myalgia (muscle ache or weakness without breakdown of skeletal muscle) that can progress to rhabdomyolysis (breakdown of skeletal muscle). Liver enzymes are initially monitored and rechecked with any increase in dosage. The creatine kinase isoenzyme, CK-MM (found in skeletal muscle), is assessed if symptoms of myopathy (e.g., muscle aches, weakness) occur.

 DRUG ALERT Simvastatin (Zocor)

- Increased risk for rhabdomyolysis when used with fibric acid derivatives (e.g., gemfibrozil [Lopid]), niacin (Niaspan), or erythromycin.
- Manifestations of rhabdomyolysis include high creatine kinase levels and muscle pain.
- Prothrombin times may increase in patients taking warfarin (Coumadin).

Niacin. Niacin, a water-soluble B vitamin, is effective in lowering LDL and triglyceride levels by interfering with their synthesis (Table 33.6). Niacin, at high doses, increases HDL levels better than many other lipid-lowering drugs. Unfortunately, side effects are common. They may include severe flushing, pruritus, gastrointestinal (GI) symptoms, and orthostatic hypotension.

 DRUG ALERT Niacin (Niaspan)

- Teach the patient that flushing (especially of face and neck) may occur within 20 minutes after taking drug and last for 30 to 60 minutes.
- Premedicate with aspirin or NSAID 30 minutes before taking to reduce flushing.
- Use of extended-release niacin may decrease side effects.

Fibric Acid Derivatives. The *fibric acid derivatives* (Table 33.6) work by aiding the removal of VLDLs. They are very effective for lowering triglycerides and increasing HDL levels. They have no effect on LDLs. Although most patients tolerate the drugs well, GI irritability is common. These drugs should be used with caution when combined with statin medications due to increased risk for myopathy.

 DRUG ALERT Gemfibrozil (Lopid)

- May increase the risk for bleeding in patients taking warfarin (Coumadin)
- Increases the risk of hypoglycemia in patients taking repaglinide (Prandin)

◆ Drugs That Increase Lipoprotein Removal

Bile Acid Sequestrants. Bile-acid sequestrants increase conversion of cholesterol to bile acids in the liver and decrease hepatic cholesterol (Table 33.6). The primary effect is a decrease in total cholesterol and LDL levels. These drugs have been associated with side effects related to taste and a variety of upper and lower GI symptoms. These include belching, heartburn, nausea, abdominal pain, and constipation. Bile-acid sequestrants decrease absorption of many other drugs (e.g., warfarin, thiazides, thyroid hormones, β-adrenergic blockers

[β-blockers]). Separating the time of giving these drugs from that of other drugs by at least 2 hours decreases this adverse effect.[7]

Proprotein Convertase Subtilisin/Kexin 9 (PCSK9) Inhibitors. PCSK9 inhibitors are a newer class of cholesterol-lowering drugs (Table 33.6). PCSK9 reduces the number of receptors on the liver that remove LDL cholesterol from the blood. By blocking PCSK9's ability to work, more receptors are available and can get rid of LDL, thus decreasing circulating LDL levels. Evolocumab (Repatha) and alirocumab (Praluent) are 2 PCSK9 inhibitors. They are given subcutaneously every 2 weeks. Evolocumab may be given every 4 weeks at a higher dose, depending on patient preference. They are not a first-line therapy. They are used in addition to diet and maximum statin therapy for adults with familial hypercholesterolemia and for patients intolerant of statin drugs. They also can be used for patients with CAD who need added LDL lowering because of inadequate treatment with statins.[7]

◆ Drugs That Decrease Cholesterol Absorption.

Ezetimibe (Zetia) selectively inhibits the absorption of dietary and biliary cholesterol across the intestinal wall (Table 33.6). It serves as an adjunct to dietary changes, especially for patients with primary hypercholesterolemia. When it is combined with a statin, either as a combination drug (e.g., ezetimibe and simvastatin [Vytorin]) or as 2 separate drugs (ezetimibe and a statin), even greater reductions in LDLs occur.

◆ Antiplatelet Therapy

Low-dose aspirin (81 mg) is recommended for people who have CAD. For people at risk but without known CAD, low-dose aspirin is recommended for adults 50 to 59 years old who have a calculated 10-year CVD risk of 10% or more, are not at increased risk for bleeding (e.g., history of GI bleeding), have a life expectancy of at least 10 years, and are willing to take low-dose aspirin for at least 10 years. For adults 60 to 69 years old who have a calculated 10-year CVD risk of 10% or more, the decision to take low-dose aspirin is an individual one made in conjunction with the HCP. Adults who have no contraindications (e.g., history of bleeding), have a life expectancy of at least 10 years, and are willing to take low-dose aspirin daily for at least 10 years are more likely to benefit. Currently there is not enough evidence to recommend low-dose aspirin for primary prevention in those younger than 50 or older than 70.[19] Clopidogrel (Plavix) is an option for people who are aspirin intolerant.[15]

Gerontologic Considerations: Coronary Artery Disease

The incidence of heart disease is greatly increased in older adults and the leading cause of death in older persons. In the older adult, CAD is often a result of the complex interaction of nonmodifiable risk factors (e.g., age) and lifelong modifiable risk behaviors (e.g., inactivity, tobacco use). Strategies to reduce CAD risk and to treat CAD are effective in this age-group.

Aggressive treatment of hypertension and hyperlipidemia helps stabilize plaques in the coronary arteries. Tobacco cessation helps to decrease the risk for CAD at any age. Similarly, encourage the older patient to consider a planned program of physical activity. Physical activity improves activity performance, endurance, and ability to tolerate stress. Positive psychologic benefits can include increased self-esteem, emotional well-being, and improved body image. For the older adult who is obese, making modest dietary changes and slowly increasing physical activity (e.g., walking) results in more positive benefits than aiming for a significant weight loss.

TABLE 33.6 Drug Therapy

Hyperlipidemia

Drug	Mechanism of Action	Side Effects	Nursing Considerations
Restrict Lipoprotein Production			
Fibric Acid Derivatives			
fenofibrate (Tricor) gemfibrozil (Lopid)	Decrease hepatic synthesis and secretion of VLDL. Reduce triglycerides by ↓ VLDL ↓ LDL ↓ Triglycerides ↑ HDL	Rashes, mild GI problems (e.g., nausea, diarrhea), high liver enzymes	May ↑ effects of warfarin (Coumadin) and some antihyperglycemic drugs. When used in combination with statins, may increase adverse effects of statins, especially myopathy.
HMG-CoA Reductase Inhibitors (Statins)			
atorvastatin (Lipitor) fluvastatin (Lescol XL) lovastatin pitavastatin (Livalo) pravastatin (Pravachol) rosuvastatin (Crestor) simvastatin (Zocor)	Block synthesis of cholesterol and increase LDL receptors in liver ↓ LDL ↓ Triglycerides ↑ HDL (small amount)	Rash, GI problems, high liver enzymes, myopathy, rhabdomyolysis	Well tolerated with few side effects. Monitor liver enzymes and creatine kinase (if muscle weakness or pain occurs).
Niacin			
Niacin (Niaspan)	Inhibits synthesis and secretion of VLDL and LDL ↓ LDL ↓ Triglycerides ↑ HDL	Flushing and pruritus in upper torso and face, GI problems (e.g., nausea and vomiting, dyspepsia, diarrhea), orthostatic hypotension	Most side effects subside with time. Taking aspirin or NSAID 30 min before drug may prevent flushing. Take drug with food. Decreased liver function may occur with high doses.
Omega-3 Fatty Acid			
icosapent ethyl (Vascepa) (contains eicosapentaenoic acid [EPA]) omega-3 acid ethyl esters (Lovaza) (contains eicosapentaenoic acid [EPA] and docosahexaenoic acid [DHA])	Inhibits synthesis and/or secretion of triglycerides ↓ Triglycerides ↑ HDL	Arthralgia Anaphylaxis, rash, taste changes, GI problems (e.g., constipation, vomiting)	Used for patients with severe hypertriglyceridemia (levels ≥ 500 mg/dL) Used for patients with high triglycerides. Give with meals and do not open or dissolve capsules
Increase Lipoprotein Removal			
Bile-Acid Sequestrants			
cholestyramine (Prevalite) colesevelam (Welchol) colestipol (Colestid)	Binds with bile acids in intestine, forming insoluble complex and excreted in feces Binding results in removal of LDL and cholesterol ↓ LDL	Unpleasant quality to taste, GI problems (e.g., indigestion, constipation, bloating)	Effective and safe for long-term use. Side effects lessen with time. Interferes with absorption of many drugs (e.g., digoxin, thiazide diuretics, warfarin, some antibiotics [e.g., penicillins])
Proprotein Convertase Subtilisin/Kexin 9 (PCSK9) Inhibitors			
alirocumab (Praluent) evolocumab (Repatha)	Inactivate PCSK9 protein ↓ LDL	Injection-site reactions, muscle pain, limb pain, and fatigue	Used with diet and maximum statin therapy to treat familial hypercholesterolemia and for those who need further LDL lowering or for those who are statin intolerant Drugs are given by injection every 2–4 wks (evolocumab may be given every 4 wks at a higher dose)
Decrease Cholesterol Absorption			
Cholesterol Absorption Inhibitor			
ezetimibe (Zetia)	Inhibits the intestinal absorption of cholesterol ↓ LDL ↑ HDL	Infrequent, but may include headache and mild GI distress	When used with a statin, further reduces LDL. Should not be used by patients with liver impairment

TABLE 33.7 Select Conditions Influencing Myocardial O₂ Needs

Decreased O₂ Supply	Increased O₂ Demand or Consumption
Cardiac	
• Coronary artery atherosclerosis	• Aortic stenosis
• Coronary artery spasm	• Cardiomyopathy
• Coronary artery thrombosis	• Dysrhythmias
• Dysrhythmias	• Left ventricular hypertrophy
• Heart failure	• Tachycardia
• Valve disorders	
Noncardiac	
• Anemia	• Anxiety
• Asthma	• Hypertension
• Chronic obstructive pulmonary disease	• Hyperthermia
	• Hyperthyroidism
• Hypovolemia	• Physical exertion
• Hypoxemia	• Substance (stimulant) abuse (e.g., cocaine, amphetamines)
• Pneumonia	
• Substance (stimulant) abuse (e.g., cocaine, amphetamines)	

TABLE 33.8 PQRST Assessment of Angina

Use the following memory aid to obtain information from the patient who has chest pain:

	Factor	Questions to Ask Patient
P	Precipitating events	What events or activities precipitated the pain or discomfort (e.g., argument, exercise, resting)?
Q	Quality of pain	What does the pain or discomfort feel like (e.g., pressure, dull, aching, tight, squeezing, heaviness)?
R	Region (location) and radiation of pain	Can you point to where the pain or discomfort is located? Does the pain or discomfort radiate to other areas (e.g., back, neck, arms, jaw, shoulder, elbow)?
S	Severity of pain	On a scale of 0 to 10, with 0 indicating no pain and 10 being the most severe pain you could imagine, what number would you give the pain or discomfort?
T	Timing	When did the pain or discomfort begin? Has it changed since this time? Have you had pain/discomfort like this before?

When planning a physical activity program, recommend: (1) longer warm-up periods, (2) longer periods of low-level activity, and/or (3) longer rest periods between sessions. Heat intolerance results from a decreased ability to sweat efficiently. Teach the patient to avoid physical activity in temperature extremes and to maintain a moderate pace. The older adult should exercise a minimum of 30 minutes on most days of the week as able.

Encouraging the older patient to adopt a healthy lifestyle may increase the quality of life and reduce the risk for CAD and fatal heart events. Older adults face many of the same challenges as younger persons when it comes to making lifestyle changes. Older adults are more likely to consider change either (1) when hospitalized or (2) when symptoms (e.g., chest pain) are the result of CAD and not normal aging (see Table 31.1). First, assess for the readiness to change and health literacy. Then, help the patient select the lifestyle changes most likely to produce the greatest reduction in risk for CAD.

CHRONIC STABLE ANGINA

CAD is a chronic and progressive disease. Patients may be asymptomatic for many years but may eventually develop chronic stable chest pain. When the demand for myocardial O₂ exceeds the ability of the coronary arteries to supply the heart with O₂, *myocardial ischemia* occurs. Angina, or chest pain, is the clinical manifestation of myocardial ischemia. It is caused by either an increased demand for O₂ or a decreased supply of O₂ (Table 33.7). The most common reason for angina to develop is significant narrowing of 1 or more coronary arteries by atherosclerosis. This leads to insufficient blood flow to the heart muscle. For ischemia to occur from an atherosclerotic plaque, the artery is usually blocked (stenosed) 70% or more (50% or more for the left main coronary artery).[20]

Chronic stable angina refers to chest pain that occurs intermittently over a long period of time with a similar pattern of onset, duration, and intensity of symptoms. It is often provoked by physical exertion, stress, or emotional upset. It is important to get an accurate assessment of the angina symptoms (Table 33.8). When asked, some patients may deny feeling pain, but

describe a pressure, heaviness, or discomfort in the chest. This discomfort is often described as a squeezing, heavy, tight, or suffocating sensation. It may be associated with other symptoms, such as dyspnea or fatigue. Chronic angina pain usually does not change with position or breathing.

Although most angina pain occurs substernally, it may radiate to other locations, including the jaw, neck, shoulders, and/or arms. Many people with angina describe a feeling of indigestion or a burning sensation in the epigastric region. The sensation may be felt between the shoulder blades (Fig. 33.3). Often, people who describe pain between the shoulder blades or indigestion type pain dismiss it as not being heart related. Some patients, especially women and older adults, report atypical symptoms of angina, including dyspnea, nausea, mid-epigastric discomfort, and/or fatigue.[13] We refer to this as an *angina equivalent.*

The pain of chronic stable angina usually lasts for only a few minutes. It often subsides when the precipitating factor is resolved (e.g., by resting, calming down, using sublingual nitroglycerin [SL NTG]) (Table 33.9). Pain at rest is unusual and may indicate UA. With ischemia, the 12-lead ECG often shows ST segment depression and/or T wave inversion. These changes represent inadequate supply of blood and O₂ to the heart muscle. ST depression is significant if it is at least 1 mm (1 small box) below the isoelectric line in at least 2 contiguous (neighboring) leads. In a normal heart, the isoelectric line should be flat (see Fig. 35.10). The ECG changes return to baseline when adequate blood flow is restored, and pain is relieved.

Chronic stable angina is controlled with drugs on an outpatient basis. Because chronic stable angina is often predictable, drugs are timed to provide peak effects during the time of day when angina is likely to occur. For example, if angina occurs when rising, the patient can take medication as soon as awakening and wait 30 minutes to 1 hour before engaging in activity. A comparison of the major types of angina is outlined in Table 33.10.

Silent ischemia refers to ischemia that occurs in the absence of any subjective symptoms. Patients with diabetes have an increased prevalence of silent ischemia. This is likely due to

- Mid sternum
- Left shoulder and down both arms
- Neck and arms

- Substernal radiating to neck and jaw
- Substernal radiating down left arm

- Epigastric
- Epigastric radiating to neck, jaw, and arms

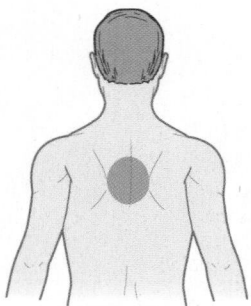

- Intrascapular

FIG. 33.3 Common locations and patterns of pain during angina or MI.

TABLE 33.9 Precipitating Factors of Angina

Physical Exertion
- Increases HR, reducing the time the heart spends in diastole (the time of greatest coronary blood flow), resulting in an increase in myocardial O_2 demand
- Isometric exercise of the arms (e.g., raking, lifting heavy objects, snow shoveling) can cause exertional angina

Temperature Extremes
- Increase the workload of the heart
- Blood vessels constrict in response to a cold stimulus
- Blood vessels dilate and blood pools in the skin in response to a hot stimulus

Strong Emotions
- Stimulate the sympathetic nervous system, activating the stress response
- Increase the workload of the heart

Consumption of Heavy Meal (e.g., holiday meals)
- Can increase the workload of the heart
- During the digestive process, blood is diverted to the GI system, reducing blood flow in the coronary arteries

Tobacco Use and Environmental Tobacco Smoke
- Decrease available O_2 by increasing the level of carbon monoxide
- Nicotine stimulates catecholamine release, causing vasoconstriction and an increased HR

Sexual Activity
- Increases the cardiac workload and sympathetic stimulation
- In a person with CAD, the extra cardiac workload may precipitate angina

Stimulants (e.g., cocaine, amphetamines)
- Increase HR and BP and increases myocardial O_2 demand
- Stimulate vasoconstriction and decreases myocardial O_2 supply
- May precipitate dysrhythmias

Circadian Rhythm Patterns
- Manifestations of CAD tend to occur in the early morning after awakening

TABLE 33.10 Comparison of Major Types of Angina

Type	Etiology	Characteristics
Chronic stable angina	Myocardial ischemia (usually from CAD) caused by an O_2 supply/demand mismatch	• Episodic pain lasting a few minutes • Provoked by exertion or stress • Relieved by rest or nitroglycerin
Prinzmetal's angina	Coronary vasospasm	• Occurs primarily at rest • Triggered by smoking and increased levels of some substances (e.g., histamine, epinephrine, cocaine) • May occur in presence or absence of CAD • Treatment may include long-acting nitrates and/or calcium channel blockers
Microvascular angina	Myocardial ischemia from microvascular disease affecting the small, distal branches of coronary arteries	• More common in women • Triggered by activities of daily living (e.g., shopping, work) vs. physical exercise (exertion) • Treatment may include nitroglycerin
Unstable angina	Rupture of unstable plaque, exposing thrombogenic surface	• New-onset angina • Chronic stable angina that increases in frequency, duration, or severity • Occurs at rest or with minimal exertion • Lasts more than 10 min

diabetic neuropathy affecting the nerves that innervate the cardiovascular system. When patients are monitored and silent ischemia occurs, ECG changes are revealed (e.g., ST depression and/or T wave inversion) (Fig. 33.4, *A*). Ischemia with pain or without pain has the same prognosis.

Prinzmetal's Angina

Prinzmetal's angina (*variant angina*) is a rare form of angina that often occurs at rest and not with increased physical demand. It is sometimes seen in patients with a history of migraine headaches, Raynaud's phenomenon, and heavy smoking. It is usually due to spasm of a major coronary artery. Strong contraction (spasm) of smooth muscle in the coronary artery results from increased intracellular calcium.[21] The spasm may occur in the presence or absence of CAD.

Factors contributing to coronary artery spasm include increased levels of certain substances (e.g., alcohol, cocaine), exposure to medications that narrow blood vessels (e.g.

FIG. 33.4 ST segment, T wave, and Q wave changes associated with myocardial ischemia (**A**), injury coronary spasm (**B**), and infarction (**C**). (From Bucher L, Melander S: *Critical care nursing*, Philadelphia, 1999, Saunders.)

sumatriptan [Imitrex]), or cold weather exposure. When spasm occurs, the patient has angina and transient ST segment elevation (not usually associated with an MI) (Fig. 33.4, *B*). The pain may occur during rapid-eye-movement (REM) sleep when myocardial O_2 consumption increases between midnight and early morning or at rest. The pain may be relieved by moderate exercise, with SL NTG, or it may disappear spontaneously. Cyclic, short bursts of pain at the same time each day may occur with this type of angina. Calcium channel blockers and/or nitrates are an option. Stopping the use of any offending substances is recommended.[22]

Microvascular Angina

In *microvascular angina*, chest pain occurs in the absence of significant CAD or coronary spasm of a major coronary artery. In these patients, chest pain is related to myocardial ischemia associated with atherosclerosis or spasm of the small distal branch vessels of the coronary microcirculation. This is known as *coronary microvascular disease* (MVD). MVD is often used interchangeably with the term *syndrome X*. It is more common in women. Often the angina is prolonged and brought on by physical exertion. These patients usually have positive stress test results and an inconsistent response to nitrates.[22] Prevention and treatment of coronary MVD follow the same recommendations as for CAD.

INTERPROFESSIONAL AND NURSING CARE: CHRONIC STABLE ANGINA

Chronic stable angina can progress or develop into UA or ACS. Therefore any change in the usual pattern of angina should be evaluated. A patient with chronic stable angina may be admitted with a change in the angina pattern. Until an assessment and diagnostic studies are completed, it may be unclear if the patient is having typical chronic stable angina, UA, or an MI.

The goal of treatment for a patient admitted with angina is to decrease O_2 demand and/or increase O_2 supply. Nursing care focuses on the priority problems of managing acute pain and anxiety while increasing O_2 delivery to the myocardium. The overall goals for a patient who presents with angina include (1) relief of pain, (2) immediate and appropriate treatment, (3) preservation of heart muscle if an MI is suspected, (4) effective coping with illness-associated anxiety, (5) participation in a rehabilitation plan, and (6) reduction of risk factors.

Acute Care

If your patient has angina, perform the following measures: (1) position patient upright unless contraindicated and apply supplemental O_2, (2) assess vital signs, (3) place patient on continuous ECG monitor, (4) obtain a 12-lead ECG, (5) provide prompt pain relief, first with NTG, followed by an IV opioid analgesic, if needed, (6) obtain cardiac biomarkers, (7) assess heart and breath sounds, and (8) obtain a chest x-ray. The patient may be anxious and may have pale, cool, clammy skin. The BP and HR may be high. Auscultation of the heart may reveal an atrial (S_4) or a ventricular (S_3) gallop. A new systolic murmur heard during an angina attack may indicate ischemia of a papillary muscle of the mitral valve, causing mitral regurgitation (the mitral valve does not close properly). The murmur may be transient and disappear when symptoms resolve.

Ask the patient to describe the pain and to rate it on a scale of 0 to 10 before and after treatment to evaluate the effectiveness of the interventions. It is important to use the same words the patient uses to describe the symptoms (e.g., tightness, pressure). Assess for other signs of pain, such as restlessness; ECG changes; high HR, respiratory rate, or BP; clutching of the bed linens; or other nonverbal cues. Support and reassure the patient. Use a calm approach to help reduce the patient's anxiety during an angina attack. If the chest pain is not related to an ACS, the patient may be discharged within 1 or 2 days. Further testing may be done during the hospitalization or as an outpatient.

> **? CHECK YOUR PRACTICE**
>
> A visitor finds you in the hallway and tells you that her father is having chest pain. The patient is not assigned to you.
> - How would you proceed?

Patient Teaching

Reassure the patient with a history of angina that a long, active life is possible. Preventing angina or at least reducing the frequency of angina is key, so teaching is important. Emphasize the importance of risk factor modification to slow the progression of CAD (Tables 33.1 and 33.11). Give the patient information about CAD, angina, precipitating factors for angina (Table 33.9) and medications to treat angina (Table 33.11).

You can provide patient teaching in a variety of ways. One-on-one contact between you and the patient is often the most effective approach. Time spent providing daily care (e.g., giving drugs) offers many teachable moments. Teaching aids, such as DVDs, heart models, and printed information, are important resources for patient and caregiver teaching (see Chapter 4).

Help the patient to identify factors that precipitate angina (Table 33.9). Tell the patient how to avoid or control these factors. For example, teach the patient to avoid exposure to extremes of weather and eating large, heavy meals. Tell the patient to rest for 1 to 2 hours after a heavy meal because blood shifts to the GI tract to aid digestion and absorption.

Help the patient to identify personal risk factors for CAD and ways to reduce modifiable risk factors (Table 33.2). Teach the patient and caregiver about diets low in salt and saturated fats (Tables 33.4 and 33.5). Maintaining ideal body weight is important in controlling angina because excess weight increases the heart's workload.

It is important that the patient has a regular, individualized program of physical activity that conditions rather than stresses the heart. For example, tell patients that walking briskly on a flat surface at least 30 minutes a day, most days of the week is recommended.

If needed, arrange for counseling to assess the psychologic adjustment of the patient and caregiver to the diagnosis of CAD and the resulting angina. Many patients feel a threat to identity, self-esteem, and the usual roles in society. These emotions are normal and real.

Drug Therapy

Drug therapy for chronic stable angina aims to reduce symptoms of and the risk for MI and death. The most common medications to optimize myocardial perfusion in chronic stable angina include nitrates, angiotensin-converting enzyme (ACE) inhibitors, β-blockers, and calcium channel blockers (Table 33.11 and Fig. 33.5). Aspirin (previously discussed) is given in the absence of contraindications (Table 33.12).

Short-Acting Nitrates. Short-acting nitrates are first-line therapy for an acute episode of angina. Nitrates produce their principal effects by the following mechanisms:

Dilating peripheral blood vessels: This results in decreased SVR, venous pooling, and decreased venous blood return to the heart (preload). Therefore myocardial O_2 demand is decreased because of the reduced cardiac workload.

Dilating coronary arteries and collateral vessels: This may increase blood flow to the ischemic areas of the heart. However, when the coronary arteries are severely atherosclerotic, coronary dilation is hard to achieve.

Sublingual Nitroglycerin. SL NTG tablets or translingual spray (Nitrolingual) usually relieves pain in about 5 minutes and lasts about 30 to 40 minutes. The recommended dose of NTG is 1 tablet taken sublingually (SL) or 1 to 2 metered sprays on or under the tongue for symptoms of angina. If symptoms are unchanged or worse after 5 minutes, the patient should repeat NTG every 5 minutes for a maximum of 3 doses. Teach the patient to contact the emergency response system (e.g., 911) if symptoms have not resolved completely after 3 doses.

Teach the patient the proper storage and use of NTG. It should be always easily accessible to the patient. Store the tablets away from light and heat sources, including body heat, to protect them from degradation. Tablets are packaged in light-resistant bottles with metal caps. Once opened, the tablets lose potency. They should be replaced every 6 months.

TABLE 33.11 Treatment of Chronic Stable Angina and Acute Coronary Syndrome

Strategies for the patient with chronic stable angina should address all the treatment elements and related patient teaching in the following mnemonic:

Element	Treatment
A	Antiplatelet/anticoagulant therapy
	Antianginal therapy
	ACE inhibitor/angiotensin receptor blocker
B	β-Blocker
	BP control
C	Cigarette smoking cessation
	Cholesterol (lipid) management
	Calcium channel blockers
	Cardiac rehabilitation
D	Diet (weight management)
	Diabetes management
	Depression screening
E	Education
	Exercise
F	Flu vaccination

Modified from Smith SC, Benjamin EJ, Bonow RO, et al: AHA/ACCF secondary prevention and risk reduction therapy for patients with coronary and other atherosclerotic vascular disease: 2011 update, *J Am Coll Cardiol* 58:2432, 2011.

Tell the patient to sit down and place the NTG tablet under the tongue and allow it to dissolve. If using the spray, the patient should direct it on or under the tongue, not inhale it. SL NTG tablets should cause a tingling sensation when taken; otherwise it may be outdated. Warn the patient that a headache, dizziness, or flushing may occur. Caution the patient to change positions slowly after NTG use because orthostatic hypotension may occur.

Teach the patient and caregiver the proper use of NTG. Patients can use NTG prophylactically before starting an activity that is known to cause angina (e.g., emotionally stressful situation, sexual intercourse). In these cases, the patient can take a tablet or spray 5 to 10 minutes before beginning the activity. Tell the patient to report any changes in the usual pattern of pain, such as increasing frequency, nighttime angina, or angina at rest.

Long-Acting Nitrates. Oral nitrates, such as isosorbide dinitrate (e.g., Isordil) and isosorbide mononitrate, are longer acting than SL or translingual NTG. They are used to reduce the frequency of angina attacks and to treat Prinzmetal's angina. The main side effect is headache from the dilation of cerebral blood vessels. Tell patients to take acetaminophen (Tylenol) to relieve the headache. Over time, the headaches may decrease, but the antianginal effects are still present.

Orthostatic hypotension is a complication of all nitrates. Monitor BP after the first dose, since the venous dilation that occurs may cause a drop in BP, especially in volume-depleted patients. Finally, tolerance to long-acting NTG can develop. To limit this, patients may have a scheduled 10- to 14-hour nitrate-free period every day. Remind patients that taking a long-acting NTG preparation should not keep them from using translingual or SL NTG if chest pain develops.

Nitroglycerin Ointment. Nitropaste is a 2% NTG topical ointment dosed by the inch. It is placed on the upper body or arm, over a flat muscular area that is free of hair and scars. Once absorbed, it prevents angina for 3 to 6 hours. The ointment

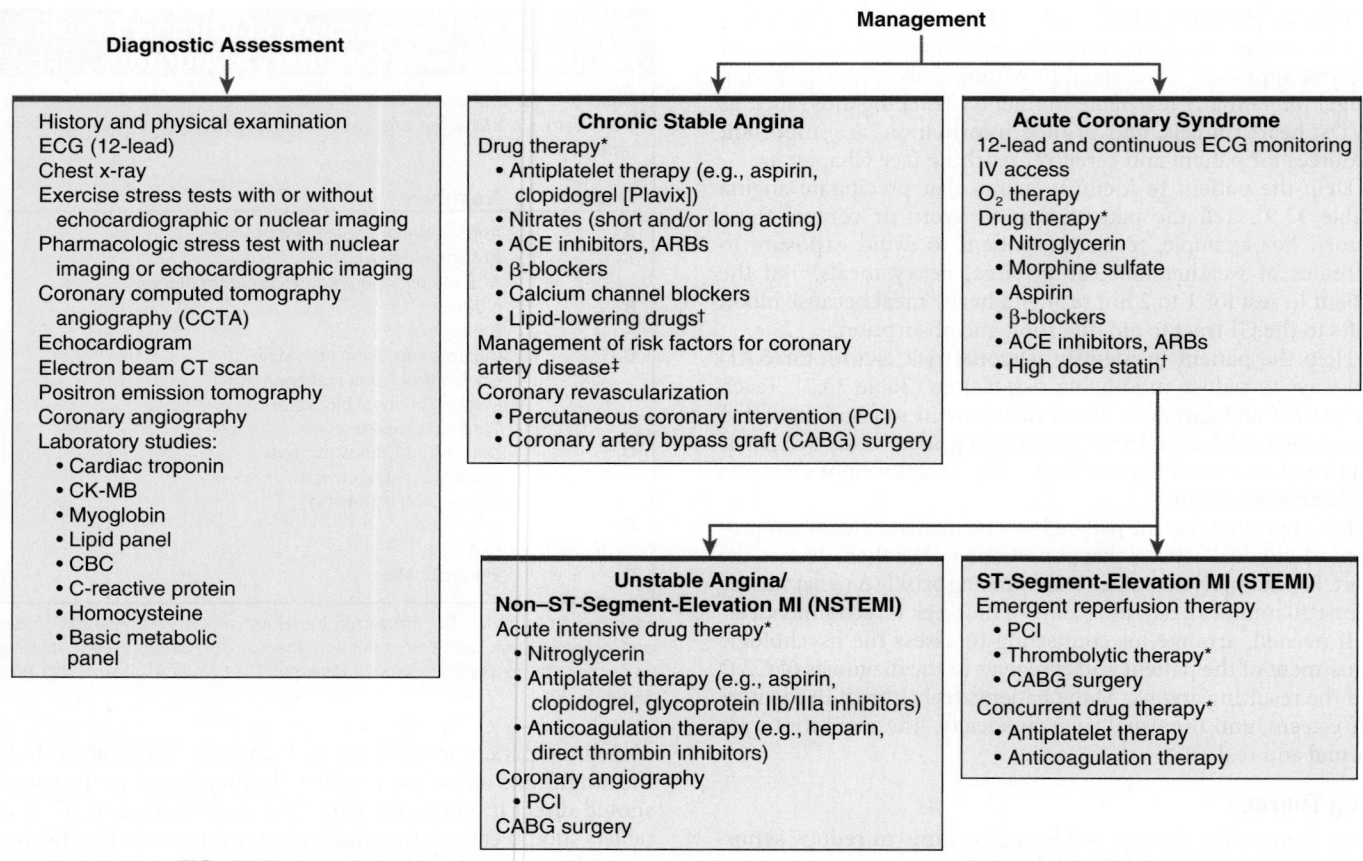

FIG. 33.5 Interprofessional care: Chronic stable angina and acute coronary syndrome. *Table 33.12. †Table 33.6. ‡Tables 33.2, 33.4, and 33.5.

should be wiped off each evening to allow for a 10- to 14-hour nitrate-free interval to prevent nitrate tolerance.

Transdermal Controlled-Release Nitrates. Currently 2 systems are available for transdermal NTG drug delivery: silicone gel and polymer matrix. These systems allow timed release of NTG over a 24-hour period. These preparations may be removed in the evening to allow for a 10- to 14-hour nitrate-free interval to reduce the risk for NTG tolerance.

💊 DRUG ALERT Nitrates

- Keep NTG tablets in a dark, airtight container to maintain potency.
- Tell patients to sit down before using short-acting nitrates.
- SL NTG must be placed under the tongue.
- Spray translingual NTG onto or under the tongue.
- Tell patient not to combine NTG with drugs used for erectile dysfunction (e.g., sildenafil [Viagra]) as severe hypotension can occur.
- Monitor for orthostatic hypotension after administration.
- Headaches are common after taking any NTG preparation.
- Caregivers should use gloves to apply and remove NTG ointment or transdermal patches to avoid contact with drug.
- Never cardiovert or defibrillate over NTG ointment or a transdermal patch.
- When using long-acting nitrates, provide a 10- to 14-hour nitrate-free period.
- Remind patient when using long-acting nitrates that short acting nitrates can still be used, if needed.

Angiotensin-Converting Enzyme (ACE) Inhibitors and Angiotensin Receptor Blockers (ARBs). Patients with chronic stable angina who have an ejection fraction (EF) of 40% or less, diabetes, hypertension, or CKD should take an ACE inhibitor

(e.g., lisinopril [Zestril]) indefinitely, unless contraindicated. Patients with chronic stable angina and a normal EF, diabetes, and 1 other CAD risk factor should also take an ACE inhibitor to decrease the risk for MI, stroke, and death.[23]

These drugs result in vasodilation and reduced blood volume. Most important, they can prevent or reverse ventricular remodeling in patients who have had an MI (see p. 725). For patients who are intolerant of ACE inhibitors (e.g., cough, angioedema), angiotensin receptor blockers (ARBs) (e.g., losartan [Cozaar]) are used. ACE inhibitors and ARBs are also discussed later in the chapter and in Chapter 32 and Table 32.6.

β-Adrenergic Blockers. β-Blockers are given for relief of angina symptoms in patients with chronic stable angina. Patients who have LV dysfunction or elevated BP or had an MI should start and continue β-blockers indefinitely, unless contraindicated. These drugs decrease myocardial contractility, HR, SVR, and BP, all of which reduce the myocardial O_2 demand and relieve angina symptoms. β-Blockers that reduce the risk for death in patients with LV dysfunction, HF, or MI include carvedilol (Coreg), metoprolol succinate (Toprol XL), and bisoprolol.[13]

β_1-Receptors are found in the heart. β_2 Receptors are found in blood vessels, lungs, and liver. Some β-blockers are called cardioselective β-blockers because they only block β_1 receptors (e.g., atenolol [Tenormin], metoprolol [Lopressor]). Some β-blockers, referred to as nonselective β-blockers, block both β_1 and β_2 receptors (e.g., nadolol [Corgard], propranolol [Inderal]). Some β-blockers block α_1, β_1, and β_2 receptors (e.g., carvedilol [Coreg], labetalol [Trandate]).

TABLE 33.12 **Drug Therapy**

Chronic Stable Angina and Acute Coronary Syndrome

Drug	Mechanism of Action and Comments
Angiotensin-Converting Enzyme (ACE) Inhibitors (See Table 32.6)	
benazepril (Lotensin) captopril enalapril (Vasotec) lisinopril (Zestril) quinapril (Accupril) ramipril (Altace)	• Prevents conversion of angiotensin I to angiotensin II, resulting in vasodilation • May prevent or limit ventricular remodeling • Decreases endothelial dysfunction • Useful with HF, decreased LV function, tachycardia, MI, hypertension, diabetes, and chronic kidney disease
Angiotensin II Receptor Blockers (See Table 32.6)	
candesartan (Atacand) irbesartan (Avapro) losartan (Cozaar) olmesartan (Benicar) valsartan (Diovan)	• Inhibits binding of angiotensin II to angiotensin I receptors, resulting in vasodilation • Used for patients intolerant of ACE inhibitors
Anticoagulant Agents (See Table 37.10)	
Direct Thrombin Inhibitors	
bivalirudin (Angiomax) argatroban	• Direct inhibition of the clotting factor thrombin • Used during PCI procedure
Low-Molecular-Weight Heparin†	
dalteparin (Fragmin) enoxaparin (Lovenox)	• Binds to antithrombin III, enhancing its effect • Heparin–antithrombin III complex inactivates activated factor X and thrombin. • Prevents conversion of fibrinogen to fibrin
Unfractionated Heparin†	
heparin	• Prevents conversion of fibrinogen to fibrin and prothrombin to thrombin
Vitamin K Antagonist†	
warfarin (Coumadin)	• Interferes with hepatic synthesis of vitamin K–dependent clotting factors • Used for patients with atrial fibrillation or those at risk for thromboembolism (large anterior wall infarctions or ventricular aneurysms) • Closely monitor for bleeding when taking with antiplatelet drugs
Antiplatelet Agents	
aspirin	• Inhibits cyclooxygenase, which in turn produces thromboxane A$_2$, a potent platelet activator • Should be given as soon as ACS is suspected, unless truly allergic
cangrelor (Kengreal)	• Inhibits platelet aggregation • Given IV • Approved for use in patients having PCI during procedure
clopidogrel (Plavix)	• Inhibits platelet aggregation • Alternative for patients who cannot take aspirin • Used in combination with low-dose aspirin to treat ACS with or without PCI and after elective PCI
prasugrel (Effient)	• Inhibits platelet aggregation • Used as an alternative to clopidogrel in combination with aspirin for patient with ACS who had PCI • Not indicated to treat ACS without PCI or for use after elective PCI

Drug	Mechanism of Action and Comments
ticagrelor (Brilinta)	• Inhibits platelet aggregation • Alternative for patient who cannot take aspirin • Used in combination with low-dose aspirin to treat ACS with or without PCI • Effectiveness may be decreased by aspirin dosages >100 mg/day
vorapaxar (Zontivity)	• Inhibits platelet aggregation • Increases risk for bleeding, including life-threatening and fatal bleeding (boxed warning) • Must not be used in people who have had a stroke, transient ischemic attack (TIA), or bleeding in the head, because the risk for bleeding in the head is too great
Glycoprotein IIb/IIIa Inhibitors	
abciximab (ReoPro) eptifibatide (Integrilin) tirofiban (Aggrastat)	• Prevents the binding of fibrinogen to platelets, thereby blocking platelet aggregation • May be used in combination with aspirin for patients with ACS or during PCI
β-Adrenergic Blockers (See Table 32.6)	
atenolol (Tenormin) carvedilol (Coreg) metoprolol (Lopressor) nadolol (Corgard)	• Inhibits sympathetic nervous stimulation of the heart • Reduces heart rate, contractility, and BP • Reduces ischemia • Decreases afterload • Cardioselective β-blockers include atenolol and metoprolol
Calcium Channel Blockers (See Table 32.6)	
amlodipine (Norvasc) diltiazem (Cardizem) felodipine nicardipine (Cardene) verapamil (Calan) nifedipine (Procardia)	• Prevents calcium entry into vascular smooth muscle cells and myocytes (cardiac cells) • May prevent or control coronary vasospasm • Promotes coronary and peripheral vasodilation • Reduces HR, contractility, and BP
Nitrates (See Table 32.6)	
Sublingual nitroglycerin (Nitrostat) Translingual spray nitroglycerin (Nitrolingual) nitroglycerin ointment Transdermal nitroglycerin isosorbide dinitrate (Isordil) isosorbide mononitrate IV nitroglycerin	• Promotes peripheral vasodilation, decreasing preload and afterload • Promotes coronary artery vasodilation • May prevent or control coronary vasospasm
Opioid	
morphine	• Functions as an analgesic and sedative • Acts as a vasodilator to reduce preload and myocardial O$_2$ consumption
Thrombolytic Agents	
reteplase (Retavase) alteplase (Activase) tenecteplase (TNKase)	• Breaks up fibrin meshwork in clots • Used only in ST-segment-elevation MI when access to a hospital with PCI capability is not available

β-Blockers have many side effects that can be poorly tolerated. These include bradycardia, hypotension, wheezing from bronchospasm, and GI effects. Many patients report weight gain, depression, fatigue, and sexual dysfunction. Absolute contraindications to using β-blockers include severe bradycardia and acute decompensated HF. Patients with asthma should avoid β-blockers, especially nonselective ones. They are used cautiously in patients with diabetes since they mask signs of hypoglycemia. β-Blockers should not be stopped abruptly without medical supervision, as this may result in an increase in the number and intensity of angina attacks.

Calcium Channel Blockers. If β-blockers are contraindicated, are poorly tolerated, or do not control anginal symptoms, calcium channel blockers are used. Their main effects are: (1) systemic vasodilation with decreased SVR, (2) decreased myocardial contractility, (3) coronary vasodilation, and (4) decreased HR. They are used to treat Prinzmetal's angina.

There are 2 groups of calcium channel blockers. The dihydropyridines (e.g., amlodipine [Norvasc], nifedipine [Procardia]) have more vasodilatory effects. The nondihydropyridines (e.g., verapamil [Calan], diltiazem [Cardizem]) have a greater effect on decreasing HR and contractility.

Side effects include fatigue, headache, dizziness, flushing and peripheral edema. The nondihydropyridines enhance the action of digoxin by increasing serum digoxin levels. Digoxin levels are closely monitored after starting these agents. Teach the patient the signs and symptoms of digoxin toxicity. Verapamil can cause severe constipation by relaxing GI smooth muscle and slowing peristalsis, especially in older adults.[7]

Lipid-Lowering Drugs. A moderate or high dose of a lipid-lowering drug is given, unless contraindicated (Table 33.6). Patients with chronic stable angina are encouraged to follow a diet low in saturated fat and cholesterol.

Sodium Current Inhibitor. Ranolazine (Ranexa), a sodium current inhibitor, is used to treat chronic angina in patients who have not had an adequate response with other antianginal medications. Although it is approved as a first-line agent, it is usually added to the medication regimen only when the angina is not well controlled. Ranolazine does not affect the BP or HR, but it can prolong the QT interval. Use it very cautiously in patients with a long QT interval or who are taking other QT-prolonging drugs (e.g., fluoxetine [Prozac]).[7] Common side effects include dizziness, nausea, constipation, and headache.

Diagnostic Studies

When a patient describes new-onset chest pain and CAD is suspected or when a patient with chronic stable angina has a change in the angina pattern, a variety of studies are done (Fig. 33.5). After a detailed health history and physical examination, a 12-lead ECG is done and compared with a previous ECG to look for changes that may indicate an ACS. Laboratory tests (e.g., cardiac biomarkers) are used to determine if the patient is experiencing an ACS. Other laboratory tests may be done (e.g., lipid profile, CRP) to identify risk factors for CAD. A chest x-ray is done to look for cardiac enlargement, aortic calcifications, and pulmonary congestion. An echocardiogram can detect resting LV wall motion abnormalities, which may suggest CAD.

If the ECG and cardiac biomarkers are negative, an exercise stress test with or without echocardiography or nuclear imaging may be done either during the hospitalization or as an outpatient. For patients with physical limitations in walking,

a pharmacologic (adenosine [Adenocard]) or dipyridamole stress test with nuclear imaging, or a pharmacologic (dobutamine) stress echocardiogram are options. Stress testing usually does not detect coronary blockages less than 70%.[13] Besides stress testing, other tests may be done if the ECG and cardiac biomarkers are negative. Electron beam computed tomography (EBCT) or coronary computed tomography angiography (CCTA or CTA) testing may be done if there is no evidence of an ACS and the patient remains free of chest pain. See Table 31.7 for more about these studies.

Cardiac Catheterization. For patients with increasing angina symptoms, a cardiac catheterization is the gold-standard test to identify and localize CAD. It is also recommended if the ECG shows ST-T wave changes (not ST elevation) and/or cardiac biomarkers are positive. This procedure should be done only if the patient is a candidate for percutaneous or surgical coronary revascularization.

If a coronary blockage is amenable to treatment, **coronary revascularization** with **percutaneous coronary intervention (PCI)** may be recommended. PCI may be done at the same time as the cardiac catheterization. During PCI, a catheter with a deflated balloon tip is inserted into the blocked coronary artery. The deflated balloon is positioned inside the blockage and inflated. This compresses the plaque against the artery wall, resulting in vessel dilation and a larger vessel diameter. This procedure is called *balloon angioplasty*.

Intracoronary stents are usually placed after a balloon angioplasty. A **stent** is an expandable mesh-like structure designed to keep the vessel open. It provides support to the arterial wall (Figs. 33.6 and 33.7). There are 2 types of stents: bare metal (BMS) and drug-eluting (DES). A DES is coated with a drug (e.g., everolimus, zotarolimus) to reduce the risk for overgrowth of the intimal lining *(neointimal hyperplasia)* within the stent. This is the primary cause of in-stent restenosis (ISR). This risk is lower with the use of a DES.

Because stents are thrombogenic, drugs are used to prevent platelet aggregation within the stent and acute stent thrombosis. Drugs commonly used during PCI are unfractionated heparin (UH) or low-molecular-weight heparin (LMWH), a direct thrombin inhibitor (e.g., bivalirudin [Angiomax]), and/or a glycoprotein IIb/IIIa inhibitor (e.g., eptifibatide [Integrilin]) (Table 33.12). After PCI, the patient receives dual antiplatelet therapy

FIG. 33.6 Placement of a coronary artery stent. **A,** The stent is positioned at the site of the lesion. **B,** The balloon is inflated, expanding the stent. The balloon is then deflated and removed. **C,** The implanted stent is left in place.

FIG. 33.7 **A,** A thrombotic occlusion of the right coronary artery is seen *(arrows).* **B,** Right coronary artery is opened and blood flow restored following angioplasty and placement of a 4-mm stent. (From Zipes DB, Libby P, Bonow RO, Braunwald E: *Braunwald's heart disease: A textbook of cardiovascular medicine,* ed 7, St Louis, 2005, Saunders.)

(DAPT) (e.g., aspirin [indefinitely] and ticagrelor or clopidogrel [Plavix]) until the intimal lining grows over the stent and provides a smooth vascular surface.

After DES placement, DAPT is used for a minimum of 12 months. The duration of DAPT for patients with a BMS is a minimum of 1 month after PCI. With the newer generation stents, 3 to 6 months of DAPT is enough to prevent stent thrombosis. Aspirin must continue forever.[24]

Potential complications from cardiac catheterization with PCI include abrupt closure from coronary artery dissection or rupture, vascular injury at the artery access site (e.g., femoral, radial), acute MI from acute stent thrombosis or from plaque dislodging and blocking the vessel distal to the catheter, stent embolization, failure to cross the blockage with a balloon or stent, coronary spasm, dye allergy, renal compromise, bleeding (e.g., retroperitoneal bleeding when the femoral artery is used or vascular access-site bleeding), infection, stroke, and emergent coronary artery bypass graft (CABG) surgery. The risk for dysrhythmias during and after the procedure is always present, so patients should be on a cardiac monitor afterwards.

More PCIs are done in the United States than CABGs.[1] PCI may not be a feasible option for all patients (e.g., patients with 3-vessel CAD [3 different coronary arteries] and/or significant left main coronary artery disease).[25] Coronary revascularization with CABG surgery may be recommended after cardiac catheterization.

Before and after cardiac catheterization and PCI, patients need frequent interventions (see Nursing Management: Cardiac Catheterization and PCI box and Table 31.9). Respiratory therapy may give prescribed therapies (e.g., nebulizer treatments) depending on the patient's past medical history.

Coronary Surgical Revascularization

In patients with chronic stable angina, coronary revascularization with CABG surgery is recommended for patients who (1) fail medical management, (2) have left main coronary artery or 3-vessel disease, (3) are not candidates for PCI (e.g., blockages are long or difficult to access), or (4) have failed PCI and continue to have chest pain. CABG also may be an option for patients with diabetes, LV dysfunction, and/or CKD.[25] CABG surgery and PCI are considered palliative treatment for CAD and not a cure. Lifestyle changes and medications may help slow the progression of the CAD and reduce the risk for recurrent events.

Traditional Coronary Artery Bypass Graft Surgery. CABG surgery consists of the placement of arterial or venous grafts to

---

■■ **NURSING MANAGEMENT**

Percutaneous Coronary Intervention

Preprocedure
- Assess for allergies, especially to contrast dye.
- Perform baseline assessment, including vital signs, pulse oximetry, heart and breath sounds, neurovascular assessment of extremities (e.g., distal pulses, skin temperature, skin color, sensation).
- Assess baseline laboratory values (e.g., cardiac biomarkers, creatinine).
- Give drugs before the procedure and stop drugs not needed for the procedure (e.g., systemic heparin is stopped right before the cardiac catheterization).
- Teach patient and caregiver about procedure and postprocedure care.

Postprocedure
- Perform assessment and compare to baseline: vital signs, pulse oximetry, heart and breath sounds, neurovascular assessment of extremity used for procedure, assessment of catheter insertion site for hematoma, bleeding, and bruit.
- Assess neurovascular status of involved extremity every 15 min for the first hour, then according to agency policy.
- Check for bleeding at catheter insertion site every 15 min for the first hour, then according to agency policy.
- Report changes in neurovascular status of involved extremity or any bleeding.
- Monitor ECG for dysrhythmias or other changes (e.g., ST segment elevation or depression).
- Monitor patient for chest pain and other sources of pain or discomfort (e.g., back, vascular access site).
- Monitor IV infusions of antianginals (e.g., nitroglycerin) and antiplatelet medications (e.g., eptifibatide).
- Teach patient and caregiver about discharge drugs (e.g., aspirin, clopidogrel, lipid lowering drugs).
- Teach patient and caregiver about discharge care, including signs and symptoms to report to HCP (e.g., access site complications, return of chest pain).

Unlicensed Assistive Personnel (UAP)
- Oversee UAP:
  - Take vital signs and report increases or decreases in HR or BP to RN.
  - Report patient descriptions of chest pain, shortness of breath, and/or any other discomfort or distress to RN.
  - Report changes in neurovascular status of the involved extremity or any bleeding to the RN.
  - Help with oral hygiene and hydration, meals, and toileting.
  - Record oral intake and urine output as ordered.

---

provide blood from the aorta or a branch of a major artery that originates from the aorta (e.g., internal mammary artery) to the heart muscle distal to blocked coronary arteries. The procedure may involve one or more grafts using the internal mammary (thoracic) artery (IMA or ITA), saphenous vein, and/or radial artery (Fig. 33.8). The gastroepiploic artery, and/or inferior epigastric artery can be used as conduits but are not used as often due to the time and difficulty in harvesting those arteries.

CABG surgery requires a sternotomy (opening of the chest cavity) and *cardiopulmonary bypass* (CPB). During CPB, blood is diverted from the patient's heart to a machine where it is oxygenated and returned (via a pump) to the patient. This allows the HCP to operate on a quiet, nonbeating, bloodless heart while perfusion to vital organs is maintained. CPB is associated with postoperative neurologic dysfunction, renal problems, and systemic inflammatory response syndrome (SIRS).[25]

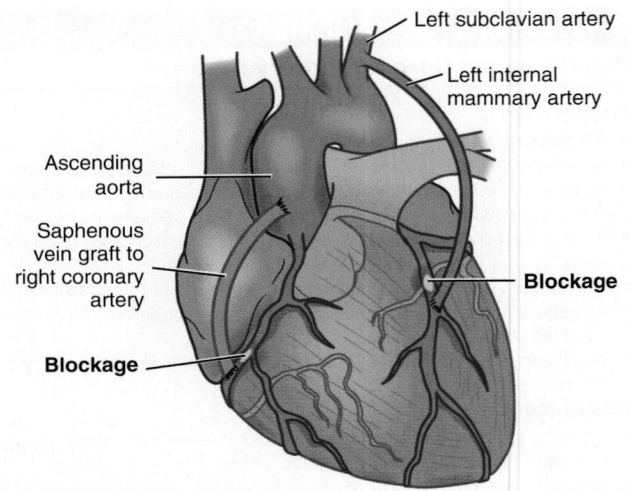

FIG. 33.8 Proximal end of the left internal mammary artery (LIMA) is left attached to the subclavian artery and the distal end of the LIMA is grafted (sutured) into the LAD artery below the blockage. Proximal end of the saphenous vein is grafted (sutured) to the aorta, and the distal end is grafted (sutured) into the right coronary artery below the area of blockage.

The IMA is the most common artery used for bypass graft. The proximal part is left attached to its origin (the subclavian artery). The distal end of the IMA is dissected from the chest wall. Next, it is *anastomosed* (sutured) to the coronary artery distal to the blockage. It usually is used to bypass the left anterior descending (LAD) artery because the LAD supplies blood to the largest part of the heart muscle (anterior wall). The IMA tends to have longer patency rates than saphenous veins (Fig. 33.8).

Saphenous veins can be used for bypass grafts. The HCP endoscopically removes the saphenous vein from one or both legs. A section is sutured into the ascending aorta near the native coronary artery opening and then anastomosed to the coronary artery distal to the blockage (Fig. 33.8). Saphenous vein grafts are more prone to develop diffuse intimal hyperplasia. This contributes to future stenosis and graft occlusion. The use of antiplatelet and statin therapy after surgery helps maintain vein graft patency.

The radial artery, another potential graft, is a thick muscular artery prone to spasm. Perioperative calcium channel blockers and long-acting nitrates can control the spasms. Patency rates are not as good as the IMA but are better than saphenous veins. Serious extremity complications (e.g., hand ischemia, wound infection) are rare after removal of the radial artery. Paresthesia and impaired sensation are common side effects after radial artery harvest.[26]

Women have higher periprocedural mortality and morbidity rates than men. This has been attributed to the late treatment of CAD in women because women first present with CAD at an older age and have more co-morbidities at the time of surgery. Other factors include smaller diameter coronary vessels, smaller body surface area, and the fact that women are less likely to be referred for catheterization.[25]

Minimally Invasive Direct Coronary Artery Bypass. *Minimally invasive direct coronary artery bypass* (MIDCAB) offers patients with disease of the LAD or right coronary artery an approach to surgical treatment that does not involve a sternotomy and CPB. The technique requires several small incisions between the ribs or a mini-thoracotomy. A thoracoscope or robotic assistance may be used to dissect the IMA from the chest wall, but usually it is done via direct visualization.[26] A mechanical stabilizer immobilizes the operative site. The IMA is then sutured to the LAD or right coronary artery. Some patients undergo hybrid procedures in which they have a MIDCAB for the LAD artery and undergo a PCI of a second or third artery later.

Off-Pump Coronary Artery Bypass. The *off-pump coronary artery bypass* (OPCAB) procedure uses a median sternotomy to access all coronary vessels. OPCAB is performed on a beating heart (no CPB) using mechanical stabilizers. OPCAB is associated with less blood loss, less renal dysfunction, less postoperative atrial fibrillation, and fewer neurologic complications.[25] Worldwide, less than 30% of CABG procedures are OPCAB procedures.[26]

Totally Endoscopic Coronary Artery Bypass. Totally endoscopic coronary artery bypass (TECAB) uses a robotic technology to perform CABG surgery. Several instrument ports in the chest are required. This procedure is done without the use of CPB or with the use of CPB using femoral access. TECAB is used for limited bypass grafting. The benefits include smaller incisions, decreased blood loss, less pain, and shorter recovery time.[26]

Transmyocardial Laser Revascularization. *Transmyocardial laser revascularization* is an indirect revascularization procedure. It is used for patients with advanced CAD who are not candidates for traditional CABG surgery and who have persistent angina despite maximum medical therapy. The procedure involves the use of a high-energy laser to create channels in the heart muscle to allow blood flow to ischemic areas. The procedure can be done using a left thoracotomy approach. It is used as an adjunctive therapy when bypass grafts cannot be placed to help reduce angina symptoms. It also can be used in combination with CABG surgery.[26]

Postoperative Care After CABG Surgery

Care after CABG surgery is provided in the intensive care unit (ICU) for the first 24 to 36 hours. Ongoing and intensive monitoring of the patient's hemodynamic status is critical. The patient will have many invasive lines for monitoring heart status and other vital functions (see Chapter 65). These include (1) hemodynamic monitoring (e.g., CO), (2) an arterial line for continuous BP monitoring, (3) pleural and mediastinal chest tubes for chest drainage, (4) continuous ECG monitoring, (5) an endotracheal tube connected to mechanical ventilation, (6) epicardial pacing wires for emergency pacing of the heart, (7) a urinary catheter to monitor urine output, and (8) a nasogastric tube for gastric decompression. Most patients are extubated within 6 hours and transferred to a step-down unit within 24 to 48 hours for continued monitoring.

Many of the postoperative complications that develop after CABG surgery relate to the use of CPB. Major complications of CPB are systemic inflammation, bleeding and anemia from damage to red blood cells and platelets, fluid and electrolyte imbalances, infections, and hypothermia (because blood is cooled as it passes through the CPB machine). Focus your care on assessing the patient for bleeding (e.g., chest tube drainage, incision sites), monitoring hemodynamics, checking fluid status, replacing blood and electrolytes as needed, and restoring temperature (e.g., warming blankets).

Postoperative dysrhythmias, especially atrial dysrhythmias (e.g., atrial fibrillation [AF]), are common. The incidence of postoperative AF after CABG surgery is 20% to 40%.[26] β-Blockers should be started or restarted as soon as possible after surgery (unless contraindicated) to reduce the incidence of AF.[25]

Discharge may be delayed in patients who develop AF in order to begin anticoagulation therapy, especially if using warfarin. (See Chapter 35 for information on treatment of AF.)

Nursing care for the patient with a CABG includes wound care for the patient's surgical sites (e.g., leg, chest, arm). Chest incisions are often closed with skin adhesive and do not need dressings after 24 hours. Management of the chest wound is similar to that of other chest surgeries (see Chapter 27). Care of the leg incision is minimal since endoscopy is used to harvest the vein.

Care of a radial artery harvest site includes monitoring sensory and motor function of the hand. The patient with radial artery harvest should take a calcium channel blocker and/or a long-acting nitrate for around 3 months to reduce the incidence of arterial spasm at the arm or anastomosis site.

Other nursing interventions include strategies to manage pain and prevent venous thromboembolism (e.g., early ambulation, sequential compression device) and respiratory complications (e.g., incentive spirometry, splinting during coughing and deep-breathing exercises). (See Chapter 19 for care of the postoperative patient.)

Patients may have some cognitive dysfunction. This includes impairment of memory, concentration, language comprehension, and social integration. Depression and anxiety are common. Patients may cry or become teary. *Postoperative cognitive dysfunction* (POCD) can manifest days to weeks to months after surgery but usually improves within a few months after surgery. However, it may become a chronic disorder.[27] POCD is discussed in Chapter 19.

In the older patient (> age 80), elective CABG is generally well tolerated. Many patients have multiple preoperative co-morbidities, so the incidence of postoperative complications (e.g., dysrhythmias, stroke, POCD, infection) is higher. Although the benefits of treatment may outweigh risks in this group, morbidity and mortality are higher than in younger persons.[25]

Postoperative nursing care of the patient with a MIDCAB, OPCAB, or TECAB procedure is similar to that for CABG surgery patients. The recovery time is shorter with these procedures. Patients often resume routine activities sooner than patients who have CABG surgery. Pain control is important regardless of the procedure. Patients generally report higher levels of pain with a thoracotomy incision than a sternotomy incision.

Alternative Therapies for Refractory Chronic Stable Angina

For patients with refractory angina, *enhanced external counterpulsation* (EECP) may be used. EECP consists of placing inflatable BP cuffs around the legs. The cuffs sequentially inflate during diastole and deflate during systole from the calves to the thighs. This action increases venous return and augments diastolic BP. This increases coronary perfusion, improves LV diastolic filling, and helps with collateral circulation. Patients get treatments 5 days a week for a total of 35 treatments. EECP is contraindicated in patients with decompensated HF, severe peripheral arterial disease, and severe aortic insufficiency.[13]

ACUTE CORONARY SYNDROME

When chest pain from ischemia is prolonged and not immediately reversible, acute coronary syndrome (ACS) may develop. ACS includes the spectrum of non-ST elevation acute coronary syndrome (*UA and non–ST-segment-elevation myocardial infarction* [NSTEMI]), and *ST-segment-elevation myocardial infarction*

FIG. 33.9 Relationships among coronary artery disease, chronic stable angina, and acute coronary syndrome.

(STEMI) (Fig. 33.9). When patients first present with chest pain, ST-elevations on the 12-lead ECG most likely indicate a STEMI (Fig. 33.4, *B*). The ECG should be compared to a previous ECG whenever possible. ST elevation represents myocardial injury that is potentially reversible, but, if not treated, will likely evolve to permanent necrosis (tissue death) of the myocardium. Patients with UA or NSTEMI may or may not have ST segment depression and/or T wave inversion on the ECG. For patients with chest pain who do not have ST segment elevation or ST-T wave changes on the ECG, it is difficult to distinguish between UA and NSTEMI until we evaluate serum cardiac biomarkers.[15]

On the cellular level, the heart muscle becomes hypoxic within the first 10 seconds of a total coronary occlusion. Heart cells are deprived of O_2 and glucose needed for aerobic metabolism and contractility. Anaerobic metabolism begins, and lactic acid accumulates. In ischemic conditions, heart cells are viable for about 20 minutes. Irreversible heart damage starts after 20 minutes if there is no collateral circulation (Fig. 33.2).[21] With restoration of blood flow (reperfusion), aerobic metabolism resumes, contractility is restored, and cellular repair begins.

ACS is caused by the decline of a once-stable atherosclerotic plaque. The previously stable plaque ruptures, releasing the lipid core into the vessel. This causes platelet aggregation and thrombus formation. The vessel may be partially blocked by a thrombus (manifesting as UA or NSTEMI) or totally blocked by a thrombus (manifesting as STEMI). We are not sure what causes the plaque to suddenly become unstable. Systemic inflammation (described earlier) may play a role. Patients with suspected ACS need immediate hospitalization.

UNSTABLE ANGINA

Unstable angina (UA) is chest pain that is new in onset, occurs at rest, or occurs with increasing frequency, duration, or less effort than the patient's chronic stable angina pattern. The pain usually lasts 10 minutes or more.

The patient with chronic stable angina may develop UA, or UA may be the first clinical sign of CAD. Unlike chronic stable angina, UA is unpredictable and must be treated immediately. The patient with previously diagnosed chronic stable angina describes a significant change in the pattern of angina. It occurs with increasing frequency and is easily provoked by minimal exertion, during sleep, or even at rest. The patient without previously diagnosed angina describes chest pain that has progressed rapidly in the past few hours, days, or weeks, often ending in pain at rest. ECG changes that may be seen with UA include ST depression and/or T wave inversion (Fig. 33.4, A). These changes are referred to as ischemic changes.

MYOCARDIAL INFARCTION: ST-ELEVATION AND NON–ST-ELEVATION MYOCARDIAL INFARCTION

A **myocardial infarction (MI)** occurs because of an abrupt stoppage of blood flow through a coronary artery with a thrombus caused by platelet aggregation. This causes irreversible myocardial cell death (necrosis) in the heart muscle beyond the blockage (Figs. 33.10 and 33.11). Serum cardiac biomarkers are released into the blood. Most MIs occur in the setting of preexisting CAD.[13]

A STEMI, caused by an occlusive thrombus, results in ST-elevation in the ECG leads facing the area of infarction (Figs. 33.12 and 33.13). ST segment elevation is significant if it is 1 mm or more above the isoelectric line in at least 2 contiguous (neighboring) leads except in V_2 and V_3, where the ST elevation must be 2 mm or more. [28]

A STEMI is an emergency. To limit the infarct size, the artery must be opened within 90 minutes of presentation to restore blood and O_2 to the heart muscle and limit the infarct size. This can be done either by PCI or with thrombolytic (fibrinolytic) therapy. PCI is the first-line treatment, if available. It confirms which artery has the occlusive thrombus so it can be opened with a balloon and stent (Fig. 33.6). Thrombolytic therapy is done in hospitals that do not have a catheterization laboratory for PCI. If the patient does not seek treatment quickly, the STEMI will evolve.

NSTEMI, caused by a nonocclusive thrombus, does not cause ST segment elevation on the 12-lead ECG. The ECG may or may not show ST depression and/or T wave inversion in the leads facing the area of infarction. NSTEMI patients usually undergo catheterization within 12 to 72 hours. Thrombolytic therapy is not indicated for NSTEMI.

With either NSTEMI or STEMI, an echocardiogram may show *hypokinesis* (worsening myocardial contractility) or *akinesis* (absent myocardial contractility) in the necrotic area(s). The degree of LV dysfunction depends on the area of the heart involved and size of the infarction.

The acute MI process evolves over time, from hours to a few days. The earliest tissue to become ischemic is the subendocardium (the innermost layer of tissue in the heart muscle). If ischemia persists, it takes around 4 to 6 hours for the entire thickness of the heart muscle to necrose. If the thrombus is not completely blocking the artery, the time to complete necrosis may be as long as 12 hours.

Most MIs affect the LV and are usually described based on the location of damage (e.g., anterior, inferior, lateral, septal, or posterior wall infarction). The location of the MI and ECG changes correlate with the involved coronary artery (Table 33.13). For example, in most people, the right coronary artery supplies blood to the inferior and posterior LV walls. Blockage of the right coronary artery results in an inferior wall and/ or posterior wall MI. Anterior wall infarctions result from blockages in the LAD artery. Blockages in the left circumflex artery usually cause lateral wall MIs. Damage can occur in more than 1 location, especially if more than 1 coronary artery is involved (e.g., anterolateral MI). Right ventricular MIs are much less common and treated differently from LV MIs. Suspect a right ventricular MI in patients who have a left inferior wall STEMI.[28]

The degree of collateral circulation influences the severity of the MI (Fig. 33.2). Not everyone develops collateral circulation. A person with a long history of CAD may develop good

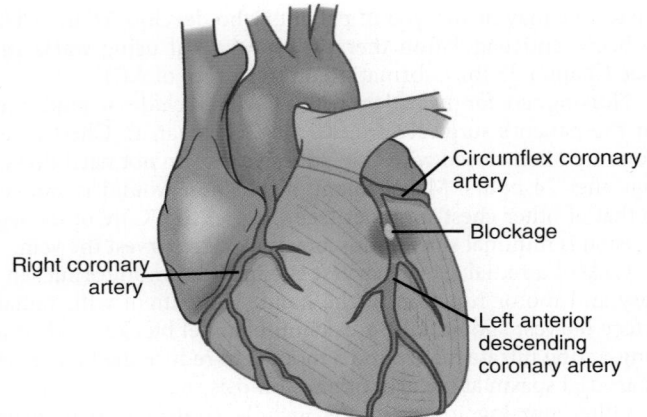

FIG. 33.10 Occlusion of the LAD coronary artery, resulting in acute MI.

FIG. 33.11 Acute MI in the posterolateral wall of the left ventricle. This is shown by the absence of staining in the areas of necrosis *(white arrow)*. Note the scarring from a previous anterior wall MI *(black arrow)*. (From Kumar V, Abbas AK, Aster JC, et al: *Robbins and Cotran pathologic basis of disease*, ed 8, Philadelphia, 2010, Saunders.)

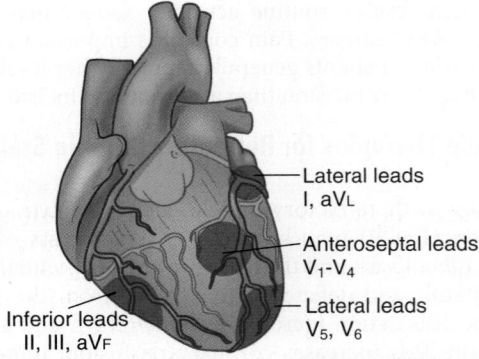

FIG. 33.12 Definitive ECG changes occur in leads that face the area of ischemia, injury, or infarction. Reciprocal changes may occur in leads facing opposite the area of ischemia, injury, or infarction.

collateral circulation to provide the area surrounding the infarction site with an adequate blood supply. This is one reason why a younger person may have a more serious first MI than an older person with the same degree of blockage.

Women who have MIs are often undertreated with guideline-based recommendations, leading to worse outcomes and increased rates of readmission, reinfarction, and death in the first year after MI.[5]

FIG. 33.13 ECG findings with anteroseptal lateral wall MI. Normally, leads I, aVL, and V_1 to V_3 have a positive R wave. Note the pathologic Q waves in these leads and the ST segment elevation in leads V_2 to V_6 *(arrows)*.

TABLE 33.13 **ECG Evidence in Acute Coronary Syndrome**

Left Ventricle Involvement	ECG EVIDENCE		Associated Coronary Artery
	Leads Facing Area	Leads Opposite Area (Reciprocal Changes)	
Septal wall	V_1, V_2	II, III, aVF	LAD
Anterior wall	V_3, V_4	II, III, aVF	LAD
Lateral wall, low	V_5, V_6	II, III, aVF	LAD or circumflex
Lateral wall, high	I, aVL	II, III, aVF	Circumflex
Inferior wall	II, III, aVF	I, aVL, V_5, V_6	Right coronary artery, posterior descending coronary artery

Clinical Manifestations of Myocardial Infarction

Pain. Severe chest pain not relieved by rest, position change, or nitrate administration may mean the patient is having an MI. Persistent and unlike any other pain, it is usually described as a heavy, pressure, tight, burning, constricted, or crushing feeling. Common locations are the substernal or epigastric area. The pain may radiate to the neck, lower jaw, and arms or to the back (Fig. 33.3). When epigastric pain is present, the patient may relate it to indigestion, take antacids without relief, and therefore delay seeking treatment. It may occur while the patient is active or at rest, asleep, or awake. It often occurs in the early morning hours. It usually lasts for 20 minutes or longer and is more severe than chronic angina pain.

Not everyone who has an MI has classic symptoms. Some patients may not have pain but may have "discomfort," weakness, nausea, indigestion, or shortness of breath. Some women may have atypical discomfort, shortness of breath, or fatigue. Patients with diabetes may have silent (asymptomatic) MIs because of cardiac neuropathy or have atypical symptoms (e.g., shortness of breath). An older patient may have a change in mental status (e.g., confusion), shortness of breath, pulmonary edema, dizziness, or a dysrhythmia.

Sympathetic Nervous System Stimulation. During the initial phase of MI, the ischemic heart cells release catecholamines (norepinephrine and epinephrine) that are normally found in these cells. This results in diaphoresis, increased HR and BP, and vasoconstriction of peripheral blood vessels. On physical examination, the patient's skin may be ashen, clammy, and cool to touch.
Cardiovascular Manifestations. In response to the release of catecholamines, BP and HR may be high initially. Later, the BP may drop because of decreased CO. If severe enough, this may result in decreased renal perfusion and urine output. Crackles, if present, may persist for several hours to several days, suggesting LV dysfunction. Jugular venous distention (JVD), hepatic engorgement, and peripheral edema may mean right ventricular dysfunction.

Examination may reveal abnormally distant heart sounds. Other abnormal sounds suggesting LV dysfunction are S_3 and S_4. A loud holosystolic murmur may occur with a ventricular septal defect, papillary muscle rupture, or mitral valve dysfunction (mitral regurgitation).
Nausea and Vomiting. The patient may have nausea and vomiting. These symptoms can result from reflex stimulation of the vomiting center by the severe pain. They can also result from

vasovagal reflexes initiated in the area of the infarcted heart muscle, especially with inferior wall MIs.

Fever. The temperature may increase to 100.4° F (38° C) within 24 to 48 hours. The temperature elevation may last for as long as 4 to 5 days. This increase in temperature is due to a systemic inflammatory process caused by the death of myocardial cells.

Healing Process

The body's response to cell death is the inflammatory process (see Chapter 11). Within 24 hours, leukocytes infiltrate the area. The dead heart cells release enzymes that are important diagnostic indicators of MI (see serum cardiac biomarkers later in this chapter). The proteolytic enzymes of the neutrophils and macrophages begin to remove necrotic tissue by the fourth day. During this time, the necrotic muscle wall is thin.

Once infarction takes place, catecholamine-mediated lipolysis and glycogenolysis occur. These processes allow the increased plasma glucose and free fatty acids to be used by the O_2-depleted myocardium for anaerobic metabolism. For this reason, serum glucose levels are often high after MI.

The necrotic zone of a STEMI is identified by ECG changes (e.g., lowering of the initially elevated ST segments, T wave inversion and/or a pathologic Q wave) within 1 or 2 days. At this point, the neutrophils and monocytes have cleared the necrotic debris from the injured area, and the collagen matrix that will eventually form scar tissue is laid down.

At 10 to 14 days after MI, the new scar tissue is still weak. The heart muscle is vulnerable to increased stress during this time. At the same time, the patient's activity level may be increasing, so special caution and assessment are necessary. By 6 weeks after MI, scar tissue has replaced necrotic tissue and the injured area is considered healed. Often the scarred area is less compliant than the surrounding area. This condition may be manifested by abnormal wall motion on an echocardiogram or nuclear imaging (e.g., hypokinesis, akinesis), LV dysfunction, altered conduction patterns, dysrhythmias, or HF. The scarred area may become an irritable focus for life-threatening dysrhythmias causing sudden cardiac death (SCD) years later (see section on SCD on pp. 730–731).

These changes in the infarcted heart muscle also cause changes in the unaffected areas. To try to compensate for the damaged muscle, the normal myocardium hypertrophies and dilates. This process is called *ventricular remodeling*. Remodeling of normal myocardium can lead to the development of late HF, especially in the person with atherosclerosis of other coronary arteries and/or an anterior MI. ACE inhibitor drugs are given to limit ventricular remodeling.

Complications of Myocardial Infarction

Dysrhythmias. Any condition that affects the heart cells' sensitivity to nerve impulses (e.g., ischemia, electrolyte imbalances, SNS stimulation) can cause dysrhythmias that adversely affect the damaged heart muscle. Dysrhythmias are the most common complication after an MI. They occur in 80% to 90% of patients. Ventricular tachycardia (VT) and ventricular fibrillation (VF) are the most common cause of death in patients in the prehospital period.

After MI, bradycardias (e.g., complete heart block) develop when key areas of the conduction system are destroyed (e.g., infarction involves the sinus or atrioventricular node). VT or VF most often occurs within the first 4 hours after the onset of pain. Premature ventricular contractions (PVCs) may precede

VT and VF. Life-threatening ventricular dysrhythmias must be treated immediately.

With reperfusion (thrombolytic therapy or PCI), it is common to see PVCs, asymptomatic nonsustained VT, and idioventricular rhythms. These rhythms are not associated with an increased risk for sudden cardiac death (SCD) and are not treated unless the patient is symptomatic.[28] See Chapter 35 for a detailed description of dysrhythmias and their management.

Heart Failure. *Heart failure* (HF) is a complication that occurs when the right or left ventricle's pumping action is reduced. Depending on the severity and extent of the injury, left-sided HF occurs initially with subtle signs, such as mild dyspnea, restlessness, agitation, or slight tachycardia. Other signs indicating the onset of left-sided HF include pulmonary congestion on chest x-ray, S_3 or S_4 heart sounds, crackles on auscultation of the lungs, paroxysmal nocturnal dyspnea (PND), and orthopnea. Signs of right-sided HF include JVD, hepatic congestion, or lower extremity edema. See Chapter 34 for information about the treatment of acute decompensated HF.

Cardiogenic Shock. *Cardiogenic shock* occurs when O_2 and nutrients supplied to the tissues are inadequate because of severe LV failure, papillary muscle rupture, ventricular septal rupture, LV free wall rupture, or right ventricular infarction.[28] This occurs less often when STEMI is treated early and rapidly with PCI or thrombolytic therapy. Cardiogenic shock, associated with a high death rate, requires aggressive management. This includes control of dysrhythmias, intraaortic balloon pump (IABP) therapy, and support of contractility with vasoactive drugs. Goals of therapy are to maximize O_2 delivery, reduce O_2 demand, and prevent complications (e.g., acute kidney injury). Cardiogenic shock is discussed in Chapter 66.

Papillary Muscle Dysfunction or Rupture. *Papillary muscle dysfunction* may occur if the infarcted area includes or is near the papillary muscle that attaches to the mitral valve (see Fig. 31.2). Suspect papillary muscle dysfunction if you hear a new systolic murmur suggestive of mitral regurgitation at the cardiac apex. An echocardiogram confirms the diagnosis.

Papillary muscle rupture is a rare and life-threatening complication. It causes acute and massive mitral valve regurgitation with no time for the heart to compensate. Dyspnea, pulmonary edema, and decreased CO result from the backup of blood in the left atrium. This condition aggravates an already damaged LV by reducing CO even further. The patient undergoes rapid clinical decline. Treatment includes afterload reduction with nitroprusside (Nipride) and/or IABP therapy and immediate cardiac surgery with mitral valve repair or replacement. (See Chapter 36 for discussion of valve disorders.)

Left Ventricular Aneurysm. *Left ventricular aneurysm* results when the infarcted heart wall is thin and bulges out during contraction. This can develop within a few days, weeks, or months. It is more common with anterior MIs.[28] The patient with a ventricular aneurysm may develop HF, dysrhythmias, and angina. Besides ventricular rupture, which is usually fatal, ventricular aneurysms can hide thrombi that can lead to an embolic stroke. Anticoagulation therapy is recommended for these patients unless contraindicated.

Ventricular Septal Wall Rupture and Left Ventricular Free Wall Rupture. A new loud systolic murmur heard in patients with acute MI may signal ventricular septal wall rupture. Depending on the size of the defect and degree of right and LV dysfunction, HF and cardiogenic shock may occur. The patient must undergo emergency repair, either surgically or percutaneously. The defect can quickly expand and lead to hemodynamic compromise.[28]

LV free wall rupture is an emergent clinical situation. Rapid hemodynamic compromise and death ensues if not treated immediately. Although this is a rare complication, death rates are high. Free wall rupture is seen more often in patients after their first MI, patients with anterior MIs, older adults, and women.[28]

Pericarditis. *Acute pericarditis,* an inflammation of the visceral and/or parietal pericardium, may occur 2 or 3 days after an acute MI. Pericarditis is characterized by mild to severe chest pain that increases with inspiration, coughing, and movement of the upper body. Sitting in a forward position often relieves the pain. The pain is usually different from pain associated with an MI.

Assess the patient with suspected pericarditis for the presence of a friction rub over the pericardium. The sound is best heard with the diaphragm of the stethoscope at the mid to lower left sternal border. It may be persistent or intermittent. Fever may be present. The patient may have hypotension and/or a narrow pulse pressure if it is accompanied by significant pericardial effusion or cardiac tamponade. Asymptomatic pericardial effusions are common after STEMI.[28]

Diagnosis of pericarditis can be made with the 12-lead ECG. Typical ECG changes include diffuse ST segment elevations in many leads (with STEMI, ST elevation occurs in the leads facing the infarcted wall). This reflects the inflammation of the pericardium. Treatment includes pain relief with high doses of aspirin (e.g., 650 mg every 4 to 6 hours). Nonsteroidal antiinflammatory drugs (NSAIDs) and corticosteroids are avoided in the first 4 weeks after MI because they can interfere with myocardial scar formation.[21,28] Pericarditis is discussed in Chapter 36.

Dressler Syndrome. *Dressler syndrome* is pericarditis and fever that develop 1 to 8 weeks after MI. Although the cause is unclear, it may be an autoimmune reaction to the necrotic heart muscle. The patient has chest pain, fever, malaise, a pericardial friction rub, and arthralgia. A pericardial effusion may be present. Laboratory findings include a high white blood cell count and sedimentation rate. High-dose aspirin is the treatment of choice.

DIAGNOSTIC STUDIES: ACUTE CORONARY SYNDROME

In addition to the patient's history of pain, risk factors, and health history, the primary diagnostic studies used to determine whether a person has UA or an MI (STEMI or NSTEMI) include a 12-lead ECG and serum cardiac biomarkers.

Electrocardiogram Findings

The ECG is one of the primary tools to diagnose UA or an MI (STEMI or NSTEMI). Whenever possible, it should be compared to a previous ECG. Changes in the QRS complex, ST segment, and T wave caused by injury, ischemia, and infarction can develop slowly or quickly with UA and MI. The pattern of ECG changes among the 12 leads provides information on the coronary artery involved in ACS (Table 33.13).

The ECG must be read carefully since changes can be absent or subtle at first. For this reason, serial 12-lead ECGs are done. For diagnostic and treatment purposes, it is important to distinguish between STEMI and NSTEMI/UA. STEMI patients usually have a complete coronary occlusion. ST elevation in the leads facing the infarcted wall is seen first on the 12-lead ECG

(Figs. 33.4, *B*, 33.12, and 33.13 and Table 33.13). ST segment elevation is significant if it is 1 mm or more above the isoelectric line in at least 2 contiguous leads. Within a few hours to days, the ST segments begin to lower, with T wave inversion and pathologic Q waves developing in the same leads (Fig. 33.4, *C*). The Q wave is the first negative deflection after a P wave (Fig. 33.4, *A*). A pathologic Q wave is defined as a deep Q wave, greater than or equal to one-third the height of the R wave in the same lead. The pathologic Q wave will remain on the ECG forever. T wave inversion may persist for months after a STEMI. With early reperfusion, Q waves may not develop.

Patients with NSTEMI or UA usually have transient thrombosis or incomplete coronary occlusion. ECG changes with UA or an NSTEMI include ST depression and/or T wave inversion in the leads facing the area of infarction (Figs. 33.4, 33.12, 33.14, and Table 33.13). Both groups of patients may present with angina and have the same ECG changes. The only way to tell if the patient is experiencing an NSTEMI or UA is by drawing cardiac biomarkers. The biomarkers will be high in the NSTEMI patient but normal in the patient with UA. These patients do not develop pathologic Q waves on the ECG.

Because MI is a dynamic process that evolves over time, serial ECGs are done to show the evolution of ischemia, injury, infarction, and resolution of the infarction.

Serum Cardiac Biomarkers

Serum cardiac biomarkers are proteins released into the blood from necrotic heart muscle after an MI (see Table 31.6). These biomarkers are important in the diagnosis of MI. The onset, peak, and duration of levels of these biomarkers are shown in Fig. 33.15.

Cardiac-specific troponin has 2 subtypes: cardiac-specific troponin T (cTnT) and cardiac-specific troponin I (cTnI). These biomarkers are highly specific indicators of MI and have greater sensitivity and specificity for myocardial injury than creatine kinase MB (CK-MB). Serum levels of cTnI and cTnT increase 4 to 6 hours after the onset of MI, peak at 10 to 24 hours, and return to baseline over 10 to 14 days. Sets of serial cardiac biomarkers are drawn over 24 hours (e.g., every 6 hours × 3). The presence of biomarkers helps distinguish between UA (negative biomarkers) and NSTEMI (positive biomarkers). A newer high-sensitivity troponin test is available that provides more rapid detection of cardiac necrosis at an earlier time than traditional troponin assays, allowing for a quicker diagnosis.

CK levels begin to rise about 6 hours after an MI, peak at about 18 hours, and return to normal within 24 to 36 hours. The CK enzymes are fractionated into bands. The CK-MB band is specific to heart muscle cells and helps to quantify myocardial damage. CK-MB is a less sensitive marker for myocardial injury compared to troponin.[15] Therefore troponin is the best biomarker for diagnosis of acute MI.[28]

Myoglobin is released into the circulation within 2 hours after an MI and peaks in 3 to 15 hours. Although it is one of the first serum cardiac biomarkers to appear after an MI, it lacks cardiac specificity. It has a limited role in diagnosing MI.

Cardiac Catheterization

The patient with a STEMI must undergo cardiac catheterization within 90 minutes of presentation or receive thrombolytic therapy within 30 minutes in agencies without PCI capability. The goal is to open the totally occluded artery and limit the infarction size. The patient with UA or NSTEMI usually undergoes

FIG. 33.14 ECG findings with anterior and lateral ischemia or an NSTEMI. Note the ST depression in the lateral leads (lead I, aVL, V5 and V6 [black arrows]) and the T wave inversion in I, aVL, V5 and V6 [red arrows]. These leads face the lateral wall. Note the ST depression in 2 anterior leads (V3 and V4 [black arrows]) and the T wave inversion in V3 and V4 [red arrows]. These leads face the anterior wall.

FIG. 33.15 Serum cardiac biomarkers found in the blood after MI.

cardiac catheterization during the hospitalization to diagnose and evaluate the extent of the disease. Guidelines suggest that it is reasonable to do cardiac catheterization on stable but high-risk patients with UA or NSTEMI within 12 to 72 hours after presentation.[15] If appropriate, a PCI is performed at this time. Depending on the findings and many factors, some patients may be treated with medical therapy and some patients may be referred for CABG surgery.

INTERPROFESSIONAL CARE: ACUTE CORONARY SYNDROME

It is extremely important to quickly diagnose and treat a patient with ACS to preserve heart muscle. Initial management of the patient with chest pain most often occurs in the ED. Table 33.14

presents the emergency care of the patient with chest pain. Obtain a 12-lead ECG and start continuous ECG monitoring. Position the patient in an upright position unless contraindicated and start O_2 by nasal cannula to keep O_2 saturation above 93%. Obtain IV access for drug administration. Give SL NTG and 162 to 325 mg of chewable aspirin if not given before arrival at the ED. Morphine is given for pain unrelieved by NTG. A high-dose statin (e.g., atorvastatin [Lipitor]) is given.

If the ECG shows ST elevation, the patient is taken directly for cardiac catheterization in PCI-capable hospitals. Thrombolytic therapy is started if the patient is unable to be quickly transported to a PCI-capable hospital. If the ECG shows ST depression and/or T wave inversion, the patient is usually transferred to an ICU or telemetry unit for ongoing care. Dysrhythmias are treated according to agency protocols. Serial cardiac biomarkers are drawn until the peak level drops off. UA and NSTEMI patients are started on heparin. Some patients with UA or NSTEMI start on glycoprotein IIb/IIIa inhibitors (e.g., eptifibatide [Integrilin]) either before catheterization or at the time of PCI. Glycoprotein IIb/IIIa inhibitors may be used during PCI for STEMI patients. Fig. 33.5 shows the interprofessional care of ACS.

Emergent PCI

Emergent PCI is the first line of treatment for patients with confirmed STEMI (i.e., ST-elevation on the ECG and positive cardiac biomarkers). The goal is to open the blocked artery within 90 minutes of arrival to an agency that has an interventional cardiac catheterization laboratory to limit the infarction size. In this case, the patient undergoes a cardiac catheterization to locate and assess the severity of the blockage(s), determine the presence of collateral circulation, and evaluate LV function. During the procedure, a bare metal stent (BMS) or drug-eluting

✚ TABLE 33.14 Emergency Management

Chest Pain

Etiology	Assessment Findings	Interventions
Cardiovascular • Aortic aneurysm • Aortic valve disease • Dysrhythmia • MI • Myocardial ischemia • Pericarditis **Respiratory** • Costochondritis • Pleurisy • Pneumonia • Pneumothorax, hemothorax • Pulmonary edema • Pulmonary embolus **Chest Trauma** • Cardiac tamponade • Flail chest • Great vessel injury • Hemothorax • Pulmonary contusion • Rib/sternal fracture **Gastrointestinal** • Cholecystitis • Esophagitis • GERD • Hiatal hernia • Peptic ulcer **Others** • Acute anxiety • Drugs (e.g., cocaine) • Strenuous exercise • Stress	• Pain in chest, neck, jaw, arm, or shoulder • Cold, clammy skin • Diaphoresis • Nausea and vomiting • Epigastric pain • Indigestion, heartburn • Dyspnea, tachypnea • Weakness • Anxiety • Feeling of impending doom • Tachycardia, bradycardia • Irregular HR, murmurs • Palpitations • Dysrhythmias • Decreased or increased BP • Narrowed pulse pressure • Unequal BP readings in upper extremities • Syncope, loss of consciousness • Decreased O$_2$ saturation • Decreased or absent breath sounds • Pericardial friction rub	**Initial** • If unresponsive, assess circulation, airway, and breathing. • If responsive, monitor airway, breathing, and circulation (ABC). • Position patient upright unless contraindicated. • Give O$_2$ by nasal cannula or nonrebreather mask. • Obtain baseline vital signs, including O$_2$ saturation. • Auscultate heart and breath sounds. • Obtain 12-lead ECG. • Insert 2 IV catheters. • Assess pain using PQRST mnemonic (Table 33.8). • Medicate for pain as ordered (e.g., nitroglycerin, morphine). • Start continuous ECG monitoring and identify underlying rhythm. • Obtain baseline blood work (e.g., cardiac biomarkers, CBC, basic metabolic panel, coagulation studies). • Obtain portable chest x-ray. • Assess for contraindications for antiplatelet, anticoagulant, or thrombolytic therapy, or PCI as appropriate. • Give aspirin for heart-related chest pain unless contraindicated. • Give a high-dose statin. • Give antidysrhythmic drugs for life-threatening dysrhythmias. **Ongoing Monitoring** • Monitor ABCs, vital signs, level of consciousness, heart and breath sounds, heart rhythm, and O$_2$ saturation. • Assess and record response to drugs (e.g., decrease in chest pain) and remedicate or titrate drugs (e.g., nitroglycerin) as needed. • Provide reassurance and emotional support to patient and caregiver. • Explain all interventions and procedures to patient and caregiver in simple terms. • Anticipate need for intubation if respiratory distress is evident. • Prepare for CPR and defibrillation if cardiac arrest is evident. • Anticipate need for transcutaneous pacing for symptomatic bradycardia or heart block.

stent (DES) is inserted into the blocked coronary artery (Figs. 33.6 and 33.7). PCI should not be done on a noninfarct artery during the same urgent procedure if the patient is hemodynamically stable.[28] Patients with severe LV dysfunction may require IABP therapy and/or inotropes (e.g., dobutamine). A small percent of patients may need emergent CABG surgery.

The advantages of PCI (compared to CABG surgery) include (1) it allows for faster reperfusion to limit infarction size; (2) it provides an alternative to surgical intervention; (3) it is performed with local anesthesia; (4) the patient is ambulatory shortly after the procedure; (5) the length of hospital stay is about 3 to 4 days after MI compared with the 4 to 6 days with CABG surgery, thus reducing hospital costs; and (6) the patient can return to work several weeks sooner after PCI, compared with a 6- to 8-week convalescence after CABG.

Complications of PCI that may lead to emergent CABG include dissection or rupture of the coronary artery, abrupt artery closure, acute stent thrombosis, and failure to cross the blockage with a balloon or stent. There is a risk that the infarction could be extended if a part of the plaque dislodges and blocks the vessel distal to the catheter.

In stent restenosis, ISR is a potential problem whenever stents are placed in a coronary artery. ISR is the build-up of scar tissue inside the stent (referred to as neointimal hyperplasia). ISR usually occurs within a few months to a year after stent placement.

Stent thrombosis is the other potential problem with stents, so DAPT is required up to 12 months post procedure.

❓ CHECK YOUR PRACTICE

Your patient underwent an emergent PCI 2 days ago for a STEMI. You are about to give him his morning medications, which include clopidogrel and aspirin. The patient asks you if he will need to take these medications forever.
• What would you tell the patient?

Thrombolytic Therapy

Thrombolytic (fibrinolytic) therapy is indicated only for patients with a STEMI. Advantages include availability and rapid administration in agencies that do not have an interventional cardiac catheterization laboratory or when one is too far away to transfer the patient quickly. Patients who are admitted to non–PCI-capable hospitals can be moved to a PCI-capable hospital if the first medical contact to balloon inflation (PCI) time can be done within 120 minutes.[28] Treatment of STEMI with thrombolytic therapy aims to limit the infarction size by dissolving the thrombus in the coronary artery to reperfuse the heart muscle. The goal is to give the thrombolytic within 30 minutes of the patient's arrival to the ED.

TABLE 33.15 Contraindications for Thrombolytic Therapy

Absolute Contraindications
- Active internal bleeding or bleeding diathesis (excluding menstruation)
- History of intracranial hemorrhage
- Intracranial or intraspinal surgery within 2 mo
- Known structural or vascular abnormality (e.g., arteriovenous malformation)
- Known intracranial cancer (primary or metastatic)
- Recent (within past 3 mo) ischemic stroke
- Severe uncontrolled hypertension
- Significant closed-head or facial trauma within past 3 mo
- Suspected aortic dissection
- For streptokinase, prior treatment within the past 6 mo

Relative Contraindications
- Active peptic ulcer disease
- Current use of oral anticoagulants
- Dementia
- History of chronic, severe, poorly controlled hypertension
- Known intracranial pathology not covered in absolute contraindications
- Major surgery (<3 wks)
- Noncompressible vascular punctures
- Pregnancy
- Prior ischemic stroke (>3 mo ago)
- Recent (within 2-4 wks) internal bleeding
- Significant hypertension on presentation (SBP >180 mm/Hg or DBP >110 mm/Hg)
- Traumatic or prolonged (>10 min) cardiopulmonary resuscitation

Source: O'Gara PT, Kushner FG, Ascheim DD, et al: 2013 ACCF/AHA guideline for the management of ST-elevation myocardial infarction: A report of the ACCF/AHA Task Force on Practice Guidelines, *Circulation* 127:e362, 2013.

Indications and Contraindications. All thrombolytics (e.g., tenecteplase, alteplase) are given IV (Table 33.12). The cost, efficacy, and ease of administration guide the choice of a thrombolytic agent. Although these drugs have different pharmacokinetics, they all open the blocked artery by lysis of the thrombus. Because thrombolytics lyse the pathologic clot, they may also lyse other clots (e.g., a postoperative site). Therefore patient selection is important because minor or major bleeding can be a complication of therapy.

Inclusion criteria for thrombolytic therapy are (1) chest pain less than 12 hours with 12-lead ECG findings consistent with acute STEMI and (2) no absolute contraindications (Table 33.15). Patients with chest pain lasting 12 to 24 hours with ECG changes supporting STEMI may be considered for thrombolytic therapy.[28]

Procedure. Each hospital has a protocol for giving thrombolytic therapy, but 2 steps should be completed before thrombolytic therapy is started: (1) draw blood to obtain baseline laboratory values and (2) start 2 or 3 lines for IV therapy. Perform all other invasive procedures before giving the thrombolytic agent to reduce the risk for bleeding.

Depending on the drug selected, therapy is given in 1 IV bolus or over time (30 to 90 minutes). Note the time at which therapy begins and monitor the patient during and after the thrombolytic. Assess heart rhythm, vital signs, and pulse oximetry. Assess the heart and lungs often to evaluate the patient's response to therapy. Regularly assess for changes in neurologic status that may indicate cerebral bleeding.

When reperfusion occurs (e.g., a blocked coronary artery is opened and blood flow is restored to the heart muscle), several clinical signs can be seen. The most reliable sign is the return of the ST segment to baseline on the ECG. Other signs include resolution of chest pain and an early, rapid rise of the serum cardiac biomarkers within 3 hours of therapy, peaking within 12 hours. These levels increase as the necrotic heart cells release proteins into the circulation after perfusion is restored to the area. The presence of *reperfusion dysrhythmias* (e.g., accelerated idioventricular rhythm) is a less reliable sign of reperfusion. These dysrhythmias are generally self-limiting and do not require aggressive treatment. (See Chapter 35 for management of dysrhythmias.)

A major concern with thrombolytic therapy is reocclusion of the artery. The site of the thrombus is unstable, and formation of another clot or spasm of the artery may occur. Therefore IV heparin therapy is started. If another clot develops, the patient will describe similar chest pain symptoms and ECG changes will return. Patients receiving thrombolytic therapy should be moved to an agency with PCI capabilities as soon as possible so PCI can be performed if thrombolytic therapy fails.

The major complication with thrombolytic therapy is bleeding. Ongoing nursing assessment is essential. Minor bleeding (e.g., surface bleeding from IV sites or gingival bleeding) is expected and controlled by applying manual pressure followed by a pressure dressing or ice packs.

> ⚠ **SAFETY ALERT Thrombolytic Therapy**
> - Minor or major bleeding can occur with thrombolytic drugs.
> - Place 2 or 3 IV lines before thrombolytic therapy is started.
> - If signs and symptoms of major bleeding occur (e.g., drop in BP, increase in HR, sudden change in the patient's mental status, blood in the urine or stool), stop the drug and notify the HCP.

Drug Therapy

When a patient presents with suspected ACS, antiplatelet therapy (e.g., chewable aspirin for UA patients plus clopidogrel or ticagrelor [for STEMI and NSTEMI patients]), IV NTG, and atorvastatin are drug treatments of choice. Since STEMI patients are taken directly to cardiac catheterization, systemic anticoagulation with either subcutaneous LMWH or IV UH is used only for UA and NSTEMI patients. Glycoprotein IIb/IIIa inhibitors may be given if PCI is anticipated. DAPT should continue for 1 year after an MI whether the patient receives a stent or not. Aspirin should never be stopped. Oral β-blockers are given within the first 24 hours if there are no contraindications (e.g., HF, heart block, hypotension). Calcium channel blockers are used if the patient cannot tolerate β-blockers. These drugs must be used cautiously after MI because they can decrease contractility. ACE inhibitors are added after an MI if there are no contraindications. Nitrates may be used for persistent chest pain.

Table 33.12 and Fig. 33.5 present drug therapy for patients with chronic stable angina and ACS. These drugs are discussed on p. 713. Drugs specifically used to treat ACS are discussed in this section.

IV Nitroglycerin. IV NTG is used in the initial treatment of the patient with ACS. SL NTG can be used until the IV NTG is prepared. The goal of therapy is to reduce angina pain and improve coronary blood flow. IV NTG decreases preload and afterload while increasing the myocardial O_2 supply. The onset of action is immediate. Titrate NTG to eliminate chest pain. Because hypotension is a common side effect, closely monitor BP. Patients who become hypotensive may be volume depleted and may benefit from an IV fluid bolus. Closely assess for volume overload after the bolus (e.g., crackles on lung auscultation).

Morphine. Morphine is the drug of choice for chest pain that is unrelieved by NTG. As a vasodilator, it decreases cardiac workload by lowering myocardial O_2 consumption, reducing contractility, and decreasing BP and HR. In addition, morphine can help reduce anxiety and fear. In rare situations, morphine can depress respirations. Monitor patients for signs of bradypnea or hypotension, which are conditions to avoid in myocardial ischemia and infarction.

β-Adrenergic Blockers. β-blockers decrease myocardial O_2 demand by reducing HR, BP, and contractility. The use of these drugs in patients who are not at risk for complications of MI (e.g., cardiogenic shock, bradycardia, hypotension) reduces the risk for reinfarction and the development of HF. Therapy continues indefinitely.

Angiotensin-Converting Enzyme Inhibitors and Angiotensin Receptor Blockers. ACE inhibitors should be started within the first 24 hours if the BP is stable and there are no contraindications. They are continued indefinitely in patients recovering from STEMI or NSTEMI, with HF, or an EF of 40% or less. The use of ACE inhibitors can help prevent ventricular remodeling and prevent or slow the progression of HF. For patients who cannot tolerate ACE inhibitors (e.g., angioedema, cough), ARBs should be considered.

Antidysrhythmic Drugs. Dysrhythmias are the most common complications after an MI. In general, they are self-limiting and not treated aggressively unless they are life threatening (e.g., sustained ventricular tachycardia). Chapter 35 discusses the drugs used in the treatment of dysrhythmias.

Lipid-Lowering Drugs. A lipid panel is done on all patients with ACS. Patients with ACS or CAD should receive lipid-lowering drugs indefinitely, unless contraindicated (Table 33.6).

Stool Softeners. After an MI, the patient may be predisposed to constipation because of bed rest and opioid drugs. Stool softeners (e.g., docusate sodium [Colace]) prevent straining and the resultant vagal stimulation from the *Valsalva maneuver*. Vagal stimulation produces bradycardia and can provoke dysrhythmias. A laxative may be used, if needed.

Nutritional Therapy

Initially, patients may be NPO (nothing by mouth) except for water until stable (e.g., pain free, nausea resolved). Advance the diet as tolerated to a low-salt, low-saturated-fat, and low-cholesterol diet (Tables 33.4 and 33.5).

❖ NURSING MANAGEMENT: ACUTE CORONARY SYNDROME

◆ Nursing Assessment

Table 33.16 presents the subjective and objective data to obtain from a patient with ACS.

◆ Nursing Diagnoses

Nursing diagnoses for the patient with ACS may include:
- Impaired cardiac output
- Acute pain
- Anxiety
- Activity intolerance

More information on nursing diagnoses of patients with ACS is presented in eNursing Care Plan 33.1 available on the website for this chapter.

TABLE 33.16 Nursing Assessment
Acute Coronary Syndrome

Subjective Data
Important Health Information
Past health history: Previous history of CAD, chest pain/angina, MI, valve disease (e.g., aortic stenosis), heart failure, or cardiomyopathy. Hypertension, diabetes, anemia, lung disease, hyperlipidemia
Medications: Use of antiplatelets, anticoagulants, nitrates, ACE inhibitors, β-blockers, calcium channel blockers, antihypertensive drugs, lipid-lowering drugs, over-the-counter drugs (e.g., vitamin and herbal supplements)
History of present illness: Description of events related to current illness (Table 33.9), including any self-treatments and response

Functional Health Patterns
Health perception–health management: Family history of heart disease. Sedentary lifestyle, tobacco use, exposure to environmental smoke
Nutritional-metabolic: Indigestion, heartburn, nausea, belching, vomiting
Elimination: Urinary urgency or frequency, straining at stool
Activity-exercise: Palpitations, dyspnea, dizziness, weakness
Cognitive-perceptual: Substernal chest pain or pressure (squeezing, constricting, aching, sharp, tingling), radiation to jaw, neck, shoulders, back, or arms (Table 33.8)
Coping–stress tolerance: Stressful lifestyle, depression; anger, anxiety. Feeling of impending doom

Objective Data
General
Anxious, fearful, restless, distressed

Integumentary
Cool, clammy, pale skin

Cardiovascular
Tachycardia or bradycardia, pulsus alternans (alternating weak and strong heartbeats), pulse deficit, dysrhythmias (especially ventricular), murmur, S_3, S_4, ↑ or ↓ BP

Possible Diagnostic Findings
Positive serum cardiac biomarkers, ↑ serum lipids; ↑ WBC count. Positive exercise or pharmacologic stress test and thallium scans. Pathologic Q wave, ST segment elevation, and/or ST-T wave abnormalities on ECG. Cardiac enlargement, calcifications, or pulmonary congestion on chest x-ray. Abnormal wall motion with stress echocardiogram or resting echocardiogram. Positive coronary angiography.

◆ Planning

Nursing care focuses on the priority problems of acute pain and decreased CO. The immediate goals for a patient with ACS include (1) relief of pain, (2) quick and appropriate treatment, and (3) preservation of heart muscle. During the hospitalization, the overall goals include: (1) effective coping with illness-associated anxiety, (2) participation in a rehabilitation plan, and (3) reduction of risk factors. The Joint Commission has identified a core measure set in the management of patients with an acute MI (AMI) to reflect standards of evidence-based care.

◆ Nursing Implementation

Acute Care. When the patient is admitted to the intensive care or telemetry unit, monitor vital signs and pulse oximetry frequently (e.g., every hour) during the first few hours after admission and closely thereafter, according to agency protocol. Start continuous ECG monitoring. Obtain serial 12-lead ECGs, and draw serial cardiac biomarkers Maintain bed rest and limit activity for 12 to 24 hours, with a gradual increase in activity unless contraindicated.

For patients with UA and NSTEMI, heparin (UH or LMWH) is recommended to prevent microemboli from forming and causing further chest pain. DAPT (e.g., aspirin and clopidogrel or ticagrelor [Brilinta]) (Table 33.12) also is recommended for NSTEMI patients (with or without a stent). UA patients receive aspirin alone unless they have a stent placed; then DAPT is used. Cardiac catheterization is an option for both UA and NSTEMI patients once the patient is stabilized and angina is controlled or if angina returns or increases in severity. Depending on the results, options include medical management, PCI, or CABG surgery.

For patients with STEMI, reperfusion therapy is started as soon as possible. *Reperfusion therapy* includes emergent PCI (preferred, for PCI-capable hospitals) or thrombolytic therapy (in hospitals not capable of performing PCI). The goal in the treatment of STEMI is to save as much heart muscle as possible. Technical advances in PCI technology have almost eliminated CABG surgery as the primary treatment for patients with STEMI unless there is another reason to perform surgery (e.g., ventricular septal rupture, papillary muscle rupture).

◆ **Pain.** Provide NTG, morphine, and supplemental O_2 as needed to eliminate or reduce chest pain. Ongoing evaluation and documentation of the effectiveness of the interventions is important. Once pain is relieved, some patients interpret the absence of pain as an absence of heart disease. Provide information about the importance of continued therapy to limit myocardial damage.

◆ **Monitoring.** Maintain continuous ECG monitoring while the patient is in the ED and ICU and after transfer to a step-down unit. Treat life-threatening dysrhythmias quickly. During the initial period after MI, ventricular fibrillation is the most common lethal dysrhythmia. In many patients, premature ventricular contractions or ventricular tachycardia (VT) precedes this dysrhythmia. Isolated PVCs are not usually treated. VT may or may not be treated depending on whether it is sustained VT or nonsustained VT and depending on the patient's hemodynamic status. Using the bedside ST segment monitor, assess the patient's ST segments for reinfarction or ischemia (ST segments will shift above or below the baseline of the ECG). Silent ischemia, noted only by ST segment changes, can occur without subjective symptoms (e.g., chest pain). Notify the HCP if you see ST segment changes with or without clinical symptoms. (See Chapter 35 for a complete discussion of ECG monitoring.)

Perform a physical assessment to detect changes from the patient's baseline findings. Assess heart and breath sounds and for signs of early HF (e.g., dyspnea, tachycardia, pulmonary congestion, distended neck veins). In addition to routine vital signs, monitor intake and output.

Assessment of the patient's oxygenation status is important. If a nasal cannula is used to deliver O_2, check the nares for irritation or dryness, which can cause considerable discomfort.

◆ **Rest and Comfort.** It is important to promote rest and comfort for the patient with any degree of heart damage. Bed rest may be ordered for the first few days after a large MI. A patient with an uncomplicated MI (e.g., angina resolved, no signs of complications) may rest in a chair within 8 to 12 hours after the event. Prolonged bed rest is not recommended. The use of the bathroom, a commode, or a bedpan is based on patient preference and hemodynamic status.

TABLE 33.17 Phases of Rehabilitation After Acute Coronary Syndrome

Phase I: Hospital
- Occurs while the patient is still hospitalized
- Activity level depends on severity of angina or MI
- Patient may first sit up in bed or chair, perform range-of-motion exercises and self-care (e.g., washing, shaving), and progress to walking in hallway and limited stair climbing
- Attention focuses on management of chest pain, anxiety, dysrhythmias, and complications

Phase II: Early Recovery
- Begins after the patient is discharged
- Usually lasts from 2-12 weeks and is held in an outpatient facility but may be done in the home
- Activity level is gradually increased under the supervision of the cardiac rehabilitation team and with ECG monitoring
- Team may suggest that physical activity (e.g., walking program) be started at home
- Information about risk factor reduction is provided at this time

Phase III: Late Recovery
- Long-term maintenance program
- Individual physical activity programs are designed and implemented at home, a local gym, or the rehabilitation center
- Patient and caregiver restructure lifestyles and roles
- Therapeutic lifestyle changes should become lifelong habits
- Medical supervision recommended

When sleeping or resting, the body requires less work from the heart than it does when active. It is important to plan nursing and other interventions to ensure adequate rest periods free from interruption. Comfort measures that can promote rest include a quiet environment, use of relaxation techniques (e.g., music therapy, guided imagery), and assurance that staff is nearby and responsive to the patient's needs.

It is important that the patient understand the reasons why activity is limited. Gradually increase the patient's heart workload through more demanding physical tasks. Before discharge, it is important that the patient achieve an activity level adequate for home care. Cardiac rehabilitation should be discussed and encouraged as an outpatient. Table 33.17 outlines the phases of cardiac rehabilitation.

◆ **Anxiety.** A degree of anxiety is present in all patients with ACS. Your role is to identify the source of anxiety and assist the patient in reducing it. If the patient is afraid of being alone, allow a caregiver to sit by quietly and check the patient frequently. If a source of anxiety is fear of the unknown, explore these concerns with the patient. For anxiety caused by lack of information, provide teaching based on the patient's stated need and level of understanding. Answer the patient's questions with clear, simple explanations.

❓ CHECK YOUR PRACTICE

You are walking in the hallway with a 64-yr-old woman who had an MI 3 days ago. She is scheduled for discharge tomorrow. She is visibly anxious and irritable, wringing her hands, and talking very fast. She tells you, "My heart is pounding." You do not know if she is anxious or about to have another MI.
- What should you do?

TABLE 33.18 Psychosocial Responses to Acute Coronary Syndrome

Anger and Hostility
- Is often expressed as, "Why did this happen to me?"
- May be directed at family, staff, or medical regimen

Anxiety and Fear
- Fears long-term disability and death
- Overtly displays apprehension, restlessness, insomnia, tachycardia
- Less overtly displays increased verbalization, projection of feelings to others, hypochondriasis
- Fears activity
- Fears recurrent chest pain, heart attacks, and sudden death

Denial
- May have history of ignoring signs and symptoms related to heart disease
- Minimizes severity of health condition
- Ignores activity restrictions
- Avoids discussing illness or its significance

Dependency
- Totally reliant on staff
- Unwilling to perform tasks or activities unless approved by HCP
- Always wants to be monitored by ECG
- Hesitant to leave the intensive care or telemetry unit or hospital

Depression
- Mourns loss of health, altered body function, and changes in lifestyle
- Realizes seriousness of situation
- Begins to worry about future implications of health problem
- Shows manifestations of withdrawal, crying, apathy
- May be more evident after discharge

Realistic Acceptance
- Focuses on optimum rehabilitation
- Plans changes compatible with altered cardiac function
- Actively engages in lifestyle changes to address modifiable risk factors

It is important to start teaching at the patient's level rather than to present a prepackaged program. For example, patients generally are not ready to learn about the pathology of CAD. The earliest questions usually relate to how the disease affects perceived control and independence. Examples include:
- When will I leave the intensive care unit?
- When can I be out of bed?
- When will I be discharged?
- When can I return to work?
- How many changes will I have to make in my life?
- Will this happen again?

Tell the patient that more complete teaching will begin once the patient is feeling stronger. Often the patient may not be able to ask the most serious concern of ACS patients: Am I going to die? Even if a patient denies this concern, it is helpful for you to start a conversation by remarking that fear of dying is a common concern among most patients who have had ACS. This gives the patient "permission" to talk about an uncomfortable and fearful topic.

◆ **Emotional and Behavioral Reactions.** Patients' emotional and behavioral reactions vary, but often follow a predictable response pattern (Table 33.18). Your role is to understand what the patient is currently experiencing and to support the use of constructive coping styles.

Assess the support structure of the patient and caregiver. Determine how you can help maximize the support system. Often the patient is separated from the most significant support system at the time of hospitalization. Talk with the caregiver(s) about the patient's progress. Allow the patient and caregivers to interact as necessary and support the caregivers who will provide the necessary assistance to the patient. Open visitation is helpful in decreasing anxiety and increasing support for the patient with ACS.[29] It is important for you to help the patient identify additional support systems (e.g., spiritual care, Mended Hearts) that can assist during the hospital stay and/or after discharge.

◆ **Patient Teaching.** Patient teaching is needed at every stage of the patient's hospitalization and recovery (e.g., ED, telemetry unit, home). Give patients and caregivers the tools they need to make informed decisions about their health. For teaching to be meaningful, the patient must be aware of the need to learn. Careful assessment of the patient's health literacy and learning needs helps you set realistic goals (see Chapter 4).

The timing of the teaching is important. When patients and caregivers are in crisis, they may not be ready to learn new information. Answer the patient's questions in simple, brief terms. The answers often need repetition. When the shock accompanying a crisis subsides, the patient and caregiver are better able to focus on new and more detailed information.

Limit your use of medical terms. For example, you are caring for a patient with UA who asks you why he has chest tightness when he climbs stairs. Begin by explaining that the heart is a muscle that works as a pump. Like all muscles, it needs O_2 to work (or pump) properly. When blood vessels supplying the heart muscle with O_2 are blocked by fat and cholesterol, less O_2 is available to the muscle. As a result, the pump cannot work well. Tell the patient that the chest tightness (angina) is the heart's message that it is having trouble doing its work. Use a model of the heart to support what you are explaining.

Anticipatory guidance involves preparing the patient and caregiver for what to expect during recovery and rehabilitation. By learning what to expect, the patient gains a sense of control.

The idea of perceived control is operationalized as the process by which the patient makes decisions by cutting back. Cutting back is one way of reducing the psychologic and physiologic losses after ACS (or any other life-changing event). For example, a middle-aged man who smokes 2 packs of cigarettes a day, is 20 lb overweight, and gets no physical exercise may feel overwhelmed. He may decide that he can live with a weight reduction plan and will get more exercise (although perhaps not daily) but that it is not possible for him to quit smoking. He believes that because he is changing 2 of his 3 risk factors, he will be healthier. Ideally, the tobacco risk factor should be a priority for this patient. If the information about risks and effects of tobacco use is not accepted, you must respect the patient's choices.

In addition to teaching the patient and caregiver what they wish to know, several types of information are essential in achieving optimal health. Table 33.19 presents a teaching guide for the patient with ACS and the caregiver.

◆ **Physical Activity.** Physical activity, an integral part of rehabilitation, is necessary for optimal physiologic functioning and psychologic well-being. It has a direct, positive effect on maximal O_2 uptake, increasing CO, decreasing blood lipids, decreasing BP, increasing blood flow through the coronary arteries, increasing muscle mass and flexibility, improving the

TABLE 33.19 Patient & Caregiver Teaching

Acute Coronary Syndrome

Include the following information in the teaching plan for the patient with acute coronary syndrome and the caregiver:

- Signs and symptoms of angina and MI and what to do should they occur (e.g., how to take nitroglycerin)*
- When and how to seek help (e.g., contact 911)*
- Anatomy and physiology of the heart and coronary arteries
- Cause and effect of CAD
- Definition of terms (e.g., CAD, angina, MI, heart failure)
- Identification of and plan to decrease risk factors* (Tables 33.1, 33.2, 33.4, and 33.5)
- Reasons for tests and treatments (e.g., ECG monitoring, blood work, angiography), activity limitations and rest, diet, and drugs*
- Appropriate expectations about recovery (anticipatory guidance)
- Resumption of work, physical activity, sexual activity
- Measures to promote recovery and health (e.g., cardiac rehabilitation)
- Importance of the gradual, progressive resumption of activity*

*Identified by patients as most important to learn before discharge.

TABLE 33.20 Energy Expenditure in Metabolic Equivalents (METs)

Low-Energy Activities (<3 METs or <3 cal/min)
Activities in Hospital
- Eating
- Resting supine
- Washing hands, face

Activities Outside Hospital
- Driving a car
- Painting, seated
- Sewing by machine
- Sweeping floor

Moderate-Energy Activities (3–6 METs or 3–5 cal/min)
Activities in Hospital
- Showering
- Sitting on bedside commode
- Using bedpan
- Walking at 3–4 mph

Activities Outside Hospital
- Cycling at 5.5 mph on level ground
- Going up a flight of stairs
- Golfing
- General gardening
- Ironing, standing
- Painting, standing

High-Energy Activities (6–8 METs or 6–8 cal/min)
- Mowing lawn using walking mower
- Performing carpentry
- Walking 5 mph

Very-High-Energy Activities (>9 METs or >9 cal/min)
- Cross-country skiing
- Cycling at >13 mph
- Running at >6 mph
- Shoveling heavy snow

psychologic state, and assisting in weight loss and control. A regular schedule of physical activity, even after many years of sedentary living, is beneficial.

One method of identifying levels of physical activity is by using metabolic equivalent (MET) units: 1 MET is the amount of O_2 needed by the body at rest—3.5 mL of O_2 per kilogram per minute, or 1.4 cal/kg of body weight per minute. The MET determines the energy costs of various exercises (Table 33.20).

In the hospital, the activity level is gradually increased so that by the time of discharge the patient can tolerate moderate-energy activities of 3 to 6 METs. Many patients with UA or an uncomplicated MI are in the hospital for 3 or 4 days. By day 2, the patient can walk in the hallway and begin climbing a few steps. Because of the short hospital stay, it is critical to give the patient specific guidelines for physical activity so that overexertion will not occur. Tell the patient to always "listen to what your body is saying"—the most important aspect of recovery.

Teach patients that 30 to 60 minutes of moderate-intensity aerobic activity (e.g., brisk walking) at least 5 days a week is recommended by the AHA. For patients who have been hospitalized for a coronary event (e.g., PCI, UA, NSTEMI, STEMI), they must "work up" to 30 minutes of exercise per day. An exercise stress test may be ordered after hospitalization to assess for chest pain with activity and help guide physical activity. The patient who has been physically inactive and just starting an exercise program should do so under supervision whenever possible. Cardiac rehabilitation, either in a group setting or home-based setting, is recommended.[15,28]

Teach patients to check their HR. Some patients may use technology (e.g., cell phone applications, fitness trackers) to check their HR. The patient should know the limits within which to exercise. Tell the patient that the heart rate should return to the resting HR within a few minutes of stopping the exercise. Tell the patient to stop exercising and rest if chest pain or shortness of breath occurs. The key factor is the patient's response to physical activity in terms of symptoms rather than absolute HR, especially since many patients are taking β-blockers and may not be able to reach a target HR. This point cannot be overstressed. Basic physical activity guidelines for patients after ACS follow the FITT formula (Table 33.3).

The basic categories of physical activity are isometric (static) and isotonic (dynamic). Most daily activities are a mixture of the two. *Isometric activities* involve the development of tension during muscular contraction but produce little or no change in muscle length or joint movement. Lifting, carrying, and pushing heavy objects are isometric activities. These activities are associated with the Valsalva maneuver and may cause a vasovagal response. Because the HR and BP change rapidly during isometric work, isometric exercises should be limited.

Isotonic activities involve changes in muscle length and joint movement with rhythmic contractions at relatively low muscular tension. Walking, jogging, swimming, bicycling, and jumping rope are examples of activities that are mostly isotonic. Isotonic exercise can put a safe, steady load on the heart and lungs and improve the circulation to other organs.

Women who have an MI often have poor adherence to a regular physical activity program.[4] Women often are the caregivers for everyone else and do not take good care of themselves. They may prioritize a physical activity program as less important than caring for others. Often women describe continued fatigue. Another factor linked to poor adherence to a physical activity program after MI is depression. Depression is common among patients with CAD, especially in women.[4] Routinely screen for depression in patients with CAD/ACS and recommend referral for treatment as appropriate.

◆ **Cardiac Rehabilitation.** *Cardiac rehabilitation* is the restoration of a person to an optimal state of function in 6 areas: (1) physiologic, (2) psychologic, (3) mental, (4) spiritual, (5) economic, and (6) vocational.

Discuss participation in an outpatient cardiac rehabilitation program with patients who have had UA, an MI, a PCI, or CABG surgery (Table 33.17). These programs are helpful, but not all patients choose or are able to take part in them due to cost, location, and travel limitations. Home-based cardiac rehabilitation programs can provide an alternative. Physical activity guidelines are developed for the patient and staff to maintain ongoing contact (e.g., telehealth, exercise logs, Internet). Maintaining contact with the patient is a key to the success of these programs.

Many patients recover physically from ACS or CABG surgery but do not attain psychologic well-being. All patients should be referred to an outpatient or home-based cardiac rehabilitation program because exercise-based cardiac rehabilitation is a Class I recommendation from the ACC/AHA for any patient with HF or who had a cardiac event.[13,15,20] Despite the proven beneficial effects of cardiac rehabilitation, it is often not recommended, and participation is less than optimal.

In considering rehabilitation, the patient must recognize that CAD is a chronic disease. It is not curable. Therefore basic changes in lifestyle must be made to promote recovery and future health. Tell patients that recovery takes time and resuming physical activity after ACS or heart surgery is slow and gradual. However, with appropriate and adequate supportive care, recovery is more likely.

◆ **Resuming Sexual Activity.** It is important to include sexual counseling for heart patients and their partners. This often-neglected area of discussion may be difficult for both the patient and HCP to approach. However, the patient's concern about resumption of sexual activity after hospitalization for ACS often produces more stress than the physiologic act. Most patients change their sexual behavior because they are concerned about sexual inadequacy, death during intercourse, and impotence. A concerned and knowledgeable HCP can clarify any misconceptions with specific counseling.

Before providing guidelines on resumption of sexual activity, it is important to know the patient's physiologic status, physiologic effects of sexual activity, and psychologic effects of having an MI. Sexual activity for most middle-aged men and women with their usual partners is considered a moderate-energy activity equivalent to climbing 2 flights of steps or walking briskly.[30]

You may be uncertain of how and when to begin counseling about resumption of sex. It is helpful to consider sex as a physical activity and to discuss or explore feelings in this area when discussing other physical activities. One helpful approach is, "Many people who have had a heart attack wonder when they will be able to resume sexual activity. Has this been of concern to you?" You may also state, "Sexual activity, like other forms of activity, should be gradually resumed after MI. If your ability to perform sexually is concerning you, the energy you use is likely no more than climbing 2 flights of steps or walking briskly." Facilitate discussion by providing the patient with reading material on resumption of sexual activity. Say something such as, "If resuming sexual activity has been of concern to you, this information should be helpful." This type of nonthreatening statement brings up the topic, allows the patient to explore personal feelings, and gives the patient an opportunity to raise questions with you or another HCP. Common guidelines are outlined in Table 33.21.

TABLE 33.21 Patient & Partner Teaching
Sexual Activity After Acute Coronary Syndrome

Include the following information in the teaching plan for the patient and his/her partner after an acute coronary syndrome:
- Resume sexual activity at a level that relates to sexual activity before experiencing ACS.
- Physical training may improve the physiologic response to intercourse. Encourage daily physical activity during recovery.
- Consumption of food and alcohol should be reduced before intercourse is anticipated (e.g., waiting 3–4 hr after eating a large meal before engaging in sexual activity).
- Familiar surroundings and a familiar partner reduce anxiety.
- Masturbation may be a useful sexual outlet and may reassure the patient that sexual activity is still possible.
- Avoid hot or cold showers just before and after intercourse.
- Foreplay is desirable because it allows a gradual increase in HR before orgasm.
- Positions during intercourse are a matter of individual choice.
- Orogenital sex places no undue strain on the heart.
- A relaxed atmosphere free of fatigue and stress is optimal.
- Prophylactic use of nitrates to decrease chest pain during sexual activity may be suggested.
- Use of erectile agents (e.g., sildenafil) is contraindicated if taking nitrates in any form.
- Avoid anal intercourse because of the chance of inducing a vasovagal response.

Tell the patient that the inability to perform sexually after MI is common and that sexual dysfunction usually disappears after several attempts. Reinforce the idea that patience and understanding usually solve the problem. However, many male patients may be interested in using drugs to correct erectile dysfunction. Warn the patient that these drugs are not to be used with nitrates because severe hypotension, and even death, have been reported. Tell patients to discuss the use of these drugs with their HCP.

It is common for a patient who has chest pain on physical exertion to have some angina during sexual stimulation or intercourse. The patient may take NTG prophylactically if he is not using erectile dysfunction medications. Tell the patient to delay sex after a heavy meal or excess alcohol intake, when extremely tired or stressed, or with unfamiliar partners. Patients should avoid anal intercourse because of the chance of eliciting a vasovagal response.

Tell the patient that resumption of sex depends on the patient and partner's emotional readiness and on the HCP's assessment of the extent of recovery. It is generally safe to resume sexual activity 7 to 10 days after an uncomplicated MI. However, some HCPs think that the patient should decide when to resume sex. Others think patients must be asymptomatic during moderate-energy activities before resuming sexual activity.[30]

◆ **Evaluation**

The expected outcomes are that the patient with ACS will
- Maintain stable signs of adequate cardiac output
- Have relief of pain and/or shortness of breath
- Report decreased anxiety and increased sense of self-control
- Achieve a realistic program of activity that balances physical activity with energy-conserving activities
- Describe the disease process, measures to reduce risk factors, and rehabilitation activities necessary to manage the therapeutic regimen

Participating in Cardiac Rehabilitation

You are caring for M.M., a 76-yr-old male who had a NSTEMI and PCI with stent placement 3 days ago. The HCP prescribed cardiac rehabilitation 3 times per week for 12 weeks, to begin in 4 weeks. M.M. and his wife live in a rural area and express concern that it will be hard for M.M. to travel to attend the nearest center-based program 40 minutes from their home. They ask you if M.M. needs to take part in the rehabilitation program or if there are other options they can pursue.

Making Clinical Decisions
Synthesis of Best Available Evidence
Cardiac rehabilitation programs help to aid in recovery and prevent further cardiac events. They typically include exercise, healthy lifestyle education, and/or psychologic interventions, such as stress reduction counseling. Programs are available in supervised centers or in the home (home-based). Home-based programs have been introduced to increase access and participation in cardiac rehabilitation. The programs are similar in terms of outcomes of mortality, exercise capacity, and health-related quality of life.

Clinician Expertise
You know that taking part in a home-based or center-based cardiac rehabilitation program will help to aid in recovery and prevent further cardiac events after a NSTEMI.

Patient Preferences and Values
M.M. and his wife want him to take part in cardiac rehabilitation but express concern about attending a hospital-based program.

Implications for Nursing Practice
1. What strategies may be useful in encouraging M.M. to take part in a program?
2. Why is it important to reinforce the benefits of adhering to a recommended exercise program?
3. What would you suggest since they are concerned about not being able to travel to a center-based program?

Reference for Evidence
Anderson L, Sharp GA, Norton RJ, et al.: Home-based versus centre-based cardiac rehabilitation, *Cochrane Database Syst Rev* 6:CD007130, 2017.

SUDDEN CARDIAC DEATH

Sudden cardiac death (SCD) is a sudden, unexpected death resulting from a variety of cardiac causes. Around 350,000 adults experience SCD yearly.[1]

Etiology and Pathophysiology

SCD is defined as sudden unexpected death occurring within 1 hour of symptom onset. In SCD, a sudden disruption in heart function from a life-threatening dysrhythmia produces an abrupt loss of CO and cerebral blood flow. The affected person may or may not have a known history of heart disease. CAD is the main cause of SCD in the United States, especially in adults over 35 years of age.[31] Black women have a higher incidence of SCD as the first manifestation of CAD than white women.[5] SCD is the initial manifestation of CAD or structural heart disease in up to 50% of people; however, SCD can occur without evidence of CAD.[31]

Acute ventricular dysrhythmias (e.g., ventricular tachycardia, ventricular fibrillation) cause most cases of SCD. With the use of implantable cardioverter-defibrillators (ICDs), the incidence of SCD from VT and VF is declining.[31] These dysrhythmias may or may not be associated with an acute MI. Many SCD survivors have a history of a prior (old) MI.

Besides patients with CAD, patients with LV dysfunction and structural heart disease are at risk for SCD. Structural heart disease includes LV hypertrophy, myocarditis, and hypertrophic cardiomyopathy. Hypertrophic cardiomyopathy is a risk factor for SCD, especially in young, athletic people.

Some cases of SCD (especially in people less than age 45) occur in the absence of structural heart disease, LV dysfunction or CAD. These involve changes in the conduction system (e.g., prolonged QT syndrome, Wolff-Parkinson-White syndrome complicated by atrial fibrillation, Brugada syndrome).

Clinical Manifestations and Complications

Some people have symptoms within 1 hour of an SCD event, such as angina, palpitations, dizziness, or lightheadedness. People who experience SCD because of CAD fall into 2 groups: (1) those who had a prior (old) MI and (2) those who had an acute MI. SCD is more common in people who had a prior (old) MI. Those who had a prior MI and survive SCD are at risk for another SCD event because of the continued electrical instability from the scarred heart muscle that caused the first event to occur. They are usually referred for an ICD. Patients who have SCD associated with an acute MI undergo at least 40 days of maximal medical therapy to see if there is recovery in the EF before an ICD can be implanted.[32]

Most SCD patients have a lethal ventricular dysrhythmia that is associated with a high incidence of recurrence. It is difficult to know who is at high risk for SCD. However, LV dysfunction (EF < 30%) is the most commonly used tool to help guide decisions about ICD implantation.[31]

❖ Interprofessional and Nursing Care

People who survive an SCD event need a diagnostic workup to determine whether they had an acute MI. Serial analysis of cardiac biomarkers and ECGs are done to rule out ACS. Because some people with SCD have undiagnosed CAD, cardiac catheterization is done to identify if significant CAD (e.g., greater than 70% stenosis in multiple coronary arteries) was the cause of the SCD event. PCI or CABG surgery may be indicated because significant CAD may be a reversible cause of SCD.

If no reversible cause is identified and the EF is low normal, it is useful to know if these patients are likely to have a recurrence. Assessment of dysrhythmias in these patients may include obtaining an electrophysiology study (EPS).[32] EPS is done under fluoroscopy. Pacing electrodes are placed in various intracardiac areas and stimuli are selectively used in an attempt to reproduce life-threatening dysrhythmias. See Chapters 31 and 35 for a discussion of EPS.

For patients with syncope with the suspected cause of ventricular dysrhythmias, an outpatient wearable monitor (e.g., Holter monitor) can be used for up to 48 hours or a Mobile Cardiac Outpatient Telemetry (MCOT) (e.g., CardioNet) may be worn up to 30 days. An implantable cardiac monitor (e.g., LINQ) may be implanted and left in place up to 3 years.

The most common approach to preventing a recurrence of SCD is the use of an ICD. It has been shown that an ICD improves survival.[31,32] (See Chapter 35 for a discussion of ICDs.) Drug therapy with amiodarone may be used with an ICD to decrease episodes of ventricular dysrhythmias if the patient is receiving multiple ICD shocks from the dysrhythmias.

Some patients at risk for SCD (e.g., during the time when a patient with an MI and low EF must wait at least 40 days on maximum medical therapy to see if there is improvement in LV function) are recommended to use a wearable cardioverter-defibrillator (e.g., LifeVest) as a bridge to ICD or heart transplantation.[33] The wearable cardioverter-defibrillator is a personal external defibrillator that has 2 main parts: a garment and monitor. The garment is worn under clothing and has electrodes that continuously record the patient's ECG. The monitor is worn around the waist or from a shoulder strap. If the patient has ventricular tachycardia or ventricular fibrillation, the device sounds an alarm to confirm that the patient is unresponsive. If the patient is conscious, the patient can press 2 buttons to stop the shock. If the patient does not respond, the device warns bystanders that a shock is about to be delivered. If the dysrhythmia continues and the patient still does not respond, a treatment shock is delivered through the electrodes.[33]

Teaching people about the care of SCD victims and the actions to take can save lives. Rapid cardiopulmonary resuscitation (CPR) and defibrillation with an automatic external defibrillator (AED), combined with early advanced cardiac life support, has improved long-term survival rates for a witnessed arrest due to ventricular dysrhythmias.

When caring for these patients, be alert to the patient's psychosocial adaptation to this sudden "brush with death." Many patients develop a "time bomb" mentality. They fear the recurrence of cardiac arrest and may become anxious, angry, and depressed. Their caregivers are likely to have the same feelings. Patients and caregivers may need to deal with other issues, such as driving restrictions, role reversal, and change in occupation. The grief response varies among patients and caregivers. Be attuned to the specific needs of the patient and caregiver. Teach them accordingly while providing emotional support.

CASE STUDY

Myocardial Infarction

(© iStockphoto/ Thinkstock.)

Patient Profile

D.M., a 51-yr-old, white, small business owner, is rushed to the ED by ambulance with crushing, substernal chest pain that radiates down his left arm. He reports dizziness and nausea.

Subjective Data

- Short of breath, nauseous
- History of chronic stable angina and hypertension
- States he is "borderline diabetic"
- Overweight, but recently lost 10 lb
- Rarely exercises
- Has 3 teenage children who are causing "problems"
- Recently lost his best friend and business partner, who died from cancer

Objective Data

Physical Examination

- Diaphoretic
- BP 165/100 mm Hg, pulse rate 120/min, respiratory rate 26/min

Diagnostic Studies

- 12-lead ECG shows sinus tachycardia with occasional premature ventricular contractions and ST elevation in leads II, III, aV$_F$, V$_5$, V$_6$ consistent with an inferolateral wall MI
- High cardiac-specific troponin I level
- Total cholesterol 350 mg/dL (9.1 mmol/L)
- Hb A1C 9.0%

Interprofessional Care

- ED: Notify the cardiac catheterization laboratory of patient with STEMI:
  - O$_2$ 2 L/min via nasal cannula, titrate to keep O$_2$ saturation above 93%
  - Continuous ECG monitoring
  - 2 IV access sites
  - Aspirin 325 mg (chewable)
  - Atorvastatin (Lipitor) 80 mg PO
  - Eptifibatide (Integrilin) IV (this should *not* delay the patient getting to the cardiac catheterization laboratory)

- Weight-based heparin IV (only used if the patient does not go directly to cardiac catheterization)
- SL NTG until an IV line is placed, then titrate nitroglycerin IV to relieve chest pain; hold for systolic BP below 100 mm Hg
- Morphine 2 mg IV q5–15 min as needed for chest pain unrelieved by NTG
- Vital signs (including pulse oximetry) every 10 minutes
- Prepare patient for cardiac catheterization with possible PCI

Discussion Questions

1. Which coronary artery(ies) is (are) most likely occluded in D.M.'s coronary circulation?
2. Explain the pathogenesis of CAD. What risk factors contribute to its development? What risk factors were present in D.M.'s life?
3. What is angina? How does chronic stable angina differ from angina associated with acute coronary syndrome?
4. Explain the pathophysiologic basis for the clinical manifestations that D.M. exhibited.
5. Explain the significance of the results of the laboratory tests and the 12-lead ECG findings.
6. Give a rationale for each treatment measure ordered for D.M.
7. ***Priority Decision:*** Based on the assessment data presented, what are the priority nursing diagnoses? Identify any collaborative problems.
8. ***Priority Decision:*** What are the priority nursing interventions for D.M. before PCI? Immediately after his PCI?
9. ***Collaboration:*** Identify activities that can be delegated to unlicensed assistive personnel (UAP).
10. ***Evidence-Based Practice:*** Two days after an uncomplicated PCI and the placement of 2 stents, D.M. wants to know what the most effective strategies are to prevent another MI. Based on his clinical situation, what would you tell him?
11. ***Quality Improvement:*** What outcomes would show that the interdisciplinary care was successful?
12. Develop a conceptual care map for D.M.

Answers and a corresponding conceptual care map available at *http://evolve.elsevier.com/Lewis/medsurg*.

BRIDGE TO NCLEX EXAMINATION

The number of the question corresponds to the same-numbered outcome at the beginning of the chapter.

1. In teaching a patient about coronary artery disease, the nurse explains that the changes that occur in this disorder include *(select all that apply)*
   a. diffuse involvement of plaque formation in coronary veins.
   b. abnormal levels of cholesterol, especially low-density lipoproteins.
   c. accumulation of lipid and fibrous tissue within the coronary arteries.
   d. development of angina due to a decreased blood supply to the heart muscle.
   e. chronic vasoconstriction of coronary arteries leading to permanent vasospasm.

2. After teaching about ways to decrease risk factors for CAD, the nurse recognizes that further instruction is needed when the patient says
   a. "I can keep my blood pressure normal with medication."
   b. "I would like to add weight lifting to my exercise program."
   c. "I can change my diet to decrease my intake of saturated fats."
   d. "I will change my lifestyle to reduce activities that increase my stress."

3. A hospitalized patient with a history of chronic stable angina tells the nurse that she is having chest pain. The nurse bases his actions on the knowledge that ischemia
   a. will always progress to myocardial infarction.
   b. can be relieved by rest, nitroglycerin, or both.
   c. is often associated with vomiting and extreme fatigue.
   d. indicates that irreversible myocardial damage is occurring.

4. The nurse is caring for a patient who is 2 days post MI. The patient reports that she is experiencing chest pain when she takes a deep breath. Which action would be a *priority*?
   a. Notify the provider STAT and obtain a 12-lead ECG.
   b. Obtain vital signs and auscultate for a pericardial friction rub.
   c. Apply high-flow O_2 by face mask and auscultate breath sounds.
   d. Medicate the patient with as-needed analgesic and reevaluate in 30 minutes.

5. A patient is admitted to the ICU with a diagnosis of NSTEMI. Which drugs(s) would the nurse expect the patient to receive? *(select all that apply)*
   a. Oral statin therapy
   b. Antiplatelet therapy
   c Thrombolytic therapy
   d. Prophylactic antibiotics
   e. Intravenous nitroglycerin

6. A patient is recovering from an uncomplicated MI. Which rehabilitation guideline is a *priority* to include in the teaching plan?
   a. Refrain from sexual activity for a minimum of 3 weeks.
   b. Plan a diet program that aims for a 1- to 2-lb weight loss per week.
   c. Begin an exercise program that aims for at least 5 30-minute sessions per week.
   d. Consider the use of erectile agents and prophylactic NTG before engaging in sexual activity.

7. The most common finding in people at risk for sudden cardiac death is
   a. aortic valve disease.
   b. mitral valve disease.
   c. left ventricular dysfunction.
   d. atherosclerotic heart disease.

1. b, c, d, 2. b, 3. b, 4. b, 5. a, b, e, 6. c, 7. c

For rationales to these answers and even more NCLEX review questions, visit *http://evolve.elsevier.com/Lewis/medsurg*.

---

e EVOLVE WEBSITE/RESOURCES LIST

http://evolve.elsevier.com/Lewis/medsurg
Review Questions (Online Only)
Key Points
Answer Keys for Questions
  - Rationales for Bridge to NCLEX Examination Questions
  - Answer Guidelines for Case Study on p. 731
Student Case Study
  - Patient With Coronary Artery Disease and Acute Coronary Syndrome
Nursing Care Plan
  - eNursing Care Plan 33.1: Patient With Acute Coronary Syndrome
Conceptual Care Map Creator
  - Conceptual Care Map for Case Study on p. 731
Audio Glossary
Content Updates

REFERENCES

1. World Health Organization: Cardiovascular diseases. Retrieved from *www.who.int/mediacentre/factsheets/fs317/en/*.
2. Benjamin EJ, Blaha MJ, Chiuve SE, et al: Heart disease and stroke statistics—2017 update: A report from the AHA, *Circulation* 135:e146, 2017.
3. Lilly LS: *Pathophysiology of heart disease: A collaborative project of medical students and faculty*, ed 6, Philadelphia, 2016, Wolters Kluwer.
*4. McSweeney JC, Rosenfeld AG, Abel WM, et al: Preventing and experiencing ischemic heart disease as a woman: State of the science: A scientific statement from the AHA, *Circulation* 133:1302, 2016.
*5. Mehta LS, Beckie TM, DeVon HA, et al: Acute myocardial infarction in women: A scientific statement from the AHA, *Circulation* 133:916, 2016.
6. Girelli D, Piubelli C, Martinelli N, et al: A decade of progress on the genetic basis of coronary artery disease, *Euro J Int Med* 1:10, 2017.
7. Brenner GM, Stevens CW: *Pharmacology e-book*, ed 5, Philadelphia, 2018, Elsevier.
*8. Stone NJ, Robinson JG, Lichtenstein AH, et al: 2013 ACC/AHA guideline on the treatment of blood cholesterol to reduce atherosclerotic cardiovascular risk in adults: A report of the ACC/AHA Task Force on Practice Guidelines, *Circulation* 129:S1, 2014. (Classic)

*9. Jellinger PS, Handelsman Y, Rosenblit PD, et al: American Association of Clinical Endocrinologist and American College of Endocrinology guidelines for management of dyslipidemia and prevention of cardiovascular disease, *Endocr Pract* 23:S1, 2017.

*10. Whelton PK, Carey RM, Aronow WS, et al: 2017 ACC/AHA/AAPA/ABC/ACPM/AGS/APhA/ASH/ASPC/NMA/PCNA guideline for the prevention, detection, evaluation, and management of high blood pressure in adults: A report of the ACC/AHA Task Force on Clinical Practice Guidelines, *Journal of the American College of Cardiology* 71:e127, 2018.

*11. James PA, Oparil S, Carter BL, et al: 2014 Evidence-based guideline for the management of high blood pressure in adults: Report from the panel members appointed to the Eighth Joint National Committee, *JAMA* 311:507, 2014. (Classic)

*12. Bhatnagar A, Whitsel LP, Ribisl KM, et al: Electronic cigarettes: A policy statement from the AHA, *Circulation* 130:1418, 2014. (Classic)

*13. Fihn SD, Blankenship JC, Alexander KP, et al: ACC/AHA/AATS/PCNA/SCAI/STS focused update of the guideline for the diagnosis and management of patients with stable ischemic heart disease: A report of the ACC/AHA Task Force on Practice Guidelines and the American College of Physicians, AATS, PCNA, SCAI, and STS, *Circulation* 130:1749, 2014. (Classic)

14. Bottaccioli AG: The role of stress and emotions in cardiovascular disease. In *Integrative cardiology: A new therapeutic vision*, New York, 2017, Springer.

*15. Amsterdam EA, Wenger NK, Brindis RG, et al: 2014 ACC/AHA guideline for the management of patients with non–ST-elevation acute coronary syndromes: A report of the ACC/AHA Task Force on Practice Guidelines, *Circulation* 130:e344, 2014. (Classic)

16. Havakuk O, Rezkalla SH, Kloner RA: The cardiovascular effects of cocaine, *JACC* 70:101, 2017.

17. American Heart Association: Fish and omega-3 fatty acids. Retrieved from *www.heart.org/en/healthy-living/healthy-eating/eat-smart/fats/fish-and-omega-3-fatty-acids*.

*18. Naylor M, Vasan R: Recent update to the US cholesterol treatment guidelines: A comparison with international guidelines, *Circulation* 133:1795, 2016.

*19. Bibbins-Domingo K, Grossman DC, Curry SJ, et al: Aspirin use for the primary prevention of cardiovascular disease and colorectal cancer: U.S. Preventive Services Task Force recommendation statement, *Ann Intern Med* 164:836, 2016.

*20. Levine GN, O'Gara PT, Bates ER, et al: 2015 ACC/AHA/SCAI focused update on primary PCI for patients with ST-elevation myocardial infarction: An update of the 2011 ACCF/AHA/SCAI guideline for PCI and the 2013 ACCF/AHA guideline for the management of ST-elevation myocardial infarction, *Circulation* 133:1135, 2016.

21. Mann DL, Zipes DP, Libby P, et al: *Braunwald's heart disease: A textbook of cardiovascular medicine*, ed 10, St Louis, 2015, Saunders. (Classic)

*22. Naderi S: Microvascular coronary dysfunction: An overview, *Curr Atheroscler Rep* 20:7, 2018.

*23. The Heart Outcomes Prevention Evaluation (HOPE) Study Investigators: Effects of an angiotensin-converting-enzyme inhibitor, ramipril, on cardiovascular events in high-risk patients, *N Engl J Med* 342:145, 2000. (Classic)

*24. Levine GN, Bates ER, Bittl JA, et al: 2016 ACC/AHA guideline focused update on duration of dual antiplatelet therapy in patients with coronary artery disease: A report of the ACC/AHA Task Force on Clinical Practice Guidelines, *Circulation* 134:e123, 2016.

*25. Hillis LD, Smith PK, Anderson JL, et al: 2011 ACCF/AHA guideline for coronary artery bypass graft surgery: A report of the ACC Foundation/AHA Task Force on Practice Guidelines, *Circulation* 124:e652, 2011. (Classic)

26. Cohn LH: *Cardiac surgery in the adult*, ed 8, New York, 2012, McGraw-Hill.

27. Sauër AC, Veldhuijzen DS, Ottens TH, et al: Association between delirium and cognitive change after cardiac surgery, *Brit J Anaesth* 119:308, 2017.

*28. O'Gara PT, Kushner FG, Ascheim DD, et al: 2013 ACCF/AHA guideline for the management of ST-elevation myocardial infarction: A report of the ACC Foundation/AHA Task Force on Practice Guidelines, *Circulation* 127:e362, 2013. (Classic)

29. American Association of Critical-Care Nurses: Family presence: Visitation in the adult ICU. Retrieved from *www.aacn.org/clinical-resources/practice-alerts/family-presence-visitation-in-the-adult-icu*.

*30. Levine GN, Steinke EE, Bakaeen FG, et al: Sexual activity and cardiovascular disease: A scientific statement from the AHA, *Circulation* 125:1058, 2012. (Classic)

31. Mitrani RD, Myerburg RJ: Ten advances defining sudden cardiac death, *Trends Cardiovasc Med* 26:23, 2016.

*32. Al-Khatib SM, Stevenson WG, Ackerman MJ, et al: 2017 AHA/ACC/HRS guideline for management of patients with ventricular arrhythmias and the prevention of sudden cardiac death: a report of the ACC Foundation/AHA Task Force on Clinical Practice Guidelines and the Heart Rhythm Society, *Circulation* 138:e272, 2018. Retrieved from *www.ahajournals.org/doi/pdf/10.1161/CIR.0000000000000549*.

33. Ferrick AM, Tian D, Vudathaneni V, et al: Wearable cardioverter defibrillators, *Cardiology in Review* 24:282, 2016.

*Evidence-based information for clinical practice.

34

Heart Failure

Vera Barton-Maxwell

There is no exercise better for the heart than reaching down and lifting people up.

John Holmes

(e) http://evolve.elsevier.com/Lewis/medsurg/

CONCEPTUAL FOCUS

Fatigue
Fluids and Electrolytes

Functional Ability
Hormonal Regulation

Self-Management

LEARNING OUTCOMES

1. Compare the pathophysiology of heart failure with reduced ejection fraction (HFrEF) and heart failure with preserved ejection fraction (HFpEF).
2. Relate the compensatory mechanisms involved in heart failure (HF) to the development of acute decompensated heart failure (ADHF) and chronic HF.
3. Describe appropriate nursing and interprofessional care to manage the patient with ADHF.

4. Describe appropriate nursing and interprofessional care to manage the patient with chronic HF.
5. Discuss advanced therapeutic options for patients with stage D HF.
6. Describe the indications for heart transplantation and the nursing care of heart transplant recipients.

KEY TERMS

acute decompensated heart failure, p. 738
cardiac resynchronization therapy, p. 741
heart failure (HF), p. 734

heart failure with reduced ejection fraction (HFrEF), p. 734
heart failure with preserved ejection fraction (HFpEF), p. 734

heart transplantation, p. 750
orthopnea, p. 740
paroxysmal nocturnal dyspnea (PND), p. 740
pulmonary edema, p. 739

HEART FAILURE

Heart failure (HF) is a complex clinical syndrome that develops in response to myocardial insult. It results in the inability of the heart to provide sufficient blood to meet the oxygen (O_2) needs of tissues and organs. The decreased cardiac output leads to decreased tissue perfusion, impaired gas exchange, fluid volume imbalance, and decreased functional ability. This chapter discusses the nursing and interprofessional care of patients with HF.

The *percentage* of the total blood volume in the left ventricle (LV) at the end of diastole that is pumped out of the LV with the next systole is called the left ventricular ejection fraction (LVEF). HF manifestations occur due to a defect in either ventricular systolic function/LV contraction (**heart failure with reduced ejection fraction [HFrEF]**) and/or a defect in ventricular diastolic function/filling (**heart failure with preserved ejection fraction [HFpEF]**).[1]

HF is associated with many cardiovascular diseases (CVDs), particularly long-standing hypertension (HTN), coronary artery disease (CAD), and myocardial infarction (MI). HF is increasing in incidence and prevalence. This is partially due to better survival after cardiac events and the aging population. HF is primarily a disease of older adults. The incidence is similar in men and women.[2]

HF is a major health problem in the United States. The number of people diagnosed with HF has increased from 5.7 million (2009–2012) to 6.5 million (2011–2014). That number is projected to rise 46% by 2030.[2] HF is the most common reason for hospital admission in adults over the age of 65. This places a significant economic burden on the health care system.[1] The complex, progressive nature of HF often results in poor outcomes, such as hospital readmissions. Around 25% of patients discharged with a primary diagnosis of HF are readmitted within 30 days. The total cost of HF care exceeds $40 billion annually, with over half of these costs spent on hospitalizations.[2]

Etiology

HTN and CAD are the primary risk factors for HF. HTN is a modifiable risk factor that should be aggressively treated and managed. Long-term treatment of HTN reduces the incidence of HF by 50%.[1] Co-morbidities, such as diabetes, metabolic syndrome, advanced age, tobacco use, and vascular disease, contribute to the development of HF. Other causes of HF include congenital abnormalities (e.g., septal defects), infiltrative cardiomyopathies (e.g., sarcoidosis), infections and inflammatory processes (e.g., viral myocarditis), persistent dysrhythmias, and toxins (e.g., alcohol, drug use, chemotherapy).[3]

🌐 PROMOTING HEALTH EQUITY
Heart Failure

- Black and Hispanic Americans develop HF at an earlier age, are admitted to the hospital more often, and have higher mortality rates related to HF as compared to whites.
- Hispanic Americans have more CVD risk factors but are 25% less likely to die of heart disease than whites.[4]

Any interference with the normal mechanisms regulating cardiac output (CO) may cause HF. CO depends on (1) preload, (2) afterload, (3) myocardial contractility, and (4) HR. These factors affect stroke volume (SV), which is the amount of blood pumped per heartbeat. Thus the equation: CO = SV × HR. Preload and afterload are discussed in Chapter 31. Any changes in these factors can lead to decreased ventricular function and HF.

The major causes of HF are divided into 2 subgroups: (1) primary causes (Table 34.1) and (2) precipitating causes (Table 34.2). Precipitating causes often increase the workload of the heart, resulting in an acute condition and decreased heart function.

Genetic Link

Several different forms of heart disease are passed down in families. Research suggests that 1 form of HF partially depends on a genetic predisposition. Mutations in more than 30 genes can cause the familial form of cardiomyopathy, a group of diseases that weaken the heart muscle. These genes provide the instructions for cardiomyocyte (heart muscle cell) proteins. The body's largest known protein, *titin,* responds to such a mutated gene. Titin mutations impair sarcomere function and disrupt chemical signaling, which negatively affects ventricular structure and stability.[5] Specific genes and gene mutations are linked to the development of HTN and CAD, known risk factors for HF (see Chapters 32, 33, and 36). Research into the effects of gene mutations on the incidence of HF is ongoing.

Pathophysiology

HF is a complex clinical syndrome that develops in response to myocardial injury and results in decreased heart function. Manifestations of HF are the result of neurohormonal compensatory mechanisms activated in response to myocardial

dysfunction, leading to *remodeling* of myocardial structure and function (Fig. 34.1).

Left-Sided Heart Failure. The most common form of HF, left-sided HF, results either from the inability of the LV to (1) empty adequately during systole or (2) fill adequately during diastole. We can further classify left-sided HF as HFrEF (systolic HF), HFpEF (diastolic HF), or a combination of the two.

Heart Failure With Reduced EF (Systolic Failure). HFrEF results from an inability of the heart to pump blood effectively. The hallmark of HFrEF is a decrease in the LVEF. Normal LVEF is 55% to 65%. Patients with HFrEF generally have an LVEF < 40%. It can be as low as 5% to 10%. HFrEF is caused by impaired contractile function (e.g., MI), increased afterload (e.g., HTN), cardiomyopathy, and mechanical abnormalities (e.g., valvular heart disorders).[3]

The LV in HFrEF loses the ability to generate enough pressure to eject blood forward through the aorta. Over time, the LV becomes dilated and hypertrophied. The weakened heart muscle cannot generate adequate SV, which impairs CO. Because the LV cannot effectively push blood forward, end diastolic volumes and pressures in the LV increase. When the LV fails, blood backs up into the left atrium (LA). This causes fluid accumulation in the lungs. The increased pulmonary hydrostatic pressure causes fluid leakage from the pulmonary capillary bed into the interstitium and then the alveoli. This results in pulmonary congestion and edema (Fig. 34.2, *A* through *D*). Fortunately, there are many therapies that reduce morbidity and mortality in HFrEF.

Heart Failure With Preserved EF (Diastolic Failure). HFpEF results from the inability of the ventricles to relax and fill during diastole. About 50% of patients with HF have HFpEF. HTN is the primary cause of HFpEF.[1] Other risk factors include older

TABLE 34.1 Primary Causes of Heart Failure

- Cardiomyopathy (e.g., viral, postpartum, substance use)
- Congenital heart defects (e.g., ventricular septal defect)
- CAD, including MI
- HTN, including hypertensive crisis
- Hyperthyroidism
- Myocarditis
- Pulmonary HTN
- Rheumatic heart disease
- Valvular disorders (e.g., mitral stenosis)

TABLE 34.2 Common Precipitating Causes of Heart Failure

Cause	Mechanism
Anemia	↓ O_2-carrying capacity of the blood stimulating ↑ in CO to meet tissue demands, leading to increase in cardiac workload and increase in size of LV
Bacterial endocarditis	*Infection:* ↑ metabolic demands and O_2 requirements *Valvular dysfunction:* causes stenosis or regurgitation
Dysrhythmias	May ↓ CO and ↑ workload and O_2 requirements of myocardial tissue
Hypervolemia	↑ Preload causing volume overload on the RV
Hypothyroidism	Indirectly predisposes to ↑ atherosclerosis. Severe hypothyroidism decreases myocardial contractility.
Infection	↑ O_2 demand of tissues, stimulating ↑ CO
Nutritional deficiencies	May ↓ cardiac function by ↑ myocardial muscle mass and myocardial contractility
Obstructive sleep apnea	Frequent nighttime apnea results in ↑ afterload, intermittent hypoxia, and ↑ sympathetic nervous system activity.
Paget's disease	↑ Workload of the heart by ↑ vascular bed in the skeletal muscle
Pulmonary embolism	↑ Pulmonary pressure resulting from obstruction leads to pulmonary HTN, ↓ CO.
Thyrotoxicosis	Changes the tissue metabolic rate, ↑ HR and workload of the heart

FIG. 34.1 Pathophysiology of HF. *Ang I*, Angiotensin I; *Ang II*, angiotensin II; *ADH*, Antidiuretic hormone; *ET*, endothelin; *HFpEF*, HF with preserved ejection fraction; *HFrEF*, HF with reduced ejection fraction; *LVEDP*, left ventricular end-diastolic pressure; *MR*, mitral regurgitation; *NO*, nitric oxide; *PVR*, pulmonary vascular resistance; *RAAS*, renin-angiotensin-aldosterone system; *SCD*, sudden cardiac death; *SNS*, sympathetic nervous system; *VHD*, valvular heart disease.

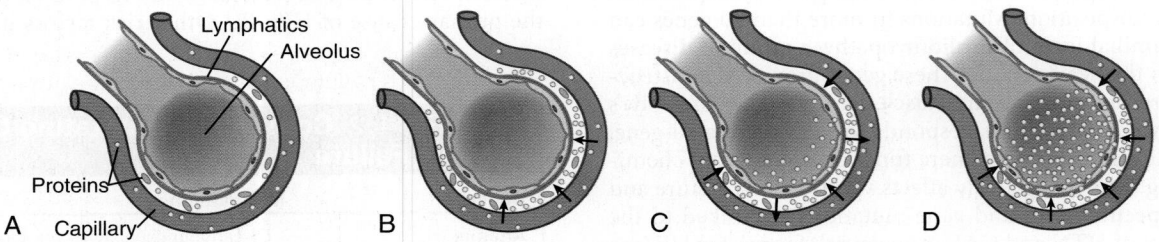

FIG. 34.2 As pulmonary edema progresses, it inhibits O_2 and CO_2 exchange at the alveolar-capillary interface. **A,** Normal relationship. **B,** Increased pulmonary capillary hydrostatic pressure causes fluid to move from the vascular space into the pulmonary interstitial space. **C,** Lymphatic flow increases to try to pull fluid back into the vascular or lymphatic space. **D,** Failure of lymphatic flow and worsening of left-sided HF result in further movement of fluid into the interstitial space and into the alveoli. (Modified from Urden LD, Stacy KM, Lough ME: *Critical care nursing: Diagnosis and management*, ed 6, St Louis, 2010, Mosby.)

age, female gender, diabetes, and obesity (see Gender Differences box). In HFpEF, the LV is generally stiff and noncompliant, resulting in high filling pressures. Decreased filling of the ventricles results in decreased SV. The eventual result of HFpEF is the same as that of HFrEF, a reduced CO leading to fluid congestion. The diagnosis of HFpEF is based on (1) signs and symptoms of HF, (2) normal LVEF, and (3) evidence of LV diastolic dysfunction by echocardiography or cardiac catheterization. Therapies are targeted at reducing underlying risk factors, treating co-morbidities, and reducing symptoms.[6]

Borderline HFpEF describes HF patients with LVEF 41% to 49%. Characteristics and therapies are like those for patients with HFpEF.[1] The patient with ventricular failure of any type may have low BP, low CO, and poor renal perfusion. Poor exercise tolerance and heart dysrhythmias are common. The patient may arrive at this point acutely from an MI or chronically from

GENDER DIFFERENCES
Heart Failure

Men
- Have HFrEF more often than women.
- Ischemic heart disease (MI, CAD) is the most common cause of HF in men.
- ACE inhibitor therapy reduces mortality more in asymptomatic HFrEF for men than women.

Women
- Underrepresented in major clinical trials about CVD making gender comparison conclusions difficult.
- Have HFpEF more often than men.
- HTN is the most common cause of HF in women.
- Women with HF tend to be older as compared to men.
- Higher risk of ACE inhibitor–related cough than men.[4]

worsening cardiomyopathy or HTN. In both acute and chronic causes of HF, the body's response to low CO is to mobilize its compensatory mechanisms to maintain CO and BP.[3]

Right-Sided Heart Failure. Right-sided HF occurs when the right ventricle (RV) does not pump effectively. When the RV fails, fluid backs up into the venous system. This causes movement of fluid into the tissues and organs (e.g., peripheral edema, abdominal ascites, hepatomegaly, jugular venous distention [JVD]).

The most common cause of right-sided HF is left-sided HF. As the LV fails, fluid backs up into the pulmonary system, causing increased pressures in the lungs. The RV must work harder to push blood to the pulmonary system. Over time, this increased workload weakens the RV and gradually it fails. Other causes of right-sided HF (independent of the function of the LV) include RV infarction, pulmonary embolism, and *cor pulmonale* (RV dilation and hypertrophy caused by pulmonary disease) (see Chapter 27).

Biventricular Failure. Biventricular failure includes both LV and RV dysfunction, the inability of both ventricles to pump effectively. Because of decreased contractility, fluid build-up and systemic venous engorgement occur. Inadequate CO results in decreased perfusion to vital organs.[3]

Compensatory Mechanisms. HF can have an abrupt onset as with acute MI, or it can be a subtle process resulting from slow, progressive changes. The overloaded heart uses compensatory mechanisms to try to maintain adequate CO. The main compensatory mechanisms include (1) neurohormonal responses: renin-angiotensin-aldosterone system (RAAS) and the sympathetic nervous system (SNS); (2) ventricular dilation; and (3) ventricular hypertrophy.

Neurohormonal Response

Renin-angiotensin-aldosterone system. The renin-angiotensin-aldosterone system (RAAS) is a regulatory system that works to maintain normal homeostasis. The goal of RAAS activation is augmentation of preload and ventricular contractility to maintain CO. RAAS activation promotes retention of fluid and sodium. The juxtaglomerular apparatus in the kidneys senses decreased renal perfusion from a falling CO. In response, the kidneys release renin, which converts angiotensinogen to angiotensin I (see Chapter 44 and Fig. 44.4). Angiotensin I is next converted to angiotensin II by a converting enzyme made in the lungs. Angiotensin II is a potent vasoconstrictor that stimulates renal water and sodium retention and the release of aldosterone from the adrenal gland. Aldosterone acts in the nephron to stimulate sodium retention and potassium excretion and promoting myocardial fibrosis in the failing heart.

Continuous activation of the RAAS and SNS in HF leads to increased levels of antidiuretic hormone (ADH). ADH regulates water retention by stimulating renal tubular reabsorption. It is released in response to arterial low pressure/under filling via baroreceptor signals. It causes vasoconstriction and increases BP and central venous pressure (CVP). The consequences are fluid congestion and hyponatremia.[7] Chronic activation of the RAAS can cause harmful effects, such as cardiac myocyte apoptosis (programmed cell death), hypertrophy, and fibrosis. These cause the burdensome signs and symptoms that develop with HF.[8]

Sympathetic nervous system. Baroreceptors sense low arterial pressure, stimulating the SNS to try to maintain CO. Catecholamines (epinephrine and norepinephrine) are released. Stimulation of β-adrenergic receptors increases HR *(chronotropy)* and ventricular contractility *(inotropy)*. Ultimately, chronic SNS stimulation increases myocardial O_2 demand on the already weakened heart.

Continuous activation of the neurohormonal responses (RAAS and SNS) in HF leads to high levels of ADH, endothelin, and proinflammatory cytokines. Together, these factors further increase in the heart's workload, intensify ventricular dysfunction, and force ventricular remodeling.[3,7]

Peptides and Cytokines.
Endothelin, a vasoconstrictor peptide made by the vascular endothelial cells, is stimulated by hypoxia, ischemia, neurohormones, and inflammatory cytokines. Although endothelin stimulates contraction in most smooth muscles, it has the opposite effect on the heart, acting as a negative inotrope. This serves to decrease ventricular contractility in the failing heart.

Proinflammatory cytokines are released by myocytes in response to heart injury (e.g., MI, HF). Two cytokines, tumor necrosis factor (TNF) and interleukin-1 (IL-1), further depress heart function by exerting a negative inotropic effect, causing myocyte hypertrophy and apoptosis. Over time, a systemic inflammatory response also occurs.[9] High levels of endothelin and proinflammatory cytokines result in an increase in the heart's workload, progressive LV dysfunction, myocyte hypertrophy, and *ventricular remodeling*.[3,8]

Ventricular Adaptations

Dilation. *Dilation* is an enlargement of the heart chambers (Fig. 34.3, *A*). It occurs when pressure in the heart chambers (usually the LV) is elevated over time. The heart muscle fibers stretch in response to the volume of blood in the heart at the end of diastole. According to the *Frank-Starling Law,* the strength of the heart's contraction is directly proportional to its diastolic expansion. The implication is that increased preload (a greater influx of blood into the ventricle during diastole) will cause a more forceful contraction. This increased contraction initially leads to increased CO and maintains BP and perfusion. Dilation starts as an adaptive mechanism to cope with increasing blood volume. However, excessive preload exhausts the Frank-Starling mechanism, cardiac muscle fibers are overstretched, and further increases in preload no longer increase CO.

Hypertrophy. *Hypertrophy* is an adaptive increase in the muscle mass and heart wall thickness as a slow response to overwork and strain (Fig. 34.3, *B*). It occurs slowly because it takes time for this increased muscle tissue to develop. Initially, the increased contractile power of the muscle fibers leads to an increase in CO and maintains tissue perfusion. Over time, hypertrophic heart muscle has poor contractility, needs more O_2 to perform work, has poor coronary artery circulation (tissue becomes ischemic more easily), and is prone to dysrhythmias.

Remodeling. Pathologic ventricular *remodeling* is an actual change in the structure (dimensions, mass, shape) of the heart. Ventricular remodeling in HF occurs over time in response to pressure or volume overload and/or cardiac injury and the subsequent compensatory mechanisms. These include neurohormonal, ET, and cytokine activation and ventricular adaptations, including dilatation and hypertrophy. This altered shape of the ventricles eventually leads to increased ventricular mass, increased wall tension, increased O_2 consumption, and impaired contractility. The actual shape of the heart becomes less elliptical and more spherical. Although the ventricles become larger, they become less effective pumps. The LVEF further declines due to loss of mechanical advantage from altered

Enlarged atria

Enlarged ventricles

Thickened heart muscle

FIG. 34.3 A, Dilated heart chambers. B, Hypertrophied heart chambers.

ventricular geometry. Increases in angiotensin II, aldosterone, and cytokines stimulate collagen synthesis leading to fibrosis and further impaired pumping ability.[10] Ventricular remodeling is a risk factor for life-threatening dysrhythmias and sudden cardiac death (SCD). Drug therapies to prevent or reverse remodeling and decrease mortality are recommended. These include ACE inhibitors, β-adrenergic blockers (β-blockers), and aldosterone antagonists.

Beneficial Counterregulatory Mechanisms. The body tries to maintain balance through several beneficial counterregulatory processes. Natriuretic peptides (atrial natriuretic peptide [ANP] and brain [b-type] natriuretic peptide [BNP]) are hormones made by the heart muscle. ANP is released from the atria and BNP is released from the ventricles in response to increased blood volume and ventricular wall stretching.[11]

The natriuretic peptides have beneficial renal, cardiovascular, and hormonal effects. Renal effects include: (1) increased glomerular filtration rate and diuresis and (2) excretion of sodium (natriuresis). Cardiovascular effects include vasodilation and decreased BP. Hormonal effects include (1) inhibition of aldosterone and renin secretion and (2) interference with ADH release. The combined effects of ANP and BNP help to counter the adverse effects of the SNS and RAAS.[11] We can measure serum BNP levels. High serum BNP corresponds proportionally with fluid retention and is a predictor of mortality in HF.

Nitric oxide (NO) and prostaglandin are counterregulatory substances released from the vascular endothelium in response to the compensatory mechanisms activated in HF. NO and prostaglandin work to relax the arterial smooth muscle, resulting in vasodilation and decreased afterload.[10]

Compensated HF occurs when compensatory mechanisms succeed in maintaining an adequate CO that is needed for tissue perfusion. *Decompensated HF* occurs when these mechanisms can no longer maintain adequate CO and inadequate tissue perfusion results.

Classifications of Heart Failure

New York Heart Association Classes of Heart Failure. The New York Heart Association (NYHA) Functional Classification places patients in 1 of 4 categories (I–IV) based on physical activity limitation due to symptom burden.[1] NYHA class designation changes based on worsening or improving symptoms.

The Stages of Heart Failure. The American College of Cardiology Foundation and the American Heart Association (ACCF/AHA) more recently developed a staging system (A–D) that emphasizes the evolution and progression of HF as well as treatment strategies.[1] This system identifies people at risk for developing HF who do not currently have heart disease (stage A). This classification encourages clinicians to actively address the patient's risk factors and treat any existing conditions to prevent further disease progression. This staging system is progressive and unidirectional. Patients advance to a higher (worse) stage as the disease progresses. Table 34.3 compares the NYHA classification and ACC/AHA staging system.

Clinical Manifestations: Acute Decompensated Heart Failure

Acute decompensated heart failure (ADHF) is an increase (usually sudden) in symptoms of HF with a decrease in functional status, often requiring rapid escalation of therapy and hospital admission. ADHF is the most common cause of hospitalization for older Americans.[12] The presentation of ADHF typically includes symptoms and signs related to pulmonary congestion and volume overload. Neurohormonal activation leads to impaired regulation of sodium excretion through the kidneys that results in sodium and fluid accumulation. The lungs become less compliant. There is increased resistance in the small airways. To help compensate, the lymphatic system increases its flow to help maintain a constant volume of the pulmonary extravascular fluid (Fig. 34.1, A and B). This early stage is clinically associated with a mild increase in the respiratory rate (RR) and a decrease in partial pressure of O_2 in arterial blood (PaO_2).

If pulmonary venous pressure continues to increase, the increase in intravascular pressure causes more fluid to move into the interstitial space than the lymphatics can remove resulting in *interstitial edema* (Fig. 34.1, C). Tachypnea develops, and the patient becomes symptomatic (e.g., short of breath). If the pulmonary venous pressure increases further, the alveoli lining cells are disrupted, and fluid moves into the alveoli (*alveolar edema*). This is accompanied by a worsening of the arterial

TABLE 34.3 Comparison of ACCF/AHA Stages of Heart Failure and NYHA Functional Classifications

ACCF/AHA Stages of Heart Failure (HF)		NYHA Functional Classifications	
A	At high risk for HF, but without structural heart disease or symptoms of HF	None	
B	Structural heart disease, but without signs or symptoms of HF	I	No limitation of physical activity. Ordinary physical activity does not cause symptoms of HF.
C	Structural heart disease with prior or current symptoms of HF	I	No limitation of physical activity. Ordinary physical activity does not cause symptoms of HF.
		II	Slight limitation of physical activity. Comfortable at rest, but ordinary physical activity results in symptoms of HF.
		III	Marked limitation of physical activity. Comfortable at rest, but less than ordinary activity causes symptoms of HF.
		IV	Unable to carry on any physical activity without symptoms of HF, or symptoms of HF at rest
D	Refractory HF requiring specialized interventions	IV	Unable to carry on any physical activity without symptoms of HF, or symptoms of HF at rest

Reprinted with permission. *Circulation* 128:e240-e327, 2013. © 2013 American Heart Association, Inc.
ACCF, American College of Cardiology Foundation; *AHA*, American Heart Association; *NYHA*, New York Heart Association.

TABLE 34.4 Clinical Profile in Acute Decompensated Heart Failure

		CONGESTION (WET)	
		No	**Yes**
LOW PERFUSION (COLD)	**No**	**Dry-Warm** • PAWP normal • CO normal • Signs and symptoms: none	**Wet-Warm** • PAWP ↑ • CO normal • Signs and symptoms: dyspnea, edema, orthopnea
	Yes	**Dry-Cold** • PAWP ↓ or normal • CO ↓ • Signs and symptoms: edema, hypotension, cool extremities	**Wet-Cold** • PAWP ↑ • CO ↓ • Signs and symptoms: altered mental status, decreased O_2 saturation, reduced urine output, shock

PAWP, Pulmonary artery wedge pressure.

chance of cardiogenic shock. Cool extremities occur with low CO and poor perfusion. Skin pallor or mottling may be present. They result from peripheral vasoconstriction and shunting of blood to the central circulation. Sometimes, hoarseness may be present because of compression of the recurrent laryngeal nerve from an enlarged LA (Ortner sign).

Patients with ADHF are categorized into 1 of 4 groups based on hemodynamic and clinical status: dry-warm, dry-cold, wet-warm, and wet-cold (Table 34.4).[1] The most common presentation in patients with ADHF is the wet and warm patient. A patient is "wet" due to volume overload (e.g., congestion, dyspnea) but "warm" due to adequate perfusion (warm skin, positive pulses).

❓ CHECK YOUR PRACTICE

You are assigned to a patient with ADHF who was admitted to the HF unit. Your assessment reveals that the patient has bilateral crackles in the mid-lower lung fields and dyspnea on exertion (e.g., moving from the bed to the commode). The patient's skin is warm, and pulses are present in all extremities. Your preceptor asks you to categorize your patient based on the classification systems in Tables 34.3 and 34.4.
- In what NYHA class would you place your patient?
- In what ACCF/AHA stage would you place your patient?
- What ADHF clinical profile does your patient best fit?

blood gas values (i.e., lower PaO_2, increased $PaCO_2$, progressive respiratory acidosis).

ADHF can manifest as **pulmonary edema**. This is an acute, life-threatening situation, in which the lung alveoli become filled with serosanguineous fluid (Fig. 34.1, *D*). The most common cause of pulmonary edema is left-sided HF. Other causes of pulmonary edema are listed in Table 27.24.

Manifestations of pulmonary edema include acute manifestations of left HF, such as dyspnea, *orthopnea*, and *paroxysmal nocturnal dyspnea*. JVD is often present and is the most sensitive and specific sign for elevated LV filling pressures. Coughing may provide an early clue to developing pulmonary edema in patients with chronic HF. The patient is usually anxious and pale and may be cyanotic. The RR is often > 30 breaths per minute. You may see use of accessory respiratory muscles. Pink, frothy sputum may be present in patients with severe disease. Auscultation of the lungs may reveal crackles and wheezes throughout. The absence of crackles does not rule out ADHF as many patients with a history of chronic HF develop increased lymphatic drainage of the alveolar edema. The patient's HR is often rapid, and an abnormal S_3 or S_4 heart sound may be heard (Table 31.4). BP may be high or decreased depending on the severity of the HF. Hypotension indicates severe LV systolic dysfunction and the

Clinical Manifestations: Chronic Heart Failure

Chronic HF is a progressive syndrome characterized by reduced CO and increased venous pressure, associated with underlying molecular changes that result in the death of cardiac muscle cells. The compensatory mechanisms in response to this reduced CO include neurohormonal and hemodynamic reactions to maintain major organ perfusion through vasoconstriction and SNS stimulation, an inflammatory response involving cytokines, and ventricular remodeling. These physiologic responses are responsible for the manifestations of chronic HF. Many therapies for chronic HF work by counteracting these mechanisms. Table 34.5 lists the manifestations of right-sided and left-sided chronic HF.

Fatigue. Fatigue following usual daily activities can be an early symptom of chronic HF. As the falling CO cannot sustain

TABLE 34.5 Manifestations of Heart Failure

Right-Sided Heart Failure	Left-Sided Heart Failure
Signs	
• Right ventricular heaves	• Left ventricular heaves
• ↑ HR	• ↑ HR
• Murmurs	• Pulsus alternans (alternating pulses: strong, weak)
• Jugular venous distention	• PMI displaced inferiorly and left of the midclavicular line (LV hypertrophy)
• Edema (e.g., pedal, scrotum, sacrum)	
• Weight gain	• ↓ PaO_2, slight ↑ $PaCO_2$ (poor O_2 exchange)
• Ascites	
• Anasarca (massive generalized body edema)	• Crackles (pulmonary edema)
• Hepatomegaly (liver enlargement)	• S_3 and S_4 heart sounds
	• Pleural effusion
	• Changes in mental status
	• Restlessness, confusion
	• Shallow respirations up to 32–40/min
	• Dry, hacking cough
	• Frothy, pink-tinged sputum (advanced pulmonary edema)
Symptoms	
• Fatigue	• Weakness, fatigue
• Anxiety, depression	• Anxiety, depression
• Right upper quadrant pain	• Dyspnea
• Anorexia and GI bloating	• Paroxysmal nocturnal dyspnea
• Nausea	• Orthopnea
	• Nocturia

PaCO₂, Partial pressure of CO_2 in arterial blood; *PaO₂*, partial pressure of O_2 in arterial blood; *PMI*, point of maximal impulse.

activities, fatigue eventually limits activities. Anemia, common in HF, is another potential cause of fatigue.

Dyspnea. Dyspnea is the most common manifestation of chronic HF. It is caused by increased pulmonary pressures from interstitial and alveolar edema. Dyspnea can occur early in the HF disease process with mild exertion. As HF progresses, dyspnea develops with less exertion until dyspnea occurs at rest.

Orthopnea, or dyspnea in the recumbent position, suggests HF. Orthopnea occurs due to redistribution of fluid from the lower extremities into the lungs while in a supine position. The dyspnea is usually relieved with sitting up. Asking the patient about the number of pillows used under the head while sleeping or about sleeping in a recliner can reveal adaptive behaviors that aid breathing.

Paroxysmal nocturnal dyspnea (PND) is episodic, sudden dyspnea that wakes a patient at night. PND is caused by fluid accumulation in the lungs entering the alveoli while the patient is supine. The patient can awaken in a panic with feelings of suffocation and a strong desire to sit or stand to aid breathing.

Cough. A chronic, nonproductive cough that is worse in the recumbent position is often associated with pulmonary congestion and can be a sign of HF. Other potential causes of cough include gastric conditions, medications (e.g., ACE inhibitors due to increased bradykinin levels), and pulmonary conditions.

Tachycardia. Tachycardia is an early sign of HF. One of the body's first responses to compensate for a reduced CO is to increase the HR via activation of the SNS. At first, this compensatory response has a favorable effect on CO. But over time, persistent tachycardia is harmful and may worsen HF and the accompanying manifestations. Adequate HR control in patients with chronic HF has been associated with better clinical outcomes, including decreased hospitalizations and mortality.[1]

Palpitations. Palpitations, or an irregular heartbeat, can occur due to dysrhythmias that occur with chronic HF. Atrial fibrillation (AF) is the most common of these dysrhythmias. Patients may report a fast or irregular heartbeat, a fluttering sensation, or "skipped beats" that may be intermittent. Palpitations may be accompanied by dyspnea, lightheadedness, or near syncope if the dysrhythmia further decreases CO.

Edema. Edema is a common sign of HF. It may occur in dependent body areas (peripheral edema), liver (hepatomegaly), abdominal cavity (ascites), and lungs (pulmonary edema and pleural effusion). If the patient is in bed, dependent sacral and scrotal edema may develop. Pressing the edematous skin with the finger may leave a depression *(pitting edema)*. Accumulation of extravascular fluid in the lower extremities can indicate volume overload and be a sign of ADHF. It is important to note that not all lower extremity edema is a result of HF. Hypoproteinemia, renal insufficiency, cellulitis, venous stasis, cirrhosis, and certain drugs can cause peripheral edema.

Changes in Urine Output. Urine output may be decreased because of decreased renal perfusion. HF patients often develop resistance to diuretics, which can result in a drop in urinary output. *Nocturia* is the tendency to urinate excessively during the night due to increased renal perfusion in the supine position.

Skin Changes. A low CO can result in decreased perfusion to the skin of the extremities resulting in *mottling*, a blue or gray coloring. A coolness or clammy feeling to touch can occur with poor perfusion. Because tissue capillary O_2 extraction is increased with chronic HF, the skin may appear dusky. Chronic edema can result in pigment changes. The skin can become dry from overdiuresis. It is important to recognize integumentary signs of other conditions, such as venous stasis, peripheral arterial disease, and cellulitis.

Neurologic Manifestations. Dizziness, lightheadedness, near syncope, or syncope can occur due to reduced CO and hypoperfusion to the brain or dysrhythmias that often occur with chronic HF. Hypotension secondary to HF medications and hypovolemia are common causes of neurologic symptoms in chronic HF.

Mental Status and Behavioral Changes. Cerebral hypoperfusion may occur because of hypoxia to the brain from decreased CO. The patient or caregiver may report confusion, forgetfulness, inattentiveness, and restlessness. A thorough assessment is needed to evaluate for possible confounding conditions, including psychologic disorders (especially depression and anxiety) or neurologic disorders, such as stroke or transient ischemic attack (TIA). Around 1 in 5 patients with HF have clinical depression, which confers a twofold risk of mortality and higher readmission rates.[13] Patients with psychologic disorders have poorer adherence to treatment plans. All HF patients should be screened for depression or coexisting mental health conditions.

Sleep Problems. Snoring and daytime sleepiness can indicate sleep apnea, a common confounding condition with chronic HF. Sleep apnea screening questions include those about daytime sleepiness and falling asleep, feeling rested in the morning, frequent nighttime awakenings, and history and results of a sleep study. Alternatively, insomnia could be due to psychologic issues, including anxiety or depression, or due to excessive daytime napping. The need to void often with nocturia may disturb the patient's rest.

Chest Pain. Chest pain or angina can be the result of the reduced CO associated with HF compounded with CAD. Chest pain in HF can also occur due to myocardial stretch from volume overload. Careful questioning and assessment will help distinguish among the many potential causes for chest pain in the patient with chronic HF.

Weight Changes. Many factors contribute to weight changes. Progressive weight gain in the patient with chronic HF may indicate fluid retention. Renal failure may contribute to fluid retention. Abdominal fullness from ascites and hepatomegaly often causes anorexia and nausea. As HF advances, the patient may have cardiac *cachexia* with muscle wasting and fat loss. This can be masked by the patient's edematous condition and may not be evident until the edema subsides.

Complications of Heart Failure

Pleural Effusion. *Pleural effusion,* fluid between the 2 tissue layers (pleura) that cover the lung and line the chest wall, is a common complication in HF. Increased capillary hydrostatic pressure in the systemic or pulmonary circulation from HF causes fluid leakage into the pleural space. Pleural effusions may result in symptoms of dyspnea, cough, and chest pain. Pleural effusion is discussed in Chapter 27.

Dysrhythmias and Dyssynchronous Contraction. Both atrial and ventricular dysrhythmias are common in HF. Structural changes, including myocardial stretch, fibrosis, and chamber dilatation, alter the electrical paths of the heart. Early and delayed depolarizations, both common in HF, can trigger dysrhythmias. AF is quite common in patients with HF, and the prevalence increases as the severity of HF increases. AF occurs when numerous sites in the atria fire spontaneously and rapidly, and organized atrial depolarization (contraction) no longer occurs. Loss of "atrial kick" during systole may contribute to decreased CO and worsening HF symptoms.

AF promotes thrombus formation within the atria. Thrombi can break loose and form emboli, placing patients at significant risk for stroke. Treatment with anticoagulation should be a priority if there are no significant contraindications. Treatment with drugs to achieve HR control is important. Restoring normal sinus rhythm with cardioversion and ablation may be considered. Atrial fibrillation is discussed in Chapter 35.

An enlarged LV and very low LVEF also increase the risk for thrombus formation in the LV. Anticoagulant therapy may be considered for patients with these problems.

Patients with HF are at risk for dangerous ventricular dysrhythmias (e.g., ventricular tachycardia [VT], ventricular fibrillation [VF]). SCD (sudden loss of cardiac function due to a fatal ventricular tachyarrhythmia), is a major cause of death in the HF population. Patients with HFrEF are at greatest risk for SCD. Guidelines recommend implantation of a prophylactic implantable cardioverter-defibrillator (ICD) for patients with an LVEF < 35%, who are NYHA Class II or III.[1] SCD is discussed in Chapter 33. Dysrhythmias are discussed in Chapter 35.

Ventricular remodeling can lead to dyssynchrony in ventricular contractions. One ventricle may contract prior to the other ventricle, leading to suboptimal ventricular filling (preload), reduced force of ventricular contraction (systole), and severe mitral regurgitation (MR). This worsens HF symptoms. **Cardiac resynchronization therapy (CRT)** in the form of implantable cardiac devices can significantly improve morbidity and mortality for these patients. Many HF patients receive a combination ICD and CRT device, discussed later in the chapter.

Hepatomegaly. HF can lead to severe hepatomegaly. The liver becomes congested with venous blood from right HF or ADHF. The hepatic congestion can lead to impaired liver function. Eventually liver cells die, fibrosis occurs, and cirrhosis can develop (see Chapter 43).

Cardiorenal Syndrome. Reduction in CO results in decreased renal perfusion, decreased glomerular filtration rate, and increased serum creatinine. Neurohormonal activation causes sodium and water retention, worsening HF symptoms and renal function. Impaired renal function with HF is an independent risk factor for HF morbidity and mortality.

Anemia. The primary cause of anemia in chronic HF is chronic kidney insufficiency due to the renal vasoconstriction that often occurs with HF. This vasoconstriction results in reduced erythropoietin production in the kidney, leading to anemia. Excessive cytokine production also can reduce erythropoietin secretion. The anemia itself can worsen cardiac function due to increased cardiac workload through tachycardia, fluid retention, and increased SV. Because anemia can reduce renal blood flow, it adds further stress to the heart and worsens fatigue and other manifestations of chronic HF.

Diagnostic Studies

Diagnosing HF can be challenging. Signs and symptoms are not highly specific and may mimic many other medical conditions (e.g., anemia, lung disease). Diagnostic tests for ADHF and chronic HF are outlined in Table 34.6. A primary goal in diagnosis is to find the underlying cause of HF.

An echocardiogram is a valuable, noninvasive diagnostic tool used in patients with HF. The echocardiogram gives information about chamber size and function, LVEF, heart valve function, wall thickness and motion, presence of effusion or thrombus, and intracardiac and pulmonary pressures. This test helps to distinguish between HFrEF and HFpEF. Other useful tests include 12-lead ECG, ambulatory heart monitors, chest x-ray, 6-minute walk test, multigated acquisition (MUGA) scan, cardiopulmonary exercise stress test, cardiac MRI, and cardiac catheterization/angiogram. Polysomnography studies for obstructive sleep apnea may be done. An endomyocardial biopsy may be done as part of a heart catheterization to evaluate for infective or infiltrative disease in acutely ill patients who develop unexplained, new-onset HF unresponsive to usual care.

Laboratory studies aid in the diagnosis of HF. In general, BNP and N-terminal prohormone of BNP (NT-proBNP) levels correlate positively with the degree of LV failure.[11] Levels are temporarily higher in patients receiving nesiritide (Natrecor) and may be high in patients with chronic, stable HF. So, it is important you know the baseline levels. Increases in BNP or NT-proBNP levels can be caused by conditions other than HF, including pulmonary embolism, renal failure, and acute coronary syndrome.

Interprofessional Care: Acute Decompensated Heart Failure

Mortality and readmission rates for ADHF remain unacceptably high. Professional HF organizations have developed quality improvement initiatives, such as "Get with the Guidelines" and the Acute Decompensated HF Registry (ADHERE), to help clinicians and agencies improve HF outcomes.[1]

Goals of therapy for the patient hospitalized with ADHF include (1) symptom relief; (2) optimizing volume status; (3) supporting oxygenation, ventilation, CO, and end organ

TABLE 34.6 Interprofessional Care

Heart Failure

Both ADHF and Chronic HF	ADHF	Chronic HF
Diagnostic Assessment		
• History and physical examination	• Measure LV function	• Cardiopulmonary exercise stress test
• Determine underlying cause	• Hemodynamic monitoring	• 6-minute walk test
• Serum chemistries, cardiac biomarkers, BNP or NT-proBNP level (see Table 31.6), liver function tests, thyroid function tests, CBC, lipid profile, kidney function tests, urinalysis	• Endomyocardial biopsy in select patients	• Sleep studies in select patients
• Chest x-ray		
• 12-lead ECG		
• 2-dimensional echocardiogram (see Table 31.7)		
• Nuclear imaging studies (see Table 31.7)		
• Cardiac catheterization (see Table 31.8)		
Management		
• Treatment of underlying cause	• High-Fowler's position	• Cardiac resynchronization therapy with biventricular pacing and internal cardioverter-defibrillator
• Drug therapy (Table 34.7)	• Noninvasive positive pressure ventilation	• Heart transplantation
• Circulatory assist devices (e.g., ventricular assist device)	• Circulatory assist device: intraaortic balloon pump	• Rest-activity periods
• Daily weights	• Endotracheal intubation and mechanical ventilation	• Dietitian consult
• Sodium- and possibly fluid-restricted diet	• Vital signs, urine output at least q1hr until stable	• Physical/occupational therapy consult
• O_2 by mask or nasal cannula if indicated	• Continuous ECG and pulse oximetry monitoring	• Cardiac rehabilitation
	• Hemodynamic monitoring (e.g., intraarterial BP, PAWP, CO)	• Home health nursing care (e.g., tele-health monitoring)
	• Cardioversion (e.g., atrial fibrillation)	• Palliative and end-of-life care
	• Ultrafiltration	

BNP, b-type natriuretic peptide; *LVAD*, left ventricular assist device; *NT-proBNP*, N-terminal prohormone of BNP; *PAWP*, pulmonary artery wedge pressure.

perfusion; (4) identifying and addressing the cause of the ADHF; (5) avoiding complications; (6) providing patient teaching addressing factors that precipitated HF exacerbation; and (7) discharge planning.

Patients with ADHF need ongoing monitoring and assessment of vital signs, O_2 saturation, weight, mentation, ECGs, and indicators of volume overload and decreased organ perfusion. Assessment findings indicating fluid volume overload include edema, ascites, JVD, a positive hepatojugular reflux test, an S_3 heart sound, crackles, hypoxia, and worsening renal function.

Stable patients with ADHF may be treated in the emergency department (ED) or admitted to a telemetry unit. Assess these patients every 4 hours (e.g., vital signs, pulse oximetry) for adequate oxygenation. Record intake, output, and daily weights to evaluate fluid status. If the patient has dyspnea, place in a high-Fowler's position with the feet horizontal in the bed or dangling at the bedside. This position helps decrease venous return because of the pooling of blood in the extremities. This position also increases the thoracic capacity, allowing for improved breathing.

If unstable, these patients are managed in an intensive care unit (ICU). In addition to continual ECG and O_2 saturation monitoring, vital signs and urine output are assessed at least hourly. Indicators of decreased perfusion include hypotension, decreased urine output, cool extremities, altered mentation, heart murmur, dysrhythmias, and worsening renal and liver function tests. The patient may have hemodynamic monitoring, including arterial BP and pulmonary artery pressures. If a pulmonary artery (PA) catheter is placed, CO and pulmonary artery wedge pressure (PAWP) are routinely monitored. PAWP is an indirect measurement of LA filling pressure measured from the tip of the PA catheter when inflated in a capillary artery. A normal PAWP is 6 to 15 mm Hg. Patients with ADHF

may have a PAWP as high as 30 mm Hg. Therapies are adjusted to maximize CO and reduce PAWP. Hemodynamic monitoring is discussed in Chapter 65.

Supplemental O_2 is provided to help increase the PaO_2. O_2 therapy is discussed in Chapter 28. In severe pulmonary edema, the patient may need noninvasive positive pressure ventilation (e.g., bilevel positive airway pressure [BiPAP]) or intubation and mechanical ventilation. BiPAP also decreases preload. Ventilatory support is discussed in Chapter 65.

Nonpharmacologic Therapies. *Ultrafiltration,* or *aquapheresis,* is an option for the patient with volume overload when diuretics have not been effective.[1] It can rapidly remove intravascular fluid volume and excess sodium from the patient's blood while maintaining hemodynamic stability. Hemodialysis can be used for volume overload with concomitant renal failure. They are discussed in Chapter 46.

Implantation of CRT, a biventricular pacemaker, may be considered for patients with ADHF who meet specific criteria and do not respond to more traditional therapies.

In the ICU, *mechanical cardiac assist devices* are used temporarily to manage patients with worsening HF. The intraaortic balloon pump (IABP) is a device that increases coronary blood flow to the heart muscle and decreases the heart's workload through a process called *counterpulsation.* The IABP is useful in hemodynamically unstable patients because it can decrease pulmonary artery pressures and systemic vascular resistance (SVR), leading to improved CO. Ventricular assist devices (VADs) can help maintain the pumping action of a weakened heart. A VAD is a surgically implanted mechanical pump. IABPs and VADs are discussed in Chapter 65.

Drug Therapy. Drug therapy is essential in treating ADHF (Table 34.7).

TABLE 34.7 Drug Therapy

Heart Failure

Drug	Mechanism of Action
Anticoagulants (see Table 37.10)	• Prevent thromboembolism • Recommended for patients with an ejection fraction <20% and/or atrial fibrillation
Antidysrhythmic Drugs (see Table 35.9)	• Prevent or treat dysrhythmias
β-Adrenergic Blockers (see Table 32.6) bisoprolol (Zebeta) carvedilol (Coreg) metoprolol succinate (Toprol XL)	• Promote reverse remodeling • Decrease afterload • Inhibit SNS • Reverse cardiac remodeling • Reduce mortality and morbidity in patients with chronic HF
Diuretics (see Table 32.7) *Loop Diuretics* bumetanide (Bumex) furosemide (Lasix)	• Block absorption of sodium and chloride in the kidneys at the loop of Henle • Increase urine output • Decrease fluid volume • Decrease preload • Decrease pulmonary venous pressure • Relieve symptoms of fluid congestion
Thiazide Diuretics hydrochlorothiazide metolazone (Zaroxolyn)	• Affect electrolyte reabsorption at the distal renal tubule resulting in sodium and chloride excretion • Increased urine output (milder diuretic effect than loop diuretics) • Decrease blood pressure
Aldosterone Antagonists (Potassium-Sparing Diuretics) eplerenone (Inspra) spironolactone (Aldactone)	• Inhibit aldosterone that causes sodium and water retention and antiinflammatory responses in HF • Prevent potassium loss by inhibiting sodium and potassium exchange in the distal tubule • Mild diuretic effect • Reduce mortality and HF hospitalizations in patients with chronic HF
Morphine morphine (MS Contin, Duramorph, Embeda, Kadian)	• Binds to opioid receptors • May decrease the chemoreceptor response to hypoxia, and/or cause vasodilation reducing pulmonary congestion • Reduces anxiety
Neprilysin-Angiotensin Receptor Inhibitors sacubitril/valsartan (Entresto)	• Sacubitril inhibits neprilysin, decreasing natriuretic degradation which promotes diuresis, natriuresis • Valsartan selectively blocks angiotensin II receptors • Lower blood pressure • Dilate venules and arterioles • Improve renal blood flow • May decrease mortality and hospitalizations in patients with chronic HF

Drug	Mechanism of Action
Positive Inotropes *β-Adrenergic Agonists** dobutamine dopamine	• Increase contractility (positive inotropic effect) • Increase CO • May reduce PAWP • May cause dysrhythmias • Increase myocardial O_2 demand
Digitalis Glycoside digoxin	• Weak positive inotrope mostly at higher doses • Reduce effects of RAAS and SNS • May reduce HF symptoms and hospitalization if added to standard therapy for chronic HF
Phosphodiesterase Inhibitor* milrinone	• Produce mild vasodilation • Increase SV and CO • Promote vasodilation
Renin-Angiotensin-Aldosterone System Inhibitors (see Table 32.6) *ACE Inhibitors* benazepril (Lotensin) captopril (Capoten) enalapril (Vasotec) *Angiotensin II Receptor Blockers* losartan (Cozaar) valsartan (Diovan)	• Dilate venules and arterioles • Reduce afterload and SVR • Improve renal blood flow • May relieve HF symptoms • Promote reverse remodeling • May reduce morbidity, mortality, and HF hospitalizations in patients with chronic HF
Selective SA Node Inhibitor ivabradine (Corlanor)	• Selectively inhibits the I *f*-current in the SA node • Decreases heart rate • May reduce CVD death and HF hospitalizations in patients with HFrEF in sinus rhythm with a HR ≥70 bpm • Used only for patients with chronic HF
Vasodilators isosorbide dinitrate/hydralazine (BiDil) neseritide (Natrecor)* nitrates (e.g., nitroglycerin [Nitro-Bid], isosorbide dinitrate [Isordil]) nitroprusside (Nitropress)*	• Reduce afterload • Dilate the arterioles of the kidneys, leading to increased renal perfusion and fluid loss • Decrease BP • Decrease preload • Neseritide may reduce PAWP • May relieve HF symptoms (e.g., dyspnea) • Isosorbide dinitrate/hydralazine, fixed dose, may reduce morbidity and mortality in blacks with HFrEF and NYHA Class III–IV symptoms

*Used for ADHF only.

Diuretics. Diuretics are the first line for treating patients with volume overload. They decrease sodium reabsorption at various sites within the kidneys, enhancing sodium and water loss. Decreasing intravascular volume with diuretics reduces volume returning to the LV (preload). This allows for more efficient LV pumping, decreased pulmonary vascular pressures, and improved alveolar gas exchange. IV administration of loop diuretics (e.g., furosemide) by bolus or infusion is preferred. We evaluate effectiveness by increased urine output, decreased symptoms, and fluid weight loss. Serum potassium and magnesium levels are continually monitored.

Vasodilators. Vasodilators are used to treat ADHF in the absence of hypotension. IV nitroglycerin (NTG) is a primary venodilator that reduces circulating blood volume. It also improves coronary artery blood flow by dilating the coronary arteries. So, NTG reduces preload, slightly reduces afterload (in high doses), and increases myocardial O_2 supply. Tolerance often develops with continued IV use, requiring higher doses. When titrating IV NTG, monitor BP often (every 5 to 10 minutes) to avoid hypotension. Patients on IV vasodilators may have an indwelling arterial line or continuous noninvasive blood pressure monitoring.

Sodium nitroprusside (Nitropress) is a potent IV arterial vasodilator that reduces both preload and afterload, thus improving myocardial contraction, increasing CO, and reducing pulmonary congestion. Complications of therapy include hypotension and, at high doses, thiocyanate (cyanide) toxicity. It is given in an ICU.

 DRUG ALERT Sodium Nitroprusside (Nitropress)

- Record baseline BP and continuously monitor during administration.
- Arterial BP monitoring is recommended during drug infusion.
- Too rapid rate of IV infusion can reduce BP too quickly and cause hypotension.
- Headache, dizziness, nausea, agitation, and restlessness can occur.
- Monitor thiocyanate (drug by-product) levels if infusion is greater than 3 mcg/kg/min, as toxicity can occur.

IV nesiritide is a recombinant form of BNP used for short-term treatment of ADHF after a failed response to IV diuretics.[1] As a venous and arterial vasodilator, its main effects include a reduction in PAWP and decrease in dyspnea. Because the primary adverse effect is symptomatic hypotension, BP is carefully monitored.

Morphine. Morphine dilates pulmonary and systemic blood vessels, reducing preload and afterload. It is often given in small IV boluses for the dyspnea associated with ADHF. Cautious use and close monitoring are advised. Morphine has serious adverse effects, including respiratory depression, which can require mechanical ventilation.

Positive Inotropes. Inotropic drugs increase myocardial contractility and are used for patients with evidence of cardiogenic shock or with low CO. Drugs include β-agonists (e.g., dopamine, dobutamine, norepinephrine [Levophed]) and phosphodiesterase inhibitors (milrinone). β-Agonists are used as a short-term treatment of ADHF. In addition to increasing myocardial contractility and SVR, dopamine dilates the renal blood vessels and enhances urine output. Unlike dopamine, dobutamine is a selective β-agonist that works mainly on the β₁-receptors in the heart and does not increase SVR. Effectiveness of inotropes is evaluated by assessing for improved CO, BP, urine output, and reduced filling pressures.

 DRUG ALERT Dopamine

- Monitor IV site. Tissue necrosis and sloughing can occur with drug extravasation.
- High doses may produce ventricular dysrhythmias.

Milrinone has both inotropic and vasodilator properties. Milrinone improves myocardial contractility, increases CO, and reduces BP (decreases afterload). Like dopamine and dobutamine, this drug is available only for IV use. Adverse effects include dysrhythmias, thrombocytopenia, and hepatotoxicity.

Digitalis is a weaker positive inotrope that can be added if symptoms persist after other medications have been started. Digoxin can mildly increase contractility but also increases myocardial O_2 consumption. It can optimize heart rate, especially in those with atrial fibrillation. We monitor digoxin levels and make dose adjustments based on renal function. Serum potassium and magnesium levels must be maintained.

Current evidence recommends the use of inotropic therapy only for the short-term management of patients with ADHF who have not responded to conventional drug therapy (e.g., diuretics, vasodilators, morphine).[1] Continuous cardiac monitoring is necessary with all positive inotropic drugs as they can cause life-threatening dysrhythmias.

! **SAFETY ALERT** Infusion Pumps

- To control the rate and assist with titration, use an infusion pump whenever you are giving IV vasodilators and inotropes.
- Ideally, pumps that have drug libraries can help to avoid rates and dosages that are out of the safe range for the drug.

Interprofessional Care: Chronic Heart Failure

The evolution of evidence-based medication and device therapies over the last few decades has dramatically improved the potential for better patient outcomes with chronic HF. The Heart Failure Society of America (HFSA) and the AHA have regularly published and updated guidelines on therapies for HF. Specialized inpatient, transitional, and ambulatory HF units have emerged. These units are staffed with interprofessional HF teams (Table 34.6).

Chronic HF therapies are tailored to the individual patient based on co-morbid conditions. The goals of chronic HF therapies include (1) optimal symptom management, (2) mortality and morbidity benefit, (3) minimizing side effects, and (4) monitoring responses to therapies. Specifically, these therapies treat the underlying cause and contributing factors, maximize CO, improve ventricular function, improve quality of life (QOL), and preserve target organ function.

In a person with HF, the blood may not be adequately oxygenated, resulting in reduced O_2 saturation. The use of supplemental O_2 improves saturation and helps meet tissue O_2 needs. This helps to relieve patient dyspnea and fatigue. Ongoing pulse oximetry monitors the need for and effectiveness of O_2 therapy.

Physical and emotional rest allows the patient to conserve energy and decreases the need for more O_2. The degree of rest recommended depends on the severity of HF. A patient with severe HF may be on bed rest. A patient with mild to moderate HF can be ambulatory with restricted activity. Urge the patient to take part in prescribed activities, allowing for adequate recovery periods. A structured exercise program, such as cardiac rehabilitation, should be considered for all patients with chronic HF. These programs are associated with decreased hospitalizations, reduced mortality, improved QOL, and less depression.[1,14]

Drug Therapy. The cornerstone of drug therapy in chronic HF is neurohormonal blockade. The result of neurohormonal blockade is decreased plasma aldosterone levels, decreased SNS activity, vasodilation, and sodium and water excretion. Each class of evidence-based medications has been shown to decrease mortality and morbidity in patients with chronic HFrEF. Recommendations for HFpEF primarily address symptoms and co-morbid conditions. Drug therapy for chronic HF is outlined in Table 34.7.

Evidenced-Based Medications for HFrEF

ACE inhibitors. ACE inhibitors are first-line drugs for chronic HFrEF. They decrease mortality, morbidity, hospitalizations, and symptoms in patients with HFrEF.[1] ACE inhibitors block the RAAS by inhibiting the conversion of angiotensin I to angiotensin II. They reduce afterload and SVR and inhibit the development of ventricular remodeling by inhibiting ventricular hypertrophy.

Major side effects include symptomatic hypotension, intractable cough, hyperkalemia, angioedema (allergic reaction involving edema of the face and airways), and renal insufficiency (when used in high doses). Aging and renal insufficiency slow the metabolism of ACE inhibitors and may lead to increased serum drug levels. We monitor renal function and serum potassium levels. Examples of ACE inhibitors are listed in Table 34.7. More information about ACE inhibitors is found in Chapter 32.

 DRUG ALERT Captopril

- Severe hypotension and hyperkalemia may occur.
- Monitor patient for first-dose hypotension (first-dose syncope).
- Skipping doses or discontinuing the drug can result in rebound HTN.
- Angioedema, a rare adverse effect, can develop suddenly and be life-threatening.

Angiotensin II receptor blockers. For patients who are unable to tolerate ACE inhibitors, angiotensin II receptor blockers (ARBs) (see Table 32.6) are recommended.[1] They prevent the vasoconstrictor and aldosterone-secreting effects of angiotensin II by binding to the angiotensin II receptor sites. ARBs promote afterload reduction and vasodilation. The side effects are similar to those of ACE inhibitors except that ARBs do not typically cause a cough. Angioedema is less common. Monitoring is similar to that for ACE inhibitors.

Neprilysin-angiotensin receptor inhibitors. Sacubitril/valsartan (Entresto) is a combination of a neprilysin inhibitor (sacubitril) and an ARB (valsartan). This drug provides dual blockade of the RAAS and the natriuretic peptide system. Sacubitril, a recombinant form of BNP, inhibits neprilysin, an enzyme that degrades natriuretic peptides. Sacubitril inhibition allows for more available circulating BNP. This results in decreased SVR, afterload, and CVP and increased natriuresis and diuresis. This drug is an alternative to ACE inhibitors and ARBs in patients meeting criteria with symptomatic HFrEF and reduces death and hospitalization. Patients are monitored for hypotension, renal insufficiency, and angioedema.[15]

Aldosterone antagonists. Spironolactone (Aldactone) and eplerenone (Inspra) are potassium-sparing diuretics that inhibit aldosterone activation. These drugs work by binding to receptors at the aldosterone-dependent sodium-potassium exchange site in the distal renal tubule, where they have a mild diuretic effect.

They may prolong survival in patients with HFrEF.[1] It is critical to carefully monitor serum potassium levels and renal function in patients taking aldosterone antagonists.

 DRUG ALERT Spironolactone (Aldactone)

- Monitor potassium levels during treatment.
- Use with caution in patients taking digoxin, since hyperkalemia may reduce the effects of digoxin.
- Teach patient to avoid foods high in potassium (e.g., bananas, oranges).
- Assess male patients for gynecomastia, a common side effect of long-term use of spironolactone.

β-adrenergic blockers. β-Blockers directly block the negative effects of the SNS (e.g., increased HR) on the failing heart. Three β-blockers decrease mortality in patients with HFrEF: metoprolol succinate (Toprol XL), bisoprolol (Zebeta), and carvedilol (Coreg). These β-blockers may also increase LVEF. The improvement in LVEF is dose-related, so the highest tolerated dose should be given.[1] However, because β-blockers can reduce myocardial contractility, care must be taken in patients with volume overload. They are usually started at low dose, then the dosage is increased every 2 weeks as tolerated. Major side effects include worsening of HF symptoms, hypotension, fatigue, and bradycardia.

 DRUG ALERT Carvedilol (Coreg)

- Obtain standing BP 1 hr after dosing to assess tolerance.
- Overdose can cause profound bradycardia, hypotension, bronchospasm, and cardiogenic shock.
- Abrupt withdrawal may result in sweating, palpitations, and headaches.

Ivabradine (Corlanor). Ivabradine selectively inhibits a particular sodium/potassium current in the SA node, resulting in a decreased HR. It can decrease hospitalizations in patients with HFrEF who are in sinus rhythm with an HR greater than 70 bpm and have symptoms despite optimal doses of other medications. Monitor patients for bradycardia and lightheadedness.[15]

Hydralazine/isosorbide dinitrate combination (Bidil). This drug is a fixed combination of the vasodilator hydralazine and isosorbide dinitrate. It can significantly reduce mortality and improve LVEF and exercise tolerance by reducing afterload through blood vessel vasodilation. The drug is specifically effective in blacks with HFrEF already receiving optimal doses of other evidence-based medications.[1] Although non-black patients do not see the same benefit, it may be used in any patient with HFrEF already on evidence-based medication. Major side effects include hypotension and headache. Like other nitrates, it should not be used with phosphodiesterase inhibitors, such as sildenafil (Viagra).

Digitalis. Digitalis (digoxin), a weak positive inotrope, acts primarily as a neurohormonal modulator that reduces the effects of the SNS and suppresses renin secretion from the kidneys. Low-dose digitalis decreases HF hospitalizations and symptoms in patients who are still symptomatic despite standard HF therapies.[1,12] No mortality benefit has been found. Better outcomes occur with digoxin serum levels of <0.9 ng/ml. Higher serum doses are associated with increased mortality rate and digoxin toxicity. Dose should be based on body mass, renal function, and concomitant medications. The usual maintenance dose in HF is 0.125 mg daily. Monitor renal function and serum potassium levels of all patients taking digitalis. Concerns about digoxin toxicity are abated by the subtherapeutic dosing in HF.

Medications for Symptom Management

Diuretics. Diuretics reduce symptoms of fluid overload and congestion in both HFrEF and HFpEF. Diuretics reduce edema, pulmonary venous pressure, and preload (see Table 32.7). These drugs act on the kidney by promoting excretion of sodium and water. Loop diuretics (e.g., furosemide (Lasix) and bumetanide [Bumex]) act on the ascending loop of Henle to promote sodium, chloride, and water excretion. Problems in using loop diuretics include low serum potassium levels, ototoxicity, and possible allergic reaction in patients sensitive to sulfa-type drugs. Thiazide diuretics inhibit sodium reabsorption in the distal tubule, promoting excretion of sodium and water. They also can severely lower potassium levels.

In chronic HF, the lowest effective dose of diuretic should be used. Side effects of diuretics include dehydration, hypotension, orthostasis, renal dysfunction, and electrolyte abnormalities. Diuretic resistance can occur in HF patients, necessitating dosing augmentation and the addition of different diuretic classes.

Device Therapy. Patients with HFrEF may benefit from implantable cardiac devices. HF patients must be on appropriate therapies before becoming a candidate for device therapy. Patients with an LVEF < 35% are at significant risk for SCD. An ICD is recommended for primary prevention of SCD in these patients.[1] In patients with a LVEF <35%, neurohormonal effects and cardiac remodeling can result in dyssynchronous contraction of the LV and RV, contributing to poor ventricular filling and reduced CO. CRT is recommended for these patients.[1] With CRT, an extra pacing lead is placed through the coronary sinus to a coronary vein of the LV. This lead coordinates right and left ventricular contractions (Fig. 34.4). Patients with symptomatic HFrEF often need both CRT and an ICD. Combination implantable devices are available. (Pacemakers and defibrillators are discussed in Chapter 35.) Mechanical assist devices available to sustain HF patients with deteriorating function and those awaiting cardiac transplant will be discussed later in the chapter.

❓ CHECK YOUR PRACTICE

Your patient is scheduled for a biventricular pacemaker for her worsening HF. She currently has a demand pacemaker and asks you why she needs this new one.
- How would you respond to her question?

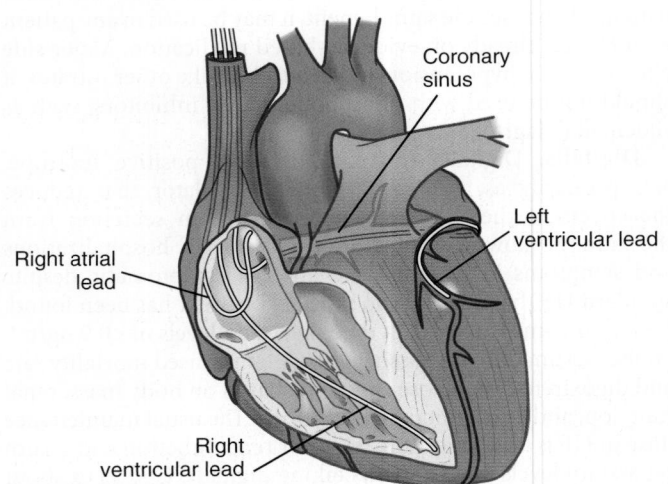

Right atrial lead

Coronary sinus

Left ventricular lead

Right ventricular lead

FIG. 34.4 Placement of pacing leads in cardiac resynchronization therapy.

Remote Monitoring of Physiologic Data

Implanted ICD and CRT devices can be used for remotely monitoring HF patients. Physiologic parameters of worsening HF known to change prior to symptom emergence can predict HF decompensation and help with clinical decision making. Information from these devices can be retrieved electronically via secure websites. Examples of parameters we can remotely follow are BP, weight, HR trends (can evaluate adequacy of beta blockade, increasing HR can indicate worsening HF), HR variability (HRV, a reduction is associated with higher risk for exacerbation and hospitalization), patient activity level, dysrhythmias, and intrathoracic impedance (an indicator of intrathoracic fluid level providing early detection of impending ADHF).[16] Implantable hemodynamic monitoring is also possible. A pulmonary artery sensor can be implanted in the pulmonary artery during a right heart catheterization. It can provide information about HR, systolic, diastolic, and mean pulmonary artery pressure. Detection of early hemodynamic and fluid status changes can allow for proactive management to reduce fluid overload, which decreases hospitalizations in patients with HFrEF. [17]

Nutritional Therapy

Poor adherence to a low-sodium diet and failure to take prescribed medications as directed are the most common reasons for readmissions of HF patients to the hospital. It is critical that you accurately assess a patient's diet and teach both the patient and caregiver about the importance of diet.

Take a detailed diet history. Determine not only what foods the patient eats, but also when, where, and how often the patient dines out. Assess the cultural value of food. Use this information to help the patient in making appropriate dietary choices when developing an individualized and culturally sensitive diet plan. The AHA website has helpful dietary guidelines for HF patients.

HF guidelines vary with regard to sodium restriction in HF management. There is agreement that excess sodium may worsen HF symptoms and facilitate an exacerbation. A low sodium intake may lead to higher adverse event rates in later stages of HFrEF. The degree of sodium restriction depends on the severity of the HF and the effectiveness of diuretic therapy. Generally, sodium intake is restricted to 2 grams per day (Table 34.8). Teach the patient what foods are low and high in sodium content and how to read labels. Review how to find sodium content per serving and the number of servings per package (Fig. 34.5). Teach ways to enhance food flavors without the use of salt (e.g., substituting lemon juice, various spices). Discuss the high sodium content of most restaurant foods.

Fluid restrictions are not often prescribed for the patient with mild to moderate HF. However, fluid restrictions may be needed for stage D HF patients with persistent fluid retention despite appropriate sodium restriction.

To monitor fluid status, tell patients to weigh themselves at the same time each day. To ensure valid trending, this should be before breakfast, using the same scale, and wearing the same type of clothing. For patients with visual limitations, suggest scales with larger numbers or an audible response. Tell patients to call the HCP about a weight gain of 3 lb (1.4 kg) over 2 days or a 3- to 5-lb (2.3-kg) gain over a week.[12]

❖ NURSING MANAGEMENT: HEART FAILURE

◆ Nursing Assessment

Subjective and objective data that you should obtain from a patient with HF are shown in Table 34.9. Carefully review the

TABLE 34.8 Nutritional Therapy

Low-Sodium Diets

General Principles

- Do not add salt or seasonings containing sodium when preparing foods.*
- Do not use salt at the table.*
- 1 tsp of salt equals 2.3 g of sodium.
- Avoid high-sodium foods (e.g., canned soups, processed meats, cheese, frozen meals).
- Limit milk products to 2 cups daily.

Sample Menu Plans for 2400-mg Sodium Diet

Breakfast	Sodium (mg)
⅔ cup bran cereal	161
(⅔ cup Shredded Wheat cereal)†	3
1 slice whole-wheat bread	149
1 medium banana	1
6 oz fruit yogurt, fat free	85
1 cup fat-free milk	126
2 Tbsp jelly	5
Coffee, 8 oz	5

Lunch	
Chicken breast sandwich	
2 slices (3 oz) chicken breast, skinless	65
2 slices whole wheat bread	299
1 slice (¾ oz) American cheese	328
(1 slice [¾ oz] Swiss cheese, natural)†	54
Large-leaf romaine lettuce	1
2 slices tomato	90
1 Tbsp mayonnaise, low fat	90
1 medium peach	7

Dinner	
¾ cup vegetarian spaghetti sauce	459
(6 oz no-salt-added tomato paste)†	260
1 cup spaghetti	1
3 Tbsp parmesan cheese	349
Spinach salad	
1 cup fresh spinach leaves	24
¼ cup fresh carrots (grated)	10
¼ cup fresh mushrooms (sliced)	1
2 Tbsp vinaigrette dressing	0
½ cup canned pears, juice pack	4
½ cup corn, cooked from frozen	4

Snack	
⅓ cup almonds	4
¼ cup dried apricots	3
6 oz fruit yogurt, fat free	85

*1 tsp of salt equals 2.3 g of sodium.
†Substitutes to reduce to 1500-mg sodium diet.

TABLE 34.9 Nursing Assessment

Heart Failure

Subjective Data

Important Health Information

Past health history: CAD (including recent MI), HTN, cardiomyopathy, valvular or congenital heart disease, diabetes, hyperlipidemia, renal disease, thyroid or lung disease, rapid or irregular heart rate
Medications: Use of and adherence with any heart drugs. Use of diuretics, estrogens, corticosteroids, NSAIDs, OTC drugs, herbal supplements

Functional Health Patterns

Health perception–health management: Fatigue, depression, anxiety
Nutritional-metabolic: Usual sodium intake. Nausea, vomiting, anorexia, stomach bloating. Weight gain, ankle swelling
Elimination: Nocturia, decreased daytime urine output, constipation
Activity-exercise: Dyspnea, orthopnea, cough (e.g., dry, productive). Palpitations, dizziness, fainting
Sleep-rest: Number of pillows used for sleeping. Paroxysmal nocturnal dyspnea, insomnia, sleep apnea
Cognitive-perceptual: Chest pain or heaviness. RUQ pain, abdominal discomfort. Behavioral changes, visual changes

Objective Data

Integumentary

Cool, diaphoretic skin. Cyanosis or pallor. Peripheral edema (right-sided HF)

Respiratory

Tachypnea, crackles, wheezes. Frothy, blood-tinged sputum

Cardiovascular

Tachycardia, S_3, S_4, murmurs. Pulsus alternans. PMI displaced inferiorly and posteriorly, lifts and heaves, jugular venous distention

Gastrointestinal

Abdominal distention, hepatosplenomegaly, ascites

Neurologic

Restlessness, confusion, decreased attention or memory

Possible Diagnostic Findings

Altered serum electrolytes (especially Na^+ and K^+), ↑ BUN, creatinine, or liver function tests. ↑ NT-proBNP or BNP. Chest x-ray showing cardiomegaly, pulmonary congestion, and interstitial pulmonary edema. Echocardiogram showing increased chamber size, decreased wall motion, decreased LVEF or normal LVEF with evidence of diastolic dysfunction (abnormal relaxation/filling). Atrial and ventricular enlargement on ECG. ↓ O_2 saturation

---

problems as they may exacerbate HF, affecting the plan of care and the timing and choice of therapies. For example, a patient with sleep apnea may not use a continuous positive airway pressure device at night. This can worsen pulmonary or systemic HTN and lead to an exacerbation of HF.

◆ Nursing Diagnoses

Nursing diagnoses for the patient with HF include:

- Impaired gas exchange
- Impaired cardiac output
- Fluid imbalance
- Activity intolerance

Additional information on nursing diagnoses and interventions for the patient with HF is presented in eNursing Care Plan 34.1 on the website for this chapter.

---

patient's current prescription and over-the-counter (OTC) drugs. Chronic HF patients often take multiple other medications for co-existing conditions and underlying CVD. OTC medications known to pose significant risk to people with HF include nonsteroidal antiinflammatory drugs (NSAIDs), higher-than-prescribed aspirin doses, ephedrine, pseudoephedrine, and diet pills. NSAIDs can contribute to sodium retention and an exacerbation of HF.

Review the patient's dietary habits to identify issues related to an exacerbation of HF. Explore the patient's chronic health

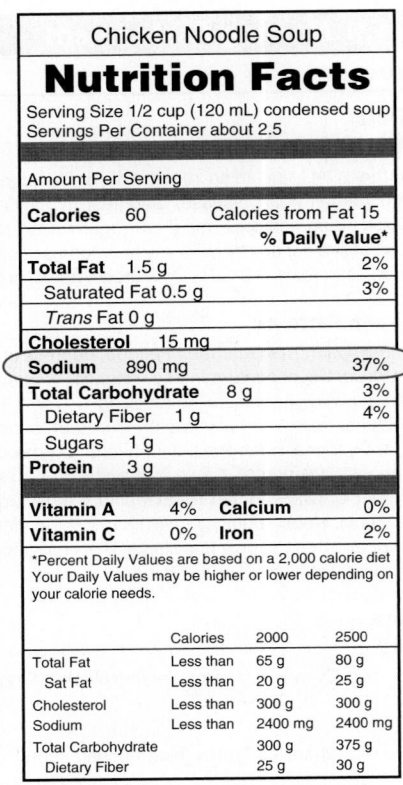

Chicken Noodle Soup		
Nutrition Facts		
Serving Size 1/2 cup (120 mL) condensed soup Servings Per Container about 2.5		
Amount Per Serving		
Calories 60	Calories from Fat 15	
		% Daily Value*
Total Fat 1.5 g		2%
Saturated Fat 0.5 g		3%
Trans Fat 0 g		
Cholesterol 15 mg		
Sodium 890 mg		37%
Total Carbohydrate 8 g		3%
Dietary Fiber 1 g		4%
Sugars 1 g		
Protein 3 g		
Vitamin A 4%	**Calcium**	0%
Vitamin C 0%	**Iron**	2%
*Percent Daily Values are based on a 2,000 calorie diet Your Daily Values may be higher or lower depending on your calorie needs.		

		Calories	2000	2500
Total Fat	Less than		65 g	80 g
Sat Fat	Less than		20 g	25 g
Cholesterol	Less than		300 g	300 g
Sodium	Less than		2400 mg	2400 mg
Total Carbohydrate			300 g	375 g
Dietary Fiber			25 g	30 g

FIG. 34.5 Typical nutrition label. Note that a single serving (½ cup) provides more than one third of the daily recommended intake of sodium.

◆ Planning

Nursing care focuses on the priority problems of decreased CO, impaired oxygenation, fluid overload, intolerance of physical activity and managing a complex medication regimen. The overall goals for the patient with HF include (1) decrease in symptoms (e.g., shortness of breath, fatigue); (2) decrease in peripheral edema; (3) increase in exercise tolerance; (4) adherence with the treatment plan, including appropriate evidence-based medication and device therapies; and (5) no complications related to HF.

◆ Nursing Implementation

Health Promotion. Communication and joint decision making among the patient, caregiver, and interprofessional team are integral to high-quality, patient-centered care. Currently, the emphasis is on aggressively identifying and treating risk factors in the patient with stage A HF to prevent or slow the progression to symptomatic HF.[18] By identifying patients with obesity, metabolic syndrome, diabetes, HTN, and hyperlipidemia as already having stage A HF, goals related to a heart-healthy lifestyle can be given deserved urgency. Recommended lifestyle modifications begin with weight management, diet, and regular exercise. Often, medications are needed. Encourage patients to get influenza and pneumococcal vaccinations. Patients with valvular disease that may be contributing to HF should be evaluated for valve repair or replacement procedures. Coronary revascularization procedures should be considered in patients with CAD. Antidysrhythmic drugs or pacing therapy may be indicated for patients with serious dysrhythmias or conduction disturbances.

◆ Acute Care. Many persons with HF have 1 or more episodes of ADHF. Common precipitating factors to HF hospitalization

include respiratory infections, dysrhythmias, acute coronary syndrome, uncontrolled HTN, and nonadherence to medications and/or diet. Patients with ADHF are usually admitted through the ED, stabilized, then cared for in an ICU, intermediate care unit, or specialized HF unit with continuous ECG monitoring capability.

Successful HF care depends on several important principles: (1) HF is a progressive disease; (2) treatment plans are established with QOL goals; (3) symptom management depends to a significant degree on adherence to self-management protocols (e.g., daily weights, diet, exercise, recognizing signs and symptoms of decompensation); and drug and device therapies; (4) precipitating factors, etiologies, and contributing comorbid conditions must be addressed; (5) complex care needs often require care in multiple settings, increasing risk for fragmented care; and (6) support systems are essential to the success of the entire treatment plan.

◆ Ambulatory Care. Transitional care programs and protocols are designed to ensure coordination and continuity of health care as patients transfer between care settings. Programs that include comprehensive discharge planning, collaboration among providers, and planned, prompt follow-up with HCPs have shown reduced readmission rates.[19]

Goals of ambulatory HF care include symptom management, QOL maintenance, morbidity and mortality benefit from therapy, identifying and mitigating factors precipitating ADHF and hospitalization, and closely monitoring responses to and potential side effects of therapies. HF is a chronic and progressive condition that will require lifelong therapies. It is important to include the patient and caregiver(s) in the overall care plan. Help them develop a clear action plan for response to increased signs and symptoms of impending exacerbation. A patient and caregiver guide for the patient with HF is shown in Table 34.10.

Effective home health (HH) care can prevent future hospitalizations by providing ongoing assessments (e.g., monitoring vital signs and weight, evaluating response to therapies) and followup.[19] HH nurses often use individualized care protocols coordinated with the patient and HCP. The protocols allow the nurse and patient to identify signs and symptoms of worsening HF (e.g., weight gain, increased dyspnea). Many agencies offer specialized HF programs. Telehealth and device remote monitoring technology (e.g., electronic scale, BP cuff, pulse oximeter) can collect physiologic and symptom data (Fig. 34.6).[15,16] Results can be sent to the HCP via telephone or secure website. In response to collected data, therapeutic interventions, such as a temporary increase in diuretic therapy, can be implemented to improve functional capacity and prevent rehospitalization.

Teach the patient the basic mechanism of action of medications and signs of drug toxicity in easily understood terms. Effective self-care includes proper technique in taking a pulse (for a full minute) and use of home BP monitor and device remote monitoring equipment. The patient should understand specific HCP instructions on when to hold heart rate–lowering medications, such as β-blockers and digoxin. If patients are taking diuretic and/or potassium supplement medications, teach them the signs and symptoms of hypokalemia and hyperkalemia, including weakness, fatigue, constipation, and muscle cramping.

Exercise training (e.g., CR) can improve symptoms of chronic HF. Exercise for patients with HF has been found to be safe and to improve overall sense of well-being. It has been associated

TABLE 34.10 Patient & Caregiver Teaching

Heart Failure

Include the following instructions when teaching the patient and caregiver about the management of heart failure:

Dietary Therapy
- Consult the diet plan and list of permitted and restricted foods.
- Adhere to specific sodium restriction guidelines outlined by your HCP.
- Examine labels to determine sodium content. Also examine the labels of over-the-counter drugs, such as laxatives, cough medicines, and antacids for sodium content.
- Avoid using salt when preparing foods or adding salt to foods.
- Weigh yourself at the same time each day, preferably in the morning, using the same scale and wearing similar clothes.
- Eat small, frequent meals.

Activity Program
- Increase walking and other activities gradually, provided they do not cause fatigue or dyspnea.
- Consider a cardiac rehabilitation program.
- Avoid extremes of heat and cold.

Ongoing Monitoring
- Know the signs and symptoms of worsening HF, including increasing dyspnea, cough, orthopnea, PND, weight gain, edema, fluid retention, fatigue, and tiredness with physical activity.
- Recall the symptoms when illness began. Reappearance of previous symptoms may indicate a recurrence.
- Report at once any of the following to the HCP:
  - Weight gain of 3 lb (1.4 kg) in 2 days, or 3–5 lb (2.3 kg) in a week
  - Difficulty breathing, especially with activity or when lying flat
  - Waking up breathless at night
  - Frequent dry, hacking cough, especially when lying down
  - Fatigue, weakness
  - Swelling of ankles, feet, or abdomen. Swelling of face or difficulty breathing (if taking ACE inhibitors)
  - Nausea with abdominal swelling, pain, and tenderness
  - Dizziness or fainting

- Follow up with HCP on regular basis.
- Consider joining a local support group with your family members and/or caregiver(s).

Health Promotion
- Obtain annual influenza vaccination.
- Obtain pneumococcal vaccine (see Table 27.5 for guidelines on pneumococcal vaccination).
- Develop plan to reduce risk factors (e.g., BP control, tobacco cessation, blood glucose/Hb A1C control, weight reduction).

Rest
- Plan a regular daily rest and activity program.
- After exertion, such as exercise and ADLs, plan a rest period.
- Consider shorter working hours or schedule rest period during working hours.
- Avoid emotional upsets. Share any concerns, fears, feelings of depression, etc. with HCP.

Drug Therapy
- Take each drug as prescribed.
- Develop a system (e.g., daily chart, weekly pillbox) to ensure drugs are taken.
- Count pulse rate each day before taking drugs (if appropriate). Know the limits that your HCP wants for your pulse rate.
- Take BP at determined intervals (if appropriate). Know your target BP limits.
- Know signs and symptoms of orthostatic hypotension and how to prevent them (see Table 32.12).
- If taking anticoagulants, know signs and symptoms of internal bleeding (bleeding gums, increased bruises, blood in stool or urine) and what to do.
- Know your INR and target range if taking warfarin (Coumadin) and how often to have blood checked.

ACE, Angiotensin-converting enzyme; *INR,* international normalized ratio.

FIG. 34.6 Home-based telehealth monitoring unit. (Used with permission from Honeywell HomMed.)

with reduced mortality.[1,14] Tailor exercise programs based on what the patient most enjoys doing. Teach the patient about the importance of rest periods, especially after exertion, and energy-conserving behaviors. Changes may be needed if environmental conditions involve an increased cardiac workload (e.g., frequent climbing of stairs). Consultation with a physical therapist or occupational therapist may be appropriate.

Mechanical Circulatory Support Devices in End-Stage Heart Failure. Therapeutic options for stage D HF patients include: (1) chronic inotropic therapy, (2) mechanical circulatory support (MCS) devices, (3) palliative care and hospice that may or may not include ICD deactivation, and (4) heart transplant. MCS devices can be beneficial to carefully selected patients for short-term management, long-term and bridge-to-transplant management, or as destination therapy.[12] Patients who are ineligible for heart transplant may be candidates for lifelong MCS. Short-term MCS include IABP, extracorporeal membrane oxygenation (ECMO), and various continual flow pumps. The limitations of bed rest and the risk for infection and vascular complications prevent long-term use of these devices.

Long-term MCS devices include LV assist devices (VADs), including percutaneous devices (PVAD) and transplanted devices (LAVDs, BiVADs) (see Chapter 65). VADs provide highly effective long-term support and have become standard care in many heart transplant centers. The heart pump runs via a driveline that exits the abdominal wall and attaches to a system controller with patient specific settings. VADs operate on AC current or batteries (Fig. 34.7). Morbidity and mortality is significantly reduced if MCS is started before onset of severe right HF and systemic organ failure.[12]

FIG. 34.7 Left ventricular assist device. (Reprinted with the permission of Thoratec Corp.)

TABLE 34.11 Common Indications and Contraindications for Heart Transplantation

Indications
- End-stage HF refractory to medical care
- Severe, decompensated, inoperable, valvular heart disease
- Recurrent life-threatening dysrhythmias not responsive to maximal interventions, including defibrillators
- Any other heart abnormalities that severely limit normal function and/ or have a mortality risk of more than 50% within 2 years

Absolute Contraindications
- Chronologic age over 70 years or physiologic age over 65 years
- Life-threatening illness (e.g., cancer) that will limit survival to <5 years despite therapy
- Advanced cerebral or peripheral vascular disease not amenable to correction
- Active infection, including HIV infection
- Severe pulmonary disease that will likely result in the patient being ventilator-dependent after transplant

Relative Contraindications
- Severe obesity
- Psychologic impairment
- Active substance use (e.g., alcohol, drugs, tobacco)
- Uncontrolled diabetes with vascular and neurologic complications
- Irreversible liver or kidney dysfunction not explained by HF
- Evidence of noncompliance with accepted medical practices
- Lack of social support network that can make long-term commitment for patient's welfare
- Unrealistic expectations by the patient or caregiver about transplant, its risks, and its benefits

◆ **Palliative and End-of-Life Care.** HF mortality rates are still high. One in 5 persons with HF die within a year of diagnosis. The estimated 5-year survival rate is worse than for most types of cancer. Repeated hospitalizations and ED visits for ADHF can be predictive of end-stage HF.[1,15,19]

The ACCF and AHA provide guidelines for patients with end-stage HF (stage D).[1] End-of-life discussions and management are emphasized, including advanced directives and information about advanced HF therapies (e.g., VADs, heart transplants), palliative care, and hospice.

Palliative care may be appropriate earlier in the course of the illness in conjunction with other therapies intended to prolong life. Palliative nursing care of the HF patient emphasizes (1) unifying the patient, family, and health care team in formulating a plan of care; (2) aggressive symptom management; (3) avoiding therapies that are no longer appropriate or effective and may prolong suffering; (4) integrating emotional and spiritual support for patient and family; and (5) determining when a patient may be ready to consider hospice care.

Patients with advanced CVD are eligible for hospice when (1) an HCP certifies that a life expectancy of 6 months or less is expected assuming the disease takes its normal course, (2) the patient has received optimal medical treatment and is not a candidate for further invasive procedures, and (3) the patient is assessed at NYHA Class IV. End-stage HF patients who meet hospice criteria are often referred late or not at all. Challenges in referring these patients to hospice include (1) difficulties with accurate life expectancy prediction, (2) reluctance to accept a DNR order due to multiple resuscitation survivals and implantable devices, and (3) a lack of patient and family understanding as to the chronic and terminal nature of HF.[20,21]

End-of-life nursing care of HF patients includes ongoing assessment and evaluation of interventions for effectiveness. Strategies include patient and caregiver support, drug therapies, and nondrug therapies. Palliative and end-of-life care are discussed in Chapter 9.

◆ **Evaluation**

The expected outcomes are that the patient with HF will
- Maintain adequate O_2/CO_2 exchange at the alveolar-capillary membrane to meet O_2 needs of the body
- Maintain adequate blood pumped by the heart to meet metabolic demands of the body
- Reduction or absence of edema and stable baseline weight
- Achieve a realistic program of activity that balances physical activity with energy-conserving activities

HEART TRANSPLANTATION

Heart transplantation is the transfer of a healthy donor heart to a patient with a diseased heart. It is done to treat a variety of terminal or end-stage heart conditions (Table 34.11). In the United States, about 3000 patients are awaiting heart transplants. However, an average of only 2000 hearts become available. The 1-year transplant survival rate is 85% to 90%, while the 3-year survival rate is about 75%.[22,23] A heart transplant is a gold standard therapy for some patients in end-stage HF.

Criteria for Selection

A careful selection process ensures that hearts are distributed fairly and to those who will benefit most from the donor heart. The United Network for Organ Sharing (UNOS) oversees a system to allocate donor organs. UNOS and transplantation are discussed in Chapter 13.

Indications and contraindications for a heart transplant are outlined in Table 34.11. Once a person meets the criteria for a transplant, an exhaustive physical examination and diagnostic workup are done. Heart function, vascular and immune systems are assessed. The patient and caregiver undergo a comprehensive psychologic evaluation that assesses coping skills, support systems, and commitment to follow a rigorous life-long regimen. The complexity of the transplant process may be overwhelming to a patient without an adequate support system and understanding of the needed lifestyle changes.

Donor and recipient matching is based on body and heart size and an immunologic assessment. That assessment includes ABO blood type, antibody screen, panel of reactive antibody (PRA) level, and human leukocyte antigen typing.

ETHICAL/LEGAL DILEMMAS
Competence

Situation

M.T., a 60-yr-old man, has been awaiting heart transplantation for 6 months. He has been in the ICU for 1 month since he needed a VAD for his failing heart. He recently had a stroke, which is a complication of the device. It left him paralyzed on his right side. He is only able to answer yes/no questions by shaking his head. He has needed mechanical ventilation since his stroke. For the past 2 weeks, he has needed hemodialysis because of renal failure. Recently, when you suction him, he turns his head away from you and bites down on the endotracheal tube. Although he does not have an advance directive, his wife and daughter tell you that, on many occasions before these events, he expressed that he would not want to live if he lost his independence. His wife and daughter request to have the mechanical ventilator withdrawn.

Ethical/Legal Points for Consideration

- Decisional capacity for informed consent related to treatment decisions involves 4 elements: (1) information provided about possible treatment options must be understood by patients, (2) patients must have the capacity to deliberate about the treatment choices and their consequences, (3) patients' treatment decisions must be freely chosen and made without coercion, and (4) patients must be able to communicate their decisions.
- Legal competence, as determined by the courts, has a low threshold. The ability to respond to questions by signaling a yes or no may be enough to prove understanding of the questions, ability to discriminate between choices, and ability to communicate choices, providing that the answers make sense and are appropriate. Review how your state defines legal competence.
- Next of kin are the legal decision makers in the absence of advance directives if the patient is unable to make decisions for himself. Decisional capacity should be tested without assuming it is absent.
- Some courts have accepted past assertions of preferences, past behavior, and assertions of their parties as evidence to support end-of-life preferences in the absence of advance directives.
- Know your agency's policies and the local jurisdiction's laws and regulations about informed consent and end-of-life decision making.

Discussion Questions

1. What would you do next given M.T.'s behavior and the information you obtained from his wife?
2. What are your feelings and concerns about caring for a patient for whom withdrawal of treatment will result in death?

A person accepted as a transplant candidate is placed on a transplant list. This may happen quickly during an acute illness or after a longer period. Stable patients may wait at home and receive ongoing medical care. If unstable, a patient may be hospitalized for more intensive therapy. Unfortunately, the overall waiting period for a new heart is long. Many patients die while waiting for a transplant.

Surgical Procedure

The transplant donor is someone who has irreversible brain injury. A surgical team goes to the hospital of the donor to remove donated organs after the declaration of brain death. The retrieved organs are transported on ice until they can be implanted. For the heart, this is optimally less than 4 hours. Often the donor heart is flown to the recipient's hospital. The donor heart is then implanted into the recipient using 1 of 2 approaches. In the biatrial approach, the recipient's damaged heart is removed at the midatrial level and the donor heart connected at the LA, pulmonary artery, aorta, and RA. In the bicaval approach, the RA of the recipient's heart (with the SA node and atrial conduction intact) is preserved and then the donor heart is connected. Cardiopulmonary bypass is needed during the surgical procedure to maintain oxygenation and perfusion to vital organs.

Posttransplantation

After cardiac transplant, a variety of complications can occur, including a risk for SCD. Acute rejection is an immediate posttransplant complication, and immunosuppressive therapy is the key in posttransplant management. In the first year after transplantation, the major causes of death are infection and acute rejection.

Most immunosuppressive regimens include corticosteroids, calcineurin inhibitors (tacrolimus); and antiproliferative drugs (mycophenolate mofetil). The mechanisms of action and side effects of these and other immunosuppressants are discussed in Chapter 13 and Table 13.17. Because of the use of immunosuppressive therapy, infection is a primary concern after transplant surgery. On a long-term basis, immunosuppressive therapy increases the risk for cancers, especially lymphomas, and cardiac vasculopathy (accelerated CAD).[23]

To detect rejection, an endomyocardial biopsy is done on a weekly basis for the first month, monthly for the next 6 months, and yearly thereafter. In this procedure, the HCP inserts a catheter into the jugular vein and moves it into the RV. The catheter uses a bioptome, a device with 2 small cups that can be closed, to remove small samples of heart muscle for analysis.[23]

Nursing management throughout the posttransplant period focuses on promoting patient adaptation to the transplant process, monitoring heart function, managing lifestyle changes, and providing ongoing teaching of the patient and caregiver.

CASE STUDY

Heart Failure

(© iStockphoto/ Thinkstock.)

Patient Profile

J.E. is a 70-yr-old Hispanic woman who was admitted to the intermediate care unit with a report of increasing shortness of breath, fatigue, and weight gain.

Subjective Data

- History of HTN for 20 yrs
- History of MI at 58 yrs of age
- Has increasing shortness of breath, fatigue, and an unexplained 11-lb weight gain during the past 2 wks
- Had a respiratory tract infection 2 wks ago; has persistent cough and edema in legs
- Cannot climb a flight of stairs without getting short of breath
- Sleeps with head elevated on 3 pillows
- Lives alone, does not always remember to take medication

Objective Data

Physical Examination

- Moderate respiratory distress, use of accessory muscles, respiratory rate 36 breaths/min
- Systolic heart murmur
- Bilateral crackles in all lung fields
- Cyanotic lips and extremities
- Skin cool and diaphoretic

Diagnostic Studies

- Chest x-ray results: cardiomegaly with right and left ventricular hypertrophy; fluid in lower lung fields
- Echocardiogram results: ejection fraction 20%

Interprofessional Care

- Furosemide (Lasix) 40 mg IV twice daily
- Potassium 40 mEq PO twice daily
- Enalapril (Vasotec) 5 mg/day PO
- Nesiritide (Natrecor) 2 mcg/kg IV bolus followed by a continuous infusion of 0.01 mcg/kg/min
- Continuous ECG monitoring
- Diet: 2-gram sodium diet
- Titrate O_2 to keep O_2 saturation >93%
- Monitor intake and output, and daily weights
- Serum electrolytes; cardiac biomarkers q8hr × 3

Discussion Questions

1. Explain the pathophysiology of J.E.'s heart disease and symptoms.
2. What clinical manifestations of ADHF did J.E. exhibit?
3. What is the significance of the findings of the diagnostic studies?
4. How would a serum NT-proBNP be beneficial in the diagnosis of ADHF?
5. Provide the rationale for each of the HCP's orders prescribed for J.E.
6. **Priority Decision:** Based on the assessment data presented, what are the priority nursing diagnoses? Identify any collaborative problems.
7. **Priority Decision:** What are your priority nursing interventions for J.E.?
8. **Collaboration:** Which interventions could be delegated to UAP or other members of the interprofessional team?
9. **Patient-Centered Care:** What priority patient teaching measures should be instituted to prevent recurrence of ADHF and prepare J.E. for discharge?
10. **Evidence-Based Practice:** J.E. asks you why it is so important to "watch her salt." She tells you that food tastes better with salt. How would you respond to her?
11. Develop a conceptual care map for J.E.

Answers and a corresponding concept map available at *http://evolve.elsevier.com/Lewis/medsurg.*

BRIDGE TO NCLEX EXAMINATION

The number of the question corresponds to the same-numbered outcome at the beginning of the chapter.

1. Which statements accurately describe heart failure with preserved ejection fraction (HFpEF)? *(select all that apply)*
   a. Uncontrolled hypertension is the primary cause.
   b. Left ventricular ejection fraction may be within normal limits.
   c. The pathophysiology involves ventricular relaxation and filling.
   d. Multiple evidence-based therapies have been shown to decrease mortality.
   e. Therapies focus on symptom control and treatment of underlying conditions.

2. What compensatory mechanism involved in both chronic heart failure and acute decompensated heart failure leads to fluid retention and edema?
   a. Ventricular dilation
   b. Ventricular hypertrophy
   c. Increased systemic blood pressure
   d. Renin-angiotensin-aldosterone activation

3. The nurse is caring for a patient with acute decompensated heart failure who is receiving IV dobutamine. Why would this drug be prescribed? *(select all that apply)*
   a. It dilates renal blood vessels.
   b. It will increase the heart rate.
   c. Heart contractility will improve.
   d. Dobutamine is a selective β-agonist.
   e. It increases systemic vascular resistance.

4. A patient with chronic heart failure and atrial fibrillation is treated with low-dose digitalis and a loop diuretic. What does the nurse need to do to prevent complications of this drug combination? *(select all that apply)*
   a. Monitor serum potassium levels.
   b. Teach the patient how to take a pulse rate.
   c. Withhold digitalis if pulse rhythm is irregular.
   d. Keep an accurate measure of intake and output.
   e. Teach the patient about dietary potassium restrictions.

5. A barrier to hospice referrals for patients with stage D heart failure is
   a. family member refusal.
   b. scarcity of hospice facilities.
   c. history of pacemaker placement.
   d. difficulty in estimating prognosis.

6. Patients are at risk for which complications in the first year after heart transplantation? *(select all that apply)*
   a. Cancer
   b. Infection
   c. Rejection
   d. Vasculopathy
   e. Sudden cardiac death

1. a, b, c, e; 2. d; 3. c, d; 4. a, b; 5. d; 6. b, c, e

For rationales to these answers and even more NCLEX review questions, visit *http://evolve.elsevier.com/Lewis/medsurg.*

EVOLVE WEBSITE/RESOURCES LIST

REFERENCES

*1. Yancy CW, Jessup M, Bozkurt B, et al: 2013 ACCF/AHA guideline for the management of heart failure: executive summary: a report of the American College of Cardiology Foundation/AHA Task Force on Practice Guidelines, *Circulation* 128:1810, 2013. (Classic)

2. Benjamin EJ, Blaha MJ, Chieve SE, et al: Heart disease and stroke statistics—2017 update: A report from the AHA, *Circulation* 135:e146, 2017.

3. Reddy Y, Lewis G, Shoh S, et al: Heart failure pathophysiology, *Circ Heart Fail* 10:e003862, 2017.

*4. Pandey A, Omar W, Ayers ML, et al: Sex and race differences in lifetime risk of heart failure with preserved ejection fraction and heart failure with reduced ejection fraction, *Circulation* 137:117, 2018.

*5. Tayal U, Prasad S, Cook SA: Genetics and genomics of dilated cardiomyopathy and systolic heart failure, *Gen Med* 9:20, 2017.

*6. Redfield MM: Heart failure with preserved ejection fraction, *New Engl J Med* 375:1868, 2016.

*7. Lueder T, Kotecha D, Ator D, et al: Neurohormonal blockade in heart failure, *Card Fail Rev* 3:19, 2017.

*8. Hartupee J, Mann DL: Neurohormonal activation in heart failure with reduced ejection fraction, *Natl Rev Cardiol* 14:30, 2017.

*9. Zhang Y, Bauersachs J, Langer H: Immune mechanisms in heart failure, *Eur J Heart Fail* 19:1379, 2017.

*10. Chirinos J, Akers S, Trieu L, et al: Heart failure, left ventricular remodeling and circulating nitric oxide metabolism, *J AM Heart Assoc* 5:3004133, 2016.

*11. Silver MA, Maisal A, Yancy CW, et al: BNP Consensus Panel 2004: A clinical approach for the diagnostic, prognostic, screening, treatment monitoring, and therapeutic roles of natriuretic peptides in cardiovascular diseases, *Conges Heart Fail* 10:1, 2004. (Classic)

*12. Lindenfeld J, Albert N, Boehmer JP, et al: HFSA 2010 comprehensive heart failure practice guidelines, *J Card Fail* 16:e1, 2010. (Classic)

*13. Gathright EC, Goldstein CM, Josephson RA, et al: Depression increases the risk of mortality in patients with heart failure: A meta-analysis, *J Psychosom Res* 94:82, 2017.

14. Volterrani M, Iellamo F: Cardiac rehabilitation in patients with heart failure: New perspectives in exercise training, *Card Fail Rev* 2:63, 2016.

*15. Yancy CW, Jessup M, Bozkurt B, et al: 2017 ACC/AHA/HFSA focused update of the 2013 ACCF/AHA guidelines for the management of heart failure: A report of the ACC/AHA Task Force on Clinical Practice Guidelines, *Circ* 136:e137, 2017.

16. Abraham W, Perl L: Implantable hemodynamic monitoring for heart failure patients, *J Am Col Card* 70:389, 2017.

*17. Abraham WT, Adamson PB, Bourge RC, et al: Wireless pulmonary artery hemodynamic monitoring in chronic heart failure: A randomized controlled trial, *Lancet* 377:658, 2011. (Classic)

18. Schocken DD, Benjamin EJ, Fonarow G, et al: Prevention of heart failure: A scientific statement from the AHA Councils on Epidemiology and Prevention, Clinical Cardiology, Cardiovascular Nursing, and High Blood Pressure Research, *Circulation* 117:2544, 2008. (Classic)

*19. Desai AS: Intensive management to reduce hospitalizations in patients with heart failure, *Circulation* 133:1704, 2016.

20. Kavalieratos D, Gelfman L, Tycon L, et al: Palliative care in heart failure: Rationale, evidence, and future priorities, *J Am Col Card* 70:1919, 2017.

*21. Hamel A, Gaugler J, Porta C, et al: Complex decision making in heart failure: a systematic review and thematic analysis, *J Card Nurs* 33:225, 2017.

22. Stehlik J, Edwards LB, Kucheryavaya AY, et al.: The registry of the International Society of Heart and Lung Transplantation: Twenty Eighth Adult Heart Transplant Report—2011, *J Heart Lung Tran* 30:1078, 2011. (Classic)

*23. Wilhelm M: Long term outcomes following heart transplantation: A current perspective, *J Thorac Dis* 7:549, 2015. (Classic)

*Evidence-based information for clinical practice.

35

Dysrhythmias

Kimberly Day

*All I ever wanted was to reach out and touch another
human being not just with my hands but with my heart.*

Tahereh Mafi

e http://evolve.elsevier.com/Lewis/medsurg

CONCEPTUAL FOCUS

Fluids and Electrolytes   Perfusion

LEARNING OUTCOMES

1. Examine the nursing care of patients needing continuous electrocardiographic (ECG) monitoring.
2. Distinguish the clinical characteristics and ECG patterns of normal sinus rhythm, common dysrhythmias, and pacemaker rhythms.
3. Describe the nursing and interprofessional management of patients with common dysrhythmias.
4. Compare and contrast defibrillation and cardioversion, including indications for use and physiologic effects.
5. Describe the nursing and interprofessional management of patients with pacemakers and implantable cardioverter-defibrillators.
6. Select appropriate interventions for patients undergoing electrophysiologic testing and radiofrequency catheter ablation therapy.

KEY TERMS

asystole, p. 768
atrial fibrillation, p. 763
atrial flutter, p. 763
automatic external defibrillator (AED), p. 769

cardiac pacemaker, p. 771
complete heart block, p. 766
dysrhythmias, p. 754
premature atrial contraction (PAC), p. 762

premature ventricular contraction (PVC), p. 766
telemetry monitoring, p. 757
ventricular fibrillation (VF), p. 768
ventricular tachycardia (VT), p. 767

This chapter describes basic principles of electrocardiographic monitoring and the recognition and treatment of common dysrhythmias. Adequate perfusion requires the heart to generate sufficient cardiac output (CO) to distribute blood to the body tissues. Abnormal heart rhythms, called dysrhythmias, can directly decrease CO by changing stroke volume and heart rate (HR). For example, tachycardia from a fever may decrease CO and cause hypotension. Your ability to recognize normal heart rhythms and dysrhythmias is an essential nursing skill.[1] Prompt recognition of a dysrhythmia and assessment of the patient's response to the rhythm is critical to maintaining adequate perfusion.

RHYTHM IDENTIFICATION AND TREATMENT

Conduction System

Four properties of heart cells allow the conduction system to start an electrical impulse, send it through the heart tissue, and stimulate muscle contraction (Table 35.1). The heart's conduction system consists of specialized neuromuscular tissue found throughout the heart (see Fig. 31.4, *A*). A normal impulse starts in the sinoatrial (SA) node in the upper right atrium near the entrance of the vena cava. It spreads over the atrial myocardium

via interatrial and internodal pathways, causing atrial contraction. The impulse then travels to the atrioventricular (AV) node, through the bundle of His, and down the left and right bundle branches to the Purkinje fibers, which transmit the impulse to the ventricles.

Nervous Control of the Heart

The autonomic nervous system plays a vital role in the rate of impulse formation, speed of conduction, and strength of cardiac contraction. The parts of the autonomic nervous system that affect the heart are the vagus nerve fibers of the parasympathetic nervous system and the nerve fibers of the sympathetic nervous system.

Stimulation of the vagus nerve slows firing of the SA node and slows impulse conduction of the AV node. This decreases heart rate. Stimulation of the sympathetic nerves increases SA node firing, AV node impulse conduction, and cardiac contractility. This increases heart rate.[2,3]

Electrocardiographic Monitoring

The *electrocardiogram* (ECG) is a graphic tracing of the electrical impulses produced in the heart. The waveforms on the ECG represent the electrical activity of depolarization and

TABLE 35.1 Properties of Heart Cells

Property	Definition
Automaticity	Ability to initiate an impulse spontaneously and continuously
Excitability	Ability to be electrically stimulated
Conductivity	Ability to transmit an impulse along a membrane in an orderly manner
Contractility	Ability to respond mechanically to an impulse

FIG. 35.1 Phases of the cardiac action potential. The electrical potential, measured in millivolts (mV), is indicated along the vertical axis of the graph. Time, measured in seconds (sec), is indicated along the horizontal axis. The action potential has 5 phases, labeled *0* through *4*. Each phase represents a specific electrical event or combination of electrical events. Phase 0 is the upstroke of rapid depolarization and corresponds with ventricular contraction. Phases 1, 2, and 3 represent repolarization. Phase 4 is known as complete repolarization (or the polarized state) and corresponds to diastole. *RP,* Resting membrane potential; *TP,* threshold membrane potential.

repolarization produced by the movement of ions across the membranes of heart cells (see Fig. 31.4, *B*).

The membrane of a heart cell is semipermeable. This allows it to maintain a high concentration of potassium and a low concentration of sodium inside the cell. Outside the cell, a high concentration of sodium and a low concentration of potassium exist. The inside of the cell, when at rest or in the polarized state, is negative compared with the outside. When a cell or groups of cells are stimulated, the cell membrane changes its permeability. This allows sodium to move rapidly into the cell, making the inside of the cell positive compared with the outside *(depolarization)*. A slower movement of ions across the membrane restores the cell to the polarized state, called *repolarization*. Fig. 35.1 describes the phases of the cardiac action potential.[1,2]

A 12-lead ECG view of the heart is helpful in assessing dysrhythmias. Six of the leads measure electrical forces in the frontal plane. These are bipolar (positive and negative) leads I, II, and III and unipolar (positive) leads aVR, aVL, and aVF (Fig. 35.2, *A* and *B*). The remaining 6 unipolar leads (V_1 through V_6) measure the electrical forces in the horizontal plane (precordial leads) (Fig. 35.2, *C*). The 12-lead ECG may show changes suggesting structural changes, conduction changes, damage (e.g., ischemia, infarction), electrolyte imbalance, or drug toxicity. Fig. 35.3 is an example of a normal 12-lead ECG.

We can use one or more ECG leads to continuously monitor a patient. The most common leads used are leads II and V_1 (Fig. 35.4). A modified chest lead (MCL_1) is used when only 3 leads are available for monitoring. MCL_1 is similar to V_1. Accurate interpretation of an ECG depends on the correct placement of the leads on the patient. The monitoring leads used are determined by the patient's clinical status.[4,5]

The ECG monitor continuously displays the heart rhythm. Paper attached to the monitor records the ECG (i.e., rhythm strip) to provide a record of the patient's rhythm. It allows for measurement of complexes and intervals and for assessment of dysrhythmias.

To correctly interpret an ECG, measure time and voltage on the ECG paper. ECG paper consists of large (heavy lines) and small (light lines) squares (Fig. 35.5). Each large square consists of 25 smaller squares (5 horizontal and 5 vertical). Horizontally, each small square (1 mm) represents 0.04 second. This means

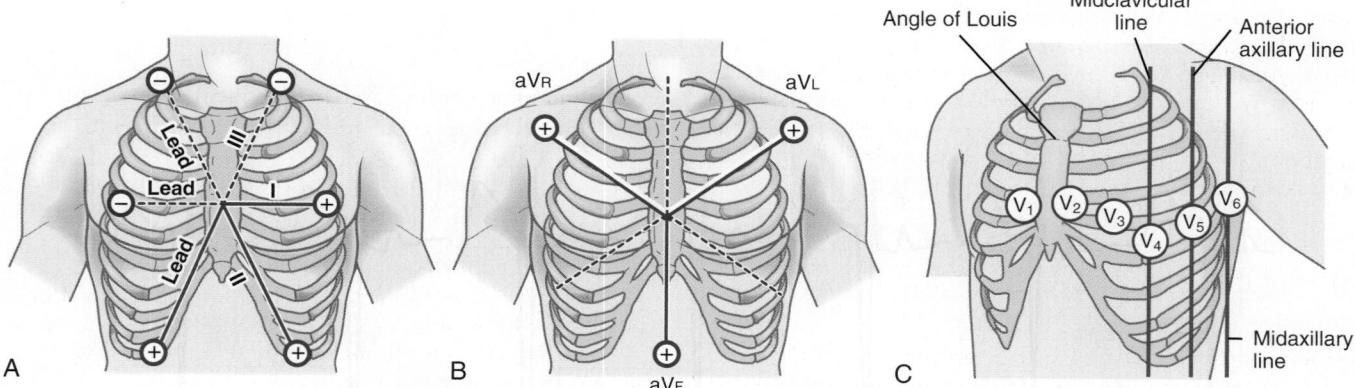

FIG. 35.2 **A,** Limb leads I, II, and III. These bipolar leads are placed on the extremities. Shown are the angles from which these leads view the heart. **B,** Limb leads aVR, aVL, and aVF. These unipolar leads use the center of the heart as their negative electrode. **C,** Placement for the unipolar chest leads: V_1, 4th intercostal space at the right sternal border; V_2, 4th intercostal space at the left sternal border; V_3, halfway between V_2 and V_4; V_4, 5th intercostal space at the left midclavicular line; V_5, 5th intercostal space at the left anterior axillary line; V_6, 5th intercostal space at the left midaxillary line.

FIG. 35.3 12-lead electrocardiogram showing a normal sinus rhythm.

FIG. 35.4 A, Lead placement for V₁ using a 5-lead system. B, Typical ECG tracing in lead V₁. *V,* Chest lead; *LA,* left arm; *LL,* left leg; *RA,* right arm; *RL,* right leg.

that 1 large square equals 0.20 second and that 300 large squares equal 1 minute. Vertically, each small square (1 mm) represents 0.1 millivolt (mV). This means that 1 large square equals 0.5 mV. Use these squares to calculate the HR and measure time intervals for the different ECG complexes.

You can use a variety of methods to calculate the HR from an ECG. The most accurate way is to count the number of QRS complexes in 1 minute. However, because this method is time consuming, you can use a simpler process. Note that every 3 seconds a marker appears on the ECG paper (Fig. 35.5). Count the number of QRS complexes in 6 seconds and multiply that number by 10. This is the estimated number of beats per minute (Fig. 35.6).

Another method to calculate the HR is to count the number of small squares between 1 R-R interval. Divide this number into 1500 to get the HR. Last, you can count the number of large squares between 1 R-R interval and divide this number into 300 to get the HR (Fig. 35.6). All these methods are more accurate when the rhythm is regular.[1,2]

Another way to measure distances on the ECG strip is to use calipers. Often a P or R wave will not fall directly on a light or heavy line. Place the fine points of the calipers exactly on the parts you need to measure and then move to another part of the strip for a more precise time measurement.

Fig. 35.7 shows the components of a normal ECG tracing. Table 35.2 describes ECG waveforms and intervals, normal durations, and possible sources of changes in each. Table 35.3 presents a systematic approach to assessing a heart rhythm.

ECG leads consist of an electrode pad fixed with electrical conductive gel. Before placing these on the patient, properly prepare the skin. Clip excess hair on the chest wall with scissors. Gently rub the skin with dry gauze until slightly pink. If the skin is oily, wipe with alcohol first. If the patient is diaphoretic, apply a skin protectant before placing the electrode.

Artifact is a distortion of the baseline and waveforms seen on the ECG (Fig. 35.8). It is hard to accurately interpret heart rhythm when artifact is present. You will see artifact on the monitor when leads and electrodes are not secure, the conductive gel is becoming dry, and there is muscle activity (e.g., shivering, ambulating) or electrical interference. If artifact occurs, check the connections in the equipment. Replace the electrodes if the conductive gel has dried out.

Telemetry Monitoring. Telemetry monitoring is the observation of a patient's HR and rhythm at a site distant from the patient. This technology can help rapidly identify dysrhythmias, ischemia, or infarction. There are 2 types of systems for telemetry monitoring. The first type is a centralized monitoring system. It requires you or a telemetry technician to continuously observe a group of patients' ECGs at a central location. The second system of telemetry monitoring does not require constant surveillance. These systems have the capability of detecting and storing data. Advanced alarm systems provide different levels of detection of dysrhythmias, ischemia, or infarction.

FIG. 35.5 Time and voltage on the electrocardiogram; 6-sec strip. (Modified from Wesley K: *Basic dysrhythmias and acute coronary syndromes,* ed 4, St Louis, 2011, Mosby JEMS.)

INFORMATICS IN PRACTICE

Wireless ECG Monitoring

- Wireless ECG monitoring systems continuously monitor and interpret the findings, sending an alert when a patient's rhythm and/or measurements fall outside of set parameters.
- Early detection of abnormal heart rhythms allows you time to assess the patient for signs of hemodynamic instability (e.g., chest pain, hypotension, palpitations, dyspnea) and determine the need to intervene (e.g., call the rapid response team).
- These systems can automatically save the pre-event portion of the ECG while continuing to record the post-event portion and send all the information to the HCP.
- Computerized monitoring systems are not fail-proof. Frequently assess all monitored patients for signs of hemodynamic instability.

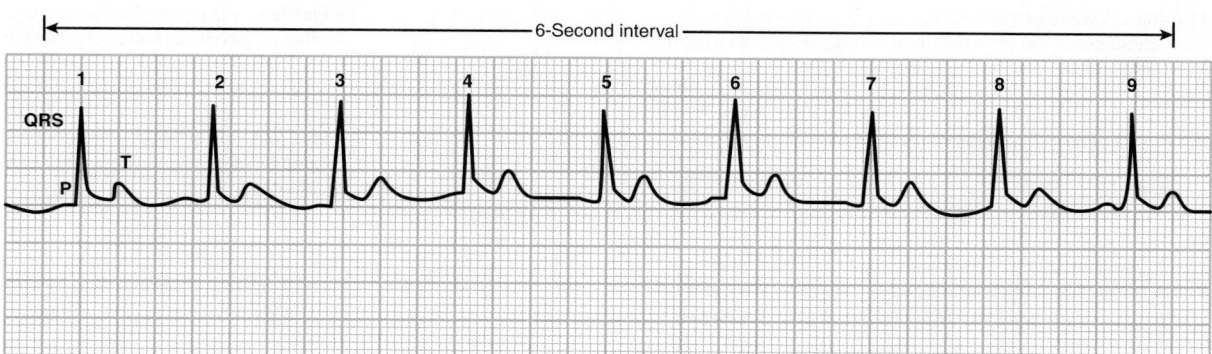

FIG. 35.6 When the rhythm is regular, heart rate can be easily determined by counting the number of "R" waves. The estimated heart rate is 90 beats/min. NOTE: Recorded from lead II.

Electrophysiologic Mechanisms of Dysrhythmias

Dysrhythmias result from disorders of impulse formation, impulse conductions, or both. The heart has specialized cells in the SA node, atria, AV node, bundle of His, and Purkinje fibers (His-Purkinje system), which can fire (discharge) spontaneously. This is termed *automaticity*. Normally, the SA node is the natural pacemaker of the heart. It spontaneously fires 60 to 100 times per minute (Table 35.4). A secondary pacemaker from another site may fire in 2 ways. If the SA node fires more slowly than a secondary pacemaker, the electrical signals from the secondary pacemaker may "escape." The secondary pacemaker will then fire automatically at its intrinsic rate. These secondary pacemakers may start from the AV node at a rate of 40 to 60 times per minute or the His-Purkinje system at a rate of 20 to 40 times per minute.

Another way that secondary pacemakers can start is when they fire more rapidly than the normal pacemaker of the SA node. *Triggered beats* (early or late) may come from an *ectopic focus* or *accessory pathway* (area outside the normal conduction pathway) in the atria, AV node, or ventricles. This results in a dysrhythmia, which replaces the normal sinus rhythm.

The impulse started by the SA node or an ectopic focus is conducted to the heart cells. The property of myocardial tissue that allows it to be depolarized by a stimulus is called *excitability*. The level of excitability is determined by the length of time after depolarization before the tissues can be restimulated. The recovery period after stimulation is the *refractory phase* or period. The *absolute refractory phase* or period occurs when excitability is zero and the heart cannot be stimulated. The *relative refractory period* occurs slightly later in the cycle, and excitability is more likely. In states of *full excitability,* the heart is completely recovered. Fig. 35.9 shows the relationship between the refractory period and ECG.

If conduction is depressed and some areas of the heart are blocked (e.g., by infarction), the unblocked areas are activated earlier than the blocked areas. When the block is unidirectional,

FIG. 35.7 Normal sinus rhythm. Note: Recorded from lead II.

TABLE 35.2 ECG Waveforms and Intervals*

Description	Normal Duration (sec)	Source of Possible Variation
P Wave Represents time for the passage of the electrical impulse through the atrium causing atrial depolarization (contraction). Should be upright	0.06–0.12	Problem in conduction within atria
PR Interval Measured from beginning of P wave to beginning of QRS complex. Represents time taken for impulse to spread through the atria, AV node and bundle of His, bundle branches, and Purkinje fibers, to a point immediately before ventricular contraction	0.12–0.20	Problem in conduction usually in AV node, bundle of His, or bundle branches but can be in atria as well
QRS Complex *Q wave:* First negative (downward) deflection after the P wave, short and narrow, not present in several leads	<0.03	MI may result in development of a pathologic Q wave that is wide (≥0.03 sec) and deep (≥25% of the height of the R wave)
R wave: First positive (upward) deflection in the QRS complex *S wave:* First negative (downward) deflection after the R wave	Not usually measured Not usually measured	
QRS Interval Measured from beginning to end of QRS complex. Represents time taken for depolarization (contraction) of both ventricles (systole)	<0.12	Problem in conduction in bundle branches or in ventricles
ST Segment Measured from the S wave of the QRS complex to the beginning of the T wave. Represents the time between ventricular depolarization and repolarization (diastole). Should be isoelectric (flat)	0.12	Changes (e.g., elevation, depression) usually caused by ischemia, injury, or infarction
T Wave Represents time for ventricular repolarization. Should be upright	0.16	Changes (e.g., tall, peaked; inverted) usually caused by electrolyte imbalances, ischemia, or infarction
QT Interval† Measured from beginning of QRS complex to end of T wave. Represents time taken for entire electrical depolarization and repolarization of the ventricles. Normal adult women have slightly longer QT intervals than men.	0.34–0.43	Problems usually affecting repolarization more than depolarization and caused by drugs, electrolyte imbalances, and changes in heart rate

*Heart rate influences the duration of these intervals, especially the PR and QT intervals (e.g., QT interval shortens in duration as heart rate increases).
†A corrected QT interval (QTc) is calculated to account for the influence of heart rate.

TABLE 35.3 Approach to Assessing Heart Rhythm

When assessing a heart rhythm, use a consistent and systematic approach. One such approach includes the following:

1. Look for the P wave. Is it upright or inverted? Is there 1 for every QRS complex or more than 1? Are atrial fibrillatory or flutter waves present?
2. Evaluate the atrial rhythm. Is it regular or irregular?
3. Calculate the atrial rate.
4. Measure the duration of the PR interval. Is it normal duration or prolonged? Is the duration consistent before each QRS?
5. Evaluate the ventricular rhythm. Is it regular or irregular?
6. Calculate the ventricular rate.
7. Measure the duration of the QRS complex. Is it normal duration or prolonged?
8. Assess the ST segment. Is it isoelectric (flat), elevated, or depressed?
9. Measure the duration of the QT interval. Correct for heart rate (cQT) to determine if it is normal or prolonged.*
10. Note the T wave. Is it upright or inverted?

Other questions to consider include:

1. What is the dominant or underlying rhythm and/or dysrhythmia?
2. What is the clinical significance of your findings?
3. What is the treatment for the particular rhythm?

*A website for calculating the cQT interval for heart rate can be found at *www.mdcalc. com/corrected-qt-interval-qtc.*

FIG. 35.8 Artifact. A, Muscle tremor. B, Loose electrodes.

TABLE 35.4 Intrinsic Rates of the Conduction System

Part of Conduction System	Rate
SA node and atria	60–100 times/min
AV node and bundle of His	40–60 times/min
Bundle branches and Purkinje fibers	20–40 times/min

this uneven conduction may allow the initial impulse to reenter areas that were previously not excitable but have recovered. The reentering impulse may be able to depolarize the atria and ventricles, causing a premature beat or rapid rhythm.

Evaluation of Dysrhythmias

Dysrhythmias occur as the result of various abnormalities and disease states. Assess the heart rhythm, any changes in rhythm, and the patient's clinical status. Determining the cause of dysrhythmias is a priority. The cause influences the patient's treatment. Table 35.5 presents common causes of dysrhythmias.

FIG. 35.9 Absolute and relative refractory periods correlated with the heart muscle's action potential and with an ECG tracing. (Modified from Urden LD, Stacy KM, Lough ME: *Critical care nursing: Diagnosis and management,* ed 6, St Louis, 2010, Mosby.)

TABLE 35.5 Common Causes of Dysrhythmias

Heart Conditions
- Accessory pathways
- Cardiomyopathy
- Conduction defects
- Heart failure
- Myocardial ischemia, infarction
- Valve disease

Other Conditions
- Acid-base imbalances
- Alcohol
- Caffeine, tobacco
- Connective tissue disorders
- Drowning
- Drug effects (e.g., antidysrhythmic drugs, stimulants, β-blockers) or toxicity
- Electric shock
- Electrolyte imbalances (e.g., hyperkalemia, hypocalcemia)
- Emotional crisis
- Herbal supplements (e.g., areca nut, wahoo root bark, yerba maté)
- Hypoxia
- Metabolic conditions (e.g., thyroid dysfunction)
- Sepsis, shock
- Toxins

Dysrhythmias occurring in nonmonitored settings present management challenges. If the patient becomes symptomatic (e.g., chest pain, syncope), determination of the rhythm by heart monitoring is a high priority. Activate the emergency response system (ERS). Table 35.6 outlines the emergency care of the patient with a dysrhythmia.

In addition to continuous ECG monitoring during hospitalization, several other tests can assess dysrhythmias and the effectiveness of antidysrhythmic drug therapy. An electrophysiologic study, Holter monitoring, event monitoring (or loop recorder), exercise treadmill testing, and signal-averaged ECG can be done on an inpatient or outpatient basis (see Tables 31.7 and 31.8 for nursing care related to these tests).

An *electrophysiologic study* (EPS) can identify the causes of heart blocks, tachydysrhythmias (dysrhythmias with rates greater than 100 beats/min), bradydysrhythmias (dysrhythmias

✚ TABLE 35.6 Emergency Management
Dysrhythmias

Assessment Findings	Interventions
• Irregular rate and rhythm; tachycardia, bradycardia • Chest, neck, shoulder, back, jaw, or arm pain • Cold, clammy skin • Decreased level of consciousness, confusion • Decreased or increased BP • Decreased O_2 saturation • Decreased peripheral pulses • Diaphoresis • Dizziness, syncope • Dyspnea • Extreme restlessness, anxiety • Feeling of impending doom • Nausea and vomiting • Numbness, tingling of arms • Pallor • Palpitations • Weakness and fatigue	**Initial** • If unresponsive, assess circulation, airway, and breathing (CAB). • If responsive, monitor airway, breathing, and circulation (ABC). • Apply O_2 via nasal cannula or nonrebreather mask. • Take baseline vital signs, including O_2 saturation. • Obtain 12-lead ECG. • Begin continuous ECG monitoring. • Identify underlying rate and rhythm. • Identify dysrhythmia. • Establish IV access. • Obtain baseline laboratory studies (e.g., CBC, electrolytes). **Ongoing Monitoring** • Monitor ABCs, vital signs, level of consciousness, O_2 saturation, and heart rhythm. • Anticipate need for antidysrhythmic drugs and analgesics. • Anticipate need for intubation if respiratory distress occurs. • Anticipate need to begin advanced cardiovascular life support (e.g., CPR, defibrillation, transcutaneous pacing).

with rates less than 60 beats/min), and syncope. An EPS study can locate accessory pathways and determine the effectiveness of antidysrhythmic drugs.

The Holter monitor continuously records the ECG while the patient is ambulatory and performing daily activities. The patient keeps a diary and records activities and any symptoms. Events in the diary are correlated with any dysrhythmias seen on the ECG. Use of event monitors has improved the evaluation of dysrhythmias in outpatients. Event monitors are recorders that the patient activates only when he or she has symptoms. New technology using smart phone apps can obtain and save ECG recordings and even detect some dysrhythmias (e.g., Kardia at *https://itunes.apple.com/us/app/aliveecg/id579769143?mt=8*).

Exercise treadmill testing evaluates the patient's heart rhythm during exercise. Any exercise-induced dysrhythmias or ECG changes that occur can be evaluated for treatment.

The signal-averaged ECG identifies *late potentials,* which suggest that the patient may be at risk for developing serious ventricular dysrhythmias. (See Chapter 31 for a discussion of diagnostic procedures for assessment of the cardiovascular system and related nursing care.)

Overview of Cardiac Rhythms
Figs. 35.10 to 35.21 give examples of the ECG tracings of common normal cardiac rhythms and dysrhythmias. Table 35.7 presents the characteristics of each.
Normal Cardiac Rhythms
Normal Sinus Rhythm. Normal sinus rhythm refers to a rhythm that starts in the SA node at a rate of 60 to 100 beats/min and

follows the normal conduction pathway (Fig. 35.10). The P wave is normal, precedes each QRS complex, and has a normal shape and duration. The PR interval is normal. The QRS complex has a normal shape and duration. Normal sinus rhythm implies that cardiac electrical activity is normal.

Sinus Arrhythmia. In *sinus arrhythmia,* the conduction pathway is the same as that in sinus rhythm, but the SA node fires irregularly. This often results from changes in intrathoracic pressure during breathing. The HR increases slightly during inspiration and decreases slightly during exhalation. It remains 60 to 100 beats/min. It is common in healthy adults.

Types of Dysrhythmias
Sinus Bradycardia. In *sinus bradycardia,* the conduction pathway is the same as that in sinus rhythm, but the SA node fires at a rate less than 60 beats/min (Fig. 35.11, *A*). *Symptomatic bradycardia* refers to a HR that is less than 60 beats/min and causes the patient to have symptoms of inadequate perfusion (e.g., fatigue, dizziness, chest pain, syncope).

Clinical Associations. Sinus bradycardia may be a normal sinus rhythm in aerobically trained athletes and in some people during sleep. It also occurs in response to carotid sinus massage, Valsalva maneuver, hypothermia, increased intraocular pressure, vagal stimulation, and certain drugs (e.g., β-blockers, calcium channel blockers). Common disease states associated with sinus bradycardia are hypothyroidism, increased intracranial pressure, and inferior myocardial infarction (MI).

ECG Characteristics. In sinus bradycardia, the HR is less than 60 beats/min and rhythm is regular. The P wave precedes each QRS complex and has a normal shape and duration. The PR interval is normal. The QRS complex has a normal shape and duration.

Clinical Significance. The significance of sinus bradycardia depends on how the patient tolerates it. Manifestations of symptomatic bradycardia include pale, cool skin; hypotension; weakness; angina; dizziness or syncope; confusion or disorientation; and shortness of breath.

Treatment. If bradycardia is due to drugs, these may have to be held, stopped, or reduced. For the patient with symptoms, treatment consists of giving IV atropine (anticholinergic drug). If atropine is ineffective, transcutaneous pacing or a dopamine or epinephrine infusion are options. The patient may need a permanent pacemaker.

Sinus Tachycardia. The conduction pathway is the same in *sinus tachycardia* as that in normal sinus rhythm. The discharge rate from the sinus node increases because of vagal inhibition or sympathetic stimulation. The sinus rate is 101 to 180 beats/min (Fig. 35.11, *B*).[2]

Clinical Associations. Sinus tachycardia is associated with physiologic and psychologic stressors, such as exercise, fever, pain, hypotension, hypovolemia, anemia, hypoxia, hypoglycemia, myocardial ischemia, heart failure (HF), hyperthyroidism, anxiety, and fear. It can be an effect of drugs, such as epinephrine, norepinephrine (Levophed), atropine, caffeine, theophylline, or hydralazine. In addition, many over-the-counter cold remedies have active ingredients (e.g., pseudoephedrine) that can cause tachycardia.

ECG Characteristics. In sinus tachycardia, the HR is 101 to 180 beats/min and rhythm is regular.[2] The P wave is normal and precedes each QRS complex. The PR interval is normal. The QRS complex has a normal shape and duration.

TABLE 35.7 Characteristics of Common Dysrhythmias

Pattern	Rate and Rhythm	P Wave	PR Interval	QRS Complex
Normal sinus rhythm (NSR)	60–100 beats/min and regular	Normal	Normal	Normal
Sinus bradycardia	<60 beats/min and regular	Normal	Normal	Normal
Sinus tachycardia	101–180 beats/min and regular	Normal	Normal	Normal
Premature atrial contraction (PAC)		Abnormal shape	Normal	Normal (usually)
Paroxysmal supraventricular tachycardia (PSVT)	151–220 beats/min and regular	Abnormal shape, may be hidden in the preceding T wave	Normal or shortened	Normal (usually)
Atrial flutter	*Atrial:* 200–350 beats/min and regular *Ventricular:* > or <100 beats/min and may be regular or irregular	Flutter (F) waves (saw-toothed pattern); more flutter waves than QRS complexes; may occur in a 2:1, 3:1, 4:1, etc., pattern	Not measurable	Normal (usually)
Atrial fibrillation	*Atrial:* 350–600 beats/min and irregular *Ventricular:* > or <100 beats/min and irregular	Fibrillatory (f) waves	Not measurable	Normal (usually)
Junctional dysrhythmias	40–180 beats/min and regular	Inverted, may be hidden in QRS complex, or behind the S wave	Shortened, if present	Normal (usually)
First-degree AV block	Normal and regular	Normal	>0.20 sec	Normal
Second-degree AV block				
• **Type I** (Mobitz I, Wenckebach heart block)	*Atrial:* Normal and regular *Ventricular:* Slower and irregular	Normal	Progressive lengthening (longer, longer, longer, drop, now you have a Wenckebach)	Normal QRS width, with pattern of 1 nonconducted (blocked) QRS complex
• **Type II** (Mobitz II heart block)	*Atrial:* Usually normal and regular *Ventricular:* Slower and regular or irregular	More P waves than QRS complexes (e.g., 2:1, 3:1)	Normal or prolonged but consistent for every QRS	Widened QRS, preceded by ≥2 P waves, with nonconducted (blocked) QRS complex
Third-degree AV block (complete heart block)	*Atrial:* Regular but may appear irregular due to P waves hidden in QRS complexes *Ventricular:* 20–60 beats/min and regular	Normal, but no connection with QRS complex	Inconsistent	Normal or widened, no relationship with P waves
Premature ventricular contraction (PVC)	Underlying rhythm can be any rate, regular or irregular rhythm, PVCs occur at variable rates	Not usually visible, hidden in the PVC	Not measurable	Wide and distorted
Ventricular tachycardia (VT)	150–250 beats/min and regular or irregular	Not usually visible	Not measurable	Wide and distorted
Accelerated idioventricular rhythm	40–100 beats/min and regular	Not usually visible	Not measurable	Wide and distorted
Ventricular fibrillation (VF)	Not measurable and irregular	Absent	Not measurable	Not measurable

FIG. 35.10 The ECG tracing as seen in normal sinus rhythm. *1*, P wave; *2*, PR interval; *3*, QRS complex: Q wave, R wave, S wave; *4*, ST segment; *5*, T wave; *6*, QT interval. Isoelectric (flat) line or baseline represents the absence of electrical activity in the heart cells. (See Table 35.2 for timing of intervals.)

FIG. 35.11 A, Sinus bradycardia. B, Sinus tachycardia.

FIG. 35.12 Premature atrial contractions *(arrows)*.

FIG. 35.13 Paroxysmal supraventricular tachycardia (PSVT). *Arrows* indicate beginning and ending of PSVT.

Clinical Significance. The clinical significance of sinus tachycardia depends on the patient's tolerance of the increased HR. The patient may have dizziness, dyspnea, and hypotension because of decreased CO. An increased HR increases myocardial oxygen (O_2) consumption. Angina or an increase in infarction size may occur with sinus tachycardia in those with coronary artery disease (CAD) or an acute MI.

Treatment. The underlying cause of tachycardia guides the treatment. For example, if the patient has tachycardia from pain, effective pain management is important to treat the tachycardia. In clinically stable patients, vagal maneuvers can be tried. IV β-blockers (e.g., metoprolol), adenosine (Adenocard), or calcium channel blockers (e.g., diltiazem) can reduce HR and decrease myocardial O_2 consumption. Clinically unstable patients may need synchronized cardioversion. Cardioversion is discussed on p. 770.

Premature Atrial Contraction. A premature atrial contraction (PAC) is a contraction starting from an ectopic focus in the atrium (i.e., a location other than the SA node) sooner than the next expected sinus beat. The ectopic signal starts in the left or right atrium and travels across the atria by an abnormal pathway. This creates a distorted P wave (Fig. 35.12). At the AV node, it may be stopped (nonconducted PAC), delayed (lengthened PR interval), or conducted normally. If the signal moves through the AV node, in most cases it is conducted normally through the ventricles.

Clinical Associations. In a normal heart, a PAC can result from emotional stress or physical fatigue, or from caffeine, tobacco, or alcohol use. A PAC can also result from hypoxia, electrolyte imbalances, hyperthyroidism, chronic obstructive pulmonary disease (COPD), and heart disease, including CAD and valvular disease.

ECG Characteristics. HR varies with the underlying rate and frequency of the PAC. The rhythm is irregular. The P wave has a different shape from that of a P wave originating in the SA node, or it may be hidden in the preceding T wave. The PR interval may be shorter or longer than the PR interval coming from the SA node, but it is within normal limits. The QRS complex is usually normal. If the QRS interval is 0.12 second or more, abnormal conduction through the ventricles is occurring.

Clinical Significance. In persons with healthy hearts, isolated PACs are not significant. Patients may report palpitations or a sense that the heart "skipped a beat." In persons with heart disease, frequent PACs may indicate enhanced automaticity of the atria or a reentry mechanism. Such PACs may warn of or start more serious dysrhythmias (e.g., supraventricular tachycardia).

Treatment. Treatment depends on the patient's symptoms. Withdrawal of sources of stimulation, such as caffeine or sympathomimetic drugs (e.g. epinephrine, dopamine), may be needed. β-Blockers may be used to decrease PACs.

Paroxysmal Supraventricular Tachycardia. *Paroxysmal supraventricular tachycardia* (PSVT), also known as supraventricular tachycardia (SVT) or atrial tachycardia, is a dysrhythmia starting in an ectopic focus anywhere above the bifurcation of the bundle of His (Fig. 35.13). Identifying the ectopic focus is often hard even with a 12-lead ECG since it requires recording the dysrhythmia as it starts.

PSVT occurs because of a reentrant phenomenon (reexcitation of the atria when there is a 1-way block). Usually a PAC triggers a run of repeated premature beats. *Paroxysmal* refers to an abrupt onset and ending. A brief period of *asystole* (absence of all cardiac electrical activity) may follow the termination. AV block may prevent some of the impulses from being conducted to the ventricles. PSVT can occur with Wolff-Parkinson-White (WPW) syndrome or "preexcitation" with extra conduction or accessory pathways.

Clinical Associations. In the normal heart, PSVT is associated with overexertion, emotional stress, deep inspiration, and stimulants, such as caffeine and tobacco. PSVT is also associated with rheumatic heart disease, digitalis toxicity, CAD, and cor pulmonale.

ECG Characteristics. In PSVT, the HR is 151 to 220 beats/min. The rhythm is regular or slightly irregular. The P wave may have an abnormal shape or be hidden in the preceding T wave. The PR interval may be shortened or normal. The QRS complex is usually normal.

Clinical Significance. The significance of PSVT depends on the associated symptoms. A prolonged episode and HR greater than 180 beats/min will cause decreased CO because of reduced stroke volume. Manifestations include hypotension, palpitations, dyspnea, and angina.

Treatment. Treatment for PSVT includes vagal stimulation and drug therapy. Common vagal maneuvers include Valsalva, carotid massage, and coughing. IV adenosine is the drug of choice to convert PSVT to a normal sinus rhythm (Fig. 35.14). This drug has a short half-life (10 seconds) and is well tolerated.[6] IV β-blockers and calcium channel blockers (e.g., diltiazem, verapamil) are options. If the patient becomes hemodynamically unstable, synchronized cardioversion is done.[7] Cardioversion is discussed on p. 770.

💊 DRUG ALERT Adenosine (Adenocard)

- Explain that the patient may feel chest pressure after the medication is given.
- Injection site should be as close to the heart as possible (e.g., antecubital area).
- Give IV dose rapidly (over 1 to 2 sec) and follow with a rapid 20-mL normal saline flush. Use a stopcock setup to make sure adenosine gets to the heart quickly.
- Monitor patient's ECG continuously. Brief period of asystole is common (Fig. 35.14).
- Assess the patient for flushing, dizziness, chest pain, or palpitations.

Treatment of recurring PSVT and PSVT in patients with WPW syndrome includes radiofrequency catheter ablation of the accessory pathway.[7] Catheter ablation therapy is discussed on p. 773.

Adenosine (6 mg)

FIG. 35.14 Administration of adenosine rapid IV push. Note that SVT is followed by a brief period of asystole before the return to normal sinus rhythm. This is a common occurrence after adenosine.

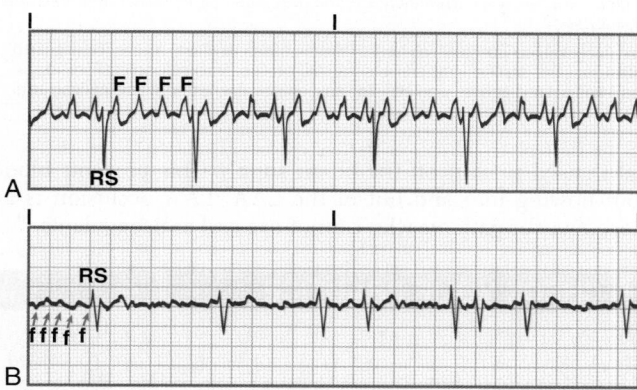

F F F F

RS

A

RS

f f f f f

B

FIG. 35.15 A, Atrial flutter with a 4:1 conduction (4 flutter [F] waves to each QRS complex). B, Atrial fibrillation with a controlled ventricular response. Note the chaotic fibrillatory (f) waves (arrows) between the RS complexes. NOTE: Recorded from lead V₁.

Atrial Flutter. Atrial flutter is an atrial tachydysrhythmia identified by recurring, regular, sawtooth-shaped flutter waves that originate from a single ectopic focus in the right atrium or, less often, the left atrium (Fig. 35.15, A).

Clinical Associations. Atrial flutter rarely occurs in a healthy heart. It is associated with CAD, hypertension, mitral valve disorders, pulmonary embolus, chronic lung disease, cor pulmonale, cardiomyopathy, hyperthyroidism, and the use of drugs, such as digoxin, quinidine, and epinephrine.

ECG Characteristics. Atrial rate is 200 to 350 beats/min. The ventricular rate varies based on the conduction ratio. In 2:1 conduction, the ventricular rate is typically around 150 beats/min. Atrial and ventricular rhythms are usually regular. The atrial flutter waves represent atrial depolarization followed by repolarization. The PR interval is variable and not measurable. The QRS complex is usually normal. There is usually some AV block in a fixed ratio of flutter waves to QRS complexes because the AV node can delay signals from the atria.

Clinical Significance. The high ventricular rates (greater than 100 beats/min) and loss of the atrial "kick" (atrial contraction coordinated with ventricular contraction) that are associated with atrial flutter decrease CO. This can cause serious problems, such as HF, especially in the patient with underlying heart disease. Patients with atrial flutter have an increased risk for stroke because thrombi (clots) can form in the atria from the stasis of blood. Warfarin or another anticoagulant is given to prevent stroke in patients who have atrial flutter.[8] (See Chapter 37 for discussion of anticoagulation therapy.)

Treatment. The primary goal in treatment of atrial flutter is to slow the ventricular response by increasing AV block. Drugs used to control ventricular rate include calcium channel blockers and β-blockers. Electrical cardioversion may be done to convert the atrial flutter to sinus rhythm in an emergency (i.e., when the patient is clinically unstable) and electively. Antidysrhythmic drugs can convert atrial flutter to sinus rhythm (e.g., ibutilide [Corvert]) or to maintain sinus rhythm (e.g., amiodarone, flecainide).[6,8]

Radiofrequency catheter ablation in an EPS laboratory is the treatment of choice for atrial flutter.[8] The procedure involves placing a catheter in the right atrium. Low-voltage, high-frequency electrical energy is then used to ablate (or destroy) the ectopic foci. This should restore normal sinus rhythm. (Catheter ablation is discussed on p. 773.)

Atrial Fibrillation. Atrial fibrillation is characterized by a total disorganization of atrial electrical activity because of multiple ectopic foci. It results in loss of effective atrial contraction (Fig. 35.15, B). The dysrhythmia may be paroxysmal (i.e., beginning and ending spontaneously) or persistent (lasting more than 7 days).[1] Atrial fibrillation is the most common, clinically significant dysrhythmia with respect to morbidity and mortality rates and economic impact. Its prevalence increases with age.[8]

Clinical Associations. Atrial fibrillation usually occurs in a patient with underlying heart disease, such as CAD, valvular heart disease, cardiomyopathy, hypertensive heart disease, HF, and pericarditis. It often develops acutely with thyrotoxicosis, alcohol intoxication, caffeine use, electrolyte problems, stress, and heart surgery.

ECG Characteristics. During atrial fibrillation, the atrial rate may be as high as 350 to 600 beats/min. Chaotic, fibrillatory waves replace the P waves. Ventricular rate varies, and the rhythm is usually irregular. When the ventricular rate is between

60 and 100 beats/min, it is atrial fibrillation with a *controlled ventricular response*. Atrial fibrillation with a ventricular rate greater than 100 beats/min is atrial fibrillation with a *rapid (or uncontrolled) ventricular response*. The PR interval is not measurable. The QRS complex usually has a normal shape and duration. At times, atrial flutter and atrial fibrillation coexist.[1]

Clinical Significance. Atrial fibrillation results in a decrease in CO because of ineffective atrial contractions (loss of atrial kick) and/or a rapid ventricular response (RVR). Thrombi may form in the atria because of blood stasis. An embolized clot may move through arteries to the brain, causing a stroke. Atrial fibrillation accounts for as many as 20% of all strokes.[9]

Treatment. The goals of atrial fibrillation treatment are to decrease the ventricular response (to less than 100 beats/min), prevent stroke, and convert to sinus rhythm, if possible. Ventricular rate control is a priority. Drugs used for rate control include calcium channel blockers (e.g., diltiazem), β-blockers (e.g., metoprolol), amiodarone, and digoxin (Lanoxin).

Some patients need drug or electrical conversion of atrial fibrillation to a normal sinus rhythm (e.g., reduced exercise tolerance with rate control drugs, contraindications to warfarin). The most common antidysrhythmic drug used for conversion to and maintenance of sinus rhythm is amiodarone.[8]

Electrical cardioversion may convert atrial fibrillation to a normal sinus rhythm. If a patient is in atrial fibrillation for longer than 48 hours, anticoagulation therapy with warfarin is needed for 3 to 4 weeks before the cardioversion.[1,8] Anticoagulation therapy continues for several weeks after because the procedure can cause the clots to dislodge, placing the patient at risk for stroke. A transesophageal echocardiogram may be done to rule out clots in the atria. If no clots are present, anticoagulation therapy may not be needed before the cardioversion.

If drugs or cardioversion does not convert atrial fibrillation to normal sinus rhythm, the patient needs long-term anticoagulation therapy (Table 35.8). Warfarin is often used, and we monitor for therapeutic levels (e.g., international normalized ratio [INR]). Alternatives to warfarin are available that do not require routine laboratory testing. Examples include dabigatran (Pradaxa), apixaban (Eliquis), and rivaroxaban (Xarelto).[8] See Chapter 37 for discussion of anticoagulation therapy.

For symptomatic patients with atrial fibrillation refractory to drugs or electrical conversion, radiofrequency catheter ablation (similar to procedure for atrial flutter), AV nodal ablation, and the Maze procedure are further options. AV nodal ablation involves the destruction of the AV node and insertion of a permanent ventricular pacemaker.[8]

The Maze procedure is a surgical intervention that stops atrial fibrillation by interrupting the ectopic foci that are causing the dysrhythmia. Incisions are made in both atria, and *cryoablation* (cold therapy) is used to stop the formation and conduction of ectopic signals and restore normal sinus rhythm.

Left atrial appendage occlusion. The left atrial appendage (LAA) is a pouch that extends off the left atrium. The LAA is known to trigger atrial fibrillation. It is a common source of blood clots in patients with atrial fibrillation. LAA occlusion is a treatment strategy to prevent blood clot formation in patients who have atrial fibrillation. Removing or occluding the LAA can decrease the incidence of strokes.

A special stapler can be used to remove the LAA. Or, the LAA can be occluded manually with sutures or an LAA occlusion device (e.g., Amplatzer, Lariat, Watchman). These devices are positioned around the LAA and then closed, like a clamp

TABLE 35.8 Drug Therapy

Antithrombotic Therapy for Atrial Fibrillation and Atrial Flutter

Risk Category	Recommended Therapy
Mechanical heart valve	Warfarin (target INR 2.5–3.5)
CHA$_2$DS$_2$-VASc* score of 0	No therapy recommended
CHA$_2$DS$_2$-VASc score of 1	No therapy recommended. An oral anticoagulant or aspirin (e.g., 81–325 mg/day) may be considered
CHA$_2$DS$_2$-VASc score of ≥2 or a history of prior stroke or transient ischemia attack (TIA)	Warfarin (target INR 2.0–3.0) Apixaban (Eliquis) Dabigatran (Pradaxa) Rivaroxaban (Xarelto)
CHA$_2$DS$_2$-VASc score of ≥2 and end-stage kidney disease or on hemodialysis	Warfarin

Source: Heidenreich PA, Solis P, Estes N, et al: 2016 ACC/AHA clinical performance and quality measures for adults with atrial fibrillation or atrial flutter, *J Am Coll Cardiol* 68:525, 2016.
*The CHA$_2$DS$_2$-VASc score for nonvalvular atrial fibrillation stroke risk can be calculated at *www.mdcalc.com/cha2ds2-vasc-score-for-atrial-fibrillation-stroke-risk/*.
CHA$_2$DS$_2$-VASc, Congestive heart failure; hypertension; age ≥75 (doubled); diabetes; prior stroke, transient ischemic attack, thromboembolism (doubled); vascular disease; age 65–74; sex, *INR*, international normalized ratio.

that is used to shut off the blood supply. This prevents blood from flowing into and out of the LAA. LAA occlusion is an alternative for patients who cannot use oral anticoagulants.[10]

? CHECK YOUR PRACTICE

You are caring for a 72-yr-old female patient who was admitted with chest pain. She has continuous EGG monitoring. You are concerned because you think her ECG tracing is hard to interpret and she may be in atrial fibrillation. Your preceptor tells you that there is a lot of artifact present.
- What can you do to improve the ECG tracing?
- How would you determine the patient's rhythm?

Junctional Dysrhythmias. *Junctional dysrhythmias* start in the area of the AV node to the bundle of His known as the AV junction. They result because the SA node does not fire or the signal is blocked. When this occurs, the AV node becomes the pacemaker of the heart. The impulse from the AV node usually moves in a retrograde (backward) fashion. This produces an abnormal P wave that occurs just before or after the QRS complex or is hidden in the QRS complex. The impulse usually moves normally through the ventricles. Junctional premature beats may occur. They are treated in a manner similar to that for PACs. Other junctional dysrhythmias include junctional escape rhythm (Fig. 35.16), accelerated junctional rhythm, and junctional tachycardia. Their treatment depends on the patient's tolerance of the rhythm and the patient's clinical condition.

Clinical Associations. Junctional dysrhythmias are often associated with CAD, HF, cardiomyopathy, electrolyte imbalances, inferior MI, and rheumatic heart disease. Certain drugs (e.g., digoxin, nicotine, amphetamines, caffeine) can also cause junctional dysrhythmias.

ECG Characteristics. In junctional escape rhythm, the HR is 40 to 60 beats/min. It is 61 to 100 beats/min in accelerated

FIG. 35.16 Junctional escape rhythm. P wave is hidden in the RS complex. NOTE: Recorded from lead V₁.

junctional rhythm and 101 to 180 beats/min in junctional tachycardia. The rhythm is regular. The P wave is abnormal in shape and inverted, or it may be hidden in the QRS complex (Fig. 35.16). The PR interval is less than 0.12 second when the P wave precedes the QRS complex. The QRS complex is usually normal.

Clinical Significance. Junctional escape rhythms serve as a safety mechanism when the SA node has not been effective. Escape rhythms like this should not be suppressed. Accelerated junctional rhythm is due to sympathetic stimulation to improve CO. Junctional tachycardia indicates a more serious problem. This rhythm may reduce CO, causing the patient to become hemodynamically unstable (e.g., hypotensive).

Treatment. Treatment varies according to the type of junctional dysrhythmia. If a patient has symptoms with a junctional escape rhythm, atropine can be used. If accelerated junctional rhythm or junctional tachycardia are caused by drug toxicity, the drug is stopped. In the absence of digitalis toxicity, β-blockers, calcium channel blockers, and amiodarone are used for rate control. Cardioversion is not done.

First-Degree AV Block. *First-degree AV block* is a type of AV block in which every impulse is conducted to the ventricles, but the time of AV conduction is prolonged (Fig. 35.17, *A*). After the impulse moves through the AV node, the ventricles usually respond normally.

Clinical Associations. First-degree AV block is associated with increasing age, MI, CAD, rheumatic fever, hyperthyroidism, electrolyte imbalances (e.g., hypokalemia), vagal stimulation, and drugs, such as digoxin, β-blockers, calcium channel blockers, and flecainide.

ECG Characteristics. In first-degree AV block, the HR is normal. The rhythm is regular. The P wave is normal. The PR interval is prolonged (greater than 0.20 second). The QRS complex usually has a normal shape and duration.

Clinical Significance. First-degree AV block is usually not serious. Patients are asymptomatic.

Treatment. There is no treatment for first-degree AV block. Treatment of associated conditions may be considered. Monitor patients for changes in heart rhythm (e.g., more serious AV block).

Second-Degree AV Block, Type I. *Type I second-degree AV block (Mobitz I or Wenckebach heart block)* includes a gradual lengthening of the PR interval. AV conduction time is increasingly prolonged until an atrial impulse is nonconducted and a QRS complex is blocked (missing) (Fig. 35.17, *B*). Type I AV block most often occurs in the AV node, but it can occur in the His-Purkinje system.

Clinical Associations. Type I AV block may result from drugs, such as digoxin or β-blockers. It may be associated with CAD and other diseases that can slow AV conduction.

ECG Characteristics. Atrial rate is regular, but ventricular rate may be slower because of nonconducted or blocked QRS

FIG. 35.17 Heart block. A, First-degree AV block with a PR interval of 0.40 sec. B, Second-degree AV block, type I, with progressive lengthening of the PR interval until a QRS complex is blocked. C, Second-degree AV block, type II, with constant PR intervals and variable blocked QRS complexes. D, Third-degree AV block. Note that there is no relationship between P waves and QRS complexes.

complexes resulting in bradycardia. Once a ventricular beat is blocked, the cycle repeats itself with progressive lengthening of the PR intervals until another QRS complex is blocked. Think of the phrase, "longer, longer, longer, drop, now you have a Wenckebach." The rhythm appears on the ECG in a pattern of grouped beats. Ventricular rhythm is irregular. The P wave has a normal shape. The QRS complex has a normal shape and duration.

Clinical Significance. Type I AV block is usually a result of myocardial ischemia or inferior MI. It is generally transient and well tolerated. However, in some patients (e.g., acute MI) it may be a warning sign of a more serious AV conduction problem (e.g., complete heart block).

Treatment. A symptomatic patient may need atropine or a temporary pacemaker to increase HR, especially if the patient has had an MI. If the patient is asymptomatic, observe the rhythm closely and have a transcutaneous pacemaker on standby. Bradycardia is more likely to become symptomatic when hypotension, HF, or shock is present.

Second-Degree AV Block, Type II. In *type II second-degree AV block (Mobitz II heart block)*, a P wave is nonconducted without progressive PR lengthening. This usually occurs when a block in 1 of the bundle branches is present (Fig. 35.17, *C*). On conducted beats, the PR interval is constant. Type II second-degree AV block is a more serious type of block because a certain number of impulses from the SA node are not conducted to the ventricles. This occurs in ratios of 2:1, 3:1, and so on (i.e., 2 P waves to one QRS complex, 3 P waves to 1 QRS complex). It may occur with varying ratios.

Clinical Associations. Type II AV block is associated with rheumatic heart disease, CAD, anterior MI, and drug toxicity.

ECG Characteristics. Atrial rate is usually normal. Ventricular rate depends on the degree of AV block. Atrial rhythm is regular, but ventricular rhythm may be irregular. The P wave has a normal shape. The PR interval may be normal or prolonged in duration and remains constant on conducted beats. The QRS complex is usually greater than 0.12 second because of bundle branch block.

Clinical Significance. Type II AV block often progresses to third-degree AV block and is associated with a poor prognosis. The reduced HR often results in decreased CO with subsequent hypotension and myocardial ischemia. Type II AV block is an indication for a permanent pacemaker.

Treatment. Transcutaneous pacing or the insertion of a temporary pacemaker may be needed before inserting a permanent pacemaker if the patient becomes symptomatic (e.g., hypotension, angina).[1,11] (Temporary pacemakers are discussed on pp. 772–773.) Atropine is not an effective treatment.

Third-Degree AV Block. Third-degree AV block, or **complete heart block**, is a form of AV dissociation in which no impulses from the atria are conducted to the ventricles (Fig. 35.17, *D*). The atria are stimulated and contract independently of the ventricles. The ventricular rhythm is an escape rhythm. The ectopic pacemaker may be above or below the bifurcation of the bundle of His.

Clinical Associations. Third-degree AV block is associated with severe heart disease, including CAD, MI, myocarditis, cardiomyopathy, and some systemic diseases, such as scleroderma. Some drugs can cause third-degree AV block, such as digoxin, β-blockers, and calcium channel blockers.

ECG Characteristics. The atrial rate is usually a sinus rate of 60 to 100 beats/min. The ventricular rate depends on the site of the block. If it is in the AV node, the rate is 40 to 60 beats/min. If it is in the His-Purkinje system, it is 20 to 40 beats/min. Atrial and ventricular rhythms are regular but unrelated to each other. The P wave has a normal shape. The PR interval is variable. There is no relationship between the P wave and the QRS complex. The QRS complex is normal if the escape rhythm starts at the bundle of His or above. It is widened if the escape rhythm starts below the bundle of His.

Clinical Significance. Third-degree AV block usually results in reduced CO with subsequent ischemia, HF, and shock. Syncope from third-degree AV block may result from severe bradycardia or even periods of asystole.

Treatment. Symptomatic patients need a transcutaneous pacemaker until a temporary transvenous pacemaker can be inserted.[1,11] (Types of temporary pacemakers are discussed on pp. 772–773.) The use of drugs such as dopamine and epinephrine is an interim measure to increase HR and support BP until temporary pacing is started.[11] Patients need a permanent pacemaker as soon as possible. Atropine is not an effective treatment.

Premature Ventricular Contractions. A **premature ventricular contraction (PVC)** is a contraction coming from an ectopic focus in the ventricles. It is the premature (early) occurrence of a QRS complex. A PVC is wide and distorted in shape compared with a QRS complex coming down the normal conduction pathway (Fig. 35.18). PVCs that have the same shape are *unifocal*

FIG. 35.18 Various types of premature ventricular contractions (PVCs).

FIG. 35.19 R-on-T phenomenon. The "shock" occurred on the T wave leading to ventricular tachycardia.

PVCs. PVCs that arise from different foci appear different in shape from each other. These are *multifocal* PVCs. When every other beat is a PVC, the rhythm is called *ventricular bigeminy*. When every third beat is a PVC, it is called *ventricular trigeminy*. We call 2 consecutive PVCs a *couplet*.

Ventricular tachycardia (VT) occurs when there are 3 or more consecutive PVCs. *R-on-T phenomenon* occurs when a PVC falls on the T wave of a preceding beat (Fig. 35.19). This is especially dangerous because the PVC is firing during the relative refractory phase of ventricular repolarization. Excitability of the heart cells increases during this time, and the risk for the PVC to start VT or ventricular fibrillation (VF) is great.

Clinical Associations. PVCs are associated with stimulants, such as caffeine, alcohol, nicotine, aminophylline, epinephrine, and isoproterenol. They are also associated with electrolyte imbalances, hypoxia, fever, exercise, and emotional stress. Disease states associated with PVCs include MI, mitral valve prolapse, HF, cardiomyopathy, and CAD.

ECG Characteristics. HR varies according to intrinsic rate and number of PVCs. Rhythm is irregular because of premature beats. The P wave is rarely visible. It is usually lost in the QRS complex of the PVC. Retrograde conduction may occur with the P wave seen after the ectopic beat. The PR interval is not measurable. The QRS complex is wide and distorted in shape, lasting more than 0.12 second. The T wave is generally large and opposite in direction to the major direction of the QRS complex.

Clinical Significance. PVCs are usually not harmful in a patient with a normal heart. PVCs in CAD or acute MI indicate ventricular irritability. PVCs may reduce the CO and lead to angina and HF for those with heart disease, so assess the patient's physiologic response. Take the patient's apical-radial pulse rate and determine the pulse deficit, since PVCs often do not generate a sufficient ventricular contraction to result in a peripheral pulse.

Treatment. Treatment relates to the cause of the PVCs (e.g., O_2 therapy for hypoxia, electrolyte replacement). Assessing the patient's hemodynamic status is important to determine if treatment with drug therapy is needed. Drug therapy includes β-blockers, lidocaine, or amiodarone.

Accelerated Idioventricular Rhythm. An *accelerated idioventricular rhythm* (AIVR) can develop when the intrinsic pacemaker (SA node or AV node) rate becomes less than that of a ventricular ectopic pacemaker. The rate is between 40 and 100 beats/min.

Clinical Associations. It is most often associated with acute MI and reperfusion of the myocardium after thrombolytic therapy or percutaneous coronary interventions (e.g., angioplasty). It can occur with digitalis toxicity.

Treatment. In the setting of acute MI, AIVR is usually self-limiting and well tolerated, and it needs no treatment. If the patient becomes symptomatic (e.g., hypotensive, chest pain), atropine is an option. Temporary pacing may be needed. Drugs that suppress ventricular rhythms (e.g., amiodarone) should not be used since they can further reduce the HR.

Ventricular Tachycardia. A run of 3 or more PVCs defines **ventricular tachycardia (VT)**. It occurs when an ectopic focus or foci fire repeatedly and the ventricle takes control as the pacemaker. Different forms of VT exist, depending on QRS configuration. *Monomorphic* VT (Fig. 35.20, *A*) has QRS complexes that are the same in shape, size, and direction. *Polymorphic* VT occurs when the QRS complexes gradually change back and forth from one shape, size, and direction to another over a series of beats. *Torsades de pointes* (French for "twisting of the points") is polymorphic VT associated with a prolonged QT interval of the underlying rhythm (Fig. 35.20, *B*).

VT may be sustained (longer than 30 seconds) or nonsustained (less than 30 seconds). The development of VT is an ominous sign. It is a life-threatening dysrhythmia because of decreased CO and the possible development of VF, which is lethal.

Clinical Associations. VT is associated with MI, CAD, significant electrolyte imbalances, cardiomyopathy, long QT syndrome, drug toxicity, and central nervous system disorders. It can occur in patients who have no evidence of heart disease.

ECG Characteristics. Ventricular rate is 150 to 250 beats/min. Rhythm may be regular or irregular. AV dissociation may be present, with P waves occurring independently of the QRS complex. The atria may be depolarized by the ventricles in a retrograde fashion. The P wave is usually buried in the

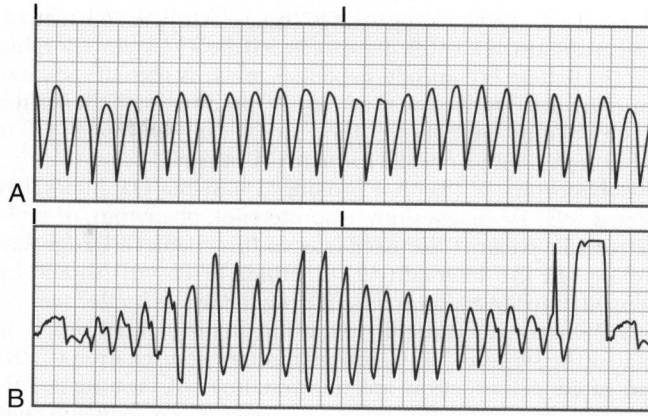

FIG. 35.20 Ventricular tachycardia. **A,** Monomorphic. **B,** Torsades de pointes (polymorphic).

QRS complex. The PR interval is not measurable. The QRS complex appears distorted and wide (greater than 0.12 second in duration). The T wave is in the opposite direction of the QRS complex (Fig. 35.20).

Clinical Significance. VT can be stable (patient has a pulse) or unstable (patient is pulseless). Sustained VT causes a severe decrease in CO because of decreased ventricular diastolic filling times and loss of atrial contraction. This results in hypotension, pulmonary edema, decreased cerebral blood flow, and cardiopulmonary arrest. VT must be treated quickly, even if it occurs only briefly and stops abruptly. Episodes may recur if prophylactic treatment is not started. VF may develop.

ETHICAL/LEGAL DILEMMAS
Scope and Standards of Practice

Situation

A young woman is admitted to the intensive care unit (ICU) after having several episodes of nonsustained VT credited to a history of viral cardiomyopathy. While she is being stabilized, she codes (pulseless VT) and needs intubation. A nurse anesthetist tries to intubate her 3 times unsuccessfully. There is an unforeseen delay in the arrival of the anesthesiologist. P.F., an ICU nurse who is a paramedic certified in advanced trauma life support (ATLS) and advanced cardiovascular life support (ACLS), tries to intubate the patient and does so successfully. The next day the nursing supervisor questions P.F. about intubating the patient since this is not within the scope of practice for an ICU nurse.

Ethical/Legal Points for Consideration

- The RN *Scope of Practice,* including rules and regulations that guide practice, are defined by individual state boards of nursing and can vary from state to state.
- Individual agencies have policies and procedures that describe the scope of practice for nurses. These can be more restrictive than those of the state.
- P.F. has had training, education, and certification beyond the usual nursing role.
- The life-threatening situation is an extenuating circumstance.
- Negligence may have been a factor if P.F., who is a nurse with training and experience, had not acted.

Discussion Questions

1. What would you have done in this situation?
2. How would you respond to the nursing supervisor?
3. What are the legal ramifications for P.F. in this situation?
4. What are the ethical issues in this situation?

Treatment. Precipitating causes (e.g., electrolyte imbalances, ischemia) must be identified and treated. If the VT is monomorphic and the patient is clinically stable (i.e., pulse is present) and has preserved left ventricular function, IV procainamide, lidocaine, or amiodarone are options. These drugs can be given if VT is polymorphic with a normal baseline QT interval.

Polymorphic VT with a prolonged baseline QT interval is treated with IV magnesium, isoproterenol, phenytoin, or antitachycardia pacing (discussed later in this chapter). Drugs that prolong the QT interval (e.g., dofetilide [Tikosyn]) should be stopped. Cardioversion is used if drug therapy is ineffective.

VT without a pulse is a life-threatening situation. It is treated the same as VF. Cardiopulmonary resuscitation (CPR) and rapid defibrillation are the first lines of treatment, followed by the administration of vasopressors (e.g., epinephrine) and antidysrhythmics (e.g., amiodarone) if defibrillation is unsuccessful.[11]

> **? CHECK YOUR PRACTICE**
>
> You are assigned to a 69-yr-old male patient on a telemetry unit who is recovering from colon surgery. He has a history of 2 MIs and he has 3 coronary stents in place. You hear his ECG monitor alarm and see what looks like ventricular tachycardia on the screen.
> - What should you do?

Ventricular Fibrillation. Ventricular fibrillation (VF) is a severe derangement of the heart rhythm characterized on ECG by irregular waveforms of varying shapes and amplitude (Fig. 35.21). This represents the firing of multiple ectopic foci in the ventricle. Mechanically, the ventricle is simply "quivering," with no effective contraction, and so no CO occurs. VF is a lethal dysrhythmia.

Clinical Associations. VF occurs in acute MI and myocardial ischemia and in chronic diseases such as HF and cardiomyopathy. It may occur during cardiac pacing or cardiac catheterization procedures because of catheter stimulation of the ventricle. It may also occur with coronary reperfusion after thrombolytic therapy. Other causes are electric shock, hyperkalemia, hypoxemia, acidosis, and drug toxicity.

ECG Characteristics. HR is not measurable. Rhythm is irregular and chaotic. The P wave is not visible. The PR interval and the QRS interval are not measurable.

Clinical Significance. VF results in an unresponsive, pulseless, and apneic state. If VF is not treated quickly, the patient will not recover.

Treatment. Treatment consists of immediate initiation of CPR and ACLS with the use of defibrillation and definitive drug therapy (e.g., epinephrine, amiodarone). There should be no delay in starting chest compressions and using a defibrillator once available.

Asystole. Asystole is the total absence of ventricular electrical activity. Occasionally, P waves are seen. No ventricular contraction occurs because depolarization does not occur. Patients are unresponsive, pulseless, and apneic. Asystole is a lethal dysrhythmia that needs immediate treatment. VF may masquerade as asystole. Always assess the rhythm in more than 1 lead. The prognosis of a patient with asystole is extremely poor.

Clinical Associations. Asystole is usually a result of advanced heart disease, a severe cardiac conduction system problem, or end-stage HF.

Clinical Significance. Generally, the patient with asystole has end-stage heart disease or has a prolonged arrest and cannot be resuscitated.

FIG. 35.21 Ventricular fibrillation.

Treatment. Treatment consists of CPR with ACLS measures. These include definitive drug therapy with epinephrine and intubation.

Pulseless Electrical Activity. *Pulseless electrical activity* (PEA) is a situation in which organized electrical activity is seen on the ECG, but there is no mechanical heart activity and the patient has no pulse. It is the most common dysrhythmia seen after defibrillation. Prognosis is poor unless the underlying cause is quickly identified and treated. Common causes of PEA include hypovolemia, hypoxia, metabolic acidosis, hyperkalemia, hypokalemia, hypoglycemia, hypothermia, toxins (e.g., drug overdose), cardiac tamponade, thrombosis (e.g., MI, pulmonary embolus), tension pneumothorax, and trauma. Treatment begins with CPR, followed by drug therapy (e.g., epinephrine) and intubation. Correcting the underlying cause is critical to prognosis.

Sudden Cardiac Death. The term *sudden cardiac death* (SCD) refers to death from a cardiac cause. Most SCDs result from ventricular dysrhythmias, specifically VT or VF. SCD is discussed in Chapter 33.

Prodysrhythmia. Antidysrhythmic drugs can cause life-threatening dysrhythmias similar to those for which they are treating. We call this a *prodysrhythmia.* The patient who has severe left ventricular dysfunction is the most susceptible to prodysrhythmias. Digoxin and class IA, IC, and III antidysrhythmic drugs can cause a prodysrhythmic response.[6] The first several days of drug therapy are the vulnerable period for developing prodysrhythmias. For this reason, many patients start oral antidysrhythmic drugs in a monitored hospital setting.

INTERPROFESSIONAL AND NURSING CARE: DYSRHYTHMIAS

Antidysrhythmic Drug Therapy

Table 35.9 shows antidysrhythmic drugs by their primary effects on the heart cells and the ECG.

Before giving any *antidysrhythmic drug,* perform a thorough assessment with a complete physical assessment, health history, and medication history. Assess for contraindications, cautions, and drug interactions. Obtain a baseline ECG. Assess vital signs, heart and lung sounds, and pulse rate, rhythm, and quality. Assess for signs and symptoms associated with decreased CO because of the dysrhythmia, such as restlessness, syncope, chest pain, dyspnea, and crackles. Review laboratory studies, including electrolytes, and liver and kidney function tests.

When giving antidysrhythmics, closely monitor the ECG and vital signs, especially BP and pulse rate. Continue to perform an ongoing physical assessment. Monitor laboratory studies as needed. Give specific instructions for each drug. Teach the patient that oral forms are often better tolerated if taken with food and fluids to help decrease GI upset. Tell patients to avoid alcohol, caffeine, and tobacco.

TABLE 35.9 Drug Therapy

Antidysrhythmic Drugs

Drug	Effects on the Action Potential	Effects on ECG
Class I: Sodium Channel Blockers	Decrease impulse conduction in the atria, ventricles, and His-Purkinje system	
Class IA disopyramide (Norpace) procainamide quinidine	Delay repolarization	Widened QRS and prolonged QT interval
Class IB lidocaine mexiletine phenytoin (Dilantin)	Accelerate repolarization	Little or no effect on ECG
Class IC flecainide propafenone (Rythmol)	Decrease impulse conduction	Pronounced prodysrhythmic actions, widened QRS, prolonged QT interval
Class II: β-Adrenergic Blockers esmolol (Brevibloc) metoprolol (Lopressor) propranolol (Inderal)	Decrease automaticity of the SA node, slow impulse conduction in AV node, reduce atrial and ventricular contractility	Bradycardia, prolonged PR interval, AV block
Class III: Potassium Channel Blockers amiodarone dofetilide (Tikosyn) ibutilide (Corvert) sotalol* (Betapace)	Delay repolarization, resulting in prolonged duration of action potential and refractory period	Prolonged PR and QT intervals, widened QRS, bradycardia
Class IV: Calcium Channel Blockers diltiazem (Cardizem) verapamil	Decrease automaticity of SA node, delay AV node conduction; reduce myocardial contractility	Bradycardia, prolonged PR interval, AV block
Other Agents adenosine (Adenocard) digoxin (Lanoxin)	Decrease conduction through AV node, reduce automaticity of SA node	Prolonged PR interval, AV block
dronedarone (Multaq)†	Suppress atrial dysrhythmias though mechanism is unknown	Prolonged QT interval
magnesium	Decrease impulse conduction through AV node	AV block

*Sotalol has both class II and class III properties.
†Dronedarone has class I through IV properties.

Defibrillation

Defibrillation is the treatment of choice to end VF and pulseless VT. It is most effective when the myocardial cells are not anoxic or acidotic. Rapid defibrillation (within 2 minutes) is critical to a successful patient outcome. Defibrillation involves the passage of an electric shock through the heart to depolarize the myocardial cells. The goal is that after repolarization, the SA node will be able to resume the role of pacemaker.

Defibrillators deliver energy using a monophasic or biphasic waveform. Monophasic defibrillators deliver energy in 1 direction. Biphasic defibrillators deliver energy in 2 directions (Fig. 35.22). The shocks delivered are at lower energies and with fewer post-shock dysrhythmias than monophasic defibrillators.

We measure the output of a defibrillator in *joules,* or watts per second. The recommended energy for initial shocks in defibrillation depends on the type of defibrillator. Biphasic defibrillators deliver the first and any successive shocks using 120 to 200 joules. Recommendations for monophasic defibrillators include an initial shock at 360 joules. After the first shock, start CPR immediately beginning with chest compressions.

We can perform rapid defibrillation using a manual or automatic device (Fig. 35.23). Manual defibrillators require you to interpret heart rhythms, determine the need for a shock, and deliver a shock. An **automatic external defibrillator (AED)** can detect heart rhythms and tell the user to deliver a shock using hands-free defibrillator pads. Proficiency in AED use is part of the basic life support course for health care professionals. Be familiar with the operation of the type of defibrillator used in your clinical setting.

The following general steps are taken for defibrillation: (1) continue CPR until the defibrillator is charged; (2) turn the defibrillator on, and select the proper energy level; (3) check to see that the synchronizer switch is turned off (discussed later); (4) apply conductive materials (e.g., defibrillator gel pads) to the chest, one to the right of the sternum just below the clavicle, and the other to the left of the apex; (5) charge the defibrillator using the button on the defibrillator or the paddles; (6) position the paddles firmly on the chest wall over the conductive material (Fig. 35.22); (7) call and look to see that everyone is "all clear" to ensure that staff are not touching the patient or the bed at the time of discharge; and (8) deliver the charge by depressing buttons on both paddles simultaneously.

Hands-free, multifunction defibrillator pads are available. We place them on the chest as described earlier. Hands-free pads decrease the risk for injury compared to paddles. Connect the cables from the pads to the defibrillator. Charge and discharge the defibrillator using buttons on the defibrillator. It is still essential to ensure that all staff are clear before discharging the defibrillator.

! SAFETY ALERT Defibrillation and Cardioversion
- Check that the synchronizer switch is OFF for defibrillation.
- Turn the synchronizer switch ON for a cardioversion.
- Never apply defibrillator pads over a pacemaker or implantable cardioverter-defibrillator.
- Be certain that personnel are "all clear" before discharging the device.

FIG. 35.22 Paddle placement and current flow in monophasic defibrillation (A) and biphasic defibrillation (B).

FIG. 35.23 LifePak contains a monitor, defibrillator, and transcutaneous pacemaker. (Courtesy Medtronic Physio-Control, Redmond, Wash.)

Synchronized Cardioversion. *Synchronized cardioversion* is the therapy of choice for the patient with ventricular tachydysrhythmias (e.g., VT with a pulse) or supraventricular tachydysrhythmias (e.g., atrial flutter with a rapid ventricular response). A synchronized circuit in the defibrillator delivers a shock on the R wave of the QRS complex of the ECG. The synchronizer switch must be turned on when performing cardioversion.

The procedure for synchronized cardioversion is the same as for defibrillation with a few exceptions (Table 35.10). If synchronized cardioversion is done on a nonemergency basis (i.e., the patient is awake and hemodynamically stable), we sedate the patient with IV agents (e.g., midazolam, fentanyl) beforehand.

TABLE 35.10 Nursing Management

Assisting With Cardioversion

Preprocedure

- Obtain 12-lead ECG and initiate ECG monitoring.
- Perform baseline assessment, including vital signs, pulse oximetry, noting any manifestations of the dysrhythmia.
- Withhold food and fluids per institution policy.
- Assess baseline laboratory values (e.g., cardiac biomarkers, electrolytes).
- Teach patient and caregiver about procedure and postprocedure care.
- Remove all metallic objects, dentures, and transdermal patches. Clipping or removing chest hair may be needed.
- Establish IV access.
- Give sedative and other drugs, as ordered.

Postprocedure

- Maintain patent airway and administer O_2 as needed.
- Monitor ECG for dysrhythmias or other changes (e.g., ST segment elevation).
- Perform assessment and compare to baseline: vital signs, pulse oximetry, and heart and breath sounds.
- Assess level of consciousness and reorient as needed.
- Administer IV dysrhythmic and analgesic medications as ordered.
- Assess for burns and provide skin care.

Strict attention to maintaining the patient's airway is critical. If a patient with supraventricular tachycardia or VT with a pulse becomes hemodynamically unstable, synchronized cardioversion should be done as quickly as possible. Start the initial energy for synchronized cardioversion at 50 to 100 joules (biphasic defibrillator) and 100 joules (monophasic defibrillator) and increase if needed. If the patient becomes pulseless or the rhythm changes to VF, turn the synchronizer switch off and perform defibrillation.

Implantable Cardioverter-Defibrillator. The *implantable cardioverter-defibrillator* (ICD) is an important technology for patients who (1) have survived SCD, (2) have spontaneous sustained VT, (3) have syncope with inducible VT or VF during EPS, or (4) are at high risk for future life-threatening dysrhythmias (e.g., have cardiomyopathy). The use of ICDs has significantly decreased mortality rates in these patients.[12]

The ICD consists of a lead system placed via a subclavian vein to the endocardium. A battery-powered pulse generator is implanted subcutaneously, usually over the pectoral muscle on the patient's nondominant side. The pulse generator is similar in size to a pacemaker. Most systems are single-lead systems (Fig. 35.24). The ICD sensing system monitors the HR and rhythm and identifies VT or VF. After the sensing system detects a lethal dysrhythmia, the device delivers a 25-joule or less shock to the patient's heart. If the first shock is unsuccessful, the device recycles and can continue to deliver shocks.

In addition to defibrillation capabilities, ICDs have *antitachycardia* and *antibradycardia pacing* capabilities. These devices use algorithms that detect dysrhythmias and determine the appropriate response. They can start *overdrive pacing* of supraventricular tachycardia and VT, sparing the patient painful defibrillator shocks. They can provide backup pacing for bradydysrhythmias that may occur after defibrillation. Nursing care of the patient undergoing ICD placement is similar to the care of a patient undergoing permanent pacemaker implantation (see p. 771).

Patients with structural or congenital cardiac anomalies may receive a totally subcutaneous ICD (S-ICD).[13] The S-ICD pulse

FIG. 35.24 A, The implantable cardioverter-defibrillator (ICD) pulse generator from Medtronic, Inc. (Courtesy Medtronic, Inc., Minneapolis, Minn.) B, The ICD is placed in a subcutaneous pocket over the pectoral muscle. A single-lead system is placed transvenously from the pulse generator to the endocardium. The single lead detects dysrhythmias and delivers an electric shock to the heart muscle.

generator is placed under the skin on the left side of the chest with the electrode under the skin above the sternum. The system delivers a shock if it detects VT or VF. Since the S-ICD does not have any electrodes implanted in the heart, it has no pacing capability.[13]

Teaching the patient who is receiving an ICD and the caregiver is extremely important. Patients may have a variety of emotions, including fear of body image change, fear of recurrent dysrhythmias, expectation of pain with ICD discharge (described as a feeling of a blow to the chest), and anxiety about going home. Encourage patients and caregivers to take part in local or online ICD support groups.[14] Table 35.11 presents a teaching guide for the patient with an ICD and the caregiver.

Pacemakers

The artificial **cardiac pacemaker** is an electronic device used to pace the heart when the normal conduction pathway is damaged. The basic pacing circuit consists of a power source (battery-powered pulse generator) with programmable circuitry, 1 or more pacing leads, and the myocardium. The electrical signal (stimulus) travels from the pulse generator, through the leads, to the wall of the myocardium. The heart muscle is "captured" and stimulated to contract (Fig. 35.25).

Current pacemakers are small, sophisticated, and physiologically precise. They pace the atrium and/or 1 or both ventricles. Most pacemakers are *demand pacemakers*. This means that they sense the heart's electrical activity and fire only when the HR drops below a preset rate. Demand pacemakers have 2 distinct features: (1) a sensing device that inhibits the pacemaker when the HR is adequate and (2) a pacing device that triggers the pacemaker when no QRS complexes occur within a preset time.[1]

In addition to antibradycardia pacing, devices now include antitachycardia and overdrive pacing. *Antitachycardia pacing* involves the delivery of a stimulus to the ventricle to end tachydysrhythmias (e.g., VT). Overdrive pacing involves pacing the atrium at rates of 200 to 500 impulses per minute to try to stop atrial tachycardias (e.g., atrial flutter with a rapid ventricular response).[15,16]

Permanent Pacemaker. A *permanent pacemaker* is totally implanted within the body (Fig. 35.26). The power source is placed subcutaneously, usually over the pectoral muscle on the patient's nondominant side. The pacing leads are placed

TABLE 35.11 Patient & Caregiver Teaching

Implantable Cardioverter-Defibrillator (ICD)

Include the following information in the teaching plan for a patient receiving an ICD and the patient's caregiver:

1. Follow up with your HCP for routine checks of the function of the ICD. This is often done by interrogating the device using a telephone.
2. Report any signs of infection at incision site (e.g., redness, swelling, drainage) or fever to your HCP at once.
3. Keep incision dry for 4 days after insertion or as instructed.
4. Avoid lifting arm on ICD side above shoulder until approved.
5. Discuss resuming sexual activity with your HCP. It is usually safe to resume sexual activity once your incision is healed.
6. Do not drive until cleared by your HCP. This decision is usually based on the ongoing presence of dysrhythmias, the frequency of ICD firings, your overall health, and state laws about drivers with ICDs.
7. Avoid direct blows to ICD site.
8. Avoid large magnets and strong electromagnetic fields because these may interfere with the device.
9. You should not have an MRI unless the ICD is approved as MRI safe or there is a protocol in place for patient safety during the procedure.
10. Travel is not restricted. Tell security (e.g., airport, train station, public buildings) of presence of ICD because it may set off the metal detector. If hand-held screening wand is used, it should not be placed directly over the ICD. Manufacturer information may vary about the effect of metal detectors on the function of the ICD.
11. Do not stand near antitheft devices in doorways of stores and public buildings. You should walk through them at a normal pace.
12. If your ICD fires once, call your HCP right away. If you feel sick or if it fires more than once, contact the emergency response system.
13. You should always wear a Medic Alert ID device.
14. Always carry the ICD identification card and a current list of your drugs.
15. Consider joining an ICD support group (e.g., *www.icdsupportgroup. org/*).
16. Caregivers should learn cardiopulmonary resuscitation (CPR).

Pacemaker spike

FIG. 35.25 Ventricular capture (depolarization) secondary to signal *(pacemaker spike)* from pacemaker lead in the right ventricle.

transvenously to the right atrium and/or 1 or both ventricles and attached to the power source. Common reasons for insertion of a permanent pacemaker are found in Table 35.12.

New technology and research are focused on miniaturized, leadless permanent pacemakers. Single-component devices have the battery, sensors, electronics, and stimulating electrodes in a small capsule that is placed in the ventricle using a deflatable sheath. A multicomponent device has a small "seed" that is placed in a cardiac chamber. It acts as an energy transducer while an outside piece beams ultrasound (or radio waves) to the seed. The seed converts the energy to a pacing pulse.[15] The lack of a transvenous lead and subcutaneous pulse generator is

A   B   Right ventricle

FIG. 35.26 A, A dual-chamber rate-responsive pacemaker from Medtronic, Inc., is designed to treat patients with chronic heart problems in which the heart beats too slowly to support the body's circulation needs. (Courtesy Medtronic, Inc., Minneapolis, Minn.) B, Pacing leads in both the atrium and the ventricle enable a dual-chamber pacemaker to sense and pace in both heart chambers.

TABLE 35.12 **Indications for Permanent Pacemakers**
• Acquired AV block
• Second-degree AV block
• Third-degree AV block
• Atrial fibrillation with a slow ventricular response
• Bundle branch block
• Cardiomyopathy
• Dilated
• Hypertrophic
• HF
• SA node dysfunction
• Symptomatic bradycardia with unknown cause
• Tachydysrhythmias (e.g., ventricular tachycardia)

a major shift in cardiac pacing.[16] Other research is focusing on making permanent pacemakers without batteries.

Cardiac Resynchronization Therapy. *Cardiac resynchronization therapy* (CRT) is a pacing technique that resynchronizes the heart cycle by pacing both ventricles *(biventricular pacing).* This promotes improvement in ventricular function (Fig. 34.4). Most HF patients have intraventricular conduction delays causing abnormal ventricular contraction. This causes dyssynchrony between the right and left ventricles and results in reduced systolic function, pump inefficiency, and worsened HF. For patients with severe left ventricular dysfunction, devices that combine CRT with an ICD provide maximum therapy.[15,16]

Temporary Pacemaker. A *temporary pacemaker* is one that has the power source outside the body (Fig. 35.27). There are 3 types of temporary pacemakers: transvenous, epicardial, and transcutaneous. Table 35.13 lists common reasons for temporary pacing.

A *transvenous pacemaker* consists of a lead or leads that are threaded transvenously to the right atrium and/or right ventricle and attached to the external power source (Fig. 35.28). Most of these pacemakers are inserted in the ED or ICU in emergency situations. They provide a bridge to insertion of a permanent pacemaker or until the underlying cause of the dysrhythmia is resolved.

Epicardial pacing involves attaching an atrial and ventricular pacing lead to the epicardium during heart surgery. The leads are passed through the chest wall and attached to the external power source. Epicardial pacing leads are placed prophylactically in case a bradydysrhythmia or tachydysrhythmia occurs in the early postoperative period.[15,16]

FIG. 35.27 Temporary external, dual-chamber demand pacemaker. (Courtesy Medtronic, Inc., Minneapolis, Minn.)

TABLE 35.13 **Common Indications for Temporary Pacemakers**
• Maintain adequate HR and rhythm during special circumstances
• During surgery and postoperative recovery
• During cardiac catheterization or coronary angioplasty
• With drug therapy that may cause bradycardia
• Before implantation of a permanent pacemaker
• Prophylaxis after open heart surgery
• Acute anterior MI with second- or third-degree AV block or bundle branch block
• Acute inferior MI with symptomatic bradycardia and AV block
• EPS to evaluate patient with bradydysrhythmias and tachydysrhythmias

A *transcutaneous pacemaker* (TCP) can provide adequate HR and rhythm to the patient in an emergency. Placement of a TCP is a noninvasive, temporary procedure used until a transvenous pacemaker can be inserted or more definitive therapy is available.[1,11]

The TCP consists of a power source and a rate- and voltage-control device that attaches to 2 large, multifunction electrode pads. Position 1 pad on the anterior part of the chest, usually on the V_4 lead position, and the other pad on the back between the spine and left scapula at the level of the heart (Fig. 35.29). When programming the TCP, use the lowest current that results in a ventricular contraction (capture) to minimize patient discomfort.

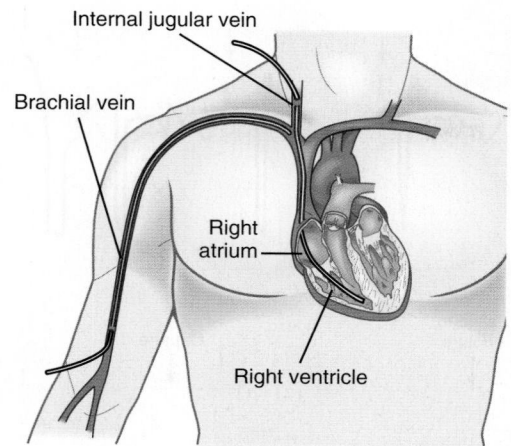

FIG. 35.28 Temporary transvenous pacemaker catheter insertion. A single lead is positioned in the right ventricle through the brachial, subclavian, jugular, or femoral vein.

FIG. 35.29 Transcutaneous pacemaker. Pacing electrodes are placed on the patient's anterior (A) and posterior (B) chest walls and attached to an external pacing unit (C).

Before starting TCP therapy, it is important to tell the patient what to expect. Explain that the muscle contractions created by the pacemaker when the current passes through the chest wall are uncomfortable. Reassure the patient that the TCP is temporary, and that it will be replaced by a transvenous pacemaker as soon as possible. Whenever possible, provide analgesia and/or sedation while the TCP is in use.

Monitoring of Patients With Pacemakers. Patients with temporary or permanent pacemakers are ECG monitored to evaluate the status of the pacemaker. Pacemaker malfunction involves a failure to sense, a failure to capture, or a failure to pace. *Failure to sense* occurs when the pacemaker does not recognize spontaneous atrial or ventricular activity, and it fires inappropriately (Fig. 35.30, A). This can result in the pacemaker firing during the excitable period of the cardiac cycle, resulting in VT. Failure to sense is caused by fibrosis around the tip of the pacing lead, battery failure, sensing set too high, or dislodgment of the electrode.

Failure to capture occurs when the electrical charge to the myocardium is insufficient to produce atrial or ventricular contraction (Fig. 35.30, B). This can result in serious bradycardia or asystole. Failure to capture is caused by pacer lead damage, battery failure, dislodgment of the electrode, electrical charge set too low, or fibrosis at the electrode tip.

Failure to pace occurs when the pacemaker does not initiate an electrical stimulus when it should fire (Fig. 35.30, C). This can happen from a wire fracture, lead displacement, oversensing, or electrical interference. Table 35.14 describes pacemaker troubleshooting.

Complications of invasive temporary (i.e., transvenous) or permanent pacemaker insertion include infection and hematoma formation at the insertion site, pneumothorax, failure to sense or capture, perforation of the atrial or ventricular septum by the pacing lead, and appearance of "end-of-life" battery power on testing the pacemaker. Several measures can prevent or assess for complications. These include prophylactic IV antibiotic therapy before and after insertion, postinsertion chest x-ray to check lead placement and to rule out a pneumothorax, careful observation of insertion site, and continuous ECG monitoring of the patient's rhythm.

After pacemaker insertion, the patient can be out of bed once stable. Have the patient limit arm and shoulder activity on the operative side to prevent dislodging the newly implanted pacing leads. Observe the insertion site for signs of bleeding and check that the incision is intact. Note any temperature elevation or pain at the insertion site and treat as ordered. Most patients are discharged by the next day if stable.

Table 35.15 outlines patient and caregiver teaching for the patient with a pacemaker. The patient with a newly implanted pacemaker and the caregiver may have questions about activity restrictions and concerns about body image. The goals of pacemaker therapy include enhancing physiologic functioning and quality of life. Emphasize this to the patient and caregiver and provide specific advice on activity restrictions.

After discharge, patients need to check pacemaker function on a regular basis. This can include outpatient visits to a pacemaker clinic or home monitoring using telephone transmitter devices. Another method to evaluate pacemaker performance is noninvasive program stimulation. This procedure is done on an outpatient basis in the EPS laboratory.

Radiofrequency Catheter Ablation Therapy

Radiofrequency catheter ablation therapy uses electrical energy to "burn" or ablate areas of the conduction system. Ablation therapy is done after EPS has identified the source of the dysrhythmia. An electrode-tipped ablation catheter ablates accessory pathways or ectopic sites in the atria, AV node, and ventricles. Catheter ablation is a definitive treatment for tachydysrhythmias. It is the nonpharmacologic treatment of choice for atrial dysrhythmias resulting in rapid ventricular rates and AV nodal reentrant tachycardia refractory to drug therapy.[8]

The ablation procedure is an effective treatment with a low complication rate. Nursing care of the patient after ablation therapy is similar to that of a patient undergoing cardiac catheterization (see Chapter 31 and Table 31.9).

SYNCOPE

Syncope is a brief lapse in consciousness accompanied by a loss in postural tone (fainting). The causes of syncope can

FIG. 35.30 Causes of pacemaker malfunction. **A,** Failure to sense: the pacemaker does not sense the patient's own cardiac rhythm and initiates an electrical impulse. Failure to sense manifests as pacer spikes that fall too closely to the patient's own rhythm, earlier than the programmed rate (see *arrows*). **B,** Failure to capture: a pacer spike is noted but is not followed by a P wave (atrial pacemaker) or a QRS complex (ventricular pacemaker). **C,** Failure to pace: the pacemaker fails to initiate an electrical stimulus when it should fire.

TABLE 35.14 **Nursing Management**

Troubleshooting Pacemakers

Problem	Potential Solution
Identified initial concern about pacemaker function	• Monitor continuous ECG and patient's vital signs while troubleshooting pacemaker problems • Call emergency response services if needed • Contact HCP immediately if basic troubleshooting does not work, as patient could have a lead wire displaced or a defective lead wire
Temporary pacemaker not firing	• Check to make sure all connections are hooked up correctly and tight • Ensure that hands-free pads have contact with the skin (shave excess hair, dry off perspiration) • Check that the generator has power (plug in the equipment or use a new battery each time)
Temporary pacemaker not capturing	• Check connections • Check for generator power • Turn up the milliamps on the generator, look for capture and set 10 milliamps above capture • Place patient on left side to promote contact of the transvenous pacing wire with the epicardium
Temporary pacemaker not sensing patient's underlying rhythm	• Check connections • Check for generator power • Turn up sensitivity • Place patient on left side
Permanent pacemaker not working	• Contact HCP • Contact pacemaker company for service if requested by HCP

TABLE 35.15 Patient & Caregiver Teaching

Pacemaker

Include the following information in the teaching plan for a patient with a pacemaker and the patient's caregiver:

1. Maintain follow-up care with your HCP to begin regular pacemaker function checks. This is often done by checking the device using a telephone.
2. Report any signs of infection at incision site (e.g., redness, swelling, drainage) or fever to your HCP at once.
3. Keep incision dry for 4 days after implantation, or as ordered.
4. Avoid lifting arm on pacemaker side above shoulder until approved by your cardiologist.
5. Avoid direct blows to pacemaker site.
6. Avoid close proximity to high-output electric generators since these can interfere with the function of the pacemaker.
7. You should not have an MRI unless the pacemaker is approved as MRI safe or there is a protocol in place for patient safety during the procedure.
8. Microwave ovens are safe to use and do not interfere with pacemaker function.
9. Avoid standing near antitheft devices in doorways of department stores and public libraries. You should walk through them at a normal pace.
10. Travel is not restricted. Tell security (e.g., airport, train station, public buildings) of presence of pacemaker because it may set off the metal detector. If hand-held screening wand is used, it should not be placed directly over the pacemaker. Manufacturer information may vary about the effect of metal detectors on the function of the pacemaker.
11. Monitor pulse and tell your HCP if heart rate drops below predetermined rate.
12. Always carry your pacemaker information card and a current list of drugs.
13. Always wear a Medic Alert ID device.
14. Consider joining a pacemaker support group (e.g., *www.pacemakerclub.com/*).

be cardiovascular or noncardiovascular. The most common cause of syncope is cardioneurogenic syncope, or "vasovagal" syncope (e.g., carotid sinus sensitivity). Other cardiovascular causes relate to dysrhythmias (e.g., tachycardias, bradycardias), prosthetic valve malfunction, pulmonary emboli, and HF. Noncardiovascular causes vary and include stress, hypoglycemia, dehydration, stroke, and seizure.[17]

A diagnostic workup for a patient with syncope from a suspected heart cause begins with ruling out structural and ischemic heart disease. This is done with echocardiography and stress testing. EPS is used to diagnose atrial and ventricular tachydysrhythmias and conduction problems causing bradydysrhythmias, all of which can cause syncope. These problems can be treated with antidysrhythmic drug therapy, pacemakers, ICDs, and/or catheter ablation therapy.

A patient without structural heart disease or in whom EPS testing is not diagnostic may have a *head-up tilt-test*. Normally, an upright position results in gravity displacing 300 to 800 mL of blood to the lower extremities. Specialized nerve fibers called mechanoreceptors are found throughout the vascular system. These respond to the increased blood volume by starting a reflex increase in sympathetic stimulation and decrease in parasympathetic output. The end results are a slight increase in HR and diastolic BP, and a slight decrease in systolic BP.[17,18]

In cardioneurogenic syncope, the increase in venous pooling that occurs in the upright position reduces venous return to the heart. This results in a sudden, compensatory increase in ventricular contraction. The brain mistakenly thinks this is a hypertensive state and stops sympathetic stimulation. This produces a paradoxical vasodilation and bradycardia (vasovagal response). The end results are bradycardia, hypotension, cerebral hypoperfusion, and syncope.

In the head-up tilt-test the patient is placed on a table supported by a belt across the torso and feet. Baseline ECG, BP, and HR are obtained in the horizontal position. Next, the table is tilted 60 to 80 degrees and the patient is kept in this upright position for 20 to 60 minutes. ECG and HR are recorded continuously. BP is measured every 3 minutes throughout the test. If the patient's BP and HR responses are abnormal and clinical symptoms occur (e.g., faintness), the test is positive. If after 30 minutes there is no response, the table is returned to the horizontal position and an IV infusion of low-dose isoproterenol may be started to try to provoke a response.

Other diagnostic tests for syncope can include various recording devices (e.g., Holter monitor or event monitor/loop recorder, discussed in Chapter 31 and Table 31.7), blood volume determination, hemodynamic testing, and autonomic reflex testing. About 30% of those who have 1 episode of syncope have a recurrence. The underlying cause of syncope and the patient's age and co-morbidities affect the patient's treatment and prognosis.[17,18]

CASE STUDY

Dysrhythmia and Cardiac Arrest

(© iStockphoto/Thinkstock.)

Patient Profile

J.M., a 68-yr-old white, retired postal worker, was admitted to the telemetry unit with a diagnosis of acute decompensated heart failure (ADHF). He had a cardiac arrest (pulseless ventricular tachycardia [VT]) and was successfully defibrillated after 1 shock. He was transferred to the cardiac care unit. J.M. is awake but lethargic and responds appropriately to questions.

Subjective Data

- History of hypertension, CAD, 2 MIs, and chronic HF
- Reports shortness of breath at rest and in an upright position

Objective Data

Physical Examination

- Appears weak, anxious
- BP 102/60 mm Hg, pulse 70/min, respirations 26/min
- Lungs: bilateral coarse crackles in the bases
- Heart: S_3 gallop at apex

Diagnostic Studies

- Echocardiogram: severe left ventricular dysfunction with ejection fraction of 24%
- Serum potassium: 2.9 mEq/L (2.9 mmol/L)
- Serum cardiac biomarkers: negative
- Serum b-type natriuretic peptide (BNP): 1852 pg/mL

CASE STUDY—cont'd

Dysrhythmia and Cardiac Arrest

Interprofessional Care

• Continuous ECG monitoring

• Amiodarone infusion
• Cardiac rehabilitation consult
• Dietary consult

Discussion Questions

1. Why is J.M. at risk for sudden cardiac death?
2. Explain the reason for using amiodarone after cardiac arrest.
3. What methods are used to assess the effectiveness of the antidysrhythmic therapy?
4. Interpret the rhythm strip.
5. Explain the significance of the diagnostic studies and other interprofessional care orders.
6. Why would J.M. be a candidate for CRT and an ICD?
7. *Priority Decision:* Based on the assessment data provided, what are the priority nursing diagnoses?
8. *Priority Decision:* What are the priority nursing interventions for J.M.?
9. *Collaboration:* Which tasks could be delegated to UAP?
10. *Evidence-Based Practice:* Once J.M. is stable, he is scheduled for the insertion of a CRT/ICD. On your rounds, he asks you why he needs 2 devices. How would you respond?

Answers available at *http://evolve.elsevier.com/Lewis/medsurg.*

▌ BRIDGE TO NCLEX EXAMINATION

The number of the question corresponds to the same-numbered outcome at the beginning of the chapter.

1. A patient admitted with syncope has continuous ECG monitoring. An examination of the rhythm strip reveals the following: atrial rate 74 beats/min and regular; ventricular rate 62 beats/min and irregular; P wave normal shape; PR interval lengthens progressively until a P wave is not conducted; QRS normal shape. The *priority* nursing intervention would be to
   a. give epinephrine 1 mg IV push.
   b. prepare for synchronized cardioversion.
   c. observe for symptoms of hypotension or angina.
   d. apply transcutaneous pacemaker pads on the patient.
2. The ECG monitor of a patient in the cardiac care unit after an MI shows ventricular bigeminy with a rate of 50 beats/min. The nurse would
   a. perform defibrillation.
   b. administer IV amiodarone.
   c. prepare for temporary pacemaker insertion.
   d. assess the patient's response to the dysrhythmia.
3. In the patient with supraventricular tachycardia, which assessment indicates decreased cardiac output?
   a. Hypertension and dyspnea
   b. Chest pain and palpitations
   c. Abdominal distention and tachypnea
   d. Bounding pulses and a systolic murmur
4. The nurse prepares a patient for synchronized cardioversion knowing that cardioversion differs from defibrillation in that
   a. defibrillation delivers a lower dose of electrical energy.
   b. cardioversion is a treatment for atrial bradydysrhythmias.
   c. defibrillation is synchronized to deliver a shock during the QRS complex.
   d. patients should be sedated if cardioversion is done on a nonemergency basis.

5. Which patient teaching points should the nurse include when providing discharge instructions to a patient with a new permanent pacemaker and the caregiver? *(select all that apply)*
   a. Avoid or limit air travel.
   b. Take and record a daily pulse rate.
   c. Obtain and wear a Medic Alert ID device at all times.
   d. Avoid lifting arm on the side of the pacemaker above shoulder.
   e. Do not use a microwave oven because it interferes with pacemaker function.
6. Important teaching for the patient scheduled for a radiofrequency catheter ablation procedure includes explaining that
   a. ventricular bradycardia may be induced and treated during the procedure.
   b. catheter will be placed in both femoral arteries to allow double-catheter use.
   c. the procedure will destroy areas of the conduction system that are causing rapid heart rhythms.
   d. general anesthetic will be given to prevent the awareness of any "sudden cardiac death" experiences.

1. c, 2. d, 3. b, 4. d, 5. b, c, d, 6. c

For rationales to these answers and even more NCLEX review questions, visit *http://evolve.elsevier.com/Lewis/medsurg.*

ⓔ EVOLVE WEBSITE/RESOURCES LIST

http://evolve.elsevier.com/Lewis/medsurg
Review Questions (Online Only)
Key Points
Answer Keys for Questions
- Rationales for Bridge to NCLEX Examination Questions
- Answer Guidelines for Case Study on p. 775

Case Study
- Patient With Atrial Fibrillation

Conceptual Care Map Creator
Audio Glossary
Content Updates

REFERENCES

1. Sole ML, Klein DG, Moseley MJ: *Introduction to critical care nursing*, ed 7, St Louis, 2017, Elsevier.
2. Wesley K: *Huszar's ECG and 12-lead interpretation*, ed5, St Louis, 2017, Elsevier.
3. Franciosi S, Perry FK, Roston TM, et al: The role of the autonomic nervous system in arrhythmias and sudden cardiac death, *Auton Neurosci-Basic* 205:1, 2017.
*4. American Association of Critical-Care Nurses: AACN practice alert: Ensuring accurate ST-segment monitoring. Retrieved from *www.aacn.org/~/media/aacn-website/clincial-resources/practice-alerts/stsegmentmonitoring.pdf.*
*5. American Association of Critical-Care Nurses: AACN practice alert: Accurate dysrhythmia monitoring in adults. Retrieved from *www.aacn.org/clinical-resources/practice-alerts/dysrhythmia-monitoring.*
6. Clayton BD, Willihnganz MJ: *Basic pharmacology for nurses*, ed 17, St Louis, 2017, Elsevier.
*7. Page RL, Joglar JA, Caldwell MA, et al: 2015 ACC/AHA/HRS guideline for the management of adult patients with supraventricular tachycardia, *Circulation* 133:e471, 2016.
*8. Heidenreich PA, Solis P, Estes NA, et al: 2016 ACC/AHA clinical performance and quality measures for adults with atrial fibrillation or atrial flutter, *J Am Coll Cardiol* 68:525, 2016.
*9. Center for Disease Control: Atrial fibrillation fact sheet. Retrieved from *www.cdc.gov/dhdsp/data_statistics/fact_sheets/fs_atrial_fibrillation.htm.*
10. American College of Cardiology: Left atrial appendage closure. Retrieved from *www.acc.org/latest-in-cardiology/articles/2016/09/20/06/41/left-atrial-appendage-closure-in-2016.*
*11. Sinz E, Navarro K, Soderberg ES: *Advanced cardiovascular life support: Provider manual 2015*, Dallas, 2015, American Heart Association. (Classic)
12. Mulpuru SK, Madhavan M, McLeod CJ: Cardiac pacemakers: Function, troubleshooting, and management, *J Am Coll Cardiol* 69:189, 2017.
13. Boersma L, Barr C, Knops R: Implant and midterm outcomes of the subcutaneous implantable cardioverter-defibrillator registry, *J Am Coll Cardiol* 70:830, 2017.
14. ICD Support Group. Retrieved from *www.icdsupportgroup.org/board/.*
15. Madhavan M, Mulpuru SK, McLeod C, et al: Advances and future directions in cardiac pacemakers, *J Am Coll Cardiol* 69:211, 2017.
*16. Reddy VY, Miller MA, Neuzil P, et al: Cardiac resynchronization therapy with wireless left ventricular endocardial pacing: the SELECT-LV study, *J Am Coll Cardiol* 69:2119, 2017.
*17. Shen WK, Sheldon RS, Benditt DG: 2017 ACC/AHA/HRS guideline for the evaluation and management of patients with syncope, *Circulation* 136:e25, 2017.
18. Cleveland Clinic: Syncope. Retrieved from *https://my.clevelandclinic.org/health/diseases/17536-syncope.*

*Evidence-based information for clinical practice.

36

Inflammatory and Structural Heart Disorders

Patricia Keegan

A kind heart is a fountain of gladness, making everything in its vicinity freshen into smiles.

Washington Irving

(e) http://evolve.elsevier.com/Lewis/medsurg

CONCEPTUAL FOCUS

Fatigue

Functional Ability

Inflammation

Perfusion

LEARNING OUTCOMES

1. Describe the pathophysiology, clinical manifestations, and interprofessional and nursing management of the patient with infective endocarditis or pericarditis.
2. Describe the pathophysiology, clinical manifestations, and interprofessional and nursing management of the patient with myocarditis.
3. Distinguish the etiology, pathophysiology, and clinical manifestations of rheumatic fever and rheumatic heart disease.

4. Describe the interprofessional and nursing management of the patient with rheumatic heart disease.
5. Describe the pathophysiology, clinical manifestations, and interprofessional and nursing management of patients with various types of valvular heart disease.
6. Relate the pathophysiology, clinical manifestations, and interprofessional and nursing management of patients with different types of cardiomyopathy.

KEY TERMS

aortic regurgitation (AR), p. 790
aortic stenosis (AS), p. 789
cardiac tamponade, p. 783
cardiomyopathy (CMP), p. 794
chronic constrictive pericarditis, p. 784
dilated cardiomyopathy, p. 794

hypertrophic cardiomyopathy, p. 795
infective endocarditis (IE), p. 778
mitral valve prolapse (MVP), p. 789
myocarditis, p. 785
pericardiocentesis, p. 784
pericarditis, p. 782

regurgitation, p. 788
rheumatic fever (RF), p. 785
rheumatic heart disease, p. 785
stenosis, p. 788

This chapter describes the pathophysiology and management of patients with select inflammatory and structural heart problems. Conceptually, these problems can adversely affect perfusion. Inflammatory, infectious, and structural problems result in impaired cardiac output (CO), which leads to decreased tissue perfusion and impaired gas exchange. The patient may have pain, hyperthermia, and decreased functional and cognitive ability. The nurse plays a key role in providing patients with the education needed to manage problems and their effects.

INFLAMMATORY DISORDERS OF HEART

INFECTIVE ENDOCARDITIS

Infective endocarditis (IE) is a disease of the endocardial layer of the heart. The *endocardium* is the innermost layer of the heart (Fig. 36.1) and heart valves. IE most often affects the aortic and mitral valves. In the United States, there are around 40,000 to 50,000 new cases of IE per year.[1] The 1-year mortality of IE has not changed in the past 20 years.[1]

Classification

We often classify IE based on the cause (e.g., IV drug use IE [IVDA IE], fungal IE) or site of involvement (e.g., prosthetic valve endocarditis [PVE]). In the past, we have described IE as subacute or acute. The *subacute form* affects those with preexisting valve disease over a period of months. In contrast, the *acute form* affects those with healthy valves and appears as a rapidly progressive illness.

Etiology and Pathophysiology

IE occurs when blood flow allows organisms to contact and infect previously damaged heart valves or other endothelial surfaces. About 30% of cases are caused by *Staphylococcus aureus*.[1] Other bacterial causes include *Streptococcus viridans* and coagulase-negative staphylococci. The organisms make biofilms, which protect the organisms from immune defenses and make antimicrobials less effective.[2]

Persons with a variety of underlying cardiac and noncardiac conditions can develop IE (Table 36.1). Patients are stratified into categories of high, moderate, or low risk for developing

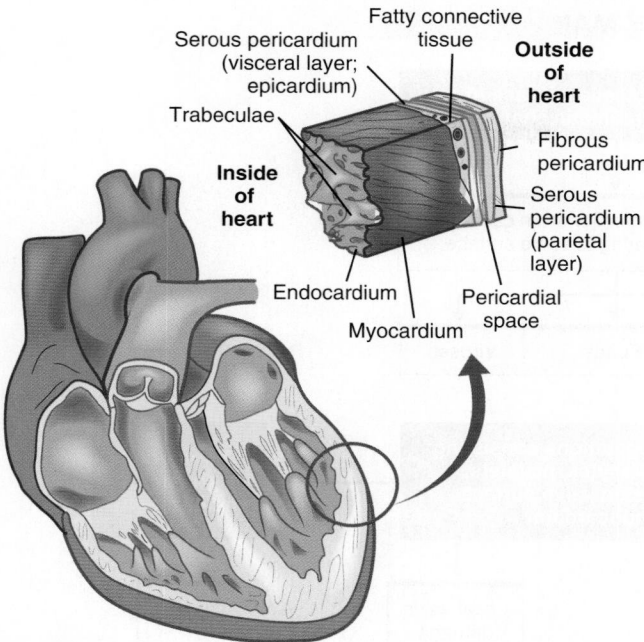

FIG. 36.1 Layers of the heart muscle and pericardium. The section of the heart wall shows the fibrous pericardium, the parietal and visceral layers of the serous pericardium (with the pericardial sac between them), the myocardium, and the endocardium. (Modified from Patton KT, Thibodeau GA: *The human body in health and disease*, ed 5, St Louis, 2010, Mosby.)

TABLE 36.1 Common Risk Factors for Endocarditis

Cardiac Conditions
- Acquired valve disease (e.g., mitral valve prolapse with regurgitation, calcified aortic stenosis)
- Cardiomyopathy
- Congenital heart disease
- Heart lesions (e.g., ventricular septal defect, asymmetric septal hypertrophy)
- Marfan's syndrome
- Pacemaker
- Prior IE
- Prosthetic heart valve(s)
- Rheumatic heart disease (e.g., mitral valve regurgitation)

Noncardiac Conditions
- Hospital-acquired bacteremia
- IV drug use

Procedure-Associated Risks
- Intravascular devices (e.g., central venous catheter)
- Procedures listed in Table 36.2

IE or having a poor outcome.[2] Rheumatic heart disease used to be the most common cause of IE. Now, it accounts for less than 20% of cases. The main risk factors for IE include (1) aging (more than 50% of older people have calcified aortic stenosis), (2) IV drug use, (3) having a prosthetic valve, (4) use of intravascular devices resulting in health care–associated infections (e.g., methicillin-resistant *S. aureus* [MRSA]), and (5) renal dialysis.[1]

IE typically develops in 3 stages: (1) bacteremia, (2) adhesion, and (3) vegetation.[1] *Vegetations,* the primary lesions of IE, consist of fibrin, leukocytes, platelets, and microbes that stick

FIG. 36.2 Bacterial IE of the mitral valve. The valve is covered with large, irregular vegetations *(arrow)*. (From Damjanov I, Linder J: *Pathology: A color atlas*, St Louis, 2000, Mosby.)

to the valve surface or endocardium (Fig. 36.2). The loss of parts of these fragile vegetations into the circulation results in *emboli*. Up to 30% of persons with IE develop embolization.[3] This occurs when left-sided heart vegetation moves to various organs (e.g., brain, kidneys, spleen) and to the extremities, causing limb infarction. Right-sided heart lesions move to the lungs, resulting in pulmonary emboli.

The infection may spread locally and damage the valves or their supporting structures. This causes dysrhythmias, valve dysfunction, and invasion of the myocardium, leading to heart failure (HF), sepsis, and heart block (Fig. 36.3).

Clinical Manifestations

The manifestations of IE are nonspecific and can involve multiple organ systems. Most patients have fever.[3] Fever may be low grade or may be absent in older adults or those who are immunocompromised. Other symptoms include chills, weakness, malaise, fatigue, and anorexia. Patients may have arthralgias, myalgias, back pain, abdominal discomfort, weight loss, headache, and clubbing of fingers in subacute forms of IE.[4]

Vascular signs include *splinter hemorrhages* (black longitudinal streaks) in the nail beds. Petechiae from microembolization of vegetative lesions can occur on the conjunctivae, lips, buccal mucosa, and palate and over the ankles, feet, and antecubital and popliteal areas. *Osler's nodes* (painful, tender, red or purple, pea-size lesions) are found on the fingertips or toes. *Janeway's lesions* (flat, painless, small, red spots) may be seen on the fingertips, palms, soles of feet, and toes. Eye examination may show hemorrhagic retinal lesions called *Roth's spots*.

Most patients have a new or worsening systolic murmur. Murmurs are usually absent in tricuspid IE because right-sided heart sounds are too low to be heard. HF is common, occurring in up to 80% of patients with aortic valve IE and 50% of those with mitral valve IE.[3]

Septic embolism is a potential complication of IE. Embolic events occur in more than half of patients.[3] The central nervous system (CNS) is the most often affected organ system, followed by extremities, spleen, and kidney.

Diagnostic Studies

The health history is important in assessing IE. Ask patients if they have had any recent (within the past 3 to 6 months) dental, urologic, surgical, or gynecologic procedures, including obstetric delivery. Note any history of IVDA, heart disease, recent heart catheterization, heart surgery, intravascular device

PATHOPHYSIOLOGY MAP

FIG. 36.3 Pathogenesis of IE.

placement, renal dialysis, or infections (e.g., skin, respiratory, urinary tract).

Three blood cultures drawn over a period of 1 hour from 3 different sites will be positive in most patients with IE.[4] Culture-negative IE is associated with antibiotic usage within the previous 2 weeks or results from a pathogen not easily detected by standard cultures A mild leukocytosis occurs in acute IE. The erythrocyte sedimentation rate (ESR) and C-reactive protein (CRP) levels may be increased. Echocardiography can show vegetations.

Guidelines for the diagnosis of IE are based on the Duke Criteria. The patient must have 2 major criteria and 1 minor criterion, or 1 major and 3 minor, or 5 minor criteria. Major criteria include positive blood cultures, typical microorganism for IE from 2 separate blood cultures, evidence of endocardial involvement, and new valvular vegetation. Minor criteria include predisposing heart condition or IV drug use, vascular phenomena, immunologic phenomena, microbiologic evidence, or echocardiographic findings consistent with IE but not meeting major criteria.[5]

A chest x-ray may show *cardiomegaly* (an enlarged heart). An electrocardiogram (ECG) may show first- or second-degree atrioventricular (AV) block because the heart valves lie close to conductive tissue, especially the AV node.

Interprofessional Care

Prophylactic Treatment. Situations and conditions that require antibiotic prophylaxis are detailed in Table 36.2.

TABLE 36.2 Antibiotic Prophylaxis to Prevent Endocarditis

Target Groups for Prophylactic Antibiotics

People with the following heart conditions should receive prophylactic antibiotics when they have the conditions or procedures listed below:

- Prosthetic heart valve or prosthetic material used to repair heart valve
- History of infectious IE
- Congenital heart disease (CHD)
  - Unrepaired cyanotic CHD (including palliative shunts and conduits)
  - Repaired congenital heart defect with prosthetic material or device for 6 mo after the procedure
  - Repaired CHD with residual defects at the site or next to the site of prosthetic patch or prosthetic device
- Heart transplant recipients who develop heart valve disease

Conditions or Procedures Requiring Antibiotic Prophylaxis

When the target groups have the following conditions or procedures, they need prophylactic antibiotics:

- Oral
  - Dental manipulation involving the gums or roots of the teeth
  - Dental manipulation involving puncture of the oral mucosa
- Respiratory
  - Respiratory tract incisions (e.g., biopsy)
  - Tonsillectomy and adenoidectomy
- Surgical procedures that involve infected skin, skin structures, or musculoskeletal tissue

Source: Nishimura RA, Otto CM, Bonow RO, et al: 2014 AHA/ACC guidelines for the management of patients with valvular heart disease: executive summary—A report of the American College of Cardiology/AHA Task Force on Practice Guidelines, *Circulation* 129:2440, 2014.

Drug Therapy. Accurately identifying the causative organism is the key to successful treatment of IE. Long-term treatment is needed to kill dormant bacteria within the valvular vegetations. Complete removal of the organism generally takes weeks. Relapses are common.[5]

Antibiotic therapy is based on blood culture results. The effectiveness of therapy is assessed with subsequent blood cultures. Cultures that stay positive indicate inadequate or inappropriate antibiotics, an aortic root or myocardial abscess, or the wrong diagnosis (e.g., an infection elsewhere). It is reasonable to obtain 2 sets of blood cultures every 24 to 48 hours until the infection is cleared.[3] After completion of antibiotics, follow-up echocardiogram and inflammatory markers are done at 1, 3, 6, and 12 months.[4]

Fungal IE and PVE respond poorly to antibiotic therapy alone. Early valve replacement followed by prolonged (6 weeks or more) antibiotics is needed in these situations. Valve replacement surgery (discussed later in this chapter) is done in 50% to 60% of cases of IE. Three reasons to perform surgery are for valve dysfunction leading to HF, to prevent embolization, or for uncontrolled infection.[4]

Fever that persists after treatment has been started is managed with aspirin, acetaminophen, fluids, and rest. Complete bed rest is usually not needed unless the temperature stays elevated or there are signs of HF. IE with HF responds poorly to drug therapy and valve replacement, so it can be life threatening.

 SAFETY ALERT Communicating Test Results
- If blood culture results for a patient diagnosed with IE show that the organism is not susceptible to the ordered antibiotic, immediately notify the HCP.
- A National Patient Safety Goal stresses the importance of communicating critical test results to the right HCP in a timely manner.

❖ NURSING MANAGEMENT: INFECTIVE ENDOCARDITIS

◆ Nursing Assessment

Subjective and objective data to obtain from a patient with IE are found in Table 36.3. Assess vital signs together with heart sounds to detect a murmur, a change in a preexisting murmur, and extra sounds (e.g., S_3).

Arthralgia (joint pain) and myalgias are common. Assess the patient for joint tenderness, decreased range of motion (ROM), and muscle tenderness. Examine the patient for petechiae, splinter hemorrhages, and Osler's nodes. Complete a general systems assessment to determine any hemodynamic or embolic complications.

◆ Nursing Diagnoses

Nursing diagnoses for the patient with IE include:
- Impaired cardiac output
- Activity intolerance

More information on nursing diagnoses and interventions for the patient with IE is in eNursing Care Plan 36.1 on the website for this chapter.

◆ Planning

The overall goals for the patient with IE include (1) normal or baseline heart function, (2) ability to perform activities of daily living (ADLs) without fatigue, and (3) an understanding of the treatment plan to prevent recurrence.

TABLE 36.3 Nursing Assessment
Infective Endocarditis

Subjective Data
Important Health Information
Past health history: Valvular, congenital, or syphilitic heart disease, including valve repair or replacement. Previous IE, childbirth, staphylococcal or streptococcal infections, hospital-acquired bacteremia
Medications: Immunosuppressive therapy
Surgery or other treatments: Recent obstetric or gynecologic procedures. Invasive procedures, including catheterization, cystoscopy. Recent dental or surgical procedures, GI procedures (e.g., endoscopy)

Functional Health Patterns
Health perception–health management: IV drug use, alcohol use. Malaise
Nutritional-metabolic: Weight gain or loss, anorexia. Chills, diaphoresis
Elimination: Bloody urine
Activity-exercise: Exercise intolerance, generalized weakness, fatigue. Cough, dyspnea on exertion, orthopnea, palpitations
Sleep-rest: Night sweats
Cognitive-perceptual: Chest, back, or abdominal pain. Headache, joint tenderness, muscle tenderness

Objective Data
General
Fever

Integumentary
Osler's nodes on extremities, splinter hemorrhages under nail beds, Janeway's lesions on fingertips, palms, soles of feet, and toes. Petechiae of skin, mucous membranes, or conjunctivae. Purpura, peripheral edema, finger clubbing

Respiratory
Tachypnea, crackles

Cardiovascular
Dysrhythmia, tachycardia, new murmurs, S_3, S_4. Retinal hemorrhages

Possible Diagnostic Findings
Leukocytosis, anemia, ↑ ESR, ↑ CRP and cardiac biomarkers. Positive blood cultures, hematuria. Echocardiogram showing chamber enlargement, valvular dysfunction, and vegetations. Chest x-ray showing cardiomegaly and pulmonary infiltrates. ECG showing ischemia and conduction defects. Signs of systemic embolization or pulmonary embolism

◆ Nursing Implementation

◆ Health Promotion. Teaching the patient at high risk for IE (Tables 36.1 and 36.2) helps reduce the incidence and recurrence of IE. Tell the patient to avoid people with infections, especially upper respiratory tract infections, and to report cold, flu, and cough symptoms. Stress the importance of avoiding excessive fatigue, planning rest periods, using good oral hygiene, and scheduling regular dental visits.[5]

Tell the patient to inform HCPs scheduling invasive procedures about the history of IE, as prophylactic antibiotic therapy may be needed. Refer the patient with a history of IVDA for drug rehabilitation.

Ambulatory Care. A patient with IE has many problems that need nursing management. IE generally requires treatment with antibiotics for 4 to 6 weeks. After initial treatment in the hospital, the patient may continue treatment at home if hemodynamically stable and adherent. Assess the home setting for adequate support. Patients who receive outpatient IV antibiotics need vigilant home nursing care.

Assessment findings are often nonspecific (Table 36.3). Tell the patient and caregiver about the importance of monitoring body temperature. Persistent temperature elevations may mean that the antibiotic is ineffective. Patients are at risk for life-threatening complications, such as stroke, pulmonary edema, and HF. Teach patients and caregivers to recognize signs and symptoms of these complications (e.g., change in mental status, dyspnea, chest pain, unexplained weight gain).

The patient needs adequate periods of physical and emotional rest. Bed rest may be needed when the patient has fever or complications (e.g., heart damage). Otherwise, the patient may perform moderate activity. To prevent problems related to decreased mobility, have the patient to wear elastic compression stockings, perform ROM exercises, and deep breathe and cough every 2 hours. The patient may have anxiety and fear. You must recognize this and begin strategies to help the patient cope with the illness.

Monitor laboratory data, including blood cultures, to determine antibiotic effectiveness. Assess IV lines for patency and signs of complications (e.g., phlebitis). Give antibiotics as prescribed. Monitor the patient for any adverse drug reactions.

Teach the patient and caregiver the nature of the disease and on how to reduce the risk for reinfection. Explain the relationship of follow-up care, good nutrition and dental care, and prompt treatment of common infections (e.g., colds) to stay healthy. Teach the patient about symptoms to report that may indicate another infection (e.g., fever, fatigue, chills). Finally, explain the importance of prophylactic antibiotic therapy before certain invasive procedures (Table 36.2).

◆ Evaluation

The expected outcomes are that the patient with IE will
- Maintain adequate tissue and organ perfusion
- Maintain normal body temperature
- Report an increase in physical and emotional comfort

ACUTE PERICARDITIS

Pericarditis is a condition caused by inflammation of the pericardial sac (pericardium), often with fluid accumulation. The pericardium is composed of the inner serous membrane (visceral pericardium) and the outer fibrous (parietal) layer (Fig. 36.1). The pericardial space between these 2 layers normally holds 10 to 15 mL of serous fluid. The pericardium anchors the heart, provides lubrication to decrease friction between heart contractions, and helps to prevent excess dilation of the heart during diastole.

Etiology and Pathophysiology

Common causes of acute pericarditis are listed in Table 36.4. Most often the cause of acute pericarditis is *idiopathic* (unknown) or viral.[6] The coxsackievirus B is the most commonly identified virus.[7]

There are 3 types of pericarditis: acute, subacute, and chronic. Acute pericarditis develops rapidly, causing the pericardial sac to become inflamed and leak fluid (pericardial effusion). The characteristic pathologic finding in acute pericarditis is inflammation. There is an influx of neutrophils, increased pericardial vascularity, and eventually fibrin deposition on the epicardium (Fig. 36.4). Subacute pericarditis occurs weeks to months after

an event. We refer to pericarditis lasting more than 6 months as chronic.[7]

Myocardial infarction (MI) causes 5% to 8% of acute pericarditis cases. Post-MI syndrome (Dressler syndrome) pericarditis can occur 4 to 6 weeks after transmural MI (see Chapter 33). This syndrome is more common after a large anterior infarct.[6] Viral pericarditis is often seen after respiratory or GI illness.[6]

Clinical Manifestations

Clinical symptoms include progressive, severe, sharp chest pain.[6] The pain is generally worse with deep inspiration and when lying flat. Sitting up and leaning forward relieves the pain.

TABLE 36.4 Common Causes of Pericarditis

Infectious
- Bacterial: Pneumococci, staphylococci, streptococci, *Neisseria gonorrhoeae*, *Legionella pneumophila*, *Mycobacterium tuberculosis*, septicemia from gram-negative organisms
- Fungal: Histoplasma, *Candida* species
- Viral: Coxsackie A and B virus, echovirus, adenovirus, mumps, hepatitis, Epstein-Barr, varicella zoster, human immunodeficiency virus
- Others: Toxoplasmosis, Lyme disease

Noninfectious
- Acute MI
- Cancers: Lung, breast, leukemia, Hodgkin's lymphoma, non-Hodgkin's lymphoma
- Dissecting aortic aneurysm
- Myxedema
- Radiation
- Renal failure
- Trauma: Thoracic surgery, pacemaker insertion, cardiac diagnostic procedures

Hypersensitive or Autoimmune
- Dressler syndrome
- Drug reactions (e.g., procainamide, hydralazine)
- Postpericardiotomy syndrome
- Rheumatic fever
- Rheumatologic diseases: Rheumatoid arthritis, systemic lupus erythematosus, systemic sclerosis (scleroderma), ankylosing spondylitis

---

FIG. 36.4 Acute pericarditis. Note shaggy coat of fibers covering surface of heart. (From Damjanov I, Linder J: *Pathology: A color atlas*, St Louis, 2000, Mosby.)

The pain may radiate to the neck, arms, or left shoulder, making it hard to distinguish from angina. One distinction is that the pain from pericarditis can be referred to the trapezius muscle (shoulder, upper back). Dyspnea is related to the patient's breathing in rapid, shallow breaths to avoid chest pain. Fever and anxiety may worsen dyspnea.

The hallmark finding in acute pericarditis is the *pericardial friction rub*. The rub is a scratching, grating, high-pitched sound believed to result from friction between the roughened pericardial and epicardial surfaces. It is best heard with the stethoscope at the lower left sternal border of the chest with the patient leaning forward. Since it is hard to tell a pericardial friction rub from a pleural friction rub, ask the patient to hold their breath. If you still hear the rub, it is cardiac. Pericardial friction rubs may be hard to identify because they are often intermittent.

Complications

The major complications are pericardial effusion and cardiac tamponade. *Pericardial effusion* is a build-up of fluid in the pericardium. It can occur rapidly (e.g., chest trauma) or slowly (e.g., tuberculosis pericarditis). Large effusions compress nearby structures. Pulmonary tissue compression can cause cough, dyspnea, and tachypnea. Phrenic nerve compression can cause hiccups. Compression of the laryngeal nerve may result in

hoarseness. Heart sounds are generally distant and muffled. BP is usually maintained.

Cardiac tamponade develops as the pericardial effusion volume increases and compresses the heart. The speed of fluid accumulation affects the severity of clinical signs. Cardiac tamponade can occur acutely (e.g., rupture of heart, trauma) or subacutely (e.g., from renal failure, cancer).

The patient with cardiac tamponade may report chest pain and is often confused, anxious, and restless. As the compression of the heart increases, there is decreased CO, muffled heart sounds, narrowed pulse pressure, tachypnea, and tachycardia. Neck veins are markedly distended because of increased jugular venous pressure. *Pulsus paradoxus,* if present, is a large decrease in systolic BP during inspiration (Table 36.5). In a patient with a slow onset of a cardiac tamponade, dyspnea may be the only manifestation.

Diagnostic Studies

The ECG is useful in diagnosing acute pericarditis, with changes noted in 90% of cases. The most sensitive ECG changes include diffuse (widespread) ST segment elevations. This reflects the abnormal repolarization from the pericardial inflammation. These changes are different from the ST changes seen in MI. In myocardial ischemia, there are usually localized ST segment changes. In acute pericarditis serial ECGs do not show evolving changes, such as those with MI.

An echocardiogram can determine the presence of a pericardial effusion or cardiac tamponade. Doppler imaging and color M-mode can assess diastolic function and diagnose constrictive pericarditis (discussed later in the chapter). A CT scan and MRI can visualize the pericardium and pericardial space. Chest x-ray findings are generally normal, but a large pericardial effusion may appear as cardiomegaly (Fig. 36.5).

Common laboratory findings include leukocytosis and increased CRP and ESR. Troponin levels may be increased in patients with ST segment elevation and acute pericarditis, which could indicate concurrent heart damage. Fluid obtained during pericardiocentesis or tissue from a pericardial biopsy may be studied to determine the cause of the pericarditis.

Interprofessional Care

Management is aimed at identifying and treating the underlying problem and symptoms (Table 36.6). Antibiotics treat

---

TABLE 36.5 Measurement of Pulsus Paradoxus

1. Position the patient in a semirecumbent position.
2. Have patient breathe normally.
3. Using a manually operated BP cuff, measure systolic BP.
4. Inflate BP cuff at least 20 mm Hg above systolic BP.
5. Deflate cuff slowly until you hear sounds throughout the respiratory cycle (inspiration and expiration) and note the pressure.
6. Determine the difference between the measurements taken in steps 4 and 5. This will equal the amount of paradox:

Sounds heard on expiration at	110 mm Hg
Sounds heard throughout cycle at	−82 mm Hg
Amount of paradox	28 mm Hg

The difference is normally <10 mm Hg. If the difference is >10 mm Hg, cardiac tamponade may be present.

FIG. 36.5 A, X-ray of a normal chest. B, Pericardial effusion is present, and the cardiac silhouette is enlarged with a globular shape *(arrows).* (From Guzzetta CE, Dossey BM: *Cardiovascular nursing: Holistic practice,* St Louis, 1992, Mosby.)

bacterial pericarditis, and nonsteroidal antiinflammatory drugs (NSAIDs) (e.g., salicylates [aspirin], ibuprofen) control the pain and inflammation. Corticosteroids are used for patients with pericarditis from systemic lupus erythematosus, patients already taking corticosteroids for autoimmune conditions, or patients who do not respond to NSAIDs. They are used cautiously because of their many side effects (see Chapter 49). Colchicine, an antiinflammatory drug used for gout, may help patients who have recurrent pericarditis.[6]

Pericardiocentesis is usually done for pericardial effusion with acute cardiac tamponade, purulent pericarditis, or suspected cancer. Hemodynamic support for the patient before the procedure may include giving volume expanders and inotropic agents (e.g., dopamine) and stopping any anticoagulants. The procedure is done rapidly and safely using a percutaneous approach guided by echocardiography (Fig. 36.6). A needle is inserted into the pericardial space to remove fluid for analysis and relieve heart pressure. Complications include dysrhythmias, further cardiac tamponade, pneumomediastinum, pneumothorax, myocardial laceration, and coronary artery laceration.

A *pericardial window* is a surgical procedure for diagnosis or drainage of excess fluid. Cutting a "window," or part of the pericardium, allows the fluid to drain continuously into the peritoneum or chest.

TABLE 36.6 Interprofessional Care
Acute Pericarditis

Diagnostic Assessment	Management

• History and physical examination (assess for pericardial friction rub, pulsus paradoxus)
• Laboratory: CRP, ESR, white blood cell count
• ECG
• Chest x-ray
• Echocardiogram
• CT scan
• MRI
• Pericardiocentesis, pericardial window
• Pericardial biopsy
	• Treatment of underlying disease
	• Bed rest
	• Drug therapy
	  • NSAIDs
	  • Corticosteroids
	• Pericardiocentesis (for tamponade)
	• Pericardial window (for tamponade or ongoing pericardial effusion)

CRP, C-reactive protein; *ESR*, erythrocyte sedimentation rate.

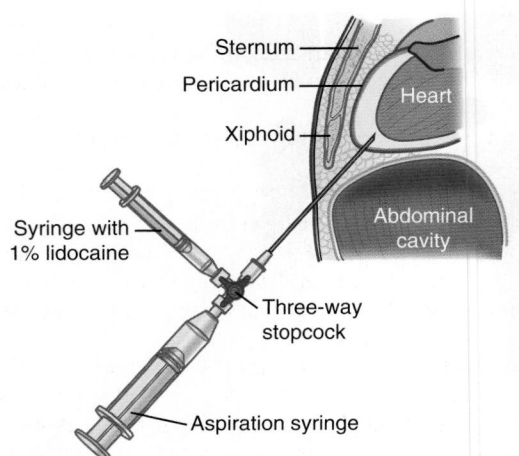

FIG. 36.6 Pericardiocentesis performed under sterile conditions in conjunction with ECG and hemodynamic measurements.

❖ NURSING MANAGEMENT: ACUTE PERICARDITIS

Managing the patient's pain and anxiety during acute pericarditis is your key nursing consideration. Assess the pain to distinguish angina (myocardial ischemia) (see Table 33.8) from the pain of pericarditis. Pericarditis pain is usually found in the precordium or left trapezius region and has a sharp quality that increases with inspiration. Pain is often relieved when the patient sits up or leans forward and is worse when lying flat.

Pain relief measures include keeping the patient on bed rest with the head of the bed raised to 45 degrees and providing an overbed table for support. Antiinflammatory drugs can help control the pain. Give these drugs with food or milk. Tell the patient to avoid alcohol because of the risk for GI bleeding. Other drugs, such as a proton pump inhibitor (e.g., pantoprazole, omeprazole), can reduce stomach acid.

Provide simple, complete explanations of procedures and possible causes of the pain to help reduce anxiety. These explanations are particularly important when the patient is undergoing testing and for the patient who has previously had angina or an MI.

The patient with acute pericarditis is at risk for cardiac tamponade and decreased CO. Monitor for manifestations of tamponade and prepare for possible pericardiocentesis.

❓ CHECK YOUR PRACTICE

You are assigned to a 58-yr-old male patient who had an MI 3 days ago. He has now developed pericarditis. When you are making rounds, you assess that the patient is slightly confused and has prominent neck veins. His heart rate is 118 beats/min.
• What should you do next?

CHRONIC CONSTRICTIVE PERICARDITIS
Etiology and Pathophysiology

Chronic constrictive pericarditis results from fibrotic thickening and rigidity of the pericardium, usually after an episode of acute pericarditis. It is characterized by fibrin deposition and pericardial effusion. Reabsorption of the effusion slowly follows, with progression to fibrous scarring, thickening of the pericardium from calcium deposits, and eventual destruction of the pericardial space. The fibrotic, thickened, and adherent pericardium encases the heart and prevents adequate atrial and ventricular stretch.

Clinical Manifestations and Diagnostic Studies

Manifestations of chronic constrictive pericarditis occur over time. They mimic HF and cor pulmonale. Decreased CO accounts for many of the manifestations. These include dyspnea on exertion, peripheral edema, ascites, fatigue, anorexia, and weight loss. The most prominent finding on physical examination is jugular venous distention (JVD). Unlike with cardiac tamponade, the presence of pulsus paradoxus (greater than 10 mm Hg) is not common.[6]

ECG changes are often nonspecific in chronic constrictive pericarditis. The heart on the chest x-ray may be normal or enlarged. Echocardiography findings may show a thickened pericardium but without a large pericardial effusion. CT and MRI can measure pericardial thickness and assess diastolic filling patterns.

❖ Interprofessional and Nursing Care

The treatment of choice for symptomatic chronic constrictive pericarditis is a *pericardiectomy*. This involves complete resection of the pericardium through a median sternotomy with the use of cardiopulmonary bypass (see Chapter 33). Some patients show immediate improvement, but others may take weeks. The prognosis improves when the patient has surgery before becoming clinically unstable.

MYOCARDITIS

Etiology and Pathophysiology

Myocarditis is a focal or diffuse inflammation of the myocardium. Causes include viruses, bacteria, fungi, radiation therapy, and pharmacologic and chemical factors. Coxsackie A and B viruses are the most common causative agents. Autoimmune disorders (e.g., polymyositis) have been linked with the development of myocarditis. It also may be idiopathic.

When the myocardium becomes infected, the causative agent invades the myocytes and causes cellular damage and necrosis. This activates the immune response. Cytokines and O_2 free radicals are released. As the infection progresses, an autoimmune response is activated. This causes further destruction of myocytes. Myocarditis results in heart dysfunction. Dilated cardiomyopathy can occur (discussed later in this chapter).[8]

Clinical Manifestations

The features of myocarditis vary from a benign course without any overt symptoms to progressive HF, dysrhythmias, or sudden cardiac death (SCD).[8] Fever, fatigue, malaise, myalgias, pharyngitis, dyspnea, lymphadenopathy, and nausea and vomiting are early manifestations of the viral illness.

Early cardiac signs appear 7 to 10 days after viral infection because pericarditis often accompanies myocarditis. These include pleuritic chest pain with a pericardial friction rub and effusion. Late cardiac signs relate to the development of HF and include an S_3 heart sound, crackles, JVD, syncope, peripheral edema, and angina.

Diagnostic Studies and Interprofessional Care

The ECG changes with myocarditis are often nonspecific but reflect associated pericardial involvement (e.g., diffuse ST segment changes). Dysrhythmias and conduction problems may be present. Laboratory findings are often inconclusive. They may include mild to moderate leukocytosis and atypical lymphocytes, elevated viral titers, and increased ESR, CRP levels, and levels of cardiac biomarkers, such as troponin. The virus is generally present in tissue and pericardial fluid samples only during the first 8 to 10 days of illness.

Endomyocardial biopsy provides histologic confirmation of myocarditis.[8] A biopsy is most diagnostic during the first 6 weeks of acute illness, when lymphocytic infiltration and myocyte damage are present. Nuclear scans, echocardiography, and MRI are used to assess heart function.

Treatment consists of managing symptoms. Angiotensin-converting enzyme (ACE) inhibitors and β-adrenergic receptor blockers (β-blockers) are used if the heart is enlarged or to treat HF (see Chapter 34). Diuretics reduce fluid volume and preload. If the patient is not hypotensive, IV drugs such as nitroprusside and milrinone reduce afterload and improve CO by decreasing systemic vascular resistance. Digoxin (Lanoxin) improves heart contractility and reduces HR. It is used cautiously in patients with myocarditis because of increased sensitivity to the adverse effects (e.g., dysrhythmias) and the potential toxicity. Anticoagulation reduces the risk for clot formation from blood stasis in patients with a low ejection fraction (EF).

 DRUG ALERT Digoxin (Lanoxin)

- Use cautiously in patients with myocarditis.
- Myocarditis predisposes to drug-related dysrhythmias and toxicity.

Myocarditis with an autoimmune basis is treated with immunosuppressive agents. These drugs reduce heart inflammation and damage. However, the use of these drugs for the treatment of myocarditis is controversial because they may lead to recurrence.[8] In some instances, antivirals may be used as adjunct therapy to treat myocarditis.

General supportive measures include O_2 therapy, bed rest, and restricted activity. In cases of severe HF, intraaortic balloon pump therapy and ventricular assist devices (VAD) may be needed (see Chapters 34 and 65).

❖ NURSING MANAGEMENT: MYOCARDITIS

Focus your interventions on improving CO and managing the signs and symptoms of HF. Select nursing measures to decrease cardiac workload. These include placing the patient in a semi-Fowler's position, spacing activity and rest periods, and providing a quiet environment. Carefully monitor drugs that increase the heart's contractility and decrease preload, afterload, or both. Evaluate the effectiveness of your interventions on an ongoing basis.

The patient may be anxious about the diagnosis of myocarditis. Assess the level of anxiety, take measures to decrease anxiety, and keep the patient and caregiver informed about the therapeutic plan.

The patient who receives immunosuppressive therapy is at increased risk for infection. Monitor for complications and provide the patient with proper infection control procedures.

Although most patients recover spontaneously, some develop dilated cardiomyopathy (discussed later in this chapter). If severe HF occurs, the patient may need a heart transplant.

RHEUMATIC FEVER AND RHEUMATIC HEART DISEASE

Rheumatic fever (RF) is an acute inflammatory disease that can involve all the heart layers. RF occurs most often between the ages of 5 and 15.[9] Rheumatic heart disease is a chronic scarring and deformity of the heart valves resulting from RF.

Etiology and Pathophysiology

RF occurs as a complication 2-3 weeks after a group A streptococcal pharyngitis. Signs of RF appear to be from an abnormal immune response to bacterial antigens.[9] RF affects the heart, skin, joints, and CNS. Rheumatic heart disease, caused by RF, primarily affects young adults.

RF has declined in developed countries because of the effective use of antibiotics to treat streptococcal infections. However, it is an important public health problem in developing countries.[9] Risk factors include age, gender, and environmental factors.[10]

Cardiac Lesions and Valve Deformities. About 50% of RF episodes are *rheumatic pancarditis,* involving all layers of the heart (endocardium, myocardium, and pericardium) (Fig. 36.1).[11]

Rheumatic IE is found mainly in the valves, with swelling and erosion of the valve leaflets. Vegetation forms from deposits of fibrin and blood cells in areas of erosion. The lesions initially create thickening of the valve leaflets, fusion of commissures and chordae tendineae, and fibrosis of the papillary muscle. Valve leaflets may become calcified, resulting in stenosis. The less mobile valve leaflets may not close properly, resulting in regurgitation. The mitral and aortic valves are most often affected.

Nodules, called *Aschoff's bodies,* are formed by a reaction to inflammation with swelling and destruction of collagen fibers. As the Aschoff's bodies age, they become more fibrous, and scar tissue forms in the myocardium. Rheumatic pericarditis develops and affects both layers of the pericardium. The layers become thick and covered with a fibrinous exudate. A serosanguineous pericardial effusion may develop. When healing occurs, fibrosis and adhesions develop that partially or completely destroy the pericardial sac. Damage to the heart begins during the first attack of RF. Recurrent infections cause further structural damage.

Extracardiac Lesions. The systemic lesions of RF involve the skin, joints, and CNS. Painless subcutaneous nodules, arthralgias or arthritis, and chorea may develop.

Clinical Manifestations

Jones criteria are used to diagnose acute RF.[9] The presence of 2 major criteria or 1 major and 2 minor criteria plus evidence of a preceding group A streptococcal infection indicate a high probability of acute RF (Table 36.7).

Major Criteria. *Carditis* is the most important manifestation of RF. It results in 3 signs: (1) heart murmur or murmurs of mitral or aortic regurgitation, or mitral stenosis; (2) heart enlargement and HF from myocarditis; and (3) pericarditis resulting in muffled heart sounds, chest pain, pericardial friction rub, or signs of effusion.

Monoarthritis or *polyarthritis* is the most common finding in RF, occurring in up to 75% of patients.[9] The inflammatory process affects the synovial membranes of the joints. This causes swelling, heat, redness, tenderness, and limitation of motion. The larger joints, particularly the knees, ankles, elbows, and wrists, are most often affected.

Sydenham's chorea is the major CNS manifestation.[9] It is characterized by involuntary movements, especially of the face and limbs; muscle weakness; and speech and gait problems.

Erythema marginatum lesions are a less common feature of RF. They only occur in less than 10% of RF patients.[10] The bright pink, nonpruritic, maplike macular lesions occur mainly on the trunk and proximal extremities. They intensify with heat (e.g., warm bath). *Subcutaneous nodules* associated with severe carditis are small, hard, painless swellings found over extensor surfaces of joints, particularly the knees, wrists, and elbows.

Minor Criteria. Minor clinical manifestations (Table 36.7) are helpful in diagnosing the disease. The minor criteria confirm the presence of RF when only 1 major criterion is present.

Evidence of Infection. In addition to the major and minor criteria, there must be evidence of a preceding group A streptococcal infection. Table 36.7 lists the various laboratory tests used to confirm evidence of infection.

Complications

Chronic rheumatic carditis results from changes in valve structure months to years after an episode of RF. Rheumatic IE can result in fibrous tissue growth in valve leaflets and chordae tendineae with scarring and contractures. The mitral valve is most often involved. The aortic and tricuspid valves may be affected.

Diagnostic Studies and Interprofessional Care

No single diagnostic test exists for RF. An echocardiogram may show valvular insufficiency and pericardial fluid or thickening.[11] A chest x-ray may show an enlarged heart. The most consistent ECG change is a prolonged PR interval from delayed AV conduction.

Treatment consists of drug therapy and supportive measures (Table 36.8). Antibiotic therapy does not change the course of the acute disease or the development of carditis. It eliminates residual group A streptococci in the tonsils and pharynx and prevents the spread of organisms to close contacts. Salicylates, NSAIDs, and corticosteroids are the antiinflammatory agents most widely used to control the fever and joint manifestations.[10]

TABLE 36.7 Revised Jones Criteria for Diagnosing Rheumatic Fever*

Major Criteria
- Carditis: Clinical and/or subclinical
- Arthritis
  - Monoarthritis or polyarthritis
  - Polyarthralgia
- Erythema marginatum
- Subcutaneous nodules
- Sydenham's chorea

Minor Criteria
- Monoarthralgia
- Fever
- Laboratory findings: ↑ ESR and/or ↑ CRP
- ECG findings: Prolonged PR interval after accounting for age variability (unless carditis is a major criterion)

Evidence of Group A Streptococcal Infection
- Laboratory findings
  - ↑ Antistreptolysin-O titer, positive throat culture, or positive rapid antigen test for group A streptococci

Modified from Gewitz MH, Baltimore RS, Tani LY, et al: Revision of the Jones criteria for the diagnosis of acute rheumatic fever in the era of Doppler echocardiography: A scientific statement from the AHA, *Circulation* 131:1806, 2015.

*Criteria apply to initial episode of rheumatic fever in moderate- or high-risk populations as defined by an all-age prevalence of rheumatic heart disease of ≥1 per 1000 population per year.

TABLE 36.8 Interprofessional Care

Rheumatic Fever

Diagnostic Assessment	Management
• History and physical examination	• Bed rest or limited activity
• Laboratory studies (Table 36.7)	• Drug therapy
• Chest x-ray	• Antibiotics
• Echocardiogram	• NSAIDs
• ECG	• Salicylates
	• Corticosteroids

❖ NURSING MANAGEMENT: RHEUMATIC FEVER AND RHEUMATIC HEART DISEASE

◆ Nursing Assessment

Table 36.9 presents the subjective and objective data to obtain from a patient with RF and rheumatic heart disease.

Inspect the patient's skin for subcutaneous nodules and erythema marginatum. Palpate for subcutaneous nodules over all bony surfaces and along extensor tendons of the hands and feet. The nodules range in size from 1 to 4 cm and are hard, painless, and freely movable. Erythema marginatum can occur on the trunk and inner aspects of the upper arm and thigh. Assess for these bright pink maculae in good light because the rash is hard to see, especially in dark-skinned patients.

◆ Nursing Diagnoses

Nursing diagnoses for the patient with RF and rheumatic heart disease include:
- Impaired cardiac output
- Activity intolerance

TABLE 36.9 Nursing Assessment
Rheumatic Fever and Rheumatic Heart Disease

Subjective Data

Important Health Information
Past health history: Recent streptococcal infection, history of RF or rheumatic heart disease

Functional Health Patterns
Health perception–health management: Family history of rheumatic fever. Malaise
Nutritional-metabolic: Anorexia, weight loss
Activity-exercise: Palpitations, generalized weakness, fatigue, impaired coordination
Cognitive-perceptual: Chest pain, widespread joint pain and tenderness (especially large joints)

Objective Data
General
Fever

Integumentary
Subcutaneous nodules and erythema marginatum

Cardiovascular
Tachycardia, pericardial friction rub, muffled heart sounds, murmurs, peripheral edema

Neurologic
Chorea (involuntary, purposeless, rapid motions; facial grimaces)

Musculoskeletal
Signs of monoarthritis or polyarthritis, including swelling, heat, redness, limitation of motion (especially of knees, ankles, elbows, shoulders, wrists)

Possible Diagnostic Findings
Cardiomegaly on chest x-ray. Prolonged PR interval on ECG. Valve abnormalities, chamber dilation, and pericardial effusion on echocardiogram. ↑ Antistreptolysin-O titer, positive throat culture, positive rapid antigen test for group A streptococci, ↑ ESR, ↑ CRP, leukocytosis

◆ Planning

The goals for a patient with RF and rheumatic heart disease include (1) normal or baseline heart function, (2) resumption of daily activities without joint pain, and (3) ability to manage the long-term antibiotic therapy.

◆ Nursing Implementation

◆ Health Promotion. Early detection and immediate treatment of group A streptococcal pharyngitis can prevent RF. Treatment with oral penicillin V (Penicillin-VK) or amoxicillin for 10 days is recommended.[9] If the patient is allergic to penicillin, a narrow-spectrum cephalosporin (e.g., cephalexin), clindamycin (Cleocin), or azithromycin (Zithromax) is used.[12] Therapy requires strict adherence to the full course of treatment. Teach people in the community to seek prompt medical care for symptoms of streptococcal pharyngitis.

◆ Acute Care. Give antibiotics as prescribed to treat the streptococcal infection. Teach the patient that completing the full course of antibiotics is vital to successful treatment.

Promote optimal rest to reduce cardiac workload and the body's metabolic needs. Position painful joints for proper alignment and apply heat for comfort. Give salicylates, NSAIDs, and corticosteroids as prescribed for joint pain.

After the acute symptoms subside, the patient without carditis can walk. The patient with carditis with HF may be restricted to bed rest (see Chapter 34 for care of a patient with HF). Stress the importance of gentle activities during recovery.

❓ CHECK YOUR PRACTICE

Your 28-yr-old male patient is recovering from carditis after RF. As you are preparing him for discharge from the hospital, he is pacing the floor and seems quite upset. You ask him to sit down so you can talk. He tells you, "I'm a cardiac cripple. I'll never be able to play ball with my sons or go skiing again. I might as well just go to bed and stay there."
- What are the key elements to include in your teaching plan?

◆ Ambulatory Care. The aim of secondary prevention is to stop the recurrence of RF. Prior history of RF makes the patient more susceptible to a second attack after a streptococcal infection. The best prevention is treatment with prophylactic antibiotics. Patients with RF without carditis need prophylaxis until age 20 and for a minimum of 5 years. Patients with rheumatic carditis and residual heart disease (e.g., persistent valve disease) need lifelong prophylaxis.[12]

Teach the patient with a history of RF about the disease process and the need for ongoing antibiotic prophylaxis. Teach the patient about good nutrition, hygienic practices, and adequate rest. Caution the patient about the possible development of heart valve disease. Tell the patient to seek medical care for symptoms, such as excessive fatigue, dizziness, palpitations, unexplained weight gain, or exertional dyspnea.[12]

◆ Evaluation

The expected outcomes are that the patient with RF and rheumatic heart disease will
- Be able to perform ADLs with minimal fatigue and pain
- Adhere to treatment regimen
- Express confidence in managing disease
- Use measures to prevent complications

VALVULAR HEART DISEASE

Two AV valves (mitral and tricuspid) and 2 semilunar valves (aortic and pulmonic) control blood flow through the heart (see Fig. 31.1). Valvular heart disease is defined by the valves affected and the type of dysfunction: stenosis or regurgitation (Fig. 36.7).

The pressure on either side of an open valve is normally equal. However, in a stenotic valve, the valve opening is smaller. The forward flow of blood is impaired. This creates a difference in pressure on the 2 sides of the open valve. The amount of stenosis (constriction or narrowing) is seen in the pressure differences (i.e., the higher the difference, the greater the stenosis). When regurgitation occurs (referred to as *incompetence* or *insufficiency*), there is incomplete closure of the valve. This results in the backward flow of blood.

Congenital heart conditions are the most common cause of valve disorders in children and adolescents. Aortic stenosis and mitral regurgitation (MR) often occur in older adults who have some form of heart disease. Other causes of valve disease in adults are related to acquired immunodeficiency syndrome and the use of some antiparkinsonian drugs.[12]

MITRAL VALVE STENOSIS

Etiology and Pathophysiology

Worldwide, the most common cause of mitral stenosis is rheumatic heart disease.[13] Rheumatic mitral stenosis is widespread in developing countries. Less common causes are congenital mitral stenosis, rheumatoid arthritis, radiation exposure, and systemic lupus erythematosus. Rheumatic IE causes scarring of the valve leaflets and the chordae tendineae. Contractures and adhesions develop between the commissures (the junctional

areas). The stenotic mitral valve takes on a "fish mouth" shape because of the thickening and shortening of the mitral valve structures. Severe mitral annular calcification is another cause in the aging population.

These deformities block the blood flow and create a pressure difference between the left atrium and left ventricle during diastole. As a result, left atrial pressure and volume increase, causing higher pulmonary vasculature pressure. The overloaded left atrium places the patient at risk for atrial fibrillation. In chronic mitral stenosis, pressure overload occurs in the left atrium, pulmonary bed, and right ventricle.

Clinical Manifestations

The main symptom of mitral stenosis is exertional dyspnea caused by reduced lung compliance (Table 36.10). Heart sounds include a loud first heart sound and a low-pitched, diastolic murmur (best heard at the apex with the stethoscope). Less often, patients may have hoarseness (from atrial enlargement pressing on the laryngeal nerve), hemoptysis (from pulmonary hypertension), and chest pain (from decreased CO and coronary perfusion). Emboli can form in the left atrium from atrial fibrillation and cause a stroke.[13] Fatigue and palpitations from atrial fibrillation may occur.

MITRAL VALVE REGURGITATION

Etiology and Pathophysiology

Mitral valve function depends on intact mitral leaflets, mitral annulus, chordae tendineae, papillary muscles, left atrium, and left ventricle. A defect in any of these structures can cause regurgitation. MR may result from problems with the leaflets or from the surrounding structures. In primary (degenerative) MR, a problem with the leaflets causes the regurgitation. In secondary

FIG. 36.7 Valvular stenosis and regurgitation. **A,** Normal position of the valve leaflets, or cusps, when the valve is open and closed. **B,** Open position of a stenosed valve *(left)* and closed position of regurgitant valve *(right)*. **C,** Hemodynamic effect of mitral stenosis. The stenosed valve is unable to open sufficiently during left atrial systole, inhibiting left ventricular filling. **D,** Hemodynamic effect of mitral regurgitation. The mitral valve does not close completely during left ventricular systole, letting blood reenter the left atrium. At the same time, blood is moving forward through the aortic valve. (From McCance KL, Huether SE: *Pathophysiology: The biologic basis for disease in adults and children,* ed 6, St Louis, 2010, Mosby.)

TABLE 36.10 **Manifestations of Valvular Heart Disease**	
Type	**Manifestations**
Mitral valve prolapse	Palpitations, dyspnea, chest pain, activity intolerance, syncope, holosystolic murmur
Mitral valve regurgitation	*Acute:* Generally poorly tolerated. New systolic murmur with pulmonary edema. Cardiogenic shock develops rapidly
	Chronic: Weakness, fatigue, exertional dyspnea, palpitations, S_3 gallop, holosystolic murmur
Mitral valve stenosis	Dyspnea on exertion, hemoptysis, fatigue. Atrial fibrillation on ECG. Palpitations. Loud, accentuated S_1. Low-pitched, diastolic murmur
Aortic valve regurgitation	*Acute:* Abrupt onset of profound dyspnea, chest pain, left ventricular failure and cardiogenic shock
	Chronic: Fatigue, exertional dyspnea, orthopnea, PND. Water-hammer pulse, heaving precordial impulse, decreased or absent S_1, S_3, or S_4. Soft high-pitched diastolic murmur, Austin Flint murmur
Aortic valve stenosis	Angina, syncope, dyspnea on exertion, HF, normal or soft S_1, decreased or absent S_2, systolic murmur, prominent S_4
Tricuspid and pulmonic stenosis	*Tricuspid:* Peripheral edema, ascites, hepatomegaly. Diastolic low-pitched murmur with increased intensity during inspiration
	Pulmonic: Fatigue, loud midsystolic murmur

PND, Paroxysmal nocturnal dyspnea.

(functional) MR, myocardial disease causes the regurgitation.[13] Most cases of MR are caused by MI, chronic rheumatic heart disease, mitral valve prolapse, ischemic papillary muscle dysfunction, and IE. MI with left ventricular failure increases the risk for rupture of the chordae tendineae and acute MR.

MR allows blood to flow backward from the left ventricle to the left atrium because of incomplete valve closure during systole. Both the left ventricle and left atrium must work harder to preserve an adequate CO. In acute MR, the sudden increase in pressure and volume transmits back to the pulmonary bed. This results in pulmonary edema and, if not treated, cardiogenic shock. In chronic MR, the added volume results in left atrial enlargement, left ventricular dilation and hypertrophy, and, finally, a decrease in CO.

Clinical Manifestations

The nature of its onset determines the clinical course of MR (Table 36.10). Patients with acute MR have thready peripheral pulses and cool, clammy extremities. A low CO may mask a new systolic murmur. Rapid assessment (e.g., heart catheterization) and intervention (e.g., valve repair or replacement) are critical.

Patients with chronic MR may remain asymptomatic for many years. Early symptoms of left ventricular failure may include weakness, fatigue, palpitations, and dyspnea. These gradually progress to orthopnea, paroxysmal nocturnal dyspnea, and peripheral edema. Increased left ventricular volume leads to an audible third heart sound (S_3), even with normal left ventricular function. The murmur is a loud holosystolic murmur at the apex radiating to the left axilla. Patients with asymptomatic MR must be monitored carefully.

Treatment for MR depends on the cause of the regurgitation. Primary MR typically requires valve repair or replacement before significant left ventricular failure or pulmonary hypertension develop.[14] Medical management includes standard HF therapy.[13]

MITRAL VALVE PROLAPSE

Etiology and Pathophysiology

Mitral valve prolapse (MVP) is an abnormality of the mitral valve leaflets and the papillary muscles or chordae that allows the leaflets to prolapse, or buckle, back into the left atrium during systole (Fig. 36.8). MVP affects 2% to 3% of the general population.[15]

The use of the term *prolapse* can be misleading because it is used even when the valve is working normally. MVP is usually benign, but serious complications can occur, including MR, IE, SCD, HF, and cerebral ischemia.

Genetic Link

Although the cause of MVP is unknown, there is an increased familial incidence. The genetic inheritance is often autosomal dominant (see Chapter 12). MVP in this group results from a connective tissue defect affecting only the valve, or as part of Marfan's syndrome or other hereditary conditions that affect collagen structure.

Clinical Manifestations

MVP has a broad range of severity. Most patients are asymptomatic for their entire lives. About 10% of those with MVP become symptomatic. A characteristic of MVP is a regurgitation murmur that is louder during systole. MVP does not alter S_1 or S_2 heart sounds. Severe MR is an uncommon but serious complication of MVP.

M-mode and 2-D echocardiography are used to confirm MVP. Dysrhythmias, such as premature ventricular contractions, paroxysmal supraventricular tachycardia, and ventricular tachycardia, may cause palpitations, light-headedness, and syncope. IE may occur in patients with MR associated with MVP.

Patients may have chest pain.[15] The cause of the chest pain may be the result of abnormal tension on the papillary muscles. Chest pain episodes tend to occur in clusters, especially during periods of emotional stress. Dyspnea, palpitations, and syncope sometimes accompany the chest pain and do not respond to antianginal treatment (e.g., nitrates). β-Blockers may control palpitations and chest pain. Encourage the patient to stay hydrated, exercise regularly, and avoid caffeine.

Most patients with MVP have a benign, manageable course. For those who do develop symptomatic MR, no current therapy delays the need for valve surgery.[16] A teaching plan for patients with MVP is outlined in Table 36.11.

AORTIC VALVE STENOSIS

Etiology and Pathophysiology

Congenital aortic stenosis (AS) is generally found in childhood, adolescence, or young adulthood. In older adults, AS is a result of RF or degeneration, similar to coronary artery disease. AS is the

FIG. 36.8 Mitral valve prolapse. In this valvular abnormality, the mitral leaflets have prolapsed back into the left atrium. There is hooding *(arrow)*. The left ventricle is on the right. (From Kumar V, Abbas AK, Aster JC, et al: *Robbins and Cotran pathologic basis of disease*, ed 8, Philadelphia, 2010, Saunders.)

TABLE 36.11 Patient & Caregiver Teaching
Mitral Valve Prolapse
Include the following information in the teaching plan for a patient with mitral valve prolapse (MVP) and the patient's caregiver: • Take drugs as prescribed (e.g., β-blockers to control palpitations, chest pain).   • Adopt healthy eating habits.   • Avoid caffeine because it is a stimulant and may worsen symptoms.   • If you use diet pills or other over-the-counter drugs, check for common ingredients that are stimulants (e.g., caffeine, ephedrine), since these can worsen symptoms.   • Begin, or maintain, an exercise program to achieve optimal health.   • Contact the HCP or emergency response system (ERS) if symptoms develop or worsen (e.g., palpitations, fatigue, shortness of breath, anxiety).

most frequent degenerative valve disorder, affecting 3% of people over 65 years of age.[17] In rheumatic valve disease, fusion and calcification cause the valve leaflets to stiffen and retract, resulting in stenosis. AS due to rheumatic heart disease accompanies mitral valve disease. Isolated AS is usually nonrheumatic.

AS causes obstruction of blood flow from the left ventricle to the aorta during systole. The result is left ventricular hypertrophy and increased myocardial O_2 consumption because of the increased myocardial mass. As the disease progresses and compensation fails, reduced CO leads to decreased tissue perfusion, pulmonary hypertension, and HF. Left untreated, severe AS has a poor prognosis.[18]

Clinical Manifestations

Manifestations of AS (Table 36.10) develop when the valve orifice becomes about one-third its normal size. They include the classic triad of angina, syncope, and exertional dyspnea, reflecting left ventricular failure.[17] Auscultation often reveals a normal or soft S_1, a decreased or absent S_2, and a crescendo-decrescendo systolic murmur, with radiation to the carotids.

Some patients may be asymptomatic. The prognosis is poorer for patients with symptoms and those whose valve obstruction is not fixed. Nitroglycerin is used cautiously to treat angina, since the drug can significantly reduce BP and worsen chest pain.

 DRUG ALERT Nitroglycerin

- Use cautiously in patients with AS since significant hypotension may occur.
- The drug can worsen chest pain due to the decrease in preload and drop in BP.

AORTIC VALVE REGURGITATION

Etiology and Pathophysiology

Aortic regurgitation (AR) may be the result of primary disease of the aortic valve leaflets, the aortic root, or both.[19] Trauma, IE, or aortic dissection can cause acute AR, which is a life-threatening emergency. Chronic AR generally results from rheumatic heart disease, a congenital bicuspid aortic valve, syphilis, a connective tissue problem, or a postsurgical cause.[19]

AR causes retrograde (backward) blood flow from the ascending aorta into the left ventricle during diastole. This results in volume overload. The left ventricle initially compensates for chronic AR by dilation and hypertrophy. Myocardial contractility eventually declines, and blood volume in the left atrium and pulmonary bed increases. This leads to pulmonary hypertension and right ventricular failure.

Clinical Manifestations

Patients with acute AR have sudden signs of cardiovascular collapse (Table 36.10). The patient develops severe dyspnea, chest pain, and hypotension indicating left ventricular failure and cardiogenic shock, a life-threatening emergency.

Patients with chronic, severe AR develop a *water-hammer pulse* (strong, quick beat that collapses immediately). Heart sounds may include a soft or absent S_1, S_3, or S_4 and a soft, high-pitched diastolic murmur.

The patient with chronic AR generally is asymptomatic for years.[19] Exertional dyspnea, orthopnea, and paroxysmal nocturnal dyspnea develop only after considerable heart dysfunction has occurred (Table 36.10). Angina occurs less often than in AS.

TRICUSPID AND PULMONIC VALVE DISEASE

Etiology and Pathophysiology

Tricuspid regurgitation (TR) can be primary or secondary. Primary TR is less common and is typically due to IE. Secondary TR is caused by right ventricular (RV) dilatation from pulmonary hypertension, cor pulmonale, or pulmonary outflow tract obstruction. The patient does not show JVD, enlarged liver, and peripheral edema until regurgitation is severe. Diagnosis is made by history and physical as well as echocardiogram. The prognosis is poor for severe TR.

Tricuspid stenosis is almost always caused by RF. Signs and symptoms include a fluttering discomfort in the neck, fatigue, and possible right upper quadrant pain.

Pulmonary regurgitation is often asymptomatic. A crescendo-decrescendo murmur is present. Potential causes include pulmonary hypertension, surgical repair of tetralogy of Fallot (TOF), or congenital valve disease. It can cause RV dilation.

Pulmonic stenosis is almost always a congenital part of TOF. It results in right ventricular hypertension and hypertrophy (Table 36.10). It is largely asymptomatic. When symptoms develop, they are similar to those of AS (syncope, dyspnea, angina). Symptoms typically do not present until adulthood.

DIAGNOSTIC STUDIES: VALVULAR HEART DISEASE

Diagnosis of valvular heart disease includes information from the history and physical examination and a variety of tests (Table 36.12). An echocardiogram shows valve structure, function, and heart chamber size. Transesophageal echocardiography

 TABLE 36.12 Interprofessional Care

Valvular Heart Disease

Diagnostic Assessment
- History and physical examination
- Chest x-ray
- Complete blood count
- ECG
- Echocardiography (Doppler and transesophageal)
- Heart catheterization

Management
Conservative Therapy
- Prophylactic antibiotic therapy (Table 36.2)
  - Rheumatic fever
  - IE
- Sodium restriction
- Drug therapy to treat or control HF
  - Vasodilators* (e.g., nitrates, ACE inhibitors)
  - Positive inotropes (e.g., digoxin)
  - Diuretics
  - β-Blockers
- Anticoagulation therapy (see Table 37.10)
- Antidysrhythmic drugs (see Table 35.9)
- Percutaneous transluminal balloon valvuloplasty
- Percutaneous valve replacement

Surgical Therapy
- Valve repair
  - Annuloplasty
  - Commissurotomy (valvulotomy)
  - Valvuloplasty
- Valve replacement

*Use cautiously in patients with aortic stenosis.

and Doppler color-flow imaging help diagnose and monitor valvular heart disease progression. Real-time 3-D echocardiography can help assess mitral valve and congenital heart disease.

Chest x-ray shows the heart size, altered pulmonary circulation, and valve calcification. An ECG identifies HR, rhythm, and any ischemia or ventricular hypertrophy. Heart catheterization detects pressure changes in the heart chambers, records pressure differences across the valves, and measures the size of valve openings.

INTERPROFESSIONAL CARE: VALVULAR HEART DISEASE

Conservative Therapy

Overall treatment focuses on preventing exacerbations of HF, acute pulmonary edema, thromboembolism, and recurrent RF and IE (Table 36.12). HF is treated with vasodilators, positive inotropes, β-blockers, diuretics, and a low-sodium diet (see Chapter 34).

Atrial dysrhythmias are common. They are treated with calcium channel blockers, β-blockers, antidysrhythmic drugs, or electrical cardioversion (see Chapter 35). Anticoagulant therapy is used in patients with atrial fibrillation to prevent systemic or pulmonary emboli.

Percutaneous Transluminal Balloon Valvuloplasty

An alternative treatment for some patients with valvular heart disease is *percutaneous transluminal balloon valvuloplasty* (PTBV). During PTBV, the fused commissures are split open. Balloon valvuloplasty treats mitral, tricuspid, pulmonic, and AS.[14]

The PTBV procedure is done in the heart catheterization laboratory. It involves threading a balloon-tipped catheter from the femoral artery or vein to the stenotic valve. The balloon is inflated to separate the valve leaflets. A single- or double-balloon technique may be used. Using a single Inoue balloon with hourglass shape allows sequential inflation. This technique is the most popular because it is easy and has good results with few complications (Fig. 36.9).

Like PTBV, the Sapien Transcatheter Heart Valve (THV) is used for select patients with AS. The THV is inserted through the femoral artery and moved to the heart. It is released and expanded with a balloon in the location of the aortic valve. This procedure is limited to patients who are eligible for surgery but who are at high risk for surgical complications (e.g., those with multiple co-morbidities).

Surgical Therapy

The decision for valve repair or replacement depends on the patient's symptoms using the New York Heart Association classification system for functional disability (see Table 34.3).[14] The procedure used depends on the (1) valves involved, (2) pathology and severity of the disease, and (3) patient's clinical condition.

Valve Repair. Valve repair is preferred over replacement when clinically appropriate. Repair has a lower operative mortality rate than valve replacement. It is often used in mitral or tricuspid valve disease.[14] Although repair avoids the risks of replacement, it may not restore total valve function.

FIG. 36.9 Mitral valvuloplasty performed by the Inoue technique. The catheter is placed in the mitral valve and the distal part of the Inoue balloon inflated (**A**). The balloon is then pulled back in the mitral valve and inflated for 10 to 15 sec under fluoroscopic control (**B**) until the waist of the balloon is no longer visible (**C**) and the balloon falls back into the left atrium. (From Crawford MH, DiMarco JP, Paulus WJ: *Cardiology*, ed 3, Edinburgh, 2010, Mosby.)

Open surgical *valvuloplasty* involves repair of the valve by suturing the torn leaflets, chordae tendineae, or papillary muscles. It is primarily used to treat mitral or tricuspid regurgitation.

Minimally invasive valve surgery involves a mini-sternotomy or parasternal approach. It may include robotic and thoracoscopic surgical systems. Advantages include shorter lengths of stay, fewer blood transfusions, less pain, and lower risk for sternal infection and postoperative atrial fibrillation.

For patients with mitral or tricuspid regurgitation, further valve repair or reconstruction using annuloplasty is an option. *Annuloplasty* involves reconstruction of the annulus, with or without the aid of prosthetic rings.

Valve Replacement. Valve replacement may be needed for mitral, aortic, tricuspid, and pulmonic valve disease. A wide variety of prosthetic valves are available. Desirable valves are nonthrombogenic, are durable, and create minimal stenosis. Valves are either mechanical or biologic (tissue) valves (Fig. 36.10).

Mechanical valves are made from artificial materials. They consist of combinations of metal alloys, pyrolytic carbon, and Dacron. *Biologic valves* are made from bovine, porcine,

FIG. 36.10 Edwards Sapien 3 Transcatheter Heart Valve. (Courtesy Edwards Lifesciences LLC, Irvine, CA.)

and human (cadaver) heart tissue. They usually contain some human-made materials. A "decellularizing" process removes the cadaver cells from the valve to lower the risk for tissue rejection. Biologic valves are asymmetric in shape. They produce a more natural pattern of blood flow compared with mechanical valves.

Mechanical valves are more durable and last longer than biologic valves. However, they have an increased risk for thromboembolism. Patients need long-term anticoagulation therapy, which increases the risk of bleeding.[13] Anticoagulation therapy is not needed with biologic valves because of their low thrombogenicity. However, they are less durable and tend to cause early calcification, tissue degeneration, and stiffening of the leaflets. Both valve types are subject to leaking and risk of IE.

Transcatheter therapies are another option for treating valvular heart disease. They are used to treat patients at high risk for surgery who have aortic or mitral bioprosthetic valve failure. Transcatheter pulmonary valve replacement is approved for use in pediatric and adult patients with pulmonary valve disease caused by congenital heart disease.

Transcatheter aortic valve replacement (TAVR) is an option for patients with severe, symptomatic AS who are at intermediate risk or higher for surgical aortic valve replacement (SAVR).[20] Symptomatic AS has a poor prognosis if left untreated. The procedure is ideally done using a transfemoral approach. The evaluation for TAVR includes echocardiogram, coronary CT angiogram, heart catheterization, and pulmonary function testing.[21] Imaging can determine valve size and plan the procedure. Currently, there are 2 TAVR valves in the United States. The Edwards Sapien 3 valve is made of bovine pericardial tissue. It is a balloon expandable valve (Fig. 36.10).[22] The CoreValve transcatheter aortic valve is a self-expanding valve made of porcine pericardial tissue (Fig. 36.11, *D*).[23]

Long-term anticoagulation is needed for those patients with biologic valves who have atrial fibrillation. Some patients with biologic valves or annuloplasty with prosthetic rings may need anticoagulation the first few months after surgery until the suture lines are covered by endothelial cells (endothelialized).

The choice of valves depends on many factors. A mechanical valve may be best for a younger patient because it is more durable. If a patient cannot take an anticoagulant (e.g., women of childbearing age), a biologic valve is considered. Frail patients with co-morbidities should be referred to a qualified heart team for a full evaluation before considering surgery.[20] Encourage patients to discuss short- and long-term consequences of valve choices with their HCPs.[21]

FIG. 36.11 Types of prosthetic heart valves. **A,** Starr-Edwards caged ball valve. **B,** St. Jude bi-leaflet valve. **C,** Carpentier-Edwards porcine valve. **D,** CoreValve transcatheter aortic valve (CV26 Hero), Medtronic 2015. (*A, B,* and *C,* From Bonow RO, Mann DL, Zipes DP, et al: *Braunwald's heart disease: A textbook of cardiovascular medicine,* ed 9, Philadelphia, 2012, Saunders.)

Heart Surgery Videos

Many patients prefer to watch recorded videos instead of reading educational pamphlets. For a patient facing heart surgery, these formats can be effective tools to teach the patient and caregiver what to expect before and after the procedure.
- Remember that the recorded video is not the teacher.
- Beforehand, discuss what the video presentation will cover.
- Encourage the patient and caregiver to write down questions or note what they do not understand.
- After the patient and caregiver view the material, answer any questions they have. Reinforce important information.

❖ NURSING MANAGEMENT: VALVULAR DISORDERS

◆ Nursing Assessment

Table 36.13 presents the subjective and objective data to obtain from a patient with valve disease.

◆ Nursing Diagnoses

Nursing diagnoses for the patient with valvular heart disease include:
- Impaired cardiac output
- Activity intolerance
- Fluid imbalance

More information on nursing diagnoses and interventions is in eNursing Care Plan 36.2, available on the website for this chapter.

◆ Planning

The overall goals for the patient with valve disease include (1) normal heart function, (2) improved activity tolerance, and (3) an understanding of the disease process and health maintenance measures.

◆ Nursing Implementation

◆ **Health Promotion.** Encouraging early treatment of streptococcal infections and providing prophylactic antibiotics for patients with a history of RF are critical to prevent acquired rheumatic valve disease. The patient at risk for IE and any patient with certain heart conditions must receive prophylactic antibiotics (Table 36.2). Teach the person with a history of RF, IE, or congenital heart disease the symptoms of valvular heart disease to report.

◆ **Acute Care and Ambulatory Care.** A patient with progressive valvular heart disease may need outpatient care or hospitalization for management of HF, IE, embolic disease, or dysrhythmias. HF is the most common reason for ongoing medical care.

Design activities considering the patient's limitations. An appropriate exercise plan can increase cardiac tolerance, but activities that cause fatigue and dyspnea should be limited. Tell the patient to avoid strenuous physical exercise because damaged valves may not handle the increased CO demand. Develop your patient's care plan to emphasize conserving energy, setting priorities, and taking planned rest periods. Discourage tobacco use. Consider a referral to a vocational counselor if the patient has a physically or emotionally demanding job.

Perform ongoing cardiac assessments to monitor the effectiveness of drugs. Teach the actions and side effects of drugs to increase adherence. The patient must understand the importance of prophylactic antibiotic therapy to prevent IE (Table 36.2).

When valvular heart disease can no longer be managed medically, surgery is needed (see Chapter 33 for the care of a patient having heart surgery). The patient on anticoagulants (e.g., warfarin) after surgery for valve replacement must have the international normalized ratio (INR) checked regularly to determine proper dosage and adequacy of therapy. INR values of 2.5 to 3.5 are therapeutic for patients with mechanical valves.

A teaching guide related to anticoagulation therapy is found in Table 37.14. Teach the patient to follow up with an HCP regularly and when to seek urgent medical care. Tell the patient to notify the HCP of any signs of infection, HF, or bleeding and any planned invasive or dental work. Last, encourage patients to wear a Medic Alert device or bracelet and carry the manufacturer's valve information card.

◆ Evaluation

The expected outcomes are that a patient with valvular heart disease will
- Maintain adequate tissue and organ perfusion
- Achieve fluid balance
- Achieve optimal level of activity
- Describe disease process and measures to prevent complications

---

TABLE 36.13 Nursing Assessment
Valvular Heart Disease

Subjective Data
Important Health Information
Past health history: RF, IE; congenital defects, heart attack, chest trauma, cardiomyopathy; syphilis, Marfan's syndrome, streptococcal infections

Functional Health Patterns
Health perception–health management: IV drug use, fatigue
Activity-exercise: Palpitations, generalized weakness, activity intolerance, dizziness, fainting, dyspnea on exertion, cough, hemoptysis, orthopnea
Sleep-rest: Paroxysmal nocturnal dyspnea
Cognitive-perceptual: Angina or atypical chest pain

Objective Data
General
Fever

Integumentary
Diaphoresis, flushing, cyanosis, clubbing, peripheral edema

Respiratory
Crackles, wheezes, hoarseness

Cardiovascular
Abnormal heart sounds, including murmurs, S_3, and S_4. Dysrhythmias, including atrial fibrillation, premature ventricular contractions. Tachycardia. ↑ or ↓ in pulse pressure, hypotension, water-hammer or thready peripheral pulses

Gastrointestinal
Ascites, hepatomegaly, unexplained weight gain

Possible Diagnostic Findings
Cardiomegaly on chest x-ray. ECG abnormalities specific to involved valve. Echocardiogram (valve disorders, chamber dilation), heart catheterization (abnormal valves, chamber pressures, CO, and blood flow, depending on involved valve)

CARDIOMYOPATHY

Cardiomyopathy (CMP) is a group of diseases that directly affect myocardial structure or function. CMP is classified as primary or secondary. *Primary CMP* refers to those conditions in which the cause is idiopathic. The heart muscle is the only part of the heart involved, and other heart structures are unaffected. In *secondary CMP*, the cause of the myocardial disease is known and is due to another disease process. Common causes of secondary CMP are listed in Table 36.14.

Three major types of CMP are dilated, hypertrophic, and restrictive. Each type has its own pathogenesis, clinical presentation, and treatment protocols (Tables 36.15 and 36.16). CMP that leads to cardiomegaly and HF is the main reason for heart transplants.

Takotsubo cardiomyopathy is a transient heart syndrome that mimics acute coronary syndrome. Patients often have chest pain, ST segment elevation on ECG, and elevated cardiac biomarkers consistent with an MI. However, when the patient undergoes heart catheterization, there is no significant coronary artery disease. It is an acute, stress-related syndrome that is more common in postmenopausal women. Most patients recover rapidly without lasting symptoms.[24]

DILATED CARDIOMYOPATHY

Etiology and Pathophysiology

Dilated cardiomyopathy is the most common type of CMP, with a prevalence of 5 to 8 cases per 100,000 people in the United States. It causes HF in 25% to 40% of cases and occurs more often in middle-aged blacks and men. Dilated CMP often follows an infectious myocarditis. Some evidence links dilated CMP with an autoimmune process or genetic causes.[25] Alcohol-related dilated CMP has its own unique presentation and treatment.[21] Other common causes of dilated CMP are listed in Table 36.14.

Dilated CMP appears with diffuse inflammation and rapid degeneration of heart fibers. This results in ventricular dilation, impaired systolic function, atrial enlargement, and blood stasis in the left ventricle. SCD from dysrhythmias is a leading cause of death in idiopathic dilated CMP.[26] Ventricular dilation causes *cardiomegaly* (Fig. 36.12) and contractile dysfunction. In contrast to HF, the walls of the ventricles do not hypertrophy.

Clinical Manifestations

The signs and symptoms of dilated CMP may develop acutely after an infection or slowly over time. Most people eventually develop HF. Symptoms can include decreased exercise capacity, fatigue, dyspnea at rest, paroxysmal nocturnal dyspnea, and orthopnea. As the disease progresses, the patient may have a

TABLE 36.14 **Causes of Cardiomyopathy**	
Dilated	**Hypertrophic**
• Cardiotoxic agents: alcohol, cocaine, doxorubicin	• Aortic stenosis
• Coronary artery disease	• Genetic (autosomal dominant)
• Genetic (autosomal dominant)	• Hypertension
• Hypertension	**Restrictive**
• Metabolic problems	• Amyloidosis
• Muscular dystrophy	• Cancer
• Myocarditis	• Endomyocardial fibrosis
• Pregnancy	• Post-radiation therapy
• Valve disease	• Sarcoidosis
	• Ventricular thrombus

TABLE 36.15 **Types of Cardiomyopathy**		
Dilated	**Hypertrophic**	**Restrictive**
Cardiac Output		
Decreased	Normal or decreased	Normal or decreased
Cardiomegaly		
Moderate to severe	Mild to moderate	Mild
Contractility		
Decreased	Increased or decreased	Normal or decreased
Dysrhythmias		
Sinus tachycardia, atrial and ventricular dysrhythmias	Atrial and ventricular dysrhythmias	Atrial and ventricular dysrhythmias
Major Manifestations		
Fatigue, weakness, palpitations, dyspnea	Exertional dyspnea, fatigue, angina, syncope, palpitations	Dyspnea, fatigue
Outflow Tract Obstruction		
None	Increased	None
Valvular Incompetence		
Atrioventricular (AV) valves, especially mitral	Mitral valve	AV valves

TABLE 36.16 **Interprofessional Care**
Cardiomyopathy
Diagnostic Assessment
• History and physical examination
• ECG
• b-Type natriuretic peptide (BNP)
• Chest x-ray
• Echocardiogram
• Nuclear imaging studies
• Heart catheterization
• Endomyocardial biopsy
Management
• Drug therapy
• Nitrates (except in hypertrophic cardiomyopathy)
• β-Blockers
• Antidysrhythmics
• ACE inhibitors
• Diuretics
• Digitalis (except in hypertrophic CMP unless used to treat atrial fibrillation)
• Anticoagulants (if indicated)
• VAD
• Cardiac resynchronization therapy
• Implantable cardioverter-defibrillator
• Surgical repair
• Heart transplant
• Cardiac rehabilitation
• Palliative and hospice care

dry cough, palpitations, abdominal bloating, nausea, vomiting, and anorexia. Signs can include an abnormal S_3 and/or S_4, dysrhythmias, heart murmurs, pulmonary crackles, edema, weak peripheral pulses, pallor, hepatomegaly, and JVD. Decreased blood flow through an enlarged heart promotes stasis and blood clot formation and may lead to systemic embolization.

Diagnostic Studies

The diagnosis of dilated CMP is based on the patient's history and exclusion of other causes of HF. Doppler echocardiography is usually the basis for diagnosing dilated CMP. Echocardiography can assess EF. EF less than 20% is associated with a 50% mortality rate within 1 year. The chest x-ray may show cardiomegaly with signs of pulmonary venous hypertension and pleural effusion. The ECG may show tachycardia, bradycardia, and dysrhythmias with conduction problems. Laboratory studies may show increased b-type natriuretic peptide (BNP) levels if HF is present.

Heart catheterization confirms or rules out coronary artery disease. An endomyocardial biopsy done at the time of the right-sided heart catheterization will identify any infectious organisms or other causes of disease.

❖ Interprofessional and Nursing Care

Interventions focus on controlling HF by enhancing heart contractility and decreasing preload and afterload. This is similar to the management of chronic HF. Treatment guidelines are based on the specific stage of disease progression (see Table 34.3). Treatment of patients with Class IV (stage D) HF is more palliative than curative.

Several different types of drugs are available to manage HF (see Table 34.7). Nitrates (e.g., nitroglycerin) and diuretics (e.g., furosemide) decrease preload. ACE inhibitors reduce afterload. β-Blockers (e.g., metoprolol [Lopressor]) and aldosterone antagonists (e.g., spironolactone [Aldactone]) control the neurohormonal stimulation that occurs in HF. Dysrhythmias are treated with the appropriate antidysrhythmic (see Chapter 35). Anticoagulation therapy reduces the risk for systemic embolization from clots that form in the heart chambers.

FIG. 36.12 Dilated cardiomyopathy. The dilated left ventricular wall has thinned *(arrow)*, and the chamber size and volume are increased. (From Kumar V, Abbas AK, Aster JC, et al: *Robbins and Cotran pathologic basis of disease,* ed 8, Philadelphia, 2010, Saunders.)

Drug and nutritional therapy and cardiac rehabilitation may help (1) lessen symptoms of HF and (2) improve CO and quality of life. A patient with secondary dilated CMP is treated for the underlying disease process. For example, teach the patient with alcohol-related dilated CMP to abstain from alcohol. (See Chapter 10 for more on alcohol use.)

Unfortunately, dilated CMP does not respond well to therapy and patients have multiple episodes of HF. Patients may be hospitalized for infusions of dobutamine or milrinone, followed by aggressive diuresis. Sometimes these treatments are done in an outpatient setting or in the home under nursing supervision. After treatment, many patients see an improvement in symptoms for several weeks. Medical management is based on clinical guidelines for HF.[27] Statins may be helpful (see Table 33.6).

Patients may benefit from nondrug therapies. A VAD allows the heart to rest and recover from acute HF. It may also serve as a bridge to a heart transplant. Other options include cardiac resynchronization therapy and an implantable cardioverter-defibrillator (ICD) (see Chapter 34).

The patient with terminal or end-stage CMP may consider a heart transplant. A permanent, implantable VAD, known as *destination therapy,* is an option for patients with advanced disease who are not candidates for a heart transplant (see Chapter 34). Currently, about 50% of heart transplants are done to treat CMP. Heart transplant recipients have a good prognosis. However, donor hearts are hard to obtain, and many patients with dilated CMP die before receiving a heart.

Patients with dilated CMP are very ill and have a grave prognosis. Your expert nursing care is critical. Observe for signs and symptoms of worsening HF, dysrhythmias, embolus formation, and drug effectiveness. The goals of therapy are to keep the patient at an optimal level of functioning and out of the hospital. Always include caregivers when planning a patient's care. Encourage caregivers to learn cardiopulmonary resuscitation (CPR). Teach them when and how to access emergency care.

Home health and hospice nursing can provide the patient and caregiver with palliative care. This includes strategies to maximize and maintain functional status or end-of-life care to prepare for a peaceful death.

HYPERTROPHIC CARDIOMYOPATHY

Etiology and Pathophysiology

Hypertrophic cardiomyopathy is asymmetric left ventricular hypertrophy without ventricular dilation.[28] In one form of the disease, the septum between the 2 ventricles becomes enlarged and blocks the blood flow from the left ventricle. We call this *hypertrophic obstructive cardiomyopathy* (HOCMP) or *asymmetric septal hypertrophy* (ASH).

Hypertrophic CMP occurs less often than dilated CMP. It is more common in men than in women. It is usually diagnosed in young adults and, most often, in active, athletic persons. Hypertrophic CMP is the most common cause of SCD in otherwise healthy young people. It accounts for 3% of deaths in young competitive athletes.[29] There is a link between genetic mutations and HOCMP. MYH7 and MYBPC3 are the 2 most common genes involved. They are found in about 50% of cases of HOCMP.[29]

Early identification is important (Table 36.14). The 4 main characteristics of hypertrophic CMP are (1) massive ventricular hypertrophy; (2) rapid, forceful contraction of the left ventricle; (3) impaired relaxation (diastole); and (4) obstruction to aortic outflow (not present in all patients). Ventricular hypertrophy is associated with a thickened intraventricular septum and ventricular wall (Fig. 36.13). The result is poor filling of the stiff ventricle. Decreased ventricular filling and obstruction to outflow can result in decreased CO, especially during exertion.

Clinical Manifestations

Patients with hypertrophic CMP may be asymptomatic or may have exertional dyspnea, fatigue, angina, and syncope. The most common symptom is dyspnea caused by an elevated left ventricular diastolic pressure. Fatigue occurs because of the resulting decrease in CO and in exercise-induced flow obstruction. Angina can occur and is often caused by the increased left ventricular mass or compression of the small coronary arteries by the hypertrophic ventricular myocardium. The patient may have syncope from obstruction to aortic outflow during increased activity. This results in decreased CO and cerebrovascular circulation. Syncope also can be caused by dysrhythmias, such as supraventricular tachycardia, atrial fibrillation, ventricular tachycardia, and ventricular fibrillation (see Chapter 35).

Diagnostic Studies

Clinical findings on examination may be unremarkable. On chest palpation the apical impulse can be exaggerated and displaced to the left. Auscultation may reveal an S_4 and a systolic murmur between the apex and sternal border at the fourth intercostal space. ECG findings usually show ventricular hypertrophy, ST-T wave abnormalities, prominent Q waves in the inferior or precordial leads, and dysrhythmias (see Chapter 35).

The echocardiogram is the main diagnostic tool used to confirm hypertrophic CMP. It may show wall motion abnormalities and diastolic dysfunction. Heart catheterization and nuclear stress testing may help diagnose and guide the treatment of hypertrophic CMP.

FIG. 36.13 Hypertrophic cardiomyopathy. There is marked left ventricular hypertrophy *(arrow)*, with decreased chamber size and volume. (From Kumar V, Abbas AK, Aster JC, et al: *Robbins and Cotran pathologic basis of disease,* ed 8, Philadelphia, 2010, Saunders.)

❖ Interprofessional and Nursing Care

Goals of care are to improve ventricular filling by reducing ventricular contractility and relieving left ventricular outflow obstruction. These can be achieved with β-blocker (e.g., metoprolol) or calcium channel blocker (e.g., verapamil) therapy. Digitalis is considered if needed to treat atrial fibrillation. Amiodarone or sotalol (Betapace) are effective antidysrhythmic drugs. However, their use does not prevent SCD. Patients at risk for SCD need a cardioverter-defibrillator (see Chapter 35).

AV pacing is helpful for patients with hypertrophic CMP and outflow obstruction. When the ventricles are paced from the apex of the right ventricle, septal depolarization occurs first. This allows the septum to move away from the left ventricular wall and reduces the degree of obstruction of the outflow tract.

Some patients with severe symptoms unresponsive to therapy may be candidates for surgical treatment of their hypertrophied septum. A *ventriculomyotomy and myectomy* involves cutting into the thickened septal muscle and removing some of the ventricular muscle. Most patients have an improvement in symptoms and exercise tolerance after surgery.

An alternative nonsurgical procedure to reduce symptoms and the left ventricular outflow obstruction is alcohol-induced *percutaneous transluminal septal myocardial ablation* (PTSMA). This procedure consists of injecting alcohol into the first septal artery branching off the left anterior descending artery to cause ischemia and septal wall infarction. Ablation of the septal wall decreases the obstruction to flow, and the patient's symptoms decrease. The procedure can improve HF symptoms and exercise capacity.[29] Potential complications of PTSMA include conduction problems (e.g., heart block) and MI.

Nursing interventions for hypertrophic CMP focus on relieving symptoms, observing for and preventing complications, and providing emotional support. Focus your teaching on helping patients plan to avoid strenuous activity and dehydration. Any activity that causes an increase in systemic vascular resistance (thus increasing the obstruction to forward flow) is dangerous. Rest and elevation of the feet to improve venous return to the heart can help manage chest pain. Vasodilators, such as nitroglycerin, may worsen the chest pain by decreasing venous return and further increasing obstruction of blood flow from the heart.

RESTRICTIVE CARDIOMYOPATHY

Etiology and Pathophysiology

Restrictive cardiomyopathy is the least common type of CMP. It is a disease of the myocardium that impairs diastolic filling and stretch. Systolic function stays unchanged. Although the specific cause of restrictive CMP is unknown, several pathologic processes may be involved in its development. Myocardial fibrosis, hypertrophy, and infiltration produce stiffness of the ventricular wall with loss of ventricular compliance. Secondary causes of restrictive CMP include amyloidosis, endocardial fibrosis, sarcoidosis, and radiation to the thorax. With restrictive CMP, the ventricles are resistant to filling and demand high diastolic filling pressures to maintain CO.

Clinical Manifestations and Diagnostic Studies

Classic manifestations of restrictive CMP are fatigue, exercise intolerance, and dyspnea. These occur because the heart cannot increase CO by increasing the HR without further compromising ventricular filling. Other symptoms may include angina, orthopnea, syncope, and palpitations. The patient may have signs of HF, including dyspnea, peripheral edema, weight gain, ascites, hepatomegaly, and JVD.

The chest x-ray may be normal, or it may show cardiomegaly from atrial enlargement. Pleural effusions and pulmonary congestion may occur as the patient progresses to HF. The ECG may show mild tachycardia at rest. The most common dysrhythmias are supraventricular (atrial fibrillation) or AV block. Echocardiography may show a left ventricle that is normal size with a thickened wall, slightly dilated right ventricle, and dilated atria. Endomyocardial biopsy, CT scan, and nuclear imaging may help in the diagnosis.

❖ Interprofessional and Nursing Care

There is no specific treatment for restrictive CMP. Interventions are aimed at improving diastolic filling and the underlying disease process. Treatment includes conventional therapy for HF and dysrhythmias. Heart transplant may be an option. Nursing care is similar to the care of a patient with HF. As in the treatment of patients with hypertrophic CMP, teach the patient to avoid situations that impair ventricular filling and increase systemic vascular resistance, such as strenuous activity and dehydration.

Nursing care of a patient with CMP includes individualized teaching based on the patient's manifestations. All patients with CMP are at risk for IE from any procedure that may cause bacteremia. Teach the patient about the need for prophylactic antibiotics (Table 36.2). A guide for patient and caregiver teaching is outlined in Table 36.17.

TABLE 36.17 Patient & Caregiver Teaching

Cardiomyopathy

Include the following information in the teaching plan for a patient with cardiomyopathy and the patient's caregiver.

1. Take all drugs as prescribed and regularly follow up with HCP.
2. Follow a low-sodium diet (if prescribed) and read all product labels (food and over-the-counter drugs) for sodium content.
3. Drink 6 to 8 glasses of water a day unless fluids are restricted.
4. Achieve and maintain a reasonable weight and avoid large meals.
5. Avoid alcohol, caffeine, diet pills, and over-the-counter cold medicines that may contain stimulants.
6. Balance activity and rest periods.
7. Avoid heavy lifting or vigorous isometric exercises and check with HCP for exercise guidelines.
8. Use stress management techniques: relaxation breathing, guided imagery.
9. Report any signs of HF to HCP, including weight gain, edema, shortness of breath, and increased fatigue.
10. Encourage caregivers to learn CPR because of the potential for cardiac arrest (see Appendix A).
11. Access emergency response system (ERS) according to the HCP's instructions.

CASE STUDY

Valvular Heart Disease

(© JennaDub/iStock/Thinkstock.)

Patient Profile

R.B., a 50-yr-old white man, is admitted to the hospital for acute decompensated HF due to valvular heart disease.

Subjective Data

- History of IV drug use
- Reports current regular alcohol intake of 1 pint of whiskey per day
- States, "I'm short of breath all the time. I can't sleep when I lay down."
- Describes chest pain with minimal exertion
- Recently unemployed
- States, "I'm always tired."
- States, "The drugs are too expensive. I can't afford them."
- Smokes a pack of cigarettes a day for past 35 years

Objective Data

Physical Examination

- Third heart sound (S₃)
- Loud holosystolic murmur of mitral regurgitation
- Missing all teeth from periodontal disease
- Vital signs: temperature 99.0° F (37.2° C); apical-radial pulse equal at 110 beats/min, irregular; respirations 24; BP 104/58

Diagnostic Studies

- ECG shows atrial fibrillation with a rapid ventricular response
- Chest x-ray shows pulmonary congestion and cardiomegaly
- Transesophageal echocardiography shows left atrial and ventricular hypertrophy and mitral and aortic regurgitation. EF 30%

Discussion Questions

1. Identify the cause and course of R.B.'s disease based on his history and current examination.
2. Distinguish between mitral and aortic regurgitation.
3. What medical treatments or surgical procedures will R.B. probably need as his condition worsens?
4. *Priority Decision:* Identify the priority nursing interventions for R.B.
5. *Safety:* What safety precautions should be initiated for R.B.?
6. *Collaboration:* Identify the tasks that you could delegate to unlicensed assistive personnel (UAP).
7. *Evidence-Based Practice:* R.B. asks you why he needs to be on "blood thinners" after his valves are replaced. How would you respond?

Answers are available at *http://evolve.elsevier.com/Lewis/medsurg.*

BRIDGE TO NCLEX EXAMINATION

The number of the question corresponds to the same-numbered outcome at the beginning of the chapter.

1. Which signs and symptoms should the nurse expect to find when assessing a patient with infective endocarditis who uses IV cocaine? *(select all that apply)*
   a. Retinal hemorrhages
   b. Splinter hemorrhages
   c. Presence of Osler's nodes
   d. Painless nodules over bony prominences
   e. Erythematous macules on the palms and soles

2. *Priority* nursing management for a patient with myocarditis includes interventions related to
   a. meticulous skin care.
   b. antibiotic prophylaxis.
   c. tight glycemic control.
   d. oxygenation and ventilation.

3. When teaching a patient about the long-term consequences of rheumatic fever, the nurse should discuss the possibility of
   a. valvular heart disease.
   b. pulmonary hypertension.
   c. superior vena cava syndrome.
   d. hypertrophy of the right ventricle.

4. Which is a *priority* nursing intervention for a patient during the acute phase of rheumatic fever?
   a. Giving IV antibiotics as prescribed
   b. Managing pain with opioid analgesics
   c. Encouraging fluid intake for hydration
   d. Performing frequent active range-of-motion exercises

5. A patient is diagnosed with mitral stenosis and new-onset atrial fibrillation. Which interventions could the nurse delegate to unlicensed assistive personnel (UAP)? *(select all that apply)*
   a. Obtain and record daily weight.
   b. Determine apical-radial pulse rate.
   c. Observe for overt signs of bleeding.
   d. Teach the patient how to get a Medic Alert device.
   e. Obtain and record vital signs, including pulse oximetry.

6. The nurse is caring for a patient newly admitted with heart failure secondary to dilated cardiomyopathy. Which intervention would be a *priority*?
   a. Encourage caregivers to learn CPR.
   b. Consider a consultation with hospice for palliative care.
   c. Monitor the patient's response to prescribed medications.
   d. Arrange for the patient to enter a cardiac rehabilitation program.

1. a, b, c, e; 2. d; 3. a; 4. a; 5. a, c, e; 6. c

For rationales to these answers and even more NCLEX review questions, visit *http://evolve.elsevier.com/Lewis/medsurg.*

ⓔ EVOLVE WEBSITE/RESOURCES LIST

http://evolve.elsevier.com/Lewis/medsurg
Review Questions (Online Only)
Key Points
Answer Keys for Questions
- Rationales for Bridge to NCLEX Examination Questions
- Answer Guidelines for Case Study on p. 797
Student Case Study
- Patient With Rheumatic Fever and Heart Disease
Nursing Care Plans
- eNursing Care Plan 36.1: Patient With Infective Endocarditis
- eNursing Care Plan 36.2: Patient With Valvular Heart Disease
Conceptual Care Map Creator
Audio Glossary
Supporting Media
- Audio
  - Pericardial Friction Rub
Content Updates

REFERENCES

*1. Cahill T, Baddour L, Habib G, et al: Challenges in infective endocarditis, *JACC* 69:324, 2017.

*2. Thornhill M, Jones S, Predergast B, et al. Quantifying IE risk in patients with predisposing cardiac conditions, *Eur Heart Journal* 39:586, 2018.

3. Wojda T, Cornejo K, Lin A, et al: Septic embolism: A potentially devastating complication of infective endocarditis. Retrieved from *www.intechopen.com/books/contemporary-challenges-in-endocarditis/septic-embolism-a-potentially-devastating-complication-of-infective-endocarditis.*

4. Cahill T, Predergast B: Infective endocarditis, *The Lancet* 387:882, 2016.

*5. Baddour LM, Wilson WR, Bayer AS, et al: Infective endocarditis in adults: Diagnosis, antimicrobial therapy, and management of complications, *Circulation* 132:e215, 2015. (Classic)

6. Rahman A, Sarawat A: Pericarditis, *Am Family Physician* 46:810, 2017.

7. Doctor N, Shah A, Coplan B, et al: Acute pericarditis, *Prog Cardiovasc Dis* 59:349, 2017.

8. Fung G, Luo H, Qiu Y, et al: Myocarditis, *Circ Res* 118:496, 2016.

9. Carapetis JR, Beaton A, Cunningham MW, et al: Acute rheumatic fever and rheumatic heart disease, *Nat Rev Dis Primers* 2:150, 2016.

10. Sika-Paotonu D, Beaton A, Raghu A, et al: *Acute rheumatic fever and rheumatic heart disease,* Oklahoma City, 2017, University of Oklahoma Press.

*11. Gewitz MH, Baltimore RS, Tani LY, et al: Revision of the Jones criteria for the diagnosis of acute rheumatic fever in the era of Doppler echocardiography: A scientific statement from the AHA, *Circulation* 131:1806, 2015. (Classic)

12. Wallace, M: Antibiotics for rheumatic fever. Retrieved from *https://emedicine.medscape.com/article/236582.*

13. Holmes K, Gibbison B, Vohra H: Mitral valve and mitral valve disease, *BJA Education* 17:1, 2017.

*14. Nishimura RA, Otto CM, Bonow RO, et al: 2014 AHA/ACC guideline for the management of patients with valvular heart disease: Executive summary: A report of the American College of Cardiology/AHA Task Force on Practice Guidelines, *Circulation* 129:2440, 2014. (Classic)

15. Jelani Q: Mitral valve prolapse. Retrieved from *https://emedicine.medscape.com/article/155494.*

16. Deeling F, Rong J, Larson M, et al: The evolution of mitral valve prolapse: Insights from the Framingham Heart Study, *Circulation* 133:1688, 2016.

17. Kamperidis V, Delgado V, van Mieghem N, et al: Diagnosis and management of aortic valve stenosis in patients with heart failure, *Euro Journal HF* 18:469, 2016.

18. Marquis-Gravel G, Redfors B, Leon MN, et al : Medical treatment of aortic stenosis, *JASE* 124:1766, 2016.

19. Wang SS: Aortic regurgitation. Retrieved from *https://emedicine.medscape.com/article 150490.*

*20. Nishimura RA, Otto CM, Bonow RO, et al: 2017 ACC/AHA focused update of the 2014 guidelines for the management of patients with valvular heart disease, *Circulation* 135:e1159, 2017.

*21. Bonow RO, Brown AS, Gillam C, et al: AUC for treatment of patients with severe aortic stenosis, *JASE* 31:117, 2018.

22. Edwards Lifesciences: TAVR with the Sapien 3 Valve. Retrieved from *https://tavrbyedwards.com/.*

23. Medtronic; Evolut TAVR Platform, CoreValve® Transcatheter Aortic Valve Implantation (TAVI) platform. Retrieved from *www.medtronic.com/us-en/healthcare-professionals/therapies-procedures/cardiovascular/transcatheter-aortic-valve-replacement.html.*

24. Lyon A, Bossone E, Schneider B, et al: Current state of knowledge on Takotsubo syndrome, *Eur J Heart Fail* 18:8, 2016.

25. Pinto Y, Elliott P, Arbustini E, et al: Proposal for a revised definition of DCM, *Eur Heart J* 37:1850, 2016.

*26. Al-Zaiti SS, Fallavollita JA, Cantry JM, et al: Electrocardiographic predictors of sudden and non-sudden cardiac death in patients with ischemic cardiomyopathy, *Heart Lung* 43:527, 2014. (Classic)

27. Bozkurt B, Colvin M, Cook J, et al: Current diagnostic and treatment strategies for specific DCM, *Circulation* 134:e579, 2016.

28. Hensley N, Deitrich J, Nyhan D, et al: Hypertrophic cardiomyopathy: A review, *Anesth Analg* 120:554, 2015. (Classic)

29. Marian A, Brunwald E: Hypertrophic cardiomyopathy: Genetics, pathogenesis, clinical manifestations, diagnosis, and therapy, *Circ Res* 121:749, 2017.

*Evidence-based information for clinical practice.

37

Vascular Disorders

Kimberly Day

Be the reason someone believes in the goodness of people.

Karen Salmansohn

(e) http://evolve.elsevier.com/Lewis/medsurg

CONCEPTUAL FOCUS

Clotting
Glucose Regulation

Perfusion
Tissue Integrity

LEARNING OUTCOMES

1. Relate the etiology and pathophysiology of peripheral artery disease (PAD) to the major risk factors.
2. Describe the clinical manifestations and interprofessional and nursing management of the patient with PAD of the lower extremities.
3. Plan appropriate nursing and interprofessional management for the patient with acute arterial ischemic disorders of the lower extremities.
4. Distinguish the pathophysiology, clinical manifestations, and nursing and interprofessional management of the patient with thromboangiitis obliterans (Buerger's disease) and Raynaud's phenomenon.
5. Distinguish the pathophysiology, clinical manifestations, and interprofessional and nursing management of patients with different types of aortic aneurysms.
6. Select appropriate nursing interventions for a patient undergoing an aortic aneurysm repair.

7. Describe the pathophysiology, clinical manifestations, and interprofessional and nursing management of the patient with aortic dissection.
8. Evaluate the risk factors predisposing patients to develop superficial vein thrombosis or venous thromboembolism (VTE).
9. Distinguish between the clinical characteristics of superficial vein thrombosis and VTE.
10. Outline the interprofessional and nursing management of patients with superficial vein thrombosis and VTE.
11. Prioritize the key aspects of nursing management for the patient receiving anticoagulant therapy.
12. Relate the pathophysiology and clinical manifestations to the interprofessional care of patients with varicose veins, chronic venous insufficiency, and venous leg ulcers.

KEY TERMS

Problems of the vascular system include disorders of the arteries, veins, and lymphatic vessels. These problems can result in decreased perfusion to the peripheral tissues, causing ischemia. Patients often have pain and difficulties with mobility and taking part in activities of daily living. Education is a key part of management. Proper nutrition, smoking cessation, and exercise are important health promotion behaviors. Following measures to promote safety, especially for those on anticoagulant therapy, is critical.

We classify arterial disorders as atherosclerotic, aneurysmal, and nonatherosclerotic vascular diseases. Atherosclerotic vascular disease is divided into coronary, cerebral, peripheral, mesenteric, and renal artery disease.[1] This chapter discusses peripheral artery disease, aortic aneurysm and dissection, and venous diseases.

PERIPHERAL ARTERY DISEASE

Peripheral artery disease (PAD) involves thickening of artery walls. This results in a progressive narrowing of the arteries of the upper and lower extremities. PAD prevalence increases with age. It typically becomes symptomatic between ages 50 and 70 years. In people with diabetes, PAD occurs earlier. In the United States, about 8.5 million people over age 40 have PAD, with higher prevalence in blacks.[2,3]

PAD is strongly related to other types of cardiovascular disease (CVD) and their risk factors. Patients with PAD have a significantly higher risk for mortality (in general), CVD mortality, major coronary events, and stroke.[3] PAD is a marker of advanced systemic atherosclerosis. Patients with PAD are more likely to have coronary artery disease (CAD) and/or cerebral artery disease.

Unfortunately, many people in the United States are unaware of PAD and its risk factors. PAD remains underdiagnosed and undertreated.

Etiology and Pathophysiology

The leading cause of PAD is *atherosclerosis,* a gradual thickening of the *intima* (the innermost layer of the arterial wall) and *media* (middle layer of the arterial wall). This results from cholesterol and lipids deposited within the vessel walls and leads to narrowing of the artery (see Fig. 33.1). Although the exact cause of atherosclerosis is unknown, inflammation and endothelial injury play a major role (see Chapter 33). Atherosclerosis often affects certain segments of the arterial tree. These include the coronary, carotid (see Chapter 57), and lower extremity arteries.

Other risk factors for PAD are similar, but not identical, to those for CAD. Important risk factors for PAD are tobacco use (most important), diabetes, hypertension, high cholesterol, and age over 60.[2] The presence of multiple risk factors dramatically increases the risk for PAD, especially in blacks.[2] Symptoms occur when vessels are 60% to 75% blocked.

GENDER DIFFERENCES
Vascular Disorders

Men
- Thromboangiitis obliterans (Buerger's disease) occurs most often in men younger than 40 yrs of age.
- Abdominal aortic aneurysms (AAAs) and aortic dissections are more common in men.
- Men with AAAs are more likely to undergo endovascular aneurysm repair or open aneurysm repair than women.
- Sexual dysfunction in male patients is common after aortic surgery.

Women
- Women with PAD have poorer physical and social functioning and higher rates of depression than men with PAD.[4]
- Women with PAD have faster functional decline and greater mobility loss than men with PAD.
- Raynaud's phenomenon occurs primarily in women between 15 and 40 yrs of age.
- Risk for venous thromboembolism (VTE) is greater in women over age 35 who use tobacco and oral contraceptives or oral hormone therapy, are pregnant or postpartum, or have a family history of VTE.
- Primary varicose veins are more common and more symptomatic in women than men.
- Risk for varicose veins is greater in multiparous women.
- Women with AAAs are at higher risk for rupture.
- In-hospital mortality is higher in women undergoing revascularization than men, regardless of disease severity or procedure done.
- Women, particularly black and Hispanic women, have more graft thrombosis and amputation after lower extremity bypass surgery than men.

PERIPHERAL ARTERY DISEASE OF THE LOWER EXTREMITIES

Lower extremity PAD may affect the iliac, femoral, popliteal, tibial, or peroneal arteries, or any combination of these arteries (Fig. 37.1). The femoral popliteal area is the most common site in nondiabetic patients. Patients with diabetes tend to develop PAD in the arteries below the knee. Those with advanced PAD often have multiple arterial occlusions.

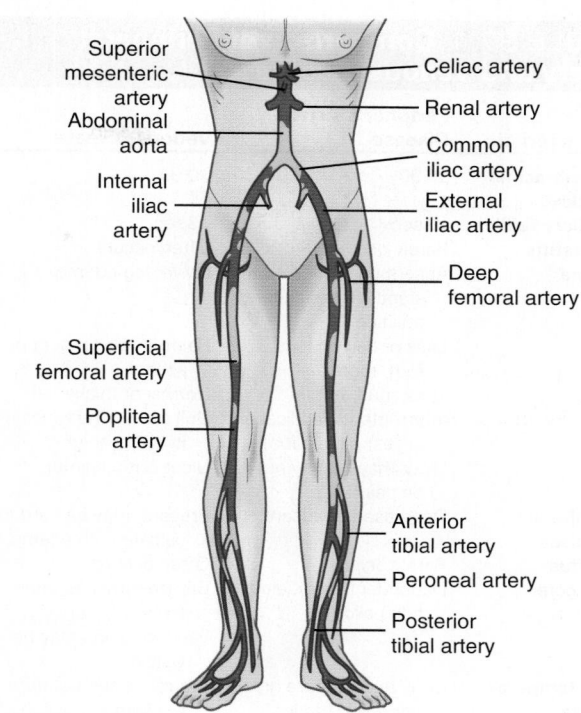

FIG. 37.1 Common anatomic locations of atherosclerotic lesions (shown in *yellow*) of the abdominal aorta and lower extremities.

Clinical Manifestations

The severity of PAD symptoms depends on the site and extent of the blockage and the amount of collateral circulation. The classic symptom of lower extremity PAD is **intermittent claudication**. This ischemic muscle pain is caused by exercise, resolves within 10 minutes or less with rest, and is reproducible. The ischemic pain is due to the buildup of lactic acid from anaerobic metabolism. Once the patient stops exercising, the lactic acid clears, and the pain subsides. PAD of the iliac arteries causes claudication in the buttocks and thighs. Calf pain indicates femoral or popliteal artery involvement.

As many as one third of patients with PAD report classic symptoms. Others have no symptoms or present with atypical leg symptoms (e.g., burning, heaviness, pressure, soreness, tightness, weakness) in atypical locations (e.g., ankle, foot, hamstring, hip, knee, shin). PAD involving the internal iliac arteries may result in erectile dysfunction.

Paresthesia (numbness or tingling) in the toes or feet may result from nerve tissue ischemia. True peripheral neuropathy occurs more often in patients with diabetes (see Chapter 48) and in those with long-standing ischemia. Neuropathy causes severe shooting or burning pain in the extremity. It does not follow particular nerve roots and may be present near ulcerated areas. Gradual, reduced blood flow to neurons causes loss of pressure and deep pain sensations. So, patients may not notice lower extremity injuries.

The limb's appearance gives vital information about reduced blood flow. The skin becomes thin, shiny, and taut. The lower legs lose their hair. Pedal, popliteal, or femoral pulses are decreased or absent. Pallor (blanching of the foot) develops when the leg is elevated (*elevation pallor*). Conversely, *reactive hyperemia* (redness of the foot) develops when the limb is in a dependent position (*dependent rubor*) (Table 37.1).

TABLE 37.1 Comparison of Peripheral Artery and Venous Disease

Characteristic	Peripheral Artery Disease	Venous Disease
Ankle-brachial index	≤0.90	>0.90
Capillary refill	>3 sec	<3 sec
Dermatitis	Rarely occurs	Often occurs
Edema	Absent unless leg constantly in dependent position	Lower leg edema
Hair	Loss of hair on legs, feet, toes	Hair may be present or absent
Nails	Thickened, brittle	Normal or thickened
Pain	Intermittent claudication or rest pain in foot	Dull ache or heaviness in calf or thigh
	Ulcer may or may not be painful	Ulcer often painful
Peripheral pulses	Decreased or absent	Present, may be hard to palpate with edema
Pruritus	Rarely occurs	Often occurs
Skin color	Dependent rubor, elevation pallor	Bronze-brown pigmentation
		Varicose veins may be visible
Skin temperature	Cool, temperature gradient down the leg	Warm, no temperature gradient
Skin texture	Thin, shiny, taut	Skin thick, hardened, and indurated
Ulcer		
• Location	Tips of toes, foot, or lateral malleolus	Near medial malleolus
• Margin	Rounded, smooth, looks "punched out"	Irregularly shaped
• Drainage	Minimal	Moderate to large amount
• Tissue	Black eschar or pale pink granulation	Yellow slough or dark red, "ruddy" granulation

TABLE 37.2 Interprofessional Care

Peripheral Artery Disease

Diagnostic Assessment
- Health history and physical examination, including palpation of peripheral pulses
- Doppler ultrasound studies
- Segmental BPs
- ABI (Table 37.3)
- Duplex imaging
- Angiography
- Magnetic resonance angiography

Management
- CVD risk factor modification
  - Tobacco cessation
  - Regular physical exercise
  - Achieve or maintain ideal body weight
  - Follow Dietary Approaches to Stop Hypertension (DASH) diet
  - Tight glucose control with diabetes, including Hb A1C monitoring
  - Tight BP control
  - Treatment of hyperlipidemia and hypertriglyceridemia (see Table 33.6)
  - Antiplatelet agent (aspirin, clopidogrel [Plavix])
  - ACE inhibitors (see Table 32.6)
- Treatment of claudication symptoms
  - Structured walking or exercise program
  - Cilostazol or pentoxifylline
- Nutritional therapy
- Physical/occupational therapy
- Proper foot care (see Table 48.21)

Surgical Therapy
- Percutaneous transluminal balloon angioplasty with or without stent
- Percutaneous transluminal atherectomy
- Percutaneous transluminal cryoplasty
- Peripheral artery bypass surgery
- Patch graft angioplasty, often in conjunction with bypass surgery
- Endarterectomy (for localized stenosis; rarely done as a stand-alone procedure)
- Thrombolytic therapy or mechanical clot extraction therapy (for acute ischemia only)
- Sympathectomy (for pain management only)
- Amputation

As PAD progresses and involves multiple arterial segments, continuous pain develops at rest. *Rest pain* most often occurs in the foot or toes. It is worse with limb elevation. Rest pain occurs when blood flow is insufficient to meet basic metabolic requirements of the distal tissues. Rest pain occurs more often at night because cardiac output tends to drop during sleep and the limbs are at the level of the heart. Patients often try to achieve pain relief by gravity, dangling the leg over the side of the bed or sleeping in a chair.

Critical limb ischemia (CLI) is a condition characterized by chronic ischemic rest pain lasting more than 2 weeks, nonhealing arterial leg ulcers, or gangrene of the leg from PAD. Patients with PAD who have diabetes, heart failure (HF), and a history of a stroke are at increased risk for CLI.[3]

Complications

Lower extremity PAD progresses slowly. Prolonged ischemia leads to atrophy of the skin and underlying muscles. Minor trauma to the feet (e.g., stubbing one's toe, blister from shoes) can result in delayed healing, wound infection, and tissue necrosis, especially in the patient with diabetes. Arterial (ischemic) ulcers most often occur over bony prominences on the toes, feet, and lower legs (Table 37.1). Nonhealing arterial ulcers and gangrene are the most serious complications. If PAD develops over an extended period, collateral circulation may prevent gangrene.

Amputation may be needed if adequate blood flow is not restored or if severe infection occurs. Uncontrolled pain and severe, spreading infection are indicators for amputation in people who are not candidates for revascularization.

Diagnostic Studies

Various tests assess blood flow and the vascular system (Table 37.2). Doppler ultrasound with duplex imaging maps blood flow throughout the entire region of an artery. When palpating a peripheral pulse is hard because of severe PAD, Doppler ultrasound can determine the degree of blood flow. A palpable pulse and a Doppler pulse are not equivalent, and the terms are not interchangeable.

Segmental BPs are obtained using Doppler ultrasound and a sphygmomanometer at the thigh, below the knee, and at ankle level while the patient is supine. A drop in segmental BP of greater than 30 mm Hg suggests PAD. Angiography and magnetic resonance angiography show the location and extent of PAD (see Table 31.7).

The *ankle-brachial index* (ABI) is a PAD screening tool. It is done using a hand-held Doppler. The ABI is calculated by

TABLE 37.3 Interpreting Ankle-Brachial Index Results

Ankle-Brachial Index (ABI)	Clinical Significance
>1.30	Noncompressible arteries
1.00–1.30	Normal ABI
0.91–0.99	Borderline ABI
≤0.90	Abnormal ABI
Classification of PAD Severity	
0.90–0.71	Mild PAD
0.70–0.41	Moderate PAD
≤0.40	Severe PAD

dividing the ankle systolic BPs (SBPs) by the higher of the left and right brachial SBPs. PAD guidelines recommend uniform reporting of ABI results (Table 37.3).[3] Calcified and stiff arteries in older patients and those with diabetes often show a falsely elevated ABI.

Interprofessional Care

Table 37.2 outlines the interprofessional care for a patient with PAD.

Risk Factor Modification. The first treatment goal for patients with PAD is to reduce CVD risk factors regardless of the severity of symptoms. Encourage risk factor modification with both drug therapy and lifestyle changes (see Tables 33.2 to 33.5). Hypertension is another well-known risk factor for PAD progression. Encourage reducing dietary sodium and following the Dietary Approaches to Stop Hypertension (DASH) diet. Chapter 32 discusses hypertension.

Tobacco cessation is essential to reduce the risk for CVD events, PAD progression, and death. This is a complex, difficult process with a high incidence of relapse. Suggest comprehensive tobacco cessation strategies (see Tables 10.3 to 10.6).

Diabetes is a major risk factor for PAD and increases the risk for amputation. Patients with diabetes should maintain a glycosylated hemoglobin (A1C) below 7.0% and, optimally, as near as possible to 6.0%.[5] Chapter 48 discusses diabetes.

Support aggressive lipid management for all patients with PAD. Both dietary interventions and drug therapy are needed. Statins (e.g., simvastatin [Zocor]) and a fibric acid derivative (gemfibrozil [Lopid]) may be used (see Table 33.6).

Drug Therapy. Angiotensin-converting enzyme (ACE) inhibitors (e.g., ramipril [Altace]) can reduce PAD symptoms. Antiplatelet agents are critical for reducing the risks for CVD events and death. Oral antiplatelet therapy should include low-dose aspirin therapy. Aspirin-intolerant patients may take clopidogrel (Plavix) daily. Combination antiplatelet therapy with aspirin and clopidogrel may be used by select high-risk patients. Anticoagulants (e.g., warfarin [Coumadin]) are not recommended for prevention of CVD events in patients with PAD.

DRUG ALERT Clopidogrel (Plavix) and Omeprazole (Prilosec)

- Antiplatelet effect of clopidogrel is reduced by about half when given with omeprazole.
- This reduced effect increases the risk for myocardial infarction (MI) and stroke.

Two drugs are available to treat intermittent claudication: cilostazol and pentoxifylline. Cilostazol, a phosphodiesterase inhibitor, inhibits platelet aggregation and increases vasodilation.

Pentoxifylline, a xanthine derivative, improves the flexibility of RBCs and WBCs and decreases fibrinogen concentration, platelet adhesiveness, and blood viscosity. It is not as effective as cilostazol. Cilostazol is usually stopped within 3 months due to side effects.[3]

 DRUG ALERT Cilostazol

- Contraindicated in patients with HF.

Exercise Therapy. A supervised exercise program is recommended as part of the initial treatment for all patients with intermittent claudication. Exercise should be done for 30 to 45 min/day, at least 3 times/week, for a minimum of 3 months. Although walking is most commonly prescribed, other modes of exercise (e.g., cycling) improve walking ability and quality of life.[3]

Encouraging taking part in exercise is particularly important for women with PAD. Women have faster functional decline and greater mobility loss than men with PAD. Overall, patients with PAD who have higher levels of daily physical activity have better survival rates.[3,4]

Nutritional Therapy. Teach patients with PAD to maintain a body mass index (BMI) less than 25 kg/m^2 and a waist circumference less than 40 inches for men and less than 35 inches for women. Even modest, sustained weight loss of 3% to 5% yields important reductions in triglycerides, glucose, A1C, and the risk for developing type 2 diabetes. Greater weight loss has greater benefits.[5] Recommend a diet reduced in calories and salt for obese or overweight persons.[5]

Complementary and Alternative Therapies. Patients taking antiplatelet agents, nonsteroidal antiinflammatory drugs (NSAIDs) (e.g., ibuprofen), and anticoagulants (e.g., warfarin) should consult with their HCP before taking any dietary or herbal supplements because of potential interactions and bleeding risks.[6,7] See the Complementary & Alternative Therapies box on p. 818.

Care of the Leg With Critical Limb Ischemia. Optimal therapy for the patient with CLI is revascularization via bypass surgery using an *autogenous* (native) vein. An alternative is percutaneous transluminal angioplasty (PTA).[3,8] Patients with CLI who are not candidates for surgery or PTA may receive IV prostanoids (e.g., iloprost [Ventavis]). However, the FDA has not approved this drug for CLI treatment.[3,8] Patients with CLI should continue optimal drug therapy (e.g., statin, antiplatelet, ACE inhibitor, β-blocker) to reduce the risk for a CVD event.

Conservative management includes protecting the extremity from trauma, decreasing ischemic pain, preventing and controlling infection, and improving perfusion. Carefully inspect, cleanse, and lubricate feet to prevent skin cracking and infection. Avoid lubrication between the toes and soaking the patient's feet to prevent skin *maceration* (or breakdown). Keep the affected foot clean and dry. Cover any ulcers with a dry, sterile dressing. Deep ulcers are treated with a variety of wound care products. Healing is unlikely without increasing the blood flow.

Encourage the patient to wear soft, roomy, and protective footwear and avoid extremes of heat and cold. Keep the patient's heels free of pressure. Place a pillow under the calves so that the heels are off the mattress or use a commercially available heel protection device. Giving analgesics and placing the bed in the reverse Trendelenburg position may control pain and increase perfusion to the lower extremities.

Spinal cord stimulation may help manage pain for patients with CLI. Other promising strategies include growth factors and gene and stem cell therapy to stimulate blood vessel growth *(angiogenesis).* Unfortunately, almost half of the patients with CLI will die within 5 years.[8]

Interventional Radiology Catheter-Based Procedures. Interventional radiology catheter-based procedures are alternatives to open surgery for treatment of lower extremity PAD. These procedures take place in a catheterization laboratory rather than in an operating room.

All these procedures are similar to angiography in that they involve the insertion of a specialized catheter into the femoral artery. The PTA procedure uses a catheter that has a balloon at the tip. The end of the catheter is moved to the narrowed (stenotic) area of the artery. The balloon is then inflated, compressing the atherosclerotic intimal lining.[3]

Stents, expandable metallic devices, are placed within the artery after the balloon angioplasty. The stent holds the artery open. Angioplasty balloons and peripheral stents may be coated with a drug (e.g., paclitaxel) to limit the growth of new tissue in the treated area and improve long-term patency rates.[3,9]

Atherectomy is the removal of the obstructing plaque. A directional atherectomy device uses a high-speed cutting disk that cuts long strips of the atheroma. Laser atherectomy uses ultraviolet energy to break up the atheroma. Other types of atherectomy catheters have a diamond-coated tip that rotates at a high speed (like a dental drill).

Cryoplasty combines PTA and cold therapy. A specialized balloon is filled with liquid nitrous oxide, which changes to gas as it enters the balloon. Expansion of the gas results in cooling to 14° F (−10° C). The cold temperature limits restenosis by reducing smooth muscle cell activity.

Nursing care is the same as for diagnostic angiography (see Tables 31.7 and 31.8). Antiplatelet agents are needed postprocedure to reduce the risk for restenosis. Long-term, low-dose aspirin therapy or clopidogrel is recommended.

Surgical Therapy. Various surgical approaches can be used to improve blood flow beyond a blocked artery. When possible, peripheral artery bypass surgery is done with an autogenous vein to bypass (carry blood around) the lesion (Fig. 37.2).

FIG. 37.2 A, Femoral-popliteal bypass graft around an occluded superficial femoral artery. **B,** Femoral–posterior tibial bypass graft around occluded superficial femoral, popliteal, and proximal tibial arteries.

Synthetic grafts are used for long routes, such as an axillary-femoral bypass. When a person's own vein is not available, human umbilical vein or a composite sequential bypass graft (native vein plus synthetic graft) can be used.[3] PTA with stenting also may be done in combination with bypass surgery.

Other surgical options include *endarterectomy* (opening the artery and removing the obstructing plaque) and *patch graft angioplasty* (opening the artery, removing plaque, and sewing a patch to the opening to widen the lumen). In-hospital mortality is higher in women undergoing revascularization than men, regardless of disease severity or procedure done.[4]

Amputation may be needed if tissue necrosis is extensive, gangrene or osteomyelitis develops, or all major arteries in the limb are blocked. We make every effort to preserve as much of the limb as possible to improve rehabilitation potential. Amputation is discussed in Chapter 62.

❖ NURSING MANAGEMENT: LOWER EXTREMITY PERIPHERAL ARTERY DISEASE

◆ Nursing Assessment

Table 37.4 presents subjective and objective data that you should obtain from a patient with PAD.

◆ Nursing Diagnoses

Nursing diagnoses for the patient with PAD may include:
- Ineffective tissue perfusion
- Activity intolerance

Additional information on nursing diagnoses and interventions for the patient with PAD of the lower extremities is presented in eNursing Care Plan 37.1 on the website for this chapter.

◆ Planning

Nursing care focuses on the priority problems of poor tissue perfusion and pain. The overall goals for the patient who has lower extremity PAD include (1) adequate tissue perfusion; (2) relief of pain; (3) increased exercise tolerance; (4) intact, healthy skin on the extremities; and (5) increased knowledge of disease and treatment plan.

◆ Nursing Implementation

◆ **Health Promotion.** Assess the patient for and provide instructions on how to control CVD risk factors (see Table 33.2). Teach diet modification to reduce cholesterol, saturated fat, and refined sugars (see Tables 33.4 and 33.5). Teach proper foot care and injury prevention. Encourage patients with positive family histories of cardiac, diabetes, or vascular disease to obtain regular follow-up care.

◆ **Acute Care.** After surgical or radiologic intervention, observe the patient in a recovery area. Check the operative extremity every 15 minutes initially and then hourly for color, temperature, capillary refill, presence of peripheral pulses, and sensation and movement. Immediately notify the HCP of any loss of palpable pulses or change in the Doppler sound over a pulse. Postoperative ABI measurements are not obtained as they place the patient at risk for graft thrombosis. Compare assessment findings with the patient's baseline and with findings in the opposite limb.

PAD patients with a history of chronic ischemic rest pain may have developed a tolerance to opioids. Thus aggressive pain management may be needed after surgery.

After the patient leaves the recovery area, continue to monitor extremity perfusion. Assess for complications, such as bleeding,

TABLE 37.4 Nursing Assessment

Peripheral Artery Disease

Subjective Data

Important Health Information

Past health history: Tobacco use, diabetes, hypertension, hyperlipidemia, hypertriglyceridemia, hyperuricemia, impaired renal function, obesity. ↑ High-sensitivity C-reactive protein, homocysteine, or lipoprotein (a) [Lp(a)] levels. Positive family history, sedentary lifestyle, stress

Functional Health Patterns

Health perception–health management: Family history of CVD. Tobacco use, including exposure to environmental smoke

Nutritional-metabolic: High sodium, saturated fat, and cholesterol intake. Elevated Hb A1C

Activity-exercise: Exercise intolerance

Cognitive-perceptual: Buttock, thigh, or calf pain that is precipitated by exercise and that subsides with rest (intermittent claudication) or progresses to pain at rest. Burning pain in feet and toes at rest. Numbness, tingling, sensation of cold in legs or feet. Progressive loss of sensation and deep pain in extremities

Sexuality-reproductive: Erectile dysfunction

Objective Data

Integumentary

Loss of hair on legs and feet. Thick toenails. Pallor with elevation. Dependent rubor. Thin, cool, shiny skin with muscle atrophy. Skin breakdown and arterial ulcers, especially over bony areas. Gangrene

Cardiovascular

Decreased or absent peripheral pulses. Feet cool to touch. Capillary refill >3 seconds. Bruits may be present at pulse sites.

Neurologic

Mobility or sensation impairment

Possible Diagnostic Findings

Arterial stenosis evident with duplex imaging, ↓ Doppler pressures, ↓ ABI, angiography shows peripheral atherosclerosis

---

hematoma, thrombosis, embolization, and compartment syndrome. A dramatic increase in pain, loss of previously palpable pulses, extremity pallor or cyanosis, numbness or tingling, or a cold extremity suggests graft or stent blockage. Report these findings to the HCP at once.

Do not place the patient in a knee-flexed position except for exercise. Turn the patient and position frequently with pillows to support the incision. On postoperative day 1, assist the patient out of bed several times. Walking even short distances is desirable. A walker may be helpful, especially for frail, older patients. Discourage prolonged sitting with legs lowered, since it may cause pain and edema, increase the risk for venous thrombosis, and place stress on the suture lines. Graduated compression stockings may help control leg edema. If edema develops, position the patient supine, and elevate the leg above heart level.

CHECK YOUR PRACTICE

You are caring for a 74-yr-old male patient who is recovering from left femoral-popliteal bypass graft surgery. When you respond to the patient's call bell, the patient reports severe pain in the operative leg. On assessment, you note that the dorsalis pedis and posterior tibial pulses are no longer palpable and the foot is cold to touch.

• What are your next actions?

Surgical site infection (SSI) is a serious complication. Careful postoperative assessment and wound care are important. SSIs are associated with early graft loss, longer hospitalizations, reoperation, and sepsis. If no complications occur, discharge occurs 3 to 5 days after surgery.

◆ **Ambulatory Care.** Assess for CVD risk factors. Be alert for opportunities to teach patients health promotion strategies. Continued tobacco use dramatically decreases the patency rates of grafts and stents and increases the risk for an MI or stroke.

Long-term antiplatelet therapy with aspirin or clopidogrel is used after surgery. Patients having distal peripheral bypass surgery (i.e., below the knee) using synthetic graft materials receive dual antiplatelet therapy (clopidogrel plus aspirin) for 1 to 3 months, followed by lifelong single antiplatelet therapy.[10]

Encourage supervised exercise training after revascularization. Explain that exercise decreases CVD risk factors, including hypertension, hyperlipidemia, obesity, and glucose levels. Teach foot care to all patients with PAD. Meticulous foot care is especially important in the patient with diabetes and PAD (see Table 48.21). Diabetic neuropathy increases the patient's risk for injury and results in delay in seeking treatment. Tell patients to inspect their legs and feet daily for changes in skin color or texture. Show patients how to check skin temperature and capillary refill and to palpate pulses. Stress reporting any changes in these findings or the development of ulceration or inflammation to the HCP.

Thick or overgrown toenails and calluses are potentially serious and need regular attention by an HCP (e.g., podiatrist). Patients who have poor eyesight, back problems, obesity, or arthritis may need help with foot care. Encourage patients to wear clean, all-cotton or all-wool socks and comfortable shoes with rounded (not pointed) toes and soft insoles. Tell patients to lace shoes loosely and to break in new shoes gradually (Table 37.5).

◆ **Evaluation**

The expected outcomes are that a patient with PAD of the lower extremities will have

• Adequate peripheral tissue perfusion
• Increased activity tolerance
• Effective pain management
• Knowledge of disease and treatment plan

ACUTE ARTERIAL ISCHEMIC DISORDERS

Etiology and Pathophysiology

Acute arterial ischemia is a sudden interruption in the arterial blood supply to a tissue, an organ, or an extremity that, if left untreated, can result in tissue death. It is caused by embolism, thrombosis of an atherosclerotic artery, or trauma. *Embolization* of a thrombus from the heart is the most frequent cause of acute arterial occlusion. Heart conditions in which thrombi can develop include infective endocarditis, mitral valve disease, atrial fibrillation, cardiomyopathies, and prosthetic heart valves. Noncardiac sources of emboli include aneurysms, ulcerated atherosclerotic plaque, recent endovascular procedures, and venous thrombi.

Thrombi that originate in the left side of the heart may dislodge and travel anywhere in the systemic circulation. Most emboli block an artery of the leg where vessels branch (e.g., iliofemoral, popliteal, tibial) or narrow. Sudden local thrombosis may occur at the site of an atherosclerotic plaque. Hypovolemia

TABLE 37.5 Patient & Caregiver Teaching

Peripheral Artery Bypass Surgery

Include the following information in the teaching plan for a patient undergoing peripheral artery bypass surgery and the patient's caregiver:

1. Reduce risk factors by stopping the use of all tobacco products, controlling blood glucose levels with diabetes and BP, lowering cholesterol and triglyceride levels, achieving or maintaining ideal body weight, and exercising regularly.
2. Provide teaching about the basic mechanism of action (why prescribed for patient) and side effects of drugs, such as antiplatelets, antihypertensives, lipid-lowering therapy, and pain medication.
3. Eat healthy—it is essential to recovery. Drink plenty of fluids, eat a well-balanced diet (e.g., foods high in protein, vitamins C and A, and zinc; high-fiber foods; fresh fruits and vegetables), eat fewer high-fat foods, and reduce salt intake.
4. Take part in a supervised exercise program or take a daily walk. In the beginning, take several short walks a day and rest between activities. Gradually increase your walking to 30 to 40 min/day, 3 to 5 days/wk.
5. Care for feet and legs. Inspect feet and wash them daily. Wear clean cotton or wool socks and well-fitting shoes. File toenails straight across. Avoid sitting with legs crossed, extreme hot and cold temperatures, and prolonged standing.
6. Follow routine postoperative wound care that includes keeping incision clean and dry; do not disturb Steri-Strips (if present).
7. Monitor for signs and symptoms of impaired healing or infection of the leg incision, and notify HCP if any of the following occur:
   * Prolonged drainage or pus from the incision
   * Increased redness, warmth, pain, or hardness along incision
   * Separation of wound edges
   * Temperature >100° F (37.8° C)
8. Keep all follow-up appointments with HCP.
9. Notify HCP at once of increased leg or foot pain or a change in the color or temperature of leg or foot.

(e.g., shock), hyperviscosity (e.g., polycythemia), and hypercoagulability (e.g., chemotherapy) predispose a person to thrombotic arterial occlusion.

Traumatic injury to an extremity may cause partial or total arterial blockage. Acute arterial occlusion may develop from arterial dissection in the carotid artery or aorta or from a procedure-related arterial injury (e.g., after angiography).

Clinical Manifestations

Manifestations of acute arterial ischemia include the *6 Ps: pain, pallor, pulselessness, paresthesia, paralysis,* and *poikilothermia* (adaptation of the limb to the environmental temperature, most often cool). If you detect these signs, immediately notify the HCP. Without immediate intervention, ischemia may progress to tissue necrosis and gangrene within a few hours.

Paralysis is a late sign of acute arterial ischemia and signals the death of nerves supplying the extremity. Foot drop occurs from nerve damage. Because nerve tissue is extremely sensitive to hypoxia, limb paralysis or ischemic neuropathy may persist even after revascularization.

Interprofessional Care

Early diagnosis and treatment are essential to keep the affected limb viable during acute arterial ischemia. Anticoagulant therapy with IV unfractionated heparin (UH) is started to prevent thrombus growth and inhibit further embolization. In patients undergoing embolectomy, UH should be followed by long-term anticoagulation (see discussion of anticoagulant options later in this chapter).

To restore blood flow, the thrombus is removed as soon as possible. Options consist of surgical thrombectomy (recommended procedure), percutaneous catheter-directed thrombolytic therapy, percutaneous mechanical thrombectomy with or without thrombolytic therapy, or surgical bypass.

Percutaneous catheter-directed thrombolytic therapy using alteplase or urokinase is recommended for acute arterial ischemia of less than 14 days. The HCP inserts a catheter into the femoral artery and moved it to the site of the clot, and the thrombolytic drug is continuously infused. Thrombolytic agents work by directly dissolving the clot over a period of 24 to 48 hours. (Chapter 33 discusses thrombolytic therapy.) Close monitoring is required to make sure the catheter does not move and the patient does not bleed from the site of the catheter insertion.

Surgical revascularization may be used in a patient with trauma (e.g., laceration of the artery) or with significant arterial blockage. Amputation is reserved for patients with ischemic rest pain and tissue loss in whom limb salvage is not possible. If the patient is at risk for further embolization from a persistent source (e.g., chronic atrial fibrillation), long-term anticoagulation is recommended.[6,10]

THROMBOANGIITIS OBLITERANS

Thromboangiitis obliterans (Buerger's disease) is a nonatherosclerotic, segmental, recurrent inflammatory disorder of the small and medium arteries and veins of the arms and legs. Rarely, cerebral, coronary, mesenteric, pulmonary, and/or renal arteries may be involved. The disease occurs mostly in men younger than 45 years of age with a long history of tobacco and/or marijuana use without other CVD risk factors (e.g., hypertension, hyperlipidemia, diabetes).[11]

In the acute phase of Buerger's disease, an inflammatory thrombus blocks the vessel. Over time, the thrombus becomes more organized and the inflammation in the vessel wall subsides.[11] During the chronic phase, thrombosis and fibrosis in the vessel cause tissue ischemia.

The symptoms of Buerger's disease often are confused with PAD and other autoimmune diseases (e.g., scleroderma). Patients may have intermittent claudication of the feet, hands, or arms. As the disease progresses, rest pain and ischemic ulcerations develop. Other signs and symptoms may include color and temperature changes of the limbs, paresthesia, superficial vein thrombosis, and cold sensitivity.

There are no laboratory or diagnostic tests specific to Buerger's disease. The diagnosis is based on age of onset; history; symptoms; involvement of distal vessels; presence of ischemic ulcerations; and exclusion of autoimmune disease, diabetes, thrombophilia (inherited tendency to clot), and other sources of emboli, such as atherosclerosis and aneurysm.[11]

The main treatment for Buerger's disease is the complete cessation of tobacco and marijuana use in any form. Use of nicotine replacement products is contraindicated.

Conservative management includes avoiding limb exposure to cold temperatures, a supervised walking program, antibiotics to treat any infected ulcers, and analgesics to manage the ischemic pain. Teach patients to avoid trauma to the extremities.

IV iloprost (Ventavis), a prostaglandin analog that promotes vasodilation, is used to manage rest pain, promote healing of ischemic ulcers, and decrease the need for amputation.[11] Surgical options include lumbar sympathectomy (transection of a nerve, ganglion, and/or plexus of the sympathetic nervous system), implanting a spinal cord stimulator, microsurgical flap and omental transfer, bypass surgery, and stem cell therapy.[11] Sympathectomy and a spinal cord stimulator can improve distal blood flow, reduce pain, and decrease the rate of amputation, but neither alters the inflammatory process. Bypass surgery typically is not an option because of the involvement of smaller, distal vessels. It may be used in select patients with severe ischemia. Stem cells can differentiate into specialized adult cells, with the potential to become any tissue in the human body. Stem cell therapy promotes ulcer healing, new blood vessel formation, and nerve cell regeneration.[11]

Painful ulcerations may require finger or toe amputations. Amputation below the knee may be needed in severe cases. The rate of amputation in those who continue tobacco or marijuana use after diagnosis is much higher than in those who stop.[11]

RAYNAUD'S PHENOMENON

Raynaud's phenomenon is an episodic vasospastic disorder of small cutaneous arteries, most often involving the fingers and toes. It occurs more often in women, especially those between 15 and 40 years of age. The pathogenesis of Raynaud's phenomenon is due to abnormalities in the vascular, intravascular, and neuronal mechanisms that cause vasodilation.[12]

Raynaud's phenomenon may occur in isolation (primary Raynaud's phenomenon) or with an underlying disease (e.g., thyroid conditions, scleroderma, systemic lupus erythematosus) (secondary Raynaud's phenomenon). Other contributing factors include the use of vibrating machinery or work in cold environments, exposure to heavy metals (e.g., lead), and high homocysteine levels.

Diagnosis is based on persistent symptoms for at least 2 years. Patients with Raynaud's phenomenon should have routine follow-up to monitor for development of connective tissue or autoimmune diseases.

Raynaud's phenomenon is characterized by vasospasm-induced color changes of fingers, toes, ears, and nose (white, blue, and red). Decreased perfusion results in pallor (white). The digits then appear cyanotic (bluish purple) (Fig. 37.3). These changes are followed by rubor (red), a hyperemic response when blood flow is restored. The patient usually describes coldness and numbness in the vasoconstrictive phase. This is followed by throbbing, aching pain, tingling, and swelling in the hyperemic

FIG. 37.3 Raynaud's phenomenon. (From James WD, Elston DM, Dirk M: *Andrews' diseases of the skin clinical atlas*, St Louis, 2018, Elsevier.)

phase. An episode usually lasts only minutes but may last for several hours. Exposure to cold, emotional upsets, tobacco use, and caffeine often bring on symptoms.

After frequent, prolonged attacks, the skin may become thickened and the nails brittle. Sometimes, complications include *punctate* (small hole) lesions of the fingertips and superficial gangrenous ulcers.

Patient teaching is the focus of nursing care for Raynaud's phenomenon. Focus your instructions on preventing episodes. Tell patients to avoid temperature extremes and wear loose, warm clothing as protection from the cold, including gloves when handling cold objects. The patient should stop using all tobacco products and avoid caffeine and other drugs that have vasoconstrictive effects (e.g., cocaine, amphetamines, ergotamine, pseudoephedrine). Provide patients with appropriate stress management strategies. Immersing hands in warm water often decreases the vasospasm.

Sustained-release calcium channel blockers (e.g., nifedipine [Procardia]) are the first-line drug therapy. They relax smooth muscles of the arterioles by blocking the influx of calcium into the cells. This reduces the frequency and severity of vasospastic attacks. If symptoms persist, other vasodilators (e.g., phosphodiesterase-5 inhibitors [sildenafil]) or topical nitroglycerin 2% ointment may be used. Calcium channel blockers can be taken with nitroglycerin topical ointment. Phosphodiesterase-5 inhibitors are not used with topical nitroglycerin due to risk for hypotension.[12]

Prompt intervention is needed for patients with digital ulceration or critical ischemia. Treatment options include prostacyclin infusion therapy (e.g., iloprost), antibiotics, analgesics, and surgical debridement of necrotic tissue. Botulinum toxin A and statins may lessen the severity of Raynaud's phenomenon.[12] Sympathectomy is done only in severe cases refractory to medical treatment where digit survival is threatened.

AORTIC ANEURYSMS

The aorta is the largest artery and supplies O_2, nutrients, and blood to all vital organs. One of the most common problems affecting the aorta is an **aneurysm**, which is a permanent, localized outpouching or dilation of the vessel wall. Aneurysms occur in men more often than in women and in whites more often than blacks. The incidence increases with age.[3,13] Aneurysms may occur in more than 1 location.

Etiology and Pathophysiology

Aortic aneurysms may involve the aortic arch and thoracic and/or abdominal aorta. Three fourths of aortic aneurysms occur in the abdominal aorta (Fig. 37.4) and one fourth in the thoracic aorta. Most abdominal aortic aneurysms (AAAs) occur below the renal arteries.

A variety of disorders are associated with aortic aneurysms. The main causes are classified as degenerative, congenital, mechanical (e.g., penetrating or blunt trauma), inflammatory (e.g., aortitis [Takayasu's arteritis]), or infectious (e.g., aortitis [*Chlamydia pneumoniae*, human immunodeficiency virus]).

Risk factors for aortic aneurysms include age, male gender, hypertension, CAD, family history, tobacco use, high cholesterol, lower extremity PAD, carotid artery disease, previous stroke, and obesity. Tobacco use is the most important modifiable risk factor.[1,13] The larger the aneurysm, the greater is the risk for rupture.

FIG. 37.4 Angiography showing fusiform abdominal aortic aneurysm. Note calcification of the aortic wall *(arrows)* and extension of the aneurysm into the common iliac arteries. (Courtesy Jo Menzoian, Boston, MA.)

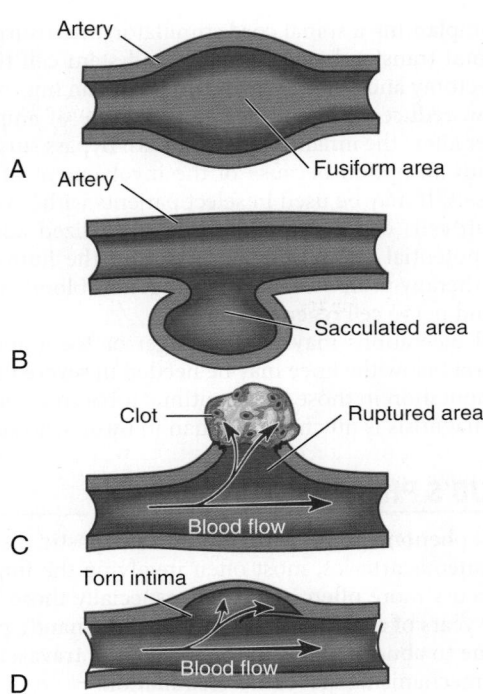

FIG. 37.5 A, True fusiform abdominal aortic aneurysm. B, True saccular aortic aneurysm. C, False aneurysm, or pseudoaneurysm. D, Aortic dissection.

 ### Genetic Link

Both aortic aneurysm and aortic dissection has a strong genetic component. The familial tendency is related to several congenital anomalies. Examples include bicuspid aortic valve, coarctation of the aorta, Turner syndrome, autosomal dominant polycystic kidney disease, specific collagen defects (e.g., Ehlers-Danlos syndrome), and premature breakdown of vascular elastic tissue (e.g., Marfan's syndrome).[1,13]

Classification

Aneurysms are classified as true or false aneurysms (Fig. 37.5, A to C). A *true aneurysm* is one in which the wall of the artery forms the aneurysm, with at least 1 vessel layer still intact. True aneurysms are subdivided into fusiform and saccular types. A *fusiform aneurysm* is circumferential and relatively uniform in shape. A *saccular aneurysm* is pouchlike with a narrow neck connecting the bulge to 1 side of the arterial wall.

A *false aneurysm,* or *pseudoaneurysm,* is not an aneurysm. It is a disruption of all arterial wall layers with bleeding that is contained by surrounding anatomic structures. False aneurysms may result from trauma, infection, peripheral artery bypass graft surgery (at the site of the graft-to-artery anastomosis), or arterial leakage after removal of cannulae (e.g., femoral artery catheters, intraaortic balloon pump devices).

Clinical Manifestations

Thoracic aortic aneurysms (TAAs) are often asymptomatic. When present, symptoms include deep, diffuse chest pain that may extend to the interscapular area. Ascending aorta and aortic arch aneurysms can cause (1) angina from decreased blood flow to the coronary arteries; (2) transient ischemic attacks from decreased blood flow to the carotid arteries; and (3) coughing, shortness of breath, hoarseness, and/or difficulty swallowing from pressure on the laryngeal nerve. If the aneurysm presses on the superior vena cava, decreased venous return can result in jugular venous distention and edema of the face and arms.

AAAs are often asymptomatic. They are often found during routine physical examinations or evaluations for an unrelated problem (e.g., abdominal x-ray, CT scan). A pulsatile mass in the periumbilical area slightly to the left of the midline may be present. Bruits may be auscultated over the aneurysm. Physical findings may be hard to detect in obese persons.

AAA symptoms may mimic pain associated with abdominal or back disorders. Compression of nearby anatomic structures and nerves may cause symptoms, such as back pain, epigastric discomfort, altered bowel elimination, and intermittent claudication. Sometimes, aneurysms spontaneously embolize plaque, causing "blue toe syndrome" (patchy mottling of the feet and toes in the presence of palpable pedal pulses).

Complications

Aneurysm rupture is the most serious complication. It is more likely to occur in people who smoke tobacco.[13] If rupture occurs into the retroperitoneal space, bleeding may be controlled by surrounding anatomic structures, preventing exsanguination and death. In this case, the patient often has severe back pain. Back or flank ecchymosis *(Grey Turner sign)* may be present.

If rupture occurs into the thoracic or abdominal cavity, patients can die from massive hemorrhage. The patient who reaches the hospital will be in hypovolemic shock with tachycardia, hypotension, pale clammy skin, decreased urine output, altered level of consciousness, and abdominal tenderness. (Shock is discussed in Chapter 66.) In this situation, simultaneous resuscitation and immediate surgical repair are needed. For patients admitted to the hospital with a ruptured AAA, in-hospital mortality is high at 53%.[13]

Diagnostic Studies

Chest x-rays are done to reveal abnormal widening of the thoracic aorta. An abdominal x-ray may show calcification within the aortic wall. An ECG may rule out MI, since thoracic aneurysm or dissection symptoms can mimic angina.

Echocardiography assesses the function of the aortic valve. Ultrasound is useful for aneurysm screening and to monitor aneurysm size. A CT scan or MRI can diagnose and assess the location and severity of aneurysms. Angiography gives helpful information by using contrast imaging to map the entire aortic system. (Chapter 31 and Table 31.7 discuss angiography.)

Interprofessional Care

The main goal of interprofessional care is to prevent the rupture of an aneurysm. Early detection and prompt treatment are essential. Conservative medical therapy of small, asymptomatic AAAs (less than 5.4 cm) is the best practice.[13] This consists of risk factor modification (ceasing tobacco use, decreasing BP, optimizing lipid profile, gradually increasing physical activity).[13] Patients should receive medical management for hypertension, hyperlipidemia, diabetes, and other CVD risk factors. A statin and an ACE inhibitor could prove to be beneficial. Those with small aneurysms, 4.0 to 5.4 cm, should have monitoring of aneurysm size using ultrasound or CT every 6 to 12 months. Ultrasound monitoring every 3 years is done for patients with AAAs smaller than 4.0 cm in diameter.

Surgical repair is recommended in patients with asymptomatic aneurysms 5.5 cm in diameter or larger. Surgical intervention may occur sooner if the patient has a genetic disorder (e.g., Marfan's, Ehlers-Danlos syndrome), the aneurysm expands rapidly, the patient becomes symptomatic, or the risk for rupture is high.[13] A careful review of body systems is needed to identify any co-morbidities as they affect the patient's surgical risk. Correcting existing carotid or coronary artery blockages may be needed before aneurysm repair.

Surgical Therapy. For elective aneurysm repair surgery, the patient should be well hydrated with normal electrolytes, coagulation, and hematocrit. If the aneurysm ruptures, emergent surgery is required.

Open aneurysm repair (OAR) involves a large abdominal incision through which the surgeon (1) cuts into the diseased aortic segment, (2) removes any thrombus or plaque, (3) sutures a synthetic graft to the aorta proximal and distal to the aneurysm, and (4) sutures the native aortic wall around the graft to act as a protective cover (Fig. 37.6). For iliac artery aneurysms, a bifurcated graft replaces the entire diseased segment. With saccular aneurysms, it may be possible to excise only the bulbous lesion and repair the artery by primary closure (suturing the artery together) or applying an autogenous or synthetic patch graft.

All OARs require aortic cross-clamping proximal and distal to the aneurysm. Most resections are done in 30 to 45 minutes, then the clamps are removed and blood flow is restored. The risk for postoperative complications, such as acute kidney injury, increases in patients who have OAR of AAAs above the level of the renal arteries.

Endovascular Graft Procedure. Minimally invasive endovascular aneurysm repair (EVAR) is an alternative to OAR for select patients. Eligibility criteria include iliofemoral vessels that allow for safe graft insertion and vessels of sufficient length and width to support the graft.[13]

EVAR involves the placement of a sutureless aortic graft into the abdominal aorta inside the aneurysm via the femoral artery. Grafts are made of various materials, such as a Dacron cylinder consisting of several sections, and supported with multiple rings of flexible wire.

FIG. 37.6 Surgical repair of an abdominal aortic aneurysm. **A,** Incising the aneurysmal sac. **B,** Insertion of synthetic graft. **C,** Suturing native aortic wall over synthetic graft.

The main section of the graft is bifurcated. It is delivered through a femoral artery catheter. The second part of the graft is inserted through the opposite femoral artery. When all graft components are in place, they are deployed against the vessel wall by balloon inflation. The blood then flows through the endovascular graft, preventing further expansion of the aneurysm (Fig. 37.7).

Angiography is done afterward to check for any leaks and to confirm patency of all stent-graft components. The aneurysmal wall shrinks over time because the blood is diverted through the endograft.

Complications. EVAR is less invasive than OAR and requires a shorter hospital stay. EVAR also has fewer complications, such as paraplegia and death.

The most common complication of AAA repair is *endoleak,* the seepage of blood back into the old aneurysm. This may result from an inadequate seal at either graft end, a tear through the graft fabric, or leakage between overlapping graft segments. Repair may require coil embolization (insertion of beads) for hemostasis.

Other complications include aneurysm growth above or below the graft, aneurysm rupture, aortic dissection, bleeding, renal artery occlusion caused by stent migration, graft thrombosis, incisional site hematoma, and incisional infection. Patients undergoing EVAR need periodic imaging for the rest of their lives to monitor for an endoleak, document stability of the aneurysm sac, and determine the need for surgical intervention.

A potentially lethal complication in an emergency repair of a ruptured AAA is the development of *intraabdominal hypertension* (IAH) with associated *abdominal compartment syndrome.* Persistent IAH reduces blood flow to the viscera. Abdominal compartment syndrome refers to the impaired organ perfusion caused by IAH and resulting multisystem organ failure. IAH is confirmed by measuring the patient's intraabdominal pressure indirectly through a catheter and transducer system.

Treatment goals include control of situations that lead to IAH. Interventions include open (surgical) decompression,

Renal artery

FIG. 37.7 Bifurcated (2-branched) endovascular stent grafting of an aneurysm. **A,** Insertion of a woven polyester graft covered by a tubular metal web (stent). **B,** The stent graft is inserted through a large blood vessel (e.g., femoral artery) using a delivery catheter. The catheter is positioned below the renal arteries in the area of the aneurysm. **C,** The stent graft is slowly released into the blood vessel. When the stent comes in contact with the blood vessel, it expands to a preset size. **D,** A second stent graft can be inserted in the opposite vessel, if needed. **E,** Fully deployed bifurcated stent graft.

percutaneous drainage, and percutaneous drainage combined with a thrombolytic infusion. Conservative measures, such as intubation, ventilation, patient positioning, gastric decompression, cautious fluid resuscitation, pain management, and temporary hemofiltration, are used.

❖ NURSING MANAGEMENT: AORTIC ANEURYSMS

◆ Nursing Assessment

Begin by performing a thorough history and physical assessment. Because atherosclerosis is a systemic disease, look for signs of coexisting cardiac, pulmonary, cerebral, and lower extremity vascular problems. Monitor the patient for signs of aneurysm rupture. These include diaphoresis; pallor; weakness; tachycardia; hypotension; abdominal, back, groin, or periumbilical pain; changes in level of consciousness; or a pulsating abdominal mass.

Establish baseline data to compare with later assessments. Pay special attention to the character and quality of the patient's peripheral pulses and renal and neurologic status. Before surgery, mark pedal pulse sites (dorsalis pedis, posterior tibial) with a single-use marker and document any skin lesions on the lower extremities.

◆ Planning

The overall goals for a patient undergoing aortic surgery include (1) normal tissue perfusion; (2) intact motor and sensory function; and (3) no complications related to surgical repair, such as thrombosis, infection, or rupture.

◆ Nursing Implementation

◆ **Health Promotion.** To promote overall health, encourage the patient to reduce CVD risk factors (see Table 33.2), including controlling BP, ceasing tobacco use (see Chapter 10), and maintaining normal body weight and serum lipid levels. These measures also help ensure continued graft patency after surgical repair. Counsel the patient about taking part in moderate physical activity.

◆ **Acute Care.** Before surgery, provide emotional support and teaching to the patient and caregiver. Preoperative teaching includes a brief explanation of the disease process, the planned surgical procedure(s), preoperative routines, what to expect right after surgery (e.g., recovery room, tubes, drains), and usual postoperative timelines. Specific routines vary by agency and HCP. In general, aortic surgery patients have a bowel preparation and skin cleansing with an antimicrobial agent the day before surgery, have NPO after midnight the day of surgery, and receive IV antibiotics before the incision is made. Patients with a history of CVD should receive a β-blocker (e.g., metoprolol [Lopressor]). Scheduling a preoperative visit to the ICU may be helpful to the patient and caregiver.

After surgery, patients typically go to an ICU for 24 to 48 hours for close monitoring. When the patient arrives in the ICU, various devices are in place. These include an endotracheal tube for mechanical ventilation, an arterial line, a central venous pressure (CVP) catheter, peripheral IV lines, an indwelling urinary catheter, and a nasogastric (NG) tube. The patient needs continuous ECG and pulse oximetry monitoring. If the thorax is opened during surgery, chest tubes will be in place. The patient may have a lumbar catheter draining cerebrospinal fluid to prevent neurologic deficits. Pain medication is given via subcutaneous infusion into incision site (e.g., On-Q pain pump), epidural catheters, or IV patient-controlled analgesia (PCA).

In addition to the usual goals of care for a postoperative patient (e.g., maintaining adequate respiratory function, fluid and electrolyte balance, and pain control [see Chapter 19]), check for graft patency and renal perfusion. Watch for and intervene to limit or treat cardiac ischemia, dysrhythmias, infections, VTE, and neurologic complications. eNursing Care Plan 37.2 for the patient with an aneurysm repair or other aortic surgery is available on the website for this chapter.

Graft Patency. An adequate BP is important to maintain graft patency. Prolonged low BP may result in graft thrombosis. Give IV fluids and blood components as ordered to maintain adequate blood flow. Monitor CVP or PA pressures and urine output hourly in the immediate postoperative period to assess the patient's hydration and perfusion status.

Avoid severe hypertension, which may stress the arterial anastomoses, resulting in leakage of blood or rupture at the suture lines. Drug therapy with IV diuretics (e.g., furosemide) or IV antihypertensive agents (e.g., labetalol, metoprolol, hydralazine, sodium nitroprusside [Nipride]) may be indicated.

Cardiovascular Status. Myocardial ischemia or infarction may occur in the perioperative period because of decreased myocardial O_2 supply or increased myocardial O_2 demands. Dysrhythmias may occur because of electrolyte imbalances, hypoxemia, hypothermia, or myocardial ischemia. Nursing interventions include continuous ECG monitoring; frequent electrolyte and arterial blood gas determinations; O_2 administration, IV antidysrhythmic and antihypertensive drugs, and electrolytes as needed; adequate pain control; and resumption of cardiac drugs.

Infection. A prosthetic vascular graft infection is a rare but potentially life-threatening complication. Nursing interventions to prevent infection include giving a broad-spectrum antibiotic as prescribed. Assess temperature regularly, and promptly report elevations. Monitor laboratory results for a high WBC count, which may be the first sign of an infection. Ensure adequate nutrition and assess the surgical incision for signs of infection (e.g., redness, swelling, drainage). Keep surgical incisions clean and dry and perform wound care as prescribed.

Use good hand-washing and strict aseptic technique in the care of all peripheral, arterial, and CVP catheter insertion sites, since these are ports of entry for bacteria. Meticulous perineal care for the patient with an indwelling urinary catheter and early catheter removal are essential to minimize the risk for urinary tract infection.

Gastrointestinal Status. After OAR, postoperative ileus may develop because of anesthesia and the handling of the bowel during surgery. The intestines may become swollen and bruised, and peristalsis ceases for variable intervals. A retroperitoneal surgical approach decreases the risk for bowel complications.

An NG tube may be present and connected to low, intermittent suction to decompress the stomach, prevent aspiration of stomach contents, and decrease pressure on suture lines. Record the amount and character of the NG output. While the patient is NPO, provide frequent oral care. Ice chips or lozenges can help soothe a dry or irritated throat. Assess for bowel sounds every 4 hours. Note the passing of flatus as it signals returning bowel function. Encourage early ambulation since this will help the return of bowel function. A postoperative ileus rarely lasts beyond the 4th postoperative day.

If the blood supply to the bowel is disrupted during surgery, ischemia or infarction (death) of intestinal tissue may result. Manifestations of this rare, but serious, complication include absent bowel sounds, fever, abdominal distention and pain, diarrhea, and bloody stools. If bowel infarction occurs, immediate reoperation is needed to restore blood flow, with resection of the infarcted bowel.

Neurologic Status. Neurologic complications can occur after aortic surgery. When the ascending aorta and aortic arch are involved, assess the patient's level of consciousness, pupil size and response to light, facial symmetry, tongue position, speech, upper extremity movement, and quality of hand grasps). When the descending aorta is involved, perform a neurovascular assessment of the lower extremities. Record all assessments and report changes from baseline to the HCP immediately.

Peripheral Perfusion Status. The location of the aneurysm determines what type of peripheral perfusion assessment to do. Check and record all peripheral pulses hourly for several hours and then routinely (based on agency policy). When the ascending aorta and aortic arch are involved, assess the carotid, radial, and temporal artery pulses. For surgery of the descending aorta, assess the femoral, popliteal, posterior tibial, and dorsalis pedis pulses (see Fig. 31.6). You may need a Doppler to assess peripheral pulses. Check skin temperature and color, capillary refill time, and sensation and movement of the extremities.

Sometimes, lower extremity pulses may be absent for a short time after surgery because of vasospasm and hypothermia. A decreased or absent pulse together with a cool, pale, mottled, or painful extremity may indicate embolization or graft occlusion. Report these findings to the HCP at once. Graft occlusion requires reoperation if identified early. It is essential to compare your findings with the preoperative status to determine the cause of a decreased or absent pulse and the proper treatment. In some patients, pulses may have been absent before surgery because of coexistent PAD.

Renal Perfusion Status. The patient will have an indwelling urinary catheter after surgery. In the immediate postoperative period, record hourly urine output. Further evaluate renal function by monitoring daily BUN and serum creatinine levels. CVP pressures give vital information about hydration status. Maintain accurate fluid intake and output and record daily weights until the patient resumes a regular diet.

Decreased renal perfusion can occur from embolization of an aortic thrombus or plaque to 1 or both renal arteries. This causes ischemia of 1 or both kidneys. Hypotension, dehydration, prolonged aortic clamping during surgery, or blood loss can lead to decreased renal perfusion. Irreversible renal failure may occur after surgery, particularly in high-risk people (e.g., patients with diabetes). (Acute kidney injury is discussed in Chapter 46.)

◆ **Ambulatory Care.** Teach the patient and caregiver to gradually increase activities once home. Fatigue, poor appetite, and irregular bowel patterns are common. Have the patient avoid heavy lifting for 6 weeks after surgery. Report any redness, swelling, increased pain, drainage from incisions, or fever greater than 100° F (37.8° C) to the HCP.

Teach the patient and caregiver to look for changes in color or warmth of the extremities. Patients and caregivers can learn to palpate peripheral pulses to assess changes in their quality.

Sexual dysfunction in male patients is common after aortic surgery. A referral to a urologist and counseling may be useful if erectile dysfunction occurs.

◆ **Evaluation**

Expected outcomes are that the patient who undergoes aortic surgery will have:
• Patent arterial graft with adequate distal perfusion
• Adequate urine output
• No signs of infection

AORTIC DISSECTION

Aortic dissection, often misnamed *"dissecting aneurysm,"* is not a type of aneurysm. Rather, dissection results from the creation of a false lumen between the intima (inner lining) and the media (middle layer) of arterial wall (Figs. 37.5, *D*, and 37.8). Aortic dissection is classified based on the location of the dissection and duration of onset. *Type A dissection* affects the ascending aorta and arch, requiring emergency surgery. *Type B dissection* begins in the descending aorta, allowing for potential conservative management. We also describe dissections as acute (first 14 days), subacute (14 to 90 days), or chronic (greater than 90 days) based on symptom onset.[14,15]

Etiology and Pathophysiology

Nontraumatic aortic dissection is caused by weakened elastic fibers in the arterial wall. Chronic hypertension hastens this process. In aortic dissection, a tear develops in the inner layer of the aorta. Blood surges through this tear into the middle layer of the aorta, causing the inner and middle layers to separate (dissect). If the blood-filled channel ruptures through the outside aortic wall, aortic dissection is often fatal.

As the heart contracts, each pulsation increases the pressure on the damaged area and worsens the dissection. Extension of the dissection may cut off blood supply to the brain, kidneys, spinal cord, and extremities. The false lumen may remain patent, become thrombosed (clotted), rejoin the true lumen by way of a distal tear, or rupture.

Men are at a higher risk for developing aortic dissection than women.[15] Women who develop aortic dissection are older and more likely than men to present with HF, coma, or altered mental status.[15] Hypertension is the most important risk factor for aortic dissection.[15] Other predisposing factors include age, aortic diseases (e.g., aortitis, coarctation, arch hypoplasia), atherosclerosis, blunt trauma, tobacco use, cocaine or methamphetamine use, congenital heart disease (e.g., bicuspid aortic valve), connective tissue disorders (e.g., Marfan's syndrome), family history, history of heart surgery, and pregnancy.[15]

Clinical Manifestations

About 80% of patients with an acute Type A aortic dissection report an abrupt onset of severe anterior chest or back pain.

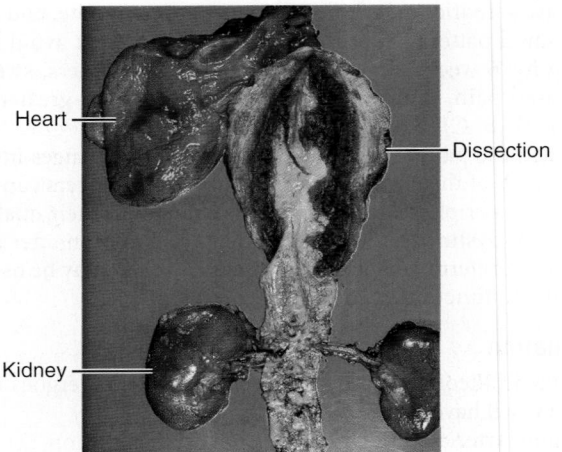

FIG. 37.8 Aortic dissection of the thoracic aorta. (From Damjanov I, Linder J, editors: *Anderson's pathology,* ed 10, St Louis, 1996, Mosby.)

Patients with acute Type B aortic dissection are more likely to report pain in their back, abdomen, or legs. Pain location may overlap between Type A and B dissections. The pain may be described as "sharp" and "worst ever," or as "tearing," "ripping," or "stabbing."

Dissection pain can be distinguished from MI pain, which is more gradual in onset and has increasing intensity. As the dissection progresses, pain may follow the path of the dissection. Older patients are less likely to have an abrupt onset of pain and more likely to have hypotension and vague symptoms. Some patients have a painless aortic dissection, emphasizing the importance of the physical examination.

If the aortic arch is involved, the patient may have neurologic deficits. These include altered level of consciousness, weakened or absent carotid and temporal pulses, and dizziness or syncope. Type A aortic dissection usually disrupts blood flow in the coronary arteries and causes aortic valve insufficiency. When either subclavian artery is involved, the radial, ulnar, and brachial pulse quality and BP readings may be different between the left and right arms. As the dissection progresses down the aorta, the abdominal organs and lower extremities show evidence of decreased tissue perfusion.

Complications

A severe and life-threatening complication of an acute ascending aortic dissection is *cardiac tamponade.* This occurs when blood from the dissection leaks into the pericardial sac. Manifestations of tamponade include hypotension, narrowed pulse pressure, jugular venous distention, muffled heart sounds, and pulsus paradoxus (see Chapter 36).

An aorta weakened by dissection may rupture. Hemorrhage may occur into the mediastinal, pleural, or abdominal cavities. Aortic rupture typically results in exsanguination and death.

Aortic dissection can lead to occlusion of the blood supply to vital organs. Spinal cord ischemia leads to weakness and decreased sensation and rarely to complete lower extremity paralysis. Renal ischemia can lead to renal failure. Abdominal (mesenteric) ischemia can occur and cause abdominal pain, decreased bowel sounds, altered bowel function, and bowel necrosis.

Diagnostic Studies

Diagnostic studies to detect aortic dissection are similar to those for suspected aneurysms (Table 37.6). An ECG can help

TABLE 37.6 Interprofessional Care

Aortic Dissection

Diagnostic Assessment	Management
• Health history and physical examination • ECG • Chest x-ray • CT scan • Transesophageal echocardiogram • MRI	• Bed rest • Pain relief with opioids • Blood transfusion (if needed) ***Drug Therapy (see Table 32.6)*** • IV β-blockers • IV calcium channel blockers • ACE inhibitors ***Surgical Therapy*** • Endovascular aortic dissection repair • Open surgical repair

rule out cardiac ischemia. A chest x-ray may show a widening of the mediastinum and pleural effusion. MRI, 3-D CT scanning, and transesophageal echocardiography (TEE) are equally reliable for the diagnosis of acute aortic dissection. A CT scan or MRI can give more detailed information on the severity of the dissection and related complications (e.g., pericardial effusions, carotid dissection). TEE is preferred in very unstable patients or those with contraindications to CT or MRI (e.g., those with metal implants, allergies to contrast material).[15]

Interprofessional Care

Patients with acute aortic dissection are managed in the ICU. The initial goals of therapy for acute aortic dissection without complications are heart rate (HR) and BP control and pain management. HR and BP control reduces aortic wall stress by decreasing SBP and myocardial contractility (Table 37.6). An IV β-blocker (e.g., esmolol [Brevibloc]) is titrated to a target HR under 60 beats/min or SBP between 100 and 110 mm Hg.

A calcium channel blocker (e.g., diltiazem) can be used to lower HR if a β-blocker is contraindicated. Reducing the HR, BP, and myocardial contractility limits extension of the dissection. Morphine decreases sympathetic nervous system stimulation and relieves pain. Supportive treatment for an acute aortic dissection serves as a bridge to surgery.

Conservative Therapy. The patient with an acute or chronic Type B aortic dissection without complications can be treated conservatively. Conservative treatment includes pain relief, HR and BP control, and CVD risk factor modification with close surveillance imaging with CT or MRI.

Endovascular Dissection Repair. Endovascular repair is a treatment option for acute Type B aortic dissections with complications (e.g., hemodynamic instability) and chronic Type B aortic dissection with complications (e.g., peripheral ischemia). Thoracic endovascular aortic repair (TEVAR) is similar to EVAR. Fewer postsurgical complications occur with TEVAR. However, TEVAR does not prevent the risk for renal failure, paraplegia, or stroke.[16] A lumbar spinal drain may be inserted to help decrease or prevent neurologic complications. If a lumbar drain is used, strict aseptic technique is essential to prevent infection.

Surgical Therapy. An acute Type A aortic dissection is a surgical emergency. Mortality rate is 50% within 48 hours of symptom onset. Otherwise, surgery is indicated when conservative therapy is ineffective or when complications (e.g., HF) occur. Open surgical repair is recommended for patients with a chronic dissection who have a connective tissue disorder or an aneurysm greater than 5.5 cm.[13,15]

The aorta is fragile after dissection. Surgery is delayed, when possible, to allow time for edema to decrease and to permit blood clotting in the false lumen. Surgery involves resection of the aortic segment with the intimal tear and replacement with a synthetic graft. Even with prompt surgical intervention, the in-hospital mortality is high.[15,16] Causes of death include aortic rupture, mesenteric ischemia, MI, sepsis, stroke, and multiorgan failure.

❖ NURSING MANAGEMENT: AORTIC DISSECTION

Preoperative nursing care includes keeping the patient in bed in a semi-Fowler's position and maintaining a quiet environment. These measures help to keep the HR and SBP at the lowest possible level that maintains vital organ perfusion (typically HR less than 60 beats/min; SBP between 100 and 120 mm Hg). Give opioids and sedatives as ordered. Manage pain and anxiety because they can cause elevations in the HR and SBP.

Titrating IV antihypertensive agents requires careful supervision, including continuous ECG and arterial BP monitoring. Monitor vital signs frequently, sometimes as often as every 2 to 3 minutes, until target HR and BP are reached. Look for changes in peripheral pulses and signs of increasing pain, restlessness, and anxiety. Postoperative care is similar to that after OAR (see earlier section on nursing management of aortic aneurysms).

In preparation for discharge, focus on patient and caregiver teaching. All patients with a history of aortic dissection require long-term health care to control HR and BP. Help patients understand that they need to take antihypertensive drugs daily for the rest of their lives. β-Blockers are used to control HR and BP and decrease myocardial contractility. ACE inhibitors (e.g., lisinopril [Zestril]) are given if the patient cannot tolerate β-blockers. It is important that patients understand the drug regimen and side effects (e.g., dizziness, depression, fatigue, erectile dysfunction). Tell the patient to discuss any side effects with the HCP before stopping any medication.

Follow-up with regularly scheduled MRIs or CTs is essential. The most common cause of death in long-term survivors is aortic rupture from redissection or aneurysm formation. Tell patients that if the pain or other symptoms return, they should activate the emergency response system (ERS) for immediate care.

ACUTE AND CHRONIC VENOUS DISORDERS

PHLEBITIS

Most hospitalized patients have an IV catheter inserted for fluids and/or drugs. *Phlebitis* is an acute inflammation of the walls of small cannulated veins of the hand or arm. Manifestations include pain, tenderness, warmth, erythema, swelling, and a palpable cord. Risk factors are mechanical irritation from the catheter, infusion of irritating drugs, and catheter location. Severe phlebitis is more likely to occur in areas of flexion (e.g., wrist and antecubital area). Avoid IV catheter insertion in this area whenever possible.

Phlebitis is rarely infectious and usually resolves quickly after catheter removal. If edema is present, elevate the extremity to promote reabsorption of fluid. Apply warm, moist heat and give oral NSAIDs (e.g., ibuprofen) or topical NSAIDs (e.g., diclofenac gel) to relieve pain and inflammation.

VENOUS THROMBOSIS

Venous thrombosis involves the formation of a *thrombus* (blood clot) with vein inflammation. It is the most common disorder of the veins. We classify it as either superficial vein thrombosis or deep vein thrombosis. **Superficial vein thrombosis** is the formation of a thrombus in a superficial vein, usually the greater or lesser saphenous vein. **Deep vein thrombosis (DVT)** involves a thrombus in a deep vein, most often the iliac and/or femoral veins. **Venous thromboembolism (VTE)** is the preferred terminology. It represents the spectrum from DVT to pulmonary embolism (PE) (Table 37.7). (Chapter 27 discusses PE.)

Superficial vein thrombosis is serious. Nearly 25% of patients with superficial vein thrombosis have a DVT or PE at the time of diagnosis. Further, these patients are at risk for developing recurrent VTE.

Etiology

The 3 key factors (called **Virchow's triad**) that cause venous thrombosis are (1) venous stasis, (2) damage of the endothelium (inner lining of the vein), and (3) hypercoagulability of the blood (Fig. 37.9). The patient at risk for developing VTE usually has predisposing conditions to these 3 disorders (Table 37.8).

TABLE 37.7 Comparison of Superficial Vein Thrombosis and Venous Thromboembolism

	Superficial Vein Thrombosis	Venous Thromboembolism (VTE)
Usual location	Typically, superficial leg veins (e.g., varicosities). Sometimes superficial arm veins.	Deep veins of arms (e.g., axillary, subclavian), legs (e.g., femoral), pelvis (e.g., iliac), vena cava, and pulmonary system.
Clinical findings	Tenderness, itchiness, redness, warmth, pain, inflammation, and induration along the course of superficial vein. Vein appears as a palpable cord. Edema rarely occurs.	Tenderness to pressure over involved vein, induration of overlying muscle, venous distention. Edema. May have mild to moderate pain, deep reddish color to area caused by venous congestion. Some have no obvious physical changes in the affected extremity.
Sequelae	If untreated, clot may extend to deeper veins and VTE may occur.	Embolization to lungs (PE) may occur and may result in death. Pulmonary hypertension and post-thrombotic syndrome with or without venous leg ulceration may develop.

Venous Stasis. Normal venous blood flow depends on the action of muscles in the extremities and the function of venous valves, which allow flow in one direction. *Venous stasis* occurs when the valves are dysfunctional or the muscles of the extremities are inactive. Venous stasis occurs most often in people who are obese or pregnant, have chronic HF or atrial fibrillation, have been traveling on long trips without regular exercise, have a prolonged surgical procedure, or are immobile for long periods (e.g., spinal cord injury, fractured hip, limb paralysis).[17]

Endothelial Damage. Damage to the endothelium of the vein may be caused by direct (e.g., surgery, intravascular catheterization, trauma, burns, prior VTE) or indirect (chemotherapy, diabetes, sepsis) injury. Damaged endothelium stimulates platelet activation and starts the coagulation cascade. This predisposes the patient to thrombus development.

Hypercoagulability of Blood. Blood hypercoagulability occurs in many disorders. These include severe anemias, polycythemia, cancers (e.g., breast, brain, pancreas, GI tract); nephrotic syndrome; high homocysteine levels; and protein C, protein S, and antithrombin deficiency.[17] A patient with sepsis is predisposed to hypercoagulability because of endotoxins released from bacteria. Some drugs (e.g., corticosteroids, estrogens) predispose a patient to thrombus formation.

Women who use tobacco, are of childbearing age and take estrogen-based oral contraceptives, are postmenopausal on oral hormone therapy, are over 35 years old, and have a family history of VTE are at a very high risk for VTE.[17] Women who use oral contraceptives with tobacco double their risk. Smoking causes hypercoagulability by increasing plasma fibrinogen and homocysteine levels and activating the intrinsic coagulation pathway.

Pathophysiology

Localized platelet aggregation and fibrin entrap RBCs, WBCs, and more platelets to form a thrombus. A frequent site of

FIG. 37.9 Pathophysiology of venous thromboembolism.

TABLE 37.8 Risk Factors for VTE

Endothelial Damage
- Abdominal and pelvic surgery (e.g., gynecologic, urologic surgery)
- Caustic or hypertonic IV drugs
- Pelvis, hip, or leg fractures
- History of VTE
- Indwelling, peripherally inserted central vein catheter
- IV drug abuse
- Trauma

Venous Stasis
- Advanced age
- Atrial fibrillation
- Bed rest
- Chronic heart failure
- Fractured leg or hip
- Long trips without adequate exercise
- Obesity
- Orthopedic surgery (especially hip or lower extremity)
- Pregnancy and postpartum period
- Prolonged immobility
- Spinal cord injury or limb paralysis
- Stroke
- Varicose veins

Hypercoagulability of Blood
- Antiphospholipid antibody syndrome
- Antithrombin III deficiency
- Cancer (especially breast, brain, hepatic, pancreatic, GI)
- Dehydration or malnutrition
- Elevated (clotting) factor VIII or lipoprotein (a)
- Erythropoiesis-stimulating drugs (e.g., epoetin alfa [Procrit])
- High altitudes
- Hormone therapy
- High homocysteine levels
- Nephrotic syndrome
- Oral contraceptives, especially in women older than 35 years who use tobacco
- Polycythemia vera
- Pregnancy and postpartum period
- Protein C deficiency
- Protein S deficiency
- Sepsis
- Severe anemias
- Tobacco use

thrombus formation is the valve cusps of veins, where venous stasis occurs. As a thrombus enlarges, increased numbers of blood cells and fibrin collect behind it. This makes a larger clot with a "tail" that eventually blocks the lumen of the vein.

If a thrombus only partially blocks the vein, endothelial cells cover the thrombus and stop the thrombotic process. If the thrombus does not become detached, it undergoes lysis or becomes firmly organized and adherent within 5 to 7 days. The organized thrombus may detach and result in an embolus. Turbulence of blood flow is a major factor in embolization. The thrombus can become an embolus that flows through the venous circulation to the heart and lodges in the pulmonary circulation, becoming a PE.

Superficial Vein Thrombosis

Clinical Manifestations. The patient with superficial vein thrombosis may have a palpable, firm, subcutaneous cordlike vein (Table 37.7). The area surrounding the vein may be itchy, painful to the touch, reddened, and warm. A mild temperature elevation and leukocytosis may be present. Extremity edema may occur. Lower extremity superficial vein thrombosis often involves 1 or more varicose veins.

Risk factors include increased age, pregnancy, obesity, cancer, recent fracture(s), estrogen therapy, recent sclerotherapy (e.g., treatment for varicose veins), recent surgery or long-distance travel, hypercoagulability, and a history of chronic venous insufficiency (CVI), superficial vein thrombosis, or VTE.[18] It can occur in people with endothelial problems (e.g., Buerger's disease).

Interprofessional Care. Ultrasound is used to confirm the diagnosis (clot 5 cm or larger) and to rule out clot extension to a deep vein.[18] If the superficial vein thrombosis affects a very short vein segment (less than 5 cm) and is not near the saphenofemoral junction, anticoagulants may not be needed and oral NSAIDs can ease symptoms. Other interventions include telling the patient to wear graduated compression stockings or bandages, apply warm compresses, elevate the affected limb above the level of the heart, apply topical NSAIDS, and perform mild exercise, such as walking.

Venous Thromboembolism

Clinical Manifestations. The patient with lower extremity VTE may or may not have unilateral leg edema, pain, tenderness with palpation, dilated superficial veins, a sense of fullness in the thigh or the calf, paresthesias, warm skin, erythema, or a systemic temperature greater than 100.4° F (38° C) (Table 37.7). If the inferior vena cava is involved, both legs may be edematous and cyanotic. About 10% of VTEs involve the upper extremity veins and may extend into the internal jugular vein or superior vena cava.[17] If the superior vena cava is involved, similar symptoms may occur in the arms, neck, back, and face. Diagnosis of an initial VTE is based on the assessment combined with D-dimer testing and/or ultrasound.

Complications. The most serious complications of VTE are PE, chronic thromboembolic pulmonary hypertension, post-thrombotic syndrome, and phlegmasia cerulea dolens. Post-thrombotic syndrome (PTS) occurs in 8% to 70% of patients. It results from chronic inflammation and chronic venous hypertension. Chronic venous hypertension is caused by vein wall and vein valve damage (from acute inflammation and thrombus reorganization), venous valve reflux, and persistent venous (outflow) obstruction. Symptoms include pain, aching, fatigue, heaviness, sensation of swelling, cramps, pruritus, tingling, paresthesia, bursting pain with exercise, and venous claudication.[19]

Manifestations include persistent edema, spider veins (telangiectasia), venous dilation (ectasia), redness, cyanosis, increased pigmentation, eczema, pain during compression, atrophie blanche (white scar tissue), and *lipodermatosclerosis* (Fig. 37.10). Venous ulceration can occur with severe PTS. Signs of PTS typically begin within a few months to a few years of a VTE. Risk factors include persistent leg symptoms 1 month after VTE, proximal VTE location (e.g., near the iliofemoral junction), extensive VTE, recurrent ipsilateral (same side) VTE, residual thrombus, obesity, older age, poor INR control, daily tobacco use before pregnancy, increased D-dimer levels, elevated inflammatory markers, varicose veins, and asymptomatic VTE.[17-19]

Phlegmasia cerulea dolens (swollen, blue, painful leg) is a rare complication of a severe lower extremity VTE(s). It involve(s) the major leg veins, causing near-total occlusion of venous outflow. Patients typically have sudden, massive swelling; deep pain; and intense cyanosis of the extremity. If untreated, the venous obstruction causes arterial occlusion and gangrene, requiring amputation.

Diagnostic Studies. Table 37.9 presents the diagnostic studies used to determine the site or location and extent of a VTE.

Interprofessional Care

Prevention. All members of the interprofessional team have important roles in VTE prevention. VTE prevention is a core measure of high-quality health care in high-risk hospitalized patients developed by The Joint Commission (TJC) and the National Quality Forum. There are 3 VTE measures. TJC recommends that hospitals have a policy that addresses

VTE prevention on admission of all adult patients. In patients at risk for VTE, interventions used are based on bleeding and thrombosis risk, past medical history, current drugs, medical diagnoses, scheduled procedures, and patient preferences.

Early and aggressive mobilization is the easiest and most cost-effective method to decrease VTE risk. Patients on bed rest should change position at least every 2 hours. Unless contraindicated, teach patients to flex and extend their feet, knees, and hips at least every 2 to 4 hours while awake. Patients who can get out of bed need to be in a chair for meals and walk at least 4 to 6 times per day. Tell the patient and caregiver about the importance of these measures. Early and frequent ambulation is sufficient prophylaxis for patients at very low risk for VTE who

FIG. 37.10 Lipodermatosclerosis. Skin on lower leg becomes scarred, and the leg becomes tapered like an "inverted bottle." Hallmark signs are leathery skin, brown discoloration, changes in pigmentation, and circumferential or near circumferential scarring and shrinking of the extremity. (From Etufugh CN, Phillips TJ: Venous ulcers, *Clin Dermatol* 25[1]:125, 2007.)

had minor surgical procedures.[20] Anticoagulation and mechanical prophylaxis are not recommended for acutely ill medical patients at low risk for VTE.

Graduated compression stockings (e.g., thromboembolic deterrent [TED] hose) are a part of VTE prevention in hospitalized patients. VTE prevention is enhanced if the stockings are used along with anticoagulation. Proper stocking use means any toe hole is under the toes, the heel patch is over the heel, a thigh gusset is on the inner thigh (thigh length only), and there are no wrinkles. The stockings should not be rolled down, cut, or otherwise altered. If the stockings are not fitted and worn correctly, venous return is impeded. This can cause arterial ischemia, edema, skin breakdown, and VTE. Stockings are not recommended if the patient already has a VTE.[20]

Intermittent pneumatic compression devices (IPCs) use inflatable sleeves or boots to compress the calf and thigh and/or foot and ankle to improve venous return. The sleeves apply external pressure through an electric pump. IPCs may be used with graduated compression stockings. Ensure correct fit of IPCs by accurately measuring the extremities. IPCs will not be effective if they are not applied correctly, if the fit is incorrect, or if the patient does not wear the device continuously while at rest. The IPCS can be removed for bathing, skin assessment, and ambulation. IPCs are not worn when a patient has an active VTE because of the risk for PE.[20]

Drug Therapy. Anticoagulants are used routinely for VTE prevention and treatment. The regimen depends on the patient's VTE risk. The goal of anticoagulant therapy for VTE prevention is to prevent clot formation. The goals for treatment of a confirmed VTE are to prevent new clot development, spread of the clot, and embolization.[20]

The 3 major classes of anticoagulants available are (1) vitamin K antagonists (VKAs), (2) thrombin inhibitors (both indirect and direct), and (3) factor Xa inhibitors (Table 37.10).[21]

TABLE 37.9 Diagnostic Studies

VTE

Study	Description and Abnormal Findings
Blood Laboratory Studies	
ACT, aPTT, INR, bleeding time, Hgb, Hct, platelet count	Altered if patient has underlying blood dyscrasia (e.g., increased Hgb and Hct in patient with polycythemia)
D-dimer	Fragment of fibrin formed from fibrin degradation and clot lysis. High results suggest VTE. *Normal results:* <250 ng/mL (<250 mcg/L)
Fibrin monomer complex	Forms when concentration of thrombin exceeds that of antithrombin. Presence is evidence of thrombus formation and suggests VTE. *Normal results:* <6.1 mg/L
Noninvasive Venous Studies	
Duplex ultrasound	Combination of compression ultrasound with spectral and color flow Doppler. Veins examined for compressibility and intraluminal filling defects to help determine location and extent of thrombus (most widely used test to diagnose VTE).
Venous compression ultrasound	Evaluation of deep femoral, popliteal, and posterior tibial veins. *Normal finding:* Veins collapse with application of external pressure. *Abnormal finding:* Veins do not collapse with application of external pressure. Failure to collapse suggests a thrombus.
Invasive Venous Studies	
Computed tomography venography (CTV)	Uses spiral CT to evaluate veins in the pelvis, thighs, and calves after injection of contrast material. May be done simultaneously with CT angiography of pulmonary vessels for patients being evaluated for VTE.
Magnetic resonance venography	Uses MRI with specialized software to evaluate blood flow through veins. Can be done with or without contrast. Highly accurate for pelvic and proximal veins. Less accurate for calf veins. Can distinguish acute and chronic thrombus
Contrast venography (phlebogram)	X-ray determination of location and extent of clot using contrast media to outline filling defects. Identifies the presence of collateral circulation. Once the gold standard, but now rarely done

ACT, Activated clotting time.

TABLE 37.10 Drug Therapy

Anticoagulant Therapy

Drug	Route of Administration	Considerations
Vitamin K Antagonists (VKA)		
warfarin (Coumadin)	PO	INR used to monitor therapeutic levels. Give at the same time each day. Variations of certain genes (e.g., *CYP2CP, VKORC1*) may influence response to drug. *Antidote:* Vitamin K. For VKA-related bleeding, treatment with prothrombin complex concentrate (human) (Kcentra), IV vitamin K and/or fresh frozen plasma is recommended.
Thrombin Inhibitors: Indirect		
Low-Molecular-Weight Heparin (LMWH)		
dalteparin (Fragmin) enoxaparin (Lovenox)	Subcutaneous	Routine coagulation tests typically not needed. Monitor CBC count at regular intervals. Do not expel air bubble from prefilled syringe. If giving subcutaneously, inject deep into subcutaneous tissue (preferably into the abdominal fatty tissue or above the iliac crest), inserting the entire length of the needle. Hold skinfold during injection but release before removing needle. Do not aspirate. Do not inject IM. Do not rub site after injection. Rotate sites. Reduced dosage needed in patients with renal impairment. Use extreme caution in patients with a history of HIT. *Antidote:* Protamine neutralizes the effects of LMWH.
Unfractionated Heparin (UH)		
heparin sodium	Continuous IV Intermittent IV Subcutaneous	Therapeutic effects measured at regular intervals by the aPTT or ACT. Monitor CBC counts at regular intervals and titrate according to parameters. Follow administration guidelines for LMWH if giving subcutaneously. *Antidote:* Protamine neutralizes the effect of UH.
Factor Xa Inhibitors		
apixaban (Eliquis) betrixaban (Bevyxxa) edoxaban (Savaysa) fondaparinux (Arixtra) rivaroxaban (Xarelto)	PO PO PO Subcutaneous PO	All are approved for VTE prevention and treatment. Routine coagulation tests not needed. Monitor CBC and creatinine at regular intervals. May cause thrombocytopenia. Do not expel air bubble before giving fondaparinux. Follow administration guidelines as described for subcutaneous LMWHs. *Antidote:* Andexanet alfa (Andexxa) reverses the effects of rivaroxaban and apixaban.
Thrombin Inhibitors: Direct		
Hirudin Derivatives		
bivalirudin (Angiomax) desirudin (Iprivask)	IV Subcutaneous	Therapeutic effect measured by ACT or aPTT. Used in patients with HIT when anticoagulation is needed. *Antidote:* None.
Synthetic Thrombin Inhibitors		
argatroban (Acova) dabigatran (Pradaxa)	IV PO	Argatroban therapeutic effect measured by aPTT. No routine coagulation tests needed for dabigatran. Used in patients at risk for or with HIT, for VTE prevention in joint replacement surgery, stroke prevention in nonvalvular atrial fibrillation *Antidote:* Idarucizumab (Praxbind) neutralizes the effect of dabigatran only.

ACT, Activated clotting time; *HIT,* heparin-induced thrombocytopenia.

Anticoagulant therapy does not dissolve the clot. Clot lysis begins naturally through the body's intrinsic fibrinolytic system (see Chapter 29).

Vitamin K antagonists. The oral anticoagulant for long-term or extended anticoagulation is warfarin, a VKA. Warfarin inhibits activation of the vitamin K–dependent coagulation factors II, VII, IX, and X and the anticoagulant proteins C and S. (See the list of clotting factors in Table 29.2. Fig. 29.4 shows the clotting pathways.) Warfarin begins to take effect in 48 to 72 hours. It then takes several more days to achieve a maximum effect. Thus an overlap of a parenteral anticoagulant (e.g., UH or low-molecular-weight heparin [LMWH]) and warfarin typically is required for 5 days. The level of anticoagulation is monitored daily using the INR. The INR is a standardized system of reporting prothrombin time (PT) (Table 37.11). The antidote for

warfarin-related bleeding is vitamin K, prothrombin complex concentrate (human) (Kcentra), or fresh frozen plasma (FFP).

Take a careful history before starting warfarin. Do not give antiplatelet drug or NSAIDs with warfarin as these increase bleeding risk.[21] Many other drugs, vitamins, minerals, and dietary and herbal supplements interact with warfarin (see the Complementary & Alternative Therapies box). A diet that varies in vitamin K intake (e.g., green leafy vegetables) can make it hard to achieve and maintain a target INR level. Genetic variants in the genes *VKORC1* and cytochrome P450 2C9 (*CYP2C9*) may influence how some people respond to warfarin (see Table 12.5 and Fig. 12.7).

Thrombin inhibitors. There are 2 major classes of *indirect thrombin inhibitors*: UH and LMWHs. UH (e.g., heparin) affects both the intrinsic and common pathways of blood coagulation

TABLE 37.11   Blood Coagulation Tests

Test and Drugs Monitored	Normal Value	Therapeutic Value
Activated Clotting Time (ACT)	70–120 sec*	>300 sec
• Hirudin derivatives (e.g., bivalirudin [Angiomax])		
• Synthetic thrombin inhibitors (e.g., argatroban [Acova])		
• Unfractionated heparin (e.g., heparin [Hep-Lock])		
Activated Partial Thromboplastin Time (aPTT)	30–40 sec	46–70 sec
• Hirudin derivatives		
• Synthetic thrombin inhibitors		
• Unfractionated heparin		
Anti-Factor Xa		
• Factor Xa inhibitors (e.g., fondaparinux [Arixtra], rivaroxaban [Xarelto])	0 units/mL 0 units/mL	0.6–1.0 units/mL 0.2
• Low-molecular-weight heparin (e.g., enoxaparin [Lovenox])		1.5 units/mL
International Normalized Ratio (INR)	0.75–1.25	2–3
• Vitamin K antagonists (e.g., warfarin [Coumadin])		

*Varies based on type of system and test reagent or activator used.

🌿 COMPLEMENTARY & ALTERNATIVE THERAPIES

Herbal and Dietary Supplements That May Affect Clotting

Scientific Evidence

Many herbs and dietary supplements may affect blood clotting. These include bilberry, black cohosh, chamomile, chondroitin sulfate, dehydroepiandrosterone (DHEA), feverfew, garlic, ginger, ginkgo biloba, ginseng, goldenseal, grapeseed extract, green tea, horse chestnut seed extract, melatonin, niacin, omega-3 fatty acids, psyllium, red yeast rice extract, saw palmetto, soy, turmeric.

Nursing Implications

• Tell patients that taking these herbs or dietary supplements may increase their risk for bleeding.
• Caution patients with bleeding disorders about using these herbs and dietary supplements. Teach them to consult with their HCP before using these substances.

by way of the plasma antithrombin. Antithrombin inhibits thrombin-mediated conversion of fibrinogen to fibrin by affecting factors II (prothrombin), IX, X, XI, and XII (see Fig. 29.4).

Heparin can be given subcutaneously for VTE prevention or by continuous IV infusion for VTE treatment. When given IV, heparin requires frequent monitoring of clotting status as measured by activated partial thromboplastin time (aPTT) (Table 37.11). Protamine sulfate reverses the effect of heparin.

One serious side effect of heparin is *heparin-induced thrombocytopenia* (HIT). HIT is an immune reaction to heparin. It causes a severe, sudden reduction in the platelet count along with a paradoxical increase in venous or arterial thrombosis. HIT is diagnosed by measuring the presence of heparin antibodies in the blood. Treatment includes immediately stopping heparin therapy and, if further anticoagulation is needed, using a non-heparin anticoagulant (e.g., fondaparinux).[21] Another side effect of long-term heparin therapy is osteoporosis.

LMWHs (e.g., enoxaparin [Lovenox]) are derived from UH. They have more predictable dose response, longer half-life, and fewer bleeding complications than UH. LMWHs are less likely to cause HIT and osteoporosis. LMWHs typically do not require ongoing anticoagulant monitoring and dose adjustment. Their antiinflammatory properties may help prevent PTS and venous ulcer development.[21] Protamine neutralizes the effect of LMWH.

Direct thrombin inhibitors are classified as hirudin derivatives or synthetic thrombin inhibitors. Hirudin is made using recombinant deoxyribonucleic acid (DNA) technology. It binds specifically with thrombin and directly inhibits its function without causing plasma protein and platelet interactions. Hirudin derivatives (e.g., bivalirudin [Angiomax]) are given by continuous IV infusion. Bivalirudin is approved for patients with or at risk for HIT having a percutaneous coronary intervention. Anticoagulant activity is monitored using aPTT or activated clotting time (ACT) (Table 37.11). If bleeding occurs, there is no antidote for hirudin derivatives.

Argatroban, a synthetic direct thrombin inhibitor, hinders thrombin. Like bivalirudin, it is an alternative to heparin for the prevention and treatment of HIT and for patients with or at risk for HIT needing percutaneous coronary interventions. The effect of argatroban is not reversible. Its anticoagulant effect is monitored using aPTT or ACT.

Dabigatran (Pradaxa) is an oral direct thrombin inhibitor. It is used for VTE prevention after elective joint replacement, for stroke prevention in nonvalvular atrial fibrillation, and as a treatment for VTE. Idarucizumab (Praxbind) neutralizes the effect of dabigatran. Dabigatran has 5 major advantages compared to warfarin: rapid onset, no need to monitor anticoagulation, few drug-food interactions, lower risk for major bleeding, and predictable dose response.[21]

Factor Xa inhibitors. *Factor Xa inhibitors* inhibit factor Xa directly or indirectly, producing rapid anticoagulation. These include fondaparinux (Arixtra), rivaroxaban (Xarelto), apixaban (Eliquis), and edoxaban (Savaysa). All are used for both VTE prevention and treatment. Fondaparinux is given subcutaneously. It is contraindicated in patients with severe renal disease. Rivaroxaban, apixaban, and edoxaban are oral drugs. Although coagulation monitoring or dose adjustment is not needed, the drug's anticoagulant activity can be measured using anti-Xa assays (Table 37.11). If uncontrollable bleeding occurs, recombinant factor VIIa may be useful. Andexanet Alfa (Andexxa) reverses the effects of rivaroxaban and apixaban.

Anticoagulant therapy for VTE prevention. For VTE prevention in the hospitalized medical patient at risk for thrombosis who is not bleeding, low-dose UH, LMWH, or fondaparinux is used. If the patient is at low VTE risk, drug prophylaxis is not needed. Patients with moderate VTE risk (e.g., general, gynecologic, urologic surgery) should receive either UH or LMWH. Patients with high VTE risk (e.g., trauma) should receive UH or LMWH until discharge. Patients having abdominal or pelvic surgery for cancer or major orthopedic surgery (e.g., total knee or hip replacement) should receive VTE prophylaxis.[20]

Anticoagulant therapy for VTE treatment. Patients with confirmed VTE should receive initial treatment with either LMWH, UH, or an oral factor Xa drug. Oral VKA therapy may be an option. A therapeutic INR is maintained between 2.0 and 3.0 if VKA therapy is used. Active treatment of VTE should continue for at least 3 months and may continue longer in some patients.[20]

Patients with multiple co-morbidities, complex medical issues, or a very large VTE usually are hospitalized for treatment.

Parenteral administration of UH is the typical initial treatment. Depending on the presentation and home situation, patients may be safely and effectively managed as outpatients.

Thrombolytic therapy for VTE treatment. Another treatment option for patients with a thrombus is catheter-directed administration of a thrombolytic drug (e.g., urokinase, tPA). It dissolves the clot(s), reduces the acute symptoms, improves deep venous flow, reduces valvular reflux, and may help to decrease the incidence of PTS. Catheter-directed thrombolysis is an option for select patients who are at a low bleeding risk and present with an acute, extensive, symptomatic, proximal VTE. Systemic anticoagulation is needed before, during, and after catheter-directed thrombolysis. (Chapter 33 discusses thrombolytic therapy.)

❓ CHECK YOUR PRACTICE

Your 55-yr-old female patient is admitted with an extensive VTE in her right leg. She is receiving weight-based IV heparin per agency protocol: 18 units/kg/hr. You receive the following critical laboratory result: aPTT 122 seconds.
• Describe your next actions.

Surgical and Interventional Radiology Therapies. A few patients with extensive, acute, proximal VTE who are not candidates for catheter-directed thrombolysis and/or interventional radiology therapies (due to bleeding risk) may have surgery.[3,16] Surgical options include open venous thrombectomy and inferior vena cava interruption. *Venous thrombectomy* involves the removal of a clot through a vein incision. Anticoagulant therapy is used after venous thrombectomy.

Vena cava interruption devices (e.g., Greenfield, Vena Tech, TrapEase filters) can be placed percutaneously through the right femoral or right internal jugular veins. The filter device is opened, and the spokes penetrate the vessel walls (Fig. 37.11). The filters act as a "sieve-type" device, allowing filtration of clots without interruption of blood flow. Complications after the insertion are rare but include air embolism, improper placement, migration of the filter, and perforation of the vena cava with retroperitoneal bleeding. Over time, clots can clog the filter and completely block the vena cava, requiring filter removal and replacement. A filter device is recommended with acute PE or proximal VTE of the leg in patients with active bleeding or if anticoagulant therapy is contraindicated or ineffective.

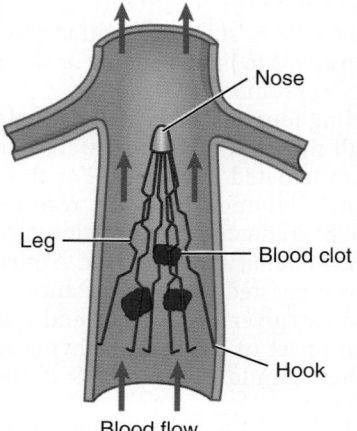

FIG. 37.11 Inferior vena cava interruption technique using Greenfield stainless steel filter to prevent pulmonary embolism. As blood travels up the vena cava, clots are trapped in the filter.

Percutaneous endovascular interventional radiology procedures can be used along with catheter-directed thrombolytic therapy, especially for severely symptomatic patients with iliocaval or iliofemoral obstruction.[17] The interventional radiology procedures are like those used in the treatment of lower extremity PAD. The difference is accessing an occluded vein instead of an artery. Options include mechanical thrombectomy, pharmaco-mechanical devices, and post-thrombus extraction, angioplasty, and/or stenting.[17] Anticoagulation therapy is recommended after an iliofemoral interventional radiology procedure. Postprocedure nursing care focuses on (1) maintaining catheter systems (if continuous infusions); (2) monitoring for bleeding, embolization, and impaired perfusion; and (3) VTE prevention teaching.[17]

❖ NURSING MANAGEMENT: VENOUS THROMBOEMBOLISM

◆ Nursing Assessment

Table 37.12 presents the subjective and objective data to obtain from a patient with VTE.

TABLE 37.12 Nursing Assessment

VTE

Subjective Data
Important Health Information (Table 37.8)
Past health history: Trauma to vein, intravascular catheter (e.g., peripherally inserted central catheter), varicose veins, pregnancy or recent childbirth, bacteremia, obesity, prolonged bed rest, irregular heartbeat (e.g., atrial fibrillation), COPD, HF, cancer, coagulation disorders and hypercoagulable states, systemic lupus erythematosus, MI, spinal cord injury, stroke, prolonged travel, recent bone fracture, dehydration
Medications: Use of estrogens (including oral contraceptives, hormone therapy), tamoxifen, raloxifene (Evista), corticosteroids, excessive amounts of vitamin E, erythropoiesis-stimulating drugs
Surgery or other treatments: Any recent surgery, especially orthopedic, gynecologic, GI, or urologic. Previous surgery involving veins. Central venous catheter

Functional Health Patterns
Health perception–health management: IV drug abuse, tobacco use, obesity
Activity-exercise: Inactivity
Cognitive-perceptual: Pain in area on palpation or ambulation

Objective Data
General
Fever, anxiety, pain

Integumentary
Increased size of extremity when compared with other side. Taut, shiny, warm skin, erythematous, tender to palpation. No physical changes in the affected extremity in some patients

Cardiovascular
Distention and warmth of superficial veins in affected area. Edema and cyanosis of extremities, neck, back, and face (if superior vena cava involvement)

Possible Diagnostic Findings
Leukocytosis, abnormal coagulation, anemia or ↑ hematocrit and RBC count, ↑ D-dimer level, positive venous compression on duplex ultrasound study; positive CT venogram, magnetic resonance venogram, or contrast venogram study

◆ Nursing Diagnoses

Nursing diagnoses and collaborative problems for the patient with VTE include:

- Acute pain
- Impaired tissue integrity
- Impaired physical mobility
- Risk for bleeding

◆ Planning

The overall goals for the patient with VTE include (1) pain relief, (2) decreased edema, (3) increased knowledge of disorder and treatment plan, (4) no skin ulceration, (5) no bleeding complications, and (6) no evidence of PE.

Nursing Implementation

◆ **Acute Care.** Focus your nursing care for the patient with VTE on preventing thrombi and reducing inflammation. Review with the patient any drugs, vitamins, minerals, and dietary and herbal supplements that may interfere with anticoagulant therapy (see the Complementary & Alternative Therapies box on p. 818). Depending on the anticoagulant ordered, monitor INR, aPTT, ACT, anti-factor Xa levels, complete blood count (CBC), creatinine, factor X levels, hemoglobin, hematocrit, platelet levels, and/or liver enzymes.[21] Monitor platelet counts for patients getting UH or LMWH to assess for HIT. Titrate doses of UH, warfarin, and direct thrombin inhibitors based on results of blood studies and agency protocols. Direct thrombin inhibitors may need adjustment for patients with renal or liver disease. Check the results of pertinent tests before starting, giving, or changing anticoagulant therapy.

Monitor for and reduce the risk for bleeding with anticoagulant therapy (Table 37.13). Bleeding risk is greater in people receiving LMWH or UH with an active gastroduodenal ulcer, prior bleeding history, low platelet count, hepatic or renal failure, rheumatic disease, cancer, or age greater than 85 years.[21] Patients receiving warfarin with an INR of 5.0 or more are at increased risk for bleeding. In case of anticoagulation above target goals, give reversal agents (e.g., protamine, vitamin K) or make dosage adjustments as prescribed.

 DRUG ALERT Anticoagulant Therapy

- Avoid IM injections.
- Observe closely for any signs of bleeding: hypotension, tachycardia, hematuria, melena, hematemesis, petechiae, bruising, oozing or visible bleeding from trauma site or surgical incision.
- Tell patients to report bleeding: black or bloody stools, bleeding gums, bloody urine or sputum, coffee-ground or bloody vomit, excessive bruising, nosebleeds, excessive menstrual bleeding.
- Assess for mental status changes, especially in the older patient, since this may indicate cerebral bleeding.
- Tell patients to avoid taking aspirin, NSAIDs, fish oil supplements, garlic supplements, ginkgo biloba, and certain antibiotics (e.g., sulfamethoxazole and trimethoprim [Bactrim]).

Early ambulation does not increase the short-term risk of a PE in patients with VTE. In addition, early ambulation after acute VTE results in a more rapid decrease in edema and limb pain, fewer PTS symptoms, and better quality of life. Teach the patient and caregiver the importance of physical activity. Help the patient ambulate several times a day. For patients with acute VTE with severe edema and limb pain, bed rest with limb elevation may initially be prescribed.

◆ **Ambulatory Care.** Focus discharge teaching on modifying VTE risk factors, monitoring laboratory values, dietary and drug instructions, and guidelines for follow-up. If appropriate,

TABLE 37.13 Nursing Management

Patients Receiving Anticoagulants

Assessment

- Monitor vital signs as indicated.
- Examine urine and stool for overt and occult signs of blood.
- Inspect skin often, especially under any splinting devices.
- Evaluate platelet count for signs of heparin-induced thrombocytopenia.
- Evaluate appropriate laboratory coagulation tests for target therapeutic levels.
- Evaluate lower extremity for bruising or hematoma development if intermittent pneumatic compression device used.
- Perform assessments frequently for signs and symptoms of bleeding (e.g., hypotension, tachycardia) or clotting.
- Notify the HCP of any abnormalities in assessments, vital signs, or laboratory values.

Injections

- Avoid IM injections.
- Minimize venipunctures.
- Use small-gauge needles for venipunctures unless therapy requires a larger gauge.
- Apply manual pressure for at least 10 minutes (or longer if needed) on venipuncture sites.

Patient Care

- Avoid restrictive clothing.
- Apply moisturizing lotion to skin.
- Use electric razors, not straight razors.
- Perform physical care in a gentle manner.
- Tell patient not to forcefully blow nose.
- Avoid removing or disrupting established clots.
- Humidify O_2 source if supplemental O_2 is ordered.
- Use soft toothbrushes or foam swabs for oral care.
- Reposition the patient carefully at regular intervals.
- Limit tape application. Use paper tape as appropriate.
- Give stool softeners to avoid hard stools and straining.
- Lubricate tubes (e.g., suction catheter) adequately before insertion.
- Use support pads, mattresses, bed cradles, and therapeutic beds as indicated.
- Apply graduated compression stockings or intermittent pneumatic compression devices (if ordered) and with attention to proper size, application, and use.
- Perform risk for fall and skin breakdown assessments per agency policy and implement safety and preventive measures as needed.

suggest the patient stop smoking and avoid all nicotine products. Teach the patient to avoid constrictive clothing. Tell women with a history of VTE to stop oral contraceptives or hormone therapy. Teach patients to limit standing or sitting in a motionless, leg-dependent position.

When traveling long distances, tell patients to frequently exercise the calf muscles, take short walks, and drink nonalcoholic, noncaffeinated beverages. For those at high risk for VTE who are planning a long trip, recommend properly fitted, knee-high graduated compression stockings during travel to decrease edema and VTE risk. Aspirin or anticoagulant use is not suggested for long-distance travelers. Teach the patient and caregiver about signs and symptoms of PE, such as sudden onset of dyspnea, tachypnea, and pleuritic chest pain. They should contact ERS if these symptoms occur.

Review drug dosage, actions, and side effects; the need for routine blood tests; and what symptoms need immediate medical attention (Table 37.14). Devices are available for home monitoring of INR. Teach patients taking LMWH or fondaparinux

NURSING MANAGEMENT

Caring for the Patient With Venous Thromboembolism (VTE)

- Assess patients for VTE risk and monitor for VTE in at-risk patients.
- Teach patients who are at risk for VTE about preventive measures, such as increasing mobility, using graduated compression stockings and IPCs, and taking anticoagulant drugs.
- Measure patients for graduated compression stockings and/or IPCs.
- Assess for the use of dietary supplements or herbs that may affect the coagulation status before the start of anticoagulant therapy.
- Give prescribed oral, subcutaneous, and IV anticoagulants.
- Evaluate the effect of anticoagulant drugs by monitoring appropriate laboratory results and side effects of therapy.
- Assess for complications of VTE, including PE and chronic venous insufficiency.
- Teach the patient and caregiver the manifestations of PE and the need to contact the ERS if these occur.
- Provide discharge teaching about use of graduated compression stockings, anticoagulant drugs, diet, laboratory testing, and subcutaneous anticoagulant therapy (if needed).
- Teach safety precautions to prevent falls or other injuries that might result in bleeding.
- Discuss how to use pressure to stop bleeding and to contact ERS for persistent bleeding.
- Teach the patient about lifestyle measures to prevent VTE, including leg exercises, ambulation, and avoiding nicotine and oral contraceptives.
- Oversee the UAP:
  - Reposition patients who are on bed rest at least every 2 hrs.
  - Remind patients about the need to flex and extend the legs and feet at least every 2 hrs while in bed.
  - Help ambulatory patients to walk at least 4 to 6 times daily.
  - Help patients with putting on graduated compression stockings.
  - Apply IPCs.
- Collaborate with the physical therapist:
  - Assess patient's mobility status.
  - Develop exercise/muscle strengthening program as needed.
- Collaborate with the dietitian:
  - Assess patient's diet and nutritional status.
  - Provide diet teaching as needed.

TABLE 37.14 Patient & Caregiver Teaching

Anticoagulant Therapy

Include the following information in the teaching plan for a patient receiving anticoagulant therapy and the patient's caregiver:

1. Give reasons for and action of anticoagulant drug and how long therapy will last.
2. Take drug at the same time each day (preferably in afternoon or evening).
3. Depending on drug prescribed, obtain blood tests to assess therapeutic effect of the drug and whether change in dosage is needed.
4. Contact ERS immediately for any of the following adverse side effects of drug therapy:
   - Blood in urine or stool; or black, tarry stools
   - Vomiting blood, coffee-grounds emesis
   - Unusual bleeding from gums, skin, or nose, or heavy menstrual bleeding
   - Severe headaches or stomach pain
   - Chest pain, shortness of breath, palpitations (heart racing)
   - Weakness, dizziness, mental status changes
   - Cold, blue, or painful feet
5. Avoid any trauma or injury that may cause bleeding (e.g., vigorous brushing of teeth, contact sports, rollerblading, use of straight razor).
6. Avoid all aspirin-containing drugs and NSAIDs.
7. Limit alcohol intake to small to moderate amounts (12 oz beer, 4 oz wine, 1 oz hard liquor/day).
8. Wear a Medic Alert device saying what anticoagulant drug is being taken.
9. If taking warfarin (Coumadin), avoid frequent or dramatic changes in eating foods high in vitamin K (e.g., broccoli, spinach, kale, greens). Do not take supplemental vitamin K.
10. Consult with HCP before beginning or stopping any drug, vitamin, mineral, or dietary or herbal supplement (see Complementary & Alternative Therapies box on p. 818).
11. Inform all HCPs, including dentist, of anticoagulant therapy.
12. Correct dosing is essential. Provide supervision if patient has confusion or cognitive impairment.

and their caregivers how to give the drug subcutaneously. Active or young patients need to avoid contact sports and activities with high risk for trauma (e.g., skiing). Teach older patients about safety precautions to prevent falls (e.g., avoid use of throw rugs). Tell the patient and caregiver to apply pressure for 10 to 15 minutes if bleeding occurs (e.g., nosebleed).

A well-balanced diet is important. Teach patients taking warfarin to follow a consistent diet of foods containing vitamin K and to avoid any supplements containing vitamin K (e.g., vitamins, green tea). Tell the patient to avoid excess amounts of vitamin E and alcohol. Encourage proper hydration to prevent hypercoagulability of the blood, which may occur with dehydration.

The overweight patient needs to limit carbohydrates and total caloric intake and increase physical activity to achieve and maintain desired weight. Exercise may help patients with VTE and PTS.[17,20] Help the patient develop an exercise program with an emphasis on leg strength training and aerobic activity. An exercise program also improves the patient's quality of life.

Graduated compression stockings reduce symptomatic swelling in patients with a proximal VTE.[17,20] Alternatively, IPCs may be used for patients with significant edema and moderate to severe PTS. The long-term use of graduated compression stockings may not prevent PTS development.

◆ Evaluation

The expected outcomes are that the patient with VTE will have
- Minimal to no pain
- Intact skin
- Increased knowledge of disorder and treatment plan
- No signs of hemorrhage or occult bleeding

VARICOSE VEINS

Varicose veins, or *varicosities*, are dilated (3 mm or larger in diameter), tortuous superficial veins often found in the saphenous vein system. Varicosities may be small and harmless or large and bulging. *Primary varicose veins* (idiopathic) are due to a weakness of the vein walls. They are more common in women. *Secondary varicose veins* result from direct injury, a previous VTE, or excessive vein distention. Secondary varicose veins may occur in the esophagus (esophageal varices), vulva, spermatic cords (varicoceles), and anorectal area (hemorrhoids), and as abnormal arteriovenous (AV) connections.

Congenital varicose veins result from chromosomal defects that cause abnormal development of the venous system.[22] *Reticular veins* are smaller varicose veins that appear flat, less tortuous, and blue-green in color. *Telangiectasias* (often called spider veins), are small visible vessels (generally less than 1 mm in diameter) that appear bluish black, purple, or red.

Etiology and Pathophysiology

Superficial veins in the lower extremities become dilated and tortuous in response to backward (retrograde) blood flow and increased venous pressure. Risk factors include family history of chronic venous disease, weak vein structure, female gender, tobacco use, increasing age, obesity, multiparity, history of VTE, venous obstruction resulting from extrinsic pressure by tumors, thrombophilia, phlebitis, previous leg injury, and occupations that require prolonged standing or sitting.[22,23]

In primary varicose veins, weak vein walls allow the vein valve ring to enlarge, so the leaflets no longer fit together properly (incompetent). Incompetent vein valves allow backward blood flow, particularly when the patient is standing. This results in increased venous pressure and further venous distention. High pressure in the superficial veins also can be caused by vein valve dysfunction in the deep veins or perforator veins (veins that perforate the deep fascia of muscles to connect the superficial veins to the deep veins).

Clinical Manifestations and Complications

Discomfort from varicose veins varies among people and tends to be worse after episodes of superficial vein thrombosis. Symptoms affect women more often than men.[23] The most common symptoms include a heavy, achy feeling or pain after prolonged standing or sitting, which is relieved by walking or limb elevation. Some patients feel pressure or an itchy, burning, tingling, throbbing, or cramp-like leg sensation. Swelling, restless or tired legs, fatigue, and nocturnal leg cramps may occur.

Superficial venous thrombosis is the most frequent complication of varicose veins. It may occur spontaneously or after trauma, surgical procedures, or pregnancy. Rare complications include rupture of the varicose veins resulting in external bleeding and skin ulcerations.

Diagnostic Studies and Interprofessional Care

Superficial varicose veins often can be diagnosed by careful physical examination. Duplex ultrasound imaging is the gold standard to evaluate venous anatomy, valvular competence, and venous obstruction.[22] Conservative treatment involves rest with limb elevation; graduated compression stockings; leg strengthening exercise, such as walking; and weight loss, if indicated.

Drug Therapy

Venoactive drugs, derived from plant extracts, are powerful antioxidants that work by stimulating release of chemicals within the vein walls to strengthen the circulation and reduce inflammation and edema. Several natural and synthetic venoactive agents have been used to treat varicose veins and advanced chronic venous disease. These include micronized purified flavonoid fraction, rutosides (e.g., horse chestnut seed extract [*Aesculus hippocastanum*]), proanthocyanidins (from grapes and apples), and *Ruscus* (butcher's broom).[23]

Therapeutic benefits of venoactive drugs include pain relief, edema reduction, and decreased leg cramping and restless legs. These drugs are widely used in Europe. They are not approved by the FDA. However, many are available over the counter as dietary or herbal supplements.

   DRUG ALERT Horse Chestnut Seed Extract (*Aesculus hippocastanum*)

- May interact with lithium and antidiabetes, antiplatelet, and anticoagulant drugs.
- Should not be taken by persons with liver or kidney disease or with a latex allergy.

Interventional and Surgical Therapies

Sclerotherapy involves the direct IV injection of a liquid or foam sclerosing substance (e.g., hypertonic saline, polidocanol, glycerin) that chemically ablates (destroys) the treated veins. Sclerotherapy can be used on telangiectasias, perforator veins, reticular veins, varicose veins 5 mm in diameter or smaller, and venous malformations (Fig. 37.12). This procedure is done in an office setting and causes minimal discomfort.

The most common complications of sclerotherapy are residual pigmentation, matting (new telangiectasias develop in the area), thrombophlebitis, and ulcers.[23] After injection, a graduated compression stocking or compression bandage is worn. Patients should not travel long distances during the first week after sclerotherapy to minimize the risk for a VTE.

Other noninvasive options include transcutaneous laser therapy for telangiectasias and high-intensity pulsed-light therapy for reticular veins. Transcutaneous laser or light therapy is used for patients in whom sclerotherapy is contraindicated or has been ineffective.[23] Vascular lasers work by heating the hemoglobin in the vessels, resulting in vessel sclerosis. Complications of these therapies include pain, blistering, hyperpigmentation, and superficial erosions.

A minimally invasive treatment option for saphenous vein reflux is endovenous ablation using thermal energy from radiofrequency or laser therapy. The HCP inserts a catheter into the vein to heat the vein wall, which then causes the vein to collapse. Complications include bruising, skin burns, hyperpigmentation, infection, paresthesia, superficial or deep vein thrombosis, and pulmonary embolism. Graduated compression stockings or bandages are worn afterwards. Endovenous thermal ablation may be done in combination with surgical ligation or phlebectomy.

FIG. 37.12 A, Lateral aspect of varicose veins before treatment. B, Lateral aspect of varicose veins 2 years after initial treatment with sclerotherapy. (From Goldman MP, Guex JJ, Weiss RA: *Sclerotherapy: Treatment of varicose and telangiectatic leg veins,* ed 5, Philadelphia, 2011, Mosby.)

Surgical intervention is needed for recurrent superficial venous thrombosis or when symptoms cannot be controlled with other therapy. The traditional surgical intervention involves ligation of the entire vein (usually the greater saphenous vein) and removal of its incompetent branches. An alternative but time-consuming technique is *ambulatory phlebectomy*. This involves pulling the varicosity through a "stab" incision followed by excision of the vein. *Transilluminated powered phlebectomy* involves the use of a tissue resector to destroy clusters of varicosities and removes the pieces via aspiration. Complications include bleeding, bruising, and infection.

NURSING MANAGEMENT: VARICOSE VEINS

Prevention is a key factor related to varicose veins. Tell the patient to avoid sitting or standing for long periods, maintain ideal body weight, take precautions against injury to the extremities, avoid wearing constrictive clothing, and walk daily.

After vein ligation surgery, encourage the patient to deep breathe, which promotes venous return. Check the extremities regularly for color, movement, sensation, temperature, edema, and quality of pedal pulses. Some bruising and discoloration are normal. Elevate the legs 15 degrees to limit edema. Apply graduated compression stockings or bandages. Remove them every 8 hours for short periods and then reapply.

Long-term management of varicose veins is directed toward improving circulation and appearance, relieving discomfort, and avoiding complications and ulceration. Varicosities can recur in other veins after surgery. Teach the patient the proper use and care of custom-fitted graduated compression stockings. The patient should apply stockings in bed before rising in the morning.

Emphasize the importance of periodic positioning of the legs above the heart. The overweight patient may need help with weight loss. The patient with a job that requires long periods of standing or sitting needs to frequently flex and extend the hips, legs, and ankles and change positions. Remind patients to consult with their HCP before taking any dietary or herbal supplements to avoid drug interactions.

CHRONIC VENOUS INSUFFICIENCY AND VENOUS LEG ULCERS

Chronic venous insufficiency (CVI) describes abnormalities of the venous system that result in advanced signs and symptoms, such as edema, skin changes, and/or venous leg ulcers.[22] CVI can lead to *venous leg ulcers* (formerly called *venous stasis ulcers* or *varicose ulcers*). Although CVI and venous leg ulcers are not life-threatening diseases, they are painful, slow to heal, debilitating, and costly conditions that adversely affect patients' quality of life. They are a common problem in older adults.

Etiology and Pathophysiology

Both long-standing primary varicose veins and PTS can progress to CVI. *Ambulatory venous hypertension* causes serous fluid and RBCs to leak from the capillaries and venules into the tissue. This causes edema and chronic inflammatory changes. Enzymes in the tissue eventually break down RBCs, causing the release of *hemosiderin,* which causes a brownish skin discoloration. Over time, fibrous tissue replaces the skin and subcutaneous tissue around the ankle. This results in thick, hardened, contracted skin. Although the causes of CVI are known, the exact pathophysiology of venous leg ulcers is unknown.

Clinical Manifestations and Complications

In patients with CVI, the skin of the lower leg is leathery, with a characteristic brownish or "brawny" appearance from the hemosiderin deposition. Edema usually has been persistent for a prolonged period. Eczema with itching and scratching is often present (Table 37.1).

Venous ulcers classically occur above the medial malleolus (Fig. 37.13). The ulcer is often quite painful, particularly when edema or infection is present. Pain may be worse when the leg is in a dependent position. If the venous ulcer is untreated, the wound becomes wider and deeper, increasing the risk for infection.

Interprofessional and Nursing Care

Compression is essential for venous ulcer healing and preventing venous ulcer recurrence.[22,23] A variety of options are available for compression therapy. These include custom-fitted graduated compression stockings, elastic tubular support bandages, a Velcro wrap (CircAid), IPCs, and multilayer (3 or 4) bandage systems (e.g., Profore).[22,23] Evaluate patients individually when choosing a compression method. Before starting compression therapy, assess the arterial status to make sure that PAD is not present. An ABI of 0.4 or less suggests severe PAD, and the patient should not have any type of compression therapy.[3] Show how to correctly apply the compression therapy and have the patient "show back" the skill. Stockings should be worn daily to prevent recurrent leg ulcers. Tell the patient to replace stockings every 4 to 6 months.

Discuss activity guidelines and proper limb positioning. Tell patients with CVI to avoid standing or sitting for long periods, which decreases blood return from the lower extremities. Teach patients to frequently elevate their legs above the level of the heart to reduce edema. Encourage patients to begin a daily walking program once an ulcer heals. Tell the patient and caregiver to avoid trauma to the limbs. Teach proper foot and leg care to avoid more skin trauma.

Moist environment dressings are the basis of wound care. A variety of dressings are available. These include transparent film dressings, hydrocolloids, hydrogels, foams, alginates, gauze, and combination dressings. Dressing decisions should be based on wound characteristics, cost, best evidence, and clinician judgment. Chapter 11 and Table 11.9 discuss dressings.

Evaluate the nutritional status of a patient with a venous ulcer. A balanced diet with adequate protein, calories, and

FIG. 37.13 Venous leg ulcer. (From Mosti G: Compression and venous surgery for venous leg ulcers, *Clin Plast Surg* 39:269, 2012.)

nutrients is essential. Foods high in protein (e.g., meat, beans, cheese, tofu), vitamin A (green leafy vegetables), vitamin C (citrus fruits, tomatoes, cantaloupe), and zinc (meat, seafood) are most important for healing. For patients with diabetes, maintaining normal blood glucose levels aids the healing process.

Though venous leg ulcers are colonized by bacteria, routine use of antibiotics is not indicated. Signs of infection include change in quantity, color, or odor of the drainage; pus; erythema of the wound edges; change in sensation around the wound; warmth around the wound; increased local pain, edema, or both; dark-colored granulation tissue; induration around the wound; delayed healing; and cellulitis. If signs of infection occur, obtain a wound culture. Culture results guide antibiotic therapy. The usual treatment for infection is wound debridement, wound excision, and systemic antibiotics.

If the ulcer does not heal with conservative therapy, drug therapy should be considered. Pentoxifylline or micronized purified flavonoid fraction (Daflon) is recommended with compression therapy to improve healing.[23] Pentoxifylline minimizes WBC activation and adhesion to capillary endothelium and decreases oxidative stress. Micronized purified flavonoid fraction acts on WBCs to decrease inflammation and edema.[23]

Other treatments are considered for large venous leg ulcers that do not respond to standard therapy after 4 to 6 weeks. These include coverage with a skin replacement or substitute, such as split-thickness skin grafts or artificial bioengineered skin.[22] (Chapter 24 discusses skin grafting.) Although grafts may aid with healing, they do not replace the need for lifelong compression therapy.

Patients with CVI have dry, flaky, itchy skin. Daily moisturizing decreases itching and prevents skin cracking. Contact dermatitis may result from contact with sensitizing products, such as topical antimicrobial agents (e.g., gentamicin); additives in bandages or dressings (e.g., adhesives); ointments containing lanolin, alcohols, or benzocaine; and over-the-counter creams or lotions with fragrance or preservatives. Assess wounds for signs of infection with each dressing change.

NURSING MANAGEMENT
Caring for the Patient With Chronic Venous Insufficiency

Many patients with CVI and venous ulcers receive outpatient care. The registered nurse (RN) does the initial wound assessment, develops and implements the plan of care, and periodically evaluates the patient and venous ulcer. Routine wound care can be done by LPN/VNs and UAP depending on the state nurse practice act and agency policy.

- Assess the patient for increases in edema, eczema, and venous leg ulcers.
- Assess diet and nutritional status and make referrals as needed.
- Assess for the use of venoactive dietary supplements or herbs that may adversely affect co-morbid conditions and/or prescription drugs.
- Choose best options for compression therapy and wound care.
- Give prescribed analgesics, antibiotics, or other drugs.
- Apply compression therapy.
- Provide wound care for venous leg ulcers.
- Evaluate for the effectiveness of therapies and need for alternative approaches.
- Teach patient and caregiver about the manifestations, complications, and treatment of venous insufficiency.
- Oversee the UAP in providing care:
  - Aid patients in elevating legs to reduce edema and pain.
  - Apply graduated compression stockings.
- Collaborate with the dietitian:
  - Assess diet and nutritional status.
  - Provide diet education as needed.

CASE STUDY
Peripheral Artery Disease

(© IPGGutenber-gUKLtd/iStock/Thinkstock.)

Patient Profile

S.J., a 73-yr-old black man, is admitted to the hospital with rest pain in both legs and a nonhealing ulcer of the big toe on the right foot.

Subjective Data

- History of a myocardial infarction, stroke, hypertension, HF, and type 1 diabetes
- Underwent a left femoral-popliteal bypass 5 yrs ago
- Has a 45-pack-yr history of tobacco use
- Has been using insulin for 30 yrs
- Reports sudden, intense increase in right foot pain for past 2 hrs
- Has slept in recliner with right leg in dependent position for several months to decrease leg pain

Current Medications

- Furosemide (Lasix) 40 mg/day PO
- Isosorbide dinitrate/hydralazine hydrochloride (BiDil) 1 tablet every 8 hr
- Aspart (NovoLog) insulin with meals
- Glargine insulin 50 units/day subcutaneously
- Diltiazem sustained release (Cardizem LA) 240 mg/day PO
- Aspirin 325 mg/day PO
- Fish oil daily (self-prescribed)

Objective Data

Physical Examination

- BP 148/92 mm Hg, irregular apical HR 90/min, respiratory rate 22/min, temperature 97.9° F (36.6° C)
- Alert and oriented, anxious, with no apparent physical or mental deficits from stroke
- Has 1+ right femoral pulse, popliteal pulse by Doppler only, posterior tibial pulse by Doppler only, and dorsalis pedis pulse absent (not palpable or present by Doppler). Left leg pulses are 1+
- Right leg ABI: 0.20. Left leg ABI: 0.68
- Has a 2-cm necrotic ulcer on tip of right big toe
- Has thickened toenails. Shiny, thin skin on legs. No hair on both lower legs
- Right foot is very cool, pale, and mottled in color with decreased sensation
- No peripheral edema
- Bedside glucose measurement 298 mg/dL (last meal 4 hrs before admission)

Discussion Questions

1. Assess S.J.'s risk factors for PAD.
2. Distinguish S.J.'s signs and symptoms of chronic PAD and acute arterial ischemia.
3. Identify the possible cause(s) for the sudden, intense increase in right foot pain.
4. How would you interpret S.J.'s ABI findings?

Continued

CASE STUDY

Peripheral Artery Disease—cont'd

5. What other diagnostic tests can be done to assess the extent of his PAD?
6. Given the physical examination data, what initial drug(s) would you expect the HCP to prescribe?
7. What treatment modalities are possible for S.J.?
8. **Priority Decision:** Based on the assessment data presented, what are the priority nursing diagnoses?
9. **Priority Decision:** What are the priority nursing responsibilities in caring for S.J.?

10. **Collaboration:** Identify activities that can be delegated to UAP.
11. **Evidence-Based Practice:** When teaching S.J., what evidence-based advice would you give him about the use of dietary supplements, such as fish oil?
12. **Safety:** To ensure S.J.'s safety, what nursing interventions are necessary to initiate?

Answers available at *http://evolve.elsevier.com/Lewis/medsurg.*

▮ BRIDGE TO NCLEX EXAMINATION

The number of the question corresponds to the same-numbered outcome at the beginning of the chapter.

1. A 50-year-old woman who weighs 95 kg has a history of tobacco use, high blood pressure, high sodium intake, and sedentary lifestyle. Which is the *most important* risk factor for peripheral artery disease (PAD) to address in the nursing plan of care?
   a. Salt intake
   b. Tobacco use
   c. Excess weight
   d. Sedentary lifestyle

2. When teaching a patient about rest pain with PAD, what should the nurse explain as the cause of the pain?
   a. Vasospasm of cutaneous arteries in the feet.
   b. Decrease in blood flow to the nerves of the feet.
   c. Increase in retrograde venous perfusion to the lower legs.
   d. Constriction in blood flow to leg muscles during exercise.

3. A patient with infective endocarditis develops sudden left leg pain with pallor, paresthesia, and a loss of peripheral pulses. What should be the nurse's *initial* action?
   a. Notify the HCP of the change in perfusion.
   b. Start anticoagulant therapy with IV heparin.
   c. Elevate the leg to improve the venous return.
   d. Position the patient in reverse Trendelenburg.

4. Which clinical manifestations can the nurse expect to see in both patients with Buerger's disease and patients with Raynaud's phenomenon? *(select all that apply)*
   a. Intermittent low-grade fevers
   b. Sensitivity to cold temperatures
   c. Gangrenous ulcers on fingertips
   d. Color changes of fingers and toes
   e. Episodes of superficial vein thrombosis

5. A patient is admitted to the hospital with a diagnosis of abdominal aortic aneurysm. Which signs and symptoms would suggest that the aneurysm has ruptured?
   a. Rapid onset of shortness of breath and hemoptysis.
   b. Sudden, severe low back pain and bruising along his flank.
   c. Gradually increasing substernal chest pain and diaphoresis.
   d. Sudden, patchy blue mottling on feet and toes and rest pain.

6. What are the *priority* nursing interventions 8 hours after an abdominal aortic aneurysm repair?
   a. Assessing nutritional status and dietary preferences
   b. Initiating IV heparin and monitoring anticoagulation
   c. Administering IV fluids and watching kidney function
   d. Elevating the legs and applying compression stockings

7. What is the *first* priority of interprofessional care for a patient with a suspected acute aortic dissection?
   a. Reduce anxiety.
   b. Monitor chest pain.
   c. Control blood pressure.
   d. Increase myocardial contractility.

8. Which patient is at *highest* risk for venous thromboembolism (VTE)?
   a. A 62-yr-old man with spider veins who is having arthroscopic knee surgery
   b. A 32-yr-old woman who smokes, takes oral contraceptives, and is planning a trip to Europe
   c. A 26-yr-old woman who is 3 days postpartum and received maintenance IV fluids for 12 hours during her labor
   d. An active 72-yr-old man at home recovering from transurethral resection of the prostate for benign prostatic hyperplasia

9. Which clinical findings should the nurse expect in a person with an acute lower extremity VTE? *(select all that apply)*
   a. Pallor and coolness of foot and calf
   b. Mild to moderate calf pain and tenderness
   c. Grossly decreased or absent pedal pulses
   d. Unilateral edema and induration of the thigh
   e. Palpable cord along a superficial varicose vein

10. Which treatment should the nurse anticipate for an otherwise healthy person with an initial VTE?
    a. IV argatroban as an inpatient
    b. IV unfractionated heparin as an inpatient
    c. Subcutaneous unfractionated heparin as an outpatient
    d. Subcutaneous low-molecular-weight heparin as an outpatient

11. Which instruction is a *key* aspect of teaching for the patient on anticoagulant therapy?
    a. Monitor for and report any signs of bleeding.
    b. Do not take acetaminophen (Tylenol) for a headache.
    c. Decrease your dietary intake of foods containing vitamin K.
    d. Arrange to have blood drawn twice a week to check drug effects.

12. The nurse is planning care and teaching for a patient with venous leg ulcers. What is the *most* important patient action in healing and control of this condition?
    a. Following activity guidelines.
    b. Using moist environment dressings.
    c. Taking horse chestnut seed extract daily.
    d. Applying graduated compression stockings.

1. b, 2. b, 3. a, 4. b, c, d, 5. b, 6. c, 7. c, 8. b, 9. b, d, 10. d, 11. a, 12. d

For rationales to these answers and even more NCLEX review questions, visit *http://evolve.elsevier.com/Lewis/medsurg.*

ⓔ EVOLVE WEBSITE/RESOURCES LIST

http://evolve.elsevier.com/Lewis/medsurg

Review Questions (Online Only)

Key Points

Answer Keys for Questions

- Rationales for Bridge to NCLEX Examination Questions
- Answer Guidelines for Case Study on p. 824
- Answer Guidelines for Managing Care of Multiple Patients Case Study (Section 8) on p. 827

Student Case Studies

- Patient With Abdominal Aortic Aneurysm
- Patient With Chronic Peripheral Artery Disease

Nursing Care Plans

- eNursing Care Plan 37.1: Patient With Peripheral Artery Disease of the Lower Extremities
- eNursing Care Plan 37.2: Patient After Surgical Repair of the Aorta

Conceptual Care Map Creator

Audio Glossary

Content Updates

REFERENCES

*1. Creager MA, Belkin B, Bluth EI, et al: 2012 ACCF/AHA/ACR/SCAI/SIR/STS/SVM/SVN/SVS key data elements and definitions for peripheral atherosclerotic vascular disease: a report of the ACCF/AHA Task Force on clinical data standards, *Circulation* 125:395, 2012. (Classic)

2. Centers for Disease Control and Prevention: Peripheral arterial disease (PAD) fact sheet. Retrieved from *www.cdc.gov/DHDSP/data_statistics/fact_sheets/fs_PAD.htm.*

*3. Gerhard-Herman M, Gornick H, Barrett C, et al: 2016 AHA/ACC guideline on the management of patients with lower extremity peripheral artery disease: Executive summary, *Circulation* 135:e686, 2017.

*4. Roumia M, Herbert H, Soukas P, et al: Sex differences in disease-specific health status measures in patients with symptomatic peripheral artery disease: Data from the PORTRAIT study, *Vasc Med* 22:103, 2017.

*5. American Diabetes Association: Standards of medical care in diabetes 2018. Retrieved from *http://care.diabetesjournals.org/content/41/Supplement_1.*

6. Di Minno A, Frigeri o B, Spadarella G, et al: Old and new anticoagulants: Food, herbal medicines, and drug interactions, *Blood Rev* 31:193, 2017.

7. Dowd F, Johnson B, Mariotti A: Use of herbs and herbal dietary supplements in dentistry. In *Pharmacology and therapeutics for dentistry*, ed 7, St Louis, 2017, Elsevier.

*8. Terra M, Conte M, Moll F, et al: Critical limb ischemia: Current trends and future directions, *JAHA* 5:002938, 2016.

9. Bunte M, Shisehbar M: Next generation endovascular therapies in peripheral artery disease, *Prog Cardiovasc Dis* 60:593, 2018.

*10. Hess C, Norgren L, Ansel G, et al: A structured review of antithrombotic therapy in peripheral artery disease with a focus on revascularization: A TASC initiative, *Circulation* 135:2534, 2017.

*11. Cacione D, Moreno D: Stem cell therapy for treatment of thromboangiitis obliterans (Buerger's disease), *Cochrane Database Syst Rev* 10:CD012794, 2018.

*12. Stringer T, Femia A: Raynaud's phenomenon: Current concepts of skin and systemic manifestations, *Dermatology* 36:498, 2018.

*13. Chaikof EL, Dalman RL, Eskandari MK, et al: The Society of Vascular Surgery practice guidelines on the care of patients with an abdominal aortic aneurysm, *J Vasc Surg* 67:1, 2017.

*14. Rylski B, Perez M, Beyersforg F, et al: Acute non-A non-B aortic dissection: Incidence, treatment and outcome, *Eur J Cardiothorac Surg* 52:1111, 2017.

15. Gawinecka J, Schonrath F, von Eckardstein A: Acute aortic dissection: Pathogenesis, risk factors, and diagnosis, *Swiss Med Weekly* 147:1, 2017.

*16. Li FR, Wu X, Yuan J, et al: Comparison of thoracic endovascular aortic repair, open surgery, and best medical treatment for type B aortic dissection: A meta-analysis, *Int J Cardiol* 250:240, 2018.

*17. Hattab Y, Kung S, Fasanya A, et al: Deep venous thrombosis of the upper and lower extremity, *Crit Care Nurs Q* 40:230, 2017.

18. Evans N, Rachford E: Superficial vein thrombosis, *Vasc Med* 23:187, 2018.

*19. Wik H, Enden T, Ganima W, et al: Diagnostic scales for the post thrombotic syndrome, *Thromb Res* 164:110, 2018.

*20. Kearon C, Aki E, Orneals J, et al: Antithrombotic therapy for VTE disease: CHEST guideline and expert panel report, *CHEST* 149:315, 2016.

21. Burcham JR, Rosenthal LD: *Lehne's pharmacology for nursing care*, ed 10, St Louis, 2019, Elsevier.

*22. Ito T, Kukino R, Takahara M, et al: Guidelines for the management of lower leg ulcers/varicose veins, *J Dermatol* 43:853, 2016.

*23. Chen JC: Current therapy for primary varicose veins, *BC Med J* 59:418, 2017.

*Evidence-based information for clinical practice.

CASE STUDY
Managing Care of Multiple Patients

You are working on the cardiovascular stepdown unit and have been assigned to care for the following 6 patients. You have 1 LPN and 1 UAP assigned to help you.

Patients

(© Jupiterimages/ Banana-Stock/ Thinkstock.)

L.P. is a 63-yr-old Asian American man who came to the ED with chest pain, shortness of breath, and palpitations. L.P.'s CK-MB and troponin levels are within normal limits. His ECG showed atrial fibrillation with a rapid ventricular response. He has been on IV diltiazem and IV heparin for 24 hr. Although his heart rate has decreased to 102 beats/min, the atrial fibrillation persists.

(© iStockphoto/ Thinkstock.)

J.E. is a 70-yr-old Hispanic woman admitted with increasing shortness of breath, fatigue, and weight gain. She has a systolic murmur and bilateral crackles. Her ejection fraction is 20%. She is receiving IV furosemide, oral potassium and enalapril (Vasotec), and a continuous infusion of nesiritide (Natrecor). She has O_2 at 6 L via nasal cannula to keep her O_2 saturation >93%. Normal initial set of cardiac enzymes.

(© iStockphoto/ Thinkstock.)

D.M. is a 51-yr-old man who was admitted 2 days ago with a suspected inferolateral wall MI. His cardiac-specific troponin I level was high, and the ECG showed marked ST segment elevation in the inferior leads. Cardiac catheterization showed a 90% blockage of his left anterior descending (LAD) artery. Coronary angioplasty was done, and 2 stents inserted. He is now 2 days post-PTCA, has had no recurrence of his chest pain, and is to be discharged today.

(© JennaDub/ iStock/ Thinkstock.)

R.B. is a 50-yr-old man admitted for HF due to valvular heart disease. He has a history of IV drug and alcohol use. He reports chest pain with minimal exertion. He has atrial fibrillation with a rapid ventricular response. His rhythm converted to normal sinus rhythm after receiving IV amiodarone. TEE shows left atrial and ventricular hypertrophy and mitral and aortic regurgitation.

(© iStockphoto/ Thinkstock.)

J.M. is a 68-yr-old man admitted 3 days ago with a diagnosis of acute decompensated HF. He had a cardiac arrest (pulseless VT) and was successfully defibrillated after 1 shock. He underwent electrophysiology studies and implantation of an implantable cardiodefibrillator (ICD). He now is being treated for HF.

(© IPGGutenberg-UKLtd/iStock/ Thinkstock.)

S.J. is a 73-yr-old black man admitted with rest pain in both legs and a nonhealing ulcer of the big toe on the right foot. He has history of an MI, stroke, hypertension, and type 1 diabetes. He had a left femoral-popliteal bypass 5 years ago. His right foot is cool, pale, and mottled in color with decreased sensation. He has a 1+ right femoral pulse, right popliteal and posterior tibial pulses only obtained by Doppler, and his right dorsalis pedis pulse is absent (not palpable or present by Doppler). His left leg pulses are 1+. His right leg ABI: 0.20; left leg ABI: 0.68.

Discussion Questions

1. ***Priority Decision:*** After receiving report, which patient should you see first? Second? Provide a rationale for your decision.
2. ***Collaboration:*** Which tasks could you delegate to the LPN? *(select all that apply)*
   a. Monitor L.P.'s heparin infusion.
   b. Report changes in pain or sensation of S.J.'s legs.
   c. Teach D.M. about activity restriction after PTCA.
   d. Administer prescribed medications to R.B. and J.M.
   e. Hook up J.M. to 12-lead ECG and monitor for dysrhythmias.
3. ***Priority Decision and Collaboration:*** As you are assessing L.P., the LPN tells you that S.J. is diaphoretic and reports chest pain. Which initial action would be *most* appropriate?
   a. Ask the LPN to notify S.J.'s HCP.
   b. Have the LPN administer prescribed nitroglycerin to S.J.
   c. Leave L.P.'s room to perform a focused assessment on S.J.
   d. Finish assessing L.P. while the UAP obtains a 12-lead ECG on S.J.

Case Study Progression

S.J. rates his chest pain as a 9/10. His blood pressure is 110/70, heart rate 110, respiratory rate 26, and O_2 saturation 93% on room air. You obtain a 12-lead ECG and administer 0.4 mg SL nitroglycerin with minimal pain relief after 5 minutes. The 12-lead ECG shows new ST elevation in leads II, III, and aVF.

4. Which interventions would you expect the HCP to order for S.J.? *(select all that apply)*
   a. IV nitroglycerin
   b. IV morphine sulfate
   c. Emergent cardiac catheterization
   d. Furosemide 40 mg IV push STAT
   e. Increase the O_2 flow rate to 12 L/min
5. What would you include in teaching about ICDs with J.M. and his family?
   a. Avoid air travel.
   b. Avoid driving for 6 weeks.
   c. Avoid any sexual activity in case the ICD discharges.
   d. Avoid standing near antitheft devices in stores and public buildings.
6. J.E is receiving nesiritide. What information is the priority to monitor?
   a. Blood pressure
   b. Respiratory rate
   c. b-Natriuretic peptide (BNP) level
   d. Troponin and CK-MB laboratory values
7. ***Priority Decision:*** You are preparing to give morning medications. Which patient's medication should be given first?
   a. Oral potassium and enalapril to J.E.
   b. Oral metoprolol, aspirin, and clopidogrel to D.M.
   c. IV furosemide, oral enalapril and metoprolol to R.B.
   d. Subcut Novolog, oral diltiazem and furosemide to S.J.
8. ***Management Decision:*** You ask the UAP to take D.M.'s vital signs before and after having him walk 300 feet. When reviewing the patient's chart, you note record of the patient's walk but not his vital signs. What is your initial action?
   a. Report the incident to the charge nurse for follow-up.
   b. Talk to the UAP about why the vital signs were not recorded.
   c. Walk D.M. yourself again and take his vital signs pre- and post-activity.
   d. Ask the LPN to ambulate D.M. and obtain his vital signs before and after.

Answers and rationales available at *http://evolve.elsevier.com/Lewis/medsurg*.

Note: Disorder names and key terms are in **boldface**. Page numbers in **boldface** indicate main discussions. Page numbers followed by *f* or *b* indicate figures or boxes/tables, respectively.

ABBREVIATIONS

ABG	arterial blood gas
ACE	angiotensin-converting enzyme
ACLS	advanced cardiac life support
ACS	acute coronary syndrome
ACTH	adrenocorticotropic hormone
ADH	antidiuretic hormone
AED	automatic external defibrillator
AIDS	acquired immunodeficiency syndrome
AKA	above-knee amputation
AKI	acute kidney injury
ALI	acute lung injury
ALL	acute lymphocytic leukemia
ALS	amyotrophic lateral sclerosis
AMI	acute myocardial infarction
ANA	antinuclear antibody
ANS	autonomic nervous system
AORN	Association of periOperative Room Nurses
APD	automated peritoneal dialysis
aPTT	activated partial thromboplastin time
ARDS	acute respiratory distress syndrome
ATN	acute tubular necrosis
BCLS	basic cardiac life support
BKA	below-knee amputation
BMI	body mass index
BMR	basal metabolic rate
BMT	bone marrow transplantation
BPH	benign prostatic hyperplasia
BSE	breast self-examination
BUN	blood urea nitrogen
CABG	coronary artery bypass graft
CAD	coronary artery disease; circulatory assist device
CAPD	continuous ambulatory peritoneal dialysis
CAVH	continuous arteriovenous hemofiltration
CBC	complete blood count
CCU	coronary care unit; critical care unit
CDC	Centers for Disease Control and Prevention
CIS	carcinoma in situ
CKD	chronic kidney disease
CLL	chronic lymphocytic leukemia
CML	chronic myelocytic leukemia
CMP	cardiomyopathy
CN	cranial nerve
CNS	central nervous system
CO	cardiac output
COPD	chronic obstructive pulmonary disease
CPAP	continuous positive airway pressure
CPR	cardiopulmonary resuscitation
CRRT	continuous renal replacement therapy
CRNA	certified registered nurse anesthetist
CSF	cerebrospinal fluid
CT	computed tomography
CVA	cerebrovascular accident; costovertebral angle
CVAD	central venous access device
CVI	chronic venous insufficiency
CVP	central venous pressure
D&C	dilation and curettage
DDD	degenerative disk disease
DI	diabetes insipidus
DIC	disseminated intravascular coagulation
DJD	degenerative joint disease
DKA	diabetic ketoacidosis
DM	diabetes mellitus; diastolic murmur
DRE	digital rectal examination
DVT	deep vein thrombosis
ECF	extracellular fluid
ECG	electrocardiogram
ED	emergency department; erectile dysfunction
EEG	electroencephalogram
EMG	electromyogram
EMS	emergency medical services
ENT	ear, nose, and throat
ERCP	endoscopic retrograde cholangiopancreatography
ERT	estrogen replacement therapy
ESKD	end-stage kidney disease
ESR	erythrocyte sedimentation rate
ET	endotracheal
FEV	forced expiratory volume
FRC	functional residual capacity
FUO	fever of unknown origin
GCS	Glasgow Coma Scale
GERD	gastroesophageal reflux disease
GFR	glomerular filtration rate
GH	growth hormone
GI	glycemic index
GTT	glucose tolerance test
GU	genitourinary
GYN, Gyn	gynecologic
HAI	health care–associated infection
HAV	hepatitis A virus
Hb, Hgb	hemoglobin
HBV	hepatitis B virus
Hct	hematocrit
HCV	hepatitis C virus
HD	hemodialysis, Huntington's disease
HDL	high-density lipoprotein
HF	heart failure
HIV	human immunodeficiency virus
H&P	history and physical examination
HPV	human papillomavirus
HSCT	hematopoietic stem cell transplantation
IABP	intraaortic balloon pump
IBS	irritable bowel syndrome
ICP	intracranial pressure
I&D	incision and drainage
IE	infective endocarditis
IFG	impaired fasting glucose
IGT	impaired glucose tolerance
INR	international normalized ratio
IOP	intraocular pressure
IPPB	intermittent positive-pressure breathing
ITP	idiopathic thrombocytopenic purpura
IUD	intrauterine device
IV	intravenous
IVP	intravenous push; intravenous pyelogram
JVD	jugular venous distention
KS	Kaposi sarcoma
KUB	kidney, ureters, and bladder (x-ray)
KVO	keep vein open
LAD	left anterior descending
LDL	low-density lipoprotein
LGV	lymphogranuloma venereum
LLQ	left lower quadrant